# Dictionary of World Biography

# The 20th Century

**Dictionary of World Biography**

The Ancient World
The Middle Ages
The Renaissance
The 17th and 18th Centuries
The 19th Century, 2 volumes
The 20th Century, 3 volumes
Index

# Dictionary of World Biography

## Volume 9
# The 20th Century

## O-Z

Frank N. Magill, *editor*

Christina J. Moose, *managing editor*

Alison Aves, *researcher and bibliographer*

Mark Rehn, *acquisitions editor*

FITZROY DEARBORN PUBLISHERS
CHICAGO • LONDON

SALEM PRESS
PASADENA • HACKENSACK, NJ

*Dictionary of World Biography* is a copublication of Salem Press, Inc. and Fitzroy Dearborn Publishers

For information, write to:
SALEM PRESS, INC.
P.O. Box 50062
Pasadena, California 91115

or
FITZROY DEARBORN PUBLISHERS
919 N. Michigan Ave., Suite 760
Chicago, Illinois 60611
USA

or
FITZROY DEARBORN PUBLISHERS
310 Regent Street
London W1R 5AJ
England

**Library of Congress Cataloging-in-Publication Data**

Dictionary of world biography / editor, Frank N. Magill ; managing editor, Christina J. Moose ; researcher and bibliographer, Alison Aves ; acquisitions editor, Mark Rehn.

v. cm.

A revision and reordering, with new entries added, of the material in the thirty vols. comprising the various subsets designated "series" published under the collective title: Great lives from history, 1987-1995.

Includes bibliographical references and indexes.

Contents: v.9. The twentieth century.

ISBN 0-89356-323-4 (v. 9 : alk. paper)
ISBN 0-89356-320-X (v. 7-9 set : alk paper)
ISBN 0-89356-273-4 (vol. 1-10 set : alk. paper)

1. Biography. 2. World history. I. Magill, Frank Northen, 1907-1997. II. Moose, Christina J., 1952- . III. Aves, Alison. IV. Great lives from history.

CT104.D54 1998
920.02—dc21 97-51154
CIP

British Library Cataloguing-in-Publication Data is available.
Fitzroy Dearborn ISBN 1-57958-048-3

First Published in the U.K. and U.S., 1999
Printed by Sheridan Books

Cover design by Peter Aristedes.

First Printing

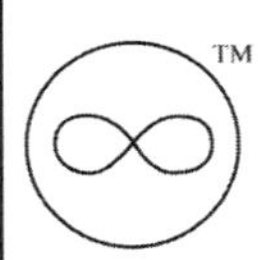

The paper used in this book meets the minimum requirements of American National Standard for Information Sciences – Permanence of Paper for Printed Library Materials. ANSI Z39.48-1984.

# CONTENTS

## LIST OF ENTRANTS

# HERMANN OBERTH

*Born:* June 25, 1894; Hermannstadt, Siebenburgen, Transylvania

*Died:* December 29, 1989; Nürnberg, West Germany

*Area of Achievement:* Aeronautics

*Contribution:* Oberth is one of the three great pioneers of the sciences of astronautics and modern rocketry. Along with Konstantin Tsiolkovsky and Robert Goddard, he is credited with developing the principles behind rocket-powered flight beyond Earth's atmosphere, liquid-fueled rockets, a manned Earth orbital space station, and manned interplanetary flight.

## Early Life

Hermann Julius Oberth was born on June 25, 1894, in Hermannstadt, Siebenburgen, Transylvania, a part of what is modern Romania. His father, Julius, was a physician who stressed learning to his son from an early age. The younger Oberth attended elementary and high school in the town of Schaessburg until 1913, when he entered the University of Munich to study medicine, as had his father. Oberth, like fellow rocketry pioneers Konstantin Tsiolkovsky in Russia and Robert Goddard in the United States, was heavily influenced in his formative years by the emerging genre of science fiction in the late nineteenth and early twentieth centuries that detailed possible methods of traveling into space. Indeed, in his later years Oberth acknowledged that his mother's gift of Jules Verne's books in his eleventh year helped shape the course of the rest of his life.

When World War I started in 1914, the twenty-year-old Oberth joined the German army's medical service. This experience gave him a strong distaste for the healing arts and convinced him to pursue another area of endeavor as his life's work. Turning to his childhood fascination with the concept of spaceflight, he chose mathematics and physics to be his new fields of study.

After leaving the army medical service, Oberth returned to the University of Munich and began his studies. He also studied at Göttingen and Heidelberg before receiving his schoolmaster's diploma in July, 1923. Returning to Siebenburgen, he began work as a fifth-grade teacher of mathematics and physics. Later he taught in the German town of Mediasch, where he made his home until 1938. He later took German citizenship. It was during his service in Germany in World War I that he unsuccessfully proposed that the German government build liquid-fueled bombardment missiles, the forerunners of the modern Intercontinental Ballistic Missiles.

Oberth continued to read and theorize about the prospects of rocket-powered space flight. This avocation led to the publication of his first and most well known work on astronautics, *Die Rakete zu den Planetenräumen* (1923; the rocket into interplanetary space). It was this seminal work's worldwide popularity that gave Oberth an international reputation as an expert in astronautics.

## Life's Work

Oberth's *Die Rakete zu den Planetenräumen* and an expanded version of the book published in 1929, *Wege zur Raumschiffahrt* (*Ways to Spaceflight*, 1972), put forth numerous ideas that were to form the basis of the German missile program in World War II and the ongoing American and Soviet manned and unmanned space programs. These included the theory that a liquid-fueled rocket could propel an object through the airless void of space and that the vehicle could develop sufficient velocity and centrifugal force to counterbalance Earth's gravity and remain in orbit around the planet. He also theorized that the vehicle could move quickly enough to break free of Earth's gravity and move into interplanetary space.

Moving beyond the theory of propulsion, Oberth hypothesized the potential effects of space travel on the human body and was the first to coin the phrase "space station" to mean a permanent manned facility in Earth orbit. Although he developed his theories independently of his peers, Oberth's two books confirmed both Tsiolkovsky's theoretical work on rocket propulsion and Goddard's practical experience in rocketry, and moved Oberth to the pinnacle of the rapidly developing field. Both before and after the publication of his first books he maintained active correspondence with both men until their deaths.

In 1928, Oberth was given the chance to put the theories he had developed into practice when he became the technical adviser to the famous film director Fritz Lang and the Ufa film company for the motion picture *Die Frau im Mond.* As part of his

service to Ufa, he was asked to build and fly a liquid-fueled rocket to promote the film. Unfortunately, the rocket Oberth constructed was unable to fly, and the film company ran out of development funds before he was able to correct the design. Oberth was, however, able to test-fire a rocket engine successfully in 1930 as part of the project.

An active and vocal proponent of space exploration, Oberth helped found in 1929 the Verein fur Raumschiffahrt (VfR), Germany's first society for space travel. In addition to Oberth, who was elected the society's first president, the group's first members included such pioneers of aeronautics and rocketry as Willy Ley and an eighteen-year-old student of Oberth by the name of Wernher von Braun. The VfR's development paralleled the founding of similar groups elsewhere in the world, including the Moscow Group for the Study of Reactive Propulsion, whose members included the future chief designer of the Soviet space program, Sergei Korolev, and aircraft designer Andrei Tupolev. The VfR and other of these groups both built and flew rudimentary rockets and sponsored public displays on rocketry such as the one built by Oberth and von Braun in a Berlin department store to educate the public about their work.

In 1930, the VfR was given a parcel of land outside Berlin to conduct practical experiments in rocketry. This empty field, which was once an ammunition dump for the German army, was called Raketenflugplatz Berlin (rocket field Berlin). Oberth and the VfR spent the next two years conducting experiments there before the German army developed an interest in their work and recruited several of the VfR's members into service developing ordnance. During this period, Oberth supported himself by teaching mathematics and physics at the technical universities in Vienna and Dresden, as well as by publishing his research in astronautics in numerous books and articles. In 1941, he went to work for his former student von Braun as a member of the team of scientists at the German rocket-development center in Heeresversuchsstelle, Peenemünde.

At Peenemünde, von Braun and Oberth developed and then successfully launched the Vengeance weapons, the V-1 and V-2 rockets. The V-1 "Buzz Bomb" was a short-range, rocket-powered winged bomb, while the V-2 was a powerful ballistic missile able to span hundreds of miles to deliver its deadly payload. With the approval in June, 1943, of Adolf Hitler, the V-2 went into mass production. The first operational V-2 missile was launched on September 8, 1944, at London, England, from The Hague, The Netherlands.

In 1943, Oberth transferred to the Rheinsdorf aircraft facility near Wittenberg, Germany, where he remained for the duration of World War II. After the war, he left Germany unnoticed by the Allies and moved to Switzerland, where he lived in seclusion until 1949. Oberth's research into rocketry resumed in 1949 at Oberried am Brienzer Lake and, later, for the Italian navy at La Spezia, Italy. During these years, he also gained considerable recognition from the growing international community of rocket scientists. His theories were being put to use by both the United States with its early V-2 tests and its own Viking rocket, and by the Soviet Union under Sergei Korolev and his larger, more powerful rockets.

During these years and later, Oberth continued to publish both technical materials and popular treatises on practical concepts of space travel. His later books and articles, including *Menschen im Weltraum* (1954; men into space) and *Stoff und Leben* (1959; matter and life), were well received both by the scientific community and by the general public. He was the recipient of numerous awards during his long career, including the REP Hirsch Award of the Société Astronomique de France, of which he was the first to be so honored in 1925, and the coveted Galabert Prize in 1962. As one of the pioneers of space travel, he was also invited to lecture and participate in many international conferences and programs on astronautics and rocketry. One of the honors he is known to have most prized, however, was having been invited to participate in the realization of his dream of interplanetary space travel as a witness to the launch of Apollo 11, the first manned landing on the moon, in 1969.

In 1955, Oberth again went to work for his former student von Braun at the Technical Feasibility Studies Office of the Ordnance Missile Laboratories in the United States. In 1956, he transferred to the Army Ballistic Missile Agency with von Braun to assist in the development of the Redstone Rocket, one of the United States' first liquid-fueled boosters and the backbone of the early U.S. space program. Two years later, Oberth returned to Germany in semiretirement.

### Summary

Hermann Oberth was one of the first great idealists of space travel in the modern age. He, along with his contemporaries Tsiolkovsky and Goddard, had the knowledge and the passion to take the fantasy of science fiction and turn it into the reality of science fact. Through their vision, they forged a new understanding of their world. Oberth's theories, enumerated in his books, showed how the laws of physics could be put to use to conquer the heavens. He theorized about the first space station and gave a detailed, startlingly accurate account of how microgravity would affect the human body on long space voyages. These writings, along with his seminal works about reaction propulsion of a space vehicle and liquid-fueled rockets, gave future engineers and scientists a path to follow in making space travel a reality.

While his work at Peenemünde helped develop weapons of destruction, he was a man who believed deeply in the peaceful pursuit of space. He urged international cooperation between the United States and the Soviet Union in the early days of the space race, even going so far as asking Nikita Khrushchev to allow him to work with Sergei Korolev in the development of the Soviet space program. One of Oberth's most direct contributions to the progress of space travel was the encouragement he gave to the rocketry enthusiasts of his day, such as Wernher von Braun. Von Braun took the knowledge he gained from Oberth, expanded upon it, and made space travel a reality by developing the launch vehicles that carried men to the moon and the unmanned probes that traveled beyond the solar system.

### Bibliography

Braun, Wernher von, and Frederick I. Ordway III. *The History of Rocketry and Space Travel.* 3d ed. New York: Crowell, 1975. As one of the unequaled giants in modern rocketry, von Braun brings to this well-written and easily understandable compendium a unique and fascinating perspective. An excellent starting point for the layperson for information on the early days of the American space program.

Freeman, Marsha G. "The Father of Spaceflight." *World and I* 9, no. 12 (December, 1994). Profile of Oberth that includes information on his book *The Rocket into Interplanetary Space* and the scientific community's reaction to it.

Hurt, Harry, III. *For All Mankind.* New York: Atlantic Monthly Press, 1988; London: Queen Anne Press, 1989. Gives an overview of the American space program through the Apollo lunar landings. An accompanying volume to a documentary on the men who flew the lunar landing missions.

Huzel, Dieter K. *Peenemünde to Canaveral.* Englewood Cliffs, N.J.: Prentice-Hall, 1962. This insider's account of the German rocket program during World War II is fast-paced and reads like a novel. Of interest to anyone who wishes to learn more about the proving ground for much of the technology in use in the modern space race.

McAleer, Neil. *The Omni Space Almanac: A Complete Guide to the Space Age.* New York: World Almanac, 1987. A compendium of information about the major developments of the space age, with emphasis on the modern years and their import for the future.

Neufeld, M.J. "Weimar Culture and Futuristic Technology: The Rocketry and Spaceflight Fad in Germany, 1923-1933." *Technology and Culture* 31, no. 4 (October, 1990). Focuses on the German interest in spaceflight in the 1920s and 1930s, including contributions by Oberth.

Oberth, Hermann. *Man into Space: New Projects for Rocket and Space Travel.* Translated by G. P. H. De Freville. London: Weidenfeld and Nicolson, and New York: Harper, 1957. This book, one of Oberth's last, is a scholarly approach to space travel, written on the eve of the modern space age. While it contains some technical information, the book is written in easily understandable language for the layperson or amateur space enthusiast.

Stuhlinger, Ernst, et al., eds. *Astronautical Engineering and Science: From Peenemünde to Planetary Space, Honoring the 50th Birthday of Wernher von Braun.* New York: McGraw-Hill, 1963. Written by von Braun's colleagues from Peenemünde, the U.S. Army missile program, the Marshall Space Center, and Cape Canaveral, this collection of essays on space technology and exploration is excellent. Oberth contributed a paper on an electrical rocket engine that is well written and informative.

*Eric Christensen*

## ÁLVARO OBREGÓN

*Born:* February 17, 1880; Hacienda Siquisiva, Sonora, Mexico

*Died:* July 17, 1928; Mexico City, Mexico

*Areas of Achievement:* The military, government, and politics

*Contribution:* Obregón emerged from humble beginnings to become the most successful and celebrated general of the Mexican Revolution. Elected President of Mexico after ten years of civil war, Obregón worked from 1920 to 1924 to pacify his country by a program of demilitarization, support for public education, and recognition by the U.S. government.

### Early Life

Álvaro Obregón, the eighteenth and youngest child of Francisco Obregón and Cenobia Salido, was born to a respectable family fallen on hard times. Francisco had been a successful businessman but lost most of his holdings because his business partner had supported the emperor Maximilian. The family was reduced to living on their Sonoran ranch, which was ruined by a series of disasters, including Indian uprisings and floods. Francisco died a few months after his youngest son's birth.

Obregón spent his early years at Siquisiva, living there until his mother moved the family to the town of Huatabampo, Sonora. Three elder sisters, Cenobia, María, and Rosa, assisted his mother in rearing him. He would remain close to his sisters for the rest of his life. These sisters, all schoolteachers, gave him his essential education. He received little formal education, attending the primary school in Huatabampo, run by his brother José, for only a few years. He was a voracious reader and largely self-educated.

By the age of thirteen Obregón had left school in order to begin making a living. He tried his hand at various jobs and money-making schemes: growing tobacco and making cigarettes, organizing a family orchestra, photography, and carpentry. He discovered that he had natural mechanical talent and began to get jobs taking care of machinery on large plantations in the region. In his early twenties, he turned to farming, after also having been a traveling salesman and schoolteacher.

In 1903, Obregón married Refugio Urrea, by whom he would have four children. By 1906, Obregón had become successful enough to buy a small farm of his own. He gave this place a whimsical name, "La Quinta Chilla," which translates as "the broken down farm" or "penniless farm." In 1907 tragedy struck. His wife and two of his children, including the eldest, died. His sisters stepped in to help rear his remaining children. In 1909, Obregón achieved his first real success, inventing a chickpea planter which was soon adopted by most of the local growers. This allowed him to become modestly prosperous. After an unsuccessful attempt to gain a state office, Obregón, by a small margin, was elected *presidente municipal* (mayor) of Huatabampo during the presidency of Francisco Madero. His interests as mayor centered on public education and public works.

### Life's Work

Obregón did not participate in Madero's 1910-1911 rebellion against Porfirio Díaz, citing his parental responsibilities as his reason for abstaining. Later he would regret his actions, which he considered cowardly. When the next opportunity came to fight, he came forward. In April, 1912, he was called upon as mayor to raise troops to fight Pascual Orozco, then in rebellion against Madero's government. Obregón recruited three hundred men and was named Lieutenant Colonel of the Fourth Sonoran Irregular Battalion. During the following months, Obregón demonstrated his courage and natural military ability in the successful campaign against Orozco, earning the rank of colonel.

Obregón had no previous military training or experience but from the first displayed a natural talent for tactics and leadership. He was shrewd, intelligent, and blessed with a prodigious memory. He used these talents to his advantage. Obregón's forte was in assessing troop and material strengths, evaluating terrain, and patiently waiting to do battle when the enemy could be maneuvered into maximum disadvantage. He was a master of the bluff and used his superior knowledge of the situation to trick the enemy into defeating itself. Obregón was also an innovator. His men were using individual foxholes for protection several years before World War I made this technique well known. A pilot in Obregón's army made the first aerial bombardment of gun emplacements in 1914. Such abilities and innovations permitted Obregón a string of uninterrupted victories during the Mexican Revolution.

In December, 1912, Obregón returned to farming, only to take up arms again after Madero's overthrow by General Victoriano Huerta in February, 1913. By August of 1914, Obregón, fighting for the constitutionalist cause organized by Venustiano Carranza, had fought his way from Sonora to Mexico City. Along the way the victorious warrior was made first a brigadier general (May, 1913), and then commander in chief of the Army of the Northeast by Carranza, the head of the constitutionalist forces.

The young general was an attractive figure. Obregón was taller than average and stockily built. His wide, handsome face, with large green eyes, brown hair, and light complexion, reflected his Hispanic heritage. He possessed a lively and creative intelligence and, despite his lack of formal education, was renowned for his prodigious memory. He had a reputation of being a cheerful, frank, and congenial person with a good sense of humor. He was a good conversationalist, much given to telling jokes and humorous stories, often with himself as the butt of the humor. He was abstemious in his personal habits, neither smoking nor drinking. Yet, Obregón was a man of contradictions, and there was a darker side to his personality as well. His genial demeanor masked a driving ambition and ruthlessness. He would not hesitate as the revolution progressed to deal harshly with his enemies and former allies if he deemed it expedient.

After the victory over Huerta, the constitutionalist forces fell into factionalism. General Obregón attempted to serve as conciliator between Carranza, Pancho Villa, and Emiliano Zapata, but without success. Obregón had to defeat Zapata and Villa's forces in battle to end their challenge to Carranza's dominance. He accomplished this but at great personal cost. It was during this campaign, at the Battle of León in June, 1915, that Obregón was wounded and lost his right arm. He became not only the revolution's most successful general but also something of a martyr.

After recovering from his wound, Obregón continued his campaign against Villa. He was made secretary of war by Carranza in March of 1916 to facilitate the campaign. Nevertheless, a rift was growing between the first chief of the Revolution and his best general. By 1916, Obregón's military successes, his reputation as a peacemaker and negotiator among the revolutionaries, his position in the government, and his personal charisma had given him a powerful position. Carranza began to see Obregón as a potential rival and to fear his growing power. For his part, Obregón was increasingly critical of his chief's lack of social conscience. Yet, each needed the other, and this postponed an open break between them until 1917.

Obregón used his position as secretary of war to begin the reorganization and professionalization by which he planned to eliminate the military from politics. He took an active, though indirect, interest in the constitutional convention which met in Querétaro from December, 1916, to January, 1917. Although not a delegate and frequently absent on military business, Obregón associated himself at the convention with the radicals, who were responsible for the inclusion of innovative articles in the constitution regarding the Church, labor, and landownership. Obregón emerged from the convention with a reputation as a champion of radical causes.

Having waited until the ratification of the new constitution and Carranza's election as president under it, in May, 1917, Obregón resigned from the cabinet and returned to private life. He and his second wife, María Tapia, whom he had married in 1916, returned to La Quinta Chilla. There, Obregón pursued numerous economic activities. He grew chickpeas, founded a cooperative agricultural society for chickpea growers, acquired additional land, raised cattle, and opened an import-export firm. He grew wealthy from his business interests and began to age rapidly, growing fat and gray by the age of forty.

By 1919, Obregón was preparing himself to run for the presidency. He had not directly challenged Carranza, preferring to bide his time until the 1920 election. President Carranza, however, attempted to block Obregón's ambitions, believing that his former subordinate lacked both an understanding of national problems and a program for dealing with them. Obregón increasingly saw Carranza as an obstructionist and reactionary who lacked commitment to the revolutionary principles embodied in the constitution. The showdown began when Obregón announced his candidacy in June, 1919. Carranza realized that Obregón, an energetic and effective campaigner, was the popular candidate and would win unless he could be eliminated from the race. Therefore, in April, 1920, Carranza pushed Obregón and his supporters into armed rebellion, hoping to eliminate the threat once and for all. Within a month, however, Carranza was dead, and the rebels triumphed. This paved the way for Obregón's landslide election to the presidency.

Obregón was inaugurated President of Mexico on December 1, 1920, inheriting a nation in chaos. While committed to implementing the provisions of the 1917 constitution, he was at heart a pragmatist. His main objective as president was the pacification of Mexico after ten bloody years of civil war. To achieve this, he needed to strengthen the central government, eliminate the military from politics, and begin the economic and social regeneration of Mexico. Strengthening and legitimizing the regime was of paramount importance if the revolution was to endure. To do this, Obregón had to compromise the constitution's nationalist principles regarding foreign investors and make an accommodation with the United States. The Bucareli Agreements of 1923 granted concessions to American companies and investors but obtained American recognition. This was an important deterrent to the success of future rebellions against the regime, because American arms and support would be withheld from the rebels. He began the forced professionalization of the army, making limited but significant gains in depoliticizing its leadership. To check the power of the military, he built new bases of regime support among urban labor and the rural peasantry by beginning the implementation of the labor and agrarian reforms outlined in the constitution. Obregón reduced military spending and increased the government's commitment to education, hoping to build Mexico's future on an educated citizenry. Obregón's presidency paved the way for the more rapid and complete implementation of the constitution under his successors.

After defeating a major military rebellion in 1923, Obregón finished his full term of office—the first Mexican president to do so since 1910—and handed power to his elected successor Plutarco Elías Calles. He then returned to farming. Helped by government loans, he further expanded his business interests. For a time he was content living in Sonora, enjoying his return to private life surrounded by his wife and children, but by 1926 he was spending increasing amounts of time in the capital. In October, 1926, the congress, after stormy debate, changed the constitution to pave the way for Obregón's reelection as president. This triggered discontent among the military chieftains. After having dealt harshly and efficiently with them, Obregón ran unopposed in 1928. He did not, however, live to take office a second time. After surviving a series of assassination attempts in 1927 and 1928, President-elect Obregón met his death at

a banquet in Mexico City in July, 1928. José de León Toral, a young Catholic fanatic posing as a caricaturist, shot Obregón at point blank range as he sat at the head table. In keeping with his wishes, Obregón was buried in his home state of Sonora.

### Summary

Álvaro Obregón's career represented both the good and bad aspects of the Mexican Revolution. He was a member of the new elite, which came to power as a result of the revolutionary struggle. A moderately successful farmer before the Revolution, he considered himself a citizen-soldier compelled to arms in order to champion the interests of the Mexican people. He risked his life to topple the entrenched interests that had perpetuated a life of misery for so many of his countrymen. He supported the writing of a constitution that would build a new, more equitable Mexico from the ashes of the old regime. As president, he worked to institutionalize the revolutionary regime and to build the mechanism needed to create that new nation. He is justly considered one of the great heroes of the Revolution.

He was, however, a flawed hero. Obregón also used the revolution for self-aggrandizement. The upheaval created opportunities for him to feed his driving ambition for power and influence. He used his success as a military leader to become the most powerful man in Mexico, despite the fact that he considered the military in politics to be the major threat to the stabilization of the country. He ruthlessly eliminated his rivals for power if they did not step aside. He forced the amending of one of the most cherished provisions of the revolutionary constitution—prohibiting the reelection of presidents to prevent dictatorships—because it stood in the way of his personal ambition. In the end, he met the fate of most revolutionary generals who survived the Revolution, death by assassination in the political struggles that followed.

**Bibliography**

Bailey, David C. "Obregón: Mexico's Accommodating President." In *Essays on the Mexican Revolution*, edited by George Wolfskill and Douglas W. Richmond. Austin: University of Texas Press, 1979. A short piece focusing on Obregón's contributions as president of Mexico. Bailey believes that Obregón's willingness to compromise made possible the institutionalization of revolutionary goals.

Dillon, E. J. *President Obregón: A World Reformer.* London: Hutchinson, and Boston: Small Maynard, 1923. An idealized and uncritical study of Obregón by a journalist who traveled with his retinue. Dillon presents Obregón as a statesman who, among others, holds out hope for the future of Western civilization.

Dulles, John W. F. *Yesterday in Mexico: A Chronicle of the Revolution, 1919-1936.* Austin: University of Texas Press, 1961. Dulles uses interviews with survivors, published memoirs, and newspaper accounts to construct a narrative of the rise and fall of the three great Sonoran revolutionary leaders: Obregón, Huerta, and Calles. Valuable for its coverage of Obregón's presidential years.

Hall, Linda. *Alvaro Obregón: Power and Revolution in Mexico, 1911-1920.* College Station: Texas A&M Press, 1981. Extensively researched and well balanced, this is the best work in English on Obregón. Hall covers Obregón's rise to presidential power through military success and political infighting. Unfortunately, Hall does not extend the work to Obregón's presidency.

———. "Alvaro Obregón and the Agrarian Movement 1912-20." In *Caudillo and Peasant in the Mexican Revolution*, edited by David Brading. Cambridge and New York: Cambridge University Press, 1980. An article focusing on Obregón's relations with the peasantry. Hall sees Obregón not as a typical caudillo but as a leader with broader based support.

Hansis, Randall. "The Political Strategy of Military Reform: Alvaro Obregón and Revolutionary Mexico 1920-1924." *The Americas: A Quarterly Review of Inter-American Cultural History* (October, 1979): 197-233. Highlights Obregón's program of military reform during his presidency.

Lieuwen, Edwin. *Mexican Militarism: The Political Rise and Fall of the Revolutionary Army, 1910-1940.* Albuquerque: University of New Mexico Press, 1968. This work describes how the revolutionary army of Mexico seized power, the role it played in social reform, and how it was gradually forced to surrender its power to civilian politicians. Obregón as president was a key figure in professionalizing and depoliticizing the army, although the task would be completed by his successors.

Ruiz, Ramón Eduardo. *The Great Rebellion: Mexico, 1905-1924.* New York: Norton, 1980; London: Norton, 1982. Contains a chapter devoted to Obregón. Ruiz sees him not as a revolutionary nor even much of a reformer, despite his political reputation. Instead, he finds Obregón's political philosophy (as reflected in his actions) to be more in keeping with nineteenth century liberal notions about individualism and capitalism.

*Victoria Hennessey Cummins*

# FLANNERY O'CONNOR

*Born:* March 25, 1925; Savannah, Georgia
*Died:* August 3, 1964; Milledgeville, Georgia
*Area of Achievement:* Literature
*Contribution:* In her short lifetime, Flannery O'Connor created a small but significant body of fiction and nonfiction unique in American literature, Southern literature, Catholic literature, and feminist literature.

## Early Life

Mary Flannery O'Connor was born in Savannah, Georgia, on March 25, 1925, the only child of Edward Francis O'Connor, Jr., and Regina Cline O'Connor, both of whom came from prominent Southern Catholic families. Flannery was a happy, sensitive, and independent child. When she was twelve, her father became critically ill with disseminated lupus, a rare and incurable metabolic disease, and the family moved from Savannah into the Cline home in Milledgeville, which formerly had been the governor's mansion (when Milledgeville was the capital of Georgia). Three years later her father died.

O'Connor attended Catholic elementary schools, Peabody High School, and Georgia College (then Georgia State College for Women) in Milledgeville, receiving an A.B. degree in 1945. While in college, she served as art editor and cartoonist for the school newspaper, editor of the literary quarterly, and feature editor of her yearbook.

She received a scholarship to study for an M.F.A. degree at the University of Iowa's School for Writers, under the direction of Paul Engle. In 1946, while still a student, she published her first short story, "The Geranium," in *Accent* magazine. She began work on her first novel, *Wise Blood*, which won her the Rinehart-Iowa Fiction Award in 1947. In 1947 and 1948, four short stories from her master's thesis, "The Heart of the Park," "The Train," "The Peeler," and "The Turkey," were published in prestigious "little magazines."

## Life's Work

Flannery O'Connor's accomplishments in college and graduate school won for her a place in the fall of 1948 as writer-in-residence at Yaddo, an artists' colony in Saratoga Springs, New York. There she met writers Robert Lowell, Edward Maisel, and Elizabeth Hardwick. That year she also engaged Elizabeth McKee as her literary agent. She was then twenty-three years old.

Early in 1949, political turmoil at Yaddo surrounding the well-known journalist Agnes Smedley led many of the artists, including O'Connor, to withdraw. She returned briefly to Milledgeville, spent the summer writing in a furnished room in New York, and then moved in September to the Ridgefield, Connecticut, home of Robert Fitzgerald, a well-known poet and translator, and Sally Fitzgerald, also a writer.

O'Connor worked on her novel *Wise Blood* while helping the Fitzgeralds with the care of their children. During the train ride home to Milledgeville during the Christmas holidays in 1950, she suffered her first severe, almost fatal, attack of what was later diagnosed as disseminated lupus. With the help of ACTH, a cortisone derivative, O'Connor slowly recovered, and in July, 1952, she and her mother moved to their family farm, Andalusia, outside Milledgeville.

O'Connor gradually adjusted to her circumstances and organized her life around her work. She drew on her daily experience for the materials of her stories, entertained a wide variety of visitors, wrote numerous letters, and delighted in raising ducks, geese, and peacocks. While she was able, she accepted invitations to lecture at colleges and libraries. By 1955, the weakness of her bones made it necessary for her to use crutches, and except for one trip to Europe, she rarely left Andalusia.

During the first year of her illness, O'Connor completed revisions of *Wise Blood*. After five years' work and some unpleasant controversy with Rinehart over publishing rights, the novel was published in 1952 by Harcourt, Brace. Puzzling, misunderstood by many, considered by turns repulsive, dull, and precocious, *Wise Blood* marks the beginning of O'Connor's mature work.

In the next three years, O'Connor published a number of short stories in magazines and literary journals. In 1955, Harcourt, Brace collected these into *A Good Man Is Hard to Find and Other Stories*. The collection was greeted with critical acclaim. O'Connor's stories were characterized as violent, grotesque, and outrageously funny. Although readers praised her keen ear for the rhythms of Southern speech and her sharp eye for telling detail, many failed to appreciate or understand the or-

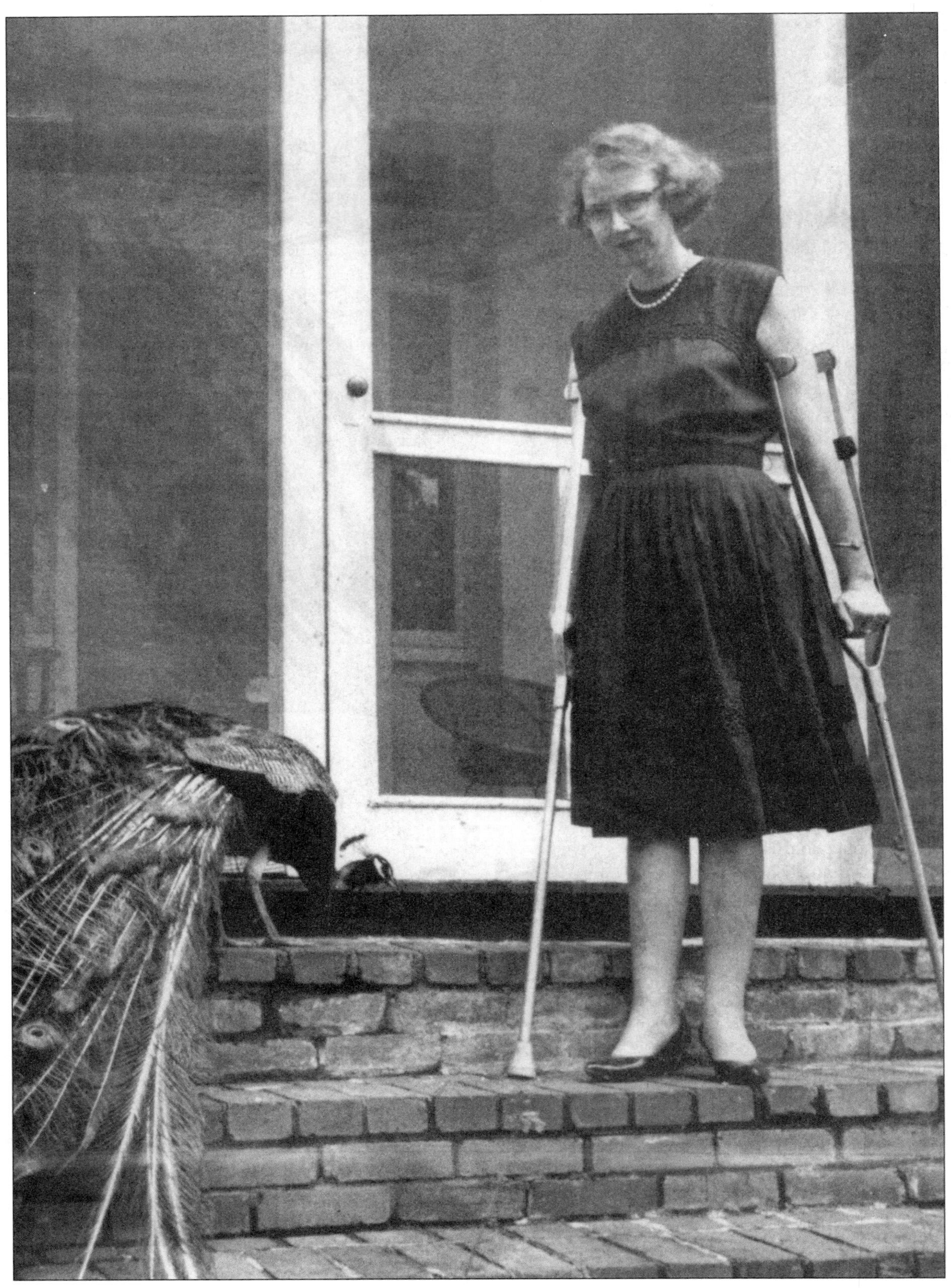

thodox Christianity that formed the foundation of her work.

In 1960, Farrar, Straus, and Cudahy published O'Connor's third book and second novel, *The Violent Bear It Away*. Like *Wise Blood*, the novel is condensed, intense, and poetic. Clearly more mature in vision and artistry than her earlier novel, it brought mixed reviews from secular readers and greater appreciation from Christians.

While working on the stories that constituted her second collection, *Everything That Rises Must Converge*, O'Connor's health began to fail. Farrar, Straus, and Giroux published the book in 1965, the year after O'Connor's death from kidney failure. The book was highly praised.

Other writings published after her death reveal the many facets of her genius and enhance her literary reputation. In 1969, Sally Fitzgerald and Robert Fitzgerald gathered O'Connor's lectures and miscellaneous nonfiction into *Mystery and Manners: Occasional Prose*. These writings, which are models of nonfiction prose style, provide insight into O'Connor's views on art, religion, and education. Also included in the collection is the lengthy introduction O'Connor wrote to *A Memoir of Mary Ann*, the true story of a remarkable little girl who suffered facial disfigurement and terminal illness with dignity and grace.

*Flannery O'Connor: The Complete Stories* appeared in 1971. This collection of thirty-one pieces includes twelve previously uncollected stories. O'Connor's first published story, "Geranium," and her last, "Judgment Day," a reworking of "Geranium," provide a framework for the chronologically ordered collection. The book received the National Book Award in 1972.

*The Habit of Being: Letters* (1979), edited by Sally Fitzgerald, is an extensive collection of personal and professional letters spanning O'Connor's adult life, from 1948 to 1964. These letters reveal something of the depth and details of Flannery O'Connor's rich personality, her numerous personal and professional relationships, and her religious faith, as well as her wide-ranging reading, her linguistic playfulness, and her sense of humor. Her letters are essential reading for anyone who wants to understand Flannery O'Connor and her work.

In 1983, Leo J. Zuber compiled *The Presence of Grace and Other Book Reviews*, a collection of the numerous book reviews O'Connor wrote for local publications. *Collected Works*, published by Literary Classics of the United States, appeared in 1988, thus firmly establishing O'Connor's place in American literature.

**Summary**

Critics have variously labeled Flannery O'Connor a black humorist, a regionalist, a Southern lady, and a Roman Catholic novelist. If she had to be labeled, she chose that of Christian realist. Working within the prevailing currents of prose fiction, O'Connor recognized her debt to such writers as Henry James, Joseph Conrad, Nathanael West, and Nathaniel Hawthorne. She profoundly interiorized her sense of place, the American South in which she was born and bred and whose idioms, cadences, and concerns she expressed. Her ultimate commitment was to what she might do with "the things of God" within the tradition of an orthodox Catholic faith. These three strands of her reality—literature, the South, and Catholicism—converged in her to produce a body of work that remains unique in American literature, in Southern literature, in Catholic literature, and in feminist literature.

Although no one has yet emerged to attempt a similar synthesis, the thirty years since O'Connor's death have brought increasing appreciation, understanding, and valuing of her life and work. The future will surely recognize her significant contribution in at least three areas: the understanding of the human condition, the appreciation of the relationship between art and religion, and the valuing of women as writers. As human beings acknowledge, accept, and understand the reality of spirit permeating matter, Flannery O'Connor's clarity and depth of vision will continue to attract new generations of admirers. As artists continue to address in their work the problem of the relationship between art and belief, Flannery O'Connor's "habit of art" will continue to evoke new depths of creativity. As women continue to claim their "true country" and their true voices, Flannery O'Connor's commitment, integrity, and faith will continue to inspire in them a transformed "habit of being."

**Bibliography**

Asals, Frederick. *Flannery O'Connor: The Imagination of Extremity.* Athens: University of Georgia Press, 1982; London: University of Georgia Press, 1987. Asals finds that the power of O'Connor's fiction springs from a passion for extremes, the tension of opposites. His work explores some of these tensions. As O'Connor's work changed and developed, the focus of her imagination on extremes remained constant.

Bacon, Jon Lance. *Flannery O'Connor and Cold War Culture*. Cambridge and New York: Cambridge University Press, 1993. Bacon considers O'Connor from a wide perspective, delving into the effects of politics, social issues, the Cold War, and other issues on her writing.

Coles, Robert. *Flannery O'Connor's South*. Baton Rouge: Louisiana State University Press, 1980; London: University of Georgia Press, 1993. Coles, a highly regarded social psychologist, draws on O'Connor's letters and extensive interviews with Southerners to discuss O'Connor's social, religious, and intellectual milieu.

Feeley, Kathleen. *Flannery O'Connor: Voice of the Peacock*. 2d ed. New York: Fordham University Press, 1982. Feeley, a Catholic nun, studies the marked passages in O'Connor's personal books to uncover the theological foundations of her writing. Doing so, she discerns six recurring themes in O'Connor's art and belief and concludes that O'Connor saw reality through the eyes of an Old Testament prophet.

Fickett, Harold, and Douglas R. Gilbert. *Flannery O'Connor: Images of Grace*. Grand Rapids, Mich.: Eerdmans, 1986. This critical-biographical essay traces O'Connor's artistic development and the treatment of sin and salvation in her writings. More than thirty photographs of O'Connor, including one self-portrait, and the people and places close to her illustrate the text.

Friedman, Melvin J., and Beverly L. Clark, eds. *Critical Essays on Flannery O'Connor*. Boston: Hall, 1985. This collection includes representative reviews of most of O'Connor's works, four of the most moving posthumous tributes, and a dozen outstanding critical essays, presented in the order of their first appearance. It concludes with a bibliography, annotated in depth, of diverse and innovative criticism intended for beginning as well as experienced readers of O'Connor.

Getz, Lorine M. *Flannery O'Connor: Her Life, Library, and Book Reviews*. New York: Mellen Press, 1980. This indispensable book for serous students of O'Connor includes perhaps the best chronological account of O'Connor's life and work, a descriptive list of her personal library, and a list of her published book reviews.

Golden, Robert E., and Mary C. Sullivan. *Flannery O'Connor and Caroline Gordon: A Reference Guide*. Boston: Hall, 1977. This annotated guide to reviews, articles, and books about O'Connor and her work, published between 1952 and 1976, is especially helpful in interpreting her work and tracing the development of her literary reputation in the early years.

Hendin, Josephine. *The World of Flannery O'Connor*. Bloomington: Indiana University Press, 1970. Hendin provides a provocative reading that takes issue with much earlier criticism, downplaying O'Connor's Catholicism and contending that she wrote out of rage at the disease that was consuming her.

Hyman, Stanley E. *Flannery O'Connor*. Minneapolis: University of Minnesota Press, 1966. This is a brief, often controversial overview of O'Connor's imagery, symbols, and themes. It includes a biographical sketch and places O'Connor in a modern literary context.

Kreyling, Michael. *New Essays on Wise Blood*. Cambridge and New York: Cambridge University Press, 1995. A collection of essays on Wise Blood.

McFarland, Dorothy T. *Flannery O'Connor*. Modern Literature Monographs. New York: Ungar, 1976. McFarland provides an excellent overview for undergraduate students, including a biographical sketch, contextual background, and brief but comprehensive discussions of O'Connor's style, techniques, imagery, and major concepts.

Orvell, Miles. *Invisible Parade: The Fiction of Flannery O'Connor*. Philadelphia: Temple University Press, 1972; London: University Press of Mississippi, 1996. Orvell establishes several contexts for O'Connor's works—the South, Christianity, and literature—and then examines individual works within those contexts. This book may provide a good orientation to O'Connor, especially for those who are uncomfortable with her religious beliefs.

*Christian Koontz*

# SANDRA DAY O'CONNOR

*Born:* March 26, 1930; El Paso, Texas
*Areas of Achievement:* Government and politics and law
*Contribution:* O'Connor was the first woman appointed to serve on the Supreme Court of the United States.

## Early Life

Born on March 26, 1930, in El Paso, Texas, Sandra Day was brought up on a rustic cattle ranch in southeastern Arizona. The oldest of three children, she proved to be a hardworking and self-reliant young woman. By age ten, Sandra was riding horses, repairing fences, and driving tractors. She also developed studious habits as a youngster, reading the many magazines and books provided by her parents. Encouraged to value education by her college-educated mother, Ada Mae Wilkey Day, Sandra was sent to live with her maternal grandmother in order to attend a private girls' school in El Paso. Between the ages of six and fifteen, Sandra alternated between spending summers with her parents on the ranch and school months away. She was graduated from high school in Austin, Texas, at the relatively young age of sixteen.

A very mature young student, Sandra Day entered prestigious Stanford University in California at age sixteen. She completed both her undergraduate and law degrees by the time she was twenty-two. Her progress through school was both rapid and marked by high achievement. She attained magna cum laude status for her B.A. degree in economics, and she ranked third in her law school's graduating class. She was chosen to be a member of the Society of the Coif, an exclusive honorary society for superior law students, and she served on the staff of the highly regarded *Stanford Law Review.* There she met, and shortly thereafter married, John O'Connor, who later was to become a senior partner in an Arizona law firm.

## Life's Work

Despite her considerable academic achievements, Sandra Day O'Connor was unable to obtain a position in one of the traditionally all-male private law firms in California, except as a legal secretary. Denied this opportunity, O'Connor began what would turn out to be an extraordinary career in public service. She served briefly as deputy attorney for San Mateo County in 1952-1953 before moving to West Germany because of her husband's Army assignment. Upon returning to the United States, she proceeded to have and rear three sons, while maintaining a busy schedule of volunteer activities in Phoenix, Arizona. Still unable to secure a law firm position, she devoted herself to public service, becoming one of Arizona's assistant attorney generals in 1965 and then a state senator in 1969. She later became the first woman to hold the majority leader position in a state senate.

Although she enjoyed the respect of her senate colleagues and the support of her constituents, O'Connor preferred the intellectual challenge of the judiciary to the social demands of the legislature. She successfully sought election in 1974 as a state trial judge, and four years later she was appointed by Governor Bruce Babbitt to the Arizona Court of Appeals. As both a state legislator and a judge, she developed a reputation as an extremely diligent, intelligent, and fair-minded public servant. Influenced as a youth by her father, Harry Day, who had an intense dislike for Franklin Delano Roosevelt and the policies of the Democratic Party, O'Connor became a loyal Republican Party activist, serving on the Arizona committee to reelect President Richard M. Nixon in 1972 and working for Ronald Reagan's presidential nomination in 1976. Her judicial temperament, fidelity to the Republican Party, impressive academic credentials, and impeccable moral character made her a prime candidate for a federal court appointment.

Since its opening session in 1789, and for almost two hundred years thereafter, no woman had served on the Supreme Court of the United States. In fulfillment of a campaign pledge to appoint a qualified woman to the U.S. Supreme Court, President Ronald Reagan nominated Sandra Day O'Connor on July 7, 1981, to become the 106th justice in the Court's history. This historic decision by President Reagan followed a three-month-long search headed by Attorney General William French Smith, who, ironically, had been a partner in one of the California law firms that had refused to hire O'Connor years before. Despite some questions that were raised about her relatively brief experience as an appellate court judge, her nomination was enthusiastically supported by both conservatives and liberals. O'Connor impressed members of the Senate Judiciary Committee with her careful and prudent approach to such controversial legal

issues as abortion and the death penalty, and she made clear her strong conservative belief that judges ought to restrain themselves from injecting personal values into their judicial decisions. Her merit being obvious to all, she was confirmed by the U.S. Senate by a vote of 99 to 0 in September of 1981. O'Connor's womanhood, for so long an obstacle to career advancement, now provided the occasion for her rise to the pinnacle of the legal profession.

Sandra Day O'Connor is a distinguished and highly respected associate justice of the Supreme Court. She immediately impressed colleagues with her disciplined work habits and dignified yet congenial manner. Shortly after arriving, she initiated an aerobics class in the Supreme Court gymnasium for all women employees, which she attends faithfully. Although slowed by a bout with breast cancer in 1988, O'Connor maintains one of the most grueling work schedules of any justice. Journalists often note that she is exceedingly well prepared for each case, citing the incisive questions she poses to counsel when the Court conducts oral arguments.

On the Supreme Court, O'Connor has had a significant influence on some of the most controversial issues in constitutional law. Her moderately conservative judicial opinions have been particularly important in the areas of abortion, religion, affirmative action, federalism, and women's rights. On the nine-member Court, she has often cast the deciding vote, repeatedly discovering some reasonable middle-ground position between her more ideological liberal and conservative brethren.

O'Connor has defined the standard by which states must abide as they devise ways to regulate abortion. Rejecting both the arguments of conservatives that the Constitution does not prevent states from prohibiting abortions and the arguments of liberal feminists that states could place no constitutional restrictions on a woman's right to choose an abortion, she argued persuasively in *Planned Parenthood of Southeastern Pennsylvania v. Casey* (1992) that states could regulate abortion up to the point that these restrictions become an undue burden on the woman seeking the abortion.

In the controversial area of religion, O'Connor has again been a voice of moderation. Against liberals who advocate a virtually total separation of religion from state activities and against conservatives who argue that the Constitution allows active government support and encouragement of religion so long as the government does not establish one preferred religion, O'Connor has articulated the position that a government policy violates the Constitution if it intends, or appears, to endorse religion. She has said, however, that government ought not to impede private citizens who wish to engage in religious activity, even within public institutions.

O'Connor has actively participated in moving the Court to a more conservative stance on affirmative action even while defending such programs against more conservative justices who would abolish them in all circumstances. In a case that displayed her sensitivity to discrimination against women as well as her support for some types of affirmative action programs, she argued in *Johnson v. Transportation Agency of Santa Clara County* (1987) against the complaint of a white male who was passed over for a skilled job in favor of a woman who, though well qualified, scored slightly lower on an interview score. At the time, none of the 237 skilled positions in the agency was held by a woman. For O'Connor, this was sufficient evidence that the county had discriminated against women. In subsequent cases, she has tried to limit government affirmative action programs only to those circumstances in which they function as a remedy for evident, actual race or gender discrimination. Justice O'Connor has taken increasingly conservative positions in other areas of civil rights, such as voting rights. In 1993, for example, she ruled in *Shaw v. Reno* against the reorganization of legislative districts to maximize the voting power of African Americans.

O'Connor is the only one of her colleagues on the Court to have been an elected state legislator. This fact, combined with her fundamentally conservative values, has made O'Connor a strong advocate of limits on the power of the federal government over the states. This stance is reflected in her ardent defense of state court jurisdiction over criminal justice matters such as capital punishment. Her conservative views on federalism have emerged in such important decisions as *Gregory v. Ashcroft* (1991), in which, writing for the majority of the Court, O'Connor ruled that Missouri's constitutional requirement of mandatory retirement for judges did not violate the federal Age Discrimination in Employment Act. Similarly, in *New York v. U.S.* (1992), O'Connor's majority opinion declared that the federal government could not order state governments to assume ownership of nuclear waste if they failed to create adequate disposal sites as required by federal law. Justice O'Connor has become the leading judicial proponent of state sovereignty.

As for women's rights, O'Connor has stood forcefully for certain principles—that the Constitution mandates gender equality and that civil rights laws protect women against discrimination in education and employment. As a state senator, she supported the Equal Rights Amendment. In 1993, Justice O'Connor wrote an opinion for a unanimous court in *Harris v. Forklift Systems* which made sexual harassment in the workplace easier to prove. Although she is not a liberal feminist, O'Connor's efforts to preserve a woman's constitutional right to choose abortion, her votes on the Court to end discrimination against pregnant workers, and her opposition to the exclusion of women from men's private clubs demonstrate her commitment to gender equality.

### Summary

Sandra Day O'Connor's pathbreaking rise to the Supreme Court was a significant moment in the greater transformation of women's lives in American society during the last half of the twentieth century. Her celebrated nomination to the Court, applauded by people of all political views, reflected the growing consensus that women were deserving of high political office and that they had been unjustly excluded from these positions for far too long. Her appointment to the Court also coincided with the increase in popularity of conservative political ideas in the 1980's, to which trend she contributed.

O'Connor's accomplishments go beyond the circumstances of her appointment. On the Court, she has influenced many important areas of American law, often casting pivotal votes in highly controversial cases. Scholars have proposed that O'Connor brings a uniquely feminine perspective to cases heard by the Court, marked in part by her consistent ability to see both sides of complex issues and her tendency to forge a reasonable compromise that is consistent with her basic conservative values. Other scholars have documented the fact that several of the justices became noticeably more receptive to arguments in favor of gender equality after O'Connor's arrival on the Court. O'Connor was joined by the second woman justice after President Bill Clinton nominated Ruth Bader Ginsburg to fill a vacancy on the Supreme Court in 1993.

Although women continue to be underrepresented in political office, O'Connor retains a unique public profile as one of the most popular and readily recognized Supreme Court Justices ever. Her determination to succeed in the predominantly male world of law and politics, and her ability to combine motherhood and family with a career dedicated to public service, make her a positive role model for many young women.

### Bibliography

Abraham, Henry J. *Justices and Presidents*. 3d ed. New York: Oxford University Press, 1992. Contains a detailed and perceptive analysis of the political circumstances surrounding O'Connor's appointment to the Supreme Court, written by one of the best Supreme Court scholars.

Behuniak-Long, Susan. "Justice Sandra Day O'Connor and the Power of Maternal Legal Thinking." *The Review of Politics* 54 (Summer, 1992): 417-444. One of the more accessible scholarly analyses of O'Connor's jurisprudence. The author argues that O'Connor has a particularly feminine, though not feminist, perspective that influences her adjudication of legal controversies.

O'Connor, Sandra Day. "Portia's Progress." *New York University Law Review* 66 (December, 1991): 1546-1558. An illuminating lecture given by the justice in 1991 on the subject of women in the legal profession. O'Connor reviews her personal experience with societal discrimination and the history of Supreme Court cases dealing with women. She also explains how her views differ from those of many feminists.

Savage, David G. "Sandra Day O'Connor." In *Eight Men and a Lady: Profiles of the Justices of the Supreme Court*. Edited by the staff of the National Press. Bethesda, Md.: National Press, 1990. The best short biography of O'Connor, with a fine account of her appointment to the Court and an analysis of her decisions through her first four years on the Court.

———. *Turning Right: The Making of the Rehnquist Supreme Court*. New York: Wiley, 1992; Chichester: Wiley, 1993. Biographical information on O'Connor and analyses of her votes in key cases are presented in the context of a comprehensive and penetrating journalistic account of the Supreme Court in action from 1986 to 1992.

Sullivan, Patricia A., and Steven R. Goldzwig. "Abortion and Undue Burdens: Justice Sandra Day O'Connor and Judicial Decision-Making." *Women and Politics* 16, no. 3 (Summer 1996). Focuses on O'Connor's work on abortion cases, which the author argues "resists the oversimplification of complex issues."

Van Sickel, Robert W. *Not a Particularly Different Voice: The Jurisprudence of Sandra Day O'Connor*. New York: Lang, 1998. Van Sickel focuses on the legal opinions of O'Connor, avoiding a stereotypical approach to her work that would link her opinions to her gender.

*Philip Zampini*

## THOMAS POWER O'CONNOR

*Born:* October 5, 1848; Athlone, Ireland
*Died:* November 18, 1929; London, England
*Areas of Achievement:* Government, politics, journalism, and publishing
*Contribution:* As a member of Parliament and as a journalist, O'Connor was able to advance the Irish cause and effect change without violence.

### Early Life

Thomas Power O'Connor was born of poor but educated parents in Athlone, County Westmeath, Ireland. His mother was the daughter of an officer in the duke of Wellington's army in Spain. A few years after O'Connor's birth, the family moved to Galway, where O'Connor spent his early life. His parents, who were determined to give their son a good education, enrolled him at the Immaculate Conception College in Athlone. A few years later, he transferred to Queens University in Galway, where he excelled as a classical scholar, mastered French and German, and gained recognition as a formidable member of the debating society. He was only eighteen when he earned his bachelor of arts degree.

During his lifetime, O'Connor was subject to bouts of melancholy. He was also troubled by chronic digestive problems that would come on with regularity two or three hours after each meal. He did not take regular exercise and drank very little. He spent money as he received it and was extremely generous, especially toward members of his family.

His first employment was as a reporter for *Saunders Newsletter* in Dublin. The newsletter had a strong Tory and Orange bias, which ran contrary to O'Connor's Catholicism and Irish nationalist convictions. Later in life he related his feelings and experiences while attending ultra-Tory meetings and listening almost nightly to denunciation, in no sparing terms, of the Church in which he had been raised. He succeeded in listening with equanimity and recording them with accuracy.

After three years, he quit this job and went to London in an attempt to advance himself in his career. He was never to reside in Ireland again. He had no friends or contacts in London and spent weeks seeking employment while his meager funds were diminishing. Near destitution, he obtained a position as a reporter for the *Daily Telegraph*. This was at the beginning of the Franco-Prussian War, and O'Connor's assignment was to read through the French, German, and Austrian newspapers and supplement the brief reports from correspondents of the newspaper.

O'Connor left the *Daily Telegraph* when he failed to get the increase in salary that he requested. He was soon hired by the *New York Herald Tribune* at the salary he had requested at the *Daily Telegraph*. After a year and a half at this position, he was laid off as part of a cost reduction effort at the London office. At the time, he had two sisters and a brother who resided with him and depended upon him for support. Lacking salaried employment, he tried to earn a living by freelance reporting, feature writing, and just about any type of literary work. During this time, he often found himself in dire need of food and other necessities. However, he often attended sessions of the House of Commons, where the picturesque figure of the Tory prime minister Benjamin Disraeli captured his interest.

### Life's Work

Disraeli became the subject of O'Connor's first book, *Life of Lord Beaconsfield* (1876). This unflattering biography was assailed with special virulence by the Tory press but was extolled by the opposition Whigs. The controversy surrounding the book gave the heretofore obscure and impoverished O'Connor name recognition. Disraeli admitted to having read the book and surprisingly said it was not scurrilous, as his sycophants had claimed, since it was all true. This established O'Connor as a writer whose pen possessed a power worthy of respect.

In 1880 O'Connor was asked to stand for election to the House of Commons for the Galway district in Ireland. O'Connor was an Irish nationalist and identified himself with the Parnell faction of the Irish party. This group, led by Charles Stewart Parnell, was an uncompromising advocate of home rule for Ireland and land reform that would enable the tenant farmers to become proprietors. To accomplish these objectives, the group resorted to militant and obstructionist tactics in Parliament. They were determined to destroy that section of the Irish party that sided with the governing William Gladstone ministry. Their objective was to form a bloc of votes that would be delivered only in exchange for legislation favorable to Ireland.

In a close election, O'Connor was victorious. This was the beginning of a career in Parliament that was to last for almost a half century and eventually earned O'Connor the title "father of the House of Commons." Despite his initial fears, O'Connor was able to obtain employment as a journalist when he returned to London as a member of Parliament. He got a job as a parliamentary reporter for the *Pall Mall Gazette*. After parliamentary sessions were concluded for the day, he would begin writing around midnight and have his copy ready for delivery to the newspaper before 7:00 A.M.

O'Connor put his English connections to good use. In 1883 he was elected president of the Irish National League of Great Britain. This was the vehicle used to mobilize the vote of the immigrant Irish in Great Britain for the Irish cause. In 1885 he stood for election in Liverpool in the so-called Scotland division. This district had a heavy concentration of Irish immigrants and their descendants. He was also a candidate for reelection for his Galway seat. He won in both districts, and he decided to take the Liverpool seat. This left a vacancy in Galway. Parnell, fearing a disclosure of his love affair with Katie O'Shea, insisted that this seat be filled by his lover's estranged husband, Captain William O'Shea, much to the consternation of party supporters. O'Connor, however, chaired the meeting that managed to impose this unpopular choice.

In June of 1885, O'Connor impetuously married Elizabeth Pascal Howard, an American who had two previous marriages. She was a gracious hostess, but O'Connor sought to avoid London social life as an embarrassment to his political image. It became clear by the end of the 1890's that they were not suited for each other. A formal separation did not occur until about 1905.

Throughout his lengthy parliamentary career, O'Connor remained a journalist. He could utilize this talent to market his ideas and, as a skilled politician, carry them into execution. In 1888 he founded the *Star*, an impressive radical newspaper. This newspaper was quite successful, but O'Connor had differences with the board of directors that caused him to sell his interest at a substantial profit. He later founded the *Sunday Sun* (1891), which was changed to the *Weekly Sun* in 1893. The publication, however, was not a financial success. Another O'Connor publishing venture was *T. P.'s Weekly*, first issued in November, 1902. This literary magazine included contributions from such noted authors as H. G. Wells, Arnold Bennett, Joseph Conrad, and G. K. Chesterton. O'Connor remained nominal editor of this magazine until his death in 1929.

Along with his journalistic career, O'Connor continued to be reelected to his Liverpool seat in the House of Commons, usually by a substantial margin. He made numerous trips to the United States to raise funds for the Irish cause. After two previous defeats, passage of a home-rule bill appeared to be secured in 1914. However, the start of World War I and the Ulster question delayed its implementation. The Ulster unionists insisted that all of Ulster be excluded, while the extreme Irish nationalists would not agree to any exclusion. O'Connor, the practical politician, believed that each county in Ulster should to be given the option to be included.

The Easter Rising of 1916 came as a surprise to O'Connor, who viewed the Dublin rebellion as irrational since it was without any chance of success. Irish public opinion was indifferent at first but turned strongly in favor of the Sinn Féin rebels following the executions of the leaders of the uprising. The election of 1918 proved to be a disaster for O'Connor's nationalist party. Sinn Féin won seventy-three seats in the south of Ireland, while O'Connor's party won only one seat. O'Connor held his seat in Liverpool by an overwhelming margin but could no longer be regarded as a spokesman for the Irish since he no longer had a political base. The newly elected Sinn Féin members would not attend Parliament.

Politically isolated, O'Connor continued to serve in Parliament. His last years were interrupted by crippling bouts of rheumatism and diabetes. He died in London on November 18, 1929.

## Summary

For centuries the plight of the Irish was excoriated by the activities of violent groups that merely reacted to grievances. Their uprisings and terrorist acts lacked direction and any reasonable chance of success. Likewise, the large number of Irish elected to Parliament in the early and mid-nineteenth century were ineffective as they failed to unite into a formidable bloc. They were content, for the most part, to be good members of the Whig or Liberal party with the hope or assurance that they would later be awarded a lucrative public office.

This all changed with the election of men like Thomas Power O'Connor. Initially led by Charles Stewart Parnell, they devised a strategy to obtain home rule and land reform for Ireland. This strategy included obstructing all proceedings in Parliament, if need be. There was to be tight party discipline among the Irish members and a strict policy against accepting any office or favor from the government. This solidarity meant that the Irish bloc had a strong negotiating position. At times they held the balance of power in Parliament and were able to bring down the ruling ministry.

As a respected journalist and publisher, O'Connor was able to articulate the Irish position to the British public. This intellectual force expressed itself through the political clout of the Irish parliamentary party to effect peaceful social and political change. Unlike other members of his party who remained part of an Irish ghetto, O'Connor was regarded as a leading member of Parliament from an English constituency. Of the Irish members of Parliament, he was the only one who figured in the intellectual and social life of London and who gave attention to matters outside the House of Commons.

**Bibliography**

Brady, L. W. *T. P. O'Connor and the Liverpool Irish.* London: Royal Historical Society, and Atlantic Highlands, N.J.: Humanities Press, 1983. This is the most readily available book written about O'Connor. While worthwhile to the researcher, it is not written in an interesting or popular style.

Fyfe, Hamilton. *T. P. O'Connor.* London: Allen and Unwin, 1934. This interesting and easily read biography of O'Connor was written shortly after his death in 1929. It captures a contemporary perception of O'Connor but unfortunately is not too readily available.

Kee, Robert. *The Green Flag: The Turbulent History of the Irish National Movement.* New York: Delacorte Press, 1972; London: Penguin, 1989. Kee provides a thorough account of the Irish struggle for home rule and land reform. A must read to obtain the historical background to understand the Irish cause as advanced by O'Connor.

O'Connor, T. P. *Lord Beaconsfield.* 8th ed. London: Unwin, 1905. First published in 1876, this unauthorized biography of Benjamin Disraeli, the famous Tory prime minister not much admired by O'Connor, launched O'Connor on a political as well as literary career.

———. *The Parnell Movement.* London: Unwin, 1889; New York: Cassell, 1891. O'Connor relates his early years in Parliament under the leadership of Charles Stewart Parnell. Also contains a short biography of the early life of the author by Thomas Nelson Page.

———. *Memoirs of an Old Parliamentarian.* London: Benn, and New York: Appleton, 1929. Although it is not an autobiography, this two-volume work sets forth O'Connor's analysis of events that occurred during his long parliamentary career. An excellent source for up-close and candid observations of the leading personalities O'Connor knew both in and out of Parliament.

*Gilbert T. Cave*

# SADAHARU OH

*Born:* May 10, 1940; Tokyo, Japan
*Area of Achievement:* Sports
*Contribution:* Oh hit more home runs, 868, than any other man in organized baseball while playing twenty-two years with the Yomiuri (Tokyo) Giants in the Central League in Japan. When he retired, he also held the Japanese career records in runs batted in, runs scored, and total bases as well as the second highest marks in doubles and games played.

## Early Life

Sadaharu Oh was born in the Sumida-ku section of Tokyo, Japan, on May 10, 1940. His father was a Chinese immigrant restaurant owner. During the war, his father was imprisoned for several months and permanently scarred during questioning as a possible Chinese agent. Oh is still technically a Chinese national with permanent working rights in Japan. His heritage and the availability of food gave him the size (5 feet, 10 inches, and 175 pounds) that made him very large for Japanese players and certainly contributed to his power hitting.

The family survived the fire-bombing of Tokyo, though their restaurant was destroyed and had to be reestablished after the war. During the occupation, Oh's elder brother was a star on an amateur baseball team and introduced him to baseball. Since he had never seen a left-handed batter, Oh first batted right-handed even though he pitched left-handed. When Oh was in the eighth grade, he was converted to a left-handed batter at the suggestion of Hiroshi Arakawa, a major league outfielder.

Oh's father had high ambitions for his sons. The eldest son became a medical doctor, and Oh was being prepared for a career as an engineer. He did not, however, make a high enough score on the entrance exam to get into the exclusive local high school and instead was accepted at Waseda Commercial High School, far across the city. High school baseball is one of the major sporting events in Japan, and Waseda always had a good team. Oh was persuaded, as a highly rated young player, to travel long hours to and from school to participate.

The climax of the high school baseball season each year is the National High School Tournament at Koshien Stadium in Osaka. There are fifty thousand spectators for each game and each is nationally telecast. In 1956, Waseda reached the national finals for the seventeenth time in thirty-eight years. They won their first game, but Oh, the starting pitcher in the second game, was unable to do well and the team was eliminated. The next year, Waseda reached the finals again, and this time Oh was their only pitcher. He had two badly injured fingers on his pitching hand with deep blisters that bled as he pitched. He managed to pitch three straight complete games to reach the climactic game. Oh won the final game 4-2 and was lauded by the newspapers for his fighting spirit. Soon afterward, he was refused the right to participate in the Kokutai (National Amateur Athletic Competition), because he was a Chinese national. In his last year in school, Waseda was beaten in their last game in Tokyo and failed to reach the Koshien tournament.

## Life's Work

In 1959, Oh joined the Yomiuri Giants, signing a bonus contract for sixty thousand yen after a bidding war in which considerably higher sums were offered by other teams. He began practice as an eighteen-year-old rookie on the veteran team of the Japanese leagues and was almost overwhelmed by all the activity, particularly since Shigeo Nagashima, a college graduate and the most popular player in Japanese baseball history, had enjoyed a brilliant rookie year in 1958. Quickly Oh earned a reputation for being very hardworking, even for a Japanese player, all of whom worked much longer hours than American players. During the first year, he lived in the dormitory for younger players. Often he practiced from eight o'clock until noon with them, in the afternoon with the Giants, and in the evening he played in a game. Throughout his career, he never took less than forty minutes of batting practice on a game day and carefully drank a secret blend of Korean ginseng before each game. The first year Oh batted .161 with only seven home runs and twenty-five runs batted in in ninety-four games, making the Giants decision to convert him to a first baseman seem quite questionable. Though he did so poorly, it was prophetic that his first hit was a home run. The next year he did improve to .270 with seventeen home runs and seventy-one runs batted in, leading the league in bases on balls for the first of nineteen times. The third year, Oh slumped again to .253 with only thirteen home runs and fifty-three runs batted in.

In the spring of 1962, Manager Kawakami of the Giants hired Hiroshi Arakawa as his batting coach.

For the next nine years, Arakawa would almost completely dominate Oh's life. He had been told to turn Oh into a .280 hitter with twenty home runs a year, a goal that Arakawa considered modest from the start. The training regimen established included work in the traditional Japanese martial arts and philosophy and orders to give up visiting the bars in the Ginza and all tobacco products. Then began intensive instruction for both of them in Zen and in the martial art called Aikido, the latter under the direction of the founder of the school Ueshiba. Aikido is based on the idea that the power of the opponent is absorbed and put to one's own use. Arakawa would always emphasize that Oh should use this technique with the pitcher, so that each at bat would be like a samurai sword fight or a sumo wrestling match—a battle between two individuals that affects all that is around them.

Arakawa also began instructing Oh in his theory of hitting, which was down swinging, or hitting downward through the ball, so that is was met at the nadir of the swing as it started upward, with the wrists exploding forward after contact was made. Moving pictures of Oh after he established his style show a swing that looks remarkably like that of a professional golfer with an elaborate backswing, downswing through the ball, and a high followthrough. The wrist explosion technique is very similar to the technique of Hank Aaron, the greatest American home run hitter.

In spite of Arakawa's help, the early part of 1962 was a disaster for Oh. Then in June, Arakawa ordered Oh to bat one-footed, holding his right, or front, foot off the ground. It was an extreme measure to solve a hitch, a double back-swing, that Oh had developed. Because he would have fallen down if he tried a double back-swing, it worked. He got a single and a home run the first two at bats, and Oh's famous "flamingo," or scarecrow, stance was born. By the end of the year, Oh was hitting .272 and led the league in home runs (38), games played (134), runs scored (79), total bases (281), runs batted in (95), walks (84), and intentional walks (9). It was a stunning turnaround. There developed the so-called O-N Cannon, the middle of the order for the Giants featuring first baseman Oh and third baseman Nagashima. They were the equivalent of Babe Ruth and Lou Gehrig for the Yankees, completely dominating the batting crowns for Japan's leagues.

From 1962 to 1979, Oh dominated Japanese baseball, leading the league each year in at least one, and usually in several, categories. He was extremely durable, playing every game eleven of his twenty-two years and never missing more than ten games in a season. He led the league in home runs thirteen straight times and fifteen in total. In 1964, he hit 55 home runs in a 140 game season, equal to Ruth's pace in his 60 in 154 games. From 1962 to 1980, he never hit less than thirty home runs in a season, including two other fifty-plus seasons and ten more in the forties. In the same years that he led in home runs, he also led the league in runs scored, thus benefitting from Nagashima's runs batted in ability. Oh himself led the league in runs batted in thirteen times, including a run of eight straight as Nagashima aged and retired. Oh also led the league in bases on balls nineteen times out of twenty-two years, including sixteen years in intentional walks. This occurred because of his fearsome reputation and his excellent eye. He was often compared to Ted Williams for his refusal to swing at a ball that was out of the strike zone. Surprisingly, he never led the league in strikeouts, and, as he matured, his strikeouts decreased. Five times he hit more home runs that he struck out, a very unusual feat for a power hitter in any league. He also led in total bases twelve times, in hits three times, and in doubles once. The most underrated part of Oh's game was his fielding. Nine times he won the golden glove as the first baseman with the highest fielding average, and his career fielding average was .994. He was the Gil Hodges of Japan, a fine power hitter who was slow afoot but graceful and quick and so knowledgeable about the game that he almost never made an error. Yet in Oh's autobiography, or in any other publication in English, this ability is never mentioned. Philosophically, Oh was a hitter who played first base so that he would be allowed to hit.

From 1965 to 1973, the Giants won both the Central League pennant and the Japan Series, the longest run of success in Japanese baseball history, surpassing the runs of the great Yankee teams of the 1930's and 1940's. In 1973 and 1974, Oh reached his zenith with back-to-back triple crowns, leading the league both times in home runs, runs batted in, and batting average, something no other player has ever done in any league.

By 1975, Oh's goal became surpassing Babe Ruth in home runs and, if possible, his friend Hank Aaron, who was still playing and with whom Oh put on some famous home run exhibition contests. On October 11, 1976, Oh hit home run number

715, surpassing Ruth. In the same month, Aaron retired, giving Oh a definite goal for the overall record. On September 3, 1977, Oh hit his 756th home run, surpassing Aaron. There was a tremendous outpouring of acclaim, particularly throughout Asia, where he was seen as a continent-wide hero. By the time Oh retired, he had hit 868 home runs with an average of one home run to every 10.7 at bats, a better average than either Ruth or Aaron. He had been an All Star for eighteen years and most valuable player in Japan's Central League nine times.

When Oh began to have vision and coordination problems, he tailed off to .236 in 1980, though he still hit thirty home runs. He retired at the end of the year and was named assistant manager of the Giants. At the end of the 1983 season, he became the manager. Originally, like so many other all-stars who became managers, he had problems, but in 1988 he led the Giants to their first pennant in several years and seems to have built another dynasty. His managerial style is a combination of Japanese hard work and discipline with the understanding of how to use star players to the best of their ability.

### Summary

By consensus, Sadaharu Oh was the greatest player in Japanese baseball history, the only one whom all observers agree could have been a star in the American major leagues. He hit more home runs, 868, than any other man in organized baseball while playing twenty-two years with the Yomiuri Giants in the Central League in Japan. When he retired, he also held the Japanese career records in runs batted in, runs scored, and total bases as well as the second highest marks in doubles and games played.

No one ever dominated an organized baseball league so completely for so long. Ruth won twelve home run titles and Aaron won four, but Oh won that title in the Central League fifteen times. His domination in runs batted in is actually even more astounding: He won the title thirteen times. His 2,504 bases on balls are more than 400 more than any other player, and no American player has won the Most Valuable Player Award more than three times—Oh won it nine times.

Philosophically and psychologically, Oh's dedication to Japanese self-discipline and martial arts was quite significant in enhancing not only his own reputation but also that of those aspects of life. Yet at the same time, his continuing status as a Chinese national remains one of the principal symbols of the Japanese internationalization movement. Nothing can be more symbolic of the tremendous popularity that Oh, more than any other player and manager, brought to Japanese baseball than the Tokyo Dome, which opened in the spring of 1988. It is the "House that Oh built."

### Bibliography

"Bambino San." *Psychology Today* 25, no. 3 (May-June, 1992). Discusses Oh's use of martial arts to enhance his performance in the game of baseball.

Deford, Frank. "Move Over for Oh-san." *Sports Illustrated* 47 (August 15, 1977). This is an excellent summary of Oh's life and hitting techniques. It emphasizes heavily his Chinese heritage and the discrimination that has been occasioned by that heritage. It was written just before Oh broke Aaron's record.

McCallum, Jack, and Richard O'Brien. "Hall *Oh* Fame." *Sports Illustrated* 86, no. 1 (January 13, 1997). The author argues that Oh should be admitted to the U. S. Baseball Hall of Fame.

Obojski, Robert. *The Rise of Japanese Baseball Power.* Radnor, Pa.: Chilton, 1975. Much more popularistic than Whiting, this book deals often with Oh. There is, however, no specific section outlining his life and accomplishments.

Oh, Sadaharu, and David Falkner. *Sadaharu Oh: A Zen Way of Baseball.* New York: Times, 1984. This is Oh's autobiography, written while he was still an assistant manager. He emphasizes Japanese philosophy and martial arts as well as baseball. In many ways it is a tribute to Arakawa, but it also includes excellent statistics and an appendix giving the opinions of many American major leaguers about Oh. It is by far the most comprehensive of all books.

Whiting, Robert. *The Chrysanthemum and the Bat: Baseball Samurai Style.* New York: Dodd Mead, 1977. This is the best overview of Japanese baseball in English. It devotes one section to Oh who, though not yet retired, is seen as the most outstanding of all Japanese players. He also appears many other times in the book. It is only here that one can learn that Oh was extremely well-paid with a total income of some $400,000 a year in the mid 1970's. Oh is also shown as modest, hardworking, and extremely popular.

———. "The Master of Besaboru." *Sports Illustrated* 71 (August 21, 1989): 68-69. This is a short section of a major summary of Japanese sports. It is the best commentary in English on Oh's managerial style. Oh is the only Japanese baseball player or manager mentioned by name.

*Fred S. Rolater*

# GEORGIA O'KEEFFE

*Born:* November 15, 1887; Sun Prairie, Wisconsin
*Died:* March 6, 1986; Santa Fe, New Mexico
*Area of Achievement:* Art
*Contribution:* Breaking with European traditionalism, Georgia O'Keeffe pointed to new ways to perceive the world about her, creating precise, sometimes stark depictions of nature and of urban scenes.

## Early Life

For her first twenty-eight years, Georgia Totto O'Keeffe was an artistic revolution waiting to erupt. Georgia, the second of seven children born to Francis and Ida Totto O'Keeffe in rural Wisconsin, was fascinated by art. By age ten, she wanted to be a painter, although she did not know what that entailed. When people pressed her to tell them what kind of painter she wanted to be, she invariably replied, "A portrait painter."

O'Keeffe's early training in art began with a local art teacher and continued in a parochial school. When the nun who taught art told the impressionable child that she was painting things too small, Georgia obliged by painting her subjects large, sometimes so large that her pictures overflowed their boundaries, as many of her later floral paintings would.

In 1905-1906, O'Keeffe attended the Art Institute in Chicago, where she was embarrassed to paint nude men and where she was schooled in an ultraconservative, highly traditional European style of painting. She spent the following year at the Art Students League in New York City, where, as had been the case in Chicago, her painting received favorable comment and won prizes.

O'Keeffe, however, was not receiving the kind of instruction she needed. Unwilling to go through life painting dead rabbits and pastoral scenes, she gave up painting in 1908, becoming a commercial artist in Chicago. She designed the rosy-cheeked girl who still graces cans of Dutch Cleanser. O'Keeffe hated commercial art but, needing to earn a living, she stayed with it until she fell ill, suffering a temporary impairment to her vision. She returned to her family, who had relocated in Virginia in 1903.

During this interval, O'Keeffe took a summer course at the University of Virginia, which did not admit women but allowed them to study in summer school. The instructor, Alon Bement, was a disciple of Arthur Dow of Columbia University, an artist who, influenced by Oriental art, had broken away from European artistic conventions. O'Keeffe eventually studied with Dow, who changed forever the way she saw things and re-created them.

From 1912 to 1914, O'Keeffe taught art in Amarillo, Texas, where she was intrigued by the big sky and the broad, seemingly endless plains. In 1915, she spent an abortive semester teaching at Columbia College in South Carolina, but the following fall she became an art instructor at West Texas State Normal School in Canyon.

It was during this teaching stint that O'Keeffe sent some of her charcoal drawings to her New York friend Anita Pollitzer, who showed them to photographer Alfred Stieglitz. He exhibited them in 1916—without O'Keeffe's knowledge or consent—at his 291 Gallery. This showing marked the beginning of Georgia O'Keeffe's future as an artist.

## Life's Work

When Georgia O'Keeffe, recently arrived from Texas to continue her studies with Arthur Dow, learned that Alfred Stieglitz had shown her work without authorization, she stormed into his studio to confront him. When the two met, however, Stieglitz's enthusiastic assessment of her work mollified her.

Stieglitz, whose reputation in the art world was solid, held another exhibition of O'Keeffe's work in 1917. She was in Texas when this exhibition was held, but Stieglitz won O'Keeffe's heart by rehanging the entire exhibition for her alone when she arrived in New York shortly after the closing.

During her years in west Texas, O'Keeffe imbibed its stark landscape and intense colors, regularly painting the nearby Palo Duro Canyon, a favorite subject. Her artwork, always precise, began to show a new depth and originality in both its use of light and its angularity.

O'Keeffe was developing one of her most significant skills, an ability to paint something as static as a tree or flower yet imbue the painting with incredible motion and dynamism. Nothing in an O'Keeffe still life is at rest; everything moves. The charcoal sketches that first attracted Stieglitz's attention reflect this motion, but as O'Keeffe experimented with color and light, the motion in her still lifes became explosive.

By 1918, O'Keeffe was ready to leave west Texas. When Stieglitz arranged for her to receive a subvention in support of her painting, she willingly moved to New York and soon was living with Stieglitz. Her years in west Texas did much to shape O'Keeffe's later work. She had discovered the unique quality of light in the southwestern desert. Also, in search of objects for her students to paint, she stumbled upon the notion of using sun-bleached animal bones, which were plentiful in the surrounding desert.

Although she did not herself begin to paint animal skulls and pelvises until more than a decade later, she had gained an appreciation for the kind of patina that sun-drenched bones acquire and for their translucence. For the next decade, however, O'Keeffe, who had first visited Santa Fe, New Mexico, just before her return to New York, remained in the East. In 1924, she was married to Stieglitz, now divorced from the wife he had left in 1918.

The life O'Keeffe and Stieglitz had established in 1918—summers at the Stieglitz family home at Lake George in New York's Adirondack Mountains, winters in New York City—continued throughout the 1920's. O'Keeffe, Stieglitz's favorite model, spent much of her time and creative energy posing for his photographs, which he exhibited widely.

O'Keeffe was finding subjects for her own painting both at Lake George and in New York City. In 1925, the couple moved into an apartment on the thirtieth floor of Lexington Avenue's Shelton Hotel from which O'Keeffe commanded a view that extended to the East River. Here she painted her famed New York cityscapes.

Her paintings of industrial scenes along the East River and of various buildings in New York City marked a new direction in O'Keeffe's career as an artist and reflected the influence of John Marin, whose paintings of industrial scenes impressed her when she first saw them in 1915.

In the 1920's, O'Keeffe also painted many still lifes—particularly flowers—and scenes from the Lake George summers. Perhaps the most interesting of her urban paintings is *The Shelton with Sunspots* (1926). The towering building in which O'Keeffe and Stieglitz lived springs from the bottom of the canvas like the prow of a ship, many of its details obscured by blinding sunspots that bounce off the hotel's windows. O'Keeffe imbues this painting of a bland, commonplace skyscraper with conflict. It has been suggested that O'Keeffe, who suffered from migraine headaches, replicated in this picture the play of light that sometimes accompanies that malady.

In 1929, Mabel Dodge Luhan invited Georgia O'Keeffe, who by now was well known, to visit her ranch in Taos, New Mexico. Because Stieglitz refused to venture west of the Hudson River, O'Keeffe went to New Mexico alone, remaining at the Luhan ranch from April until August. This trip heralded a new direction in O'Keeffe's life and work.

From that point on, she would spend most of her summers in New Mexico, doing so until 1946, when Stieglitz died. O'Keeffe moved permanently to Abiquiu, north of Santa Fe, in 1949. She had bought a house at Ghost Ranch, fifteen miles north of Abiquiu, in 1940 and occupied both houses until encroaching feebleness necessitated her final move to Santa Fe in 1984.

In Taos, O'Keeffe learned to drive and bought a car. Every day during her New Mexican summers, she packed her equipment into her car, which rode high off the ground, and drove into the desert to paint. When the desert heat oppressed O'Keeffe, she stretched out beneath the car's chassis.

The desert paintings represent a large portion of O'Keeffe's most celebrated work. Her paintings of animal bones—*Cow's Skull: Red, White, and Blue* (1931), *Ram's Head with Hollyhock* (1937), and *Pelvis with Moon* (1943)—representing an extended period in her artistic career, are among her most puckish works.

O'Keeffe enjoyed painting the soft, flowing lines and angles of adobe buildings, as seen in such paintings as her *Ranchos Church* (1930) or *Black Patio Door* (1955), to which such Lake George paintings as her *Stables* (1932) and *Barn with Snow* (1933) contrast sharply.

After Stieglitz's death, O'Keeffe became a world traveler. Many thought she had now entered her abstract period. Actually, many of the paintings she produced between 1946 and 1980 were photographically realistic representations of scenes she observed from more than 30,000 feet up as she jetted across the sky. Among her most famous paintings of this period is an enormous canvas, *Sky Above Clouds II* (1963).

Living to be nearly a hundred, Georgia O'Keeffe painted until failing eyesight forced her into a brief retirement with her companion, Juan Hamilton, and his family in Santa Fe. There she died quietly on March 6, 1986.

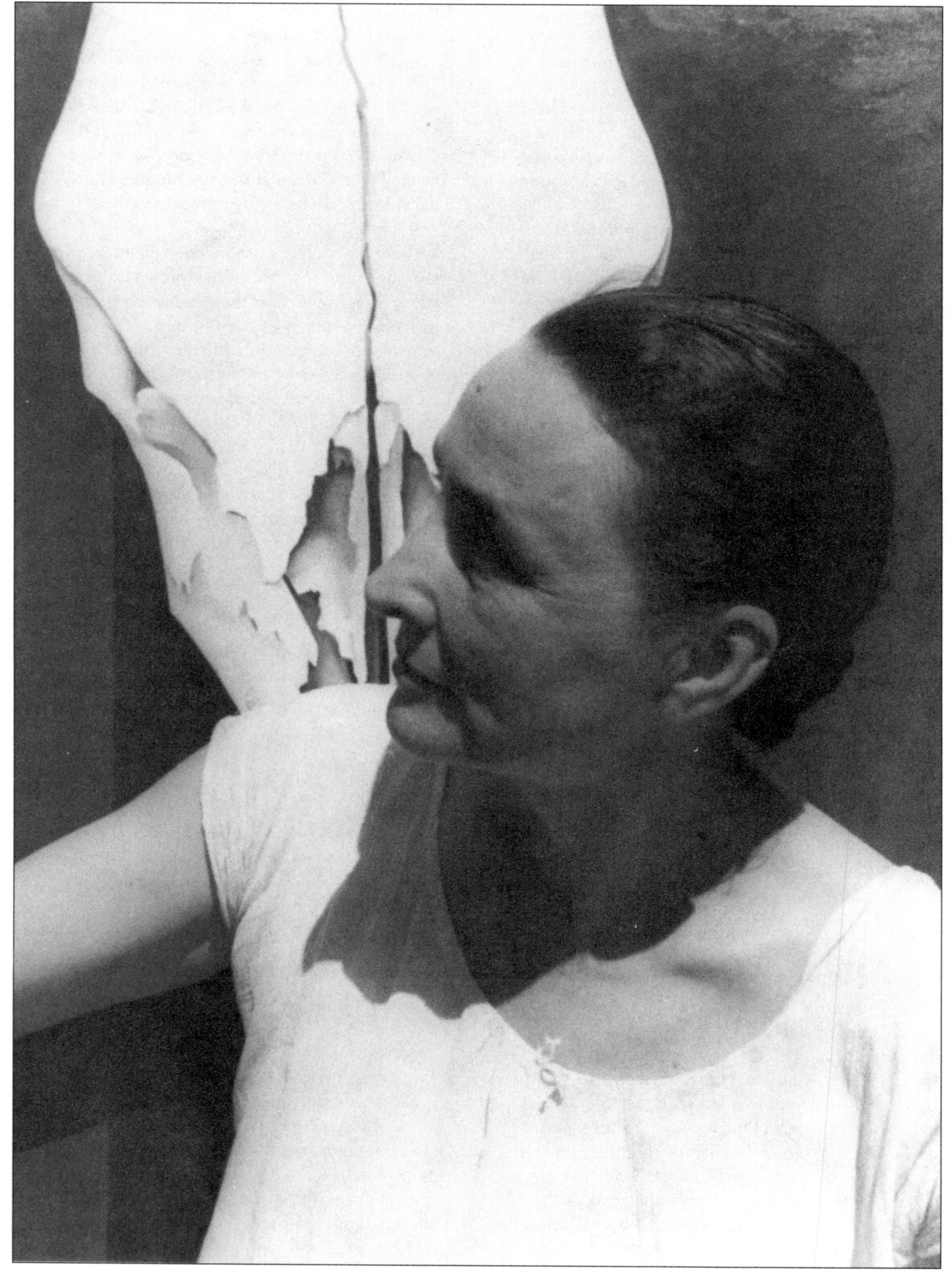

### Summary

Georgia O'Keeffe always insisted that she was an artist, not a woman artist. She denied that gender had much to do with accomplishment and, from her earliest exhibitions, demonstrated that she could hold her own with her masculine competitors. Indeed, as an artist, she was superior to most of them.

During nearly a century of life, Georgia O'Keeffe continually grew professionally. She constantly tried new things. She considered no subject lacking in artistic potential, as her preoccupation with bones, paper flowers from New Mexican graveyards, conventional urban buildings, and scenes of smokestack industries clearly demonstrates.

O'Keeffe saw things as no one else saw them. Many subsequent artists have tried to imitate her floral paintings, for example, producing huge flowers crammed into canvases too small to accommodate them. Somehow, O'Keeffe could do that and, in the process, communicate something about the essence of a flower that no one had captured before. Her imitators end up with crowded canvases that look cramped. Perhaps an artist's imitators suggest more accurately than words can the true greatness of the artist they seek to copy.

In O'Keeffe's work, one finds the zeal for life that so well characterized her as a person. O'Keeffe left a legacy of hope to artists in all fields who dare to deviate drastically from artistic convention. O'Keeffe neither disparaged her predecessors nor imitated them. She was truly and completely her own person.

### Bibliography

Ciboire, Clive, ed. *Lovingly, Georgia: The Complete Correspondence of Georgia O'Keeffe and Anita Pollitzer*. New York: Simon and Schuster, 1990. Georgia O'Keeffe maintained a correspondence with Anita Pollitzer, a classmate at Columbia University, for more than forty years. Much of it is reproduced here.

Didion, Joan. *The White Album*. New York: Simon and Schuster, and London: Weidenfeld and Nicolson, 1979. Didion's "Georgia O'Keeffe" discusses O'Keeffe's reaction to "the men," the power structure that determined the artistic and aesthetic principles of the art world of her day.

Dijkstra, Bram. *Georgia O'Keeffe and the Eros of Place*. Princeton, N.J.: Princeton University Press, 1998. The author challenges the generally accepted view that O'Keeffe's work was influenced by modernists, claiming that her American upbringing was the more significant force.

Eisler, Benita. *O'Keeffe and Stieglitz: An American Romance*. New York: Doubleday, 1991. Eisler provides crucial insights into the sometimes stormy but always symbiotic relationship that existed between O'Keeffe and Stieglitz for the forty years they knew each other. Contains many of Stieglitz's photographs of O'Keeffe.

Eldredge, Charles C. *Georgia O'Keefe: American and Modern*. New Haven, Conn.: Yale University Press, 1996. Eldredge focuses on O'Keeffe's work and her interest in Freudian theory, transcendentalism, and feminism.

Lisle, Laurie. *Portrait of an Artist: A Biography of Georgia O'Keeffe*. New York: Seaview, 1980. A sensitive and accurate biography of O'Keeffe. The author understands the artist's artistic orientation and how she uses her environment artistically.

Messinger, Lisa Mintz. *Georgia O'Keeffe*. New York: Metropolitan Museum of Art, 1988; London: Thames and Hudson, 1989. This book, aside from O'Keeffe's autobiography, contains the best reproductions of O'Keeffe's work. It offers reproductions of the twenty-nine works in the collection of the Metropolitan Museum of Art. Well written and insightful.

O'Keeffe, Georgia. *Georgia O'Keeffe*. New York: Viking Press, 1976; London: Penguin, 1983. If one could read only one book relating to O'Keeffe, this autobiography would be the sensible choice. An indispensable book for anyone seriously interested in O'Keeffe.

Peters, Sarah Whitaker. *Becoming O'Keeffe: The Early Years*. New York: Abbeville Press, 1991. Peters offers a sensitive and spirited look into the making of an artist. Excellent illustrations.

Robinson, Roxana. *Georgia O'Keeffe: A Life*. New York: Harper, 1989; London: Bloomsbury, 1990. The most comprehensive biography of Georgia O'Keeffe to date. Well written and amply illustrated. The illustrations, however, do not include reproductions of O'Keeffe's work, which are readily available in the autobiography.

Shuman, R. Baird. *Georgia O'Keeffe*. Vero Beach, Fla.: Rourke, 1993. Intended for the nonspecialist, this book contains excellent illustrations, a chronology, and an annotated bibliography. It provides accurate coverage of O'Keeffe's life and work.

*R. Baird Shuman*

# SEÁN T. O'KELLY

*Born:* August 25, 1882; Dublin, Ireland
*Died:* November 23, 1966; Dublin, Ireland
*Areas of Achievement:* Diplomacy, government, and politics
*Contribution:* O'Kelly was one of the pioneers of the Gaelic Revival and the Irish Independence movement. After independence had been secured for the southern twenty-six counties of Ireland, O'Kelly emerged as a mainstay of the Fianna Fail Party and a leading statesmen for the Irish Free State and the Republic of Ireland. He culminated his public career with two terms as president of Ireland.

## Early Life

Seán Thomas O'Kelly was born in Dublin, Ireland, into a Catholic working-class family. His father was Samuel O'Kelly, a bootmaker by profession, and his mother was Catherine O'Dea. The family was always in straitened circumstances, and Seán's education was adequate, at best: He attended Christian Brothers' School (St. Mary's Place) and O'Connell Schools (North Richmond Street). He achieved a major breakthrough in 1898 when, at the age of sixteen, he was employed at the National Library of Ireland on Kildare Street in Dublin as a messenger and errand boy. During his term of employment at the library (1898-1902), he profited from its facilities and largely educated himself, developing his writing skills to the extent that he was able to practice freelance journalism and, in 1903, become a full-time journalist.

The Gaelic Nationalist Revival, which blossomed in Ireland in the years after the eclipse of Charles Stewart Parnell's constitutional nationalist movement in 1891, exerted a major influence upon the young O'Kelly, who adopted it as his life's cause. The broadly based Gaelic Revivalist phenomenon encompassed culture (literature, art, drama, language, and sports), religion, and politics, and O'Kelly flung himself into each of these. In 1903, he had come to the notice of nationalist leader Arthur Griffith and joined Griffith's Sinn Féin Party, which at that stage advocated the creation of a dual monarchy on the Austro-Hungarian model for Britain and Ireland.

As an active member of the Gaelic League (Conradh na Gaelige), which focused upon language revival, O'Kelly became managing editor for its publication *An Claidheamh* while regularly contributing to Griffith's paper, *United Irishman*. In 1905, Griffith made him a full journalistic associate.

## Life's Work

In 1906, O'Kelly ran for Dublin City Council on the Sinn Féin ticket and was elected, launching what would be a fifty-three-year political career. He was to serve on the Dublin Council until 1932. O'Kelly became honorary secretary for Sinn Féin from 1908 to 1910 and would serve as general secretary for the Gaelic League from 1915 to 1920.

As hopes for a constitutional solution through Home Rule establishing a separate Irish Parliament under the Crown were repeatedly frustrated, first by recurring vetoes of the Home Rule Bill by the Conservative-dominated House of Lords and then by Ulster Protestant resistance, Sinn Féin drifted away from dual monarchy to a more radical revolutionary nationalism centering on the establishment of an independent Irish republic. The Parliament Act of 1911 curtailed the House of Lords' veto power. Instead of a permanent, absolute veto as before, the upper house could now only delay the passage of a bill for two successive parliamentary sessions. If a bill could pass the House of Commons in three successive sessions, it would automatically become law. The Irish Home Rule Bill carried the House of Commons in 1912 and 1913 and appeared destined for certain passage during the summer of 1914. However, Ulster Unionist Protestants swore to oppose the implementation of the bill by armed force if necessary. By 1913 they had assembled a paramilitary force named the Ulster Volunteers, which numbered some ninety thousand members armed with rifles that had been illegally smuggled into the port of Lame, County Antrim. In response, Irish nationalists formed their own counterparamilitary force, the Irish Volunteers, in November of 1913; O'Kelly, who was one of its founders, played a crucial role in smuggling in arms through Kilcoole, County Wicklow.

The Ulster Resistance and the outbreak of World War I caused the British government to delay its plans for Home Rule. Though most of the Irish seemed to accept the situation, a radical minority within the Irish Volunteers led by Patrick Pearse and numbering O'Kelly among their supporters favored an immediate uprising against British rule. During the consequent Easter Rebellion of 1916,

*Seán T. O'Kelly (center), at a formal reception.*

O'Kelly participated as Pearse's staff captain and was held in Richmond Prison, Dublin, upon the rebellion's collapse. Upon Pearse's execution and the assumption of the Sinn Féin presidency by Eamon De Valera, O'Kelly became one of De Valera's chief lieutenants. Sent to continued imprisonment in Wales, O'Kelly was released, then quickly rearrested, but he managed to escape by May of 1917 and successfully campaigned for a parliamentary seat for County Longford.

In 1918 he was named director in charge of organizing Sinn Féin's general elections campaign; it was an overwhelming success, and O'Kelly was himself elected a member of Parliament for College Green, Dublin. He therefore sat on the first independent Irish Dail, as Sinn Féin members of Parliament styled themselves, on January 21, 1919. During the War for Irish Independence, O'Kelly served as Dail Speaker and as Irish emissary to both Italy and France, where he unsuccessfully attempted to present his country's case before the Versailles Conference. O'Kelly joined De Valera in opposition to the Anglo-Irish Treaty and Partition of 1921-1922, serving the Republican cause during the Irish Civil War of 1922-1923. Incarcerated by the victorious Free State forces, he was released before the end of 1923.

When De Valera formed the Fianna Fail Party in opposition to the governing Cumann na Gael group, which had established the Irish Free State, O'Kelly became its deputy leader in 1926 and was elected to the Dail the following year. In De Valera's first Fianna Fail government, O'Kelly served as minister of local government and public health (1932-1939). In 1932 he also relinquished his place on Dublin City Council, having served almost continually since 1906. In at least one significant respect, O'Kelly's first ministerial tenure marked a continuation of his efforts at city council level. He had always advocated programs for improved housing for lower-income families (perhaps as a result of his family's situation during his own formative years) and, as minister, implemented the building of working-class cottages. During this time, O'Kelly was instrumental in the drawing up and ratification of the Eire Constitution of 1937, which personified his dreams and those of De Valera for a Catholic, theoretically self-sufficient, rural Ireland where Gaelic would be as much (if not more) a part of everyday speech as English. It was a constitution that assigned a favored position to the Catholic Church and specifically reasserted the Irish government's claim to sovereignty over the six counties of Northern Ireland.

In 1939, O'Kelly was given the ministerial portfolio for Education, which he held for only a few weeks before being transferred to head the Ministry for Finance from 1939 to 1945. In 1945, Douglas Hyde, who was the first president of Ireland elected under the Irish Constitution of 1937, declined to run for a second seven-year term, and O'Kelly was convincingly elected under the Fianna Fail banner. He served two terms, from 1945 to 1959, after being reelected without opposition in 1952. His role as president included presiding over the change from the Free State (Eire) to establishing the Republic of Ireland in 1949. He also assumed a nonpolitical, conciliatory role as far as attempting to distance the country from the lingering animosities of Partition and civil war.

O'Kelly married twice, first to Mary Kate Ryan, daughter of John Ryan of Tomcoole, County Wexford, from 1918 to 1934, when she died. Two years later, he married her younger sister, Phyllis. There were no children from either marriage. In 1959 O'Kelly refused to run for a third term and retired to his home in Roundwood, County Wicklow, while De Valera succeeded to the presidency. O'Kelly died in Dublin on November 23, 1966, and was survived by his second wife.

### Summary

Seán T. O'Kelly was one of those figures whose effective work was largely accomplished behind the scenes. In a better sense, he conducted his career as the ideal "right-hand man," first for Griffith, then Pearse, and finally De Valera. His preferred role was as a backroom negotiator, conciliator, and power broker who shunned the limelight and deferred to his more flamboyant superiors. O'Kelly's contribution is thus often difficult to gauge. One is often at a loss to know where his ideas and those of De Valera began and ended; the two men were nearly identical as far as their political and social vision of the nature of an independent Ireland.

The De Valera-O'Kelly vision has been a mixed legacy for Ireland. The dominant role assigned to the Catholic faith as stated in the 1937 constitution, the clerical legislation enacted under the auspices of De Valera's ministries, and the continuing claims of the Irish Republic over Ulster have undoubtedly contributed to subsequent Protestant Unionist resistance, the resurgence of nationalist violence, and the troubles in the North. The Irish language, though rescued from extinction, did not supplant English as Ireland's dominant spoken or written language, and a rural, self-sufficient Ireland never seems to have been a practical aspiration. In recent years there has been a repudiation of O'Kelly's romantic vision: The Catholic clergy is held in lesser esteem, divorce and birth control have been legalized, Ireland has experienced increasing economic diversification, and the republic has been integrated into the European Community. It was during his tenure as president that O'Kelly achieved the detachment from the political arena that enabled him to come more into his own and to independently become a voice for conciliation. As ceremonial head of state, he was also able to represent his country abroad and establish the Irish presidency as a viable part of the government.

### Bibliography

Allen, Kieran. *Fianna Fail and Irish Labour: 1926 to the Present*. London and Chicago: Pluto Press, 1997. Though somewhat specialized and thus at times peripheral to the "grand scheme" of Irish political history, this monograph is important for the insights into the ruralist attitudes of the leaders of the Fianna Fail Party toward the very urbanized phenomenon of the Irish working class.

Bowman, John. *De Valera and the Ulster Question: 1917-1923*. Oxford and New York: Clarendon Press, 1982. Sheds a great deal of light on the inner workings of the early Republican Movement and the shaping of sentiment regarding the counties of Northern Ireland and the 1922 Partition.

Dunphy, Richard. *The Making of Fianna Fail Power in Ireland: 1923-1948*. Oxford: Clarendon Press, and New York: Oxford University Press, 1995. Offers the best and most detailed examination of the philosophy, composition, and strategy of De Valera's Party and the most definitive view of the significant contribution rendered by O'Kelly in his role as deputy leader.

Lawlor, Sheila. *Britain and Ireland: 1914-1923*. Dublin: Gill & Macmillan, 1983. Scholarly, objective summary of all aspects of the fragile relationship between Britain and Ireland, including evidence of O'Kelly's persistent, behind-the-scenes activities during an early stage of his career.

Lee, J. J. *Ireland, 1912-1985: Politics and Society.* Cambridge and New York: Cambridge University Press, 1989. Broadest account of the overall politics and personalities of the Irish Free State and the early Republic of Ireland.

Macardle, Dorothy. *The Irish Republic*. London: Gollancz, 1937; New York: Farrar Straus, 1965. Covers the years 1916 to 1923. Though heavily biased in favor of the anti-Treaty views of De Valera and O'Kelly, Macardle provides some useful information for the student of this period.

Martin, F. X., T. W. Moody, F. J. Byrne. *The Course of Irish History.* Rev. ed. Cork, Ireland: Mercier Press, 1984. This is still the most informative book as far as providing a background and placing the early twentieth century events into the broad sweep of Irish history. Though it falls short of detailed explanation in certain respects, the book commends itself as an adequate reference for beginners.

*Raymond Pierre Hylton*

## SIR LAURENCE OLIVIER

*Born:* May 22, 1907; Dorking, Surrey, England
*Died:* June 11, 1989; near Ashurst, West Sussex, England
*Areas of Achievement:* Theater and cinema
*Contribution:* Widely considered the greatest twentieth century actor in the English-speaking world, Olivier has also been a distinguished theater manager and stage and film director and producer who has done more than anyone else to bring William Shakespeare's works to the screen.

### Early Life

The third and youngest child of the Reverend Gerald Olivier, Laurence Olivier grew up in a series of Anglican parsonages in and around London. The ritual and pageantry of Anglican worship gave young Laurence, a choirboy, a sense of the theatrical. At the age of nine, he entered All Saints School in London and the next year played Brutus in Shakespeare's *Julius Caesar.* In the audience were the great players Ellen Terry and Sir Johnston Forbes-Robertson, who found Olivier's performance remarkable and saw him as a potentially great actor. Later, at school, Olivier played Maria in *Twelfth Night* and Katharina in *The Taming of the Shrew.* The latter show was so impressive that it was put on again at the Shakespeare Memorial Theatre at Stratford-upon-Avon, Olivier's first appearance in a professional theater. In 1921, Olivier entered St. Edward's School, where he was cast as Puck in *A Midsummer Night's Dream.* When his older brother went off to India, Olivier wanted to follow him, whereupon his father said, "Don't be such a fool; you're not going to India, you're going on the stage." Accordingly, Olivier studied under Elsie Fogerty at the Central School of Speech Training and Dramatic Art. Upon graduation, he started off as callboy, bit player, and understudy in various theaters; toured with the Lena Ashwell Players; acted with Sybil Thorndike and Lewis Casson; and, in 1927, joined the Birmingham Repertory. In Birmingham and London, he played a great variety of roles, taking advantage of all opportunities. Olivier's break came when a London theater club put on a new play by R. C. Sherriff, then an unknown author. In *Journey's End,* directed by James Whale, Olivier played the lead of Captain Stanhope, trying to survive the stress of command in the trenches during World War I. Instantly hailed as a masterpiece, *Journey's End* has come to be considered one of the great war plays of all time. Olivier's performance made him a star. The play was slated for a brief run, however, and Olivier had auditioned for and been selected to play the lead in a stage version of P. C. Wren's *Beau Geste. Beau Geste* failed dismally, while a professional revival of *Journey's End,* now starring Colin Clive, became an immense hit, ran for several years, and was filmed. At first Olivier seemed to have made a fatal mistake, but as it turned out, he may have done well after all, for while Clive played Stanhope repeatedly, Olivier was able to play a variety of roles and established himself as a versatile and dynamic performer.

### Life's Work

The most notable of Olivier's early roles was Victor Prynne opposite Noël Coward and Gertrude Lawrence in Coward's *Private Lives.* In 1933, Olivier starred as a neurotic homosexual in a stage adaptation of Louis Bromfield's novel *The Green Bay Tree* in New York. Motion-picture producers had noticed him, and beginning in 1929, he began a film career, starring in a number of competent but undistinguished films in both England and the United States. Hollywood then saw him as another Ronald Colman, and in fact, Olivier wore a Colman mustache and admits to imitating Colman during the late 1920's and early 1930's. Olivier was tested for the lead opposite Greta Garbo in *Queen Christina* (1933), a part that might have elevated him to stardom, but Garbo was dissatisfied with his audition and had him replaced with her frequent costar John Gilbert. Olivier's film career slipped back into mediocrity.

Onstage, Olivier continued to make a strong impression, in such roles as Tony Cavendish, a satiric portrait of John Barrymore, in Edna Ferber and George S. Kaufman's *Theatre Royal* (1934; directed by Coward). His major break came in 1935, when John Gielgud, who had directed him as Bothwell in Gordon Daviot's *Queen of Scots* the year before, invited him to alternate with him as Romeo and Mercutio in the production of *Romeo and Juliet* that Gielgud was directing. Gielgud, a few years older than Olivier, was then considered the great Shakespearean actor of the time, and alternating roles with him gave Olivier a chance to showcase his talent. Their performances were quite different,

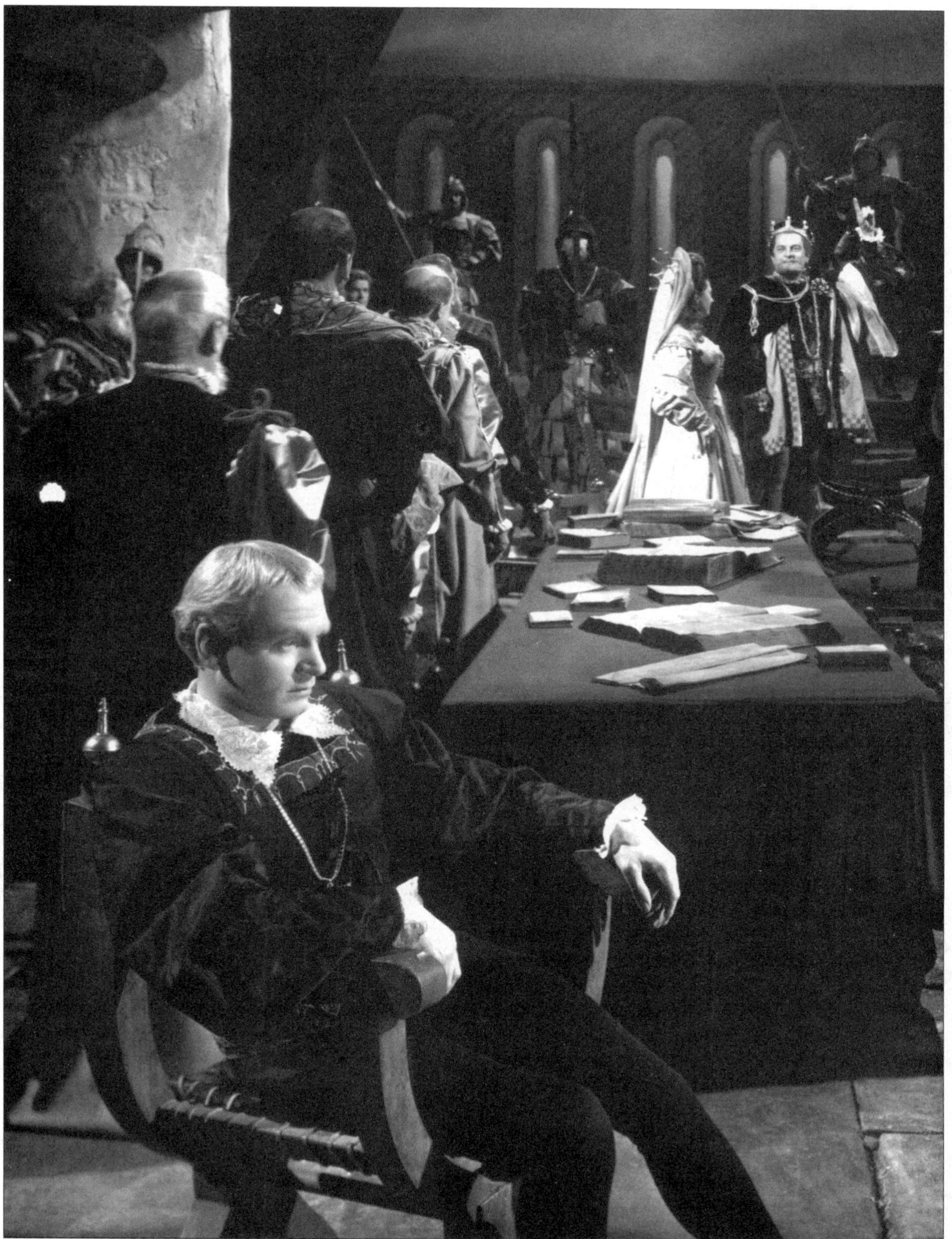

*Sir Lawrence Olivier as the title character in* Hamlet.

Gielgud almost singing his lines with a flutelike voice, while Olivier played with a raw, realistic energy and sexuality that disturbed some traditional critics but excited audiences. *Romeo and Juliet* was Olivier's first professional appearance in Shakespeare; he would go on to become the leading Shakespearean actor of the century on both stage and screen.

Olivier made his first Shakespearean film the next year as Orlando in *As You Like It* (1936), costarring Elisabeth Bergner and directed by her husband Paul Czinner. The film has considerable charm but is flawed by Bergner's German accent. Olivier thought it a failure, but in his later Shakespeare films he cast some of its players and commissioned scores by its composer, William Walton. Also in 1936, Olivier appeared in J. B. Priestley's *Bees on the Boat Deck*, a forgettable work, but notable for its casting of Olivier for the first time with Ralph Richardson, with whom he would act frequently and who became one of his closest friends. With *As You Like It*, Olivier's film career began to pick up. The next year, he was cast as the swashbuckling hero of *Fire over England* (1936), a historical epic about the Spanish Armada. Playing Queen Elizabeth was Flora Robson, who would be a frequent costar of Olivier. Cast opposite him as the female romantic lead was Vivien Leigh, a rising young star. Though she was married to barrister Leigh Holman and Olivier in 1930 had married actress Jill Esmond, by whom he had a son, Tarquin, Leigh had announced to a friend, when she first saw Olivier onstage in 1934, that she was going to marry him. During the filming of *Fire over England*, they became lovers.

In 1937, Olivier joined London's Old Vic Company, of which he was to be a member off and on until 1949. His first role with the company was Hamlet, under the direction of Tyrone Guthrie; after a successful London engagement, it was performed on the play's actual location, Elsinore Castle in Denmark. Leigh appeared as Ophelia. Also for the Old Vic in 1937, Olivier played Sir Toby Belch in *Twelfth Night* and the title roles in *Henry V* and *Macbeth*. The next year he played Coriolanus and was Iago to Ralph Richardson's Othello. Within three years, he had demonstrated an amazing versatility and established himself as the leading young Shakespearean actor.

The year 1937 saw him in the romantic comedy *The Divorce of Lady X*, his first film in color and the first in which he played opposite Richardson. His costar was Merle Oberon. When William Wyler cast Oberon as Cathy in Samuel Goldwyn's film of *Wuthering Heights* (1939), he cast Olivier as Heathcliff. In the role of the foundling stable boy who, alternately loved and spurned by Catherine Earnshaw, disappears, to return as a mysteriously wealthy gentleman determined to win her back from Edgar Linton, the man she married during his absence, Olivier made a dynamic impact and became an international star. Heathcliff is one of the roles for which he is best known, yet he almost failed in the part. Olivier confesses to having scorned filmmaking up to that time and to overacting shamelessly until director Wyler taught him to restrain his performance, to respect the medium, and to think in cinematic terms. From Wyler, Olivier learned film acting and direction. As Heathcliff, he won his first Academy Award nomination as best actor but lost to Robert Donat. The Best Actress Oscar that year went to Leigh in *Gone with the Wind* (1939). Suddenly, Heathcliff and Scarlett, lovers in private life, became the hottest romantic performers in motion pictures.

In 1940, the two actors capitalized on their popularity by costarring on the American stage in a production of *Romeo and Juliet* directed by Olivier. Surprisingly, it was a commercial failure, in which they lost most of their savings. To recoup, they returned to films, and in 1940, each of them had a great hit, Leigh in *Waterloo Bridge* and Olivier as the moody Maxim de Winter in Alfred Hitchcock's *Rebecca*, for which he received his second Oscar nomination. Also in 1940, Olivier played Mr. Darcy opposite Greer Garson as Elizabeth Bennett in a superb film version of *Pride and Prejudice*. That year, having divorced their respective spouses, Olivier and Leigh secretly married at Colman's ranch and honeymooned on his yacht.

World War II had erupted in Europe, and to boost morale for the British war effort, Olivier and Leigh played Lord Nelson and Lady Hamilton in Alexander Korda's *That Hamilton Woman* (1941), with a literate script by Walter Reisch and Sheriff, climaxed by a spectacular Battle of Trafalgar. As the illicit and tragic lovers, the stars were at their best; the picture remains one of the great romantic films and is reputed to have been Winston Churchill's favorite film. Returning to England in 1940, Olivier joined the Royal Navy Fleet Air Arm from 1940 to 1944, serving as a pilot except for two stints in propaganda films. The first was *49th Parallel* (1941), in which he plays a French Canadian trapper shot by the invading crew of a Nazi submarine. In the second, *The Demi-Paradise* (1943), he plays a Soviet engineer who goes to England to invent a propeller that will enable ships bringing supplies to Russia to navigate the ice to Archangel and Murmansk.

Olivier's greatest propaganda film, however, and one of the greatest films ever made, is *Henry V* (1944), which he produced, starred in, and directed. Because of wartime economy, little money could be used to make the film, but Olivier turned the budgetary limitations into an artistic triumph. "On your imaginary forces work," says Shakespeare's chorus, and Olivier developed the concept to its fullest potential. He opens the film in 1600 at its first performance in the Globe Theatre, showing how plays were performed in Shakespeare's day. One sees a panoramic view of Tudor London, then moves into the theater, sees the audience gathering, vendors selling oranges, the actors preparing, the orchestra playing the overture. Then the players perform the first few scenes in the Globe itself. Not until the Chorus's second invocation of the imagination does the film shift to the fifteenth century, as one sees the king taking sail at Southhampton. Thereafter, instead of building lavish sets, Olivier used obviously painted backdrops that resembled the medieval illuminations *Les Très Riches Heures de Duc de Berry*. The result was a work of consummate artistry. He filmed the battle of Agincourt in Ireland, and the charge of the French knights, cut down by a hail of English arrows, is one of the most exciting moments in film. The acting was flawless; Olivier's performance ranged from regal dignity to sinister irony to the tense quiet of the night before the battle to ringing battlefield exhortations to the romantic humor of his wooing the French princess. Filmed in color, *Henry V* has the look of a sumptuous epic, despite its pinched budget. It was first shown to the troops in Europe, who supposedly took heart from such lines as "Once more into the breach" and "God for Harry, England, and Saint George!" Not until 1946 did it play in New York, but there it ran a record forty-six weeks. Olivier won a special Academy Award for "outstanding achievement as an actor, producer and director in bringing *Henry V* to the screen."

Meanwhile, Olivier returned to the stage with equal success. In June of 1944, he took a five-year contract as director of the Old Vic, where he and Ralph Richardson starred in hit after hit. In 1944-1945, Olivier played the Button Moulder in *Peer Gynt*, Sergius in George Bernard Shaw's *Arms and the Man*, and had a stunning success as Richard III, one of his greatest roles. The next year, he played Astrov in Anton Chekhov's *Uncle Vanya*, Hotspur in *Henry IV, Part I*, and Justice Shallow in *Henry IV, Part II*, opposite Ralph Richardson's Falstaff, and did a double bill of Sophocles' *Oedipus Rex*, followed by Mr. Puff in Richard Brinsley Sheridan's satiric farce *The Critic* in the same evening. These enormous successes he followed with the title role in *King Lear* (1946), with Alec Guinness as the Fool. In 1948, Olivier and Leigh toured Australia and New Zealand, with Olivier playing Sir Peter Teazle in Sheridan's *The School for Scandal*, an encore of *Richard III*, and Mr. Antrobus in Thornton Wilder's *The Skin of Our Teeth*.

Meanwhile, Olivier was preparing another Shakespearean picture, *Hamlet* (1948), which he filmed in black and white, dying his own hair blond to look Scandinavian. Though *Hamlet* is Olivier's favorite of his Shakespeare films and though it won the Academy Award for Best Picture of 1948 and for Olivier as Best Actor, it is not as successful as *Henry V*. Olivier cut several key soliloquies and instead spent much time having the camera move around the gloomy corridors of the castle, and his Freudian interpretation of the relationship between Gertrude and Hamlet is questionable. Nevertheless, Olivier's *Hamlet* is one of the most dynamic productions ever, stunningly directed and acted, with Olivier himself as an intense, brooding, ironic, dashing, even swashbuckling prince, who at the end makes a spectacular swan dive off a fifteen-foot wall onto the murderous king. More accessible to audiences than the experimental *Henry V*, *Hamlet* was even more popular. In addition to winning the Oscar for it, Olivier received a knighthood.

Back on the stage, Olivier directed Leigh in Tennessee Williams' *A Streetcar Named Desire* and then became manager of London's St. James Theatre, where he directed Christopher Fry's *Venus Observed* and played the role of the Duke of Altair. Next, opposite Leigh as Cleopatra, he was Caesar in Shaw's *Caesar and Cleopatra* and Antony in Shakespeare's *Antony and Cleopatra*, playing on alternate nights at the St. James, followed by a run in New York.

Aside from a cameo as a Cockney policeman in *The Magic Box* (1951), Olivier made no films for four years. In 1952, he returned to the screen as Hurstwood in Wyler's *Carrie*, adapted from Theodore Dreiser's *Sister Carrie* (1900). Olivier's first Hollywood film in twelve years, *Carrie* was a failure, despite brilliant performances by Olivier and Jennifer Jones and sterling direction by Wyler, because of the script by Ruth and Augustus Goetz, which turned Dreiser's grimly naturalistic novel into a romantic love story full of noblesse oblige. Olivier then coproduced and starred in Peter Brook's technicolor film of the eighteenth century musical drama *The Beggar's Opera* (1952), in which Olivier did his own singing and turned in a dashing performance as Macheath the highwayman. Though the script cuts some of playwright John Gay's more ironic dialogue and lyrics, the film has much brilliance and is by far the best cinematic rendering of an eighteenth century play. Unfortunately, it was caviar to the general and failed at the box office.

For the next two years, Olivier did no acting. One reason was Leigh, who for some years had been suffering from a manic-depressive illness and who broke down while filming *Elephant Walk* (1954) in Ceylon and had to be flown home. By 1955, she had recovered sufficiently to costar with Olivier during the summer season at Stratford-upon-Avon. Olivier played a hilarious Malvolio in *Twelfth Night*, a profoundly tragic king in *Macbeth* (hailed by many critics as the best Macbeth within memory), and a harrowing Titus in *Titus Andronicus*, with Vivien Leigh as a sprightly Viola, a sinister Lady Macbeth, and a suffering Lavinia. It was possibly the best summer Stratford ever had.

Meanwhile, Olivier had been at work directing *Richard III* (1955) as a technicolor film drenched in blood red. For film audiences, he repeated his sensational performance as Richard, with Richardson as Buckingham, Gielgud as Clarence, and Claire Bloom as Lady Anne. Though it rivals *Henry V* as Olivier's best Shakespearean film, it failed at the box office, partly because Olivier blundered by having it shown first on American black-and-white television, thus undercutting the potential theatrical audience. Olivier won another Oscar nomination but lost to Yul Brynner in *The King and I* (1956).

Olivier wanted to film *Macbeth* next but needed a commercial film first to make money and so agreed to direct and star opposite Marilyn Monroe in Terence Rattigan's *The Sleeping Prince*, a play he had done four years earlier. Unfortunately, he found Monroe quite difficult to work with; she was tardy, temperamental, and instead of taking Olivier's direction, turned to Paula Strasberg, wife of the dean of Method acting, Lee Strasberg, whom she had brought to coach her and lend moral support. A master of thespian technique, Olivier had no use for Method acting's dialectic and mumbling search for motivation. Consequently, though Monroe looked ravishing, the film, retitled *The Prince and the Showgirl* (1957), had the wrong chemistry, and it, too, failed at the box office, destroying Olivier's hopes of getting funding to film *Macbeth.*

At that point, Olivier turned from the classics to a work by John Osborne, England's angriest angry young playwright. In *The Entertainer* (1957-1958), Olivier was Archie Rice, a seedy, middle-aged, music-hall song-and-dance man whose lost popularity parallels the decline of the British Empire and its humiliation during the Suez Crisis, in which Archie's son is killed. Doing his own song-and-dance numbers, Olivier gave a brilliantly rancid performance that some critics still rank as his best. In 1959, he was Coriolanus again, at Stratford-upon-Avon, and the next year, directed by Orson Welles, he played Berenger in Eugène Ionesco's *Rhinoceros* on the London stage.

Meanwhile, films lured him back to Hollywood, as General Burgoyne in *The Devil's Disciple* (1959) and Crassus, opposite Kirk Douglas, in Stanley Kubrick's Roman epic *Spartacus* (1960). In 1960, Olivier repeated his role of Archie Rice in Tony Richardson's film *The Entertainer* and got yet another Oscar nomination.

Cast as Archie Rice's daughter was a young actress named Joan Plowright, with whom Olivier fell in love. His marriage to Leigh had been battered by her manic-depressive behavior and her intermittent affair with actor Peter Finch. Though the Oliviers had been England's "Theatre Royal" for two decades, their marriage was falling apart, and in 1961 they were divorced. Ten days later, Olivier married Joan Plowright. The marriage endured and produced three children.

Meanwhile, Olivier, always ready for something new, was one of the first British stars to act for television, playing the title role in Henrik Ibsen's *John Gabriel Borkman* in 1950, the Gauguin-type painter in the stage adaptation of W. Somerset Maugham's *The Moon and Sixpence* in 1959, and the whiskey priest in a stage version of Graham Greene's novel *The Power and the Glory* in 1961. He did much distinguished work on television, hosting as well as acting in some programs and playing myriad roles, including James Tyrone in

*Long Day's Journey into Night* in 1972, Shylock in *The Merchant of Venice* in 1973, Big Daddy in *Cat on a Hot Tin Roof* in 1976, and Lear in *King Lear* in 1983.

On the stage, Olivier played Becket and then King Henry in Jean Anouilh's *Becket* in Detroit and New York (1960-1961). The next year, he directed the Chichester Festival, where he starred in John Ford's seventeenth century tragedy *The Broken Heart* and repeated his role of Astrov in *Uncle Vanya*, a part he also played on television in 1963, under his own direction. Olivier's work as director of the Chichester Festival Theater led to his appointment in 1962 as first director of the newly created National Theater of Great Britain. Olivier collected a company of some of the finest performers in England, managed the National's seasons, directed Chekhov's *Three Sisters*, and acted in numerous plays.

In 1964, Olivier undertook one of his most demanding and controversial roles: Othello. Twenty-six years earlier, he had played Iago; now he would be the Moor himself. With a voice that critics have called trumpetlike, Olivier worked to lower his range an octave and develop a cellolike sound. With Maggie Smith as Desdemona, Frank Finlay as Iago, and Derek Jacobi as Cassio, the show was extremely popular with audiences. Yet by 1964, with civil rights battles being fought and won by blacks, there was some controversy over a white performer acting in blackface. Hostile critics charged that Olivier played Othello like a Harlem Negro, but in fact, his Othello—in voice, facial expressions, and movement—was an uncanny reproduction of an African from a country such as Nigeria. When the production was filmed in 1965, Olivier won another Oscar nomination. For the film, however, Olivier's larger-than-life performance was almost too large; had he, instead of Stuart Burge, directed it and designed it in cinematic terms rather than as a filmed stage play, it might have ranked with his three great Shakespeare films; as it is, the filmed *Othello* is not wholly satisfactory. An interesting pendant to Olivier's Othello was his performance as the Sudanese Mahdi who defeats General Gordon in *Khartoum* (1966).

So far, Olivier had been boundlessly energetic and a remarkably athletic performer. In 1967, however, his health began to deteriorate. He was diagnosed as having cancer of the prostate. He conquered that disease, however, and when he had an appendectomy in 1967, the surgeon found the cancer completely gone. Yet thrombosis and eye trouble began to slow his pace. From 1966 to 1972, he played mainly cameo roles in films, though he managed such demanding stage roles as Edgar in August Strindberg's *The Dance of Death* (1967), a performance that some critics considered his greatest; Shylock in *The Merchant of Venice* (1970); and James Tyrone in Eugene O'Neill's *Long Day's Journey into Night* (1971). In 1972, he played his first starring film role in seven years in *Sleuth*, in which he and Michael Caine were the only actors; it was an immense hit and won for Olivier yet another Oscar nomination.

In 1970, Olivier was elevated to the peerage as Lord Olivier of Brighton, the first actor ever to enter the House of Lords. Unfortunately, his days on the stage were numbered. In 1974, Olivier was diagnosed as having dermatopoly-myocitis, a muscle-wasting disease. He combated it by taking steroids and exercising, swimming fifty laps a day, and he fought it to a standstill. Yet the disease made him unable to sustain a long stage role. In 1973, he played his last role onstage and resigned as director of the National. Afterward, he threw himself into film and television work with a vengeance, making twenty-nine motion pictures and television films between 1975 and 1987, playing such diverse roles as a Nazi war criminal, a hunter of Nazi war criminals, a rabbi, a Parisian boulevardier, a vampire hunter, Douglas MacArthur, Zeus, and King Lear. Some of these roles were for potboilers, such as *The Betsy* (1977), from Harold Robbins' novel, but for *The Marathon Man* (1976) and *The Boys from Brazil* (1978), Olivier won two more Oscar nominations, making him the most nominated actor in history, while for *Brideshead Revisited*, he won a television Emmy. In the 1980's, he turned to writing, producing his autobiographical *Confessions of an Actor* (1982) and *On Acting* (1986). Olivier died in July of 1989.

## Summary

Sir Laurence Olivier was a titanic figure in the theater, comparable in the twentieth century to Richard Burbage in the sixteenth, Thomas Betterton in the seventeenth, David Garrick in the eighteenth, and Edmund Kean in the nineteenth; in some ways he surpassed them all, since he did groundbreaking work in motion pictures and television as well as on the stage. One can debate whether he was the greatest actor in English; Gielgud, Richardson, and

Guinness have sometimes rivaled him. Yet Olivier has shown greater range and daring than any of them. Not only was he a consummate character actor in such diverse roles as Archie Rice, Justice Shallow, Mr. Creakle, Dr. Chebutikin, and a host of others, but also, unlike Gielgud, Richardson, and Guinness, he was able to play intense romantic figures and larger-than-life heroic and demoniac ones. He played all the great tragic Shakespearean roles (Hamlet, Lear, Macbeth, Othello, Antony, Coriolanus, Brutus, Titus Andronicus, Shylock), the consummate villains Richard III and Iago, such heroic figures as Henry V and Hotspur, and comic ones such as Malvolio and Sir Toby Belch. Though he did most of the great classics, he did not hesitate to take on avant-garde works and to play such non-classic roles as a cockney cop or a seedy music-hall song-and-dance man. His repertory ran from Sophocles to Sheridan to Chekhov to Strindberg to Shaw to Osborne. Besides acting, Olivier was a great theater director-producer-manager who established Great Britain's National Theatre. The three great Shakespearean films that he produced, directed, and starred in have been cinematic landmarks that made Shakespeare viable on film and led to subsequent Shakespearean films by Grigori Kosintsev, Franco Zeffirelli, Joseph Mankiewicz, Roman Polanski, Akira Kurosawa, and others. Olivier was the only actor ever to have been made a lord and life peer of the realm.

**Bibliography**

Barker, Felix. *The Oliviers*. London: Hamilton, and Philadelphia: Lippincott, 1953. A joint biography of Olivier and Leigh, dated but reliable as far as it goes. Illustrated.

Cottrell, John. *Laurence Olivier*. London: Weidenfeld and Nicolson, and Englewood Cliffs, N.J.: Prentice-Hall, 1975. The definitive scholarly biography for the first sixty-eight years of Olivier's life. Illustrated, with an extensive bibliography.

Dent, Alan. *Hamlet, the Film and the Play*. London: World Film, 1948. A study of Olivier's film of *Hamlet*. Illustrated.

Edwards, Anne. *Vivien Leigh*. London: Coronet, and New York: Simon and Schuster, 1977. A biography of Olivier's second wife and frequent costar. Thorough and readable, but gushing and "pop" in style. Illustrated.

Gourlay, Logan, ed. *Olivier*. London: Weidenfeld and Nicolson, 1973; New York: Stein and Day, 1974. A collection of interviews with Olivier's theatrical friends, associates, directors, and fellow players. Illustrated.

Morley, Margaret. *The Films of Laurence Olivier*. New York: Citadel Press, 1978. A volume in the "Films of . . ." series, with a comprehensive, illustrated history of Olivier's films and television performances through 1978, in addition to an article by Olivier on filming *Hamlet*.

Olivier, Laurence. *Confessions of an Actor: An Autobiography*. London: Weidenfeld and Nicolson, and New York: Simon and Schuster, 1982. Concentrates on the author's personal life, with less space devoted to his interpretation of roles as actor and director. Illustrated.

———. *On Acting*. London: Weidenfeld and Nicolson, and New York: Simon and Schuster, 1986. Supplements *Confessions of an Actor* by concentrating on Olivier's work on stage and screen, with detailed analysis of his key roles and of his Shakespeare films. Illustrated.

Spoto, Donald. *Laurence Olivier: A Biography*. London: HarperCollins, 1991; New York: HarperCollins, 1992. This volume recounts Olivier's affair with Danny Kaye and provides information on Olivier's wives and his sexual insecurities.

Tynan, Kenneth. *"Othello": The National Theatre Production*. London: Rupert-Hart-Davis, and New York: Stein and Day, 1966. A history and analysis by the literary manager of the National Theatre. Illustrated.

*Robert E. Morsberger*

# JACQUELINE KENNEDY ONASSIS

*Born:* July 28, 1929; Southampton, New York
*Died:* May 19, 1994; New York, New York
*Area of Achievement:* Government and politics
*Contribution:* Jacqueline Kennedy was one of the most famous First Ladies of the twentieth century. The American people associate her with the glamour and excitement of her husband's brief presidency, his tragic death, and the troubled history of her celebrated family.

## Early Life

Jacqueline Lee Bouvier was born on July 28, 1929, to John Vernou Bouvier III and Janet Lee Bouvier in Southampton, Long Island, New York. Her father was a stockbroker and a member of a wealthy Roman Catholic family of French heritage. Her mother came from a prominent family in New York whose wealth was based on banking. During her early years, Jacqueline and her younger sister, Lee, grew up in comfortable circumstances. A local reporter covered her second birthday party, and the press noted her appearances in horse shows with her mother.

The Bouvier marriage encountered problems during the mid-1930's. After several separations, the couple divorced in 1940. Jacqueline and Lee lived with their mother but saw their father on weekends. His lessons about social behavior and the way that young women interacted with men made a great impression on Jacqueline. Her mother later married Hugh D. Auchincloss, also a prosperous stockbroker. Jacqueline attended Miss Chapin's School in New York City and entered Miss Porter's School in Connecticut when she was fifteen. She was presented to society in 1947. One columnist named her his "Debutante of the Year."

Jacqueline entered Vassar College in 1947. She spent her junior year in France, attending the University of Grenoble and the Sorbonne in Paris. She finished her college education at George Washington University, from which she was graduated in 1951. She won *Vogue* magazine's Prix de Paris contest but declined the award. After a summer trip to Europe in 1951, she worked at the *Washington Times-Herald* as the Inquiring Photographer, asking questions and taking pictures for a daily feature column. John F. Kennedy was one of the people she interviewed. She was briefly engaged to John G. W. Husted, Jr., but they ended the engagement by mutual agreement.

In 1951, friends introduced Jacqueline to Congressman John F. Kennedy of Massachusetts. They met again the following year, when Kennedy was a candidate for the United States Senate. After his victory in November of 1952, they saw each other more frequently. Their engagement was announced on June 24, 1953. They were married on September 12, 1953, with 750 wedding guests, 3,000 spectators, and extensive news coverage.

## Life's Work

The early years of her marriage to John F. Kennedy were not easy ones for Jacqueline Kennedy. She did not like politics or the routine of campaigning, at which her husband excelled. The senator's health was also poor, and she helped him recover from surgery in 1954 and 1955. Jacqueline provided particular assistance in the writing of his Pulitzer Prize-winning book *Profiles in Courage* (1956). She also had two miscarriages before her first child, Caroline, was born on November 27, 1957.

As John F. Kennedy made his run for the White House in 1960, his wife participated grudgingly in the early days of primary campaigning. Despite her reluctance to do so, she proved to be very popular with the people who saw her. The announcement of her pregnancy during the summer of 1960 enabled her to limit her campaign activities. A "Campaign Wife" newsletter, written for her by Kennedy aides, radio broadcasts, and several news conferences were her direct contribution to John Kennedy's narrow victory over Richard M. Nixon. Following the election, her son, John F. Kennedy, Jr., was born on November 25, 1960.

Jacqueline Kennedy had mixed feelings about her ceremonial role as the president's wife. She disliked the term "First Lady" and asked the White House staff not to use it. She was also unwilling to meet on any regular basis the various social and charitable delegations that came to the White House or sought her patronage. In her place, she sent the wife of the vice president, Lady Bird Johnson. Jacqueline Kennedy's relations with the press were often strained. She would have preferred that reporters not attend White House parties, and she sometimes referred to female journalists as "harpies."

Other aspects of her new position engaged Jacqueline Kennedy's enthusiastic interest. She re-

garded the White House itself as a potential national showplace for art and culture that previous administrations had ignored. She told her staff that she intended to make the mansion a grand place for the American people. Over the next three years, Jacqueline embarked on an ambitious program to obtain antiques and historical artifacts that would transform the White House into a replica of what existed during the era of Thomas Jefferson.

Jacqueline called upon wealthy friends to assist her in locating antiques suitable for the White House. The mechanism for receiving these funds and carrying on her work was the White House Historical Association. She obtained legislation from Congress that declared White House furnishings to be government property. To finance her campaign, the First Lady arranged for the sale of guidebooks to the White House. Jacqueline displayed what she had done when she conducted a televised tour of the White House on February 14, 1962. The program received critical praise for her taste and skill. Popular interest in the White House grew dramatically during the early 1960's because of Jacqueline Kennedy's efforts.

A related part of her agenda as First Lady was to promote cultural events. She and the president hosted more informal evenings than their predecessors had, and noted artists and performers entertained the dignitaries. Among those who appeared were noted cellist Pablo Casals, violinist Isaac Stern, and actor Frederic March. The social side of John Kennedy's "New Frontier" was a glittering success, and invitations to the Kennedy evenings at the White House became highly sought after.

Jacqueline Kennedy traveled with the president on some of his foreign tours and made several trips abroad on her own as well. When President Kennedy went to Paris in 1961, Jacqueline was such a success that her husband wryly remarked: "I am the man who accompanied Jacqueline Kennedy to Paris—and I have enjoyed it." The First Lady's trip to India in 1962 was another popular triumph for her.

Recent research has revealed that Jacqueline Kennedy was more of an adviser to the president than had been known previously. She attended some meetings of the National Security Council as an observer, and John Kennedy trusted her judgment on numerous issues. Though their marriage had experienced strain because of the president's infidelities, the couple drew closer together during their years in the White House. The death of their son Patrick in August of 1963, shortly after his birth, was a source of sadness.

Jacqueline Kennedy was riding with her husband in Dallas on November 22, 1963, when he was killed by an assassin. She supervised the details of the funeral in a way that made the ceremonies a moment of intense national mourning. Her stoic bearing and graceful dignity during the aftermath of the tragedy and through the funeral that followed impressed the world. In a conversation with a journalist shortly thereafter, she described her husband's presidency as an American "Camelot" and asked that his memory be preserved.

The five years after her husband's murder saw Jacqueline Kennedy endeavor to build a new life for herself and her children amid unrelenting newspaper publicity about her every move. She left Washington and lived in New York City. A difficult controversy with author William Manchester about the accuracy of his book on President Kennedy's death underscored her unique position with the public. Seeking to escape the constant scrutiny that followed her everywhere, she was married to Aristotle Onassis, a wealthy Greek ship owner, on October 20, 1968. The news shocked a nation that had regarded her as a perpetual presidential widow and thus recoiled from what appeared to be a marriage of convenience.

Her marriage to Onassis lasted for seven years, until he died in 1975. Publicity and photographers still surrounded her, and every aspect of Jacqueline Onassis' life was discussed in the media. In the years after the death of her second husband, she worked as an editor for several publishers in New York City and produced some best sellers for these firms. Her two children grew up, and she became a grandmother. In her mid-sixties, she was still a favorite subject for magazine covers and media attention. She refused to give interviews, wrote no memoirs, and made no comments on the many books written about her life and her years as Mrs. John F. Kennedy.

In January of 1994, Jacqueline Kennedy Onassis began to receive treatments for non-Hodgkin's lymphoma, a form of cancer. Her lymphoma was highly aggressive, and she died at home in New York City on May 19, 1994. She was buried in Arlington National Cemetery in Washington, D.C., next to her first husband, John F. Kennedy.

### Summary

Jacqueline Kennedy Onassis was one of the most popular and famous of all First Ladies. She is forever associated in the public mind with the brief years of the Kennedy presidency and its tragic conclusion. During the early 1960's, her restoration work at the White House, the glittering parties that she and her husband gave, and the image of worldly sophistication that she presented took the role of the First Lady to levels of international prominence that it had never previously attained. Her gallant bearing in the aftermath of her husband's murder gained for her a unique place in American social consciousness.

During the three decades between November of 1963 and her death in 1994, Jacqueline Kennedy Onassis saw her public image shift from the negative reaction when she married Aristotle Onassis in 1968 to a more positive assessment since the mid-1970's. Her success as a mother, editor, and cultural figure kept her in the news. Biographies and articles about her continued to attract a large readership. Jacqueline Kennedy Onassis's life offers striking evidence of the extent to which fame and celebrity have shaped the way in which Americans evaluate First Ladies as historical figures.

### Bibliography


Abbott, James, and Elaine Rice. *Designing Camelot: The Kennedy White House Restoration.* New York: Van Nostrand Reinhold, 1997. The first volume to cover in detail the Kennedy restoration of the White House. Includes anecdotes and many photographs.

Andersen, Christopher. *Jackie after Jack: Portrait of the Lady.* New York: Morrow, 1998. Andersen's research into recently declassified government documents and previously unavailable archives produces an in-depth portrait of Onassis's last 30 years.

Anthony, Carl Sferrazza. *First Ladies: The Saga of the Presidents' Wives and Their Power.* 2 vols. New York: Morrow, 1990-1991. Contains a sympathetic evaluation of Jacqueline Kennedy as First Lady.

Birmingham, Stephen. *Jacqueline Bouvier Kennedy Onassis.* New York: Grossett and Dunlap, 1978; London: Fontana, 1979. A thoughtful and well-written biography that relies heavily on the work of other authors for its factual information.

Caroli, Betty. *2d ed. First Ladies.* 2d ed. New York: Doubleday, 1993. An overview of the institution of First Ladies with some interesting insights about the performance of Jacqueline Kennedy in the White House.

Davis, John H. *The Bouviers: Portrait of an American Family.* New York: Farrar Straus, 1969. Davis is a member of the Bouvier family, and his access to important source materials and insights make this a very valuable volume about the Bouviers.

Gutin, Myra G. *The President's Partner: The First Lady in the Twentieth Century.* New York: Greenwood Press, 1989. Focusing on First Ladies as communicators and political surrogates for the president, this book appraises the impact of Jacqueline Kennedy's White House years.

Heymann, C. David. *A Woman Named Jackie.* Secaucus, N.J.: Carol, and London: Heinemann, 1989. A full biography that mixes original research in Jacqueline Kennedy's White House

Social Files at the Kennedy Library with an equal amount of gossip.

Kelley, Kitty. *Jackie Oh!* Secaucus, N.J.: Stuart, and London: Granada, 1978. A sensationalized biography that includes every lurid tale about its subject that the author could find. Some anecdotes may be true, but the book should be used cautiously.

Smith, Nancy, and Mary C. Ryan, eds. *Modern First Ladies: Their Documentary Legacy.* Washington, D.C.: National Archives and Records Administrations, 1989. This book of essays has an illuminating chapter on Jacqueline Kennedy's records at the John F. Kennedy Library and further information that helps to place her role as First Lady in historical context.

Thayer, Mary Van Rensselaer. *Jacqueline Kennedy: The White House Years.* Boston: Little Brown, 1971. This volume draws extensively on Jacqueline Kennedy's Social Office Files at the John F. Kennedy Library. It is a valuable source, since so many of those files are still unavailable for research.

*Lewis L. Gould*

## EUGENE O'NEILL

*Born:* October 16, 1888; New York, New York
*Died:* November 27, 1953; Boston, Massachusetts
*Area of Achievement:* Drama
*Contribution:* O'Neill is commonly considered a great American playwright, honored as a writer who experimented ambitiously in a variety of dramatic modes.

### Early Life

Eugene Gladstone O'Neill was born in a Broadway hotel at a corner of Times Square on October 16, 1888. His father, James O'Neill (1846-1920), came to the United States from Ireland when he was ten and established himself as a talented Shakespearean actor, expected to inherit the mantle of Edwin Booth. In 1883, the elder O'Neill opened as the protagonist Edmond Dantès in a dramatization of *The Count of Monte-Cristo* (1844-1845), by Alexandre Dumas, *père*. The play proved a spectacular success, and James O'Neill toured with it for the next fifteen years, earning up to forty thousand dollars annually to assuage his incessant fear of poverty. Later, the father came to believe that he had sacrificed his opportunity for greatness upon the altar of materialism. His son took this regret as a cautionary lesson and resolved never to compromise his artistic integrity for money.

Eugene's mother, Ellen Quinlan O'Neill (1857-1922), was a devout Catholic, educated in a convent in South Bend, Indiana, where she won a medal for her piano-playing but seriously considered becoming a nun. She fell in love with the dashing James O'Neill when his company toured South Bend. She accompanied her husband on his road trips for many years, all the while resenting their nomadic itinerary of frequent one-night stands, hotel rooms, and irregular meals. Eugene, once established as a playwright, developed an emphatic fondness for settled routine and a detestation of trains and hotels.

Ellen O'Neill found an escape from her aversion to theatrical traveling by becoming an increasingly addicted morphine user. She withdrew from many of her child-rearing responsibilities, leaving Eugene to be mothered, during his first seven years, by a Cornish nursemaid, Sarah Sandy, who exposed her charge to sensational horror stories. The elder O'Neill sent his son to Catholic preparatory schools in New York and Connecticut. In 1906, Eugene entered Princeton University, drank heavily, and studied very little; after a brick-throwing episode, he was failed in all of his courses and never returned to the university. For the next two years, he spent most of his time touring Manhattan in the company of his alcoholic older brother, James, Jr. (1878-1923).

On October 2, 1909, Eugene secretly married the non-Catholic Kathleen Jenkins, the beautiful daughter of a once-wealthy New York family. Two weeks later, the bridegroom left her to prospect for gold in Honduras. There he found not shining metal but a severe case of malaria; he was to use his knowledge of the tropical jungle in *The Emperor Jones* (1920). Even though Kathleen gave birth to a son, Eugene, Jr., on May 5, 1910, O'Neill refused to live with them upon his return, ignoring his firstborn until after the child's eleventh birthday. On July 10, 1912, Kathleen Jenkins was awarded an interlocutory divorce decree.

The year 1912 proved to be the crucial year of Eugene O'Neill's life: The nuclear O'Neill family—father, mother, two sons—spent the summer together in O'Neill's parents' New London, Connecticut, home, with Eugene writing for the local paper. In December, 1912, he was diagnosed as tubercular; Ellen O'Neill refused to accept the physician's findings, withdrawing into morphine-induced fantasies. Miserly James O'Neill first placed Eugene in Connecticut's Fairfield County State Sanatorium, a bleakly depressing charity institution, many of whose patients died. After staying there from December 9 to 11, Eugene had himself discharged. On Christmas Eve, James entered his son in a private institution, Gaylord Farm, which proved distinctly more therapeutic: Eugene was discharged as an arrested case on the third of June, 1913; *The Straw* (1921), one of his most deeply felt early plays, is a heavily autobiographical depiction of his stay there.

### Life's Work

During his sanatorium stay, O'Neill crystallized his career goal: he would be a playwright. His most pervasive influence was the intense, self-tortured, somber Swedish writer, August Strindberg. In his acceptance speech for the Nobel Prize for Literature, awarded to him in 1936, O'Neill singled out Strindberg as "that greatest genius of all modern dramatists.... It was reading his plays ... that, above all else, first gave me the vision of what modern

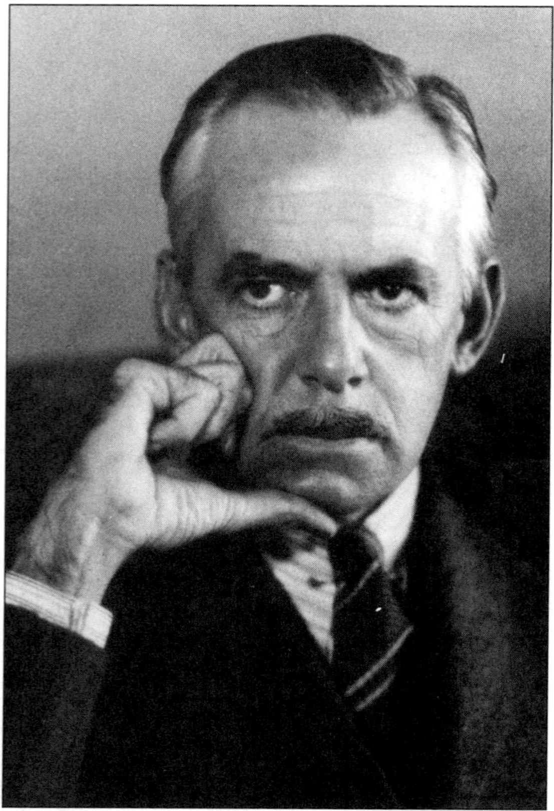

drama could be, and first inspired me with the urge to write for the theater myself."

After his discharge from the institution, O'Neill boarded for a year with a private family and used this time to write thirteen plays, of which he included six one-act plays in a volume, *Thirst* (1914), subsidized by his father; he later disowned this collection, preventing its republication during his lifetime. From September, 1914, to May, 1915, he was a student in Professor George Pierce Baker's playwriting class at Harvard, remembered by classmates as handsome, thin, shy, and restless.

In 1916, O'Neill fell in love with the high-spirited journalist Louise Bryant, already the mistress and soon to be the wife of the celebrated war correspondent John Reed (1887-1920). The two men liked each other, and the trio formed a turbulent triangle which persisted close to the day of O'Neill's second marriage to Agnes Boulton on April 12, 1918. Indeed, Agnes reminded O'Neill of Louise: Both women were slender, pretty, and sophisticated; Agnes, however, was quiet and softly feminine, in contrast to Louise's strident manner. The marriage to Agnes Boulton lasted eleven years; its first two years are vividly described in her account, *Part of a Long Story* (1958). The union resulted in two children. Shane O'Neill (1919-1975) was never able to settle on a career and became a hopeless heroin addict. Oona O'Neill (born 1925) married Charles Chaplin (1889-1977). O'Neill's firstborn son, Eugene O'Neill, Jr., tall and handsome with a resonant voice, began a brilliant career as a classicist at Yale but turned increasingly alcoholic, resigned his academic post, and, in his fortieth year, committed suicide. O'Neill held himself apart from his children throughout his life, although he did make sporadic, intense, but always short-lived attempts to reach them intimately.

O'Neill's first important play, *The Emperor Jones*, dramatizes, in eight scenes, Brutus Jones's fall from "emperor" of a West Indian island to a primitive savage who is slaughtered by his rebellious people. Jones is a former Pullman porter who escapes imprisonment for murder, finds his way to the island, and there establishes himself as a despot by exploiting the natives' fears and superstitions. While the play's first and last scenes are realistic, the intervening six are expressionistic, consisting of Jones's monologues and the visions of his fearful mind as he struggles through a tropical jungle. O'Neill manages to merge supernatural beliefs with psychological effects in a powerful union that shows his dramatic affinity with two noted German expressionists, Georg Kaiser (1878-1945) and Ernst Toller (1893-1939).

*Desire Under the Elms* (1924) is usually considered O'Neill's finest play of the 1920's, his first in the classic Greek mode. It is a modern treatment of the Phaedra-Hippolytus-Theseus myth, set on a New England farm in 1850. The father, seventy-five-year-old Ephraim Cabot (Theseus), returns to his farm with a passionate new wife, thirty-five-year-old Abbie (Phaedra), who falls in love with her twenty-five-year-old stepson, Eben (Hippolytus). Like Phaedra, Abbie confronts the young man in a superb scene; unlike Phaedra, Abbie wins him. They become lovers and have a child, which Abbie kills in infancy to demonstrate her primary love for Eben. He insists on sharing her guilt; they go to jail together, remorseful over their infanticide but not over their adultery. O'Neill dramatizes in this play not only sexual but also materialistic desire: Desire for the farm causes Abbie to marry old Ephraim; resentment of his father's usurpation of the farm from his abused, dead mother causes Eben to exact vengeance upon the father he hates. The play's multiple setting effectively counterpoints the older and younger generations, external nature and domestic temperament.

Determined to compress within his career virtually all stages of drama, O'Neill challenged Aeschylus with his longest work, *Mourning Becomes Electra* (1931), a thirteen-act trilogy. The action is a modern adaptation of the *Oresteia* (458 B.C.), with O'Neill following *Agamemnon* faithfully with his *The Homecoming*, and *Libation Bearers* fairly closely with *The Hunted*, but departing freely from *Eumenides* in *The Haunted*. The Trojan War becomes the American Civil War, with the Mannon family (House of Atreus) awaiting the return from the fighting of Ezra Mannon (Agamemnon). The daughter, Lavinia (Electra), has discovered that her mother, Christine (Clytemnestra), has been having an affair with Adam Brant (Aegisthus). In *The Haunted*, the playwright abandons Aeschylus in favor of Freud by having Orin (Orestes), racked by remorse for his mother's suicide, not murder (as in Aeschylus), but transfer his incestuous feelings for his mother to his sister, who has come to resemble his mother. Lavinia rejects him, Orin commits suicide, and Lavinia realizes that she has always loved her father and hated her mother. She closes the drama by rejecting marriage to a loyal suitor, instead immuring herself, with the Mannon dead, alone in the Mannon house. This work had the most laudatory initial reception of any O'Neill play, but a number of critics have since tempered the original enthusiasm, deploring the drama's implausibly implacable determinism, the overly clinical, self-analytic speeches of its leading characters, and the absence of even the slightest elements of humor or warmth.

From 1934 to 1946, O'Neill did not have a play produced. He spent these years largely in a Chinese-style mansion, Tao House, built to his specifications in Contra Costa County, California. He devoted most of his work to an ambitious cycle of eleven related plays dealing with the rise and fall of an American family from 1775 to 1932, to be called *A Tale of Possessors Self-Dispossessed*, which would offer his adverse judgment on America's increasing enslavement to possession and greed. "We are the clearest example," he declared, "of 'For what shall it profit a man if he gain the whole world and lose his own soul?' " The only play of this cycle surviving in completed form is *A Touch of the Poet*, set in a Massachusetts tavern in 1828 and treating the marriage of Sara Melody, of Irish descent, and Simon Harford, of Yankee stock. O'Neill wrote various drafts of the cycle's other plays but, fearing that they might eventually be performed in unfinished form, he and his third wife, Carlotta, burned the manuscripts during the winter of 1952-1953. A third draft of *More Stately Mansions* escaped the flames and was produced in 1967.

O'Neill had met Carlotta Monterey when she played the society girl in his *The Hairy Ape* (1922). She was a sultry brunette, usually cast as the sexually magnetic adventuress eventually to be overcome by the virtuous wife. She and O'Neill began their romance in 1928 and married in 1929, three weeks after Agnes Boulton had been granted a Reno divorce. Carlotta loved O'Neill deeply but possessively, routinized his life, limited his contacts with friends, and helped estrange him from his children, whom he disinherited in his will, making her his literary executor. In his middle and later years, O'Neill both impressed and often intimidated people with his "black Irish" appearance: dark, brooding eyes; spare, rangy, five-foot, eleven-inch frame; quiet, deep voice; and mysterious, reserved, often morose temperament. From 1944 to his death in 1953, an uncontrollable hand tremor, similar to that caused by Parkinson's disease, forced him to stop writing; he tried to dictate but found that method unworkable. His final years were marked not only by physical pain but also by increasing trouble with his children and dissension with his wife. He died of bronchial pneumonia, just past the age of sixty-five.

Most critics regard two plays written at the end of the 1930's as O'Neill's greatest, comparable to the finest dramatic achievements of the twentieth century. The first, *The Iceman Cometh* (1946), is one of his bleakest dramas, set in a squalid barroom in 1912 and portraying more than a dozen drunken wrecks who alternately feed upon and poison one another's illusions. The sum of their pipe dreams represents the total content of man's capacity for deception and repudiates any affirmation. The play's theme—that human beings cannot live without illusions, no matter how ill-founded—parallels that of Henrik Ibsen's *The Wild Duck* (1884). Opposing the alcoholic customers of Harry Hope's saloon in this work is a hardware salesman, Hickey, who kicks away their crutches of self-deception out of professed confidence that the truth shall set them free. Yet Hickey turns out to have murdered his long-betrayed wife, not only out of love—as he at first insists—but also out of a lifetime of hatred and self-loathing. Hickey, the derelicts discover, has been a false messiah; they gladly relapse into their drunken delusions. O'Neill has here written a despairing masterpiece about the impossibility of salvation in a man-centered world.

O'Neill's other, perhaps even more magnificent, achievement is the confessional family play he prepared himself for many years to write, *Long Day's Journey Into Night* (1956). This is O'Neill's most personal play: The O'Neills are called the Tyrones. His father and elder brother retain their own first names, James. Ellen O'Neill becomes Mary Tyrone, while Eugene names himself Edmund—the name of the O'Neill brother who died in infancy. Did O'Neill, as he claims in his preface, "face [his] dead at last . . . with deep pity and understanding and forgiveness for all the four haunted Tyrones"? A qualified yes is in order, for the author represses the painful data of his first marriage, first son, and first divorce, instead portraying himself as a sensitive, irresponsible, twenty-three-year-old would-be poet without commitments.

The play lives up to its title: It consumes the time from 8:30 A.M. to midnight on a day in August, 1912, in New London—The O'Neill/Tyrone summer residence. It has the unified formality of French classical drama, with the Tyrone quartet bound together by links of resentment, grief, guilt, and recrimination, yet also by tenderness, compassion, and love. Two events charge the action: Mary Tyrone's final relapse into morphine addiction and the diagnosis of Edmund as tubercular. In the day's course, she moves away from the other three but especially from her younger son; he moves toward her, in vain agony. Who is to blame for their maladies? All, replies O'Neill—and no one. As Mary says,

> None of us can help the things life has done to us. They're done before you realize it, and once they're done they make you do other things until at last everything comes between you and what you'd like to be, and you've lost your true self forever.

### Summary

In power, insight, scale, and ambition, Eugene O'Neill is unsurpassed among American dramatists. He began as a realist-naturalist in a native tradition that includes Edwin Arlington Robinson and Robert Frost in poetry, and Frank Norris, Stephen Crane, and Theodore Dreiser in fiction. His middle period is marked by intermittently effective plays, influenced by many European modes, particularly expressionism, and by the ideas of Friedrich Wilhelm Nietzsche, Sigmund Freud, and Carl Gustav Jung. His last work is both his best and his most characteristically American: It demonstrates a fierce determination to dig beneath the illusions and lies of everyday behavior, to assert a profoundly tragic sense of man's shortcomings, and to reconcile himself to the melancholy state of a flawed and often unjust universe. Like tragedians from Aeschylus to Samuel Beckett, O'Neill has a desolate view of life. His talent in dramatizing that view was often flawed by self-conscious portentousness. In at least two plays, however—*The Iceman Cometh* and *Long Day's Journey Into Night*—O'Neill climbed dramatic heights unscaled by any other American and rivaled by only a handful of world-renowned modern playwrights: Henrik Ibsen, August Strindberg, Anton Chekhov, George Bernard Shaw, Bertolt Brecht, and Samuel Beckett.

### Bibliography

Alexander, Doris. *The Tempering of Eugene O'Neill*. New York: Harcourt Brace, 1962. This biography treats O'Neill's life and career up to *Anna Christie* (1921). Alexander devotes several chapters to O'Neill's parents and brother, follows him to Greenwich Village and Provincetown, then to his marriage to Agnes Boulton and his first dramatic successes. The book stresses O'Neill's maturation as an artist.

Bogard, Travis. *Contour in Time: The Plays of Eugene O'Neill*. Rev. ed. New York: Oxford University Press, 1988. A study of O'Neill's works that unites theatrical knowledge with finely honed critical insights. Professor Bogard also provides illuminating accounts of both the American and European theaters in the first half of the twentieth century.

Boulton, Agnes. *Part of a Long Story*. London: Davies, and New York: Doubleday, 1958. Boulton begins with her first meeting of the twenty-nine-year-old playwright in 1917 and stops with the birth of their son Shane in October, 1919. A promised second volume was never written. She relates not only the first years of O'Neill's second marriage but also his version of his first marriage and suicide attempt.

Bowen, Croswell. Assisted by Shane O'Neill. *The Curse of the Misbegotten*. New York: McGraw-Hill, 1959; London: Hart-Davis, 1960. Bowen is a journalist and biographer who is here considerably assisted by O'Neill's younger son. The "curse" is the inability of the O'Neills to tell one another their love and concern, thus dooming themselves to emotionally impoverished lives. Much valuable material about Eugene O'Neill's life.

Gallup, Donald C. *Eugene O'Neill and His Eleven-Play Cycle: A Tale of Possessors Self-Dispossessed.* New Haven, Conn., and London: Yale University Press, 1998. Focuses on O'Neill's set of plays that followed a family through several generations. The author presents the story of this project based on research into unpublished scenarios, outlines, and notes.

Gassner, John, ed. *O'Neill: A Collection of Critical Essays.* Englewood Cliffs, N.J.: Prentice-Hall, 1964. Gassner, an eminent authority on drama, has collected fifteen essays on O'Neill's achievement. Included are adverse views from distinguished critics such as Eric Bentley, as well as laudatory articles by Stark Young, John Henry Raleigh, Travis Bogard, and others. A discriminating selection.

Gelb, Arthur, and Barbara Gelb. *O'Neill.* London: Cape, and New York: Harper, 1962. This volume of more than one thousand pages treats O'Neill's life and works in monumental detail. The writing is often pedestrian, but the information is usually fascinating enough to maintain the reader's interest.

Manheim, Michael, ed. *The Cambridge Companion to Eugene O'Neill.* Cambridge and New York: Cambridge University Press, 1998. A collection of essays on O'Neill's life, his productions, and his critics.

Sheaffer, Louis. *O'Neill: Son and Artist.* Boston: Little Brown, 1973; London: Elek, 1974.

———. *O'Neill: Son and Playwright.* Boston: Little Brown, 1968; London: Dent, 1969. These two volumes comprise close to thirteen hundred pages and will be the definitive O'Neill study for many years. Shaeffer, a former journalist, devoted sixteen years to this titanic labor; they were worth it. He emphasizes a wealth of biographical lore, obtained not only from documents but also from personal interviews. Indispensable.

*Gerhard Bran*

## THOMAS PHILIP O'NEILL, JR.

*Born:* December 9, 1912; Cambridge, Massachusetts

*Died:* January 5, 1994; Boston, Massachusetts

*Areas of Achievement*: Government and politics

*Contribution:* O'Neill was a lifelong defender of social legislation and an energetic leader of the House of Representatives whose ten years as Speaker saw a resurgence of congressional authority.

### Early Life

Thomas Philip (Tip) O'Neill, Jr., was born on December 9, 1912, in Cambridge, Massachusetts, the son of Thomas Philip and Rose Ann (Tolan) O'Neill. O'Neill was nicknamed "Tip" after baseball player James Edward O'Neill of the St. Louis Browns, who was famous for hitting foul tip after foul tip until he was finally walked to first base. His father, Thomas, Sr., was the son of an immigrant bricklayer from County Cork, Ireland, and a dedicated member of the Democratic Party. Beginning in 1900, Thomas, Sr., served six years as an elected member of the Cambridge City Council. As a result of his upbringing, Thomas, Jr., remained close to his Irish-immigrant, working-class, and Democratic roots throughout his public career.

Educated exclusively in Catholic schools, O'Neill began his education at St. John's Grammar School and continued at St. John's Parochial School, where he was considered an average student at best. Equally unimpressive in athletics, he nevertheless was elected captain of both the football and basketball teams. At the age of fifteen, O'Neill experienced his first taste of politics when he campaigned for the Catholic Democratic candidate Al Smith in his unsuccessful bid for the presidency in 1928.

After his graduation from secondary school in 1931, O'Neill enrolled at Boston College. During his senior year, he ran for city council and lost; this would prove to be the only electoral defeat of his entire career. He lost by only 160 votes, largely because he had taken his own neighborhood for granted and had failed to solicit votes there. This loss, accompanied by his father's advice that "all politics is local," formed a lesson O'Neill would never forget.

After graduating from Boston College in 1936, O'Neill was elected to the Massachusetts state legislature. While serving there, he married his sweetheart of many years, Mildred Miller, in June, 1941. As a legislator during President Franklin D. Roosevelt's New Deal, O'Neill formed his liberal democratic principles. By such acts as arranging jobs for out-of-work constituents and advocating quality education for the working class, O'Neill earned a reputation as a friend of the people. As a result, in 1948 he was made the youngest majority leader in Massachusetts history. As leader, he pushed through a broad program of social legislation popularly known as the "Little New Deal."

When then Congressman John Fitzgerald Kennedy launched his senatorial campaign in 1952, O'Neill decided to run for the vacant position. Enjoying strong support from the heavily Democratic Irish and Italian working-class wards of the Eleventh Congressional District, O'Neill was easily elected to the U.S. Congress.

### Life's Work

O'Neill's ascension to the U.S. House of Representatives marked the start of over three decades of service in Washington. As the protégé of House Democratic Whip John W. McCormick, a fellow Bostonian, O'Neill was quickly introduced to the House power structure. Soon, O'Neill was invited to Speaker of the House Sam Rayburn's informal "board of education" meetings, held after-hours for congressional leaders and friends. At these meetings, congressional business was discussed in casual detail, allowing O'Neill an inside track in the rough-and-tumble world of Washington politics.

These contacts would gain him a coveted position on the House Rules Committee in only his second term, a rare appointment for a freshman congressman. The committee regulated the flow of legislation to the House floor, exposing O'Neill to all facets of the legislative process and helping to make him a more well-rounded, less parochial congressman. Following Sam Rayburn's advice—"If you want to get along, go along"—O'Neill proved himself an adept compromiser, able to steer his bills around the deadlocks resulting from the 1950's split between liberals and conservatives.

In keeping with his roots, Congressman O'Neill routinely voted along liberal Democratic lines, casting votes in favor of housing redevelopment, expansion and improvement of mass-transit facilities, the Economic Opportunity Act, and the Civil

Rights Acts of 1956, 1957, and 1964. His advocacy of adequate health care, education, and increased worker opportunities all reflected his New Deal roots. Later, O'Neill supported strict gun-control laws, busing to achieve racial equality in schools, and strong environmental legislation.

By the mid-1960's, the Vietnam War had come to dominate the national consciousness. Initially, O'Neill backed President Lyndon B. Johnson's Southeast Asia policies, as did most of O'Neill's blue-collar constituents. Eventually, however, O'Neill reconsidered his position at the urging of both his own children (Thomas III, Christopher, Michael, Susan, and Rosemary) and the intellectual communities of Harvard University and the Massachusetts Institute of Technology, both of which were in his district. After much soul-searching, O'Neill concluded that Vietnam was a civil conflict from which the United States needed to withdraw. He made his opinion known to President Johnson in 1967, long before "dovish" (antiwar) positions were popular, and he backed the Democratic peace candidate Eugene McCarthy in the 1968 presidential primaries.

Thereafter, O'Neill worked to withdraw American troops from Southeast Asia. In March, 1971, he cosponsored a bill setting a date for U.S. withdrawal contingent upon the release of American prisoners of war. He also supported legislation in August, 1973, that would have cut off funds for the continuation of air raids against North Vietnam. In November, O'Neill voted to override President Richard Nixon's veto of the War Powers Bill, which effectively limited the executive's war-making powers.

O'Neill's opposition to the Vietnam War eventually gained him the respect and support of many younger members of Congress, who would be largely responsible for his rise to the speakership. O'Neill's rise began in 1971, when he was appointed majority whip. When majority leader Hale Boggs died in a plane crash the following year, O'Neill assumed his position.

O'Neill was pivotal in leading the charge for House reform. He lessened the autocratic power of committee chairpersons, pushed for the publication of committee votes, and advocated limiting the number of chairs a representative could hold. O'Neill also urged Congress to embrace its responsibility to oversee the actions of the other branches of the federal government, a desire reflected in his calls for the investigation and impeachment of President Nixon when the Watergate scandal broke in 1973.

O'Neill's ability to compromise, along with his affability and overwhelming popularity, led in December, 1976, to his election by acclamation as Speaker of the House. In 1977, in the shadow of Watergate, O'Neill helped to pass a far-reaching government ethics bill as his first official act as Speaker.

Jimmy Carter entered the White House at about the same time that O'Neill became Speaker. During Carter's four years as president, it seemed that the two men shared only their party affiliation. As politicians, they were direct opposites: Carter a Washington outsider elected to office on his anti-politician credentials, O'Neill a politician who had raised himself through the party ranks. Yet despite their differing views, O'Neill as a loyal Democrat felt bound to support Carter. This he did by backing the president's foreign-policy initiatives (such as the Camp David Peace Accords between Israel and Egypt) and by pushing for passage of Carter's energy legislation.

Carter's defeat in the 1980 presidential election brought to Washington the former governor of California, Ronald Reagan. On the surface, O'Neill and Reagan had many similarities. Both were from blue-collar, Irish backgrounds and had outgoing personalities; they also shared an interest in sports and were the same age. The similarities ended there, however; according to O'Neill, Reagan had forgotten his roots. From 1981 to 1987, O'Neill led congressional opposition to the Republican president.

The remainder of O'Neill's career as Speaker was largely spent performing damage control, as the Reagan Administration worked to slash spending on government social programs—including Social Security, Medicare, employment-training programs, and college-aid programs—and increase defense spending. O'Neill constantly reminded members of Congress and the public that it was these programs that had enabled many people to rise to their current status, and he implored them not to deny these same benefits to others. By stressing the theme of fairness, he resisted Reagan's efforts to slash social programs and helped to preserve New Deal legislation, much of which O'Neill himself had originally helped to implement.

On October 18, 1986, O'Neill retired from the House of Representatives, bringing his fifty-year career in politics to a close. Thirty-four of those years were served as a member of Congress, and ten as Speaker of the House of Representatives—the longest continuous term of any Speaker in history. Throughout, O'Neill made certain he never lost touch with his roots. On January 5, 1994, he died in his hometown of Boston at the age of eighty-one.

### Summary

A liberal New Deal reformer in the Roosevelt mold, O'Neill never forgot his origins. Having grown up in a working-class community, he worked tirelessly to raise men and women out of poverty by way of social legislation. Believing the federal government to be the only body capable of creating a solid middle class, O'Neill stuck by these principles even when they were unpopular. Above all, O'Neill stressed fairness. His generation had been saved from the depths of the Depression by government intervention, and a solid middle class had been created. To O'Neill, it was unfair for these very people to kick out from behind them the ladder that had allowed their ascent, denying others the same opportunity for upward mobility. As Speaker, he headed a resurgent Congress no longer willing to concede all initiative and authority to the president. Tip O'Neill fought his entire life to assure people their government's help in achieving the American Dream.

### Bibliography

Clancy, Paul R., and Shirley Elder. *Tip: A Biography of Thomas P. O'Neill, Speaker of the House.* New York: Macmillan, 1980. A comprehensive and readable biography that follows O'Neill's development as a politician from childhood to the Speakership. Provides a solid bibliography to aid further research on O'Neill's life, career, and influence on American politics.

Kennon, Donald R., ed. *The Speakers of the U.S. House of Representatives: A Bibliography.* Baltimore: John Hopkins University Press, 1986. Provides a brief synopsis of O'Neill's career up until 1984, followed by a comprehensive bibliography. Organized by topic; easy to follow.

O'Neill, Tip, with Gary Hymel. *All Politics Is Local: And Other Rules of the Game.* New York: Times, 1994. A guide to politics as envisioned by O'Neill. Provides insight into his life, political tactics, and relationships; also useful as a guide to modern U.S. politics.

O'Neill, Tip, with William Novak. *Man of the House: The Life and Political Memoirs of Speaker O'Neill.* New York: Random House, 1987; London: Bodley Head, 1988. A valuable primary source that provides a careful and detailed personal recollection of O'Neill's life from his boyhood to his retirement.

Peters, Ronald M., ed. *The Speaker: Leadership in the United States House of Representatives.* Washington, D.C.: Congressional Quarterly, 1994. Describes and reviews the Speaker's role in the House. Specific contributions are also made by former Speakers such as O'Neill, his predecessor Carl Albert, and his successor Jim Wright. Delineates these men's various views on politics and on how power should be used in the House.

Vogler, David J. *The Politics of Congress.* 6th ed. Madison, Wis.: Brown and Benchmark, 1993. Provides a good overview of the workings of Congress. More specifically, however, it shows the tremendous influence O'Neill had on Congress, especially during his years as Speaker.

*James Edward Zacchini*

# JAN HENDRIK OORT

*Born:* April 28, 1900; Franeker, The Netherlands
*Died:* November 5, 1992; Leiden, The Netherlands
*Area of Achievement:* Astronomy
*Contribution:* Oort was one of the most significant astronomers of the twentieth century. He was the first to postulate the vast swarm of comets known subsequently as the Oort cloud. He was one of the pioneers of radio astronomy, and he was one of the leaders in establishing the structure of the Milky Way Galaxy.

## Early Life

Jan Hendrik Oort was born in Franeker, The Netherlands, on April 28, 1900, the son of Abraham Hermanus Oort, a physician, and Ruth Hannah Faber Oort. His grandfather, a professor of Hebrew at the University of Leiden, was one of the translators of the Bible into the Dutch Leiden edition.

Following his graduation from the Leiden *Gymnasium* in 1917, Oort enrolled in the University of Gröningen, where he studied under the prominent astronomer Jacobus Kapteyn. He spent the years 1922 to 1924 in the United States as a research assistant at Yale University and became familiar with Harvard University astronomer Harlow Shapley's study of the Galaxy. Upon his return to The Netherlands, Oort began working at the University of Leiden, an association that would last throughout his career. He was appointed an instructor in 1926, after receiving his Ph.D. from the University of Gröningen with a dissertation on high-velocity stars.

Oort married Johanna Maria Graadt van Roggen on May 24, 1927. In that same year, he began establishing his reputation as a major scholar with the presentation of two papers on the rotation of the galactic system.

## Life's Work

Although it hardly reflects the full range of his accomplishments in the world of astronomy, Oort's name and reputation are guaranteed longevity through the Oort cloud—the conglomeration of comets he hypothesized in 1950—and, to a lesser extent, by the Oort constants of galactic rotation and Oort's limit, the value of density near the Galaxy's midpoint. Despite the public recognition inherent in the name of the comet cloud, however, Oort's greatest achievements lie in his contributions to an understanding of the structure and function of the Galaxy.

Oort began his career by studying under Jacobus Kapteyn, one of the pioneers of galactic research. By 1922, Kapteyn had spent sixteen years mapping the Galaxy. Although Kapteyn's map showed the Galaxy as only half its actual size, he was correct in his assessment of its shape as a disk with a central bulge narrowing toward the edges (something like a discus). After sharing the Bachiene Foundation Prize in 1920 for his paper on stars of the F, G, K, and M types, Oort turned his attention to Kapteyn's researches. Oort began studying stars of high velocity, which had proved difficult to reconcile with a galactic model that had the Sun near its center. His analysis of high-velocity stars and his close observation of Shapley's work during his research assistantship in the United States convinced Oort that the Galaxy was much larger than Kapteyn had assumed.

Oort's two 1927 papers furthered the work of Bertil Lindblad of the Stockholm Observatory. The papers argued that the Galaxy rotates not as a unit but more like the solar system, with those stars far from the center moving slower and those close to the center, faster. Through elaborate calculations involving rotational velocities of various stars, Oort was able to estimate the galactic mass, the number of stars, and the dimensions of the Galaxy. As Bengt Stromgren observed in awarding the Vetlesen Prize to Oort, ". . . it was only through Professor Oort's detailed analysis . . . that the hypothesis was finally proved. This is an example of one paper changing the whole outlook of the astronomical community."

In 1935, Oort was promoted to professor of astronomy, and, during that decade, he turned his attention to the distribution of stars in the Galaxy, realizing that Kapteyn's problem had been the interstellar dust that obscures the view of the distant parts of the Galaxy. Although Oort's theory of galactic structure was accepted by the scientific community, it was not possible to test his hypothesis until the development of radio astronomy. During World War II, with the occupation of The Netherlands by the Nazis, the Leiden Observatory was closed, and Oort and his colleagues continued their work only with the greatest of difficulties. Nevertheless, one of the most important discoveries for modern astronomy was made by Oort's colleague Hendrik Van de Hulst. Van de Hulst's work was based upon the principle that the hydrogen atom periodically emits radio waves at a constant wavelength of 21 centimeters. Though this characteristic is useless in local applications, in the vastness of space there is a sufficient number of atoms to be measured. Immediately following the war, Oort and Van de Hulst began working toward a test of Van de Hulst's hypothesis, but it was not until 1951 that they were able to do so. The theory, which had been independently reached by the Soviet scientist I. S. Shklovsky, proved to be true and, coupled with the building of large radio telescopes, led to the establishment of radio astronomy, the most important step in studying the Galaxy. The 21-centimeter waves pass through the dust and gas and allow astronomers to "see" as they cannot with optical telescopes. Meanwhile, also in collaboration with Van de Hulst, Oort, who had been appointed director of the Leiden Observatory following the war, in 1946 published a study of the clouds of gas and dust and subsequently showed that these clouds surrounding bright, hot stars can provide the material for the spontaneous formation of new stars.

In 1950, Oort made public the theory that led to the naming of the Oort cloud. His observations of the actions of nineteen long-period comets led him to the conclusion that there is a vast body of comets—in the trillions—consisting largely of debris from the disintegration of a planet. As a result of gravitational forces from various stars, comets are periodically thrust into orbits that bring them into the solar system. Oort theorized that there must be a swarm of these comets extending almost to the nearest stars, but their tie to the solar system suggests that they were formed soon after the planetary system itself. It is again a measure of Oort's careful reasoning and analysis that his theory is accepted almost universally despite the total absence of visual evidence.

By 1954, Oort and Van de Hulst had completed a map of the spiral structure of the Galaxy's outer region based on their radio-wave analysis. Oort also showed that the part of the Galaxy that is visible is far too small to account for its gravitational attraction on distant stars—evidence of a black hole in the Galaxy. In 1956, Oort and Van de Hulst revealed the discovery of radio signals produced by ionized hydrogen in space. Further investigation showed that these emissions occurred across the Galaxy, and, using the 21-centimeter wavelength, they established the rotational period of the Galaxy at 225,000,000 years.

In 1956, with T. Walraven, Oort engaged in the first extensive examination of the light polarization in the Crab nebula, a gaseous mass assumed to be the result of the fabled supernova of A.D. 1054. In a 1957 article in *Scientific American*, Oort argued that the light of this nebula consists of synchrotron radiation produced by high-velocity electrons spiraling about large magnetic fields, in accordance with a theory of Shklovsky. This phenomenon is believed to be responsible for the significant radio-wave radiation from the Crab nebula and other radio sources in space.

In the late 1950's, Oort and Australian Frank Kerr discovered that the galactic core consists of "turbulent" hydrogen that is constantly expanding outward only to be replaced by other hydrogen falling back into the center from the top and bottom of the central bulge. Oort's observations suggest that a massive explosion in the core of the disk, perhaps ten million years ago, produced this turbulence. Further radio analysis allowed him to establish the Galaxy as a rapidly whirling disk with a jagged edge produced by the juxtaposition of rapidly rotating material on the inside and material of slow rotation on the outside. In 1964, Oort and G. W. Rougoor discovered a ring of neutral hydrogen 3,000 parsecs from the galactic center. These gases, which form the spiral arms of the Galaxy, are expanding rapidly outward and also provide support for the hypothesis of a major explosion.

Oort then began studying the space through which the Galaxy moves, both on its own and as part of the cluster of galaxies to which it belongs. His most significant observation was the nearly limitless clouds of hydrogen through which the Galaxy moves. He hypothesized, from the fact that the densest part of this hydrogen corona was above, that the Galaxy was moving upward. He also theorized that while some gas was absorbed and other gas was moving outward, the fact that some was moving inward would double the mass of the Galaxy every three billion years and also effect a change in its shape.

In addition to his duties in Leiden, Oort served from 1935 to 1948 as general secretary of the International Astronomical Union and from 1958 to 1961 as its president. He received numerous honorary degrees and other awards, including the 1942 Bruce Medal from the Astronomical Society of the

Pacific, the Gold Medal of the Royal Astronomical Society in 1946, and the Vetlesen Prize (established to supplement the Nobel Prizes in areas where they are not awarded) in 1966.

### Summary

Jan Hendrik Oort's long and distinguished career was characterized by steady progress toward the solutions to the problems which he undertook. From the beginning, he demonstrated the ability to work well with his colleagues and students. From his first modification of Kapteyn's galactic model, he demonstrated the capacity for detailed and painstaking research even—as in the case of the German Occupation—in the face of exceptional difficulty. While the ever more sophisticated methods of modern astronomy have modified or enhanced some of his theoretical work, his methods were so precise, his research so painstaking, and his arguments so convincing that the scientific mainstream accepted his theories even when no direct visual evidence existed.

Highly respected by his contemporaries, Oort cast a long shadow. His galactic formulations and his pioneering work in radio astronomy, his postulation of the comet cloud and his analysis of the Crab nebula, his administrative work, and his encouragement of others justify Carl Sagan's assertion that "Jan Oort . . . perhaps more than any other person in the twentieth century has revolutionized our knowledge of the Galaxy."

### Bibliography

Pfeiffer, John. *The Changing Universe: The Story of the New Astronomy.* London: Gollancz, and New York: Random House, 1956. A good popular introduction to radio astronomy. The author devotes several pages to the work of Oort and Van de Hulst.

Ritchie, David. *Comets: The Swords of Heaven.* New York: New American Library, 1985. One of the better books to capitalize on the arrival of Halley's Comet. Contains a brief discussion of the Oort cloud.

Sagan, Carl, and Ann Druyan. *Comet.* London: Joseph, and New York: Random House, 1985. In one of his best-selling scientific works, Sagan and his novelist wife have assembled an impressive study of comets from both a scientific and a cultural perspective. Their discussion of Oort and the Oort cloud is outstanding. Profusely illustrated, this is a truly beautiful book.

Stromgren, Bengt. "An Appreciation of Jan Hendrik Oort." In *Galaxies and the Universe*, edited by Lodewijk Woltjer. New York: Columbia University Press, 1968. The Vetlesen tribute to Oort by the eminent Danish astronomer is an excellent commentary on Oort's career to that point.

Struve, Otto. "The Origin of Comets." In *The Origin of the Solar System*, edited by Thornton Page and Lou Williams Page. New York: Macmillan, 1966. This article, which first appeared in 1950, summarizes one of Oort's papers, which concluded with the theory of the comet cloud.

Tayler, R. J. *Galaxies: Structure and Evolution.* Rev. ed. Cambridge and New York: Cambridge University Press, 1993. This book in the Wykeham Science series is aimed at high school seniors and first-year undergraduates. The book presents the full mathematical details and applications of both Oort's constants and Oort's limit.

*Daniel J. Fuller*

# ALEKSANDR IVANOVICH OPARIN

*Born:* March 2, 1894; Uglich, Russia

*Died:* April 21, 1980; U.S.S.R.

*Areas of Achievement:* Biochemistry, botany, and biology

*Contribution:* Oparin was the principal pioneer in theorizing on the origins of life on Earth from inorganic matter. Of major importance also were his works which dealt with the biochemistry of plant material, from which he successfully developed the principles of Soviet biochemistry based on biocatalysis.

## Early Life

Born on March 2, 1894, in the small village of Uglich, near Moscow, Aleksandr Ivanovich Oparin was the youngest of three children in a typical Russian family. Because the area lacked a secondary school, Oparin's family moved to Moscow when he was nine, making it possible for him to continue his education. Details of his younger years are scant until he reached college age. Attaining a complete secondary education, in which he distinguished himself by his abilities in science, Oparin decided to attend Moscow State University. There he became interested in plant physiology, studying in the natural sciences department of the physico-mathematical faculty. While at the school, he became associated with and greatly influenced by K. A. Timiryazev, who had known Charles Darwin and was a determined exponent of his theory of evolution. Oparin himself was drawn to Darwin's theory of natural selection, a viewpoint that would dominate his later career and be a special feature of his theory of the beginnings of life.

## Life's Work

Impressed with the ideas inherent in contemporary Darwinian thinking, particularly that of selection for characteristics best adapted to a specific environment, Oparin began to extend the theory of evolution to the possible biochemical origin of life. Graduated in 1917, Oparin worked in several research institutes and institutions of higher learning, doing research under A. N. Bakh in biochemistry and botany. In 1922, his ideas, already in a concrete form, were presented at a meeting of the Russian Botanical Society, causing quite a stir, particularly among critics of the idea that life could form from nonliving chemicals. The entire topic of life's original beginnings had been ignored for years because of a basic biological assumption that "life begets life," which was prevalent since Louis Pasteur's experiments put the final demise to the idea of spontaneous generation of organic bodies, and also because of the tremendous philosophical and religious issues inherent in the subject. With the collapse of the vitalistic theory, removing the need for a spiritual force animating matter to distinguish it from nonliving material, it became possible to explain life exclusively in terms of chemistry and physics, an outlook readily adopted by members of the physical sciences.

Oparin's theory was based on three premises, derived from his ideas on how life might have arisen in the primitive conditions that existed on Earth some three billion years previously. He assumed that the first organisms arose between 4.7 and 3.2 billion years ago in the ancestral world seas. The oceans, in the process, had derived the necessary chemicals for complete organic synthesis from the primordial atmosphere, consisting of methane, hydrogen, ammonia, and water, much like the atmospheres today encircling the giant planets Jupiter and Saturn. These earliest organisms would not have been able to synthesize their own food but rather must have been heterotrophs, deriving nutrients from the surrounding medium or from consuming each other—this was in conflict with the then-current idea that all the early life-forms were autotrophs, making their own food supplies. Second, Oparin speculated that there was a virtually unlimited, continual supply of energy usable by the organisms, most likely in the form of sunlight, particularly ultraviolet, but also possibly from other sources (including volcanoes, lightning discharges in electrical storms, meteoric actions, and cosmic rays). Since this energy was continually added, life forming was not limited by the second law of thermodynamics acting in a closed system. Finally, Oparin postulated that life had to be characterized by a high degree of structural and functional organization before it could be called alive. This last point stood strongly at odds with the prevailing view that life was basically molecular in nature. To back up his arguments, he showed, by using well-known chemical reactions, how molecules might combine to form the important organic molecules and amino acids needed. Through painstaking laboratory experiments, he was able definitively to answer his critics, particularly as to the feasibility of reactions being caused by energy from either electrical storms or ultraviolet radiation from the sun. His findings, although they did not answer the question of how primitive organisms could reproduce, suggested that the necessary degree of order in protein structure probably resulted from restrictions imposed on the binding of amino acids through their shapes and electric charge distribution. Oparin showed conclusively that enzymes, as proteins, functioned much more efficiently in synthetic cells than in an ordinary aqueous solution. This idea was critical to later experiments with microscopic droplets, called "coacervates," of gelatin and gum arabic that demonstrated that the droplets, in a water and sugar solution, would grow and continually reproduce by budding.

Oparin's basic theory, published in 1924, reached the general public in 1936 in *Vozniknovenie zhizni na zemle* (*The Origin of Life*, 1939). This single work stimulated great interest and was first tested analytically in 1953 by S. L. Miller and Harold Urey. These two scientists used a mixture of Oparin's gases to simulate the early atmosphere of primordial Earth with electrical discharges, simulating lightning bolts for energy that ran through the circulating gases. After the test period of two weeks, the chemicals that were turning the water turbid were found to be compounds of sugars, complex carbohydrates, and amino acids, the latter being the basic material for producing proteins and enzymes. Additional confirmation of Oparin's idea came almost at the same time, with the discovery of fossilized amino acids in rocks dating some three billion years old. C. Ponnamperuna complemented Oparin's theory by performing the same experiments but altering the original mixture of gases, adding other compounds and molecules quite regularly found in volcanic discharges. He showed that, in support of Oparin's ideas, one could easily make nucleotides, dinucleotides, and ATP (adenosine triphosphate, the energy molecule in the cells)—more organic materials necessary for life. Oparin himself carried the work forward when he was able in the laboratory to polymerize adenine to form droplets that he called protobionts. These droplets carried out many of the normal processes associated with life such as absorbing molecules from the surrounding media, metabolizing those molecules, recombining the ingredients in their own structures, and reproducing by division. Oparin believed that these early creations were alive because of their spectacular ability to reproduce and to take in and use foodstuffs.

In 1929, Oparin became professor of plant biochemistry at Moscow State University. In 1935, he helped found, with the botanist Bakh, the Bakh Institute of Biochemistry at the Academy of Sciences of the Soviet Union in Moscow. He was appointed by the government to be deputy director of the institute until 1946, when he became the director, a position he held until his death in April, 1980. From 1948 to 1955, Oparin also served as the academician-secretary of the department of biology of the Soviet Academy of Sciences. For his work, he was the noteworthy recipient of the A. N. Bakh Prize in 1950 and the Élie Metchnikoff Gold Prize in 1950.

### Summary

Aleksandr Ivanovich Oparin became one of the best-known Soviet biochemists internationally. After being graduated from Moscow State University in biological chemistry, he helped cofound the Institute of Biochemistry. His main works dealt with the development of biochemical principles necessary for processing plant raw materials, processes vital to the economy of his country. He became greatly interested in the enzymatic activities in plants, the study of such enzymes leading to his work on the origin of terrestrial life. He was able to show through scientific experiments that biocatalysis was the basis of the production in nature of a large number of food products, the combined operation of molecules and enzymes together being necessary for the formation of starches, sugars, and other carbohydrates and proteins found in usable plants. Virtually alone, he developed the principles of Soviet technical botanical biochemistry.

He is best known worldwide for his hypotheses on the origin of life on the planet, first made available in 1922, and for *The Origin of Life*. According to his theory, life originated on Earth as a result of evolution acting on molecules formed from simpler combinations created in Earth's primordial atmosphere by violent energy discharges. Such complex molecules, raining down on the oceans, came together to react and produce structures with the basic characteristics of life, including, as he showed in the laboratory, the ability to grow, metabolize, and reproduce. Subsequent work by others has given credence to many of his ideas.

As a result of his work, Oparin was elected president in 1970 of the International Society for the

Study of the Origin of Life, becoming honorary president in 1977. Over the years, he has been a member of numerous scientific societies, including the academies of Bulgaria, East Germany, Cuba, Spain, Italy, and the Leopoldine German Academy of Researchers in the Natural Sciences. He received numerous awards and medals including one as Hero of Socialist Labor (1969), the Lenin Prize (1974), five Orders of Lenin, two other Soviet orders, and many foreign awards. He was a member of the Soviet Committee in Defense of Peace and a member and vice president of the International Federation of Scientists. Oparin's participation contributed to his belief in world peace and a harmony well worth looking for overriding the magnificence of nature.

### Bibliography

Bernal, J. D. *The Origin of Life.* London: Weidenfeld and Nicolson, and Cleveland: World, 1967. Provides a detailed review of the known characteristics of life and the various solutions that have been proposed to account for its origin. Many ideas are presented as extensions of those of Oparin. The importance of primeval conditions is stressed. Includes an extensive bibliography and a very usable glossary of necessary terms.

Cairns-Smith, A. G. *The Life Puzzle: On Crystals and Organisms and on the Possibility of a Crystal as an Ancestor.* Edinburgh: Oliver and Boyd, 1971. An investigative account of how life could have arisen from developments within crystalline matter. Stressing the relationships between inorganic crystals and organic forms, the author clearly presents the rationale for the belief that life could arise from nonliving forms.

Calvin, Melvin. *Chemical Evolution: Molecular Evolution Towards the Origin of Living Systems on the Earth and Elsewhere.* Oxford and New York: Oxford University Press, 1969. An older book that presents in detail the evidence, both chemical and physical, for life arising in the past from inorganic materials. Traces the early finds of fossils to substantiate ideas such as Oparin's.

Fox, Sidney W. *Molecular Evolution and the Origin of Life.* Rev. ed. New York: Dekker, 1977. This well-written work presents a detailed view of how, once chemical molecules of sufficient complexity are formed, processes associated with evolution take over to lead to life. Fox details many theories of life's formation, including the data and problems with each theory. Includes comprehensive references.

Futuyma, Douglas J. *Evolutionary Biology.* 3d ed. Sunderland, Mass.: Sineuer, 1998. A detailed explanatory treatment of how evolution works, starting from the formation of life molecules through the processes that have acted on Earth for four billion years. Encompasses a wide range of evolutionary thought and covers Oparin and others speculating on life's origins. Very well written and illustrated.

Hoyle, Fred. *The Intelligent Universe.* London: Joseph, 1983; New York: Holt Rinehart, 1984. A very enjoyable and well-illustrated book that explains how life might have formed anywhere in the universe as a result of chemical reactions occurring on Earth and in the depths of space. Presents scenarios dealing with the evolution of life under diverse conditions and the possible transmittal of life elsewhere in the galaxy.

Oparin, Aleksandr Ivanovich. *The Origin of Life on the Earth.* London: Oliver and Boyd, and New York: Academic Press, 1957. The original work on the possible causes and mechanisms for organic molecule formation early in Earth's history. Presents all Oparin's major ideas, including a discussion of molecular formation, energy sources, and reactions observed in the laboratory.

*Arthur L. Alt*

## J. ROBERT OPPENHEIMER

*Born:* April 22, 1904; New York, New York
*Died:* February 18, 1967; Princeton, New Jersey
*Area of Achievement:* Physics
*Contribution:* As director of the Los Alamos Laboratories, Oppenheimer was in charge of the team of scientists who developed the nation's first nuclear weapons.

### Early Life

J. Robert Oppenheimer was born April 22, 1904, in New York City, the firstborn son of wealthy Jewish parents. Oppenheimer and his younger brother Frank were educated at the New York Society for Ethical Culture, where Oppenheimer became interested in science and literature. An aloof, serious young boy, he did poorly in sports but loved sailing and horseback riding.

In 1922, Oppenheimer entered Harvard, where he majored in chemistry and was introduced to physics. After graduating, Oppenheimer went to England in 1925, to study physics at Cambridge. Oppenheimer had planned to study experimental physics but proved inept at laboratory work. Theoretical physics fascinated him, but the creative, sustained, and solitary mental effort necessary for effective work drove him to the point of mental collapse. After a summer's vacation, however, Oppenheimer recovered his stability. Realizing that he was not cut out for lab work, he left Cambridge to study at the University of Göttingen, Germany, then a center for theoretical physics.

Oppenheimer made a reputation at Göttingen, writing papers dealing with aspects of the then new theory of quantum physics. In 1927, Oppenheimer was awarded a doctorate from Göttingen. After a year's further study with leading European physicists, he returned to the United States in 1929.

### Life's Work

Oppenheimer hoped to build an American center for the study of physics. In 1929, he was appointed assistant professor of physics at the University of California, Berkeley, where Ernest Lawrence was building a reputation as one of the nation's leading experimental physicists. Together, Oppenheimer and Lawrence made Berkeley the best-known graduate school for physics in the nation during the 1930's.

At Berkeley, Oppenheimer became a famous, charismatic teacher. Tall, thin, with striking blue eyes, he stood before the blackboard with chalk in one hand and an ever-present cigarette in the other. He was best known for his ability to communicate abstruse theoretical material clearly. Although some found Oppenheimer an arrogant intellectual snob, to favored students he was "Oppie," a charming mentor who introduced them to art, Eastern literature, gourmet foods, and fine wines as well as physics.

Independently wealthy, Oppenheimer had lived a sheltered life and paid little attention to economic or world events. In the 1930's, as the Great Depression worsened and Adolf Hitler came to power in Germany, Oppenheimer began to take more interest in politics. Also in the 1930's, he became involved with various local reform groups, many of which were affiliated with the Communist Party. Communism was popular among many intellectuals because it seemed to offer hope for social justice at home and resistance to Fascism overseas. Many of Oppenheimer's friends were leftists. His brother, Frank, became a Communist Party member.

In November, 1940, Oppenheimer married Kathryn Puening. She had been married three times before, once to a dedicated Communist who had been killed during the Spanish Civil War; she was also a Party member.

In 1942, the United States, at war with the Axis, began a crash program to produce an atomic weapon. Oppenheimer was chosen to head the Los Alamos Laboratories, near Santa Fe, New Mexico, where the proposed weapon would be assembled and tested. At Los Alamos, Oppenheimer coordinated the work of more than three thousand scientists, technicians, and military personnel. His performance as director of the Los Alamos scientific staff, which included past and future Nobel Prize winners, was superb. His skills as a communicator helped him coordinate the project that produced the first nuclear weapon.

On July 16, 1945, the first atom bomb was tested. Oppenheimer said later that, as the first mushroom cloud rose above the New Mexico desert, he recalled a line from the Hindu scriptures, "I am become death, the shatterer of worlds." In August, 1945, American bombers dropped atomic weapons on Hiroshima and Nagasaki, and World War II was brought to an end by the Japanese surrender.

After the war, Oppenheimer returned to academic life, first teaching at Berkeley and then moving

to Princeton, New Jersey, where he was appointed director of the Institute for Advanced Study. His service at Los Alamos had made him one of the nation's most famous scientists, and he was in demand as a government consultant on atomic energy. From 1947 to 1952, he was chairman of the General Advisory Committee of the Atomic Energy Commission.

In the postwar years, Oppenheimer often spoke publicly about his fear that nuclear energy would lead to world destruction unless controlled and shared. He and other influential scientists hoped that the new discoveries in physics would become an international resource, controlled and used for the good of the world as a whole. Yet as the Cold War between the United States and the Soviet Union worsened, such hopes faded.

In 1950, the Soviet Union exploded a hydrogen bomb. Shortly thereafter, Americans were shocked to learn that a member of the British delegation to Los Alamos during World War II, Klaus Fuchs, had admitted to passing information about the project to the Soviets. After these revelations, government security became much tighter, and demagogues seized on public concern to whip up hysteria about possible Soviet sympathizers in the State Department, in the public entertainment industry, and among the nation's scientists.

Oppenheimer's left-wing connections had been well-known when he was chosen to head the Los Alamos project. He had been under Federal Bureau of Investigation surveillance for years and had continued to work on highly secret projects. In December, 1953, at the height of the Cold War hysteria, Oppenheimer's security clearance was suspended.

In the spring of 1954, the Personnel Security Board of the Atomic Energy Commission conducted hearings on the Oppenheimer case. His old associations were rehashed. He was also accused of injuring American security by being less than enthusiastic about the development of the hydrogen bomb. Despite a parade of character witnesses which included many prominent scientists, the board voted in June, 1954, to revoke Oppenheimer's security clearance. Oppenheimer returned to Princeton, where he continued to serve as director of the Institute for Advanced Studies until his retirement in 1966.

In 1963, he was given the Enrico Fermi Award by the United States government. This award was given to those who had made contributions to "development, use, or control of atomic energy." The presentation to Oppenheimer has been seen as a gesture of rehabilitation by the government. Yet his security clearance was not restored. Oppenheimer died February 18, 1967, of cancer, at his home in Princeton.

### Summary

Oppenheimer is famous for two things: He directed the project which produced the first atom bomb, and he was stripped of his security clearance during a period of national paranoia. Those who denied him access to the nation's technological secrets did not allege that he was a Soviet spy or that he had at any point violated the trust placed in him. Rather, he was accused of having had Communist friends, relatives, and students, of having failed to be sufficiently security-conscious, and of failing to support the development of the hydrogen bomb.

The Oppenheimer case remained a *cause célèbre* for many years. The inherent drama of Oppenheimer's rise and fall made the case a fitting subject for a play, a television documentary, and, in the 1980's, a British Broadcasting Corporation television miniseries.

Oppenheimer's most lasting contribution was scientific. His ability to communicate, to direct, to teach in the true sense—drawing from each member of his team and incorporating all insights into a working whole—made the achievement at Los Alamos possible.

Oppenheimer himself was aware of the irony of that achievement. A man dedicated to the pursuit of knowledge, he could yet be appalled at the cost of the pursuit. In 1946, in a farewell address to the staff at Los Alamos, he said, "If atomic bombs are to be added to the arsenals of a warring world, or to the arsenals of nations preparing for war, then the time will come when mankind will curse the names of Los Alamos and Hiroshima." He went on to express the hope that the world would unite "before this common peril, in law, in humanity."

**Bibliography**

"Brotherhood of the Bomb: Two Flinty Physicists Struggle over Their Terrifying Legacy." *U.S. News and World Report* 125, no. 7 (August 17, 1998). Examination of the relationship between Oppenheimer and Edward Teller and their involvement in the development of the hydrogen and atom bombs.

Curtis, Charles P. *The Oppenheimer Case: The Trial of a Security System.* New York: Simon and Schuster, 1955. A journalistic and declamatory account of Oppenheimer's 1954 hearing.

Davis, Nuel Pharr. *Lawrence and Oppenheimer.* New York: Simon and Schuster, 1968; London: Cape, 1969. A highly readable popular biography of Berkeley's two leading physicists; also gives a good picture of the scientific community at mid-century. Good bibliography.

*The Day After Trinity: J. Robert Oppenheimer and the Atomic Bomb.* Produced by Jon Else and KTEH-TV; written by Janet Peoples, David Peoples, and Jon Else. Santa Monica, Calif.: Pyramid Films, 1981. Video recording. This excellent documentary film focuses on Los Alamos and the World War II years.

Goodchild, Peter. *J. Robert Oppenheimer: Shatterer of Worlds.* London: BBC, 1980; Boston: Houghton Mifflin, 1981. Published in conjunction with the BBC series on Oppenheimer, this is an objective, often critical analysis of Oppenheimer's personality and of United States security. Copiously illustrated.

Kunetka, James W. *Oppenheimer: The Years of Risk.* Englewood Cliffs, N.J.: Prentice-Hall, 1982. A concise, well-balanced biography dealing with Oppenheimer's public service from 1942 to 1954. Describes the postwar controversies over security and the development of the hydrogen bomb in some detail.

Oppenheimer, J. Robert. *Robert Oppenheimer: Letters and Recollections.* Edited by Alice Kimball Smith and Charles Weiner. Cambridge: Harvard University Press, 1980. Letters from Oppenheimer to friends and colleagues interspersed with biographical information.

Szasz, Ferenc Morton. *The Day the Sun Rose Twice: The Story of the Trinity Site Nuclear Explosion.* Albuquerque: University of New Mexico Press, 1984. A short history of the successful first test of the atom bomb, using Manhattan Project papers. Not about Oppenheimer per se, but deals with his role at the test.

Taylor, Bryan C. "The Politics of the Nuclear Text: Reading Robert Oppenheimer's Letters and Recollections." *Quarterly Journal of Speech* 78, no. 4 (November, 1992). The author considers Oppenheimer's writings from a post-structuralist perspective.

*Jeanette Keith*

# JOSÉ CLEMENTE OROZCO

*Born:* November 23, 1883; Ciudad Guzmán, Mexico

*Died:* September 7, 1949; Mexico City, Mexico

*Area of Achievement:* Art

*Contribution:* Orozco was one of the greatest muralists of the twentieth century and was considered the foremost to work in fresco. He was among the earliest Mexican artists to break away from European conventionalism and treat purely Mexican themes: The silent, suffering masses became a recurring interest in his art, reflecting his deep humanitarian concern and empathy for his people.

## Early Life

José Clemente Orozco was born into a respected middle-class family on November 23, 1883, in Ciudad Guzmán in the coastal state of Jalisco in west-central Mexico. When he was two, the family moved to Guadalajara and then in 1890 to Mexico City, where he would grow up with his sister, Rosa, and brother, Luis. While attending primary school, Orozco passed by the workshop of Mexico's finest engraver, José Guadalupe Posada, and frequently stopped to watch as Posada produced caricatures for news stories, illustrations for children's books, and traditional Mexican folk art. By Orozco's own admission, it was Posada's work that first awakened his own artistic talents and taught him his earliest lessons about using color. He began to sketch and soon was enrolled in night classes in drawing at the Academy of Fine Arts of San Carlos, but Orozco's art studies were interrupted in 1897 when his family sent him to the School of Agriculture in San Jacinto.

Orozco was bored with his agrarian training, but it did give him some practical experience, and he was able to earn money drawing topographical maps. During this period, an accident damaged his eyes (he wore thick glasses), and his left hand became a fingerless stump (probably the reason for his preoccupation with hands in his paintings). He next entered the National Preparatory School, where he studied architecture for four years, but his obsession with painting eventually led him back to the Academy of Fine Arts in 1905. Since his father had died, Orozco earned his way by working as a draftsman and doing architectural drawings. At the academy, he had only a brief introduction to the methods of Antonio Fabrés, a masterful academic Spanish painter, but embraced wholeheartedly the latter's insistence on intense training, discipline, and photolike exactness in reproducing nature.

While at the academy, Orozco met Gerardo Murillo, recently returned from studies in Rome and Paris. A radical student who rejected conventional artistic views and Mexican subservience to Spain and Europe, Murillo had taken an Aztec name, calling himself "Dr. Atl." Atl's violent anticolonial views began to sway Orozco and other students away from dependence on a European style and toward Mexican-oriented themes in art. For the first time, Mexican painters began to look to their own country for inspiration, and a purely Mexican style of art began to emerge. For Orozco, a strong, dramatic style began to overwhelm his earlier traditionalist training.

## Life's Work

In 1910, with Atl as their leader, Orozco and other emerging "Mexican" artists gave their first exhibit at a state exhibition to celebrate the first hundred years of Mexican independence. Originally, the exhibit was to feature only Spanish artists, but Atl objected and conducted negotiations that enabled the group to show their art also. The exhibit—the first of Mexican artists—met with unexpected success. The group next formed a society called the Artistic Center and secured wall space from the government to paint murals. Just as work was beginning at the amphitheater of the National Preparatory School, the Revolution of 1910 began on November 20, and the project was necessarily shelved.

Orozco showed little interest in the new government of Francisco Madero, believing it offered nothing new. When student strikes closed the academy, he spent the winter of 1911-1912 doing anti-Madero caricatures for an opposition newspaper, claiming he was an artist and had no political convictions. When the academy reopened in 1913, Orozco gave the new curriculum a try but soon left, unimpressed, disliking the emphasis on French Impressionists. He began to find inspiration for his developing expressionist style in the brothels and dark streets of the Mexico City counter-culture and produced a series of watercolors of prostitutes—who became a major symbol in his art—and their environs known collectively as the *House of Tears.*

Civil war erupted in 1914. Orozco's damaged hand foiled every attempt to draft him, but he produced satirical caricatures for *La Vanguardia*, a pro-revolutionary newspaper, which supported the cause of General Venustiano Carranza and was edited by Dr. Atl. There were moments when Orozco could not help but be amused by the confused antics of the dissident generals, but the violence, bloodshed, terror, and mutilated and mangled bodies he personally observed were what he remembered and what affected his art. In 1916, Orozco had his first one-man exhibit, which included *House of Tears*, and, the following year, he produced a series of watercolors called *Sorrows of War.*

Critics and moralists did not react favorably to his work, and insecure politicians winced at his earlier published cartoons and caricatures. Orozco found it opportune to spend several years in the United States. He lived in San Francisco and New York, where he had a brief meeting with David Siqueiros, another of Mexico's emerging artistic giants. These years were not happy ones for Orozco, but what he observed was not lost on his artist's eye.

In 1920, Orozco returned to Mexico, where he found the new government of Álvaro Obregón sympathetic with the old ideas of the Artistic Center. The "Mexican Muralist" movement began in 1922 when Orozco, Diego Rivera, Siqueiros, and others were commissioned by the minister of education to adorn the walls of the National Preparatory School. Lacking experience, the artists' first results were disappointing, and much in the murals betrayed a European rather than Mexican style of execution. The murals were disliked and defaced by students, who drove Orozco and Siqueiros out. In 1926, Orozco was invited back to complete his frescoes. He gradually developed his own personal, distinctive style, exemplified in the finest of his early work, *The Trench*, and also in *Cortes and Malinche*. During this period, Orozco also completed *Omniscience* (1925) in the House of Tiles, and *Social Revolution* (1926) in Orizaba at the Industrial School.

The agitation caused at home by the unpopular art and views of Orozco and his fellow artists, as well as a growing family (he had married Margarita Valladares on November 23, 1923) that was becoming more difficult to support (his third child had just been born), prompted him to leave for New York, where he arrived in December, 1927.

He was promised a three-month subsidy by the secretary of foreign relations. While in New York, he met Mrs. Alma Reed and Madame Sikelianos, whose spacious house on Fifth Avenue had become an international salon for intellectuals, poets, artists, and revolutionaries. The women were interested in Orozco's paintings and sketches of revolution and exhibited them in their house; they also influenced him with their own interest in Greek culture and classical scholarship. Through their patronage, Orozco became better known. An exhibition at the Marie Sterner Gallery (1928) was followed by a showing of his earlier fresco studies for the National Preparatory School by the Art Students' League (1929). Reed dedicated her new Delphic Studios to Orozco and exhibited his paintings of New York and Mexico.

In 1930, Orozco received his first commission to do a mural in the United States from Pomona College in Claremont, California, which wanted a Mexican artist to decorate the student refectory. There he would execute his *Prometheus*, departing temporarily from Mexican subjects and social criticism in favor of a classical and more universal theme (reflecting the influence of Reed's salon). The colossal figure of the immortal, self-sacrificing Titan, leaning on one knee, his curved body and muscular shoulders stretching upward with their burden, recalls Michelangelo and El Greco. Holding it aloft in his hands, the bright gift of fire emerges from the browns and grays of the lower mural to offer liberation, enlightenment, and purification. Yet, fire can also destroy. Fire became a major symbol in Orozoco's work. The *Prometheus* is less stylized and more expressionistic than earlier frescoes. At the time, only his sponsors were pleased with the result, and Orozco earned little money for his efforts.

Unfortunately, Orozco became overly technical in his next set of murals at the New School for Social Research (1930-1931) in New York City. Influenced by a then-current theory known as "dynamic symmetry," his execution of themes concerned with universal brotherhood, world revolution, and arts and sciences was rigid and mechanical, a disappointing sequel to the *Prometheus*. Orozco followed this project with a brief trip to Europe to see the great paintings in the museums and churches of England, France, Italy, and Spain. When he returned, he began decorating the library at Dartmouth College in New Hampshire (1932-1934), where he incorporated much of what he had recently observed overseas, presenting his worldview in two main scenes entitled *The Coming of Quetzalcoatl* and *The Return of Quetzalcoatl*. The Mexican Revolution, the Great Depression, and an impersonal, industrialized urban society had provoked Orozco to contrast a primitive, non-Christian paradise of the past with a modern-day, Christian, capitalist hell.

By 1934, Orozco's reputation had been firmly established. He triumphantly returned to Mexico and painted a huge single mural, *Catharsis*, in the Palace of Fine Arts. In 1936, he was in Guadalajara, where he executed what most consider his greatest murals at the University of Guadalajara, the Governor's Palace (1937), and in the chapel at the orphanage of Hospicio Cabañas (1938-1939). Historical themes illustrating inhumanity developed in earlier works are repeated here, with greater negativity. In the Hospicio dome, Orozco painted the *Man of Fire*, the logical culmination of his art and thought, and a composition some regard as unique in the history of art. Here is represented a figure engulfed in flame with light radiating all about him—embodying hope, salvation, and creativity, it is a meditation on human existence itself.

No later murals match the emotional intensity of the Guadalajara group, and universal themes took a second place to nationalistic ones, perhaps because of World War II and contemporary events in Mexico. Orozco painted frescoes in the Ortíz Library (in Jiquílpan) in 1940 and, during the same year, painted a mural for the New York Museum of Modern Art, which he entitled *Dive Bomber*, a work not as powerful in form as his others, more abstract and with delicate colors. Returning to Mexico City in 1941, he adorned the walls of the Supreme Court Building. He never finished his project in the Chapel of Jesus Nazarene (1942-1944). His last murals were at the National School of Teachers (1947-48), the Museum of History at Chapultepec (1948), and in the Government Palace in Guadalajara (1948-1949). In 1947, he received his government's highest award for cultural achievement during the preceding five-year period. While Orozco's murals constitute the heart of his work, his easel paintings alone would have established his reputation as a great artist. His *Zapatistas*, for example, captures some of the essence of his murals but lacks the grandeur that only a large-scale painting can convey. The abstract quality and hint of mysticism in his work toward the end of his life suggest to some that he was on the verge of an artistic breakthrough when he died on September 7, 1949, at age sixty-five.

### Summary

José Clemente Orozco was one of the monumental painters of the twentieth century and was foremost in reviving and perfecting the art of the mural, especially frescoes. He was one of the small group of Mexican artists who were the first to break with European colonial tradition and produce a purely Mexican, nationalistic art. Orozco believed that his paintings should convey ideas rather than stories. The bold form, social content, mordant colors, and revolutionary nature of his paintings made him unpopular in his own country, but Orozco persevered, developing his own expressionistic style. He finally found fame in the United States, where his work took on a more mature and international flavor, represented best in his work at Pomona College and, especially, the Dartmouth murals. His genius was finally recognized internationally.

A sensitive man who was deeply disturbed by the Mexican Revolution, the Great Depression,

World War II, and other less traumatic but nevertheless horrifying aspects of the human condition, Orozco empathized with the suffering masses, decried inhumanity, and viewed modern industrial society as a seemingly godless, capitalistic wasteland compared to the paradise of primordial, non-Christian times. Yet in his paintings there is usually a glimmer of hope—if humankind will recognize and be guided by it. His greatest work was produced in Guadalajara from 1936 to 1939, culminating in what is perhaps his most representative painting, the *Man of Fire* in the dome of the Hospicio Cabañas. Few artists have had such an impact on their craft, yet because of Orozco's Mexican origins and socialistic tendencies, his name is not as well known as that of other artistic giants of this century, who are from Europe and the United States.

### Bibliography

Charlot, Jean. *The Mexican Mural Renaissance, 1920-1925*. New Haven, Conn.: Yale University Press, 1963. Contains two chapters on Orozco and some illustrations. Good brief survey of his role in Mexican mural painting by a French muralist who knew him.

Edwards, Emily. *Painted Walls of Mexico*. Austin: University of Texas Press, 1966. A survey from prehistoric to modern times. Includes a general discussion of Orozco's life, highlighting the major events and contributions. Contains some illustrations.

Fernandez, Justino. *A Guide to Mexican Art from Its Beginnings to the Present*. Translated by Joshua C. Taylor. Chicago: University of Chicago Press, 1969. Under the section on "Contemporary Art," this work devotes pages 161-170 to Orozco's life and work. Contains some illustrations. Good for a quick summary.

Folgarait, Leonard. *Mural Painting and Social Revolution in Mexico, 1920-1940: Art of the New Order*. Cambridge and New York: Cambridge University Press, 1998. This volume is an in-depth study of Mexican art between 1920 and 1940. The murals of Orozco and other artists are discussed with emphasis on the effects of cultural issues on their works.

Helm, MacKinley. *Man of Fire: J. C. Orozco*. New York: Harcourt Brace, 1953. An interpretive memoir by a person who knew Orozco. The earliest major work on the artist, MacKinley's book attempts to understand the man and his art.

Orozco, José Clemente. *An Autobiography*. Translated by Robert C. Stephenson. Austin: University of Texas Press, 1962. Orozco's own account of his life to 1936. Indispensable but lacking pertinent detail.

———. *José Clemente Orozco*. Introduction by Alma Reed. New York: Delphic Studios,1932. An illustrated collection of Orozco's work to 1932. Minimal textual matter.

Polcari, Stephen. "Orozco and Pollock: Epic Transfigurations." *American Art* 6, no. 3 (Summer 1992). The author considers the influence of Orozco on the work of Jackson Pollock.

Reed, Alma M. *Orozco*. New York: Oxford University Press, 1956. A biography written by Orozco's New York patron and friend, who first introduced him to American art circles and was largely responsible for launching his international career.

*Robert B. Kebric*

## KATHERINE DAVALOS ORTEGA

*Born:* July 16, 1934; Tularosa, New Mexico
*Area of Achievement:* Government and politics
*Contribution:* As one of the first Latinas to hold a high government position, Ortega provided a role model and example for all women with political aspirations.

### Early Life

Donaciano Ortega and Catarina Davalos, the parents of Katherine Davalos Ortega, were from pioneer families that in the 1800's settled in what later became the state of New Mexico. The couple married and had nine children, with Katherine the youngest. Donaciano held many different jobs, including that of deputy U.S. marshal, which he began at the age of sixteen. He also worked at a copper mine, had a blacksmith shop, and did carpentry work. The family moved to Tularosa, a town with fewer than three thousand inhabitants, so that the children could attend high school. The family owned and operated a restaurant and dance hall in Tularosa, then a restaurant and a furniture store in nearby Alamogordo, New Mexico. Katherine's oldest sister, Ellen, founded the Otero Savings and Loan Association there in 1974. The businesses were moderately successful, but the family had a modest income.

Working in the family restaurant provided Katherine with early training in business skills. Even at the age of ten, she showed such facility with numbers that she was allowed to work the cash register. All the Ortega children participated in the family business, and each had a say in its operation.

Donaciano Ortega encouraged his children to learn English, though Spanish was their first language, and Katherine attended schools where Spanish was used rarely or never. While a senior in high school, she worked at the Otero County State Bank in Alamogordo. After high school, she worked in a bank for two years to save money to pay her college tuition.

Katherine Ortega was graduated with honors from Eastern New Mexico University in 1957 with a bachelor's degree in business and economics. She also studied secondary education, giving some thought to teaching high school business courses, but she was told not to bother applying for jobs in the eastern part of the state because her Hispanic background would disqualify her. She decided to abandon teaching, disgusted with the discrimination that kept her from pursuing her preferred career to the level of her ability and in a location of her choice.

### Life's Work

Soon after her graduation, Katherine Ortega started an accounting firm in Alamogordo with her sister, Ellen. She held several accounting positions in New Mexico and later in California, after she moved to Los Angeles in 1967. From 1969 to 1972, she worked as a tax superviser with Peat, Marwick, Mitchell and Company, one of the largest accounting firms in the United States. In 1972, Ortega was recruited by Pan American National Bank of Los Angeles to serve as its vice president and cashier. Her accounting skills and bilingualism aided in her work with the local Hispanic community. In December, 1975, she was selected as president and director of the Hispanic-owned Santa Ana State Bank, becoming the first woman to be president of a commercial bank in California. In 1978, respecting the wishes of her mother, who was in ill health, Ortega returned to New Mexico. She became a consultant to the family-owned Otero Savings and Loan Association, which grew to have assets of $20 million while she was associated with it. She became a certified public accountant (CPA) in 1979.

Ortega had been active in the Republican Party since college and had joined the Young Republicans soon after graduation. Following her return to New Mexico, Ortega's involvement in politics intensified. She worked as a precinct chair for the party in Alamogordo and assisted in the campaign of Senator Pete Domenici. The Republican Party called on her to serve as a liaison with Hispanic and women's organizations.

Ortega was rewarded for service to the Republican Party in April, 1982, with her first presidential appointment, when Ronald Reagan named her to the ten-member Advisory Committee on Small and Minority Business Ownership. In December of that year, she was appointed to the five-person Copyright Royalty Tribunal, which was created in the late 1970's to set royalty fees that cable television systems had to pay to copyright holders of broadcast programs. Among other duties, the tribunal also set the fees that jukebox operators paid to copyright holders of music.

While Ortega was serving on the Copyright Royalty Tribunal, Reagan recognized her professional abilities. On September 12, 1983, on the recommendation of Senator Domenici, who was then chair of the Senate Budget Committee, Reagan nominated Ortega as treasurer of the United States. Ortega would replace Angela M. Buchanan, who left office after the birth of her first child. The nomination came at a ceremony marking the beginning of Hispanic Heritage Week. Reagan's nominating speech pointed out the positive influence of the strength and decency of the Hispanic family. At the ceremony announcing her nomination, Ortega stressed the opportunities increasingly becoming available to women but noted the importance of self-reliance.

Ortega was sworn in on October 3, 1983, becoming the thirty-eighth holder of the position of treasurer of the United States. After being sworn in by Treasury Secretary Donald T. Regan, she signed special forms that were later used to add her signature to printing plates from which U.S. currency would be produced. Ortega was the tenth woman, and the second Latina, to be U.S. treasurer, following Romana Acosta Bañuelos, who served in the position from 1971 to 1974. Beginning in the mid-twentieth century, the position traditionally was given to a woman as a reward for service to her party and to the president. Ortega's new appointment made her the highest-ranking Hispanic in the Reagan Administration.

As U.S. treasurer, Ortega supervised the Bureau of Engraving and Printing, the U.S. Mint, and the U.S. Savings Bond Division. At the time of her appointment, Ortega oversaw five thousand employees and a budget of $220 million; her salary was $63,800 per year. The treasurer is a senior member of the staff of the secretary of the treasury, who is a member of the president's cabinet. The Bureau of Engraving and Printing produces U.S. currency as well as other documents and postage stamps. Ortega's signature soon began to appear in the lower left-hand corner on the front of each unit of U.S. paper currency. In 1985, Ortega was given the responsibility of promoting the sale of U.S. Liberty Coins, special gold and silver commemorative coins designed to raise $40 million to pay some of the costs of restoring the Statue of Liberty.

During 1984, Ortega traveled around the country speaking to various Hispanic and Republican groups. Although hers was not a policy-making position, she was important in articulating the Republican Party position on policy issues. Ortega's most important speaking engagement came at the end of the year, when she was chosen to give the keynote address at the Republican National Convention in Dallas, Texas. This honor recognized her accomplishments as a government official. She noted at the time that she was firmly committed to Reaganomics and the Republican Party, saying that she was "born a Republican." Political analysts widely expected a woman to be chosen to deliver the keynote address, but Senator Nancy Kassebaum and cabinet members Elizabeth Dole and Margaret Heckler, all with much more tenure at high levels of the federal government, were considered more likely to be chosen for the honor. In her speech, Ortega referred several times to her Hispanic heritage, and she included several phrases in Spanish. She noted how many people of Hispanic descent were leaving the Democratic Party and welcomed them to the Republican fold.

Ortega's high profile at the convention served to dispel complaints that the Reagan Administration was not committed to appointing women to high positions. Ortega made a point in her many speeches of emphasizing the many subcabinet positions that Reagan had filled with women.

Ortega served as treasurer of the United States from 1983 to 1989. She was married to Lloyd J. Derrickson on February 17, 1989. After leaving government service, she was primarily self-employed. She also served as an alternative representative to the United Nations and was on the boards of directors of several major corporations, including Ralston Purina Company and the Kroger Company.

### Summary

Katherine Davalos Ortega serves as an example of how determination and hard work can lead to success in a chosen field. Although she came from a modest background and suffered discrimination that made her abandon teaching, her first career choice, she earned professional credentials and through her dedicated work won the recognition of the Republican Party. She was well qualified when President Reagan looked for a candidate, preferably a Hispanic woman, to fill the position of U.S. treasurer.

In that position, Ortega was one of the highest ranking Hispanic members of the Reagan Administration. She provided a positive role model, and her service likely played some part in the increasing numbers of appointments of people of Hispanic descent to high government positions. The administration of President Bill Clinton, for example, included two Latinos, Henry G. Cisneros and Federico F. Peña, in cabinet-level positions as secretary of Housing and Urban Development (HUD) and secretary of transportation, respectively.

Ortega's life achievements and government service have been recognized and honored by many groups. She was given the 1977 Outstanding Alumni Award from Eastern New Mexico State University and also earned the California Businesswoman's Achievement Award and the Damas de Comercio Outstanding Woman of the Year Award. She was willing to serve as an example to other Hispanics, noting that everyone encounters obstacles of some sort. When faced with discrimination, she chose a career path on which her abilities would speak for themselves.

**Bibliography**

Brownstein, Ronald, and Nina Easton. *Reagan's Ruling Class: Portraits of the President's Top One Hundred Officials*. Washington, D.C.: Presidential Accounting Group, 1982. Provides details about the people with whom Ortega worked in Washington, D.C., but does not discuss her. Useful for providing context on Reagan's other appointees.

Clines, Francis X. "Reagan Names Hispanic Woman as Treasurer of the United States." *The New York Times*, September 13, 1983, p. B14. Brief article announcing Reagan's nomination of Ortega. Notes that the announcement, made at a White House ceremony for Hispanic Heritage Week, came at a time that the Republican Party was trying to attract Hispanic voters.

Edmunds, Lavinia. "Women to Watch at the Republican National Convention." *Ms.* 13 (August, 1984): 22. Places Ortega in the context of women at the convention, at which the Republican Party had vowed to have about half of its delegates be women. Notes that Ortega was firmly committed to Reaganomics and that cabinet members Elizabeth Dole and Margaret Heckler, along with Senator Nancy Kassebaum, had been considered more likely to be chosen as keynote speaker.

Gonsior, Marian C. "Katherine D. Ortega." In *Notable Hispanic American Women*, edited by Diane Telgen and Jim Kamp. Detroit: Gale Research, 1993. A three-page biography of Ortega. Useful for details about her early life, with many of Ortega's thoughts included as quotations. The volume as a whole provides an overdue look at the contributions of Hispanic American women.

McFadden, Robert. "Choice for Treasurer: Katherine Davalos Ortega." *The New York Times*, September 13, 1983, p. B14. A brief biography with some quotations from Ortega regarding her background.

Morey, Janet, and Wendy Dunn. "Katherine Davalos Ortega." In *Famous Mexican Americans*. New York: Cobblehill, 1989. An eight-page biography, containing details of the duties of the U.S. treasurer. Appropriate for middle-school readers. Contains a photograph of Ortega as treasurer of the United States.

Salkowski, Charlotte. "GOP Keynoter Radiates Self-Help Ideals." *The Christian Science Monitor*, August 17, 1984, pp. 1, 32. An article about Ortega written near the time of her keynote address at the Republican National Convention. Notes her modest background and opinions concerning the character-building nature of hard work and self-sufficiency.

*A. J. Sobczak*

## JOSÉ ORTEGA Y GASSET

*Born:* May 9, 1883; Madrid, Spain
*Died:* October 18, 1955; Madrid, Spain
*Areas of Achievement:* Philosophy and journalism
*Contribution:* Ortega's books, journalism, and lectures commanded attention throughout Europe. His renown helped to bring Spain out of a long period of cultural isolation, and his thought contributed greatly to his country's intellectual reawakening.

### Early Life

José Ortega y Gasset was born in Madrid, Spain, on May 9, 1883. His father, José Ortega y Munilla, was a novelist and had formerly been editor of *El Imparcial*, a leading Madrid newspaper founded by his grandfather. He was first taught by private tutors. Subsequently, like so many European intellectuals before him, he was schooled by Jesuits, at the College of Miraflores del Pala in Málaga. He later studied at the University of Madrid and at the universities of Leipzig, Berlin, and Marburg in Germany. In 1904, he received a doctorate in philosophy and literature from the University of Madrid, and in the German years that followed he deeply imbibed neo-Kantian philosophy. Ortega was named professor of metaphysics at the University of Madrid in 1910-1911. His association with that institution was to continue until 1936, when he went into self-imposed exile during the Spanish Civil War.

The same year that he received his chair, he founded *Faro* (beacon), a philosophical review. Shortly thereafter, he founded a second, *Europa*. These were the first of many periodicals he was to found during his long journalistic career. By roughly the age of thirty, Ortega was well launched upon his multifaceted career as philosopher, journalist, author, educator, and statesman. Having spent the years 1905-1907 at German universities, he had become conversant with northern European ideas. He believed that Spanish thought would tend to be superficial as long as Spain remained cut off from the cultural roots of Europe. In his own journals and in the newspapers, he tirelessly argued for a reintegration. By the time Spain's intellectual reawakening came to pass, Ortega was famous throughout the Spanish-speaking world.

### Life's Work

For several years, Ortega had been writing on Spanish problems, in his own reviews and in *El Imparcial*, but it was a speech he made in 1914 that catapulted him into national prominence. The speech, entitled "Old and New Politics" and delivered at the Teatro de la Comedia, denounced the monarchy. Shortly thereafter, the League for Political Education was founded, and Ortega participated in the establishment of its monthly organ, *España*.

Also in 1914, Ortega published *Meditaciones del Quijote (Meditations on Quixote*, 1961), which contains the germs of his philosophy. The work contrasts the depth and profundity of German culture with the perceived superficiality of Spanish and Mediterranean culture. At this same time, the German writer Thomas Mann was exploring in fiction the different frames of mind in northern and southern Europe. In 1917, Ortega conducted a lecture tour in Argentina. Upon his return to Spain, he became one of the founders of the liberal newspaper *El Sol*. The paper was intended to counter the conservatism of *El Imparcial*, which his father had once edited.

The 1920's were a period of great literary productivity for Ortega. The title of *España invertebrada* (1921; *Invertebrate Spain*, 1937) is a metaphor for the nation's lack of an intellectual elite that could lead it out of its morass. Many essays that Ortega originally wrote for *El Sol* appear in this book and in *El tema de nuestro tiempo* (1923; *The Modern Theme*, 1931). The latter explores the different concepts of relativity that have influenced the author and states his philosophy more systematically than do his first two books. Also in 1923, Ortega founded yet another magazine: *La Revista de Occidente*, a literary monthly that soon came to be held in very high regard. It was in this journal that many European writers first appeared in Spanish.

By the end of the decade, Ortega and his fellow philosopher Miguel de Unamuno y Jugo were recognized as the foremost intellectuals in Spain. In 1928, Ortega again traveled in South America, where he was even more popular than Unamuno. His reception there was tremendously enthusiastic, but he soon returned to Spain to participate in the revolution that would lead in 1931 to the exile of King Alfonso XIII. In the same year, principally because of his work in the Association for Service to the Republic, he was elected deputy for León.

Ortega's political career was short-lived. In 1929, he had published *La rebelión de las masas*

*(The Revolt of the Masses*, 1932), destined to become a best-seller in its English translation. This book, like the earlier *Invertebrate Spain*, had predicted that the hegemony of mass man would have dire consequences. When the republican movement rapidly proceeded far to the left of mere liberalism, Ortega broke with it. He also did not support the loyalists when civil war finally came. He fled to France instead.

His stated longings for the leadership of an intellectual aristocracy misled the theoreticians of the Falange, the Spanish Fascist organization. They believed that his sympathies were being altered in their favor, while he still desired a rule of enlightened liberalism. After the forces of Francisco Franco had triumphed, Ortega was offered a position as Spain's official philosopher. The regime also offered to publish a deluxe edition of his works, provided that he would delete certain essays and certain passages from others. He declined and remained abroad. He moved to Argentina, where earlier he had been well received, and in 1941 became professor of philosophy at the University of San Marcos, in Lima, Peru. This was a difficult period for Ortega. All of his political impulses were liberal, but he feared the results of an undifferentiated egalitarianism. Thus, he was condemned by the Right and Left alike. He did not return to his native country until 1945.

During his exile of almost a decade, Ortega had also lived in The Netherlands and Portugal. Upon his return to Spain, he chose not to reclaim his chair at the University of Madrid, although technically he still held the rank of professor there. Instead, he and Julián Marías founded a private institution of higher learning, the Instituto de Humanidades in Madrid.

In the same year (1948), his influential treatise on modern art, *La deshumanización del arte, e Ideas sobre la novela*, 1925, was translated into English under the title *The Dehumanization of Art and Notes on the Novel*. His interests continued to be wide-ranging. Toward the middle of his career, he had offered his theories on higher education—*Misión de la universidad* (1930; *Mission of the University*, 1944). During the last fifteen years of his life, he also addressed the daunting subjects of love—*Estudios sobre el amor* (1939; *On Love*, 1957)—and history—*Historia como sistema y Del imperio romano* (1941; *Toward a Philosophy of History*, 1941).

Ortega y Gasset was an intensely private man. Beyond his writings, he revealed little of himself to his readers. He was described physically by observers as a small, well-proportioned man, with dark olive features and bright, arresting eyes. During his last years, he lectured throughout Europe. He died in the city of his birth on October 18, 1955.

### Summary

José Ortega y Gasset is acknowledged to be a beautiful stylist. Some critics have found his individual books disappointing and have implied that his style is superior to his thought. Julián Marías, however, who edited several volumes of his posthumous works, asserts that, despite surface indications, Ortega's philosophy is highly systematic. He saw no transcendent purpose in life and, since it consists of the present only, he argued that one should approach life as one approaches a game. Ortega's insistence that man must remain totally free, so that he can create his own life, has caused his name to be linked with existential philosophy. He held life to be the relationship between the individual and his environment—that is, each person is the ego plus its circumstances. He believed, therefore, that Aristotelian reason must be sometimes subordinated to the intuition and spontaneous insight that comes from life experiences. His adjective for this kind of biological reason is translated as "vital" or "living." Commentators have identified various influences upon Ortega's thought, foremost among them the differing relativities of Albert Einstein and Oswald Spengler.

Ortega's extensive use of the essay form meant that of necessity he often could not rigorously pursue ideas to their ultimate conclusions, in the manner of a dissertation. Yet his breadth of interests and mastery of language have earned for him a readership much larger than most serious philosophers can attract. An excellent example of both the benefits and hazards of his method is *The Dehumanization of Art and Notes on the Novel*. While it is one of the most influential statements on the art of the twentieth century, it is also—say many commentators—widely misunderstood. In books, journals, magazines, and newspapers, Ortega tirelessly sought to Europeanize Spain. Certainly not the least of his accomplishments was his profound effect upon the culture of his nation.

### Bibliography


Díaz, Janet Winecoff. *The Major Themes of Existentialism in the Work of José Ortega y Gasset.* Chapel Hill: University of North Carolina Press, 1970. Examines Ortega's major works against the background of the existentialist tradition. Also contains a survey of the critical reaction to these works.

Ferrater Mora, José. Ortega y Gasset: An Outline of His Philosophy. Rev. ed. New Haven, Conn.: Yale University Press, 1963. This sixty-nine-page book uses a biographical method as the best approach to Ortega's nonsystematic philosophy.

Frank, Joseph. *The Widening Gyre: Crisis and Mastery in Modern Literature.* New Brunswick, N.J.: Rutgers University Press, and London: Yale University Press, 1963. In his chapter "The Dehumanization of Art," Frank notes that the influential essay of that name is universally accepted as a defense of modern art, while Ortega insisted that he was acting as neither judge nor advocate. Frank attempts to reassess Ortega's observations from a more balanced perspective.

Gray, Rockwell. *The Imperative of Modernity: An Intellectual Biography of Ortega y Gasset.* Berkeley: University of California Press, 1989. Coming as it does almost thirty-five years after the death of the subject, this biography benefits from the accumulated scholarship.

Huéscar, Antonio R. *José Ortega y Gasset's Metaphysical Innovation: A Critique and Overcoming of Idealism.* Edited and translated by Jorge García-Gómez. Albany: State University of New York Press, 1995. This volume is praised by critics as one of the best English-language expositions on Ortega y Gasset's work.

McClintock, Robert. *Man and His Circumstances: Ortega As Educator.* New York: Teachers College Press, 1971. This massive work (648 pages) studies Ortega's role as an educator. McClintock emphasizes the philosopher's view of the future of Western society.

Marías, Julián. *José Ortega y Gasset: Circumstance and Vocation.* Translated by Frances M. López-Morillas. Norman: University of Oklahoma Press, 1970. This exhaustive study (479 pages) originally appeared in 1960 under the title *Ortega, Revista de Occidente.* The work is considered the single most important treatment of Ortega's philosophy.

Ouimette, Victor. *José Ortega y Gasset.* Boston: Twayne, 1982. This is a comprehensive survey of Ortega's works, including the collections of his later and posthumous essays. Ouimette argues that, while Ortega almost always fails to see his insights through to their logical conclusions, he is consistently evocative.

Tuttle, Howard N. *The Crowd Is Untruth: The Existential Critique of Mass Society in the Thought of Kierkegaard, Nietzsche, Heidegger, and Ortega y Gasset.* New York: Lang, 1996. Tuttle considers the philosophical approaches of Ortega y Gasset and three others to the sociological concept of the masses.


*Patrick Adcock*

# GEORGE ORWELL
## Eric Arthur Blair

*Born:* June 25, 1903; Motihari, Bengal, India
*Died:* January 21, 1950; London, England
*Area of Achievement:* Literature
*Contribution:* Orwell's uncompromising ideals, reflected consistently in the enormous and diverse body of his works, entitle him to be considered among the most personally courageous writers in the history of British letters, one whose social concern and distinctive style can be compared only to those of the eighteenth century political and social satirist Jonathan Swift.

### Early Life

George Orwell was born Eric Arthur Blair on June 25, 1903, at Motihari, Bengal, in India. His father, Richard Walmesley Blair, was a relatively minor official in the Opium Department, the British civil service agency which regulated legalized opium trade with China as a government monopoly. Orwell's mother, born Ida Mabel Limouzin, was of English-French background. She had lived in Moulmein, Burma, where her French father was a teak trader and boat builder and was eighteen years younger than her husband, whom she had married in 1896. Their first child, Marjorie, was born at Tehta, Bihar, India, in 1898. After Eric was born, the elder Blair's almost annual changes in posting, often to remote towns within India, coupled with possibilities of better schooling, caused Ida Blair's return to England with the children. Richard Blair did not see his family again until 1907 on a three-month leave; their last child, Avril, would be born as a result of this visit.

Orwell's early childhood was, consequently, essentially a fatherless one. This was not a particularly unusual situation among overseas service families, but the need to maintain two residences on a meager civil service stipend meant that finances always remained tight and luxuries few. Though Orwell was born to what he refers to in *The Road to Wigan Pier* (1937) as the "lower-upper-middle" class, he appears to have become aware of his "shabby gentility" only upon attending St. Cyprian's, a new but successful preparatory school, at age eight. St. Cyprian's was considered "successful" because of its boys' record of gaining admission to the "great" public schools, such as Eton and Harrow. "Such, Such Were the Joys," an essay of uncertain date (internal features allow arguments for as early as 1938, though it was not submitted for publication until 1947), is a polemic on the ruthless class distinctions and favoritism in such privately founded schools.

Clearly, Orwell was never happy at St. Cyprian's. Mr. and Mrs. Vaughan Wilkes, its founders (who also taught at the school), gauged its curriculum toward a successful outcome on the public school examinations. (In Great Britain, "public" schools are what in the United States are called "private" schools.) There was, accordingly, next to no instruction in authors after John Milton and precious little in history beyond dates of the British monarchs. In addition, Mr. Wilkes told Orwell when prepping him for the Eton exam that he had been given a half-scholarship to St. Cyprian's because of his family's financial circumstances, and that the now thirteen-year-old boy therefore had a special obligation to the school as well as to his parents to win his scholarship. The pressures on him were certainly unremitting, and two concerns which would dominate his works, money and the politics of the British class structure, have their origins in this period of Orwell's life.

Orwell placed fourteenth on the King's Scholars examination; this was not high enough to ensure a place at Eton for the fall, 1916, election, though it would mean acceptance by as early as Christmas of that year if a place became available. (The King's Scholars could number no more than seventy, with between ten and thirteen in each "election," or year; thus, availability depended upon how many boys left Eton during a given year.) Wilkes was pleased at the boy's performance, nevertheless, and Orwell finished the year at St. Cyprian's and spent nine miserable weeks of the winter, 1917, term at Wellington, a military school, waiting to hear from Eton.

By May, 1917, Orwell was at Eton, a member of the school's intellectual elite, known as "College." The boys of this group were marked to fill the most important positions in the intellectual and political life of Great Britain; nevertheless, Orwell's resentment of class distinctions coupled with Eton's rigid curriculum and his own free spirit led him to elect a large number of courses outside College among the regular students known as "Oppidans." His me-

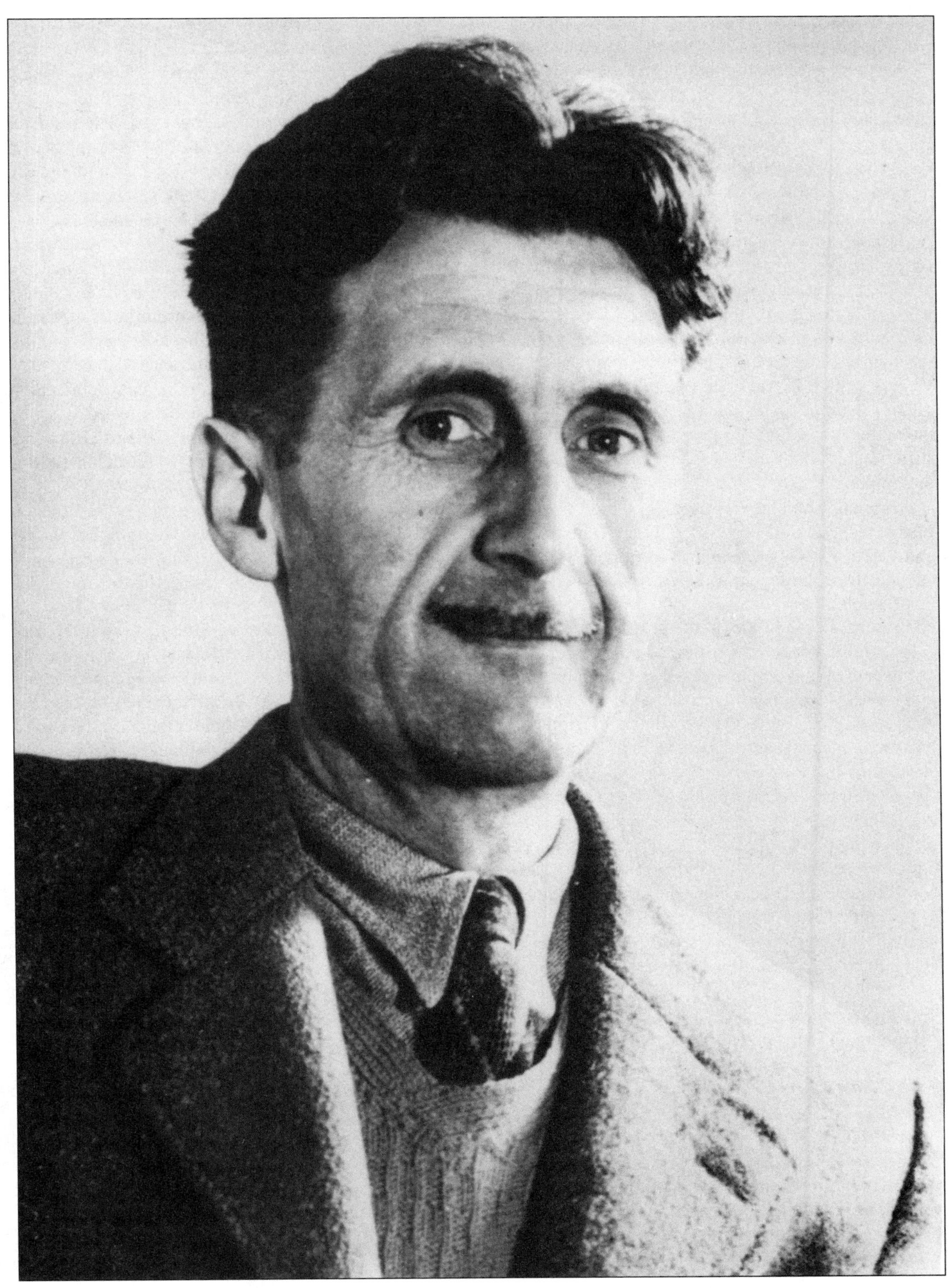

diocre performance even in these made a first-class diploma impossible and a scholarship to one of the Oxford colleges unobtainable. Thus, Orwell was graduated from Eton in December, 1921, with relatively poor prospects, despite what, by contemporary American standards, was an astoundingly deep knowledge of British literature and history for a young man only eighteen years old.

It was partly because of his father's refusal (or inability) to finance an Oxford education and in part because of his lackluster record that Orwell went to a "crammer" for six months starting in January, 1922, to prepare for the India Office's examinations. Class distinctions dogged Orwell's steps whether he liked it or not, and the foreign civil service was the only realistic career option for him given his family background. Even Eton did not guarantee him a place in the civil service. He was still required to sit for a week of two-hour examinations in English, English history, mathematics, and French, plus three options (in Orwell's case, Latin, Greek, and drawing). The exams were equivalent to "O" ("ordinary" as opposed to advanced) level college entrance tests. Thus it was that Orwell, in late October, 1922, came to be posted in Burma as an officer in the provincial police.

Even in Burma, Orwell's limited finances as well as his own inclination to solitariness led him to remain by himself, reading as usual and spending what money he could on books and subscriptions, mostly on history and politics. He wrote some poetry during his five years in Burma, but Orwell was still Eric Blair and had no pretensions toward a career as a writer until recurring bronchitis, a complaint which had appeared as early as his school days, forced his return to England in 1927. It was at this time that he resigned from the service, much to his family's dismay, not so much for health reasons as from a distaste for the nature of his work. He could not see himself as a preserver of the British Empire. This theme would ultimately emerge in his novel *Burmese Days* (1934) and essays such as "Shooting an Elephant."

## Life's Work

August, 1927, found Orwell unemployed with few prospects, twenty-four years old, with an undistinguished school record, ill but with the announced intention of becoming a writer. One can imagine his family's exasperation, particularly that of his father, who had viewed the Burma service as his son's last chance to salvage some sort of future. Still, Orwell began to write that winter, not with the style and ease of his mature years and not about Burma or the British Empire as one might expect, but about poverty and degradation. The old Etonian lived among, dressed as, and associated with the poorest element of the British and French working class in 1928 and 1929, gathering material for what would eventually be published as *Down and Out in London and Paris* (1933). Meanwhile, Orwell wrote sketches and "potboilers," with only indifferent success. Even *Down and Out in London and Paris* caused problems of publication, for its disjointed incidents fell somewhere between autobiography and the novel. The essay "How the Poor Die" was written as a result of his stay in a charity ward in a Paris hospital as he was felled again by the bronchitic condition which would afflict him throughout his life. It was published late in 1929 in Max Plowman's magazine *The Adelphi*, and Orwell began a long though never lucrative association with that publication.

The pseudonym "George Orwell" was chosen to conceal the author's identity and avoid embarrassment for his family upon publication of *Down and Out in London and Paris*. It came from a list of names which included P. S. Burton (the name Orwell actually used when tramping), Kenneth Miles, and H. Lewis Allways, and was mutually agreed upon by the author and Victor Gollancz, the book's publisher. The Orwell was a river the author liked and knew well, and he believed that the whole name had a solid working-class ring to it. Even after he became an established author, however, Orwell never formally changed his name, and he continued to be called Eric Blair by those who had known him before his success.

By the mid-1930's, Orwell's works, among them numerous essays and reviews, began to find a small but faithful audience. He was still unable to live on his writing alone, since first printings were small and his essays and reviews poorly paid, so beginning in late April, 1932, and for the next several years, Orwell taught school, first at The Hawthorns in Middlesex. Fourteen to sixteen boys between the ages of ten and sixteen were in his charge each term. Former students recall that he was an enthusiastic teacher, and they remember long nature walks through the Middlesex countryside as part of the curriculum. Evidently, Orwell was determined that his boys would not have to face an ordeal similar to his own at St. Cyprian's.

During these years, Orwell wrote *A Clergyman's Daughter* (1935) and *Keep the Aspidistra Flying* (1936). These works, ultimately repudiated and not reprinted during the author's lifetime, at his request, develop themes of clashes between the social orders that would find deeper expression and broader public acceptance in his nonfictional work *The Road to Wigan Pier* and the novel *Coming Up for Air* (1939). Orwell increasingly realized, in these works particularly, a deepening concern with social questions: unfulfilled lives, rife commercialism, poverty among the working class, and the instinctual but futile attempt to find meaning in a simpler life. His themes were those of a twentieth century Jonathan Swift, and though Orwell's self-effacing personality would never have allowed him to make the comparison himself, it would have pleased him.

By no means wealthy but with at least the assurances of a small income and a loyal and growing audience, Orwell left a job as bookshop clerk and with an advance of five hundred pounds on his *The Road to Wigan Pier* began planning his marriage to Eileen Maud O'Shaughnessy, then a student at University College, London. The two were married on June 9, 1936, in a simple Anglican ceremony and moved soon after to Wallington, Herfordshire, two miles off the main London road to Cambridge. Known as the Blairs by villagers, the two supplemented Orwell's small income by converting a room of their nonelectrified, corrugated iron-roofed cottage to a general store.

The Independent Labour Party (ILP), Socialist in its general outlook, held summer meetings in nearby Letchworth, and Orwell attended several of these, lending his name to the group for fund-raising. As all these changes were occurring in Orwell's personal life, he came to take great interest in the Republican cause in Spain. Not waiting for the ILP to raise its own contingent, Orwell left on his own and arrived as a volunteer in late December, 1936. He joined the United Marxist Workers Party's contingent known as POUM (Partido Obrero de Unificación Marxista) and served with distinction until a throat wound nearly cost him his life. He returned to England in late spring, 1937, to recuperate, and he immediately began his memoir *Homage to Catalonia* (1938), detailing the factionalism between Communist and Marxist elements which ultimately destroyed the Republican cause. Orwell remained committed to socialism until his death (contrary to what particularly American critics of the 1950's have written), but the intrigues of the Communist faction in Spain, backed by Stalin's Russia, made him firmly anti-Communist as early as 1937. As a result, all of his political works, including his masterpiece, *Animal Farm* (1945), and his much-acclaimed final work, *Nineteen Eighty-Four* (1949), were soundly attacked in the Communist press. It was a bitter irony that some rightists in the Cold War period which followed World War II made Orwell their champion. This role is one he adamantly refused to accept.

The years of World War II were personally frustrating for Orwell. He was repeatedly refused for military service because of his recurring lung ailment, and the throat wound inflicted in Spain made his voice rasping and difficult to control. Even civilian war work was denied him at first, probably because his political affiliations were considered suspect. Ironically, Orwell had resigned from the ILP because of its refusal to support the war. He was willing to fight for Great Britain, both because he saw its imperialism as less malignant than Fascism and because he realized that the British Empire could not survive the war unaltered. Eventually, Orwell was given the opportunity to host a program of commentaries and interviews for the Eastern Service of the British Broadcasting Corporation (BBC), but the signals of these broadcasts (primarily to India) were weak, and they were offered at bad times to gather an audience. During the London blitz, when Great Britain expected an imminent German invasion, Orwell organized a squadron of the Home Guard among residents of his London neighborhood. His experience in Burma and Spain made him especially fit for this task.

In March, 1945, Orwell was offered a chance to become war correspondent for *The Observer*. Despite his own health, which was never good, and although he and Eileen had just adopted a son, Richard, even though Eileen was about to have what he believed was minor surgery, Orwell could not resist the opportunity to see the last phase of the war. Eileen, realizing how much an active life meant to him, encouraged him to go. Having weighed these considerations, he set out on March 15 for Paris, writing all along the way; he even met Ernest Hemingway in a Paris hotel room and had with him an amiable discussion about the works of Charles Dickens, Rudyard Kipling, and Gerard Manley Hopkins. On March 29, however, he received a wire from *The Observer* reporting that Eileen had died under anaesthesia while undergoing surgery for a malignant tumor. Clearly she had suspected the worst, even before entering the hospital; this explains her reluctance to adopt a child the year before.

Orwell lived a lonely life in the years following the war. There were governesses for Richard, ultimately Orwell's sister Avril. He divided his time in the final years of his life between London and an isolated retreat on the island of Jura in the Scottish Hebrides. It was consummate irony that *Animal Farm*, just published and already a widely translated best-seller, now provided him the financial security he had sought throughout his career. It is equally ironic, perhaps even an indication of Orwell's hubris, that with his own health declining he decided to move to a place without doctor, telephone, or regular boat service to the mainland.

By the summer of 1946, Orwell was established on Jura, in a neglected farmhouse called Barnhill on the north of the island, and was hard at work on what would be his last and most widely read work, *Nineteen Eighty-Four.* He completed this project in the following year in great pain from his steadily worsening lung ailment, and by Christmas Eve, 1947, he found himself in Hairmyres Hospital near Glasgow, Scotland. Tuberculosis had done extensive damage to his left lung and had affected the right as well. After seven months of convalescence in Hairmyres and various nursing homes, he was finally transferred to University College Hospital, London, on September 3, 1949. He was forbidden and unable to do any serious writing in these final months, but two events cheered him: the immediate international success of *Nineteen Eighty-Four* and his marriage to Sonia Brownell, performed in the hospital on October 13. Marriage in these circumstances was a practical as well as a romantic consideration. Orwell needed a literary executor as well as a guardian for his son, and Sonia, in her mid-twenties at the time of their marriage and with extensive experience in editing and publishing, was a fortunate choice. The two had known each other for several years through *Horizon* magazine, where she worked and to which he had contributed. They had, since that time, felt a deep mutual affection.

Orwell's death occurred suddenly and quietly on the night of January 21, 1950, just before he was to be transferred to a treatment center in Switzerland. Until the end, he was hoping for a remission of his disease.

### Summary

Photographs of George Orwell taken at various stages of his life testify to the cumulative effects on this artist of ill health and turbulent times, from which Orwell never shied away. Early photographs show a round-faced Orwell in Edwardian ruffles, sailor suit, and, in his teens, country tweeds. He was, in his own words, a chubby boy. Eton photos reveal a thinner but by no means slight young man in rugby jersey or bathing suit, tall and with deep-set features. A photograph taken while he was training in Burma shows Orwell at his full height (six feet, two inches) but without his distinctive mustache, which appears only in photographs of the mid-1930's. His police uniform is ill-fitting compared to those of other trainees, and badly tailored clothes are the first thing one notices in all the later photographs. His face is deeply lined in all pictures taken after 1933. Orwell is much thinner in the photos taken after his tramping experiences and looks at least ten years beyond his true age. A famous series of photographs taken in London in the last year of the war shows him at work and leisure, always with a self-rolled cigarette of black-shag tobacco and wearing the dark-blue shirts he always preferred in the war years. He was forty-two when these pictures were taken; he looks at least past fifty.

Orwell's is a prime example of a short and difficult but well-lived life. He set his ideals high: social justice with freedom of opportunity for every human being. He was willing, furthermore, to sacrifice his life for what he believed. Orwell came to realize, especially after his experiences in Spain, that the best chances for reform lay neither in ideology nor in anarchy, and he incurred the lasting enmity of Stalinists as well as the undesired and repudiated adulation of the political right wing. Even on his deathbed, Orwell denounced those who misinterpreted *Nineteen Eighty-Four* as a tract on Stalinist Russia or an unalterable prophecy.

It is amazing how far Orwell traveled and how much he accomplished in his forty-six years. Born into a solidly middle-class Anglo-Indian family, reared and educated as a young man destined for privilege, he refused to become either a tool of British imperialism or a dupe of communism. His socialism was ethical rather than ideological, and he held to it consistently at the cost of friendships and potential supporters who could have smoothed the path of his career.

Orwell was not, however, so solitary as to be friendless. His first wife, Eileen, consistently supported him, even placing herself in jeopardy by traveling to Spain to return him to England after he had been seriously wounded. Cyril Connolly, the eminent man of British letters and a fellow student of Orwell at Eton, remained Orwell's friend throughout his life and introduced him to Sonia Brownell, the young woman who would brighten Orwell's last months and become his second wife and capable literary executor.

As great as many of Orwell's works are, one cannot help but sense that the life of the man was even greater. It would not be incorrect to say that his art combined with his personal courage to create a truly distinctive writer comparable only to Swift.

### Bibliography

Crick, Bernard. *George Orwell: A Life*. Boston: Little Brown, 1980; London: Secker and Warburg, 1981. This first complete biography remains the classic study of Orwell's life and times. It is scholarly with full notes, index, and photographs but is completely readable and rewarding for both scholars and general readers.

Gross, Miriam, ed. *The World of George Orwell*. New York: Simon and Schuster, 1971; London: Weidenfeld and Nicolson, 1972. A collection of essays by those who knew Orwell, covering each phase of his life. Essentially, these are unscholarly appreciations illustrated with photographs. The collection is interesting, nevertheless, even if sentimental and highly subjective.

Meyers, Jeffrey. "George Orwell: A Bibliography." *Bulletin of Bibliography* 31 (July-September, 1974): 117-121.

———. "George Orwell: A Selected Checklist." *Modern Fiction Studies* 21 (Spring, 1975): 133-136. These two bibliographies list nearly every important article and book written to the mid-seventies and include non-English Orwell criticism as well.

———. *A Reader's Guide to George Orwell*. London: Thames and Hudson, 1975; Totowa, N.J.: Littlefield Adams, 1977. Analyzes Orwell's books and major essays in context of his period and considers his position in English and French letters.

———, ed. *George Orwell: The Critical Heritage*. London and Boston: Routledge, 1975. Contains a broad survey of reviews, most contemporary with the works they discuss, by a number of celebrated critics. The collection is chronologically arranged and includes translations of foreign-language reviews as well.

Orwell, George. *The Collected Essays, Journalism, and Letters of George Orwell*. Edited by Sonia Orwell and Ian Angus. 4 vols. London: Secker and Warburg, 1968. Supplements the uniform edition (1948-1965) of the novels and is distinct from the Penguin one-volume *Collected Essays* (1970). Harcourt Brace Jovanovich published the American edition.

Pearce, Robert. "Revisiting Orwell's Wigan Pier." *History* 82, no. 267 (July, 1997). Considers Orwell's book *The Road to Wigan Pier* as a source for study of the Depression

Rodden, John, ed. *Understanding Animal Farm: A Student Casebook to Issues, Sources and Historical Documents*. Westport, Conn.: Greenwood Press, 1999. This casebook includes a literary analysis of *Animal Farm* and several chapters covering the historical and political issues that influenced the author. Extensive reference work for a full study of this novel.

Zwerdling, Alex. *Orwell and the Left*. New Haven, Conn.: Yale University Press, 1974. Discusses Orwell's works in the context of his political involvements, arguing that Orwell tried to reform the Left from within and illustrating how he often managed to blend political writing with high art.

*Robert J. Forman*

## THOMAS MOTT OSBORNE

*Born:* September 23, 1859; Auburn, New York
*Died:* October 20, 1926; Auburn, New York
*Area of Achievement:* Social reform
*Contribution:* Osborne's theories of limited self-government encouraged prisoners to be responsible for their own group discipline. His plan reduced problems within the American prisons where he worked and German prisons in the 1920's and 1930's.

### Early Life

Born into a wealthy family in western New York, Thomas Mott Osborne had the opportunity to travel widely and receive a college education at Harvard. After graduating cum laude in 1884, he worked in his father's agricultural implement business, managing it for several years until he sold it to International Harvester in 1903. Retiring from business gave him more time to pursue his civic interests.

His first civic involvement came as a member of the Auburn, New York, school board from 1885 until 1891 and then again from 1893 to 1895. Next he served as mayor of Auburn from 1903 until 1906. By fulfilling these offices with integrity and honesty, he became a leader in upstate Democratic politics. He served in a variety of appointed positions, including one as a delegate to the national Democratic conventions.

Following his wife's death in 1896, Osborne became interested in the George Junior Republic, a youth movement emphasizing self-government. Osborne served as a member and later as chairman of its governing board. This, along with his early associations with Auburn Prison, located in his hometown, led to his interest in prison reform. In 1906 he addressed the National Prison Association, emphasizing the need for prisoners to be given the most freedom possible so that they could return to society as contributing members.

### Life's Work

Osborne's major contribution to prison reform began in 1912 when he read Donald Lowrie's *My Life in Prison* (1912). Although he had long been interested in prison reform, it was not until this point that Osborne began to devote his life to improving the condition of the incarcerated. He firmly believed that the function of prison was twofold: First, it protected society by removing the individual from its midst; second, incarceration provided the opportunity for prisoners to reform those areas of their lives that had led to their imprisonment.

Osborne, a gifted lecturer, increased public interest in prison reform. In 1913 Osborne met with the newly elected governor of New York State to propose a commission to investigate prison conditions. The governor accepted the suggestion and appointed Osborne to chair the New York State Prison Reform Commission. Osborne had a deep interest in prison reform and a sympathy for the prisoner but neither education nor experience in the area of adult corrections. In an unusual and exceptionally bold move, Osborne proposed that he investigate prison conditions from the inside by becoming a prisoner at Auburn, which served as a national model of harsh treatment.

With the consent of both the warden and the superintendent of prisons, Osborne addressed the fourteen hundred inmates at Auburn prison on Sunday, September 28, 1913, and told them his plan. He expected to be treated as one of them, wearing what they wore, sleeping where they slept, eating what they ate, and doing what they did. He realized, however, that since he could be released at any moment he could not completely share their experiences. To make the situation as realistic as possible, Osborne assumed the identity "Tom Brown." As such, the guards treated Brown as they did any other prisoner. He dressed in a grey striped uniform, walked in the required lock step, worked in the prison shop, and abided by the silent system.

Although he remained incarcerated for only one week, the experience reaffirmed Osborne's belief that prisoners remained people with the same emotions, dreams, hopes, and fears as those who were free. More important, he realized that the silence and monotony of prison life did nothing to prepare the inmate to return to society. Even though the press was not particularly enthusiastic about Osborne's week in prison, he became a national figure in prison reform.

The experience at Auburn gave Osborne the chance to introduce the basic principles of his Mutual Welfare League. A few months after his "release," the inmates at Auburn voted to establish a league at their prison. For the first time in any American prison, the inmates had a chance to participate in their own management. As a result of a secret ballot, forty-nine prisoners were elected to a constitutional convention that established the basis for the league. Meeting without interference from prison guards or officials, they determined that an executive committee and five grievance committees would be formed to assist with the management of Auburn Prison. As time went by, the warden granted more and more power to the league, allowing it to help maintain order and discipline within the prison. It negotiated Sunday afternoon meetings for its members and oversaw the movement of men to meals and to work. When these concessions caused no disruptions, the warden agreed to allow the league to oversee order in the shops; as a result, the guards were withdrawn.

In 1914, Osborne moved to Ossining, New York, to become the warden of Ossining Correctional Facility (also known as Sing Sing). There he ended the Golden Rule Brotherhood, which was similar to the Mutual Welfare League but was introduced and managed by prison authorities rather than the inmates themselves. When he replaced it with a league, he witnessed the same improvement in prison discipline and inmate morale that took place at Auburn. Even though the buildings at Ossining were old and there had been riots shortly before Osborne took over, the situation improved dramatically. Despite the mixing of young and old criminals in overcrowded conditions, the riots ended. Assaults and fights declined, as did the incidence of drug abuse. The prisoners dealt severely with any infractions of the rules, and the prison industries became more productive. Clearly, the participation of inmates in the management of the institution proved to be worthwhile for both the inmates themselves and the prison administration.

However, Osborne soon ran into trouble. Unaccustomed to dealing with the prison bureaucracy as an employee, he freely criticized his superiors and their management. He stopped the graft that has existed at Sing Sing for decades. Furthermore, he was an upstate Democrat, and his position normally went to a local official of the dominant Republican Party. After one year in office, the local grand jury indicted him for perjury and neglect of his duties. In a politically motivated action, the grand jury accused Osborne of failing to exercise supervision over the prison, of undermining discipline, and of not acting in a manner worthy of respect and confidence.

Refusing to resign, Osborne took a six-month leave of absence and returned in July, 1916. Inmate morale continued to improve during that time as the interim warden maintained the Mutual Welfare League, proving that the creative platform upon which it was built could operate with any caring, intelligent warden. The case against Osborne never went to trial. The court dismissed it because of insufficient evidence. When Osborne returned to Sing Sing, the inmates honored him with a grand demonstration. Prison officials passed laws designed to hamper the working of the Mutual Welfare League; realizing the action was directed against him, Osborne resigned as warden three months later.

Upon leaving Sing Sing, Osborne accepted an appointment from the secretary of the Navy to study its prison system. As with Auburn, Osborne studied the situation from the inside. He joined the Navy and deserted, thus ending up first on a prison ship and then at the main prison in Portsmouth, Virginia. Osborne concluded that the Navy's prison system was a failure. Most of the men, incarcerated for minor violations, received a dishonorable discharge, which deprived the Navy of their services and which followed the men for the rest of their lives. He thought it would be better if the naval prison could return the men to active military duty when they completed their sentences.

The secretary of the Navy was so impressed with the report that he invited Osborne to take over the prison at Portsmouth, a radical decision given that Osborne was a civilian. In August, 1917, as a newly commissioned officer in the Naval Reserve, Osborne took charge of the prison. He held the position until March of 1920. During this time, Osborne dismissed the guards who had worked inside the compound and allowed the prisoners to establish a Mutual Welfare League. Of six thousand men held in the prison during Osborne's three years as warden, only eight escaped. More important, he convinced the Navy to allow worthy men to return to service upon completion of their sentence. As a result, some four thousand men returned to active duty. Upon his resignation, the secretary of the Navy commended Osborne for mending rather than breaking men.

When Osborne left Portsmouth in 1920, he ended his active involvement with individual prisons, but he continued to lecture, write, and conduct prison investigations. In 1922 he helped organize the National Society for Penal Information, designed to acquaint the public with the workings of the prison system. After his death, the organiza-

tion's name was changed to the Osborne Association as a memorial to his work.

Thomas Mott Osborne died on October 20, 1926. The next morning, the guards opened the cells at Auburn and announced that Tom Brown had died. At a funeral service held in the prison chapel on October 23, fourteen hundred of the prison's sixteen hundred inmates filed past the casket to say a last goodbye to their greatest supporter.

### Summary

Thomas Mott Osborne displayed an interest in the humanity of inmates. He believed that the best way to teach them to return to society as productive citizens rather than as criminals was to give them a chance to participate in managing their own behavior and to be accountable for their actions while in prison. He influenced both the prisoners and the authorities with whom he worked. His work came at the end of a period in American penology during which the emphasis was on reform of the convict. From the late 1860's to the early twentieth century, Americans accepted the theory that society was responsible for reforming its criminals, an idea that fit with the nation's optimism. Osborne's reforms also coincided with the Progressive Era in U.S. history, during which the nation extended its interest in reform to all aspects of society, including prisons. Following Osborne's retirement, however, the nation shifted away from reform. State legislatures moved toward a policy centered on punishment—a view supported by the general public—leaving the league with little authority. Many prisons in Germany experimented with implementing Mutual Welfare Leagues in the 1920's and early 1930's with prisoners who were close to release.

### Bibliography

Chamberlain, Rudolph W. *There Is No Truce: A Life of Thomas Mott Osborne*. New York: Macmillan, 1935; London: Routledge, 1936. A factual, clearly sympathetic biography of Osborne.

Johnson, Herbert A. *History of Criminal Justice*. 2d ed. Cincinnati, Ohio: Anderson, 1988. Criminal justice from ancient time to the present with a brief mention of Osborne.

McKelvey, Blake. *American Prisons*. Chicago: University of Chicago Press, 1936. A classic analysis of the prison system in the United States.

Osborne, Thomas Mott. *Prisons and Common Sense*. Philadelphia and London: Lippincott, 1924. Osborne's perspective on prison management as well as the operation of the Mutual Welfare League.

———. *Society and Prisons*. New Haven, Conn.: Yale University Press, 1916. A clear presentation of Osborne's prison philosophy.

———. *Within Prison Walls*. New York and London: Appleton, 1914. A graphic account of "Tom Brown's" week as a prisoner in Auburn.

Pisciotta, Alexander. *Benevolent Repression: Social Control and the American Reformatory Prison Movement*. New York: New York University Press, 1994. An analysis of the attempts on reform in American prisons.

Tannenbaum, Frank. *Osborne of Sing Sing*. Chapel Hill: University of North Carolina Press, 1933. A biography focusing on Osborne's prison reform activity.

*Duncan R. Jamieson*

## WILHELM OSTWALD

*Born:* September 2, 1853; Riga, Latvia
*Died:* April 4, 1932; Grossbothen, near Leipzig, Germany
*Areas of Achievement:* Chemistry, physics, and philosophy
*Contribution:* Ostwald's most notable work was in the field of chemistry, in which he is considered to be the "father" of physical chemistry and in which he was awarded the 1909 Nobel Prize. He was later nominated for a second Nobel Prize, this time in physics, for his work in the field of color science.

### Early Life

Friedrich Wilhelm Ostwald, son of Gottfried Wilhelm and Elisabeth Leuckel Ostwald, was born in Riga, Latvia, on September 2, 1853, and spent the first thirty-four years of his life there and in nearby Dorpat (now Tartu). At the *Realgymnasium* at Riga, Ostwald required seven years to complete the curriculum normally finished in four. This delay can be attributed to the wide range of his interests, because during this period young Ostwald pursued studies in music, becoming proficient on both piano and viola; studied painting and handicrafts under the tutelage of his father; and set up a private laboratory in which he experimented in chemistry and physics, became an accomplished amateur photographer and film processor, and manufactured fireworks. The near disasters that accompanied the fireworks project taught him the need for more than a recipe and a desire. He knew he needed an understanding of what was occurring.

In 1872, following graduation from the *Realgymnasium*, Ostwald left Riga to attend the University of Dorpat and studied chemistry under Carl Schmidt and Johann Lemberg and physics with Arthur von Öttingen. More focused on his pursuits, Ostwald finished this part of his chemical education in only three years. Thereafter, he took positions as an unpaid assistant, first to Öttingen and later to Schmidt. Ostwald credited these two men as the main influences on his chemistry. Ostwald also realized the need for a strong mathematical background and proceeded to teach himself from a textbook by Karl Snell. Ostwald later gave Snell credit both for his sound mathematics and for his direction into the field of philosophy. He was awarded the doctorate in chemistry by the University of Dorpat in 1878 with a dissertation whose subject was optical refraction as a way to assess chemical affinity. Ostwald stayed in Dorpat, assisting at the university and teaching at the *Realgymnasium.*

In 1880, Ostwald married Helen von Reyher. Their marriage produced two daughters and three sons. His son, Karl Wilhelm Wolfgang, followed in his father's footsteps and was a prominent chemist, and one of his daughters, Grete, published an Ostwald biography, *Wilhelm Ostwald: Mein Vater* (1953; Wilhelm Ostwald, my father). In 1881, Ostwald returned to Riga as professor of chemistry at the Polytechnic Institute. While holding this position, Ostwald began making scientific contributions that brought him to the attention of the world's chemists.

### Life's Work

The branch of chemistry known as physical chemistry originated in a series of lectures on chemical affinity that Ostwald presented at the University of Dorpat in 1876. Notes from that series were expanded by research and reading and published as Ostwald's first book, *Lehrbuch der allgemeinen Chemie* (1885-1887; textbook of general chemistry), which presented a new organization of chemistry.

In 1881, Ostwald accepted the professorship of chemistry at the Riga Polytechnicum. At Riga, Ostwald became interested in Svante Arrhenius' ionic dissociation theory, and in 1886 Arrhenius accepted an invitation to work with Ostwald. The two worked closely, but on different problems, for years. Jacobus H. van't Hoff's publications on chemical dynamics were also noted by Ostwald. It was the importance of these new concepts of Arrhenius and of van't Hoff that Ostwald recognized and promoted in his writing. The controversy generated by Ostwald's "new chemistry" brought him wide recognition and the appointment as professor of physical chemistry at the University of Leipzig in 1887.

Ostwald organized the Department of Physical Chemistry and spent the years until 1906 strengthening it. The department was at its prime in 1899, and it was common to have forty students from around the world in Ostwald's laboratory. Research on such a large scale required special methods, and those developed by Ostwald are still seen in university research groups. Mature scientists

acted as assistants to Ostwald and as liaison officers between Ostwald and the students. Each problem to be studied was chosen by consultation between Ostwald and the student. There were weekly seminars to present and discuss research progress. This way Ostwald exerted his influence on each investigation, though he did not directly participate in each one.

Many to-be-famous chemists worked in Ostwald's laboratory. Among them were Arrhenius (Nobel Prize in 1903), van't Hoff (Nobel Prize in 1901), Walther Hermann Nernst (Nobel Prize in 1920), and Americans Theodore William Richards, Arthur Amos Noyes, and Gilbert Newton Lewis. This succession of scientists solidified physical chemistry as a new branch of chemistry.

Ostwald was greatly involved with communicating knowledge. He published forty-five books, five hundred scientific papers, and fifty thousand reviews and in 1887 founded, jointly with van't Hoff, the *Zeitschrift für physikalische Chemie* (journal of physical chemistry). Ostwald continued as editor of this publication through the first one hundred volumes, stepping down in 1922. In 1894, Ostwald's *Die wissenschaftlichen Grundlagen der analytischen Chemie* (*The Scientific Foundations of Analytical Chemistry Treated in an Elementary Manner*, 1895) appeared and revolutionized analytical chemistry. From that time on, analytical chemistry was taught in terms of physical chemistry, and the measurement of physical properties became the common thread in all of chemistry.

Ostwald's 1901 discovery of a method to manufacture nitric acid is his only notable commercial contribution. The process freed Germany from dependence on foreign sources of nitrates for munitions manufacture, an important freedom to have as the world was building toward war.

At the turn of the century a confrontation occurred between two camps in the scientific world. Ostwald headed the "energetics" and Ludwig Boltzmann, also at Leipzig, headed the "atomistics." Ostwald and his followers claimed to represent "science without suppositions" and demanded that science be purely descriptive and deal only with correlating observable data. As late as 1904, Ostwald did not believe in the existence of atoms and would not use them, even as models, in explaining chemical observations. At some later date, he did relent and accept atoms as models, but he never did rely on them in his own work.

Ostwald was also involved outside chemical research, teaching, and publication. He published books and lectured internationally about methods of teaching, philosophy, painting, and educational reform and published a number of biographies. These activities caused Ostwald to be away from Leipzig much of the time and strained the relationship between Ostwald and his colleagues. This strain was relieved in 1906 when he admitted that he had become exhausted and had lost all interest in doing chemistry and resigned.

Ending his career at the university did not mean a quiet retirement. He had shown an interest in philosophy in publications at the turn of the century, and through these works, and others, Ostwald founded a branch of philosophy—natural philosophy. He led the movement for monism, a doctrine that stated that there is only one kind of substance or ultimate reality, and that reality is one unitary organic whole with no independent parts. To Ostwald, the ultimate was energy, as it had been in all of his chemical researches. He wrote and spoke widely on this topic from 1910 to 1914, when World War I brought the effort to an end.

Ostwald put his organizational abilities to work on the national and international scale. In Germany, he founded what became the Kaiser Wilhelm Institute, a national bureau of chemistry. He served on the International Commission for Atomic Weights from 1916 to 1932. He cooperated in the founding of the International Association of Chemical Societies in 1911.

The importance of Ostwald's discoveries in catalysis to the war effort is ironic, because he was an ardent pacifist. He considered war a horrible waste of energy and regularly attended and addressed peace congresses. His pleas for voluntary disarmament fell on deaf ears, however, and war came. Ostwald took no part in the war and was mentioned by some as a candidate for a Nobel Peace Prize.

Always interested in painting, Ostwald, in 1914, turned his skills to the study of color. He devised ways of measuring color, invented the instruments needed, set the standards, and wrote books that were accepted as the classics in the study of color. Ostwald believed that his work on color was his greatest contribution, and there were those in agreement who nominated him as a candidate for a Nobel Prize in Physics. Ostwald died on April 4, 1932, at his home, "Landhaus Energie," at Grossbothen, near Leipzig.

## Summary

Wilhelm Ostwald contributed to scientific knowledge with several very sound pieces of chemical research, but his major impact was by way of his organizational skills, his skills as a systematizer, and his writing skills. Chemical knowledge in the 1880's was expanding at a fast pace and was branching out into considerable new ground. The niche that Ostwald chose to fill was that of synthesizer of this new knowledge to the end that it could be taught and built upon.

Wilder D. Bancroft, a student of Ostwald in 1892, distinguished three classes of scientists. The first group is composed of those who make great discoveries, the second those who see the importance and bearing of the discoveries and promote them, and the third the group who have to have discoveries explained to them. Ostwald stood at the head of the second group as a great protagonist and inspiring teacher, more greatly loved and greatly followed than any chemist of his time.

In matters not strictly in the field of chemistry, Ostwald also had vital ideas. He preached the need to conserve natural energy resources, promoted the organization of scientific work as the means to attain solutions to problems, and recognized that new ideas need a champion to push for their acceptance. In each of these ideas, Ostwald stands out as being well ahead of his time.

## Bibliography

Bancroft, Wilder D. "Wilhelm Ostwald: The Great Protagonist." *The Journal of Chemical Education* 10 (1933): 539-542, 609-613. Bancroft was a doctoral student with Ostwald in the late 1880's and writes about Ostwald as chemist, as teacher, and as synthesizer of diverse information. This is the best and most personal comment, published in English, about Ostwald. This was published just following Ostwald's death.

Deltete, Robert J., and David L. Thorsel. "Josiah Willard Gibbs and Wilhelm Ostwald: A Contrast in Scientific Style." *Journal of Chemical Education* 73, no. 4 (April, 1996). Compares and contrasts the research and teaching styles of Ostwald and Gibbs including their students' perceptions of them.

Farber, Eduard. *Nobel Prize Winners in Chemistry.* Rev. ed. London and New York: Schuman, 1963. This text contains a chapter concerning Ostwald. Within the chapter there is a short biographical sketch, a description of the prizewinning chemistry, and an analysis of the consequence of that chemistry.

Harrow, Benjamin. *Eminent Chemists of Our Time.* 2d ed. New York: Van Nostrand, 1927. Although Ostwald is not treated in a separate chapter in this text, much of his impact on the structure of chemistry in his day is shown through the discussions of his contemporaries.

———. "The Meeting of Ostwald, Arrhenius, and van't Hoff." *The Journal of Chemical Education* 7 (November, 1930): 2697-2700. Utilizing the recently published autobiography of Ostwald, Harrow concentrates on the details dealing with the way in which a remarkable friendship grew among the three founders of physical chemistry. This short article gives a close look into the meetings that led to Nobel Prizes for each of these men.

Hauser, Ernst A. "The Lack of Natural Philosophy in Our Education: In Memoriam of Wilhelm Ostwald." *The Journal of Chemical Education* 28 (September, 1951): 492-494. This article concerns itself with the philosophical aspect of Ostwald's life. It contains an extensive quotation translated from Ostwald's *Grundriss der Naturphilosophie* (1908).

Jaffe, George. "Recollections of Three Great Laboratories." *The Journal of Chemical Education* 29 (May, 1952): 230-238. Jaffe was the last personal student of Ostwald and writes of his recollections of the man and the laboratory. Jaffe also met van't Hoff and Arrhenius during this period and writes about the interrelationship of these three winners of the Nobel Prize in Chemistry.

Moore, Forris J. *A History of Chemistry.* 3d ed. New York and London: McGraw-Hill, 1939. Presents a concise biography of Ostwald and places his work in the context of the developing chemistry of that era.

Stock, John T. "The Pathway to the Ostwald Dilution Law." *Journal of Chemical Education* 74, no. 7 (July, 1997). Discusses Ostwald's dilution law and traces his work back to 1872.

Wall, Florence E. "Wilhelm Ostwald: A Study in Mental Metamorphosis." *The Journal of Chemical Education* 42 (January, 1948): 2-10. As the title suggests, this article follows the life of Ostwald from his earliest years through his chemical interests and on to the later eclectic years. There is a very good listing of relevant literature included with this article.

*Kenneth H. Brown*

# J. J. P. OUD

*Born:* February 9, 1890; Purmerend, The Netherlands
*Died:* April 5, 1963; Wassenaar, The Netherlands
*Area of Achievement:* Architecture
*Contribution:* Oud is one of the founders of functional modern architecture, which through subtle techniques he imbued with an elegance and style achieved by few other architects. With a pronounced social commitment, Oud specialized in handsome yet low-cost housing and public buildings.

## Early Life

Jacobus Johannes Pieter Oud showed an interest in architecture at an early age. Possibly because of the ferment involving architectural styles at the turn of the century as well as a decided turn toward social commitment by the more progressive European states, an architect friend of his father suggested the son concentrate on the technical rather than aesthetic aspects of architecture. Consequently, Oud studied at the Rijks Normal School for Drawing Masters in Amsterdam and the Technical School of the University of Delft. He then worked as a designer with architectural firms in both The Netherlands and Germany. His basic training was thorough, especially in the technical aspects of architecture and in the knowledge of building materials. While still a student, Oud designed his first building for a member of his family.

While at Delft, Oud came under the influence of Hendrik Petrus Berlage, an early functionalist and considered to be the father of modern Dutch architecture. Berlage emphasized structural rationalism in architecture involving simplicity of form and clarity of structure. According to Berlage, the aesthetic qualities of a building should derive from these guidelines and the building materials themselves rather than from deliberate ornamentation. A pioneer in city planning and an early environmentalist, Berlage stressed continuity and harmony in the urban fabric. His most noted building, the massive Stock Exchange in Amsterdam, while completely modern in concept, in its use of plain and glazed brick, hewn stone, and iron visually was in harmony with the existing buildings of the old city. Probably the greatest influence Berlage had on his pupil was his firm belief that architecture is art, not technology and engineering. It was an admonition that Oud never forgot.

## Life's Work

In 1913, Oud established himself as an independent architect. His early designs were derivative, reflecting Berlage's influence: handsome and functional but not particularly distinguished. The change came in 1915, when Oud became aware of the work of the cubists and their message that it was not the object that was important but the emotion it transmitted to the spectator. To impart the message effectively, the cubists designed a universal language of fundamental forms: the cube, sphere, triangle, and circle. At this time, Oud met the aesthetic theorist Theo van Doesburg. Their friendship and collaboration effected the change in Oud's architectural style. In 1917, with other architects and artists, notably the abstract painter Piet Mondrian, they formed a revolutionary art group called *De Stijl* (the style) and published a magazine by the same name. Although Oud would become known as a *De Stijl* architect, the greatest influence on him would come from Mondrian's adaptation of cubism called neoplasticism. Neoplasticism did not make use of figurative elements but restricted design to the right angle in horizontal-vertical relation to the frame using primary colors together with white, black, and grey. In 1917, Oud designed a group of seaside houses for an esplanade above the beach at Scheveningen which were little more than cubic masses clearly showing the influence of neoplasticism. The project was never executed and probably could not have been without extensive modifications. The one building that Oud designed and had built completely in the neoplastic manner was the Café de Unie in Rotterdam, now destroyed.

In 1918, Oud became the architect for the City of Rotterdam; he was commissioned to help solve an acute housing shortage. At the time he had become aware of the *Neue Sachlichkeit* (new reality) movement in architecture—precursor of the International Style—and its message that the course of architecture would be determined by social and technological forces necessitating the development of the techniques of standardization and mass production.

Between 1918 and 1925, various socialistic Dutch governments sponsored comprehensive building programs whose primary objective was making housing for everyone a social right. The programs helped Oud achieve the architectural designs for which he is best known: three low-cost housing projects. All showed the *De Stijl* influence yet demonstrated the basic precept of functionalism, namely that form follows function, and as such Oud's designs were integrated into the broader more practical idiom of the International Style. The projects were working-class housing in the Hook of Holland (1924), residential housing in Kiefhoek (1925), and experimental housing the Weissenhof Settlement, Stuttgart, Germany (1927). Oud's sound technical training enabled him to make the often impractical *De Stijl* ideas reality. Although starkly austere, the designs of all three projects differed from the often impersonal rectangular International Style in that they bore the unmistakable Oud touch: meticulous workmanship, exquisite proportioning, and subtle, integrated ornamentation. Rounded corners softened the angularity of the buildings of the Hook of Holland project; integrated gardens lent a bucolic aspect to the Kiefhoek development; and even though the Weissenhof project, with its severe carefully syncopated geometric forms, most clearly showed the cubist influence, it was limited to the street façade. The rear had charming gardens overlooked by traditional balconies. It was at Weissenhof that Oud raised the minimal worker's dwelling to a work of art.

The Stuttgart exhibition, coordinated by Mies van der Rohe, was devoted to single family houses designed by the leading architects of the time, including Walter Gropius and Le Corbusier. Oud's project was among the most admired, and in 1932, when the New York Museum of Modern Art mounted its seminal exhibit that defined modern architecture and the International Style, Oud was one of four European architects whose works were displayed.

In 1933, Oud resigned as architect for the City of Rotterdam and resumed private practice. In 1938, his admirers were startled and some outraged by his design for a massive building in The Hague housing the offices of the Shell Oil Company. The *De Stijl* manner had given way to monumentality, symmetry, and ornamentation. Over a concrete skeleton, Oud fashioned a mantle of wheat-colored, hand-fired bricks, sandstone, and Majolica in novel decorative patterns. Toward the end of his life, Oud explained that his stockpile of ideas needed to be expanded and that the dispute between the old-fashioned and modern in architecture must end. It is a tribute to the greatness of Oud as an architect that in his Shell building he anticipated and was a pioneer in a movement in architecture beginning in the 1940's called "The New Empiricism" marked by a movement from established modernity and the enrichment of newer structures with patterns and traditional styles.

Between 1938 and his death in 1963, Oud either designed or designed and completed fourteen major projects. Among these was the charming Bio Resort Village near Arnhem for spastic children and the Congress Building in The Hague, a major complex incorporating assembly halls, theaters, recreational areas, and a hotel. The "village" is an exercise in miniature of city planning as can be seen in the organic relationship of the buildings. The cubist influence can be seen in the geometric forms of the buildings. Oud's fondness for integrated ornamentation can be seen in the mosaic that he commissioned from the Dutch artist Karel Appel and incorporated into the circular conical-roofed central administration building.

In 1955, Oud was given an honorary doctorate by the Technical University of Delft. The year before, he had moved to Wassenaar near The Hague, where he continued to practice architecture until his death in 1963.

### Summary

J. J. P. Oud's greatness is derived from not only his skill as an architect in the modern manner but also his demonstrating that such architecture, while functional, can also be handsome and individualistic. Because of the relatively small number of buildings designed by Oud, there is a tendency among some critics to dismiss him as a major architect. What is overlooked is that in his work Oud was always the artist and the meticulous craftsman. Each work was an individual creation, not to be altered to meet later exigencies. To be admired is Oud's strong social commitment, especially in the design of public housing that was not only serviceable and handsome but also, through techniques such as prefabrication and the innovative use of space, remarkably inexpensive. Another indication of Oud's greatness as an architect is his versatility, his ability to move from the stark rigidity of neoplasticism to the more traditional New Empiricism with no loss of artistic integrity.

### Bibliography

Langmead, Donald. *J. J. P. Oud and the International Style: A Bio-Bibliography.* Westport,

Conn.: Greenwood Press, 1999. Excellent volume for those seeking a guide to the archives, collections, and books in Oud's own library. Includes a biographical essay.

Museum of Modern Art. *Modern Architecture International Exhibition.* New York: Museum of Modern Art, 1932. Although Oud's professional career had not reached the halfway point at the time this important exhibition was mounted, the projects for which he is most admired were completed. The book has a well-written essay by Russell Hitchcock on Oud, especially on his development as a *De Stijl* architect. The book contains a series of excellent black-and-white photographs of Oud's major works.

"Recent Works of a Pioneer: J. J. P. Oud." *Progressive Architecture* 42 (June, 1961): 72. Enthusiasm for Oud's earlier works often obscures the fact that he worked steadily until the time of his death on major projects that would have daunted a much younger man. Photographs and models for his Resort Village in Arnhem and the Congress Hall in The Hague, unfinished at the time of Oud's death, illustrate his mastery of conceptualizing large complexes.

Tafuri, Manfredo, and Francesco Dal Co. *Modern Architecture.* Translated by Robert Erich Wolf. New York: Abrams, 1979; London: Academy, 1980. Throughout his professional life, Oud either worked with or was influenced by other artists and architects. This work is particularly valuable in differentiating modern architecture with which Oud is associated from earlier movements. It also gives details on the influence of other architects such as Berlage and the nature of his associations with the *De Stijl* group.

Wiekart, K. *J. J. P. Oud.* Translated by C. de Dood. Amsterdam: Meulenhoff, 1965. Probably the only available work in English on Oud that spans his entire career. Contains an excellent monograph on Oud's aesthetic and professional development. Of particular interest are the details of Oud's designing techniques: his attention to the most minute details in a design, even to the size of kitchen tiles; his selection of materials; and his specifications of workmanship. Contains an extensive bibliography, a list of all of Oud's projects and completed works, and forty-four black-and-white photographs of completed works, projects, and plans.

"The Work and Writings of J. J. P. Oud." *Architectural Design* 33 (July, 1963): 308-309. Oud was a prolific writer as well as a shrewd and witty observer. Unfortunately, few of his writings have been translated from Dutch and German, both of which he utilized. This article contains selections from his writings dating from 1918 to 1957 and gives a valuable insight as to his reasons for modifying his architectural styles. There are twelve photographs of his works, including furniture and the delightful but now-destroyed Café de Unie.

*Nis Petersen*

# JESSE OWENS

*Born:* September 12, 1913; Oakville, Alabama
*Died:* March 31, 1980; Tucson, Arizona
*Area of Achievement:* Sports
*Contribution:* The winner of four gold medals at the Berlin Olympics in 1936, Owens served as an inspirational model of success for American blacks, and later became a symbol and eloquent spokesman for America as a land of opportunity for all.

## Early Life

James Cleveland Owens was born on September 12, 1913, in Oakville, Alabama, a remote little farm community on the northern edge of the state. His father, Henry Cleveland Owens, and his mother, née Mary Emma Fitzgerald, were sharecroppers, descendants of slaves. James Cleveland, the last of nine children who survived infancy, was called J. C. When he was eight or nine years old, the family moved to Cleveland, Ohio, for better work and educational opportunities. On his first day of school, he introduced himself as "J. C.," but his teacher misunderstood him to say "Jesse." The young Owens bashfully accepted the mistake, thus taking on the name by which he would become famous.

At Fairmount Junior High School his exceptional athletic ability caught the eye of a physical education teacher, Charles Riley. A white man, Riley became Owens' coach, his moral monitor, and his surrogate father, teaching him citizenship as well as athletic techniques. Riley worked long hours with his pupil and continued to do so through high school. While on his high school track team, Jesse set several interscholastic records. In 1932, he failed to win a place on the United States Olympic squad, but by the time he had finished high school, in 1933, he had won much acclaim as a track athlete of extraordinary promise.

Owens wished to attend the University of Michigan. No track scholarships were available in that day, however, and Jesse's parents could not afford tuition. He therefore matriculated at Ohio State University, athletic boosters having arranged for him to work at part-time jobs to pay his expenses. He waited on tables in the dining hall, operated an elevator in the State House, and served as a page boy for the Ohio legislature.

Poorly prepared for college work and distracted by athletics, he was never a good student. After his first term he was constantly on academic probation; once he had to sit out the indoor track season because of bad grades. All the while he excelled in sports, setting numerous Big Ten and national track records. His finest day was May 25, 1935, at the Big Ten championships in Ann Arbor. Within a single hour he set new world records in the 220-yard sprint, the 220-yard hurdles, and the long jump, and tied the world record in the 100-yard dash. Well over a year before the Berlin Games of 1936, Owens emerged as a young man destined for Olympic fame.

His physique, style, and personality made him a sportswriter's dream. He carried about 165 pounds on a compact frame of five feet, ten inches. A model of graceful form, he ran so smoothly that each performance seemed effortless. Whether on or off the track, he frequently flashed a warm, spontaneous smile. Never did he refuse an interview or autograph. In the face of racial insults and discrimination, he kept a mild, pleasant demeanor. Like most blacks of his generation, Owens survived by turning the other cheek, by presenting himself as a modest individual who did not openly retaliate against the bigotry of his day.

At the Olympic trials in the summer of 1936, he finished first in all three of the events he had entered. Several weeks later, he took the Berlin Olympics by storm. First, he won the 100-meter dash in 10.3 seconds, equaling the world record. Next he took the gold medal in the long jump with a new Olympic distance of 8.06 meters. Then he won the gold in the 200-meter race with a new Olympic mark of 20.7 seconds. Toward the end of the week, he was unexpectedly placed on the American team for the 400-meter relays. He ran the opening leg in yet another gold-medal, record-making effort.

By the end of that fabulous week in Berlin, an attractive yarn attached itself to the name of Jesse Owens. Supposedly, he was "snubbed" by Adolf Hitler, who reportedly refused to congratulate him publicly after his victories. Actually, the story was concocted by American sportswriters, who were all too willing to read the worst of motives into Hitler's behavior and to assume innocent excellence from America's newest hero. Although it had no basis in fact, the story of "Hitler's snub" was repeated so often that people took it as truth. It remains one of the great anecdotes of American popular culture.

## Life's Work

For several years after the Berlin Olympics, life did not go smoothly for Owens. American officials had planned a barnstorming tour for the track team immediately after the Berlin Games. At first, Owens cooperated, running exhibitions in Germany, Czechoslovakia, and England. Having received numerous offers from the United States to capitalize on his Olympic fame, he balked when the team departed from London for a series of exhibitions in Scandinavia. The Amateur Athletic Union suspended him from any further amateur competition.

Accompanied by his Ohio State coach, Larry Snyder, Owens returned to the United States only to find that all the "offers" were phony publicity stunts by unscrupulous entrepreneurs. They never seriously intended to give a young black man—not even an Olympic hero—a steady job at decent pay. Instead, Owens found a lucrative assignment in the presidential campaign of Alf Landon, who paid him to stump for black votes. That turned out to be a futile effort but no more futile than a subsequent string of unsatisfactory jobs. For a time, Owens directed a band for Bill "Bojangles" Robinson on the black nightclub circuit. Tiring of that, he organized traveling basketball and softball teams, raced against horses at baseball games and county fairs, served for a summer as a playground director in Cleveland, and briefly worked as a clothes salesman. He suffered his biggest failure in a dry-cleaning venture that went bankrupt within six months.

Now married with three young daughters, Owens at twenty-seven years of age returned to Ohio State to finish his baccalaureate degree. Unfortunately, he could not bring his grade average up sufficiently to earn his degree. At the outbreak of World War II, he took a government appointment as director of a physical fitness program for blacks. Two years later, he took a job with Ford Motor Company in Detroit, in charge of Ford's black labor force. Dismissed from that position at the end of the war, by 1946 Owens no doubt winced when he looked back on the ten years since his Olympic victories. During that decade he had held ten jobs or so, all confined to the segregated black community.

Finally, in the 1950's, Owens broke out of that ghetto existence. When, after the onset of the Cold War, America needed a successful black to display to the world as an exemplar of the cherished American ideal of equal opportunity, Jesse Owens fit the bill. Having moved to Chicago in 1949, he worked with the Southside Boys Club and gave addresses to both black and white audiences in the greater Chicago area. Soon, he was in great demand throughout the United States as a spokesman for American patriotism and the American Dream. In 1951, he returned to Berlin with that message. In 1955, he toured India, Malaya, and the Philippines under the sponsorship of the United States Department of State, and the following year, he attended the Melbourne, Australia, Olympic Games as a personal representative of President Dwight D. Eisenhower. Never again would Owens be shunted aside as a black man in a white man's world. For the last two decades of his life, he gave more than one hundred speeches a year in praise of athletics, religion, and the flag.

Becoming politically more conservative as he got older, Owens refused to join the Civil Rights movement. His moderate position put him out of touch with the younger, angrier generation of blacks. He was rejected as an "Uncle Tom" in the 1960's. After Tommie Smith and John Carlos gave their world-famous black-fist salutes at the Olympic Games held in Mexico City in 1968, Owens demanded apologies, but to no avail.

He received numerous honors during his final years. In 1974, the National Collegiate Athletic Association presented him its highest recognition, the Theodore Roosevelt Award for distinguished achievement. Two years later, President Gerald R. Ford bestowed on him the Medal of Freedom Award for his "inspirational" life, and in 1979, Democratic president Jimmy Carter honored him with the Living Legends Award for his "dedicated but modest" example of greatness. Less than a year later, on March 31, 1980, Jesse Owens died of lung cancer. Ironically, America's greatest track and field athlete fell victim to a twenty-year habit of cigarette smoking.

## Summary

When Jesse Owens achieved stardom in the Berlin Olympics of 1936, rigid racial segregation pervaded baseball, football, and basketball in the United States. Owens and Joe Louis stood virtually alone as black athletes who had excelled against whites. Black Americans viewed them as examples of success, inspirational models of black ability, symbols of racial pride and dignity.

Although he was America's first Olympic superstar, Owens did not become a widely acclaimed

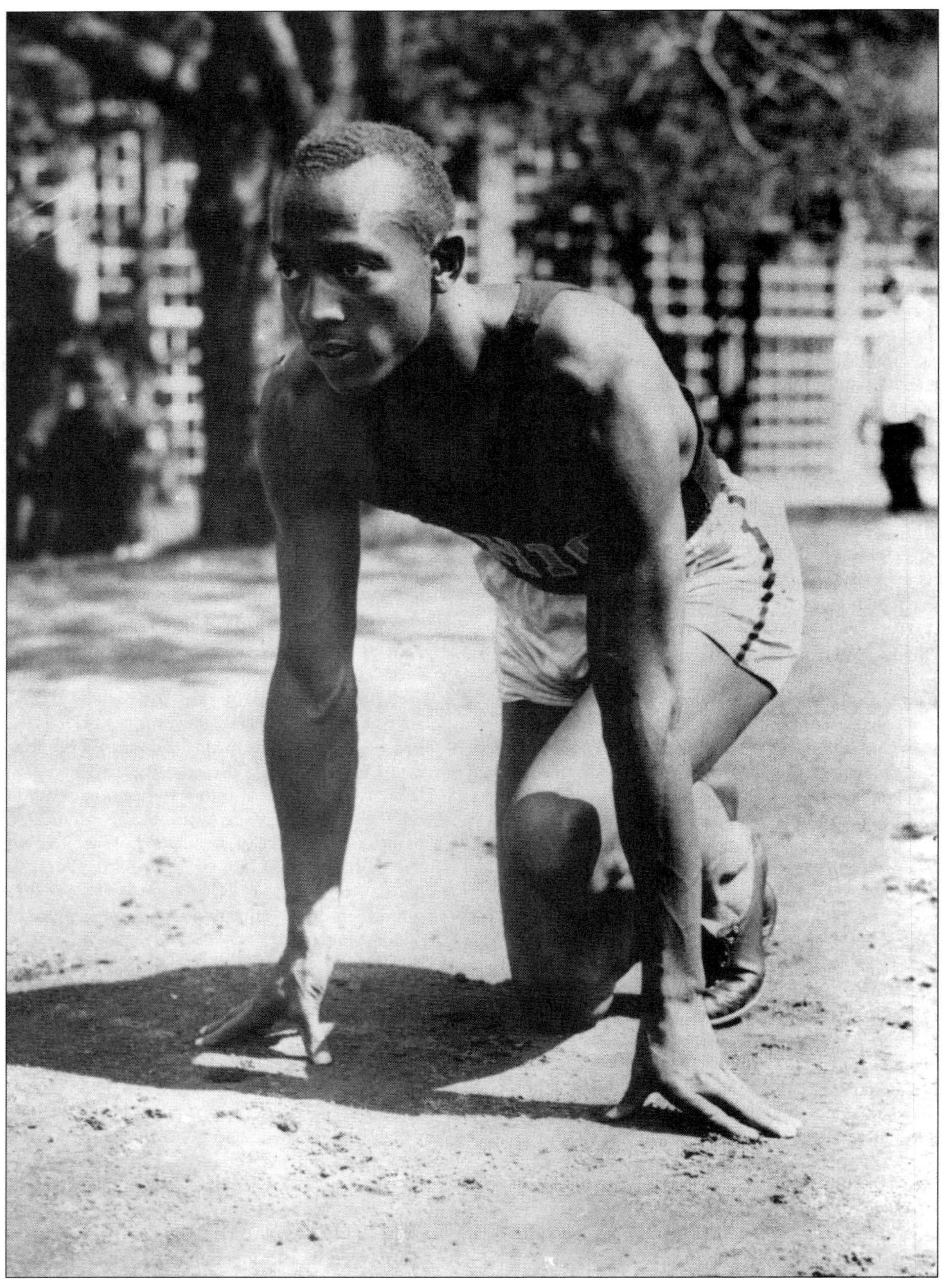

hero until after World War II. As Americans transposed their hatred of Hitler and the Nazis to Stalin and the Communists, Owens' rags-to-riches story confirmed American values as superior to Communist claims to a better way of life. "In America, anybody can become somebody," Owens often said, and American politicians, the media, and the public at large loved him for it. Especially to people in the nonaligned Third World, he was an effective spokesman for American democracy.

Four years after Owens' death, the 1984 Los Angeles Olympics demonstrated his perennial popularity. At Los Angeles, Carl Lewis won gold medals in the same four events that Owens had dominated half a century earlier, with much better statistical results. Yet Owens' fame remained undiminished. Each time Lewis won a race, he was compared to Owens. Old film clips from the Berlin Games were aired repeatedly on television, showing the graceful Owens in action. Numerous interviews with family and friends kept his memory alive. Arguably, Jesse Owens was the posthumous star of the Los Angeles Olympics.

His life illustrates the principle that an athlete becomes a national hero only when his achievements, personality, and image coincide with momentous events to fulfill a cultural need beyond the athletic arena. So long as people struggle against the odds of racial prejudice and economic deprivation, the story of Jesse Owens will be told. He overcame the odds.

### Bibliography


Baker, William J. *Jesse Owens: An American Life.* New York: Free Press, and London: Macmillan,1986. The only complete, critical biography available. Based on archival research, the black press, interviews with family and friends, and FBI files on Owens, all fully documented. A candid appraisal of Owens' limitations and vices as well as his achievements and virtues, set against the background of American society.

———. *Sports in the Western World.* Totowa, N.J.: Rowman and Littlefield, 1982. Places Owens in the larger context of sport history, briefly focusing on his Olympic victories in the face of Hitler's ambitions in 1936. A survey, undocumented, but with a good critical bibliography of sport history.

Bennett, Lerone, Jr. "Jesse Owens' Olympic Triumph over Time and Hitlerism." *Ebony* 51, no. 6 (April, 1996). Profile of Owens focusing on his participation in the 1936 Olympics.

Edwards, Harry. *The Revolt of the Black Athlete.* New York: Free Press, and London: Macmillan, 1970. A firsthand account of the movement for black athletes' rights in the 1960's by the leader of the revolt that culminated in Mexico City. Depicts Owens as a lamentable representative of an older generation's acquiescence to racial abuse. A fiery, argumentative treatise.

Gilmore, Al-Tony. "Black Athletes in an Historical Context: The Issue of Race." *Negro History Bulletin* 58, no. 3-4, (October-December, 1995). Short study on African American athletes in the United States and the obstacles they have faced.

Mandell, Richard D. *The Nazi Olympics.* New York: Macmillan, 1971; London: Souvenir Press, 1972. The best treatment of the Berlin Games of 1936. Strong on Nazi ideology and technical efficiency behind the Games, also on daily events and profiles of athletes. Well documented from German as well as English sources, a gem of cultural history.

Owens, Jesse, with Paul Neimark. *Blackthink: My Life as Black Man and White Man.* New York: Morrow, 1970. A tirade against black power advocates, especially against black athletes who openly protested American racism. Mostly autobiographical, with Owens illustrating his own acquaintance with bigotry, concluding that patience and moral character rather than angry rebellion would produce social change. Evoked hostile response from black readers, prompting Owens to collaborate once again with Paul Neimark to produce *I Have Changed* (New York: William Morrow and Co., 1972), another collection of stories from his life to explain his present point of view.

———. *Jesse: A Spiritual Autobiography.* Plainfield, N.J.: Logos International, 1978. An indulgent use of anecdotes in the service of homilies. As always, Owens' recollections cannot be taken at face value. Some are outright fabrications; most are romantically embellished.

———. *The Jesse Owens Story.* New York: Putnam, 1970. A lightweight, ghost-written autobiography directed towards a teenage readership. More inspirational than factually accurate; anecdotal, not analytical. Undocumented and untrustworthy, the Jesse Owens story as Owens himself wanted it told.

Quercetani, Roberto L. *A World History of Track and Field Athletics, 1864-1964*. London and New York: Oxford University Press, 1964. Useful reference for Owens' achievements in comparison with other athletes before and since his day. Covers his intercollegiate as well as his Olympic victories.

*William J. Baker*

# VIJAYA LAKSHMI PANDIT

*Born:* August 18, 1900; Allahabad, India
*Died:* December 1, 1990; Dehra Dun, India
*Areas of Achievement:* Diplomacy, government, and politics
*Contribution:* Pandit served as post-independence India's foremost diplomatic representative, holding the highest positions in international councils and in many ways helping to reconcile the bitter and deep disputes between India, its neighbors, and its former rulers.

## Early Life

Vijaya Lakshmi Pandit was born on August 18, 1900, the eldest daughter of Motilal Nehru, a prosperous attorney, in the city of Allahabad. Her name at birth, Swarup Kumari ("Beautiful Princess"), was changed, according to the Hindu custom, upon her marriage at the age of twenty to Ranjit Sitaram Pandit, but as a child and throughout her life she was known by the nickname "Nan." Her elder brother, Jawaharlal Nehru, served as India's prime minister, and Pandit, along with her entire family, was an active participant in the Indian political struggles of the day to separate India from the British Empire.

Pandit's early life reached a watershed in 1920 during the turmoil following the Amritsar Massacres. The action by British General Reginald Dyer of allowing his troops to fire on demonstrators protesting British rule, killing 372 and wounding thousands, caused Pandit, along with the other members of her previously politically moderate family, to shift her allegiance to Mahatma Gandhi's satyagraha movement, which aimed through nonviolent methods to force the British from India completely. Given Pandit's upbringing with a Westernized and Anglophilic environment, however, such a high degree of political involvement might not have been expected. Still, while embracing the West, her family were members of the Kashmiri Brahman, and the family was correspondingly conservative in attitude.

Pandit was educated at home by English governesses and later attended finishing school in Switzerland. She was taken by her father on a visit to England when she was five and was encouraged in her studies, but it is unlikely that she hoped for any kind of scholarly future—within the family most expectations were for Jawaharlal. She did begin writing for Hindu periodicals at about the age of fifteen, at much the same time as the divisions between Indian nationalists and the British were gaining strength. This division, marked by the participation of her father in the Indian National Congress meetings of 1915, led to Pandit's first introduction to Gandhi.

Pandit's marriage, unlike that of many upper-class Hindus of the time, was not arranged. Her husband was an attorney and as well a highly educated scholar who had studied abroad. He shared the Nehru family's political interests, and the couple worked together in Allahabad toward Indian independence. Pandit, her husband, her brother, and his wife journeyed to Switzerland in 1926, where they were joined by Pandit's father the next year. Pandit's three daughters—Chandalekha, born in 1924, Nayantara, born in 1927, and Rita Vitasta, born in 1929—were in their own right to carry on the family traditions of active political involvement in Indian politics. Further, after her sister-in-law's death, Pandit was to help rear her niece, Indira Gandhi, India's future prime minister.

## Life's Work

It was during the 1920's that Pandit, by then accustomed to the highest levels of political discourse, began her own active participation. By the end of her public career, she had held more key diplomatic and political positions, both appointed and elected, then any other Indian woman of the twentieth century. Pandit's background in Indian politics lay in both Gandhi's "Quit India" movement, directed against the British, and in the All-India Women's Conference. This latter affiliation culminated in her organization, with her sister-in-law Kamala Nehru, of the women's general boycott of British goods, which spread outward from Allahabad throughout the entire province now known as Uttar Pradesh. She spoke vigorously at public gatherings, advocating the complete withdrawal of the British.

It was not until the 1930's, however, that Pandit's activities began seriously to alarm the British. In January, 1932, she and her sister Krisha (also a member of the All-India Women's Conference, and Pandit's junior by seven years) were forbidden to take part in any more political meetings, under threat of confinement. On Independence Day, January 26, 1932, the two deliberately participated in just such a meeting and were promptly arrested by the British authorities. This

marked Pandit's first term of imprisonment, when she was sentenced to serve one year. The political punishment was served at Lucknow Prison and was extremely rigorous.

Released in 1933, Pandit rejoined the independence movement. Her political fervor had been heightened not only by her imprisonment but also by the public reaction that had followed her father's death in 1932. The funeral had been marked by the presence of Gandhi, whose eulogy for Nehru was heard by thousands gathered on the banks of the Ganges River. It had become clear that the politicization of India against the British occupation was increasing at a very swift pace.

While it would be incorrect to speak of this period of Indian history as somehow indicating the "inevitable" withdrawal and defeat of the British, once the influential Indian upper classes had reached out and connected with the middle and lower classes on a unified political basis, the relatively small British ruling class was faced with very difficult choices. In an attempt to maintain the status quo, there were increased numbers of political arrests, interdictions of free speech, and military action. In response, the Indian political activists used Great Britain's own traditions. The independence movement participants chose to join the existing governmental bodies, campaigning in and winning election after election, leaving the British in a position of appearing to oppose legitimately chosen representatives with legitimate grievances.

Pandit's participation within government began when she stood as the Congress candidate for the Allahabad Municipal Board and won. In 1935, a year later, she was elected Chairman of the Board and served two years. During her membership, her chief concern was with local public institutions, particularly in the social services areas. In the time she was a member of the board, she was instrumental in turning the local "night schools" into the focus of Allahabad's advanced study of literary and political issues. This change in emphasis reflected a worldwide movement in adult education, and allowed, often for the first time, workers in the city access to education beyond a primary or vocational level.

In 1936, Pandit won a seat during the general elections of that year, standing for Kanpur. In that rural district, she won a majority of about ten thousand from an electorate of thirty-eight thousand. In 1937, still representing the Congress Party, she capped her local governmental career by her unopposed election as the Minister of Local Self Government and Public Health for the United Provinces.

During the 1930's, Pandit consolidated her political position, standing firmly for the independence goals of the Congress Party and as well for the rights of women within the "new" India. It was a time of advancement for women throughout the world, but it is significant that within India women, from the first of the independence movement, were an integral part. Rather than having to assert a separate role, Indian women political activists were accorded a fully equal position in the struggle against British rule. Not only were they admitted to strategic and political associations but also they suffered the same consequences in terms of imprisonment and censure by the British. Thus, women's rights in India have not generally been a separate issue, at odds with mainstream political objectives. Pandit's place within India was won with the assistance of the emerging political power of the Congress Party and the leaders of India. Consequently, after independence, her role as ambassador must be seen as fully representative of India's nationalist political opinion and not as a concession to her position as Prime Minister Nehru's sister.

When independence came in 1947, Pandit's career as an international spokeswoman for India was well under way. After her husband's death in 1944, which had left her without financial resources, she had decided to go to the United States and lecture; she was accepted as India's representative at the Pacific Relations Conference held by the Council for World Affairs. Her background as the former president of the All-India Women's Conference (1940-1942) had validated her right to speak at such an international meeting and marked the beginning of her association with world figures. At the end of the war, she became the leader of the Indian delegation to the inaugural meetings of the United Nations (1946) and continued to serve in that position in 1947 and 1948. Her prestige was such that in 1949 she was appointed Indian Ambassador to the United States, where she remained until 1951.

In 1947, however, she served as Indian Ambassador to the Soviet Union, initiating a pattern that typified her public life. Pandit frequently held more than one post for the government at a time, and the 1940's and 1950's saw her moving between one responsibility and another. For example, in 1952 she headed the Indian "Goodwill Mission" to China during the extremely tense political atmosphere that had resulted from Sino-Indian border disputes and that same year was again leader of the Indian United Nations delegation. During the Eighth Assembly (1952-1953), she was elected president of the General Assembly and had become the acknowledged leader of the newly emerging Arab-Asian bloc.

It was in 1954 that Pandit served in what may have been the most remarkable position of her career. In that year, she became India's High Commissioner to Great Britain, consolidating the former colony's new status as an independent and equal state within the community of nations. Her work in the United Kingdom marked the conclusion of much of the enmity that had resulted from the conflict of the two nations and can be viewed not only as the high point of her career but also as an illustration of the ways in which colonial relationships could develop into effective partnerships.

### Summary

While Vijaya Lakshmi Pandit was most actively representing India internationally during the 1950's, it was after the death of her brother that it became clear that she saw herself first and foremost as a servant of India, rather than as a world figure. When she left the High Commission to Great Britain in 1961, it had been her intention to resume private life, but she soon realized that this would be impossible. Between 1961 and 1964, she was her brother's unofficial link to European opinion, most significantly during private talks with Chancellor Konrad Adenauer. By 1963, she gradually reentered official life, serving as leader of the Indian United Nations mission. She was eventually recalled to India to become the appointed governor of Maharashtra Province.

This largely ceremonial position occupied her only until it became clear that her prestige and the respect in which she was held made it necessary that she stand in the by-election at Phulpur, for the seat her brother had held until his death. Pandit won the election with a huge majority of more than fifty-eight thousand votes, preserving the seat for the Congress Party and continuing thereby to ensure the presence of her family in Indian politics.

Pandit's position in Indian government virtually paralleled that country's own growth and development in the twentieth century. From her early life as a traditional member of the upper classes, through her participation in the effort to free India from the British, to her successful attempts to have India received into the community of nations, Pandit always stood for the betterment of the people of India.

### Bibliography

Andrews, Robert Hardy. *A Lamp for India: The Story of Madame Pandit*. London: Barker, and Englewood Cliffs, N.J.: Prentice-Hall, 1967. A very admiring biography, with photographs and an index, which takes the story of Pandit's life past her brother's death, particularly noting her role as negotiator during the Pakistan-Indian conflicts of the 1960's.

Bowles, Chester. *Ambassador's Report*. London: Gollancz, and New York: Harper, 1954. This former Ambassador of the United States recounts his time spent in India during the early 1950's and provides an insight into Pandit's circle during the post-independence period. Contains many unique photographs that more than convey the flavor of the period.

Brittain, Vera. *Envoy Extraordinary: A Study of Vijaya Lakshmi Pandit and Her Contribution to Modern India*. London: Allen, and South Brunswick, N.J.: Barnes, 1965. A well-written, accessible biography by a contemporary and friend. This account is intended for the general reader with some knowledge of the times and concentrates on the feelings and personal behavior of Pandit.

George, T. J. S. *Krishna Menon: A Biography*. London: Cape, 1964; New York: Taplinger, 1965. This biography of Pandit's sometime friend and sometime enemy contains in-depth discussion of the United Nations period and is particularly useful when discussing how the conflicts between the two emerged.

Guthrie, Anne. *Madame Ambassador: The Life of Vijaya Lakshmi Pandit*. New York: Harcourt Brace, 1962; London: Macmillan, 1963. Intended for younger readers, the author relies heavily on anecdotal accounts and personal information. Still, her retelling of Pandit's early life and how she gradually became political is most evocative.

*A. J. Plotke*

# EMMELINE PANKHURST

*Born:* July 14, 1858; Manchester, England
*Died:* June 14, 1928; London, England
*Area of Achievement:* Social reform
*Contribution:* Pankhurst fought to attain the vote for British women during the early years of the twentieth century, organizing the militant Women's Social and Political Union into an effective tool for obtaining women's rights.

## Early Life

Emmeline Pankhurst was born in Manchester, England, on July 14, 1858, the eldest daughter (third of eleven children) of Robert Goulden and his wife, née Sophia Jane Craine. Her father was the owner of a calico-printing and bleach works located outside Salford, the industrial twin city to Manchester. Emmeline's education was typical of a girl of her class. She attended a girls' boarding school in Manchester and then, at the age of fifteen, was sent to Paris to attend a finishing school, the École Normale, from which she was graduated at the age of nineteen. More important than formal schooling in the development of the future political agitator was her informal education. Her father taught her to read at an early age, and in her autobiography she tells how she was inspired by reading Thomas Carlyle's *History of the French Revolution* (1837). Moreover, both of her parents had been actively involved in liberal and radical reform movements, among them women's suffrage. At the age of fourteen, Emmeline was taken to her first suffrage meeting in Manchester, then a center of the women's emancipation movement, with an active chapter of the Manchester Women's Suffrage Committee. One of the founders of that committee was Richard Marsden Pankhurst, a barrister and author of Great Britain's first women's suffrage bill. They were married in 1879. Emmeline Pankhurst almost immediately became a member of the Manchester Women's Suffrage Committee; she and her husband supported the Married Women's Property Bill, which he had helped draft in 1882. Their home was a gathering center for political reformers; the Pankhursts entertained such individuals as James Keir Hardie (who would become a Member of Parliament for the Labour Party), Annie Besant, and Sir Charles Dilke. After Prime Minister William E. Gladstone indicated his refusal to support women's suffrage as part of the general reform legislation of 1884, the Pankhursts left the Liberal Party. They became members of the Fabian Society, believing that "mild socialism" offered much more hope for the future than did Liberalism.

Five children were born to the couple, three daughters and two sons. The two boys, Henry and Frank, died early in life. The girls reached maturity and all, especially Christabel and Sylvia, associated with their mother's cause. Emmeline Pankhurst at this time was an elegant woman, with raven black hair, an olive complexion, and expressive blue-violet eyes. She was an effective speaker, with a melodious voice, and she had the ability to command almost complete loyalty from her close acquaintances.

The Pankhursts remained in Manchester into the mid-1880's. Richard Pankhurst was an unsuccessful candidate for the House of Commons in Manchester in 1883. When he was approached by the Liberal and Radical Association of Rotherhithe to run for the Commons from that constituency, the family moved to London, where Richard Pankhurst was again unsuccessful. This election, however, was instrumental in contributing to the outlook of Emmeline Pankhurst and her future activities. She was disturbed by the refusal of those in favor of Irish home rule to vote for her husband, who had been a vocal supporter of their cause. When Charles Stewart Parnell explained the reasons for his opposition to Liberals, Emmeline Pankhurst grudgingly recognized the correctness of a militant policy, which by constant obstruction would wear down a government and produce its defeat, a valuable political lesson that Pankhurst would later put into practice.

In 1893, the Pankhursts returned to Manchester, and she resumed her association with Suffragists in that city. The death of her husband in 1898 was both an emotional and a financial blow for Pankhurst, who was in the difficult position of having to support herself and four children (the youngest, Frank, had just died).

## Life's Work

When the family returned to Manchester, Pankhurst was selected to serve in the unsalaried position of a member of the Board of the Poor Law Guardians. As she notes in her autobiography, her experiences here opened her eyes to wider issues. She had always lived in relatively comfortable sur-

roundings, but as a Poor Law Guardian she came in contact with women's broader needs and concluded that these needs would not be met until women gained the vote. In the past, Pankhurst had seen suffrage as a basic right that ought to be honored; from this point onward, she was convinced that it was a practical necessity. In 1898, she was appointed Registrar of Births and Deaths in Manchester, a salaried position. She held this position until 1907, when she resigned to devote herself fully to the suffrage movement.

Agitation for women's political rights had emerged in the middle of the nineteenth century, with two contrasting approaches manifesting themselves rather early. The more moderate approach was that of the National Union of Women's Suffrage Societies, established and led by Lydia Becker in 1867, during the period of the second Reform Bill. This group was willing to work with and cooperate with the establishment in the attainment of women's suffrage. The Women's Social and Political Union (WSPU), founded and led by Pankhurst and her eldest daughter, Christabel, followed a militant line in the attainment of its aim. The WSPU was organized while Pankhurst was still associated with the Independent Labour Party. Indeed, one of the goals in the formation of the Union was to assist women industrial workers. The goal of the WSPU, like that of other suffrage associations, was "to secure for women the parliamentary vote as it is or may be granted to men." Completely independent of any and all established political parties, it opposed any government that was in power and in elections opposed all government candidates. In these tactics the clear influence of Parnell can be seen. To attain its goals, the Union sought to utilize all means available to educate the public, including public meetings, demonstrations, debates, and distribution of literature.

Attacks upon the government and its ministers at elections became a basic tactic of the WSPU. The nature of the constitution before World War I played right into the hands of the suffragettes; a Member of Parliament accepting an appointment as a minister had to resign his seat in the Commons and stand for election. Pankhurst and her followers could thus be more selective in their agitation and concentrate their efforts on the ministers. The heckling of ministers began in 1905, when Sir Edward Grey was queried about his stance on the vote. When no answer was forthcoming and the question was repeated, the questioners (including Christabel Pankhurst) were forcibly ejected from the hall; a subsequent protest meeting in the street outside resulted in arrest and imprisonment for Christabel Pankhurst. It soon became clear that the publicity resulting from militancy gained for the WSPU far more news coverage than years of peaceful agitation would have gained. Militancy paid off.

Early militancy was characterized by confrontations with the police, but without damage to property. Generally, at the opening of each parliament, a Women's Parliament would meet in nearby Caxton Hall, followed by a procession to Westminster to present (always unsuccessfully) a petition to the prime minister. Clashes with the police, arrests, and court trials followed, all of which added to coverage of the cause in the newspapers. A second phase of militancy started in the summer of 1909, with attacks on property; the first target was the official residence of the prime minister. The purpose of this violence was twofold: to lodge a symbolic protest against the government and to shorten the struggle with the police and thus lessen the possibility of violence being committed against women. Militant tactics were escalated; soon, any form of violence or destruction short of injury to persons was acceptable to the group.

Members of the WSPU allowed themselves to be imprisoned in order to attract the notice of newspapers. If given the choice of a fine or incarceration, the women chose jail, where they would engage in hunger strikes. Pankhurst herself refused food (and later food and drink) when sentenced to Holloway for her part in public demonstrations. Pankhurst insisted that women be treated equally with men who had been jailed under similar circumstances; men had been treated as political prisoners, while women were categorized as common criminals. Since the government did not want to create martyrs, women were released from prison well before they had served their full time. This policy was legislated in the so-called Cat and Mouse Act of 1913, allowing the temporary release of prisoners who were not well with the threat of being arrested and incarcerated again if their health improved or if they made any trouble for the authorities. The process—arrest, hunger strike, release, and possible rearrest—kept the women's movement in the public's eye. Pankhurst and her organization made the most of it. There were, however, indications that the militancy of the WSPU and the dictatorial leadership of Pankhurst had become counterproductive by the beginning of 1914 and that support was weakening.

The outbreak of war in Europe in 1914 brought an end to active agitation for women's rights. For the entire period of the war, Pankhurst devoted herself to patriotic endeavors, perhaps inspired by the ardent anti-German feelings which were a legacy of her Parisian schooling. She recruited women to work in munitions factories, and in 1916, when the issue of women's suffrage became prominent, she took no part in the agitation. Two years later, the movement gained a partial victory as women were allowed to vote at the age of thirty. Soon after the war, Pankhurst visited Canada, but she returned to England in 1926 and joined the Conservative Party. She was adopted by that party as a candidate for Parliament to present Whitechapel, but she was defeated. Pankhurst died in London, on June 14, 1928, shortly after women had gained the vote on a par with men.

**Summary**

Emmeline Pankhurst's career illustrates one kind of response by individuals to social and political injustice. Seeking to remedy a situation that they had come to regard as intolerable, Pankhurst and her followers initially sought reform through normal channels. When these channels were exhausted, Pankhurst and her organization took a militant stance, and like other social movements, such as the Irish home rule movement, turned to violence and obstruction. The suffrage movement also had more than a merely superficial resemblance to the Civil Rights movement in the United States. Both women and blacks were clearly identified physically and emerged from a condition in which they were regarded as inferior beings. In both, attempts to persuade peacefully evolved into violent agitation. Ultimately, both movements were incorporated into the mainstream culture.

Interestingly, Pankhurst's tactics were those utilized by the Liberals and the Chartists to promote parliamentary reform in the nineteenth century. When persuasion failed, unrepresented men used violence, initially window-breaking and then arson, in the pursuit of their goals; the destruction in Bristol in support of the Reform Bill of 1832 well illustrates this trend. Pankhurst may have taken a perverse pleasure in using the same tactics that the detested Liberal Party had countenanced earlier.

Pankhurst's most productive years fall into a brief time span—a decade only—the years between the founding of the WSPU and the outbreak of World War I. While the first forty-five years of her life were significant in the formation of her attitudes, her leadership of the radical suffragettes who alternately challenged, amused, frustrated, and disgusted the British establishment before 1914 represents Pankhurst's true heroic impact on Great Britain.

**Bibliography**

Dangerfield, George. *The Strange Death of Liberal England, 1910-1914*. New York: Smith, 1935; London: Constable, 1936. Dangerfield's classic study associates the increasing irrationalism on the part of the suffragettes and their opposition with the general breakdown of the Liberal consensus.

Fletcher, Ian Christopher. "'A Star Chamber of the Twentieth Century': Suffragettes, Liberals and the 1908 'Rush the Commons' Case." *Journal of British Studies* no. 4 (October, 1996). Discussion of the Bow Street case of 1908 involving Pankhurst and prison treatment of suffragettes.

Harrison, Brian. *Separate Spheres: The Opposition to Women's Suffrage in Britain*. London: Croom Helm, and New York: Holmes and Meier, 1978. Although clearly sympathetic to the women's cause, the author studies the roots and the nature of the ideological and political opposition to women's suffrage, which produced a National League Opposing Women's Suffrage with a greater membership in 1914 than the WSPU.

Mackenzie, Midge. *Shoulder to Shoulder: A Documentary*. London: Allen Lane, and New York: Knopf, 1975. Gives a flavor of the time and the movement with judicious selections from the writings of the participants. More than three hundred illustrations contribute to the usefulness of this volume.

Pankhurst, E. Sylvia. *The Life of Emmeline Pankhurst*. London: Laurie, 1935; Boston: Houghton Mifflin, 1936. A largely uncritical biography by Pankhurst's second daughter, as much an autobiography of the author as it is a study of the mother.

Pankhurst, Emmeline. *My Own Story*. London: Nash, and New York: Hearst's, 1914. A propagandistic autobiography written for the third of Pankhurst's visits to the United States to explain to Americans the cause of the suffragettes.

Rosen, Andrew. *Rise Up, Women: The Militant Campaign of the Women's Social and Political*

*Union, 1903-1914*. London and Boston: Routledge, 1974. A highly detailed chronological account of the suffrage campaign, emphasizing the anger, frustration, and prejudices on both sides of the question.

Rover, Constance. *Women's Suffrage and Party Politics in Britain, 1866-1914*. London: Routledge, and Toronto: University of Toronto Press, 1967. A carefully documented analysis of the political campaign to gain the vote for women and the obstacles to be overcome in this endeavor, emphasizing the lack of total commitment in either party and the suspicion of Liberals and Tories over potential women's voting patterns, which delayed the ultimate successful conclusion.

*Ronald O. Moore*

## FRANZ VON PAPEN

*Born:* October 29, 1879; Werl, Westphalia, Germany

*Died:* May 2, 1969; Obersasbach, Baden-Württemberg, West Germany

*Areas of Achievement:* The military, government, and politics

*Contribution:* After serving six months as German chancellor in 1932, Papen masterminded the backstairs appointment of Adolf Hitler to power on January 30, 1933. In the years that followed, he served the Third Reich as vice-chancellor (1933-1934) and ambassador to Austria (1934-1938) and Turkey (1939-1944).

### Early Life

Franz von Papen was born in Werl, Westphalia, on October 29, 1879. A child of aristocratic privilege, he grew up the third of five children in a Catholic family that traced its noble ancestry back four centuries. As a younger son with no claim to the family estate, he was guided into a military career by his father, a retired officer. Beginning at age eleven in Bensberg Cadet School and culminating with three years of training at Gross-Lichterfeld Academy near Berlin, the young Papen dutifully learned the military discipline and bearing, commitment to national service, and loyalty to the Hohenzollern monarchy that were to shape his political outlook and future. After graduation in 1898, he was posted to his father's former regiment in Düsseldorf, the Fifth Westphalian Uhlans, as a second lieutenant. There he developed the professional expertise, social graces, and personal contacts essential for a successful military career in imperial Germany.

His marriage in 1905 to Martha von Boch-Galhua, the daughter of a wealthy and influential Saarland industrialist, added important new dimensions to Papen's life. Besides responsibility for a wife and eventually five children, the marriage brought him into contact with Francophile in-laws who persuaded him to view French culture and Franco-German friendship in a more positive light. His father-in-law's admiration for the German General Staff also encouraged Papen to seek appointment to this powerful military circle, a goal he realized in 1913 with his promotion to captain.

By prewar standards, Papen's military career was modestly successful. Peacetime promotion came too slowly for this ambitious young officer, however, and so he used his personal contacts to secure appointment to the German embassy in Washington as military attaché He was expelled in 1915 for directing anti-Allied espionage and sabotage operations covering the United States and Canada. Much to Papen's future embarrassment, moreover, check stubs documenting agent payoffs were confiscated from his luggage by British authorities during his return to Germany and reproduced in a British white paper that questioned his personal integrity and respect for international law.

Papen fought with conspicuous courage on the Western Front in World War I, winning the Iron Cross (First Class) in 1916 while commanding a regiment on the Somme River. Transferred to Turkey in 1917, he served bravely in the Middle Eastern campaign as both a political officer and field commander, attaining the rank of major. With the collapse of the Central Powers in 1918, Papen was forced to return to civilian life in Germany.

### Life's Work

Unable to remain idle for long, Papen turned to politics in 1921, trading in the life of a country gentleman on his Westphalian estate for a seat in the Prussian state diet representing the Catholic Center party. The Westphalian Centrists who recruited him were impressed by Papen's conservative orientation, agricultural interests, strong Catholic beliefs, independent wealth (inherited mostly from his wife's family), and influential contacts.

They were less familiar with his political views. An obdurate reactionary, Papen bitterly rejected the new Weimar Republic and parliamentary democracy in favor of the discarded military monarchy of the kaisers. He believed that true political leadership had to come from an experienced ruling elite standing above partisan, interest-oriented parties. In his mind, the fundamental duty of government was not to promote majority rule or social reform but to defend the authoritarian state from the dangers of socialism and Asiatic Bolshevism. Measured even by the standards of conservative Westphalian Centrists, Papen's views were narrow and extreme.

Yet this extremity was not immediately apparent to party leaders. In the early 1920's, he worked hard for Centrist causes, especially agricultural issues important to him and his Westphalian constituents. By 1924, however, as his dissatisfaction with the Center Party's republican ties mounted,

Papen turned his energies to separating the Center Party from its Socialist and democratic allies and aligning it with the conservative Right. His uncompromising persistence in this crusade gradually alienated party colleagues and cost him his diet seat between 1928 and 1930, and again in 1932.

Exclusion from Center Party politics did not end Papen's public career. Even as Germany was slipping into the Great Depression, he kept in touch with forces of the Right through private associations such as the Herrenklub in Berlin. To those who would listen, he repeatedly warned of the dangers of communism, urged rapprochement with France—something most conservatives eschewed—and called for the establishment of an authoritarian dictatorship of the Right. Yet he rarely attracted wider attention in the years between 1928 and 1932.

It thus came as a stunning surprise in June of 1932 when President Paul von Hindenburg, the aging World War I hero, asked Papen to form a national government. In reality, it was not Hindenburg who had picked Papen but General Kurt von Schleicher, a backstairs intriguer who planned to use the little-known Papen as a figurehead chancellor for a cabinet under his command. Papen accepted the offer, noting in his memoirs that he could hardly disobey an order from his wartime commander Hindenburg, a man he deeply admired.

Yet Papen's "cabinet of barons" did little during its six-month tenure to ease Germany's growing political crisis. The new chancellor negotiated the end of reparations, but neither this nor his reactionary domestic policies produced enough political or popular support to end the parliamentary stalemate paralyzing the German government. Above all, Papen failed to deal decisively with the growing National Socialist movement. Like his predecessor, he was also handicapped by his dependence on presidential emergency powers rather than a Reichstag majority. As Germany's domestic crisis worsened, Schleicher finally realized that he had misjudged Papen's usefulness and, over the angry objections of President Hindenburg, brought the Papen government down in December.

In the critical weeks that followed, as Schleicher formed his own government and struggled to cope with the Depression and the Nazis, Papen embarked on a fateful venture that was to bring Adolf Hitler to power. Determined to regain power and repay Schleicher's disloyalty, he secretly reopened negotiations with Hitler and the Nazis toward the formation of a new government of national concentration. He arduously patched together a coalition of three Nazis and eight non-Nazis headed by Hitler as chancellor and himself as vice-chancellor. Then he convinced the reluctant Hindenburg to accept and support it. In the end it was Papen more than any other person who masterminded Hitler's legal appointment as German chancellor on January 30, 1933.

Shortly thereafter, Papen predicted that "in two months we'll have pushed Hitler into a corner so hard he'll be squeaking." Yet the new vice-chancellor did not know Hitler as well as he believed. Within weeks all the safeguards he had erected to contain Nazi excesses were brushed aside, and Hitler was wresting absolute power into his own hands. The vice-chancellor and non-Nazi cabinet members were left reeling, often confused or bypassed by the lightning pace of events. Thus the conservative revolution envisioned by Papen actually took place according to the revolutionary precepts of Hitler and the Nazis.

In the tragedy that followed, Papen seemed unable to separate himself from the dictatorship he had helped to install. Because he saw only what he wanted and dismissed Nazi excesses as temporary, he defended Hitler's coalition throughout the Nazi consolidation of power in 1933-1934. His negotiation of a concordat between Germany and the Vatican in 1933 may even have helped in the process by winning the Catholic church's blessing for the Third Reich. Papen did, to be sure, speak out courageously against Nazi illegalities and cruelty on June 17, 1934, at the University of Marburg. Thereafter he kept silent, intimidated perhaps by threats of Brownshirt violence.

Papen claims in his memoirs that he served Hitler and the Third Reich out of a sense of national loyalty, a loyalty instilled in him by his aristocratic origins, military service, and deep Catholic faith. Whatever the reasons, he did publicly represent Nazi Germany for most of its existence. When Hitler offered him the post of Ambassador to Austria in 1934, he accepted, working for four years to improve Austro-German relations, strengthen the Austrian Nazis, and prepare the groundwork for the 1938 Anschluss that unified the two countries. When Hitler sent him as ambassador to Turkey in 1939 during the Albanian Crisis, he took up his new duties eagerly, engaging once again as he had earlier in espionage activities. This time, however, his intrigues were more successful, providing Ger-

many with invaluable intelligence on Allied operations in the Middle East.

Captured by U.S. forces at the end of the war, Papen was held for trial at Nürnberg, where he was cleared of all charges by the War Crimes Tribunal. He was subsequently sentenced to eight years' hard labor by a Bavarian denazification court, but punishment was suspended in 1949. Papen devoted the last years of his life to writing his memoirs, trying unsuccessfully to rehabilitate his reputation, and seeking the pension he believed due him for service in the Prussian army.

### Summary

Franz von Papen's archaic aristocratic creed and reactionary political views remained unchanged throughout his entire life. These, combined with his vanity and lack of political acumen, made it relatively easy for others to use him for their own questionable purposes. His mistake was to believe that he, relying on his social charm and aristocratic standing, could outplay his rivals at their own game. Without the selfish machinations of this short-sighted, devious man, National Socialism might not have found the road to power in 1933. Papen compounded his fateful mistake by refusing to recognize the Third Reich for what it really was: a criminal conspiracy. His myopic support made it easier for other conservatives, aristocrats, and officers to tolerate National Socialism, even when they found certain aspects distasteful. In the end, Papen's biography demonstrates not only the importance of reactionary monarchists in Hitler's rise to power but also the susceptibility of people like Papen to political manipulation and expedience.

### Bibliography

Blood-Ryan, H. W. *Franz von Papen: His Life and Times*. London: Rich and Cowan, 1940. One of several contemporary journalistic biographies covering the pre-1940 period. The absence of footnotes and a bibliography, glaring omissions, and the anti-German predisposition make it necessary to use this work with caution.

Dorpalen, Andreas. *Hindenburg and the Weimar Republic*. Princeton, N.J.: Princeton University Press, 1964. Possibly the best general discussion of Papen's role in 1932 and 1933, especially for his maneuvers to bring Hitler to power at the head of a coalition of the Right. Carefully documented, extremely well written, highly analytical, and accurate.

Papen, Franz von. *Memoirs*. Translated by Brian Connell. London: Deutsch, 1952; New York: Dutton, 1953. The most important primary source available on Papen's life and politics. Filled with inaccuracies, attributable partly to the destruction of Papen's papers at the end of the war and partly to his notoriously subjective approach, it nevertheless provides a valuable insight into this debonair nobleman's outlook and life.

Rolfs, Richard W. *The Sorcerer's Apprentice: The Life of Franz von Papen*. Lanham, Md.: University Press of America, 1996. Rolfs offers the first complete biography of Hitler's vice chancellor and his contributions to the success of Nazism.

Shirer, William L. *The Rise and Fall of the Third Reich*. London: Secker and Warburg, and New York: Simon and Schuster, 1960. Shirer incorporates Papen's role into a broader history of the Third Reich, focusing appropriately on his role as chancellor, political mediator, and ambassador. In Shirer's view, this vain and incompetent man was "more responsible than any other individual for Hitler's appointment as Chancellor."

Turner, Henry Ashby, Jr. *German Big Business and the Rise of Hitler*. New York: Oxford University Press, 1985; Oxford: Oxford University Press, 1987. Shows convincingly that big business played a far smaller role in Papen's actions than many historians have believed.

Wheaton, Eliot B. *Prelude to Calamity: The Nazi Revolution 1933-35, with a Background Survey of the Weimar Era*. New York: Doubleday, 1968; London: Gollancz, 1969. Provides a brief analysis of Papen's role in Nazi politics and assesses him as an amateur who underestimated Hitler.

*Rennie W. Brantz*

## CHARLIE PARKER

*Born:* August 29, 1920; Kansas City, Kansas
*Died:* March 12, 1955; New York, New York
*Area of Achievement:* Music
*Contribution:* Through mastery of the alto saxophone and broad knowledge of modern and contemporary music, Parker established himself as a virtuoso performer. He began as a bebop musician and soon earned, through his innovations in harmony and diverse improvisations, a lasting reputation as a key figure in the emergence of modern jazz.

### Early Life

Charles Christopher Parker, Jr., also known as Yardbird or Bird, was the son of Charles Parker, Sr., an African American vaudeville entertainer who hailed from Mississippi and Tennessee, and Adelaide Bailey Parker, a woman of African American and Choctaw Indian heritage. Charles Parker, Sr., drank to excess, and his marriage to Adelaide deteriorated. When Parker was eight years old, his father separated from his mother and took John, Parker's half brother, with him. Although Parker rarely saw his father again, he maintained respect and, on exceptional occasions, managed to visit his father, who worked as a waiter or chef for the railroads.

Adelaide moved to Kansas City, Missouri, where Parker attended elementary school and high school. At Lincoln High School under the direction of Alonzo Lewis, Parker participated in various school bands, playing alto and baritone horn. Parker often cut classes in high school and made little progress. In about 1933, Parker's mother bought him an alto saxophone, but he loaned the instrument to a friend, leaving himself to play (most probably on a school instrument) in a school band with Lawrence Keyes, a classmate who became a bandleader. Parker developed as a musician by eavesdropping on professional performances in Kansas City and listening to music on records and the radio. He applied what he heard to long hours of practice.

In 1935, Parker dropped out of school and sought professional status as a jazz musician in Kansas City. The jazz world was mixed with a world of prostitution and drugs, and Parker, still only fifteen, acquired the heroin habit that plagued him throughout his short life. Nevertheless, Parker played with the Deans of Swing, led by Lawrence Keyes. At jam sessions at the Reno Club, Parker faced the challenge of jamming with older and more experienced musicians; because they playfully mocked him, Parker intensified his determination to succeed in music. Even Parker's marriage in 1936 to his high school sweetheart, Rebecca Ruffin, did not swerve him from his goal: He spent his days playing saxophone and piano and his nights prowling the jazz scene in Kansas City.

### Life's Work

During the summer of 1937, Parker played dates at resorts in the Ozark Mountains with a band led by singer George E. Lee. The escape from the Kansas City scene enabled Parker to completely focus on music. In addition to the performances, Parker studied the recordings of Count Basie and mastered the featured solos of Lester Young. After returning to Kansas City from the mountains, Parker had achieved a level of professionalism that made him worthy of work with bands led by Henry "Buster" Smith and Jay McShann. Unfortunately, even as this significant musical advance occurred, Parker indulged in counterproductive behavior, including heroin addiction and marital infidelity.

Determined to fulfill his potential, Parker traveled to New York City around 1939. To establish himself, he was forced to accept work first as a cleaning man at a Harlem club and later as a dishwasher at Jimmy's Chicken Shack, where Art Tatum, the gifted pianist, was a featured performer. Perhaps Tatum influenced Parker by introducing him to techniques involving variations from an established key and superimpositions of alternative chords upon established chord sequences. Parker played at numerous clubs in Harlem, often combining with guitarist Biddy Fleet. Distinguishing themselves from lesser players, Parker and Fleet experimented with popular songs in unfamiliar keys. In particular, Parker recalls a night in December, 1939, when he was playing "Cherokee" with Fleet; Parker remarked, "I found that by using the higher intervals of a chord as a melody line and backing them with appropriately related changes, I could play the thing I'd been hearing. I came alive."

In 1940, Parker began an extended association with the Jay McShann Band, playing tenor sax in an eight-piece band that was based in Kansas City but toured extensively. Band members devoted

many hours to rehearsal and jamming, and they drew inspiration from Parker's fresh outlook. Parker intensified his study of music as a written form and composed an arrangement for "What Price Love." McShann's band regularly performed the piece, and Parker later recorded the arrangement with the title "Yardbird Suite." Parker also began to demonstrate amazing resourcefulness on saxophone as he exploited his wide knowledge of melodies by gracefully inserting bits of melodic lines that his fellow musicians recognized as commentaries on someone or something in the immediate environment.

Parker acquired the nickname "Yardbird" (or sometimes "Bird") during his association with the Jay McShann Band. According to McShann, the band's car ran over a chicken during a road trip, and Parker insisted on going back to pick up the bird. He later gave it to a cook to be prepared. Parker was already known for his references to chicken as "yardbird," and soon the name became tied to Parker himself.

Near the end of 1941, the Jay McShann Band entered the New York scene and played engagements at the Savoy that were broadcast on the radio. Parker became famous for extraordinary soloing on "Cherokee," which Charlie Barnet's band had often played with much less invention. During the period at the Savoy, Dizzy Gillespie sat in with the band, and Parker began playing at after-hours clubs uptown, enhancing his reputation among New York musicians.

As 1942 ended, McShann's band was on a multicity tour. Parker's heroin addiction led to a collapse during a performance in Detroit, Michigan, and McShann found it necessary to dismiss Parker. After returning to New York, Parker drew interest from Earl Hines, whose big band included Gillespie, Billy Eckstine, and Sarah Vaughan. Parker played tenor sax and basked in the opportunity to exchange musical ideas, both in the big band with Gillespie and at after-hours clubs such as Minton's and Monroe's.

Hines's band eventually broke up, but as 1943 progressed, Eckstine formed a bebop big band that included Gillespie, Vaughan, and Parker. The discipline required of a big-band member did not suit Parker, and by 1945 he was ready to move on to a quintet directed by Gillespie that played at the Three Deuces. Parker also experimented with a trio at the Spotlite, where Miles Davis joined with Parker for the first time in September, 1945.

Gillespie received an offer to play eight weeks in Los Angeles, California, and invited Parker to join him. Parker went, but he had difficulty satisfying his addiction and soon suffered an emotional breakdown that led to treatment at Camarillo State Hospital in California in 1946. Parker recuperated and returned to New York in January, 1947, to form a quintet with Davis, Max Roach, Duke Jordan, and Tommy Potter. Recordings of this quintet were prime examples of Parker's musicianship in both studio and live versions. This quintet enjoyed enduring popularity, successful tours, lucrative and distinguished engagements, and various performances on radio.

In spite of continuing problems with drugs, alcohol, and mental health, Parker expanded his successes. A recording agreement with Norman Granz provided for enhanced distribution on the Mercury Records label. In 1948, Parker was named the top alto saxophone player in *Metronome* magazine's readers' poll and retained that honor each year through 1952. In May, 1949, the quintet traveled to Europe for the International Festival of Jazz. In December, 1949, Birdland, a nightclub named in Parker's honor, opened in New York. In 1950, *Down Beat* magazine published a readers' poll in which Parker was voted the top alto saxophone player; he retained that status until he died.

Tragedy touched Parker in March, 1954, when Pree, the child of Parker and Chan Richardson, succumbed to heart problems. Parker was devastated and descended further into drug and alcohol abuse. He tried to kill himself on two occasions and was a patient at Bellevue Hospital various times. He performed at Birdland with Kenny Dorham, Bud Powell, Charles Mingus, and Art Blakey on March 4 and 5, 1955. On March 9, struggling to get to an engagement in Boston, Massachusetts, he stopped at the Stanhope Hotel, where Panonica de Koenigswarter, a jazz enthusiast known for her support of musicians, maintained an apartment. Parker became ill, and de Koenigswarter called her physician, who recommended hospitalization. Parker refused. With rest at de Koenigswarter's apartment, he seemed to improve over the next few days, but on March 12, 1955, he died.

### Summary

Charlie Parker's approach to music influenced all of modern jazz, not just for saxophonists but also for players of all other jazz instruments. Parker's mastery of the saxophone enabled him to play at any speed he chose. His photographic memory enabled him to retain a score after a single reading, and his mind was a storehouse of melodies. He had an extraordinary capacity to flawlessly integrate his improvisations into songs. The depth of his knowledge of harmony combined with his extensive knowledge of musical selections to make him incredibly adept and resourceful in creating "musical conversation." His recordings reveal the breadth of his musicianship; selections such as "'Round Midnight," "Relaxin' at Camarillo," "Ornithology," "Yardbird Suite," and many others earned him legendary status. Literary figures of the 1950's and 1960's Beat generation such as Jack Kerouac and Allen Ginsberg admired Parker's artistry and sought to imitate musical improvisations and immediacy in novels and poetry.

Parker's death at age thirty-five is perhaps the end of what should be a cautionary story, a warning about the destruction of a genius by alcohol and drugs, but his end resulted in his immortality. Although news coverage generally ignored Parker's artistic excellence and emphasized the image of the "cool cat" with beret, shades, and goatee, the words his devotees painted on the walls around New York City ultimately proclaimed the truth about Charlie Parker: "Bird lives."

### Bibliography

Giddins, Gary. *Celebrating Bird: The Triumph of Charlie Parker.* London: Hodder and Stoughton, and New York: Beech Tree, 1987. This study of Parker's life, career, and significance in the history of music is the basis for a documentary video with the same title. The video includes commentary by Jay McShann, Dizzy Gillespie, Chan Parker, Rebecca Parker Davis, and Roy Haynes.

Gitler, Ira. "Reflections of Bird: On the 75th Anniversary of His Birth, Charlie Parker's Legacy Burns Strong." *Down Beat* 62, no. 8 (August, 1995). Several of Parker's contemporaries offer their thoughts on his work and lifestyle.

Harrison, Max. *Charlie Parker.* London: Cassell, 1960; New York: Barnes, 1961. A compact review of Parker's life and musical output. Includes several black and white photographs and a select discography.

Komara, Edward M. *The Dial Recordings of Charlie Parker: A Discography.* Westport, Conn.: Greenwood Press, 1998. This volume includes a detailed catalog of Parker's ten Dial recording sessions along with historical information on Dial Records and its dealings with Parker.

Reisner, Robert, ed. *Bird: The Legend of Charlie Parker.* London: Quartet, and New York: Citadel Press, 1962. A collection of remembrances of Charlie Parker, including an extended piece by the editor and numerous shorter pieces by other writers, among them Miles Davis, Billy Eckstine, Dizzy Gillespie, Charlie Mingus, and Jay McShann. Includes many black and white photographs, a chronology, and a discography.

Russell, Ross. *Bird Lives! The High Life and Hard Times of Charlie (Yardbird) Parker.* London: Quartet, and New York: Charter House, 1973. A thorough biographical study focusing on the development of Parker's musical career. Includes black and white photos, a bibliography, a discography, and an index.

Woideck, Carl. *Charlie Parker: His Music and Life.* Ann Arbor: University of Michigan Press, 1996. Part 1 provides a compact biography, and part 2 presents Parker's music divided into four key periods. Includes a select discography and transcriptions of four of Parker's famous solos. Also includes a bibliography and an index.

*William T. Lawlor*

# DOROTHY PARKER

*Born:* August 22, 1893; West End, New Jersey
*Died:* June 7, 1967; New York, New York
*Area of Achievement:* Literature
*Contribution:* Parker's ironic wit, astute observations, and acute verse, along with her place at the Algonquin Round Table, made her one of the twentieth century's most popular writers.

## Early Life

Dorothy Rothschild was born on a rainy August night in 1893, at her family's summer home on the shore of West End, New Jersey. Her father, Jacob Henry Rothschild, was the son of German-Jewish immigrants who came to the United States in the wake of the revolutions that spread across Europe in 1848. J. Henry, as he preferred to be known, joined his father in the men's furnishings business. In 1868, he fell in love with his neighbor, Eliza Annie Marston, the daughter of Christian English gun merchants. The disapproval of her family kept the two apart for ten years, during which time Eliza took a job teaching public school; they finally married in 1878.

Dorothy, who was born when Eliza was forty-two years old, was the last of four children. The family lived the comfortable lives of the upper middle class, hiring Irish maids and residing on the fashionable Upper West Side. Disaster, however, does not acknowledge wealth: On July 20, 1898, when Dorothy was four years old, Eliza died of a combination of acute colic and heart disease.

Within less than two years, Henry married another well-educated gentile, Eleanor Francis Lewis. Dorothy cordially despised both her and the Blessed Sacrament Academy where Eleanor convinced Henry to enroll her as a day student. Eleanor's determination to see Dorothy accept Christian dogma kept the two at constant loggerheads. Their struggles ended in April, 1903, when Eleanor died suddenly of a cerebral hemorrhage.

After Eleanor's death, Dorothy attended the academically rigorous Miss Dana's School in Morristown, New Jersey, where she learned Latin and French and was required to recite poetry. She graduated in 1911. From that moment until her father's death in 1913, Dorothy's social life revolved around tedious parties, piano playing, and composing silly rhymes to send to her father while she sat on the wide verandas of various seaside hotels.

Henry's death on December 28, 1913, marked the end of Dorothy's comfortable, middle-class life for a time. After the siblings divided up the household goods, Dorothy was forced to support herself by playing the piano at various Manhattan dance schools. She amused herself in the off-hours by writing light verse. Although she professed not to think of verse as a serious vocation, she thought enough of her efforts to send pieces to various publishers, including Franklin Pierce Adams, writer of the newspaper column "The Conning Tower," and to Frank Crowninshield at *Vanity Fair.*

Acceptance finally came in 1914, when Crowninshield sent a letter accepting Dorothy's poem "Any Porch" and a payment of twelve dollars. Thrilled, Dorothy immediately proposed that he might offer her a job as well. When he declined, she continued banging out tunes for would-be flappers. A few months went by, followed by another letter from Crowninshield, this time offering Dorothy a job at *Vanity Fair*'s sister publication *Vogue.* Her career was about to begin.

## Life's Work

At *Vogue*, Dorothy's wit showed itself in the advertising copy and picture captions she was assigned to write. "Brevity," she quipped in one of her most-quoted captions, "is the soul of lingerie." During this period, she met her first husband, a handsome young stockbroker named Edwin Pond Parker II. The two married over the protests of his well-connected Protestant family but lived together only briefly; Parker enlisted as an ambulance driver and shipped out to the battlefields of Europe almost immediately.

By 1918, Parker's clever way with words had finally earned her a position on the editorial staff of *Vanity Fair.* Only twenty-four years old, Parker became New York's only woman drama critic, replacing P. G. Wodehouse during his leave of absence. The reviews she wrote, penned in her highly individual style, attracted her first broad audience and put her name on the lips of sophisticated New Yorkers.

At *Vanity Fair*, Parker met two lifetime friends, Robert Benchley and Robert Sherwood, witty, relatively unknown writers who, like Parker, were poised on the brink of success. The three went everywhere together, including the first luncheon of the group that was to become the renowned Algonquin Round Table. Alexander Woolcott, Edna Ferber, Harpo Marx, George Kaufman, Irving Berlin, and many other celebrated authors, critics, artists, and songwriters gathered around this table for daily, lunchtime exchanges of ideas, observations, and witty repartee. Parker was reputedly the wittiest of the bunch, waiting calmly in the midst of the daily babble until she saw an opening for her deadly, often profane barbs, which the petite brunette delivered in a soft, cultivated voice.

Parker was fired by Crowninshield in 1920 for writing unfavorable reviews of three plays produced by prominent advertisers. Her marriage was also in trouble. Her husband, always a heavy drinker, had not stayed sober in Europe; in fact, his troubles with alcohol accelerated and became further complicated by his introduction to opiates. By the time he returned home in 1919, he and Dorothy had become strangers. By 1920, he was one of her most useful humorous topics at the Round Table; they separated in 1922 and divorced in 1928.

The friendships she developed at the Round Table and the ability of her friends to keep her name in the public eye helped Parker begin her long and successful freelance career. Harold Ross begged her to join the founding board of *The New Yorker*, where, under the pseudonym "The Constant Reader," she wrote book reviews. Her short stories and verse appeared in a large number of publications, including *The American Mercury*, *The Bookman*, "The Conning Tower," and others. In 1929, her short story "The Big Blonde" won the O. Henry Prize. All told, between 1926 and 1933 she published three collections of verse—*Enough Rope* (1926), *Sunset Gun* (1928), and *Death and Taxes* (1931)—which, along with two collections of short stories, *Laments for the Living* (1930) and *After Such Pleasures* (1933), captured the spirit of the times and enjoyed outstanding sales.

Parker's life always contained heartaches as well as triumphs. She learned from her former husband the art of drinking to avoid pain; during the 1920's, she and her Algonquin compatriots made cocktail hour a day-long experience. Her love life was flamboyant; she boasted of her many lovers, preferred men younger than herself, and knew no moderation in her feelings. When her relationship with playwright Charles MacArthur ended in abortion and abandonment, she attempted suicide, an act that she repeated four times between 1923 and 1932. The first time, she slashed her wrists with a razor; later, she tried Veronal, barbiturates, and

even a bottle of shoe polish. The pain and confusion in her life provided the material for her short stories. Her technique seduced her readers into laughter at human foibles that transformed, at the story's resolution, into an anguished cry of despair. Parker turned even suicide into laughter: "Resume," one of her best-known verses, lists methods of self-annihilation and their drawbacks, finally concluding, with regret, "You might as well live."

Writing was never an easy process for Parker; even during the productive 1920's, she struggled over every word. As her life progressed, her output declined. She often missed deadlines, and she produced, over the course of her lifetime, a surprisingly small volume of work. What she did write, however, spoke volumes about the rage in her life, which, as she aged, turned from gender issues to social injustice. In 1927, she marched through the streets of Boston, protesting the pending execution of Sacco and Vanzetti. She was arrested on charges of "public sauntering" and reported from inside the prison on the course of the execution.

The decade of the 1930's, which for most Americans held the hardships of the Great Depression, were years of wealth and happiness for Parker. In 1933, at the age of forty, she married Alan Campbell, a handsome actor eleven years her junior. They moved from New York to Hollywood, where they were paid exorbitantly as a screenwriting couple, at one point making a combined salary of $5,200 a week. They were hired because of Parker's fame, but many people attribute their success to Campbell's powers of organization and careful tending to Dorothy's every need. Together they worked on dozens of screenplays, the most famous of which was made into the 1937 hit, *A Star is Born*.

In 1937, during the height of the Spanish Civil War, Parker and Campbell went to Spain. Parker's experiences there, immortalized in her short story "Soldiers of the Republic," further radicalized her. She returned to the United States determined to raise money to feed the starving children she had encountered. This involvement blossomed over the years into work opposing Nazi Germany. She conducted her political work largely by serving as a figurehead and public speaker for organizations she found worthy. In the 1950's, this involvement resulted in threats from the House Committee on Un-American Activities, which considered her a communist. Although this charge was never proved, Parker was blacklisted in Hollywood.

By the 1940's, Parker's career and her marriage to Campbell had disintegrated. The couple divorced in 1947. Parker wrote a play based on the life of Charles Lamb, *The Coast of Illyria*, with beau Ross Evans in 1949, but it never made it to Broadway. She and Campbell remarried in 1950. They separated less than a year later, then reunited briefly in 1960, near the end of Campbell's life. Writing became more difficult with the passing years; Parker wrote book reviews for *Esquire* but accomplished little creative work on her own. The years of high earnings in Hollywood had been accompanied by years of lavish spending. After Campbell's death, Parker lived alone in two rooms at the Volney Hotel in New York City, strapped for money and starved for company. Typically, she immortalized this life in a play written with Arnaud d'Usseau, *Ladies of the Corridor*. Parker died of a heart attack on June 7, 1967.

Upon her death, Parker left her estate of $20,000 to the Reverend Martin Luther King, Jr., naming the National Association for the Advancement of Colored People (NAACP) as the residual beneficiary. Lillian Hellman, her fellow writer and longtime friend, was named Parker's literary executor.

### Summary

Dorothy Parker flourished as a professional writer at a time when women's lives and interests were still largely confined to their homes. She provided readers with brilliant, witty descriptions of her world and the people who inhabited it, painting their foibles and her own in a clear, unsentimental light. She has been praised for the economical language of her stories, for her evocative and funny verse, and for the sparkle of her conversation. She drew a compelling portrait of women in a rapidly changing world.

Despite her continual drinking, ruinous love affairs, and a tendency to waste her talents in endless hours of self-hatred, she created a body of work that has lasted well beyond her lifetime. The works collected into *The Portable Dorothy Parker* have proved to be enduring favorites, keeping Parker's work in print for more than fifty years. Readers looking for insight into the literary world of the early twentieth century would do well to study Dorothy Parker, whose trenchant observations bring that world alive in a way unmatched by the work of her peers.

### Bibliography

Acocella, Joan. "After the Laughs." *The New Yorker* 69 (August 16, 1993): 76-81. A critical and biographical article in which the author argues that Parker let her personal insecurities cloud her artistic potential.

Calhoun, Randall. *Dorothy Parker: A Bio-Bibliography.* Westport, Conn.: Greenwood Press, 1993. Excellent bibliography including primary and secondary sources, a biographical piece, and opinion pieces by three of Parker's contemporaries.

Keats, John. *You Might as Well Live: The Life and Times of Dorothy Parker.* New York: Simon and Schuster, 1970; London: Secker and Warburg, 1971. This work, the first popular biography of Parker, is both thorough and readable. Contains an index and a bibliography.

Kinney, Arthur F. *Dorothy Parker.* Boston: Twayne, 1978; London: Prentice Hall, 1998. Kinney combines a brief biography with detailed literary criticism of Parker's work.

Meade, Marion. *Dorothy Parker.* London: Heinemann, and New York: Villard, 1988. A thorough biography that places Parker squarely in the middle of New York's literary society. The author stresses the personal side of Parker's life, referring to Parker's literary work only to illustrate biographical material.

Melzer, Sondra. *The Rhetoric of Rage: Women in Dorothy Parker.* New York: Lang, 1997. Melzer examines Parker's work, the manner in which it reflects her life, and the evidence in it of anger toward a male-dominated society.

Parker, Dorothy. *The Portable Dorothy Parker.* Rev. ed. New York: Viking Press, 1973. Parker's own selections of her work to be included in the Viking edition of 1944 are joined here with new material and introductions by Brendan Gill and W. Somerset Maugham.

*Susan E. Keegan*

# ROSA PARKS

*Born:* February 4, 1913; Tuskegee, Alabama
*Area of Achievement:* Civil rights
*Contribution:* Rosa Parks, who is well known for her refusal to relinquish her bus seat to a white passenger in Montgomery, Alabama, on December 1, 1955, was a civil rights advocate before she committed her historic and heroic act.

## Early Life

The oldest of two children, Rosa Lee McCauley was born on February 4, 1913, to Leona Edwards McCauley and James McCauley. Her mother was an educator; her father, a carpenter. The influences in young Rosa's life included her mother and her grandparents. According to Parks, half of her life was spent in a segregated South that "allowed white people to treat black people without any respect." Rosa's parents were separated a great deal of the time. His occupation in carpentry and construction took James away from home often. Her mother resented being left alone. By the time her brother was born, her parents had separated. She did not see her father again until she was five. Rosa, her mother, and her brother moved in with her maternal grandparents. They lived in Pine Level, Alabama, where Rosa was to spend her formative years. Her brother, who was two years and seven months younger, doted on Rosa's every word and action. She became his protector and primary caretaker while her mother worked.

Rosa was small for her age. Her health was poor and her growth appeared to be stunted. She also suffered from chronic tonsillitis. These problems kept her out of school for a year.

Rosa observed the many differences between the white and black schools. Blacks had to build and heat their own schools, whereas white schools were funded by the town, county, or state. There were no buses to transport blacks, and black children attended school for five months, while white students went for nine. Such a discrepancy existed because the majority of black parents were sharecroppers, and their children were needed in the spring and fall to plow, plant, and harvest.

Rosa's great-grandfather (her grandmother's father) was a Scots-Irishman who migrated to the United States in the nineteenth century. He was an indentured servant who married an African slave. He and Mary Jane Nobles married and had two daughters and one son before slavery was abolished in 1865. After emancipation, six other children were born to the couple. Rosa grew up in a home where family history was important. She listened to stories about slavery, segregation, and the Ku Klux Klan.

As a young girl, Rosa worked as a field hand, tended to household chores, and cared for her ill grandparents. Her mother spent much of her time teaching. Soon, her mother decided that Rosa should go to a nine-month school. This could only be done if Rosa moved away from Pine Level. Consequently, Rosa was shipped to Montgomery, Alabama, to live with her maternal aunt. She attended a private girls' school. While enrolled in the Montgomery Industrial School for Girls, Rosa was responsible for doing household chores and domestic work outside the home.

By the time she was eleven, Rosa's childhood seemed far behind. She cleaned two classrooms at her school in exchange for free tuition. After graduation, she enrolled in Booker T. Washington High School. After her mother became ill, she dropped out of school to care for her. Rosa's outlook on discrimination and segregation was influenced by family stories, her tenure at the Montgomery Industrial School for Girls, and her experiences as a child. She detested the plight of blacks and the advantages that whites possessed, often at the expense of African Americans.

As a teen, she sewed, read, and attended the local African Methodist Episcopal (A.M.E.) church. Her love for singing and praying continued throughout her life. Active in the Allen Christian Endeavor League, Rosa kept busy as a member of the A.M.E. church.

In her nineteenth year, Rosa met Raymond Parks through a mutual friend. Both had been previously unlucky in love, and they did not pursue a romantic relationship immediately. Raymond Parks was a barber and an active participant in the Civil Rights movement. Rosa resisted his advances, but his persistence wore her down. Their common interest in civil rights tended to bond them. During their many conversations, she discovered that their interests and backgrounds were often the same. Both were born in February in the segregated South, were committed to the advancement of the black race, and were of mixed racial heritage. Like herself, Raymond cared for an ill mother and grandmother.

*Rosa Parks being fingerprinted by a deputy in 1956.*

They both shared a love of God, and like Rosa, Raymond was an active participant in his church.

In December of 1932, Rosa and Raymond were married in her mother's house. In 1933, she obtained her high-school diploma at the age of twenty. The couple settled in Montgomery, Alabama. Rosa engaged in a variety of occupations in an effort to augment her spouse's income. She became a seamstress, a domestic, and an office clerk. She became the secretary of the Montgomery chapter of the National Association for the Advancement of Colored People (NAACP) in 1943. She was also an adviser to youth organizations. She became a member of the Montgomery Voters League and began to encourage blacks to become politically empowered. Her thirst for education continued. She attended seminars and workshops whose topics dealt with the civil rights struggle. Rosa waged her own personal battle against segregation. Instead of riding on segregated buses, she often opted to walk home. She went out of her way to avoid drinking from segregated water fountains. At the age of forty, Rosa was a well-known civil rights activist in her community.

### Life's Work

"The only tired I was, was tired of giving in." These were the words spoken on Thursday, December 1, 1955, by Rosa Parks. Parks was returning home from her job as a seamstress. She boarded the segregated bus in the manner usual to Montgomery. Blacks would enter the front, pay, get off, and reenter to take their seats through the back door. The front of the bus was reserved for whites, while African Americans occupied the rear. On this particular day, however, the front of the bus quickly filled up. The area where blacks were designated to sit would have to be vacated. A white male passenger required a seat and there was none available in the white section. Consequently, the blacks in the front of the black section were asked to move. They were told by the driver to relinquish their seats. All complied except for Rosa. She was dealing with the same driver who had evicted her more than a decade earlier from his bus. Rosa remained adamant on this occasion. This particular request was not to be taken lightly.

The majority of the riders were black. The black patrons believed that they were within their rights in requesting better treatment in exchange for their consistent patronage. Other blacks in the community had defied the driver's requests to move. Rumblings of boycotts and demonstrations ensued, but there was no mass organized effort. Parks was arrested on the evening of December 1, 1955, for refusing to relinquish her seat to a white patron, thereby violating the segregation laws of Montgomery, Alabama. A white lawyer, Clifford Durr, was hired to take her case. She was released on a one-hundred-dollar bond.

The African American community quickly mobilized. An organization called the Women's Political Council passed out thousands of pamphlets, asking for a one-day bus boycott. A community meeting was held on December 5 in the Holt Street Baptist Church. The Montgomery Improvement Association was created, and a young, charismatic minister, the Reverend Martin Luther King, Jr., was elected its president. Rosa agreed to allow her case to serve as the focus of the civil rights struggle. The one-day bus boycott was considered a success. By the time Rosa was tried and found guilty, the boycott was in its second month. The cooperation of the black ridership was 100 percent. Rosa was fined ten dollars and told to pay an additional four dollars in court fees. She refused to pay and appealed.

Because seventy-five percent of Montgomery's ridership was black, the bus company was quickly sliding into bankruptcy. Rosa and her husband lost their jobs. They were harassed with phone calls, letters, verbal threats, and intimidation. As a result of 381 days of boycotting, segregation was banned on municipal buses. On December 21, 1956, Rosa sat in the front of the newly integrated city buses in Montgomery, Alabama. As a result of her part in the boycott, Rosa and her husband were unemployable.

Because she was unable to find work, and with Raymond suffering from ill health, Rosa, her mother, and Raymond moved North. They settled in Detroit, where her brother Sylvester resided. After spending a year there, Rosa opted to take a job at the Hampton Institute in Virginia as a hostess in the Holly Tree Inn. The inn was a residence and guest house on the historically black college campus. Thinking that her husband and mother would find positions in Virginia, Rosa took the position, but the job market in Virginia was not as favorable as she had hoped. Raymond and Leona remained in Detroit for the year Rosa was in Virginia. She returned to Detroit in 1959 and took a position as a seamstress. She continued her work in the African American community, joining another civil rights group, the Southern Christian Leadership Conference.

On March 1, 1965, Rosa was hired as a staff assistant to U.S. Representative John Conyers. She worked for him for twenty-three years. During her tenure in Conyers' employ, Rosa lost her brother, spouse, and mother. Raymond's demise came in 1977 after a five-year struggle with cancer. Three months later, her brother Sylvester met the same fate. In 1979, her mother, Leona, also died of cancer. Having had no children, Rosa was left alone, except for distant relatives. Despite personal tragedy and failing health, Rosa continued to work tirelessly for the rights of all people. In August of 1994, Parks was briefly hospitalized for injuries she sustained after a thief broke into her Detroit home, robbed her of fifty dollars, and hit her. Community outrage over her assault led to the quick arrest of her assailant.

### Summary

Hailed as the Mother of the Civil Rights movement, Rosa Parks has garnered a place in human history. The recipient of innumerable awards, Rosa maintains that she is unaccustomed to being a public person. By her own admission, she possesses more honorary degrees, awards, and plaques than she is able to count. Yet she continues to accept all invitations to speak, lecture, or simply be honored. She humbly accepts her status as a national treasure and symbol. Her many awards include the Spingarn Medal (1979), the Martin Luther King, Jr., Nonviolent Peace Prize (1980), and the Eleanor Roosevelt Women of Courage Award (1984). She possesses more than ten honorary degrees. On February 28, 1991, the Smithsonian Institution unveiled a bust of her. She has established the Rosa and Raymond Parks Institute for Self-Development. She continues to raise funds for the NAACP and is an active member of her church and of the Southern Christian Leadership Conference. It is the latter organization that has sponsored the Rosa Parks Freedom Award, which is awarded annually. Streets in Detroit and in Montgomery, Alabama, have been renamed Rosa Parks Boulevard. The African-American Museum in Detroit unveiled her portrait in January of 1988, in time for her seventy-fifth birthday. She was honored in 1990 at the Kennedy Center in Washington, D.C. Her eightieth birthday was spent in California, where she was on a national tour to promote her autobiography.

Parks remains a dignified individual who continues to influence society. She symbolizes many things to many people. For those in the 1950's and 1960's, she ignited a movement that was dormant for far too long. For individuals in the 1990's, she is important because of her tireless efforts to alter society for the better. Future generations will still feel her influence. Her courage has inspired others to take chances, work for the betterment and advancement of all people, and continue to challenge and change society's foibles and discriminatory actions.

### Bibliography

Massaquoi, Hans J. "Rosa Parks: Still a Rebel with a Cause at 83, Civil Rights Icon Refuses to Rest on Her Laurels." *Ebony* 51, no.5 (March, 1996). Profile of Parks, her origins, her courageous acts, and her continued promotion of civil rights.

Metcalf, George R. *Black Profiles*. New York: McGraw-Hill, 1968. This book documents the life and contributions of black individuals. Parks is one of the featured individuals.

Miller, Judi. *Women Who Changed America*. New York: Manor, 1976. This anthology discusses women in America, including Parks, who have contributed to American life. It demonstrates how these women altered life in the United States in a positive manner.

Parks, Rosa. *Rosa Parks: My Story*. New York: Dial, 1992. This autobiography is an insightful look into the life, times, and experiences of Rosa Parks. Through her own works, Parks reminisces about her childhood, family influences, marriage, and civil rights activities.

Robinson, Jo Ann. *The Montgomery Bus Boycott and the Women Who Started It*. Edited by David J. Garrow. Knoxville: University of Tennessee Press, 1987. This text focuses on the historic 381-day boycott. Parks is discussed in this book in great detail.

Smith, Jessie Carney, ed. *Notable Black American Women*. Detroit: Gale Research, 1992. The lives and contributions of African American women in all fields are highlighted. Parks is one of hundreds discussed.

Sparks, Holloway. "Dissident Citizenship: Democratic Theory, Political Courage, and Activist Women." *Hypatia* 12, no. 4 (Fall 1997). The author considers the role of dissidents in democratic society using the story of Parks as a basis for discussion.

*Annette Marks-Ellis*

# VERNON L. PARRINGTON

*Born:* August 3, 1871; Aurora, Illinois
*Died:* June 16, 1929; Winchcombe, England
*Areas of Achievement:* American history and literature
*Contribution:* Parrington's three-volume *Main Currents in American Thought* (1927-1930) was a landmark work that not only helped shape how the generation coming to maturity in the 1930's viewed the United States' past but also did much to stimulate interest in American intellectual history as a field of study.

## Early Life

Vernon Louis Parrington was born August 3, 1871, in Aurora, Illinois, the son of John William and Louise (McClellan) Parrington. A graduate of Waterville (modern Colby) College in his native Maine, Parrington's father had moved to Illinois and, after a stint as a school principal, began the practice of law. He served as an officer in the Union Army during the Civil War, and then, after moving to Kansas in 1877, he farmed and was elected judge of the local probate court. Vernon attended the preparatory department of the College of Emporia and then its collegiate division before transferring to Harvard as a junior. Given his upbringing on the Western plains, he had an unhappy two years at Harvard—an experience that did much to shape his hostility to the upper-class Eastern establishment. After he was graduated from Harvard in 1893, Vernon returned to the College of Emporia as an instructor in English and French and there received an M.A. in 1895. In 1897, he began work at the University of Oklahoma as an instructor in English and modern languages. The following year, he was promoted to professor of English. In 1908, however, Parrington lost his job when the newly elected Democratic governor fired the president and fourteen faculty members—including Parrington—who were deemed insufficiently politically sound or religiously orthodox by Southern Methodist standards.

Parrington managed to find a position as assistant professor of English at the University of Washington in Seattle. In 1912, he was promoted to full professor. He was a highly popular teacher whose courses on American literature and thought drew impressive enrollments. He appears to have begun work in 1913 on what would become *Main Currents in American Thought: An Interpretation of American Literature from the Beginnings to 1920* (1927-1930). A related article, "The Puritan Divines, 1620-1720," appeared in the first volume of *The Cambridge History of American Literature* (1917). He edited and wrote the introduction to *The Connecticut Wits*, published in 1926. Apart from *Main Currents in American Thought*, Parrington's other publications did not amount to much: an occasional review, a few encyclopedia articles, a brief appreciation of the novelist Sinclair Lewis, and an essay, "The Development of Realism," in *The Reinterpretation of American Literature* (1928). Parrington married Julia Rochester Williams on July 31, 1901; the couple had two daughters and a son.

## Life's Work

As a student at the College of Emporia, Parrington had accepted without question his father's allegiance to the Republican Party, the school's Presbyterian religious orthodoxy, and belief in the inevitability of progress. At Harvard, exposure to Darwinian ideas eroded his religious faith. During his first years of teaching, his interests were primarily literary and aesthetic. Parrington dabbled at writing poetry, and he was strongly impressed by English Utopian Socialist William Morris' attacks upon the shoddiness and commercialism of the machine age and extolling of the work of the Middle Ages, which Morris romanticized as the time when craftsmanship reigned supreme. By the late 1890's, however, under the impact of the agrarian revolt that swept over Kansas, the major focus of Parrington's interest had shifted to reform politics. "I become," he confessed in 1918, "more radical with each year, and more impatient with the smug Tory culture. . . . " His Populist sympathies shaped his approach in *Main Currents in American Thought.* "The point of view from which I have endeavored to evaluate the materials," he admitted, "is liberal rather than conservative, Jeffersonian rather than Federalistic. . . . "

The first volume, dealing with the period from settlement to 1800, was turned down by the first two publishers to whom Parrington submitted the manuscript, because of doubts about its sales potential. He was so discouraged that he abandoned work on the projected second volume. The literary critic and historian Van Wyck Brooks, however, who had read and liked the manuscript, interested

Alfred Harcourt of Harcourt, Brace and Company. Harcourt agreed to publish the work if Parrington would finish the second volume carrying the story to 1860. The two volumes appeared in 1927, with the first bearing the subtitle "The Colonial Mind: 1620-1800" and the second "The Romantic Revolution in America: 1800-1860." The work was an immediate success; Charles A. Beard spoke for most of the reviewers when he hailed Parrington for writing "a truly significant book . . . that promises to be epoch-making, sending exhilarating gusts through the deadly miasma of academic criticism." *Main Currents in American Thought* was awarded the Pulitzer Prize for history in 1928. When liberal or left-wing intellectuals were polled in the late 1930's about the authors who had most influenced their thinking, Parrington's name was prominent among those listed. As late as 1952, when a sample of American historians were asked to name their "most preferred" American histories published between 1920 and 1935, *Main Currents in American Thought* received more votes than any other.

*Main Currents in American Thought* had the subtitle "An Interpretation of American Literature," and the larger part of the text was devoted to literary figures. Yet Parrington had scant interest in literature as literature. "With aesthetic judgments," he confessed in the foreword to volume 2, "I have not been greatly concerned. I have not wished to evaluate reputations or weigh literary merits. . . . " When dealing with the work of literary figures, he focused primarily upon their political and social views. Writers who had been uninvolved with such issues were summarily dismissed. Thus, he devoted less than three pages to Edgar Allan Poe and still less to Henry James. He brushed aside criticism upon this point with the reply that he was not writing the history of American literature but was rather concerned "with the total pattern of American thought." As an intellectual historian, however, Parrington had major blind spots. As a later critic pointed out, "he showed slight interest or competence in metaphysics and theology; he scarcely touched scientific thought and development, or the rise of the social sciences; he ignored legal thought, intellectual institutions, and the nonliterary arts."

Parrington had been much influenced by the emphasis placed by the French historian Hippolyte Taine in his book *History of English Literature* (1863-1864) upon the role of the social environment in shaping literary expression. "Ideas are not godlings that spring perfect-winged from the head of Jove," he wrote in an unpublished essay of 1917. Rather, "they are weapons hammered out on the anvil of human needs." Accordingly, the historian's task was "to understand how ideas are conditioned by social forces." The most important social force was economics—the "subsoil" upon which literature and ideas rested. Unfortunately, Parrington was not consistent in applying this economic determinism. On the one hand, he dismissed ideas that he disliked as rationalizations of selfish interests. On the other, he extolled those with whom he sympathized for their "creativity" and "originality." Increase Mather, for example, was a supporter of the established order because he was "a beneficiary of things as they were, certain to lose in prestige and power with any relaxing of the theocracy"; Roger Williams, however, was "a social innovator on principle, . . . and his actions were creatively determined by principles the bases of which he examined with critical insight."

In sum, *Main Currents in American Thought* amounted to a catalog of Parrington's biases. He pictured American history as a struggle between two sets of forces: the aristocracy versus the democratic majority; the defenders of selfish privilege against the champions of the rights of man and social justice; the capitalists versus the farmers and laborers. The work was organized around a series of biographical-critical sketches of individuals representing those conflicting forces: John Cotton versus Roger Williams; Alexander Hamilton versus Thomas Jefferson; Henry Clay versus Andrew Jackson; Daniel Webster versus Ralph Waldo Emerson. The metaphor of a ship's voyage was utilized to provide a unifying theme. The ideas with which Parrington sympathized were the progressive currents carrying the vessel forward; those to which he was hostile were "reefs," "barriers," a "dragging anchor." Similar value judgments were freely applied to individuals. The target of his animus would be described as "the victim of a decadent ideal," "studiously conventional," or so closed-minded as to be "shut up within his own skullpan"; the object of his favor would be pictured as an "unshackled thinker," "an adventurous pioneer," or a man of "fine idealism."

Parrington directed his sharpest barbs against the Puritans—perhaps a reflection of the slights of which he believed himself the object while at Harvard. Typical was his portrayal of Cotton Mather:

"What a crooked and diseased mind lay back of those eyes that were forever spying out occasions to magnify self! He grovels in proud self-abasement. He distorts the most obvious reality. . . . His egoism blots out clarity and even the divine mercy." More broadly, he juxtaposed Puritanism to the liberating force of the Enlightenment. Puritanism represented "an absolutist theology that conceived of human nature as inherently evil, that postulated a divine sovereignty absolute and arbitrary, and projected caste divisions into eternity." By contrast, the Enlightenment

> asserted that the present evils of society are the consequence of vicious institutions rather than of depraved human nature; and that as free men and equals it is the right and duty of citizens to re-create social and political institutions to the end that they shall further social justice, encouraging the good in men rather than perverting them to evil.

In his treatment of the Founding Fathers, Parrington took the view put forward by his friend and University of Washington colleague J. Allen Smith in his book *The Spirit of American Government* (1907) that the framers of the Constitution had as their major purpose to clip the wings of a threatening democracy. He portrayed Hamilton as "a high Tory." "Accepting self-interest as the mainspring of human ambition," he elaborated, "Hamilton accepted equally the principle of class domination." Parrington did feel an almost grudging admiration for John Adams: "A stubborn intellectual independence and a vigorous assertiveness were his distinguishing characteristics. . . . He was no believer in unchecked government by wealth. His honest realism taught him the sophistry of Hamilton's assumption that gentlemen of property are equally gentlemen of principle, and that wealth voluntarily abdicates selfish interest. He feared the aggressions of the rich as much as the turbulence of the poor." Parrington's special hero was Thomas Jefferson:

> To all who profess faith in the democratic ideal Jefferson is a perennial inspiration. A free soul, he loved freedom enough to deny it to none; an idealist, he believed that the welfare of the whole, and not the prosperity of any group, is the single end of government.

Parrington pictured the conflict between Henry Clay and Andrew Jackson as a continuation of the struggle over the Constitution and the Hamilton-Jefferson battle of the 1790's. At a philosophical level, Parrington portrayed the issue as a clash between the egalitarian and humanitarian idealism of the Rousseauian tradition in French Romantic thought and the cold, calculating rationalism of English liberalism, represented by Adam Smith, with its exaltation of the beneficent workings of the pursuit of self-interest. He lamented the growing ascendancy of the belief in what he sarcastically termed "the natural right of every free citizen to satisfy his acquisitive instinct by exploiting the natural resources in the measure of his shrewdness." Even in the West, where once the democratic frontiersman had held sway, egalitarianism gave way to get-rich-quick "speculative psychology" under the impact of "abundant wild lands, rapid increase in population, and an elastic credit, operating on a vast scale." Even Abraham Lincoln was found to have had his "instinctive democracy" compromised by the new Whiggish "philosophy of progress [that] had displaced the older agrarianism."

Parrington died on June 6, 1929, while on vacation in England, before completing a third volume that would have continued the history to the 1920's. Parrington's publisher issued the unfinished and in parts fragmentary manuscript in 1930 under the subtitle "The Beginnings of Critical Realism in America." The volume exuded a mix of pessimism and hope. The pessimism grew out of the reign of plunder carried on by business in the years since the Civil War—what Parrington, in one of his most striking metaphors, called "The Great Barbecue." Nevertheless, he was optimistic that the revolt underway among American intellectuals during the 1920's against middle-class philistinism might yet manage "to unhorse the machine that now rides men and to leaven the sodden mass that is industrial America." He simultaneously reaffirmed his faith that "Jeffersonian democracy still offers hope." He was, however, ambivalent about what substantive policies were required. In correspondence, he expressed a vague sympathy with Marxism, but *Main Currents in American Thought* resounded with hostility to "the coercive state." Parrington even eulogized the Southern spokesmen for states' rights as "the best liberals of the time." He thus remained trapped in what he saw as the irresolvable dilemma facing the would-be reformer: "We must have a political state powerful enough to deal with corporate wealth, but how are we going to keep that state with its augmenting power from being captured by the forces we want it to control?"

## Summary

The popularity of *Main Currents in American Thought* owed much to the fit of Parrington's prejudices with those of American intellectuals and would-be intellectuals of the time. In the 1920's, the Puritans were the favorite target of the self-consciously enlightened as the source of all the shortcomings found in American life: sexual repression, Prohibition, religious Fundamentalism, the Ku Klux Klan, and the middle-class philistinism that Sinclair Lewis satirized in *Babbitt* (1922). Here, then, Parrington was simply reinforcing existing stereotypes. His animus against business would similarly fit the mood of the Depression years. Parrington is typically linked with Frederick Jackson Turner and Charles A. Beard as one of the founders of so-called Progressive history, but he had neither their intellectual power nor their longterm influence. Later scholarship has left most of his interpretations in shambles; even his style, with its melodramatic rhetoric, appears contrived and overdone to the modern reader. The most generous appraisal of his lasting contribution is that he directed the attention of scholars to American intellectual history as a legitimate and important field of study.

## Bibliography

Colwell, Stephen. "The Populist Image of Vernon Louis Parrington." *Mississippi Valley Historical Review* 49 (52-66. According to Hofstadter, "corrects certain notions about Parrington's Populist activities in the 1890's, but only at the cost of minimizing the impact of Populism on his thinking."

Gabriel, Ralph H. "Vernon Louis Parrington." In *Pastmasters: Some Essays on American Historians*, edited by Marcus Cunliffe and Robin W. Winks. New York: Harper, 1969. A rambling and disjointed sympathetic appraisal.

Harrison, Joseph B. *Vernon Louis Parrington: American Scholar.* Seattle: University of Washington Book Store, 1929. A brief appreciation that is gushingly admiring of Parrington as a "humanist and liberal."

Hofstadter, Richard. *The Progressive Historians: Turner, Beard, Parrington.* New York: Knopf, 1968. Contains the fullest available account of Parrington's life. Hofstadter makes a valiant effort to treat Parrington as a major thinker but is sufficiently astute an analyst to recognize that he was not.

Skotheim, Robert A. *American Intellectual Histories and Historians.* Princeton, N.J.: Princeton University Press, 1966. Includes an examination of Parrington's place in the development of American intellectual history that is devastating on the shortcomings of *Main Currents in American Thought.*

*John Braeman*

## DOLLY PARTON

*Born:* January 19, 1946; rural Locust Ridge, Sevier County, Tennessee

*Area of Achievement:* Music

*Contribution:* A major force in bringing women to the forefront of country music, Parton also fashioned successful pop music as well as films and television.

### Early Life

A true child of Appalachia, Dolly Rebecca Parton was born in Eastern Tennessee, in the foothills of the Smoky Mountains, the fourth of twelve children. In her family's one-room cabin, there was no electricity, running water, or indoor plumbing.

Her father was a farmer and construction worker, and although the Parton family was quite poor, this did not seem to doom young Dolly to an unhappy life. Her mother was a singer of ballads and old-time songs, and as a very young child, Dolly Parton made up songs for her mother. In time, Dolly Parton took up playing the guitar and banjo on the local radio and, later, on television in nearby Knoxville. She was the first member of her family to graduate from high school.

She had appeared on the Grand Ole Opry as a child and thereafter knew what she wanted to do with the rest of her life. Dolly Parton was nothing if not determined, so in June of 1964, immediately after she was graduated from high school, she took a bus to Nashville to make her name in the country music business.

### Life's Work

With her move to Nashville, Dolly Parton struggled to make herself a star. The way for women to succeed in country music had been demonstrated by Kitty Wells, Patsy Cline, and Loretta Lynn. At first, Dolly Parton lived with her uncle, Bill Owens, with whom she wrote songs. In 1966, when Bill Phillips made a minor hit of Dolly Parton's composition *Put It off Until Tomorrow*, her career as a songwriter formally commenced.

Parton's husband Carl Dean (they were married in 1966) always played a supportive role in helping her professional career. Her performing career took off in 1967, when she had hits with two novelty songs: *Dumb Blonde* and *Something Fishy*. That same year, she joined the Porter Wagoner television show as a female soloist and frequent duet partner with Wagoner.

During this part of her career, Dolly Parton sang as a high soprano; there was a sharp contrast between the lyrics she sang, which were about hardship and pain, and her delicate singing voice. In a short time, "Porter and Dolly," as they were known to their legions of fans, became country music's top duo, winning national awards in 1968, 1970, and 1971.

Wagoner helped Dolly Parton secure a contract with RCA, and she began to fashion her career as a recording artist. By the mid-1970's, singing songs she claimed she had made up while trying to survive growing up in grinding poverty, Parton, with her sensitive lyrics and fragile vocal stylings, became a star. At this point in her career, she was trying to find her own style, exploring a wide variety of themes and sounds. Among her early recordings were conventional hymns, moral tales, and the usual country music stories of love lost. She seemed to be trying everything and anything that had worked for women in country music since the days of Kitty Wells, whom Dolly Parton had admired.

Dolly Parton was not satisfied with being atop the country music charts. She set out to map territory that only Patsy Cline before her had tread—stardom in pop music. She left Wagoner in 1974 and a few years later made her move with a series of Los Angeles-influenced albums. In 1977, when Dolly Parton recorded *Here You Come Again*, written by veteran New York City pop music writers Barry Mann and Cynthia Weill, the song rose to number three on the mainstream pop charts and set in motion a whole new career for Dolly Parton.

Dolly Parton wanted to put behind her the traditional country associations she had worked so successfully to build up in the years with Porter Wagoner. No one mistakes her later duets—with Kenny Rogers and the BeeGees—for hard-core hillbilly music. The new Dolly Parton was aimed directly at mainstream musical tastes.

Dolly Parton's new goal was to become a film star. In the late 1970's, she hired an agent, and soon she was appearing regularly on *The Tonight Show with Johnny Carson*. She formally began working in films in 1980, when she gave an engaging performance as a Southern secretary opposite Lily Tomlin and Jane Fonda in *Nine to Five*. Dolly Parton also wrote and sang the film's title song, which earned for her an Oscar nomination, a Grammy award, and a hit album—on both country and pop charts.

The song "Nine to Five" has a big-band introduction and two basic melodies as it liltingly expresses working-class frustration. A full studio backup band (no country music combo here) beats at a disco-like pace. This song, the ultimate crossover hit, contains elements of most forms of pop music of the late 1970's and early 1980's, from disco to country-pop. Thereafter, Dolly Parton continued to work regularly in Hollywood, starring (and frequently singing as well) in *The Best Little Whorehouse in Texas* (1982), *Rhinestone* (1984), and *Steel Magnolias* (1989).

As her career prospered, Dolly Parton took full control of her business, creating, with her manager Sandy Gilmore, Sandollar Production Company and, in 1986, opening her own theme park, Dollywood, located in the Smoky Mountains, not far from where she was born. Dolly Parton has regularly graced the covers of *Redbook*, *Vanity Fair*, and *People* magazines. She has been as famous as any Hollywood personality during the closing years of the twentieth century.

Dolly Parton even had her own television series from late September of 1987 through May of 1988 on the ABC television network. The network brass were looking for someone to revive the variety show genre, which had been moribund since the demise of *The Carol Burnett Show*. ABC made a two-season, $44 million commitment to *Dolly*, believing that Parton could cross over the generation gap and make a hit. Dolly Parton sang from her rustic living room, complete with a roaring fire, and *Dolly* seemed to be the perfect show for the nostalgic Reagan era of the 1980's. Unfortunately for both ABC and Dolly Parton, the glitzy, big-budget hour finished forty- seventh in the ratings for its first and only season. If anything, Dolly Parton's considerable talents and appeal were overused; she appeared in every segment, singing duets with guest stars and performing in comedy skits. Indeed, except for a four-man vocal harmony group called the A Cappellas, Dolly Parton was the lone show regular.

In 1991, Parton starred in a critically acclaimed made-for-television film about battered women: *Wild Texas Wind*. In 1992, she starred in and helped to produce the film *Straight Talk*. Parton continued to release new albums and singles, including duets with young country singers such as Randy Travis, Ricky Van Shelton, and Billy Ray Cyrus; some of her songs were produced as videos that were aired on television video programs such as VH-1 and The Nashville Network. In the fall of 1994, HarperCollins published Parton's autobiography, *Dolly*.

### Summary

The life of Dolly Parton is a wonderful version of the all-American success story. As the "Cinderella of the South," Dolly Parton started with almost nothing, save her talent and iron will to succeed. Before she turned thirty, she had become a national star. By the time she was forty, she was a millionaire.

She became a tough businesswoman, a very talented songwriter and singer, and a television and film star. In the long term, Dolly Parton should be remembered as a songwriter whose lyrics expressed the feelings of children and women in contemporary rural and urban American society.

A major force in bringing women to the forefront of country music, Dolly Parton followed the stylings of Kitty Wells and Patsy Cline. Fashioning a smooth sound to traditional country music instrumentation, she created a popular commercial product intended to appeal to a national pop music audience. In turn, she inspired a score of country-pop female singers, including Emmy Lou Harris and Linda Ronstadt, with whom she recorded the highly successful album *Trio* in 1987.

As a recording artist, Dolly Parton moved ever further into the heart of the pop music tradition, abandoning her earlier pure country style, much to the sorrow of many critics. These traditional critics argue that to appreciate Dolly Parton's genius fully one has to go back to two pathbreaking albums from the early 1970's: *Coat of Many Colors* and *My Tennessee Mountain Home*. The song "Coat of Many Colors" carefully tells the tragic story of a rag coat that Dolly Parton's own mother made for her poor young child one winter. The album also includes a dark song dealing with madness, "If I Lose My Mind," and a pondering of religion, mountain style, in "The Mystery of the Mystery." *My Tennessee Mountain Home* presents a wonderfully engaging oral history lesson complete with a vision of Nashville ("Down on Music Row"), a pair of musical essays about hard times and grinding poverty ("Daddy's Working Boots" and "In the Good Old Days"), and a trio of lyrical oral histories ("Dr. Robert F. Thomas," "I Remember," and "My Tennessee Mountain Home").

Despite her widespread popularity, Dolly Parton is a real country artist. This petite (five feet, two

inches) blonde woman, with her towering wigs and skin-tight fashions, seems to epitomize that curious mixture of hillbilly fashion and heartfelt singing that Nashville likes to project.

People who know little about country music frequently underestimate Dolly Parton. She embodies conservatism, the all-American virtues of family, and down-home music, but she was able to become a pop cultural icon. Country stars before her have become famous, but few have matched the range and level of success as a performer that Dolly Parton has achieved.

**Bibliography**

Brown, Charles T. *Music U.S.A.: America's Country and Western Tradition*. Englewood Cliffs, N.J.: Prentice-Hall, 1986. This valuable survey of the history of country music in the United States includes a major section on Dolly Parton. The best part of this well-illustrated book is its musical analysis of top country hits, including "Nine to Five."

Bufwack, Mary A., and Robert K. Oermann. *Finding Her Voice: The Saga of Women in Country Music*. New York: Crown, 1993. A well-documented history of the impact of women in the field of country music. The bibliography is extensive. Chapter 14 is the best piece yet written about the latter part of the career of Dolly Parton. Well illustrated.

"Dolly Parton." *Country Music* no. 187 (September/October, 1997). Short profile of Parton including lists of her achievements and songs.

Kingsbury, Paul, and Alan Axelrod, eds. *Country: The Music and the Musicians*. New York and London: Abbeville Press, 1988. Do not be fooled by the appearance of this lavish, beautifully illustrated, oversized picture book. Its sixteen essays cover all the basics of the history of country music. Chapter 16 examines Dolly Parton.

Malone, Bill C. *Country Music U.S.A.* Rev. ed. Austin: University of Texas Press, 1985. This is the standard one-volume scholarly history of country music. Its detailed bibliography and guide to recordings ought to be required reading for anyone seriously interested in this genre of popular music. The career of Dolly Parton is treated in considerable detail.

Nash, Alanna. *Dolly*. Los Angeles, Calif.: Reed Books, 1978; London: Panther, 1979. A popular biography with a number of color photographs, a score of black-and-white photographs, and a short discography—only reference material is lacking. This is the best full biography of Dolly Parton, although it does not cover her career beyond 1978.

Parton, Dolly. *Dolly*. New York and London: HarperCollins, 1994. Parton's autobiography is a frank account of the singer's life—one that, if not entirely revealing, at least provides a glimpse of the hardship and challenges that Parton overcame in her quest to succeed in the world of country music and beyond.

Scobey, Lola. *Dolly: Daughter of the South*. New York: Kensington, 1977. This popular biography is inferior to Alanna Nash's *Dolly*. There are few details, and only a handful of black-and-white photographs are included. No footnotes, bibliography, or discography.

Wilson, Pamela. "Mountains of Contradictions: Gender, Class, and Region in the Star Image of Dolly Parton." *South Atlantic Quarterly* 94, no. 1 (Winter 1995). Discusses Parton's public image, its development, and its impact.

*Douglas Gomery*

# BORIS PASTERNAK

*Born:* February 10, 1890; Moscow, Russia
*Died:* May 30, 1960; Peredelkino, near Moscow, U.S.S.R.
*Area of Achievement:* Literature
*Contribution:* Pasternak was a leading Russian poet, a particularly gifted translator, and a writer of prose, most notably the novel *Doctor Zhivago*, for which he was offered the Nobel Prize in 1958. His highly cultured talent managed to find both expression and influence despite severe adversity in the Soviet literary climate.

## Early Life

Boris Leonidovich Pasternak was born on February 10, 1890, in Moscow, the first child of Leonid Osipovich Pasternak, an artist renowned for his portraiture, and Rosa Isidorovna Pasternak (née Kaufman), a talented pianist. In their youth, Boris, his brother Alexander, and his two sisters, Josephine and Lydia, were exposed to a richly cultured environment of art, music, and literature. The famous author, Leo Tolstoy, was an admirer of Leonid's work and sat for one of his most prominent portraits. The Pasternaks were, as a result, visitors on several occasions to Tolstoy's Moscow residence and to his estate near Tula. The effect of this contact was to be felt in Pasternak's later religious and philosophical views. The German poet Rainer Maria Rilke, who twice visited the Pasternaks, influenced young Boris to appreciate the role of the poet in society—a role he later assumed. It was the eccentric composer Aleksandr Scriabin who most determined Pasternak's youthful endeavors. Under his influence, Pasternak studied music composition while attending Moscow's German Classical Grammar School. At school, Pasternak enjoyed foreign languages, especially German, and philosophy. He took an interest in the poetry of the Russian Symbolists Innokenty Annensky and Aleksandr Blok. Through his father he met the founder of the Soviet literary doctrine of Socialist Realism, Maxim Gorky, both in Moscow and in Berlin, to which the Pasternaks traveled in 1905 after the failed Russian revolution attempt of that year. In 1907, the family returned to Moscow, and in 1908 Pasternak was graduated from school with a gold medal for excellence.

In 1909, Pasternak entered Moscow State University as a law student, but he soon transferred to philosophy. He began to participate in a literary circle called "Serdarda," which was devoted to poetic innovation. Other members of this group, notably Sergei Makovsky and Sergei Bobrov, recognized Pasternak's talent for poetry and urged him to give up his work in music composition to focus on poetry. In 1912, Pasternak traveled to Germany to study philosophy under the Neo-Kantian leader Hermann Cohen at the University of Marburg. He was unhappy over his relationship with Ida Davidovna Vysofskaya, the daughter of wealthy family friends. He had fallen in love with her while tutoring her. She visited him in Marburg and there rejected his proposal of marriage. He then withdrew from the university and returned to Moscow, intent on devoting himself more exclusively to literary pursuits.

## Life's Work

In 1913, Pasternak had five of his poems published in a Moscow almanac called *Lirika.* The group that sponsored this almanac soon merged with a Futurist group, Centrifuge, through which Pasternak came under the influence of Vladimir Mayakovsky, the revolutionary poet who had been a passing acquaintance of Pasternak in school. In 1914, Russia's participation in World War I began, and Pasternak was drafted for service; he was soon exempted, however, because of his leg, which had improperly healed after a fracture sustained in a fall from a horse in 1903. In 1914, his first collection of verse, *Bliznets v tuchakh* (twin in the clouds), was published, and, while staying on the estate of the Lithuanian poet Jurgis Baltrushaitis, he translated Heinrich von Kleist's *Der zerbrochene Krug* (1808; *The Broken Jug*, 1930) into Russian. By the time his translation was published with Gorky's personal editorship in *Sovremennik* (the contemporary) in 1922, Pasternak was roundly acclaimed as an author and a poet. Early prose writings such as "Apellesova cherta" (1918; the mark of Apelles) and especially "Detstvo Liuvers" (1922; the childhood of Liuvers), with its depiction of a child's growing awareness of an adult world, established Pasternak as a leading stylist. His collections of verse, *Poverkh bari erov* (1917; *Above the Barriers*, 1959, 1964) and *Sestra moia zhizn* (1922; *My Sister, Life*, 1959, 1964), demonstrated his transcendence of Mayakovsky's revolutionary Futurism and his coming into his own as a major modern poet.

Like many of the leading artistic intellectuals with whom he was acquainted, Pasternak's initial enthusiasm for the Russian Revolution of 1917 was short-lived. In 1921, his parents and his sisters emigrated to Germany, never to return. He remained in the family house in Moscow with his brother Aleksandr, and, in 1922, married a talented painter, Evgenia Vladimirovna Lourié. Together they traveled several times to Germany and to France, where he met with prominent émigré poets such as Andrei Biely, Vladislav Khodasevich, and especially the ill-fated Marina Tsvetayeva, with whom he was to maintain a long mutual admiration by correspondence. Pasternak's son Evgeny was born in 1923.

After a successful collection of lyric verse published in 1923, *Temy i variatsii* (*Themes and Variations*, 1959, 1964), Pasternak attempted to explore the revolutionary ethic in the narrative poems "Devyatsot pyaty god" (1926; the year 1905) and "Lyutenant Shmidt" (1927; Lieutenant Schmidt). In his prose story "Vozdushnye puti" (1924; aerial ways) and in his novel-in-verse *Spektorsky* (1931), however, Pasternak's problems in viewing the poet as a revolutionary became clear. Pasternak's poet-heroes were prone to passivity in the buffetings of historical change. They martyred themselves to serve as witnesses to the personal consequences of global events. In this they presaged the character of Yuri, his hero in *Doktor Zhivago* (1957; *Doctor Zhivago*, 1958).

In 1931, Pasternak left his wife and took a residence with Zinaïda Nikolaevna Neuhaus, the wife of an acquaintance. He published his unconventional autobiography *Okhrannaya gramota* (*Safe Conduct*, 1945) in the same year. Travel to the Caucasus and meetings with Georgian poets inspired the verse collection *Vtoroye rozhdeniye* (1932; *Second Birth*, 1959, 1964). Yet the increased strictures on literature after the formation of the Union of Soviet Writers in 1932 kept Pasternak from publishing original work throughout the remainder of the 1930's. Although he did serve as a delegate of the Union of Soviet Writers to a Paris conference in 1935, he was privately dismayed at Stalinist tyranny in the arts. On one occasion detailed by the poet Osip Mandelstam's widow, Joseph Stalin personally telephoned Pasternak to gain assurance that Mandelstam "was a great poet." Inevitably Mandelstam perished in the labor camps. Pasternak was able to find a safer livelihood by translating into Russian the works of Johann Wolfgang von Goethe, Friedrich Schiller, George Gordon, Lord Byron, John Keats, Paul Verlaine, and especially William Shakespeare, the major tragedies of whom he published during World War II.

Pasternak married Neuhaus in 1934, and a second son, Leonid, was born three years later. In 1937, he refused to sign a letter in *Pravda* denouncing the purged General Mikhail Tukhachevsky, but colleagues protectively signed his name anyway. In 1939, his mother died in London, and Tsvetayeva returned from emigration only to commit suicide in the Yelabuga labor camp two years later. The need to impress literature into the service of the country during World War II enabled the publication of Pasternak's own patriotic collections *Na rannikh poezdakh* (1943; *On Early Trains*, 1959, 1964) and *Zemnoy prostor* (1945; *The Vastness of Earth*, 1959, 1964). The postwar clampdown, however, ceased for Pasternak all but the publication of translations until the death of Stalin in 1953.

In 1945, Pasternak's father died in Oxford, England. The next year, Pasternak fell in love with Olga Vsevolodovna Ivinskaya, a worker in the offices of the literary journal *Novy mir* (new world). In 1947, he excused himself from participating in the Union of Soviet Writers' condemnation of Anna Akhmatova and Mikhail Zoshchenko. Soon after Ivinskaya's arrest in 1949, Pasternak had a serious heart attack, and while convalescing he worked on the poems and the prose of his novel *Doctor Zhivago.* Ivinskaya refused to incriminate Pasternak in "activities against the state" and was transferred to a labor camp only to be released in 1953. The stress of Pasternak's literary plight, combined with his being torn between his family and his lover, eroded his health and necessitated prolonged periods of rest.

The thaw that followed the death of Stalin and Nikita S. Khrushchev's subsequent denunciation of the cult of Stalin in 1956 gave Pasternak hope that his novel *Doctor Zhivago*, which he had completed the previous year, would be accepted for publication. Indeed several of the poems that were to accompany it were accepted and published by *Znamya* (the banner) in 1954. Thus encouraged, he sent a complete manuscript to Feltrinelli Publishers in Italy. When Communist Party officials decided not to allow the publication of *Doctor Zhivago* in the Soviet Union, Pasternak tried to recall his manuscript from Italy, but Feltrinelli published it anyway in 1957. The novel, describing the harried life of Dr. Yuri Zhivago, a physician and poet caught up in the monumental events of Russia's first third of the twentieth century—war, revolution, civil war, and the radical transformation of Russian society—was an international sensation. Translated into many languages, *Doctor Zhivago* was admired by all who appreciated the travail inflicted by the clash of political ideologies on sensitive and creative individuals of conscience. Abroad Pasternak was acclaimed. In Stockholm, the Nobel Prize Committee voted to award him the 1958 Nobel Prize in Literature. Within a day of this announcement letters denouncing Pasternak as a "Judas who has shut his eyes to the transformation of his country by victorious socialism" appeared in the Soviet press. Not only was he expelled from the Union of Soviet Writers but also a petition of more than eight hundred Moscow writers requested that the government deprive him of his Soviet citizenship. Ill and harassed, Pasternak telegrammed to Stockholm his refusal to accept the Nobel Prize, and, a few days later, wrote a letter to Khrushchev asking that he not be separated from his native land.

In the year and a half left in Pasternak's life, he tried to have his works *Kogdá razguliayetsa* (1959; *When the Skies Clear*, 1959, 1964), a collection of reflective verse, and *Avtobiograficheskiy ocherk* (1958; *I Remember: Sketch for an Autobiography*, 1959) published in the Soviet Union as they had been abroad. His historical drama *Slepaya krasavitsa* (1969; *The Blind Beauty*, 1969) was left incomplete at his death. In his last days the Soviet authorities cut off his royalties from foreign publications and continued their personal harassment of his family and his loved ones. He died of a weakened heart and of lung cancer on May 30, 1960. At a sparsely attended funeral his poem "Hamlet" from the *Doctor Zhivago* cycle was read. His home in the writer's colony at Peredelkino has become a kind of shrine for visiting literati, students, and tourists.

### Summary

Boris Pasternak left a legacy of poetic achievement. Through his poetry he labored to create something profound and beautiful—a different way of appreciating reality given to the reader. He was unable to make his poetry adapt to the rigors of social utility and so he escaped into translation, the competence of which still enriches Russian-speaking peoples everywhere. The work for which he is best known is his novel *Doctor Zhivago*, the political impact of which stands in ironical juxtaposition to its content—a veritable paean to the apoliticality of artistic achievement. Banned from publication in its native land for almost a quarter century—only in 1989 was a Russian version printed in the Soviet Union—*Doctor Zhivago*'s characters and poems are nevertheless widely known and held in high esteem.

### Bibliography

Barnes, Christopher. *Boris Pasternak: A Literary Biography.* Vol. 1. Cambridge and New York: Cambridge University Press, 1989. Barnes's study may be termed a second-generation biography, building on others done soon after Pasternak's death and having available more recently published memoirs (such as the memoirs of Ivinskaya, who was arrested and sent back to the camps after Pasternak's death), and archival materials. Volume 1 of this work covers Pasternak's life and works to 1928, and volume 2 will cover the rest. Detail is superb.

Carlo, Testa. "Doktor Zhivago: Values Versus Voodoo." *Russian Review* 56, no. 3 (July, 1997). Examination of Pasternak's novel *Doktor Zhivago* and its commentary on Russian economics.

Dyck, J. W. *Boris Pasternak.* New York: Twayne, 1972. This is an important overall survey of Pasternak's life and works that endeavors to explain Pasternak's complexities of both philosophy and style to the layperson. A useful chronology of Pasternak's life is included for ease of reference.

Gifford, Henry. *Pasternak: A Critical Study.* Cambridge and New York: Cambridge University Press, 1977. Gifford's work frames the events of Pasternak's life well within the literary context of his times. The chronological table, for example, lists the suicides or grim deaths of a dozen of Pasternak's literary compatriots. The literary works are deeply and clearly analyzed, with citations given in both Russian and English.

Hingley, Ronald. *Pasternak: A Biography.* London: Weidenfeld and Nicolson, and New York: Knopf, 1983. Hingley's biography focuses on Pasternak's personal motivations for his reactions to the forces that molded Soviet literature and, indeed, Soviet culture in this century.

Hughes, Olga R. *The Poetic World of Boris Pasternak.* Princeton, N.J.: Princeton University Press, 1974. An examination both thematic and structural of Pasternak's peculiar perception as expressed in his poetry is the strength of this work by Hughes. The scholarly apparatus of this work is particularly useful, with the frequent Russian citations given insightful translations.

Mallac, Guy de. *Boris Pasternak: His Life and Art.* Norman: University of Oklahoma Press, 1981; London: Souvenir Press, 1983. This is a very detailed narration of Pasternak's life with included critical treatments of his works. The book is wonderfully illustrated as well and features the most complete capsulized chronology available.

Payne, Robert. *The Three Worlds of Boris Pasternak.* London: Hale, and New York: Coward-McCann, 1961. This work, by a very experienced biographer, was produced soon after Pasternak's death. It attempts to sketch Pasternak's life as a poet, prose writer, and political figure for the lay audience, giving insightful explanations of Russian historical context.

Sicher, Efraim. *Jews in Russian Literature after the October Revolution: Writers and Artists between Hope and Apostasy.* Cambridge and New York: Cambridge University Press, 1995. The author examines the works of four Jewish writers including Pasternak, with emphasis on their places in Revolutionary Russia.

*Lee B. Croft*

# VALLABHBHAI JHAVERBHAI PATEL

*Born:* October 31, 1875; Nadiād, Gujerāt, India
*Died:* December 15, 1950; Bombay, India
*Areas of Achievement:* Government and politics
*Contribution:* Patel's uncanny ability to inspire political cooperation among disparate personalities and groups served as the single most important element in the post-independence Indian government's successful integration of the various princely states into a single national unit.

## Early Life

Vallabhbhai Jhaverbhai Patel was born in the province of Gujerāt, the son of a fairly prosperous farmer of the peasant class. Within the family there was a tradition of opposition to the occupying British administration; Patel's father had been involved in the Mutiny of 1857, although it has never been clear how far his participation went. Nevertheless, Patel and his elder brother Vithalbai were sent for their educations to the Nadiād and Baroda high schools, where the standard subjects were presented. After this level of education, Patel very much wished to study law and to that end inquired about the various criteria that would be necessary in England. The reply to his letter was apparently addressed to him by his initial, and his brother, who was also considering law, prevailed on Patel to sponsor his study in England first.

While Vithalbai studied in England, Vallabhbhai studied for and passed the local district pleaders' examinations and set up his first practice at Godhra. He later moved his practice to Borsad, where he specialized in criminal law. To a degree this specialization was less a matter of personal interest than of opportunity, since the Borsad region was notorious as a criminal center.

In 1913, Patel was finally able to attend the Middle Temple in London, where his already well-developed legal talents allowed him to be called to the bar in two rather than the customary three years. When he returned to India, he decided to establish his practice at Ahmadabad, where as a defense counsel he was very much sought after. His practice very quickly made him quite wealthy, and, since much of his prosperity was dependent on the goodwill of those connected with the British administration, he was more than a little reluctant to participate in activities that might have jeopardized the relationship. Patel was during this period fully Westernized in attitude and behavior and was quite willing to allow the debates about nationalism and independence to take place without him.

At least part of Patel's reluctance to involve himself in the political controversy was his doubt that men such as Gandhi could succeed against the pragmatic British. Thus, while Patel actually met Gandhi in 1915, it was not until some two years later that Patel was able to reconcile his personal doubts as to Gandhi's nonviolent campaign with his understanding of the campaign's potential implementation. It was in 1917, at the time that Gandhi refused to abide by a judicial order, that Patel realized that other areas of Indian life might be equally susceptible to a policy of refusal. It was this realization that spurred Patel's organization of the no-tax campaign for Gandhi, his participation as an advocate representing those accused by the British authorities of taking part in self-government activities, and his prominent role in local Gujerati politics. Between about 1917 and 1928, Patel's activities in support of Gandhi's effort to gain Indian freedom gradually expanded outside the province of Gujerāt, and his reputation as a pragmatic and astute political strategist was enhanced nationally.

## Life's Work

After Patel's four-year term as president of the Ahmadabad municipality (1924-1928), he began to try to apply the principles of public responsibility and governmental obligation to a wider area. Committed to the ideas of Indian self-government, he led a massive civil disobedience campaign in the district of Surat in 1928, largely on behalf of small landowners of the class from which he had come. In this case, too, the matter at issue seems to have appealed to his legal experience, in that the farmers, having been severely overtaxed and underrepresented, chose tax refusal as the best method of fighting the injustice.

While Patel customarily chose legalistic and specific methods of depriving the British authorities, his methods were not without risk. His actions during the national civil disobedience campaign of 1930 caused his first imprisonment by the British, and he was jailed again in January, 1932. His prominence within the independence movement was recognized in 1931 when he was elected president of the Congress Party.

Patel during the 1930's was largely responsible for the strategic foundations that were to allow the Congress Party to form an effective government as the British were gradually forced from power. His position on the 1935 parliamentary subcommittee meant that he, along with others similarly involved in long-range political planning, was to guide most of the decisions about the ways in which Hindus and Muslims within India were to cooperate within the government. Unfortunately, Patel and the subcommittee chose not to share their power with Muslim proponents of independence, a decision that was to have brutal consequences after partition.

Up until the outbreak of the war, Patel continued his work within the Congress Party, but when war was declared in 1939 all Congress ministries resigned and effectively cut off Patel and the party from further hope of reconciliation under any circumstances. Patel was again imprisoned, in 1940. By that time the activities of Congress and the independence movement generally had reached such a pitch that approaches to the Japanese were made in an attempt to force the British from India. The 1942 "Quit India" movement was the culmination of Congress' hostility toward the British occupation, and the campaign's planning was in very large part that of Patel. For the campaign, along with what Great Britain perhaps properly viewed as extraordinary disloyalty in time of war, Patel and other Congress leaders were imprisoned until June, 1945.

Thus, it was only in 1945, after some twenty-five years of active resistance, that the British finally began negotiations that would lead to their departure from India. At that time, and until the final transfer of power in August, 1947, Patel played his most important role, both behind the scenes and as a member of the interim form of government that was established in 1946. Eventually, Patel was to become, first, minister for the states and then deputy prime minister. The second position, which he achieved directly after independence, gave him authority over home affairs, information and broadcasting, and the matters that concerned the Indian states.

It was during the period immediately following independence that Patel's talents in organization, conciliation, and political compromise were most used by President Jawaharlal Nehru and the Congress Party generally. His pragmatism and sense of expedience in service of the goals of creating a unified India were of enormous value. The civil disorder that followed independence could have aborted Indian political unity completely; instead, Patel, as deputy prime minister, insisted on and achieved a level of discipline within the government that has not subsequently been matched. This discipline was especially important following partition, when the bitterness and violence that partition caused among both Muslims and militant Hindus threatened to destroy India altogether.

As part of his responsibilities as deputy prime minister, Patel was in charge of maintaining civil order as much as possible. In a real sense, his position may have been unique within modern politics. Essentially, as one of the leaders of a national revolution as expressed through the "Quit India" movement, he was then called upon to restructure the revolution, halt the protests that had almost become a way of Indian life, and rechannel an entire pattern of conduct directed against authority; in short, he was asked to create methods for a newly independent nation to function within its ideology.

Without Patel, it is unlikely that India would have survived the extremely difficult period after partition. Further, he also had the responsibility for somehow unifying the Indian princedoms, which composed in large measure the political superstructure that had sustained the independence movement. That superstructure was certainly unwieldy, and the powers of the princes were such that very few were willing to give them up easily; Patel, however, was determined that the nearly six hundred different jurisdictions be forced into orderly and mutually supportive units.

If Patel's work in maintaining order was difficult, the work he undertook to reorganize the princely political states was virtually overwhelming, although for rather different reasons. Since the eighteenth century, most of these states had been granted treaty privileges that gave them legal paramountcy within their borders. These rights were not automatically transferred to a central Indian government when independence came, and as a result each had to be dealt with separately by the Nehru government. Patel's methods of dealing with the states was utterly straightforward—they were merged into larger administrative units, the larger states became provincial units, and princes themselves were retired or became elected officials. In some cases Patel took military or police action against recalcitrant states, and the central government occupied the district. The entire national realignment took him two years, but at its conclusion India was indeed a single, independent nation, and the real threat that it would simply collapse into anarchy.

In this administrative work, Patel had the support of Nehru and the other members of the government, but it is doubtful that he was entirely influenced by Nehru's sometimes more expedient point of view. Patel was ruthless in his belief that the consolidation of the various political structures had to be accomplished as quickly as possible. He was not prepared to allow any interference with the achievement of that end goal, regardless of whether it might be temporarily desirable. Perhaps of greater importance, given the likelihood of such a philosophy being perverted toward personal gain, Patel was instead completely focused on the benefits to be accrued for India. He was ready to abandon his own views when they came into conflict with the greater ambitions that the Congress held for the nation.

### Summary

Vallabhbhai Jhaverbhai Patel, called "Sardar," or leader, by his peers, was that most unique political figure, the intellectual pragmatist. In his early life, he put his family responsibilities before his own preferences; in his active life within the Congress Party and later the Indian government, he was able to see consequences and effects of actions where others saw only short-term benefits or losses. In the largest sense, Patel was India's *éminence grise* after independence, allowing Nehru to present as accomplished fact what Patel forced into creation: a unified India.

Patel's private behavior was always secondary to the necessities of public life, so much so that he gained a reputation for both cynicism and coldness. He has been compared to Otto von Bismarck in his ruthless suppression of the princely resistance; if the comparison is apt, then it is so because after independence India desperately needed a Bismarck. He was in many ways an idealist, but of a kind specifically necessary to his time and completely without the sentimentality that did affect other Congress leaders. Patel took up the cause of an independent India early in his life and never varied his belief that it was both politically and emotionally achievable. His early training and natural disposition toward order, when combined with an overwhelming sense of public duty and responsibility, illuminated the path for India to follow into the modern political structure.

### Bibliography

Ahluwalia, B. K., ed. *Facets of Sardar Patel.* Delhi: Kalyani, 1974. A collection of personal and political assessments of Patel and of all facets of his life, this volume tries to present the whole man within the context of his political importance. Included are reminiscences by Vapal P. Menon, B. Shiva Rao, and the Earl Mountbatten of Burma. An invaluable portrait of Patel as both his friends and opponents saw him.

Menon, Vapal P. *The Transfer of Power in India.* London and New York: Longman, 1957. In this volume, written at the behest of Patel, Menon examines India's constitutional history and the mechanisms that Patel and others used to effect a transfer of power from Great Britain to the centralized Indian government. Menon's account is straightforward, devoid of unnecessary wordage, and a valuable and scholarly record of events that were at the time often confusing.

Moraes, Frank. *Witness to an Era: India 1920 to the Present Day.* London: Weidenfeld and Nicolson, 1973; New York: Holt Rinehart, 1974. Moraes, former war correspondent for the

*Times* of India, was present at almost every step of India's road to independence and offers a personal account of the leadership of the movement. His insights and recollections of Indian life before and after independence are accessible, and his understanding of Patel's difficult position enlightening.

Patel, Sardar. *Sardar Patel: In Tune with the Millions.* Edited by C. M. Nandurkar. Ahmadabad: Navajivan Press, 1975. A chronological collection of Patel's speeches and writings during the period 1947-1950. Nandurkar has selected those writings that shed the most light on Patel's work across India to unify the nation and has traced Patel's attitudes toward those who placed personal gain above that unity. While a difficult volume if used as an introduction to Patel, it provides much primary information on the way in which Patel's mind worked and his hopes for India's future.

Subramanya Menon, K.P. *Homage to Sardar Patel.* Bombay: Patel Institute, 1976. Menon's extensive examination of the relationship between Nehru and Patel and his role as the "Bismarck of India." Menon dwells on Patel's devotion to India and his loyalty to principle, although he points out it was often at odds with Nehru's convictions.

*A. J. Plotke*

# ALAN PATON

*Born:* January 11, 1903; Pietermaritzburg, Natal, South Africa

*Died:* April 12, 1988; Botha's Hill, Natal, South Africa

*Areas of Achievement:* Literature and social reform

*Contribution:* Through his writings and political work, Paton both foresaw and helped to effect fundamental changes in the shape of South African society.

## Early Life

Alan Stewart Paton was born in Pietermaritzburg, Natal, South Africa, on January 11, 1903. His father James was a stern authoritarian from Scotland, and his mother Eunice was a mild schoolteacher of British ancestry. The family was of the Christadelphian faith, which Alan would leave as a young man. A good student, Alan attended the Berg St. Girls School, a coeducational facility, and accelerated quickly. Though timid and shy, he enjoyed performing and role-playing. In 1914, Paton earned a scholarship to attend Maritzburg College, one of South Africa's oldest schools. He graduated at the age of fifteen with many prizes and honors.

In 1919 Paton entered Natal University College on an Education Department bursary to become a science teacher. While there, he published poems in the *Natal Witness* and the campus magazine, acted in plays, began a novel, and was active in the debating society. Paton developed a circle of friends known for their puns and clever repartee. He joined the rugby, tennis, and cricket clubs and was selected as a dapper dresser by a campus journal. Though short of stature—he never grew taller than 5 feet 7 inches—his pale blue eyes and straight brown hair made him a fairly attractive man.

While at the university, Paton abandoned Christadelphianism, thus distancing himself from his family. He became president of the Students Representative Council and in July 1924 was their delegate to an Imperial Conference in England. It was his first trip abroad, and it opened his eyes to how other nations regarded his country's treatment of Africans, Indians, and other nonwhites.

## Life's Work

An interesting series of jobs helped Paton develop into a world-renowned author and social reformer. In 1925, fresh out of the university, Paton had great ambition but no clear path. He took his first position as a teacher in Ixopo, a village southwest of Pietermaritzburg. His three years there were challenging, and he was known more for his strict disciplinary practices than for his effectiveness as an instructor. In 1928, Paton accepted a post teaching at his alma mater, Maritzburg College. He joined a Christian men's organization, Toc H, that focused on community and social service and soon becoming a senior administrator. Paton remained active with the organization through much of his life.

He continued writing poetry while aspiring to become a headmaster at the college. He befriended and deeply admired Jan Hendrik Hofmeyr, a rising politician who eventually became prime minister, and hoped to follow his mentor into politics as well. However, though Paton dropped many hints over the years, Hofmeyr, in his ascendance to higher and higher posts, never saw fit to offer preferment. In 1930, Paton enrolled for a master's degree at Natal University College and joined the South African Institute of Race Relations, a small group of liberal thinkers addressing issues of race in the nation. His awareness of the injustices of South African society was growing steadily. Throughout his thirties, Paton wrote poems, short stories, and the beginnings of plays and novels that never reached fruition.

His career took a turn in 1935 when he applied for and was appointed headmaster at Diepkloof, a black prison that was being changed into a reformatory. Located outside of Johannesburg, Diepkloof was a shambles of squalor and filth when Paton arrived. With a clear mandate and strong pedagogical vision, he set about transforming Diepkloof into a civilized institution, using fairly radical theories that emphasized freedom over captivity and incorporated personal psychology as a factor in the teacher-student relationship. Under Paton's leadership, Diepkloof saw a great drop in the rate of escapes and the successful implementation of many innovative techniques. Paton wrote little at Diepkloof but gathered mental prototypes for characters that would later appear in his fiction. He considered his thirteen years at Diepkloof some of the happiest and proudest of his life.

In 1946, Paton began to foresee the end of his tenure at Diepkloof. The rise of the Nationalist Party to political power promised a rollback of the reforms that Paton had modeled so successfully. He traveled on sabbatical to visit prisons in

Britain, Sweden, Norway, and the United States. He was also considering what his next career move would be.

It was in a hotel in Trondheim, Norway, that Paton penned the words that would become the first paragraph of *Cry, the Beloved Country.* The novel deals with a Zulu pastor, his son, and the ambitions and crimes that engulf them on their separate journeys from rural Ixopo to the great city of Johannesburg. It is a very South African novel, and the injustices of race and apartheid are central themes. Paton completed the novel during his travels. While in the United States in 1947, friends referred his manuscript to Charles Scribner's Sons, a prestigious publishing house, and he returned to South Africa with a book deal. *Cry, the Beloved Country* was published in the United States on February 1, 1948, and subsequently in England and South Africa. Its reception was better than Paton or his publishers could have imagined. Paton was hailed for his astounding insights, his melodious prose, and his compelling story. The book went into its sixth printing within three months and was translated into nine languages within two years.

Paton's life changed irreversibly. Income from the novel made him relatively rich. He decided to focus on writing, but a second novel was not immediately forthcoming. Over the next few years, *Cry, the Beloved Country* was adapted for both stage and screen. Paton traveled and spoke widely and continued his work with various organizations. In 1951, he began work on a new novel about a white police officer's desire for an African woman. *Too Late the Phalarope* was published in 1953 to equally enthusiastic response. Paton's income and reputation were now firmly established.

Meanwhile, the increasingly powerful Nationalists were passing more and more laws ensuring the separation of the races in South Africa. Angered by the injustice and idiocy of these laws, Paton turned to political activism. He helped to form and then assumed leadership roles in the Liberal Party, the only multiracial party in the country, devoting heart and soul to it for the next fifteen years. While never running for office himself, Paton was a ubiquitous spokesman for the cause. He met with many key public figures, including Albert Lutuli of the African National Congress and Senator Robert Kennedy of the United States. Always a moderate, Paton opposed violent means for political ends. He was hounded by the police, arrested and fined for political organizing in 1957, and deprived of his passport in 1960. Nevertheless, he spoke out for a unified society and worked with such groups as the Defence and Aid Fund to channel international financial support to liberal causes.

Paton continued to write. He produced numerous poems on political themes. Larger writings include *The Land and People of South Africa* (1955); *Last Journey* (1958), a play about the loyalty of explorer David Livingstone's Zulu servants; a libretto for the musical *Mkhumbane* (1960), about an African suburb near Durban (1960); *Tales from a Troubled Land* (1961), a collection of short stories; *South African Tragedy: The Life and Times of Jan Hofmeyr* (1965), a biography of his friend and mentor; *Instrument of Thy Peace* (1968), a collection of meditations; and *Apartheid and the Archbishop* (1974), a biography of Geoffrey Clayton, archbishop of Cape Town.

By 1963, Paton was gray-haired and slump-shouldered. Violent resistance was becoming more common, and the middle road advocated by Paton and the Liberal Party seemed to satisfy neither radical Africans nor conciliatory white people. Paton continued to travel and lecture as much as he could but was losing hope that the changes he envisioned would happen within his lifetime. *The Long View*, an anthology of his articles for the Liberal Party magazine *Contact*, was published in 1968.

In 1967, after a long battle with lung disease and emphysema, Paton's wife Dorrie passed away. Though their marriage had not been without difficulty, he missed her tremendously and commemorated her in a unique volume of intimate recollections entitled *For You Departed*, published in 1969. During the course of his later life, Paton earned honorary doctorates in literature and divinity from twelve universities, including Yale, Michigan, and Edinburgh. He won many awards, including the American Freedom Award and *The Sunday Times* Book Award for *Cry, the Beloved Country*.

In 1974 Paton began his autobiography. The first half, recounting his life through 1948, was published in 1980 under the title *Towards the Mountain*. That same year, he unexpectedly started another novel, a historical narrative of South Africa in the 1950's. *Ah, but Your Land Is Beautiful* (1981), the first of a projected trilogy, met mixed reviews, and Paton never wrote the sequels. His health began to fail him, and his pace slowed as he entered his ninth decade. *Save the Beloved Country*, a collection of lectures and writings, was published in 1987. Through the 1980's, Paton worked assiduously to complete his autobiography. In March of 1988, a tumor was discovered in Paton's esophagus. After an unsuccessful operation, he developed pneumonia. Paton died at his home on April 12, 1988, at the age of eighty-five. The second half of his autobiography, *Journey Continued*, appeared posthumously later that same year.

### Summary

Throughout his life, Alan Paton wrote and spoke of the inevitable dissolution of the system of apartheid. Through his work with Toc H, the Students Christian Association, the Institute of Race Relations, the Liberal Party, Diepkloof Reformatory, and numerous other organizations, Paton put his beliefs into action. With the wealth received from his writings, Paton funded many projects and initiatives, and independently sponsored the welfare and education of many young Africans. He was also known to be a captivating speaker.

Though Paton himself never saw the dismantling of apartheid, his books served as agents for social change. *Cry, the Beloved Country* sold more than fifteen million copies in twenty languages by the time of his death; along with *Too Late the Phalarope*, it movingly informed readers around the world about the plight of South Africa's ethnic majorities and thus fueled the international sentiment that eventually helped to transform South African society.

### Bibliography

Alexander, Peter F. *Alan Paton: A Biography*. Oxford and New York: Oxford University Press, 1994. This comprehensive biography of Paton draws deeply on Paton's writings as well as interviews and correspondence with family, friends, colleagues, former students, and others. Alexander deftly interweaves Paton's life with the larger threads of change in South African society. The style is unpretentious, though the accumulation of names, dates, and events is sometimes dense. Includes sixteen photographs, a bibliography, and a good index.

Armstrong, Rye. "Arrested Development." *Biblio* 3, no. 11 (November, 1998). A discussion of *Cry, the Beloved Country* and Paton's feelings as he wrote this novel.

Callan, Edward. *Alan Paton*. Rev. ed. Boston: Twayne, 1982. The first book of criticism of Paton's work, written by an American friend and colleague. The volume is both sympathetic and scholarly. Callan effectively combines critical readings of Paton's work with a deep understanding of the South African psyche and political system.

Gray, Stephen. *Southern African Literature: An Introduction*. London: Collins, and New York: Barnes and Noble, 1976. An overview of the literature of southern Africa in the twentieth century. Gray is very conscious of the divisions and connections between white and nonwhite authors and the role of race in the shaping of literary tradition. Includes occasional references to Paton and his works.

Jordan, John O. "Alan Paton and the Novel of South African Liberalism: 'Too Late the Phalarope.'" *Modern Fiction Studies* 42, no. 4 (Winter 1996). Paton has a commentary on the culture and ideologies that helped establish apartheid.

Paton, Alan. *Journey Continued*. Oxford: Oxford University Press, and New York: Scribner, 1988. The second part of Paton's autobiography traces his life from 1948 through 1968. Paton recounts the parallel strands of his later life: his development as a writer and his role in the political evolution of South Africa. Paton's sincere and poetic style provides a smooth and engaging narrative.

———. *Save the Beloved Country.* New York: Scribner, 1987. A collection of Paton's articles and essays expressing his vehement antiapartheid opinions. Includes articles on South African statesmen such as Albert Luthuli, Nelson Mandela, Hendrik F. Verwoerd, and Jan Christian Smuts.

———. *The Long View.* London: Pall Mall Press, and New York: Praeger, 1968. This is a collection of sixty essays written for the magazine *Contact* between 1958 and 1966. They include some of Paton's most pointed and provocative writing, challenging apartheid and the consequent evils of South African society.

———. *Towards the Mountain.* New York: Scribner, 1980; Oxford: Oxford University Press, 1981. The first installment of Paton's autobiography recounts his life from birth through 1948. The memoir is especially valuable for its insights into Paton's childhood, his work at Diepkloof, and the creative process that led to *Cry, the Beloved Country.*

*Barry Stewart Mann*

## GEORGE S. PATTON

*Born:* November 11, 1885; San Gabriel, California
*Died:* December 21, 1945; Heidelberg, Germany
*Area of Achievement:* The military
*Contribution:* Though never a theoretician, Patton was a masterful tactician who demonstrated the advantages of mobility and aggressive offensive action as essential elements of modern warfare.

### Early Life

George Smith Patton, Jr., was born on November 11, 1885, in San Gabriel, California. His father, George Smith Patton, was descended from a well-established Virginia family rooted in the culture of genteel Southern aristocracy and steeped in the military tradition one commonly associates with that class. His mother, Ruth Wilson, was the daughter of B. D. Wilson, a California businessman who made a sizable fortune in the winery business. Owing to the affluence of his family, Patton's childhood was happy and largely carefree. He did suffer from dyslexia, and as a result his parents decided to enroll him in a private school just prior to his twelfth birthday. His classmates represented some of the wealthiest families in Southern California, but it was with the tradition of his paternal forebears that Patton's affinities lay.

The year 1902 proved to be critically important in Patton's early life. He had decided to pursue a career in the military and thus sought appointment to the United States Military Academy at West Point, New York. He also met Beatrice Banning Ayer, the daughter of Frederick Ayer, a wealthy industrialist from Massachusetts. She would later become his wife—and her marriage to him would on more than one occasion prove beneficial to Patton's career. There were no senatorial or congressional vacancies available at West Point in 1902, so Patton enrolled for one year at Virginia Military Institute, his father's alma mater. During that year, Patton's father worked untiringly to ensure his son's appointment to West Point, and his efforts were rewarded the following year.

At nineteen, Patton was tall—slightly over six feet—very athletic, and quite handsome. An arm injury prevented his playing varsity football, but he took up the broadsword, excelled in the high hurdles, and became a skilled horseman. In fact, three years after graduating from West Point, he competed in the Modern Pentathlon event in the 1912 Stockholm Summer Olympics and finished fifth. Patton had two physical traits, however, which were of great concern to him—a high-pitched, almost squeaky voice, and a very fair and placid facial expression. To correct the latter he practiced in front of a mirror to develop what he called "my war face." There was little that could be done about his voice, but his frequent use of profanity may well have been designed to compensate for what he considered to be a flaw.

### Life's Work

Patton was graduated from West Point in June, 1909. He married Beatrice in May of the following year, and in March, 1911, their first daughter, Beatrice, was born. Following his initial assignment at Fort Sheridan, near Chicago, Patton utilized family influence to secure a tour of duty at Fort Myer in Washington, D.C. Knowing that advancement in the peacetime army would be painfully slow, Patton actively sought to make contact with the "right people." His personal wealth and family connections certainly facilitated his efforts—a fact well illustrated in 1915, when he secured an assignment to a cavalry regiment at Fort Bliss, Texas, while the rest of his outfit went to the Philippines. It proved to be a particularly fortuitous assignment for Patton, who met and served as aide to General John J. Pershing when the latter was ordered into Mexico in 1916. Patton, who served with distinction in Mexico, regarded Pershing as a model soldier and continued to serve as his aide when the latter was chosen to head the American Expeditionary Force to France in 1917.

Once in France, Patton relinquished his staff position for a combat command. He was particularly interested in the tank, which promised to be the cavalry arm of the modern army. His dream of leading a tank unit in combat became a reality during the St. Mihiel campaign. During one engagement he was wounded, but he continued to direct his tanks to their targets by runners. When the newspapers ran the story of the "Hero of the Tanks" who directed his men while lying wounded in a shellhole, Patton became an instant hero. His actions won for him the Distinguished Service Cross and the Distinguished Service Medal. Later, he would admit to his father that he had always feared that he was a coward but had now begun to doubt it.

The peacetime army was a difficult place for Patton. He tried desperately to gain appointment as

commandant to West Point and even sent a personal letter to Pershing in which he poignantly argued that he could transmit his ideal of "blood and gutts [*sic*]" to the cadets under his command. The argument failed, but the sobriquet remained for all time.

Denied West Point, Patton pursued the course one might expect of an ambitious young officer on the rise. In 1923, he attended the Command and General Staff College at Fort Leavenworth, Kansas, and in 1931, he entered the Army War College. During the intervening years, he served tours of duty in Hawaii and in Washington, D.C. His commanding officer in Hawaii described him as "invaluable in war . . . but a disturbing element in time of peace," a prescient evaluation, indeed. Patton lost his father in 1927 and his mother the following year. He consoled himself with the knowledge that he had not been a failure in their eyes and had achieved more, perhaps, than they had dreamed for him. Now he was free to fulfill his own destiny.

In 1938, Patton was ordered back to Fort Myer to replace General Jonathan Wainwright. He was fifty-three years old at the time, and although the war clouds were gathering in Europe and Asia, it seemed likely that age alone might preclude his being considered for a possible combat command. Following the outbreak of war in Europe, however, two decisions by Army Chief of Staff George Marshall changed all that. The German blitzkrieg convinced Marshall that the United States Army needed an armored force. He ordered the creation of two armored divisions and chose Patton to command the Second Armored Division—destined to win fame as "Hell on Wheels." Patton, obviously elated, wrote to his friend and army colleague, Terry Allen, "Now all we need is a juicy war."

Patton got his war and saw his first action in North Africa when, as part of Operation "Torch," his forces landed on the beaches of Morocco. Following the debacle at Kasserine Pass in Tunisia, he was ordered to assume command of the United States Second Corps. He chose Omar N. Bradley as his deputy and initiated a program of rigid training and discipline designed to redeem the valor of American arms. His subsequent victory over the Germans at Al-Guettar was therefore a source of great satisfaction to him. As initially planned, Patton gave up the Second Corps to Bradley to assume command of the Seventh Army which was to participate in the invasion of Sicily.

The Sicilian campaign was one of triumph and tragedy for Patton. Convinced that American forces had been assigned a subordinate role in the operation, he nevertheless managed to turn adversity into advantage by taking the historic town of Palermo and then beating General Bernard Law Montgomery and the vaunted British Eighth Army to Messina. Unfortunately, his shining victories were soon tarnished by the revelation of the famous slapping incident—actually two of them—wherein he struck two enlisted men who had been hospitalized for "battle fatigue." Patton's violent temper and his susceptibility to radical shifts in mood were well-known. Some of his biographers have suggested that he may have suffered from what is known as subdural hematoma, the result of head injuries sustained in falls from and kicks by some of his horses. Whatever the cause, the results were devastating.

Bradley was chosen to command American ground forces preparing for the Normandy invasion, and it was not until the summer of 1944 that Patton was given command of the newly activated Third Army. Determined to redeem himself, Patton's accomplishments as commander of the Third Army were truly remarkable. His forces liberated almost all of France north of the Loire River and were responsible for relieving the besieged 101st Airborne Division at Bastogne during the Ardennes Offensive. Patton considered the latter to be the Third Army's most brilliant operation and "the most outstanding achievement of this war."

As the war began to wind down, Patton expressed his fear of the "horrors of peace." His intemperate remarks expressing hatred of the Russians and contempt for the Jews were most embarrassing to the American High Command. Consequently, when the press subsequently reported that he had compared the Nazi Party to the Democratic and Republican parties, Dwight Eisenhower, Supreme Allied Commander in Europe, had little choice but to relieve him of command. On December 9, 1945, the day before he was to leave to return to the United States, the car in which he was riding slammed into a truck. Patton suffered severe lacerations, a broken nose, and two fractured vertebrae. At best it was feared that he would be a semi-invalid, but that was not to be. He died on December 21, 1945, and was buried in Hamm, Luxembourg.

### Summary

The name of George Patton is and perhaps always will be synonymous with war—particularly World War II. No doubt Patton would have relished that association. He regarded war as the greatest of human endeavors and the battlefield as a place of honor. Patton idolized the great military leaders of the past—Hannibal, Caesar, and Napoleon—and spent much of his life preparing himself to be a worthy follower of the tradition they represented. Like them he would one day lead great numbers of men into battle. It was his destiny.

Patton achieved his destiny, though he did so late in life. World War II was his stage, and though he occupied it for only a brief period of time and never in more than a supporting role, he created a legend. He played to an appreciative audience as a tenacious, innovative, and daring battlefield commander. Had he lived, years of peace might have dimmed the luster of his star. Death intervened to prevent that, and before the applause faded, George Patton was born into immortality.

His death prompted a flood of praise, most of which paid tribute to his skills as a great fighting general. Perhaps the accolade he would have appreciated most, however, came from a former adversary, Field Marshal Gerd von Rundstedt, who, in a postwar interview with American military personnel, said simply, "Patton was your best."

### Bibliography

Ayer, Fred, Jr. *Before the Colors Fade: Portrait of a Soldier, George S. Patton, Jr.* Boston: Houghton Mifflin, 1964. An attempt to analyze Patton the man rather than the legendary battlefield general. This work, authored by Patton's nephew, is highly impressionistic and rather superficially researched.

Blumenson, Martin. *Patton: The Man Behind the Legend, 1885-1945.* New York: Morrow, 1985: London: Cape, 1986. Blumenson's skills as a writer and military historian are evident in this biography. The author reminds his readers that the Patton legend was molded from human clay.

———, ed. *The Patton Papers: 1885-1940.* 2 vols. Boston: Houghton Mifflin, 1972. Blumenson's judicious selection from the voluminous Patton Papers allows the reader to see Patton as he saw himself and to know his fears, failures, strengths, and weaknesses.

Essame, Herbert. *Patton: A Study in Command.* New York: Scribner, 1974. This very favorable biography of Patton focuses on his talents as a battlefield commander. Based exclusively on published sources, this synthetic work adds little that is new to the general's life story.

Farago, Ladislas. *The Last Days of Patton.* New York: McGraw-Hill, 1981. Focusing on the events surrounding Patton's tragic death in December, 1945, Farago attempts a more detailed investigation of the incident than was conducted at the time.

———. *Patton: Ordeal and Triumph.* New York: Obolensky, 1963; London: Barker, 1966. Considered by many to be the definitive biography of George Patton, this impressive work was the basis for the critically acclaimed film *Patton*, released in 1970.

Patton, George S. *War as I Knew It.* London: Allen, and New York: Houghton Mifflin, 1947. This work is best when viewed as a critique of the role of the battlefield general and the problems associated with high command. As military history it suffers from too much detail.

Rickard, John Nelson. *Patton at Bay: The Lorraine Campaign, September to December 1944.* Westport, Conn.: Praeger, 1999. Rickard examines Patton's conduct of the Lorraine Campaign and argues that there were shortcomings in his approach.

Sobel, Brian. *The Fighting Pattons.* Westport, Conn.: Praeger, 1997. This is the first book to present Patton together with his son and includes previously unpublished information, commentary from his son and daughter, and interviews with individuals such as Richard Nixon, Jimmy Doolittle, and General William Westmoreland.

*Kirk Ford, Jr.*

# PAUL VI
## Giovanni Battista Montini

*Born:* September 26, 1897; Concesio, near Brescia, Italy
*Died:* August 6, 1978; Castel Gandolfo, Italy
*Areas of Achievement:* Religion and church reform
*Contribution:* Paul VI convened the last three sessions of the historic Second Vatican Council (1962-1965), which brought the Roman Catholic church into constructive engagement with the modern world. His abiding concern for the poor and for human rights and social justice and his extensive travels reinforced the progressive influence of the Vatican Council.

### Early Life

Giovanni Battista Montini was born on September 26, 1897, in Concesio, a small village near Brescia, in the province of Lombardy, Italy. He was the second son of Giorgio and Giuditta Alghisi Montini. The Montinis were a prosperous aristocratic family, deeply devoted to the Roman Catholic church. Giorgio was one of the founders of Sa Paolo Bank of Brescia, La Scuola Publishing Union, and the Morcelliana publishing house. A successful journalist, he edited the daily *Il Cittadino di Brescia* between 1881 and 1912. Giorgio was also very active in Italian politics, defending the interests of the Catholic church. Pope Benedict XV appointed him to the leadership of the Catholic Electoral Union of Italy. After World War I, when Catholics were allowed to participate in Italian politics, Giorgio Montini became active in the Popular Party. He was elected to represent Brescia in three legislatures prior to the party's suppression in 1926 by Benito Mussolini. Giovanni's mother, Giuditta, was also from an aristocratic family. She was noted in Brescia as a leader of the Catholic women of the area and for her generosity to the poor. Thus, Giovanni's parents provided a home atmosphere that emphasized education and a lively interest in the social and political issues of the turn of the century.

Giovanni suffered from chronic ill health as a child. Much of his early education was provided at home. Until 1914, he was enrolled at the Institute Cesare Arici, an elementary school operated by the Jesuits. Between 1914 and 1916, he was privately tutored in preparation for final examinations at the Liceo Arnaldo de Brescia, which he passed with "highest honors." Because of his health, Giovanni was not called up for military service along with his classmates in 1916. Instead, he began studying for the priesthood. He was ordained on May 29, 1920. After his ordination, Father Montini took up the study of philosophy at the Jesuit Gregorian University in Rome, while simultaneously becoming enrolled at the University of Rome.

Father Giovanni Montini's talents and potential were soon recognized by those close to the papal throne. In 1922, during the first year of Pope Pius XI's reign, he was asked to prepare himself for service in the Vatican's diplomatic corps. It was the first step in a career that led to his election as Pope Paul VI, forty-one years later.

### Life's Work

Montini's first appointment in the Vatican's diplomatic corps came in 1923, when he was sent to Warsaw, Poland, as attaché on the staff of the apostolic nunciature (papal ambassador). Ill health cut short his appointment. Within a year, he was back in Rome. It was a propitious move, for it returned Montini to the very center of power at the Vatican. He rose steadily over the next thirty years from one post to another in the Vatican Secretariat of State. In addition to his duties at the secretariat, Montini was active in the Catholic student movement during the 1920's and 1930's. In 1924, he was appointed chaplain at the University of Rome. During the following year, he was appointed national ecclesiastical assistant to the Federation of Italian Catholic University Students (FUCI), a post he held until early 1933. During those years, Montini led the FUCI in active opposition to the Fascist University Youth. The struggle for the hearts and minds of Italian youth was often a violent one. By his leadership, Montini won the respect and admiration of many individual Catholic students who would later play key roles in postwar Italian politics.

In 1937, Cardinal Eugenio Pacelli, secretary of state, appointed Montini to his personal staff. The two worked closely together. In 1938, when Pacelli was appointed the papal legate to the Eucharistic Congress in Budapest, Hungary, Montini accompanied him. Their collaboration continued after Pacelli's election as Pope Pius XII in 1939. They worked together so harmoniously that the Roman press referred to Montini as "the right eye of the

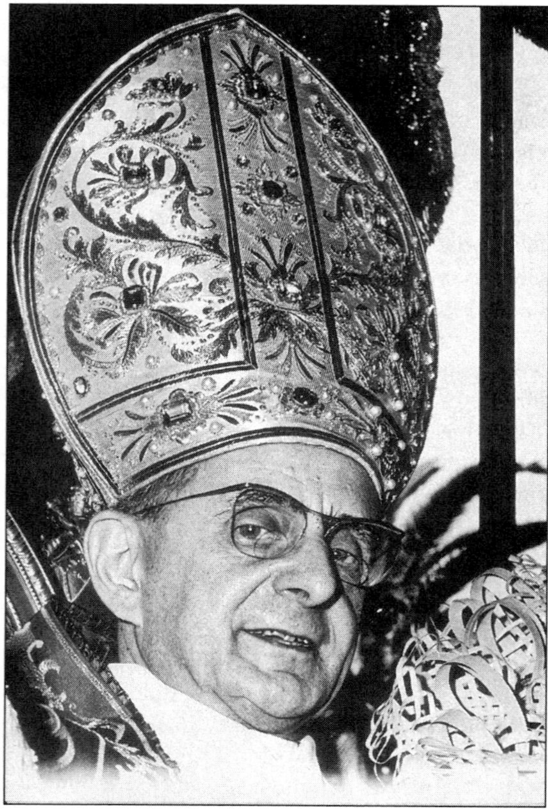

Pope." Pius appointed Montini undersecretary of state in 1939, acting secretary of state for ordinary (that is, nondiplomatic) affairs in 1944, and prosecretary of state in 1953. Pius wanted to elevate him to the Sacred College of Cardinals, but Montini declined the honor.

Throughout his years in Rome, Montini served the poor as a parish priest. It was in recognition of his interest in the working classes that Pius appointed him Archbishop of Milan in 1954. For the next nine years until his election as pope, Montini labored to win the workers of Milan to the Catholic church. It was not an easy task. Milan during the 1950's was a heavily industrial area and a regional stronghold of the Communists.

With the death of Pius XII in 1958, Cardinal Angelo Giuseppe Roncalli was elected Pope John XXIII. Montini's name was the first on a list of twenty-three prelates named by John to the Sacred College of Cardinals in December, 1958. Montini supported the progressive policies of the new pope, including John's call for an ecumenical council to revitalize the Roman Catholic church. The first session of the historic Second Vatican Council convened on October 11, 1962. On June 3, 1963, shortly before the second session was to convene on September 29, John died. On June 21, the College of Cardinals chose Cardinal Giovanni Montini to succeed John as Pope Paul VI.

Paul's background in diplomacy prepared him for the difficult task of leading the Roman Catholic church during the remaining years of the Second Vatican Council and afterward. His leadership was conservative in that he sought to keep the Church faithful to past traditions, except where those traditions were hopelessly out of tune with the twentieth century. The progressive nature of Paul's leadership both during and after the Second Vatican Council can be seen in the reforms he instituted and the causes he championed. Among the former were creation of a Synod of Bishops, replacement of the Latin Mass with the vernacular, and reforms of the papal curia. Even his style was progressive. He was the first pope whose reign was covered by television, as he led the papacy into the center of world religious and political affairs. He traveled extensively, being the first pope to travel by airplane.

Paul also used his influence to promote the cause of human rights and social justice, values he learned in his parents' home and which he never abandoned. In 1967, he issued a papal letter, *Populorum Progressio* (progress of the peoples), which was such a departure from the Vatican's traditional conservative stance on social justice that *The Wall Street Journal* called it "warmed-over Marxism." In the interest of world peace and social justice, Paul addressed the United Nations General Assembly in 1965 and made journeys to Asia, Africa, and Latin America.

Paul was noted for his faithfulness to what he believed to be right, even when it put him at odds with his own clergy and laity. In March, 1964, against the strong opposition of the German bishops, Paul welcomed a delegation from the West German Social Democratic Party (SPD) to the Vatican. It was a recognition of both the efforts of the SPD on behalf of German workers and the progress the SPD was making in moving away from its Marxist origins.

Paul's conservatism can be seen in his steadfast resistance to all efforts to change the Church's position on such key issues as artificial birth control and priestly celibacy. In July, 1968, he issued the papal encyclical *Humanae Vitae* (of human life), which upheld the Church's ban on all forms of artificial birth control. In *Sacerdotalis Caelibatus* (sacerdotal celibacy), issued in June, 1967, Paul reaffirmed the church's stand on clerical celibacy, while condemning the "spiritual and moral collapse" of priests who abandoned their ministries for marriage. Both encyclicals evoked some of the most serious attacks on papal authority in modern history, but Paul stood firm.

Paul is perhaps best remembered as the "pilgrim pope," who reached out to Christians as well as nonbelievers with an ecumenical spirit. He met with the Greek Orthodox patriarch of Constantinople while on a pilgrimage to the Holy Land in 1964 and again in 1967 while on a journey to Turkey. In 1969, he visited the headquarters of the World Council of Churches in Geneva, Switzerland. Yet his ecumenism was not restricted to Christians alone. He reached out to Jews, nonbelievers, and adherents of non-Western religions, also. He established a Vatican Secretariat for Nonbelievers and a Secretariat for Relations with Non-Christian Religions. Throughout his pontificate, Paul followed an exhausting schedule. When he died on August 6, 1978, at Castel Gandolfo, his summer retreat, he was one of the most significant popes of the Roman Catholic church in modern history.

### Summary

Paul VI was undoubtedly one of the most significant popes of the twentieth century. It was John XXIII who called for the changes that brought the Roman Catholic church into the modern world, but it was Paul who saw the changes implemented. His constructive and conservative leadership enabled the Church to undergo revolutionary changes without being rent asunder or breaking its continuity with the past.

Paul's personal contribution, aside from his conservative leadership, was to make the Church an active participant in the struggle for social justice and world peace. On May 15, 1971, the eightieth anniversary of Pope Leo XIII's historic social encyclical *Rerum Novarum* (new things), Paul issued a papal letter calling upon all people, whatever their religious beliefs or positions in life, to seek out practical means by which they could work for world peace and justice. Yet, he did more than call for involvement. He set an example that others could follow.

In one respect, however, Paul's legacy was a mixed one. By upholding the Church's traditional stance on such controversial issues as birth control and clerical celibacy, he contributed, some believe, to the weakening of papal authority. Others believe just as strongly that by his defense of what he held to be true doctrine, he enhanced papal authority within the Church. Perhaps the Second Vatican Council and Paul's strong leadership enabled the Roman Catholic church to change without experiencing the physical schism and fragmentation that had rent a more rigid Church in the sixteenth century.

### Bibliography

Andrews, James F., ed. *Paul VI: Critical Appraisals.* New York: Bruce, 1970. Seven distinguished Catholic and Protestant scholars, theologians, and journalists assess Paul's policies on such key issues as birth control, celibacy, and ecumenism. It also contains a brief biography and a chronological outline of his reign through 1969.

Clancy, John G. *Apostle for Our Time: Pope Paul VI.* New York: Kenedy, 1963; London: Collins, 1964. Published in the year Paul began his reign, this standard biography is especially good for his early life. The influence of his parents in developing his concern for social justice is well covered. Clancy is clearly one who admired Paul.

Curran, Charles E. "Humanae Vitae: Still Controversial at 30." *National Catholic Reporter* 34, no. 35 (July 31, 1998). The author examines Pope Paul VI's 1968 encyclical against contraception.

Gremillion, Joseph. *The Gospel of Peace and Justice.* New York: Orbis, 1976. Part 1 is a summary and analysis of Catholic social teaching during the reigns of John XXIII and Paul VI. Part 2 contains some 550 pages of papal documents (for example, *Humanae Vitae* and Paul's address to the United Nations) in English.

Hebblethwaite, Peter. *The Year of Three Popes.* London: Collins, 1978; Cleveland, Ohio: Collins, 1979. Although a somewhat dry and fact-laden account of the careers of Paul VI, John Paul I, and John Paul II, this book is particularly good for an understanding on how a pope is elected. It provides a balanced and sympathetic assessment of Paul's reign.

Holmes, J. Derek. *The Papacy in the Modern World, 1914-1978.* London: Burns and Oates, and New York: Crossroad, 1981. This is a highly readable history of the Papacy during the years when Giovanni Montini rose from parish priest to supreme pontiff. The latter chapter covers the Second Vatican Council.

Serafian, Michael. *The Pilgrim.* London: Joseph, and New York: Farrar Straus, 1964. A critical analysis of Paul's role in the Second Vatican Council by a Roman Catholic diplomat writing under a pseudonym. The emphasis is on Paul's role during the second session of the Council.

Waibel, Paul R. "Politics of Accommodation: The SPD Visit to the Vatican, March 5, 1964." *The Catholic Historical Review* 65 (April, 1979): 238-252. This essay provides an example of how Paul could influence the course of politics within a nation simply by granting an audience to a visiting delegation. Paul's act meant that the Geman bishops could no longer influence Catholic voters not to vote for the Social Democrats.

*Paul R. Waibel*

# ALICE PAUL

*Born:* January 11, 1885; Moorestown, New Jersey
*Died:* July 9, 1977; Moorestown, New Jersey
*Area of Achievement:* Women's rights
*Contribution:* The leader of the radical wing of the woman suffrage movement that helped pass the Nineteenth Amendment, Paul also introduced the Equal Rights Amendment.

### Early Life

Born on January 11, 1885, in a farmhouse near Moorestown, New Jersey, to a wealthy Quaker (Society of Friends) family, Alice Paul entered the women's movement at a very early age. Her father, William Paul, served as president of the Burlington County Trust Company, and her mother, Tacie Parry Paul, was clerk of the Moorestown Friends' Meeting. Both strongly encouraged young Alice's interest in equal rights.

Alice's early life focused almost entirely upon her Quaker heritage. The Friends created a humane, optimistic religion during the seventeenth century, and they were one of the few sects that preached equality between the sexes. The fact that the Quakers allowed women to become missionaries and ministers created a unique religious environment. Although not much is known about Alice Paul's childhood, many scholars agree that it was the egalitarian, flexible, and tolerant nature of Quaker society that allowed her to develop as perhaps America's greatest radical feminist.

Although both of Alice's parents encouraged her independent attitudes, her mother served as her chief mentor. Alice's father died before she reached adulthood. Tacie Paul was one of many Quaker women (such as Lucretia Mott) who were involved in the nineteenth century American woman suffrage movement.

Alice followed in her mother's footsteps, enrolling in the Moorestown Quaker school and later graduating from another Friends' institution, Swarthmore College. During these formative years, Alice also used Lucretia Mott as her role model. Mott, one of the founding mothers of the American woman suffrage movement, helped organize the first women's rights convention in 1848 at Seneca Falls, New York, where she and Elizabeth Cady Stanton wrote the Declaration of Sentiments. Alice began her great crusade for equal rights as a graduate student at England's Woodbridge Quaker College and the London School of Economics, where she joined Emmeline, Christabel, and Sylvia Pankhurst, the radical British feminists who taught her the aggressive tactics that later produced American congressional support for the Nineteenth Amendment.

During Paul's years in Britain, she formed a close, lifelong friendship with another American suffragist, Lucy Burns, who also belonged to the Pankhursts' Women's Social and Political Union. Nearing the end of this political apprenticeship, Paul resolved to bring confrontational feminism to the United States.

### Life's Work

When Alice Paul returned to the United States in 1910, she found Susan B. Anthony's bill granting women the right to vote still stalled in a congressional committee. Even though Anthony had submitted her bill in 1896, American women still lacked "The Franchise." Paul concluded that the situation in America called for drastic measures.

Paul persuaded the National-American Woman Suffrage Association (NAWSA) to allow her to coordinate its lobbying effects in Congress and promptly organized a huge march on the White House backed by a suffrage army estimated at a half-million people. Her dramatic entrance into Washington politics duly impressed the new president, Woodrow Wilson, whose inauguration occurred the next day. Immediately after the opening of the new Congress, Paul employed her aggressive tactics on the returning politicians in order to secure the Anthony Bill's release from committee to the floor of the House of Representatives. It would have been an overwhelming task for any lobbyist. Given Paul's extreme shyness, introverted Quaker personality, and lack of rhetorical skills, the bill that Congress passed, the president signed, and the states ratified became a signal triumph for her organizational genius.

During World War I, Paul quickly became the radical leader of the feminist movement. First, she changed NAWSA's lobbying focus from the states to the national legislature. She became a public relations expert at a time in history when such experts were rare. Paul's training in British circles enabled her to overcome opposition from the Washington, D.C., police, who wanted her marchers to parade on Sixteenth Street in front of the foreign embassies (instead of picketing the White

House). She stood her ground, insisting that the ladies must be seen by President and Mrs. Wilson. She won the debate—the first of many such victories resulting in the ratification of the Nineteenth Amendment to the Constitution.

In 1917, when the United States declared war on Germany and President Wilson declared that the "world must be made safe for democracy," Paul decided that the time was right for another parade and picketing of the White House. "Why should American women support the war to make the world safe for democracy," her pickets emphatically asked, "when they have no democracy since they cannot vote?" When the White House called the police, Paul and her loyal "soldiers," facing arrest and imprisonment, followed tactics learned in England and refused to eat. Force-fed by law enforcement officials afraid of the possible public outcry produced by the hospitalization or death of a suffragist, Paul turned that tactic as well to the advantage of her cause.

Not everyone in the suffrage movement approved of Paul's tactics. More radical than the mainstream NAWSA's moderate leadership, she organized the National Woman's Party in 1913. The Quaker activist incorporated the party on September 20, 1918, but kept it largely inactive until the passage of the Nineteenth Amendment became a certainty.

After the Congress and the states approved woman suffrage, Paul reactivated the National Woman's Party in 1921. Although most women perhaps believed that equal rights would result automatically from the ratification of the Nineteenth Amendment, Paul and her colleagues remained unconvinced.

The principal philosophical ideas Paul wrote into the National Woman's Party platform reflected her skepticism that voting rights would lead to equal rights. Women, she argued, would no longer constitute the "governed half" of the American people. In the future, they would participate equally in all aspects of life.

The National Woman's Party organized most of the serious agitation—such as jail-ins, marches, fasts, and picketing—that occurred before the ratification of the Nineteenth Amendment. When ratification occurred, the more moderate NAWSA transformed itself into the League of Women Voters. Paul, however, believed that the battle would not be over until equal rights had been achieved for all Americans, regardless of sex.

For Alice Paul, true freedom extended far beyond the simple attainment of suffrage. She single-mindedly pursued the goal of removing all legal obstacles for women throughout the United States. After careful consideration and examination of the tactics and strategies that won the battle for woman suffrage, she concluded that the only means to legal equality was the passage of a federal Equal Rights Amendment (ERA). This was an extremely radical idea when Paul introduced it in 1923 at Seneca Falls, New York, where the first women's rights convention had been held in 1848. The central point she expressed focused on the philosophy that women would never be subjugated again "in law or in custom, but shall in every way be on an equal plane in rights." In this way, her Woman's Party gave birth to the Equal Rights Amendment.

Paul's proposed amendment split the women's movement. Some women believed that voting rights naturally would produce equality, making a second amendment unnecessary. Since the ERA radically redefined power relationships between men and women, even stronger opposition than originally existed to the Nineteenth Amendment developed within the male establishment.

Critics dismissed Paul as either a harmless but misguided "bleeding heart liberal" or a dangerously deranged radical. Democrats and Republicans alike warned the public against being receptive to her ideas. As the nation turned more conservative during the 1920's, with the election of President Warren Harding and the widespread repudiation of progressivism, the popularity of Alice Paul and her party declined, and she did not resurface as a significant force until the reintroduction of the ERA in 1972.

Following Paul's creation of the National Woman's Party and the introduction of the Equal Rights Amendment, the popularity of women's rights declined in the United States during the Depression of the 1930's. As the fight for jobs excluded more and more American women, Alice took her campaign to Europe, where she founded the World's Woman's Party. Since Paul always expressed strong opposition to the League of Nations' failure to allow female political participation, she continued her lobbying efforts on behalf of women until the organization collapsed during World War II. When the League gave way to the United Nations, Paul played a key role in introducing an equal rights provision in the preamble to the U.N. charter.

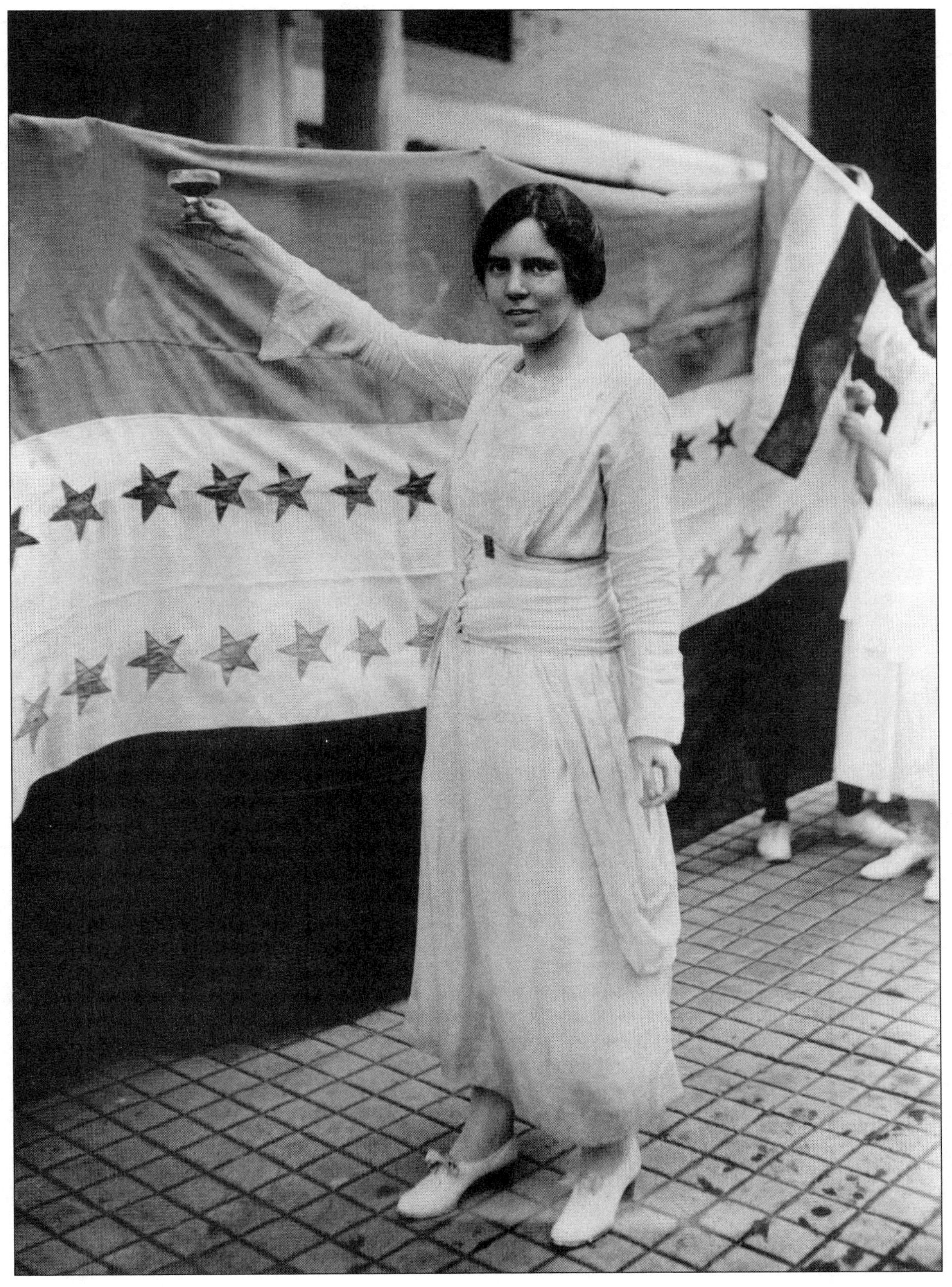

Following Paul's European experiment, she returned to the United States, where she resumed her efforts to pass the new, revamped Equal Rights Amendment. During the late 1960's, Paul campaigned against the Vietnam War while working for the ERA. Still marching and fighting for equal rights at the age of eighty-five, she finally surrendered to old age and moved to a Quaker nursing home in her native Moores-town, New Jersey, where America's great radical feminist died on July 10, 1977, at the age of ninety-two. She never lived to see the passage of the amendment to which she had devoted her entire life.

### Summary

Few leaders in the politics of women's liberation were more significant than Alice Paul. Her longevity and radical proclivities outdistanced others who garnered more press and historical notice. For sixty-five years, from 1912 until her death in 1977, Paul stood ready to give her best to the cause of equal rights.

Despite her reputation for radical measures, Paul was not an abrasive personality. Although some thought her insensitive, perhaps what they perceived was the absent-mindedness of an intellectual who received her Ph.D. in sociology in 1912, before she launched her suffrage career. She understood both the politics and the economics of equal rights. The real struggle, she once argued, would not be won in state or even national legislatures. Women would have to win economically before they could win politically. Political forms would crystallize, she hypothesized, only when women had gained economic power. More important, she emphasized that having money was not enough. Knowing how to use money to attain political ends was the key.

Paul was not as well known as other feminists of her day—Susan B. Anthony, Lucretia Mott, and Elizabeth Cady Stanton. Her strategies and tactics, however, have since been considered to have been paramount in obtaining the Nineteenth Amendment to the Constitution. Although she died without realizing victory in her struggle to institute the Equal Rights Amendment, many of the goals she sought came to pass nevertheless, partly because of the half-century of supreme effort she exerted in order to realize her great dream.

### Bibliography

Barker-Benfield, G. J., and Catherine Clinton. *Portraits of American Women: From Settlement to the Present*. New York: St. Martin's Press, 1991; London: Oxford University Press, 1998. A collection of scholarly articles on significant American women from Pocahontas to Betty Friedan. The article on Alice Paul by Christine A. Lunardini presents a particularly effective analysis.

Becker, Susan D. *The Origins of the Equal Rights Amendment: American Feminism Between the Wars*. Westport, Conn.: Greenwood Press, 1981. An analysis of Paul's postsuffrage role in reorganizing the women's movement along the international lines of the World's Woman's Party.

Flexner, Eleanor. *Century of Struggle: The Woman's Rights Movement in the United States*. Rev. ed. Cambridge, Mass.: Belknap Press of Harvard University Press, 1975. A classic history of the women's movement (highlighting Alice Paul's role) by one of the great feminist historians.

Gallagher, Robert S. "I Was Arrested, of Course . . ." *American Heritage* 25, no. 2 (February, 1974): 16-24, 92-94. A fascinating and penetrating interview conducted with Paul three years before her death.

Irwin, Inez Haynes. *The Story of Alice Paul and the National Woman's Party*. Fairfax, Va.: Denlinger's, 1977. This is the primary history of the National Woman's Party.

Morgan, David. *Suffragists and Democrats: The Politics of Woman Suffrage in America*. East Lansing: Michigan State University Press, 1972. This is a narrow British interpretation of the politics of the American woman suffrage movement.

Stevens, Doris. *Jailed for Freedom*. New York: Boni and Liveright, 1920. This primary source focuses on the militant feminists who campaigned for the vote between 1913 and 1919. The work includes a valuable chapter on "General Alice Paul."

Thomas, M. "How We Didn't Get There." *Ms.* 1, no. 5 (March/April, 1991). Thomas considers the obstacles to ratification of the Equal Rights Amendment and includes information on Alice Paul.

*J. Christopher Schnell*

# WOLFGANG PAULI

*Born:* April 25, 1900; Vienna, Austria
*Died:* December 14, 1958; Zurich, Switzerland
*Area of Achievement:* Physics
*Contribution:* Pauli's discovery of the exclusion principle, which asserts the individuality of electrons, revolutionized atomic physics. He is also responsible for the electron theory of metals, which led to the development of transistors, and for proposing the existence of neutrinos.

## Early Life

Wolfgang Pauli was born on April 25, 1900, in Vienna, Austria. His father, also named Wolfgang, was a distinguished professor of colloid physics at the University of Vienna. Although Pauli received his formal education in the Viennese school system, he was also informally instructed by his father, who often discussed questions relating to physics with his son. Because of his proficiency in higher mathematics, he read such works as Camille Jordan's *Cours d'analyse* (1882) during dull classroom periods in high school. Yet it was Albert Einstein's theory of relativity that had the most profound effect on Pauli's development. Once he was satisfied that he understood Einstein's theory and had acquired an adequate background in classical physics, he decided to embark on a career as a physicist.

When he was nineteen, Pauli enrolled at the University of Munich. His mentor at this time was Arnold Sommerfeld, the most prestigious teacher of theoretical physics in Germany. Under Sommerfeld's supervision, Pauli acquired the analytical skills that he was to put to good use years later. At the age of twenty, Pauli was assigned the task of submitting an article on relativity theory for the *Encyklopädie der mathematischen Wissenschaften* (encyclopedia of mathematical knowledge). Pauli's article became a 250-page monograph which is both an informative introduction to relativity theory and a history of the mathematical foundations of the theory. The art with which Pauli presented science in this early work was to characterize everything that he wrote thereafter.

At the same time that he was working on the relativity theory, Pauli also became familiar with the quantum theory at the University of Munich. He was strongly influenced by the different approaches to the structure of the atom to which Sommerfeld had introduced him. Whereas Niels Bohr's theory attempted to reconcile the differences between the laws of quantum theory, Sommerfeld's theory tried to interpret atomic phenomena through the direct application of integral numbers. The revolutionary nature of quantum theory was quite shocking to someone such as Pauli, who had been steeped in classical physics.

In 1921, Pauli became an assistant in theoretical physics at the University of Göttingen. Not only did he meet the noted physicists Max Born and James Franck, who were teaching there at the time, but also he came into personal contact with Bohr, who delivered a series of lectures there in 1922. Pauli was particularly impressed with Bohr's attempts to explain why electrons in an atom are distributed in definite groups throughout the atom's structure instead of clustering within the shell closest to the nucleus.

## Life's Work

After obtaining his doctorate, Pauli immediately initiated the projects from which emerged his most significant hypothesis. In 1922, Pauli tried to explain why the spectrum lines of atoms do not always split into three lines when exposed to a strong magnetic field. After spending considerable time probing this phenomenon, known as the Zeeman effect, Pauli postulated that the quantum properties of the atomic core were permanent. This theory had far-reaching consequences, both for Pauli's own research and for the field of physics in general, because it suggested that every electron could be described by quantum numbers. Pauli was not any closer to solving the Zeeman effect a year later, when he went to the University of Hamburg as an assistant in theoretical physics. Soon after his arrival there, he was promoted to the position of assistant professor, and he spent the next few months reexamining the standard explanations for the anomalous splitting of the spectrum lines.

In 1925, Pauli's research culminated in an argument that he proposed in an article in *Zeitschrift für Physik* (periodical for physics). In this article, he stated that a new quantum theoretic property of the electron was necessary before the Zeeman effect could be properly understood. The publication of this opinion gave him the resolve he needed to complete his research into the phenomenon. That same year, Pauli discovered the final clue to the problem's solution in a paper by the English physicist Edmund Stoner. By way of explaining Stoner's

rule, Pauli developed his famous exclusion principle, which states that no two electrons can have the same energy in an atom. Pauli's description of the exclusion principle in the *Handbuch der Physik* (handbook of physics) in 1926 paved the way for the development of mathematically consistent quantum mechanics through research conducted by Werner Karl Heisenberg, P. A. M. Dirac, and Erwin Schrödinger.

Pauli left Hamburg in 1928 to assume the position of professor of theoretical physics at the Federal Institute for Technology in Zurich, Switzerland, which became his home for the next twelve years. Together with his friend George Wentzel, a professor at the University of Zurich, Pauli taught a seminar for many years in which all areas of theoretical physics were discussed. During his first ten years in Zurich, he was fortunate enough to have students such as R. Kronig, Rudolf Peierls, H. B. G. Casimir, and V. F. Weisskopf as his assistants, all of whom later went on to become prominent physicists in their own right.

While Pauli was in Zurich, he produced one of his most important theories, the neutrino hypothesis. In a letter that he wrote to Lise Meitner in 1930, he reported that a neutron is emitted along with an electron when certain subatomic particles decay. Although Enrico Fermi later christened this neutron the "neutrino," it is also referred to in some circles as the "Paulino," since Pauli made this observation before Sir James Chadwick had discovered the neutron in the nucleus. Pauli published his proposal in the report of the Solvay Congress in 1933.

Much of Pauli's research in this period was also devoted to the development of relativistic quantum electrodynamics in an effort to explain the infinite self-energy of the electron. This work led Pauli into a study of wave mechanics. In an article Pauli wrote for *Handbuch der Physik* in 1933, he expanded the scope of wave mechanics to include not only a single particle but the interaction of an indefinite number of particles as well.

In the late 1930's, Pauli's work began to take him away from Zurich. Between 1935 and 1936, he was appointed visiting professor of theoretical physics at the Institute for Advanced Study in Princeton, New Jersey. Then, in 1940, the Institute for Advanced Study once again summoned him to Princeton, largely because of the Nazi invasion of Norway and Denmark. In 1945, while he was still a temporary member of the institute's faculty, Pauli received a Lorentz Medaille and, later, the Nobel Prize in Physics.

In 1946, at the end of the war, Pauli returned to Zurich with his wife, Franciska, whom he had married in April, 1934. He spent the remainder of his life in a heavily forested area called "Zollikon," where he often took long walks. During this time, he also became a Swiss citizen.

In the last years of his life, Pauli began to reflect seriously on the meaning of scientific activity; this new interest manifested itself in a number of essays, lectures, and a book coauthored with C. G. Jung—*Naturerklärung und Psyche* (1952). He even looked to Chinese philosophy for answers. Actually, though, Pauli had hoped all along that physics would reveal the harmony between God and nature. Pauli became seriously ill in December, 1958, and he died on December 14.

### Summary

Wolfgang Pauli's impact on the world of physics can be traced to the scientific method that he employed throughout his career. His solid background in classical physics, which he had acquired from his father and from his own reading, became the standard against which he weighed all hypotheses, his own as well as those of others. As a student at the University of Munich, Pauli was willing to exchange some of the principles of classical physics for the quantum theory of Niels Bohr and Sommerfeld only after he was convinced that quantum theory could solve some of the mysteries of the atom, such as the Zeeman effect. For the most part, though, his classical training acted as a buffer, protecting him from obscure argument and superficial speculation.

Pauli's research laid the foundation for a new physics at the same time that it was shaking the very foundation of the old. His exclusion principle demonstrated the individuality of electrons and thus solved a problem—the Zeeman effect—that had puzzled physicists since Pieter Zeeman first observed it in 1892. The principles of relativistic quantum electrodynamics, which had been the focus of much of Pauli's work, were finally accepted after twenty years of skepticism and inquiry. Pauli's discovery of the neutrino set the stage for further investigations by Sir James Chadwick and Enrico Fermi. Finally, his hypothesis for the permanence of quantum numbers permitted the development of a periodic table.

Yet Pauli's influence goes beyond physics. His concern with finding an ethical basis for scientific inquiry had a lasting effect on both his students and his colleagues. He was truly, as Victor Weisskopf eulogized at Pauli's funeral, "the conscience of theoretical physics."

### Bibliography

"Atom Bomb Nobelists." *Science News Letter* 48 (December 1, 1945): 141-142. Announces the awarding of the Nobel Prize in Physics in 1945 to Wolfgang Pauli. Explains very clearly what Pauli meant by the "rugged individualism" of electrons.

*Current Biography: Who's Who and Why.* New York: Wilson, 1947. A short but fairly detailed account of Pauli's life and work. A very good introduction to his career.

Fierz, Marcus. "Wolfgang Pauli." In *Dictionary of Scientific Biography*, vol. 10. New York: Scribner, 1974. An excellent account of Pauli's most important hypotheses and their impact on the field of physics. The entry also discusses Pauli's philosophical views regarding science. The scientific sections are fairly technical and would, therefore, appeal to a reader with a solid background in physics.

Fierz, Marcus, and V. F. Weisskopf, eds. *Theoretical Physics in the Twentieth Century: A Memorial Volume to Wolfgang Pauli.* New York: Interscience, 1960. Contains a series of articles ranging from first-person accounts from Pauli's coworkers to a complete listing of Pauli's books, articles, and studies. Provides useful insights into Pauli's personality as well as short, technical discussions of his theories, some of which are in German.

Goudsmit, S. A. "Pauli and Nuclear Spin." *Physics Today*, June, 1961: 18-21. Written by one of Pauli's colleagues, the article disputes Pauli's contention that Goudsmit and Ernst Back had been influenced by a paper of Pauli published in 1924 regarding the angular momentum of the atomic nucleus.

Laurikainen, Kalervo V. *The Message of the Atoms: Essays on Wolfgang Pauli and the Unspeakable.* New York: Springer, 1997. The author considers the subject of quantum mechanics, using Pauli's writings as basis for analysis.

"The Weight of the Evidence." *Economics* 334, no. 7901 (February 11, 1995). This article focuses on the neutrino.

*Alan Brown*

# LINUS PAULING

*Born:* February 28, 1901; Portland, Oregon
*Died:* August 19, 1994; Big Sur, California
*Areas of Achievement:* Chemistry, biology, medicine, and world peace
*Contribution:* Pauling is the only person to have won two unshared Nobel Prizes, and these prizes, in chemistry and in peace, symbolize his contributions. In the 1930's and 1940's his scientific discoveries helped to make the United States an important center for structural chemistry and molecular biology. In the 1950's and 1960's his activities in the peace movement helped to mobilize the American public against the atmospheric testing of nuclear weapons.

## Early Life

Linus Carl Pauling was born in Portland, Oregon, on February 28, 1901, the son of Herman William Pauling and Lucy Isabelle (Darling). His mother was a daughter of Oregon pioneers who could trace their ancestry in America to the seventeenth century. His father's family was German and had come to the United States after the revolutionary upheavals of 1848 in Europe. During childhood, Pauling and his two younger sisters led a peripatetic existence as their father, a traveling drug salesman, tried to find a position that suited him. The family eventually settled in Condon, Oregon, where, in a two-room schoolhouse, Linus' education began. Life in Condon proved to be financially unrewarding, however, and in 1909, the Paulings moved back to Portland. Shortly after settling in a new drugstore, Herman died suddenly of a perforated gastric ulcer. He was only thirty-two years old.

Herman's death created severe difficulties for the family. Linus became a shy adolescent who spent most of his time reading. His intellectual energies also found an outlet in schoolwork, and he moved at an accelerated pace through Portland's individualized grammar-school system and through Washington High School. The most important event of this period occurred when Lloyd Jeffress, a friend, showed him how sulfuric acid could turn white sugar into a steaming mass of black carbon. So excited was Linus by what he saw that he decided then and there to become a chemist.

Pauling was able to pursue a career as a chemical engineer at Oregon Agricultural College by working at various jobs during the school year and in the summer. Because of the need to support his mother, he was forced to interrupt his education for a year and teach quantitative analysis. This hiatus gave him time to read science journals, and he came across papers on the chemical bond by Irving Langmuir and Gilbert Newton Lewis. These papers provoked his lifelong interest in chemical bonding and structure. In his senior year, he met Ava Helen Miller, a freshman in the general chemistry class he was teaching. At first she was not attracted to this curly-haired, blue-eyed young man who was "so full of himself," and Pauling, though attracted to her, was reluctant to show it because of his position as a teacher. After the course was over, and by the time of Pauling's graduation from college in 1922, they were very much in love.

Pauling's graduate career took place at the California Institute of Technology (CIT) in Pasadena, where three professors, Arthur A. Noyes, Roscoe G. Dickinson, and Richard C. Tolman, helped to shape his career. Noyes acted as Pauling's father figure, and behind the scenes he made sure that his protégé remained a chemist (Pauling was being tempted by theoretical physics). Dickinson trained Pauling in X-ray diffraction, a technique for discovering the three-dimensional structures of crystals. Tolman was Pauling's mentor in theoretical physics. After a successful year at CIT, Pauling returned to Oregon to marry Ava Miller. She returned with him to Pasadena, where they began a close relationship that continued until her death fifty-seven years later.

After receiving his Ph.D. from CIT in 1925, Pauling spent a brief period as a National Research Fellow in Pasadena. He was then awarded a Guggenheim Fellowship to study quantum mechanics in Europe. He spent most of his year and a half abroad at Arnold Sommerfeld's Institute for Theoretical Physics in Munich, but he also spent a month at Niels Bohr's institute in Copenhagen and a few months in Zurich. Upon his return to California in 1927, Pauling began a career as teacher and researcher at CIT that would last for thirty-six years.

## Life's Work

Structure was the central theme of Pauling's scientific work. Most of his early research focused on the determination of the structures of molecules, first by directing X-rays at crystals, later by directing electron beams at gas molecules. As these X-rays and electron techniques provided Pauling with experimental tools for discovering molecular structures, so quantum mechanics gave him a theoretical tool. For example, he used quantum mechanics to explain why the carbon atom forms equivalent bonds. In 1939, he wrote about many of his structural discoveries in *The Nature of the Chemical Bond and the Structure of Molecules and Crystals*, one of the most influential scientific books of the twentieth century.

Pauling's interest in biological molecules began in the 1930's with his studies of the hemoglobin molecule, whose striking red color and property of combining with oxygen appealed to him. Interest in hemoglobin led naturally to an interest in proteins, and with Alfred Mirsky he published a paper on the general theory of protein structure in which they suggested that proteins had coiled configurations that were stabilized by weak intermolecular forces and hydrogen bonds.

On one of Pauling's visits to the Rockefeller Institute to visit Mirsky, he met Karl Landsteiner, the discoverer of blood types, who introduced him to another field—antibodies. Pauling's first paper on antibody structure appeared in 1940. During World War II, his work shifted toward practical problems, for example, the discovery of an artificial substitute for blood serum. This was only part of the extensive work that he did for the government. He also invented an oxygen detector, a device that depended on oxygen's special magnetic properties and that found wide use in airplanes and submarines. He also spent much time studying explosives and rocket propellants. At the end of the war, he became interested in sickle-cell anemia, which, he speculated, might be a molecular disease caused by an abnormal hemoglobin molecule. Working with Harvey Itano, Pauling showed in 1949 that this indeed was the case.

While a guest professor at Oxford University in 1948, Pauling returned to a problem that had occupied him in the late 1930's—to find precisely how the chain of amino acids in proteins is coiled. By folding a piece of paper on which he had drawn such a chain, he discovered the alpha helix, a configuration of turns held together by hydrogen bonds, with each turn having a nonintegral number of amino-acid groups. Pauling and Robert B. Corey published a description of the helical structure of proteins in 1950, and this structure was soon verified experimentally.

During the early 1950's, Pauling became interested in deoxyribonucleic acid (DNA), and in February, 1953, he and Corey published a structure for DNA that contained three twisted, ropelike strands. Shortly thereafter, James Watson and Francis Crick published the double-helix structure, which turned out to be correct. Watson and Crick profited from X-ray photographs of DNA taken by Rosalind Franklin, a research tool denied Pauling because of the refusal of the United States State Department to grant him a passport for foreign travel. He was finally given a passport when he received the 1954 Nobel Prize for Chemistry for his research into the nature of the chemical bond.

With the heightened publicity given him by the Nobel Prize, Pauling began to devote more of his attention to humanitarian issues connected with science. For example, he became increasingly involved in the debate over nuclear fallout and in the movement against nuclear-bomb testing. In 1958, he and his wife presented a petition signed by more than eleven thousand scientists from around the world to Dag Hammarskjöld, secretary-general of the United Nations. Pauling defended his petition before a congressional subcommittee in 1960, and he risked going to jail by refusing to turn over his correspondence with those who helped to circulate the petition. For all these efforts, he was awarded the Nobel Peace Prize for 1962 on October 10, 1963, the day that the partial nuclear test-ban treaty went into effect.

Through the mid-1960's, Pauling was a staff member at the Center for the Study of Democratic Institutions (CSDI). He had left CIT primarily because of the negative reaction of many members of the CIT community to his peace efforts, and in Santa Barbara he hoped to be able to work effectively in both areas, science and peace. While at CSDI, he participated in discussions on peace and politics, and he proposed a new model of the atomic nucleus in which protons and neutrons were arranged in clusters.

Pauling left Santa Barbara in 1967 to become research professor of chemistry at the University of California at San Diego, where he published a paper on orthomolecular psychiatry that explained how mental health could be achieved by manipulating the concentrations of substances normally present in the body. During this time, Pauling's interest became centered on a particular molecule—ascorbic acid (vitamin C). He examined the published evidence about vitamin C and came to the conclusion that ascorbic acid, provided that it is taken in large enough quantities, helps the body fight off colds and other diseases. The eventual outcome of Pauling's work was the book *Vitamin C and the Common Cold*, published in 1970, while he was a professor at Stanford University. This interest in vitamin C in particular and orthomolecular medicine in general led to his founding in 1973 the institute that now bears his name: the Linus Pauling Institute of Science and Medicine. During his tenure at the institute, Pauling was involved in a controversy about the relative benefits and dangers of the ingestion of large amounts of vitamins. In the early 1970's, he became interested in using vitamin C for the treatment of cancer, largely through his contact with the Scottish physician Dr. Ewan Cameron. Their collaboration resulted in a book, *Cancer and Vitamin C* (1979), in which they marshaled evidence for the effectiveness of vitamin C against cancer. In the 1980's Pauling obtained financial support to have his ideas about vitamin C and cancer tested experimentally in his own laboratory as well as in the laboratories of the Mayo Clinic. Positive results were obtained in animal studies at the Linus Pauling Institute, but negative results were obtained with human cancer patients in two Mayo Clinic studies, and so the controversy remained unresolved.

### Summary

Throughout his life Pauling saw himself as a Westerner, with a strong belief in those values that Frederick Jackson Turner called the "traits of the frontier": self-sufficiency, strength combined with inquisitiveness, a masterful grasp of material things, restless nervous energy, and love of nature and hard work. One can see these traits in Pauling's scientific work, as his curiosity drove him from one area to another. He liked to work on the frontiers of knowledge, not in crowded fields, and many of his greatest discoveries occurred in the area between disciplines—between chemistry and physics, chemistry and biology, chemistry and medicine.

A master showman, Pauling cleverly fought for the recognition of his ideas. He was passionate in defending his scientific views, even when most of his colleagues did not accept them, as in his ideas about vitamin C. Despite his involvement in many scientific controversies, scientists have recognized the overwhelming importance of his contributions. On the occasion of Pauling's eighty-fifth birthday, Crick called him "the greatest chemist in the world." When Pauling was born, chemistry was a discipline dominated by Europeans, mainly Germans. Pauling's work symbolized and helped to make real the dominance of chemistry by Americans.

Pauling's influence on America was not restricted to chemistry. J. D. Bernal stated that if one person could be given credit for the foundation of molecular biology, that person would be Linus Pauling. Another field—molecular medicine—was created by Pauling's discovery of the first molecular disease, sickle-cell anemia. Besides helping revolutionize and found several scientific disciplines, Pauling had a major influence on American society through his many speeches and writings on peace. He helped to change the climate of American public opinion on nuclear weapons, which made the 1963 test-ban treaty possible. In fact, he was prouder of his efforts on behalf of peace than he was of his scientific accomplishments. Yet he did not see these contributions as separate: They were both part of his single-minded quest for truth.

### Bibliography

Davenport, Derek A. "Letters to F. J. Allen: An Informal Portrait of Linus Pauling." *Journal of*

*Chemical Education* 73, no. 1 (January, 1996). Profile of Pauling drawing from his correspondence with Frederick J. Allen.

Judson, Horace Freeland. *The Eighth Day of Creation: Makers of the Revolution in Biology.* London: Cape, and New York: Simon and Schuster, 1979. The story of molecular biology told mainly in the words of the people who created it. Judson interviewed Pauling, and the book contains a good account of Pauling's work in molecular biology.

Kauffman, George B., and Laurie M. Kauffman. "An Interview with Linus Pauling." *Journal of Chemical Education* 73, no. 1 (January, 1996). Interview in which Pauling discusses his greatest achievements.

Olby, Robert. *The Path to the Double Helix.* London: Macmillan, and Seattle: University of Washington Press, 1974. In terms of scientific accuracy and objectivity, Olby's is probably the best historical account of the discovery of the double helix. The book has a good discussion of Pauling's research on the alpha helix and DNA.

Pauling, Linus. "Fifty Years of Progress in Structural Chemistry and Molecular Biology." *Daedalus* 99 (Fall, 1970): 988-1014. This article is also available in a book, *The Twentieth-Century Sciences: Studies in the Biography of Ideas*, edited by Gerald Holton (New York: Norton, 1972). The article contains the most extensive autobiographical reminiscences that Pauling has ever written. The emphasis is on his scientific work, and the account is intended for the general reader.

———. *The Nature of the Chemical Bond and the Structure of Molecules and Crystals: An Introduction to Modern Structural Chemistry.* 3d ed. Ithaca, N.Y.: Cornell University Press, 1960. Pauling's magnum opus, and the best summary of his work in structural chemistry. The book is intended for students of chemistry, and it has become a classic.

———. *No More War!* New York: Dodd Mead, and London: Gollancz, 1958. The best extended treatment of Pauling's thinking about war, nuclear weapons, and peace. This edition contains an addendum to each chapter in which Pauling reflects on the changes, for better or worse, that have occurred in the quarter century since the first edition.

Pauling, Linus, and Roger Hayward. *The Architecture of Molecules.* San Francisco: Freeman, 1964. This book gives an excellent introduction to Pauling's structural imagination. Roger Hayward was a distinguished scientific illustrator, and the book has fifty-seven full-color illustrations of molecular structures accompanied by Pauling's clear and incisive discussions.

Rich, Alexander, and Norman Davidson, eds. *Structural Chemistry and Molecular Biology: A Volume Dedicated to Linus Pauling by His Students, Colleagues, and Friends.* San Francisco: Freeman, 1968. A festschrift for Pauling on his sixty-fifth birthday. J. H. Sturdivant's discussion of Pauling's scientific work is particularly good.

White, Florence Meiman. *Linus Pauling: Scientist and Crusader.* New York: Walker, 1980. This short biography is intended for young people ten years of age and older, but because it was written with the cooperation of Linus and Ava Helen Pauling, it contains some interesting anecdotes about and insights into the human side of its subject.

*Robert J. Paradowski*

# LUCIANO PAVAROTTI

*Born:* October 12, 1935; Modena, Italy
*Area of Achievement:* Music
*Contribution:* Possessing a rigorously trained voice of exceptional beauty, Pavarotti became the leading lyric tenor of his time and a musical superstar who reached a larger audience than any classical artist who preceded him.

## Early Life

Operatic tenor Luciano Pavarotti was born on October 12, 1935, in Modena, Italy. His father, Fernando, a baker with a strong tenor voice, sang as a soloist and a choir member with the local church but was too shy to attempt a singing career. Fernando collected recordings of his favorite singers, including the famed Italian tenors Enrico Caruso, Beniamino Gigli, Tito Schipa, and Mario del Monaco. His son would carry on the lyric legacy of these great singers. During his boyhood, Pavarotti was surrounded by doting girls and women who populated the modest apartment house in which his family lived. He was a particular favorite of his grandmother Giulia, who cared for him while his mother worked in a local cigar factory to supplement the family income. During World War II, the Pavarotti family faced dangers and privation, but on the whole, they led a normal life in wartime Italy.

An indifferent student at the local Modena school, Pavarotti was fond of sports and music, although his vocal talent was not generally recognized. At age twelve he attended a live concert by fifty-seven-year-old Gigli and was impressed by Gigli's discipline and dedication to practice. At age nineteen, Pavarotti considered whether to attend college in order to become a mathematics teacher or to prepare for a singing career. Though they were by no means affluent, his parents agreed to support him for ten years while he studied music and attempted to establish himself as a singer.

In 1954, Pavarotti secured a local voice teacher, Arrigo Pola, who worked with him intensively for two and one-half years on breathing technique, scales, and vocalizing. A promising pupil, Pavarotti applied himself and attempted to master the art of singing. He accepted the view that the tenor voice is not natural but is rather an artificial creation that requires rigorous discipline and careful nurturing in order to develop properly.

While his temporary jobs such as part-time teaching and insurance sales helped ease the financial burden on his family for a brief time, Pavarotti eventually found it necessary to devote all his energy toward developing his voice. After studying with Pola in Modena, he became the pupil of Ettore Campogalliani, who lived in nearby Reggio Emilia and who was also the teacher of the soprano Mirella Freni.

In 1961, Pavarotti began giving concerts; during that year, he won first place in a singing contest held in Reggio Emilia. The prize was the lead tenor role of Rodolfo in Giacomo Puccini's opera *La Bohème* (1869), scheduled for production at the Teatro Municipale in Reggio Emilia on April 29, 1961. Following a moderately successful debut, Pavarotti appeared in operas chiefly in Italian provincial towns over the next three years.

Before becoming a seasoned performer, Pavarotti experienced both disappointment and good fortune in his early recitals and operatic performances. At times his voice did not function well, whereas on other occasions it was comparable to the best tenor voices. At one performance, however, a talent agent who was interested in signing the baritone offered instead to become Pavarotti's agent after hearing the tenor for the first time. On other occasions, Pavarotti received encouragement from contemporary tenors Giuseppe di Stefano and Ferruccio Tagliavini and famed conductor Tullio Serafin.

## Life's Work

While singing in the Dublin Opera Company in 1963, Pavarotti received the break that led to stardom. The manager of England's Royal Opera Company, Covent Garden, believed it prudent to secure a backup singer for tenor di Stefano, whose voice had become somewhat inconsistent, and Pavarotti was chosen. Summoned to London, he assumed the role of Rodolfo in Puccini's *La Bohème* in the middle of a performance after di Stefano could not continue. He subsequently sang the role for three additional scheduled performances and was warmly received by the London audience.

After di Stefano canceled a live appearance on England's top televised variety show, Pavarotti was invited to sing to an audience that numbered in the millions. He sang with an especially good voice, and the event introduced him to the general public, as opposed to the few who attended operas. Similar media successes would be repeated many times over as he presented outdoor concerts before mass audiences and sang in televised galas and operatic performances.

Following these experiences, Pavarotti was selected by the leading soprano, Joan Sutherland, to sing tenor roles opposite her during a tour of Australia in 1965. Before leaving on tour, Pavarotti made his first American appearance. In Miami and Fort Lauderdale, Florida, Pavarotti and Sutherland starred in Gaetano Donizetti's *Lucia di Lammermoor* (1835). The operas selected for performance on the tour offered tenor roles especially congenial to Pavarotti, the bel canto parts in operas by composers Vincenzo Bellini, Donizetti, and Giuseppe Verdi. Perhaps more important, Pavarotti improved his breathing technique by working with Sutherland.

After the successful Australian tour, Pavarotti began receiving invitations to sing worldwide and signed a lucrative contract with Decca Records for a series of recordings. His debut with the Metropolitan Opera in New York City in 1968 as Rodolfo in *La Bohème* was clouded by a case of the flu, which caused him to cancel several performances. Even so, the New York critics and audience were highly favorable in their responses. Four years later, he returned to the Metropolitan Opera in triumph, singing his famous role in Donizetti's *La Fille du régiment* (1840). He was to become a leading tenor at the Metropolitan Opera for more than twenty-five years, specializing in lyric roles.

Along with operatic performances, Pavarotti continued singing concerts and recitals worldwide, reaching huge audiences and travelling as far as Moscow, Russia, and Beijing, China. His repertoire included well-known arias, Italian songs, and sacred music. His highly successful recordings and television appearances brought what critics call "the Pavarotti sound" to millions who had never attended an opera or a live classical performance. His televised *Three Tenors Concert in Rome* (1990), made with colleagues José Carreras and Placido Domingo, broke all previous sales records for a classical program. Reprises of the event in Los Angeles (1994) and Paris (1998) repeated the spectacular success of the first event.

### Summary

The Pavarotti sound is unmistakable, a large-volume lyric tenor voice with an even vibration, slight nasality, and strength on every note in his range of more than two octaves. His delivery features precise tones; crisp, clear articulation; and an unbroken legato line. While he sometimes lengthens high notes to please the audience, his singing remains free of distracting mannerisms that marred the performance of such great singers as Gigli. At the same time, he is somewhat limited in color tones so that purity of tone takes precedence over emotional effect.

Always emphasizing practice, breathing technique, and vocal training, Pavarotti has been careful in selecting operatic roles suitable to his voice. This, combined with careful warmups before performances, has sustained his career for much longer than the normal tenor career. His inclination toward skillful covering of notes, barely noticeable in a voice as strong and precise as his, has also helped prolong his vocal career.

At the same time, the quality of his voice and an inclination toward caution have limited his versatility. Although he accepted the most challenging lyric roles and even sang roles so difficult that they had rarely been performed, he generally avoided the spinto and dramatic roles that require a heavier voice with tones darker than his. He declined offers to sing parts that he knew might damage his voice.

Yet during the latter part of his career he was willing to undertake carefully selected spinto and verismo roles.

Never known for his acting ability, Pavarotti has nonetheless always been a favorite with audiences, who respond to his warm personality as well as his art. Like other great singers, he realized that, if performed properly, emotion is conveyed by the music, not the acting. In live performance, he seems to give his all, whether the audience numbers a few hundred or several hundred thousand. This impression is enhanced by his larger-than-life physical presence that dominates the stage and by his habit of extending his large arms as if to embrace the audience. He is known for remaining hours after a performance to sign programs for eager fans, something that few artists have the inclination to do.

Pavarotti increased his popular appeal by singing light classical songs and appearing in films without compromising his vocal standards. It was his good fortune that throughout the peak years of his career, stereophonic and digital recordings were at a high level of technical excellence, and thus his recordings will preserve the full range of his talent. He will be remembered as the leading lyric tenor of the final third of the twentieth century and the most popular opera singer of his time.

**Bibliography**

Hastings, Stephen. "The Art of Luciano." *Opera News* 60 (April 13, 1996): 18-20. Hastings praises Pavarotti's vocal instrument and his musicality and assesses his appeal to mass audiences. The author concludes that audiences influence Pavarotti's singing style.

Kesting, Jürgen. *Luciano Pavarotti: The Myth of the Tenor.* Translated by Susan H. Ray. Boston: Northeastern University Press, 1996. Kesting's somewhat questionable thesis is that the art of tenor singing peaked in the late nineteenth century and was sustained through the period of Enrico Caruso, followed by a long decline. Kesting finds the superstar status of Pavarotti corrosive to art and stresses Pavarotti's limited range of nuanced singing and roles. However, in an extensive critique of the tenor's recordings, he finds more to praise than to blame.

Mayer, Martin. *Grandissimo Pavarotti.* New York: Doubleday, 1986; London: Hale, 1987. Offering a discography and a list of Pavarotti's opera appearances, concerts, and recitals, Mayer gives a highly informative account of the singer's career. In addition, he provides a brief history of tenor singing and places Pavarotti within the context of the tenor tradition, naming other past and present stars. Numerous illustrations.

Pavarotti, Adua. *Pavarotti: Life with Luciano.* London: Weidenfeld and Nicolson, and New York: Rizzoli, 1992. This richly illustrated book by the tenor's wife of many years offers a glimpse of his home life in his native land and clarifies the demands of his career on his family. Useful perspective on the tenor's personality, domestic life, and interactions with others.

Pavarotti, Luciano, and William Wright. *Pavarotti: My Own Story.* New York: Doubleday, 1981. This book is an account of Pavarotti's life and career in his own words that offers his reflections on the art of singing. It also includes chapters about the tenor written by associates, friends, and colleagues.

———. *Pavarotti: My World.* New York: Crown, and London: Chatto and Windus, 1995. This second book by the famous tenor is both inspirational and sentimental and offers the reader a rare glimpse of the singer's love of life.

Remnick, David. "The Last Italian Tenor." *The New Yorker* 69 (June 21, 1993): 36-46. Remnick explores Pavarotti's repertoire and place within the world of opera, finding him the essential Italian tenor. He laments the commercialism surrounding the singer and finds him on the decline.

*Stanley Archer*

## IVAN PETROVICH PAVLOV

*Born:* September 26, 1849; Ryazan, Russia
*Died:* February 27, 1936; Leningrad, U.S.S.R.
*Areas of Achievement:* Physiology and medicine
*Contribution:* Pavlov is best known for developing the theory of conditioned reflexes, which he demonstrated by teaching a dog to salivate when it heard a bell. He also performed important experiments to determine the connection between human behavior and the nervous system; he won the Nobel Prize in Physiology or Medicine in 1904 for his work on the digestive tract.

### Early Life

Ivan Petrovich Pavlov was born on September 26, 1849, in Ryazan, Russia, the eldest son of parents of peasant stock. His father, Peter Dmitrievich Pavlov, was a village priest, who emphasized family, hard work, reading, and education. His mother, Varvara Ivanovna Pavlov, supported his father in these efforts. Pavlov was born into a large family of eleven children, six of whom died in childhood.

Pavlov's education began when he was seven years old; at home, he was taught to read and write. When he was ten years old, he had an accident that weakened him physically, and the effects of the accident lasted throughout the remainder of his childhood. When he was eleven years of age, his parents entered him in the second grade at the local parish school to begin his formal education. Four years later, in 1864, he entered the theological seminary of Ryazan, where he received a classical education of the day in preparation for the priesthood. It was there that he developed his first genuine interest in science. In 1870, he decided not to become a priest and left the seminary to enroll at the University of St. Petersburg, where he studied science. There he pursued inorganic chemistry, organic chemistry, and physiology under such renowned professors as Dmitry Mendeleyev, Aleksandr Butlerov, and Ilya Tsion.

Pavlov completed his studies at the University of St. Petersburg in 1875 and entered the Medico-Chirurgical Academy (later renamed the Military Medical Academy), where he worked as a laboratory assistant while earning his medical degree. In 1877, he published his first work of substance; the subject was the control of blood circulation by reflexes. He completed his course of study and became a full physician in 1879 at thirty years of age. Four years later, in 1883, he completed his dissertation. In the meantime, he met and married Serafima Karchevokaya, a friend of Fyodor Dostoevski. Theirs was a good, supportive marriage.

### Life's Work

Pavlov's three main areas of investigation and physiological inquiry include blood circulation, food digestion, and conditioned reflexes. These three matters provide a convenient way of discussing his life's achievements, as he took these up in turn.

After completing his medical dissertation in 1883, Pavlov and his wife spent two years in Germany, where Pavlov studied cardiovascular physiology under Carl Ludwig and gastrointestinal physiology under Rudolf Heidenhain. Upon his return to St. Petersburg in 1886, Pavlov began his first major, sustained research; his efforts were directed to understanding cardiac physiology and regulating blood pressure. His success is greatly attributable to his surgical skills. Pavlov was able to enter a catheter into the femoral arteries of dogs and cats with little pain and no anesthesia; thus, he was able to observe and record the effects of various stimuli on the blood pressure of the animals. By working carefully and repeatedly, he was eventually able to determine which nerves controlled the pulsation and magnitude of the heartbeat. Dissection further assisted him in verifying his findings, as did the use of drugs, cutting nerves, and making permanent openings into the digestive tract.

At about the time Pavlov completed his work on blood circulation, he was appointed to a position at the Military Medical Academy, where he had earlier been a medical student. First, he served as an instructor of pharmacology; he then became director of a new surgical department of the school called the Institute of Experimental Medicine, where he conducted his scientific studies for the next several decades. To his credit, Pavlov was consistently humane in his treatment of his subjects, that is, his dogs and cats. His leadership provided for a system under which pain during surgery and other study was minimized, and the animals received the best of care after procedures were completed.

Pavlov had already been at work on the digestive tract before he finished his work on blood circulation. For some ten or twelve years after the formation of the Institute of Experimental Medicine under his direction in 1891, Pavlov and his researchers determined a number of things about

the digestive system. They were able to do so primarily because Pavlov perfected a surgical technique of creating a kind of separate stomach in dogs, which made it possible for investigators to monitor secretions and other activity of the digestive process. He was able to determine the function of nerves in controlling digestion, and he discerned a wealth of other information about processes of the alimentary canal. In 1888, he discovered the secretory nerves of the pancreas; in 1889, he studied the function and activity of other gastric glands. His work on digestion continued for decades, but in 1897 he published his findings on the principal digestive glands. This demonstrated existence of secretory nerves to the digestive tract resulted in Pavlov's receiving the Nobel Prize in Physiology or Medicine in 1904.

Pavlov and researchers under his guidance at the Institute of Experimental Medicine never discontinued their study of digestion. Yet at some point in the early 1900's, Pavlov became absorbed with the effects of the brain upon learned behavior. He became almost completely concerned with what came to be known as his theory of conditioned reflexes. Early in his career, Pavlov had realized that dogs would secrete saliva and other digestive fluids throughout the alimentary canal before they actually received food. He noticed this occurrence when dogs would hear the timely approach of laboratory assistants who might or might not be bringing food to the animals. In one of the most famous scientific experiments ever conducted, Pavlov trained (that is, he conditioned) dogs to salivate at the sound of a bell, when they learned that the bell indicated that food was soon coming. Some critics immediately dismissed his theory, or at least the relevance thereof, claiming that Pavlov had simply given terminology to what every dog trainer already knew. In general, though, Pavlov had demonstrated clearly that there is an explicit connection between physiological function and learned behavior, the ramifications of which have never been fully explained. His experiment, perhaps, left more of a mark on psychology than it did on physiology. In general, he showed that the theory of muscular reflexes of the nervous system could be expanded to include mental reflexes; thus, his experiments put forth the question as to what extent human behavior is controlled by learned mental patterns and responses.

Beginning in 1918 and for several years thereafter, Pavlov studied the behavior patterns of several mentally ill patients in an attempt to treat them. He believed he could alter the behavior of the insane by using a physiological method that primarily involved removing the patient from any physiological stimuli which might be considered harmful. In other words, insanity was treated with quiet and solitude.

At the end of his career, Pavlov used his beliefs about conditioned reflexes to explore the differences between mankind and animals. He came to regard human language itself as the most advanced and complicated form of conditioned reflex. He found both in mankind and among the animals a commonality in some matters of reflexes but not in all. Man is thus viewed as a kind of advanced species, different from other creatures primarily because the brain and nervous system accommodate more complicated, conditioned reflexes. Pavlov remained in general good health until 1935, when he first began to fall ill. He recovered somewhat to live until February 27 of the next year, when he died of pneumonia.

## Summary

Given the extreme advance of modern medicine in the second half of the twentieth century, Ivan

Petrovich Pavlov's discoveries about blood circulation and digestion seem to be rather basic, if not primitive, contributions to modern science. Such a judgment, however, does injustice to both Pavlov and his work. Readers should remember that in the late 1800's, medicine had only lately rediscovered that the blood circulates. For Pavlov to succeed in determining causes for both the rhythm and strength of the heartbeat was quite a feat in the medicine of his time. Pavlov's perfection of surgical techniques and his enthusiasm for studying the previously unexamined matter of digestion also qualify him as one of the great scientists of the twentieth century. His humane treatment of the animals that served as the subjects of his studies further adds credit to his name.

In his personal life, Pavlov must be repeatedly credited for doing what he believed was morally right regardless of consequences. In 1895, he had open conflict with his superior at the Military Medical Academy, and consequently his promotion from professor of pharmacology to professor of physiology was delayed for two years. His most noteworthy of moral actions occurred, however, in his resistance to the Communists after their rise to power in 1917. In 1922, because of a food shortage, Pavlov requested permission of Vladimir Ilich Lenin to relocate the Institute of Experimental Medicine abroad. Lenin denied the request but did offer Pavlov more food for himself. Angrily, Pavlov refused to accept the food until it was available for everybody working at the laboratory. He later publicly accused the Bolsheviks of conducting a social experiment with Communism, and he added that for the value of this experiment he would not sacrifice so much as a frog's hind leg; the statement became the most famous he ever uttered. In 1924, when the sons of priests were collectively expelled from the Military Medical Academy, Pavlov resigned from the Institute of Experimental Medicine, a division of that school, reminding the government that he, too, was the son of a priest. The government permitted these instances of resistance undoubtedly because it thought Pavlov's theories and research into human behavior would be useful for its own purposes. At the same time, Pavlov gradually mellowed toward the government and its policies, although he never joined the Communist Party.

Pavlov was wrong in thinking that psychology would eventually become a subset of physiology. This, however, does not undercut the validity of his theory of conditioned reflexes; nor does it diminish the effects of his own theories on later thinkers in other disciplines of study. Pavlov's works provided the foundation upon which the subsequent study of human behavior has been conducted. His methods and approaches, though not all of his theories, are still intact and in practice in research laboratories throughout the world.

## Bibliography

Babkin, Boris P. *Pavlov: A Biography.* Chicago: University of Chicago Press, 1949; London: Gollancz, 1951. Babkin, who was one of Pavlov's pupils, has provided one of the best biographies of Pavlov. Much of the biography is given to personal anecdote. Babkin also uses information gathered from A. A. Savich, one of Pavlov's colleagues, and Pavlov's widow.

Dewsbury, Donald A. "In Celebration of the Centennial of Ivan P. Pavlov's (1897/1902): 'The Work of the Digestive Glands.'" *American Psychologist* 52, no. 9 (September, 1997). Commemorates the 100th anniversary of the publication of Pavlov's work on digestion and its contribution to psychology.

Gantt, W. Horsley. "I. P. Pavlov: A Bibliographical Sketch." In *Lectures on Conditioned Reflexes*, by Ivan Petrovich Pavlov. Translated by W. Horsley Gantt. New York: International, and London: Lawrence and Wishart, 1928. Gantt, a friend and student of Pavlov, has written an excellent short biography of the scientist. Information about Pavlov's life is accurate and is provided in some detail. Modern readers of biography will not appreciate the patronizing, self-serving flavor of Gantt's approach.

———. "Physiology Since Pavlov." *The New Republic* 105 (1941): 728-731. In this article, Gantt traces developments in physiology in the five years following Pavlov's death. He reports on the connection between the amount of external stimulus and brain activity; he also takes up the formation of neuroses.

Grigorian, N. A. "Ivan Petrovich Pavlov." In *Dictionary of Scientific Biography*, edited by Charles Coulston Gillispie, vol. 10. New York: Scribner, 1974. After a brief biographical sketch, this article provides a straightforward account of Pavlov's work, emphasizing his methodological innovations. Strongly disputes the popular image of Pavlov as "a mechanist who saw complex behavior as the sum of individual conditioned reflexes." Includes a bibliography.

Pavlov, I. P. *Conditioned Reflexes: An Investigation of the Physiological Activity of the Cerebral Cortex*. Translated by G. V. Anrep. Oxford: Oxford University Press, and New York: Dover, 1927. Anrep's translation of Pavlov's work on conditioned reflexes is one of the best and most reliable available. Pavlov's own lectures, rendered into English here, remain the best introduction to the man and his life and theories. The book contains a rather extensive bibliography for those who would further study conditioned reflexes.

Straus, Erwin. *The Primary World of Senses*. Translated by Jacob Needleman. New York: Free Press, 1963. One of Straus's main objections to Pavlov's theories is that "man thinks, not the brain." The critic's perspective essentially is that of a psychologist.

Wells, Harry K. *Ivan P. Pavlov: Toward a Psychology and Psychiatry*. New York: International, 1956. Wells primarily treats Pavlov in the light of the theories of Sigmund Freud; he defines the roles of psychology and psychiatry in the context of theories presented by both thinkers.

Windholz, Goerge. "Pavlov's Conceptualization of the Dynamic Stereotype in the Theory of Higher Nervous Activity." *American Journal of Psychology* 109, no. 2 (Summer 1996). The author examines Pavlov's theory of higher nervous activity and its critics.

*Carl Singleton*

# ANNA PAVLOVA

*Born:* February 12, 1881; St. Petersburg, Russia
*Died:* January 23, 1931; The Hague, The Netherlands
*Area of Achievement:* Dance
*Contribution:* Pavlova was widely regarded as the greatest embodiment of ballet in her lifetime, and she became a symbol of the best the ballet has known after her death. She spread knowledge of and interest in ballet through her worldwide tours.

## Early Life

Anna Pavlovna Pavlova was born in St. Petersburg, on February 12, 1881. Her parents were poor, and her father died when she was only two. Her mother sent her to live in the country with her grandmother. In Ligovo, she led a simple life with a grandmother who was totally devoted to caring for her. Her favorite amusement was seeking flowers in the woods. She developed a deep love of nature and of this landscape in particular. When she was eight years old, her mother took her to see the ballet at the Maryinsky Theater. The performance of *La Belle au Bois Dormant* (Sleeping Beauty) captured her imagination, and she told her mother that she wanted to become a ballerina and dance that role. At Anna's insistence, her mother applied to the Imperial Theater School, but she was told they would take no children under ten. After waiting for two years, they applied again. She passed the examination and entered the school in 1891.

At the school, her teachers were Christian Johannsen, a former pupil and dancer of the Danish master, Auguste Bournonville, and Pavel Gerdt. She also studied with E. P. Sokolova, a former prima ballerina of the Maryinsky, and Enrico Cecchetti, the great Italian teacher. The Imperial Theater School gave instruction in general education and religion as well as dance. The full program took seven years to complete. In addition to ballet, the students learned historical and national dances and practiced long hours on their own. Pavlova was graduated and made her debut at the Maryinsky on June 1, 1899. She immediately moved into small parts rather than the *corps de ballet* and moved steadily through the ranks of the company from second soloist (1902) to first soloist (1903), ballerina (1905), and prima (1906). Before becoming a ballerina, she spent more time studying with Cecchetti to perfect her technique. By that time, she had appeared in all the major ballerina roles and had attracted a loyal following.

## Life's Work

Two of the great themes of Pavlova's life became apparent very early in her career. In 1907, she created the title role in *The Dying Swan*, choreographed by Michel Fokine, and in 1908, she began to tour abroad. Throughout her life, though she performed with companies and organized and led her own, she was best known for her solo and duet roles, in which her individual artistry as a performer shone clearly. Her tours throughout the world helped to make ballet universal and an international language of art.

In her early years as prima ballerina with the Maryinsky company, she created her major solo roles. In 1907, she premiered Fokine's *Pavillon d'Armide*, in 1908, *Egyptian Nights*, and also in 1908, Fokine's second version of *Chopiniana*. After she began to tour outside Russia in 1908, she remained a member of the Maryinsky company but spent continually less time there. Eventually, she would return only after long tours and would study again with her teachers to refresh her technique. Her performances at the Maryinsky ended when she officially left the company in 1913.

Her first foreign tour took her to Scandinavia, Leipzig, Prague, and Vienna. She was immediately successful and acclaimed wherever she performed. In Stockholm, young men unharnessed the horses from her carriage and led it back to her hotel themselves—a tribute paid to only a few nineteenth century ballerinas and an exuberant beginning to her international career. In 1909, she performed with Sergei Diaghilev's company, the Ballets Russes, in Paris. She made her debut in Berlin, in 1909, and in New York and London, in 1910, all with the Ballets Russes. Her last appearance with Diaghilev's company was in London, in 1911. London was to be her home; in 1912, she and her husband, Victor Dandré, purchased Ivy House on Hampstead Hill. She had a particular love for the gardens and pond at the home.

She formed her own company in 1914, a more difficult path to choose than to stay within the Maryinsky or to continue with Diaghilev. Yet, she assembled a company and led it on world tours as though given a mission to take ballet and her own dancing presence to every country on the earth.

Her company repertoire was drawn from the classics, sometimes in abbreviated versions. The choreography was by Jean Coralli, Marius Petipa, and Lev Ivanov. The repertoire also included the dances by Fokine in which she created her great roles. Newer work was contributed by Uday Shankar, among others. Her attention to Shankar, an Indian artist studying painting in London, led to their performances together of dances inspired by classical Indian dance. Pavlova encouraged Shankar to leave ballet and develop and renew the Indian art form. As Shankar was greatly responsible for the renaissance of classical dance in India, Pavlova can be credited with urging him to do so.

Pavlova's repertoire also included works that she herself choreographed. Among the most popular was *Autumn Leaves* (1919), set to music by Frédéric Chopin, the only full company ballet she choreographed. Similar to her other works, it developed from an intense appreciation of nature. All of her work was inspired by nature, and her artistic gift was to appear actually to become the flower, dragonfly, swan, or human emotion that she portrayed. To her audience, she seemed to create a miracle in each performance, transcending her own being and transporting the members of the audience from their own time and place as well. She believed that expressing beauty so that the audience might experience it in an immediate way was the goal of her art and also the source of hope for humanity.

As her performances featured duets and solos, Pavlova had a series of male partners who were famous dancers in their own right. The first was Mikhail Mordkin, who partnered her at the Maryinsky; Laurent Novikov became her partner in 1911 and Pierre Vladimirov in 1927. Although her first set of dancers were mostly Russian, once she fully organized her company they were drawn mainly from England and other European countries. The company members were influential in spreading her philosophy and style and the Cecchetti-influenced technique. Many European dancers left the company to remain as teachers and performers in the United States, and many Americans who returned home after being in her company gained fame on their return. They became important not only in ballet but also in theatrical and popular dance.

Pavlova's touring was tireless and covered great distances on the globe at a time when the only means of travel was ocean liner. She and her company spent the period of World War I in South America, where they had been conducting an extensive series of performances when the war broke out. Her company danced not only in the great capitals of Europe but also in provincial towns. Their travels also took them to then-exotic places such as Egypt and Australia.

Pavlova made one film and a series of test shots in Hollywood. In 1915, she portrayed Fenella in *The Dumb Girl of Portici.* The test shots, filmed in 1924, included excerpts from some of her most popular dances: *Christmas, The Dying Swan, Oriental Dance, Rose Mourante, Fairy Doll, The Californian Poppy,* and *Columbine.* These were arranged for a film, *The Immortal Swan*, in 1956, the twenty-fifth anniversary of her death.

This pioneer of world dance suffered somewhat from the fluctuations of fashion. She kept to her classical repertoire throughout the time that Diaghilev's innovations became popular. Thus, there was little enthusiasm among the patrons of the high culture in London for her production of *Giselle*, for example, in the late 1910's and early 1920's. At that time, most of the classics of Russian ballet, the works of Petipa, were out of favor. After her death, the importance of the classics was restored as they took their places in repertoires alongside modern additions. Pavlova's faith in the classics did not come from a lack of curiosity or a limited imagination; rather, she believed that these ballets and her own dances were the best way to touch the hearts of the broadest range of people. To bring ballet to the world did not mean to her to limit it to an aesthetic elite. In 1915, she considered experimenting with dance without music but decided it would be too strange to attract "the masses." She wanted to reach the people and was in turn embraced by them. She truly believed that she could provide joy for the people of the world and through dance give them relief from the sorrows of life.

Her wide appeal affected many future dancers and dance lovers. Sir Frederick Ashton, who was to become one of the great twentieth century ballet choreographers, saw her dance when he was a young man in Lima, Peru; her performances helped lead him to a life in ballet. He always considered himself a follower of the tradition of the great Russian choreographers Fokine and Petipa, but with a sense of theater that might be traced to Pavlova. He remembered her exceptionally expressive hands and feet and the sensitivity and unique "plasticity" of her movement. Although questions have been raised about the purity of her technique—was hers the greatest or was it merely equally great as that of other ballerinas?—Ashton and other exemplars of ballet, such as Margot Fonteyn, have maintained that her technique was fine but so surpassed by her magical presence that it cannot be considered separately. Hers was a total performance. Ashton claimed that she was the "greatest theatrical genius" that he had ever seen and that she was able to create more beauty and emotion from her slight dances than could be achieved in full-scale ballets.

Pavlova's death came tragically early, in 1931, after she became ill while on tour in The Netherlands. She continued with her rehearsal preparations despite her illness. One of her company members who was with her at the time recalled that after she was forced to bed by a high fever, doctors pierced her back in order to drain fluid from her lungs; she died soon after this treatment. It is said that her last words were a request for her swan costume. At her funeral in London near Ivy House, she was mourned by many who had never known her but had believed in the beautiful legend she had become.

### Summary

Anna Pavlova became the image and spirit of ballet during her lifetime. Her name continues to be synonymous with greatness not only as a dancer but also as an artist who gave her whole life to her art. There was nothing in her life that did not contribute in some way to her perfection of her dancing or to the furthering of the art. She traveled at least three hundred thousand miles at a time when travel was difficult. While acknowledged as the world's greatest dancer, she took her performances to remote places and was said never to find them anything less than stimulating and a source of joy. She called herself "a sower." Through her work and her travels, she not only allowed vast numbers of people to share the pleasure of her performances but also spread the knowledge and love of ballet. She was physically beautiful but did not stop at portraying prettiness; according to Ashton, her performances could make the audience uncomfortable because of her powerful presence and uncompromising presentation of emotional truth. She stirred her audiences more than she entertained them. Even in choreography that would not have been meaningful without her performing it, she created profound illustrations of life. No one could be indifferent to her. As a woman leading her own company around the world with her husband assisting, she presented a strong image of courage and confidence. It is to her credit, through her own performances and the legend she created, that ballet is performed and applauded on every continent.

### Bibliography

Algeranoff, Harcourt. *My Years with Pavlova.* London: Heinemann, 1957. A narrative by a company member of Pavlova's work with her companies on tour.

Beaumont, Cyril W. *Anna Pavlova.* London: C. W. Beaumont, 1938. A brief biography and appreciation of Pavlova by a ballet lover who admired her greatly and promoted her legend after her death.

Dandré, Victor. *Anna Pavlova in Art and Life.* London: Beaumont, 1932. A detailed biography by Pavlova's husband. In this book, Dandré frequently tries to correct what he believes to have been mistaken ideas about Pavlova's life.

Fonteyn, Margot. *Pavlova: Portrait of a Dancer.* New York: Viking, 1984. A remarkable collection of photographs from all stages of Pavlova's life accompanies a text drawn greatly from Pavlova's interviews and letters. The commentary by Dame Margot Fonteyn is helpful but never intrusive and serves to illustrate the continued admiration for Pavlova in the ballet world.

Kent, Allegra. "Anna Pavlova: The Swan." *New York Times Magazine* (November 24, 1996). Short profile with career highlights.

Lazzarini, John, and Roberta Lazzarini. *Pavlova: Repertoire of a Legend.* New York: Schirmer, and London: Macmillan, 1980. A large-format picture book that focuses on photographic studies from Pavlova's repertory. The authors are the curators of the Pavlova Society and offer reliable discussion of the works.

*Leslie Friedman*

## ROBERT EDWIN PEARY

*Born:* May 6, 1856; Cresson, Pennsylvania
*Died:* February 20, 1920; Washington, D.C.
*Area of Achievement:* Arctic exploration
*Contribution:* After several unsuccessful attempts, Peary became the first man to reach the geographic North Pole, on April 6, 1909.

### Early Life

Robert Edwin Peary was born on May 6, 1856, in Cresson, Pennsylvania, a backwoods farm community. His New England forebears were Frenchmen (Peary is an American modification of the Gallic Pierre) who had made barrel staves for their livelihood. His father died when he was three and his mother, Mary Peary, was forced to rear her only child on meager resources.

His mother was extremely possessive and forced her son to dress in girlish clothes. Robert was nicknamed "Bertie" and he was regarded as a sissy by his peers. He would spend the remainder of his life attempting to compensate for his tortured early years.

Peary studied civil engineering at Bowdoin College in Brunswick, Maine, and resolved to outdo his rivals. He became active in sports, drama, and debate. Symbolically, he dressed up as Sir Lancelot at his college fraternity masquerade party. For graduation exercises, he composed an epic poem in which he imagined himself to be Sir Roland.

### Life's Work

Peary received a degree in civil engineering in 1877 from Bowdoin College. After his graduation, he served as a draftsman for the United States Coast and Geodetic Survey. While in that position, he applied for and received a commission in the Civil Engineer Corps of the United States Navy in 1881.

In 1886, Peary borrowed five hundred dollars from his mother, took a summer leave of absence from the navy, gathered a crew, and embarked on what would be the first of eight expeditions to the Arctic. Peary, along with a Danish skiing companion, made a one-hundred-mile journey over the inland ice from the southwest coast of Greenland. The purpose of his first expedition was to acquire some fame by discovering what existed on north Greenland's ice cap: Was Greenland an island continent, or did it, as some geographers believed, thrust its ice cap right up to the North Pole? This expedition accomplished little. Yet Peary quickly learned what he needed to do in the future, and when his leave of absence expired, he returned to duty in Nicaragua with an obsession to return to the Arctic and to continue his quest for fame.

His second expedition was delayed until 1891. In 1888, he returned to his navy job on the Nicaraguan canal route for what would be a two-year tour. That same year, Peary married Josephine Diebitsch, the daughter of a professor at the Smithsonian Institution. She was a tall, spirited woman whose appearance closely resembled his mother's. Peary's mother moved in with the newlyweds. This uncomfortable arrangement lasted a year. Josephine soon realized that her husband was really married to his Arctic adventures; to solve her dilemma, she accompanied him on his second expedition. By this point, Peary had become skillful in getting what he needed to continue his explorations. He pulled strings and used his gifted oratorical skills and enormous self-confidence to obtain ten thousand dollars from financial backers and an eighteen-month leave of absence from the navy.

The stern, blue-eyed Peary sported a reddish-blond mustache; despite his serious nature, his overall appearance resembled that of the walruslike Ben Turpin, the silent-screen comedian. His face was already wrinkled from his time in Nicaragua and from exposure to Arctic blizzards and sun. His sixfoot, sturdy physique, with broad shoulders and narrow hips, his finely tuned body which had already passed its thirty-fifth birthday, was ready for the mental and physical challenges ahead.

For his second trip to the Arctic, which began in 1891, his strategy was to take with him a party of six "campaigners," including Dr. Frederick Cook, and a seventh person, his wife, Josephine. Josephine attracted much attention from the newspapers: She would be the first white woman to winter at such a high altitude in Greenland. Once in position, Peary planned to conduct a "white march" over the great ice of northeast Greenland and to claim for the United States a highway to the North.

On June 6, 1891, the *Kite* sailed from Brooklyn, destined for the northwest coast of Greenland. Cook, nicknamed the Sigmund Freud of the Arctic, proved to be a helpful passenger; his obsession to reach the North Pole went back to his own deprived childhood, during which he won prizes in geography and worked in his free time to help support his poverty-stricken family. To pay for medical school, he had worked nights as a door-to-door milkman.

The *Kite* was in the process of ramming its way through the ice of Baffin Bay when Peary broke his lower right leg by striking it against the iron tiller. Cook quickly set the leg in splints, and Josephine relieved Peary's pain with morphine and whiskey. Peary would later praise Cook as a helpful and tireless worker who was patient and cool under pressure.

On July 30, 1891, the party landed on the foot of the cliffs in Inglefield Gulf, immediately north of Thule, the United States Greenland military base. With his right leg strapped to a plank, Peary continued to demonstrate leadership as he carried a tent ashore and supervised the construction of a prefabricated, two-room cabin named Red Cliff House. As the party settled in for the long polar night, the Etah Eskimos flocked from hundreds of miles away to see the first white woman to come to their country.

Peary soon began to recover from his broken leg. Josephine recorded in her journal that, within three months, he had discarded his crutches and had begun running foot races with Cook to build up his leg. The Eskimos watched as the white man took snow baths in subzero temperatures. To demonstrate his endurance to the Eskimos, he wore a hooded parka and caribou socks and slept in the open all night without a sleeping bag.

Peary realized that, to endure in the Arctic, he would have to adopt the survival techniques of the Eskimos. He learned from the Eskimos that expeditions required dog teams, sleighs, fatty meat for nourishment, and light fur garments. Yet he treated the Eskimos, who would continually come to his aid, as subhumans. He refused to learn their language, in contrast to Cook and Matthew Henson, and he rejected the hospitality of their igloos.

During May of 1892, Peary set out eastward, on his white march across the ice cap of north Greenland. Initially, the Eskimos and Cook accompanied him. Cook had gone ahead as a forward scout. When the two men rendezvoused, Peary ordered Cook to return to look after Josephine. The Eskimos feared that the evil spirit Tormarsuk presided in the interior, and they departed with Cook.

Peary and Eivind Astrup, a Norwegian ski champion, proceeded forward. In sixty-five days, the two men completed the unbelievable distance of six hundred miles over unknown terrain. On July 4, he named an easterly inlet Independence Bay, planted two American flags, and held a small celebration with the Norwegian skier. After they had rested, they turned around to retrace the six hundred miles back.

The trip would bring Peary fame; yet he had made costly cartographic errors that would eventually cause the death of a Danish scientist who attempted to confirm Peary's "discoveries." From Navy Cliff, Peary had believed that he had seen the Arctic Ocean, but he had actually been one hundred miles from the coast. Independence Bay had not been a bay but rather a deep fjord, and his conclusion that Peary Channel marked the northern boundary of the Greenland mainland was erroneous. In 1915, the United States government withdrew Peary's maps of Greenland, and Peary's reckless, unscientific behavior became legend.

When he returned, Peary raised twenty thousand dollars on the lecture circuit. Cook resigned from Peary's organization when Peary refused to allow him to publish ethnological findings on the Eskimos. No one in the group was allowed to publish anything, except in a book bearing Peary's name as author.

Peary's next expedition included Josephine, who was pregnant, a nurse, an artist, eight burros, and a flock of carrier pigeons. On September 12, 1893, Josephine gave birth to the first white child to be born at that altitude. The Peary's nine-pound daughter was named Marie Ahnighito Peary; her middle name came from the Eskimo woman who had chewed bird skins to make diapers for the blue-eyed child, nicknamed the Snow Baby.

The birth of the child was the only happy event of this expedition, as discontent broke out among the crew. Peary's drive and relentless nature began to cause problems. Astrup had a nervous breakdown and committed suicide on a glacier. Most of the remainder of the crew could no longer tolerate Peary, and they took the next supply ship back to the United States, as did Josephine, her child, and her nurse.

On future expeditions, Eskimos would lose their lives for Peary; Peary himself lost eight of his toes to frostbite. Now a near cripple, he simply stuffed his boots with tin-can lids to protect his stumps. Nothing short of death itself would stop Peary's single-minded quest.

Peary's first serious attempt to reach the North Pole began during the four-year expedition starting in 1898. Matthew Henson, a black who had mas-

tered the skills of Arctic exploration, was the only member from the original crew. The 1898-1902 mission failed to get to the North Pole, but Peary was able in 1902 to travel to eighty-four degrees, seventeen minutes north. On his seventh mission, in 1905-1906, Peary reached eighty-seven degrees, six minutes north, only 174 nautical miles from the North Pole, before having to retreat.

In 1908, Peary, though crippled, aging, and weatherbeaten, knew that he had the physical and mental resources for one final attempt to reach the North Pole. It would be his eighth and final trip. Several millionaires in the Peary Arctic Club pledged $350,000 for the final outing and *The New York Times* paid four thousand dollars in advance for the exclusive story. The National Geographic Society of Washington and the American Museum of Natural History in New York bestowed their prestige on him. The United States Navy once again released him with pay after President Theodore Roosevelt personally intervened.

In 1905, at a cost of $100,000, Peary had built, according to his own design, a schooner-rigged steamship named the *Roosevelt*. He took six men with him, the most loyal being Matthew Henson, who had nursed Peary and had saved his life on numerous occasions. A remarkable man, he had mastered everything for the mission, including the language of the Eskimos, who worshiped him as the Maktok Kabloonna (black white man). Both Peary and Cook, who was involved in a rival expedition, believed that the best companion for such an outing was a nonwhite, since whites, ultimately, could not seem to get along.

The flag-decorated *Roosevelt* got under way from New York Harbor on the steamy afternoon of July 6, 1908. At Oyster Bay, Long Island, President Roosevelt came aboard and shook hands with every member of the crew. At Sydney, Nova Scotia, Peary's wife Josephine, fourteen-year-old Marie, and five-year-old Robert, Jr., once again bade farewell to Peary. At Anoatok, on the northwest coast of Greenland, the Eskimos reported to Peary that Cook had already passed westward on his march to the Big Nail.

Peary ordered Captain Bob Bartlett to begin ramming the *Roosevelt* through the ice packs and to head toward Cape Sheridan, the proposed wintering berth, which was 350 miles away. On September 5, the *Roosevelt* had reached her goal of eighty-two degrees, thirty minutes latitude—a record north for a ship under her own steam.

Cape Sheridan became home base. Ninety miles northwest lay Cape Columbia, which Peary decided would be the ideal jumping-off spot. Four hundred and thirteen miles of Arctic Ocean ice separated Cape Columbia from Peary's goal, the North Pole, the Big Nail, ninety degrees north latitude.

Peary was ready for the final chance to realize the greatest dream of his life. On the appointed Sunday morning, twenty-four men, 133 dogs, and nineteen sleighs departed. The expedition was broken up into five detachments: Each one would break trail, build igloos, and deposit supplies in rotation. Peary would follow the group from the rear as each exhausted team rotated back toward land.

On April 1, Bartlett took a navigational fix and determined a reading of eighty-seven degrees, forty-seven minutes north latitude. He took no longitudinal reading, which made his determination dubious, but Peary was convinced that he was 133 nautical miles on a direct beeline to the North Pole. Peary then surprised and disappointed Bartlett and ordered him home. The only qualified nautically trained witness who might verify the North Pole sighting finally departed.

Peary continued on with Henson, four Eskimos, five sleighs, and forty dogs. On April 6, 1909, at ten in the morning, after a labor of twenty years, Peary became the only white man to reach the North Pole. Once there, Peary draped himself in the American flag. Henson later recalled in his memoirs that his fifty-three-year-old commander was a dead-weight cripple, a mere shadow of the civil engineer in Nicaragua. One of the Eskimos remarked, "There is nothing here. Just ice!"

### Summary

En route from his last mission to the Arctic, Peary learned that Cook had claimed to reach the Pole on April 21, 1908, nearly a year before Peary. Later, Cook was so hounded by the press and others that he took to wearing disguises and left the country for a year. When he returned, he spoke in his defense on the lecture circuit. Ultimately, his claims were disregarded, but the controversy was kept alive by the press because the dispute made a good story. Peary's claims were not scientifically documented. The National Geographic Society did a hasty, perfunctory examination of Peary's trunk of instruments in the middle of the night in a railway baggage station and agreed that Peary had discovered the North Pole.

In the 1930's, Dr. Gordon Hayes, an English geographer, scrupulously and fairly examined Cook's and Peary's claims. He concluded that neither one had got within one hundred miles of the North Pole. Nevertheless, Peary is credited with reaching the North Pole, attaining the fame he so desperately desired. After much lobbying and a congressional hearing, Peary was promoted to rear admiral. Peary served for a year as chairman of the National Committee on Coast Defense by Air during World War I. He retired and received a pension of sixty-five hundred dollars a year. He had achieved his goal, and the United States and the world recognized him for the twenty years of supreme sacrifices he had made.

Shortly after his return from the Arctic, Peary began suffering from anemia. On February 20, 1920, he died from that affliction at the age of sixty-four. He was buried with full honors at Arlington National Cemetery in Washington, District of Columbia. His casket was draped with the remnants of the American flag with which he had covered himself as he stood atop the world on the North Pole. The National Geographic Society constructed a huge globe of white granite, representing the Earth and inscribed with Peary's motto, "I shall find a way or make one," and a legend proclaiming him Discoverer of the North Pole.

**Bibliography**

Clark, T. "The Prisoner of Eagle Island." *Yankee* (April, 1989). Clark offers a brief biography of Peary including his claim that he reached the North Pole in 1909, his personal life, and the Frederick Cook controversy.

Cook, Frederick A. *My Attainment of the Pole*. New York: Polar, 1911; London: Kennerly, 1912. Cook's own descriptions of his expedition. Some claim that it was a hoax and others state that he only got to within a hundred miles of the North Pole.

Diebitsch-Peary, Josephine. *My Arctic Journal: A Year Among Ice-Fields and Eskimos*. New York: Contemporary, and London: Longman, 1893. Peary's wife gives her account. Includes "The Great White Journey."

Henson, Matthew A. *A Black Explorer at the North Pole: An Autobiographical Report by the Negro Who Conquered the Top of the World with Admiral Robert E. Peary.* Foreword by Robert E. Peary. Introduction by Booker T. Washington. New York: Walker, 1969. Henson's account. Henson began his life in poverty, attained fame, and ended his life as a parking attendant and a seventeen-dollar-a-week messenger in Brooklyn. He lived to be eighty-eight, and in his last years he suffered extreme poverty.

Hunt, William R. *To Stand at the Pole: The Dr. Cook-Admiral Peary North Pole Controversy.* New York: Stein and Day, 1982. Contains detailed account of the controversy over which man (Cook or Peary) got to the North Pole first. The mystery is not answered. Contains an excellent bibliography.

Peary, Robert E. *The North Pole*. London: Hodder and Stoughton, and New York: Stokes, 1910. Peary wrote three books—the others are *Nearest the Pole* (Doubleday, 1907) and *Northward over the "Great Ice"* (Stokes, 1898). *The North Pole* is Peary's own account of reaching the Pole. Exciting as an account but criticized by others.

Rasky, Frank. *Explorers of the North: The North Pole or Bust*. New York: McGraw-Hill, 1977. Chapters 10 and 11 are devoted to Peary. A human account of the explorer, warts and all. Short, readable, extremely detailed report of the important events. Good starting point.

Rawlins, Dennis. *Peary at the North Pole: Fact or Fiction?* Washington, D.C.: Luce, 1973. Argues that Peary never made it to the North Pole.

Salewicz, Gary. "Polar Opposites." *Canadian Geographic* 116, no. 2 (March-April, 1996). Salewicz examines the navigation techniques used by Peary and Richard Weber to reach the North Pole.

*John Harty*

# I. M. PEI

*Born:* April 26, 1917; Canton (now Guangzhou), China

*Area of Achievement:* Architecture

*Contribution:* Through his designs for major public buildings, Pei helped shape architectural design in the second half of the twentieth century. Equally skilled in the conceptual process of design, urban development, and client and community politics, he succeeded in completing buildings under complicated and difficult urban situations.

### Early Life

Ieoh Ming Pei was born to Tsuyie and Lien Kwun Pei in 1917. In the Chinese calendar, 1917 was a year of the snake, and individuals born under this symbol are traditionally characterized by wisdom, charm, and intuition. Pei's father, a prosperous banker, was descended from an ancient family of almost mandarin standing. His banking responsibilities moved the family from Canton to Hong Kong and then to Shanghai, where Pei attended a Western missionary school. Though he passed the entrance examinations for Oxford University, Pei insisted, against paternal advice, on attending college in the United States. He entered the Massachusetts Institute of Technology (MIT) in 1935, where he was an outstanding student. He received his bachelor's degree in architectural design in 1940.

He had met Eileen (Ai-Ling) Loo, another student from China, in 1938. She was attending Wellesley College for Women, but her interest in landscape architecture led to associations with the Harvard School of Design. Through Loo, Pei was introduced to the school, where he rapidly received the support and mentorship of Walter Gropius and Marcel Breuer, leading Bauhaus figures who had relocated to the United States because of the outbreak of World War II in Europe. The Bauhaus ideals that these men brought with them to the United States were critical to Pei's intellectual and architectural development. They taught that architecture was a force for social change and that "authentic" architecture developed its visual forms from its social functions and exploited the most up-to-date technology. Furthermore, architecture in the Bauhaus scheme was an art of teamwork in which design, engineering, urban planning, and landscape design each played its part. Pei was recruited to the graduate design program, and he received his master's degree in 1946. He also taught at the Harvard Graduate School of Design until 1948. Pei and Loo were married in 1942.

In 1948 Pei became the in-house architect for William Zeckendorf, a real estate developer and speculator in New York. This was a risky move, but it gave Pei opportunities unavailable to other young architects. He gained invaluable real-world experience dealing with large-scale projects of urban redevelopment. He designed projects in Denver, New York, Montreal, and Washington, D.C. During the twelve years of his association with Zeckendorf, he learned to design by adapting site and function, and he learned how to cajole, convince, and outlast bureaucratic opposition. He also put together the architectural team with which he would work for the rest of his career. His association with Zeckendorf ended in 1960.

### Life's Work

The split with Zeckendorf was a difficult but necessary step in Pei's development. As long as he remained identified with the entrepreneurial requirements of a single patron, prestigious public commissions and recognition would continue to elude him. Beginning in 1961, a series of early and important clients risked hiring Pei. In these early independent commissions, the elegant, personally reticent, and almost obsequious Pei showed himself extremely adept at working personally with his patrons and at the social and bureaucratic maneuvering required to bring controversial programs to completion. These skills almost outshone his technical and aesthetic solutions. With his design for the East Building of the National Gallery of Art in Washington, D.C., however, he became recognized as a major architect whose work was characterized by clean, geometric forms subtly adapted to the particular site, function, and infrastructural needs of the commission.

During its first decade as an independent firm, I. M. Pei and Associates worked on a number of public commissions. Most of these were won by the firm because of Pei's successful courting of clients who had the power of sole approval. The National Center for Atmospheric Research (NCAR; 1961-1967) demonstrated Pei's ability to blend a large (223,220 square feet), multifunction structure with a pristine natural site in the foothills above Boulder, Colorado. Based on both the modernist tradition and pre-Columbian architecture, the building has been characterized as both a fortress and a monastery, and it shows Pei's abiding preference for juxtaposed geometric forms.

Based on the modest successes of the NCAR building, the Luce Chapel in Taiwan (1954-1963), and several university buildings, Pei was selected in 1966 to build the Dallas Municipal Administrative Center. Characteristically, he envisioned the final project as more sweeping than its originators had, and there were enormous cost overruns by the time the building opened in 1977. In true, if lingering, Bauhaus fashion, Pei's design—horizontal and dynamic—reflected his concept of appropriate government (democratic and active), and its formal contrast to the many private skyscrapers that it balanced embodied his view of the relationship between the public and the private in the modern metropolis.

The commissions of the 1960's also demonstrated the bureaucratic and technical difficulties that large-scale projects faced. In 1964 Pei was chosen by Jacqueline Kennedy Onassis to design the Kennedy Library and Museum. Though his original design and siting were masterful—it was the first appearance of the glass pyramid in his work—community opposition delayed work for years and eventually forced major changes in both site and design. The building was finally completed in 1979. The John Hancock Tower in Boston (1966-1976), considered by some architectural critics at the time as a fiasco, is now seen as an elegant, defining feature of the Boston skyline. Though not of Pei's own design, its history significantly affected the firm's image. Pei and Associates was inexperienced in skyscraper design when it took on the task, and the Hancock Corporation's desire to surpass its rival, the Prudential Tower, in height forced the design beyond the specifications of the materials and perhaps beyond the firm's technical competence. The building was first built with a thin, double-layer glass sheathing that, in 1973, began cracking and, in some cases, falling to the street below. There were also concerns about the building's overall stability in unusually high winds. Much energy went into settling numerous lawsuits, and Pei's firm suffered badly. Pei received no large corporate commissions in the United States for almost a decade.

The lasting triumphs of Pei's career have been in the field of museum design. His reputation was established with the Kennedy project, and numerous smaller art facilities appear on his list of completed projects, including the Everson Museum in Syracuse, New York (1961-68), and the Miho Museum near Kyoto in Japan (1997). However, he will remain best known for his designs for the East Building of the National Gallery of Art in Washington, D.C. (1968-1978), and for the entrance to the Grand Louvre in Paris (1983-1989).

The East Building of the National Gallery of Art is Pei's best-known American work. Collaborating closely with donor Paul Mellon and museum experts, Pei created a striking, functional, and beautifully sited building. It represents his mature style: Clean, almost crystalline geometric forms and a large glass curtain wall create an imposing atrium space, while the exterior defines the urban relations around it. It is one of the most frequently visited buildings in the nation's capital.

Pei's design expertise and his skill at bureaucratic maneuvering were fully called upon during the "Battle of the Pyramid," as the public and governmental debates surrounding the project for the Louvre Museum in Paris were called. Part of the furor centered on Pei himself (a Chinese-born U.S. citizen designing a cultural monument in the heart of France), and part focused on the audacity of the design. Pei reworked the necessary infrastructure to house art objects and to serve huge numbers of people, but all of that was concealed underground in the great Cour Napoleon. What appeared to the public was an unforgivingly modern glass pyramid, 116 feet on a side and 71 feet high. Pei patiently outlasted his critics and even survived changes in government. As is typical of his designs, early negative public sentiment about the pyramid has been replaced by almost universal praise. The pyramid of the Louvre has come to stand with the Eiffel Tower as one of the defining features of Paris.

As a mature architect, Pei returned to Asia to blend his modernist vision with local traditions and functions. In addition to the early Luce Chapel, his Asian commissions include the Overseas-Chinese Banking Corporation Building in Singapore (1970-1976); Raffles City (a hotel and office complex), also in Singapore (1973-1986); Sunning Plaza in Hong Kong (1977-1982); the Fragrant Hill Hotel in Beijing (1979-1982); the Bank of China Building in Hong Kong (1982-1990); the Shinji Shumeikai bell tower (1988-1990); and the Miho Museum (1997) in Shiga, Japan.

A selection from among his many honors includes the Thomas Jefferson Medal for Architecture (1976), La Grande Medaille D'or d'Architecture (1981), the Pritzker Prize (1983), the Medal of Liberty (1986), the Medal of the French Legion of Honor (1988), the Praemium Imperial of the Japanese Art Association (1989), and the Medal of Freedom (1993).

### Summary

I. M. Pei has made a lasting contribution to the architecture of the twentieth century, not only in the United States but also worldwide. His visual elegance and love of modernist geometry is matched by his grasp of urban site planning and his ability to provide adequate infrastructural support for large public projects. Furthermore, his career is a model of the architect as astute politician.

His most successful works—NCAR, the National Gallery addition, the Grand Louvre project, and the Miho Museum—express his sculptural sensitivity while fulfilling the functional demands of the commission. His own grasp of architecture is so artistic that it is on these art-oriented projects that he excels. To the extent that his projects fail, they do so because the commission cannot accept the lofty artistic ideals he imposes on it. As author Peter Blake points out, the firm of I. M. Pei and Associates is an entity that was designed to continue on after the death of its leader. The team concept that Pei created and sustained is one that has changed American architectural practice.

### Bibliography


Adams, Eric. "Letting in the Light." *Architecture* 87, no. 1 (January, 1998). The author examines Pei's design for the Miho Museum in Japan and its construction.

Blake, Peter. *Form Follows Fiasco: Why Modern Architecture Hasn't Worked*. Boston: Little Brown, 1977. This essay takes modern American architecture to task for its adherence to Bauhaus ideals. The book discusses the structural failure of the Hancock Tower as a symptom of modern architecture.

Cannell, Michael. *I. M. Pei: Mandarin of Modernism*. New York: Southern, 1995. This chatty biography stresses Pei as a mix of American exuberance and Chinese control. Cannell discusses Pei from a personal and social point of view rather than addressing his structural solutions to architectural problems. This book lacks the elegant photographs of other works.

Dean, Andrea O. "Conversations: I. M. Pei." *AIA Journal* 68 (June, 1979): 61-67. Dean's interview with Pei explores Pei's personal history, influences (especially Mies van der Rohe and Le Corbusier), and view of architecture.

Diamonstein, Barbaralee. *American Architecture Now*. New York: Rizzoli, 1980. This is a book of interviews with leading late twentieth century architects. Diamonstein leads Pei to consider his own sense of debt to his Asian heritage, his personal philosophy of public buildings, and the organization of his firm.

"I. M. Pei: A Feeling for Technology and Art." *Technology Review* 98, no. 3 (April, 1995). Interview with Pei in which he discusses his career and design techniques.

Marder, Tod A. *The Critical Edge: Controversy in Recent American Architecture*. Cambridge, Mass.: MIT Press, 1985. In a chapter devoted to Pei's East Building of the National Gallery of Art, Marder uses contemporary critical reactions both during the construction of the buildings and after its completion to explore the press as an arbiter of public taste and the community's reception of new architecture. This is a study in what is frequent in the reception of Pei's designs: early negativism replaced by general praise once the building is functioning.

Ryback, Timothy. "From Villain to Hero: I. M. Pei's Louvre Odyssey." *ARTnews* 94 (Summer, 1995): 96-103. Ryback recounts the political debates surrounding the commission and the change in critical and public perception of the design over the course of the construction of the building.

Wiseman, Carter. *I. M. Pei: A Profile in American Architecture*. New York: Abrams, 1990. This is probably the most basic and easily available book on Pei. It is more of a biography of the man and his social context than a study of his designs and structure. The book includes copious and beautiful architectural photographs of Pei's buildings, a useful bibliography, and a valuable chronology of the building commissions of the firm.

*Jean Owens Schaefer*

# PELÉ
## Edson Arantes do Nascimento

*Born:* October 23, 1940; Três Corações, Minas Gerais, Brazil

*Area of Achievement:* Sports

*Contribution:* Probably the greatest soccer player of all time, Pelé starred on the Brazilian national teams that won the World Cup in 1958, 1962, and 1970. Following his retirement, the New York Cosmos of the North American Soccer League lured him to the United States, where he did much to popularize soccer. After retiring from the field, Brazil's greatest goodwill ambassador also became his nation's Sports Minister.

### Early Life

Pelé, christened Edson Arantes do Nascimento, was born October 23, 1940, in Três Corações, Minas Gerais. His father, João ("Dondinho") Ramos do Nascimento, was a popular minor league soccer player in a nation where soccer was a consuming passion. The young black considered Dondinho the greatest player in the world and wanted to be like him, but his mother, Celeste Arantes, hoped for a better career for her son than that of itinerant soccer player. Although Edson attended school until the fourth grade, it held little interest for him. At age ten, he quit school and, when not working as a two-dollar-a-month shoemaker's apprentice, spent his days playing soccer with the neighborhood boys. The games provided a carefree interval in a life of poverty and insecurity, made worse when his father suffered a serious knee injury.

Young Edson had natural gifts unlike anything his chums brought to their makeshift field. In Bauru, São Paulo, he and his friends played in the streets, with sticks or rocks marking the goals and rags tied up with string serving as the ball. One day they pilfered a cargo of raw peanuts and then roasted and sold them in the streets to raise money for a real ball and some faded uniforms. A local promoter organized them into a team, and for two years they won the children's championship of Bauru. By this time, Edson had acquired his famous nickname: "Pelé" is meaningless in Portuguese although probably derived from the verb *pelejar*, to battle. Pelé also caught the attention of Valdemar de Brito, a former member of the Brazilian national team and coach of the Bauru Athletic Club. Brito offered Pelé a contract to play for his club's youth team, and the boy led the team to three championships.

### Life's Work

Pelé was almost fifteen when Brito took him to Santos for a tryout with the team there, a major Brazilian club. Although a slender 130 pounds and awed by the big city, Pelé managed to impress the coach. For several months, he played on the junior squad, but, on September 7, 1956, he substituted in the second half for an injured player and scored his initial first-division goal. By early 1957, still only sixteen years old, he was a striker on the starting team, and the goals had begun to accumulate.

Brazilians loved graceful, elegant, attacking soccer, and Pelé gave it to them. As his body matured, he stood five feet, nine inches and weighed 165 pounds. A superb athlete, he had a powerful kick with either foot, remarkable peripheral vision, great leaping ability, and amazing skill in feinting

and dribbling. Pelé was creativity on the field, using acrobatic moves to manufacture seemingly impossible shots and passes. Most important, he used his individual skills to improve the play of his teammates.

Pelé won international recognition in 1958, when he was chosen at age seventeen to play on the Brazilian national team in the World Cup competition held in Sweden. Suffering from a knee injury, he did not participate in Brazil's first two games of the tournament. In the quarterfinal match against Wales, however, he gave the Europeans a taste of the spectacular: Receiving a high pass on his chest, he used his foot to lift the ball over the onrushing defender's head and then blasted it past the goalkeeper without the ball ever hitting the ground. The goal gave Brazil a 1-0 victory. He marked three goals in Brazil's 5-2 win over France in the semifinal. Pelé's two goals in the final against Sweden helped give Brazil a 5-2 victory and its first world championship.

Pelé's success in Sweden and the elegance and showmanship of Brazilian soccer made his Santos club a tremendous draw on the international circuit during the following years. A group of Italian clubs offered Santos one million dollars in 1960 for Pelé, and the Brazilian congress responded by declaring him a "non-exportable national treasure." With Pelé leading the way, Santos won the world club championship in 1962 and 1963.

In 1962, Brazil gained its second World Cup triumph, this time in Chile. Pelé scored once and assisted on Brazil's other goal in its 2-0 victory over Mexico in its initial match, but, in the second game against Czechoslovakia, he severely pulled a muscle. Fortunately for Brazil, the team had good depth, and Garrincha, Pelé's sidekick in the forward line, emerged as the star of the tournament. Pelé's injury kept him out of action for several weeks after Brazil's 3-1 defeat of Czechoslovakia for its second consecutive championship.

The 1962 World Cup gave a taste, however, of the new levels of violence to which international soccer had sunk and to which Pelé would be subjected. The increasing intrusion of politics and nationalism into international competition and the financial rewards for success added to the tendency for teams to seek victory at any price. Stars such as Pelé became marked men, subject to brutal, vicious tackling, which in his eyes seemed even worse because his style of play emphasized elegance and agility.

The Brazilian national team headed to England in 1966 in search of its third consecutive world championship, but the fates were unkind. At the peak of his game, Pelé went into the competition on a wave of international acclaim and national euphoria. Brazil's midfielders were past their prime, however, and the tournament was being played in northern Europe, on the English fields where soccer had originated. Sir Stanley Rous, English president of the International Soccer Federation, which conducted the tournament, had allegedly instructed referees to let the northern Europeans play their style of soccer rather than penalizing them for defensive aggressiveness. Brazil defeated Bulgaria 2-0 in its first match, but a savage tackle left Pelé injured for the remainder of the tournament. Without Pelé, the Brazilians then lost to Hungary. Trying to save the team from elimination, Pelé attempted to play against Portugal. Savagely fouled, Pelé was reinjured. In the wake of Brazil's defeat, Pelé's spirit was shattered, and he vowed not to play in another World Cup competition as a protest against the mounting violence.

Back home in Brazil, his love for the game gradually revived, and besides he had contractual obligations with Santos that carried him around the world and earned for both him and the club huge sums for exhibition matches. On November 19, 1969, he scored the thousandth goal of his career against Vasco da Gama in Rio de Janeiro. The country nearly stopped in adulation, he received equal billing in the newspapers with an American moon landing, and Brazil rushed out a postage stamp commemorating his achievement.

The following year brought his crowning feat. Having put the misery of 1966 behind him, Pelé agreed to play once again for Brazil in World Cup competition in Mexico. While he had never been strictly an individualist on the field, Pelé recognized that opponents would attempt to brutalize him again, and so he became the consummate team player in 1970. He flicked pinpoint passes to streaking teammates when defenses collapsed on him; he fought valiantly on defense; and he still marked marvelous goals. The final against Italy pitted the defensive, counterattacking strategy of European soccer with the slashing, offensive flair of the Brazilians. Pelé and his teammates won 4-1, retiring the Jules Rimet cup that belonged to the first country to win three championships.

The triumph in Mexico left Pelé with little to achieve on the field. He announced his retirement from the national team on June 18, 1971, to the consternation of Brazilians who hoped he would help defend the title again in 1974. Then on October 2, 1974, he retired from Santos, intending to devote greater attention to his family. After a secret six-year engagement to Rosemari Cholby, a blond bank employee, the couple had married in 1966; they had two children, Kelly Cristina, born in 1967, and Edson, born in 1970. Pelé's business activities outside soccer were also time-consuming. He had invested in several industries and companies, starred as a detective in a television series, acted in movies, and performed songs that he had written. Manufacturers of clothing, watches, chocolate, soccer equipment, soft drinks, and bicycles all sought his endorsement. He was probably the wealthiest athlete in the world and certainly the most famous.

As it turned out, his soccer career was not finished. In 1975, he shocked the soccer world by signing a seven-million-dollar, three-year contract to play for the New York Cosmos of the North American Soccer League (NASL). He needed the money to offset business losses but was also motivated by love for his country and for soccer. He saw the Cosmos' offer as an opportunity to be a goodwill ambassador for Brazil in the United States and at the same time popularize soccer there, where it had always been a minor sport. While some Brazilians were initially upset that their hero was leaving to play in the United States, his countrymen came to take great pride in his achievements among the Yankees. During the three seasons he played, Pelé was by far the greatest draw of the NASL. The Cosmos set attendance records wherever they played, and Pelé retained enough of his skills to awe American crowds. When he retired in 1977, his final opponent was the Santos club from Brazil. At halftime, he put on his famous Santos shirt and finished his career playing for his old team. When the match ended, both teams carried him off the field on their shoulders to the chant of "Pelé! Pelé!" from the seventy-six thousand Americans who had braved a rainstorm to witness history.

### Summary

Gracious and accommodating to his fans, Pelé was idolized throughout the world. Brazilians regularly talked about electing him president, and Pelé was the most recognized figure in the country. In black Africa he was a demigod, the pride of the entire subcontinent. The Nigerians and Biafrans halted their war for a day so that Pelé could play an exhibition there. Popes and heads of state asked to meet him, curious about the man who attracted such universal acclaim. A few Brazilians quietly criticized him for not being more of a social reformer, for not taking bolder stands on behalf of his country's poor and blacks, but such activism would have been out of character. Instead, he was an outstanding role model for children, setting a good moral example and devoting much time to his fans. He also returned to his studies and received a university degree.

During his twenty-two-year career, Pelé played 1,363 games and scored 1,281 goals, twice as many as anyone else in the world's most popular team sport. From 1957 to 1966, for ten consecutive years, he was the leading scorer in the tough São Paulo League, yet he also stood at the top in 1974, when he retired in Brazil. The youngest to play on a World Cup winner, he was also the only person to win the World Cup three times. In addition, Pelé scored what was reputed to be the greatest goal in the history of the game: Taking the ball in his own penalty area, he dribbled the length of the field, eluding nine defenders, and scored. Brazilian television replayed a tape of that goal every day for the next year. Altogether, Pelé played soccer in eighty-eight different countries. His ability to create goals for teammates and make seemingly impossible shots set him apart as a genius in stark contrast to the trend of modern soccer to become more and more conservative and defensive, avoiding risk and subduing individualism. That genius and his long career exalted Pelé above all others who have played the game.

### Bibliography

Bodo, Peter, and David Hershey. *Pelé's New World*. New York: Norton, 1977. A biography that focuses primarily on Pelé's years playing for the Cosmos.

Lever, Janet. *Soccer Madness*. Chicago: University of Chicago Press, 1983. In this study of soccer's sociological impact on Brazil, Lever discusses Pelé's popularity and his symbolic importance to the game and his country.

Morris, Desmond. *The Soccer Tribe*. London: Cape, 1981. Morris portrays soccer as a tribal sport that demands intense loyalties from players and fans. He makes numerous references to Pelé.

Pelé, with Robert L. Fish. *My Life and the Beautiful Game: The Autobiography of Pelé*. New

York: Doubleday, and London: New English Library, 1977. Movingly written by Fish, this book is the place to start for anyone interested in Pelé.

"Pelé on American Soccer and the World Cup!" *Scholastic Coach* 63, no. 5 (December, 1993). Interview with Pelé in which he discusses his early life in Brazil, his career, soccer in general, and the World Cup.

Rosenthal, Gary. *Everybody's Soccer Book.* New York: Scribner, 1981. A good history of the World Cup, including references to Pelé's participation.

Rote, Kyle, and Basil G. Kane. *Kyle Rote Jr.'s Complete Book of Soccer.* New York: Simon and Schuster, 1978. This general overview of soccer contains numerous references to Pelé, particularly in the chapter tracing the history of the World Cup.

Swift, E. M. "A Dream Come True." *Sports Illustrated* 80, no. 24 (June 20, 1994). The author discusses the life and career of Pelé.

Thébaud, François. *Pelé.* Translated by Leo Weinstein. New York: Harper and Row, 1976. A French sports writer who saw Pelé play many times and interviewed him wrote this biography and analysis of Pelé's place in the soccer pantheon.

Trevillion, Paul. *"King" Pelé.* London: Paul, 1971. This short biography is aimed at juvenile readers and contains illustrations and a section on soccer techniques.

*Kendall W. Brown*

## P'ENG TE-HUAI

*Born:* c. October 24, 1898; Xiangtan county, Hunan Province, China

*Died:* November 29, 1974; Beijing, China

*Area of Achievement:* The military

*Contribution:* P'eng was a soldier for his entire adult career, all but the first few years of that career spent in the highest echelons of the Chinese Communist army. Despite making an immense contribution to the military victory of communism in China, P'eng became the victim of political purges carried out by Mao Tse-tung in 1959 and spent his last years in official disgrace.

### Early Life

P'eng Te-huai was born in Hunan Province, China, very near to the village birthplace of his later comrade-in-arms Mao Tse-tung. One's class background could be very important in later years, especially in the Cultural Revolution, in determining one's political reliability—the presumption being that higher social origins made one more unreliable. P'eng described his family as "lower-middle peasant," and clearly his family suffered severe hardships in his youth. It is not surprising then that he made the same career choice as other impoverished peasant boys—military service. At the age of eighteen, he joined one of the many warlord armies that dominated the political and military scene in China from 1916 to 1928. He was to remain a soldier for the next forty-three years of his life, until he fell victim to purges carried out by Mao in 1959.

In 1922, P'eng was able to gain admission to the Hunan Provincial Military Academy to receive professional training. After nine months of training, P'eng was graduated and was appointed captain and commander of the very unit he had joined as a recruit seven years earlier. In 1926, the army that P'eng served went over to the Nationalist army under Chiang Kai-shek, who had just launched the Northern Expedition aimed at eliminating the warlord menace. Though not an official member of the Nationalist army, P'eng regarded himself as a "follower" for the next two years, during which time he rose to the rank of colonel in the Nationalist army. In early 1928, he applied for membership in the Chinese Communist Party (CCP), and in April of that year his entrance into the Party was approved. What prompted his transfer of allegiance from the Nationalist (KMT) cause to the Communists was not ideology so much as a rebellious spirit and the conviction that the CCP and not the KMT was committed to a struggle against rural poverty.

### Life's Work

Much of P'eng's career, especially his later years, would be characterized by an antagonistic relationship with his fellow Hunanese, Mao Tse-tung. In the earlier years, conflicts, while frequently evident, were moderated. Building an army from scratch, challenging the much superior forces of the KMT, and, in the 1930's, mobilizing resistance against the invading Japanese—these challenging tasks overshadowed the factional struggling that often went on behind the scenes.

Though not one of the founders of the Chinese Red Army—it was organized in the year before P'eng joined the CCP—P'eng was one of the major figures in developing the guerrilla tactics that the CCP used to defend itself against the "annihilation campaigns" launched against it by Chiang Kai-shek's forces in the period from 1930 to 1934. Like nearly all the subsequent leadership of the CCP, P'eng was present on the yearlong (1934-1935) retreat called the "Long March," which took the Communists on a six-thousand-mile journey from their bases in the south of China to a new headquarters in Shensi Province. They had barely dug in at their new base at the city of Yen-an when war erupted with Japan.

The eight-year-long Sino-Japanese War, 1937-1945, would prove to be a key factor in determining the fortunes of the CCP. At the beginning of the war, the CCP, weak and exhausted after having barely survived the ordeal of the Long March, controlled the single base at Yen-an and commanded the allegiance of no more than a million Chinese. At the end of the war, in 1945, the CCP, thanks to perfecting tactics of guerrilla warfare and mobilizing masses of China in the patriotic resistance cause, had expanded its network of bases to nineteen and controlled a population of about one hundred million. Throughout that war, P'eng was deputy commander of the Eighth Route Army, the formal designation of the Chinese Red Army. While the commander, Chu Teh, was a towering figure in the army and highly respected, P'eng is often given credit for carrying the main responsibility of the frontline direction of the war of resistance against Japan.

The defeat of Japan did not bring peace to China for long. In 1946, one year after Japan's surrender, a three-year civil war between Chiang's Nationalists and Mao's Communists swept over China. The now largely expanded Communist armies were reorganized and named the People's Liberation Army (PLA); Chu continued as commander, with P'eng as his deputy. As commander in chief of the First Field Army, P'eng was responsible for the victorious offensive against the KMT armies in the northwest of China.

In 1950, one year after the establishment of the People's Republic of China (PRC), China found itself involved in the Korean War. As American forces drove into North Korea toward the Yalu River boundary with the PRC in November, 1950, P'eng was called upon to lead the "Chinese People's Volunteers" into engagement with American forces. For the next three years, until the war ended in a stalemate in 1953 near the original thirty-eighth parallel, P'eng remained in Korea directing the Chinese effort there. He was the only first-rank PLA veteran to participate in the Korean War. In 1954, P'eng became both the de facto commander in chief of the PLA and the minister of defense. One year later he was elevated to the newly created rank of marshal.

It was exactly at this time that P'eng launched a campaign to modernize the army, a venture that was eventually to arouse Mao's suspicion. To modernize meant to professionalize and that required trimming the ranks of the PLA, which had ballooned in size. What was needed, P'eng believed, was a relatively small, highly trained elite establishment rather than a mass army steeped in guerrilla traditions. Compulsory military service was substituted for the old "volunteer" system. Insignia of rank were introduced in the PLA, and distinctive uniforms and caps, modeled on those of the Soviet Red Army, were issued. It is a wonder that P'eng's reforms saw the light of day, for they contradicted Mao's dicta that men were more important than weapons, that the guerrilla traditions of the Yen-an days had to be preserved, that political indoctrination was more important than technical training, and that political commissars were at least as important as good professional officers.

The chairman's response came in 1958, when Mao moved to check P'eng's professionalization drive by promoting his own militia movement under the slogan "Every man a soldier." While only a limited number of the so-called core militiamen would be issued rifles and live ammunition, a second armed force was being created. In addition to this frontal challenge to P'eng's professional military convictions, Mao's Great Leap Forward, launched in 1958, caused the rift between Mao and P'eng to widen. Inspection trips into the countryside in that year caused P'eng to recoil at the veritable chaos caused by the sudden rush into the communes and frenzied campaigns to increase steel production in the backyard furnaces that became the hallmark of the Great Leap Forward.

The issue came to a head at historic meetings attended by the entire top level of party leadership in the resort area of Lushan in the summer of 1959. By that time, bogus statistics and heroic slogans could no longer conceal the economic dislocations and plunging national morale that were the main legacy of the Great Leap Forward. It was P'eng who stepped forward at the conference to offer the most frontal challenge to Mao's personal leadership and policies by anyone from the Party's inner circle in the twenty-four years since the chairman had assumed unchallenged control during the Long March.

Many ranking Party members endorsed P'eng's views, and in fact the Party did move decisively away from the Great Leap Forward programs after the Lushan Conference. Nevertheless, Mao had a score to settle with his defense minister, and he moved swiftly to force P'eng into ignominious retirement in September, 1959. During the next seven years, from 1959 to 1966, he was mentioned only once in the official media.

A worse fate was to befall P'eng during the Cultural Revolution. In December, 1966, as that decade-long upheaval began to sweep over China, P'eng was arrested. The final eight years of his life were a nightmare of imprisonment, physical abuse, and character assassination—as it was for most of Mao's rivals in the Party. P'eng died of the effects of his imprisonment and medical neglect on November 29, 1974, an all but forgotten "nonperson." In 1978, two years after Mao's death and the end of the Cultural Revolution, China's new leadership, under Teng Hsiao-p'ing, posthumously "rehabilitated" P'eng and restored his good name.

## Summary

In his judiciously balanced biography of P'eng Te-huai, Jürgen Domes argues that much of P'eng's success as a military leader must be explained by his character. He won the loyalty of his subordinate officers and troops because of his personal qualities. He led a simple, frugal life, worked hard, and was straightforward in his dealings with both superiors and subordinates. While P'eng was courageous in battle and a good campaigner and tactician, Domes concludes that he was "at best a fair if not a mediocre strategist."

P'eng's career is of great interest as a case study in intraparty conflict. Mao's purge of P'eng from the very highest ranks of the military establishment in 1959 came at a time when there was widespread dissatisfaction with Mao's policies and tyrannical methods. Mao's response to P'eng's challenge was to issue an ultimatum to the Party leadership: If it and the PLA accepted P'eng's views, Mao would split the Party by going to the countryside and mobilizing the peasants in his own private army to maintain control. The specter of such a civil war was apparently enough to isolate P'eng from his supporters and leave him to face Mao's wrath alone.

P'eng's fate illustrates the ability of the government of the PRC to reverse the public image of one of its most important leaders overnight. From being recognized as a hero of the revolution for decades, P'eng was transformed overnight into an archvillain, a "great conspirator, a great ambitionist," who had joined the movement only to advance his career and achieve fame for himself. Then, after Mao's death, P'eng's reputation was soon elevated to almost superhuman heights. The power of a regime to manipulate personal images in such an arbitrary fashion should give caution to those seeking to separate fact from fiction in the careers of men such as P'eng.

## Bibliography

Domes, Jürgen. *Peng T-huai: The Man and the Image*. London: Hurst, and Stanford, Calif.: Stanford University Press, 1985. This brief volume, the only biography of P'eng in English, is an engrossing study of the man and his relationship to the political and military development of China with an especially good analysis of the intraparty conflict which swirled around P'eng and Mao after 1959.

Griffith, Samuel B., II. *The Chinese People's Liberation Army*. New York: McGraw-Hill, 1967; London: Weidenfeld and Nicolson, 1968. A well-respected standard authority on China's army written by a United States Marine Corps general with long years of experience in China and considerable academic expertise as well. Includes valuable organizational charts and biographical sketches of all important PRC military leaders including P'eng.

Joffe, Ellis. *Between Two Plenums: China's Intraleadership Conflict, 1959-1962*. Ann Arbor, Mich.: Center for Chinese Studies, University of Michigan, 1975. A highly specialized study of the three-year period of conflict touched off by P'eng's challenge of Mao at the Lushan Conference; by a recognized expert on Chinese military history.

Klein, Donald W., and Anne B. Clark, eds. *Biographic Dictionary of Chinese Communism, 1921-1965*. Cambridge, Mass.: Harvard University Press, 1971. Volume 2 contains a richly detailed and largely factual account of P'eng's career, though information on the post-1959 years is scanty. Contains a good bibliography.

Snow, Helen Foster. *The Chinese Communists: Sketches and Autobiographies of the Old Guard*. Westport, Conn.: Greenwood Press, 1972. This is a highly personal account of the early years of P'eng and other Communist leaders based on interviews conducted in Yen-an in 1937. Includes a glossary of terms and a chronology.

*John H. Boyle*

# JAVIER PÉREZ DE CUÉLLAR

*Born:* January 19, 1920; Lima, Peru

*Areas of Achievement:* Diplomacy, government, and politics

*Contribution:* Javier Pérez de Cuéllar served as Secretary-General of the United Nations from 1982 to 1992, focusing on the development of global social and economic policies and resolving a variety of international crises that emerged during his two terms in office.

## Early Life

Born into the bustling city of Lima, Peru, with its large import market, Javier Pérez de Cuéllar gravitated to other cultures and languages at an early age. Most of his ancestors and some contemporary family members had come to Peru from Spain, bringing a European culture and perspective that would influence him throughout his life. Because the family was economically comfortable, Pérez de Cuéllar was able to collect coins and stamps from foreign lands and even sought out a French tutor at a young age. Prophetically, the young Pérez de Cuéllar used to engage the tutor, who was from Alsace, France, in heated discussions of Adolf Hitler and the Nazi activities in Germany.

As a university student, Pérez de Cuéllar studied law and literature and, through a student intern program, became a clerk in the Peruvian Foreign Ministry. Although his aspirations at the time were not political and certainly not international, this position piqued his interest in the area and provided him with important contacts in the diplomatic field. After earning his law degree in 1944, Pérez de Cuéllar entered the diplomatic service as third secretary and, with the help of a family friend who was then the deputy foreign minister of Peru, earned an assignment to Paris and the French culture that had always intrigued him.

One year later, World War II ended and preparations were under way to create the new world organization of the United Nations (U.N.). Pérez de Cuéllar was assigned to the Peruvian delegation of the Preparatory Commission of the United Nations. Still relatively new to international politics, Pérez de Cuéllar was amazed by the number of world leaders flooding into London for the preparations and by the frenetic activity that was taking place, but the experience prepared him well for the climb to positions of leadership in Peru's Foreign Ministry and later the United Nations.

## Life's Work

Pérez de Cuéllar received his first ambassadorial position in 1962, becoming Peru's ambassador to Switzerland. In 1964, he returned to Peru to assume the prestigious title of deputy foreign minister. The year 1968 brought dramatic changes to both Peru and Pérez de Cuéllar's career in the form of a coup d'etat. The new regime established diplomatic relations with the Soviet Union, although Peru had never maintained permanent relations with czarist Russia or the Soviet bloc in previous years. The new government appointed Pérez de Cuéllar as its ambassador to the Soviet Union in 1969. Although Pérez de Cuéllar's personal politics were conservative, he felt it was his duty to facilitate relations between his nation and the Moscow leadership, a move that would aid his negotiations with the Soviets in later years.

In 1971, the leadership of Peru sent Pérez de Cuéllar to New York as its permanent representative to the United Nations in hopes of strengthening the international position of Peru. During this period, Pérez de Cuéllar served two terms as president of the security council and held several other positions within the United Nations dealing with specific international crises.

In 1981, Kurt Waldheim's second term as secretary general of the United Nations was coming to a close. Although Waldheim was actively campaigning for a third term, Salim Salim of Tanzania ranked as a strong challenger, supported by those who wanted a leader from the Third World. However, as it became clear that the People's Republic of China would not accept a third term from Waldheim and the United States would not accept the communist ally Salim, Pérez de Cuéllar emerged as a compromise candidate. Pérez de Cuéllar began the first of his two terms as secretary general in 1982.

Some of the most persistent challenges during Pérez de Cuéllar's administration involved the political conflicts of the Middle East. When Palestinian refugees poured into Lebanon, the nation erupted in civil war. The Palestine Liberation Organization (PLO) began launching attacks against the Israelis in 1978, and Israel responded by sending occupation forces into Lebanon. When Pérez de Cuéllar took office in 1982, he sought to diminish the still-lingering effects of this violence by using U.N. forces to protect the Lebanese civil-

ians and Palestinian refugees caught in the morass. He further sought to bring the United Nations into the resolution of these conflicts, although his efforts were often thwarted by the lack of cooperation not only between the Arab nations and Israel but also between the United States and the Soviet Union.

The Persian Gulf War and the success of Operation Desert Storm in reinstating the territorial integrity of Kuwait brought renewed hope to those seeking a peaceful settlement to the Middle East situation. Pérez de Cuéllar furthered these efforts by initiating a relationship with PLO leader Yasir Arafat to ensure the latter that any United Nations-led peace settlement would take into consideration the rights and needs of the Palestinian people. Although Pérez de Cuéllar felt that he had failed in his attempts to bring peace to the Middle East, he did increase the role of the United Nations as moderator in these conflicts.

Pérez de Cuéllar also played a role in the efforts to free hostages in Lebanon. He personally contacted political and underground leaders in Lebanon, Iran, and Syria in an attempt to negotiate the release of hostages such as the late British journalist Alec Collett and Lieutenant Colonel William R. Higgins, as well as other Westerners being held in the region. Although these efforts were not entirely successful, even the surviving family members credited Pérez de Cuéllar and the United Nations with extraordinary persistence in pursuing the hostages' release.

Pérez de Cuéllar's involvement in the Cypriot crisis predated his tenure as secretary general. Pérez de Cuéllar characterized the problem as a seemingly simple one consisting of hammering out appropriate representation of both the Turkish Cypriot minority and the Greek Cypriot majority, yet one that has defied resolution for over thirty years. Ironically, however, the continued presence of what has become the longest U.N. peacekeeping mission in history has actually established an environment peaceful enough that no official resolution has been required.

The African continent called upon Pérez de Cuéllar for assistance as well. Namibia, South Africa, Angola, Mozambique, and the Western Sahara all suffered severe political crises during the 1980's. Drought and famine brought disease and economic collapse, which in turn contributed to political upheaval and civil war, creating floods of refugees and continuing the cycle of famine and political strife. Namibia's problems stemmed from its status as a territorial possession of South Africa. Although South African control of Namibia had technically ended in 1966, in reality little had changed by the time Pérez de Cuéllar became secretary general. Furthermore, South Africa had extended its racial policies of apartheid to Namibia. Although Namibia's independence had been largely planned by this time, U.N. involvement in negotiating cease-fires and actually implementing independence became crucial. Under Pérez de Cuéllar, the United Nations was also instrumental in coordinating international pressure on South Africa to withdraw the apartheid policies against its own people.

The conflict between Angola and Mozambique proved more complex for Pérez de Cuéllar. Angola's government received support from the Soviet Union and Cuba, while Mozambique benefited from the aid of South Africa and what was then Southern Rhodesia. Meanwhile, Angola was engaged in repelling invasions from Namibian and South African forces. Although the United Nations was not the primary actor in the peaceful resolution of these conflicts, its peacekeeping missions played an important role in creating an environment for national negotiators to act. In contrast, Pérez de Cuéllar was largely responsible for the establishment of the Western Sahara's independence from Morocco.

Latin America presented similar challenges to Pérez de Cuéllar. British possession of the Falkland Islands had long been a thorn in the side of Argentina and had remained a matter of mediation before the United Nations from 1965 to 1982. In addition to the lack of cooperation between Great Britain and Argentina, the eagerness of the United States, the Organization of American States (OAS), and various Latin American countries to help resolve the conflict only served to complicate the negotiation process and thwart the efforts of the United Nations. Ultimately, the Falkland Islands War resolved the issue but not in the peaceful manner anticipated by Pérez de Cuéllar.

U.N. efforts to establish peace in Central America met similarly unintentional resistance through the active intervention of the United States, the OAS, and other nongovernmental institutions. However, the nations of Central America, in conjunction with U.N. guidance, were able to organize and resolve some of their problems before resorting to open warfare, although not without overcoming a number of coups and short-lived military regimes.

### Summary

Javier Pérez de Cuéllar remains a staunch defender of the integrity and effectiveness of the United Nations and in his autobiography notes that even though the much-maligned staff of the Secretariat comes from over 150 different countries with varying work cultures and management styles, they have been able to adapt remarkably well to what is largely an American model of bureaucracy.

Coming from the Third World, Pérez de Cuéllar understands the importance of economic and social development in resolving and preventing these types of crises, and thus the United Nations' failures in these areas have been particularly frustrating for him. In his autobiography, he points out that the Economic and Social Council (ECOSOC) of the United Nations has never possessed authority to create or coordinate global policies, nor has it ever been able to control powerful agencies such as the International Monetary Fund or the World Bank. Instead, Pérez de Cuéllar emphasizes the importance of nongovernmental institutions, whose independence from governmental and bureaucratic constraints allows them to respond to potential problems long before intergovernmental institutions are able to take action. Pérez de Cuéllar credits organizations such as the Red Cross and Save the Children with providing qualified and well-trained staff members who are often familiar with local problems and can adapt to varying local needs.

### Bibliography

Bennett, A. Leroy. "The Search for Leadership in International Organizations." In *International Organizations: Principles and Issues*. 6th ed. Englewood Cliffs, N.J.: Prentice-Hall, 1995. Bennett discusses the role of leadership in the United Nations and the diplomatic style of various secretary generals, including Javier Pérez de Cuéllar.

Everitt, Anthony. "Designer Global Culture." *New Statesman and Society* 9 (February 2, 1996): 31-32. Addresses Pérez de Cuéllar's efforts to promote the study and preservation of indigenous cultures in developing nations, which are often subordinated to the needs of economic development in the Third World.

Hourong, Liu. "UN's Role in Solving Regional Conflicts Enhanced." *Beijing Review* 35, no. 4 (January 27, 1992). The author considers the role of Pérez de Cuéllar in successfully mediating international conflicts.

Isar, Raj. "Janvier Perez de Cuellar." *UNESCO Courier* (September, 1996). Interview with Pérez de Cuéllar in which he discusses economic issues.

"New Wave." *The Economist* 331 (June 25, 1994): 42-43. Discusses Pérez de Cuéllar's loyalty to Peru and his continued efforts to improve the social and economic development of Latin America through a bid for the Peruvian presidency in 1994.

Pérez de Cuéllar, Javier. *Pilgrimage for Peace: A Secretary-General's Memoir.* London: Macmillan, and New York: St. Martin's Press, 1997. This book presents Pérez de Cuéllar's views on international relations and the role of the United Nations in contemporary politics, focusing on the author's experiences in handling international crises over a decade.

*UN Chronicle*. (December, 1989). Discusses the political crisis in Namibia and Pérez de Cuéllar's role in protecting refugees and encouraging a democratic voting process.

———. (March, 1992). Summarizes the two-term tenure of Pérez de Cuéllar as secretary general of the United Nations, following his initial efforts to guide international relations within the confines of the Cold War through his final years dealing with the fragmentation of Eastern Europe.

*Margaret C. Gonzalez*

# FRANCES PERKINS

*Born:* April 10, 1880; Boston, Massachusetts
*Died:* May 14, 1965; New York, New York
*Area of Achievement:* Government and politics
*Contribution:* Perkins, as secretary of labor for twelve years under President Franklin Delano Roosevelt, was the first woman to serve in a president's cabinet. As secretary of labor, she was instrumental in developing legislation to improve labor conditions for workers. Her most notable achievement was to chair the committee responsible for developing the social security system.

## Early Life

Frances Perkins was born on April 10, 1880, in Boston, Massachusetts. In 1882, her family moved to Worcester, Massachusetts, where her father prospered in the stationery business. Known as Fannie Coralie Perkins until her twenty-fifth year, she was raised in the fashion typical of middle-class girls of her generation. Her conservative, New England family upbringing influenced her early life. She was taught to behave like a lady, to be seen but not heard, and to accept her father's authority on all matters. Her childhood was comfortable and sheltered. She learned to read at a young age and was encouraged to do so by her father. Although she was extremely shy as a young girl, at school she discovered her ability to express herself through words.

School broadened her range of experiences, and she was very involved in a variety of activities. Her ability to debate enabled her to pass her courses with ease, and she was graduated from high school in 1898. Not sure what she wanted to do with her life, Perkins decided that she would pursue teaching because that was an acceptable occupation for a woman of her time. She convinced her father that attending college would help her find a good teaching position, so he agreed to let her attend Mount Holyoke College in western Massachusetts.

Perkins entered Mount Holyoke with no particular direction for her studies. After taking a required chemistry course, however, she discovered her skills and interest in the sciences. She pursued chemistry as her major, but in her last year at Mount Holyoke she took a course that changed her life. It was an economics course, but unlike other courses, it involved the direct observation of factories and industry. Perkins was deeply affected by the working conditions of women and children in the factories. This experience gave Perkins an awareness of social conditions that affected her the rest of her life.

After she was graduated in 1902, Perkins taught briefly at several girls' schools until finding a permanent job teaching chemistry at Ferry Hall School in Lake Forest, Illinois, outside of Chicago. Although it was far from her family, her father agreed to let her go, and in 1904 she left for Chicago.

Perkins taught for two years, spending her free time in Chicago working with many of the social reformers there. She was greatly inspired by the efforts of settlement workers, and in 1906, she left teaching to live at Hull House, the settlement house founded by Jane Addams. Although she was there for only six months, the time greatly influenced her, and Perkins was convinced that her calling was to strive to change working conditions for laborers, particularly women and children.

## Life's Work

Frances Perkins' first paid employment in reforming labor conditions came in 1907, when she left Chicago to become the secretary of the Philadelphia Research and Protection Association. The organization helped immigrant girls from Europe and African American girls from southern states who came to Philadelphia looking for work. The young girls were often preyed upon by unscrupulous employers or forced into prostitution. As secretary, Perkins was responsible for gathering facts and using them to pressure city officials to legislate changes in employment practices. In this first job, Perkins developed skills she used throughout her professional life. She learned to gather data on working conditions and use it to influence policymakers to develop laws to protect workers. Perkins felt that the best way to help workers and the poor was through government action.

Perkins left in 1909 and went to study at the New York School of Philanthropy. In 1910, she graduated with a master's degree in political science from Columbia University. With her social work and political science training, she was well prepared to follow her chosen path of working for labor reform and rights. Perkins became the executive secretary of the New York City Consumers' League in 1910. In this position, she was responsible for investigating the conditions that existed in industries domi-

nated by women workers. Living in Greenwich Village near many of the factories, Perkins witnessed the Triangle Shirtwaist Factory fire of 1911, the worst factory fire in New York history. The sight of young women jumping out of windows because there were no fire escapes reinforced Perkins' commitment to social and labor reform. After witnessing that event, she realized that organizing and union efforts, while important, were not enough. She became convinced that only through the power of legislation could there be real change.

The aftermath of the Triangle Shirtwaist Factory fire did bring legislative action. The New York State assembly founded the New York State Factory Commission in 1911. Perkins was director of investigation for the commission until 1913.

In 1912, while serving on the State Factory Commission, Perkins took the position of executive secretary of the New York Committee on Safety. Already experienced in lobbying from her work with the Consumers' League, she was active in influencing the passage of numerous regulations protecting workers and improving labor conditions. Included in her legislative efforts were reorganizing the state labor department and limiting the workweek for women to fifty-four hours. These were the first legislative efforts at labor reform by any state.

In 1913, Perkins married Paul Wilson, an economist and budget expert with the Bureau of Municipal Research. As intensely private people who were committed to their work, they kept their personal lives separate from their public lives. Perkins chose to keep her birth name, for she felt she had made much progress and saw no reason to take her husband's name. Over the next few years, she maintained her work with the Committee on Safety. In 1916, after experiencing two unsuccessful pregnancies, she gave birth to a daughter Susanne, her only child. Perkins limited her travels and lobbying, but stayed with the Committee on Safety until 1917.

Perkins' years with the Consumers' League and work on state commissions brought her close to a number of New York politicians. In 1918, she campaigned for Al Smith, a legislator who had supported her early labor reform efforts. Smith was elected governor of New York and after he took office in 1919, he appointed Perkins to her first public position, as a member of the New York State Industrial Commission. Perkins served in Smith's administrations until 1929. During those years, she mediated strikes between workers and management, improved factory inspections, regulated working conditions, and administered workers' compensation. When Smith, who ran unsuccessfully for president, was replaced as governor by Franklin D. Roosevelt, Perkins was appointed industrial commissioner of the State of New York. Perkins thus became the first woman to serve on a governor's cabinet.

With the full support of Roosevelt, Perkins was able to make significant reforms in working conditions in New York. She expanded employment services, increased factory investigations, and created data-gathering systems to provide information necessary to support legislative change. Among her legislative initiatives were reducing the work week for women to forty-eight hours, creating a minimum wage, and developing unemployment insurance. These efforts proved to be the blueprint for the work she did with Roosevelt years later in Washington.

Perkins served under Governor Roosevelt until his election as president of the United States. Without hesitation, President Roosevelt asked Perkins to serve as his secretary of labor. In 1933, Frances Perkins became the first woman ever to be appointed to a cabinet-level position. She accepted the position with the understanding that she was free to pursue the social reforms she had begun in New York and had advocated throughout her professional career.

Initially, labor and business leaders were critical of the idea of a female secretary of labor. Fully aware of that fact, Perkins developed a leadership style that brought together labor and management through cooperation and conciliation. As secretary of labor, Perkins also tried to bring together different factions of the labor movement. With the Great Depression looming, Perkins viewed reforming labor conditions as a way to improve economic conditions.

Over time, Perkins was successful in facilitating legislative reforms. Major relief legislation passed during Perkins' first years included the establishment of the Federal Emergency Relief Administration, the Civilian Conservation Corps, and the Public Works Administration. These programs represented the first major employment efforts by the federal government. Additional legislation was passed to regulate minimum wages, child labor, and work hours.

Perkins' major contributions as secretary of labor were the development of a data system to track statistics on employment and unemployment, standardization of state industrial legislation, and the development of the social security system. Perkins chaired the Committee on Economic Security, which crafted the Social Security Act of 1935. For both Perkins and Roosevelt, the Social Security Act represented a major accomplishment because it established minimum securities for workers through national insurance. In 1938, Perkins realized another major labor reform through the Fair Labor Standards Act, which set minimum wages, maximum work hours, and child labor prohibitions.

Perkins remained secretary of labor throughout Roosevelt's years as president. She resigned in 1945 and served on the U.S. Civil Service Commission until 1953. Her last years were spent writing and teaching at Cornell University. Frances Perkins died on May 14, 1965, in New York City.

### Summary

Frances Perkins' work demonstrated a rare blend of social concern and political action. Her early years in settlement houses and investigating working conditions propelled her to work toward changing the American labor system and improving the lives of working women and men. Perkins was convinced that what the labor system needed was legislative reform, not a complete overhaul. She devoted her professional career to influencing legislation that supported the needs of workers, particularly women and their families.

Perkins' role as a member of the presidential cabinet paved the way for future women to be directly involved in government action. She held public office before women could even vote. As a lobbyist and public official, she was instrumental in establishing government as a developer and regulator of legislation to protect workers. Under her influence, programs such as workers' compensation, unemployment insurance, minimum wages, and social security were formed. Such social legislation changed the face of labor forever and formed the foundation of modern workers' rights.

### Bibliography

Greengard, Samuel. "Twenty-five Visionaries Who Shaped Today's Workplace." *Workforce* 76, no. 1 (January, 1997). Greengard looks at the contributions of several individuals, including Perkins, Bill Gates, and Betty Friedan, in the creation and transformation of the workplace.

Martin, George W. *Madam Secretary.* Boston: Houghton Mifflin, 1976. A comprehensive and extensive biography based on Perkins' oral history, this book provides a very personal view of Perkins' life.

Mitchell, Donn. "Against Privatization: The Genius of Social Security." *Christian Century* 115, no. 25 (September 23, 1998). Mitchell evaluates the theory of privatization of Social Security and its original intent as created by Perkins.

Mohr, Lillian Holmen. *Frances Perkins: That Woman in FDR's Cabinet!* Croton-on-Hudson, N.Y.: North River Press, 1979. A biography of Perkins with some emphasis on the role of Perkins as a woman in government.

Severn, Bill. *Frances Perkins: A Member of the Cabinet.* New York: Hawthorn, 1976. Chronicles Perkins' life from her youth throughout her years in government.

Sternsher, Bernard, and Judith Sealander, eds. *Women of Valor: The Struggle Against the Great Depression as Told in Their Own Life Stories.* Chicago: Dee, 1990. This collection of essays by various women includes a piece by Perkins, excerpted from her book *The Roosevelt I Knew.* It gives insight into the kind of government official she was.

Wandersee, Winifred D. "I'd Rather Pass a Law than Organize a Union: Frances Perkins and the Reformist Approach to Organized Labor." *Labor History* 34, no. 1 (Winter, 1993): 5-32. Describes Perkins' approach to working with organized labor during her cabinet years.

*Elizabeth A. Segal*

# EVA PERÓN

*Born:* May 7, 1919; Los Toldos, Argentina
*Died:* July 26, 1952; Buenos Aires, Argentina
*Areas of Achievement:* Government and politics
*Contribution:* Eva Perón's partnership with her husband, president Juan D. Perón, brought the laboring masses of Argentina into politics for the first time but also laid the foundation for a corrupt and brutal dictatorship.

## Early Life

Eva "Evita" Maria Duarte de Perón was born María Eva Duarte in 1919 in the small rural town of Los Toldos, located some one hundred miles east of the Argentine capital city of Buenos Aires. She was the fifth and last child of Juan Duarte, an agricultural estate manager, and his mistress, Juana Ibarguren. At the time of Eva's birth, Duarte was already married to another woman by whom he had three daughters, and none of his children with Juana was legitimate. One year later he returned to his wife, and Juana was left alone to raise the children while bearing the brunt of neighborhood gossip. A critical turning point in Eva's life came with the death of her father in 1926. Duarte's legal family forbade Juana and her children from attending the funeral mass, and the attendant at the church would only allow them to follow the procession to the cemetery at a "respectable" distance from the heirs. The shame and trauma associated with this snub may have ignited Eva's identification with the poor and excluded.

Eva received little formal education, and her exposure to the world outside of Los Toldos came chiefly through the cinema. At age sixteen she migrated to Buenos Aires. Her physical beauty made her stand out in the city then known as the Paris of South America. Her most prominent feature was her platinum-blond hair, so important in a nation whose elite claimed descent from European conquerors. The girl's constitution was frail, however, and her voice was soft but distinctive. In the company of others she was a natural conversationalist who was little intimidated by rank or money, yet her illegitimate birth made her distrustful of strangers and gave her a marked tendency toward paranoia.

Staying in flophouses and tenements, Eva worked with small theater companies performing in forgettable productions. Her big break came in 1940 when her brother Juan landed her a job as an actress on a radio soap opera. Eva soon became nationally famous, but her ventures into cinema, while granting her greater public exposure, were not commercially successful, and she seemed destined to spend her life playing mediocre roles.

## Life's Work

Eva's turn from show business to politics came almost by chance. On January 15, 1944, a powerful earthquake struck the northeastern town of San Juan, killing an estimated ten thousand people. Colonel Juan Domingo Perón, a prominent member of the military junta that ruled Argentina, was put in charge of organizing a national charity drive to aid the survivors. Perón asked artists and entertainers to help collect funds for the relief effort, and it was in his office in Buenos Aires a few days after the earthquake that the forty-nine-year-old army officer and the radio actress first met. Perón later recalled that what he immediately noticed about Eva, then twenty-five years old, was her intelligence and determination in trying to help the unfortunate. While this account sounds self-serving, there were solid political as well as personal reasons for Perón to link himself to this young woman.

Perón had played a minor role in the coup d'état that had brought the armed forces to power in 1943. Whereas his fellow officers took lucrative positions in the new regime, however, he claimed the post of minister of labor and social welfare. Argentina's trade unions, ravaged by years of government persecution and the aftershocks of the global depression of 1929, counted for little with the military but could still mobilize millions of members. Perón, eager to run for president once civilian rule was restored, used his office to get close to the country's impoverished day laborers, *los descamisados* ("the shirtless ones"), figuring he could rely on their votes. However, as an officer serving a repressive government, he was distrusted by the union rank and file. The colonel needed a political ally well known to the urban masses who could speak to them in their own language. Eva fit the bill perfectly: She was an established media personality, and her own life served as a powerful symbol of how Argentina's forgotten ones could triumph over adversity. What she saw in Perón was the redeemer and avenger of Argentina's working class against the oligarchy of landowners, capital-

ists, and nouveaux riche who stomped on the dreams of the poor. Making their first joint appearance at an outdoor rally for the earthquake victims, the new "power couple" of Buenos Aires began to live together in mid-1944.

Eva soon threw herself back into radio work, this time with a political mission; when Perón assumed the additional offices of vice president and minister of war in 1945, she made broadcasts on behalf of her lover, the self-proclaimed champion of Argentina's workers, soldiers, wives, and mothers. Perón returned the favor by making Eva head of the union of radio employees, a step that alarmed the military establishment, already nervous about her populist-flavored tirades.

The couple's domestic life also elicited official censure. That an army colonel should keep a mistress was not sufficient cause for public scandal in Buenos Aires. What did raise a stir was the way Eva insisted on all the prerogatives of a wife: to be received by officers and their spouses, entertain politicians and business people at home, and stand side-by-side with her lover at public functions. Government ministers jealous of Perón's rising influence among the working class used the couple's "scandalous" relationship as an excuse to order his arrest on October 12, 1945. Eva kept in touch with Perón in his jail cell by correspondence, and through her he gave instructions to the trade unions to rally and demand his release. The armed forces, reeling from factional infighting and a postwar economic crisis, were obligated to grant his freedom on October 17. Nine days later, Perón married Eva and announced his candidacy for the presidential elections scheduled for February of 1946.

Perón swept into the presidency on a record vote, although allegations of electoral fraud marred his victory. His new bride became Argentina's second most important political figure. The president gave her virtual veto power over appointments to key cabinet positions, including the Ministry of the Interior, which controlled the national police. Eva also became owner of an influential newspaper, *Democracia*, transforming it into an organ of pro-Perón propaganda. After the government granted suffrage to women in 1946, she took charge of the Feminine Branch of the Peronist party to mobilize female support for her husband. She also played an active role in the General Trade Union Confederation (CGT) by handpicking its secretary general. Her influence extended equally into foreign affairs: In 1947 she made a much-publicized tour of Spain, France, Italy, and the Vatican to shore up support for Perón in the face of mounting opposition from the United States, which was angry over Argentina's nationalization of U.S. property.

Eva's most important function, however, was to cement the ties between Perón and the working class. In impassioned speeches given from balconies, she reminded the Peronist faithful that their day of delivery had come and that through her person every Argentine laboring man was the leader's comrade and every woman his bride. The Eva Perón Foundation (FEP), which was subsidized by the government, dispersed food, clothing, and medicine to the needy and built thousands of hospitals and schools in poor districts. However, Perón's critics charged the foundation with corruption and Eva herself of embezzlement. Her extravagance in clothing and home decoration did not fit well with her stated goal of uplifting the masses, and the ongoing political and economic turmoil that befell the Peronist regime after 1949 made her an easy target for slander.

Perón's first administration (1946 to 1955; he returned to power from 1973 to 1974) greatly improved life for Argentine workers in the form of higher wages, shorter hours, and medical care, but his mismanagement of the economy resulted in food shortages, strikes, lockouts, and high inflation. His attempt to regulate agricultural production led landowners to cut back on supplies to the cities. Nationalized industries such as railroads and banks were badly directed. Foreign investors stayed away from Argentina, while domestic manufacturers suffered from low customs and tariff duties. Critics of the regime were imprisoned or exiled, and opposition newspapers were shut down. By 1951, although Perón had won reelection as president, a mighty coalition of aristocrats, bankers, the Catholic Church, and old rivals from the military joined together to press for his resignation. Then, while fighting for his political life, he lost his wife and most important ally.

As her husband's fortunes declined, Eva's speeches took a hysterical turn, denouncing enemies of Perón everywhere. Listeners could tell something was amiss. By late 1951 her public appearances became less frequent and her voice, although still full of passion, had lost its once-commanding power. Finally, the president was forced to announce that Eva was suffering from uterine cancer and did not have long to live. A death watch started in nearly all corners of the country, with public prayers, pilgrimages, and masses. Eva passed away on July 26, 1952, leaving her husband alone to wage a losing fight to stay in office. Under pressure from the military, Perón left Argentina in 1955, taking Eva's body with him into exile in Europe.

### Summary

Few figures in modern times have passed so easily from history into myth as Eva Perón. Vain, egotistical, jealous, charismatic, generous, and deeply patriotic, she was Latin America's first true political celebrity, acting out in real life the cinema roles she had always coveted. The myth, however, has obscured much about her historical significance. To her followers she represented the populist side of Peronism, but she was no democrat; her manner in dealing with political opponents was dictatorial and deceitful. She championed the female vote but disdained feminism, insisting that everything she did was for the sake of Perón. She lived nearly all her life in public, often gripped by scandal, but advised women to be good homemakers and moral paragons.

Her tragic death at age thirty-three turned her into an instant icon, but she failed to pass on an exemplary political legacy. Railing against anyone who stood against her as a traitor, Eva poisoned the atmosphere of a country already sick of politics as a grubby business. With her death and Perón's banishment into exile, Argentina entered into a dark age, during which brutal military regimes alternated with incompetent civilian governments. Meanwhile, the Peronist party and trade unions lay frozen, longing for their departed father and mother.

### Bibliography

Barnes, John. *Evita: First Lady.* New York: Grove Press, 1978. A laudatory volume written for a popular audience, Barnes's book stresses Eva's devotion to the poor. Contains an index but no notes or bibliography.

Flores, María. *The Woman with the Whip: Eva Perón.* New York: Doubleday, 1952. Written by an Argentine woman who relocated to the United States to escape the Peronist dictatorship, this is the earliest and still the most hostile of all full-length biographies of Eva. Although it is a telling example of how Eva was regarded by the educated middle-class of her country, this volume lacks credibility because it does not include notes or a bibliography.

Fraser, Nicholas, and Marysa Navarro. *Eva Perón.* London: Deutsch, 1980; New York: Norton, 1981. The authors aim to separate the woman from the myth, relying heavily on interviews with participants in Argentine politics from the 1930's to the 1950's. Includes notes, a thorough bibliography, and an index.

Guillermoprieto, Alma. "Little Eva: Evita Made Herself, but What Are We to Make of Her?" *New Yorker* 72, no. 37 (December 2, 1996). Profile of Perón, her transformation from actress to politician, and her senseless death.

Ortiz, Alicia Dujovne. *Eva Perón.* New York: St. Martin's Press, 1996. This pedestrian biography written in novelistic prose contains photos and a short bibliography but no notes. It is interesting only for trying to convey the elegance of Evita.

Perón, Eva D. *In My Own Words: Evita.* New York: New Press, 1996. This volume includes Eva Perón's 1951 autobiography and her deathbed manuscript titled "My Message," originally suppressed by Juan Perón because of its criticism of the military.

Savigliano, Marta E. "*Evita:* The Globalization of a National Myth." *Latin American Perspectives* 24, no. 6, (November, 1997). This article considers the movie musical Evita and its romantic portrayal of Perón, who was much different in reality.

Taylor, J. M. *Eva Perón: The Myths of a Woman*. Chicago: University of Chicago Press, 1979. An anthropological study of Evita as myth and symbol. Utilizes periodicals from the 1940's and 1950's and interviews with an Argentine working-class family to gauge popular perceptions and interpretations of the "cult" of Evita. Includes notes, a bibliography, an index, and reproductions of photographs and posters from the Perón era.

*Julio César Pino*

## JUAN PERÓN

*Born:* October 8, 1895; Lobos, Buenos Aires Province, Argentina

*Died:* July 1, 1974; Buenos Aires, Argentina

*Areas of Achievement:* Government and politics

*Contribution:* More than any other figure, Perón dominated the history of twentieth century Argentina. He participated in coups that toppled the government in 1930 and 1943. With support from the armed forces and organized labor, he governed as president from 1943 to 1955 and 1973 to 1974. His legacy continued to divide Argentina long after his death in 1974.

### Early Life

Juan Domingo Perón was born in the town of Lobos in Buenos Aires Province on October 8, 1895. His restless father, Mario Tomás Perón, had given up the study of medicine to live as a minor government bureaucrat and tenant rancher. In 1890, at Lobos, he met Juana Sosa Toledo, a farm girl, and they had a son the following year. Juan was the second born, although the couple still had not married. In 1900, the family moved to Patagonia, but four years later his parents sent the boy to Buenos Aires to begin elementary school while living with some of his father's relatives.

Large for his age and increasingly self-reliant, Perón stayed on in the city with brief visits to his family, until in 1911 he entered the Military College, a prerequisite for a career in the armed forces. An average student as a cadet, Perón was commissioned a second lieutenant in 1913. By 1929, he was a captain, and his career had been routine and apolitical. Charismatic, hardworking, and energetic, Perón showed talent as a teacher and athlete. He also received an appointment to the Escuela Superior de Guerra (war academy) for three years of intensive study (1926-1929). On January 5, 1929, he married Aurelia Tizón, from a respectable middle-class Buenos Aires family.

### Life's Work

The depression of 1929 provoked a crisis in Argentina that brought Perón into politics. Appointed to the army's general staff, he joined in conspiracies against the government of President Hipólito Yrigoyen, culminating in the 1930 military coup. Although Perón's role was a small one, he did perceive an important lesson: The armed forces succeeded in overthrowing the government, he believed, only because a large number of civilians in Buenos Aires took up arms in support of the coup. The Revolution of 1930 subverted the Argentine political system, and constitutional rule came to an end. Perón became a professor of military history at the war academy, improved his didactic and speaking skills, and published several books. Promoted to lieutenant colonel in 1936, he served as a military attaché in Chile. His wife's death from cancer on September 10, 1938, ended a happy marriage, which had produced no children.

Perón then received orders to go to Italy, an assignment that shaped his political philosophy and later guided his policies as president of Argentina. His experiences in Italy, Germany, and Spain convinced him that some form of Fascism would dominate the future, although his own predilection was for a state similar to Francisco Franco's Spain rather than Nazi Germany. Perón's reading of military theory, much influenced by German writers, had persuaded him that war was an inevitable state of society. He admired the way that Adolf Hitler and

Benito Mussolini had mobilized and organized their peoples, especially through the use of trade unions, mass demonstrations, and appeals to anticommunism.

After spending 1939 and 1940 in Europe, he returned to Argentina, was promoted to full colonel, and began to conspire with fellow officers against the civilian government. The conspirators' organization was the Group of United Officers (GOU), an extremely secret faction probably founded by Perón. When President Ramón S. Castillo unconstitutionally tried to name his successor, it provoked the GOU into action. On June 14, 1943, a military faction led by General Arturo Rawson forced Castillo's resignation. Perón, who had been deeply involved in the conspiracy, did not participate in the military action. He usually disappeared when physical danger threatened.

Perón emerged from the coup as chief aide to General Edelmiro J. Farrell, the new minister of war. As the only leading officer who had a clear idea of what to do with the government, Perón appealed for working-class support. On October 27, 1943, he became minister of the National Labor Department and converted it into a nearly independent Secretariat of Labor and Social Welfare. He simultaneously courted factions within the military and gained support from the workers by according them respect. He encouraged them to organize, aided older unions that supported his policies, and oversaw the implementation of new laws favorable to the working class. Anarchist, socialist, and communist union leaders were repressed. In July, 1944, Perón became vice president under President Farrell, while retaining his other positions. Yet his mounting power threatened his rivals and the United States government, which mistakenly considered him a Nazi.

The end of World War II forced the military government to relax its most authoritarian measures, but more political freedom allowed opponents of the regime to organize. Anti-Peronist elements in the military seized power on October 9, 1945, arrested Perón, and imprisoned him on Martín García Island. When the workers saw that the anti-Peronist faction intended to erase most of the gains that Perón had granted, they rallied to his support. Resorting to mass demonstrations and violence on October 17, the working class forced the opposition to back down, release Perón, and permit free elections for the presidency in 1946. Meanwhile, Perón's mistress, actress Eva ("Evita") Duarte, had shored up his courage, but she had nothing to do with the popular demonstrations despite later myths to the contrary. Although Perón and Evita had flaunted their relationship since early 1944, to the scandal of straitlaced Argentines, they married shortly after his release, in part to enhance Perón's chances in the presidential election.

With the campaign under way, both the opposition and the United States government underestimated the depth of Perón's support. His opponents, ranging from the Radicals to the Communists, coalesced in the Democratic Union, confident of victory. Meanwhile, United States Assistant Secretary of State Spruille Braden made public a compilation of anti-Perón propaganda, the "Blue Book," intended to portray Perón as a Nazi and discredit him with Argentine voters. Braden's ploy backfired, however, because Argentine nationalists resented American intervention. Charismatic and forceful, Perón attracted huge crowds and mounting support. In the freest election up to that point in Argentine history, Perón won 54 percent of the popular vote and decisive control of both houses of congress. He took office on June 4, 1946.

On the surface, Perón ruled for the next nine years as a populist president, playing to nationalist sentiments. He used foreign reserves accumulated during the war to repatriate railroads, utilities, and other holdings from foreign investors. For the first time, Argentine manufacturers benefited from a high protective tariff, along with the governmental measures to stimulate industrialization. The government invested great sums in heavy industry, building the nation's first steel plant and subsidizing automobile manufacturing. Perón also spent huge sums to provide new equipment for the armed forces.

Perón called his political philosophy *Justicialismo*, a muddled theory that neither he nor his followers ever clearly defined. It was allegedly a middle position between capitalism and communism. Perón was no democrat despite his reliance upon the working class for support, yet neither did he espouse an ideologically consistent form of dictatorship. While his attitudes favored the lessons learned in Italy and Spain, his only consistent policy was Argentine nationalism, much to the chagrin of the United States. The new constitution of 1949, which abolished the proscription upon a president's succeeding himself and permitted Perón's reelection in 1951, gave women the right to vote and established ten basic rights of workers.

Evita played an important but not crucial role in Perón's rule. She was the de facto head of the labor department, provided an important link to the common people and to female voters, and ran the Eva Perón Welfare Foundation, a graft-ridden charitable institution that enriched its namesake. Evita derived her power from her husband, however, and, as a female involved in politics, was barely tolerated by Perón's military supporters. Her campaign for the vice presidency in 1951 had to be aborted when the military balked. Her death from cancer on July 26, 1952, deeply affected Perón.

Perón's regime was also in crisis. Public spending had outstripped revenues, causing serious inflation. Livestock and grain production fell because of Perón's economic policies. Enemies spread rumors about Perón's alleged sexual orgies with young girls. As discontent mounted, he became more dictatorial inside Argentina but began to soften his xenophobia in the hope of obtaining international aid. Although Perón and the Roman Catholic church had initially supported each other, a bitter conflict broke out between the two erstwhile allies, with the government of Argentina making divorces easy to obtain, legalizing prostitution, and limiting the Church's role in education. When the regime arrested and exiled two bishops, the papacy excommunicated the officials responsible. The next day, June 16, 1955, factions within the armed forces attempted a coup against the Peronist government, but it failed because it lacked the army's support. Perón responded fearfully, however, and made a number of concessions to the opposition. He seemed afraid to fight and claimed later that he was trying to avoid a civil war. When sectors of the army joined a second coup on September 16, 1955, Perón went into exile, leaving a bitterly polarized nation.

Perón first sought refuge in Paraguay, later drifted through Venezuela, Panama, Nicaragua, and the Dominican Republic, and eventually took up permanent residence in Spain. Peronists never abandoned hope, however, that their hero would govern Argentina once again. In 1964, he made a semiserious attempt to return but upon his arrival in Brazil was prevented from embarking for Argentina and was sent back to Madrid. Even from Spain, however, he exerted great influence over the Peronists, directing their political activities and preventing anyone from challenging his position as leader of the movement. Meanwhile, political chaos engulfed Argentina, with neither the armed forces nor civilians able to govern. Beginning in 1969, terrorism and turmoil mounted until the military decided to permit a free election, even if it might permit a Peronist victory and the return of Perón himself to Argentina.

Perón arrived in November, 1972, too late to be a candidate, but his lieutenant, Hector Cámpora, won the presidency. Cámpora soon resigned, and Perón was elected on September 27, 1973, with his third wife, Isabel Martínez de Perón, as vice president. Yet during his eighteen-year exile, Peronism had changed. Organized labor remained loyal, but many intellectuals, students, and others dissatisfied with Argentine politics, including some terrorists such as the Montoneros and Peronist Youth, also looked to Perón for leadership. Once in office again, Perón sought national reconciliation and seemed committed to democratic rule. The conflicting aims of his own supporters made government difficult, however, and his health failed before he even took office. Perón died on July 1, 1974.

### Summary

Juan Perón's first administration attempted to deal with important obstacles to Argentine development. He played to the interests of organized labor and accorded women new political rights. He attempted to break the rural elite's control over the economy by subsidizing industrialization. His nationalism carried popular support. Yet his dictatorial method and lack of fiscal restraint, his grandiose but xenophobic foreign policy, the continued enmity of the rural oligarchs, and the regime's failure to achieve long-lasting social and economic reform undercut his accomplishments. Argentina was far more polarized when he fell in 1955 than it had been when he took office.

By the 1970's, Perón was the only person with a chance of healing Argentina's wounds, and his death, followed by the shortlived rule of his third wife, touched off a downward spiral into military dictatorship, leftist- and state-sponsored terrorism, and military debacle in the Falkland Islands.

### Bibliography

Alexander, Robert J. *Juan Domingo Perón: A History.* Boulder, Colo.: Westview Press, 1979. A short biography, with bibliography, by an author who has written extensively on various facets of the Peronist years in Argentina.

Crassweller, Robert. *Perón and the Enigmas of Argentina.* New York: Norton, 1987. This well-written biography argues that Perón achieved great popularity in Argentina, despite accomplishing little, because he embodied the cultural ethos of Hispanic and creole Argentina. Contains a good bibliography and photographs.

Falcoff, Mark. "Perón's Nazi Ties." *Time International* 152, no. 18 (November 9, 1998). The author considers Perón's Nazi ties, Argentine concealment of ex-Nazis, political crimes, and more.

Fraser, Nicholas, and Marysa Navarro. *Eva Perón.* London: Deutsch, 1980; New York: Norton, 1981. Generally balanced in its treatment of Evita, this biography strips away much of the myth surrounding Perón's wife and shows her political contributions.

Madsen, Douglas, and Peter G. Snow. *The Charismatic Bond: Political Behavior in Time of Crisis.* Cambridge, Mass.: Harvard University Press, 1991. The authors continue Max Weber's study of Perónism.

Page, Joseph A. *Perón: A Biography.* New York: Random House, 1983. The best biography of Perón available, this is a lengthy, thorough treatment of his entire career and is more sympathetic to its subject than most studies.

Rock, David. *Argentina, 1516-1982: From Spanish Colonization to the Falklands War.* Berkeley: University of California Press, 1985; London: Tauris, 1986. This excellent overview of Argentine history devotes extensive coverage to Perón, including photographs and bibliography.

Turner, Frederick C., and José Enrique Miguens, eds. *Juan Perón and the Reshaping of Argentina.* Pittsburgh: University of Pittsburgh Press, 1983. Offers the flavor of Perón's thought through translations of speeches, lectures, essays, and addresses.

*Kendall W. Brown*

# H. ROSS PEROT

*Born:* June 27, 1930; Texarkana, Texas

*Areas of Achievement:* Business, industry, government, and politics

*Contribution:* An immensely successful entrepreneur, Perot spent his first sixty years dedicated to improving American business. Thereafter he devoted his life to political reform and making government responsible to the people.

## Early Life

Henry Ross Perot was born on June 27, 1930, in Texarkana, Texas, a quiet cotton-dependent town that lay on the state line between Texas and Arkansas. His father Gabriel earned his living as a cotton broker in Texarkana, where he met and married Lulu May Ray, a secretary for a local lumber company. Because of Gabriel's skills as a merchant, the Perot family lived comfortably despite the Great Depression. He and Lulu also provided hot meals to the poor from their back door.

Gabriel Perot taught his son the importance of relationships in business, stressing that a businessman's good word allowed him to continue to do business. From his father, Ross learned to love the art of buying and selling. An equal influence on Ross was his mother, Lulu May, a strong and spiritual woman who demanded honesty, uprightness, and perfect manners from her children. Instead of whipping her children when they misbehaved, she chose to lecture them for their punishment. She taught him the importance of setting high standards for himself and of judging himself rather than waiting for others to judge him.

When he turned eighteen, Perot began sending letters to congressmen, seeking an appointment to the U.S. Naval Academy. After several rejections, Perot received an appointment and was sworn in on June 27, 1949. He was graduated only 454th in a class of 925 graduates, but his leadership record was impeccable; he served as class president and as head of the school's honor committee. While at the academy, he met Margot Birmingham, a student at Goucher College, on a blind date, and they were married in 1956 in Greensburg, Pennsylvania.

Upon his graduation in June, 1953, Perot was assigned to the destroyer USS *Sigourney* as an assistant fire-control officer, and the ship headed across the Pacific to take part in the Korean War. On the way, however, a truce was signed between Allied and Communist forces, and the ship headed home by continuing west through the Suez Canal and into the Mediterranean Sea. For his second assignment, Perot served as assistant navigator aboard the aircraft carrier USS *Leyte*. While escorting visitors aboard ship, Perot met an International Business Machines (IBM) executive who suggested that Perot interview with the company. Following his discharge in 1957, Perot and Margot left for Dallas, Texas, where IBM accepted Perot as a trainee.

## Life's Work

Perot proved extremely successful selling computer systems for IBM. He consistently achieved 100 percent of his yearly sales quota and persuaded difficult accounts to sign with IBM; however, he became irritated that his supervisors would not listen to his suggestions. In 1962, therefore, Perot formed Electronic Data Systems Corporation (EDS) with only $1,000 in initial capital. His sales pitch was simple but effective: Rather than selling customers computer systems that they would not know how to operate, he proposed to do the computing and data processing for them.

In February, 1963, Perot landed his first contract, with Frito-Lay; other contracts soon followed. EDS's profits remained modest until 1965, when the passage of Medicare legislation suddenly increased the demand for computers, programmers, and storage—all of which Perot and EDS provided. Demand for the company's services was extremely high, and there was little competition. Because of the tremendous growth, Perot began selling stock to the public in September, 1968. The shares sold quickly, giving EDS $5 million in capital and Perot $5 million in cash; he became a millionaire nearly overnight. Only two years later, Perot's portion of the stock had risen in value to $1.4 billion.

In 1969, Perot received a call from Secretary of State Henry Kissinger asking for his assistance in getting the North Vietnamese to improve the conditions for U.S. prisoners of war. In response, Perot formed the United We Stand committee to collect money and buy advertising to pressure North Vietnam into improving prison conditions. A week before Christmas in 1969, Perot announced that United We Stand would deliver Christmas dinners to the POWs. Suspicious, the North Vietnamese refused to admit the United We Stand representatives, however, and the mission failed. Perot, nevertheless, remained deeply committed to the effort to locate POWs.

EDS broke into the international market with a $41 million contract with the Iranian social security system in November, 1976. An exciting situation turned critical in December, 1978, when revolutionary officials began jailing many Iranian officials with whom EDS had dealt. Partly in reaction, EDS notified the government that it was suspending operations. Soon afterward, Perot ordered all EDS workers and dependents out of Iran, except for the company's top officials. Without warning, Iranian revolutionaries arrested the EDS manager in Iran, Paul Chiapparone, and his assistant Bill Gaylord on charges that EDS had diverted millions from the Iranian treasury, a claim that was never proven. When diplomacy failed to get the two released, Perot sent ex-Green Beret colonel Arthur D. Simons and a team of EDS executives to try to free them from an Iranian prison. The executives were released by mistake before the team could implement its plan, but Perot's agents did succeed in getting them safely out of the country. Novelist Ken Follett later chronicled the effort in his 1983 nonfiction account *On Wings of Eagles*.

In June, 1984, Perot agreed to a merger between EDS and General Motors (GM). He was given a position on the GM board of directors and was allowed to run EDS as a separate organization within GM. Soon, however, differences emerged between Perot and Roger Smith, GM's chairman and chief executive. Perot disagreed with the way GM was being run, and Smith disliked the amount of independence Perot demanded. Finally, after Perot publicly criticized GM in November, 1986, the board of directors agreed to buy out Perot's interest for $742.8 million.

In the years following his ouster, Perot began to receive pressure from various sources to run for president. On February 20, 1992, he appeared on the *Larry King Live* television show on the Cable News Network (CNN) to state how he thought America could be "fixed." Throughout the interview, Perot claimed that the American people needed to take back control of their government, and he hinted that if the public gave him sufficient encouragement, he would run as an independent candidate. Although he never declared himself as an official candidate, Perot funded a campaign to get himself on the ballot in all fifty states. By late June, many polls showed that Perot would win a substantial number of votes. On July 17, however, he withdrew his name from candidacy, stating that the Democrats had begun to address his concerns. Following his withdrawal, his supporters formed an organization called United We Stand America, which continued to work to get Perot's name on the ballot in every state, and he continued to fund these efforts.

Stating that he wanted the campaign to focus on economic issues, Perot reentered the race on October 1. He appeared on television in paid commercial spots in which he presented his plan for saving the American economy and reforming the government.

Ultimately, though, Perot was unable to regain the political strength that he had shown in the summer. Nevertheless, he finished with 19 percent of the popular vote, the strongest showing by a third-party candidate since 1912, and many political analysts claimed that Perot's candidacy contributed to Bill Clinton's victory.

In January, 1993, Perot announced that United We Stand America would continue to receive new members and would become a nonprofit citizens' action group. Perot planned for the organization to pressure lawmakers for political reform and debt reduction. The group, however, failed to work together as he had hoped. Members of United We Stand America's volunteer staff complained that the Dallas headquarters acted in a dictatorial fashion, and the movement weakened.

Over the next three years, Perot continued his watchdog tactics. In June, 1995, he invited President Clinton and the principal contenders for the Republican nomination to a conference in Dallas. The convention met in August with political leaders such as Jesse Jackson, House Speaker Newt Gingrich, and Senator Bob Dole in attendance. The Republicans were particularly interested in pleasing Perot in order to keep him from running for president in 1996. Perot, however, claimed dissatisfaction with both the Democrats and the Republicans, and he announced in September that he would be forming a new, independent Reform Party for the 1996 election.

In the first months of 1996, Perot again hinted that he would run for president if his name could be listed on the ballots of all fifty states. On July 11, two days after former Colorado governor Richard Lamm announced that he would seek the Reform Party's presidential nomination, Perot declared his own intention to seek the party's nomination. After bitter arguments between Lamm and

Perot in the months leading to the August convention, Perot handily won the nomination with 65.2 percent of the vote, and he soon launched another series of television spots. In September, however, his campaign was crippled when the Commission on Presidential Debates barred him from participating in the televised debates between Clinton and Republican nominee Bob Dole; Perot then lost a court appeal to allow him to engage in the debates. Ultimately, Perot's campaign never gained the momentum of his 1992 effort, and he finished a distant third, with only 8 percent of the popular vote. Following the elections, he stated that his party would continue to pressure the government, but renewed divisions within the party led to questions about its direction and leadership.

### Summary

A controversial figure throughout his life, H. Ross Perot used his early business success to allow him to bring certain issues, such as the status of American prisoners in Vietnam, into the national spotlight. He used the publicity generated by the Iran rescue to foster a positive public image, appearing as a national hero and a father figure determined to take care of his employees. All these factors played an important role when he decided to become involved in presidential politics.

Regardless of his motives, Perot has undeniably contributed a new popular vitality to politics that had been lacking in previous presidential elections. In 1992, he helped to turn the focus of the campaign from character questions to the American economy. In 1996, he forced the candidates to talk about political reform. Although many Americans disagreed with Perot's views, he did succeed in getting many people to start talking about the issues. More important, he also helped to empower many people, giving them the feeling that they could reclaim their government from special interests and regular party politics. In addition, although the Reform Party did not rival the strength of the Democratic or Republican Parties, his grassroots campaigns helped to strengthen and legitimize third-party politics.

### Bibliography

Barta, Carolyn. *Perot and His People: Disrupting the Balance of Political Power.* Fort Worth, Tex.: Summit Group, 1993. A lengthy and detailed account of Perot's 1992 presidential campaign. Besides narrating the campaign, the book critically examines Perot's influence in the election's outcome and weighs the possible positive and negative effects of Perot's bid on future elections. Charts list state-by-state election statistics.

Follett, Ken. *On Wings of Eagles.* London: Collins, and New York: Morrow, 1983. Commissioned by Perot to detail his and EDS's role in the rescue of two EDS employee hostages in Iran in 1979, this entertaining and popular work is decidedly biased in Perot's favor.

Koch, Jeffrey. "The Perot Candidacy and Attitudes Toward Government and Politics." *Political Research Quarterly* 51, no. 1 (March, 1998). The author discusses the historical relationship between U.S. voter discontent and support for a third political party, focusing on Perot's 1992 campaign.

Levin, Doron P. *Irreconcilable Differences: Ross Perot vs. General Motors.* Boston: Little Brown, 1989. An account of Perot's dealings with General Motors, particularly useful for its discussion of the formation of EDS and the personal disagreements that led to Perot's buyout at GM. Includes photographs of Perot and the major figures involved in the GM crisis.

Livengood, R. Mark. "Pitching Politics for the People: An Analysis of the Metaphoric Speech of H. Ross Perot." *Western Folklore* 56, no. 3-4 (Summer-Fall 1997). Discussion of Perot's rhetoric in the 1992 presidential campaign that served to align him with blue- and white-collar voters.

Mason, Todd. *Perot: An Unauthorized Biography.* Homewood, Ill.: Irwin, 1990. As suggested by the subtitle, this business biography does not use interviews with Perot but depends on interviews with his competitors at GM and EDS. Covers Perot from his earliest years to the EDS suit against him in 1989.

Posner, Gerald. *Citizen Perot: His Life and Times.* New York: Random House, 1996. A relatively objective biography, with particular emphasis on Perot's formation of EDS and his dealings with GM. Especially useful for its balanced and unbiased account of the 1992 election.

*Michael R. Nichols*

# AUGUSTE PERRET

*Born:* February 12, 1874; near Brussels, Belgium
*Died:* February 25, 1954; Paris, France
*Area of Achievement:* Architecture
*Contribution:* Perret's great contribution was the utilization, refinement, and promotion of reinforced concrete, or ferroconcrete, which he was convinced was the building material of the future.

## Early Life

Auguste Perret, the eldest of three brothers, was born near Brussels of French parentage. His father, descended from a long line of master stonemasons, had been a successful building contractor in Paris. His involvement in the Communist uprising against the government in 1871 forced him to leave France for Belgium, where he reestablished himself as a contractor. In 1881, however, after a general amnesty, he and his family returned to Paris, where he successfully continued his career as a building contractor, training his sons to do the same.

In 1891, Auguste Perret was enrolled in the École des Beaux-Arts, the leading architectural school of its time. The training was theoretical, and the curriculum stressed classical designs. Perret was a diligent student, earning a series of first prizes. He always considered the architect Eugène Viollet-le-Duc (1814-1879), known for his restoration work on ancient French monuments, to have been his great inspiration. Not only did Viollet-le-Duc respect traditional architecture but also he stressed the importance of unity between design and execution.

While at the Beaux-Arts, Perret continued to work for his father in construction. He left the school without completing the final project for his diploma. The move was deliberate. By law, a licensed architect could not be a building contractor. Perret wanted to build what he designed. Therefore, for the next sixty years one of France's leading architects was known simply as a contractor.

At the time Perret was at the Beaux-Arts, François Hennebique patented a process for creating a concrete frame structure reinforced by embedded iron or steel rods. He constructed several buildings in Paris with a reinforced concrete core but with exposed surfaces covered with traditional building materials. Perret recognized both the potentials and faults of the new material; he was determined to improve it and to utilize it honestly as an inexpensive, versatile, and potentially handsome building material.

## Life's Work

Perret's first major use of reinforced concrete was in 1899 at the municipal casino in St. Malo, where he installed a clear span reinforced concrete beam sixty feet long. The pivotal structure, the one to establish Perret's reputation as a great architect, was the rue Franklin apartment house in Paris built in 1903, the first to be built completely of reinforced concrete with its basic lines revealed rather than hidden. The site with its limited area would have been unsuitable for conventional building materials. Using more compact and stronger reinforced concrete solved the problem.

Perret designed what appeared to be a conventional, handsome seven-story and penthouse apartment building architecturally in harmony with those it abutted. Technically, the design was revolutionary. All the light for the apartments came from the street side. Since the walls were non-load-bearing because of the reinforced concrete frame, more window space was available. To secure even more lighting, Perret recessed part of the façade as a light well and compensated for the lost space by cantilevering the lateral bay windows of the apartments. The services were in the rear, where light was secured by embedded hexagonal glass bricks. The interior walls too were non-load-bearing and thus could be rearranged at will. The only concession Perret made to conventional architecture was in covering the exposed concrete with colorful faience tiles. The concrete was not impervious to moisture—a shortcoming Perret was determined to correct. The tiles, however, followed the building lines.

The elder Perret, who had neither sympathy for nor understanding of reinforced concrete and forced the son to use a subcontractor for the rue Franklin building, died in 1905. The firm now became Perret Brothers: Auguste and his two brothers Gustave and Claude. The same year, the new firm built another concrete frame building, a garage. Then for seventeen years, Perret would not build another, although his firm often constructed skeletal reinforced concrete frames upon which a veneer of conventional building material would be placed—a process Perret considered dishonest.

In 1913, Perret was involved in a major building project that would enhance his reputation as an innovative builder, for he had to accept with modification a design already accepted. The building was the Théâtre Champs-Élysées in Paris. Again there were difficulties: groundwater and an irregular building site. Perret overcame the former by floating the theater on a concrete pontoon; he overcame the latter by the use of concealed reinforced concrete arches, which enabled him by the process of cantilevering and suspending to construct three separate theaters, each capable of being used independently.

The war years of 1914-1918, while inhibiting conventional architectural design, afforded Perret the opportunity of improving reinforced concrete and demonstrating its versatility. At the great docks constructed in Casablanca, Morocco, his reinforced concrete vaulting was in places less than two inches thick yet incredibly strong. In a clothing factory completed in 1919, Perret created the greatest amount of unobstructed floor space yet known through the use of gigantic freestanding reinforced concrete arches.

By this time, through consultation and experimentation, Perret had succeeded in making reinforced concrete moisture-resistant. He achieved this innovation by vibrating the composition before it had hardened in order to increase its density. The improved concrete was used to construct in 1922-1923 the church of Notre-Dame at Le Raincy, for many Perret's greatest masterpiece. Dedicated to French soldiers who had fallen in the Battle of Ourq in World War I, built in record time and with limited funds, the church was made entirely of exposed reinforced concrete. In form, the church followed that of the traditional cathedral, but its execution was unique. A single great barrel vault spanned the nave, which was separated from the side aisles by slender columns added for dramatic effect. The glory of the church was the walls constructed of precast concrete grilles in geometric patterns. Into the openwork Perret had inserted colored glass arranged according to the spectrum. The effect was overwhelmingly magnificent. In the words of one critic, concrete had at last come of age.

The time of the building of Notre-Dame at Le Raincy marked a turning point in Perret's professional career. His reputation now firmly established, he could devote himself to honest reinforced concrete constructions. The architectural avant-garde ignored him, but businessmen and governmental bureaucrats liked him, seeing him as a dependable architect who never exceeded cost estimates.

Between 1923 and his death in 1954, Perret completed more than seventy projects in addition to numerous plans. Three bear mentioning because they demonstrate advances in Perret's professional career. The Mobilier National Building of 1934, built to house the costly official furniture and furnishings of the French government, again had to be built on an irregular site and for multiple functions ranging from monumental exhibition halls to domestic quarters for curators. Perret created a harmonious design incorporating features of traditional French architecture. Because of the increased density and strength of the concrete, the unattractive layer of mortar that rises to the surface once concrete is poured could now be removed. Perret executed this innovation through a bushhammering technique, and the concrete looked like traditional dressed stone.

Since the bushhammering revealed the pebble and stone content of the concrete or its aggregate, Perret now sought to improve its appearance. One method involved graduated sizes in the pebbles and stone. Another mixed colored stone chips with a white matrix or cement binder, thus achieving a pointillistic effect. The best examples of his experimentations are to be seen in the composition of the columns of the Museum of Public Works built facing the Place de la Concorde in Paris. Perret's columns harmonized with those on the splendid eighteenth century buildings. By carefully controlled formwork, Perret also succeeded in achieving beautiful profiling for the building in the form of subtle curves.

Perret's last major project was the rebuilding of the port city of Le Havre, whose center had been demolished by Allied bombing during World War II. In his design, Perret showed the influence of the great city planners of the seventeenth and eighteenth centuries whose ideas Perret had adapted to the twentieth. His plan called for grand avenues connecting principal buildings with the spaces between filled with parks, squares, and streets laid out in grid fashion. He designed both the new city hall and the monumental church of St. Michael.

Official recognition and honors for Perret came late. At the age of seventy-one, he was finally permitted to call himself an architect and was made president of the newly formed Order of Architects. He became a professor at the Beaux-Arts, was elected to the Institute of France, and was appointed officer of the Legion of Honor. In 1948, he was awarded the Gold Medal by the Royal Institute of British Architects; in 1953, he was awarded the Gold Medal by the American Institute of Architects. Perret died the following year as he would have wished, in a luxurious apartment in a building he had himself constructed—of reinforced concrete.

### Summary

Auguste Perret's professional career as an architect can best be summed up by viewing him essentially as an innovator and compromiser. The innovation was the utilization, refinement, and promotion of reinforced concrete. Through processes such as vibrating, bushhammering, constituting, and profiling, Perret succeeded in making it not only an inexpensive and incredibly strong but also a handsome building material. In a sense, he accomplished in a lifetime for concrete what it had taken countless generations of others to do for stone. As a compromiser, Perret in his designs tried to draw what was useful from the past and adapt it to the present. He viewed much of the work of his architectural contemporaries as unwarranted displays of egotism. He always maintained that the architect was limited by the laws of nature regarding the properties of materials, the vagaries of climate, the rules of optics, and the sense of lines and forms. Ignoring these limitations produced designs that fatigued the eye and were transitory. In the last analysis, what was to be sought was environmental harmony.

### Bibliography

Benevolo, Leonardo. *History of Modern Architecture.* Translated by H. J. Landry. 2 vols. London: Routledge, and Cambridge, Mass.: MIT Press, 1971. Benevolo explains how Perret, despite his reputation as a "classical" architect, through subtle refinements and true originality fits into the 1890-1914 avant-garde movement of European architecture.

Bosworth, William Wells. "Perret, the Innovator, a Professional Study." *American Society Legion of Honor Magazine* 26 (Summer, 1955): 141-148. Bosworth knew Perret well. They were both members of the Institute of France. The article has interesting quotes from various authorities on Perret. Bosworth singles out the Museum of Public Works as Perret's most significant work and explains why.

Collins, Peter. *Concrete: The Vision of a New Architecture.* London: Faber, and New York: Horizon Press, 1959. The most comprehensive work available in English on Perret. The book is divided into three sections. The first deals with the historic development of the use of concrete; the second with the technological evolution of reinforced concrete or ferroconcrete in the nineteenth century; the third section and principal part of the book deals with the work of Perret. Collins divides Perret's career into two parts: the formative and the definitive, with 1928 as the dividing line. It was in the latter period that Perret came into his own. Of particular value are the 156 black-and-white photographs of all of Perret's principal works as well as related works and designs of other architects.

Goldfinger, Ernö. "The Work of Auguste Perret." *Architectural Journal* 70 (January, 1955): 144-156. Goldfinger knew Perret for nearly a quarter century and had worked in his office. This article is a transcript of a speech Goldfinger delivered to a meeting of the British Architectural Association shortly after Perret's death. Goldfinger divides Perret's career into four parts: search for a medium, adventures in tectonic truth, search for a French style, and the final achievement. The comments of some of the members of the association who also knew Perret are also interesting.

Tafuri, Manfredo, and Francesco Dal Co. *Modern Architecture.* Translated by Robert Erich Wolf. New York: Abrams, 1979; London: Academy, 1980. The book gives probably the best concise overall account of Perret's career from the building of the rue Franklin apartment house to the plan for the rebuilding of Le Havre. Of particular interest is the description of French politics that prevented Perret from receiving commissions he deserved.

*Nis Petersen*

# FRED PERRY

*Born:* May 18, 1909; Stockport, Cheshire, England
*Died:* February 2, 1995; Melbourne, Australia
*Area of Achievement:* Sports
*Contribution:* Between 1933 and 1936, Perry won all the world's major tennis championships and led the British team to victory in the Davis Cup, thereby restoring British tennis prestige.

## Early Life

Frederick John Perry, born May 18, 1909, to Hannah and Sam Perry, spent most of the first decade of his life in Stockport, Bolton, and Wallasey, towns in Cheshire and Lancashire, where his father, a cotton spinner, was involved with the Cooperative Party and the Labour Party. When World War I ended, his father was transferred to Ealing in west London, though as a Labour candidate he was later elected Member of Parliament for Stockport.

Perry showed ability at the leading sports in Ealing County School, as a forward on the soccer team and wicket keeper on the cricket team. Disenchanted with getting knocked around at soccer and hit by the hard cricket ball, he turned to concentrating on what he really preferred: individual, as opposed to team, sports.

Hating homework, in the evenings Perry would push the kitchen table up against the wall, put up a table-tennis net, and hit a ball over it and back off the wall. The repetitious noise was nerve-racking for his family, but through this drill he acquired the knowledge of spins, quick reflexes, and sense of rhythm that were to enable him ultimately to win world championships at both table tennis and tennis. He adopted a comparable kind of tennis drill against the outside wall of his home after he had discovered tennis during a summer holiday at Eastbourne while he was fourteen. Perry's interest was sparked when he learned that the expensive cars at Devonshire Park were owned by the elegantly dressed players on the tennis courts.

Owning only one tennis racket, which his father bought him for five shillings, he began playing in junior tournaments and reached the singles final and won the doubles at the Middlesex Championships. Concurrently, he developed his table-tennis skills, was selected at age nineteen to play for England, and the following year he won the men's singles at the 1929 World Championships in Budapest.

## Life's Work

Having become world champion at table tennis at age twenty, Perry decided to retire while at the top and to switch all of his attention to tennis. The same year, he qualified for Wimbledon and won two rounds before being beaten. His father offered to support him financially for a year while he sought success at tennis. Fred spent the winter of 1929-1930 working at taking the ball as early as possible after the bounce, a technique adapted from table tennis. In 1930, he reached the final of the British Hard Court Championships and the fourth round at Wimbledon, beating the world's fourth-ranked player and gaining the praise of Bill Tilden, who won the title again that year. These achievements earned for him a place on the English team touring the Americas, during which he won the championship of Argentina without losing a set.

In 1931, Perry reached the semifinals at Wimbledon, where he lost to the American Sidney Wood (who then won the title by the default of the injured Frank Shields). Perry beat Wood but lost to Shields in the semifinals of the Davis Cup team competition, as the British eliminated the Americans. In the Challenge Round, Perry beat Jean Borotra but lost to Henri Cochet, the French thus retaining the Cup. On tour of the United States, Perry reached the semifinals of the United States National Championships, where he lost to Ellsworth Vines, who went on to win the final.

In 1932, Perry lost the deciding singles in a Davis Cup match against Germany and was beaten by Sidney Wood in the United States National Championships, each time in the fifth set. Always furious at losing, Perry resolved to increase his already notable fitness. He did not drink alcohol, and although he toyed with a pipe, it was usually unlit. Before a match, he avoided shaking hands so that he would not lose feeling in his hand. Partly for psychological and theatrical effect, he would come onto the court immaculate in white blazer and long white flannel trousers. (He never wore shorts on court until one night late in his career as a professional, when a rip at the knee obliged him to cut off the torn trouser leg and then the other to match.) At the end of a long match, he would leap over the net in order to impress the image of his fitness on his opponent's memory.

After a disappointingly short run at Wimbledon, Perry made 1933 a banner year. In the Davis Cup Interzone Finals against the United States, he defeated Wilmer Allison and Ellsworth Vines and then in the Challenge Round against France, he beat Henri Cochet and André Merlin, thereby bringing the Davis Cup back to Great Britain after twenty-one years. In the next three years, he also won all of his matches, thereby helping to keep the cup in Great Britain. His record in David Cup singles was thirty-four wins in thirty-eight matches.

In September, 1933, Perry acquired the first of his eight Grand Slam singles titles (the Australian, French, Wimbledon, and United States Championships). In the final of the United States Championship, Jack Crawford of Australia seemed to be on the verge of becoming the first person ever to win all four Grand Slam titles in the same year, as he led Perry by two sets to one, but the supremely fit Perry swept the last two sets, 6-0, 6-1.

Perry opened 1934 by defeating Crawford in three straight sets to win the Australian Championship and repeated the feat in the Wimbledon finals. He retained his United States title by defeating Allison in five sets in the final. In 1935, he lost his Australian title to Crawford in four sets in the final. He then beat Crawford in straight sets in the semifinals of the French Championships and won the title by defeating the elegant German Gottfried von Cramm in four sets. At Wimbledon, Perry retained his title by beating von Cramm in straight sets. In the United States Championship, he lost his title when, during the first set of his semifinal against Allison, he fell and his racket handle drove into his chest. Despite the pain of what turned out to be a broken rib, he played to the finish. In 1936, he lost his French title to von Cramm in a five-set final, then beat him in the Wimbledon final with the loss of only two games, von Cramm struggling with a pulled leg muscle. Perry regained the United States Championship by defeating Don Budge 10-8 in the fifth set.

Although he often did not participate in doubles matches, Perry did win each of the Grand Slam doubles championships at least once. With Sarah Palfrey, he won the United States mixed doubles title in 1932 and with Dorothy Round the Wimbledon mixed doubles in 1935 and 1936. With G. P. Hughes he won the French men's doubles in 1933, the Australian in 1934, and eleven out of fourteen Davis Cup doubles matches.

This extraordinary sequence of triumphs meant that Perry was constantly being offered lucrative contracts to turn professional. He declared that he believed that he owed British tennis, in particular the Davis Cup team, his continued participation. By remaining in amateur competition after reaching the top, he risked losing his championships and with them his value on the professional market, as had happened to Vines. Eventually, citing his obligations as a recently married man, Perry turned professional in late 1936.

His professional debut was against the hard-hitting Vines at Madison Square Garden on January 6, 1937. Some eighteen thousand spectators were present, an indoor match record which lasted thirty-six years, and they paid $58,120 for their seats. Perry won in four sets. This match inaugurated their North American tour, in which Vines won thirty-two matches and Perry twenty-nine. The tour grossed more than $412,000; under his guarantee, Perry received $91,335 of this and Vines got $34,195. They toured again in 1938, Vines winning, 48-35. The tour grossed $175,000, and the two split the purse, $34,000. Then Don Budge turned professional after becoming the first person to win all four Grand Slam titles in the same year, and in 1939 he defeated Vines, 21-18, and Perry, 18-11. The tour grossed more than $204,000, of which Budge was guaranteed $75,000. Perry won the United States Professional Championships in 1938 and 1941. His competitive career came to an abrupt end on December 26, 1941, in Madison Square Garden, when, playing the new professional Bobby Riggs, Perry's foot got caught in a hole in the canvas surface and he fell and smashed his right elbow. His playing arm remained partially disabled. Yet in 1948, he won a professional tournament in Scarborough, England, beating Yvon Petra, who had won Wimbledon in 1946.

During the war, Perry, who had become a United States citizen in November, 1938, served in the United States Air Force, chiefly in public relations and rehabilitation work. His business ventures included tennis resorts and a very successful line of tennis clothing and footwear. He and Vines used their tour earnings to buy into the Beverly Hills Tennis Club, where they played exhibitions with Charlie Chaplin, Groucho Marx, Errol Flynn, and other Hollywood celebrities. By invitation, Perry partnered King Gustav of Sweden and helped develop tennis programs in Egypt and the Soviet Union. He married four times, the first three ending in divorce: first to the Hollywood actress Helen Vinson, a few hours after breaking his rib in the United States Championship semifinals of 1935; then to an American model, Sandra Breaux, in 1941 and, after the war, to Lorraine Walsh. In 1952, he married Barbara Riese.

### Summary

Tall, dashing, fit, and confident, Fred Perry won the world table-tennis championship and went on to dominate lawn tennis in the mid-1930's. He had a feared forehand and no weaknesses.

Perry is the only man from England to have won all four of the world's major tournaments. He is the only Englishman since 1909 to have won Wimbledon, and he won it for three straight years, a record in modern tennis until Bjorn Borg's five wins after Open tennis began in 1968. He is the only Englishman to have won the French Championship, on the clay courts of Roland Garros Stadium. He is one of two Englishmen to have won the United States Championship, and he did so three times—a number equalled by few players. He led the British team to victory in the Davis Cup for four years, the only British victories since 1912.

Even after he won Wimbledon, some of the British tennis authorities still took snobbish exception to his social background and disliked what they considered to be his brashness. Fifty years later, His Royal Highness the Duke of Kent presided at the unveiling of a statue of Perry in the Wimbledon grounds and the designating of the Somerset Road entrance as the Fred Perry Gates. No British athlete better deserves such commemoration.

### Bibliography


Clerici, Gianni. "Fred Perry, the Son of a Labour M.P." In *The Ultimate Tennis Book*. Translated by Richard J. Wiezell. Chicago: Follett, 1975. A lively chapter, emphasizing Perry's personality and well illustrated with photographs.

Grimsley, Will. *Tennis: Its History, People, and Events*. Englewood Cliffs, N.J.: Prentice-Hall, 1971. One chapter, "Fred Perry—The British Master," summarizes Perry's amateur career. Another, "Fred Perry," in the section entitled "Styles of the Great" by Julius D. Heldman, gives a detailed account of Perry's strokes and playing style.

Hart, Stan. *Once a Champion: Legendary Tennis Stars Revisited*. New York: Dodd Mead, 1985. The chapter "Fred Perry: 'Showing the Flag'" recounts the author's 1984 visit to and spirited discussion with Perry at his Florida home and includes three jaunty photographs.

Perry, Fred. *Fred Perry: An Autobiography*. London: Hutchinson, 1984. A candid discussion of his tennis career, business ventures, and personal and marital relationships, and a shrewd analysis of the state of the game and its exponents, such as Borg, John McEnroe, and Ivan Lendl.

———. *My Story*. London: Hutchinson, 1934. Written in the year of Perry's first Wimbledon victory.

———. *Perry on Tennis: Expert Advice for All on Lawn Tennis*. London: Hutchinson, 1936; Chicago: Winston, 1937. An instructional guide to playing the game.

Rosenbaum, D. "War and Remembrance." *World Tennis* 39, no. 2 (July, 1991). Excerpts from an interview with Perry (at age 82) in which he discusses World War II and his three Wimbledon championships.

Shippey, Kim. "In the Press Box with Tennis Great Fred Perry." *Christian Science Monitor* 87, no. 147 (June 26, 1995). Profile of Perry's life, temperament, and ties to Wimbledon.


*Christopher Armitage*

## JOHN J. PERSHING

*Born:* January 13, 1860; Laclede, Missouri
*Died:* July 15, 1948; Washington, D.C.
*Area of Achievement:* The military
*Contribution:* A career soldier, Pershing was ready when called upon to lead the American Expeditionary Force to Europe in World War I, helping to preserve democracy in the first global conflict.

### Early Life

The oldest of John and Elizabeth Pershing's nine children, John Joseph Pershing was born in Laclede, Missouri, in the year preceding the outbreak of the Civil War. Tensions ran high in this Midwestern state, and Pershing's father suffered for his staunch support of the Union, which he served as a sutler. Pershing early aspired to a career in law, and initially his goal appeared attainable. A brief period of postwar prosperity, however, soon gave way to virtual bankruptcy for the family, and when Pershing's father gave up storekeeping to work as a traveling salesman, John took to farming and odd jobs. One of them, as janitor for the nearby black school in Prairie Mound, led to a permanent position as a teacher there. In 1882, he attended the Normal School in Kirksville, obtaining a bachelor's degree in elementary didactics. That same year, he took the test for appointment to the United States Military Academy and received a nomination. To meet the age limitation for entrants, he changed his birth month from January to September.

After a month in a Highland Falls, New York, preparatory school, Pershing enrolled with 129 other young men at West Point. Somewhat older than his classmates, he commanded their respect, holding his five-foot, ten-inch frame ramrod-straight and casting a stern glance at the world from steel-gray eyes; the mustache and silvered hair would come later. Pershing proved an adequate student and a first-rate leader, whom schoolmates elected class president each year. In each of his four years, he held the top position for cadets, culminating in his selection as first captain of the Corps of Cadets in his final year. In 1886, he was graduated and commissioned a second lieutenant of cavalry.

### Life's Work

A career as a soldier did not hold great promise in the late nineteenth century. Pershing spent his first years with the Sixth Cavalry, fighting in the last of the Indian Wars. Later, he commanded a troop in the Tenth Cavalry, an all-black unit with whom Pershing gained unusually good rapport. His service on the frontier was broken by a tour at the University of Nebraska, where he transformed a slovenly cadet corps into one of the country's finest detachments of college trainees. During his off-duty time, he earned a law degree and gave serious thought to resigning. In 1898, he returned to his alma mater as a tactical officer, instructing West Point cadets in the fundamentals of soldiering. In that year, troubles with Spain over Cuba erupted into a war, and Pershing sought duty with the force being organized to invade the Caribbean island.

Unable to go to Cuba as a cavalryman, Pershing obtained a temporary assignment as a quartermaster. In that position, he gained important insight into the follies of the army's system for providing supplies to its line units. That lesson was stored away for future use in Europe during the first global conflict of the twentieth century.

Pershing was promoted to captain in 1901, fifteen years after he was commissioned. Because promotions were based on seniority, he expected little further advancement. The early years of the new century saw him in the Philippines, leading American soldiers in a pacification effort against nationals who resisted the United States government's efforts to bring Western-style democracy to the islands. Pershing earned a reputation as a successful negotiator with Philippine leaders, and his remarkable march around Lake Lanao was noted not only in the Philippines but also in Washington, D.C.

A tour on the newly formed general staff gave Pershing the opportunity to meet the woman he would eventually wed: Frances Warren, daughter of Wyoming senator Francis E. Warren, a Republican and member of the Senate's military committee. Pershing and Frances were married in January, 1905, and left almost immediately for Japan, where Pershing was to serve as a military observer during the Russo-Japanese War.

Then, in 1906, Pershing's efforts on behalf of his country were generously rewarded. In an unusual move, President Theodore Roosevelt nominated the captain for promotion to brigadier general, allowing him to jump over almost a thousand officers senior to him and bypass the field grade ranks (major, lieutenant colonel, and colonel). The new general spent much of the next decade in the Philippines, returning to the United States for assignment at the Presidio, San Francisco, in 1914. Almost immediately, Pershing left for El Paso, Texas, to organize a force that would invade Mexico to capture the bandit Pancho Villa.

While Pershing was in Texas, his family, which now included three girls and a boy, remained in California. On August 26, 1915, tragedy struck the Pershings. Coals ignited wax on the ground floor of their wood-frame quarters, and Frances and the three girls perished in the ensuing fire; only Pershing's son, Warren, was saved. With stoic courage, Pershing made his way to California, accompanied the bodies to Wyoming for burial, then returned to his troops on the Mexican border.

The Punitive Expedition which Pershing commanded from 1915 to 1917 was ostensibly organized in retaliation for raids conducted by Villa within the United States city of Columbus, New Mexico. Pershing's force of twenty thousand men traversed the Mexican desert for months, while political negotiations continued between President Woodrow Wilson and the various factions trying to seize permanent control of the government in Mexico. The force withdrew in 1917, when the war in Europe forced Wilson to shift his attention to that region of the world.

In May, 1917, Pershing was notified that he had been selected to organize an American force for duty with the Allied forces in Europe. Hastily assembling a small staff, he traveled to England and then to France, where he spent a year shaping a force that would ultimately consist of more than one million Americans. Handpicked subordinates wrestled with problems of obtaining supplies, coordinating troop movements, quartering the divisions and separate units, feeding and clothing the newly arrived recruits, and training men to survive as individuals and fight as units. Pershing's time was occupied in constant inspections and in wrangling with Allied commanders, especially marshals Philippe Petain of France and Douglas Haig of England, both of whom wanted to detail small American units for duty with French and British units already employed on line against the Germans. Convinced that Americans should fight in American units, commanded by American officers, Pershing held out against their constant requests. Only reluctantly did he finally commit some battalions of the First Infantry Division for duty with the French. His strategy paid off in the late summer of 1918, when the American First Army achieved smashing victories against the Germans along the Saint-Mihiel salient and then in the Meuse-Argonne area of France.

The entrance of American forces into the war helped deal the final death blow to Germany's hopes for conquest. In November, 1918, the Germans agreed to the terms of surrender, and Pershing was faced with the problems of dismantling the huge military machine he had worked so hard to assemble. For the better part of the next two years, he was engaged in returning troops to America and drafting detailed reports of the actions of his army during the war. In 1920, Congress passed a law designating Pershing general of the armies, allowing him to keep the four-star rank that had been bestowed upon him temporarily while he was in command of the American Expeditionary Force (AEF). There was some talk of Pershing running for president, and he allowed his name to appear on the ballot in the Nebraska primary as a favorite son candidate; a poor showing convinced him, however, to abandon that campaign.

In July, 1921, President Warren G. Harding and Secretary of War John Weeks named Pershing chief of staff of the army. In that position, the hero of World War I fought a three-year battle against the Congress and a large contingent of American people who wanted to return the American military to its prewar position: small and poorly funded. Pershing argued (in vain) for larger permanent forces and an active program to train men for future service through the National Guard and Army Reserve. Despite his pleas, the size of the army shrunk, its budget dwindled, and its capability to mobilize evaporated. In September, 1924, Pershing retired.

The following years were far from quiet ones, though, since duty with various government commissions kept the general busy. In 1924, he served with the delegation trying to resolve the Tacna-Arica boundary dispute between Peru and Chile. He later served with the American Battle Monuments commission and continued to provide sage advice to his successors in the office of the chief of staff. In 1936, Pershing became seriously ill, but he recovered and once again offered his services to the country when America became embroiled in World War II. President Franklin D. Roosevelt sought his advice, and in fact Pershing helped convince the president to keep General George C. Marshall in Washington, D.C., rather than let him assume field command in Europe. Marshall, a protégé of Pershing who had been a key staff officer in the AEF, often consulted his mentor during World War II.

Pershing received special honors when the Congress ordered a medal struck in his honor in 1946. He died on July 15, 1948. In accordance with his wishes, he was buried at Arlington National Cemetery, under a simple headstone, among the soldiers whom he had led in "the Great War."

## Summary

Pershing's lifelong career of service to his country has secured for him a place among American military heroes. The epitome of the American soldier-leader, he was purposely self-effacing when placed in political circles, remaining true to the principle of military subordination to civilian control with great conviction. His efforts as a stern disciplinarian, a brilliant organizer of large forces, and a staunch believer in the capabilities of the American soldier were a vital element in the Allied success in World War I. In addition, his consistent support for the citizen-soldier helped set the model for future generations of planners and shaped the future of American military organization for the remainder of the century. Finally, his sagacious tutelage of subordinates such as George C. Marshall and George S. Patton provided America the military leadership it needed to rise to the challenge posed by Adolf Hitler and his confederates in World War II.

## Bibliography

*American Military History.* Washington, D.C.: Office of the Chief of Military History, 1969. Official history of American military involvement at home and abroad; includes accounts of the Indian Wars, the Punitive Expedition in Mexico, and World War I, providing excellent background and highlighting Pershing's contributions when in command.

Cooke, James J. *Pershing and His Generals: Command and Staff in the AEF.* Westport, Conn.: Praeger, 1997. Considers Pershing's work in developing the AEF.

Editors of *Army Times. The Yanks Are Coming: The Story of General John J. Pershing.* New York: Putnam, 1960. Short biography, with many photographs. Good summary of Pershing's major accomplishments.

Goldhurst, Richard. *Pipe, Clay and Drill: John J. Pershing: The Classic American Soldier.* New York: Reader's Digest Press, 1977. A solid biography that places Pershing's actions within the larger context of American political enterprises. Detailed chapters on the Punitive Expedition.

Liddell-Hart, Basil Henry. *Reputations Ten Years After.* Boston: Little Brown, 1930. Hart's chapter on Pershing provides an antidote to hagiographic portraits that were popular immediately after the war and points out Pershing's difficulties in dealing with high-ranking officials of Allied forces.

O'Connor, Richard. *Black Jack Pershing.* New York: Doubleday, 1961. An objective biography, highly readable and informative, of modest length.

Smith, Gene. *Until the Last Trumpet Sounds: The Life of General of the Armies John J. Pershing.* New York: Wiley, 1998. Excellent biography of the United States' only six-star general.

Smythe, Donald. *Guerrilla Warrior: The Early Life of John J. Pershing.* New York: Scribner, 1973. A detailed, scholarly account of the early years of Pershing's life through his participation in the Punitive Expedition.

———. *Pershing: General of the Armies*. Bloomington: Indiana University Press, 1986. With this volume, Smythe concludes his definitive biography of Pershing. Focuses on Pershing's role as commander in chief of the American Expeditionary Force in World War I and his tenure as chief of staff of the army.

Vandiver, Frank. *Black Jack: The Life and Times of John J. Pershing*. 2 vols. College Station: Texas A & M University Press, 1977. A comprehensive biography, based largely on records in the Library of Congress, National Archives, and other collections. Places Pershing's actions in the context of America's coming of age as a world power.

Weigley, Russell A. *A History of the United States Army*. New York: Macmillan, 1967; London: Batsford, 1968. A scholarly yet highly readable account of the growth of the American military establishment; chapter on World War I provides excellent summary of Pershing's actions and an assessment of his accomplishments as commander of the American Expeditionary Force.

*Laurence W. Mazzeno*

# PHILIPPE PÉTAIN

*Born:* April 24, 1856; Cauchy-à-la-Tour, France

*Died:* July 23, 1951; Port-Joinville, Île d'Yeu, France

*Areas of Achievement:* The military, government, and politics

*Contribution:* During World War I, Pétain was one of the few prominent military commanders to discard the massive offensive as a desired operational method. His skill at defensive warfare contributed to the Allies' eventual defeat of Germany in 1918. Pétain later entered politics and served as the controversial Vichy chief of state during the entire German Occupation of France.

## Early Life

Henri-Philippe Pétain was the third of five children born to the peasants Omer-Verant and Clotilde Pétain. Clotilde died in 1857, and Omer-Verant remarried less than two years later. Three more children followed in rapid succession as the Pétains managed an austere living in the Artois region of northern France. Like most peasant children of the middle-nineteenth century, Pétain spent much of his early childhood working on the family farm and attending a local school.

At the age of eleven, Pétain left home to attend school full-time. From 1867 to 1875, he lived at the Collège Saint-Bertin, where he received an education dominated by religious deference and military discipline. Upon the urging of several maternal relatives, Pétain eventually decided upon a military career. Pétain realized that the first step in this direction was his attendance at the Imperial Special Military School of Saint-Cyr. Despite a poor performance on the entrance examination, Pétain was admitted to Saint-Cyr in 1877. Pétain did not excel at Saint-Cyr; the school's engineering curriculum frequently baffled him. Saint-Cyr's moral lessons did, however, help forge an emerging character. By the time of his graduation, Pétain had developed a strong sense of duty and honor. Concerned more with these attributes than career advancement, Pétain entered the army as a second lieutenant in 1878.

## Life's Work

In the early part of 1914, Pétain was apparently nearing the end of an undistinguished military career. Since 1878, he had capably served France, but nothing stood out to indicate greatness. In the age of some of his country's biggest imperial ventures, Pétain had never left France. He had commanded troops, but a majority of his service was as an instructor at the École de Guerre in Paris. While a teacher, Pétain acquired the reputation of being a military nonconformist when he condemned the French reliance upon offensive doctrine. Having studied the then-recent Boer and Russo-Japanese wars, Pétain dismissed large-scale offensive tactics as useless in the era of the modern machine gun. This position, coupled with his blunt personality, made Pétain extremely unpopular at France's war ministry. His future promotions were therefore severely hindered. By 1914, Pétain was an obscure colonel with thirty-six years of service who awaited retirement in two short years.

The outbreak of World War I, however, quickly changed Pétain's military and political destiny. The German invasion of Belgium and France in the late summer of 1914 provided Pétain with the opportunity to practice his unorthodox defensive theories. Pétain was a success, and he gained rapid promotion to the rank of general.

Throughout the war Pétain outperformed his peers. In February, 1916, the Germans launched a massive offensive that threatened the capture of Paris. Standing firm on the Meuse River at the town of Verdun, Pétain organized and inspired the French in a bloody defense that lasted until December, 1916. With this victory, the once unpopular Pétain was now known throughout a grateful France as the "Hero of Verdun."

Appointed the commander of all French armies in May, 1917, Pétain faced another crisis. Approximately 350,000 frontline troops throughout the army had mutinied. Sacrificed in innumerable assaults that served to accomplish no apparent objectives, French soldiers simply left the trenches in droves. Pétain quickly assumed control of a situation that had the potential to spell the defeat of France. Leaders of the uprising were arrested and publicly sentenced to death. Although few of the mutineers were actually executed, this response helped squelch the disorder. In other actions, the commanding general gained the cooperation of his soldiers by visiting their outposts, listening to their complaints, and promising to end useless attacks. Once he had restored order, Pétain led the French army to victory in 1918.

At the close of the war, Pétain remained France's leading military figure. He was made a Marshal of France and placed on the influential peacetime army council, Conseil Supérieur de la Guerre. French citizenry and politicians revered the "Hero of Verdun" and generally followed his military pronouncements. In his most significant decision of the interwar period, Pétain called for the fortification of France's eastern border against future German attacks. Built at the expense of weapons modernization, this costly series of forts and entrenchments—called the Maginot Line—did not include the border with Belgium. Pétain concluded that this heavily forested area between France and Belgium was impregnable and therefore not in need of fortification. In 1940, this assumption would prove tragically incorrect, but in the interwar years France clung to the strategies of its most popular marshal.

Although war minister for a short period in 1934, Pétain remained outside active French politics. His lack of participation did not, however, represent political apathy. He believed that republican politics and socialism were weakening France. Interestingly, he continued to avoid others' attempts to draft him into political office. An ambassador to Spain in 1940, Pétain was called home when Adolf Hitler's German armies easily bypassed the Maginot Line and invaded France through the Ardennes Forest. As the armies collapsed, France turned to Pétain as a symbol of greatness and power to save the crumbling nation. In May, 1940, and at eighty-four years of age, Pétain acquiesced to these wishes. He formed a new government and acquired the authorization to abolish the Third Republic and create a new constitution.

Almost immediately Pétain proclaimed defeat, and he negotiated an armistice with Germany that split France into occupied and unoccupied zones. Pétain remained the "chief of state" of the unoccupied territory, which had its capital at Vichy in southern France. Unlike many resisting Frenchmen, Pétain saw no sense in continuing a guerrilla war after the nation had been defeated. He reasoned that only a functioning French government could help rebuild the shattered country.

Although Pétain was allowed to rule over southern France, Germany exacted many demands upon Pétain's government that forced Vichy into increased collaboration with the enemy. In 1940 and 1941, Pétain maintained some form of autonomy. He was able to purge his cabinet of radical collaborationists such as Pierre Laval and still court the United States as an ally. By 1942, however, Pétain drifted into the role of aging figurehead. Germany installed Laval as first premier, while giving him absolute power to run the government. Decisions now drifted from Pétain's control. By the end of the war, Vichy would cooperate with Germany in such endeavors as Jewish persecution, munitions exchanges, and recruitment of men to serve with the German armies on the Eastern Front.

During World War II, Pétain resisted any idea of fleeing France and what he perceived as his duty. Even as the Allies invaded France and his government collapsed, Pétain desired to remain at his post. Detained by the Germans as they fled eastward in late 1944, Pétain protested this treatment. In April, 1945, his captors relented, and he was allowed to return to France. Once on native soil, Pétain was promptly placed on trial by Charles de Gaulle's new French government for his leadership of the collaborationist government. On August 15,

1945, the deaf Marshal of France was found guilty and sentenced to death and national degradation. De Gaulle commuted the sentence to life imprisonment on the Île d'Yeu off the Mediterranean coast of France, Pétain remained imprisoned on this island until pulmonary failure ended his life on July 23, 1951.

### Summary

Philippe Pétain is a controversial figure in French history. During World War I, he received the highest accolades a country can offer. He was then strictly an army officer, and his contribution to the military science of the early twentieth century was enormous. Twenty-seven years later, however, and in the twilight of his life, Pétain suffered national humiliation. Vichy was in shambles, and Pétain bore the stain of leading France along the path of Nazi collaboration.

A stubborn sense of duty had guided Pétain to his greatest triumphs, and it now contributed to the disaster of Vichy. Pétain did not espouse Fascism or even crave power; he simply believed himself the only man capable of saving France. The country needed a leader, and his concept of duty would not permit him to back down from his challenge. He therefore offered himself to the nation as a persevering moral example of past glory. Only by such a sacrifice did Pétain think that he could both acquit his duty and return France to the country's former prominence.

Pétain's estimation of this situation was wrong, and it altered his place in history. The Vichy experiment demonstrated a failed chapter in Pétain's life, but it does not detract from either his military reputation or his personal character. Trained to place duty above self-interest, Pétain left a legacy of having struggled in two separate conflicts to save France. At his death, he was most proud of this simple fact.

### Bibliography

Atkin, Nicholas. *Pétain.* London and New York: Longman, 1998. Atkins places Pétain's life and career in the historical context of two wars.

Griffiths, Richard. *Marshal Pétain.* London: Constable, 1970. The best analysis in any language of Pétain's military and political career. The book contains eighteen illustrations and a select bibliography.

Horne, Alistair. *The Price of Glory.* London: Macmillan, and New York: St. Martin's Press, 1962. The definitive account of the Battle of Verdun. This book contains an extensive sketch of Pétain and his role during the battle. Horne's treatment of Verdun provides an excellent beginning for studies into the tactics of World War I.

Lottman, Herbert R. *Pétain, Hero or Traitor.* London: Viking, and New York: Morrow, 1985. Based upon previously sealed archives, Lottman's work frequently delves into the personal life and character of Pétain. The narrative reads extremely well, but it lacks both illustrations and bibliography.

Paxton, Robert O. *Vichy France.* London: Barrie and Jenkins, and New York: Knopf, 1972. This is a comprehensive account of Vichy. The book provides an overview of life, economics, and politics in unoccupied France during Pétain's period in office. The bibliographic essay contains detailed references for further research.

Spears, Sir Edward. *Two Men Who Saved France.* London: Eyre and Spottiswoode, and New York: Stein and Day, 1966. This is a fine account of Pétain during the mutiny of 1917. The volume contains an eyewitness account plus Pétain's own version of the crisis.

Vinen, R. "Vichy." *History Today* 40, no. 6 (June, 1990). Analysis of Pétain's French government of 1940, including his political legacy.

*Kyle S. Sinisi*

# JEAN PIAGET

*Born:* August 9, 1896; Neuchâtel, Switzerland
*Died:* September 16, 1980; Geneva, Switzerland
*Areas of Achievement:* Biology, education, and philosophy
*Contribution:* Piaget was awarded an honorary degree from Harvard University in 1936, the Sorbonne in 1946, and the University of Brussels in 1949 for his work on the evolution of intelligence in the human young. He found in developmental psychology a link between the biological adaptation of organisms to the environment and the philosophical quest for the source of knowledge.

## Early Life

Jean Piaget was born the first of three children and only son of Arthur and Rachel Piaget. Arthur was devoted to medieval literature, and Rachel, although energetic and intelligent, suffered from poor mental health. As a young child, Piaget was interested in mechanics, birds, sea shells, and fossils. At the age of ten, he went to Latin School and after school hours helped the director of the Natural History Museum put labels on collections in exchange for rare species, which he added to his own collection. Piaget began writing when he was seven, and a short essay on an albino sparrow was published when he was eleven. By the age of fifteen, he was writing a series of articles in the *Swiss Review of Zoology* and was receiving letters from foreign scholars who expressed a desire to meet him. They did not, of course, realize how young he was.

Piaget might have pursued his career as a naturalist had it not been for several events that occurred when he was between fifteen and twenty years of age. His mother insisted that he take religious instruction, and, by doing so, he became interested in philosophy. His godfather, a philosopher, believing that Piaget's education needed to be broadened, invited him to spend time with him. While Piaget looked for mollusks along a lake, his godfather talked with him about the teachings of Henri Bergson. It was through this experience that Piaget decided to devote his life to a biological explanation of knowledge. Even though he received the doctor's degree in his early twenties in the natural sciences with a thesis on mollusks, Piaget was more interested in the relationship of biology and philosophy. He decided that if he obtained work in a psychological laboratory, he could better research this epistemological problem.

Piaget's first experience in a laboratory was in 1918 in Zurich, where he was introduced to psychoanalysis by Eugen Bleuler and Carl Jung. He pursued psychoanalysis diligently, partly in an effort to understand his mother's illness and partly to use the therapeutic approach with mental patients. In 1919, he went to Paris, where for two years he adapted the clinical technique to questioning schoolchildren at the Alfred Binet Institute. His assignment at the institute, given to him by Theodore Simon, was to standardize Sir Cyril Burt's reasoning tests. By listening to the verbal responses of the children, he was able to probe such areas as the child's understanding of space, time, numbers, physical causality, and moral judgment. He became fascinated with the question of why children up to the age of eleven or twelve have great difficulty with certain intellectual tasks that adults assume children should be able to do. He noticed that the difficulty seemed to be the child's inability to

relate adequately the parts of the problem to the whole. Logic apparently is not inborn but develops little by little with time and experience. Here was the embryology of intelligence fitting in with his biological training.

### Life's Work

Piaget came to believe that knowledge is not a subjective copy of an external world but rather is invented or constructed by the developing human organism. The child assimilates meaningful information from the environment and actively accommodates to that information by adapting to new situations. A person's intellectual or cognitive understanding determines other aspects of life as well: emotions, humor, moral development, and social interaction. Thinking precedes language and derives from human action upon the environment, so, in order to understand the origins of intelligence, it is necessary to study the behaviors of the young child rather than to ask questions of children already in school.

The opportunity to observe infants presented itself when he became the father of three children: two girls and a boy. He and his wife, a young woman he had met at the Jean-Jacques Rousseau Institute in Geneva, where he was named director in 1921, spent considerable time observing the behaviors of their babies and submitting them to various tasks. Three volumes were published dealing with the genesis of intellectual conduct based on these experiments. Other books written during this time are entitled *Le Langage et la pensée chez l'enfant* (1923; *The Language and Thought of the Child*, 1926), *Le Jugement et le raisonnement chez l'enfant* (1924; *Judgement and Reasoning in the Child*, 1928), *La Représentation du monde chez l'enfant* (1926; *The Child's Conception of the World*, 1929), and *La Causalité physique chez l'enfant* (1927; *The Child's Conception of Physical Causality*, 1930). The central theme running through all this work is that in every area of life—organic, mental, or social—there exist totalities qualitatively distinct from their parts and imposing upon the parts a particular organization. Growth or development, with roots in biological morphogenesis, is a striving for the equilibrium of these structures of the whole.

Not only was Piaget director of the Rousseau Institute, a post he held until his death, but also, from 1925 to 1929, he taught classes in child psychology and the philosophy of science at the University of Neuchâtel. In 1929, he became director of the International Bureau of Education, a position he retained for almost forty years. This led to his becoming president of the Swiss Commission of the United Nations Educational, Scientific, and Cultural Organization. At the bureau, he contributed to the improvement of pedagogical methods based on the mental development of the child. In 1929, he was also named professor of the history of scientific thought at the University of Geneva. Ten years later, he became professor of sociology and a year after that, professor of experimental psychology at that same institution. His special research interests between 1929 and 1939 were the study of scientific epistemology, both autogenetic and phylogenetic; the development of the concepts of numbers, space, and time in children ages four to eight; and the formation of the idea of preservation or constancy, which he labeled "concrete operations."

The standardization of Burt's reasoning tests with schoolchildren in Paris, the careful observation of his own children as infants, continued research at the Rousseau Institute, and numerous teaching duties resulted in Piaget's recording voluminous amounts of information on the evolution of thought in the child. Piaget wrote that there are four major stages of cognitive development. These stages are invariant, hierarchical, and seen in children universally. Every normal child goes through the same sequence because every person is genetically programmed to do so. The first is a period of sensorimotor intelligence and takes place from birth to approximately two years of age. The newborn is provided with such reflexes as sucking, swallowing, and crying, the bases of later adaptation tasks. The infant understands the world only as he acts upon it and perceives the consequences of those acts. By the age of two, he begins to invent solutions by implicit as well as explicit trial and error. He can "think" as well as act.

The second stage occurs between the ages of two and seven and is called preconceptual or intuitive intelligence. The advent of language brings mental images of events. Yet the child understands these events only from his own perspective and experience and is therefore unable to take the viewpoint of others. Error is perceptual in nature in that the child is influenced by the way objects appear to him: If a sausage-shaped piece of clay appears to be more when it is broken into small pieces, then it is more. This faulty relation of parts to the whole disappears sometime during concrete operational intelligence, when the child is in elementary school. He now can compare classes and relationships, and thought no longer centers on one salient characteristic of an object. He discovers that things are not always what they appear to be. What he knows, however, is still tied to the concrete world. It is not until eleven years of age or older that he reaches the fourth stage of formal operational intelligence, in which hypothetico-deductive thinking is possible. The orientation is toward problem solving rather than toward concrete behavior. The adolescent is full of ideas that go beyond his present life and enable him to deal through logical deduction with possibilities and consequences.

From 1938 to 1951, Piaget was a professor of psychology and sociology at the University of Lausanne. This post, in addition to his teaching at the University of Geneva and his duties as coeditor of the *Archives de psychologie* and the *Revue Suisse de psychologie*, did not lessen his productivity in research and writing. In the 1940's, his major concerns were the relationship of perception and intelligence and the testing of the claims of Gestalt psychology. By the 1950's and through the 1960's and 1970's, Piaget was surrounded by an ever-increasing number of assistants and colleagues. His professorships, including one in child psychology at the Sorbonne in 1952, and his directorships, including that of director of the International Center for Genetic Epistemology at the University of Geneva funded by the Rockefeller Foundation in 1955, provided him with eager scholars who collaborated with him on his studies. Men and women from around the world and representing many disciplines—biology, psychology, philosophy, mathematics, and linguistics—gathered to learn from him and to engage in research.

Piaget wrote in his autobiography that solitude and contact with nature were as essential to his well-being as hard work. After a morning of interaction with academicians, he would take long walks, collect his thoughts, and then write for the remainder of the afternoon. Summertime found him in the mountains of Switzerland, hiking and writing. He remained physically and mentally active in his eighties.

### Summary

Jean Piaget has been called a biologist, a logician, a sociologist, and a psychologist, but he is best known as a genetic epistemologist, for he spent a lifetime studying the origins of human knowledge. Over a seventy-year period, he wrote fifty books and monographs and hundreds of articles, as well as lecturing in French to audiences all over the world. Unlike B. F. Skinner, who focused on environmental influences, or Sigmund Freud, who emphasized emotions and instincts, Piaget selected for his topic the rational, perceiving child who has the capacity to make sense of the world about him. Knowledge is a process, not a product; it is dynamic, never static, self-regulatory rather than imposed from without. Even as mollusks taken from the lake of Neuchâtel and placed in an aquarium change very little after five or six generations, the human organism has a built-in blueprint that determines the course of cognitive evolution, a course not unlike that of the evolution of scientific thought.

Piaget's later writings refined and helped to explain his previous studies, yet it is the earlier works that have received the greatest attention. From these writings, parents have been encouraged to provide a rich, supportive environment for the child's natural propensity to grow and learn. Educators have been exposed to child-centered classrooms and "open education," a direct application of Piaget's views. Lawrence Kohlberg's paradigm of moral reasoning, itself fostering hundreds of studies in moral cognition, has as its basis Piaget's study of the moral judgment of the child. A child prodigy, Piaget used his superior intellect to examine the evolution of human thought from birth to adulthood, and the interdisciplinary nature of his work has, in turn, influenced many areas of inquiry.

### Bibliography

Cohen, David. *Piaget: Critique and Reassessment.* London: Croom Helm, and New York: St. Martin's Press, 1983. An outline of Piaget's career and the main elements of his theory are given, including the moral development of the child. Several major criticisms are offered as well as studies that run counter to Piaget's ideas.

Flavell, John H. *The Developmental Psychology of Jean Piaget.* Princeton, N.J.: Van Nostrand, 1963. This volume is a groundbreaking attempt to organize, for the English-speaking world, Piaget's ideas from the viewpoint of a developmental psychologist.

Furth, Hans G. *Piaget and Knowledge: Theoretical Foundations.* 2d ed. Chicago: University of Chicago Press, 1981. This book deals with Piaget's basic theoretical positions, including the biological, logical, and epistemological dimensions of human knowledge. Piaget's final work in the area of equilibration is explained in the last chapter.

Piaget, Jean. *The Essential Piaget*, edited by Howard E. Gruber and J. Jacques Venèche. London: Routledge, and New York: Basic, 1977. An anthology of Piaget's writings organized by time periods and topics. Essays published prior to 1922 were translated from the French especially for this volume. The editors' introductory notes to each section are insightful and informative.

———. "Jean Piaget." In *A History of Psychology in Autobiography*, edited by Edwin G. Boring, Herbert S. Langfield, H. Werner, and Robert M. Yerkes, vol. 4. Worcester, Mass.: Clark University Press, 1952. A fascinating account of Piaget's life and work until 1950. The variety and enormity of his interests and responsibilities come through in this autobiography.

Wadsworth, Barry J. *Piaget's Theory of Cognitive and Affective Development: Foundations of Constructivism.* 5th ed. New York: Longman, 1996. The author provides an introduction to Piaget's theory of cognitive development, a short biography, and a discussion of his research methods.

*Bonnidell Clouse*

# ÉMILE PICARD

*Born:* July 24, 1856; Paris, France
*Died:* December 11, 1941; Paris, France
*Areas of Achievement:* Mathematics, physics, and engineering
*Contribution:* Picard's theories advanced research into analysis, algebraic geometry, and mechanics.

## Early Life

Émile Picard's mother was the affluent daughter of a doctor from France's northern provinces. His father, from Burgundy, was a textile manufacturer, who died during the Franco-Prussian War of 1870. Picard demonstrated brilliance early in his life. While in school, he developed interests in varied subjects such as literature, languages, and history. His accomplishments in these areas of scholarship were enhanced by his love for books and reading and by his exceptionally powerful memory. One theme that appears throughout Picard's life is his broad range of interests. He was an athlete as well as a scholar. Throughout his life, he maintained a love for such rigorous physical activities as gymnastics and mountain climbing.

Given the fact that Picard was a generalist, it was difficult for him to choose any one field in academics on which to focus. In fact, he only decided to study mathematics at the end of his secondary studies. The reason for this decision came from his having read an algebra book. After making the decision to study mathematics, Picard committed himself to this pursuit with a devotion that is rarely matched. Indeed, by 1877, at age twenty-one, he had already made a major contribution to the development of a portion of mathematics that focused on the theory of algebraic surfaces. He had also received, by this time, the degree of doctor of science.

Picard's scholarship was recognized by many important members of the academic community. One of the great French mathematicians of the time, Charles Hermite, became his mentor and lifelong friend. In fact, Picard's development as a mathematician was strongly guided by Hermite. In 1881, with support from Hermite, he was appointed to a professorship at the Sorbonne, and during the same period he married Hermite's daughter.

## Life's Work

The diversity that marked his life also marked his professional development. His early career emphasized research and focused on algebra and geometry. Some of his major contributions came in the field of algebraic geometry. He soon, however, began to pursue other interests in mathematics. By 1885, he had begun to pursue work in the field of differential and integral calculus. Picard was elected to the chair of this subject at the Sorbonne during this period.

Picard's most famous work came from his investigations of differential equations. Indeed, one theorem for which he is still remembered in modern texts of all languages is Picard's theorem, a method for approximating the solution to a differential equation. More important, however, is the work that Picard did in trying to develop a general framework for finding solutions to differential equations.

In addition to his work in differential equations, Picard did work in complex analysis. In this area, he helped to extend the research of his colleague Henri Poincaré. The work on which he focused involved functions of two complex variables. Picard

termed these functions hypergeometric and hyperfuschian. The work that he did here was collected in a two-volume set entitled *Théorie des fonctions algébriques de deux variables indépendantes* (1897, 1906). This work was coauthored by the mathematician Simart.

At the turn of the century, Picard was engaged in the study of algebraic surfaces. This series of investigations was inspired by his previous work on the nature of complex functions. One of the interesting side effects of Picard's career as a generalist is the fact that his investigations frequently led him into other areas of study.

Another interesting facet of Picard's career is the fact that it touched so many areas that one would not expect. For example, he was the chairman of many government commissions, including the Bureau of Longitudes. Also, the quality and the variety of his scholarship led to his permanent election as the secretary to the Academy of Sciences. Picard's wide-ranging scholarship reached even into areas such as physics and engineering. His researches included the application of mathematical methods to physics problems of elasticity, heat, and electricity. One subject to which Picard added significantly was the way in which electrical impulses moved along wires. In engineering, Picard, who had originally begun as a theoretician in mathematics, developed into an excellent teacher and eventually became responsible for training ten thousand French engineers between 1894 and 1937.

It should be emphasized that the quality of Picard's scholarship did not suffer because of its variety. During the course of his career, he was responsible for the development of more than three hundred papers on various subjects. His *Traité d'analyse* (1891-1896) is considered a classic book on mathematics. At one time, this monumental work was considered required reading for obtaining a thorough background in mathematics.

Picard also published materials that were, strictly speaking, outside the realm of mathematics. He was, for example, responsible for collecting and editing the works of Charles Hermite, his mentor. In addition, he published a number of works on the philosophy of science and the scientific method, the majority of these after 1900.

Picard's career was long as well as productive. Many mathematicians find their most productive years early. Picard was a notable exception to this pattern. Again following his early path of intellectual diversity, he made significant contributions to the development of mathematical concepts such as similarity and homogeneity well after he was eighty years old. These concepts are important in algebra and engineering.

Picard's investigations were particularly significant in their effects on his fellows and successors in his field. Among those influenced by him were Henri-Léon Lebesgue, Émile Borel, and Otto von Blumenthal. Picard was one of the most honored scientists of his generation. In 1924, he was elected to the Academy of France. In 1932, he received the Gold Cross of the Legion of Honor. In 1937, he received the Mittag-Leffler Gold Medal from the Swedish Academy of Sciences. All told, he was awarded honorary doctorates by universities in five foreign countries.

In contrast to his almost unbroken string of professional successes, Picard had a personal life that was filled with tragedy. War was a common theme in the litany of misery that filled his personal existence. Besides the death of his father in the Franco-Prussian War, he lost a daughter and two sons during World War I. During World War II, his grandsons were wounded in the invasion of France. The personal tragedy under which Picard lived was emphasized by the fact that he died while France was still under German occupation. Yet he had lived as one of the most productive and honored mathematicians in a period known for the brilliance of its mathematical researchers.

## Summary

Émile Picard was, in all ways, a generalist. Many would have termed him a Renaissance man. This diversity of interests was reflected in his work both in and out of mathematics. In mathematics, his research involved such varied areas as geometry, algebra, differential equations, and complex analysis. It is extremely rare to encounter mathematicians in the modern world who make significant contributions in more than one specialty. Picard's most significant work was in differential equations. It is here that the mathematical world outside France most commonly remembers the great Parisian. Modern works still make reference to Picard's theorem for approximating solutions to differential equations, and these new efforts still mention Picard groups as a way of categorizing the transformations that can occur in linear differential equations.

In areas outside mathematics, Picard was known as a teacher, writer, editor, and administrator. He published an important survey of mathematics in

France. He headed both the Academy of Sciences and the Society of Friends of Science, a group interested in helping needy scientists. Picard was not only a great mathematician and scientist, he was a great man as well. In an age that is characterized by the specialist, it is good to reflect that men such as Picard have lived.

**Bibliography**

Bell, Eric T. *The Development of Mathematics.* 2d ed. New York and London: McGraw-Hill, 1945. This is a particularly good discussion of the history of mathematics from a developmental standpoint. Consequently, Picard gets fairly good treatment. This book also discusses Hermite fairly extensively.

———. *Men of Mathematics.* London: Gollancz, and New York: Simon and Schuster, 1937. Picard is mentioned only slightly in this text. Yet it provides an excellent look at one of his most famous colleagues, Henri Poincaré. It gives a good view of the flavor of the times and the problems that were faced by mathematicians.

Boyer, Carl B. *A History of Mathematics.* 2d ed. New York: Wiley, 1989. Picard is referenced several times in footnotes in this work. Why he receives no discussion in the text is hard to understand. These footnotes help to place Picard's work in relationship to other important works of mathematics.

Considine, Douglass M., ed. "Picard's Theorem." In *Van Nostrand's Scientific Encyclopedia.* 8th ed. New York: Van Nostrand Reinhold, 1995. This includes a good discussion of Picard's theorem.

Griffiths, Phillip. "Œuvres de Émile Picard, Tome II." *Dialog Math-Sci Database*, February, 1989. A review of the collected works of Picard. It discusses the material addressed by Picard during his researches. It also includes a good discussion of his life. The review is in English. Unfortunately, the book that it covers is not.

Hadamard, J. "Émile Picard." *Journal of the London Mathematical Society* 18 (1943). This biographical sketch, published not long after Picard's death, is the best description of his life.

*Lyndon Marshall*

# PABLO PICASSO

*Born:* October 25, 1881; Málaga, Spain
*Died:* April 8, 1973; Mougins, France
*Area of Achievement:* Art
*Contribution:* The most prolific and famous artist of his time, Picasso was crucial to the development of modern art. He was an inventor of cubism and one of the prime practitioners of academic realism, Postimpressionism, art nouveau, expressionism, Fauvism, abstract expressionism, Surrealism, and Futurism. A skilled craftsman, he was the master of many mediums.

## Early Life

Pablo Ruiz Picasso first learned how to draw from his father, José Ruiz Blasco, an art teacher and curator of the local museum. Don José was also a skilled painter, and he recognized early that his son possessed considerable artistic talent, potentially vaster than his own. As an old school pedagogue, he saw to it that Pablo became well grounded in the classical style of art, insisting that he copy the works of the masters with meticulous fidelity and pay close attention to the traditional laws of proportion and harmony of color. So formidable a draftsman did Pablo become that Don José abandoned his own painting and gave his son all of his materials. Pablo was then only thirteen years old.

In 1895, the family moved to Barcelona, where Pablo's father was to teach at the local School of Fine Arts and where he had his son enrolled to perfect his skills. Pablo stayed at his father's school for two years and was then sent to continue his studies in the more prestigious Royal Academy of San Fernando at Madrid. Yet Pablo's developing personal style and growing professional confidence put him increasingly at odds with the strictures of art currently taught by his hidebound professors. Taking advantage of a brief illness, he quit the Madrid academy to return to Barcelona.

The art scene in Barcelona was then in the throes of a modernist revolution, just the sort of atmosphere to stimulate experimentation and independence. Despite such positive reinforcement, Pablo still felt constrained. He wanted to leave, to go to London, and he persuaded his father to come up with the money. On the journey to Great Britain, however, he stopped off in Paris. The city so impressed him that he decided to go no farther. Although he returned to Spain from time to time, the French capital henceforth became his home and continued to be so during the most creative periods of his life. At this time, he definitively adopted his mother's maiden name as his own, Picasso being less common than Ruiz. The change also dramatically symbolized the artistic break that he was making with the academic and, for him, stultifying artistic values of his father.

This initial association with Paris, and with it a deeper exposure to the works of Edgar Degas, Paul Gauguin, and Henri de Toulouse-Lautrec, led Picasso to modify his artistic style. He eliminated the bright colors from his palette and began painting in monochromatic blue. At the same time, he exchanged his carefully modeled figures for flatter, more solid surfaces. The Blue Period—prompted by the suicide of a friend—is appropriately one of deep melancholy in which Picasso showed his compassion for the Paris poor, its downcast and destitute. To emphasize this sense of desolation, Picasso elongated the bodies of his subjects, making them bony and angular in the style of El Greco, thereby accentuating their condition of hopelessness.

Picasso, however, could not remain faithful to any one style for long. By 1904, his mood had changed; he had fallen in love for the first time in his life, and, abandoning his cold colors, he now used warmer, more romantic tones. His subject matter also became more joyful, as revealed in a series of paintings of circus performers. These works are painted with great skill and sensitivity and with more dimensionality than those of his previous period. Yet soon this Rose Period also disappeared. During a visit to Spain, he used more earth colors. His figures became more classically ponderous, perhaps more naïve, in their reflection of prehistoric art. These paintings exude a strong, sensual vitality. The twenty-four-year-old Picasso seemingly had established himself in a style that he might exploit for years to come. He was on the verge, however, of a sudden change in direction that would lay the foundations of modern art.

## Life's Work

During the last half of the nineteenth century, French artists had discovered new ways of expression, either by depicting light through color or by distorting perspective to transform shape and form. Picasso had been influenced by these new directions but until 1906 had yet to go beyond them. In that year, however, he began working on a canvas that would end any associations with the traditional spatial organization of the past. In *Les Demoiselles d'Avignon* (the young ladies of Avignon), painted on a canvas nearly eight feet square, he showed the distorted anatomy of five nude women in a jarring assemblage of disorderly facets, triangular and rectangular wedges, and other confusing geometric shapes. Two of the figures are wearing hideous African-like masks. The other three have eyes on different levels and noses jutting out like pieces of architecture. The painting has no rational focus of attention, the viewer being forced to look everywhere as if at pieces of broken glass. Yet *Les Demoiselles d'Avignon* is now recognized as the first true painting of the twentieth century. When Picasso showed the painting to his friends, however—none of whom was exactly a rustic when it came to accepting new ideas—the reaction was almost universally negative. As a result, Picasso rolled up the canvas and refused to exhibit it publicly, thereby removing its direct influence on the course of the modern movement. Nevertheless, it had firmly established Picasso's new artistic direction, marking his great adieu to the past.

In embarking on this more hazardous artistic journey, Picasso had been strongly influenced by the works of Paul Cézanne, who in his mature works had also distorted shapes and contours and broken-down images into an infinite series of individual geometric perceptions. Picasso, with the close collaboration of Georges Braque, who had been heading in the same direction, broke down his figures into a series of flat tonal planes that in succeeding pictures became progressively more abstract. He also reduced his palette to only several colors. So close was Picasso's association with Braque that it was often difficult to tell which painter painted which canvas. The outbreak of World War I, and Braque's departure for military service, however, ended their partnership.

Although Picasso continued to paint in the cubistic manner, he also returned to realistic portraiture, thus continuing to fluctuate between the academic realism of his youth and the modernist synthesis of his early adulthood. Many of his more traditional figure paintings reflect his interest in sculpture, frequently the subjects being inspired by classical mythology. Sometimes he would do a portrait in one style and follow it by doing one in another. He reintroduced perspective depth into his later cubist paintings, rendering figures less abstract yet more fantastic, a characteristic that pointed the way to yet another direction.

Picasso's ensuing productivity is almost impossible to classify neatly. Throughout the interwar years, he continued to distort the human anatomy, reemploying a technique he had developed in his early cubist days: the rearrangement of pictorial features so that one part of the anatomy is seen simultaneously from many angles.

*Guernica* (1937), his most famous painting of this period, shows his preoccupation with violence. The masterpiece, nearly twelve by twenty-six feet, was reputedly inspired by the German bombing of that Basque city during the Spanish Civil War. It is, however, a universal statement of human anguish, heightened by terrorized people and animals. In its exaggerations and distortions—its overlapping planes and absence of modeling—it reveals both the influences of cubism and expressionism, but without the latter style's lurid colors. The painting was Picasso's contribution to the Spanish Pavilion of the 1937 International Exposition held in Paris, where it became the center of controversy.

Picasso had become sufficiently famous that anything he did became noteworthy: his many affairs with women, his membership in the Communist Party, his friendships with writers and movie stars, his habits of work and tastes in food. Dora Maar, his mistress during the *Guernica* days, said that during Picasso's postcubist days, his style was determined by the woman he loved, the place where he lived, the circle of his friends, poets, and his dog.

Picasso lived frugally and was reluctant to sell many of his finished works. Consequently, the greatest collector of Picassos was Picasso himself. When the artist died, the French government in lieu of collecting monetary death duties, selected over a thousand of the choicest paintings, drawings, and pieces of sculpture—about one-fourth of the entire treasure trove—and made them the nucleus of a special Picasso museum in Paris.

## Summary

In Western society, which so highly prizes artistic change, diversity, and innovation, Pablo Picasso stands forth as the quintessential creative genius. A master in every medium to which he put his hand—painting, sculpture, graphics, ceramics—he, more than any other single artist of his age, was responsible for altering the way people approach, view, and accept art. Constantly moving from one style to another, he destroyed forever the hold that

Renaissance concepts of pictorial space held over artists, especially their devotion to the canon that flat images on a canvas are given dimensionality and perspective through diminution in size and change in coloristic atmosphere. Picasso broke his figures into fragments, split them into geometric shapes, and had them occupy diverse planes, ignoring any rational relationship they had to their environment. He made his images exist independently of nature, giving them no unifying point of view and no fixed perspective. He even made them completely abstract. By forging a new tradition, Picasso revealed a more profound reality. He recognized that the human eye is highly selective, that it often glances at objects haphazardly, focusing on bits and pieces, looking at things selectively, highlighting parts and planes and aspects, and divorcing the particular from the totality, independent of any natural arrangement of shapes and lines and colors. Thus, Picasso was able to transcend the times in which he lived. His talent remained fresh and young throughout his entire professional life of more than sixty years. In addition, his creations, despite their great diversity, always remained unified in the strength of his own remarkable personality and vast talent for regeneration.

**Bibliography**

Brassai. *Conversations with Picasso.* Translated by Jane M. Todd. Chicago: University of Chicago Press, 1999. Brassai, famed author and photographer of avant-garde Paris, offers records of his meetings with Picasso between 1943 and 1946 that provide an intimate look at the artist's day-to-day life.

Cirlot, Juan-Eduardo. *Picasso, Birth of a Genius.* London: Elek, and New York: Praeger, 1972. This sumptuous volume was published on the occasion of the lavish donation of his works that the artist made to the city of Barcelona to memorialize his friend Jaime Sabartés. Thus, it serves as a catalog of that collection but also provides a complete record of the development of the artist during his crucial formative period before the birth of modernism to the period of World War I. The collection is particularly strong in sketches and drawings. Cirlot organizes his study around the way Picasso worked rather than where he worked.

Daix, Pierre, and Georges Boudaille, with Joan Rosselet. *Picasso, The Blue and Rose Periods: A Catalogue Raisonné of the Paintings, 1900-1906.* Translated by Phoebe Pool. 2d ed. Greenwich, Conn.: New York Graphic Society, and London: Adams and Mackay, 1967. More than a listing of the paintings of that important period in Picasso's creative life, this study also deals with the development of the early modern art movement and discusses Picasso's relation to its formation. Lavishly illustrated.

Duncan, David Douglas. *The Private World of Pablo Picasso.* New York: Harper, 1958. This study is by a famous photographer who, upon Picasso's invitation, lived as Picasso's guest for three months during the artist's seventy-fifth year. The several hundred photos that illustrate Picasso in the act of creativity and at play and relaxation—there is even a shot of him in the bathtub—is a distillation of the more than ten thousand that Duncan took. Duncan's worship of his subject is evident from his opening sentence: "Maybe this is the happiest house on earth." As a photographic record of the object of this veneration, it is a true tour de force.

Elgar, Frank, and Robert Maillard. *Picasso.* Translated by Francis Scarfe. Rev. ed. London: Thames and Hudson, and New York: Tudor, 1972. The premise that Picasso's art cannot be understood without reference to the society in which he lived gives shape to this outline of his corpus, in which the biographical study of Maillard is conveniently juxtaposed with a study of his work by Elgar.

Gedo, Mary Mathews. *Picasso: Art as Autobiography.* Chicago: University of Chicago Press, 1980; London: University of Chicago Press, 1981. Gedo looks at the artist from a psychodramatic point of view. She considers how the experiences, emotions, and images of his childhood relate to his artistic vision. She maintains that his frequent change of artistic vision corresponded to some alteration or disruption in his life at the time. This central theme of "partnership" is varied and complex and is more related to other men of genius than to women.

Granell, Eugenio Fernandez. *Picasso's "Guernica": The End of a Spanish Era.* Ann Arbor, Mich.: UMI Research Press, 1967. Through analysis of one of Picasso's masterpieces, Granell seeks to understand the culture and tradition that gave it life, claiming that its inspiration emanates from two Spanish myths: the myth of Epiphany, which expresses the irrational and passive proclivities of Spanish society, and the myth of the bullfight, which expresses the irrational but active attitudes. In any case, the author rejects the common assumption that the painting represents an episode in the Spanish Civil War.

Klüver, Billy. *A Day with Picasso.* Cambridge, Mass., and London: MIT Press, 1997. Through exhaustive research, Klüver has reconstructed an afternoon in the life of Picasso and several of his friends (including Max Jacob, Moise Kisling, and Modigliani) from a set of photographs taken by Jean Cocteau.

Penrose, Roland. *Picasso: His Life and Work.* 3d ed. London and New York: Granada, 1981. Penrose provides an outline of the artist's works from style to style and period to period. While establishing Picasso's talent as a main part of the landscape of modern art, he reveals the artist's lack of interest for that period's continual factional quarrels and any intellectual theorizing.

Wertenbaker, Lael. *The World of Picasso.* New York: Time-Life, 1967. A worthy addition to the acclaimed series of the Time-Life Library of Art. The commentary is perceptive and the illustrations first-rate.

*Wm. Laird Kleine-Ahlbrandt*

# AUGUSTE AND JEAN-FELIX PICCARD

## Auguste Piccard

*Born:* January 28, 1884; Basel, Switzerland *Died:* March 24, 1962; Lausanne, Switzerland

## Jean-Felix Piccard

*Born:* January 28, 1884; Basel, Switzerland *Died:* January 28, 1963; Minneapolis, Minnesota

*Areas of Achievement:* Aviation, space exploration, oceanography, and physics

*Contribution:* The Piccards designed hot-air balloons and piloted them into the stratosphere to study cosmic rays and atmospheric electricity and to encourage high-altitude flight. Auguste also developed a bathyscaphe in which he reached unprecedented ocean depths, while Jean-Felix's discovery that certain types of molecules split apart in solution was named the Piccard Effect in his honor.

### Early Lives

Jules Piccard, head of the Department of Chemistry at the University of Basel in Switzerland, and his wife Hélène were overjoyed at the birth of twin sons, Auguste and Jean-Felix, on January 28, 1884. The parents had no difficulty telling the identical blue-eyed, blond-haired boys apart: Auguste was left-handed, and Jean-Felix was right-handed. The twins had frequent contact with visiting professors and scientists as well as with their uncle Paul Piccard, who helped design and build the turbines at Niagara Falls. This exposure stimulated the boys to conduct experiments in heat and electricity, but when, at the age of fourteen, they saw a hot-air balloon in their hometown, the Piccards turned their attention to ballooning. Their first attempt to construct a balloon ended in failure when the alcohol lamp used to heat the air ignited the paper envelope, but their fascination with French author Jules Verne's writings, combined with a driving spirit to explore the remaining frontiers beyond the earth's already mapped land area, motivated the Piccards to continue their interest in ballooning. When they worked on sketches and plans to explore the ocean depths using the principles of ballooning, the Piccards realized they did not have the technical knowledge needed for such an undertaking and postponed the project until a later date.

After graduation from the local *Ober Realschule*, the Piccards entered the Federal Institute of Technology at Zurich, where Auguste received a degree in mechanical engineering, and Jean-Felix received a degree in chemical engineering. Both earned doctorates at the institute and turned to teaching, Auguste at Zurich (1907-1922) and Brussels Polytechnic Institute (1922-1954) and Jean-Felix at Munich (1914), Lausanne (1914-1916, 1919-1925), Chicago (1916-1918), and the University of Minnesota (1936-1952). Jean-Felix also held positions with the Hercules Powder Company in Delaware and the Bartol Foundation of the Franklin Institute in Philadelphia, Pennsylvania.

In preparation for their ballooning experiments, the Piccards studied the history of human flight, weather forecasting, and writings on the stratosphere and cosmic rays (Auguste's particular interest). In 1913 they made their first balloon ascent, a sixteen-hour flight from Zurich across parts of Germany and France during which they measured the density and pressure of gases within the balloon. During World War I, they briefly served in the Swiss Army Lighter-Than-Air Service in an auxiliary capacity because they did not meet the army's physical requirements. The Piccard's collaboration ended when Jean-Felix moved to the United States, where he established himself as a respected chemist, married Jeanette Ridlon in 1919, and became a citizen in 1931. Auguste married Marianne Denis in 1920 and assumed the position of professor of physics in Brussels in 1922.

### Life's Work

Auguste believed that a manned balloon could provide better scientific data on cosmic rays than an unmanned ascent, but he knew the perils involved in high-altitude flights. English meteorologist James Glashin, who, in 1862, had lost consciousness at 29,000 feet, demonstrated the risk of using an open-air gondola above that altitude, but Auguste wanted to study cosmic rays in the stratosphere, where the pressure and mass of the earth's atmosphere would not distort measurements. Additionally, he wanted to induce the air services to travel at higher altitudes, where they could achieve higher speeds because rarefied air offered less resistance. Funds from Belgium's King Albert and the Fonds National de la Recherche Scientifique allowed Auguste to design a balloon able to withstand the rigors of travel into the stratosphere and an enclosed gondola that held two men and instruments and provided protection from cold, radiation, and lack of oxygen. The airtight aluminum sphere he developed was light enough for a heavily rubberized cotton bag filled with hydrogen to lift, yet substantial enough to maintain a constant air pressure. To keep the gondola at a relatively constant temperature, Auguste painted it half white and half black and installed a motor to rotate it so the sphere would alternately absorb and reflect the sun's heat. He and his assistant, Paul Kipfer, lifted off from Augsburg, Germany, in the 150-foot-high balloon, named *FNRS* in honor of the funding organization, on May 27, 1931. The eighteen-hour flight, the first one in a pressurized cabin, was fraught with difficulties, but the men achieved a maximum altitude of 51,762 feet, a new record for manned flight. When members of the Swiss Aero Club congratulated Auguste on his feat and expressed the hope that no one would surpass his record for many years, Auguste answered that his aim was not to maintain records but to open the stratosphere to scientific research and aerial navigation.

Auguste installed a radio and additional instruments for measuring radioactivity, atmospheric electricity, and cosmic rays. On August 18, 1932, he and a Belgian colleague, Max Cosyns, ascended to a record height of 55,563 feet. A deterioration of the balloon and lack of money hampered further experiments in the *FNRS*. Auguste made several more balloon flights before retiring from the activity in 1937. For his development of an enclosed gondola that enabled travel into the stratosphere, the Belgian Aero Club presented him with a gold medal.

Jean-Felix, who had moved permanently to the United States in 1926 to take a position as a research instructor at the Massachusetts Institute of Technology, did not forget his love of ballooning. After Auguste's successful flights, Jean-Felix decided to test several of his own theories of atmospheric electricity and cosmic rays in a similar manner. The Franklin Institute agreed to oversee the project and provide Geiger counters to study cosmic rays. Numerous corporations and individuals supplied the funds to refurbish an old balloon and gondola. Jean-Felix invented a method that used explosive charges to quickly dump the ballast. He and his wife Jeanette, who served as pilot, made the first successful stratospheric flight through clouds on October 23, 1934, ascending to a height of 57,579 feet. With them went a sack of specially franked U.S. mail. The information gathered on the flight showed positively that cosmic rays were not "rays" but high-energy particles that traveled at speeds approaching that of light.

*Auguste Piccard*

Jean-Felix believed that a cluster of balloons rather than a single one would allow for safer and easier control. After moving to the University of Minnesota, he tested his theory on July 18, 1937. *The Pleiades*, an open-air gondola attached to one hundred balloons, climbed to over 11,000 feet, but a fire during the landing destroyed it. Jean-Felix had demonstrated that a complex balloon could maneuver well and stated that ascensions to altitudes of 17 to 20 miles were entirely possible. While at the University of Minnesota, Jean-Felix developed balloons made of plastic film, a frost-resistant window for balloon gondolas, and an electronic system for emptying ballast bags.

After Auguste retired from ballooning, he turned his attention to his other childhood dream—to plunge into the sea deeper than any person had done before. However, World War II postponed his research. He returned home to work in the Swiss aluminum industry designing precision instruments for physicists, and after the war he resumed his teaching position and research at Brussels. Auguste's goals were to beat William Beebe's 1934 record of 3,028 feet for an ocean descent, investigate oceanic conditions at great depths, take photographs, and possibly catch some fish that dwelled at deep levels in the ocean. He was convinced that he could use the same techniques to investigate the high-pressure ocean depths that he and his brother had used to study the low-pressure stratosphere.

To descend to the ocean's depths, Auguste designed a two-part diving bell called a bathyscaphe. The upper part consisted of a 5,200-cubic-foot, cigar-shaped metal tank containing heptane to provide buoyancy for the vessel. Suspended from this was a watertight steel sphere cabin built to withstand 12,000 pounds of pressure per square inch. The self-powered bathyscaphe used iron pellets as ballast, which it would dump in order to rise, just as balloons did. The first test of the bathyscaphe *FNRS 2* came in October, 1948, off the coast of West Africa, where it managed to dive only one mile below sea level. The project floundered until industrialists in the city of Trieste, Italy, offered Auguste's son Jacques, an economist at the University of Geneva, funds to build a new bathyscaphe. In August, 1953, Auguste and Jacques descended in the *Trieste* to a depth of 10,330 feet, the greatest depth humans had ever reached. The United States Navy bought the *Trieste* in 1958, and in 1960 Jacques and Donald Walsh, an American submarine officer, piloted the Auguste-designed bathyscaphe to a depth of 35,800 feet in the Marianas Trench off Guam. Two years later, on March 24, 1962, Auguste died of a heart attack at the age of seventy-eight in Lausanne, Switzerland. The following year, his brother Jean-Felix also died of heart trouble on his birthday in Minneapolis.

### Summary

The ballooning records the Piccards established did not stand for long because they inspired others to ascend higher into the stratosphere to explore it in greater detail. A few years after Auguste's journeys into the stratosphere, the United States, the Soviet Union, and Poland developed balloons that traveled even higher. A U.S. balloon achieved an altitude of 72,395 feet in 1935, and by the 1960's heights of over 100,000 feet had been reached.

The Piccards realized earlier than most men that the stratosphere, with its relatively stable temperature and lack of storms, would be ideal for air travel, and their most enduring legacy may be the creation of equipment to explore its environs and beyond. Auguste's greatest contribution was the development of a pressurized, airtight cabin that became essential for the airline industry and space flight. Jean-Felix's invention of the plastic-film balloon proved invaluable to all sorts of scientific work, especially modern weather research, and the space program incorporated his idea of using explosives to direct an aircraft's course into their vehicles.

Just as the Piccards' ballooning innovations opened the upper atmosphere to study, Auguste's development of the bathyscaphe afforded scientists the opportunity to explore the geology and biology of the ocean depths to give insight into the earth's origins. It also enabled them to locate sunken vessels, such as the U.S. submarine *Thresher*, which the *Trieste* located 8,500 feet below the ocean's surface a few months after it sank in 1963.

### Bibliography

De Grummond, Lena Young, and Lynn De Grummond Delaune. *Jean Felix Piccard: Boy Balloonist.* Indianapolis: Bobbs-Merrill, 1968. This book, part of the Childhood of Famous Americans series designed for young readers, relates the childhood and early adult life of the Piccard twins and the ballooning exploits of Jean-Felix. It contains a few illustrations but no bibliography.

"High Drama." *Wilson Quarterly* 15, no. 4, (Autumn 1991). This article focuses on space flight in the 1930s, including Auguste Piccard's flight of the Explorer II.

Honour, Alan. *Ten Miles High, Two Miles Deep: The Adventures of the Piccards.* New York: Whittlesey House, 1957. Designed for teen readers, this book details the twins' early lives, both brothers' research in ballooning, and Auguste's development and testing of the bathyscaphe.

Malkus, Alicia. *Exploring the Sky and Sea: August and Jacques Piccard.* Chicago: Encyclopaedia Britannica, 1961. Malkus's book, part of the Britannica Bookshelf Great Lives for Young Americans series, devotes only one chapter to ballooning, concentrating on Auguste's and his son Jacques's development and testing of the bathyscaphe. Includes a few illustrations.

Piccard, Auguste. *Earth, Sky and Sea*. Translated by Christina Stead. New York: Oxford University Press, 1956. Although Piccard devoted most of this personal account to the bathyscaphe, one chapter contains a narrative, sketches, and pictures of Piccard's 1931 balloon ascent and gives an insight into Piccard's reasons for exploration.

Stehling, Kurt R., and William Beller. *Skyhooks*. New York: Doubleday, 1962. Stehling and Beller summarize the most significant balloon flights from 1783 to 1960 and devote one chapter to Auguste's 1931 flight. Includes a chronology of balloon flights and several photographs.

*Anthony N. Stranges and Marlene Bradford*

# MARY PICKFORD

*Born:* April 8, 1892; Toronto, Ontario, Canada
*Died:* May 29, 1979; Santa Monica, California
*Area of Achievement:* Film
*Contribution:* Early in the history of the film industry, Pickford established herself as the first name box-office draw, and hence the first star, of American cinema. While the attraction of her name and image shaped the economics of motion pictures for decades, Pickford also became an early role model for independent women who took charge of their own destinies.

## Early Life

The actress known as Mary Pickford was born Gladys Louise Smith on April 8, 1892, in Toronto, Canada. Poverty and early widowhood led Gladys' mother, Charlotte Hennessey Smith, to place her children on the stage. In 1898, at the age of six, Gladys appeared in *The Silver King* at Toronto's Princess Theatre. Her early success on the stage, and her mother's example, soon made the little girl the principal source of income for her family, a burden, she wrote later, that she felt keenly at an early age. This sense of fiscal responsibility led to an early maturity in which the young performer fought aggressively for salary increments and contract rights.

Gladys' theater career began in earnest when she appeared with the Valentine Stock Company's production of *The Little Red Schoolhouse* in April of 1901; her performance earned for her a part in the touring version of that play, which went on the road in November of 1901. During the next four years, Gladys went on tour—usually accompanied by her mother Charlotte—with several plays. Touring companies in those days followed a hard schedule, frequently playing one night and then moving on, staying in cheap hotels. Gladys endured, however, even though she never had time for more than six months of formal education, because even as a child she was determined to keep her family out of poverty. She educated herself on the road and somehow learned to read.

Sometimes her success led to parts for her mother or her brother and sister, Jack and Lottie, but it was Gladys' ability and determination that enabled the family to stay together. Devoted to her career, Gladys worked hard, observing the work of established performers whenever possible. By the age of about twelve, she decided that she would try to become a "success" by the age of twenty.

## Life's Work

In fact, Gladys did not need to wait that long. Although she was suffering from exhaustion in 1907, a successful audition with David Belasco, a famous Broadway producer, brought her a part in *The Warrens of Virginia*. Belasco also urged Gladys to find a more appealing stage name. In those days, a part with Belasco was a sign that an actress had "arrived," and this association was to be a launching pad for the Belasco actress now known as Mary Pickford.

In 1909, when Pickford found herself temporarily out of work, her mother urged her to talk to the director D. W. Griffith, who had begun making "flickers" for Biograph studios in New York. Although Pickford was reluctant—stage actors considered work in films to be a sign of failure—she was not only able to find work with Griffith at a salary higher than that she had earned with Belasco, but she was also able to dictate her own terms to Griffith, who was more than pleased to have a Belasco veteran in his company. Pickford's determination at age sixteen to have some control over her work was to be a hallmark of the rest of her career.

Griffith did not allow his players to be known by name, fearing that prominence would lead them to demand more money, but Mary Pickford, known to audiences as "Little Mary" (the name of one of her screen characters) or "The Girl with the Golden Curls," soon became popular anyway. Her fame during this period came partially from her appearances in child roles, which, because of her slight physical stature and youthful looks, she was able to play until well into her thirties.

In 1911, Pickford left Biograph for IMP pictures, but she returned in 1912; shortly thereafter, she left to join Adolph Zukor's Famous Players, where she established herself as the industry's first individual box-office draw, or "star." Pickford demanded and got from Zukor the unprecedented salary of five hundred dollars a week; moreover, her growing popularity led to a series of raises, and by 1916 she was earning ten thousand dollars a week plus bonuses. In 1917, Zukor created Artcraft Pictures Corporation, a division of Famous Players-Lasky, to produce Mary Pickford films exclusively. By now, Pickford was making feature-length films (as opposed to shorts) that were commercial as well as artistic successes; *Poor Little Rich Girl* (1917) was the first of these films.

*Poor Little Rich Girl* was one of many period melodramas that appealed to the values of middle and working classes, but it was also distinguished by the cine- matographic art of director Maurice Tourneur, who was breaking new ground with lighting, camera angles, and dream sequences. The film's ultimate success, however, was equally the result of Pickford's comedic scenes (such as a mudfight), which relieved the film's otherwise somber tone and which Pickford inserted over director Tourneur's objections.

Pickford's control over this film is another hallmark of her career. When she began her next film for Zukor, *Rebecca of Sunnybrook Farm* (1917), she demanded—and got—Marshall Neiland as director and Frances Marion as writer. In 1918, Mary Pickford obtained the rights to scripts for *Pollyanna* and *Daddy Long-Legs* and demanded complete control, with Famous Players-Lasky functioning solely as distributor. When Zukor balked, Pickford signed with First National, which formed its own division, Mary Pickford Co., which had complete control over production.

Two years later, Pickford and her husband Douglas Fairbanks joined with Griffith and Charlie Chaplin to form United Artists Corporation, a company that served as a distributor for independent producers, frequently the stars themselves, who were able to keep the profits from each picture, select or reject any role, and control publicity. By contrast, 1930's stars who worked for large studios such as Metro-Goldwyn-Mayer (MGM) or Twentieth Century-Fox worked under contracts that paid them a straight salary for a given number of pictures, with acting roles being chosen by the studio heads or their subordinates. During the early days of United Artists (UA), Pickford produced some of her most famous films: *Pollyanna* (1920), *Little Lord Fauntleroy* (1921), and *Rosita* (1923). A less-known but critically acclaimed UA production was *Sparrows* (1926), which was noted for its gothic texture and brooding cinematography. In all, Pickford acted in sixteen films for United Artists between 1920 and 1933; after her acting career ended, she produced several other films during the thirties and forties.

The late twenties and early thirties were a difficult time for Mary Pickford. Her marriage to Douglas Fairbanks was becoming shaky, and the advent of "talking pictures" threatened many actors whose careers were built in the silent era. Pickford's first talkie, *Coquette* (1929), was a commercial success that won her the first Academy Award for Best Actress, but it was a critical failure that even horrified Pickford herself, who did not like what the new sound technology did to her voice. The only film Pickford and Fairbanks did together, an adaptation of Shakespeare's *The Taming of the Shrew* (1929), was a failure with the critics and at the box office, as were Pickford's remaining talkies. Although the Depression was probably partly responsible for the commercial failure of these films, Pickford, always insecure even at the height of her success, halted production before her last film, *Secrets*, was completed. The film was never released, and Pickford, only forty-two in 1933, never acted again. She was disheartened by her commercial failures, as well as by the death of her mother—whose business sense had helped to build Pickford's wealth—and the impending collapse of her marriage to Fairbanks.

In 1936, she and Fairbanks were divorced, and Pickford married Buddy Rogers, her former leading man who had remained devoted to her. Rogers and Pickford adopted two children, and she was able finally to play in real life the mother role she had played in films such as *Sparrows*. Although she continued to produce films, with indifferent success, Pickford gradually retired from public life, secluding herself at Pickfair, the estate she and Fairbanks had once shared, as she grew older. In 1953, she and Chaplin, the surviving founders, relinquished control of United Artists. In 1977, a few years before her death, Mary Pickford was given a Life Achievement Academy Award, but even this did not draw her out of seclusion, and the award ceremony had to be filmed at Pickfair.

## Summary

Mary Pickford's contributions to the film industry are manifold. Her curly-headed "Little Mary" character became the prototype for child stars of later years; Shirley Temple was only the first in a long line that includes recent roles on television situation comedies. In all of her roles, moreover, Pickford's acting style created an important bridge between the silent and sound period; critics have noticed that Pickford could convey emotions in the silent films with subtle gestures and facial expressions, unlike the exaggerated styles of many silent actors.

Pickford's greatest contribution to the film industry was her popular appeal. The rise of stars such as Pickford and Chaplin, with whom audiences could identify, led to the growth of the film industry from a curiosity featuring short films to a serious art form with feature-length productions. Her independence paved the way for United Artists, which she cofounded, and which provided opportunities for creative producers such as Alexander Korda, David O. Selznick, and Samuel Goldwyn.

For women, moreover, Pickford was a trailblazer. Although she probably never considered herself a feminist (she was very conservative politically and socially), her life and work nevertheless provided a valuable role model for women. On the screen, her interpretation often gave her heroines a kind of plucky independence despite the overlay of middle-class conventionality that her audiences demanded. In an era when Victorian mores still predominated, she emerged as one of the few financially independent women of her era, one who had earned her fortune through hard work and gritty determination. For the time in which she flourished, that was a considerable achievement.

**Bibliography**

Balio, Tino. *United Artists: The Company That Changed the Film Industry.* Madison: University of Wisconsin Press, 1987. Although the focus of this treatment is on the history of United Artists after Pickford and Chaplin sold their interest in 1951, it still offers a good, if brief, perspective on the early years.

Eyman, Scott. *Mary Pickford: America's Sweetheart.* New York: Fine, 1990. A thorough treatment of Pickford's life, with a critical discussion of her major films and her artistic contributions. More than forty photographs illustrate Pickford's life from childhood to old age. Probably the best treatment of Pickford's life and work, this book has few competitors.

Gomery, Douglas. *The Hollywood Studio System.* London: Macmillan, 1985; New York: St. Martin's Press, 1986. Case histories of each of the five major studios (Twentieth Century-Fox, Paramount, MGM, RKO, Warner Bros.) are followed by an eight-page, concise history of United Artists (under "Specialized Studios"), with an account of the founders' roles in its successes and failures.

Herndon, Boonton. *Mary Pickford and Douglas Fairbanks.* New York: Norton, 1977; London: Allen, 1978. An examination of Pickford's and Fairbanks' careers, emphasizing their married years. A good supplement to Eyman's book.

Pickford, Mary. *Sunshine and Shadow.* New York: Doubleday, 1955; London: Heinemann, 1956. Pickford's autobiography, although subjective and not always entirely reliable, remains one of the principal sources of information on her life.

Schickel, Richard. *D. W. Griffith: An American Life.* New York: Simon and Schuster, 1984. A detailed biography of the director who brought Pickford to the screen as "Little Mary," did much to shape her career, and later joined her as cofounder of United Artists. This book is valuable for its bibliography alone.

Tibbetts, John C. "Coquette: Mary Pickford Finds a Voice." *Films in Review* 48, no. 1-2 (January-February, 1997). Focuses on Pickford's most popular movie, *Coquette.*

Whitfield, Eileen. *Pickford: The Woman Who Made Hollywood.* Lexington: University Press of Kentucky, 1997. After eight years of research and financial losses, Whitfield completed this biography of Pickford that situates the actress at the center of Hollywood's creation.

*Timothy C. Frazer*

## SUSAN LA FLESCHE PICOTTE

*Born:* June 17, 1865; Omaha Indian Reservation, Nebraska

*Died:* September 18, 1915; Walthill, Nebraska

*Areas of Achievement:* Medicine and social reform

*Contribution:* As the first female Native American physician, Picotte served her tribe as medical missionary and community leader for twenty-five years.

### Early Life

Susan La Flesche was born June 17, 1865, on the Omaha Indian Reservation in northeast Nebraska. Her father, chief Joseph La Flesche (also known as Iron Eye), was the son of a French fur trader and his Indian wife. Adopted by Omaha chief Big Elk, Iron Eye succeeded him as one of the two principal chiefs of the tribe in 1853. Susan's mother, Mary Gale La Flesche (also known as One Woman), was the daughter of a white army surgeon and his Omaha wife. The La Flesches believed that some accommodation to the ever-advancing white world was essential if their tribe were to survive. As the youngest of Iron Eye's four remarkable daughters, Susan grew up in a family much influenced by assimilation-oriented missionaries. Her parents converted to Christianity, adopted the white man's lifestyle, and encouraged their children to seek formal education. Her oldest sister, Susette (Bright Eyes), ultimately gained fame as a speaker, journalist, and Indian rights advocate; Rosalie enjoyed a successful business career in the livestock industry; and Marguerite became a teacher among the Omahas.

Reared on the reservation, Susan attended agency day schools run by Quaker and Presbyterian missionaries. At the age of fourteen, she and seventeen-year-old Marguerite traveled to New Jersey to attend boarding school at the Elizabeth Institute for Young Ladies, returning home to Nebraska two and a half years later. From 1882 to 1884, Susan taught at the mission school before continuing her education at the Hampton Normal and Agricultural Institute in Virginia. Established in 1868 to educate freed slaves (and later, Indians as well), Hampton emphasized vocational training; however, Susan and Marguerite could read and write English fluently and were encouraged to pursue an academic program. Susan was graduated second in her class in 1886. Urged to study medicine by the school physician, Dr. Martha Waldron, she eagerly accepted a scholarship to Woman's Medical College of Pennsylvania. On March 14, 1889, Susan was graduated at the head of her class of thirty-six women, becoming the first female Native American to acquire a medical degree.

### Life's Work

Following a four-month internship at Women's Hospital in Philadelphia, Susan La Flesche accepted the position of government physician to the Omaha agency school. Of all the Nebraska tribes, the Omahas were considered the most successful in trying to accommodate to white ideas of "progress." The Omaha Allotment Act of 1882 had divided much of the reservation into individual farms, and more and more Indian families were sending their children to the agency school. Despite this seeming progress, drought, grasshoppers, unscrupulous white neighbors, and inept government agents all combined to create desperate poverty among the Omahas. With this social upheaval and deprivation came malnutrition and disease. Influenza, dysentery, and tuberculosis were endemic on the reservation, as were periodic outbreaks of cholera, smallpox, diphtheria, and typhoid fever. Within weeks of her arrival, the twenty-four-year-old La Flesche also took on the arduous task of treating the entire adult population, giving her a patient load of more than twelve hundred.

The size of the reservation—thirty by forty-five miles—and the absence of paved roads forced La Flesche to travel huge distances by horse and buggy or on horseback, often in severe weather. In 1891, the Women's National Indian Association, which had financed her medical training, asked her to take on additional duties as their medical missionary to the tribe. That same year, she gained membership in the Nebraska State Medical Society. Soon La Flesche experienced the first of several bouts with osteomyelitis, a painful infection of her facial bones which later caused deafness and eventually led to her premature death. Exhausted and temporarily bedridden by the disease, she resigned as agency doctor in October of 1893.

Despite her frail health and enormous professional responsibilities, La Flesche became increasingly involved in tribal and family affairs during the 1890's. Ever the missionary, she taught Sunday school at the Presbyterian church, acted as interpreter for non-English speaking Omahas, and worked closely with Marguerite to upgrade sanitary conditions on the reservation. To everyone's surprise, on June 30, 1894, she married Henry Picotte, an uneducated French-Sioux from the Yankton Agency who was a brother of Marguerite's late husband, Charles. The Picottes settled for a time in Bancroft, on the southern edge of the reservation, where Henry farmed the La Flesche allotment and Susan bore two sons: Caryl, born in 1895, and Pierre, born in 1898. While rearing her children and caring for her ailing mother, she continued to practice medicine, treating both Indian and non-Indian patients. Before long she was also nursing Henry, whose excessive drinking undermined his health and ultimately caused his death in 1905.

For Susan Picotte, the scourge of alcoholism went beyond the boundaries of a personal family tragedy. Her father had waged a successful campaign against whiskey peddlers and liquor consumption on the Omaha reservation. After Iron Eye's death in 1888, however, the situation deteriorated. Picotte eventually came to regard "demon rum" as the principal health hazard threatening her people. In temperance lectures, newspaper articles, and letters to government officials, she argued that alcohol abuse not only increased violence and crime but also made her tribesmen easy prey for all sorts of deadly diseases, especially tuberculosis and pneumonia. Moreover, she charged, local politicians and bootleggers routinely used whiskey to cheat tribal members out of their allotments. She lobbied the Bureau of Indian Affairs (BIA) for stricter enforcement of the 1897 congressional ban on selling liquor to Indians. By 1906, she had convinced the secretary of the interior to ban all liquor sales in any new town carved out of the Omaha reservation.

Picotte and her sister Marguerite (who had remarried) bought property in the new town of Walthill, where, in 1906, they each built modern homes. Over the next nine years, Picotte actively participated in the civic and professional life of the community, despite her own failing health. The Presbyterian Board of Home Missions hired her as their missionary to the Omahas, the first nonwhite to hold such a post. She served several terms on the Walthill Board of Health, during which time she led campaigns to eradicate the communal drinking cup and the household fly as agents of disease. She organized the Thurston County Medical Association, served a three-year term as state chair of the Nebraska Federation of Women's Clubs' public health committee, and began an intensive study of tuberculosis.

In 1909, the Omaha tribe sought Picotte's help in solving serious problems arising out of the allotment system. By law, individual allotments were to be held in trust by the government for twenty-five years, until Native American owners were deemed sufficiently "assimilated" to handle their own financial affairs. Meanwhile, government red tape and dictatorial agency control deprived tribal members of desperately needed trust funds. Making matters worse, the BIA instituted new restrictions in 1909; consolidated the Omaha and Winnebago agencies; and announced plans to extend the trust period an additional ten years, despite the Omahas' high literacy rate and well-educated leadership. Picotte wrote a series of blistering newspaper articles protesting the BIA's conduct. In February of 1910, barely recovered from a near-fatal attack of neurasthenia, she headed up a tribal delegation sent to Washington, D.C., to fight the new policies. Unsuccessful in getting the old agency restored, Picotte did persuade the secretary of the interior to cancel the ten-year trust extension, thus granting most Omahas control over their own property.

Picotte's main dream was to erect a centrally located hospital where she could provide better medical care for her Indian patients. Through her efforts, the Presbyterian Church provided $8,000, and Quakers gave an additional $500. Marguerite and her husband donated the land, and various other friends agreed to purchase the equipment. After Walthill Hospital opened in January of 1913, Picotte was able to practice there for only two years. The bone disease in her face and neck spread, taking her life on September 18, 1915. Her funeral was conducted jointly by Presbyterian clergy and a tribal elder; the medical facility she built was renamed the Dr. Susan Picotte Memorial Hospital.

### Summary

As practicing physician, missionary, social reformer, and political leader, Susan La Flesche Picotte had a profound effect on the lives of her people. By 1915, there was scarcely an Omaha alive who had not been treated by her; even those who did not embrace all of her reformist ideals trusted her. As the Omahas' unofficial but clearly recognized spokesperson, Picotte defended their interests in the white world, even as she devoted her energies to their physical well-being at home. Beyond modern medical care, public health improvements, and vigorous leadership, she provided her tribe—and the larger world—with a vibrant example of what late nineteenth century reformers hoped to accomplish with their assimilationist policies. Like her father, Picotte believed that education, Christian principles, and legal rights were the key to her tribe's advancement. That she and her non-Indian mentors underestimated the difficulties facing Native Americans and overestimated the virtues of forced acculturation does not detract from her achievement. Susan Picotte walked with grace in two worlds; assimilated into middle-class mainstream American culture, she never abandoned her tribal roots or her overriding concern for her people. Few women, Indian or white, have left such an indelible mark on their communities.

### Bibliography

Clark, Jerry E., and Martha Ellen Webb. "Susette and Susan La Flesche: Reformer and Missionary." In *Being and Becoming Indian: Biographical Studies of North American Frontiers*, edited by James A. Clifton. Chicago: Dorsey Press, 1989. Contrasting the lives of the two best-known La Flesche sisters, the authors conclude that both women were thoroughly assimilated into white culture; Susan, however, participated more directly in tribal life and harbored less bitterness toward non-Indians.

Green, Norma Kidd. *Iron Eye's Family: The Children of Joseph La Flesche*. Lincoln, Ne.: Johnsen, 1969. The pioneering work on the La Flesche family, and still the best source of detailed information on Picotte's life. Green explores the achievements of three generations of this large and fascinating clan. Included are the children of Iron Eye's secondary wife, Ta-in-ne, as well as a glimpse of the adult lives led by Picotte's two sons, Caryl and Pierre.

Hauptman, Laurence M. "Medicine Woman: Susan La Flesche, 1865-1915." *New York State Medical Journal* 78 (September, 1978): 1783-1788. Focuses on Picotte's experiences in medical school, emphasizing her enthusiasm and scientific curiosity. Hauptman makes good use of her correspondence to convey the image of a supremely self-confident young woman who also possessed a wry sense of humor.

Mathes, Valerie Sherer. "Dr. Susan La Flesche Picotte: The Reformed and the Reformer." In *Indian Lives: Essays on Nineteenth- and Twentieth-Century Native American Leaders*, edited by L. G. Moses and Raymond Wilson. Albuquerque: University of New Mexico Press, 1985. Mathes portrays Picotte's life and work as a manifestation of the late nineteenth century female reform tradition. This article also gives the most up-to-date diagnosis of the physician's own perplexing health problems.

Milner, Clyde A. *With Good Intentions: Quaker Work Among the Pawnees, Otos, and Omahas in the 1870's*. Lincoln: University of Nebraska Press, 1982. Places the La Flesche family's advocacy of accommodation in the larger context of the Quaker-inspired "Peace Policy" adopted by the government in 1869. For the Omahas' role within this framework, Milner relies heavily on a landmark study of the tribe published in 1911 by Picotte's half brother, ethnologist Francis La Flesche.

Wilson, Dorothy Clarke. *Bright Eyes: The Story of Susette La Flesche, an Omaha Indian*. New York: McGraw-Hill, 1974. Romanticized biography of Picotte's older, more famous sister. There is little material here on Susan herself, but more on her mother, Mary Gale, than is available elsewhere.

*Constance B. Rynder*

## LUIGI PIRANDELLO

*Born:* June 28, 1867; Girgenti (now Agrigento), Italy
*Died:* December 10, 1936; Rome, Italy
*Area of Achievement:* Literature
*Contribution:* Pirandello revolutionized modern drama by creating innovative plays that explored the nature of drama itself. He created an intellectual drama that redefined the nature of the self and examined in detail the effects of relativity on the human psyche.

### Early Life

On June 28, 1867, in the midst of a cholera epidemic, Luigi Pirandello was born prematurely at Il Caos, in Girgenti, Sicily. He was a fragile, weak, and lonely child. Unable to communicate with his authoritarian father, he felt isolated and turned rebellious. This feeling of isolation became a central theme in his creative work. Pirandello was also influenced by his Sicilian background. Sicily's hierarchical, almost feudal, society demanded restrictive codes of honor and strict adherence to convention, which led to repressed emotions and acts of violence. This conflict between individual desires and repressive social norms would become a recurring motif in Pirandello's work.

As a student, Pirandello read classical and Italian literature, and at fifteen he wanted to be a poet. His early poetry already showed his preoccupation with the themes of death and madness. After an unsuccessful venture into his father's business, he pursued his academic studies at the University of Rome and at the University of Bonn, where he earned a doctorate in philology.

After completing his education, Pirandello returned to Rome and became involved in the literary circle of the realist author Luigi Capuana. He then began to focus on his prose writing and published a collection of his short stories, *Amori senza amore* (1894; loves without love). In 1893, he began to formulate his artistic credo. He saw modern humanity trapped in a maze and believed that the old social norms were disintegrating, leaving the world in a state of uncertainty.

At twenty-six, Pirandello entered into an arranged marriage with Antonietta Portulana, the daughter of his father's business partner and a woman he hardly knew. Four years later, he began teaching in Rome at the Instituto Superiore Magistero, a teacher's college for women. In 1903, his father's sulfur mine was destroyed in a flood, leaving the family bankrupt. Distraught by these events, his wife was stricken by hysterical paralysis and later went insane. She became obsessively jealous, tried to stab Pirandello, and accused him of incest with his daughter. After many years of torment, he finally put her in a clinic in 1919. From living with a madwoman, he learned that reality was a matter of perception and that in the eyes of his demented wife, he could become many different people. These experiences would influence his writing.

### Life's Work

Pirandello soon began to establish himself as a noted writer of short stories, novels, and most significantly, dramas. With his novel *Il fu Mattia Pascal* (1904; *The Late Mattia Pascal*, 1923), he gained recognition both within Italy and abroad. In the novel, he shows how the modern individual tries both to escape the conventional roles placed on him and to free himself from social restraints. The attempt is a failure. Mattia, an insignificant, unheroic man, always questioning his own actions, finds out that he cannot exist outside the bounds of society, nor can he return to a role he once had.

In *Si gira . . .* (1916; *Shoot, The Notebooks of Serafino Gubbio, Cinematograph Operator*, 1926), Pirandello continues to treat the themes of alienation and loss of identity. In this novel, he uses the diary form to trace the fragmented impressions of a cameraman who tries to become a detached recorder of the lives of glamorous movie stars. In *Uno, nessuno centomila* (1925; *One, None, and a Hundred Thousand*, 1933), he foreshadows the modernist novel. The work is composed of long interior monologues, lengthy self-reflexive digressions, and an unreliable narrator who cannot certify what he has seen.

Throughout his career, Pirandello continued to publish short stories, 233 in all. He had planned to do twenty-four volumes but completed only fifteen. His stories reflect a pessimistic worldview tinged with a sense of tragicomic irony. As journeys in search of the unattainable, they bring out the humor in the disparity between human ideals and the cruel realities of experience.

Pirandello was to reach the height of his artistic genius as a dramatist. In 1915, Angelo Musco coaxed Pirandello into writing for the Sicilian theater. Writing plays in the Sicilian dialect, he began

to achieve popular success as a playwright, and drama became the perfect medium for him to explore his vision. Between 1916 and 1924, Pirandello made his most significant contribution to modern drama in particular and world literature in general. In *Così è (se vi pare)* (1917; *Right You Are (If You Think So)*, 1922), he shows how a husband who separates his wife and his mother-in-law can lead a whole town into confusion as both the mother-in-law and the husband claim that they are playing along with the deluded perceptions of the other. In this play and in subsequent dramas of this period, Pirandello turns the well-made play of the nineteenth century against itself. His dramas thrust bizarre characters into fantastical situations that lead to explosive climaxes built around ironic twists. As each character gives his own conflicting view of what has happened, the facts blur, and truth becomes a matter of individual perception. Pirandello's plays use passionate confrontations to examine one of the major philosophical issues of modern times: the relativity of truth.

In *Sei personaggi in cerca d'autore* (1921; *Six Characters in Search of an Author*, 1922), Pirandello achieved his greatest success. This play was so unconventional that at its first performance in Rome in 1921, it precipitated a riot in the theater. Pirandello was hissed off the stage and slipped out a back entrance, pursued by a mob crying "Madhouse!" Despite the initial reaction, the play achieved international fame. Between 1922 and 1925, it was translated into twenty-five languages. Pirandello's fame eventually spread to England and the United States, where one theater devoted an entire season to his plays. *Six Characters in Search of an Author* tells the story of six unfinished characters who interrupt the rehearsal of a Pirandello play and insist on acting out their drama. In this play, Pirandello not only examines the psychology of the twentieth century individual but also dissects the nature of theater itself. Theater becomes a distorting mirror through which actions are viewed from various perspectives. Each character interprets his actions differently so that reality becomes a matter of perception. As the professional actors try to play the parts of the characters, the characters begin to see distorted views of themselves as others interpret them. Thus, all human beings are seen as actors who play a variety of roles and who constantly try to adjust their perceptions of themselves to the way others see them.

In *Enrico IV* (1922; *Henry IV*, 1923), Pirandello continues to depict the uncertain nature of the self. The play shows how a man masquerading as an emperor receives a blow on the head, goes insane, and believes that he actually is the emperor. The play depicts the desperate quest of the modern individual to create a life of his own in a world that is constantly changing. It is the tragedy of a man who has remained frozen and static behind a mask while the rest of the world has changed around him.

Pirandello's later plays take on a mythical dimension as he confronts universal problems. In *La nuova colonia* (1928; *The New Colony*, 1958), he treats the impossibility of the Utopian myth. In *Lazzaro* (1929; *Lazarus*, 1952), he focuses on the nature of the religious experience. Finally, in his unfinished work, *I giganti della montagna* (act 1 published in 1931, act 2 in 1934, and act 3 in 1937; *The Mountain Giants*, 1958), he confronts the nature of art itself. His final plays have a more fantastical, visionary, and even allegorical quality.

Pirandello not only wrote plays but also produced and directed them. In 1925, he established the Arts Theater, in which he tried to combine the energetic improvisatory style of Italian acting with the more disciplined approach of the new schools of realistic acting. The Arts Theater toured Europe and South America before it was disbanded in 1928 for financial reasons.

In the latter part of his life, Pirandello achieved popular success. In France, he was awarded the Legion of Honor medal. In the United States, he was greeted with accolades. In Italy, he became a member of the Italian Academy, and, in 1934, he won the coveted Nobel Prize in Literature. Yet, to the very end, he believed himself to be an alienated man. In his will, he stated that he wanted his death unannounced, his naked body wrapped in a winding sheet, his remains cremated, and his ashes scattered in the wind so that nothing of himself would remain. His ashes were preserved and finally buried in his birthplace in Il Caos. Pirandello was, indeed, what he had called himself, the "Son of Caos."

## Summary

Luigi Pirandello is one of the leading writers of the modernist period. His drama and fiction focus on the relativity of truth and the impossibility of certainty in an age of anxiety. He examines in detail the disintegration of the self, the fragmentation of human experience, the unreliability of rational thought, and the impossibility of language to communicate. His self-conscious, tortuously analytical antiheroes constantly confront the dilemmas of an indifferent universe. His use of parody and farce to undercut the tragedy of existence in a world without hope foreshadows contemporary absurdist literature. The existentialist philosopher and playwright Jean-Paul Sartre found him the most timely dramatist of the post-World War II era. His influence on the French dramatists Jean Giraudoux, Jean Anouilh, and Eugène Ionesco is extensive. More than any other playwright, he is responsible for the self-reflexive theatricality of the modern era that has given us everything from the optimistic panoramas of Thornton Wilder to the absurdist dramas of Samuel Beckett. The famous poet, playwright, and critic T. S. Eliot wrote: "Pirandello is a dramatist to whom all dramatists of my own and future generations will owe a debt of gratitude. He has taught us something about our own problems and has pointed to the direction in which we can seek a solution to them."

## Bibliography

Bassnett-McGuire, Susan. *Luigi Pirandello.* London: Macmillan, and New York: Grove Press, 1983. Briefly discusses the political and personal influences on Pirandello's work and concentrates on a detailed analysis of the major plays grouped according to themes. Also touches on Pirandello's one-act plays and mentions his use of stage directions. Contains photographs of international productions and a bibliography.

Bentley, Eric. *The Pirandello Commentaries.* Evanston, Ill.: Northwestern University Press, 1986. A series of articles by an eminent critic and theorist of modern drama, spanning a lifetime's work of penetrating insights into Pirandello's major dramas. The articles include a short biographical profile of Pirandello.

Caesar, Ann H. *Characters and Authors in Luigi Pirandello.* Oxford and New York: Clarendon Press, 1998. Caesar considers the importance of characters and the author's relationship to them in this examination of Pirandello's work.

Cambon, Glauco, ed. *Pirandello: A Collection of Critical Essays.* Englewood Cliffs, N.J.: Prentice-Hall, 1967. A diverse collection of critical articles, including Adriano Tilgher's influential analysis of Pirandello's drama, Wylie Sypher's discussion of Pirandello's cubist approach to drama, Thomas Bishop's article tracing Pirandello's influence on French drama, and A. L. de Castris' dissection of Pirandello's experimental novels. Includes a detailed chronology of Pirandello's life and a selected bibliography of critical works on Pirandello.

Giudice, Gaspare. *Pirandello: A Biography.* Translated by Alastair Hamilton. London and New York: Oxford University Press, 1975. One of the more comprehensive biographies of Pirandello even though an abridged version of the original. Details much of Pirandello's personal life using quotations from personal correspondence and other primary sources. Includes extensive descriptions of Sicilian life-styles and a good analysis of the political climate in Italy during Pirandello's lifetime.

Oliver, Roger W. *Dreams of Passion: The Theater of Luigi Pirandello.* New York: New York University Press, 1979. This study demonstrates a connection between Pirandello's theory of humor and his drama. Oliver shows how Pirandello makes a distinction between the surface awareness of contrary events in comic situations and a more internal awareness experienced by an audience when it is cognizant of the "sentiment of the contrary." Presents a close analysis of five major plays.

Paolucci, Anne. *Pirandello's Theater: The Recovery of the Modern Stage for Dramatic Art.* Carbondale: Southern Illinois University Press, 1974. A literary and theatrical analysis of Pirandello's major plays and some of his minor dramas arranged thematically. The introduction discusses most of the major themes in his works, and the individual chapters—each preceded by brief synopses of the plays discussed—focus on the development of those themes.

Pirandello, Luigi. *Pirandello's Love Letters to Marta Abba.* Edited and translated by Benito Ortolani. Princeton, N.J.: Princeton University Press, 1994. This volume contains the letters between Pirandello and Abba, tracing their dreams for the Italian theater and their love.

Starkie, Walter. *Luigi Pirandello.* 2d ed. London: Murray, and New York: Dutton, 1937. A very thorough literary biography. Discusses various literary movements in Italy that influenced Pirandello's writings and outlines the primary themes that run throughout his work. Also discusses Pirandello's place in world literature as well as his influence on other playwrights. Well organized, with a good but dated bibliography.

*Paul Rosefeldt*

# DOMINIQUE PIRE

*Born:* February 10, 1910; Dinant, Belgium
*Died:* January 30, 1969; Louvain, Belgium
*Area of Achievement:* Social reform
*Contribution:* Pire received the Nobel Peace Prize for his work among World War II refugees in Europe, particularly those who were aged, crippled, or without those skills that could assure them acceptance by a receiving country.

## Early Life

Georges Charles Clement Ghislain Eugène François Pire was born in Dinant, Belgium, in 1910, the first of seven children. His father was a schoolmaster in the nearby village of Leffe. Pire was four years old when World War I began. In 1914, German troops marched into Belgium, and Pire fled with his parents to France, where they remained as refugees until 1918. When he arrived in his hometown again after the war, Pire returned to a family house which had been burned to the ground.

Pire attended school in Leffe and, after learning classics and philosophy at the Collège de Bellevue at Dinant, decided in 1926 to become a priest. He was sixteen years old. As Brother Henri Dominique, he entered the Couvent de la Sarte, a Dominican monastery in Huy, where he studied philosophy for four years. Pire took his final vows on completion of his studies in 1932 and during the same year went to Rome to attend the Angelicum, the Dominican university. While pursuing doctoral work there, he was ordained into the priesthood (1934) and became Father Pire. He was ordered back to the Couvent de la Sarte monastery at Huy, where he continued work on his dissertation, receiving the doctorate of theology in 1936. At that time, the assignment came to teach the Dominican brothers at Huy. At the age of twenty-six, Pire believed himself to be too young and inadequate to assume those duties and requested further preparation. He studied social and political sciences at the University of Louvain in 1937 and then returned to Huy to begin work as a teacher of moral philosophy and sociology at the Couvent de la Sarte.

When German troops marched into Belgium in 1940, Pire fled to France with other Belgian refugees. When France itself was occupied, he returned to Belgium and resumed his lectures at Huy.

## Life's Work

Aside from teaching, Pire spent the war years trying to obtain sufficient food from the countryside for the children in the villages. He served as chaplain to patriots of the Belgian underground and as an intelligence officer for the resistance, carrying messages and using his proximity to vital information to serve the cause. Pire also assisted downed Allied airmen in escaping German occupied territory and reported German V-1 launches on the Strait of Dover to Allied authorities. For his work, he was honored with several national medals.

Already in 1938, Pire had established a mutual aid society for poor families in rural areas, and, by 1945, his open-air camps in the country had supplied homes for thousands of children from bombed Belgian and French cities and towns. In 1949, on hearing an address by Colonel Edward F. Squadrille, formerly of the United Nations Relief and Rehabilitation Administration, Pire expanded his commitment to charitable work and assistance to the homeless. Squadrille had resigned his post with the United Nations out of frustration, citing enormous difficulties in placing stateless and destitute refugees who were old, handicapped, or without marketable skills. Although most of the eight million displaced persons of World War II had been settled by relief and relocation organizations, approximately 150,000 remained uprooted. These were the "hard-core" refugees who had little to offer receiving countries.

Pire began writing letters to such refugees and visited an Austrian camp in which sixty thousand of them awaited relocation. Noting the toll that years of insecurity, lack of privacy, and reliance on charity had taken on their lives, he began disseminating information about their plight, encouraging more fortunate people to develop relationships by writing letters and sending packages, and calling on others to assist in programs to resolve the displaced persons' problems. In 1950, Pire opened the first of four homes in Belgium for elderly refugees who were no longer able to care for themselves. To rekindle self-worth, these people were encouraged to cultivate old and vanishing skills, such as embroidery, to offer for sale.

The priest's major task was locating refugees in communities where they could participate productively in mainstream European life. Pire believed that reestablishing roots was the fundamental need of displaced persons, and he conceived of small villages near cities where refugees would gradually

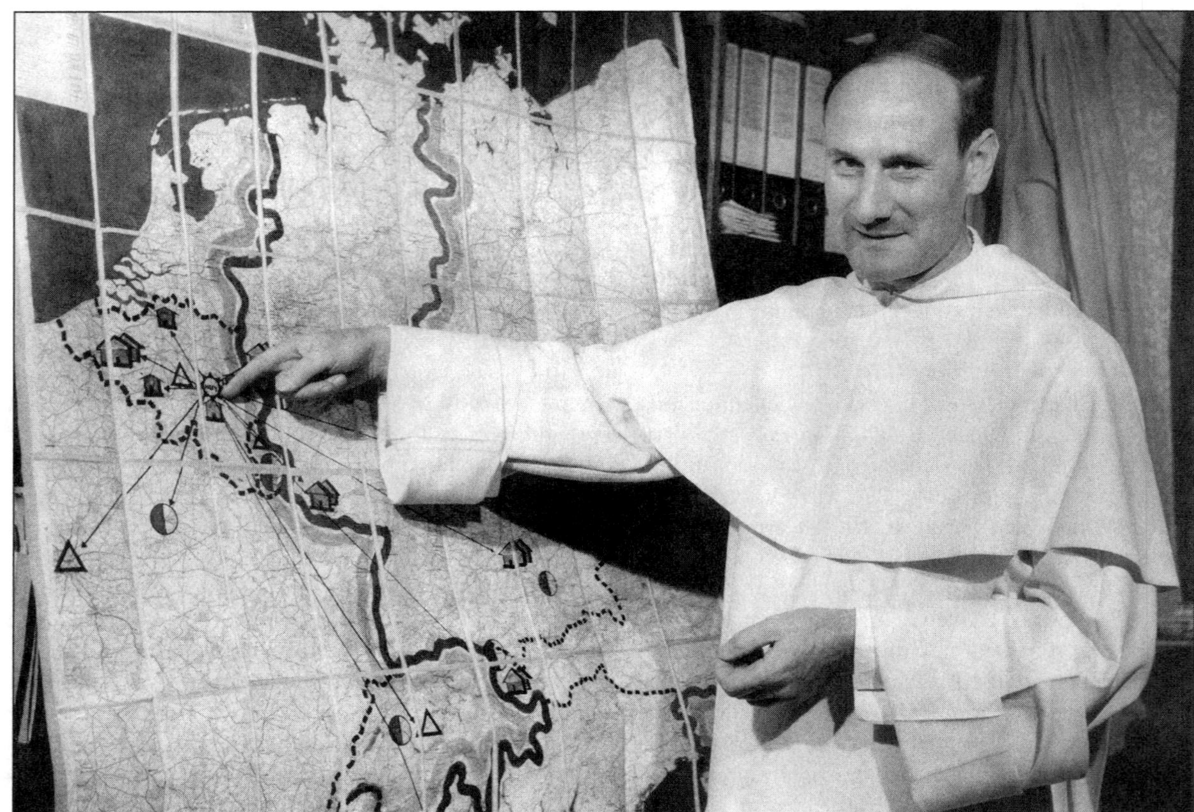

be integrated into local life. After convincing citizens that their cities would not be negatively impacted by such groups, Pire began establishing his "European Villages," consisting of 150-200 refugees and largely supported by private funds. Eventually there were six such villages, and members ultimately became self-supporting.

It was through his efforts to establish the sixth village that Pire received the Nobel Peace Prize. Short of funds, Pire applied to the Nobel Foundation for support but was informed that the organization only disbursed money as prizes. The priest found a person qualified to nominate him for a prize, and in 1958, Pire received an invitation to come to the Norwegian Embassy to present his work to Nobel Foundation representatives. Later, he traveled to Oslo for further discussions, and, in 1958, Pire was awarded the Nobel Peace Prize for his efforts to help refugees, especially the "hard core," leave their camps and return to lives of freedom and dignity.

Pire extended his efforts to achieve peace through creating contacts and understanding among people from different parts of the world by beginning his Open Heart to the World organization in 1960. The major operation of the organization was the Mahatma Gandhi International Peace Center, which later became known as the University of Peace. Located in Huy, the university held seminars designed to help men, women, and youth to engage in positive peace activism. Additionally, the organization sponsored the World Friendships initiative, which encouraged exchanges between people of varied backgrounds; the World Sponsorship system, which provided aid for Asian and African refugees; and the Peace Islands in East Pakistan and India, which provided education, medical assistance, and help in developing more effective agricultural methods. Pire died at the age of fifty-eight in Louvain, Belgium, of a heart attack while recovering from surgery.

## Summary

Dominique Pire's commitment to social justice pivoted on interaction between individuals of varied backgrounds. Beginning with a recognition of both the fundamental diversity and unity of humankind, Pire promoted the equality of all persons in respect to their dignity and rights. In order to achieve that level of mutual esteem as a practical reality, he developed a style of communication that he referred to as "fraternal dialogue." This form of exchange was characterized by listening, openness, and unselfishness on both sides of the dialogue, and Pire advanced it through his writings and teachings as the sure means of achieving internal as well as external peace.

Pire was one of several post-World War II peace activists who went beyond nationality, race, and creed to seek solutions to the destructive capabilities and the competitiveness that his generation had experienced in human relations. Although his goals were regarded by some as idealistic, the priest's simple and practical program for achieving them united with useful results to gain international recognition. Pire described himself as being prohumankind and not "anti" anything. Because his agenda included the advancement in dignity of all categories of people, Pire's views obtained widespread currency and support.

### Bibliography

Gray, Tony. *Champions of Peace.* New York: Paddington Press, 1976. The story of Alfred Nobel, the Nobel Peace Prize, and its recipients is described in this work. Gray analyzes the political and social milieu in which Pire worked and how that environment impacted the decision to award him the prize.

Houart, Victor. *The Open Heart.* London: Souvenir Press, 1959. Houart focuses on the evolution of Pire's "European Villages" but includes substantial information on the priest's childhood and early adult years.

Northcott, Cecil. "Profile: Father Dominique Pire." *Contemporary Review* 202 (September, 1962): 130-131. This article deals with the University of Peace and the philosophy and approach of the person who founded it.

Pire, Dominique. *The Story of Father Dominique Pire.* Translated by John L. Skeffington. New York: Dutton, 1961. This work provides Pire's autobiography and includes editorial comments from Hugues Vehenne, the person to whom Pire told the story. The engaging and reflective account is enriched by photographs of family, friends, refugees, and the villages that Pire founded.

Wintterle, John, and Richard S. Cramer. *Portraits of the Nobel Laureates in Peace.* London and New York: Abelard-Schuman, 1971. The chapter on Pire contains an interesting analysis of how he obtained the Nobel Peace Prize and addresses the question of whether he was an appropriate recipient.

*Margaret B. Denning*

# THE PIRELLI FAMILY

## Giovanni Battista Pirelli

*Born:* December 27, 1848; Varenna, Austrian Empire *Died:* October 20, 1932; Milan, Italy

## Piero Pirelli

*Born:* January 27, 1881; Milan, Italy *Died:* August 7, 1956; Milan, Italy

## Alberto Pirelli

*Born:* April 28, 1882; Milan, Italy *Died:* October 19, 1971; Casciano, Italy

*Areas of Achievement:* Business, industry, government, politics, invention, and technology

*Contribution:* The Pirelli family was a group of Italian industrialists who furthered the development, production, and trade of rubber goods, electric wire, and electric cables. The family also figured significantly in nineteenth and twentieth century Italian and international politics.

### Early Lives

Giovanni Battista Pirelli was born in Varenna, Como, then part of the Austrian Empire, in December, 1848. He attended schools in Como and later entered the Facolta de Matematica in Pavia, from which he went on to the Politechnico of Milan. During the years of the Italian unification, Giovanni fought with the Italian patriot Giuseppe Garibaldi, serving as a guerrilla Red Shirt at Trentino and in the Battle of Mentana. He later served as a senator in the Italian government.

In 1870, Giovanni traveled to Switzerland and Germany to learn about the rubber industry, which, like other forms of industry, was little developed in Italy. He returned to Milan and, in 1872, started a rubber hose factory to combat domination of the market by the French, Italy's erstwhile enemy. He opened a shop in Milan with forty-two thousand dollars in borrowed capital, thirty-five workers, and some experience in vulcanization, the process whereby rubber is hardened to prevent melting at high temperatures. It was the first business of its kind in Italy and one of the first in Europe.

### Lives' Work

The firm developed specialties in wires, insulated cables, and eventually automobile tires. It produced some of the earliest telegraph and telephone wires for Italy's new army. In 1879, Giovanni extended his enterprise to the production of electrical conductors. He later produced cables whose design and construction stood far in advance of anything obtainable at the time. In 1883, Milan inaugurated the Edison Central Electric Station, the first station of its scale in Europe. The Pirelli firm supplied the rubber-coated wires used in the new installations, its first customer being the Milanese opera house, La Scala. The company pioneered the manufacture of electric cable and, in 1887, began producing and installing underwater cables as well. The firm had a subsidiary factory in Barcelona for the production of electric cables by 1902, making Pirelli the first Italian industrialist to establish plants outside Italy. In 1917, when a Pirelli engineer patented an oil-insulated cable that could carry far more than the limit then in effect, Pirelli became a leader in the high-tension cable business. The Pirelli firm entered the pneumatic tire business in 1890 with production of its first air-filled bicycle tires. As Italy's automobile industry began increased development, Pirelli moved into the pneumatic automobile tire market in 1899.

Giovanni's son, Piero, joined the firm in 1901. Born in Milan in 1881, Piero received an LL.D. at the University of Genoa. Alberto, a second son, joined the business in 1903. To promote the automobile tire industry, Alberto helped sponsor the eight-thousand-mile Peking-to-Paris automobile race of 1907, which was won by the Italian driver Prince Borghese in a car fitted with Pirelli tires. Alberto built dirigibles for North Pole explorations during the 1920's. The Pirelli *Norge* was the first lighter-than-air craft to succeed in reaching the pole, making a more than eight-thousand-mile voyage from Rome to Teller, Alaska, in 1926. The crew, which included Roald Amundsen, saw and photographed parts of the globe never before seen by human eyes.

By 1914, the Pirelli company was the largest Italian manufacturer of rubber goods. It had built an industrial system that was virtually independent of the Italian state, linking its strength to foreign markets without Italian favors. Pirelli plants could be found in many parts of Italy and the world.

Both Piero and Alberto participated actively in promoting Italian business and international trade. Piero assisted greatly with the development of the Italian telephone service, represented Italy in many important international financial negotiations, and served as vice president of the Confederation of Italian Industries. Alberto was chosen by Benito Mussolini to represent Italy at the important post-World War I conferences. The younger Pirelli brother was a member of the Supreme Economic Committee of Versailles, Italian delegate to the first International Labor Office of Geneva, and a member of the League of Nations Economic Committee. Between 1928 and 1932, Alberto served as president of the International Chamber of Commerce. He served on the Dawes Committee, bringing to bear his concern for the impact of reparations payments on international trade. Alberto became Mussolini's trusted financial and economic adviser. He was a member of the National Council of Corporations and a commissioner of the General Fascist Confederation of Industries, two syndicates through which the Italian government controlled industry.

Giovanni died in 1932. Piero was then serving as managing director of the Pirelli organization and, after his father's death, became chairman of the board. Alberto assumed management of the business that year.

Pirelli plants were destroyed during World War II, but Marshall Plan funds assisted in building five new factories and refurbishing old ones; the business flourished again. To counter the growing communist influence among workers during the 1950's, Alberto began a progressive program that brought higher wages, increased benefits, and greater worker satisfaction to the business, resulting in the decline of communist influence and an increase in worker productivity. Pirelli workers gained a free medical, surgical, and hospital plan, low-cost modern housing options, a free home for retirees on Lake Como, and free vacation camps on the Italian Riviera. During one eight-year period, Pirelli wages increased 96 percent vis-à-vis the 28 percent Italian cost-of-living rise.

By the mid-1960's, Pirelli had become the second-largest tire and rubber company outside the United States and shared a close race with a British company for the position as the world's largest producer of electric cable. It sold more abroad than any other Italian company and had eighty-one plants in thirteen different countries. It was also the second-largest stockholder in Italy's Fiat automobile company.

The Pirelli organization continued innovation in the tire industry. In 1953, radial-ply tires using textile belts were introduced, giving much greater vertical flexibility. During the 1970's, Pirelli improved wet traction by modifying rubber formulas, and the company's methods of measuring vehicle handling came to be considered the most professional in the world. In 1971, the firm merged with Great Britain's Dunlop Holding, Ltd., a union designed to join the resources of Europe's two largest tire and rubber companies, while maintaining their status as separate holding companies and retaining their own trademarks. The merger was dissolved in 1981. Its failure has been attributed to greater competition in the industry and to higher production costs emerging from increased oil prices. Today Pirelli is an international holding company with operations in Europe, North and South America, the Middle East, and New Zealand.

Piero died in 1956. His younger brother, Alberto, retired in 1965 and died six years later after a long illness. The direction of the Pirelli company remained in the hands of Alberto's second son, Leopoldo, who modernized the organization's management structure and conducted the firm as the chief executive of the vast and highly organized stockholder organization that it had already become.

### Summary

Giovanni Pirelli, his sons, and the firm they established were both cause and effect in the industrialization of Italy during the late nineteenth and early twentieth centuries. Giovanni brought to Italy the production practices of that part of Europe north of the Alps. His sons Alberto and Piero played a large role in the political and industrial advancement of Italy as a substantial international power.

The Pirelli family, particularly Alberto, pushed rubber technology to the limit. Besides innovative research and application in the tire industry and with rubber-insulated electric cables, the Pirelli organization has produced countless rubber items, including skin diving equipment, raincoats, elastic thread, plastic food bags, baby bottle nipples, rubber hoses, and drive belts.

**Bibliography**

Coates, Austin. *The Commerce in Rubber: The First 250 Years.* New York: Oxford University Press, 1987. Coates's interesting and comprehensive history of the world rubber industry places the Pirelli organization in the larger context of that trade. The chapter entitled "Europe-electricity and tyres-Pirelli-Dunlop-Michelin" is particularly relevant.

*Fortune*, Editors of *Businessmen Around the Globe.* Englewood Cliffs, N.J.: Prentice-Hall, 1967. The article on Leopold Pirelli, who assumed leadership of the Pirelli organization in 1965, contains a brief account of Giovanni's founding of the business.

Nobile, Umberto. "Navigating the *Norge* from Rome to the North Pole and Beyond." *National Geographic Magazine* 52 (August, 1927): 177-215. Nobile was an Italian Air Force general who codirected the Pirelli-sponsored dirigible flight over the North Pole. The body of the *Norge* was constructed of rubberized, triple-ply fabric.

Pirelli, Alberto, Josiah C. Stamp, and Count A. de Chalendar. *Reparation Payments and Future International Trade.* Paris: International Chamber of Commerce, 1925. This report by the Economic Restoration Committee of the International Chamber of Commerce contains the study of the possible effects of the German reparation payments on international trade. Pirelli served on the subcommittee and helped compose part 1 of the report.

Ridgeway, George L. *Merchants of Peace: Twenty Years of Business Diplomacy Through the International Chamber of Commerce.* New York: Columbia University Press, 1938. Ridgeway describes the evolution and work of the International Chamber of Commerce, whose president from 1928 to 1932 was Alberto Pirelli. The chapter on the business settlement of reparations also describes the work of the Dawes Committee, on which Alberto also served.

Webster, Richard A. *Industrial Imperialism in Italy 1908-1915.* Berkeley: University of California Press, 1975. Webster's research provides a valuable description of the environment in which Italian companies such as the Pirelli organization worked during the decade preceding World War I. The chapter dealing with non-trust industries is the most pertinent.

*Margaret B. Denning*

# HENRI PIRENNE

*Born:* December 23, 1862; Verviers, Belgium
*Died:* October 24, 1935; Ukkel, Belgium
*Area of Achievement:* Historiography
*Contribution:* Pirenne altered extant periodization of European history and altered the thinking of medievalists by reminders of the influences of Islam and Byzantium on Western history and of all historians by diverting them from undue emphasis on institutional (legal), political, and religious events. The "Pirenne Thesis" has been a major influence on professional historical thinking.

## Early Life

Jean Henri Otto Lucien Marie Pirenne was the first, and ultimately the most distinguished, child born into an unusual bourgeois family on December 23, 1862, in Verviers, Belgium. His father, Lucien Henri, a hard-driving industrialist who operated Belgium's technically most advanced woolen manufactory, was also bookish, polylingual, learned, and widely traveled. Young Henri's mother, Marie Duesberg, was the accomplished daughter of his paternal grandfather's business partner. She came from a less fervently economic, more intellectual lineage than her husband. Since the marriage, which joined Verviers's two most respected families, was less a marriage of convenience than one based on mutual respect and affection, young Henri enjoyed a nourishing familial environment.

Romantic, bookish, but gregarious and observant, Pirenne not only came to know Verviers's urban workers but also explored the surrounding Franchimont region, whose peasants had always been freemen. At seven, his formal education began at the local Collège Communal, pedagogically French, where he displayed a remarkable memory and prizewinning excellence in Latin, German, Greek, French, geography, and history, but notable weakness in mathematics, thus aborting his father's hopes that he would proceed to engineering, helping to upgrade the mill's technology. Pirenne's father, therefore, suggested that his son study law at the University of Liège.

Matriculating in 1879, Pirenne subsequently performed brilliantly in all subjects but swiftly came under the influence of historians Godefroid Kurth and Paul Fredericq: Kurth was fervently Catholic, and Fredericq was vociferously Protestant. Each taught superbly, however, and both, trained in the new critical German historical methodologies, identified with Leipzig's great Theodor Mommsen and Berlin's masterful Leopold von Ranke, helped further a renaissance in Belgian university life. Not less propitious was the amazing Belgian archival collection somewhat earlier assembled by Paris-born and self-taught Prosper Gachard. It was invaluable to the Liège historians—later, most particularly to Pirenne.

In 1881, Pirenne qualified with greatest distinction (by examination) to proceed toward the doctorate; directed by Kurth, he published his first monograph at the age of nineteen in 1882. Completing his doctorate in 1883, he was urged by his mentors to continue medieval studies in Paris at the École Pratique des Hautes Études and the École des Chartres, which, after extensive scholarly travels, he did, again performing with excellence. Essentially his career was well launched with a scholarship to study at the very heart of the modern revolution in historical studies: in Germany at the University of Leipzig, then at the University of Berlin.

## Life's Work

Berlin meant Pirenne's direct contact with the elite of nineteenth century historians: Ranke, Gustav von Schmoller, Georg Waitz, and a host of young rising historians. Then in 1885, through the indefatigable efforts of Kurth, Pirenne received a professorship at the University of Liège, teaching Latin paleography and diplomatic as well as historical exercises for the humanities division. Master of French, German, Dutch, Latin, and Greek, he also read Italian and English; master too of paleography, philosophy, and toponomy (the origins of regional place names and languages), he had, as they expected, excelled his mentors. However distinguished a future awaited him at Liège, he was within a year "stolen" by Fredericq for a post in the less distinguished University of Ghent, where he would remain until retirement in 1930. Advancement in academic rank was one reason for the move but was less important than Fredericq himself and the opportunity to teach his own courses on medieval history and the history of Belgium—of which in time he would be applauded as the nation's premier historian.

Two loves pinned Pirenne to Ghent: first, as a medievalist, his recognition of its immense economic importance from the twelfth into the fourteenth centuries—and the economic revivification it again was enjoying while he was there—and second, his marriage in 1887 to Jenny Vanderhaegen, an alert, shrewd, gracious woman who industriously protected and advanced her husband's career. They would have four sons, one a historian of note.

Thus settled, Pirenne extended associational activities promoting collections of Belgian historical documents, added the teaching of urban economic history, and published a series of originally documented monographs, which exposed previous scholarship as myth and thereby promoted controversies of the sort that would mark his entire career. He also produced a monumental Belgian bibliography of extant documents from dozens of fields up to the year 1580 plus a history of Belgium and the Low Countries up to 1830 that instantly won international acclaim. Further, his monographic history on medieval Dinant became a model of urban history because of its concentration upon social, political, legal, and economic affairs—a precursor of total history, later to characterize the Annales school of historical research that has enjoyed international recognition.

Disciplined, a splendid teacher—whose students' scholarly careers confirmed this—active in meliorating German and French scholars after embitterments of the Franco-Prussian War, active also in a host of professional associations, Pirenne, with the publication in the *Revue historique* of his "L'Origine des constitutions urbaine au moyen âge," by 1893 ranked among the greater European historians. Already he had established the thesis that urban development was the key to understanding the history not only of Belgium and The Netherlands but also of European civilization in general. Additionally, besides scores of book reviews, lectures, and meetings, he published eighteen major articles on aspects of the Middle Ages between 1894 and 1899.

Of these articles, the most important conveyed Pirenne's conviction that European urban life, based largely on Roman towns, was virtually extinguished between the sixth and eighth centuries and that a general economic revival in the tenth and eleventh centuries produced and centered on the town, a new institution in the Middle Ages, one that precipitated the decline of feudal institutions and social structure. The second portion of the article (1895) focused on historical forces that he regarded as responsible for the rise of the town and the emergence of the bourgeoisie.

While this so-called mercantile-settlement theory gained some adherents, it initially was rebuffed by most French historians, while those in Great Britain clung to earlier Germanic explanations of town origins. Nevertheless, it commenced another of Pirenne's shifts of historians' emphases. This theory was also incorporated into the first of what eventually became seven volumes of his *Histoire de Belgique* (1900-1932; history of Belgium); the initial volume alone made him Belgium's national historian and a figure of international professional renown, with accompanying honors and awards. His writing continued, of which the most significant was his *Les Anciennes Démocraties des Pays-Bas* (1910; *Belgian Democracy: Its Early History*, 1915). He continued in these works to reject traditional history as mere chronologizing, as a lexicon of biographies, or tales of politics and wars, rather emphasizing that events were best depicted as a complex interweaving of a people's collective activities.

Congenitally optimistic, a meliorist through his professional contacts of Franco-German-Belgian relations, he naïvely dismissed possibilities of war in 1914, let alone the invasion of Belgium, or the instant obedience that German historians lent their government. For passive resistance, both Pirenne and Fredericq were arrested in 1916 and confined in German camps. There, over the next thirty-two months, Pirenne learned Russian, expanded his perspectives beyond Western Europe, and became intrigued with comparative interactions of Eastern and Western cultures.

Free in 1918, Pirenne continued to ask when historically the break came between the Roman world and "the First Europe," a query he answered in his *Les Villes du moyen age: Éssai d'histoire économique et sociale* (1927; *Medieval Cities: Their Origins and the Revival of Trade*, 1925). His next major study, partially completed after his retirement in 1930, *Mahomet et Charlemagne* (1937; *Mohammed and Charlemagne*, 1939), demonstrated that the Roman world lasted longer than traditional histories indicated and that it was Islam, not the Germanic invasions, that finally destroyed it. He was unable to revise the work, for, stricken with pneumonia, this distinguished, indomitable, unassuming man died of heart failure on October 24, 1935, in Ukkel, Belgium.

### Summary

In an era of great historians, Henri Pirenne ranks among the greatest for his dramatic and provocative thesis that the accepted periodization of European history was erroneous; that the Roman world lasted centuries longer than had been believed; that its disruption was the work of militantly spreading Islam, not a consequence of the Germanic invaders—who, in his view, assimilated quite readily into Roman civilization; and that the revival of Europe from rather backward agrarianism was the result of a revival of trade, responsibility for which should be assigned to the emergence of new European urban life and the activities of its commercial (or bourgeois) citizenry. While controversy still continues over his thesis and there have been factual revisions of some of its elements, most of its main features are widely viewed as basically sound. Few historical perspectives have so dramatically changed historical thinking and research or so massively shifted the focus of professional attention to economic and social history away from literal chronologization and literal political and institutional history. Historians accept superannuation of their research and syntheses; undoubtedly, Pirenne would have agreed that on very minimal available evidence on the Merovingian and Carolingian periods, he at times both overstated and understated his basic thesis. Yet he unquestionably raised and substantially answered fresh questions on medieval history and decisive changes within the Mediterranean-European world and altered perspectives in the profession to which he so decently and devotedly committed his life.

### Bibliography

Boyce, Gray C. "The Legacy of Henri Pirenne." *Byzantion* 15 (1940-1941): 449-464. An early, scholary, well-written, appreciative but by no means uncritical analysis of Pirenne's studies upon medieval studies as well as upon the historical profession in general.

Havighurst, Alfred F., ed. *The Pirenne Thesis: Analysis, Criticism, and Revision.* 3d ed. Boston: Heath, 1976. With excellent introductory materials, fine footnoting throughout, and excellent bibliographical references, this brief volume not only includes excerpts from Pirenne's work but also compacts a distinguished range of fine, very readable scholarly reactions to it.

Lyon, Bryce. *Henri Pirenne: A Biographical and Intellectual Study.* Ghent, Belgium: Story-Scientia, 1974. A major work and as fine a study as exists on any major modern historian. Contains a superb summation of the strengths, weaknesses, and legacies of Pirenne's work in chapters 11 and 12. Includes photographs, citation footnotes, an excellent select bibliography, and an index.

———. *The Origins of the Middle Ages: Pirenne's Challenge to Gibbon.* New York: Norton, 1972. Well written by an authoritative Pirenne expert and medievalist in his own right, this work provides excellent perspective on problems of reinterpreting or delineating the origins of the Middle Ages. Contains a good bibliography and an index.

Pirenne, Henri. *Medieval Cities: Their Origins and the Revival of Trade.* Translated by Frank D. Halsey. Princeton, N.J.: Princeton University Press, 1925. For all of his immense scholarship, Pirenne wrote in order to be read by intelligent publics. It is essential for serious readers to read Lyon's biography, but there is no substitute for reading the master himself. As was usual in his writing, the text itself generally suffices for documentation; there are few notes, only a modest select bibliography and index.

Riising, Anne. "The Fate of Henri Pirenne's Thesis on the Consequence of Islamic Expansion." *Classica et Mediaevalia* 13 (1952): 87-130. Riising, a Danish journalist, here examines in greater detail than anyone the arguments pro and con respecting this critical aspect of Pirenne's major thesis about the severance of Europe from the Roman Mediterranean world in the Merovingian and Carolingian periods. Her purpose, since she agrees that the last word has not been said, is to review the extant evidence, which she manages with great skill and clarity.

*Clifton K. Yearley*

# PIUS XI
## Ambrogio Damiano Achille Ratti

*Born:* May 31, 1857; Desio, Italy
*Died:* February 10, 1939; Vatican City, Italy
*Areas of Achievement:* Religion and diplomacy
*Contribution:* Pius XI was forced to deal with the problems emerging from World War I, especially the rise of communism and the various forms of right-wing totalitarianism (including Fascism and Nazism), along with the economic dislocation that affected Europe throughout the interwar period. His efforts not only allowed the Catholic church to regain respect but also restarted the Church's public involvement in social and political issues.

### Early Life

Ambrogio Damiano Achille Ratti was the son of a well-to-do manufacturer in northern Italy. His scholastic brilliance and encyclopedic mind were recognized early and, probably partially through the influence of his uncle, an important priest in his home diocese, Ratti was admitted to the famous Roman seminary of Lombard College and was ordained in December, 1879. While he continued his studies in Rome, taking graduate degrees in canon law, theology, and philosophy, Ratti was also pursuing his hobby of mountain climbing, tackling several technically difficult peaks and later producing a small book of memoirs on the subject.

In 1882, Ratti became an instructor at the seminary in Milan. Seven years later, he transferred to the famous Milanese library, the Biblioteca Ambrosiana, starting the field of work that would occupy him for most of the rest of his life. He reached the pinnacle of his field within the Catholic church in 1914, when Pope Pius X appointed him to serve as the prefect of the Vatican Library.

For reasons known only to himself, the next pope, Benedict XV, chose his librarian to head a diplomatic mission to Warsaw in the spring of 1918, anticipating the formation of a united Poland out of the chaos of war-torn Eastern Europe. The Catholic church would become one of the forces that helped the Poles create a unified nation after having been split by Russia, Austria, and Prussia in the 1790's.

The three years in Poland when Ratti was the apostolic envoy and then nuncio were filled with problems. Besides the great economic problems, Poland also launched an attack on the areas immediately to the east and southeast. Unfortunately, the new Soviet Union was also interested in regaining its lost provinces, and so the two states were quickly fighting each other. Poland lost the war, but Ratti gained some fame for being one of the few diplomats who refused to flee Warsaw when the Soviet troops nearly surrounded the city. This episode also led to Ratti's personal dislike for the Soviet Union, in addition to the religious objections all Church leaders had for the officially atheistic state.

In recognition of his service, Benedict recalled Ratti late in 1921, made him a cardinal, and posted him to the Diocese of Milan, one of the most important posts within the Church. Ratti had little time to do anything as Archbishop of Milan, however, because of Benedict's death on January 22, 1922. On February 6, Ratti was elected pope, taking the name Pius XI.

### Life's Work

Pius started his reign with an important gesture. Ever since the new Italian nation had taken over Rome and the Papal States more than fifty years before, the popes had acted as "prisoners of the Vatican," meaning that they refused to accept the loss of the papal territory, recognize the Italian state, or leave the area of the Vatican. Pius made his first appearance as pope on an outside balcony, as a symbolic opening of the Vatican. Pius was determined to bury the feud with the Italian state, which would enable the Papacy to move on to some of the other problems that it faced in the twentieth century.

Pius was sincere in his desire to reestablish the Vatican as a force in the modern world, and he made more concordats (Church-state agreements) in his reign than had ever been made before, a total of twenty-five. He also opened numerous diplomatic missions to countries with small, almost forgotten, Catholic minorities, especially in the Balkan region. Other signs of Pius' desire to bring the Church into the modern world include his establishment of Vatican Radio (a worldwide shortwave service) in the 1930's, the establishment of new orders within the Church whose prime service goals were to publicize the faith, and his many encyclicals on the state of the world, beginning with *Ubi Arcano Dei* (where God's silence) in 1923, which discussed the state of post-World War I Europe, and ending with his trio of antidictatorial statements in 1937.

*Pope Pius XI posing for a portrait in 1924*

Unfortunately, Pius is best known for two of his concordats: the 1929 concordat with Benito Mussolini's Italy and the 1933 agreement with Nazi Germany. The Italian concordat established Vatican City, and some other Church property, as an independent state, while the one with Nazi Germany (which was more of a culmination of a decade-long process than a quick agreement with the new German regime) promised noninterference with the internal workings of the Church; neither concordat, however, would prevent the two Fascist states from persecuting the Catholic church during the 1930's.

Pius' 1937 encyclical *Divini Redemptoris*, refuting the claims of historical inevitability that the Soviets were then making, is still probably his best-known work. Because it is so well known and so often quoted and reprinted, *Divini Redemptoris* overshadows Pius' other social and political commentaries, at times to the point at which he has been accused of ignoring the threats of Fascism in general and Nazism in particular and concentrating only on the threat from the far Left.

Pius did condemn the far Left and not only in *Divini Redemptoris.* He also condemned the left-wing Mexican Revolution in 1937 and the left-wing government in Spain during the mid-1930's. On the other hand, he also restated Pope Leo XIII's 1891 condemnation of the exploitation of the working classes by capital in his 1931 encyclical *Quaragesimo Anno* and condemned Mussolini's Fascism in his other 1931 encyclical *Non Abbiamo Bisogno* and the Nazi movement with the first of his 1937 condemnations, *Mit brennender Sorge.* Both of these last two encyclicals had to be smuggled out of Italy in order to be published. Taking all twenty-nine of the pope's encyclicals together (the most written by one pope until that time and dealing with problems and developments from politics to the film industry), it can be seen that, while he was most concerned about the dangers from the far Left, Pius was also concerned about the other problems facing interwar Europe, including the dangers posed by the Right.

Besides the many social and political problems that Pius saw emerging during his time as pope, he also dealt with a number of other issues. One, as befitting the former head of the Vatican library, was the sponsoring of a number of new intellectual agencies, including the Pontifical Academy of Sciences (which recognizes the achievements of non-Catholic as well as Catholic scientists), the reform of some older ones, and an increased support by the Church to regional literary, religious, and scientific conferences and congresses. Pius also enlarged the Vatican Library and encouraged Catholic seminaries to update their curricula to include more science and social science.

Pius was also interested in opening dialogues with other religious leaders, especially those within the Orthodox churches. While a little progress was made with some of the Eastern Orthodox churches, the effort did not go very far during this period, since neither side was willing to make concessions to the other, nor was the Russian Orthodox church, perhaps the largest of the Orthodox churches and completely under the authority of the Soviet government, interested in making any contacts at all. These attempts mark the start of the dialogue that has lasted until today between the Catholic church and the Orthodox churches.

Late in 1936, the seventy-nine-year-old pope became very sick, and the press of the world set up a sort of "death watch" to cover the expected funeral and subsequent papal election. Pius recovered from that illness by the Easter of 1937 and returned to working full-time. Rumors started circulating in late 1938 and early 1939 that Pius was going to issue a new, stronger, condemnation of either Fascism or Nazism, perhaps both. These rumors increased when the entire Italian episcopate was ordered to come to Rome to hear a major papal address on February 11, and Pius was known to be working hard on the texts of two speeches. What those speeches might have been are unknown. Pius fell ill with a cold on February 7 and died of complications on February 10.

### Summary

Pius XI faced many problems during his reign, most of them having to do with the political and social problems that Europe faced during the period between the world wars. He was, perhaps, hampered with a determination to maintain, if not increase, the traditional powers of the pope while having to face the fact that the Papacy no longer had any secular power base. Pius condemned the evils of his time, but, like all the other leaders of the period, secular and religious alike, his reputation has suffered since because he was unable to stop the coming of World War II and the Holocaust that accompanied it.

Autocratic, brilliant, and determined, Pius never stopped working to improve the social and political climate around him until his death. In the short run, Pius can be said to have failed, since World War II and its attendant horrors started six months after his death. The failure, however, was not so much Pius', since he did more than most leaders of the period to point out the evils that were growing, as it was that of Europe as a whole. Unable to recover from the political and economic ruin of World War I, most European societies opted during the interwar period for solutions that would lead to World War II.

### Bibliography

Brown, Frederick. "The Hidden Encyclical: The Contradictions of Catholic Anti-Semitism." *The New Republic* 214, no. 16 (April 15, 1996). Discusses Pius XII's quashing of Pius XI's encyclical "The Unity of the Human Race" in an effort to promote an air of Vatican neutrality.

Browne-Olf, Lillian. *Pius XI: Apostle of Peace.* New York: Macmillan, 1938. A very sympathetic, well-researched biography of Pius, written just before his death. Writing from the viewpoint of the 1930's, Browne-Olf's judgment of Pius is all the more favorable because of the lack of hindsight that has tarnished the reputations of most of the world leaders from the interwar period.

———. *Their Name Is Pius.* Milwaukee, Wis.: Bruce, 1941. A study of five of the seven popes who chose the name Pius since 1775. Pius VIII, who was pope for only eight months, and Pius XII, who had just started his pontificate when the book was written, are omitted.

Coppa, Frank J. "The Hidden Encyclical of Pius XI against Racism and Anti-Semitism Uncovered—Once Again!" *Catholic Historical Review* 84, no. 1 (January, 1998). This article deals with Pius XI's encyclical attacking anti-Semitism and racism.

The Daughters of St. Paul. *Popes of the Twentieth Century.* Boston: St. Paul Editions, 1983. A short work that serves as a favorable introduction to the twentieth century popes, laying out the salient facts of each one's biography and life's work.

Kent, Peter C. *The Pope and the Duce.* London: Macmillan, and New York: St. Martin's Press, 1981. This is a monograph on the relationship between the foreign policies of the Vatican and Fascist Italy during the period 1922-1935. The author's thesis is that these foreign policies at times came together and worked in concert, especially when most of Europe was fearing possible rising support for Communism during the early years of the Depression, although the Vatican ultimately took a strong stand against both Fascist Italy and Nazi Germany, as well as the Soviet Union.

Murphy, Francis X. *The Papacy Today.* London: Weidenfeld and Nicolson, and New York: Macmillan, 1981. A concise history of the internal and external political evolution of the Papacy during the first eighty years of the twentieth century.

Teeling, William. *Pope Pius XI and World Affairs.* New York: Stokes, 1937. Although this is a very biased work, based on a fundamental anti-Catholic worldview, this work is valuable because it shows how the theory of Pius' alleged pro-Fascist and pro-Nazi views became widespread.

*Terrance L. Lewis*

# PIUS XII
## Eugenio Maria Giuseppe Pacelli

*Born:* March 2, 1876; Rome, Italy

*Died:* October 9, 1958; Castle Gandolfo, near Rome, Italy

*Areas of Achievement:* Diplomacy, religion, and theology

*Contribution:* Pope Pius XII preserved the Church as an institution during the crisis of World War II. He upheld traditional Catholic doctrine in an era of difficult economic, political, and social change.

### Early Life

Eugenio Maria Giuseppe Pacelli (the future Pope Pius XII) was born in Rome, Italy, on March 2, 1876. His parents were Filippo Pacelli and the former Donna Virginia Graziosi, and he was the second of their four children. He was baptized March 26, 1876, at the Church of Saints Celso and Giuliano as Eugenio Maria Giuseppe Giovanni. The Pacellis were an old Roman family with a long tradition of service to the Vatican in key positions. Eugenio's grandfather, Marcantonio Pacelli, helped found *L'Observatore Romano* in 1861 and served as Papal Minister of the Interior. Filippo Pacelli, a lawyer, served as Dean of the Lawyers of the Consistory and president of a Catholic action group. His family's traditions ensured that Pacelli was reared in an atmosphere of religious devotion and scholarship. He continued a long tradition of service to the Vatican.

After finishing studies at the Lyceum Visconti with an excellent academic record, Pacelli decided to become a priest in October, 1894. After further education at the Capranica, a Roman college, the papal Athenaeum of St. Apollinare, and the Gregorian University, he was ordained to the priesthood on April 2, 1899. Although serious health problems had threatened his ability to continue his duties, he had achieved his first major goal. His ordination did not end Pacelli's education. He added a doctorate in canon and civil laws to the doctorate in sacred theology that he had already received.

### Life's Work

After his ordination, Pacelli served briefly as a substitute canon at the Chapter of St. Mary Major. This period was his only direct experience as a local pastor. In February, 1901, he received an appointment in the Papal Secretariat of State in the section called the Congregation of Extraordinary Ecclesiastical Affairs. This appointment marked the beginning of a long career as a Church diplomat.

Pacelli's intelligence and hard work received quick recognition, and the future Pius XII rose rapidly in rank. He became a monsignor in 1904 and a Domestic Prelate in 1905. On May 13, 1917, Pope Benedict XV consecrated him Titular Archbishop of Sardes. In the reign of Pope Pius XI, the future pope became a cardinal on December 15, 1929. Pacelli was Benedict's nuncio to Munich, Bavaria, and he became Apostolic Nuncio of Germany on June 22, 1920, when the nunciature moved to Berlin. He earned the respect of the German people, who regretted his departure for Rome in 1929.

While Pacelli did not secure the approval of the Kaiser for a peace proposal supported by Benedict, he did secure a "solemn agreement" between Prussia and the Holy See on June 14, 1929, which was ratified on August 14, 1929. While his critics contend that his German experience biased his later actions, the agreement did give the Vatican certain

legal rights, which helped protect Church interests in the Adolf Hitler era. During the 1930's, Pius XI used the future Pius XII as Cardinal Secretary of State from 1930-1939. Pacelli did much traveling to represent the Vatican in countries as diverse as Argentina, Hungary, and the United States.

When Pius XI died on February 10, 1939, his successor, Eugenio Cardinal Pacelli, called the consistory that was to elect him pope. Pius XI's trust in the then Cardinal Pacelli had resulted in his appointment as camerlengo. The camerlengo administers the Vatican during an interregnum period. On March 2, 1939, Eugenio Cardinal Pacelli, was elected pope. Many observers believed that this election fulfilled the wishes of his predecessor.

Pius XII was soon required to put his diplomatic talents to use. The outbreak of World War II put the Vatican in a difficult position, since it was an island in Fascist Italy. As war began Pius XII watched in horror as the devoutly Catholic population of Poland suffered under Nazi occupation. By 1942, the Vatican had clear proof that the Jewish population of Europe was threatened.

Despite his pity for the victims of the Nazis, Pius XII decided that the interests of Catholic Europe required that the Vatican maintain strict neutrality. The Vatican's firm neutrality angered Sir Winston Churchill and Franklin D. Roosevelt, and New York's Cardinal Francis Joseph Spellman warned the pope that many American Catholics were seriously alienated by Vatican neutrality.

Unfortunately for his historical reputation, Pius' actions during World War II have obscured his achievement as a scholar, teacher, and theologian. Papal critics who believe that Pius should have been a prophet or martyr during World War II tend to ignore his achievements in other areas and see him as a callous, cold bureaucrat, who preserved the institutional Church at the expense of the ideals of Jesus Christ.

Pius probably took more pleasure in his role as a teacher and theologian than in any other aspect of his papal duties. Among his outstanding pronouncements were *Mystici Corporis Christi* (1943), *Mediator Dei* (1947), *Humani Generis* (1950), *Menti Nostrae* (1950), *Munificentissimus Deus* (1950), *Musicae Sacrae Disciplina* (1955), *Haurietis Aquas* (1956), and *Miranda Prosus* (1957). *Mystici Corporis Christi* attempted to define the nature of the Church's role as the Mystical Body of Christ. *Mediator Dei* served to stimulate the liturgical movement. Pius always had a strong interest in the proper forms for Christian worship. *Humani Generis* hoped to correct what Pius saw as errors in modern theology. In this encyclical, Pius limited the ability of Catholic theologians to question the historical validity of parts of the Old Testament. In *Menti Nostrae*, Pius stressed the necessity of sound education, obedience to proper authority, and holy living for priests. *Munificentissimus Deus*, which may have been the most important encyclical of Pius' reign, proclaimed that the Virgin Mary had been assumed body and soul into heaven. In this encyclical, Pius broke important doctrinal ground. In *Miranda Prosus*, Pius considered both the blessings and the problems that radio and television brought to Catholic life. He urged priests to master the use of communication.

While Vatican II radically changed Catholic life, the teaching of Pius did not lack enduring value. Pius was an important transitional figure, who preserved the Catholic church in an era of economic, political, and social turmoil.

### Summary

Pius XII's career reflected the upheaval experienced by European society during the first half of the twentieth century. As a skilled diplomat, he consistently sought peace. As a pastor, he tried to relieve the sufferings of the poor and the persecuted. Since he did not speak out strongly to condemn Nazi atrocities against Jews during World War II, many postwar writers have condemned his failure to protest Fascist actions vigorously and publicly. His critics have contended that strong action by Pius might have saved many innocent Jewish lives.

Pius agonized over his actions in World War II, and he was aware that the strict neutrality maintained by the Vatican during the war angered the Allies and those involved in anti-Nazi movements. His priorities clearly stressed the preservation of the Church as an institution and opposition to the spread of communism. These priorities caused him to believe that condemning Nazi atrocities in the early 1940's would jeopardize the Church, and he also contended that he could not condemn Nazi atrocities without condeming Soviet atrocities.

Given his priorities, Pius' actions are understandable. His long-term, historical reputation, however, has suffered greatly from what critics see as pro-German bias, cowardice, and even anti-Semitism. Many historians share the conviction that Pius could have and should have done more to aid the victims of Hitler and defend the European Jewish community.

### Bibliography

Alvarez, David J. "The Vatican and the Far East, 1941-1943." *Historian* 40 (1978): 508-523. This excellent article focuses on the Vatican's relations with Japan and its concern for the Philippines.

Byers, Catherine. "Pius XII and the Jews." *Indiana Social Studies Quarterly* 31 (1978-1979): 57-67. Byers provides an excellent bibliography of writings on the life and pontificate of Pius.

Dietrich, Donald J. "Historical Judgements and Eternal Verities." *Society* 20 (1983): 31-35. Dietrich disagrees with Rolf Hochhuth to some extent. He does, however, believe that Pius should have spoken out against Nazism to his bishops from 1941 to 1943 and to European Catholics generally in 1944.

Friedlander, Saul. *Pius XII and the Third Reich: A Documentation*. Translated by Charles Fullman. London: Chatto and Windus, and New York: Knopf, 1966. Friedlander collects German documents from 1939 to 1944. His brief conclusion is unsympathetic to Pius, whom he regards as pro-German and overly anti-Bolshevik. In Friedlander's view, Pius' silence over the extermination of Jews is almost inexplicable.

Herber, Charles J. "Eugenio Pacelli's Mission to Germany and the Papal Peace Proposals of 1917." *Catholic Historical Review* 65 (1979): 20-48. Herber provides a solid account of Pius' role in World War I peace efforts at the behest of Benedict XV.

Hochhuth, Rolf. *The Deputy*. Translated by Richard Winston and Clara Winston. Preface by Albert Schweitzer. New York: Grove Press, 1964. This critically acclaimed drama attacks Pius for his silence during World War II.

Lipstadt, Deborah E. "Moral Bystanders." *Society* 20 (1983): 21-26. Lipstadt supports Hochhuth's accusations against Pius. She states that "by maintaining its thunderous silence and refusing to act, the Vatican bestowed a certain degree of legitimacy on Nazi atrocities and the inaction of other "bystanders."

O'Carroll, Michael. *Pius XII, Greatness Dishonored: A Documentary Study*. Chicago: Franciscan Herald Press, 1980. O'Carroll attempts to defend Pius against Hochhuth.

Pawlikowski, John. "Pius XII and the Jews: Further Research, Please." *Commonweal* 125, no. 13 (July 17, 1998). Considers Pius XII's reputation following the discovery of his decision to withhold publication of Pius XI's encyclical against racism and anti-Semitism. Pawlikowski argues for further research into the issue.

Sanchez, Jose M. "The Enigma of Pope Pius XII." *America* 175, no. 6 (September 14, 1996). Examines Pius XII's personality, perceptions of him, and his critics.

Smit, Jan Olav. *Angelic Shepherd: The Life of Pope Pius XII*. New York: Dodd, Mead, 1950. This sympathetic biography was written during the lifetime of Pius.

Tinnemann, Ethel Mary. "The Silence of Pope Pius XII." *Journal of Church and State* 21 (1979): 265-285. In an article focused on Eastern Europe, Tinnemann, a nun, condemns Pius for what she sees as his failure to denounce Nazi atrocities in Germany, Poland, and Czechoslovakia forcefully.

*Susan A. Stussy*

## MAX PLANCK

*Born:* April 23, 1858; Kiel, Schleswig
*Died:* October 4, 1947; Göttingen, West Germany
*Areas of Achievement:* Physics, philosophy, and religion
*Contribution:* Planck's discovery in 1900 that light consists of infinitesimal "quanta" and his articulation of the quantum theory replaced classical physics with modern quantum physics. This work not only resulted in Planck's receiving the Nobel Prize in Physics for 1918 but also became a major enabling factor in the work of many other Nobel laureates.

### Early Life

Born into an intellectual family in Kiel, Schleswig, Max Karl Ernst Ludwig Planck spent most of his early life in Munich, where the family moved in the spring of 1867, when he was nine. Planck's father, Johann Julius Wilhelm von Planck, was a professor of civil law at the university in Kiel, whose second wife, Emma Patzig, was Max's mother. Max's forebears included many lawyers and clergymen, a fact which helps explain Planck's lifelong respect for the law and interest in religion.

In May, 1867, Planck was enrolled in Munich's Konigliche Maximilian-Gymnasium, a classical *Gymnasium*, where he came under the tutelage of Hermann Müller, a mathematician who took an interest in the youth and taught him astronomy and mechanics as well as mathematics. It was from Müller that Planck first learned the principle of the conservation of energy that underlay much of his future work in thermodynamics and quantum theory.

Upon completion of the *Gymnasium* in 1874, Planck was at a personal crossroads. He was gifted in music and humanities as well as in mathematics and the sciences. He concluded ultimately that his music talents were insufficient to justify his continuing in that field. When he entered the University of Munich in October, 1874, he concentrated on mathematics. At Munich, however, his interest in physics grew, although his mathematics professors tried to dissuade him, arguing that nothing new remained to be discovered in the field.

Planck became ill as he was completing his first year at Munich and missed two years of school. In the winter term of 1877-1878, when he was well enough to resume his studies, he entered the University of Berlin, where he decided to study theoretical physics because of the order and logic that discipline demanded. Planck yearned to study the nature of the universe. Theoretical physics offered him his most sensible foothold for achieving that goal.

In Berlin, Planck studied with Hermann von Helmholtz, Gustav Kirchhoff, and Rudolf Clausius. Only Clausius was a gifted teacher, although the other two were able physicists. Planck learned much on his own through reading. Although his doctoral dissertation, on the second law of thermodynamics, was undistinguished, he was graduated summa cum laude in 1879. He taught mathematics and physics briefly at his former secondary school in Munich and in 1880 was appointed a privatdocent at the University of Munich. At that time, theoretical physics was viewed as an unpromising field, so his future seemed less than bright.

In 1885, Planck became an associate professor of physics at the University of Kiel, where he remained until 1888, when he was appointed assistant professor and director of the Institute for Theoretical Physics, to replace Kirchhoff, who had died. He rose to professor in 1892 and remained at Berlin until his retirement in 1926.

### Life's Work

Planck's early work in the laws of thermodynamics and his early interest in the principle of the conservation of energy figured largely in his research from his early teaching days at Kiel through his first decades at the University of Berlin. Although he had been reared on classical physics and was a conservative at heart, Planck began to realize that the laws of classical physics deviated greatly from results obtained in experimental physics. He found the greatest disparities not in the field of optics but in that of thermodynamics. The problems stemmed from the measurement of radiant energy in the frequency spectrum of black bodies.

Kirchhoff deduced that radiant energy is independent of the nature of its radiating substance, reasoning that black bodies that absorb all frequencies of light should therefore radiate all frequencies of light. Energy at that time was considered infinitely divisible, a theory that led to many anomalies and seeming contradictions in physics. The problem arose because the lower-frequency range has a smaller number of frequencies than the higher-frequency range.

Important physicists working on this problem reached conflicting conclusions. Wilhelm Wien devised an equation that explained the emissions at high frequencies but not at low frequencies. John William Strutt, Third Baron of Rayleigh devised an equation that worked for low frequencies but not for high frequencies. Work in the field was at an impasse when Planck devised a classically simple equation that explained the distribution of radiation over the full range of frequencies, basing his equation on the daring supposition that energy is not an indivisible flow but is composed of tiny particles, or "quanta," for the Latin word meaning "How many?" Incidental to this discovery was his discovery of a means of measuring the absolute weight of molecules and atoms, in itself a major breakthrough.

Planck's theory showed that the energy of various frequencies of light from violet to red contain different energies, a quantum of violet containing twice the energy of a quantum of red and requiring twice the energy to radiate from a blackbody, making such radiation improbable. So pristine and uncluttered was Planck's theory that he himself was suspicious of it.

Other scientists, however, began to realize its validity, and soon Albert Einstein based much of his work on photoelectric effect, which classical physics could not explain, on quantum theory. Planck embraced Einstein's theory of relativity eagerly because of its absolutism and because of its presentation of the velocity of light.

Now firmly established at the University of Berlin, Planck was instrumental in bringing Einstein to the Berliner Academie in 1914 as a professor without teaching obligations and as director of the embryonic Kaiser Wilhelm Institute for Physics, which Planck himself eventually headed. Planck also nominated Einstein for the Nobel Prize in Physics in 1921, a year in which the award was withheld. In 1922, however, partly at Planck's urging, Einstein received the 1921 prize a year late.

Max Born, Theodor von Kármán, and Peter Joseph Wilhelm Debye began to study the problem of the dependence of specific heat on temperature from the standpoint of quantum theory and soon articulated a law that made it possible to ascertain the variation in specific heat with temperature from the elastic constants in any substance. The field of quantum mechanics became the most important field of physics in the first half of the twentieth century, followed closely by the field of quantum electrodynamics, both developments that evolved from Planck's original insights and from his expression of the ratio between the size of a quantum and its frequency by the symbol $h$, which expresses a universal quantity.

Planck, a balding, bespectacled man with heavy brows, a dark mustache, and grayish eyes, spent nearly four decades at Berlin, teaching extensively and carrying heavy administrative responsibilities. He apparently was a splendid, well-organized teacher, who was clear in his presentations and interested in students. His life during these years was not easy. His wife died in 1909, and, in the next decade his son was killed in World War I and his two daughters died in childbirth.

With Adolf Hitler's rise to power, Planck decided that he had to remain in Germany, although he deplored what was happening. His respect for the law was deeply ingrained, and he felt duty-bound as a citizen to live within the laws but to work from within to change them. He intervened unsuccessfully for Jewish friends and colleagues who were being sent to death camps.

As a Nobel laureate of enormous prestige, Planck scheduled an interview with Hitler and tried to dissuade him from the genocide that was overwhelming Nazi Germany. Hitler, upon learning why Planck had come to see him, began a diatribe that lasted for hours; Planck's intervention did not deter Hitler from his disastrous course. Before the end of the war, Planck, in his eighties, had lost his home and all of his papers to a bombing raid, had once been trapped for several hours in a collapsed air-raid shelter, and, worst of all, had suffered the execution by the Nazis of his son Erwin, a secretary of state before Hitler's ascension, who had been accused of plotting to assassinate Hitler.

### Summary

Max Planck lived for twenty-one years after his retirement. These were troubled years in Germany. The search for the meaning of the universe and for the nature of existence that had led him into physics, where he hoped he would discover absolutes to help answer his questions, persisted in his later years. He wrote on general subjects, developing some of his earlier lectures and essays into fuller works.

In 1930, Planck became president of the Kaiser Wilhelm Society of Berlin, which was renamed the Max Planck Society in his honor. In his final postwar years, he again became president of the society, agreeing as he approached his ninetieth year to assume the post until a permanent president could be found.

Five volumes of Planck's work in theoretical physics were published in English under the title *Introduction to Theoretical Physics* (1932-1933). His highly philosophical *Physikalische gesetzlichkeit im lichte neuer forschung* (1926) and *Das Weltbild der neuen Physik* (1929; combined in *The Universe in the Light of Modern Physics*, 1931) were released and showed a search for absolutes in a broadly religious context, although Planck sought a prime cause more than for an anthropomorphic god.

His general works, *Where Is Science Going?* (1932) and *Wege zur Physikalischen Erkenntnis* (1933; *The Philosophy of Physics*, 1936) were combined with *The Universe in the Light of Modern Physics* and published in English under the title *The New Science* (1959). Planck's autobiography, entitled *Wissenschaftliche Selbstbiographie* (1948; *Scientific Autobiography and Other Papers*, 1949), was published posthumously.

When the Allies came into Germany in May, 1945, Planck, who, with his second wife, had fled to Magdeburg to live with friends after the destruction of their home near Berlin, was again homeless. The area was overrun with Allied soldiers, and Planck had no place to live. American soldiers rescued him and had him sent to a hospital in Göttingen, the city in which he lived for the two and a half years remaining to him. He continued his professional activities, giving his last public lecture—on pseudoproblems—in 1946.

## Bibliography

Hermann, Armin. *The Genesis of Quantum Theory (1899-1913).* Cambridge, Mass.: MIT Press, 1971. This careful study of the pioneering work Planck did in the late 1880's and in the 1890's as he moved toward the discovery of quanta is a complex, thorough book that definitely is best for readers with some background in physics, particularly in thermodynamics and optics.

Hiebert, Erwin N. "The Concept of Thermodynamics in the Scientific Thought of Mach and Planck." *Wissenschaftlicher Bericht, Ernst Mach Institute* 5 (1968). This article demonstrates the marked differences between classical physics as represented by Ernst Mach, a leading Austrian physicist, and the quantum physics of Planck. Mach refused to accept the atomic theory and degraded it as a retrogression that undermined the philosophical development of physics.

Hirosige, T., and S. Nisio. "The Genesis of the Bohr Atom Model and Planck's Theory of Radiation." *Japanese Studies in the History of Science* 9 (1970): 35-47. In this article, Planck is viewed as a catalyst who made Niels Bohr's model of the atom possible. This highly technical article illustrates how quantum mechanics was integral to nearly every major occurrence in physics after Planck's discovery.

Mulligan, Joseph F. "Max Planck and the 'Black Year' of German Physics." *American Journal of Physics* 62, no. 12 (December, 1994). Planck referred to 1935 as the "black year" in German physics as a result of the loss of three important physicists. Mulligan looks at the contributions of Heinrich Hertz, August Kundt, and Hermann von Helmholtz and Planck's evaluation of them.

Planck, Max. *The New Science.* New York: Meridian, 1959. This book is valuable for its preface by Albert Einstein and its splendid introduction by James Franck. This compact volume contains three of Planck's most important general works: *Where Is Science Going?, The Universe in the Light of Modern Physics*, and *The Philosophy of Physics.* A reasonable starting point for intelligent readers with minimal background in physics.

Rosenfeld, Leon, et al., eds. *Max Planck Festschrift.* Berlin: Veb Deutscher Verlag der Wissenschaften, 1958. Eleven of this memorial volume's thirty-one essays are in English, including important contributions by Linus Pauling, Herbert Fröhlich, and Hannes Alfvén, each contribution being directly pertinent to understanding Planck's scientific impact.

Sweet, Geoffrey. "'Historismus' and Experimental Philosophy." *Modern Language Review* 90, no. 4 (October, 1995). Discusses approaches to continuity in historiography and philosophy, including the writings of Planck and Friedrich Meinecke.

*R. Baird Shuman*

## SYLVIA PLATH

*Born:* October 27, 1932; Boston, Massachusetts
*Died:* February 11, 1963; London, England
*Area of Achievement:* Literature
*Contribution:* As both poet and novelist, Plath adopted a self-analytical style that helped to inspire the "confessional" school of literature in the decade following her death.

### Early Life

When Sylvia Plath was eight years old, her father died after a long illness. This early loss of a loved one affected Plath's poetry in a way that would be unparalleled by any other event in her life. Otto Emil Plath had been fifteen years old when he came to the United States from Grabow, a town near the Polish-German border. When Sylvia was an infant, he taught biology at Boston University and came to be nationally recognized as an authority on bees. After her father's death in 1940, Sylvia moved with her mother, the former Aurelia Shrober, and her younger brother, Warren (born April 27, 1935), to the Boston suburb of Wellesley, Massachusetts. There Sylvia's mother found work as a teacher, her grandmother took care of their home, and her grandfather helped to support the family by working as a maître d'hôtel at the Brookline Country Club.

At about the time of her father's death, Plath began writing poetry and short fiction. Her works won several newspaper contests and, in August of 1950, she sold her first story ("And Summer Will Not Come Again") to *Seventeen* magazine. A year later, another short story ("Sunday at the Mintons") won a fiction contest sponsored by *Mademoiselle* magazine.

In September of 1950, Plath began attending Smith College on a fellowship endowed by Olive Higgins Prouty, the author of *Stella Dallas* (1922). In 1952, Plath was one of two fiction authors to win a contest sponsored by *Mademoiselle* magazine. She spent the next summer as the student editor of *Mademoiselle*'s annual college issue. *Harper's* magazine also began to display an interest in Plath's work, paying $100 for three of her poems.

Despite this appearance of initial success, however, Plath fell into a deep depression. Hiding herself in an isolated part of the cellar, Plath took an overdose of sleeping pills. She was rescued in time and began to receive psychiatric treatment, including electroshock therapy.

Plath's initial suicide attempt and the incidents surrounding it were to become the basis for her autobiographical novel *The Bell Jar* (1963). Some of Plath's medical expenses following her attempted suicide were paid by Olive Higgins Prouty. Prouty had taken an interest in Plath as one of the recipients of the scholarship that she had endowed at Smith College. The older novelist's generosity toward Plath was to be repaid uncharitably when Plath caricatured Prouty as the novelist Philomena Guinea in *The Bell Jar.*

### Life's Work

Appearing to be cured, Sylvia Plath returned to Smith College and was graduated summa cum laude with a Bachelor of Arts degree in 1955. The following year, she received a Fulbright Fellowship enabling her to go to England, where she attended Newnham College of Cambridge University. There Plath met the poet Ted Hughes; after a brief romance, they married in London on June 16, 1956. To Plath, Hughes—who was self-assured, decisive, and authoritarian—seemed to possess the qualities that she had both admired and feared in her father. In her later poetry, she described her initial attraction to Hughes as an attempt to bring her dead father back into her life.

In 1957, Plath received her master's degree from Cambridge and, with Hughes, returned to the United States. Later that same year, she took a teaching position at Smith College, her alma mater. Soon, however, Plath began to find that teaching did not satisfy her creative desires, and she decided to devote her full attention to writing. She attempted to find a publisher for the book of poems that would eventually become *The Colossus and Other Poems* and was disappointed to have it rejected a number of times. She continued to revise these poems and, in December of 1959, returned to England with Hughes. The following April, their daughter, Frieda Rebecca, was born.

In 1960, *The Colossus and Other Poems* was finally published by William Heinemann. With one major work already accepted for publication and with ideas for several others, Plath, in May of 1961, applied for a Eugene F. Saxton Fellowship with the intention of writing a novel. On November 6, 1961, Plath received a grant of $2,080 that would enable her to work on *The Bell Jar.* The year 1962 was a period of incredible activity for

Plath. On January 17, she gave birth to her son, Nicholas Farrar, and less than a month later reported to the Saxton committee that the first eight chapters of her novel were in their final form. Despite a number of illnesses, Plath continued to work on *The Bell Jar* steadily throughout the year. She also accepted several assignments for the British Broadcasting Corporation and, in June, began to write the poems that would be published after her death as *Ariel*.

On August 1, 1962, Plath reported to the Saxton committee that she had begun the final stages of *The Bell Jar*. Suddenly, however, after a vacation in Ireland, Plath's world of hard work and domestic harmony began to unravel. In autumn, after learning that Hughes had been having an affair with the Canadian poet Assia Wevill, Plath separated from her husband. She moved to London, submitted the final draft of *The Bell Jar* for publication, and found an apartment in a house that had once belonged to the Irish poet William Butler Yeats.

The final months of Plath's life were marked by a prodigious amount of literary activity. Working each morning from four o'clock until seven (when her children awoke), Plath began writing far more spontaneously than she had ever done before. Abandoning the ornate and polished style of *The Colossus*, Plath produced several poems a day, in a remarkable burst of creativity that she began to refer to as the "blood jet." The works of this final period of her life are marked by natural, unpolished rhythms and are often attempts to work out her deep-seated feelings of loss, frustration, and anger.

In January of 1963, *The Bell Jar* was published, not under Plath's own name but under the pseudonym of "Victoria Lucas." Plath considered *The Bell Jar* to be a mere "potboiler . . . not serious work" and wanted her real name to be associated only with her poetry. In addition, Plath hoped to spare the feelings of friends and members of her family who appear in the novel thinly disguised as fictional characters.

The narrator of *The Bell Jar*, Esther Greenwood, is based upon Plath herself, and many incidents in the novel were drawn from the poet's own life. Esther loses her father at an early age, wins a number of writing contests, and undergoes psychiatric treatment for suicidal tendencies. Initial reviews of *The Bell Jar* were generally positive, but Plath's attention seemed drawn only to the criticism that the book received. Although appearing to be under

great pressure, Plath gave her friends no indication of the severity of her depression. On February 11, 1963, she entered the kitchen of her apartment, placed towels around the doors to protect her children, and then committed suicide by turning on the gas.

Ever since her first suicide attempt at the age of twenty, death had been a frequent theme in Plath's writings. She occasionally referred to suicide as an act of purification and viewed death as merely another form of birth. In the late poem "Daddy" (written 1963; first published 1965), she describes her first attempt at suicide as a desire to return to the father who had been taken away from her in her youth. The imagery of rebirth and emergence from the womb also appears in *The Bell Jar*, where Plath describes the efforts to revive her after she has taken an overdose of sleeping pills.

A consistently high level of symbolism is found throughout all Plath's works. In *The Bell Jar*, for example, the electrocution of convicted spies Julius and Ethel Rosenberg in the summer of 1953 serves the young protagonist as an image for her own electroshock treatments. In many of her poems (such as the title work in *Ariel*), the symbols of speed—figures rushing headlong toward an undefined, distant object—appear. Some critics have interpreted these symbols as Plath's own movement toward her inevitable suicide. Suicide itself appears as a frequent theme in much of Plath's poetry, as in "The Manor Garden" and "Suicide Off Egg Rock," both of which were first published in *The Colossus*. In her late poetry, Plath began to deal with the pain resulting from her father's death, occasionally depicting her father as a Nazi and herself as a Jew. In each of these cases, the symbolism transforms events occurring in Plath's own life into something more universal, a general image in which readers can find their own meaning.

### Summary

The period of Sylvia Plath's greatest impact came only after her death. In retrospect, even her earliest poems were seen as providing insight into her troubled personality and the reasons for her eventual suicide. The autobiographical nature of *The Bell Jar* and the introspective glimpses provided by many of her later poems, which were published after her death in *Ariel* (1965) and *Crossing the Water* (1972), gave a new impetus to the "confessional" style of poetry. Leading figures of this literary movement included Robert Lowell, who wrote the introduction to *Ariel*, and May Sarton, the author of *A Private Mythology* (1966).

Plath's writing has also been important in feminist circles. Though Plath herself displayed little interest in feminist causes, her struggles to find a role for herself, reflected through the eyes of Esther Greenwood in *The Bell Jar*, made her works influential to feminists throughout the early 1970's. Furthermore, Plath's negative treatment of male figures in much of her later poetry has caused the poet to be adopted by feminists as a tragic symbol of male oppression.

### Bibliography

Broe, Mary Lynn. *Protean Poetic: The Poetry of Sylvia Plath*. Columbia: University of Missouri Press, 1980. Broe traces the development of Plath's literary style and concludes that there is a consistent use of imagery and of "female personae" throughout her works. Contrary to the generally accepted view, Broe argues that even the late poems do not indicate that Plath's suicide was inevitable.

Bundtzen, Lynda K. *Plath's Incarnations: Woman and the Creative Process*. Ann Arbor: University of Michigan Press, 1983. Offering a feminist perspective of Plath's poetry, this analysis explores the ways in which her works were written from a distinctly female perspective. It also includes a feminist interpretation of the symbols in Plath's poetry.

Bundtzen, Lynda K. "Poetic Arson and Sylvia Plath's 'Burning the Letters.'" *Contemporary Literature* 39, no. 3 (Fall 1998). The author focuses on the controversial relationship between Ted Hughes and Plath, arguing that Plath's poem "Burning the Letters" is a symbolic attack on Hughes' aesthetics.

Hall, Caroline King Barnard. *Sylvia Plath*. Boston: Twayne, 1978. Taking a traditional biographical and literary approach, this work places Plath's poetry firmly in the context of the "confessional" school of literature.

Holbrook, David. *Sylvia Plath: Poetry and Existence*. London: Athlone Press, and Atlantic Highlands, N.J.: Humanities Press, 1976. This work adopts a psychoanalytical approach to provide a biographical profile of Plath as well as a literary analysis of her novel and poetry. Holbrook is especially interesting in his discussion of how the layer of fiction separating Plath from Esther Greenwood in *The Bell Jar* ultimately breaks down.

Kroll, Judith. *Chapters in a Mythology: The Poetry of Sylvia Plath*. New York: Harper, 1976. Kroll argues that the autobiographical elements of Plath's poetry are always viewed impersonally and are given a larger, symbolic dimension.

Newman, Charles Hamilton, ed. *The Art of Sylvia Plath: A Symposium*. London: Faber, and Bloomington: Indiana University Press, 1970. This collection of biographical and literary essays provides an analysis of all the major aspects of Plath's life and poetry. It also includes a useful bibliography and an appendix of Plath's unpublished works.

Rose, Jacqueline. *The Haunting of Sylvia Plath*. London: Virago, 1991; Cambridge, Mass.: Harvard University Press, 1993. Rose's analysis focuses on the sexuality, fantasy, and ambiguity in Plath's work.

Wagner-Martin, Linda. *"The Bell Jar": A Novel of the Fifties*. New York: Twayne, 1992. Providing a thorough literary analysis of *The Bell Jar*, this work examines the novel's imagery and literary form, and interprets it in its historical context.

———, ed. *Sylvia Plath: The Critical Heritage*. London and New York: Routledge, 1988. This excellent collection of essays includes biographical portraits by individuals who knew Plath and literary analyses by several important critics.

*Jeffrey L. Buller*

## GARY PLAYER

*Born:* November 1, 1935; Johannesburg, South Africa

*Area of Achievement:* Sports

*Contribution:* Player is one of only four men to achieve golf's Grand Slam, and at twenty-nine the youngest player to do so. He won numerous championships worldwide and helped to promote golf as an athletic sport.

### Early Life

Gary Jim Player was the youngest of three children born to Francis Harry Audley Player and Muriel Marie Ferguson in Johannesburg, South Africa. His father was a foreman in a gold mine for more than thirty years. The Player family was not destitute, but the financial resources were never abundant during Player's childhood. When Player was eight years old, his mother died of cancer. This tragedy proved to be an almost devastating blow to the young Player. Player, however, surmounted the loss. Thus, Player began a lifelong struggle to conquer whatever challenge or challenger loomed in his path. This determination to succeed was fueled by his elder brother, Ian, who encouraged him to excel despite his diminutive stature. Spurred by his determination to triumph over those bigger than himself, which was just about everyone, Player launched himself into athletic competition. Goaded by his brother's fraternal intolerance, Player was ultimately voted all-round athlete at King Edward School in Johannesburg.

Since his father was a two-handicap golfer, it was perhaps inevitable that Player would seek parental approval by taking up the game. In his first round, the unskilled, self-taught player of fifteen shot par on the first three holes. This achievement caught the eye of the club professional, Jock Verwey. Simultaneously, Verwey's daughter, Virginia, came to Player's attention. Virginia Verwey quickly provided Player with a powerful stimulus to pursue the sport.

Verwey put Player to work as an assistant, while providing lessons to the intense young man courting his daughter. Player began to compete at the amateur level, and, even though he had not won a tournament, he was convinced that competition golf was his goal in life. Determined to turn professional, even though he was only seventeen, Player left school. He practiced constantly and followed a carefully constructed plan of physical exercise and diet to compensate for his relative lack of size and strength.

### Life's Work

When he was nineteen, Player won the East Rand Open. This victory served to persuade his father to finance his first foray outside South Africa. He entered the Egyptian Match Play Championship that same year (1955). Player won again and used his prize money to fuel an assault on the British golf tour. Player spent five months on the British tour and posted not a single victory. Still, he did garner enough in prize money to cover his expenses—a considerable achievement.

The next year, 1956, Player won the Ampol Tournament (Australia) and promptly married Virginia. He thereupon began the practice of a lifetime by leaving his young bride to return to the professional circuit. This time, Player made his mark with a win at the British Dunlop Tournament, which he followed with the first of his many victories in the South African Open.

From 1957 to 1959, Player competed around the world from Great Britain to the United States and on to Australia and South Africa. If Player did well in Australia and South Africa, his performance in the United States and Great Britain was rather lackluster. He did win the Kentucky Derby Open (1957) and made a surprisingly good showing in the 1958 U.S. Open. Still, he was only barely making his expenses on the American tour. Yet, if Player was absent from the winner's circle on the Anglo-American tour, he constantly improved the quality of his game. Moreover, his victories elsewhere, when combined with a frugal life-style, an unexpected benefit of his concern with his diet and physical well-being, enabled him to support his growing family and continue to pursue a professional career in golf.

Then came the breakthrough victory in the British Open in 1959. Player became the youngest golfer to capture that Grand Slam event since 1868. In 1961, Player determined to make a concentrated effort on the prize-laden American tour. He entered all twelve tournaments sponsored by the Professional Golfers' Association of America (PGA) between January and April. He finished in the top five in seven of the tournaments and won two—the San Francisco Open and the Sunshine Open. Player then joined the gathering of men in Augusta, Georgia, for the 1961 Masters Tournament.

Player arrived in Georgia fresh from a one-stroke victory over the defending Masters champion, the redoubtable Arnold Palmer. Needless to say, Palmer was expected to retain his title—most especially against a relatively unknown golfer from South Africa. In one of the most dramatic finishes in the history of the competition, however, Player edged Palmer yet again, by one stroke. Player did not win another tournament on the American tour that year, though he did take first prize in tournaments in Japan and Australia. On the other hand, while Player was not victorious in the United States, he was in the money on several occasions. In consequence, he ended the year as the leading money winner on the American tour—a first for an overseas-based player.

The euphoria engendered by his triumph in the American Masters Tournament soon, however, turned to despair. Player was suddenly in the midst of a slump so profound that he went fifteen months without a single win. He became so depressed by his failure that he seriously contemplated leaving the tour and returning home for good. Before he could implement his retirement plans, Player captured the PGA Championship (1962). Player now had three of the four events necessary to achieve the Grand Slam of golf to his credit and every reason to continue with the tour. Player was undoubtedly a force to reckon with on the international circuit during the 1960's. On the American circuit, he shared the honors with Jack Nicklaus and Arnold Palmer, particularly the former, as the essential component of the "Big Three" of the modern era. Furthermore, while Player won far more tournaments away from the American tour than in the United States, he consistently placed in the top five when he did play there. In 1965, Player won the U.S. Open and completed the Grand Slam.

In the years following the completion of the Grand Slam, Player seemed to vanish from the American tour—not in the sense of failing to compete, but rather the absence of victories. Indeed, from 1966 to 1969, Player went without a first-place finish on the American tour. He did repeat his victory in the British Open (1968), however, and announced his pursuit of a second Grand Slam. Nevertheless, throughout this period Player continued to win outside the United States. Moreover, he continued to make money on the American tour by placing near the top in those tournaments he entered.

In 1972, a second victory in the PGA Championship put him on the road to a second, unprecedented, Grand Slam. Unfortunately, he underwent serious surgery in 1973, and for a time he wondered if he would ever recover his skill. If Player, and others, wondered if his career was finally over, the answer came in 1974. In that year, he took the U.S. and British Open championships. A second U.S. Open continued to elude him, however, and Player capped his active career on the American tour with a victory at the American Masters Tournament. At forty-two, Player was the oldest player to accomplish that feat.

In 1985, Player joined the Senior Tour sanctioned by the PGA. Once again he became a fixture in the winner's circle with his triumph in the PGA Senior Championship. In 1988, Gary Player was voted "player of the year" by his competitors on the senior circuit.

Player was always a subject of controversy. He definitely upset the staid world of British golf with his many questions and his requests for free lessons from his fellow professionals when he joined the tour in 1956. In fact, one British professional informed Player that inasmuch as he was so poorly prepared, perhaps he should abandon the game altogether. Player, however, if he was nothing else, was tenacious. Player persevered and survived to confound his critics. He ended most tournaments with a lengthy practice session to correct defects and deficiencies he had observed in the course of tournament play. Informed by seemingly knowledgeable observers that he lacked the physical stamina or the size to prosper on the professional circuit, he intensified his already rigorous physical regime. Moreover, he supplemented his campaign for physical fitness with an attention to his diet that was quite exceptional at the time. Actually, it must be said that Player pioneered the concept of the golfer as an athlete. He ignored the doomsayers and the faint-hearted to pursue his dream of being a "world" golfer.

Player's decision did not come without problems. For one thing, continued residency in South Africa meant long periods of inactivity while in transit to almost any tournament. Moreover, travel across multiple time zones exacted a physical toll from Player. A further complication was the effect of international competition on his family. His wife was required to function as a single parent for all practical purposes. Finally, although it was not a problem initially, there was the question of international perceptions of his country. The mere fact that he was a South African citizen subjected Player, over the years, to criticism as the visible representative of a governmental policy (apartheid) that an increasing number of people found objectionable. He was physically abused during the 1969 PGA Championship and was forced to deal with protesters during the 1979 French Open.

### Summary

There were more than a few who insisted in 1961 that Gary Player's surprising victory in that year's Masters Tournament was a fluke. Surely, it was asserted, this largely self-taught golfer with a questionable grip and a swing that no one cared to copy was nothing more than a flash in the pan. Yet, in the final analysis, no one can gainsay the fact that in his active career on the international tour Player compiled an impressive record. He won nine major tournament titles as well as the Grand Slam of golf. He not only won more than 120 tournaments worldwide, including twenty-one PGA tour events, but also was the first overseas-based player to head the American money list.

Player began his career determined to be a world golfer, the best there was, and in that he posted a remarkable success. Yet, in typical fashion, Gary Player was not content to rest on his laurels. Once he became eligible to participate in the PGA Senior Tour he returned to vigorous competition with all the enthusiasm he had demonstrated on what he fondly called the "junior" tour. Indeed, the continued expansion of the Senior Tour was largely the result of Player's activities.

Player triumphed over adversity by turning seemingly insurmountable deficiencies into apparent assets. He continued, despite his years and accomplishments, to play the game he truly loved. It is doubtful that his donation of his entire purse from the 1965 U.S. Open (twenty thousand dollars to the American junior golf program and five thousand dollars to cancer research) was simply a public relations gesture. Player most definitely adhered to the principle that from those to whom much is given, much is expected.

### Bibliography

Callahan, Tom. "Memories for Cushions." *Golf Digest* 49, no. 12 (December, 1998). Profile of Player, including his relationship with Jack Nicklaus and Arnold Palmer and his career achievements.

"Gary Player Swinging Hard On Life's Course." *Psychology Today* 32, no. 2 (March, 1999). Discussion of Player's training and practice regimes.

Hobbs, Michael. "Gary Player." In *Fifty Masters of Golf.* Ashbourne, Derbyshire: Moorland, 1983. This work offers a technical assessment of Player as a golfer. The centerpiece of the article is an analysis of Player's performance in a 1965 match with Tony Lema.

McCormack, Mark H. *The Wonderful World of Professional Golf.* New York: Atheneum, 1973. A general book about professional golf, this work contains many references to Player and discussion of all the major tournaments up to the time of its publication. Includes a good appendix.

McDermott, Barry. "No Such Word as Can't." *Sports Illustrated* 48 (May 1, 1978): 16-19. A portrait of Player after he had won three tournaments in a row. Describes his family life and exercise and diet regimen.

McDonnell, Michael. "Gary Player." In *Golf: The Great Ones.* London: Pelham Books, 1971; New York: Drake, 1973. This piece, by the golf correspondent for the London *Daily Mail*, attempts to determine exactly what makes Player tick.

———. "The Man in Black." *Golf Magazine* (November, 1985): 58-59, 94-96. This is a retrospective on Player's career at the moment he was eligible to join the Senior Tour. Once again, the author addresses himself to the why and less to the what.

Moritz, Charles, ed. *Current Biography Yearbook, 1961*. New York: Wilson, 1962. A fairly in-depth look at Player's life up to 1961.

Player, Gary, with Floyd Thatcher. *Gary Player, World Golfer.* Waco, Tex.: Word Books, 1974; London: Pelham, 1975. An as-told-to autobiography composed with the help of Thatcher. This work is written in a conversational tone and does not diverge from the portrait that has appeared in countless magazines and interviews.

*J. K. Sweeney*

# RAYMOND POINCARÉ

*Born:* August 20, 1860; Bar-le-Duc, France

*Died:* October 15, 1934; Paris, France

*Areas of Achievement:* Government and politics

*Contribution:* Poincaré was perhaps the most important political figure of the French Third Republic (1871-1940). He had the distinction of moving from the premiership to the presidency before World War I and back to the premiership twice in the 1920's. He and Georges Clemenceau struggled to defend France against Germany during World War I and by the Treaty of Versailles, and Poincaré attempted to enforce or at least salvage part of the treaty during the postwar decade.

## Early Life

Raymond Poincaré was born during the summer of 1860 in Lorraine in northeastern France, exactly a decade before the outbreak of the Franco-Prussian War. Nevertheless, his was a secure and comfortable childhood in the bosom of a prosperous bourgeois family. He was a highly competitive and talented student, who started keeping a journal when he, his mother, and his brother fled Bar-le-Duc as the German troops advanced into their province. The brilliant lad would be haunted by the memory of the German occupation for the rest of his life. The evacuation of his province in 1874, after the French had paid a war indemnity of one billion dollars, was also etched in his mind. The young man, a cousin of the distinguished mathematician Henri Poincaré, was educated in Bar-le-Duc and Paris, where he studied law and was admitted to the bar.

Poincaré was introduced to politics in 1886 when he was appointed chief assistant to the minister of agriculture. That same year he was elected to the general council of the Meuse department and the following year to the Chamber of Deputies. During these turbulent years of the Boulanger crisis and the forced retirement of Jules Grévy from the French presidency, he seldom addressed the Chamber. In 1893, he was offered the Ministry of Finance in a "Progressist," or Moderate, government; however, he chose that of public instruction. The government resigned after a few months, but he became minister of finance the following year, when he was only thirty-four. He displayed typical nineteenth century bourgeois liberalism as he favored governmental economy and opposed an income tax. He returned to the education ministry for several months in 1895 and attempted unsuccessfully a reorganization of the French university system. He was highly acclaimed for his many polished and erudite speeches, which he wrote rapidly and delivered from memory. At the funeral of Louis Pasteur in October, 1895, he gave the only eulogy before an immense crowd in front of Notre Dame Cathedral. The premier, the press, and the public acclaimed his oration, but three days later the cabinet fell. Nevertheless, Poincaré's second tenure at the education ministry greatly increased his prestige.

## Life's Work

Disenchantment with politics and financial need prompted Poincaré to develop his legal practice and reject cabinet positions from 1896 to 1906. The Dreyfus affair was raging during these years, and he reluctantly but dramatically broke with the "Progressists" in November, 1898, and cautiously supported the Radicals when he realized that Cap-

tain Alfred Dreyfus had been unjustly convicted. Early the next year, he and several friends founded the Democratic Alliance, a loose grouping of "liberals" who advocated patriotism, religious and educational freedom, and opposition to socialism. His dissatisfaction with the extreme anticlerical legislation and socialist ties of the Radical cabinets from 1899 to 1905 led him often to abstain from important votes in the Chamber of Deputies. Therefore he was happy to accept election to the senate in 1903. The following year he married the divorcée Henriette Benucci in a civil ceremony, much to his pious mother's displeasure. Benucci's divorce and Poincaré's anticlerical politics prevented a sacramental wedding even if the couple had desired it.

The Agadir crisis with Germany during 1911 undermined the government of Joseph Caillaux and helped provoke a passionate upsurge of French patriotism in many quarters. This carried Poincaré to the premiership in January, 1912. As both foreign minister and premier, he vigorously sought to restrain Russia in the Balkans but also to strengthen the alliance with Russia and the entente with Great Britain. During late 1912, Poincaré began to consider running for the presidency and was elected by the National Assembly to this largely symbolic office.

Poincaré's major domestic goal in 1913 was to increase universal military service from two years to three. The Germans had twice in two years enlarged their standing army until it was virtually double the size of the French. In midsummer, the "three years law" was passed over the opposition of most Radicals and all the Socialists. An income tax and the "three years law" were the chief issues in the 1914 spring elections for the Chamber of Deputies. These were won by the leftists, but the European war prevented a return to two-year military service.

Poincaré was certainly not responsible for the outbreak of World War I, despite some postwar accusations. Poincaré successfully increased presidential power, his major reason for seeking the office, during 1913 and the first three years of war. He played a very active role in military and foreign affairs and was not an impotent "prisoner in the Élysée" palace, as he often complained. He, of course, selected the premiers but also influenced ministerial choices and policy decisions as he presided over the Council of Ministers. Yet the great popularity that he had enjoyed in 1912 and 1913 evaporated, and he was often criticized for his leadership and even ridiculed for his "chauffeur's uniform," which he adopted to visit the troops.

In his memoirs, Poincaré called 1917 the *année trouble* (the confused year), but it was also a troubled year for France, with widespread French mutinies and three ineffectual cabinets. During November, Poincaré was confronted with an unpalatable choice for premier, either the defeatist Joseph Caillaux and a possible compromise peace or the domineering Georges Clemenceau and bloody war until victory. Clemenceau in his newspaper had constantly criticized the government and especially Poincaré. The president, however, inevitably chose the "tiger," who would become a great popular hero as "Father Victory," whereas Poincaré would be somewhat forgotten. Poincaré had very little influence on the peace conference, since Clemenceau, David Lloyd George, and Woodrow Wilson made the decisions. The president thought the final treaty was a poor one and that Clemenceau had won the war but lost the peace.

Centrist cabinets, attempting to lead a rightist Chamber of Deputies after the December, 1919, elections, were confronted with a Germany determined to avoid reparations and a Great Britain concerned about alleged French hegemony in Europe. Several ephemeral ministries were finally replaced in February, 1922, by a Poincaré government that survived for twenty-six months. He was once again widely popular, for it was believed that he would enforce the Treaty of Versailles. Poincaré is probably best known outside France as the "man of the Ruhr," the Frenchman who occupied the Ruhr Valley and tried to obtain reparations by coercion. There is general agreement that he did this as a last resort. In 1922, French per capita taxes were almost twice those in Germany, and French per capita governmental debt was greater than that across the Rhine River. Poincaré's goals in the Ruhr have been questioned, but undoubtedly he wanted German payments so that the French budget, overburdened by reconstruction costs, could be balanced.

The occupation began in January, 1923, after the Reparation Commission found Germany in default; therefore, Poincaré had sound legal if not wise diplomatic grounds for action. Poincaré's Ruhr policy fractured the entente with the British and triggered vitriolic attacks upon him by Parisian intellectuals and French Communists. Nevertheless, he was generally popular and had a large majority in the Chamber of Deputies. German surrender, Anglo-American hostility, and French fiscal problems led Poincaré to accept an international investigation and eventually the Dawes Plan. Most French conservatives thought he had won the Ruhr "war" but lost the peace. Moreover, Poincaré insisted upon a 20 percent tax rise in March, 1924. The increase was not to pay for the Ruhr occupation, which was profitable, but to cover the budget deficit and reverse the critical decline of the franc.

Not surprisingly, the Cartel des Gauches (cartel of leftists) of Socialists and Radicals won a majority in the 1924 spring elections as Frenchmen voted against Poincaré's higher taxes. The leftist government of Édouard Herriot was divided on financial policy and soon confronted a dangerous flight of capital abroad. The franc, stable since 1924, began to fall precipitously. In April, 1925, Poincaré vigorously attacked Herriot in the senate and provoked his resignation. A series of Cartel ministries failed to stanch the fiscal hemorrhage as the franc fell to fifty to the dollar in July, 1926.

Poincaré, the "man of the Ruhr," now became the "savior of the franc." He was sixty-six years of age but still had an impeccable memory and prodigious energy for work. He formed a government containing Herriot and four other former premiers, representing all parties except the extremes of Left and Right. Following the recommendations of a committee of experts, excise taxes were raised, expenses were reduced, and a budgetary deficit became a surplus. Higher interest rates coaxed fugitive French capital to return, and within several months the franc had risen to twenty-five to the dollar. The premier wisely stabilized it officially in 1928 at that rate. Stabilization was achieved smoothly after Poincaré's supporters in the chamber were successful in the spring elections. The committee of experts had also urged ratification of treaties regularizing the repayment of French war debts to Great Britain and the United States. Poincaré sought ratification by the National Assembly for several weeks in the summer of 1929, but he became seriously ill in July and was forced to resign permanently from the cabinet and active political life.

### Summary

Raymond Poincaré has been described as a petit bourgeois, a grand bourgeois, or even a bourgeois king who fought valiantly for his nation. Certainly he exemplified many characteristics of the French bourgeoisie with his probity, diligence, intelligence, dignity, and ardent republican patriotism. He was considered to be a genie who saved France in time of crisis. On the eve of World War I, he incarnated and led the national revival, and in 1923 he attempted to ensure reparations. He was the savior of the franc in 1926, but, more important, he rescued a floundering parliamentary republic.

His career may appear to have been a failure. France was victorious by 1918 but proportionately suffered the heaviest manpower losses. The Ruhr was occupied, but reparation payments were never very productive and ceased by 1932. Then the liberal Third Republic collapsed in 1940 from the onslaught of Adolf Hitler, the very antithesis of Poincaré. Nevertheless, all nations can profit from Poincaré's method of approaching problems with studious, precise analysis and solving them by the honest, equitable administration he practiced throughout his life.

### Bibliography

Carley, Michael Jabara. "The Shoe on the Other Foot: A Letter from Raymond Poincaré to Alexandre Millerand, December, 1922." *Canadian Journal of History* 26, no. 3 (December, 1991). This article presents a letter written by Poincaré to then French Prime Minister Alex Miller concerning presidential power, neutrality, and foreign and domestic matters.

Gooch, George P. *Before the War: Studies in Diplomacy.* London and New York: Longman, 1936. This book contains a lengthy sixty-three-page essay on Poincaré's conduct of foreign policy as premier and foreign minister during 1912. Gooch admires Poincaré's ability and integrity and says that he did not desire or work for war but sought to maintain the balance of power by closer cooperation with Russia and Great Britain.

Huddleston, Sisley. *Poincaré: A Biographical Portrait.* London: Unwin, and Boston: Little Brown, 1924. This book by a correspondent of *The Times* of London is not a biography of Poincaré. It is a journalistic account that stresses his honesty, patriotism, incredible memory, and legalistic attitude. It was written during the Ruhr occupation but has limited value.

Keiger, John F. V. *Raymond Poincaré.* Cambridge and New York: Cambridge University Press, 1997. This is the first new Poincaré biography in 35 years. Keiger has researched new archival materials on various facets of World War I and provides a clearer vision of an enigmatic personality.

McDougall, Walter A. *France's Rhineland and Diplomacy, 1914-1924*. Princeton, N.J.: Princeton University Press, 1978. This excellent study describes the failure of the French, in their view, to secure a satisfactory peace and then the failure of their allies to help enforce the treaty. Most of the book is devoted to Poincaré's Rhenish policy and occupation of the Ruhr. The author argues that, as a result of British opposition and German passive resistance, Poincaré sought to revise the treaty. There is an exhaustive bibliography.

Martin, Benjamin F. *Count Albert de Mun: Paladin of the Third Republic*. Chapel Hill: University of North Carolina Press, 1978. This valuable biography of an aristocratic Catholic leader describes his change from a royalist to a moderately conservative supporter of the republic. There is considerable information about Poincaré during the decade before World War I and an extensive bibliography.

Poincaré, Raymond. *The Memoirs of Raymond Poincaré*. Translated by George Arthur. 4 vols. London: Heinemann, and New York: Doubleday, 1926-1931. Covers the years 1912 through 1918. Unfortunately, this English edition of the memoirs has been adapted and compressed, but it does include most of Poincaré's first seven volumes.

Schuker, Stephen A. *The End of French Predominance in Europe: The Financial Crisis of 1924 and the Adoption of the Dawes Plan*. Chapel Hill: University of North Carolina Press, 1976. This superbly researched book presents essential economic information about reparations, the occupation of the Ruhr, the French financial crisis of 1924, and the Dawes Plan. Schuker revises Poincaré's reputation upward and Herriot's downward. There is an extensive bibliography.

Weber, Eugen J. *The Nationalist Revival in France, 1905-1914*. Berkeley: University of California Press, 1959. Weber argues that patriotism became respectable and widespread after 1905 because of domestic and foreign factors. Concern about German aggressiveness resulted in widespread chauvinistic nationalism after November, 1911. Poincaré is often mentioned as a patriotic leader.

Wright, Gordon. *Raymond Poincaré and the French Presidency*. Stanford, Calif.: Stanford University Press, and London: Oxford University Press, 1942. Wright's book is not a biography even for the years 1913 to 1920; it is a detailed consideration of Poincaré's attempt to strengthen the presidency without constitutional amendment. Nevertheless, it is a well-documented account of his presidential activities and includes a helpful biography.

*Malcolm M. Wynn*

# JACKSON POLLOCK

*Born:* January 28, 1912; Cody, Wyoming
*Died:* August 11, 1956; East Hampton, Long Island, New York
*Area of Achievement:* Art
*Contribution:* A central figure in the New York School of Abstract Expressionists during the late 1940's and early 1950's, Pollock, through his "drip" painting, produced some of the most distinctive and unique work in the history of American art.

## Early Life

Paul Jackson Pollock was born January 28, 1912, on the Watkins Ranch at Cody, Wyoming. Both his mother, née Stella May McClure, and his father, LeRoy Pollock, were of Scotch-Irish ancestry and had been born and reared in Tingley, Iowa. The elder Pollock worked at various jobs during his lifetime (ranch hand, dishwasher, truck farmer, plasterer, and surveyor) but listed his occupation as "stone mason and cement work" on Jackson's birth certificate. By the time Jackson had reached ten years of age, his family (he had four older brothers) had moved six times and had lived in San Diego, Chico, Janesville, Orland, Riverside (all in California), and Phoenix, Arizona.

Pollock entered Manual Arts High School in Los Angeles in 1928 and came under the influence of an art teacher named Frederick John de St. Vrain Schwankovsky, who encouraged his growing interest in art and sparked his attachment to Eastern mysticism. Although he already knew by this time that he wanted to be "an artist of some kind," he had personal difficulties in high school (he was temporarily expelled in early 1929) and eventually left without being graduated in 1930. He then followed his older brothers, Charles and Frank, to New York City in the fall of 1930, where he joined the Art Students League and took classes from Thomas Hart Benton, John Sloan, and Robert Laurent. Benton was strongly impressed with Pollock's talent, especially his use of color; became his mentor; and continually urged the young man to pursue a career in art. Although they rarely saw each other after 1937, this close relationship between teacher and student would persist, via letters and the telephone, until Pollock's death in 1956.

During this early New York period, Pollock appeared to be the typical all-American young man: well built (although slightly thin), with a mop of auburn hair, rough-hewn good features, and a vague pugnacious air about him. Only later would the creeping effects of alcoholism and hard living be reflected in his appearance: Photographs from the 1940's and 1950's show a paunchy and balding man, his face increasingly lined and depressed. The seeds of these personal and physical problems had already been planted in the 1930's; Pollock was arrested in July, 1937, for public intoxication and disturbing the peace, and he entered treatment for alcoholism, once in 1937, again in 1938, and again in 1939.

The first public exhibition of Pollock's work came in February, 1935, when he showed a work entitled *Threshers* at the Eighth Exhibition of Watercolors, Pastels, and Drawings by American and French Artists, held at the Brooklyn Museum. He also joined the Federal Art Project of the Works Project Administration (WPA) in 1935, earning approximately ninety-five dollars per month in exchange for submitting one painting every eight weeks. He would remain with the Federal Arts Project until early 1943 and produced more than fifty paintings during this time. Only two of them are known to exist today.

In April, 1941, Pollock was classified IV-F and declared unfit for military service by his local draft board. He also met Lenore (Lee) Krasner that year at an exhibit at the McMillen gallery. He had been introduced to her briefly in 1935, but this time the relationship flowered. They became constant companions and finally married on October 25, 1945, at Marble Collegiate Church in New York City.

Pollock's career also began to flower during the early 1940's. He attracted the attention of Peggy Guggenheim, an art collector, patron, and owner of a newly established museum-gallery in New York called Art of this Century. After inviting him to submit a collage for a show in her gallery in 1943, she issued him a one-year contract which guaranteed him $150 a month plus a negotiated bonus if she sold more than twenty-seven hundred dollars' worth of his paintings during that year. She also gave him a one-man show at her gallery in November, 1943, and commissioned him to paint a mural for the entrance hall of her town house. Guggenheim's patronage allowed Pollock to give up the custodial job he had obtained after the end of the Federal Arts Project and devote himself full-time to painting. Pollock's reputation and creativity soared from this point onward.

### Life's Work

With the financial security provided by his connection with Peggy Guggenheim, Pollock entered the most creative period of his career. Show followed show as he exhibited his work at such prestigious galleries and museums as the New York Museum of Modern Art (1944-1945), the Cincinnati Art Museum (1944), the David Porter Gallery in Washington, District of Columbia (1945), The Arts Club of Chicago (1945), the San Francisco Museum of Art (1946), and the Whitney Museum of American Art in New York (1946). He sold his first painting to a museum during this period. In 1944, the Museum of Modern Art, acting on the advice of Alfred Barr, purchased Pollock's *The She-Wolf* for its permanent collection. He also received increasingly favorable notices in the art press, which praised his sense of color and surface, his fluent design, and his "exuberance, independence, and native sensibility."

Pollock's work underwent a clear creative evolution during this period. His work during the 1930's revealed the strong influence of Benton and David Alfaro Siqueiros, both advocates of the social realism school of art that attracted so many young painters during the difficult years of the Depression. Although often heavily stylized in their portrayal of reality, the social realists insisted that art carry a clear social or political message and thus serve a "useful" purpose. Paintings such as *Going West* (1934-1935) and *The Covered Wagon* (1934) demonstrate the impact of social realism on Pollock's early work. Yet as he entered the 1940's, Pollock became more and more interested in the work of such painters as Pablo Picasso, Joan Miró, Piet Mondrian, Henri Matisse, Wassily Kandinsky, and Hans Hofmann, and his work became increasingly abstract and, according to many critics, surrealistic. Yet his paintings from this period, such as *The She-Wolf, Guardians of the Secret* (1943), *The Troubled Queen* (1945), and *Red* (1946), show the gradual development of a style that, while reflecting the influence of other abstract painters, was also uniquely his own.

As Pollock evolved into a mature and unique artist, his personal life continued along its rather rocky course. In the fall of 1945, he and Lee left New York City and purchased (with a loan from Peggy Guggenehim) a farmhouse, barn, and five acres of land on Fireplace Road in East Hampton, Long Island. He would live and work there for the remainder of his life. Two years later, in 1946, Guggenheim closed her gallery and planned to return permanently to Europe. Before leaving, she arranged for the art dealer Betty Parsons to take over Pollock's contract and market his work. Pollock renewed this contract in 1949, but, when it expired in January, 1952, he signed an exclusive agreement with the Sidney Janis Gallery in New York City. He would remain with Janis until his death. Pollock also continued to suffer from alcoholism throughout these years and entered treatment with an East Hampton doctor in 1948, to arrest his chronic drinking. Thanks to this doctor's efforts, Pollock did manage to stay sober until 1950 but then reverted to his old behavior. From this point onward, he would visit a series of doctors and psychiatrists in an effort to cure his problem, but permanent success eluded him.

Beginning in 1946 or 1947, Pollock began experimenting with what would become his most important contribution to modern art, his "drip" or "action" painting. Action painting was a style pioneered by Hans Hofmann, who insisted that a finished painting is only the record of the intense personal feelings that an artist experienced while creating it. Moreover, the painting should also reflect the spontaneous, uncontrolled, and prerational actions that the artist made during the creative process. In this sense, the action of painting became more real and important than the painting itself. Pollock carried this idea to new extremes. He would roll out a large canvas on the floor of his East Hampton studio and drip and splatter paint on its surface as he worked in an energetic frenzy around its border. Pollock argued that the finished product was not accidental, that his actions were guided by internal psychic forces that were unleashed while he worked, and thus the painting represented a manifestation of his inner being on canvas. Examples of work produced during his drip period include *Lucifer* (1947), *Number 5* (1948), *Birds of Paradise* (1949), *Lavender Mist* (1950), *Autumn Rhythmn* (1950), and *Number 8* (1950), and all demonstrate a spontaneous freshness of statement and an exciting combination of dynamic composition and color. Many sophisticated art critics recognized the creative genius at work in these paintings and hailed Pollock as the most important American artist of the era. Critics for the popular press, however, generally dismissed him as

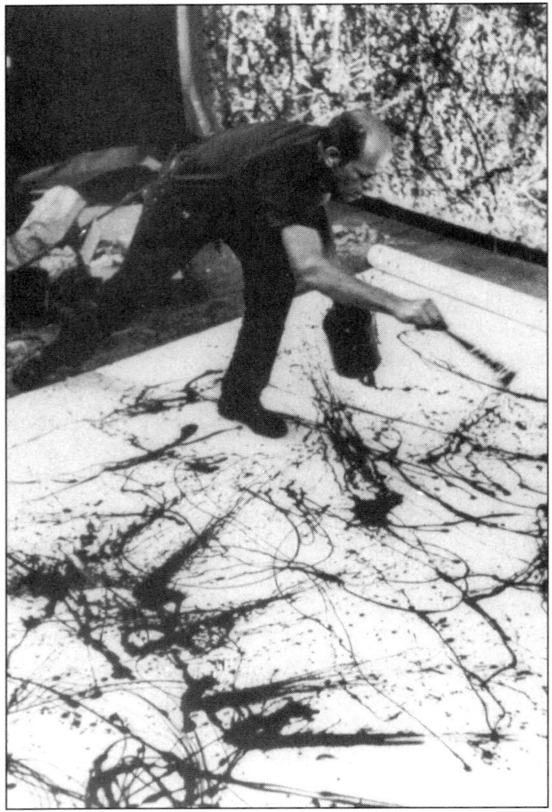

a fraud and claimed that any three-year-old child could produce a Pollock " dribble" painting. The general public tended to agree with this assessment, and Pollock's work became the target for numerous jokes, cartoons, and ridicule. As a result, he continued to have difficulty selling his paintings and had to rely on the generosity of his patrons and an occasional grant to make ends meet.

Beginning in 1953, Pollock began to explore other styles of painting, as represented by his *Easter and the Totem* (1953) and *Sleeping Effort* (1953), but he still frequently returned to his drip technique in such works as *White Light* (1954) and *Scent* (1955). Yet this later work was produced during the all-too-brief creative spurts that punctuated an otherwise protracted period of artistic inactivity. In 1954, for example, Pollock produced only a handful of paintings and, in 1955, he hardly painted anything at all because, as he told a friend, he wondered whether he could say anything with his art anymore. He even contemplated a trip to Europe to renew his creativity but never went beyond obtaining a passport. Although his standing among knowledgeable art critics continued to escalate, his well of inspiration had dried up because of the severity of his alcoholism. His personal behavior had also become increasingly belligerent, as demonstrated by the fights he often provoked at the various taverns he frequented.

The year 1956 initially seemed to hold out some promise for Pollock. In May of that year, the New York Museum of Modern Art notified him that it was planning a one-man show of his work to honor him at midcareer. His wife was sufficiently satisfied that he had his drinking under control that she left for a vacation in Europe in July. A month later, on August 11, Pollock, with two female friends, lost control of his car on Fireplace Road and crashed into a clump of trees. One of the passengers survived but Pollock and the other passenger were killed instantly. He was buried at Green River Cemetary in Springs, Long Island, on August 15, 1956.

### Summary

As with many artists before him, and undoubtedly many after, appreciation for what Jackson Pollock had accomplished during his short career grew after his death. By defying all traditional conventions and taking tremendous artistic and aesthetic risks, especially with his drip paintings, Pollock shattered old barriers and expanded the horizon of modern art into realms that few even dreamed existed. He also freed American art from its dependence on European innovation and at least temporarily pushed it to the forefront of the art world's avant-garde. In the process, he paved the way for the recognition of American artists within the international art community and helped create a market for their work. Many younger American artists, such as Robert Rauschenberg, Claes Oldenburg, Roy Lichtenstein, and Andy Warhol, benefited from his fearless desire to do what no one else had ever done, to push art beyond all previous limits, no matter what the cost.

That cost proved to be extraordinarily high. Public rejection and ridicule, alcoholism, eventual creative burnout, and a tragic death proved to be the price Pollock paid for his artistic courage. In many ways, he epitomized the rootless and innovative artists who were attracted to New York City at the end of World War II, young artists who celebrated absolute freedom and art as an intense personal commitment in their work but who ultimately fell victim to a society that neither understood nor appreciated them during their lifetimes. Jackson Pollock and his colleagues tried to stimulate the aesthetic imagination of the America of Disneyland, backyard barbecues, and television game shows. They lost in the short term, but their long-range influence would prove to be both liberating and exciting.

**Bibliography**

Doyon-Bernard, Suzette. "Jackson Pollock: A Twentieth-Century Chavin Chaman." *American Art* 11, no. 3 (Fall 1997). The author argues that Pollock's fascination with Chavin's artistic styles did not disappear from his work in the early 1940s, as is widely believed, but was merged with other influences.

Friedman, B. H. *Jackson Pollock: Energy Made Visible*. New York: McGraw-Hill, 1972; London: Weidenfeld and Nicolson, 1973. Highly opinionated account of Pollock's life and work by a friend who met the artist late in the latter's career. Despite a rather confusing and overly dramatic style, the author provides some interesting insight into Pollock's personal demons.

Hunter, Sam. *Jackson Pollock*. New York: Museum of Modern Art, 1956. Originally intended to be a catalog to accompany Pollock's one-man show at the Museum of Modern Art in 1956, this book was expanded after the artist's death to be a retrospective of his entire career.

Leja, Michael. *Reframing Abstract Expressionism: Subjectivity and Painting in the 1940s*. New Haven, Conn.: Yale University Press, 1993. The author argues that the approaches of Pollock and many of his abstract expressionist contemporaries mirrored those of the period's writers, filmmakers, and philosophers.

Motherwell, Robert, and Ad Reinhardt, eds. *Modern Artists in America: First Series*. New York: Wittenburg Schultz, 1951. Includes an excellent analysis of what Pollock was trying to say in his drip paintings. Motherwell always held Pollock in high regard.

O'Connor, Francis V. *Jackson Pollock*. New York: Museum of Modern Art, 1967. This book was published to supplement a major retrospective exhibit of Pollock's art in 1967. It includes a detailed chronology of Pollock's life and career, numerous excerpts from his correspondence, and black-and-white reproductions of most of his important work.

O'Hara, Frank. *Jackson Pollock*. New York: Braziller, 1959. An appreciation of Pollock's career by a noted poet who also worked as a staff member at the Museum of Modern Art. This book provides a concise and intelligent survey of Pollock's place in American art. An excellent starting point.

Potter, Jeffrey. *To a Violent Grave: An Oral Biography of Jackson Pollock*. New York: Putnam, 1985. These reminiscences, gathered from many sources by a friend of Pollock, document his problems with alcoholism, his troubled personal life, and his self-obsession. The book is valuable as a supplement to other studies, but it sheds little light on Pollock's art.

Robertson, Bryan. *Jackson Pollock*. London: Thames and Hudson, and New York: Abrams, 1960. A massive collection of black-and-white and color reproductions of Pollock's paintings and drawings. Little biographical information on Pollock is included in this volume.

Rubin, William S. "Jackson Pollock and the Modern Tradition." *Artforum* 5 (February-May, 1967): 14-22, 28-37, 18-31, 28-33. A highly esoteric examination of Pollock's art that attempts to clarify the influences upon which he drew and his impact on the development of modern art in the United States.

*Christopher E. Guthrie*

# GEORGES POMPIDOU

*Born:* July 5, 1911; Montboudif, France
*Died:* April 2, 1974; Paris, France
*Areas of Achievement:* Government and politics
*Contribution:* Of the eighteen years during which Gaullism was in power in France, Pompidou was premier from 1962 to 1968 and president from 1969 to 1974. Gaullism stabilized France, renewed its pride, and restored its stature in the world.

## Early Life

Born of peasant stock in the small village of Montboudif, Georges Pompidou spent much of his early life in nearby Albi, where his mother's family were linen cloth merchants. His father, Léon, and his mother, née Marie-Louise Chavagnac, were both schoolteachers. Molded by the parish church, the communal school, and his parents's wish that he succeed as an educator, Pompidou studied at Lycée d'Albi, Lycée de Toulouse, and Lycée Louis-le-Grand at Paris, emphasizing French literature, Greek, Latin, and history. Having performed brilliantly, he then went to the École Normale Supérieure in Paris. He received his *agrégé des lettres* in 1934, the *diplôme* of the Institute of Political Studies in 1934, and the *breveté* of the Centre des Hautes Études Administratives in 1947.

After obligatory military service, Pompidou was named professor of French, Latin, and Greek at Lycée Saint-Charles in Marseilles in 1935 and then married Claude Cahour, the daughter of a physician. In 1938, he was invited to teach at Lycée Henry IV in Paris. The Pompidous began a social pattern that continued when he was a banker. They frequented art galleries, bookstores, bistros, films, concerts, the theater, and played tennis, skied, and vacationed in Saint-Tropez. Pompidou had a reputation for indolence, but he had leisure time because he did his work quickly, effortlessly, and yet effectively.

In August, 1939, Pompidou was a second lieutenant with the 141st Infantry regiment from Marseilles, assigned first to the Italian frontier, then Alsace, Lorraine, and the Somme. Pompidou heard and was deeply moved by de Gaulle's radio appeal from London urging that Frenchmen outside France continue the war against the Germans, but he went back to Paris to the *lycée* to teach a class preparing students for colonial service. His son, Alain, was born in 1942.

## Life's Work

Pompidou was present at de Gaulle's liberation march down the Champs Élysées in 1944, and with the help of a friend was put in charge of school and university problems in de Gaulle's provisional government. From February, 1946, to 1949 he was assistant to the director of the Commission of Tourism for the national government. Although he had not studied law, from September, 1949, to 1954 he was one of a number of *maîtres des requêtes* preparing reports for the Conseil d'état, an administrative court. He became secretary-general in 1951 of his colleagues' association.

In January, 1946, the de Gaulle family put him in charge of their charitable foundation. After de Gaulle organized the Rassemblement du Peuple Français, Pompidou began assisting de Gaulle in various other ways. In 1953 Pompidou handled the negotiations for publication of the first volume of de Gaulle's war memoirs. Working on de Gaulle's finances in 1951, Pompidou met the director-general of the Rothschild Bank and in 1953 helped him become a senator. Leaving the Conseil d'état, in February, 1954, Pompidou became director of a railroad company and, in July, of an import-export company—both affiliates of the bank. In 1956, he became director-general of the bank, and, until 1962, he also administered several of the bank's affiliated companies. Rothschild was especially interested in mining ventures in Africa. While still at the bank, Pompidou resumed giving lectures at the Institute des Sciences Politiques and helped de Gaulle put together his new government in May, 1958.

On leave from the bank, he served from June 1, 1958, to January 8, 1959, as de Gaulle's principal private secretary. While back again at the bank, he was appointed as a member of the Conseil Constitutional. He also continued his writing. He was not a creator of literature, but he was an appreciator. Having specialized in Jean Racine's tragedies, he published *"Britannicus" de Jean Racine* (1944) and edited two books for use in secondary school instruction. While at the bank he edited *Anthologie de la poésie française* (1961), giving much space to Charles Baudelaire. His last book was *Le Nœud gordien* (1974), discussing values and events, with references, among others, to Niccolò Machiavelli, Blaise Pascal, and Paul Valéry. Some effort was made after his death to compile a record of political thought, though he was not prone to original thinking, nor was he given to theorizing. These included a two-volume compilation of his speeches, *Entretiens et discours, 1968-1974* (1975) and *Pour rétablir une vérité* (1982).

De Gaulle had chosen Pompidou as his confidential agent because he made quick decisions; was a good judge of men; was loyal, discreet, and diplomatic; and made himself indispensable by efficiently taking care of numerous details. In 1961, de Gaulle sent him to negotiate in Switzerland with the chiefs of the Algerian rebels. De Gaulle began using Pompidou as de facto premier in March, 1962, and formally made him premier on April 16, 1962. The new premier was assigned jurisdiction over financial and domestic policies and politics while de Gaulle personally directed the army, the department of justice, and colonial and foreign affairs.

Pompidou had not come up through the ranks of politics, but he proved to be skillful at directing election campaigns. He had not had experience in front of television cameras, but he became effective at using that medium. When he began to think of himself as successor to President de Gaulle, this did not please the president, who had valued him for his self-effacing services. By 1966, de Gaulle began to think of replacing Pompidou, especially as Pompidou's public popularity grew. The turbulence of student rebellions and a general strike in May, 1968, gave de Gaulle the occasion he needed. When Pompidou left the government on July 10, 1968, he had been premier longer than any Frenchman except François Guizot.

Pompidou remained remainer on the municipal council at Carjac (Lot) to which he had been elected in March, 1965, and remained a deputy to the National Assembly from Cantal. The other Gaullist deputies made him their honorary president. While Couve de Murville was premier, the Gaullist party organization and parliamentary group were dominated by Pompidou's men.

De Gaulle left office on April 28, 1969. Pompidou was elected president of France on June 15, 1969. His first premier was Jacques Chaban-Delmas, who launched a program for a "new society." Pompidou was more conservative than his premier and gave top priority to making French industries more internationally competitive. He wanted France to grow richer. In 1972, he replaced Chaban-Delmas with Pierre Messmer. While de Gaulle was still alive, until November 9, 1970, Pompidou could not be sure that de Gaulle would not intervene, and he had to satisfy the Gaullists who deplored any deviation

from the general's policies. Pompidou's first cabinet was full of the barons of Gaullism. He made a point of making speeches echoing de Gaulle's views about French nationalism and Europe as a combine of nations.

Most of the Gaullist objectives remained, but the language and methods were new. Astute, realistic, down to earth, prudent, calm, courteous, and patient, Pompidou was more pragmatic than doctrinaire. Unlike de Gaulle, he preferred to achieve cordial understandings through negotiations, and he was less likely to resort to de Gaulle's brand of political theater. By temperament he favored stability, tranquillity, and maintenance of the social order. He valued traditions and also believed in freedom, for which he thought the state was essential as a guarantor. Man is neither angel nor beast, he said, but a little of both.

He negotiated with the Soviet Union's Leonid Brezhnev, though he profoundly distrusted communism. He did not share de Gaulle's hostility toward the Anglo-Saxons, but he believed Spain and Portugal would be useful counterweights to the north in the European Common Market. He was criticized by the French Communist Party for supporting American Vietnam policies in 1972. He took an interest in Francophone Africa and thought Israel should trade land for peace. He leaned toward economic liberalism and believed that the solution to France's problems was economic growth, but he did not propose to denationalize state-owned industry. His government promoted new technology. His government also sought to modernize Paris, to make it a counterweight to London in the expanded Common Market. An underground shopping center was placed where Les Halles had been, new office towers rose at La Défense, and the striking Pompidou Center was built. In the midst of all the rebuilding, there was a scandal about real estate speculation. When he died on April 2, 1974, of cancer of the bone marrow, he left an unfinished term as president.

### Summary

Georges Pompidou's most notable achievement was as a sustainer of the Gaullist regime. Although he was a banker, he was not a banking technician. Although he worked in government commissions concerned with law, he was not a legal technician. Although he won elections, he was not a politician. His posts were gained through personal contacts. Although he socialized with fashionable and artistic people, he never lost the aspect of a peasant. Although his father was a Socialist, Pompidou was unwilling to complete de Gaulle's plan for greater worker participation in decision-making.

Pompidou was loyal to his friends, able to assess situations quickly and accurately, and able to resolve problems quietly and effectively. These qualities induced de Gaulle to turn to him for help from 1946 onward. De Gaulle believed that his premier was practical and prudent. As president, Pompidou demonstrated that his concerns in foreign affairs were closer to those of Europe and less global than de Gaulle's had been. He continued support for nuclear defense. One of the roles of a president is to symbolize France, and he did do that. Blessed with a keen intelligence, Pompidou loved poetry and understood people.

### Bibliography


Alexandre, Philippe. *The Duel: De Gaulle and Pompidou*. Translated by Elaine P. Halperin. Boston: Houghton Mifflin, 1972. This is the best available account in English of the subtleties of personal relationship between the two men. It is highly readable.

Bomberger, Merry. *Le Destin secret de Georges Pompidou*. Paris: Fayard, 1965. This book is very readable and gives a thorough account of his life up to the early stages of his roles as premier.

Cogan, C. G. "The Break-Up: General de Gaulle's Separation from Power." *Journal of Contemporary History* 27, no. 1 (January, 1992). This article considers the disappearance of Charles de Gaulle and includes information on his relationship with Pompidou.

Roberts, Frank C. *Obituaries from the Times, 1971-1975*. Reading: Newspaper Archive Developments, and Westport, Conn.: Meckler Books, 1978. Written from an American viewpoint, this assessment concentrates on Pompidou's foreign policies as President of France. He improved relations between France and Great Britain, especially in terms of Great Britain's membership in the European Economic Community. The article states that he did not like sweeping social reforms.

Roussel, Eric. *Georges Pompidou*. Paris: Jean-Claude Lattès, 1984. To read about the rest of Pompidou's career, as well as the earlier stages, turn to this book. It has photographs, lists the ministers of his cabinets when he was premier and president, and contains a bibliography.

Werth, Alexander. *De Gaulle*. New York: Simon and Schuster, 1966; London: Penguin, 1967. This book is about de Gaulle but contains a number of references to Pompidou, including a short biography. Mention is made that Pompidou was a Socialist in his youth but became a neo-capitalist—that is, someone who believed that modernization of France could best be achieved through a combination of big business and state capitalism. An explanation is given of why de Gaulle picked him to be prime minister, and there is a description of the parliament's initial dissatisfaction with the appointment.

Williams, Philip M. *French Politicians and Elections, 1951-1969*. Cambridge: Cambridge University Press, 1970. Williams describes de Gaulle's selection of Pompidou as prime minister and Pompidou's subsequent role in elections and in the events of May, 1968.

Williams, Philip M., and Martin Harrison. *Politics and Society in de Gaulle's Republic*. London: Longman, 1971; New York: Doubleday, 1972. This book contains numerous scattered references to Pompidou, including a description of his conciliatory gestures as prime minister.


*Corinne Lathrop Gilb*

## COLE PORTER

*Born:* June 9, 1891; Peru, Indiana
*Died:* October 15, 1964; Santa Monica, California
*Area of Achievement:* Music
*Contribution:* Porter was a composer and lyricist whose individuality and imagination brought a new facet to Broadway and Hollywood musicals.

### Early Life

Cole Albert Porter was the third and only surviving child of an overprotective mother named Kate Porter and an ineffectual father. His grandfather, J. O. Cole, was one of the wealthiest men in Indiana. Kate used her father's money to see that her son had the best of everything. She was determined to see that he became a member of the social circle that she herself could not seem to enter.

Though tiny and fragile at birth, Porter grew into a healthy child. At the age of six, Kate signed her son up for piano lessons, enforcing two-hour practices each day. She often sat with Porter and parodied the popular songs of the day. These sessions helped Porter develop his own style of humorous and playful lyrics. His first "published" work was a composition he wrote for his mother when he was ten, "The Bobolink Waltz." Kate had one hundred copies made and sent it to family and friends.

Porter was a solitary child who spent most of his time with his mother or his music. He was not allowed to play baseball or other sports, but instead learned how to ride horses. Porter's small circle of friends increased when he entered Worcester Academy at the age of fourteen. His quick smile and sparkling personality soon endeared him to both students and faculty. He did well in school, joining the Glee Club, Mandoline Club, the debate team, and various school theater productions. Although his performances earned him positive reviews, Porter did not care for acting and chose music and composing as his profession.

After graduating from Worcester, Porter took the entrance exams for Yale, mainly to please his grandfather. He passed on his second try and entered the university in the fall of 1909. Porter was more concerned with his music, joining clubs, and making friends than he was in his studies. During his years at Yale, Porter wrote over three hundred songs, including the fight song "Bingo Eli Yale." At the insistence of his grandfather, Porter entered Harvard Law School. His head, however, was not in it. At the suggestion of the dean of the law school, Porter switched his studies to the Harvard Graduate School of Arts and Science, where he lasted only one year before turning his sights to New York society and Broadway.

### Life's Work

Porter's professional career started on Broadway when he composed music for *See America First* in 1916. Although this production did not receive very good reviews, thirteen of Porter's songs were published. Perhaps because of his disappointment in the musical, Porter traveled to Paris in 1917. He claimed to have joined the French Foreign Legion during World War I, but there are no records to prove this. He also fabricated the story that he was awarded the French Croix de Guerre. After the war, Porter decided to stay in France, where he enjoyed his life as a wealthy American in Paris society. In 1918, he met Linda Lee Thomas. Known as one of the greatest beauties of the time, Thomas was the epitome of style and grace and became an important influence in Porter's life. She was also his introduction into the world of high society. Thomas saw great potential in Porter's music and became one of his greatest supporters.

In 1919, Porter returned to the United States. On the ship he met a producer and, with Thomas's help, found himself hired. He went on to write the words and music for *Hitchey-Koo* (1919), his second Broadway musical. Porter's song "Old-Fashioned Garden" quickly caught on and became his first big hit. Sales from the song enabled Porter to return to France and propose to Thomas. They were married on December 19, 1919. The couple, both wealthy in their own right, owned homes in New York and France. They hosted extravagant parties for friends and nobility alike. It was at parties such as these that Porter came up with many of the ideas for his songs.

Through the 1920's, Porter provided songs for several unsuccessful productions. He began to have self-doubts, but in 1928, his luck began to change. He produced a steady flow of songs that caught the public's attention. With his involvement in the successful musical *Paris*, Porter felt he had finally arrived as a Broadway composer. In 1929, Porter was busy with the Broadway productions *Wake Up and Dream* and *Fifty Million Frenchmen*. He was also involved with the motion picture *The Battle of*

*Paris*. Porter spent a good deal of his time studying other composers and working on his own style. He was years ahead of his colleagues with his sophisticated and worldly lyrics. "Love for Sale", from *The New Yorkers* (1930), was banned from the radio for its suggestive lyrics.

While at Yale, Porter had started the practice of tailoring his songs to fit the performers who would sing them. He played up their strong points and minimized their weak ones. This was an effective way of getting excellent results out of everyone. He used this method when he wrote "Night and Day" for Fred Astaire to sing in the film *The Gay Divorcee* (1934). Astaire did not have a very good voice, but Porter's song fit him perfectly and it became an instant hit.

When the theater began to suffer because of the Depression, Porter accepted an offer to work for Metro-Goldwyn-Mayer (MGM) studios in Hollywood, California. In late 1935, he and Linda made the temporary move west. Porter had no trouble fitting into the flamboyant Hollywood lifestyle. Linda, however, did not care for it and returned to France, visiting Porter every few months.

In 1937, Porter suffered a serious horse-riding accident. After being thrown from his horse, the animal rolled over him and crushed both of his legs. Upon hearing of the accident, Linda quickly returned to his side. She and Kate convinced the doctors not to amputate, knowing how important Porter's appearance was to him. Despite the doctors' best efforts, Porter ended up crippled; he wore leg braces and was in constant pain for the rest of his life. In spite of his accident, Porter continued to work. During the late 1930's and early 1940's, he alternated between writing for Broadway and Hollywood. This was the high point of his musical career. In 1945, Porter authorized the filming of the motion picture *Night and Day* (1946). Intended as a biography of Porter, it did little to portray his actual life. It left out important parts such as his pampered childhood, his alternative lifestyle, and his questionable military career.

With the beginning of the 1950's, Porter felt he was losing his creative flair. He suffered from severe headaches, sleeplessness, and moodiness. Three of the people he counted on most for support—his mother, his wife, and his good friend Howard Sturgis—all died during this time. These personal losses hit Porter hard and threatened his personal life. His professional life also began to suffer. After the premier of the musical *Silk Stockings* (1955), Porter vowed never to write another Broadway musical. His last film, *High Society* (1956), earned him an Oscar nomination for his song "True Love." The last thing Porter ever wrote was for the television musical production *Aladdin* in 1958. The songs were not up to his usual originality and fire.

In 1958, Porter was admitted to the hospital to have his right leg amputated. The loss of his leg was difficult for Porter and left him feeling like "half a man." He became despondent, and depression set in during the 1960's. In 1964, Porter entered the hospital once again, this time to have a kidney stone removed. The operation was successful, but Porter had lost his will to live. He died on October 15, 1964.

### Summary

Cole Porter was well liked among his peers and contemporaries. Those who knew Porter considered him complex and somewhat distant, yet polite and devoted to family and friends. Those fortunate enough to work with him considered him a gentleman who never said an unkind word or raised his voice.

Even after his accident, during the most painful time of his life, Porter continued to work. His method of writing was not common. He would think through the lyrics and melody away from the piano. Only when he was satisfied would he try the song on the piano. It was also Porter's practice to read the script of a show so his songs could closely match the dialogue. Of the five most popular song writers of the first half of the twentieth century—George Gershwin, Irving Berlin, Jerome Kern, Richard Rodgers, and Cole Porter—Porter was the only one who wrote both words and music.

### Bibliography

Citron, Stephen. *Noel and Cole: The Sophisticates.* London: Sinclair-Stevenson, 1992; New York: Oxford University Press, 1993. Composer and lyricist Citron has produced a skillful dual biography of Porter and Noel Coward based on previously unpublished manuscripts, letters, and many interviews. Includes chronologies and analysis of songs.

Eells, George. *The Life That Late He Led.* London: Allen, and New York: Putnam, 1967. This was the first full-length biography of Porter, as told by a personal friend. The author uses a chatty, conversational style that tends to ramble. This publication includes anecdotes and interviews with Porter's friends and colleagues.

Forte, Allen. "Secrets of Melody: Line and Design in the Songs of Cole Porter." *Musical Quarterly* 77, no. 4 (Winter 1993). In-depth, technical analysis of Porter's songs.

Grafton, David. *Red, Hot & Rich!* New York: Stein and Day, 1987. This is a revealing oral history of Porter that includes quotations and reminiscence from those who knew him. The author also includes his own personal recollections, having met Porter a number of times.

Schwartz, Charles. *Cole Porter: A Biography.* New York: Dial Press, 1977; London: Allen, 1978. Revealing, comprehensive, and objective study of who Porter really was, including his relationships with his mother, wife, and close friends. Includes detailed description of Porter's musical style, as told by another musician.

*Maryanne Barsotti*

## KATHERINE ANNE PORTER

*Born:* May 15, 1890; Indian Creek, Texas
*Died:* September 18, 1980; Silver Spring, Maryland
*Area of Achievement:* Literature
*Contribution:* An important modernist writer, Porter was a fiercely independent and exacting artist whose life and work influenced many writers who followed her.

### Early Life

During Katherine Anne Porter's unhappy early life, she received little encouragement to become a creative writer, yet her very misery may have spurred this sensitive and strong-willed young girl to greatness. Born Callie Russell Porter in a log cabin on the Texas frontier, she lost her mother, Mary Alice Jones Porter, when she was only two and struggled through poverty and the humiliation of being a motherless child. Her father, Harrison Boone Porter, seems to have lost his will to provide for himself and his family after his wife's death. Thus, the burden of raising Porter, her brother, and two sisters fell to her father's mother, Catherine Anne Porter, otherwise known as Aunt Cat, who had reared nine children of her own.

Moved to her grandmother's house in Kyle, Texas, Porter was sensitive to the crowded conditions and the fact that neighbors regarded her and her siblings as charity cases. Her biographer, Joan Givner, believes that her father's neglect left Porter with a yearning for affection from men that eventually led to four marriages and innumerable affairs, often with men whose circumstances almost guaranteed instability. Her grandmother's strength of character, however, was a lifelong influence, and Porter eventually adopted her name, with a slight spelling difference, perhaps in an effort to internalize that strength. In later years, when asked about her early life, Porter frequently suppressed painful details and transformed them into more palatable ones. She was furious when researchers discovered her original name. Instead of dirt-poor Callie Russell Porter, she wished to be remembered as Katherine Anne, descendant of a long line of southern aristocrats.

Aunt Cat's death when Porter was eleven deprived her of her only source of stability. After they had lived for a time with Porter's aunt Ellen on a farm near Buda, Texas, which was probably the setting for the short novel "Noon Wine," Porter's father moved the family to San Antonio, where she attended the Thomas School, a private institution that introduced her to drama. Her marriage at age fifteen to John Henry Koontz was partially motivated by a desire to escape from the poverty and unhappiness of her home life. Although she later termed the marriage "preposterous," it lasted nine years, longer than any of her subsequent ones. After she divorced Koontz, she felt liberated from marital restrictions, much as her autobiographical protagonist Miranda Gay felt in "Old Mortality," one of her fine short novels:

> She would have no more bonds that smothered her in love and hatred. She knew now why she had run away to marriage, and she knew that she was going to run away from marriage, and she was not going to stay in any place, with anyone, that threatened to forbid her making her own discoveries, that said "No" to her.

After a failed attempt to earn a living as an actress in Chicago in 1914, she eventually moved to Dallas seeking office work. There she contracted tuberculosis. In the hospital, she befriended Kitty Barry Crawford, one of the first newspaperwomen in Texas. From her she learned of Jane Anderson, Kitty's college roommate and a war correspondent in Europe. Jane's and Kitty's examples suggested journalism as a career. Consequently, after leaving the sanatorium in 1917, Porter worked for the Fort Worth *Critic* as a society columnist and theater reviewer. When Jane and Kitty moved to Colorado, she went there too and eventually got a job on the Denver *Rocky Mountain News*. In 1918, just two years after her bout with tuberculosis, she was victimized by an influenza epidemic that was sweeping the country. Hospitalized with a temperature of 105 degrees for nine days and with death imminent, she was saved by an experimental dosage of strychnine. The near-death experience caused by the strychnine would eventually be immortalized in the excellent short novel "Pale Horse, Pale Rider." She herself regarded the incident as an important dividing line in her life, after which she devoted herself more purposefully to her writing career.

### Life's Work

In 1919, Katherine Anne Porter moved to New York's Greenwich Village, where she was surrounded by artists like herself who were committed to their work. She found work with a magazine promoting Mexico and was soon asked to visit that country as part of her assignment. This began a long relationship with Mexico that influenced several of her works, including her first important story, "Maria Concepcion" (1922). This character study of a strong Indian woman, who is generous despite being oppressed and who is wronged but does something about it, earned her $600 from *Century* magazine and launched Porter's fiction writing career.

She had numerous affairs in New York and Mexico, and in 1926 she was married to Ernest Stock, an Englishman. The marriage lasted only a short time. In 1928, in an episode that was characteristic of her behavior of plunging into love with a man very soon after a breakup with another, she met and had an affair with Matthew Josephson, who was married. Porter was impressed by the fact that his first interest was in her writing: "From a man I surely never had that before." A writer himself, Josephson provided Porter with encouragement and literary guidance that helped her develop confidence in her work.

She began a biography, "The Devil and Cotton Mather," on which she worked periodically for the rest of her life but which she never completed. She was drawn to the subject because of her interest in the phenomenon of mass hysteria as manifested in the revival meetings of her youth, Adolf Hitler's Germany, and Mather's Puritan New England during the witch trials. Another manifestation of mass hysteria and social injustice that attracted her passionate interest was the case of Nicola Sacco and Bartolomeo Vanzetti, Italian immigrants who had been accused of murder. Porter and others believed that the two men were condemned because of their anarchist political beliefs rather than on the basis of legitimate evidence. On the night of their execution in 1927, she took part in a group vigil outside the prison. It would take her many years, but she would eventually publish her account of that event in *The Never-Ending Wrong* (1977).

Porter was exacting in her craft and uncompromising in her artistic vision. She would forgo the large sums of money paid by commercial magazines in order to prevent her works being edited for mass consumption. Thus, many of her finest works were published in "little magazines"; that is, small-circulation journals specializing in experimental writing that would not appeal to the general public. In the company of some of the finest writers of 1920's and 1930's America, Porter published "The Jilting of Granny Weatherall" and "Magic" in *Transition*; "Theft" in *Gyroscope*; "Flowering Judas" in *Hound and Horn*; "Circus," "Old Mortality," and "Pale Horse, Pale Rider" in *Southern Review*; and "The Grave," "That Tree," "Two Plantation Portraits," and "Hacienda" in *Virginia Quarterly*. Most of the books published by Porter consist of collections of these scattered stories. *Flowering Judas and Other Stories* (1930) was published in a limited edition by Harcourt, Brace, then expanded and reissued four years later. Three short novels—"Old Mortality," "Noon Wine," and "Pale Horse, Pale Rider"—were published under the title *Pale Horse, Pale Rider* (1939), and another volume appeared under the title *The Leaning Tower and Other Stories* (1944).

Although her stories featured many themes, one of the major ones was her view that the dark side of human life was an important part of reality even though many of her characters attempted to evade it. She had an interest in evil characters, but she seemed to be more fascinated by the innocent bystander who effectively collaborates with evil by allowing it to perpetuate itself. She attributed the successes of Adolf Hitler, Benito Mussolini, Joseph McCarthy, and Huey Long to the tacit consent of bystanders who had the moral sense to know that these men were wrong. Both "Theft" and "Flowering Judas" exhibit this theme. To complicate matters, as often as not, the evil person is on the "right" side of a particular cause. Her Homer T. Hatch of "Noon Wine," for example, is evil in spite of the ostensible justice of his attempt to reincarcerate a man convicted of criminal conduct; likewise, the men who visit Miranda in "Pale Horse, Pale Rider" to ask why she has not bought liberty bonds are ostensibly working for a good cause, the U.S. war effort, but are clearly portrayed as the basest form of humanity. Porter was convinced that evil, because it was innate in humans, manifested itself everywhere, even in the best of causes or institutions.

Returning to Mexico in 1930 for her health, she met Eugene Dove Pressly, a dozen years her junior, to whom she was eventually married in Paris in 1933. Long wanting to go to Europe, she sailed with him for Germany in 1931. This trip and the diversity of persons aboard the ship provided much of the inspiration for *Ship of Fools* (1962), which would take another thirty years to complete. Her only full-length novel, it attempted to expose the flaws in Western society that had led to two world wars within three decades. Porter was deeply influenced by her visit to 1930's Germany, for during this period Hitler's rise to power had begun. Her impressions of the weakness at the base of Germany's empire-building are recorded in "The Leaning Tower."

Porter loved and needed men, but she was never able to maintain a long-term relationship. According to Givner, she sought two attributes in men: They had to be willing to take care of her and they had to be interested in her work. Whereas Matthew Josephson had satisfied the second but not the first of these criteria, Eugene Pressly satisfied the first but not the second. After several years in Europe, she separated from him. Returning to the United States in 1936, she visited with her father in Indian Creek. As was her pattern, soon after deciding to divorce Pressly, she fell in love with another man, Albert Erskine. A graduate student at Louisiana State University, business manager of the *Southern Review*, and young enough to be her son, he was a friend of her good friends, the writers Allen Tate and Caroline Gordon. After their marriage in 1938, Erskine was horrified to discover that she was nearly fifty years old, while he was in his mid-twenties. She left him just two years later.

Porter had many female friends. From Kitty Barry Crawford and Jane Anderson, early role models, to several younger women who looked up to her, she formed friendships with women who were as committed to their work as she was to hers. Among the most famous of these women were the writers Caroline Gordon, Josephine Herbst, and Eudora Welty. She firmly rejected the advances of lesbians such as Carson McCullers, whose behavior repulsed her. As had been the case with her male friends, personality conflicts often led to permanent breaks in her relations with female friends. She condemned Josephine Herbst for being a dupe of the communists, and, according to Herbst's biographer, even went so far as to denounce her former friend to the Federal Bureau of Investigation (FBI).

Although she leaned toward the Left, Porter rejected involvement with the Communist Party because she did not want to be made a propagandist and lose her artistic freedom. Furthermore, she believed that evil existed in every political movement, even those with which she sympathized: "the mere adoption of a set of ideas, no matter how good the ideas may be, is [no] cure for the innate flaws of the individual." This innate depravity "accounts for the comparative failure of all movements towards human improvement."

Like many artists, Porter struggled to earn enough money to buy the freedom to write what she wanted. In 1940, she spent some time at Yaddo, the

writers' colony in New York, took a salaried job in Washington, D.C., assisting Allen Tate at the Library of Congress in 1944, and even went to Hollywood to be a screenwriter at $1,500 a week in 1945. Financial security, however, came only with the increased recognition she received in her later years. The long-awaited publication of *Ship of Fools* in 1962, more than any other event, secured her reputation and ended her financial worries.

After the publication of *Ship of Fools*, Porter increasingly became a public figure. She was a visiting professor at various universities, was awarded several honorary degrees, and was sought after to appear on panels with other literary figures. She even became a guest in the White House of John F. Kennedy and Lyndon Johnson. She did little new writing in her later years, spending most of her time reaping benefits from past work. At the age of seventy-six, for example, she won the Pulitzer Prize and the National Book Award for the *Collected Stories of Katherine Anne Porter* (1966).

Her spirit did not abate with old age. In her sixties and seventies she had affairs with younger men. As had been the case in her earlier years, when these relationships did not work out, she became as passionate an adversary as she had been a lover. Even in her seventies and eighties, she hired younger men as personal assistants to keep her literary and legal affairs in order, and she carried on at least platonic love affairs with them. She also remained passionate about her artistic independence. At eighty, she was enraged when her publisher wrote an acknowledgment to several of her friends who, in the publisher's view, had helped to collect the works in *The Collected Essays and Occasional Writings of Katherine Anne Porter* (1970). Feeling betrayed, she wrote indignant remarks on copies of this book to the effect that her publisher was impudent for believing that she could not conduct her own affairs and that it was ludicrous to suggest that the men who had been acknowledged were competent to put together a book for her.

A series of strokes paralyzed her writing hand and impaired her speech when she was eighty-seven, and she eventually died in 1980, at ninety years of age. Her body was cremated and buried alongside her mother's grave in Indian Creek.

### Summary

Rising from artistic isolation and an unhappy childhood, Katherine Anne Porter became one of the most conscientious of literary craftsmen. Nearly all of her fictional works, despite their relative brevity, took many years to complete. Finely crafted and intensely focused, her small body of writings has been inspiring to other artists, just as her life story has been. Fiercely independent yet also strongly desiring love and care, she vacillated between her role as artist and southern belle. The conflicts that she experienced regarding gender roles are effectively sublimated into much of her fiction and, along with her interests in other aspects of human nature, create a lasting testament to Porter's life and imagination.

### Bibliography

Bloom, Harold, ed. *Modern Critical Views: Katherine Anne Porter*. New York: Chelsea House, 1986. This is a book of twelve interpretations of Porter's fiction. It also includes a chronology of her life and a bibliography.

DeMouy, Jane Krause. *Katherine Anne Porter's Women: The Eye of Her Fiction*. Austin: University of Texas Press, 1983. An analysis of feminine psychology in the fiction, particularly the protagonists' conflicting desires for the security of a traditional female role and for the freedom from convention necessary to be an artist.

Givner, Joan. *Katherine Anne Porter: A Life*. Rev. ed. Athens: University of Georgia Press, 1991. The most thorough account of Porter's personal and professional life, this excellent biography often dispels myths propagated by Porter herself.

———. "Letters to Lodwick: Uncovering the Hidden Life of Katherine Anne Porter." *Southwest Review* 81, no. 1 (Winter 1996). Focuses on Porter's relationship with Lodwick Hartley, one of her biographers.

———, ed. *Katherine Anne Porter: Conversations*. Jackson: University Press of Mississippi, 1987. Porter sometimes fictionalized her life story. This collection of interviews with the author provides her view of her life and art.

Hendrick, Willene, and George Hendrick. *Katherine Anne Porter*. Rev. ed. Boston: Twayne, 1988. An overview of Porter's life and work, this carefully researched book provides a chronology of imsportant dates, a bibliography of works by and about her, and chapters of her life and major works. A good place to begin study.

Porter, Katherine Anne. *The Collected Essays and Occasional Writings of Katherine Anne Porter*. New York: Delacorte Press, 1970. According to Porter, these essays were the opposite of her fiction in that they were limited by time, space, and subject requirements. They range from the personal and biographical to criticism of other writers' works.

Unrue, Darlene Harbour. "Katherine Anne Porter, Politics, and Another Reading of 'Theft.'" *Studies in Short Fiction* 30, no. 2 (Spring 1993). The author considers the political overtones in Porter's work.

———. *Truth and Vision in Katherine Anne Porter's Fiction*. Athens: University of Georgia Press, 1985. An interpretation of Porter's fiction that stresses her exploration of the dark side of life and humankind's vain effort to evade it.

Warren, Robert Penn, ed. *Katherine Anne Porter: A Collection of Critical Essays*. Englewood Cliffs, N.J.: Prentice-Hall, 1979. These essays on Porter's work include contributions from some of the most influential interpreters of twentieth century writing: Warren, Cleanth Brooks, Eudora Welty, V. S. Pritchett, Edmund Wilson, and Mark Schorer, among others.

*William L. Howard*

# BEATRIX POTTER

*Born:* July 28, 1866; South Kensington, Middlesex (now London), England

*Died:* December 22, 1943; Near Sawrey, Lancashire, England

*Areas of Achievement:* Art, literature, and social reform

*Contribution:* Potter, an English writer and illustrator of such children's books as *The Tale of Peter Rabbit*, was also an early member of England's National Trust for the preservation of properties of historic value or natural beauty. She donated four thousand acres of Lake District farmland to preserve the area's rural quality of life.

## Early Life

Helen Beatrix Potter was born to middle-class parents in a fashionable rural suburb of London in 1866 at the very height of Victorian England's prosperity and dominance on the world stage. Her father, Rupert Potter, was a barrister who had studied law at Lincoln's Inn, and her mother was the daughter of a prosperous Lancashire cotton merchant. Their four-story Kensington house, bought especially to prepare for raising a family, had a staff of six servants, with a young Scottish nanny added after Beatrix's birth. A brother, Bertram, followed not quite six years later.

As a child, Potter was shy, delicate, and often ill. She seldom ventured out into London, except for walks in Kensington Gardens with her nurse and her first dog, Sandy. She learned to read, she recalled, by painfully spelling her way through the Scottish novelist Sir Walter Scott's *Rob Roy* (1817), then *Ivanhoe* (1819), then *The Talisman* (1825), and then back to *Rob Roy*, which she could suddenly read. Rupert had been an amateur artist as a student and took up collecting, especially the drawings of Randolph Caldecott, the children's illustrator for whom the Caldecott Medal was named, given annually since 1938 to the best-illustrated children's book. Rupert was friends with the painter John Everett Millais and Prime Minister William Gladstone, whom he photographed.

The formative experience of Potter's childhood was the family's annual three-month vacation in Scotland, a ritual that began when Potter was five and lasted for the next eleven years. Each summer, Rupert would lease Dalguise House, a large country estate, where the adults would shoot grouse and fish for salmon while Potter would explore the meadows and woods collecting specimens, drawing and painting, and imagining Scottish lords and ladies walking alongside her. She and Bertram brought back pets from their expeditions—frogs, lizards, snakes, newts, bats, rats, hedgehogs, and rabbits—which they often smuggled into their upstairs rooms in the London house. Potter meticulously sketched and painted these animals. She did not like to draw people, nor did she draw them well. Her parents, fearful of germs and bad influences, kept the children isolated from other playmates. Potter's substitutes for human warmth were her pets and her imagination. She began a journal when she was fifteen, written in a secret code to ensure privacy, which was her chief confidante until she was over thirty.

## Life's Work

It was through her continued attention to the writing and drawing that were the companions of her long and lonely childhood that Potter eventually produced the children's books for which she is most famous. Her first attempts at serious work were as a scientific illustrator. She had become fascinated by fungi during the family's Scottish vacations, befriending a shy postman who taught her much about local mycological lore. Back in London, she spent long afternoons at the nearby Natural History Museum studying and drawing specimens, producing over one hundred watercolors that she hoped to have published as a book. However, they were rejected by the director of the Royal Botanical Gardens at Kew.

Potter was pointed in a new direction by the happy accident of her family's change of summer vacation locales. Beginning in 1882, when the Dalguise House was no longer available to rent, the family began summering in the Lake District, first renting a Victorian mansion called Wray Castle on the shores of Lake Windermere. The local vicar, Canon Rawnsley, was an amateur naturalist and conservationist deeply concerned about the despoilation of the lakes by tourism and its accompanying development. (In 1895 he succeeded in cofounding the National Trust, largely to protect the Lake District.) In 1890, upon seeing Potter's drawings, he suggested offhandedly that she might illustrate birthday cards or nursery rhymes with one of the new foreign firms in London such as Hildesheimer & Faulkner. With Bertram's help, she sent off six designs for

Christmas cards, using their pet rabbit Benjamin Bouncer as a model. She received a check for six pounds and, for the next two years, poured herself into illustration work for the firm. The work, however, was not aesthetically satisfying.

About that time she began writing "picture letters" to the small children of one of her former governesses, now Mrs. Moore. In 1893, one of these letters to the oldest child, Noel, then five, began, "I don't know what to write to you, so I shall tell you a story about four little rabbits, whose names were Flopsy, Mopsy, Cottontail and Peter." This was the beginning of what was to become her most famous book, *The Tale of Peter Rabbit* (1900). The Moore children kept all of the picture letters that Potter sent each summer. She was now nearly thirty but was still a devoted daughter living with her stern and proper Victorian parents. Bertram had escaped by buying a farm in the Scottish Border country and secretly marrying, though he dutifully turned up for the annual summer holidays.

By this time, Potter had found a particular village in the Lake District that seemed to her the most beautiful of all called Near Sawrey. She often visited a farm there called Hill Top and told the farmer's children the same stories she was telling the Moore children. Perhaps because of the appreciative responses she was getting from so many children, the idea of a book occurred. She wrote Noel Moore, now twelve, to ask if he had saved the Peter Rabbit picture letters, which she had. Potter expanded the story, sent if off to six publishers, received six rejections, and decided to self-publish the book in 1900 with money her father had given her. It was a great success not only with friends and kind aunts but also with a wider audience, including Sir Arthur Conan Doyle, who bought it for his children. At this point, the publisher Frederick Warne agreed to bring out an edition if she would supply color rather than black-and-white illustrations.

There followed a long and profitable relationship with Warne, who published, among other books, *The Tale of Peter Rabbit* (1902), *The Tailor of Gloucester* (1903), *The Tale of Squirrel Nutkin* (1903), *The Tale of Benjamin Bunny* (1904), *The Tale of Two Bad Mice* (1904), *The Tale of Mrs. Tiggy-Winkle* (1905), *The Tale of Mr. Jeremy Fisher* (1906), *The Tale of Tom Kitten* (1907), *The Tale of Jemima Puddle-Duck* (1908), and *The Tale of Pigling Bland* (1913). The youngest son of the Warne family, Norman, who had been made responsible for the "rabbits" account, proposed marriage to Potter, by letter, on July 25, 1905. She was on the annual summer holiday with her parents. They insisted that it would be beneath her to marry "into trade," but Potter accepted the proposal, though for the sake of her parents did not disclose this outside of the two families. Norman fell ill, however, and exactly one month later, on August 25, he died of leukemia.

Potter was grief-stricken that her last letter to him had been chattily unaware of how seriously ill he was. Despite his death, however, his proposal did help free her from her parents. With the royalties from her books, she decided to buy a farm in the Lake District. By chance, Hill Top itself was for sale. She purchased it and allowed the farm family she had known there to remain as caretakers. She spent only one month per year there, however, for her parents were increasingly ill, and she felt responsible for managing their London house. Then came the great crisis that finally changed her narrow and enclosed life. The local solicitor who had helped her buy Hill Top and other properties proposed marriage in 1913. Her parents would not allow it, though Potter was in her late forties. She fell deathly ill of pneumonia until help came from her brother Bertram, who finally revealed to their parents that he had married a shopkeeper's daughter eleven years before. Her parents acquiesced, and Potter became Mrs. William Heelis. From that moment on, she ceased to use any other name.

Though she produced a few more books for Warne and continued to license merchandise using the images of her creations, Potter enter full-heartedly into the life of a married countrywoman. She became especially interested in restoring the native breed of sheep to the Lake District and became a breeder and shower of Herdwick sheep. She often regarded the children's stories from the most creative period of her life, her thirties and forties, with distaste, considering them reminders of a life lived in the imagination as compensation for not living in the world. She refused all interviews and publicity and donated her farms to the National Trust on her death.

### Summary

Beatrix Potter's stories have become classics of children's literature. This is partly because of the charm of the illustrations, in which animals are dressed in clothes but otherwise unsentimentalized—indeed, she had to fight battles against censorship when she had her animals undress themselves. Her stories do not shy away from difficult words whose sound Potter liked. They are often tales of escape or domestic happiness, the most meaningful of themes for Potter and many children and adults.

Her legacy also includes a marketing strategy, which is not surprising for the daughter and wife of lawyers: She created the first Peter Rabbit doll in 1903 and licensed Wedgewood's to produce nurseryware. Her characters have inspired a ballet, animated films, a British postage stamp, an exhibition at the Tate Gallery, a Beatrix Potter Society, and tourist brochures marketing the Lake District as Peter Rabbit Country. Her most lasting legacy, however, may turn out to be her donations of property and royalties to the National Trust, which has subsidized the continuance of sheep farming in the Lake District, which otherwise would have given way long ago to commercial development and the disappearance of the way of life she loved.

### Bibliography

Frey-Ridgway, Susan. "Beatrix Potter: An Annotated Bibliography." *Reference Services Review* 24, no. 3 (1996). An annotated bibliography covering Potter's writing, art, and life.

Jay, Eileen, Mary Noble, and Anne Hobbs. *A Victorian Naturalist*. London: Warne, and New York: Penguin, 1992. While quite young, Potter made frequent trips to the Natural History Museum near her London home, making serious watercolor studies of animals and, oddly, fungi, reproduced in this book.

Lane, Margaret. *The Magic Years of Beatrix Potter*. London and New York: Warne, 1978. A study of Potter's most creative years, during her late thirties and early forties, by her first biographer. Illustrated.

———. *The Tale of Beatrix Potter*. London and New York: Warne, 1946. The first biography, written with the cooperation of Potter's husband, William Heelis.

Linder, Leslie. *The History of the Writings of Beatrix Potter*. Rev. ed. London and New York: Warne, 1987. A study of Potter's writings using the previously unavailable journal material.

Peck, Robert McCracke. "Beatrix Potter, Scientific Illustrator." *Magazine Antiques* 146, no. 6 (June, 1996). Profile of Potter discussing her talent as a wildlife artist, her childhood love of animals, and her ability to create personalities in her animal characters.

Potter, Beatrix. *Beatrix Potter's Letters*. Edited by Judy Taylor. London: Warne, 1989. A selection of some four hundred letters.

———. *The Journal of Beatrix Potter from 1881-1897*. Edited and transcribed by Leslie Linder. Rev. ed. London: Warne, 1989. A transcript of Potter's encrypted journal, finally decoded by Linder.

Taylor, Judy. *Beatrix Potter: Artist, Storyteller and Countrywoman*. Rev. ed. London and New York: Warne, 1996. A lavishly illustrated biography containing a useful bibliography and many photographs.

Taylor, Judy, Irene Whalley, Anne Hobbs, and Elizabeth Battrick. *Beatrix Potter 1866-1943: The Artist and Her World*. London: Warne, and New York: Penguin, 1987. The catalogue for the Beatrix Potter exhibition at the Tate Gallery, London, in 1987. This is the chief reference work available on Potter.

*James Persoon*

# FRANCIS POULENC

*Born:* January 7, 1899; Paris, France
*Died:* January 30, 1963; Paris, France
*Area of Achievement:* Music
*Contribution:* Poulenc gradually came to be recognized by many as perhaps the greatest twentieth century exponent of the art song and, toward the latter part of his career, as the composer of deeply felt religious music.

## Early Life

Francis Poulenc was born in Paris on January 7, 1899, to wealthy parents. From his father, Émile Poulenc, a manufacturer of pharmaceuticals, he inherited affluence, which allowed him to devote his life to music, and a profound Catholicism, which manifested itself strongly in his music by his late thirties. His musical interests were awakened as a small child by his mother, the former Jenny Royer, an excellent pianist who gave him his first lessons. At eight, Poulenc studied with Mademoiselle Boutet de Monvel, César Franck's niece. About this time, as he later noted, he was profoundly moved upon hearing a composition by Claude Debussy.

In 1915, Poulenc's pianistic education was turned over to the Spanish virtuoso Richard Viñes, who, realizing that Poulenc's ambition was to compose rather than perform, provided him a sound training in the classics and encouraged his interest in modern music. Poulenc had already become acquainted with and been moved by the music of Igor Stravinsky, Erik Satie, and Debussy. An even older musical influence was *Die Winterreise*, Franz Schubert's song cycle, which encouraged Poulenc's lyrical gifts and romantic tendencies as well as his later passion for writing songs. In addition to his musical studies, Poulenc, at his father's insistence, remained in school until he was graduated from the Lycée Condorcet.

## Life's Work

Poulenc's first compositions were for the piano, written early in 1917, the year his father died, leaving him financially independent. He achieved success the same year with *Rapsodie nègre*, an unusual work for chamber ensemble which anticipated the Dada movement. The text of this composition consisted of a verse from *Les Poésies de Makoko Kangourou*, supposedly the work of a Liberian black but in fact a hoax. The success of the rhapsody, with its verse of sheer gibberish, attracted the attention of the public and critics to Poulenc for the first time. He never completely abandoned the levity of this piece, continuing to produce from time to time compositions in which mockery and laughter were the keynotes.

In January of 1918, Poulenc was drafted into the French army. After spending six months at Vincennes and three in an antiaircraft battery in the Vosges, he was in Chalons-sur-Marne when the war ended. Instead of being demobilized, he was sent to Paris to work as a typist in the Ministry of Aviation. He was discharged in October of 1921. While still in the army, he composed a number of tongue-in-cheek works. His three *Mouvements perpétuels* for piano, in which his indebtedness to Satie is obvious, were introduced by Viñes in 1919.

Poulenc's first songs also came in 1919—the cycles *Le Bestiaire* (to poems by Guillaume Apollinaire) and *Cocardes* (to poems by Jean Cocteau), both characterized by a rich irony. It was soon afterward that the critic Henri Collet, in a review of a new music concert promoted by cellist Félix Delgrange, half-jokingly dubbed Poulenc, along with his associates Louis Durey, Georges Auric, Arthur Honegger, Darius Milhaud, and Germaine Tailleferre, "Les Six," a label that stuck with them long after they had drifted apart. The group worked together long enough to create (minus Durey) a scandal with contributions to *Les Mariés sur la tour Eiffel*, Cocteau's rather loony ballet of June, 1921. Of "Les Six," Poulenc for a time was the one who remained most faithful to such principles as directness, simplicity, and economy as well as to the idea of everyday music for ordinary people. All of this was a reaction to German post-Romanticism and French Impressionism.

By 1921, Poulenc, who thus far had produced nothing of substance, had begun to feel a need for some formal instruction. Seeking a sympathetic teacher, he found one in Charles Koechlin, with whom he worked for four years. During this period, he produced his first major work, the music for the ballet *Les Biches*, commissioned by Sergei Diaghilev for the Ballets Russes de Monte Carlo in 1923. Poulenc's score consisted of a suite of dances, each complete and self-sufficient. The ballet was a major success when it was presented in Paris on January 6, 1924. It was also about this time that Poulenc traveled with Milhaud to Rome and Vienna to meet the leading musical figures in those cities.

Poulenc followed *Les Biches* with other important works, also in a light and graceful vein. He wrote *Concert champêtre*, for harpsichord and orchestra, for Wanda Landowska, who introduced it on May 3, 1929, with the Paris Philharmonic, under Pierre Monteux. About this time, he bought an estate at Noizay, on the Loire River near Amboise—more for the sake of privacy than its rural location, he being a boulevardier at heart (he kept a Paris apartment on the Left Bank near the Luxembourg Gardens after 1935). In 1929, Poulenc was the piano soloist in his ballet score *Aubade* for piano and eighteen winds. First presented at the International Society for Contemporary Music festival in Venice on September 5, 1932, Poulenc's Concerto in D Minor for Two Pianos and Orchestra is characterized by its wit projected through a number of popular tunes and rhythms.

Poulenc reached a new maturity around 1935, precipitated by his reacquaintance with the baritone singer Pierre Bernac and the death in a car accident of his friend Pierre-Octave Ferroud. In August of 1935, Poulenc appeared as a piano accompanist of Bernac in song recitals at Salzburg, Austria. It marked the first of many similar recitals in the major music centers of Europe and the United States. These recitals played a major role in Poulenc's growth as a composer of art songs. He maintained that he learned the art of writing songs through his accompaniment of Bernac in the great literature of the French and German schools. From his association with Bernac, Poulenc went on to write songs that won him acclaim as one of the greatest twentieth century composers of such music. His 1935 musical setting of five poems by Paul Éluard was followed in 1937 with a setting for Éluard's cycle *Tel jour, telle nuit.* From the late 1930's to 1956, Poulenc wrote about a hundred songs, most of them to poems by Éluard and Apollinaire. The best of these are noted for the sensitivity and poetic beauty of their melodies and for the rich invention of the piano accompaniment, as well as for Poulenc's gift for projecting subtle nuances, feelings, and atmospheres.

The death of Ferroud in 1935 and a consequent visit to Notre Dame de Rocamadour restored Poulenc to his paternal Roman Catholic faith. The first fruits of this restoration were *Litanies à la vierge noire* (1936), for children's (or women's) voices and organ, and the Mass in G Major (1937) for four-part a cappella mixed chorus. These works give expression to deep religious convictions; they combine serenity with spiritual ardor and humility with sweetness, traits characteristic of Poulenc's greatest religious compositions. In 1938, Poulenc wrote the Concerto in G Minor, for organ and orchestra, for the Princesse Edmond de Polignac, at whose salon it was premiered the same year. Though wit is given free rein, there are solemn, perhaps ominous, passages that portend a new and more serious direction for the composer.

The outbreak of World War II in 1939 called the forty-year-old composer back to the antiaircraft guns. He was in Bordeaux when the French military collapsed the following summer; instead of heading for the border, he returned to Paris. Poulenc remained in occupied France for the war's duration, demonstrating his "resistance" by musical means. The war years invested his music with increasing expressiveness and intensity. In 1943, Poulenc wrote a poignant Sonata for Violin and Piano, inspired by and dedicated to Federico García Lorca, the Spanish poet who had been murdered by the Falangists. Its first performance was given on June 21, 1943, in Paris, with the composer at the piano. During the same year, Poulenc finished *Figure humaine*, one of his greatest works for chorus, to a poem by Éluard. Deeply moving and tragic, this music, which concludes with a mighty hymn to human liberty, expressed the suffering of every Frenchman as well as his will to resist. In 1944, Poulenc completed his first opera, *Les Mamelles de Tirésias*, a one-act Surrealist fantasy based on a play by Apollinaire. It received its first performance in 1947 at the Opéra-Comique in Paris, where it became a center of violent criticism. Satirizing a French campaign to increase the population, it caused shock and dismay by some of the items discussed in the text, such as the way by which one of the characters changes his sex. This latter work, which had its American premiere on June 13, 1953, at the second annual Festival of the Creative Arts in Waltham, Massachusetts, demonstrates that, despite the increasing seriousness and sobriety of purpose in many of his works after 1935, Poulenc had not altogether deserted an iconoclastic attitude and the light touch.

It was from a Bernac-Poulenc recital in Paris just after the war that the general recognition of Poulenc's songs as the finest since Gabriel Fauré's arose. In 1948, Poulenc and Bernac received an enthusiastic welcome on the first of several visits to the United States. The world premiere of Poulenc's piano concerto was given in Boston by the composer and the Boston Symphony on January 6, 1950.

Poulenc spent the years 1953-1956 at work on his first full-length opera, *Dialogues des carmélites*, which deals with the self-sacrifice of a group of Carmelite nuns during the French Revolution. It is possibly Poulenc's greatest single work in any medium. First produced with outstanding success at La Scala in Milan on January 26, 1957, it is characterized by exalted spirituality, expressive lyricism, and shattering tragedy. An American premiere of the opera followed in September of the same year in San Francisco. In 1958, it was telecast by an American television network and received the New York Music Critics Circle Award. Poulenc had no librettist for either *Les Mamelles de Tirésias* or *Dialogues des carmélites*. Preferring to deal directly with the original texts, he skillfully condensed the originals by excising unessential details and repetitions. He retained the beauty and force of the original language and the logic of the original dramatic structure.

Trouble over the rights of *Dialogues des carmélites* in 1954 put Poulenc under severe nervous strain, but he made a complete recovery. In 1958, he composed another unorthodox opera, *La Voix humaine*. A tour de force, but this time on a note of tragedy, it is a one-character opera with a libretto by Cocteau. First heard at the Paris Opéra-Comique on February 9, 1959, it concerns the reactions of a woman who is being spurned by her lover. The heartbreak of the deserted woman is effectively captured by the declamatory style of most of the music. In 1960, Poulenc made another successful tour of North America with Denise Duval.

It is the serious and religious side of Poulenc that is encountered in his last important compositions. The six-part Gloria, for chorus and orchestra, was commissioned by the Koussevitsky Music Foundation and introduced on January 21, 1961, by the Boston Symphony. His last major completed work was the vocal-orchestral *Sept Répons des ténèbres* (1961), which was posthumously premiered on April 11, 1963, by the New York Philharmonic to help celebrate its opening season at the Lincoln Center for the Performing Arts. Poulenc was working on a fourth opera based on Cocteau's *La Machine infernale* (1934; *The Infernal Machine*, 1936) when he died.

Poulenc's death from heart failure on January 30, 1963, was unexpected. He had never married. It is said that he loved only one woman in his life. She was Raymonde Linaissier, with whom he had grown up. He was deeply attached to her, but she died prematurely in 1930. Every song Poulenc wrote in which the word "face" appeared in the title was dedicated to her memory. Bernac survived Poulenc by sixteen years and published a useful guide to the songs, most of which he recorded with the composer.

**Summary**

Francis Poulenc did not care for abstract ideas or philosophy. He was essentially a sensualist and was sentimental as well. A musical natural, Poulenc probably composed more from aural experience and instinct than any other major composer of the twentieth century. During the first half of Poulenc's career, critics frequently failed to consider him as a serious composer because of the directness and simplicity of his writing. Gradually, it became clear that the lack of linguistic complexity in his music in no way indicated the absence of technique or feeling.

In addition to exhibiting a kind of classical simplicity, Poulenc's music often emphasizes the unexpected. Even though these traits can be found in music by Stravinsky, Maurice Ravel, and Satie—all of whom influenced Poulenc's style—he probably came to them more directly through the work of such writers as Apollinaire, Éluard, and Cocteau. They provided an aesthetic with which he could identify and furnished the texts for many of his best vocal pieces.

In Poulenc's music, melody is always the dominant element. His songs often begin immediately with the voice. His religious music, for which he became known as a distinguished master, is imbued with an almost medieval quality of naïveté and candor because of this samze lyricism. A five-record collection of all Poulenc's songs (released in France in 1980)—performed by Elly Ameling, Nicolai Gedda, Gérard Sougay, and others—strengthened Poulenc's reputation as perhaps the foremost twentieth century composer of the art song.

**Bibliography**

Bernac, Pierre. *Francis Poulenc: The Man and His Songs.* Translated by Winifred Radford. London: Gollancz, and New York: Norton, 1977. The unrivaled interpreter of Poulenc's songs provides a detailed and lucid analysis of all Poulenc's piano-accompanied songs. Having had the unique advantage of concertizing repeatedly with Poulenc, Bernac provides interesting insights in two chapters on Poulenc "the man" and "the composer."

Daniel, Keith W. *Francis Poulenc: His Artistic Development and Musical Style.* Ann Arbor, Mich.: UMI Research Press, 1982. Five biographical chapters are followed by material on Poulenc's style and compositions.

Ellison, Cori. "Cafes and Catechisms." *Opera News* 58, no. 12 (March 5, 1994). The author looks at the major influences in the life of Poulenc.

Hell, Henri. *Francis Poulenc.* Translated by Edward Lockspeiser. London: Calder, and New York: Grove Press, 1959. First published in France in 1958 as *Francis Poulenc, musicien français*, this is a good study of Poulenc and his work.

Mellers, Wilfrid Howard. *Francis Poulenc.* Oxford and New York: Oxford University Press, 1993. Mellers traces Poulenc's development as a composer and examines the reasons why his music has endured.

Myers, Rollo. *Modern French Music, from Fauré to Boulez.* New York: Praeger, 1971. A good account of French music in the twentieth century. Helps place Poulenc and his music in its historical context.

Poulenc, Francis. *My Friends and Myself: Conversations with Francis Poulenc.* Translated by James Harding. London: Dobson, 1978. Conversations originally broadcast by Suisse-Romande Radio between 1953 and 1962. Poulenc discusses his youth, early studies, "Les Six," his secular and religious works, and friends ranging from Satie and Éluard to Honegger and Stravinsky.

Roy, Jean. *Francis Poulenc: L'Homme et son œuvre.* Paris: Seghers, 1964. Available only in French, this work contains a complete list of Poulenc's works and a discography.

*L. Moody Simms, Jr.*

# COLIN L. POWELL

*Born:* April 5, 1937; New York, New York
*Area of Achievement:* Military affairs
*Contribution:* The first African American to become chairman of the Joint Chiefs of Staff, Colin Powell successfully organized and supervised American military operations in the Gulf War of 1991.

## Early Life

Colin Powell was born in New York City on April 5, 1937. His parents, Luther Powell and Maud McKoy, were both immigrants from Jamaica who had come to the United States in the 1920's. Both worked in Manhattan's garment district. Their first child, a daughter, was born in 1931; five and a half years later, Colin Powell was born. In 1940, the Powells moved from Manhattan to the Bronx and settled in Hunt's Point, an ethnically mixed working-class section of the city. Colin's boyhood friendships reflected that ethnic mixture, experiences that may have contributed to his attitudes about race.

Powell attended neighborhood public schools. The New York City school system was then among the strongest in the country, and although Powell did not stand out scholastically, he benefited from the high quality of his teachers. In high school, he took the college preparatory program; as a senior, he applied for admission to New York University and to the City College of New York. Admitted to both, he elected to attend City College, at that time the only free public university in the United States.

City College of New York (CCNY) was a remarkable school. It attracted first- and second-generation students from every immigrant group arriving in New York. Its alumni flocked to graduate and professional schools in greater numbers than from any other undergraduate institution. Powell began as an engineering student but switched to geology when, as he later put it, he could not manage to "visualize a plane intersecting a cone in space." The highlight of Powell's university career was his service in the Reserve Officers Training Corps (ROTC). In the ROTC, Powell found himself in his element. He enjoyed every aspect of his military training and became a member of the Pershing Rifles, an elite military fraternity. Powell was graduated in June, 1958, his degree in geology less important to him than his commission as a second lieutenant in the U.S. Army.

## Life's Work

A few days after his graduation, Powell traveled to Fort Benning, Georgia, for five more months of military training, including attendance at the Infantry Officer Basic Course. He volunteered for and successfully completed Ranger School and Airborne (parachute) training. His first full duty assignment was in Germany as a platoon leader in the Second Armored Rifle Battalion of the Forty-eighth Infantry. As the reports of his superiors confirmed, he was an able and adaptable officer from the beginning of his military career. His record was typical of officers who are on the "fast track"—that is, who are marked for early promotion because of their exceptional abilities.

On his return from Germany, Powell was assigned to the Fifth Infantry Division at Fort Devens, Massachusetts. While there, he met Alma Johnson, a young woman working as an audiologist with the Boston Guild for the Hard of Hearing. Johnson and Powell began dating, and they were married shortly before he received orders that would send him to Vietnam.

Powell served two tours of duty in Vietnam. During the first, in 1962 and 1963, he worked as adviser to a South Vietnamese army battalion in the A Shau Valley, one of the hottest areas of the war. His unit saw a great deal of action, and Powell suffered a wound from a Viet Cong booby trap. During his second Vietnam tour, in 1968 and 1969, Powell was already a major, senior enough to be a battalion executive officer. When the division's commander, Major General Charles Gettys, learned that Powell had been the second-ranking graduate of the Army's Command and General Staff College at Fort Leavenworth, he assigned Powell to be the staff operations officer for the entire division. Powell was successful in this position, but his tour of duty ended when he suffered a broken ankle in a helicopter crash. His two tours in Vietnam persuaded him that war must have clear political and military objectives and a definable end—a belief that would help to shape his later service.

After Vietnam, Powell served in a variety of military and political positions. His introduction to the civilian side of senior leadership occurred when he was awarded a White House Fellowship in 1972. These fellowships are awarded on a competitive basis to a select group of young professionals. Powell's assignment as a White House Fellow was to the Office of Management and Budget under Caspar Weinberger, who later became secretary of defense; Weinberger's deputy, Frank Carlucci, also later went on to become secretary of defense. Powell learned about budgeting, the importance of press relations, and, more generally, how to handle himself in the senior political world. The White House Fellowship marked Powell, both in the Army and in the government, as a rising young officer. The contacts he made at the Office of Management and Budget were also to serve him well in later years.

After his fellowship year, Powell received assignments of increasing responsibility. He commanded a brigade of the 101st Airborne Division in 1976 and 1977. He was military assistant to the deputy secretary of defense from 1979 to 1981 and to the secretary of defense from 1983 to 1986. Later in 1986, he was given overall command of the Army's V Corps in Europe. From 1987 to 1989, he served as President Ronald Reagan's National Security Adviser, working on the most delicate matters of national security policy. Among these were such issues as nuclear disarmament and the U.S. stance toward the dissolution of the Soviet Union. During his service as National Security Adviser, Powell continued to impress those with whom he was working, among them Vice President George Bush.

In 1988, Bush was elected to succeed Reagan, and he became president in January, 1989. Powell refused several jobs in the new administration, including that of director of the Central Intelligence Agency (CIA). He preferred to return to the Army, and he was promoted to full general and put in charge of Forces Command. Ten months later, when Admiral William Crowe retired as chairman of the Joint Chiefs of Staff, Powell was the obvious choice for the position. Although he was the most junior of the fifteen existing four-star generals, he had a unique combination of civilian and military service, a record of success in every job he had undertaken, and excellent personal and professional relations with other senior members of the defense and foreign-policy establishment. After a brief period of consideration, President Bush nominated him for the chairmanship, and the appointment was quickly confirmed by the Senate.

Powell's new job did not involve the direct command of troops. The chairman, however, is the head of the Joint Chiefs of Staff and the principal military adviser to the president and the secretary of defense. It is a unique position; the chairman has immense power and influence. Powell determined to use this influence to prevent unwise military entanglements—the lesson of Vietnam remained vivid to him—and to promote his conception of the size and organization of the U.S. military establishment in the wake of the Soviet collapse.

He had hardly settled into his new office when a crisis developed in Panama. The Bush Administration had been awaiting an opportunity to depose Panamanian president General Manuel Noriega, who was deeply involved in the international drug business. On Powell's second day in office, reports were received that an anti-Noriega coup was imminent. Should the United States enter the fray? Powell and his senior colleagues decided that the reports were too fragmentary and the probability of success too remote. In the event, they were proved right; the coup collapsed after only a few hours.

Two months later, however, after Panamanian soldiers shot and killed an American serviceman and beat another, the Bush Administration acted. U.S. forces invaded Panama, routed the Panamanian military, and captured Noriega within a few days. The operation was conducted in compliance with Powell's prerequisites for the use of U.S. forces: There must be attainable military objectives and a way out of the commitment after the objectives are achieved.

Powell's greatest accomplishment as chairman of the Joint Chiefs of Staff was the successful organization and implementation of U.S. strategy during the 1991 Persian Gulf War. On August 2, 1990, Saddam Hussein's Iraqi forces invaded Kuwait and threatened the security of Saudi Arabia. For a variety of reasons, President Bush determined that the United States could not tolerate these extensions of Iraqi power. The U.S. military response, code-named "Operation Desert Shield," began almost immediately, and American forces were sent to Saudi Arabia to protect it from a potential Iraqi attack. Within a few months, the American commitment of forces to Desert Shield amounted to nearly 250,000 troops. Simultaneous economic and diplomatic pressures were applied to Iraq in order to persuade Hussein to withdraw from Kuwait. When it became clear that these were not succeeding, Bush ordered preparations for "Operation Desert Storm"—the forcible expulsion of Iraqi troops from Kuwait—to begin. Overall responsibility for these operations fell to Colin Powell, and the buildup of U.S. forces continued. Eventually, half a million American troops reached Saudi Arabia, where they were joined by detachments sent by many U.S. allies, including a number of Arab countries.

Powell was instrumental in insisting to his superiors that the military and political objectives be clearly defined. Moreover, he worked closely with General Norman A. Schwarzkopf, the field commander, to assure that the strategy of attack did not involve costly frontal assaults on fortified positions. In January, 1991, air attacks began against Iraq and Iraqi forces. In February, a ground assault was launched. Four days of fighting were sufficient to clear Kuwait of the invaders and destroy most of Iraq's heavy armored divisions. President Bush, Secretary of Defense Dick Cheney, and Powell halted the war immediately thereafter to prevent further slaughter.

Powell's term as chairman lasted into the Bill Clinton Administration. When his term expired, he retired from the Army. In 1996, there was intense speculation about whether Powell would accept a vice-presidential nomination on the Republican presidential ticket, but he declined to be considered.

### Summary

Colin Powell's career has been marked by a number of notable achievements. He was the first African American to achieve the highest position in the U.S. military. Some observers pointed to Powell's success as a sign that racial barriers were continuing to disappear; others remarked that the rise of an African American to the very top of the military establishment was appropriate for an Army that is disproportionately black. Powell also helped to restore confidence and pride in the American armed forces, among both the general public and the troops themselves, as the Gulf War victory helped to assuage the bitterness that had been the legacy of Vietnam. For this, some of the credit belongs to Powell, one of the principal architects of the resounding victory. In addition, his efforts to reduce the size of America's standing forces in the wake of the Soviet Union's collapse met with general approval as an appropriate step toward a more realistic and affordable military policy for the United States. Finally, Powell's insistence that military objectives be defined and attainable helped to put national foreign policy on a more realistic basis.

### Bibliography

Alter, Jonathan. "Powell's New War." *Newsweek* 129, no. 17 (April 28, 1997). Examines Powell's participation in the President's Summit for America's Future, which will assist fifteen million U.S.children to become more employable.

Means, Howard. *Colin Powell: Soldier/Statesman, Statesman/Soldier.* New York: Fine, 1992. Although marred by minor factual errors, this biography is based on interviews with many of Powell's closest associates and friends. Contains numerous quotations.

Powell, Colin L., with Joseph E. Persico. *My American Journey.* New York: Random House, 1995. Powell's own summation of his life. Especially strong on the details of his military career. Although Powell was assisted by Joseph Persico, enough of his own character and personality come through to make the book worthwhile.

Romano, Gerry. "Never Walk Past a Mistake." *Association Management* 50, no. 10 (October, 1998). An interview with Powell in which he discusses his management principles and style.

Roth, David. *Sacred Honor: A Biography of Colin Powell.* San Francisco: HarperCollins, 1993. Roth, one of Powell's public affairs officers after the Gulf War, has prepared this admiring biography of the general. Contains discussions of Powell's character and religious views that are not found in other works about him.

Schwarzkopf, H. Norman. *It Doesn't Take a Hero.* New York and London: Bantam, 1992. General Schwarzkopf's autobiography is strong in its coverage of the relationship between the field commander—Schwarzkopf—and the overall strategist—Powell—in the planning and execution of the Gulf War, although Schwarzkopf naturally focuses on his own activities.

Woodward, Bob. *The Commanders.* New York: Simon and Schuster, 1991. Focuses on the decision-making process in Washington, especially regarding the Panamanian and Iraqi operations during Powell's tenure as chairman. Much of the material comes from anonymous sources.

*Robert Jacobs*

## LUDWIG PRANDTL

*Born:* February 4, 1875; Freising, Germany
*Died:* August 15, 1953; Göttingen, West Germany
*Areas of Achievement:* Physics and aerodynamics
*Contribution:* Prandtl was one of the fathers of theoretical aerodynamics and is credited with discovering many of the pivotal concepts upon which modern aviation is based. He was also the founder of the highly acclaimed school of aerodynamics and hydrodynamics at the University of Göttingen and the first director of what would become the Max Planck Institute for Fluid Mechanics.

### Early Life

Born in the town of Freising, Germany, on February 4, 1875, Ludwig Prandtl took an early interest in the forces and characteristics of nature as a result of the strong influence of his father, Alexander Prandtl, who was a professor of engineering at a college in Weihenstephan, Germany. Magdalene, Ludwig's mother, played a lesser role in her son's life because of her extended periods of chronic illness. Ludwig took an early interest in science and engineering, deciding in 1894 to study the latter as his major at the Munich Technische Hochschule, a facility for higher education at the time, comparable to a modern college or university. He successfully completed the course of study and, in 1898, went on to earn his doctorate in physics.

Prandtl's doctoral thesis, an experimental study in the distribution of tension and torque along a beam arranged at right angles from its source, became an important work in the field of the mechanics of solids. It was an indication of his exceptional abilities as a scientist that his first major paper—and one in an area that would be of peripheral interest in his later work—would generate significant interest from the contemporary scientific community.

His doctoral thesis and the help of his mentor, a noted German physicist, August Foppl, would earn for him a job upon graduation as an engineer in the Augsburg-Nürnberg Machine Factory. It was at the factory that Prandtl was introduced to the study of the characteristics of the flow of air over objects, otherwise known as fluid mechanics. This emerging science was in its infancy at the turn of the century, with the first practical wind tunnels and heavier-than-air craft only slowly coming into use. (Prandtl himself would later in his life be responsible for the construction of the first functional wind tunnel in Germany in 1909.) Prandtl's own introduction to the field came as a result of a project to refit a vacuum device used in the factory. Prandtl's work at the factory would be the last he would undertake outside the world of academia, but it led to his most important discoveries and to a brilliant career as a founder of an emerging modern science.

### Life's Work

In 1901, to allow him to continue his studies into fluid mechanics, Prandtl accepted a position as a professor at the Technische Schule in Hannover. His first observations at Hannover involved the flow of thin liquids through a pipe. He noticed that the shape of the liquid flow did not fully conform to the shape of the pipe through which it flowed. A minute layer of liquid, no matter how low in viscosity the substance, would always form between the interior surface of the pipe and the main body of the liquid. This layer between the wall and the fluid actually controlled the pressure of the liquid flow and, consequently, the rate of flow itself. In practical terms, this boundary of stationary fluid is much the same as the layer of air that forms on a wing or airfoil in flight. This boundary actually helps to provide the lift and drag of an air wing necessary to control its movement through the air. Prandtl's discovery of the boundary theory, as he named it, would be his single most meaningful discovery and would revolutionize powered aviation, leading to major innovations in the streamlining of aircraft wing and fuselage designs.

In 1904, shortly before Prandtl's publication of his paper on the boundary theory, he was invited to head a new Institute for Technical Physics at the University of Göttingen. The institute would serve as Prandtl's primary base of operations for the remainder of his life and would become one of the world's leading centers for theoretical research into fluid mechanics. At Göttingen, Prandtl addressed many of the theoretical questions about manned flight that were arising as a result of the breakthroughs in aviation technology. He conducted research into, among many subjects, the characteristics of airflow around a body traveling at either subsonic or supersonic speeds. He directed research projects by the institute's graduate students into wing drag, the mechanics of solids, and other areas. Part of his work during the years before World War I also involved developing testing procedures for electrical fans for the German government and in-

dustry. In 1909, Prandtl married Gertrude Foppl, the daughter of his former mentor August Foppl. The couple eventually had two daughters.

Prandtl's mathematical theories also played a significant part in the advent and popular acceptance of the single-winged airplane. He was himself an advocate of the controversial design concept, in direct conflict with the prevailing opinion held by the aircraft design community in favor of bi- and tri-winged aircraft. He also contributed through his theoretical discoveries to improvements in the design of lighter-than-air craft known as dirigibles, which were commonly in use in the early years of the century as both civilian and military air carriers.

After World War I, in 1918-1919, Prandtl published a breakthrough paper on the way in which air flows around airplane wings of a finite span. The paper, which duplicated and expanded on work done simultaneously by a British physicist named Frederick W. Lanchester, became known as the Lanchester-Prandtl wing theory, one of many theoretical innovations that would bear Prandtl's name over the next several years.

In the mid-1920's, Prandtl and other researchers in Göttingen and elsewhere undertook the study of air turbulence created by a body moving through the air. In conjunction with another scientist, Theodor von Kármán, a former student of Prandtl, he developed a device for analyzing the distance turbulent air travels before its motion is dissipated. Prandtl's paper on the subject, presented in 1933, led to radical changes in accepted theories about air turbulence and to concepts used by pilots around the world. Prandtl also conducted extensive studies into the question of how objects traveling at high subsonic speeds are compressed by the air flow over their surfaces. This theory, known as the Prandtl-Glaubert rule, along with his other research into supersonic airflow, played a vital role in developing successful designs for supersonic aircraft.

During the same period, Prandtl, already a world-renowned pioneer in his field, was named to head a technical facility in Germany that would later be known as the Max Planck Institute for Fluid Mechanics. Part of this facility, following Prandtl's leadership and inspiration, would later become a major engineering design center and, in the 1970's and 1980's, an important contributor of spaceflight hardware and support services to the National Aeronautics and Space Administration (NASA) of the United States and to the European Space Agency.

Although it was not his area of primary investigation, Prandtl was also interested in questions concerning the elasticity and plasticity of a variety of solids, and the reaction of solid structures to torsion forces. In the latter, he developed a soap-film analogy that was found to be exceptionally useful in analyzing the effects of torsion forces on structures with noncircular cross sections. Prandtl's work often centered on the equipment and mathematical models for use in testing natural reactions and design concepts. Such devices include the tubes that bear his name used in the measurement of the static and complete pressure of a liquid flow at any point. He was also instrumental in advancing the development of air-tunnel technology and other equipment used in aerodynamic testing and design.

Unlike many of the scientists in Germany during the years between World War I and the end of World War II, Prandtl managed to avoid responding to political pressure from the ruling Nazi Party and to maintain civilian control over his work. He also continued to publish technical papers on his work regularly and to receive widespread attention from the international scientific community. In later years, after World War II, Prandtl expanded his efforts to include meteorology, a subject on which he published a paper in 1950. On August 15, 1953, Prandtl died in Göttingen, West Germany.

### Summary

Ludwig Prandtl was one of a generation of scientific pioneers whose practical innovations during and after the Industrial Revolution made possible many of the conveniences known to modern mankind. As the father of several pivotal theories of fluid mechanics used in the production of aircraft, he helped create the age of rapid, safe air transportation. Prandtl is known as the father of aerodynamics, because he developed some of the fundamental concepts upon which modern air travel is based. There is, however, much more to his story than the list of his singular accomplishments. Prandtl both developed numerous theories and helped create much of the basic methodology used by both his own students and others in the generation of physicists who followed him. Men such as Kármán, although only slightly younger than Prandtl, owed much of their understanding of how to approach theoretical problems to the training and example of Prandtl. Prandtl's contributions extend into education as well as science. He helped build two institutions, the Institute for Technical Physics at the University of Göttingen and the Max Planck Institute for Fluid Mechanics, both of which have made significant contributions to science during and after Prandtl's time.

Beyond his accomplishments, Prandtl was one of a class of scientists in the late nineteenth and early to mid-twentieth centuries who possessed an extraordinarily single-minded drive to advance their areas of investigation. Konstantin Tsiolkovsky in Russia, Pierre and Marie Curie in France, and Robert Hutchings Goddard in the United States were chronologic and spiritual contemporaries of Prandtl, who worked not only to solve individual scientific questions but also to create a new field of study and to advance the broader body of mankind's knowledge. It was the collegial perspective that also helped build an international scientific community that could coordinate and fully exploit limited financial, human, and natural resources to the best, most productive end.

As part of this community, Prandtl focused his efforts on practical, technological questions, the solutions for which could be put to direct use in aircraft design and other areas. Prandtl and his contemporaries were part of the modern class of scientists who used their studies to solve problems that derived from practical, secular needs. In this regard, Prandtl's discoveries are every bit as significant as those of more visible inventors such as Orville and Wilbur Wright.

### Bibliography

Lienhard, John H. "Ludwig Prandtl." In *Dictionary of Scientific Biography*, edited by Charles Coulston Gillispie, vol. 11. New York: Scribner, 1975. This reference series includes concise, well-written biographies of many scientific figures. Listings are generally confined to basic facts about the individual's life and works, with minimal coverage of the motives or reasons behind the person's work.

Liepmann, H. W., and A. Roshko. *Elements of Gasdynamics.* New York: Wiley, 1957. This book illustrates the role that Prandtl played in the theory of compressible flow.

Prandtl, Ludwig. *Applied Hydro- and Aeromechanics: Based on Lectures of Ludwig Prandtl.* Translated by J. P. Den-Hartog. New York and London: McGraw-Hill, 1934. This collection of technical lectures given by Prandtl is one of the earliest English-language versions of his works still readily available.

———. *Essentials of Fluid Dynamics, with Applications to Hydraulics, Aeronautics, Meteorology, and Other Subjects.* London: Blackie, and New York: Hafner, 1952. This technical volume provides an in-depth look at Prandtl's work in fluid dynamics and other areas of interest to him throughout his long career. One of the few more readily available English-language works of Prandtl.

Schlichting, Hermann. *Boundary Layer Theory.* Translated by J. Kestin. 4th ed. New York: McGraw-Hill, 1960. This work includes many references to Prandtl and to his students. Contains a good discussion of his involvement in the viscous flow theory.

Sundaram, T. R. "The Father of Aerodynamics." *World and I* 12, no. 11 (November, 1997). Profile of Prandtl, his early work in air flow modeling, boundary layer theory, and his later career.

———. "Friends and Foes." *World and I* 12, no. 11 (November, 1997). Focuses on Prandtl's relationship with Theodore von Karman.

*Eric Christensen*

# ELVIS PRESLEY

*Born:* January 8, 1935; Tupelo, Mississippi
*Died:* August 16, 1977; Memphis, Tennessee
*Area of Achievement:* Music
*Contribution:* Fusing the legacies of black and white American music, Presley helped create the cultural phenomenon of rock and roll and became its most famous and influential performer.

## Early Life

Elvis Aron Presley was the son of Gladys and Vernon Presley; his twin brother, Jesse Garon Presley, died at birth and was buried in an unmarked grave in a local cemetery. There were no other children in the Presley family, and Elvis grew up especially close to his mother. His father held a variety of jobs, none very successfully, and served time in the state penitentiary for check forgery. While not actually poverty-stricken, the Presley family was poor.

In 1948, they moved to Memphis, Tennessee. Presley had already demonstrated a talent for singing, particularly in church, and in Memphis he won first place at his high school's annual variety show. He had already assimilated much of the rich musical tradition of the South: the blues and spirituals; gospel and country music, some of it reaching back to the English folk tradition; and contemporary American song, including jazz and the first stirrings of what he would help transform into rock and roll. With no formal training, Presley combined these varied influences through his inborn gifts.

After high school, Presley became a truck driver for the Crown Electric Company in Memphis. In 1953, he paid to record a single at a local studio; Sam Phillips, the owner of Sun Records, heard this single and recognized the immense talent Elvis possessed. In July, 1954, Presley recorded his first commercial tapes with Phillips for Sun Records in Memphis.

As he began his career, Presley was of average height, and his dark hair was worn rather long for the period, with sideburns. He had full lips, which would later become famous for his "sneer," a slight lifting as he talked or sang. His eyes were dark, penetrating, and heavy-lidded. As he grew older, he would have increasing problems with his weight. When he performed, he moved freely, even wildly, about the stage; his pronounced hip movements while singing earned for him the nickname "Elvis the Pelvis." His most remarkable characteristics were his fine singing voice and his intense, charismatic presence.

## Life's Work

For Sun, Presley recorded a song called "That's All Right Mama," which was released in July, 1954. Played on the local radio stations, it became an immediate hit. Other records followed, equally successful, and Presley rapidly became a regional sensation. In 1955, Phillips sold his contract with Presley to Radio Corporation of America (RCA), and Colonel Tom Parker became Elvis' manager; Parker would retain almost complete control of all financial matters until long after Presley's death.

Presley's fame spread rapidly as more and more radio stations aired his records, and his recognition spread beyond the South. He appeared on major television shows, including the Dorsey brothers' *Stage Show*, the *Milton Berle Show*, and the *Steve Allen Show*. His real explosion into national prominence came with his three appearances on the popular *Ed Sullivan Show*, between September 8, 1956, and January 6, 1957. In the last of these, Presley was shown only from the waist up, to avoid complaints over his wild gyrations. Older viewers were astonished, younger ones delighted, and almost everyone recognized that a new era in popular music had been inaugurated by this skinny Southern boy.

The years between 1955 and 1958 were the most creative and important of Presley's career. It was during this time that he recorded music the likes of which had never been heard before, and which transformed American popular songs. Violence, tragedy, and lost love mingled with unlimited promise and undefeated optimism in these songs, as Presley's remarkable performances drew upon the musical heritage he had known and then transcended it. His immensely popular recordings included "Mystery Train," "Heartbreak Hotel," "Blue Suede Shoes," "Shake, Rattle and Roll," "Teddy Bear," and what became the song most closely associated with him, "Hound Dog." The pulsing, infectious rhythm of these songs, a combination of all the songs and singers Presley had known growing up in the South, swept across the country with unprecedented popularity.

Such popularity was soon translated into films. Presley signed a contract with Hal Wallis of Paramount Studios, and, in 1956, he began filming

*Love Me Tender*, the first of his thirty-three films. His early films were his best, especially *Jailhouse Rock* (1957), a gritty film which used prison as a metaphor for the fate of the popular artist, and *King Creole* (1958), in which Presley was given the opportunity to display his real, if limited, dramatic abilities. His later films were repetitious in plot and mechanical in production; they were always set in some exotic location—Hawaii, Arabia, Las Vegas—and used a breezy, romantic story line on which to hang a half dozen forgettable songs. These songs were written specifically for the films and were far removed from the energetic recordings of Presley's first years as an artist.

In 1957, Presley received his induction notice from the Memphis draft board, and in March, 1958, he entered the United States Army. While stationed at Fort Hood, Texas, for his basic training, Presley received emergency leave to visit his mother in a Memphis hospital. Gladys Presley died on August 14, 1958, at the age of forty-six. The cause of death was a heart attack, complicated by hepatitis. His mother's death was a severe blow to Presley. The huge mansion he had built for her in Memphis, Graceland, would be his home for the remainder of his life.

Stationed in Germany, Presley met Priscilla Beaulieu, the teenage daughter of a career army officer. They began dating, and after his duty in the service, Presley convinced the Beaulieus to permit Priscilla to move into Graceland. His grandmother served as chaperone while Priscilla completed high school. Presley and Priscilla were married on May 1, 1967, in Las Vegas, Nevada. Nine months later, on February 1, 1968, their daughter and only child, Lisa Marie Presley, was born.

Presley was discharged from the army in March, 1960. There was some concern that his absence from the musical scene would have erased or diluted his popularity, but his reception by two thousand fans at Fort Dix, New Jersey, was an indication that such fears were groundless. He was soon in the studio recording new tracks for an album, and he appeared in a television special entitled *Frank Sinatra's Welcome Home Party for Elvis Presley*. It was soon apparent that Presley's time in the army had not weakened his hold on the popular imagination.

Changes were made, however, under the direction of Presley's manager, Parker. In March, 1961, Presley gave a memorial concert; it would be his last for eight years. Instead of live appearances, he concentrated on films, making an average of two a year. His records consisted mostly of songs written for the films—the title track and a variety of forgettable tunes. On occasion, he recorded some gospel albums, such as the powerful *How Great Thou Art* (1967), which demonstrated his mastery of that musical genre. The RCA record label also released collections of his best-selling hits.

During the 1960's, however, Presley displayed none of the galvanic, revolutionary musical energy that had captured the attention of millions at the start of his career. That energy still had its effect, however, as an entire generation of performers, American and British, followed in his path. Groups such as the Beatles and the Rolling Stones, and individual artists such as Bob Dylan, expanded in their own ways the musical frontier which Presley had first marked out. Ironically, the originator of this movement was conspicuous by his absence.

In 1968, Presley returned to public performances. He first recorded a television program called, simply enough, *Elvis*. The success of the program led to live appearances in resort hotels in Las Vegas and a series of concert tours across the United States. The act Presley presented in these concerts was totally different from that of his early days: He now had a large, carefully rehearsed orchestra, sizable numbers of background singers, and increasingly elaborate costumes. His popularity, always high, increased; his records began to appear at the top of the music charts for the first time since the early 1960's. In 1973, his television special *Elvis: Aloha from Hawaii via Satellite* was broadcast to forty countries throughout the world.

During the 1970's, Presley toured heavily, as well as performing regularly in Las Vegas. In part because of his schedule, in part for personal reasons, the Presley marriage deteriorated, and on August 18, 1972, Presley filed for divorce on the grounds of irreconcilable differences. The divorce was granted on October 9, 1973.

Over the years, Presley had come to rely increasingly on a wide variety of drugs: stimulants for the concerts, depressants for sleep, painkillers for comfort. His behavior became occasionally erratic and irrational, and at times, even violent. He took to carrying pistols and other weapons, insulting or attacking longtime friends, and afterward presenting them with automobiles or other expensive gifts. Some attributed these actions to regret over the failure of his marriage or to a long-standing depression at the death of his mother; other observers blamed the peculiar lifestyle imposed upon such a hugely popular entertainer, or the influence of drugs.

Despite these problems, and perhaps to avoid them, Presley continued to tour. In the summer of 1977, he planned another national circuit, to begin with a concert on August 17. On the afternoon of August 16, Presley was discovered unconscious in a bathroom of Graceland. Efforts by paramedics at the mansion failed to revive him, as did further attempts by doctors at Baptist Memorial Hospital. Although his death was apparently drug-related, the official statement gave the cause as heart disease.

His body was viewed by thousands as he lay in state in his mansion, and thousands more formed the miles-long procession to the cemetery. His body was later moved to Graceland, where he was buried beside his mother. Elvis Presley was forty-two years old when he died.

### Summary

The career of Elvis Presley and his impact on modern culture transcend the outlines of biography and defy analysis. Rising from poverty and obscurity, Presley became a major force in shaping contemporary popular music; indeed, for some, he was the essential inspiration and source of rock and roll. While this claim may be extreme, there is little doubt that Presley was the focus that brought together the various traditions which united to produce America's most energetic and perhaps most typical music.

With his background in Southern gospel, black soul and blues, and traditional country music, Presley was able to forge something new yet totally familiar. His music was instantly recognized as the work of genius, even if the work was denounced as obscene or attacked as primitive. In its truest sense, it was primitive, because it went to the very roots of American culture.

President Jimmy Carter attempted to express this feeling in his tribute to Presley when he said that his music and his personality, fusing the styles of white country and black rhythm and blues, permanently changed the face of American popular culture. His following was immense and he was a symbol to people the world over of the vitality, rebelliousness, and good humor of his country.

Perhaps the truest summary came from rock and roll critic Greil Marcus, who wrote of the relationship between the performer and the United States: "At his best Elvis not only embodies but personalizes so much of what is good about this place."

Presley's impact is even more remarkable when it is noted that his period of truly creative work fell within the relatively short period of the late 1950's. During these years, he recorded his most memorable and influential songs, the songs for which he will always be remembered. The path to both Woodstock and Abbey Road begins at Sun Records in Memphis. This period ended with his induction into the army; following his return to civilian life, Presley spent most of the 1960's making films and recording sound tracks; he remained popular but distant from his public. It was not until 1968 that he staged a triumphant comeback and resumed live performances. Clearly, however, he had either lost or muted his energy and his unpredictable, even dangerous, appeal. Just as clearly, it made little difference, for his image had become reality to his fans.

Presley was undoubtedly the most famous entertainer in the world, known to millions only as Elvis. Others knew him as The King, perhaps of rock and roll, perhaps of entertainment, and perhaps, in some mysterious way, king of the complex experience of America itself, which he summed up so well in his performances and his presence.

### Bibliography

Cotten, Lee. *All Shook Up: Elvis Day-by-Day, 1954-1977.* Ann Arbor, Mich.: Pierian Press, 1985. An exhaustive chronology of Presley's activities during his career. Proof that Presley was undoubtedly the most closely observed of contemporary performers.

Dundy, Elaine. *Elvis and Gladys.* New York: Macmillan, and London: Weidenfeld and Nicolson, 1985. The influence of Gladys Presley on her son, and his relationship to her, has been an issue which has always fascinated both fans and more neutral observers. This book gives a generally balanced account.

Goldman, Albert. *Elvis.* New York: McGraw-Hill, 1981; London: Penguin, 1982. A long, unfriendly look at Presley—the man, the performer, and the music. Although Goldman seems to have done extensive research, his dislike for his subject is apparent on every page.

Hopkins, Jerry. *Elvis: A Biography.* New York: Simon and Schuster, 1971; London: Open Gate, 1972. A well-researched, solid life of Presley, good especially for his early life and his career from the years with Sun Records to his semiseclusion in the 1960's. Contains much useful information.

———. *Elvis: The Final Years.* New York: St. Martin's Press, and London: Allen, 1980. Takes up where Hopkins' earlier book left off, and completes the life. The work is carefully documented and free of sensationalism.

Marcus, Greil. *Dead Elvis: A Chronicle of a Cultural Obsession.* New York and London: Viking Press, 1991. The author examines the continuing fascination with Presley after his death.

———. *Mystery Train.* 4th ed. London: Penguin, 1991; New York: Plume, 1997. In general, this is one of the best books yet written about rock and roll, and the section on Presley is a sharp, penetrating analysis of both the individual performer and his place in modern American music.

Miller, Jim, ed. *The Rolling Stone Illustrated History of Rock and Roll.* Rev. ed. New York: Random House, 1980; London: Pan, 1981. The article on Presley by Peter Guralnick is a well-balanced and informative survey of the performer's career and influence and provides an excellent, short biography.

Opdyke, Steven. *The Printed Elvis: The Complete Guide to Books about the King.* Westport, Conn.: Greenwood Press, 1999. An annotated guide to more than 400 books written about Presley.

*Michael Witkoski*

# LEONTYNE PRICE

*Born:* February 10, 1927; Laurel, Mississippi
*Area of Achievement:* Music
*Contribution:* Internationally acclaimed soprano of the operatic and concert stage, Leontyne Price paved the way for many subsequent black classical performers. The fifth black singer to appear at the Metropolitan Opera, she was the first to sustain a long career there. During her thirty-four-year history at the Met, she became the most sought after prima donna at the opera house.

## Early Life

Mary Violet Leontine Price was born to James Anthony and Katherine Baker Price on February 10, 1927, in the city of Laurel, a county seat in southeastern Mississippi. In college, she changed the spelling of her name to Leontyne. The Prices' family life was centered around the church where Leontyne and her brother George spent much of their time. Music was always an integral part of home and church life. Leontyne's father played tuba in the church band, and her mother sang in St. Paul's choir. Leontyne exhibited unusual musical instincts at an early age and her mother immediately sought musical training for her. At three-and-one-half years old, Leontyne began piano lessons with the local music teacher, Mrs. Hattie V. J. McInnis. In school, she sang in choral groups and as school soloist while also excelling in dance and acrobatics. By age eleven, she played regularly for Sunday school and church services.

The first major event that affected Leontyne's future musical career was a trip to Jackson, Mississippi, to hear a concert by the black contralto, Marian Anderson. Impressed by the beauty and power of communication of Anderson's voice, nine-year-old Leontyne at once aspired to a stage career. Her first solo concert was performed on December 17, 1943, in Sandy Gavin School Auditorium, where she played classical piano selections and sang for an audience that demanded several curtain calls.

Leontyne attended Oak Park Vocational High School in Laurel and continued to perform both as a singer and as pianist for the school choirs. Upon graduation, Leontyne won a four-year scholarship to Central State College in Wilberforce, Ohio. She was graduated from Wilberforce in 1948 certified to teach public school music. Recognizing her remarkable gift, however, her teachers had encouraged Leontyne to pursue a performance career. With the advice of her voice teacher, Catherine Van Buren, and the college's president, Dr. Charles Wesley, she obtained a full scholarship to attend the Juilliard School of Music in New York. Additional money for living expenses was contributed by Elizabeth Chisholm, a musician and wealthy white resident of Laurel for whom Leontyne's aunt worked. Mrs. Chisholm had recognized the girl's talent and often paid Leontyne to entertain for occasions in her home. Even when financial support was no longer needed, she remained a lifelong friend and patron. Another important contributor to Price's scholarship fund was celebrated baritone Paul Robeson, who, after hearing Leontyne sing, agreed to perform a benefit concert in Dayton Memorial Hall. She also appeared on this concert program, from which $1,000 was raised for her education.

## Life's Work

Leontyne Price entered Juilliard in 1948 and was placed in the voice studio of Florence Page Kimball. Kimball remained a friend, adviser, and voice coach long after her student left Juilliard. It is she whom Price credits for her basic knowledge of vocal technique. Several milestones in Price's career came as a result of her Juilliard work. In 1952, Price was cast in her first major operatic role as Mistress Ford in the Juilliard production of Giuseppe Verdi's *Falstaff*. At these performances, the soprano was heard by numerous important musicians. Virgil Thomson, a noted composer and music critic, was assembling a cast for an International Music Festival production of his opera *Four Saints in Three Acts*. Price was chosen to sing St. Cecilia at the opera's New York opening and later in Paris, marking the beginning of her international appearances. Robert Breen and Blevins Davis were also present at her Juilliard performance in *Falstaff* and immediately offered her a contract as Bess in the 1952 revival of George Gershwin's opera *Porgy and Bess*. *Porgy and Bess* made an international tour sponsored by the U.S. State Department and, in 1953, was produced on Broadway. Price remained with the cast for two years and received wide acclaim for her portrayal of Bess. During the rehearsals for *Porgy and Bess*, Price met baritone William Warfield, who portrayed Porgy. On August 31, 1952, the couple was married. Sadly, professional demands on the two performers over-

whelmed the relationship, and they separated physically in 1959, not to separate legally until 1967. They remained friends, however, as well as mutually supportive colleagues.

American composer Nicolas Nabokov, who was also impressed with Price's *Falstaff* performance, introduced her to one of the most influential figures of her professional life—composer and pianist Samuel Barber. Barber heard Price in a performance of *Porgy and Bess* in 1953 when composing his cycle of *Hermit Songs*, and he completed them with Price's voice in mind. He accompanied her when she sang them for the first time at the Library of Congress in Washington, D.C., and later the same year at the Twentieth Century Music Conference in Rome. He then arranged for her to sing his *Prayers of Kierkegaard* in her debut with the Boston Symphony Orchestra. In 1954, Barber was also pianist for the *Hermit Songs* during Price's Town Hall debut recital in New York. This long and valuable association continued throughout their careers.

The year 1955 marked the most radical turning point in Price's career. Upon hearing her in *Porgy and Bess*, Peter Herman Adler cast Price in the role of Floria Tosca in the NBC Opera Company production of *Tosca*, breaking the color barrier in the operatic world, especially in the United States. Although not carried by twelve NBC affiliate stations in the South, the production was still a major success, and the young black soprano was no longer an unknown to the operatic world.

Following *Tosca*, Price's career opportunities multiplied rapidly. She signed a management contract with André Mertens of Columbia Artist Management, who introduced her to conductor Herbert von Karajan. Karajan, then conductor of the Berlin Philharmonic, introduced Price to European opera audiences. After she refused his offer to sing the demanding title role in *Salomé* by Richard Strauss, he presented her instead in a production of Giuseppe Verdi's *Aida* with the Vienna State Opera in 1959, in which she was an enormous success as the Egyptian princess. Just prior to singing Aida, Price made her American operatic stage debut on September 20, 1957, with the San Francisco Opera as Madame Liodine in Francis Poulenc's *Dialogues of the Carmelites*. She continued to appear in San Francisco throughout her career and performances included roles in *Aida* and *Il Trovatore* by Verdi, Carl Orff's *The Wise Maiden*, and as Donna Anna in Wolfgang Amadeus Mozart's *Don Giovanni*. She also appeared in the title role in Jules Massenet's *Thaïs* and as Liù in Giacomo Puccini's *Turandot* at the Lyric Opera of Chicago in 1959.

Leontyne Price was becoming known the world over for her ravishing, warm lyric soprano voice that proved to be the perfect instrument for the works of Verdi and Puccini. She became the most celebrated Verdi singer of her era. The role of Aida, especially, became synonymous with Price, not only for the ethnic heritage that helped make her ideal for the role but also because of the sumptuous quality of her voice, which was able to soar with the drama. When approached by the Metropolitan Opera in 1961, after several previous attempts to schedule a debut performance for her had failed, she chose to portray Leonora in Verdi's *Il Trovatore* so as to avoid making her debut in what the public might interpret as a role for "black sopranos." Her debut, with its forty-five-minute ovation, made sensational headlines. Price sang five major roles with the Metropolitan Opera in her first season—Leonora (*Il Trovatore*), Aida (*Aida*), Donna Anna (*Don Giovanni*), Cio-Cio-San in Puccini's *Madama Butterfly*, and Liù in *Turandot*. Although Price's voice was recognized as lighter in quality than voices of singers often heard in those roles, it had a special quality that projected a highly charged emotional element and adequate power to fill the opera house. In 1962, she had the honor of singing the opening night of a new production of Puccini's *The Golden Girl of the West*. She continued to sing with the Met and in Chicago, San Francisco, Paris, Cologne, Berlin, and the Soviet Union. In 1964, Leontyne Price was doubly honored for her work: She received a Spingarn Medal from the National Association for the Advancement of Colored People (NAACP), and President Lyndon B. Johnson awarded her the Presidential Medal of Freedom.

The highest honor in Leontyne Price's career came in 1966 when she was chosen to star in Samuel Barber's opera, *Antony and Cleopatra*, which had been commissioned for the opening of the new Metropolitan Opera House at Lincoln Center for the Performing Arts in New York. Barber wrote the role of Cleopatra especially for Price, and the music was ideally suited to her voice. Reviews of the performance were mixed as a result of production problems attributed to designer Franco Zeffirelli; nevertheless, references to Price's singing of Cleopatra were glowing. Her repertoire began to include new roles such as Fiordiligi in Mozart's *Cosí fan tutte*, Ariadne in Richard Strauss's *Ariadne auf Naxos*, and Manon in Puccini's *Manon Lescaut*.

In 1985, Price retired from the operatic stage in order to devote more time to concerts, recitals, and master classes while her talent was still at its peak. Appropriately, she chose Aida for her farewell role. Her personal identification with the role focused upon freedom and loyalty to family and country created a special attachment for her to Aida. On January 4, 1985, she had the distinction of singing her last performance as a live telecast from the stage of the Metropolitan Opera.

In addition to opera, oratorio, and recital performances, Price maintained an active recording schedule throughout her career. All of her major roles have been recorded, and more than ten of these recordings earned Grammy Awards.

### Summary

Leontyne Price was recognized first for her extraordinary artistry and additionally for the exposure she afforded other African American singers as a result of opening many doors that had previously been closed to them throughout the world. Price was acutely aware of her black heritage and made careful decisions about career issues that she believed would ultimately make life better for minorities. She had friends among the major civil rights leaders of the United States such as Martin Luther King, Jr., and Robert F. Kennedy and supported and worked through organizations such as the American Civil Liberties Union and the NAACP. In 1969, Rust College in Mississippi (where her mother attended school) named a new library in honor of her.

Leontyne Price was the most celebrated American diva of her time. Her presence was demanded on stages internationally. She treated her artistic gift with great respect, using it to communicate messages of love, beauty, and freedom to people all over the world. As an American, as a black woman, and as a consummate artist, she charted new courses and earned the admiration of all who knew her work.

### Bibliography

Garland, Phyl. "Leontyne Price: Getting out at the Top." *Ebony* 40 (June, 1985): 31-34. In an intimate interview, Garland explores Price's background, career, and plans following her operatic retirement.

Hughes, Langston, and Milton Meltzer. *Black Magic: A Pictorial History of the Negro in American Entertainment*. Englewood Cliffs, N.J.: Prentice-Hall, 1967. A detailed history, written by noted author Langston Hughes, includes Price among famous African American artists that have made significant contributions to the field of American entertainment.

Jackson, Jacquelyn. "Leontyne Price." In *Epic Lives: One Hundred Black Women Who Made a Difference*, edited by Jessie Carney Smith. Detroit: Visible Ink Press, 1993. This profile, included as part of a select collection on prominent African American women, provides a concise overview of Price's life and accomplishments. Price's appearance in this collection places her within the broader historical context of achievements by women who struggled to overcome unfair limitations placed upon them because of their gender and their race.

Jacobson, Robert. "Collard Greens to Caviar." *Opera News* 50 (July/August, 1985): 18-23, 28-33. Following her farewell appearance at the Metropolitan Opera, Price discusses at length various aspects of her career and personal life, projecting plans for her future.

Lyon, Hugh L. *Leontyne Price: Highlights of a Prima Donna*. New York: Vantage Press, 1973. This thorough biography of Price is filled with personal and professional details which give the reader an understanding of her artistic development as well as a sense of the soprano as a warm, generous personality.

Price, Reynold. "Bouquet for Leontyne." *Opera News* 59, no. 14 (April 1, 1995). Tribute to the voice and career of Price, who, the author argues, is not properly appreciated in the United States.

Roach, Ronald, and Max Taylor. "The Price of Operatic Success." *Black Issues in Higher Education* 15, no. 20 (November 26, 1998). The authors report on a master's class in voice given at Harvard University by Price.

Sargeant, Winthrop. *Divas*. New York: Coward McCann, 1973. Sargeant devotes separate chapters to the lives and professional accomplishments of Leontyne Price, as well as Marilyn Horne, Beverly Sills, Birgit Nilsson, Joan Sutherland, and Eileen Farrell.

Story, Rosalyn M. *And So I Sing: African-American Divas of Opera and Concert*. New York: Warner, 1990. A comprehensive historical view of African American divas, this book includes information from research and personal interviews with a separate chapter on Price.

*Sandra C. McClain*

## SERGEI PROKOFIEV

*Born:* April 23, 1891; Sontsovka, Ukraine, Russian Empire

*Died:* March 5, 1953; Moscow, U.S.S.R.

*Area of Achievement:* Music

*Contribution:* Prokofiev is one of the two most successful Soviet composers of the twentieth century; he also ranks with the half dozen leading composers of the century. Although he first gained notice as an extraordinary pianist, he eventually created masterpieces in most major musical forms; in particular, in *Peter and the Wolf*, *Alexander Nevsky*, and *Romeo and Juliet*, he wrote three of the most celebrated works of his time.

### Early Life

Sergei Prokofiev was born on April 23, 1891, on an isolated estate in the remote Ukraine, where his father managed agricultural production. Born to his parents only after fourteen years of marriage and two earlier pregnancies that had failed, Prokofiev experienced both the advantages and the disadvantages of an only and long-desired child. He enjoyed much attention, stimulating his creativity; he was treated overindulgently, which made him self-centered and demanding. Because of the remoteness of the area, all of his early education was at home, supplemented by summer excursions to Moscow and especially St. Petersburg, his mother's family home, one marked by intellectual upward striving. An enthusiastic amateur pianist herself—she played regularly for her unborn child—she was overjoyed when her five-year-old son said that he wanted to learn the piano. Shortly thereafter he declared that he wanted to write his own music; he proceeded to do so, inventing his own notation in the process. Yet, although his family encouraged this musical precocity, his father insisted that he acquire a rigorous standard academic background. At nine, his parents took him to his first opera; he returned home to write and stage his own opera, with neighbor children and servants taking the roles. The following year he was introduced to the head of the Moscow Conservatory, who recommended that a professional tutor be hired to teach him the fundamentals of composition and theory.

At considerable sacrifice, his parents decided to follow this advice. For two summers, beginning in 1902, they hired the young composer Reinhold Gliere, who proved the perfect mentor for a talented child for whom music was both a complex mathematical game and the basis of a spectacle. At the same time, his father continued to insist on his general education. His mother, however, determined that he was destined for music; from this point she managed his education so that he would qualify for admission to the St. Petersburg Conservatory, the most prestigious in the country, at the earliest possible moment. He took the examinations in August, 1904, and was admitted at the age of thirteen. He would remain there for ten years, though he would gain his first degree in 1911.

As a student, Prokofiev was both precocious and obnoxious; he early formed the habit of doing his exercise compositions the way his professors insisted he do them, while working on his own compositions in private. Entering the conservatory as a prodigy of sorts did little for his social development; in fact, for a while it intensified his obstinacy and irritability, since he felt different from everyone else. Still, Prokofiev grew up at the conservatory, both socially and musically. Socially, he passed through adolescence there, developing a fondness for women, with whom he always got along better than men. Musically, he was instructed by Aleksandr Glazunov, Nikolai Tcherepnin, and Nikolay Rimsky-Korsakov, among others. He largely ignored them, however, concentrating more on developing a reputation as a spoiled prodigy. Within four years, he was performing his own compositions in conservatory and city concert series. He became a sensation; no other conservatory student gained public notice at such an early age. His remaining years as a student saw him building on his early successes. When he left in 1914, he was ready to step into the front ranks of performers and composers.

### Life's Work

Before Prokofiev left the conservatory at the age of twenty-three, he had already begun his career as a published composer and had gained a national reputation as a performer. His list of compositions was already impressive: He had before graduation completed a number of piano pieces, including a set of études and three sonatas; two chamber works; a fairy tale for voice and piano; two sets of songs; a sinfonietta; two symphonic sketches; two piano concerti; and an opera. Not all of these saw publication, but the list is intimidating and ambitious.

Yet at that point his celebrity was primarily as a performer. He had premiered both of his piano concerti in Moscow and St. Petersburg, causing a sensation with each appearance. These were the most controversial entrances onto the Russian musical scene of the period; single-handedly they catapulted Russian music into the twentieth century. To be sure, he was following the lead of Stravinsky, who had caused a riot with the premiere of *The Rite of Spring* in 1912; that was in Paris, however, and besides Stravinsky had turned his back on Russia. Prokofiev brought the modernist revolution to Russia.

During the four years following—the years of the outbreak first of World War I and then of the Russian revolutions—Prokofiev consolidated his position. Just prior to the beginning of hostilities, Prokofiev toured Europe, in the course of which he met Sergei Diaghilev, the famous impresario of the Ballets Russes and the primary vector of the modernist movement in Paris; he also introduced both his performance technique and his music to Europe. After hearing the Paris premiere of the second piano concerto, Diaghilev commissioned a ballet score from the young composer. Prokofiev completed a version within a year, but it proved unsatisfactory, whereupon Diaghilev commissioned another. This became *The Buffoon*, which he finished quickly. Simultaneously he developed the *Scythian Suite* out of the rejected ballet, and this was a triumph. He also finished a second opera, *The Gambler*, based on a Fyodor Dostoevski novel but unproduced until 1929; a first symphony, the *Classical*, a sensation then and popular ever since; a first violin concerto, another success; two more piano sonatas; two sets of songs; and a cantata. Yet making a living through music in war- and revolution-afflicted Russia was dubious at best, and in 1918 Prokofiev decided to leave for the West. His visit—intended at first to last only a few months—extended in the end to seventeen years.

Those years constitute Prokofiev's middle period, during which he gradually shed his bad-boy image and established his position as one of the world's leading composers. During that period, he tried living in a variety of places before finally settling on Paris. Before leaving Russia he had introduced his *Classical* symphony (No. 1), modeled on his notion of what Joseph Haydn might have done with the harmonic modifications of the twentieth century. Because of the turmoil in Europe, he traveled across Siberia, itself in disarray because of the revolution; from Japan, where he concertized to replenish his finances, he sailed to the United States. He spent most of the following three and a half years in that country, performing often, introducing his works as he composed them, but getting mixed responses—regularly cool in New York and hot in Chicago. He also traveled to the Continent, where he renewed connections with Diaghilev. The major achievements of his American years were the opera *Love for Three Oranges*, which is still performed and from which a more popular suite was extracted; the ballet *The Buffoon*; and the Third Piano Concerto.

From 1922 to late 1935, Prokofiev lived in Europe, for two years in Austria and then semipermanently in Paris. In 1923, he married Lina Codina, a young American singer of Cuban, Spanish, and Polish background whom he had met in New York in 1918 and with whom he had often performed. The couple had two sons, both born in Paris, Sviatislav in 1924 and Oleg in 1928. Although the strain of supporting a family—which in those days included relatives—at first proved difficult, these years witnessed a series of successes, which confirmed Prokofiev's eminence. In 1927, he returned to the Soviet Union for the first time in nine years, tentatively attempting to repair connections, but the financial attractions of the West still proved too tempting. Thereafter he would return to Russia regularly. Yet for the next several years, his triumphs occurred in the West, which saw several major works premiered: the ballets *Le Pas d'acier* (1927), *The Prodigal Son* (1929), and *On the Dnepr* (1932); the opera *The Gambler* (1929); the film score for *Lt. Kije* (1933), which also furnished material for a popular suite and which introduced Prokofiev to the medium of film composition; the Fourth Symphony (1930); two piano concerti (1931 and 1932); the Second Violin Concerto (1935); and a profusion of chamber, solo instrument, and vocal works.

By 1935, Prokofiev had decided that his future lay in returning to the Soviet Union. The Depression (1929-1941), while limiting opportunities in the West, had had little effect on the Soviet economy, and Prokofiev had begun to believe that his soul was rooted in Russia. This return inaugurated his Soviet period (1935-1953), the years of his greatest achievements as well as his greatest humiliations. For he returned just as Stalin began putting into practice his program for turning artists into propaganda-mongers. For musicians as for others this meant subordinating creative impulses to socially and politically acceptable work. At first Prokofiev fit smoothly into this regimen. He had always worked well in response to specific directions, and the commissars required much work to order. His first years were extraordinarily productive: He completed the ballet *Romeo and Juliet* (1937) and the three suites drawn from it; *Peter and the Wolf* (1938), a children's fable for narrator and orchestra; film scores for *Queen of Spades* (1938) and *Alexander Nevsky* (1939), the latter also developed into a cantata; and his First Cello Concerto (1939).

These were also the years immediately preceding World War II, years of intensifying tension and suspicion. Some of this fell on Prokofiev because of his long absence from the country during its formative years. As a result, he experienced some negative criticism, hostile reactions he did not expect in his homeland. The outbreak of war affected him both professionally and personally. Like most Soviet artists, Prokofiev was expected to produce works that would help rally the Soviet people. Seizing the opportunity, Prokofiev chose the classic text for an opera aimed at that end, Leo Tolstoy's *Voyna i mir* (1865-1869; *War and Peace*, 1886), although it was not produced until 1946. He also composed a number of classic film scores, most notably that for Sergei Eisenstein's monumental *Ivan Grozny* (1944-1946; *Ivan the Terrible*). With Russian success in the war, he returned to the ballet score *Cinderella* (1945), another wonderful work. The premiere of his epic fifth symphony was appropriately symbolic; its performance was delayed by cannon salvos signaling the beginning of Russia's final victorious offensive of the war.

The war also brought the dissolution of his first marriage and his liaison with and eventual marriage to Mira Mendelson. His remarriage in 1948 accompanied significant changes: He was humiliated before and censured by a congress of Soviet composers as part of Stalin's program to establish absolute rule. Simultaneously his first wife, Russian only by naturalization, was sentenced to hard labor in a Siberian prison camp for supposed disloyalty. His health broke in this crisis; the last five years showed a lingering decline. He continued composing to the end; though his final works are not among his finest, they do include the bold Sinfonia Concertante for Cello and Orchestra (1948); the broad and affirmative Sixth Symphony (1949); the Cello Sonata, his most accessible chamber work; and the somewhat less effective Seventh Symphony (1950). Broken by hypertension and high blood pressure, hounded by the attacks of ideological commissars, Prokofiev died in Moscow on March 5, 1953, at very nearly the same time that his prosecutor, Joseph Stalin, died.

### Summary

By all accounts one of the most brilliant and successful composers of the twentieth century, Sergei Prokofiev is in some respects more remarkable because of his interaction with Russian culture and the evolving Soviet state. His cultural heredity determined the orientation of his music and shaped his life. His most popular and enduring works grow out of and reflect the Russian soul: historically in *Alexander Nevsky* and *Ivan the Terrible*, folkloristically in *Peter and the Wolf*, artistically in *Romeo and Juliet* and *Cinderella*, narratively in *Lt. Kije* and *War and Peace*. He is the prototypical iconoclastic Russian artist, shattering idols in an orgy of self-expression yet reserving his best work for command performances and made-to-order scores. Throughout his life he remained Russian, returning home at a hard time because he believed it was home and expending his energies in really trying to express the Russian soul in his music.

Some critics have contended that Prokofiev's return to the Soviet Union and voluntary submission to creative controls stunted his creative growth and limited the music he could have composed. Throughout his career, however, Prokofiev did his best work in response to strict directions. Probably for this reason he is indisputably the master film-score composer; no other craftsman proved more adept at creating the perfect aural analogue for a visual image. Similarly, no other attempt at creating a musical illustration for a fable has succeeded like *Peter and the Wolf*, which has entered the common consciousness as few classical compositions have. Undoubtedly Prokofiev suffered from the strictures clamped on him, but what he achieved is unprecedented and will endure.

### Bibliography

Dunnett, R. "Sergei and the Wolf." *New Statesman and Society* 4, no. 176 (November 8, 1991). Dunnett describes the rise and fall of Prokofiev.

Karl, Gregory. "Organic Methodologies and Non-Organic Values: The 'Andante Caloroso' of Prokofiev's Seventh Piano Sonata." *Journal of Musicological Research* 18, no. 1 (Winter 1999). Discussion and analysis of Prokofiev's Seventh Piano Sonata.

Krebs, Stanley Dale. *Soviet Composers and the Growth of Soviet Music*. London: Allen and Unwin, and New York: Norton, 1970. This is the best general account of the impact of socialist ideology on Russian composers up to 1960. Quite useful because it sets Prokofiev squarely in his cultural context, this work offers interesting comparisons of Prokofiev with other composers. The book perhaps overstresses the negative aspects of Stalinism.

Nestyev, Israel. *Prokofiev*. Translated by Florence Jonas. Stanford, Calif.: Stanford University Press, 1960. An authorized Soviet biography with full apparatus, this work presents much detailed information through the distorting lens of ideological preconception. Nestyev's basic view is that Prokofiev's music was perverted by his stay in the West.

Robinson, Harlow. *Sergei Prokofiev*. London: Hale, and New York: Viking, 1987. This book is the single indispensable work on the composer, a complete and evenhanded scholarly biography with full critical materials, including an annotated bibliography. Robinson presents all the information available with clarity and grace, leaving readers to draw their own conclusions.

Samuel, Claude. *Prokofiev*. Translated by Miriam John. London: Calder and Boyars, and New York: Grossman, 1971. A readable and well-focused biography, this book is particularly useful for the general reader. It is, however, colored by a pro-Western bias and is somewhat limited in technical musical information.

Savkina, Natalia. *Prokofiev*. Translated by Catherine Young. Neptune City, N.J.: Paganiniana, 1984. A translation of an authorized Soviet biography of 1982, this presents a revisionist Soviet view of the composer and his sufferings under Stalin. More objective and pictorial than Nestyev, this account is slighter and less substantial, and still exhibits a pro-Russian bias.

Seroff, Victor. *Sergei Prokofiev: A Soviet Tragedy*. London: Frewin, and New York: Funk and Wagnalls, 1968. As the title indicates, this book is less objective biography than the Western entry in an ideological conflict. It is well written, however, and contains some good illustrations.

*James Livingston*

## MARCEL PROUST

*Born:* July 10, 1871; Auteuil, France
*Died:* November 18, 1922; Paris, France
*Area of Achievement:* Literature
*Contribution:* Proust is the most celebrated French writer of the twentieth century. His masterwork in seven volumes, the novel *À la recherche du temps perdu* (1913-1927; *Remembrance of Things Past*, 1922-1931, 1981) broke new ground in its explorations of the nature of individual identity, its psychology of space and time, and its stylistic and thematic expansiveness. Proust's fiction and his criticism have helped widen the traditional perspectives of literary criticism.

### Early Life

Marcel Proust was born in Auteuil, a suburb of Paris, on July 10, 1871. Proust's father, Adrien Proust, a medical doctor and professor, had received the Légion d'Honneur the previous year for his theoretical and practical efforts to halt the spread of epidemics. Dr. Proust's success lent his family stature, but, because Proust's mother was Jewish, he was also something of an outsider in Parisian society. Proust was a weak child, plagued by asthma, which intesified when he was a teenager and limited his activities for most of his life. During his childhood, his family divided its time between Paris, Auteuil, and Illiers, a village southwest of Paris. Despite the security of his father's prestige and his family's wealth, Proust was tormented by his poor health and by a strained, although loving, relationship with his parents. In 1882, he entered the Lycée Condorcet, a private secondary school, where he pursued the chief interests of his life: the theater, reading, and writing. In 1889, Proust received a baccalaureate degree from the *lycée;* in the examinations, he took a first prize in French composition.

Proust had no plans for a career when he left the *lycée.* He spent a voluntary year of military service with the Seventy-sixth Infantry in Orléans, where, despite his weak constitution, he delighted in the routine and the camaraderie. Pressure from his family to settle on an occupation led him to study law at the Faculté de Droit at the Sorbonne and diplomacy at the École des Sciences Politiques, but much of his energy was devoted to the Parisian social scene. Proust began by frequenting bourgeois literary salons, gatherings at the homes of prominent society matrons that attracted figures from the arts. At first, Proust gained entry only to salons linked to school and family friends. Eventually, however, he was accepted into some of the most exclusive salons in the Faubourg Saint-Germain, representing the highest level of French nobility. At the same time, Proust continued writing short stories and essays like those he had contributed to magazines at the *lycée.* He passed the law examination in 1893, but he never practiced the profession. In the eyes of family members and acquaintances, he was a dilettante. Even the publication in 1896 of his early stories and sketches, under the title *Les Plaisirs et les jours* (*Pleasures and Regrets*, 1948), failed to win for him a reputation as a serious writer. Doubtless his negligent attitude toward an unpaid position at a library, which he often abandoned to travel with friends, suggested that he was more interested in gossip and play than in producing substantial work. The deaths of his father in 1903 and his mother in 1905, however, served as catalysts to Proust's literary efforts.

### Life's Work

Despite appearances to the contrary, the influences and the aborted beginnings that would eventually culminate in Proust's *Remembrance of Things Past* can be traced through the ten years before his parents' deaths. The nature of aesthetic experience fascinated Proust. Before the turn of the century, he became interested in the work of the English art critic and historian John Ruskin. Despite Proust's relatively meager knowledge of English, he translated some of Ruskin's work and wrote prefaces, published in 1904 and 1905, that explore the nature of reading and its effect on the reader. Proust valued reading not for its power to educate but for its power to send the reader deep within himself. For Proust, reading is communication "in the midst of solitude," and therefore is divorced from ordinary, daily life. Allied to Proust's conception of reading was his determination to change the assumptions and the nature of French literary criticism. In a book written during this period but not published until 1954, *Contre Sainte-Beuve* (*By Way of Sainte-Beuve*, 1958), Proust takes exception to the views of the most influential nineteenth century French critic, Charles Sainte-Beuve. Proust argues in opposition to Sainte-Beuve that a book should not be judged by its author or an author by his book. Instead, he argues, the author and the book represent two distinct selves. A book presents the elusive inner self that cannot be glimpsed in the daily life of the author, but, in Proust's view, that glimpse should push the reader to plumb his own elusive self. Thus, the key to truth is not in any book, but within each individual.

*Remembrance of Things Past*, which Proust wrote and rewrote over a span of at least fourteen years, also draws on narrative material from several earlier efforts: the aborted novel *Jean Santeuil* (English translation, 1955) probably written largely between 1895 and 1899, but not published until 1952; "Sur la Lecture" (1905; "On Reading," 1971), his preface to his translation of Ruskin's *Sesame and Lilies* (1865), and *Contre Sainte-Beuve.* In 1909, incorporating parts of these works, Proust wrote the beginning and end of *Remembrance of Things Past.* What he intended in 1912, the year the first volume, *Du côté de chez Swann* (1913; *Swann's Way*, 1922), was published, to be three volumes eventually became seven, as Proust added hundreds of thousands of words. The novel's seemingly infinite expandability reflects Proust's addition of new layers to his narrator's life. The added length intensifies one of the novel's key processes: forgetting and remembering. Proust writes in the last volume, *Le Temps retrouvé* (1927; *Time Regained*, 1931), "[T]he true paradises are the paradises that we have lost."

The plot of *Remembrance of Things Past* is a transmuted version of Proust's life. The narrator begins by remembering a time when his life was disordered, when he was plagued by memories. One memory, an unconscious memory, sparked by a cup of tea and a madeleine, a shell-shaped French pastry, conjures up a vivid memory of his childhood; from that memory, the main narrative begins. The narrator presents his life in a roughly chronological order, with digressions and some hints of the future. His life is one of repeated disappointments in himself and in others: in his parents, in the wealthy bourgeois aesthete Swann, in the aristocratic Guermantes family, and in the enigmatic Albertine, the narrator's great love, who may represent a combination of women the homosexual Proust admired and men he loved. Seemingly like Proust, the narrator feels lost, unsure of his life's work. The novel's sheer mass occasions in its reader the same divorce from the past experienced by the narrator. Finally, in the last volume, the narrator experiences a series of revelations that highlight his error in searching for truth in others instead of seeking it within himself. He discovers himself and his past anew and, in an effort to resurrect all the selves buried within him, he determines to write the book that the reader has now finished.

*Remembrance of Things Past* is autobiographical, but its clues to Proust's life are of secondary importance. More significant, drawing in part on the ideas of the French philosopher Henri Bergson, Proust's novel asserts in both its narrative form and its theme the need for a "three-dimensional psychology, one that adds to the traditional points in space and time a movement through time: what Bergson calls 'duration.' " Proust's literary theory and technique might be compared to a cubist painter's representation of movement or changes in perspective in a medium generally considered two-dimensional. In an attempt to create duration in fiction, Proust turned to a variety of techniques, including cutting back and forth between memories in a quasi-cinematic fashion and undermining narrative tension by prematurely revealing future events.

Proust had difficulty finding a publisher for his novel and therefore paid for the printing of the first volume. When it was published, however, its value was soon recognized. Printing difficulties and the outbreak of World War I delayed publication of subsequent volumes until after the war's end, but the delay proved fortuitous because it allowed Proust the time to expand and revise the novel. When he was awarded the prestigious Goncourt Prize in 1917 for the second volume, Proust was lionized.

Stories abound of Proust's eccentricities during the years he spent writing *Remembrance of Things Past.* He usually slept during the day and wrote at night. To shield himself from urban noise, he had a cork lining applied to the bedroom walls of one apartment he occupied during those years. His guilt over his homosexuality sometimes led him toward sadomasochism, but he was not a recluse, as he is sometimes claimed to have been. He emerged often to dine at the Ritz, he still sometimes attended society soirées, and he occasionally patronized the ballet and the theater. His true devotion, however, was to his work. When he was dying of pneumonia, too weak to write in his own hand, he insisted on dictating textual additions to his housekeeper. At Proust's death on November 18, 1922, the last three volumes of *Remembrance of Things Past* remained unpub-

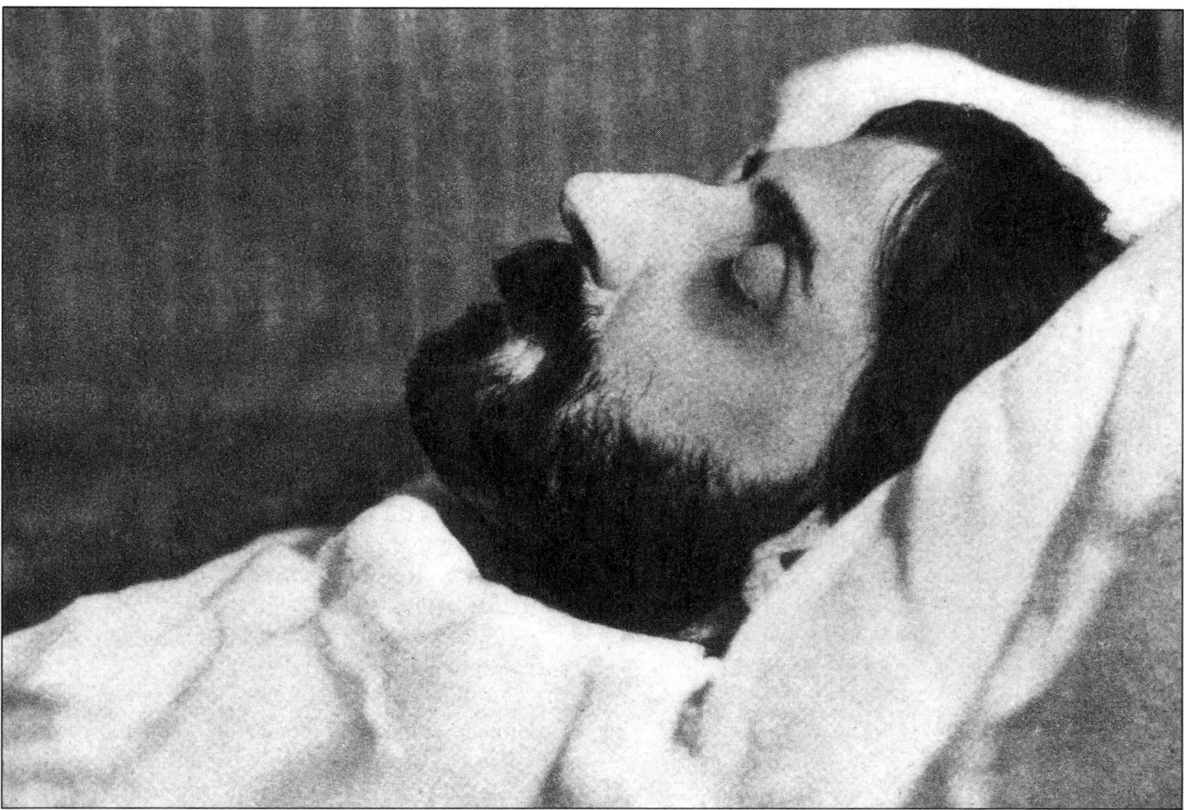

lished. Doubtless Proust would have revised them if he had lived longer, but their published forms complete his design.

### Summary

Marcel Proust's *Remembrance of Things Past* is valuable in all its facets: as a panorama of French society of his time, ranging through all economic and social classes and illustrating changes in fashion, technology, psychology, philosophy, and politics; as a treatise on the psychology of the self and the relation of the individual to society; and as an exemplum of literary modernism in its isolation and elevation of the individual consciousness. Proust's influence on both criticism and literature has been powerful. Although no single author can be credited with spawning new schools of criticism, a comprehensive review of criticism would suggest that Proust's experiments with narrative and his three-dimensional psychology deserve some part of the credit for the development of branches of criticism such as structuralism and narratology. In literature, Proust's influence is clearly evident in the work of a number of major figures who have followed him, including Samuel Beckett, whose debt to Proust would be obvious from a look at his characters lost in time even if he had not written about Proust himself, and Alain Robbe-Grillet, whose dismembered narratives and amnesiac narrators represent extreme versions of Proust's narrative cross-cutting and his forgetful narrator. Like the work of most great innovators, Proust's novel *Remembrance of Things Past* is part of a historical complex of interrelated ideas. That complex has shaped the psychology and the values of the twentieth century.

### Bibliography

Beckett, Samuel. *Proust.* London: Chatto and Windus, and New York: Grove Press, 1931. A brief but fascinating book by the premier playwright of the second half of the twentieth century, who explores the nature of habit and its role in *Remembrance of Things Past.*

Brée, Germaine. *The World of Marcel Proust.* London: Chatto and Windus, and Boston: Houghton Mifflin, 1966. One of a number of books by a prominent critic of Proust, this work explains the problems and joys of reading Proust.

Finn, Michael R. *Proust, the Body and Literary Form.* Cambridge and New York: Cambridge University Press, 1999. Examination of the nineteenth century French fixation with nervous physical conditions and its effect on Proust's work.

Genette, Gerard. "Time and Narrative in *À la recherche du temps perdu.*" In *Aspects of Narrative,* edited by J. Hillis Miller. New York: Columbia University Press, 1971. A seminal article on Proust's narrative techniques by one of the French literary critics who have helped shape the branch of criticism called narratology.

Kilmartin, Terence. *A Reader's Guide to "Remembrance of Things Past."* New York: Random House, 1983. Four indexes to characters, historical figures, places, and themes in *Remembrance of Things Past,* compiled by the most recent translator of the novel.

Ladenson, Elisabeth. *Proust's Lesbianism.* Ithaca, N.Y.: Cornell University Press, 1999. The author examines lesbianism as a central element in the works of Proust.

Painter, George. *Proust: The Early Years.* Boston: Little Brown, 1959.

———. *Proust: The Later Years.* Boston: Little Brown, 1965. An exhaustive two-volume biography that is especially helpful about Proust's historical context and the correspondences between Proust's life and the plot of *Remembrance of Things Past.*

Poulet, Georges. *Studies in Human Time.* Translated by Elliott Coleman. Baltimore: Johns Hopkins University Press, 1956; London: Johns Hopkins University Press, 1970. A widely cited critical work that helped open a new sphere of inquiry for criticism by identifying one of Proust's methods as the "spatialization of time."

Proust, Marcel. *Letters of Marcel Proust.* Translated and edited by Mina Curtiss. New York: Random House, 1949; London: Chatto and Windus, 1950. Although not the most recent selection of Proust's letters, this book includes a range of letters from all periods of his life as well as notes and photographs.

Shattuck, Roger. *Proust's Binoculars.* London: Chatto and Windus, and New York: Random House, 1963. A thought-provoking book by a prominent critic of French literature, who here outlines Proust's use of optical and cinematic images and techniques in *Remembrance of Things Past.*

*Helaine Ross*

# GIACOMO PUCCINI

*Born:* December 22, 1858; Lucca, Italy
*Died:* November 29, 1924; Brussels, Belgium
*Area of Achievement:* Music
*Contribution:* Born into a Tuscan family with almost a dynastic tradition in musical composition and instruction, Puccini became a leading member of a talented group of Italian composers of opera in the generation succeeding Giuseppe Verdi. Many of Puccini's operatic works have proved to be among the most popular in the twentieth century operatic repertory.

## Early Life

Tradition and expectation are reflected in the names given the fifth child of Michele and Albina Puccini: Giacomo Antonio Domenico Michele Secondo Maria Puccini. The child's great-great-grandfather, Giacomo Puccini, had studied music at Bologna, then returned to Lucca to become organist and choirmaster at this Tuscan city's cathedral (San Martino) and prolific composer of sacred and civic music. His son Antonio also studied at Bologna, returned to Lucca to compose sacred music and assist, then succeed, his father as choirmaster. His son Domenico followed study at Bologna with a musical apprenticeship at Naples (under the operatic composer Giovanni Paisiello), then returned to Lucca to assist his father and compose an occasional opera. Domenico's son Michele studied music first at Lucca with his father, then at Bologna with a contemporary master of opera, Gaetano Donizetti, and at Naples with Giuseppe Mercadante, composer of operatic and choral music. Michele then became choirmaster and organist at San Martino and wrote an opera on a historical theme (1884) and texts on counterpoint and harmony.

The child Giacomo was therefore expected to study music, and his skill was such—and the family tradition so strong—that at his father's death (1864), the Luccan authorities reserved the post of organist and choirmaster until the eight-year-old Giacomo should come of age. By age fourteen, Giacomo was sufficiently adept to become organist at San Martino and other local churches. He was also pianist for several nearby resorts, taverns, and (some said) a brothel. Additional funds came from the sale of organ pipes that he and his friends stole from churches.

Meanwhile, Puccini continued musical studies with his father's sometime pupils, then entered the local musical academy. There he studied Verdi's operas—a performance of Verdi's *Aida* (1876) in nearby Pisa inspired in Puccini a vow of composing opera himself—and composed minor orchestral and choral works. His final exercise, a *Mass of Glory* (1880), was performed amid praise for the young musician's skillful writing for chorus and solo voices. With a relative's aid and a royal scholarship, Puccini, in the fall of 1880, commenced advanced study at the Milan Conservatory. There his work was directed by a leading operatic composer, Amilcare Ponchielli. In July, 1883, Puccini was graduated with the performance of his *Capriccio sinfonico*, which was praised for its orchestration and melody. Now Puccini would compose an opera.

## Life's Work

Puccini's first opera, *Le Villi*, with a libretto by the dramatist Ferdinando Fontana, used a story that Adolphe Adam had already exploited for his popular ballet *Giselle* (1841): A peasant girl's spirit haunts the lover who abandoned her. Puccini submitted his work for a Milanese competition and was rebuffed, primarily because his score was illegible. Yet the respected composer Arrigo Boito heard Puccini play his score at the piano, promptly raised funds for a production, and convinced the Milanese editorial firm of Ricordi to publish the opera. *Le Villi* was performed to great acclaim at the Teatro dal Verme in Milan on May 31, 1884.

Sorrow, scandal, and defeat followed. Puccini's mother died in the summer of 1884; shortly thereafter, he eloped from Lucca with Elvira Bonturi Gemignani, who was already married, with two children. (She would not marry Puccini until her husband's death in 1903.) In January, 1885, *Le Villi* was poorly received in Naples and at La Scala, the premier Milanese opera house.

Puccini and Elvira lived in poverty in Milan for the next several years, supported by a stipend from Ricordi, their difficulties compounded by the birth of a son, Antonio, in 1886. Puccini's second opera, *Edgar*, with a libretto by Fontana, intentionally resembled Georges Bizet's popular *Carmen* (1875). Yet while Puccini's score was pleasant, the drama (a fourteenth century youth is seduced by a Gypsy girl) was dull. A lukewarm reception greeted the premiere at La Scala on April 21, 1889.

Encouraged by Ricordi, Puccini had started yet another opera on an unpromising subject. Abbé

Prévost's novel *Histoire du chevalier des Grieux et de Manon Lescaut* (1731, 1733, 1753; *Manon Lescaut*, 1734, 1786) had already been the subject of at least three operas, including Jules Massenet's great Parisian success, *Manon* (1884). Puccini's opera had a difficult birth, requiring several librettists. The result was an incoherent plot overwhelmed by music of great passion and memorable melody. The premiere, at the Royal Theater of Turin, February 1, 1893, was a popular success.

*Manon Lescaut* provided financial freedom. Puccini acquired a villa at Torre del Lago, by a scenic lake between Pisa and Lucca, where he would compose and, for relaxation, hunt wild fowl. In March, 1893, Puccini learned that a rival, Ruggiero Leoncavallo, planned an opera based on Henri Murger's novel and play, *Scènes de la vie de bohème* (1847-1849). Puccini hastened to complete his opera on the same subject, choosing as librettists the noted playwrights Giuseppe Giacosa and Luigi Illica. Both had worked on *Manon Lescaut*; both would collaborate on Puccini's next two operas. *La Bohème* had a favorable premiere at Turin on February 1, 1896, with a conductor, Arturo Toscanini, who commenced a lifelong friendship with Puccini. Critics noted the trivial plot, but all were impressed by this work's drama and powerful music, especially in the heroine's death scene.

Puccini had long been interested in an opera based on Victorien Sardou's play *La Tosca* (1887; English translation, 1925), as popularized by the French actress Sarah Bernhardt. Ricordi acquired the rights to the play, arbitrated quarrels among librettists and composer, and urged completion. Puccini's version of this melodrama set in Rome, 1800, was presented at Rome's Teatro Costanzi, January 14, 1900—and for twenty more performances. Critics have often deplored the plot of *Tosca*, "that shabby little shocker," but none denies the dramatic tension imparted by Puccini's music.

From a factual magazine article by John Luther Long, the American impresario David Belasco produced a popular play (1904) about a Japanese woman's love betrayed by an American naval officer. Puccini saw the play in London, was fascinated by the exotic setting, and his version, *Madama Butterfly*, first appeared at La Scala on February 17, 1904. The critical reception was devastatingly negative (Toscanini hated the opera), but it has become Puccini's most popular. Meanwhile, Puccini's own life came to resemble a melodrama. His constant womanizing drove Elvira to jealous rages; she, in turn, drove Puccini's servant girl to suicide—tragically, for the girl was innocent of dallying with Puccini. The composer could focus on no project, until 1907, when he saw in New York another Belasco play, *The Girl of the Golden West* (1905). Puccini's version, *Fanciulla*, with libretto by Guelfo Civinini, was presented first at the New York Metropolitan Opera, with Toscanini conducting, December 10, 1910. Technically perfect, the opera was well, but not enthusiastically, received. Igor Stravinsky described it as "a remarkably up-to-date television horse opera," without noting that the plot was far from common in 1910.

Puccini's earlier operas had now become widely popular, frequently performed in Italy, elsewhere in Europe, and in North and South America. Puccini convinced himself that he should now compose a romantic opera similar to the popular operettas of Franz Lehár. A new librettist, Giuseppe Adami, assisted the completion of *La Rondine* (the swallow). Puccini intended a premiere in Lehár's city, Vienna, but war interfered. This slight work was staged to modest acclaim in Monte Carlo, March 27, 1917, and has never been popular. Puccini was already busy with a plan to render in opera the scheme of the French Grand Guignol: a tragedy, a sentimental drama, a comedy. Librettists were found: Adami (again) and G. Forzano. *Il Trittico* (the triptych) was staged in New York, December 14, 1918. The first two episodes—*Il Tabarro* (the cloak), a horrific tragedy, and *Suor Angelica* (Sister Angelica), a miraculous tale with a heroine bearing some resemblance to Puccini's sister, Mother Superior Iginia—were poorly received. The third, *Gianni Schicchi*, a black comedy based on Dante's *Inferno* (canto 30), was popular. All three episodes have magnificent arias for the female voice. Critics have come to appreciate Puccini's dramatic and musical skill in constructing this complex work.

Puccini chose as his next subject a drama by the Venetian playwright Carlo Gozzi: a bloody, romantic fairy tale set in exotic China. The librettists Renato Simoni and Adami set to work. Puccini composed, while complaining of throat pains. In the autumn of 1924, cancer of the throat was diagnosed. Puccini, accompanied by his son, went to Brussels for radioactive therapy. The treatment seemed successful, but a heart attack brought death on November 29. The body was returned to Milan for temporary burial in the Toscanini family tomb. On the day of national mourning, Benito Mussolini

delivered the obituary. In 1926, Puccini was interred at Torre del Lago.

Toscanini conducted the premier of the unfinished *Turandot* at La Scala on April 25, 1926. When he reached the end of Puccini's score, Toscanini turned to the audience, said, "Here ends the opera, which remains incomplete because of the composer's death," and left the stage in silence.

### Summary

*Turandot* was completed from Giacomo Puccini's notes by Franco Alfano and forms part of the standard operatic repertory, as does *Manon Lescaut. La Bohème, Tosca*, and *Madama Butterfly* have become favorites with American and European audiences. *Fanciulla* and *Il Trittico* are occasionally presented as curiosities, the latter often to critical acclaim.

Contemporary and later critics debated whether Puccini was the true heir of Verdi. He was not. Puccini's plots lacked the heroic and nationalistic themes that Verdi favored; Puccini was an exponent of *opera verismo*: human characters caught in more or less realistic situations. Indeed, Puccini's best vocal writing was consistently for the vulnerable woman caught in plausible tragic circumstances. Furthermore, the springs of Puccini's music were not fed by Verdi. His skillful orchestral harmonies and lyrical choral passages came from experience, education, and family tradition. Contemporary composers also contributed to Puccini's craft: From *Fanciulla* on, the influence of Claude Debussy and Richard Strauss is apparent, while Stravinskian rhythms enhance *Turandot*. Above all, Puccini learned from Richard Wagner: The continuous melodic line (constant musical background) in Puccini's operas derives from Wagner's *Tristan and Isolde*. Puccini's strong theatrical sense owes something to Wagner's music-dramas, as does Puccini's careful attempt to fit music to words—hence the great emotive power of his music, which often seems to drive his characters to a desired action. Critics said that a craftsman's operatic music should reflect, not force, the characters' actions. The emotive power of Puccini's music is so strong that his melodies have been appropriated for everything from film soundtracks to television commercials.

### Bibliography

Ashbrook, William. *The Operas of Puccini*. New York: Oxford University Press, 1968; London: Cassell, 1969. A detailed discussion of the composition, structure, and production of each opera, set within the framework of a biography. Includes notes, a bibliography, an excellent index, and full summaries of each opera.

Carner, Mosco. "Giacomo Puccini." In *The New Grove Masters of Italian Opera*, edited by Philip Gosset et al. London: Macmillan, and New York: Norton, 1983. This is an excellent, brief monograph distilled from the work listed below. Part 1 is a brief biography; part 2 discusses (thematically, not by opera) Puccini's music. Includes photographs of Puccini, a bibliography, an index, and a detailed chronology of Puccini's musical works.

———. *Puccini: A Critical Biography*. 3d ed. London: Duckworth, and New York: Holmes and Meier, 1992. The standard scholarly discussion, with separate sections on biography, Puccini the artist, and detailed musicological treatment of his works. Includes full reference notes, a bibliography, a detailed index, and selected illustrations, primarily of Puccini and his family.

Casali, Patrick Vincent. "The Pronunciation of 'Turandot': Puccini's Last Enigma." *Opera Quarterly* 13, no. 4 (Summer 1997). Detailed historical consideration of whether or not the final "t" should be silent in the pronunciation of Puccini's opera "Turandot."

Gentry, Theodore. "Musical Symbols of Death in 'Tosca.'" *Opera Quarterly* 14, no. 4 (Summer 1998). Examines the musical symbolism used by Puccini and others to foreshadow death.

Marek, George R. *Puccini*. New York: Simon and Schuster, 1951; London: Cassell, 1952. An anecdotal biography incorporating substantial material from letters by, to, and about the composer. The other biographies listed here offer a more sophisticated discussion of Puccini's music. Contains an excellent index and selected illustrations of Puccini and his associates.

Mordden, Ethan. *Opera Anecdotes*. New York: Oxford University Press, 1985; Oxford: Oxford University Press, 1988. A humorous book with a wealth of reliable information. Mordden supplies serious and sound introductory essays to the subjects and personalities treated. Contains an index.

Osborne, Charles. *The Complete Operas of Puccini*. London: Gollancz, 1981; New York: Atheneum, 1982. Similar to the work by Ashbrook, but written with a lighter touch, this biography is organized as background to a discussion of each opera in chronological order. Osborne stresses Puccini's works as musical theater. Contains a brief bibliography, an index, and selected illustrations of items (scores, sets, and the like) pertinent to Puccini's life and work.

Specht, Richard. *Giacomo Puccini: The Man, His Life, His Work*. Translated by Catherine Alison Phillips. London: Dent, and New York: Knopf, 1933. A personal assessment of Puccini's work by one who knew the composer (but not well). Specht's study reflects the ambiguity that contemporary Europeans felt concerning Puccini's life, personality, and musical tastes. The index is inadequate and the few illustrations are poorly reproduced.

Weaver, William. *Puccini: The Man and His Music*. London: Hutchinson, and New York: Dutton, 1977. A superb collection of photographs of Puccini, his family, friends and associates, and productions (mostly at the Metropolitan Opera) of his operas. The text should be supplemented by Carner's essay. Contains plot summaries of the operas and a brief bibliography.

*Paul B. Harvey, Jr.*

# MUAMMAR AL-QADDAFI

*Born:* 1942; near Surt, Libya
*Areas of Achievement:* Government and politics
*Contribution:* As the leader of the Free Unionist Officers, Qaddafi demolished the monarchical *ancien régime* of Libya, founded the Libyan Arab Republic, launched a relentless struggle against Western imperialism, and enunciated a sacred ideology by blending the precepts of Islam and Arab nationalism.

## Early Life

Muammar al-Qaddafi was born in a poor family belonging to the Arabized Berber Qaddafadam tribe of the Surt Desert between Tripolitania and Cyrenaica, two of the three main geographical zones of Libya. Though himself virtually illiterate, Muammar's father arranged for his seven-year-old son's education at home under a Koran teacher. He went to Sirte elementary school at the age of nine. After facing discrimination as a Bedouin minority at school, Muammar began to develop a deep aversion to inequality and a strong sense of self-reliance and leadership. Four years later, his family relocated to Sabha, the main town of the Fezzan district, where he enrolled in a secondary school.

At Sabha, the teenage Qaddafi was deeply influenced by the Arab leadership of Gamal Abdel Nasser, who had ended monarchical rule and corrupt party politics in Egypt and acquired a reputation as new leader of the Arab world. In 1956 Nasser nationalized the Suez Canal Company and confronted a joint attack by England, France, and Israel, finally emerging from the crisis as a strong Arab nationalist. Qaddafi admired Nasser's pan-Arab foreign policy and his strong socialist domestic program. In 1958 Qaddafi celebrated the union of Egypt and Syria as the United Arab Republic (UAR) with his cohorts at school; three years later he organized a demonstration at Fezzan protesting against Syria's secession from the UAR and consequently courted expulsion from school. He had to move to Misrata in Tripoli to finish his secondary education in 1963.

## Life's Work

Qaddafi formed his first effective political movement for Arab unity at Misrata. He envisioned a massive sociopolitical revolution to liberate Libya from internal corruption and external exploitation. He was convinced that the success of this program called for a corps of disciplined and dedicated military officers committed to Arab unity and emancipation. After high school, he and his close associates joined the military academy at Benghazi, where Qaddafi formed the movement of the Free Unionist Officers, modeled after Nasser's Free Officers in Egypt. This movement was divided into one civilian section and one, more important, military section with a central committee comprising highly disciplined and puritanical military officers serving as the vanguard of the projected revolution.

Qaddafi graduated from the academy in 1965 and the following year visited the Sandhurst Military College in England on a short study program with the Royal Corps of Signals. Upon his return from England four months later, Qaddafi entered the university to study history while continuing his career in the army. Qaddafi's experience in England convinced him of the material success of the Western countries and the need for an all-encompassing revolutionary change in his own country.

Until modern times, Libya possessed neither national nor territorial identity. It formed a part of some other territorial unit and was often subjected to foreign political domination. However, control was limited only to the accessible coastal regions, while the Berbers of the interior remained free from outside control and influence—political or cultural—they being, to a great extent, Arabized and Islamized since the seventh century. Coastal Libya, around Tripoli, belonged to the Ottoman Empire. However, in the area of northern Cyrenaica, an Algerian reformist Islamic movement, the Sanusiya, had taken root. The movement turned militant as a response to the European imperialist activities to the north and west. The Italian conquest of Libya began in 1911 as part of Italy's design to create a "Fourth Shore" of a new Roman Empire, though the Italian conquest was confined to Tripoli and a few other locations by the Ottoman garrison and the Sanusi warrior monks. After the defeat of the Ottomans as a member of the Central Powers in World War I, the Italian Fascist leader Benito Mussolini conquered Libya in 1932. Italian imperialism in Libya was gallantly resisted by the Sanusi leader Sheikh Omar Mukhtar, who became Libya's first national hero after his martyrdom through execution at the hands of the Italians in 1931.

During World War II, the British defeated the Germans (Axis ally of the Italians) and occupied northern Libya, while the army of France (one of the Allied powers) occupied the Fezzan. The United States later built the Wheelus Air Base near Tripoli. The Allies could not come to an agreement concerning Libya's political future after the war, so the problem was referred to the United Nations General Assembly, which approved a resolution for an independent Libyan kingdom under the Grand Sanusi Idris of Cyrenaica. Under King Idris, Libya became a constitutional monarchy, though it did not achieve a strong national identity and remained an extremely poor country economically and an underdeveloped nation politically. The only period of relative reform and prosperity was the regime of Abdul Hamid al-Bakkush, who was appointed by the king as his prime minister in October, 1967, in an attempt to shore up Libyan national identity in the context of the shattered pan-Arab dream following the disastrous Six-Day Arab-Israeli War of June. Unfortunately, Bakkush was replaced in September, 1968, and the family of King Idris began to confront increasing opposition from the powerful and ambitious Shalhi family bent on capturing leadership of post-Idris Libya.

The Six-Day War triggered Qaddafi's coup. Under his command, the Free Unionist Officers in the army ousted King Idris, who was visiting Turkey at the time for a medical checkup, and established the Libyan Arab Republic. Qaddafi had planned to turn his coup into a revolution signifying an all-around material, moral, and spiritual conquest that would transform Libya into a modern, progressive state. He suspended the constitution, outlawed all political parties, and put his twelve-man Revolutionary Command Council (RCC) in charge of carrying out the required structural changes. Qaddafi's stated objective was to undo the acts that had "shattered . . . [Libya's] honor." The three fundamental ideals of the revolution were announced by the RCC: individual and national liberty, Arab unity, and Islamic socialism. Accordingly, the new government pledged to expel the Italian Libyans, evacuate the foreign military bases, maintain its neutrality between the superpowers, and achieve national unity and Arab unity. His economic measures included rent reductions, doubling of minimum wage, and conversion of foreign banks into Libyan joint-stock companies. All place and street names were rewritten in Arabic, alcoholic beverages were banned, Sanusi activities were restricted, and non-Muslim religious institutions were closed.

Colonel Qaddafi's revolution could be conveniently divided into three stages. The first and formative stage, the phase of the RCC, extended from September, 1969, to April 15, 1973. The initial RCC efforts did not register satisfactory progress, and thus the revolutionary committee proclaimed the organization of the Arab Socialist Union (ASU)—a quasipolitical organization seeking to provide for popular participation in the decision-making process—on June 11, 1971. On April 15, 1973, Qaddafi proclaimed the Popular Revolution that was to lead the formation of structures for a people's republic during the second phase.

The second stage, extending from April 15, 1973, to March 2, 1977, commenced with the appearance of the three-volume work entitled *Kitab al-akhbar* (*The Green Book*, 1976, 1980) which described Qaddafi's vision of the appropriate political system for Libya. The first volume of *The Green Book* seeks to proffer a solution to the problem of democracy and guidance for the liberation of human societies from oppressive political systems and provides the blueprint for a new form of government (*adat al-hukm*). The second volume seeks to provide a philosophy of "new socialism" to achieve economic freedom. The final volume analyzes the social problems of humanity and enjoins readers to remain free from all human-made laws and artificial social systems and structures.

The second phase of the revolution saw the rise of the populist society of the masses, the *Jamahiriyah*, and witnessed the formation of people's congress, committees, and unions. In September, 1976, the General People's Congress (GPC) was formed to replace the RCC as the supreme authority in the country. This concept of direct democracy was based on Qaddafi's Third Universal Theory, which posits that religion and nationalism are the driving forces of history. Neither capitalism nor communism is capable of solving human problems. What is needed is a middle way that will harness religion and nationalism; Islam, which Qaddafi considers a complete civilization, is the source of that middle way because it "is a universal religion which explains the phenomena of the universe and life, as well as the life of its community at the same time."

The new experiment in direct democracy was legislated by the GPC on March 2, 1977, as "the sole foundation of the new political system in the Socialist People's Libyan Arab *Jamahiriyah*." In the state of *jamahir* ("masses"), there is complete equality. The founding of the *Jamahiriyah* was followed by the abolition of the RCC. Meanwhile, in the early 1970's, Qaddafi gradually began divesting himself of official titles. A decree in April, 1974, relieved him of all political, administrative, and protocol functions. He was designated general secretary of the GPC, a post he gave up in February of 1979. He did, however, retain his position as the commander in chief of the armed forces and adopted the title "leader of the revolution."

### Summary

Though the third phase of Qaddafi's revolution, the post-*Green Book* phase, continues to unfold, it can safely be said that Qaddafi has been the subject of a multidimensional mythology in the Western world for his active support of Arab national struggles (especially that of the Palestinians) and his defiance of Israel. Both stances have brought Western, chiefly American, allegations against him for his complicity with and support for state-sponsored terrorism. Consequently, his life has remained under constant threat, though he remains a proud and patriotic Libyan who has succeeded in instilling "self-confidence and dignity on all levels of Libyan society." As one American-Arab scholar has observed, Qaddafi's appearance on the Middle East scene was timely, especially in the aftermath of the Arab-Israeli War of 1967, when "the Arab world desperately needed a psychological boost." Qaddafi and his fellow officers who had wrought a new Libya out of the quagmires of history have appropriately been called by a distinguished Arab journalist "the post-setback generation, the new hope of the Arab world."

### Bibliography

Ayoub, Mahmoud. *Islam and the Third Universal Theory: The Religious Thought of Mu'ammar al-Qadhdhafi*. London: Kegan Paul, and New York: Routledge, 1987. A thoroughly researched, "non-apologetic but positive" analysis of Qaddafi's religious and political ideology as well as a succinct biography by a distinguished scholar.

Bianco, Mirella. *Gadafi: Voice from the Desert*. Translation. London: Longman, 1975. A highly personal profile of the Libyan leader by a sympathetic but scholarly author who had personal access to Qaddafi and his family.

Carlberg, Russell. "Escapade in Hell: Reading the Short Stories of Colonel Kadhafi." *Antioch Review* 56, no. 1 (Winter 1998). Considers the short stories written by Qaddafi and their political and anti-American themes.

First, Ruth. *Libya: The Elusive Revolution*. London and Baltimore: Penguin, 1974. First, a renowned South African journalist, provides a somewhat biased but valuable critical examination of the early days of the revolution.

Harris, Lillian Craig. *Libya: Qadhafi's Revolution and the Modern State*. London: Croom Helm, and Boulder, Colo.: Westview Press, 1986. Harris is highly critical of Qaddafi and his revolution but provides a very helpful bibliography of materials available in English.

El-Khawas, Mohamed A. *Qaddafi: His Ideology in Theory and Practice*. Brattleboro, Vt.: Amana, 1986. A balanced review of Qaddafi as a man and as a statesman. A sound study by a serious historian.

St. John, Ronald Bruce. *Qaddafi's World Design: Libyan Foreign Policy, 1969-1987*. London and Atlantic Highlands, N.J.: Saqi Books, 1987. This interesting study by a specialist is especially useful for Qaddafi's Third Universal Theory.

Takeyh, Ray. "Qadhafi and the Challenge of Militant Islam." *Washington Quarterly* 21, no. 3 (Summer 1998). The author examines the affects of Islamic fundamentalism on Qaddafi's regime.

Tremlett, George. *Gadaffi: The Desert Mystic*. New York: Carroll and Graf, 1993. This absorbing account is written by a British television journalist who is detached from Western propaganda, which continually seeks to stereotype Qaddafi.

*Narasingha P. Sil*

# ISIDOR ISAAC RABI

*Born:* July 29, 1898; Rymanow, Austria-Hungary
*Died:* January 11, 1988; New York, New York
*Areas of Achievement:* Physics and statesmanship
*Contribution:* Rabi developed the magnetic resonance method to measure with unprecedented accuracy the properties of atomic nuclei. After World War II, he used the international nature of science to bring peoples of the world together, himself becoming a world figure in the process.

## Early Life

Isidor Isaac Rabi was born July 29, 1898, in the town of Rymanow, in Galicia, the northeasternmost province of the old Austro-Hungarian Empire. After World War I, the town of Rymanow became a part of Poland. His father, David Rabi, left Galicia soon after Rabi's birth and came to the United States. Within a matter of months, David sent for his wife, Sheindel, and his infant son.

The Rabi family settled in the Lower East Side of New York City, a Jewish ghetto. While the Rabis had little money, there was a richness to their life that came from their devotion to the traditions and practices of Orthodox Judaism. The turning point in Rabi's life came when he was only nine years old. After his family moved to Brownsville, a community in the New York borough of Brooklyn, Rabi discovered the public library, where he came upon a little book on astronomy. In the pages of this book, Rabi read about the Copernican solar system with the planets orbiting around the sun. Suddenly, he understood the seasons of the year and the phases of the moon. With equal suddenness, Rabi recognized a natural explanation for events that previously had been explained only in terms of divine causes. The focus of Rabi's life then began to change from Orthodox Judaism to science.

Rabi entered Cornell University in 1916, and three years later, he was graduated with a major in chemistry. Chemistry did not inspire him, however, and Rabi spent the three years after graduation living at home, doing little besides reading in the New York Public Library. In 1922, he returned to Cornell as a graduate student of chemistry and soon discovered that the part of chemistry he liked was called physics. He transferred to the physics department at Columbia University in 1923 and obtained his doctorate in 1926. The day after he submitted his doctoral dissertation, he married Helen Newmark.

As a graduate student, Rabi knew that the most exciting physics research was occurring in Europe, where quantum mechanics was being created. In 1927, Rabi obtained a fellowship, went to Europe, and studied with Niels Bohr, Werner Heisenberg, Wolfgang Pauli, and Otto Stern. While he was in Zurich with Pauli, he received an offer from Columbia University to join the physics faculty. He returned from Europe in 1929 and began his career as a lecturer, the lowest academic rank. Thirty-nine years later, Rabi, a university professor, retired from Columbia, the first Columbia professor to hold that prestigious rank.

## Life's Work

Throughout the decade of the 1930's, Rabi was consumed by physics. In 1931, he turned the molecular beam method from the study of atoms (as he had learned it during 1928 in Stern's Hamburg laboratory) to the study of atomic nuclei. In the molecular beam method, a stream of atoms or molecules move through a highly evacuated chamber. Within this chamber, the beam passes between the poles of a magnet designed so that magnetic forces are exerted on individual atoms or molecules. With Rabi's method, the responses of atoms or molecules to these subtle magnetic forces revealed basic, and unknown, properties of the nucleus. Like a virtuoso, Rabi brought modification after modification to Stern's basic method and brought the uncertainties in the data coming from his laboratory from ten percent down to five percent and ultimately to less than one percent.

The climax of Rabi's molecular beam work was the molecular beam magnetic resonance method. In this method, atoms or molecules passed, in succession, between the poles of three magnets. The second of these magnets produced an oscillating magnetic field. For certain frequencies of this oscillating field, atoms or molecules were ejected from the beam by the third magnet and thus were not registered by the detector. As the frequencies could be measured with great accuracy, this enabled properties of the nucleus to be determined with corresponding accuracy. The new precision led to unanticipated discoveries such as the quadrupole moment of the heavy hydrogen nucleus.

For this work, Rabi was awarded the Nobel Prize for Physics in 1944.

World War II brought Rabi's molecular beam research to a sudden halt. Long before the United States entered the conflict, physicists had an insider's view of events in Europe. Jewish physicists were being displaced from their academic positions in Europe, and many of them came to England and the United States. Added to the concern of American physicists was the discovery of nuclear fission by the Austrian physicists Lise Meitner and Otto Frisch. With this discovery, it became apparent that a new energy, nuclear energy, was potentially available: The question was, what were German scientists doing about it?

During the summer of 1940, a magnetron—a powerful source of microwave radiation recently invented in England—was secretly brought to America by a delegation of British physicists. They wanted to enlist the aid of American physicists in the development of microwave radar. In rapid succession, the magnetron was demonstrated, the Massachusetts Institute of Technology (MIT) Radiation Laboratory was established, and Rabi left Columbia University for the Radiation Laboratory in Cambridge.

Rabi became the head of the research division and later the associate director of the laboratory. He took it upon himself to anticipate the course of the war and to anticipate the type of radar that would be needed by the military services. By the time the United States entered the war in December of 1941, a variety of radar systems had been developed, and as the conflict proceeded, radar systems from the MIT Radiation Laboratory were being used by the Allied forces in every theater of the war.

In 1943, another wartime laboratory was established in Los Alamos, New Mexico. The director of the Los Alamos laboratory, the laboratory founded to develop the atomic bomb, was J. Robert Oppenheimer. Rabi and Oppenheimer had first met in Europe in 1929, and their friendship was based on deep mutual respect. Oppenheimer wanted Rabi as his associate director, but to Rabi, the radar project was more important to the war effort, and he retained his position at the Radiation Laboratory. Rabi, however, became one of two senior advisers to Oppenheimer (the other one was Niels Bohr) and in this capacity made important contributions to the development of the atomic bomb.

When the war ended in 1945, the world was faced with a powerful new energy, and it was a matter of great importance to establish policies to control this new power. During December of 1945, Rabi and Oppenheimer spent a long day talking in Rabi's living room. During that day, a set of ideas was formulated that in the spring of 1946 became the Acheson-Lillienthal Report. This incredible document proposed to place atomic energy in the hands of an international agency and thereby to dissociate the energy of the atom from any nation's interests. In June, 1946, these ideas were presented to the United Nations by the United States' delegate, Bernard Baruch. To Rabi's great disappointment, the Russian delegate, Andrei Gromyko, rejected this proposal. Three years later, the Russians detonated their first atomic bomb, and the arms race was under way.

The Russian achievement prompted a few influential Americans to propose a crash program to develop the hydrogen bomb. Rabi was then a member of the General Advisory Committee of the Atomic Energy Committee. This committee, chaired by Oppenheimer, was called into session to consider the question of a fusion-bomb program. The committee unanimously opposed the development of such a weapon, and Rabi and Enrico Fermi wrote a minority opinion in which they expressed their moral revulsion to a weapon that cannot be confined to any military target. Once again, Rabi was on the losing side: The United States detonated a fusion bomb in 1952; nine months later, the Russians followed suit.

Throughout the postwar years, the culture of science was for Rabi a means for bringing peoples of the world together. In 1950, as a United States delegate to the fifth General Assembly of the United Nations Educational, Scientific, and Cultural Organization (UNESCO) held in Florence, Italy, Rabi proposed that European nations unite in the formation of a scientific laboratory. Two years later, the decision was made to establish the Center for European Nuclear Research (CERN) in Geneva, Switzerland. Today CERN is one of the foremost physics laboratories in the world, and Rabi is regarded as its father.

In 1954, Rabi proposed an international conference on the peaceful uses of atomic energy. This proposal, which was inspired by a speech given by President Dwight D. Eisenhower before the United Nations, was, at Eisenhower's direction, presented to the United Nations by Secretary of State John Foster Dulles. Dag Hammarskjöld, secretary-general of the United Nations, was an enthusiastic supporter of the idea. Rabi and Hammarskjöld together promoted the idea, and in 1955, the first International Conference on the Peaceful Uses of Atomic Energy was held in Geneva. This conference was, according to Hammarskjöld, the beginning of détente.

During the mid-1950's, Rabi was the chairman of the Science Advisory Committee (SAC) of the Office of Defense Mobilization. Rabi was concerned because SAC did not have direct access to the president and, as a result, the scientific implications of various policies were not adequately understood by the president. The Russian launch of *Sputnik* in 1957 prompted Eisenhower to seek the advice of SAC. Rabi proposed six specific actions, all of which Eisenhower accepted immediately. Rabi suggested that SAC needed direct access to the president (thus, SAC became PSAC, President's Science Advisory Committee) and that the president needed a science adviser. James Killian became the first assistant to the president for science and technology. Rabi remained a member of PSAC until the committee was dissolved by the Nixon Administration.

On the evening of October 21, 1986, at the Weizmann National Dinner, Rabi, as guest of honor, shared the head table with the president of Israel and many other dignitaries. In his response to the honor bestowed upon him that evening, Rabi proposed that Israel build a laboratory to be shared, as the European nations share CERN, with nations of the Middle East. At the age of eighty-eight, Rabi was still using science to bridge national, religious, and ideological differences.

### Summary

When Rabi returned from his studies in Europe in 1929, he was determined, as were others, to bring American physics out from the shadows of European physics. This determination paid dividends: By the end of the 1930's, American physics was preeminent. Rabi's influence in American physics is pervasive; his research contributions are cited by contemporary physicists. His influence, however, transcends physics. He saw clearly the significance of science in the modern world and used the international character of science in the pursuit of peace.

### Bibliography

Bernstein, Jeremy. *Experiencing Science: Profiles in Discovery*. New York: Dutton, 1978; London: Burnett, 1979. The first significant overview of Rabi's work. Originally appeared in *The New Yorker*.

Kevles, Daniel J. *The Physicists: The History of a Scientific Community in Modern America*. New York: Knopf, 1978; London: Harvard University Press, 1995. This book, inspired by Rabi, is an intriguing account of the development of American physics.

Killian, James R., Jr. *Sputnik, Scientists, and Eisenhower: A Memoir of the First Special Assistant to the President for Science and Technology*. Cambridge, Mass., and London: MIT Press, 1977. Killian describes the formation of the President's Science Advisory Committee (PSAC)—a committee proposed by Rabi—and its activities during his tenure as Eisenhower's science adviser.

Rabi, Isidor Isaac. *Science: The Center of Culture*. New York: World, 1970. Rabi's insight and wisdom are revealed in this collection of his articles and speeches.

Rigden, John S. "The Birth of the Magnetic-Resonance Method." In *Observation, Experiment, and Hypothesis in Modern Physical Science*, edited by Peter Achinstein and Owen Hannaway, 205-237. Cambridge, Mass.: MIT Press, 1985. This article traces the development of Rabi's powerful magnetic-resonance method.

———. *Rabi: Scientist and Citizen*. New York: Basic, 1987. The definitive biography of Rabi traces his life and work.

*John S. Rigden*

# SERGEI RACHMANINOFF

*Born:* April 1, 1873; Semyonovo, Novgorod District, Russia
*Died:* March 28, 1943; Beverly Hills, California
*Area of Achievement:* Music
*Contribution:* Rachmaninoff is best remembered as the composer who was the last great figure in the Romantic tradition and the leading pianist of his era. His music is noted for melancholy and long melodic line.

## Early Life

Sergei Vasilyevich Rachmaninoff was born near Novgorod in 1873, the offspring of two noble families. His father was a spendthrift who by 1882 had squandered the family fortune, forcing him to take a flat in St. Petersburg, where he soon deserted his family. Rachmaninoff received a scholarship and attended the St. Petersburg Conservatory. He had shown an early aptitude for the piano. Because of his idle nature, Aleksandr Ziloti, his cousin, suggested that Rachmaninoff study with Nikolai Zverev. In 1885, Rachmaninoff moved into Zverev's apartment. Zverev was a hard taskmaster and, as a result, Rachmaninoff's technique and musical knowledge improved rapidly, especially by playing symphonies in four-hand arrangements and attending concerts.

The Zverevs spent their summers in the Crimea, and it was there that Rachmaninoff, in 1886, first tried his hand at composition. His first surviving composition was the Scherzo in D Minor for orchestra of 1887. In 1888, he studied composition with Ziloti, counterpoint with Sergei Taneyev, and harmony with Anton Arensky. After an argument with Zverev, he went to live with his aunt, Varvara Satin, whose daughter, Natalie, he married in 1902.

In 1890, Rachmaninoff received his first commission for a piano reduction of Peter Ilich Tchaikovsky's *Sleeping Beauty*, though it had to be improved by Ziloti. Rachmaninoff took his graduation examinations one year early and passed with the highest scores. In the summer of 1891, he worked on his First Piano Concerto as well as on the first movement of his Symphony No. 1 in D Minor. For his final presentation at the Conservatory, he presented a one-act opera, *Aleko*, receiving a gold medal for it. That fall he composed his famous Op. 3 for solo piano, *Morceaux de Fantaisie*, in which both the Prelude in C-sharp Minor (No. 2) and the No. 4, the *Polichinelle* in F-sharp Minor, are included. The former piece made him immediately famous. For millions of piano students, this is his quintessential piece because of its melancholia and grandiose style. This piece became the necessary encore at all of his concerts.

It was at this time that Rachmaninoff wrote an orchestral fantasy, *The Rock* (Op. 7), as well as finished his First Symphony, performed on March 27, 1897. This symphony was a colossal failure, and that deeply disturbed him. So great was his despondency that the Satins sent him for psychiatric treatment with Nikolai Dahl. Dahl's treatment was successful, and he dedicated to Dahl one of his best loved works, the Piano Concerto No. 2 in C Minor, which he introduced on October 17, 1901. It was a great success and marks his return to music as an acknowledged master.

The Piano Concerto No. 2 begins with nine unaccompanied chords on the piano and then the entrance of the orchestra with arpeggios played on the piano. It has a passionate second theme followed by a march and a coda. The second movement, the one that took the world by storm, has a nocturnal Russian-like song in the flutes and broken chords from the piano. The finale of the work is martial in character with bravura passages for the soloist. This work is considered his "signature" piece.

## Life's Work

In March, 1902, Rachmaninoff completed his choral work, *Spring*, and in both 1905 and 1906 he won the Glinka Award. During 1905, he and his family left revolutionary Russia and lived in Dresden. It was there that he began sketching his Symphony No. 2 in E Minor, which he conducted in St. Petersburg on February 8, 1908. It is the most celebrated of his symphonic works because of its spontaneity and sincerity, directness, and musical balance. Throughout there is a stepwise shape to his themes. This structure is the key to his mature style.

Early in 1909, Rachmaninoff was back in Dresden, where he began a symphonic poem, *The Isle of the Dead*, inspired by Arnold Boeklin's famous painting of the same name. The 1880 painting is a famous mood piece with a dreamlike island cemetery toward which Charon rows a boat across the River Styx, which holds a flag-draped coffin presided over by a mourner. The island rises steeply with grottos in its tall cliffs, bathed in an eerie glow of the setting sun. High, deep-green cypresses crowd the center, and overhead there is an oppressive purple sky. Rachmaninoff set out to capture Boeklin's morbid sensitivity. The gloom is captured by the composer's quote of the *Dies irae* chant in chromatic figures. As Charon's boat nears the isle, the music climaxes in E minor, seemingly reaching out to the high granite cliffs of the painting itself. The 5/8 bars end and the rowboat drifts to its destination. The piece concludes with the soul of the departed recalling its anguished life, used as a contrast of textures between death and life. This piece has had enormous popular success.

In the summer of 1909, Rachmaninoff prepared for his first American tour, and for this occasion he composed his Concerto No. 3 in D Minor, first performed in New York City on November 28, 1909. Although this piece illustrates his great gifts for long phrased melodies, the music has never enjoyed the success of the Second Concerto. In 1910, he completed the Thirteen Preludes of his Op. 32 and his largest unaccompanied choral work, the *Liturgy of St. John Chrysostom*, Op. 31.

In the winter of 1912, after suffering from a stiffening of his fingers, Rachmaninoff took a vacation in Rome, where he began his largest orchestrated choral work, *The Bells*. The previous summer he had received a copy of Konstantin Balmont's translation of Edgar Allan Poe's poem of the same name. He completed the work while still in Rome. The first movement is full of vigor and a symbol of youth. The second movement, a soprano solo with choral interjections in a rocking figure, is for the golden bells of marriage. He gives this movement a passionate melodic line for the solo voice. The third movement, a scherzo, is without solos and depicts a relentless terror. The finale is quite still and with a solo baritone and recurring chords suggesting the approach of death. In fact, the central part of the section uses a chromatism for Poe's lines about the fiend who dwells in the belfry, and then it ends on the serenity of D flat on the last verse of Poe's poem.

World War I, his father's death in 1916, and the Bolshevik Revolution of 1917 were extremely hard on Rachmaninoff. He and his family left Russia permanently just before Christmas of that year. First they went to Scandinavia, and then to the United States, where he took up a performing career that would last for the rest of his life. During the 1920's and 1930's, he became an incomparable pianist whose theory of a performance centered on making every piece have a culminating point that had to be approached with exact calculation. His playing always had, in addition, a pronounced rhythmic drive, precision, and clarity.

In the United States, Charles Ellis arranged his tours and Victor-RCA did all of his recordings. From 1924 onward, he began to alter his American tours so as to spend time in Europe, first at Dresden; then finally he made Lucerne, Switzerland, his home. It was also at this time that he founded a musical publishing house in Paris called Tair. When, in 1930, he coauthored a letter to *The New York Times* that was critical of the Soviet Union, his music was condemned by the Soviets. In 1931 he resumed composing after a ten-year dry spell. This work was a solo set of variations for the piano on a theme of Marie Corelli and inaugurates his last creative period.

In 1933, Rachmaninoff began work on his *Rhapsody on a Theme by Paganini*, which he finished in August of 1934, giving its first performance on November 7. This piece was an immediate success and is technically his finest work. The rhapsody was written in a loose concerto form of three movements, or twenty-four variations: fast (1-10), slow (11-18), fast (19-24). They are all variations on Paganini's Violin Caprice in A Minor, which Rachmaninoff fully quotes in the second variation. In Variation 7 we get the *Dies irae* theme, which also ends the tenth variation. In Variation 14, the theme is inverted. Variation 17 is a darkly moving passage which leads to the central variation, 18, a highly lyrical modified inversion. Variation 19 starts the last section as a toccata with the rest of the variations increasing in crescendo to the *Dies irae* restatement concluding Variation 24. This is the most melodic and lyrical of all Rachmaninoff's music.

Rachmaninoff returned to Switzerland, and from June to August of 1937 he wrote his Third Symphony. In 1940, he finished his last masterwork, the *Symphonic Dances* of the Op. 45. It was first performed by Eugene Ormandy and the Philadelphia Orchestra on January 3, 1941. Here is a piece of deep chromaticism and contrasting textures. It is especially famous for its long melodic lines in the central section carried by the solo alto saxophone. It ends, humorously, with a quote from his failed First Symphony.

Rachmaninoff's health collapsed in 1942, and in February of 1943 he was brought to his home in Beverly Hills, where he died of lung cancer on March 28, 1943.

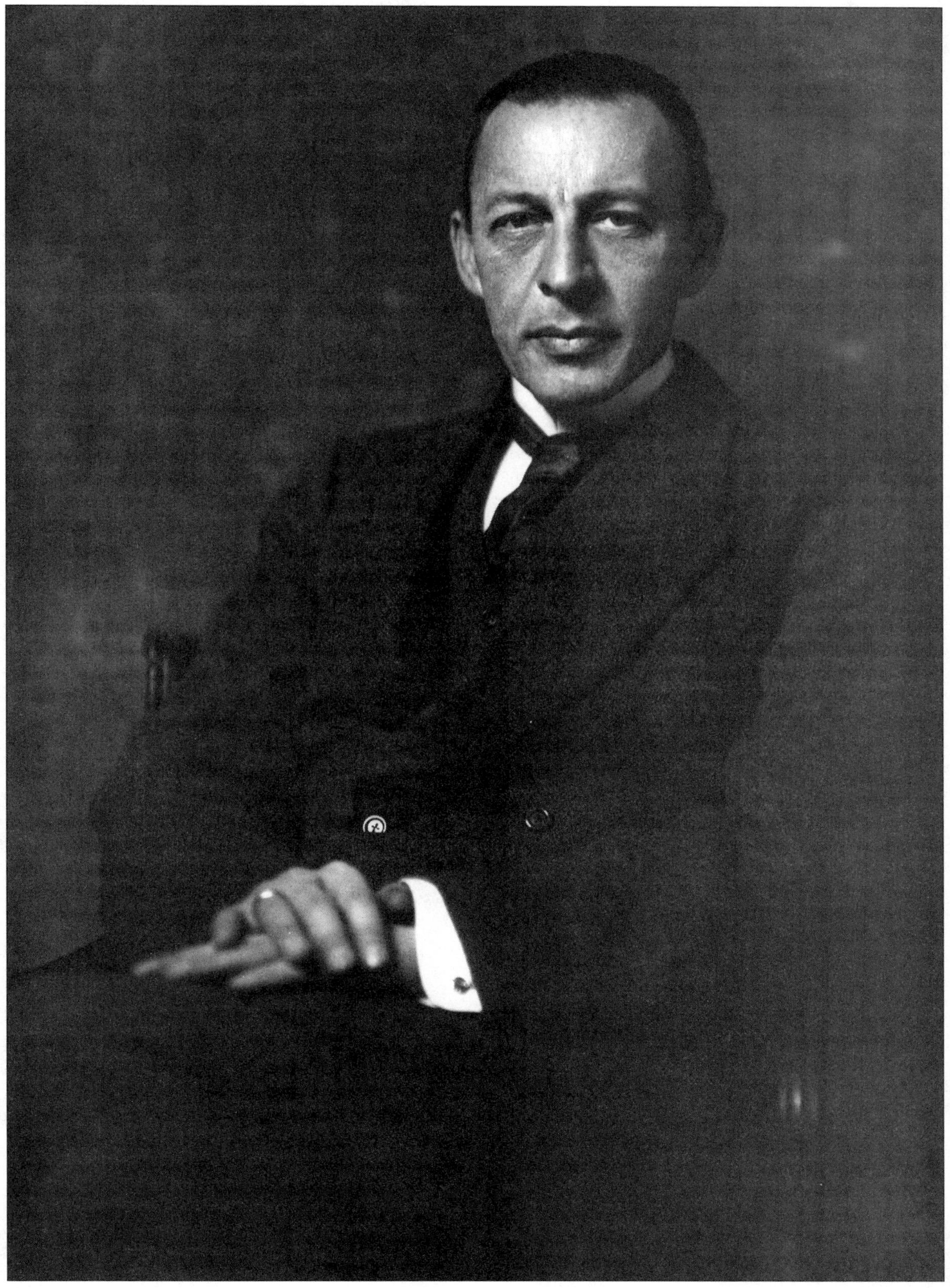

### Summary

Sergei Rachmaninoff's career has all of the pathos of a Romantic novel wherein the hero is at first accepted, then rejected for another lover, undergoes much travail, and is finally reaccepted. After the ups and downs of Rachmaninoff's career, can anyone wonder why this Romantic hero of music is renowned for his compositions of deep melancholy and a rich lyricism of unremitting sadness? Rachmaninoff's music deeply reflects the inner torment of his own soul's journey through life. It was truly his own life that he saw in Boeklin's picture, *The Isle of the Dead* of 1880, that found such a responsive chord for Rachmaninoff's work of 1909. Perhaps it is because human life oscillates between hope and despair that Rachmaninoff's music will always touch the heart of humanity. Rachmaninoff may be considered the last romanticist. His music is melodic and melancholic. Though he was out of joint with twentieth century music and disliked by two other émigré Russian composers, Sergei Prokofiev and Igor Stravinsky, his music is so lush and beautifully moving that he has found a permanent place in the contemporary repertoire.

### Bibliography

Bertensson, Sergei, and Jay Leyda. *Sergei Rachmaninoff: A Lifetime in Music*. New York: New York University Press, and London: Allen and Unwin, 1956. This is the definitive biography of Rachmaninoff and is must reading for anyone interested in the composer. The research on this book is extraordinary and the whole benefits from the intimate recollections of Rachmaninoff's cousin, Sophia Satina.

Cross, Milton, and David Ewen. *Encyclopedia of the Great Composers and Their Music*. Vol. 2. Rev. ed. New York: Doubleday, 1962. Pages 598-608 are an excellent and succinct starting place for those who enjoy Rachmaninoff's music. The "analytical notes" on the composer's major works are particularly helpful for the nonspecialist.

Norris, Geoffrey. *Rachmaninoff*. London: Dent, 1976; New York: Schirmer, 1994. This book is well worth the reader's effort. It is conveniently divided into a biography and a thoroughgoing analysis of Rachmaninoff's works, including useful piano parts. Also, there is a biographical calendar and a very useful catalog of his works.

Rachmaninoff, Sergei. *Rachmaninoff's Recollections*. Translated by Dolly Rutherford. New York: Macmillan, and London: Allen and Unwin, 1934. This is a controversial book, because, after the composer's many conversations with the editor, the final product angered Rachmaninoff. Nevertheless, it is a very personal account, especially of his early life with a very important chapter on his psychiatric treatment by Dahl.

Seroff, Victor I. *Rachmaninoff*. New York: Simon and Schuster, 1950; London: Cassell, 1951. A popular and very readable account of the composer's life. It is especially noteworthy for its photographic album of the composer.

Wright, David. "Rachmaninoff Makes Converts of His Critics." *New York Times* 147, no. 51153 (May 10, 1998). Detailed analysis of selected Rachmaninoff compositions.

*Donald E. Davis*

## SIR CHANDRASEKHARA VENKATA RAMAN

*Born:* November 7, 1888; Trichinopoly (Tiruchirapalli), India

*Died:* November 21, 1970; Bangalore, India

*Areas of Achievement:* Physics, physiology, and education

*Contribution:* Raman, the first internationally acclaimed Indian physicist to be entirely educated within India, was awarded the Nobel Prize in Physics in 1930 for his discovery of important characteristics of light scattering. Raman also made significant contributions to the education of Indian students, establishing the Raman Research Institute in Bangalore in 1948.

### Early Life

Sir Chandrasekhara Venkata Raman was born in Trichinopoly, India, on November 7, 1888. He was born into a family of academicians. His father, Chandrasekhara Iyer, was a professor of mathematics and physics, and his mother, the former Parvathi Ammal, was from a family of well-known Sanskrit scholars. His family's income was considered modest at that time in India, and Raman was the second eldest of eight children.

In 1892, while Raman was still a child, his father accepted a position at Mrs. A. V. N. College in the city of Vishakhapatnam, in Andhra Pradesh Province. There, Raman early demonstrated his academic prowess, finishing his secondary education at eleven years of age and immediately entering Mrs. A. V. N. College. Raman completed two years there and entered Presidency College in Madras. Raman continued to manifest his brilliance, receiving his B.A. with honors in English and physics at age fifteen. Raman was not well enough to travel abroad to study as did his peers. Instead, he pursued his postgraduate education at Presidency College, completing his M.A. in 1907, again with honors at the top of his class.

By the time Raman had completed his M.A., he had already begun intense study of available literature on physics, with special interest in the physics of light and of stringed instruments. In November, 1906, Raman saw his first paper published in the British *Philosophical Magazine* on "unsymmetrical diffraction bands caused by a rectangular aperture, observed when light is reflected very obliquely at the face of a prism."

Yet Raman had exhausted the available educational routes in India. Since he was unable to travel, his academic career essentially ended, he applied to take the examination in the Indian civil service, on which he scored top marks. Such positions were highly respected and well paid. Before entering the civil service, Raman married Lokasundari Ammal and in late 1907 moved his new family to Calcutta, where he had been assigned assistant accountant general.

Before the end of 1907, Raman discovered that only a few blocks from his residence was the Indian Association for the Cultivation of Science. The association had fallen on hard times, chiefly because of lack of interest and attention. Raman changed all that, spending nearly all of his spare time at the association for the next ten years and actively pursuing his own research interests in a carefully defined research program that he designed chiefly on his own initiative. During those years, Raman published frequently in his chosen area—primarily the physics of stringed instruments and acoustics—in such publications as *Nature, Bulletin of the Indian Association for the Cultivation of Science, Physical Review,* and the *Philosophical Magazine.*

### Life's Work

By 1917, Raman's reputation had been well established so that he was offered the Sir Tarakanath Palit chair in physics at the University of Calcutta. Again, however, Raman was required to study abroad and he refused. Vice Chancellor Asutosh Mookerjee judiciously recognized Raman as the ideal person to occupy the newly established position and was so impressed by Raman's expertise that he waived the requirement, allowing Raman to accept the post.

Raman's move to the University of Calcutta signaled significant changes in his life. He could no longer claim the leadership position at the Indian Association for the Cultivation of Science, and his salary was reduced by at least three quarters. He also moved from a path of studies on the physics of stringed instruments and drums to focus on the physics of light and optics.

Four years after he entered the University of Calcutta, he had become a fully participating faculty member, teaching, lecturing, and helping to establish a fully developed graduate curriculum. For the first time in his career, in 1921, Raman traveled outside India to the Congress of Universi-

ties of the British Empire in Oxford. In England, Raman presented the first of his many lectures to be given abroad to the Physical Society about his research activities. On his return to Calcutta, he made the observation that would ultimately lead him to win the Nobel Prize in Physics.

As his ship plowed the blue waters of the Mediterranean Sea, Raman commented on its "wonderful blue opalescence." He also recognized that the blue was a result of the scattering of the light by the water itself and not the reflection of the sky, as was widely accepted at the time. This single observation would focus his career. Even as his ship headed toward home, Raman conducted a simple experiment that confirmed his suspicion. Soon after his return to Calcutta, he published a paper in *Proceedings of the Royal Society* entitled, "On the Molecular Scattering of Light in Water and the Colour of the Sea." He was so delighted at uncovering this apparently pristine area of scientific investigation that he began to focus nearly all of his research in uncovering other aspects of the physics of light.

In 1923, Raman and graduate student K. R. Ramanathan were conducting observations in light scattering through highly purified glycerine, when a phenomenon that would later be called the Raman effect was first discovered. It was a barely detectable trace of light, shifted to either side of the primary optical spectra of the glycerine.

Raman and his associates first suspected that these very weak secondary reflections that were shifted off the primary spectral trace were the result of impurities in the glycerine. They went to great lengths to purify the glycerine before the light was passed through again. Yet the secondary reflections were still present and undiminished no matter how pure the substance. It became obvious to Raman that these secondary reflections were the result of an inherent characteristic of the matter under investigation. Similar results could be observed in liquids, solids, and gases, but the effect was so weak that conventional methods could not magnify the reflections sufficiently for detailed study.

As Raman's group raced to understand the effect, they discovered that if they used a mercury arc lamp, which produced a very intense beam of monochromatic light (light of a single wavelength), they could study the fractional secondary wavelengths reflected. They soon discovered that these secondary reflections revealed aspects of the molecular structure itself. It was a tool of immense importance to physicists and chemists. In 1928, Raman and his colleagues published their results in the *Indian Journal of Physics.* His discovery was of such consequence that, in only a year's time, he was designated a Knight of the British Empire. In 1930, Sir Raman was awarded the Hughes Medal from the Royal Society and won the Nobel Prize in Physics on December 10, 1930, in Stockholm, Sweden.

Raman was ever devoted to the education of Indian students and knew well that the prominence of his nation in the world largely depended on its scientific literacy. Raman would state, "There is only one solution for India's economic problems, and that is science, science and still more science." Raman had already founded the *Indian Journal of Science* and in 1934 would found the Indian Academy of Sciences and its publication *Proceedings.*

In 1933, Raman left his university post to accept the directorship of the Indian Institute of Science in Bangalore. There, he poured the full intensity of his personality to gather a world-class faculty. Unfortunately, his personality did not harmonize with those of the board of directors, and, after only three years as its director, Raman was forced to resign, becoming a professor there. He resigned that post also in 1948.

That year, Raman accepted the directorship of the newly created Raman Research Institute in Bangalore. India had just become independent from Great Britain, and Raman was named national professor. Raman and his students continued studies in optics and reflected light. As he studied the reflection of color from roses in his rose gardens, he became fascinated with the physiology of vision. By 1968, on his eightieth birthday, he had published forty-three papers on vision in a book entitled *The Physiology of Vision.*

Still building the Raman Research Institute and maintaining an active lecture and teaching schedule, he was awarded in 1954 the highest honor of the Indian people—the "Bharat Ratna," or "The Jewel of India." Raman died while still active on November 21, 1970, at the age of eighty-two. He was cremated in one of his rose gardens, as he had requested.

## Summary

Sir Chandrasekhara Venkata Raman has been described as one of the last true "natural philosophers of science." He was able to blend a conscious love for nature into a fully developed scientific investigation as was evidenced by his observations of the blue of the sea, of stringed musical instruments, and even of the color of roses and how it relates to the act of vision. Raman's guileless approach to science formed the basis for his life's work, but the consequences of his life's work carried other, far-reaching impressions.

Raman's insistence on remaining in India to complete his education later became the foundation for his motivation to make Indian educational institutions second to none and to provide world-class institutions of learning for Indian students. Raman's influence on science, education, and the spirit of nationalism in the newly independent nation of India was far-reaching. His personal work in establishing so many of India's influential publications and institutions has had a profound impact on India's economic development and social evolution in the world. The Raman effect has experienced a resurgence of interest. With the advent of the laser, a very powerful, monochromatic beam of light, the Raman effect has been used extensively to investigate the molecular characteristics of many substances.

## Bibliography

Blanpied, William A. "Pioneer Scientists in Pre-Independent India." *Physics Today* 34 (May, 1986): 36-49. Depicts the life of Raman in a historical perspective in reference to his peers. Demonstrates how Raman influenced his nation's political affairs.

Jayaraman, Aiyasami, and Anant Krishna Ramdas. "Chandrasekhara Venkata Raman, India's Great Savant of Science." *Physics Today* 41 (August, 1988): 56-64. This article was written by one of Raman's close associates and one of his students. It details, in a close and intimate account, the life of Raman. Displays Raman in a very personal way from his early years to his death.

Mehra, Jagdish. "Raman, Chandrasekhara Venkata." In *Dictionary of Scientific Biography*, edited by Charles Coulston Gillispie. New York: Scribner, 1984. This widely referenced account of Raman's life involves some technical references about his work and chronologically details his life for the general reader. The emphasis is on the details of his life but it does list some relevant equations connected to the Raman effect and other work.

Weber, Robert L. *Pioneers of Science: Nobel Prize Winners in Physics.* London: Institute of Physics, 1980. Details in a chronological order all the winners of the Nobel Prize in Physics to 1980. Provides a sketch of Raman and with the adjoining references shows the applications of his work.

*Dennis Chamberland*

# A. PHILIP RANDOLPH

*Born:* April 15, 1889; Crescent City, Florida
*Died:* May 16, 1979; New York, New York
*Areas of Achievement:* Trade unionism and civil rights
*Contribution:* Having a passionate desire for economic justice and an unwavering advocacy for social and political equality among all persons, A. Philip Randolph improved significantly the status of Afro-American labor and greatly advanced the civil rights of minority people throughout the United States.

## Early Life

Asa Philip Randolph was born April 15, 1889, in Crescent City, Florida. His mother, Elizabeth, was from Baldwin, Florida, and the youngest of four daughters born to James and Mary Robinson. A devoted member of the African Methodist Episcopal (AME) church, Elizabeth was an intelligent and proud woman who deeply resented bigotry and segregation. James Robinson, independent and resourceful, supported his family by running a small lumber business which supplied pine logs, crossties, pulpwood, and other materials for the railroads and papermills in northern Florida. Philip's father, James William Randolph, was born in 1864, a descendant of slaves who worked for the Virginia planter, John Randolph. James acquired a rudimentary education from Northern missionaries who came South after the Civil War. He became an accomplished tailor and AME minister, serving several poor congregations in Jefferson County, Florida. Outraged by the failure of Reconstruction to secure full racial equality for black people, the itinerant preacher militantly fought to defend his community's newly acquired political rights. James was also strongly influenced by Henry McNeal Turner, the AME bishop and Georgia legislator who sought better wages and living conditions for black workers. Elizabeth and James were married in 1885. They were to have two sons, James William, Jr. (1887), and later A. Philip. In 1891, the Randolphs moved to Jacksonville, Florida, where the family lived frugally in a modest home enriched with purpose, respect, and love.

Several influences shaped Philip's formative years. He greatly admired his brother, a brilliant student, whom Philip readily acknowledged he "loved very much." As youngsters, they often played roles championing the rights of blacks. They remained close friends until William's death in 1928. Philip also revered his father and often accompanied him on house visits to his congregation. The boy basked in the prestige and respect shown his father throughout the community. His father's moving speeches and effective sermons taught young Philip the value of having a social consciousness. Contributing to the family income, Philip worked at a number of jobs including store clerk, newsboy, errand runner, boxcar loader, and railroad section hand. He attended Cookman Institute High School in Jacksonville (later Bethune-Cookman College), where he took the classical course. A diligent student, he developed his elocution skills and did much reading both in and outside class. After graduation he decided to leave the South and go North; his move was an individual example of the great migration undertaken by thousands of other Afro-Americans at the turn of the century to improve themselves economically.

## Life's Work

In 1911, Randolph arrived in New York City and found residence in the Harlem section of upper Manhattan. During the day he worked odd jobs as a porter, waiter, elevator operator, and switchboard operator. In the evenings he enrolled in courses at the City College of New York; there he became interested in literature, especially the works of William Shakespeare, and honed his oratorical talent. He gave readings of the classics to church groups, to literary clubs, and at public forums. He took courses in history, political science, and economics. College life introduced him to socialism, the cause of the Industrial Workers of the World, the ideas of William D. ("Big Bill") Haywood, Eugene V. Debs, and Elizabeth Gurley Flynn. While growing up in Jacksonville, he had read the works of Booker T. Washington and W. E. B. Du Bois, but now he discovered Marxism and other radical approaches to ameliorating the difficulties facing the laboring classes.

Tall and handsome, he was a meticulous, clean-cut dresser who paid careful attention to his grooming. As he matured into a confident yet disciplined young man, his baritone voice and sharp intellect presented a figure of considerable dignity whose presence commanded one's undivided attention. He married Lucille Campbell Green in 1915, an attractive, socially exuberant manager of a Madam C.J. Walker beauty salon. Although six years his senior, she shared his interest in socialism, the classics, the welfare of Afro-Americans, and concern for the working poor. They remained together until her death in 1963.

The seminal event that launched Randolph's career as a labor and political activist occurred when he took a job as a waiter on the Fall River Line which transported people from New York to Boston. Appalled at the cramped, squalid quarters of the employees, the long hours, and the low pay, he attempted to organize his fellow workers, whereupon he was fired by the steamboat company. Undaunted, he joined the Brotherhood of Labor Organization and helped to establish the Independent Political Council (1912).

In 1915, Randolph met Chandler Owen, a brilliant young intellectual who studied social sciences at Columbia University. They held similar political views and became great friends. It was a time of radical protest against brutal, intolerable working conditions in mills, mines, factories, and railroads across the nation. They joined the Socialist Party and believed that the only way to end black racial oppression in America was to attack the capitalistic economic system, which exploited both white and black workers by pitting them against one another, driving wages and living conditions down. Appeals to religious sentiment or humanistic ideals of fair play and equity were viewed as vacuous and pusillanimous. The majority of blacks were politically disfranchised. A successful strategy, they reasoned, must appeal to the economic self-interests of the parties involved. The solution was to forge black-white labor unity, have the laboring masses take control of the economic system from the capitalist classes, and establish a more equitable social system. Pragmatic and militant, their plan of action was to educate and organize Afro-American workers. Randolph spoke from street-corner soapboxes, rallied opponents in social clubs, and debated opponents in public forums.

With Owen, Randolph published a monthly periodical, *Messenger*, subtitled "The Only Radical Negro Magazine in America." In editorials they treated many issues: the need for solidarity among black and white workers, impotent black leadership, the Socialist critique of capitalism, and creative use of boycotts by blacks to achieve their goals. For example, one 1919 editorial succinctly put it, in part:

> Black and white workers should combine for no other reason than that for which individual workers should combine, viz., to increase their bargaining power, which will enable them to get their demands.Second, the history of the labor movement in America proves that the employing class recognize no race lines. They will exploit a white man as readily as a black man. They will exploit women as readily as men. They will even go to the extent of coining the labor, blood and suffering of children into dollars. The introduction of women and children into the factories proves that capitalists are only concerned with profits and that they will exploit any race or class in order to make profits, whether they be black or white men, black or white women or black or white children.

As a pacifist, Randolph opposed the United States' participation in World War I and was jailed for a short period of time because of his antiwar position. Randolph and Owen charged that W. E. B. Du Bois had failed as a theorist and offered no sound solutions to Afro-American problems. They counseled blacks to eschew the National Association for the Advancement of Colored People (NAACP) because it was "controlled and dominated by a group who was neither Negro nor working people." The editors claimed that capitalism was the real culprit responsible for the lynchings of more than three thousand Afro-Americans that occurred between 1890 and 1920; they advocated the use of armed resistance to end this barbaric extralegal practice. Despite having fundamental political differences with Marcus Garvey, Randolph worked for a while with him and his Universal Negro Improvement Association (UNIA). Although Randolph staunchly opposed Communism, he believed that the Russian Revolution was "the greatest achievement of the twentieth century." Responding to Red-baiters who made no distinction between his support for socialism and disapproval of Communism, he remarked:

> If approval of the right to vote, based upon service instead of race and color is Bolshevism, count us as Bolshevists. If our approval of the abolition of pogroms is Bolshevism, stamp us again with that epithet. If the demand for political and social equity is Bolshevism, label us once more . . . .

For several years during and after the Great War, Randolph worked to organize several trade unions, with little success. In 1925, he took up the causes of the porters and maids on the Pullman railroad cars who had failed in their attempts to organize. The problems confronting these largely black workers were shocking. They labored between three hundred and four hundred hours a month barely earning seventy-five dollars monthly in good years. These workers had to pay for their dining-car meals, uniforms, lodging, and other expenses while supporting families and homes. To gain better wages and shorter hours, Randolph and less than a dozen men formed The Brotherhood of Sleeping Car Porters union, with *Messenger* as its official organization. By 1928, a majority of the maids and porters had joined the union. Randolph was labeled a dangerous agitator, Red, atheist, and radical—an outsider who never had worked as a Pullman porter. The American Federation of Labor (AFL) refused to support the union, and the Railroad Labor Board would not protect it. The Interstate Commerce Commission declined to investigate labor complaints. The Brotherhood lost its first attempt to win concessions from the Pullman Company. While a solid core remained loyal, membership in the union declined thereafter. During the Great Depression, when the New Dealers sought to protect the rights of labor to bargain collectively with their employers, porters once again began joining The Brotherhood and by 1935 voted to have the union represent them. By 1937, the union secured an important contract with the Pullman Company, reducing hours to 240 a month, better working conditions and much higher pay. In less than twenty years, the union grew to become the most successful black labor organization in the nation, and Randolph was invited in 1957 to become a vice president of the newly merged AFL-CIO.

Randolph showed as much interest in politics as he had in labor organizing. While serving as president of the Joint Committee on National Recovery (JCNR) in 1935, he called for a united front of all black organizations (civic, labor, political) to abolish Jim Crow laws, attain civil rights, oppose Fascism, and improve the economic status of Afro-Americans. "True liberation," he maintained,

> can be acquired and maintained only when the Negro people possess power; and power is the product and flower of organization—organization of the masses, the masses in the mills and mines, on the farms, in the factories, in churches, in fraternal organizations, in homes, colleges, women's clubs, student groups, trade unions, tenant's leagues, in cooperative guilds, political organizations and civil rights associations.

With the coming of World War II, Afro-Americans were still being denied fair employment opportunities, and those working were not receiving the same pay as their white counterparts for doing the same work. Randolph made a bold yet brilliant move by threatening a massive nonviolent march on Washington to protest job discrimination. As enthusiasm for the protest grew, fear of hampering the nation's war economy led President Franklin D. Roosevelt to issue Executive Order 8802, forbidding racial discrimination in employment by companies having defense contracts. A Fair Employment Practices Commission (FEPC) was established to monitor the order and investigate violations.

During the late 1940's, Randolph called for the complete desegregation of the United States armed forces. An ardent spokesman for the Committee Against Jim Crow in Military Service and Training, he warned the government that he would lead a civil disobedience campaign to refuse registration and resist conscription into a Jim Crow army. Randolph's popular support no doubt influenced President Harry S Truman to begin desegregation of the military. In 1950, Randolph, along with others, established the Leadership Conference on Civil Rights (composed of more than 157 national organizations representing blacks, Hispanics, Asians, labor, major religious denominations, women, the handicapped, and the aged) to guide President Truman's efforts to achieve racial equality. The Negro American Labor Council was founded in 1960 because Randolph, as its president (from 1960 to 1966), believed that the AFL-CIO was doing "little more than paying lip service to desegregation in unions." He was the prime mover behind the historic March on Washington for Civil Rights in 1963 involving a quarter of a million people.

Randolph retired from active political and labor work in 1968 to join for a brief period the A. Philip Randolph Institute, a labor research and information center directed by Bayard Rustin.

### Summary

In numerous ways, A. Philip Randolph sought to secure economic opportunities, political power, and social justice for Afro-Americans in particular and for all exploited and oppressed people in general. If the common people, the workers, unified and organized themselves, he believed that they would have the power in a democracy. In the early years, he had insisted that all ethnic groups and genders must fight together for their common rights. Although he continued to call for interracial solidarity throughout his life, he seemed to have lost faith that most white Americans would ever overcome their bigotry and racism. By the late 1930's, he put less emphasis on his earlier belief in a united labor party and urged the formation of a "tightly organized Negro non-partisan bloc."

With this concept, he galvanized the Afro-American community for the threatened 1941 March on Washington. His masterful tactic was the most significant achievement initiated by any Afro-American to achieve racial equality since Emancipation. Extraordinary indeed, the federal government acceded to black demands. Although President Roosevelt's Executive Order 8802 was grossly undermined and the FEPC lacked strong enforcement power, for the first time in the nation's history, Afro-Americans by themselves had successfully compelled an administration to take action to improve their socioeconomic condition. It was a momentous event that marked a turning point in black-white relations. If for no other reason, this feat alone guaranteed Randolph an indelible place in the pages of United States history.

A. Philip Randolph was the consummate black political organizer of his age. He labored unrelentingly to get individuals and groups to put aside their divisive, parochial, and often petty concerns and close ranks in the formation of a mass movement for the common good. The foremost architect of the modern Civil Rights movement, he urged boycotts in the South against Jim Crow trains, buses, schools, and businesses. "Nonviolent Good Will Direct Action" is what he labeled his movement to gain social equality decades before Martin Luther King, Jr., and others emerged on the 1960's political scene. If not the man himself, then his influence and ideas were at home at the forefront of virtually every civil rights campaign from the 1930's through the 1960's, including desegregation of public accommodations and schools, ending of restrictive covenants, the Montgomery bus boycott, and the 1957 March on Washington. Randolph is to be credited for his role in passage of the 1957, 1960, and 1964 civil rights acts and the voting rights bill of 1965 as well. As one award stated: "No individual did more to help the poor, the dispossessed and the working class in the United States and around the world than A. Philip Randolph."

### Bibliography

Anderson, Jervis. *A. Philip Randolph: A Biographical Portrait*. New York: Harcourt Brace, 1973. This work is the most complete treatment of the life and work of Randolph. Although a sympathetic account, a wide variety of sources, particularly useful interviews with Randolph and others, were used. A strength of this biography is the author's conscientious effort to provide the historical background at each phase of Randolph's long and illustrious career.

Chenoweth, Karin. "Taking Jim Crow Out of Uniform: A. Philip Randolph and the Desegregation of the U.S. Military." *Black Issues in Higher Education* 14, no. 13 (August 21, 1997). Discusses Randolph's successful campaigns to integrate the military and the federal workforce.

Foner, Philip S., and Ronald L. Lewis, eds. *The Black Worker: A Documentary History from Colonial Times to the Present*. Vol. 6, *The Era of Post-War Prosperity and the Great Depression, 1920-1936*, and Vol. 7, *The Black Worker from the Founding of the CIO to the AFL-CIO Merger, 1936-1955*. Philadelphia: Temple University Press, 1983. These works contain an invaluable collection of primary documents on a wide range of labor issues, not only those involving Randolph. The documents give an indispensable account of the difficulties and aspirations of black trade unionism.

Garfinkel, Herbert. *When Negroes March: The March on Washington Movement in the Organizational Politics for FEPC*. New York: Atheneum, 1959. This is the first major treatment of the proposed March on Washington in 1941, initiated by Randolph. It is a well-reasoned, thoroughly documented examination of the central event in Randolph's career and should be read by all scholars of the period.

Harris, William H. *Keeping the Faith: A. Philip Randolph, Milton P. Webster, and The Brotherhood of Sleeping Car Porters, 1925-37*. Urbana: University of Illinois Press, 1977. Harris' study of the origins of The Brotherhood of Sleeping Car Porters is the best scholarly account of the creation and development of the union. The author's thorough research and thoughtful analysis of the problems, mistakes, and successes of this organization tell much about black trade unionism in particular and national opposition to it in general.

Marable, Manning. "A. Philip Randolph: A Political Assessment." In *From the Grassroots: Essays Toward Afro-American Liberation*. Boston: South End Press, 1980. Marable's essay is a critical analysis of Randolph, suggesting that the leader became increasingly cautious and conservative as he won modest victories for labor and achieved limited civil rights reforms. A provocative essay, it deserves a careful reading.

Meier, August, Elliott Rudwick, and Francis L. Broderick, eds. *Black Protest Thought in the Twentieth Century.* 2d ed. Indianapolis: Bobbs-Merrill, and London: Macmillan, 1971. Several primary documents spanning Randolph's career in labor and politics from 1919 to 1963 are made available in this collection. The volume is also useful for ideas and insights into other significant figures.

Pfeffer, Paula F. *A. Philip Randolph, Pioneer of the Civil Rights Movement.* Baton Rouge: Louisiana State University Press, 1990. Thoughtful biography arguing that Randolph's beliefs and strategies gave birth to the mid-twentieth century civil rights movement.

Rustin, Bayard. *Down the Line: The Collected Writings of Bayard Rustin*. Chicago: Quadrangle, 1971. This collection of essays has several partisan articles on various aspects of Randolph's philosophy and activities. Most of the selections on Randolph deal with his later years and offer an interesting, if not polemical, interpretation of the labor leader by his longtime colleague and friend.

*Lamont H. Yeakey*

# JEANNETTE RANKIN

*Born:* June 11, 1880; near Missoula, Montana
*Died:* May 18, 1973; Carmel, California
*Areas of Achievement:* Government and politics and social reform
*Contribution:* Rankin devoted her life to women's rights and peace. She was the first woman elected to Congress and the only member to vote against the entry of the United States into both world wars.

## Early Life

Born in a ranch house near Missoula, Montana, on June 11, 1880, Jeannette Rankin was the eldest of seven children. Her father, John Rankin, the son of Scottish immigrants, moved into Montana in the late 1860's. After prospecting for gold, he settled in Missoula, became a builder and contractor, and played a central role in the town's political and economic development. Jeannette's mother, Olive Pickering, migrated from New Hampshire to Missoula in 1878 and served the town as its schoolteacher until her marriage to John Rankin the following year. John developed a lucrative business and purchased a ranch for cattle raising and farming.

The Rankin family was close-knit and loving but fostered each member's individuality. Evenings were often spent in lively discussion and hearing stories of gold prospecting and Indian warfare in the Montana Territory. The family was also very religious, and its beliefs formed the values by which Jeannette lived her entire life.

Although she loved to read, public school bored Jeannette. She found more satisfaction in learning practical skills from her parents. From her mother, Jeannette learned sewing, and she became an expert seamstress. She studied carpentry with her father and constructed a sidewalk in downtown Missoula.

Jeannette entered Montana State University in 1898, but her college experience was as frustrating as her earlier schooling had been. Because the university was located in Missoula, the change of scenery that she desired was impossible, and because the campus was regional, little opportunity existed to meet students from diverse backgrounds. Moreover, she frequently complained that her classes were uninteresting. She completed her studies, was graduated in 1902, and for a short time taught school.

Looking for something more challenging than teaching, Jeannette drifted from one job to another—dressmaker, sawmill supervisor, and furniture builder. In 1904, Jeannette visited her brother at Harvard College in Boston. She found the city exhilarating but was shocked by the slum conditions and the extent of poverty, overcrowded dwellings, and poor health among ·working-class residents. Repulsed by what she witnessed, Jeannette committed herself to social work.

## Life's Work

In 1908, Jeannette Rankin enrolled in the New York School of Philanthropy to study social issues and social work. After completing the program in 1910, she secured employment in a Spokane, Washington, children's home. At that time the state of Washington was considering woman suffrage. Volunteering her services, she distributed leaflets, canvassed voters door-to-door, and delivered speeches in favor of the state suffrage amendment. Washington granted women the right to vote in No-

vember, and her participation sparked an enthusiasm that placed Jeannette on a crusade for woman suffrage and social reform.

Rankin returned to Montana in December, 1910, for the Christmas holidays and learned that her home state had scheduled debate on a suffrage amendment for January. She quickly organized the Equal Franchise Society, requested and received an invitation from the state assembly to speak on behalf of the amendment, and presented a well-received argument for woman suffrage. Although the amendment was not passed until 1913, Jeannette was instrumental in its eventual victory.

Having gained a taste for social reform politics, Jeannette Rankin became a member of the National-American Woman Suffrage Association (NAWSA) and joined organizations in several states. By autumn of 1914, she had lobbied and spoken before the legislatures of ten states, marched in rallies in major cities, and petitioned Congress for a national woman suffrage amendment. Rankin was quickly becoming a national personality.

In 1914, war erupted in Europe. Although the United States was not involved, Rankin feared that it might be unable to remain neutral. War, she reasoned, would shift the public's attention from social issues and slow the movement for woman suffrage. While in New York, Rankin helped to form the Women's Peace Party in January, 1915, and lobbied Congress to stay out of the European conflict. Although she spent the next summer in Montana organizing "good government clubs" designed to eliminate corruption and to increase women's rights, she devoted most of her time to speaking and writing against American entry into World War I.

In 1916, the likelihood of war led Jeannette Rankin to take the boldest step of her career. Against the advice of Republican Party leaders, Rankin announced her candidacy for election to the U.S. House of Representatives. Her personal platform reflected her professional goals—an amendment to the U.S. Constitution for woman suffrage, child protection laws, social justice, and good government. She was most demanding regarding continued American neutrality. Her antiwar views, which most Montana voters shared, brought her victory in November. Jeannette Rankin was the only Republican to win office in Montana that year and the first woman in American history to take a seat in the United States Congress.

Jeannette Rankin took the oath of office on April 1, 1917, but the warm welcome she received did not last long. On April 5, the House of Representatives commenced debate on American entry into the Great War. Special attention was focused on Rankin. She symbolically represented all women in the nation. Her vote for or against war would be interpreted as a woman's ability to deal with political crises.

The House debated the war resolution throughout the night. Rankin chose to remain silent but listened intently to the heated arguments. Tensions rose as opponents of war were jeered, hissed, and verbally branded as unpatriotic. When the House voted, Jeannette Rankin rose to her feet. "I want to stand by my country," she said, "but I cannot vote for war. I vote no." She found herself in the minority. Three hundred seventy-four representatives supported the resolution, while only fifty voted against war. On April 7, 1917, President Woodrow Wilson declared war on Germany.

Hannah Josephson stated in her biography *Jeannette Rankin, First Lady in Congress* (1974) that Rankin was warned before the vote that she might lose reelection because of her antiwar stance. Her opposition to war was far more important to her than her concern for reelection. The public's response was swift. Rankin was labeled unpatriotic and a disgrace to women nationwide. Even the National-American Woman Suffrage Association claimed that her vote against war would lose supporters for a constitutional suffrage amendment. Rankin later said that her vote against war was the most significant one she ever made. Women, she believed, had to take the lead to end war.

Once the nation was committed to war, Jeannette Rankin supported American troops, worked in Congress to protect civil liberties, and pushed for social reform. She championed legislation authorizing the government to hire more women workers, to provide financial relief to families of soldiers, to improve conditions for imprisoned women, and to guarantee food, clothing, shelter, and health care for children living in poverty. She participated in congressional debates on a federal amendment for woman suffrage, which Congress finally sent to the states for approval in 1918. As her term in the House of Representatives ended, however, Rankin's antiwar vote resurfaced and caused her defeat for reelection.

During the twenty years which followed, Rankin toured the nation promoting feminist issues. She served the National Consumers' League, which advocated federal child labor laws, better working conditions, and increased women's rights. Most of her energy, however, was directed toward achieving international peace.

The horrors of World War I still vivid in her mind, and aware that social justice could never be attained as long as money was spent on defense and warfare, Rankin helped to form the Women's International League for Peace and Freedom and volunteered her services to numerous other peace organizations. She campaigned against Reserve Officers Training Corps programs on college campuses. She was a central figure at the Conference on the Cause and Cure for War, participated in the Peace March on Chicago, lobbied congressmen to introduce legislation to outlaw war, and advocated the creation of a National Peace Party to challenge both Republicans and Democrats in state and federal elections. As the 1930's drew to a close and the prospect for another world war seemed likely, Rankin intensified her efforts.

In November, 1940, at age sixty, Jeannette Rankin was again elected to Congress on a peace platform. She proposed bills to prevent the sending of American troops abroad and to require a national vote before war could be declared. Neither measure passed, but she persisted throughout 1941. Despite Japan's attack on Pearl Harbor on December 7, Rankin stood for peace regardless of personal consequences. On December 8, Congress voted for war. This time, Rankin cast the only vote in opposition. As before, Rankin received the brunt of public criticism and was not reelected the following year.

Until her death in 1973, Jeannette Rankin traveled the world. The extent of global poverty and injustice she witnessed intensified her belief that only in a peaceful world could social problems be resolved. Based on this view, she condemned America's war in Vietnam throughout the 1960's. In January, 1968, she participated in an antiwar march on Washington. The Jeannette Rankin Brigade, so named by her admirers, petitioned Congress to end the war and "heal a sick society at home."

### Summary

Until her death on May 18, 1973, Jeannette Rankin pressed her demands for an end to war, protection of civil liberties, and direct popular vote on critical national issues. She never realized her dream to end war, but she was responsible, directly or indirectly, for the creation of many laws. Her efforts resulted in voting rights for women, support for dependents of servicemen, free postage for members of the armed forces, retention of citizenship for women who marry aliens, child labor and protection laws, and women's rights. Throughout her life she spoke on behalf of labor, for child welfare, for social justice and greater democracy, and against racial prejudice. She further advocated multimember congressional districts, a unicameral Congress, direct election of the president, and the restructuring of the U.S. military into a purely defensive force. Her two elections to Congress opened avenues for women nationally in politics and business. Although she was labeled an idealist and was criticized severely for her antiwar position, Jeannette Rankin possessed the courage to remain true to her convictions and dedicated her life to the betterment of American society and the human race.

### Bibliography

Anderson, Kathryn. "Steps to Political Equality: Woman Suffrage and Electoral Politics in the Lives of Emily Newell Blair, Anne Henrietta Martin, and Jeannette Rankin." *Frontiers* 18, no. 1 (January-April, 1997). Discusses the lives and achievements of three noted women's rights activists, including Rankin.

Chafe, William H. *The American Woman: Her Changing Social, Economic, and Political Roles, 1920-1970*. New York: Oxford University Press, 1972; London: Oxford University Press, 1974. Chafe develops a thorough, detailed study of American feminism in the twentieth century, illuminating its development, course, and reception by American society. This work has become a standard in the field and accurately presents Rankin's era.

*Dedication of the Statue of Jeannette Rankin*. Washington, D.C.: Government Printing Office, 1986. This publication includes a biographical sketch of Rankin and speeches given by prominent political figures in remembrance of her advocacy of women's rights and an end to war. Included is a time line of Jeannette Rankin's life.

Fenton, Matthew McCann. "'I Can't Stand Being a Worm.'" *Biography* 1, no. 5 (May, 1997). Profile of Rankin, including her views on gender, equality, and social issues.

Josephson, Hannah. *Jeannette Rankin, First Lady in Congress*. Indianapolis: Bobbs-Merrill, 1974. Although many prominent and influential women with whom Rankin worked receive limited attention and the broad context in which Rankin operated is somewhat vague, Josephson has presented a complete, well-researched biography of Jeannette Rankin. The author's twenty-year personal relationship with Rankin makes the work most insightful and revealing.

Libby, Frederick J. *To End War.* Nyack, N.Y.: Fellowship, 1969. Libby surveys the patterns of antiwar thought and peace organizations in twentieth century America.

Noble, David W. *The Progressive Mind, 1890-1917.* Rev. ed. Minneapolis, Minn.: Burgess, 1981. This work provides an overview of the intellectual foundations of the Progressive Era and the evolution in thought of Progressives themselves. One chapter devoted exclusively to women of the period adequately highlights the feminist movement.

*Kenneth W. Townsend*

# KNUD JOHAN VICTOR RASMUSSEN

*Born:* June 7, 1879; Jakobshavn, Greenland
*Died:* December 21, 1933; Gentofte, Denmark
*Areas of Achievement:* Exploration, geography, and anthropology
*Contribution:* A pioneer Arctic explorer, Rasmussen was best known for his seven Thule expeditions. In the fifth, the most famous of these, he crossed North America from Greenland to the Bering Strait. A celebrated ethnographer, Rasmussen studied the folkways of the Eskimos and published many works about the peoples and places of Arctic America.

## Early Life

Knud Johan Victor Rasmussen was born on June 7, 1879, in the Lutheran parsonage at Jakobshavn, Greenland. This Danish settlement was situated halfway up the western coast of Greenland. The eldest son of Christian Rasmussen, a Danish missionary in Greenland for twenty-eight years, who later became a lector in Greenlandic studies at the University of Copenhagen, Knud was exposed to exploration and ethnography in early childhood. His father took as his parish the entire northern half of colonized Greenland, often working his way by dogsled up the west coast of the island to visit his five remote preaching stations. An excellent linguist who later produced both a Greenlandic grammar and dictionary, the elder Rasmussen taught Knud to regard all Greenlanders as his brothers, and Knud responded by learning their ways and developing a love for them that never waned.

Rasmussen's mother was herself part Eskimo. Her father, Knud Fleischer, had been born in Greenland of Norwegian parents. Becoming a colonial administrator for the Danes as well as a successful trader, Fleischer married an Eskimo woman. Young Rasmussen grew up celebrating his dual heritage—the Scandinavian (Danish and Norwegian) and the Eskimo.

Rasmussen recalled his childhood as a happy one. From the parsonage, he could view Disko Island, the largest off the coast of Greenland, as well as the great glacier and the spring icebergs. Fascinated by the North, Rasmussen rejoiced in a childhood trip with his father and Riis Carstensen, an explorer, to visit his uncle, Carl Fleischer, who headed the Danish settlement at Qeqertak. This Greenland childhood determined the direction of Rasmussen's later life. Two additional influences affected Rasmussen's development. In 1888, Fridtjof Nansen attempted the first complete crossing of Greenland, an adventure that had a profound influence on the lad. The impact of his Aunt Helga, his first teacher, was equally decisive. It filled him with a profound love for the ways of Greenland.

Reluctantly, Rasmussen left Greenland for Denmark. Failing his entrance examinations for the Herlufsholm School, Rasmussen studied in Copenhagen. He was not a particularly good student. Completing his baccalaureate education at the University of Copenhagen (Rasmussen later was awarded a Ph.D. by his alma mater and an LL.B. by the University of Edinburgh), Rasmussen flirted with several occupations, such as acting, singing, and journalism. As a correspondent for the *Christian Daily* and the *Illustrated Times*, he went to Stockholm to cover the Nordic games; then, at age twenty-one, he went to Lapland to study reindeer breeding. Travels in Scandinavia's Northland, to Narvik and Tomso, reinforced his fascination with the Arctic.

## Life's Work

At age twenty-three, Rasmussen began his life's work. He joined the Danish Literacy Expedition of Mylius-Erichsen, an ethnographer, Jorgen Brønland, a catechist, Count Harald Moltke, a painter and illustrator, and Alfred Bertelsen, a doctor, on an expedition to visit the most northern tribe in the world, the Polar Eskimos of upper Greenland. This voyage of 1902-1904 was followed in 1905 by an assignment from the Danish government to travel in Greenland with a group of Lapps to determine the feasibility of introducing the reindeer as an addition to the Eskimo economy. For the next two years, 1906-1908, Rasmussen lived among the Polar Eskimos, studying their folklore. By then it was becoming obvious that Rasmussen's ability to travel and hunt like the Eskimos was a phenomenal asset. He could speak their languages fluently and maintain friendly relations with them. Rasmussen was able to record much of their oral tradition before it disappeared with the onset of modern civilization.

Returning to Denmark in 1908, Rasmussen married Dagmar Andersen, daughter of Niels Andersen, state counselor, chairman of the Employers' Association, and considered one of Denmark's major entrepreneurs. Friends considered this marriage a

*Knud Rasmussen (third from left)*

major source of strength for Rasmussen. Within a year, Rasmussen had returned to the Arctic, serving the Danish government on an expedition for educational purposes in 1909. This fired his imagination and caused him to envision the possibility of founding a permanent base for additional explorations.

At the age of thirty, in 1910, Rasmussen established Thule, a center for trade and exploration among the Polar Eskimos. Trade in manufactured goods provided the economic support, but the real purpose of this base on the northwest coast of Greenland was not commercial but scientific. Thule became the starting point for seven expeditions. Rasmussen's timing was excellent. The discovery of the North Pole in 1909 had aroused considerable interest in the Arctic. Danish claims to the north of Greenland were being contested, and Rasmussen saw such a settlement as Thule as critical to establishing Danish sovereignty over the region. This opinion was vindicated in 1933, when the International Court of Justice at the Hague ruled against Norway and in favor of Denmark, recognizing Copenhagen's claims to all of Greenland. Following a lecture tour to raise funds for building Thule, Rasmussen sailed to the Arctic. The harbor at Thule was open only twenty-five days of the year (August 1-25), and the environment was harsh. Rasmussen coped with these conditions and became the first to cross Melville Bay by sledge, demonstrating the feasibility of exploration from Thule.

On April 8, 1912, together with explorer Peter Freuchen, a longtime friend, Rasmussen led the first Thule expedition, crossing the Greenland ice cap from Thule to Independence Fjord. This feat had been attempted only once before, by Nansen in 1888, an event that had inspired Rasmussen as a child. This trip allowed Rasmussen to study Eskimo life and to formulate his theory as to their origins. Postulating their Asian origin, Rasmussen believed that American Indians and Eskimos were descended from prehistoric immigrants who came to the Americas across the Bering Strait. Upon the completion of the first Thule expedition, Rasmussen returned to Denmark to report on his scientific progress and to see his three-year-old daughter for the first time.

Though Denmark remained neutral during World War I, the European conflagration had consequences for the far North. Rasmussen continued his work, however, and a mapping expedition in 1914 was followed in 1916-1918 by a survey of the north coast of Greenland. In 1918, following a visit to Denmark, Rasmussen set out for Angmagssalik in eastern Greenland on an ethnographic expedition to collect Eskimo tales. This was completed in 1919. On the two-hundredth anniversary of the arrival in Greenland of Hans Egede, the pioneer Lutheran missionary, there was a royal visit by the King of Denmark to the island. This event in 1921 honoring "the Apostle of Greenland" encouraged Rasmussen to think in terms of further discoveries.

The fifth Thule expedition, Rasmussen's most famous journey, lasted from 1921 to 1924, and he explored Greenland, Baffin Island, and the Arctic Coast of America, the longest dogsled journey in history. Rasmussen traversed the American Arctic from the Atlantic to the Pacific, conducting a scientific study of virtually every Eskimo tribe in that region. The expedition began on September 7, 1921, at Upernavik and went from Greenland to the Bering Strait, arriving at Point Barrow, Alaska, on May 23, 1924. During this trip, Rasmussen traced Eskimo migration routes and observed the essential unity of Eskimo culture.

Rasmussen was an excellent communicator, and his works were widely published in Danish, Greenlandic, and English translation. Rasmussen's works included travelogs, collections of Eskimo mythology and songs, and scientific texts, as well as writings of cartographic, ethnographical, and archaeological significance. *Under nordenvindens svobe* (1906) and *Nye mennesker* (1905) appeared in English translation in 1908 under the single title *The People of the Polar North: A Record* and established his reputation. *Grønland Langs Polhavet: Udforskningen af Grønland fra Melvillebugten til Kap Morris Jesup* (1919; *Greenland by the Polar Sea: The Story of the Thule Expedition from Melville Bay to Cape Morris Jessup*, 1921) introduced the earth's largest island to readers throughout the Western world and was followed within the decade by his account of the most extensive expedition yet to explore the Arctic, published as *Fra Grønland til Stillehavet* (1925; *Across Arctic America: Narrative of the Fifth Thule Expedition*, 1927). Rasmussen's work also included collections of Native American literature such as *Myster og sagn fra Grønland* (1921-1925; myths and sagas from Greenland).

### Summary

Knud Johan Victor Rasmussen was honored by the world for his many scientific contributions and was a Knight of the Royal Order of Dannebrog (Denmark), a Commander of the Order of Saint Olav (Norway), a Commander of the White Rose (Finland), a Knight of the Royal Order of the North Star (Sweden), and a recipient of a Golden Medal of Merit from the Danish king, among other awards. Rasmussen was a member of many distinguished learned societies, including the Norwegian Geographical Society and the equivalent geographical societies of Sweden, Italy, and the United States as well as the Explorers' Club of New York and the Scientific Society in Lund, Sweden.

Explorer of the Arctic and famed ethnographer of the American Eskimos, Rasmussen was honored with doctorates from Danish and British universities and the Knud Rasmussen room in the National Museum in Copenhagen recalls his memory. More than sixteen thousand artifacts in that museum testify to the thoroughness of his work. On December 21, 1933, Rasmussen died near Copenhagen, at Gentofte, Denmark, of food poisoning contracted during his final expedition, complicated by influenza and pneumonia.

### Bibliography

Croft, Andrew. *Polar Exploration.* 2d ed. London: Black, 1947. More than a general survey of polar expeditions, this volume focuses on the more prominent explorations of the Arctic regions in the twentieth century. With eight maps and twenty-two illustrations, this text is organized into two parts. Part 1, entitled "The Arctic Regions," is especially relevant to the life of Rasmussen; it surveys the scientific exploration of the North and contains valuable discussion of Rasmussen's contribution to geographical knowledge in Greenland and Canada.

Freuchen, Peter. *Arctic Adventure: My Life in the Frozen North.* New York: Farrar and Rinehart, 1935; London: Heinemann, 1936. Freuchen was Rasmussen's best friend, and together they shared many interests and experiences. Enhanced with illustrations and maps, this book is more than a recollection of one man's life in the Arctic. Contains interesting vignettes of the region, its conditions, and peoples. Invaluable personal recollections and anecdotes.

———. *I Sailed with Rasmussen.* New York: Messner, 1958. This work is not an exhaustive scholarly work on Rasmussen but rather a collection of impressions of a dear friend. A vivid description that is supplemented by useful illustrations.

Stefansson, Vilhjalmur. *Greenland.* New York: Doubleday, 1942; London: Harrap, 1943. An older work, this history of Greenland from the earliest times until the start of the 1940's remains a valuable introduction to the world that Rasmussen knew and loved. Readable and reliable, Stefansson's survey conveys a feel for a region that is as large as the combined twenty-six states east of the Mississippi. Particularly helpful are references to Rasmussen's works.

Williamson, Geoffrey. *Changing Greenland.* Introduction by Ole Bjørn Kraft. London: Sidgwick and Jackson, 1953; New York: Library Publishers, 1954. This survey of the history of Greenland from the arrival of the Vikings to the major changes of the 1950's is organized into two main sections. Part 1, entitled "Old Orders," helps place the life and labors of Rasmussen in proper chronological and sociological context.

*C. George Fry*

## WALTER RAUSCHENBUSCH

*Born:* October 4, 1861; Rochester, New York
*Died:* July 25, 1918; Rochester, New York
*Areas of Achievement:* Religion and social reform
*Contribution:* Moving away from individualism, Rauschenbusch formulated a social gospel which influenced the Church and society to accept responsibility for social and economic injustice and to institute social reform.

### Early Life

Walter Rauschenbusch was born on October 4, 1861, in Rochester, New York, of German immigrant parents. His father, August Rauschenbusch, came from a Lutheran background but became an Orthodox Baptist minister. In 1865, Rauschenbusch traveled with his mother and two sisters to Germany, where his father joined them in 1868. He attended public school there, but when the family returned to New York in 1869, he attended a private school and the Free Academy, both in Rochester.

From 1870 to 1879, Rauschenbusch enjoyed summer farm work in Pennsylvania. The farmer who employed him was kind and the work pleasant. At a farm in New York, however, he experienced at first hand unfair labor practices. The farmer kept him at hard work for long hours, feeding and paying him very little. This influenced his later thoughts on economic injustice.

Healthy and bright, Rauschenbusch was a mischievous boy but eager to work and learn. His mother encouraged in him a sense of humor, courtesy, an appreciation of beauty, and a love of nature. Rauschenbusch was taught to attend Sunday school and church and to read the Bible and pray, but the family religion did not include an interest in social issues. At the age of seventeen, he underwent a spiritual awakening and had a personal experience with God.

After his conversion and baptism, he concluded work at the Free Academy. From 1879 to 1883, he studied and traveled in Europe. He completed courses at the Evangelical Gymnasium of Gütersloh and the University of Berlin. Although urged to enter other work, he continued to move toward the ministry.

When he returned home, he studied at the University of Rochester and Rochester Theological Seminary from 1883 until 1886. During this time, another spiritual experience inspired him to resolve to live entirely by the spirit and teachings of Jesus Christ.

During the summer of 1884, Rauschenbusch pastored a German Baptist Church in Louisville, Kentucky. He found a small, neglected congregation with internal disharmony and a poor reputation with outsiders. Shy and sensitive but upright and determined, he began to raise the spiritual standards of the congregation. When he left at summer's end, he had settled disputes, united members, and nearly doubled the congregation.

When he completed his seminary studies, Rauschenbusch was six feet tall with a mustache, sideburns, and hazel eyes that sparkled with humor. His close friends were of exceptional character and ability. He applied for the mission field with the American Baptist Foreign Mission Society but was turned down, apparently because of his liberal views concerning the Old Testament.

### Life's Work

When the Second German Baptist Church in New York City asked Rauschenbusch to be their pastor, he accepted and began work on June 1, 1886. The church, located in a tough West Side neighborhood known as Hell's Kitchen, was filled with discouragement and need.

At the start, he planned to preach and pastor, bringing individuals to salvation and then nurturing their faith. He soon realized, however, that Christians were unsafe in the city because of oppressive social conditions. In his church families, he saw the effects of poverty, unemployment, and malnutrition. Disease and crime were widespread in the overcrowded slum tenements. As he developed a plan of social action, he became convinced that capitalism was causing the injustice. He began to see Christian socialism as a cure for economic injustice.

Also, he recognized that one's acceptance of Christ gave one inner strength but did not change the unfair political and economic system that was ruining families. His gospel needed to expand to provide for the redemption of society. In his search for a principle to encompass the salvation of individuals and society, he studied the writings of economists, political activists, socialists, and other social reformers. He also read Jesus' teachings and the Old Testament Book of Amos.

Long hours in study and church work weakened his health, and he became ill with Russian influenza in 1888. Unwilling to neglect his parishioners, he returned to work too soon and a relapse left him

deaf. Although his deafness caused him suffering and loneliness, he did not allow it to ruin his friendships or his work. In three years, the church membership increased from 143 to 213 and a new building was erected.

While developing his ideas of social reform, Rauschenbusch began to write for newspapers and journals. In 1889, he helped found *For the Right*, a monthly paper for working people that discussed their questions in terms of Christian socialism.

When the last issue was published in March, 1891, Rauschenbusch sailed for Europe. While exploring social and economic conditions in Europe, he hoped to discover new ways to serve the poor. He investigated the Salvation Army but concluded that it was treating symptoms of poverty, while he wanted to eliminate the cause.

While in Germany, Rauschenbusch formulated his idea of the Kingdom of God, the organization of society in obedience to God's will. The individual is converted and receives the power and responsibility to participate in the redemption of society. Worldwide missions would extend the Kingdom to every institution and group, and society would move progressively toward unity. God's will—justice and righteousness—would be done on earth as in Heaven. He returned home in 1891 and formed the Brotherhood of the Kingdom, whose members were committed to obeying the ethics of Jesus and spreading the spirit of Christ throughout the political, industrial, social, and scientific life of society.

At a conference of German Baptists, Rauschenbusch met Pauline Rother, a Milwaukee schoolteacher, and married her on April 12, 1893. It was a happy marriage, and Pauline became an active partner in his ministry at the New York church. Intelligent and well educated, she shared his views on Christianity and social reform. Her ability to communicate with her husband enabled her to help him in conversations and meetings. The couple had five children, and Rauschenbusch was devoted to his family.

As Rauschenbusch continued his difficult but successful work with the church in New York, he was becoming well-known as an activist and as a speaker on social reform. He also participated in the Baptist Congress, a liberal forum for Baptist leaders.

In 1897, Rauschenbusch left the pastorate to teach in the German Department of Rochester Theological Seminary. He taught German Americans to pastor the German Baptist churches, but under him many students became too liberal for the churches. Five years later, he became a professor of church history and continued teaching there until his death in 1918.

In 1907, Rauschenbusch gave *Christianity and the Social Crisis* (1907) to a publisher and sailed for Europe. When he returned, he was famous, in great demand for sermons and lectures. His book explored the biblical history of social ethics, described the need for reform, and urged Christians to promote social justice.

Personal prayer was the source of Rauschenbusch's vitality, and that part of his spiritual life is revealed in his book, *For God and the People: Prayers of the Social Awakening* (1910). It includes a collection of prayers written for various situations and an essay on the Lord's Prayer. *Christianizing the Social Order* (1912) gives a detailed and systematic explanation of his views on social problems and their relationship to Christianity. *A Theology for the Social Gospel* (1917) was written to provide a theological and intellectual basis for the social gospel. Not a substitute for the individual gospel, the social gospel expands it to include the good news of redemption for society.

The world was at war when Rauschenbusch finished his last book, and he knew that there could be no immediate regeneration of society. Seriously ill and saddened by the war, he died on July 25, 1918.

### Summary

Working across denominational lines, Walter Rauschenbusch influenced and changed the thinking of American Protestantism. He moved Christianity away from individualism and into the area of social consciousness. Churches could no longer ignore the poverty and injustice around them but were made aware of their responsibility to change oppressive social and economic conditions. His theory of social ministry became the basis for the social creeds adopted by major Protestant denominations.

Rauschenbusch and his writings were instrumental in the formation of the Federal Council of the Churches of Christ in America. The organization has given leadership to the Christian movement and worked for unity, social justice, and international goodwill. The Federal Council was the forerunner of the National Council of Churches.

The direction of the work of the Young Men's Christian Association and the Young Women's Christian Association was also influenced by Rauschenbusch's teachings. He provided religious justification for their outreach to humanity and encouraged the provision of a Christian social environment.

By speaking and writing of the oppressive conditions in the cities and fighting for reform, Rauschenbusch made the public aware of the needs of the poor. The labor movement, public park movement, and Christian socialism were all influenced by his teachings. After his first book was published, he was accepted as the chief spokesman for the American Social Gospel movement. His views on social change have become a part of American Christianity and social service.

### Bibliography

Dorn, Jacob H. "The Social Gospel and Socialism: A Comparison of the Thought of Francis Greenwood Peabody, Washington Gladden, and Walter Rauschenbusch." *Church History* 62, no. 1 (March, 1993). Considers the relationship between Christianity and socialism from the perspective of three Social Gospel theologians.

Handy, Robert T., ed. *The Social Gospel in America*. New York: Oxford University Press, 1966. Biographical sketches and selected writings of three prominent leaders of the Social Gospel movement: Washington Gladden, Richard T. Ely, and Rauschenbusch. Depicts the growth and development of the social gospel.

Hopkins, Charles Howard. *The Rise of the Social Gospel in American Protestantism: 1865-1915*. New Haven, Conn.: Yale University Press, and London: Oxford University Press, 1940. The relationship between Christianity and society's moral and ethical problems is explored in this comprehensive chronicle of the Social Gospel movement. Describes how the industrial revolution, social injustice, and an interest in reform led to the theology of the social gospel.

Lasch, Christopher. "Religious Contributions to Social Movements: Walter Rauschenbusch, the Social Gospel, and Its Critics." *Journal of Religious Ethics* 18, no. 1 (Spring 1990). Examines the achievements of Rauschenbush and compares his thoughts to those of Reinhold Niebuhr.

Macfarland, Charles S. *Christian Unity in the Making*. New York: Federal Council of the Churches of Christ in America, 1948. Traces the development of the Federal Council of the Churches of Christ in America from the first attempts to unify the denominations to the establishment of the organization in 1908 and includes its history through 1930. Details the work and purpose of the council and its progress in working with various denominations and interdenominational groups.

Mowry, George E. *The Era of Theodore Roosevelt: 1900-1912*. London: Hamilton, and New York: Harper, 1958. Only briefly covering the Social Gospel movement, Mowry gives insight into the social, political, and economic problems of the early 1900's and why reform was needed. Explores conservatism, liberalism, Progressivism, and socialism.

Rauschenbusch, Walter. *Christianity and the Social Crisis*. New York and London: Macmillan, 1907. First of a series of major works which contributed to a social awakening and the humanization of theology in America. Examines the social ethics of the Old Testament and Jesus' teachings. Describes the need for reform and offers suggestions for change.

———. *Christianizing the Social Order*. New York: Macmillan, 1912. Most complete and systematic explanation of Rauschenbusch's position. Specifically discusses social problems and changes needed in religion and the economic system to resolve them.

———. *A Rauschenbusch Reader.* Edited by Benson Y. Landis. New York: Harper, 1957. Compilation of selected Rauschenbusch writings, abridged but including main points. Preceding each chapter, Landis remarks on then-prevailing issues and describes the chapter selection.

Sharpe, Dores Robinson. *Walter Rauschenbusch.* New York: Macmillan, 1942. Comprehensive biography by his secretary and longtime friend. Sharpe portrays Rauschenbusch as a scholar, a loving husband and father, a pastor who cared deeply for his struggling parishioners, and a creative thinker who penned the theology of a social gospel. Summarizes and comments on Rauschenbusch's most important writings.

White, Ronald C., and C. Howard Hopkins. *The Social Gospel.* Philadelphia: Temple University Press, 1976. Restatement of the social gospel and expansion of its definition and history, including criticisms, personalities, and lasting effects. Examines the influence of the Social Gospel movement on issues such as human rights, social injustice, ecumenism, and social action.

*Elaine Mathiasen*

# MAURICE RAVEL

*Born:* March 7, 1875; Ciboure, France
*Died:* December 28, 1937; Paris, France
*Area of Achievement:* Music
*Contribution:* Ravel was one of the most important composers during the first third of the twentieth century, working in many styles and in many different forms.

## Early Life

Joseph Maurice Ravel was the first son of a French-Swiss engineer and a Basque woman he had met while working in Spain. After Ravel was born, he and his family moved to Paris. Although he would later write music based on Spanish and Basque themes and travel throughout Europe and the United States, Ravel would remain, at heart, a Parisian. Ravel's parents recognized and appreciated their son's early interest in music and spared no effort to send him to the best teachers they could find, starting at the age of six. From the ages of six through sixteen, Ravel moved quickly through the steps of a sound education in piano and music theory, gaining entrance into the Paris Conservatory in 1891. By 1895, when he left the conservatory, Ravel had already set his own style, which would upset the musical establishment.

## Life's Work

Ravel was an active composer for forty years (1893-1932) before ill health prevented him from composing during the last five years of his life. Most of those forty years were spent ignoring the critics and fellow composers, who usually heaped abuse upon him from all sides until after his death. Many of the more avant-garde members of the musical scene before World War I either tended to criticize Ravel for being a poor copy of Claude Debussy or criticized both men for not following the lead of the German composers of the Richard Wagner school, while the establishment critics saw all the above, including Ravel, as a threat to the music with which they had grown up. After the war, Ravel was often considered old-fashioned by the more radical composers, who were looking at jazz, Dada, or the works of Arnold Schoenberg for their inspiration.

Ravel was not interested in composing in the grand Romantic and chromatic style of the German school, and, while he admired Debussy and Schoenberg, he had no desire to imitate them. Instead, Ravel sought inspiration in the French baroque and in Spanish and Basque folk music. Yet, while his inspirations were often found in the past, his musical language was near the cutting edge of the avant-garde. Performers, especially pianists, often found his music to be exactly what they were looking for when they looked for the best contemporary music. His major works, including *Pavane pour une infante défunte* (1899), *Sonatina* (1905), *Valses noble et sentimental* (1911), *Le Tombeau de Couperin* (1917), and many others remain in the standard literature, while *Pavane pour une infante défunte* and *Le Tombeau de Couperin*, later orchestrated by Ravel, are also in the standard symphonic repertoire.

Ravel did not seek out publicity, but he nevertheless often found himself in the middle of controversy. In retrospect this is not surprising, since the French artistic scene at the turn of the century until the outbreak of World War I is now famous for its squabbling and even riots at premieres of new works of music and art. Perhaps the most famous controversy in which Ravel found himself was over the 1905 competition for the Prix de Rome (a contest in which a musician would be sent to study and compose in Rome for a year). The rejection of his work led to a major scandal fought out in the national press, which resulted in the resignation of the head of the Paris Conservatory.

Ravel also found himself in the middle of another scandal in early 1907. He had composed five humorous settings for five rather obscurely written poems by Jules Renard, which Ravel entitled *Histoires naturelles*, and in January, 1907, they were performed at the National Society of Music, most of whose members preferred the music of Wagner to that of the emerging school of French modernists. Most of the audience hissed at the work, and the critics lambasted it, one implying the music was a bad echo of Debussy. All those who did not like the music missed the humor, perhaps because they had made so much noise they had not really heard the music. Again the French newspapers took sides, and Ravel's music was debated for weeks. Ravel ignored the entire affair and spent the time finishing his comic opera *L'Heure espagnole*, although it was not produced until 1911. Ravel continued this basic pattern up until World War I, composing works that would stir up opposition when they were first performed, even if they

gained almost immediate acceptance by musicians, while he went on to produce another work. While Ravel was never a prolific composer, the years 1905-1914 were easily his most productive.

World War I changed Ravel's personal world, just as it changed Europe. Ravel was not physically fit for the French army, but he managed to use his influence and was allowed to go to a training camp in 1915 with the possibility of later joining the new air force. Ravel never got to join the air force, but he did join the Motor Transport Corps as a driver in March, 1916. By May, his health had started to give way, and he was in various hospitals and rest camps for the rest of 1916. The year 1917 started with the death of his mother, something from which the very attached Ravel never completely recovered, and Ravel never really was active in the military afterward, as he suffered from insomnia and general poor health. It was during 1916, however, that Ravel, along with most other French musicians, opposed a plan to ban German music from France for the duration of the war. The letter Ravel wrote on the subject was one of the better-known objections to the plan.

Although Ravel wrote two of his most famous works, *Le Tombeau de Couperin* and *Le Valse* (1919), and the first versions of his Sonata for Violin and Cello (1920, 1922) and his second opera, *L'Enfante et les sortilèges* (1920, 1925), between 1917 and 1920, his musical output had slowed down, his health never completely recovered, and he would only get progressively worse as the years went by. Although Ravel would still produce a few more masterpieces (two piano concertos, a sonata for violin, and, in 1928, his famous short ballet piece *Bolero*), he worked less and less, until, by 1933, Ravel was unable to complete any more projects, although he occasionally thought about trying to start one. At times, especially in the middle of 1933, he was unable even to sign his name.

Ravel spent the last few years of his life traveling and receiving friends at his house outside Paris, although he at times seemed unaware of his surroundings. He had undergone various medical treatments, but none had had any positive effect. As his health became worse, it was decided to operate on Ravel for a possible brain tumor on December 19, 1937. No evidence of a tumor was found, and Ravel's decline increased. He died nine days after the operation.

### Summary

Maurice Ravel's works are some of the most important French compositions of the early twentieth century as well as the hardest to define. In many respects, Ravel's music encompasses French music since the early baroque, and European music since Hector Berlioz. Elements and forms from all these styles, as well as Spanish and Basque folk elements, were quoted or used by Ravel throughout his career. So while in some respects Ravel was near the forefront of musical exploration, his use of these conservative elements disturbed most radicals, even as the way he used them bothered the musical establishment of his era. Ravel was determined to compose music that he believed would project the mood and themes he wished to convey, rather than being consistent within any set style.

For the most part, Ravel worked mainly in the areas of vocal, chamber, and piano music, and it is in these works that Ravel's many varieties of style show themselves best. For the most part, as far as the general musical audience is concerned, he is best known for his larger symphonic works such as *Bolero* and for the orchestrations he made, for his own piano works and those of others, especially Modest Mussorgsky's *Pictures at an Exhibition* (1922).

Ravel's direct influence was limited to a small group of students, best known as interpreters of Ravel and other twentieth century piano composers. His indirect influences, especially in the area of orchestration, are harder to define yet are nevertheless important. His compositions were meant to illustrate ideas and feelings, not to overwhelm the senses as much music of the previous generation had. At the same time, Ravel meant to stay within the basic confines of French music, although he felt free to recombine those elements as he saw fit. His genius was his eclecticism and taste.

### Bibliography

Demuth, Norman. *Ravel.* London: Dent, 1947; New York: Farrar Straus, 1956. Part of the Master Musicians series, this work has a short but complete biography of the composer but devotes more than three-quarters of the volume to competent academic analyses of Ravel's music.

James, Burnett. *Ravel, His Life and Times.* Tunbridge Wells, Kent: Midas, and New York: Hippocrene, 1983. A successful attempt to integrate Ravel's life and music with the more general social and cultural context of the composer's life.

Jankélévitch, Vladimir. *Ravel.* Translated by Margaret Crosland. New York: Grove Press, 1959. Although it has a short biography, this work is distinguished by its musical and dramatic critiques of Ravel's music, especially the ballets. The analysis comes more from a romantic tradition than an academic one and includes a detailed chronology of Ravel's work.

Larner, Gerald. *Maurice Ravel.* London: Phaidon, 1996. A Ravel biography by the *London Times* critic that sheds light on the composer's elusive personality. Focuses in part on his parents' influence on his music.

Myers, Rollo H. *Ravel.* London: Duckworth, and New York: Yoseloff, 1960. Although the biographical and analytical sections are fairly standard, this work also includes Alexis Roland-Manuel's 1937 memorial essay and Ravel's 1916 letter from the Western Front opposing the ban of German music from performance in France.

Nichols, Roger, ed. *Ravel Remembered.* London: Faber, 1987; New York: Norton, 1988. Ravel's life as told through letters, diaries, and other accounts by those who knew him. Nichols places these anecdotes into context when necessary but prefers to let the memories speak for themselves as much as possible.

Orenstein, Arbie. "Maurice Ravel." *American Scholar* 64, no. 1 (Winter 1995). Profile of Ravel focusing on his relationship to his mother and his family background.

———. *Ravel: Man and Musician.* New York: Columbia University Press, 1975; London: Columbia University Press, 1977. Although the biographical section is only a standard account, this work does include more than forty illustrations. More important, it contains excellent discussions of Ravel's musical aesthetics and creative process.

Roland-Manuel, Alexis. *Maurice Ravel.* Translated by Cynthia Jolly. London: Dobson, 1947; New York: Dover, 1972. An interesting and honest appraisal of Ravel's life and work, originally written in French in 1938 and translated in 1947. Roland-Manuel was both a pupil and friend of Ravel, and the book includes a detailed list of Ravel's compositions.

*Terrance L. Lewis*

# SATYAJIT RAY

*Born:* May 2, 1921; Calcutta, India
*Died:* April 23, 1992; Calcutta, India
*Area of Achievement:* Film
*Contribution:* Ray was India's most distinguished film director, responsible for gaining Indian cinema international recognition and rescuing it from a reputation for indiscriminate productivity and vulgar escapism. For more than thirty years, his films not only established him as a moving force in world cinema but also provided Western audiences with profound insights into Indian life and inspired a generation of Indian filmmakers to follow his lead in producing films of serious social comment.

## Early Life

Satyajit Ray came from a distinguished Bengali family whose members have made lasting contributions to the intellectual life of their country. His grandfather, Upendra Kishore, was an artist and illustrator who established a publishing house (U. Ray and Sons), which Ray's father, Sukumar, later headed. Upendra was friendly with Rabindranath Tagore, Bengal's most distinguished intellectual and social visionary, who would later take an interest in the education of his friend's grandson. Both Upendra and Sukumar were directly influenced by a group of Bengali reformers known as the Brahmo Samaj, who in the late nineteenth century tried to introduce into their society progressive European ideas (notably relating to the education of women and the condition of the underclass) without disturbing the best of native traditions. Satyajit Ray inherited much of his own universalism and concern over the tensions between ancient and modern social forces from the tradition of Brahmoism.

Ray was only two years old when his father, who had already established a considerable reputation as an artist and publisher, died; the press had to be sold to pay the family's debts. He and his mother, Suprabha, went to live with her brother and his family. Like his grandfather, Ray completed his secondary education and higher education at Presidency College in Calcutta, from which he was graduated in economics in 1940. He was then persuaded to go to Santineketan, the art center founded by Tagore for the purpose of creating a new generation of Bengali artists and intellectuals who would make careers for themselves faithful to the tenets of the progressive spirit of Brahmoism. Ray spent two and a half years in this intellectually encouraging atmosphere, gradually developing his inherited talent as an artist and deepening his acquaintance with the major figures in world cinema. Leaving Santineketan during World War II, Ray eventually found work as a commercial artist for the British firm of J. Keymer, for whom he worked until he turned his attention entirely to filmmaking.

Various events confirm a move in this direction in the years around Indian independence (1948). In 1947, he helped to establish the Calcutta Film Society and began to try his hand at writing articles on film. He was further encouraged by the arrival in Calcutta in 1950 of Jean Renoir to film *The River.* Finally his firm sent him to London for six months in 1950, where by his own account he saw ninety-nine films: among them were several Italian neorealist films, including Vittorio De Sica's *The Bicycle Thief* (1948), wherein Ray noted the potency of a family drama springing from an immediate economic crisis and the appeal of using nonprofessional actors. By the time he returned to Calcutta in late 1950, Ray not only knew he was to be a film director but also already had a complete draft of his first screenplay: an adaptation of a very popular Bengali novel, Bibhuti-Bhusan Banerji's *Pather panchali* (1929; *Pather Panchali: Song of the Road*, 1968).

## Life's Work

The film *Pather Panchali* was only completed in 1955 after enormous difficulties (including the pawning of family jewelry and books). This unblinkingly honest portrayal of life in an Indian village won immediate international acclaim in New York and at the 1956 Cannes Film Festival. It gave Ray the confidence (and funds) he needed to complete the trilogy on the life of his hero Apu from birth to maturity. His second film, *Aparajito* (1956; *The Unvanquished*), moves from the death of the father to Apu's education in Calcutta. It won the Golden Lion in Venice, 1957. The final film of the trilogy is *Apu Sansar* (1959; *The World of Apu*), which shows the hero as an aspiring novelist, the circumstances of his marriage, and the tragic death of his young wife.

Before completing the Apu trilogy, Ray made a subtle masterpiece in *Jalsaghar* (1958; *The Music Room*). Music and cultural reference are the means whereby the director dramatizes the decline of a representative of the landowning class in the 1920's. Characteristic of Ray is his sympathy for a character whose indolence brings about his own tragedy.

Social tensions within the Indian past are the inspiration of *Devi* (1960; *The Goddess*) and the superb *Charulata* (1964; *The Lonely Wife*). The former takes controversial issue with religious fanaticism. A zamindar (feudal landlord) drives his favorite daughter-in-law, Daya, to madness and death through his obsessive conviction that she is the reincarnation of the goddess Kali. The latter, set in Calcutta in 1879, is a profound study of a wife neglected by her publisher husband and drawn to his sensitive cousin Amal. Clearly Ray did not see the problems of women imprisoned by the taboos of Indian society as frozen in the historical past but as unresolved contradictions in independent India.

As part of the centenary of the birth of Tagore, Ray was commissioned to make a documentary of the poet's life: *Rabindranath Tagore* (1961). The completed film is a reminder of the debt that all Bengalis owe to this protean artist and of the personal relationship between the Rays and the Tagores. Among the themes of progressive Brahmoism both inherited and embodied by Tagore is that of the rights of women; this idea is precisely what is incorporated into Ray's first color film, *Kanchenjungha* (1962), and *Mahanagar* (1963; *The Big City*). From the interwoven crises of the vacationing family in *Kanchenjungha* may be isolated the gentle rebellion of a younger daughter strong enough to choose continuing education over an arranged marriage and the sense of the decline of a once-dominant paternal authority. *Mahanagar* concentrates on the economic struggles of the lower-middle class, with a wife leaving prejudice and her own fears behind to find a job and enjoy her new independence. She must also face unaccustomed problems in the commercial world, such as defending a fired coworker and fending off the boss.

The late 1960's was a time of turmoil in Bengal, seeing rising unemployment, ethnic and religious violence, and food riots in Calcutta. The tensions of an unwieldly twenty-year-old democracy were threatening its stability. None of these social conflicts is directly observed in Ray's films, a fact that brought him into polemical discussion with such overtly political filmmakers as Mrinal Sen. Ray, however, was neither aesthete nor escapist. To chronicle social change over a vast historical canvas—and via psychological relationships—requires a measure of serene detachment. His hollow men of *Kapurush-o-Mahapurush* (1965; *The Coward and the Saint*) and *Nayak* (1966; *The Hero*) are both products of a modern world that demands compromise and punishes forthrightness. At least twice Ray escaped into fantasy: *Goopi Gyne Bagha Byne* (1969; *The Adventures of Goopi and Bagha*) and *Hirok Rajar Deshe* (1980; *The Kingdom of Diamonds*). Based on stories by his grandfather Upendra Kishore, they reflect a fidelity to a family tradition of writing and drawing for children. Both Ray's grandfather and father published a children's magazine, *Sandesh*, which Ray revived in the early 1960's.

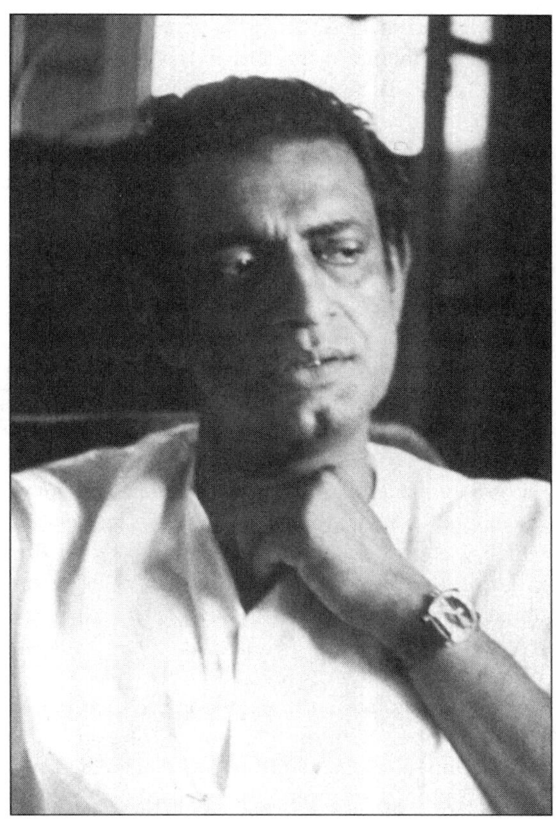

Ray's experience in the business world lay behind an informal trilogy made in the early 1970's based on studies of a confused Calcutta intelligentsia trying to define its place in a world that belittles tradition and proclaims self-interest above conscience. These films are *Aranyer din Ratri* (1970; *Days and Nights in the Forest*), *Pratidwandi* (1970; *The Adversary*), and *Simabaddha* (1971; *Company Limited*). To these one can add an epilogue,

*Dahana-Aranja* (1975; *The Middleman*), a variation on the theme of modern forms of corruption. *Days and Nights in the Forest* was Ray's finest film since *The Lonely Wife.* It is a film of dislocation: Four self-satisfied urban professionals are removed to a natural setting and observed as they come face to face with their limitations. The results are unsettling but not without some salutary chastening.

*Ashani Sanket* (1973; *Distant Thunder*) reveals the dramatic impact of war on a distant Bengal village. The images of starvation serve as a reminder that no one is immune to historical upheaval and as a response to Ray's critics, who had accused him of remaining aloof from the world's problems. "Outside observers" is an accurate description of the protagonists of Ray's film *Shatranj ke Kilhari* (1977; *The Chess Players*). This historical drama, which was produced in color, was Ray's first film in Urdu, the purpose being to attract a larger national audience.

With *Ghare-Baire* (1984; *The Home and the World*), Ray's career came full circle. He had first written an adaptation of this important Tagore novel in 1948, but, with thirty-six years of experience behind him, produced a far more sophisticated version. The film's structure, like the title, is dialectical, juxtaposing the values of domestic retirement and political commitment. The husband, Nikhil, urges his wife, Bimala, to interest herself in public events and introduces her to a friend, Sandip, a leader of the Swadeshi movement promoting independence from Great Britain (the year is 1905). Bimala soon recognizes that Sandip is a ruthless manipulator. In her understanding of her own independence and of the dangers of the charismatic Sandip one can sense the beliefs of Ray himself: his support of women's emancipation and his doubts regarding forms of political extremism.

### Summary

Satyajit Ray was primarily a Bengali artist whose films successfully reflect the past and the present of his native land. He was in a direct line from those artists and intellectuals (in particular Rabindranath Tagore) who promoted the Bengali renaissance, which aimed at a vibrant renewal of the culture as well as progressive social reforms. In a country whose official language is Hindi and where the capital of the film industry is Bombay, Ray's fidelity to his native Bengali in his films limited the countrywide appeal of his work. Nevertheless, his international standing as the man who liberated Indian cinema from its vacuous escapism made of him a spokesman and informal ambassador abroad. Such prominence did not come smoothly. He came under fire for overexposing India's problems of poverty, religious excess, and the status of women, while from the Left he had to answer charges of aloofness or political indifference.

Ray's life, like that of most Indians, revolved around his family, a fact that gives a particular flavor to his films, which are so often studies of the intimate dynamics of family groups and married couples. The family serves as a microcosm of the world's events, the conflicts between parents and children or man and wife reflecting those between classes and competing ideologies. Undoubtedly this concentration on the small but accessible unit of human experience has enhanced the appeal of his films outside India to audiences in Europe and the United States. There was something familial, too, about his working methods, in the fidelity of a small number of inseparable associates with whom he worked after the Apu trilogy, whose contributions to his work added to its consistency and wholeness. However rooted he was in his native traditions, however provincial his stories seem to be, Ray invested his characters and their lives with a universal humanity that viewers from East and West instantly recognize.

### Bibliography

Cooper, Darius. "The Indian Woman in the Bengali/Hindu Dollhouse: Satyajit Ray's 'Charulata' (1964)." *Women's Studies* 25, no. 2 (January, 1996). Discussion of Ray's film *Charulata,* which is based on a novel by Rabindranath Tagore. Unlike the novel, the film suggests that there is hope for women relegated to the fringes of Indian society.

Das Gupta, Chidananga. *The Cinema of Satyajit Ray.* New Delhi: Vikas, 1980. A book written by a critic personally close to Ray and one of several publications timed to coincide with the twenty-fifth anniversary of the completion of *Pather Panchali.* Das Gupta places Ray firmly in the context of Bengali culture, emphasizing the importance of the late nineteenth century Bengal renaissance and the influence of Tagore.

Micciollo, Henri. *Satyajit Ray.* Lausanne: Éditions l'Âge d'Homme, 1981. A book designed to fill a void in European critical attention paid to Third World cinema, and in particular that of Ray. Includes a lengthy introduction placing Ray in the context of his own national cinema and interviews with Ray himself. Each film—up to *Pikoo's Day* (1980)—is given an extended sequence-by-sequence plot summary, followed by a lengthy formal and thematic analysis.

Nyce, Ben. *Satyajit Ray: A Study of His Films.* New York: Praeger, 1988. This is the first full-length study of Ray's film by an American critic, including analyses of his rarely seen documentaries and short subjects and a final chapter on *The Home and the World.* There is a brief recapitulation of biographical material and some clear notes on the director's cultural and historical roots.

Ray, Satyajit. *Satyajit Ray: An Anthology of Statements on Ray and by Ray.* Edited by Chidanada Das Gupta. New Delhi: Directorate of Film Festivals, Ministry of Information and Broadcasting, 1981. An indispensable volume for the student of Ray's career, published at the time of a complete retrospective of the director's work presented at the Bangalore Film Festival of 1980. Part 1 includes a summary of the plots of every film up to *Pikoo's Day,* followed by lengthy extracts from contemporary reviews, Indian and Western. The final section is an anthology of statements by Ray on all aspects of his art and working habits. No clearer summary of his career has been published.

Sen, Amartya. "Our Culture, Their Culture: Satyajit Ray and the Art of Universalism." *New Republic* 214, no. 14 (April 1, 1996). Discusses several of Ray's films and their treatment of cultural differences.

Seton, Marie. *Portrait of a Director: Satyajit Ray.* London: Dobson, and Bloomington: Indiana University Press, 1971. While much of the material here has been outdated by later studies and developments in Ray's career itself, this remains the definitive biography up to the period of *Days and Nights in the Forest.* It includes a detailed account of Ray's ancestry and family history and of the way he lives and works. Provides fascinating background information on the production history and problems of the individual films. Includes interviews with Ray, articles by him, examples of his artwork and illustrations, and many excellent photographs.

Wood, Robin. *The Apu Trilogy.* New York: Praeger, 1971; London: November, 1972. A purely critical and largely formalist study of the Apu trilogy alone by a prolific critic and long-time associate. Those encountering the trilogy for the first time will find it a valuable introduction.

*Harry Lawton*

# RONALD REAGAN

*Born:* February 6, 1911; Tampico, Illinois
*Area of Achievement:* Government and politics
*Contribution:* After a succession of failed presidencies over two decades, Reagan stemmed the general feeling of instability that had begun to surround the office. Almost by sheer personality and by effortlessly exuding an enormous self-confidence, Reagan reversed many of the negative images of the presidency.

## Early Life

Ronald Wilson Reagan was born February 6, 1911, in Tampico, Illinois. He was the younger of two sons; his brother John Neil Reagan was born on September 3, 1909. His father, John Edward Reagan, was born July 13, 1883, in Fulton, Illinois; his father's parents were born in County Cork, Ireland. His mother, Nelle Clyde Wilson Reagan, of English-Scottish ancestry, was born July 24, 1885, in Fulton, Illinois. When Reagan was ten years old, his family settled in Dixon, Illinois, after living in several other rural Illinois towns. Reagan's father was a shoe salesman who was troubled by alcoholism and had difficulty holding a job. His mother loved the theater, and it was in Dixon, while attending high school, that Reagan first participated in acting. In 1928, he was graduated from high school, where he played basketball and football and was on the track team; he was also president of the student body. For seven summers during his high school and college years, he worked as a lifeguard at Lowell Park near Dixon.

Reagan won a scholarship which paid half of his living expenses, tuition, and fees at Eureka College, where he majored in sociology and economics. At Eureka, he participated in student politics, athletics, and theater, playing the lead in several college productions and winning honorable mention in a drama competition sponsored by Northwestern University. He won varsity letters in football, swimming, and track, and, as in high school, was elected president of the student body. After receiving a B.A. degree on June 7, 1932, he was hired as a sports announcer for station WOC in Davenport, Iowa. WOC was a five-thousand-watt station which shared its wavelength with WHO in Des Moines; both stations became part of the NBC network within a year after Reagan's initial employment. By 1937, his coverage of major league baseball, Big Ten Conference football, and other sports events had earned for him a national reputation as a sportscaster. While covering the Chicago Cubs' training camp at Catalina Island, he was introduced to a Los Angeles motion picture agent who succeeded in getting him a screen test at the Warner Bros. studio. In 1937, he signed a two-hundred-dollar-per-week, seven-year contract with Warner Bros.

## Life's Work

Reagan's first film, the 1937 production *Love Is on the Air*, was well received, with Reagan cast as a radio commentator. He played in more than twenty B pictures before his performance as George Gipp, the famous Notre Dame football star, in *Knute Rockne, All American* (1940) established his reputation as a serious actor. In 1940-1941, he was chosen one of the "Stars of Tomorrow" in an exhibitor's poll. Reagan's most memorable film role was probably that of Drake McHugh, the victim of a sadistic surgeon, in *King's Row* in 1942. This was an excellent film, directed by Sam Wood, and Reagan's performance was generally described as excellent by reviewers. In all, Reagan, generally regarded as a competent but not outstanding actor, made fifty-five feature-length films, mostly for Warner Bros., between 1937 and 1964. Reagan left Warner Bros. in the 1950's and free-lanced among several studios for a few years; his career was to be rescued by television.

On April 14, 1942, Reagan had entered the United States Army as a second lieutenant of cavalry in reserve; poor eyesight disqualified him for combat duty. Until his discharge as a captain on December 9, 1945, he made training films for the army in California. It was after his three-year stint in the army that Reagan began to give serious attention to the politics of the film industry. He took fewer roles as an actor after he was elected as president of the Screen Actors Guild (SAG) in 1947. SAG was one of the major labor unions in the industry; Reagan was elected to six one-year terms as president, in which capacity he successfully negotiated several significant labor contracts. In October, 1947, he appeared before the House Committee on Un-American Activities (HUAC, as it became popularly known) as a friendly witness in its investigation of communist influence in the film industry. He came to view HUAC and its chairman, Congressman J. Parnell Thomas, and their questionable tactics, how-

ever, with enough wariness that he did not name names of suspected communists.

Reagan started his political life as a liberal Democrat who ardently supported Franklin D. Roosevelt. In the 1940's, however, his political outlook became much more conservative. His movement to the right of center politically came during his experience from 1954 to 1962 when he was employed by the General Electric Company, as host, program supervisor, and occasional actor on the weekly television show *General Electric Theater.* Between television appearances, Reagan traveled throughout the country for General Electric's personnel relations division. He spoke at the company's 135 plants and addressed thousands of its workers. In these speeches he often repeated the themes of the American need for free enterprise while warning against the evils of big government. In 1962, Reagan became the host of the weekly television program *Death Valley Days*; he remained with that show until he entered the race for governor of California in 1965.

Reagan switched to the Republican Party in 1962, although he had campaigned as a Democrat for Dwight Eisenhower in 1952 and 1956, and again for Richard Nixon in 1960. He had supported Harry S Truman in 1948. In October, 1964, Reagan's prerecorded speech on behalf of Barry Goldwater, "A Time for Choosing, " was well received by viewers and resulted in a huge surge in campaign contributions. Reagan's friendly, low-key delivery suggested a reassuring, plain patriotism that became a hallmark of his appeal to voters in the future.

In November, 1966, Reagan defeated incumbent Democratic Governor Edward G. "Pat" Brown by more than a million votes. Reagan stumped the state with his basic speech, essentially unchanged from his days with General Electric. He called on voters to bring "common sense" back to government. He was reelected four years later when he defeated Democratic State Assembly Speaker Jesse Unruh by more than a half-million votes.

As governor, Reagan mastered the art of compromise with state legislators and was more restrained and pragmatic than his conservative rhetoric suggested. He took a hard line toward dissident students in the state's educational system, particularly at the University of California in Berkeley. He also reduced expenditures in a number of areas, including social services and education, in order to fulfill his campaign promise to reduce the size of government. These cuts, along with a prosperous state economy, resulted in substantial surpluses in the state government's revenues. In 1973, he was able to begin generous programs of income tax rebates and credits as well as significant property tax relief. A major tax law was passed during his tenure as governor which corrected a regressive state revenue system. A major achievement of Reagan's second term was the passage of the California Welfare Reform Act of 1971. This law reduced the numbers of people on the welfare rolls while increasing payments to those in need, notably those recipients of Aid for Families with Dependent Children. His successes as a governor led many political observers to regard him as a leading contender for the GOP presidential nomination in 1968.

Reagan's first run for the presidency, however, was too tentative to stop Richard M. Nixon in 1968, and he accordingly requested that the convention make Nixon's nomination unanimous. He next campaigned for the presidency against Gerald R. Ford, beginning with the New Hampshire primary in February, 1976. Reagan narrowly lost the nomination to Ford at the Republican Convention in Kansas City, Missouri; the delegate vote was 1,187 for Ford to Reagan's 1,070. Nevertheless, Reagan had laid the groundwork for 1980 by his strong showing, especially with voters in the South, and in July of that year he arrived unopposed at the Republican National Convention. In his acceptance speech, Reagan pledged to support a conservative platform which called for voluntary prayer in public schools, tuition credits for private school tuition, and strong opposition to school busing, abortion, and the Equal Rights Amendment. Reagan overcame questions about his age with a vigorous campaign against incumbent Jimmy Carter, and his disarming and engaging performance in televised debates helped him to defeat Carter at the polls on November 4, 1980. His margin in the popular vote was substantial, and he received 489 votes to Carter's 49 in the electoral college.

Ronald Wilson Reagan was inaugurated as the fortieth president of the United States at 11:57 A.M. on Tuesday, January 20, 1981, with Chief Justice Warren Burger administering the oath of office. For the first time, the ceremony was held at the West Front of the Capitol, in a symbolic allusion to Reagan's Western roots. The president gave a twenty-minute address calling for "an era of national renewal." Minutes afterward, he fulfilled a campaign promise by placing a freeze on government hiring. As the president concluded his address, at 12:33 P.M., the Iranian government released the American hostages whom they had held for 444 days. The news added to the festive spirit of the occasion.

Reagan is six feet, one inch tall and weighs 185 pounds, with light-brown hair and blue eyes. He has worn contact lenses for many years, is a nonsmoker, and drinks only on occasion. He retreats often to his ranch, Rancho del Cielo, near Santa Barbara, California. He enjoys horseback riding, chopping wood, and watching television and privately screened motion pictures. In 1994, he was diagnosed with Alzheimer's disease and has since made few public appearances.

Reagan was married for the first time on January 24, 1940, to actress Jane Wyman, whom he had met while they were both appearing in films for Warner Bros. From that marriage, which ended on July 19, 1949, they had a daughter, Maureen Elizabeth, and an adopted son, Michael Edward. On March 4, 1952, Reagan married actress Nancy Davis, the daughter of Dr. Loyal Davis, a prominent Chicago neurosurgeon. They had two children, Patrician Ann and Ronald Prescott. Reagan was the first president to have been divorced.

Reagan was shot in the chest as he left the Washington Hilton Hotel at about 2:30 P.M. on March 30, 1981, after addressing a group of union officials. His assailant, John Hinckley, Jr., was overpowered and arrested at the scene of the crime. The president was rushed to nearby George Washington University hospital, where he later was operated on to remove a bullet from his left lung. On April 11, 1981, after a remarkably quick recovery, he returned to the White House.

During his first term, Reagan concentrated on a strategy of cutting taxes for economic growth stimulation, holding back increases in government spending, and an expensive buildup of American defenses throughout the world. By 1984, inflation was under control, interest rates moved down, though not low enough, employment was up significantly, and generally the economy was upbeat. Difficult problems remained, however, such as the huge size of the federal deficit, a somewhat myopic view of government's role in domestic matters, and a Supreme Court which was perhaps too conservative in such a complex, modern world. Solutions for the plight of minorities and the American farmer remained to be found. Nevertheless, the Reagan presidency set standards against which present and future programs will be judged.

### Summary

Ronald Reagan has fashioned two careers in his long years in the public eye. He has held only two public offices, first as governor of the largest state in the union, then as President of the United States; he began his second career at the top. His years in the governor's mansion in Sacramento coincided with an era of national protest, foreign war, and social change; his years in the White House have been marked by economic recession and recovery, problems of unemployment, complicated foreign affairs, and expanding American military buildup.

Yet Ronald Reagan was well known to the public before he undertook a career in public service in the 1960's. His first career was in film and television, and most voting-age Americans initially encountered him in the darkened film theater or at home on television. It was during the Hollywood years that Reagan's vision of America was formed. He learned more in the film world than simply acting: He acquired an easy way with an audience, and also experienced the competition and studio politics that led him into the larger arenas of the New Deal, SAG, and HUAC—all of which constituted the apprenticeship for his second career.

Reagan's optimistic attitude appealed to voters, and his conservatism produced a number of programs that have changed American government in fundamental ways. By June, 1986, public approval of President Reagan's performance was higher than ever before, according to a Gallup Poll. The poll also found that Reagan was more popular than any previous President in the second year of his second term since World War II. A crest of public support in 1981, when fifty-eight percent of Americans approved of his performance, had tapered off in 1982 and 1983 to forty-four percent, rising again in 1984 to fifty-six percent approval and sixty-one percent in 1985. Despite the Iranian arms crisis which marred the later half of his second term, few presidents in the twentieth century have demonstrated such staying power in the polls, including Dwight Eisenhower and Franklin D. Roosevelt. Indeed, perhaps Reagan's greatest achievement is to have restored the office of President of the United States to a position of power and prestige.

### Bibliography

Adler, Bill. *Ronnie and Nancy: A Very Special Love Story.* New York: Crown, 1985. The most interesting part of this book follows Reagan's career from Hollywood actor and political activist to television personality and General Electric spokesman and on to governor of California and president. There are fascinating glimpses into the inside workings of campaigning and, to a lesser extent, life in the White House. There is also a frank discussion of the most successful public marriage in recent American history.

Cannon, Lou. *President Reagan: The Role of a Lifetime*. New York: Simon and Schuster, 1991; London: Simon and Schuster, 1992.

———. *Reagan*. New York: Putnam, 1982. This substantial and highly critical biography is the work of a veteran reporter and White House correspondent for *The Washington Post*. Although dated—writing his conclusion midway through his subject's first term, Cannon confidently assesses him as a one-term president—it provides a perspective on Reagan to be considered with other, more positive viewpoints. Illustrated and well documented, with an extensive bibliography.

Evans, Rowland, and Robert Novak. *The Reagan Revolution*. New York: Dutton, 1981. An informed analysis of the Reagan administration, which the authors portray as "revolutionary"; they favorably compare Reagan's first one hundred days in office to that celebrated span in Franklin D. Roosevelt's first term. In seeking the presidency, the authors suggest, Reagan hoped to restore the United States to world leadership, to halt the pervasive growth of government, and to revive free enterprise.

Gelb, Leslie H. "The Mind of the President." *The New York Times Magazine*, October 6, 1985, sec. 6: 20-24, 28-32, 103, 112-113. The author concludes that Reagan is unique in the history of American presidents because he alone possesses the mind of both an ideologue and a politician. Reagan "has all the moral force and power that swell from absolute conviction." His success stems from the fact that he is a "natural horsetrader" who has mastered the art of political compromise in order to achieve his own political ends.

Greenstein, Fred I., ed. *The Reagan Presidency: An Early Assessment.* Baltimore: Johns Hopkins University Press, 1983. A collection of scholarly essays that came out of a November, 1982, conference at Princeton University on the first two years of the Reagan presidency. The authors attempt to judge Reagan's performance in four major policy areas—fiscal, foreign, defense, and domestic. They examine Reagan's ideological objectives and the ways in which they have been translated into public policy.

Hannaford, Peter. *The Reagans: A Political Portrait.* New York: Coward McCann, 1983. Written by a former aide, this book provides many details about Reagan's political life, including a thorough treatment of his days as Governor of California. The author reveals the intense struggle between Reagan's 1980 campaign manager John Sears and the others in the candidate's inner circle of advisers. An interesting portrait written from the standpoint of an "insider."

Reagan, Ronald, with Richard G. Hubler. *Where's the Rest of Me?* New York: Duell Sloan, 1965. Reagan wrote this autobiography long before he dreamed of becoming President of the United States. It is a frank, witty, and moving account of his life. The title comes from his most famous line from his best movie, *King's Row*, in 1942. The book reveals much of the charm, optimism, and common sense that made him such a phenomenally successful politician.

Ritter, Kurt W., and David Henry. *Ronald Reagan: The Great Communicator.* Westport, Conn.: Greenwood Press, 1992. Comprehensive study of Reagan the orator from his years in Hollywood to his terms as president. Includes analysis of selected speeches and a detailed bibliography.

Schaller, Michael. *Reckoning with Reagan: America and Its President in the 1980s.* New York: Oxford University Press, 1992. Schaller offers a comprehensive overview of the Reagan presidency, focusing on the image that allowed him to bond strongly with the American people despite failures.

Schmertz, Eric J., et al. *Ronald Reagan's America.* Volumes 1 and 2. Westport, Conn.: Greenwood Press, 1997. In-depth consideration of the Reagan presidency and its effect on the economy, the national debt, and society as a whole.

Thomas, Tony. *The Films of Ronald Reagan*. Secaucas, N.J.: Citadel Press, 1980. The only book-length study of Reagan's film career. Reagan took his acting seriously, in spite of what his political opponents may say. He was an able actor usually assigned to poor roles. Workmanlike in his professional duties, he was seldom criticized for being less than convincing within his acting range. The author concludes that Reagan's career was a respectable one.

Weintraub, Bernard. "The Reagan Legacy." *The New York Times Magazine*, June 22, 1986, sec.

6: 12-21. This article examines Reagan's firm belief that his impact on America will prove to be just as far-reaching as Franklin Roosevelt's. The author concludes that Reagan has reestablished the primacy of the presidency as an institution after nearly two decades of White House disarray. Weintraub quotes Senator Edward M. Kennedy, who, despite his frequent criticism of Reagan's economic, social, and civil-rights policies, acknowledges that "he has contributed a spirit of good will and grace to the presidency and American life generally and turned the presidency into a vigorous and forceful instrument of national policy."

*Arthur F. McClure*

## WILLIAM H. REHNQUIST

*Born:* October 1, 1924; Milwaukee, Wisconsin
*Area of Achievement:* Law
*Contribution:* Rehnquist served as solicitor general, associate justice, and chief justice of the United States. He supported and presided over the Court's conservative shift during his tenure.

### Early Life

William Hubbs Rehnquist was born in Milwaukee, Wisconsin, in 1924 and was raised in Shorewood, a middle-class suburb. His father was a paper salesman. The Rehnquist household was politically conservative; Alf Landon, Herbert Hoover, and Wendell Wilkie, all Republican candidates for the presidency, were much admired. Rehnquist was educated in the public schools and finished one semester at Kenyon College in Gambier, Ohio, before enlisting in the Army Air Corps in 1943. He served as a weather observer in North Africa for the duration of World War II. On his return to the United States, he resolved to pursue his education in a warmer climate than his native Wisconsin, and so he enrolled at Stanford University in Palo Alto, California. His education was financed by scholarship money provided under the G.I. Bill. He studied political science, earning both bachelor and master of arts degrees. He was an excellent student and was elected to Phi Beta Kappa in 1948. In 1950 he returned to Stanford Law School and graduated first in his class. Sandra Day O'Connor, later to be a colleague on the United States Supreme Court, was one of his classmates.

Rehnquist's reputation as a brilliant legal thinker brought him an interview with United States Associate Justice Robert Jackson, who was sufficiently impressed with Rehnquist to offer him an eighteen-month clerkship. On the completion of his clerkship with Jackson in 1953, Rehnquist moved to Phoenix, Arizona, which he had chosen for its mild climate and conservative political leanings. He married Natalie Cornell that year, and they eventually raised a son and two daughters. In Phoenix, Rehnquist became associated with the firm of Evans, Kitchel & Jenckes. He practiced law in Phoenix for the next seventeen years, specializing mostly in litigation and establishing a reputation for integrity and professional competence. He also became active in Republican Party work—following advice that Justice Felix Frankfurter had given him—and became a local party official. He supported Barry Goldwater's presidential campaign in 1964 and, during this period, became closely associated with Richard Kleindienst, who later became attorney general of the United States. When Richard Nixon became president of the United States in 1969, Kleindienst suggested that Rehnquist be appointed to the Justice Department's Office of Legal Counsel. Rehnquist got the job, and when Justice John M. Harlan retired in 1971, Nixon chose Rehnquist to fill the vacated seat. His nomination was overwhelmingly approved by the Democratic Senate despite his known conservative philosophy and want of judicial experience. Rehnquist took the oath of office as an associate justice of the United States on January 7, 1972.

### Life's Work

When Rehnquist came to the Supreme Court, he was practically the only voice of judicial conservatism on the Court despite the presence of three other Republican appointees. The Court's liberal wing, led by Justices William J. Brennan, Hugo

Black, William O. Douglas, and Thurgood Marshall, dominated the Court's jurisprudence. Rehnquist became known as an outspoken dissenter against many of the Court's most liberal decisions. He opposed the expansion of federal power, argued for limits on the scope of the Fourteenth Amendment's due-process guarantee, and strongly advocated states' rights. He rarely prevailed in his early years on the Court, but his opinions were later to have a powerful influence as the composition of the Court changed in the years after his appointment.

Rehnquist's judicial and political conservatism evidenced itself from the very beginning of his judicial career. His philosophy was based on three related constitutional ideas. The first of these was "strict construction," which meant that judges should decide cases as closely in accord with the text of the Constitution as possible. "Judicial deference," Rehnquist's second tenet, implied that judges should not use their power to determine whether a law is wise or not—that is, judges should not second-guess Congressional determinations. "States' rights" was the third idea. Rehnquist believed that too much power had flowed from the state governments to the federal government, distorting the constitutional balance established by the framers of the Constitution in 1787. He read the Fourteenth Amendment, which limits the powers of state governments, as narrowly as possible. For Rehnquist, as for Thomas Jefferson, the principle of states' rights was supreme among the intentions of the framers and thus should be strictly adhered to.

Over the years, Rehnquist was remarkably consistent and persuasive in applying these principles. They led him to tend to resolve conflicts between individuals and the government in favor of the government, conflicts between state and federal authority in favor of the states, and questions of the exercise of federal jurisdiction against its exercise when possible. Thus he dissented in the abortion case *Roe v. Wade* (1973), accusing the liberal majority of interpreting the law to suit its own preferences when it took the power to regulate abortion away from the states. Another significant early dissent was in *United Steelworkers of America v. Weber* (1979), in which Rehnquist opposed giving broad effect to affirmative action rules and again castigated the majority for reading its own substantive opinions into the Constitution. Rehnquist also dissented from the majority in a variety of cases in which Congress had sought to apply federal laws directly to state governments.

By 1975 the growing conservatism of the Court allowed Rehnquist to prevail more frequently. He wrote for the majority in *National League of Cities v. Usery* (1975), which barred federal regulation of core state government functions. For Rehnquist, this was a great victory that presaged increased influence in the Court. As the more liberal justices left the Court and were replaced by new members appointed by Presidents Richard Nixon, Gerald Ford, and Ronald Reagan, Rehnquist's influence and reputation grew. Upon the retirement of Chief Justice Warren Burger in 1986, President Reagan promoted Rehnquist to fill the vacancy. Liberals howled in protest. Many depicted Rehnquist as a racist and conservative extremist. Several unproven charges were leveled at Rehnquist during the confirmation struggle, but despite these, he was eventually confirmed by a solid majority of the United States Senate on September 17, 1986.

Rehnquist had always been an affable and popular man. His informality and unpretentious lifestyle brought a more relaxed and pleasant atmosphere to the Supreme Court. Indeed, Rehnquist's ability to prevail in the Court's deliberations rested in part on the genuine warmth and respect felt for him among his colleagues and others who worked at the Court as well as on his extraordinary persuasive powers and knowledge of constitutional law. After his promotion, Rehnquist's view of the law and the Constitution prevailed in more than three-quarters of the cases in which he participated. He managed court affairs efficiently and also showed some moderation of this conservatism by voting with liberals to protect free speech and gay rights. In 1987 Rehnquist published *The Supreme Court: How It Was, How It Is*, a graceful and clear exposition of the Court's history and traditions that can be read with pleasure by lay people. Rehnquist's book sold well and further enhanced his reputation.

Despite some amelioration, the Court under Rehnquist's leadership moved constitutional interpretation consistently toward the conservative side of the spectrum. "Original intention" prevailed most obviously in the areas of federal-state relations in which exercises of federal power and federal court jurisdiction over state governments was limited again and again. Among the most notable of these decisions was *New York v. United States* (1992), in which a federal law requiring state governments to assume responsibility for low-level radioactive wastes was held unconstitutional because it invaded state sovereignty. A similar ruling in *Printz v. United States* (1997) held that there was no federal power to compel local elected sheriffs to perform the background checks required for handgun purchases under the Brady Bill.

One issue in which Rehnquist's views did not prevail was the matter of abortion rights. Rehnquist, who dissented in *Roe v. Wade*, continued to vote and argue against abortion rights at every opportunity, but he was unable to establish a coalition or majority in the Court to agree with him.

The most stunning and significant decision of the Rehnquist Court took place in 1995 in *United States v. Lopez*. The Court, for the first time in nearly sixty years, declared a federal statute unconstitutional because it was beyond the power of the federal government altogether and not because the law conflicted with some constitutional right. In the Gun-Free School Zones Act of 1990, Congress had made it a federal offence for a person to possess a firearm within a school zone. Like most federal social or economic legislation, the constitutional basis for this statute was the federal power to regulate interstate commerce. Ever since the New Deal, the Supreme Court had approached this kind of case with the utmost deference to Congress' opinion about whether an activity affected interstate commerce. This is very important constitutionally because an activity may be regulated by the federal government only if commerce is affected. In *Lopez*, however, the court held by 5-to-4 that mere possession of a firearm near a school had no connection with interstate commerce and consequently could not be regulated. Chief Justice Rehnquist wrote the majority opinion in the case that may turn out to establish the high-water mark of federal power expansion in the United States. Rehnquist's opinion in the case contained a brilliant summary of the rules and precedents for commerce-clause jurisprudence. His classification of these rules is likely to guide commerce-clause jurisprudence for many years to come.

### Summary

William H. Rehnquist's tenure on the Supreme Court allowed him to observe and, at least partly, to direct, a substantial change in political and constitutional ideology. From his early struggle as a dissenter—often alone—against a liberal majority through his role as chief justice and the leader of a conservative coalition, Rehnquist consistently and successfully fought for his ideas. Under his leadership, the number of unanimous or near-unanimous decisions made by the Court increased, thus enhancing the public's perception of the level of professionalism among the justices. By seeking compromise rather than confrontation, Rehnquist was able to maintain high credibility for the Court. The public perception of judicial unity contributed to the success of the court's conservative shift, and although the appointment of two liberal justices by President Bill Clinton's administration balanced the conservative wing of the court to some extent, Rehnquist's popularity with his colleagues assured that his conservative views would remain strong on the court for a long time.

### Bibliography

Boles, Donald E. *Mr. Justice Rehnquist, Judicial Activist*. Ames: Iowa State University Press, 1987. Boles singles out federalism and separation of powers as areas in which Rehnquist operated as a judicial activist rather than deferring to Congress.

Davis, Derek. *Original Intent: Chief Justice Rehnquist and the Course of American Church/State Relations*. Buffalo, N.Y.: Prometheus, 1991. Davis provides an insightful discussion of how Rehnquist's underlying idea of "original intent" affects his views and votes in religious freedom cases.

Davis, Sue. *Justice Rehnquist and the Constitution*. Princeton: Princeton University Press, 1989. This is a good, clear summary of Rehnquist's constitutional views. At 247 pages, it is fairly short, but Davis covers most of the important areas.

Jenkins, John A. "The Partisan: A Talk with Justice Rehnquist." *The New York Times Magazine* 134 (March 3, 1985): 28-35, 88, 100-101. This clear discussion of Rehnquist's opinions emphasizes the strength and consistency of his views.

Rehnquist, William H. *The Supreme Court: How It Was, How It Is*. New York: Morrow, 1987. This partly autobiographical and partly historical discussion of the Supreme Court's traditions and internal patterns is clearly and simply written. It may be the best available introduction to the Court and to Rehnquist.

Rosen, Jeffrey. "Rehnquist's Choice: How Will the Chief Justice Preside over the Trial of the President?" *New Yorker* 74, no. 41 (January 11, 1999). Rosen considers Rehnquist's prospective handling of President Clinton's impeachment trial, highlighting Rehnquist's own problems with respect to accusations of lying under oath prior to his confirmation hearings in 1986.

Wagner, David. "The Rehnquist High Court?" *Insight on the News* 13, no. 27 (July 28, 1997). Wagner presents an overview of the 1997 Supreme Court rulings that reflect the conservative leanings of Rehnquist.

*Robert Jacobs*

# FIRST BARON REITH OF STONEHAVEN

*Born:* July 20, 1889; Stonehaven, Kincardineshire, Scotland

*Died:* June 16, 1971; Edinburgh, Scotland

*Area of Achievement:* Broadcasting

*Contribution:* Reith created in the British Broadcasting Corporation the world's most famous radio broadcasting system, in which was combined high culture and moral uplift as well as entertainment.

## Early Life

John Charles Walsham Reith was born on July 20, 1889, in Stonehaven, Kincardineshire, Scotland. His father, the Reverend George Reith, of the Scottish Free Church, was a prominent Glasgow minister, and his grandfather, also George Reith, had been an engineer and manager of the Clyde Navigation Trust. His mother, Adah Mary, was the daughter of a London stockbroker. Reith was the last of seven children, born when his parents were in their forties. He attended Glasgow Academy until the age of fifteen and then a minor public school in England for two years. Reith was an indifferent student, and although he hoped to attend Oxford or Cambridge, he instead entered Glasgow Technical College and in 1908 was apprenticed as an engineer.

Reith's was a somewhat lonely childhood because of his father's busy ministry and the fact that most of his brothers and sisters were near adulthood when he was born. His parents were loving but strict, and at an early age Reith felt the weight of living up to their ideals. Theirs was a very religious household; Scottish Presbyterianism, with its Calvinist foundations, played an important part in Reith's character. Something of a dreamer, he felt driven to accomplish great things, called both by God and by the example of his father and grandfather. Throughout his life, in spite of his accomplishments, he often feared that he had not responded sufficiently.

In Glasgow, during his engineering apprenticeship, Reith joined the Officers' Training Corps and received a commission in the territorial reserves in 1911. When World War I broke out in August, 1914, Reith was mobilized and sent to France as a transport officer. Like so many men of his generation, he matured in No Man's Land. Reith was an imposing figure, more than six feet, six inches in height and with beetling brows; he was an able officer, popular with the men under him, but he often came into conflict with his superiors. Combat ended for Reith in October, 1915, when he was shot through the head by a German sniper and was permanently scarred. After he recovered, he was sent to the United States in 1916 as part of the British war effort to facilitate the purchase of weapons from American manufacturers. He also discovered, when he talked about the war to American audiences, that he could be an inspiring speaker. He came very much to admire America, its energy, its efficiency, and particularly its people, and in later years he occasionally voiced the wish to emigrate to the United States. Reith never did so.

When the United States entered the war in April, 1917, Reith returned to London. During the rest of the war, he worked as an engineer for the military, and after the armistice he helped to liquidate munitions contracts. Like so many former soldiers, Reith felt frustrated about the future, and his belief that he had been called to do great things made that feeling more intense. Although before the war was over he had fallen in love with Muriel Odhams, daughter of a London publisher, he postponed their marriage until 1921 because he considered his life to be too unsettled. Unable to find a challenging position in London, he returned to Glasgow in 1920 to manage a manufacturing firm. Reith was very successful in reorganizing the factory, but the company eventually failed, and, in 1922, leaving his wife in Glasgow, Reith returned to London to what he hoped was a political career. In the election which followed, the fall of David Lloyd George's coalition government, Reith served as a secretary for a London Member of Parliament and met a number of important politicians. Nevertheless, it was not politics which would be his destiny.

## Life's Work

During the election campaign, Reith answered a newspaper advertisement seeking a manager for a new firm, the British Broadcasting Company (BBC). Reith knew nothing about broadcasting but his experience as an engineer and manager and his recent political contacts were sufficient, and he began work in December, 1922. Although Reith would become known as the father of the BBC, he came to broadcasting only after many earlier developments. In the United States, as in Great Britain, wireless broadcasting had been taken over by the government during World War I. After the war, however, it was demanded that the government end its monopoly and allow private enterprise to develop radio broadcasting, and by 1924, 530 broadcasting stations had been established in the United States. The lack of governmental control and the size of the country led to considerable chaos. Developments in England were different, where the tradition of government involvement was much greater. The Post Office had been given power over the telegraph in 1869, and early in the twentieth century, the same department was given control over wireless transmissions. By early 1922, radio manufacturers and prospective listeners were pressing the British government to allow more wireless broadcasting. The result was the formation of the BBC, a private company, but one which had a monopoly in the United Kingdom, operating under a license granted by the Post Office and funded in part by license fees paid by listeners. Reith became its first manager; he had found that for which he had long been looking.

In the early years of the BBC, Reith was given considerable freedom; the directors, representing the manufacturers, were more concerned with selling radios than broadcasting, and generally the Post Office officials did not interfere. Initially, both in the United States and in the United Kingdom, there was a reluctance to use the medium for advertising purposes; in both countries, there was also a belief that the new technology should be used for public service and should be educational, not simply entertaining. In the United States, however, entertainment quickly dominated and advertisers were soon selling their wares over the airwaves. With Reith's influence, though, mere entertainment came second on the BBC, for Reith had always been a person of strong opinions, and his opinions about radio broadcasting reflected his middle-class, Christian background. He believed that broadcasting should be, in a broad sense, morally uplifting and educational, and until he retired in 1938, Reith was able to dictate both policy and performance on the BBC. Advisory committees were established in such areas as religion and the arts in order to ensure the moral and intellectual quality of the broadcasts. Many members of the staff came from Reith's own background, often from Cambridge and Oxford, and there soon developed a recognizable BBC style of speech. His announcers wore dinner jackets when broadcasting over the radio, and not only were the shows to be of high moral content, so was the staff: Personal moral lapses were not tolerated. Reith was successful in molding the BBC to his view both because of his own vision and energy and because the British middle classes and politicians of the day shared his values.

Reith and the BBC did have their opponents. At first, the company was forbidden to report news, a protection which the powerful newspaper publishers demanded. Moreover, there were complaints about the company's monopoly status. After several governmental commissions had examined the status of the BBC, in 1926 it was decided that the company should divest itself of its private business character and become instead a public corporation: As a result, the British Broadcasting Company became the British Broadcasting Corporation, headed by a board of governors appointed by the government and still funded from listeners' license fees. Reith became the first director general, and in 1927 he was awarded a knighthood. Reith had accepted the restrictions against news reporting, but the BBC was forced into it suddenly in May, 1926, as a result of a general strike, launched by trade unions at the urging of the coal miners. Most of the major newspapers shut down, and Reith reluctantly stepped into the communications vacuum. In reporting the strike, Reith saw it as his duty, and the duty of the BBC, to be as objective as possible and not simply to take the side of the government against the strikers, but it was not an easy task. The Chancellor of the Exchequer, Winston Churchill, opposed that approach and never forgot Reith's unwillingness to support the authorities more fully.

As the years passed, the BBC became more and more Reith's creation. He continued to oppose advertising and the development of any competing broadcasting system; under Reith, the BBC retained its monopoly. It increased in staff and in functions, establishing both television and foreign-language facilities, and became more bureaucratic in nature. Although Reith usually picked excellent subordinates, and on paper he delegated responsibility, because of his domineering personality the corporation somewhat stagnated during the 1930's. Still, the BBC under Reith's leadership had become one of the most important institutions in Great Britain, and it was greatly admired, if not always emulated, throughout the world. Reith, having once found his destiny, was reluctant to allow his grown child to continue on its own; it was not until the eve of World War II that he left the BBC, to take over Imperial Airways, and when he left it was with an angry emptiness. Reith felt like a rejected father.

### Summary

With the outbreak of World War II in September, 1939, the first Baron Reith of Stonehaven prayed that Prime Minister Neville Chamberlain would give him a task commensurate with his abilities; after a few months, Reith was made minister of information and was necessarily elected to the House of Commons. Before he could implement needed reforms, Chamberlain was replaced by Winston Churchill, in May, 1940. Reith unwillingly became minister of transport and then, after a few months, minister of works. He was forced to give up his seat in the Commons and became instead Baron Reith of Stonehaven, with a seat in the House of Lords. In early 1942, Churchill, in a cabinet reshuffle, removed Reith from the government. Although Reith had wanted to go into politics as a young man, he would have made a poor professional politician; he lacked the ability to compromise, and he was unable to disguise his feelings about his colleagues. Churchill remembered Reith's part in the General Strike and also blamed Reith for not allowing him more speaking time on the BBC during the 1930's, but it was probably as much Reith's failures as Churchill's memory which destroyed Reith's ministerial career.

Deeply hurt, Reith joined the Royal Navy, and, although not a senior officer, he was responsible for bringing together the ships and matériel necessary for the successful D-day invasion of 1944. In 1945, Churchill was defeated by the Labour Party, and Reith briefly hoped that the new prime minister, Clement Attlee, might appoint him to office. Reith's lack of a proper grasp of political realities was again apparent, however, as he was not a member of the Labour Party and refused to join. In the late 1940's, he was chairman of the National Film Finance Board as well as holding what he believed to be were other minor positions. During the 1950's, he directed the government's Colonial Development Corporation and did much to reverse that institution's difficulties. Through it all, Reith continued to hope that he would be once again summoned for a great task, but the call never came. Although he was made Knight of the Thistle, the highest royal order for a Scotsman, and though he became Lord High Commissioner of the Church of Scotland, in his old age he looked back on his life with a sense of failure. In the 1920's, Reith had created out of his own vision and need the most famous broadcasting system in the world and one of the most important institutions in twentieth century Great Britain, but that was not enough for him; he spent the rest of his life attempting unsuccessfully to recapture that earlier sense of achievement.

### Bibliography

Boyle, Andrew. *Only the Wind Will Listen*. London: Hutchinson, 1972. This is the only complete biography of Reith, and it relies heavily on Boyle's personal discussions with Reith toward the end of his life. Because of this, the volume reflects Reith's own attitudes in his old age as he looked back at his childhood and his days at the BBC.

Briggs, Asa. *The History of Broadcasting in the United Kingdom*. 4 vols. London and New York: Oxford University Press, 1961-1979. Briggs has written a masterful and comprehensive study of broadcasting. The first volume takes the story to 1926 and the establishment of the public corporation, and the second volume goes to the eve of World War II. Reith is a dominant subject in both volumes. The third volume covers the war years, and Reith plays some small part when minister of information.

Reith, J. C. W. *Into the Wind*. London: Hodder and Stoughton, 1949. This is Reith's own autobiography, written in the years after World War I. It shows the author's attitudes at that time, but it is not always entirely accurate when discussing the events of his earlier life. Nevertheless, it is absolutely necessary for any understanding of Reith.

———. *The Reith Diaries*. Edited by Charles Stuart. London: Collins Sons and Co., 1975. Reith kept a diary for more than fifty years, which eventually resulted in many volumes of manuscript. Unfortunately, the result was somewhat superficial and formless. Stuart has sifted the whole and has produced the best single volume on the life of Reith. Stuart's editorial comments are extremely helpful.

———. *Wearing Spurs*. London: Hutchinson, 1966. Although not published until late in his life, here Reith wrote of his experiences in the Great War. As such, it belongs to the genre of personal accounts of World War I, but it does not achieve the literary level of Robert Graves's *Goodbye to All That* (1929).

Taylor, A. J. P. *English History, 1914-1945*. Oxford: Clarendon Press, and New York: Oxford

University Press, 1965. This volume in the Oxford History of England series is perhaps the best. It is a brilliant if somewhat controversial account of British history from the beginning of World War I through the conclusion of World War II. Taylor is not particularly an admirer of Reith, but this book is the place to begin any study of the history of England during the first half of the twentieth century.

*Eugene S. Larson*

## ERICH MARIA REMARQUE

*Born:* June 22, 1898; Osnabrück, Germany
*Died:* September 25, 1970; Locarno, Switzerland
*Area of Achievement:* Literature
*Contribution:* Remarque's novel *Im Westen nichts Neues* (1929; *All Quiet on the Western Front*, 1929), a realistic account of a soldier's life during World War I, is perhaps the most widely read and highly influential war novel of all time.

### Early Life

Erich Paul Remark, as he was known before changing his name to Erich Maria Remarque in 1920, was born on June 22, 1898, in Osnabrück, Germany. His father was a bookbinder. The family was poor and moved often; as a result, young Erich attended several different schools.

Remarque was talented in music, art, and literature, and even thought to become a professional musician. Instead, he chose to enter teacher's training. In 1916, before he was able to begin his career as a teacher, he was drafted into the army at a time when World War I was raging. He was sent to Flanders on the western front. On July 31, 1917, he was wounded and sent to a hospital to recover. Remarque's mother, who had been ill for some time with cancer, died while her son was in the hospital. This death appears to have profoundly affected Remarque.

During his hospital stay, Remarque began his writing career, completing a novel called *Die Traumbude* (1920; the dream room). The novel was published after the war, and Remarque had to sell his piano to cover printing costs. The novel, a sentimental and romantic account of his circle of friends, later proved an embarrassment to Remarque, who found the writing to be lacking in quality and maturity.

After his release from the hospital, Remarque had some trouble with authorities for wearing a lieutenant's uniform and medals he had not earned. By all accounts a handsome young man, the medal incident demonstrated Remarque's tendency toward flamboyance. During the early 1920's, Remarque had several jobs before becoming an editor of *Sport Im Bild* (sport in pictures) in 1925. It was at this time that he married Jutta Ilse Zambona, his first wife.

### Life's Work

While at *Sport Im Bild*, Remarque began publishing articles and stories. No one could have predicted from these, however, that he would produce a work of such stature as *All Quiet on the Western Front*. Reportedly, Remarque began to suffer from depression in 1927. He attributed his depressed state to his war experiences and found that many of his former comrades were also suffering negative emotional effects. Consequently, he began working on *All Quiet on the Western Front* for cathartic purposes. He believed that if he committed his memories to paper, he could overcome the depression they caused. The book was completed in six weeks, but Remarque was unable to find a publisher for it. Initially, *All Quiet on the Western Front* was serialized in the paper *Vossische Zeitung* in November and December of 1928 and excited a great deal of public interest.

Remarque attempted to describe his project in the brief preface to *All Quiet on the Western Front*: "This book is to be neither an accusation nor a confession, and least of all an adventure for death is not an adventure to those who stand face to face with it. It will try simply to tell of a generation of men who, even though they may have escaped shells, were destroyed by the war." For Remarque, the most important message of his novel was that war destroys more men than it kills.

Remarque set *All Quiet on the Western Front* during the last two years of World War I along the German lines in France. During this time, the Germans were losing strength just as the Americans entered the war. The novel tells the story of young Paul Bäumer and his acquaintances who enlist in the German army at the urging of their teacher, Kantorek. The young recruits soon learn that war is not the glorious, heroic experience their elders have proclaimed but is instead a brutal, futile business. Remarque's story is told from the point of view of a German foot soldier; however, his descriptions of the horrors of war transcend national boundaries. Allied and German veterans alike recognized their experiences in Remarque's novel.

In the opening chapters of *All Quiet on the Western Front*, the young men spend most of their time behind the front lines recalling the past. Although they have become fairly cynical, they have not yet been subjected to the horrors of trench warfare. Then they participate in a horrendous battle that Remarque describes in graphic detail. After this first battle, Paul goes home on leave. While at home, he begins to realize that he can no longer communicate with members of his family or with others at home who have not experienced the war. Ironically, it is the visit home that demonstrates the isolation of the frontline soldier; his experiences in the war render him unable to live among the people he is fighting for. Paul returns to the front after a wrenching farewell with his mother, who is dying of cancer. From this point until the end of the book, the men are engaged in almost constant fighting. Most of the main characters die. Paul can no longer find any meaning in life. All events and all deaths seem meaningless and random, and he loses hope. He also knows that those who will suffer most from the war are the ones who survive it. Finally, on a day very nearly at the end of the war, a day when all is quiet, Paul is killed by a random bullet.

After its serialization, *All Quiet on the Western Front* was published in book form in January, 1929, and was an immediate best-seller. Some attribute the success of the book to the massive publicity campaign undertaken by the publisher prior to the book's release. However, most critics agree that the book touched a nerve among not only the German people but also veterans all over the world. Although the book was wildly popular, it generated considerable controversy. As a result of his book's publication, Remarque became the subject of intense media and political scrutiny. Most notably, the Nationalist Socialist German Workers' Party, or the Nazi Party, rabidly criticized the book for its pacifist philosophy and for its supposedly negative picture of German soldiers. Remarque was accused of being a French Jew whose name was really "Kramer" (Remark spelled backward). In fascist Italy, the book was banned almost as soon as it was printed. In 1933, the Nazis publicly burned the book.

In addition, a German-born American filmmaker Carl Laemmle acquired the rights to *All Quiet on the Western Front* soon after its publication. By 1930, the motion picture version was released to instant critical and commercial acclaim. The film, starring Lew Ayres and Lewis Milestone, won several Academy Awards and is considered to be a landmark in filmmaking.

Meanwhile, Remarque began working on his next book, a sequel to *All Quiet on the Western Front* called *Der Weg zurück* (1931; *The Road Back*, 1931). In this book, he follows a group of veterans after the war, demonstrating the ways in which their lives had been destroyed. The novel was not the commercial success of *All Quiet on the Western Front* and received a more positive critical response in the United States than it did in Germany. After completing the book, Remarque realized that the growing power of the Nazis endangered him. After moving his money out of Germany, he moved to Switzerland, where he remained until 1939. During this time, he and his wife divorced, only to remarry in order to expedite her emigration from Germany. In 1938, the Germans took away his German citizenship.

While in Switzerland, Remarque continued his writing career, publishing a novel entitled *Drei Kameraden* (1938; *Three Comrades*, 1937). The German edition of the book was published in Amsterdam, Holland, as were many novels by German émigré writers. In this novel, Remarque details the lives of three Germans between the years 1923 and 1930, again returning to themes of friendship and displacement that had so marked his earlier work. Film versions of both *The Road Back* (1937) and *Three Comrades* (1938) were made in the United States and enjoyed commercial, if not critical, success.

In 1939, Remarque moved to the United States, living first in Los Angeles, California, and then New York City. During these years he wrote a number of novels and worked as a screenwriter. After divorcing Jutta Ilse Zambona a second time, he married the actor Paulette Goddart in 1958. The couple spent their time in New York, Italy, and Switzerland. In 1970, after a period of failing health, the seventy-two-year-old writer died in a hospital in Locarno, Switzerland.

### Summary

Erich Maria Remarque was certainly not the most talented writer of his generation, nor has all of his work stood the test of time. Indeed, without *All Quiet on the Western Front*, Remarque might be relegated to the status of an interesting period writer. Further, while critics may not view *All Quiet on the Western Front* as one of the greatest works of literature produced during the twentieth century, none deny that it is an extremely important book. Thus, the impact of *All Quiet on the Western Front* on society, politics, film, and literature confers on Remarque a higher status than he might otherwise have achieved. Throughout the novel, Remarque provides a ghastly look at the realities of war. Perhaps more important, this book has come to define the experience of World War I not only for Germans but also for all who fought in the war. Like its predecessor, Stephen Crane's *The Red Badge of Courage* (1895), *All Quiet on the Western Front* stands as a monument to those destroyed by the war.

### Bibliography


Barker, Christine R., and R. W. Last. *Erich Maria Remarque*. London: Wolff, and New York: Barnes and Noble, 1979. A solid, thorough introduction to Remarque's life and work. The writers argue that Remarque's best quality as a writer is his "overt admission" that the meaning of life is beyond human understanding.

Berson, Arnold. "Erich Maria Remarque." *Films in Review* 45, no. 9-10 (September/October, 1994). The author examines movies made from Remarque's books, including *All Quiet on the Western Front,* and focuses on Remarque's success with war stories.

Chambers II, John Whiteclay. "'All Quiet on the Western Front' (1930): The Antiwar Film and the Image of the First World War." *Historical Journal of Film Radio and Television* 14, no. 4 (1994). In-depth study of *All Quiet on the Western Front,* its portrayal of Remarque's experiences, and its historical authenticity.

Firda, Richard. *Erich Maria Remarque: A Thematic Analysis of His Novels*. New York: Lang, 1988. Although the book claims to analyze Remarque's novels, it generally provides little more than plot summaries. However, it provides a good deal of useful biographical detail and is especially useful in its discussion of Remarque's later novels.

Owen, C. R. *Erich Maria Remarque: A Critical Bio-Biography.* Amsterdam: Rodopi, 1984. Although this source provides little direct information on Remarque (apart from introductory materials), it is of considerable use to students assembling materials on Remarque's life and work.

Remarque, Erich Maria. *All Quiet on the Western Front*. Translated by A. W. Wheen. Boston: Little Brown, and London: Putnam, 1929. An autobiographical novel of World War I based on Remarque's experiences in the trenches of the Western Front. Any student studying Remarque should begin with this work, his masterpiece.

Taylor, Harley U. *Erich Maria Remarque: A Literary and Film Biography.* New York: Lang, 1989. An accessible introduction to Remarque's life. Although the book provides adequate plot summaries of the novels, it offers little analysis. It is most useful in its treatments of the film versions of Remarque's novels.

Wagener, Hans. *Understanding Erich Maria Remarque*. Columbia: University of South Carolina Press, 1991. A well-balanced, well-written introduction to Remarque's work. The book includes a full chapter on *All Quiet on the Western Front* and emphasizes the theme of exile that runs through Remarque's novels.


*Diane Andrews Henningfeld*

# JANET RENO

*Born:* July 21, 1938; Miami, Florida

*Areas of Achievement:* Law and government and politics

*Contribution:* As Florida's first female state attorney, Janet Reno focused on the root causes of criminal behavior, instituting programs to change the social and personal conditions that lead people to commit crimes. As the first woman attorney general of the United States, she declared her intention to reorient the national crime policy in the same way—toward prevention first, and then punishment.

## Early Life

Janet Reno was born on July 21, 1938, in the Coconut Grove section of Miami, Florida. Her father, Henry Reno, was a Danish immigrant who worked as a police reporter for the *Miami Herald* for forty-three years until his death in 1967. Her mother, Jane Wood Reno, was an investigative reporter for the *Miami News*. Her maternal grandmother was Daisy Sloan Hunter Wood, a genteel southern lady who instilled in her children and grandchildren a passionate commitment to duty and family.

Janet was the oldest of the Renos' four children, each born a year apart. In 1946, the family bought twenty-one acres on what was then the edge of the Everglades, twenty miles outside Miami. Jane Reno built the family house, where Janet still lives and where she lived with her mother until the latter's death on December 21, 1992. The house became a symbol to Janet that she could do anything she really wanted, if it was right, and if she put her mind to it.

The house had no air conditioning or central heating, and no television. Janet spent much of her time outdoors and developed a love of camping and canoeing. Her family's love of books, poetry, world affairs, and music linked her to the outside world.

While Janet got much of her independent spirit from her mother, who did not tolerate cosmetics, organized religion, or racism, she was also greatly influenced by her father. He was a gentle man who understood protocol. He taught his children compassion and social justice, always treating people with respect and dignity. He told his children stories of police officers, judges, and officials, most of whom were wise, compassionate, and honorable. Janet was drawn to government by the judges and police officers Henry brought home.

Janet attended public schools in Dade County, Florida. In 1960, she graduated from Cornell University with a bachelor's degree in chemistry. At Cornell, she was president of the Women's Student Government and earned her spending money by working as a waitress. She received her LL.B. degree in 1963 from Harvard Law School, where she was one of sixteen women in a class of 500.

Denied a position in one of Miami's large law firms because she was a woman, she took a position in a smaller firm. In 1971, she received her first political appointment as staff director of the Judiciary Committee of the Florida House of Representatives. In 1972, she ran for a seat in the state legislature and lost, but cheered herself with the knowledge that Abraham Lincoln had also lost his first election.

## Life's Work

Janet Reno's career in public service began to flourish when she joined the state attorney's office in Dade County, Florida, in 1973. While there, she was assigned to organize a juvenile division within the prosecutor's office. It was at this time that she began developing views about preventive crime-fighting through services to children and rehabilitating delinquent youths. From 1976 to 1978, she left public service briefly to become a partner in the Miami-based law firm of Steel, Hector and Davis, the same firm that refused to give her a job thirteen years earlier because she was a woman. In 1978 she was appointed by the governor of Florida to serve as Dade County State Attorney, becoming Florida's first female state attorney.

Janet Reno was elected five times to the post of state attorney for Dade County, running as a Democrat in a heavily Republican district. She believed that the first objective of a prosecutor should be to make sure innocent people do not get charged. The second objective should be to convict the guilty according to due process.

Reno took office when racial tension, drug trafficking, and illegal immigration from Cuba, Haiti, and South America were all on the rise. She gained widespread criticism in 1980, when her office failed to convict four white police officers who had been charged with beating to death a black insurance salesman. Miami's black community erupted into three days of rioting and black community leaders called for her resignation.

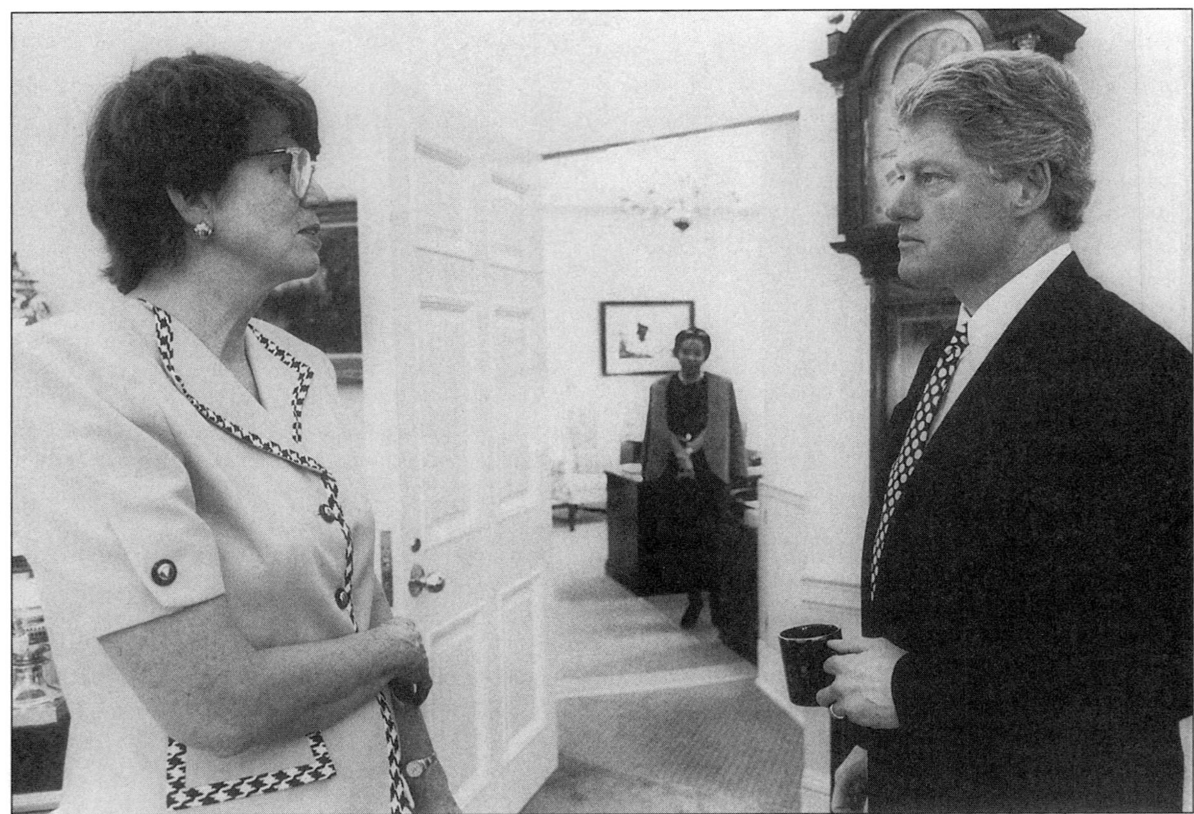

*Janet Reno outside the Oval Office with President Clinton*

Reno systematically set out to mend fences with the black community. She attended social functions and meetings, listened to their opinions as well as their anger, and took the time to explain her decisions. She marched in the Martin Luther King, Jr., Day Parade every year following the riots. Her office hired more blacks and Latinos and tackled issues important to minorities. Her policy of pursuing delinquent fathers for child support also helped her gain widespread respect in the black community. When she marched in the Martin Luther King, Jr., Day Parade five years after the Miami riots, she received a standing ovation.

As Dade state attorney she reformed the juvenile justice system, and began aggressively prosecuting child abuse cases. She also instituted a domestic-violence intervention program that relied heavily on counseling for victims and abusers. Beginning in the mid-1980's, she advocated a new approach to the prosecutor's traditional mission, one best described as preventive crime-fighting by trying to get at the root cause of crime. Since most people who go to jail eventually return to their communities, Reno chose to emphasize the importance of rehabilitation. She stated her view that imprisonment cannot serve as the ultimate solution to crime, although she did support life imprisonment sentences for the most violent criminals.

During her term in office, Reno developed a community policing team that helped clean up a crime-ridden Miami housing project. In 1989, she established Miami's innovative drug court, which offered first-time drug offenders a chance to wipe their records clean if they completed a year-long treatment program. Approximately sixty percent of those who start the program finish it, and ninety percent of those who finish remained trouble-free a year later. The court became a model for dozens of others around the country.

In 1990, Reno extended her office's pioneering approach to justice still further, offering young, nonviolent offenders a chance to avoid confinement and a criminal record by undertaking a program of rehabilitation which may include making restitution to their victims.

Reno's accomplishments and support for law and order issues brought her to the attention of the Clinton Administration. On March 12, 1993, Janet

Reno was sworn in as the seventy-eighth Attorney General of the United States, the first woman ever to hold that post. Following her swearing-in ceremony, in her first act as attorney general, she told reporters that she intended to protect women who sought abortions from harassment by anti-abortion protesters.

She made perhaps the most difficult decision of her career in April, 1993, when she ordered the Federal Bureau of Investigation (FBI) to launch an assault on the Branch Davidian cult compound outside Waco, Texas. The FBI and representatives of the Bureau of Alcohol, Tobacco, and Firearms (ATF) had been locked in a tense confrontation with the cult and its leader, David Koresh, for several weeks; Reno believed the children in the compound were being physically abused. In the end, eighty-six people, including seventeen children, died in the fire that followed. Shortly thereafter, Reno, visibly distraught, took full responsibility for the tragedy. Her earnest manner and the fact that she did not pass blame impressed both Washington officials and ordinary citizens.

As attorney general, Reno sought to revolutionize how American's think about law enforcement. She encouraged government agencies, federal, state, and local, to work together to address the root causes of crime. She suggested starting with good prenatal care, continuing to ensure that all children will have adequate health care, education, supervision, jobs and job training. She advocated flexible workdays so that parents can be home when their children get out of school.

She acknowledged that most of the country's successful crime programs come from local communities, not the federal government, but believed that one of her responsibilities is to keep talking about her crime prevention ideas in order to promote an ongoing, national dialogue. Her enormous influence on the criminal justice debate outside Washington cut across the political spectrum. She persuaded the American Bar Association to broaden its criminal studies by examining the needs of children.

### Summary

In her years as Florida state attorney for Dade County, Janet Reno gained a reputation as a hardworking prosecutor with a social conscience, and fought for better children's services as a way of preventing crime. In addition, she instituted innovative rehabilitation programs for first-time offenders.

As the first woman attorney general of the United States, Reno brought unquestioned integrity to the office and was recognized nationally for her strength and honesty. She became known as a direct, strong-willed, but compassionate politician with a record of attacking the root causes of criminal behavior. In a break with her Republican predecessors, Reno envisioned her preeminent role as reorienting national crime policy, calling for comprehensive programs that provide a balance between punishment and prevention. Believing society's resources should go toward better education, housing, and health care, not more jails, Reno also stated that she believed hardened criminals should be locked up permanently. As the people's lawyer, she stated her desire to be accessible to all citizens and to know what is happening on the streets of America, not just in the Justice Department. By implementing her plans to shift national crime-fighting priorities from punishment of crime to crime prevention, Reno established her mark on law enforcement nationwide.

In 1995, two years after being named attorney general, Reno had to face a personal, rather than professional, challenge when she was diagnosed with Parkinson's disease.

The longest-serving U.S. attorney general, Reno survived the usual cabinet purge as Bill Clinton began his second term as president. Ironically, her reappointment was almost assured because she had opened investigations into a number of cabinet members; her dismissal would appear to be an attempt to evade scandal. Already known for her independent style, Reno faced criticism from Democratic colleagues who opposed the numerous independent councils she agreed to appoint during her tenure; yet Republicans were frustrated by her disinclination to pursue charges where she determined the evidence did not warrant further investigation. She twice ended investigations into Vice President Al Gore's fund-raising activities, infuriating Republicans in Congress. Nevertheless, her appointment of Kenneth Starr to investigate the many allegations against the president led to a crucial moment in U.S. history—the impeachment and trial of President Clinton.

### Bibliography

Anderson, Paul. *Janet Reno: Doing the Right Thing*. New York: Wiley, 1994. Written by a reporter for the *Miami Herald* who observed Reno for many years, this first book-length biography chronicles Reno's lively family history (her immigrant grandfather discarded his Rasmussen surname in favor of "Reno" upon his arrival), her college and law school years, and her legal career. Emphasizes Reno's integrity, common sense, and strong work ethic.

Gibbs, Nancy. "Truth, Justice and the Reno Way." *Time* 142 (July 12, 1993): 20-27. Provides an indepth overview of Reno's history and her plans for the Justice Department, specifically focusing on her advocacy for children and cooperation among government agencies as a way to prevent crime.

Gordon, Diana R. "Can Reno Be the People's Lawyer? Justice Watch." *Nation* 258, no. 11 (March 21, 1994). Evaluation of Reno as attorney general after her first year in office. Places her actions in context within the Clinton administration.

Laughlin, Meg. "Growing up Reno." *Lear's* 6 (July, 1993): 48-51. Written by a Miami-based writer, the article focuses on Reno's upbringing, yet also includes brief highlights of her career.

Reno, Janet. "A Common-Sense Approach to Justice." *Judicature* 77 (September, 1993): 66-67. An edited transcript of Reno's address to the annual dinner of the American Judicature Society, August 6, 1993. Reno discusses her goals as attorney general and the role of lawyers in society.

———. "As State Prosecutor: Respected, Abused, Liked and Hated." In *Women Lawyers: Perspectives on Success*, edited by Emily Couric. New York: Harcourt Brace, 1984. Reno discusses her job as Florida state attorney for Dade County, covering the years 1978-1982. Readable, concise explanation of her thoughts and the philosophy behind some of her actions.

Reske, Henry J. "Talking with Attorney General Janet Reno." *ABA Journal* 79 (June, 1993). Interview with Reno in which she discusses her hopes of forging a partnership between police and social authorities to curb youth violence.

Simon, Charnan. *Janet Reno: First Woman Attorney General*. Chicago: Children's Press, 1994. One of the first juvenile biographies about Reno to appear in print, this work provides a useful introduction to Reno's life and career up through her first year as attorney general.

Wood, Chris. "World: America's Top Cop." *Maclean's* 106 (April 5, 1993): 18-20. Discussion of Reno as Florida state attorney for Dade County. Includes information on various programs instituted by Reno to prevent crime, such as Miami's drug court.

*Sarah Thomas*

# JEAN RENOIR

*Born:* September 15, 1894; Paris, France
*Died:* February 12, 1979; Los Angeles, California
*Area of Achievement:* Film
*Contribution:* Considered by many to be the world's greatest film director, Renoir explored his characters' relations to society and nature and their humanity during his forty-five-year career.

## Early Life

Jean Renoir was born September 15, 1894, in Paris. His father, the Impressionist painter Pierre-Auguste Renoir, had married his mother, Aline Charigot, a dressmaker's assistant, in 1890, although the couple's first child, Pierre, had been born in 1885. Among the many artist friends of the elder Renoir who visited his country house at Essoyes were Edgar Degas and Claude Monet. Renoir later described growing up amid an extended family of artists, models, art dealers, relatives, and their children as the happiest time of his life. By 1901, his immediate family included his younger brother, Claude.

Beginning in 1903, the Renoirs lived much of the year at Les Collettes, a villa in Cagnes-sur-Mer near Nice, where Jean attended school. He was always a poor, restless student, and his parents hoped he would eventually find some career working with his hands. In 1913, after finishing his studies in philosophy at the Nice extension of the University of Aix-en-Provence, Renoir joined the cavalry, hoping to become an officer. He was a sergeant when World War I broke out, and, after being kicked by a horse, he transferred, over his parents' objections, to the infantry as a sublieutenant. In April, 1915, his thighbone was fractured by a bullet. Since Renoir's wound left him with a slight limp, he was unable to return to the infantry. With time on his hands, he began going to films and soon became addicted, seeing as many as twenty-five American movies a week. He persuaded his father (his mother died in 1915), confined to a wheelchair, to buy a projector so that they could watch Charlie Chaplin films together.

In 1917, Renoir fell in love at first sight with Andrée Heurschling, one of his father's models. Pierre-Auguste Renoir died in December, 1919, and Jean married Andrée on January 24, 1920. After working in ceramics with his brother Claude at Cagnes-sur-Mer for a while, Renoir moved to Paris in 1921, had a kiln built, and started a pottery enterprise. Ceramics did not fulfull Renoir's need to create, and the inheritance from his father afforded him the freedom to take his time deciding what to do with his life. His only child, Alain, was born in 1922. By 1923, he had decided to make films.

## Life's Work

Through his brother Pierre, who had become an actor, Renoir met Albert Dieudonné, later the star of Abel Gance's *Napoléon* (1927), who wanted the wealthy young man to finance a film for him. Renoir wrote *Une Vie sans joie* (1924; *A Joyless Life*), and Dieudonné directed and costarred, against her will, with Renoir's wife, now known as Catherine Hessling. Renoir and Dieudonné quarreled over the melodrama, leading to the latter's reediting the film and rereleasing it in 1927 as *Catherine.* Not discouraged by this experience, Renoir immediately directed his first film, beginning his lifelong custom of filling the cast and crew with his friends, making the experience of filming a friendly collaboration. (Renoir would direct thirty-six films, writing or cowriting twenty-eight of them.) Through such early works as *La Fille de l'eau* (1924), he learned the techniques of filmmaking, taking great pleasure, as an artisan, in creating scale models of landscapes and streets.

Inspired by the force of the director's personality in Erich von Stroheim's *Foolish Wives* (1922), Renoir made the most expensive French film up to 1926, adapting *Nana* from the novel by Émile Zola. The stylization of *Nana*, especially in Catherine Hessling's pantomime-like performance, indicated Renoir's originality and maturing talent, but, as with several later films, its quality was not recognized in France at the time. His next film, *Charleston* (1927), a dance fantasy shot in four days, also failed at the box office. The release of *La Petite Marchande d'allumettes* (1928; *The Little Match Girl*), from the story by his beloved Hans Christian Andersen, was delayed by a plagiarism suit brought by two writers who had created a stage version of the story. In the interim, talking pictures arrived, and Renoir was forced to add a bad sound track. After making two commissioned silent films, he played opposite his wife in two films directed by his friend Alberto Cavalcanti. Because he loved actors so much, Renoir believed he should try acting. He and Catherine separated in 1930.

Unlike many French directors, Renoir welcomed the advent of sound as offering new possibilities to the art of the cinema. He directed *On purge bébé* (1931), based on a Georges Feydeau farce, just to prove he could make a sound film quickly and cheaply. He deliberately chose a less commercial project as his next effort. The producers were so shocked by *La Chienne* (1931) that they drove him from the studio and called the police to keep him out. When they were unable to reedit the film, Renoir was allowed to restore his version. This early example of *film noir*, now considered one of Renoir's masterpieces, was another commercial failure.

*La Nuit du carrefour* (1932), an adaptation of a Georges Simenon novel, with Pierre Renoir as Inspector Maigret, was also a failure. Renoir considered it such a mess that even he did not understand it. Among his assistants on this film were his brother Claude and Jacques Becker, later a prominent director himself, whose sense of order helped compensate for Renoir's more informal approach to his work. In explaining his seemingly haphazard methods, Renoir said, "[Y]ou discover the content of a film in the process of making it." He followed with another masterpiece, *Boudu sauvé des eaux* (1932; *Boudu Saved from Drowning*), in which he continued the use of deep-focus cinematography, a technique he helped pioneer. Such films, with their fluid, seemingly improvisational styles, led the French cinema away from an overreliance on dialogue.

Despite such artistic successes, Renoir continued having difficulty with the practical side of filmmaking. Because *Madame Bovary* (1934), his adaptation of Gustave Flaubert's novel, was more than three hours long, the distributors shortened it into a largely incoherent state. Once again, the director recovered with a notable achievement, *Toni* (1934), the first of several films focusing on the individual's relation to society. His friendship with the Groupe Octobre, writers and artists with Communist leanings, influenced *Le Crime de M. Lange* (1936; *The Crime of Monsieur Lange*), in which workers form a cooperative to save a failing business.

Renoir combined his concern with society and his passion for nature in *Une Partie de campagne* (1946; *A Day in the Country*). The 1936 filming went more chaotically than usual, Renoir's usual happy family of collaborators turned against one other, and the director abandoned the film before it was completed. After World War II, Marguerite Renoir reedited it from the uncut negative saved by Henri Langlois, director of the Cinémathèque Française, and the film was finally released in 1946. (Marguerite Mathieu lived with Renoir from 1935 to 1940 and used his name even though they never married.) Despite all the problems, this bittersweet film is one of Renoir's most charming.

After *Les Bas-Fonds* (1936; *The Lower Depths*) got a lukewarm reception, the director made one of his most lasting achievements, *La Grande Illusion* (1937; *Grand Illusion*). Censors altered Renoir's version, and, while critics were enthusiastic about it, the public, anticipating another war, was disturbed by its pacifist message. The film was better received in the United States, running for twenty-six weeks at a New York theater. Using an uncut negative found in Munich by the American army, Renoir finally restored it to his original intentions in 1958.

After *La Marseillaise* (1938), his interpretation of the French Revolution, and *La Bête humaine* (1938; *The Human Beast*), another Zola adaptation, Renoir created *La Règle du jeu* (1939; *The Rules of the Game*), considered by many to be his finest film. It was made in typical Renoir fashion with the director and his collaborators writing the dialogue and choosing the locations as they needed them. Once the film was made, Renoir had to overcome editing problems and legal difficulties to arrive at his 113-minute cut. Distributors trimmed *La Règle du jeu* to eighty-five minutes, and it was eventually banned by the Vichy government as demoralizing and by the Nazi occupiers. The original negative was destroyed when the Allies bombed the Boulogne studios, but Renoir's version was restored in 1956 from more than two hundred cans of film and bits of sound track. Because of the film's reputation as one of the greatest ever made, the public perception of Renoir the person is as he appears here in his most notable acting performance. Tall, plump, energetic, with thinning reddish-blond hair, a perpetual gleam in his eye, and a gravelly voice, Renoir has been likened by critic Andrew Sarris to a dancing bear.

In 1939, France, fearing that Italy would side with Germany in the coming war, sent Renoir on an artistic diplomatic mission to Rome to teach a course in directing and make a film of Giacomo Puccini's opera *Tosca.* When Italy entered the war in June, 1940, he returned to Paris, leaving *Tosca* to be finished by Carl Koch, who had worked with Renoir on two earlier films. In February, 1941, Renoir sought refuge from the war by going to the

United States accompanied by Dido Freire, script girl for *La Règle du jeu* and niece of Alberto Cavalcanti. They were married February 6, 1944, without realizing that his divorce from Catherine was legal only in America. Renoir had a villa built in Beverly Hills near the home of his cousin Gabrielle and her husband, the American painter Conrad Slade.

Beginning at Twentieth Century-Fox, Renoir the improviser had difficulty working in the highly structured Hollywood studio system. He surprised the Fox executives by rejecting their scripts dealing with French or European history, choosing instead a screenplay set in Georgia, and shocked them by choosing to film *Swamp Water* (1941) in the Okefenokee Swamp instead of on a Hollywood soundstage. He missed, however, working with his family of collaborators and later said his five American films "don't even come close to any ideal I have for my work" because of the studios' reluctance to take chances. He made only *The Diary of a Chambermaid* (1946) with his typical approach.

Instead of returning to France after this bitter experience, Renoir chose to make another English-language film, *The River* (1951), an adaptation of a Rumer Godden novel set in India. His first color film, with his nephew Claude, Pierre's son, as cinematographer, *The River* is one of his most beautifully lyrical works. After going to Italy for another visually striking film, *Le Carrosse d'or* (1953; *The Golden Coach*), Renoir finally returned to France, directing his play *Orvet* (1955) in Paris. He continued experimenting with color in his first French film in sixteen years, *French Cancan* (1955), but his poetic lyricism proved unfashionable in an age of cinematic realism. French critics attacked him for being more sentimental than he had been before the war. His next four films were also badly received, seemingly showing a loss of his former surety of tone and lightness of touch.

In 1960, he taught a theater course at the University of California, Berkeley, where his son was a professor of medieval literature. He published his first novel, *Les Cahiers du Capitaine Georges* (the notebooks of Captain Georges), in 1966 and wrote a biography of his father. His final cinematic work, *Le Petit Théâtre de Jean Renoir* (*The Little Theatre of Jean Renoir*), consisting of four short films, each introduced by Renoir, was released in 1970. He claimed he directed as much with his legs as with his head, and the pain from his old wound would no longer allow him to make films. He received a special Academy Award in 1975 and the French Legion of Honor in 1977 and spent his last decade writing his memoirs and three more novels.

Renoir became a naturalized American citizen in 1946 while maintaining his French citizenship. He lived in both Beverly Hills and Paris thereafter and died of a heart attack in Los Angeles on February 12, 1979. He was buried at Essoyes.

### Summary

During the 1930's, Jean Renoir was considered one of the major French directors, along with Marcel Carné, René Clair, Jacques Feyder, and Julien Duvivier, although his work was believed to lack the polish and moral certainty of his rivals' work. By the 1950's, the auteur critics, including such future directors as Eric Rohmer, Jean-Luc Godard, and François Truffaut, paved the way for recognizing Renoir's genius. Truffaut, later speaking for his fellow New Wave directors, called Renoir "the father of us all." As films such as *La Grande Illusion* and *La Règle du jeu* were rereleased, filmgoers had the opportunity to see his best work as he intended it to be seen. Renoir's causal techniques and groping after tenuous truths appealed to the New Wave and to sophisticated audiences. For the most part, however, critics agree only that his films of the 1930's are masterpieces. The critical consensus is that while his movies after 1939 are interesting in the context of his entire output and are striking in places, they are inferior to his earlier work, often self-indulgent and aimless.

In addition to his effect on the New Wave directors, Renoir influenced the future directors who worked as his assistants, including such diverse talents as Luchino Visconti, Robert Aldrich, and Satyajit Ray. Those who have called him the greatest film director include Renoir's own idol, Charlie Chaplin. For critic Pierre Leprohon, Renoir is the true poet of the cinema, adhering to no theories, imitating no one, creating his art out of his experiences, his love of an imperfect world.

### Bibliography

Bazin, André. *Jean Renoir.* Edited by François Truffaut. Translated by W. W. Halsey II and William H. Simon. New York: Simon and Schuster, 1973; London: Allen, 1974. Affectionate analysis of Renoir's work by the critic most responsible for the reevaluation of his career. May have become the definitive study had Bazin not died before completing it.

Bergstrom, Janet. "Jean Renoir's Return to France." *Poetics Today* 17, no. 3 (Fall 1996). Discusses Renoir's film *Cancan,* in which he attempted to merge American film style with the desires of French audiences.

Braudy, Leo. *Jean Renoir: The World of His Films.* New York: Doubleday, 1972; London: Robson, 1977. Focuses on the contrasts in Renoir's films between theatricality and naturalism, improvisation and order, social commitment and aesthetic detachment. Good balance between considering Renoir as a craftsman and as a humanist. Includes a good brief summary of his life.

———. "Renoir at Home." *Film Quarterly* 50, no. 1 (Fall 1996). Includes never-before-published excerpts from a 1970 interview with Renoir.

Durgnat, Raymond. *Jean Renoir.* Berkeley: University of California Press, 1974; London: Studio Vista, 1975. Lengthy critical biography. Gives considerable background about the making of the films. Summarizes what other critics have said about Renoir. Perhaps the best all-round study of the director.

Leprohon, Pierre. *Jean Renoir.* Translated by Brigid Elson. New York: Crown, 1971. Excellent biographical sketch with excerpts from interviews with Renoir and commentaries by critics and friends.

Renoir, Jean. *My Life and My Films.* Translated by Norman Denny. London: Collins, and New York: Atheneum, 1974. The director recalls the people and events associated with the making of his films. Discusses the influence on his work of Charlie Chaplin, D. W. Griffith, and Erich von Stroheim. Not that specific about the details of his life. Good for conveying Renoir's personality.

———. *Renoir: My Father.* Translated by Randolph Weaver and Dorothy Weaver. London: Collins, and Boston: Little Brown, 1962. This memoir of his father is an excellent source of details about the director's childhood, some supplied by his cousin Gabrielle. Aids in understanding the father's influence on the son as artist and man.

———. *Renoir on Renoir: Interviews, Essays, and Remarks.* Translated by Carol Volk. Cambridge and New York: Cambridge University Press, 1989. Collection of his comments on his work.

Sesonske, Alexander. *Jean Renoir: The French Films, 1924-1939.* Cambridge, Mass.: Harvard University Press, 1980. This study of the first half of the director's career provides accounts of the making of the films. Good analysis of Renoir's visual style. Written with the director's cooperation, it may be too reverential.

*Michael Adams*

# WALTER P. REUTHER

*Born:* September 1, 1907; Wheeling, West Virginia
*Died:* May 9, 1970; Pellston, Michigan
*Areas of Achievement:* Labor and social reform
*Contribution:* Committed to politically active unionism, Reuther helped organize the automobile workers in the 1930's and led that union in the support of a broad range of social and economic reform in post-World War II United States.

## Early Life

Walter Philip Reuther was born September 1, 1907, in Wheeling, West Virginia, the son of a dissenting German Lutheran family. His father, Valentine Reuther, was active in local union activities and had become a convert to Debsian socialism, which advocated the gradual, democratic achievement of a humanitarian social order. The elder Reuther campaigned extensively for Eugene V. Debs for president, and he, himself, sought a state senate seat as a Socialist. He imbued his sons with the need for greater social and economic justice and the necessity of independent thinking, and he taught them the techniques of effective public speaking and debate. Valentine Reuther became convinced that the labor movement should be organized along industrial rather than craft lines and that workers should be encouraged to use the ballot box as well as the strike to advance their cause. Unions existed, he insisted, not only to promote the selfish interests of their members but also as instruments for the achievement of broad social equality and economic reform.

Young Reuther's own experiences tended to reinforce his father's teachings. At sixteen, he dropped out of school to work at Wheeling Steel Company. Excelling at die making, the production of exceptionally hard and precise steel forms for use as metal-shaping presses, Reuther was naturally attracted to Detroit, the center of the new automobile industry. Moving to Detroit in 1927, he worked briefly at Briggs Manufacturing Company before obtaining a job as a die maker at Ford Motor Company. During the five years he worked at Ford, Reuther earned relatively high wages, completed high school, and, along with his brother Victor, enrolled in classes at Detroit City College (later Wayne State University). At the same time, he noted the hectic, inhumane hours and work pace on the automobile assembly line and joined the small, ineffectual, left-wing Auto Workers Union. After 1930, while at Detroit City College, he and his brother organized a Social Problems Club, opposed the establishment of Reserve Officers' Training Corps on campus, and organized tours of the Depression-wracked city with its shantytowns and massive unemployment. They joined the Socialist Party and, in 1932, campaigned throughout southeastern Michigan on behalf of Norman Thomas, the party's presidential candidate.

Laid off from his Ford job in 1932 (in part, he thought, because of his political and union activities), Reuther and his brother traveled extensively for almost three years. They bicycled through Europe, visited relatives, and established contact with the anti-Nazi underground just as Adolf Hitler was consolidating his power in Germany. In late 1933, they arrived in the Soviet Union and worked for almost two years at a massive automobile plant in Gorki. In letters to American friends as well as in interviews with Soviet newspapers, the stocky, redheaded, brash, idealistic, and self-confident Reuther spoke out on conditions inside the Soviet Union. Like many other Americans of left-wing sympathies, he praised the heroic purposefulness of the Soviet worker. Increasingly, however, he criticized the clumsy, inefficient, overly centralized state bureaucracy which slowed progress. In the fall of 1935, after further travels in the Soviet Union, China, and Japan, Walter and Victor Reuther returned to the United States.

## Life's Work

Reuther threw himself into union activities upon arriving home. Despite New Deal legislation encouraging collective bargaining, labor organizing was a dangerous and uncertain undertaking in the mid-1930's. Industrialists in Detroit—a notoriously "open shop" city—opposed unions with all the resources at their command. When regular law enforcement personnel were not at their disposal, they sometimes employed violent gangs with underworld connections. They conducted extensive spying on union activities, fired organizers, and employed strikebreakers. Meanwhile, the work force was composed of a bewildering number of nationalities, speaking a variety of languages. Labor spokesmen, some influenced by Communist and Socialist ideologies, bitterly debated organizational strategies and engaged in internecine intrigue against one another.

Reuther became an unpaid organizer for a small United Automobile Workers (UAW) local in early 1936. At the same time, he married May Wolf, a teachers union activist and member of the Marxist Proletarian Party. He addressed a labor rally the very evening of his marriage.

A shrewd strategist, Reuther understood the use of the dramatic in building UAW membership. Named president of a newly chartered west-side local in later 1936, he orchestrated a sit-down strike at Kelsey-Hayes, a major manufacturer of wheels and brakes for Ford Motor Company. Workers, in taking physical possession of the plant, prevented the introduction of strike-breakers and police by Kelsey-Hayes, whose owners naturally feared the destruction of company property in any possible scuffle. The successful Kelsey-Hayes confrontation was followed by the celebrated General Motors (GM) sit-down strike of 1937, in which Reuther's brothers, Victor and Roy, played principal roles. The controversial sit-down strategy, ruled illegal by the Supreme Court in 1941, proved enormously helpful in building UAW membership in GM and Chrysler factories. Reuther and other UAW officials attempted to recruit Ford workers in 1937 as well but were surrounded and physically beaten by company service detectives. Not until 1941 did Ford finally capitulate to organizing efforts. Although he had only a marginal role in the GM strike, Walter Reuther had demonstrated remarkable courage and ingenuity during the organizational successes of the late 1930's.

As a labor politician, Reuther engaged in acrimonious debate with critics, both on the Left and on the Right. In the mid-1930's, he was part of the UAW's Unity Caucus, composed of moderate nonideologues as well as Communists and Socialists. In 1937, he ran with Socialist Party backing for a seat on the Detroit Common Council but resigned from the party in 1939 and subsequently supported liberal, New Deal Democrats for public office. Although continually attacked by rivals as pro-Communist because of his stands in the mid-1930's, Reuther emerged, at the end of World War II, as the leading anti-Communist spokesman within the UAW. Gradually, he fashioned a middle position, opposing both Communism and Fascism and urging a program of government-encouraged production and abundance. During the war, he advocated a plan of rapid conversion of automobile manufacturing facilities to aircraft production but opposed a piecework incentive program proposed by union Communists. In an especially bitter strike at GM in 1945-1946, Reuther attempted to speak for inflation-conscious consumers as well as union members. He demanded a "look at the books" of GM, which he said would justify his request for an hourly pay hike without a corresponding price increase to automobile buyers.

Although the postwar GM strike failed, Reuther was able to capitalize on his imaginative leadership during the dispute. In 1946, charging that Communists as well as more orthodox labor leaders had sabotaged the strike, he won the presidency of the UAW. The subsequent year, he tightened his grip upon the union, appointed persons loyal to him to influential positions, and began to commit the UAW to a broad program of political activity. In 1947, he helped form the Americans for Democratic Action (ADA), the leading liberal anti-Communist organization of the postwar period. The ADA, heavily financed by the UAW, exercised considerable influence with the Democratic Party. It backed Harry S Truman's Fair Deal programs of government-encouraged economic growth, the creation of national health care and housing plans, an attack on racial segregation, and the repeal of the probusiness Taft-Hartley Act of 1947. Reuther and the ADA argued that the best guarantee against Communism, both domestically and internationally, was the expansion of material abundance and its more equitable distribution.

By winning major concessions for union members from the prosperous postwar automobile industry, Reuther was able to deflect internal criticism of his expansive reform activities. An exceptionally skillful negotiator, he won automatic cost-of-living adjustments in UAW contracts, improved medical and dental insurance coverage, and substantially advanced retirement and unemployment benefits. Multiyear contracts, moreover, brought a measure of stability to both the industry and the UAW work force. While his Left-liberal political positions and his strident, somewhat intolerant, style would hardly engender deep affection among most UAW members, Reuther clearly commanded their respect through his intelligence and stamina at the negotiating table. His personal courage, demonstrated during his recuperation from a serious wound suffered in a 1948 assassination attempt, added to his appeal among blue-collar automobile workers.

Beginning in 1952, Reuther played a major part in the merger of the Congress of Industrial Organizations (CIO) and the American Federation of Labor (AFL). These two giant labor federations, the first based on industrial unionism and the second having its foundation in craft unionism, had been sometimes harsh rivals since the mid-1930's. With the deaths of the presidents of both organizations in 1952, serious talks about a merger became realistic. George Meany, a veteran labor politician, emerged as president of the AFL. Reuther overcame bitter opposition from the steelworkers union to become president of the CIO. (He also retained the presidency of the UAW.) Encouraged by progress in lessening interunion raiding, Meany and Reuther led their respective federations toward a merger in 1955. While Meany became president of the AFL-CIO, Reuther assumed the leadership of its Industrial Union Department and won Meany's promise to eliminate corruption and racial discrimination in the new federation and to launch a major organizational drive.

From the beginning, the AFL-CIO proved to be a disappointment for Reuther. The much vaunted organizational blitz never took place; interunion rivalries precluded a genuine merger at the local level; and the percentage of the nonagricultural work force that was unionized began a slow decline. Reuther clashed openly with Meany's visceral anti-Communism, his foot-dragging on civil rights issues, and his reluctance to commit the AFL-CIO to a massive organizational drive. Meany, a gruff, cigar-smoking bureaucrat with a more traditional view of unionism, enjoyed the good life and the annual AFL-CIO conventions at posh resort areas. He had little in common with Reuther, an abstemious (he used neither tobacco nor alcohol) idealist who continually sought to commit the labor movement to a broad program of social and economic reconstruction.

Frustrated with Meany and the AFL-CIO, Reuther enthusiastically embraced the reform policies of the John F. Kennedy and Lyndon B. Johnson administrations. A longtime advocate of programs such as the Peace Corps, he was the most vocal and visible labor leader in support of the antipoverty and civil rights legislation of the 1960's. Because of his support for Johnson's domestic agenda, he only reluctantly expressed his reservations about American participation in the Vietnam War. By 1968, however, concerned about urban rioting, the assassinations of Robert Kennedy and Martin Luther King, and the disarray within Liberal circles, Reuther moved into open criticism of the war.

His painful break with the Administration coincided with his departure from the AFL-CIO. Disputes with Meany over the Vietnam War, civil rights, and other public issues underscored fundamental differences about unionism itself. The continued rejection by the AFL-CIO of his view that unions should transcend narrow bread-and-butter issues to become instruments of broad social reform proved increasingly intolerable to him. The unwillingness of the federation to support Cesar Chavez's United Farm Workers, in which Reuther took a deep personal interest, represented only the most recent example. In 1968, Reuther took the UAW out of the AFL-CIO and entered a loose partnership with the Teamsters called the Alliance for Labor Action (ALA). In the ALA, the Teamsters agreed to respect Chavez's organizational efforts and defer to Reuther on most issues of public policy. While still groping for ways to reinstill idealism and meaning into the labor movement, Reuther and his wife were killed in an airplane crash on May 9, 1970.

### Summary

Reuther's death occurred at a time of deep division and disillusionment in the United States. Most labor leaders spurned his call to greater social activism. UAW members, mostly of post-Depression era age, cared far more about upward personal mobility than the heroic organizing struggles of the 1930's that had helped define Reuther. The American automobile industry, which had sustained high wages for the union, was plagued with antiquated productive facilities and faced increased foreign competition and a coming fuel shortage. Even Reuther's Liberal political allies, torn by war and domestic unrest, were entering a period of difficult redefinition.

While Reuther's active career spanned thirty-five years, his consciousness—thanks largely to his father—touched most of the twentieth century. He remained true to his father's Debsian Socialist vision even when circumstances and practicality mandated that he sever official ties with avowedly Socialist organizations. His goals of a purposeful, just, and humanitarian industrial order clearly date back to Valentine Reuther's teachings. His dramatic, confrontational style, molded in the contentious 1930's, remained his trademark even in the post-World War II period, when a lack of energy and idealism joined with rigid anti-Communism to produce the conservative "business unionism" of George Meany. More than any other union leader of his time, Reuther struggled to transcend narrow conceptions of legitimate union activity and to commit labor organizations to a broad, advanced program of social and economic justice.

**Bibliography**

Barnard, John. *Walter Reuther and the Rise of the Auto Workers*. Boston: Little Brown, 1983. An excellent introduction to Reuther by a respected academic historian. Especially good in defining Reuther's relationship with Debsian socialism. Barnard benefited from the extensive Archives of Labor History and Urban Affairs at Wayne State University.

Bernstein, Irving. *Turbulent Years: A History of the American Worker, 1933-1941*. Boston: Houghton Mifflin, 1969. The classic study of labor organizing efforts in the 1930's, including the passage of the Wagner Act, the rupture between the AFL and the CIO, and the growth of the UAW.

Cormier, Frank, and William J. Eaton. *Reuther*. Englewood Cliffs, N.J.: Prentice-Hall, 1970. A readable and sympathetic biography based heavily on interviews of Reuther and those close to him.

Dayton, Eldorous L. *Walter Reuther: The Autocrat of the Bargaining Table*. New York: Devin Adair, 1958. A hostile study by a right-wing writer, most useful as a summary of conservative anxieties about Reuther.

Goode, Bill. *Infighting in the UAW: The 1946 Election and the Ascendancy of Walter Reuther.* Westport, Conn.: Greenwood Press, 1994. The author provides an in-depth examination of the reasons behind Reuther's defeat of the incumbent leader of the United Auto Workers Union.

Goulden, Joseph C. *Meany: A Biography of the Unchallenged Strong Man of American Labor.* New York: Atheneum, 1972. Based heavily on interviews, this is the single best volume on Reuther's rival in the AFL-CIO. Goulden portrays Meany as a gifted labor leader, by background and temperament very different from the UAW leader.

Lichtenstein, Nelson. *The Most Dangerous Man in Detroit: Walter Reuther and the Fate of American Labor.* New York: Basic, 1995. Insightful biography of Reuther focusing on both the evolution of the labor movement and its decline in recent years.

Marquart, Frank. *An Auto Worker's Journal: The UAW from Crusade to One-Party Union*. University Park: Pennsylvania State University Press, 1975; London: Pennsylvania State University Press, 1976. A slashing indictment by an old-line UAW Socialist of Reuther's overweening control of the union. Marquart argues that Reuther rose to power within the union by Red-baiting his enemies.

Reuther, Victor G. *The Brothers Reuther and the Story of the UAW.* Boston: Houghton Mifflin, 1976. An indispensable defense. Victor Reuther emphasizes the impact of their father and the closeness with which the brothers operated. To the left of Walter on most issues, Victor Reuther was highly critical of Meany and cautioned against the merger in 1955.

Salvatore, Nick. *Eugene V. Debs: Citizen and Socialist*. Urbana: University of Illinois Press, 1982. A fascinating biography of Debs that provides excellent insights into early twentieth century American socialism.

Zieger, Robert H. *American Workers, American Unions, 1920-1985*. 2d ed. Baltimore: Johns Hopkins University Press, 1994. A first-rate historical overview of organized labor in the United States since World War I.

*William Howard Moore*

# SYNGMAN RHEE

*Born:* March 26, 1875; P'yŏngsan, Korea
*Died:* July 19, 1965; Honolulu, Hawaii
*Areas of Achievement:* Government and politics
*Contribution:* Rhee began his career as a student movement leader in the 1890's. In exile, he became the leader of an overseas movement to liberate Korea from Japanese rule between 1913 and 1945. He later became President of South Korea, holding that position throughout the Korean War.

## Early Life

Syngman Rhee was born in 1875 in P'yŏngsan, Hwanghae Province, sixty miles north of Seoul. He was the only son of Yi Kyŏng-sŏn, a descendant of King T'aejong. Though impoverished by the passage of generations, Rhee's aristocratic family helped shape his character and endowed him with certain lifelong traits: a lonely devotion to principle over practicality, a fierce pride which demanded complete loyalty from others, and a surpassing ambition to lead, whether as a student in Seoul, an exiled Korean nationalist in the West, or president of the Republic of Korea (1948 to 1960).

As a boy, Rhee was schooled in the traditional way, learning the Chinese classics. In 1894, however, he entered Paejae Boys School, run by missionaries of the American Methodist Episcopal Church in Seoul. There he became a Christian. He also achieved notoriety as a student demonstrator in the Korean reform movement and as a member of the reformist Independence Club, for which he was arrested in 1898 and imprisoned by the Korean government for six years. In 1904 when he was released, American friends arranged for him to pursue his studies in the United States. He was enrolled in George Washington University where he earned a B.A. He earned an M.A. at Harvard and went on to Princeton for a Ph.D. in political science. The distinction of being the first Korean to earn a doctorate in the West created an enormous fund of respect for him among the education-conscious Koreans, both in their homeland and in exile.

## Life's Work

In 1910, Korea was annexed to Japan and remained a colony for thirty-five years, until it was liberated by the Allied victory in 1945. Rhee spent most of this period in exile. He did return to Korea briefly after finishing his doctoral studies at Princeton and worked with the Young Men's Christian Association, but he was arrested again, this time by the Japanese during a roundup of Christian leaders who were thought to be involved in a conspiracy to assassinate the Japanese governor-general. He was soon released, but because he was a marked man his missionary associates had him sent back to the United States as a delegate to a church convention. Once in the United States he stayed there, moving to Hawaii to establish himself as a Korean community leader. He founded a school, an association (the Tongji-hoe, one of the main Korean associations in America), and a magazine (the *Pacific Weekly*, in Korean). Though he was respected for his attainments, he was also a controversial figure who fell out with rivals and found it difficult to rise above the status of faction leader.

One of Rhee's main contributions was as a representative of the Korean Provisional Government (KPG), an exiled body formed in 1919 and headquartered in Shanghai. Because of his wide reputation, Rhee was elected the KPG's first president, in 1919. He remained, however, in Washington for nearly two years, urging the case for Korean independence upon the United States Congress and various international bodies. When he finally arrived in Shanghai to assume the presidency of the provisional government, he found it very difficult to work with his compatriots and left after seventeen frustrating months. In 1921, he returned to his base in Hawaii, from which he ventured often on speaking tours to other parts of the United States, trying to influence American policy in favor of the cause of Korean independence from Japan. His campaign to get the United States government to recognize Korea in effect by treating him as an official representative was tireless and resourceful. His methods included offering to have Korean guerrillas fight the Japanese during World War II and demanding diplomatic immunity for himself when he was stopped for speeding by the District of Columbia police. Although he aroused considerable sympathy among American audiences who heard him speak, he came to be regarded as a nuisance by many in the diplomatic and policymaking establishment.

With the end of World War II and the American occupation of South Korea, however, Rhee became useful to General Douglas MacArthur, the Supreme Commander for the Allied Powers in Tokyo. He ob-

tained MacArthur's help in returning to Korea in October, 1945, and arrived back in Seoul as if to claim his destiny as leader of the independent Korean republic. Like most Koreans, Rhee was frustrated and upset by the fact that his homeland had been liberated from Japan only to be divided at the thirty-eighth parallel and reoccupied by the United States and the Soviet Union. He helped lead the fight against a short-lived proposal to put Korea under an international trusteeship. Then, as American and Soviet negotiators failed to agree on a slate of Korean leaders to form a combined Korean government, Rhee maneuvered himself into a commanding position for leadership in the south.

Rhee's rise was far from automatic. After his return in 1945, he was forced to overcome challenges from leaders of the China-based KPG and from Korean nationalist leaders who had spent the years of the Japanese occupation within Korea. He enjoyed surpassing advantages, however, in dealing with the American occupation authorities. His American training and command of English were key assets as he positioned himself. So was his political conservatism as the Americans suppressed the Left in South Korea and turned increasingly to right-wing interests to form the new government in their zone. In 1948, when a United Nations-sponsored election failed to unite Korea, separate republics were formed in the two zones. In August, Rhee was elected president by the newly formed National Assembly of the Republic of Korea (South Korea). In the same year in North Korea, the Soviet-sponsored Kim Il Sung became President of the Democratic People's Republic of Korea. By 1949, most of the American and Soviet forces had withdrawn, leaving the peninsula to the Rhee and Kim regimes.

As President of the Republic of Korea from 1948 to 1960, Syngman Rhee faced successive trials. The first was the quest for legitimacy: to be recognized as more than a factional leader domestically and an American client internationally, a quest in which he was never entirely successful. His greatest test was the Korean War (1950-1953), the direct result of the Allies' division of Korea in 1945 and Kim Il Sung's disastrous attempt to reunite the peninsula by force. The economic situation in Korea, already desperate because of the isolation of the developed north from the agricultural south, was rendered incomparably worse by the war's destruction, which flattened large areas of Seoul and the other cities (as it also destroyed the major cities in the north) and took the lives of an estimated two million Korean people. When the war ended in stalemate, again roughly along the thirty-eighth parallel, Rhee was confronted with the forbidding task of reconstruction. Although large amounts of American and international aid poured into South Korea in the 1950's, it took many years to show results. With the populace demoralized it proved to be a very poor climate in which to develop new political traditions. Corruption flourished, and as Rhee aged and grew more isolated, his political organization became more obsessed with power and its privileges. The Rhee years were marked by stolen elections, constitutional amendments to perpetuate his party in power, repression by police, and organized youth gangs that mocked the government's proclaimed ideals. In 1959, the forcible passage of a series of laws including a National Security Law that was plainly intended to punish political opponents in the name of national defense, led to a wave of popular revulsion against the Rhee regime.

The quadrennial presidential election of 1960 pitted Rhee against an opposition candidate who died of natural causes during the campaign. Rhee, at age eighty-four, therefore won a fourth term by default. The election of his vice presidential running mate, however, required widespread fraud and voter intimidation. There was so much irregularity in the voting that demonstrations broke out demanding a new election. The demonstrations turned into student-led riots in April, 1960. These were answered by police bullets and heavy loss of life on April 19. Martial law was declared, and, after attempting to bargain with the demonstrators and the National Assembly, Rhee finally was persuaded to resign the presidency. Within weeks he left Seoul for the last time and flew with his wife to Hawaii. In Honolulu, he spent his last years and died at the age of ninety, on July 19, 1965.

## Summary

Despite his flaws Syngman Rhee is remembered by Koreans with a special kind of reverence. His fiery nationalism was always a source of pride in a country so victimized by foreigners. He is admired for the years he spent in exile working in the nearly hopeless cause of Korean independence, for his leadership in the Korean-American community, and for bringing South Korea through the war. Rhee believed that the division of Korea was a great injustice. Once the Korean War began, he thought it should be won decisively. He wanted his American and United Nations allies to press the counterattack and make the sacrifice worthwhile. The decision to settle for a stalemate was a bitter blow to Rhee, and his angry rhetoric at the time expressed what many Koreans believed.

During the truce negotiations that ended the Korean War, Rhee displayed a talent for manipulating his American and United Nations allies. Though the war accomplished little but destruction in Korea, Rhee at least was able to wrest from the United States a mutual security treaty under which American forces were positioned to prevent a recurrence of the war. That guarantee enabled South Korea to develop the capability to defend itself and assured a long enough peace to begin a spectacular economic growth that Rhee did not live to see.

Rhee left Koreans with a certain cynicism about democracy. His regime was followed by a year of constitutional government under a cabinet-responsible system that was overthrown by a military coup in May, 1961, a predictable development in view of the militarization of Korea that followed the Korean War and the failure of Rhee's government to create a viable civilian tradition. Military-led dictatorships then ruled South Korea from 1961 until 1987. Only with the beginning of the presidency of former general Roh Tae Woo in 1988 was there any visible movement back to basic freedom and a reduction of the military's role in politics.

## Bibliography

Allen, Richard C. *Korea's Syngman Rhee: An Unauthorized Portrait.* Rutland, Vt.: Tuttle, 1960. A critical biography written in the aftermath of Rhee's fall from power to provide general readers with the pieces missing in Robert Oliver's earlier work.

Cumings, Bruce. *The Origins of the Korean War: Liberation and the Emergence of Separate Regimes.* Princeton, N.J.: Princeton University Press, 1981; London: Princeton University Press, 1990. The leading American historical treatment of the internal politics of South Korea under American rule. Highly critical of American political leadership and United States' sponsorship of the right.

Han, Sungjoo. *The Failure of Democracy in South Korea.* Berkeley: University of California Press, 1974. Scholarly treatment of the April, 1960, revolution, the Rhee legacy, and the regime that followed Rhee prior to the military coup of May, 1961.

Henderson, Gregory. *Korea: The Politics of the Vortex.* Cambridge, Mass.: Harvard University Press, 1968. A detailed and richly annotated analysis of the patterns in Korean politics in the mid-twentieth century by a Foreign Service officer who worked alongside the Rhee government in the 1950's.

Kim, Quee-Young. *The Fall of Syngman Rhee.* Berkeley: University of California, Institute of East Asian Studies, Center for Korean Studies, 1983. A definitive study of the events surrounding Rhee's exit from Korea, based on the author's Harvard dissertation.

———. "From Protest to Change of Regime: The 4-19 Revolt and the Fall of the Rhee Regime in South Korea." *Social Forces* 74, no. 4 (June, 1996). The author considers how protest movements evolve into revolutions by examining the revolt that ousted Rhee from power.

Lee, Hahn-Been. *Korea: Time, Change, and Administration.* Honolulu: East-West Center Press, 1968. A detailed study of public policy and administrative patterns in the Rhee years with stress on the trends leading up to the 1960 revolution.

Oliver, Robert T. *Syngman Rhee: The Man Behind the Myth.* New York: Dodd Mead, 1954; London: Hale, 1955. An authorized biography and good source of personal information, though seriously flawed by lack of critical distance and numerous errors in historical detail. A basic source of Rhee's life and movements.

———. *Syngman Rhee and American Involvement in Korea, 1942-1960: A Personal Narrative.* Seoul, Korea: Panmun, 1978. Rhee's close friend and biographer compiled this collection of Rhee documents and comments on the most controversial aspects of his relations with the United States.

Reeve, W. D. *The Republic of Korea: A Political and Economic Study.* London and New York: Oxford University Press, 1963. A comprehensive treatment of the political and economic dimensions of the Rhee years including issues relating to reconstruction and political control.

Rhee, Syngman. *Japan Inside Out.* London: Long, and New York: Revell, 1941. Rhee's estimate of Japan under the militarists' control and the likely effect of its imperial designs upon its neighbors and the West. Useful as an example of Rhee's political position and his approach to propaganda.

Sung-hwa, Cheong. "The Political Use of Anti-Japanese Sentiment in Korea from 1948-1949." *Korea Journal* 32, no. 4 (Winter 1992). Examines the use of anti-Japanese sentiment in gaining voter support during Korean elections in 1948 versus the use of anti-communist propaganda by Rhee.

*Donald N. Clark*

## ANN RICHARDS

*Born:* September 1, 1933; Lakeview, Texas
*Area of Achievement:* Government and politics
*Contribution:* A longtime activist in Texas Democratic politics, Ann Richards became Texas' second woman governor in 1990 and was the first woman to be elected to that office based on her own merit.

### Early Life

Ann Richards was born Dorothy Ann Willis on September 1, 1933, in the rural Texas town of Lakeview, near Waco. Her parents, Cecil Willis and Iona Warren Willis, were children of farmers who had been part of a wave of immigration to Texas during the late nineteenth century. Cecil's family settled on a farm in the Waco area, but Iona moved to Waco (where she met Cecil on a blind date) from Hico—a town just south of Fort Worth—to work in a dry-goods store. The move was not typical for rural Texas women, but Iona was ambitious and independent—qualities that she later instilled in her daughter Ann.

Cecil's salary as delivery truck driver was not large, but both he and Iona valued hard work. Like many people who lived through the Depression, they were also frugal. In order to give Ann all they could, they had no more children. Ann did not experience great hardship or poverty. Nevertheless, Ann was given a rather strict upbringing; she was responsible for much regular work around the house, and she was constantly given special projects to complete. There were also limits placed on the amount of time Ann was allowed to spend socializing. Her parents were active in the community, and they emphasized common-sense notions of decency and fairness in community affairs, sowing the seeds for Ann's later progressive political philosophy.

Ann attended Waco High School, where she was an outgoing student who excelled at debate. She was selected as a delegate to the Girls State mock government in Austin during her junior year, and then as one of two Texas delegates to attend Girls Nation in Washington, D.C., where she shook hands with President Harry Truman. This experience was her first real introduction to both politics and the world outside Waco. While in high school, Ann met her future husband, David Richards.

After her graduation from Waco High in 1950, Ann attended Baylor University on a debate scholarship. David Richards transferred from the University of Texas to Baylor in 1953, and he and Ann were married the same year. They both were graduated in 1954. They then moved to Austin, where David enrolled in the University of Texas Law School and Ann took graduate courses in education and earned her teaching certificate. In 1955, Ann took a job teaching social studies and history at a junior high school in Austin, a post she held until 1956.

### Life's Work

It was in Austin as a graduate student that Ann Richards first became involved in Texas politics. She and her husband became active in the University of Texas chapter of the Young Democrats, and they regularly socialized with other liberal Democrats who supported Lyndon B. Johnson, who was engaged in a power struggle with conservative Allen Shivers for control of the Texas Democratic party. In Austin, Richards made many of the political contacts on which she would later depend during her campaigns for state office.

After his graduation from law school, David Richards began work in a Dallas labor law firm, and, after giving birth at home in Waco, Ann and their new child Cecile Richards joined him there. While the two remained active in the Austin Young Democrats during this period, Ann also spent considerable time volunteering on political campaigns, such as civil rights supporter Henry Gonzalez's 1958 gubernatorial race, progressive Ralph Yarborough's 1952, 1954, and 1956 gubernatorial campaigns, and Yarborough's successful senatorial race in 1957.

It was while Ann Richards was working on the 1960 John F. Kennedy/Lyndon B. Johnson presidential campaign in Dallas that David announced they were to move to Washington, D.C., so that he could begin work as a staff attorney on the national Civil Rights Commission. The two socialized with many transplanted Texas Democrats while in the nation's capital, and they had occasion to meet Johnson while he was vice president. Nevertheless, they soon tired of life in Washington and moved back to Dallas in 1962.

While in Dallas, Ann helped form the North Dallas Democratic Women's group, and she served as its president for a time. She also helped organize the Dallas Committee for Peaceful Integration to fight for the integration of the public schools, a radical view to support in Texas at the time. Ann also continued to spend considerable time rearing her family, giving birth to her sons Clark and Dan.

Though the Richards' lives in Dallas had been rewarding, by 1969 the pull of Austin was too great, and the family moved back. Ann Richards served on the local zoning and planning commission, and, in 1971, she was asked to advise Sarah Weddington about her run for the Texas legislature. Richards devised a way to create a targeted mass mailing for the campaign, and Weddington won the election in 1972. Richards went to work as Weddington's administrative assistant. She also continued to work on other Democratic campaigns during this period, including Wilhemina Delco's successful attempt in 1974 to become the first black woman to be elected to the Texas state legislature.

In 1975, David Richards was asked to run against Johnny Voudouris in the Democratic primary for county commissioner. When David turned down the offer, Ann was asked to step in. The request was particularly unusual because the county commissioner was responsible for overseeing all county road crews, and the position had always been occupied by men. After a shrewd and targeted campaign, Ann beat three-term incumbent Voudouris in the primary and went on to win the general election in the fall.

As county commissioner, and despite initial prejudice, Ann Richards managed to cultivate good relationships with her largely conservative male employees and was able to improve the county road system. She also provided increased funding for support services through her oversight of the county Human Services division.

As a result of Richards' innovations at county Human Services, Lieutenant Governor Bill Hobby appointed her to a special committee to overhaul the delivery of human services statewide. While serving as county commissioner, Richards was asked to serve on President Jimmy Carter's Advisory Committee for Women, where she met many of the most influential women of the time, such as congressional representative Bella Abzug, while they lobbied the president for his support of the Equal Rights Amendment.

Although these years were professionally very good for Ann Richards, her marriage was under increasing stress. As the couple continued to grow apart, Ann's drinking also increased, until it became such a problem that in 1980, at the behest of David and their closest friends, she sought treatment. Although the treatment for alcoholism was successful, the marriage did not improve, and the two were separated. They were divorced in 1984.

During the separation, in 1982, Ann Richards was asked to run in the Democratic primary for state treasurer against Warren Harding. The campaign turned ugly, and Richards' alcoholism became a central issue. She remained forthright and honest about the subject, and the smear tactics backfired. Harding eventually withdrew, and Richards went on to beat Republican Allen Clark by a wide margin in November. She was the first woman to hold a Texas state office in fifty years.

Richards' reforms in the state's revenue system while treasurer—the implementation of up-to-date technology to assist depositing and processing of state money, and reductions in paper work—eventually earned for the state of Texas more than two billion dollars in nontax revenue. She was reelected in 1986.

Her performance as treasurer again brought Richards to the attention of national Democratic leaders, and she was invited to second the nomination of Walter Mondale as the Democratic candidate for president in 1984 and to give the keynote address at the 1988 Democratic National Convention. Her speech at the 1988 convention was an outright, plainspoken assault on Republican nominee George Bush, and it was a smashing success.

In 1990, Richards mounted a gubernatorial campaign to replace retiring Republican Governor William Clements. During the primary, her alcoholism again became an issue, and her reluctance to respond to questions about drug abuse hurt her popularity considerably. Yet, as before, the political mudslinging backfired when it was revealed that her opponent had himself possibly used illegal drugs. Richards won the Democratic nomination.

Her Republican opponent Clayton Williams' marked insensitivity to women's issues and Richards' strong pro-choice stance led large numbers of Republican women to vote for her, and on November 6, 1990, Ann Richards was elected governor of Texas. She was the first woman to become governor of Texas in more than fifty years and was the first ever to do so based on her own merits.

As governor, Ann Richards set a progressive agenda for the conservative state and appointed unprecedented numbers of women, Latinos, and African Americans to state offices. She also contributed to the state's economic recovery after several years of recession. In recognition of her achievements both in Texas and on the national political scene, Richards was asked to chair the Democratic National Convention in 1992. In 1994, Richards campaigned for reelection and lost to a Republican candidate whose political connections, wealth, and family name constituted a serious challenge to Richards' bid for another four-year term: George Walker Bush, the forty-eight-year-old son of former President George Bush.

### Summary

Ann Richards managed to thrive in the political environment of Texas, a state famous for its conservatism and male-dominated "old-boy" power network. While rewriting the rules of gender and power in Texas, she also managed to implement a decidedly reformist and progressive agenda to a state government woefully bogged down in "cronyism."

A tireless supporter of women's issues and civil rights, she appointed unprecedented numbers of women and minorities to positions of power. A consummate politician, Richards managed both to pierce the "glass ceiling" for women in Texas politics and to develop a power network composed of women, minorities, and liberals that rivaled that of the male-dominated, oil-industry-backed politicians who had been in control in Texas for so long.

Richards also had an impact on national politics. Her plain speaking and firecracker wit launched her into prominence on the national political scene, and, along with several other women Democrats newly elected to major offices, she helped keep the national Democratic Party focused on women's issues while proving to other women that they could succeed in politics in even the most male-dominated of arenas. Richards' forthrightness about her alcoholism and her past marital troubles also set an example for the nation. Ann Richards proved that women could be single and independent and still be successful in the public sphere.

### Bibliography

Collins, Gail. "The Unsinkable Meets the Unthinkable: Ann Richards May Have Lost Her Power Base, but Not Her Wisdom, Wit or True Grit." *Working Woman* 20, no. 3 (March, 1995). Interview with Richards a few days before leaving office as governor of Texas.

Dow, Bonnie J., and Mari Boor Tonn. "'Feminine Style' and Political Judgment in the Rhetoric of Ann Richards." *Quarterly Journal of Speech* 79 (August, 1993): 286-302. An in-depth, scholarly treatment of Richards' rhetoric and political oratory, including content analysis and a consideration of the issues of feminism and psychology.

Morris, Celia. *Storming the Statehouse: Running for Governor with Ann Richards and Dianne Feinstein*. New York: Scribner, 1992. A very detailed narrative account of the campaigns mounted by two women for the governorships of their states. The Ann Richards section does a good job of capturing the flavor of Texas politics. The work argues that Richards' and Feinstein's pursuit of higher office constitute a cultural revolution.

Richards, Ann. *Straight from the Heart*. New York: Simon and Schuster, 1989. An autobiography written in an informal style, this work reflects Richards' personality. It also provides much information about life as a liberal in Texas politics.

Smith, Evan. "Two Fisted Texans." *Mother Jones* 21, no. 2 (March-April, 1996). Interview with Richards and her daughter Cecile on the rise of the radical right.

Witt, Linda, Karen M. Paget, and Glenna Matthews. *Running as a Woman: Gender and Power in American Politics*. New York: Free Press, 1994. A journalist, a political scientist, and a historian collaborated on this narrative overview of the experiences of women candidates in American politics. Although this work focuses primarily on women candidates at the national level, the authors include Richards' comments on her early campaign work on behalf of Sarah Weddington.

*Colin Ramsey*

# HYMAN G. RICKOVER

*Born:* August 24, 1898, or January 27, 1900; Makow, Russian Empire (now Poland)

*Died:* July 8, 1986; Arlington, Virginia

*Area of Achievement:* The military

*Contribution:* A specialist in electrical engineering, Rickover became a pioneer in nuclear propulsion after World War II. He headed the project that developed the *Nautilus*, the world's first nuclear-powered submarine, and remained a dominant personality in the navy and in public life for three decades.

## Early Life

According to his public school records, Hyman George Rickover was born on August 24, 1898 (January 27, 1900, is the date of birth given by him), in the village of Makow, about fifty miles north of Warsaw, in what was then the Russian Empire. His parents were Abraham, a tailor, and Ruchal Rickover. In 1899, Abraham Rickover, like many other Jews, left the poverty and discrimination of Russia behind to try to achieve a better life in America. For several years the senior Rickover worked in New York City to save enough money to send for his wife and two children, Hyman and a daughter, Fanny. In 1904, or thereabouts (there are discrepancies surrounding many facets in Hyman Rickover's childhood), the family was reunited in New York. A second daughter, Hitel, usually known as Augusta, was born there. In 1908, the family moved to Chicago, where they settled in North Lawndale, a neighborhood of two-family homes that was a typical first step above the ghetto for families such as the Rickovers. Hyman attended public school in the neighborhood and worked at various jobs as he grew older. His high school record was by no means outstanding, but Rickover liked to think that his time-consuming work as a Western Union messenger kept him from achieving the grades of which he was capable. He did do well his final two years at John Marshall High School and was graduated early in February, 1918.

Rickover entered the United States Naval Academy later that year and graduated in 1922. Rickover's years at Annapolis were not happy ones, but as with so many other incidents in his life, inconsistencies exist between his version of events and the written record and/or the recollections of others. According to Rickover, anti-Semitism marred his years at the academy. Others recall that several Jews who were enrolled at the same time were very well liked and that Rickover was a loner because of his own desire to pass up social and athletic activities in order to study diligently. To use the slang of the time, it seems he was considered a "grind."

Of slender build and about five feet, six inches in height, Rickover never seemed to show an interest in sports or other recreational activities; he was, however, from his childhood years on, a determined worker. In Chicago, he had sometimes held two part-time jobs while attending school. At the academy, he became known for his zeal to get things done.

## Life's Work

Commissioned an ensign in 1922, Rickover served the next two years on the destroyer *LaVallette*, holding the position of engineering officer during the second half of his tour. Rickover's next assignment was as electrical officer of the battleship *Nevada*. He then undertook advanced studies, first a year's course in electrical engineering at the Naval Academy's postgraduate school and then a year at Columbia University, where he received a master's degree in engineering. He was promoted to lieutenant while at Columbia. There, Rickover met Ruth Masters, a student in international law and subsequently a recognized scholar in the field. The two carried on a courtship, largely by correspondence, and in 1931 were married by an Episcopal minister. They had one son. (Two years after Ruth Rickover's death in 1972, Rickover married Eleonore Bednowicz, then a navy nurse; she retired after their marriage.)

In 1929, Rickover was accepted into submarine school. The training program lasted six months, after which Rickover was assigned to the submarine *S-48* as engineer and electrical officer. A year later, he was named executive officer and navigator, a position which he held until 1933. Although at this time in his career he was eligible to command an older submarine or an auxiliary such as a minesweeper, he was assigned to two years of shore duty in Philadelphia, where, with the Office of Naval Matériel, he was charged with inspecting supplies and equipment being produced for use by the navy. Next, Rickover was rotated to duty at sea as assistant engineering officer of the battleship *New Mexico*. Given much latitude by his immediate superior, Rickover was able to demonstrate his zeal

for efficiency by instituting methods to save on fuel consumption. Not all of his innovations were popular, and Rickover could be hard on lax subordinates. He had the reputation for thoroughness, if not tact, and the *New Mexico* won the navy's prized E awards for efficiency in engineering each year of Rickover's tour of duty.

Ordered to the Asiatic Fleet in 1937, Rickover was promoted to lieutenant commander and given command of the old minesweeper *Finch*. This was his first and only command, and accounts differ regarding whether Rickover was merely striving to bring his customary efficiency to a ship where morale was already low or whether he bore down too hard on an otherwise decent crew. He was relieved of command after three months and assigned to the Cavite Navy Yard near Manila, in the Philippines, for duty as assistant planning officer. His responsibilities included planning the repair and overhaul of machinery for ships coming into the yard.

Rickover requested a transfer to the status of engineering duty officer, having recognized from the fact of his assignment to the *Finch* that his career as a line officer was headed toward a dead end. Since 1916 the navy had officially differentiated between line officers and EDO's. Line officers were trained, in effect, to command ships and eventually task forces and even fleets in the case of the most able. While outstanding line officers such as Chester Nimitz and Ernest King might in their younger days become expert in engineering matters, they would be rotated in the course of their careers to a variety of command and staff duties at sea and on shore so that they would be familiar with many aspects of the navy. In contrast, an engineering duty officer could design, operate, and maintain ships but could not command one.

After duty at Cavite, Rickover returned to the United States for assignment to the Bureau of Engineering, which later consolidated with another shore establishment into the Bureau of Ships in 1940. In an effort to prepare for World War II, the navy was undergoing rapid expansion. As head of the electrical section of the Bureau of Ships for much of the war, Rickover was responsible for organizing the design, construction, maintenance, and repair of the electrical apparatus in radios, radars, guns, lights, refrigerators, and propulsion. Promotion now came quickly; Rickover rose to commander in 1942 and some months later to the temporary wartime rank of captain.

Rickover's style of command was unconventional in that he ignored rank among the personnel detailed to his section, and he thought nothing of working late into the evenings or on Sundays. What mattered in wartime was that he got the job done, and he impressed his superior, Rear Admiral Earle Mills. Appealing to Mills for duty in a combat zone, Rickover, in 1945, received orders to develop and command a ship repair base on Okinawa. The war ended before the base became operational, and in a postwar navy due for retrenchment, Rickover, like many others, was an officer whose future career was uncertain.

Rickover, however, was destined to achieve fame as the father of the nuclear navy. Although the name of Rickover has become synonymous with the nuclear navy in popular accounts, the idea of a nuclear-powered submarine, a true submersible, had been batted around within the navy since 1939. Mills was certainly in favor of it, as were many experienced submariners, and so after the war, Rickover and a few other engineering officers were sent to Oak Ridge to learn about nuclear technology. Rickover assumed leadership of the group and so impressed Mills with his grasp of the subject that he became the admiral's assistant for nuclear matters until 1948, by which time the navy at last had made the decision to develop nuclear propulsion. Rickover received the two assignments that would place him at the center of what was to become the nuclear navy: head of the Nuclear Power Branch of the Bureau of Ships and, in early 1949, chief of the recently established Naval Reactors Branch of the Atomic Energy Commission.

For Rickover, there was a great advantage to the fact that he now held two positions, the former in the naval hierarchy, the latter in the civilian-run AEC: Depending on circumstances, he could initiate action either from his naval position or from the Naval Reactors Branch. Having already learned the ins and outs of military bureaucracy and how to deal with major defense contractors when he headed the electrical section of the Bureau of Ships, Rickover, still an obscure captain, became increasingly autonomous.

What became known as the Rickover style was again evident, and he gathered around him a group of bright and intensely loyal officers who worked diligently to overcome the myriad problems in harnessing a nuclear reactor for shipboard power. By the early 1950's Rickover began to receive the media attention that he worked hard to cultivate and had also made himself known to influential congressmen as an officer who got things done, perhaps the only one who could make the navy's nuclear propulsion program a success. Whether he was, he did have a demonstrated record of accomplishment and was both an engineer and an experienced submariner.

Rickover, nevertheless, had his problems, not only those involving the design of the submarine and the complex requirements for the prototype reactor to power the nuclear sub but also others involving naval politics. Twice he was passed over for promotion to rear admiral, meaning that he would have to retire; navy regulations so stipulated. His congressional supporters, however, rallied to him, and Secretary of the Navy Robert Anderson directed that a special board meet to select an engineering duty captain with experience in the nuclear field for promotion to rear admiral. As Anderson had known when he specified the criteria, Rickover was chosen. Just as this threat to Rickover's navy career was nearing resolution, the crucial Mark I nuclear reactor underwent a full-power test. Convinced that no excessive risk was involved, Rickover ignored advice to halt the test at the planned forty-eight-hour mark or less and ordered the test continued for ninety-six hours, enough time for a submarine to have crossed the Atlantic at full throttle. The successful completion of the test in June, 1953, generated much favorable publicity, soon to be surpassed by the achievements of the nuclear submarine itself.

In January, 1954, the *Nautilus*, the world's first nuclear submarine, was launched and a year later undertook her trial runs on nuclear power. The vessel was clearly a success, establishing all sorts of firsts and earning many laurels for the navy, for Rickover, and for the Eisenhower Administration, particularly with her August, 1958, submerged polar crossing. Rickover was now in a very real sense above the navy, for in a service whose personnel were routinely rotated to different assignments, he built an empire based in the Naval Reactors Branch of the AEC and in the Nuclear Power Branch of the Bureau of Ships and kept control for more than three decades. As the navy added more nuclear subs as well as surface vessels such as the cruiser *Long Beach* and the carrier *Enterprise*, Rickover was promoted to vice admiral (1958) and admiral (1973) and was continued on active duty by special presidential directive issued every two years, even after he reached the normal retirement age in 1962.

On the organization charts he was well down the chain of command. In fact, however, he was able to exert influence far beyond his official slot by insisting that safety considerations required him to approve personally the commanding officers of all nuclear-powered ships. As these officers spread throughout the navy in subsequent assignments, they carried the Rickover influence to many quarters.

By no means was Rickover's influence confined to the navy. Using reactor plans for a nuclear-powered carrier that had been cancelled, his organization, with some funding from private industry, developed for use by the Duquesne Light Company the nation's first nuclear-powered generating facility at Shippingport, Pennsylvania, in 1957. Although Rickover himself had little more to do with commercial nuclear power following the completion of the Shippingport facility, many men who learned their trade with NRB went on to become leaders in the growing nuclear power field in the 1960's.

For a time following the Soviet launching of their Sputnik satellite, Rickover also became widely known as an authority on American education.

The lamentation about the spectacular Soviet first led to an uproar about the quality of education in the United States. Rickover was ready with an answer, criticizing what he considered its shortcomings and calling for standards of excellence such as those he had always imposed on himself.

Not until 1982 was Rickover retired from duty, and even then he remained a well-known figure, ironically making the news several times in 1984 when it was revealed that he had received expensive gifts from one of the major contractors with which he had dealt. He was reprimanded by the secretary of the navy. In July, 1986, he died at his Arlington, Virginia, home.

### Summary

Hyman Rickover served on active duty longer than any previous naval officer in American history. His career was perhaps even more remarkable for its influence than for its longevity. In his tenacity and in his ability to use the media to advantage he displayed some of the characteristics of Douglas MacArthur and J. Edgar Hoover, two other public servants who far outserved most of their contemporaries.

Unlike MacArthur and Hoover, however, he labored in obscurity for a quarter of a century. Had he retired in 1945, his naval service would by no means have been without purpose, for Rickover was one of those scores of officers in such navy specialties as engineering, ordnance, logistics, and construction who, with little chance for popular recognition, provided the indispensable support for the fleets.

He became a public figure only around 1950, showing the same dedication and drive he had always demonstrated but doing it in the glamorous new area of nuclear power. Already experienced in the ways of bureaucracy, he developed a constituency among the media and in Congress and, with the support at crucial times of those who believed in him, guided the navy into the age of nuclear propulsion and made important contributions in the civilian power field as well.

Always he remained controversial. His detractors believe that by the 1960's he had become a conservative force in the navy, hindering innovation in submarine design and in the field of gas-turbine technology for surface ships. The charge has also been made that the overall strength of the navy was not what it might have been had not such emphasis been placed upon costly nuclear-powered ships at the expense of additional conventionally powered ships that could perform many missions just as well. Finally, it is charged that Rickover was vindictive to those who disagreed with him or to subordinates who failed to display the loyalty he demanded.

His admirers, however, are many. They applaud his part in the guiding of the navy into the nuclear age and his emphasis upon excellence at a time when standards throughout the armed forces and society as a whole appeared to be slipping. Whichever view more closely approximates the reality, much about the twentieth century navy cannot be understood without comprehending Hyman Rickover's role in it. A bureaucrat *par excellence*, he brought a uniquely personalized style of leadership—what has been termed a "rude genius"—to a service in the midst of technological revolution.

### Bibliography

Anderson, William R., and Clay Blair, Jr. *Nautilus—90—North*. London: Hodder and Stoughton, and Cleveland: World, 1959. Written by Anderson, second skipper of the *Nautilus*, and journalist Blair, this book relates the *Nautilus*' crowning achievement—the voyage to the North Pole—perhaps Rickover's greatest triumph.

Beach, Edward L. *Around the World Submerged: The Voyage of the Triton*. New York: Holt Rinehart, 1962; London: Hodder and Stoughton, 1963. A fascinating account by the commander of the *Triton*, one of the first nuclear subs and the largest when built. Achieved invaluable publicity for Rickover with around-the-world voyage.

Blair, Clay, Jr. *The Atomic Submarine and Admiral Rickover*. New York: Holt, 1954; London: Oldhams Press, 1955. An authorized biography, with much information made available by Rickover, written when the controversy over Rickover's retention and promotion to rear admiral was under discussion. Lauds Rickover and downplays the contributions of others to the development of the *Nautilus*. What would become known as the Rickover mystique is seen throughout the pages of this book.

Hewlett, Richard G., and Francis Duncan. *Nuclear Navy: 1946-1962*. Chicago: University of Chicago Press, 1974. Factually reliable, concise, and clearly written narrative history of the building of the nuclear navy. Perhaps the best relatively brief study of the first fifteen years of Rickover's career in the nuclear navy.

Lewis, Eugene. *Public Entrepreneurship: Toward a Theory of Bureaucratic Political Power.* Bloomington: Indiana University Press, 1980. This valuable and interesting probe into the theory of bureaucracy uses Rickover (along with J. Edgar Hoover and Robert Moses) as one of three case studies in the gaining and wielding of bureaucratic power.

Polmar, Norman, and Thomas D. Allen. *Rickover: Controversy and Genius, A Biography.* New York: Simon and Schuster, 1982. Lengthy but readable study of Rickover. By no means friendly to the late admiral, it needs to be consulted by anyone interested in him or in the nuclear navy.

Rickover, Hyman G. *Education and Freedom.* New York: Dutton, 1959. A compilation of many of Rickover's speeches on education, this volume presents Rickover's views on a topic about which he felt strongly. Rickover authored several other volumes dealing with education.

Rockwell, Theodore. *The Rickover Effect: How One Man Made a Difference.* Annapolis, Md.: Naval Institute Press, 1992. Rockwell (who worked for Rickover for fifteen years) shares behind-the-scenes stories of the emerging nuclear industry.

Zumwalt, Elmo R., Jr. *On Watch.* New York: Quadrangle, 1976. Memoirs of a former chief of naval operations who once turned down a chance to serve as executive officer of the nuclear-powered *Long Beach.* No fan of Rickover, Zumwalt devotes many pages to a critique of the Rickover style and to an appeal for a balanced navy.

*Lloyd J. Graybar*

# SALLY RIDE

*Born:* May 26, 1951; Encino, California
*Areas of Achievement:* Aeronautics and astrophysics
*Contribution:* An astronaut for the National Aeronautics and Space Administration (NASA) and the first American woman to fly in space.

## Early Life

Sally Kristen Ride was born on May 26, 1951, in Encino, a suburb of Los Angeles, California. She was the older of two daughters born to Dale B. Ride, a member of the faculty at Santa Monica Community College, and his wife, Joyce. Sally's parents were active as elders in their Presbyterian church, and Joyce Ride often volunteered her time as an English tutor to foreign-born students and as a counselor at a women's prison.

Sally's parents encouraged her competitive spirit in academics and in athletics. Sally was a born athlete and often played the rough and tumble games of football and baseball with the neighborhood boys. Ride began playing tennis, a less hazardous sport, at the request of her mother. Under the tutelage of tennis great Alice Marble, Sally quickly excelled in this sport and became proficient enough to rank eighteenth nationally. Her excellence in tennis earned her a partial scholarship to Westlake School for Girls, a private preparatory school in Los Angeles. At the preparatory school, Sally became interested in the study of physics through the influence of her science teacher, Elizabeth Mommaerts, and, for the next five years, science and tennis competed for Sally's time and attention.

In 1968, Sally enrolled at Swarthmore College in Pennsylvania as a physics major, but left after three terms to concentrate on her tennis game after winning a national collegiate tennis tournament. Although she was a top-ranked college player, she realized that she did not have the talent to advance to professional tennis. Sally returned to college in 1970 and completed a double major in English literature and physics at Stanford University in California in 1973. After graduation, she briefly considered continuing with Shakespeare in graduate school, but settled on astrophysics to further her dream of working for NASA.

## Life's Work

Sally Ride began her path to fame while completing work on her doctoral dissertation at Stanford. One day she read an announcement in the campus newspaper indicating that NASA was seeking young scientists to serve as "mission specialists." Acting on impulse, she applied to join the astronaut program, which had lifted its long-standing ban against women in order to attract additional qualified scientists willing to forgo high salaries in order to work on the new space shuttle program. To Ride's surprise, she made it through the preliminary screening process to become one of the finalists. In 1977, she was flown to the Lyndon B. Johnson Space Center outside Houston, Texas, for exhausting interviews and fitness and psychiatric evaluation tests. After three months of rigorous testing, Sally Ride officially became an astronaut. In 1978, shortly after earning her Ph.D. degree, she reported to the Johnson Space Center to begin the intensive training required of NASA mission specialists.

In the first year of training, Ride learned parachute jumping and water survival techniques, the latter for the possibility that the shuttle might be

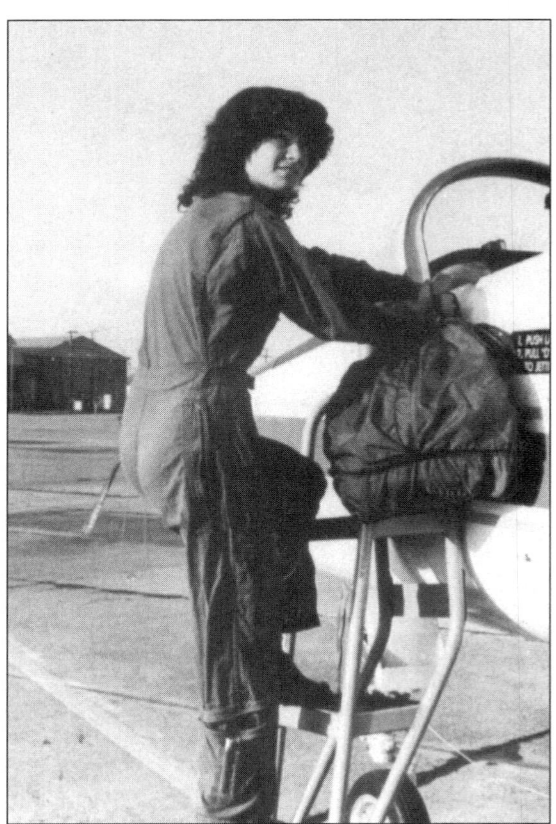

ditched in the ocean. She also became acclimated to increased gravity forces, the force encountered during acceleration and deceleration back to earth, as well as to weightlessness. Ride took courses in radio communication and navigation and learned to fly a jet. Piloting a jet proved to be an enjoyable experience for Sally Ride, and she eventually acquired a pilot's license.

Throughout Ride's entire preparation time, NASA maintained its bureaucratic composure regarding its inclusion of women in the space shuttle program. There was no flamboyant talk about one giant step for womankind. Indeed, team player that she was, Ride insisted that her participation in the flight was "no big deal." Whether she liked it or not, news of her flight brought her instant celebrity. Newspapers and television reporters interviewed her again and again, and even President Ronald Reagan gave her an extra share of attention at a White House luncheon. Composer Casse Culver wrote and recorded a song entitled "Ride, Sally, Ride" to celebrate the event, and T-shirts urged the same.

Sally Ride was specifically requested by Navy Captain Robert L. Crippen, a veteran astronaut who had piloted the first shuttle mission in 1981. Crippen said, of his choice of Ride: "She is flying with us because she is the very best person for the job. There is no man I would rather have in her place." Ride, in her unassuming manner, simply stated that she had not become an astronaut to become "a historic figure," and that she believed it was "time that people realized that women in this country can do any job that they want to do." Ride's special virtue was that she was so much like the male astronauts and so utterly and convincingly their equal. She was just as determined, just as disciplined, just as fearless, and just as predictable.

Aboard the *Challenger*, Ride had duties in addition to her scientific work. She was chosen to sit behind mission commander Crippen and copilot Frederick Hauck to act as flight engineer during takeoff and landing. During the ninety-six orbits, she and her fellow mission specialist, John Fabian, worked in weightless conditions with the complex Canadarm—a fifty-foot remote "arm" used to move payloads in and out of the shuttle cargo bay. Ride and Fabian trained for two years on the ground with the computerized arm and became experts in its operation. Another task on the mission was to place Anik-C, a Canadian domestic communications satellite, in a geosynchronous orbit hovering above the equator. This satellite was designed to handle thirty-two color television channels. A second communications satellite, named Palapa-B and owned by Indonesia, was launched into orbit to carry voice, video, and telephone signals to southeast Asia.

Forty other experiments were conducted by the *Challenger* crew. These included studies of metal alloy manufacture, solar cell testing, growth of semiconductor crystals, and glass production. One experiment, devised by high-school students, was a project sending 150 carpenter ants into orbit in the shuttle cargo bay to see how weightlessness affects their social structure. The California Institute of Technology sent an experiment in which radish seedlings were subjected to simulated gravity to find the right gravitational force for best growth. Purdue University's experiment investigated how sunflower seeds germinated in zero gravity. The highlight of the mission was the deployment of a huge free-floating satellite in order to document its position with the first in-space color photographs before recapturing it. The satellite was then released again and snared once more. The crew repeated this procedure for nine and one-half hours before Ride captured the satellite for the last time and stowed it in the cargo bay for the trip home.

Sally's ride (a pun often used by the media) was only one sign of a major change in what could no longer be called the United States manned space program. Much of the daredevil aspect had gone out of space travel. The object was not simply getting into orbit but working there. In fact, Sally Ride recommended that space be used to study the planet Earth to NASA administrator James Fletcher, who made her his special assistant for Long Range and Strategic Planning.

Being a space pioneer was more important to Sally Ride than achieving celebrity as a woman astronaut. Specialists have since been recruited from the ranks of male and female scientists. For all the merits of the scientific and experimental aspects of the Challenger voyage, it was Sally Ride who provoked the world's curiosity. Cool, calm and apparently controlled in any circumstance, Sally Kristen Ride hurtled through space aboard the 100-ton white and blue shuttle *Challenger*. Sally Ride showed that she was certainly made of "the right stuff."

### Summary

Although two Soviet women preceded Sally Ride into space, they hardly left their mark on it. About 1963, in the early days of manned spaceflight, a twenty-six-year-old textile mill worker and amateur sky diver named Valentina Tereshkova was put on a rocket by the Soviet Union as a propaganda coup. Reports of that flight say that Tereshkova was sick for most of the three-day flight.

In August of 1982, the Soviets launched the second woman cosmonaut—a thirty-four-year-old test pilot named Svetlana Savitskaya. Her presence, however, was taken lightly by her colleagues.

Ride's mission came to signify the ascendancy of the mission specialist over the pilot. The close-knit brotherhood of test and fighter pilots who made up the original astronaut corps was diluted by those having a new kind of "right stuff"—the ability to do quadratic equations and conduct scientific experiments instead of mere fancy flying. Under these new guidelines, Ride was an ideal candidate not only because of her excellent scientific background but also because she exhibited the ability to learn new skills and solve problems readily. Sally Ride's experiences on the space shuttle earned for her the trust and high regard of her colleagues as well as the admiration of an entire nation.

**Bibliography**

Begley, Sharon. "Challenger: Ride, Sally Ride." *Newsweek* 101 (June 13, 1983): 20-21. An overview of Sally Ride's life and the results of her crucial decision to join the elite NASA astronaut group in preparation for missions on the space shuttle.

Chaikin, Andrew. "Sally Ride: 1983 the First American Woman in Space." *Working Woman* 21, no. 11 (November-December, 1996). Profile of Ride, including her continuing efforts to encourage women in the space program.

Fox, Mary Virginia. *Women Astronauts Aboard the Shuttle*. Rev. ed. New York: Messner, 1987. Chronicles the experiences of the women who have been selected to participate in the space shuttle program. Aimed at young readers, this work focuses particular attention on Ride's experiences as the first American woman to fly in space while providing equally useful profiles of the various women who followed. Touches on Ride's decision to leave the astronaut program in 1987.

"From the Cosmos to the Classroom: Q and A with Sally Ride." *T H E Journal* 26, no. 8 (March, 1999). Discussion with Ride about beginning serious scientific education in elementary school.

Golden, Frederic. "Sally's Joy Ride into the Sky." *Time* 121 (June 27, 1983): 56-58. In the magazine's "Space" section, Golden tells of Ride's experiences on the second orbiting flight of the space shuttle *Challenger* and includes some of Ride's own observations regarding the public's reaction to her flight.

Otto, Dixon P. *On Orbit: The First Space Shuttle Era, 1969-1986*. Athens, Ohio: Main Stage, 1986. Aimed at a general audience, this work examines the space shuttle from its design origins through its first twenty-five flights. Contains information about the crew members, payloads, and objectives of each flight as well as many black-and-white illustrations highlighting these missions. Provides a context for understanding Ride's experiences in the space shuttle program.

Ride, Sally, with Susan Okie. *To Space and Back*. New York: Lothrop Lee, 1986. Written for a young audience, this book describes the human side of being a member of an astronaut crew. Ride shares her personal experience of space travel on the space shuttle. The book does a fine job of revealing both the remarkable talents and the more ordinary characteristics of those individuals who have chosen to become space pioneers.

Ride, Sally, and Tam O'Shaughnessy. *Voyager: An Adventure to the Edge of the Solar System*. New York: Crown, 1992. Although this work is not specifically related to her shuttle experiences, Ride does draw upon her astrophysics background in order to create this popular account of the two Voyager spacecraft that were launched during the late 1970's in order to explore and transmit images of four of the solar system's most distant planets: Jupiter, Saturn, Uranus, and Neptune.

*Jane A. Slezak*

# RAINER MARIA RILKE

*Born:* December 4, 1875; Prague, Bohemia, Austro-Hungarian Empire

*Died:* December 29, 1926; Valmont, Switzerland

*Area of Achievement:* Literature

*Contribution:* Rilke is generally considered the greatest German poet since Goethe, and his fame is by no means limited to his own country.

## Early Life

Rainer Maria Rilke was born on December 4, 1875, as a member of the German-speaking minority in Prague, then part of the Austro-Hungarian Empire. His early life reads like a Freudian case history. His father, Josef Rilke, had been frustrated in a military career and had become a minor official on the railroad. His mother was temperamental, socially pretentious, and superficially Catholic. They separated in 1884. It is natural to associate Rilke's troubled relations with his mother with his later troubled relations with other women; though he had innumerable affairs and some warm friendships, he could never settle down to a domestic relationship.

After his parents' separation, Rilke, who for his first five years had been treated almost as a girl, was sent to military schools. He later represented his life there as miserable, though his grades were good and he was encouraged to read his poems in class. After he left military school at sixteen, he spent a year in a trade school at Linz; he studied privately for his *abitur*, or *Gymnasium* diploma; and he took university courses in Prague (1896) and Munich (1897), particularly in art history. Already he was trying to establish himself as a man of letters; although neither Rilke nor his critics thought much of the work he did in the 1890's, the mere quantity of it is impressive: Not only is there a mass of poetry but also there is some fiction and ten dramatic works, a few of which were actually produced.

Before Rilke moved to Paris and began to write works of more maturity and individuality, he underwent two maturing experiences. One was his affair with Lou Andreas-Salomé, the Russian-born wife of a Berlin professor and the first biographer of Friedrich Wilhelm Nietzsche, who had proposed to her. She introduced Rilke to the Russian language and culture and took him with her on two visits to Russia, where he met Leo Tolstoy. Even after the affair ended, Lou remained Rilke's friend and confidante. The second experience was Rilke's sojourn in the artist's colony of Worpswede near Bremen. There he continued his interest in art, and there he met and married a young sculptor, Clara Westhoff. They set up housekeeping and she bore him a daughter, but they found themselves unsuited to domestic life, and, depositing the baby with Clara's parents, they took off for Paris. They never divorced but never lived together again, though they remained on good terms.

## Life's Work

Paris was Rilke's favored residence until World War I, even though its size and impersonality and the depressing scenes of poverty he witnessed at first repelled him. Much of his time, however, was spent in travel: to Scandinavia, to Berlin and Munich, to Vienna and Trieste, to Rome and Venice and Capri, to Spain and North Africa. Some of this restlessness was not a matter of either culture or curiosity. Rilke was beginning to have an income from royalties and from lectures and readings, but to the end of his life he was not really easy in the matter of money. His personal charm and aristocratic manners made him friends at the highest levels of society. It was convenient for him to be a guest in people's houses for long periods or to have the loan of a vacant apartment—or castle. A case in point is Duino, the castle of Princess Marie von Thurn und Taxis near Trieste, where he began the famous elegies.

The period in Paris was one of the most productive of Rilke's life. When he came to Paris he had a commission to do a monograph on the sculptor Auguste Rodin, who had been Clara's teacher. Rodin cooperated on the project, and the two became quite intimate; for a time, Rilke served as Rodin's secretary, handling much of his burdensome correspondence. Then came a temporary estrangement, but not before Rilke had received from the master a confirmation of his conception of the artist as one who sees creatively, as well as a conception of art as a craft at which the artist must work steadily and systematically. The monograph was well received, as was an account of the artists at Worpswede. At this period, too, Rilke was an admirer and partisan of Paul Cézanne.

The period also produced poems that were no longer immature and derivative. In *Das Stundenbuch* (1905; *The Book of Hours*, 1941), through the persona of a Russian monk, Rilke explores different conceptions of art and of God and ends by making God a creation of the artist. *Das Buch der Bilder* (1902; the book of images) is of a more miscellaneous character, though it also contains some of Rilke's most striking lyrics; one critic would see it as bound together by the recurring theme of seeing, of perception. The poems of *Neue Gedichte* (1907, 1908; *New Poems*, 1964) in keeping with this conception of poetry, take their start not from an idea or mood but from some "thing" that must be seen and understood, even if it is ugly, such as a corpse in the morgue. Many of the poems tell a story from the Bible or classical mythology, showing it in a novel light. Thus, the story of the prodigal son may emphasize the oppressiveness of family life, while the tale of Orpheus and Eurydice may turn on the reluctance of Eurydice to return to the land of the living.

To this period also belong Rilke's two important works of fiction: *Die Weise von Liebe und Tod des Cornets Christof Rilke* (1906; *The Tale of the Love and Death of Cornet Christopher Rilke*, 1932) and *Die Aufzeichnungen des Malte Laurids Brigge* (1910; *The Notebooks of Malte Laurids Brigge*, 1930, 1958). *The Tale of the Love and Death of Cornet Christopher Rilke* is a short novel or prose poem telling of the death of an ancestral Rilke at the hands of the Turks in Hungary in 1663. The night before his heroic death he spends in the bed of a countess who never learns his name. This book had sold more than a million copies by 1969; it was immensely popular with soldiers in World War I. *The Notebooks of Malte Laurids Brigge* is in a way Rilke's "portrait of the artist," but he effectively distances himself more than does James Joyce. Brigge is a Danish poet living in Paris; his notebooks record both the present and memories of the past. The past is far more glamorous than Rilke's own; Malte's father is master of the hunt to the King of Denmark; his mother is beautiful and affectionate. The sordid realities of Paris are closer to Rilke's experience, as is his conviction that he (and Malte) must learn to accept and record these realities. The realities are linked with death and Rilke's conviction that one ought to die his own individual death, which had been with him from birth. The themes of the novel are supported by much anecdotal material, both Malte's memories and (often obscure) episodes from history. The novel ends with another retelling of the prodigal son, who even in his return home asserts his own individuality. The writing of the novel left Rilke in a state of creative exhaustion. Nevertheless, in 1912, he began the Duino elegies, only to put them aside for years.

When war broke out in 1914, Rilke was in Germany and could not return to France, where he was now an enemy alien. The war years were comparatively unproductive. For a brief period in 1916, he served in the Austrian army; at the end of the war, he was an object of suspicion for his friendships with some of the leaders of a brief Bavarian Soviet. In 1919, he was invited to Switzerland to give poetry readings and remained there until his death. After the usual wanderings, he settled in the castle of Muzot, which a Swiss friend supplied free of charge. Six months after moving in, inspiration returned; he not only finished the *Duineser Elegien* (1923; *Duino Elegies*, 1930) but also wrote the related *Die Sonette an Orpheus* (1923; *Sonnets to Orpheus*, 1936). During this period, he also managed a final trip to Paris, his second since the war. His health was deteriorating, however, and he died of leukemia on December 29, 1926.

### Summary

After Rainer Maria Rilke's death, says Norbert Fuerst, "began the battle of the critics, who admired him, with the 'hagiographers,' who loved him"—though the reactions of "ordinary people" might have been closer to Rilke's heart. "Rilke is of all modern poets the one who translated the concerns of the non-poet most comprehensively, so that we do find them in his work . . . and can retranslate them into our existential concerns." Different readers will find their concerns voiced in different poems or will find that different poems concern them at different times in their lives. The fame of the *Duino Elegies* suggests an appeal to troubled intellectuals who, like Rilke, feel in their emotional conflicts envious at once of the beasts, "simple-minded, unperplexed," and of imagined angels, who represent a level at which all conflicts are resolved. In a different mood, the artist might respond to the *Sonnets to Orpheus* by feeling, in the exuberance of Rilke's verse, that he, too, might have power over trees and stones.

The shorter lyrics are more likely to voice concerns familiar to "ordinary people." One might turn to *Das Buch der Bilder*, manageable on the whole because there is likely to be only one idea expressed in each poem. Even for readers who know little German, these lyrics are best read in the original. The reader might start with such poems as "Pont du Carrousel," "Herbstag" (autumn day), "Herbst" (autumn), "Abend" (evening), or from *New Poems*, "Letster Abend" (last evening), which has been adapted by Robert Lowell. Wolfgang Leppmann, a distinguished Rilkian, says that Rilke can be and should be read for fun. "Fun" seems an odd term to use of a poet who is often difficult, yet perhaps it is an appropriate description for the satisfaction that comes from simultaneously solving a difficult puzzle and having a human concern find expression.

**Bibliography**

Brodsky, Patricia Pollock. *Rainer Maria Rilke.* Boston: Twayne, 1988. An exceptional introductory work. Not only are there accounts of the major sequences but also there are a remarkable number of analyses of individual lyrics. There is a good, short description of Rilke's life, and, in addition to the standard bibliographies of primary and secondary sources, there is a bibliography of translations.

Fuerst, Norbert. *Phases of Rilke.* Bloomington: Indiana University Press, 1958. There are eight phases, "eight of his life, eight of his work." Though the scheme is artificial and the writing somewhat impressionistic, this book is still an attractive medium-length introduction to Rilke. Fuerst tries to mediate between Rilke's critics and his "hagiographers."

Heep, Hartmut. *A Different Poem: Rainer Maria Rilke's American Translators Randall Jarrell, Robert Lowell, and Robert Bly.* New York: Lang, 1996. Heep compares the philosophies and cultures of Rilke and three poet/translators, providing new perspectives on their works.

Kleinbard, David. *The Beginning of Terror: A Psychological Study of Rainer Maria Rilke's Life and Work.* New York: New York University Press, 1993. Kleinbard presents a psychological portrait of Rilke focusing on his poetry and other writings and evaluating their reflection of his fears and fantasies, as well as the relationship between illness and genius.

Lange, Victor. Introduction to *Rainer Maria Rilke: Selected Poems.* Translated by A. E. Flemming. New York: Methuen, 1986. A brief but eloquent introduction to Rilke by a major Germanic scholar.

Leppmann, Wolfgang. *Rilke: A Life.* Translated in collaboration with the author by Russell M. Stockman. Cambridge: Lutterworth, and New York: Fromm International, 1984. A massive treatment of Rilke's life and work, thoroughly researched and annotated. There are extensive bibliographies and a very detailed chronology.

Prater, Donald. *A Ringing Glass: The Life of Rainer Maria Rilke.* Oxford: Clarendon Press, and New York: Oxford University Press, 1986. Not a "life and work" but simply a life, this book takes advantage of the enormous amount of correspondence and other material that is gradually becoming available.

Rilke, Rainer Maria. *Letters to a Young Poet.* Translated by Reginald Snell. London: Sidgwick and Jackson, 1945. Rilke's published correspondence comes to about thirty volumes in the original languages; only a few are available in English. They are a rich source of material on his life and thought and provide a basis for further interpretations of his work.

Sandford, John. *Landscape and Landscape Imagery in R. M. Rilke.* London: University of London Press, 1980. One of the many specialized works on Rilke. "Rilke's search for a home . . . is the key to his experience and description of landscape."

*John C. Sherwood*

## DIEGO RIVERA

*Born:* December 8, 1886; Guanajuato, Mexico
*Died:* November 25, 1957; Mexico City, Mexico
*Area of Achievement:* Art
*Contribution:* Rivera was a painter who at first transcended his native Mexico and its rich and diverse artistic heritage to embrace broader modern European movements. Eventually in his work, he fused the Mexican and European forms to become one of his country's greatest muralists and a giant in the world of art.

### Early Life

Diego Rivera was born on December 8, 1886, in Guanajuato, Mexico, the birthplace of Mexican independence from Spain in 1810. His father, Diego, was a schoolteacher of Spanish-Portuguese-Jewish background, and his mother was of mixed Spanish-Indian descent. A few years after he was born, Rivera's family moved to Mexico City, where he grew up.

Because of his already marked artistic leanings at an early age, in 1896, his parents entered him in the San Carlos Academy of Fine Arts before he was ten years old. There he studied under the likes of Santiago Rebull, José Salomé Peña, Felix Parra, and the great José María de Velasco until 1902, when Rebull, the rector of the academy, died, to be replaced by Antonio Fabres. The young Rivera soon rebelled against the deadening regime of realism imposed by Fabres and left the academy.

Thereafter, Rivera studied and associated with the great José Guadalupe Posada and others. At this time, he also was stirred by the monumental native Mexican architecture. His first exhibition, held in Veracruz in 1907, so impressed the local governor and others, such as the legendary artist and patron Dr. Atl (Gerardo Murillo), who recommended Rivera, that he won a scholarship to further his studies at the prestigious San Fernando Academy in Spain under Eduardo Chicarro, a member of the Spanish realist school.

### Life's Work

In Spain, Rivera came under not only the influence of his teachers in Chicarro's studio but also, perhaps more important, the work of El Greco and Francisco de Goya. Rivera's first stay in Europe lasted two years, until 1909. During this time, he often left Spain to wander through Belgium, The Netherlands, France, and the British Isles.

When he returned home, it was just in time to experience and be caught up in the Mexican Revolution, which began in earnest in 1910. Rivera's youthful, aesthetic rebelliousness was wholly compatible with the political and social struggles developing in Mexico. Although not yet really of the people, more and more his sympathies were with them. He and other prominent Mexican artists easily came to equate aesthetic freedom with political freedom and vice versa.

When he returned to Europe in 1912, this time to stay until 1921, he was already experiencing profound changes in his worldview and his art. This second European episode and the events he witnessed during it generally set his new aesthetic-political outlook. As before, he traveled extensively and associated with artists such as Pierre-Auguste Renoir, Georges Seurat, Paul Gaugin, Henri Matisse, Amedeo Modigliani, Paul Cézanne, and Pablo Picasso. He also felt comfortable among the Russian artists, communist and noncommunist, in exile in Western Europe. His art began to reflect the

work of his fellow painters, and, in Paris, he sometimes exhibited his canvases with theirs. Rivera also felt the impact of World War I and the Russian Revolution, some of which he saw firsthand.

Gradually, Rivera drifted toward cubism, to which he became completely dedicated until at least 1917. Major works such as his *Majorcan Landscape* made a significant contribution to the movement and firmly established him as a cubist of the first degree. Through Matisse, he also experimented with Fauvism. His Mexican background especially helped him appreciate the Fauvists' use of color. In fact, more and more during this period his native Mexico and its influence grew in evidence in Rivera's work.

In 1920, Rivera met the young David Alfaro Siqueiros in Paris, and, sharing a growing belief in the need for a people's art to reflect revolutionary struggle and that art was political, they began to work toward a national popular art movement for their beloved Mexico. In this, they were eventually joined and supported by many, including the third founder of the modern Mexican mural tradition and Mexican Renaissance, the great José Clemente Orozco, and the then Mexican president, Álvaro Obregón, among others. Thus, Rivera returned home to start the work.

Rivera's first products of this new mural movement appeared on the walls of the National Preparatory School (University of Mexico) in 1922 and thereafter in the new Ministry of Education building in Mexico City. Mexico and its progress were almost always his subject. In this work, the Mexican muralists gradually recovered and fused the frescoing techniques of ancient Mexico (Orozco) and the Italian Renaissance (Rivera). In 1926-1927, Rivera completed his first masterpiece, a fresco cycle in the National Agricultural School in Chapingo.

Like Picasso, Orozco, Siqueiros, and numerous other artists during the interwar period, Rivera was a Communist, at least spiritually and emotionally if not doctrinally so. He was not, however, a Stalinist. While he went to Moscow in 1927-1928 and seems to have been impressed by what he saw, his disappointment with the Soviet Union grew thereafter. In 1936, Rivera interceded with President Lázaro Cárdenas to permit the Communist dissident Leon Trotsky to come to Mexico to end his wanderings. After 1928, Rivera returned to the Soviet Union only once more, in 1956, shortly before his death, for an operation.

Upon his return from Moscow, Rivera briefly served as the director of the San Carlos Academy in 1929. A year later, he married the Mexican artist Frida Kahlo, who also on occasion served him as a model. In 1932, Rivera completed a second masterpiece, a mural depicting the industrial progress of the United States, in the patio of the Institute of Fine Arts in Detroit. Thereafter, numerous commissions in the United States followed. The most controversial of these was in the lobby of the RCA Building in New York City in 1933. Before it was completed, it had to be obliterated because it contained a portrayal of Vladimir Ilich Lenin. Rivera reexecuted the controversial mural a year later as part of a series of masterpieces in the Palace of Fine Arts in Mexico City. Other important works by Rivera include *The Bandit Augustin Lorenzo*, done in the lobby of the Hotel Reforma in 1938 and *Vision of Alameda Central* in 1948 in the Del Prado Hotel, both in Mexico City.

Near the end of his life, Rivera led a movement to ban all nuclear testing, and he became a Roman Catholic. He died on November 25, 1957, in Mexico City, survived by his then wife, Emma Hurtado, and two daughters from a previous marriage to a former model, Lupe Marin. His death brought to a close a major era in Mexican cultural history.

## Summary

Already early in his life under the influence of his native Mexico and its rich artistic heritage, and, more important, of Europe, Diego Rivera became a major painter. He was a significant cubist and a Fauvist. Under the influence of revolutionary events in Mexico and Europe and as a direct result of his collaboration with Orozco and Siqueiros, however, he changed the face of modern art.

With his work, Rivera helped to create the modern mural movement and also put art into the political arena on the side of the popular struggle for freedom and equality. Although he was foremost a Mexican nationalist, a Mexican national artist, and a founder of the Mexican Renaissance and had a profound influence on younger Mexican artists such as Siqueiros, the painter-architect Juan O'Gorman, and many others, this influence reached far beyond Mexico back to Europe and into the United States, to the New Deal Works Progress Administration of the 1930's, for example. Rivera was a true founder of the people's art movement.

**Bibliography**

Carrillo Azpéitia, Rafael. *Mural Painting of Mexico: The Pre-Hispanic Epoch, the Viceroyalty, and the Great Artists of Our Century.* Mexico City: Panorama Editorial, 1981. A good, brief, and popular study from Mexico, containing a chapter on Rivera. Straightforward treatment.

Edwards, Emily. *Painted Walls of Mexico: From Prehistoric Times Until Today.* Austin: University of Texas Press, 1966. Almost half of this standard volume is on Rivera and the other modern Mexican muralists. Profusely illustrated.

Fernandez, Justino. *A Guide to Mexican Art: From Its Beginnings to the Present.* Chicago: University of Chicago Press, 1969. Puts Rivera and his work in a broad perspective and provides a good analysis of the work.

Folgarait, Leonard. *Mural Painting and Social Revolution in Mexico, 1920-1940: Art of the New Order.* Cambridge and New York: Cambridge University Press, 1998. This volume is an in-depth study of Mexican art between 1920 and 1940. The murals of Rivera, Orozco and other artists are discussed with emphasis on the effects of cultural issues on their works.

Helm, MacKinley. *Modern Mexican Painters.* New York: Harper, 1941. Contains a good chapter on Rivera and his work prior to World War II but is dated.

Reed, Alma. *The Mexican Muralists.* New York: Crown, 1960. A good general work with a chapter on Rivera by the biographer of Orozco. Profusely illustrated.

Rivera, Diego. *My Art, My Life: An Autobiography.* New York: Citadel Press, 1960. An excellent partial autobiography of a complex artist. It is essential to a full understanding of Rivera.

Rodriguez, Antonio. *A History of Mexican Mural Painting.* London: Thames and Hudson, and New York: Putnam, 1969. Another and more important standard work with five chapters on Rivera and his art. Profusely illustrated.

Rubyan-Ling, Saronne. "The Detroit Murals of Diego Rivera." *History Today* 46, no. 4 (April, 1996). Considers the Rivera murals commissioned by the Detroit Institute of the Arts in which he depicted the good and bad in technology.

Smith, Bradley. *Mexico: A History in Art.* New York: Doubleday, 1968; London: Phaidon Press, 1975. A standard with a significant chapter on Rivera and the other modern muralists. Profusely illustrated.

Wolfe, Bertram. *The Fabulous Life of Diego Rivera.* New York: Stein and Day, 1963. Still probably the best biography of Rivera, certainly the best in English. Sympathetic, understanding, and understandable.

*Dennis Reinhartz*

# PAUL ROBESON

*Born:* April 9, 1898; Princeton, New Jersey

*Died:* January 23, 1976; Philadelphia, Pennsylvania

*Areas of Achievement:* Music, drama, and social reform

*Contribution:* A Renaissance man, Robeson made unprecedented contributions to American and world history as an athlete, intellectual, performer, and internationally renowned peace advocate. In politics, he championed the cause of human rights for black Americans and other oppressed people throughout the world.

## Early Life

Paul Bustill Robeson was born April 9, 1898, in Princeton, New Jersey, at a time when black Americans were politically disenfranchised, economically exploited, excluded from the mainstream of American life, and suffering the worst racial hostility since the abolition of slavery. Paul was the youngest of six children born to the Reverend Mr. William Drew Robeson and Maria Louisa Bustill Robeson. His mother, Maria Louisa, was a member of the prominent Bustill family of Philadelphia, some of whom were patriots in the American Revolutionary War. The Bustills helped to establish the Free African Society and produced a long line of teachers, artisans, and ministers to the Northern free black community. Paul's father, William Drew Robeson, was born a slave in Martin County, North Carolina. He fled to the North and, with the outbreak of the Civil War, joined the Union army. After the war, William Robeson attended Lincoln University and received a degree in divinity.

Paul was six years old when his mother died; the family moved to Sommerville, New Jersey, where Paul received most of his early education. The greatest influences on Paul for the remainder of his life were his family tradition, the environment of Jim Crow America, and the experience of being reared by his father. At an early age, Paul, who often worked with his father after school, sang in his father's church, listened to stories about slavery, and became imbued with several basic principles: to labor diligently in all endeavors, pursue worthwhile goals, maintain high standards, be of service to his people, and maintain his integrity.

At age seventeen, Robeson won a state scholarship to Rutgers University in New Brunswick, New Jersey. Those who knew him described him as a good-natured person who loved life. Striving for perfection in his work, this handsome six-foot, three-inch man maintained a sense of quiet, modest self-confidence. While attending Rutgers, he established an unprecedented academic record, achieving the highest grades in his class. He was also considered to be without equal in athletics.

Although football was his favorite sport, he participated in basketball, track and field, and baseball, winning an astonishing twelve major letters in four years. He was honored as the greatest athlete in Rutgers' history and elected to the All-American team twice (in 1917 and 1918) and has been called the greatest defensive back ever to tread the gridiron. Robeson brought the school national recognition by being the first player ever named All-American in any sport at Rutgers.

Robeson also loved public speaking and debate. A master in elocution contests, for four consecutive years he won first place honors in many speaking competitions, excelling in oratory, in extemporaneous speaking, and in forensics.

Robeson won admission to Rutgers' exclusive Cap and Skull honor association and the prestigious Phi Beta Kappa society. His senior thesis, "The Fourteenth Amendment: The Sleeping Giant of the American Constitution," by identifying several ways in which the law could be used to secure civil rights for black Americans, presaged by nearly forty years ideas adopted by the United States Supreme Court in the landmark decision, *Brown v. Board of Education* (1954). At commencement, he delivered the class oration, and afterward Rutgers honored him as the "perfect type of college man."

## Life's Work

In 1920, Robeson began law school at Columbia University and played a few games of professional football to finance his education. While at Columbia, he met and married Eslanda Goode Cardozo. They had a son, Paul, Jr., in 1927. After his graduation, Robeson worked briefly for a New York law firm; after encountering considerable hostility in the legal profession, however, he took up acting as a career.

During his law school days, Robeson played Simon in a benefit play, *Simon the Cyrenian* (1921), staged at the Harlem Young Men's Christian Association by the Provincetown Players, a Greenwich Village theater group. His successful performance led to other parts, and he was offered the lead in

two plays by Eugene O'Neill, *All God's Chillun Got Wings* (1924) and, in 1924, *The Emperor Jones* (1920). Robeson's acting was immediately acclaimed. He also made theater history, for that production of *All God's Chillun Got Wings* was the first in which a black man played the leading role opposite a white woman on the American stage. The young actor starred in numerous plays, including *Black Boy* (1925), by Jim Tully and Frank Dazey, *Porgy* (1927), by DuBose and Dorothy Heyward, and *Show Boat* (1927), by Jerome Kern and Oscar Hammerstein. He successfully toured Europe in the late 1920's and throughout the 1930's, drawing massive, enthusiastic crowds. Robeson played Othello in William Shakespeare's play at London's Savoy Theatre in 1930, where the opening performance received twenty curtain calls. He reached the pinnacle of his stage career in 1943-1944, with his New York performance in *Othello*, which holds the record for the longest run of any Shakespearean play produced on Broadway. His ovations were among "the most prolonged and wildest . . . in the history of the New York theatre."

In one scene from the 1924 production of Eugene O'Neill's *The Emperor Jones*, Robeson was asked to whistle; instead, he sang a black spiritual. To his listeners' delighted surprise, he had a marvelous voice. This event launched an illustrious musical career that brought additional celebrity. Robeson began augmenting his acting by singing spirituals. Robeson was the first person to give entire programs of exclusively Afro-American songs in concert to white audiences. This innovation made Robeson one of the most popular concert singers for more than a quarter of a century. Later, he broadened his repertoire to include the music of other nationalities. Accompanied on piano by Lawrence Brown, Robeson's magnificent baritone voice thrilled audiences around the world. Jerome Kern's "Ol' Man River" became his personal signature, concluding every concert.

Robeson made several films, the more significant being *The Emperor Jones* (1933), *Sanders of the River* (1935), *Show Boat* (1936), *The Song of Freedom* (1937), *King Solomon's Mines* (1937), *Jericho* (1937), and *Big Fella* (1938). He was particularly pleased with *Proud Valley* (1939), which depicted the harsh life of Welsh coal miners and gave a fair and accurate portrayal of black people, and his narration for *Native Land* (1942), a moving documentary on contemporary American life. Although British filmmakers, unlike their American counterparts, were willing to feature Robeson in major roles, with few exceptions these films depicted blacks in a demeaning manner. Disgusted at the results, Robeson picketed his own films, abandoned the cinema, and focused attention on the stage, where he could control and determine the images in every performance.

As Robeson became more successful in the theater and on the concert stage, he committed himself to improving the plight of blacks. He believed that with his singing and acting he could increase the white world's respect, knowledge, and understanding of his people. "They will," he said in 1932, "sense that we are moved by the same emotions, have the same beliefs, the same longings—that we are all humans together." Moreover, his prominence motivated him to reaffirm his black identity, and he started a campaign to educate black people about the virtues of their own cultural heritage, arguing that African history was as old and significant as that of the Chinese or Persians. Uncompromisingly, he maintained that "it should be the mission of Negro artists to earn respect as Negroes as a step toward making the white race eventually respect the black." He believed that blacks had a unique and valuable contribution to make in humanizing the world through their philosophy and art.

Robeson developed a sophisticated concept of cultural pluralism that had at its roots a deep respect for his own nationality. Living in Europe during the 1930's, he determined to use art to advance the cause of his own people and to use it on a grander scale to build a more humane world. Art would be the vehicle to unite all people against the common foes of poverty, exploitation, bigotry, political violence, and war. He began studying world cultures, history, politics, and economic and social systems, and he became fluent in more than two dozen languages, including Ashanti, Mande, Swahili, Yoruba, Hindustani, Arabic, Chinese, German, Russian, French, Spanish, and Finnish.

Robeson's cultural philosophy led him to more direct political activity. In 1934, at the invitation of Sergei Eisenstein, he made the first of several trips to the Soviet Union. He spoke out against the Fascist politics of the Nazis and was the only American entertainer to go to Spain and sing to Loyalist troops. At a rally sponsored to aid Spanish refugee children held in 1937 at London's Royal Albert Hall, he remarked, "The artist must take sides. He must elect to fight for freedom or slavery. I have made my choice." He raised money to fight the Italian invasion of Ethiopia and opposed all forms of colonialism. Robeson supported the Committee to Aid China, denounced Japanese imperialism, and made a special album of Chinese songs, *Chee Lai* (1940), which he recorded in the language to raise money for Chinese relief. The foremost spokesman against European colonialism, he led the campaign for African independence and became chairman of the Council on African Affairs, which he helped establish in 1937. With the outbreak of World War II, he supported the American effort by entertaining soldiers in camps and laborers in war industries. Many of his concerts were greeted by some of the largest military audiences and civilian workers ever assembled during wartime.

By 1946, Robeson became more determined than ever to work for an end to colonialism in Africa, Asia, and the Caribbean. For the second time in his life, black soldiers were returning from a war to preserve democracy only to be greeted with racism and bigotry. Robeson could no longer tolerate the status of second-class citizenship imposed on blacks. Jeopardizing his career and spending more than $100,000 a year, he devoted his time to campaigning for black civil rights. He spoke on behalf of trade unions who found their wartime, New Deal economic gains eroded, defended Native Americans, denounced sexism, backed Henry Wallace and the Progressive Party, and confronted President Harry S Truman, demanding that he put an end to lynchings in the South and segregation in the armed forces and that he enforce fair employment practices for minority laborers.

Disturbed by Robeson's militance, opponents labeled him a Communist to undermine his legitimate dissent and weaken his mass appeal. When Cold War tensions and McCarthyistic hysteria mounted, Robeson's detractors tried to discredit him, and on several occasions he was called to testify before government committees regarding his loyalty to the United States. Repeatedly he challenged the officials, reminding them of the unconstitutionality of these proceedings, and refused to be baited into identifying anyone of his associates or activities as being un-American.

As the fear of war between the United States and the Soviet Union escalated, Robeson, at the 1949 Paris Peace Conference, called for a cessation of hostilities and an end to the arms race. A cogent and powerful speaker, he articulated the similarities in attitude between many domestic and international policies, suggesting that the black people of the world, whether in the South or in colonies abroad, had no quarrel with Russia. Their grievance was more immediate; it was with those who oppressed them: "the senators who have just filibustered them out of their civil rights. . . . Milan in South Africa who, just like Hitler, is threatening to destroy eight million Africans and hundreds of thousands of Indians through hunger and terror."

In the 1950's, Robeson was viciously attacked for his statements. Riots occurred, disrupting his concerts in Peekskill, New York. His opposition to the United States' participation in the Korean War brought a barrage of criticism. Books and information about his achievements were removed from library circulation and stricken from histories, anthologies, and bibliographic references. Blacklisting and intimidation cost him his theatrical and concert bookings and a domestic audience. His passport was revoked, and he was barred from travel outside the United States. According to the State Department's brief, action was taken "solely because of his recognized status as a spokesman for large sections of Negro Americans . . . in view of his frank admission that he has been for years active politically in behalf of independence of the colonial people of Africa."

The government offered to return his passport if he signed a statement that he would not make any speeches while abroad; Robeson refused. He lost the lucrative income from concerts and an international forum. In the meantime, he continued to accept invitations to speak and sing before labor organizations, civic groups, and black churches. One amazing concert was mounted in 1953, when Canadians arranged to meet Robeson near the border at Blain, Washington, where he spoke and sang to nearly thirty thousand people who jammed the Peace Arch Park.

With the Supreme Court ruling in 1958, Robeson's passport was reinstated. He published his autobiography, *Here I Stand* (1958), and resumed a vigorous speaking and concert tour, traveling to Great Britain, the Soviet Union, Germany, New Zealand, and Australia. Dispelling any misconceptions about his actions, he stated, "The truth is, I am not and never have been involved in any international conspiracy or any other kind, and do not know anyone who is."

Whenever he spoke crowds gathered. Yet the physical strain of the previous decades had taken its toll. In 1961, illness caused him to retire from singing and acting, and in 1963 he returned to the United States, where he remained in seclusion until his death in 1976.

### Summary

During his life, Paul Robeson received hundreds of awards and tributes for his superlative artistic achievements, phenomenal intellectual contributions, and unparalleled political sacrifices on behalf of world freedom and international peace. The British Parliament set aside a day to honor him. He won the Donaldson Award for Best Acting Performance, received the American Academy of Arts and Sciences' Gold Medal for Best Diction, and was awarded numerous honorary degrees from colleges. He was honored with the Badge of the Veterans of the Abraham Lincoln Brigade, for those who fought for Republican Spain against Francisco Franco, the Thirtieth Annual Spingarn Medal, and the National Federation for Constitutional Liberties' award. Further, he received the Lenin Peace Prize and the African Freedom Award, as well as other international honors. His prodigious career included eleven films, five documentaries, nearly two dozen plays, and hundreds of records. His meticulous and constant scholarship resulted in three dozen articles, one book, and hundreds of addresses and speeches.

Robeson believed that he could show the world through the media of entertainment that racism and exploitation of all people had to end. For him, art had a definite purpose. Aside from offering pleasure and joy, art was enhanced when it enlightened people; this was the true essence of art's potential to uplift the human spirit.

During the 1930's, Robeson integrated his artistic career with that of a political activist, a Socialist cultural philosopher, and a peace advocate. Seeing German Fascism at first hand compelled him to fight against it. He called for "immediate action" to save the Jews of Europe even though it might mean "heavy sacrifice and death." His interest in labor organization grew out of his pioneering effort as a founder of the Unity Theatre in England.

Robeson supported popular liberation movements in Asia, Africa, and the Caribbean in the 1930's and 1940's. He wrote on behalf of Philippine independence from the United States and was the most prominent voice against colonial rule in Africa. Robeson pioneered in the antiapartheid movement, counseling in the 1940's that "we cannot afford to tolerate the advocates of White Supremacy in South Africa, any more than we can agree to the activities of the Ku Klux Klan in Georgia or Mississippi."

Robeson was without peer in championing the cause of worldwide democracy; yet he became one of the greatest casualties of the Cold War. Actions which won approval and praise in the 1920's and 1930's brought derision and enmity in the late 1940's and 1950's. (Earl Schenck Miers, at the height of Robeson's vilification, wrote in *The Nation* that, "as a product of his times, Robeson today is perhaps more All-American than he was as a member of his college.") His constitutional rights were violated, and a torrent of hostility was directed against him.

A new generation of Americans, rediscovering Robeson in the 1970's, brought increasing recognition of his achievements. No doubt they would be reassured by his last public statement just before his death: "Though I have not been able to be active for several years, I want you to know that I am the same Paul, dedicated, as ever, to the worldwide cause of humanity, for freedom, peace and brotherhood." As William Shakespeare's Othello said in his last speech before they took him away: "Soft you; a word or two before you go. I have done the state some service, and they know't." With his genius and his humanism, Paul Robeson did indeed serve the state extraordinarily well.

### Bibliography

Davis, Lenwood G. *A Paul Robeson Research Guide: A Selected Annotated Bibliography.* Westport, Conn.: Greenwood Press, 1982. All Robeson scholars must consult this very fine bibliography. Given the difficulty in identifying foreign and obscure domestic material on Robeson, this rather large compendium is a timely and essential reference.

Foner, Philip S., ed. *Paul Robeson Speaks: Writings, Speeches, Interviews, 1918-1974.* London: Quartet, and New York: Brunner/Mazel, 1978. This is an extremely valuable reader containing most of Robeson's major published material. Anyone interested in twentieth century history and politics must include this volume on his reading list.

Freedomways Associates. *Paul Robeson: The Great Forerunner.* New York: International, 1985. This anthology contains a number of short articles on various aspects of Robeson's life.

Also included are a few documents and numerous tributes to the man from friends, associates, and admirers, who appreciated his contributions to humanity.

Gilliam, Dorothy Butler. *Paul Robeson: All-American*. Washington, D.C.: New Republic, 1976. This thoughtful biography of Paul Robeson is the best of the recent surveys of his life. The author, however, fails to explain adequately political events in the 1930's or Cold War issues that shaped his thinking.

Howard, H. Wendell. "Paul Robeson Remembered." *Midwest Quarterly* 38, no. 1 (Fall 1996). Profile of Robeson as civil rights activist, performer, and writer.

Robeson, Paul. *Here I Stand*. London: Dobson, and New York: Othello, 1958. Although short and succinct, this autobiography covers Robeson's life, beginning with his family and concluding with his sixtieth birthday. This fascinating personal account should be read by everyone.

Robeson, Paul Jr. "Paul Robeson: Voice of a Century." *Black Collegian* 28, no. 2 (February, 1998). Brief tribute to Robeson.

Seton, Marie. *Paul Robeson*. London: Dobson, 1958. Seton, a longtime friend of Robeson since the early 1930's, has written the best biography of the man to date. Filled with many colorful insights, Seton endeavors to explain the origin of Robeson's radicalism in the 1930's. The work should be updated to cover the period from 1958 until his death in 1976.

Stuckey, Sterling. "'I Want to Be African': Paul Robeson and the Ends of Nationalist Theory and Practice, 1914-1945." *Massachusetts Review* 17 (Spring, 1976): 81-138. This stimulating article treats the development and expression of Robeson's cultural nationalism in the 1930's. The author is correct in asserting that the actor had a profound understanding of African culture and its possibilities as a humanistic approach to life which, if accepted by the West, might benefit the entire world.

Wright, Charles H. *The Peace Advocacy of Paul Robeson*. Detroit, Mich.: Harlo Press, 1984. This short pamphlet provides valuable insight into a hitherto misunderstood aspect of Robeson's political activities: his role as one of the world's leading antiwar pioneers at the start of the nuclear age.

———. *Robeson: Labor's Forgotten Champion*. Detroit, Mich.: Balamp, 1975. Although much has been written about Robeson, this book stands alone as the only treatment of his trade-union activities, a vital commitment to which the artist devoted much of his life. Another virtue of the book is its insight into labor's views and support for this champion of the working class.

*Lamont H. Yeakey*

## JACKIE ROBINSON

*Born:* January 31, 1919; Cairo, Georgia
*Died:* October 24, 1972; Stamford, Connecticut
*Areas of Achievement:* Sports and civil rights
*Contribution:* Robinson was the first black to play in the major leagues and as such is known for breaking the "color line" in baseball. A hero for his brilliant career with the Brooklyn Dodgers, he was elected to the Baseball Hall of Fame.

### Early Life

John Roosevelt, or Jackie (as he was known throughout his adult life), Robinson was the fifth child born to Mallie and Jerry Robinson, sharecroppers of Cairo, Georgia. Robinson's grandparents had been slaves. When he was six months old, his father abandoned the family, and a year later his mother took the family to Pasadena, California, where Robinson grew up. Although poor, Robinson's mother saved money and ultimately purchased a house in a previously all-white neighborhood. This was Robinson's first experience as a pioneer in integration. As a child, Robinson excelled in all sports. In high school, junior college, and at the University of California at Los Angeles, Robinson starred in baseball, basketball, football, and track. In 1938, at Pasadena Junior College, he broke the national junior college record for the broad jump, previously set by his older brother, Mack Robinson, who himself had won a silver medal at the 1936 Olympics. In 1939, he entered UCLA, where he became the school's first letterman in four sports. Robinson's best sport was football; in 1941, he was named an All-American. That year, he dropped out of college to earn money for his family.

In 1941, Robinson played professional football with the Honolulu Bears. Drafted in 1942, Robinson applied for Officer's Candidate School at Fort Riley, Kansas. Although admitted to the program, Robinson and the other black candidates received no training until pressure from Washington forced the local commander to admit blacks to the base's training school. Robinson's reputation as a sports hero helped to generate that pressure. As a second lieutenant, Robinson successfully challenged some of the Jim Crow policies at the base post exchange. He quit the base football team in protest when the army agreed to keep him out of a game with the nearby University of Missouri, because that school refused to play against black opponents. Transferred to Fort Hood, Texas, Robinson protested segregation on an army bus. His protests led to a court-martial, at which he was acquitted. In November, 1944, he was honorably discharged. The army had little desire to keep this black man who kept fighting against racism, and for his part, Robinson was, as he later wrote in his autobiography, "pretty much fed up with the service."

### Life's Work

Out of the army, Robinson secured a tryout with the Kansas City Monarchs, a leading team in the segregated "Negro leagues." He was quickly offered four hundred dollars a month. In August, 1945, while playing for the Monarchs, Robinson was approached by a scout for the Brooklyn Dodgers. Dodger president Branch Rickey was publicly calling for a new black baseball league, with a team to be called the Brooklyn Brown Dodgers. Rickey wanted Robinson for the team and asked him to come to Brooklyn for a meeting.

Robinson traveled to Brooklyn to meet Rickey. The twenty-six-year-old Robinson was just under six feet tall and weighed 195 pounds. He was handsome, agile, and a natural athlete of almost limitless potential. He was also intelligent and articulate and one of the best-educated black baseball players in the United States. He had grown up in an integrated world and played on integrated teams in high school and college. He was the perfect candidate for Rickey's great experiment: the integration of the major leagues.

The meeting between Robinson and Rickey is a classic in American sports. Robinson expected to talk about a new black baseball team. Instead, Rickey asked him if he had a girlfriend, and on hearing about his college sweetheart, Rachel Isum, Rickey told him to marry her. Robinson was puzzled. Rickey continued the conversation, asking Robinson if he knew why he was there. Robinson mentioned the Brown Dodgers. No, Rickey told him, Robinson was brought there to play for the real Dodgers, to integrate baseball. Rickey then began to detail Robinson's life for him. Robinson had not been scouted simply for his baseball skills; he had been scouted for his character. Rickey wanted to know if he had the courage to be the first black athlete to play in the major leagues—if he could stand the insults, the racial slurs, the beanballs, without fighting back. Rickey swore at Robinson, called him the worst possible names, and tried in other ways to anger him. The meeting was "tough" according to Robinson, but necessary, because for Robinson, baseball would not simply be a matter of box scores. That day, he signed a contract for six hundred dollars a month with a thirty-five-hundred-dollar bonus. Rickey, who was a businessman as well as a man with a strong sense of social justice, knew that Robinson had only an oral contract with the Monarchs, which was renewed monthly. Thus, Rickey never offered to pay the Monarchs for the rights to Robinson's contract.

On October 23, 1945, the Brooklyn Dodgers shocked America by announcing that Jackie Robinson would be playing for their number-one farm team, the Montreal Royals. Southerners asserted that they would never play on the same team as Robinson; white sports reporters declared that he had few baseball skills and would never make it to the major leagues; owners of other baseball teams complained about Rickey's breaking the unwritten rule against hiring blacks. The manager of the Royals, a Mississippian, privately begged Rickey not to send Robinson to his team. In spring training in Florida, Robinson faced segregation as he had never seen it before. Buses, restaurants, hotels, and all other public facilities were rigidly segregated. On the way to Florida, Robinson and his new wife were twice asked to leave their airplane seats to make room for white passengers. Later, they were forced to move to the back of a bus. These were common experiences for Southern blacks but had been unknown to the California couple. During training, Robinson could not stay with the team at a local hotel but had to live with a local black family. Tensions were high throughout the spring.

Despite a poor spring training, Robinson started at second base for the Montreal Royals in the opening game. His performance was masterful. He had four hits, including a three-run home run, scored four times, and stole two bases. His baserunning so unnerved opposition pitchers that twice they balked with Robinson on third base, which allowed him to score. This was the beginning of a promising career.

That first year, Robinson faced hateful racist crowds and opponents in a number of cities. Often this only spurred Robinson on. For example, at Syracuse, the opposing players threw a black cat on the field, yelling, "Hey, Jackie, there's your cousin." Robinson then hit a double and shouted to the Syracuse bench, "I guess my cousin's pretty happy now." Robinson was totally unnerved by the crowd, however, when he played in Louisville in a post-season championship game. The Southern crowd mercilessly booed him with "a torrent of mass hatred," as he later described it. In Montreal, on the other hand, Robinson, nicknamed the "dark dasher" for his baserunning skills, was a star and a hero. When he made the game's winning hit in the last game of the "little world series," he was carried off the field by his teammates and had to run from an adoring crowd. One sportswriter noted that it was "probably the only day in history that a black man ran from a white mob with love instead of lynching on its mind."

In 1947, Robinson started for the Brooklyn Dodgers. Enormous pressures and racial insults hampered his playing. A few Dodgers, most notably Fred "Dixie" Walker, asked to be traded. The St. Louis Cardinals, playing in a segregated city, threatened to boycott Dodger games. The manager of the Philadelphia Phillies, Ben Chapman of Alabama, became so abusive that the commissioner of baseball, himself a Southerner, intervened. By the end of the season, most of Robinson's teammates were behind him, as were many opponents. Robinson smothered his temper, absorbed insults, and fought back only with his bat, glove, and baserunning. He led the league in stolen bases that year, batted .297, and electrified fans with his baserunning, including his ability to steal home. The *Sporting News*, which had initially predicted that he would never make it to the major leagues, voted him Rookie of the Year. More significant, a public opinion poll found him the second most popular man in America, behind the singer Bing Crosby.

Two years later, in 1949, Robinson led the National League in hitting with a .342 average and was named Most Valuable Player. By then, a few other blacks, including Roy Campanella, Don Newcombe, Larry Doby, and the legendary pitcher LeRoy "Satchel" Paige, had entered the major leagues. Most major league teams were beginning to scout black ballplayers. In 1950, Hollywood gave its stamp of approval to the experiment by hiring Robinson to star in a film about himself entitled *The Jackie Robinson Story*. Robinson was now making the rather princely sum of thirty-five thousand dollars a year from the Dodgers, as well as additional income from endorsements and promotions. The Dodgers were the dominant team in their league, and Ebbets Field was attracting large crowds. The experiment seemed to be paying off

B

for all concerned. The owners of teams in the so-called Negro leagues, however, complained that their players were being stolen from them by the major league teams and that, with one or two exceptions, they were never compensated. The complaints were justified as Negro league stars such as Paige, Campanella, and Monte Irvin, and future great stars such Hank Aaron and Willie Mays, were indeed being hired by forward-thinking, previously all-white baseball teams. By the early 1950's, all but a few teams—most notably the New York Yankees and the Boston Red Sox—would have black players.

After the 1950 season, Rickey left the Dodgers and was replaced by Walter O'Malley. Robinson feuded with his new boss for the next six years. O'Malley seemed uninterested in challenging the status quo, while Robinson would no longer quietly accept racist insults. For example, O'Malley was unsympathetic to Robinson's demand that he be allowed to stay at the same hotels as his teammates. Robinson contemplated leaving baseball in 1954 and finally did so after the 1956 season. Robinson secretly sold the exclusive story of his retirement to *Look* magazine. Meanwhile, the Dodgers sold Robinson's contract to the New York Giants, their crosstown rival. Despite an offer of sixty thousand dollars a year, Robinson stuck to his plans and left baseball.

Robinson did not, however, fade from public life. He accepted a job with a New York restaurant chain and continued to work actively in civil rights causes. He became a major fund-raiser for the National Association for the Advancement of Colored People in the 1950's. In the 1960 presidential election primaries, he campaigned for Hubert Humphrey, but in a decision he later regretted, he supported Richard Nixon in the general election. Henry Cabot Lodge, Nixon's running mate, promised Robinson that Nixon would appoint a black to a cabinet position. In addition, Robinson was unimpressed with John F. Kennedy's record on civil rights. Robinson later wrote: "The Richard Nixon I met back in 1960 bore no resemblance to the Richard Nixon as President." After the 1960 election, Robinson became closely associated with Nelson Rockefeller, the New York liberal Republican governor. In 1964, he became one of Rockefeller's advisers on civil rights and a deputy director of his presidential campaign. After the nomination of Barry Goldwater, however, Robinson became national leader of the Republicans for Johnson. At about this time, Robinson also became involved in the formation of a black-owned bank in Harlem, the Freedom National Bank. Robinson correctly noted that white-owned banks offered few services to blacks, and he believed that the situation could be remedied only with black-controlled capital. In 1966, he accepted an appointment from Governor Rockefeller as a special assistant to the governor for community affairs.

While Robinson became involved in politics and business, he was never fully divorced from baseball. In 1962, he was elected to the Baseball Hall of Fame. In the early 1950's, he had publicly attacked those teams, such as the New York Yankees, which had not yet hired black players. In the late 1960's, he began to campaign for the hiring of a black manager. He accused the men of professional baseball of hypocrisy and of maintaining a double standard in allowing blacks to play but not to manage. In 1972, Robinson threw the first ball out at the World Series. Given a public forum, he declared, on national television, "I'd like to live to see a black manager; I'd like to live to see the day when there is a black man coaching at third base." When asked why he had to use the World Series to raise this issue, he responded, "What better place? What better time?" Nine days later, Robinson died at fifty-three of complications caused by diabetes.

### Summary

The significance of Jackie Robinson was twofold. First, he was an outstanding athlete and one of the most exciting baseball players of his time. In the late 1970's, the New York Mets would use pictures of Robinson in their advertising, knowing that the memory of his playing could still thrill fans. In an age of power-hitters, Robinson brought back base-stealing, bunting for hits, and finesse. His ability to unnerve pitchers was uncanny. His daring in stealing home, even in a tight World Series game, brought spectators to their feet. He was a clutch player who came through with the big hit, or the big stolen base, at a crucial moment in the game. He was a star with charisma and class. He was truly one of the greatest sports heroes of his age.

Robinson was also a pioneer. While he had the backing of Rickey and the help of many players and fans when he integrated baseball, it was Robinson who had to bear the racial slurs, duck the beanballs, and dodge spikes aimed at his body. Robinson did this with grace and dignity, but he also did it with fire. Moreover, he was able to make the transition from turning the other cheek to fighting back verbally. He was the ultimate competitor, for after his baseball career was over, he continued to fight for racial justice and equality. To the end, Robinson spoke out against all forms of segregation.

### Bibliography

Early, Gerald. "American Integration, Black Heroism, and the Meaning of Jackie Robinson." *Chronicle of Higher Education* 43, no. 37 (May 23, 1997). Short piece on Robinson including his trials, his achievements, and his feelings about later generations' ambivalence toward integration.

Frommer, Harvey. *Rickey and Robinson: The Men Who Broke Baseball's Color Line*. New York and London: Macmillan, 1982. Excellent dual biography of Branch Rickey, the owner of the Dodgers who hired Robinson, and Robinson. Follows careers of both beyond their years in baseball, to their deaths.

Kahn, Roger. *The Boys of Summer*. New York: Harper, 1972. Written by a leading sportswriter, this is warm and readable history of the Brooklyn Dodgers in the age of Jackie Robinson.

Nack, William. "The Breakthrough." *Sports Illustrated* 86, no. 18 (May 5, 1997). Focuses on Robinson's life during his first few weeks as a Brooklyn Dodger.

Peterson, Robert. *Only the Ball Was White*. Englewood Cliffs, N.J.: Prentice-Hall, 1970. History of black baseball. Contains important information on early black players and the organization of the Negro leagues.

Robinson, John Roosevelt. *Baseball Has Done It*. Edited by Charles Dexter. Philadelphia: Lippincott, 1964. Part autobiography, part history of the integration of baseball, and part a history of the blacks who played in the Negro leagues, this book is also Robinson's first long statement about race relations and integration after he left baseball. Written during the early years of the civil rights revolution, this is an important book that links civil rights to baseball. The book also gives important details about the events leading up to Robinson's breaking of the color line.

———. *I Never Had It Made*. New York: Putnam, 1972. Robinson's autobiography, published just before he died. A key source for Robinson's life, especially after he left baseball.

Rogosin, Donn. *Invisible Men: Life in Baseball's Negro Leagues*. New York: Atheneum, 1983. Study of black baseball before the integration of the major leagues. Based on extensive interviews with former players. Readable, yet scholarly.

Tygiel, Jules. *Baseball's Great Experiment: Jackie Robinson and His Legacy*. New York: Oxford University Press, 1983. Skillfully written, this is the best study of the integration of baseball. Written by a professional historian, based on archival work and interviews, this book is a joy to read and the place to start when reading about Robinson.

*Paul Finkelman*

## NORMAN ROCKWELL

*Born:* February 3, 1894; New York, New York

*Died:* November 8, 1978; Stockbridge, Massachusetts

*Area of Achievement:* Art

*Contribution:* Rockwell is one of America's most popular and best-known artists. His appeal lies in his ability to capture scenes of traditional American life in a way that needs no explanation.

### Early Life

Norman Percevel Rockwell was born in New York City on February 3, 1894. His parents were J. Waring Rockwell and Nancy Hill. He had one older brother, Jarvis. Both his father and his maternal grandfather, Howard Hill, stimulated his interest in art. Grandfather Hill, an artist born in England, came to the United States in the mid-1860's. His paintings of animals done with meticulous care impressed Rockwell, who noted in his autobiography that this inspired him to seek accurate detail in his own work. His father, who enjoyed copying illustrations from magazines, encouraged his son's talent for drawing. In the evenings, when his father read aloud from Charles Dickens, Rockwell visualized the scenes and drew the characters.

At the age of fifteen, Rockwell left high school to study art full time. He enrolled first at the National Academy of Design, where he got his first training in anatomy, drawing from plaster casts of famous classical sculpture. From there he went to the Art Students League, where his most influential teachers were George Bridgeman and Thomas Fogarty.

Rockwell's career as an illustrator started early. In 1912, he published his first work, eight book illustrations for C. H. Claudy's *Tell-Me-Why Stories about Mother Nature* and Gabrielle Jackson's *Maid of Middies Haven.* In 1913, Fogarty encouraged Rockwell to show his drawings to the editor of *Boys' Life* magazine. He was engaged to create one cover and illustrate one story per issue and was soon hired as the art editor. During his four years at the *Boys' Life*, he completed two hundred illustrations. During his last year with the magazine, he started to work for *The Saturday Evening Post.*

Rockwell's first *Saturday Evening Post* cover was published May 20, 1916, which began a forty-seven-year association with the magazine. That same year, Rockwell married Irene O'Connor, who divorced him thirteen years later. In 1930, he married Mary Barstow. They had three children—Jarvis, Thomas, and Peter—but Mary died in 1959. In 1961, Rockwell married Mary "Molly" Punderson, who survived him and died in 1985.

Rockwell lived in New York during his early years, mainly in New Rochelle. In 1939, he moved to Arlington, Vermont, and left there, in 1953, for Stockbridge, Massachusetts. Friends and neighbors in these towns became his models and posed in a great number of paintings.

### Life's Work

Rockwell's capacity for work during his seventy years of professional life was enormous. He made paintings for magazine covers and illustrations for books, stories, and advertisements. An incomplete estimate lists about four thousand works. He worked on several projects at the same time. His favorite work was creating magazine covers, which allowed him freedom to develop his own ideas. Rockwell's most famous covers were made for *The Saturday Evening Post.* The very first one, *Boy with Baby Carriage* (May 20, 1916) set the tone for most of what followed. In the painting, an elegantly dressed twelve-year-old boy is mocked by two of his buddies. They are on their way to play baseball while he must push the baby carriage. A young neighbor in Arlington, Vermont, posed for all three boys. Rockwell's last published cover for *The Saturday Evening Post* (December 14, 1963), his 322d cover, commemorated the assassinated President John F. Kennedy. Since it was a reprint from 1960 to which a black border had been added, the actual number of *Saturday Evening Post* covers was 321.

Rockwell also illustrated books, following in the tradition of great illustrators he admired such as Howard Pyle and J. C. Leyendecker. His characteristic work method was demonstrated in the assignment to illustrate Mark Twain's two classics, *The Adventures of Tom Sawyer* (1876; Rockwell edition, 1936) and *The Adventures of Huckleberry Finn* (1884; Rockwell edition, 1940). In order to get the details as authentic as possible, Rockwell read the books several times and traveled to Hannibal, Missouri, Mark Twain's boyhood town, to sketch the actual houses, streets, the river, and the cave. He even bought old clothes to take back home.

Rockwell also painted story illustrations for *The Saturday Evening Post.* The most celebrated of these are the *Four Freedoms*, inspired by President

Franklin D. Roosevelt's speech in January, 1941, to the U.S. Congress to secure the "four essential human freedoms" everywhere in the world. The paintings were published as *Freedom of Speech* (February 20, 1943), *Freedom of Worship* (February 27, 1943), *Freedom from Want* (March 6, 1943), and *Freedom from Fear* (March 13, 1943) to illustrate essays on these topics. After publication, the paintings went on a nationwide tour, the Four Freedoms War Bond Show, until May 8, 1944. About 1.2 million people saw the show and about $133 million worth of war bonds were sold to support the war effort.

In May, 1943, shortly after the War Bond tour began, Rockwell suffered a severe setback when his studio in Arlington, Vermont, was destroyed by fire. He lost everything that he had collected over the past thirty years, including the props he used in his paintings as well as finished paintings and preliminary sketches. Rather than rebuild the studio, he moved to another house in Arlington.

Despite the lighthearted appearance of Rockwell's work, he suffered through periods of restlessness and depression. Around 1952, he felt the need to consult some mental health counsellors at the Austin Riggs Center in Stockbridge. One of them was Erik Erikson, a psychoanalyst, who became a friend. Under Erikson's influence, Rockwell gradually took a new approach to his art as he became more interested in social issues such as the Civil Rights movement.

After he ended his association with *The Saturday Evening Post* in 1963, Rockwell started to work for *Look*, where he began to use his talent to illustrate serious themes, such as *The Problem We All Live With* (January 14, 1964). Also called *Ruby Bridges Goes to School*, the painting was based on an incident in the South, which was still opposed to integration ten years after the Supreme Court's decision requiring school desegregation. It depicts a shy little black girl, about six years old, being escorted to school by four tall deputy U.S. marshals. A red tomato that has just been smashed against a white wall provides a strong color accent. Another powerful painting, *Southern Justice* (June 20, 1965), reminds the viewer of the three black men who were murdered for their activism on behalf of civil rights in Mississippi.

Also alluding to the racial issue but with a positive message was *New Kids in the Neighborhood* (January 16, 1967). Three white children on the right side of the painting are looking at two black children fac-

ing them on the left. A large moving van between them is being unloaded. The five children, all about the same age, express some apprehension as well as anticipation of new playmates but no hostility. It is clear that they have several things in common. One of the white boys has baseball gloves, as does the black boy. The black girl is holding her pet, a white cat, in her arms. The white girl also has a pet, a black and brown dog, sitting at her feet. Rockwell is optimistic that all will end well.

This was a new and lesser known side of Rockwell. Although magazine editors and advertising agencies continued to commission his work, the public interest in his art had waned. In the early 1970's, however, a revival took place. It actually began in 1968, when Bernard Danenberg, a New York art dealer, arranged an exhibition in his Madison Avenue galleries. He placed *Saying Grace* (1951), voted as Rockwell's most popular painting, in the window and exhibited forty of Rockwell's paintings in the gallery. Harry N. Abrams, a publisher of art books, noticed that while long lines of people were waiting to get into an Andrew Wyeth exhibit at the nearby Whitney Museum of American Art, no one was at the Danenberg Galleries. Abrams decided to publish a book of reproductions of Rockwell's art as a sixty-year retrospective with a text by Thomas S. Buechner. Six years after the book was published, on November 8, 1978, Rockwell died in his home in Stockbridge.

### Summary

The majority of Norman Rockwell's work depicts the positive side of American middle-class life. A storyteller, Rockwell captured witty or comic situations in which viewers could recognize themselves. The public loved his pictures. He helped them see the America that he had observed and that they might not have noticed.

In the debate concerning fine arts versus commercial art, a change in attitude toward Rockwell's work is taking place, "upgrading" it to fine arts. His own appreciation of great art is evident in his painting *The Connoisseur* (1962), which depicts a huge modern painting in the style of Jackson Pollock. *The Art Critic* (1955) incorporates two seventeenth century paintings in the style of Peter Paul Rubens and Frans Hals. His *Triple Self-Portrait* (1960) includes copies of self-portraits by Albrecht Dürer, Rembrandt, and Vincent van Gogh, with a reference to a cubist portrait by Pablo Picasso.

After the Norman Rockwell Art Museum opened in 1993, it has become increasingly clear that Rockwell's place in American art history is secure. Located in Stockbridge, Massachusetts, the museum holds the world's largest collection of original Rockwell art.

### Bibliography

Buechner, Thomas S. *Norman Rockwell: Artist and Illustrator.* New York: Abrams, 1970. This book is a serious study by a Rockwell expert.

———. *Norman Rockwell: A Sixty Year Retrospective. A Catalogue of an Exhibition Organized by Bernard Danenberg Galleries, New York.* New York: Abrams, 1972. This is the catalogue for an exhibition of Rockwell's work that traveled to nine U.S. museums from February 11, 1972, to April 15, 1973.

Finch, Christopher. *Norman Rockwell's America.* New York: Abrams, 1975. Finch's richly illustrated account of Rockwell's art focuses on his magazine covers.

———. *Norman Rockwell: 322 Magazine Covers.* New York: Abbeville Press, 1979. Finch deals with Rockwell's *Saturday Evening Post* covers.

Graebner, William. "Norman Rockwell and American Mass Culture: The Crisis of Representation in the Great Depression." *Prospects* 22 (1997). Graebner considers Rockwell's work during the Depression, his experimentation with different techniques, and his final relegation to illustration.

Guptill, Arthur L. *Norman Rockwell Illustrator.* 3d ed. New York: Watson-Guptill, 1970. In the final chapter, Guptill discusses Rockwell's creative and technical procedure, his methods of study, and painting in fifteen steps from idea to delivery of the finished picture.

Marling, Karal Ann. *Norman Rockwell.* New York: Abrams in association with the National Museum of American Art, Smithsonian Institution, 1997. In this competent biography, Marling, an art historian, discusses Rockwell in the context of fine arts versus commercial art, regarding him as a great artist in both realms. Includes one hundred illustrations.

———. "Norman Rockwell: Great American Artist?" *American Enterprise* 9, no. 2 (March-April, 1998). Focuses on realism in the works of Rockwell.

Moffatt, Laura Norton. *Norman Rockwell: A Definitive Catalogue.* 2 vols. Stockbridge, Mass.: Norman Rockwell Museum at Stockbridge, 1986. Moffatt's book illustrates all of Rockwell's known finished paintings, in some cases with preliminary sketches and studies. It is a very useful work to get an overall view. Includes 3,594 illustrations and 96 color plates.

Murray, Stuart, and James McCabe, eds. *Norman Rockwell's Four Freedoms: Images that Inspire a Nation.* Stockbridge, Mass.: Berkshire House, 1993. This book includes several essays on the *Four Freedoms* and a foreword by Laurie Norton Moffatt. Richly illustrated with color plates as well as early sketches and drawings of the *Four Freedoms*, it offers a good summary of the impact of these paintings.

Rockwell, Norman. *My Adventures as an Illustrator.* New York: Doubleday, 1960. This seemingly light-hearted autobiography gives some insight into the complexity of this artist. Includes numerous illustrations, many in color, and a forward and afterward by Tom Rockwell.

———. *The Norman Rockwell Album*, New York: Doubleday, 1961. This handsome collection of Rockwell's work reveals his concern for people.

*Elvy Setterqvist O'Brien*

# RICHARD RODGERS

*Born:* June 28, 1902; New York, New York
*Died:* December 30, 1979; New York, New York
*Area of Achievement:* Musical theater
*Contribution:* In the course of his sixty-year career as a Broadway composer, Richard Rodgers helped to establish the prototype of the American musical.

## Early Life

Richard Rodgers was born in New York City at the dawn of the twentieth century. Tensions created by live-in grandparents and a competitive older brother were dispelled when Dr. William and Mamie Rodgers gathered the family around the Steinway to sing and play songs from current Broadway shows. It was here that Richard Rodgers received his first taste of the Broadway musical.

Rodgers started to play the piano at age four. Although he was given formal lessons, he was much happier picking out show tunes by ear. The family marveled at the boy's achievements, and Rodgers quickly learned that music was a sure way of getting attention.

Rodgers had been stagestruck from his first visit to the theater. When he discovered the musicals of Jerome Kern, he quickly adopted Kern's ideals as his own. Rodgers aspired to create a new form of American musical theater free from European stuffiness and grounded in a conscious attempt to relate songs to story.

Rodgers' parents encouraged their son's ambition to be a Broadway composer. When Rodgers attempted his first amateur score at the age of fifteen, his father and brother Mortimer helped with the lyrics and, through his father's efforts, he got his first copyright on a song.

In order to pursue his career, he needed a lyric writer. When a mutual friend introduced him to Lorenz Hart, the professional attraction was immediate. They not only shared a disdain of the childish, old-fashioned quality of current musicals, but they also had a mutual hero in Kern. Hart's eccentric, disheveled appearance and mercurial personality, however, were the antithesis of his new partner's dependability and practicality. (Despite his boyish face and expressive eyes, Rodgers was known for his conservative habits and sober appearance.)

In 1919, Rodgers enrolled at Columbia University, primarily to be able to write the Varsity Show with his new partner. The team soon moved from amateur status to professional when Lew Fields, a respected Broadway producer, chose songs from two of the Varsity Shows for *A Lonely Romeo* (1919) and *Poor Little Ritz Girl* (1920).

Buoyed by the encouragement of his family and friends, Rodgers left Columbia after two years to study music at Juilliard. By 1925, however, in debt to his father and frustrated by his inability to get professional recognition on Broadway, the young composer nearly took a job in the garment business. An offer to write *The Garrick Gaieties* (1925) for the Theatre Guild, one of New York's most prestigious producing organizations, became the unexpected opportunity that launched Rodgers and Hart's career on Broadway.

## Life's Work

Rodgers and Hart rapidly became one of Broadway's most important songwriting teams. Between 1925 and 1930, they wrote fifteen full scores. Most were hits. Their greatest successes were shows in which they experimented with new subjects, ranging from the American Revolution to King Arthur's court.

Rodgers married Dorothy Feiner in 1930 and, in the same year, signed a film contract and moved to Hollywood. Although he and Hart were challenged by their early work, they missed New York. Both returned to Manhattan soon after learning in the press that they had been all but forgotten on Broadway.

The late 1930's were vintage years for Rodgers and Hart. *On Your Toes* (1936) was the first musical to incorporate a ballet into the story of a musical, *The Boys from Syracuse* (1938) was the first musical inspired by one of William Shakespeare's plays, and *Pal Joey* (1940) was one of the first musicals that did not sugarcoat the disagreeable qualities of its characters.

In the early 1940's, Hart became increasingly self-destructive and unpredictable. Despite the critics's doubts about Rodgers's ability to succeed without Hart, the composer had to find another collaborator. In 1943, Rodgers teamed up with Oscar Hammerstein II (an old friend from the Varsity Shows at Columbia), and together they wrote the landmark musical *Oklahoma!*

Hammerstein was a playwright as well as a lyricist. His work with Jerome Kern on *Show Boat* (1927) had been an attempt at the kind of cohesive

musical play that Rodgers wanted to write. Their plan for *Oklahoma!* was to write a show in which the songs, story, dances, and stage design were so well integrated that no single element would overshadow any other. This not only represented a crystallization of the conceptual and structural ideals tested by Rodgers and Hart but also set a precedent for all subsequent Rodgers and Hammerstein collaborations. After Hart's death in 1943, Rodgers seized the chance for a second career with Hammerstein. Rodgers and Hammerstein also became business partners. They produced others' work in addition to their own—Irving Berlin's *Annie Get Your Gun* (1946) was their most successful venture—and established their own publishing house, Williamson Music, Inc.

In the 1940's, Rodgers and Hammerstein achieved unprecedented success. Both *Oklahoma!* (which would hold the record for the longest-running musical in Broadway history for fifteen years) and *South Pacific* (1949) received Pulitzer Prizes; *Carousel* (1945) became their most ambitious attempt at the integration of song and story; and *The King and I* (1951), following the pattern of its predecessors, became the third Rodgers and Hammerstein musical to run for more than one thousand performances.

Rodgers was operated on for cancer of the jaw in 1955 and in 1957 was treated for depression. Returning to work proved to be excellent medicine: He teamed with Hammerstein to write *Flower Drum Song* in 1958 and *The Sound of Music* in 1959. Hammerstein died ten months after the opening of *The Sound of Music*, at the age of sixty-five.

Having outlived two of the most successful collaborations in the history of Broadway, Rodgers had to find a way of continuing to work after Hammerstein's death. After a failed attempt at forming a partnership with lyricist Alan Jay Lerner, he became his own lyric writer for *No Strings* (1962), which incorporated an onstage orchestra into the plot.

In the last years of his life, Rodgers continued to find new projects and collaborators to satisfy his indefatigable need to work. A heart attack and a second bout with cancer made it difficult for him to speak clearly and walk. Although he continued to write beautiful songs, neither the scripts nor the lyrics of his final projects could compare favorably with those of his successes with Hart and Hammerstein.

After sixty years in the professional theater, Richard Rodgers died on December 30, 1979, at the age of seventy-seven—seven months after the opening of his final musical, *I Remember Mama*.

### Summary

Although the theater songs that were the result of Rodgers and Hart's twenty-five-year collaboration represent some of the best work of his career, the eighteen-year collaboration between Rodgers and Hammerstein proved to be the most influential partnership in the history of the American musical theater. As a result of the success of *Oklahoma!, Carousel, South Pacific*, and *The King and I*, the definition of the Broadway musical was irrevocably changed.

The most successful Rodgers and Hammerstein musicals were inspired by solid literary sources, were strictly American in character despite some exotic settings, and were painstakingly structured so that the songs would be believable expressions of the characters. Both men supervised every aspect of their productions and earned reputations for setting standards of excellence, fairness, and generosity in all of their dealings.

Ironically, the overwhelming popularity that came to Rodgers, combined with the disappointments of his last five musicals, generated a distorted perception of his career. Many came to view him as an outdated Establishment hero. A look at his contribution to the American musical theater from 1925 to 1962, however, reveals not only remarkable quality and quantity (he wrote fifty-nine musical scores and more than one thousand songs) but also a persistence in breaking with convention. His music has influenced generations of musical theater artists in America and has bolstered the reputation of the musical in the United States and throughout the world.

### Bibliography

Engel, Lehman. *The American Musical Theatre*. New York: Macmillan, 1975. A history of the American musical theater and the best analysis of musical and dramatic structure based on the Rodgers and Hammerstein prototype.

Ewen, David. *Richard Rodgers*. New York: Holt, 1957. Draws upon reminiscences and firsthand information from Rodgers' family, friends, and colleagues. Includes photos, a copy of Rodgers' first copyrighted song, and many useful appendices.

Green, Stanley. *The Rodgers and Hammerstein Story*. New York: Day, and London: Allen, 1963. Focuses on the parallel careers of Rodgers and Hammerstein before and after their collaboration. Includes direct quotes from recorded conversations. A provocative concept but a generally uninspired text.

———, ed. *Rodgers and Hammerstein Fact Book: A Record of Their Works and with Other Collaborators*. New York: Drama Book Specialists, 1980. The most comprehensive, meticulously researched reference book on Rodgers and Hammerstein. Includes biographical and production fact sheets and selected critical reviews from professional productions.

Hyland, William G. *Richard Rodgers*. New Haven, Conn.: Yale University Press, 1998. Comprehensive biographical study of Rodgers from his affluent childhood in then-fashionable Harlem to his collaboration with Lorenz Hart.

McConachie, Bruce A. "The 'Oriental' Musicals of Rodgers and Hammerstein and the U.S. War in Southeast Asia." *Theatre Journal* 46, no. 3 (October, 1994). The author argues that the Rodgers and Hammerstein musicals *The King and I, South Pacific,* and *Flower Drum Song* fostered the kind of American imperialistic attitudes that led to the Vietnam War.

Rodgers, Richard. *Musical Stages: An Autobiography*. New York: Random House, 1975; London: Allen, 1976. Contains useful personal anecdotes, photos, descriptions of his working methods, and analyses of some of his most successful songs. Some insight into the forces that shaped his career. Written with characteristic modesty and dry humor.

Suskin, Steven. *Show Tunes: The Songs, Shows and Careers of Broadway's Major Composers*. Rev. ed. New York: Oxford University Press, 1999. Annotated reference of all published songs. Valuable resource for musical theater scholars and enthusiasts. All entries are cross-referenced.

Wilder, Alec. "Richard Rodgers." In *American Popular Song: The Great Innovators, 1900-1950*. Edited by James T. Maher. Oxford and New York: Oxford University Press, 1972. Analysis of Rodgers' most musically satisfying songs. Author admits preference for songs written with Hart. Analysis of songs based upon their inherent musical strength, rather than their dramatic contexts.

*Marilyn Plotkins*

# WILL ROGERS

*Born:* November 4, 1879; near Oologah, Indian Territory (modern Oklahoma)

*Died:* August 15, 1935; Walakpa Lagoon (near Point Barrow), Alaska

*Areas of Achievement:* Entertainment, journalism, and humanitarianism

*Contribution:* An internationally prominent humorist and satirist, Rogers functioned as a constructive social critic and humanitarian as well as an entertainer.

## Early Life

William Penn Adair Rogers was born November 4, 1879, in the Indian Territory of the United States of America near what eventually became Oologah, Oklahoma. Both of his parents came from the Indian Territory and contributed to his status as a quarter-blood Cherokee Indian. His father, Clement Van (Clem) Rogers, was a rough and wealthy rancher, farmer, banker, and businessman, in addition to being a prominent politician. His mother, Mary Schrimsher Rogers, was a loving woman who came from a financially successful and politically powerful family. Will was the youngest of eight children, three of whom died at birth, and the only male to survive childhood.

Rogers developed a lasting love for the life and basic skills of the cowboy, horseback riding and roping, in his early years. At home, he adored his affectionate mother but developed a complex and not completely positive relationship with his father. Rogers clearly loved his father, who provided a masculine establishment figure with whom to identify. At the same time, Will possessed a strong personality which eventually clashed with that of the elder Rogers. Then, at age ten, disaster entered the young Oklahoman's life when his mother died and the closing of the open range heralded an end to the cowboy's life. These conditions changed a relatively secure and happy child into a sad wanderer who sought desperately to replace the love and sense of purpose that had been taken from him.

Tension increased between Rogers and his father in the years following Mary Rogers' death. The elder Rogers was particularly infuriated by his son's uneven performance in school. Between the ages of eight and eighteen, Rogers attended six different educational institutions and left each one under questionable circumstances. His main interests during these years were playing the class clown and participating in theatrical activities. He also developed a growing fascination with trick roping. In 1898, after running away from the last school he attended, the eighteen-year-old embarked on a seven-year odyssey. He worked variously as a wandering cowboy, as the manager of the family ranch, and as a trick-rope artist in Wild West shows, then turned to vaudeville. His travels took him literally across the globe. Such behavior merely increased the elder Rogers' dissatisfaction with his son. The son, on the other hand, manifested guilt at not having lived up to the father's expectations and example of success.

One final factor remains to be discussed in connection with Rogers' teenage and early adult years: his sensitivity to his Cherokee Indian heritage. This sensitivity was evident in his militant reaction to any criticism of Indians or those of Indian ancestry. Furthermore, because of his own Indian background, he was the victim of racial prejudice in trying to establish relationships with women.

The year 1905 proved to be a crucial one for Rogers. He went to New York and entered vaudeville as a trick-rope artist. At the same time, he began making serious proposals of marriage to Betty Blake of Roger, Arkansas, whom he had first met in 1899. When Rogers and Blake were married in 1908, the Oklahoman had taken the first step in what proved to be one of the most successful entertainment careers in American history. Perhaps more important, however, these events assisted Rogers in overcoming the sadness which had enshrouded him since youth: His marriage helped to replace the female love and sense of belonging he had lost when his mother died, while his success in show business enabled him to establish a more positive relationship with his father and compensated Rogers for the loss of the cowboy life.

## Life's Work

Will Rogers' career can be divided into four periods. During the first, from 1905 to 1915, he became a successful vaudevillian. He began his stage career with a trick-roping act, in which he lassoed simultaneously a moving horse and its rider. Gradually, the young performer began making comical remarks as his lariats whirled about. By 1911, he was a bona fide monologuist, making humorous comments about other artists and the theater world. Traveling the famous Orpheum Circuit, he used the same material each evening. Rogers also toured England and Western Europe several times. The Rogers family numbered five by 1915: Will and Betty, William Vann Rogers, Jr. (born 1911), Mary Amelia Rogers (born 1913), and James Blake Rogers (born 1915).

The next stage in Rogers' rise to prominence started in 1915, when he began performing in Florenz Ziegfeld's Midnight Frolic. The Midnight Frolic was staged on the roof of the New Amsterdam Theater in New York City, the home of the Ziegfeld Follies. Rogers encountered a problem working in the Midnight Frolic. Since it attracted many repeat customers, he had to struggle to present new material each night. Eventually, the daily newspapers provided him with constantly changing material concerning contemporary society upon which he could base his humorous monologues.

Rogers' career received a giant boost in 1916, when he joined the Ziegfeld Follies. Within two years, Rogers had finished developing the basic characteristics of his humor. Fittingly, it was at this time that the budding comedian became known as the Cowboy Philosopher and began each performance with his famous line: "Well, all I know is what I read in the newspapers." Rogers' humor was based on the following precepts: Proven material was mixed with continually changing jokes about contemporary news; neutrality on controversial topics was maintained by poking fun at all sides; truth and realism, sometimes exaggerated, provided the best foundation for humor; the comical style involved the projection of Rogers' personality. With his humor resting on these tenets, Will quickly assumed the characteristics of a cracker-barrel philosopher and satirist who functioned as a constructive social critic. As such, he became increasingly serious about what he said.

An additional facet of Rogers' life emerged during World War I: his genuine humanitarianism. He pledged one tenth of what he made during the conflict to the Red Cross and the Salvation Army, and he was extremely active in raising funds for both organizations.

The third stage of Rogers' career encompassed the years from 1918 to 1928. He became a national figure during this era, expanding into new fields of endeavor. Much of his success was a result of his physical appearance and bearing. Slender, athletic, six feet tall, with handsome facial features that reflected his Indian heritage, Rogers performed in cowboy regalia, chomping on an ever-present wad of chewing gum, and twirling ropes which he watched while making detached comments concerning contemporary events. His ungrammatical speech, Western accent, contagious smile, and unruly forelock merely added to the pretense of an illiterate, homespun yokel, perceptively satirizing society. This pose enabled Rogers to get away with saying things that other performers would never have considered saying.

In 1918, Samuel Goldwyn offered Rogers a starring role in the film *Laughing Bill Hyde*. The humorist hesitantly accepted, since the New Jersey shooting location of the film allowed him to continue working in the Ziegfeld Follies. *Laughing Bill Hyde* proved to be a reasonable success, and Goldwyn presented Rogers with a two-year contract to make motion pictures in California. He agreed to the arrangement and moved to Los Angeles. Rogers added another dimension to his work in 1919, with the publication of two books: *Rogers-isms: The Cowboy Philosopher on the Peace Conference* and *Rogers-isms: The Cowboy Philosopher on Prohibition* (1919).

The move to California was not without its troubles. The newest Rogers baby, Fred Stone Rogers, died of diphtheria when he was eighteen months old. The numerous two-reel motion pictures which Rogers made for Goldwyn did not turn the aspiring actor into a star, and when his contract with Goldwyn was not renewed in 1921, Rogers himself made three two-reel pictures in which he played the leading role. A complex set of circumstances resulted in his losing a large amount of money in the venture. Faced with bankruptcy, the determined performer left Betty and the children in California while he returned to New York and the Ziegfeld Follies. Between 1921 and 1923, Rogers launched a banquet-speaking career and began a syndicated weekly newspaper column, in addition to his work for Ziegfeld. Two years of laboring around the clock in this fashion enabled him to pay off his debts.

Rogers continued to pursue a career in motion pictures, despite his initial difficulties. Thus, in 1923, after he had taken care of his money problems, he returned to Los Angeles and signed a contract with the Hal E. Roach Studio to make a series of two-reel comedies. Thirteen films resulted from this agreement. They were more successful than the Goldwyn films but Rogers was still not a great motion-picture success. He eventually reached the conclusion that the problem resided with the unwillingness of studios and directors to allow him to

project his own personality. Frustrated, the humorist once again returned to New York and the Ziegfeld Follies. A third book, *Illiterate Digest*, composed mainly of weekly newspaper articles, appeared in 1924.

Rogers added still another dimension to his work in the mid-1920's. He began his one-person lecture tour in 1925, repeating it in 1926 and in 1927, and periodically thereafter. Additionally, the energetic satirist published a number of magazine articles for the *Saturday Evening Post* and *Life* (at that time a humor magazine). In 1926, he began his short daily syndicated newspaper column, which frequently appeared under the caption "Will Rogers Says." Two more books followed quickly: *Letters of a Self-Made Diplomat to His President* (1926) and *There's Not a Bathing Suit in Russia and Other Bare Facts* (1927). These were collections of articles he had written for the *Saturday Evening Post*, as was his 1929 offering, *Ether and Me: Or, "Just Relax."*

In the 1920's, Rogers also expanded his humanitarian efforts. While in Europe during 1926, he traveled to Dublin, Ireland, and did a benefit for the survivors of a theater fire. The same year, he took similar action to assist survivors of Florida tornadoes and Mississippi River flood victims. His daily and weekly newspaper columns complemented these efforts, repeatedly appealing for public support.

The final phase in Rogers' professional evolution covered the years from 1929 to 1935. During this time, Rogers was catapulted into the elite arena of superstardom. His salary, popularity, influence, and the range of media he employed to communicate with his massive audiences all contributed to this achievement.

Rogers made his first sound motion picture, *They Had to See Paris*, in 1929 for Fox Film Corporation. It was successful, and Rogers became a star overnight. He soon signed a two-year contract with Fox to make five pictures. A leading figure in the development of sound films, in 1934 Rogers was voted the nation's most popular box-office attraction in a poll taken among independent theater owners. It is estimated that at the time of his death in 1935, Rogers was making one million dollars a year performing in motion pictures, a sum then unsurpassed by any screen personality.

Rogers made infrequent radio appearances during the 1920's but did not feel comfortable with the medium. Nevertheless, he did seventy-five radio programs between 1927 and 1935. His radio appearances increased after 1930, when he did fourteen programs sponsored by E. R. Squibb and Sons. A longer but more sporadic series was sponsored by the Gulf Oil Corporation between 1933 and 1935. In time, Rogers became one of the most popular radio entertainers in the country; as early as 1930, he was receiving $350 per minute for his radio performances.

The onset of the Depression in 1929 elicited a predictable response from Rogers. He devoted more and more time to benefits for victims of all sorts of natural disasters and the disadvantaged. These activities took him all over the United States and as far afield as Nicaragua.

Haphazard vacation plans in August of 1935 resulted in Rogers joining the famous aviator Wiley Post on a flight in a newly constructed plane of Post's design. Plans called for the two to fly from Seattle, Washington, to Point Barrow, Alaska, with stops in between. The plane crashed on August 15, 1935, at Walakpa Lagoon, sixteen miles short of its destination. Both Rogers, age fifty-five, and Post were killed in what became one of the most famous air tragedies of the twentieth century.

### Summary

Rogers' philosophy remained consistent throughout his career. He generally sided with the disadvantaged and weak against the powerful and wealthy on both domestic and international questions. This outlook in part reflected Rogers' early experiences. His Indian heritage, for example, exposed him to racial prejudice. Having experienced such prejudice, he became more understanding of society's disadvantaged people and more supportive of the weak and the poor.

Underlying Rogers' humor was a combination of realism and optimism. Regardless of how bad the truth seemed to be, there was almost always a positive message in what he said and wrote. This quality reflected the experience of his nation and region. In both, the task of carving a civilization out of a primitive environment made reality impossible to ignore and hope necessary for survival.

In the entertainment world, Rogers established several important precedents. His method of remaining neutral on controversial topics by criticizing all involved established an approach to satire which has been employed by succeeding generations of performers. His commitment to humanitarian activities set a standard which entertainers have followed. Finally, his reliance on contemporary news as the basis for his constantly changing material has been widely imitated.

### Bibliography

Croy, Homer. *Our Will Rogers*. New York: Duell Sloan, 1953. One of the numerous biographies available on Rogers, this volume is extremely valuable because of the interviews Croy conducted. Croy also knew Rogers personally during the latter's motion-picture career.

Day, Donald. *Will Rogers: A Biography*. New York: McKay, 1962. This volume is unbalanced since it overemphasizes the importance of the early days in Rogers' relationship with his wife. Includes no footnotes or bibliography. Well written, but of questionable value for research.

Keith, Harold. *Boy's Life of Will Rogers*. New York: Crowell, 1938. A valuable work for reminiscences by hundreds of Rogers' relatives and friends, supported by the author's study of books, magazines, and newspapers that contained information by or about Rogers.

Ketchum, Richard M. *Will Rogers: His Life and Times*. New York: American Heritage, 1973. This book is well written, accompanied by an excellent collection of photographs, and based on many materials not previously used. Unfortunately, it is not documented, fails to describe causative factors in Rogers' life, and does not analyze the humorist's philosophy.

Meachum, Jon. "What Will Rogers Could Teach the Age of Limbaugh." *Washington Monthly* 26, no. 1-2 (January-February, 1994). Compares and contrasts the radio styles and messages of Rogers and Rush Limbaugh.

Milsten, David Randolph. *An Appreciation of Will Rogers*. San Antonio, Tex.: Naylor, 1935. Valuable for interviews with close friends and associates of Rogers.

Robinson, Ray. *American Original: A Life of Will Rogers*. New York: Oxford University Press, 1996. One of the few biographies of Rogers to deal successfully with his political commentary. Filled with anecdotes and information on important individuals of the time such as Flo Ziegfield and Samuel Goldwyn.

Rogers, Betty. *Will Rogers: The Story of His Life Told by His Wife*. New York: Garden City Publishing, 1943. Betty's recollection of her life with Will is a key source. Contains no footnotes or bibliography. Rogers states that her direct quotes frequently come from her husband's newspaper articles.

Rogers, Will. *The Autobiography of Will Rogers*. Edited by Donald Day. Boston: Houghton Mifflin, 1949. Day mixes in various materials from numerous other sources and does not inform the reader. The work is not documented.

———. *The Writings of Will Rogers*. 23 vols. Edited by Joseph A. Stout, Jr., Peter C. Rollins, Steven K. Gragert, and James M. Smallwood. Stillwater: Oklahoma State University Press, 1973-1984. A twenty-three-volume set of the edited, annotated writings of Rogers with some radio broadcasts included. Includes a subject index for the entire set; most of the individual volumes possess an index as well.

Rollins, Peter C. *Will Rogers: A Bio-Bibliography*. Westport, Conn.: Greenwood Press, 1984. The most significant resource for anyone doing research on Rogers. It contains a wealth of information ranging from a biographical overview to a complete listing of the available primary and secondary sources. This material is not only described, but much of it is also summarized and evaluated. A treasure trove without equal.

Trent, Spi M. *My Cousin Will Rogers: Intimate and Untold Tales*. New York: Putnam, 1938. Trent was a close companion of Rogers during the latter's youth and early adulthood. His work is a valuable source for those years. It must be used cautiously when dealing with the period after Rogers' marriage.

*S. Fred Roach*

# CHARLES STEWART ROLLS and SIR FREDERICK HENRY ROYCE

## Charles Stewart Rolls

*Born:* August 28, 1877; London, England
*Died:* July 12, 1910; Bournemouth, England

*Areas of Achievement:* Automotive engineering, aviation, and business

## Sir Frederick Henry Royce

*Born:* March 27, 1863; Alwalton, England

*Died:* April 22, 1933; West Wittering, England

*Areas of Achievement:* Automotive and aeronautical engineering

*Contribution:* Combining their talents, Royce produced, and Rolls marketed, an automobile built to the highest standards of engineering excellence. Additionally, Royce designed a series of engines which powered many of the British aircraft of the two world wars.

### Early Lives

Charles Stewart Rolls was born on August 28, 1877, at his parents' London residence on Berkeley Square. He was the third son of John Rolls, the first Baron Llangattock, and Georgiana, née Maclean, the ninth Baronet of Morvaren's daughter. Rolls was educated at Eton and then Cambridge University, receiving his B.A. (1898) and M.A. (1902) in mechanical engineering. Rolls was an avid bicyclist in college, serving as captain of Cambridge's racing team in 1897. Later, his love of sports and speed was manifested in cars, hot-air balloons, and, finally, airplanes. (At Cambridge, Rolls owned the first automobile ever seen there.) Photographs reveal a sturdy, handsome man with dark hair, a dark mustache, and dark eyes; good-looking as he was, however, Rolls was never married.

A great contrast to Rolls in background and personality was Frederick Henry Royce. He was born on March 27, 1863, near Peterborough, England, the youngest son of James Royce, a poor flour miller, and Mary, née King, a farmer's daughter. The Royce family met financial disaster when the father died in 1873, leaving Henry to fend for himself when only ten years of age, with two years' schooling. Royce worked as a newsboy and then as a messenger for a London post office; in 1877, he was apprenticed through an aunt's generosity to the Great Northern Railway's shops in Peterborough, where he worked on locomotives. Royce did not finish the apprenticeship—his aunt's money gave out—but his association with the beautifully crafted locomotives of Victorian England left him with a lifelong love of elegance expressed through machinery. In 1884, Royce set up a firm in Manchester with his friend Ernest Claremont, to manufacture electrical appliances. The firm, called F. H. Royce and Company, soon was known for its electric bell sets; by the 1890's, it was prospering, and Royce was manufacturing dynamos and electric cranes. The white-bearded Royce looked prematurely old; chronically tired and malnourished (when faced with some interesting mechanical problem he often

*Charles Stewart Rolls*

missed sleep and meals), Royce's health broke in 1911, and he never regained it.

### Lives' Work

Rolls and Royce met through Rolls's need to discover a reliable British automobile. Rolls had joined the Royal Automobile Club in 1897 and became involved in international motorcar racing—an expensive pastime. To supplement his income, in 1902 Rolls set up a car sales and repair business in London, using his wealthy friends as customers. At the turn of the century, most luxury autos were French-built but were still not very reliable. Searching for a dependable (and British) automobile, he was led to Royce through a mutual friend, Henry Edmonds, one of Royce's company directors. Royce had bought his first car in 1903, but was convinced that he could build a better one; soon, Royce had constructed a two-cylinder, ten-horsepower auto which was successfully road-tested on April 1, 1904. Edmonds persuaded Rolls to test-drive the car, although Rolls did not like two-cylinder engines, thinking that they vibrated excessively. Nevertheless, Royce's automobile appealed to him, for its well-built engine ran practically silently, with no detectable vibration. Rolls drove it from Manchester to London and ordered nineteen more to sell.

A holding company was established to market Royce's automobiles, and in November, 1906, it and Rolls's car business were united as Rolls-Royce Limited, a publicly held concern. From the beginning, all of Royce's cars were marketed with the double name. Rolls and his business manager, Claude Johnson, were excellent promoters; Rolls, an accomplished motorist, won many races with the autos, while Johnson aggressively advertised them as "The Best Cars in the World."

It was decided that Rolls-Royce would produce one standard but superb model, to escape the expenses of diversification. This was the Silver Ghost, introduced at the 1906 London Motor Show. It had a six-cylinder engine producing forty to fifty horsepower, had an eye-catching silver finish (Johnson's idea), was extremely durable, and remained in production for nineteen years—one year longer than the Model T Ford. The Silver Ghost established Rolls-Royce's reputation as the world leader in luxury cars; it was followed in production by a series of Phantoms (built from 1925 to 1939). Although Rolls-Royce was never to mass-produce automobiles, the Silver Ghost's popularity soon forced the firm to transfer the motor section to bigger quarters in Derby.

With the company's formidable reputation for motoring dependability established, Rolls turned to piloting balloons and airplanes. In 1908, he visited France to fly with Wilbur Wright and bought one of Wright's biplanes. Rolls became the first person to fly both ways across the English Channel, taking off from Dover, circling Calais, and returning to his starting point, on June 2, 1910. Rolls's life tragically ended the next month, however, when his plane's tailgear disintegrated at an air show in Bournemouth, England. The holder of so many records established another one with his death: Rolls was Great Britain's first air fatality.

Royce, meanwhile, continued as the guiding force behind the company. A designer rather than a businessman, he was eased out as head of the firm in January, 1910, and appointed "engineer-in-chief." He was shocked by Rolls's death, and his health collapsed in 1911. Henceforth, Royce shuttled between his English home at St. Margaret's Bay and a villa at Le Canadel in southern France. In this sequestered manner, Royce continued to pour out blueprints for new engines and suggestions for improvements to existing models, which were relayed to Derby for implementation. (Royce was fortunate to find a talented technical director in Ernest W. Hives, who managed the company's production until his retirement in the 1950's.)

During World War I, civilian auto production ceased, but some Rolls-Royces were converted to armored cars and saw action against German cavalry in France and, under Lawrence of Arabia, against the Turks in the Middle East. Meanwhile, the British government wanted airplane engines. Royce had never designed one and was not interested in doing so but was characteristically displeased with those existing and decided to build something better. Royce designed a series of engines, named after birds of prey. First came the Eagle, a twelve-cylinder engine, then its smaller version, the Falcon, which propelled the Bristol Fighter, then the Hawk, used for powering blimps, and finally the Condor, a large engine developing six to seven hundred horsepower, intended for use on the Handley-Page four-engined bomber (dubbed the "Bloody Paralyser" by its pilots). Altogether, Rolls-Royce built more than sixty percent of British engines which saw service in World War I; the Eagle was the most widely employed.

Rolls-Royce resumed auto production with the war's end in 1918, but Royce's design activities stayed focused on air engines. The Kestrel, introduced in 1927, was a revolutionary engine cast in aluminum which, with its small frontal profile, allowed for a sharp-nosed, more streamlined plane, thus changing aircraft design significantly. The Kestrel powered planes in many air forces, including that of the Nazis, and a derivative of the type drove a special automobile to a world land-speed record of 357.5 miles per hour in 1937 at Bonneville Salt Flats, Utah. The last engine on which Royce personally worked before his death on April 22, 1933, was a predecessor of the famous "Merlin" of World War II. Royce died before the Merlin's final development, but his design legacy proved crucial to Great Britain in World War II. Manufactured in four variants, all with twelve cylinders arranged in a "V" bank of six on each side, this engine successively powered the Hurricane and Spitfire fighters, the four-engined Lancaster bomber, the two-engined De Havilland Mosquito, and (in an American-built version) the versatile P-51 Mustang fighter. Including American production, more than 166,000 Merlins were built. British air chief Arthur William, Lord Tedder, later stated, "Three factors contributed to . . . victory—the skill and bravery of the pilots, the Rolls-Royce Merlin engine and the availability of suitable fuel."

### Summary

Charles Stewart Rolls and Sir Frederick Henry Royce had symbiotic careers; the former would have had no superlative cars to sell, the latter no clientele for whom to design them, without the other. Together, they created a firm which represented British industrial excellence to the world, and although the original company went bankrupt in 1971 as a result of faulty management, its successors (one manufacturing jet engines and gas turbines, the other Rolls-Royce cars) have continued in that tradition. Rolls appears essentially as a gifted dilettante, and Royce as perhaps the last in a long line of brilliant British mechanics and engineers, whose creations helped make England the home of the Industrial Revolution. A fanatical perfectionist, Royce designed the world's most engineering-dominated cars, with all parts of the engine and chassis able to operate indefinitely without overstress, given regular maintenance. Henry Ford once observed, "Royce was the only man to put heart into an automobile." A modest man who scarcely noticed when the grateful British government made him a baronet in 1930, Royce's life work was characterized by the motto "Whatever is rightly done, however humble, is noble."

### Bibliography


Beebe, Lucius. "The Rolls Mystique." *Horizon* (Winter, 1966): 40-48. Not directly concerned with either Rolls or Royce but a splendidly written article about their famous cars' appeal, written by a noted American railroad and automobile buff.

Fox, Mike, and Steve Smith. *Rolls-Royce: The Complete Works: The Best 599 Stories About the World's Best Car.* London and Boston: Faber, 1984. A book intended only for light reading. The compilers nevertheless give ample evidence of why Rolls-Royce cars enjoy their formidable reputation. Contains many good anecdotes, both true and apocryphal, about Rolls and Royce.

Harker, Ronald W. *The Engines Were Rolls-Royce: An Informal History of That Famous Company.* New York: Macmillan, 1979. An interesting, although partisan, history of the company, by its first test pilot, who was with Rolls-Royce from 1925 to 1971.

Keith, Sir Kenneth, Sir Stanley Hooker, and Samuel L. Higginbottom. *The Achievement of Excellence: The Story of Rolls-Royce.* New York: Newcomen Society, 1977. Consists of addresses by Keith (who served as chairman of Rolls-Royce in 1971), Hooker (who was the company's technical director), and Higginbottom (the company's president) to the Newcomen Society's annual meeting. Laudatory of the original company's achievements.

Lloyd, Ian. *Rolls-Royce: The Growth of a Firm.* London: Macmillan, 1978. Originally written as the author's Cambridge University dissertation, this scholarly work draws on company documents. Rolls and Royce are covered in the first two chapters, but the rest of the work (and its two successor volumes, *The Years of Endeavour* and *The Merlin at War*, both published also in 1978 by Macmillan) give the best description available of the great firm the two founders built.

Montagu of Beaulieu, Lord. *Rolls of Rolls-Royce: A Biography of the Hon. C. S. Rolls.* London: Cassell, 1966; South Brunswick, N.J.: Barnes, 1967. A well-written biography of Rolls. While Rolls's activities as a driver and pilot are emphasized, his relationship with Royce is covered in detail in chapter 6.

Nockolds, Harold. *The Magic of a Name: The Story of the Rolls-Royce Company.* London: Foulis, 1938. A history of Rolls-Royce's earlier years; concentrates on others besides the founders, such as Johnson and Hives.

Pemberton, Sir Max. *The Life of Sir Henry Royce: With Some Chapters from the Stories of the Late Charles S. Rolls and Claude Johnson*. London: Selwyn and Blount, 1930. The only full-length biography of the great designer; celebratory, having been written soon after his death.

*Thomas John Thomson*

## ERWIN ROMMEL

*Born:* November 15, 1891; Heidenheim an der Brentz, Württemberg, Germany

*Died:* October 14, 1944; Herrlingen, near Ulm, Germany

*Area of Achievement:* The military

*Contribution:* A legendary commander of World War II, Rommel, known as "The Desert Fox" for his cunning, achieved distinction for his actions in France and North Africa. His successes on the battlefield resulted from his courage and determination, his aggressive leadership, and his mastery of military tactics.

### Early Life

Erwin Johannes Eugen Rommel was born in Heidenheim an der Brentz, Germany, on November 15, 1891. The second son of a schoolmaster and mathematician, he was an indifferent student. A susceptibility to childhood illnesses prompted him to increase his stamina through athletic training. When he expressed an interest in a military career, his father attempted to dissuade him from a course so unpromising but later agreed to assist him. Once he had chosen a career, he sought to reach the top of his profession. He joined the Württemberg Sixth Infantry Regiment as a cadet on July 19, 1910; in the following year he entered officer training at the War Academy in Danzig. There he met Lucie Maria Mollin, the one woman in his life; they were married in 1916 while he was on military leave.

Rommel was commissioned a second lieutenant in time to enter World War I as a platoon leader. He became known for his bravery under fire and his aggressive leadership, fighting at Bleid, at Verdun, and in the Argonne, where he was awarded the Iron Cross. After recovery from a leg wound, he joined a mountain infantry division stationed in the Alps along the Romanian and Italian fronts. In a daring attack at the head of his men, who never numbered more than six hundred, he broke the Italian line, captured the strategically important Mount Matajur, and took nine thousand prisoners and quantities of matériel. For this feat he was awarded the Pour le Mérite (the "Blue Max"), Germany's highest military honor.

During the interval between wars, Rommel served as a commander of troops who put down insurrections and as a military instructor first at the Infantry School at Dresden and later at the War College, Pottsdam. His lectures were the basis of his *Infanterie greift an* (1937; *Attacks*, 1979), a book read with attention by Adolf Hitler.

### Life's Work

Rommel's career, like those of other German officers, began to advance with the rise of National Socialism and the rearming of the nation. Along with the rest of the army, Rommel took his oath of loyalty to Hitler in July, 1934. In 1935 he escorted Hitler in a review of troops at Goslar and attracted the attention of other Nazis by refusing to permit Schutzstaffel (SS) troops to take precedence over regular officers. During Hitler's trip to Czechoslovakia in 1938, he was in charge of troops providing security. When war erupted in Poland, he accompanied Hitler to the front as a staff officer. There he observed the successes of German armored (panzer) units and, when Hitler offered him his choice of commands, he selected a panzer division over infantry. He was appointed commander of the Seventh Panzer Division stationed on the Rhine River.

In the Blitzkrieg on France of May, 1940, Rommel's division crossed the Meuse and Sambre rivers, knifing through Belgium in a sweeping arc bypassing the Maginot Line. Near Arras, he encountered a sharp British counterattack that slowed the advance, but his forces prevailed over superior numbers. After a successful conclusion of the sweep, he moved south against Cherbourg, where he captured, among others, four French admirals.

Having triumphed in France, Hitler reluctantly posted two divisions to North Africa to reinforce Italian allies who had suffered a catastrophic defeat at the hands of British General Sir Archibald Wavell. Rommel, a lieutenant general, was named commander of the divisions that formed the nucleus of the Afrika Korps. Although nominally under the command of an Italian general and later under Field Marshal Albert Kesselring in a rather loose command structure, he usually had freedom of decision and independence.

The terrain of the 1941-1943 conflict in North Africa consisted largely of coastal desert stretching two thousand miles from Morocco to Egypt and up to two hundred miles inland. For Rommel it offered a vast theater in which to adapt the principles of Blitzkrieg against a British army whose leaders were trained in conventional defense and conservative attack strategy. Rommel conceived a grand ob-

jective that transcended his original purpose of assisting Italian allies. Driving eastward from Tunisia, he would capture British strongholds along the Mediterranean, until he reached Cairo. From there he would take the Suez Canal and then sweep around the east side of the Mediterranean until he reached the oil fields of Persia and Arabia.

Numerous adverse factors intervened to deny Rommel's dream of conquest. The German invasion of the Soviet Union (Operation Barbarossa) on June 22, 1941, meant that the first priority for men and matériel became the Eastern Front. Rommel's British opponents, with a well-equipped and sound army, learned how to counter his tactics and almost always outnumbered him. Further, British naval and air power in the Mediterranean, based at Malta, took a heavy toll on supplies sent to Rommel, while the British could bring their supplies around the Cape and through Suez, a longer but more reliable route.

Once in Tunisia, Rommel quickly went on the attack, driving Wavell's Eighth Army, now reduced because many units were sent to Greece, eastward toward the Gazala Line and Tobruk, the British port and stronghold. Breaking through the line, Rommel besieged Tobruk; he met a crushing counterattack in the British Operation Crusader. Both sides lost heavily, but Rommel ran short of supplies and fuel and was forced to lift the siege and withdraw to Al-Agheila in December, 1941.

In May, 1942, after resupply and reinforcements, Rommel renewed the attack on Tobruk, flanking the Gazala Line to the south with his main panzer units. In order to shorten his supply lines, he then breached the line from behind and brought through the Italian Ariete Division, placing it in a fortified defense position to the east. When British units moved up to attack and repair the break, the Ariete held while Rommel's Fifteenth and Twenty-first Panzer Divisions encircled them. In the Battle of the Cauldron, Rommel's forces inflicted losses so punishing that the British were forced to withdraw, leaving Tobruk to fall on June 20, 1942. Its cache of fuel, provisions, and vehicles resupplied Rommel's army, and the victory brought him the rank of field marshal.

Hardly pausing for rest, Rommel pressed his weary men after the retreating British and toward the next objective, Al-Alamein in western Egypt, where the British had established a strong defense line, bounded on the north by the sea and on the south by the impassable Qattara Depression. Behind extensive mine fields and obstacles, British General Sir Claude Auchinleck positioned his divisions and brigades across the desert in checkerboard fashion.

Rommel opened the attack against the southern portion of the line and made progress in swinging it back, but the British defenders did not crack. He fought doggedly on, with both sides incurring heavy losses, yet for Rommel, with his precarious resupply situation, the losses grew unsustainable. He withdrew to approximately the original points of attack and waited for supplies and reinforcements, constructing heavy defenses—mine fields and obstacles. During a three-month lull, British supply operations proved more successful, and General Bernard Law Montgomery, newly appointed commander of the Eighth Army, built an approximate two-to-one superiority in tanks, field guns, and troops.

On October 23, 1942, Montgomery opened the second Battle of Al-Alamein with a cannonade from a thousand guns massed along a five-mile stretch. In Germany for medical treatment, Rommel rushed to the front, arriving late on October 25 to find that all reserves had been committed. With his units being overpowered in all sectors, he sought permission to withdraw; in response, Hitler forbade him to retreat a yard. On the following day, November 3, with the concurrence of Field Marshal Kesselring, he ordered a fourteen-hundred-mile withdrawal toward Tunisia with only twelve tanks still operational. The retreat enabled him to save most of his army only because Montgomery was slow in pursuit.

Toward Tunisia, American forces were advancing from the west following their landings in Morocco and Algeria in Operation Torch. Realizing that the Axis faced a hopeless situation, Rommel urged Hitler to withdraw the Afrika Korps for the defense of Europe. Instead, Hitler, who had reluctantly entered Africa, now determined to hold a position there at all costs. He poured in men and matériel, including the new Mark V (Panther) and Mark VI (Tiger) tanks. Although Rommel was in command at the Battle of Kasserine Pass, where his forces mauled inexperienced American troops, his influence was waning, and he was withdrawn before the surrender of all remaining forces in May, 1943. Hitler's refusal to withdraw the Afrika Korps remained a bitter disappointment to their commander.

After minor assignments in Italy and the Balkans, Rommel was appointed deputy commander of the Western Front, in charge of coastal defenses, under the aging Field Marshal Gerd von Rundstedt. After carefully surveying coastal installations, Rommel began an extensive construction of gun emplacements, tank traps, mines, and other obstacles, and made frequent personal visits to his troops to build their morale. Realizing that Allied air supremacy would hamper any movement of forces, he believed it essential that an invasion be stopped on the beaches. His preparations were far from complete when the Normandy Invasion occurred on June 6, 1944.

Unable to contain the invasion, Rommel and Rundstedt met Hitler near the front to request reinforcements and permission to withdraw to better defensive positions; both requests were denied. By this time Rommel had reached the conclusion that only a separate peace with the Western Allies could save Germany; he further believed it necessary to replace Hitler.

Though he was drawn into the plot against Hitler, he never sanctioned assassination. When the bomb planted by Colonel Claus von Stauffenberg exploded at Hitler's headquarters on July 20, Rommel lay in a Paris hospital recovering from wounds sustained when his staff car was strafed by a British Spitfire on July 17. During the interrogations that followed, Rommel was implicated by General Heinrich von Stülpnagel, among others, and a list of offices to be filled after the demise of Hitler, which fell into the hands of the SS, showed Rommel as reich president.

As his recovery continued at his home in Herrlingen, he was visited by two SS generals, who bore a brief charging him with treason. He was offered the choice of the People's Court or suicide by poison. Since Hitler gave assurances that his family and staff would be protected if he elected to take a cyanide capsule, he accepted this course. The official explanation was that he died of a brain hemorrhage resulting from his wounds. He received a hero's funeral at Ulm, where Rundstedt read the eulogy.

## Summary

During World War II, Erwin Rommel was Germany's most celebrated commander. To his enemies and to Germany he was a legend, and at times he seemed invincible. A popular leader with his men, he insisted on commanding from the front, oblivious to personal danger and hardship. He practiced the principle he taught his cadets: to be to the men an example in both their personal and professional lives. Among the British who opposed him, he had a reputation for chivalry and for correct, even considerate, treatment of prisoners. In North Africa, he employed an astonishing variety of military tactics that worked in his favor so long as he was not overpowered by superior numbers.

Though a model soldier, Rommel was not without flaws. As a commander who insisted on being at the front, he sometimes lost contact with his headquarters. He neglected logistical problems and often attacked when his forces were poorly supplied. He demanded that his officers and men be as aggressive and efficient as he was, and he had a reputation for being tactless and somewhat abrasive with senior officers. Strong-willed and single-minded, he was politically naïve, allowing himself to be used by Nazi propaganda.

Bold and aggressive by nature, Rommel emphasized attack over defense, insisted that officers should lead attacks, and saw that success required that firepower be concentrated in the spearhead, not behind it. He grasped the concept of fluidity in military attack—the view that one does not assault fixed positions and then stop—and the importance of carefully coordinated attacking units. He developed ingenious tactics and achieved important victories over superior numbers in North Africa. Successes came to his opponents after they mastered his own art of desert warfare. In the end, Rommel lost because the opposing forces won the contest for supplies and reinforcements.

**Bibliography**

"The Atlantic Wall." *American History* 29, no. 2 (June, 1994). Focuses on Hitler's "Atlantic Wall" and the efforts of German military leaders including Rommel.

Irving, David. *The Trail of the Fox.* London: Weidenfeld and Nicolson, and New York: Dutton, 1977. Carefully researched and written in vivid detail. Highly readable, it is the most comprehensive and accurate biography.

Lewin, Ronald. *The Life and Death of the Afrika Korps.* London: Batsford, and New York: Quadrangle, 1977. A straightforward and detailed narration of the North African campaign.

Mitcham, Samuel W., Jr. *The Desert Fox in Normandy: Rommel's Defense of Fortress Europe.* Westport, Conn.: Praeger, 1997. Mitcham examines the Battle of Normandy from the German perspective, focusing on Rommel's efforts to fortify German defenses in the weeks prior to D-Day.

———. *Rommel's Desert War.* New York: Stein and Day, 1982. Chronicles the North African campaign from December, 1941, until the surrender of the Afrika Korps.

———. *Triumphant Fox: Erwin Rommel and the Rise of the Afrika Korps.* New York: Stein and Day, 1984. Beginning with a biographical account, the book chronicles Rommel's early successes in North Africa.

Rommel, Erwin. *The Rommel Papers.* Edited by B. H. Liddell Hart. Translated by Paul Findlay. London: Collins, and New York: Harcourt Brace, 1953. A collection of Rommel's memoirs, letters, and personal documents giving his own account of his campaigns.

Young, Desmond. *Rommel: The Desert Fox.* New York: Harper, 1950. A sympathetic and comprehensive biography by an English officer who fought against Rommel in Africa.

*Stanley Archer*

## ELEANOR ROOSEVELT

*Born:* October 11, 1884; New York, New York
*Died:* November 7, 1962; New York, New York
*Area of Achievement:* Social reform
*Contribution:* As First Lady and as a private citizen, Roosevelt worked for civil rights, women's rights, and domestic and international peace and justice.

### Early Life

Anna Eleanor Roosevelt, the first child of Elliot and Anna Livingston Ludlow Hall Roosevelt, was born in New York City on October 11, 1884. Her beautiful and aristocratic mother, who was only twenty years old when Eleanor was born, was more involved in the social life of her contemporaries than in the needs of her daughter. Elliot Roosevelt, although handsome and charming, was troubled by problems associated with alcoholism. As a result of her parents' self-absorption, Eleanor's early childhood was lonely and somber despite her family's wealth and social position.

Anna Roosevelt died of diphtheria in 1892, depressed and discouraged by her husband's drinking and irresponsibility. Eleanor idolized her father and imagined that she would live with him and that they would travel to exciting places together. In reality, however, Elliot's attitude toward Eleanor, although expressed in loving words, was characterized by thoughtlessness. Elliot died on August 14, 1894, of complications related to his drinking.

After her father's death, Eleanor lived with her maternal grandmother Mary Livingston Ludlow Hall. A strict disciplinarian, Hall insisted on a regimented life for her grandchildren. Despite her grandmother's insistence that she wear unfashionable clothes and a back brace to improve her posture, and despite the dreary atmosphere of Hall's New York townhouse, Eleanor's childhood was not as miserable as some writers have suggested. She had, for the first time in her life, a stable and orderly home. Her grandmother and aunts were sympathetic and supportive of her academic and athletic activities, and the family's country estate at Tivoli was a pleasant place with spacious grounds for a child to roam.

Eleanor remained in this environment until the age of fifteen, when she was sent to Allenswood, a girls' boarding school in England. Presided over by Mademoiselle Marie Souvestre, Allenswood provided a rigorous academic environment that encouraged young women to think and act independently. Eleanor came into her own at boarding school. She was an outstanding student, was active in sports, was held in the highest esteem by her fellow students, and was a protégée of Mademoiselle Souvestre. She took from Allenswood an intellectual self-possession, an increased sense of tolerance, and a commitment to public activity.

### Life's Work

At eighteen, Eleanor Roosevelt returned to New York, at her grandmother's insistence that she make her debut. Although in her own memoirs Eleanor describes herself as shy and awkward at this period of her life, her contemporaries remembered her as attractive and sought-after by the more thoughtful young men. One young man who was particularly interested was Eleanor's fifth cousin once removed, Franklin Delano Roosevelt (FDR), at the time a Harvard student. The two became secretly engaged in November, 1903, and were married in March, 1905, after a courtship during which his rather possessive mother tried to raise obstacles.

During the years before her marriage, Eleanor had become involved in volunteer work in New York City. There she had found a sense of usefulness and satisfaction that social life had never held for her. She worked with the Junior League to teach settlement house children, and she joined the Consumers' League, helping to investigate women's working conditions in factories and department stores. She had firsthand exposure to urban poverty, and Eleanor's commitment to improving the lives of the less fortunate dates from this period of her life.

After their wedding, Eleanor and Franklin settled in New York City in a townhouse adjoining his mother's home. During the next eleven years, Eleanor bore six children: Anna (1906); James (1907); Franklin (1909), who lived only seven months; Elliot (1910); Franklin, Jr. (1914); and John (1916). Her life was filled with domestic responsibilities and with her mother-in-law's interference in the younger Roosevelts' household. Those were years of little personal satisfaction for Eleanor. She had little involvement with friends or work outside her family.

In 1910, Franklin Roosevelt began his political career by winning a seat in the New York state legislature. Eleanor also began her public life. She enjoyed the role of political wife, especially because it brought her into contact with the issues and figures of the day. Contrary to some reports, Eleanor was not opposed to woman suffrage during this period. She had not given the issue much thought until FDR came out in support of votes for women in 1911. Then she realized that "if my husband were a suffragist I probably must be too."

In 1913, the Roosevelts moved to Washington, D.C., where Franklin served as assistant secretary of the Navy under President Woodrow Wilson. There, during World War I, Eleanor organized the Red Cross canteen and the Navy Red Cross. She knitted, entertained troops, and served food to servicemen. She visited soldiers in the hospital and raised money for a recreational center for wounded men. Her work often lasted from 9:00 a.m. until long past midnight. The war years also brought Eleanor heartache and disillusionment when she learned of her husband's affair with her social secretary, Lucy Mercer. Eleanor offered to divorce Franklin at this time, but he refused. Certainly, the Roosevelts' decision to continue their marriage was made partly because divorce was a serious liability in politics in the early twentieth century, but also because Franklin realized that Eleanor's special skills would be invaluable in his career. For Eleanor, the Lucy Mercer episode encouraged her to seek her own fulfillment in the world outside her marriage.

After an unsuccessful run for the vice presidency in 1920, Franklin Roosevelt developed polio in 1921. Spurred by these events, Eleanor became involved in politics both in women's issues and in the Democratic Party. During the 1920's, she became active in the League of Women Voters and the Women's Trade Union League, which supported protective legislation for women. She became acquainted with such activist women as Esther Lape and Elizabeth Read, who introduced Eleanor into a community of independent women. With her friends Marion Dickerman and Nancy Cook, Eleanor built a cottage called Val-Kill on the grounds of the Roosevelt family estate at Hyde Park. There they created a partnership that managed a furniture crafts factory and also published the *Women's Democratic News*. With her friends, Eleanor also purchased Todhunter, a private girls' school in New York City. She taught there three days a week until she became First Lady in 1933. Teaching fulfilled a dream from her days at Allenswood, gave her immense satisfaction, and brought her into contact with the young people she always loved.

With the phenomenal energy that characterized her whole life, Eleanor also entered Democratic politics, first as a representative of her husband during his convalescence and then in her own right as a spokesperson for women and social reform. She organized Democratic women in New York, traveled and spoke for Democratic Party candidates, and advocated the election of women to public office.

When Franklin was elected governor of New York in 1928 and president of the United States in 1932, Eleanor worked with the Women's Division of the Democratic National Committee to involve women in the election process and to ensure that women were appointed to positions in the administration. Among those whom Eleanor brought to her husband's attention was Frances Perkins, the secretary of labor, the first woman ever appointed to a presidential cabinet.

Eleanor had feared that the position of First Lady would mean curtailing her own political and reform activities, but she discovered new opportunities to promote her primary concerns, such as equal rights and the concerns of the poor and dispossessed. She held regular press conferences that were open only to women reporters, gave radio interviews and lectures, and wrote a syndicated newspaper column called "My Day." In addition, she supervised the responses to the thousands of letters she received, sometimes sending a personal note or a check. Eleanor also traveled throughout the country as the president's "eyes and ears," seeing for herself the conditions on farms, in mines and factories, and in the homes of the poor during the Depression. She brought representatives of excluded groups to the White House, frequently seating them next to the president so that he could hear their stories.

A primary commitment of Eleanor Roosevelt's adult life was to civil rights for African Americans. She had grown up in an isolated and prejudiced environment, but living in Washington, D.C., had made her aware of the evils of racism. Her advocacy took the form both of symbolic gestures, as when she insisted on placing her chair in the center of the aisle between black and white sections at a segregated meeting of the Southern Conference on Human Welfare in 1939, and of quiet lobbying, as in her role of messenger between her husband and the National Association for the Advancement of Colored People (NAACP). She supported federal

legislation to outlaw lynching and, during World War II, worked to eliminate discrimination in the armed forces.

During the war, Eleanor endeavored to ensure women's participation in all aspects of the mobilization, visited troops in hospitals and in the field, and sought to continue the many New Deal social reforms jeopardized by the country's focus on the international crisis.

Franklin Roosevelt died in April of 1945, during his fourth term as president. Eleanor continued her public life, perhaps feeling freer because she was no longer perceived as a politician's wife. She turned many of her efforts to international matters, an extension of her long-standing interest in building a lasting peace. She had earlier been an advocate of the League of Nations and the World Court, and now President Harry S Truman appointed her as a delegate to the newly formed United Nations, where she served until 1953. She chaired the committee that produced the 1948 Declaration on Human Rights and was nominated four times for the Nobel Peace Prize.

The "First Lady of the World" showed concern for the victims of war and oppression parallel to her continuing domestic interests in civil rights and women's issues. Her last public role was as the chairperson of President John F. Kennedy's Commission on the Status of Women, in which capacity she supported full access by women to economic and political opportunities.

She died in New York City on November 7, 1962, of a rare type of tuberculosis.

## Summary

Eleanor Roosevelt's life bore out the advice she had written to women in 1930, "to be ready to go out and try new adventures, create new work for others as well as herself, and strike deep roots in some community where her presence will make a difference in the lives of others."

She defined a new role for women in American public life. Although during much of her life she filled a position as the wife of a prominent politician, her contributions stand on their own. With compassion and a commitment to humanitarian interests, Eleanor helped to place the issues of racial and gender justice on the national agenda. She was an advocate for all excluded groups, using her public visibility as a means to bring their concerns to national attention and using her influence to promote changes in attitudes and in legislation. On the international scene, she reached out to the victims of injustice and poverty, legitimizing and promoting their well-being.

To women of future generations, Eleanor Roosevelt became a model of energy, humanity and courage. Always an example of impeccable courtesy, she could also confront leaders of the Soviet Union or the proponents of segregation and state her case. Eleanor Roosevelt demonstrated the need to redefine power as not only the authority to move armies or to control economic might but also the ability to inspire, to question the status quo, and to work for equality without the expectation of personal gain.

## Bibliography

Black, Allida M. *Casting Her Own Shadow: Eleanor Roosevelt and the Shaping of Postwar Liberalism.* New York: Columbia University Press, 1996. The author examines Roosevelt's post-White House life and career and the importance of her work in human rights and women's issues.

Cook, Blanche Wiesen. *Eleanor Roosevelt.* Vol. 1. New York: Viking, 1992; London: Bloomsbury, 1993. The first volume of a projected two-volume study, Cook's sensitive biography places Eleanor Roosevelt in the context of a rich emotional life and emphasizes her lifelong strengths.

Edens, John A. *Eleanor Roosevelt: A Comprehensive Bibliography.* Westport, Conn.: Greenwood Press, 1994. The most comprehensive listing of works by and about Roosevelt to date. Includes 3,780 sources.

Hoff-Wilson, Joan, and Marjorie Lightman, eds. *Without Precedent: The Life and Career of Eleanor Roosevelt.* Bloomington: Indiana University Press, 1984. An excellent collection of articles on Roosevelt's character and contributions. The essays introduce fine scholarship dealing with the major themes in her life.

Lash, Joseph P. *Eleanor and Franklin.* New York: Norton, 1971; London: Deutsch, 1972.

———. *Eleanor: The Years Alone.* New York: Norton, 1972; London: Deutsch, 1973. Lash was the first to write a biography of Roosevelt based on full access to her papers. His personal friendship with Roosevelt enabled him to provide a warm and comprehensive picture of her life.

Roosevelt, Eleanor. *The Autobiography of Eleanor Roosevelt.* New York: Harper, 1961. Three volumes consolidated into one, this autobiography is indispensable to the student but provides a picture that is too self-effacing.

Youngs, J. William T. *Eleanor Roosevelt: Personal and Public Life*. Edited by Oscar Handlin. Boston: Little Brown, 1985. Part of the Library of American Biography series, this is an accessible and positive short biography.

*Mary Welek Atwell*

# FRANKLIN D. ROOSEVELT

*Born:* January 30, 1882; Hyde Park, New York
*Died:* April 12, 1945; Warm Springs, Georgia
*Area of Achievement:* Government and politics
*Contribution:* Displaying extraordinary personal courage and perhaps the most astute political leadership America has ever witnessed, Roosevelt dominated American government for a longer period than has any other president of the United States.

## Early Life

Born in Hyde Park, New York, on January 30, 1882, Franklin Delano Roosevelt was a member of an American aristocratic family of great wealth. James and Sara Roosevelt, of Dutch and English ancestry, educated their only child with private tutors and European tours. At Groton School in Massachusetts, Roosevelt came under the influence of Rector Endicott Peabody, who prided himself on grooming future politicians and instilling in his charges a lifelong commitment to public service.

By 1900, when Franklin enrolled at Harvard University, he was an impressive young man—six feet two inches tall, handsome, with a patrician nose and majestically deep-set eyes. In his junior year, he fell in love with his fifth cousin, Eleanor Roosevelt, a tall, slender woman whose pleasing face was punctuated by a prominent set of Rooseveltian teeth. Eleanor was the daughter of President Theodore Roosevelt's younger brother, Elliott, who died from alcoholism when she was ten. In 1905, Franklin married Eleanor, over the objections of his mother, who tried to postpone the wedding.

Following Harvard, Roosevelt dabbled briefly with the practice of law before turning to the real love of his life: politics. In 1910, he entered the political arena for the first time, running for the New York State Senate. Fellow Democrats skeptically observed his entrance into the race for several reasons: his aristocratic bearing, his tendency to look down his nose at people, his unfamiliarity with working-class voters in the Hyde Park-Poughkeepsie area, and the fact that he was a former Republican. The political climate, however, demanded a reformer, and Roosevelt, following in the footsteps of his cousin Theodore, could fill the bill by pointing to the ugly specter of corruption within the opposition party. During the campaign, FDR (as he came to be known) showed he was different from the average "cheap-talking" politician, displaying a pragmatic unorthodoxy that later endeared him to the nation. He even campaigned for office in an automobile, an unusual political act for a time when most people eyed the horseless carriage with suspicion. Victory was his, however, and FDR became only the second Democrat elected from his district to the New York State Senate since the Civil War. He was on his way.

It was not an easy path to success. Experiences in the New York senate taught him the limits of progressive, reformistic power. When he challenged Charles F. Murphy's Tammany machine of New York City over the Democratic nomination for the United States Senate, he met defeat. He gradually learned, however, to moderate his reform tendencies. This later proved to be his first major lesson in the school of politics. Following his reelection in 1912, Roosevelt jumped at the opportunity to join Woodrow Wilson's administration in the capacity of assistant secretary of the Navy under Josephus Daniels. In doing so, young FDR may have imagined himself following the example of Theodore, who had achieved the governorship of New York, the vice presidency, and the presidency after serving in the same position. The Navy Department afforded Roosevelt a chance to hone his administrative skills and strengthen his political ties throughout the Democratic Party to the point that, by 1920, delegates to the national convention were willing to exploit his famous name by nominating him for the vice presidency as James M. Cox's running mate. Cox and Roosevelt suffered defeat in the Republican landslide that swept Warren G. Harding and Calvin Coolidge into office. FDR remained basically unchanged throughout these events, still a somewhat immature young man who maintained very few strong convictions.

All this changed in August, 1921, when Roosevelt contracted polio while vacationing at Campobello Island, his family's resort off the Maine seacoast. His health was shattered, but a new Roosevelt slowly began to emerge. Paralyzed from the waist down, and wealthy enough to retire at the age of thirty-nine, he fought to regain his vigor. First, he had to overcome the frustration that resulted from the wearing of heavy steel braces which prohibited him from walking unaided. Second, he had to ignore the pleas of his mother (whom he worshiped but who urged him to with-

draw from politics) and listen to his wife and his personal secretary, Louis McHenry Howe, who plotted to restore him to some semblance of health. During this period of recovery, Eleanor became his "legs," going where he could not go, doing what he could not do physically, and generally learning the art of politics.

### Life's Work

In 1924, FDR showed that Roosevelt the fighter had superseded Roosevelt the dedicated aristocrat when he appeared at the Democratic National Convention to give his "Happy Warrior Speech" nominating Alfred E. Smith for president. Smith lost the nomination, but Roosevelt did not lose his political career to polio. Instead, it seemed to give him a strength of character he had rarely shown before the Campobello incident. In 1928, while Smith was losing his home state of New York by 100,000 votes to Herbert Hoover, FDR was winning the governorship by twenty-five thousand, thus becoming the front-runner for the 1932 Democratic presidential nomination. Reelected by an unprecedented 725,000 votes in 1930, Roosevelt, aided by his national campaign manager, James A. Farley, began his first run for the presidency. Capturing the nomination on the third ballot, Roosevelt pledged himself to create, if elected, a "new deal" for the American people.

The 1932 presidential campaign pitted FDR against the Republican incumbent, Herbert Hoover. With the country three years into the Great Depression, Roosevelt wisely ran a pragmatic campaign—fluctuating between alternative ideological positions, allowing Hoover's record to speak for itself, and leaving the decision to the American electorate. On November 8, 1932, the people spoke—giving him a 472-59 electoral victory over Hoover. When Roosevelt took office on March 4, 1933, the nation was mired in the worst depression in American history. There were approximately thirteen million unemployed people—25.2 percent of the work force. As a mood of apprehension gripped the country, Roosevelt tried to calm the panic-stricken populace:

> First of all, let me assert my firm belief that the only thing we have to fear is fear itself—nameless, unreasoning, unjustified terror which paralyzes needed efforts to convert retreat into advance. In every dark hour of our national life a leadership of frankness and vigor has met with that understanding and support of the people themselves which is essential to victory. I am convinced that you will again give that support to leadership in these critical days.

During the crucial one hundred days that followed his inaugural speech, Roosevelt began the New Deal. He quickly satisfied the public's overwhelming desire for leadership and action by issuing executive orders and introducing legislation which a frightened Congress quickly rubber-stamped. FDR acted in four critical areas: finance, industry, agriculture, and relief (welfare). In combating the Depression, Roosevelt gave the nation no panacea but offered the means through which it might be able to survive the crisis. He did not end the Depression—but many of his programs and the laws he signed got the country through the Depression and remained an effective part of the federal government long after his death. In finance, the Emergency Banking Act (1933) and the Glass-Steagall Banking Act (1933) saved the banking structure and helped prevent a future crisis by creating the Federal Deposit Insurance Corporation. The Truth-in-Securities Act (1933) and the Securities Exchange Act (1934) brought Wall Street under tighter public regulation. In industry, the National Industrial Recovery Act (1933) offered both business and labor opportunities for greater self-government. Later, through the National Labor Relations Act (1935), he concentrated more on allowing labor unions the right to organize. In agriculture, Roosevelt tried to restore farmers' prosperity through the Agriculture Adjustment Act (1933) by subsidizing certain farm products they could not afford to sell at market prices. In relief, FDR straddled the line between welfare and public works. At first, the New Deal doled out money to unemployed people through the Federal Emergency Relief Administration (1933) and sent young men to work camps through the Civilian Conservation Corps (1933).

After the one hundred days had passed, FDR turned away from welfare and made government jobs a primary goal of his administration. Listening to his advisers, Harry Hopkins and Harold L. Ickes, Roosevelt made the federal government the employer of the last resort through the Civil Works Administration (1933), the Public Works Administration (1933), and the Works Progress Administration (1935). In particular, the WPA, which averaged 2,112,000 on its monthly payrolls from 1935 to 1941, was the largest, most visionary, and probably most effective federal relief program ever created. Perhaps the most long-lasting reform achieved by FDR was the Social Security Administration (1935), granting unemployment compensation and old-age pensions.

Roosevelt's New Deal programs generated billions of new dollars throughout the American economy, increasing incomes and causing tax revenues to "trickle up" to the federal and state governments. The jobs also raised the hopes of millions of voters who came to believe that FDR had saved them from financial disaster. He was the man who put food on their tables, shoes on their feet, and a roof over their heads. In brief, the New Deal was political dynamite, and Roosevelt was the New Deal. The president's charismatic leadership, his inspirational speeches and informal "fireside chats," made him an unbeatable campaigner, as his 1936 Republican opponent learned. Roosevelt crushed Kansas Governor Alfred M. Landon by the largest electoral margin in recent American history, 523 to 8.

In less than three years, Roosevelt created an imperial presidency and vastly enlarged the federal bureaucracy, thus prompting criticisms from conservatives and the Supreme Court. When the Court began invalidating some New Deal programs such as the National Industrial Recovery Act *(Schechter v. United States*, 1935) and the Agriculture Adjustment Act *(Butler v. United States*, 1936), he struck back. In 1937, FDR tried to pack the Court with New Dealers by introducing the Federal Judiciary Reorganization Bill. Although the bill failed to pass Congress, Roosevelt prevailed in this struggle, since the Court's later decisions proved more favorable to New Deal legislation. Still, the court-packing scheme suggested dictatorial ambitions and damaged FDR's reputation in some circles. His popularity further declined as the nation slid deeper into the Depression in 1938, and the president, determined to keep his working majority in Congress, attempted to purge conservative Democrats from his party. This tactic also failed. By 1939, the New Deal, for all practical purposes, was dead.

As the New Deal passed into history, new dangers loomed on the horizon. Totalitarian regimes in Germany, Japan, and Italy threatened America's position in the world. Roosevelt himself recognized that the leaders of these regimes, Adolf Hitler, Hideki Tojo, and Benito Mussolini, would necessitate some changes in American foreign policy when he said that "Dr. Win the War" would have to replace "Dr. New Deal." In this way, he reluctantly began to shift American diplomacy in the direction of confronting these aggressors. After Germany invaded Poland on September 1, 1939, precipitating a declaration of war by England and France, Americans debated whether their country should maintain its isolation or aid its British and French allies. While Roosevelt was preaching neutrality, he won an unprecedented third term, a 449-82 electoral victory over his 1940 Republican opponent, Wendell Willkie.

When the war came to America, it struck with a fury. Possibly no aspect of FDR's foreign policy has evoked more controversy than the role he played in leading the United States into World War II. On December 7, 1941, a little more than a year after he promised that "this country is not going to war," Japanese planes swept down on the American naval base at Pearl Harbor, Hawaii, nearly destroying the United States Pacific Fleet. The declaration of war that followed prompted his critics to complain that he had tricked his nation into war. While the Roosevelt Administration made numerous errors in judgment, FDR did not intentionally expose the military installation to attack in order to drag a reluctant and isolationistic American people into the war.

Shortly after the "day of infamy," Roosevelt met with British prime minister Winston Churchill in the first of several Washington conferences forming a "grand alliance" between the two world leaders and their nations. At the first meeting, Roosevelt agreed to the idea that the allies should place top priority on defeating Germany and Italy, while fighting a holding action against Japan in the Pacific theater. In fact, throughout the war, FDR actively planned and executed top military and diplomatic decisions that affected its outcome and the postwar world. Together with Churchill and Soviet premier Joseph Stalin, he agreed to the formulation of the United Nations. At the Yalta Conference (February, 1945), Roosevelt made another of his extremely controversial decisions that would affect public opinion long after he was gone. In return for Stalin's promise to enter the war against Japan and to allow free elections in the Soviet bloc nations, FDR acquiesced to Russia's hegemony in eastern Poland and other territories occupied by Soviet troops. Because these decisions were kept secret by the chief signatories, Roosevelt never felt the full fury of his critics before his death on April 12, 1945.

### Summary

In electing Franklin D. Roosevelt to an unprecedented four terms of office, the American people lent credence to the belief that FDR was the greatest leader ever to hold the presidency. This view was further substantiated by the 1982 survey conducted by Professor Robert K. Murray of Pennsylvania State University among a thousand Ph.D. historians; only Abraham Lincoln ranked ahead of Roosevelt as the best president in American history. Nevertheless, Roosevelt certainly had his critics, and they made valid points: He seems to have had dictatorial ambitions when he circumvented the Constitution and tried to pack the Supreme Court. FDR may have gravely damaged the national economy by allowing the national debt to grow to astronomical proportions. Other presidents followed him down the path of "deficit spending," enlarging upon the problem that he had created in order to combat the Depression. Without a doubt, Roosevelt was one of the most controversial presidents in American history.

FDR created the imperial presidency, in the process setting a precedent for leadership by which all his successors have been evaluated. He took the executive branch, which had lost much of its power and glory, and expanded it beyond the limits achieved by any twentieth century American chief executive. Circumstances such as depression and war, and the force of his indomitable personal character shaped by the adversity of polio, allowed him to restructure the office into its present form—one that casually encroaches on the normal powers and functions of Congress and the Supreme Court. In 1939, for example, in an act that escaped virtually unnoticed by the nation's press, he issued Executive Order 8248, creating the Executive Office of the President and shifting the powerful Bureau of the Budget from the Treasury Department to the White House. Then, when the time came to run for an unprecedented third term in 1940, Roosevelt occupied a perfect position to manipulate the federal economy for reelection purposes, and manipulate it he did—setting another example that his successors have followed.

Although Roosevelt's primary claim to greatness lay in domestic achievements, he made major contributions in foreign policy as well. He was the president who led America to victory over the Axis powers and then achieved the first détente with the new superpower: Soviet Russia. It was in the arena of American politics and government, however, that FDR made his greatest imprint. Even his critics must concede that his impact on the nation was extraordinary.

### Bibliography

Abbott, Philip. *The Exemplary Presidency: Franklin D. Roosevelt and the American Political Tradition*. Amherst: University of Massachusetts Press, 1990.

Burns, James MacGregor. *Roosevelt: The Lion and the Fox*. New York: Harcourt Brace and London: Secker and Warburg, 1956. The best political biography of Roosevelt. Burns stresses FDR's Machiavellian tendencies and his failure to implement an enduring reform coalition.

———. *Roosevelt: The Soldier of Freedom*. New York: Harcourt Brace, 1970; London: Weidenfeld and Nicolson, 1971. One of the best books analyzing Roosevelt's role as commander in chief during World War II.

Dallek, Robert. *Franklin D. Roosevelt and American Foreign Policy, 1932-1945*. New York: Oxford University Press, 1979; Oxford: Oxford University Press, 1981. Dallek received the Bancroft Prize in history for this excellent analytical overview of FDR's foreign policy.

Davis, Kenneth Sydney. *FDR, Into the Storm, 1937-1940: A History*. New York: Random House, 1993.

Dickinson, Matthew J. *Bitter Harvest: FDR, Presidential Power and the Growth of the Presidential Branch*. Cambridge and New York: Cambridge University Press, 1997. Examines FDR's methods for managing his presidency. The author suggests that modern presidents could benefit from similar practices, which would produce less cumbersome organizations.

Divine, Robert A., ed. *Causes and Consequences of World War II*. Chicago: Quadrangle, 1969. Very good historiographical collection of essays and accompanying bibliography focusing on the prelude to and aftermath of World War II.

Freidel, Frank. *The Apprenticeship*. Boston: Little Brown, 1952. The first of a projected six-volume biography. *The Apprenticeship* covers the period from Roosevelt's birth through his tenure as assistant secretary of the Navy. Some reviewers thought this volume suffered from an overemphasis on FDR's early life.

———. *The Ordeal*. Boston: Little Brown, 1954. The second volume covers the era from 1919 to

1928, including FDR's contracting polio in 1921, his comeback (firmly established by the "Happy Warrior Speech" in 1924), and his election as governor of New York in 1928.

———. *The Triumph*. Boston: Little Brown, 1956. The third volume addresses the subject of Roosevelt's two terms as governor of New York, culminating with his election as president of the United States in 1932. This is a very dispassionate analysis of Roosevelt's emergence as the master politician who crushed Herbert Hoover's hopes in the 1932 presidential election.

———. *Launching the New Deal*. Boston: Little Brown, 1973. Focuses on the winter of 1932-1933 through the completion of the "One Hundred Days" Congress of June, 1933. This is a very detailed, well-documented study of the early New Deal, although it omits Harry L. Hopkins' Federal Emergency Relief Administration. (Freidel's four-volume series on Roosevelt provides an unusually well-balanced account. The first three volumes constitute the definitive analysis of FDR's early years.)

———. *Franklin D. Roosevelt: A Rendezvous with Destiny*. Boston: Little Brown, 1990.

Leuchtenburg, William E. *Franklin D. Roosevelt and the New Deal*. New York: Harper, 1963. This overview of Roosevelt's foreign and domestic policy up to 1940, the best one-volume treatment of its subject, is scholarly yet highly readable.

Perras, Galen Roger. *Franklin Roosevelt and the Origins of the Canadian-American Security Alliance, 1933-1945: Necessary, but Not Necessary Enough*. Westport, Conn.: Praeger, 1998. Perras examines Roosevelt's relationship with Canada and his efforts to encourage its security awareness.

Schlesinger, Arthur M., Jr. *The Age of Roosevelt: The Crisis of the Old Order, 1919-1933*. Boston: Houghton Mifflin, 1957; London: Heinemann, 1961. This is the first of four projected volumes focusing on the changes experienced by the United States during Franklin Roosevelt's career. Essentially, the first volume analyzes the political, economic, and social currents of the 1920's, culminating with FDR's first presidential election in 1932. Somewhat flawed by the author's tendency to allow his liberalism to prejudice his historical analysis of the period.

———. *The Age of Roosevelt: The Coming of the New Deal*. Boston: Houghton Mifflin Co., 1958. The second volume of Schlesinger's series analyzes the first two years of Roosevelt's presidency and the New Deal from 1933-1935. The problem of Schlesinger's pro-Roosevelt bias is less serious in this work than in his first volume.

———. *The Age of Roosevelt: The Politics of Upheaval*. Boston: Houghton Mifflin, and London: Heinemann, 1960. The third volume (to date) of Schlesinger's multivolume study of Roosevelt carries the analysis of FDR through his reelection in 1936. As with the first and second volumes, this work is characterized by Schlesinger's highly subjective analysis of political, economic, and social history, but it solidifies Schlesinger's major contribution to the literature on Roosevelt.

*J. Christopher Schnell*

# THEODORE ROOSEVELT

*Born:* October 27, 1858; New York, New York
*Died:* January 6, 1919; Oyster Bay, New York
*Area of Achievement:* Government and politics
*Contribution:* As twenty-sixth president of the United States, Roosevelt energetically led America into the twentieth century. Popular and effective, he promoted major domestic reforms and a larger role for the United States in world affairs. In so doing, he added power to the presidential office.

## Early Life

Theodore Roosevelt, twenty-sixth president of the United States, was born October 27, 1858, to a moderately wealthy mercantile family in New York City. His father, Theodore, Sr., was of mostly Dutch ancestry; his mother, Martha Bulloch of Georgia, came from a slaveholding family of Scots and Huguenot French. (During his political career, Roosevelt would claim an ethnic relationship with practically every white voter he met; among his nicknames—besides TR and Teddy—was Old Fifty-seven Varieties.) He was educated at home by tutors and traveled with his parents to the Middle East and Europe.

As a child, Roosevelt was puny, asthmatic, and unable to see much of the world until he was fitted with thick eyeglasses at the age of thirteen. He grew determined to "make" a powerful body, and by strenuous exercise and force of will, young Roosevelt gradually overcame most of his physical shortcomings. Shyness and fear were other weaknesses he conquered. "There were all kinds of things of which I was afraid at first," he later admitted in his *Theodore Roosevelt: An Autobiography* (1913). "But by acting as if I was not afraid I gradually ceased to be afraid." Insecurity, however, was one demon which he never exorcised.

While becoming athletic and assertive, young Roosevelt retained his wide-ranging intellectual curiosity. At Harvard, from which he was graduated in 1880, his absorption with both sports and books made him something of an oddity. Yet career plans remained uncertain. Dull science classes at Harvard dimmed his earlier interest in becoming a naturalist. A year at Columbia University Law School (1880-1881) did not stimulate him toward a legal career. While attending Columbia, he married Alice Lee, completed his first book, *The Naval War of 1812* (1882), and entered politics in the autumn of 1881 by election to the New York legislature as a Republican representative from Manhattan. For the remainder of his life, except for brief military glory in the Spanish-American War, writing and politics would absorb most of his overflowing energy.

## Life's Work

At the age of twenty-three, Roosevelt, the youngest member of New York's legislature, attracted attention because of his anticorruption stance and his flair for the dramatic. He instinctively knew how to make his doings interesting to the press and the public. Personality flaws were obvious from the beginning of his political career (egotism, impulsiveness, a tendency to see everything in black or white, and occasional ruthlessness), yet Roosevelt's virtues were equally apparent and won for him far more admirers than enemies: extraordinary vitality and intelligence, courage, sincerity, conviviality, and, usually, a willingness to make reasonable compromises.

Family tragedy, the death of his young wife, prompted Roosevelt to retire from politics temporarily in 1884. During the next two years, he operated cattle ranches he owned in the badlands of the Dakota Territory, where he found time to write *Hunting Trips of a Ranchman* (1885), the first of a trilogy of books on his Western activities and observations. Ranching proved financially unprofitable, but outdoor life made Roosevelt physically more robust and helped ease the pain of Alice's death. In 1886, he returned to New York and married Edith Kermit Carow, who would bear him four sons and a daughter and rear the daughter, Alice, born to his first wife. That same year, Roosevelt was the unsuccessful Republican nominee for mayor of New York City; he also commenced work on a six-volume history of America's Western expansion, *The Winning of the West* (1889-1896).

Roosevelt did not seek another elective office until he won the governorship of New York in 1898, but in the meantime, he served in three appointive positions: member of the United States Civil Service Commission (1889-1895), president of New York City's Board of Police Commissioners (1895-1897), and assistant secretary of the navy (1897-1898). He resigned the latter post when war with Spain broke out in 1898. Eager for combat, he organized a volunteer cavalry regiment known as the Rough Riders. Most of the land fighting between the United States and Spain occurred in Cuba; the image of Colonel Roosevelt leading a charge up San Juan Hill (in actuality, Kettle Hill) became a public symbol of this brief, victorious war. "Teddy" was a national hero. In November of 1898, he was elected governor of New York and quickly published a new book, *The Rough Riders* (1899), which a humorous critic said should have been titled "Alone in Cuba."

As governor of New York (1899-1900), Roosevelt pursued a vigorous program of political reform. The Republican state machine, wanting him out of New York, promoted his nomination for vice president on the national ticket in 1900. With reluctance, thinking that office might be a dead end, Roosevelt was finally persuaded to accept the nomination, thus becoming President William McKinley's running mate in 1900.

Within a year, McKinley died by an assassin's bullet, and Theodore Roosevelt, at age forty-two, was sworn in as the youngest chief executive in the nation's history. Physically, the new president had an aura of strength despite his average height, spectacles, small hands and feet, and high-pitched voice. His wide, square face, prominent, firm teeth, and massive chest overrode any hint of weakness.

The presidency, Roosevelt once observed, was a "bully pulpit," and he wasted no time in exhorting America toward new horizons in both domestic and foreign policy. Yet Roosevelt was painfully aware that he had become president by mishap. Not until his overwhelming election to a full term in 1904 did he believe that the office was truly his.

Within the nation, President Roosevelt called for a Square Deal for both capital and labor. He saw himself as chief arbiter of conflicts between economic groups; government, he believed, should represent everyone equitably. Believing in capitalism yet convinced that big corporations were too powerful and arrogant, he began a policy of "trust busting." Roosevelt's administration was the first to use successfully the Sherman Anti-Trust Act (passed in 1890) to break up business monopolies. Actually, Roosevelt believed more in regulation than in "busting, " but he hoped to frighten big business into accepting regulation. Privately, he was convinced that, for modern America, industrial and financial combinations were inevitable; he desired to subordinate both big business and labor unions to a stronger central government, which he viewed as the proper instrument for protecting the general interest.

The Hepburn Act, which for the first time gave the Interstate Commerce Commission regulatory power over railroads, was a signal accomplishment of Roosevelt's presidency as were the Pure Food and Drug Act and the Meat Inspection Act, all passed in 1906. Conservation of natural resources was another Roosevelt goal. Over both Democratic and Republican opposition, he cajoled Congress into limiting private exploitation of the nation's wilderness, mineral, and water resources. His administration doubled the number of national parks and tripled the acreage of national forests. Fifty-one wildlife refuges were established. Conservation was probably Roosevelt's most passionate cause and one of his most enduring legacies.

In foreign policy, Roosevelt is remembered by the proverb he once used: "Speak softly and carry a big stick." In practice, however, he bifurcated that approach; he spoke softly toward nations whose power he respected, while saving the big stick for small or weak countries. High-handedly, he "took Panama"—to use his own words—away from the nation of Colombia in 1903, so as to build an isthmian canal; the next year, he proclaimed a protectorate over all of Latin America—the Roosevelt Corollary to the Monroe Doctrine. As for the Far East, Roosevelt worried over but respected the rising power of Japan. He wanted the Japanese to thwart Russian expansionism but not to dominate Asia. He assumed that Great Britain and the United States would draw closer in worldwide interests; he viewed Germany, Japan, and Russia as probable enemies of a future Anglo-American alliance.

Roosevelt did not run for reelection. He had pledged after his 1904 triumph that he would not seek or accept another nomination. It was a promise he later regretted. The Republican Party in 1908 chose Roosevelt's close personal friend William Howard Taft who, with Roosevelt's blessing, easily won the presidency. Yet Taft's troubled term (1909-1913) split the Republicans into Progressive and Old Guard wings, and by 1910, Roosevelt angrily decided that Taft had capitulated to the Old Guard. Consequently, Roosevelt attempted to regain the White House in 1912. After losing a bitter contest to Taft for the Republican nomination, Roosevelt burst into the general election as a third party (Progressive, or Bull Moose Party) candidate, thus virtually guaranteeing victory for Democratic nominee Woodrow Wilson. Roosevelt's personal popularity allowed him to finish second in the

1912 presidential election, but without a viable national organization, he lost heavily to Wilson in the electoral count. Taft ran third.

Roosevelt spent most of the remainder of his life writing books, exploring Brazil's backcountry, and criticizing President Wilson, whom he hated. He wanted to fight in World War I but was refused a commission. His health weakened by infections contracted in Brazil, Theodore Roosevelt died in his sleep on January 6, 1919, at the age of sixty.

### Summary

"The Republican Roosevelt," as one historian termed him, is usually ranked among the best American presidents. An inspirational leader and superb administrator, he revitalized the presidency. His career seemed to defy the adage that power corrupts. In mental prowess, he had few equals in American political history; indeed, Roosevelt ranks among the rarest of human types: an intellectual who was also a man of action.

Ideologically, Roosevelt defies simple definition. Whether he was an "enlightened" conservative or a "Progressive liberal" remains in dispute. Roosevelt himself refused to accept pat labels. He viewed himself as a moral leader who combined practicality and idealism for the purpose of unifying the nation's opposing economic and social interests into a mutually beneficial synthesis.

Coming to the presidency at the dawn of the twentieth century, Roosevelt understood that America was fast becoming a complex urban, industrial nation and that a new balance was needed between individualism and the collective good. In foreign policy, Roosevelt acted upon his conviction that the old isolationism was no longer possible and that the United States, because of its growing strength, was destined to be a world power.

### Bibliography


Beale, Howard K. *Theodore Roosevelt and the Rise of America to World Power.* Baltimore: Johns Hopkins University Press, 1956. Best study of Roosevelt's foreign policy. Beale demonstrates that Roosevelt had prophetic insights yet was blind toward the nationalistic aspirations of "backward" colonial peoples.

Blum, John M. *The Republican Roosevelt.* Cambridge, Mass.: Harvard University Press, 1954. "Brilliant" is the usual word for characterizing this book. Blum explains Roosevelt as an astute conservative who welcomed change as the only means of preserving what was vital from the past.

Chessman, G. Wallace. *Theodore Roosevelt and the Politics of Power.* Boston: Little Brown, 1969. Most recommended brief biography of Roosevelt. Sympathetic to Roosevelt, it is a skillful blend of narrative and analysis.

Harbaugh, William Henry. *Power and Responsibility: The Life and Times of Theodore Roosevelt.* New York: Farrar Straus, 1961. The most thorough full-length biography of Roosevelt. Judiciously balances his virtues and limitations.

Jeffers, H. Paul. *Colonel Roosevelt: Theodore Roosevelt Goes to War, 1897-1898.* New York: Wiley, 1996. Jeffers examines the Spanish-American War, Roosevelt's ambitions, and his participation in the conflict.

Morris, Edmund. *The Rise of Theodore Roosevelt.* London: Collins, and New York: Coward McCann, 1979. Splendidly written, insightful treatment of Roosevelt's life from birth to the beginning of his presidency in 1901. Especially good for Roosevelt's ranching days in the Dakota Territory and his exploits during the Spanish-American War.

Mowry, George E. *The Era of Theodore Roosevelt: 1900-1912.* London: Hamilton, and New York: Harper, 1958. The standard study of the first dozen years of twentieth century America, when Roosevelt was the central political figure. Invaluable for understanding Roosevelt's actions within the context of his time of ascendancy.

Pringle, Henry F. *Theodore Roosevelt: A Biography.* London: Cape, and New York: Harcourt Brace, 1931. This readable Pulitzer Prize biography of Roosevelt was long considered the definitive work, but later historians tended to fault Pringle for overemphasizing Roosevelt's immaturity and bellicosity.

Renehan, Edward. *The Lion's Pride: Theodore Roosevelt and His Family in Peace and War.* New York: Oxford University Press, 1998. The author focuses on Theodore Roosevelt's family, his approach to family values and wealth, and the tragic closing years of his life saddened by the effects on his sons of the war he supported.

Roosevelt, Theodore. *The Writings of Theodore Roosevelt.* Edited by William H. Harbaugh. Indianapolis: Bobbs-Merrill, 1967. An excellent one-volume anthology of Roosevelt's own words, including excerpts from his autobiography.


*William I. Hair*

## ELIHU ROOT

*Born:* February 15, 1845; Clinton, New York
*Died:* February 7, 1937; New York, New York
*Area of Achievement:* Diplomacy, government and politics
*Contribution:* As secretary of war under William McKinley and Theodore Roosevelt, Root administered territories gained at the end of the Spanish-American War and initiated reforms in army administration. He pursued a conservative line as secretary of state under Roosevelt and later as United States senator from New York, and argued for the value of international law as a political instrument.

### Early Life

Born in Clinton, New York, on February 15, 1845, Elihu Root was the third of four sons of Oren and Nancy Buttrick Root. His father was professor of mathematics at Hamilton College in Clinton, and Elihu was valedictorian of the Hamilton class of 1864. He was graduated from New York University Law School in 1867. Root's legal career was successful from the start; in time he became one of the leading members of the American bar. Specializing in cases involving large corporations, he was labeled a Wall Street lawyer. Among his corporate clients were the Havemeyer Sugar Refining Company and the traction syndicate controlled by William C. Whitney and Thomas F. Ryan. Root's success as a lawyer and later as a member of McKinley's and Roosevelt's cabinets came from his capacity to master detail, the concise and logical qualities of his written arguments, and his ready wit. Reserved and a bit stiff with those he did not know well, Root formed strong friendships with men such as Theodore Roosevelt, William Howard Taft, and Henry Cabot Lodge.

Prior to his appointment as secretary of war in 1899, Root was involved in Republican Party politics on the local and state levels. He served from 1883 to 1885 as United States attorney for the district of Southern New York; he was a manager of the New York State constitutional convention of 1894. His association with Roosevelt began around 1882, when Root provided legal advice about an obstacle to Roosevelt's running for the state legislature. Root ran Roosevelt's unsuccessful campaign for mayor of New York City in 1886, he provided advice when Roosevelt served as city police commissioner, and in 1898 he resolved a question about Roosevelt's legal residence that enabled him to run for and be elected governor.

A thin, wiry man of average height, Root had closely clipped hair and a full mustache, both of which turned white in his old age. In 1878, he married Clara Frances Wales. An attentive husband and father to his daughter, Edith, and sons, Elihu and Edward Wales, Root often made decisions about his public career based upon his wife's distaste for life in Washington, D.C.

### Life's Work

While Root declined President McKinley's offer to serve on the commission concluding a peace treaty with Spain, he accepted appointment as secretary of war in 1899. McKinley said that he wanted a lawyer in the job because of the need to administer the territories acquired during the war. The legal problems posed by the American occupation of Puerto Rico, Cuba, and the Philippines were complex, and the transition from military to civilian governments required a different solution in each case. In all three

territories, however, Root favored improvements in education, health care, and transportation.

The absence of a strong movement for independence in Puerto Rico led Root to conclude that the best solution would be an indefinite period of American control. He proposed a highly centralized governmental structure centered on a governor and legislative council appointed by the president. Root persuaded McKinley that Puerto Rico's economic well-being depended upon an exemption from the Dingley Tariff rates, but the Administration accepted a temporary lower rate in the Foraker Act of 1900. Congress also provided for a popularly elected lower house in a bicameral Puerto Rican legislature, and Root accepted the change.

The terms of the peace treaty with Spain called for Cuban independence, and by 1902 Root had established a native government for Cuba and had withdrawn American military forces. He first replaced General John R. Brooke with General Leonard Wood as the military governor, and he instructed Wood to mount a program to repair war damage and to modernize schools, roads, and systems of sanitation. A constitutional convention met in 1901; the delegates were elected by Cubans, but Root had restricted the vote to property owners, former soldiers, and those who were literate. The constitution produced by the convention contained guarantees of American interests originally outlined in the Platt Amendment to the Army Appropriation Act of March 2, 1901. The government of the United States was granted the right to buy or lease bases on Cuban soil, and it was given the right to intervene with troops if Cuban independence or the stability of the Cuban government were threatened.

Root faced a more difficult task in dealing with the situation in the Philippines. Forces led by Emilio Aguinaldo were in revolt against the American military government, and Root, as secretary of war, had both to bring home the twenty-one thousand troops in the islands whose enlistments were running out and to replace them with an effectively trained force which eventually numbered seventy-four thousand. It took two years to end the guerrilla war, and in the interval the report of a commission headed by President Jacob Schurman of Cornell led Root to conclude that the Philippines were not ready for independence or for a great degree of self-government. In 1900, McKinley and Root sent Judge William Howard Taft to Manila at the head of a second commission charged with replacing the military government. Taft became governor general, and a bicameral legislature was created. Root's instructions to the Taft commission, adopted by Congress in the Organic Act of 1902, became the formula for government of the Philippines pursued by the Roosevelt Administration.

Partly as a result of his activities as a colonial administrator, Root saw the need for reforming the army bureaucracy. He instituted a general staff system headed by a chief of staff directly responsible to the secretary of war, and he ended the practice of making permanent army staff appointments in Washington. There was a regular rotation of officers from the staff to the line. Root called for legislation which established the Army War College and which made the national guard the country's militia. He took steps to see that the guard received the same training and equipment as the regular army.

Root resigned as secretary of war on February 1, 1904, despite the objections of President Roosevelt, but he returned to the cabinet as secretary of state on July 7, 1905. He played no part in Roosevelt's arbitration of an ending to the Russo-Japanese War by means of the Treaty of Portsmouth; nor did he have anything to do with securing for the United States the right to build a canal through the Isthmus of Panama. Root's chief actions as secretary of state were designed to bolster the fabric of international agreements ensuring world peace. He placed emphasis on friendly relationships with the nations of South America, and in 1906 he undertook a lengthy personal tour of that continent which led to Latin American participation in the Second Hague Peace Conference in 1907.

In the area of Canadian-American relations, Root resolved the North Atlantic coastal fisheries dispute. With the help of Lord Bryce, the British ambassador in Washington, he found a solution to the Alaska boundary issue. Root negotiated a voluntary immigration restriction agreement with Japan after the unrest in California over Japanese labor precipitated exclusion laws. By means of the Root-Takahira agreement and an arbitration treaty concluded in 1908, he established mechanisms for consultation between the governments of the United States and Japan. Root was committed to voluntary arbitration of international disputes, and during his tenure as secretary of state, he negotiated bilateral arbitration agreements with twenty-four foreign governments. In 1912, he was awarded the Nobel Peace Prize for these efforts to move international disagreements within a judicial framework.

In the instructions that were given to the American delegates to the 1907 Hague Peace Conference, Root outlined plans for a permanent court of arbitral justice and committed the American government to its establishment. The nations represented at the conference, however, could not agree on a procedure for selecting judges. The idea was put aside until 1920, when Root, invited by the League of Nations, served on the committee that drafted the statute establishing the World Court. Root worked with President Warren G. Harding and Secretary of State Charles Evans Hughes to gain approval for American membership in the court, but congressional opposition led by Senator Henry Cabot Lodge frustrated the effort. In 1929, Root returned to Geneva to serve on the committee revising the 1920 statute, and he devised a compromise on advisory opinions, usually termed the "Root formula," meeting United States objections to certain classes of cases coming before the World Court. Delays in submitting these changes to Congress and the changing political situation led to the treaty's eventual defeat in 1935.

By that time, Root was ninety years old, and his public career was behind him. He had resigned as secretary of state on March 5, 1909, before assuming the office of United States senator, to which he had been elected by the New York State legislature. Root's career as a senator was less significant than his previous career as a member of the McKinley and Roosevelt cabinets. Root lacked sympathy with the Progressive legislation supported by William Howard Taft, Roosevelt's successor, and he grew disenchanted with Woodrow Wilson's policy of neutrality toward the conflict in Europe that developed into World War I.

Root supported Wilson's efforts to mobilize once the United States entered World War 1, and in 1917 he went to Russia as head of a mission to the Provisional Revolutionary Government. Wilson did not appoint Root as an American representative to the peace conference at Versailles, but the former secretary of state gave public support to Wilson's plan to join the League of Nations. He had reservations about Article X of the League Covenant and wanted modifications in the terms of the treaty, but he encouraged Senator Lodge to support American membership. Lodge, however, came out in opposition to both the Treaty of Versailles and membership in the League of Nations.

Elihu Root died in New York City on February 7, 1937. He was buried in the cemetery on the Hamilton College campus in Clinton, New York, his birthplace and family home.

### Summary

The achievements of Elihu Root's long period of public service fall into two categories. The first is a set of pragmatic solutions to specific problems. His differing approaches to the governing of Puerto Rico, Cuba, and the Philippines, like the reforms he initiated in the structure and training of the army, testify to his skills as a lawyer. Root's work as secretary of war demonstrates the ability of the United States at the beginning of the twentieth century to take on the responsibilities of a global power. The second category of achievement is Root's consistent efforts to forge a judicial system to interpret a growing body of international law. His work as secretary of state on a series of bilateral arbitration treaties, his support of Wilson's call for a League of Nations, and his efforts to establish the World Court testify to his commitment. Root declined an appointment to the World Court itself. Given the fact that the United States was not a party to the treaty establishing the court, he believed that it was inappropriate for him to sit as a judge.

Root's skills were best suited to administration and negotiation. In addition to his work on behalf of the League of Nations and the World Court, he was one of four American delegates to the Conference on the Limitation of Armaments held in Washington, D.C., between November 12, 1921, and February 6, 1922. He served as president or chairman of a number of the organizations founded by Andrew Carnegie, including the Carnegie Endowment for International Peace, and he advised every administration through that of Franklin D. Roosevelt in the area of foreign affairs.

### Bibliography

Coletta, Paolo E. *The Presidency of William Howard Taft*. Lawrence: University Press of Kansas, 1973. Clear account of the Roosevelt-Taft split. Notes Root's ties to both men; examines the 1912 election campaign.

Gould, Lewis L. *The Presidency of William McKinley*. Lawrence: University Press of Kansas, 1981. Gould argues that McKinley shaped military and foreign policy more aggressively than previous scholars have believed.

Jessup, Philip C. *Elihu Root*. 2 vols. New York: Dodd Mead, 1938. The most complete account of Root's public career and his political views, this book was begun during Root's lifetime and benefited from the use of his papers.

Leopold, Richard W. *Elihu Root and the Conservative Tradition*. Boston: Little Brown, 1954. Leopold traces Root's political conservatism but also shows his pragmatic interest in international law.

Millett, Allan Reed. *The Politics of Intervention: The Military Occupation of Cuba, 1906-1909*. Columbus: Ohio State University Press, 1968. This study stresses the role of the United States Army in the policy-making process which determined the nature of the American occupation of Cuba.

Mowry, George E. *The Era of Theodore Roosevelt: 1900-1912*. London: Hamilton, and New York: Harper, 1958. Granting Root's service to Roosevelt, Mowry notes that the president's growing progressivism was matched by Root's increasing conservatism.

Pratt, Julius W. *America's Colonial Experiment: How the United States Gained, Governed, and in Part Gave Away a Colonial Empire*. Englewood Cliffs, N.J.: Prentice-Hall, 1951. Pratt's study pulls together the story of America's involvement in Cuba, the Philippines, Puerto Rico, Hawaii, and Central America.

*Robert C. Petersen*

# HERMANN RORSCHACH

*Born:* November 8, 1884; Zurich, Switzerland
*Died:* April 2, 1922; Herisau, Switzerland
*Areas of Achievement:* Psychiatry and psychology
*Contribution:* Rorschach is credited with only one major scientific achievement during his short career, but this achievement was important in the development of modern psychology and had far-reaching effects on other disciplines as well. In the early 1920's, Rorschach set forth a formal method of testing personality traits by recording, timing, and interpreting a subject's reactions to a series of inkblots. The test remains one of the most valuable testing tools of psychology.

## Early Life

Hermann Rorschach was born in Zurich, Switzerland, on November 8, 1884. The psychiatrist's early preoccupation with inkblots in part came from the fact that his father, Ulrich Rorschach, was an art teacher at local schools. Early in life, he was given the nickname "Kleck," meaning inkblot in German, by companions at school. Rorschach was the eldest of three children; he had a sister, Anna, and a brother, Paul. When he was twelve years old his mother died, and six years later his father died also.

Rorschach attended local elementary and high schools and was graduated with distinction from the latter when he was nineteen years old. At this time, he decided to pursue a career in medicine and attended medical schools in Neuchâtel, Zurich, and Bern—all in Switzerland—as well as in Berlin, Germany. He completed his medical study in five years, finishing in Zurich, where he had worked at a psychiatric unit of the university hospital and had excelled as a student of Eugen Bleuler. In 1909, he secured a residency at an asylum in Munsterlingen, Switzerland; the following year, he married Olga Stempelin, a Russian who worked at the institution. They later had two children: Elizabeth, born in 1917, and Wadin, born in 1919.

In 1912, Rorschach completed all requirements for the degree of doctor of medicine from the University of Zurich. In 1913-1914, his wife and he worked at a mental institution in Moscow, Russia; they returned to Switzerland when Rorschach became a resident doctor at Waldau Mental Hospital in Bern. Some two years later, he left Bern for Appenzell, Switzerland, where he accepted a better position at the Krombach Mental Hospital. In 1919, he became the first vice president of the Swiss Psychoanalytic Society.

## Life's Work

Because of his father's influence, Rorschach had been interested in drawing and art from youth. As early as 1911, when he was completing the doctor of medicine degree at the University of Zurich, he had conducted limited research with inkblots, using schoolchildren as his subjects. As a student of psychology and psychiatry himself, Rorschach studied the works of other researchers who had conducted experiments into the possibility of determining personality traits by using inkblots; chief among these were the recorded experiments of Justinus Kerner and Alfred Binet. None of these, however, succeeded in formulating a systematic method of conducting such a test and meaningfully interpreting the results in a consistent fashion from subject to subject.

Between 1911 and 1921, Rorschach conducted extensive research (both on patients in the mental hospitals where he worked and on well-adjusted, unconfined persons) in order to develop such a test. During this period, he published several professional papers, none of which received any particular notoriety. His single contribution was his *Psychodiagnostik* (1921; *Psychodiagnostics: A Diagnostic Test Based on Perception*, 1942), written as a preliminary study upon a basic method which he expected to refine and improve. The major contribution of the work to psychiatry is that it presented what came to be known as the "Rorschach test." (Later, this phrase was changed to "projective test"; the terms are now more or less used interchangeably, although technically the Rorschach test is merely one kind of projective personality test.) Rorschach's book has usually been cited for this achievement, but in fact it contains a far grander scope than this. *Psychodiagnostics* provides an entire theory of human personality, both individual and collective. Rorschach found two major personality types, the "introversive" and the "extratensive"—roughly equivalent to "introverted" and "extroverted" in modern parlance. Introversive persons are motivated by internal factors and inclinations, finding meaning in activities of the self; extroverts, on the other hand, function under the influence of external forces and motivators and look outside themselves to find meaningful experiences. Rorschach believed that both of these types exist in each person but to different extents, in various measures, and in determinable ratios. The test he devised was intended to discover these ratios in an individual, that is, the extent of introversion and extratension. Additionally, he believed that the test could be some measure of the subject's emotional stability, intelligence, capabilities, resolve at problem solving, and general normalcy; he thought that the test would reveal with some certainty any significant psychological problems or aberrations.

The test itself is unusually simple, although recording, scoring, and interpreting the results is a complicated process, the effectiveness of which depends primarily upon the capabilities and experience of the person giving the test. The subject is shown ten cards in turn, five of which are black and white, two of which are black and white with some color, and three of which are in color. The tester maintains total neutrality when asking the subject what he sees. The inkblots themselves are meaningless in that they do not, by design, represent any known object in the physical world; however, they are symmetrical figures which are suggestive of actual physical objects. The subject's responses are carefully noted in terms of location (the part of the inkblot on which the subject's eyes focus); time (the length of time it takes the subject to see an object after the inkblot is presented to him); content (what the subject "sees"); various determinants (the subject's focus upon color, form, and shadings of the drawing); and originality (the subject's ability to see items not usually suggested). Through the years, testers have amassed a wealth of information regarding these responses. Statistical data, formulas, weighted frequencies, and the like have been developed to help ensure accuracy of test results. It is interesting also that the same ten inkblots designed by Rorschach are still in use.

When *Psychodiagnostics* first appeared in Europe in 1921, it was virtually ignored, until it was attacked. The belief of the day by the best-known psychologists and psychiatrists was that personality could not be tested. They recognized some validity in the free-association responses to inkblot drawings but were overwhelmingly skeptical of formulating a system that could be of much use. In 1922, Rorschach himself expressed to the Psychoanalytic Society his intention to change and improve his techniques. Unfortunately, this was

never to happen, because he fell prey to an attack of appendicitis and died on April 2, 1922, in Herisau, Switzerland.

### Summary

The loss to psychology wrought by Hermann Rorschach's premature death can only be guessed. He was the foremost researcher into psychological testing of his day, and he clearly had a masterful command of every facet of study in his discipline. However great the loss, there is some professional comfort in knowing that his methods were quickly adapted and adopted by his students and colleagues; consequently, his ten inkblots have been the subject of a large number of studies, publications, experiments, and applications. His program has been used in studying child development and psychology; it has also been used by employers screening job applicants, by the military to determine which soldiers would do well as commanding officers in warfare, and by prison officials, psychologists, and psychiatrists. Moreover, Rorschach's program, or a modified version thereof, has been used in anthropology, sociology, and education. Counselors and clinicians have administered the test and made use of the results in the treatment of persons with speech problems, juvenile delinquents, alcoholics, and drug abusers.

The Rorschach test has been an integral part of psychological testing and diagnosis for nearly a century, yet its validity is still subject to dispute. Some professionals maintain that personality cannot be tested; others relentlessly affirm the accuracy of a properly administered and interpreted test. Most persons who work extensively with the Rorschach test testify to its value as an indicator. They make use of it for formulating hypotheses about a particular subject's behavior and motivation, or they regard it simply as one possible test which can be successfully used as part of a psychological profile. Whatever the case, Rorschach made an enormous contribution to psychological testing, and thereby to psychoanalysis and to psychology itself, when he published *Psychodiagnostics*.

## Bibliography

Beck, Samuel J. *The Rorschach Experiment: Ventures in Blind Diagnosis*. New York: Grune and Stratton, 1960. This book is primarily concerned with assisting testers in interpreting test results. Beck relates personal experiences in instructing others in the matter of correct interpretation.

———. *Rorschach's Test*. New York: Grune and Stratton, 1944. Beck was the leading proponent of Rorschach testing in the United States during the first half of the twentieth century. The book is essentially an instruction manual on how to administer the test. Diagrams of the ten inkblots are comprehensively treated.

Bohm, Ewald. *A Textbook in Rorschach Test Diagnosis for Psychiatrists, Physicians, and Teachers*. Translated by Ann Beck and Samuel Beck. New York: Grune and Stratton, 1958. Bohm was a leader in Rorschach testing in Europe during the two or three decades after Rorschach's death. Details Bohm's experiences using the test in diagnosing particular psychological maladies.

Hirt, Michael. *Rorschach Science: Readings in Theory and Method*. Glencoe, Ill.: Free Press, 1962. This is somewhat advanced in its discussions, content, and approach, and will be of little use to a student unfamiliar with Rorschach testings. For those who are, however, it provides valuable information about problem areas of testing and interpreting test results.

Klopfer, Bruno, and Douglas Kelley. *The Rorschach Technique: A Manual for a Projective Method of Personality Diagnosis*. Yonkers-on-Hudson, N.Y.: World, 1942. This book is one of the best overall treatments of Rorschach and his testing theories. A history of projective testing is provided, and every important aspect of the testing process is examined in a readable fashion.

Larson, Cedric A. "Hermann Rorschach and the Ink-Blot Test." *Science Digest* 44 (October, 1958): 84-89. This short article provides a good general sketch of Rorschach's life and works. It is glowingly appreciative, too much in the style of the day; nevertheless, it is factually accurate.

Rabin, Albert I., ed. *Assessment with Projective Techniques: A Concise Introduction*. New York: Springer, 1981. This book contains ten articles written by professional specialists in psychological testing. The contributions represent sundry attitudes and approaches to Rorschach testing. Provides a good introduction to the field.

———. *Projective Techniques in Personality Assessment*. New York: Springer, 1968. This text is a comprehensive general introduction to projective techniques in psychological testing. It contains articles by some twenty of the best researchers of the decade.

Rickers-Ovsiankina, Maria A., ed. *Rorschach Psychology*. New York: Wiley, 1960. This book is a collection of essays written by eighteen contributors from the field of psychological testing. The text is not an introduction manual in methodology; various aspects of the testing process are critically examined.

Zulliger, Hans. *The Behn-Rorschach Test*. New York: Grune and Stratton, 1956. Hans Behn-Eschenburg recognized the need for a duplicate Rorschach test—one which is composed of a series of alternate inkblots—even before Rorschach's death. This book explains the development of this alternate series and discusses correlation and results between the two tests.

*Carl Singleton*

# PETE ROSE

*Born:* April 14, 1941; Cincinnati, Ohio
*Area of Achievement:* Sports
*Contribution:* Rose broke Ty Cobb's major league baseball record of 4,191 hits in 1985 and established a new record of 4,256 hits by the time he retired in 1986. He lost an assured place in baseball's Hall of Fame in 1989 when he was banned from the sport for allegedly betting on baseball games.

## Early Life

A native of Cincinnati, Ohio, Peter Edward Rose was born on April 14, 1941, the son of Harry Francis Rose and LaVerne Bloebaum Rose. They had four children: two girls (Jackie and Caryl) and two boys (Peter and Dave). The Rose children attended Saylor Park Elementary School. As a child, Rose was obsessed with baseball. His father Harry was a famous local athlete who, along with his uncle, Ed (Buddy) Bloebaum, devoted special time to teaching Rose how to play the game. Harry rolled and pitched baseballs to his first-born son in the back yard of the house. At the age of four, Rose hit one of his father's pitches through a back window. Harry treasured the broken pane as a sign of his son's future baseball prowess; it was covered but never replaced while the parents lived in the house.

As Rose grew older, his father began drilling him in baseball skills. They both loved to play the game, but his dad dictated that he play to win. Because of Rose's small stature, both agreed that he should work on just getting hits rather than trying to be a home-run hitter like Babe Ruth. At the age of nine, Rose became a member of the Knothole Club, which sponsored baseball leagues in Bold Face Park. He "banged out line drive after line drive" on the same diamond on which his grandfather and father once had played.

Uncle Buddy began training Rose to prepare for a professional baseball career. He and Harry decided to teach him to be a switch hitter. Before going to bed each night, Rose would swing the bat one hundred times left-handed and one hundred times right-handed. Rose worked hard to perfect the technique, as his hitting records later proved. Rose started as a catcher and, after two years, began to play third base. Yet he valued the experience behind the plate as a quick learning position for a baseball player.

Rose attended Western Hills High School. In 1955, when Rose entered his freshman year, the baseball coach was Paul "Pappy" Nohr, who had sent several high-school players into the major leagues. Counting on playing on the varsity football team as a sophomore, Rose was devastated when he was not invited to try out because of his small size. He lost interest, skipped classes and school, bummed around town, and flunked his second year. He lost a year of his eligibility and was forced to repeat his sophomore studies. He did play two years on the varsity football and baseball teams but stood on the sidelines most of his senior year.

Two baseball openings filled the void of his final year in high school. First, sports watchdog John Brosnan got Rose into a Cincinnati Reds uniform to catch fly balls during the team's batting practice when they were in town. Second, his uncle helped place him on the roster of the Lebanon team in the Dayton Amateur League. Rose loved the experience; he played at second base, and his team was soon "tearing the league apart." The day after Rose graduated from high school in 1960, his uncle and dad took him to the Reds' Crosley Field offices, where he was offered a contract to play on one of the Reds' minor league teams.

## Life's Work

Rose got an early start on his ambition to become a professional baseball player. He signed his first contract on June 18, 1960, and flew to Geneva, New York, to join the Geneva Red Legs of the Class D New York-Penn League. He earned $400 per month. The team manager moved the second baseman to third base to make room for Rose. He batted .227 and made thirty-six errors in the eighty-five games of his first season for a team that finished last in the league, yet the Reds kept him on the roster for a second season.

That winter Rose attended the Instructional League in Florida to improve his game skills, then returned to a job unloading freight cars for a Cincinnati firm to build his strength. He was able to increase his weight to 175 pounds before he reported to spring training in Tampa, Florida, where he joined the Class A Florida State League. Rose led the league with thirty triples for the year and batted .331. His third season was spent in Macon, Georgia, with the South Atlantic League, where the

Reds sent their best prospects. His credentials continued to improve: He batted .330, led the league with 136 runs and 17 triples, and hit 9 home runs.

In 1963, Rose was invited to the Reds' spring training camp along with several others from the minor league. During the opening game of the Florida preseason, manager Fred Hutchinson put Rose in as a pinch runner. He stayed in the game to hit two doubles and score the game-winning run. Hutchinson started Rose at second base in the Reds' opening-day game against the Pittsburgh Pirates in 1963 and issued him his first major-league baseball contract. When introduced to the sold-out Crosley Field audience, including his parents, he was given a standing ovation that he never forgot. Rose batted .271 his first season and won the Rookie of the Year Award for 1963. In 1965 he made the All-Star Team for the first time. During his career, he was named to the National League All-Star team sixteen times and started in five different positions.

Hutchinson died in 1964, and Dave Bristol became the Reds' manager. He moved Rose to left field to make a place for Tommy Helms. During the late 1960's, Rose won his first batting titles, hitting .335 in 1968 and .348 in 1969. Perhaps the most famous single play of his career occurred during the 1970 All-Star Game held in the new Riverfront Stadium in Cincinnati. With the score tied in the bottom of the twelfth inning, Rose singled and then moved to second base on another player's single. When Jim Hickman sent a base hit into center field, Rose took off at the crack of the bat and barreled over catcher Ray Fosse before the ball got to home plate, winning the game 5 to 4. It provided one of baseball's most famous action photographs.

Rose played for the Cincinnati Reds as a powerful switch hitter from 1963 through 1978. He was the lead-off hitter during the winning era of Cincinnati's "Big Red Machine" assembled by general manager Bob Howsam and managed by George "Sparky" Anderson, which included catcher Johnny Bench, Tony Perez, Dave Concepcion, Joe Morgan, Ken Griffey, George Foster, and Cesar Geronimo. Anderson asked Rose to be the team captain and build a sense of unity among the players. Rose moved to third base to accommodate Foster, who could then play in left field. The team won four pennants and back-to-back World Series in 1975 and 1976. Rose's 1974 fielding of .997 set a National League record for outfielders.

In 1979, as a free agent, Rose accepted a four-year contract worth $3.2 million with the Philadelphia Phillies, making him the highest salaried player in baseball. He helped the Phillies win the World Series title in 1980 and the pennant race in 1983. He moved to the Montreal Expos in 1984, only to be called back to Cincinnati later that season to lead the Reds as the player-manager. On September 11, 1985, again in a Reds uniform, Rose walloped his 4,192d hit, finally beating Ty Cobb's long-standing major-league record set in 1928. He retired from professional baseball with dozens of records and honors in 1988. During his career, Rose amassed two hundred hits or more per season ten times, averaged over .300 for nine straight years (1965-1973), and scored over one hundred runs ten times. He was voted the National League's Most Valuable Player in 1973. In 1978 he hit safely in forty-four consecutive games, setting a new National League record.

Rose married Karolyn Ann Engelhardt on January 25, 1964, in Cincinnati. They had two children: a son named Pete, Jr., and a daughter named Fawn. After their divorce in 1980, Rose married Carol Woliung on April 11, 1984, and had two children:

a boy named Tyler and a girl named Cara Chae. Pete Rose, Jr., followed his father into professional baseball and played briefly for the Reds during September, 1997, then returned to the minors. Rose's father Harry had died of a heart attack on December 9, 1970, but had lived long enough to see his son reach stardom.

In August, 1989, Baseball Commissioner A. Bartlett Giamatti banned Rose from baseball for life. Giamatti based his action on evidence from an investigation conducted by his office into charges that Rose had violated baseball rules by betting on baseball games. The "lifetime suspension" included the right to apply for reinstatement after one year. Rose accepted the agreement but denied ever betting on baseball games. A few days after the agreement was signed, Giamatti died of a heart attack at his summer home on Martha's Vineyard. As of 1998, Rose still had not been reinstated. In April, 1990, Rose also pleaded guilty to two counts of filing false federal income tax returns. His penalty included a prison sentence of five months and a fine. After his release, he returned to live with his family near Plant City, Florida.

### Summary

Pete Rose proved to be a versatile major league baseball player for twenty-four years, with his greatest achievement coming when he broke Ty Cobb's record one year before he retired in 1986. By that time, he had appeared in a record 3,562 regular season games and had amassed 14,053 at bats, 4,256 hits, and 3,215 singles. He had also accumulated twenty-three straight one-hundred-hit seasons and a lifetime batting average of .303. He continued to manage the Reds through twenty-three games during the 1988 season, when he was forced to retire. Rose has also authored or coauthored at least fourteen books.

Rose's ever-growing habit of gambling (he continues to deny ever betting on baseball games) eventually twisted his life story into a wretched morality tale, a race between good and evil running toward an inevitable judgment day. His search for the Holy Grail of baseball, the Cooperstown Hall of Fame, crashed at home plate when major league baseball's commissioner permanently banned him from the sport. The true hallmark of Rose was his gritty determination to play baseball aggressively in every inning regardless of the score. He set a keen example for the field of athletics by playing to win regardless of his own physical risk and the position assigned to him. His rambunctious and optimistic outlook characterized his actions on and off the baseball diamond. In retirement, he still believes he will be inducted into the Hall of Fame, where his fans know he belongs.

### Bibliography

Gilbert, Thomas W. *Pete Rose*. Baseball Legends Series. New York: Chelsea House, 1995. Each book in this series of short biographies of forty legendary baseball heros (to 1995) for juveniles provides a basic, well-illustrated introduction to each man's career and includes a chronology, major league statistics, and list of further reading.

Reilly, Rick. "A Rose Is a Rose." *Sports Illustrated* 79, no. 7 (August 16, 1993). Account of Rose's life after being banished from baseball and his hopes for the future.

Reston, James, Jr. *Collision at Home Plate: The Lives of Pete Rose and Bart Giamatti*. New York: Burlingame, 1991. This dual biography is the most thorough account of two Americans whose careers led to the clash between a baseball hero allegedly turned gambler and the baseball commissioner in 1989.

Rose, Pete. *The Pete Rose Story: An Autobiography*. New York: World, 1970. Almost like a Horatio Alger story, this personal recollection of Rose's "rags to riches" (he won a $100,000 contract win the Reds in 1970) story is "a testament to the fact that desire, hustle, and devotion to the sport are what make the fine athlete a superstar."

Rose, Pete, and Hal Bodley. *Countdown to Cobb: My Diary of the Record-Breaking 1985 Season*. St. Louis, Mo.: Sporting News, 1985. Another season diary by Rose that traces the events that led to his breaking Ty Cobb's hitting record while in a Reds uniform as player-manager. Full of stats for that historic season.

Rose, Pete, and Bob Hertzel. *Charlie Hustle*. Englewood Cliffs, N.J.: Prentice-Hall, 1975. Written like a diary for the troublesome 1974 season during which the Reds fought the Dodgers in a tight race for the pennant, this book gives a closeup view of Rose's reactions to the upsets of baseball players, managers, and fans.

———. *Winning Baseball*. Chicago: Regnery, 1976. This how-to volume generously condenses Rose's accumulated insights about playing baseball to win, with pertinent chapters on hitting and playing every position of the game. Fine illustrative photographs.

Rose, Pete, and Roger Kahn. *Pete Rose: My Story.* New York and London: Macmillan, 1989. This is the best baseball biography for Rose, who worked closely with Kahn for the three final years of his record-breaking athletic career. Good reading with few photographs.

Sokolove, Michael Y. *Hustle: The Myth, Life, and Lies of Pete Rose*. New York: Simon and Schuster, 1990. This caustic story presumes to be a fair judgment of Rose compared to Commissioner Giamatti but, as the title indicates, terribly damages the baseball hero's image.

*Paul F. Erwin*

# NELLIE TAYLOE ROSS

*Born:* November 29, 1876; St. Joseph, Missouri
*Died:* December 19, 1977; Washington, D.C.
*Area of Achievement:* Government and politics
*Contribution:* The first woman governor of a state (Wyoming) in the United States, Ross later served as an officer in the Democratic Party and as a director of the U.S. Mint, one of the first women to head a federal agency.

## Early Life

Nellie Davis Tayloe was born on November 29, 1876, in St. Joseph, Missouri. Her father, James Wynn Tayloe, was from a prominent Southern family, one of whose members had built the Octagon House in Washington, D.C., where President James Madison and his wife Dolley lived after the British burned the White House during the War of 1812. Her mother, Elizabeth Blair Green Tayloe, was descended from a family that claimed a distant kinship with George Washington.

Nellie attended public and private schools and had private instruction as well. Her family eventually moved to Omaha, Nebraska, where she completed a two-year program as a kindergarten teacher and taught briefly before her marriage.

While visiting relatives in Tennessee, she met and fell in love with a young lawyer, William Bradford Ross. He moved to Cheyenne, Wyoming, before marrying Nellie in 1902. The Rosses had four sons: the twins, George Tayloe and James Ambrose, born in 1903; Alfred Duff, born in 1905, who died at ten months of age; and William Bradford, born in 1912. Nellie devoted herself to her home and family during her marriage. She was active in the Cheyenne Woman's Club, which concentrated on intellectual self-improvement, and she often presented programs there.

William Ross practiced law and occasionally ran for political office. As a Democrat in a Republican state, however, he had little political success until, to his wife's dismay, he was elected governor of Wyoming in 1922 by a coalition of Democrats and Progressive Republicans. In September of 1924, he became ill and underwent an appendectomy. Complications from the surgery led to his death on October 2, 1924.

## Life's Work

Because Governor Ross's death occurred close to the upcoming general election on November 4, 1924, Wyoming law required that his successor be elected then. Democratic Party leaders in Wyoming offered Nellie Tayloe Ross the nomination to fill the remainder of her husband's term. She did not reply and the party took her silence for acquiescence, nominating her on October 14. She had no political experience except for what she had acquired as her husband's confidant and in her tenure as the governor's wife. Although she lived in a state where women had voted since 1869, she had played no role in the woman suffrage campaign. She later indicated that she had accepted the nomination because she wished her husband's programs to continue and believed that she understood what he would have done better than anyone else; she also expressed the need for some purpose in her own life as she coped with the grief of widowhood. The Republicans nominated Eugene J. Sullivan of Casper, an attorney whose ties to the oil industry may have hurt his campaign since both Wyoming and the nation were immersed in the Teapot Dome scandal in-

volving federal oil lands (including property located in Wyoming).

Nellie Ross did not campaign for office. Friends paid for a few political advertisements, and she wrote two open letters stating her intentions. She probably had two advantages in the election. The first was the sympathy of the voters for her widowhood. She indicated, and many people agreed, that a vote for her was a tribute to her deceased husband. The second advantage was the popular support among citizens for Wyoming to become the first state to elect a woman governor, since it had been first in 1869 to allow women to vote. This election would be the state's only chance to secure this distinction, since Miriam A. ("Ma") Ferguson, wife of impeached former governor James A. Ferguson, was likely to be elected governor of Texas in November. Although Ross won election easily, she did not help other Democrats in Wyoming in what was generally a catastrophic year for Democratic candidates nationwide in the wake of the crushing defeat of the party's presidential candidate by Republican Calvin Coolidge.

Nellie Tayloe Ross was inaugurated as the thirteenth governor of Wyoming on January 5, 1925, still wearing mourning clothes. In her brief address she stated that her administration would not be a new one, but rather a continuation of her husband's. She entered office with much popular sympathy and an administration in place. Since Ferguson was not sworn in as governor of Texas until January 25, Nellie Tayloe Ross was the nation's first woman governor.

When the Wyoming legislature convened in January of 1926, the new governor gave her first major speech, based on her husband's notes on his plans for that legislative session. She called for reductions in both state expenditures and taxes; for state assistance to the economically depressed agricultural industry; and for banking reform, noting the number of recently failed banks. She championed protective legislation for miners and for women and children, and she requested unsuccessfully that Wyoming ratify the federal amendment prohibiting child labor.

Ross recognized that the Republican-dominated legislature had little reason to cooperate with her. On some issues, such as banking reform, she was able to work out compromises with Republican leaders. In a few instances, she used the veto. She believed that her veto of a bill requiring a special election (rather than appointment by the governor) to fill a vacancy in Wyoming's delegation to the United States Senate caused her defeat in 1926. Wyoming's elderly Republican senator had been reelected only a short time earlier, and it was believed that he would not live to complete his term. Republicans did not want their Democratic governor to have the opportunity to appoint a Democrat to the position.

Ross was aware of the public's intense scrutiny of her actions and knew that if she made mistakes as governor, people would use them to claim that women should not hold high elective office. She found curiosity-seekers constantly in her office and on the porch of her home. Although she received invitations to speak all over the country, she declined them all. When she appeared in Calvin Coolidge's Inaugural Parade in Washington, D.C., she got the largest ovation. Many Easterners still thought of Wyoming as an uncivilized place, and its cultured, gracious governor attracted attention simply because she was so different from their expectations.

As an administrator, Ross received mixed reviews. She removed from office some administrators appointed by her husband who were not meeting her expectations. She lamented the difficulties of enforcing Prohibition and advocated better law enforcement. She stood up to the federal government on issues of federal lands and water allocation.

Nellie Ross was nominated by the Democrats for reelection in 1926, but was defeated in a close election by the Republican candidate, Frank C. Emerson. While her veto of the senatorial special election law was one issue, Republicans vaguely alluded to the idea that a man would be a better governor than a woman. Democrats tried unsuccessfully to win women voters by suggesting that a rejection of Ross would be a rejection of woman suffrage. Ultimately she probably was defeated because she was a Democrat in a Republican state and the sympathy issue that had helped her in 1924 was no longer a factor. As it was, she did better than any other statewide Democratic candidate in Wyoming.

Ross never again sought elective public office. Instead, she lectured and wrote articles for magazines. She became involved in national politics, serving as a Wyoming committeewoman to the Democratic National Committee (DNC) and then as vice chairman of the DNC, in charge of activities for women. In 1928, she seconded the presidential nomination of New York Governor Alfred E. Smith. With Eleanor Roosevelt, she headed the campaign drive launched by the party's Women's Division to generate support for Smith. Already a popular speaker, Ross traveled around the country making speeches tirelessly and unsuccessfully for Smith's election. Four years later, Ross was active in the Women's Speakers' Bureau, campaigning for the Democratic presidential nominee, Franklin D. Roosevelt.

With the election of Roosevelt as president in 1932, women became more visible in the federal government. Eleanor Roosevelt acted on her husband's behalf and publicly involved herself in policy issues to an unprecedented degree—one that was not duplicated until Hillary Rodham Clinton became First Lady in 1993.

Franklin D. Roosevelt decided that he wanted to be the first president to appoint a woman to the cabinet. Ross was considered for either secretary of the interior or secretary of labor, but Roosevelt selected Frances Perkins as secretary of labor instead. He appointed a number of women to federal office; among them were Ruth Bryan Owens as minister to Denmark (1933-1936), Josephine Roche as assistant secretary of the Treasury (1934-1937), and Nellie Tayloe Ross as director of the United States Mint.

As director of the Mint, Ross dealt with the American gold and silver bullion reserve and the minting of coins for the United States and several foreign governments. Appointed in 1933, she served as the Mint's first woman director. At that time, huge quantities of gold and silver poured into the U.S. government's coffers. Ross discovered that most of the work was still being done by hand and directed that the process be automated. She emphasized efficiency and was able to reduce the costs of her operation significantly. In 1950, she informed an astonished Congressional Appropriations Committee that she had not needed all of her previous year's appropriation and wanted to return about $1 million of her $4.8 million appropriation. Her efficiency plans reduced the labor needs of the mint and resulted in the discharge of about 3,000 of the Mint's 4,000 employees. She continued as director of the Mint in the Roosevelt and Truman administrations and was not replaced until the Republican administration of President Dwight D. Eisenhower came to power in 1952. Ross continued to make her home in Washington, D.C., until her death on December 19, 1977.

### Summary

Nellie Tayloe Ross never intended to have a political career. She believed that women belonged at home and was content there until her husband's death thrust her into politics. Her election was probably attributable to public sympathy generated by her husband's death. She was the first of many women elected to fill out their husbands' unexpired terms in office.

As the nation's first woman governor, she did not have a tremendous impact. She was probably an average governor, although she was regarded more favorably than Texas governor Miriam A. Ferguson. She achieved few of her goals because of Republican control of the legislature. Her defeat for reelection was probably the result of being a Democrat in a predominantly Republican state.

After her defeat, she focused her attention on other political matters by becoming active in the Democratic National Committee and appearing as a popular and effective speaker. Her loyalty and support for Franklin D. Roosevelt led him to consider her for several offices before appointing her the first woman director of the U.S. Mint. She administered the Mint economically and efficiently for almost twenty years. Although she was not the most visible woman in the New Deal, Ross was one of the most durable and effective.

### Bibliography

"First U.S. Woman Governor Celebrates Her Centennial During the Bicentennial." *Aging* 268 (February/March, 1977): 13-14. Aimed at a general audience, this biographical sketch provides a concise assessment of Ross's life and career. Discusses her activities after leaving office as governor, when she worked as a lecturer on the Chautauqua circuit and helped organize the women's division of the Democratic Party.

Huch, Ronald K. "Nellie Tayloe Ross of Wyoming Becomes First Female Governor." In *Great Events from History II: Human Rights*, edited by Frank N. Magill. Pasadena, Calif.: Salem Press, 1992. This is a brief, well-written account of her election as governor in 1924, with an analysis of its impact.

Othman, Frederick C. "She Makes Our Money." *Reader's Digest* 57 (November, 1950): 141-144. This condensation of a previously published newspaper article is a rare account of Ross's years as director of the Mint and is especially useful for information on her efforts to automate it.

Ross, Nellie Tayloe. "The Governor Lady." *Good Housekeeping* 85 (August, 1927), 30-31, 118-124; (September, 1927), 36-37, 206-218; (October, 1927), 72-73, 180-197. These articles provide Ross's own account of her years as governor. Except for Barbara Jean Aslakson's thesis, "Nellie Tayloe Ross: First Woman Governor" (University of Wyoming, 1960), these magazine pieces contain the best account of those years.

Ware, Susan. *Beyond Suffrage: Women in the New Deal*. Cambridge, Mass.: Harvard University Press, 1981. This is a well-researched account of influential women in the New Deal. It has information on Ross's activities in the Democratic National Committee, placing them in the context of women's roles in the New Deal.

———. *Holding Their Own: American Women in the 1930s*. Boston: Twayne, 1982. This well-documented account is useful in placing Ross's activities in the context of her times, but it has only two direct references to her.

*Judith A. Parsons*

# RONALD ROSS

*Born:* May 13, 1857; Almora, India

*Died:* September 16, 1932; Putney, London, England

*Area of Achievement:* Medicine

*Contribution:* Ross demonstrated the role of the mosquito in the transmission of malaria, proved the insect to be essential to the life cycle of the malarial parasite, and introduced the first effective preventive measures against malaria.

## Early Life

Ronald Ross was the oldest of ten children born to General Sir Campbell Claye Grant Ross, a Scotsman and British army officer in India, and Matilda Charlotte Elderton, the daughter of a London lawyer. While three Ross generations had served as fighting officers of the British Empire, a gentler stream also flowed into young Ross. His father was a skillful watercolorist of Indian scenery, and both parents loved music and poetry.

In 1865, Ross went to England for his education, living first on the Isle of Wight with an aunt and uncle and then at a school near Southampton until he was sixteen. When he left school, he showed no special promise, but he had developed a passionate interest in the arts and thought that he would be an artist. His father insisted that art was suitable only as a hobby and urged his son to enter the Indian Medical Service (IMS). Ross, with no inclination toward medicine, deferred to his father out of a sense of duty. In 1874, he began his training at London's St. Bartholomew's Medical School. He found medical studies difficult and never became a good student.

Ross needed to fulfill both surgery and medicine requirements to qualify for the IMS. He put off study until the last moment but passed the examination in surgery. This success gave him the notion that he could get away with studying even less for the medical requirement. He failed badly. After serving as ship's surgeon on a transatlantic liner, he qualified for the IMS and returned to India in 1881.

In India, Ross saw his future in terms of writing, and throughout his life, he wrote plays, romances, novels, fables, and poetry. He also threw himself into mathematics, developing a new theory of algebra. By 1885, Ross had served in Madras, Bangalore, Burma, and the Andaman Islands, enjoying the perquisites of a British officer. His novel *The Child of Ocean* (1889), set in the Andaman Islands, was highly praised by some critics, by others less so, although most thought Ross might become an important writer.

While Ross felt strongly about his writing, he was also aware of a lack of direction in his life. By 1888, he had received no promotion and no permanent position. He became despairing and neglected his medical duties. He threatened to resign unless granted a leave. His demand met, he returned to England for a year. He pursued his literary interests and took a diploma in public health. While on leave, he met and married Rosa Bloxam in 1889. They had two sons and two daughters.

Ross was powerfully built, and his wax-tipped, upturned military mustache and close-cropped hair gave him a bold appearance. He could not tolerate what he took to be stupidity or incompetence, and he lashed out at officials and fellow officers. His pugnacious and egotistical personality aroused hostility and created difficulties. Ross was also a melancholic dreamer and poet with a passionate

curiosity and could be kindly and genial. He reflected the British upper-class attitude of superiority in India. To Ross, the British were a true aristocracy ruling an inferior people.

## Life's Work

By 1890, Ross had published two volumes of poetry and two novels and had attempted to create an algebra of space and time. Medicine was secondary to him. While serving in Secunderabad, however, a large military post on a vast plain with lakes, his medical conscience awakened in the face of awesome medical problems, most especially the prevalence of malaria. He read all that he could about the disease, its symptoms, and the miasmatic theories of emanations from marshes. He read also of the 1880 discovery by Alphonse Laveran, a French army surgeon in Algeria, of a parasite in the blood cells of malarial patients. These crescent-shaped bodies on examination outside the body threw off flagella, little moving filaments. The parasites were protozoa of the *Plasmodium* genus. Ross wanted to understand malaria, and with a crude microscope, he tried to find the parasite in the blood of malaria patients, with no success. He became skeptical of its existence. He was floundering, and because the IMS did not encourage research, there was no one to advise him.

In 1894, Ross returned to England for his second leave. In London, the key figure in his career suddenly entered his life in the person of Sir Patrick Manson, an expert on tropical diseases. Manson took him to Charing Cross Hospital to show the skeptical Ross the parasite in the blood of patients. He directed Ross to publications and told him of a theory he had on how malaria was transmitted. In 1877, Manson had discovered the small parasitic worm in human blood that caused elephantiasis. Mosquitoes sucked the blood, and the worm developed in the mosquito. Manson suggested that the same might be true with malaria. Laveran's parasite might be transferred to a mosquito. Perhaps when mosquitoes laid their eggs in pools of water, the parasite escaped, and when people drank the water the parasite entered the human system to cause new cases of malaria. Ross now had an intense desire to return to India and test this mosquito theory. To replace his inadequate microscope, he invented a small portable one and had it made in London to take back with him to India. At the same time, he managed to finish two novels.

Back in India, with a promotion to major, Ross worked furiously for the next four years in his spare time from medical duties. He wrote 110 letters to Manson, pouring out his questions and difficulties; Manson replied regularly with answers, suggestions, and encouragement. At Secunderabad in 1895, Ross elaborated techniques for dissecting the internal organs of mosquitoes. Malarial patients volunteered to submit to the bites of mosquitoes captured by assistants. Ross then dissected the mosquitoes. His mosquitoes were the *Culex* and *Aëdes* types of the region. He proved that the parasite formed spheres in the stomachs of mosquitoes and that some gave off flagella, but this process took place in the blood itself when drawn from a patient. Something further must happen to the flagella, but he could find nothing. He did disprove Manson's drinking water theory; volunteers who drank water contaminated by malarious mosquitoes did not get the disease. The IMS saw no value in Ross's research and placed a series of obstacles in his way. For eighteen months, following a transfer to Bangalore to direct sanitary measures, he could do no research. During that time, however, the idea came to him that the parasite got into the healthy person the same way it got out of a sick one, by the bite of a mosquito.

In 1897, Ross returned to Secunderabad. His assistants caught some mosquitoes of a different type, not gray or brindled like the *Culex* or *Aëdes* ones but brown with dappled wings. He tested these on volunteers. With but two mosquitoes left, he dissected one on August 20, 1897 (Mosquito Day), and saw a cyst on the stomach wall, a new stage in the parasite's life. He examined his last mosquito the next day. The cells were larger; the parasite had grown. Fortunately, Manson had informed him of a recent discovery which enabled Ross to realize what he had observed. William MacCallum at Johns Hopkins that same summer saw the flagellation process and proved that the only cells which threw off flagella were male gametes, one of which penetrated a female cell and fertilized it. In addition to its asexual phase in human blood, the parasite had a sexual phase in its life history. Ross's cyst was part of that phase, and he immediately incorporated MacCallum's discovery into his research.

Ross thought that it would be a matter of a few weeks to unravel the whole life cycle of the parasite. Then came his biggest disappointment—an order to go to Bombay immediately. His research was at the breakthrough stage, but he was not to see the *Plasmodium* parasite for two years. Ross was bitter, especially since he was assigned to a small post near Bombay, simply as a replacement for an officer on leave.

In 1898, through Manson's urging, Ross was granted six months for research in Calcutta. There, however, he had no malaria cases. At Manson's suggestion, he studied avian malaria, since birds got malaria, had parasites in their blood, and were bitten by mosquitoes. He found that the gray *Culex* mosquito bit birds and carried the parasite in its stomach. He traced the full life cycle of the parasite from the fertilization of a female cell through the formation of spores which burst, releasing threads into the mosquito's body cavity and thence into the salivary gland. These germinal threads were the agents which invaded the healthy bird when the mosquito bit it. He confirmed the process by producing the disease in healthy birds by the bite of mosquitoes fed on infected birds. Ross's was the basic work in the field. Surely, the same process must take place in human blood and the dappled-wing mosquito.

When Ross requested more time for research, his superiors instead ordered him to Assam, denying him once again a chance to work on human malaria. When later in 1898 Italian scientists made the breakthrough he had hoped for by demonstrating the life cycle of the *Plasmodium* in human blood and in the *Anopheles* mosquito, Ross angrily claimed that they had stolen everything from him and refused to acknowledge the independence of their work. His bitterness was lasting. His *Memoirs with a Full Account of the Great Malaria Problem and Its Solution* (1923) is full of attacks on the Italians as thieves and pirates.

Ross decided to resign from the IMS and return to England in 1899. Publication of his avian malaria report made him famous. He planned to devote his life to the prevention of malaria; the way was clear, since the *Anopheles* mosquito was the sole mode of infection and it bred chiefly in stagnant water. He believed that it would take only a few years to rid the world of malaria by drainage and larvicide programs. He accepted an appointment as lecturer at the new Liverpool School of Tropical Medicine, the first of its kind. He used his position to undertake sanitary expeditions between 1899 and 1914. His optimism proved unwarranted; the world would not be rid of malaria in a few years. His initiatives did not proceed as quickly as he thought they should, in part as a result of the lack of cooperation by political authorities, in part because of the complexity of the problem. Nevertheless, his efforts significantly reduced the incidence of the disease, and his expeditions to malarial regions gave the Liverpool school its fame and prosperity.

In 1902, Ross received the Nobel Prize. His main contribution to the literature of malaria control was the classic, *The Prevention of Malaria* (1910), which gave a full account of antimalaria work in many countries. Ross was especially pleased when American officials cleared Panama of the mosquitoes responsible for malaria and yellow fever (1904); he believed they had set an example for the rest of the world.

In 1911, Ross received knighthood. During World War I, his first son, Ronald Campbell, an officer in the Royal Scots Regiment, was killed in action. Ross served during the war as consulting physician on tropical diseases and went overseas to deal with outbreaks of disease among British troops. His memoirs graphically depicted the torpedoing of his ship on a 1917 expedition to Greece.

In 1922, a letter signed by prominent persons on the twenty-fifth anniversary of Mosquito Day declared the importance of Ross's discoveries. The letter led to the founding in 1926 of the Ross Institute and Hospital for Tropical Diseases in Putney, near London, with Ross as director. It became an important center for malaria research, continuing its existence after 1933 as part of the London School of Hygiene and Tropical Medicine.

Although when Ross's memoirs appeared in 1923 he was full of resentment over his experiences in India and the slow progress in malaria control, his attitude changed when his pupil, Malcom Watson, went to Malaya and won an impressive victory over malaria by 1926. Ross went there to see for himself, the first example of all-out war against malaria in the British Empire.

Several of his literary endeavors were published during the 1920's, including a collected edition of his poetry, *Poems*, in 1928. The deaths of both his younger daughter and his wife preceded his death, which came after a long illness, at the Ross Institute on September 16, 1932.

## Summary

Ronald Ross's work was part of a series of investigations on malaria involving many scientists in different parts of the world and whose work linked together to unravel the nature of malarial fevers, the mode of transmission, the life cycle of the pathogen, and the measures to control the disease. His discoveries illuminated malariology profoundly, revealing the unsuspected mechanism of transmission by the mosquito and the sporogonic cycle of the parasite in it. Furthermore, Ross's work provided key insights for other investigations of tropical disease, especially yellow fever.

**Bibliography**

Bagla, Pallava. "Malaria Fighters Gather at a Site of Early Victory." *Science* 277, no.5331 (September 5, 1997). Brief story on a meeting of medical professionals commemorating Ross's discovery of the malaria parasite.

De Kruif, Paul. "Ross vs. Grassi: Malaria." In *Microbe Hunters*. New York: Harcourt Brace, 1926; London: Cape, 1963. De Kruif presents the dramatic story of both Ross and the Italians, trying to sort out who did what and what the controversy was about.

Gorgas, William C., and Fielding H. Garrison. "Ronald Ross and the Prevention of Malarial Fever." *Scientific Monthly* 3 (August, 1916): 132-150. A perceptive article by Gorgas, the leader of the mosquito campaign in Panama, and Garrison, the historian of medicine, on Ross's pioneering control efforts.

Kamm, Jacqueline. *Malaria Ross*. London: Methuen, 1963; New York: Criterion, 1964. A clear, straightforward, popular biography based on Ross's memoirs but supplemented with a valuable account of his last ten years.

Mégroz, Rodolphe L. *Ronald Ross: Discoverer and Creator*. London: Allen and Unwin, 1931. In addition to Ross's life and malaria work, this is a study of Ross as a writer, claiming he has been unduly neglected and praising him as a fine novelist and poet.

Nuttall, G. H. F. "Sir Ronald Ross." *Obituary Notices of Fellows of the Royal Society* 1 (1933): 108-115. The best account of Ross's career in the context of his time.

Nye, E. R., and Mary E. Gibson. *Ronald Ross: Malariologist and Polymath, a Biography*. London: Macmillan, and New York: St. Martin's Press, 1997. Biography of Ross including his work on tropical diseases.

Ross, Ronald. *Memoirs with a Full Account of the Great Malaria Problem and Its Solution*. London: Murray, and New York: Dutton, 1923. Indispensable reading for anyone wishing to understand the man and his lasting anger and bitterness and for the presentation of the minutest details of his research.

Russell, Paul F. *Man's Mastery of Malaria*. London and New York: Oxford University Press, 1955. A good, clear retrospective picture of malaria through history with chapters on the parasite, the mosquito, control methods, and much more. All the major figures are lucidly discussed.

Yoelli, Meir. "Sir Ronald Ross and the Evolution of Malaria Research." *Bulletin of the New York Academy of Medicine* 49 (August, 1973): 722-735. The most perceptive study on Ross and the major investigators from the point of view of medical science.

*Albert Costa*

## GEORGES ROUAULT

*Born:* May 27, 1871; Paris, France
*Died:* February 13, 1958; Paris, France
*Area of Achievement:* Art
*Contribution:* One of the greatest painters of the twentieth century, Rouault combined an existential philosophy and a strong Catholic faith with a prodigious artistic energy to amass a unique and distinctly identifiable body of work over fully seventy years of creativity.

### Early Life

Georges Rouault was born during a bombardment of Paris during the "troubled days of the Commune," his mother having taken shelter in the cellar of a house in the Belleville district. His cabinetmaker father worked at a piano factory; Rouault acquired much of his artistic taste from his maternal grandfather, Alexandre Champdavoine, a collector of the work of Honoré Daumier, Gustave Courbet, and Édouard Manet.

However oversimplified the observation may be, much of Rouault's distinct painting style can be traced to his very early apprenticeship in the stained-glass ateliers of Georges Hirsch. In his mature work, the bright colors and clearly defined shapes, separated by dark areas, are suggestive of the traditional stained-glass techniques.

Formal training came from the famous art studios at the École des Beaux-Arts, briefly under Élie Delaunay, but quickly followed by the tutelage of Gustave Moreau, whose favorite pupil he became. Rouault began his career with traditional paintings in line with the principles of the Academy painters but was encouraged by Moreau to seek his own way. His desire to find his own style can be seen as the positive outcome of his failure to win first prize in several early competitions. In 1895, encouraged by Moreau, he left the École to paint a series of sacred and profane scenes set in fantastic landscapes. A series of notebooks that the student maintained during his school years, *Souvenirs intimes* (1926; intimate memories), attest the importance on Rouault's whole aesthetic attitude of Moreau's lectures and admonitions to paint the spiritual life.

The death of Moreau in 1898 left Rouault without his best friend and spiritual adviser. Yet, in his will, Moreau arranged for Rouault to manage the archives of the Musée Gustave Moreau, thereby freeing Rouault from financial difficulties and allowing him to concentrate on his painting. Scholars have listed as Rouault's early influences the art of Daumier, Francisco de Goya, and Paul Cézanne, and the writings of Joris-Karl Huysmans, Léon Bloy, and Fyodor Dostoevski.

### Life's Work

Rouault's career parallels the Fauvist movement, but he was not among them; their descent into the primitive was contrary to Rouault's ascent into the spiritual, although their use of color bears definite similarities, with its richness and purity. Influenced by the Catholic writer Bloy (who befriended him but loathed his paintings), Rouault's work became more and more religious, sometimes in subject matter, as with his innumerable portraits of the Passion, but equally often in his approach to secular subjects. By 1905, figures such as clowns, prostitutes, and peasants, always shown in despair, never cartooned or ridiculed but depicted at a moment of deep philosophical grief, can be found in his paintings. This tendency to take seriously the angst of the common person has been connected with the existentialist philosophers of this and later periods, notably fellow Frenchmen Jean-Paul Sartre and Albert Camus, and also the earlier philosophers Søren Kierkegaard and Martin Heidegger.

Rouault's existential view, however, was a Christian one, in which suffering was humankind's earthly fate and temptations of the flesh a universal shortcoming. Almost never dealing with inanimate objects or landscapes, Rouault sought to capture the deep tragedy of human existence, expressed most succinctly in the faces of clowns, lower-class subjects, and Christ figures, often on the cross. His obsession with the crucifixion came from his acute sensitivity to the fact of Christ the man, capable of experiencing human pain and death.

Marrying, in 1908, Marthe Le Sidaner, who bore him four children, he began to settle into his working habits, a meticulous reworking of every painting and engraving over a period of years. A period of residence in Versailles in 1911 brought friendship with Jacques Maritain, who was to influence his religious views profoundly. The years until the beginning of World War I were filled with work in watercolors of a particularly brilliant palette, as he examined the themes of circus and prostitution equally fully. An extremely private man, especially for the glittering world of Parisian modern art,

Rouault needed to be sought out by his slowly growing admirers. Exhibits of his paintings were sparse on the calendars of the leading galleries, and those that did manage to acquire his work could only get hold of a few paintings at a time. In this sense, Rouault was truly an expressionist painter (another movement of this time, but centered in Germany), more concerned with putting his personal feelings onto canvas than with satisfying a commercial market.

Even though he was a prolific painter all of his life, there was a period from about 1910 to 1918 in which Rouault concentrated on other media, working in gouache, ink, and watercolor, only to return to oil painting occasionally; some years later, he again concentrated on oil, a slower, more contemplative medium.

Almost in passing, the established world of traditional art began to acknowledge Rouault's genius. The Musée d'Unterlinden in Colmar purchased his early work *Child Jesus Among the Doctors* in 1919; other museum purchases of the kind that ensured a growing reputation followed, as Rouault was preparing for his first major show, a 1924 retrospective at Bruet's Gallery in Paris, which brought together all of his scattered works from the past twenty years.

The year 1913 marked Rouault's commercial success and his first artistic commitment to a major gallery; it was the year that Ambroise Vollard bought his entire studio's output, including rights to subsequent paintings. By investing in the relatively unknown painter (Vollard had originally been attracted to some ceramic work of the artist), he made both a wise investment and a commitment to support the painter's work for life. He had previously bought the studio of Maurice de Vlaminck, who was to become a major force in the Fauvist movement, paralleling Rouault's career but separate from it.

At the center of the Vollard-Rouault relationship were two controversies. The first was artistic: Vollard commissioned a publication of a major engraving project, one hundred works originally to be called *Miserere et guerre* but later reduced by almost half and changed to *Miserere*, consisting of fifty-eight works. The project combined the energies of the two men for a period of thirty years. The project was impeded by Rouault's insistence on reworking the smallest detail of each engraving and Vollard's insistence on perfection. A similar attention to detail by both men accounts for the overlayering of paint on the canvases, resulting from the reworking of entire canvases sometimes over a period of twenty years. Other features of Rouault's style were the intense coloration of discrete segments, the outlining of areas, a frontal presentation of the subjects accompanied by a two-dimensionality common to icons, and a pronounced elongation of forms. The stained-glass windows of his youth were more than passingly instrumental in their effect on Rouault's perceptions.

The second controversy involved the right of the artist to change his work after its purchase by another party. Upon the death of Vollard in 1939, Rouault sued the estate for the return of some eight hundred paintings in Vollard's possession, claiming that they were unfinished and that his reputation as a painter would be jeopardized by their sale in the unfinished state. He won his case in 1947 and one year later, in front of horrified witnesses whose attitude was as though a wake were taking place, destroyed more than three hundred paintings, believing that he would never have a chance in his lifetime to complete them properly.

The Paris World's Fair of 1937 finally brought to Rouault the world recognition he long deserved.

Entitled "Masters of Independent Art," the exhibit came just in time, as World War II was to endanger all Paris galleries and artists alike. His popularity in the United States came rather late in life, with a traveling exhibit in 1940-1941 to Washington, Boston, and San Francisco and major exhibits at the Museum of Modern Art (a print exhibit in 1938 and a comprehensive show in 1945) and the Cleveland Art Museum, 1953.

Rouault's last works, to which he refers as the "dawn" after a lifetime of painting "twilights," were iconographic landscapes of ancient Eastern lands, with Christ and other religious figures now distantly on the horizon, receding from individuality, blending into the pastoral landscape. He died in 1958, at the age of eighty-six.

### Summary

The megalomania and egotism of the stereotypical artist were entirely absent in Georges Rouault, replaced by an intensity of commitment to perfection in everything he did. The act of painting was for Rouault an act of prayer, an intimate cry of anguish into the ontological void. Where other painters kept one eye on their commercial value, Rouault's attention to his public image was less selfish; it came from a desire to unify his artistic voice into one symphony for the eye, a kind of supplication before his Master.

That the modern art public has accepted his work as the masterpieces they are does not automatically mean it understands the man who created them. More than one art critic has noted that Rouault's life paralleled Dante's *Inferno, Purgatorio*, and *Paradiso;* the artist lived long enough to find peace in his art. Rouault is too often loved as the great religious essayists are loved: for the beauty of the form rather than the zeal of the content. It is not too much to say that Rouault prayed with his brush, or that his prayers were all one prayer: the *Miserere.*

### Bibliography

Dorival, Bernard. *Georges Rouault.* New York: Crown, 1983. This collection illustrates the variety and intensity of Rouault's work, with representatives of all styles and subjects. One reproduction, *Pierrot* (1920), is tipped in for optimum clarity. Text follows Rouault's life through the years of apprenticeship, "days of anger," during the "school of stoicism," and "en route to peace." Biographical chronicle, strong bibliography, and table of main exhibits.

Fowlie, Wallace. *Jacob's Night: The Religious Renascence in France.* New York: Sheed and Ward, 1947. Chapter 2, "Rouault: The Art of a Painter," is a discussion of Rouault's distinctly Catholic view of Sartre's existentialism, manifested in the anguished generic portraits of prostitutes, clowns, and peasants. A study of Rouault's religion, the chapter fits into Fowlie's larger discussion of the renaissance of Catholicism in early twentieth century France, indebted to the writings of Charles Péguy and Jacques Maritain. Index of last names.

Getlein, Dorothy, and Frank Getlein. *Georges Rouault's "Miserere."* Milwaukee: Bruce, 1964. A presentation of the final fifty-eight monochrome prints, with subjective and poetic commentaries by the Getleins. The long preface traces Rouault's life and concentrates on the techniques and the history of the production of the *Miserere* collection. This project took up a large part of the center of Rouault's career; the Getlein study is particularly valuable for an analysis of Rouault's Catholicism, the light shed on the Vollard-Rouault relationship, and the details of the multiple engraving techniques of this important print series, spanning thirty-five years from conception to birth.

Rouault, Georges. *G. Rouault, 1871-1958.* Text by Bernard Dorival. Translated by P. S. Falla. Manchester: Manchester City Art Galleries and the Arts Council of Great Britain, 1974. Dorival's introduction is a poetic recapitulation of Rouault's qualities. Detailed descriptions of paintings, with provenance and identifications, prove valuable to understanding his slow, meticulous processes.

Venturi, Lionelle. *Rouault: A Biographical and Critical Study.* Translated by James Emmons. New York: Skira, 1959. An appreciation by one of the first Rouault scholars, whose catalog of the 1940 exhibit still stands as the definitive Rouault biography. An introductory essay accompanies fifty-eight magnificent color reproductions, tipped in and therefore of a superior quality, but disappointingly small in size. Includes an exhaustive chronological survey with parallel artistic events, text references, bibliography, list of exhibitions, index of names, and list of color plates, all definitive and comprehensive.

*Thomas J. Taylor*

# JOSIAH ROYCE

*Born:* November 20, 1855; Grass Valley, California
*Died:* September 14, 1916; Cambridge, Massachusetts
*Area of Achievement:* Philosophy
*Contribution:* Royce was the last major philosopher of the twentieth century to integrate theological or religious topics with idealistic philosophy and to present his system to the general reader in terms of community and loyalty. He advanced philosophic idealism and played a significant role in Harvard University's intellectual development.

## Early Life

Josiah Royce was born November 20, 1855, in Grass Valley, California. His parents, Josiah Royce, Sr. (1812-1888), and Sarah Bayliss Royce (1819-1891), had come to California during the gold rush of 1849. They were pious, evangelical Christians. Since Royce's father was never successful in any of his various business activities and, as a salesman, was often absent from the home, his mother played a major role in shaping young Josiah's world. He was a sickly boy, short, freckled, with wild red hair; his mother did not allow him to play with the other children in the community. According to later autobiographical remarks, Royce was fascinated by the problem of time: He considered his hometown old, yet people referred to Grass Valley as a "new community." Meanwhile, in 1866 Royce entered Lincoln Grammar School in San Francisco, the family having moved there for better economic opportunities and educational possibilities for "Jossie." After a year at San Francisco Boy's High School, which in 1869 had a distinct militaristic manner that Royce hated, he entered the preparatory class at the University of California in Oakland. Within five years, Royce received his bachelor of arts degree in classics. As a result of his achievement, local patrons of the university sponsored him for a year's study in Germany.

Accordingly, from 1875 to 1876, Royce studied at Heidelberg, Leipzig, and Göttingen. His area of study was philosophy. His early concerns about time, the individual, and the community now found expression in his study overseas and at The Johns Hopkins University, the pioneer in graduate study and research. Enrolling in 1876, Royce completed his Ph.D. degree at Johns Hopkins within two years. Jobs teaching philosophy were scarce, and—very unwillingly—Royce returned to the University of California, where he taught English rhetoric and literature for the next four years. He did not, however, give up his study of philosophy.

In 1880, Royce married Katharine Head; the couple produced three sons. Royce kept his public role and private life separate, although the latter often indirectly revealed itself in his letters. Having met William James while at Johns Hopkins, Royce corresponded with him, and in 1883 Royce joined the Harvard faculty as a temporary replacement for James, who was on academic leave. Royce could now be a full-time philosopher.

## Life's Work

Having published fifteen articles by the time of his temporary appointment, Royce worked very hard, teaching and writing, to gain a permanent place on the Harvard faculty. Within six years he would achieve tenure and have a nervous breakdown. *The Religious Aspect of Philosophy* (1885) was based on lectures which he published as a book. This was a method he used for nearly all of his books. Exceptions were *California from the Conquest in 1846 to the Second Vigilance Committee in San Francisco, 1856: A Study of American Character* (1886), a state history, and *The Feud of Oakfield Creek* (1887), a novel; both books were early reflections of Royce's lifelong interest in community and individual behavior.

After spending most of the year 1888 traveling to Australia as a cure for his nervous condition, Royce returned to Harvard with a fuller grasp of his ideas as well as the energy to express them. After publishing *The Spirit of Modern Philosophy* (1892), he was appointed professor of the history of philosophy at Harvard. He continued to write on an extraordinary range of topics, but his basic focus was on religious values and philosophy; *The Conception of God* (1897) and *Studies of Good and Evil* (1898) were typical expressions of that focus. During the years 1894 through 1898, Royce was chairman of the Department of Philosophy, and he significantly shaped the courses and the faculty at Harvard.

Royce published his Gifford Lectures as *The World and the Individual* (1899-1901). In the last sixteen years of his life, his scholarship was truly remarkable. His writing continued to be both broad and technical; *Outlines of Psychology: An Elemen-*

*tary Treatise, with Some Practical Application* (1903), *The Philosophy of Loyalty* (1908), and *Race Questions, Provincialism, and Other American Problems* (1908) were the results of his efforts to have philosophy inform both the scholar and the general public.

While his scholarly achievements were many, in his personal life Royce suffered many setbacks. His marriage was a strain. His wife was often caustic and hypercritical, and his children disappointed him in various ways. Christopher, his oldest son, who suffered from mental illness most of his adult life, was committed to Danvers State Hospital in 1908. Christopher died two years later. A month before, William James had died; he was Royce's closest and dearest friend.

Despite these tragic events, Royce continued to work, publishing *William James and Other Essays on the Philosophy of Life* (1911). Within a year he had completed *The Sources of Religious Insight* (1912). Despite a major stroke, Royce struggled back to health and continued his philosophic work with a significant book, *The Problem of Christianity* (1913).

World War I was a philosophical crisis for Royce. After much thought, he became a strong advocate for American intervention. Worn out by personal worries and poor health, Royce died on September 14, 1916, in Cambridge, Massachusetts.

### Summary

Royce left no school of thought or prominent disciples. His philosophy of metaphysical idealism fell out of fashion as pragmatism, logical positivism, and existentialism gained currency in the academic and the larger society. His use of the German idealism of Immanuel Kant and Georg Wilhelm Friedrich Hegel also limited Royce's appeal. It would, however, be premature to downgrade Royce's lasting contributions.

In his varied writings, Royce stressed the primacy of the individual while holding fast to his emphasis on community. Royce recognized the damage done to individuals and to society by the alienation in American life. Also significant in his thought was the distinction between the world of appreciation or value and the world of factual description. The world of appreciation gives meaning, shape, and value to the human condition.

Finally, Royce was not a naïve thinker. He recognized evil in the world in various manifestations. His philosophy of the Absolute recognized three kinds of evil: metaphysical evil—anything short of the Absolute is not perfect; natural evil—anything that offends man's ethical sense or which man cannot accept because of his limited human intelligence (the problem of Job); and human evil—sin or voluntary inattention. Royce was a philosopher whose ideas have application to the modern world. Along with Charles Sanders Peirce and William James, Josiah Royce during his lifetime and in his writing contributed to the golden age of American philosophy.

### Bibliography

Buranelli, Vincent. *Josiah Royce*. New York: Twayne, 1963. In this brief biography the focus is on Royce's philosophy, particularly its origins in German idealism. According to Buranelli, Hegel was the major philosophic influence on Royce's intellectual development.

Clendenning, John. *The Life and Thought of Josiah Royce*. Rev. ed. Nashville: Vanderbilt University Press, 1998. Based essentially on Royce's letters, this biography follows a chronological scheme in which the philosopher's writings are related to the personal developments in his life. Royce's personality is clearly presented. He had a strong sense of humor and an attraction toward the ironic. The thesis is that a close relationship exists between the particulars of Royce's life and the universality of his system of thought.

Kuklick, Bruce. *Josiah Royce: An Intellectual Biography.* Indianapolis: Bobbs-Merrill, 1972. A solid history of Royce's ideas, this book relates him to the issues of his time. In the process, Royce's place in the history of American philosophy is clearly developed.

———. *The Rise of American Philosophy: Cambridge, Massachusetts, 1860-1930.* New Haven, Conn.: Yale University Press, 1977; London: Yale University Press, 1979. An outstanding history of the Department of History at Harvard University, this book clearly places Royce in the changing context of American philosophy as it moved from a gentlemanly pursuit of the truth to being part of academic professionalism. Well written; includes extensive bibliography.

Oppenheim, Frank M. *Royce's Mature Ethics.* Notre Dame, Ind.: University of Notre Dame Press, 1993. The author provides an in-depth study of Royce's ethics in his later years.

———. *Royce's Voyage Down Under: A Journey of the Mind.* Lexington: University Press of Kentucky, 1980. With a modest use of psychohistory, Oppenheim's book explores the philosophical consequences of Royce's trip to Australia as a cure for his nervous condition. In fact, Royce's greatest philosophical achievements were ahead when he returned to Harvard.

Powell, Thomas F. *Josiah Royce.* New York: Washington Square Press, 1967. A solid but brief treatment of Royce's life and thought. The later scholarship of Clendenning, Kuklick, and McDermott has undermined the importance of Powell's book.

Royce, Josiah. *The Basic Writings of Josiah Royce.* Edited by John J. McDermott. 2 vols. Chicago: University of Chicago Press, 1969. A handy introduction to Royce's writings, since some of the original editions are out of print. Organized by topic. The introduction is informative. The annotated bibliography of Royce's publication makes this book an invaluable source.

———. *The Letters of Josiah Royce.* Edited by John Clendenning. Chicago: University of Chicago Press, 1970. The introduction places the letters in their proper historical and philosophical contexts. The letters reveal a man who moved from the mundane to the sublime often in the same letter. Taken together, the letters constitute an interesting autobiography.

Royce, Sarah B. *A Frontier Lady: Recollections of the Gold Rush and Early California.* New Haven, Conn.: Yale University Press, and London: Oxford University Press,1932. A personal narrative of the Royce family overland trip to California as written by Josiah's mother. A basic document in understanding her influence on Royce's later philosophy on community and history.

"Royce's Argument for the Absolute." *Journal of the History of Philosophy* 36, no. 3 (July, 1998). Examines Royce's approach to the concept of absolute idealism.

Santayana, George. *Character and Opinion in the United States.* New York: Scribner, and London: Constable, 1920. An often caustic and ironic account of the academic world that Royce shared with Santayana, his former student and fellow faculty member.

Starr, Kevin. *Americans and the California Dream, 1850-1915.* New York: Oxford University Press, 1973. A solid presentation via cultural history and analysis and biographies of the California of Royce's youth. Starr explains how the state rapidly changed as a result of many types of influences (not the least of which was to gain wealth) and how Royce's philosophic concern for community grew out the state's colorful past.

*Donald K. Pickens*

# MURIEL RUKEYSER

*Born:* December 15, 1913; New York, New York
*Died:* February 12, 1980; New York, New York
*Area of Achievement:* Literature
*Contribution:* Known as something of a veteran literary "freedom fighter," Rukeyser helped to promote social justice in many areas and showed women how they could improve their lives by improving the lives of others.

## Early Life

Muriel Rukeyser was born in New York City on December 15, 1913. Her father, Lawrence B. Rukeyser, was a successful businessman, her mother, Myra Lyons Rukeyser, was a former bookkeeper. She grew up surrounded by skyscrapers, factories, tenements, and machinery. Muriel's spare, functional poetry was to reflect this cold, manmade environment. She entered Vassar College in the fall of 1930, when she was only seventeen. Her main interests were literature and music. Later, she attended Columbia University, but did not receive a degree.

At Vassar, she served on the *Vassar Review* and the *Vassar Miscellany News*, the two major student publications. She also had poems published in *Poetry* and in the *New York Herald Tribune*. Like many intellectuals of her generation, she developed strong left-wing political views in college. Most of her early poetry, however, was of a strictly personal nature, and she continued to write about personal themes throughout her life. One of her outstanding characteristics as a writer was her tendency to project her personality into her subject matter.

Rukeyser admired poets such as John Milton, Percy Bysshe Shelley, and Walt Whitman who wrote with the moralistic fervor of prophets. As a child, she told her father that she wanted to be "someone like Joan of Arc." It was her belief that poets were inspired leaders whose mission was to encourage humankind to realize its highest potential. She did not believe that a poet should live in an ivory tower producing art for art's sake but should be actively involved in worthy causes. As early as the age of nineteen, she caught typhoid fever while being held in a police station in Alabama, where she went to attend a protest meeting during the famous Scottsboro trial, in which eight young black men were convicted of raping two white women and sentenced to death.

Little is known about Rukeyser's personal life except for the information she revealed through her poetry. She was married for a short time and had one child by a second man whom she did not choose to marry. Her poems suggest that she was unhappy as a child and remained so most of her life. She was always remarkably candid about expressing her personal feelings, and the following lines from a poem entitled "Effort at Speech Between Two People" are quite revealing:

> When I was fourteen, I had dreams of suicide,
> I stood at a steep window, at sunset, hoping
> toward death:
> if the light had not melted clouds and plains to beauty,
> if light had not transformed that day, I would
> have leapt.
> I am unhappy. I am lonely. Speak to me.

## Life's Work

Muriel Rukeyser's life and writings were dominated by her anger at social injustice and her desire to change the world through political activism. Her career as a published poet began in 1935, when her work *Theory of Flight* was published by Yale University Press after winning the Yale Series of Younger Poets competition. For the next forty years she produced a steady steam of poetry and translated poetry from French, German, Swedish, and Italian.

Rukeyser was a Marxist-inspired activist all of her life. As such, she aroused considirable hostility from conservative critics. Even after her death, attitudes toward her writing continued to be colored by readers' political persuasions.

The following lines from "Facing Sentencing" reveal much about Rukeyser's poetry and personality:

> But fear is not to be feared
> Numbness is To stand before my judge
> Not knowing what I mean.

The indifference to orthodox punctuation, the gap in the second line indicating a pause similar to a rest in musical scoring, and the starkly prosaic diction exemplify her modernist technique; while the thought expressed represents the attitude she exhibited all of her life. She believed that a poet should be an activist, that poetry should be a way of life rather than a vocation or an avocation.

One of the most famous incidents in Rukeyser's life occurred when she went to South Korea to pro-

test the imprisonment of the poet Kim Chi-Ha. When she was refused admission to see the condemned prisoner, she stood outside the prison gates in silent protest to draw attention to the reactionary government's suppression of free speech. This incident was expressive of Rukeyser's belief that a poet should be a social activist. She describes her experiences in South Korea in her last published book of poetry, *The Gates* (1976).

Rukeyser remained remarkably active even after she became seriously ill with diabetes and had suffered two strokes. Her outstanding qualities were her strength of purpose and her powerful drive. She aspired to be a prophet rather than a mere poet. She admired and wrote about people who were innovators and revolutionaries. Perhaps the literary figure whom she most closely resembles is the illustrious John Milton, author of *Paradise Lost* (1667, 1674), who continued writing poetry and essays in the service of the cause he believed in even after he had gone completely blind and was in danger of being prosecuted for treason by the vindictive inquisitors of the restored monarchy.

Rukeyser was an experimentalist in poetry. She wrote elegies, odes, lyrics, documentary poems, epigrams, and dramatic monologues. She was more intelligent than most of her contemporaries and could not be beguiled or coerced into following any established political line. She was guided by her own intelligence and her own conscience. This attitude made her a loner and an individualist; she did not have any faction to support, encourage, or defend her and, as a result, has tended to be ignored while inferior poets receive undue praise.

Rukeyser was a prolific writer. Her collected poems, published in 1978, fill a book containing 538 pages. She also wrote a novel, some plays, television scripts, juvenile books, biographies, and essays; it is as a poet, however, that she will be remembered. She also taught writing and poetry appreciation at Vassar, Sarah Lawrence College, and the California Labor School. She gave countless campus and public readings all over the United States before her death in New York City, her lifelong home, on February 12, 1980.

### Summary

Muriel Rukeyser was a feminist poet who worked diligently on behalf of human rights. Unlike many feminists of the generation that followed hers, she did not display conspicuous hostility toward the male sex or express resentment of woman's historical role. She encouraged women writers to seek their unique feminine identities, not only through their writing but through taking active roles in the never-ending struggle for social justice. She had a strong impact as a writer, a teacher, a scholar, and a social activist. Her life demonstrated that she concurred wholeheartedly with Milton's sentiments expressed in his essay *Areopagitica* (1644):

> I cannot praise a fugitive and cloistered virtue, unexercised and unbreathed, that never sallies out and sees her adversary, but slinks out of the race, where that immortal garland is to be run for, not without dust and heat.

Rukeyser demonstrated through her life and work that writing, in order to be of value, must be an integral part of one's total life. Throughout her life, she struggled to find herself as an individual and to express that unique individuality in her writing—especially in her poetry. She believed that women had not only the ability but also the duty to influence the course of history through their activities in every field of human endeavor.

She was regarded as a courageous fighter, even by her bitter adversaries; she inspired many other women to follow her example and continues to be regarded as an influential figure in the feminist movement. Her refusal to follow any party line or subscribe to any dogma brought her into conflict with factions on both the left and right of the political spectrum. The final decision as to her importance as a poet remains unresolved, but she is sure to be remembered as an individualist with a powerful will who followed her own conscience and encouraged others to do the same.

**Bibliography**

Bernikow, Louise. "Muriel at Sixty-five: Still Ahead of Her Time." *Ms.* 7 (January, 1979): 14-18. An interview published in a popular feminist magazine not long before the poet's death. Rukeyser discusses her later poems and her views on recent developments in the feminist movement.

Cooper, Jane. "'Meeting Places': On Muriel Rukeyser." *American Poetry Review* 25, no. 5 (September-October, 1996). Discusses the republication of Rukeyser's "Life of Poetry."

Dayton, Tim. "Lyric and Document in Muriel Rukeyser's 'The Book of the Dead.'" *Journal of Modern Literature* 21, no. 2 (Winter 1997). Dayton offers analysis of Rukeyser's extended poetic work, "The Book of the Dead."

Gardinier, Suzanne. "A World That Will Hold All People: On Muriel Rukeyser." *Kenyon Review* 14 (Summer, 1992): 88-105. An in-depth discussion of Rukeyser's poetry as reflecting her life experiences and her political beliefs. Gardinier states that Rukeyser wrote "the poetry of a believer—in an age of unbelief." Many quotations from Rukeyser's early and later poems.

Kertesz, Louise. *The Poetic Vision of Muriel Rukeyser.* Baton Rouge: Louisiana State University Press, 1980. A comprehensive book about Rukeyser that traces the progress of images and themes in her work decade by decade. Explores her traditions and contemporaries and also records the critical reception of her published works over the years. Excellent bibliography and footnotes. Illustrated with photos of Rukeyser at various stages of her life.

Rich, Adrienne. "Beginners." *Kenyon Review* 15 (Summer, 1993): 12-19. In this beautifully written essay, Rich, a prominent poet herself, discusses Walt Whitman, Emily Dickinson, and Muriel Rukeyser, calling them all "beginners . . . openers of new paths . . . who take the first steps . . . and therefore seem strange and 'dreadful.'"

Rosenthal, M. L. "Muriel Rukeyser: The Longer Poems." In *New Directions in Prose and Poetry,* No. 14, edited by James Laughlin. New York: New Directions Books, 1953. A detailed examination of Rukeyser's longer poems. Rosenthal acknowledges Rukeyser's faults, such as her occasional "muddy emotionalism," but claims they are by-products of real achievements.

Rukeyser, Muriel. *The Collected Poems.* New York: McGraw-Hill, 1978. Rukeyser compiled and edited this collection of poems herself. They are drawn from twelve previously published books and represent the best single-volume collection of her poetry available. Index of titles and first lines. Some footnotes.

———. *The Life of Poetry.* New York: Current Books, 1949. Rukeyser's explanation of her conception of the role of the poet in society, drawing on such diverse authorities as English mathematician/philosopher Alfred North Whitehead, Austrian psychoanalyst Sigmund Freud, German philosopher Georg Hegel, and American physicist Willard Gibbs. As the title suggests, Rukeyser believed that poetry should be a way of life.

Untermeyer, Louis. "The Language of Muriel Rukeyser." *Saturday Review* (August 10, 1940): 11-13. A distinguished American author and editor discusses the early career of the young Rukeyser, identifying what is unique in her use of language and comparing her with poets Hart Crane and W. H. Auden.

Ware, Michele S. "Opening 'The Gates': Muriel Rukeyser and the Poetry of Witness." *Women's Studies* 22 (June, 1993): 297-308. An extensive analysis of *The Gates* (1976), the last volume of Rukeyser's new poetry to be published before her death. Praises her oracular characteristics and lyricism while maintaining the integrity of her political and social messages.

*Bill Delaney*

## GERD VON RUNDSTEDT

*Born:* December 12, 1875; Aschersleben, Germany
*Died:* February 24, 1953; Hannover, West Germany
*Area of Achievement:* The military
*Contribution:* Rundstedt, though not an innovator, supported Manstein's revolutionary strategy, which led to victory over France in 1940. He did not participate in anti-Hitler conspiracies, though he disliked the Nazis and Hitler in particular. Prussian military honor and obedience guided his professional and personal life.

### Early Life

Karl Rudolf Gerd von Rundstedt's father was a Prussian general of old Brandenburg/Prussian nobility, which had provided officers for the Prussian army for centuries. Young Rundstedt became a cadet at age sixteen and was commissioned in the infantry a year later. He served as battalion and regimental adjutant and received further training at the Kriegsakademie, the army's "graduate school." In 1907, Rundstedt entered the prestigious General Staff, Germany's military elite. After serving as company commander, Rundstedt spent the war years in General Staff positions.

Rundstedt advanced rapidly in the postwar *Reichswehr.* Initially he served as divisional chief of staff and from 1923 to 1927 as commander of an infantry regiment; in 1927, he became major general and commander of the Second Cavalry Division. In 1929, Rundstedt advanced to lieutenant general and in January, 1932, became commander of the Third Division and of the Military District (*Wehrkreis*) III (Berlin). In October, 1932, three months before Adolf Hitler assumed power, Rundstedt was promoted to general of infantry and became commander of Army Group I (Berlin), one of two Army Groups within the *Reichswehr.* Rundstedt had thus reached the highest rank within the *Reichswehr.* Rundstedt's unwilling involvement in politics began in July, 1932, when Chancellor Franz von Papen was named federal commissioner for the state of Prussia, in what history has dubbed the "Rape of Prussia": the transfer of the state's executive power to the federal chancellor. (This move put Prussia's police and executive functions under Papen's authority, a position that Hitler inherited in January, 1933, upon becoming chancellor.) As commander of Military District III (Berlin), Rundstedt exercised this executive power, in keeping with constitutional provision.

### Life's Work

Rundstedt advocated modernization of the infantry, in both equipment and training. He called for mechanization and the increase of firepower, being convinced that the tanks' function was to support the infantry, contrary to views being developed in Germany and elsewhere. Rundstedt, however, did not oppose creation of armored (tank) divisions, as long as that development did not hinder the infantry's modernization.

Rundstedt had been unhappy with the Weimar Republic's democratic nature but also quickly developed dislike for the Nazis, the "brown dirt," as he called them. In 1934, when President Paul von Hindenburg died, Rundstedt, together with the entire army, took a new personal oath to Hitler, a fact that proved to be of great consequence later. His deeply rooted, traditional Prussian sense of honor brought him into conflict with Hitler during the Fritsch Crisis in early 1938, when he protested Fritsch's dismissal as the Army's commander in chief. Thereafter, however, he urged his fellow generals to avoid the "rash actions" contemplated by some and await the outcome of legal proceedings. Hitler, who respected Rundstedt's natural dignity and military ability, promoted him to colonel general in March, 1938. During the Sudeten Crisis of October, 1938, he commanded Army Group IV of Germany's expanded *Wehrmacht.* Rundstedt did not involve himself in the incipient conspiracy against Hitler, centered on the army's former commander in chief, General Ludwig Beck, though he was aware of it. In late October, 1938, Rundstedt accepted retirement, ostensibly at his request, actually as part of a purge that removed a number of senior officers.

Within less than a year, however, Rundstedt was recalled. Neither he nor his fellow generals opposed war with Poland to recover lost territory (Versailles Treaty, 1919), especially after Hitler's treaty with Joseph Stalin made war with the Soviets unlikely. The generals, including Rundstedt, however, realized that a Polish war might lead to a wider conflict. During the Polish campaign, Rundstedt commanded Army Group South. His forces cut off the Polish retreat across the Vistula River and played a key role in the capture of Warsaw. Rundstedt vainly urged Hitler not to bombard Warsaw and to extend humane treatment to the civilian population.

Following a brief and unwelcome tenure as commander in chief east (occupation of Poland in cooperation with Germany's civilian administration of that unhappy country), Rundstedt asked for and received reassignment as commander of Army Group A facing France. Rundstedt strongly supported the revised operational plans for the western campaign (following the need to discard the original Schlieffen-like plan). The new plan, developed by General Erich von Manstein, his chief of staff in Poland and on the Western Front, called for a daring armored thrust through the Ardennes, trapping the Allied field armies in Belgium and northern France. It was on Rundstedt's advice that Hitler accepted this controversial plan, initially rejected by the army's high command.

Following the western victory, Rundstedt and eleven others were elevated to field marshals, Rundstedt being the eldest. He was slated to play a major role in Operation Sea Lion, the invasion of Great Britain. Following its cancellation, Rundstedt commanded Army Group South during the invasion of the Soviet Union in June, 1941. His task was to capture the Ukraine and the Caucasus oil fields and to penetrate as far east as Stalingrad to cut off the Soviets' southern supply route. Army Group South had an inadequate force of 750 tanks, and Rundstedt soon recognized that this task was impossible. When Hitler rejected first his request for additional forces and then his proposal to fall back on a defensive winter line, Rundstedt asked to be replaced. In December, 1941, he retired again, as part of a larger shake-up within the high command.

Despite strong differences in opinion, Hitler again recalled Rundstedt, this time as commander in chief west, to create the "Atlantic Wall." Rundstedt's Prussian sense of duty, as well as the natural ambition of military men, caused him to return to active duty again and again, even though he no longer believed in German victory.

Little was done on anti-invasion defenses until the matter became increasingly urgent in 1943. Soon a controversy arose between Rundstedt and his subordinate, General Erwin Rommel. Rommel wanted to place all reserves, especially the armored divisions, in the immediate vicinity of the potential landing sites, while Rundstedt desired to hold the reserves back. Rommel believed that the invasion could only be defeated on the beaches, and Rundstedt, though doubtful that the invaders could be stopped at all, wanted to engage them in a war of movement in the interior. General Heinz Guderian, Germany's paramount tank expert, as well as Hitler, agreed with Rundstedt. Rundstedt compromised by strengthening the forward units but retaining the armor in strategic reserve. The question of who would control these reserves, Hitler or the field commanders, produced yet another controversy.

Following the invasion and the inability to stop the Allies in Normandy, Rundstedt requested permission to withdraw behind the Seine River. Hitler refused, and, when Field Marshal Wilhelm Keitel, chief of staff of the high command, telephoned on June 29, 1944, to inquire what could be done in such a desperate situation, Rundstedt responded acidly, "Quit, you idiots! What else do you still want to do?" On July 6, 1944, Rundstedt was retired a third time.

By 1944, a determined military resistance to Hitler had coalesced. Rundstedt was in sympathy but was unwilling to commit himself to the cause, invoking his 1934 Hitler oath. Following the failed plot of July 20, 1944, Rundstedt was once more recalled, to preside over the military "Court of Honor" that had the task of dishonorably discharging the involved officers. Under Rundstedt's presidency, fifty-five officers were discharged without the opportunity to defend themselves.

In September, 1944, while the German forces in the west were in headlong retreat across northern France, Rundstedt returned as commander in chief west. Hitler's trust was not misplaced, and Rundstedt halted the rout, temporarily stabilizing the front. The attempt to turn the tide in the unsuccessful Ardennes Offensive (Battle of the Bulge) of mid-December, 1944, however, was Hitler's own plan. Following this campaign, Rundstedt was awarded the Knight's Cross with Oak Leaf and Swords.

On March 9, 1945, following the American crossing of the Rhine River at Remagen, as the Third Reich and its *Wehrmacht* were in their final death throes, Hitler dismissed Rundstedt a fourth and final time. On May 2, 1945, Rundstedt became a prisoner of war. The British intended to try him for war crimes. Those proceedings, however, were halted because of Rundstedt's ill health, and he was released in May, 1949. It is doubtful that Rundstedt was guilty of war crimes. Rundstedt died of a heart ailment in February, 1953, in Hannover.

### Summary

Gerd von Rundstedt was the product of a Prussian aristocratic upbringing and thorough General Staff

*Gerd von Rundstedt observing Allied operations during World War II*

training. His personal dignity, undisputable ability, and scrupulous devotion to duty and honor as he saw them saved him from the bitter personal criticism that Hitler heaped on other aristocratic officers. Though Rundstedt repeatedly faced Hitler early in the war and though he had a great disdain for Nazi ideology, he never forced a showdown but simply offered, or accepted, his resignation when he could no longer take responsibility for proposed actions. In July, 1944, when Rundstedt was dismissed, he told Rommel that he "was grateful not to have to experience the coming catastrophe in a position of leadership." At the Nürnberg Trial he explained that "we did our duty because Hitler had legally been made Chancellor by Hindenburg, and because, after his death, he appeared as the Führer on the basis of the [Hindenburg's] testament."

Rundstedt was a thoroughly competent military leader, though not an innovator, and is certainly counted among the war's most capable generals. General Dwight D. Eisenhower considered him the most capable German general, though that judgment might be questioned. Eisenhower never faced Manstein, Rundstedt's erstwhile chief of staff, who may well deserve that accolade. Rundstedt was always determined not to become a "political general," yet his acceptance of, and tacit support for, Hitler and his resignation from uncomfortable positions were in fact indirect support. His unwillingness to become involved in the 1938 and 1944 conspiracies constituted setbacks to these efforts precisely because his colleagues respected him. In the final analysis one cannot escape the feeling that Rundstedt was either the epitome of the honorable Prussian officer in the best sense or "an accomplished cynic, the Talleyrand of Hitler's [generals]"; maybe he was a bit of both.

**Bibliography**

"The Atlantic Wall." *American History* 29, no. 2 (June, 1994). Focuses on Hitler's "Atlantic Wall" and the efforts of German military leaders including Rundstedt.

Brett-Smith, Richard. *Hitler's Generals.* London: Osprey, 1976; San Rafael, Calif.: Presidio Press, 1977. A comprehensive treatment. Rundstedt is discussed under "The Old Guard," and there are substantial references to him throughout. Includes maps, appendices, a glossary, a bibliography, and an index.

Dziewanowski, M. K. *War at Any Price: World War II in Europe, 1939-1945.* 2d ed. Englewood Cliffs, N.J.: Prentice-Hall, 1991. A college-level textbook that put Rundstedt and the campaigns he was involved in into an overall framework. The author integrated military and nonmilitary developments and placed all in the broader global setting of the war. Excellent for general reading. Includes an extensive bibliography.

Horne, Alistair. *To Lose a Battle: France 1940.* London: Macmillan, and New York: Little Brown, 1969. An extensive discussion of the background to the war, military resistance to Hitler, and war plans. Considerable discussion of the Manstein plan, armored tactics, and Rundstedt's involvement in the western campaign. The book includes an extensive bibliography.

Liddell Hart, B. H. *The German Generals Talk.* New York: Morrow, 1948. Rundstedt is discussed in the chapter "'The Old Guard'—Rundstedt," with extensive references throughout. Includes an index and a table of the German High Command.

Mellenthin, F. W. von. *German Generals of World War II: As I Saw Them.* Norman: University of Oklahoma Press, 1977. Mellenthin served in various theaters as a German General Staff officer. The book contains separate chapters on fourteen generals, though not on Rundstedt, since Mellenthin was not directly associated with him. The book, however, contains extensive references to Rundstedt and provides an excellent discussion of command decisions in World War II.

*Frederick Dumin*

# BERTRAND RUSSELL

*Born:* May 18, 1872; Trelleck, Monmouthshire, Wales

*Died:* February 2, 1970; near Penrhyndeudraeth, Wales

*Areas of Achievement:* Philosophy, mathematics, and politics

*Contribution:* Russell's original work in the areas of logic, mathematics, and the theory of knowledge was complemented by several important volumes of philosophical popularization, and in his later years Russell emerged as a major figure in the peace movement.

### Early Life

Bertrand Arthur William Russell was born on May 18, 1872, in Trelleck, Monmouthshire, Wales. His mother, née Kate Stanley, was the daughter of the second Baron Stanley of Alderley and a leader in the fight for votes for women; his father, Lord Amberley, was the eldest son of the first Earl Russell and a freethinker who lost his seat in Parliament because of his advocacy of birth control. Both parents were considered extremely eccentric, and both died before Russell reached the age of four. Russell and his older brother were brought up by their rigidly conventional paternal grandmother, and they spent a rather solemn childhood being educated at home by a succession of governesses and tutors.

At the age of eighteen, Russell entered Trinity College, Cambridge, where it did not take him long to make a positive impression. He was taken under the wing of the philosopher Alfred North Whitehead, with whom he would later collaborate on *Principia Mathematica* (1910-1913), and was much influenced by fellow student G. E. Moore (1873-1958), who helped him to develop his early ideas on the independent existence of what is perceived by the senses. In 1894, Russell married Alys Pearsall Smith, an American Quaker five years older than he was, and in 1895 he was elected a Fellow of Trinity College for his dissertation "An Essay on the Foundations of Geometry." In the following year, he and his wife spent three months in the United States, thus beginning a lifelong interest in and involvement with American affairs.

In the late 1890's, Russell achieved wide recognition as a professional philosopher of promise, as he subjected the dominant Idealist thought of the period to an increasingly rigorous critique. His personal life revolved around the strains of a deteriorating marriage, which in 1902 reached a crisis when Russell told his wife that he no longer loved her. Although they continued to live together until 1911, the pressures of conflict at home and a demanding professional career made this the most difficult period of Russell's life. It was also, however, a very productive time for him, highlighted by the publication of perhaps his greatest single work: *The Principles of Mathematics* (1903), which took the groundbreaking step of removing metaphysical notions from the concept of numbers and arguing that logic alone could serve as the basis for a true science of mathematics. After the publication of this volume, even those who took issue with Russell's views had to acknowledge his status as a major contributor to contemporary philosophical and mathematical thinking.

Russell's striking personal appearance became part of the folklore of Cambridge. His tall, thin frame and sharply chiseled, almost hawkish facial lines were seldom observed at rest, as his penchant for vigorous intellectual disputation was matched by a passion for strenuous walking. Russell kept his distinctive looks to the end of his life, with the only significant change being a whitening of his full head of hair, which added a mature dignity to his craggy features. The heavy media coverage of his public appearances on behalf of the peace movement in the 1960's reflected the charismatic appeal of his majestically leonine figure, which seemed to many observers to possess an almost biblical air of wisdom and authority.

### Life's Work

The decade preceding the outbreak of World War II found Russell achieving success as a professional philosopher and undertaking what would be the first in a tempestuous string of love affairs and marriages. His collaboration with Whitehead on the three volumes of *Principia Mathematica* developed the ideas touched upon in *The Principles of Mathematics* into a coherent and influential formal system, and he was fruitfully stimulated by his pupil Ludwig Wittgenstein, who helped him to clarify his thoughts about the proper conduct of philosophical analysis. Russell's growing interest in the theory of knowledge resulted in his *The Problems of Philosophy* (1912), the first in what would be a series of books concerned with such perennial philosophical issues as the nature

of reality and the operations of the mind. In 1911, he began an intense love affair with Lady Ottoline Morrell, which lasted until 1916 and put an end to his first marriage.

Russell was deeply affected by the horrors of World War I and found himself compelled to become active in the pacifist movement. His *Principles of Social Reconstruction* (1916) signaled a deepening involvement with questions of human relations, and his antiwar efforts led to his being fined in 1916, imprisoned for six months in 1918, and as a result deprived of his lectureship at Trinity College. In 1916 he met and in 1921 married his second wife, Dora Black, a fellow freethinker with whom he had two children and briefly ran an experimental school at Beacon Hill. A visit to postrevolutionary Russia produced *The Practice and Theory of Bolshevism* (1920), in which he recorded his disillusionment with the gap between the Soviet Union's promise and performance, and he became somewhat notorious for his advocacy of free love—a doctrine which he practiced in a string of extramarital affairs—in the book *Marriage and Morals* (1929).

Russell continued to do serious work in philosophy during the interwar period, although his refusal to accept Trinity College's offer of reinstatement meant that he had to spend more time writing financially profitable books and journalistic articles. Thus, popularly oriented titles such as *The Conquest of Happiness* (1930) and *Education and the Modern World* (1932) were interspersed with the more technical philosophical works *Our Knowledge of the External World* (1929) and *An Inquiry into Meaning and Truth* (1940), and Russell also became a popular lecturer on topics such as divorce, sexual relations, and pacifism. His personal life continued to be turbulent, as he divorced his second wife in 1935 and married his third, Patricia Spence, in 1936, to whom a son was born in the following year.

In 1938, Russell and his new family moved to the United States, where he held several university posts and made a number of extensive lecture tours. He was in continual difficulty as right-wing pressure groups attacked his liberal views, and in 1943 he even had to go to court to collect his salary from the outraged head of a charitable foundation. The main positive result of his American sojourn was *History of Western Philosophy* (1945), a popular success whose royalties would comfortably support him for the remainder of his life. The Russells returned to England in 1944, and he decided to accept a five-year lectureship at Trinity College and endeavor to settle down into a less hectic pattern of existence.

The award of the Order of Merit in 1949 and the Nobel Prize for Literature in 1950 indicated that Russell's achievements now commanded general respect. This did not, however, seem to have a stabilizing effect upon his domestic life: He divorced his third wife in 1949 and married his fourth, Edith Finch, in 1952. Disappointed by the indifference of his academic colleagues to his last serious philosophical work, *Human Knowledge: Its Scope and Limits* (1948), Russell devoted more and more time to antiwar activities. He helped to found the Campaign for Nuclear Disarmament in 1958, organized its militant wing, the Committee of 100, in 1960, and was jailed for seven days for participating in a Whitehall sit-in in 1961. Although Russell's physical powers now began to weaken, he remained an effective propagandist for the pacifist movement and in the late 1960's was a prominent member of the international opposition to the American presence in Vietnam. His final days were spent resting quietly at his home in northern Wales, where he died on February 2, 1970.

### Summary

Bertrand Russell brought keen intellectual perception to every task that fired his imagination. As a philosopher, he was instrumental in the development of modern analytical techniques; as a mathematician, he helped to anchor speculative hypotheses on the firm ground of formal logic; and as a political activist, he cut through the verbiage of politicians with a clarion call to abandon nuclear weapons before they produced a global holocaust. Although the content of his ideas has in some cases been rejected by subsequent commentators, there is an almost universal acknowledgment of his methodological contributions to his areas of academic specialization.

Yet Russell was not merely a man with a great mind. His charismatic public persona and his ability to write for a general readership extended his influence into regions usually closed to the professional academic, and the range of his published work is extraordinarily impressive. His volatile emotional life also reflected the immense energy and appetite for new experiences that, in combination with his outstanding intellectual prowess, made Bertrand Russell one of the seminal figures of his time.

## Bibliography

Clark, Ronald W. *The Life of Bertrand Russell.* London: Cape, and New York: Knopf, 1975. A fully documented and lucidly written biography containing much material not in Russell's autobiography. Although no coherent psychological portrait emerges, the sheer amount of data makes this an important—if by no means final—addition to knowledge of its subject.

Feinberg, Barry, and Ronald Kasrils. *Bertrand Russell's America.* Vol. 1. London: Allen and Unwin, and New York: Viking Press, 1973. Covering the years 1896 to 1945, the first in what will ultimately be a two-volume work tracing Russell's attitudes toward and experiences in the United States. The authors make extensive use of previously unpublished letters and essays and succeed in presenting a comprehensive account of what are often very dramatic and at times even amusing episodes in Russell's career.

Ironside, Philip. *The Social and Political Thought of Bertrand Russell: The Development of an Aristocratic Liberalism.* Cambridge and New York: Cambridge University Press, 1996. The author focuses on the context in which Russell developed his political and social theories.

Jager, Ronald. *The Development of Bertrand Russell's Philosophy.* London: Allen and Unwin, and Atlantic Highlands, N.J.: Humanities Press, 1973. An excellent study of Russell's growth as a philosopher, aimed at the general reader as well as the specialist. Particular attention is paid to the historical influences, ranging from Plato to Wittgenstein, that affected a thinker always conscious of the rich history of his discipline.

Landini, Gregory. *Russell's Hidden Substitutional Theory.* New York: Oxford University Press, 1998. Landini studies Russell's thought on logic as expressed in his "Principles of Mathematics" and "Principia Mathmatica." The author finds that these works, historically assumed to reflect conflicting views, actually have a common thread: substitutional theory.

Nakhnikian, George, ed. *Bertrand Russell's Philosophy.* London: Duckworth, and New York: Barnes and Noble, 1974. Contains fourteen essays on various aspects of Russell's thought, from logical issues to the theory of knowledge to political philosophy. Some assume a background in philosophy, but the majority should be accessible to the nonspecialist reader. Includes an excellent bibliography.

Roberts, George W., ed. *Bertrand Russell Memorial Volume.* London: Allen and Unwin, and Atlantic Highlands, N.J.: Humanities Press, 1979. Twenty-six essays assessing Russell's achievements in philosophy, mathematics, ethics, and politics, from a distinguished group of contemporary scholars. The book is strongest on Russell's philosophical accomplishments, although its exhaustive index makes it a good source of information on almost every facet of his career.

Russell, Bertrand. *The Autobiography of Bertrand Russell.* 3 vols. London: Allen and Unwin, and Boston: Little Brown, 1967-1969. The judicious mixture of chronological narrative and extensive quotation from letters contributes to the impact made by this superb intellectual autobiography. On personal matters, the story needs to be fleshed out by the books by Clark and Tait, but for a fascinating account of the development of Russell's thought there is no better source than these eminently readable volumes.

Sainsbury, Richard Mark. *Russell.* London and Boston: Routledge, 1979. Both a presentation of Russell's ideas and an analysis of their adequacy. A reliable, clearly written, but nevertheless fairly difficult volume which does not shy away from the most complex aspects of Russell's thinking.

Tait, Katharine. *My Father, Bertrand Russell.* New York: Harcourt Brace, 1975; London: Gollancz, 1976. Tait, Russell's daughter by his second wife, concentrates upon his failures as a father and demonstrates how his self-centeredness resulted in great pain for his family. A sensitive memoir that provides an unfamiliar angle on Russell as well as some implicit criticism of his educational and social theories.

Vellacott, Jo. *Bertrand Russell and the Pacifists in the First World War.* Brighton, Sussex: Harvester Press, 1980; New York: St. Martin's Press, 1981. A welcome portrait of Russell at the beginning of his career as a political activist. The book provides much information about the origins of the pacifist movement in Great Britain, particularly its socialist and Quaker roots, and is very well researched and written.

*Paul Stuewe*

# BILL RUSSELL

*Born:* February 12, 1934; Monroe, Louisiana
*Area of Achievement:* Basketball
*Contribution:* Revolutionizing the strategy of basketball, Russell introduced to the sport a style of play never before used or advocated.

## Early Life

William Felton Russell was born February 12, 1934, in Monroe, Louisiana. His mother, Katie, who died when Bill was twelve, exerted a strong, lasting influence. She named Bill for William Felton, president of Southeastern Louisiana College, and made it clear that her children would be college graduates. Bill's father, Charles Russell, was a hardworking wage earner who held several jobs: factory laborer, truck driver, construction worker, hauling business owner, and ironworker in a foundry. He was also a semiprofessional baseball player, as had been his brother, Robert. Robert Russell, just short of making the Negro Major Leagues, blamed his failure on his being right-handed. Robert insisted that his nephew do everything with his left hand.

When Bill was nine, the family left Louisiana for better economic opportunities in Detroit, Michigan, but soon afterward moved to West Oakland, California. Bill's brother, Chuck, proved to be an outstanding athlete in baseball, football, basketball, and track. Two years older than Bill, Chuck cast a shadow over Bill through high school. Unlike Chuck, Bill was not gifted with coordination and muscle until late in his senior year. His gawkiness and awkwardness gave him a self-admitted inferiority complex which, through later athletic stardom, was replaced by an outgoing, although enigmatic, personality.

Russell, six-foot, ten-inches and 215 pounds in his prime, is noted for his fierce integrity, frequent cackling laugh, incisive wit, competitive intensity, and far-ranging, intellectual mind. His interests run from music appreciation and reading to assembling electric trains and investing in a Liberian rubber plantation. His ego was described by Boston Celtic teammate Tom Heinsohn as the largest on the team, while another Celtic teammate, Tom Sanders, emphasized Russell's capacity to needle people and keep them slightly off balance. Twice married, Russell has three children, William Felton, Jr. (called Buddha), Jacob Harold, and Karen Kenyatta.

## Life's Work

Russell's older brother, Chuck, was named to Bay Area all-star teams in basketball, football, and track, playing for Oakland Tech. When Bill enrolled at McClymonds High School, he intended to escape Chuck's shadow. Instead, coaching personnel and students expected him to lead McClymonds in similar fashion. Russell proved instead to be skinny and awkward. One sport in which Russell became proficient, however, was table tennis, which improved his reflexes and coordination. As his height and weight increased, Russell's efforts in basketball and track improved.

In his senior year, Russell was a starter as McClymonds won the Bay Area basketball championship. A winter graduation enabled him to be chosen for a California high school all-star group which toured northward into Canada, playing against top high school and even small college competition. The trip was a turning point for Russell, his play dramatically improving and his mind constantly analyzing the game. He also gained his first insight into his jumping ability.

Despite Russell's starting role on a championship team and noticeably improved play with the touring group, only the University of San Francisco offered a basketball scholarship. Russell had never heard of the school. While waiting for University of San Francisco (USF) head coach Phil Woolpert to contact him, Russell took a job as an apprentice sheet-metal worker. Playing in a McClymonds alumni game, Russell experienced a first, enjoyable and terrifying at the same time: He jumped high enough to look down into the basket. A new dimension entered Russell's expanding range of skills.

Russell's freshman coach at USF, Ross Giudice, introduced him to the hook shot and spent innumerable postpractice and weekend hours helping Russell sharpen his game. During that season, Russell averaged twenty points per game and started to develop the most remarkable defensive skills basketball would ever witness. Giudice was so impressed that he told Woolpert that the potential was there for Russell to become the greatest player in history.

Another great help to Russell was K. C. Jones, his dormitory roommate and teammate. Jones and Russell decided that basketball was a geometric game, and repeated analyses led them to develop

and redevelop concepts and strategies from that time throughout their careers. Their approach eventually revolutionized theories of rebounding and defense, but it did not result in instant success. The varsity fell well short of championship-level play. A ruptured appendix removed Jones as soon as the season started, and other illnesses and injuries depleted the roster. Russell looked back with no excuses, however, and ascribed the squad's mediocrity to lack of teamwork.

In Russell's junior year, everything changed. Jones was back, Russell was the acknowledged leader, and tough team defense keyed San Francisco to an amazing year. After losing to the University of California at Los Angeles (UCLA) in their third game of the season, the USF Dons swept their next twenty-six to win the National Collegiate Athletic Association (NCAA) championship. By then, Russell had been tabbed by Howard Dallmar, coach of Stanford and a former standout player in the National Basketball Association (NBA), as one who could stop George Mikan, then professional basketball's best. The Eastern press was not convinced, though, calling Tom Gola, senior leader of defending champion La Salle, college basketball's best player. The issue was settled in the NCAA title game. Russell scored twenty-three points, had twenty-two rebounds, and constantly harassed La Salle shooters, while teammate Jones kept Gola scoreless from the field for twenty-one minutes, in an 89-77 win. Russell tallied 118 points in five play-off games, breaking Gola's NCAA record of 114, and was named the tournament's Most Valuable Player.

Russell's defensive play had created controversy, tied to what appeared at times to be both offensive and defensive goaltending. The NCAA rules committee widened the free-throw lane from six to twelve feet, a move quickly referred to as the "Bill Russell rule." After his junior year, Russell was invited by President Dwight D. Eisenhower to the White House to discuss a national fitness program. Russell was designated the college basketball representative on a physical-fitness council, joining the likes of Willie Mays and Bob Cousy.

Russell, by then, had tried varsity track and became a friend and intense rival of another USF high jumper, Johnny Mathis, who was destined to be a popular singer. At the Modesto Relays, Russell outjumped Mathis, six feet seven inches to six feet six inches. Russell's interest in track lasted past his graduation when, intent on being a 1956 United States Olympian, he entered both the basketball and high-jump trials. The high jump narrowed to four contestants for three spots, and Russell tied Charlie Dumas—who would later be the first man to leap seven feet—for first place. Since Russell had already been selected as one of only three collegians on the twelve-man United States Olympic basketball team, he withdrew his name from the high-jump ranks.

Prior to that, Russell had led San Francisco to an undefeated season and a second consecutive NCAA title. In the process, the Dons had won fifty-five games in a row, then an NCAA record. When the NBA draft came around, Russell discovered that the Boston Celtics had dealt veteran scorer Ed Macauley and rugged Kentucky all-American Cliff Hagan to the St. Louis Hawks for their draft rights. The Rochester Royals selected first, taking Sihugo Green, a top-rated guard, bypassing Russell because they believed that Maurice Stokes, the NBA Rookie-of-the-Year, supplied them with the same kind of rebounding strength. Additionally, Russell's presence on the Olympic team would remove him from much of the regular season. It was rumored, too, that the Harlem Globetrotters would outbid any NBA team to get Russell.

Arnold "Red" Auerbach, coach of the Celtics, picked Russell anyway. His Celtics had always been a high-scoring team but needed a strong big man. Russell led an undefeated Olympic team to a gold medal and then rejected a Globetrotter offer which was well above Boston's offer. By the end of his first NBA season, Russell proved to be the Celtics' long-needed ingredient. They celebrated their first NBA championship, and Russell had turned pivot play around forever. Thus, in one year, Russell had been the dominant force on three championship teams, in the NCAA, in the Olympics, and in the NBA.

In his second year, Russell was severely injured during the third game of the championship finals. Boston, without its shot-blocking, rebounding genius, lost to the Hawks in six games. During that season, Russell set a single game rebounding record of forty-nine, which he later increased to fifty-one, set a play-off single game rebounding record, a single season's rebounding record, and was the runaway choice as the league's Most Valuable Player. Curiously, he was bypassed on the All-League team.

In the following season, Russell broke his own season's rebounding record, enjoyed a .598 shooting percentage from the field (the best of his career), and led Boston to a sweep of the Minneapolis Lakers for the league crown. He was named All-League center. Over the next seven seasons, Russell led the Celtics to eight league championships in a row and nine out of ten. During that period, Russell was constantly compared to Wilt Chamberlain, the seven-foot, two-inch record-breaking scorer whose style of play contrasted sharply with Russell's. Opinion was divided as to which powerful center was better, but Russell wore the championship rings.

In 1966-1967, Russell succeeded Auerbach as head coach and, though leading the Celtics to a 60-21 slate, finished behind the Chamberlain-powered Philadelphia 76ers, whose 68-13 mark set an NBA record. The 76ers throttled Boston four games to one in the play-offs, and many believed that Russell and the Celtics were an item of the past. Instead, Boston came back in 1967-1968, to beat Philadelphia in three straight play-off games, after being down, three games to one, and then whipped the Los Angeles Lakers in six games, for their tenth title in twelve years. When Russell took them to another title in 1968-1969, the Celtics claimed the best championship streak in sports history, eleven titles in thirteen tries, and Russell had been the central figure in each. After the season, Russell retired.

Russell took up golf, ventured into films, did several radio shows for the American Broadcasting Company, basketball broadcasts for ABC-TV, and later held television contracts with the Columbia Broadcasting System and the Turner Broadcasting System. He also did lecture tours, Bell Telephone commercials, and even served as a substitute host for Dick Cavett.

Sam Schulman, principal owner of the then hapless Seattle SuperSonics, lured Russell back into NBA coaching in 1973. In Russell's initial season, the SuperSonics won ten more than their previous year, and in 1974-1975, Seattle made the play-offs for their first time. They repeated that achievement in 1975-1976, but Russell had already started to lose faith in too many of his players. He started a fourth and final season with little determination and regretted that he had not resigned earlier.

### Summary

Russell's fame was a result of his consistently superb efforts as an unselfish team player who intimidated enemy shooters, whose blocked shots almost always triggered fast breaks for his team, whose belief in and use of psychology constantly worked to his team's advantage, and whose leadership was undenied. Auerbach, knowing the importance of winning in professional sports, guaranteed Russell that he would never talk statistics at contract time. This was exactly what Russell, the ultimate team player, wanted to hear. In his own view, he never graded himself higher than sixty-five against a perfect game standard of one hundred.

More important, Russell recognized that there was far more to life than basketball. From his pedestal of fame, he stood taller, making himself heard in matters that counted. Teammate Cousy referred to Russell as a crusader. Certainly, Russell was among the first blacks in sports to speak out on issues. He remembered his being regularly stopped on Oakland's streets as a teenager, the police routinely harassing him with racial epithets. He remembered the mayor of Marion, Indiana, presenting each Celtic with a key to the city. Then, with K. C. Jones, Russell was refused service in a restaurant. He remembered honors being given him in Reading, Massachusetts, where he lived, the citizens of a wealthy section of town then circulating a petition to keep him out, when they learned that he planned to move there. Similar hurts were experienced in his hometown of Monroe, in Lexington, Kentucky, and elsewhere. Teammate Heinsohn remarked that Russell led the league in regrets. Russell also remembered, however, his grandfather's crying when, in the Celtic locker room, he had seen white John Havlicek showering alongside black Sam Jones.

Russell spoke out against the NBA's unwritten, but patently obvious, "quota" rule, and was fined. He was among those who defended Muhammed Ali, while condemning newspapers and magazines for their yellow journalism. When he was the first black selected to the Basketball Hall of Fame, already in its fifteenth year of operation, he refused to be inducted, criticizing the hall's standards and terming their leadership racist. He took up the cudgels when he could, on one hand speaking about blacks nationally, on the other being active in Boston school issues. This is the Russell who has affected America, a sports hero who insists on being judged as a total person.

### Bibliography

Auerbach, Arnold "Red," and Joe Fitzgerald. *Red Auerbach: An Autobiography.* New York: Putnam,

1977. A breezy study which contains the drive to win not only of Auerbach, but also of his Celtics.

Brown, Clifton. "Matchup for the Ages is Revisited by N.B.A." *New York Times* 146, no. 50596 (October 30, 1996). Brown examines the relationship between Russell and Wilt Chamberlain and offers information on their careers, accomplishments, and the rift between them that lasted several years.

Cousy, Bob, with Ed Linn. *The Last Loud Roar.* Englewood Cliffs, N.J.: Prentice-Hall, 1964. A very revealing book. Cousy tells his story as frankly as any athlete ever has. Much insight into league and team methods is contained here.

Harris, Merv. *The Lonely Heroes*. New York: Viking Press, 1975. A valuable work on professional basketball's big men, dependable in its facts, written with an effort to achieve balance.

Havlicek, John, with Bob Ryan. *Hondo: Celtic Man in Motion*. Englewood Cliffs, N.J.: Prentice-Hall, 1977. Candid descriptions of Boston plus very interesting insights into Russell's youth make this a worthwhile book. As with all books by Celtic personnel, Russell's personality, as well as his value to the club, is assessed.

Heinsohn, Tommy, with Leonard Lewin. *Heinsohn, Don't You Ever Smile?* New York: Doubleday, 1976. Easily the most humorous of all Celtic literature. In his discussion of Russell, Heinsohn may get closer to the truth of how Russell and his teammates related than any other work yet written.

Hirshberg, Al. *Bill Russell of the Boston Celtics*. New York: Messner, 1963. A slick, useful study, discussing Russell's youth very well. Its value is diminished only because it was published before Russell's career had closed.

Linn, Ed. "I Owe the Public Nothing." *Saturday Evening Post* 237 (January, 1964): 60-63. An article which, because Russell spoke out so candidly, created controversy. Permits a quick study of Russell's pride and philosophy.

Montville, Leigh. "Bill Russell." *Sports Illustrated* 81, no. 12 (September 19, 1994). Brief article on Russell's career achievements in basketball.

Russell, Bill, and Taylor Branch. *Second Wind: The Memoirs of an Opinionated Man*. New York: Random House, 1979. The second of two Russell autobiographies, this concentrates considerably more on his private life and behavior and rearticulates his philosophy. This is the better of the pair.

Russell, Bill, as told to William McSweeny. *Go Up for Glory*. New York: Coward-McCann, 1966. Though surpassed by Russell's second autobiography, this stands as an outstanding work. Contains valuable statements about sports and goals achievable within competition.

Russell, Bill, with Tex Maule. "I Am Not Worried About Ali." *Sports Illustrated* 26 (June, 1967): 18-21. Concentrating on Muhammed Ali's problems, the article reveals the passion and attitudes of Russell in several matters.

*John E. DiMeglio*

# BABE RUTH

*Born:* February 6, 1895; Baltimore, Maryland
*Died:* August 16, 1948; New York, New York
*Area of Achievement:* Baseball
*Contribution:* A remarkably talented athlete with a great flair for showmanship, Babe Ruth has come to symbolize baseball, the American national pastime.

## Early Life

George Herman Ruth was born in Baltimore, Maryland. His father was George H. Ruth, Sr. (1871-1918), and his mother was Kate Schamberger (1875-1912). Some confusion exists about the younger Ruth's actual date of birth. For many years, George Ruth believed that he had been born on February 7, 1894, but his birth certificate gives February 6, 1895, as his date of birth. George Ruth was the eldest of the eight children born to the Ruths, although only he and a sister (later Mrs. Wilbur Moberly) survived to adulthood. George Ruth's mother (whose maiden name is sometimes spelled Schanberg) lived until her eldest son was thirteen. His father survived until young George's second year in the major leagues.

The Ruths attempted to support their family through the operation of a barroom. Of his childhood, the dying Ruth told Bob Considine in 1947, "I was a bad kid. I say that without pride but with a feeling that it is better to say it." Having discovered that their eldest child, George, was a fractious youth, George and Kate enrolled him in St. Mary's Industrial School in Baltimore, Maryland, in 1902. Under the direction of the Xaverian Catholic Brothers, St. Mary's served as a vocational school as well as an orphanage, boarding school, and reform school. It was at St. Mary's that young Ruth studied to become a tailor and also learned to play baseball. Brother Matthias of St. Mary's would hit fungoes to Ruth, who quickly seized upon the game as a release from the studies and chores at St. Mary's as well as a chance to demonstrate what Brother Matthias recognized as a remarkable skill in the popular game. To Ruth, Brother Matthias was not only a fielding, hitting, and pitching coach, he was also "the father I needed." Years later, at the height of his fame and popularity, Babe Ruth never forgot St. Mary's or the Xaverian Brothers who had taught him so well.

In Baltimore, in 1914, there was a professional baseball team named the Orioles. At the time, the Orioles were a minor league team, owned and managed by Jack Dunn, who, after learning about Ruth's great baseball promise, signed the young athlete to a contract. Ruth discovered that he did not have to become a tailor; he could make a living doing what he enjoyed most: playing baseball. On February 27, 1914, George Ruth left St. Mary's to join the Baltimore team. During his first few days of spring training, Jack Dunn's new "babe" was the subject of some good-natured baseball pranks. Eventually, the new arrival on the team became Babe Ruth, arguably the greatest and most colorful player in the history of the sport he loved so well.

## Life's Work

Young Babe Ruth was a left-handed pitcher, and the high prices being offered for Ruth's pitching ability soon proved too tempting for the financially distressed Orioles to resist: Ruth was sold to the Boston Red Sox in July, 1914. On July 11, 1914, Babe Ruth pitched and was victorious in the first major league baseball game he had ever played. With his tremendous speed and sharp breaking ball, Ruth impressed Red Sox manager Bill Carrigan. Still, it was clear by August that the Red Sox would not win the American League pennant from Connie Mack's Philadelphia Athletics. Ruth was therefore sent down to the Red Sox minor league team in Providence, Rhode Island, to help them win the International League pennant. Providence manager "Wild Bill" Donovan was credited by Ruth for his effective pitching coaching, later of value to Ruth in his Red Sox career.

Throughout his long and colorful career, Ruth was criticized for financial, gastronomic, and sexual excesses. As with other legendary personalities, however, his sins as well as his successes may have been exaggerated. In his major league career, spanning 1914 to 1935, the Babe (as he was called) was an exciting, intelligent, and astonishingly well-rounded ball player, suggesting that the tales about his endless hedonism were largely, if not entirely, fictitious. On October 17, 1914, Babe Ruth married Helen Woodford, a waitress whom he had met in 1914, while with the Red Sox. In 1922, the Ruths adopted a baby girl named Dorothy. In 1926, the Ruths separated; in January, 1929, Helen Ruth was killed in a tragic fire. Three months later, Ruth married a beautiful widow named Claire Merritt Hodgson and adopted her daughter Julia. Ruth remained with his second wife until his death in August, 1948.

In 1915, the Boston Red Sox won the American League pennant, winning 101 games, of which Ruth had won eighteen, and losing only fifty. In the 1915 World Series, the Red Sox defeated the Philadelphia Phillies, four games to one. In 1916, Ruth won twenty-three games—a figure he matched in 1917. Overall, Babe Ruth won ninety-two games as a pitcher, and lost only forty-four; his earned run average was a remarkable 2.24. Ruth pitched for Boston in three World Series: 1915, 1916, and 1918. He won three World Series games, lost none, and sported an earned run average of 0.87. Had he continued as a pitcher, Ruth's pitching record could have been as remarkable as his hitting record.

The Red Sox now faced a problem with Ruth. In 1918, Ruth was recognized as one of the finest pitchers in baseball. He also hit eleven home runs, knocked in sixty-four runs, and batted .300. Ruth was too good a hitter to pitch every four days, resting between starts. He was too good a pitcher, however, to play the outfield or first base every day. It is some indication of Ruth's phenomenal baseball ability that from 1914 to 1919, while he was principally a pitcher, Ruth had 342 hits in 1,110 at-bats, with forty-nine home runs and 230 runs batted in. He simply had become too powerful as a hitter to keep as a pitcher. He also had become too expensive. Babe Ruth's 1917 salary was five thousand dollars, in 1918 it was seven thousand, and by 1919, it had grown to ten thousand. In January, 1920, Babe Ruth was sold again— this time by the Red Sox to the New York Yankees. The price tag was $100,000 and a loan of $350,000.

The season of 1920 was a turning point in the history of baseball. In that season, Ruth smashed an incredible fifty-four home runs, driving in 137. A new national hero was born, and the game of baseball began to change from a short game (meaning a game of bunts, sacrifices, and steals) to a long game (meaning home runs and big-scoring innings). There had been great concern for the future of the national pastime when it was revealed that some Chicago White Sox players had been bribed in the 1919 World Series, which they lost to Cincinnati. Ruth's amazing feats, however, drove the 1919 scandal from fans' minds. As *The New York Times* reported: "Inside of a fortnight the fandom of the nation had forgotten all about the Black Sox, as they had come to be called, as its attention became centered in an even greater demonstration of superlative batting skill by the amazing Babe Ruth." In 1921, Ruth hit an astounding fifty-nine home runs and drove in 170, while batting .378. Ruth's Yankees won ninety-eight games in that season and beat their cross-town rivals, the New York Giants, five games to three, in the World Series. It was no wonder, *The New York Times* reported, that "the baseball world lay at his feet."

The Yankees won the pennant again in 1922, 1923, 1926, 1927, 1928, and 1932; they won the World Series in 1922, 1923, 1927, 1928, and 1932. In the World Series games in which he played as a Yankee, Ruth hit fifteen home runs, drove in twenty-nine runs, and hit .347. Obscured by his extraordinary totals as a hitter (and pitcher) is Ruth's fielding, throwing, and baserunning ability. Numerous baseball fans and analysts testify to Ruth's superb skills as an outfielder and daring, aggressive baserunner. Ruth's attempted steal of second base in the final game of the 1926 World Series, which the St. Louis Cardinals won, is part of baseball folklore. With two outs in the ninth inning of the deciding Series game, Ruth walked. Trailing 3-2 in the ninth inning, the Yankees had two outs, but powerful Bob Meusel was at bat. With one strike on Meusel, Ruth attempted a delayed steal of second but was thrown out. The game was over, and the Cardinals were world champions. Baseball fans still argue the wisdom of Ruth's attempted steal. There is another Ruth legend associated with the 1926 World Series, the validity of which is still debated by baseball mythologists. A young boy, John Sylvester, was seriously ill during the 1926 Series. When he asked his father for a ball autographed by Ruth, the older Sylvester wired that request to the Babe. Players of both teams autographed balls which were sent to the Sylvester home. Johnny Sylvester did recover, but reports that Ruth promised to hit a home run for Johnny which, when executed, led to the boy's recovery, are in error.

In 1927, the New York Yankees, led by Ruth's herculean hitting (sixty home runs, 164 runs batted in, batting average of .356), won the World Series in a four-game sweep of the Pittsburgh Pirates. The 1927 Yankees are properly regarded by baseball historians as the greatest of all baseball teams. Ruth had by that time accumulated 416 home runs, batted in 1,274, and was batting .349. He was regarded as the great turnstile whirler, and it seemed as though people everywhere knew of Babe Ruth. In 1927, the Yankees paid Ruth an unbelievable seventy thousand dollars—a figure they matched in

*Babe Ruth crossing home plate after hitting his first home run of the season in 1925*

1928 and 1929. In 1930 and 1931, he received eighty thousand dollars per season. Ruth's earnings over twenty-two seasons in the majors were estimated to be $896,000, in addition to World Series shares of $41,445 and approximately one million dollars from endorsements and barnstorming tours. Despite the high cost, Ruth was an asset to the Yankees: He attracted so many fans to Yankee Stadium, which opened in 1923, that it was nicknamed "the House that Ruth Built."

Although 1927 will always be associated in sports history with Babe Ruth, the years 1928-1933 are equally, perhaps even more, impressive. In those years alone, Ruth batted .341, hit 270 home runs, and drove in 852 runs. It was spectacular. It was the golden age of sports, and Babe Ruth came to symbolize it all. Americans needed a diversion: The Depression had hit, and prohibition was not repealed until December, 1933. The public followed Ruth's successes and his failures, his heroics and his occasional misconduct, with enthusiasm.

In 1934, Babe Ruth spent his last full year in the major leagues. His average sank to .288; he hit twenty-two home runs and batted in eighty-four. It would have been an excellent season for most players, but it signaled the end for Babe Ruth. In 1934, the Yankees failed again (as in 1933) to win the pennant. Ruth left the Yankees and signed on for the 1935 season with the Boston Braves of the National League. He played in only twenty-eight games for the Braves, hitting six homers, driving in twelve runs, and batting .181. Ruth never attained his goal of becoming a major league manager, although he did coach in 1938 for the Brooklyn Dodgers. Statistics do not always reliably convey the value of a ballplayer, but, in Ruth's case, the evidence is clear: In his major league career, he played in 2,503 games; he batted 8,396 times and had 2,873 hits, of which 714 were homers. His lifetime batting average was .342. At the time of his death in 1948, Babe Ruth held fifty-four major league records. Although some of those records have now been captured by more recent players, Babe Ruth, the famous Number Three of the Yankees, is still the standard against which ballplayers are measured.

In June, 1948, Ruth, a dying man, stood in Yankee Stadium to say goodbye to thousands of fans. About two months later, he died of cancer at a New York City hospital. On the evening of August 17, 1948, Ruth's body lay inside the main entrance to Yankee Stadium. It is estimated that more than 100,000 fans passed by to pay their respects. The Babe was dead, but, as Marshall Smelser put it, "one with ears tuned and eyes alert will hear or read his name almost monthly. Even without any imposing monument his memory will last in this country till memory be dead."

## Summary

In March, 1944, during the bitter fighting on Pacific Islands, Japanese soldiers attacked United States Marine positions, screaming in English: "To hell with Babe Ruth." Babe Ruth had come to symbolize not only American baseball but also America. As Robert Creamer, the baseball historian, reported, Ruth once said of himself: "I swing big, with everything I've got. I hit big or I miss big. I like to live as big as I can." Here was an indigent boy who rose from the obscurity of a Maryland boys' home to become one of the most famous Americans, whose death was reported in the headlines of *The New York Times*. Although he only lived to be fifty-three, Ruth's life seemed curiously long and complete. Ruth had a remarkable flair for the spectacular and the flamboyant. He lived his life with a zest which his countrymen seemed able to share. As he was dying, he told his biographer, Bob Considine, that "I want to be a part of and help the development of the greatest game God ever saw fit to let man invent—Baseball." Even in death, Ruth will always be associated with baseball, and with America. Marshall Smelser summarized the importance of Babe Ruth in American life thus: "[H]e is our Hercules, our Samson, Beowulf, Siegfried. No other person outside of public life so stirred our imaginations or so captured our affections."

## Bibliography


Creamer, Robert W. *Babe: The Legend Comes to Life*. New York: Simon and Schuster, 1974; London: Penguin, 1983. A very well-written and well-researched biography. A balanced account of Ruth's life, neither iconoclastic nor hagiographic. Probably the best general account of Ruth's life, although there is little documentation for the close reader.

———. "'Ruth? He Is Still in the Spotlight, Still Going Strong.'" *Smithsonian* 25, no. 11 (February, 1995). Profile of Ruth's colorful life and career.

Nack, William. "The Colossus." *Sports Illustrated* 89, no. 8 (August 24, 1998). Focuses on Ruth's 60-homerun season along with other events of 1927.

Ruth, Babe. *Babe Ruth's Own Book of Baseball*. New York and London: Putnam, 1928. No credit is given in this volume to any assistant writer, although there very probably was at least one. This is an interesting book because it contains details about Ruth's life—as well as about his baseball beliefs—which are rarely referred to elsewhere. Anecdotal. It provides an interesting view of baseball strategy in the 1920's.

Ruth, Babe, as told to Bob Considine. *The Babe Ruth Story*. New York: Dutton, 1948. A surprisingly well-done and frank account of Babe's life, written in the last months of that life. Although bowdlerized, the book contains the Babe's views of many important episodes in his life and is enjoyable reading for the Ruth fan.

Smelser, Marshall. *The Life That Ruth Built*. New York: Quadrangle, and London: University of Nebraska Press, 1993. By far the best study of Ruth yet to emerge. Balanced account, if rather forgiving of Ruth in certain areas. Superbly researched and documented. Thoughtful and analytical. Thorough. Attempts to place Ruth into his historical context. Indispensable for those wishing a deeper study of the Ruth legend.

Wagenheim, Kal. *Babe Ruth: His Life and Legend*. New York: Praeger, 1974. A very good popular account, overshadowed by Creamer's when both appeared at about the same time. Although this volume is not as thorough as Creamer's—and certainly not as thorough as Smelser's—it is a useful and readable account.

Weldon, Martin. *Babe Ruth*. New York: Crowell, 1948. A book appearing about the same time as *The Babe Ruth Story*, this book was never given close attention, but it is a short, readable account without documentation. Tends to be rather flattering of the Babe. This book, like Claire Ruth's memoir *The Babe and I* (with Bill Slocum), published by Prentice-Hall in 1959, becomes a philippic against organized baseball for not embracing Babe as a manager after his playing career was done. Useful if read with other accounts.


*James H. Toner*

# ERNEST RUTHERFORD

*Born:* August 30, 1871; Spring Grove (later known as Brightwater), near Nelson, New Zealand
*Died:* October 19, 1937; Cambridge, England
*Area of Achievement:* Physics
*Contribution:* One of the pioneers of the atomic age, Rutherford investigated the nature of the atom and of radioactivity, laying the experimental basis of the new atomic physics.

## Early Life

Ernest Rutherford was born in 1871 in a rural area of New Zealand. He was the fourth child of a family of twelve, and although his father was an engineer, the boy's early life was on a farm. He had to travel some distance to school but quickly established himself as a student of ability. In 1886, he won a scholarship to Nelson College (with a result that was a record for the times). Three years later, he won a university scholarship to Canterbury College, Christchurch, from which he was graduated in 1894 with a double first in physical sciences and mathematics.

While at Christchurch, Rutherford met Mary Newton, the only recorded romantic attachment of his life. He had, in fact, a reputation for being somewhat diffident with women. He began what was to become a six-year courtship, feeling secure enough to marry only in 1900, when he had taken a professorship in Canada, after several years in Europe.

In 1894, Rutherford won the 1851 Exhibition Scholarship, an award established to finance young graduates from the British Empire to study in England. He had already published an audacious paper challenging the leading scientists of the day, titled "Magnetisation of Iron by High Frequency Discharges." He designed and constructed the apparatus himself—no mean achievement for a twenty-three-year-old, isolated in New Zealand from the scientific community. In 1895, therefore, it was no surprise that he was courted by the Cavendish Laboratory in Cambridge; he went to study there at one of the most exciting periods in its history, working alongside such eminent scientists as James Clerk Maxwell, J. J. Thomson, and John William Rayleigh. It was the year of the discovery of X rays, a scientific development that was to point the way to Rutherford's future work.

Rutherford was at first something of an outsider in the rarefied atmosphere of Cambridge University. Not only was he not a graduate of that university, but also his New Zealand country upbringing made him appear both brash and gauche. Moreover, unlike most of his colleagues, he had no independent means, and despite various small scholarships, he had to pay his way by taking on work as a tutor. He was a large, ruddy-faced man with a directness of manner that people who did not know him well considered uncouth. It was, however, this very characteristic which later, when he ran his own laboratory, inspired loyalty among his colleagues.

His first research was on the long-distance transmission of radio waves. He had, in fact, arrived from New Zealand with a radio-wave detector that he himself had constructed. Indeed, one of Rutherford's chief characteristics was his ability to devise his own experimental apparatus to test the leading theories of the day. Although his research into radio waves was important—Guglielmo Marconi was working along similar lines at the time and a few years later developed the wireless—Rutherford's thoughts began to turn in other directions. J. J. Thomson, who was something of a mentor to the young Rutherford, was working on X rays, and Rutherford elected to join him.

## Life's Work

One of Rutherford's early experimental successes was to detect and measure the ionization caused by the passage of electricity through gases. He was working with Thomson's theory of ionization; the experiment was important in that it showed Rutherford's ability to translate theory into a measurable reality—a talent which he utilized throughout his life. In 1898, Rutherford was offered the second MacDonald Professorship of Physics at McGill University, Montreal, Canada. Although his work with Thomson at the Cavendish was over, he continued his research into what would later become known as radioactivity. A year later, he published a paper based on his work at the Cavendish, which showed that there were two distinct types of radiation: alpha and beta rays. He was working toward demonstrating that the energy of alpha and beta rays comes from within the atom. He discovered a curious "emanation" from thorium—that is, radioactivity—which decreased geometrically with time. His own discovery, however, was overshadowed by the Curies' discovery, in the same period, of radium and the half-life of its emanation. Histor-

ically, therefore, the discovery of radioactivity is ascribed to the Curies. Rutherford's greatest achievement in this field occurred when he joined forces with Frederick Soddy—an unusual combination, since Soddy was a chemist. Together they analyzed the emanation, realizing that it arose from the transformation of one element into another. That was, at the time, an outrageous suggestion, with its overtones of alchemy, but within a brief period the scientific community came to accept that radioactivity, as it was now called, was a new kind of phenomenon. In 1908, Rutherford was awarded the Nobel Prize for Chemistry for his work on radioactivity, a unique achievement for a physicist and an indication of the unorthodox combination of disciplines whereby Rutherford had achieved his goal.

In 1907, Rutherford left Canada. He had begun to feel isolated from the main centers of scientific research and turned down offers from Yale University and the Smithsonian Institution in order to return to Great Britain and take up the Chair of Physics at Manchester University. At a time when European scientists such as Werner Heisenberg and Albert Einstein were leading the world in scientific theory, Rutherford established a "school" at Manchester which set out to unite experimental and theoretical talent. Among the world-famous scientists who studied under him were Lawrence Bragg (later professor of chemistry at Manchester), Harry Moseley (who was killed during World War I), Hans Geiger (who later invented the Geiger counter), and Neils Bohr, perhaps the most brilliant scientist of the twentieth century. Under Rutherford's leadership, Manchester became one of the major scientific centers of the world.

Rutherford was now a leading figure in the scientific community, corresponding with scientists around the world, advising appointments in Europe, Australia, and North America, and playing a major part in the Royal Society. His most important international contribution at this time was to take part in the convention to establish an international radium standard. This was a very delicate task, particularly given Madame Curie's prior claims in the field. It demanded a high level of diplomacy from the normally blunt Rutherford, and the convention was eventually successful. His international standing was honored at home when he was knighted in 1914.

Rutherford now pointed his research in a slightly different direction. He had already, as has been noted, established the nature of radioactivity; now he used radioactivity to determine the nature of the atom itself. The currently accepted model was that of Rutherford's old teacher, Thomson, who visualized the atom as a kind of "plum pudding," with the atomic particles suspended haphazardly within its confines. This model, however, was at odds with Max Planck's quantum theory and could not explain the discrete units of energy emitted by atoms. Through continual correspondence and experimentation, Rutherford, Planck, and, later, Bohr (after he had left Manchester) gradually developed a new model, the one that has become generally accepted. If Planck and Bohr separately pushed out the theoretical boundaries of atomic physics, then Rutherford and his colleagues (first at Manchester, later at the Cavendish Laboratory) supplied the experimental verifications.

Bohr's suggested model of the atom is the basis of the contemporary theory. It pictures negatively charged electrons orbiting around a central nucleus composed of positively charged protons and uncharged neutrons. It was Rutherford's carefully planned experiments which provided the first indications that Bohr's theory was correct, and later, in 1917, when Rutherford smashed the atom and the predicted particles were emitted, Bohr's theory was demonstrated beyond doubt. In disproving Thomson's version, Rutherford had finally overtaken his teachers' teachings.

During World War I, Rutherford, like many of his colleagues, was called into service on behalf of the government. Rutherford's particular contribution was in the field of antisubmarine warfare, and he worked on numerous committees and with the navy to discover ways of detecting submarines underwater, concentrating on sonic methods. Once again, Rutherford's talents for diplomacy were called upon to construct a team of scientists and naval officers to work together under difficult and sometimes hostile circumstances. His experiences during that time convinced him that scientific research and government policy had to be linked both financially and in terms of priorities, and, after the war, he set out to establish more formal contacts between the two arenas. While Rutherford spent much time and energy on his war work, it was eventually superseded by his atomic work, particularly during the excitement of 1917, when it became clear that his ambition of smashing the atom was nearing fruition. As always, for Rutherford, science came first and anything else was pushed into the background when important new discoveries were on the horizon.

In 1919, Thomson resigned as head of the Cavendish Laboratory, and inevitably Rutherford was asked to take his place. As the Professor of the Cavendish, Rutherford was responsible for its postwar regeneration, and he reorganized and expanded it to become the world's leading center of experimental physics. Further, he developed it into a modern institution, in which teaching and research were planned to fulfill national needs.

Rutherford continued to play a part on the political stage in the 1930's. When many Jewish scientists were having to flee from Nazi Germany, Rutherford became a champion of the refugees, helping them in both practical and political matters; in particular, he enabled the Nobel Prize winner Max Born to work at the Cavendish until he succeeded in obtaining the chair at Edinburgh. Rutherford believed that science was an international pursuit without geographical boundaries, and these beliefs were put to a severe test when Peter Kapitsa, a brilliant student from the Soviet Union, came to study at the Cavendish in 1921. Thirteen years later, he was detained in Leningrad and not allowed to return to the West. Rutherford worked tirelessly to find a means whereby Kapitsa could continue his work in either Great Britain or the Soviet Union and finally succeeded in transferring the bulk of Kapitsa's experimental apparatus from Cambridge to Moscow—perhaps the most difficult diplomatic task of his life.

Under Rutherford's direction at the Cavendish, Sir James Chadwick organized the finances and the research policy of the laboratory, Sir John Cockcroft and E. T. S. Walton built their famous accelerator, and the Cavendish led the world in experimentation on the atom and its composition. Rutherford achieved personal honor when he was elected president of the Royal Society, a post he held from 1925 to 1930.

## Summary

Ernest Rutherford died of intestinal paralysis in 1937. During his scientific career, the theories of physics had changed beyond recognition: The discovery of radioactivity and the smashing of the atom were two of the most important milestones of the atomic age, and Rutherford had played a major part in both developments. Under his guidance, the Cavendish Laboratory had reached the limits of its experimental possibilities. The new era demanded larger and larger equipment, and only international institutes which could pool the resources of several governments could carry on the research. The unanswered questions were about the structure of the nucleus, and higher energies—requiring larger accelerators—were needed to probe its secrets. Rutherford had been one of the key experimentalists of the atomic age, but the new direction in physics were to take it into the nuclear age. Rutherford died before the major practical applications of his work, nuclear power and nuclear weaponry, were developed. Many believe that, while he would have welcomed the former, he would have striven to limit the potential of the latter. He was without doubt one of the founders of the nuclear age. He was buried in Westminster Abbey as Lord Rutherford of Nelson.

## Bibliography

Badash, Lawrence, ed. *Rutherford and Boltwood: Letters on Radioactivity.* New Haven, Conn.: Yale University Press, 1969. An important series of letters in which Rutherford describes his own research.

Birks, J. B., ed. *Rutherford at Manchester*. London: Heywood, 1962; New York: Benjamin, 1963. An important source as background to his work on the atom, especially in contributions by Niels Bohr, A. S. Russell, and Sir Charles Darwin.

Crowther, J. G. *The Cavendish Laboratory, 1874-1974*. London: Macmillan, and New York: Science History, 1974. Although the author's Marxist viewpoint has aroused some controversy, this study is universally accepted as the fullest and most detailed chronicle of the history, founding, and work of the Cavendish. Chapter 6, on the period 1895-1898, was written by Rutherford himself, and a section by J. J. Thomson is included.

Eve, A. S. *Rutherford*. Cambridge: Cambridge University Press, and New York: Macmillan, 1939. The first biography of Rutherford, and the most important one for his early work and discoveries.

Romer, Alfred. "Proton or Prouton?: Rutherford and the Depths of the Atom." *American Journal of Physics* 65, no. 8 (August, 1997). Romer focuses on Rutherford's theories on the hydrogen nucleus.

Rutherford, Lord Ernest. *The Newer Alchemy*. Cambridge: Cambridge University Press, and New York: Macmillan, 1937. Rutherford's last book was an expanded version of a memorial lecture he gave at Newnham College in 1936. Only seventy pages long and fully illustrated, it expresses in popular style the latest developments in atomic research.

———. *Radioactivity*. Cambridge: Cambridge University Press, 1904. Rutherford's first book, a summation of his work in 1904 on radioactivity. It was this work which led to his being awarded the Nobel Prize.

Thomson, J. J. *Recollections and Reflections*. London: Bell, 1936; New York: Macmillan, 1937. A series of autobiographical sketches which provide some interesting personal insights into Rutherford's work at the Cavendish Laboratory.

Trenn, Thaddeus. *The Self-splitting Atom*. London: Taylor and Francis, 1977. A major academic study on the Rutherford-Soddy partnership in Canada. Very thorough and accurate but tends to overrate Soddy's share in the partnership.

Von Baeyer, Hans Christian. "Mortal Coil." *Sciences* 38, no. 3 (May/June, 1998). Examines the concept of radioactive decay using a January 1900 report by Rutherford.

Wilson, Donald. *Rutherford: Simple Genius*. London: Hodder and Stoughton, and Cambridge, Mass.: MIT Press, 1983. A detailed survey of the life and work of Rutherford with a reevaluation of his role in public science, based on material that had only recently become available.

*Sally Hibbin*

# NICOLA SACCO

*Born:* April 22, 1891; Torremaggiore, Italy
*Died:* August 23, 1927; Boston, Massachusetts
*Area of Achievement:* Law
*Contribution:* Along with Bartolomeo Vanzetti, Sacco was charged with a payroll robbery and murder in 1920. Their trial and execution, which led to worldwide protests, are considered examples of political and ethnic bias in the criminal justice system.

## Early Life

The man who would later change his name to Nicola was born Ferdinando Sacco, the third son in a family of seventeen children, in Torremaggiore, Italy. Sacco's family were relatively prosperous farmers and olive oil merchants. His father also owned a successful vineyard. Ferdinando (Nando) was a healthy and happy child, and although he was not interested in education, he attended school up until the third grade and was literate in Italian when he emigrated to the United States. Young Sacco loved growing things and working with machines. The latter interest seemed perfect for a boy who dreamed of going to the United States and making his way in a free country.

In 1908, Sacco and his older brother Sabino sailed for the United States. An old friend of their father welcomed them to his home in Milford, Massachusetts, where they settled into a community of Italians from their home province of Foggia. After a year and a half, Sabino returned home to Italy, but Sacco stayed in Massachusetts. He worked his way from water boy at a construction site to a skilled job at the Milford Shoe Company. Sacco realized that to better himself, he needed to learn a trade, so he invested about fifty dollars of his savings and learned to become one of the best edge trimming machine operators in the business. He was considered a steady, hard-working employee and was well liked by his supervisors. He remained with the Milford Shoe Company until 1917.

Sacco attended English classes three evenings each week and enjoyed sports and socializing with friends in his free time. In 1911, the young man met sixteen-year-old Rosina Zambelli at a dance. She was a small, pretty girl with copper-colored hair. Rosina had a good mind and a good character. At this time, Sacco was described as sturdy, clean-cut, handsome, and modest. He was rather short (5 feet 5 inches tall) with dark hair and brown eyes. The couple seemed proud of each other and very much in love. They were married in 1912, and their first son, Dante, was born in 1913.

Although Sacco made good wages as a skilled machine operator, he was concerned about the economic injustice he saw around him. He worried about poverty and unemployment and looked to various radical organizations for solutions. During the 1912 textile strike in Lawrence, Massachusetts, during which Sacco supported the workers, he came into contact with a group of Italian anarchists. He joined an anarchist study group, the Circolo di Studi Sociali, and there he found fellowship and commitment to noble ideals of economic justice. Anarchism provided Sacco with an ethical framework and a focus for his life. He came to believe that capitalism was evil, that all governments were oppressive, that wars were crimes against humanity, and that liberty was the foundation of human happiness. Sacco collected money for anarchist causes and participated in demonstrations and strikes. He was not a thinker or a leader in the movement but rather a faithful foot soldier in the radical army.

With the outbreak of World War I, the anarchists faced the issue of whether registering for the draft would be a betrayal of their beliefs. Sacco was not eligible for the draft because he was an Italian citizen and also because he had a dependant wife and child. Nonetheless, the law required registration; to avoid the obligation, Sacco left the United States for Mexico. Among his companions was a new acquaintance, Bartolomeo Vanzetti.

Work was hard to find in Mexico, however, and Sacco and Vanzetti remained there only a few months. While in Mexico, Sacco used the alias Nicola Mosmacotelli. Although he resumed his surname in the United States, Sacco continued to call himself Nicola. Returning to Massachusetts, Sacco eventually found work with his old supervisor, now at the Three-K Shoe Company in Stoughton. Sacco remained at that job until May, 1920, four days before his arrest. Once again, he was considered a model employee, a hard worker, and a generous friend.

## Life's Work

During the period of U.S. involvement in World War I, the political atmosphere was characterized by hostility and suspicion toward immigrants and radicals. That attitude persisted after the war's end,

*Anarchists Nicola Sacco (center right) and Bartolomeo Vanzetti (center left) going to trial.*

as fear of uprisings in the wake of the Russian Revolution led to the Red Scare in 1919-1920. Radical publications were banned, suspicious aliens were deported, and Congress voted to restrict immigration. In this environment of antiforeign feeling, Sacco and Vanzetti were charged, tried, convicted, and executed for robbery and murder in a 1920 incident in South Braintree, Massachusetts.

On April 15, 1920, Frederick Parmenter, the paymaster for a shoe manufacturing company, and his guard, Alexxandro Berardelli, were robbed of $15,777 in cash and shot by two men with pistols. The robbers, whom witnesses described as "looking like Italians," jumped into a getaway car with several other men and drove away. The incident followed a similar attempted robbery the previous Christmas Eve in Bridgewater, Massachusetts. The police suspected Mike Boda, an Italian radical, whose car was traced to a garage where it was being repaired. They told the owner of the garage to notify them when someone came to claim the car.

On May 5, Sacco and Vanzetti, along with Boda and another associate, arrived to pick up the car. Given the political atmosphere and fearing they might be deported as dangerous aliens, they intended to use the vehicle to haul away and dispose of some anarchist and radical literature. Instead, they fell into a police trap. Both men were carrying guns when the police stopped them. Sacco had a .32 caliber Colt automatic along with twenty-three extra cartridges in his pocket. Vanzetti was carrying a .38 caliber revolver and a number of shotgun shells. Both men, fearing reprisals for their radical views, lied to the police when originally questioned. They were not informed that they were under suspicion for robbery and murder but were instead asked about their citizenship, their political affiliations, their reading habits, and their advocacy of revolution. They lied about their politics and their movements to both Police Chief Michael Stewart and District Attorney Frederick Katzmann. Their flimsy stories reinforced the theory that the district attorney would use against them throughout their trials. He believed that a group of Italian bandits was responsible for both the Bridgewater and South Braintree holdups, that Boda's car had been used in the crimes, that the stolen money had been smuggled back to Italy, that Vanzetti had been the Bridgewater thief, and that Vanzetti had been one of the shooters at South Braintree. The fact that the two men had lied to police was repeatedly cited during the trial as proof of their "consciousness of guilt."

During the following summer, Vanzetti was tried and convicted for the Bridgewater robbery. Although he had an alibi supported by many witnesses, the jury did not believe witnesses whose testimony in Italian had to be translated into English. As a first-time offender and for a crime with no injury, Vanzetti received the harsh sentence of ten to fifteen years. Based on Vanzetti's experience, supporters of Sacco and Vanzetti concluded that it would be difficult for the two men to have a fair trial in the hostile political atmosphere and so brought in Fred H. Moore, known for representing labor leaders and other militant clients, as lead defense attorney.

Moore determined to exploit the political prejudices of the prosecution by exposing the charges as an attempt to destroy the anarchist movement. He advised the defendants to admit their radical views and to insist that they were being tried for their politics, not for a crime. Outside the courtroom, he organized political meetings, contacted international organizations, raised funds from labor unions, and publicized the injustice of the case in millions of pamphlets. Meanwhile, the prosecution produced numerous witnesses, some of whom testified to the identity of Sacco and Vanzetti as the robbers and others whose identifications were thoroughly untrustworthy. They also brought ballistics experts to demonstrate similarities (although not positive matches) between the defendants' weapons and those used in the crimes. A cap found at the crime scene was put into evidence because it resembled a cap Sacco often wore. Although Sacco's own cap was found at his home, the jury was presented with the spurious cap as evidence. The prosecution repeatedly charged that the lies told by the defendants were evidence of their guilt.

Despite Sacco's alibi that he was at the Italian consulate getting a passport on the day of the robbery and despite evidence of perjury by some of the prosecution witnesses, the two men were found guilty on July 14, 1920. Demonstrations were organized around the world to protest the verdict, and crowds stormed American embassies and consulates in Europe and Latin America.

Judge Webster Thayer presided over the trial. Known for his opposition to radicalism and immigration, Judge Thayer also ruled on every appeal. In other words, the same judge who had ruled on procedures and evidence during the original trial was allowed to review those decisions on appeal. In 1924, defense attorney Moore was replaced by William G. Thompson, a respected Boston lawyer. Thompson raised many points of law—that prosecution witnesses had lied, that the police had engaged in illegal activities, that a convicted bank robber (Celestino Madeiros) had confessed to the crime, and that there was strong evidence implicating the notorious Morelli gang in the Braintree incident. Judge Thayer rejected every motion.

On April 9, 1927, Sacco and Vanzetti were sentenced to death. Public outrage at the sentence and international protests led the governor of Massachusetts, Alvan T. Fuller, to appoint a special advisory committee, chaired by the president of Harvard University, to review the case. After a superficial examination, the committee concluded that the trial had been fair and recommended that the governor not grant clemency. Sacco and Vanzetti were electrocuted on August 23, 1927. Along with an international outcry against the execution, many Americans saw the event as proof that the nation had failed to live up to its ideals of justice and equality.

**Summary**

Fifty years after the execution, Massachusetts governor Michael Dukakis declared August 23, 1977, "Nicola Sacco and Bartolomeo Vanzetti Day." Dukakis did not comment on the guilt or innocence of the two men but proclaimed instead that the atmosphere of their trial had been engulfed by "prejudice against foreigners and hostility toward unorthodox political views."

The case of Sacco and Vanzetti has continued to provoke debate since the moment of their arrest. The arguments about whether ballistics evidence proves that Sacco or Vanzetti committed the crime continue. Sacco's wife Rosina lived into her nineties, but never clarified her husband's guilt or innocence.

On the other hand, virtually everyone agrees that Sacco and Vanzetti did not receive a fair trial and that police, prosecutors, and the judge were guilty of infringing on the rights of the accused. Most agree that the men were convicted because of their politics rather than because of evidence beyond a reasonable doubt. Many see the case as an example of the unfairness of the U.S. justice system, which convicts the poor, the unpopular, and members of minority groups while the more privileged classes break the law with impunity.

**Bibliography**

Avrich, Paul. *Sacco and Vanzetti: The Anarchist Background*. Princeton: Princeton University Press, 1991. Avrich locates Sacco and Vanzetti within the context of a comprehensive examination of anarchist politics.

Cannistraro, V. "Mussolini, Sacco-Vanzetti, and the Anarchists: The Transatlantic Context." *The Journal of Modern History* 68, no. 1 (March,1996). Focuses on Benito Mussolini's use of support for Sacco and BenitoVanzetti to further his political and diplomatic aims while preserving his relationship with the United States.

Feuerlicht, Roberta S. *Justice Crucified: The Story of Sacco and Vanzetti*. New York: McGraw-Hill, 1977. Feuerlicht interprets the Sacco and Vanzetti case as a symbolic conflict between the establishment and outsiders.

Frankfurter, Felix. *The Case of Sacco and Vanzetti*. Boston: Little Brown, 1927. This book provides a meticulous examination of the legal issues involved in the case.

Joughin, G. Louis, and Edmund M. Morgan. *The Legacy of Sacco and Vanzetti*. New York: Harcourt Brace, 1948. Jouglin and Morgan place the judicial process within the social and cultural conflicts of the 1920's.

Russell, Francis. *Sacco and Vanzetti: The Case Resolved*. New York: Harper, 1986. Russell claims to have proof of Sacco's guilt based on a letter.

*Mary Welek Atwell*

# NELLY SACHS

*Born:* December 10, 1891; Berlin, Germany
*Died:* May 12, 1970; Stockholm, Sweden
*Area of Achievement:* Literature
*Contribution:* Sachs, primarily because of her focus upon the deaths of Europe's six million Jews in World War II and her anguished outcry against this ghastly event, has become known as the poet of the Holocaust. One who escaped Nazi horrors because of last-minute maneuvering on her behalf, Sachs was a witness who had to find a fitting way to commemorate the dead and engender hope despite the horror of the event; incredibly, given the difficulty of the task, Sachs succeeded brilliantly.

## Early Life

Nelly Sachs was the only daughter of humane, highly cultured parents. Her father, William, was a prosperous manufacturer living in Berlin; her mother, Margarethe, was a pleasant, refined woman. Sachs's Berlin was busy with trade and self-importance, being the arrogant new capital of a recently united Germany bent upon proving its worth to the world. Though certainly no stranger to anti-Semitism as a child, Sachs was spared an acquaintance with the rough side of life as a child and grew up in a household in which self-expression was esteemed. A member of the upper-middle class, she had ample time to create puppet plays and stories as well as write verse.

Sachs's parents sent her to fine schools and encouraged her interests, especially her love of music. Adept at dancing, she wanted to be a dancer in her teen years but also harbored the hope of becoming a mime. At age seventeen, Sachs wrote her first poetry, which was of a romantic, even florid type conventionally approved of in Berlin and therefore acceptable to the local newspapers to which she sent her poems. Berlin intellectuals, however, paid no attention to her newspaper poems, for they enjoyed the avant-garde poetry of the expressionists then in vogue. The tame and often mawkish poems of Sachs's teen years gave no hint of the powerful verse she would one day write.

Sachs's safe, secure, and pleasant Berlin began to change for the worse beginning in the pivotal year 1933, when Adolf Hitler assumed the office of German chancellor. Anti-Jewish feeling, on the rise throughout the post-World War I period, had grown intense, leading to the persecution of all Jews regardless of financial position. To escape the oppression and hatred she felt, Sachs turned to studies of such books as the Kabala, the Bible, and those of mystic writers such as Jakob Böhme.

## Life's Work

Fortunately for Sachs, she had corresponded for a long time with Swedish author Selma Lagerlöf, whose *Gösta Berlings saga* (1891; *The Story of Gösta Berling*, 1898) and other writings she passionately admired. In fact, Sachs had been writing to Lagerlöf since Sachs published her first volume of work, *Legenden und Erzählungen* (1921; legends and tales). When it became apparent that the Nazis would send Sachs and her mother to the gas chambers, Lagerlöf used whatever influence she could muster to persuade the King of Sweden to intercede for her friends in Germany—which he did. Sachs and her mother fled to Stockholm, narrowly missing being caught by the Gestapo and sent to a concentration camp.

From 1933 to 1940, the year Lagerlöf engineered Sachs's escape, Sachs had kept to herself as much as possible, fearing that contact with the world outside her home would bring disaster. Living a hermetic existence, Sachs studied Hebrew and German literature, absorbing the rhymes and rhythms found there as well as the authors' mystical sense of the world. Thwarted in her pursuit of a writer's career because of the fact that she was Jewish, Sachs put all of her energies into honing her imagination. Also during this period she fell in love with a man, though little is known about him except for the fact that the Nazis dragged him away to his death.

When she went to Sweden in 1940, she knew only one person there—Lagerlöf; yet Lagerlöf died only two months after her arrival in Stockholm, a further source of anguish for Sachs and her mother. A stranger in a strange country, Sachs, exiled from a country gone insane with blood lust and hatred of the Jews, started to write as a survivor surveying the wreckage of lives she had known. Gone were the nature poems of her youth. In their place was a new kind of poetry, a harder, tougher poetry that spoke of the unspeakable—tortures, ashes, smoking chimneys, madness, suicide, mass death, all the realities with which she was faced as a survivor of the cruelest spectacle in mankind's cruel history. In her tiny apartment she could join with her ailing mother in lamenting the loss of friends and family. In Stockholm she was alone and unknown as a writer. Her poetry became her only way out of spiritual torpor and anguish.

Out of the wartime exile came her first notable poems, those of *In den Wohnungen des Todes* (in the dwellings of death), first published in 1946, in which she discovered her true themes and poetic voice. Here she concentrated her considerable imaginative powers upon the sufferings of the people of Israel and, for the first time, took as her own responsibility the solemn, enormous task of remembering the dead victims of Hitler's tyranny. To Sachs, there could be no division between herself and those who perished; she consciously chose to craft a poetic monument worthy of them.

Writing in German and living in Sweden meant that Sachs's audience was far smaller than if she had chosen to write in Yiddish or English or lived in New York, London, or Paris. Nevertheless, German recognition came to her because she wrote in that language and later international attention was finally given her.

Her collection of poetry entitled *Sternverdunkelung* (1949; eclipse of the stars) increased her readership and gained for her some critical attention. The biblical cadence, the magnificent themes of death, life, and rebirth, and the harrowing intensity of these poems announced that the wandering Jews of Europe, those alive and those dead, had found their poetic voice. Though heartened by the critical reception of her latest poems, Sachs and her mother endured extreme economic hardship in the early phase of their exile. After her mother's death in 1950, however, Sachs's burden began to lighten as money from her translations of Swedish writers into German came in. Moreover, she was heartened by sales of *Eli: Ein Mysterienspiel vom Leiden Israels* (*Eli: A Mystery Play of the Sufferings of Israel*, 1967), a verse play written in 1943 but published in 1951 which dealt with the death of a Jewish shepherd boy at the hands of a Nazi soldier.

In Sachs's next volume, *Und niemand weiss weiter* (1957; and no one knows where to turn), she began to universalize the torments of the Jews, seeing them as part of the larger story of human suffering throughout history; by so doing, she no longer envisioned the Holocaust as the only catastrophic event in history but as the greatest of them all. This new vision of universal suffering and the searching of all people for meaning and hope found further expression in her subsequent collection, *Flucht und Verwandlung* (1959; light and change), which brought her increased critical attention, especially in Germany.

Sachs's collected poems, *Fahrt ins Staublose* (1961; journey beyond the dust), brought her new readers intrigued by her ability to ask the difficult questions of God that naturally occur after Auschwitz. Following this volume came *Zeichen im Sand: Die szenischen Dichtungen* (1962; signs in the dust), *Späte Gedichte* (1965; later poems), and *Glühende Rätsel* (1964-1966; glowinzg enigmas), in which her exploration of silence and the questions God leaves unanswered deepens. Here again is the Jewish experience translated into the experience of all human beings alive in the twentieth century—and of all who have ever lived.

To Sachs, the apocalypse that was the Holocaust is contrasted with the promise held by a resurrected state of Israel, the sorrow mitigated thought not erased by the joyful re-creation of the Jewish nation. Sustained by the hope for the future of not only Jewry but also mankind, Sachs increasingly appreciated her adopted homeland and grew ever more proficient in speaking and writing Swedish. Her Swedish admirers were many but so too were her East and West German ones. In fact, she was honored by many German societies in several cities and towns.

The culmination of her career, however, came in two ways: with her being awarded the 1966 Nobel Prize in Literature and with the publication of what would become her most noted work, the epic-length lyric *O the Chimneys* in 1967. With characteristic modesty, Sachs accepted the Nobel Prize on behalf of the millions of Jews who perished in the Holocaust and dedicated it to their memory. This award enabled Sachs once more to widen her reading public, yet she did not become a popular poet. Her works were thought by many to be far too painful or too difficult to read, their abstract quality and enormous themes tending to overwhelm first-time readers.

*O the Chimneys* is generally acknowledged as Sachs's finest poem. She labored on it for many years, trying to create a mighty epic of lasting significance. With the publication of this great poem, Sachs's reputation as the poet of the Holocaust was established for all time. Lyrical at a time when lyric poetry was thought archaic, long when brevity was sought in poetry, and biblical in tone and cadence when sophisticated readers looked for irony, *O the Chimneys* bewildered some critics and disappointed others. Yet most critics who wrote about it found it masterful. Sachs determined that this poem would be an unsentimentalized lament for a vanished people as well as a wellspring of hope for a desperate, confused world.

Sachs's final years were relatively happy ones spent in an adopted land she came to acknowledge as home, where her fellow Swedes saw her as a national treasure. Always the mystic, she spent her last years as she had spent previous ones—in contemplation. She died quietly in Stockholm on May 12, 1970, and her mourners were many.

### Summary

Nelly Sachs wrote as an outcry against horrors and evils she had known and those she had narrowly escaped knowing. In her career as a poet, she began as a romantic nature poet and ended as a portrayer of history's darkest event. Increasingly, she dealt with the biggest themes: death, life, resurrection, man's destiny, God's love, and peace, and her poetry became less and less descriptive and more abstract, even hermetic.

No other poet gave herself over so completely to the incredibly difficult task of portraying the Holocaust. Perhaps the only others who could have written about the concentration camps, gas chambers, and ovens were murdered or, if they survived, were too emotionally scarred to express their horror and outrage adequately. Postwar Europe needed a poet of Sachs's intensity to help understand the incomprehensible event that was the Holocaust. With her biblical language, Sachs gave her readers a sense of the mystery at the heart of human experience, the sense of wonder and terror one experiences when one contemplates monstrous crimes and their aftermath.

Sachs is undeservedly little known in North America, but her reputation is assured in Europe. Ironically, Germans remain her most avid readers. Her sustained vision of freedom for all people is that of a remarkable woman who never allowed hatred to dominate her life or her art. Hers is one of the twentieth century's most resonant voices, and she needs to be heard.

### Bibliography

Celan, Paul, and Nelly Sachs. *Paul Celan, Nelly Sachs: Correspondence.* Edited by Barbara Wiedemann; translated by Christopher Clark. Riverdale-on-Hudson, N.Y.: Sheep Meadow Press, 1995. The first complete publication of the correspondence between Paul Celan and Sachs between 1954 and Celan's suicide in 1970. This nicely annotated volume helps the reader to understand these two important poets on a personal level.

Kurz, Paul K. *On Modern German Literature.* Translated by Mary Frances McCarthy. 2 vols. University: University of Alabama Press, 1970-1971. The author emphasizes Sachs's considerable contribution to modern German poetry, citing her as a master of form and technique. Included is a valuable bibliography.

Opfell, Olga S. *Lady Laureates.* 2d ed. Metuchen, N.J.: Scarecrow Press, 1986. Opfell chooses Sachs as one of several seminal women writers who have earned lasting recognition. Her analysis of Sachs's inner qualities is fascinating as is her discussion of Sachs's achievements.

Rosenfeld, Alvin H. "The Poetry of Nelly Sachs." *Judaism* 20 (Summer, 1971): 356-364. Rosenfeld's article discusses Sachs being close to silence, even madness, asking unanswerable questions to an unfathomable God. He emphasizes how fragile are her abstract concepts in the face of the horror of the Holocaust.

Slater, Joseph. "From Death to Rebirth." *Saturday Review* 1 (November 4, 1967): 36. Slater discusses the various elements that make Sachs's poetry so powerful and makes a strong plea for her to be accepted by American readers.

Spender, Stephen. "Catastrophe and Redemption." *The New York Times Book Review*, October 8, 1967: 5, 34. One of Sachs's most ardent admirers, Spender compares Sachs to other notable writers of the twentieth century and finds her contribution unique. He also expounds upon the essential unity of her themes developed over the decades.

*John D. Raymer*

# ANWAR EL-SADAT

*Born:* December 25, 1918; Mit Abul-Kum, Egypt
*Died:* October 6, 1981; Cairo, Egypt
*Areas of Achievement:* Government and politics
*Contribution:* Sadat was awarded the Nobel Peace Prize in 1978 for his role in preparing the first permanent peace between Israel and an Arab country (Egypt). Beyond this recognition for his efforts as a statesman, however, there is no doubt that Sadat was an excellent military strategist, a fact that was clearly illustrated in the first stage of the October, 1973, Arab-Israeli War.

## Early Life

Anwar el-Sadat, who was destined to become President of Egypt in 1970 and to die by an assassin's hand in 1981, was born in the modest Nile delta village of Mit Abul-Kum on December 25, 1918. His father, who was then stationed with the Anglo-Egyptian army in the Sudan, had at least completed basic-level public schooling. This made it possible for him to follow his military service with an appointment as a senior clerk in the Department of Health. These modest accomplishments qualified him and his own children, all of whom also attended school, to effendi status in the eyes of Mit Abul-Kum commoners. Sadat's education began when his family moved, and he was enrolled first in the private Islamic Benevolent Society School in Cairo, then in the Sultan Hussein School. By 1930, despite the heavy weight of tuition charges for his father's modest budget, Sadat entered Fu'ād I Secondary School. It was only after considerable difficulty (and transfer to another school) that he finally earned his general certificate of education.

Sadat's first attempts to gain entry to the Royal Military Academy were unsuccessful, obliging him to fill a short interim by becoming enrolled first at the Faculty of Law and then the Faculty of Commerce. Once admitted to the military academy, and especially after being commissioned as a second lieutenant in 1938, Sadat met and conversed with a number of cadets and young officers who harbored strong nationalist political sentiments. Their aim was to rid Egypt of all remaining indirect controls that the British (foreign occupants of Egypt between 1882 and 1914, and holders of a formal protectorate from 1914 to 1922) had redefined in an Anglo-Egyptian treaty in 1936. As international conditions deteriorated and the outbreak of World War II came closer, politically active officers formed a group called the Free Officers Organization, whose members included Sadat and another officer who would become famous earliest: Gamal Abdel Nasser. This group not only believed that Egypt's vital nationalist interests demanded that it should not tie itself irrevocably to Great Britain but also that it should also deal directly with Germany, then very near to winning the North African War at Egypt's borders. Sadat's association with political nationalism led to his arrest and imprisonment in 1942, until his escape in 1944. Continued radical political activity, this time involving plots against high-level postwar Egyptian political figures, brought another two-year prison term in 1946.

Between 1948 and 1951, when Sadat renewed ties with the underground Free Officers Organization, he was reinstated in the army, rising to the rank of lieutenant colonel. By 1952, he had become one of Nasser's confidants, participating in the coup that overthrew Egypt's corrupt monarch, King Farouk I, in July, 1952. One year later, the Egyptian monarchy was abolished by the Free Officers Organization, now transformed into the Revolutionary Command Council.

## Life's Work

Sadat's political career should be divided into two main periods: from 1952 to 1970, during which time he rose gradually to become one of the most important members of the Egyptian Revolutionary Command Council organized by Nasser, and from 1970 to the end of his presidency in 1981. During the first years of the first period, Sadat held a number of significant but not key policy-making posts, including that of minister of state without portfolio (1954-1955) and secretary general of Egypt's Islamic Congress (an unprecedented and largely ineffective body). By the time of Egypt's attempted "revolutionary" union with Syria (1958-1961), he had gained enough of Nasser's confidence to serve as speaker of the union's joint parliament. From that point on, Sadat's responsibilities tied him ever more closely to Egypt's real power center. His appointment as speaker of the Egyptian National Assembly (1966) was significant but was overshadowed in real political terms by other tasks he carried out personally for Nasser. These included membership in Egypt's special delegations to both the Soviet Union and the United States in 1966.

Although Sadat played no direct role in the disaster of the Arab-Israeli War of 1967, it is clear that his predictable loyalty to Nasser was a vital support for the latter during the difficult three years to 1970. Nasser made him vice president in 1969, a responsibility that became very serious when, during Nasser's "summit" meeting with the Soviets in December, 1969, and again when the president was incapacitated by illness at several points in 1970, Sadat served as acting president.

Thus, when Nasser died (September, 1970), Sadat seemed to have many of the qualifications required to succeed him, but he also had critics and even enemies. Primary among these was another former vice president of Egypt, Ali Sabri, then head of Egypt's single revolutionary party, the Arab Socialist Union. Sabri was the primary spokesman of the pro-Soviet wing of the Egyptian regime. Within less than a year, in May, 1971, Sadat was able to isolate the political and military clique headed by Sabri and remove the members from positions of prominence, even while assuring the Soviets that his actions were not aimed against them.

Part of the reason behind Sadat's success in challenging his critics was his insistence that the "Year of Decision" in Egypt's confrontation with Israel was at hand and that internal unity of purpose had to be maintained. As the new president searched for the means to prepare for a show of force against Israel, however, he discovered that Egypt's Soviet allies, by this date engaged in the spirit of détente with Washington, were unwilling to escalate their military commitment to Cairo. Sadat made history, therefore, in deciding to expel thousands of Soviet technicians and military personnel from Egypt in 1972. During more than a year, plans were laid for a carefully coordinated surprise attack on heavily fortified Israeli positions along the Suez Canal—the opening phase of the Yom Kippur War of October, 1973.

Although the October War was not entirely successful from the Arab point of view, it had enormous consequences, especially because it caused the United States to play a more active role in seeking a negotiated settlement to the Arab-Israeli conflict. From the Egyptian point of view, these consequences would make President Sadat a figure of internationally recognized importance. Within two years of the 1973 conflict, the good offices of, among others, United States Secretary of State Henry Kissinger had led to the Sinai Agreement, providing for Israeli withdrawal to strategically defensible fortifications in the interior of the Sinai Peninsula.

Most spectacular, however, were Sadat's decisions, between 1975 and 1977, first to declare a reversal of Nasserian policies of state socialism in Egypt (which was to be replaced by economic liberalization, or "opening," with foreign assistance), and then personally to open peace negotiations with Israel. His November, 1977, visit to Jerusalem, where he addressed the Israeli Knesset, represented an unprecedented action by an Arab leader to prepare the way for a lasting peace in the Middle East. It was followed in stages by United States sponsorship, through the personal offices of President Jimmy Carter, for direct negotiations between Sadat and Israeli prime minister Menachem Begin, which took place at Carter's Camp David retreat in September, 1978. The dramatic outcome of the Camp David accords was a bilateral Egyptian-Israeli peace treaty, signed at the White House on March 26, 1979. By this treaty, Israel committed itself to withdraw from the Egyptian Sinai. Both parties were to initiate full normal bilateral relations. A separate document, which proved to be quite ineffective, called for progress toward solving the Palestinian political and territorial dilemma.

Although Sadat gained worldwide recognition for his peace initiative and was awarded the Nobel Peace Prize in 1978, Egypt's political and economic situation was not a peaceful one. In his attempt to deal with various forms of unrest at home, including criticism of the Egyptian-Israeli peace and growing religious fanaticism, Sadat assumed extraordinary presidential powers in May of 1980. In a little more than a year, following riots in June, 1981, and mass arrests in September, Sadat was assassinated by splinter elements of the extremist Islamic underground.

### Summary

Anwar el-Sadat's career illustrates several key aspects of nationalism as it has operated in the Middle East since World War II. His early career was obviously marked by extremist positions against perceived enemies of Egypt's national destiny: Great Britain, Israel, and, by 1952, insufferable internal corruption. Although Sadat followed a revolutionary path to make gains against these obstacles, ultimately he proved to be a pragmatist, tying Egypt's destiny to the necessity to compromise. This was visible not only in his dealings with Israel but also in his attempt to bring Egypt's economy, badly displaced by twenty years of revolutionary socialism and the massive costs of war, back into a situation of internal and international equilibrium. This latter decision was not an independent one but was tied to the assumption that foreign participation in Egypt's economic future would be essential.

### Bibliography

Ben Elissar, Eliahu, et al. *Sadat and His Legacy: Egypt and the World, 1977-1997: On the Occasion of the Twentieth Anniversary of President Sadat's Journey to Jerusalem.* Washington, D.C.: Washington Institute for Near East Policy, 1998. A comprehensive study and analysis of Anwar Sadat's legacy and diplomacy by several noted contributors.

Blaisse, Mark. *Anwar Sadat: The Last Hundred Days.* London: Thames and Hudson, and New York: Viking Press, 1981. This mainly pictorial volume contains a textual narrative based on the author's own conversations with Sadat.

Gazit, Mordechai. "Egypt and Israel—Was There a Peace Opportunity Missed in 1971?" *Journal of Contemporary History* 32, no. 1 (January, 1997). Gazit disputes the often-stated opinion that Sadat could have accomplished peace as early as 1971.

Hirst, David, and Irene Beeson. *Sadat.* London: Faber, 1981. Following an abbreviated summary of Sadat's earlier career under Nasser's presidency, the authors of this book offer the most detailed account of the period from the 1973 Yom Kippur War to the Egyptian-Israeli peace treaty.

Israeli, Raphael. *"I, Egypt": Aspects of President Anwar al-Sadat's Political Thought.* Jerusalem: Magnes Press, 1981. This survey of Sadat's views contains numerous citations of his speeches and writings. Commentary is organized under eight topics, including "Concepts of Leadership," "Sadat between Arabism and Africanism," and "Peace Strategy."

———. *Man of Defiance: A Political Biography of Anwar Sadat.* London: Weidenfeld and Nicolson, and Totowa, N.J.: Barnes and Noble, 1985. This not only is the most complete biography of Sadat in English but also is a quite scholarly analysis of both the men and political issues that affected his life, both in its earlier and later stages.

Sadat, Anwar el-. *In Search of Identity: An Autobiography.* London: Collins, and New York: Harper, 1978. Sadat's life based on his personal reflections. The narrative includes valuable descriptions, not only of Sadat's own personal ideas but also of the roles played in his career, up to 1977, by other Egyptian and foreign personalities.

Sadat, Camelia. *My Father and I.* New York: Macmillan, 1985. This is a combined biography/autobiography by Sadat's daughter, who was born in 1949. In addition to recollections concerning her father, it contains valuable views on the status of women in Egypt both before and during his presidency.

*Byron D. Cannon*

# CARL SAGAN

*Born:* November 9, 1934; Brooklyn, New York
*Died:* December 20, 1996; Seattle, Washington
*Areas of Achievement:* Astronomy and education
*Contribution:* One of the most well-known scientists in the twentieth century, Sagan had the unique ability to simultaneously conduct significant astronomical and planetary research and make science interesting and accessible to the general public.

## Early Life

Born in Brooklyn, New York, in 1934, Carl Edward Sagan knew from an early age that he wanted to be an astronomer when he grew up. At that time, however, astronomy was a somewhat obscure field, and when the eight-year-old Sagan asked a librarian for a book on stars, she gave him a book on Hollywood film stars. Sagan persisted and eventually found what he wanted. Fascinated by the fact that the stars are like the Earth's sun but merely farther away, he continued to read about science on his own. He also supplemented his reading with science fiction magazines, which he carefully evaluated for their scientific accuracy.

Even while avidly pursuing these interests, Sagan did not yet know that it was possible to make a living as an astronomer—he thought he would have to get a "regular" job during the day and indulge his astronomy hobby on evenings and weekends. While attending high school in Rahway, New Jersey, where his family had moved at the end of World War II, Sagan learned that it was indeed possible to pursue a career in astronomy. Fortunately, his parents supported his ambitions, and Sagan began studying physics at the University of Chicago in 1951 at the age of sixteen.

The University of Chicago, which had several Nobel Prize-winning scientists on its faculty, was an ideal environment for Sagan. He learned that other scientific fields such as biology and chemistry were also relevant to his interests, which had expanded to include the origin of life. He even organized a series of science lectures on campus, foreshadowing his later success as a popularizer of science.

Sagan continued his studies after graduation by pursuing a doctoral degree in astronomy and astrophysics under Dutch astronomer Gerard Kuiper at the University of Chicago campus in Williams Bay, Wisconsin. Before receiving his doctorate in 1960, Sagan met and married biologist Lynn Alexander, with whom he later had a son, Dorian. Sagan held academic posts at various institutions, including Harvard University, before accepting a permanent professor position at Cornell University in Ithaca, New York, in 1968, where he remained until his death.

From the beginning of his academic career, Sagan proved to be an energetic researcher and writer, publishing numerous papers and articles over the years. In 1966, he wrote a nontechnical, educational book on planets that was published as part of a Time-Life science book series. In the same year, he coauthored *Intelligent Life in the Universe* with Soviet scientist I. S. Shklovskii, an unusual collaboration in light of the Cold War hostilities between the two nations at that time. Sagan also conducted significant research on such topics as the greenhouse effect on Venus and the composition of the atmosphere of Titan, one of Saturn's moons.

## Life's Work

By this time Sagan was fairly well known in the scientific world as an expert on the possibility of extraterrestrial life. In fact, when Arthur C. Clarke and Stanley Kubrick began working on the film *2001: A Space Odyssey* (1968), they consulted with Sagan about what the alien creatures in the film should look like. Ultimately, they followed Sagan's advice and decided not to show the aliens.

Sagan's entry into the public's view, however, did not occur until 1972, when he made a brief appearance on *The Tonight Show*, hosted by comedian Johnny Carson, to promote a book of his essays titled *Cosmic Connection* (1972). Carson liked Sagan enough to invite him back a few weeks later, at which time the scientist spoke about one of his favorite topics, the history of the universe. Viewers were so enthralled with Sagan's knowledge and charisma that he became a regular guest on *The Tonight Show.* Never before had a practicing scientist become so widely known to the American public.

After his success on *The Tonight Show*, Sagan realized that the general public could indeed find science fascinating if presented to them correctly and that he had a talent for doing so without abandoning the actual research itself. The dual nature of Sagan's contributions is illustrated by the fact that he simultaneously served as editor in chief of *Icarus*, a highly technical scientific journal, and wrote several articles for *Parade*, a magazine supplement distributed in newspapers all over the United States every Sunday.

In the meantime, Sagan and his first wife had divorced, and Sagan married Linda Salzman, an artist, with whom he had two sons, Jeremy and Nicholas. In the early 1970's, Sagan and Salzman worked together with the National Aeronautics and Space Administration (NASA) on the Pioneer project. Pioneer 10 was a NASA spacecraft designed to explore the outer solar system in general and the planet Jupiter in particular before becoming the first human-made object to leave the solar system. Inspired by his interest in the possibility of alien life, Sagan came up with the idea of placing a message from humankind on the spacecraft in case it ever encountered an alien race, even though that was unlikely to happen for thousands or millions of years, if ever. NASA agreed, and Sagan began designing the message, which was placed on a gold anodized aluminum plate on the spacecraft. The basic message employed mathematic and scientific concepts, which Sagan felt were a "universal language" that could be understood by any intelligent race. Salzman contributed a drawing of two nude human figures.

Sagan's "interstellar message" received much public attention, and, in spite of some negative reactions to the nudity of the male and female figures, most people supported the idea of sending a message to the stars. In fact, the project received enough support that it was repeated on the Pioneer 11 spacecraft as well as on the two Voyager spacecraft launched in 1977. Ironically, Sagan ultimately collaborated with his third wife, Ann Druyan, on the Voyager message; Druyan's brain waves were recorded on a gold-plated phonograph record, along with greetings in dozens of languages, that was included on the Voyager spacecraft. Sagan and Druyan married in 1981, one month after his divorce from Salzman became final, and they remained married until the scientist's death in 1996. Sagan and Druyan had a daughter, Alexandra (called Sasha), and a son, Sam.

Even during the busiest periods of his life, Sagan did not neglect his writing. In 1977 he published *The Dragons of Eden: Speculation on Human Intelligence*, which spent several months on the *New York Times* best-seller list and won the Pulitzer Prize for general nonfiction. He also turned his efforts to a new medium, television. Dismayed by the relative lack of media attention given to the various NASA projects, Sagan conceived of the idea of a

regular television series about the solar system and the universe. A public television station in Los Angeles, California, agreed to sponsor a thirteen-part series called *Cosmos*, which became Sagan's most famous work. Although the project employed well over one hundred people, including Druyan as cowriter, Sagan himself narrated the series and, rather unusually, appeared on camera most of the time. The series, which was filmed at locations all over the world, took three years to produce and was aired in 1980. *Cosmos* won three Emmy Awards and was eventually seen by over 500 million viewers in sixty different countries. In addition, an accompanying book by the same title, also published in 1980, became the best-selling nonfiction science book in U.S. history up until that time.

Sagan also took on another role: public policy activist and advisor. After studying the effect of massive dust storms on Mars, Sagan began to calculate how vast amounts of dust could affect the Earth's climate. In 1983, a controversial television film, *The Day After*, gave a fictional account of the effects of nuclear war. Immediately after the show, a panel of scientists that included Sagan discussed these effects, and Sagan voiced his opinion that a "nuclear winter," brought about by debris from nuclear bombs blocking the sunlight, could completely devastate the Earth's climate and possibly cause mankind's extinction. While many scientists disagreed with Sagan's belief that the effects would be so devastating, enough people paid attention to the theory that it prompted some historians to claim that Sagan played a significant role in nuclear disarmament and the end of the Cold War.

Finally, in order to reach yet another segment of the public, Sagan published *Contact*, his first and only science fiction novel, in 1985. Because of his enormous popularity, Sagan was paid a $2 million advance for the book, an unprecedented amount for a first novel. *Contact*, a story about the first message from an extraterrestrial race, received mixed but generally positive reviews. Sagan had originally intended *Contact* to be produced as a motion picture, but after many delays he decided to turn it into a novel first. A film version starring Academy Award-winning actor Jodie Foster was finally released in 1997. Unfortunately, although Sagan worked on the film production up until the time of his death, he did not live to see its actual release. In 1995 Sagan had been diagnosed with myelodysplasia, a rare bone-marrow disorder that can lead to leukemia. Several bone-marrow transplants extended his life, but on December 20, 1996, Sagan died of pneumonia, a complication caused by the disease.

### Summary

Carl Sagan was simultaneously a scientist and a celebrity whose enormous popularity both helped and hurt his career. Although almost all scientists recognize that public awareness and support are essential to scientific research, scientists have historically shunned any colleague who receives media attention. From his early college days when he organized public science lectures at the University of Chicago, Sagan was criticized for "calling too much attention to himself" and for being too undignified for a scientist. In a commentary titled "Kinship With the Stars" in *Discover* in 1997, Jared Diamond asserted that Sagan was rejected for membership in the National Academy of Sciences—even though he had already been provisionally approved—because of his fame. The same scientists who continually bemoaned the public's lack of interest in science felt that Sagan could not possibly be a serious scientist because he spent too much time in the public eye. Eventually the academy recognized its mistake and awarded Sagan its highest honor in 1994, the Public Welfare Medal. However, their earlier rejection of Sagan may have made young scientists wary of jeopardizing their scientific careers by becoming involved in public education.

In spite of the negative attitudes directed toward him by other scientists, Sagan was very successful in the wide variety of activities he pursued and has been credited with inspiring many young people to choose science as a career path.

### Bibliography

Cohen, Daniel. *Carl Sagan: Superstar Scientist.* New York: Dodd Mead, 1987. Cohen's biography of Sagan was written for young adult readers. The book's main focus is on Sagan's unique position as a popularizer of science. Includes a bibliography and index.

Ginenthal, Charles. *Carl Sagan and Immanuel Velikovsky.* New York: Ivy Press, 1990. Ginenthal presents an overview of a highly publicized debate between Sagan and Russian-born scholar Immanuel Velikovsky, who attempted to prove that biblical events could be explained scientifically. This book is heavily biased in favor of Velikovsky but may be of interest regarding Sagan's views on psuedoscience.

Riggs, Eric M. "Toward an Understanding of the Roles of Scientific, Traditional, and Spiritual Knowledge in Our 'Demon-Haunted World.'" *American Indian Culture and Research Journal* 21, no. 1 (Winter 1998). The author examines Sagan's views on the role of science in society as discussed in his book *The Demon-Haunted World.*

Sagan, Carl. *Cosmos.* New York: Random House, 1980; London: Macdonald, 1981. The companion to Sagan's world-renowned television series, this 365-page book contains numerous color photographs and illustrations, an introduction that discusses the origin and development of the television series, and an extensive list for further reading organized in the same topic order as the book's chapters.

Sagan, Carl. Interview. *Psychology Today* 29 (January/February, 1996): 30. This informative and readable interview with Sagan touches upon many of the topics he was most passionate about: science, technology, intelligence, religion, overpopulation, and nuclear winter.

Sagan, Carl. *Billions and Billions: Thoughts on Life and Death at the Brink of the Millennium.*

New York: Random House, and London: Headline, 1997. A collection of essays by Sagan on a wide range of subjects including life on other planets, morality, various inventions, and the government.

Terzian, Yervant, ed. *Carl Sagan's Universe*. Cambridge and New York: Cambridge University Press, 1997. This book contains a collection of essays by various scientists and writers on the many areas of scientific inquiry influence by Sagan. Published shortly after Sagan's death, the book serves as a tribute to Sagan by his peers.

*Amy Sisson*

# ANDREI SAKHAROV

*Born:* May 21, 1921; Moscow, U.S.S.R.
*Died:* December 14, 1989; Moscow, U.S.S.R.
*Areas of Achievement:* Physics, civil rights, social reform, and politics
*Contribution:* Sakharov's work as a scientist and human rights activist made him an important international figure. His scientific work played a key role in the production of the first hydrogen bomb and later in the study of the structure of the universe. His calls for civil rights in the Soviet Union commanded attention and respect throughout the world and earned for him the Nobel Peace Prize in 1975.

## Early Life

Andrei Dmitrievich Sakharov was born in Moscow on May 21, 1921, son of Dmitri Sakharov, a professor of physics at the Lenin Pedagogical Institute and author of several classroom texts and popular science books. Beyond the fact that the family led a comfortable life in a large communal apartment, little is known about Sakharov's childhood. By his own account, the major influence on him, apart from his parents, was his grandmother, who read to him every evening from the Gospel and such English authors as Charles Dickens and Christopher Marlowe. The atmosphere at home, he was later to write, was pervaded by a strong, traditional family spirit, "a liking for work, and dedication to mastery of one's chosen profession."

In 1938, Sakharov completed high school and entered Moscow State University as a student of physics and mathematics. He was graduated in 1942 as one of the most brilliant students in the annals of the university and was exempted from military service. Instead, he was assigned to work as an engineer in a war plant, where he developed several inventions relating to ammunition quality control. With the end of World War II, Sakharov resumed his studies, entering the P. N. Lebedev Physics Institute of the Soviet Academy of Sciences to work under Igor Tamm, the leading Soviet scientist in the field of quantum mechanics and the head of the institute's theoretical division. In 1947, Sakharov was awarded the degree of candidate for doctor in science (roughly equivalent to the American Ph.D.) for his work on cosmic ray theory.

## Life's Work

Up to the mid-1960's, Sakharov's research focused on weapons development. In the spring of 1948, he became a member of a research team headed by Tamm, which worked under strict security on the development of a new generation of nuclear weapons. In 1950, Sakharov and Tamm achieved a breakthrough when they formulated the theoretical foundations of the hydrogen bomb. In recognition of this and other achievements in hydrogen weapons research, Sakharov was awarded the Stalin and Lenin prizes, and on three occasions he received the Order of Socialist Labor, the Soviet Union's highest civilian honor. Shortly after the first testing of the hydrogen bomb in 1953, he received the title of doctor of science and was elected to full membership in the Soviet Academy of Sciences. At the age of thirty-two, he thereby became the youngest scientist ever to have reached this prestigious position. From then to 1968, he continued his work in the secret Soviet nuclear weapons research center.

Between January and March, 1958, the Soviet Union conducted a series of atmospheric nuclear tests. When it became known that an additional series was being planned for the autumn of the same year, Sakharov wrote an article in which he warned against severe genetic damage caused by atmospheric tests; to reduce international tension and decrease the threat of nuclear war, he demanded their total cessation. The same arguments were repeated in a memorandum that Sakharov sent to the chief scientific administrator of the Soviet nuclear weapons program, and this came to the attention of the Communist Party leader Nikita S. Khrushchev. What impact if any this had on Soviet policy is unclear, but, after concluding the 1958 tests, the Soviet Union joined the United States in an informal moratorium on nuclear atmospheric tests, which lasted until the summer of 1961.

Sakharov's protest activities were soon extended beyond the issues relating to his research interests. Already in 1958 he had taken a stand against Khrushchev's proposed reforms in secondary education, which would have required all students to devote two or three years to farm or factory work before graduation. In June, 1964, he took part in a successful effort to end the politically motivated scientific research associated with Trofim Lysenko and to resist Khrushchev's demand to admit his followers to the Academy of Sciences. In so doing, he put himself squarely on the liberal side of an ideological conflict that had stunted the develop-

ment of the biological and agricultural sciences in the Soviet Union since the mid-1930's.

The year 1966 constituted a watershed in the direction of Sakharov's political activity. With the fall of Khrushchev, conservative elements in the Communist Party sought to rehabilitate Joseph Stalin. On the eve of the Party's Twenty-third Congress, Sakharov, Tamm, and twenty-three other intellectuals signed an open letter opposing the move. Later in the same year, Sakharov again joined Tamm and others in signing a collective appeal to the Supreme Soviet to prevent the approval of decrees curtailing dissent that were being added to the criminal code. In February, 1967, he sent yet another appeal to Soviet president Leonid Ilich Brezhnev, protesting the arrest of four members of the group and demanding their release. This was his first attempt to intercede on behalf of individual citizens.

Sakharov's conversion to dissidence was followed by his formulation of a theory linking his hitherto divergent social and political activities. Previously he had addressed his protests to the political and scientific elites. In 1968, however, he wrote an article that he published himself and that was smuggled to the West. The article constituted the first effort to relate the issues of civil rights in the Soviet Union to global peace and human progress. Its main thesis was that a rapprochement between the Soviet Union and the West is the only alternative to thermonuclear holocaust. Moreover, only by pooling American and Soviet resources can humankind overcome the dangers of poverty, environmental pollution, and overpopulation. Without freedom of thought, Sakharov maintained, Soviet society will never attain the stage of peaceful convergence with the democratic world. Sakharov therefore advocated ending censorship and the suppression of dissidents as a first step in an ideal process that would culminate in the formation of a world government dedicated to the advancement of humankind.

Shortly after the article was published, Sakharov's security clearance was withdrawn, and he was barred from all secret work. Earlier in the decade, he had begun research in macrophysics, resulting in several papers on the expansion of the universe and on the structure of quarks. In 1969, he continued his work on gravitation and the structure of the universe as a senior researcher in the P. N. Lebedev Physics Institute. At about the same time, he suffered a personal loss with the death of his wife, Klavidia. It was in this period too that his political perspective underwent its final evolution. Up to his dismissal from the Soviet atomic weapons program, he was "isolated from the people" by his "extraordinary position of material privileges" and tended to treat world peace and human rights as theoretical problems. With the loss of these privileges, he became more acutely aware of concrete wrongs suffered by specific individuals and groups in society. This sensitivity was heightened through the work of the Moscow Human Rights Committee, which he founded with two younger physicists in the fall of 1970 to monitor and publicize human rights violations in the Soviet Union. This sense of moral obligation and urgency led Sakharov to embark on an accelerated campaign of letters, appeals, press interviews, and protestations on behalf of Jews seeking emigration, Crimean Tatars demanding repatriation, Ukrainian and Volga German nationalists, fellow dissidents, and political prisoners. During a protest vigil outside a courthouse where dissidents were standing trial, he met Elena Bonner-Alikhanova, and the two were married in 1972.

In September, 1972, Sakharov was detained by the police after participating in a demonstration protesting the murder of Israeli athletes at the Munich Olympics. This was the first episode in a campaign of harassment and intimidation that included the expulsion of his two stepchildren from the University of Moscow, press attacks on his views and activities, and summonses to appear before the Komitet Gosudarstvennoi Bezopasnosti (KGB). In August, 1973, after he had appealed to United Nations Secretary-General Kurt Waldheim to intercede on behalf of dissidents confined to mental hospitals, Sakharov was called to a meeting with the deputy procurator-general, who threatened him with prosecution on the charges of defaming the state. A week later, in defiance of such pressures, Sakharov convened a press conference in his apartment to warn against "détente without democratization." A month later, Sakharov appealed to the U.S. Congress, calling on it to support the Jackson-Vanik Amendment linking the Soviet Union's preferred trade status to the level of Soviet emigration. In December, 1973, Sakharov was awarded the Human Rights Prize by the International League for the Rights of Man. Two years later, he became the first Soviet to win the Nobel Peace Prize. On both occasions, Sakharov was denied an exit visa to attend the ceremonies. His Nobel Prize acceptance speech was read by his wife, Bonner.

Despite Sakharov's continuous defiance, he was not arrested until 1980. In January of that year, after denouncing the Soviet invasion of Afghanistan and calling on the United Nations to persuade it to withdraw, he was stripped of his honors and banished without trial to Gorki, a military-industrial city officially closed to foreigners. Confined to the city limits, he was placed under KGB supervision, his mail was scrutinized, and he was forbidden any contact with other dissidents. Nevertheless, he continued his study of cosmology and the physics of elementary particles and was elected in 1980 and 1981 as a member of the Italian and French Academies of Sciences. At first, even his political work was not totally disrupted, for his statements and appeals were communicated to the outside world by his wife, who traveled back and forth between Moscow and Gorki. In 1984, however, Bonner too was restricted to Gorki after being accused of slandering the state.

Several days before Christmas, 1986, Soviet leader Mikhail Gorbachev in person telephoned Sakharov to announce his release from exile. Back in Moscow, Sakharov resumed his scientific and political activities. A week after his return, he appeared on American television and vowed to continue the struggle for the liberation of all "prisoners of conscience." A symbol of his changed status was the transmission of his interview through the satellite facilities of the Soviet government. Toward the end of 1988, Sakharov left the Soviet Union for the first time in his life for a tour of meetings with major European and American politicians, including United States President Ronald Reagan. While continuing his advocacy of civil rights in the Soviet Union and calling for Soviet troop cutbacks and reduction of military spending, he now called on the West to support Gorbachev's reforms. In April, 1989, he was nominated by the Soviet Academy of Sciences for a seat in the new Soviet National Congress of Deputies. There he became a leader of the Interregional Deputies Group, a faction dedicated to the acceleration of reform in the Soviet Union. Sakharov continued his political dissent to the end of his life, which occurred on December 14, 1989. Only two days before his death, he engaged Gorbachev in an angry debate, demanding the abolition of the Communist Party's monopoly of political power in the Soviet Union.

### Summary

The final assessment of Andrei Sakharov's scientific contribution must await the lifting of the veil of secrecy that still shrouds his military-related work. Nevertheless, it is clear that he played a key role in the production of the first hydrogen bomb and the industrial utilization of nuclear energy. He is also accepted as a pioneer in research into the structure of the universe and the quark phenomenon. These accomplishments were intimately related to his activities in the cause of human rights and global peace. His position at the pinnacle of Soviet society and fame as the developer of the thermonuclear bomb added weight to his arguments and enabled him, almost single-handedly, to change the dissident movement into a force that could not be ignored. He himself regarded his scientific and political endeavors as complementary aspects of a single quest for human dignity and a world in which science and technology can be harnessed for the advancement of humankind.

There is no available method by which to gauge Sakharov's impact on the policies of his government. He admitted that his struggles to remedy specific wrongs "almost always met [with a] tragic absence of positive results." Yet, perhaps his greatest achievement lies in the mere fact of his activity. He himself explained this clearly when he argued that, in a repressive society, "there is a need to create ideals even when you can't see any route by which to achieve them, because if there are no ideals then there can be no hope and then one [is left] completely in the dark. . . ." His courage, personal example, and relentless advocacy of human rights helped keep alive ideas and aspirations without which no reforms are possible. The era of *perestroika* and *glasnost*, and his election to the National Congress of Deputies, may serve as proof that his efforts were not in vain.

### Bibliography

Babenyshev, Alexander, ed. *On Sakharov.* New York: Knopf, 1982. A collection of essays, stories, and poems written by prominent Soviet dissenters and dedicated to Sakharov, offering an insider's view of the problems of the dissent movement and of Sakharov's place within it.

Bonner, Elena. *Alone Together.* Translated by Alexander Cook. London: Collins, and New York: Knopf, 1986. Written during Bonner's six-month leave of absence from Gorki, this book contains important information about the activities of the Sakharovs in the 1980's as well as interesting anecdotes about and insights into their personalities and private life.

Dorman, Peter. "Andrei Sakharov: The Conscience of a Liberal Scientist." In *Dissent in the USSR*, edited by Rudolf Tökés. Baltimore: Johns Hopkins University Press, 1975. An excellent exposition of Sakharov's social and political ideas based on his writings, statements, and activities up to 1974.

Gorelik, Gennady. "The Metamorphosis of Andrei Sakharov." *Scientific American* 280, no. 3 (March, 1999). Profile of the inventor of Russia's hydrogen bomb including his eventual remorse over its development.

LeVert, Suzanne. *The Sakharov File: A Study in Courage.* New York: Messner, 1986. Intended for young people but offers a good historical background and a clear account of Sakharov's human rights activities.

Rubenstein, Joshua. *Soviet Dissidents: Their Struggle for Human Rights.* 2d ed. Boston: Beacon Press, 1985. Explores the origins and development of the dissident movement in Moscow through the lives and activities of Sakharov and other prominent human rights activists.

Sakharov, Andrei. *Alarm and Hope.* Edited by Efrem Yankelevich and Alfred Friendly, Jr. London: Collins, and New York: Knopf, 1978. A collection of Sakharov's short writings, correspondence, and press interviews. Includes the text of his 1975 Nobel Peace Prize lecture and an appendix offering brief sketches of some of the individuals he sought to publicize and defend.

———. *Sakharov Speaks.* Edited by Harrison E. Salisbury. London: Collins, and New York: Knopf, 1974. Contains a valuable foreword by Salisbury and some of the most important early writings of Sakharov himself, notably *Progress, Coexistence, and Intellectual Freedom* and a 1973 interview with Olle Stenholm on his view of life and the goals of his human rights activities.

*Jonathan Mendilow*

# J.D. SALINGER

*Born:* January 1, 1919; New York, New York
*Area of Achievement:* Literature
*Contribution:* Although Salinger wrote only one novel and thirty-five stories, he attained a degree of international recognition and popularity that is unequaled by most twentieth century American authors.

## Early Life

Born in Manhattan, the setting (or focal point) for most of his best fiction, Jerome David Salinger was the second child and only son of Sol and Marie Jillich Salinger. His paternal grandfather, Simon, born in Lithuania, was at one time the rabbi for the Adath Jeshurun congregation in Louisville, Kentucky. His mother, reared a Christian, converted to Judaism upon marrying Sol and changed her name to Miriam. Salinger's father, an importer of meat (hams from Poland in particular), was a highly successful businessman. The family lived on Riverside Drive during Salinger's early years. The Salingers were not conventionally religious; the children were exposed primarily to the ideas of Ethical Culture. In 1930, young Salinger, or "Sonny" as he was called by his family, spent the summer at Camp Wigwam in Harrison, Maine (the probable source for the setting of his last published story).

Salinger attended Manhattan public schools until, at age thirteen, he was enrolled in the McBurney School, also in Manhattan, where he earned below-average grades but became manager of the fencing team and was elected sophomore class president in his second year there. In the fall of 1934, hoping for better academic performance from his son, Salinger's father sent him to Valley Forge Military Academy in Wayne, Pennsylvania, where he participated in all the usual activities, was literary editor of the yearbook, and maintained about a B average.

After Salinger was graduated from Valley Forge in 1936, he attended the Washington Square campus of New York University. He took the following year off to travel with his father in Austria and Poland; while in Europe, Salinger learned German and familiarized himself with the family business. This experience led him back to academe, to Ursinus College in Collegeville, Pennsylvania, in the fall of 1938. The columns that Salinger wrote for the Ursinus College newspaper reveal a very literary man most unhappy with college life. Salinger abruptly left Ursinus in December; his train voyage home to New York was perhaps the inspiration for a similar scene in *The Catcher in the Rye* (1951).

In the spring of 1938, Salinger enrolled in the Extension Division of Columbia University and attended Whit Burnett's writing class. Within a year, his first story, "The Young Folks," was published in Burnett's *Story* magazine; another appeared in the *University of Kansas City Review.* In 1941, he cracked the slick magazines, with one story each in *Collier's* and *Esquire*. Thereafter, for ten years or more, regardless of his life circumstances, Salinger regularly published stories in these and such other magazines as *The Saturday Evening Post, Good Housekeeping, Cosmopolitan, Harper's*, and *The New Yorker.* Several of Salinger's stories, even some of those written as early as 1941, concern a young man named Holden Caulfield, who would become the hero of Salinger's first and only novel, *The Catcher in the Rye*.

Meanwhile, in the spring of 1942, Salinger was drafted into the United States Army, serving first in the Signal Corps and then later in the Counter-Intelligence Corps, where he was assigned to the Twelfth Infantry Regiment of the Fourth Division. He sailed with the latter for England in January of 1944. On D-Day, Salinger, by then a staff sergeant, landed on Utah Beach with his regiment, five hours after the first assault. The fighting that Salinger witnessed provided the background for the story "For Esmé—with Love and Squalor" (1950). In August of 1944, Salinger had a friendly meeting with Ernest Hemingway, in France. Until his discharge in the spring of 1946, Salinger's duty was to interrogate captured German soldiers and French civilians. In 1945, he married a French psychiatrist, from whom he was divorced soon after.

For the next several years Salinger moved quite often; he lived first with his parents on Park Avenue, then in Westport, Connecticut, and finally in an apartment on East Fifty-seventh Street in Manhattan—all the while writing stories, cruising around Greenwich Village in his sports car, and working on the final drafts of *The Catcher in the Rye*. This remarkable novel about the odyssey of a teenage boy spiritually lost in nighttime Manhattan was an immediate popular success. Salinger obligingly sat for interviewers and photographers. One particular picture of him—the one that appeared on the dust jacket of the first printing of *The Catcher*

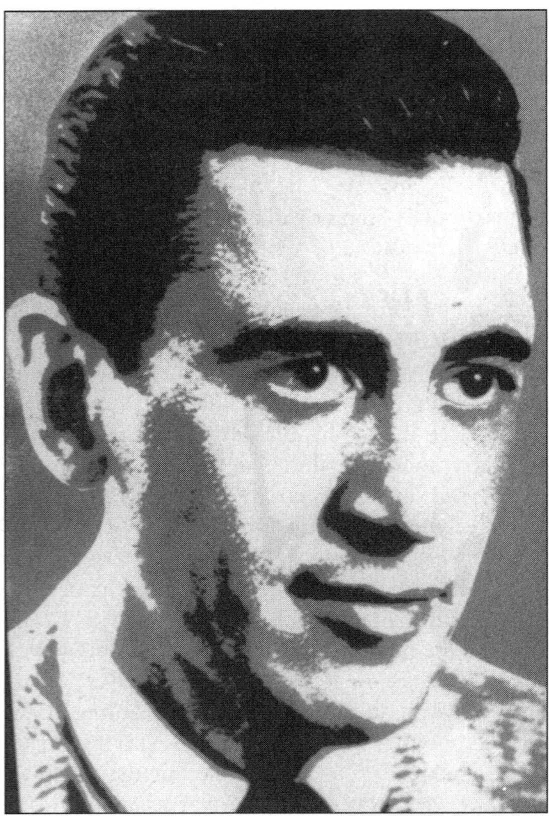

*in the Rye* (and frequently elsewhere)—became so well-known to the public that it became a kind of icon. It shows a handsome young man in three-quarters profile, with dark eyes in a slender and sensitive face and a mouth anticipating a possibly sad smile. The owner of this iconic face was six feet, two inches tall—and soon to be disillusioned about the rewards of popularity.

### Life's Work

The novel *The Catcher in the Rye* illustrates well the basic features of Salinger's art. In his novel, as in most of his short stories, Salinger identifies with the concerns of young people who suffer from the hypocrisy of the adult world, and he effectively re-creates their speech. The book also contains numerous examples of Salinger's distinctive humor—often considered vulgar—for which the book was banned from many libraries and school reading lists. Finally, in a plot development typical of Salinger's fiction, the protagonist is transformed through spiritual insight, allowing him to accept, at least temporarily, the world as it is. The quest of many of Salinger's protagonists is religious in character, usually containing elements of both Buddhism (recognition of the pain of life) and of Christianity (Holden, in his desire to protect the children in the field of rye, acting as a savior or Christ figure). Some critics found Salinger mannered, sentimental, and insufficiently interested in social questions, but readers around the world—not merely in the United States—identified strongly with Salinger's adolescent protagonist. Many readers, together with numerous magazine reporters, sought out the young writer.

To escape from his fans, Salinger ordered his portrait removed from all later printings of *The Catcher in the Rye*, refused all requests for interviews, and finally, in January of 1953, retired from the world altogether by moving to a rustic cottage near Cornish Flat, New Hampshire—located on a dirt road in the woods, about a mile from St. Gaudens Memorial Park. In the same year Salinger's collection *Nine Stories* was published, notable for its chronicles of the Glass family, its use of Zen Buddhist motifs, and for its remarkable "For Esmé—with Love and Squalor," a story which presents the agony of war, the Dostoevskian premise that hell is the suffering of being unable to love, and an offer of hope through love from a young girl in England to a battle-weary American sergeant.

Also in 1953, Salinger met nineteen-year-old Claire Alison Douglas at a party in Manchester, Vermont. An English debutante, she had studied at the best private schools and was then a top student at Radcliffe College. She was much influenced by Salinger's religious preoccupations and became in part the model for Franny Glass, the protagonist of "Franny" (1955). Franny is memorable for her antipathy toward ambitious, egotistical English instructors and for her desperate effort to escape the pain of the world by endlessly repeating the Jesus Prayer of Russian Orthodoxy. Despite her attraction to Salinger, Claire Douglas married (in August of 1953) her fiancé, Colman Mockler, a student at the Harvard Business School. Within a short time, however, this marriage was annulled. On February 17, 1955, Salinger and Claire Douglas were married. On December 10 of that year their first child, Margaret Ann, was born, and on February 13, 1960, their second and last child, Matthew Robert, was born.

During the late 1950's and early 1960's, Salinger completed his cycle of Glass family stories, publishing two stories each in the books *Franny and Zooey* (1961) and *Raise High the Roofbeam, Carpenters and Seymour: An Introduction* (1963). In 1965, he published "Hapworth 16, 1924" in *The New Yorker*, consisting chiefly of a long letter home written from camp by Seymour Glass at the age of seven. This strange and precocious document would be the last work of fiction published by Salinger, at least through the late 1980's.

In 1967, Salinger and Claire Douglas divorced. The cottage was sold. When the children were grown, Claire moved to San Francisco and established herself as a Jungian psychologist. Salinger continued to live in his hilltop chalet, writing daily and trying to avoid intrusive fans and reporters, who, once a year or so, invaded his retreat, hoping to engage him in conversation for a few minutes or at least catch a glimpse of him. To some, Salinger's withdrawal into almost total privacy seemed psychotic; he has not, however, completely isolated himself from society. For example, romantic interests have been reported in the press—with the nineteen-year-old novelist Joyce Maynard in 1973 and with actress Elaine Joyce in 1982. In 1978, he attended a testimonial dinner in Queens, New York, for an old army buddy. As to what Salinger has written since 1965, Truman Capote reported shortly before he died: "I'm told, on very good authority, that . . . he's written at least five or six short novels and that all of them have been turned down by *The New Yorker*. And that all of them are very strange and about Zen Buddhism." In 1997 Salinger surprised many by allowing a small publishing house to reprint his 1965 short story "Hapworth 16, 1924."

## Summary

Salinger's major work, *The Catcher in the Rye*, had, by the late 1980's, been translated into thirty-five languages and sold more than twelve million copies in English-language editions alone. Indeed, it is the income from such unprecedented sales that has allowed Salinger to live his monkish life and to write for himself alone, refusing to conform to the expectations of publishers. Foreign readers have found it easy to identify or sympathize with the sensitive Holden Caulfield. Russians in particular have fallen in love with the young protagonist. Many editions of *The Catcher in the Rye* (to say nothing of the stories) have been published in the Soviet Union not only in Russian but also in other Soviet languages. (A Russian edition of Salinger's collected works in one volume was published in fifty thousand copies as late as 1983.) In this way, Salinger has made an important contribution to international understanding and therefore to world peace. Indeed, *The Catcher in the Rye* has probably done more than any other American novel—in part precisely because of the attacks on it by book censors—to introduce young people to great literature.

## Bibliography

Alsen, Eberhard. *Salinger's Glass Stories as a Composite Novel*. Troy, N.Y.: Whitston, 1983. A fascinating summary and analysis of the Glass family stories. Includes a helpful chronology of events in the lives of both Buddy and Seymour, as well as of the other siblings. Although little is said about Salinger's own life, autobiographical elements in the Glass stories become apparent under Alsen's treatment. Especially useful is a list of all the books that form the basis of Seymour's (that is Salinger's) eclectic religious philosophy. All are mentioned in the Glass stories, and they are essential to Alsen's analysis of Salinger's religious views.

French, Warren. *J. D. Salinger*. Rev. ed. Boston: Twayne, 1976. Both critical and biographical. Has a useful chronology of life and work, updated from the 1963 edition, and a selected bibliography, also updated.

Grunwald, Henry Anatole, ed. *Salinger: A Critical and Personal Portrait*. New York: Harper, 1962; London: Owen, 1964. A good early collection of critical articles, most of them favorable to Salinger. A detailed "biographical collage" forms the first chapter.

Laser, Marvin, and Norman Fruman, eds. *Studies in J. D. Salinger: Reviews, Essays and Critiques of "The Catcher in the Rye" and Other Fiction*. New York: Odyssey Press, 1963. Balanced collection of critical articles which include incidental biographical information. A checklist of Salinger's work is appended.

Lundquist, James. *J. D. Salinger*. New York: Ungar, 1979. Excellent critical analysis of the fiction, with a chronology of life and work and an extensive bibliography.

Pinsker, Sanford, and Ann Pinsker. *Understanding the Catcher in the Rye: A Student Casebook to Issues, Sources and Historical Documents*. Westport, Conn.: Greenwood Press, 1999. This volume includes cultural, social, and historical information that places Salinger's classic in proper perspective, clarifying reader understanding.

Salzman, Jack. *New Essays on "Catcher in the Rye."* Cambridge and New York: Cambridge University Press, 1992. Five essays covering aspects of Salinger's *Catcher in the Rye.*

Sublette, Jack R. *J. D. Salinger: An Annotated Bibliography, 1938-1981*. New York: Garland, 1984. Well-organized bibliography of 1,462 items, with author and title indexes and a detailed chronology of life and work. Annotations are extensive, especially in the section on biography, which contains 175 entries. Sublette's bibliography essentially incorporates all previous bibliographies and is indispensable to any serious study of Salinger.

*Donald M. Fiene*

# JONAS EDWARD SALK

*Born:* October 28, 1914; New York, New York
*Died:* June 23, 1995; La Jolla, California
*Areas of Achievement:* Medicine and immunology
*Contribution:* Salk developed the first effective vaccine for polio, and he marshaled the nation's resources to help eradicate the disease.

## Early Life

Jonas Salk was the firstborn child of Daniel B. Salk and Dora Press. His father was a garment maker, and both of his parents encouraged their children to do well in school. Salk attended Townsend Harris High School for the gifted and received his B.A. from College of the City of New York in 1934. He received his M.D. from New York University in 1939 and interned at Mount Sinai Hospital, where he studied immunology. Salk was recognized as an able scientist by his teachers, and during World War II he was a participant in the army's effort to develop an effective vaccine for influenza. He continued this interest in his first academic appointment at the University of Michigan, developing such a vaccine with his more senior colleague and former mentor, Thomas Francis, Jr. This established Salk's reputation professionally as an ambitious, bright, and innovative scholar who could organize a laboratory and work well under pressure.

Salk was restless and wanted independence from the projects of his senior colleagues so that he could try out some of his own unconventional ideas. He astounded his peers by accepting a position at the University of Pittsburgh Medical School, which, at that time, had no record of basic research in medicine. Salk got the space he needed and rapidly put together a team of laboratory workers to help him study infectious diseases. Not intimidated by authority, Salk used his managerial skills and cultural breadth to convince philanthropists and university administrators to equip his laboratory. His driving energy resulted in the publication of many important papers that caught the attention of the National Foundation (March of Dimes) and its director, Daniel Basil O'Connor. The National Foundation had for many years supported treatment and rehabilitative programs for paralytic polio victims. Salk was one of many younger investigators whom O'Connor hoped to recruit for the research that would lead to a vaccine for that dreaded disease.

## Life's Work

Salk's greatest contribution to immunology was his insight that the killing of a virus by chemical treatment need not profoundly alter the antigenic properties of the virus. Any foreign material in a body can serve as an antigen and provoke the body's immune system to form antibodies to attack it. This is one of the body's major defenses against the invasion of bacteria and viruses. A virus may have complex proteins that coat its deadly infectious nucleic acid. Chemical treatment by formaldehyde may damage some of the genes of the virus so that they cannot multiply in the body, but they may not appreciably change the shape of the surface proteins of the virus. It is the surface proteins, and not the inner core of genes contained in the viral nucleic acid, that provoke antibody formation.

Salk's success in developing a vaccine for polio depended on the discoveries of many other researchers in immunology and virology. Originally polio could only be grown in live monkeys. Attempts in the 1930's to use a vaccine prepared from the killed extracts of infected monkey brains resulted in deaths of several children from meningitis and other reactions. It was also erroneously thought that polio grew only in nerve tissues, but infected humans produced large amounts of viruses in their feces, suggesting that it also grew in the intestines. John F. Enders and his colleagues succeeded in growing polio virus in tissue culture using embryonic cells, a major breakthrough that led to their being awarded a Nobel Prize in 1954. Polio also turned out not to be one virus but at least three different types of viruses, each type having many different strains, some highly infectious and others only weakly so. It was this need to type the polio viruses that brought O'Connor to Pittsburgh. Salk developed new methods to type the viruses rapidly and new methods to grow the viruses in large quantities. He realized that this work could not be done with a few animals and he organized a large laboratory, heavily funded, to maintain and use thousands of monkeys for his experiments. Salk made good use of the facilities and support; he soon proved his hunch that the antigenic properties of killed polio virus were not impaired by the formaldehyde treatment of the viruses.

Two additional findings were important for Salk's future work in developing a polio vaccine. Isabel Morgan Mountain succeeded in immunizing

monkeys against polio by using formaldehyde-killed virus. Hilary Koprowski used live viruses whose properties had been attenuated or weakened by passage through rats; he fed twenty-two human subjects with the altered virus, and none showed symptoms, although all had developed antibodies against the fully infectious strain of polio virus.

Salk rejected two prevailing views at the time. Many immunologists believed that purified antibody, gamma globulin, would be effective in preventing polio. Gamma globulin, however, was expensive, and it afforded protection for only a short time. Many other immunologists were convinced that a killed virus would not work or that it could not be purified without contamination of the proteins from the cells on which it grew. Salk proved that these two views were mistaken; with the backing of the National Foundation, he prepared the purified killed polio virus vaccines against all three types of polio. Although the virus was rendered inactive after three days, Salk kept the virus in formaldehyde for thirteen days to guarantee that no live virus was present. By 1954, all the difficulties were resolved, and Salk began the crucial human experimentation to confirm the results obtained on monkeys. He and his laboratory workers immunized themselves and their families and then began field-testing the vaccine. The virus proved better than ninety percent effective. The first seven million doses of the vaccine were administered in 1955. A contaminated source from a California pharmaceutical firm was noticed, and the trials were held up until the purification procedures were standardized. Salk then initiated a nationwide program from 1956 through 1958. Almost immediately after this massive program of immunization, the United States was polio-free.

Salk's killed virus vaccine required four injections, one for each type plus a booster. Additional boosters were necessary as the antibody levels gradually fell. The National Foundation, aware of this possibility, had also backed Albert Sabin to develop a live polio vaccine. The live vaccine, which then required fewer visits to a physician for booster doses, replaced the Salk vaccine. The killed virus vaccine does not cause polio in its recipients or in individuals who have never been vaccinated; the live vaccine, however, occasionally does cause polio in family members or neighbors who have never been vaccinated. For this reason, Salk urged the use of killed vaccine in areas where compliance with vaccination requirements was inadequate. Although live vaccine was more frequently used in the years following Salk's campaign, polio had already been defeated and in the public's mind Salk had become a national hero. Among the many honors showered on him was the Lasker Award in 1956 and the Presidential Medal of Freedom in 1977.

Salk's popularity with the National Foundation and with philanthropists led him to a second major venture. He proposed an institute for biological research which would permit the most talented scientists in the world to carry out research that would lead to new advances in knowledge beneficial to health and human happiness. The Salk Institute for Biological Studies was founded in 1960, and a building for it opened in 1963. The building, chiefly funded by the National Foundation, was constructed at La Jolla, a suburb of San Diego noted for its beautiful scenery and beachfront. The Salk Institute attracted many Nobel laureates; the freedom to do full-time research and thinking was a major feature of its design. Salk thought of the institute as an experiment in the sociology of science, with a primary mission to study and initiate modern trends in biology tempered with a conscience for humanity. Among the seven original resident fellows of the Institute was Jacob Bronowski, a mathematician turned philosopher, whose television series *Ascent of Man* reflected the optimism of the Salk Institute—the conviction that knowledge of the universe enriches both human understanding and human welfare. Salk maintained a laboratory to study multiple sclerosis, and he also devoted much of his energy to writing books about the philosophy and social role of science. In 1995, Salk emerged from retirement to develop a theraputic AIDS vaccine for HIV-positive patients.

### Summary

Salk's national immunization campaign in 1956-1958 administered more than two hundred million doses of killed vaccine without a single individual becoming infected with the disease. This remarkable achievement reflected Salk's talent for establishing quality control as he shifted from a single laboratory to the national level in carrying out his project. The disease was particularly frightening to parents, who witnessed the devastating paralysis it produced in schoolchildren and the helplessness of its most severely affected survivors, who had to live in "iron lungs," expensive and bulky machines that kept them breathing. The disease had also taken on national importance as Americans admired the courage of President Franklin D. Roosevelt, who had survived polio and went on to guide the nation through the Great Depression and World War II while confined to a wheelchair.

Salk represented a new generation of scientists who required funded research to accomplish their goals. Directing a large laboratory with many technical assistants and advanced students involves management skills, inspired leadership, the ability to write convincing grant applications and progress reports, and a personality that thrives on hard work and the occasional successes that careful scientific research yields. Jonas Salk was a model of this new breed, but he was also unique in extending his efforts to involve an entire nation in his enterprise.

### Bibliography

Carter, Richard. *Breakthrough: The Saga of Jonas Salk*. New York: Trident Press, 1965. This popular biography covers Salk's life through 1965. Salk's energy and personality are well depicted, although specific experiments are only mentioned and not analyzed.

Salk, Jonas. *Anatomy of Reality: Merging of Intuition and Reason*. New York: Columbia University Press, 1983. Salk relates metabiological ideas to biological and cultural evolution. He proposes more efforts to view life and the universe from both rational and intuitive, especially value-laden, perspectives.

———. *Man Unfolding*. Edited by Ruth N. Anshen. New York: Harper, 1972. Salk introduces the idea of biological dualisms as attributes of the human condition, whose unresolved conflicts lead to social unrest and conflict. He uses biological processes as guides or analogies for constructing psychological and social models that attempt to resolve the conflicts.

———. *The Survival of the Wisest*. New York: Harper, 1973. Salk greatly extends his concept of dualisms and introduces the idea of metabiology, a philosophic extension of the life sciences. From this perspective, Salk argues that resolution of conflicts arising from dualisms is not only possible but also necessary.

Salk, Jonas, and Jonathan Salk. *World Population and Human Values: New Reality*. New York: Harper, 1981. The ideas of Salk's metabiology are applied to the population problem. Each concept is provided a separate diagram to reinforce the verbal reasoning. A perspective on the world is attempted by use of United Nations vital statistics and population trends in different continents and cultures.

Self, Will. "Jonas Salk's Plan for Global Drug Security." *Spy Magazine* (March 1998). Profile of Salk highlighting his desire and failure to develop a vaccine against drug addiction before his death.

Sheed, Wilfred. "Virologist: JONAS SALK. Many Scientists Were Racing to Make a Polio Vaccine in the '50s—But He Got There First." *Time* 153, no. 12 (March 29, 1999). Short profile of Salk's life, career, and rocky relationships with other scientists who felt he never gave credit to others who helped him discover the polio vaccine.

*Elof Axel Carlson*

# CARL SANDBURG

*Born:* January 6, 1878; Galesburg, Illinois
*Died:* July 22, 1967; Flat Rock, North Carolina
*Area of Achievement:* Historiography and literature
*Contribution:* A prolific writer of verse and prose for adults and children, Sandburg extended the poetic techniques of free verse and glorified the American working person as its subject. He also sought to revitalize the biographical format by making it more human.

## Early Life

Second of seven children, Carl August Sandburg grew up in Abraham Lincoln country in Illinois, absorbing the Lincoln lore and the hotly argued local politics. During the Panic of 1893, fourteen-year-old Sandburg dropped out of school after finishing eighth grade to help his family financially. He did not get along with his austere Swedish immigrant father but shared his mother's love of books, learning, and word play.

In 1897, at the age of nineteen, a restless Sandburg headed West and became infatuated with the lifestyles of "gay-cats" or hoboes, who exchanged songs and stories around campfires. As he worked in the wheat fields of Kansas, chopped wood, and washed dishes along the way, he filled his pocket journal with the lingo of strangers, memorable stories, and plaintive songs of the road. His travels made him identify with working-class people and the displaced, alerted him to critical social problems of the 1890's, and provided materials for his later poetry and prose. Unwilling to settle down, Sandburg volunteered to serve in the Spanish-American War (1898-1899), which left within him a lifelong hatred of war.

As an 1899 war veteran entitled to free college tuition, Sandburg entered Lombard College in Galesburg despite not having earned a high school diploma. From 1899 to 1902, Sandburg became a good student, excelling in basketball and developing a passion for literature. He identified, in particular, with American poet Walt Whitman and imitated Whitman's free verse (poetry without predictable rhyme, meter, or format). Sandburg left Lombard College in 1902 without graduating because he took only "interesting" courses rather than those counting toward graduation. Before he left, however, he came under the tutelage of Professor Philip Wright who, recognizing Sandburg's poetic talents, later privately published Sandburg's early poems in the collection *In Reckless Ecstasy* (1904).

Between 1902 and 1908, Sandburg became a vagrant, a peddler, a fireman, a lecturer, and a writer. As he roamed the country, he stored observations in his notebooks, studied experimental poetry, and wrote biting newspaper columns on strikes, sweatshops, and socialism. In 1907, he organized workers for the Socialist Party and spoke on street corners about needed government reforms, women's rights, and child-labor exploitation. Sandburg began a six-month courtship with schoolteacher Lilian Steichen in Milwaukee, Wisconsin, resulting in marriage in 1908.

In constant need of money for his growing family, Sandburg increased his hectic pace—campaigning for socialist candidates, doing investigative journalism, lecturing, and selling advertising. From 1912 until the late 1920's, Sandburg worked as a newspaperman and movie critic, primarily in Chicago, Illinois. Late nights found him tinkering with his unconventional poems, which, when submitted to professional magazines, were rejected by unimpressed editors because they did not follow traditional expectations. Tall, gaunt, and with serious eye problems, Sandburg struggled to find his poetic niche, encouraged only by his wife.

## Life's Work

In 1913, a disheartened, thirty-six-year-old Sandburg sent a batch of his rejected poems about corrupt, energetic Chicago to a new magazine, *Poetry: A Magazine of Verse*. Editor Harriet Monroe of *Poetry*—startled by Sandburg's unorthodox poetic forms, hard style, and original subject matter, which ranged from brutal images to lyrical beauty—published his poems in March, 1914. Some Chicagoans hated Sandburg's unflattering portrait of Chicago and protested his "hog butcher" school of poetry, while others saw him as a rebel assaulting traditional poetry and weaving virility with tenderness. As a rising poet, Sandburg joined the Chicago School, a circle of American writers and poets around Chicago from 1912 to 1925 that included Sherwood Anderson, Vachel Lindsay, Edgar Lee Masters, and Theodore Dreiser. Sandburg also won the Levinson Prize in 1914 for the best American poems. After long years of apprenticeship and failure, Sandburg found success.

In 1916, Sandburg's first commercially published volume—*Chicago Poems*, which celebrated working people's loves, struggles, and tragedies—garnered good reviews and established him as the poet of industrial Chicago. Sandburg served as special correspondent for a news organization in 1917 in Sweden and Norway, ferreting out information on the Finnish and Russian revolutions during World War I. When the United States entered the war in 1917, Sandburg shifted from attacking the lunacy of war in his prose and poetry to supporting the United States' war efforts. After the war, he worked for the *Chicago Daily News*, writing columns and covering labor-management disputes. Sandburg's second book of poetry, *Cornhuskers* (1918)—a nostalgic paean for America's heartland—established him as a national poet. In addition to cross-country lecturing on Walt Whitman and labor-management conflicts, Sandburg investigated rising racial tensions and released his first commercial book of prose, *The Chicago Race Riots* (1919).

During the 1920's, Sandburg offered several other volumes of poetry: *Smoke and Steel* (1920), *Slabs of the Sunburnt West* (1922), and *Good Morning, America* (1928). In these volumes, Sandburg examined "the People" in conflict with governmental power, industrial corruption, and the emptiness of contemporary life. Critics noted Sandburg's maturing use of free verse, powerful images, and spare, economical style. Concurrently, Sandburg developed a series of children's fantasies that he had begun to entertain his own three daughters at bedtime. Disliking European fairy tales, Sandburg created a whimsical American fairyland of bizarre settings such as the Zipsap Railroad and the Village of Liver-and-Onions, populated by such strange characters as Gimme the Ax and Jason Squiff, with a popcorn hat and mittens. The results were the highly successful *Rootabaga Stories* (1922), *Rootabaga Pigeons* (1923), *Rootabaga Country* (1929), and *Potato Face* (1930).

Among Sandburg's diverse projects during the 1920's was a biography of Abraham Lincoln. Fascinated with Lincoln and the importance of the Civil War, Sandburg collected Lincoln stories, letters, and early biographies that focused on his public life. Sandburg, however, wanted to probe Lincoln's private life, the elusive core of Lincoln's character. At first, he considered writing his Lincoln book for children, but the complex material lent itself to adult fare. By 1924, Sandburg also decided that the book could only sketch Lincoln's frontier days—his early career as country lawyer and prairie politician—and would end with Lincoln becoming president in 1861. Filled with realistic details of the era, Sandburg's two-volume *Abraham Lincoln: The Prairie Years* (1926) became a best-seller. Critics gave the book mixed reviews: Some hailed it an overpowering masterpiece that captured the contradictory nature of Lincoln's character, while others objected to the book for having no footnotes and including fictitious scenes rather than verifiable facts. Above the controversy, Sandburg stood at the height of his career. He was now eagerly sought out for lectures, magazine articles, and radio programs.

During his early traveling days and into the 1920's, Sandburg collected American folk tales and ballads. He used these materials to become a charismatic lecturer-entertainer who strummed a few chords on the guitar and transfixed audiences with his craggy voice while singing spirituals and songs of the pioneers, soldiers, prisoners, and laborers. Refining the material, he brought out *The American Songbag* (1927) and made an early "talking-book" record. Overworked, ill, and driven by family demands and publishing deadlines, Sandburg suffered a nervous breakdown in 1927, which forced him to reduce his activities.

Despite his "slowdown," Sandburg produced *Steichen the Photographer* (1929), a biography of his famous brother-in-law, and coauthored *Mary Lincoln: Wife and Widow* (1932) with Paul Angle. The market crash of 1929 and the ensuing Great Depression of the 1930's deeply affected Sandburg's perspective. As his response to the calamity, he offered *The People, Yes* (1936), an epic poem that draws upon the mythic past, examines conditions of the 1930's by detailing the suffering of the exploited masses, and projects the future, affirming that "the People" will survive and thrive through their strength and heroic actions. Sandburg intertwines his own experiences with historical personages, folklore, and anecdotes. Critics generally praised the originality and scope of the poem, but some found unsettling political overtones and propaganda within the poem.

Sandburg's other major achievement during the 1930's was his four-volume *Abraham Lincoln: The War Years* (1939), which chronicled Lincoln's presidency during the Civil War and his assassination. Sandburg examined Lincoln's humor, religious behavior, humility, and mystical leanings in the midst of crisis. To stem the criticisms of poor scholarship and too much poetic license that his earlier Lincoln book had suffered, Sandburg relied on Lincoln scholars and historians to provide guidance and insight. Most critics lauded Sandburg as the foremost spokesperson on Lincoln. Sandburg received personal accolades and many honorary degrees, and, in 1940, he accepted the Pulitzer Prize in history.

Sandburg campaigned vigorously for the reelection of President Franklin Roosevelt in 1940. With the United States' entry in World War II, Sandburg worked on government propaganda films, made radio speeches, lectured, and wrote syndicated columns mainly concerned with working-people's efforts and sacrifices. He brought out *Storm over the Land* (1942), a Civil War story, and *Home Front Memo* (1943), his views on World War II in verse and prose. In 1945, as he and his family moved from the Midwest to the warmer climate of Flat Rock, North Carolina, Sandburg began his first novel at age seventy. An epic, *Remembrance Rock* (1948) spanned three hundred years of America's development, from the Mayflower and the Pilgrim years through the end of World War II. The novel sold well, but critics found it tedious and overwritten, with wooden characters steeped in allegory.

In the 1950's, Sandburg continued traveling, lecturing, and accepting more honors. He brought out *The New American Songbag* (1950) and promoted his *Complete Poems* (1950), winning a second Pulitzer Prize in 1951, this time for poetry. With the deaths of so many intimate friends, Sandburg began working on his own autobiography, culminating in *Always the Young Strangers* (1953), which described his adventures while growing up in Galesburg, Illinois.

Sandburg's final years in the 1960's were spent mainly at his estate in the Flat Rock area, where he died peacefully in 1967. His last book of poetry published before his death, *Honey and Salt* (1963), showed a mature poet at work. Several works were published posthumously: *Breathing Tokens* (1978), a collection of his poems; and *Ever the Winds of Chance* (1983), autobiographical materials drawn from 1898 to 1907.

### Summary

Carl Sandburg's poetry, according to his detractors, was crude, sentimental, and deficient in traditional forms, and his messages of social protest were often propagandistic. To his admirers, however, Sandburg's poetry celebrated the United States' agricultural and industrial power, particularly that of the Midwest. In creating over eight hundred poems, Sandburg found his subject matter mainly in the struggles of the working class, using simple situations to reveal universal themes and identifiable life experiences. Sandburg also created new poetic techniques, melding the literary tools of realism and free verse couched in everyday language. As a craftsman and endless reviser, Sandburg sought strong, simple words and short lines to convey exact images. Having a keen inner ear for appropriate cadence and an eye for visual impact on the printed page, Sandburg became a renowned poet whose goal was clarity, not obscurity.

Sandburg allowed his restless poetic imagination to interplay with his experiences as an investigative journalist, movie critic, newspaper columnist, and lecturer to produce some twenty-three books of prose. Identifying with Abraham Lincoln's rise from humble origins on the Midwest prairie and his passionate sense of social justice, Sandburg became the premier historian of Lincoln. From 1920 to 1939, Sandburg produced seven volumes for adults on Lincoln and the Civil War and one volume for teenagers, *Abe Lincoln Grows Up* (1928). He also wrote seven books for young children, a novel, several autobiographical pieces, and collected little-known American folk songs.

### Bibliography

Callahan, North. *Carl Sandburg: His Life and Works*. University Park, Penn.: Pennsylvania State University Press, 1987. Outlines Sandburg's life and the significance of his writings. Includes Callahan's personal reminiscences.

Fetherling, Dale, and Doug Fetherling, eds. *Carl Sandburg at the Movies: A Poet in the Silent Era, 1920-1927*. Metuchen, N.J.: Scarecrow Press, 1985. Selects Sandburg's best movie columns to reveal an early film critic's concern with realism, film techniques, and film serving as a social conscience. Demonstrates Sandburg's melding of his journalistic talents with artistic sensibilities.

Hendrick, George, and Willene Hendrick. *Selected Poems: Carl Sandburg 1878-1967*. San Diego: Harcourt Brace, 1996. A collection of 166 of Sandburg's poems, many of which have never been published. Sandburg revival at its best.

Niven, Penelope. *Carl Sandburg: A Biography*. New York: Scribner, 1991. Fascinating insights on the influence that Sandburg's wife and family had on the poet-writer. Includes photographs and a full listing of Sandburg's works.

Steichen, Edward, ed. *Sandburg: Photographers View Carl Sandburg*. New York: Harcourt Brace, 1966. A pictorial odyssey of Sandburg's life using excerpts from his writings to highlight his achievements.

Yannella, Philip R. *The Other Sandburg*. Jackson: University Press of Mississippi, 1996. Provides evidence from Sandburg's own writings from 1900 to 1920 that Sandburg was deeply radicalized, promoting socialism and calling for the overthrow of capitalism.

*Richard Whitworth*

# MARGARET SANGER

*Born:* September 14, 1879; Corning, New York

*Died:* September 6, 1966; Tucson, Arizona

*Areas of Achievement:* Public health and social policy

*Contribution:* Through the establishment of low-cost birth control clinics, Sanger made birth control information and contraceptive devices available to American women of all social classes.

### Early Life

Born in Corning, New York, to poor Irish parents, Margaret Higgins was the sixth of eleven children. Her mother died at the age of forty, and Margaret always believed that her mother's premature death was a consequence of excessive childbearing. During her mother's illness, Margaret acted as a nurse and also helped care for her younger siblings. Margaret enjoyed a close relationship with her father, who worked as a headstone carver. Higgins advised his resourceful children to use their minds to make a contribution to the world and to try to leave it better than they found it.

As a young girl, Margaret formed the conclusion that poverty, illness, and strife were the fate of large families, whereas small families enjoyed wealth, leisure, and positive parental relationships. Being from a large family, Margaret always felt inferior, and she longed to be rich and comfortable.

After the death of her mother, Margaret decided to become a nurse. During her final training at a Manhattan hospital, she met an architect named William Sanger, who fell in love with her at first sight. Margaret married Bill Sanger in 1902 after a six-month courtship. Over the next few years, Bill continued his work as an architect and Margaret stayed home with their three children. Sanger's restlessness and boredom in her role as a housewife led to her return to obstetrical nursing in 1912. She felt a need to regain her personal independence, and her mother-in-law agreed to move in and take care of the children. At the same time, Margaret and Bill Sanger began attending Socialist meetings in Greenwich Village. Margaret observed forceful speakers, such as Emma Goldman, who were rethinking the position of women and the future of worldwide political and economic systems. Sanger was considered a shy, delicate woman who rarely voiced her opinion at meetings.

Sanger's speaking debut was as a substitute before a group of working women. Her topic was family health. The working women liked Sanger's demeanor and believed what she said. Throughout her life, much of Sanger's impact was attributable to her personal appearance: She was petite, feminine, and demure. Sanger invariably gained support after the publication of her picture in the newspaper. Although her appearance was described as Madonna-like, Sanger was single-minded, stubborn, and intolerant; she was also charming, personable, and energetic. Sanger's personality was such that people either worshiped her or despised her.

### Life's Work

During her years as an obstetrical nurse, Sanger frequently made house calls to the Lower East Side of New York City to attend poor women who were giving birth or experiencing complications from self-induced abortions. These women were worried about the health and survival of the children they already had and were desperate to find a way to stop having more children. They would beg Sanger to tell them "the secret" of the rich women and would promise that they would not tell anyone else. Sanger would suggest coitus interruptus or the use of condoms, but she quickly realized that the women rejected initiating these methods, placing contraceptive responsibility on men. Sanger herself never believed in male-oriented contraceptives because she saw men as opponents, rather than partners, in the struggle for conception control.

A turning point in Sanger's life occurred when she met a young mother of three named Sadie Sachs. Sanger was called to nurse Sadie during the sweltering summer of 1912. Sadie had attempted an abortion and was near death when Sanger was called to the apartment. Two weeks later, Sadie was finally out of danger. Sadie believed that another pregnancy would kill her and she pleaded with the attending physician to help prevent another pregnancy. The doctor callously told Sadie that she could not expect to have her cake and eat it too. His only suggestion, jokingly added, was that she have her husband, Jake, sleep on the roof. After the doctor left, Sadie turned to Sanger, who was more sympathetic than the doctor but who had no better suggestion for contraception. Sanger promised the anguished woman that she would return at a later date and try to provide helpful information. Sanger did not return, and three months later she was again summoned to the Sachs apartment.

*Margaret Sanger on trial in New York for promoting birth control.*

Sadie was in critical condition from another abortion attempt, and this time she died minutes after Sanger arrived. Sanger was burdened with guilt over the death of Sachs and resolved that she would find out how to prevent conception so that other women would be spared the pain, suffering, and heartache of unwanted pregnancies.

After two years of research, including a trip to France, Sanger decided to publish a journal aimed at working women which would encourage them to rebel and to insist on reproductive freedom. It was at this time that Sanger coined the term "birth control." In 1914, the first issue of *The Woman Rebel* was published. Although Sanger advocated that women limit births, she was prohibited by Anthony Comstock from explaining to women the precise methodologies for limiting births. Comstock was the head of the New York Society for the Suppression of Vice, and Sanger had experienced problems with him several years earlier when she wrote articles for *The Call*, a labor publication. Sanger's health-oriented column on venereal disease was aimed at adolescent girls, but Comstock refused to allow the column to be published. He had been instrumental in seeing that no obscene materials were distributed through the United States mail, and Comstock made it clear to publishers of *The Call* that he considered Sanger's article obscene and that its publication would result in immediate revocation of their mailing permit. Both Sanger and Comstock wanted to protect America's young people. Comstock sought to protect the young by distancing them from information on venereal disease, while Sanger thought that the protection of the young could best be achieved by exposing them to and educating them about the realities, dangers, and treatment of venereal disease.

Thousands of women responded to Sanger's articles in *The Woman Rebel*, once again pleading for information about the prevention of pregnancy. Sanger wrote a pamphlet called *Family Limitation* which provided practical, straightforward information in language that women of all social classes could understand. Sanger included descriptions and drawings of suppositories, douches, sponges, and the cervical pessary. Sanger also advocated sexual fulfillment for women, which was a radical idea in the early 1900's. After twenty refusals, Sanger found a printer for *Family Limitation*. With the help of friends, Sanger began distributing the pamphlet and was arrested immediately. The possibility of prison was overwhelming to Sanger at this time, so she sailed for Europe before she came to trial, leaving her husband and children behind. She settled in London and was accepted into the intellectual circle of people on the vanguard of sexual and contraceptive thought. Sanger discovered that the Netherlands, because of an emphasis on child spacing, had the lowest maternal death rate and infant mortality rate in the world. In addition, contraceptive clinics had been in operation for thirty years. When Sanger visited the Netherlands, she received trained instruction on the fitting and insertion of the diaphragm, which came in fourteen sizes. Sanger became convinced that she not only would have to overcome the restraint on free speech in the United States but also would have to provide women with access to trained people, preferably physicians, who could fit them with contraceptives.

Sanger returned to the United States to stand trial, but the charges against her were dismissed. Anthony Comstock had died while she was away, and the mood of the people was now supportive of Sanger.

In October of 1916, Margaret Sanger opened the nation's first birth control clinic. The clinic provided birth control and venereal disease information and birth control instruction. Most important, the clinic kept detailed medical records and case histories of patients. Although Sanger and her sister Ethel Byrne were imprisoned for their role in the new birth control clinic, public sentiment was in their favor. In the next few years, Sanger began publishing the *Birth Control Review*, a scientific, authoritative journal intended for health care professionals. In 1921, Sanger organized the first national birth control conference, which attracted physicians from all over the country.

Margaret and Bill Sanger were divorced in 1920, and in 1922 Margaret married a wealthy businessman named Noah Slee. Slee contributed many thousands of dollars to his wife's cause but always stayed in the background of her life. Sanger was a national figure by this time and a frequent speaker who enthralled her audience. She traveled internationally and made a great impact on the birth control movements in both Japan and India. In her efforts to establish international unity, Sanger established a World Population Conference, and years later, in 1952, the International Planned Parenthood Federation.

Throughout her career, Sanger lamented the absence of a safe, easy, effective contraceptive. She believed that some sort of contraceptive pill would best meet the needs of women, and she called such a pill her "holy grail." When she discovered that scientists John Rock and Gregory Pincus were experimenting with hormonal methods of contraception, Sanger convinced Mrs. Stanley McCormick, a wealthy widow, to provide funding for Rock and Pincus to continue their research for a contraceptive pill.

Sanger continued to be an active force in the birth control movement until very late in her life. As a nursing home patient in Tucson, Arizona, she was irascible and stubborn and insisted that since she was rich and smart she would do exactly as she pleased. She did just that until she died in 1966 of arteriosclerosis, one week before her eighty-seventh birthday.

## Summary

In her lifetime, Margaret Sanger was jailed eight times, yet she never relented in her efforts to promote, and democratize access to, birth control. The medical records of patients visiting Sanger's birth control clinic provided the basis for the initial studies on the effects of child spacing on maternal health and marital satisfaction. These records also yielded information on the efficacy of various birth control methods for different groups of women.

Sanger's early efforts to disseminate contraceptive information were condemned by the church, the press, and the medical profession. Her belief that sex is a normal part of human life which requires a rational response led her to search for easy and safe contraceptives that would allow women to choose maternity while attaining freedom through control of their bodies. Sanger believed that in some way every unwanted child would be a social liability, and that a society should try to maximize its social assets by having children that are wanted by their parents. Sanger insisted that the best measure of the success of her work was in the reduction of human suffering.

Availability of contraceptive information and birth control devices has had widespread implications for Americans, both individually and collectively. Maternal death rates and infant mortality rates have declined, child spacing spans have increased, and total family size has decreased. Control of conception is a subject taught in classes throughout the country, and American women and men take for granted the fact that contraceptives are sold in drugstores and are easily obtained from physicians. As a result of the achievements of Margaret Sanger, control of conception has become a reality for many women throughout the world.

## Bibliography

Chandrasekhar, Sripati. *"A Dirty Filthy Book": The Writings of Charles Knowlton and Annie Besant on Birth Control and Reproductive Physiology*. Berkeley and London: University of California Press, 1981. Includes essays by Sanger's American and British predecessors who laid the foundation for her work. Provides an account of the Bradlaugh-Besant trial in 1877 and its impact on the British birth rate.

Dash, Joan. *A Life of One's Own*. New York: Harper, 1973. A somewhat psychoanalytic portrait of Sanger and the men in her life. Provides a chronological account as well as descriptions of Sanger's public and private activities.

Douglas, Emily Taft. *Pioneer of the Future*. New York: Holt Rinehart, 1970. A thorough work documenting the milestones of Sanger's life. Good in-depth account of research, events, and individuals who gave Sanger the basic knowledge, ideas, and encouragement from which to proceed.

Elvin, John. "Did Mother of Free Love Urge Selective Breeding?" *Insight on the News* 12, no. 47 (December 16, 1996). The author looks at Sanger's career leading to the creation of today's Planned Parenthood organization, and through analysis of her writings, alleges that she advocated eugenics.

Gray, Madeline. *Margaret Sanger: A Biography of the Champion of Birth Control*. New York: Marek, 1978. Excellent, well-researched biography with one of the few in-depth examinations of Sanger's later years, including her addiction to Demerol.

Kennedy, David M. *Birth Control in America: The Career of Margaret Sanger*. New Haven, Conn.: Yale University Press, 1970; London: Yale University Press, 1971. Focuses on Sanger's public career in the United States and illuminates American society in the years prior to 1945. Describes the social context in which Sanger worked and the attitudinal, behavioral, and institutional responses she evoked.

Prose, Francine. "Having It All." *The New York Times Magazine* 141 (July 26, 1992). Compares Sanger with women leaders of the 1990s, concluding that the range of acceptable behavior has narrowed.

Sanger, Margaret. *Margaret Sanger: An Autobiography*. New York: Norton, 1938; London: Gollancz, 1939. A factual description of the life of the author without much insight and introspection. Describes people who influenced Sanger, including the C. V. Drysdales and Havelock Ellis in England, and Dr. Aletta Jacobs, birth control pioneer in Amsterdam.

———. *Motherhood in Bondage*. London and New York: Brentano's, 1928. Composed of letters written to Sanger by women desperate to discover a method of preventing conception. Tragic, heart-wrenching accounts.

———. *Woman and the New Race*. New York: Brentano's, 1920; Oxford: Pergamon Press, 1969. Attempts to convince working-class women that control of reproduction is the key to a healthier, more satisfying life and a better world. Advocates rebellion in order to gain access to contraceptive information.

*Lesley Hoyt Croft*

# GEORGE SANTAYANA

*Born:* December 16, 1863; Madrid, Spain
*Died:* September 26, 1952; Rome, Italy
*Areas of Achievement:* Philosophy and letters
*Contribution:* Combining a deep sense of the enduring and ideal nature of classic Greek culture with a learned sense for the immediate and natural, Santayana produced a series of philosophical and literary works as well as personal commentaries on the life and cultures of his times. He has been deemed the "Mona Lisa" of philosophy.

## Early Life

George Santayana was born December 16, 1863, in Madrid, Spain. His mother, Spanish by birth, was first married to a member of the Sturgis family of Boston, an American merchant in the Philippines, where, until her husband's death in 1857, she lived and reared three children. Santayana's father was a friend of the Sturgis family, having served as a civil servant in the Philippines and authored a book on the natives of the Island of Mindanao. In 1862, the couple returned to Spain and were married in Madrid. Shortly thereafter, Santayana's mother returned to Boston with her older children while Santayana remained with his father in Spain. In 1872, he was brought by his father to Boston.

When Santayana arrived in Boston, he knew no English, and only Spanish was spoken in his home, but he soon picked up English outside the home and from his reading and was able to speak it without a marked accent. He attended Brimmer School, Boston Latin School and Harvard College, where he was graduated summa cum laude in 1886. In 1883, after his freshman year at Harvard, he returned to Spain to see his father. There, he considered a career in either the Spanish army or as a diplomat but decided instead to return to the United States and pursue a career as a writer. His attachment to Europe, however, remained strong.

At Harvard, Santayana had studied with both Josiah Royce and William James. Having already published since 1880 in *The Boston Latin School Register*, he became a regular contributor of cartoons and literary pieces to the *Harvard Lampoon*. He helped found *The Harvard Monthly* and provided it with a continuous flow of poetry and articles.

In physical appearance, Santayana was a gentle looking man of medium size. He had lively eyes, was bald, and for a while wore a handsome beard; later, he wore a mustache. He was fastidious about his clothes, often wearing black.

## Life's Work

Santayana's first major philosophical work, *The Sense of Beauty: Being the Outline of Aesthetic Theory*, was published in 1896 when he was thirty-three. A book of sonnets and a series of pieces of literary criticism were also published that year. This was also the year that Santayana went to study with Dr. Henry Jackson at Trinity College, Cambridge. He undertook careful examination of the works of classical Greece, particularly those of Plato and Aristotle. This experience led to the production of one of Santayana's major philosophical works, the five-volume *The Life of Reason: Or, the Phases of Human Progress* (1905-1906). In it, Santayana attempted to present a summary history of the human imagination, a panorama of the whole life of reason and of human ideas as they are generated out of and controlled by man's animal life and nature. This was Santayana's first major effort at combining a skeptical naturalism-humanism with a Platonic idealism. A variety of pieces of literary philosophical criticism followed, and in 1914 his famous piece "The Genteel Tradition in American Philosophy" appeared.

In that year, Santayana received news of a legacy. He promptly retired from Harvard at the age of fifty and in January, 1912, he left the United States for Europe, never to return. Santayana had been an extremely gifted teacher, and his sudden departure for Europe astonished his colleagues. Yet, although he was interested in his students, he disliked academic life and wished to devote himself to his writing. Also, his dual Spanish-American heritage, although contributing extraordinary range and perspective to his thinking, awoke in him conflicts from which he was thankful to escape. He went to France, Spain, and England, and finally to Rome, Italy, where he lived for eleven years in the monastery of the Blue Sisters. From there, Santayana produced a number of penetrating pieces on the life and culture of his times, including *Winds of Doctrine: Studies in Contemporary Opinion* (1913) and *Egotism in German Philosophy* (1916), a book much read by the Germans during the war, although it strongly demonstrated his loyalty to the Allied cause. In 1920, he wrote *Character and Opinion in the United States*. A major philosophical work appeared in

1923, *Scepticism and Animal Faith*, followed by his magnum opus, the four-volume *Realms of Being* (1927-1940). In 1935, he produced a novel reflective of his American experience entitled *The Last Puritan: A Memoir in the Form of a Novel*.

Santayana's *Persons and Places* (1944-1953), a kind of autobiographical travelogue, captures much of the spirit of all of Santayana's writing. It presents him as a traveler who, however appreciative or critical of the places and people encountered, is always a stranger, catching glimpses of people and places and recomposing these images as an artist would a painting. Santayana, in his work, too, conveys a constant sense of detachment, reflecting his reclusive spirit. Yet his works of speculative philosophy, with precision, depth, and coherence, elucidate complex ideas with what has been described as "luminous succinctness."

Santayana's life ended with characteristic ambiguity. Although he considered himself Catholic and lived among the nuns for eleven years, he did not officially return to the Roman Catholic Church and he did not receive the Sacraments on his deathbed. He died in September, 1952, a few months before his eighty-ninth birthday. He was buried in Rome, on ground reserved for Spanish nationals.

### Summary

To many Americans, George Santayana was a great man of letters, a civilized hermit, an isolated sage. His works were eloquent and penetrating but always a bit of a mystery. Santayana spent forty years in the United States and wrote eleven books as well as numerous other works. Yet he left the United States in 1912 never to return. As Santayana himself noted, however, his intentional detachment from America must be balanced by the fact that he was detached from every other place as well. He never did have a sense of home, yet he clearly believed that "it was as an American writer he was to be counted."

Like Ralph Waldo Emerson, Santayana was essentially concerned with the conditions of life, with the bearing of events on men, and with the emergence of values and the possibilities for happiness. His account of the many sides of human experience, ethical, social, artistic, and religious, shows an interweaving of themes normally kept separate in modern philosophy and is expressed in prose that is polished to great beauty. Although his philosophy was much influenced by classical culture, it also contains much of the dynamic, fresh, naturalistic aspects of American culture. Santayana's profound belief in the life and power of the human mind and imagination and in the creativity and freedom of the human spirit produced a series of truly noteworthy works which expressed the American spirit at its best.

### Bibliography

Cory, Daniel. *Santayana: The Later Years*. New York: Braziller, 1963. This book presents a collection of recollections by Santayana's close friend. Contains also various letters from Santayana and gives an excellent personal picture of the man and his thoughts.

Howgate, George W. *George Santayana*. Philadelphia: University of Pennsylvania Press, and London: Oxford University Press, 1938. This book deals with the various aspects of Santayana as a person and professional, namely, the poet, the critic, the moral philosopher, the writer, the metaphysician. Using abundant quotes from Santayana's writings, Howgate traces the influences that have shaped his thought and tries to show the interrelationships and underlying unity of various aspects of Santayana's personality and thought. The author also frequently takes issue with some of Santayana's opinions.

Munson, Thomas N. *The Essential Wisdom of George Santayana*. New York: Columbia University Press, 1962. This is an exposition of Santayana's philosophical positions, primarily from the viewpoint of neo-Thomist philosophy. The book is interesting in this respect and also because its appendices contain several letters from Santayana to the author raising critical questions about Munson's interpretations.

Posnock, Ross. "Genteel Androgyny: Santayana, Henry James, Howard Sturgis." *Raritan* 10, no. 3 (Winter 1991). Examines the androgyny of Santayana and two other authors, including Santayana's avoidance of self-identification.

Schilpp, Paul Arthur, ed. *The Philosophy of George Santayana*. Vol. 2. Evanston: Northwestern University Press, 1940. In this volume, the writings of Santayana are scrutinized and evaluated by eighteen of his philosophical contemporaries. Almost every aspect of Santayana's work is covered. Further, Santayana has written an *Apologia Pro Mente Sua*, in which he replies to his critics. The volume also contains Santayana's autobiography and a complete bibliography of Santayana's writings from 1880 to October, 1940.

Singer, Beth J. *The Rational Society*. Cleveland: Press of Case Western Reserve University, 1970. This book focuses on Santayana's social thought and depicts him as a metaphysician of human experience and culture. Professor Singer gives primary attention to two of Santayana's works, *Reason in Society*, a volume of *The Life of Reason*, and *Dominations and Powers* (1951). A critical and analytical study directed primarily to professional philosophers.

Singer, Irving. *Santayana's Aesthetics*. Cambridge, Mass.: Harvard University Press, 1957. This book presents Santayana's aesthetics and philosophy of art as seen in the light of his later writings on ontology and metaphysics. It also uses Santayana's work to suggest some new approaches to traditional problems in the fields of aesthetics and the philosophy of art.

Sprigge, Timothy L. S. *Santayana: An Examination of His Philosophy*. London and Boston: Routledge, 1974. A detailed examination of Santayana's philosophy, treating such topics as skepticism, animal faith, the doctrine of essence, spirit and psyche, and the material world. It also gives an outline of Santayana's philosophical development.

*Jacquelyn Kegley*

# ALBERTO SANTOS-DUMONT

*Born:* July 20, 1873; Palmira, Brazil

*Died:* July 24, 1932; Guarujá, Brazil

*Areas of Achievement:* Aeronautics, invention, and technology

*Contribution:* Santos-Dumont, a leading European aviator during the period of early development of manned flight, is recognized as an inventor and innovative designer in both major categories of flight: lighter than air (airships) and heavier than air (airplanes). Working with semirigid airships, he adapted the internal-combustion engine as a source of power for lighter-than-air vehicles, and he was the first to design, build, and fly a heavier-than-air machine in Europe. Two of the airplanes he designed and built played a major role in the development of European aviation.

## Early Life

Alberto Santos-Dumont was born in Brazil, the third son and the last of seven children of Francisca Santos and Henriques Dumont, known as the Brazilian "coffee king." An avid reader, especially of Jules Verne's science fiction, Alberto was enthralled by the idea that man might fly, and he was also fascinated by machinery. At an early age, he drove the huge steampowered tractors and locomotives that transported coffee beans to the processing plant. There, the young Santos-Dumont would observe how the machines operated, and he soon became adept at making needed repairs. During a visit to the Palace of Industry in Paris, Alberto was completely captivated by a working exhibit of an internal-combustion engine, the first he had ever seen. He bought an automobile, to which he applied his mechanical talents, and he was soon able to disassemble an engine and rebuild it perfectly. He also read every book he could find on balloons and aerial navigation. Such experiences were to influence his later work much more than did his formal education, which ended with his graduation from the academy at Minas Gerais province, although he did later take some studies in physics, mechanics, electricity, and chemistry with a private tutor in France.

In 1897, the young Santos-Dumont went to France, where he became a balloon pilot for Henri Lachambre and Alexis Machuron, whom he then commissioned to build a balloon to his design: small, light, and made of Japanese silk. Although the two experts had maintained that silk would not be strong enough, tests proved Santos-Dumont correct: The silk was stronger than the material previously used. He named his tiny balloon the *Brazil* and flew it time after time, becoming a familiar sight and a popular hero to the Parisians, who reacted enthusiastically, taking him to their hearts.

## Life's Work

Having learned to fly, Santos-Dumont turned his back on everything else and devoted all of his energies to the goal of controlled, powered flight. This dream was scoffed at by his friends, who argued that an engine mounted under a balloon would shake itself to pieces. Undeterred, Santos-Dumont experimented with a small, motor-powered tricycle, which he suspended by ropes from tree branches, finding that it vibrated less in the air than on the ground. The success of this experiment and of his first balloon encouraged the inventor to rely increasingly on his own intuition, refusing suggestions from others.

Santos-Dumont's first controllable airship was an elongated balloon with rigging lines, from which was suspended a basket on which was mounted a modified internal-combustion engine. The vehicle incorporated two control mechanisms: one a crude but movable rudder, the other a method of controlling pitch (vertical angle) by moving weights, thus allowing the pilot to climb or descend. On September 20, 1898, the designer made the first successful flight in his airship number 1. He was able to steer the ship, but its balloon envelope collapsed in midair, and he was saved from crashing only by a group of boys who grabbed the lines and ran into the wind, allowing the balloon to settle gradually to the ground.

Santos-Dumont's airship number 2, constructed from parts of number 1, also collapsed on its first flight, dumping its pilot in a tree. Undaunted, he began plans for his first semirigid airship. Its construction was similar to that of its predecessors but with a bamboo pole added to the underside of the envelope, providing some rigidity. After his first flight in number 3, the designer was ecstatic; for the first time he believed that he was mastering control of the airship. This success hardened Santos-Dumont's resolve to pursue aviation as his life's work.

In April, 1900, a prize of 100,000 francs was offered by M. Deutsch de la Meurthe to the first person to fly from the Parc d'Aérostation of the Aéro Club de France in St. Cloud, near Paris, around the Eiffel Tower, and back to the Parc d'Aérostation without landing, in thirty minutes or less. Santos-Dumont began construction of his airship number 4 immediately, using a combination of old and new ideas. The envelope was of the same basic design as number 3, with a longitudinal bamboo spar underneath to add rigidity; attached to this was an engine, mounted now as a tractor rather than a pusher. The basket was omitted, replaced by a bicycle seat mounted aft of the engine. Horizontal steering was done with controls attached to bicycle handle bars. Pitch was again controlled by shifting weights, but with a new component, water ballast, which the pilot could dump by simply turning a tap. Although Santos-Dumont made several successful flights in this airship, it lacked the speed necessary to win the Deutsch Prize.

In his next model, Santos-Dumont made four major changes. First, he built a girderlike keel of aluminum and pine, which provided a lightweight, rigid framework on which to mount the engine and basket. Second, he braced the framework with piano wire rather than rope, greatly reducing drag. Third, he enlarged the rudder for more effective control. Finally, he installed an air-cooled fifteen horsepower Buchet engine, into which he incorporated an electric ignition system. On its maiden voyage, the engine failed, and once again Santos-Dumont landed in the trees. The damage was quickly repaired, but on his next attempt the airship lost its rigidity and deflated, crashing into the Hotel Trocadero. Rescuers found the pilot perched on a windowsill high above street level; safe on the ground again, he announced that construction of number 6 would begin immediately. It took only twenty-two days, the only design change being a modified water-cooled Buchet engine. On October 19, 1901, Santos-Dumont made the round-trip flight from the Parc d'Aérostation around the Eiffel Tower and back again. Although his flight had lasted forty seconds more than the allotted time, the people of Paris demanded that he be awarded the prize, half of which he gave to the poor of Paris and the other half to his mechanics and other workers. Santos-Dumont went on to design a total of fourteen airships, of which his number 9 is considered the most successful. This short, fat vehicle, so easy and convenient to fly that he used it as his "runabout," reflected his credo of smallness, lightness, and simplicity of design.

In 1905, Santos-Dumont entered the race for prizes offered by Ernest Archdeacon, a wealthy patron of aviation, for the first heavier-than-air flight of more than twenty-five meters, and by the French Aéro Club for a flight of more than one hundred meters. His first design was an ungainly looking "canard-type" airplane, with a rectangular, fabric-covered fuselage and tail unit forward of the main wings with its propeller in the rear. Its wings, which resembled large box kites, were attached at a pronounced dihedral angle, providing lateral stability. Attached to the leading end of the fuselage was a small boxlike device that pivoted both vertically and horizontally, the sole means of control during flight. The pilot stood in a wicker basket directly in front of the engine. The airplane's first test, which involved towing by a donkey harnessed to a pulley arrangement, occasioned a series of colorful comments by observers, which were not appreciated by the designer. He then decided to suspend it from his number 14 airship, resulting in the appellation number 14-*bis* (again, twice). On October 23, 1906, at Bagatelle, near Paris, Santos-Dumont made the first successful European airplane flight, covering some sixty meters before crashing to earth. He had won the Archdeacon Prize and was the toast of Europe. To improve control, he now added ailerons, modified from an earlier design of Robert Esnault-Pelterie. Wires from the ailerons ran to a piece of metal sewn into the back of his jacket. To activate them, he shifted his body to and fro, controlling the airplane through a sort of dance. On November 12, 1906, Santos-Dumont flew his modified number 14-*bis* a distance of 220 meters, in slightly more than twenty-one seconds, to win the Aéro Club Prize of fifteen hundred francs.

Santos-Dumont forged ahead, trying to solve the still-worrisome lack of control. In March, 1909, he surprised the aviation world by unveiling a totally new design—a tractor (front propeller) monoplane with a silk-covered wing and tail surfaces and a skeletal fuselage made of bamboo. He had returned to his original criteria of small, light, and simple. This beautiful machine, powered by a Dutheil-Chambers engine which Santos-Dumont had modified extensively to give it more horsepower, was the prototype for his number 20, the *Demoiselle* (dragonfly). Incorporated into its construction were his solutions to control problems: a rudder and an elevator for control about the longitudinal and vertical axes and wing warping for lateral control. The mechanism for the latter was a pair of metal rings worn around the pilot's arms; when he wanted to turn, he moved his arms up or down, twisting the wings. The *Demoiselle*, relatively easy to construct and an excellent flying machine, was an instant success, joining Santos-Dumont's number 9 airship and his number 14-*bis* airplane as the third jewel in his crown of achievements.

In 1910, Santos-Dumont, ill with multiple sclerosis, retired from his work in aviation and, after a period of wandering, returned to Brazil. In July, 1932, despondent because the machine to which he had devoted his life was being used to kill people in war, he took his own life.

## Summary

Working independently of developments in the United States, Alberto Santos-Dumont designed and built the first airplane to fly successfully in Europe. He was the third person in the world to pilot an airplane, with only Wilbur and Orville Wright having preceded him in achieving sustained heavier-than-air flight. In early 1910, Santos-Dumont was the only aeronaut qualified to fly all four types of flying machines then in existence: balloons, airships, biplanes, and monoplanes. His major technological contributions were the design of a small, light, controllable airship, powered by an internal-combustion engine, and of a small, light, reliable airplane, the *Demoiselle*, whose ease of construction and flying helped to open the field of aviation.

A pilot, mechanic, skilled craftsman, adapter, and inventor, Alberto Santos-Dumont did not engage in systematic research in the same way as did the Wright brothers and others; rather, he built, tested, modified, and rebuilt as necessary to reach his goal. His contribution to the science of aviation is considered by historians to be minimal. Nevertheless, his influence on the development of aviation remains important. His refusal to patent any of his innovations made possible the use and development of his ideas by others, furthering the advancement and popularization of aviation, and his criteria of smallness, lightness, and simplicity became the quintessential concepts of aircraft design.

Santos-Dumont's other major contribution to aviation was his impact on people's perception of flight. Moving easily through all levels of society, he did more than any other person during the early 1900's to make Europeans "air-minded." Santos-Dumont's daring aeronautical successes thrilled people and awakened in them an overwhelming curiosity about and awareness of aviation. In a period of history erupting in technological advances, Santos-Dumont fired the imagination of a continent.

## Bibliography

Barnes, Michael. "Blimps on the Rise." *Technology Review* 97, no. 1 (January, 1994). Examines the development and many uses of blimps, including the first practical blimp designed by Santos-Dumont.

Emde, Heiner. *Conquerors of the Air: The Evolution of Aircraft, 1903-1945.* London: Stephens, and New York: Viking Press, 1968. Contains a large number of detailed drawings of airplanes, with specifications and descriptions. The short section on Santos-Dumont describes his 14-*bis* and his *Demoiselle* airplanes.

Gibbs-Smith, Charles H. *The Invention of the Aeroplane, 1799-1909.* New York: Taplinger, 1965; London: Faber, 1966. A definitive study of early aviation, in which are chronicled Santos-Dumont's achievements along with those of other early aviators. The book is essential for anyone interested in the early development of the airplane.

Napoleão, Aluizio. *Santos-Dumont and the Conquest of the Air.* 2 vols. Translated by Luiz Victor Le Cocq d'Oliveira. Rio de Janeiro: National Printing Office, 1945. Volume 1 contains a brief history of the Santos-Dumont family, followed by a detailed factual description of Santos-Dumont's work in the development of flying machines. Volume 2 is a compilation of untranslated documents on the aeronautical accomplishments of Santos-Dumont, with some explanatory annotations in English.

Page, Joseph A. "Brazil's Daredevil of the Air." *Americas* 45, no. 2 (March/April, 1993). Profile of Santos-Dumont, his career in early aviation, his aircraft designs, and his education.

Santos-Dumont, Alberto. *My Airships: The Story of My Life.* New York: Dover, 1973. An unabridged republication of the English translation originally published in 1904 by Grant Richards in London of Santos-Dumont's *Dans l'air.* Santos-Dumont's own detailed account of how he designed, constructed, and flew each of his airships. Drawings aid the reader in understanding the problems faced by the inventor, and his descriptions of his adventures make enjoyable reading.

Villard, Henry S. *Contact!—The Story of the Early Birds.* New York: Crowell, 1968; London: Barker, 1969. An excellent history of early aviation, its participants and events, by an author who knew many of the pioneers. Contains many anecdotes that add to the enjoyment of the reader.

Wykeham, Peter. *Santos-Dumont: A Study in Obsession.* London: Putnam, 1962; New York: Harcourt Brace, 1963. This entertaining, informative, and factual book is the definitive biography of Santos-Dumont, covering every aspect of his life. The major portion, however, is devoted to his aviation-related experiments, adventures, and triumphs. The author's respect and admiration for Santos-Dumont is evident throughout.

*P. John Carter*

# NATHALIE SARRAUTE

*Born:* July 18, 1900; Ivanovo-Voznessensk, Russia
*Area of Achievement:* Literature
*Contribution:* Sarraute is often called the mother of the French New Novel. The New Novel rejected nineteenth century novelistic concerns of character and plot and changed the face of French literature. After a thirty-year career of novel writing, Sarraute began playwriting and found new success on the Parisian stage.

## Early Life

The daughter of Ilya Tcherniak, a chemist and owner of a dye factory, and Pauline Chatounowski, Sarraute was born in Russia on July 18, 1900. Her parents had met in Geneva while studying at the university; they were exiled from their native Russia because Nicholas II had barred Jewish students from attending universities in Russia. When Sarraute was two, her parents were divorced, and she began an unsettled childhood, constantly on the move between Russia, France, and Switzerland. Sarraute's own mother was a writer, who, having returned to Russia with her daughter and remarried, had published a number of novels and short stories under the male pseudonym Vichrowski. At the age of eight, Sarraute was finally settled in Paris with her father in the fourteenth arrondissement, the hub of Russian émigré activity in the city.

Through the influence of her artistic mother and the vital intellectuality provided by her father and the Russian community, Sarraute came to believe that women could equal the career success enjoyed by men. Sarraute pursued her studies in English at the Sorbonne, but she also read history at Oxford, England, and sociology at the Faculty of Letters, Berlin, before entering the University of Paris law school in 1922. While Sarraute chose to lead a highly demanding academic career, she also had a family life and, in 1925, married a fellow law student, Raymond Sarraute. Sarraute was a member of the Paris bar for twelve years, during which time she became the mother of three daughters and began her career in letters.

## Life's Work

Sarraute's first work, *Tropismes* (1938, 1957; *Tropisms*, 1963), consists of a series of sketches that received a highly positive appraisal by Jean-Paul Sartre, but this one review comprised the only critical attention for the novel. This debut work already demonstrated the theoretical and innovative approach to writing that was to set Sarraute in the forefront of contemporary artists. The sketches are fragile moments in which an observer experiences alienation from another through gestures and tones of voice. Sarraute chose the term "tropism" from the field of biochemistry to describe a preverbal, instinctive, psychic movement, as primitive and imperceptible as that of a plant's response to light and water. Overt human acts or words—often those demanded by social convention—obscure these authentic responses according to Sarraute.

After the publication of *Tropisms*, Sarraute, a Jew, spent World War II posing as a governess to her children. Despite the lack of critical attention received for *Tropisms*, Sarraute began work on *Portrait d'un inconnu* (1948; *Portrait of a Man Unknown*, 1958). Sartre wrote an introduction to this second novel, which he described as an "anti-novel" because it rejected nineteenth century concepts of plot and character. Sarraute also rejects the position of omniscient narrator in the sense that she

refuses to assume authority; her writing tends to conjure up the reader's own memories as well as creating her own imaginative world; rather than imposing her own vision through artistic manipulation, she allows room for the reader's participation in her texts.

It was not until nearly twenty years after the publication of *Tropisms*, after the publication of *Portrait of a Man Unknown* in 1948, *Martereau* (English translation, 1959) in 1953, and the popular *Le Planétarium* (1959; *The Planetarium*, 1960), that Sarraute began to receive recognition by the majority of French critics and the public. Since then, Sarraute has published a novel every four or five years: *Les Fruits d'or* (1963; *The Golden Fruits*, 1964), *Entre la vie et la mort* (1968; *Between Life and Death*, 1969), *Vous les entendez?* (1972; *Do You Hear Them?*, 1973), *"Disent les imbéciles"* (1976; *"Fools Say,"* 1977), and *L'Usage de la parole* (1980; *The Uses of Speech*, 1980).

For a relaxation between novels, Sarraute turned to playwriting in the early 1960's. She transferred the preverbal "tropisms" into dialogue, at first for the radio, then for the stage. The plays' characters use everyday, conversational language that reveals deeply hidden animosities and rivalries. In order to retain the same anonymity as her characters possess in the novels, Sarraute simply provided identifying labels such as M.1 and 2, for first and second man, for example. Among her plays are *Le Silence* (1964; *Silence*, 1981), *Le Mensonge* (1966; *The Lie*, 1981), *C'est beau* (1973; *It's Beautiful*, 1981), and *Pour un oui ou pour un non* (1982).

During the 1980's, Sarraute's work began to receive recognition by readers and critics, especially feminists, outside France. A feminist criticism tends to examine her authorial refusal to manipulate the reader as well as the autobiographical work—such as *Enfance* (1984; *Childhood*, 1984)—which she has produced. Sarraute lives a hardworking and quiet life, continuing to write and publish well into her ninth decade of life.

### Summary

While Nathalie Sarraute's writing is highly experimental, she compares herself to Fyodor Dostoevski, Gustave Flaubert, Dame Ivy Compton-Burnett, and Virginia Woolf, all exceptional creators of character and all experts in the use of irony. As her career progressed, Sarraute began to distance herself from the New Novel movement. In 1963, she added a foreword to a new edition of *Tropisms* in which she denies that she wished to suggest that humans are like plants in her use of the term "tropisms": "It obviously never occurred to me to compare human beings with insects or plants, as I have sometimes been reproached with doing." In the 1970's and 1980's, feminist criticism began to explore Sarraute's writing from more useful avenues, regarding her as a major autobiographical writer, and as a novelist with particular insight into human psychology, while pursuing the twentieth century tradition of experimentation at the level of the word. Sarraute's reputation has been enhanced since she has been viewed as separate from the very school of writing she was credited with founding.

### Bibliography

Britton, Celia. "The Self and Language in the Novels of Nathalie Sarraute." *Modern Language Review* 77 (July, 1982): 577-584. This paper argues that Sarraute's novels are about language itself and, in particular, language as used in encounters between the novels' characters.

Cismaru, Alfred. "Conversation with Nathalie Sarraute." *Telescope* 4 (Spring, 1985): 17-24. An informal interview that provides a glimpse of Sarraute's rather private life and her views on writing in general.

Henderson, Liza. "Sarraute's Silences." *Theater* 20 (Winter, 1988): 22-24. A close study of Sarraute's play *Silence*, and of the drama in general as consisting of lies and silences.

Knapp, Bettina L. "Nathalie Sarraute's Between Life and Death: Androgyny and the Creative Process." *Studies in Twentieth Century Literature* 11 (Spring, 1987): 239-252. Knapp's paper examines Sarraute's novel *Between Life and Death*, its treatment of the creative process, and its creation of an archetypal writer, who creates at the level of the word as a living thing.

Minogue, Valerie. *Nathalie Sarraute and the War of the Words: A Study of Five Novels*. Edinburgh: University of Edinburgh Press, 1981. A straightforward, in-depth study of five of Sarraute's novels with an emphasis on language. Includes an extensive bibliography. An appendix adds a letter from Sarraute herself, whose theorizing about writing is always clear and illuminating.

———. "Voices, Virtualities and Ventriloquism: Nathalie Sarraute's 'Pour un oui ou pour un non.'" *French Studies* 49 no. 2 (April, 1995). The author examines Sarraute's use of imagery and metaphor in novels and the dialogue techniques used in her plays, focusing on "Pour un oui ou pour un non."

Munley, Ellen W. "I'm Dying but It's Only Your Story: Sarraute's Reader on Stage." *Contemporary Literature* 24 (Summer, 1983): 233-258. Munley argues that Sarraute's novel *The Uses of Speech* is interested in the separation of self from others, at the same time as the self becomes confused with others.

Sarraute, Nathalie. *The Age of Suspicion.* Translated by Maria Jolas. London: Calder, and New York: Braziller, 1963. Sarraute presents her own theories of narrative method in this clear collection of essays that analyze her own writing in comparison to that of others. These theories have influenced a generation of subsequent writers of the New Novel, including Alain Robbe-Grillet and Michel Butor.

Watson-Williams, Helen. *The Novels of Nathalie Sarraute: Towards an Aesthetic.* Amsterdam: Rodopi, 1981. A full-length study of Sarraute's writings and their concern with the artistic process and the value and appreciation of art in everyday life.

*Joanne E. Butcher*

# JEAN-PAUL SARTRE

*Born:* June 21, 1905; Paris, France
*Died:* April 15, 1980; Paris, France
*Areas of Achievement:* Philosophy, literature, and social reform
*Contribution:* A powerhouse of intellectual energy, French existentialist Sartre poured out novels, plays, screenplays, biographies, criticism, political essays, and philosophy. Journalist, teacher, and perennial activist, he served in the first rank of worldwide liberal causes.

## Early Life

Jean-Paul Sartre was the only child of Anne-Marie Schweitzer and Jean-Baptiste Sartre. Jean-Baptiste had been a promising naval officer, active in several engagements in China, where he contracted the enterocolitis that killed him in September, 1906. The young widow and her son, then fifteen months old, returned to her parents' home. Charles Schweitzer, Anne-Marie's father, an overbearing intellectual, undertook the education of the precocious boy, who was soon reading voraciously and writing imitations of adventure comic books. Anne-Marie kept her son in long, golden curls. When the curls were finally cut, he recognized himself as ugly, with one eye turned out and blinded by an early illness. This ugliness and his small adult stature (five feet, two inches) fueled his self-consciousness. Formal schooling was intermittent until he was enrolled in the Lycée Henri-Quatre in 1915. After a rocky start, he was academically successful and began making friends.

In 1917, Anne-Marie remarried and moved with her son and new husband to La Rochelle. The move was unhappy for Sartre, who returned to Paris in the fall of 1920 as a boarding student. Thus began a happy period of his life. He renewed and deepened his school friendships and in 1924 entered the rigorous École Normale Supérieure. He shared an interest in philosophy with several classmates and spent hours in reading and discussion, and in the fun of movies, music, jokes, and girl-watching. Sartre loved the regimented life of all-male schools with their camaraderie and emphasis on intellectual achievement. He read widely, preferring Plato or René Descartes to his living professors. He also began to develop his own philosophical attitudes.

Probably his stubborn originality lay behind his failure at the *agrégation* in 1928. Since this competitive exam was the sole entry into the national system of secondary schools and universities, failure made a would-be academic unemployable. Sartre began a year of concentrated preparation for a retake. Early in that year, he met Simone de Beauvoir, a brilliant philosophy student also preparing for the *agrégation.* Although Sartre's romantic life was already crowded, de Beauvoir soon took the central position. They became partners, each the other's first reader and critic. They openly shared all experiences, and, although each had other lovers, they never broke with each other. They took the *agrégation* in July, 1929; Sartre took first place, de Beauvoir second.

In November, 1929, Sartre was called up for military service. Trained as a meteorologist, he spent his spare time in reading and writing. Both Sartre and de Beauvoir felt driven to put everything on paper, but neither had published when he was demobilized in February, 1931. Both accepted teaching jobs, and Sartre's unconventional style made him a favorite with students. He spent 1933-1934 in Berlin, studying the works of Martin Heidegger and the phenomenology of Edmund Husserl. Sartre finally gave up teaching for professional writing in 1945.

## Life's Work

In the years before World War II, Sartre settled into a lifelong pattern of regular hours of work, often at café tables and while traveling. Very prolific, he was unconcerned with the fate of his manuscripts, losing some and leaving several works unfinished. In the years 1937-1939, he published philosophical essays on imagination, ego, and emotions. Simultaneously, he published the novel *La Nausée* (1938; *Nausea*, 1949) and a collection of short stories, *Le Mur* (1939; *The Wall and Other Stories*, 1948). These writings were well received, in spite or because of their pessimistic view of absurd human life. Albert Camus, later a close friend, was an early, enthusiastic reviewer.

Sartre was called into active service as a meteorologist on September 2, 1939, the day after German troops invaded Poland. His military duties were minimal, and he spent most of his time writing letters, a journal, and the first draft of a novel, *L'Âge de raison* (1945; *The Age of Reason*, 1947), first of the planned tetralogy, *Les Chemins de la liberté* (1945-1949; *The Roads to Freedom*, 1947-1950). Equally important was his philosoph-

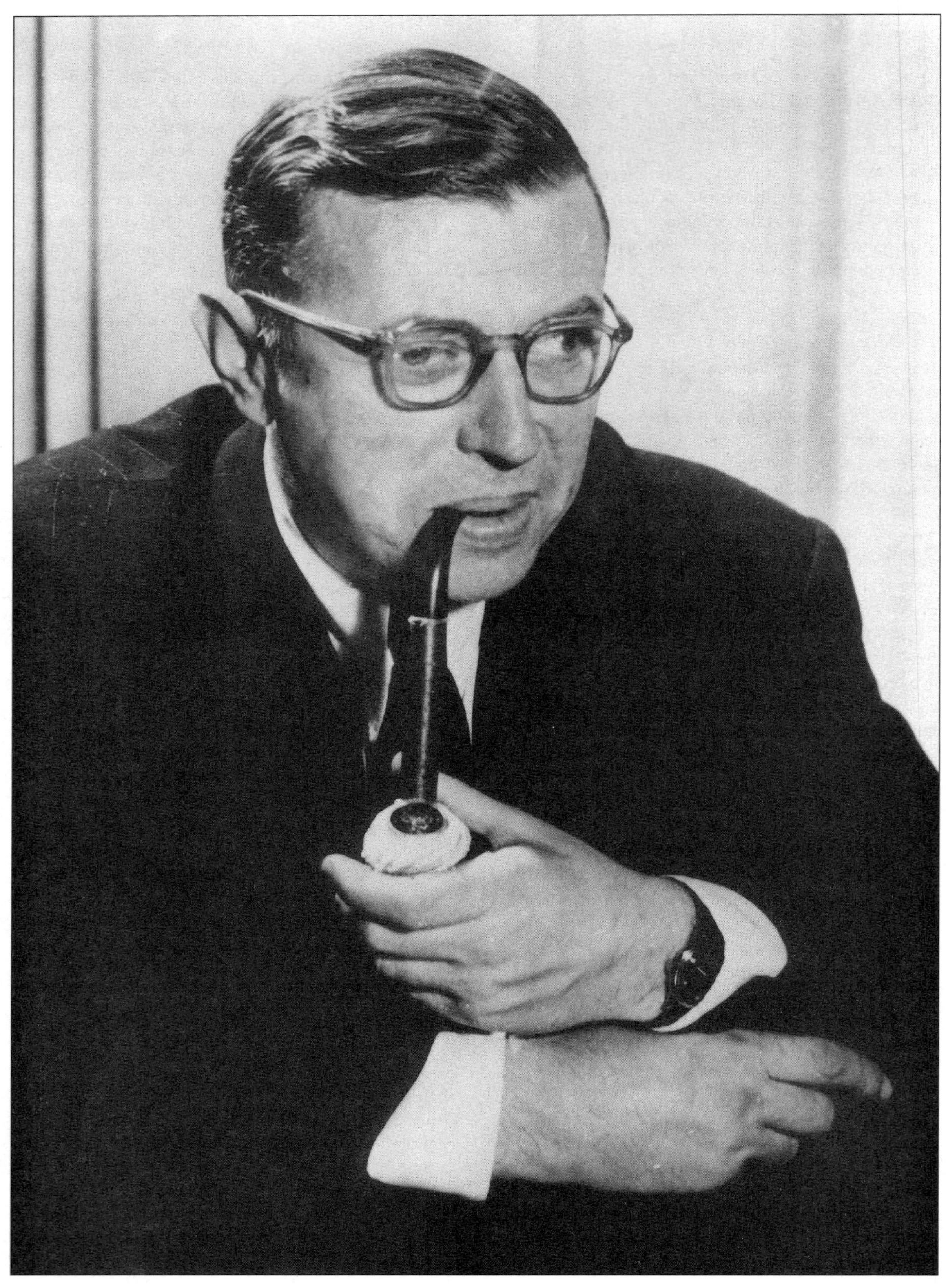

ical work *L'Être et le néant* (1943; *Being and Nothingness*, 1956), begun in the same period. In June, 1940, he was captured and sent to a German prison camp. Paradoxically, Sartre felt liberated as a prisoner. He enjoyed the solidarity of inmates against their jailers. He discussed theology and philosophy with the priests who served the camp and wrote his first play, *Bariona: Ou, Le Fils de tonnere* (1962; *Bariona: Or, The Son of Thunder*, 1970), a Christmas story published much later that camouflaged a call to resistance against foreign invasion. When he escaped in March, 1941, he returned to occupied Paris and resumed teaching.

Sartre and de Beauvoir were active in the Resistance as writers and distributors of underground material, but Sartre also continued writing philosophical and literary texts. *Being and Nothingness* was completed in October, 1942. The second novel of his tetralogy, *Le Sursis* (1945; *The Reprieve*, 1947), was finished in November, 1943. In 1943, *Les Mouches* (*The Flies*, 1946), a play based on the Greek myth of Orestes' revenge on his mother Clytemnestra, appeared in Paris, using an ancient story to mask a call to violent resistance, and passed the German censors. During rehearsals, Sartre met Camus. They became friends, and Sartre wrote for Camus's underground paper, *Combat*. In May of 1944, he presented a new play, *Huis clos* (1944; *No Exit*, 1946). The direct audience contact of the theater was congenial. As in his novels, Sartre used the conventions of plot and character to present his philosophical concepts to a wider public.

During the war, Sartre and de Beauvoir collected a family of former lovers, students, and friends who ate or starved together, with de Beauvoir coordinating the scanty rations. A social network of avant-garde artists and writers met for all-night parties in defiance of wartime curfews. Sartre, an accomplished jazz pianist, played and sang. A heavy drinker and smoker, he always preferred café atmosphere to academic circles. Shortages of food and goods meant little to him. He did not collect property. He idealized the solidarity of students, prisoners, and resistance fighters and, in the decades that followed, would yearn for and never quite recapture the euphoria of the war years. He remained on good terms with his mother and, after the death of his stepfather, shared an apartment with her from 1946 until 1961, when bomb threats made the arrangement dangerous for her. She died in January, 1969.

The end of the war coincided with Sartre's entry into full-time writing and celebrity. Between 1945 and 1965, he wrote eleven plays and filmscripts, set in times and places as disparate as occupied France and medieval Germany. He promised a study on ethics to follow *Being and Nothingness;* it never came, but many considerations of good and evil were transposed into his biography of the outlaw genius Jean Genet, *Saint Genet: Comédien et martyr* (1952; *Saint Genet: Actor and Martyr*, 1963). He published a major biographical essay entitled *Baudelaire* (English translation, 1950) in 1947, but his massive biography of Gustave Flaubert, *L'Idiot de la famille: Gustave Flaubert, 1821-1857* (3 vols., 1971-1972; *The Family Idiot: Gustave Flaubert, 1821-1857*, partial translation, 1981), was never finished. His own autobiography, *Les Mots* (1964; *The Words*, 1964), covers only the early years of his childhood. He published *La Mort dans l'âme* (1949; *Troubled Sleep*, 1950), the third volume of his tetralogy, but the projected fourth book never appeared. Even his *Critique de la raison dialectique, I: Théorie des ensembles pratiques* (1960; *Critique of Dialectical Reason I: Theory of Practical Ensembles*, 1976) was never finished, although some themes were transposed into other works. The sheer press of demands from all sides, coupled with the ferment of his ideas, made completion of these works unlikely, but their open-ended state gave an illusion of freedom; he still had the option of working on them. A series of essays, gathered in collections entitled *Situations* (1947-1976), dealt with specific issues, rather than philosophical generalizations. His emphasis was less on systematic consistency than on spontaneity of thought in relation to individual circumstances. His *Qu'est-ce que la littérature?* (1947; *What Is Literature?*, 1949) examines aesthetics, especially in literature, and makes the case for the "engaged writer," who aims at action in the world and rejects "art for art's sake."

Sartre was the most prominent of a group loosely defined under the label "existentialist," and his writings of the 1940's and 1950's most clearly define the terms of that movement in French literature, criticism, and philosophy. Sartre detested all labels. He argued that each man is responsible for himself, that the external definitions of history or religion conceal the chaos to which actions give shape, and that choice of those actions defines human liberty. To a France bowed down by the shame of defeat, existentialism offered a fresh start with a clean slate.

Immediately after the war, Sartre worked to found a new journal, *Les Temps modernes* (a bow to Charlie Chaplin), whose diverse editorial board encouraged freewheeling discussion of political and literary subjects. By the time of the French student uprisings of May, 1968, Sartre spoke a frank Maoist line and loaned his name to the editorial boards of radical underground journals, helping to distribute them in defiance of the law.

Sartre died of long-standing vascular illness on April 15, 1980. He had been virtually blind since 1973, able to work only with the help of patient friends such as de Beauvoir, who would talk with him and record his words. He had remained active, going to demonstrations and speaking at rallies, but gradually decaying flesh triumphed over will. He had been idolized and hated by a diverse, worldwide audience.

## Summary

A listing of Jean-Paul Sartre's plays, articles, biographies, philosophical studies, causes he espoused, travels, talks, demonstrations, and volatile friendships is dizzying. He declined a Nobel Prize in Literature in 1964, the first person ever to do so, because he said he preferred not to be made an institution. The example of writers of the Resistance who risked their lives in their work defined his artistic position. In a sense, Sartre always believed himself to be such a Resistance writer. As he worked for liberal causes around the world, he was never deterred by fears of ridicule. His flirtation with the French Communist Party and the governments of Cuba, the Soviet Union, and China was long-standing. A frequent apologist for Marxist movements, he still opposed oppression within the Eastern Bloc, speaking out against the Soviet use of force in Hungary and Czechoslovakia.

Sartre's ideas influenced scholars, artists, and ordinary people. The novels and plays that brought his ideas directly before the public continue to be read and studied throughout the world. Situational ethics grew out of the existentialist milieu, as did the contemporary antihero, a figure whose anguish is measured by his individual reactions to life rather than eternal standards of good and evil. Although literary and critical fashion passed him by in the 1970's, some fifty thousand people followed his funeral procession through the streets of Paris.

## Bibliography

Beauvoir, Simone de. *Adieux: A Farewell to Sartre.* Translated by Patrick O'Brian. London: Deutsch, and New York: Pantheon, 1984. A look at Sartre by his lifelong companion, de Beauvoir. If anyone can write a meaningful reflection on Sartre's life, it is de Beauvoir.

Cohen-Solal, Annie. *Sartre: A Life.* Translated by Anna Cancogni. London: Heinemann, and New York: Pantheon, 1987. A lucid, flowing account of Sartre's life, with particular attention given to the development of his interpersonal relationships. Contains illustrations, notes, a bibliography, and an index.

Gerassi, John. *Jean-Paul Sartre: Hated Conscience of His Century.* Vol 1. Chicago and London: University of Chicago Press, 1989. In a personal work, encouraged by Sartre, who knew the journalist author well, Gerassi presents the bourgeois writer on his way to revolutionary politics. The first volume covers the years before Sartre's World War II Resistance work.

Hayman, Ronald. *Sartre: A Life.* New York: Simon and Schuster, 1987. An invaluable, scholarly work, this biography focuses with particular clarity on the progression of Sartre's ideas and his changing philosophical stance. Contains illustrations, notes, a bibliography, an index, and a chronological table.

Ireland, John. "Freedom as Passion: Sartre's Mystery Plays." *Theatre Journal* 50, no. 3 (October, 1998). Considers Sartre's feelings on theater as a form of literature.

Sartre, Jean-Paul. *The Words.* Translated by Bernard Frechtman. London: Hamilton, and New York: Braziller, 1964. This autobiographical work covers the childhood years of the author, giving a hypnotic, highly impressionistic picture of his relationship to his family and to the world of words and ideas. Few hard facts, no index or bibliography, but fascinating.

Wider, Kathleen Virginia. *The Bodily Nature of Consciousness: Sartre and Contemporary Philosophy of Mind.* Ithaca, N.Y.: Cornell University Press, 1997. Wider examines Sartre's theories on consciousness, taking into account contemporary work in this area by philosophers, neuroscientists, and psychologists.

*Anne W. Sienkewicz*

# ERIK SATIE

*Born:* May 17, 1866; Honfleur, France
*Died:* July 1, 1925; Paris, France
*Area of Achievement:* Music
*Contribution:* Satie was a unique figure in French music at the beginning of the twentieth century. In the 1890's he played an important role in turning French music away from the influence of nineteenth century German Romanticism. During and after World War I, he was the major composer of the French avant-garde; he turned away from Impressionism, in which he never really took part, and prefigured the neoclassicism of the 1940's and 1950's.

## Early Life

Erik Satie was born in a coastal town in the Normandy region of France to Jules Alfred Satie, a marine broker, and Jane Leslie Anton, a Scotswoman. In 1870, at the close of the Franco-Prussian War, the family moved to Paris. When Satie's mother died two years later, he and his brother and sister returned to Honfleur to live with their grandparents, who reared them in a strict Catholic tradition. Satie attended school in Honfleur with little distinction.

In 1874, Satie's grandfather started him in piano lessons with a church organist, who introduced the boy to liturgical music, particularly Gregorian chant; this exposure influenced the full range of Satie's later work. Another notable influence at this time was an eccentric uncle, nicknamed the Sea Bird because he spent much of his time sitting in a beautifully outfitted boat that never left the dock. The Sea Bird also took young Satie to see traveling circuses and acting troupes, and the boy got a glimpse backstage while the uncle pursued various female performers.

Satie's music teacher left Honfleur in 1878, the same year his grandmother died, and shortly thereafter he returned to live with his father in Paris. At this point all aspects of his formal education languished except for music. In 1879, he entered a preparatory class at the Paris Conservatoire and began auditioning for the regular piano class. For the next seven years, he continued to take the biannual examinations with no success. In November of 1885 he finally passed the entrance exam for the intermediate class, where he spent a year working under an intolerant teacher. Throughout his conservatory experience, Satie's teachers took note of his natural talent but chastised him for laziness.

Part way through his second year of the intermediate class, Satie dropped out and volunteered for military service. This allowed him to shorten the customary five years' compulsory service to one year, but he ended his military career even earlier with a self-inflicted case of bronchitis. While convalescing he began to sketch out the *Trois Gymnopédies* and *Trois Sarabandes*, his earliest significant compositions. Later that year, 1887, Satie left his father's home and settled at the foot of Montmartre, the Bohemian section of Paris. The following year he began playing piano at the Chat Noir, a Montmartre café, and he assumed the full costume and role of a bohemian eccentric.

## Life's Work

While earning a living as a café pianist, Satie also began his career as a serious composer. With the *Trois Gymnopédies*, which he finished in 1888, and the *Trois Gnossiennes* of 1890, he prefigured many of the harmonic innovations of Claude Debussy and Maurice Ravel at a time when the German Romanticism of Johannes Brahms and Richard Wagner still dominated European music. These early works for piano combine exoticism and awkwardness into a simple but purely original style, and they set a pattern for Satie's career by anticipating popular taste by at least ten years. In fact the *Gymnopédies* did not achieve their full initial popularity until 1911.

Satie's early fascination with the mysticism and ritual of the Catholic church drew him to a brief affiliation with the Rosicrucian sect in 1890, and over the next two years he composed incidental music and fanfares for their elaborate ceremonies. He then disassociated himself from the group, but his affinity for religious pomp reasserted itself in the next few years in the form of the "Metropolitan Church of the Art of Jesus the Conductor," an imaginary institution under the auspices of which Satie published attacks on his perceived enemies and rivals in the Paris music scene. A small inheritance in 1892 allowed him to indulge such fantasies with increased vigor. He proposed himself three times for the Institut de France, an impossible honor for an obscure bohemian in his twenties, and he maintained a pose of complete seriousness throughout, all the while mocking the prosperous bourgeois self-importance of such established institutions. Thus Satie carried the bohemian ethos to fulfillment.

While performing in the cafés of Montmartre, Satie met many of the painters and poets of the artistic avant-garde that flourished in Paris from the 1890's through the 1920's. In later years, he acknowledged having spent more time with and learned more from painters than musicians. In 1891, however, while playing at the Auberge du Clou, Satie met Debussy and began a close friendship that would last thirty years. The two composers influenced each other, particularly at the beginning of their friendship, as they attempted to find a new direction for a more uniquely French music than was then being composed. Debussy had already achieved some renown as a composer, but his wider experience had exposed him to more of the Wagnerian influence then prevalent. Satie played an important role in Debussy's career by liberating his more famous friend from that tendency. Satie also met the young Ravel in the 1890's and exercised a similar influence on his development. These two composers went on to create Impressionism in music, drawing in part from Satie's earliest work.

Satie's stylistic development moved in a different direction. His music reached the height of its liturgical phase with the *Messe des pauvres* (1895) and then returned to the simplicity and playfulness of his earlier work with *Pièces froides* (1897). A year later, he moved across Paris from Montmartre to the obscure suburb of Arcueil-Cachan, where he lived in a second-floor flat over a bistro called The Four Chimneys. Although he still composed and performed popular songs in Montmartre to make his living—and in fact he made the six-mile walk twice a day—he essentially shut himself off from the frenzy of artistic activity in his former neighborhood and retreated into solitude. Over the next twelve years, Satie composed very little work of importance, and his grandiose public gestures ceased. The most notable composition of these years is *Trois Morceaux en forme de poire* (three pieces in the shape of a pear), his most ambitious work for piano. Debussy is said to have advised Satie to pay more attention to form in his composition; Satie supposedly responded to his friend's advice with *Trois Morceaux en forme de poire*, a formless piece having no relation to pears or to the number three. In fact the work is a twenty-minute conglomeration of short pieces spanning the previous fifteen years of Satie's career. In it he combined the style of his popular songs with the modal and harmonic characteristics of his more serious liturgical work.

Satie laid the foundation for the second half of his career when, nearing the age of forty and against Debussy's advice, he returned to school. In 1905, he entered the Schola Cantorum, a music school founded ten years earlier by Vincent d'Indy, and he studied counterpoint under Albert Roussel for the next three years. Satie was a diligent student; he worked with seriousness and deep conviction, and this time he earned the admiration of his teachers. Upon graduating in 1908, he received a diploma entitling him to pursue a life of composition, but at first Satie composed nothing at all. Rather, he devoted his energies in the winter of 1908-1909 to local affairs in his neighborhood of Arcueil. He joined the local Radical-Socialist Party, gave music lessons to his neighbors, and wrote a column in the local newspaper.

Satie put aside his civic activities in 1910 and returned to composition. Following his intense study of counterpoint, he now wrote in a spare, linear, contrapuntal style. His titles grew increasingly grotesque, as in *Embryons desséchés* (dried embryos), and his directions on interpretation began to mock those of Debussy: "Like a nightingale with a toothache," for example. He grew increasingly playful and humorous with the running commentary of text in his piano works: A musical quote from Chopin's funeral march appears in *Embryons desséchés* deliberately mislabeled as "a well-known mazurka by Schubert."

At the same time, Satie began to receive recognition for the compositions of his youth. Ravel and Debussy both presented such early works as *Trois Gymnopédies* in performance in 1911, praising Satie for anticipating Impressionism. The critics began to mention him favorably, and publishers began requesting new compositions. Satie's style had changed, however, and the work he submitted in response was rejected. He found it bewildering that twenty-year-old works previously considered simplistic were now considered charming, while the works he now composed were considered too complex, too academic. Ultimately Satie ignored the fashion and continued to write what have become known as his humoristic works. This period culminated in *Sports et divertissements*, a collection of twenty fragments that combines poetry, painting, and Satie's exquisite calligraphy with his music.

In 1915, the young poet Jean Cocteau heard Satie perform *Trois Morceaux* and was moved to propose a collaboration on a ballet with Sergei Diaghilev, the producer of the Ballets Russes. Pablo Picasso designed the sets and costumes, and Satie wrote a score that included parts for typewriters, sirens, and similar effects. The result was *Parade*, a rendering of cubism in music and choreography, premiered in 1917. The first performance caused a minor uproar in the audience, and Satie is said to have joined in the whistling from his seat in the balcony. The critics responded with such hostility that Satie sent one critic an insulting postcard and wound up with a damage suit that led to a stiff fine and a week's prison sentence; he avoided prison only with the urgent intercession of his friends.

*Parade* established Satie's reputation as an opponent of Impressionism and a friend to the newer schools. When Dubussy, now an invalid and nearing the end of his life, neglected to send Satie any congratulations over *Parade*, Satie took offense. As far back as the 1890's, Satie had been known for quarreling with his friends over imagined slights, and this was no exception. He wrote Debussy a reproachful letter in 1918, the year Debussy died. The two friends were never reconciled, and Satie later regretted this last falling out.

At this point Satie began to collect a following of his own; a group of young French musicians, later dubbed "Les Six," including Francis Poulenc and Darius Milhaud, were attracted as much by Satie's personality as by his music. Satie was amazed by this; he asked their advice, quarreled with them, but refused to assume the role of master of a school.

As the critics began to recognize the importance of *Parade*, Satie turned to a new form. His next major composition, *Socrate* (1919), was a musical setting of the *Dialogues* of Plato for chamber orchestra. Often called Satie's masterpiece, *Socrate* is the culmination of his spare, linear conception of music. Satie anticipated its reception with a note in the program for its premiere: "Those who are unable to understand are requested to adopt an attitude of complete submission and inferiority." In fact, part of the audience giggled at its apparent monotony, and the critics responded with both praise and scorn.

A few months later, in March of 1920, Satie engaged in an experiment with "furniture music," an idea that originated with the artist Henri Matisse, who envisioned an art without subject matter, an art similar in function to a comfortable easy-chair. At the intermission of a play by Max Jacob being performed in an art gallery, Satie and Milhaud had musicians dispersed about the gallery start playing rhythmic but purposefully inconsequential music. The audience was instructed to ignore the music, to treat it as merely a background. Thus Satie was disappointed when the audience ignored his instructions and kept silent; he rushed about the gallery, urging them to talk, move around, make noise, but not listen.

Satie further developed this approach to music several years later with background music for a Surrealist film by Renè Clair, which formed the entr'acte of his ballet *Relâche* (1924). Here the function of the music was to underline the action of the film indirectly, without drawing attention to itself. *Relâche*, subtitled *Ballet instantanéiste* (instantaneous ballet), was Satie's last work. The performance included dancers smoking cigarettes, a fireman wandering through the set, and costume changes on stage. Satie's music elicited heckling and laughter: His prelude was based on an indecent student song, and the rest was considered dull. At the end of the premiere, Satie drove on stage in a tiny automobile to take his bow. Like *Parade*, the performance was considered scandalous, and, true to form, Satie ignored the response.

Shortly thereafter Satie grew ill with cirrhosis of the liver. The illness lasted for six months, during which time he refused to see most of the old friends with whom he had quarreled, and he died in St. Joseph Hospital on July 1, 1925.

## Summary

Erik Satie has never been considered more than a minor composer. His collected works would make a slim volume, and most of his individual compositions are very short. Even now only a handful of his early piano works are regularly performed. Yet his contributions to the development of Western music in the early twentieth century are considerable. Tonal music over the preceding centuries had used chords to create motion, as one chord implies motion to another related chord. Satie ignored that tradition; he was one of the first to use chords as isolated sonorities, with no need to move in any given direction. Starting from this harmonic conception, Debussy developed a style of great complexity, while Satie's music always retained an apparent simplicity, ever avoiding grand, transcendent sentiment. Often his work took the form of parody, not only of Romanticism but also of Impressionism; in his more serious work he stripped his music of all pretension, revealing austere essence. Thus, while Debussy's music has been compared to the works of the Impressionist painters, the sonorities of his chords resembling their brushtrokes, critics have compared Satie's *Trois Gymnopèdies*, for example, to the cubist still-life paintings of Picasso and Georges Braque, not only for the motionlessness of his harmonies but also because the three movements seem to take three different perspectives on the same theme, just as the painters view their subjects from different angles and superimpose the images.

These qualities in his music combined with his eccentric social behavior, his ability to ignore current fashion and anticipate future styles, and his emphasis on graphics and textual elements to put him at the center of the Parisian avant-garde after 1910. Ultimately he outpaced the avant-garde as well: A play he wrote in 1913, *La Piège de Meduse*, anticipated the Dada movement by eight years, and it was unearthed and celebrated by the Dadaists in 1921. His later music, with its clarity, simplicity, and wit, influenced Poulenc, Milhaud, and beyond them the American neoclassical composer Virgil Thomson. The same attributes in Satie's personality set an example for the entire artistic avant-garde.

## Bibliography

Gillmor, Alan M. *Erik Satie.* London: Macmillan, and Boston: Twayne, 1988. Gillmor's biography of Satie derives mostly from Myers' (see below), but his musical analysis is excellent, providing a clear, concise, and readable discussion of technical issues. Includes a bibliography, a chronology of Satie's life, a list of works, and an excellent discography.

Harding, James. *Erik Satie.* London: Secker and Warburg, and New York: Praeger, 1975. In this biography Harding vividly portrays the spirit of Satie's times, focusing particularly on the years leading up to his collaboration with Cocteau and Diaghilev. Smoothly written and very readable, the book includes a bibliography and a catalog of Satie's published works and writings.

Myers, Rollo H. *Erik Satie.* London: Dobson, 1948; New York: Dover, 1968. This monograph was the first biography of Satie available in the English language. Short but comprehensive, it provides a balanced portrait of his life and a general introduction to his music.

Orledge, Robert. "Satie's Sarabandes and Their Importance to His Composing Career." *Music and Letters* 77, no. 4 (November, 1996). The author examines Satie's "Sarabandes," its importance to Satie's career, and the techniques used in the composition.

———. "Understanding Satie's 'Vexations.'" *Music and Letters* 79, no. 3 (August, 1998). Analysis of Satie's "Vexations," written during the break-up of a love affair.

Shattuck, Roger. *The Banquet Years: The Origin of the Avant-Garde in France, 1885 to World War I.* Rev. ed. New York: Vintage Books, 1968; London: Cape, 1969. This social history provides a detailed analysis of the French avant-garde, focusing on four of its members: the painter Henri Rousseau, the poets Alfred Jarry and Guillaume Apollinaire, and Satie. Shattuck's approach is scholarly and incisive. Includes illustrations and a bibliography with a list of principal works and published writings.

Templier, Pierre Daniel. *Erik Satie.* Translated by Elena L. French and David S. French. Cambridge, Mass.: MIT Press, 1969. This translation of the first biography of Satie, originally published in France in 1932, provides an excellent starting point. Templier gives a sympathetic analysis of Satie's character and a general description of his music. Written mostly from primary sources, the book contains excellent documentation as well as an extensive selection of Satie's illustrations and drawings, a discography, and a few pages from his original scores in sixty pages of plates.

*John Neil Ries*

# EISAKU SATŌ

*Born:* March 27, 1901; Tabuse, Japan
*Died:* June 2, 1975; Tokyo, Japan
*Areas of Achievement:* Government and politics
*Contribution:* Satō served consecutively as Prime Minister of Japan longer than any other individual. He is the only modern Japanese politician to expand the country permanently. One of the founders of the Liberal-Democratic Party, he not only followed its traditional probusiness policy but also tripled the per capita income of the Japanese. In 1974, he became the first Asian to receive the Nobel Peace Prize.

## Early Life

Eisaku Satō was born to a samurai family in Tabuse, Yamaguchi Prefecture, in southwestern Japan, far from the center of power. The family, however, was one of the leaders in that area, and his two elder brothers also became famous. The eldest was Ichiro, who ultimately became a vice admiral in the Japanese navy. The second son was adopted by his wife's family and took the name of Nobusuke Kishi. He served as Prime Minister of Japan from 1957 to 1960.

Satō was born on March 27, 1901. Relatives at first considered him as the most personable of the brothers but the least intelligent, which was not a large slight in a brilliant family. He attended the Fifth Higher School in Kumamoto (essentially a combination high school and junior college). One of the other graduates was Satō's immediate predecessor as prime minister, Hayato Ikeda.

Satō then entered the Imperial University at Tokyo (Todai), the traditional school for governmental and top business leaders in Japan. He received a law degree in 1924. His classmates included six other members of the diet, one supreme court justice, three bank presidents, Fuji Iron and Steel president Nagasno, and *Sankei Shimbun* (newspaper) president Mizuno. The latter two formed half of Satō's Koba Chu quartet, giving him in effect a joint chiefs of staff relationship to the business community during his prime ministership.

Immediately upon graduation, Satō joined the Ministry of Railways (later Transportation), for which he held a number of administrative positions. In 1926, he married the niece of the president of the Manchurian Southern Railroad. It was a typical arranged marriage, and his wife said it took her ten years to understand him. They had two sons, Roataru and Shingi, the latter of whom has a close marital relationship to Michiko, Empress of Japan. From August, 1934, to April, 1936, Satō was on a study tour of the United States, learning railroad operations and business methods. In both 1938 and 1939, he was sent to China to direct railroad construction. During World War II, he continued to operate in the ministry, trying to keep transportation going during wartime. Satō remained a part of the Asian Study Group throughout his political career.

## Life's Work

At the end of the Pacific War, Satō was not imprisoned, as was his second brother, who had served in the Tōjō cabinet. Fortunately, Satō was still at the subdirector level, whose members mostly escaped imprisonment. In 1945, he was named director of the Osaka District Railway Bureau and then vice minister of transportation in 1947. His efficiency in dealing with the construction led him to the attention of Prime Minister Shigeru Yoshida, who named him cabinet secretary in 1948. The next year he was elected to the diet as a member of the Liberal Party. Working well with the liberal, pro-United States Yoshida (the U.S. installed prime minister), Satō also served as minister of posts and telecommunications and as minister of construction. In 1953, he became the secretary-general of the Liberal Party. By now he was displaying the ability to work well with all factions in politics, which was one of his greatest assets.

In 1954, the *zosen gigoku* scandal rocked Japanese politics. Several shipping companies were accused of giving kickbacks and bribes to government officials and party leaders in return for government contracts and subsidies. Satō was involved, and a warrant was issued for his arrest; yet Prime Minister Yoshida had his minister of justice order that Satō not be arrested. Later in the year, however, Satō was indicted on charges of violating the Public Funds Regulation Law, but the case was dropped in 1956 as a part of a general amnesty celebrating Japan's entry into the United Nations. Meanwhile, in 1955, Satō had been one of the founding members of the Liberal-Democratic Party (LDP), emerging in 1957 as the head of his own faction in the party.

In 1957, Satō's brother Kishi became prime minister, and the next year brought Satō back into the cabinet as minister of finance. Satō and Kishi both strongly supported Prime Minister Ikeda from 1960 to 1964, and Satō served as minister of international trade and industry at a time when Japan was vastly increasing its international efforts. The climactic effort of Satō's early career was the directorship of the Tokyo Olympics, which is considered to be the extravaganza that notified the world of the reemergence of Japan as a major power. Certainly it was quite successful for Satō.

On July 10, 1964, Satō challenged the incumbent Ikeda for the LDP presidency and prime ministership. Also in the race was Aiichiro Fujiyama. The election was close and hard-fought, but Ikeda was reelected. Yet the fellow graduate of the Fifth Higher School in Kumamoto was stricken with terminal cancer. In October, Ikeda announced his decision to resign. There was great concern in two areas. The LDP members in the diet feared another acrimonious election. Furthermore the *zaikai*, or leaders of the community of large businesses, were fearful of both of the other major contenders, Fujiyama and Kono. Consequently the secretary-general of the party and the vice president of the party were allowed to choose the successor through consultation. Ikeda announced on November 9, 1964, that the sole candidate for the party presidency was Satō, and he was unanimously elected to begin the longest single term of any Japanese prime minister, serving until July 6, 1972.

During his prime ministership, Satō was always closely aligned with the business community, which gave him strong support and advice. The leading business club was the Choeikai, made up of approximately fifty presidents, vice presidents, and chairmen of big corporations, including the Bank of Japan, the Fuji Bank, Mitsubishi Heavy Industry, Hitachi Shipbuilding, Sony, Tokyo Gas, and Nissan, among others. The club was coheaded by the vice president of Tokyo Gas, who was the father of Satō's daughter-in-law. Yet Satō was highly unusual in one way in his relationship to business, which was a long-term LDP policy. He had approximately twenty clubs, which included a total of 280 different members from business. Even his elder brother Kishi had been unable to maintain such a pace. In fact, older *zaikai* members were quite unhappy at times with this larger advisory group, even saying that their era had ended. It was during Satō's regime, however, that *Time* magazine named the combination of business, bureaucracy, and legislative/executive leadership in Japan "Japan, Inc." Certainly, Japanese business continued to prosper and expand under the Satō administration, but it was a Japanese business of far greater diversification.

One of Satō's main interests was in party politics. He was reelected as prime minister three more times in 1966, 1968, and 1970. Only during the first election was there serious opposition, and he beat Fujiyama by 289 to 94 with 81 other scattered votes. Quickly he became known as Satō the "personnel manager" for his ability to see that each of the factions in the party, of which his was the largest, had a stake in the jobs available in the government.

As for any politician, domestic activities were extremely important to Satō. One of his major efforts was to persuade the businesses of Japan, in exchange for continued governmental assistance, to liberalize their pay policy. The average factory worker's pay went from $500 to $1,500 annually, making this a very prosperous period for the worker in Japan. Satō also increased the governmental support for the national health insurance and the rice subsidy for the farmers. Always interested in transportation, he extended the Shinkansen (bullet train) line from Ōsaka to Okayama between 1967 and 1972. Discovering that Haneda (Tokyo International) Airport was seriously overcrowded, he originated in 1966 the new Tokyo International Airport Authority, which began construction at the farming village of Narita, Chiba Prefecture, about forty miles east of Tokyo in 1969. Serious opposition developed among both local residents and the opposition parties, which led to riots and eventual suspension of construction in 1971. Eventually, the airport was completed in 1978, after Satō's death.

Satō's policy concerning atomic weapons was extremely popular in Japan. It was named Hikaku Sangensoku, or "three nonnuclear principles," and called for nonmanufacturing of atomic weapons in Japan, nonpossession of atomic weapons by Japan, and nonintroduction into Japan of atomic weapons. The latter policy, though widely popular in Japan, led to problems with the United States at times, particularly over the reversion of Okinawa to Japan. The sponsorship of the Ōsaka International Exposition (World's Fair) in 1970 was also considered a great success. These policies made Satō extremely popular in Japan and allowed him to win general elections in 1967 and 1970.

Satō is best known for his foreign policies. He was always interested in Asia, and one of his first policies was to normalize relationships with South Korea, a policy that was popular in the United States also. He also made a commitment of $800 million to build up Korea's economy. In 1967, he made two visits to Southeast Asia and began assistance to several countries there. His China policy, however, was an anomaly. Though he had expressed interest in normalized relationships earlier, his original policy was support of the isolation of China, similar to that of the United States. In 1971, however, when Richard Nixon went to China, Satō and the Japanese government were not informed of the trip, and it created what was called the Nixon Shocks. This policy seemed a great affront to a loyal ally and was considered a possible hindrance in the continuation of normal relationships. Yet Satō loyally continued to support the United States.

Much of this continued support related to the policy of reversion of Okinawa and the Ryukyu Islands. First acquired by Japanese rulers in the 1600's, the Ryukyus had come under complete Japanese control in 1895. They had been occupied by U.S. forces in 1945 and not returned to Japan. Satō made it his policy from the first to obtain their reversion. At first he was unwilling to allow continued U.S. bases there but soon relented as long as atomic weapons were not allowed. In 1968, unable to effect a treaty for these islands, he obtained a reversion of the Bonin Islands, sixty miles south of Tokyo. The next year, Nixon and Satō signed a reversion agreement for the Ryukyus, which became completely Japanese on May 15, 1972.

Having obtained the desired foreign policy result that made him the only modern Japanese politician to expand the country permanently, Satō retired on July 6, 1972. One final honor, however, awaited him. In 1974, Satō was named a cowinner, with Sean MacBride of Ireland, of the Nobel Peace Prize. Several reasons were cited for his selection, the most notable being his nonnuclear policy. Also important were his Southeast Asia support, his support for the denunciation of war as set out in the 1947 constitution of Japan, and the reversion of the Okinawa area peacefully to Japan. The honor was almost as much that of Japan as it was of Satō, since he was the first Asian to receive the Nobel Peace Prize. In his acceptance speech, Satō emphasized the ordinary people's portion in peace with their activities in art, culture, and religion, among other things, and saw himself as a practical politician who wanted to achieve policies peacefully and warned of nuclear dangers. Satō died in Tokyo on June 2, 1975.

## Summary

Eisaku Satō was a Japanese bureaucrat from a prominent country family who served continuously as prime minister from November, 1964, to July, 1972, longer than any other man in his country's history. His greatest success was in the acquisition of the Ryukyu and Bonin islands for his country; he became the only modern Japanese politician to expand Japan permanently. He was also quite successful in expanding his country's gross national product through an alliance with business, while at the same time tripling the average worker's salary. He also normalized relationships with nearby South Korea and began the policy of assistance to less developed nations. The climax of his career was the receipt of the 1974 Nobel Peace Prize.

## Bibliography

Eiji, Tominomori. "Satō's Legacy." *Japan Quarterly* 19, no. 2 (1972): 154-159. This is a summary article mostly interested in Satō's foreign policy, written just before his retirement.

Gray, Tony. *Champions of Peace*. New York: Paddington Press, 1976. This work has the best article on Satō and the Nobel Peace Prize.

Kim, Hong N. "The Satō Government and the Politics of Okinawa Reversion." *Asian Survey* 13, no. 11 (1973): 1021-1035. This article summarizes well the politics involved in persuading the United States to accept the reversion of the Ryukyus and the Japanese diet that it was permissible for the Americans to retain their bases.

Thayer, Nathaniel B. *How the Conservatives Rule Japan*. Princeton, N.J.: Princeton University Press, 1969. Written during Satō's administration, this book best summarizes Satō's political policies.

Yanaga, Chitoshi. *Big Business in Japanese Politics*. New Haven, Conn.: Yale University Press, 1968. This book, also written during Satō's administration, illustrates well his election by business and his policies toward business.

Yasutomo, Dennis T. "Satō's China Policy." *Asian Survey* 17, no. 6 (1977): 530-544. This article is mostly interested in the early China policy before the Nixon Shocks.

*Fred S. Rolater*

# FERDINAND DE SAUSSURE

*Born:* November 26, 1857; Geneva, Switzerland
*Died:* February 22, 1913; Vufflens, near Geneva, Switzerland
*Areas of Achievement:* Language and linguistics
*Contribution:* Primarily through a book written by colleagues after his death, Saussure established the foundations of twentieth century linguistics. His focus on the systematic structure of language is the fundamental principle of structuralism in linguistics, anthropology, and literary criticism, and he provided the theoretical basis of semiology—the study of signs.

## Early Life

When Ferdinand de Saussure was enrolled in chemistry and physics courses at the University of Geneva in 1875, he was following a tradition long established on his father's side of the family. Ferdinand's great-grandfather was Horace-Bénédict de Saussure, a famous scientist; his grandfather was professor of geology and mineralogy; and his father, Henri, had a doctorate in geology. Ferdinand, too, was to become a scientist, but it was the science of linguistics that captured his attention at an early age.

Adolf Pictet, a friend of the family, and Count Alexandre-Joseph de Pourtalès, Ferdinand's maternal grandfather, encouraged the young boy to study languages. By the age of twelve, Ferdinand had read chapters of Pictet's book on linguistic paleontology. He knew French, German, English, and Latin, and he began Greek at the age of thirteen. The year before entering the university, the young Saussure, on Pictet's advice, studied Sanskrit from a book by the German scholar Franz Bopp.

Saussure's career in physics and chemistry lasted for only two semesters. During that time, he continued his studies of Greek and Latin and joined the Linguistic Society of Paris. By autumn 1876, he had transferred to the University of Leipzig in Germany. For the next four semesters, Saussure attended courses in comparative grammar, history of the German language, Sanskrit, Greek, Old Persian, Celtic, Slavic languages, and Lithuanian. His teachers were the leading figures of the time in historical and comparative linguistics, including, among the younger generation, the "Neogrammarians," scholars of Indo-European who established the famous principle that sound changes in the historical development of languages operate without exception.

In the Leipzig environment of August Leskien, Hermann Osthoff, and Karl Brugmann, Saussure wrote extensively, publishing several papers through the Linguistic Society of Paris. At age twenty-one, in 1878, he produced the monograph that was to be the most famous work of his lifetime, *Mémoire sur le système primitif des voyelles dans les langues indo-européennes* (1879; memoir on the original system of the vowels in the Indo-European languages). When it appeared, he was in Berlin studying Sanskrit. Returning to Leipzig in 1880, he received his doctoral degree with honors.

## Life's Work

Saussure's *Mémoire sur le système primitif des voyelles dans les langues indo-européennes* was a daring reconstruction of an aspect of proto-Indo-European which was met in Germany with little understanding, even with hostility. Yet the work was very well received in France; in the fall of 1880, Saussure moved to Paris. He attended courses in classical languages, lectures by the leading

French linguist Michel Bréal, and meetings of the Linguistic Society of Paris. The next year, on October 30, 1881, with Bréal's strong support, he was unanimously named lecturer in Gothic and Old High German at the École des Hautes Études. His lifelong career as a teacher began a week later.

Saussure's courses dealt primarily with comparative grammar of the Germanic languages, but he was highly critical of the earlier nineteenth century German tradition in such studies. Comparison of individual words in different languages or over time within one language seemed to him haphazard, unfruitful, and unscientific. In his *Mémoire sur le système primitif des voyelles dans les langues indo-européennes*, he had used the notion of a language as a structured system in which all forms are interrelated, and this fundamental concept had led him to hypothesize forms in Indo-European that had disappeared in the languages for which there were historical records. It was a half century after the publication of the *Mémoire sur le système primitif des voyelles dans les langues indo-européennes* that evidence was discovered in Hittite proving him correct.

At the École des Hautes Études, Saussure's courses attracted substantial numbers of students, and, with Bréal, he set the foundation for comparative grammar in France. He taught Sanskrit, Latin, and Lithuanian as well, and some of his students and disciples became the most prominent French linguists of the early twentieth century. One of these, Antoine Meillet, was later to emphasize the intellectual excitement and commitment generated by Saussure in his classes. So engrossed was Saussure in his teaching during the Paris years that his publications became increasingly infrequent, but he was greatly admired, and when he left the École des Hautes Études for a position at the University of Geneva in the winter of 1891, his French colleagues nominated him for the Cross of the Legion of Honor.

At Geneva, too, students and colleagues were devoted to Saussure and committed to his teachings. Were it not for this dedication, there would be little more to say about Saussure. He married Marie Faesch; they had two sons. He entirely ceased to publish, rarely traveled, and attended only a few local scholarly meetings. From 1891 until 1899, he taught primarily comparative grammar and Sanskrit, adding a course on French verse in 1899; once in 1904, he taught a course on German legends.

Between 1906 and 1909, he conducted research on a topic that some scholars have called "esoteric"; others, more direct, labeled it "strange." Saussure believed that he had found "hidden texts" within Latin verse—deliberately concealed proper names, relevant to the meaning and repeated throughout the poems, whose spellings could be detected distributed among the words of the verse. He called these "anagrams," and he compiled more than a hundred notebooks of examples. He abandoned this work, without publishing a single paper on the topic, after receiving no response from a contemporary poet to whom he had written seeking confirmation of this poetic device.

The work on anagrams seems to have been an escape from Saussure's overriding preoccupation—probing the very foundations of the science of linguistics. Toward the end of his life, he confided to a former student that he had added nothing to his theory of language since the early 1890's, yet he struggled with the subject off and on for many years. At the University of Geneva, his teaching responsibilities for fifteen years in specific languages and comparative grammar precluded the incorporation of his general linguistic theory into his lectures. Then, in December, 1906, upon the retirement of another faculty member, Saussure was assigned to teach a course on general linguistics and the history and comparison of the Indo-European languages. He accepted the assignment reluctantly.

The course was offered three times, in alternate academic years. The first offering, in 1907, was actually only half a year, and Saussure focused almost entirely on the historical dimension. Five or six students were enrolled. In 1908-1909, there were eleven students, and, again, the emphasis was on the historical study of languages, although this time Saussure did begin with more general topics. For 1910-1911, Saussure spent the entire first semester on general linguistic theory. There were a dozen students in the course. Before he could teach the course again, Saussure fell ill in the summer of 1912. He died near Geneva on February 22, 1913, at the country home of his wife's family.

Two of Saussure's colleagues at the University of Geneva gathered the few lecture notes that Saussure had not destroyed and collected course notes from students who had attended his classes in general linguistics. Using the third offering of the course as a base, Charles Bally and Albert Sechehaye attempted "a reconstruction, a synthesis" of Saussure's thought on the science of linguistics. First published in 1916, Saussure's *Cours de linguistique générale* (1916; *Course in General Linguistics*, 1959) initially received mixed reviews and relatively little attention.

In Europe, Saussure's views on linguistics, as represented in *Course in General Linguistics*, were discussed and adopted, often with alterations, only among members of the Copenhagen, Moscow, and Prague Linguistic Circles. It was not until the 1930's that *Course in General Linguistics* had any significant effect on linguistics in France. In the United States, little attention was paid to Saussure's work until the 1941 arrival in New York of Roman Jakobson, a founding member of the Linguistic Circles of both Moscow and Prague. In the development of the discipline of linguistics, Saussure has been more acknowledged in retrospect than followed directly.

### Summary

In *Course in General Linguistics*, Ferdinand de Saussure made a sharp distinction between what he termed synchronic linguistics and diachronic linguistics. The latter is the study of change in language; to a great extent, diachronic work had dominated the nineteenth century. Synchronic linguistics, however, concentrates on a static view of language, as it exists for speakers at a particular point in time, and this became the major focus of twentieth century linguistics, particularly in the United States. Saussure also maintained that the proper object of study in linguistics should be not the actual speech of individual members of a linguistic community (which he labeled *parole*) but rather the common code, the language (*langue*), that they share. This distinction became so widely recognized that Saussure's original French terms are still in international use.

Of all the concepts for which Saussure is now known, however, the most influential has been his view of a language as a system of signs, each of which is meaningful and important only in terms of its relationships to the other signs in the system. This system of relationships constitutes a structure, and it is this notion that is the foundation of twentieth century structuralism not only in linguistics but also in anthropology and literary criticism.

In his discussion of signs, Saussure proposed that linguistics was only one dimension of a broader science of the study of signs that he called "semiology." Referred to as semiotics in the United States, this field has been all but ignored by linguists, but for many nonlinguists the name of Saussure is intricately intertwined with semiology. It is interesting, therefore, to note that semiology is mentioned in less than a dozen paragraphs in the entire *Course in General Linguistics*.

*Course in General Linguistics* has been the subject of numerous commentaries, and scholars have explored the origins of Saussure's ideas and compared the work with the notes from which it was constructed. This research shows that some of the concepts often credited to Saussure may have their origins with other nineteenth century scholars, and there has been a continuing debate about the "authenticity" of the work in representing Saussure's views. Regardless of these findings, the assessment of Saussure provided in a 1924 review of *Course in General Linguistics* by the great American linguist Leonard Bloomfield has been confirmed by the twentieth century: "He has given us the theoretical basis for a science" of language.

### Bibliography

Culler, Jonathan. *Ferdinand de Saussure.* Rev. ed. Ithaca, N.Y.: Cornell University Press, 1986. This is the most readable account of Saussure's theory and legacy in linguistics and semiotics, with suggestions for additional reading.

Gadet, Françoise. *Saussure and Contemporary Culture.* Translated by Gregory Elliott. London: Hutchinson, 1989. The first part offers extended quotations from Saussure's *Course in General Linguistics* with exegesis, while part two deals with the editorial fortunes of the book and its reception and influence.

Harris, Roy. *Reading Saussure: A Critical Commentary on the "Cours de linguistique générale."* London: Duckworth, and La Salle, Ill.: Open Court, 1987. A personal reading of Saussure with chapter-by-chapter commentary and summations of general issues by the author of a controversial translation; assumes basic background in linguistics and some familiarity with Saussure's place in intellectual history.

Hawkes, Terence. *Structuralism and Semiotics.* London: Methuen, and Berkeley: University of California Press, 1977. An overview of structuralism in linguistics, anthropology, literature, and semiotics; pages 19-28 deal specifically with Saussure, but his influence is described throughout the book. Contains a good selective bibliography of works available in English.

Koerner, E. F. K. *Ferdinand de Saussure, Origin and Development of His Linguistic Thought in Western Studies of Language: A Contribution to the History and Theory of Linguistics.* Braunschweig, West Germany: Vieweg, 1973. The most extensive biographical information available in English, with considerable coverage of possible sources of Saussure's thought; includes a substantial bibliography.

Sampson, Geoffrey. "Saussure: Language as Social Fact." In *Schools of Linguistics.* London: Hutchison, and Stanford, Calif.: Stanford University Press, 1980. Sampson provides a clear and engaging discussion of several of Saussure's most influential concepts, including the distinction between *langue* and *parole.* Other chapters treat a variety of twentieth century approaches to linguistics, most of which deal with issues raised by Saussure.

Saussure, Ferdinand de. *Course in General Linguistics.* Edited by Charles Bally and Albert Sechehaye in collaboration with Albert Reidlinger. Translated by Wade Baskin. New York: Philosophical Library, 1959; London: Owen, 1960. This is the standard English translation; also available in a number of reprintings. A book of less than 250 pages, this is the cornerstone of Saussure's influence.

Starobinski, Jean. *Words upon Words: The Anagrams of Ferdinand de Saussure.* Translated by Olivia Emmet. New Haven, Conn.: Yale University Press, 1979. Extensive extracts from Saussure's notebooks on anagrams.

*Julia S. Falk*

# JEANNE SAUVÉ

*Born:* April 26, 1922; Prud'Homme, Saskatchewan, Canada

*Died:* January 26, 1993; Montreal, Quebec, Canada

*Area of Achievement:* Government and politics

*Contribution:* As Canada's first female governor-general, Sauvé was a pioneer for women and for French-Canadians.

## Early Life

Jeanne Mathilde Benoît was born on April 26, 1922, in Prud'Homme, Saskatchewan. Her father, Charles, a building contractor, and her mother, Anna, were French Canadians who were determined to preserve their culture in the midst of the English majority. Although the Benoît family had moved from the Saskatchewan prairies to the Canadian capital of Ottawa when Jeanne was three, they still felt surrounded by English speakers. To compensate, Charles reared his children in a traditional French cultural atmosphere, based on the Roman Catholic church. Jeanne attended church school throughout her childhood and adolescence. She then attended the University of Ottawa.

Jeanne Benoît left the somewhat stifling security of her childhood world behind forever when she moved to Montreal in 1943. Montreal was then the leading city in Canada, a multiethnic, cosmopolitan metropolis. Of greatest importance to Jeanne was that Montreal was primarily French-speaking; there, she did not have to shelter herself against the majority culture. As a member of Jeunesse Étudiante Catholique, a liberal organization of young Quebecois, Jeanne made many contacts that were to prove influential in the future, among them Pierre Elliott Trudeau, who years later was to sponsor Jeanne's political career as prime minister of Canada. In 1948, Jeanne married Maurice Sauvé, an economics student. The Sauvés went to Europe, where Jeanne taught French in England and later received her baccalaureate degree at the University of Paris. Educated on two continents, Sauvé throughout her career was to impress Canadians as an unusually literate and intelligent politician and public figure. In 1952, the Sauvés returned to Canada.

## Life's Work

Jeanne Sauvé soon began a career as a journalist and television personality. Fluently bilingual, Sauvé broadcast in both English and French on the best-known Canadian and American networks. Sauvé's visibility and articulateness made her ideally suited to symbolize the aspirations of Quebec society during the 1960's. During this decade, in a process known as the "Quiet Revolution," Quebec was transformed under the leadership of Liberal premier Jean Lesage from a largely rural, conservative province to a progressive, assertive force that sought greater influence within Canada and even independence for itself. Although the conservative Union Nationale party had ruled Quebec during their youth, both Sauvés were enthusiastic about the modernizing Liberals. As Jeanne rose to fame in the media sector, Maurice was making equal headway in the political sphere, serving in prominent provincial and national posts. The Sauvés were becoming a true "power couple" in Quebec public affairs.

This career division between the couple was to end, however, when Maurice lost his seat in 1968. The national Liberal Party, Canada's governing party, which by now was headed by Sauvé's old friend Trudeau, asked Jeanne to run in his stead in the next election four years later. Sauvé won handily and moved to Ottawa to take her seat in the federal parliament for the next session. Sauvé's move into national politics paralleled a decision made earlier by Trudeau and many other Quebecois politicians of his generation to "go to Ottawa" rather than focus their governmental ambitions within the province of Quebec. The ultimate goal of this decision was to make virtually manifest the theoretical assertion of equality between French-speaking and English-speaking Canadians as the two founding languages of the Canadian confederation, to give French Canadians a position of leadership on the national scene. Trudeau, seeing in his old friend Sauvé a kindred spirit in this regard, almost immediately appointed her to a cabinet post in charge of issues relating to science and technology. Even though Sauvé was a political novice, she rose to the task impressively, exhibiting a technical proficiency and competence that went beyond mere execution of day-to-day policy. After Sauvé won reelection in 1974 in her home riding (the Canadian term for a parliamentary district) of Ahuntsic in Montreal, Trudeau promoted Sauvé to a position of more responsibility, that of minister of the environment. Sauvé's most challenging crisis in this capacity was a dispute between the American state of

North Dakota and the adjoining Canadian province of Manitoba over irrigation runoff that threatened to dump excess water from the upper Mississippi watershed into the Red River of the North Basin, largely located in Canada. Sauvé held her ground, although the dispute was resolved only after she had left office.

Sauvé's rapid advance in prominence during the 1970's was assisted by factors external to her own performance. This decade saw the large-scale revival of feminism in North America, as women began to be perceived as an interest group demanding more influence in the political process and desiring public visibility commensurate with their demographic position. Sauvé was poised to benefit from the existing power structure's need to accommodate women's interests. This era also saw the crest of a renewed Quebec nationalism. Federally inclined politicians such as Trudeau had hoped that the economic prosperity that had accompanied the modernization launched by the Quiet Revolution would bind Quebec closer to the rest of Canada. Instead, it had the opposite effect, raising nationalistic expectations in the province and ushering in an unprecedented era of Quebecois self-confidence. This was expressed politically in 1976, when the Parti Quebecois, which openly demanded political independence from Canada, won the provincial election, led by the charismatic René Levesque. Because she was a Quebec native committed to the maintenance and revitalization of the federal idea of Canada, Sauvé's presence in the cabinet became all the more crucial for Trudeau.

By this time, in one of the frequent cabinet reshuffles characteristic of Canadian politics, Sauvé had become communications minister, a task for which her media background had prepared her. This position brought her into direct conflict with Quebec nationalists. The conflict quickly became representative of the general tension in the linguistically divided Canada of the late 1970's, as Quebec premier Levesque arranged a referendum, to be held in May of 1980, that would determine whether the province would secede from Canada.

For a brief time, it seemed that Sauvé and the Liberal Party would not be in office to meet this challenge. In elections held in May of 1979, the Liberals were swept out of office by the progressive Conservatives, led by an attractive young politician, Joe Clark. Clark possessed only a minority, however, and in new elections held the following February, the Liberals were returned to office with a majority. Three months later, the independence side lost the Quebec referendum, temporarily silencing the national aspirations of the Quebec people.

Sauvé had been very active on Trudeau's behalf in both causes, and the returned prime minister rewarded her with the post of speaker in the new parliament. Unlike the American Congress, in which the speaker is the leader of the majority party, the speaker in Canada is deliberately nonpartisan; the main function of the post is to maintain decorum and process in parliamentary discussion. Sauvé's performance in this role over the next three and a half years demonstrated that she could transcend the particularities of factionalism and party interest, thus paving the way for her next position.

In December of 1983, Trudeau made history by appointing Sauvé to the position of governor-general. When Canada had entered into confederation in 1867, it had been agreed that the British sovereign would rule Canada. Because of Canada's geographical distance from London, however, the sovereign needed a representative, the governor-general, to rule on his or her behalf. From the beginning, the post had been ceremonial, as the British monarchy itself was by this time, but it was very important symbolically, and when the first Canadian entered this post in the middle of the twentieth century, it was felt that Canada's colonial status was on its way to being changed. When Trudeau appointed Sauvé, Queen Elizabeth II was the nominal Canadian head of state, with Sauvé serving as her representative in Ottawa. Theoretically, Trudeau served at Sauvé's behest, though actually the elected prime minister had all the power; Sauvé's role was wholly ceremonial.

Canadians paid more attention than usual to the appointment of this governor- general, because Sauvé was the first woman to hold the post. Sauvé plunged into her duties with gusto, immediately winning respect from the Canadian people for her bearing and dignity. The national scene, however, was shifting under Sauvé's feet, because her old friend Trudeau resigned in February of 1984, to be succeeded as Liberal leader and prime minister by John Turner. Turner lost the next federal election, in September, 1984, to the Conservative Brian Mulroney. Sauvé swore both Turner and Mulroney into office in her constitutional capacity as prime minister, and she worked smoothly with the latter man for the remainder of her five-year term, even though he was of the opposing party. Most important for the strongly Roman Catholic Sauvé, however, was the role she played in receiving Pope John Paul II when he made the first-ever papal visit to Canada in 1984.

The life of a Canadian governor-general is not particularly eventful, but Sauvé succeeded in making a marked impression on Canada during her five years in office. Remaining scrupulously nonpartisan throughout her term, Sauvé had occasion to swear in Mulroney again on his reelection in 1988. Sauvé's term ended in 1989, and she retired, spending most of her post-government years in support of the artistic charities to which she had always been dedicated. When she died in Montreal in January of 1993, she was mourned by all Canadians.

### Summary

Jeanne Sauvé's role as governor-general may have been only ceremonial, but she turned this lack of political clout into a personal advantage on the strength of her ability to relate to the Canadian people without the obtrusion of ulterior motive or political agenda. Sauvé refined the role of the governor-general, sometimes thought to be outdated and superfluous, to what it should be at its best: a cheerleader for the potential of the peoples of Canada.

Sauvé demonstrated that women had the capacity to hold supreme office in Canada. Once in the shadow of her husband, she ultimately became far more prominent than he had ever been. Sauvé's experience prepared the way for a woman who was to exercise real political power, future Prime Minister Kim Campbell. Most important, Sauvé's soothing presence and bilingual cosmopolitanism helped heal the simmering wounds that remained after the defeat of the Quebec independence referendum in 1980. Although the relationship between English and French Canadians was still bitter and unresolved, the fact that Canada remained unified as a nation was largely the result of Sauvé's quiet but determined efforts.

### Bibliography

Armour, Moira, and Pat Staton. *Canadian Women in History: A Chronology.* Toronto: Green Dragon Press, 1990. Accords Sauvé's odyssey a prominent role in its chronicling of the accomplishments of women north of the 49th parallel, though it tends to marginalize the importance of her Quebecois background.

Greenwood, Barbara. *Jeanne Sauvé.* Markham, Canada: Fitzhenry and Whiteside, 1988. This introductory book covers Sauvé in a thorough if noncontroversial manner. The spotlight is on Sauvé as female role model and as bridge-builder between the English and French communities in Canada.

Kaufman, Michael T. "Jeanne Suavé, 70, an Ex-Speaker and Governor General in Canada." *New York Times* 142, no. 49225 (January 28, 1993). Obituary of Sauvé, former speaker in Parliament and Governor General of Canada in the 1980s.

Megyery, Kathy, ed. *Women in Canadian Politics.* Toronto: Dundurn Press, 1991. This comprehensive book situates Sauvé's career in the context of the possibilities and obstacles faced by politicians of her generation and gender.

Mollins, Carl. "A Quiet Revolutionary." *Maclean's* 106 (February 8, 1993): 17. This most generous and affectionate of Sauvé's obituary notices reflects on her constitutional role and the promise she held out to Canadian women.

Wearing, Joseph. *The L-Shaped Party: The Liberal Party of Canada, 1958-1980.* New York: McGraw-Hill, 1981. This book provides crucial background on the party in which Sauvé received her political baptism and through which she rose to national prominence.

Woods, Shirley. *Her Excellency Jeanne Sauvé.* Toronto: Macmillan, 1986. The most detailed and scholarly treatment of Sauvé's life available. Although this book eventually will be surpassed by a full-scale historical biography, it is a vital prerequisite to the serious study of Sauvé's career.

*Nicholas Birns*

# MAX SCHELER

*Born:* August 22, 1874; Munich, Germany
*Died:* May 19, 1928; Frankfurt, Germany
*Areas of Achievement:* Philosophy, sociology, and religion
*Contribution:* Scheler was one of the most brilliant and creative moral philosophers of the twentieth century. His system of ethics, in sharp disagreement with Kantian ethics as well as with positivism, attempts to give the emotional life its due as an epistemologically reliable response to objective values.

## Early Life

Max Scheler was born into a family with considerable domestic tension. His father, Gottfried, died before Max entered high school, his will to live devoured by his own unhappiness and that of his wife. Although his father was of Protestant extraction and his mother was a Jewess, Scheler became a convert to Catholicism at age fourteen. He was attracted to the spirit of community that he found in the Catholic religious festivities.

While on vacation during the summer after his graduation from high school, Scheler met Amelie von Dewitz. She was married, had a small child, and was eight years older than Scheler. All this notwithstanding, she soon became his mistress. Eventually Amelie divorced her husband, and she and Scheler were married in a civil ceremony on October 2, 1899, in Berlin. The marriage was not a happy one, but it lasted for thirteen years. Amelie and Max had one child, Wolfgang, born in 1905.

In 1895, Scheler moved to Jena, where he completed a doctorate in philosophy with Rudolf Eucken as his adviser. In his dissertation, Scheler argued that values are not apprehended by the intellect but by a separate nonrational faculty in human beings that perceives values.

Scheler's second work, *Die transszendentale und die psychologische Methode* (1900; the transcendental and the psychological method), showed the continuing influence of Eucken's philosophy. This work earned for Scheler a position at Jena, where he taught ethics and the history of philosophy. Scheler was, however, gradually becoming dissatisfied with the transcendental, neo-Kantian approach of Eucken. A meeting with Edmund Husserl in 1901 sparked Scheler's own search for an enlargement of the concept of philosophical intuition.

In 1906, Scheler moved from Jena to teach at the University of Munich. The move was precipitated by marital problems. Scheler's professional life flourished in Munich, but his marriage continued to deteriorate. Within a year after the move, he was separated from his wife. Amelie avenged herself on her unfaithful husband by informing the Munich socialist newspaper that Scheler had gone into debt to support his affairs with other women, leaving her and his children in poverty. In 1910, Scheler was asked to resign from the University of Munich and was deprived of the right to teach at any German university.

Scheler moved from Munich to Göttingen, the center of the phenomenological movement in Germany, in the spring of 1911. There he quickly established himself as a phenomenologist of note and as a charismatic lecturer. Yet a falling-out with Husserl occurred at this time. Tension between Husserl and Scheler became so great that Scheler moved from Göttingen back to Munich.

## Life's Work

The personal resentment and pessimism that Scheler felt as he found himself isolated and jobless in Munich in 1911 enabled him to express the resentment and pessimism of many in Germany at the time. Wilhelmian Germany was seething with criticism of modern industrial society. It was at this time that Scheler began work on *Das Ressentiment im Aufbau der Moralen* (1912; *Ressentiment*, 1961) and other essays pointing to the need for modern society to return to precapitalistic Christian communal ideals. What the modern world was lacking, according to Scheler, was a metaphysics of community. It was only at the metaphysical level that true cooperation among human beings could take place.

Several years earlier, Scheler had met and fallen in love with Marit Furtwangler. Furtwangler's mother had forced her to separate from Scheler after the scandal of 1910, but Scheler continued to correspond with Marit, who was living in Berlin. They decided to marry as soon as Scheler could secure his divorce from Amelie. Scheler and Furtwangler were married on December 28, 1912, in the Church of St. Ludwig in Munich.

World War I had a profound impact upon Scheler's evolving political consciousness and inaugurated his years of intense literary productivity, which lasted from 1915 until his death in 1928. In *Der Genius des Krieges und der deutsche Krieg* (1915; the genius of war and the German war), Scheler praised the community-building powers of the German nation and welcomed war as a form of liberation from decadence. One year later, with the publication of *Krieg und Aufbau* (1916; war and rebuilding), he reversed both of these positions. By then he had come to see war as the evidence of decadence rather than as a means of liberation from it. He had also turned away from German nationalism to seek in the Church the community-building powers that he now failed to find in the German nation.

Most of Scheler's thought and action during the remainder of the war years was related to his reconversion to Catholicism. From 1917 until the end of the war, Scheler proclaimed the need for a universal repentance. He now saw the war as God's punishment for human greed. He lectured on such topics as "Germany's Mission and the Catholic World View," "The Contemporary Relevance of the Christian Idea of Community," and "The Renewal of European Culture."

In the postwar chaos, Germany's universities were flooded with young men returning from the army. The rector of the newly reestablished University of Cologne, Christian Eckart, found it possible to overlook the Munich indiscretions that had blocked Scheler's academic career. In January, 1919, Scheler accepted an appointment to the Sociological Institute, since the new university, supported by Cologne businessmen rather than by state funds, could not afford a chair of philosophy.

Scheler's social and political ideas suffered a drastic reorientation between 1921 and 1924. In 1919, Scheler had believed that the resolution of the conflicting religious and political ideologies in the Weimar Republic could be found in the religious sphere, specifically in the Roman Catholic faith. By 1924, Scheler had lost faith in the community-building powers of the Catholic religion. He now believed that political and ideological disunity could only be resolved by persons who had scientific knowledge of the sociological basis of ideological conflicts. Modern society had become so diversified that no religious leader, no matter how charismatic, could win the allegiance of persons from every social strata. The solution was to recognize the partial truth of every viewpoint. Political leaders must learn to develop flexible practical programs based on the conditions of the time rather than on abstract ideological principles. This was Scheler's position in 1923 when he published his pioneer work on the sociology of knowledge, *Schriften zur Soziologie und Weltanschauungslehre*. Scheler's work established sociology of knowledge as a significant field of study within German sociology for the next decade.

While he was teaching at the University of Cologne, Scheler became involved in an affair with a young, beautiful, and intelligent woman by the name of Maria Scheu. He still loved his wife but seemed powerless to break off the affair despite the fact that his marriage, his career as a Catholic philosopher, and his membership in the Catholic church were all at stake. Scheler was unable to decide between his wife and his mistress for quite a while but finally chose to divorce his second wife and marry Maria Scheu. The inner turmoil caused by this decision appears to have continued throughout the rest of his life. He continued to write to Marit and to see her until the time of his own death. After his marriage to Maria, Scheler decided that he had to leave Cologne because of difficulties with his colleagues and superiors who refused to condone his personal life-style. Catholic students, especially seminarians, were forbidden to attend his classes. Scheler, in turn, attacked the Catholic church for its crude dogmatism.

At the peril of contradicting his prewar attack on the Western scientific tradition, Scheler opposed the antirationalist tendencies of the 1920's. Before the war, Scheler had denounced the modern industrial world and idealized the community life of medieval Europe. In the 1920's, however, Scheler allied himself with the traditions of the Enlightenment. This allegiance became evident in his speech at the Lessing Institute for Adult Education in 1925 entitled *Die Formen des Wissens und die Bildung* (the forms of knowledge and culture).

In the face of the plethora of conflicting worldviews afoot in postwar Germany, Scheler adopted a relativistic approach toward truth as a sociologist, but as a philosopher he retained the insights into eternal essences offered by phenomenology. He also maintained his theory of absolute values, a product of his Catholic period. The link between his sociological and philosophical stances was provided by what be called "functionalization," the process whereby truth is splintered as it descends from its absolute realm into its concrete cultural manifestations in history. Furthermore, Scheler argued that although different people saw reality differently, it was still the same ultimate reality that they were viewing from different perspectives.

In the last years of his life, Scheler devoted himself to the construction of a metaphysics of man. Scheler died before he had a chance to put his thoughts on this topic into book form, yet some idea of his central concerns can be drawn from his articles and lectures of the mid-1920's. The human being, according to Scheler, is both a microcosm and a microtheos. The human person is a microcosm because he or she participates in all the aspects of being: physical, vital, spiritual, and personal. The human person is a microtheos, because he or she participates in the ultimate metaphysical principles of the universe, mind, and instinct. Contrary to the claims of traditional Western metaphysics, the human person is not to be viewed as merely the imitator of a world of ideas that was already present in the mind of God before creation. Rather, human persons were to be viewed as the cocreators and coexecutors of the stream of ideas that enables the Absolute to realize itself in the course of world history.

In 1928, Scheler accepted an appointment at the University of Frankfurt. He died suddenly of either a stroke or a heart attack on May 19, 1928, immediately prior to beginning his work at Frankfurt.

### Summary

Along with Edmund Husserl and Martin Heidegger, Max Scheler was one of the three founding fathers of the philosophical school known as "phenomenology." Scheler was the most versatile and comprehensive thinker of the three. Among the wide variety of topics treated in his writings are ethics, value theory, philosophy of religion, repentance, humility, the foundation of biology, psychology, metaphysics, the theory of cognition and perception, Buddhism, education, culture, philosophy of history, the sociology of knowledge, pragmatism, capitalism, the sense of suffering, love, death, awe, and shame. One of Scheler's most radically new contributions to philosophy was his development of a phenomenological theory of ethics. His theory of nonformal or "material" values situates the emotional experience of values as the primordium of all experience of reality. His ethics is based upon this nonrational, intuitive grasp of values.

Scheler also made important contributions to the sociology of knowledge, in which he struggled for a middle way between idealism (a Hegelian approach) and materialism (a Marxist, or Positivist, approach); the philosophy of religion, an area in which he has attracted a steady number of commentators, especially among Roman Catholics; and philosophical anthropology.

José Ortega y Gasset, Nicolai Hartmann, Dietrich von Hildebrand, Alois Dempf, and Paul L. Landsberg are merely a few of the thinkers who have been influenced by Scheler. Scheler's writings continue to inspire philosophers and others who are interested in the perennial and humanitarian themes of community, value, love, person, and God. Scheler offers no neat and tidy systematic treatment of any of these themes. Nevertheless, he can justly be described as an inspirational and brilliant philosopher who consistently offers creative and profound insights upon these topics.

### Bibliography

Crosby, John F. "The Individuality of Human Persons: A Study in the Ethical Personalism of Max Scheler." *The Review of Metaphysics* 52, no. 205 (September, 1998). Crosby considers Scheler's emphasis on the importance of the individual in the creation of ethical philosophy as opposed to German idealism, which focused on the universality of ideals.

Deeken, Alfons. *Process and Permanence in Ethics: Max Scheler's Moral Philosophy.* New York: Paulist Press, 1974. A systematic exposition of Scheler's ethics. Generally thorough except for the lack of any discussion of community. Includes a bibliography and indexes.

Emad, Pravis. "The Great Themes of Scheler." *Philosophy Today* 12 (Spring, 1968): 4-12. A concise summary of Scheler's philosophy. A good place for the general reader to begin.

Frings, Manfred S. *Max Scheler: A Concise Introduction into the World of a Great Thinker.* Pittsburgh: Duquesne University Press, 1965. One of the earliest studies of Scheler to appear in English. Each chapter discusses one of the fundamental ideas of Scheler's philosophy. A good overview, but lacks consideration of the chronological development of Scheler's thought. Includes a bibliography and indexes.

Kelly, Eugene. *Max Scheler.* Boston: Twayne, 1977. Despite its title, this work is not a biography. It is an analysis and critique of Scheler as a phenomenologist.

———. *Structure and Diversity: Studies in the Phenomenological Philosophy of Max Scheler.* Boston: Kluwer, 1997. The author considers the bases for Scheler's philosophies and presents the only volume to consider Scheler's manuscripts published since 1973.

Ranly, Ernest W. *Scheler's Phenomenology of Community*. The Hague: Martinus Nijhoff, 1966. This book is an outgrowth of the author's doctoral dissertation on Scheler's theory of community. It includes a careful discussion of Scheler's description of the emotions and their role in community. Contains a bibliography and an index.

Schutz, Alfred. "Max Scheler's Epistemology and Ethics." *The Review of Metaphysics* 11 (1957): 304-314, 486-501. A good, short explanatory article written by a fellow phenomenologist. Part 1 covers Scheler's epistemology, and the second part covers his ethics.

Staude, John Raphael. *Max Scheler, 1874-1928: An Intellectual Portrait*. New York: Free Press, 1967. The most detailed biography of Scheler in the English language. The author offers an insightful and generally sympathetic interpretation, although he can be critical when he deems it appropriate. Includes a bibliography and an index.

*Ann Marie B. Bahr*

# BERNHARD VOLDEMAR SCHMIDT

*Born:* March 30, 1879; Island of Naissaar, Estonia
*Died:* December 1, 1935; Hamburg, Germany
*Areas of Achievement:* Astronomy, invention, technology, and physics
*Contribution:* In 1930, Schmidt invented an optical system that revolutionized astronomy by significantly widening the field of vision of the largest telescopes then in use. The Schmidt photographic telescope used a spherical mirror in combination with a glass plate to capture celestial images on photographic plates. For the first time, wide areas of the sky could be photographed with sharp definition across the entire field, edge to edge.

## Early Life

Bernhard Voldemar Schmidt was born on Naissaar, an island in Estonia in 1879. His family was poor, and he had little formal schooling. Yet he had an early interest in science and often conducted simple experiments. One such experiment with gunpowder resulted in a disastrous explosion that cost him part of his right arm. Despite that handicap, his curiosity was undeterred, and he continued to study physical science and eventually demonstrated a strong aptitude for optical engineering, aided by an intuitive understanding of the physical nature of optical structures. While still a youth, he made his first telescope lens by cutting the bottom from a glass bottle and grinding it with sand. Schmidt was as resourceful as he was curious and conducted fairly complicated optical experiments with extremely crude instruments.

In 1900, Schmidt entered the Institute of Technology at Göteborg, Sweden, where he studied engineering. He left Göteborg, to study in Mittweida, Germany, where he became a skilled crafter of mirrors and lenses for telescopes. He remained in Mittweida after graduation and created a top-quality, fifteen-inch mirror for an observatory at Potsdam, Germany.

From the earliest days of his life, Schmidt was a loner. He was moody, difficult to approach, and often unpredictable. He worked alone at a variety of jobs until 1926 when, at the age of forty-seven, he joined the staff of the Hamburg Observatory. He was considered an eccentric by fellow astronomers. He refused to accept a conventional position with the observatory staff, preferring to continue working alone as a crafter of optical instruments. He had few, if any, friends and labored with crude equipment. Occasionally he would disappear on drinking binges that would often last for days. Despite his contrary disposition and antisocial nature, Schmidt was considered a genius in the field of optics, wherein he made the discovery that revolutionized celestial photography.

## Life's Work

Schmidt devoted his life to the development of mirrors and optic lenses for use in astronomical observatories. Late in life, he developed the optical system for which he became famous, one that was later modified and enhanced to improve significantly the field of observational astronomy. Ironically, the basis for that system came from an idea proposed by Sir Isaac Newton in the early eighteenth century, but which had been long abandoned by astronomers. Newton, better known for his study of the laws of gravity than for his lifelong work in the field of optics, recognized the need for a telescope lens that could take in a significantly larger field of view than was possible with the telescopes of his day. He designed such a lens using spherical curvature. Yet telescope-makers found the concept to be unworkable because different areas of lens received light-beams of varying length, thus causing aberrations in the focus of captured images. Schmidt overcame the problem by placing an error-correcting glass plate as far ahead of the focal point of the telescope as the spherical mirror lay behind it. Since the telescope was designed to function with a relatively short focus, the length of the tube required to house the optics was also relatively short. A curved film was placed in front of the mirror, and for the first time ever a clear, sharp image of an area of the sky greater than 20 degrees of arc could be photographed. This allowed scientists to study galactic star clusters in several wavelength ranges, while searching for young stars, the study of which is useful in understanding the structure of the universe. Before 1930, most telescopes were of the reflector or refractor type. Each was useful in the study of stars and star clusters in distant space but had the inherent disadvantage of being able to see only a small portion of the sky. Interestingly, in 1910, Kellner invented the optical components that became the basic technology incorporated in the Schmidt telescope, but it was Schmidt who actually constructed the first one.

The theory behind the Schmidt telescope, often referred to as a camera, relates to the physical properties of reflected light. Parallel light-rays reflected at the edge of a spherical mirror travel shorter distances to a medium placed above it than does light reflected from the center of the sphere. That causes the focus to be in one region of the medium, or film, rather than over its entire area. Schmidt's glass-correcting plate compensated for those variant distances, thus achieving sharp images over the full range of the area being viewed through the telescope. In later versions of the Schmidt telescope, the correcting plate was ground so thinly that very little chromatic distortion occurred at that point, making the image even sharper.

The largest Schmidt photographic telescope was installed on Mount Palomar in California. Its intended function was to do the first full-scale photographic sky mapping. It was equipped with a forty-eight-inch correcting lens and a seventy-two-inch reflecting mirror with a radius of curvature of twenty feet. The focal length was ten feet. Photographs were taken in both red and blue light, with all stars displaying luminescence down to a magnitude of 21.1 appearing on the blue plates and those down to a magnitude of 20 appearing on the red plate. More than seventeen hundred plates were required for each photographic image in order to accommodate both colors. The first photographs taken by the Schmidt camera were published in the 1950's.

It is important to note that the Schmidt telescope was used only as a camera. Photographically, the f/ratio, or focal length divided by the aperture, of the Schmidt telescope was similar to that of a fast photographic lens. That fact, combined with developments in photographic image processing, resulted in modifications to the Schmidt telescope that made the instrument more efficient and led to new estimates of the distances of galaxies far from Earth.

In spite of the breakthrough for astronomers that was embodied in the Schmidt telescope, one problem resulted from the curved photographic plates required to achieve wide-area coverage: They made it awkward for making precise determinations of distances among stellar objects. Nevertheless, the Schmidt photographic telescope became extremely popular, primarily because it was able to accomplish significantly more mapping at those infrequent times when weather conditions were ideal. Schmidt died in an asylum for the insane in Hamburg in 1935. His personal life was troubled, but his contribution to astronomy was great.

### Summary

Bernhard Voldemar Schmidt was a technician, not an astronomer. He was concerned with developing the technology of astronomy rather than with studying the universe. Yet his optical system has earned for him a place among the great astrophysicists of his time. Over the centuries prior to 1930, the study of astronomy had been carried on in much the same way. While lenses and other telescopic components had been enlarged and refined over time, the techniques of astronomical observation were much the same. The Schmidt telescope represented a major step forward, providing a means for expanding the field of celestial observation. Over a seven-year period, a giant Schmidt telescope at Mount Palomar photographed the entire sky that could be viewed from that location in California. Schmidt telescopes were later installed in other regions of the world to photograph celestial objects visible only from those regions, adding significantly to the body of knowledge about the structure of the universe.

### Bibliography

Hoyle, Fred. *Astronomy.* London: Macdonald, and New York: Doubleday, 1962. Contains several good photographs of the Schmidt telescope, an index, and an appendix.

Marx, Siegfried, and Werner Pfau. *Observatories of the World.* New York: Van Nostrand Reinhold, 1982. An excellent description of several of the important astronomical observatories of the world, including Schmidt's home observatory at Hamburg, Germany. Includes photographs and an index.

Moore, Patrick. *Men of the Stars.* New York: Gallery, 1986. Contains a brief biographical sketch and picture of Schmidt. This highly illustrated book is particularly useful to the young reader looking for a fine introduction to astronomy.

Richardson, Robert S. *The Star Lovers.* New York: Macmillan, 1967. A survey of the work of many of the best-known personalities in astronomy. Tracks the evolution of astronomy through the early 1960's and contains many useful photographs, including several of Schmidt photographic telescopes, including the one at Mount Palomar. Includes a brief passage on Schmidt's professional relationship with Walter Baade, one of the great astronomers of the early twentieth century. Includes a bibliography and an index.

Ronan, Colin A. *Changing Views of the Universe.* London: Eyre and Spottiswoode, and New York: Macmillan, 1961. An overview of developments in astronomy over the centuries as viewed from the social perspectives that prevailed at the time. Contains a passage on the significance of the Schmidt camera from a social and political context.

Rousseau, Pierre. *Man's Conquest of the Stars.* London: Jarrolds, and New York: Norton, 1961. A highly readable survey of the evolution of astronomy for the layperson. Contains no complicated, technical descriptions. Includes an index.

Shapley, Harlow, ed. *Source Book in Astronomy, 1900-1950.* Cambridge, Mass.: Harvard University Press, 1960. Contains a discussion of the instrumentation used during the first half of the twentieth century to study the solar system and the position and motion of stars.

Sidgwick, J. B. *Amateur Astronomer's Handbook.* London: Faber, and New York: Macmillan, 1955. Contains a good discussion of the technical components of astronomy: telescopic function, optics, oculars, mountings, and several modifications to the Schmidt camera, including the thick mirror Schmidt, solid Schmidt, folded solid Schmidt, off-axis Schmidt, all reflector Schmidt, Spectroscopic Schmidt, and others. Bibliography and index.

*Michael S. Ameigh*

# KARL SCHMIDT-ROTTLUFF

*Born:* December 1, 1884; Rottluff, Germany
*Died:* August 10, 1976; West Berlin, West Germany
*Area of Achievement:* Art
*Contribution:* The period 1905-1915 marked the beginning of twentieth century artistic principles. This was the decade of *Die Brücke*, an organized group of European artists and art lovers whose common interest was to encourage revolutionary methods of artistic expression. Schmidt-Rottluff, as a founding member of this influential group, maintained a lifelong dedication to its purposes.

## Early Life

Karl Schmidt-Rottluff was born Karl Schmidt. As a young man, he added "Rottluff" to his name, for the rural village, near Chemnitz (now Karl-Marx-Stadt), where he was born in 1884. Schmidt-Rottluff received his formal schooling between the years 1897 and 1905 at the *Gymnasium* in Chemnitz. He was virtually self-taught as an artist, though he received some formal training in the art classes that he attended twice weekly at the Chemnitz *Kunstverein.* As a student, he demonstrated interests in poetry, music, and the humanities as well as in art.

In 1905, Schmidt-Rottluff became a student of architecture at the Technical College of Dresden. It was in the same year that he and three of his fellow students, Ernst Ludwig Kirchner, Fritz Bleyl, and Erich Heckel, decided to terminate their formal studies and seek free expression in painting. They were the founding members of a group known as *Die Brücke* (the bridge), so named by Schmidt-Rottluff because he wanted their label to symbolize that membership would bring together not only artists but also collectors, connoisseurs, and writers—any and all who sought and appreciated fresh, new approaches to human expression.

The group of young artists painted, produced graphics, and occasionally sculpted wherever they could find space available at a price they could afford. *Die Brücke* produced an annual portfolio and sponsored group exhibitions of members' works. By 1910, the group had reached its peak as an artists' community. After that year, some members of the group moved to Berlin, where there was not the same degree of communal activity and cooperation. The year 1913 saw the dissolution of *Die Brücke.* Schmidt-Rottluff remained true to its goals, however, and attempted, in 1926, to start a new group, but his efforts were generally unsuccessful. The group and its spirit of community had been, for Schmidt-Rottluff, a most important part of his long, productive life as an artist.

## Life's Work

Schmidt-Rottluff had begun painting in oils as a high school student in Chemnitz, but he later wrote that he considered his first works to date from 1905, the year of *Die Brücke*'s creation. Erich Heckel, however, who was Schmidt-Rottluff's lifetime friend, considered the earlier works to have been very worthwhile, especially as to the use of color. By 1904, Schmidt-Rottluff had begun experimenting with woodcuts, which proved to be, for Schmidt-Rottluff, a most appropriate means of describing the relationship of plane surfaces to one another. His first were impressionistic, but within a short time he had developed a more abstract style. It was his desire, as well as that of the entire Dresden group, to create in a manner that would be in contrast with that of the previous generation, for whom painting had virtually been abandoned in favor of what was termed "Art Nouveau," the practical application of art. *Die Brücke* artists, in their youthful self-confidence, wished to preserve their naïveté and rejected the idea that in order to be an artist one must employ traditional techniques and skills.

In 1906, Schmidt-Rottluff extended, on behalf of *Die Brücke*, an invitation for membership to the artist Emil Nolde. Subsequently, Schmidt-Rottluff spent time with Nolde at his home on the North Sea island of Alsen. The wild, harsh landscape of the island had a great appeal for Schmidt-Rottluff, who loved the freedom of nature, and he began to develop a consistent need for isolated, outdoor environments in which to paint. An earlier van Gogh exhibition in Dresden had been seen by the artists of *Die Brücke*, and Schmidt-Rottluff's painting began to reflect the influence of the Dutch artist, even though he would deny that he was able to put to any use the expressionism of van Gogh in what he, himself, was attempting. Nolde hoped he could help Schmidt-Rottluff to rely less heavily on the example of van Gogh. The effects of nature notwithstanding, Schmidt-Rottluff's self-portrait of that year, with its heavy impasto brushstrokes, purposeful placement of contrasting colors—colors not necessarily descriptive of the subject—and the strong suggestion of movement in the painting, reflects a definite van Gogh influence.

Schmidt-Rottluff spent winters in Dresden, but in 1907 he made the first of what was to become an annual summer visit to the area of Oldenburg flanking the North Sea. *Windy Day*, a 1907 landscape, still reflects the van Gogh influence. It is considered a dominant work of Schmidt-Rottluff's early period. In 1908, the artist spent the period from May until October in Oldenburg. The richly textured surface of that season's *Midday on the Moor*, the intensity of color applied in broad, expressive brushstrokes, along with the resulting near absence of definition of subject continued to be reminiscent of van Gogh, though there was obviously an emerging individual style. A distinctive technique of the artist was to describe the subject in terms of its planes, sometimes emphasizing them by the use of black outlines. Schmidt-Rottluff's work in these early years focused primarily on landscape painting.

Schmidt-Rottluff was one of *Die Brücke*'s members who exhibited in 1910 with the New Secession in Berlin. The group's work received critical favor in Berlin, thus enhancing the emerging national reputation of the artists. Schmidt-Rottluff had been living in Hamburg in that year and had had a number of one-man shows in that city. The group's Dresden show of that year had been a failure. It became desirable, if the artists were to maintain their newly earned status, to move to Berlin.

In 1912, in Berlin, Schmidt-Rottluff painted *Houses at Night*. This and other paintings of that period reflected the artist's movement toward a form of expressionist abstraction. He rejected the idea, however, of totally non-representational art. He began to utilize a more precise definition of subject matter. Figures and still lifes began to appear as subjects for his development of color planes, and his brief experiment with cubism is seen in *The Pharisees* of 1912. It was during the early years in Berlin that Schmidt-Rottluff's work also reflected his exposure to the work of the Fauvists and to primitive African art. Meanwhile, Schmidt-Rottluff received wide exposure through his work published in *Der Sturm*, a Berlin weekly that promoted the new movements in art, and through his participation in several important exhibitions.

By 1914, Schmidt-Rottluff's work became more somber, perhaps in anticipation of war. Typical works of this period contain figures that have, for the first time, human expression instead of figures absorbed by nature; his landscapes of this period also are more realistic in detail. Colors are dark, emphasizing the sadness reflected in the pictures. In the final months before he entered the military, Schmidt-Rottluff painted single figures with spiritual quality; these figures filled the entire picture. *Portrait of a Girl* is typical of this brief period.

During his three years of military service, Schmidt-Rottluff produced only woodcarvings and woodcuts, many having religious themes, including a series of nine woodcuts concerning the life of Jesus. After the war, his works contained symbolism as the dominant element, reflecting the internal personal changes that his experiences as a soldier in Russia had brought about. Titles of his postwar works included *Stellar Prayer, Melancholy*, and *Conversations About Death*.

Schmidt-Rottluff settled in Berlin after World War I, but during the next ten years he traveled widely, leading study groups to Italy, Paris, Dalmatia, and Ticino. Between 1936 and 1939, the first American exhibitions of his work were held. In 1931, he had become a member of the Prussian Academy of Arts, but, along with many German artists, was removed from academy membership during the Nazi regime. As many as 680 of Schmidt-Rottluff's paintings were stripped from German gallery holdings during the twelve years of the Third Reich. Some were sold for cash; many were destroyed. In 1941, Adolf Hitler condemned Schmidt-Rottluff as one of the artists he considered decadent and therefore dangerous to the German culture. In that year, the artist was forbidden to create works of art in his own country.

After the close of World War II, in 1947 the artist, in order to pick up the pieces of his life, accepted a professorship at the Hochschule für Bildende, where he remained until his retirement. In 1974, the year of his ninetieth birthday, he was made an honorary member of the American Academy of Arts and Letters and the American National Institute of Arts and Letters for his pioneering work in expressionist art. He died in West Berlin in 1976. Having no immediate heirs, his entire estate became part of the Karl and Emy Schmidt-Rottluff Foundation, which is in the custodial care of the Brück Museum. He had helped to establish the small museum in 1967 at a site in the Grunewald landscape of Berlin. It houses a collection of *Die Brücke* artists' works that survived the purges of the Nazi regime.

## Summary

Like most *Die Brücke* artists, Karl Schmidt-Rottluff was, in the beginning, a provincial who was drawn to Dresden for professional training. He was perhaps awkward and ill-equipped as to city manners and social customs. Yet he and his colleagues brought to the world an expression and an emotion stronger than that perhaps of any other art movement. Their dependence on one another for support was in part responsible for the rapid development of each member as an accomplished artist. Audacity, originality, and emotionalism were their contribution.

The courage of these artists who survived two wars and despicable treatment by the Nazis serves as an example to all artists and patrons of the arts. Schmidt-Rottluff, as one of the survivors, left to his country and to the entire world all that he had salvaged, in order to preserve for posterity the remaining evidence of an important movement in the arts. Of his work as an individual artist, his religious woodcuts are perhaps his most important and unique contribution.

## Bibliography

Dube, Wolf-Dieter. *The Expressionists.* Translated by Mary Whittall. London: Thames and Hudson, 1972; New York: Thames and Hudson, 1985. Contains effective descriptions as well as plates of the artist's work.

Grosshans, Henry. *Hitler and the Artists.* New York: Holmes and Meier, 1983. Schmidt-Rottluff is only one of the sixteen artists who are the subject of this work. It is important, especially, because it provides a perspective of the artist in historical context as a contemporary and as a victim of Hitler, who considered himself the cultural leader of the German peoples.

Halasz, Piri. "German Expressionism, Explosive Art Movement in a Troubled Age." *Smithsonian* 11 (January, 1981): 88-95. This article describes German expressionism, its history, and its participants. In this article, Schmidt-Rottluff is placed within the movement.

Reidemeister, Leopold. *The Brücke Museum.* Translated by Margot Dembo and Edna McCowen. Fort Lee, N.J.: Penshurst, 1981. The author describes his contact with the artist and other members of *Die Brücke* and their successful establishment of a museum to house their works. With twenty-four plates of Schmidt-Rottluff's works and English-language notes.

Selz, Peter. *German Expressionist Painting.* Berkeley: University of California Press, 1957; London: University of California Press, 1974. A comprehensive study of the expressionist movement. The artist is discussed as he relates both to the group, *Die Brücke*, and to his individual work. Contains extensive notes and a bibliography as well as plates.

Willett, John. *Expressionism.* London: Weidenfeld and Nicolson, and New York: McGraw-Hill, 1970. A broad overview of the movement and its history from 1900 to the date of publication. Covers the literature, music, and drama as well as the painters and graphic artists of the movement. Contains a discussion of each artist, his work, and the sociocultural context.

*P. R. Lannert*

# ARNOLD SCHOENBERG

*Born:* September 13, 1874; Vienna, Austro-Hungarian Empire
*Died:* July 13, 1951; Los Angeles, California
*Area of Achievement:* Music
*Contribution:* Schoenberg was the leading composer of the second Viennese school, a manifestation of the expressionist movement in music. By breaking from the tradition of tonality, a process he later codified in his twelve-tone method, Schoenberg introduced compositional techniques and aesthetic principles that became pervasive throughout the first half of the twentieth century.

## Early Life

Arnold Franz Walter Schoenberg (originally Schönberg) was born in Vienna on September 13, 1874. His parents were Jewish and reared their three children in this heritage. Samuel, his father, owned a small shoe shop. The family was never wealthy, and Samuel's death in 1890 forced Schoenberg to leave school in order to support his family. Neither Samuel nor his wife Pauline (née Nachod) was particularly musical, although Samuel had sung in amateur choirs, and the Nachod family had for generations provided cantors for synagogues in their native Prague. The main cultural influence in Schoenberg's youth was his uncle Friedrich (Fritz) Nachod, who taught the young Schoenberg poetry, drama, and French.

There was no piano in the Schoenberg home; Arnold began his musical training at age eight on the violin, later switching to viola and a homemade cello. He immediately began to compose violin duets to play with his teacher; as his circle of musical friends grew, so did his early compositional efforts, which soon included string quartets, songs, and piano pieces. While Schoenberg was essentially self-taught as a composer, his musical friendships played an important role in his early development and throughout his career. One friend, the philosopher Oskar Adler, became his first true music teacher, providing instruction in harmony and ear training. Most influential, however, was the composer/conductor Alexander von Zemlinsky, who met Schoenberg while conducting an amateur orchestra. Schoenberg's elder by two years, Zemlinsky had been trained at the Vienna Conservatory and had attracted the attention of Johannes Brahms. While later recollections as to the nature of the tutelage differ, it appears that Zemlinsky not only offered specific compositional advice but also brought to Schoenberg's attention the rich possibilities of combining the then-opposed Brahmsian and Wagnerian traditions. The two friends became brothers-in-law in 1901, when Schoenberg married Zemlinsky's sister Mathilde; Zemlinsky remained a lifelong friend and advocate of Schoenberg's music.

It was through Zemlinsky that Schoenberg's music received its first public performance; his String Quartet in D Major (1897) was presented in 1898 by the Wiener Tonkünstlerverein. The next year, however, this same organization rejected Schoenberg's first mature composition, the string sextet *Verklärte Nacht*, Op. 4 (1899; transfigured night), on the basis of a single unconventional chord. This sort of misguided rejection proved to be the first indication of the harsh and shortsighted criticism that would continue to be levied against Schoenberg throughout his career.

## Life's Work

Schoenberg's career has often been described in terms of four stylistic periods: the tonal, late-Romantic works of 1899-1908; the expressionist, atonal works of 1909-1920; the application of the twelve-tone method in the works of 1920-1936; and a broader, more eclectic approach that evolves in the works from the mid-1930's onward. Such delineations do not merely serve to categorize Schoenberg's works; rather, they highlight the continuity of his development. The stylistic diversity of his oeuvre is paralleled by its breadth, which encompasses important operas, orchestral works, chamber music, songs, and theoretical treatises.

Schoenberg never considered his own work to be revolutionary. Rather, he viewed it as descendant from the German late-Romantic tradition of Richard Strauss and Gustav Mahler (the latter of whom, like Zemlinsky, grew to be a close friend and professional ally). While such stylistic derivation was overlooked by the critics of the time, Schoenberg's early works are now understood in this light. *Verklärte Nacht* adopts the nineteenth century genre of the tone poem, projecting imagery of transfigured love through broad melodic lines and a rich harmonic palette. Similar musical and symbolic richness characterizes the orchestral tone poem *Pelleas und Melisande*, Op. 5 (1903) and the setting of Jens Peter Jacobsen's *Gurrelieder*

(1900-1911), a massive song cycle that calls for five soloists, multiple choirs, and a huge orchestra.

Schoenberg soon found such grandiose gestures to be at odds with the goal of immediate and direct expression and adopted a leaner, more transparent style, apparent in the String Quartet in D Minor, Op. 7, No. 1 (1904-1905), and particularly in the First Chamber Symphony, Op. 9 (1906), the culmination of his first period. The instrumental forces here have been trimmed to fifteen solo winds and strings, allowing for greater clarity within the highly contrapuntal texture. Melodic and harmonic aspects coalesce through the motive manipulation of whole-tone collections and superimposed fourths. Yet the work remains ostensibly tonal, although resolutions to tonal centers are relegated to mark only the major structural divisions. While the contrapuntal complexity, the rapid rate of motive development, and the extension of tonality all proved to be stumbling blocks for critics of the time, these traits have come to be seen as progenitors of Schoenberg's subsequent development.

It was immediately following this period, in which he was reevaluating the efficacy of various means of musical expression, that Schoenberg became increasingly active as a painter. He studied with the young Richard Gerstl (with whom Mathilde would subsequently have a devastating affair) and developed sufficiently to mount a one-man exhibition in 1910. Through these activities, Schoenberg became active in the burgeoning expressionist movement, befriending such important painters as Wassily Kandinsky and Oskar Kokoschka; Schoenberg contributed to the Blaue Reiter (Blue Rider) exhibition of 1912. While his interest in painting as his principle means of artistic expression soon waned, Schoenberg's foray into this medium helped to solidify the aesthetic principles that continued to form the basis of his musical style.

Similar to the expressionist painters who sought to convey directly the innermost essence of the human experience (as was recently being examined in the work of Sigmund Freud), Schoenberg sought to bring similar depth to musical expression, resulting in the remarkable series of works that inaugurate his second period. First apparent in the final two movements of the String Quartet, Op. 10, No. 2 (1907-1908), which incorporate a soprano singing texts by Stefan George, these musical advances coalesce in the mystifying and delicate song cycle *Das Buch der hängenden Gärten*, Op. 15 (1908-1909; the book of the hanging gardens), also on texts by George, and in the Three Piano Pieces, Op. 11 (1909). Most harrowing, however, is the synergy of Marie Pappenheim's text and Schoenberg's music in the creation of the angst-filled nightmare world of the monodrama *Erwartung*, Op. 17 (1909; expectation), where all distinction between reality and hallucination is lost. Similar effect describes the parodic dreamworld of *Pierrot Lunaire*, Op. 21 (1912; moonstruck Pierrot), a cycle of twenty-one rondels by Albert Giraud scored for *Sprechstimme* (a hybridization of speech and song) and five instruments, which remains one of Schoenberg's most popular works and epitomizes the style of his second period.

The sound of these works is quite unlike that of any other music in history, but it is born of the same artistic impulse and musical language that shaped Schoenberg's first period. Motive manipulation has become the paramount means of direct expression, with reference to tonal centers, previously relegated to background structural functions, dispensed. Although the outmoded tonal system is no longer operative, the label "atonal," often applied pejoratively, was dismissed by Schoenberg as being nonsensical, for the purity of the tones and their interrelationship as motives remain. The music thus develops in accordance with its own inherent logic, not that of an applied hierarchical system, thereby representing direct, unencumbered artistic expression.

The ramifications of this stylistic direction were never fully explored by either Schoenberg or his growing coterie of students (the two most important of whom, Alban Berg and Anton von Webern, became known along with Schoenberg as the second Viennese school), for World War I interrupted much of the artistic activity in Europe. Schoenberg was called up twice, but was at first rejected for goiter and later released because of asthma, a problem that plagued his entire life. The interwar years were marked by other hardships as well, including continued financial difficulties; further critical rejection, which he attempted to counter through the formation in 1918 of the Verein für musikalische Privataufführungen (the Society for Private Musical Performances); and the death of Mathilde in 1923. He married Gertrud Kolisch, sister of his student Rudolf Kolisch, in 1924. The difficulties of this period continued to motivate the evolution of his religious beliefs (he had converted to Lutheranism in 1898 and would reconvert to Judaism in 1933), apparent in the influence of August Strindberg and Emanuel Swedenborg in the text of the incomplete oratorio *Die Jakobsleiter* (1917-1922; Jacob's ladder). This work also proves to be an important musical link, for in retrospect it displays the beginnings of serial compositional processes that would soon develop into Schoenberg's most widely known contribution: the twelve-tone (dodecaphonic) method of composition.

The new method brought to fruition Schoenberg's continual search for the complete integration of linear and vertical musical dimensions. The twelve notes of the chromatic scale are ordered to form a tone row, from which the melodic and harmonic materials of a composition are sequentially drawn; the continued manipulation of a single row throughout the course of a piece contributes to its structural unity. The formalization of the technique in the Five Piano Pieces, Op. 23 (1920-1923) and the Suite for Piano, Op. 25 (1921-1923) demonstrates the new structural order, for these works no longer rely upon the framework of a text as had many of the earlier, freely atonal expressionist works.

It is ironic that the twelve-tone method has often been maligned as being a stylistic determinant rather than a compositional device. In fact, the new syntactic logic that the method provided allowed Schoenberg's work to adopt neoclassical formal models in the piano pieces as well as in the Variations for Orchestra, Op. 31 (1926-1928) and the Third String Quartet, Op. 30 (1927). A broadening perspective is found in later works such as the Fourth String Quartert Op. 37 (1936), but the method's stylistic adaptability is most readily demonstrated in the delicate pointillism of Webern's application as compared to the lush lyricism of Berg. In the opera *Moses und Aron* (1930-1932), Schoenberg draws upon the full richness of the method. While the music to the short third act was never composed, the first two acts stand both dramatically and musically complete, portraying the trials of the prophet being compelled to accept his task. Such a subject calls for great breadth in its treatment, which the vast technical and artistic resources of Schoenberg's development could supply; the resultant work remains Schoenberg's monumental profession of faith.

As with the earlier stages of stylistic evolution, the growing eclecticism apparent in the works from the mid-1930's onward reflects in part Schoenberg's reactions to the continuous upheavals of the world around him. The growing anti-Semitism in Germany caused him to flee to the United States in 1933; the three late works for speaker and ensemble, *Kol Nidre*, Op. 39 (1938), *Ode to Napoleon*, Op. 41 (1942), and particularly the chilling *A Survivor from Warsaw*, Op. 46 (1947), reflect the profound effect that the horrors of World War II had on his Jewish consciousness. Poor health prompted him to move from Boston to Los Angeles in 1934; the compelling String Trio, Op. 45 (1946), which followed a near-fatal heart attack, presents his personal reflection on mortality and death. Along with poor health, the poverty and critical misunderstanding that he had endured throughout his life plagued him to the end; he was retired at age seventy from teaching at the University of California at Los Angeles with a pension of only thirty-eight dollars a month, only to be refused in 1945 for a grant from the Guggenheim Foundation that would have allowed him to complete *Die Jakobsleiter*, *Moses und Aron*, and a series of theoretical textbooks. He died in Los Angeles on July 13, 1951; the last word that he spoke was "harmony."

## Summary

Since his death, recognition of the importance of

Arnold Schoenberg's work has superseded the indictment of his contemporaries. He now stands regarded as one of the great innovators in the history of music who, similar to Johann Sebastian Bach, stood at the juncture of two distinct stylistic eras yet incorporated characteristics of each. Thus arises the paradox of his apparent revolutionary stature with his self-assessment of continuing the German Romantic tradition.

Similar paradoxes characterize much of Schoenberg's life and career, reflecting his intellectually curious yet fiercely independent nature. Essentially self-taught as a composer, he went on to become one of the most influential teachers of his era. Yet, as innovative as his own compositional work was, his approach to teaching was thoroughly grounded in the traditional practices of tonal harmony and counterpoint; he never taught the twelve-tone method to his students and rarely lectured or wrote about it. Yet it is precisely for this method that Schoenberg is best known; his music has unfortunately been more widely analyzed than performed.

In both his teaching and compositional practices, Schoenberg's ultimate goal was clarity of expression and a compelling sense of inevitability through structural logic and coherence. This objective outlook was balanced by his view of music as reflecting the innermost psyche, as the intensity of works such as *Erwartung* testifies. Constant self-evaluation contributed to the continual evolution of both his musical style and his personal beliefs, journeys perhaps reflected in the reluctantly prophetic stance of the protagonists of both *Die Jakobsleiter* and *Moses und Aron*. Yet, through the many disappointments that marked his life, Schoenberg held tenaciously true to the tenet that underscored his life and work: complete honesty to the integrity of one's own artistic convictions.

**Bibliography**

MacDonald, Malcolm. *Schoenberg*. London: Dent, 1976. A balanced account of Schoenberg's life, works, beliefs, and musical style. Four chapters give a biographical overview; eleven discuss his artistic ideals and describe his work by genre. The appended calendar, catalog of works, personalia, and bibliography prove useful.

Neighbour, Oliver. "Arnold Schoenberg." In *Second Viennese School: Schoenberg, Webern, Berg*. Vol. 16 in *The New Grove Dictionary of Music and Musicians*, edited by Stanley Sadie. Washington, D.C.: Grove's Dictionaries of Music, and London: Macmillan, 1980. *Second Viennese School* is part of the New Grove's Composer Biography series. This article provides a concise yet thorough survey of Schoenberg's life and work. Separate sections discuss his life, beliefs, and works in chronological order. The appended list of works and bibliography are among the most comprehensive available.

Reich, Willi. *Schoenberg: A Critical Biography*. Translated by Leo Black. London: Longman, and New York: Praeger, 1971. Reich, a student of Berg and Webern, provides an in-depth look at Schoenberg's personality and his relationship to those around him through plentiful quotations from letters and commentaries, given in the context of a general biographical overview. Much emphasis is placed on contemporary criticism of Schoenberg's work and his reaction to it. Five long essays, a short bibliography, and a list of works are appended.

Rognoni, Luigi. *The Second Vienna School*. Translated by Robert W. Mann. London: Calder, 1977. A study of the stylistic derivation of expressionism, and its relationship, as applied by Schoenberg, Berg, and Webern, to other artistic trends of the era. Schoenberg's works are discussed in terms of genre and period, the emphasis being stylistic description rather than biographical delineation.

Rosen, Charles. *Arnold Schoenberg*. Edited by Frank Kermode. New York: Viking Press, 1975. Part of the Modern Masters series, this is a concise discussion of the stylistic traits that characterize Schoenberg's music: expressionism, atonality, serialism, and neoclassicism. By describing these traits in artistic and historical perspective, Rosen emphasizes the inseparable relationships of musical form, function, and expression.

Schoenberg, Arnold. *Style and Idea*. Edited by Leonard Stein. Translated by Leo Black. London: Faber, and New York: St. Martin's Press, 1975. This collection of writings and lectures, spanning forty years, provides great insight into Schoenberg's complex and often paradoxical beliefs. The balance of technical topics, artistic discussion, critical commentary, and personal reflection presents a very human view of the multifaceted composer.

Simms, Bryan R., ed. *Schoenberg, Berg and Webern: A Companion to the Second Viennese School.* Westport, Conn.: Greenwood Press, 1999. A collection of essays examining the development of modern Viennese composition in the early twentieth century including comparisons of music to other arts of the period.

Stuckenschmidt, Hans Heinz. *Schoenberg: His Life, World, and Work*. Translated by Humphrey Searle. London: Calder, and New York: Schirmer, 1977. One of the longest and most thorough, if wide-ranging, biographies available. Provides a detailed account of Schoenberg's life, personal and professional relationships, documentation, and the artistic and historical atmosphere that shaped these events. Includes numerous photographs, an analytical essay on Schoenberg's process of motive manipulation, translations of a number of documents and lectures, a list of works, and a select bibliography.

Van den Toorn, Pieter. "What's in a Motive? Schoenberg and Schenker Reconsidered." *The Journal of Musicology* 14, no. 3 (Summer 1996). Considers motive and imagination in the atonal musical compositions of Schoenberg and Schenker.

*Paul A. Siskind*

## ERWIN SCHRÖDINGER

*Born:* August 12, 1887; Vienna, Austro-Hungarian Empire

*Died:* January 4, 1961; Alpbach, Austria

*Areas of Achievement:* Physics and philosophy

*Contribution:* Schrödinger invented wave mechanics in 1926, for which he received the Nobel Prize in Physics (along with Paul Adrien Maurice Dirac) in 1933, and he helped to develop the formal equations that are central to quantum mechanics. His pioneering work on the relationship between physics and living systems influenced the growth of molecular biology.

### Early Life

Erwin Schrödinger was born on August 12, 1887, the only child of a well-to-do Viennese family. The Schrödinger family was part of the intellectual life of Vienna during a period when scholarly attainment was regarded as a loftier goal than material or political well-being. Erwin's father, Rudolf Schrödinger, operated a prosperous linoleum business, but he managed to find time in his schedule to pursue studies in Italian painting, in botany, and in chemistry.

With the exception of a brief stay at a public elementary school in Innsbruck, Erwin was educated by a tutor who visited the family home twice a week. His maternal grandmother was British, and fluency in English gave his studies a considerable boost; as he matured, Schrödinger added proficiency in German, French, and Spanish to his arsenal of languages. Until the age of eleven, Erwin's primary educational influence was his father, who proved to be an invaluable sounding board on a host of subjects. At this time, Erwin entered the academic *Gymnasium* at Vienna and commenced a program of studies in the classics and in mathematics and physics.

Schrödinger entered the University of Vienna in 1906. The following year, he began to attend lectures in theoretical physics. In 1910, he received his doctorate and assumed a position as assistant to Franz Exner at the university's Second Physics Institute, where he remained until the outbreak of World War I. During this period, Schrödinger published papers on a range of subjects, including magnetism, radioactivity, X rays, and Brownian motion. Exner was heavily influenced by Ludwig Boltzmann, an influence which carried over to Schrödinger's later work. When Schrödinger was awarded the Nobel Prize in 1933, he declared that "his [Boltzmann's] line of thought may be called my first love in science. No other has ever thus enraptured me or will ever do so again."

Following an undistinguished service in the military, brief appointments at Jena, Stuttgart, and Breslau culminated with Schrödinger's appointment in 1921 to the chair of theoretical physics in Zurich, a position formerly held by Albert Einstein. Prior to his stay in Jena, he had married Annemarie Bertel of Salzburg on June 6, 1920. During this period, his papers touched on a number of subjects, including general relativity, probability theory, a lengthy review of dielectric phenomena, and a series of papers on three- and four-color theories of vision. Schrödinger's main efforts, however, were targeted on atomic theory. The papers that secured his reputation were composed in a half-year's flourish of creativity before he left Zurich. It was there in 1926 that Schrödinger, at the relatively advanced age of thirty-nine, invented wave mechanics and published what is known as the Schrödinger wave

equation, the formalism which is the foundation of modern quantum mechanics.

### Life's Work

Schrödinger's invention of wave mechanics represented an attempt to overcome some difficulties generated by Niels Bohr's theory of the hydrogen atom. In particular, attempts to construct a theory of a stable system of more than two particles (such as the helium atom, with a nucleus and two electrons) had failed. The inspiration for Schrödinger's wave mechanics was Louis de Broglie's suggestion that particles are nothing more than a wave crest on a background of waves. De Broglie supposed that electrons display wave features, and, in order to support this thesis, he attempted to fit a whole number of wavelengths into each electron orbit, in a way which precluded the possibility of in-between orbits. He concluded that both wave and particle behavior are inextricably combined in the case of the electron. On behalf of his thesis, de Broglie predicted that matter-waves would be detected by diffracting a beam of electrons from a crystal. Even as de Broglie was formulating his ideas, this effect was observed in 1922 by Charles Kunsman and Clinton Davisson.

Schrödinger used the mathematics of waves in a way which attempted to eliminate quantum jumps, or the notion that electrons move instantaneously from one level to another. He sought to represent this quantum transition as the passage of energy from one vibrational form into another, rather than as the jumping of electrons. The transition of an electron from one energy state to another, Schrödinger believed, was akin to the change in the vibration of a violin string from one note to another. These results were announced by Schrödinger in four seminal papers published in the *Annalen der Physik* early in 1926, the first of which contains his famous wave equation.

Schrödinger's wave mechanics was eagerly embraced by numerous scientists who had been puzzled by the emerging atomic theory and regarded the model of a wave as furnishing a realistic account of microprocesses; it was also criticized on a number of counts. It was not clear, for example, how an entity such as a wave could make a Geiger counter click as though a single particle were being recorded. Furthermore, it was not evident how black-body radiation was to be explained in terms of Schrödinger's waves. A further wrinkle was added when Carl Eckart and Paul Adrien Maurice Dirac showed that Werner Heisenberg's equations (which were based on the supposition that electrons are particles) were equivalent to Schrödinger's theory that electrons are waves.

Bohr suggested that both models, particle and wave physics, were valid and complementary descriptions of the world—that there are some cases when it is appropriate to utilize the particle concept and other cases when it is better to use the wave concept. Max Born's suggestion that Schrödinger's wave function expressed the probability of finding a particle at a given point in space furnished support for Bohr's resolution to the controversy. The location of a particle cannot be ascertained with certainty, but the wave function enables one to work out the probability that the particle will be found in a certain place. Finally, Heisenberg suggested in 1926 that scientists cannot measure both the position and the momentum of an electron at the same time. The more one knows about its position, the less one knows about its momentum, and vice versa.

These developments were largely accepted by the time Schrödinger succeeded Max Planck in 1927 in the renowned chair of theoretical physics at the University of Berlin. This position allowed Schrödinger to enjoy the intellectual companionship of the greatest collection of physicists anywhere in the world, and his working environment was second to none; yet quantum mechanics was completed in other centers, primarily because the Berlin group, including Schrödinger, was opposed to the statistical and dualistic aspects of quantum theory as it was being developed in these other centers.

In Berlin, Schrödinger enjoyed a fruitful period until Adolf Hitler assumed the reins of power in 1933, the same year that Schrödinger and Dirac received the Nobel Prize. Schrödinger's background ensured that his position was secure. His opposition to the Nazi regime, however, induced him to give up his post. Schrödinger settled in Oxford for a brief and unproductive period, but in 1936 he succumbed to homesickness and accepted a position in Graz, Austria. This decision was imprudent, since his opposition to the Nazi regime was common knowledge, and he was dismissed from his position without notice in 1938. With no recourse, he fled Austria when Hitler's forces invaded later the same year.

During 1935, Schrödinger had published a paper that criticized the current state of quantum theory. In quantum mechanics, the laws of physics are governed by probability; a radioactive atom might decay and emit an electron, or it might not. Schrödinger was upset by the absurdity of this implication and framed a famous thought experiment designed to expose it. In this experiment, he envisioned a box that contains a radioactive source, a device for detecting the presence of radioactive particles, a live cat, and a container of poison. The experiment is constructed such that the detector is switched on long enough so that there is a fifty-fifty chance that one of the atoms in the radioactive material will decay and that the detector will record the presence of a particle. If the detector does record such an event, the poison container is broken and the cat dies. If the detector does not record the presence of a particle, the cat lives.

In the world of ordinary experience, there is a fifty-fifty chance that the cat will be killed. Without examining the contents of the box, it is safe to assert that the cat is either dead or alive. In the world of quantum physics, neither of these two possibilities has any reality unless it is first observed. The atomic decay has neither occurred nor not occurred. Since the fate of the feline is tied to the state of the radioactive material, one cannot say that the cat is dead or alive until the inside of the box is examined. This implication, Schrödinger declared, reveals the absurdity of quantum mechanics. It is one thing to conceive of an elementary particle such as an electron being neither here nor there but quite another to conceive of a concrete thing such as a cat in this indeterminate state.

Schrödinger was encouraged in his decision to leave Graz by a message from Eamon de Valera, the President of Ireland, who invited him to serve as the first director of the school of theoretical physics at the Dublin Institute for Advanced Studies. The intellectual atmosphere of Dublin was fruitful for Schrödinger because its mandate was to foster breadth of interest and intellectual speculation. Among the eminent mathematical physicists at the time, Schrödinger most aptly fulfilled these criteria. During this period, Schrödinger published many works on the application and statistical interpretation of wave mechanics, and on problems concerning the relationship between general relativity and wave mechanics. As senior professor, it was Schrödinger's pleasant duty to give a series of lectures from time to time. Four of his books, *What Is Life?* (1944), *Science and Humanism: Physics in Our Time* (1951), *Nature and the Greeks* (1954), and *Mind and Matter* (1958), were written for these lecture series. The most famous was his lecture series "What Is Life?" presented in 1944 to a large and enthusiastic audience. The thesis of these lectures is that quantum physics is required for understanding biological replication. Although his theme was controversial, it aroused much interest among many promising young physicists, such as Francis Crick, and encouraged them to turn to biology.

In 1956, near the end of Schrödinger's stay in Dublin, asthma and bronchitis curtailed his productivity. His friend, Hans Thirring, arranged a special chair for him as professor emeritus of theoretical physics at the University of Vienna. He wrote only two articles during this period, one on the interpretation of quantum mechanics and a second on the problem of nature and the self. Schrödinger died after a prolonged illness at the age of seventy-three.

### Summary

Erwin Schrödinger is primarily known for inventing wave mechanics and for the equation which bears his name, but his legacy is much greater. His collected papers include important contributions to virtually every branch of physics, and he constantly encouraged physicists to examine the foundations of their discipline and its relationship to other scientific endeavors. As a philosopher, he was worried about the problems of knowers in a world governed by probabilistic laws. Schrödinger was also interested in the classics and in poetry, and he even tried his hand at sculpture.

While his interests knew no bounds, Schrödinger was somewhat narrow in his outlook on questions of physics. His conservativeness was not surprising granted that, when he made his most important contributions during the mid-1920's, he was already a senior member of the scientific community and steeped in traditional concepts and theories. Indeed, Schrödinger resisted the new innovations of indeterminacy and the instantaneous jumping of electrons from one state to another to the end of his days. His most important contribution—the wave mechanics—attempted to describe atomic structures in terms of waves, an established model in the scientific community. Schrödinger furnished scientists with invaluable tools for problem-solving, but his wave mechanics represented a return to nineteenth century ideas.

**Bibliography**

Atkins, Kenneth R. *Physics: Once Over Lightly.* New York: Wiley, 1972. This book is a serious guide to modern physics for the casual reader or the nonscience major. It is invaluable as an aid to further study.

Born, Max. *The Restless Universe.* 2d ed. New York: Dover, 1951. One of the best contemporary accounts of the new physics by one of its central participants. This is a popular book about the birth of modern physics that can be read for profit by the nonspecialist.

Crow, James F. "Erwin Schrödinger and the Hornless Cattle Problem." *Genetics* 130, no. 2 (February, 1992). Although awarded the Nobel Prize in Physics, Schrödinger is noted by geneticists for his book *What is Life?* The author looks at the influence of this book on the work of several scientists and its contributions to the field of molecular biology.

Gribbin, John. *In Search of Schrödinger's Cat: Quantum Physics and Reality.* London: Wildwood House, New York: Bantam Books, 1984. The author believes that Schrödinger's wave mechanics attempted to restore nineteenth century concepts, an assessment first made by some of Schrödinger's contemporaries, such as Born. This book provides a historical backdrop for the development of the central concepts of quantum mechanics, and it contains a useful bibliography.

Haroche, Serge. "Entanglement, Decoherence and the Quantum/Classical Boundary." *Physics Today* 51, no. 7 (July, 1998). Examines Schrödinger's cat gedankenexperiment where he theorized that a cat could become entangled with an individual atom, using the principles of quantum mechanics.

Schrödinger, Erwin. *What Is Life? The Physical Aspect of the Living Cell.* Cambridge: Cambridge University Press, and New York: Macmillan, 1944. This book was very influential on an entire generation of scientists, including Crick, who unraveled the structure of the living molecule. It is mistaken on some key points, but it stands as a testament to the importance of quantum theory for genetic engineering.

Scott, William T. *Erwin Schrödinger: An Introduction to His Writings.* Amherst: University of Massachusetts Press, 1967. An invaluable account of Schrödinger's life and work. Many of the chapters are highly technical, but the first chapter gives a good synopsis of Schrödinger's life and work. The bibliography of Schrödinger's publications is indispensable for additional research.

*Brian S. Baigrie*

# KARL SCHWARZSCHILD

*Born:* October 9, 1873; Frankfurt am Main, Germany
*Died:* May 11, 1916; Potsdam, Germany
*Area of Achievement:* Astronomy
*Contribution:* Schwarzschild developed a new use for photography, as a tool for measuring the brightness of stars, particularly variable objects. He was the first scientist to develop a solution for Albert Einstein's general relativity field equations, dealing with gravity around a star of such intensity that it becomes a black hole, surrounded by a boundary known as the Schwarzschild radius.

## Early Life

Karl Schwarzschild was the eldest child of six children. His father, a prosperous businessman in Frankfurt, encouraged Karl's early interest in science, particularly astronomy. He was the first of his family to be interested in science; indeed, he wrote and published his first two astronomical papers, on the topic of double-star orbits, when he was only sixteen. While in school, he was introduced to J. Epstein, a mathematician with a private observatory. From Epstein's son, Schwarzschild learned to make and to use a telescope, and studied advanced mathematics and celestial mechanics. After education at the local level, he spent two years at the University of Strasbourg (1891), then two more at the University of Munich. He received his doctorate from that university in 1896, graduating summa cum laude. The thesis for his Ph.D. was on the application of the theory of stable configurations in rotating bodies, developed by Henri Poincaré, to investigations of tidal deformation in satellites and the validity of Pierre-Simon Laplace's theory for the origin of the solar system. He also invented a multislit interferometer for measuring separation of double stars.

## Life's Work

Schwarzschild was interested in observational astronomy. In the early 1890's, he developed the use of photography, later called photographic photometry, to measure the apparent magnitude of stars using a photographic plate to substitute for the human eye at the telescope. Using his new method of measuring the image densities on the plates, he was able to establish the magnitude of 367 stars; he used those results to get a teaching position at the University of Munich. In all, he worked on thirty-five hundred stellar objects of magnitude greater than 7.5, at the same time showing conclusively that there was a vast difference between visual (with the unaided eye) and photographic magnitude or brightness, a difference later known as the star's color index. His results also led him to suggest that periodic variable stars behaved as they did, going through a regular cycle of maximum and minimum brightness, because of periodic temperature changes. In turn, this hypothesis led to further work on Cepheid variables by the famous astronomer Sir Arthur Eddington.

From 1896 to 1899, Schwarzschild worked as an assistant at the Kuffner Observatory in Vienna. After some time spent lecturing and writing (his lectures conveyed the excitement of astronomy to nonastronomers to such an extent that the lectures would become famous), he received an associate professorship in 1901 from the University of Göttingen. A year later, he became a professor of astronomy there, and was also made director of its observatory. In 1909, he succeeded Hermann Vogel as the director of the Astrophysical Observatory in Potsdam.

Schwarzschild worked extensively in theoretical astronomy and also in subjects as diverse as orbital mechanics, the curvature of space throughout the known universe, stellar energy production, and the surface structures of the Sun. In 1900, he suggested that the geometry of space did not necessarily have to conform to Euclidean geometry, in which two parallel lines are forever parallel, and the sum of interior angles of a triangle is always 180 degrees. Light rays from a star hitting Earth's orbit at two widely separated points form an overextended triangle. By measuring the interior angles of such a hypothetical structure, he attempted to determine the curvature of space, since he knew that, if the angles added up to more or less than 180 degrees, he would be dealing with non-Euclidean space. He concluded, from his experimental results, that if space were curved, it had an extremely large radius of curvature, so large as to be unnoticeable in as small a region as the solar system.

In 1906, Schwarzschild worked diligently on a paper showing that a star should not be considered as a simple gas held together by its own gravity. Thermodynamical properties, particularly concerning the transfer of heat inside the stellar surface by both convection and radiation, had to be present. To deal effectively with this situation, he invented the concept of radiative equilibrium in astrophysics, a balance of the energy flowing inward and outward to help maintain the star's stability. He showed how, mathematically, radiative processes would be important in conveying heat in stellar atmospheres—how energy could be transferred at and near the Sun's surface. Many of his ideas were stimulated by his observation of the total solar eclipse in 1905, an event he photographed with a newly devised instrument, one forming spectrograms from an objective prism at the eyepiece of the telescope. This instrument allowed him to derive information on the chemical composition of various areas at differing depths in the Sun's atmosphere.

Among the topics to which he contributed was stellar statistics, how to deal with large numbers of stars and their associated data. The methods and techniques he developed are now standard in graduate stellar astronomy courses. He designed, as a new tool for analysis, a spectrographic objective that provided a reliable means of determining a star's radial velocity, the speed and direction in which it is moving. Many new contributions to geometric optics stemmed from this fertile period.

Schwarzschild volunteered for military service in 1914, at the start of World War I, spending his time first in Belgium manning a weather station, then transferring to France for the job of calculating the trajectories for long-range cannon shells. Craving action, he managed to get transferred again, to Russia. While in Russia in 1916, he heard of Albert Einstein's new general theory of relativity. As a result, Schwarzschild wrote two papers on the theory, both published that year. He provided a solution, the first to be found, to the complex partial differential equations fundamental to the theory's mathematical basis. Schwarzschild solved the Einstein equation for the exterior space time of a spherical nonrotating body. He showed that when a star is contracting under the influence of gravity, a result of the amount of mass present, if it reaches a particular radius, the gravitational potential, representing the energy needed to escape from the object, becomes infinite in quantity. This solution showed that there is an enormous redshift, virtually infinite, when a body of large mass contracts to that certain radius, a size known as the Schwarzschild radius. The value of that size is easily calculated by a simple astrophysical formula he derived, relating the

radius to the universal gravitational constant, the star's mass, and the speed of light (*R* = *2GM/c*[2]). Surprisingly, he showed that the general theory of relativity gave basically the same results as Isaac Newton's more common theory of gravitation, but for different reasons. When the mass of the object is measured in units of the Sun's mass, the Schwarzschild radius is neatly given by three times the ratio of the mass to the Sun's mass, the answer expressed in kilometers (*R* = 3 x *M/M* [Sun]). If the Sun were contracted to a radius of 3 kilometers, it would be of the right size to be labeled a "black hole." A body becomes a black hole when it shrinks to a radius of less than the critical radius; at that point, nothing, including light, will have enough energy ever to escape from the body—hence the name "black hole," since no light escapes and anything falling in remains. Earth's mass is such that it would have to contract to a radius of approximately one centimeter to become such a glorified vacuum cleaner for the universe.

The theoretical study of black holes and the continuing search for them has become an important field in modern astronomy, particularly since they can be used to solve some of the most fundamental problems of stellar, galactic, and cosmological astronomy.

While in Russia, Schwarzschild contracted pemphigus, an incurable metabolic disease of the skin. He was an invalid at home in 1916 when he died. For his service in the war effort, he was awarded an Iron Cross. In 1960, he was honored by the Berlin Academy, which named him the greatest German astronomer of the preceding century.

## Summary

Karl Schwarzschild, as an astronomer and theoretician, achieved many great things in his chosen field, despite his short life. As a final contribution to history, he was father to Martin Schwarzschild, born in 1912, who has done his own great work in astronomy, primarily on the theory of stellar structure and evolutionary dynamics.

Schwarzschild early developed the kind of flair for science of which many scientists only dream. His practical skill he demonstrated by the superb and innovative instruments he designed and built, including astrophotographic tools, spectral analysis instruments, and many important contributions to the theory and design of geometrical optics. With his exceptional mathematical ability, he was able to contribute greatly to theoretical astronomy, in subjects including celestial mechanics, stellar physics, solar dynamics, thermodynamics of stellar interiors, and applications of the theory of relativity, all of which are important fields of research in modern astronomy.

Schwarzschild attached great importance to lecturing and writing on popular astronomy. He attempted to make difficult subjects in physics and astronomy more lucid, presenting pictures with words that the average nonscientist could understand. He was equally at home with his scientific associates, ready to discuss and extend any conjecture or idea. As a theoretical astrophysicist, he was one of the great promoters of Niels Bohr's theory of atomic spectra, presented in 1913, a theory that he believed would solve most of the analytic problems of stellar spectral analysis. While on his deathbed, Schwarzschild finished a famous paper on that subject, in which he developed the rules of quantization, work that, developed independently by Arnold Sommerfeld, provided for the theory of the Stark effect and the quantum theory of molecular structure. Perhaps he expressed his wonderment at nature best regarding relativity and the curvature of space when he wrote: "One finds oneself here, if one will, in a geometrical fairyland, but the beauty of this fairy tale is that one does not know but that it may be true." One wonders how far he might have gone if war had not ended his brilliant career so early.

## Bibliography

Bergmann, Peter G. *The Riddle of Gravitation*. Rev. ed. New York: Scribner, 1987. A detailed study of the effects of gravity in the universe, from the viewpoints of Newton and Einstein. A major portion of the book is spent on the role of gravity in the operation of stars and the formation of black holes. Excellent glossary and extensive pictures. Some mathematics; difficult reading.

Bowers, Richard, and Terry Deeming. *Astrophysics*. Vol. 1, *Stars*. Boston: Jones and Bartlett, 1984. A detailed excursion into the features and history of stellar bodies. Beginning with observational data, the work proceeds with the life history of stars, to the endpoints, including black holes, supernovas, and white dwarfs. Very detailed in mathematics; recommended for the advanced layperson. References.

Calder, Nigel. *Einstein's Universe*. London: BBC, and New York: Viking Press, 1979. A brief but clearly written account of how the universe works under the actions of the special and general theories of relativity. Deals with the origin of the universe and the evolution of stars to the black-hole stage. Interesting discussion of the curving of space as a result of effects of large masses. Good diagrams and pictures; easy reading.

Hartmann, William K. *Cycles of Fire*. New York: Workman, 1987; London: Aurum Press, 1988. An immensely enjoyable book dealing with the stars. Covers their origins and lives, to the end when they die, by using basic telescopic data to explain, in simple terms, basic astrophysics. Also deals with possible planetary systems and life-forms. Fantastic pictures and paintings. Additional references and a well-written glossary.

Kaufmann, William J., III. *Black Holes and Warped Spacetime*. San Francisco: Freeman, 1979. A book for the layperson on the general theory of relativity and its consequences, particularly in terms of star deaths. Extensive section on the Schwarzschild radius and its importance in forming black holes, altering the space around the star. Well written, with a comprehensive nonmathematical treatment.

Kippenhahn, Rudolf. *100 Billion Suns*. London: Weidenfeld and Nicolson, and New York: Basic, 1983. A well-written overview of the development of knowledge of stellar astronomy. Using extensive drawings, Kippenhahn details the evolution of stars, from original dust clouds collapsing, through middle age, to the death throes of various-sized objects. Black-hole formation is nicely discussed. Numerous pictures and drawings, and extensive references.

*New Frontiers in Astronomy: Readings from "Scientific American."* San Francisco: Freeman, 1975. A collection of major articles from the magazine representing the major areas of research in astronomy. Excellent sections on stars, black holes, and the role of relativity in the universe. Written for the advanced layperson. Additional bibliographies for each article. Numerous pictures and explanatory diagrams.

Schwarzschild, Karl. *Gesammelte Werke—Collected Works.* Edited by H.H. Voight. New York: Springer, 1992. Three-volume set of the complete works of Schwarzschild accompanied by biographical information, comments by contemporary experts, and an essay by Nobel laureate S. Chandrasekhar.

Verschuur, G. L. *The Invisible Universe Revealed.* New York: Springer-Verlag, 1987. Using the previously unknown parts of the electromagnetic spectrum, this work traces the development of radio astronomy and its offshoots. Details the types of observations made and the nature of the data gathered on black holes, quasars, galaxies, nebulas, and stellar objects. Excellent and extensive collection of pictures; extensive references.

*Arthur L. Alt*

## ALBERT SCHWEITZER

*Born:* January 14, 1875; Kaysersberg, Germany
*Died:* September 4, 1965; Lambaréné, Gabon
*Areas of Achievement:* Theology, peace advocacy, philosophy, music, and medicine
*Contribution:* Schweitzer, a renowned organist, student of the music of Bach, and an unorthodox biblical scholar, dedicated himself as a medical missionary to the natives of Africa, a decision that led to a fifty-year career that captured the admiration of many people and led to his receiving the Nobel Peace Prize. He also actively urged the public, politicians, and statesmen to come to grips with the threat of nuclear war and work for peace.

### Early Life

Albert Schweitzer was born in Kaysersberg, Haute Alsace, on January 14, 1875. During that year his father, Louis Schweitzer, a liberal protestant, became pastor of the village church in Gunsbach, Alsace. There in what today is the Rhineland of France, Schweitzer grew up. Alsace has in its history been alternately governed by France and Germany. Because of this background Schweitzer spoke both French and German fluently. He studied and wrote in both languages.

Schweitzer's father began teaching him to play the piano and organ when he was five and eight years old, respectively. At nine he occasionally substituted for the regular organist in his father's church. When he was ten, he was sent to school in Mulhouse, where he lived with a great uncle and began taking music lessons from Eugene Munch. It was during the eight years he spent in Mulhouse that his creative, intellectual, and musical abilities blossomed.

In order to follow in the footsteps of his father, he was enrolled in the University of Strasbourg as a student of theology and philosophy at the Theological College of St. Thomas. He did not, however, give up his new love, music. It was music, particularly the editing of the organ works of Johann Sebastian Bach, and his organ playing, building, and restoring abilities that supported Schweitzer through much of his life and brought him international acclaim. His college career was interrupted when he was drafted into the infantry. He, however, did not leave his mind at home. He took what he had learned at St. Thomas and a copy of the Greek New Testament with him. He spent many hours thumbing through it, reading and meditating on the words of Jesus in the light of the modern historical criticism he had been taught.

Immediately after graduation, Schweitzer entered a postgraduate program in philosophy that took him to the Sorbonne in Paris, the University of Berlin, and finally back to the University of Strasbourg, which awarded him the doctor of philosophy degree for his treatise on the religious philosophy of Immanuel Kant. He believed that he was ready to begin working toward a doctor of theology degree, which he completed one year later. In September, 1900, he was ordained at St. Nicholas Church in Strasbourg and the following spring received an appointment to the faculty of the Theological College of St. Thomas at the University of Strasbourg, a post he held for six years. During this time he continued his study of the organ and gained quite a reputation as a performer.

### Life's Work

Schweitzer, on his thirtieth birthday, informed his friends that he had decided to devote the rest of his life to the natives of Africa as a doctor of medicine. This created quite a stir among family and friends, most of whom thought he had lost his mind. He was not to be dissuaded. While continuing his duties as a faculty member and completing a biography of Bach, Schweitzer began taking the science courses needed to enter medical school. He made contact with the Paris Missionary Society, whose newsletter containing an article on the need for medical missionaries in Africa had inspired him, volunteering his services as a medical missionary. To his surprise, he was not readily accepted, because of his unorthodox biblical views. He finally convinced the Paris Missionary Society to grant him permission to set up a medical facility for them when he promised not to preach but only to serve as a medical doctor.

From 1906 to 1912, Schweitzer studied medicine at the University of Strasbourg, all the time teaching religion at the university, preaching at St. Nicholas, giving organ concerts, working with Charles Widor on an edition of Bach's organ works, writing several books and treatises, and making plans for his work in Africa. In 1912, he resigned his positions at the University of Strasbourg and St. Nicholas Church and on June 18, 1912, married Helene Bresslau, the daughter of a Jewish colleague and professor of history. In February, 1913, he completed his internship in tropical medicine, finished his thesis on the psychiatric study of Jesus, and received his M.D. degree. On March 26, 1913, he and his wife, who had become a nurse in order to work with him, set sail from Bordeaux, France, to set up a hospital on the land of the Paris Missionary Society in Lambaréné, French Equatorial Africa, today known as Gabon. This trip was the first of his many trips between Europe and Africa and marks the end of Schweitzer's life of preparation for service and the beginning of his life of service to Africans.

Schweitzer's life in Africa can be divided into four periods, each of which was marked by three events over which he had no control: World War I, World War II, and the death of his wife. Schweitzer had barely established his hospital when he was put under house arrest in Lambaréné by the French. He was considered an enemy alien because he was German and came from German Alsace. In 1917, he and his wife were transferred to France, where they were interned in two different prison camps for civilian aliens. It was to be ten years before he was able to return to Lambaréné. When he did so, this time without his wife, he found his hospital in ruins.

During the years from 1927 to 1947, Schweitzer built a new hospital at a new location not far from the first site. He traveled back and forth to Europe four times. One additional trip was cut short—so short, in fact, that the same boat that took him to Europe took him back to Africa. He was afraid that Hitler would attack France and somehow, perhaps because he was now considered a French citizen or perhaps because he had a Jewish wife, prevent him from returning to French Equatorial Africa. There were four reasons for these frequent trips: to visit his wife; to give concerts in order to raise the money he needed to operate his hospital and support himself; to deliver lectures to gather charitable support; and to recruit doctors and nurses to serve with him in Africa.

Schweitzer's longest sojourn in Africa took place during World War II. He was hard pressed to keep his hospital afloat. His concert tours in Europe could not be held, medical supplies were consumed by the war, and his supporters in Alsace were surrounded by the war. Fortunately, a speaking tour that his wife made in the United States brought his cause to the attention of some Americans who raised money and sent medical supplies to him when the people of Europe could not do so.

The years between 1947 and 1957 Schweitzer spent mostly in Europe. During this time he was in great demand as a lecturer and organist. Both of these activities brought him and his work into the public eye, and support for his work was no longer in question. During this time he was idolized by Europeans and Americans alike. He was courted by people seeking support for their own causes. In 1952, he was awarded the Nobel Peace Prize. Perhaps it was his experiences with war, perhaps it was his Christianity, perhaps it was both and more—in any case he gave wholehearted support to the antinuclear protests of the late 1950's. He made only four short stays in Africa. Unfortunately, it was during the last sojourn that his wife died. Shortly after Helen's death, he made one more trip to Europe when, besides the usual public appearances, he put his European house in order. Schweitzer brought his wife's ashes with him to Africa and buried them on his hospital grounds in Lambaréné. This time he returned to stay. He no longer felt the need to visit Europe. Support for his work was assured, and he wanted to see his hospital, especially his leprosarium, developed in his way. Now, more than ever before, people came to see him and his hospital at Lambaréné. The hospital they saw was not necessarily what they expected, but Schweitzer, himself, disappointed only those who had come with their own agenda. He had fought his own battles; he was now an old man too occupied with his work to take up causes other than his own.

In July, 1964, Schweitzer designated Walter Munz as chief of staff of his hospital. On August 28, 1965, Schweitzer appointed his daughter, Rhena Schweitzer-Eckert, as administrator of the hospital. On September 4, 1965, his house in order, Schweitzer died. African drums, similar to those that told the Africans that he had arrived in Lambaréné more than a half a century earlier, now told of his death. Modern forms of communication spread the news throughout Gabon to the rest of the world.

### Summary

It is really incorrect to say, as many do, that Albert Schweitzer's life's work began with his first trip to Africa. Everything he did leading up to that time and everything he did from then until his death revolved around his work in Africa. The proceeds of his books on the life of Bach financed his personal expenses for the first years in Lambaréné. He sup-

ported himself while in Africa by writing about his work there, by writing on theology, philosophy, and music for book publishers and magazines. He kept up his skills as an organist by practicing in Africa on a piano outfitted with organ pedals so that he could give organ concerts while visiting Europe. All this made it possible for him to care for the sick, operate on the ill and injured, comfort the dying, plan and supervise the construction of his hospital, and recruit people with medical skills to his hospital.

It was Schweitzer's theology that led him to his interpretation of Jesus' command, "Follow me." He traced his ethical philosophy back to Jesus' teaching to love your neighbor. Schweitzer was a man of heroic proportions, yet he was human and had human failings. This plus the human failings of others caused him to be subjected to a fair amount of unkind and unjustified criticism. This criticism never seriously affected him or his reputation. His place in history seems secure.

### Bibliography

Anderson, Erica. *The Schweitzer Album: A Portrait in Words and Pictures*. New York: Harper, 1965. This work strives to explicate Schweitzer's thought through quotations from his conversations, speeches, and letters. Also contains many photographs of Schweitzer.

———. *The World of Albert Schweitzer: A Book of Photographs*. New York: Harper, 1955. This book is an excellent place to start a study on the life of Schweitzer. Contains pictures taken by Anderson during the several trips she made to Lambaréné plus many others she selected in order to complete this photographic essay.

Brabazon, James. *Albert Schweitzer: A Biography*. New York: Putnam, 1975; London: Gollancz, 1976. A long, balanced, and well-written biography published ten years after Schweitzer's death. Its strength is in its discussion of the last part of Schweitzer's life. It has an epilogue about life in Lambaréné after Schweitzer. The book contains photographs, a bibliography, scholarly notes, and an index.

Cousins, Norman. *Dr. Schweitzer of Lambaréné*. New York: Harper, 1960; London: Black, 1961. An account of Cousins' visit to Schweitzer's hospital in Lambaréné during January, 1957. The appendix contains Schweitzer's radio broadcast, "Peace or Atomic War." The book contains photographs of the persons and sights to be seen at the Schweitzer Hospital. It gives insight into Schweitzer's work and accomplishments during the last years of his life.

Hagedorn, Hermann. *Prophet in the Wilderness: The Story of Albert Schweitzer*. New York: Macmillan, 1947. An early, popular account of Schweitzer's life. It has bibliographic references to English works about Schweitzer and to English translations of Schweitzer's books that were published before 1947.

Marshall, George, and David Poling. *Schweitzer: A Biography*. Rev. ed. New York: Macmillan, 1954. If only one book about Schweitzer can be read, this one should be considered. It tells the story of his life and evaluates him as a man and as a world citizen. This book contains a chronological biography, an index, a bibliography of English translations of Schweitzer's books, collections based on his works, selected biographies of Schweitzer, and recordings by and films about him. The bibliography is annotated and includes references to two books containing negative criticism.

Payne, Robert. *The Three Worlds of Albert Schweitzer*. Translated by Edward Fitzgerald. New York: Nelson, 1957. This book is less on the life and more on the thought of Schweitzer. It is an examination of Schweitzer's writings on Kant, Jesus, Paul, and Johann Wolfgang von Goethe. It discusses his music, ethics, and theological views on the "Kingdom of God."

Peddle, Francis K. "Albert Schweitzer and the Transcendence of History." *Modern Age* 39, no. 3 (Summer 1997). Considers Albert Schweitzer's thoughts on history as a basis for philosophical truth and ethical behavior.

Schweitzer, Albert. *Music in the Life of Albert Schweitzer with Selections from His Writings*. Edited by Charles R. Joy. New York: Harper, 1951; London: Black, 1953. Schweitzer was renowned as a performer of music. This book, however, concentrates on his thoughts on music, organs and organ building, and his writings about Bach. While it does this, it is not just a book for musicians. It, like most books about him from the 1950's, was written to satisfy the curiosity of people who wanted to know more and more of the person about whom everyone was talking.

———. *The Wit and Wisdom of Albert Schweitzer*. Edited by Charles R. Joy. Boston: Beacon Press, 1949. A topically arranged collection of quotations, some short, some longer, which show the wide range of Schweitzer's interests. The book contains a bibliography of Schweitzer's writings and a good chronology of Schweitzer's life up until October, 1949.

Seaver, George. *Albert Schweitzer: The Man and His Mind*. 6th ed. London: Black, 1969. This work devotes equal time to Schweitzer's biography and to a discussion of his writings. Appendixes 1 and 3 feature Schweitzer's thoughts on colonization, race relations, and religion (ethics) in modern civilization, areas of thought where Schweitzer is most controversial.

*Theodore P. Aufdemberge*

# GLENN THEODORE SEABORG

*Born:* April 19, 1912; Ishpeming, Michigan

*Areas of Achievement:* Nuclear science and education

*Contribution:* Codiscoverer of ten transuranium elements and numerous radioisotopes with wide applications in research, medicine, and industry, Seaborg served under five United States presidents in establishing policy regarding the role of science and uses of atomic energy.

## Early Life

Glenn Theodore Seaborg was born in Ishpeming, Michigan, a small iron-mining town on the Upper Peninsula, in April, 1912. His mother, Selma O. Erickson, came through Ellis Island from Sweden in 1904 to join family members in a predominantly Swedish immigrant section of Ishpeming. There she met and married his father, Herman Theodore Seaborg, whose father and mother had moved from Sweden to Michigan in 1867 and 1869. Young Glenn's first language was Swedish, and his early years were strongly influenced by Swedish cultural traditions.

When he was ten years old and starting the fifth grade, his parents decided to leave Michigan and move to Southern California to take advantage of a better climate and broader opportunities for their children. They settled in Home Gardens (now South Gate), which, as a brand-new subdivision, did not have any schools during their first year there. Seaborg and his younger sister, Jeanette, attended part of a year of grammar school and, later, four years of high school in the Watts district of Los Angeles. His schoolmates in Watts came from many different ethnic backgrounds: European, Chinese, Mexican, Japanese, black, Filipino. This early exposure to different cultures may have contributed to Seaborg's later facility in getting along well and communicating effectively with a wide range of people.

Seaborg was urged by his parents to undertake a commercial course in high school, which they believed was the most secure route to a respectable, white-collar job, their fondest dream for the son of a long line of machinists. Seaborg, however, elected to take college preparatory courses and, in his final two years of high school, thanks to the inspiration of a fine science teacher, discovered the excitement of science, in which he would make his career.

When Seaborg started college in 1929 at the University of California, Los Angeles (UCLA), there were only four permanent buildings and much mud at the newly established Westwood campus. There were, however, gifted teachers who encouraged his scientific curiosity and told him about the thrilling new discoveries being made in the field of nuclear science in Europe and at the Berkeley campus. He became determined to work in this new frontier.

After earning his undergraduate degree in chemistry from UCLA in 1934, the tall (six-foot, three-inch), lanky young man moved north to Berkeley to undertake graduate work. Berkeley was a mecca for scientists; its chemistry and physics faculties were among the finest in the world, with such notable pioneers as the chemist Gilbert N. Lewis and the physicist Ernest O. Lawrence. Intense and hardworking, Seaborg could hardly believe his good fortune. At weekly seminars, he was enthralled by reports of the results being obtained by Lawrence at the twenty-seven-inch cyclotron and delighted to have the chance of working the graveyard shift to complete experiments for his thesis on the inelastic scattering of neutrons, for which he earned his Ph.D. in chemistry from University of California, Berkeley, in 1937. During the years immediately following, he developed two associations which would have great influence on his life: He served as personal research assistant to Lewis, and he met and courted Lawrence's secretary, an attractive woman named Helen Griggs.

His career as a published nuclear scientist actually began in 1936 when physicist Jack Livingood asked him to perform the chemical separations on a target just bombarded at the cyclotron in order to identify the radioisotopes it had produced. During the ensuing five years of collaboration with Livingood, they discovered or identified a number of radioisotopes (iodine-131, iron-59, cobalt-60) which are still widely used in medicine for diagnosis and therapy. In 1938, with Emilio Segre, Seaborg discovered technetium-99m, which is the most widely used diagnostic radioisotope in nuclear medicine.

Seaborg has often described the exhilaration he and his colleagues felt when they learned in 1939 about the experiments Otto Hahn and Fritz Strassman were performing in Germany, which gave the first evidence of a nuclear fission reaction. The next year, Edwin M. McMillan and Philip Abelson discovered the first transuranium element, element 93, which they named neptunium. McMillan then began the search for element 94, but was called away in 1940 to work on important war research on the East Coast. As a young assistant professor, Seaborg took over this work and enlisted the help of his graduate student Arthur C. Wahl and a fellow chemistry instructor, Joseph W. Kennedy. In February, 1941, through bombarding uranium with deuterons in the sixty-inch cyclotron, they discovered element 94, plutonium, in the form of plutonium-238. With the added collaboration of Segre, they discovered plutonium-239, which proved to be a fissionable isotope that might serve as the explosive ingredient in a nuclear weapon and as a nuclear fuel. In 1942, John W. Gofman, Raymond W. Stoughton, and Seaborg created and identified a second major source of nuclear energy, the isotope uranium-233, which is the key to the use of the abundant element thorium as a nuclear fuel.

On his thirtieth birthday, April 19, 1942, Seaborg arrived at the University of Chicago Metallurgical Laboratory to join the Manhattan Project as leader of the group working on the chemical extraction of plutonium. This began his long career as a scientific leader, employing his gift for communication and talent for administration as well as his instinct for science.

### Life's Work

Seaborg has often described the years in Chicago working on the Manhattan Project as the most exciting and most challenging of his life. The team of dedicated scientists worked around the clock in what they believed was a race against the Nazis to produce the first atomic bomb and, later, an attempt to save thousands of lives in the Pacific theatre. In June, 1945, when their part of the project was successfully completed, Seaborg joined six colleagues in signing the Franck report, which recommended that the bomb be demonstrated, rather than used against a civilian Japanese population. Nevertheless, President Harry S Truman made the decision to go ahead and drop the bomb. The second atomic bomb, dropped on Nagasaki, Japan, on August 9, 1945, was fueled with plutonium. The "Atomic Age" had begun, and Seaborg shared the conviction of others that control of nuclear weapons was now the most critical question of our times. He joined in the debate about implications for the future of our planet and served on the first General Advisory Committee to the Atomic Energy Commission, participating in difficult decisions about the development of more advanced nuclear weapons (for example, the hydrogen bomb) and in explorations of the peaceful uses of atomic energy.

During the years in Chicago, Seaborg and his coworkers also discovered two new transuranium elements, americium (element 95) and curium (element 96). He holds patents on these elements, making him the only man ever to hold a patent on a chemical element. In 1944, he formulated the actinide concept of heavy element electronic structure, which accurately predicted that the heaviest naturally occurring elements together with synthetic transuranium elements would form a transition series of actinide elements in a manner analogous to the rare earth series of lanthanide elements. This concept, the most significant change in the periodic table since Dmitri Mendeleev's nineteenth century design, shows how the transuranium elements fit into the periodic table and thus demonstrates their relationships to other elements.

When Seaborg returned to Berkeley in 1946 with his wife, Helen, whom he had married on a brief return visit to Berkeley in June, 1942, he dedicated himself to two efforts: establishing the world's premier research group working on transuranium elements and starting a family. Now a full professor of chemistry at the University of California and soon to become associate director of the Radiation Laboratory, he brought back from Chicago with him a number of the brightest young scientists in the nation, and together, this team discovered six more transuranium elements, elements 97 through 102. He and Helen were also successful in attaining their goal of a large family— they had six children. A highlight of the first years back in Berkeley was the receipt of the Nobel Prize for Chemistry with McMillan in 1951 for their work on the chemistry of the transuranium elements. The visit to Stockholm to receive the prize from the King of Sweden was a dream come true for this son of a Swedish immigrant.

In 1958, Seaborg's talents as an administrator were presented with a new challenge. He became the second chancellor of the University of California, Berkeley, and served during a period (1958-1961) of tremendous growth and development at the university. The Master Plan for Higher Education in California (1959) set an ambitious agenda for the state university and college systems. A long-range physical plan was developed for the Berkeley campus, which was undergoing an unprecedented period of building; the College of Environmental Design and the Space Sciences Laboratory were both established at that time. Students were beginning to shake off postwar apathy and became actively involved with such issues as free speech, the draft, and racial discrimination in housing.

Caricatures of Seaborg at this time began to make use of his dramatic bushy eyebrows, yet these depictions were generally in good humor. Seaborg somehow had a talent for keeping people on opposite sides of fences talking to one another and seeking compromise solutions to problems. Some of these negotiating techniques were no doubt the result of experience leading groups of scientists with diverse interests and opinions; his interpersonal skills had been further honed by serving as faculty athletic representative for the Berkeley campus during an era of corruption and controversy in the Pacific Coast Intercollegiate Athletic Conference, which ended with the establishment in 1959 of a new conference: the Athletic Association of Western Universities (now known as the Pac Ten), of which Seaborg was chief architect.

The Soviet launch of Sputnik in 1957 provoked a wave of concern in the United States about the need for improved science education for schoolchildren. Chancellor Seaborg, who had always had a particular interest in this area, served as a leader in the movement to improve science education. He served as chairman of the Steering Committee for CHEM Study (an innovative new chemistry curriculum still widely used throughout the world), as chairman of the Panel on Basic Research and Graduate Education of President Eisenhower's Science Advisory Committee, as a member of a national committee on the application of the National Defense Education Act of 1958, as a member of the Board of Directors of the National Educational Television and Radio Center, and as initiator and chairman of a committee to establish a memorial for Ernest Lawrence (who died in August, 1958) on the Berkeley campus.

In 1961, Seaborg was appointed Chairman of the Atomic Energy Commission (AEC), a position in which he served for ten years. The AEC engaged in a wide range of activities: the development and testing of nuclear weapons; the sponsorship of nuclear energy as a source of electricity; the production of nuclear material; the conduct of reactor research and development for the armed services (including the nuclear navy); the sponsorship of research in high-energy and low-energy nuclear

physics, in chemistry, and in biology; the support of educational activities in schools; the production and sale of radioisotopes for use in medicine, agriculture, industry, and research; the licensing of the use of nuclear materials for power plants and other peaceful purposes; and international cooperation in science. Seaborg was responsible for overseeing all these varied activities, supported by a budget of two and a half billion dollars.

As a chief adviser to the president, Seaborg also played an important role in establishing policy regarding arms control agreements. He went to Moscow as a part of the American delegation for the signing of the Limited Nuclear Test Ban Treaty of 1963, which prohibited the testing of nuclear weapons in the atmosphere, in outer space, and underwater. He also participated in laying the groundwork for the Non-Proliferation Treaty of 1970 by helping to establish safeguards that would assure that nuclear materials intended for peaceful uses were subject to appropriate inspections and controls by the International Atomic Energy Agency and to ensure that they were not diverted for military purposes. During his ten years as

Chairman of the AEC, Seaborg traveled to more than sixty countries, promoting international cooperation in science.

After he returned to his professorship at the University of California in 1971, University Professor of Chemistry Seaborg continued to pursue the goals of international cooperation in science and the attainment of arms control agreements. He helped to establish the International Organization for Chemical Sciences in Development (IOCD), which facilitates collaboration between chemists in developed countries and chemists in developing countries in the search for solutions to Third World problems, and became its president in 1981. He has written and lectured extensively about the need for a comprehensive test ban treaty, which would extend the prohibition of testing of nuclear weapons to underground testing. Among the many books he has authored are two on the subject of arms control history: *Kennedy, Khrushchev and the Test Ban* (1981, describing the negotiations during the Kennedy Administration for the Limited Test Ban Treaty) and *Stemming the Tide: Arms Control in the Johnson Years* (1987, featuring a description of the negotiations that led to the Non-Proliferation Treaty).

In 1974, Seaborg's research group at the Lawrence Berkeley Laboratory discovered element 106, which was officially named "seaborgium" in 1997. Seaborg continues to work as an active research scientist, helping to direct a research group in the search for new isotopes and new elements at the upper end of the periodic table, including a search for the "superheavy" elements. The group is also investigating the mechanism of the reactions of heavy ions with heavy element target nuclei. Another aspect of the research program is concerned with the determination of the chemical properties of the very heaviest synthetic chemical elements.

Deeply involved in the effort to improve mathematics and science education, Seaborg has served as President of Science Service from 1966 and as head of the Lawrence Hall of Science since 1982. He also served on the National Commission on Excellence in Education, which published the much-publicized report, "A Nation at Risk," in 1983.

He began keeping a diary at the age of fourteen and has maintained a detailed record of his daily activities since that time. This personal historical record (which also contains less significant childhood entries such as "took a bath") is a valuable resource for his work on the history of science, recording much about critical decisions in the nuclear age. An avid hiker, he also served as vice president of the American Hiking Society, helped to establish the "Golden State Trail," the California segment of a cross-country hiking route, and is an eloquent supporter of conservation of natural resources and protection of wilderness areas.

### Summary

Seaborg's discovery of several radioisotopes has revolutionized medical science. Seventy percent of all diagnosis and treatment in the United States employs nuclear techniques. By 1970, ninety percent of the eight million administrations per year of radioisotopes in the United States utilized cobalt-60, iodine-131, or technetium-99m. Technetium-99m is the workhorse of nuclear medicine; in 1985, it accounted for more than seven million diagnostic procedures per year in bone, liver, lung, thyroid, cardiovascular, and brain scanning and imaging. Millions of people have already benefited (including Seaborg's own mother) and will continue to benefit directly from his research and from his support of research and development during his chairmanship of the AEC through advanced diagnostic and therapeutic applications.

It is impossible to overstate the impact of the discovery of the element plutonium on our times. It has been argued that the existence of weapons of mass destruction has acted as a deterrent and prevented the outbreak of a major conflict between the superpowers for a longer period than at any other time in history. Certainly, knowledge of the potential for destruction of our planet has cast a pall over the lives of all human beings. The other side of the coin is the potential which plutonium has to serve as a virtually inexhaustible source of electrical energy, on which the world depends more each day. Considering the horrifying threat of nuclear war, Seaborg's efforts to prevent the development of still more potent weapons (the Limited Test Ban Treaty of 1963) and to limit the spread of ownership of these weapons to more countries (the Non-Proliferation Treaty of 1970) are of critical importance to the world's future. In Seaborg's view, the need to control nuclear weapons is urgent. The epilogue of his book, *Kennedy, Khrushchev and the Test Ban*, ends thus:

> [W]e are negotiating at a higher and more dangerous level. If we allow the present opportunity to slip away, however, the next one, if there is a next one, will be at a level still higher and more dangerous. The hour is late. Let us hope not too late.

## Bibliography

Seaborg, Glenn T. *Nuclear Milestones: A Collection of Speeches*. San Francisco: Freeman, 1972. A unique compilation of historical insights with many unpublished photographs of the scientists and laboratories responsible for the nuclear age. In this book, through a selection of speeches he gave while chairman of the Atomic Energy Commission, Seaborg tries to present some of the reminiscences and reflections of the scientific accomplishments to advance mankind.

———. *The Transuranium Elements*. New Haven, Conn.: Yale University Press, 1958. Seaborg tells for the first time the full and dramatic story of plutonium, with emphasis on the men who did the work.

Seaborg, Glenn T., with Benjamin S. Loeb. *Kennedy, Khrushchev and the Test Ban*. Berkeley: University of California Press, 1981. Seaborg tells the story that made the signing of the Limited Test Ban Treaty on August 5, 1963, possible.

———. *Stemming the Tide: Arms Control in the Johnson Years*. Lexington, Mass.: Lexington Books, 1987. A description of the efforts in arms control during the Johnson administration, including the attainment of the Non-Proliferation Treaty of 1970.

*Sherrill Whyte*

# HANS VON SEECKT

*Born:* April 22, 1866; Schleswig, Prussia
*Died:* December 27, 1936; Berlin, Germany
*Area of Achievement:* The military
*Contribution:* Seeckt reshaped Germany's small post-1918 *Reichswehr* on modern lines, emphasizing the principles of mobility and combined attack later employed in the Blitzkrieg victories of 1940.

## Early Life

Johannes (Hans) Friedrich Leopold von Seeckt was born on April 22, 1866, the second surviving child and only surviving son of Captain (later General) Richard von Seeckt, and Auguste von Seeckt aus Greifswald. *Gymnasium*-educated and more intellectual than athletic, Hans joined the select Alexander Guards Regiment of the Prussian army as an ensign in 1885 and made second lieutenant in 1887. Hard work and intelligence earned for him a year at the War Academy in 1893, promotion to first lieutenant in 1894, General Staff assignments in 1897, and appointment to the German General Staff, with subsequent promotion to captain in 1899. Seeckt worked on the mobilization of the 1900 China Expedition and was promoted to major in 1906.

In 1893, Seeckt married Dorothea Jacobson Fabian, of German-Jewish middle-class background, in a happy though childless union. Seeckt's foreign observer assignments plus holidays provided the couple with travel experience in Europe, North Africa, the Middle East, and India. Their Berlin home became a center for a varied society with broad cultural interests. By 1914, the slim, monocled, somewhat elegant major already had much the appearance of his later years.

In the War of 1914, Lieutenant Colonel von Seeckt planned the attack at Soisson well enough to be promoted to colonel and was sent to the Eastern Front as chief of staff for the Eleventh Army and Mackensen's Army Group. Seeckt's spectacular success in the Gorlice-Tarnow breakthrough of May, 1915, earned for him a promotion to major general but also the lasting jealousy of Paul von Hindenburg and Erich Ludendorff. In 1916 and 1917, as chief of staff for Archduke Karl of Austria and later Archduke Joseph, he coordinated Austro-German operations in Southeastern Europe. In 1918, Seeckt served as a lieutenant general in, and chief of staff for, the Turkish army under Enver Pasha.

## Life's Work

Late in 1918, General von Seeckt returned to a Germany shaken by the November collapse of the *Kaiserreich.* He strongly urged the view that the new *Reichswehr* was the legitimate heir to the old army rather than simply a creation of President Friedrich Ebert's hastily contrived Weimar Republic. As organizer of Northeastern defenses, Seeckt successfully pushed the recapture of Riga to show that Germany still counted in Eastern Europe. As an adviser, however, on the 1919 Treaty of Versailles settlement, he found the Allies adamant on German disarmament, which included abolishing the General Staff and reducing the army to four thousand officers plus ninety-six thousand men, all on long-term enlistments.

Seeckt preserved a de facto General Staff through the *Truppenamt* (troops bureau), which he headed after the retirement of Hindenburg and General Wilhelm Gröner in 1919. General Walther Reinhardt became army commander, and with him, and under Defense Minister Gustav Noske, Seeckt shared the tumultuous domestic and *Freikorps* conflicts of 1919 and 1920.

Such a conflict brought Seeckt to national prominence in March of 1920, when the right-wing Kapp Putsch in Berlin threatened to overthrow the republic. Seeckt consistently opposed this attempt, in which General Ludendorff was a chief figure, but he refused to sanction divisive bloodshed. His persistent "*Reichswehr* do not shoot *Reichswehr*" line of argument preserved army unity, and, after civil officials and labor unions thwarted the putsch, the government promoted Seeckt to army commander in place of Reinhardt. Seeckt's subsequent leniency toward some former putschists has been criticized.

Shaping Germany's 100,000-man army into a credible military force was now the great task confronting Seeckt. The insignificance in numbers was compounded by Treaty of Versailles prohibitions on military aircraft, tracked vehicles, heavy guns, and trained reserves. What officer of ability and ambition would join an army incapable of beating any country worth calling an enemy? The situation required imaginative alternatives, political as well as military. Seeckt turned to Russia in 1921 to establish in that diplomatically isolated country some jointly owned factories for tank and airplane design. These covert projects were small, but their experimental planes and tanks loomed large in

Seeckt's military thinking. Also, this not totally secret prelude to the Rapallo Pact (1922) gave the German generals a sense of direction. Any Russo-German cooperation endangered Poland, and thereby weakened the French alliance structure in Eastern Europe.

In the Silesian border plebiscite of March, 1921, Seeckt sanctioned unofficial *Freikorps* activities, and these increased in scope during the 1923 French occupation of the Ruhr and the Rhineland Republic attempt. With the skyrocketing inflation of 1923, the economic and political weakness of the Weimar Republic invited a renewal of the "putsch politics" to which the *Freikorps* leaders gravitated. Seeckt adroitly squelched the Küstrin-Spandau Officers' Putsch of September 30 and forcibly suppressed the Leipzig "Red Militia" in October. In the November, 1923, Munich Putsch, Seeckt strung out negotiations until, with emergency powers and Hindenburg's support, he persuaded the Bavarian separatist leaders and the *Reichswehr* commanders to acknowledge and uphold the authority of the republic. This did not prevent Ludendorff and Adolf Hitler from leading a November 9, 1923, "March," but its suppression by the local authorities seemed at the time a vindication of Seeckt's methods.

There was in early 1924 some press speculation that Seeckt might use his emergency powers to make a putsch of his own, but Seeckt's special powers had been conditioned on clear and public promises to support the republic. Seeckt may have intended to position himself for a presidential try in 1926, but on Ebert's unexpected death in 1925, the patriotic candidate elected to be Reich president was Field Marshal Hindenburg. Seeckt was now no longer "the coming man" in politics, or at the top of army authority, but was henceforth an unnecessary and even inconvenient figure in both fields.

In February of 1926, Seeckt gave an incautious casual agreement to Crown Princess Cecilie's request that her eldest son, Prince Wilhelm, be allowed to take part in some *Reichswehr* exercises. Seeckt's staff failed to keep this participation (September 13-21) as discreetly obscure as he had ordered, and German news stories inspired foreign fears of a Hohenzollern restoration. Worse, when War Minister Otto Gessler asked for an explanation, Seeckt penned such an unsatisfactory reply that Gessler asked for his resignation. Seeckt appealed to the president, but Hindenburg accepted Seeckt's resignation on October 8.

The last decade of Seeckt's life was active but less influential. After travel vacations with his wife, Seeckt wrote several books and articles and was from 1930 to 1932 a People's Party member of the Reichstag. The 1932 reelection of Hindenburg and the 1933 accession to power of the Nazis ended his political activities. Still nominally an "adviser" to the *Reichswehr*, from 1933 to 1935 he established the German military mission to the Chinese Nationalist Government of Chiang Kai-shek. In 1935, Seeckt returned to Germany in ill health, and the final year of his life was one of ceremonies and tributes, in great part from the Nazi leaders who now controlled the Reich. Seeckt died in Berlin on December 27, 1936.

### Summary

The narrative of Hans von Seeckt's political fortunes accounts for much of his career, but the task of rebuilding the army was the work for which he was, and remains, celebrated. Briefly, Seeckt rejected the World War I overemphasis on mass armies and entrenched defensive firepower and proposed a mobile offensive with new technology to win by disorganizing the enemy's power to resist. Effective general staff control of war policy was a key to success, and the preserving, organizing, and directing of this staff was an immediate priority for Seeckt. The mobile offensive involved a coordinated firepower concentration with a capacity to advance in the course of battle. The airplanes, tanks, gun carriers, and even cavalry of the attack must be accompanied or closely followed by men, ammunition, and fuel. The mechanization, motorization, and radio command of the next war would impose a speed of action controllable only by a staff of highly trained professionals. Seeckt evidently had no exact blueprint for the practical details and technical problems involved, to the frustration of many of his staff, who had to prepare "maneuvers" with conspicuously imaginary weapons. Seeckt's general concept of the next war was not unique among contemporary military theorists, but his fellow visionaries in France and Great Britain were not in command, and their supreme commanders did not share the vision, with results made manifest in 1940.

In restoring the morale of a defeated army, Seeckt succeeded beyond all expectations, as the dispirited though dogged style of 1919 steadily improved into the energetic and purposeful confidence of 1926. This was a morale that refused to accept the defeat of 1918 as final and that defied the 1919 treaties. These sentiments were felt, or at least understood, by most Germans. The burdens of Versailles, weakness of the League of Nations, and Allied hypocrisy on "disarmament" seemed to justify Seeckt in making Germany's small army at least one that was ready to fight. The later political developments of the 1930's were not then anticipated.

Politics, indeed, were not Seeckt's métier. His ability at logical deduction from fixed principles, perhaps useful in his idea of an army-state, was ill-suited to Germany's experiment in democracy. As a monarchist and authoritarian, Seeckt could not love the republic, although he served it better than some of his critics have admitted. Like many others, Seeckt in 1932 believed that Hitler might be the leader Germany needed and learned better only when it was too late.

Seeckt was not by training or nature an innovator, and his turn of thought was contemplative rather than original or creative, a fact that limited his capacity for inventing new mobile offensive tactics for practical operations. He saw with logical clarity that the accepted objectives and principles of warfare were lost sight of in World War I's "strategy of attrition," which opposed modern technology with great human numbers until the side with more lives to spend became the winner. For soldiers to exploit the technology of war rather than to be exploited by it was the useful premise of Seeckt's thinking.

### Bibliography

Carsten, Francis L. *The Reichswehr and Politics, 1918-1933.* Oxford: Clarendon Press, and Berkeley: University of California Press, 1966. Best account of army politics in the Seeckt era. This is not a biography or a sympathetic look at Seeckt's politics but a detailed and scholarly work drawn from extensive research in the papers of many army leaders.

Corum, James S. *The Roots of Blitzkrieg: Hans von Seeckt and German Military Reform.* Lawrence: University Press of Kansas, 1992. Corum examines the contributions to military science made by von Seeckt.

Craig, Gordon A. *The Politics of the Prussian Army, 1640-1945.* Oxford: Clarendon Press, and New York: Oxford University Press, 1955. A moderately critical history by an American scholar; provides a useful introduction and background.

Dupuy, T. N. *A Genius for War: The Germany Army and General Staff, 1807-1945.* London: Macdonald, and Englewood Cliffs, N.J.: Prentice-Hall, 1977. This general work includes a good two-page biography of Seeckt plus a readable account of Seeckt's political career, with a practical sense of the normal military role.

Goerlitz, Walter. *History of the German General Staff, 1657-1945.* London: Hollis and Carter, and New York: Praeger, 1953. Standard general history by a respected German scholar; gives a good introduction and background.

Gordon, Harold J. *The Reichswehr and the German Republic, 1919-1926.* Princeton, N.J.: Princeton University Press, 1957. Best defense of Seeckt's politics by an American scholar. Well documented. Critical of the republic's antimilitary bias. Overlooks some points covered by Carsten and is too credulous of police reports but gives more inside information than most authors attempt.

Salomon, Ernst von. *The Outlaws.* Translated by Ian F. D. Morrow. London: Cape, 1931; Millwood, N.Y.: Kraus, 1983. A *Freikorps* member's memoir. Distasteful, but generally authentic, and an essential supplement to academic studies of *Freikorps* politics.

Seeckt, Hans von. *Thoughts of a Soldier.* Translated by Gilbert Waterhouse. London: Benn, 1930. This is the most useful of several short works published in English. Seeckt's style does not translate easily.

Wheeler-Bennett, Sir John Wheeler. *The Nemesis of Power: The German Army in Politics, 1918-1945.* London: Macmillan, and New York: St. Martin's Press, 1953. The most widely read and broadly informative version of the thesis that the German generals undermined the republic and sold out to Hitler. The chapter on Seeckt presents more interpretation than research.

*K. Fred Gillum*

# ANDRÉS SEGOVIA

*Born:* Probably February 17, 1893; Linares, Spain
*Died:* June 2, 1987; Madrid, Spain
*Area of Achievement:* Music
*Contribution:* Renowned as one of the foremost concert performers of the twentieth century, Segovia is responsible for establishing the guitar as a serious musical instrument. In addition to adapting works of Mozart, Haydn, Bach, and others for the classical guitar, Segovia stimulated modern composers to write new works for his instrument.

## Early Life

Andrés Segovia was born in Linares, Spain, in mid-February, 1893. A baptismal certificate suggests that the date was probably February 17, but various sources list dates ranging from February 17 to 23. His parents were Rosa Torrez Cruz and Bonifacio Segobia y Montoro, but Segovia was adopted at an early age by an aunt and uncle in Granada. (Although his father's name is spelled with a "b" on the baptismal certificate, he has been universally known as Segovia.) He was interested in music as a child and received instruction in piano, violin, and cello, but none of these inspired him. The guitar became Segovia's choice as soon as he heard a flamenco guitarist play. In fact, after the performance at a friend's home, the guitarist is said to have given Segovia his first lesson, though he could, in fact, teach the boy very little. Segovia's interest was at first clandestine, because the guitar was thought to be appropriate only for flamenco or folk music, as an accompaniment for exuberant singing and dancing. Despite opposition from family and teachers at the Granada Music Institute, young Segovia pursued his instrument. The first techniques he learned, and later had to unlearn, were those used by flamenco players. When Segovia could not find a qualified teacher, he taught himself. He applied his previous musical knowledge—particularly piano techniques—to the guitar, and his principles of fingering are said to stem from this early period. During his teenage years, Segovia became increasingly familiar with the works of Johann Sebastian Bach, Ludwig van Beethoven, Wolfgang Amadeus Mozart, and others and became aware of guitar virtuosos of the nineteenth century such as Fernando Sor, Julian Arcas, and Francisco Tárrega.

Although Segovia acknowledged the influence of these early masters, he developed a style and a technique that were essentially his own and distilled his program from various sources, transcribing and adapting lute, vihuela, and early guitar compositions. The encouragement of a young aristocrat, Rafael de Montis, based on what Segovia considered to be more cosmopolitan standards than the praise of the local people, helped convince him to attempt a concert career. In 1909, at the age of sixteen, Segovia made his public debut in Granada under the auspices of a local cultural organization, Circulo Artístico. He eventually moved to Madrid, where he heard musicians of international reputation perform, and Segovia considered that his "real debut" took place in 1916 at the Madrid Ateneo, the Spanish equivalent to Carnegie Hall. In 1919, he toured in Latin America, playing for enthusiastic Spanish-speaking audiences who were already inclined toward the guitar and, until 1923, performed only for such audiences.

## Life's Work

The year 1924 was pivotal in Segovia's career. He performed at the home of well-known French musicologist Henri Prunières, who had invited top musicians to hear Segovia play this instrument, which was still considered unusual; the positive reception set the stage for Segovia's most important early success: his Paris debut in April, 1924. At this debut, arranged with the encouragement of fellow countryman Pablo Casals, Segovia played to a large audience that included such musical dignitaries as Paul Dukas, Joaquín Nin, Albert Roussel, Miguel de Unamuno y Jugo, Manuel de Falla, and Madame Debussy. Unveiling the brilliance of the Spanish guitar, Segovia was an immediate sensation with the general public and critics alike. In 1924, he also made successful debuts in Berlin and London, and he undertook a second Latin American tour including Argentina, Mexico, and Cuba (where he had his first recording session). In that same year, Segovia met George Krick, an American who later persuaded impresario Sol Hurok to arrange a recital tour in the United States.

By this time, Segovia's international reputation was firmly established, and he was attracting composers such as Federico Moreno Torroba, Joaquín Turina, Roussel, Manuel Ponce, Gustave Samazeuilh, Alexandre Tansman, and de Falla, who were stimulated to compose original works that liberated the guitar from the restrictions of its past.

During the next four years, Segovia gave concerts in Spain, France, England, Italy, Germany, Scandinavia, and the Soviet Union. In 1926, the first editions of Schott's Segovia Guitar Archive Series were published, an important event in the guitar's history. While on tour in Germany, Segovia came across a complete edition of Bach's compositions for lute, which he transcribed for guitar and later became a familiar part of his repertoire. Several of these were published in 1928 in the Segovia Guitar Series, and, in 1934, Segovia's most important transcription of Bach was published as his edition of the "Chaconne." For some musicians, transferring this piece written for violin to the guitar amounted almost to blasphemy, but mastery of Segovia's edition eventually became a standard by which classical guitarists were measured.

In January, 1928, Segovia undertook his first performance tour in the United States. His first engagement was an intimate recital in Proctor, Massachusetts. His U.S. concert debut was at the Town Hall in New York City, with a program that included music by Bach and Joseph Haydn. Critics praised him highly, some even comparing him with Casals and Fritz Kreisler. He played five more sell-out concerts and then toured about forty other American cities in eleven weeks. For the next ten years, Segovia toured annually in the United States and developed an enthusiastic following. In 1928, he also toured in the Far East and again in Latin America. Segovia made his first trip to Japan in 1929 and subsequently performed there regularly. In the twenty years since his first public debut at age sixteen, Segovia rose from obscurity to international acclaim, and his reputation was to grow still more over the next years, as he continued to give concerts and recitals, transpose and adapt compositions for guitar, and inspire composers to compose original works for him.

In 1932, Segovia traveled to Venice with Falla and attended the International Festival of Music. While there, he met Mario Castelnuovo-Tedesco, a leading Italian composer, who became a great guitar enthusiast and composed for Segovia until he died in 1968. By the 1930's, many composers were writing for the guitar. Those such as Castelnuovo-Tedesco, Ponce, Joaquín Rodrigo, and Heitor Villa-Lobos introduced woodwind, brass, and percussion into guitar compositions, a practice that soon became popular with both guitarists and audiences. Then, Segovia's life in Spain was disrupted by the Spanish Civil War. In 1938, he left his home in Barcelona and lived away from his native land for the next sixteen years. After a brief stay in Italy, Segovia established residence in Montevideo, Uruguay, and toured extensively from there, though, during the years of World War II, Segovia did not perform in Europe. In 1943, he returned to the United States after a hiatus of five years. It seemed at first that Segovia had been almost forgotten by the public, but his popularity was soon reestablished, and he was also introduced to a wide American audience through the medium of television. During the 1940's, the guitar world experienced two important technological events, and Segovia incorporated both advances into his work. The first was Albert Augustine's introduction of nylon guitar strings, which gave the instrument a more reliable sound than gut strings. The second was the invention of the long-playing (LP) record; the LP recordings that Segovia made in the 1950's are considered some of his finest. Segovia gave about one hundred concerts each year during the 1950's and 1960's and performed in almost every non-Communist country.

By this time, through Segovia's influence, the repertoire for the guitar had become rich in depth and scope. Composers, both old and new, wrote for Segovia and his instrument. The unrivaled master of classical guitar, Segovia inspired and challenged the next generation of guitarists. He taught at Santiago de Compostela in Spain, the Academy Chigi in Siena, Italy, and the University of California, Berkeley, among other schools, and helped to establish the guitar as a respected part of the curriculum at music schools throughout the world. In addition, he made numerous recordings, including a wide range of composers and periods from classical to romantic to modern. Into his seventies and eighties, Segovia continued to perform internationally. Even into his nineties, he was still playing up to sixty concerts each year—though in his later years he decided to forego concert tours to faraway places—and he conducted master classes into the final months of his life. Segovia's commitment to the guitar as the central focus in his life never wavered; in recognition of his service to music, he received many honors, including two dozen Grand Crosses and Medals and many honorary doctorate degrees. He was also made an honorary citizen of several cities.

Segovia preferred to discuss his instrument rather than himself, and thus many details about his personal life are not well documented. Segovia married three times. His final marriage was to a former stu-

dent in 1960, and he and his wife Emilie had a son, Carlos, in 1970. Segovia's autobiography indicates that one previous marriage was to pianist Paquita Mardiguera, and he also had a son Andres and a daughter Beatrice. Throughout his long and celebrated career, Segovia was nourished by his music. He said that he belonged to "that small minority of artists that toil in good faith. Around these the world of phenomenal vanishes, and happens to mystics when they give themselves to prayer." On June 2, 1987, Segovia died in Madrid at age ninety-four. His musical tradition lives on, especially through celebrated guitarists such as Julian Bream, John Williams, and Alirio Diaz, who themselves continued to perform Segovia's masterpieces and inspire composers to write for classical guitar.

### Summary

Andrés Segovia has been called the founding father of the modern guitar movement. Almost singlehandedly, he elevated the guitar to the status of solo concert instrument, achieving a brighter sound by plucking with his fingernails rather than playing with his fingertips in the traditional manner. He established a wide repertoire, arranging works for the classical guitar himself, encouraging others to do so, and inspiring composers to compose original works. Segovia dedicated himself to the creation of beauty, even though he lived through times of great international unrest; his music reflects order in the midst of chaos. In recitals that delighted audiences and critics, Segovia filled huge concert halls with the intimate sounds of the guitar, which he called an orchestra in miniature, and classical guitar study became widely available through the efforts of this tireless master who generously encouraged young artists.

Segovia stated in *Guitar Review* that he had five ambitions in life:

> To extract the guitar from the noisy and disreputable folkloric amusements . . . to create a wonderful repertoire for my instrument . . . to make the guitar known by the philharmonic public all over the world . . . to provide a unifying medium for those interested in the development of the guitar . . . [and] to place the guitar in the most important conservatories of the world for teaching the young lovers of it, and thus securing its future.

During his lifetime, Segovia achieved his goals. In later years, he was pleased by the instrument's expanding popularity but remained steadfastly opposed to electronic amplification of the guitar. "The real music lover wants to hear the small instrument speaking straight to the heart of the people," he said. Fortunately, numerous recordings are available so that Segovia will continue to speak to the hearts of people for generations to come.

**Bibliography**

Chotzinoff, Samuel. *A Little Nightmusic.* London: Hamilton, and New York: Harper, 1964. This volume presents seven interviews with distinguished musicians. The thirteen-page chapter on Segovia, written in an informal style, describes a lunch with Segovia in 1961 and offers a glimpse of Segovia's charming personality and wit as he discusses his early influences and recollections.

Clinton, George, ed. *Andrés Segovia: An Appreciation.* London: Musical News Services, 1978. This collection of facts, opinions, and anecdotes contains articles and reviews published in *Guitar* as well as previously unpublished interviews, essays, and reminiscences from Julian Bream, Alirio Diaz, John Duarte, Christopher Nupen, Alice Artzt, John Williams, Vladimir Bobri, Akinabu Matsuda, and Ivor Mairants.

Gavoty, Bernard. *Andrés Segovia.* Geneva: Rene Kister, 1955. Written by the then music critic of *Figaro*, this pamphlet presents an intimate portrait of Segovia illustrated with twenty-three photographs by Roger Hauert and three drawings. Part of the Great Concert Artists series, it includes a selected list of Segovia's Decca recordings as well as a copy of a handwritten letter from Segovia to Gavoty and its English translation.

Gelatt, Roland. *Music Makers.* New York: Knopf, 1953. This volume includes twenty-one entries on musicians who interested the author. The chapter on Segovia gives a brief account of his life to 1950, which includes interesting detail as well as thoughtful commentary by Gelatt.

Purcell, Ronald C. *Andrés Segovia, Contributions to the World of Guitar.* 2d ed. Melville, N.Y.: Belwin Mills, 1975. This is a compilation of Segovia's many contributions to the world of music. Its forty pages include listings of articles by Segovia, books and articles about Segovia, his music editions, and his discography. It is illustrated with five photographs and an unusual line drawing of Segovia by Bobri.

Segovia, Andrés. *Andrés Segovia: An Autobiography of the Years 1893-1920.* Translated by W. F. O'Brien. London: Boyars, and New York: Macmillan, 1976. Segovia intended to publish several volumes of memoirs, but this indexed first volume is the only one he completed. Written without a ghostwriter, its two hundred pages present a fascinating picture of Segovia's life, and the reader comes away realizing that it is the guitar that is really the main character.

Wade, Graham. *Segovia: A Celebration of the Man and His Music.* London: Allison and Busby, and New York: Schocken, 1983. Although it does offer some biographical details, the volume focuses on aspects of Segovia's development that had previously been unexplored, such as Segovia's relationship with flamenco and the influence of Spanish literary and artistic figures on his life. Illustrated with photographs, it includes lists of Segovia's honors, his principal recordings, and composers' works recorded by him. It also includes a listing of his music editions, a representative selection of his recital programs from 1936 to 1982, and a bibliography.

*Jean C. Fulton*

# MAURICE SENDAK

*Born:* June 10, 1928; Brooklyn, New York
*Area of Achievement:* Art
*Contribution:* Sendak was one of the twentieth century's best-known illustrators of children's books. He received the international Hans Christian Andersen Award in 1970 in recognition of his major contribution to children's literature.

## Early Life

Maurice Bernard Sendak was the youngest of three children born to Polish-Jewish immigrants. Childhood influences included his parents' old-world traditions of Jewish village life and the urban society of the United States in the 1930's—two very different, and often conflicting, cultures. His father was an especially gifted storyteller who related many tales of life in Poland. Sendak has identified these stories as important early sources for the development of his own work. Another important influence was the family's weekly visit to the local cinema, where young Maurice saw musicals, monsters, comedies, and Walt Disney's *Fantasia* (1940), which he later described as the most aesthetic experience of his childhood. Mickey Mouse became one of the dominant figures of Sendak's youth, "an early best friend" as he later recalled, as well as the subject of his earliest extant color drawing, done in 1934 at age six.

Sendak, a frail child plagued with various, often severe, illnesses, has stated that as a result of his delicate health, he was terrified of death because he heard talk of it all around him. Unable to take part in many strenuous outdoor activities, he stayed indoors drawing pictures and developing a talent for the acute observation of people and events. Although the adult Sendak overcame the illnesses of his childhood, these early experiences undoubtedly shaped his life attitudes in significant ways, as indicated by the personalities of some of his characters, who tend to be passive, introverted, or lonely. Additionally, Sendak frequently refers to the boredom and loneliness of children, especially during the endless days of city summers. He has, however, described his own childhood as an essentially happy time with his parents and siblings. He disliked some of his other relatives, however, and on their Sunday visits to the Sendak household, Maurice observed them closely, noting every unflattering detail. These observations were used later in the creation of the "wild things."

Sendak disliked school, believing that the regimen of public education stifled creativity. In high school, however, he contributed drawings for the school newspaper, yearbook, and literary magazine. After graduation in 1946, he worked for a window-display company, and in 1947, his first published illustrations appeared in the textbook *Atomics for the Millions*.

## Life's Work

From 1948 to 1952, Sendak worked at F.A.O. Schwarz as an assistant window-display designer. He had access to the extensive children's book department and was exposed to the works of many different illustrators. The nineteenth century artists George Cruikshank, Walter Crane, and Randolph Caldecott became most important to him. While working days at F.A.O. Schwarz, Sendak began his only formal art training by attending night classes at the Art Students League. His favorite instructor, John Groth, taught him to achieve motion and liveliness in drawing, an approach seen in his illustrations for Ruth Sawyer's *Maggie Rose: Her Birthday Christmas* (1952) and Meindert DeJong's *Shadrach* (1953) and *Hurry Home, Candy* (1953). After two years, Sendak left the Art Students League, a decision he regretted later, feeling that his work matured slowly because of his lack of formal training.

In 1950, Sendak met Ursula Nordstrom, the children's-book editor at Harper and Brothers publishing company, who commissioned him to illustrate Marcel Ayme's *The Wonderful Farm* (1951). Sendak has said that this work made him an official presence in the children's book market and also marked the beginning of a professional relationship that influenced his entire career as an illustrator.

In 1952, Nordstrom gave Sendak the opportunity to illustrate Ruth Krauss's *A Hole Is to Dig*, an innovative approach to children's literature in which plot was replaced by concept—the concept in this case being a series of definitions that children might make, such as "hands are to hold" or "dogs are to kiss people." The book's success and the critics' enthusiastic acclaim for Sendak's work placed him among the major illustrators of children's books. He left F.A.O. Schwarz and became a freelance illustrator.

Although Sendak's work in the next several years lacked the visual sophistication and polish that

marked his mature style, he evidenced an unusual ability to depict characters of all ages with equal sympathy and without any taint of mawkish sentimentality. The talent for observation that he had developed in his childhood was put to good use. As his work progressed, he began to establish the precepts that would guide him throughout his career. For example, Sendak always insisted upon interpretive illustrations that expanded and enriched the meaning of a text rather than narrative pictures that merely reflected the words of the text or pictures that provided simple graphic decoration. He felt strongly that the illustrator's contribution to a book was as important as the author's. He declared that to be an illustrator was to be a participant.

Sendak never followed the mainstream style of American children's book illustration. In the 1950's, when most illustrators were creating dazzling technical displays of abstract designs in bold color and large formats influenced by contemporary advertising, Sendak's work was reminiscent of nineteenth century wood engravings, an effect achieved by the consistent use of crosshatching—examples include E. H. Minarik's "little bear" series (1957-1968), Jack Sendak's *Circus Girl* (1957), his own *Kenny's Window* (1956) and *Where the Wild Things Are* (1963), and *The Juniper Tree and Other Tales from Grimm* (1973). Sendak created his own personal language by borrowing styles and techniques from those artists he most admired, including William Blake, Thomas Rowlandson, George Cruikshank, Randolph Caldecott, Walter Crane, Arthur Hughes, Samuel Palmer, and Winsor McCay.

As Sendak's graphic work became more assured and polished from the mid-1950's through the early 1960's, he began to write as well as illustrate. His first book, *Kenny's Window*, introduced a theme that reappeared often in his work, which he defined as "children who are held back by life, but, one way or another, manage miraculously to find release from their troubles." There are many aspects of Sendak's own childhood in *Kenny's Window*, as the young hero tries to reconcile his fantasies with his real life. Autobiographical content is also found in *Higglety Pigglety Pop! Or, There Must Be More to Life*, which he wrote and illustrated in 1967 as a tribute to his beloved pet and "best friend," a Sealyham terrier named Jennie.

By 1962, at age thirty-four, Sendak had illustrated fifty books, seven of which he had also written. He next published four miniature volumes—*Alligators All Around*, *Chicken Soup with Rice*, *One Was Johnny*, and *Pierre*—entitled *The Nutshell Library* (1962). Response was very positive, with one critic proclaiming him "the Picasso of children's books." He also received the American Library Association Notable Book Award and, in 1975, produced an animated film featuring the Nutshell Kids that was broadcast on television.

In 1963, Sendak created his most successful, and most controversial, work—*Where the Wild Things Are*. Initial critical appraisal was favorable, with the book being labeled "refreshingly imaginative," although some parents and educators expressed concern that the fearsome wild things, with sharp teeth and claws, might scare children. The most outrageous criticism came, however, from a child psychologist named Bruno Bettelheim, who had not even read the book before pronouncing it a document of parental desertion that would produce anxiety in a child (the young hero Max is sent to bed without his supper). Thus the book was not initially popular with the general public, although librarians supported it. This first resistance was overcome when, in 1964, Sendak received the Caldecott Medal for the best picture book; from that time, *Where the Wild Things Are* began to be considered a classic; by its twenty-fifth anniversary, it had sold two million English copies, it had been translated into sixteen languages, and it had been adapted into an opera.

*In the Night Kitchen* (1970) was another controversial work, with objections centering primarily on what American educators labeled the book's blatant sensuousness and suggestive sensuality stemming from the frontal nudity of the young hero, Mickey. International response was favorable, however, and Sendak became the first American illustrator to be given the prestigious Hans Christian Andersen Award.

With his position as one of the foremost writers and illustrators of children's literature now secure, Sendak worked harder than ever. He illustrated several volumes of Brothers Grimm stories (*The Juniper Tree and Other Tales from Grimm*; *King Grisly-Beard*, 1973), worked with contemporary authors (Randall Jarrell's *Fly by Night*, 1976), and continued to illustrate his own stories (*Some Swell Pup: Or Are you Sure You Want a Dog?*, 1976; *Seven Little Monsters*, 1977; and *Outside Over There*, 1981). In 1970, he stated that he was now looking for a form of expression beyond simple illustration or even writing. He began to think of combining music and words to produce a more exciting method of creativity; in the late 1970's, he collaborated with Frank Corsaro on the production and staging of six operas, including Wolfgang Amadeus Mozart's *The Magic Flute* for the Houston Grand Opera and Sergei Prokofiev's *Love for Three Oranges*, performed in England and New York City. In 1979, the United Nations Educational, Scientific, and Cultural Organization (UNESCO) commissioned an opera of *Where the Wild Things Are* for the International Year of the Child and, in 1985, the British Broadcasting Corporation (BBC) commissioned an opera of *Higglety Pigglety Pop!*

## Summary

The philosophy underlying Maurice Sendak's work was greatly influenced by his own childhood spent between two conflicting cultures. In both his illustrations and his stories, he combines seemingly incongruous traditions and fuses images of death and mortality with those that celebrate life. The whole truth must be revealed, however and wherever it is to be found. In order to accomplish this, he has made use of diverse styles and techniques, from Disney to William Blake to Randolph Caldecott. Sendak stated that Caldecott's greatness lay in the wholeness of his personal vision of life, in his refusal to dilute the truth. Much the same could be said of Sendak's work, for he has declared that even though his stories are essentially dream or fantasy, all successful fantasy must be rooted in living fact. He has explained that when he tries to draw the way children feel, or the way he imagines they feel, it is the way he knows he felt as a child. He has said many times that he has an endless fascination and absorption with childhood and an obsession with his own childhood. As one writer has observed, Sendak's fascination and absorption has put thousands of adults in closer touch with their own childhoods and has enriched the fantasy lives of children everywhere.

## Bibliography

Bader, Barbara. "Maurice Sendak." In *American Picturebooks from Noah's Ark to the Beast Within*. New York: Macmillan, 1976. This essay contains an in-depth discussion of the eclecticism of Sendak's style that documents the evolution of his art.

Ball, John Clement. "Max's Colonial Fantasy: Rereading Sendak's 'Where the Wild Things Are.'" *ARIEL* 28, no. 1 (January, 1997). Analysis of Sendak's acclaimed children's book, Where the Wild Things Are, including the developmental and philosophical characteristics of the protagonist, Max.

DeLuca, Geraldine. "Progression through Contraries: The Triumph of the Spirit in the Work of Maurice Sendak." In *Triumphs of the Spirit in Children's Literature*, edited by Francelia Butler and Richard Rotert. Hamden, Conn.: Library Professional Publications, 1986. DeLuca traces and discusses Sendak's ambivalent vision of childhood throughout his works.

Deverraux, Elizabeth. "In the Studio with Maurice Sendak." *Publishers Weekly* 240, no. 44 (November 1, 1993). Profiles of Sendak including his sources of inspiration, his techniques, and the seriousness of his book *We Are All in the Dumps with Jack and Guy.*

Hentoff, Nat. "Among the Wild Things." *The New Yorker* (January 22, 1966): 39-73. Hentoff discusses the critical and public response to Sendak's work and traces the influences on his art from his early beginnings through his mature style.

Kloss, Robert. "Fantasy and Fear in the Work of Maurice Sendak." *Psychoanalytic Review* 76 (Winter, 1989): 567-579. In this essay, Kloss examines Sendak's transformation of the psychoanalytic vision of experience into fiction and art.

Lanes, Selma. *The Art of Maurice Sendak*. New York: Abrams, 1980; London: Bodley Head, 1981. This extensive, well-illustrated biography examining Sendak's life and work contains many direct quotes taken from interviews with Sendak, discussions of his major works, and a chronology.

Sonheim, Amy. *Maurice Sendak*. New York: Twayne, 1991. Sonheim analyzes Sendak's work from several eclectic approaches: biographical, linguistic, art historical, and generic. The author attempts to discover the intricacies of Sendak's verbal and visual styles, but the book contains no reproductions of his visual works. It does, however, contain a lengthy bibliography of both primary and secondary sources.

*LouAnn Faris Culley*

# LÉOPOLD SENGHOR

*Born:* October 9, 1906; Joal, Senegal

*Areas of Achievement:* Literature, government, and politics

*Contribution:* Senghor, one of Africa's leading poets and intellectuals, is best known for having helped create and having greatly contributed to the *négritude* movement begun in the 1930's. A writer of rich, complex poems illuminating his love for his native Senegal as well as that for his beloved France, Senghor was also both a diplomat representing colonial Senegal in the French National Assembly and the President of Senegal after its independence in 1960. He has been a forceful, intelligent, influential pro-African leader respected throughout the world.

## Early Life

Léopold Sédar Senghor was born in Joal, a Senegalese town on the Atlantic Coast of Africa to a well-to-do Christian merchant from a minority tribe. Much of his youth was spent at various schools, the first of which was a Roman Catholic mission school, where he was given the standard fare of French colonial education. In such schools, French rather than African culture was highlighted, and one learned about French geography, politics, and history. A devout Catholic, Senghor was a bright, avid pupil, though his teachers failed to comprehend how special were his talents.

Senghor spent four years at a seminary in Dakar, yet left after he found he had no calling to the priesthood. Thereafter, he was allowed to attend the Dakar *lycée*, a secondary school administered by French people, which he entered in 1928. There he studied the standard French course offerings. His command of the French language combined with scholarly prowess led to his being sent to Paris, first to the Lycée Louis-le-Grand and then to the famous École Normale Supérieure of the University of Paris. At the latter, he received the sought after *agrégation* designation, which made him the first West African to be so honored.

His Parisian studies were the most formative of his career, but simply being in Paris, and therefore in contact with brilliant thinkers from around the world, was just as important for Senghor. At the university were other colonial intellectuals who did much to encourage his mental restlessness and his burgeoning interest in African life and culture. To this young outsider, Paris was not only the center of the France that exploited Africans but also an alluring, often enchanting city. Senghor participated in the life of the city as teacher, writer, and seminal thinker whose ideas about African culture and black identity became part of the *négritude* movement that flourished in the 1930's.

In Paris, Senghor, together with such fellow intellectuals as Aimé Césaire from Martinique, boldly postulated that black people the world over were not merely equal to whites but in some ways their superiors. In an influential review they helped establish, *L'Étudiant noir*, Senghor and Césaire came to believe that, in fact, blacks would offer the world an alternative to the destructive whites who, in Europe during World War I, created a truly fallen world of hatred and despair. Unlike the death-dealing, mechanical culture of whites, black culture was, in their estimation, happy, spontaneous, alive to possibilities, and invigorating—a true life force in a world ruled by death and destruction.

## Life's Work

The 1930's was a decade of dissatisfaction for black members of the French intelligentsia like Senghor, a time when colonialism with its assumptions of European superiority over nonwhite cultures became increasingly resented and even hated by African, Caribbean, and American black people. Senghor's feelings about France were pained and decidedly mixed: He appreciated the cultural offerings and opportunities in his adopted country, yet felt disparaged and belittled by French condescension toward anything African. To his despair, Senghor realized that white Europeans would continue to scorn African history and culture unless someone could boldly and graphically assert the power and beauty of African literature, art, and tribal existence.

Out of Senghor's association with writers Césaire and Léon Dumas came the concept of *négritude*, which became a major force behind revolutionary worldwide developments such as the independence movement in Africa and the Caribbean and the Black Pride movement in the United States. Nevertheless, Senghor, for all of his bitterness toward France for its racism and despoilation of part of the African continent, still continued to have a profound respect for French civilization and the positive things that French civilization had wrought in Senegal.

It became Senghor's passion to fuse his Senegalese experience with that of his French life into a meaningful synthesis wherein French themes and motifs were interwoven with those of Africa. In Senghor's poetry of the 1930's, African masks and ancestor worship make their appearance, especially in his first volume of poetry, *Chants d' ombre* (1945), in which he contrasts his pastoral childhood village life with the harsh, mechanized reality of Parisian life and the alienation he sometimes feels there. In trying to fuse Senegal and France into a coherent vision of life, Senghor deviated from what his black contemporaries were doing in their verse. Césaire and Dumas, for example, found little or nothing worth writing about in European culture and were unhappy with Senghor's "colonialist" values.

After his student days ended, Senghor served in the French army during World War II, an experience that disturbed him greatly; yet, as always, he found his reactions mixed. On one hand, he felt vaguely hopeful that France's taste of German occupation would lead to its freeing the African colonies, yet intuitively he realized that it would take more than the Occupation to free the Africans from their oppression. Senghor, horrified by the widespread destruction of the war, looked even more longingly to Africa and black people the world over for answers to European soul-sickness.

As *négritude* gathered momentum after the war and the desire of French colonies to free themselves from colonial rule became keen, Senghor became Senegal's delegate in the French parliament, wherein he received considerable praise for giving graceful, powerful, authoritative speeches. This marked the beginning of a political career as distinguished as Senghor's career as a writer. He found to his joy that he could not only influence people with his considerable literary gift but also exhort them in oratory to recognize black Africa's need for recognition and freedom. Senghor's demands for change were among the most eloquent heard in the National Assembly.

Increasingly in the years between 1945 and 1958, Senghor's reputation as a forceful advocate of the rights of Senegalese grew to the point where he eclipsed such rivals as Lamine Guèye. Elected in 1951 and 1956, he also was appointed to Edgar Fauré's cabinet in 1955. Out of this period of maturation, Senghor produced some of his more noted poems, including those in the collections entitled *Hosties noires* (1948), *Chants pour Naëtt* (1949), and *Éthiopiques* (1956). In *Hosties noires*, he contrasts his growing love for France with his fading memories of a Senegal only seen upon rare occasions, a problem of allegiance created by his having to live in France in order to serve as a delegate. Senghor, because he could not repudiate France, remained a man caught between worlds; his poetry reflects the tensions of his predicament.

After 1958, Senghor's attentions turned toward Senegal. He returned home after a long absence and rediscovered his home and people. He gained political support, first becoming president of the legislative assembly in the Mali Federation of which Senegal was a part, then President of Senegal Republic when Senegal broke away from the federation in 1960. Always working for African unity, Senghor was popular within and without Senegal, particularly in many West African countries. He was reelected president in 1963, 1968, and 1973.

Beginning with his rivalry with Mamadou Dia, who, as the original cabinet minister of Senegal, shared power with Senghor, a rivalry that created a 1962 *coup d' état* attempt, Senghor has not been universally admired: considerable countergovernment activity resulted from his concentrating all power in Progressive Union Party hands, and he had to worry constantly about being ousted from office. In 1967, his fears proved justified when there was an attempt on his life. Senghor's best poetry was behind him at this point in his life. Perhaps the fecundity of his imagination had been diminished by the strain of political life as some critics maintain.

### Summary

Léopold Senghor will continue to be remembered as the spokesman of the *négritude* movement who did some of his best, most moving work in the form of verse. His strong, sensual, vibrant early poetry is his best, and in it resonates the life of Senegal and, by extension, that of Africa itself. Without Senghor's unique ability to deal with French people on their own soil, it is questionable whether Césaire and other intellectuals caught up in the notion of *négritude* would have been as successful in drawing attention to their beliefs. With Senghor as spokesman, the movement had a strong voice to proclaim the importance of the African experience and African culture and the need for Africans to pursue their own destinies.

Senghor's verse, appreciated around the world, teems with African masks and the scents and sounds of African rivers and savannahs, bold African tribal women of powerful sexual presence, a paean to Africa, the mysterious mother and necessary restorer of the human race, the force for peace, justice, and harmony in the world. Yet his France, if not equally compelling as his Africa, is certainly a kind of homeland of the heart, a mother of culture and a teacher of the Christian religion to those lacking spiritual guidance. Thus Senghor will always be seen as one of the intermediaries between Europe and Africa, explaining each to each. In this role, Senghor records the creative tensions existing between these two worlds in a way no other French-speaking colonial poet has done. By not limiting his cultural horizon to Senegal, Senghor has served as a bridge connecting European writing with that of Africans and, as such, has interested the world outside Africa in its poetry.

Senghor did more for *négritude* than did most other writers, for he refused to address himself to an exclusively black audience but rather chose to write for all people interested in serious poetry. As a Senegalese politician of considerable presence and ability, he was able to lead his country into nationhood and out of colonialism, a complex and difficult process. His life story is one of remarkable achievement.

### Bibliography

Allen, Samuel. "Négritude, Africa, and the Meaning of Literature: Two Writers, Senghor and Soyinka." *Negro Digest*, June, 1967: 54-67. Allen offers readers one of the finest essays on the subject of how the ideas arising from the *négritude* movement influenced the writing of Senghor's poetry. His discussion of theme is particularly useful.

Anyinefa, Koffi. "Hello and Goodbye to Negritude: Senghor, Dadie, Dongala and America." *Research in African Literatures* 27, no. 2 (Summer 1996). The author considers the writings of three Sengalese writers: Senghor, Bernard Dadie, and Emmanuel B. Dongala, all of whom spent time in the United States; and analyzes their views on race, America, and African Americans.

Bâ, Sylvia Washington. *The Concept of Négritude in the Poetry of Léopold Sédar Senghor.* Princeton, N.J.: Princeton University Press, 1973. Bâ's account is an enriching, engaging study of the tensions within Senghor because of his divided allegiance. She delves into the origins of *négritude* and proves it to be a powerful influence upon Senghor's poetry.

Cartey, Wilfred. *Whispers from a Continent: The Literature of Contemporary Black Africa.* London: Heinemann, and New York: Random House, 1969. A classic study of African literature, this book deals with, among other things, the *négritude* movement as it pertains to the poetry of Senghor and others earmarked as key African writers.

Hymans, Jacques L. *Léopold Sédar Senghor: An Intellectual Biography.* Edinburgh, Scotland: Edinburgh University Press, 1971. Hyman's superb study does give Senghor proper credit for being a leading poet who is also a fine statesman. Here Senghor is portrayed as a complex, often troubled human being who had a vision of what black Africa could become.

Kluback, William. *Léopold Sédar Senghor: From Politics to Poetry.* New York: Lang, 1997. A collection of fantasy conversations between Senghor and several noted twentieth century philosophers.

Peters, Jonathan A. *A Dance of Masks: Senghor, Achebe, Soyinka.* Washington, D.C.: Three Continents Press, 1978. A West African himself, Peters offers a lively study (complete with useful bibliography) of Senghor's development as an artist. His discussion of the *négritude* movement is enlightening and includes a discussion of Senghor's cultural context.

Spleth, Janice. *Léopold Sédar Senghor.* Boston: Twayne, 1985. Part of the Twayne World Authors series, this book is a good introduction to Senghor's life and works. Contains a fairly in-depth biographical essay, basic discussion of his major writings and influences, a selected bibliography, notes, and an index.

*John D. Raymer*

# ANNE SEXTON

*Born:* November 9, 1928; Newton, Massachusetts
*Died:* October 4, 1974; Weston, Massachusetts
*Area of Achievement:* Literature
*Contribution:* Despite a modest education and her lifelong struggle with mental illness, Anne Sexton became a poet who was celebrated by critics, academics, and the public as a new voice in literature and the cause of feminism.

## Early Life

Anne Gray Harvey was born on November 9, 1928, the youngest of three daughters born to Ralph Harvey and Mary Gray Staples Harvey. Although Ralph Harvey had only a high school education, he did well in the New England wool business and opened his own firm shortly after Anne was born. Anne's mother, Mary Gray Staples, was born into a Maine family whose members held important positions in state politics and journalism. An adored only child, Mary Gray was sent to boarding school and completed three years at Wellesley College.

The three Harvey daughters were never close, and Anne grew up a lonely child. Ralph Harvey was fastidious of appearances, and Anne's messy clothes and loud voice failed to please him. Years after her sisters were permitted to join their parents at the dinner table, Anne continued to eat in the breakfast room with the nurse. Her parents went out most nights, threw large parties, and drank constantly. Anne's only happy memories were of summers at the Squirrel Island, Maine, vacation home with her mother's extended family. A great-aunt, Anna Dingley, who had lived abroad and later become a reporter for her father's newspaper, provided Anne's greatest family affection. Despite her full life, Dingley, called "Nana" by the children, played the family spinster. She moved in with the Harveys when Anne was eleven, and Anne remembers her as the only person who provided a parent's unconditional love.

Anne bloomed during her teenage years. Her mother, hoping to remedy her "boy-crazy" behavior, sent her to Rogers Hall, a girls' boarding school in Lowell, Massachusetts. Although she was an indifferent student, Anne published early poems in the school yearbook. She went on to Garland School, a finishing school in Boston, and became engaged. While still engaged, she met Alfred Muller Sexton II, called "Kayo," a young man from a prosperous Boston suburb, and eloped with him on August 16, 1948. Their first daughter, Linda Gray Sexton, was born in the summer of 1953, and Joyce Ladd Sexton was born two years later. Kayo accepted a job as wool salesman from his father-in-law, and the young family settled down near Boston, close to their childhood homes.

Despite the idealized roles of housewife and mother in the 1950's, Anne was severely depressed after the birth of her second child. She suffered terrors and fits of rage during which she abused the children and even attempted suicide. Her family paid first for household help, then for psychiatric help. While the children lived with relatives, Anne began treatment first with Martha Brunner-Orne in 1955, and later with her son, Martin Orne. Recognizing Anne's creative potential, he encouraged her to write. After another suicide attempt in May, 1957, Orne told her that she couldn't kill herself; she had too much to give through her poetry. Anne Sexton, the poet, was born.

## Life's Work

With Martin Orne's encouragement, Anne Sexton enrolled in an evening poetry workshop and began to send her poems out for possible publication. More important, however, was the bond she formed with another student in the workshop, Maxine Kumin, which was to become the most fruitful poetic relationship in Sexton's life. The well-educated Kumin was three years older than Sexton, also had small children, and published regularly. Her instant recognition of Sexton's gift cemented a friendship that would comfort Sexton for the rest of her life.

By spring of 1958, Sexton was taking a new antidepressant drug and felt well enough for her daughter, Joy, to come home to live. She received occasional acceptances from prestigious magazines such as *Harper's* and *The New Yorker.* Her poetry was developing in new directions, partly as a result of her encounter with "Heart's Needle," a poem by William DeWitt Snodgrass which was seminal in what was to become known as "confessional" poetry. This poetry addresses the "unpoetic" themes in a person's life: domestic struggles, personal failure, and mental illness. At its best, it is well crafted and formally polished. Sexton attended the Writer's Conference at Antioch College in Ohio, where Snodgrass led a week's workshop.

This marked the start of a long correspondence in which Snodgrass helped her find an authentic voice and encouraged her tendency to use poems as vehicles of autobiography and self-analysis. Her connection with Snodgrass led to an acceptance in Robert Lowell's famous writing seminar at Boston University, where she became friendly with poet Sylvia Plath. It was here that Sexton started her first major poem, "The Double Image," which established her among the new "confessional" poets.

In May of 1959, Houghton Mifflin accepted Sexton's first book, *To Bedlam and Part Way Back*. Even before it appeared, Sexton was in demand for readings at Harvard and for a series of recordings at Yale. The book came out in April, 1960, and received wide attention, partly because of Sexton's honesty in speaking of her mental illness. On the strength of the book, she was one of the first to apply to a new program at Radcliffe College designed for women whose careers had been interrupted. When Sexton received an acceptance the day after her friend, Kumin, received hers, she was jubilant. An honorarium of $2,000 that came with it was used to convert the back porch to a study for her use, but the biggest difference was in her relationship to her family. They finally considered her work respectable. Sexton felt well during this period and started to enjoy being with her family, particularly around their new swimming pool. Kumin frequently joined her with her children, and their friendship deepened. In the fall of 1961, *Newsweek* featured Sexton in an article on Radcliffe's new program, and soon afterward *The New Yorker* offered her a coveted "first reader" agreement. Some of her strongest poems date from this time, including "The Fortress," which was written for her daughter Linda.

*All My Pretty Ones*, her second collection, came out in October of 1962 and won mostly rave reviews. On the short list for the National Book Award, it established the themes she was to write about for the rest of her life: mental illness, sexual love, and spiritual anguish. A new orientation to her themes was to come with her growing interest in the feminist movement, triggered by the landmark publication of Betty Friedan's *The Feminine Mystique* (1963).

The suicide of her friend Sylvia Plath in 1963 affected her badly, and to make matters worse, she became involved in an affair with her new therapist. She worked on a long-abandoned play, but broke down and was hospitalized briefly. Her doctor prescribed Thorazine, which produced severe, long-term side effects. Nevertheless, Sexton continued to write. A new poetry collection called *Live or Die* came out in September of 1966 to mixed reviews. That same autumn, Sexton's therapist, Ollie Zweitung, terminated their affair. Distraught, she fell down the stairs at home and broke her hip.

After a long winter of convalescing, Sexton received heartening news: She had won a Pulitzer Prize. During this period, Sexton completed work for her next collection, *Love Poems*, which appeared in 1968. The following year there was some interest in her play *Mercy Street*, and she received a Guggenheim Foundation award that would help fund production. The play opened in October of 1969 at the American Place Theater in New York to mixed reviews, and had a brief run. A more successful venture was *Transformations*. Intended to be a popular poetry book of black humor, it took the form of fairy tales that Sexton transformed from the traditional ones. In September, 1972, Sexton was appointed part-time professor at Boston University, and she also accepted an appointment in literature at Colgate University, which required a long weekly journey to teach two days of classes in New York. In spite of her teaching commitments, she completeds *The Book of Folly* and continued to work on *The Death Notebooks*, which turned out to be the last collection published during her lifetime.

Professional success did not alleviate her inner turmoil. During twenty days in January, 1973, that included two days in a mental hospital, Sexton wrote thirty-nine poems that were to make up a posthumous volume: *The Awful Rowing Towards God*. The poems came from a sudden frenzy of energy that resulted in bursts of images, and it was Kumin's encouragement that guided Sexton in the editing that completed the book. During the same surge of energy, Sexton made a decision to divorce her husband, an act that enraged her family.

After the publication of *The Death Notebooks* in February, 1974, Sexton was bombarded with requests for personal appearances. The high point of that winter was a reading in March arranged by the Harvard Literary Club, which was to be the Boston debut of *The Death Notebooks*. It turned out to be a triumph. Nevertheless, she was becoming more unstable, and she made another suicide attempt. Increasingly isolated from her family and old friends, she began to drink heavily and engaged in casual affairs with strangers. On Friday, October 4, 1974, she had a last working lunch with Kumin, then went home and committed suicide.

### Summary

Anne Sexton's poetry was particularly important to young women in the 1960's and 1970's because of its intimate nature and feminist themes. She illustrated the problematic position of women at the time, the struggle to create an identity beyond what was recognized as "women's place in society." Another important feminist theme grew from Sexton's relationship with her mother and daughters. Some of Sexton's poems suggest that a woman *is* her mother and open the way for a new evaluation of the mother-daughter connection. Sexton wrote of menstruation, abortion, incest, adultery, and drug addiction when such topics were not considered suitable for poetry, particularly by male critics. Always grateful for the support of other women poets, she had much in common with Sylvia Plath, Maxine Kumin, May Swenson, Adrienne Rich, and Denise Levertov.

Sexton's poetry often addresses the sexual stereotyping of women and other themes that were central to the emerging feminist movement. As Sexton struggled with these issues in her own life, she confronted problems that she could not solve, but she was able to use them in her art. Contemporary women's poetry owes a debt to Sexton's pioneering work, which gave women the courage to think about their own lives honestly and courageously.

### Bibliography

George, Diana Hume, ed. *Sexton: Selected Criticism*. Urbana: University of Illinois Press, 1988. Hume has collected eighteen essays that represent diverse perspectives and conclusions, although they all approach Sexton's work from a feminist viewpoint. Some are published here for the first time.

Hall, Caroline King Barnard. *Anne Sexton*. Boston: Twayne, 1989. Part of Twayne's United States Authors series, this volume studies Sexton's poetry chronologically with the aim of acquainting the reader with the whole work of an important poet. Hall examines the poet as the subject of her poems. This volume is a useful introduction, providing a framework for more advanced study.

Long, Mikhail Ann. "As If Day Had Rearranged into Night: Suicidal Tendencies in the Poetry of Anne Sexton." *Literature and Psychology* 39, no. 1-2 (Spring-Summer 1993). Considers the evidence of suicidal tendencies in Sexton's poetry, based on the female suicidal paradigm advanced by Charles Neuringer.

Markey, Janice. *A New Tradition? The Poetry of Sylvia Plath, Anne Sexton, and Adrienne Rich*. New York: Lang, 1985. This valuable textual analysis tries to fit the three poets' work into the literary tradition. The relationship between feminism and poetry that characterizes the work of all three poets is discussed at length.

Middlebrook, Diane Wood. *Anne Sexton: A Biography*. London: Virago, and Boston: Houghton Mifflin, 1991. Both comprehensive and controversial, Middlebrook's sources include tapes from Sexton's psychotherapy sessions with Martin Orne. The biographer uses them to illustrate the inextricable connection between the poet's illness and her writing.

Sexton, Linda Gray, and Lois Ames, eds. *Anne Sexton: A Self-Portrait in Letters*. Boston: Houghton Mifflin, 1977. Among these letters are intimate writings to her family as well as more formal correspondence to some of the major figures of twentieth century literature. The editors provide a helpful commentary.

Slorczewski, Dawn. "What Prison Is This? Literary Critics Cover Incest in Anne Sexton's 'Briar Rose.'" *Signs* 21, no. 2 (Winter 1996). The author provides analysis of Sexton's "Briar Rose," a poem about incest and its societal and cultural effects.

*Sheila Golburgh Johnson*

# GEORGE BERNARD SHAW

*Born:* July 26, 1856; Dublin, Ireland

*Died:* November 2, 1950; Ayot St. Lawrence, Hertfordshire, England

*Areas of Achievement:* Literature, theater, and social philosophy

*Contribution:* Shaw was not only England's greatest modern playwright but also a dazzlingly versatile and witty showman of ideas.

## Early Life

George Bernard Shaw was born in Dublin of English Protestant stock, one of a brilliant group of literary Anglo-Irishmen (others include Jonathan Swift, Richard Brinsley Sheridan, and William Butler Yeats). His father, George Carr Shaw, was a chronic alcoholic—pleasant, cheerful, but a failure at gainful employment. His mother, Lucinda Elizabeth Gurley, was a shabbily genteel, cold person who neglected her family in favor of cultivating her voice, hoping to shine on the concert stage. The Shaw household was largely sustained by a singular music master, Vandeleur Lee, who made Mrs. Shaw his protégée and even got the Shaws to move into his commodious house. When Lee moved to London to promote his career, Mrs. Shaw followed him with her daughter Lucy, forsaking her husband and her then sixteen-year-old son.

The young Shaw left school at fifteen and worked as a real estate clerk. He hated his job, and in 1876, he went off to London to join his mother, even though he had not heard from her for four years. She received him with little affection. Nevertheless, he lived with her for twenty-two years, until his marriage in 1898.

At twenty, Shaw was tall, gangly, thin, pale, and red-haired, with sharp gray eyes, projecting ears, prominent brows, and an even more prominent nose. Five years later, he was to grow the forked beard that was to become one of his marks. After months of inactivity except for heavy reading, he agreed to ghostwrite for Lee the weekly articles of music criticism for which Vandeleur had contracted with *The Hornet.* England's economic depression in the mid-1880's made jobs extremely difficult to obtain for a young man without regular education or connections. Shaw, therefore, spent most of his days in the reading room of the British Museum, studying many texts on philosophy and economics, particularly the works of Karl Marx and Henry George. Evenings he often devoted to attending the discussion groups which flourished all over London; there he began to hone his skills as a debater and publicist, heroically overcoming his natural shyness and instead cultivating what he himself called "an air of impudence."

At twenty-three, Shaw believed that he was ready to write full-time. He began broadcasting articles to newspapers and periodicals, and composed his first novel, *Immaturity* (1930), in 1879; nine publishers rejected it. Undismayed, he wrote four more novels in as many years; all failed initially to find a publisher. The most successful (and perhaps worst) of his novels proved to be *Cashel Byron's Profession*, finally issued by a leftist publisher in 1886. At thirty, Shaw had at last become an established author.

In 1884, Shaw joined the newly formed Fabian Society, widening his views considerably. This group included a galaxy of brilliant Socialists who dedicated themselves to reforming English society thoroughly, but gradually, in the spirit of their Roman namesake, Fabius Maximus; many of their policies were eventually enacted by the Labour Party. In 1885, Shaw had met William Archer, then a book reviewer, who was to remain his steadfast friend. When Archer soon moved to *The World* as drama critic, he arranged for Shaw to be the paper's art critic, a post Shaw filled with little distinction for three years. In 1888, a radical journal began publication as *The Star.* In February, 1889, Shaw became the paper's music critic, filling that post with great distinction until October, 1890, when he switched to the better-paying *The World*, writing a weekly musical critique for it until 1895.

As a music critic, Shaw admired Wolfgang Amadeus Mozart, George Frideric Handel, Ludwig van Beethoven, Giuseppe Verdi, and Edward Elgar, while deprecating Johannes Brahms, Franz Schubert, and such avant-garde composers as Gustav Mahler, Jean Sibelius, and Richard Strauss. Shaw was one of Richard Wagner's earliest champions, eventually coming to regard him as the greatest modern composer. In 1898, he published an essay, *The Perfect Wagnerite* (1898), which hailed Wagner's Ring cycle for its romantic, Schopenhauerian metaphysics and Socialist politics—values which Shaw strongly shared. Even readers who disagreed with Shaw's musical opinions were often delighted by his graceful prose style, Augustan in its ease, clarity, and polish, operatic in its climactic constructions, and always witty and epigrammatic.

In January, 1895, Shaw was engaged by Frank Harris to write drama criticism for a newly organized weekly, the *Saturday Review*; he held this position until May, 1898, for the first time signing his articles G. B. S. By that time, Shaw had also begun writing plays, so that his standing as a critic-dramatist was a complex one in the London theater. He proved to be an admirably discriminating and incorruptible drama reviewer. By the time he resigned his job, he had also written seven plays, few of which had been staged, none of which had been a commercial success. Yet when he wrote his valedictory to his readers in the *Saturday Review*'s May 21, 1898, issue, Shaw proclaimed, with typical audacity:

> For ten years past, with an unprecedented pertinacity and obstination, I have been dinning into the public head that I am an extraordinarily witty, brilliant and clever man. That is now part of the public opinion of England; and no power in heaven and earth will ever change it.

### Life's Work

The theater which Shaw inherited in the 1890's was mediocre at best, controlled by a small group of unimaginative professionals. They catered to the sentimental, melodramatic, middle-class tastes of their uncultivated public, which cherished moralistic conventions and the uncontested superiority of British ways under God's Providence. London's theatrical managers preferred to import the well-made French farces of Eugène Scribe and Victorien Sardou, virtually ignoring the late nineteenth century plays of the great Continental masters of modern drama—Henrik Ibsen, August Strindberg, Gerhart Hauptmann, and Anton Chekhov.

Not so Shaw. Archer had induced Shaw to read Ibsen's works from the mid-1880's onward, and Shaw soon interpreted the Norwegian author as a Fabian Socialist resembling himself in his radical politics, passionate realism, and championship of women's rights in such works as *Et dukkehjem* (1879; *A Doll's House*, 1880). Shaw amplified these views in an 1891 essay, *The Quintessence of Ibsenism*, which selectively tailored Ibsen's drama to Shaw's didactic measures. Throughout his career, Shaw preferred the drainpipes of a social reformer to the panpipes of a poet. He regarded the pursuit of art for its own sake as escapist self-indulgence and considered his art as didactic, aimed at reforming the moral and intellectual sentiments of his audience. It is fair to call him the most intellectual of major playwrights, dedicated to persuading his public of the reasonableness of a regiment of ideas ranging from Marxism to Lamarckism to eugenic breeding to innumerable other areas of politics, medicine, science, law, religion, and above all, ethics.

Shaw began in 1885 to collaborate with Archer on "an original didactic realistic play," *Widowers' Houses* (1892). Composition was frequently interrupted and not concluded until 1892, with Archer by then a reluctant partner, unconvinced of Shaw's dramatic talent. The play ran for two performances. Shaw's first important drama was *Mrs. Warren's Profession* (1898), which was banned by the Lord Chamberlain because it dealt with prostitution; although it was presented at the New Lyric Club in London in 1902, it was not publicly performed until 1905 at New Haven, Connecticut. Mrs. Warren, in her mid-forties, has become the head of a syndicate of flourishing brothels in Europe. Her highly cultivated daughter, Vivie, discovers both her mother's profession and the identity of her would-be fiancé as her half brother. She disowns both, to embark on her own career as a legal actuary. While somewhat squeamish about prostitution, Shaw takes pains to show it as a preferable alternative to poverty and sweatshop degradation. Both mother and daughter prove to be hardheaded career women, dominating an unsentimental work.

Shaw's next substantial drama was his fifth, *Candida: A Mystery* (1897). Like *A Doll's House*, it seems to lead up to the emancipation of an intelligent, dignified wife, Candida, from her matrimonial bond to her shallow husband, the Christian Socialist clergyman Morrell. In a climactic auction scene, Morrell demands that his wife choose between him and the dreamy, brilliant eighteen-year-old poet Marchbanks. She replies that she will select the weaker of the two—and picks her husband. Allegorically, she is the Holy Mother preferring the Father to the Son. In Shaw's evolutionary philosophy, Candida's destiny is to fulfill herself as a woman, not by leaving her family, as Ibsen's Nora does, but by rearing her children with a reliable consort, as Candida decides to do.

*Caesar and Cleopatra* (1901) is designed as a contrast to William Shakespeare's tragedy. Whereas Shakespeare's Caesar was an ambitious, cruel would-be dictator, Shaw's is a sage, humane elder statesman, a Victorian empire builder of extraordi-

nary wisdom and efficiency. Shaw omits any mention of Caesar's liaison with Cleopatra. While Shakespeare's Cleopatra is an intensely voluptuous woman with unrestrained passions, Shaw's is a spoiled, kittenish child queen whose petty tantrums require Caesar to father and educate her.

In May, 1898, Shaw suffered from necrosis of the bones in his left foot, was seriously ill for months, and obtained the nursing services of Charlotte Payne-Townshend, a wealthy yet Socialist Irish heiress, shy, philanthropic, a good friend of the distinguished Fabian couple Sidney and Beatrice Webb. She and Shaw were married June 1, 1898, with the stipulation that their union would never be consummated, since sex filled her with horror and him with uneasiness. For the first time in his life, Shaw was financially secure; he immediately abandoned journalism to devote himself to serious writing.

Shaw's relations with women usually bear upon them the stamp of comedy. He was a virgin until his twenty-ninth birthday, when a widow fifteen years his senior, Jane Patterson, got him to spend the night in her house. As an eloquent, dashing Fabian publicist he often attracted susceptible young women; his biographers are divided, however, as to whether the Mephistic-looking Shaw was indeed a devil with the ladies. The preponderant evidence indicates that he was not. In 1895, he began what was to become a famous epistolary courtship of the great actress Ellen Terry. They made soaring love to each other in the four-year correspondence but never forgot that they were hardheaded professionals primarily dedicated to their careers. In his introduction to their published letters, Shaw summarized their relationship candidly: "It must be borne in mind . . . that we were both comedians, each acting as audience to the other . . . without ulterior motives or what matchmaking mothers call intentions."

The only serious amatory event in Shaw's life was his infatuation with another fine actress, Mrs. Patrick Campbell, whom Shaw persuaded in 1912 to play the part of Liza Doolittle in *Pygmalion*. He wrote her poignant love letters for more than a year but had no intention of leaving his wife for her. The day before *Pygmalion*'s premiere, Campbell married an impecunious boulevardier. Two days later, Shaw gallantly took the newlyweds to lunch.

Shaw's first indubitably great play was *Man and Superman* (1903), an ambitious attempt to dramatize his views of what he called the Life Force. The work is really two plays: a romantic comedy reminiscent of William Congreve's *The Way of the World* (1700) and a long, dazzling, dialectical interlude, "Don Juan in Hell," which dominates the third act. The pattern of the comedy is that of a Scribean farce in four neatly arranged acts, with the plot centering on those old reliables, love and money. In the main plot, the emancipated Ann Whitfield inherits her father's money in act 1 and gets the radical John Tanner to propose marriage to her in act 4. In the minor plot, the even more emancipated Violet Robinson has made a secret marriage even before act 1 and gets her husband's rich Irish-American father to bless the union financially in act 4.

The dream sequence in act 3, which takes place in Shaw's version of Hell, is far more interesting. It may well be the most stimulating dialogue of ideas in English drama. In it, John Tanner has become the legendary Don Juan Tenorio; Ann Whitfield, Doña Ana; Ann's reactionary coguardian, Roebuck Ramsden, the Commendatore whom Don Juan slew; a romantic brigand, Mendoza, is now the suave Devil. Shaw's Hell is the ordinary person's idea of Heaven: a haven for escapists and hedonists. Shaw's Heaven is more complex: It is a home for those who will work and strive and contemplate, who will let the evolutionary Life Force guide them into creating nature's supreme achievement, the philosophic man. Don Juan chooses to ascend to Heaven so that he can toil in its workshop. Ana joins him, to help create "a father for the Superman!" Shaw has succeeded—through dramatic fireworks, if not intellectually—in transforming Don Juan from a mythical exploiter of women into a Puritan ascetic, in desexualizing a profligate debaucher into an appealing victim of female wiles.

With *Man and Superman*, Shaw began twenty vintage years during which he wrote his finest works, including *Major Barbara* (1905), *The Doctor's Dilemma* (1906), *Androcles and the Lion* (1912 in German, 1913 in English), *Pygmalion, Heartbreak House* (1919), *Back to Methuselah* (1921) and *Saint Joan* (1923).

On November 14, 1914, Shaw published a thirty-five-thousand-word pamphlet, *Common Sense About the War*. In it, he said that the war had been fomented by fanatic militarists in England as well as Germany and Austria-Hungary. He also discharged barbed arrows against what he saw as the devious diplomacy of British Foreign Secretary Sir Edward Grey. Virtually all Britons were outraged by Shaw's document. His cold rationalism was wholly out of step with a public mood of frenzied jingoism. Friends avoided him; booksellers and librarians removed his texts from their shelves; editorials vilified him as a traitor. Shaw felt deeply misunderstood and frustrated.

In this saddened, disillusioned, bitter mood he wrote, from 1913 to 1916, *Heartbreak House*, subtitling it "A Fantasia in the Russian Manner on English Themes." The action transpires on a single September day in an unreal atmosphere of boredom and upper-class leisure. A group of English gentry have assembled in old Captain Shotover's country house in Sussex, engaging in useless though sophisticated private amusements. The characters possess a dreamlike quality; the plot is rife with implausible reversals and recognition scenes. Resentments, indifference, and irresponsibility fill the haunted, tortured, ominous air of the play. The dialogue, instead of being exuberantly witty, is ambiguous, portentous, and heavily charged with overtones. All the plot's love actions turn out badly. The drama is Shaw's parallel to Anton Chekhov's *Vishnyovy Sad* (1904; *The Cherry Orchard*, 1908), a *Götterdämmerung* for England's governing class, a warning that its ship of state is about to wreck on the rocks of mental stagnation, moral flabbiness, and loss of political will. Shaw's implied solution is stated by Captain Shotover: "learn your business as an Englishman . . . Navigation. Learn it and live; or leave it and be damned." As in Chekhovian drama, Shaw forsakes rhetoric for genuine dramatic poetry, suggesting the dispersion and destruction of a class for having lived badly. For once, Shaw has dropped his mask of amiable, confident reformer. He soon resumed it, wearing it tightly except for one tragic scene in *Saint Joan*.

In a one-hundred-page preface to *Back to Methuselah*, Shaw concluded, wistfully yet cheerfully, "My powers are waning; but so much the better for those who found me unbearably brilliant when I was in my prime." He still had thirty years left to live. During them, he published seventeen more books, which neither diminished nor magnified his stature. He also wrote thousands of letters and postcards, received the Nobel Prize for Literature in 1925, traveled extensively, and garnered enormous publicity as a world figure on an Olympian plateau with Mahatma Gandhi, Albert Einstein, and Sigmund Freud. Occasionally, he used his high platform for foolish pronouncements, as when he praised Adolf Hitler, Benito Mussolini, and Joseph Stalin, shrugging off the horrors that their regimes perpetrated. Shaw's wife died in September, 1943, after a four-year period as an invalid. Shaw reduced the protein content of his vegetarian diet and went on writing and talking. In September, 1950, he fractured his thigh falling in his garden, failed to rally from resulting complications, and died on November 2, at age ninety-four. His body—like his wife's—was cremated.

### Summary

Indubitably, George Bernard Shaw is England's greatest modern dramatist. As a writer of high comedy, he has no twentieth century peer. As a wit and pamphleteer, a virtuoso of the language of assertion and dialectic, he also has no equal. Essentially, Shaw was a Platonist, convinced that the appetites of the mind are stronger, and its passions deeper, than those of other human faculties. He was a remarkably pure intellectual, certain that the drama of ideas is the only one worth writing, and that his gospel of Creative Evolution, part progressive socialism and part neo-Lamarckian biological theory, is the only one worth propagating. He was a marvelously entertaining showman of ideas.

Shaw was far less successful, however, when dealing with feelings: With the exception of *Heartbreak House* and parts of *Saint Joan*, he is too remote from his characters' emotions. Humanity and its future are everything to him; the individual, nothing. Moreover, his rational relativism caused him to ignore or dismiss the dark side of human nature. He has no evil people among his characters—only unenlightened ones. He makes little effort to sound the depths of the soul below the rational threshold that he intends to educate with his instructive discussions. For these reasons Shaw, while a dazzling wizard of language, ranks below the very greatest of modern playwrights: Ibsen, Strindberg, and Chekhov.

### Bibliography

Bentley, Eric. *Bernard Shaw, 1856-1950*. Rev. ed. New York: New Directions, 1957. An incisively probing and concisely written critical study, hailed by Shaw when its first edition was published in 1947.

Ervine, St. John. *Bernard Shaw: His Life, Work, and Friends*. London: Constable, and New York: Morrow, 1956. Ervine was an Irish-born dramatist and critic who became one of Shaw's few close friends. His 600-page work contains many anecdotes, told in a spirit of admiring affection.

Innes, Christopher, ed. *The Cambridge Companion to George Bernard Shaw.* Cambridge and New York: Cambridge University Press, 1998. A collection of essays by a team of scholars on a wide range of subjects concerning Shaw's drama.

Irvine, William. *The Universe of G. B. S.* New York: Whittlesey House, 1949. A first-rate interpretation of Shaw's writings from the perspective of a distinguished historian of ideas.

Shaw, George Bernard. *Bernard Shaw's Plays: Major Barbara, Heartbreak House, Saint Joan, Too True to Be Good.* Edited by Warren S. Smith. New York: Norton, 1970. This is a Norton Critical Edition and therefore includes helpful criticism of these texts, as well as five comprehensive essays on Shaw's works.

———. *Collected Letters.* Edited by Dan H. Laurence. 3 vols. New York: Dodd Mead, and London: Bodley Head, 1965-1985. Laurence has devoted forty years to chronicling and editing Shaw's plays, prefaces, essays on music, and letters. To date, three volumes of a quartet selecting twenty-five hundred of Shaw's letters and postcards have been published. They are admirably chosen and edited.

———. *The Portable Bernard Shaw.* Edited by Stanley Weintraub. New York: Penguin, 1977. Weintraub, an authoritative Shavian, has included all of *Pygmalion, Heartbreak House, The Devil's Disciple* (1897), *In the Beginning* (1921), and *Shakes Versus Shav* (1949), as well as the "Don Juan in Hell" interlude and a choice assortment of Shaw's reviews, articles, and letters.

———. *Shaw, Lady Gregory and the Abbey: A Correspondence and a Record.* Edited by Dan H. Laurence and Nicholas Grene. Gerrards Cross, Buckinghamshire: Smythe, 1990. The collection of the complete surviving correspondence between Lady Gregory and Shaw along with other letters, diaries, and private papers presents a clear picture of this friendship. Of interest to any theater afficionado.

Valency, Maurice. *The Cart and the Trumpet: The Plays of George Bernard Shaw.* New York: Oxford University Press, 1973. Valency's study is erudite and eloquently written. In a long concluding chapter he illuminatingly establishes Shaw's place in modern drama.

Wilson, Edmund. "Bernard Shaw at Eighty." In *The Triple Thinkers.* London: Oxford University Press, and New York: Harcourt Brace, 1938. The great critic attacks Shaw for what he claims to be the confusion and contradiction of his ideas. He does respect Shaw, however, as "a considerable artist."

*Gerhard Brand*

# ALAN SHEPARD

*Born:* November 18, 1923; East Derry, New Hampshire

*Died:* July 21, 1998; Monterey, California

*Areas of Achievement:* Aviation and space exploration

*Contribution:* Shepard flew the first U.S. manned space flight in 1961 and became the only Mercury astronaut to walk on the Moon.

## Early Life

Alan Bartlett Shepard, Jr., was born to Colonel Alan B. Shepard and his wife in East Derry, Hew Hampshire. After attending primary school in East Derry, Shepard graduated from Pinkerton Academy in Derry. He spent a year studying at Admiral Farragut Academy in Toms River, New Jersey, prior to his acceptance into the United States Naval Academy. After several years of distinguished military service, Shepard studied at the Naval War College in Newport, Rhode Island, graduating in 1958.

The National Aeronautics and Space Administration (NASA), created on October 1, 1958, received primary authority for Project Mercury, which attempted to send the first humans into space. As a result, astronauts were required. Military service files of test pilots were studied, invitations for application were sent, and NASA accumulated a large set of candidates. Following rigorous medical examinations, psychological tests, and personal interviews, seven individuals were selected as the original Mercury astronauts. Alan Shepard was among that select group.

NASA announced on February 22, 1961, that three astronauts—John Glenn, Gus Grissom, and Alan Shepard—had been selected to train for the first suborbital Mercury flight. Which astronaut would make that first flight was not revealed until Shepard emerged from the Astronaut Quarters on May 2, 1961, fully suited, only to have poor weather prevent launch that day. By that time, NASA had lost the race to send the first human into space. On April 12, 1961, Soviet cosmonaut Yuri Gagarin had orbited Earth once in Vostok 1 before landing within the Soviet Union.

## Life's Work

Shepard's next launch attempt came on May 5, 1961. Before sunrise, Shepard rode out to Pad 5-6. Leaving his transfer van, he paused to look up at the Redstone rocket about to hurtle him down the Atlantic Missile Range. Shepard slipped into his Mercury-Redstone 3 (*Freedom 7*) spacecraft and was hooked up to life support and communications systems therein. Technicians bolted closed the hatch. Minor difficulties were encountered during the remainder of the countdown. Each was overcome, but each delayed liftoff. The last, a faulty pressure gauge reading, surfaced less that three minutes before liftoff. Once resolved, the countdown continued until, at 9:34 A.M. eastern daylight time (EDT), the Redstone rocket rose from its pedestal. Shepard was on his way. The Redstone exhausted its fuel a little over two minutes into flight. *Freedom 7* separated from the spent booster, and the escape tower jettisoned. Shepard assumed manual control and reoriented his spacecraft for retrofire.

Shepard briefly viewed the Earth below using a periscope extended from *Freedom 7*'s hull. He experienced five minutes of weightlessness before reentry, reaching a maximum altitude of 115 miles. Three retrorockets fired in turn, and then the retropack on which they were located separated from *Freedom 7*. The spacecraft hit the upper atmosphere at over five thousand miles per hour, slowing down to about three hundred miles per hour over the next minute, the result of which was to subject Shepard to ten times normal Earth gravity.

Parachute deployments occurred normally, and, at 9:50 A.M., *Freedom 7* splashed down about one hundred miles from Grand Bahama Island. NASA's first manned space flight lasted fifteen minutes, twenty-two seconds. The spacecraft traveled 302 miles downrange from Cape Canaveral (now Cape Kennedy). Based on Shepard's success, a prior chimpanzee (Ham) flight, and a subsequent suborbital flight by Virgil "Gus" Grissom (*Liberty Bell 7*), NASA was confident to move ahead with orbital missions, beginning with John Glenn's three-orbit flight on February 20, 1962.

Later, as Project Gemini (the stepping stone between Mercury missions and Apollo lunar flights) evolved from design to test-flight stages, Shepard was considered for an early flight assignment. However, he was dropped from active astronaut status in 1963 and restricted to flying conventional aircraft only with a copilot, having developed Menniere's syndrome, an inner-ear condition capable of inducing nausea, ringing ears, and vestibular disturbances. Shepard assumed the role of chief of

*Alan Shepard is hauled aboard a helicopter after landing his space capsule in the ocean, May, 1961.*

the Astronaut Office but clung to hopes of flying in space again. In 1968 he secretly underwent an experimental surgical procedure. Detailed postsurgical testing by NASA doctors found no evidence of Menniere's syndrome, and Shepard lobbied for active flight status restoration and assignment to a lunar landing. He received command of Apollo 13. NASA management did not approve and suggested that Shepard needed additional training time because he had been inactive so long. He and fellow crew members Edgar Mitchell and Stuart Roosa were bumped back to Apollo 14, and James Lovell, Fred Haise, and John Swigert moved up to the ill-fated Apollo 13 mission.

Apollo 13's lunar landing site, the Fra Mauro highlands, was considered too scientifically significant to be missed. Fra Mauro held promise for sampling bedrock material excavated from deep below the lunar surface during the formation of Cone Crater. Originally, Apollo 14 was to land near the crater Censorinus in Mare Tranquilitatis relatively close to where Apollo 11 landed. Fra Mauro became Apollo 14's landing site. Apollo 14 carried tremendous responsibility for continuing Moon flights in the aftermath of Apollo 13. Budget considerations had already cut three previously planned landings. NASA could not survive another aborted flight and maintain sufficient congressional support for the remaining Apollo missions.

Apollo 14 launched from Cape Canaveral at 4:03 P.M. on January 31, 1971, the thirteenth anniversary of Explorer 1, United States' first orbital satellite. Ascent into orbit and subsequent translunar injection to boost Apollo 14 toward the Moon were both normal. A series of serious problems arose shortly thereafter, the first when the command and service module (*Kitty Hawk*) attempted to dock with the lunar module (*Antares*). Contact was made, but not a latched mating. If the two vehicles could not rigidly dock, Apollo 14's lunar landing was impossible. On the sixth attempt, *Kitty Hawk* and *Antares* achieved hard dock and separated from their Saturn 5 rocket's spent third stage.

Apollo 14 entered lunar orbit on February 4 amid concern over a suspect docking apparatus. Examination of the command module's probe failed to relieve that concern or identify the cause of earlier difficulties. *Kitty Hawk* dropped down to an orbital low point of only eleven miles above the surface, the point from which *Antares* would begin its powered descent to touchdown.

On February 5, *Antares* separated from *Kitty Hawk*, but before its braking engine could fire, a major computer problem required resolution. A false signal was being sent to *Antares*' guidance computer, one that would automatically trigger an abort twenty-six seconds after power descent initiation and send the astronauts back up to orbit. After two hours, Massachusetts Institute of Technology (MIT) computer specialists devised a software patch that circumvented that action. Then, as *Antares* steadily descended toward the lunar surface, the radar altimeter failed to lock on and provide critical altitude data to the guidance computer. After technicians recycled the radar's circuit breaker, critical data started flowing at an altitude of just 2,500 feet.

*Antares* touched down at 4:17 A.M., resting in a small depression tilted 8 degrees. Five and one-half hours later, Shepard and lunar module pilot Mitchell stood on the surface at Fra Mauro to begin the first of two moonwalks, the primary focus of which was to assemble a small science station that would provide data for months after the astronauts returned home. One experiment required active data collection. Shepard and Mitchell fired small pyrotechnics while a seismometer registered subsurface vibrations. Before concluding the first moonwalk, there was time for collecting geological samples.

The second moonwalk began at 3:10 A.M. on February 6, this one dedicated to careful geological sampling during a traverse to the rim of Cone Crater. Shepard pulled behind him a special rickshawlike transporter in which he stored tools and samples during the climb up Cone Crater's slope. The slope of the crater proved steeper than anticipated, and determination of position among the boulders and depressions was difficult. Shepard and Mitchell terminated their ascent and settled for sampling a promising boulder field just short of Cone Crater's rim. Before returning to *Antares*, Shepard, an avid golfer, took time to chip a pair of golf balls using a sample-collecting tool affixed with a club head. With limited moon-suit mobility, Shepard could only swing one arm, but the balls went quite far in the reduced lunar gravity.

*Antares* lifted off from the Moon carrying Shepard, Mitchell, and 108 pounds of lunar samples at 1:49 P.M. on February 6. This time, docking was trouble free, and the journey home was devoid of nagging problems. Apollo 14 ended after slightly more than nine days with a gentle ocean splashdown.

Shepard returned to his post of chief astronaut, remaining in that capacity from June, 1971, until August 1, 1974. Shepard retired simultaneously from NASA and the Navy (at the rank of rear admiral) to enter private enterprise, joining the Marathon Construction Company in Houston, Texas. Shepard had other business ventures in his post-Apollo period and served as president of Seven-Fourteen Enterprises in Houston. He was instrumental in several different efforts to both memorialize early space flights and educate young people. Shepard, along with the other Mercury, Gemini, and Apollo astronauts, was inducted into the Astronaut Hall of Fame in Titusville, Florida, where the *Kitty Hawk* is on display.

Shepard had planned to be present at the Kennedy Space Center to view his former colleague John Glenn's historic return to space after thirty-six years when the space shuttle Discovery launched in late 1998. Unfortunately, the United States' first man in space succumbed to leukemia and passed away at age seventy-four on July 21, 1998. That passing was noted by all major Western media news services with great nostalgia and respect for Shepard's contributions to the early years of the U.S. space program.

## Summary

The name and contributions of Alan Shepard loom large in the U.S. space program's early history. His laurels include being the original Mercury astronaut, the first American in space, the seventh man to walk on the Moon, and the first astronaut to be posted as chief of the Astronaut Office. Shepard's suborbital Mercury flight came three weeks after Russian cosmonaut Yuri Gagarin became the first human to orbit the Earth. Although Shepard's flight only lasted fifteen minutes, *Freedom 7* provided enough confidence for President John F. Kennedy to challenge the Soviets to achieve a manned lunar landing before the end of the 1960's. That challenge was issued nine months before NASA was even able to match Gagarin's orbit with John Glenn's Friendship 7 flight.

## Bibliography

Caidin, Martin. *Man Into Space*. New York: Pyramid, 1961. Perhaps somewhat difficult to locate, this book provides an excellent account of the early days of the space program leading up to and including Shepard's suborbital *Freedom 7* flight told from that period's viewpoint. The author is a noted writer of historical spaceflight books for the general audience.

Carpenter, M. Scott, et al. *We Seven*. New York: Simon and Schuster, 1962. The original Mercury astronauts provided insight from personal experience as part of the first U.S. manned space program. Four sections and one entire chapter were provided by Shepard. The chapter chronicles his *Freedom 7* suborbital flight.

Durocher, Cort. "A Legend in Our Time." *Aerospace America* 36, no. 9 (September, 1998). Brief obituary with highlights of the life of the first man to walk on the moon.

Shepard, Alan, et al. *Moon Shot: The Inside Story of America's Race to the Moon*. Atlanta: Turner, and London: Virgin, 1994. Plenty of texts chronicle the United States' race to the Moon from an engineering, exploration, or political viewpoint. Written by two astronauts instrumental in the rich story of Apollo, assisted by two of the most experienced space journalists, this book provides the inside story of NASA's golden age of manned spaceflight, detailing Shepard's participation in and supervision of that effort. A video version of this material is also available.

Slayton, Deke, with Michael Cassutt. *Deke! U.S. Manned Space: From Mercury to the Shuttle*. New York: Forge, 1994. Although an autobiography of Deke Slayton, this book also provides plenty of insight into the life of Alan Shepard, who, like Slayton, was an original Mercury astronaut and suffered a long period during which a medical condition forced him off active flight status. Slayton and Shepard developed a close friendship working together in the Astronaut Office.

Wohleber, Curt. "Alan Shepard." *American Heritage* 42, no. 7 (November, 1991). Brief profile of Shepard from his days as a Navy test pilot to his walk on the moon.

*David G. Fisher*

# DMITRI SHOSTAKOVICH

*Born:* September 25, 1906; St. Petersburg, Russia
*Died:* August 9, 1975; Moscow, U.S.S.R.
*Area of Achievement:* Music
*Contribution:* Shostakovich was a first-rank composer in the Soviet Union for a full five decades. He adroitly balanced the insistent requirements of totalitarian political dictatorship over artistic culture with his own irrepressible inspiration for superb creativity to win worldwide acclaim.

## Early Life

Dmitri Dmitrievich Shostakovich grew up in a musical family, adopting a musical vocation quite naturally. His mother, a product of the St. Petersburg Conservatory, was a piano teacher. Amateur musical evenings in the family home were a regular part of Shostakovich's childhood. At the age of fourteen, Shostakovich himself entered the conservatory, where he studied piano and composition. Already he had displayed a talent for composition with pieces, as their titles suggest (*Soldier* and *In Memory of the Heroes Who Fell in the October Revolution*), that manifested another of his natural inclinations, namely the reflection of contemporary political conditions in his creative productions.

Shostakovich acquired international fame early with his symphony (1925), written as his graduation composition when he was only nineteen. After Bruno Walter introduced it in Berlin in 1927, performance of the symphony soon spread around the world and contributed to a positive view of artistic creativity in Soviet music during the New Economic Policy (1921-1928). The government showed its recognition of Shostakovich's potential value to it by subsidizing a European tour in 1927, during which he received an award in the International Chopin Competition as a pianist. Presently he made the decision to concentrate his talents upon composition at the expense of piano performance.

## Life's Work

The 1920's in the Soviet Union was a period of experimentation in all aspects of human social existence. Shostakovich celebrated the new society in his compositions. His second (1927) and third (1929) symphonies carried explicitly political titles, *October* and *May Day*, respectively, and expressed the optimistic triumphalism of the revolutionary milieu with bold instrumental and grandiose choral movements. Shostakovich ventured into the arena of social criticism with modernist ballets—*The Golden Age* (1928), *The Bolt* (1930), and *The Limpid Stream* (1935)—and operas—*The Nose* (1928) and *Lady Macbeth of Mtsensk* (1932)—that satirized bourgeois values, some of which he found surviving in Soviet Russia.

Of his ballets and operas, only *Lady Macbeth of Mtsensk* earned sustained critical praise, but it was also the work that brought him into collision with the Stalinist regime that put an end to the opportunity for artistic experimentation that the 1920's had afforded. After the opera enjoyed numerous successful performances for two years in both the Soviet Union and abroad, Joseph Stalin attended a performance in January, 1936. The Communist Party daily *Pravda* published a vicious attack upon it under the rubric "chaos instead of music." The work was condemned as discordant, incomprehensible, and pornographic, whose true meaning was revealed by the approval it won among capitalist enemies. The shock of the *Pravda* attack changed Shostakovich's behavior, and his composing became cautious. He withdrew his fourth symphony (1936) from rehearsal, and it waited until the cultural thaw of 1961 for its premiere. With his fifth symphony (1937), Shostakovich adopted a new, more straightforward and traditional compositional style. The success of the symphony established his position as the preeminent Soviet composer.

After the German invasion in 1941, Shostakovich wrote two patriotic symphonies (seventh, 1942, and eighth, 1943) in which the world heard the inspirational celebration of the heroism and courage of the Soviet people. Shostakovich's world fame reached its greatest height. Western appreciation of Shostakovich waned after the war. One reason for the fading of his luster was the recognition that the wartime symphonies were not great compositions by modern aesthetic standards. Another reason was the imposition of stifling artistic restrictions in the Soviet Union by Stalin's cultural dictator, Andrei Zhdanov.

In January, 1948, Zhdanov staged an event that actually amounted to a trial of Shostakovich, at which he was accused, in effect, of possessing musical talent that was appreciated in the rest of the world. Zhdanov assembled a conference of composers at which, in the guise of an exchange of opinions about Soviet music, he set the example for a parade of speakers who attacked Shostakovich for his failure to "reform" in the years since 1936. Oth-

er composers also were attacked, but Shostakovich was the principal target. Although he was defended by the courageous intervention of such talented musicians as Aram Khachaturian and Visarion Shebalin, Shostakovich meekly requested that the Party explain what he must do. That explanation came on February 10, 1948, in the form of a resolution of the Party Central Committee that condemned the "formalism" and obedience to Western artistic standards of Shostakovich and the composers who defended him. The resolution declared socialist realism the only style that could be tolerated in the country, and that meant that music must be simple and straightforward enough to be enjoyed by unsophisticated laborers, that it must be tuneful, harmonious, and elevating.

The resolution's effect was like that of the *Pravda* article in 1936. Other musicians spoke against Shostakovich's "formalistic" work, especially his sixth (1939), eighth, and ninth (1945) symphonies, and Shostakovich recanted. In a public statement, he acknowledged that the Party had criticized him justly because his music had failed to speak the idiom of the people. He offered as propitiation civic music—*Song of the Forests* (1949)—and patriotic film scores—*The Fall of Berlin* (1949) and *The Unforgettable Nineteen-Nineteen* (1951)—all of which heaped exaggerated praise upon Stalin, who did not fail to show his appreciation. Shostakovich not only was permitted to retain his privileged living conditions in Moscow but also could travel to Western countries and was awarded the Stalin prize. Yet in the period between the resolution and Stalin's death, the musical compositions that Shostakovich published were artistically inferior.

Only after Stalin's death did Shostakovich unfetter his talent. The tenth symphony, which premiered in December, 1953, proved its worth in both the acclaim it won at home and abroad and the controversy it stirred. For it, Shostakovich won the highest honor that the Soviet Union bestows on an artist, the title "People's Artist of the Soviet Union." The 1948 resolution that had cast a shadow over Shostakovich was substantially rescinded by formal action of the Central Committee in 1958.

In the circumstances of the post-Stalin cultural "thaw," Shostakovich regained his artistic footing to become the moral leader of Soviet music. His best years were the ten between 1954 and 1964. In February, 1954, Shostakovich published an article condemning the Party's dogmatic and brutal imposition of ideological strictures on artistic creativity. This article served as a manifesto upon which Shostakovich based his repeated advocacy of the right of the Soviet composer to experiment with modern techniques. At the same time, Shostakovich balanced his appeals for freedom of the creative spirit with forthright recognition of the artist's social responsibility, which meant, for Shostakovich, that the musician was morally obligated to promote the just society toward which the Communist Party aspired. He confirmed this recognition by his successful application for membership in the Communist Party in 1960.

Shostakovich excelled in creative production in this period with artistically successful grand works. These included his eleventh (1957) and twelfth (1961) symphonies (the latter dedicated to Lenin's memory), the second concerto for piano, and a magnificent concerto for cello (1959). He added to the body of his successful quartets by writing the worthy seventh and eighth (1960) quartets. He made an especially bold statement with his thirteenth symphony (1962), which carried the title "Babi Yar," the name of a palace in the Ukraine where Germans had conducted a mass slaughter of

Jews. Shostakovich teamed with the anti-Stalinist poet Yevgeny Yevtushenko to produce this patriotic piece, which also directed a clear attack upon anti-Semitic manifestations that remained vigorous within Soviet society even at the time of the composition. Further evidence of Shostakovich's rehabilitation was the production of the very opera that had occasioned his first brutal censure in 1936. In 1963, *Lady Macbeth of Mtsensk* returned to the Soviet theater, renamed *Katerina Izmailova*. Yet soon the reality that he was not entirely free manifested itself. Khrushchev banned the thirteenth symphony after only two performances, and it was withdrawn from the repertoire.

About one year before his death, as the maestro Mstislav Rostropovich (for whom Shostakovich wrote two cello concertos) was in the process of emigrating from the Soviet Union because of restrictions on his artistic expression, Shostakovich addressed the fifth congress of the Union of Composers (April, 1974) with words that repeated his formal adherence to the Soviet artistic standard. It is immoral, he declared, for music to satisfy the tastes of the elite or merely to entertain. The composer is ethically bound to direct his art to the construction of Communism and to the creation of hope and happiness for humankind. When he died of heart disease in the Kremlin hospital on August 9, 1975, Shostakovich was honored officially as a "true son of the Communist Party" and a "civic-minded artist." After a week of official mourning, Shostakovich was buried at the Novodevichy Cemetery.

### Summary

The date of Dmitri Shostakovich's death marked the end of an era of Russian music history. Shostakovich was a composer very much in tune with his own time and his native society. Shostakovich provided resounding refutation of a widely held belief that a great artist could not prosper publicly in a society dominated by a Communist Party that aspired to totalitarian control and that great art could not be produced by someone who sincerely supported the social vision that Party promoted. Although he was rebuffed repeatedly because of the directions in which his creative genius drove him, he consistently sought to restore harmony between himself and the revolutionary transformations that surrounded him. He was a man of his own people, even while he reserved to himself the right to protest against society, with its vulgarity, anti-Semitism, and bloody suppression of human value.

Shostakovich's fifth symphony (1937) can be taken as a touchstone of interpretation of his significance as a composer. He himself named it a "response to just criticism" of the *Pravda* article on *Lady Macbeth of Mtsensk*. Widely acknowledged as a superb technical masterpiece of the symphonic form, it also has been criticized as an unfortunate abandonment of the avant-garde directions implied in works immediately preceding it. Political convictions appear to bias unavoidably the evaluations of even the most sophisticated critics. While most acknowledge the work as a masterpiece, some see in it a maturing of the talent of an artistic genius informed by patriotism, while others excoriate a craven submission to politically inspired cultural terrorism. In its grandiose and precise dimensions, it mirrors the new society toward which the Stalinist regime aspired, yet this frankly political statement was achieved without compromise of aesthetic excellence. Such was Shostakovich's distinct achievement throughout his life.

### Bibliography

Avrutin, Lilia. "Shostakovich on Screen: Film as Metatext and Myth." *Russian Review* 56, no. 3 (July, 1997). Examines "The Viola Sonata," a 1980 experimental film about the life of Shostakovich that was banned due to Soviet fears about its content.

Karl, Gregory and Jenefer Robinson. "Shostakovich's Tenth Symphony and the Musical Expression of Cognitively Complex Emotions." *Journal of Aesthetics and Art Criticism* 53, no. 4 (Fall 1995). Focuses on the connection between music and emotion.

Kay, Norman. *Shostakovich*. London and New York: Oxford University Press, 1971. A brief but useful biography of Shostakovich, in the Oxford series of composers, which will serve satisfactorily until the definitive scholarly treatment of Shostakovich is prepared.

Norris, Christopher, ed. *Shostakovich: The Man and His Music*. London: Lawrence and Wishart, and Boston: Boyars, 1982. A collection of scholarly essays evaluating Shostakovich's compositions, with separate treatments of the various forms in which he wrote.

Schwarz, Boris. *Music and Musical Life in Soviet Russia*. Rev. ed. Bloomington: Indiana University Press, 1983. A detailed treatment of Soviet musical history in which the figure of Shostakovich looms large.

Seroff, Victor Ilyich, with Nadejda Galli-Shohat. *Dmitri Shostakovich: The Life and Background of a Soviet Composer*. New York: Knopf, 1943. This book, written in collaboration with Shostakovich's aunt, is a detailed biography up to the year of its publication. Includes appendices, an index, and photographs.

Sollertinsky, Dmitri, and Ludmilla Sollertinsky. *Pages from the Life of Dmitri Shostakovich*. Translated by Graham Hobbs and Charles Midgley. New York: Harcourt Brace, 1980; London: Hale, 1981. A highly laudatory yet complete biography. Includes several photographs and an index.

*Paul D. Steeves*

# JEAN SIBELIUS

*Born:* December 8, 1865; Tavastehus, Finland
*Died:* September 20, 1957; Järvenpää, Finland
*Area of Achievement:* Music
*Contribution:* Closely identified with Finnish nationalism, Sibelius not only is a national hero in his own country but also is considered by many to have been the greatest symphonic composer of the twentieth century.

## Early Life

Johan "Jean" Julius Christian Sibelius was born in the house of his father, a surgeon of the Tavastehus territorial army battalion, on December 8, 1865. His family was of mixed Swedish and Finnish ancestry, and like most middle- and upper-class Finns, he grew up speaking Swedish as his first language. When Johan was less than three years old, his father died during a cholera epidemic, and the boy was reared by his mother and grandmother. As a youth, he took the first name of an uncle who had been a sea captain and was ever after known as "Jean."

Like many great composers, Sibelius displayed a precocious talent: He was playing the violin and had composed his first piece (a duet for violin and cello) by age ten. He began formal studies in violin and composition at fourteen, hoping, at least for a time, to become a great violin virtuoso. During his teens, he wrote numerous chamber works and also developed a deep interest in the *Kalevala*, the Finnish national epic collected from traditional ballads in the 1860's. This was later a great inspiration to him, as was his passionate love of nature.

Though his family enjoyed his music, his mother wanted him to have a more secure profession, and he acceded to her wishes by entering the law school of the University of Helsinki in 1885. Somewhat covertly, however, he also took courses in the school of music, and, after a year, gave up the law for full-time training on the violin and in music theory. His teacher, Martin Wegelius, was a versatile and widely experienced composer, pianist, and conductor, who recognized Sibelius' talents and took the young musician under his wing. Sibelius was also befriended by the Italian composer Ferruccio Busoni, who was teaching at the time in Helsinki.

After three years of Wegelius' patient encouragement, Sibelius left for Berlin to study with the famous theorist Albert Becker, a thorough and demanding teacher. He also indulged a taste for high living, hard drinking, and financial extravagance. Apparently, this lifestyle led to problems, and, after only a year, he left for Vienna to study with Karl Goldmark, a popular Romantic composer. Under Goldmark's tutelage, he expanded his studies from solo and chamber music and began to work toward composing for the orchestra.

In 1891, Sibelius returned to Finland, possibly because his high-society lifestyle had exhausted his resources. He made his living by teaching, but most of his energies were directed toward the composition of his first orchestral work, *Kullervo*, based on the *Kalevala.* In view of the fact that Sibelius had only recently had any training in writing for the orchestra, *Kullervo* seems little short of miraculous. Not only is it a work of very large proportions—more than an hour long—but also it includes a highly dramatic central movement with vocalists. Once *Kullervo* had received its first performance, in April, 1892, Sibelius' position as the

leading Finnish composer was never again seriously questioned.

### Life's Work

A few months after the premiere of *Kullervo*, Sibelius was married to Aino Järnefelt, the daughter of a prominent Finnish nationalist. Since 1809, Finland had been an autonomous grand duchy, with its own popular assembly, under the sovereignty of the Russian Empire. A movement for independence had started in the 1870's, gaining momentum toward the end of the century because of the czarist government's attempt to impose the Russian language and culture on the Finns. Sibelius had always been strongly patriotic, and, following the success of *Kullervo*, he expressed these feelings in a series of powerful orchestral works based on Finnish legends. Among these were the well-known *En saga* and a group of four tone poems called the *Lemminkäinen.* In 1899, he composed *Finlandia*, a short tone poem that remains his most famous and popular work. It has been claimed that this piece did more to promote Finnish independence than a thousand speeches and pamphlets. Many Americans, in fact, have mistakenly assumed that it is the national anthem of Finland.

By the 1890's, Sibelius had developed a very personal style of composition. Most composers are affected, at least to some extent, by models from the past, and Sibelius was no exception. His early works reveal the influence of his studies of Peter Ilich Tchaikovsky, Edvard Grieg, Joseph Haydn, and even Richard Wagner, though he rejected Wagner's dense, grandiose orchestral textures by the turn of the century. The most important factor in the evolution of Sibelius' musical style, however, was his fascination with the natural landscapes and folk culture of his country. In 1892, he had visited Karelia, a somewhat primitive area of eastern Finland, where he absorbed the rhythms and harmonies of native folksinging. Though Sibelius always insisted that he had never used any actual folk tunes in his works, their spirit, at any rate, can be clearly discerned. Most of his later music evokes images from the myths of the ancient Finns, as well as the mystery and power of Finland's primeval forests and lakes.

In 1897, in acknowledgment of his achievements, the Finnish assembly granted Sibelius a state pension. Though this was not a large amount, and certainly not enough to support the composer's expensive tastes, it did free him to begin work on his greatest compositions, the seven symphonies. The first of these was created in 1899, after Sibelius returned from a tour of Italy and Germany. Though both his first and second symphonies are relatively conventional works in the late Romantic idiom, already Sibelius was moving toward a sparseness of texture and condensation of form that would later be referred to as "neoclassicism." It has been said that Sibelius had a natural affinity for the processes of musical logic and development, which is demonstrated by his ability to weld coherently short, even fragmentary, motives into great organic structures full of dramatic tension and momentum.

Around the turn of the century, Sibelius began to achieve international fame. When the Helsinki Philharmonic Orchestra toured Europe in 1900, several of Sibelius' tone poems were on its program, and concert audiences loved them. Over the next few years, Sibelius himself was invited to conduct performances in cities throughout the Continent. By 1903, however, his insouciant lifestyle began to catch up with him, and his mounting debts and episodes of drunkenness seem to have provoked changes in both his personal life and his method of composition. In 1904, he bought a plot of land at Järvenpää, in the forests outside Helsinki, and he had a villa built there. Though he continued to travel until the beginning of World War I, much of the rest of his life was spent in seclusion in this new home.

In his next major works, the Violin Concerto (1903) and Symphony No. 3 (begun in 1904, but not completed until 1907), Sibelius turned away from the exuberant nationalism of his earlier music, and both of these pieces create instead a moody, somber sense of loneliness and dissonant energy. Such feelings are fully realized in Symphony No. 4, finished in 1911. Highly dissonant, even savage, harmonies dominate, and, of all Sibelius' symphonies, the fourth comes closest to the atonal and twelve-tone systems that would soon characterize much of European serious music. Yet, in this symphony, as in everything he wrote, Sibelius clearly demonstrated total independence from any "school" or movement: His style was uniquely his own.

Throughout the period before the beginning of World War I, Sibelius' international reputation continued to grow, and he was honored in England, France, and Austria. In 1914, he made a triumphant visit to the United States, where he was amazed by his popularity. This was his last major tour for many years; the beginning of the war disrupted international travel, and, by its end, Sibelius had largely retired from the world.

Seclusion did not, however, end his artistic activity. His expansive, uncomplicated Fifth Symphony was finished in time for his fiftieth birthday celebration in December, 1915; this was treated in Finland as a national holiday. Sibelius continued to revise this symphony, though, as he did many of his works, and it did not reach its final form until three years later, by which time his world had been completely disrupted.

The Russian Revolution of October, 1917, led Finland to declare its independence, but, early in the following year, Communist Red Guards invaded the country and provoked a civil war. Sibelius, whose sympathies were not only nationalist but also anticommunist, was forced to flee Järvenpää when the Red Army invaded his home. He did not return until after the war, and, from that time onward, he composed less and less. The Sixth Symphony, not completed until 1923, may reveal his feelings in this era, for in it Sibelius again eschews any nationalist exuberance or heroism; its themes are bleak and full of anguish. Though it is the least popular of his major works, many music critics regard the Sixth Symphony as Sibelius' greatest achievement, the most complete demonstration of his mastery of orchestral technique.

Both the Sixth and Seventh symphonies have been characterized as being "religious" in spirit, and Sibelius himself has been said to have had the sensibilities of religion but not the faith. The Seventh Symphony (1924), especially, seems to have left Finland—and perhaps even the earth itself—behind, for it suggests a kind of final cosmic vision of the reaffirmation of life. In fact, the seventh symphony seems also to signal the end of Sibelius' creative inspiration, for he wrote only one other major work, *Tapiola*, a tone poem for orchestra, in 1926. Tapio was the ancient forest god of Finland, and *Tapiola*, like some of Sibelius' earlier pieces, portrays the awesome mystery of the Finnish forests and the power of the spirits said to inhabit them. Unlike his earlier images, however, the world depicted in *Tapiola* is one of desolate isolation, an appropriate, but nevertheless devastating, portrait of life in the twentieth century.

After the completion of *Tapiola*, Sibelius' musical voice was stilled, and his last published work, a group of relatively insignificant pieces for piano, appeared in 1929. Though his sixtieth and seventieth birthdays were, like his fiftieth, celebrated in Finland as national holidays, Sibelius seldom ventured from the seclusion of his country villa. His last concert tour occurred in 1921; after conducting several of his symphonies in London, Rome, and Göteborg, Sweden, he returned permanently to Järvenpää, where he died of a cerebral hemorrhage on September 20, 1957, only three months short of his ninety-second birthday.

## Summary

Though for many years, especially in England and the United States, Jean Sibelius' music enjoyed great critical acclaim, an apparently inevitable reaction set in among critics on the Continent. In Germany and France, particularly, music was now dominated by the cerebral, acrid dissonances of composers such as Arnold Schoenberg, Igor Stravinsky, and the French group known as "Les Six." Though he expressed an affinity with a few of the "modernists," among them Béla Bartók, Sibelius generally rejected the avante-garde movements. They, in turn, rejected him as representing an obsolete tradition of tonality and emotionalism. Perhaps most damning, Sibelius' music remained popular with concert audiences, a sure sign that he was not "in tune" with the latest trends in serious music.

Throughout his productive life, Sibelius had pursued what may be seen as two creative paths. One of these is expressed in his "lesser works," the nationalistic tone poems and other popular pieces such as the *Valse triste*, a beautifully lyrical work composed in 1904. His first and second symphonies might also be considered as following this more accessible, popular style. His other approach may be seen in the Fourth, Sixth, and Seventh symphonies, as well as certain tone poems, such as *Barden* (1913) and *Tapiola.* These pieces demonstrate both Sibelius' mastery of classical technique and his success in concentrating melodic and harmonic development into austere, unaffected motives of great clarity and classical purity.

Yet to attempt to classify or categorize Sibelius' works into any kind of consistent "system" would have repelled him, for, as many critics have noted, with particular reference to his symphonies, each is unique, a theoretical and creative unity unto itself, expressing a deeply personal concept of symphonic structure. As a result, no other twentieth century composer has excited such deep and enduring controversy. Writers of the "modernist" schools have often viciously attacked Sibelius as trite, sentimental, and old-fashioned, and his retention of the tonal system—despite the highly innovative ways in which he used it—has been regarded as showing his lack of originality. Some have relegated him to the nineteenth century as a "late Romantic" or purely "nationalist" composer, or have even chosen to dismiss him altogether. On the other hand, to many critics, especially in England and the United States, Sibelius remains the finest symphonic composer of the twentieth century and one whose individuality stands above the transient fads and intellectualism of much of today's serious music. In any case, his works remain extremely popular with audiences, and their many recordings assure Sibelius of a prominent and permanent place in the history of great music.

**Bibliography**

Abraham, Gerald, ed. *The Music of Sibelius.* London: Drummond, and New York: Norton, 1947. A compilation of eight essays. Only the first, by Ralph Hill, is biographical. The others analyze Sibelius' music, classifying it by type. Therefore, much of this volume may be beyond those without musical training. It does include, however, a very useful bibliography, a chronology, and an indexed list of compositions.

Ekman, Karl. *Jean Sibelius: His Life and Personality.* Translated by Edward Birse. London: Wilmer, 1936; New York: Tudor, 1946. Ekman is Sibelius' principal biographer. Since he was a close friend of Sibelius, and because this work was written before the composer's death, it can hardly be called "objective." Sibelius was often given to somewhat melodramatic and less-than-accurate claims about himself and his music, all of which Ekman faithfully recorded as truth. Nevertheless, this is a valuable and entertaining account of Sibelius' creative life.

Goss, Glenda Dawn, ed. *The Sibelius Companion.* Westport, Conn.: Greenwood Press, 1996. A collection of research and analysis that radically alters understanding of Sibelius and his music. The volume includes analysis of vocal music, biographical data, analysis of well-known works, a bibliography, and more.

Lambert, Constant. *Music Ho! A Study of Music in Decline.* 3d ed. London: Faber, 1966. Lambert, himself a prominent British composer before his premature death in 1951, offers a challenging view that dissents from the critical bombast, gnosticism, and pedantry that has often characterized discussions of "revolutionary" twentieth century music. Lambert was one of Sibelius' most enthusiastic critics, and he suggests that it is Sibelius, rather than Schoenberg or other "modernists," who should offer a model for the music of the future.

Layton, Robert. "Jean Sibelius." In *Schuetz to Spinto*, vol. 17 in *The New Grove Dictionary of Music and Musicians*, edited by Stanley Sadie. Washington, D.C.: Grove's Dictionaries of Music, and London: Macmillan, 1980. Though articles in this set are often too technical for those without musical training, this essay on Sibelius is among the best brief sources available. While some sections will be difficult for general readers, the wealth of biographical information, as well as the clarity and balance with which it is presented, make this article well worth the effort. Contains an extensive bibliography.

Machlis, Joseph. *Introduction to Contemporary Music.* 2d ed. London: Dent, and New York: Norton, 1979. Essential for general readers interested in twentieth century music. Introduces modern music through comparison with earlier periods, providing a painless introduction to music theory. European and American composers are grouped by types; each receives a concise biographical treatment and analysis of important works. Includes an excellent bibliography, discography, and texts and translations of vocal works.

Mellers, Wilfrid. *Romanticism and the Twentieth Century, from 1800.* Rev. ed. London: Barrie and Jenkins, 1988. An excellent analysis of romantic music in the late nineteenth century and its relationship to twentieth century music. Useful comparisons and contrasts of twentieth century composers, especially those considered to be inheritors of the Romantic tradition. Sibelius is discussed in this framework as a nationalist and "naturist" composer.

Ross, Alex. "Prospero's Songs: A Season of Sibelius Teaches Us to Take the Finnish Composer Seriously." *The New Yorker* 73, no. 42 (January 12, 1998). Examines the revival of interest in the works of Sibelius including not only his well-known pieces, but more obscure works as well.

*Thomas C. Schunk*

# NORODOM SIHANOUK

*Born:* October 31, 1922; Phnom Penh, Cambodia
*Areas of Achievement:* Government and politics
*Contribution:* King of Cambodia from 1941 to 1955, then alternately prime minister, head of state, and leader of various opposition movements, Sihanouk could for many years be found at the center of Cambodia's fractious and highly controversial politics.

## Early Life

Norodom Sambeth Preah Sihanouk's privileged position in Cambodian politics came in part because his parents were direct descendants of modern Cambodia's two main royal lines. Sihanouk's father, Prince Norodom Suramarit, was the grandson of King Norodom (reigned 1860-1904), the man who first welcomed the French colonization of his country but then became bitterly disillusioned and hence a popular symbol of Cambodian nationalism. His mother, Princess Kossamak Neareath, was the granddaughter of two kings named Sisowath who ruled between 1904 and 1927, and 1927 and 1941, respectively. Sihanouk's parents separated, and his childhood was apparently not a happy one. While still a student at the exclusive Lycée Chausseloup Laubat in Saigon (now Ho Chi Minh City), Vietnam, Sihanouk was unexpectedly chosen by the French resident general to succeed his uncle as king, apparently in hopes that he would be easy to control. Sihanouk instead made efforts to rule well, refusing, among other things, the annual French gift of opium. He also took advantage of the Japanese takeover of the French colonial administration between March and October, 1945, to press for independence. Sihanouk angered more radical nationalists by compromising when French troops returned in 1946, but he again pressed his case when the French were doing badly in their war against Ho Chi Minh in neighboring Vietnam. Full independence was finally granted in the multination Geneva Conference of July, 1954.

## Life's Work

Sihanouk's major concern over the next decade and a half appeared to be to keep Cambodia out of the rapidly escalating conflict in neighboring Vietnam between the American-backed South Vietnamese government on the one hand and the National Liberation Front (often crudely called "Viet Cong") and North Vietnamese Communist forces led by Ho Chi Minh on the other. Abdicating the throne to his father in 1955, Sihanouk soon founded the Sangkum Reastre Niyum, or "People's Socialist Community" organization, that was designed to spread his own mix of capitalist and Marxist elements in what he liked to call a unique form of "Buddhist Socialism." Energetically touring the country distributing gifts and giving long-winded and apparently quite earthy speeches in his rather unique high-pitched voice, Sihanouk had much appeal in the countryside. Even in the cities he remained powerful, however, both because he could be ruthless toward his enemies and because few of Cambodia's constantly squabbling politicians could agree on who should take his place.

Sihanouk initially tried to be neutral toward the United States, refusing both as king and prime minister to join the Southeast Asia Treaty Organization (SEATO), yet accepting United States military aid and advisers. In 1963, he veered sharply to the left, nationalizing the import-export trade and Cambodia's banks, while also cutting off all U.S. aid and, indeed, breaking relations with the United States in 1965. Sihanouk took these actions in part because he blamed the United States Central Intelligence Agency (CIA) for supporting Son Ngoc Thanh's Khmer Serei ("Free Khmer," or "Free Kampuchean People") movement, in part because he was horrified by the apparent U.S. involvement in the overthrow and subsequent assassination of the South Vietnamese prime minister Ngo Dinh Diem and his brother Nhu, and in part, some argued, because he simply was convinced that the North Vietnamese and National Liberation Front troops were going to win. Fully aware that only French colonial rule had previously kept the traditional Vietnamese enemy at bay, Sihanouk in this period was now busy emphasizing his Socialist credentials.

In 1966, Sihanouk was forced to move back toward a more conservative position, in part because of the fact that Cambodia's more wealthy urban elite, and particularly the military, resented the loss of U.S. aid and because the protests reflected anger at the new opportunities for corruption that Sihanouk's nationalization schemes provided. Sihanouk himself also appears to have been bothered by a revolt against high taxes that took place in Battambang Province in 1967, and he may also have concluded that the arrival of U.S. troops in Vietnam in 1965 and the U.S. policy of bombing

North Vietnam made it advisable for Cambodia to move a bit away from the Left. For complex reasons, then, Sihanouk did not prevent the conservative general Lon Nol and many of his supporters from winning seats in the National Assembly in 1966, nor did he object to Lon Nol's brutal suppression of the Battambang Revolt the following year. He apparently agreed to allow the North Vietnamese and National Liberation Forces to send supplies through Cambodia to their troops in return for guarantees of Cambodia's borders, yet he also allegedly sanctioned the United States's secret bombing raids against those forces as long as these were not brought to his official attention. Intensive U.S. bombing soon began.

Try as he might, then, Sihanouk was unable to prevent Cambodia from becoming sucked into the increasingly violent war in Vietnam. On the one hand, leftists such as Khieu Samphan, Hou Youn, and Hu Nim no longer believed that they could work safely with Sihanouk, and they therefore fled to the jungles, where they joined a revolt of certain Cambodian Communists (called by Sihanouk himself the Khmer Rouge, or "Red Khmers") led by a radical leader named Pol Pot. Rightists, on the other hand, objected to what they believed was increasingly erratic and even bizarre behavior by their long time leader. The last straw in this process may well have been the opening of a gigantic gambling casino in Pnompenh in 1969, most of the profits of which appeared to be somehow connected to previous corruption schemes by Sihanouk's Eurasian wife, Monique. As the Cambodian economy deteriorated, the corruption and maneuvering that appeared to surround Sihanouk's rule became all the more alarming.

In 1970, therefore, Lon Nol took advantage of Sihanouk's visit to France to proclaim a new and more conservative government. The U.S. government apparently had advanced notice of the coup, may have supported it, and certainly did little to work out a compromise between the more actively anticommuist Lon Nol and their nemesis Sihanouk. Sihanouk, therefore, repaired to the Chinese capital of Peking, where the Chinese foreign minister Chou En-lai quickly gave him enthusiastic support. Swinging again leftward, Sihanouk now embraced the Khmer Rouge cause and hence gave the leftists far more support among the peasants and moderates within Cambodia. Fighting between the Lon Nol and Khmer Rouge forces continued to be bitter for the next five years, with little quarter asked or given. Finally Lon Nol was defeated, and a new government headed by Pol Pot and Khieu Samphan took over the country in 1975.

During the next three years, Sihanouk first briefly toured a number of foreign countries to proclaim the worthy social purposes of the new regime and then returned to Pnompenh to announce a new constitution that ended his role as head of state and placed him under virtual house arrest. During this time, the Khmer Rouge emptied the cities of almost all of their residents, executed thousands of "class enemies," and forced most of the people to work exhausting hours on ambitious but cruelly misplanned agricultural collectivization schemes. The historically deep hatred of the Vietnamese was used to rally support for the new regime, and border incidents were gradually increased until a full-scale war erupted between Vietnam and Cambodia in 1978. Only after the Pol Pot regime had been quickly defeated and forced back into the craggy jungles on the border with Thailand was Sihanouk finally released by the Khmer Rouge. His job now was to be at the United Nations to make sure that the new government installed by the Vietnamese invaders did not get Kampuchea's seat in the United Nations.

Throughout the 1980's Sihanouk tried hard to find an acceptable political future for Cambodia. During this time, the People's Republic of Kampuchea ("Kampuchea" being the name originally given Cambodia by the Communist regime), led by Hun Sen and backed by the Vietnamese, made slow but steady progress in restoring a more normal economy and providing a reasonable amount of security in all but the more rural areas near Thailand. Vietnamese occupying forces, meanwhile, began a plan of total withdrawal that was to be completed by the end of 1989. Against them, Sihanouk's Coalition Government of Democratic Kampuchea consisted of an uneasy coalition of Sihanouk's own forces, Son Sann's Khmer People's National Liberation Front, and the slightly modified Khmer Rouge. Each of these groups had its own army, and each accused the others of ruthlessness, corruption, or betrayal. United in their hatred of the Vietnamese-backed Hun Sen government, yet quite distinct in their ideas about what should replace it, each had different major powers on its side. A country that had once been a symbol of apparent pastoral bliss was now a perfect example of the cruelties to which human beings can sink.

By 1993, elections had been held, resulting in a tenuous government headed by Sihanouk's son Ranariddh as "first premier" and Hun Sen as "second premier." A new constitution was written and Sihanouk was officially made king. He was nevertheless without real authority, and a power struggle between Ranariddh and Hun Sen led to renewed bloodshed.

### Summary

Norodom Sihanouk appears to have been at the center of most every major event in Cambodia since 1941 and hence to be indistinguishable from the modern history of Cambodia. His detractors would deplore this history and point a major finger of blame at Sihanouk. The sometime-king was enormously vain and erratic, they would say. He dabbled in films, played the saxophone, and boasted of his successes with women when he should have been running the country. The father of many children by several wives and mistresses—including his mother's half sister—he was not considered to be a very good parent. Fond of giving moral lectures, he nevertheless tolerated an extraordinary amount of corruption, particularly by his mother, Kossamak, and by his Eurasian wife, Monique. Sihanouk could be ruthless to the point of foolishness, as, for example, when his police humiliated the future Khmer Rouge leader Khieu Samphan by leaving him naked in the street. Not surprisingly, one of Sihanouk's last Western advisers found him an erratic man who was alternately a "Prince Charming" and a "Prince of Darkness."

Supporters of Sihanouk could find much to respect in Sihanouk's boundless energy and his repeated attempts to preserve the security of a very small nation surrounded by extremely hostile neighbors. Dismissing Sihanouk's personal foibles as either typical of Cambodian males or of little consequence in the life of the nation, supporters of Sihanouk instead saw the Cambodian tragedy as part of a "proxy war" in which the United States both inflicted terrible damage by bombing an enraged Khmer Rouge and supported unsatisfactory right-wing regimes that would help its cause in Vietnam, in which China inspired radical reforms and kept the Khmer Rouge supplied with arms so as to hurt the Vietnamese, and in which the Russians supported Vietnamese efforts to establish a friendly regime. Since Cambodia was caught in the middle of a major struggle between the great powers of the world, the wonder is that Sihanouk was able to do as much as he did to preserve the fragile nation's independence. Sihanouk perhaps put it best himself when he said that the "great misfortune" of the Cambodian people "is that they always have terrible leaders who make them suffer. I am not sure that I was much better myself, but perhaps I was the least bad."

### Bibliography

Chandra, Nayan. "The Centre Cannot Hold: Sihanouk Fears for the Future of His Country." *Far Eastern Economic Review* 157, no. 20 (May 19, 1994). Interview with Sihanouk in which he discusses the future of Cambodia, the threat of the Khmer Rouge, and his desire to establish elite army units to fight the Khmer.

Kiernan, Ben. *How Pol Pot Came to Power.* London: Verso, 1985. Though primarily a history of Cambodian Communism, this book does deal with Sihanouk's rule.

Kissinger, Henry. *The White House Years*. London: Weidenfeld and Nicolson, and Boston: Little Brown, 1979. Kissinger's eloquent defense of his dealings with Sihanouk should be read in conjunction with the William Shawcross book listed below to understand the complex relations between United States policy and Sihanouk's rule.

Lacouture, Jean. *The Demigods: Charismatic Leadership in the Third World*. Translated by Patricia Wolf. New York: Knopf, 1970; London: Secker and Warburg, 1971. Lacouture's work emphasizes Sihanouk's appeal to peasants rather than his use of power and his corruption.

Lancaster, Donald. "The Decline of Prince Sihanouk's Regime." In *Indochina in Conflict*, edited by Joseph J. Zasloff and Allan E. Goodman. Lexington, Mass.: Lexington Books, 1972. An attempt by one of Sihanouk's last Western advisers to convey the complexity of Sihanouk's personality.

Osborne, Milton. *Before Kampuchea: Preludes to Tragedy*. London and Boston: Allen and Unwin, 1979. This useful recounting of the author's experiences and observations helps explain the later tragedy.

———. *Politics and Power in Cambodia: The Sihanouk Years*. Camberwell, Australia: Longman, 1973. A more formal history than the 1979 book, hence a useful supplement full of valuable information.

Shawcross, William. *Sideshow: Kissinger, Nixon, and the Destruction of Cambodia*. Rev. ed. London: Hogarth, 1986; New York: Simon and Schuster, 1987. This controversial book blaming U.S. policy for the Khmer Rouge has much information on Sihanouk's role. The new edition responds to Secretary of State Henry Kissinger's comments.

Sihanouk, Norodom, as related to Wilfred Burchett. *My War with the CIA: The Memoirs of Prince Norodom Sihanouk*. London: Penguin, and New York: Pantheon, 1973. Written between the 1970 coup and the Khmer Rouge victory in 1975, this work reflects one of Sihanouk's anti-American periods and makes a number of disturbing charges about U.S. policy.

Thayer, Nate. "End of the Line: Can the Monarchy Survive Beyond Sihanouk?" *Far Eastern Economic Review* 158, no. 9 (March 2, 1995). Considers the activities of the Cambodian People's Party (CPP) with respect to Sihanouk.

*Peter K. Frost*

# FRANK SINATRA

*Born:* December 12, 1915; Hoboken, New Jersey
*Died:* May 14, 1998; Los Angeles, California
*Area of Achievement:* Music
*Contribution:* Perhaps the most popular singer of his generation, Sinatra recorded definitive renditions of many popular American songs. His personal sense of style extended to performances on stage and screen, making him an icon of American culture.

## Early Life

Francis Albert Sinatra, the son of Italian immigrants, was born in the blue-collar town of Hoboken, New Jersey, and grew up during the Great Depression. He dropped out of high school determined to become the next great crooner. Bing Crosby set the model for him, as he in turn would set the model for younger singers such as Vic Damone.

Sinatra got his first break when he appeared on an amateur hour on national radio in 1935. With Sinatra as the lead singer and spokesman, the Hoboken Four proved so popular that they were invited back regularly. They used the name of a different New Jersey town each week in order to preserve their image as amateurs. Later, Sinatra began singing at the Rustic Cabin, a tavern near the George Washington Bridge. Because there was a radio hookup with WNEW in New York City, his voice was on the air several times per week. In June, 1939, the great trumpeter Harry James listened to a broadcast and liked what he heard. James had just left the band of Benny Goodman to form his own group, and he soon signed Sinatra as his "boy singer."

James had exceptional breath control and a snappy sense of rhythm. He would draw out a line where others would cut it off and would rush or lag the next line to syncopate the beat. Sinatra learned a lot from him, and their best-known recording, "All or Nothing at All," has a phrasing that amounts to an interpretation of the lyrics. By the time he left James to join Tommy Dorsey's orchestra, Sinatra was a respected singer as well as a new celebrity.

## Life's Work

Sinatra's recording career is conveniently divided into his years with several major recording companies. His first hit recordings were made with Tommy Dorsey's group on the RCA Victor label. "I'll Never Smile Again," recorded May 23, 1940, topped the *Billboard* chart for twelve consecutive weeks. Backed up by a female group, the Pied Pipers, Sinatra's voice projected all the sweet sadness of a world at war, setting the mood for a wonderful trombone solo by Dorsey. Like James, Dorsey had remarkable breath control, and his long lines challenged Sinatra to develop the clear, apparently effortless style of singing that he displayed in "Without a Song" and "In the Blue of Evening." By the mid-1940's, Sinatra had a huge following, especially of young women. *Newsweek* called him the "Swami of Swoon." Sinatra, sometimes known as "Swoonatra," was ready to go out on his own.

Sinatra signed a contract with Columbia Records, where he worked with the gifted arranger and conductor Axel Stordahl. With Stordahl, he recorded songs by some of the best-loved composers of Broadway show tunes: George and Ira Gershwin ("Embraceable You"), Oscar Hammerstein and Jerome Kern ("The Song Is You"), Irving Berlin ("Always"), Cole Porter ("Night and Day"), and Johnny Mercer ("Fools Rush In"). Most of these were old favorites by the time Sinatra got to them: The Gershwins and Porter had written their songs for films of the previous decade, and Mercer's song was in Dorsey's repertoire when Sinatra joined the group. However, Sinatra managed to make each his own by adding a unique phrasing.

Sinatra was everywhere in the 1940's: at popular night clubs such as the Copacabana, on the radio show *Your Hit Parade*, on the early television program *The Lucky Strike Hour*, in musical films such as *Anchors Aweigh* (1945), and in public-service advertisements calling for racial tolerance. He moved from New York to Hollywood, California, and romanced the film stars, divorcing his first wife to marry the beautiful actor Ava Gardner in 1951. However, the wheel of fortune continued to turn, and he was soon nearing the bottom. The House Committee on Un-American Activities investigated his possible ties to left-wing organizations. He lost his voice after a grueling series of performances and was losing his hair too. Columbia Broadcasting System (CBS) canceled his television show, while Columbia Records, unwilling to put up with his moods and demands, dropped him from their list of artists. Even worse, Ava Gardner dropped him as well.

Capitol Records signed Sinatra in 1953, and he stayed with them until he organized his own recording company, Reprise Records, in 1960. The Capitol years were perhaps Sinatra's greatest as a singer. His voice had lost some range and sweetness but had gained darker tones that allowed him to explore the experiences of midlife. Self-described as "an eighteen-carat manic depressive," Sinatra was either up or down, "swinging" or "blue," and the new long-play (LP) recording technology enabled him to extend the mood beyond the single song rendition. His main arranger at Capitol was Nelson Riddle, a former trombone player with the Glenn Miller Orchestra. Riddle wanted to produce a theme or concept album with a group of songs connected by a single mood and by a core of musicians backing up Sinatra. While Sinatra chose the songs, many of them from his club repertoire, Riddle made the arrangements. The LP gave new control over sequence and transition. Sinatra's first venture in the new genre was *Songs for Young Lovers* (1953) with eight songs by the Gershwins, Porter, and others.

For many fans, Sinatra's finest hour came at quarter to three in the morning, when he probed the depths in torch songs such as "I See Your Face before Me" by Jimmy Van Heusen on *In the Wee Small Hours* (1955) and saloon songs such as "One for My Baby" by Johnny Mercer on *Sings for Only the Lonely* (1960). Sinatra recorded two other saloon songs by Mercer: "Drinking Again" and "Empty Tables." If he had a problem with alcohol—he certainly had a fondness for Jack Daniel's whisky—he also had uncanny knowledge of the culture that depended on it.

Sinatra's claim as "The Come-Back Kid" was secured when he won an Academy Award for his performance as Maggio, the off-beat Italian American soldier in the film *From Here to Eternity* (1953). His film career continued with serious dramas such as *The Man with the Golden Arm* (1955) and *The Manchurian Candidate* (1962) but moved increasingly toward typecast roles with a musical dimension. The delightful *Robin and the 7 Hoods* (1964), which ends with the song "My Kind of Town," resembles the Hollywood musicals of his early career.

After Sinatra formed the Reprise label in 1960, he worked with a wide variety of musicians and styles. He hated racial intolerance and worked with legendary black performers when other white performers would not. Although he disliked rock and roll, he admired the Beatles as songwriters and dabbled in soft rock. Indeed, he tried everything from folk (*September of My Years*, 1965) to bossa nova (*Francis Albert Sinatra and Antonio Carlos Jobim*, 1967). He added newly composed numbers to his repertoire, including "My Way" and "New York, New York," but increasingly sang the songs that had made him famous. His last major effort was a collection of duets (1993) performed with the top singers of the younger generation.

Even new technology did not leave him behind. With the advent of the compact disc (CD) in the 1980's, his works were reengineered, and old albums were enriched with the addition of previously omitted studio sessions; for example, the CD of *Nice 'n' Easy* (1960), Sinatra's last project with Nelson Riddle, includes a haunting rendition of "The Nearness of You" that was omitted from the original album at the last minute to make room for the title song.

### Summary

In a career spanning more than five decades, Frank Sinatra made some 1,800 recordings for which he won many Grammys (including a Grammy Legends Award and a Grammy Lifetime Achievement Award). He appeared in some sixty film credits, earning two Academy Awards. As an actor he was often typecast, but as a singer he chose his own material. At a time when popular singers tended to avoid old songs, Sinatra recorded whatever he liked. His total body of recorded work provides a cross-section of the best American music of his era.

A New York disk jockey, William B. Williams, gave Sinatra the moniker by which he would be known for the last four decades of his life: Chairman of the Board. The name was appropriate in the conservative 1950's, when Sinatra had, in Williams's words, the "most imitated, most listened to, most recognized voice" in the world. This became increasingly true as Sinatra aged with the century.

After two strokes and hints of Alzheimer's disease left him a lonely celebrity, Sinatra died of heart failure at Cedars Sinai Hospital in Los Angeles in May, 1998. The outpouring of affection was almost unparalleled, even in an age of celebrity. Radio and television stations around the country played his records and films. Sales of his recordings reached all-time highs. Perhaps most to the point, *Time* magazine chose him as "The Singer of the Century" in its list of the entertainers of the twentieth century.

**Bibliography**

Friedwald, Will. *Sinatra: The Song Is You*. New York: Scribner, 1995. This book, based on interviews with the musicians who helped make Sinatra's records, includes a defining essay on "The Sinatra Style" and a "Consumer's Guide with Compact Discography."

Kelley, Kitty. *His Way: The Unauthorized Biography of Frank Sinatra*. New York: Bantam, 1986. Sinatra tried to block publication of this controversial "tell-all" by the writer of "unauthorized" lives of Jacqueline Kennedy Onassis and Nancy Reagan. Later exposés modify certain of Kelley's claims.

Lahr, John. *Sinatra: The Artist and the Man*. New York: Random House, 1997. This sympathetic essay was written by a drama critic for *The New Yorker*, where it was first published in a shorter version. Profusely illustrated with black-and-white photographs, many in full-page format.

Mustazza, Leonard. *Sinatra: An Annotated Bibliography, 1939-1998*. Westport, Conn.: Greenwood Press, 1999. Comprehensive bibliography including a diverse group of sources and more than 200 notable essays written about Sinatra after his death.

Mustazza, Leonard, ed. *Frank Sinatra and Popular Culture: Essays on an American Icon*. Westport, Conn.: Praeger, 1998. A collection of essays on Sinatra, his contributions, and his life. A unique collection of interest to fans and covering the development of his image, his music, and the way he was viewed by those who knew him.

O'Brien, Ed, and Robert Wilson. *Sinatra 101: The 101 Best Recordings and the Stories Behind Them*. New York: Boulevard, 1996. Detailed production notes on Sinatra's best-known renditions, arranged chronologically.

Petkov, Steven, and Leonard Mustazza, eds. *The Frank Sinatra Reader*. New York: Oxford University Press, 1995; Oxford: Oxford University Press, 1997. One of two anthologies compiled on the occasion of Sinatra's eightieth birthday. Many of the items first appeared in newspapers and magazines, assessing Sinatra's success at different stages.

Taraborrelli, J. Randy. *Sinatra: Behind the Legend*. Secaucus, N.J.: Carol, 1997. Taraborrelli's exposé has information on Sinatra's gangland ties and Hollywood romances. The author preserves Sinatra's tough-guy language, which some readers will find offensive, but presents him as a vulnerable and very human being.

Vare, Ethlie Ann, ed. *Legend: Frank Sinatra and the American Dream*. New York: Boulevard, 1995. This is the second of two anthologies that were compiled as Sinatra turned eighty. Arranged chronologically, the items follow Sinatra through his career.

Zehme, Bill, and Phil Stern. *The Way You Wear Your Hat: Frank Sinatra and the Lost Art of Livin'*. New York: HarperCollins, 1997. The worshipful book is based on an *Esquire* interview with Sinatra and members of his "Rat Pack."

*Thomas Willard*

# UPTON SINCLAIR

*Born:* September 20, 1878; Baltimore, Maryland

*Died:* November 25, 1968; Bound Brook, New Jersey

*Areas of Achievement:* Government, politics, literature, and social reform

*Contribution:* Sinclair was a prolific writer, a champion of social justice, a socialist reformer, and a 1934 Democratic candidate for governor of California. His greatest impact came from his muckraking novel *The Jungle* (1906), which stirred America's conscience, strengthened the Progressive reform movement, and brought about national consumer legislation.

### Early Life

Upton Beall Sinclair, Jr., born in Baltimore and raised there until age eight, was an only child. His father's family, Virginia aristocrats and naval officers who sided with the Confederacy during the 1800's, lost everything in the Civil War. Sinclair's father, too young to fight and unable, as an adult, to adjust to his family's downfall, failed as a businessman and succumbed to alcoholism. Dragging his drunken father from saloons would lead Sinclair to favor temperance, fostering a lifelong tendency toward reform.

His dominant, upper-middle-class mother, Priscilla Harden, daughter of a successful Maryland railroad executive and Methodist leader, taught him morality and resistance to temptations (especially sexual ones), instilling a sense of Christian social justice and duty. She often read to Sinclair, who was so captivated by stories that he taught himself to read by age five. Reading became the basis of his early education (he did not attend school until age ten) and offered an escape from his harsh, emotionally contradictory childhood.

Whether in Baltimore or later in New York City, his parents often lived in squalor, moving from one cheap boarding house or hotel to another and sharing rooms with rats and bedbugs. Compared to the homeless children he saw everyday, Sinclair felt fortunate but also angry. During most summers he lived luxuriously in the country with his mother's wealthy family. This contrast, which instilled a deep antipathy toward the wealthy, heightened his sense of social injustice and his duty to reform society.

After moving to New York City, Sinclair found religious and educational guidance under the influence of William Moir, an Episcopalian minister. Attending public school for the first time, he was ready for college in just two years. At age fourteen he entered a five-year program at the City College of New York, where Sinclair rejected Moir's theology (but not Jesus Christ) and explored philosophy, literature, and poetry. His greatest sources of inspiration throughout his school years remained Jesus and the English poet Percy Bysshe Shelley. His later idealistic, romantic, and missionary socialism would stem more from these two heroes than from any systematic doctrine.

During his first year at City College, Sinclair, at age fifteen, stumbled upon professional writing as his life's work when, in financial need, he sent a children's story to *Argosy* magazine, which published it and paid him twenty-five dollars. Thereafter he wrote numerous other children's stories and became a joke writer. The latter paid well, with *Life*, *Puck*, and the *Evening Journal* buying his humor. His income kept the family afloat. At age seventeen he got his own apartment but continued sending most of his income to his parents.

### Life's Work

Sinclair, a physically fit and rather attractive man of medium stature, graduated from City College in 1897. He considered but rejected a law career, instead entering Columbia University to study philosophy and literature. After three years, he moved to Canada where, living in a cabin, he began writing his first novel. Around this time he also met an attractive young woman named Meta Fuller, the daughter of a friend of his mother. The two fell in love and, after much indecision, married in 1900.

Sinclair's first novel, *Springtime and Harvest* (1901), failed both commercially and artistically, even when reissued as *King Midas*. His marriage to Meta, complicated by the birth of a son, David, in 1901 and by Sinclair's sexual hang-ups, ended in divorce in 1911. By that time Sinclair's literary career had been established, but only after two more unsuccessful novels, *Prince Hagen* (1903) and *The Journal of Arthur Stirling* (1903). Arthur Stirling, a poet of genius who represents Sinclair, commits suicide in the novel, signaling Sinclair's abandonment of his identity as an American Shelley.

Having jettisoned the poet as well as the priest, Sinclair hungered for a new faith. He found it in socialism, introduced to him by Leonard D. Abbot,

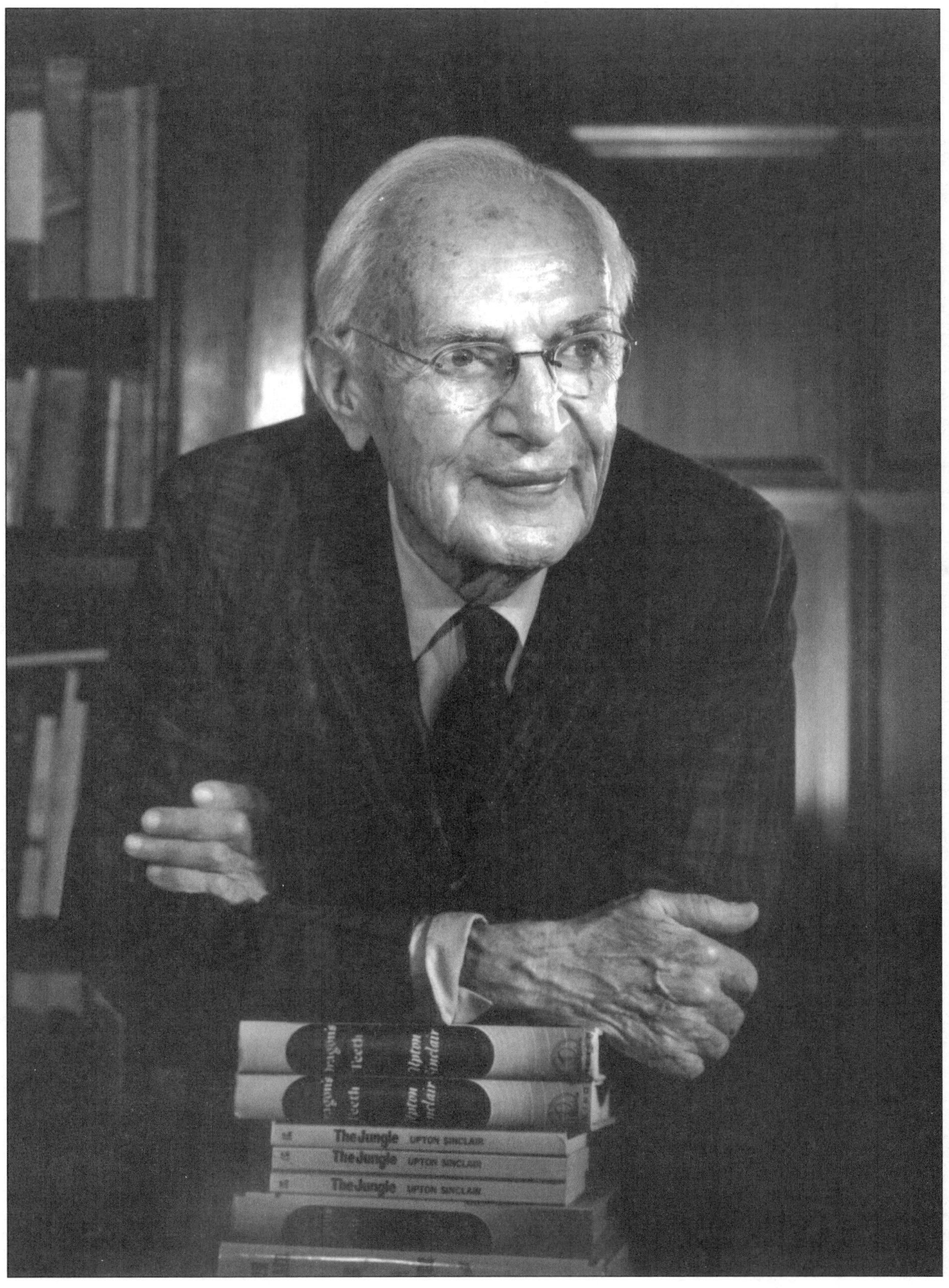
The Jungle UPTON SINCLAIR
The Jungle UPTON SINCLAIR
The Jungle UPTON SINCLAIR

Gaylord Wilshire, and George D. Herron. These middle- and upper-class Christian socialists transformed Sinclair's notion of radical politics as something vulgar into a conception of nobility and justice, with socialism redefined in terms Sinclair understood—a fulfillment of Christianity. Sinclair became a literary realist and resolved to make his writing a force for social justice. He honed his newly adopted literary realism in a novel about the Civil War, *Manassas* (1904). The book's condemnation of slavery and its support for abolitionism as a holy crusade foreshadowed the author's mature muckraking style by linking 1850's abolitionism with early twentieth century Progressivism. *Manassas* marked Sinclair's entry into American radicalism and led directly to *The Jungle*.

Fred D. Warren, editor of the United States' premier socialist journal, *Appeal to Reason*, read *Manassas* and suggested that Sinclair produce a book detailing the horrors of wage slavery as convincingly as he had done with antebellum slavery. *Appeal to Reason* gave Sinclair a $500 advance, with which he moved his family to a New Jersey farm and then traveled alone to Chicago to investigate the economic, social, and environmental conditions facing the city's meat packers.

When Sinclair arrived in Chicago late in 1905, the Meat Trust was still under fire for the Spanish-American War "embalmed meat" scandals, and it had further fanned the flames of discontent by crushing a meat packers' strike just weeks earlier. Chicago citizens eagerly supplied Sinclair with information. His investigation lasted about two months. He stayed in workers' homes (both native-born and immigrant); interviewed meat packers, barkeeps, social workers, doctors, policemen, politicians, and journalists; and prowled the neighborhoods and stockyards. He also inspected the packing plants, first as an official visitor and then, in muckraker fashion, disguised as a worker. His findings shocked him.

After returning to New Jersey, Sinclair wrote one of the most influential books in American history, *The Jungle* (1906), which Jack London called the *Uncle Tom's Cabin* of wage slavery. *The Jungle* exposed the dehumanizing, despairing world of the working class. Its story centers on Jurgis Rudkus, a Lithuanian immigrant, and his young wife Ona, who have come to the United States seeking their dream only to find a nightmare. After Jurgis is hurt at work and laid up, he loses his meat packer's job. He finds another job, but it pays far less, while Ona, also underpaid, is forced into prostitution by her boss under threat of dismissal. Jurgis discovers this, beats her boss, and lands in jail. After weeks in prison, he returns to find his family homeless and his wife dying in childbirth. He continues struggling until his oldest son, still a child, drowns in Chicago's unpaved streets. Jurgis then gives up, becoming a bum, thief, even a strikebreaker. Sinclair's clear message is that in capitalist society, workers have no hope and no chance. In the concluding chapters, however, Jurgis discovers socialism, and with it all problems are solved, Jurgis is happy, and hope reigns.

While the American public rejected Sinclair's socialist solution, they totally accepted his powerful exposé of the Meat Trust. Sinclair's graphic depiction of meat processing, which included the use of rotten meat disguised with chemicals, general filth, and dead rats, dung, and even human appendages thrown into the meat, appalled the nation. Sinclair knew he had missed his mark when he said, "I aimed at the public's heart and by accident hit it in the stomach." In doing so, Sinclair struck a blow worldwide for consumer rights. After reading *The Jungle*, President Theodore Roosevelt demanded meat inspection and pure food and drug legislation. As Progressivism's new champion, Sinclair became famous, wealthy, and admired.

In 1913, Sinclair married poet Mary Craig Kimbrough, and the couple moved to California in 1915. Sinclair continued to write realist, socialist-inspired novels. Three of his best works were written in the 1910's and 1920's: *King Coal* (1917), which explored labor issues in the Western mines; *Oil!* (1927), based loosely on the Teapot Dome scandal, which French critics considered a masterpiece; and *Boston* (1928), a powerful treatment of the Nicola Sacco and Bartolomeo Vanzetti case, which led Arthur Conan Doyle to label Sinclair America's Émile Zola.

During the 1930's, Sinclair's writing became more political as he attempted to win election as governor of California. With the Great Depression gripping the nation, left-wing voices rose in protest while capitalism faltered and democratic governments, even Franklin D. Roosevelt's New Deal, responded slowly to human needs. In 1934, after being approached by a California businessman, Sinclair shocked his friends and admirers by abandoning the Socialist Party, registering as a Democrat, and running in the primary election. Behind a program entitled End Poverty in California (EPIC),

Sinclair defeated eight other Democrats and won the nomination.

EPIC, based on Sinclair's book *I, Governor of California—And How I Ended Poverty* (1934), powerfully indicted capitalism and vaguely outlined a socialist plan for redistributing wealth. Sinclair's vision, power of persuasion, moral character, and deep belief carried him far. Yet the forces aligned against him: Big money men and film moguls who conducted a multimillion-dollar smear campaign and threatened to fire actors who supported Sinclair proved too powerful. Roosevelt's refusal to endorse Sinclair as a Democrat also hurt badly. Sinclair lost the election (by about 200,000 out of about 2.3 million votes cast), but in another sense he carried the day, locally and nationally, as the Republican winner, Frank Mirriam, and President Roosevelt later signed into law a number of programs strongly resembling Sinclair's proposals.

Following the election, Sinclair returned to fiction writing, composing more than thirty new novels during the next three decades. Included in this long list were the commercially successful Lanny Budd novels: eleven historical narratives, written from 1940 to 1953, covering the years from World War I to the early Cold War. In these books Sinclair becomes increasingly sympathetic toward capitalism, hostile toward communism, and lukewarm toward reform socialism. In his post-Lanny Budd novels, Sinclair even questions the power of reform literature and his life's work. A teetotaler, nonsmoker, and vegetarian, he died in 1968 at age ninety.

### Summary

Although he wrote over eighty books, Upton Sinclair is not considered one of the literary giants of twentieth century America. His fiction was sometimes stylistically and structurally shallow but nevertheless had distinctive strengths. A successful popularizer of ideas more than an original thinker, a journalist more than a poet, Sinclair was a diligent realist who used interviews, notes, and world events as sources. His novels more often than not accurately reflected the United States' social and cultural landscape. As historical fiction, Sinclair's books are among the twentieth century's best in their depiction of events and in their ability to evoke thought and, sometimes, action.

Working for social justice and against abusive power was his life's mission. His literary skill was almost single-mindedly harnessed to this purpose. He exposed abuses, evoked sympathy for those suffering injustice, and elicited societal reform. Nowhere was this more visible than in *The Jungle*, with its ability to bring about consumer protection legislation. Though Sinclair has been downgraded as a literary figure and his novels go largely unread, continued twentieth century demands for consumer protection legislation remains as Sinclair's lasting testimonial.

### Bibliography

Bloodworth, William A. *Upton Sinclair.* Boston: Twayne, 1977. This short, sympathetic, yet balanced literary biography examines Sinclair's place in American literary radicalism and the writer as social activist. Includes a bibliography.

Dell, Floyd. *Upton Sinclair: A Study in Social Protest.* New York: Doran, 1927. A sympathetic contemporary biography with a strong Freudian critique that nevertheless applauds Sinclair's vision and protests.

Derrick, Scott. "What a Beating Feels Like: Authorship, Dissolution, and Masculinity in Sinclair's 'The Jungle.'" *Studies in American Fiction* 23, no. 1 (Spring 1995). The author offers analysis of Sinclair's novel *The Jungle,* dealing with the threat of feminine reproductive power in traditional male-centered societies.

Gentry, Curt. ". . . Right Back Where We Started From." *Columbia Journalism Review* 31, no. 3 (September-October, 1992). Examines the tactics used by Sinclair in his bid for governor of California and the threats they represented to California business and economic interests.

Harris, Leon. *Upton Sinclair: American Rebel.* New York: Crowell, 1975. At 435 pages, this thorough, well-researched, and sympathetic biography relies heavily on Sinclair's own words and emotions. Extensive annotated notes included.

Mitchell, Greg. *The Campaign of the Century.* New York: Random House, 1992. At 665 pages, this excellently researched book details Sinclair's 1934 gubernatorial campaign from August to November, stressing the media's key role in defeating Sinclair and ushering in a new era of media politics. Includes notes.

Sinclair, Upton. *The Jungle.* Girard, Kans.: Wayland, 1905; London: Heinemann, 1907. Sinclair's great muckraking novel on meat packing that spurred consumer legislation and gave him worldwide notoriety.

———. *The Autobiography of Upton Sinclair.* New York: Harcourt Brace, 1962; London: Allen, 1963. At 342 pages, this is the most important source on Sinclair's early life and a useful mirror of his personality.

*Ken Millen-Penn*

# B. F. SKINNER

*Born:* March 20, 1904; Susquehanna, Pennsylvania
*Died:* August 18, 1990; Cambridge, Massachusetts
*Areas of Achievement:* Psychology and literature
*Contribution:* By developing a variety of effective techniques for behavioral modification, Skinner radically transformed the science of psychology and thereby exerted a profound influence in the fields of psychiatry and pedagogy. His ideas, moreover, have been popularized through nontechnical writings of his own, including a utopian novel entitled *Walden Two*.

## Early Life

In the spring of 1902, William Arthur Skinner and Grace Madge Burrhus were married in Susquehanna, Pennsylvania. He was a twenty-five-year-old attorney with political aspirations, while she was a twenty-one-year-old legal secretary of remarkable beauty. The first of the couple's two children was born on March 20, 1904, and was formally named Burrhus Frederic Skinner. He was, however, soon called "Fred" by everyone. A second son was born two and a half years later. Mr. Skinner did not believe that children should be baptized until they were old enough to appreciate the full significance of this sacred rite. In the case of his elder son, that day never arrived. Despite all attempts to indoctrinate him into the Presbyterian faith, the boy became a freethinker by the time he reached puberty.

Throughout his twelve years at grade and high school, Fred Skinner proved himself to be academically gifted in a variety of areas. He was extraordinarily adept not only in mathematics and other scientific subjects but also in the humanities. Above all, Skinner loved literature, and he even began to write stories and poems of his own at an early age. Although the public school system in Susquehanna offered no courses in music within its educational curriculum, Skinner nevertheless managed to accrue much expertise in this area as well. His mother, who was an accomplished amateur musician in her own right, arranged for him to take piano lessons early in life, and he later studied the saxophone of his own volition when an opportunity to receive free instruction presented itself. Skinner was sufficiently proficient on both instruments to be paid for performing on them. For a time he was a saxophonist in a jazz band that played at various dance halls and was also a pianist in another group that provided background music for silent films at a local motion-picture theater. In his junior and senior years in high school, furthermore, Skinner discovered the world of art and began to paint watercolors, and draw in charcoal. He thereupon put his artistic talent to use for monetary purposes by lettering advertising show cards. His chief job during his high school years, however, was at a shoe store, where he developed a speciality of fitting arch supports. Throughout his life, Skinner was to retain this penchant for putting his expertise to practical use.

When Skinner was graduated from high school, he ranked second in a class of seven seniors. Oddly enough, both of his parents achieved a similar class ranking at their own respective high school graduations. Much to the disappointment of his mother, Skinner was short in stature when he reached maturity. His bone structure, however, was delicate to the point of being birdlike and was admirably suited to his slender build. Skinner's facial features were, moreover, both regular and pleasing. These physical traits, including a full hairline and a slim figure, were to change very little throughout the years that followed his graduation from high school.

It had always been assumed that Skinner would go on to college, and he duly matriculated at Hamilton College in Clinton, New York, for the purpose of acquiring a bachelor's degree in English. His college years proved to be socially pleasant and academically profitable. Despite the fact that Skinner never shied away from taking difficult courses, he still managed to maintain a grade point average sufficiently high to qualify him for election to Phi Beta Kappa. Ironically, he had previously written a piece for the college paper in which he contemptuously dismissed the majority of its members as "key chasers."

During his college years, Skinner's prime interest lay in creative writing, and to further these skills he went to Vermont in the summer between his junior and senior years for the purpose of studying at Middlebury College's Bread Loaf School of English. There he met Robert Frost, who lived nearby at Ripton, and the celebrated poet suggested that the young man submit some of his work to him for the sake of a critical appraisal. Upon his return to Hamilton College, he sent Frost three short stories and received a warm letter of encouragement in response. He thereupon resolved to pursue a career as a free-lance writer. After his

graduation from Hamilton College in 1926, Skinner moved back into his parents' house and built for himself a study where he could work undisturbed. About a year later, however, it became evident to him that his writings were totally devoid of significant content. After a feeble attempt to become a journalist, he finally decided to abandon his literary ambitions entirely for the sake of a career in psychology. Admitted as a graduate student at Harvard University for the fall semester of 1928, Skinner first spent a few months in New York's Greenwich Village, where he led the customary bohemian life, and then toured several countries in Western Europe, part of the time in the company of his parents.

### Life's Work

Skinner had always been interested in human behavior. In his endeavor to become a writer, he read very extensively and gradually came to the conclusion that psychology is superior to literature as a method of investigating this topic. It was, above all, the writings of Ivan Petrovich Pavlov on conditioned reflexes and those of John Broadus Watson on the new psychology of behaviorism that particularly intrigued him. Oddly enough, Bertrand Russell's articles attacking behaviorism, published in various magazines during the 1920's, served only to strengthen Skinner's commitment to this doctrine and its basic premise that animal and human behavior may be explained entirely in terms of responses to objectively observable external stimuli. Skinner henceforth never wavered in his adherence to the tenet that behavior is shaped and maintained by its consequences. Owing to his boyhood fondness for observing animal life and tinkering with mechanical devices, he was, moreover, ideally suited to devise laboratory experiments aimed at the conditioning of rats and pigeons through behavioral technology.

Even though the Harvard Graduate School curriculum in psychology was predominantly mentalist in orientation, Skinner encountered few obstacles in completing the requirements for the master's degree in 1930 and for the doctorate in 1931. He was able to remain at Harvard as a National Research Council Fellow for the next three years and as a Harvard Junior Fellow for an additional two years. In 1936, Skinner joined the faculty of the University of Minnesota and soon thereafter married a young lady named Yvonne Blue, who had majored in English at the University of Chicago. Two daughters were subsequently born, Julie in 1938 and Deborah in 1944. During World War II, Skinner worked on a project sponsored by the United States Office of Scientific Research and Development in which he trained pigeons to guide missiles and torpedoes to their targets, but owing to official skepticism this scheme was never actually implemented. In 1945, he accepted an appointment at Indiana University as chairman of its psychology department. Three years later, Skinner joined the faculty of Harvard University, where he became Edgar Pierce Professor of Psychology in 1953. In the mid-1960's, Skinner terminated his research activities in order to devote all of his time to writing and lecturing. He eventually retired, in 1975, with the honorary title of Professor Emeritus.

Skinner's first major publication, essentially a revised version of his doctoral dissertation, appeared in 1938 under the title *The Behavior of Organisms*. Most noteworthy among his other professional writings are *Science and Human Behavior* (1953), *Verbal Behavior* (1957), and *The Technology of Teaching* (1968). The lay public first became aware of his work through an article entitled "Baby in a Box" that was published in the October, 1945, issue of *Ladies' Home Journal*. There, Skinner describes how he reared his infant daughter Deborah in a temperature-controlled air crib that came to be popularly known as a "Skinner-Box." Skinner became even more widely known through the publication of *Walden Two* in 1948. This controversial utopian novel is essentially a fictional elaboration of the oft-quoted proposition made by Watson in 1925, in which he declared: "Give me a dozen healthy infants, and I'll guarantee to take any one at random and train him to become any type of specialist I might select—doctor, lawyer, even beggarman and thief, regardless of his talents, penchants, tendencies, abilities." It was not until 1971, however, that Skinner offered the public a comprehensive nonfictional account of his views on the application of behavioral technology to social planning in a book entitled *Beyond Freedom and Dignity*, a work which became the subject of a cover story in the September 20, 1971, issue of *Time* magazine. His efforts at popular exposition were to culminate in 1974 with the publication of *About Behaviorism*, in which he presents a masterful defense of the behaviorist position in psychology.

Throughout his career, Skinner, like his compatriots Thomas Alva Edison and Henry Ford, manifested a characteristically American propensity to translate ideas into practical use for the benefit of the masses. Far from content to write theoretically about designing new cultures, he worked with great dedication over the years to transform the methods of instruction traditionally employed by educational institutions both in the United States and abroad. To this end, Skinner insisted that all instruction, whether in the form of textbooks or teaching machines, be based on two fundamental principles: first, incremental learning (that is, the material to be taught is broken down into such small steps as to preclude the possibility of error on the part of the pupil), and second, immediacy of reinforcement (the student is routinely reassured that his answers are correct after the completion of each of these small steps). Whereas it is theoretically possible to employ negative reinforcement in the pedagogical process, Skinner is totally opposed to the use of punishment and insists that the bestowal of rewards is a far more effective means of social conditioning. This aversion to negative reinforcement appears to have had its roots in his early childhood, a period during which neither of his parents employed punishment as a disciplinary measure. (The time when his mother washed his mouth out with soap for telling a lie constitutes a solitary exception.) Skinner prefers to designate his method of behavior modification as "operant conditioning" in order to distinguish it from "reflex conditioning." The essential distinction between these two methods is that the subject experiences the one as voluntary and the other as involuntary. In contrast to the automatic nature of reflex behavior, Skinner asserts that "operant behavior is felt to be under the control of the behaving person and has traditionally been attributed to an act of will." The term "operant," moreover, underscores the fact that the process of conditioning espoused by Skinner is entirely overt, observable, and measurable. The efficacy of operant conditioning was perhaps most strikingly demonstrated by Skinner's own success in teaching pigeons to play Ping-Pong. The merit of the Skinnerian principle that behavior can be predicted and controlled in terms of its consequences has also been amply vindicated by his numerous disciples in such fields as sociology, psychiatry, and penology, who have applied it in their endeavors to solve a wide variety of societal problems.

### Summary

Skinner has always been a controversial figure in the field of psychology because the behaviorist movement itself is controversial. Since its theoretical frame of reference excludes all consideration of consciousness and introspection, it constitutes a radical departure from the long-established mentalist orientation of traditional psychology. Even though the behaviorist movement has antecedents in the work of certain European psychologists, the first comprehensive explication of its basic tenets was set forth by John Watson in a series of lectures given at Columbia University during the winter of 1912-1913. Watson's views enjoyed a degree of notoriety from the outset, but it is primarily because of the research activities on the part of Skinner and his collaborators that behaviorism has finally attained academic respectability. It has, however, won relatively few formal adherents outside the United States and may consequently be viewed as a characteristically American phenomenon. The objective of transforming psychology into a scientifically rigorous discipline through the elimination of all subjective factors is, moreover, another manifestation of the pragmatic temperament that is the common denominator of so many individuals who have made significant contributions to the intellectual climate in the United States. With respect to Skinnerian operant conditioning itself, its current popularity as a means of behavior modification stems in large measure from the widespread dissatisfaction with the ineffectual procedures employed in conventional psychotherapy. Through the systematic manipulation of the consequences of previous behavior, operant conditioning has proven to be far less time-consuming and costly than those methods based on the attainment of self-knowledge on the part of the individual being treated. Because of this, Skinner has become the most influential psychologist that the United States has thus far produced.

**Bibliography**

Epstein, Robert. "Skinner as Self-Manager." *Journal of Applied Behavior Analysis* 30, no. 3 (Fall 1997). The author provides analysis of Skinner's theories on determinism and self-control.

Geiser, Robert L. *Behavior Mod and the Managed Society.* Boston: Beacon Press, 1976. A work that relates how Skinner's concept of operant conditioning has been applied to societal problems. It focuses on the uses of behavior modification in schools, prisons, hospitals, industry, and elsewhere.

Jensen, Robert, and Helene Burgess. "Mythmaking: How Introductory Psychology Texts Present B.F. Skinner's Analysis of Cognition." *Psychological Record* 47, no. 2 (Spring 1997). The authors examine fifteen psychology textbooks to determine the accuracy and completeness of the books' presentations of Skinner's theories on cognitive processes.

Kinkade, Kathleen. *A Walden Two Experiment: The First Five Years of Twin Oaks Community.* New York: Morrow, 1973. A candid assessment of the problems encountered at Twin Oaks, a 123-acre farm situated in the Piedmont region of Virginia, where an attempt to establish a commune modeled after the utopian society depicted in *Walden Two* was initiated in 1967. Written by one of its founders and accompanied by an optimistic preface by Skinner himself.

Sagal, Paul T. *Skinner's Philosophy.* Washington, D.C.: University Press of America, 1981. The author persuasively argues that Skinner's philosophy has been unjustifiably neglected by both professional philosophers and psychologists alike. This perceptive analysis will be especially helpful to those readers about to embark on a study of *Beyond Freedom and Dignity.*

Skinner, B. F. *Particulars of My Life.* London: Cape, and New York: Knopf, 1976. Skinner's own account of his early life from the time of his birth in 1904 to his matriculation as a graduate student of psychology at Harvard University in 1928. Includes intimate portraits of his parents and grandparents as well as a detailed record of his intellectual and sexual maturation.

———. *The Shaping of a Behaviorist.* New York: Knopf, 1979. Here, Skinner delineates his intellectual and professional development from the time of his arrival at Harvard University as a graduate student to his return as tenured member of its faculty some twenty years later. Especially noteworthy are Skinner's extensive comments dealing with the air crib that he designed for his daughter Deborah as well as those pertaining to the ideology that underlies the utopian society depicted in *Walden Two.*

———. *A Matter of Consequences.* New York: Knopf, 1983. Spanning a period of more than three decades, this volume is intended as the final installment of Skinner's autobiography and constitutes an apologia for both his life and work. Much of the information purveyed here pertains to his lifelong interests in music, literature, drama, and art.

Weigel, John A. *B. F. Skinner.* Boston: Twayne, 1977. An excellent introduction to Skinner's scientific and philosophical works that also offers a reasoned response to his critics. A brief biographical sketch precedes the author's discussion of Skinner's ideas.

*Victor Anthony Rudowski*

# FIRST VISCOUNT SLIM

*Born:* August 6, 1891; Bishopston, near Bristol, England

*Died:* December 14, 1970; London, England

*Area of Achievement:* The military

*Contribution:* After conducting a fighting retreat from Burma in early 1942, Slim was chosen to command the British Fourteenth Army, which in the succeeding years defeated the Japanese invasion of India, destroyed the main Japanese army of Southeast Asia, and reconquered Burma.

## Early Life

In his early years, William Joseph Slim suffered such disadvantages as to make his later career seem virtually impossible. One of these was social standing. He had no connections with the army or with the officer class. While his great contemporary Field Marshal Bernard Law Montgomery was the son of a bishop, Slim was the son of a self-employed metalworker. When he left school, the only job he could get was as an elementary teacher in a Birmingham slum; from that he went on to be a junior clerk. It was not an impressive background, and even after his greatest victories Slim was exposed to upper-class English snobbery and distrust, shown even by Winston Churchill.

A further and almost literally crippling disadvantage resulted from war wounds. Slim had managed, though not a university student, to join the Birmingham University Officer Training Corps, and with the outbreak of World War I he was gazetted to the Royal Warwickshire Regiment. He was sent to Gallipoli in July, 1915, and during an assault in which every officer of the Ninth Warwicks was killed or wounded, was shot inches from his heart. The final, official diagnosis was that he would lose a lung and be unable ever to use his left arm. Slim, however, refused to have the suggested operation, recovered by himself, and by means still unclear returned to active service in Mesopotamia. There he was wounded again by a shell splinter, causing considerable official disapproval as soon as his records were inspected. While a Brigadier in Eritrea in 1941, he was once again shot (in the buttocks) by an Italian fighter plane: only a flesh wound, perhaps, but inflicted by three bullets, one armor-piercing, one incendiary, and one explosive. At several moments of his life Slim came very close to being "invalided out" of the army.

To complete the list of disadvantages, with the end of World War I Slim's chance of staying on in the shrinking British army was zero, his Military Cross won in 1917 being no match for his non-regular-officer background. He transferred accordingly to the Indian army and became an officer in the Gurkha Rifles. "Indian" generals, however, though often more efficient and practical than their British army equivalents, were usually distrusted by British headquarters and politicians; they were believed to be second rate and middle class. This, too, affected Slim's later career.

Yet in other ways all three disadvantages contributed greatly to Slim's eventual success. With his own troops he was unquestionably the most popular British commander of the century, known to all as "Uncle Bill." The reasons for this were obvious. He had not a trace of snobbery; his army chauffeur was under standing orders always to pick up soldier hitchhikers. He had a healthy distrust of bureaucrats, official channels, and rear-echelon planners. He insisted with all the force of his ex-

tremely forceful personality that everything had to be subordinated to the welfare of frontline troops, taking particular interest in hospitals. The men of the Fourteenth Army soon called themselves "the Forgotten Army," alluding to their low status on equipment priority lists drawn up in Washington or Whitehall. They knew, however, that their army commander remembered them all the time, and so did his staff. Slim's rule was that if any troops went on half rations as a result of supply shortages, so did he and his headquarters. Very little space was wasted on paper. In the Fourteenth Army, all documents were sorted once a fortnight, and everything not immediately vital was burned.

Slim also benefited enormously from twenty years of "peacetime" service with the Indian army. He saw further active service against the able and dangerous Afghan tribesmen of the Indian Northwest Frontier. He also made many friends among the professional imperial officer corps. Mainly, however, he saw service with an elite volunteer force which in many ways combined the professionalism of a European army with the speed of movement, flexibility, and ruthlessness of what would now be called a guerrilla army. Service with the Gurkhas was excellent training for service against their Mongolian cousins, the Japanese.

### Life's Work

After the outbreak of World War II, Slim was sent first to command the Tenth Indian Brigade against the Italians in Eritrea, and after recovery from his wound, to command the Tenth Indian Division in Iraq, Syria, and Iran. Slim himself described his invasion of Iran as "comic opera," in that the highly equipped Iranian army (largely equipped, at the expense of the Indian army, by the British government) collapsed immediately under serious threat. Nevertheless, he learned one lesson from these experiences—never to break off a successful assault simply because of administrative shortages. On one occasion, he ordered all unnecessary vehicles to have their gasoline siphoned off to supply his spearhead. Defeat for him then would have led to total disaster; his actual success meant that his stranded forces could be refueled quietly and at leisure. Moreover, the determination he showed gave him *iqbal*, as his Indian and British-Indian soldiers called it: the aura of success. He was to need that desperately.

From February, 1942, the British Empire in the East was to face far more serious enemies. The Japanese had overwhelmed Singapore and the Royal Navy. In February, 1942, they broke into Burma, where with their combination of high morale, jungle tactics, and modern equipment, they showed every sign of destroying the static and unprepared British forces. Slim was moved to Burma and—after strange delays and confusion, caused partly by the fact that Slim was an "unknown" to Whitehall—was placed in command of the First Burma Corps.

The situation was, however, already irretrievable. The Japanese had, or would soon gain, total command of the air, total command of the jungle, and strong support from the native Burmese population, who viewed them (for a while) as liberators. Slim's corps was in effect bundled out of Burma, losing men and equipment all the way, completing the final stages of its retreat in atrocious weather, across appalling country, with no food, ammunition, gasoline, transport, or protection from malaria, typhus, and other endemic diseases. Simply holding his men together was a major achievement for Slim.

The real difficulties, however, were still to be faced during the period from mid-1942 to late 1943. At this stage, Slim had still to expect a probable invasion of India by an army thought to be invincible, with total command of sea and air. He had to do it with troops who had 120 cases of disease for every battle casualty; without material support; in what has been called the worst country in the world, where men without packs cannot average a mile an hour; and at the end of a supply line consisting of mud tracks and a single-line, narrow-gauge, incomplete railway. He also had the specter of rebellion at his back. Many Indians believed that the Japanese would also "liberate" them. Many British doubted the loyalty even of the Indian army. No retreat was possible for British women and children in India, since the Japanese controlled the sea-lanes. It was also well-known to everyone what the experience had been of European and Australian soldiers and civilians captured in the countries already overrun. Slim's forces in fact faced a fight to the death, with no prospect of retreat or surrender. Their defeat would lead to collapse and massacre on an appalling scale.

Slim's greatest achievement was perhaps to remotivate and retrain his forces during this period. He received little help from above, where grandiose plans abounded for defeating the Japanese without effort—by persuading Chinese armies to attack them from the north, by landing airborne forces in their rear to make them panic, by organizing amphibious invasions. All these plans were to founder on the fact that the Japanese did not panic and could beat almost any army brought against them. Instead, Slim organized massive self-help schemes. The Fourteenth Army—which he commanded from October, 1943—eventually ran its own duck and fish farms for protein, maintained its own front-line kitchen gardens for vitamins, made its own parachutes from jute (since silk was unobtainable), commissioned its own navy, ran its own rafts and railways, and fought its own battles, usually without or even against superior orders. At the same time, the whole army became jungle-wise. Slim's orders were quite simple: There were to be no noncombatants, all units were to protect and patrol their own areas (and this included headquarters staff and hospitals), the Japanese were to be beaten on foot, in the jungle, man to man. The difficulty, initially, was in having these orders obeyed.

One more failure was still to take place. Slim's predecessor as army commander, Lieutenant General Noel Irwin, ordered a counterattack in Arakan in early 1943. Slim was not given operational command until too late, and the attack was a failure. Irwin tried to dismiss Slim in May but was dismissed himself, eventually (after some months of indecision) for Slim to take over. Slim then waited, with his retrained army, for the Japanese "March on Delhi."

This confrontation came in early 1944. In the Second Battle of Arakan, a Japanese assault was for the first time held and destroyed. Undeterred by the failure of *Ha-Go*, the Japanese launched the *U-Go* offensive on Slim's forces, meaning to seize his tiny railhead at Dimapur and destroy his army as it tried to flee. In the twin battles of Imphal and Kohima, it was instead the Japanese army which was destroyed. Slim counted on several new factors. First, his own troops were now untroubled by attacks from the rear. They knew that in jungle fighting there was no rear, and that either side could consider the other "surrounded." Second, the Japanese were overconfident. The high command relied on capturing stores from the British. If this plan failed, troops would then be left to starve in the jungle or to make increasingly suicidal assaults. Third, and most important, the British and Indian soldiers of the Fourteenth Army were now as anxious to fight things out as the Japanese, their morale perversely heightened by the many war crimes committed against them.

From March to July, 1944, desperate fighting took place at Imphal and Kohima, between forces of approximately the same size (perhaps 100,000 men each, all that could be supplied). First both sides had to get their forces into position. Then the Japanese strained every nerve to destroy the Fourteenth Army, in point-blank fighting—their high point at Kohima, for example, being the deputy commissioner's tennis court, where they held one baseline and the British the other. Then the British and Indians began to counterattack their weakening enemies. Finally, even Japanese determination failed, and they attempted to withdraw—though, since they had gone on too long, they suffered appalling casualties in retreat. It has been estimated that not one man in ten of the Japanese involved in *Ha-Go* and *U-Go* survived to return to Japan.

The Japanese army in Burma was in fact broken at Imphal and Kohima. As it retreated, the Fourteenth Army followed, to force its way across the Irrawaddy River and win further battles at Meiktila and Mandalay, and to continue unrelenting pressure until Rangoon was reached in May, 1945. The Japanese continued to fight fanatically, and Slim was faced with immense problems of supply (losing seventy-five precious Dakotas in December, 1944, for example, drawn off to another "sideshow" with no warning given to him other than the sight of the planes passing overhead). After mid-1944, however, there was no chance of serious reverse. The war in Southeast Asia was won in a thousand close-range infantry encounters at Imphal and Kohima, by men who until then had known nothing but defeat.

## Summary

First Viscount Slim was in most ways an orthodox commander, with no great respect for "special forces" or unconventional tactics. He did the basics well. Like other Allied commanders, he had to beat a fanatically courageous enemy. Unlike them, he had to do so with no advantage in numbers or matériel. He fought an Asiatic war against an Asiatic enemy, with a largely Asiatic army. His experiences and published conclusions are of striking relevance to the American experience in Vietnam.

After the capture of Rangoon, Slim was, typically, replaced as army commander for no clear reason, though the order caused such general fury that it was reversed. On retirement he remained immensely popular with the general public, the British overseas, and the royal family, and was correspondingly out of favor with politicians. He was made a viscount, became Governor General of Australia, Constable of Windsor Castle, and eventually Governor of the Order of the Garter: though with his three corps commanders he had been knighted already, for valor, on the field of battle at Imphal. Slim died in London on December 14, 1970.

**Bibliography**

Allen, Louis. *Burma: The Longest War, 1941-1945.* London: Dent, and New York: St. Martin's Press, 1984. A recent and thorough single-volume account of fighting on all the Indo-Burmese fronts, including those not controlled by Slim.

Evans, Sir Geoffrey. *Slim as Military Commander.* London: Batsford, and Princeton, N.J.: Van Nostrand, 1969. An attempt at a technical evaluation of Slim, written by the commander of the Seventh Indian Division.

Evans, Sir Geoffrey, and Anthony Brett-James. *Imphal.* London: Macmillan, and New York: St. Martin's Press, 1962. Close study of an almost unsummarizable battle, authored once more by a major participant.

Lewin, Ronald. *Slim: The Standard Bearer.* London: Cooper, 1976. The standard biography, covering Slim's early and late years as well as his short period of critical command.

Masters, John. *The Road Past Mandalay.* London: Joseph, and New York: Harper, 1961. Before becoming a best-selling novelist, Masters was a long-service officer of the Gurkha Rifles. This autobiography includes the best firsthand account of Fourteenth Army fighting, with many interesting sidelights on Slim's style of leadership, and on the difficulties he faced.

Slim, Sir William. *Defeat into Victory.* London: Cassell, 1956. The most modest, and also the best written, volume of memoirs produced by any Allied general. Slim's amusement at the "strategic direction" of his superiors is rarely concealed.

———. *Unofficial History.* London: Cassell, 1959; New York: McKay, 1962. A collection of stories written for money under a pseudonym during the between-war years. Largely autobiographical, they convey vividly the Indian Army ethos, and form an excellent antidote to "official history."

*T. A. Shippey*

# ALFRED E. SMITH

*Born:* December 30, 1873; New York, New York
*Died:* October 4, 1944; New York, New York
*Area of Achievement:* Government and politics
*Contribution:* Smith was a leading figure in the Democratic Party during the Progressive Era and the 1920's. He represented the urban, immigrant Roman Catholic, and relatively liberal interests of the party at a time when it was deeply divided along regional, cultural, and ideological lines.

## Early Life

Alfred Emanuel Smith was born the first of two children to a poor but not impoverished Irish-American family on the Lower East Side of New York City, in 1873. His sister Mary was born two years later. Smith's father, also named Alfred Emanuel Smith, was a "truckman" (driver of a horse-drawn wagon); he and Smith's mother, Catherine Mulvehill Smith, were the New York-born children of Irish immigrants.

Smith grew up in a mixed though primarily Irish and German neighborhood in the Battery section of New York, on the banks of the East River. His early youth was a happy one, although never without money worries, revolving around his close and warm family and the Roman Catholic Church. Smith served as an altar boy throughout his adolescence and was educated at the local parish school. His parents, particularly his mother, worked hard at rearing a "respectable" boy who was immune to the bad influences common in their kind of neighborhood.

Smith was not a particularly strong student; books would never play an important role in his life. He did like elocution, however, a not unusual interest among those who would ultimately enter politics. Nevertheless, young Smith stayed in school until completing the eighth grade. His father having recently died, Smith went to work at a wide variety of jobs over, roughly, the next six years. At seventeen, he got a job at the Fulton Fish Market as "assistant bookkeeper," and despite its title, much of the work was hard labor. At the same time, he expanded his interest in amateur drama and considered a career on the stage. Ultimately, however, this was neither respectable enough nor sufficiently sure as an escape from poverty.

Politics pervaded Smith's neighborhood, centering on Tammany Hall, the leading Democratic organization in New York City. Tammany's reputation for corruption went against Smith's strong personal ethical sense, but it was the only route to political preferment available to a young man with his lower-class, Irish Catholic background.

Smith began active political participation before he could vote, rapidly developing a reputation as a popular speaker, a reputation which his dramatic background served well. He steadily increased his involvement in party and Tammany activities and was rewarded, at twenty-one, with his first political job, as an investigator in the office of the commissioner of jurors. It paid eight hundred dollars per year and was his first white-collar job. During this period, Smith also courted a young woman of a middle-class Irish family from the Bronx, Catherine Dunn, whom he married in 1900. It was a strong, happy marriage, blessed with five children: Emily, Catherine, Arthur, Alfred, Jr., and Walter.

Tammany Hall was in disarray in the 1890's. Scandals associated with Boss Richard Croker not only permitted the reformers to take over City Hall but divided the Democratic Party and Tammany it-

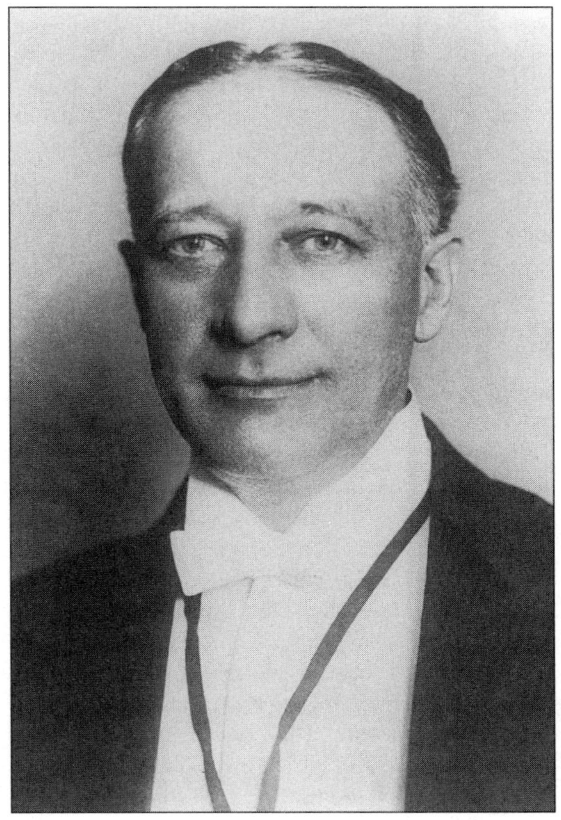

self into bitterly opposed factions. Smith, through both good luck and his own sense of propriety, ended up on the right side among these factions, so that in the post-Croker period, when Charles Francis Murphy came to rule Tammany Hall, his reputation and potential were unblemished.

Finally, after loyal party work for more than a decade, Smith got what he wanted: party nomination for the state assembly in 1903. Once nominated, he easily won the election with seventy-seven percent of the vote in his overwhelmingly Democratic district. His electoral career had begun.

### Life's Work

Smith found legislative life difficult, given his lack of schooling and of social contact outside his narrow Lower East Side milieu. He was a hard worker, however, and a quick learner. He taught himself both sufficient law and sufficient social graces to be able to fit in and function well in the Albany environment. He became a close friend of another Tammany legislator, future New York State and United States senator Robert F. Wagner, and both of them gradually developed reputations as unusually honest and competent Tammany legislators. Smith also developed a sense of bipartisanship and was able to work well with the Republicans, who generally controlled the assembly at the time.

The early twentieth century was still a period of much corruption in New York politics but also of increasing interest in reform. Smith, while maintaining his loyalty to Tammany, began to develop an identification with reform as well, particularly in the area of controlling large business interests, such as the utility companies, and defending the "little man." Steadily, his reputation grew and he became a leader of the Democratic Party in the legislature, straddling the growing division between Tammany and the reform Democrats, who were led by a new breed such as State Senator Franklin D. Roosevelt. In 1911, Smith became the Democratic leader of the assembly.

Smith's career continued to progress as he became steadily closer to the political and social reformers of the day. A highlight of this period was his leading role in the state constitutional convention of 1915, in which he demonstrated his expertise in state government and won the praise of both parties and numerous interests. Smith's contribution to the convention led to his nomination and election as sheriff of New York County in 1915, an extremely lucrative post that provided him with financial security for the first time in his life; it also widened his recognition among voters. In 1917, Smith ran for and was elected president of the Board of Aldermen, New York City's second most powerful position.

Smith ran for and was elected governor of New York in 1918. He was defeated for reelection in the Republican landslide year of 1920 but came back two years later and won three gubernatorial elections in a row; Smith completed a total of four terms as New York's governor. His gubernatorial years were successful, as he continued to use bipartisanship and negotiation among Democratic factions to create effective coalitions in the legislature.

Always a fiscal conservative, Governor Smith pared government finances. At the same time, however, he pursued an ambitious legislative program. Most notable was a spate of administrative reform and social legislation, which put his administration clearly in the progressive mainstream of the time. Financial reform, conservation, public health laws, workmen's compensation, and child labor reform were all among the measures of his governorship. He filled the state's administrative apparatus with first-rate personnel, a number of whom, such as Frances Perkins, would later distinguish themselves in Roosevelt's New Deal.

In 1924, Smith campaigned for the Democratic presidential nomination. The national convention saw bitter division between the more rural, Protestant, prohibitionist South and West, on the one hand, and the urban, ethnically heterogeneous, antiprohibitionist Northeast, on the other. Smith, representing the latter and being the first serious Roman Catholic candidate for a presidential nomination, was able to stalemate the former's candidate, William Gibbs McAdoo, but could not get the requisite two-thirds majority for himself.

In 1928, Smith once again fought for the nomination and got it. His unsuccessful campaign against Republican Herbert Hoover was an emotional one; his Tammany and New York background, opposition to Prohibition, and, especially, his Catholicism, alienated many voters. These same characteristics were very attractive to voters in the cities, however, and among newer Americans and the working class. Consequently, Smith's candidacy was important in beginning the swing of those groups toward the Democratic Party, groups which Roosevelt would soon turn into a Democratic majority.

After the 1928 campaign, Smith entered private business, serving as president of the Empire State

Building and in a number of other ventures. He prospered but still sought the presidency, and contested Roosevelt in the 1932 Democratic National Convention. Beaten badly there, his long friendship with Roosevelt came to an end, the break exacerbated by Roosevelt's failure to request Smith's involvement in the New Deal.

Both his personal alienation from the Administration and his traditional fiscal conservatism rendered Smith less and less happy with the New Deal as its programs developed. By the mid-1930's, he became a leading figure in the virulently anti-Roosevelt Liberty League, which was trounced by the president in the elections of 1936. Smith remained moderately active in Democratic conservative politics for a few more years, but his public life had really come to an end with the election of 1936. In the spring of 1944, Smith's beloved wife died, and he followed her to the grave six months later.

### Summary

In his early public years, Smith was one of those Democrats who brought their party into the mainstream of political reform that had been primarily the province of the Republicans. Throughout his career, he represented, and to some degree sought to enhance the position of, the newer elements in American society: workers, immigrants, Catholics and Jews, and the nonpowerful generally. This was, however, always within the constraints of a cautious, even conservative ideology.

Smith's presidential campaigns highlighted the contemporary divisions between newer and older groups of Americans and were a frustration to the former. At the same time, they illustrated the rising power of the cities and their people, whose political time did in fact come in 1932. Smith played an important role in the development of that voter coalition, which would dominate American politics from the Great Depression through the 1970's.

Smith's alienation from the New Deal was typical of old Progressives of both parties—their definition of reform did not include all the elements of mid-twentieth century American liberalism. By the 1930's, Smith was politically outmoded, but his role in the political developments of the 1910's and 1920's was considerable.

### Bibliography

Allswang, John M. *A House for All Peoples: Ethnic Politics in Chicago, 1896-1936*. Lexington: University Press of Kentucky, 1971. A case study of Smith's role in the development of the "Roosevelt coalition" of urban, ethnic, and working-class voters in the Democratic Party.

Handlin, Oscar. *Al Smith and His America*. Boston: Little Brown, 1958. An interpretive biography, sketchy in some parts, but also perceptive. Focuses on the religious and ethnic aspects of Smith's career and his presidential campaign.

Hapgood, Norman, and Henry Moskowitz. *Up from the City Streets: A Biographical Study in Contemporary Politics*. New York: Harcourt Brace, 1927. A laudatory study by two men who worked with Smith in New York. Useful for its contemporary nature, and because of the authors' closeness to Smith.

Josephson, Matthew, and Hannah Josephson. *Al Smith: Hero of the Cities*. Boston: Houghton Mifflin, 1969; London: Thames and Hudson, 1970. Based primarily on the Frances Perkins papers and research Perkins had done for a planned Smith biography. Well researched and interesting reading.

O'Connor, Richard. *The First Hurrah: A Biography of Alfred E. Smith*. New York: Putnam, 1970. A general but fairly thorough biography. Based primarily on secondary materials but balanced and informative.

Pringle, Henry F. *Alfred E. Smith: A Critical Study*. New York: Macy-Masius, 1927. Written before the 1928 presidential race; Pringle was a poor predictor. The book is quite personal and interpretive, balanced in its view of Smith, and still worth reading.

Roberts, S. "Albany Redux: Faith and Politics Are in Conflict." *New York Times* 139, no. 48154 (February 22, 1990). The author comments on New York Governor Mario Cuomo's conflict with the Catholic church over abortion in comparison to Smith, governor 65 years previously.

Smith, Alfred E. *Up to Now*. New York: Viking Press, 1929. A straightforward autobiographical narrative for the period through the 1928 presidential campaign. Not overly critical but honest and factually reliable.

Warner, Emily Smith. *The Happy Warrior*. New York: Doubleday, 1956. An affectionate and approving biography by a devoted daughter. It is worth reading, as she was close to her father and was in his confidence.

*John M. Allswang*

## BESSIE SMITH

*Born:* April 15, 1894; Chattanooga, Tennessee
*Died:* September 26, 1937; Clarksdale, Mississippi
*Area of Achievement:* Music
*Contribution:* The first internationally popular female blues singer, Bessie Smith paved the way for later female blues and gospel singers such as Billie Holiday, Ella Fitzgerald, and Mahalia Jackson.

### Early Life

Bessie Smith was born into abject poverty in Chattanooga Tennessee. Her parents, William and Laura Smith, had a total of seven children in what Bessie later described as "a little ramshackle cabin." William was a part-time Baptist minister who ran a small mission but had to support his family by doing manual labor. He died shortly after Bessie was born, and her mother died by the time Bessie was eight or nine years old. Bessie and the other children were reared by their oldest sister Viola, who became an unwed mother at an early age, adding another hungry mouth to the family.

Bessie realized at an early age that she had an exceptional voice. She used to sing on the streets of Chattanooga with her brother Andrew accompanying her on the guitar. Then another brother got her a job with the Moses Stokes traveling minstrel show, and she began appearing with the legendary blues singer, Gertrude "Ma" Rainey. Their audiences were predominantly black because African American music was yet to be discovered by most white Americans. For many years, Bessie toured the South with the Rabbit Foot Minstrels under the tutelage of Ma Rainey, who is generally considered a blues singer second only to Bessie Smith.

It was a hard life, with exhausting schedules, segregated accommodations, humiliating encounters with bigoted white police officers, late hours, casual sex, gambling, fighting, and plenty of drinking. Bessie did not use hard drugs, but she enjoyed smoking marijuana, which was considered fairly innocuous and did not become illegal under federal law until 1937. Bessie picked up many bad habits from the people she associated with, who included gangsters, prostitutes, pimps, gamblers, dope peddlers, con artists, and assorted grifters, along with the hard-boiled booking agents who paid starvation wages to their overworked performers.

Bessie's early life taught her to be tough in a tough world. She was a big, strong woman who weighed approximately 210 pounds; she became notorious for her dangerous temper as well as her powerful voice. Her singing has been described as rough, coarse, low-down, and dirty, but her voice was a perfect instrument for the earthy blues songs that would eventually make her world famous.

### Life's Work

Bessie Smith's big break came in 1923, when she was discovered by Frank Walker, a talent scout for Columbia Records. Her recording of "Downhearted Blues" sold three-quarters of a million copies, a fantastic achievement in those early days of wind-up phonographs and primitive recording equipment. In that one year she sold more than two million records. Some of her other famous recordings were "Jealous Hearted Blues" and "Jailhouse Blues." The power of Smith's singing is impossible to describe in words. Fortunately, her recordings are readily available throughout the United States, Europe, and elsewhere.

During the next decade, Bessie Smith recorded approximately 160 songs, accompanied by some musicians who also made music history, including trumpeter Louis Armstrong and pianist-bandleader Fletcher Henderson. At the peak of her career, during the Roaring Twenties, she was making as much as two thousand dollars a week from personal appearances and had a large additional income from royalties on record sales. It was her recordings that first brought her to the attention of white listeners in America and Europe; the affluence of this new audience made her rich and famous.

The titles of some of Smith's most popular songs provide an idea of the nihilistic philosophical background of the blues, which appealed so strongly to white audiences during the lawless Prohibition Era. One famous song was "'T'ain't Nobody's Bizness If I Do." Another was "Nobody Knows You When You're Down and Out." The standard twelve-bar form consisted of four bars per line, with the first line of the lyrics repeated, as in the following stanza:

> I cried and worried, all night I laid and groaned,
> I cried and worried, all night I laid and groaned,
> I used to weigh two hundred, now I'm down to skin and bone.

Many citizens, both black and white, regarded the blues as "devil's music" because it seemed so hopeless and negative, and because it frequently

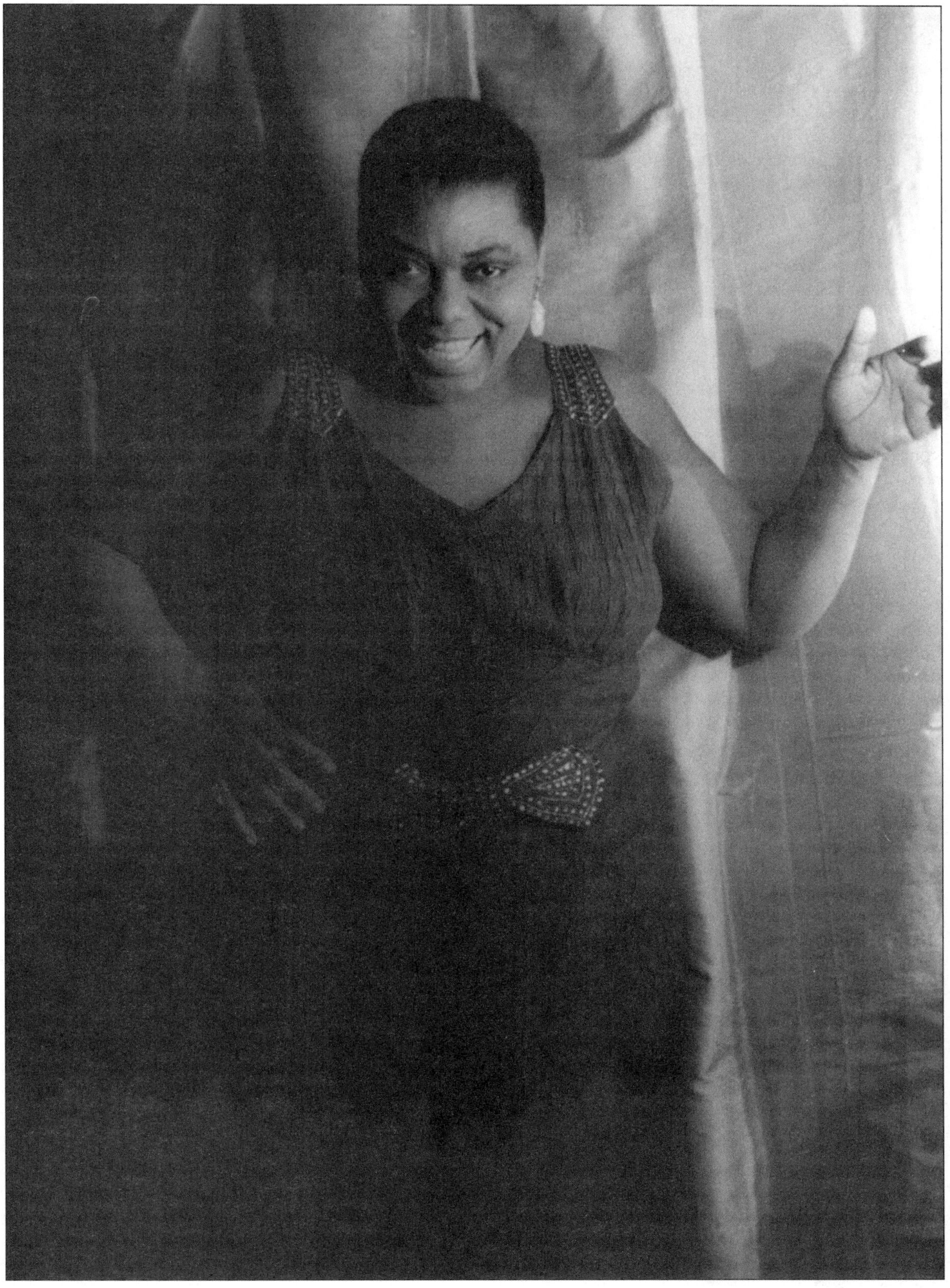

celebrated such activities as drinking and having sex. Nevertheless, it appealed to many people who were disillusioned with traditional religion and were becoming pessimistic about the human condition in an era of gangsterism, predatory laissez-faire capitalism, and crooked politics. The blues had an influence not only on popular music but also on poetry, fiction, drama, and other art forms.

Bessie Smith lavished her money on her husband Jack Gee, an enormous man with a temper matching Smith's own. He had been a Philadelphia policeman but left the force to manage—or mismanage—his wife's business affairs. Jack was not faithful to his wife, and she was not faithful to him. She was sexually attracted to women as well as men and suffered many beatings from her husband, who was extremely jealous in addition to being concerned about guarding the source of his income. They separated in 1930 but remained on reasonably good terms until her death.

Bessie Smith's life ended abruptly in a tragic automobile accident on a narrow Louisiana road in the dead of night. The driver of her car did not see a truck that was blocking part of the road; they crashed into it at full speed, and the singer suffered numerous serious injuries, including a nearly severed arm. The aftermath has been the subject of many conflicting stories. Some people claim that Smith died from loss of blood because she was refused admittance at a racially segregated hospital. For more than thirty years she lay in an unmarked grave. Then in the 1960's, the famous white rock 'n' roll singer Janis Joplin, acknowledging her debt to Smith's inspirational example, paid to have a headstone created bearing the epitaph "The Greatest Blues Singer in the World Will Never Stop Singing."

When Bessie Smith died in 1937, her career was on the decline. Record sales had collapsed with the advent of the Great Depression after the stock market crash in October of 1929. New kinds of popular music were being developed to suit the younger generation and the more sophisticated, urbane spirit of the 1930's. Swing, as exemplified by such big bands as those of Glenn Miller, Count Basie, and Tommy Dorsey, had stolen the spotlight from blues and jazz, and Smith could not adapt to this type of music. Alcoholism was another important factor in destroying her illustrious career. She acquired a bad reputation for not showing up for engagements or for being too intoxicated to perform when she finally arrived.

## Summary

Bessie Smith is generally considered the greatest blues singer who ever lived and is still referred to as the "Empress of the Blues." Before her time, most blues singers had been men. Smith not only became a great blues singer in her own right but also feminized the musical form so that the way was opened for many women to follow in her footsteps. Some of America's most famous popular female vocalists owe their success to the model provided by Bessie Smith. Among those others are Billie Holiday, Mahalia Jackson, and Janis Joplin, but there were also countless others whose careers were not as brilliant or dramatic. She also influenced the musical styles of such famous jazz musicians as Louis Armstrong, Bix Beiderbecke, and Jack Teagarden, among many others.

Bessie Smith was the first blues singer to achieve popularity with white audiences. This occurrence brought the wonderfully expressive musical form of the blues to the attention of the entire world. She introduced the blues to the new media of phonograph records, radio, and talking pictures, which had the capability of reaching vast numbers of people. Her recordings made white audiences in the United States and Europe conscious of the important contributions of African Americans to popular art and inspired musicologists to scour the South in search of great folk musicians who were still living in poverty and obscurity.

It was many years, however, before another new generation rediscovered Smith through her recordings and gave her the credit she richly deserved for her contributions to popular music. In 1970, Columbia Records initiated one of the biggest reissue projects in recording history. The company released Bessie Smith's entire output on five double albums. Two hundred thousand copies of these albums were snapped up within two years, and her recordings continue to be played on radio broadcasts and featured in record stores all over the world.

The blues expressed the suffering of African Americans and made other people more conscious of the injustice that this minority group had experienced since the settlement of the American Colonies began. Black women were an oppressed minority within a minority because they often bore the burden of providing all the financial and moral support for their families. Smith's beautiful blues songs carried the implicit message that racial injustice was responsible for much of the pain they expressed. Because of the many recordings Bessie Smith made during her lifetime, she became better known after her death than she was at the height of her career. Great art always has the power to bring people closer together, and Bessie Smith continues to influence people all over the world in that positive way.

**Bibliography**

Albee, Edward. *The Death of Bessie Smith*. New York: New American Library, and London: French, 1960. This one-act play by a famous American author helped to spread Bessie's reputation to a wider audience and also helped to perpetuate the legend that she had died of injuries because she was refused admittance to a white hospital in Tennessee.

Albertson, Chris. *Bessie Smith, Empress of the Blues*. New York: Schirmer, 1975. A carefully researched biography written by an authority on Bessie Smith's music and told in an interesting, anecdotal fashion. Liberally illustrated with black-and-white photographs of Bessie Smith taken throughout her life. Contains a valuable discography of Bessie Smith's recordings as well as those of Ma Rainey and other significant blues artists.

Azerrad, Michael. "Rock and Roll Hall of Fame." *Rolling Stone* (February 9, 1989): 93. A section on inductees to the Rock and Roll Hall of Fame discusses the meteoric career of "the Empress of the Blues" and the great musical artists with whom she worked. Contains a portrait of Bessie Smith.

Brooks, Edward. *The Bessie Smith Companion: A Critical and Detailed Appreciation of the Recordings*. New York: Da Capo Press, and Wheathampstead, Herts: Cavendish, 1982. This book represents many years of intense work by a Bessie Smith enthusiast who offers a detailed analysis of 159 recordings by the singer along with discussions of her life and the characteristics of her various accompanists. The best Bessie Smith discography available.

Feinstein, Elaine. *Bessie Smith*. Londdon: Penguin, and New York: Viking, 1985. A short, well-written biography covering all the main details of Bessie Smith's life. This book is part of Viking's Lives of Modern Women series. Contains photographs, a chronology, a bibliography, and some information about available recordings.

Jones, Hettie. *Big Star Fallin' Mama: Five Women in Black Music*. Rev. ed. New York: Viking Press, 1995. This excellent small volume contains chapters devoted to Ma Rainey, Bessie Smith, Mahalia Jackson, Billie Holiday, and Aretha Franklin, focusing on their influences on one another as well as their contributions to popular music. Contains good photographs of all five world-famous women.

Marvin, Thomas F. "'Preachin' the Blues': Bessie Smith's Secular Religion and Alice Walker's 'The Color Purple.'" *African American Review* 28, no. 3 (Fall 1994). Compares Smith to Alice Walker's character (in The Color Purple) of blues singer Shug Avery.

McCorkle, Susannah. "Back to Bessie." *American Heritage* 48, no. 7 (November, 1997). Comprehensive look at the impact of Smith on blues and jazz music.

Mezzrow, Milton. *Really the Blues*. New York: Random House, and London: Secker and Warburg, 1946. One of the best books ever written about the history and meaning of the blues. Mezzrow was a white musician who knew most of the early blues and jazz artists in Chicago and New York, including Bessie Smith. Discusses the early use of drugs by musicians and the precarious lives they led on the road.

Moore, Carmen. *Somebody's Angel Child: The Story of Bessie Smith*. New York: Crowell, 1969. A short biography containing excerpts from the lyrics of Bessie Smith's blues songs. Emphasizes how the songs reflected her life experiences. Contains a discography and a bibliography.

Terkel, Studs. *Giants of Jazz*. New York: Crowell, 1957. A famous American writer discusses the careers of thirteen great jazz artists with perception and sincere appreciation. He devotes one chapter to Bessie Smith.

*Bill Delaney*

# MARGARET CHASE SMITH

*Born:* December 14, 1897; Skowhegan, Maine
*Died:* May 29, 1995; Skowhegan, Maine
*Area of Achievement:* Government and politics
*Contribution:* As the first leading American stateswoman to be elected in her own right to both houses of the United States Congress, Margaret Chase Smith focused her attention on improving the status of women, military preparedness, and defense of free speech and democratic values.

## Early Life

Margaret Madeline Chase was born in Skowhegan, Maine, on December 14, 1897. Skowhegan, a mill and factory town in west-central Maine, provided a small-town atmosphere in which her parents George Emery and Carrie Murray Chase reared their six children. Margaret was the eldest of the four who survived. Her father, a barber from Irish and English background, was a hardworking family man whose own father had fought in the Civil War before taking his position as a Methodist minister in Skowhegan. Her mother took jobs occasionally to supplement family income while instilling in her children the importance of family life and independence.

While pursuing a commercial course of study in high school Margaret worked as a clerk in the local five-and-dime store, was employed as a telephone operator, and was hired to record tax payments in the town books during her senior year. She shook hands with President Woodrow Wilson on her senior class trip to Washington, D.C. After her graduation from Skowhegan High School in 1916, Margaret taught in the one-room Pitts School outside Skowhegan. Seven months later she returned to Skowhegan to accept a full-time telephone operator's job for Maine Telephone and Telegraph Company.

In 1919, she began an eight-year job at the town's weekly newspaper, the *Independent Reporter*, which Clyde Smith (her future husband) coowned. Rising to circulation manager, she continued to meet influential people and cultivate her skills in public relations. She drew on these skills in 1922, when she organized the Skowhegan chapter of the Business and Professional Women's Club. Margaret was named president of the Maine Federation of the Business and Professional Women's Clubs the following year. In 1928, she served as Office Manager for the Daniel E. Cummings Company, a Skowhegan woolen mill. Her early working experiences not only taught her how to get along with people but also instilled in her a respect for working people that influenced her subsequent pro-labor record in the United States Congress.

In 1930, Margaret Chase married Clyde H. Smith, a respected and experienced Maine politician who was twenty-two years her senior. From 1930 to 1936, she supported his energetic public career while learning the basic skills for campaigning and public service. During this period, she also served as a member of the Maine Republican State Committee. Clyde Smith was elected to the United States House of Representatives in 1936. Margaret served as his secretary in Washington, D.C., until his death in April, 1940.

## Life's Work

Margaret Chase Smith won a special election in the spring of 1940 to fill her husband's vacated seat in the House of Representatives. As a candidate for the succeeding full term in office, Smith scored an impressive electoral victory in the September general election. Her eight years as the congresswoman from Maine's Second Congressional District were highlighted by her interest in military affairs. In her first term she broke with the Republican Party and voted for the Selective Training and Service Act to draft men for the upcoming war. She was the only member of the Maine delegation to vote for Lend Lease in 1941 and she broke with her party to support a bill to arm American merchant ships. In 1943 she was appointed to the House Naval Affairs Committee which was later merged into the Armed Services Committee.

Many of Smith's concerns focused on the status of women in the civilian workforce and in the military. In 1944, she was appointed by Secretary of Labor Frances Perkins to serve as technical adviser to the International Labor Organization, which explored the role of women in employment planning after World War II. Smith worked to improve the status of women in the military by introducing the Army-Navy Permanent Nurse Corps Bill to grant women permanent status in the military. This bill was signed into law by President Harry S Truman in April of 1947. Smith toured the South Pacific naval bases and sponsored legislation which would permit women to serve overseas during war. She gained passage for the Women's Armed Services Integration Act of 1948 which gave women equal pay, rank and privileges. Her desire to see the United States exert leadership in world affairs enabled her to support U.S. membership in the United Nations and the European Recovery Plan.

Senator Smith favored domestic legislation to improve the conditions of the working class and women. She helped to defeat the Tabor Amendment which had proposed to halve the funds designated for community service programs such as child care. In 1945 and 1949 she cosponsored a proposed Equal Rights Amendment which did not get the necessary two-thirds majority votes in Congress to be submitted to the states for ratification. She voted with the Democrats against the Smith-Connally Anti-Strike bill. In economic matters she opposed a bill to freeze the social security tax and voted for federal pay raises. In 1947 she voted against a Republican proposal to cut President Truman's budget. That same year she voted with her party in supporting the Taft-Hartley Act, which placed specific limits on labor. She had been named chair of the Maine State Republican Convention in 1944 to prepare her to chair the national Republican Party conference in 1967.

Margaret Chase Smith ran for election to the U.S. Senate in 1948 winning by a record plurality. Though her opponents charged her with being a party maverick by calling attention to the votes that she cast contrary to her party, she produced a House voting record that aligned with her party ninety-five percent of the time. Her election to the United States Senate in 1948 made her the first woman in United States history to be elected in her own right without prior service by appointment to serve in the U.S. Senate and the first woman to be elected to both houses of Congress. Her four terms in the Senate from 1948 to 1972 acquainted her with six presidents among whom were Dwight D. Eisenhower and John F. Kennedy.

In 1949 Senator Smith began a daily newspaper column, *Washington and You*, which was syndicated nationally for five years. She was named to the prestigious Senate Republican Policy Committee. She won the Associated Press award for Woman of the Year in politics in 1948, 1949, 1950, and 1957. She delivered her famous "Declaration of Conscience" speech on June 1, 1950 as a response to the abuses of Senator Joseph R. McCarthy's inquisitions into communism in the United States. She courageously opposed McCarthy's negativism and demeaning of Americans at a time when most Republicans in the Senate were either too afraid to oppose him or somewhat supportive of his extremist anticommunist activities. Her "Declaration of Conscience" speech still has appeal as a defense of American values and the importance of free speech to the maintenance of American democratic processes.

She traveled to Florence, Italy, in 1950 as U.S. delegate to the UNESCO conference. She was also appointed as a lieutenant colonel in the U.S. Air Force Reserves. After winning reelection to the Senate in 1954 she embarked on a twenty-three nation world tour to see how U.S. foreign aid money was being used. She interrupted her trip to return to the United States to cast her censure vote on Joseph R. McCarthy. In 1956 Senator Smith campaigned for Dwight Eisenhower, the Republican presidential candidate. She debated in his defense with Eleanor Roosevelt on CBS television's *Face the Nation*. As someone who enjoyed new experiences, Smith had by this time been the first woman to ride on an American destroyer in wartime, spend a day on an aircraft carrier at sea, and in 1957 to fly as a passenger in a F-100 jet fighter which broke the sound barrier.

In 1960, Smith won a hotly contested election over another female candidate, the first time two women had run against each other for a Senate seat. That same year she won *Newsweek* magazine's press poll rating as Most Valuable Senator. Upon resuming her duties in the Senate, she agonized over her vote on Kennedy's Limited Nuclear Test Ban Treaty. Her concern for national security won out in her vote against both the treaty and most of her Party. Her vote put her on the same side as Barry Goldwater, who became the Republican party presidential nominee for 1964. Although Margaret Chase Smith was touted as a potential candidate for vice president in 1964, she earned the distinction that year of becoming the first woman nominated for president by a major U.S. political party.

She supported the 1964 Civil Rights Act using her influence in the Republican Conference to keep the provision barring sex discrimination in employment in Title VII intact. Smith won an unprecedented fourth term for a woman to the Senate in 1966. In 1967 she was elected chair of the Conference of Republican Senators. The next year she had to miss her first roll call vote in her thirteen years in Congress because of hip surgery. She held the record for 2,941 consecutive roll call votes. In the remaining two years of her tenure in the Senate, Margaret Chase Smith cast important votes against President Richard Nixon's nominations of Clement F. Haynesworth and G. Harold Carswell for the U.S. Supreme Court. Demonstrations protesting the Vietnam War, especially on college campuses, led her to make her second "Declaration of Conscience" speech on June 1, 1970.

In her final campaign for reelection to the Senate in 1972, Smith was defeated by her Democratic opponent, William D. Hathaway. During her Senate career she served on the powerful Armed Forces, Appropriations, Government Operations and Rules Committees and showed strong support for the space program as a charter member of the Senate Aeronautical and Space Committee. She also sponsored legislation for government support of medical research. Senator Smith used her considerable influence to look out for the seafaring interests and industries of the state of Maine and to cast votes on issues critical to the well-being of the Republican Party and the future course in world politics for the United States.

After she left public office, Smith focused on a second career as a visiting professor and lecturer with the Woodrow Wilson National Fellowship Foundation and at numerous college and university campuses. In the course of her career, she received ninety-five honorary doctoral degrees and more than 270 other awards and honors. In 1989, she was awarded the Presidential Medal of Freedom, the nation's highest civilian honor. The Northwood Institute, Margaret Chase Smith Library in Skowhegan, Maine, was dedicated in 1982 to serve as a congressional research library and archives. This library houses the papers, political memorabilia, and documents that Smith accrued in her thirty-two years in Congress. In 1990 she was honored by the dedication of the Margaret Chase Smith Center for Public Policy at the University of Maine.

### Summary

Margaret Chase Smith's long and distinguished public service career furthered the interests of national security, especially military affairs. She pioneered legislation to further the status of women in domestic issues, military status, and internationally. She was a model of decorum and earned a reputation for integrity, honesty, and independence of judgment. As a servant of the people in Congress, she put first priority on her duties in office. She campaigned vigorously and without accepting campaign contributions.

### Bibliography

Fleming, Alice. *The Senator from Maine*. New York: Crowell, 1969. This is a well-written book highlighting the life of Margaret Chase Smith from childhood through her activities in Congress. Somewhat historically fictionalized, the book is suitable for grades six through eight.

Gould, Alberta. *First Lady of the Senate: Life of Margaret Chase Smith*. Mt. Desert, Maine: Windswept House, 1990. This work presents a juvenile level review of the public career of Margaret Chase Smith. The author emphasizes Smith's personal values, public integrity, independent judgment, and contributions to public life.

Graham, Frank, Jr. *Margaret Chase Smith: Woman of Courage*. New York: Day, 1964. This readable biography describes Smith's professional life in the Senate. The author emphasizes her accomplishments as a woman in national politics—at that time, an arena dominated almost exclusively by men. Presents clear explanations of how the U.S. government works.

Meisler, Stanley. "Margaret Chase Smith: The Nation's First Woman Senator Reflects Back over a Capitol Life." *Los Angeles Times*, December 8, 1991, p. M3. A brief interview with Smith in which she reminisces about her experiences as a politician in Washington, D.C. Places her accomplishments within the context of women's efforts to gain greater political representation during the 1990's.

Sherman, Janann. "'They Either Need These Women or They Do Not': Margaret Chase Smith and the Fight for Regular Status for Women in the Military." *Journal of Military History* 54 (January, 1990): 47-78. A scholarly analysis of Smith's stance on the issue of equitable status and treatment for women in the military. Amplifies her views on a topic that continues to generate interest among American military leaders and the general public.

Smith, Margaret Chase. *Declaration of Conscience*. New York: Doubleday, 1972. This book, composed by Smith with the assistance of her legislative aide, William C. Lewis, Jr., focuses on her three decades of public service. It contains important source material including the text of her famous speeches and other important legislative statements.

Vallin, Marlene B. *Margaret Chase Smith: Model Public Servant.* Westport, Conn.: Greenwood Press, 1998. The author offers critical analysis of speeches made by Smith and focuses on the various facets of her political persona.

Wallace, Patricia W. *Politics of Conscience: A Biography of Margaret Chase Smith.* Westport, Conn.: Praeger, 1995. The first biography of Smith to make use of her personal papers and of interviews with both Smith and her cohorts in Congress.

Witt, Linda, Karen M. Paget, and Glenna Matthews. *Running as a Woman: Gender and Power in American Politics*. New York: Free Press, 1993. A journalist, a political scientist, and a historian collaborated on this sweeping narrative of the experiences of female candidates in American politics. Written from the vantage point of 1992's "Year of the Woman," the book contains various references to Smith's trailblazing efforts in Congress and a telling assessment of public opinion regarding her chances of becoming president in 1964.

*Willoughby G. Jarrell*

# THEOBALD SMITH

*Born:* July 31, 1859; Albany, New York
*Died:* December 10, 1934; New York, New York
*Areas of Achievement:* Microbiology and animal pathology
*Contribution:* Considered to be the most distinguished American microbiologist and probably the leading comparative pathologist in the world, Smith made discoveries fundamental to theoretical biology, public health, and veterinary medicine, and opened new vistas in disease control.

## Early Life

Theobald Smith's parents, Philipp Schmitt and Theresia Kexel, emigrated from Germany following their marriage and settled in Albany, New York, where Schmitt became a tailor. Their only son was baptized in his mother's Roman Catholic faith and given the surname of his godfather, Jacob Theobald. (He later abandoned Catholicism and became a Unitarian.) Smith's mother, a fine musician, provided musical training for him, and his favorite recreation throughout life was playing the piano.

Smith began his education in a German-speaking private academy; in 1872, he enrolled at the Albany Free Academy. An exceptional student, he received a state scholarship, and this, plus earnings from piano lessons and playing the chapel organ, enabled him to attend Cornell University. He was graduated with honors in 1881, enrolled in the Albany Medical College, and received the M.D. in 1883 at the top of his class.

Smith felt neither inclined nor ready to practice medicine, preferring a research career. Wealthier Americans in this situation pursued furthur studies in Europe and returned with a Ph.D. and a professorship in an American university. Smith, however, needed a job, and, on the recommendation of the Cornell microscopist Simon Gage, took a position with the Department of Agriculture's Bureau of Animal Industry in Washington, D.C., established in 1884 by Congress to combat the economically devastating diseases infecting farm animals. He knew no bacteriology, very little about pathology, and nothing at all about the diseases of farm animals, but he learned in these fields by reading the papers of Louis Pasteur, Robert Koch, and other pioneers in microbiology. He taught himself the culture-plate methods of Koch and even improved upon them. Thus, Smith learned bacteriology as it was quickening into an exciting new field.

On May 17, 1888, Smith married Lilian Hillyer Egleston of Washington, D.C., the daughter of a clergyman and chief of forestry in the Bureau of Forestry. It was a happy marriage; his wife supported him through the hardships and dissatisfactions which he endured during his early career. They had three children.

Smith matured into a slender, bearded man, with a long, gentle face; he was a simple, companionable, unpretentious, and guileless person, so self-effacing that, despite his achievements, he was virtually unknown to the American public.

## Life's Work

Smith quickly appreciated the significance of microbiology for the bureau's task of finding the causes of diseases which attack farm animals. The head of the bureau, Daniel Salmon (after whom the *Salmonella* group of bacteria is named) assigned him to sorting out the chaos of information on swine diseases; Smith demonstrated the presence of two diseases, hog cholera and swine plague, as

the major causes of death, and tracked down the microbes involved. In 1886, he disclosed that hog cholera bacterial cultures which had been killed conferred immunity, preparing the way for the development of a new type of vaccine.

Overshadowing all else during his tenure at the bureau was his six-year investigation of Texas cattle fever and the publication of the remarkable *Investigations into the Nature, Causation and Prevention of Texas or Southern Cattle Fever* (1893). Smith discovered that a protozoan microparasite destroyed the red blood cells of cattle. In a long series of beautifully planned experiments, he clearly described the parasite, providing the first clear demonstration of a protozoan disease in higher animals. Moreover, he was the first to trace the exact path by which an agent of disease went from one animal to another: It was transmitted to susceptible cattle by the offspring of bloodsucking ticks. The complex, meticulously verified tick-borne mechanism astounded scientists. The long-term consequences were the saving of the cattle industry by tick-eradication programs and, of greater significance, the revelation that insects carry deadly germs; as a result of this discovery, over the next two decades investigators were able to demonstrate how insects transmit the germs of malaria, yellow fever, sleeping sickness, typhus, and bubonic plague.

By the 1890's, Smith had acquired an international reputation in science, his work having been published in German journals. There was disharmony at the bureau, however, as Salmon attempted to divert credit for Smith's work to himself and his associates. Smith saw Salmon overgenerously make F. L. Kilborne, the superintendent of the experimental farm, coauthor of the cattle fever monograph. He chafed under the repeated injustices and waited for an opportunity to leave the bureau.

Meanwhile, Smith developed ingenious methods for culturing and differentiating microorganisms. He investigated the bacteriology of water supplies, and the American Public Health Association incorporated his techniques and studies into its *Standard Methods for the Examination of Water and Waste Water* (1905). Smith organized the first department of bacteriology in an American medical school at the National Medical College of Columbian University (later renamed George Washington University) and aided in the organization of the department at Cornell.

Smith's association with the Bureau of Animal Industry ended in 1895 upon the acceptance of a dual appointment in Boston as a Harvard professor in comparative pathology and director of the antitoxin laboratory of the Massachusetts State Board of Health, the nation's first effective state health board. In Boston, Smith roamed widely with no end to his enthusiasm, investigating sewage disposal, control of water supplies, transmission of typhoid fever by milk, and many topics in host-parasite relationships.

In 1898, Smith published a classic paper differentiating human and bovine tuberculosis. Koch, the discoverer of the tubercle bacillus, believed the bacilli infecting humans and cattle were identical; Smith demonstrated their differences in virulence, structure, and growth. Two years earlier, he had met Koch in Germany and told him of his ongoing research on the two varieties. In 1901, Koch reversed his opinion and confirmed Smith's findings but appropriated the discovery as his own, not acknowledging Smith's priority until 1908.

Smith's primary duty at the antitoxin laboratory was the supervision of smallpox vaccine production and the newly introduced diphtheria antitoxin. He made many improvements in vaccines, notably the use of slightly unbalanced mixtures of toxin-antitoxin for the active immunization against diphtheria. He discovered that such mixtures incite antibody production in guinea pigs and greatly enhance immunity. This prophylactic effect, once perfected for human use, was to be of enormous benefit to American children.

In 1904, Smith observed what was for many years known as the "Theobald Smith phenomenon": anaphylaxis in guinea pigs. They became acutely ill when given a second injection of a toxin-antitoxin mixture several days after the first. This was the first recorded observation of hypersensitivity and the basis for the study of hypersensitivity in clinical medicine.

In 1914, Smith resigned his positions to accept the directorship of the new animal pathology laboratory of the Rockefeller Institute for Medical Research. He had been offered the directorship of the institute on its founding in 1901 but refused, not wanting to be primarily an administrator. (He was, however, on its board of scientific directors from inception to 1933 and served as its president in 1933.) The institute, needing a place outside New York City for research on animal diseases, purchased farmland near Princeton, New Jersey, with Smith largely responsible for the planning and design of the laboratories and animal quarters.

With a group of young, eager scientists, the new department at first restricted itself to confirming the details of pathological and bacteriological knowledge, but it shortly became the scene of important new developments.

Smith investigated turkey blackhead, a fatal disease ruining the turkey breeding industry in the eastern states. In 1920, he found the cause to be a protozoan parasite transmitted by ingestion of embryonated eggs of a small roundworm. His work provided all the information necessary to keep turkeys healthy and, in addition, revealed an important and novel cycle of transmission and parasitism.

With a large dairy herd at his disposal, Smith studied brucellosis, the infectious abortion in cows which was responsible for losses of twenty percent in calf generation. In 1926, he induced protection by vaccination of heifers with a living, attenuated *Brucella abortus* culture and also found a hitherto unrecognized spiral microbe, *Vibrio fetus*, responsible for infection of the placentum and fetal membranes and one out of four abortions.

In 1929, the seventy-year-old scientist retired as the institute's director while continuing to work at the laboratory. During 1934, he grew progressively weaker and died of heart failure during the administration of ether incident to an exploratory operation for intestinal cancer. At the time of his death, his peers regarded him as America's greatest medical scientist, comparable to Pasteur and Koch. Never widely known outside scientific circles, honors came late in life. A lecture series at Princeton in 1933 led to his only book written for the lay reader, *Parasitism and Disease* (1934). He was recommended several times for the Nobel Prize, but, although deserving, he never received the award. Active in organizing the American Academy of Tropical Medicine and elected its first president, he did not attend its first meeting as he was stricken with the illness that led to his death. The society created the Theobald Smith Medal for notable contributions in the field. His portrait hangs at the entrance to the Theobald Smith Building of Rockefeller University in New York.

### Summary

Smith summarized his own work as "a study of the causes of infectious diseases and a search for their control." He was the first American to do important work in bacteriology and immunology, demonstrating that infectious disease could be insect-borne and that killed bacterial cultures may produce immunity, a find which was the basis for protective vaccination against several diseases. He brought attention to the hypersensitive condition and established culture methods for the bacteriological examination of milk, water, and sewage. In the development of American science, he was a major force in the professional development of bacteriology at a time when the United States was considered backward in the laboratory sciences. He brought medical science to bear on public health and its need to adapt to new findings on the sources and transmission of infectious diseases and to developments in immunology, which together resulted in the great elongation in the average life span of Americans living in the twentieth century.

### Bibliography

Clark, Paul Franklin. "Theobald Smith, Student of Disease." *Journal of the History of Medicine and Allied Sciences* 14 (October, 1959): 490-514. A clear, straightforward treatment of Smith's research career.

Corner, George W. *A History of the Rockefeller Institute, 1901-1953*. New York: Rockefeller Institute Press, 1964. An informative account of the creation and activities of the institute; it documents Smith's role on the board of directors and as head of the animal pathology department.

De Kruif, Paul. "Theobald Smith: Ticks and Texas Fever." In *Microbe Hunters*, New York: Harcourt Brace, 1926; London: Cape, 1963. A vivid, popular, readable account of Smith's most famous investigation. Subsequent chapters show how scientists followed Smith's lead in investigating other insect-borne diseases.

Gage, Simon Henry. "Theobald Smith, Investigator and Man." *Science* 84 (August 7, 1936): 117-122. A brief but perceptive essay written by Smith's Cornell professor and lifelong friend.

Winslow, Charles-Edward Amory. "The Insect Host." In *The Conquest of Epidemic Disease*, Princeton, N.J.: Princeton University Press, 1943. Less dramatic than the work by De Kruif but beautifully written, instructive, and rich in interpretation and insights.

Zinsser, Hans. "Biographical Memoir of Theobald Smith." *Biographical Memoirs. National Academy of Sciences* 17 (1937): 261-303. There is no full biography of Smith. This is the best study and includes a bibliography of 247 of his publications.

*Albert B. Costa*

# JAN CHRISTIAN SMUTS

*Born:* May 24, 1870; Bovenplaats, near Riebeeck West, Cape Colony, (now in South Africa)

*Died:* September 11, 1950; Irene, near Pretoria, South Africa

*Areas of Achievement:* Government, politics, and the military

*Contribution:* In addition to a distinguished military career in three wars, Smuts helped create the South African Union and integrate it within the British Commonwealth; he influenced the shaping of the League of Nations and the United Nations.

## Early Life

Jan Christian Smuts was born May 24, 1870, on the farm of his parents, Jacobus Abraham Smuts and "Tante (Aunt) Cato," Catharina Petronella de Vries, near Riebeek West, a rural community north of Cape Town in what was then the British Cape Colony in South Africa. Up to the age of twelve, when he was finally sent to school after the death of his older brother Michiel, Smuts lived the life of an illiterate farm boy and developed a love for the outdoors which would stay with him as a sophisticated general and statesman.

As soon as he entered school, the farm boy transformed into an avid reader and studious loner; Smuts did so well that he was admitted to Victoria College, Stellenbosch, from which he was graduated with highest honors in both science and literature at the age of twenty-one in 1891. Winning a scholarship, Smuts sailed to England to attend Christ's College, Cambridge; he performed so brilliantly that 1894 became known as "Smuts's year" at Cambridge. Yet while Smuts showed scholarly excellence throughout his academic career, he always remained isolated from his peers, who did not share a distaste for sports and less healthy pastimes with this lean, pale student, whose tall stature and blond hair betrayed his primarily Dutch ancestry.

Choosing to return to Cape Town rather than accepting a professorship at Cambridge, Smuts learned that his lack of social graces barred him from becoming a successful lawyer; his colleagues as well as his potential clients came to dislike his aloofness and impatience with any signs of inefficiency. By cultivating a second occupation as a journalistic writer and taking his first steps as a politician for the Afrikaner Bond Party, however, Smuts aroused the interest of Sir Cecil Rhodes, then Prime Minister of the Cape Colony, who had already noticed the brilliance of the boy during a prior visit to Stellenbosch.

It was Rhodes who used the young Afrikaner Smuts in a tactical maneuver to placate the Boers of Transvaal shortly before springing a surprise attack on them. Rightly feeling betrayed by Rhodes, Smuts left the Cape Colony for the South African Republic in Transvaal under President Paul "Ohm" Kruger in Pretoria. After a short and again unsuccessful spell as a lawyer in the "boom town" of Johannesburg, Smuts became state attorney of the republic at age twenty-eight and abandoned his British nationality. The outbreak of the Boer War in 1899 saw him in Pretoria with his wife Sibella Margaretha "Isie" Krige, a fellow student at Victoria College, whom he had married in 1897 and with whom Smuts stayed close throughout his life. Six of their children survived infancy.

## Life's Work

After the regular forces of the Boers were defeated by the British, Smuts was made general and given a commando group which in 1901 and 1902 embarked on a course of raids which led them dangerously close to Cape Town. During this time, Smuts emerged as an excellent leader of men: The pale scholar felt at home again in the outdoors, and his men quickly came to admire their somewhat reclusive and demanding general. At the peace conference in 1902, Smuts showed the first signs for his vision of a British Commonwealth which should replace the Empire; he decided to trust the promise of the British commander in chief, Lord Kitchener, for a constitution for South Africa and negotiated peace. This achievement also laid the foundations of a lifelong love-hate relationship between Smuts and his fellow Afrikaners; nevertheless, Het Volk (the people), the Boer party after 1902, elected Smuts to go to England in order to achieve "responsible government," a form of limited self-government, from the new British prime minister Henry Campbell-Bannerman.

After his success in England, Smuts teamed up with the congenial Louis Botha in order to achieve his next great goal. While the popular Botha was elected prime minister of Transvaal, as colonial secretary Smuts tirelessly worked for the formation of the Union of South Africa. Established in 1910, the Union had a strong central government and

granted equal rights to British and Boer subjects. For almost ten years, the Union was successfully led by Smuts's alliance with Botha, who "reigned" as prime minister, while the general applied himself to both grand-scale projects and daily administrative duties as minister with no less than three portfolios: mines, defense, and the interior.

Smuts's use of force to restore order in the face of increasing labor conflicts in the gold and diamond mines brought him in conflict with the South African Labour Party; the question of the treatment of the Indians brought Smuts the enmity of Mohandas K. (later Mahatma) Gandhi. Yet after a prolonged industrial dispute in 1913 and 1914, World War I temporarily ended the interior strife and saw General Smuts's return to the battlefield as the second youngest general in the British army.

In a quick campaign against inferior forces, Smuts's relentlessly driven troops helped Botha to conquer German South West Africa in 1915; in 1916, against a similarly outclassed opponent in German East Africa, Smuts's extraordinarily executed strategy of outflanking the enemy, and his success in hostile tropical conditions, secured large territorial gains and the *de facto* defeat of his adversary. Following this, though still only thirty-seven, Smuts was sent to London to represent South Africa at an imperial conference and in the Imperial War Cabinet in 1917. He swiftly became instrumental in the organization of the Royal Air Force, before turning his mind toward peace. He helped American president Woodrow Wilson clarify his ideas regarding a League of Nations, and at Versailles he spoke for a nonvindictive peace.

Back in South Africa, Botha died and Smuts became prime minister for four crucial years in 1919. His party suffered when J. B. M. Hertzog and his Nationalists engineered a breakaway by the right-wingers, and South Africa was plagued by a recurrence of the prewar social unrest. On the international front, Smuts successfully negotiated the discussions leading toward the Anglo-Irish Treaty. His plan for the inclusion of Southern Rhodesia in the Union was defeated, however, two years before a poorly timed general election sent him into a long period of opposition, during which he wrote his philosophical work, *Holism and Evolution* (1926).

It was another war which returned Smuts to the helm of South Africa; willing to declare war on Nazi Germany in 1939, Smuts replaced Hertzog and led his country into World War II on the side of the Allies. As British field marshal, Smuts advised Winston Churchill on a strategy for the repulse of the Axis in North Africa, and after Erwin Rommel's defeat, he stressed the importance of a second front in Italy and the Balkans, an idea which was finally responsible for the British intervention in Greece. Peace brought Smuts to San Francisco in 1945, where the Charter of the United Nations was drafted. Sadly, at home his defeat in 1948 brought to power the Nationalists and their fateful policies. Still active in policies of the Commonwealth, but from a position of opposition to the new government of South Africa, Smuts died on his farm, Irene, on September 11, 1950. He was eighty years old.

### Summary

Throughout his life, Jan Christian Smuts proved himself to be one of the best supporters of the idea of the British Commonwealth. His political vision always focused on the concept of a larger political organization comprising independent units contributing to the whole, and in his philosophical works, he identified himself as a "holist." Contrary to the claim of the Afrikaners, some of whom never forgave the general his seeming "betrayal" of his special obligations to his people, Smuts always kept in mind the interest of the Afrikaners in the context of a large political unit, the Commonwealth.

Smuts fought exceedingly well in the Boer War, which was made unavoidable by the intransigence of the British high commissioner for South Africa, Lord Milner, who rejected all conciliatory compromises, most of which were drafted by Smuts, at the Bloemfontein Conference in 1899. After this war, Smuts directed all of his energies toward the formation of a strong, unified South Africa, which was meant to become one of the cornerstones of the Commonwealth; he understood that in order to succeed as a union of different nations governed by a shared political idea of individual freedom and common responsibility in world affairs, the British Empire had to transform itself, giving its members constitutions of their own, self-government, and limited autonomy.

Brave and capable in war, Smuts showed himself generous and farsighted in peace; twice he advocated clemency for a defeated enemy, and twice his belief in a community of all responsible nations led him to advocate the idea of a world organization. In racial questions, Smuts was not ahead of his time, yet he fought the Nationalists in 1948 and opposed the implementation of their apartheid policies.

### Bibliography


Crafford, F. S. *Jan Smuts*. New York: Doubleday, 1943; London: Allen and Unwin, 1946. Impartial biography by an Afrikaans-speaker; paints Smuts "warts and all." As a result of its wartime origin, Crafford's study overemphasizes Smuts's role in World War II and overindulges in prophecy toward the end; overall, useful and accurate.

Friedlander, Zelda, ed. *Jan Smuts Remembered*. London: Wingate, 1970. Collection of eighteen essays by people associated with Smuts. Covers the full range of his achievements and interests; perceptive and varied portrait enhanced by photographs which bring Smuts the man to life. Mostly well written and enjoyable.

Friedman, Bernard. *Smuts: A Reappraisal*. London: Allen and Unwin, 1975; New York: St. Martin's Press, 1975. Friedman's work is not a biography; it severely criticizes Smuts for a perceived lack of sympathy for the natives' cause.

Haarhoff, T. J. *Smuts the Humanist*. Oxford: Blackwell, 1970. Focuses on Smuts's philosophical work and his political vision. Somewhat dry on his relation to the classics but otherwise a perceptive portrait of Smuts as a thinker. Includes a useful bibliography.

Hancock, W. K. *Smuts*. Vol. 1, *The Sanguine Years, 1870-1919*. Vol. 2, *The Fields of Force, 1919-1950*. Cambridge: Cambridge University Press, 1962, 1968. The definitive biography of Smuts. Clearly written and historically accurate, it draws on the primary material contained in the Smuts Archive at Cape Town. Hancock's emphasis is on Smuts in his historical context, not on his personal life.

Kruger, D. W. *The Making of a Nation: A History of the Union of South Africa (1910-1961)*. London: Macmillan, 1969. Solid background information; Smuts's historical role is discussed in the light of the challenge of his times.

Millin, Sarah G. *General Smuts*. 2 vols. London: Faber, and Boston: Little Brown, 1936. Millin gets off to a rather novelistic start with her first volume, but recovers thereafter and succeeds in painting a perceptive, open, and sympathetic view of Smuts, whom she clearly admires.

Owen, Frank. *Tempestous Journey: Lloyd George, His Life and Times*. Vol. 5. London: Hutchinson, 1954; New York: McGraw-Hill, 1955. Relates Smuts's importance and influence under David Lloyd George, the British prime minister during World War I; puts in context the general's military and political achievements in that era.

Smuts, J. C. *Jan Christian Smuts*. London: Cassell, and New York: Morrow, 1952. Accurately written by Smuts's son; reveals Smuts the father as well as the public man. At times too flattering, but not a eulogy.


*Reinhart Lutz*

# NATHAN SÖDERBLOM

*Born:* January 15, 1866; Trönö, Sweden
*Died:* July 12, 1931; Uppsala, Sweden
*Areas of Achievement:* Religion and peace advocacy
*Contribution:* Söderblom, as Archbishop of Uppsala, was a principal promoter of the Universal Christian Conference on Life and Work. He was awarded the Nobel Peace Prize for his work in promoting international understanding through the ecumenical movement. He is also noted for his work on behalf of war prisoners and displaced persons following World War I. A prolific writer, he emphasized the need to reunite Christianity and make it a practical, humanitarian movement.

## Early Life

Lars Olaf Jonathan Söderblom was born on January 15, 1866, at Trönö, Gävleborg's Län, Sweden. At an early age, he determined to pursue the same calling as his father, a Lutheran pastor. He also chose to shorten his name and became known as Nathan for the rest of his life. Söderblom earned his licentiate of theology at the University of Uppsala. Consecrated a Lutheran minister in 1893, he served briefly as chaplain of the Uppsala Mental Hospital. In 1894, he began graduate studies at the famed Sorbonne in Paris, where he earned the highest academic honor granted by the Protestant theological faculty. He was the only Swede ever to be so honored. His specialties were comparative religions with emphasis on the Persian Zoroastrianism. At the Sorbonne he was influenced by the liberal Protestants, especially by Auguste Sabatier, under whom he studied. Because of this influence, he became interested in the ecumenical movement and a reunification of the Christian denominations.

Söderblom was able to pursue his studies by serving as pastor of the Swedish legation in Paris from 1894 to 1901. Among those who consistently supported the Swedish church in Paris was Alfred Nobel, the inventor-philanthropist, who was often referred to as an atheist. The two men became close friends, and Nobel donated generously to the Swedish congregation. When Nobel died in 1896 at his villa in San Remo, the youthful Söderblom officiated at the funeral services.

## Life's Work

Upon receiving his doctorate of theology in 1901, Söderblom returned to Sweden to become a professor of the history of religions at the University of Uppsala. From 1912 to 1914, he was an instructor at the University of Leipzig. In 1914, he was nominated to become Archbishop of Uppsala and primate of the Church of Sweden, the most prestigious ecclesiastical position in Lutheranism. As archbishop he transformed the archdiocese at Uppsala into a center of world ecumenism. Together with the Archdiocese of Canterbury, England, the Archdiocese of Uppsala was the ecclesiastical center of world Protestantism.

The terrors of World War I occupied the first four years after Söderblom became archbishop. Because of the years spent in France and Germany, Söderblom was intimately acquainted with many of the battle sites, and he grieved over the loss of lives. An outspoken pacifist and proponent of Christian unity, he intervened on behalf of war prisoners and displaced persons. This was the beginning of his many efforts to unite Christianity for the purpose of saving lives and promoting social justice.

Even before the war began, Söderblom actively helped form a "General World Union of Churches for International Understanding." It closed with the outbreak of war. Undaunted, he tried to continue by working with a Norwegian and Danish bishop. A planned conference for 1917 failed to materialize, however, so a purely Nordic Conference was held at Uppsala from September 14 to 16, 1917. At this conference, a manifesto, clearly inspired by Söderblom, was drafted and issued. The churches, it declared, must work to remove the causes of war, and each religion must strive to understand the differences of other beliefs. In 1920, he managed to convoke an international meeting in Geneva, where the foundations were laid for an ecumenical conference in Stockholm. After five years of very careful preparation, the Universal Christian Conference on Life and Work was convened. Nearly six hundred delegates from thirty-one Protestant and Orthodox church communities in thirty-seven different nations attended. The Roman Catholic church did not attend.

Although interested in the ecumenical "Faith and Order Movement" begun in Scotland in 1910, Söderblom insisted that the Stockholm Conference be separate from the World Conference held at Lausanne in 1927. "Doctrine divides—Service unites," he wrote, and he intended the churches to provide the necessary leadership to encourage social justice, not to squabble over doctrinal traditions. After the Stockholm Conference, a continuation committee was named to pursue the objectives of the conference and plan for later meetings. Söderblom was its first president. It was this committee that in 1930 became a permanent organization with the title, the Universal Christian Council for Life and Work.

Despite his demanding tasks as archbishop, Söderblom found time to write in the fields of theology, church history, the history of religions, and the reinterpretations of the life and thought of Martin Luther. His numerous publications included *Religion problemst inom Katolicism och Protestantism* (1910; the religious problem of Catholicism and Protestantism) and *Humor och melankoli och andra Lutherstudier* (1919; humor and melancholy with other studies of Luther). Although he was definitely high church, his writings show considerable liberal influence. He firmly espoused ecumenism, or the reunion of all Christianity to meet the social justice, economic, and civil rights needs of the world as well as to establish international peace. All religion depended on revelation, he wrote, but the "reality of revelation," as he perceived it, was the manifestation of godliness through the genius and leadership abilities of extraordinary people in all civilizations. Finally, he saw the practical application of Christianity to the needs of modern man as the "social justice" for which he worked.

Because of his unfailing determination to promote international understanding through the church, Söderblom was awarded the Nobel Peace Prize in 1930. He was also invited to deliver the famous Gifford lectures on natural theology at Edinburgh, Scotland, in 1931. A brief illness led to his death on July 12, 1931, only a few weeks after those lectures.

### Summary

Nathan Söderblom was honored with the highest academic honors at the Sorbonne, and, when he returned to Sweden, he became the first to occupy the chair of chief professor in the religious history department. As archbishop, he also served as vice chancellor of the University of Uppsala. Söderblom's influence was not restricted to Sweden or Scandinavia. The 1925 Stockholm Conference was a seminal conference for the international ecumenical movement, and he was a dominant figure at that meeting. As one of the founding fathers and pioneers, he sought cooperation of all Christian denominations in solving social problems and in serving society without consideration of doctrinal differences. Largely because of his work, the Universal Christian Council on Life and Work came into being. This movement was one of two that in 1948 merged in the World Council of Churches.

Söderblom did not perceive himself as merely archbishop of Uppsala; his parish was the world. He envisioned a united Christendom providing social justice and international peace. For these efforts, he was the first Swedish churchman to receive the Nobel Peace Prize. The reason for his being so honored was his promotion of international understanding through the church. His prominent role in the spiritual and intellectual life of Sweden was given recognition by his election to the Swedish Academy of Sciences in 1921. Ironically, this academy was one of those prescribed by Nobel as the selectors of the Nobel Prize recipients. The contributions of the archbishop were recognized before the Nobel Prize was awarded, for he was accorded honorary doctorates from eleven universities and membership in numerous learned societies.

### Bibliography

Curtis, C. J. *Contemporary Protestant Thought.* New York: Bruce, 1970. This work presents an excellent definition of Söderblom's ecumenical theology. It presents a foundation for the so-called Life and Work movement of practical Christianity that became Söderblom's preoccupation. The work includes a brief biographical sketch.

Duff, Edward. *The Social Thought of the World Council of Churches.* London and New York: Longman, 1956. This is an excellent source of the history, development, and goals of the World Council of Churches. Söderblom's stellar role as a pioneer in establishing the Conference of Life and Work is put in context with the larger World Council, or ecumenical movement.

Kaplan, Flora, comp. *Nobel Prize Winners: Charts, Indexes, Sketches.* Chicago: Nobelle, 1941. This collection of short biographies includes a brief sketch of Söderblom and the reasons for which he was awarded a Nobel Peace Prize. It includes a complete (through 1938) listing of all prize-winners.

Nobelstiftelsen. *Nobel: The Man and His Prizes*, edited by H. Schuck et al. 2d ed. New York: Elsevier, 1962. This book presents a history of Nobel, his bequests, and the selection process of recipients of this coveted award. It includes the brief relationship of the priest Söderblom and the philanthropist Nobel. Both men desired world peace, Nobel through the encouragement of peacemakers, Söderblom through the Church. Details the actions and contributions that earned the archbishop the nomination for the Peace Prize.

Pfisterer, K. Dietrich. "Söderblom." *The McGraw-Hill Encyclopedia of World Biography*, vol. 10. New York: McGraw-Hill, 1973. A brief biographical essay on Söderblom that relates the major events of his life and encapsulates his ideas. Includes a list of further reading.

Sharpe, Eric J. *Nathan Söderblom and the Study of Religion.* Chapel Hill: University of North Carolina Press, 1990. Well-written, scholarly treatment of Söderblom and his achievements.

*H. Christian Thorup*

## ALEKSANDR SOLZHENITSYN

*Born:* December 11, 1918; Kislovodsk, U.S.S.R.

*Areas of Achievement: Literature, government, politics, and social reform*

*Contribution:* One of three persons to hold honorary U.S. citizenship, Solzhenitsyn has produced a striking body of literature and has led a long, heroic life, working for freedom in the Soviet Union. His nomination for the Lenin Prize affected de-Stalinization, and his Nobel Prize has positively influenced East-West relations.

### Early Life

Aleksandr Isayevich Solzhenitsyn scarcely had a childhood. He was born during the Russian Civil War as White and Red armies raced back and forth across the Caucasus, where his family had long resided. His understanding of family history and of the father who died in a freak hunting accident six months before Solzhenitsyn was born are detailed in *Avgust chetyrnadtsatogo* (1971, 1983; *August 1914*, 1971, 1989). His earliest memory (1921) is of Soviet soldiers looting a church. Growing up fatherless and with a mother (born Taissa Zakharovna Shcherbak) struggling to hold any kind of a job—her family's wealth, although confiscated, made her "a social alien"—encouraged in Solzhenitsyn precocity, self-reliance, and self-discipline. Living in harsh circumstances was valuable preparation for the rigors of war and the camps. Private penury merged with public penury after termination of the New Economic Policy in 1928, giving Solzhenitsyn another reason to feel sorry for the Soviet Union (the reason his father had enlisted) and to be attracted to the vision of Leninism.

Solzhenitsyn labored harder on household chores than most boys, read voraciously, always made top marks in school in Rostov-on-Don, and wrote tales and journals regularly from age ten. He read Leo Tolstoy's *Voyna i mir* (1865-1869; *War and Peace*, 1886) ten times and drank in Vladimir Dahl's collection of Russian proverbs. Other of his favorites were William Shakespeare, Friedrich Schiller, Charles Dickens, Jack London, and the Russian poet Sergei Yesenin. Though Solzhenitsyn idolized Tolstoy, he termed Maxim Gorky Russia's greatest writer. In 1936, Solzhenitsyn began to research World War I in preparation for a history of the Russian Revolution, his main task in life, as he had known from early childhood.

Top marks earned for Solzhenitsyn admittance to the University of Rostov on scholarship and without entrance examinations or inquiry into his social origins, and continued top marks along with his activities in Komosol (youth wing of the Communist Party) earned for him a Stalin scholarship paying two and a half times as much. In the summer of 1939, he was enrolled in the Moscow Institute of Literature, Philosophy, and History (MILFI), and he was moved by his first visit to that city. On April 27, 1940, he married fellow-student Natalia Reshetovskaya. He was graduated from the University of Rostov in June, 1941, and applied for a position as a village schoolmaster instead of for one of the prestigious positions that his top marks warranted. On June 22, 1941, war was declared. Solzhenitsyn was not permitted to enlist, because of an old groin injury, but total mobilization on October 16, 1941, made him a private soldier.

### Life's Work

Solzhenitsyn's military career began as a farce and

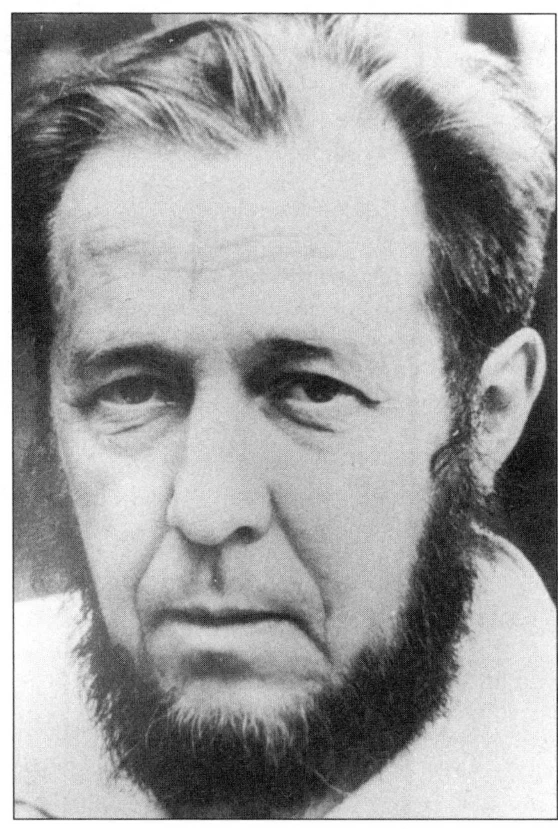

ended as a tragedy, but he regarded it as a central part of his life's work. He was defending the Soviet Union and Leninism, and he studied and wrote, not knowing his letters were being intercepted. Assigned to the Seventy-fourth Horse-Drawn Transport Battalion of the Stalingrad Command, Solzhenitsyn spent the winter mostly mucking stables. On March 22, 1942, he learned through an old friend of the need of a courier to Stalingrad. Solzhenitsyn volunteered and managed to get assigned to artillery school. Commissioned as a lieutenant in October, 1942, Solzhenitsyn served in several locations through the winter and in April, 1943, was assigned to Orel, about midway between Rostov and Moscow. Now a battery commander, he was always on the front lines, because his mission was to locate enemy gun positions by measuring their sounds. He served in the decisive Battle of Orel in July, 1943, was decorated with the Order of the Patriotic War, and pursued the Germans toward Poland. The Soviets crossed the Dnieper River in February, 1944. Solzhenitsyn was wounded and promoted to captain, and the advance continued. "The Last Offensive," aimed at Berlin, began in January, 1945. Solzhenitsyn, disobeying Stalin's orders to loot everything in just revenge, felt sympathy for conquered peoples and restrained his battery, although he did take some rare Russian books from a house and appropriated stacks of white, blank paper from a Prussian post office. Solzhenitsyn was stunned by the sight of liberated Soviet prisoners of war and was totally shocked on February 9, 1945, to be summoned to his commanding general's office, where he was arrested by Smersh agents and stripped of his insignia.

Solzhenitsyn arrived at the famous Lubyanka Prison in Moscow on February 20, 1945, where procedures for receiving prisoners had been crafted into a fine art over twenty-five years. The process is described in the arrest of Volodin at the end of *V kruge pervom* (1968; *The First Circle*, 1968). Solzhenitsyn was charged with creating anti-Soviet propaganda (disparaging remarks about Joseph Stalin had been found in his letters) and of founding a hostile organization. On July 27, 1945, he was sentenced to eight years by the Special Court.

Solzhenitsyn served eight years in various prison camps, which are immortalized in *The First Circle*, the three volumes of *Arkhipelag GULag, 1918-1956: Opyt Khudozhestvennogo issledovaniya* (1973-1975; *The Gulag Archipelago, 1918-1956: An Experiment in Literary Investigation*, 1974-1978), and other writings. Like Gleb Nerzhin in *The First Circle*, he accommodated himself to camp society. Seen from outside, Nerzhin's life was unhappy—nearly hopeless—but he was secretly happy in that unhappiness. In the camps he got to know people and events he could have learned nowhere else. Solzhenitsyn's sentence was officially ended February 9, 1953, and he was exiled in perpetuity to Kok Terek, Kazakhstan, 250 miles from China. He slept in ecstasy in the open on March 5, 1953, heard of Stalin's death the next day, and wrote the poem "The Fifth of March." After administrative technicalities, in May, 1953, he began teaching math, physics, and astronomy in the high school at Kok Terek, population four thousand, about equally divided between natives and exiles. His teaching was interrupted at the end of 1953 by the diagnosis of cancer and by his two treatments in Tashkent, a thousand miles to the west, in 1954. It is not known how literally autobiographical the case of Oleg Kostogolotov in *Rakovy Korpus* (1968; *Cancer Ward*, 1968) is, but his own tumor was most serious (one had been removed in the camps) and treatment and recovery were difficult.

The political climate changed in 1956, beginning with the secret speech of First Secretary Nikita S. Khrushchev admitting crimes of Stalin and announcing the end of Gulag and exile. In April, 1956, Solzhenitsyn's sentence and exile were ended. He went to Moscow and was amazed to find bureaucrats almost friendly and to be able to see his file in Lubyanka Prison and to see a prosecutor laugh at it. Solzhenitsyn found a teaching job in Torfoproduct on the rail line a hundred miles east of Moscow. Natalia joined him there, and they were remarried February 2, 1957. In 1958, Boris Pasternak was awarded the Nobel Prize, and there was a furor in the Soviet Union. While polishing *The First Circle*, Solzhenitsyn began a tale entitled "One Day in the Life of a School Teacher"—Solzhenitsyn was then an excellent and happy teacher—but in May, 1959, he changed the title to *Shch-854* and the scene to a labor camp in Ekibastuz. He completed it in six weeks, burned the drafts, and hid the finished copy. His first published writing "Post Office Curiosities," on the failings of the Soviet postal service, appeared in *Priokskaya Pravda* in Ryazan in March, 1959, and a year later the newspaper *Gulok* published his article on rail service. Times were changing, yet *Literaturnaya Gazeta*, the organ of the Union of

Soviet Writers, and other periodicals rejected his work. Solzhenitsyn had read the journal *Novy mir* since December, 1953, when an article entitled "On Sincerity in Literature" had appeared in it and on November 4, 1961, he took *Shch-854* to *Novy mir* in Moscow. The editor of *Novy mir* loved the story. How it became *Odin den' Ivana Denisovicha* (1962; *One Day in the Life of Ivan Denisovich*, 1963) and got on Khrushchev's desk is legendary and embellished, but it was printed in *Novy mir* in November, 1962, and was nominated for the Lenin Prize in 1964. The vote was close, but conservatives, fearing that de-Stalinization was proceeding too rapidly, struck it from the list. Even so, Solzhenitsyn was now famous, and publishers scrambled for his works. Publication of his works in the Soviet Union, however, was denied.

Solzhenitsyn's works circulated in *samizdat* (underground literary network), *The First Circle* and *Cancer Ward* were published in the West without authorization, and he was expelled from the Union of Soviet Writers in 1969. He refused to go to Sweden in 1970 to receive his Nobel Prize in fear of not being readmitted to the Soviet Union. In 1974, he was arrested and exiled. After a brief time in West Germany, he moved to Zurich, Switzerland. In 1976, he settled in a rural retreat in Vermont, where he made his home in closely guarded privacy with his second wife, Natalia Svetlova (they had met in 1967), until returning to his homeland in 1994 following the collapse of the Soviet Union.

While in exile, Solzhenitsyn began working on a project that he first conceived in 1937, when he was still in his teens: a multivolume fictional chronicle of Russian history in the years leading up to the Revolution of 1917. To write this massive work, collectively entitled *Krasnoe koleso* (*The Red Wheel*), he assembled a historical archive that includes documents of all kinds from that period. The first installment, or "knot" (*uzel*), to use Solzhenitsyn's own term, is the revised version of *August 1914*, which is more than half again the length of the original. The second knot, *Oktiabr shestnadtsatogo* (1984; October, 1916), was actually published after the third, *Mart semnadtsatogo* (1983; March, 1917). *Aprel' semnadtsatogo* appeared in 1991. In general, critical reaction to this ambitious work, which the author regards as his most important, has been very negative. In response, Solzhenitsyn has said that he is writing for readers fifty or a hundred years in the future.

**Summary**

Students and critics will be sorting out Solzhenitsyn's distinctive contributions for some time to come. The volume of his works, the copies sold, and the different languages into which his works have been translated are enormous and growing. Solzhenitsyn is a poet and a prophet; he is a master storyteller with an incredible capacity for details; he is accomplished in many genres; and he has a mission to tell the truth about what happened in the Soviet Union in his lifetime. Solzhenitsyn believes that his experiences and knowledge of eyewitness sources justify the placing of *August 1914* and subsequent volumes in a category beyond historical fiction. Perhaps critics will invent a genre or perhaps Solzhenitsyn will remain his own genre.

**Bibliography**

Allaback, Steven. *Alexander Solzhenitsyn.* New York: Taplinger, 1978. A short discussion of Solzhenitsyn's four best-known works, this work provides an easy way to become acquainted with the basics of these stories by Solzhenitsyn.

Berman, Ronald, ed. *Solzhenitsyn at Harvard: The Address, Twelve Early Responses, and Six Later Reflections.* Washington, D.C.: Ethics and Public Policy Center, 1980. This work is important to any student of world affairs. Most Americans were hurt that the famous victim of Soviet dictatorship did not love the United States as much as he hated dictatorship. Most of Solzhenitsyn's points are probably more valid than they were ten years ago; much of the criticism is less relevant.

Brown, Edward J. *Russian Literature Since the Revolution.* Rev. ed. Cambridge, Mass.: Harvard University Press, 1982. Describes the literary environment in which Solzhenitsyn wrote and provides helpful background and context. Solzhenitsyn's prose is discussed. Contains a selected bibliography.

Burg, David, and George Feifer. *Solzhenitsyn.* London: Hoddder and Stoughton, and New York: Stein and Day, 1972. The best early biography, clearly written and easy to read. Written while Solzhenitsyn was still in Russia, so it is incomplete in several respects. Includes a short bibliography, eight pages of illustrations, and a very helpful chronology.

Clément, Olivier. *The Spirit of Solzhenitsyn.* Translated by Sarah Fawcett and Paul Burns. London: Search Press, andd New York: Barnes and Noble, 1976. A thought-provoking thesis on the universality of Solzhenitsyn seeing him as speaking for every man, for everyone's freedom to speak the truth.

Dunlop, John B., Richard S. Haugh, and Alexis Klimoff, eds. *Aleksandr Solzhenitsyn: Critical Essays and Documentary Materials.* 2d ed. New York: Collier, 1975.

Dunlop, John B., Richard S. Haugh, and Michael Nicholson, eds. *Solzhenitsyn in Exile: Critical Essays and Documentary Materials.* Stanford, Calif.: Hoover, 1985. These works constitute an excellent source for the serious student. Contains a select bibliography.

Medvedev, Roy. "A Prophet and His Country . . . " *Russian Life* 40, no. 11 (November, 1997). The author discusses the life and works of Solzhenitsyn.

Scammell, Michael. *Solzhenitsyn: A Biography.* New York: Norton, 1984; London: Hutchinson, 1985. As close to a definitive biography as can be done of a living and working writer in only a thousand pages. Thoroughly researched, including interviews with Solzhenitsyn, and remarkably dispassionate in treating controversies. Very helpful in translating and explaining terms and things Russian. Includes an excellent bibliography and an excellent index.

Yakolev, Yegor, et al. "Solzhenitsyn Turns 80: Tributes, Appraisals." *Current Digest of the Post-Soviet Press* 50, no. 50 (January 30, 1999). Considers the tributes presented by Russian journalists on Solzhenitzyn's eightieth birthday.

*Frederic M. Crawford*

# GEORGES SOREL

*Born:* November 2, 1847; Cherbourg, France
*Died:* August 30, 1922; Boulogne-sur-Seine, France
*Areas of Achievement:* Social reform and philosophy
*Contribution:* Sorel was the leading spokesman for revolutionary syndicalism in the first two decades of the twentieth century.

## Early Life

Georges-Eugène Sorel was born in Cherbourg, Normandy, in the coastal region of western France, on November 2, 1847. His parents were Catholic and middle-class; his father was the director of a business concern, and his mother was the daughter of an army officer. Georges, the second of three sons, had a traditional education with an emphasis on the utilitarian rather than the philosophical. School records indicate that he did especially well in mathematics. The capstone of this was his graduation from the École Technique in 1867. He then worked as a civil engineer for the government for the next twenty-five years in the Department of Roads and Bridges. Most of these years were spent outside Paris in Corsica, Algeria, and in Perpignan.

As was the case with most young men of his generation in France, Sorel was deeply disturbed by the French defeat in the Franco-Prussian War of 1870-1871. The crisis was compounded by the bloodshed and violence of the civil war that followed; the suppression of the Paris Commune had a lasting effect on Sorel's concept of politics and society.

Sorel took early retirement from his government job in 1892, rejected his pension, and devoted the remainder of his life to writing at his home in Boulogne-sur-Seine near Paris. The ideas expressed by Sorel in the next thirty years were shaped by his own background in engineering, by his twenty-year association with Marie David, and by his reading of the works of Alexis de Tocqueville, Pierre Proudhon, and Karl Marx. Sorel, the student of the proletariat, got to know the proletariat intimately from 1875 until 1897 in the person of Marie David. She was, he once said, part of his existence as a socialist writer. His first work, published before his retirement, *Le Procès de Socrate* (1889; the trial of Socrates) was closer to the Tocqueville tradition, but in his second publication, *D'Aristote à Marx* (1894; from Aristotle to Marx), Sorel was moving toward socialism.

## Life's Work

The major crisis of French politics that attracted the interest of all writers in the 1890's was the Dreyfus affair. Sorel joined with other radicals and socialists to defend Alfred Dreyfus, who was unjustly accused of selling military secrets to the Germans. After a ten-year struggle in the courts and in the press, Dreyfus was exonerated and his defenders triumphant. Sorel, however, did not see this victory in the same light as did Jean Jaurès and many other socialists. Socialist politicians were, Sorel believed, as corrupt and deceitful as bourgeois politicians. What was needed was a complete transformation of society through class war and the general strike. The working class was now ready to seize power for itself.

By the turn of the century, Sorel was a well-known Parisian, usually seen in the Bibliothèque Nationale, at the Sorbonne, or around the office of the *Cahiers de la quinzaine*, whose editor and founder was his friend, Charles Péguy. The major theme in his own writings had become the decadence of bourgeois society. Sorel considered himself a Marxist but found himself at odds with both the orthodox Marxists and the revisionists. For Sorel, Marxism, though a useful analytical tool, was not a science. It was social poetry, a body of imprecise meanings couched in symbolic forms. The cure for modern society would not come from middle-class intellectuals such as Marx but from the *syndicats*, or trade unions. These themes are the basis of his two major works: *Les Illusions du progrès* (1908; the illusions of progress) and *Réflexions sur la violence* (1908; *Reflections on Violence*, 1912). Violence for Sorel was not simply method but morality. It was not to be confused with brute force that trampled liberty. Sorel saw violence as a creative force that rejected the immoral concessions made by most politicians.

*Reflections on Violence* remains the one successful Sorelian work out of some dozen publications. It went through several editions and printings before World War I and had considerable influence. This book stresses the importance of the "social myth"—legends of the 1789 revolution, for example, which contain the strongest inclination of a people to act. This he believed was now summed up in revolutionary syndicalism, a heroic struggle in the best interests of civilization. In this book, Sorel also labels his method of analysis, *diremp-*

*tion*, which is best translated as abstraction. *Diremption* was used to describe the relationship of institutions and society, keeping in mind that both are continually changing. This allows the investigator to isolate and examine an institution, but the distinctiveness discovered is somewhat artificial since one has to ignore temporarily the institution's interaction with its social environment to do this. Sorel's work was closely related to the origins of modern sociology as an independent discipline. He attended Émile Durkheim's defense of his doctoral dissertation in 1893, and he published critiques of Durkheim, Jean-Gabriel de Tarde, Gustave Le Bon, and Cesare Lombroso.

Sorel's call for a true social war went unanswered despite the general turmoil in the unions in France and other European countries in the decade before World War I. Instead of a social war among the classes, Europe was plunged into a war between the nations. The internationalism of socialism broke down in the face of a new fanatic wave of patriotism, which took Jaurès' life and ruined Sorel's revolutionary syndicalism. The revolution that Sorel had hoped for seemed shattered by the war, but he was enthusiastic about events in Russia and applauded the overthrow of the Romanovs in 1917. A new edition of *Reflections on Violence* was published in 1919 and dedicated to Vladimir Ilich Lenin. In approving Lenin's Bolshevik Russia (Sorel called Lenin the new Peter the Great), he was going against much of what he had said earlier about working-class leadership. Lenin's vanguard of the proletariat was not Sorelian, not even good Marxism perhaps, but Sorel was an old man desperate for some kind of change in a bourgeois, chauvinistic Europe, and so he gave the new revolution his wholehearted support.

This kind of support was never tendered to Benito Mussolini. Sorel had followed Mussolini's career both as a Marxist and as a syndicalist. He had as early as 1912 predicted victory for Mussolini's faction, but Mussolini's subsequent identification with Italian nationalism and the war saw their paths diverge. Nevertheless Sorel did not oppose Mussolini in the same sense that his friend and longtime correspondent, Benedetto Croce, did. Sorel did not share Croce's admiration for the old Italian liberal government and believed that Mussolini, like Lenin, was an extraordinary man. Mussolini claimed at one time that he was a disciple of Sorel, but Sorel never acknowledged this. Whether Sorel would ever have approved the new Fascist Italy is impossible to say, since he died two months before Mussolini actually came to power in October, 1922. The considered opinion of most commentators today is that Sorel would not have supported Fascism. He may have been a critic of democracy, but he loved liberty and he was careful to make a distinction between the two. Liberty would best be preserved by the *syndicats* that he had proposed in his earlier writings. The *syndicats* were designed to help the worker realize his potential in the political and socioeconomic spheres. The *syndicat* was at the heart of Sorel's concept of proletarian socialism; he sometimes compared the role of the *syndicats* to the role of the monasteries in the early history of the Church. Mussolini's syndicats were controlled by the middle-class capitalists in union with the Fascist state and did not further liberty.

Sorel's reputation has suffered partly from these suspicions about his link to Communism and to Fascism but mainly from his attacks on elitists and intellectuals. Unfortunately for Sorel, it was the intellectuals, not the proletariat, who would pass judgment in print on his career and his contribution to society. They were bound to have their revenge. So the legend of the guru of terrorism and totalitarianism was born; the *Reflections on Violence* was posited as their bible.

### Summary

Interpretations of *Reflections on Violence* and of Georges Sorel's ideas in general have ranged widely from outright condemnation by many who have been quick to label and to classify, to praise from others who valued Sorel's insights into the nature of revolution and the relationship between thought and action. Closely related to this is the question of Sorel's place in the history of political thought. He was certainly closer to the Left than the Right, despite his lukewarm support of the Third French Republic and a brief flirtation with Charles Maurras's movement called Action Française. Sorel was above all else an independent thinker, a kind of "wild Marxist" who never fully agreed with anyone else. There were two basic themes in all he wrote: first, a rejection of bourgeois society and bourgeois values, and second, a rejection of the supreme role of reason and of the intellect. The anti-intellectualism of Sorel was first developed in his book on Socrates. Socrates was not a hero for the people but a man like John Calvin, who tried to force his ideas on others. Sorel carried this argument over to apply to most of the politicians and the writers of his day. Government by the totality of its citizens was the ideal, not government by the few members of the intelligentsia.

**Bibliography**

Curtis, Michael. *Three Against the Third Republic: Sorel, Barrès, and Maurras*. Princeton, N.J.: Princeton University Press, 1959. Contrasting the leaders of the Left and the Right, Curtis provides insights into the complexities of Sorel's views and concludes that Sorel was inconsistent, moving from Marxism to finally ally himself with nationalists and monarchists.

Horowitz, Irving L. *Radicalism and the Revolt Against Reason: The Social Theories of Georges Sorel*. London: Routledge, and New York: Humanities Press, 1961. A penetrating analysis of Sorel's basic ideas, but the book is difficult to read owing to the profusion of names. The inclusion of the author's translation of Sorel's *La Décomposition du Marxisme* (1908; *The Decomposition of Marxism*) is helpful.

Humphrey, Richard. *Georges Sorel: Prophet Without Honour.* Cambridge, Mass.: Harvard University Press, 1951. The author makes a convincing case that Sorel should not be viewed as an advocate of violence or as the ideological source of Bolshevism or Fascism. He does an excellent job of presenting the essential Sorel, the "metaphysician of syndicalism," who searched all of his life for a humane social morality.

Jennings, J. R. *Georges Sorel: The Character and Development of His Thought*. London: Macmillan, and New York: St. Martin's Press, 1985. Most recent assessment of Sorel's ideas and influence. Scholarly study that tries to explain the many transitions in Sorel's life and work. Sorel, he concludes, had a tendency to pluralize rather than to simplify or unify.

Meisel, James. *The Genesis of George Sorel*. Ann Arbor, Mich.: Wahr, 1951. This doctoral thesis turned into a book by an obscure publisher has value if one overlooks the pretentiousness of the author. Especially good on the correspondence of Sorel with Croce, Robert Michels, and other intellectuals of the day.

Portis, Larry. *Georges Sorel*. London: Pluto Press, 1980. This book was written for a Marxist audience and places Sorel clearly in that tradition. He sees Sorel and Sartre as the most profound French Marxists and calls Sorel's revolutionary syndicalism the most legitimate realization of a Marxist revolutionary strategy.

Roth, Jack J. *The Cult of Violence: Sorel and the Sorelians*. Berkeley: University of California Press, 1980. Best single volume on the Sorelians—syndicalists, integral nationalists, Fascists—all advocates of violence and direct action, who claimed Sorel as their master.

Vernon, Richard. *Commitment and Change: Georges Sorel and the Idea of Revolution*. Toronto: University of Toronto Press, 1978. One of the best discussions of Sorel's ideas and the influence of Henri Bergson and Proudhon on Sorel. The author fails to examine fully Sorel's concept of revolution. Camus is seen as Sorel's successor.

*Norbert J. Gossman*

# JOHN PHILIP SOUSA

*Born:* November 6, 1854; Washington, D.C.
*Died:* March 6, 1932; Reading, Pennsylvania
*Areas of Achievement:* Music and literature
*Contribution:* Sousa profoundly affected the development of American musical taste. One of his era's finest bandmasters, he was renowned as a composer of infectious marches and other musical pieces and was, at one time, the most popular musician in the world.

## Early Life

John Philip Sousa was born November 6, 1854, in Washington, D.C. He was the oldest boy among ten children born to Maria Elisabeth Trinkhaus, a Bavarian immigrant, and John Antonio Sousa, born in Spain of Portuguese descent. The senior Sousa, who played the trombone in the United States Marine Band and in marching bands of the Civil War, influenced his son's love of band music profoundly. The boy began music lessons at age six and was later enrolled in the Esputa Conservatory of Music in Washington, where he studied violin, piano, winds, and brass. He also took trombone lessons with his father. At age eleven, as first violinist, Sousa formed a quadrille dance orchestra with seven men. When Sousa was thirteen, his father enlisted him in the United States Marine Band as an apprentice musician to dissuade the boy from joining a circus band. Concurrently, Sousa took private theory and violin lessons with George Felix Benkert. By age twenty, he was playing violin in Benkert's small symphony and in the Ford's Theater orchestra, as well as conducting and playing first violin with the Washington Theatre Comique.

Sousa continued to play with the marines for seven years. Moving to Philadelphia, he won a position to play first violin in the 1876 Centennial Exhibition orchestra, which for a time was conducted by Jacques Offenbach. Sousa was also influenced by the conducting styles of Theodore Thomas and Patrick S. Gilmore. Sousa's natural understanding of composition was further developed through his work as an arranger for two music publishers in Philadelphia, J. M. Stoddart and Co., and W. F. Shaw Publishing Co. In addition to private teaching, he directed an amateur opera company, which specialized in the works of Gilbert and Sullivan. These experiences in Philadelphia developed for him a growing reputation and culminated in his decision to devote his talents to commercial entertainment. In 1879, he married Jane van Middlesworth Bellis, a soprano in the opera company and the daughter of a carpenter. The next year, the couple moved to Washington, D.C.; Sousa had accepted the directorship of the United States Marine Band from Corps officials, who had been impressed with his work in Philadelphia. The Sousas would have three children: John Philip, Jr., Jane Priscilla, and Helen.

## Life's Work

Sousa's unprecedented success as a bandmaster began upon his second enlistment in the Marine Corps in 1880. For the next twelve years, he rigidly directed the Marine Band, turning it into a professional organization of national renown. During this time, Sousa composed some of his most famous marches: *The Gladiator* (1886); *Semper Fidelis* (1888), named for the Marine motto Always Faithful and adopted by the Corps as its official march; and *The Washington Post* (1889), which received internation-

al popularity and won for its composer the title "The March King." Sousa's directorship was further distinguished with the Marine Band's first national tours in 1891 and 1892 and when the band made cylinder recordings for Columbia Phonograph Co. in 1890-1892, recordings which were among the first ever produced.

In 1892, David Blakely, a talented promoter who handled the Marine Band's 1891 tour and had formerly managed Gilmore's renowned band, advised Sousa to resign from the Corps and form his own band. As the new organization's manager and financier, Blakely promised the bandmaster six thousand dollars a year—four times his annual military salary—plus twenty percent of all profits. He accepted, and in the summer of 1892 formed Sousa's New Marine Band. Soon renamed Sousa's Grand Concert Band, the organization premiered September 26, 1892, in Plainfield, New Jersey. In early 1893, the New Jersey Phonograph Co. (Newark) began recording the new band, and in time, the group recorded in both cylinder and disk technologies for all the major companies, including Columbia, the National Phonograph Co. (of Thomas Edison), and the Victor Talking Machine Co. The new band found early success by playing in the 1893 Chicago World's Fair, the 1896 Cotton State's Exposition in Atlanta, the 1901 Pan American Exposition in Buffalo, New York, the 1904 St. Louis World's Fair, and annually during summers at the Manhattan Beach Hotel resort in Brooklyn. By 1897, Sousa's annual income was approximately fifty thousand dollars.

The Sousa Concert Band, which averaged seventy members after 1897, was distinguished by the virtuosity of its players, many of whom were the eminent soloists of their day: coronetists Herbert L. Clarke and Frank Simon, "Paganini of the Trombone" Arthur W. Pryor, tuba player William J. Bell, "Saxophone King" E. A. Lefebre, soprano Estelle Liebling, violinist Maud Powell, euphonium player Simone Mantia, and bass drum legend Gus Helmecke. Their conductor directed with a rigid professionalism and demanded perfection. He claimed to know precisely what each member of the band was doing each second during a performance, because it was he who commanded them to action. His every arm movement or finger twitch was a directive to an individual player or to the group.

A short man with a high-pitched voice, piercing black eyes, and a subtle wit, Sousa was beloved and respected by his band. He was repelled by profanity and religious prejudice and enjoyed a reputation as a wholesome, healthy man's man who delighted in work. Frail as a child, he excelled in sports, especially trapshooting, horseback riding, and baseball (the Sousa Band had its own team). Distinctive in appearance, the bandmaster wore gold-rimmed glasses and dressed, like the players in his band, in immaculate uniforms. For most of his adult life, Sousa wore a beard, and while he insisted on new white kidskin gloves for almost every performance, he used inexpensive wooden batons. Strong-willed, he appeared before his adoring public only ten weeks after breaking his neck in a fall from a horse, leading people to believe that he had only broken his arm.

The Sousa Band and its conductor, much like one of the era's presidents, Theodore Roosevelt, quickly achieved the phenomenon of celebrity and were closely associated with American nationalism. They played to capacity audiences throughout the band's thirty-nine-year existence and traveled more than a million miles in annual North American tours, four European tours (1900, 1901, 1903, 1905), and a world tour in 1910-1911. The Sousa Band was a concert band—it marched only seven times in its existence. The band traveled six to ten months each year, frequently appearing in two towns per day. In addition to the tours were the regular summer season concerts at Ocean Grove, New Jersey, the New York Hippodrome, and Willow Grove, Pennsylvania. Weekly attendance in New York alone from 1911 to 1914 exceeded sixty thousand. The concerts were fast-paced; the bandmaster would allow only twenty to thirty seconds to lapse between each piece until intermissions. Yet the concerts often lasted three hours, and true to Sousa's preference for entertainment over education, the program was generous with light tunes and many encores, usually Sousa pieces. Nevertheless, he exposed many Americans for the first time to the music of Richard Wagner, Gioacchino Antonio Rossini, Richard Strauss, Edward Elgar, and other classical composers.

The phenomenal popularity of Sousa and his band corresponds closely with the rise of American imperialism and cultural nationalism. Above all, Sousa was a patriot, evidenced even in the titles of his marches: *America First* (1916), *The Invincible Eagle* (1901), *The Liberty Bell* (1893), and of course, *The Stars and Stripes Forever* (1896), which was first heard at the George Washington Centennial, May 14, 1897, with President William McKinley attending. The public's intoxication with this piece was immediate and soon it became a national symbol, especially during the Spanish American War in 1898. Congress twice entertained resolutions to make it the national anthem. The piece was played at least once in every future Sousa Band concert; audiences often demanded it several times.

When the United States was drawn into World War I in 1917, Sousa, at age sixty-two, enlisted as a lieutenant in the United States Naval Reserve to lead the navy band on national tours to support the Red Cross, recruitment, and Liberty Loan bonds. During the summers, he was allowed leave to tour with his own band. The sparkle and verve of Sousa's compositions and performances raised more than twenty-one million dollars for the war effort. After the war, Sousa was promoted to lieutenant commander and released from duty, but his audiences saw him in his uniform for most of his remaining concerts. The Sousa Band continued to tour into the 1920's, though their tours were tapering off by 1926 and were much less frequent in 1929. The band broke up in 1931 after the Great Depression no longer made concerts profitable. On March 6, 1932, the March King died of a heart attack in Reading, Pennsylvania, while preparing for a guest appearance. After lying in state in the Marine Barracks, Washington, District of Columbia, his body was buried in the Congressional Cemetery.

## Summary

Sousa's popularity rested upon his musical genius and disciplined conducting and upon the virtuosity of his musicians. His belief in musical variety pleased most everyone, and his sensitivity to audience response and use of encores after each programmed piece easily cultivated enthusiasm. Yet the phenomenon of his celebrity was also a consequence of the time in which he lived: Sousa was a symbol of patriotism, discipline, and Victorian respectability and order in an age of rapid social change. His popularity rose concurrently with the rise of American imperialism and commercialism. Sousa's concerts provided a vibrant outlet for nationalism while enhancing American prestige, for he stressed American composers and uplifted the reputation of American music. His image was much the result of the mass publicity efforts and promotional techniques of professional managers such as David Blakely, who advertised his client with illustrated posters, magazine and newspaper articles, photographs, and local interviews.

In an age preceding radio and the high-fidelity phonograph, Sousa provided countless Americans with their first experience of professional music. Although his bands' recorded works were pioneer efforts in the development of the phonograph, Sousa was openly hostile toward mechanically reproduced music. He standardized the march form, though his output was hardly limited to that genre. Indeed, his oeuvre shows not only variety but also immense productivity: 136 marches, fifteen operettas, seventy songs, eleven waltzes, thirteen dances, eleven suites, twenty-seven fantasies, fourteen humoresques, twelve trumpet and drum pieces, twenty-five miscellaneous pieces, and 322 arrangements and transcriptions. A man of letters, Sousa also wrote seven books, including an autobiography and three novels, and 132 journalistic articles.

Sousa's philosophy of music centered on a belief that entertainment was of more real value than a technical education in music appreciation. His mission, as he saw it, was "to move all America, while busied in its various pursuits, by the power of direct and simple music. I wanted to make a music for the people, a music to be grasped at once." He chose as his medium the concert band at a time when bands and band music were Americans' favorite sources of musical expression; the march was not only a popular parade and military piece but also a fashionable song, hymn, and dance number. Sousa consciously designed his career to cater to the millions rather than to the few. Ironically, he was critical of both the phonograph and the radio (which enabled popular entertainers such as Sousa to reach the widest possible audience) because, for him, music had to be live. The spirit of music—the interaction between audience and performers—could not be recorded and was in danger of being lost through mechanical reproduction. With Victor Herbert, he also led the fight in 1909 to convince Congress to pass a new copyright law that forced recording companies to pay royalties to composers upon the sale of their recorded pieces.

Sousa's legacy is many-faceted. He aided the development of bands in high schools not only through inspirational example but also through financial contributions, by donating royalties from *The Northern Pines* (1931) to a scholarship fund for the National High School Orchestra and Band Camp at Interlochen, Michigan. He provided the fledgling recording industry with celebrity sales but also helped secure composers' rights regarding royalty payments. He contributed significantly to

American musical theater with his operettas. The straight-belled tuba, dubbed the "sousaphone," was his design. He helped to bring ragtime to Europe and make jazz respectable in America. He contributed to the rise of mass publicity and commercialism, aided the development of American musical culture, and discouraged musical snobbery. The Sousa Band alumni effectively influenced the development of bands and band music in the United States long after his death. His music, aural artifacts that provide a living link to a younger America growing to world power, remains infectious to modern audiences, who find their own toes and fingers unalterably moved to tapping during concerts. The American composer William Schuman called Sousa the American spirit in music, able to invoke shared inheritances in his audiences and allow them a sense of self-recognition. This, perhaps, is Sousa's most significant, yet most ambiguous, legacy.

**Bibliography**


Bierley, Paul E. *John Philip Sousa: American Phenomenon*. New York: Appleton-Century-Crofts, 1973. The best single work on the composer and his band, but obviously written by a Sousa devotee. Examines the Sousa phenomenon within the context of the rise of American nationalism. Well indexed, extensively illustrated, contains a good bibliography and useful appendices outlining Sousa's works, family, and military career.

———. *The Works of John Philip Sousa*. Columbus, Ohio: Integrity Press, 1984. An annotated bibliography of Sousa's complete writings—the musical compositions as well as his articles, novels, and other works. Excellent supplemental reading to help gauge Sousa's literary contribution; provides useful insight into the variety of musical pieces.

Danner, Phyllis. "John Philip Sousa: The Illinois Collection." *Notes* 55, no. 1 (September, 1998). Discusses the library of military and symphonic band music left to the University of Illinois by Sousa.

Goldman, Richard Franko. *The Concert Band*. New York: Rinehart, 1946. Traces the development of the concert band, its instrumentation and music, and analyzes the functions of the various instruments. A useful reference that puts the Sousa Band into context with the concert band tradition. Somewhat technical and audience-specific. Includes a bibliography.

Helmecke, August, et al. "Sousa: A Symposium." *The Instrumentalist* 5 (March, April, 1951): 12-17, 34-37. A variety of articles written by Sousa family and band alumni as an outgrowth of a Sousa Band clinic at the University of New Hampshire, January 13, 1951, devoted to preserving and recapturing the composer's style and intent.

Hess, Carol A. "John Philip Sousa's 'El Capitan': Political Appropriation and the Spanish-American War." *American Music* 16, no. 1 (Spring 1998). Discusses Souza's operetta, "El Capitan," a popular piece due to its pro-U.S. message in a time of anti-Hispanic sentiment.

Lingg, Ann M. *John Philip Sousa*. New York: Holt, 1954. Written for the high school audience, reads well, and recounts Sousa's accomplishments as a musician. Useful for gaining insight into the bandmaster's era but is a laudatory account and not deeply analytical. Bibliography included.

Newsom, Jon, ed. *Perspectives on John Philip Sousa*. Washington, D.C.: Library of Congress, 1983. A useful collection of articles that will help bring about a better understanding of Sousa's great talent and popularity, his era, and the contribution of David Blakely, manager of the Sousa Band. Authors include composer William Schuman, John Philip Sousa III, musicologists James R. Smart and Pauline Norton, and historians Frederick Fennell, Margaret L. Brown, and Neil Harris. Extensively illustrated and documented.

Quayle, Nolbert Hunt. "Stars and Stripes Forever: Memories of Sousa and His Men." *The Instrumentalist* 9 (September, October, November, December, 1954) and 10 (January, February, March, April, 1955). A long-running series of articles about Sousa Band members and their era. Aids in understanding the personality of the band and the virtuosity of the players. Includes illustrations.

Schwartz, Harry Wayne. *Bands of America*. New York: Doubleday, 1957. A colorful, balanced, and well-researched account of American bands at the turn of the century. Analysis of Sousa and his contemporaries, such as Gilmore, Pryor, Allesandro Liberati, some of whom were Sousa Band alumni. Treats the decline of band popularity and offers technical information about the instrumental organization of the various bands. Includes a good index, a bibliography, and illustrations.

Smart, James, R., comp. *The Sousa Band: A Discography.* Washington, D.C.: Library of Congress, 1970. Chronicles Sousa's recording history with the Marine Band, the Sousa Band, and the Rapid Transit Co. Band on cylinder and disk technologies. The discography is annotated. Instructive account of Sousa and his relationship with the phonograph and early recording industry. Indexed by composers, conductors, and soloists.

Sousa, John Philip. *Marching Along*. Rev. ed. Westerville, Ohio: Integrity Press, 1994. The March King's own story. Useful insight into Sousa's life and philosophy, but primarily offers a collection of memories rather than any attempt at analysis. Nevertheless, a primary source. Chronology can become confusing, but the book is good reading. It is illustrated.

*Craig H. Roell*

# WOLE SOYINKA

*Born:* July 13, 1934; Abeokuta, Nigeria
*Area of Achievement:* Literature
*Contribution:* The first African ever to win the Nobel Prize in Literature, Soyinka is generally held to be Nigeria's foremost contemporary dramatist and possibly the most influential of all black African playwrights. Although he has earned high praise equally for his poetry, fiction, and literary criticism, it is as a playwright that Soyinka has distinguished himself.

## Early Life

Akinwande Oluwole Soyinka (pronounced Shoy-ink-a) was born July 13, 1934, in Abeokuta in Western Nigeria, to Ayo and Eniola Soyinka. His mother was a successful businesswoman, his father the headmaster of the local missionary school, which Soyinka attended as a child. Describing his earliest memories in an autobiographical work, *Aké: The Years of Childhood* (1981), Soyinka remembers that his father seemed to be on a first-name basis with God; he recalls that his mother was nicknamed "the Wild Christian," for her flamboyant faith.

The young Soyinka was exposed early to Christian ideas and English language and culture. He attended St. Peter's School and Abeokuta Grammar School in his hometown before transferring to Government College in Ibadan. His undergraduate education began at University College, Ibadan (later to become the University of Ibadan), where he studied from 1952 to 1954. Interestingly his classmates number among them such future literary giants as Chinua Achebe and Christopher Okigbo. Soyinka traveled abroad to England to complete his undergraduate degree, graduating from the University of Leeds in 1957 with a B.A. in English. It was at Leeds that he met G. Wilson Knight, a noted scholar, whose influence started Soyinka on a lifelong interest in the metaphysical and the imagistic.

After graduation, Soyinka spent two years working as a play reader at the Royal Court Theatre, where he was exposed to the experimental and innovative of some of Great Britain's best young playwrights, among them Harold Pinter, John Osborne, Samuel Beckett, and John Arden. His experience at the Royal Court rounded out his academic and professional training in drama and theater. During these years, Soyinka wrote his first plays: *The Swamp Dwellers* (1958), about one community's history; *The Invention* (1959), a one-act satire comparing the leaders of South Africa's apartheid system to mad scientists conducting horrible experiments; and *The Lion and the Jewel* (1959), a comedy. *The Invention* was performed at the Royal Court Theatre in November, 1959, as part of a program which also featured excerpts from *A Dance of the Forests* (1960). That same year, *The Swamp Dwellers* was produced in London and in Ibadan, where *The Lion and the Jewel* was also performed.

Even as a child Soyinka had felt drawn to his Yoruba roots despite the Christian environment in which he was reared and educated. His grandfather had initiated him into adulthood through the traditional ritual incisions on the wrists and ankles to prepare him to face the world. As an adult, Soyinka realized that his dream of a thriving black African theater tradition required his immersion in traditional African culture, and in 1960 he returned to Nigeria with the support of a Rockefeller Research Fellowship. Although the fellowship attached him to

the University of Ibadan, he spent much of his year as a fellow in an intensive study of Nigerian culture. He traveled widely throughout the country to participate in community rituals and traditional festivals, and he experimented with ways to combine native traditions with Western culture. At the end of his fellowship year, Soyinka accepted a position as lecturer at the University of Ife in Ibadan. Since that time, he has held various faculty positions at universities all over the world. In 1998 he returned to his homeland amid renewed hopes that the long era of military rule in Nigeria was nearing an end.

## Life's Work

Soyinka returned home to a Nigeria which had no native dramatic tradition in English. Theatrical productions were limited to William Shakespeare's plays and other English classics, or to European plays in English translation. Nothing on stage had any bearing on the average playgoer's life; the only extant Nigerian play in English was written in Elizabethan speech. In 1960, Soyinka created "The 1960 Masks," a theater company composed of professionals and civil servants who were interested—if untrained—amateurs. Formed in Lagos primarily to perform in Soyinka's *A Dance of the Forests* for Nigerians' independence year celebrations, The 1960 Masks was that country's first English-language theater company—although its amateur composition kept it from being the theater group that Soyinka had dreamed of forming. The year 1960 also saw the production of two more Soyinka plays: *The Trials of Brother Jero* and *Camwood on the Leaves*, a radio script.

Because the actors involved in The 1960 Masks were dependent for their livelihoods on their positions in the civil service and in the schools, Soyinka was hesitant about involving them in political drama for fear that their participation would cost them their careers. Consequently, in 1964, he formed the Orisun Theatre group, composed of theater professionals who could present his political revues as well as his longer plays.

For Soyinka, the decade or so from the mid-1960's to the mid-1970's proved to be a period of intense and fruitful playwriting during which he wrote many of his most important and most strongly political works for theater: *The Strong Breed* (1964), his most frequently anthologized play, is a portrayal of the individual sacrifices necessary for the atonement of communal guilt, a dramatization of the ancient scapegoat ritual; *Kongi's Harvest* (1964) is a scathing indictment of Africa's new politicians who are driven by their passion for authority; *The Road* (1965) depicts a society moving inexorably toward death and destruction; *Madmen and Specialists* (1970) focuses on the gradual deterioration of humanity, which is subjected to the rigid control of an authoritative society; *Jero's Metamorphosis* (1973) is a cynical satire on the excesses of right-wing military dictatorships; and *Death and the King's Horseman* (1976) returns to the same symbiosis of rhetoric with ritual that informs the earlier *The Strong Breed*. Two plays from this period are interesting for their fusion of Western dramatic forms with Yoruba concepts and performance elements: *The Bacchae* (1973), an adaptation of the Euripides play, changes the original ending to allow for a positive interpretation inspired by Yoruba folk ritual, and *Opera Wonyosi* (1977), which caricatures modern African despots, is taken from Bertolt Brecht's *Die Dreigroschenoper* (1928; *The Threepenny Opera*, 1949).

Although Soyinka believes—as do many of his admirers—that his Nobel Prize commemorates his dramatic work, he has also earned praise for his poetry and fiction, for his autobiographical work, as well as for his essays on literary criticism. His first collection of poetry, published early in his career, featured the long poem "Idanre" (1967), which celebrates the Yoruba god Ogun, who figures prominently in a number of Soyinka's other works, including another long poem, "Ogun Abibiman" (1977). Imprisoned for two years for his outspokenness about human rights violations, Soyinka detailed the trauma of his solitary confinement in two more collections of poetry, *Poems from Prison* (1969) and *A Shuttle in the Crypt* (1972), and in his prison diary, published in 1972 as *The Man Died*. Also a product of his own experience is *Aké: The Years of Childhood*, a warm but unsentimental memoir of his childhood.

Soyinka's two novels—unlike the rest of his literary output—have elicited strongly contradictory commentary from serious students of African literature. *The Interpreters* (1965), a hilarious exposé of decadent modern African society, is the focus of much of the controversy; while some readers believe the novel to be nothing less than a masterpiece, others point out that both the language and the structure are so convoluted and dense that whole sections of the book succeed only in confusing the reader. *Season of Anomy* (1973) is a much grimmer and more artistically successful novel that deals with the horrible consequences of the lust for power displayed by dictatorial rulers.

In the field of literary criticism, Soyinka has proven himself to be a formidable theorist and thinker with his *Myth, Literature, and the African World* (1976), a collection of essays originally delivered as lectures at the University of Cambridge, and with various individual pieces, most notably "The Fourth Stage," in which he outlines a theory of Yoruba tragedy based on Yoruba theology and concepts of existence.

Soyinka's later work is more focused on the modern world and its evils, and somehow less pervaded by traditional Yoruba cultural motifs. Nevertheless, Soyinka still displays a concern with the human race's capacity for both creation and destruction. *A Play of Giants* (1984) explores the notion of power and how it is wielded for good or evil; the play is a satire on Africa's self-appointed "presidents-for-life"—men such as Idi Amin and Jean-Bedel Bokassa—who used their power to destroy anyone who dared question their authority. A more humorous piece, *Requiem for a Futurologist* (1986), takes on television charlatans and their gullible public and proves that human beings are the potential victims of their own cleverness.

### Summary

Whatever the focus of any specific piece of his writing, Wole Soyinka manifests a passionate concern for his society and for the fate of the human race. Much of his work is political, arising from his own outspokenness against human rights violations and from his own experience—several incarcerations in Nigerian prisons, exile, and denunciation by the corrupt powers-that-be in his own country. Out of the crucible of his own life, Soyinka has distilled his most pervasive and powerful themes: the struggle for selfhood and national identity, the cost of that struggle, the need for sacrifice and purging of collective guilt in the quest for progress, the duty of the artist, and the relationship between the health of the state and individual liberties.

Awarded the Nobel Prize in Literature in 1986, Soyinka was praised by the Nobel Committee for a body of work that is "vivid, often harrowing, but also marked by an evocative, poetically intensified diction." Soyinka's work is the artistic contribution of a man who courageously shares his vision of salvation for humanity and his denunciation of oppression in spite of harassment and persecution from the very society he seeks to serve. Characteristically, he sees the Nobel Prize not as an award for his own artistry but as a recognition of the African cultural traditions that have made his work possible.

### Bibliography

Coger, Greta M. K. *Index of Subjects, Proverbs, and Themes in the Writings of Wole Soyinka.* London and New York: Greenwood Press, 1988. A valuable key to references and allusions in much of Soyinka's work. The introduction is particularly useful for its brief discussion of connections between works, for its descriptions of topics of interest to Soyinka, and for its commentary on Soyinka's use of Yoruba proverbs and rituals.

Garrett, Shawn-Marie. "A World of Amusement and Pity." *Theater* 28, no. 1 (Spring 1997). Interview with Soyinka in which he discusses the role of theater in improving multiculturalism and whether it can affect the attitudes of governments.

Gibbs, James. *Wole Soyinka.* London: Macmillan, and New York: Grove Press, 1986. Part of the Macmillan Modern Dramatists series, this is a very detailed source that follows Soyinka's career from his earliest plays. Contains some good biographical information, illustrations, a bibliography, and an index.

———, ed. *Critical Perspectives on Wole Soyinka.* Washington, D.C.: Three Continents Press, 1980; London: Heinemann, 1981. A collection of essays by various scholars on different aspects on Soyinka's work. The introduction provides a concise overview of Soyinka's life and career.

Graham-White, Anthony. *The Drama of Black Africa.* New York: French, 1974. A chronological survey of the development of a dramatic tradition in black Africa. Beginning with a chapter on "The Origins of Drama in Africa," the author points out that drama as a literary genre in Africa has its roots in the period of European colonization and that Soyinka alone of black African playwrights claims to write a new kind of drama drawn from native culture.

Jaffrey, Zia. "Wole Soyinka: 'This Regime Just Does Not Believe in Innocence.'" *The Progressive* 61, no. 8 (August, 1997). Interview with Soyinka, exiled from Nigeria since 1994 and charged with treason by its government. The winner of the 1986 Nobel Prize for literature talks of the Nigerian death squads that have targeted him.

Jones, Eldred Durosimi. *Wole Soyinka.* 3d. ed. London: Currey, and Portsmouth, N.H.: Heinemann, 1988. An introductory critical-analytical study of Soyinka's career, including biographical, cultural, and historical material essential to an appreciation and understanding of Soyinka's work.

Katrak, Ketu H. *Wole Soyinka and Modern Tragedy: A Study of Dramatic Theory and Practice.* Westport, Conn.: Greenwood Press, 1986. An analysis of the principles of Yoruba tragedy as articulated and applied by Soyinka. Katrak focuses on the major themes of Yoruba tragedy and on the influences—Yoruba and Western—on Soyinka's tragic plays.

Palmer, Eustace. *The Growth of the African Novel.* London and Exeter, N.H.: Heinemann, 1979. Includes an excellent chapter on two of Soyinka's novels—the humorous early work, *The Interpreters,* and the darker *Season of Anomy.*

*E. D. Huntley*

# PAUL-HENRI SPAAK

*Born:* January 25, 1899; Schaerbeek, Belgium
*Died:* July 31, 1972; Brussels, Belgium
*Areas of Achievement:* Government and politics
*Contribution:* A Socialist member of the Belgian Chamber of Deputies, Spaak was prime minister on three occasions and foreign minister in many cabinets. He successfully opposed the return of King Leopold III to the Belgian throne following World War II. The implementor of Belgium's policy of voluntary neutrality before the war, Spaak subsequently advocated European integration and international cooperation. He shaped treaties and served in multiple international posts in service to this goal.

## Early Life

Paul-Henri Charles Spaak's legal and political career reflected family tradition. His father, Paul Spaak, was a lawyer who turned to literature and drama and became director of the Brussels opera. His mother, Marie (Janson) Spaak, was a Socialist who in 1921 became the first woman member of the Belgian parliament. His maternal grandfather, Paul Janson, was a leader of the Belgian Liberal Party; his uncle, Paul-Émile Janson, served as prime minister for the Liberals on several occasions. Reared in a free-thinking anticlerical tradition and educated in French-language schools, as a resident of the capital city region Spaak was less involved in the linguistic divisions of his country than were the militant Flemings and Walloons of other regions. His patriotism was strong. At the age of seventeen, during World War I, he attempted to escape from German-occupied Belgium to join the remnants of the nation's army. Detained by the Germans, he was placed in a prison camp for two years.

Spaak studied law at the Free University of Brussels and was admitted to the Brussels bar, serving for some time as counselor for the commune of Forest. More athletic than his later stout figure would suggest, Spaak was a member of the 1922 Belgian Davis Cup tennis team. In 1922, he married Marguerite Malevy, the daughter of a Liberal senator. They were to have one son and two daughters. A year following Marguerite's death in 1964, Spaak married Simonne Deal.

## Life's Work

In 1921, Spaak made the crucial decision to become active in the Socialist rather than the Liberal Party. The Socialist demand for justice for all was appealing. The chance to assume a leadership position quickly also lay more with the Socialists than with the aging Liberals. By 1925, Spaak was *chef de cabinet* for a Socialist minister. A year later, however, Spaak resigned rather than serve under a Catholic Party prime minister in a cabinet of national union. He founded a small paper, the *Bataille socialiste*, and became the spokesperson of the left wing of the Socialist Party. In November, 1932, he was elected to the Belgian Chamber of Deputies from Brussels. His former paper now defunct, he and friends founded the weekly *Action socialiste.* Spaak's radical views offended moderate members of his party, and in 1934 he barely escaped expulsion from the party.

Spaak's socialism was inspired more by his own sense of justice and concern for the common person than by any deep conviction concerning Marxism. He was later to admit that his extremism was in part a tactical move to break into politics. It therefore was not difficult for Spaak to come under the partial influence of Belgian socialist theorist Henri de Man. Accepting that "integral socialism" was only a distant hope, Spaak followed Man's espousal of Keynesian economics and the view that capitalism, instead of being overthrown, should be transformed into an instrument for service to the working class. Spaak decided his left-wing predilections were not so strong as to prevent him from taking in 1935 the post of minister of transport and communications in a cabinet headed by the Catholic Paul van Zeeland. He soon was recognized for his moderation and collegial collaboration.

In 1936, in his mid-thirties, Spaak became foreign minister in a cabinet led by his uncle, Paul-Émile Janson. With the chambers and populace so riven by the Flemish-Walloon language disputes that passage of a military bill was impossible as long as the Flemings believed Belgium to be linked to French foreign policy, the cabinet opted for a policy of independent neutrality. Spaak carried out the negotiations associated with this course. In May, 1938, he became the youngest prime minister in the history of his country. He left the post in February, 1939, but again became foreign minister in November. His sharp interruption of the German ambassador's announcement of the Nazi invasion on May 10, 1940, reflected his passionate nature

and became a rallying point for Belgian pride in the dark years of World War II.

Spaak and other members of the government fled to France before the German onslaught. Spaak and the prime minister, Hubert Pierlot, disapproved of King Leopold's personal decision to remain in occupied Belgium. The Germans later moved Leopold to Austria. With a few compatriots, Spaak and Pierlot escaped to form a government-in-exile in London. Reflection there confirmed Spaak's sense of the need for international cooperation. The first step was to defeat the Axis powers. When approached by the British and Americans, desperate for uranium in their effort to construct an atomic bomb, he granted them first option for ten years on the world's prime source of uranium in the Belgian Congo.

A man of action, Spaak did what he could to support both his own country and the concept of internationalism in practical terms. During the war, he held preliminary negotiations with The Netherlands, which led to the Belgium-Netherlands-Luxembourg Economic Union (Benelux) Treaty of 1947. He was chief of the Belgian delegation to the conference at San Francisco that drafted the charter for the United Nations Organization. In 1946, Spaak was elected the first president of the United Nations General Assembly. Spaak declined the position for the assembly's 1947 session, for he had again become Belgian prime minister. He had also occupied that post briefly in March, 1946; this time he would remain in office into June, 1949.

In the months after he left the government, the Belgian royal question reached its climax. Spaak opposed bitterly any return of the monarch to the Belgian throne and led a massive street demonstration. Among his several objections to Leopold was the manner in which the king took crucial actions as commander in chief of the army in the crucial days before and after the outbreak of war without consulting fully with the civilian government. On July 16, 1951, Leopold relinquished the royal prerogative to his son Baudouin I.

When British foreign minister Ernest Bevin in January, 1948, called for a consolidation of Western Europe, his Belgian counterpart responded quickly. Spaak's influence speeded creation in March, 1948, of a Western European Union that entailed more political and economic cooperation, as well as military cooperation, than the British and the French had initially contemplated. Spaak also signed on behalf of Belgium the 1949 Treaty of Washington, forming the North Atlantic Treaty Organization (NATO). He took pride in Article 9 of that treaty; the permanent council it authorized provided for more continuing political and economic consultation among the members of the organization than did traditional military alliances. Spaak returned to the Belgian foreign ministry in 1954 but left the office to serve as secretary-general of NATO from 1957 to 1961. Spaak did yeoman service there by restoring confidence in the alliance shaken by the Suez crisis of 1956.

Spaak's interest in European political and economic collaboration is also reflected in the other posts that he held. He chaired from 1948 to 1950 the Council of the Organization for European Economic Cooperation, the European arm of the United States European Recovery Program (Marshall Plan). At the end of 1949, he was elected first president of the Consultative Assembly of the newly formed council of Europe. Disheartened by the failure of the council to press firmly toward economic and political integration, Spaak resigned the position in December, 1951. His efforts then turned to encouraging the integration of a smaller grouping of six nations in the nascent European Coal and Steel Community (ECSC), serving as president of its common assembly from May, 1953, to April, 1954. In 1955, Spaak was selected by his colleagues in the ECSC to chair a committee that would recommend steps to bring about a common economic market among the six. The recommendations of the "Spaak Report" became the foundation for the 1957 Treaties of Rome creating the European Economic Community and the European Atomic Energy Community.

Spaak's skill as foreign minister was once more called upon in April, 1961. The newly independent Congo had broken relations with Belgium, the province of Katanga was in secession, U.N. troops were intervening, and Belgian nationals in the Congo appeared in danger. After many difficulties, Spaak improved relations with both the Congo and the United Nations, saw the secession ended, and encouraged restoration of order in the former colony. In February, 1966, the coalition cabinet in which Spaak was serving was overthrown. That June, in the midst of a political scene dominated by the linguistic question, the Socialist Party refused to back Spaak when he urged that it support the government, which sought to host the Supreme Headquarters of the Allied Powers in Europe. Discouraged by this lack of vision by his party, Spaak retired from politics.

### Summary

Paul-Henri Spaak served in the Belgian government for more than twenty-two years, holding the foreign ministry portfolio for most of that time. His influence was great, for the paths he set were usually followed by those who briefly relieved him at the post. His energy in promoting a united Europe was indefatigable. Spaak's skill as a diplomat lay in finding those points that brought people together. His vision was wide and ambitious, but he was willing to work patiently and determinedly to reach his goals through cumulative small steps. His sense of timing was good, and in both domestic and international politics he was not afraid to propose bold moves when he thought the moment right. His ability to extract the best from his collaborators, his straightforwardness, his clarity of expression, and even his emotional personality all contributed to his success. Frequently he led others to make efforts that they had not originally contemplated. He suffered in reappraising his prewar policy and his relations with Leopold, yet learned from his experience and did not shrink from the consequences of his conclusions. The nature of post-World War II Europe was permanently altered by his efforts. While he believed that European unity and economic and political integration had not proceeded fast or far enough by the time of his retirement, he had earned the sobriquet by which he was then widely known: Mr. Europe.

### Bibliography

Arango, E. Ramón. *Leopold III and the Belgian Royal Question.* Baltimore: Johns Hopkins University Press, 1961. The best-balanced account of this affair in English, it describes well the view of the Socialists and Spaak.

Helmreich, Jonathan E. *Belgium and Europe: A Study in Small Power Diplomacy.* The Hague: Mouton, 1976. The last chapters provide a general review of Belgian foreign policy and Spaak's role from 1936 to 1964.

———. *Gathering Rare Ores: The Diplomacy of Uranium Acquisition, 1943-1954.* Princeton, N.J.: Princeton University Press, 1986. Though written from the viewpoint of U.S. policy, the book tells much about Spaak's role in the uranium negotiations of this period.

Huizinga, James H. *Mr. Europe: A Political Biography of Paul Henri Spaak.* London: Weidenfeld and Nicolson, and New York: Praeger, 1961. The greatest portion of this book by a Dutch journalist focuses on the evolution of Spaak's views on socialism and his breach with Leopold. The development of both Spaak's character and internationalism is well illuminated.

Spaak, Paul-Henri. *The Continuing Battle: Memoirs of a European, 1936-1966.* Translated by Henry Fox. London: Weidenfeld and Nicolson, and Boston: Little Brown, 1971. The English version slightly abridges the French text. The focus is on Spaak's work for European unity; no references are made to personal or family events or to those preceding 1936. The period of neutralism and the royal controversy are covered succinctly. Spaak demonstrates his priorities, includes quotations from significant documents and speeches, and presents incisive descriptions of international figures.

*Jonathan E. Helmreich*

# BENJAMIN SPOCK

*Born:* May 2, 1903; New Haven, Connecticut
*Died:* March 15, 1998; San Diego, California
*Areas of achievement:* Education, medicine, and social reform
*Contribution:* Through his advocacy, publications, and activities related to child care and developmental psychology, Spock sought to advise parents on matters and issues previously ignored by mainstream pediatric medicine. As a social activist, he called for socialized medicine, an end to U.S. military police action abroad, and nuclear disarmament.

### Early Life

Benjamin McLane Spock was the oldest of six children of Benjamin Ives Spock, a conservative Connecticut railroad lawyer, and Mildred Louise Stoughton, a native of Vermont. As a child, he attended Hamden Hall and Phillips Academy in Andover, Massachusetts. Upon graduation from Phillips Academy, Spock entered Yale College, where he majored in English and minored in history. A very tall young man (six feet four inches) with an athletic build and broad shoulders, Spock was a member of the Yale crew that won a gold medal in the 1924 Olympics held in Paris. He went on to study at the Yale Medical School for two years before transferring to the Columbia University College of Physicians and Surgeons, receiving his medical degree in 1929. He interned at Presbyterian Hospital in New York, was a pediatrics resident at the New York Nursery and Child's Hospital, and spent ten months as a psychiatry resident at New York Hospital. The first individual ever to train professionally in both pediatrics and psychoanalysis, he also received training at the New York Psychoanalytic Institute from 1933 to 1938. He later attributed much of his professional success to the psychoanalytic training he received during the 1930's.

Spock began his medical career in 1933 as a pediatrician in New York City. The first few years of his practice were difficult. The Depression made collection of payment for services extremely difficult. The three to five dollars he charged for office visits, about average for the time, was difficult for the average citizen to afford, especially considering the fact that about one in four Americans was unemployed. He received few patients from referrals during those early years and barely paid his expenses. His eventual success as a physician, despite the overwhelming difficulties, was partly because of his extensive knowledge of medicine and partly because of his unique bedside manner. He wore a business suit instead of the typical white doctor's coat, an effort to make patients feel more at ease. He continued to make house calls long after most in the profession had discontinued the practice. He supplemented his income during those early years as an instructor of pediatrics at Cornell Medical College, an assistant attending physician at New York Hospital, the part-time school doctor at the Brearley School, and a consultant for the New York City Health Department. His relaxed, conversational lecture style put listeners at ease while garnering increasing respect in the medical community.

### Life's Work

In 1943 Spock began writing *The Commonsense Book of Baby and Child Care*, the book that would eventually make him the best-known doctor in America. He spent three years dictating it to his first wife, Jane Davenport Cheney, whom he had married in 1927. She typed as he spoke, and she edited the text. Spock was drafted into the Navy in 1944 and worked as a psychiatrist in military hospitals on both the East and West Coasts, but he continued to write. More than half of his tenure in the military was at the U.S. Naval Hospital, St. Alban's, in Queens, New York. The assignment allowed him to live with his family in Manhattan and continue working on the book. He left the Navy in 1946, the same year *The Commonsense Book of Baby and Child Care* was published.

*The Commonsense Book of Baby and Child Care* advocated previously controversial methods of child care. Spock stressed the psychological state of being in child development and progressive childhood guidance at every stage of development. For example, Spock wrote that it was not necessary for mothers to stick to rigid feeding schedules for their babies and that it was unnatural for a mother to have to wait for an established feeding time while her baby cried. Such statements contradicted conventional medical practice. The accompanying illustrations, by Dorothea Fox, complemented the text and comforted the reader.

Spock's well-received book gave parents much more information than any previous publication on child care and sold 750,000 copies in its first year.

During the following six years, the book sold more than four million copies and was eventually translated into forty-two languages. Pocket Books, which had originally convinced Spock to write the book, published it in paperback as *The Pocket Book of Baby and Child Care*. At three dollars per copy, the original hardcover edition was considered expensive for a young family, but the twenty-five cent paperback version was easily affordable and in great demand. Later editions were also titled *Baby and Child Care*, as well as *Dr. Spock's Baby and Child Care*. By the mid-1950's, the popularity of Spock's work was such that it was often referenced on popular prime-time television programs such as *I Love Lucy*.

After quitting his New York practice in 1947, Spock joined with the Mayo Clinic in Rochester, Minnesota, where he also served as associate professor of psychiatry at the University of Minnesota Mayo Graduate School of Medicine. He later went on to serve for four years as professor of child development at the University of Pittsburgh and twelve years at Case Western Reserve University in Cleveland. He constantly wrote articles and books about child care and child development during the 1950's and frequently spoke at professional conferences.

Spock first became openly involved in presidential politics in 1952 when he endorsed Democratic candidate Adlai Stevenson. He later supported John Kennedy and Lyndon Johnson before becoming disenchanted with the two major political parties. Disturbed by President Kennedy's 1962 announcement that the United States had to resume nuclear testing to stay ahead of the Soviet Union, he emerged as a vocal opponent of nuclear testing. He served as the primary spokesperson for the National Committee for a Sane Nuclear Policy, warning of the possible risks of radiation exposure. He went on to become cochair of the committee from 1962 to 1967. It was also during the early 1960's that Spock became an outspoken antiwar activist, an opponent of the draft, and a critic of the United States' involvement in Southeast Asia.

An advocate of civil disobedience for just causes, Spock was arrested at numerous protest demonstrations, the first time in 1967. One year later a Boston court convicted him, along with four others, of conspiracy to counsel, aid, and abet evasion of the draft. He and all but one of the "Boston Five" were found guilty, sentenced to two years in prison, and fined $5,000. The decision, however, was later reversed by the United States Court of Appeals for the First Circuit for lack of ample evidence.

Spock was the 1972 presidential nominee for the People's Party, a coalition of radical left-wing organizations from ten states. The People's Party platform called for an end to the military draft, nuclear disarmament, the elimination of property and sales taxes, and the immediate withdrawal of U.S. military personnel from foreign countries. Spock's campaign proved to be a dismal failure. His name was only on the ballot in ten states and he received less than eighty thousand votes. In 1976 he was the People's Party candidate for vice president with similar results. That same year he divorced his first wife, Jane.

Although very much involved in the social activism of the day, Spock never neglected to revise his book over the years. The fourth edition, published in 1976, was revised in an effort to eliminate the sexist language so prevalent in his earlier editions. The move was a response by Spock to quell increasing criticism from Gloria Steinem and other feminist leaders of the women's liberation movement. The fifth and sixth editions, which appeared in 1985 and 1992 respectively, were coauthored with Dr. Michael B. Rothenberg, professor of pediatrics and psychiatry at the University of Washington's medical school. The fortieth anniversary edition (1985) included a completely updated medical-pediatric section written by Rothenberg. The seventh edition, by Spock and Boston pediatrician Steven J. Parker, was published in 1995. Over the years Spock was the author or a coauthor of thirteen other books (including two autobiographies) and numerous magazine articles. He wrote columns for some of the most widely circulated magazines in the United States, including *Redbook*, *Ladies Home Journal*, and *Parenting*.

### Summary

In 1976 Spock married Mary Morgan, a native of Arkansas. Spock and Morgan coauthored his 1989 autobiography entitled *Spock on Spock: A Memoir of Growing Up with the Century*. In the final chapters of the book, Spock discussed, at length, his views on death and dying, including the role of doctors in assisted suicide. He also commented on the hospice movement sweeping through the United States. Spock attributed his longevity to good genes inherited from his mother, diet, and meditation. Always the social activist, he continued his criticism of the United States government for

spending "trillions of dollars on arms" while eliminating programs to help the poor, the elderly, and children.

By the mid-1990's Spock's health began to decline considerably. He was diagnosed with pneumonia six times during the final year of his life. By the time of his death in 1998, *The Commonsense Book of Baby and Child Care* had sold more than forty million copies worldwide.

### Bibliography

Bloom, Lynn Z. *Dr. Spock: Biography of a Conservative Radical*. Indianapolis: Bobbs-Merrill, 1972. Contains very detailed information about the early career of the noted child-care expert. Published just as Spock began his run for the presidency and his subsequent divorce, much of his later social activism is not included.

Hulbert, Ann. "Dr. Spock's Baby." *The New Yorker* 72, no. 12 (May 20, 1996). Discusses the six revisions of Dr. Spock's famous book, *Baby and Child Care.*

Michalek, Irene R. *When Mercy Seasons Justice: The Spock Trial*. Boston: Branden Press, 1972. Offers interesting insight into the social activism of the 1960's and 1970's as well as the government response to such activities.

Morgan, Mary, and Benjamin Spock. *Spock on Spock: A Memoir of Growing Up with the Century*. New York: Pantheon, 1989. Spock's autobiography, coauthored with his wife, offers interesting insight into his career and personal life. Acknowledgments and preface written by Mary Morgan. The text is complemented by personal family photographs as well as those from other sources.

Spock, Benjamin M. *The Common Sense Book of Baby and Child Care*. Rev. ed. New York: Dutton, 1985. Any of the numerous editions of the now-famous book are worthy of review. Readers should be sure to note the evolution of thought by the author toward child rearing as reflected in each subsequent edition.

———. *Decent and Indecent: Our Personal and Political Behavior*. New York: McCall, 1970. Often referred to as the author's spiritual autobiography, this is a hodgepodge of thought on the problems faced by modern society.

Torrey, E. Fuller. "Oedipal Wrecks: Has a Century of Freud Bred a Country of Narcissists?" *Washington Monthly* 24, no. 1-2 (January-February, 1992). The author discusses the psychoanalytic practices of Spock and Sigmund Freud, whose writings influenced Spock.

*Donald C. Simmons, Jr.*

# JOSEPH STALIN
## Joseph Vissarionovich Dzhugashvili

*Born:* December 21, 1879; Gori, Georgia, Russian Empire

*Died:* March 5, 1953; Moscow, U.S.S.R.

*Areas of Achievement:* Government and politics

*Contribution:* Stalin succeeded Lenin as leader of the Soviet Union. During Stalin's twenty-five years in power, the Soviet Union was transformed from a backward agricultural society into one of the world's superpowers. This was achieved through a combination of Marxist-Leninist ideology, police terror, and sheer political will.

### Early Life

Joseph Vissarionovich Dzhugashvili, known by his revolutionary name of "Stalin," was born in Gori in the Russian province of Georgia on December 21, 1879. His father worked in a shoe factory, expecting his son to follow in his footsteps. His mother, Ekaterina Geladze, pious and hardworking, was determined that her only surviving child should escape the family's cycle of poverty, labor, and ignorance. Since education was to her the key to success, she enrolled Joseph in a Russian Orthodox church elementary school, hoping that he would become a priest. Upon graduation in 1894 he was enrolled in a theological seminary located in the Georgian capital of Tiflis. There he was converted to Marxism, leading a Marxist study group among the local railway workers when he was only eighteen years old. His revolutionary activities caused growing friction with the clerical staff of the seminary and led to his expulsion in May, 1899.

Stalin then found employment as a clerk at the Tiflis Geophysical Observatory, continuing revolutionary agitation among the workers, which led to his arrest in 1902. During his first imprisonment, the historic split in the Russian Social Democratic Workers' Party occurred, and Stalin found his sympathies with the Bolshevik (later "Communist") radicalism of Vladimir Ilich Lenin.

Between 1902 and 1917, Stalin spent almost nine years in either czarist prisons or internal exile. When not incarcerated, he helped organize bank robberies in his native Caucasus to secure money for the Bolsheviks and continued his underground activities as a Marxist propagandist. By 1912 his loyalty came to the attention of Lenin, and Stalin began his steady rise in the Party hierarchy. In 1913, Lenin asked him to compose an article on the problems of national minorities in the Russian Empire. The resulting essay, *Marksizm i natsional'nyi vopros* (1914; *Marxism and the National and Colonial Question*, 1934), while it represents the longest piece of writing he ever did, actually reflects Lenin's ideas on the subject. Stalin argued the right of nationalities occupying contiguous territory to their own language but condemned too much decentralization as unsuited for a modern industrial state. This view foreshadowed future Communist policy: the promise of cultural autonomy behind which was political centralization and rule by the Party. By the time the essay was published, however, Stalin was again under arrest and remained in Siberian exile until the overthrow of the czar in March, 1917.

### Life's Work

Stalin's considerable organizational skills and willingness to take on seemingly onerous desk jobs resulted in his appointment to a number of important Party offices. Between 1917 and 1922, he served as a member of the Bolshevik General Staff and Central Committee Politburo, and as Commissar of Nationalities, Commissar of the Army, director of the Workers' and Peasants' Inspectorate, and member of the government's organizational bureau. Yet his most important office was to be general secretary of the Communist Party, a post to which he was appointed in 1922 and from which he would eventually control the Party and the nation.

By the time of Lenin's death in 1924, Stalin had emerged as a major rival for power. Using his numerous political skills through his Party and government offices, he was by 1929 the undisputed leader of the Soviet Union. This power struggle was hidden behind numerous policy debates concerning the future of the socialist state. Stalin supported the concept of "socialism in one country," arguing that the Soviet Union, surrounded by hostile capitalist nations, needed to defend the revolutionary base and become the model for future socialist societies. This was his most important contribution to Marxist-Leninist theory and provided the ideological framework for his future transformation of the Soviet Union. Beginning in

1929, he began the struggle to create a socialist society in a backward agrarian country and carried it out in the face of massive popular opposition, forcibly changing the lives of millions of people, and thrusting the Soviet Union into the forefront in international leadership.

First, Stalin called for collectivization of agriculture in order for the state to gain control of the grain supply, the Soviet Union's major export item. When the peasantry resisted, Stalin unleashed the full coercive apparatus of the state, resulting in open warfare in the countryside. Party members, city workers, and police and army units were all mobilized. Faced with the loss of their homes and land, the peasants fought back by burning their crops and slaughtering their livestock, but in the end Stalin won. Those peasants who survived were banished to Siberia or dispatched to the numerous forced labor camps. By 1936 more than 90 percent of Soviet peasant households were forced to live and work on closely supervised collective or state farms.

The destruction wrought by the peasants in their struggle with the Soviet state had lasting repercussions for the rural economy. One of the main justifications for collectivization was replacement of the old-fashioned, unmechanized, individually managed peasant farm with a centralized, highly mechanized agricultural system worked by a collectivized peasantry. This new system was to produce the grain necessary to finance the purchase abroad of the heavy machinery needed for the massive industrialization effort going on at the same time. Because of the tragic nature of the collectivization process, this goal was never achieved. Instead, the Soviet people paid for industrialization through personal sacrifice, increasing regimentation, and a lower standard of living.

Collectivization was a part of the First Five-Year Plan, which called for a massive drive that would increase overall industrial production by some 250 percent, with heavy industry increasing by 330 percent. Such figures implied a social change of unimaginable scope. In actuality the plan was meant to outline and control massive changes in all aspects of the economy and society, and Stalin and his supporters in the Party could not foresee the ramifications of such a plan. Between 1928 and 1932, heavy industry more than doubled. Still, Stalin kept urging an ever more accelerated tempo. Under this kind of prodding, fulfillment of quotas became more important than quality of product. Those enterprises achieving their targets were given new and higher ones. In such an environment, force and compulsion became the rule of both industry and agriculture as the entire society was whipped forward by the general secretary.

Such a social transformation created enormous pressures. From 1929 to 1933, the urban population increased from some twenty-seven million to more than forty million, straining city services to the breaking point. The harshness of life in the city, coupled with the forced collectivization of the countryside, gave rise to various kinds of opposition. To combat this, the coercive arm of the state expanded, both through the power of the police and through Party control over all social institutions. When opposition appeared within the Party itself, the ever-suspicious Stalin unleashed the terror of the mid- and late-1930's.

While collectivization and industrialization changed the economic base of the Soviet Union, the terror transformed society. Party members associated with Lenin were purged from the ranks, and many were later executed. The terror struck the ordinary Soviet citizen as well, however, as it did all institutions of society. More than eight million people were arrested, tortured, and sentenced to hard labor as they were terrorized into sullen submission to the will of the leader.

While the 1930's witnessed the transformation of the Soviet Union from a weak, agrarian, underdeveloped state into an industrialized, collectivized, socialist giant, the 1940's would make the Soviet Union into a world power. First, however, it had to withstand military invasion by Nazi Germany. The ensuing struggle was of titanic proportions within the larger framework of World War II. By May, 1945, however, Soviet troops were in Berlin, and the Red Army had liberated most of the German-occupied countries of Eastern Europe.

With the end of the war, the Soviet Union faced a massive rebuilding effort. Now an increasingly irrational and suspicious man, Stalin reinstituted the five-year plans and recollectivized agriculture in those areas that had been under German control, all accompanied by the omniscient terror. By the end of his life, Stalin ruled over a massive socialist empire that extended beyond its European frontier into the satellite states of Poland, Romania, Bulgaria, Czechoslovakia, Hungary, and East Germany. The Soviet Union had become the main actor with the United States in a bipolar world. When Stalin died on March 5, 1953, he left a powerful but morally and physically exhausted state.

### Summary

The language used by Joseph Stalin was, as that of Lenin before him, the language of Karl Marx. They were after the same goal, a communist society in which the basic goods and services would be available to all without exploitation by one dominant class. Marx talked about achieving this through the working out of economic laws. Yet Stalin inherited from Lenin a Soviet Union still in the first stages of industrialization and surrounded by much more advanced economic societies. Therefore, Stalin accelerated the pace of industrial development in the Soviet Union via a series of five-year plans forced upon a reluctant society through the use of police terror. In agriculture he forced the peasants onto collective farms, which, like the urban factories, were controlled and run by the Party leadership in far-off Moscow. Where Marx emphasized the forces of history to construct communism, Stalin emphasized the political will of the Party.

While Stalin's industrialization effort in the building of socialism did make the Soviet Union a major superpower in the wake of World War II, it was accomplished at incredible sacrifice on the part of the Soviet people. In one generation, despite a devastating war, the Soviet Union increased its overall production fourfold and heavy industry ninefold. The methods used, however, were those that echoed Russia's autocratic past from Ivan the Terrible to Peter the Great.

### Bibliography

Adams, Arthur E. *Stalin and His Times.* New York: Holt Rinehart, 1972. A readable history of the Soviet Union during the time of Stalin, meant for the general reader already familiar with the basic outlines of twentieth century history. Helps in understanding why Stalin was successful in achieving his objectives.

Conquest, Robert. *The Great Terror: Stalin's Purges of the Thirties.* Rev. ed. London: Penguin, 1971; New York: Macmillan, 1973. A thorough and very detailed analysis of the purges and terror through which Stalin came to dominate and mold the Communist Party and Soviet society. Discusses the means by which the terror was accomplished and the reasons Stalin believed it was necessary.

Deutscher, Isaac. *Stalin: A Political Biography.* 2d ed. London and New York: Oxford University Press, 1967. This has become a classic biography, although dated. Emphasis is on Stalin's political skills in rising to the top of the Communist Party, especially the reasons behind his victory in the power struggle after Lenin's death.

McNeal, Robert H. *Stalin: Man and Ruler.* London: Macmillan, and New York: New York University Press, 1988. A solid and well-written biography by a longtime specialist in the field. By examining the known available source material, McNeal attempts to evaluate Stalin's contribution to Soviet history from the perspective of the late twentieth century.

Thurston, Robert W. *Life and Terror in Stalin's Russia, 1934-1941.* New Haven, Conn.: Yale University Press, 1996. A well-written book with an unconventional approach to the study of Stalinist terrorism that advances the theory that the dictator did not need to terrorize the Soviet state because many agreed with his basic ideas.

Tucker, Robert C. *Stalin as Revolutionary, 1879-1929.* New York: Norton, 1973; London: Chatto and Windus, 1974. The first of a projected two-volume biography by a well-known expert in the field. This volume, spanning the first fifty years of Stalin's life, attempts to analyze those ingredients in his formative years that eventually created a dictator.

Ulam, Adam B. *Stalin: The Man and His Era.* New York: Viking Press, 1973; London: Allen Lane, 1974. A thorough, well-written biographical study by a noted Sovietologist, this work examines Stalin's life against a larger world background. Includes an excellent treatment of the development of the terror as a technique of government.

Ward, Chris, ed. *The Stalinist Dictatorship.* London: Arnold, and New York: Oxford University Press, 1998. This collection looks at the Stalinist dictatorship from the perspectives of Stalin's character, his role within the Soviet Union, and the effects of socialism on the people.

Wolfe, Bertram D. *Three Who Made a Revolution.* 4th ed. New York: Dial Press, 1964. This is a classic study of the lives of Lenin, Leon Trotsky, and Stalin, and an excellent introduction to the subject of Soviet history. Its emphasis is on the formative years of Russian Marxism up to the 1917 Revolution.

*Jack M. Lauber*

# KONSTANTIN STANISLAVSKY
## Konstantin Sergeyevich Alekseyev

*Born:* January 17, 1863; Moscow, Russia

*Died:* August 7, 1938; Moscow, U.S.S.R.

*Areas of Achievement:* Theater and acting

*Contribution:* The founder (with Vladimir Nemirovich-Danchenko) of the Moscow Art Theater, director of the plays of Anton Chekhov, and writer of the most influential acting lessons in modern times, Stanlislavsky is the father of modern acting techniques; all modern actors, directors, and acting schools owe a great debt to Stanislavsky's methods, which revolutionized the theater in the early twentieth century.

### Early Life

Born Konstantin Sergeyevich Alekseyev, into an affluent and cultured Russian family, Stanislavsky participated in amateur dramatic entertainments at his family's estate from a very early age, putting on small plays and musical pieces with his brothers and sisters, for family guests. The Alekseyev Circle, a group of amateur players largely recruited from Stanislavsky's immediate family, provided not only the entertainments for his parents and friends but also the first school of dramatic theory for young Stanislavsky. As visiting actors from Moscow and from foreign companies visited the country estate and participated in the productions (sometimes only as audience members), Stanislavsky gleaned more and more about their techniques for creating and sustaining stage characters. Their criticism after performance, whether positive or negative, helped Stanislavsky gradually form an idea about how to approach the actor's art.

This combination of experiences was to feed him as he moved from family entertainment to amateur acting in other parts of Russia. His merchant "aristocracy" prevented his turning professional, but the amateur status did not deter him from playing important roles in major professional productions in his early life. It was necessary for Stanislavsky to assume a stage name to avoid embarrassment to his family; the profession of actor was held in low esteem in this period, especially in contrast to the prestige his father enjoyed as owner of a gold- and silver-thread manufacturing company.

A unique combination of happenstances and personal traits was to lead to the wide-ranging and even more widely accepted "method" of acting that Stanislavsky left as his heritage. His impressionable temperament, together with his absolutely ruthless ability to examine his own imperfections, caused him to examine in close study every actor he saw on stage or in society. He copied the external features of their acting styles and at the same time struggled with his external discipline to achieve the characterizations he saw and admired on stage. Rather than compromising his standards or causing him to give up, each frustrated attempt prodded Stanislavsky to try harder and harder to reconcile all the disparate influences bombarding him. Further, being of independent means, he did not have the economic burden of self-sustenance that plagues so many theater figures.

Stanislavsky's first experiments with acting styles, as well as the forming and running of his first acting companies, have been well documented, especially in his own autobiography, *My Life in Art* (1924), more an explanation of his theater philosophies than a personal memoir. Subsequent biographers traced every detail of Stanislavsky's early roles, the development of his talent and skills, and the reaction of audiences (often friends and family members) who saw him emerge as one of Moscow's finest actors, amateur or professional.

One of the most influential factors in his development was the Meiningen players (whose 1890 tour Stanislavsky saw), a German acting company, from whom Stanislavsky learned the power of crowd scenes, the importance of overall mood, and the value of a rigid discipline among the actors. He quickly was to refine his own ideas, however, past the militaristic limitations of the company's regisseur, Ludwig Kronegk.

### Life's Work

Stanislavsky's work truly began with the formation of the Moscow Art Theater in 1898, with Vladimir Nemirovich-Danchenko, a literary figure and regisseur already enjoying Moscow success. That partnership began on June 22, 1897, after a now-famous eighteen-hour marathon discussion of the principles of the ideal theater. The division of labor was interesting—Stanislavsky was to deal with the artistic considerations while Nemirovich-Danchenko would be the businessman and the literary adviser (the term "dramaturge" expresses his contributions well). More accurately, each man had veto power in his particular area, but their work was a cooperative collaboration from the start. For Stanislavsky, it was the culmination of several earlier attempts at producing and honing his skills as "director," a term not fully in use at that time.

The Moscow Art Theater was propelled by the combined efforts of these two men of the theater and one great Russian writer. The playwright whose name was to be permanently linked with the Moscow Art Theater was Anton Chekhov, already a successful short-story writer and medical doctor. His plays, only five in number but central to modern drama from his time on, were produced at the Moscow Art Theater in a way that demonstrated Stanislavsky's approach to theater production and the new realistic acting style that was to become his trademark.

It was the Moscow Art Theater's production in 1898 of Chekhov's *Chayka* (1896; *The Sea Gull*, 1909) that marked the beginning of its successful relationships with the playwright. This production was the second one for the play; it had failed in St. Petersburg when a talented but misguided group of professionals tried to find its essence without understanding that this new kind of writing called for a new kind of acting. The Moscow Art Theater's production, which did in fact combine the realistic acting style with the new play script, was moderately successful, but the marriage of literary idea and theatrical realization was so ideal that the theater took the seagull as its insignia. To this day, the stylized seagull figure from the first production flies on the flag over the theater. Subsequent productions of Chekhov's plays, notably *Dyadya Vanya* (1897; *Uncle Vanya*, 1914) in 1899, *Tri Sestry*, (*Three Sisters*, 1920) in 1901, and *Vishnyovy sad* (*The Cherry Orchard*, 1908) in 1904, were unqualified critical successes.

Stanislavsky's international popularity was determined by the many visitors to Moscow who saw and were astounded by his theater accomplishments. When the company toured (to Germany in 1906, and to the United States in 1922), an even larger audience appreciated the care, attention to detail, absolute discipline, and intelligence of the productions.

Stanislavsky's accomplishments with the Moscow Art Theater and Chekhov would have ensured him an international reputation all by themselves, even without his subsequent accomplishments with acting style, developed and practiced on stage, in rehearsals, and in the studios and classrooms of the theater. This style, actually a system of preparation, development, and performance, is usually referred to simply as The System (not to be confused with its American offshoot, "The Method"). It was designed gradually over the full length of Stanislavsky's career; he constantly rethought, revised, and upgraded his ideas, working in notebooks.

His complete works, published in many volumes in Russian, have come to English-speaking audiences in bits and pieces, not necessarily in the order of their composition but roughly in the order of their intended application by the individual actor. In their first English edition, they are *An Actor Prepares* (1936), *Building a Character* (1949), *Stanislavski's Legacy* (1958), and *Creating a Role* (1961). This series of theoretical speculations, illustrated and demonstrated out of Stanislavsky's own theater experiences, is considered a must-read for all modern actors. The books deal with each distinct step in the actor's art: preparing one's body, voice, and mind for roles in general, constructing a characterization from the clues of the text, and working in an actual production. Together with his analytical mid-life autobiography, *My Life in Art*, these books constitute the "bible" of acting the Stanislavsky System.

The American tour marked a major schism in the Moscow Art Theater that was not so much artistic as it was geographic. Some of Stanislavsky's best actors chose to stay behind and open schools of acting and directing in New York. As a result, a second and third generation of Stanislavsky's ideas were spread by his own students, who naturally altered the basic principles with refinements of their own, sometimes adding a vocabulary that clarified for some and obfuscated for others the original intent of the acting system Stanislavsky propounded.

Stanislavsky ended his own acting career in 1928 but actively continued to revise his theories right up to his death in 1938. Near his death, he had been discussing ideas with one of his students, Vsevolod Meyerhold, whose earlier experiments with expressionist stage techniques had temporarily estranged him from his teacher. On the day Stanislavsky died, his thoughts were on Nemirovich-Danchenko, also estranged from him over aesthetic differences. Despite these differences, Stanislavsky was deeply respected by all of his peers for his monumental contributions to and love of his art and his uncompromising zeal for truth in the theater.

### Summary

Today's acting teachers can trace a direct line through the American acting schools and companies such as the Actor's Studio and the Group Theatre, through the Russian students of Konstantin Stanislavsky such as Michael Chekhov (Anton Chekhov's nephew) and Richard Boleslavsky, back to the Moscow Art Theater's American and European tours of that period. N. M. Gorchakov took elaborate notes of Stanislavsky's directing methods at the height of his powers; these, too, are studied by today's student directors and teachers, whose mentors in turn, such as Elia Kazan and Lee Strasberg, owe a great debt to their exposure to the Moscow Art Theater.

The Stanislavsky heritage, as Christine Edwards describes it in her book of that name, is the belief "that the actor must experience real emotion, that he must identify with the character he is portraying, that he may use his own past emotional experiences, and above all, that he must learn to speak and behave naturally, as a human being in life." The fact that it is inconceivable to challenge such a statement today is convincing testament to the ubiquitous influences of Stanislavsky on modern theater.

### Bibliography

Benedetti, Jean. *Stanislavski: A Biography.* New York: Routledge, 1988; London: Methuen, 1990. An updated version of the standard biography by David Magarshack (see below), this study offers new translations of new letters and documents. It follows Magarshack's work a little too closely, reworking his anecdotes in several places. Contains twenty-nine illustrations (mostly production stills and portraits in character), a select bibliography, a chronology of roles and productions, and an index.

———. *Stanislavski: An Introduction.* New York: Theatre Arts Books, and London: Methuen, 1982. A slim, handy introduction to "The System," weaving biographical material into an explanation of how the system functions. Of value to the actor looking for an entry into the complexities of the multivolume work of Stanislavsky himself. Includes a chronology, an index, and a list of topics discussed in the text.

Carnicke, Sharon Marie. "Stanislavsky." *The Drama Review* 37, no. 1 (Spring, 1993). Examination of past publications of Stanislavsky's collected works and the new uncensored editions that offer clearer representations of his writings. Includes information on Stanislavsky's critics and the history of the publication of his writings in the West.

Edwards, Christine. *The Stanislavsky Heritage: Its Contribution to the Russian and American Theatre.* New York: New York University Press, 1965; London: Owen, 1966. Puts Stanislavsky's work in the context of two important movements: traditional Russian stage practice and the emerging and developing American theater in the first half of the twentieth century. The very considerable influence of The System on the American "method" is well chronicled here. Includes a bibliography, an appendix, and an index.

Genard, Gary. "The Moscow Art Theatre's 1923 Season in Boston: A Visit from on High?" *Theatre History Studies* 16, no. 15 (June, 1996). Discusses the influence of Stanislavsky's theories on actor training and theater practices as a result of his Moscow Art Theatre's tour of the United States in 1923.

Magarshack, David. *Stanislavsky: A Life.* London: Macgibbon and Kee, 1950; New York: Chanticleer Press, 1951. Still the authoritative study, not only of Stanislavsky but also of the theater itself; contains a good balance of personal and professional information and is careful in the details of production. Particularly valuable is the discussion of how Stanislavsky gradually found the vocabulary to express and teach his acting system. Includes twenty illustrations and an index.

Nemirovich-Danchenko, Vladimir. *My Life in the Russian Theatre.* Translated by John Cournos. Boston: Little Brown, 1936; London: Bles, 1937. Stanislavsky always insisted that the Moscow Art Theater was founded by both him and Nemirovich-Danchenko. This autobiography puts the dramaturge's experiences in the context of a longer, more varied career. Literary and sophisticated compared with Stanislavsky's autobiography.

Sayler, Oliver M. *Inside the Moscow Art Theatre.* New York: Brentano's, 1925. This study was conducted during the height of Stanislavsky's success and after two American tours. Following a preliminary chapter on the effect of these tours on the temperament of the company, Sayler offers the most complete and respectful record in print of the theater's accomplishments. Full informative photographs and illustrations throughout, including marvelous portraits of leading actors, valuable production stills, a flow chart of the management, and an index.

Senelick, Laurence. *Gordon Craig's Moscow Hamlet: A Reconstruction*. Westport, Conn.: Greenwood Press, 1982. A book-length examination of the monumental production at the Moscow Art Theater in 1912, in which Stanislavsky and Edward Gordon Craig, two geniuses of the modern theater, met and worked together in what should have been but could never be the ideal collaboration. An excellent way to understand Stanislavsky's way of working on classics. Includes illustrations, two appendices, notes, a bibliography, and an index.

Wiles, Timothy J. *The Theater Event: Modern Theories of Performance*. Chicago: University of Chicago Press, 1980. One-third of this important study of modern performance theories is dedicated to Stanislavsky, especially his work on Chekhov's *The Three Sisters*. Examines the common ground between Stanislavsky's system and Chekhov's intentions; Wiles believes Chekhov may have feared that the Moscow Art Theater and Stanislavsky "constantly misinterpreted" his plays, turning his comedies into tragedies.

*Thomas J. Taylor*

# JOHANNES STARK

*Born:* April 15, 1874; Schickenhof, Germany
*Died:* June 21, 1957; Traunstein, West Germany
*Area of Achievement:* Physics
*Contribution:* Stark's detection of the Doppler effect in a terrestrially generated light source led to his discovery that a strong electric field will split the spectral lines of chemical elements. Stark's experiments provided confirmation of Albert Einstein's special theory of relativity and evidence for the controversial quantum theories of Max Planck.

### Early Life

Johannes Stark was born in Schickenhof on April 15, 1874. His father was a landed proprietor, as was his maternal grandfather. The young Stark demonstrated early scholarly promise and eventually attended the *Gymnasiums* of Bayreuth and Regensburg before entering the University of Munich in 1894. After studying chemistry, crystallography, mathematics, and physics courses for three years, he received his doctorate for a dissertation entitled *Untersuchung über Russ* (1897; investigations into lampblack). Stark successfully completed the state examinations required for teaching higher mathematics in 1897 and assumed the post of assistant to Eugen Lommel of the Physical Institute at the University of Munich in October of that year. Shortly thereafter, he married Luise Uepler, who eventually bore him five children.

In 1900, Stark became a privatdocent at the University of Göttingen, the beginning of a tumultuous career in higher education that lasted until 1922. Stark never got on well with his coworkers or superiors, which led to frequent moves from one university to another. In 1906, he received an appointment as professor extraordinary at the Technical High School in Hannover, where he incurred the enmity of his immediate superior, Julens Precht, who eventually managed to have Stark transferred to Griefswald in 1907 and to Aachen in 1909. In 1917, Stark returned to Griefswald as a full professor. Two years later, he took a similar position at the University of Würzburg, where he remained until 1922, when he resigned and left academia permanently.

### Life's Work

Stark's productive career spanned approximately the years 1902-1928. After 1920, he became increasingly involved in what might be called the racial politics of German science, a matter in which he had already become bitterly embroiled during his earlier years.

Stark's most important work involved the electrical conduction in gases, which was the subject of his first published book, *Die Elektrizität in Gasen* (1902). Stark's discoveries were based on the Doppler effect. Johann Doppler predicted as early as 1842 that a luminous object moving toward a stationary observer would appear to be a different color than the color the same object would appear to be if it were moving away from the observer. Doppler theorized that all stars emit neutral or white light and that their apparent colors to an earthly observer are caused by their relative velocities toward or away from the earth. Doppler's theory was modified in 1845 and again in 1848 by other physicists and finally confirmed in 1870 with advances in spectroscopy.

It was not possible to detect the Doppler effect with any sources of light generated on Earth until

the twentieth century, because no earthly light source could attain sufficient velocity. In his 1902 book, Stark correctly predicted that the Doppler effect might be observed in canal rays. Eugen Goldstein discovered in 1896 that, by placing the cathode in a cathode ray tube in such a way that it divides the tube into two equal parts and then piercing the cathode with a number of holes, one can observe many bright-colored rays traveling in straight lines and entering the space behind the cathode through the holes. Goldstein named these rays *Kanalstrahlen*, or canal rays.

A number of physicists subjected these canal rays to intense investigation in the early part of the twentieth century, but it fell to Stark to demonstrate the Doppler effect in canal rays in an ingenious experiment which showed it in the hydrogen lines. Stark immediately proposed his experiment as a proof of Einstein's then-new (1906) theory of special relativity and a year later as evidence for quantum theory. In 1904, Stark had founded the *Jahrbuch der Radioaktivität und Elektronik*, a scientific journal which he edited until 1913. In 1907, he became the first editor to request an article from Albert Einstein concerning relativity. In 1907, he also proposed that his experiments furnished proof of Planck's quantum theories. He was thus in the forefront of what he later contemptuously dismissed as "Jewish physics," where he remained a champion of the new hypotheses until 1913. In that year, his animosity toward Jews increased to grotesque proportions, a result in part of personal rivalries and professional jealousy.

From 1913 until his death, Stark opposed what he perceived to be the pernicious Jewish influence in science which perverted and debilitated the discoveries and course of so-called Germanic science. After 1913, he vitriolically denounced quantum theory, the special theory of relativity, and the Jewish champions of those theories from every forum to which he had access. His reactionary position regarding the new physics and his open Judeophobia combined to make for him many enemies in German academia and ultimately led to denial of his becoming a member of the two most prestigious scientific organizations in Germany and to his first retirement in 1922.

Despite his racial philosophy, Stark was accorded many honors in the international scientific community. He was awarded the Baumgartner Prize by the Vienna Academy of Sciences in 1910, and in 1914 won both the Vahlbruch Prize of the Göttingen Academy of Sciences and the Matteucci Medal of the Rome Academy. In 1919, he was honored with the Nobel Prize in Physics. Of all the recipients of the Nobel Prize, Stark was undoubtedly the most ignored by the world media and the international scientific community, which only confirmed him in his growing Judeophobia. In 1922, he resigned his university post in disgust at what he perceived to be the growing Jewish dominance in German academic life and retired to the area in which he was born to pursue private research.

His last important scientific work, *Atomstruktur und Atombindung*, appeared in 1928. The book confirmed the Judeophobic stand that had made him unpopular with many of his colleagues and had forced his retirement. Stark would almost certainly have remained in an obscure retirement and would have had no more impact on German science after 1922 had circumstances not brought Adolf Hitler to power in 1933.

The Nazis brought Stark out of retirement and appointed him president of the Physikalisch-Technische Reichsanwalt on April 1, 1933. This position gave him considerable influence over appointments to academic positions in German universities and the allocation of research funds. His enemies within the academy nevertheless prevented his election as president of the German Physics Association that year and prevented his gaining membership in the prestigious Prussian Academy the next. In June, 1934, however, the Nazis appointed Stark president of the German Research Association. His two presidencies and the concurrent passage of the so-called Nuremberg Laws allowed Stark to exercise enormous influence on the course of physics research and teaching in Germany. The Nuremberg Laws established that only "Aryans" were citizens of the Reich, and that a noncitizen could not hold a government post. Since professors were government employees, the laws gave Stark legal authority to purge the German universities of most Jewish professors. A few "non-Aryans" were able to keep their jobs because of stipulations in the laws that those noncitizen government employees who had served honorably on the front lines during the war or whose fathers had died in that war could retain their posts.

After the outbreak of widespread anti-Jewish violence in Germany on the *Kristallnacht* in 1938, Stark was able to retire the remaining Jewish professors supposedly for their own protection. In 1938-1939, he waged a heated campaign against what he called the "viceroys of the Einsteinian spirit," the "white Jews of science," and their continued championing of the new physics. Stark's definition of Jewish physics was an "un-German" predilection for theory over experiment. He was never able to remove all of his opponents from their positions, but he did much to retard the acceptance of theories which contained within them the seeds of the atom bomb.

Stark was instrumental in the exodus to the United States of the German physicists, both gentile and Jewish, who provided invaluable aid to the Allies during World War II toward the development of the first atom bomb in 1945. Concurrently, he was more than somewhat responsible for the failure of German physicists to supply that same weapon to Hitler, although that surely was not his intention.

Several influential German physicists opposed Stark's attacks against other scientists to the point that he was obliged to retire again from public life in 1939. In 1947, Stark stood trial before a de-Nazification court for his activities on behalf of the Third Reich and his attacks on Jewish academics. The court found him guilty and sentenced him to four years in a labor camp. Stark served the entire term despite his advanced years. He died at his home in Traunstein on June 21, 1957.

### Summary

Johannes Stark's formidable accomplishments as a scientist have been greatly overshadowed by the ignominy attached to his name by his affiliations with the Nazis. He exerted a considerable positive influence on physics during his early years but an even greater negative influence later in his life. From 1900 to 1913, he was in the vanguard of the new physics. His championing of the theories of Einstein, Planck, and others was a powerful force in the international acceptance of those ideas. His own experiments provided much of the practical underpinnings which validated the theoretical work of the men who laid the foundations for modern physics. Even though the Stark effect is considered of comparatively little practical value by contemporary physicists in the analyses of complex spectra or atomic structure, it nevertheless represents a milestone in atomic research. Unfortunately, he is best remembered not for these accomplishments but for his political activities.

Stark will be remembered most vividly as the Nazis' "tame physicist," as a victim or a harbinger of the ideology that swept his country and the world into a holocaust of previously unimaginable proportions.

### Bibliography


Beyerchen, Alan D. *Scientists Under Hitler: Politics and the Physics Community in the Third Reich.* New Haven, Conn.: Yale University Press, 1977. Beyerchen's book virtually ignores Stark's early contributions to science, concentrating instead on his support for Hitler and the Nazi movement and his attacks on non-Aryan physics. Beyerchen's accounts of Stark's feud with Einstein, of his efforts to cleanse German physics of Jewish influence, and of the consequences of those efforts are the most complete available in English.

Cohen, I. Bernard. *Revolution in Science.* Cambridge, Mass.: Harvard University Press, 1985. Cohen's book is a literate and compelling history of science centered on the theme of scientific revolutions that have often mirrored political and social revolution. Cohen evaluates Stark's contribution to modern physics and places him squarely in the camp of scientific reactionaries.

Hartshorne, Edward Yarnall, Jr. *The German Universities and National Socialism.* London: Allen and Unwin, and Cambridge, Mass.: Harvard University Press, 1937. This book, written during the period when Stark was attempting to purge German physics of Jewish influence, is of interest because it contains an English translation of parts of an address delivered by Stark at the University of Heidelberg in 1935. The address includes an attack on the Jewish Einsteinian influence in German physics, which was still being championed by some German scientists, notably Max von Laue, Max Planck, and Werner Heisenberg, all Nobel laureates in their own right and old enemies of Stark.

Heathcote, Niels Hugh de Vaudrey. *Nobel Prize Winners in Physics, 1901-1950.* New York: Schuman, 1953. Heathcote accords Stark only seven pages in his account of the first fifty Nobel laureates in physics, one of the shortest entries. In the biographical sketch that introduces each laureate, there is no mention of Stark's Nazi affiliations, nor is there any reference to the books Stark wrote defining and contrasting German and Jewish physics.

Hermann, Armin. "Johannes Stark." In *Dictionary of Scientific Biography,* edited by Charles

Coulston Gillispie, vol. 11. New York: Scribner, 1975. Hermann's brief sketch of Stark's career includes a considerable amount of information concerning the many feuds between Stark and his contemporaries in the scientific community, both in Germany and around the world. He explains Stark's complete reversal of position concerning the theory of relativity, not as a result of his Judeophobia but of his compulsion always to oppose the accepted point of view.

MacDonald, James Keene Lorne. *Stark-Effect in Molecular Hydrogen in the Range of 4100-4700 A.* Montreal: McGill University Publications, 1931. MacDonald's discussion of the Stark effect is much too technical for all but those with an advanced knowledge of physics. It does contain some biographical details about Stark and the research that led to his discovery of the Stark effect.

*Paul Madden*

# ERNEST HENRY STARLING

*Born:* April 17, 1866; London, England
*Died:* May 2, 1927; near Kingston, Jamaica
*Area of Achievement:* Medicine
*Contribution:* Starling discovered the mechanisms that regulate the output of the heart and the flow of lymphatic fluid and discovered the role of hormones in the control of organ function.

## Early Life

Ernest Henry Starling was born on April 17, 1866, in London and was reared there by his mother and a Canadian governess because his father was the Clerk of the Crown in Bombay, India, and returned to Great Britain on leave only once every three years. Despite the infrequent contact between father and son, the elder Starling is said to have influenced his son toward a career in medicine. Starling's choice of a career in physiology was an extremely unlikely one in the educational setting of late nineteenth century Great Britain. Education for everyone up to the age of ten became compulsory in 1876; any training beyond that age was mainly in the classics, with little emphasis on modern languages and even less on natural science. In later life, Starling was to criticize severely the limited and regressive educational system of his youth. At age thirteen, he enrolled in King's College School and studied divinity, Greek, Latin, French, ancient history, English, and mathematics. He distinguished himself in university entrance examinations and entered Guy's Hospital Medical School in 1882.

Starling's outstanding examination scores set him apart from his classmates and brought him to the attention of Leonard Charles Wooldridge, the demonstrator in physiology and later physician in chief at the hospital. Wooldridge introduced Starling to German experimental physiology and arranged for his protégé to spend a summer in Heidelberg studying under Wilhelm Kühne. The exciting discoveries of the German physiologists persuaded Starling to concentrate on physiology rather than opt for a medical practice. At the end of his clinical training in 1889 Starling accepted Wooldridge's former position as demonstrator and began to lay the groundwork for modern cardiovascular physiology. In this role, he was to employ fully his rare intellect and fulfill his deep commitment to the advancement of medical practice through fundamental research.

Several years later, the presence of the brilliant William Maddox Bayliss at University College drew Starling to Guy's Hospital's rival laboratory. It would prove to be a fruitful partnership. Starling was a forceful visionary, innovative and impatient, while Bayliss was deliberate, cautious, methodical, and kind. Together they would collaborate on some of the most important discoveries in the field of physiology.

## Life's Work

Starling's first publication with Bayliss, written while he was still at Guy's Hospital, described the earliest successful attempt to record a mammalian electrocardiogram and showed that contraction began at the base of the heart and proceeded to the apex. This study disproved the then-accepted hypothesis that all parts of the heart contracted simultaneously.

Starling next became interested in the formation of lymphatic fluid and the physical processes of secretion and absorption of this fluid in the cavities of the body. After four years of work with Bayliss, Starling showed that pressure inside a capillary determined the rate at which lymph transuded into the tissues, and that protein colloid determined the reabsorption of the lymphatic fluid from the tissues back into the capillary by osmotic pressure. Once this theory was established, Starling developed a model for heart failure in which the failing heart, unable to maintain arterial and capillary pressure, allows lymphatic fluid to enter the circulation under the influence of unopposed osmotic pressures. This model accounted for the dilated heart associated with heart failure, and Starling studied the significance of this dilation in his later work.

In 1897, a new physiology laboratory opened at Guy's Hospital, but these new facilities were not sufficient inducements for Starling to remain separated from Bayliss; in 1899, Starling accepted the Jodrell Chair of Physiology at University College. In the same year, he was elected Fellow of the Royal Society, at the age of thirty-three.

The two researchers next worked on intestinal function and in 1902 concentrated on pancreatic secretion. Injecting acid into a segment of jejunum, completely isolated except for its blood supply, resulted in copious pancreatic secretion. In the absence of any other connection between jejunum and pancreas, the unknown messenger had to be carried through the blood; the chemical messenger was named secretin. To describe such chemical messengers, Starling coined the word "hormone" in 1905. He noted that the pancreas produced a hormone which regulated the ability of tissue cells to utilize glucose. Having come so close to discovering insulin, Starling turned away from research into chemical control and resumed his investigation of the heart.

As Jodrell Professor, Starling did very little active research between 1904 and 1909. Instead, during this time he successfully sought funding for a new physiology building at University College and took elocution lessons to improve his public speaking, for he was frequently called to address large audiences. More important, Starling was now in a position to modify the empirical, practical nature of British medical education. In 1903, his idea of a curriculum emphasizing basic science and a medical school with its own hospital for teaching and research was published in the *British Medical Journal*.

This publication marked Starling's appearance as a man of ideas outside the laboratory, and in this role he became an effective public opponent of the antivivisection movement a few years later. The Antivivisection Law of 1876 had constrained the work of British physiologists during the last quarter of the nineteenth century, but the antivivisectionists now found the law inadequate and agitated to strengthen it. In 1903, Stephen Coleridge, the leader of the antivivisectionists, publicly accused Starling and Bayliss of dissecting an unanesthetized dog, a criminal offense. Bayliss failed to obtain a retraction from Coleridge and filed suit against him. As the dog had indeed been anesthetized, the jury awarded two thousand pounds and costs to Bayliss. This award was used to set up a research fund at University College.

As a result of these agitations, in 1906 Parliament set up a royal commission to investigate Coleridge's criticisms of the 1876 act; Starling chaired a committee to select witnesses from the scientific community on behalf of scientific investigation. The committee ensured that the scientists' views were well stated, and Starling himself testified before the commission, to great effect. As a result of Starling's efforts, the commission almost completely rejected the charges of the antivivisectionists.

Starling's second great productive period, leading to his formulation of the "law of the heart," began in 1911. Starling and his associates used an isolated heart-lung preparation. They showed that

within certain limits the output of the isolated heart is independent of arterial resistance and proportional to venous inflow. In 1914, Starling demonstrated that beyond these limits cardiac output falls, despite further increases in venous inflow to the heart. His first plots of ventricular function curves appeared in 1914. These discoveries were made at a time when many doubted that cardiac output rose during exercise, and when no one had thought of focusing on venous inflow as the prime determinant of the output of the heart.

Having established that, within limits, the heart would eject whatever blood flowed into it, Starling elucidated the mechanism of this response. He showed that, like a stretched spring, the force of the contraction of the heart muscle was proportional to the length of the muscle fibers when the heart was filled with blood immediately before a contraction. As a fiber was stretched, more chemically active contractile surface was exposed in the fiber, and the force of contraction became stronger. Thus the explanation was complete; the heart contracted more forcefully when stretched by increased blood flowing in, and within limits, the heart would succeed in ejecting whatever blood flowed to it from the veins. This law of the heart is Starling's greatest contribution to clinical medicine, for it dictates the principles of the diagnosis and treatment of heart failure.

World War I interrupted this work. Starling served in the Royal Army Medical Corps after being dissuaded from enlisting as an infantryman. He advocated the use of mustard gas as a weapon fifteen months before the Germans used it, but his foresight antagonized his superiors, and he was promoted and sent to Salonika, with nothing to do. While in Salonika, he was awarded the Order of St. Michael and St. George, the only award he ever received from the state. Frustrated, he resigned his commission in 1917 and returned to London.

In 1919 and 1920, Starling turned to an angry denunciation of British secondary education and the system that supported it. Perhaps the futility of his military experience stimulated these thoughts. He criticized the time spent on Latin and Greek in schools and the failure to teach a useful knowledge of either language in nine years or more of schooling, and advocated studies in English, modern languages, and science. Such education, he believed, would help prevent another war by preparing a generation to take its part in international endeavors. In the light of events of the 1930's, 1940's, and later, the tragic import of these thoughts is obvious.

Starling resigned his professorship at University College in 1922 and became the Fullerton Research Professor of the Royal Society. At this time a new anatomy building and an extension to the physiology department were built at University College, and he saw his efforts to develop the medical school move closer to fruition. Bayliss died in 1924, and Starling wrote the anonymous obituary of his partner which appeared in *The Times*.

In the next two years, Starling worked on renal function, showing that the glomerulus is in fact a simple filter and that the renal tubule actively secretes some substances into the urine while reabsorbing others. Discouraged about his health, in 1927 Starling took a cruise to the West Indies and died unexpectedly on board ship near Kingston, Jamaica.

## Summary

Ernest Henry Starling did not make every important discovery in physiology, but if his work were to be removed, the resulting void would be enormous. He overcame an educational system seemingly designed to prevent students from learning anything of science and, fortunate in his mentors, turned to his own uses a university system that was disinterested in his gifts. In so doing, he improved British medical schools for all students who followed him.

Starling made an astonishing series of discoveries in physiology, and his central ideas on hormones, lymphatic flow, and autoregulation of the heart have stood the test of time. Moreover, he criticized a system and a society in which ignorance was prized, amateurism valued, muddling through was a virtue, and practical knowledge of the natural world was denigrated. His life's work was a forceful statement of the opposite principle, for, based on reason and knowledge of natural phenomenan, he made discoveries that were to prevent or relieve immeasurable human suffering.

## Bibliography

Chapman, Carleton B. "Ernest Henry Starling: The Clinician's Physiologist." *Annals of Internal Medicine* 57, suppl. 2 (August, 1962): 1-43. An excellent account of Starling's life, setting his accomplishments against the background of early twentieth century British society. The details of experiments are clearly described, and a complete chronological annotated bibliography is included

"Ernest Henry Starling (1866-1927): The Clinician's Physiologist." *Journal of the American Medical Association* 214 (November 30, 1970): 1699-1701. An overview of Starling's life and work, including a brief section on his impact on medical education.

Fye, W. Bruce. "Ernest Henry Starling: His Law and Its Growing Significance in the Practice of Medicine." *Circulation* 68 (November, 1983): 1145-1147. After a brief overview of Starling's life, the author shows how Starling's basic scientific discoveries have become increasingly important to clinical medicine and uses Starling's work to illustrate the ways in which advances in clinical medicine depend on basic research done many years earlier.

*James A. Cowan*
*Abraham Verghese*

# HERMANN STAUDINGER

*Born:* March 23, 1881; Worms, Germany
*Died:* September 8, 1965; Freiburg im Breisgau, West Germany
*Area of Achievement:* Chemistry
*Contribution:* Staudinger became the father of a novel branch of chemistry when he conceived of and proved the existence of macromolecules. This work laid the foundation for the technological achievements in the plastics and high polymer synthetics industries. In addition, Staudinger contributed to the fields of organic chemistry and molecular biology.

## Early Life

Hermann Staudinger, the winner of the 1953 Nobel Prize in Chemistry, was born in Worms, Germany (modern West Germany) in 1881. He was the son of Auguste Staudinger and Franz Staudinger, a neo-Kantian philosopher. Staudinger's primary education took place at a local *Gymnasium* in Worms from which he was graduated in 1899. When he began his secondary education at the University of Halle, he was interested in botany; however, he switched his major to chemistry upon the advice of his father, who had been told that his son must first master the basic principles of science to understand plant life adequately. This interest in botany remained throughout his life and surfaced in his later work. Almost immediately, he transferred to Darmstadt after his father was appointed to a teaching position there. Staudinger pursued advanced studies at Munich (briefly) and at Halle, where he wrote his dissertation on the malonic esters of unsaturated compounds under the direction of Daniel Vorlander. He received his Ph.D. in organic chemistry on August 3, 1903.

Staudinger continued his research at the University of Strasbourg to obtain his teaching qualification, which he received in 1907. It was at Strasbourg, working under Johannes Thiele, that Staudinger made his first important discovery, the ketene, a highly reactive unsaturated form of ketone. Having earned his teaching qualification, he became an assistant professor at the Technische Hochschule in Karlsruhe, where he remained until 1912, when he succeeded Nobel laureate Richard Willstätter at the Eidgenossische Technische Hochschule in Zurich. Because of the shortages of World War I, Staudinger's work at Karlsruhe and Zurich kept very much in touch with the needs of industry and Germany. Staudinger worked on the synthesis of rubber and, with his student, Leopold Ružička, studied the composition of the insecticide pyrethrin and developed an artificial pepper. With the help of another student, Tadeusz Reichstein, Staudinger succeeded in synthesizing the aroma of coffee, a commodity cut off from wartime Germany. Yet Staudinger's main thrust of research during these early years remained the study of ketenes, about which he published *Die Ketene* (1912), a book which is still considered a standard. In 1926, Staudinger left Zurich to accept a position as a lecturer of chemistry at the University of Freiburg im Breisgau, where he remained until his retirement in 1951.

In 1927, Staudinger married Magda Woit, a Latvian plant physiologist, with whom he coauthored many papers. They had no children.

## Life's Work

Staudinger, educator, author, inventor, and researcher, made his greatest contribution to science by enunciating and proving the macromolecular theory, which states that rubber, plastics, and similar substances (polymers) are composed of long chain molecules having hundreds of repeating units connected by primary covalent bonds. For these molecules, which can have indefinitely large molecular weights, Staudinger coined the term "macromolecule."

Prior to 1920, the relatively insoluble, uncharacterizable resinous substances which organic chemists frequently found on the bottom of their reaction flasks were an enigma, although they were suspected to be polymeric (having chains composed of repeating units) in nature. This group of substances, of which rubber is a member, displays a nonlinear relationship between viscosity and concentration, nonstoichiometry, an inability to crystallize and in general a failure to adhere to the same physical laws as conventional molecules.

There were two prevailing theories at the time, the most popular of which was the micellar theory of the German chemist Carl Harries, who believed that these substances were physical aggregates of low-molecular-weight polymers held together by weak residual forces, and the theory of Samuel Pickles, who believed that the substances were composed of long chain molecules held together by primary chemical bonds. In 1910, while work-

ing under Carl Engler at Karlsruhe, Staudinger discovered a new way to synthesize isoprene, the structural unit of synthetic rubber, and was thereby introduced to this controversy. Harries thought that the weak secondary forces which held the isoprene rings of rubber together arose from their unsaturated double bonds, so Staudinger devised an experiment to test this theory. Harries predicted that removal of the double bonds by hydrogenation would restore the native, conventional properties of these molecules, causing them to form liquid hydrocarbons, but a series of experiments carried out in 1922 by Staudinger gave no such results. Staudinger's saturated synthetic hydrorubbers were nondistillable, colloidal, and differed little from natural rubber. It was this experiment which caused him to embark on an ambitious new area of research to prove his macromolecular theory.

In an attempt to avoid the experimental difficulties associated with natural polymers, Staudinger, in the early 1920's, chose to extend his studies to the polymers of styrene and oxymethylene (the solid form of the preservative formalin), synthetic models of rubber and cellulose, respectively. The physical properties of the homologous series of paraffin waxes, long chain hydrocarbons having the general formula $C_nH_{2n+2}$, vary with chain length. Staudinger, recognizing that styrene behaves in a similar manner to these paraffins, came to the conclusion that polystyrene is also one member of a homologous series, the properties of which depend on the average chain length.

This inspiration led Staudinger to engage in a series of experiments to measure the viscosity of polymers, a technique well established as being sensitive to the molecular weight of small molecules. In this work, Staudinger indeed found a direct correlation between the viscosity and the length of the polystyrene samples from which he was able to calculate the molecular weight of the polymer molecule. The results indicated an extremely large chain, which was presented as strong evidence for his macromolecular concept. This work, as well as his hydrogenation experiments, were published in his classic book *Die hochmolekularen organischen Verbindungen, Kautschuk und Cellulose* (1932; the high-molecular organic compounds, rubber and cellulose).

Staudinger presented his results on three important occasions from 1924 to 1926, but they were not well received. Especially the last two times, at the meeting of the Zurich Chemical Society and the Düsseldorf meeting of the Association of German Natural Scientists and Physicians, Staudinger encountered vigorous opposition from the proponents of the micellar aggregate theory. In fact, Staudinger once stated that he only convinced one person at the Düsseldorf meeting, Richard Willstätter. They did not believe that Staudinger's viscosity measurements were a reliable indicator of molecular weight but thought rather that his results reflected a state of aggregation of numerous molecules. Furthermore, the well-respected mineralogist Paul Niggli insisted that a molecule with dimensions larger than the unit cell obtained by X-ray diffraction could not exist. The scientific community would not be convinced of the existence of macromolecules unless they could be sure that Staudinger was looking at a pure sample instead of an aggregate of many molecules.

At this point, some events began to turn in Staudinger's favor. Toward the end of the 1920's, Theodor Svedberg and Robin Fåhraeus conducted experiments to measure the equilibrium sedimentation of oxyhemoglobin and carbonylhemoglobin using an ultracentrifuge, a powerful new tool for determining molecular weights. From these experiments, hemoglobin was found to have a very high molecular weight of about sixty-five thousand, four times higher than that given from elementary analysis. Furthermore, this was a sharply defined molecular weight, without the spread that would be expected if hemoglobin were an aggregate. The recognition of a high-molecular-weight compound in protein chemistry by an independent method lent welcome support to Staudinger's macromolecular theory.

Staudinger hoped to measure the molecular weight of synthetic and natural polymers by this method, so he applied for a grant to purchase an ultracentrifuge for Freiburg. His grant was turned down, however, a reminder of the skepticism Staudinger and his concepts endured. In a fit of depression over this event, Staudinger turned again to viscosity measurements and in 1929, working with two students, R. Nodzu and E. Ochiai, he showed that for linear molecules the viscosity of their solutions is proportional to the number of residues in the chain. This relationship between the specific viscosity and the molecular weight is known as Staudinger's law and is widely used in industry wherever there is polymer research in progress.

Finally, other evidence emerged to support the existence of macromolecules. Flow birefringence experiments conducted by R. Signer showed that polymers in solution had very large length to breadth ratios; the American chemist W. H. Carothers succeeded in synthesizing nylon by a condensation polymerization reaction which liberated an amount of water equal to the number of residues in the product; and X-ray crystallographers at last realized that a molecule could be larger than the unit cell. With this work accomplished, Staudinger was finally able to concentrate on his first love, biology, for which he had been preparing himself for thirty years.

Staudinger's youthful interest in biology emerged in 1926, when he began studies on the structure and function of macromolecular compounds in living systems. At a lecture delivered in Munich in 1936, Staudinger stated, "Every gene macromolecule possesses a quite definite structural plan, which determines its function in life." This statement was perceptive in the light of the fact that the genetic code was not understood until 1953. Some of Staudinger's ideas in biology were simplistic, however, and he clearly lacked a strong understanding of biological concepts. For example, he took the macromolecular concept to an extreme when he calculated the molecular weight of a bacterium. In 1947, Staudinger published *Makromolekulare Chemie und Biologie*, which gives his view of future developments in molecular biology.

With the help of his wife, Magda, Staudinger spent the last part of his career working on biologically related topics and using the phase-contrast microscope to visualize macromolecules. This work ended when Freiburg was bombed in 1944 during World War II. Staudinger's energies had been spent by this time and he retired in 1951. Staudinger died of a heart condition at the age of eighty-four.

## Summary

By the time Hermann Staudinger began his work on macromolecules, he was already forty and had a considerable reputation as an organic chemist. Indeed, his colleagues could not understand why a man of his stature would want to do research in an area they called "grease chemistry." It is fortunate, however, that Staudinger did take up the challenge, for a less persistent, less eloquent, or less respected chemist could not have endured the attacks and controversy surrounding the macromolecular theory. Unfortunately, there was even conflict among the supporters of the macromolecular theory. Herman Mark and Frederick Eirich believed that polymers could be flexible chains and form micellelike bundles while still being macromolecules, a view which proved to be correct, but Staudinger rejected the micellar theory so completely that he believed that macromolecules could be nothing but rigid rods. Because of this controversy, Staudinger was not awarded the Nobel Prize until 1953.

Staudinger was a prolific writer, having published more than five hundred papers and books. He also founded and became the editor of the journal *Die Makromolekulare Chemie* in 1947. Staudinger was the founder of macromolecular chemistry, and his work laid the foundation for a tremendous polymer industry. In addition, his students and disciples formed the core of this area of research. Besides the Nobel Prize, Staudinger won many other prizes for scientific achievement as well as two honorary degrees.

Although best remembered for his pioneering work in polymer chemistry, Staudinger was also a first-rate teacher and administrator. Students came from all over the world to work under him; he was so successful at inspiring in others his talent for creative thinking that two of his students, L. Ružička and T. Reichstein, each won the Nobel Prize. His students remember him as a quiet man who was fond of explosions.

### Bibliography

Borman, Stu, et al. "Chemistry Crystallizes into Modern Science." *Chemical and Engineering News* 76 no. 2, (January 12, 1998). Discusses some of the inventions and discoveries of the last 75 years in the chemical area including Staudinger's 1920 work with macromolecules which laid a foundation for biotechnology.

Furukawa, Yasu. *Staudinger, Carothers, and the Emergence of Macromolecular Chemistry.* Ann Arbor: University Microfilms International, 1983. A dissertation by Furukawa for his doctorate in the history of science. This book describes in detail Staudinger's education and work and puts them into their proper historical perspective. References are included.

Morawetz, Herbert. *Polymers: The Origins and Growth of a Science.* New York: Wiley, 1985; London: Constable, 1995. The publication of this book was suggested by Staudinger's wife, Magda. The chapter "Staudinger's Struggle for Macromolecules" gives the best step-by-step account of the battle to prove the macromolecular theory.

Olby, Robert. "The Macromolecular Concept and the Origins of Molecular Biology." *Journal of Chemical Education* 47 (1970): 168-174. A lucid account of the intellectual battles fought in the effort to establish the macromolecular concept in the field of molecular biology.

Quarles, Willem. "Hermann Staudinger: Thirty Years of Macromolecules." *Journal of Chemical Education* 28 (1951): 120-122. A summary of Staudinger's life's work, written in honor of his seventieth birthday. The article emphasizes Staudinger's early years. It describes his manner, teaching accomplishments, and his relationship with his students, some of whom became Nobel laureates. A portrait is included.

Staudinger, Hermann. *From Organic Chemistry to Macromolecules.* New York: Wiley, 1970. An autobiography based heavily on Staudinger's scientific publications. This book has the best account of Staudinger's early work and explains the motivations for his choice of research projects. Explains Staudinger's line of reasoning and why he was convinced that his macromolecular concept was correct. Contains almost all the references to Staudinger's scientific publications as well as portraits of him and of some of the men he admired.

*Kenneth S. Spector*

# EDWARD STEICHEN

*Born:* March 27, 1879; Luxembourg
*Died:* March 25, 1973; West Redding, Connecticut
*Area of Achievement:* Photography
*Contribution:* Steichen was a gifted and remarkably versatile photographer and a visionary editor, who did more than any single individual in developing the range of photography's possibilities as an expressive medium.

## Early Life

Éduard (it became Edward early in his career) Jean Steichen was born March 27, 1879, in Luxembourg, the only son of Jean-Pierre and Marie Kemp Steichen. In 1881, the Steichens emigrated to Hancock, Michigan; two years later, their daughter Lillian was born. (She would later marry the poet Carl Sandburg, with whom Steichen would become close friends.) A hardworking and precociously inquisitive boy, Steichen once took apart his Western Union delivery bicycle and put it together again; he did the same with a watch and got it to run with two pieces left over. When a teacher at his college preparatory school praised one of his drawings, his mother—who owned a hat shop and was the family's chief breadwinner after her husband's health declined from work in the copper mines—determined that her son would become a great artist.

Steichen got his first camera at the age of sixteen. Eagerly, he took a roll of fifty pictures, but when the film came back, only one of them had been clear enough to print. His mother said that the one picture was so beautiful it was worth the forty-nine failures, and, bolstered by her encouragement, Steichen taught himself photography (at the time, there were no classes and few books on the subject). His formal education having ended at the age of fifteen, he was then working as an apprentice at a Milwaukee lithography firm that supplied posters and display cards for packers and flour mills. Always interested in finding a new and better way of doing things, Steichen persuaded his superiors to let him photograph their subjects so the drawings made of them would be more accurate (they had been using outdated woodcuts as models). Also a talented designer, he won a prize for his design of an envelope, and one of his illustrations was reproduced on posters across the country.

Painting and sketching in his spare time, he organized the Milwaukee Art Students League in 1897 and became its first president. Tall, with a prominent nose, striking blue eyes, and unruly hair, he had, as a local newspaper would later declare, the looks of an artist. Fascinated with the romantic subjects of twilight and moonlit scenes in his paintings, Steichen wrestled with the problem of communicating mood and emotion in his photographs. Through persistence and an ability to convert failure into success (an accidental kick to the tripod blurred the image but succeeded in conveying the mood), Steichen created new, experimental photographs. He achieved his first recognition as a photographer when two prints he submitted were selected to appear in the Second Philadelphia Salon in 1899.

His entries in the Chicago Salon in 1900 brought a letter of encouragement from prominent photographer Clarence White, who also wrote about him to Alfred Stieglitz, another leading photographer. On his way to Europe at the age of twenty-one, Steichen stopped in New York and met with Stieglitz, who bought three of his prints. Steichen had quit his job as a commercial artist (against his father's wishes but with his mother's support) to devote himself to fine art. While in Europe, he continued to paint, and, as he had hoped, met with and photographed many prominent writers and artists, among them the sculptor Auguste Rodin. Steichen had his first major showing in the New School of American Photography in London in 1901 and his first one-man showing of paintings and photographs in Paris in 1902.

## Life's Work

Steichen returned to New York in 1902 and supported himself through commercial portrait photography—one of his most famous photographs was of J. P. Morgan, the powerful financier. Steichen was taking it for a portrait painter who found Morgan too restless to sit still. Carefully preparing the shot and lighting beforehand with a janitor as stand-in, Steichen accomplished the job using only three minutes of Morgan's time; the pleased Morgan rewarded Steichen with a roll of hundred-dollar bills—yet more valuable was the lesson the experience had taught him. He had asked Morgan to strike a particular pose, which Morgan complained was uncomfortable, but when Steichen told him to pose the way he wished, Morgan returned to that same "uncomfortable" position, only this time with an air of defiance and irritation that brought out his true

personality. Steichen realized that when some live moment was brought to a sitting, it could change a picture from simply an image into a portrait that revealed character. He would use that insight to great advantage in a later phase of his career.

In 1905, along with Stieglitz, Steichen established "The Little Galleries of the Photo-Secession" in his former studio at 291 Fifth Avenue. The Photo-Secessionists were committed to promoting modern art and, in particular, to winning respect for photography as an art form (when photographs had been shown at an art museum for the first time seven years earlier, the exhibition had stirred quite a controversy). The group published the influential *Camera Work* from 1903 to 1917; its cover was designed by Steichen, and his photographs, which Stieglitz considered proof that photography was an art, appeared in numerous issues. Steichen, feeling stifled by the routine of commercial photography, returned to Paris in 1906. From there, he sent back America's first glimpses of European modernism, arranging for exhibitions at "291" of Rodin, Henri Matisse, Paul Cézanne, and Pablo Picasso. He returned to the United States when war broke out in 1914; soon afterward, his friendship with Stieglitz ended over differing views about the war—in particular, about how artists should respond to the world crisis.

In 1917, then thirty-eight, Steichen volunteered for the United States Army and was put in charge of the Photographic Division of Aerial Photography for the American Expeditionary Forces; it was the first time that aerial photography was used for reconnaissance and intelligence purposes. Steichen proved to be a remarkably able commander, skilled at solving the large-scale organizational problems of wartime as well as the technical difficulties of shooting clear pictures from a moving airplane. After the war, he made a decisive change in the direction of his career. Steichen gave up painting—dramatically burning all of his paintings in a bonfire in his garden—and devoted himself exclusively to photography, through which, he reasoned, he could reach a wider audience and make an affirmative contribution to the world. His experience in aerial photography had given him a renewed appreciation for the medium; he entered into a second apprenticeship in photography, determined to master its range of technical possibilities. He worked with patient dedication—in one experiment, taking more than one thousand shots of a white cup and saucer to study various arrangements of light; he also worked with abstract symbolism and design, bringing a new sense of shape and form into his work.

Steichen returned to New York in 1923 and was hired by Conde Nast to do fashion and portrait photography for *Vogue* and *Vanity Fair* magazines (his lucrative contract made him the most highly paid photographer in the world). His fashion photographs were distinguished by a strong sense of design and dramatic lighting; his portraits of celebrities (among them actors Greta Garbo, Marlene Dietrich, and Charles Chaplin) were often considered the best ever taken of the stars because of Steichen's gift for putting his subjects at ease and then finding the moment when their faces were lit with character. He also did advertising work—photographing silks, creams, and vacuum cleaners—for the J. Walter Thompsen agency. He devoted his spare hours to his longtime hobby of breeding delphiniums (the Museum of Modern Art displayed his hybrids in 1936). When Steichen found that his work was becoming too repetitious, he closed his New York studio in 1938.

At the outbreak of war in 1941, the then sixty-two-year-old Steichen volunteered for service, was initially refused because of his age, but eventually succeeded in receiving a commission as lieutenant commander, in charge of all navy combat photography. He assembled a unit of top photographers and instructed them to focus on the human aspects of war. He supervised a navy film, *The Fighting Lady*, and directed two photographic exhibitions for the Museum of Modern Art: "Road to Victory" (1942) and "Power in the Pacific" (1945). Coordinating the work of many photographers around a single theme, these exhibitions introduced a new concept of photographic presentation that was both visually and emotionally compelling.

In 1947, he was appointed director of the department of photography of the Museum of Modern Art; he temporarily gave up his own work to gain more objectivity in judging the work of others. He organized numerous exhibitions; the most notable was "The Family of Man," a collection of more than five hundred photographs from around the world, selected to convey the essential unity of humankind. In honor of his eighty-second birthday the museum gave him a large retrospective exhibition in 1961. He became director emeritus of the department in 1962, and in 1963, he wrote his autobiography, *A Life in Photography*. In his advanced years, he continued to take pictures, experimenting with a movie camera and color photography. He was married three times and had two daughters. He died at his home in 1973, two days before his ninety-fourth birthday.

### Summary

Steichen's list of achievements is so extensive that it could easily have been the work of several men rather than one. His tremendous vitality, his ambitious pursuit of change, and his drive to find new expressions mirrored the spirit of America at the beginning of the twentieth century—and consistently placed him at the leading edge of photography's evolution. The young painter-photographer who in 1898 thrilled at the news that photographs were being shown in an art museum might never have dreamed that he would be named a director of photography at a major museum in his later years. Yet not only did Steichen play a significant role in winning this respect for photography as an art form, but also he pioneered the movement of photography back out of the museum and into the public eye for more popular and widespread consumption. He was often criticized as having sold out his artistic instincts for his commercial work, to which he responded:

> If my technique, imagination and vision are any good I ought to be able to put the best values of my noncommercial and experimental photographs into a pair of shoes, a tube of tooth paste, a jar of face cream, a mattress or any object that I want to light up and make humanly interesting in an advertising photograph.

For more than half a century, his creativity and technical mastery set a new standard of excellence which revolutionized each of the fields he entered—portraiture, the military, fashion, and advertising—literally changing the way Americans saw themselves.

It took a visionary spirit to bring, as he did, the first examples of modernist art to the American continent; in a real sense, he ushered the culture into the twentieth century. Later, responding to the shattering side effects of two world wars on the American psyche, he was, as an editor and director of exhibitions, essentially a humanist, bringing to the public a view of man that was both compassionate and ennobling. His "The Family of Man" exhibition was viewed by more than nine million people in more than sixty-nine countries. He had indeed realized his goal of making, through photography, an affirmative contribution to the world.

### Bibliography

Green, Jonathon, ed. *Camera Work: A Critical Anthology.* New York: Aperture, 1973. A valuable resource for anyone interested in studying the Photo-Secessionists, with commentary, excerpts from issues, photographs, an extensive bibliography, and biographies of contributors.

Harrison, Martin. "Art: Vintage Fashion Photography." *Architectural Digest* 51, no. 10, (October, 1994). Discusses the development of fashion photography, including Steichen's platinum prints.

Longwell, Dennis. *Steichen: The Master Prints, 1895-1914: The Symbolist Period.* London: Thames and Hudson, and New York: Museum of Modern Art, 1978. Focuses on Steichen's early career as an art photographer. Though Longwell's thesis linking Steichen to the Symbolist movement is of limited value, the seventy-two prints and accompanying commentary and selections from letters are worth viewing.

Newhall, Beaumont. *The History of Photography from 1839 to the Present Day.* 5th ed. New York: Museum of Modern Art, 1997. A comprehensive look at the development of photography, its technology and major figures. Scattered references to Steichen.

Parsons, Melinda Boyd. "'Moonlight on Darkening Ways': Concepts of Nature and the Artist in Edward and Lilian Steichen's Socialism." *American Art* 11, no. 1 (Spring 1997). Examines the evidence of socialist ideals in Steichen's landscapes of the 1890s.

Phillips, Christopher, comp. *Steichen at War.* New York: Harry N. Abrams, 1981. The focus is on Steichen's years as commander of navy photography in World War II. Text and photographs are excellent.

Sandburg, Carl. *Steichen the Photographer.* New York: Harcourt Brace, 1929. An affectionate and anecdotal look at Steichen's life by his brother-in-law. Survives its early publication date quite well. Though this edition is difficult to find, a large portion of it is reprinted in *The Sandburg Range*, published in 1957 by Harcourt, Brace and Co.

Steichen, Edward. *A Life in Photography.* London: Allen, and, New York: Doubleday, 1963. The best account of Steichen's life is his own. Steichen wrote the text and selected the 249 photographs that accompany it. Also included is a valuable biographical outline.

———, ed. *The Family of Man*. New York: Museum of Modern Art, 1955. Contains the photographs from Steichen's popular exhibition, with a brief prologue by Sandburg and an introduction by Steichen.

*Dana Gerhardt*

# EDITH STEIN

*Born:* October 12, 1891; Breslau, Germany (now Wrocław, Poland)

*Died:* August 9, 1942; Auschwitz, Poland

*Areas of Achievement:* Philosophy, theology, religion, and women's rights

*Contribution:* Stein, a disciple of the phenomenologist Edmund Husserl, became herself a leading proponent of his method of philosophy. Alongside her spiritual evolution from Judaism to atheism to Catholicism, she tried, in her writings, to relate phenomenology to personalism, Thomism, the Catholic tradition on women, and the mystical theology of Saint John of the Cross.

## Early Life

On the Day of Atonement, the tenth day of the seventh month (Tishri) in the Jewish calendar (October 12, 1891, in the Christian calendar), Edith Stein was born in Breslau. She was the youngest of eleven children, and Auguste Stein, her intelligent and devout mother, thanked the God of Israel in her synagogue for this sign of the special election of her last child. The Steins were merchants who had come to Breslau from Silesia in central Europe (now in southwestern Poland) when the family's lumber business failed. Soon after he had settled in Breslau, Edith Stein's father, who was only forty-eight, died of a stroke. Edith was only a year old, and her mother was left with the management of a debt-ridden lumber business and the care of seven children (four had died before Edith arrived).

With Auguste Stein's energies absorbed by her duties as principal provider, Else, her eldest daughter, assisted with the children's upbringing. Edith was a gifted but high-strung young girl, difficult to control. She possessed an agile mind and an independent spirit, which she enjoyed exhibiting by reciting poems and making witty remarks. Around the age of seven, however, she isolated herself from her family, perhaps because they treated her as "Edith, the smart one." This characterization hurt her feelings, since she recognized, even then, that being good was much more important than being smart. She did not reveal these emotional undercurrents of her interior world to her sisters or mother, and her great firmness of will allowed her to construct a placid temperament for the exterior world.

Her formal education began at the Viktoriaschule ("Victoria School") in Breslau, where, at her own insistence, she was admitted early. She quickly established herself as the best student in the class, a position she maintained throughout her schooling. She once said that she felt more at home in school than in her own family. In fact, in her need to nourish her hungry mind, she turned her home into a school by her voracious reading. Her academic success made it all the more shocking to her family when, at thirteen, she announced that she was leaving school. Unknown to her mother, Edith was passing through an adolescent religious crisis. Though remaining publicly observant, she no longer believed in God and had abandoned private prayer. The family attributed her change in personality to frail health, and she was sent to recuperate to the home of her sister Else in Hamburg (Else had married a doctor and already had three children).

After an eight-month hiatus, Edith returned to the Victoria School to recommence a college-preparatory program, for she had decided to become a teacher and dedicate herself to the discovery and communication of truth. In choosing teaching as a career, she was being faithful to the evolution of her personality as she experienced it in her thoughts, feelings, and abilities. Despite her youth, she manifested a remarkable insight into her own intellectual development and a daring independence from her family, religion, and society.

## Life's Work

Stein entered the University of Breslau in 1911, and not long after, she came into contact with phenomenology, the philosophy that was to dominate her intellectual life. Her path to phenomenology began when she attended lectures in psychology. She hoped to discover through this "science of the soul" the undergirding coherence of human existence, but the course, which emphasized experimental psychology, disappointed her because the teacher completely ignored the soul. Amid this disillusionment, she read *Logische Untersuchungen* (1900; logical investigations), by Edmund Husserl, phenomenology's founder, and this experience revolutionized her thinking. While attending classes at the university, Stein lived at home, but her enthusiasm for phenomenology grew so keen that she soon expressed her strong desire to leave Breslau and to study with Husserl at the University of Göttingen. By this time her mother had become aware of her daughter's apostasy from Judaic beliefs and her recent conversion to a modern philosophy, and she was deeply disappointed, but she did not prevent her daughter from transferring to Göttingen.

As one of the first women admitted to Göttingen, Stein stood out at the university, but she found a comfortable philosophical home with the phenomenologists. She had come to Husserl searching for truth, and he convinced her that phenomenology, when practiced rigorously, would lead to the truth. In her early days as a phenomenologist, Stein found that empathy was her key to the truth.

Although Stein became friendly with several Catholics at Göttingen, her main entré into Catholicism came through Max Scheler, one of Husserl's Jewish pupils who would later convert to Catholicism. His lectures on religious philosophy, which were attended by Stein, made her an admirer of the spiritual beauty of Catholicism. She was sympathetic with Scheler's attempt to rank values hierarchically, ascending from sensory through life to spiritual values. Scheler held that religious values make a person fully human, and the empathic heart of Stein responded to the message of Christianity, even though it led her to acknowledge her own spiritual poverty. Adolf Reinach, another phenomenologist who would later convert to Christianity, also helped her to start the internal transformation that would bring her to the Christian faith.

When World War I began in the summer of 1914, Stein, who had absorbed an intense patriotism from her family, felt a sense of duty to her country. She volunteered her services and was assigned to a hospital for infectious diseases in Austria, where she cared for soldiers suffering from typhus, dysentery, and cholera. After the hospital closed in 1915, she returned to Göttingen and resumed her doctoral studies. Building on her concrete wartime experiences, she was able to probe the subject of empathy more pointedly as a special kind of knowing involving the entire human person. Husserl was very impressed by her work and called her the best doctoral student he had ever had (which was high praise, indeed, since Martin Heidegger was also his student at the time). When Husserl was offered a professorship at the University of Freiburg in 1916, he asked Stein to come with him as his graduate assistant. During her first summer in Freiburg, she completed her dissertation, "The Problem of Empathy," and after its successful defense, she was awarded her doctoral degree summa cum laude. She then became a member of Freiburg's faculty and quickly gained a reputation as one of the university's leading philosophers. Her main duties were to initiate new students into the strange world of phenomenology and to edit Husserl's manuscripts.

At the end of 1917, she received the sad news that Reinach had been killed on the battlefield of Flanders, and, while attending his funeral, Stein was approached by Frau Reinach to put her husband's papers in order. Stein discovered that many of Reinach's writings were concerned with the person of Jesus Christ, and this caused her to read the New Testament. The experience of Frau Reinach's faith at the funeral and of Jesus Christ's message in the Gospels led her to abandon her atheism, and she began to wonder whether she would eventually convert to Lutheranism or Catholicism. Although intellectually convinced of God's existence and the Incarnation, she nevertheless found herself unable to take the practical step of conversion.

Upon her return to Freiburg, she applied to the University of Göttingen, where she wanted to work on her *Habilitationsschrift* (a second dissertation that would qualify her as a university lecturer), but, despite a laudatory recommendation from Husserl, Göttingen's reluctance to hire a woman professor proved to be unconquerable. Thus, in 1919, Stein returned to Breslau, where she gave lessons and continued her philosophical research. A turning point in her life occurred during the summer of 1921, when she was visiting friends at Bergzabern in southeastern Germany. She happened to pick up the autobiography of Saint Teresa of Avila, which so fascinated her that she continued reading it all night. On completing it in the morning, she had an overwhelming sense that the Catholic Christianity that guided Teresa was the truth for which she had been searching. She immediately bought a catechism and went to her first Mass. She wanted to be baptized, but the local priest informed her that a preparation period was required. She returned to Breslau and continued her teaching and research, but she returned to Bergzabern to be baptized on January 1, 1922. Prior to her conversion to Catholicism, she had always assumed that she would eventually marry, but with faith had come a call to consecrate herself to God as a nun. Realizing that her mother would have serious problems accepting her conversion, she postponed her entrance into the religious life. She continued to attend synagogue services with her mother, who was surprised that the Psalms in her daughter's breviary were the same as the Jewish Psalms.

Having abandoned her past plans for an academic career, Stein accepted a position as a German teacher at a girls' school run by Dominican sisters at Speyer in the Rhineland. Her life became a blend of teaching and prayer, and she enjoyed sharing the life of a religious community. Though not a Dominican, she lived as one, refusing to accept any salary beyond what she needed for room, board, and clothing. In 1925, Erich Przywara, a Jesuit priest and philosopher, encouraged her to resume her research, and she began to translate from Latin into German a treatise by Saint Thomas Aquinas on truth. Through Aquinas, she became familiar with Scholasticism, a philosophical approach developed in the Middle Ages to help Christians obtain a deeper understanding of revealed truth. Przywara and Aquinas helped her realize that God could be served through scholarship. Aquinas, like Teresa of Avila, effectively communicated his personal experience of God in his writings, and his example facilitated Stein's own spiritual development through her writings on phenomenology and Aquinas.

Stein's philosophical writings and translations attracted the attention of many groups, especially associations of Catholic women, and she received numerous invitations to speak on women's issues in Germany, Switzerland, and Austria. So popular did she become as a lecturer that Przywara set up periodic tours for her. Stein's success as a lecturer convinced her that she had outgrown the small school at Speyer, which she left in March, 1931, to devote herself to the writing of her *Habilitationsschrift* on phenomenology and Scholasticism. Unable, because of male chauvinism and anti-Semitism, to obtain a position at Freiburg or Breslau, she became, in 1932, a lecturer at the Educational Institute in Münster. Before moving there, she again investigated the possibility of entering a contemplative religious order, but her spiritual advisers counseled her that she could best serve the Catholic church as a teacher and lecturer. Yet after a decade's hiatus from university work and secular life, she found it difficult to reroot herself into a modern world that increasingly horrified her. She witnessed Jews being attacked, and she worried about her family in Breslau. She was a vehement opponent of Nazism, and when Adolf Hitler came to power in 1933, she, like many others of Jewish descent, lost her position.

Anti-Semitic persecution contributed to Stein's realization of her unique vocation—the reconciliation of Judaism and Christianity. She began writing *Aus dem Leben einer Jüdischen Familie* (1965; *Life in a Jewish Family*, 1986), in which she tried to show young Germans that Jewish families shared the same joys and frustrations in their daily lives as their Christian neighbors. She finally decided that the time had come for her to carry out her long-held wish to enter the Carmelite Order. After applying to the convent in Cologne, she worried that, at age forty-two, she might be judged too old, but the sisters were impressed with her, and the notification of her acceptance came in June, 1933. She finally faced the soul-shattering task of telling her mother that she would be leaving her forever for a life that she knew her mother would never understand.

Many friends and relatives predicted that she would become discontented in a cloistered life with nuns of constricted intellectual interests, but she adjusted surprisingly quickly to her new environment. She found the Carmel community full of solicitous love, and, although her fellow novices were much younger than she was, she was stimulated by their sense of spiritual adventure. Stein took Teresa Benedicta a Cruce as her religious name to express her gratitude for the spiritual patronage of Saint Benedict and Saint Teresa of Avila and also to reflect her special devotion to the Passion of Christ.

At the request of her superiors, she returned to her philosophical research and writing. Most of her efforts centered on her synthesis of the major ideas of Husserl and Aquinas in a study begun several years before and now called *Endliches und ewiges Sein* (1950; finite and eternal being). Her religious experiences had changed her, however, and she no longer shared the aversion of most phenomenologists to metaphysical assertions. Consequently, she incorporated theological truths into her discussions without supporting Phenomenological analysis. Despite problems of lack of an adequate library and of opportunities to consult with other philosophers, she completed her account in the summer of 1936. While awaiting news from a German publisher, she learned that her mother had died, unreconciled to her daughter's vocation, on September 14, 1936, the Feast of the Holy Cross. More bad news arrived soon after, when she was told that anti-Jewish laws prevented the publication of her book.

In the winter following her mother's death, Stein's spirits revived on hearing that her sister Rosa had entered the Catholic church, but the situation in Europe was so distressful that her happiness was short-lived. She saw the sufferings of the Carmelites in Spain during the Civil War as a harbinger of what the German Carmelites could expect. These upheavals made her eager to pronounce her solemn vows as quickly as possible. On November 8, the so-called Kristallnacht occurred, when many windows of synagogues and Jewish businesses were smashed and many Jews were beaten. Stein was aghast at the abyss of sinfulness revealed by these attacks on her fellow Jews. Many of her relatives applied to emigrate to America, and some of them were fortunate enough to escape, but others had their applications turned down. Stein herself, who had explored the possibility of emigrating to a Carmelite convent in Palestine, left Cologne on December 31, 1938, for the Carmelite convent in Echt in The Netherlands. Leaving the Cologne Carmel was difficult, since she felt so much a part of the community, but she knew that her presence there would endanger her fellow nuns. She had no illusion that she was escaping to safety, however, for in a final testament that she wrote in 1939 she stated her acceptance of the death that she believed God was preparing for her.

In 1940, Stein's sister Rosa, fleeing from the Nazis, joined her in Echt, where she became portress at the convent. Their joy of reunion soon turned to anxiety when the Nazis overran The Netherlands. Edith and Rosa again faced the threat of anti-Semitic persecution. Under the constant danger of being taken from her convent, Stein tried to continue with her life. A new superior assigned her to teach the postulants Latin, and Edith began instructing Rosa in the basics of the Carmelite life. Stein's superior also asked her to write a book on Saint John of the Cross, the great Carmelite mystic, in commemoration of the four hundredth anniversary of his birth. She devoted much time and thought to *Kreuzewissenschaft: Studie über Joannes a Cruce* (1950; *The Science of the Cross: A Study of Saint John of the Cross*, 1960), a phenomenological study of the saint's life and work.

During the summer of 1942, the Nazis began to deport Jews from The Netherlands. Throughout 1942, Stein had been desperately trying to get a Swiss visa to transfer to a Carmelite convent in Switzerland, but she was unable to make arrangements for her sister, and she refused to go without her. In July, as the deportations increased, the situation of the Stein sisters grew more critical. On August 2, Gestapo officials came to the Carmel cloister of Echt and arrested Edith and Rosa Stein. From Echt, the sisters were driven to local police headquarters for questioning and then taken to a concentration camp at Amersfoort, several miles northeast of Utrecht. While at Amersfoort, Stein gathered with other religious people to pray and to care for the sick. She was soon transported with twelve hundred fellow Jews to Westerbork, the central detention camp in the north of The Netherlands. Meanwhile, the efforts of the Carmelites at Echt and Catholic officials to obtain permission for Edith and Rosa to emigrate to Switzerland proved fruitless. By August 7, Stein and her sister were deported to Auschwitz in Nazi-occupied Poland. Stein's long-nourished sense that she would be asked to sacrifice her life intensified during these last days. Despite her fear, she approached death with serenity and in the spirit of atonement. Not much is known of her final hours, except that she was probably killed in an Auschwitz gas chamber on August 9, 1942, along with her sister and hundreds of other Jews. Her body, like the others, was initially thrown into a mass grave, but later in the year, to obliterate evidence of their crimes, the Nazis exhumed and cremated the remains.

Stein was beatified by Pope John Paul II at a ceremony in Cologne on May 1, 1987. She was proclaimed a martyr for her Catholic faith, an action that deeply disturbed those Jews who considered her an apostate as well as others who were convinced that she was murdered because she was Jewish and not out of hatred for her Catholic faith. The pope, who was an admirer of phenomenology and of Stein's personalism, wanted to make her a modern saint, but he also wanted to soothe bruised Jewish feelings. He emphasized that she had shared the fate of the Jewish people.

## Summary

Edith Stein's life was an intellectual and spiritual odyssey toward the truth. A highly intelligent and sensitive woman, she first became thoroughly familiar with scientific truth, but she soon discovered that this truth did not deserve her absolute devotion. Furthermore, it did not coincide with her experience of truth incarnated in persons. She once compared philosophy to a walk along the edge of an abyss, and she saw her philosophical and spiritual commitments as matters of life and death. Although she always maintained a scholar's appreciation for the value of scientific and philosophical findings, she increasingly centered her quest on spiritual truth, even when this cost her dearly. She identified herself with Jesus Christ, a deeply spiritual Jew, and she became a prayerful woman—some say a mystic—who continued to be an active and influential philosopher.

In the period following World War II, Stein's importance as a phenomenologist was overshadowed by the circumstances of her death. Many of the German Catholic women's organizations for whom she once lectured made her martyrdom into a symbol of Christian solidarity with Jews murdered in the Holocaust. Some Catholic scholars thought that her lack of theological training weakened the import of her writings, and to secular philosophers, many of whom had moved away from the phenomenological approach to a concern with language analysis, her attempt to link phenomenology and a philosophy of being seemed to be religious apologetics, with little to say to the modern world. Stein, who believed that she was living in a spiritually impoverished age, would have understood this neglect of her ideas. More recently, some scholars have begun to see her importance in the light of her work rather than in terms of her death. In this reevaluation, she emerges as a superb scholar and translator as well as a woman of penetrating moral acumen.

### Bibliography

Baseheart, Mary C. *Person in the World: Introduction to the Philosophy of Edith Stein.* Boston: Kluwer, 1997. Discusses the nature of the human being, which the author identifies as the common thread that runs through all of Stein's work and provides a basis for further study.

Graef, Hilda C. *The Scholar and the Cross: The Life and Work of Edith Stein.* Westminster, Md.: Newman Press and London: Longman, 1955. Graef, a British writer, based her account of Stein's life on a German biography written by the prioress of the Cologne Carmel and on new material gathered from several sources, including collections of manuscripts at Louvain and the personal reminiscences of Stein's friends and colleagues. The biography is strongest on the period after Stein's conversion to Catholicism.

Herbstrith, Waltraud. *Edith Stein: A Biography.* Translated by Bernard Bonowitz. 2d ed. San Francisco: Ignatius Press, 1992. Herbstrith, a Carmelite nun who knew Stein, presents an affectionate portrait of her as a Jew, a phenomenologist, and a Carmelite. She intersperses her largely chronological account with ample quotations from Stein's letters and writings as well as with analyses of her philosophy, theology, and interior development. The book contains notes to primary and secondary sources, a selected bibliography, and an index.

Nota, John H. "Misunderstanding and Insight About Edith Stein's Philosophy." *Human Studies* 10 (1987): 205-212. Attempts to correct a widespread misunderstanding about Stein's use of phenomenology after she became a Catholic (several philosophers have remarked that she was lost to the phenomenological movement after her conversion). The author's thesis is that Stein remained faithful to phenomenology throughout her life and that her Catholicism made her a better phenomenologist than she had been before her conversion.

Oben, Freda Mary. *Edith Stein: Scholar, Feminist, Saint.* New York: Alba House, 1988. Oben, like Stein, is a convert from Judaism to Catholicism. Her biography, the first written since Edith Stein was beatified by John Paul II in 1987, seeks to answer the question of why Stein is more famous now than during her lifetime. Oben's work gives a balanced treatment of Stein as a Jew, philosopher, Catholic convert, educator, feminist, Carmelite nun, and martyr.

Posselt, Sister Teresia Renata de Spiritu Sancto. *Edith Stein.* Translated by Cecily Hastings and Donald Nicholl. London and New York: Sheed and Ward, 1952. During the years after World War II, Teresia Renata, the prioress of the Carmelite convent in Cologne, collected the biographical data then available about Stein. She published this biography—mostly a collection of reminiscences and testimonies—in Nürnberg in 1948. It proved successful, and it had gone into a fifth printing and four translations by 1950, when Cecily Hastings and Donald Nicholl made this English translation for an American audience.

*Robert J. Paradowski*

# GERTRUDE STEIN

*Born:* February 3, 1874; Allegheny, Pennsylvania
*Died:* July 27, 1946; Neuilly-sur-Seine, France
*Area of Achievement:* Literature
*Contribution:* A literary innovator, Gertrude Stein captured the dialogue of common people and significantly influenced the writing of post-World War I authors.

## Early Life

Born into an affluent family that traded in imported fabrics, Gertrude Stein was the last child of Daniel and Amelia Stein, who vowed to have five children. Gertrude recommended being the youngest child in the family, contending that it saved one considerable bother.

Daniel Stein, having quarreled with his brother and business partner Solomon, took his family to Vienna in 1875, remaining abroad until Gertrude was five. She grew up fluent in French and German as well as English.

In 1880, the Steins moved to Oakland, California, where Gertrude grew up. In 1888, Amelia Stein died, followed by Daniel in 1891. Gertrude's brother Michael became her legal guardian. Her brother Leo, then nineteen, transferred from the University of California at Berkeley to Harvard. Gertrude followed as soon as she could, entering Radcliffe College (then known as "Harvard Annex") in 1893 as a special student because she failed the entrance examination.

At Radcliffe, Gertrude studied philosophy and psychology with Harvard professor William James, becoming his star student. She received the bachelor's degree magna cum laude in 1898. Returning to Baltimore, where much of her family lived, Stein began a medical degree at The Johns Hopkins University in 1897, continuing her studies until 1901, whereupon, although she had succeeded during her first three years as a medical student, she lost interest, failed courses, and left school a few months short of receiving the M.D.

Gertrude Stein's life took its most significant turn in 1903, when she went to Paris. There she fell in with the sisters Etta and Claribell Cone, textile heiresses who were involved in the art world. Leo came to Paris where he and Gertrude, comfortable from their inheritance, took an apartment at 27 rue de Fleurus. Gertrude lived there until 1937, when the owner reclaimed the apartment for a relative.

On September 8, 1907, Gertrude Stein met Alice Babette Toklas, newly arrived in Paris from San Francisco. From that day until Stein's death almost forty years later, the two were inseparable. Alice managed Gertrude's life, keeping house, shopping, cooking, and guarding Gertrude's privacy so zealously that no one could see Gertrude before passing muster with Toklas.

When interesting people arrived for the weekly salons at 27 rue de Fleurus, Toklas shepherded away the women, whom Gertrude called totally uninteresting, so that Stein could engage their men—including such luminaries as Pablo Picasso, Jo Davidson, Henri Matisse, Juan Gris, Ernest Hemingway, Ford Madox Ford, F. Scott Fitzgerald, Thornton Wilder, and Sherwood Anderson—in animated conversation. Stein, who enjoyed husbands, found wives boring. When she toured America in 1934-1935, she stipulated that she would speak to no strictly female audiences.

## Life's Work

Although Leo and Gertrude Stein were not enor-

mously rich, Paris in the early twentieth century offered inexpensive living in a sophisticated European capital. The Steins lived from trust distribution to trust distribution, but after meeting their fixed expenses, they had enough left over to haunt the shops of art dealers and buy paintings that eventually were worth millions: works by Picasso, Matisse, Gris, and others who emerged as the most significant painters of the period.

Gertrude formed close friendships with the artists whose work she collected. Reflecting on the philosophy that underlay much Impressionist and post-Impressionist art, Stein began to transform elements of that aesthetic into a literary theory that determined the course her writing took.

Misunderstood by literary audiences that expected authors to tell their tales directly, presenting largely observable surface realities, Gertrude Stein moved in her own direction. By doing so, she led the way for more than a generation of later writers.

Stein's was a singularly original mind, given to abstraction. Her undergraduate work in psychology and her subsequent training in medicine helped Stein become attuned to nuances in human behavior—especially in the ways that people use language—that few people perceived.

Just as the artists she admired distorted reality to achieve artistic ends, so did Stein begin to work with language in untried ways. Whereas most people are concerned with words as purveyors of meaning, Stein considered words also as sounds and shapes. That she became concerned with essences is evident in her line from "Sacred Emily" in *Tender Buttons* (1914), "Rose is a rose is a rose is a rose."

Hardly a horticultural description of a rose or a visual depiction of the color rose or an insight into a person named Rose, Stein's sentence forces conscientious readers to nudge into their consciousness all that they know about the word "rose." Stein plants a seed that she invites readers to cultivate.

Stein's first book, *Three Lives* (1909), is generally called a novel, although one must stretch the definition to call it one. This book contains sketches of three women, each a domestic servant. The first and third sketches, "The Good Anna" and "The Gentle Lena," are considerably shorter than the central sketch, "Melanctha," a name meaning "black earth." The good Anna is a German woman, bossy but with a kind heart. Lena is as submissive as Anna is domineering, but both women have two things in common: They work hard to survive, and they talk not as previous literary figures have spoken but as people of their social class actually talk. Their dialogue is filled with endless repetitions and non sequiturs, peppered with drivel—irrelevant details, middle-class moral judgments.

If readers object to this sort of dialogue (and most readers, on first exposure to *Three Lives*, find the dialogue bewildering), they should listen carefully to a typical conversation among working people riding home on a crowded bus or subway train after a day's work. Stein, who, as a medical student, did field work among Baltimore's working people, was attuned to their way of speaking. In *Three Lives*, she captures the everyday speech of common people with a verisimilitude that most authors of the day would have replaced with more conventional, literary dialogue.

*Three Lives*, using a stream-of-consciousness approach, broke new literary ground not only because it used three ordinary women as the protagonists of their respective stories but also because it devoted the longest of the three segments to a black protagonist, Melanctha Herbert, whom Stein presents not specifically as a black but as an ordinary working woman. Elements of Melanctha's black culture resonate in the story, but this segment is more than story of a working woman than that of a black woman—and "Melanctha" is the centerpiece of Stein's book.

Gertrude Stein's books seldom sold well. Some were printed at the author's expense. Publishers who accepted them usually ended up with mountains of copies that had not sold. *Tender Buttons*, a unique book of poetry employing collage and imposing the tenets of Cubism and Expressionism upon literature, and *Geography and Plays* (1922), a collection of short pieces, an almost surrealistic venture into the possibilities of language, followed *Three Lives*. Stein had also written a huge novel, *The Making of Americans* (1925), which traced three generations of a German American family not unlike her own.

No one wanted to publish this unwieldy book, which is still generally considered one of the most unreadable novels in the English language, although it is historically significant for its inventions in language and structure. In 1924, Ernest Hemingway, by now a close friend of Stein, persuaded Ford Madox Ford to serialize some of *The Making of Americans* in his *transatlantic review*, which ceased publication before Stein could be paid for her work. Finally, after years of trying, Stein got Robert McAlmon to publish her long manuscript in Paris.

Ten more of Stein's books were published before she experienced commercial success with *The Autobiography of Alice B. Toklas* (1933), which remains her most accessible book. It is fascinating for its glimpses into post-World War I Paris, culturally vibrant, filled with exciting American expatriates whom Stein labeled members of the "lost generation." Stein, who had always encouraged Alice to write her autobiography, finally did it for her in a book that is whimsical, factual, and delightful.

After three decades abroad, Gertrude Stein returned with Alice B. Toklas to the United States to lecture. They stayed from October, 1934, until May, 1935. Following *The Autobiography of Alice B. Toklas*, Gertrude published eleven more books. Gertrude and Alice sat out the Nazi occupation of France in the countryside where they usually spent their summers. The Nazis apparently overlooked Gertrude's Jewish heritage.

Gertrude developed cancer after the armistice. When her condition worsened, she was hospitalized in Paris, where she died in 1946, Toklas at her side. Alice remained in Paris, dying there on March 7, 1967, two months before her ninetieth birthday.

### Summary

Some would say that Gertrude Stein had more impact as a personality than as a writer. Certainly, her force of personality drew people to her and, eventually, drove most of the same people away from her. It is the reflection of Stein's dynamic personality in *The Autobiography of Alice B. Toklas* that accounted for the initial success of that book and that accounts for its continued acceptance.

Like most highly original artists, Stein did not feel bound by what had gone before her. It is doubtful that she was well read in the classics, although she had a considerable understanding of modern literature, perhaps more through knowing its creators than through reading it systematically.

From 1903 on, Stein imbibed a way of life in Paris that stimulated all of her aesthetic sensibilities. She made a unique contribution in appropriating from the graphic arts ideas she could translate into her own form of artistic expression, writing. She also moved beyond writing when, with Virgil Thomson, she collaborated in setting her words to music, in producing with Thomson the opera *Four Saints in Three Acts* (1934).

Stein was forever attuned to nuances. Her field work in Baltimore exposed her to artistic possibilities in ordinary speech. Her understanding of the human brain provided her with insights into characters such as Melanctha Herbert, one of her most sensitively drawn protagonists.

Above all else, Gertrude Stein was her own person—brilliant, talented, prickly, self-assured, opinionated, and devoted to language in all its unique possibilities. Stein's advice to young writers, had she deigned to offer it, would probably have been "Live, live, live"; she would have followed this advice, however, with the admonition "Write, write, write!"

### Bibliography

Bloom, Harold, ed. *Gertrude Stein*. New York: Chelsea House, 1986. Part of the Modern Critical Views series, this work contains fifteen essays on Stein, a chronology, and a bibliography. A balanced selection. A good starting point for beginners.

Bridgman, Richard. *Gertrude Stein in Pieces*. New York: Oxford University Press, 1970. Bridgman offers one of the fullest analyses of the overall structure and style of Stein's writing. The book is carefully conceived and clearly presented.

Hemingway, Ernest. *A Moveable Feast*. New York: Scribner, and London: Penguin, 1964. Hemingway gives his side of the story about his relationship with Gertrude Stein and about its fracture. His view is biased but interesting.

Hobhouse, Janet. *Everybody Who Was Anybody: A Biography of Gertrude Stein*. London: Weidenfeld and Nicolson, and New York: Putnam, 1975. This book gives a good rundown of the significant people who frequented 27 rue de Fleurus and both Stein and Toklas' opinions of them. Well illustrated.

Hoffman, Frederick J. *Gertrude Stein*. Minneapolis: University of Minnesota Press, 1961; London: Prior, 1976. This brief overview provides basic, salient details biographical and critical.

Mellow, James R. *Charmed Circle: Gertrude Stein and Company*. New York: Praeger, 1974. This book, rich with illustrations, captures the vibrant spirit of the exciting circle of painters, sculptors, writers, and fascinating passersby that came within the Stein-Toklas social orbit before and after World War I.

Miller, Rosalind S. *Gertrude Stein: Form and Intelligibility.* New York: Exposition Press, 1949. Miller presents the first sustained assessment of Gertrude Stein's conscious artistry in lucid detail. This book remains important despite its age.

Moore, George B. *Gertrude Stein's The Making of Americans: Repetition and the Emergence of Modernism.* New York: Lang, 1998. Moore is the first to study Stein's novel *The Making of Americans* and relate it to the development of the author's aesthetics.

Souhami, Diana. *Gertrude and Alice*. London: Pandora, 1991; San Francisco: Pandora, 1992. The most frank account of Gertrude Stein's long-standing lesbian relationship with Alice B. Toklas, this book shows how strong Alice was and how she dominated many aspects of her forty-year marriage to Stein.

Sprigge, Elizabeth. *Gertrude Stein: Her Life and Work*. London: Hamilton, and New York: Harper, 1957. Like Mellow's book, this well-written biography is replete with excellent illustrations. It and Mellow's biography remain among the most valuable resources for Stein scholars and enthusiasts.

Stein, Gertrude. *The Letters of Gertrude Stein and Thornton Wilder.* Edited by Edward Burns et al. New Haven, Conn.: Yale University Press, 1997. Wonderful, fully-annotated chronicle of the friendship/mentorship of these two successful writers and their support for one another.

*R. Baird Shuman*

# JOHN STEINBECK

*Born:* February 27, 1902; Salinas, California
*Died:* December 20, 1968; New York, New York
*Area of Achievement:* Literature
*Contribution:* Steinbeck has given to the American consciousness a permanent portrait of America's rural and immigrant underclasses, especially during the years of the Great Depression.

## Early Life

John Ernst Steinbeck was born in 1902 in Salinas, California, of German and Irish parentage. His father was of German origin and was variously a bookkeeper, accountant, and manager, and he eventually became the treasurer of Monterey County. The elder Steinbeck was an avid gardener (throughout his life, his son would always have to have a garden wherever he lived) and a somewhat introspective man. Steinbeck's mother was of Irish descent, a woman of energy and determination, emotional and sensitive to art, and fond of stories of fantasy and enchantment. The later dichotomies observed in Steinbeck, between the romantic and the hardheaded naturalist, between the dreamer and the masculine tough guy, may be partly accounted for by inheritance from the Irish and German strains of his parents.

The young Steinbeck had a local reputation as a loner and a bit of a dreamer. He read much on his own, his favorite writings being those of Robert Louis Stevenson, Alexandre Dumas *père*, Sir Walter Scott, the Bible, and especially *Le Morte d'Arthur* (1485), by Sir Thomas Malory. This last would remain an influence throughout his life, with many of his stories displaying Arthurian parallels and influences; the work which occupied much of his time in the last years of his life was a translation or redaction of the Arthurian stories, unfinished at his death.

Steinbeck grew to be a tall, gangly youth with broad shoulders, a barrel chest, and a large head. He early developed a fondness for words and a passion for language that was never to leave him. He was independent-minded, not to say stubborn, and as a freshman in high school determined to be a writer. He was graduated from high school in 1919, at best an average student and athlete. For the next six years, he attended Stanford University on and off but never took a degree. As in high school, he took what interested him and cared little for other courses, even if required; the courses he took were those he thought would help him in his writing.

During his many vacations from Stanford Steinbeck worked for the local sugar company in the field and in the office; he also worked on ranches, on a dredging crew, and in the beet harvest. He came to know well the Mexican-American workers alongside whom he labored. He rather enjoyed working with his hands and was certainly throughout his life never afraid of hard work; he also became a notable handyman and maker of gadgets. After leaving Stanford for good in 1925, he worked sporadically during the next three years at a lodge in the High Sierra near Lake Tahoe as a caretaker and handyman. The job gave him much time, especially in the winter, for writing. Steinbeck briefly sought his fortune in New York, where he worked on construction and as a cub reporter. He returned to California in the summer of 1926.

Since his early years in high school, Steinbeck had been writing. His first published stories were in a Stanford literary magazine; his first paid story, "The Gifts of Iban," was published pseudonymously in 1927. By 1930, his apprenticeship could be said to be over: In that year, his first novel, *Cup of Gold*, was published, he married Carol Henning, and he met Edward F. Ricketts, who was to have a notable effect upon the ideas and content of his further work.

## Life's Work

*Cup of Gold* was not widely noticed, and Steinbeck and his new wife, while not subjected to grinding poverty, did live a rather hand-to-mouth existence. The publication of *Pastures of Heaven* (1932) and *To a God Unknown* (1933) increased his critical reputation in narrow circles but did little for his finances or fame. Finally, the publication of *Tortilla Flat* (1935) made the breakthrough; the book was a best-seller and brought Steinbeck fame and money. Though Steinbeck complained about lack of money for the rest of his career, after this date he was never in any financial distress. This book was the first full-length presentation of those themes and characters that have come to be particularly associated with Steinbeck. He turned away from the mythic and legendary materials of *Cup of Gold* and *To a God Unknown* and dealt with contemporary issues, especially the plight of the socially and economically dispossessed. Like the great majority of

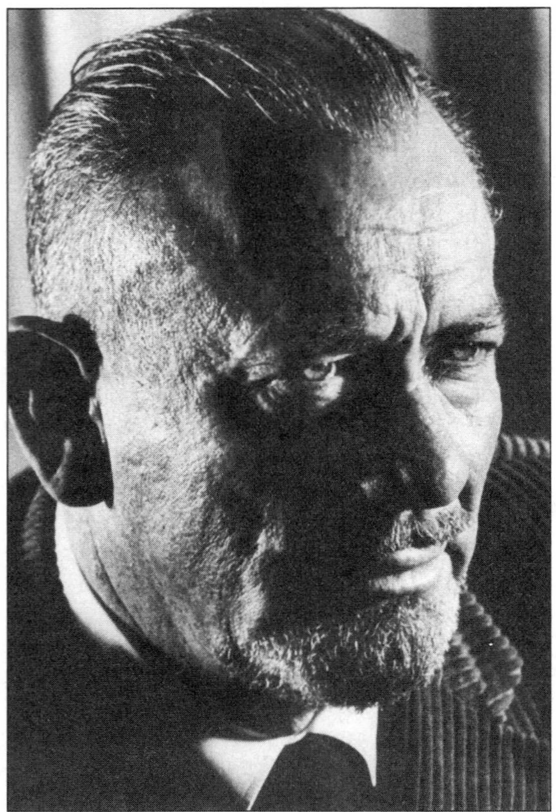

Steinbeck's works, *Tortilla Flat* presents familiar, ordinary characters based on his own firsthand acquaintance. His next major works, *In Dubious Battle* (1936), *Of Mice and Men* (1937), and *The Grapes of Wrath* (1939), would continue to exploit these characters and themes.

These works also displayed some of the effects of Steinbeck's friendship with Ed Ricketts (1897-1948), a marine biologist. Steinbeck had earlier been interested, if only haphazardly, in natural science. His naturalistic view of men, especially in groups, was at least reinforced by his friendship with Ricketts. Ricketts was an exponent of nonteleological thinking (seeing what *is* rather than what might be, should be, or could be). This attitude accorded well with Steinbeck's own naturalistic impulses, at least as fictional method; Steinbeck did not always accept the grim conclusions implicit in a naturalistic view of man and maintained his belief in human progress and free will. The most straightforward presentation of such views may be found in *The Log from the Sea of Cortez* (1951), by both Steinbeck and Ricketts. The book provides the philosophical and organizational background for a tidepool collecting and survey trip taken by Ricketts and Steinbeck in 1940 in the Gulf of California.

During World War II, Steinbeck produced only a few minor works until *Cannery Row* (1945). He served for a few months as a war correspondent in Europe, was divorced in 1942, and married Gwyndolen Conger in 1943. He moved to New York and for the remainder of his life traveled frequently with New York as a base. During these years he also spent much of his time writing film scripts and stage plays based on his works. As much as any other American novelist, Steinbeck was attracted to and involved in the stage and the cinema.

After the war, he began the major work that critics and the public were expecting after *The Grapes of Wrath*. The work was eventually to be *East of Eden* (1952), a long generational novel into which Steinbeck poured much of his own personal experience and which he regarded as his major work and expression of whatever he had learned over the years. The public did not share Steinbeck's regard, and the novel is perhaps best known today in its film version, starring the cult figure James Dean. Before *East of Eden* appeared, however, Steinbeck had published *The Wayward Bus* (1947), which was a Book-of-the-Month Club selection, and *Burning Bright* (1950). After *East of Eden*, Steinbeck published only three more novels: *Sweet Thursday* (1954), *The Short Reign of Pippin IV: A Fabrication* (1957), and *The Winter of Our Discontent* (1961). The latter is considered to be the best of the three and expresses Steinbeck's view of the malaise into which postwar America had fallen.

Steinbeck had divorced his second wife in 1948 and was remarried, in 1950, to Elaine Scott. In the postwar years he traveled often, seeming unable to settle down in a single place. He went several times to Russia, Europe, and especially England, but when abroad he would frequently long for home. After *East of Eden*, Steinbeck became preoccupied with nonfiction work. He wrote regular editorials for *The Saturday Review*, his wartime dispatches were published (1958), he published *Travels with Charley* (1962, a record of a three-month trip by truck around America with his dog), and he completed the essays that compose *America and Americans* (1966), designed to accompany a series of photographs showing the spirit and diversity of America and its people. In 1967, Steinbeck, who had done some speech-writing for President Lyndon B. Johnson, went to Vietnam at the request of the president and recorded his views and impressions in a series of newspaper reports. His long career as a writer was capped in 1962 with the award of the Nobel Prize for Literature. He died of coronary disease in New York in December, 1968, and his ashes were later scattered with the wind on the California coast.

In the course of his career, Steinbeck was held to be a sentimental romantic and a grim naturalist, a Communist and a Fascist, a mere journalist and the spokesman of a generation. It is a tribute to the man that his work has inspired such varying views; clearly, he has made a mark on American consciousness. Steinbeck was the writer (he disliked the word "author") of at least one major masterpiece—*The Grapes of Wrath*—and several excellent works of lesser scope: *Tortilla Flat*, *Of Mice and Men*, *The Red Pony*, *In Dubious Battle*, and *Cannery Row*. All, except perhaps the last, are standard readings in high school and college English courses, as well as the subject of a large and growing body of critical analysis and opinion.

His particular contribution to the American ethos was to make uniquely his own the portraits of migrant workers, the dispossessed, dirt farmers, and manual laborers. He provided authentic portraits of a class of people seldom seen in fiction before his day. His pictures of stoop laborers, strikes, and the Depression are today the standard images by which those things are known and imagined. *The Grapes of Wrath* has become not only an artistic creation but also an authentic view of many of the plagues of the 1930's. For most people, *The Grapes of Wrath* is what the Depression was, at least in the Western United States.

Perhaps the greatest general qualities of Steinbeck's work, qualities which help his works continue to interest, are life and immediacy. Steinbeck was enamored of life and gloried in it. He recreated it vividly in many of his works, with color and accuracy. He took great pains to research most of his works and believed he was thus attaining to some sort of truth, as well as reality. His generally nonteleological view of life led him to concentrate on the moment, on what *is*. At his best, mostly in works before World War II, he re-created authentic American types and characters and placed them in contexts which partook of the great myths and patterns of life and literature: the Bible, the Arthurian myths, the eternal cycles of nature. He had a strong faith in the natural processes of renewal and continuity and thus expanded his tales of the small and the insignificant to give them resonance and universality.

His accuracy and realism can perhaps best be seen in his care for the dialogue of his novels, even to the extent, in his later works, of reading into a tape recorder his own dialogue and playing it back for himself until he felt he had got it right, testing it constantly on the ear. It was probably this attention to authentic speech which made so many of his novels good candidates for stage and screen. None of his novels made bad films and some were outstanding, notably *The Grapes of Wrath* and *Of Mice and Men*. With only a few exceptions, his characters and events were equally genuine, dealing as they did with specifically American and specifically contemporary events.

Finally, Steinbeck was a patriot, but not of the flag-waving, jingoist persuasion. He displayed a deep feeling for the American people and the land both early and late in his career. He saw the values—perhaps felt them would be more correct—of family and social cohesion. He saw man as a part of a whole, often against a background of the disintegration of larger social and economic units and systems. At roughly the same time as Sinclair Lewis was skewering the middle class of America, Steinbeck was giving his public an equally authentic view of a very different class of Americans, though with less satire and more affection.

### Bibliography

Astro, Richard. *John Steinbeck and Edward F. Ricketts: The Shaping of a Novelist*. Minneapolis: University of Minnesota Press, 1973. Indispensable work on Steinbeck's friendship with the man who is often given credit for supplying Steinbeck with important elements of his philosophy and view of man. Astro's conclusion, that the force of Rickett's personality was largely responsible for Steinbeck's success as a writer, is greatly overstated.

Benson, Jackson J. *The True Adventures of John Steinbeck, Writer*. London: Heinemann, and New York: Viking Press, 1984. Complete biography, detailing Steinbeck's life virtually day-by-day. Draws on many unpublished letters and personal interviews. Steinbeck's works are viewed in relation to his life, but detailed analyses are not provided; indispensable for correcting many myths and misconceptions about Steinbeck.

Fontenrose, Joseph. *John Steinbeck: An Introduction and Interpretation*. New York: Holt Rinehart,

1963. Considers Steinbeck an eminent novelist; emphasizes the conflict in Steinbeck between myth (especially biblical and Arthurian) and the biological basis of his fiction (especially the view of society as a group organism). One of the earliest full-length studies to take Steinbeck seriously as an artist.

French, Warren. *John Steinbeck*. Rev. ed. Boston: Twayne, 1975. A semipopular introduction to Steinbeck for the student and general reader by a noted Steinbeck critic. It supplies a brief biography and novel-by-novel analyses and introduces the reader to the complexity, universality, and general characteristics of Steinbeck.

Hayashi, Tetsumaro, ed. *A Study Guide to Steinbeck: A Handbook to His Major Works*. Metuchen, N.J.: Scarecrow Press, 1974. Well-organized, invaluable work for students and teachers; chapters on each work supply background, plot synopses, critical explications, and a selected bibliography. This volume covers most of the major novels.

———. *A Study Guide to John Steinbeck, Part II*. Metuchen, N.J.: Scarecrow Press, 1979. Covers *East of Eden* and a number of minor works. Hayashi is a member of the Steinbeck Society, Ball State University, Indiana, which sponsors conferences and publishes a monograph series on Steinbeck.

Johnson, Claudia Durst. *Understanding "Of Mice and Men," "The Red Pony," and "The Pearl": A Student Casebook to Issues, Sources and Historical Documents*. Westport, Conn.: Greenwood, 1997. This volume provides information on the cultural, social, economic, and historical issues that influenced the writing of three of Steinbeck's most famous novellas and includes many sources not available elsewhere.

McElrath, Joseph R, Jr., et al, eds. *John Steinbeck: The Contemporary Reviews*. Cambridge and New York: Cambridge University Press, 1996. The first collection of critiques of Steinbeck's work by his contemporaries from 1920 forward.

Timmerman, John H. *John Steinbeck's Fiction: The Aesthetics of the Road Taken*. Norman: University of Oklahoma Press, 1986; London: Eurospan, 1987. A full-length critical study; deals more with literary craftsmanship than with Steinbeck's social thought. Puts in perspective his agnosticism and his fascination with biblical symbolism. Also discusses Steinbeck's concern for "authenticity," particularly for realistic dialogue.

*Gordon Bergquist*

# GLORIA STEINEM

*Born:* March 25, 1934; Toledo, Ohio

*Areas of Achievement:* Women's rights and journalism

*Contribution:* A leading proponent of the twentieth century feminist movement, Steinem was also a founder of *Ms.* magazine. Her outspoken advocacy for women has made her a nationally known figure.

## Early Life

Gloria Steinem was born on March 25, 1934, to Ruth Nuneviller Steinem and Leo Steinem. Leo was a buyer and seller of antiques who traveled around the country with his family during the winter months. Their summers were spent at Ocean Beach Pier, an entertainment hall that Leo owned and managed at Clark Lake, Michigan. Before Gloria reached her teens, however, her parents separated and then divorced, and her older sister Sue went to college, leaving Gloria to take care of her mother, who was mentally ill with anxiety neurosis and agoraphobia. The two lived in the rundown little Toledo, Ohio, house in which Gloria's mother had grown up.

Gloria spent her teen years in Toledo, trying to balance schoolwork, social life, dancing lessons, and taking care of her mother, who was kept reasonably calm but also disoriented by tranquilizing drugs. When Gloria was seventeen, with their house increasingly dilapidated and their furnace condemned, she was feeling desperate until the church next door offered to purchase the house. After a great deal of persuasion, her father agreed to care for Ruth for one year so that Gloria could finish high school in Washington, D.C., where her sister Sue was living.

The following year, 1952, she entered Smith College, while Sue cared for their mother. After being graduated as a Phi Beta Kappa majoring in government in 1956, she broke a college engagement and went to India on a year's fellowship. Upon her return, unable to get a job as a writer, she spent two years working for the Independent Service for Information, a youth outreach organization that she later discovered was funded by the Central Intelligence Agency. Beginning in 1960, she worked in New York as a freelance writer and assistant for *Help!* magazine.

In 1964, she received national attention as a writer for the short-lived comedy television show *That Was the Week That Was*. She was still frustrated, however, because, although her interests were serious—politics, civil rights, the Vietnam War, world issues—she was limited because of her sex to writing about light topics such as fashion and celebrities. In 1968, however, she joined with Clay Felker in founding the magazine *New York*, becoming one of its writers and editors. Finally, she was able to write about political issues, and for that magazine she published articles about serious events in the country and the world.

## Life's Work

Gloria Steinem's feminist consciousness began developing in 1969, when she realized that her concern with society's disenfranchised groups stemmed from the fact that she too was part of an oppressed group: women. She began in that year to talk with women who had experienced abortions, as she had herself before her trip to India, and she became an advocate for legalized abortion, coining the phrase "reproductive freedom."

In 1969, she won the Penney-Missouri Journalism Award for her article in *New York* entitled "After Black Power, Women's Liberation," one of the first serious journalistic reports on the new feminist movement. She marched in New York City's Women's Strike for Equality, a rally held in 1970 to celebrate fifty years of women's right to vote. Her writing became more and more focused on feminist issues, and she began lecturing with Dorothy Pitman Hughes, a black feminist, about the new movement and its importance. She became part of the National Women's Political Caucus, which had been founded in 1971 to try to involve women in politics and government.

In 1971, she became a cofounder, with Brenda Feigen, of the Women's Action Alliance, an organization whose purpose was to develop educational programs geared toward women's personal and economic equality. Members of the Alliance, meeting in Steinem's apartment, came up with the idea of a feminist-oriented national magazine for women.

At first, the women were unable to obtain funding for their venture, but then Clay Felker offered to put out a first issue as a supplement to *New York*. It was a great success, and with additional articles, it was republished as the preview edition of *Ms.* magazine, in January of 1972. In the midst of a publicity trip, Steinem began receiving complaints

that the magazine was not available at newsstands. Assuming that it had not been delivered, Steinem called the home office, only to find that the entire first issue, three hundred thousand copies, had sold out in eight days. It was clear that Steinem and her associates were offering something that American women desperately wanted. Ultimately, Warner Communications agreed to finance *Ms.* while allowing the female editorial board complete control of the magazine. *Ms.* has the distinction of being the first national magazine to be run and controlled entirely by women.

Continuing her concern with politics, Steinem was elected in 1972 to the Democratic National Convention as a delegate for Representative Shirley Chisholm. That same year, she was chosen "Woman of the Year" by *McCall's* magazine. Still concerned that women would never be equal until the politics not only of the nation but also of their personal lives were changed, she and some of her *Ms.* colleagues founded the Ms. Foundation for Women, whose purpose is to provide grants to grass-roots, self-help projects for women. In 1974, she helped found the coalition of Labor Union Women. Gloria Steinem had become one of the most prominent spokespersons for the women's movement, and her name had become a household word.

In 1974, *Ms.* launched a television talk show called *Woman Alive*, which was hosted by Steinem. In 1975, she attended the International Women's Year conference in Mexico City, though not as a delegate. Like many others, she was disappointed that women's real concerns were largely ignored in favor of nationalistic issues and divisive propaganda. Two years later, as a member of President Jimmy Carter's national commission to organize an American Conference on Women to be held in Dallas in 1977, Steinem traveled the country speaking about feminist concerns and organizing state conferences that would elect delegates to the national meeting.

Throughout the 1970's, she was active in the effort to ratify the Equal Rights Amendment (ERA). It had passed Congress in 1972 and had received the ratifications of several states, but in an increasingly conservative time it failed to receive sufficient votes to pass by its original deadline in 1979 or even by an extended deadline in 1982. In 1978, in an effort to publicize the importance of the amendment and to extend the ratification period, Steinem helped to organize the extremely successful ERA Extension March in Washington, D.C.

In 1978, Steinem moved to Washington to research the effects of feminism on political theory, financed by a Woodrow Wilson Fellowship from the Smithsonian Institution. This fellowship gave her a chance to spend more time with her sister Sue, as well as her mother, who had finally received hospitalization and treatment and was now living independently.

In 1983, Steinem published her first book, *Outrageous Acts and Everyday Rebellions*, a collection of essays such as a feminist analysis of her mother's life, an undercover exposé of the Playboy Club written in 1963, and a fantasy about what life would be like if men could menstruate. Steinem had long encouraged women to commit "outrageous acts," no matter how small, to change the world, so the title was apt.

*Ms.* magazine, which had ceased publication in 1989, resumed in 1990 as a no-advertising, editorially free feminist publication, and it has been extremely popular despite the fact that the lack of advertising has increased the cost to subscribers. In the first issue, Steinem wrote an essay explaining the effect advertising has on women's magazines and the effect it had had in previous years on *Ms.* magazine, requiring the watering down of its message. Now published six times yearly, the new *Ms.* can include whatever its editors deem appropriate.

The year 1992 saw the publication of another book by Steinem, *Revolution from Within: A Book of Self-Esteem*. In this book, which utilizes some of the tools of the self-help movement that became popular in the 1980's, Steinem explores the issue of self-esteem for women, probing her own life as well as the stories of others to show the importance of high self-esteem for women as they struggle for equality in American society.

### Summary

Gloria Steinem insists that she is an ordinary woman and that her concern has always been with ordinary women. Although she is a celebrity, she believes that the most important issues are those of the grass roots. She believes, passionately, that the personal is political, that changing the world begins by changing lives and the interactions of individuals, and that political power for women will mean nothing if their daily lives are filled with sexist oppression. Therefore, even as a celebrity, she is able to be a spokesperson for everyday people with everyday lives.

Her writing is insightful and brings readers frequently to the "click" experience (the "click" is a moment, identified and made famous in *Ms.* magazine, when the light comes on in one's mind and a new insight comes into focus—when something is thought about in a whole new way). Some of the phrases that she has coined have passed into the popular jargon and are considered part of the folk wisdom of the feminist movement. Some examples are "A woman without a man is like a fish without a bicycle." "We have become the men we wanted to marry." "Most of us are only one man away from welfare."

Although Steinem's time in the limelight was the 1970's, when she was most publicly active and at the helm of *Ms.* magazine, she is still known and respected as an outspoken leader of the second wave of the feminist movement.

## Bibliography

Cohen, Marcia. *The Sisterhood: The True Story of the Women Who Changed the World.* New York: Simon and Schuster, 1988. This study of the feminist movement of the 1970's and beyond begins with an analysis of the post-World War II social factors that spawned the movement. It also weaves together biographical accounts of the lives of a number of feminist leaders, including several very informative sections on Gloria Steinem.

Davis, Flora. *Moving the Mountain: The Women's Movement in America Since 1960.* New York: Simon and Schuster, 1991; London: Simon and Schuster, 1992. This history of thirty years of the feminist movement will help the reader understand the events and issues with which Gloria Steinem has been deeply involved. She is mentioned several times in the book, which illustrates how her journalistic and political work relates to the efforts of others.

Henry, Sondra, and Emily Taitz. *One Woman's Power: A Biography of Gloria Steinem.* Minneapolis, Minn.: Dillon Press, 1987. Written for younger students, this biography takes the reader from Steinem's childhood through her years as a young journalist, the founding of *Ms.*, and her political activism to the publication of *Outrageous Acts and Everyday Rebellions.*

Gorney, Cynthia. "Gloria: At 61, Steinem Wants Straight Talk, More Fun, and a New Congress." *Mother Jones* 20, no. 6 (November-December, 1995). Interview with Steinem in which she discusses right-wing politics, low voter turnout, her problems with trigeminal neuralgia, and her feelings toward recent feminist writings.

Myers-Parrelli, Anna, and Gloria Steinem. "Steps toward Transformation: A Conversation with Gloria Steinem." *Women and Therapy* 177, no. 3-4 (Winter 1995). Interview with Steinem where she discusses her achievements, her organizational skills, and marriage concepts that require men to share equally in raising children.

Steinem, Gloria. *Outrageous Acts and Everyday Rebellions.* 2d ed. New York: Holt, 1995. Steinem's first book, this is a collection of essays written at various points in her career as a journalist and feminist activist. Many of the pieces are personal and reveal a great deal about the author's own life. The thread binding these disparate essays together is Steinem's conviction that women matter and that women's needs are important.

———. *Revolution from Within: A Book of Self-Esteem.* Boston: Little Brown, and London: Bloomsbury, 1992. This book is an examination of the importance of self-esteem in women's lives. Using much of the language and many of the concepts of the self-help movement of the 1980's and 1990's, this book is self-revealing as well as analytical.

Yates, Gayle Graham. *What Women Want: The Ideas of the Movement.* Cambridge, Mass.: Harvard University Press, 1975. This early analysis of feminist principles and activity includes a brief section on Gloria Steinem's ideals and her beliefs about the possibility of creating a feminist utopia in which men and women would be equal and gender differences would be minimized.

*Eleanor B. Amico*

# ADLAI E. STEVENSON

*Born:* February 5, 1900; Los Angeles, California
*Died:* July 14, 1965; London, England
*Area of Achievement:* Government and politics
*Contribution:* Although unsuccessful in his repeated bids for the presidency, Stevenson inspired a new generation of liberals who would write the agenda for the New Frontier and Great Society during the 1960's; he brought to the American political scene an all too uncommon blend of integrity, high intelligence, and humane values.

## Early Life

Adlai Ewing Stevenson II was born on February 5, 1900, in Los Angeles, California, where his father, Lewis Stevenson, managed the Hearst mining and newspaper interests. Stevenson's family, however, was based in Bloomington, Illinois, and the marriage of his parents had united the town's leading Republican and Democratic families. The Stevensons and their relatives had long been active in Illinois political affairs. His great-grandfather, Jesse Fell, was a founder of the Republican Party and a political confidant of Abraham Lincoln. His grandfather, after whom he was named, was an Illinois Democrat who had served as Grover Cleveland's vice president during the 1890's.

This family history influenced Stevenson's formative years. In 1906, his family returned to Bloomington, where his father owned and managed several farms, became a noted agricultural reformer, and was active in state and national politics. Consequently, Adlai became acquainted with such political giants as William Jennings Bryan and, most notably, Woodrow Wilson, whose moral vision and internationalism became guideposts for his subsequent political career. Although he enjoyed a happy childhood in Bloomington, he became an indifferent student in the town's primary and secondary schools. This idyllic period was shattered in December, 1912, when he accidentally shot and killed his cousin. Stevenson was so shattered by the tragedy that he could never speak of it until it became part of the 1952 presidential campaign.

In 1916, Stevenson attended Choate School in Connecticut in order to prepare for the entrance examinations for Princeton University. He entered Princeton in 1918 and was graduated four years later with average grades. He was very active in student affairs and was managing editor of *The Princetonian*. At his father's insistence, Stevenson enrolled at Harvard Law School, where he was miserable; his grades declined accordingly. In 1926, he completed his legal training at Northwestern Law School. During this period, he met with Supreme Court Justice Oliver Wendell Holmes, Jr., which proved to be one of the most satisfying experiences of his life.

By this time, Stevenson had decided to make law his life's work. He had been considering seriously becoming a newspaper publisher, and he enjoyed working on the school press in Choate and Princeton as well as editing the family's Bloomington newspaper. In 1926, Stevenson made one last effort in the newspaper business by hiring out as a reporter for the International News Service to enter the Soviet Union and obtain an interview with Foreign Minister Georgi Chicherin. Stevenson traveled by train from the Black Sea through Kharkov and Kiev to Moscow, and his observations of life under the Bolshevik regime colored his attitude toward the Soviet system for the remainder of his life.

In 1927, Stevenson became a member of a prestigious Chicago law firm, and in the following year, he married Ellen Borden, a Chicago heiress with literary interests. They produced three sons, Adlai III, Borden, and John Fell, and established a home in the small community of Libertyville, Illinois.

## Life's Work

In 1929, the United States suffered the greatest economic contraction in its history, with devastating social, economic, and political consequences. In 1932, voters turned to the Democratic Party under Franklin D. Roosevelt, who promised the country a "new deal." Stevenson became one of the New Deal's bright young attorneys who swarmed into Washington, D.C., to write, enact, and administer myriad administration programs. In 1933, he served as special counsel to the Agricultural Adjustment Administration under George Peek; then, a few months later, he joined the Alcohol Control Administration as special counsel to handle price codes and tax problems following the repeal of Prohibition. During the course of his brief service, Stevenson became acquainted with such figures as George Ball, Alger Hiss, James Rowe, and Tommy Corcoran, who played significant roles in American history.

Although Stevenson had left government service, he became increasingly active in politics. In 1930, he had joined the Council on Foreign Relations, where he honed his oratorical skills on behalf of Wilsonian internationalist principles. In 1939, he joined the Committee to Defend America by Aiding the Allies to counter the isolationist mood of the country. His support of Roosevelt's mobilization efforts, including the "destroyer deal" and the Lend-Lease program, reflected his belief that Great Britain was fighting the American fight against totalitarian aggression.

After the United States entered World War II in December, 1941, Stevenson became assistant secretary of the navy under his close friend Frank Knox, a Republican newspaper publisher from Chicago. Stevenson handled the press, wrote Knox's speeches, and promoted desegregation of the navy. In 1943, he led a mission to Italy to plan the Allied occupation of that country. As the war concluded, he was made a member of the United States Strategic Bombing Survey and then became assistant secretary of state under Edward L. Stettinius and James F. Byrnes, Jr. Finally, he became press officer of the United States delegation to the United Nations conference at San Francisco in 1945.

These posts served as a proving ground for Stevenson's meteoric rise in Illinois and national politics during the late 1940's and the 1950's. In Illinois, the incumbent Republican governor had been compromised by corruption in his administration, and Democratic boss Colonel Jacob M. Arvey of Cook County needed strong reform candidates to capture the state house and the Senate seat. Arvey selected Stevenson for governor and Paul H. Douglas for the Senate. In 1948, Stevenson campaigned as a political amateur and pledged honest government. He won by more than 500,000 votes, helping to bring in not only Douglas but also President Truman in one of the country's greatest political upsets. This victory made Stevenson one of the "class of '48," a group of moderates and liberals who would dominate national politics into the 1970's.

Although his political career led to the breakup of his marriage, Stevenson was an effective liberal governor during a period of anti-Communist hysteria known as McCarthyism. Stevenson appointed businessmen, Republican and Democratic, to state positions, terminated commercial gambling, placed the Illinois state police on civil service, built new highways, streamlined state government, and increased education appropriations. On the debit side, however, was his failure to persuade the state legislature to enact a permanent fair employment practices commission and to authorize a state convention to revise an archaic state constitution.

As a result of his gubernatorial performance, Stevenson became a favorite for the Democratic presidential nomination in 1952. The Democrats had been in power since 1933, and its domestic record and Cold War policies made it vulnerable to a conservative attack. The Truman Administration, in fact, had become so unpopular that the president declined to seek reelection. Instead, Truman placed strong private and public pressure on Stevenson to make the race. The problem was that Stevenson did not want the position; he wanted to be reelected governor of Illinois. Moreover, he believed himself to be too inexperienced for the office. Stevenson's hesitation led to the charge that he was indecisive, which was to haunt him for the rest of his career. In the end, he was nominated for president in a movement that came as close to a draft as any in the twentieth century.

The 1952 campaign between Stevenson and General Dwight D. Eisenhower, an enormously popular war hero, became a classic confrontation. Behind in the polls from the beginning, Stevenson pledged to "talk sense" to the American people and offered no panaceas for the nation's troubles. His position on the issues revealed him to be a moderate liberal on domestic matters and a cold warrior in foreign affairs. His penchant for writing his own speeches, his wit and erudition, his use of Lincolnian and Holmesian anecdotes, and his humility charmed millions of voters. When his opponents condemned him for appealing to intellectuals, he responded, "Eggheads of the world, unite! You have nothing to lose but your yolks!"

Although the early stages of the campaign showed promise, a number of factors combined to bring the Stevenson effort to a bitter conclusion. Stevenson's humor, intellectualism, and Hamlet-like posturing before the nominating convention made many voters suspect that he did not lust for the office. Moreover, the Republican attack of "K1C2" (Korea, Communism, corruption) proved to be very effective with the voters. Stevenson's entanglement with the Alger Hiss controversy did nothing to refute the charge that he was "soft on Communism." Additionally, his support for federal over states' rights on the tidelands issue cost him significant support in such states as Louisiana,

Texas, and California. The *coup de grace* to the campaign, however, proved to be Eisenhower's pledge to "go to Korea" and bring that stalemated conflict to an end. On election day, Stevenson lost by 33,936,252 to 27,314,992 votes, including the electoral votes of four Southern states.

Stevenson declined to disappear from public view during the 1950's. He became a world traveler, met world leaders, and solidified his credentials in foreign affairs. He also maintained a rigorous speaking schedule at home, campaigned for Democrats in the congressional elections of 1954 and 1958, and published several books on contemporary issues. In 1956, he was renominated for president by his party and campaigned on the theme of a "New America." Although he proved to be more liberal on civil rights than Eisenhower, he badly mishandled the *Brown v. Board of Education* decision (1954), which struck down segregation. Seeking to prevent national divisiveness on this issue, he declared that he would not use federal troops to desegregate public schools. He later recovered somewhat by pledging to enforce the decision if it was defied by state authorities. More controversial, however, were his proposals to end the draft and nuclear testing. Whatever chance he had for success was undermined in late October and November, 1956, by the Suez Canal and Hungarian crises. The electorate declined to change leaders, and Stevenson lost by an even greater margin, by 35,590,472 votes to 26,029,752.

By now, Stevenson's career had crested. In 1960, die-hard Stevenson loyalists made a "last hurrah" for their hero at the Democratic National Convention in Los Angeles, but the party turned to John F. Kennedy and a younger generation for leadership. Following Kennedy's narrow election victory, Stevenson hoped to be appointed secretary of state, only to be bitterly disappointed by his nomination for ambassador to the United Nations. Kennedy softened the disappointment by making the position cabinet-level and promising Stevenson a role in the National Security Council.

Stevenson's expertise on world affairs and his relationships with world leaders made him a popular and effective representative for the United States. His confrontations with his Soviet counterpart, Valerian Zorin, were tough and dramatic. In April, 1961, Stevenson's prestige tumbled when he denied that the United States had aided the Bay of Pigs invasion in Cuba by Cuban exiles. When President Kennedy took full responsibility for the incident, Stevenson was badly embarrassed and

contemplated resignation. This action was averted when Kennedy promised to keep him fully informed on foreign policy decisions and even to seek his counsel.

This led to Ambassador Stevenson's superb performance in October, 1962, over the Cuban missile crisis when he successfully challenged Zorin's denial of Soviet insertion of missiles inside Cuba. His calm presentation of the evidence and his vow to wait until "hell freezes over" for the Soviet response won for him great praise at home and abroad. Unfortunately, this bravura performance was tarnished by administration insiders who leaked to journalists that Stevenson had acted the role of appeaser toward the Soviets. Although Stevenson and the Kennedy Administration denied the story, it once again reinforced the public's perception of Stevenson's passivity.

Stevenson clearly was unhappy serving under Kennedy and Johnson. His admirers encouraged him to resign with a denunciation of their foreign policies, but he could not bring himself to take that step. While he did criticize Johnson's intervention in the Dominican Republic in 1965, he continued to support the containment, limited war, and collaborative aspects of American diplomacy developed during the Truman Administration. He even supported basic American policies in South Vietnam. On the afternoon of July 14, 1965, Stevenson collapsed and died of a heart attack on a street in London.

### Summary

Adlai Stevenson had acquired the reputation of a political loser, but his career should elicit admiration rather than contempt. He brought to public life the highest ideals and standards and never wavered in their defense. He did not seek easy answers to complex issues. He was an enigmatic political leader, a man who sought the nation's highest office yet appeared indifferent when it was within his grasp. It has been said that Stevenson lacked the ruthlessness to become president, but it may also be that he wanted the office on his terms. It seems ironic that he received his highest accolades not from his fellow citizens but from the people of the world who saw him as the best that America could produce.

A politician's success can be measured in many ways. Stevenson's "New America" campaign of 1956 anticipated much of the social and economic legislation of the New Frontier and Great Society in the 1960's. He inspired and brought into the political system millions of voters who had never before participated. He stood up to McCarthyism and practiced a disciplined civility in politics to which all politicians should aspire.

Stevenson belongs to the tradition of pragmatic reform characteristic of the twentieth century. His admirers saw him as a political leader with a moral vision for economic and social justice at home and abroad. In foreign affairs, he represented the tradition of Wilsonian internationalism, with its respect for international law, collective security, nuclear arms limitation, and human rights. He was, at heart, an optimist, a gentle and wise man who believed in strong and compassionate government and the nurturing of democratic principles throughout the world.

### Bibliography

Baker, Jean H. *The Stevensons: A Biography of an American Family.* New York: Norton, 1996. Baker covers four generations of the Stevenson family, relating each to its times.

Brown, Stuart Gerry. *Adlai E. Stevenson, a Short Biography: The Conscience of the Country.* Woodbury, N.Y.: Barron's Woodbury Press, 1965. A popular biography by a Stevenson admirer. Based on secondary sources as well as interviews with the subject and his friends and colleagues.

Cochran, Bert. *Adlai Stevenson: Patrician Among the Politicians.* New York: Funk and Wagnalls, 1969. Interprets Stevenson's life and career within the context of upper-class reform dating to the Gilded Age. Includes commentary on the role of intellectuals in the Cold War era.

Johnson, Wallace, and Carol Evans, eds. *The Papers of Adlai E. Stevenson, 1900-1965.* 8 vols. Boston: Little Brown, 1972-1979. Correspondence and papers dealing with the life and career of Stevenson. Reflects Stevenson's wit, intelligence, and character. A significant source of primary materials for students of post-World War II politics.

Martin, John Bartlow. *Adlai Stevenson of Illinois: The Life of Adlai Stevenson.* New York: Doubleday, 1976.

———. *Adlai Stevenson and the World: The Life of Adlai Stevenson.* New York: Doubleday, 1977. An objective and scholarly two-volume biography of Stevenson by a longtime friend and associate. Volume 1 covers the formative years through the 1952 presidential campaign. Volume 2 discusses Stevenson's political decline and his influence in world affairs. A sympathetic portrait.

Ramsey, Edward W. "The Has-Been." *American Heritage* 47, no. 6 (October, 1996). The author recalls his accidental meeting with Stevenson at the 1964 Democratic National Convention.

Severn, Bill. *Adlai Stevenson: Citizen of the World.* New York: McKay, 1966. A popular biography useful for readers with little background in modern American political history. An admiring treatment.

Stevenson, Adlai E. *Call to Greatness.* New York: Harper and Brothers, and London: Hart-Davis, 1954. A candid nonpartisan assessment of the United States' position in world affairs during the 1950's. Emphasizes the destabilizing impact of nationalist and independence movements in the underdeveloped world. Urges Americans to be more mature in their hopes and aspirations for a stable and peaceful world order.

———. *Friends and Enemies: What I Learned in Russia.* New York: Harper, and London: Hart-Davis, 1959. Commentary on his observations while in the Soviet Union in 1958. Notes that the Soviet regime is here to stay but states that the Soviet Union and the United States can maintain a peaceful coexistence. Typical of Stevenson's elegance of expression and clarity of style.

Whitman, Alden, and *The New York Times*. *Portrait: Adlai E. Stevenson, Politician, Diplomat, Friend*. New York: Harper, 1965. Drawn largely from the files of *The New York Times*. A flattering account of Stevenson's career, especially from his Illinois gubernatorial campaign until his death. Views Stevenson as a great, but flawed, man and emphasizes his growing estrangement from the Kennedy and Johnson administrations.

*Stephen P. Sayles*

# JAMES STEWART

*Born:* May 20, 1908; Indiana, Pennsylvania
*Died:* July 2, 1997; Beverly Hills, California
*Areas of Achievement:* Film, military affairs, theater, and entertainment
*Contribution:* Stewart was one of the most successful and enduring actors in the history of American motion pictures.

## Early Life

James Maitland Stewart was born on May 20, 1908, in the small town of Indiana, Pennsylvania. His father, Alex, owned a local hardware store where Stewart worked as a young man. His mother, Elizabeth, was a homemaker and church organist. Stewart's only contact with the theater as a young man was the plays he staged in the family basement with his two younger sisters, Mary and Virginia. As a child, he attended Indiana's Model School, then Mercersburg Academy. Upon graduation from high school, he went to his father's alma mater, Princeton University, to study architecture.

While at Princeton, Stewart met future theatrical writer-producer Josh Logan, who encouraged him to appear in university main-stage productions. Shortly after graduation in 1932, Stewart accepted Logan's invitation to join him at a local theatrical group, the University Players, and played a number of small roles in summer stock productions. At the end of the summer, Princeton University offered Stewart a scholarship to pursue a master's degree in architecture. Instead, he traveled to New York with the University Players to appear in the Broadway opening of *Carry Nation*, a play loosely based on the life of the outspoken nineteenth century temperance leader. Though the play closed shortly after it opened, Stewart never returned to Princeton University.

## Life's Work

Stewart stayed in New York after *Carry Nation* closed. He spent the next two years looking for stagework to help pay rent for the small apartment he shared with fellow struggling actors Josh Logan and Henry Fonda. Stewart's first successful stage appearance was as Sergeant O'Hara, a soldier volunteer for Walter Reed's malaria experiments, in *Yellow Jack*. Though *Yellow Jack* was also short-lived, Stewart received good critical reviews. He also received favorable notice from critics for his performance in *Divided by Three*. It was during the run of *Divided by Three* that a talent scout for Metro-Goldwyn-Mayer (MGM), the largest and most prestigious film studio in California, spotted Stewart's performance and arranged for a series of screen tests. Stewart signed a contract with MGM for $350.00 per week and moved to California.

In June of 1935, Stewart arrived in Hollywood and once again shared rent with Fonda and a series of other newly arrived actors. Over the next few years, Stewart appeared in a wide variety of roles while MGM tried to find a character type that would succeed with film audiences. He played a fugitive on the run in *Rose Marie* (1936), Jean Harlow's boyfriend in *Wife vs. Secretary* (1936), a murderer in *After the Thin Man* (1936), a sewer worker in *Seventh Heaven* (1937), a botany professor in *Vivacious Lady* (1938), and even sang a couple songs in *Born to Dance* (1936). He was also paired with former University Player Margaret Sullivan in a series of popular romantic comedies, including *The Shopworn Angel* (1938), *The Shop Around the Corner* (1940), and *The Mortal Storm* (1940). During this time, Stewart was also a frequent voice on radio, performing shortened versions of popular films and plays.

Stewart's screen personality—the sweet, small-town, dependable good guy—developed during the late 1930's. He made his mark with film critics in 1938 when he played Tony Vanderhoff in the screen adaptation of George Kaufman's Pulitzer Prize-winning play *You Can't Take It With You*. The film won the Academy Award for Best Picture, and Stewart's characterization of Tony charmed film audiences. In 1939, Stewart was paired with boisterous Marlene Dietrich as a sheriff in a comedy western *Destry Rides Again*, which showed off Stewart's comedic flair. He received critical acclaim for holding his own against Dietrich's enormous screen presence.

In 1939, Stewart was cast as Jefferson Smith in *Mr. Smith Goes to Washington*, directed by Frank Capra. His performance as young and idealistic Jefferson Smith cemented Stewart's good-guy image. In the film, Smith is a small-town boy elected to serve in the United States Congress who is unjustly accused of criminal activity. Smith discovers corruption and loses his political innocence while sponsoring a bill to establish a boys' camp. The film was popular with audiences and critics alike, and Stewart received his first Best Actor Oscar nomination.

*James Stewart and Marlene Dietrich in the comic western film* Destry Rides Again.

In 1940, Stewart appeared in *The Philadelphia Story* with Katherine Hepburn and Cary Grant. Hepburn played Tracy Lord, a rich divorcee on the eve of her second marriage who has difficulty deciding among her fiancé, her ex-husband, and Mike Conner, a visiting reporter played by Stewart. *The Philadelphia Story* was a huge box-office success, and Stewart received the 1940 Academy Award for Best Actor for his performance.

As Stewart's acting career reached new heights, his life took an unexpected turn. When conflicts that precipitated World War II erupted in Europe, Stewart enlisted in the United States Army. Initially turned down for service because he was underweight, Stewart went on a high-calorie diet and reported for duty on March 22, 1941. Already a licensed pilot, he was assigned to the Army Air Corps. Stewart received his wings and commission as a second lieutenant within weeks of the Japanese attack on Pearl Harbor that brought the United States into World War II. He received heavy-bomber instruction at Kirkland Field in New Mexico and trained as a B-17 commander at Hobbs Air Force Base. In 1943, Captain Stewart was transferred to Boise, Idaho, where he trained young bomber pilots. He also appeared on recruiting tours, traveled on bond drives to raise funds for the war effort, and made instructional films for the army, a project he would continue for the next four decades.

In 1943, Stewart was transferred to Tibenham, England, to command the 703d Squadron of the 445th Bombardment Group of B-24 Liberators. He led nearly twenty bombing missions against the Germans in a total of 1,800 flying hours and was promoted to the rank of major. For his wartime service, Stewart was awarded the Air Medal, an Oak Leaf Cluster for leadership, the Distinguished Flying Cross, and the French Croix de Guerre. Early in 1944, Colonel Stewart became operations officer for the 453d Bombardment Group before returning to the United States in August of 1945. After the war ended, Stewart remained in the Air Force Reserves and eventually achieved the rank of brigadier general.

Stewart returned to Hollywood after the war unsure of the status of his acting career. In 1946, he quickly accepted an invitation from director Frank Capra to star in a small black-and-white film for Radio-Keith-Orpheum (RKO). At the time of its release, the film received some critical favor but only mediocre audience response, yet years later, Stewart proclaimed *It's a Wonderful Life* (1947) to be his favorite motion picture. Stewart played George Bailey, a small-town man who longs for adventure but is seemingly stuck in an uneventful life. Matters degenerate, and George contemplates suicide before an angel named Clarence shows George what his family and friends would be like if he had never been born.

In the summer of 1948, Stewart met Gloria Hatrick at a dinner party given by Gary Cooper. Gloria was a recently divorced mother of two small boys. The two were married on August 9, 1949, at the Brentwood Presbyterian Church, ending the career of Hollywood's most eligible bachelor and beginning a long, successful marriage. In addition to Gloria's two boys, the Stewarts had twin girls in 1951.

After the release of *It's a Wonderful Life*, Stewart tried to find his place in postwar American film by playing a variety of characters through the late 1940's. He was a newspaper reporter in *Call Northside 777* (1948), a public relations man in *Magic Town* (1947), and a detective in *Rope* (1948), which teamed him with director Alfred Hitchcock for the first time.

Stewart was the summer Broadway replacement for Frank Fay, who played the part of Elwood P. Dowd in *Harvey* twice during the later 1940's. Stewart enjoyed the role and successfully campaigned to play Dowd in the 1950 film version. *Harvey* marked the beginning of the most successful decade of Stewart's life. Dowd is a quiet, tipsy man who spends his day with his best friend, an invisible rabbit named Harvey. Stewart received another Oscar nomination for the role and for years to come was associated with the harmless nut with his rabbit friend.

Stewart appeared in a number of westerns during the 1950's and 1960's. The sweet, small-town man became a hardened cowboy, and audiences loved it. Stewart appeared in *Winchester 73* (1950), *Bend of the River* (1952), *The Naked Spur* (1953), *The Far Country* (1955), and *The Man From Laramie* (1955). Stewart teamed with director John Ford for *The Man Who Shot Liberty Valance* (1962) and played Wyatt Earp in *Cheyenne Autumn* (1964). For every western, Stewart insisted on working with his favorite horse, Pie, which he credited with making him look like a real cowboy. In 1965, he played a stoic Virginia farmer determined to keep his six sons out of the Civil War in the popular film *Shenandoah*. The film was the number-one box-office draw for the year. He also portrayed a number of real-life heroes: He appeared as popular band leader Glenn Miller in *The Glenn Miller Story* (1954); baseball player Monty Stratton, who lost his leg in a hunting accident, in *The Stratton Story* (1949); and Charles Lindbergh in *The Spirit of St. Louis* (1957).

In 1954, Stewart teamed with director Alfred Hitchcock to make the very successful film *Rear Window*. Stewart played a photojournalist who breaks his leg. Housebound and bored, he takes interest in the lives of the neighbors he watches through his rear window. Convinced that one neighbor has murdered his wife, he involves his girlfriend, played by Grace Kelly, and his nurse in the intrigue. He teamed with Hitchcock again for *The Man Who Knew Too Much* (1956), in which Stewart played Dr. Ben McKenna, a vacationer in North Africa who finds himself thrust into murderous events over which he has little control. He played an ex-policeman plagued by a fear of heights in *Vertigo* (1958) and received another Oscar nomination for the role of a small-town lawyer in *Anatomy of a Murder* (1959), directed by Otto Preminger.

Stewart appeared in fewer films during the 1970's and 1980's but starred in the television detective series *Hawkins*. He made frequent appearances at award ceremonies in his honor. He received an honorary Academy Award, was inducted into the American Film Institute, and was honored by the Kennedy Center. As a frequent guest on *The Tonight Show* with Johnny Carson, Stewart sometimes read poems he had written. They were so popular with audiences that he published a book of his poetry called *Jimmy Stewart and His Poems* (1989). Stewart's last film role was the voice of Wylie Burp in the animated *An American Tail 2: Fievel Goes West* (1991). Stewart's wife Gloria died of cancer in 1994, and Stewart remained reclusive until his death in 1997 at the age of 89.

### Summary

Jimmy Stewart was one of the most popular and beloved actors of the twentieth century. Theater revivals and videotapes served to increase his popularity. *It's a Wonderful Life* was rediscovered in the

1970's and became a traditional Christmas favorite. Stewart's portrayal of small-town good guy George Bailey is perhaps his most memorable performance and creates a new generation of Stewart fans each year.

### Bibliography


Bingham, Dennis. *Acting Male: Masculinities in the Films of James Stewart, Jack Nicholson, and Clint Eastwood*. New Brunswick, N.J.: Rutgers University Press, 1994. Bingham studies different acting styles and male portrayals among three leading actors.

Coe, Jonathan. *Jimmy Stewart: A Wonderful Life*. New York: Arcade, 1994. Coe concentrates on Stewart's film and stage career.

Dewey, Donald. *James Stewart: A Biography*. Atlanta: Turner, 1996. This book studies Stewart's life from his small-town upbringing to his life as an actor, father, and military pilot.

Fonda, Henry, as told to Howard Teichmann. *Fonda: My Life*. New York: New American Library, 1981; London: Allen, 1982. This book, written by Stewart's best friend, gives special insight into Stewart's personal life.

Lacayo, Richard. "Tall in Every Sense: Jimmy Stewart Didn't Just Play Laconic Heroes. He Was One." *People Weekly* 48, no. 3 (July 21, 1997). Detailed profile of the life and work of Stewart.

Molyneaux, Gerard. *James Stewart: A Bio-Bibliography*. Westport, Conn.: Greenwood Press, 1992. A detailed biography accompanies this extensive bibliography covering Stewart's credits in movies and on the stage, radio, and television.

Pickard, Roy. *Jimmy Stewart: A Life in Film*. New York: St. Martin's Press, 1993. Pickard focuses on Stewart's film work with a good chronology of film and television appearances.


*Leslie Stricker*

## ALFRED STIEGLITZ

*Born:* January 1, 1864; Hoboken, New Jersey
*Died:* July 13, 1946; New York, New York
*Area of Achievement:* Photography
*Contribution:* Stieglitz was a central figure in the development of early twentieth century photography, in the introduction of modern art to the American people, and, most important, in the discovering and fostering of an indigenous American culture.

### Early Life

In 1849, Edward Stieglitz came to America from Hannover-Münden, Germany. After marrying Hedwig Werner in 1862, this German-Jewish immigrant became a successful woolen merchant. On New Year's Day, 1864, Hedwig gave birth to their first child, Alfred, in Hoboken, New Jersey. Within seven years, the Stieglitz family grew to include two additional sons and three daughters. In 1872, Edward moved his family to Manhattan, New York, where Alfred grew to early manhood. In Manhattan, as in Hoboken, Alfred was infused with an appreciation for art by his family and surroundings. His father, an amateur artist, socialized with artists and decorated his home with prints and art objects of the artists of the day.

Alfred's interest in photography was indicated at a very early age. At the age of two, he was obsessed with a photograph of his cousin; he carried it with him at all times. At age nine, he encountered his first photographer. The child was completely fascinated with the magical process of film development. When, however, the photographer put carmine on the cheeks of the faces on the tintype and explained that this touch-up made the subjects look more natural, Alfred disagreed, stating that this effect merely spoiled the clarity of the images photographed. This insistence upon honesty in photography intensified as Alfred grew.

As a youth, Alfred was considered different. He was intensely observant and sensitive to others' feelings. Inquisitive and precocious, he spoke German and French as well as English by age seven. He had well-developed feelings of honor and responsibility. Although Alfred rejected many of the values and attitudes of his family, like his father he was driven by a need to rid himself of every fault; he demanded honesty and perfection in those around him as well. He was unpredictable and sociable, yet lonely and brooding, and his appearance reflected his nature. His deep-set, dark, piercing eyes seemed to penetrate rather than simply observe; his lips were thin and finely curved, with a slight blue tinge and an almost imperceptible quiver; and he was thin with pale, fine skin. He always wore a mustache and, later in life, wire-rimmed frames. His coarse, dark hair was usually tousled—the image of a mythological creator/god.

In 1879, Alfred entered City College in New York. As the lad showed no interest in any one profession, Edward decided his eldest son should pursue a career in chemistry or engineering. Alfred had attended City College for two years when his father retired and temporarily moved the family to Germany. Thus, in 1881, Alfred enrolled in the Realgymnasium at Karlsruhe, Germany. In 1882, he transferred to the University of Berlin to study mechanical engineering.

As a college youth, he became an ardent collector of art books. He soon acquired an extensive, carefully selected library, which he studied at his leisure. This portable gallery was unique in its stylistic and geographic diversity, which helped Stieglitz develop very eclectic tastes.

In July, 1890, Alfred returned to America unwillingly. At his father's insistence, he entered the photoengraving business with Joseph Obermeyer (who was to become his brother-in-law) and Louis Schubart. Together with financial help from Edward, they bought the Heliochrome Company and renamed it the Photochrome Engraving Company. Alfred was a partner in this unsuccessful business for five years, contributing very little.

On November 16, 1893, Alfred (because of family pressures) married Emmeline Obermeyer. Although this union was to last twenty-five years, it brought him little happiness. His wife neither shared his interest in photography nor accepted or understood his friends. On September 27, 1898, Alfred's only child, Katherine (Kitty), was born. She, too, proved to be something of a disappointment to him.

### Life's Work

Although Stieglitz's interest in photography was evident when he was a child, it was not until 1883 that he obtained his first camera, purchased on impulse while shopping in Germany. Shortly thereafter, he made his first print. He soon abandoned his dictated career and began studying photography. He enrolled in Professor Hermann Wilhelm Vogel's photochemistry class. Vogel, an author and the editor of the German journal *Photographische Mitteilungen*, soon became Stieglitz's mentor.

Stieglitz's passion for photography grew into an obsession. During the early 1880's, he traveled throughout Europe, photographing much of it. By the mid-1880's, he began contributing articles to Germany's photographic publications (the first of more than two hundred articles to be written in his lifetime).

From 1885 to 1887, Stieglitz worked compulsively on his photography. In 1887, he received his first official recognition in the photographic world when he won the first-place award of a silver medal and two guineas in the Holiday Work Competition, sponsored by *The Amateur Photographer* (a British publication). Within a brief period of time, he received more than 150 such awards.

Alfred's failing photoengraving business and his unhappy marriage encouraged him to spend much of his time taking pictures and experimenting with technique. His work advanced both the art and the science of photography. His work was exhibited frequently, and his artistic integrity soon made him famous in America as well as in Europe.

From 1887 to 1911, Stieglitz's main goal was to establish photography as a valid form of artistic expression—separate from and equal to painting. In accomplishing this goal, he also worked to develop a uniquely American art form. At this time, American photographers were dependent upon Europe for ideas for style and content. The European style stressed a hazy and blurry finished product, and the subject was usually pretty and serene. The idea was to make the photograph look like a painting.

Stieglitz, however, did not think that photographs should look like a painter's work. To this end, and partly because of his search for America's essence, he began shooting photographs of the streets of New York City. He sought unusual subject matter, such as workhorses, muddy streets, and emigrants in steerage, trying to record the feeling of life within his photographs. He began to break conventions by insisting upon clarity and detail and by experimenting with unusual uses of light. His trademark was sharp contrasts of black and white. Stieglitz also realized that fewer objects in a picture drew more attention to the subject; too many objects diffused the impact. He began to study form rather than subject matter. Stieglitz believed that the function of photography was to provide visual truths, not to give aesthetic pleasure.

In 1891, he joined the Society of Amateur Photographers, and in 1893, he became an editor of *American Amateur Photographer.* As Stieglitz was a born propagandist, he sought to reform the art of photography by taking pen in hand. From 1887 to 1902, he directed his writings to the general public and the amateur photographer. In 1896, he resigned his position as editor of *American Amateur Photographer* and began editing *Camera Notes*, the quarterly journal of the Camera Club.

In 1902, Stieglitz, disgusted with the crass commercialism associated with his trade, began a revolution in the world of art. The movement, with Stieglitz as its leader and director, was known as the Photo-Secession. The aims of the movement were to draw together Americans interested in art, to advance photography as applied to pictorial expression, and to hold exhibitions of all artwork. Stieglitz provided the ideological framework for the movement, and it became a very powerful artistic and political influence in the world of photography. Stieglitz's stand against standardization, institutionalism, and commercialism, as well as his high standards and convictions, attracted talented young people to his group.

Stieglitz's new publication, *Camera Work* (1903 to 1915), complemented the Photo-Secession movement. He began to direct his writings to the more artistic photographer. This journal was one of the most important forces in American cultural life at this time. Through it, Stieglitz provided America with a visual record of the achievements of American and European photographers and provided an accurate history of the Photo-Secession. It was later used to explain and discuss theories behind the work of Paul Cézanne, Henri Matisse, and other modern artists.

In 1905, Stieglitz founded 291, also known as the Little Galleries of the Photo-Secession. (It was referred to as 291 because of its address, 291 Fifth Avenue.) Because of his hatred for commercialism, Stieglitz's galleries were strictly nonprofit establishments. He received a modest income of twelve hundred dollars a year from his father's estate; the money received from any works sold went to the artist—Stieglitz took no commission. He did not classify himself as a dealer or a businessman. In fact, he often supported the artists in his group so that they could concentrate on their art.

By this time, Stieglitz had been successful in raising American photography to an international level and was soon identified with various schools of art. Because his subjects were everyday, urban scenes, he was associated with the New York Realists (later to be called the Ash Can school). His work resembled that of the Impressionists to the extent that they, too—with their unorthodox practice of painting in the open air—sought to capture the momentary impression. By 1910, Stieglitz saw a definite connection between his work and that of the Cubists. While he and the Cubists presented two opposite ways of seeing the objective world, both saw art as representing more than a material presence. Stieglitz realized that art in its abstract form was a true medium of expression and that it was antiphotographic. He believed that photography freed artists from the need to depict reality. Painting and photography were not equal; they were antithetical.

From 1908 through 1911, he introduced the work of such innovative artists as Henri Matisse, Henri Toulouse-Lautrec, Paul Cézanne, and Pablo Picasso, to an initially unreceptive American public. Stieglitz soon convinced the cultural elite that modern art was indeed worth more than the canvas upon which it was painted. By 1913, he had become the leading spokesman for avant-garde art in America. He was also the first in America to publish the literary works of innovative writers such as Gertrude Stein. Stieglitz recognized that all of the arts were important and interrelated. His main concern was that all work should show honesty, vitality, intensity of feelings, and originality.

In 1915, Stieglitz stopped regular publication of *Camera Work*. From 1915 to 1916, he edited and published a more radical magazine, *291* (printed in both English and French). It was satirical and critical and exhibited a proto-Dada spirit.

In 1917, with the involvement of the United States in World War I, Stieglitz closed 291 and issued the last special edition of *Camera Work*. The center for artists now shifted to Greenwich Village. Stieglitz's active role was suspended until 1925, but his influence continued. Stieglitz turned his attention to the work of a young artist, Georgia O'Keeffe. It was not until 1916, when he met Georgia O'Keeffe, that Stieglitz found true happiness. This fifty-two-year-old found a new source of inspiration in his twenty-eight-year-old mistress. Six years later, he received his divorce from Emmeline and married O'Keeffe. Stieglitz had finally found a woman who was a gifted artist and one he could photograph.

In 1924, the Royal Photographic Society of Great Britain awarded the Progress Medal to Stieglitz for his work in establishing American pictorial photography and for his contribution in *Camera Work*. In 1940, he received an honorary fellowship from the Photographic Society of America.

In 1925, Stieglitz opened the Intimate Gallery. In 1928, he suffered a heart attack which left him partially disabled. Nevertheless, he continued presenting exhibits, and in 1929 he replaced the Intimate Gallery with An American Place, dedicating this new gallery exclusively to exhibiting the work of American artists.

Upon his death on July 13, 1946, in New York City, O'Keeffe donated most of his work to various museums, as he had instructed. His remains were cremated, his ashes secretly dispersed at Lake George, New York, a family retreat which he had loved.

## Summary

Stieglitz photographed from the mid-1880's until 1937. He believed that photography was rooted in external reality. He wanted to photograph what he saw, but, in his mind, he never achieved that goal.

His contributions to the art world and to American culture in general are nevertheless profound.

His most important achievements in the art world were his innovations in photography and his exhibitions of modern art in America. He helped explain art to the American public and change America's taste in art. He helped young American artists by sponsoring and encouraging them, encouraging them to follow and trust their instincts. Only by doing this could an artist achieve his best work. He preached that in order for art in any form to be good, it must have some measure of vital essence; it must be alive. Stieglitz is considered one of the most important humanists of his time because of his insistence upon art for *life's* sake.

To America, Stieglitz gave his love and devotion; he considered himself as one of the leading spiritual forces of this country. He had a strong belief in his own genius, and he also had an overwhelming sense of mission. At a time when America was shifting to mass production and trying to manufacture more (rather than better) products, Stieglitz was still seeking quality and excellence. This search for excellence, combined with his role in fostering a new art form, helped America create its own cultural identity.

### Bibliography

Bry, Doris. *Alfred Stieglitz: Photographer.* Boston: Museum of Fine Arts, 1965. Brief biographical sketch of Stieglitz from 1883 to 1937. The author discusses Stieglitz's growth as a photographer and his contributions to photography. Contains sixty-two photos (housed at the Museum of Fine Arts in Boston) which are considered among Stieglitz's best work. Offers a good selected bibliography which emphasizes sources dealing with Stieglitz as a photographer.

Dijkstra, Bram. *Cubism, Stieglitz, and the Early Poetry of William Carlos Williams: The Hieroglyphics of a New Speech.* Princeton, N.J.: Princeton University Press, 1969. Although the major theme of this book is Stieglitz's influence upon other disciplines, it provides an excellent brief biographical sketch of Stieglitz and presents an interesting concept of translating Stieglitz's photography into written language. A working knowledge of French is helpful, as the author sometimes quotes in French without translating.

Doty, Robert. *Photo-Secession: Stieglitz and the Fine-Art Movement in Photography.* New York: Dover, 1978. The major emphasis of this brief monograph is on the background, origin, and work of the Photo-Secession movement. The work discusses the relationship of this movement and Stieglitz to the history of photography. The text is based primarily on original documents, and the reproductions in the portfolio section are taken from Stieglitz's publication *Camera Work.* Doty also includes a list of Photo-Secession members.

Greenough, Sarah, and Juan Hamilton. *Alfred Stieglitz: Photographs and Writings.* Washington, D.C.: National Gallery of Art, 1983. Concentrates mostly on Stieglitz's work as a photographer rather than as a publisher or gallery director. Explains the evolution of Stieglitz's understanding of the "idea photography." The work contains seventy-three Stieglitz photos (presented at the National Gallery of Art in Washington, D.C.). The authors also include selected letters and articles (presented in chronological order) written by Stieglitz on photography. Very well documented.

Haines, Robert E. *The Inner Eye of Alfred Stieglitz.* Washington, D.C.: University Press of America, 1982. As suggested by the title, this book is not a study of Stieglitz's work but a discussion of his metaphysics and of his influence as a symbol. Examines Stieglitz's impact (upon literary figures as well as artists) as a catalyst, critic, and leader. Very well documented, with an extensive bibliography.

Homer, William Innes. *Alfred Stieglitz and the American Avant-Garde.* London: Secker and Warburg, and Boston: New York Graphic Society, 1977. Deals with the basic goals and principles of the Photo-Secession movement and presents an excellent biography of Stieglitz. Provides biographical sketches of Stieglitz's associates and the members of his circle of friends. Also discusses the rivals of 291.

———. *Alfred Stieglitz and the Photo-Secession.* Boston: Little, 1983. A comprehensive study of the Photo-Secession movement. Concentrates not only on the major members but also on some of the minor ones. While the major emphasis is on the movement, the work examines Stieglitz's life through 1917, particularly his role as the political and artistic leader of the movement.

Lowe, Sue Davidson. *Stieglitz: A Memoir/Biography.* London: Quartet, and New York: Farrar Strauss, 1983. Stieglitz's grandniece presents an excellent and delightful anecdotal biography of him. She depicts the private side of this public figure. The author provides an interesting insight into Stieglitz as only a family member might. Extensive use of primary sources. Not in exact chronological order, but interesting reading.

Norman, Dorothy. *Alfred Stieglitz: An American Seer.* New York: Aperture, 1973. Very good chronology; excellent source for high school level because of the simplicity of the presentation—more a dialogue than a narrative. The book is concerned primarily with Stieglitz's career rather than his personal life, concentrating on his spirit and motivations. Based on conversations the author had with Stieglitz from 1927 to 1946.

Stieglitz, Alfred. *Alfred Stieglitz: Photographs from the J. Paul Getty Museum.* Malibu, Calif.: J. Paul Getty Museum, 1995. Includes 93 of Stieglitz's more obscure images and an essay by the museum's curator arguing that the photographer's best work was done later in life at his family retreat in Lake George, New York.

Stieglitz, Alfred, and Pam Roberts. *Camera Work: The Complete Illustrations 1903-1917.* New York: Taschen, 1997. Comprehensive look at fifty issues of *Camera Work,* Stieglitz's journal of photography. Roberts offers an essay on the significance of both the photographer and his journal.

Thomas, F. Richard. *Literary Admirers of Alfred Stieglitz.* Carbondale: Southern Illinois University Press, 1983. Concentrates on the impact Stieglitz and photography have had upon the way people see, think, and write, discussing the influence Stieglitz and his work had upon such literary figures as Gertrude Stein, William Carlos Williams, Hart Crane, and Sherwood Anderson. Provides a working knowledge of terminology needed to understand Stieglitz's work.

*Charles A. Dranguet, Jr.*

# HENRY L. STIMSON

*Born:* September 21, 1867; New York, New York
*Died:* October 20, 1950; Huntington, New York
*Area of Achievement:* Diplomacy, government and politics
*Contribution:* Serving as secretary of war during the years 1909 to 1913 and again during World War II, and serving as secretary of state from 1929 to 1933, Stimson helped to define the United States' transition from isolationism to world responsibility.

## Early Life

Henry L. Stimson's ancestors arrived in the New World from England as part of the Massachusetts migration of the seventeenth century. From his father, who made and lost a fortune on Wall Street before devoting the remainder of his career to surgery, Stimson learned the Presbyterian values of simplicity, hard work, and frugality. Stimson's mother died when he was nine. He spent the next four years living with his grandparents. At thirteen, his father sent him to private schools that profoundly shaped his outlook: Phillips Academy, Yale, and finally Harvard Law School. Stimson credited Yale with giving him an appreciation for corporate class spirit and democracy; Harvard, with impressing upon him the values of individualism and competition.

Leaving law school in 1890, Stimson joined a firm headed by Elihu Root (who later joined President Theodore Roosevelt's cabinet). He soon entered local politics. Disgusted with what he considered to be the low ethical level of party leaders, Stimson helped to engineer a minor political revolt in 1897. This included attempts to eliminate financial corruption, to reform primary and election laws, and to select honest men to run for public office. Stimson's efforts brought him considerable influence in a revitalized Republican Party. His work was typical of Progressive reformers of that period.

Stimson's stern Presbyterian background helped to make him a patriot as well as a reformer. To his dying day, Stimson, like his hero Theodore Roosevelt, admired the military virtues. He joined the National Guard at the outbreak of the Spanish-American War in 1898. Sent to Puerto Rico, he arrived too late to see active service; nevertheless, he remained in his squadron for nine years after returning to the practice of law. In 1905, in part because of his association with Root, who had just become secretary of state, and in part because of his friendship with President Roosevelt, which began during his reform period in New York, Stimson was appointed United States attorney for the Southern District of New York (which included New York City). At age thirty-eight, the national phase of his career was about to begin.

## Life's Work

Stimson's work as United States attorney involved prosecutions of many corporations during a period when the government began to serve as a counterweight to the influence of big business. By the time he resigned in 1909, he had gained both a zest for public life and a modest national reputation.

He also had gained Roosevelt's admiration, and in 1910 the former president handpicked Stimson to run as the Republican candidate for governor of New York. This was Stimson's one campaign for elective office. He did not enjoy the experience, and he lost the election. Stimson was ill-suited to popular campaigns. He was erect, mustasched, conservatively dressed, and self-consciously digni-

fied; in fact, Stimson was rather cold and reserved. He resented telling crowds what they wanted to hear. Those who worked with him often found him distant and domineering, even arrogant.

His conservative brand of Progressive politics, however, met with the approval of both Roosevelt and his successor, William H. Taft, leading to Stimson's appointment as secretary of war in 1911. He served in the office for two years, initiating changes in the army that proved of value during World War I. Most notably, he increased the authority of the General Staff over the politically sensitive bureaus, and he modernized training procedures.

The political and administrative skirmishes that characterized Stimson's tenure in the War Department were forgotten when World War I arrived. Stimson had admired President Woodrow Wilson's domestic program, and he supported Wilson's defense of American neutrality. Stimson, however, increasingly deplored Wilson's refusal to prepare for war and openly opposed sending American troops to Mexico in 1915 because, he felt, the real enemy was in Europe. Only Wilson's Declaration of War ended Stimson's anger. He applied for a commission in the army and went to Europe as a colonel in the artillery. "Wonderfully happy," he later recalled of these days. His friends called him "Colonel" for the remainder of his life.

After the war, Stimson returned to the practice of law. His developing interest in international affairs was greatly sharpened by the debate over American membership in the League of Nations. Together with Elihu Root, who authored the charter of the World Court, Stimson became a leading Republican supporter of international organization. Regretting the Senate's rejection of League membership, Stimson in 1922 helped to found the Council on Foreign Relations in order to stem a national return to isolationism.

It is not surprising, therefore, that Stimson's subsequent public service occurred in the area of international affairs. During 1927, he accepted a presidential appointment as a special envoy to Nicaragua. He helped to protect American economic interests by ending a revolutionary challenge to the authority of the government, a process aided by the presence of American Marines. During the next two years, he accepted appointment as governor general of the Philippines. There he encouraged programs of economic development and became an influential opponent of those who wanted to grant independence to the islands.

Shortly after Stimson returned home, President-elect Herbert Hoover offered him the post of secretary of state. It was in the State Department that Stimson learned the lessons that shaped his approach to foreign policy for the rest of his life. The American public's preoccupation with the Great Depression, reinforcing popular disillusionment with the United States' involvement in World War I, undermined his efforts to generate a policy of international cooperation. Moreover, Stimson's own plans concerning the American role in both Europe and the Far East were much less clear than he later suggested in his memoirs.

These matters were not academic. In 1931, Japanese army units began the occupation of Manchuria in China, undermining the post-World War I peace settlement and beginning the process that led to World War II. In the years after he left the State Department, Stimson became one of the most articulate champions of collective security (that is, the use of collective force to keep the peace).

Just before the Manchurian Crisis, however, Stimson had been ambivalent about the League of Nations and collective security, preferring to see the League as useful in Europe alone. Even as he brought the United States into closer cooperation with the League following the Japanese occupation of Manchuria, he did so with a divided mind. He was fearful about becoming involved in war against Japan and uneasy about the isolationist sentiments of both President Hoover and the American public. Moreover, he was troubled by his own failure to reconcile conflicts among his Far Eastern priorities—protection of American economic interests, preservation of the postwar treaties and the League, and maintenance of peace with Japan. Even his greatest accomplishment—the famous Non-Recognition Doctrine of 1932, which held that the United States would not recognize political change made in violation of existing treaties—illustrated his failure: Japan subsequently ignored this doctrine, and friendly countries such as Great Britain and France viewed it as overly moralistic and rhetorical.

Henry Stimson learned from his failures. Between 1933 and 1939, while out of public office, he strongly advocated a policy of collective security that went far beyond nonrecognition. These were years that witnessed the rule of Adolf Hitler in Germany, the invasion of Ethiopia by Italy, and the expansion of Japanese control over China. Consequently, when the Democratic President

Franklin D. Roosevelt in mid-1940 needed to personify his own commitment to the principles of bipartisanship and collective security after Hitler's armies invaded France, he invited a Republican, Stimson, to serve again as secretary of war.

Stimson headed the War Department from 1940 to 1945. He helped to streamline the lines of military command and brought a number of extraordinary subordinates into the War Department at a critical time in the nation's history. He worked well with Chief of Staff George C. Marshall, and he maintained a trusted relationship with President Roosevelt, whose domestic policies were at odds with his own. Stimson did not always prevail on issues of policy. He favored opening a second front in France in 1943 rather than 1944, as was finally done, and he respected General Charles de Gaulle more than did Roosevelt, who distrusted the leader of the Free French forces. He was rebuffed on strategic issues related to such things as his advocacy, in 1942, of the use of Army Air Forces for antisubmarine duty and his proposals in 1944 to increase the size of the army rather than merely replace units in the field.

Most of his recommendations, however, were accepted. He fully supported the "Europe first" strategy of defeating Germany before turning the weight of American military might against Japan. He reluctantly approved the removal of Japanese Americans from their homes on the West Coast, and he prevailed in his opposition to Secretary of the Treasury Henry Morgenthau's plan to convert postwar Germany into a strictly agricultural society. He oversaw the Manhattan Project, which produced the first atom bomb, and successfully chaired the Interim Committee that devised the strategy for using that terrible new instrument of war. Stimson understood the implications of the bomb better than most officials, and in 1946 he called for international cooperation regarding its development. In this quest he failed. Out of this failure would, in part, grow the Cold War.

### Summary

Stimson left government service in 1945. His direct influence on military and foreign policy thereby ended, but his indirect influence as embodied in the work of his subordinates continued to affect policy for many more years. In many ways, Stimson's early contributions were made possible by his well-placed connections with men such as Elihu Root and Theodore Roosevelt. He did the rest on his own. Stimson was neither brilliant nor charismatic. He was, however, loyal, forceful, and strong-minded. His failures were often the product of an overly moralistic approach to politics, a trait that was especially evident in his service as secretary of state during the Manchurian Crisis.

Yet Stimson's failures prepared the way for his successes. If he failed in diplomacy, he came to symbolize collective security during a period when the diplomacy of appeasement gradually yielded to a recognition of the need for military defense. As secretary of war a second time, his administrative and military talents paid great dividends. There is no reason to think that the outcome of World War II would have been any different had someone other than Henry Stimson headed the War Department. Nevertheless, there is every reason to think that he effectively administered both the hugely complex war machinery between 1940 and 1945 and the planning for the postwar period, in which his moralism gave way to a more realistic appreciation of the behavior of great powers.

### Bibliography

Bernstein, Barton J. "Seizing the Contested Terrain of Early Nuclear History: Stimson, Conant, and Their Allies Explain the Decision to Use the Atomic Bomb." *Diplomatic History* 17, no. 1 (Winter, 1993): 35-73.

Current, Richard N. "Henry L. Stimson." In *An Uncertain Tradition: American Secretaries of State in the Twentieth Century*, edited by Norman A. Graebner, 168-183. New York: McGraw, 1961. This is the best short overview of Stimson in the State Department. The author views Stimson's moralistic approach to diplomacy as creating more problems than it solved, and emphasizes the differences between Stimson and President Hoover.

———. *Secretary Stimson: A Study in Statecraft*. New Brunswick, N.J.: Rutgers University Press, 1954. This critical appraisal faults Stimson for pursuing a policy that the author views as erratic and excessively moralistic.

Ferrell, Robert H. *American Diplomacy in the Great Depression: Hoover-Stimson Foreign Policy, 1929-1933*. New Haven, Conn.: Yale University Press, and London: Oxford University Press, 1957. The author contends that the Depression prevented Hoover and Stimson from taking an assertive stance against the enemies of peace.

———. *Frank Kellogg and Henry L. Stimson*. New York: Cooper Square, 1953. The author views Stimson as unnecessarily accommodating in respect to the action of Japan in Manchuria.

Gullan, Harold I. "Expectations of Infamy: Roosevelt and Marshall Prepare for War, 1938-41." *Presidential Studies Quarterly* 28, no. 3 (Summer 1998). Examines President Franklin Roosevelt's role in the preparation of the United States for World War II and includes the importance of Secretary of War Henry Stimson.

Morison, Elting E. *Turmoil and Tradition: A Study of the Life and Times of Henry L. Stimson*. Boston: Houghton Mifflin, 1960. In the most comprehensive biography of Stimson, Morison provides a somewhat uncritical account of his career. The author relies heavily on the material in Stimson's own memoirs.

Ostrower, Gary B. *Collective Insecurity: The United States and the League of Nations During the Early Thirties*. Lewisburg, Pa.: Bucknell University Press, 1979. This work focuses on Stimson as the key figure in the transition of American diplomacy from isolationism to collective security.

———. "Henry L. Stimson and the League of Nations." *Historian* 41 (1979): 467-482. The author argues that Stimson was less consistent in his support for the League than his memoirs and most conventional accounts suggest.

Sherwin, Martin J. *A World Destroyed: The Atomic Bomb and the Grand Alliance*. New York: Knopf, 1975. A brilliant analysis of the way in which the Bomb affected wartime diplomacy, and the part Stimson played in this drama.

Stimson, Henry L. *The Far Eastern Crisis: Recollections and Observations*. New York and London: Harper, 1936. Stimson wrote this book as a lesson for those who would deal with aggression in the future. His book is a plea for the democratic states to cooperate within the framework of a collective-security system.

Stimson, Henry L., and McGeorge Bundy. *On Active Service in Peace and War.* London: Hutchinson, and New York: Harper, 1948. A gracefully written memoir which benefited greatly from the existence of extensive diaries composed by Stimson. This volume emphasizes the period since 1929.

Stimson, Henry. "Stimson Doctrine, 1931." *Essential Documents in American History,* 1999. Transcript of the text of the Stimson Doctrine, sent on January 7, 1932, to Japan and China by Stimson. The doctrine stated the U.S. position with respect to attempted limitations on its treaty rights.

*Gary B. Ostrower*

# KARLHEINZ STOCKHAUSEN

*Born:* August 22, 1928; Mödrath, near Cologne, Germany

*Area of Achievement:* Music

*Contribution:* Stockhausen is one of the most innovative and influential composers of his time, successfully bridging the gap between technology and creative endeavor and integrating a wide spectrum of musical and nonmusical concepts into his work.

## Early Life

Karlheinz Stockhausen was born on August 22, 1928, in the village of Mödrath, near Cologne in northwestern Germany. He was the first of three children born to Simon Stockhausen, a schoolteacher, and his wife Gertrud. When Karlheinz was only four years old, his mother, who suffered from depression, entered a sanatorium. Soon after, Simon was forced to become an active member of the Nazi Party because of his status as a teacher, and Karlheinz was occasionally pressed into service as a party messenger for his father.

Upon starting primary school in the village of Altenberg, Stockhausen began the study of the piano with the organist of the village church. Since he was gifted musically and seemed also to have inherited from his father a capacity for study, he soon was recommended for study at a secondary school in a nearby town, from which he progressed in 1941 to a teacher training college at Xanten, which lay downstream on the Rhine River from his native region.

The college in Xanten was a somewhat harsh environment where military rigor was imposed upon the students' lives. Fortunately, music was not proscribed, and Stockhausen began lessons on the violin as well as the oboe, which he played in the college wind band. His earliest contact with jazz music also dates from his three years at Xanten. During these years, Stockhausen was largely cut off from his family. His father had entered the army, and in 1942 Stockhausen learned that his mother had been put to death under the terms of a government policy to create more space for military hospitalization.

Leaving Xanten in October, 1944, Stockhausen became a stretcher-bearer in a military hospital, where he came into contact with wounded and dying American and English soldiers as well as those of the German army. He saw his father for the last time shortly before the end of the war; Simon Stockhausen is believed to have died in service on the Hungarian front.

After the war, Stockhausen found work on a farm, and soon his evenings were occupied in assisting a local operetta society in preparing performances. Qualifying in February, 1946, for entrance as a senior student at a school in Bergisch Gladbach, he supported himself with miscellaneous musical jobs until his graduation the following year. Now nineteen years old, Stockhausen was enrolled in the four-year course of the State Academy of Music in Cologne and simultaneously took courses in musicology and philosophy at the University of Cologne. At the academy, his principal areas of study were piano and school music, but in 1950 he had several lessons in composition from the Swiss composer Frank Martin, who had joined the faculty at the academy. Several short works by Stockhausen survive from these years, including *Chore für Doris* (1950; chorus for Doris), for unaccompanied chorus, and *Drei Lieder* (1950; three songs), for alto voice and orchestra. In his final year at the academy, Stockhausen was engaged largely in composing and in preparing his final examination thesis. In the midst of this demanding academic activity, the young musician continued to work nights as a jazz pianist in local bars.

In 1951, Stockhausen met the Cologne music critic Herbert Eimert, who was in charge of a series of evening broadcasts of contemporary music on North-West German Radio. Finding in the young composer both musical talent and a strong personality, Eimert arranged the first radio performance of a Stockhausen work and invited the composer to become a regular contributor to his program. Eimert also introduced Stockhausen to the Darmstadt New Music Courses, which in 1951 included a seminar by Eimert and others on music and technology. That same year at Darmstadt, the French composer Pierre Schaeffer contributed a lecture-demonstration on the activities of a Paris group pursuing the concept of *musique concrète*, electronic music employing manipulated tape-recorded sounds of the everyday, "concrete" world.

Following the Darmstadt course in the summer of 1951, Stockhausen returned to Cologne to prepare for state examinations to qualify as a secondary school music teacher, which he passed with distinction. In November, he completed his first

major composition, *Kreuzspiel* (crossplay), which he dedicated to Doris Andreae, a fellow student at the academy. On December 29, Stockhausen and Doris were married (four children were born to the couple between 1953 and 1961), and in January, 1952, he went to Paris for further study.

### Life's Work

In the early 1950's, Parisian musical life, like that of many European centers, was dominated by the example of the composer Anton Webern, whose radically distilled works were based upon the concept of "serialism." Serialism, an evolution of developments initiated earlier in the century by Arnold Schoenberg, dictated that unity in musical composition was to be sought by rigorously and systematically interrelating musical elements such as pitch, harmony, rhythm, and instrumental tone-color. After Webern's premature death, the serialist banner was carried into the postwar period by the influential French composer Olivier Messiaen, whose music Stockhausen heard at Darmstadt in 1951. Already influenced by Messiaen's *Mode de valeurs et d'intensités* (1949; mode of values and intensities), which Stockhausen likened to "star music," the young German determined to attend Messiaen's course in analysis and aesthetics during 1952-1953.

Paris offered more to Stockhausen than just the stimulus of Messiaen's powerful musical thinking. He also worked with the *musique concrète* group, producing his first tape composition, *Étude* (1952; study), and investigated the synthesis of sound spectra by the combination of pure sounds produced electronically, thus laying the foundation for his early electronic compositions. The best-known work of Stockhausen's Parisian year is *Kontra-Punkte* (1952-1953; counterpoints), a composition of a type called "pointillist." This term, loosely derived from the technique of painting in small dots of color, is intended to evoke the sense of the free distribution of notes across a continuum of pitch and time. Pointillist form was intended as a rejection of many of the compositional ideas of European music, such as theme, contrast, and rhythmic sequence. Accordingly, Stockhausen's early compositions, like those of many of his contemporaries, were not well received by the general public, which had difficulty perceiving the constructive artistic intent behind the wholesale transformation of musical language.

In 1953, Stockhausen returned to Germany and became a collaborator at the studio for electronic music at West German Radio in Cologne, where he began work on *Electronishe Studien I and II* (1953 and 1954; electronic studies I and II), his first exclusively electronic compositions. The first of these is made up of combinations of pure sine-wave tones in fixed proportions; the second is derived from sine tones acoustically manipulated to create an element of indeterminate pitch, or "noise." The second study is historically significant in that it was the first electronic composition to be published as a score, and it was one of the first to be brought out on record. Both compositions display a nearly total "serialization" of the process of composition, in which a set of rules determines the musical content. In works such as this, a blurring of distinctions between "form" and "material" is brought about that, in theory, might render the music wholly abstract and mechanical, but Stockhausen's inventiveness and his grasp of the psychology of perception allowed him to maintain the vividness of musical experience.

While at work on the second study, Stockhausen undertook further academic study under Werner Meyer-Eppler of the University of Bonn. Lecturing on communication theory and phonetics, Meyer-

Eppler provided Stockhausen with new perspectives on the physical and structural potential of sound. The result of Stockhausen's study can be heard in his *Gesang der Jünglinde* (1956; songs of the youths), which is widely regarded as one of the major early achievements of electronic music.

Stockhausen's activities outside the realm of composition continued with his participation in the journal *Die Reihe*, which first appeared in 1955 under his joint editorship with Eimert, who had also founded the Cologne Electronic Studio. Still only in his late twenties, Stockhausen was already widely recognized as a leading figure in contemporary music, and the influence of this musical thinking had begun to spread. In 1953, he began collaborating in the "International Vacation Courses for New Music" in Darmstadt, and in the 1960's, he was to lecture at universities in the United States, where his articulate and compelling exposition of his own work brought him to the attention of a widening audience.

The composition *Zeitmasze* (1956; tempi) began a new period of instrumental composition for Stockhausen. This dense, many-layered work, scored for flute, oboe, English horn, clarinet, and bassoon, represents a reassessment of the pointillist style that had been the mainstay of European avant-garde music in the early 1950's. *Zeitmasze* maintains the composer's characteristic formal rigor while allowing the physical and psychological vitality of live musical performance to take on new importance. A fundamental conception of the work is that independently varying measures of time can be made to interact in a manner that necessitates a "distributive" and "statistical," rather than a thematic and metrical, perception of musical material. To a degree, *Zeitmasze* represents the adaptation of abstract theory to an appreciation of the perception of music; its jazzlike flux of instrumental sound-events lends it a quality distinct from intellectualized, conventional serialism.

In the late 1950's, Stockhausen sought out new avenues of musical organization that often led to larger-scale works, though piano composition remained an important element in his overall development. *Gruppen* (1957; groups), employing three spatially separated orchestras directed by three conductors, signals a shift toward what has been called "group form," in which sound events can be resolved into identifiable microstructures with collective properties capable of either logical or imaginative organization. *Gruppen* seems to embody musical analogues of natural phenomena, and the composer has likened audible structures in this work to the outlines of mountains he observed in Switzerland during its composition.

Stockhausen's increasing confidence in composing large-scale works is shown by *Carré* (1960; square), written for four orchestras and four choirs, *Kontakte* (1960; contacts), for electronic sounds, piano, and percussion, and *Momente* (1964; moments), for solo soprano, four choral groups, and thirteen instrumentalists. The composer has written that *Carré* arose out of a new experience of time gained while flying for hours at a time while on tour in the United States. With his ear to the window, Stockhausen studied the vibrations coming from the engines of the propeller-driven airplanes and later composed the work as an exploration of fluctuations of continuous sounds. A notable development of *Kontakte* is the "contact" and interaction of electronic and instrumental sounds. As in *Carré*, the distribution of sound in space is a cardinal feature of the work.

In many of the compositions of the late 1950's and early 1960's, Stockhausen considered the problem of the audience's involvement in the often sterile concert environment of modern music. Surrounding the audience with moving sound, as in *Carré*, was a technical and aesthetic venture of great consequence, but he explored other ways of breaking down barriers between composer, performer, and audience. *Momente*, a work ultimately of some popularity, goes to the extreme of providing instructions to the choir to supply some of the heckling often associated with performances of contemporary music. Yet, characteristically, this somewhat ironic gesture fits seamlessly into the purely musical fabric of the composition.

*Momente* embodies in its title one of Stockhausen's most important aesthetic principles, that of "moment form." Although distinctions between pointillist form, group form, and moment form are often difficult, the composer's own explanation is that each "moment" is an individual and self-regulated state or process that neither depends on a previous musical form nor dictates a subsequent one but has an integrity in the present transcending the everyday experience of sequential time. "Moment form" is clearly a concept with a philosophical as well as a technical grounding, and it has underlain most of Stockhausen's later work.

Stockhausen was as unceasingly productive in the 1960's as in the previous decade. One of the most significant developments of these years was his turning toward Asian culture for inspiration. The year 1966 brought commissions from the national broadcasting corporation of Japan, including *Telemusik.* In 1970, Stockhausen was commissioned by the West German government to produce a work for a spherical auditorium at the World's Fair in Osaka. During a period of 183 days, more than one million visitors heard the composer and his ensemble perform his compositions in an environment designed especially for them.

Increasingly, Stockhausen's compositions have embraced intuition, performer interaction, and open forms of organization in an effort to refine the humanistic goals of his music. *Hymnen* (1967; hymns), a composition of electronic and concrete music, is a tapestry of electronically transformed national anthems that embodies, in a general way, a message of universal toleration and diversity. *Stimmung*, completed in 1968 (the composer notes that the title may be translated in various ways, including "spiritual harmony" in addition to the conventional "tuning"), is an appealing work in which precise, demanding vocal technique is used to create a meditative atmosphere.

In 1967, Stockhausen married the painter Mary Bauermeister, with whom he subsequently had two children. Several of the composer's children became involved in the composer's artistic projects, particularly Marcus Stockhausen, a talented trumpeter.

Stockhausen's "intuitive music" reached its greatest intensity in the work entitled *Aus den sieben Tagen* (1968; from the seven days), which seems to embody the resolution of a spiritual crisis that the composer experienced in 1968. *Aus den sieben Tagen* is not composed in musical notation but exists instead as a set of fifteen texts written by Stockhausen that communicate states of mind and spiritual aspirations. These have titles such as "Right Duration," "Intensity," and "Set Sail for the Sun," which essentially direct the performer toward his own musical and spiritual resources. When played by musicians attuned to its demands, *Aus den sieben Tagen* can result in improvisation of substance and beauty, but few performing artists have the courage to proceed on the instruction "Play in the rhythm of the Universe," as one of the pieces suggests.

During the next decade, Stockhausen continued his research and speculation in the structuring and presentation of music. From this period, *Mantra* (1970) is widely regarded as a masterpiece that unites technological sophistication and creative inspiration. Much of the composer's work immediately following was on a smaller scale and had more specific objectives than his work of the 1960's, but in 1977 he began an ambitious series of compositions that would continue to occupy him for many years. The projected cycle is called *Licht, die sieben Tagen der Woche* (light, the seven days of the week), and when completed it will contain seven components, designated as operas, one corresponding to each day of the week. The first section of the work to be completed was *Donnerstag aus Licht* (Thursday from light); it was composed between 1978 and 1980 and was first performed at La Scala in Milan, Italy, in 1981. The next two years were taken up with the composition of *Samstag aus Licht* (Saturday from light), which was produced with Stockhausen's active participation in 1984 by the La Scala organization at a sports stadium in Milan. These works have proven very elaborate and demanding as stage productions; in them the composer continues to be the same uncompromising executant of his own works that he has been throughout his career.

### Summary

Karlheinz Stockhausen's compositional output is remarkable by any measure of creative endeavor, and, though questions of quality in twentieth century musical culture are as difficult to formulate as they are to answer, the status of many of his works is unquestioned with respect to musical integrity, inventiveness, and influence. A true burden of creative innovation in music after World War II has fallen on relatively few shoulders. Among Stockhausen's contemporaries perhaps only his friend and colleague Pierre Boulez bears comparison with him in these terms.

The complex evolution of Stockhausen's music has encompassed the analysis and electronic creation of sounds, the electronic shaping of musical material and its integration into the more familiar world of live musical performance, the reshaping of the concept as well as the experience of time in music, and the revision of the relation of the composer to performer and audience. In broad terms he has developed from an artist following intellectual models to one capable of a powerful synthesis of objective and subjective materials and processes. An appearance of calculated impersonality noted in his earlier career by some critics has yielded to a willingness to engage openly issues of deep significance, and in his advocacy of personal and social transformation he sometimes seems almost to be an elder statesman of pluralist, humanist culture. Without question, Stockhausen has attempted to restore the image of the artist as culture-hero but only by first establishing a solid foundation in musical practice.

**Bibliography**

Bergstein, Barry. "Miles Davis and Karlheinz Stockhausen: A Reciprocal Relationship." *Musical Quarterly* 76, no. 4 (Winter 1992). Considers the influence that Miles Davis and Stockhausen had on each other's work.

Brindle, Reginald Smith. *The New Music: The Avant-Garde Since 1945.* 2d ed. Oxford and New York: Oxford University Press, 1987. This survey, in which Stockhausen figures very prominently, draws refreshing distinctions between the claims made by composers for their music and its actual expressive achievements. The author, himself a composer, treats technical matters with clarity and common sense.

Coenen, Alcedo. "Stockhausen's Paradigm: A Survey of His Theories." *Perspectives of New Music* 32, no. 2 (Summer 1994). The author offers analysis of Stockhausen's music based on Thomas Kuhn's model theory of knowledge and argues that the consistency derived from the model is valuable in musical composition.

Cott, Jonathan. *Stockhausen: Conversations with the Composer.* New York: Simon and Schuster, 1973; London: Robson, 1974. The author is a poet and veteran journalist who knows how to elicit a colorful response from Stockhausen, who is here an almost ideal interview subject. This book is one of the best documents of the postwar musical avant-garde.

Harvey, Jonathan. *The Music of Stockhausen.* London: Faber, and Berkeley: University of California Press, 1975. This book presents Stockhausen's work with insight but with only intermittent sympathy for the nontechnical reader. Alone among books on the composer and his works, this one features an attractive design.

Heikinheimo, Seppo. *The Electronic Music of Karlheinz Stockhausen: Studies on the Esthetical and Formal Problems of Its First Phase.* Helsinki: Suomen Musiikkitieteellinen Seura, 1972. Although this is a highly technical examination of a narrow range of the composer's works, many of the central issues in Stockhausen's earlier music are lucidly presented. The translation from Finnish is excellent.

Maconie, Robin. *The Works of Karlheinz Stockhausen.* 2d ed. Oxford: Clarendon Press, and New York: Oxford University Press, 1990. The author greatly admires Stockhausen's music, and this book embodies committed study of individual works and their complex interrelationships. A high degree of technical detail is enhanced by excerpts of scores and graphic notation of the works, and the book is made especially useful by the inclusion of exhaustive performance and recording data accompanying each entry.

Stuckenschmidt, H. H. *Germany and Central Europe.* Vol 2 in *Twentieth Century Composers.* London: Weidenfeld and Nicolson, 1970; New York: Holt Rinehart, 1971. Stuckenschmidt here devotes a reliable chapter of his survey to Stockhausen's career to about 1963, but he is unable to convey the complexity of the composer's work because of limitations of space. A sense of Stockhausen's status as a German cultural figure may be gained by comparing him with other composers represented.

———. *Twentieth Century Music.* Translated from the German by Richard Deveson. London: Weidenfeld and Nicolson, and New York: McGraw-Hill, 1969. This excellent survey of the field has a particular value in detailing the thought of the Russian-born musicologist Joseph Schillinger, whose advanced theories on the relation between mathematics and music seem to have greatly influenced Stockhausen.

Tannenbaum, Mya. *Conversations with Stockhausen.* Oxford: Clarendon Press, and New York: Oxford University Press, 1987. Translated by David Butchart. Consisting of texts of interviews conducted from 1979 to 1981, this is an often amusing look at both the mundane and exalted concerns of the composer as he struggles to arrange performances of his opera *Donnerstag aus Licht.*

Wörner, Karl Heinrich. *Stockhausen.* London: Faber, and Berkeley: University of California Press, 1973. Translated and edited by Bill Hopkins. This book consists of a 1963 text that was updated by the author in the late 1960's, combined with descriptions by Stockhausen of most of his early works. The book is a mine of information but is loosely organized. Like most authors listed here, Wörner enjoyed the composer's cooperation in the preparation of the book.

*C. S. McConnell*

# HARLAN FISKE STONE

*Born:* October 11, 1872; Chesterfield, New Hampshire
*Died:* April 22, 1946; Washington, D.C.
*Areas of Achievement:* Education and law
*Contribution:* As Associate and then Chief Justice of the United States Supreme Court, Stone advocated a philosophy of moderation that combined judicial restraint and liberal nationalism with a concern for civil and political liberties. His integrity and persistence contributed significantly to the Court's dramatic shift in 1937 from hostility to sympathy for the liberal nationalism of New Deal legislation, thereby avoiding a major constitutional crisis over the Court's powers.

## Early Life

On October 11, 1872, Harlan Fiske Stone became one of the fifth generation of his family to be born in Chesterfield, New Hampshire. His father, Frederick Stone, was a farmer and trader of moderate wealth. His mother, née Ann Sophia Butler, a former schoolteacher, was also from an old Chesterfield family. In 1874, the Stone family bought a new farm and moved to Amherst, Massachusetts, so that Harlan and his older brother, Winthrop, could eventually attend college there. Here Harlan grew up and developed his love of nature, although he never cared much for farm work.

Early in school Stone displayed above-average mental abilities, and with only two years of high school he entered Massachusetts Agricultural College in 1888, as a premedical student. He was expelled toward the end of his second year for participating in a student brawl, but he convinced his father to give him a second chance and was accepted by Amherst the next fall. He gave up science for a liberal arts curriculum and was graduated in 1894. Stone was active in student affairs at Amherst and served as class president for three years, won awards in declamation, worked on the student newspaper, was elected to Phi Beta Kappa, and played football.

In appearance, Stone was large of frame, five feet and eleven inches in height, 175 pounds in weight, and had an ordinary but friendly look and an easy manner. After he was graduated from Amherst, he spent a year as science teacher and football coach at Newburyport High School, before enrolling in Columbia University's law school. Although not always especially articulate, his persistence, self-confidence, and willingness to work hard allowed him to overcome this difficulty, earning for him the respect of his law professors. He was graduated in June of 1898, at the age of twenty-six, and joined the New York City law firm of Satterlee and Canfield. Three years later he was made a full partner. In December of 1898, he accepted a part-time appointment as professor of law at Columbia. Stone began his career full of idealism and optimism for his chosen profession, but over the years he came to realize that few other lawyers perceived the profession as a noble, idealistic calling.

Stone had known Agnes Harvey of Chesterfield, New Hampshire, the daughter of his mother's best friend, since early childhood. They pledged themselves to each other in 1890 and maintained a regular correspondence thereafter. Early in 1899, Stone thought himself well enough settled to give her an engagement ring, and they were married September 7 of that year at her home in Chesterfield. They had two sons, Marshall, born in 1903, and Lauson, born in 1904. It was a long and happy union.

## Life's Work

By 1910, Stone had achieved a good reputation as a practicing lawyer and was recognized as a superior law professor. In his practice he stressed preventing future legal problems rather than waiting until trouble occurred. As a teacher, he believed that the lecture method had become obsolete with the printing press, and he emphasized the Socratic case method in order to stress to his students the importance of learning how to reason like a lawyer. On July 1, 1910, he assumed a position with the law school as professor and dean. He soon began making administrative and curricular improvements, insisting on high scholarly standards from students and faculty, allowing elective courses for seniors, and publishing scholarly articles regularly. Under Dean Stone's leadership, Columbia Law School became one of the leading American institutions.

As dean and as legal scholar, Stone began to attract national attention. During World War I, he distinguished himself for fairness as a member of a special board of inquiry to consider whether those military draftees who claimed to be conscientious objectors were legitimate. He also gained recognition as an advocate of civil rights and justice for dissenters by protesting the harassment of professors for antiwar views and the witch-hunts of Attorney General A. Mitchell Palmer, who had rounded up thousands of suspects and deported hundreds of alleged politically radical recent immigrants in 1919 and 1920, without the benefit of any kind of hearing. This was not because Stone agreed with the radicals. He had fully supported the American war effort, was disturbed by violent political and labor protests, and was skeptical of their theories of social justice. Yet he maintained his perspective and understood that it was dangerous for a society to permit the violation of a minority's civil rights in the name of protecting the majority. Furthermore, by the end of his tenure as dean he had developed some sympathy for the radicals' theory of sociological jurisprudence. He became involved in several projects to reform the law so that it would better serve the needs of the new urbanized, industrialized age. In 1923, Stone decided to resign as dean. Too much administrative work and too many disagreements with Columbia's President Nicholas Murray Butler had left him feeling thwarted, and he elected to devote his time to practicing law. Six months later he was in Washington, D.C.

In March of 1924, Attorney General Harry M. Daugherty was forced to resign by President Calvin Coolidge. Rumors of his involvement in the scandals surrounding former president Warren G. Harding led to an attempt by Congress to investigate his conduct in office. President Coolidge, in need of an attorney general who was not only capable but also of untarnished reputation, offered the job to Stone, who accepted. His first problem was to clear out the numerous incompetent political and volunteer appointees in the Washington and regional offices and replace them with trained people who would remain apart from politics and conduct themselves according to high professional standards. One of his early decisions was to appoint J. Edgar Hoover as temporary chief of the Bureau of Investigation (later the Federal Bureau of Investigation). In time Stone concluded that this bright young lawyer was the right person and made the appointment permanent. There were complaints from members of the Senate and the House over the firings and over Stone's strict enforcement of various laws, especially antitrust and prohibition laws. Stone ignored the complaints and remained characteristically persistent in his efforts, and the operation of his department began to show marked improvement.

On January 5, 1925, the public learned that President Coolidge had nominated Stone to succeed Joseph McKenna as Associate Justice of the Supreme Court. His selection was undoubtedly the result of the president's respect for Stone's vigorous and impartial conduct of affairs as attorney general, the broad respect commanded by Stone from his professional colleagues, and the president's personal regard for Stone. A few senators whose interests had been harmed by Stone as attorney general tried to obstruct his nomination, but they were too few and their cause too suspect to prevent confirmation on February 5, 1925.

Stone was well suited in temperament and training for the Supreme Court. He did not have a mind that quickly grasped all the ramifications of an idea or that was absorbed with fundamental philosophical issues. He was at his best proceeding slowly, as a court does, case by case, cautiously building interpretations of law and avoiding careless, sweeping generalizations that would rebound and cause trouble later. When Stone joined the Supreme Court, the United States appeared to be in the midst of an economic boom based on an unprecedented number of new inventions and products. To Stone, with his frugal New England habits, this rampant materialism seemed to threaten the nation's spiritual values. He never idolized big business as so many of his contemporaries did, nor did he approve of those lawyers who seemed so willing to place their talents in the service of business without concern for matters of conscience or ethics. He feared lawyers had become thoroughly commercialized, to the detriment of professional standards. Throughout his long career on the bench, Stone was more concerned in economic issues about problems of the general welfare than he was about the interests or rights of the individual, an attitude which colored many of his decisions.

The social and economic stress on American society from the Great Depression worried Stone, although he had sheltered his own investments. As a friend and supporter of President Herbert Hoover, he was concerned about Hoover's lack of initiative in dealing with the crisis. The election to the presidency of Franklin D. Roosevelt in 1932 did not fill Stone with hope, and while he applauded the moderate economic experimentation of the New Deal and voted to uphold some measures, several important laws were clearly unconstitutional in his opinion. On May 27, 1935, known as Black Monday, Stone voted with the other justices to declare two major New Deal laws unconstitutional, the National Industrial Recovery Act (NIRA) and the Frazier-Lemke Act (in *Schechter v. United States* and *Louisville Bank v. Radford*, respectively). The extent of the delegation of legislative authority to the executive branch of the government and the cavalier attitude of the New Deal NIRA law appalled Stone. He also agreed that the Frazier-Lemke Act constituted the taking of private property without compensation. The response of President Roosevelt to these and other cases in which the Court had declared parts of the New Deal unconstitutional was his famous Court Packing Plan. Even though Roosevelt experienced one of the major defeats of his career on this issue, several factors presented him with a Supreme Court more sympathetic to New Deal experimentalism. First, several members of the Court, including Stone, began to retreat from their position and give the establishment of economic policy to Congress out of fear that the New Deal Congress might agree to a major restructuring of the Court should the justices continue their opposition. There was no certainty that public opinion would save the Court again. Second, several justices retired, giving President Roosevelt enough appointees on the Court to ensure that his program would receive a favorable hearing in the future. Finally, the Court had already dealt with the most radical parts of the New Deal and found the remaining laws more moderate measures and, therefore, easier to accept.

By virtue of his seniority in service and his long history of dissent on behalf of liberal nationalism and judicial restraint on economic questions, Stone had become the intellectual spokesman of the Supreme Court by 1940. When Chief Justice Charles Evans Hughes resigned in 1941, it was no surprise to anyone that Roosevelt nominated Stone as his successor. The Senate readily consented. Although the whole Court was now sympathetic to liberal nationalism, factions had emerged, and Roosevelt seems to have believed that Stone was the best person to bring harmony. In fact, however, Stone found it necessary to become a restraining influence to prevent serious damage to the Constitution and the American concept of free government. Stone feared the Court would give up too much to Congress, and he began to sound a new theme in his writings. In his opinion, it was appropriate to permit Congress wide latitude in setting economic policy because economic rights were inferior to political and civil freedoms; the Court must look closely at any law limiting civil or political rights and narrowly construe the constitutional powers of Congress. Stone found himself writing minority opinions again. It should be noted, however, for reasons that have never been clear, that Stone's defense of civil and political liberty did not extend to their suppression by the military during World War II. This lapse was especially notable in those cases dealing with the internment of the Japanese on the West Coast.

Stone had begun to think about retirement as early as 1945. He wanted to leave before he could no longer carry out his duties. His health remained good, however, and he had not set a date. Events made the decision for him. On April 22, 1946, just as he was about to read three decisions in formal court session that he had prepared, Stone slipped into a state of unconsciousness from which he never recovered. He died at 6:45 P.M. at home with his wife and sons by his side, of a massive cerebral hemorrhage. The state funeral services were held in the Washington Cathedral on April 25.

### Summary

In two major respects, Harlan Fiske Stone was a man ahead of his time. In his early years as an Associate Justice of the Supreme Court, often joining Oliver Wendell Holmes, Jr., and Louis D. Brandeis in dissents from the majority's opinion, he elaborated a theory of judicial restraint to allow experimentation by Congress and state legislatures in establishing policies to cope with the massive changes permeating American society from industrialization and urbanization. He also believed the Court should consider the full historical context of events surrounding cases and not base decisions solely on the narrow reasoning of previous cases and legal doctrines from the past. He saw the Constitution as a starting point, not a discrete document. This loose handling of the concept of constitutionalism was a serious breach of American political and constitutional philosophy to many. During the crisis of the Great Depression, however, it provided a rationale for the Court to withdraw from the battles over economic legislation and survive with its powers intact.

As senior Associate Justice and then Chief Justice of the Supreme Court, Stone found it necessary to urge the Court to reassert itself on behalf of civil and political liberties. His opinions contained ideas and precedents that were again ahead of their time. They would not become popular until the later struggles over civil rights in the 1950's. Both these achievements came at the cost, however, of demoting the economic and property rights of the individual to a secondary status. Yet as Stone himself said, the justices on the Court are never free to decide the present without the past. The Court must move one step at a time.

### Bibliography

Burns, James MacGregor. *Roosevelt: The Lion and the Fox*. London: Secker and Warburg, and New York: Harcourt Brace, 1956. Probably the best single-volume political biography of FDR; covers the political-constitutional issues of the New Deal with much insight, though it is very favorable to Roosevelt.

Engdahl, David E. "The Necessary and Proper Clause as an Intrinsic Restraint on Federal Lawmaking Power." *Harvard Journal of Law and Public Policy* 22, no. 1 (Fall 1998). Discusses the Necessary and Proper Clause as the foundation for Congress's power over interstate commerce. Focuses on the history of the clause and its reestablishment by Stone in the 1941 case *U.S. v. Darby*.

Konefsky, Samuel J. *Chief Justice Stone and the Supreme Court*. New York: Macmillan, 1945. A study of Stone's philosophy of constitutional interpretation, as it evolved in his written opinions from 1925 to 1943, by a contemporary. Dated but still useful for its coverage of specific issues and analysis of Stone's jurisprudence.

Link, Arthur S., and William B. Catton. *American Epoch: A History of the United States Since 1900*. 2 vols. 7th ed. New York and London: McGraw-Hill, 1993. Volume 1 covers the years 1900 to 1945 and is one of the best general histories of the period available. Stone is mentioned only briefly.

Linzer, Peter. "The Carolene Products Footnote and the Preferred Position of Individual Rights: Louis Lusky and John Hart Ely vs. Harlan Fiske Stone." *Constitutional Commentary* 12, no. 2 (Summer 1995). Considers the development and criticism of Stone's footnote to the *Carolene Products v. United States* decision which dealt with the treatment of individual and economic rights in assessing the constitutionality of government regulation.

McCloskey, Robert G. *The American Supreme Court*. 2d ed. Chicago: University of Chicago Press, 1994. A good short interpretive history of the Supreme Court, but tends to be biased in favor of the rise of liberal nationalism. Stone is mentioned only briefly.

Mason, Alpheus Thomas. *Harlan Fiske Stone: Pillar of the Law*. New York: Viking Press, 1956. Full of detail on Stone's life and the only full-length biography in print, but overly favorable to Stone and lacking in-depth analysis of the significance of Stone's constitutional philosophy.

———. *The Supreme Court from Taft to Warren*. 3d ed. Baton Rouge and London: Louisiana State University Press, 1979. Survey history of the Supreme Court from 1921 to 1967. While somewhat biased toward liberal nationalism in its account, this is still a useful summary of Court history. Contains a chapter on Stone.

Murphy, Paul L. *The Constitution in Crisis Times, 1919-1969*. New York: Harper, 1972. Excellent, scholarly history of the Supreme Court from 1914 to 1969. Describes in some detail the hostility of the Supreme Court toward the New Deal before 1937 and the changes that followed the Judicial Revolution of 1937. Mentions Stone only in passing.

Schwartz, Bernard. *The Supreme Court: Constitutional Revolution in Retrospect*. New York: Ronald Press, 1957. A good coverage and analysis of the impact of the New Deal on the Supreme Court and the results of the Judicial Revolution of 1937 over the succeeding twenty years. Mentions Stone briefly.

Swindler, William F. *Court and Constitution in the Twentieth Century*. 2 vols. Indianapolis: Bobbs-Merrill, 1969. A sound, detailed, scholarly history of the Supreme Court from 1889 to 1968, which mentions Stone and his role in the development of constitutional doctrine.

*Richard L. Hillard*

## MARIE STOPES

*Born:* October 15, 1880; Edinburgh, Scotland
*Died:* October 2, 1958; Norbury Park, near Dorking, Surrey, England
*Areas of Achievement:* Social reform and sex research
*Contribution:* A pioneer in sex education and birth control, Stopes emphasized the importance of happiness in human relationships.

### Early Life

Marie Charlotte Carmichael Stopes was born October 15, 1880, in Edinburgh, Scotland. Her father, Henry Stopes, was an architect. Her mother, née Charlotte Carmichael, was the first woman in Scotland to take a university certificate and a respected Shakespearean scholar. The family moved to London soon after Marie's birth. She was educated by her mother at home until she was twelve, when she entered St. George's School in Edinburgh, where her unconventional early schooling made it difficult for her to compete with girls her own age. She soon transferred to North London Collegiate, where she blossomed academically.

She enrolled in the science faculty of University College, shifting from her first love, chemistry, to botany, where she was allowed to pursue an honors program. She passed her final B.Sc. examination in 1902, with first-class honors in botany and third-class honors in geology. Her father died in 1902, leaving the family in a precarious financial condition. Marie used her studies of the reproductive habits of cycads to pursue a doctorate in paleobotany at the Botanical Institute at Munich University in Germany. In 1904, she received her Ph.D. degree, magna cum laude.

Marie Stopes was small, with a slender, uncorseted figure, dark chestnut hair (later dyed red), and large, expressive, greenish-hazel eyes. She preferred flowing silk gowns in unusual colors and wore large hats, jangling jewelry, and voluminous furs. She was self-confident to the point of arrogance and quickly grew intolerant of anyone who opposed her. Her own sexual attractiveness was important to her, especially as she grew older.

### Life's Work

In 1905, Stopes became the first woman on the science faculty at Manchester University. Also in 1905, she became the youngest doctor of science in Great Britain (London University). Among her interests were the study of coal and the origins of angiosperms. A grant from the Royal Society financed an eighteen-month expedition in 1907-1908 to Japan, the first such award to a woman.

Upon her return to England she resumed her position at Manchester, moving to London in 1911 and lecturing in paleobotany at University College, London, from 1913 to 1920. During those years, she published several scientific works, including *Ancient Plants* (1910), *The Constitution of Coal* (with R. V. Wheeler, 1918), and *The Four Visible Ingredients in Banded Bituminous Coal: Studies in the Composition of Coal* (1919).

It was for her work in sex education and birth control, rather than her work as a scientist, however, that Stopes became best known. This work grew at least partially out of difficulties in her personal relationships.

On March 18, 1911, Stopes married Canadian botanist Reginald Ruggles Gates in Montreal. They set up housekeeping in London. Stopes, whose knowledge of human sexuality at that time was as-

tonishingly meager, did not at once realize that Gates was impotent. When she realized the nature of the problem, she read medical and legal books to prepare an annulment suit on the grounds of nonconsummation; the annulment was granted in 1916.

Her own unhappiness may have contributed to her first book on sex, *Married Love* (1918). The book, directed toward an educated, middle-class audience, emphasized the romantic aspects of marriage with what was for the time an unusually frank discussion of sexual relations. Publishers were reluctant to handle such a controversial book, and Stopes needed financial backing which she could not obtain until she met Humphrey Verdon Roe, a wealthy aviator who was already an advocate of birth control. He lent her the money she needed to publish *Married Love* (which she repaid). Stopes and Roe married in a registry office on May 16, 1918, with a church ceremony at St. Margaret's, Westminster, on June 19, 1918. She retained use of her maiden name in both of her marriages.

*Married Love* was an immediate success and generated, as did most of her books on sex, a tremendous mail response mostly requesting contraceptive information. She responded with *Wise Parenthood* (1918), offering contraception information and detailed drawings of the human reproductive systems. Stopes recommended a cervical cap with a quinine pessary as the preferred method of birth control (and never recognized its limitations). In 1919, Stopes published her first book for working-class women, *A Letter to Working Mothers*. In March, 1921, she and Roe opened the Mother's Clinic in London, the first birth control clinic in Great Britain. Later in 1921, Stopes became president of the newly organized Society for Constructive Birth Control and Racial Progress. Among Stopes's other books were *Radiant Motherhood* (1920) and *Enduring Passion* (1928).

Opposition to Stopes as the best-known advocate of contraception came from many sources, including religious and medical groups. At a 1921 medical and legal meeting in London, a professor of obstetrics and gynecology attacked the rubber cap advocated by Stopes as the method of birth control most harmful to women. Soon afterward, Halliday Sutherland, a Roman Catholic physician, wrote *Birth Control: A Statement of Christian Doctrine Against the Neo-Malthusians* (1922), alleging that Stopes exploited the ignorance of the poor by using them in birth control experiments. Stopes sued Sutherland for libel. In the trial, both sides presented expert medical testimony. The presiding judge ruled in favor of Sutherland. Stopes won the first appeal but lost when Sutherland appealed the case to the House of Lords. She responded to the Church's opposition by writing *Roman Catholic Methods of Birth Control* (1933). As a result of the trial publicity, Stopes's public speaking career blossomed.

In July, 1919, at the age of thirty-nine, Stopes gave birth to her first child, a stillborn son. Stopes blamed the doctor, and only the threat of legal action stopped her accusations. She never again trusted doctors. In March, 1924, she was delivered by cesarean section of a son, Harry Stopes-Roe, on whom she doted.

After 1938, Stopes grew disenchanted with humanity. When she was in her late fifties, she began writing love poems. She concentrated on literary pursuits during the last years of her life despite unfavorable critical reviews and poor sales. Among her books at this time were *Love Songs for Young Lovers* (1939), *We Burn* (1950), and *Joy and Verity* (1952).

Stopes separated from Roe about 1938 and lived alone at Norbury Park, near Dorking. She became estranged from her son, Harry, when he married against her wishes, a break which was mended slightly but never healed. In her later years, Stopes wrote poetry, maintained a voluminous correspondence, supported her mothers' clinic, and fought lost causes, such as her unsuccessful battle to win a state pension for poet Lord Alfred Douglas.

Convinced that she would live to be 120 and suspicious of physicians, Stopes ignored the early signs of illness. When she sought medical attention, her doctors found advanced breast cancer. She researched the subject carefully and briefly took holistic treatment in Switzerland. She died at Norbury Park on October 2, 1958. She left the bulk of her estate to the Royal Society of Literature, with only a small portion of the estate going to her family.

### Summary

Marie Stopes moved into realms traditionally closed to women—higher education, science, and sexual research. She wrote the first popular marriage manual and opened the first birth control clinic in Great Britain. Although her ideas were rarely original, she put the ideas of others into understandable, if flowery, language in a readily available form. Stopes put forth the radical idea that people, especially women, have the right to happiness (sexual and otherwise) in marriage. Although her books were innocuous by later standards, they shocked many of her contemporaries, and she both reveled in and suffered from the response of her critics. She was so controversial that many newspapers refused any mention of her (*The Times* even refusing to print the announcement of her son's birth).

Stopes saw herself as a pioneer in sex education and birth control and the only true expert in the field. She refused to acknowledge others in the field and never recognized that no one method of birth control was right for everyone. She quarreled with virtually everyone working in either sex research or birth control.

She had other quarrels as well, including a serious one with the Roman Catholic church, which opposed her work in contraception. The Church supported and helped finance Sutherland in his libel litigation with Stopes. It banned her books and her film, *Maisie's Marriage* (1923). British newspapers refused advertisements for her books lest the police in Roman Catholic Eire confiscate those issues. Her early battles with the Church eventually led her to a sense of persecution verging on paranoia, seeing almost any misfortune as part of a Roman plot against her.

Stopes also faced medical opposition. Many doctors opposed Stopes's use of nurse-midwives instead of doctors to dispense contraceptives in her clinics. Others saw birth control as a threat to practices heavily dependent on deliveries and the gynecological problems resulting from frequent pregnancies. Still others resented Stopes's encroachment into what they regarded as their territory (neither of her doctorates was a medical one).

Her dislike and suspicion of physicians stemmed only in part from this medical opposition. Later, as new knowledge about sex emerged, Stopes refused to admit that her ideas were outdated and viewed all other research in sex and birth control as a personal attack against her. She saw herself as the ultimate expert on virtually everything and considered her own regimen of a daily glass of sea water and cold baths sufficient to maintain good health.

Stopes's flamboyance, her outdated factual data, and her outspoken advocacy of such later-discredited causes as eugenics have drawn attention from her accomplishments. She had a genuine and deserved reputation as a paleobotanist. She dared to advocate marital happiness and talk about sex when almost no one else would do so. The wide sales of her books testified to the genuine needs they addressed for people of all classes throughout the world. She often said that she wished to give twenty years of her life to science, twenty years in service to humanity, and twenty years to literature. She came close to doing just that.

## Bibliography

Adam, Corinna. "The Disappointed Prophetess." *New Statesman* 78 (August 8, 1969): 177-178. Reassessment of Stopes which concludes that she was a distinguished scientist and a great humanitarian whose contentious personality diminished her influence. Contends that her major contribution was hastening people's knowledge of how to achieve happiness in sexual relationships.

Blythe, Ronald. "Dinner with Dr. Stopes." *New Statesman* 57 (January 31, 1959): 140-142. Brief account of Stopes's lecture before a local literary society shortly before her death. Vivid depiction of her personal appearance and personality in the latter years of her life, showing her literary preoccupation and her disenchantment with humanity.

Briant, Keith. *Passionate Paradox: The Life of Marie Stopes*. New York: Norton, 1962. Written by a close friend soon after Stopes's death with some use of her papers. Generally favorable and reflects closely Stopes's own perceptions of herself. Less laudatory than Aylmer Maude's book, but not as complete as Ruth Hall's.

Geppart, Alexander C.T. "Divine Sex, Happy Marriage, Regenerated Nation: Marie Stopes's Marital Manual 'Married Love' and the Making of a Best-Seller, 1918-1955." *Journal of the History of Sexuality* 8, no. 3 (January, 1998). The author considers the reasons for the popularity of Stopes' book *Married Love*.

Hall, Ruth. *Passionate Crusader: The Life of Marie Stopes*. London: Deutsch, and New York: Harcourt Brace, 1977. Thorough biography of Stopes. Sometimes critical but generally balanced account which uses the Stopes and Stopes-Roe papers extensively. Heavy emphasis on personal life and its effect on her professional life.

Hauck, Christina. "Through a Glass Darkly: 'A Game of Chess' and Two Plays by Marie Stopes." *Journal of Modern Literature* 21, no. 1 (Summer 1997). Compares Stopes' plays *Vectia* and *Our Ostriches* with T.S. Eliot's "A Game of Chess" (from *The Waste Land*) These works were published within two years of each other and commented on a postwar rise in promiscuity.

Maude, Aylmer. *The Authorized Life of Marie C. Stopes*. London: Williams and Norgate, 1924. Earliest biography of Stopes, written by a close friend (with considerable help from Stopes) in response to criticism of her early works on sex. Tells nothing Stopes did not want known, including her date of birth.

Sawin, Lewis. "Alfred Sutro, Marie Stopes, and Her *Vectia*." *Theatre Research International* 10 (1985): 59-71. Concerns *Vectia: A Banned Play and a Preface on the Censorship* (1926), Stopes's only written account of her disastrous first marriage. Reveals both Stopes's version of the events and her attitude.

Stopes-Roe, Harry Verdon, with Ian Scott. *Marie Stopes and Birth Control*. Hove, East Essex: Wayland, 1974. Written for young adults by Marie Stopes's son. Balanced account of her role in sex education and birth control. Extensive illustrations, including many not found in other biographies.

*Judith A. Parsons*

# RICHARD STRAUSS

*Born:* June 11, 1864; Munich, Bavaria, Germany

*Died:* September 8, 1949; Garmisch-Partenkirchen, West Germany

*Area of Achievement:* Music

*Contribution:* The symphonic poems composed by Strauss in the last years of the nineteenth century won for him early fame and fortune. He was widely regarded by the music community as one of the brilliant young men destined to lead music into the twentieth century.

## Early Life

Richard Strauss was born in Munich, Bavaria, on June 11, 1864. He was the elder and only son of two children born to Franz Strauss, a professional horn player, and Josephine Pschorr, whose family owned and operated the Pschorr Brewery. From the beginning, there was little doubt about Richard's future. The combination of the Pschorr family wealth and Franz Strauss's position as a virtuoso performer afforded Richard every opportunity to pursue a career in music. Franz, who was the principal hornist of the Munich Court Orchestra, carefully supervised the early music training of his son. He arranged for Richard to study with various members of the Munich Orchestra. Richard studied piano with August Tombo, violin with Benno Walter, and music theory with F. W. Meyer. Since Franz Strauss disliked the music of the late Romantics, it is no surprise that his son was solidly grounded in the classics, studying the music of such composers as Joseph Haydn, Wolfgang Amadeus Mozart, and Ludwig van Beethoven. His earliest composition was a Christmas song composed when he was only six years old.

Strauss studied at the *Gymnasium* in Munich until he was eighteen years old. He did not take specialized training in music at the Munich Conservatory upon his graduation from the *Gymnasium*. Instead, he was enrolled at the University of Munich, where he took courses in the humanities. In fact, Strauss's performance skills at the keyboard were regarded as respectable, but not exceptional. Strauss's father had been more intent upon encouraging and developing the compositional talents of his son rather than performance skills.

Strauss's first composition for orchestra, entitled *Festival March*, was composed in 1876 when he was only twelve years old and was actually published by Breitkopf and Hartel, attributable more to the influence of his mother's family than the merit of the piece. Another early work, the *Serenade for Wind Instruments in Eb*, was more important because it attracted the attention of Hans von Bülow, one of the more colorful figures in the history of music, who was a virtuoso pianist and a respected conductor. He was the conductor of the Meiningen Orchestra when Strauss's piece came to his attention. Bülow became one of Strauss's earliest and strongest supporters and, when the position of assistant conductor at Meiningen became vacant, Bülow recommended the twenty-one-year-old Strauss for the position, thus embarking him upon a dual career as a composer and conductor that was to continue throughout his life.

## Life's Work

When Strauss accepted the position of assistant conductor at Meiningen in 1885, he was a conservative composer who knew next to nothing about conducting. Upon arrival at Meiningen, Strauss entered an intensive apprenticeship under the tutelage of Bülow, and, when Bülow resigned his position as conductor a few months later, he was appointed Bülow's successor. His appointment as first conductor at Meiningen may have been ill-timed in respect of his experience as a conductor, and he resigned that position several months later, early in 1886, to accept another position as third conductor at Munich. During the remaining years of the nineteenth century, Strauss was to hold the position of conductor at Weimar, a second term at Munich, and at Berlin, all the while steadily growing in confidence and stature as a conductor and as a composer.

While at Meiningen, Strauss had become good friends with and had fallen under the influence of a violinist named Alexander Ritter, who was an ardent Wagnerite. It was during this time that Strauss began to move away from the conservative camp and became interested in the music of Wagner and his followers. His first composition in the new style was a symphonic fantasy entitled *Aus Italien*, first performed in Munich in 1887, and was an outgrowth of a vacation he had taken in Italy prior to the assumption of his duties at Munich. This work was followed by a series of symphonic poems, or tone poems, as he preferred to call them, all composed in the last years of the nineteenth century, that rocked the music community and cat-

apulted him to international fame as a composer. These works established his reputation as a radical modern composer.

Strauss was unsurpassed in his day for the creative and imaginative way he skillfully wrote for the orchestra, placing unprecedented technical demands upon the performers, creating sensitive and subtle nuances of color, and always striving to depict musically the subject content in a realistic manner. Numbering among his finest works in this genre are *Don Juan, Till Eulenspiegels lustige Streiche*, and *Ein Heldenleben*.

Strauss's output in the area of choral music remains generally neglected today, possibly because of the great difficulty in the performance of most of these works. Of the roughly two hundred songs that he composed, many were for soprano voice and written for Pauline de Ahna, who was a graduate of the Munich Conservatory. Strauss had met Ahna, a member of a respected and titled family, in the summer of 1887. A courtship ensued that extended over a period of years, and they eventually married in 1894. Some of Strauss's best efforts in this genre, such as *Standchen* and *Morgen*, were composed during the years of courtship and early marriage. Early in their relationship, Ahna actually sang roles in some of the operas that Strauss conducted, and, over the years, she would often sing his songs in recitals with him accompanying her on the piano. Their only child, Franz Alexander Strauss, was born in 1897.

Strauss's creative focus changed in the early twentieth century. He moved away from compositions for orchestra and began to concentrate on opera. The change was not as drastic as it would appear on the surface in view of the highly poetic and dramatic content of his symphonic poems, his familiarity and understanding of the voice, and his, by now, extensive experience as a conductor of opera. His earliest attempt was *Guntram*, first performed in Weimar in 1894; it was poorly received by the public and the critics, a fact he never understood or forgot.

Strauss's first major success, and one of his most powerful works, was *Salome*, which was first performed in Dresden in 1905. It was a one-act opera based on the Oscar Wilde play of the same name. The subject of the opera, which dealt with Salome's obsession with John the Baptist, proved to be quite controversial and was regarded as scandalous in some circles. The subject pushed Strauss to new artistic heights as he strived to portray musically the characters and to capture the intensity of their feelings in the music. The music can be characterized by the extreme demands placed upon the singers and the extensive use of the orchestra for coloristic effects. The high point of the opera came at the end with Salome's dance of the veils and then her kissing of the head of John the Baptist.

Strauss's next opera, *Elektra*, first performed in Dresden in 1909, marks the beginning of his collaboration with Hugo von Hofmannsthal. Hofmannsthal remained Strauss's librettist until his death in 1929. *Elektra*, which dealt with a woman's obsession with revenge, paralleled *Salome* in that it was also a very intense psychological drama. Again, Strauss placed great demands upon the singers and utilized a very large orchestra. With this work, Strauss had moved to the brink of atonality, thus maintaining a reputation as one of the more radical composers of his day.

*Der Rosenkavalier*, on a libretto by Hofmannsthal, was first performed in 1911 and marks a strong break with *Salome* and *Elektra*. The subject, which deals with the aristocracy of eighteenth century Vienna, has nothing of the brooding darkness and violence of the earlier works. In this work, Strauss returns the voice to its normal position of prominence, making use of duets and trios and using the orchestra in a more traditional role. *Ariadne auf Naxos*, which followed in 1912, confirmed the change in style. Strauss was to maintain this style, as reflected in *Rosenkavalier* and *Ariadne auf Naxos*, with little change for the rest of his career. Other operas deserving of mention with Hofmannsthal as librettist are *Die Frau ohne Schatten*, *Intermezzo*, and *Arabella*.

Strauss enjoyed an international reputation as one of the great German composers of his time. It is for this reason that the Third Reich, wanting to receive approval and support from some sectors of the German intellectual and creative community, appointed Strauss as president of the Reich Chamber of Music in 1933. Strauss was forced to resign that position in 1935 over a dispute involving his Jewish librettist, Stefan Zweig, but the damage had been done. World opinion had shifted against him, and, when the war ended in 1945, he was, for a period of time, before being cleared of all charges, regarded as a Nazi supporter. He spent his final years in his villa in Garmisch-Partenkirchen. His last composition was four songs for soprano and orchestra entitled *Vier letzte Lieder* (four last songs). Strauss died at his villa in Garmisch-Partenkirchen, Bavaria, on September 8, 1949, survived by his wife, who was to die a year later, and his son, Franz.

### Summary

The twentieth century has not been an easy time in which to live for many artists, including Richard Strauss. He was reared in an environment of wealth, security, and opportunity. The early years were exciting and promising ones that saw him achieve national and even international prominence as a conductor and as the composer of the tone poems and the early operas. These were the good times for Strauss.

As did so many composers, he flirted with atonality, one of the major controversies for composers and audiences in the early 1900's, and rejected it, preferring to work within a tonal framework. Thus, Strauss, who was one of the radical young leaders of the new music at the turn of the century, became one of the conservatives over a period of time, a defender of the status quo. Those who were disappointed with that decision have claimed that he abandoned his artistic principles for fame and fortune. His reputation has suffered for this in past years, but, in the long term, history will judge him most favorably, not only for his many orchestral masterpieces but also as one of the major composers of opera in the twentieth century. He found and rightfully understood that his strength of musical expression lay in the tonal language of the post-Wagnerian era, and, in this idiom, he was the undisputed master.

### Bibliography

Del Mar, Norman. *Richard Strauss: A Critical Commentary on His Life and Works*. 3 vols. London: Barrie and Rockliff, and Philadelphia: Chilton, 1969-1973. Remains the best general study. This work discusses Strauss's compositions in some detail. Accessible to the general reader, it is recommended only to those interested in an in-depth study of Strauss.

Gilliam, Bryan. *Richard Strauss's Elektra.* Oxford: Clarendon Press, and New York: Oxford University Press, 1991. Gilliam provides a comprehensive study of Strauss's opera *Electra* including analysis of the music and its place in music history.

Griffiths, Paul. "The Turn of the Century." In *Music Guide: An Introduction*. Edited by Stanley Sadie with Alison Latham. Englewood Cliffs, N.J.: Prentice-Hall, 1986. This chapter by Griffiths provides an excellent overview of music in the late nineteenth and early twentieth centuries. Strauss and other composers contemporary with him are covered. Highly recommended to the general reader.

Kennedy, Michael. "Richard Strauss." In *New Grove Dictionary of Music and Musicians*, edited by Stanley Sadie, vol. 18, 6th ed. Washington, D.C.: Grove's Dictionaries of Music, and London: Macmillan, 1980. The author provides a thorough discussion of Strauss's life and works. The works are discussed by genre. A list of his compositions is provided at the end of the article along with an excellent bibliography.

Marek, George. *Richard Strauss: The Life of a Non-Hero*. London: Gollancz, and New York: Simon and Schuster, 1967. This is a good account of Strauss's life. It is rich in factual material but does not make any attempt at analysis of Strauss's style or any of his works. An excellent source for the general reader.

Rolland, Romain. *Richard Strauss and Romain Rolland: Correspondence*. Edited by Rollo Meyers. Berkeley: University of California

Press, and London: Calder and Boyars, 1968. Contains a translation of letters exchanged between Strauss and Rolland, a professor at the Sorbonne and a French musicologist. Also included are excerpted fragments from Rolland's diary that are of some interest in respect to Strauss.

Strauss, Richard. *Recollections and Reflections*. Edited by Willi Schuh. Translated by L. J. Lawrence. London: Boosey and Hawkes, 1953; Westport, Conn.: Greenwood Press, 1974. Often very short comments written in response to a wide variety of issues and concerns, these writings allow the reader a very special private insight into Strauss, the artist and the man. Excellent source for the general reader.

Williamson, John. *Strauss: "Also Sprach Zarathustra."* Cambridge and New York: Cambridge University Press, 1993. Study of Strauss's most controversial work.

*Michael Hernon*

# IGOR STRAVINSKY

*Born:* June 17, 1882; Oranienbaum, Russia
*Died:* April 6, 1971; New York, New York
*Area of Achievement:* Music
*Contribution:* Summarizing and consummating the history of Western music, Stravinsky, reacting against the growing chaos of late nineteenth century Romanticism, reintroduced principles of order and expanded the horizons of music.

## Early Life

Igor Fyodorovich Stravinsky was born in a small resort town some thirty miles west of St. Petersburg, the capital of the Russian Empire. His father, Fyodor, first basso with a St. Petersburg opera company, was also a gifted amateur painter and well-known bibliophile. He was a man of formidable temper; the home atmosphere was not warm, nor were young Igor's school years happy ones, either emotionally or academically. His fluency in German and French owed as much to the household domestic staff and prolonged family vacations in Western Europe as to his schooling.

Stravinsky's earliest musical memories were connected with country holidays when he heard the unison singing of peasant women returning from the fields. Piano lessons began when he was nine, later followed by study of harmony and counterpoint. The teenage Stravinsky absorbed the capital's rich musical life—concerts, opera, ballet. At his family's insistence, Stravinsky entered St. Petersburg University to study law, but most of his time was devoted to musical studies under composer Nikolay Rimsky-Korsakov. Rimsky-Korsakov's sons stood as Stravinsky's best men when he married his childhood friend and first cousin, Ekaterina (Catherine) Nossenko, in 1906. His first composition to gain public attention, the orchestral fantasy *Fireworks* (1908), was in honor of the marriage of Rimsky-Korsakov's daughter.

Turn-of-the-century Russia was experiencing an artistic renaissance, now called its Silver Age. This flowering was perhaps best embodied in the gifted group surrounding Sergei Diaghilev, who had launched a spectacularly successful career as the impresario of Russian culture in Paris. Diaghilev liked Stravinsky's *Fireworks* and decided to invite his participation. Then, planning the 1910 Paris season for his Ballets Russes, the impresario wanted a new work based on the Russian folktale, "The Firebird." Stravinsky completed the commission, and in May, 1910, went to Paris to help prepare the performance of the piece. The premiere was a triumph, and the twenty-eight-year-old composer was to remain a celebrity for sixty-one years.

Pictures of Stravinsky in 1910 are immediately recognizable to those who knew the man at eighty. At five feet, two inches tall, he was a slender, wiry man with a forward-craning head suggesting his impatient and sometimes imperious nature. The face, narrow with a very prominent nose and ears and a neatly trimmed mustache, was dominated by the high forehead over his glasses and below a vanishing hairline. In dress, he was stylish, as might be expected of an intimate of the French designer Gabrielle Chanel.

Stravinsky's personality, like his music, was in stark contrast to the Romantic stereotype of the artist. His work habits, like his personal ones, were disciplined, precise, and methodical. His public manner was severe, elegant, and often acerbic. Typical was his response to someone informing him that the "great success" of a premiere would

subsequently be "tremendous" were he to sanction minor changes. His reply: "Satisfied with great success."

## Life's Work

*The Firebird* (1910) marked the beginning of a new international existence for Stravinsky and his family. It was followed by two more landmark ballets staged by Diaghilev's company: *Petrushka* (1911), based on traditional Russian puppet theater, and two years later, Stravinsky's most famous work, *Le Sacre du printemps* (1913), known in English as *The Rite of Spring*. The ballet is based on pagan folklore evoking the sudden, violent advent of the northern Russian spring—the most loved of Stravinsky's childhood memories. The music is exotic, barbaric, dissonant, and still disturbing to the listener after many decades. Its Paris premiere remains one of the great scandals of musical history, for audience reaction was so vociferous that the music was barely audible. Some fifty people who disrobed in protest were arrested.

World War I curtailed European musical life, and Stravinsky's ties with Russia (and the income from his Russian possessions) ended with the Bolshevik Revolution in 1917. From 1910 to 1920, the family resided mainly in Switzerland, and then, until 1939, in France. The most famous of Stravinsky's works from the war years is *The Soldier's Tale* (1918). Like most of his music until 1920, this piece, designed as a traveling show, was based on Russian folktales.

Stravinsky's popular fame rests largely on these early works, but his growth as a composer was only beginning. Around 1923, Stravinsky turned to very different musical models as a source of inspiration. While musical modernism's other avatar, the Austrian Arnold Schönberg, had undertaken radical experiments based on atonality and serialism, Stravinsky now undertook a reexamination of the "classical" eighteenth century and still earlier musical periods. The resulting compositions, such as Sonata for Piano (1924), inaugurated his "neoclassical" period, which extended for thirty years. Audiences that had responded enthusiastically to Stravinsky's early, exotically flamboyant innovations were often dismayed.

Stravinsky increasingly appeared as a conductor and as a performer of his own work—in part for financial reasons. For his tours, he composed a number of piano works, some of which were reserved for his own concert use. Contact with the United States began with a tour in 1925 and a commission for his classically oriented ballet *Apollo Musagetes* (1928), first performed at the Library of Congress three years later. Others of his neoclassical works are the opera-oratorio *Oedipus Rex* (1927), done in collaboration with Jean Cocteau, and the melodrama *Perséphone* (1934), done in collaboration with Nobel Prize laureate André Gide. The composer's reawakened religious feeling found major expression in the *Symphony of Psalms* (1930) commissioned for the fiftieth anniversary of the Boston Symphony Orchestra. This chef d'oeuvre was one of a growing number devoted to religious themes. Stravinsky's American reputation was further enhanced by a festival dedicated to his work and that of choreographer George Balanchine at the Metropolitan Opera in 1937. *The Card Party: A Ballet in Three Deals* (1937) was commissioned for the occasion by Lincoln Kirstein, codirector of the newly formed American Ballet.

Stravinsky, well established in French cultural life and a French citizen since 1934, was troubled by the ominous political scene in Europe. Family tragedy augmented his forebodings when tuberculosis claimed his long-ill wife and eldest daughter. Stravinsky himself spent several months of 1939 in a sanatorium together with his remaining daughter, also tubercular. These somber events were, however, accompanied by others that indicated a brighter future. While working on his Symphony in C Major (1940) for the Chicago Symphony Orchestra, Stravinsky, still in the sanatorium, received news of his one-year appointment to the Charles Eliot Norton Chair at Harvard University.

In September, 1939, Stravinsky, age fifty-seven, arrived in his new homeland. He was soon joined by his close companion of nearly twenty years, Vera Sudeikin, whom he married in 1940 before establishing permanent residence in Los Angeles. They became American citizens in 1945. Stravinsky quickly entered the mainstream of American life. Shortly before his arrival, the composer had reluctantly agreed to Walt Disney's proposal to use portions of *The Rite of Spring* to accompany the early, "primeval" section of the Disney classic *Fantasia* (1940). Even more surprising was a Barnum and Bailey commission for *Circus Polka* (1942), a short ballet for fifty elephants performed under the big top. Other popular ventures were the ballet sequence done for Broadway producer Billy Rose's revue *The Seven Lively Arts* (1944), and the *Ebony Concerto* (1945) for a Woody Herman Carnegie Hall performance. Stravinsky also continued his more serious work: Symphony in Three Movements (1946), the ballet *Orpheus* (1947), once again with Balanchine, and his longest single work, the opera *The Rake's Progress* (1951), inspired by William Hogarth engravings and done in conjunction with poet W. H. Auden.

Stravinsky met the young American conductor Robert Craft in the late 1940's. Craft, a man of great cultural breadth and a specialist in contemporary music, especially the serialists Schönberg, Alban Berg, and Anton von Webern, soon became a member of the Stravinsky household and, eventually, the composer's alter ego. Craft's presence contributed to the launching of the third phase of Stravinsky's musical development at seventy-one. The music of the earlier Russian and neoclassical periods had been experimental, sometimes radical, but always rooted in traditional tonality. The composer's shift to an atonal, serial mode of composition again bewildered much of his audience. New works followed, all in the serial mode: the ballet *Agon* (1953), the religious choral works *Canticum Sacrum* (1956) and *Threni* (1958), and *Movements* (1960) for piano and orchestra. *The Flood* (1962), Stravinsky's last dramatic work, was written for television.

Stravinsky, at eighty, still awesomely active as a composer and touring conductor, was a living legend. In 1962, he was a White House guest of John and Jacqueline Kennedy, and later that year, he accepted an invitation from the Soviet Union for an emotional visit to the country he had left a half century before. His last compositions were completed in 1966: the song *The Owl and the Pussy-Cat*, dedicated to his wife Vera, and the *Requiem Canticles*, heard at the services following his death on April 6, 1971. He was buried in his beloved Venice.

### Summary

Stravinsky's career summarizes and culminates twentieth century music. His music, which includes more than one hundred compositions, spans sixty years, during much of which he was the world's best-known serious composer.

Through all three, radically different phases of his musical career, certain Stravinskian constants are evident: shifting, syncopated rhythms; exotic, highly colored instrumental voicings; a relatively high degree of dissonance that was, until the last period, always based upon a perceptible basic tonality. The music is marked by precision and emotional coolness. Stravinsky held that composition is a discipline, and the act of composition is the solution of a problem according to certain rules, though the rules may change. Although his compositions were often integrated with other artistic media, Stravinsky was adamant about the absolute independence and integrity of music: It means and expresses nothing beyond itself. Stravinsky spent half his creative life in the United States, and his ties with the country's music were deep. In his early European music, there are traces of quintessential American forms such as ragtime and jazz. Stravinsky entered more deeply into American popular consciousness than any other composer, even among those with little interest in serious music. In the late 1950's, Stravinsky and his collaborator Robert Craft began publishing a series of "conversations" that were eventually gathered and published in six books. These witty, elegant, and often caustic recollections and reflections of an original, iconoclastic mind brought the composer the admiration of a wide circle of readers. Often displaced by the turbulent events of his century, Stravinsky found a permanent home in the United States, where he reshaped the musical and cultural life not only of America but also of the world.

### Bibliography


Cross, Jonathan. *The Stravinsky Legacy.* New York: Cambridge University Press, 1998. Cross examines the legacy of Stravinsky and his impact on twentieth century music, with emphasis on several specific composers. Includes analysis and historical commentary.

Druskin, Mikhail S. *Igor Stravinsky: His Life, Works and Views*. Translated by Martin Cooper. Cambridge and New York: Cambridge University Press, 1983. A fine study of Stravinsky's musical development by a Soviet musicologist. Especially strong on Russian aspects.

Routh, Francis. *Stravinsky.* London: Dent, 1975. This concise, well-informed work is probably the best starting point for the novice. The first half sketches the life, and the second analyzes the music by categories. Appendices include a useful calendar of Stravinsky's life, a catalog of his music, a somewhat erratic "Who's Who?" and a bibliography.

Stravinsky, Igor. *The Poetics of Music in the Form of Six Lessons*. Cambridge, Mass.: Harvard University Press and Oxford: Oxford University Press, 1947. The best personal statement of Stravinsky's musical aesthetic.

———. *Stravinsky: An Autobiography.* New York: Norton, 1962; London: Calder and Boyars, 1975. A rather austere and impersonal account of the first half of Stravinsky's professional life.

Stravinsky, Igor, and Robert Craft. *Conversations with Igor Stravinsky.* London: Faber, and New York: Doubleday, 1959. The first of the six Stravinsky-Craft collaborations discussed above.

Stravinsky, Vera, and Robert Craft. *Stravinsky in Pictures and Documents.* New York: Simon and Schuster, 1978; London: Hutchinson, 1979. A vast treasure house of Stravinskiana lovingly compiled by the composer's wife and longtime associate. Until a definitive biography appears, this is the best book on Stravinsky's life. Accurate, judicious, and entertaining.

Walsh, Stephen. *The Music of Stravinsky.* London and New York: Routledge, 1993. Walsh offers a critical study of Stravinsky's entire volume of work. Arranged chronologically, this is a significant research tool for students and scholars alike.

White, Eric Walter. *Stravinsky: The Composer and His Works.* 2d ed. London: Faber, and Berkeley: University of California Press, 1979. A basic reference work combining a rather mechanical biography and an excellent "Register of Works" giving detailed information on all aspects of the compositions. Essential for the serious student.

*D. Barton Johnson*

# GUSTAV STRESEMANN

*Born:* May 10, 1878; Berlin, Germany
*Died:* October 3, 1929; Berlin, Germany
*Areas of Achievement:* Government and politics
*Contribution:* Although unenthusiastic in his support for a German republic, Stresemann nevertheless served the Weimar Republican government as chancellor and foreign minister during the 1920's. As foreign minister, he was able to revise portions of the Treaty of Versailles and help to bring Germany into the mainstream of European diplomacy.

## Early Life

Gustav Stresemann was born on May 10, 1878, in Berlin. He was the youngest child of Ernst Stresemann, an innkeeper and beer distributor in the southern section of Berlin. His mother died while he was a teenager. Gustav attended the Andreas Realgymnasium in Berlin, where the headmaster placed a heavy emphasis on humanistic scholarship. Records indicate that Stresemann developed an interest in mathematics and literature. He read the great works in Latin, German, French, and English, and seemed especially impressed with the style of Thomas Macaulay. His greatest fascination as a young student was modern history. He was intrigued by the origin and consequences of great events and with the lives of people who stood above everyday routine. He put Johann Wolfgang von Goethe and Napoleon I in this category. As both of his headmasters in the Realgymnasium were trained as pastors, it is not surprising that while a schoolboy Stresemann had strong religious convictions.

In 1897, Stresemann began his advanced studies at the University of Berlin, where he escaped the solitude that had marked his younger years. At first, he concentrated on literature and history, but later, hoping to improve his business prospects, he devoted more time to economics. To pursue this interest, he moved to the University of Leipzig. He took an active part in student life by writing lighthearted articles for the *University Gazette* and by joining the Reform Burschenschaften, an offshoot of the original national liberal organization founded in the early nineteenth century. Within a short time, Stresemann was elected by the association to be chairman of its general conference. In this position, he was introduced to parliamentary style debate and to the give-and-take of politics. He also began to write some serious articles.

It had been Stresemann's plan to earn a doctoral degree with a dissertation heavy on economic theory. By this time, Stresemann had come under the influence of Karl Bucher, who urged him to tackle a "practical" topic for his dissertation. Accordingly, Stresemann produced a thesis entitled "The Development of the Bottled Beer Industry in Berlin, an Economic Investigation." Based on his knowledge of his father's business, the thesis describes with bitterness the decline of Berlin's independent middle class in the face of large commercial concerns. The dissertation, with its underlying call for social justice, was later used against him by right-wing elements.

After earning his doctorate in 1900, Stresemann moved to Dresden and quickly established himself in the business world. From 1901 to 1904, he was a minor administrator in the German Chocolate Maker's Association. In 1902, he founded the Saxon Manufacturer's Association and remained its chief representative until 1911. In 1903, he married Kathe Kleefeld, the daughter of Berlin industrialist Adolf Kleefeld. They had two sons, Wolfgang and Joachim. Kathe was highly visible in Berlin society of the 1920's. It was also in 1903 that Stresemann joined the National Liberal Party, in which he frequently found his support for social measures out of step with the party's right wing. In 1906, he became a Dresden city councillor, and this experience whetted his appetite for a more important career in national politics. It led to his candidacy for a seat in the Reichstag (parliament) in 1907.

## Life's Work

In January, 1907, Stresemann began his career in the Reichstag as a National Liberal delegate from Annenberg, a district in the mining region. He argued that Germany should be strong militarily while taking care of the poor at home. At age twenty-eight he became the youngest member of the Reichstag. In his first five years in the Reichstag, Stresemann gave most of his attention to advanced economic questions: how to reform taxation, how to apportion taxation equitably, and how to create an awareness that all classes in Germany were interdependent. His first parliamentary speech (April 12, 1907) dealt with the need for the state to provide effective national social legislation for German workers. Outside the Reichstag, Stresemann wrote many articles for newspapers and periodicals

dealing with economic policy. In addition, he edited a journal he had founded, *Saxon Industry*, in which he published essays regarding the relationship between workers and industry.

Stresemann's staunch support for commercial interests alienated the right wing of his party as well as conservative supporters in Annenberg. As a result, he lost his seat in the Reichstag elections of 1912. He then visited the United States to learn something of commerce and industry there. His journey took him to such industrial and commercial centers as Boston, Detroit, Chicago, and Pittsburgh. On this trip he met the future president, Woodrow Wilson, for whom Stresemann developed great admiration.

In these years just prior to World War I, Stresemann gave support to the government's military spending. He believed that Germany must prepare for a defensive war, and he was not alarmed when the war began. In December, 1914, he was returned to the Reichstag in a by-election for the district of Aurich. He was, during the war years, an eloquent spokesman for the annexationists—those who wished to claim for Germany territory in Poland, Russia, France, and Belgium. By 1916, Stresemann had become an advocate for the views of Field Marshal Paul von Hindenburg and General Erich Ludendorff in the Reichstag. He was, as well, a proponent of the disastrous unrestricted submarine warfare policy pushed by Admiral Alfred von Tirpitz.

Appalled that conservative Chancellor Theobald von Bethmann Hollweg could not prevent the Reichstag from considering a resolution for peace offered by Matthias Erzberger in July, 1917, Stresemann played a major role in forcing Bethmann Hollweg from office. Stresemann did not comprehend Germany's weakened military circumstances until a month before the November, 1918, armistice. He was further shocked by the collapse of the monarchy and Emperor William II's abdication on November 9. It was difficult for Stresemann to adjust to a republican Germany under the Social Democratic Party. In February, 1919, he founded the German People's Party, a right-wing elite organization aimed at blunting the Social Democrats' plan for economic reconstruction. Stresemann engaged in a heated debate with Walther Rathenau over how to revive Germany's economy, with Stresemann emphasizing the role of the individual and Rathenau arguing that the state had to take the lead.

It was not until after the failure of the right wing Kapp Putsch in March, 1920, that Stresemann was fully reconciled to a republican government. In 1920, Stresemann was returned to the Reichstag. He became chancellor in August, 1923, as a result of a coalition of deputies from the Social Democratic, Center, German Democratic, and People's parties. Stresemann remained chancellor for only four months, but it was a time of great crisis for Germany as ruinous inflation brought misery and social disorder. Although historians generally give Stresemann high marks for his brief tenure as chancellor (especially for the way in which he stabilized the currency), he was not able to hold the coalition together and resigned after a vote of no confidence.

In the new government, Stresemann stayed on as foreign minister, a post he held through various administrations until he died in 1929. In this office he had his greatest achievements. He dedicated himself to revising the Treaty of Versailles, a treaty he despised. He wished to achieve reconciliation with the Western powers. In return, he thought it was time to reduce Germany's reparation payments and allow his country to join the League of Nations. His successes began in 1924 when the

Dawes Plan was signed reducing the reparations payment. The Pact of Locarno followed in 1925. This guaranteed the French-German borders and prevented the Allies from making further demands upon Germany. On September 10, 1926, Germany was admitted to the League of Nations, a proud day for Stresemann's strategy of reconciliation. After the League meeting, Stresemann and the French foreign officer, Aristide Briand, held discussions at Thoiry about the need to continue to establish goodwill between France and Germany. Both men were now extremely popular, and they shared the 1926 Nobel Peace Prize. Although nothing of substance came from the Thoiry meeting, they continued a spirit of optimism about the future. In 1928, the peak of this optimism was reached when Germany signed the Kellogg-Briand Pact, an agreement to outlaw war approved by more than fifty nations. Stresemann's health was in decline for most of 1928, and he died the next year on October 3, 1929.

### Summary

Gustav Stresemann's most effective years as a politician came while he served as foreign minister during the 1920's. His successful efforts to return Germany to the community of European nations stands as his single greatest achievement. With French statesman Aristide Briand, he helped to create a period of hope about the future of French-German cooperation and, indeed, about the prospects of avoiding European wars of any kind. On the other hand, as historian Henry Turner observes, in giving all of his attention to revising the Treaty of Versailles, Stresemann failed to be attentive to domestic politics. Whereas he, as a conservative leader, could have helped to strengthen the middle in German politics, he chose to stand aloof. Hence, by the time of his death in 1929, the right wing stood ready to dominate German politics.

Although Stresemann devoted the last six years of his life to international concerns, he was not transformed into an internationalist. He remained a defender of Germany's goals in Europe, including rearmament and the recovery of Danzig, the Polish Corridor, and Upper Silesia. Germany could no longer gain these ends by force, but could do so, he believed, through finesse. Rearmament was illegal by the terms of Versailles, but Stresemann was involved in the rearming that occurred during the Weimar era. His statecraft, in the end, bore a resemblance to that of the German politician he most admired: Otto von Bismarck. Like Bismarck, Stresemann was a wholly pragmatic politician who believed that Germany was destined to be the arbiter of Central and Eastern European politics.

### Bibliography

Bretton, Henry L. *Stresemann and the Revision of Versailles.* Stanford, Calif.: Stanford University Press, 1953. This study brought renewed scholarly interest in Stresemann's career. It is well worth reading.

Dorpalen, Andreas. *Hindenburg and the Weimar Republic.* Princeton, N.J.: Princeton University Press, 1964. Hindenburg was President of the Weimar Republic from 1925, and Dorpalen discusses the very restrained support that Stresemann received from the president between 1925 and 1929. This is a highly readable and respected account of the collapse of the republic.

Gatzke, Hans. *Stresemann and the Rearmament of Germany.* Baltimore: Johns Hopkins University Press, 1954. In this excellent monograph, Gatzke gives a critical account of Stresemann's years as foreign minister. He provides substantial information regarding Stresemann's role in the illegal rearming of Germany in the 1920's.

Rheinbaben, Rochus, Baron von. *Stresemann: The Man and the Statesman.* Translated by Cyrus Brooks and Hans Herzl. New York and London: Appleton, 1929. This is an uncritical account written in cooperation with Stresemann shortly before his death. The book does provide much information about Stresemann's early life and influences that is not available elsewhere.

Turner, Henry Ashby, Jr. *Stresemann and the Politics of the Weimar Republic.* Princeton, N.J.: Princeton University Press, 1963. This is the best overall account of Stresemann's service to the Weimar Republic. Turner generally gives Stresemann high marks for his tenure as chancellor and foreign minister. He questions, however, Stresemann's handling of domestic politics after 1925.

*Ron Huch*

# AUGUST STRINDBERG

*Born:* January 22, 1849; Stockholm, Sweden
*Died:* May 14, 1912; Stockholm, Sweden
*Area of Achievement:* Literature
*Contribution:* Sweden's Strindberg stands, with the Norwegian Henrik Ibsen, as Scandinavia's greatest dramatist. He introduced both naturalism and expressionism to the modern European stage; considered to be the father of Swedish literature, with dozens of novels, essays, and scientific treatises as well as more than fifty plays to his credit, he never received that country's Nobel Prize but permanently influenced the shape of twentieth century world theater.

## Early Life

Born into a successful merchant family, the third son of Carl Oscar Strindberg and Ulrika Eleonora Norling, Johan August Strindberg enjoyed an orderly, if emotionally undemonstrative, childhood, until his mother's death when he was only thirteen. His father's coldness and hasty marriage to Strindberg's governess were, according to some biographers, the precipitating factors in Strindberg's lifelong anxieties about his place in society and his ambivalent relationships with the women in his life. His teen years became a series of explorations into literature, the occult, and science, always motivated by the emptiness he felt from the loss of his mother. He attended several schools, finally seeking a medical education at the university at Uppsala, but dropped out suddenly in 1872.

A prolific letter-writer, Strindberg chronicled his own early life in correspondence to his brothers and friends and wrote a fictionalized autobiography entitled *Tjänstekvinnans son: En själs utvecklingshistoria* (4 volumes, 1886; *The Son of a Servant: The Story of the Evolution of a Human Being*, 1966, first volume only), from which many of the details of his youth are taken. Contact with the Royal Theater of Stockholm, first as a bit-part actor and then as a playwright, began his interest in drama; his first production was of his play, *I Rom* (1870). His early writing included journalistic essays on contemporary political topics, a combative habit that was to continue throughout his life.

## Life's Work

Although not his first commercial work, Strindberg's play *Fröken Julie* (1888; *Miss Julie*, 1912) first brought him international recognition as a playwright in the new naturalistic vein, a trend in theater owing its popularity in large part to the independent theater movement advocated in France by André Antoine, in Germany by Otto Brahm, and in England by Jacob Thomas Grein. This one-act play (with a balletic interlude), not only a model of naturalistic pyschological characterization but also a miniature portrait of Strindberg's subsequent thematic preoccupations, was performed throughout Europe whenever the independent theater's repertory needed a new play. In this first wave of mature creativity, Strindberg fed the new theater (again alongside Ibsen) with *Fadren* (1887; *The Father*, 1899) and, after a period of instability (his "Inferno"), two other plays on the battle of marriage, *Dödsdansen första delen* (1901; *The Dance of Death I*), and *Dödsdansen, andra delen* (1901; *The Dance of Death II*, 1912), while at the same time publishing several novels, most notably the autobiographical *Inferno* (1897; English translation, 1912), in which he describes this most tumultuous period of his life.

The explosive and egoistic personality of Strindberg was often combined with his exaggerated sense of self-righteousness to produce a public image of a fiery, tyrannical man of letters; in private life he was shy, insecure, and constantly enthralled by his affection for others, first fantasizing about love affairs, next perceiving slights to his honor, and finally living in a dream construction made of his own psychological delusions. His behavior, typically artistic in that he always walked a fine line between creativity and madness, became erratic enough in the years from 1892 to 1898, especially 1895-1896, that scholars divide his life work at that point, referring to pre-and post-Inferno outlooks and styles. These years, often called the "Inferno Crisis," marked a change in Strindberg's dramatic style; whether his new attitude reflected a conversion or a regression is a matter of contention, but he clearly altered his view of stage language, if not his major themes.

He emerged from that period with even greater creative powers, turning out the three-part play *Till Damaskus* (1898-1904; *To Damascus*, 1913), *Ett drömspel* (1902; *A Dream Play*, 1912), and several other works in the first few years of the twentieth century. His dramatic style during this outburst was markedly different from the earlier naturalism: Now Strindberg moved almost cinematically from scene to scene, dealing with personal and universal symbols in great sweeps of ideas, depicting historical and archetypal characters, trying out a fragmented, internalized communication of character, theme, and plot that eventually earned the name "expressionism" and became the major framework of German drama between the world wars.

In addition to his literary contributions to the theater, Strindberg established the "intimate" theatrical style, in which a small audience experienced plays in "chamber"-sized settings. Strindberg, along with August Falck, an actor and producer who had toured *Miss Julie* to great acclaim in 1906, founded the Intimate Theater in Stockholm, contributing play after play to its repertory. In its first few seasons, Maurice Maeterlinck's *L'Intruse* (1890; *The Intruder*, 1891) was the only non-Strindberg play in the repertory.

Part of Strindberg's fascination with the theater included his love of actresses, three of whom he married: Siri von Essen (married to Strindberg from 1877 to 1892), Frida Uhl (1893-1897), and Harriet Bosse (1901-1904). His major female roles (usually in combat with a Strindbergian alter-ego) were invariably written with one or another actress specifically in mind, and today modern actresses are challenged to bring these characters to life in Strindberg's conception.

Strindberg retired to apartments in Stockholm, which he referred to as "The Blue Tower," during the last years of his life (1908-1912), and he was cared for in an ambiguous relationship with Fanny Falkner, also a young actress. There, too, his output was prodigious, but none of these works, possibly excepting one of his last plays, *Stora landsvägen* (1909; *The Great Highway*, 1954), enjoyed the same notoriety as his earlier work. The disappointment of being rejected for the Nobel Prize (probably political in motivation) was greatly relieved by the spontaneous homage paid to him on his sixtieth birthday by the workers of Stockholm, who saw Strindberg as a champion of the working class. Strindberg referred to this acclamation as the "anti-Nobel" prize.

After one last politically explosive series of his journal articles was published in Stockholm, Strindberg succumbed to stomach cancer in 1912, leaving behind a vast canon of fiction, drama, and essays as well as private correspondence that would become multivolume editions after his death. In his obsessive, almost paranoiac behavior, his unrealistic view of the secret power of women against men, and his tyrannical condescension to his peers, Strindberg never gained during his lifetime the respect afforded him after his death.

### Summary

Among the great names in modern theater, August Strindberg is known for his psychological insight into the workings not only of women but also of the men they dominate in his dramas. While his naturalistic plays are still performed with regularity, the more expressionistic plays are neglected, partly because of the financially exhausting demands of the multiple stage sets and large casts and partly because the matrices of symbols the plays present have lost their universality and stageability in the light of modern aesthetic sensibilities. Strindberg has become more interesting to critics and scholars employing a psychological approach to literature than he has to theater practitioners, and his unequivocal condemnation of the feminine mystique has weakened his contemporary currency. Nevertheless, theater and drama from World War I to the present day have taken shape largely through the influence of Strindberg on his followers, in the areas of naturalistic characterization and in the free-form, subjectively presented, "theatrical" styles of contemporary auteur directors. Anticipating the filmic language of cuts, zooms, segues, and similar cinematic syntax, Strindberg broke the mold he himself had helped to create. Subsequent playwrights have seen in Strindberg's life itself the raw material for dramatic presentation—Friedrich Dürrenmatt, with *Play Strindberg: Totentanz nach August Strindberg* (1969; *Play Strindberg: The Dance of Death*, 1971), and Michael Meyer (a Strindberg scholar), with *Lunatic and Lover* (1981), are examples.

**Bibliography**

Brandell, Gunnar. *Strindberg in Inferno*. Translated by Barry Jacobs. Cambridge, Mass.: Harvard University Press, 1974. A psychoanalytical study of Strindberg's turbulent middle life, illuminating the substance and power of his later writing. Brandell, considered Sweden's leading Strindberg expert, traces the playwright's path both into and out of the crisis, adding a valuable description of the works generated from 1893 to 1898. Includes notes, a bibliography, and an index of names.

Davy, Daniel. "Strindberg's Unknown Comedy." *Modern Drama* 40, no. 3 (Fall 1997). Discusses Strindberg's 1902 play *Crimes and Crimes,* public opinion on the play, and the comments of critics.

Johannesson, Eric O. *The Novels of August Strindberg: A Study in Theme and Structure*. Berkeley: University of California Press, 1968. A good introduction to the prose work, which in turn informs the plays. Discusses fourteen novels available in English, examining the metaphoric language and the techniques of the novels' construction, noting Strindberg's difficulties with muddling "illusion and reality." Includes a bibliography and index of proper names.

Johnson, Walter. *Strindberg and the Historical Drama*. Seattle: University of Washington Press, 1963. Literary analysis of Strindberg's neglected (in the United States) history plays, especially those written after the Inferno period, that casts light on Strindberg's erudition, craft, and nationalistic zeal. Johnson finds lasting literary merit in at least twelve of the "dynamic" historical plays. Includes bibliographic and other notes and an index.

Lagercrantz, Olof. *August Strindberg*. Translated by Anselm Hollo. London: Faber, and New York: Farrar Straus, 1984. Strindberg's life described as a series of psychological explanations for his creative output. Oddly sparse, even cavalier, regarding the details of Strindberg's theatrical and dramatic activity. Includes sixty-three illustrations throughout the text, biographical notes on figures mentioned in the text, a select bibliography of Strindberg editions, and an index.

Lamm, Martin. *August Strindberg*. Translated and edited by Harry G. Carlson. New York: Blom, 1971. Written in the classic literary biography form, the two parts of this thorough study—"Before the Inferno Crisis" and "After the Conversion"—anticipate the major division of all subsequent Strindberg scholarship. Lamm analyzes the work from a literary rather than a theatrical viewpoint but adds some interesting details concerning the Scandinavian Experimental Theater of Denmark (Strindberg lived in Copenhagen from 1887 to 1889) and the Intimate Theater of his later years. Includes notes, a bibliography, and an index.

Morgan, Margery. *August Strindberg*. London: Macmillan, and New York: Grove Press, 1985. Part of the Modern Dramatists series. A brief biography followed by a thorough critical overview of Strindberg's work as theatrical script, not merely as literature. A full description of the canon (concentrating on the dramas), with contemporary interpretation, plus a valuable section on Strindberg as director of the Intimate Theater. Contains fifteen illustrations, including a photographic self-portrait with his daughters, an appendix, notes, a valuable bibliography, and an index.

Mortensen, Brita M. E., and Brian Downs. *Strindberg: An Introduction to His Life and Work*. Cambridge: Cambridge University Press, 1949. A centenary introduction to the man and his work, divided into four periods and four genres—plays, novels, short stories, and autobiographical writings—with an added chapter on miscellaneous works. Includes a good conclusion, a select bibliography, and an index.

Ollén, Gunnar. *August Strindberg*. Translated by Peter Tirner. New York: Ungar, 1972. Part of the World Dramatists series. Bracketed by a brief biography and an overview of Strindberg's stage work, a capsule description of each of the plays in almost encyclopedic form, in the order of their composition, is presented. This is a useful quick reference to specific titles. Includes a chronology, a bibliography, and an index.

Reinert, Otto, ed. *Strindberg: A Collection of Critical Essays*. Englewood Cliffs, N.J.: Prentice-Hall, 1971. An introduction by the editor, followed by twelve articles in three sections: "The Divided Self," "A New Theater," and "Some Major Plays." A good overview of how scholars discuss Strindberg's work, ranging from Robert Brustein's study of *The Father* to Brian Rothwell's essay on the chamber plays. Includes a chronology of important dates, notes on the editor and contributors, and a selected bibliography.

Steene, Birgitta. *The Greatest Fire: A Study of August Strindberg*. Carbondale: Southern Illinois University Press, 1973. This study moves away from the common psychological (and therefore "sour") approach to Strindberg, concentrating instead on the innovations and craft in his work and its importance in studying modern playwrights such as Edward Albee, Harold Pinter, even Tennessee Williams. Includes notes, a selected bibliography, and an index.

Strindberg, August. *Inferno, Alone, and Other Writings*. Edited by Evert Sprinchorn. New York: Doubleday, 1968. An accessible selection of Strindberg's autobiographical work, which alters facts into a fiction more true than the original. A substantial introduction defends Strindberg's genius.

———. *Letters of Strindberg to Harriet Bosse*. Edited and translated by Arvid Paulson. New York: Grosset and Dunlap, 1959. A collection of letters to his third wife, written from 1900 (before their marriage in 1901) to 1908, when she remarried. Her personal comments and ten letters to Strindberg, are included. A frighteningly personal entry into Strindberg's mentality. Includes a brief introduction, a biographical note on Harriet Bosse, notes, and an index.

Tornqvist, Egil. "The Strindbergian One-Act Play." *Scandinavian Studies* 68, no. 3 (Summer 1996). Examines the format and structure of Strindberg's one-act plays and their impact on modern drama.

Valency, Maurice. *The Flower and the Castle: An Introduction to Modern Drama*. New York: Macmillan, 1963; London: Macmillan, 1967. On Ibsen and Strindberg, this important critical discussion of the sweeping changes in theater history from Eugène Scribe's "well-made play" to realism is a central study for both authors and for the period. Of Strindberg's neurotic predilections he remarks, "At bottom the subject matter of his plays is almost invariably the same." Of his style, it "is at the opposite pole from that of Ibsen." Includes notes, an extensive bibliography, and an index.

*Thomas J. Taylor*

# SUKARNO

*Born:* June 6, 1901; Surabaya, Dutch East Indies (now Indonesia)

*Died:* June 21, 1970; Jakarta, Indonesia

*Areas of Achievement:* Government and politics

*Contribution:* A superb orator and a charismatic leader, Sukarno raised Indonesian national consciousness while providing a rudimentary administrative infrastructure under Dutch colonial and Japanese occupational forces. After the Japanese defeat in 1945, he declared his nation's independence and served as president and strongman until 1965, when involvement in a Communist-inspired coup undermined his authority.

## Early Life

According to his autobiography, Sukarno was the child of a Balinese mother of the House of Singaradja and a Javanese father who was a descendant of the Sultan of Kediri. Other accounts regard him variously as the illegitimate son of a Dutch coffee planter and a native peasant girl, the offspring of a Eurasian plantation overseer, and the son of Sunan Pakubuwono X of Surakarta, spirited away from the palace to escape death. The circumstances of Sukarno's birth are obscured by these and similar contradictory stories. There is no question, however, that Sukarno grew up in abject poverty. The Sukarno family of four—he had a sister two years his senior—lived on a monthly income of the Dutch equivalent of twenty-five rupiahs. Sukarno's father, Sukemi, a strict schoolteacher and a Muslim, made sure that his son received a good education at his own school in reading, writing, and mathematics, as well as being trained in the Islamic faith, the Indonesian culture, and the Western sciences. Sukarno was graduated from his father's school in 1914.

While instruction in Islamics and *gotong royong* (the Indonesian principle of mutual assistance) was readily available, access to Western thought was not. Dutch regulations allowed only a few native students to attend the Dutch schools that were a stepping stone to higher education in The Netherlands. In spite of financial difficulties, Sukemi sent Ahmad to the Dutch-language elementary school and after two years enrolled him in the Hogere Burger School in Surabaya. Umar Sayed Tjokroaminoto, who had helped Sukemi enroll his son, provided room and board for young Sukarno. Entrance difficulties paled in comparison with the ordeal of a brown Indonesian youth coping with white Dutch schoolboys. Sukarno managed, but he developed a distinct abhorrence for the culture that Dutch education at Surabaya projected. His abhorrence was enhanced by his surroundings at Tjokroaminoto's, which were suffused with discussions of colonial exploitation of ignorant masses. He was graduated from the Hogere Burger School in 1921.

Following China, India, and the Philippines, Indonesia began its movement for independence in 1908 with the *Budi Umoto* (pure endeavor) leading to Sarekat Islam (islamic union) in 1912. Headed by Tjokroaminoto, Sarekat attracted a wide spectrum of rural and urban Indonesians. Its membership included the union's founding merchant class, urban workers, and religious personages. At the time Sukarno arrived in Surabaya, the union claimed eighty branches throughout the archipelago with close to two million members. The contending factions for the union's leadership were the scripturalists and the Marxists. The former, descendants of Muslim sea merchants who had brought Islam to Indonesia in the fourteenth century, defended the feudal system encompassing Java, Sumatra, Malaya, and Borneo. The latter wished to internationalize the party, educate Indonesia's peasants, and help them arrive at self-rule. The Marxists' bid for leadership resulted in the expulsion of Communists from the party in 1920. The party's subsequent policy of refusing membership to Communists depleted Sarekat's ranks so that it was clearly on the decline by the time Sukarno left Surabaya.

In 1921, Sukarno moved to Bandung to study engineering at its newly established technical college. The city teemed with political activity, especially among Indonesian youth who had graduated from Dutch universities and who were back home, anxious to effect change. Drawing on this body, and equipped with a wealth of political savvy from Tjokroaminoto's cookshop of nationalism, Sukarno founded a Study Club in 1925 and transformed it into a political forum, the Nationalist Party of Indonesia (NPI), in 1927. The NPI platform advocated intense struggle for national independence through noncooperation with the Dutch Indies government. Sukarno was elected the party's chairman.

Initially, the Dutch exercised a policy of permissiveness. This allowed the NPI to become the hub of a still larger national coalition, the Association of Political Organizations of Indonesian People. Later, however, to put an end to Sukarno's bold activities, the Dutch government changed its stance so that, in 1929, governmental troops surrounded the house where Sukarno was a guest, arrested him, and, following a public trial, put him in prison for the next two years. Soon after his release from prison, Sukarno resumed his previous activities as the leader of the NPI. Arrested again in 1933, he was exiled without trial to Flores; he remained there until 1942, when Japanese forces invading the islands freed him.

### Life's Work

Sukarno emerged from exile a distinguished politician. Capitalizing on the Japanese need to reach his masses, he negotiated his way into Indonesian politics by agreeing to cooperate with the Japanese as long as they regarded him as the leader of his country's nationalists. He also received high-level assurances that he could promote his political aims, which culminated in an independent Indonesia. Satisfied that the Japanese would provide necessary means of communication to educate and unify the Indonesian masses, Sukarno began the distasteful task of placing his people as *romushas* (male laborers) at the service of the Japanese. Soon after, he founded an advisory council and established the Indonesian military force, Peta. While engaged in administering Japanese affairs, he strengthened his own position as well by placing longtime associates like Mohammad Hatta in important positions throughout the nationalist administrative hierarchy.

By early 1945, it became reasonably clear that Japan could not win the war. To prevent Indonesia's reversion to its past colonial status, the Japanese established a committee, chaired by Sukarno, to study the implications of making Indonesia independent. The committee recommended Sukarno's *pantja sila*—nationalism, internationalism, democracy, social democracy, and belief in God—as the operative principles for Indonesian *merdeka* (independence). Soon after, Sukarno and Hatta jointly proclaimed Indonesia's independence.

The entrance of the Allied armies into the Pacific theater strengthened the Dutch position enough to try to reestablish colonial rule in the archipelago. Sukarno and the nationalists resisted this in the face of Western-inspired embargoes and held steadfastly to their revolutionary capital of Jogjakarta. Furthermore, with world public opinion on

their side, they forced the Dutch to accept the United States of Indonesia in 1949 and the Republic of Indonesia in 1950. Sukarno moved to Jakarta and became president of the republic. Sukarno preferred an executive presidency, but, considering that Hatta and others had won the negotiations in The Hague, he conceded most of the power to them. Hatta became the vice president, governing a rather large parliament and interacting with a burgeoning system of parties. Hatta's task was difficult: He and the president had long-standing differences of opinion on the course that Indonesia should take.

In 1960, Sukarno's disagreements with Hatta culminated in the latter's dismissal and the abolition of the one-hundred-member cabinet and the parties. Sukarno then instituted his guided democracy. Based on *gotong royong*, guided democracy allowed all interested political factions to contribute their views. Unlike Western democracies, however, it did not call for a vote and a resolution. Rather a strongman, in this case Sukarno, weighed those views in private and issued a decree.

Once established as the ultimate authority in domestic affairs, Sukarno directed his attention to international politics. Even though since 1956 the United States had contributed close to one billion dollars to the Indonesian economy, Sukarno all but broke with the United States, saying, "to hell with their dollars!" By siding with Communist China in the Sino-Soviet split, he also affronted Moscow, which had poured close to a billion dollars in armaments into Indonesia. Finally, he recalled his ambassador from the United Nations, claiming that in the dispute between Indonesia and Malaysia the United Nations had sided with Malaysia to appease the capitalists and strengthen their encirclement of the Archipelago.

Although he was neglectful of the results, Sukarno's activities on the international scene impacted his decisions at home. He could no longer administer *gotong royong* impartially and properly. He consistently found himself at odds with the army, which resented the president's attitude toward the Communists. For their part, the Communists supported Sukarno's policies, even his senseless wars, and applauded his decisions. Furthermore, freed from contending with the president, the Communists used their energies in penetrating all levels of the civil and military administration that Sukarno had painstakingly put in place over forty years.

The Communist Party of Indonesia (PKI) was founded in 1914 as a block within the Sarekat Islam on which it drew for membership as well. In spite of factionalism and many setbacks, it successfully fought nationalism and Islam so that by the 1950's it was already a force with which to be reckoned. The movement came fully into its own under Dipa Nusantara Aidit, a pro-Moscow member who adopted and promoted Sukarno's philosophy and politics. Within five years of Aidit involvement, the PKI had mustered enough strength in the army alone to attempt a coup in 1965. Ostensibly its purpose was to strengthen Sukarno's position, but the PKI's real goal was to bring Indonesia under Communist rule before the ailing president's death. The coup was not successful. Implicated in the overthrow attempt, Sukarno reverted to the figurehead that he had been before the introduction of guided democracy. Over the next months, the Communist Party was subjected to a systematic bloodbath. Sukarno's pleas to stop the bloodshed fell on deaf ears, while in Java and Bali between 250,000 and 300,000 Indonesians lost their lives. General Suharto became the acting president in 1967 and the president of Indonesia in 1968. Sukarno sank into disgrace and dotage.

Sukarno died of acute kidney poisoning at the age of sixty-nine. Rather than being buried in the garden of his Batu Tulin home as he had wished, he was interred next to his mother at Biltar, perhaps to prevent the institution of a pilgrimage place close to Jakarta. Nevertheless, Indonesians attended his funeral in droves and a magnificent mausoleum was dedicated to his efforts. Sukarno wore dark glasses, the black cap of the peasant, and the uniform of the military. His countrymen never questioned his revolutionary zeal. To them he was affectionately known as Bung Karno, Bapak, and the lifetime president of the republic. His personal life was as colorful as his public life. His love for women was proverbial. He married seven times, four of the marriages allowed by Islam. He was survived by his only son and several daughters.

## Summary

Sukaro and Indonesia grew up together from poverty to presidency and independence respectively. The colorful and charismatic Sukarno, who claimed he was at once Christian, Muslim, Hindu, and Marxist, made it possible. As a child Sukarno was attracted to the world of the *wayang* (shadow play). In that world the *dalang* (showman) always found a common denominator and made the diversity of the real blend and blend until it assumed the uniformity of the unreal or the shadow. The *dalang* created harmony among opposing factors. Sukarno's approach to politics included elements of the *wayang.* As a Muslim, he exercised *mushavirat* (discussion and deliberation) and *ittifaq* (consensus); as an Indonesian, he practiced *gotong royong*, and as a Marxist he interpreted the outcome as would a socialist. He then expected his people to agree with his views and, more important, to implement them.

*Gotong royong*, however, belonged to the polity of traditional Java. It could not find its proper place in the 1960's international arena when Indonesian nationalism was no longer a monolithic opposition of the oppressed against colonialism. Concrete, diverse, and diametrically opposing forces were at work both within and outside Indonesia. Internally, the country cried for economic reform and military discipline. Internationally it needed a ruler who could harness and utilize the potential benefits of Islam, Western technology, marketing, and Communism, all contending fiercely for attention in the archipelago. The 1965 coup was Indonesia's first encounter with international politics.

**Bibliography**

Benda, Harry J. *The Crescent and the Rising Sun: Indonesian Islam Under the Japanese Occupation, 1942-45.* New York: Institute of Pacific Relations, 1958. A well-documented account of Indonesian Islam under Japanese rule, this book combines careful historical research with sociological insight. The chapters on "The Colonial Legacy" are especially important for understanding Sarekat Islam and its role in Sukarno's life. Includes copious notes, a comprehensive bibliography, and an index.

Brackman, Arnold C. *The Communist Collapse in Indonesia.* New York: Norton, 1969. Brackman concentrates on the dynamics of power in Southeast Asia during the Vietnam War. The book also includes a comprehensive account of the rise of Aidit and of his role in the 1965 coup. Contains notes, an annotated bibliography, and a map.

———. *Indonesian Communism: A History.* New York: Praeger, 1963. The first full-length history of the Communist Party of Indonesia, this book deals with the genesis of the movement and analyzes its turbulent course between 1920 and 1963. Must reading for understanding how the political parties reacted to the Dutch, the Japanese, and Sukarno.

Crouch, Harold. *The Army and Politics in Indonesia.* Rev. ed. Ithaca, N.Y.: Cornell University Press, 1988. Crouch provides an in-depth examination of the role of the army in Indonesian politics and discusses the various ways whereby the army expanded its civil interests under Sukarno's guided democracy before 1965. After the coup, Crouch says, the army furthered its socioeconomic gains. Includes a comprehensive bibliography and an index.

Dahm, Bernhard. *Sukarno and the Struggle for Indonesian Independence.* Ithaca, N.Y.: Cornell University Press, 1969. Dahm studies Sukarno's complex character in the context of the Indonesian concept of *Ratu Adil* (just savior). His book is a scholarly account of the development of young Sukarno's career and of his thought before Indonesian independence. Includes a glossary, a bibliography, and an index.

Fischer, Louis. *The Story of Indonesia.* London: Hamilton, and New York: Harper, 1959. A journalist with exclusive access to Sukarno, Fischer provides a balanced view of Indonesia's past and its revolutionary present through interviews with the country's leaders. Copiously illustrated with a bibliography and an index.

Geertz, Clifford. *Islam Observed.* New Haven, Conn.: Yale University Press, 1968. Geertz views Islam in Indonesia as an understanding of Islamic principles rather than as a set of accepted dogma. In this context, his discussion of Sukarno differs from those of most other writers. Includes two maps, an annotated bibliography, and an index.

Hughes, John. *Indonesian Upheaval.* New York: David McKay, 1967. This firsthand report deals exclusively with the students' campaign against Sukarno after the 1965 coup and with the slaughter that ensued. Contains an index.

Legge, John D. *Sukarno: A Political Biography.* London: Allen and Unwin, and New York: Praeger, 1972. A complete biography of Sukarno, this book first surveys Sukarno's actions and words in a general context and then follows with an in-depth analysis of specific questions and issues. This work is necessary reading for understanding Sukarno's motives, accuracy of his judgment, and leadership capability. Includes an annotated bibliography and an index.

Liu, Hong. "Constructing a China Metaphor: Sukarno's Perception of the PRC and Indonesia's Political Transformation." *Journal of Southeast Asian Studies* 28, no. 1 (March, 1997). This article discusses Sukarno's views on China, the People's Republic of China, and how they influenced his politics and evolution.

Penders, C. L. M. *The Life and Times of Sukarno.* London: Sidgwick and Jackson, and Rutherford, N.J.: Farleigh Dickinson University Press, 1974. Penders based his biography of Sukarno on statements made by Sukarno's associates, especially Abu Hanifa and Hatta, and on the president's autobiography and speeches. Illustrated, with notes, a bibliography, and an index.

Poulgrain, Greg. "Sukarno and the New Frontier." *Australia and World Affairs* 32 (Fall 1997). Examines Sukarno's term in office, his relationship with U.S. President Kennedy, social and economic problems in Indonesia, and more.

Sukarno, Ahmad. *Sukarno: An Autobiography as Told to Cindy Adams.* Indianapolis: Bobbs-Merrill, 1965. This is a standard autobiography, written in the president's casual style. It includes a wealth of information on Indonesian culture, politics, and Islam. Factual, readable, but not always accurate and reliable. Contains a glossary and an index.

Wilhelm, Donald. *Emerging Indonesia.* 2d ed. London: Quiller Press, 1985. This book includes four chapters on the rise and fall of Sukarno. Chapter 4, "The Grand Conspiracy," deals with Sukarno's involvement in the 1965 Communist coup, leading to his dismissal from office. Illustrated with a good index and map.

*Iraj Bashiri*

# HARRY STACK SULLIVAN

*Born:* February 21, 1892; Norwich, New York
*Died:* January 14, 1949; Paris, France
*Area of Achievement:* Psychiatry
*Contribution:* The life of Sullivan, the formulator of the interpersonal theory of psychiatry, marks an outsider's triumph over personal adversity. A former schizophrenic, Sullivan broke through his loneliness to deliver rich insights into the human psyche and schizophrenia.

## Early Life

As Clara Thompson, a close friend and colleague of Sullivan, stated: "Harry Stack Sullivan was a lonely person from his earliest childhood." He was born in Norwich, New York, on February 21, 1892. His grandparents had immigrated to the United States from Ireland. When Sullivan was three years old, his family moved from the county seat to a farm located near the village of Smyrna. Not many relationships with other children were possible, especially since the Sullivans, a Catholic family, were the only people of their faith in a Yankee Protestant community. Because Sullivan was the only surviving child—two other children had died in infancy—he knew isolation at an early period of his life.

Sullivan's family environment was not a healthy one for his later maturation. His mother, who believed that she had married beneath her station, was a nagging semi-invalid with deep resentment toward her status of wife to a humble farmer. She transmitted little warmth to young Harry. Through these difficult years, Sullivan harbored the belief that if he could only reach his father, he would know understanding and warmth. This did, indeed, occur, but only in adult life and after his mother's death.

It has long been believed that Sullivan's sole early associations were with the animals on the family farm. Though a bright pupil, he found it difficult making friends during his early school years. Thanks to his definitive biographer, Helen Swick Perry, it is now known that Sullivan did develop a friendship with an older boy, Clarence Bellinger, who also later became a psychiatrist. No doubt it was this relationship which prompted the mature Sullivan to emphasize the necessity for a young boy to have a "chum," a close association with another boy.

This chum relationship did not, however, serve to socialize Harry, for his later youth was spent in conflicted isolation. Sent to Cornell University to study physics, Harry remained an outsider and was suspended from school for poor grades. This trauma set the stage for emotional suffering in a period that is still clouded in mystery. Later, Sullivan would confide to his assistant, Perry, that during his youth he had a schizophrenic reaction. In preparation for her biography of Sullivan, Perry searched in vain for a hospital record of his illness but came to accept its occurrence and concluded that Harry had probably been confined to Bellevue. On the other hand, Silvano Arieti, in his book *Creativity: The Magic Synthesis* (1976), declares that "Sullivan had several schizophrenic episodes."

Although he never completed college, Sullivan, determined to study medicine and psychiatry, entered the Chicago College of Medicine and Surgery, where he received the M.D. in 1917. According to his colleague Clara Thompson, "he finally got to medical school, where his poverty and his feeling of not knowing how to belong kept him still isolated from his contemporaries."

Although Sullivan's grades in medical school were mediocre, he read widely in the works of Sigmund Freud and others.

During World War I, Sullivan served as a lieutenant and as a junior member of the Board of Examiners for the medical corps of Sixth Service Command. After being discharged from army service, he was determined to enter psychiatry. In 1919, he was called to become assistant medical officer in the Eighth District Headquarters of the Rehabilitation Division of the Federal Board for Vocational Education. In 1920-1921, he served as executive medical officer of the division. In these positions, Sullivan drafted recommendations for the treatment of military men who had been disabled by psychiatric traumata.

Having returned to Chicago, Sullivan, in 1922, became United States Veterans Bureau liaison to St. Elizabeth's Hospital. At last, he was launched on a career in psychiatry. In 1923, he was appointed assistant physician at Sheppard and Enoch Pratt Hospital in Baltimore, Maryland. In 1925, Sullivan was named Director of Clinical Research, with unlimited power to investigate schizophrenic disorders.

## Life's Work

Freud's psychoanalysis, which in Sullivan's day was winning broad support in psychiatric circles, gave up on the schizophrenic as untreatable. Sullivan, in turn, though he at first attempted to use psychoanalysis in the treatment of psychotics, "humanized" schizophrenia and argued that it was treatable. Not only did he modify Freud in his approach to the disorder, but also he claimed that the malady was treatable by psychotherapy because there was no divorce between the characteristics of most schizophrenics and "normal" neurotics. Indeed, Sullivan's insistence on schizophrenia as a human process led him to a theme which undergirds all of his efforts: the One-Genus Postulate. This postulate holds that all human beings are much more similarly human than otherwise, and the true aim of psychiatry is to develop a science of human similarities rather than individual differences.

Freud's emphasis was on the intrapsychic, the struggle of the individual against his antisocial biological instincts. Sullivan's emphasis was on the external shaping of the human psyche through interpersonal relations going back to the mothering one in infancy and extending through the patient's mature life. Sullivan also came to stress the cultural and social milieu in which the patient's interpersonal relations developed. This cultural orientation led Sullivan to reach out to the great social scientists of America: Edward Sapir, Charles H. Cooley, Ruth Benedict, and Harold D. Lasswell. Indeed, Sullivan, who envisioned a fusion of psychiatry with the social sciences, was moving toward social psychology.

In Freud's psychoanalysis, the therapist attempts an objective and largely passive treatment of the patient. Sullivan, on the other hand, depicted the therapist as a "participant observer" who enters into the interpersonal nexus of the patient. By conscious awareness of his participatory role, the psychiatrist seeks to penetrate and reorient the schizophrenic's distorted symbolic thinking.

Sullivan was a brilliant and compassionate clinician to the "lonely ones," as he referred to the schizophrenics, and the remission rate of patients at Sheppard and Enoch Pratt Hospital was little short of amazing. While Sullivan was a harsh mentor to medical students and a waspish colleague to other psychiatrists, he, according to Thompson, "had another side—a gentle, warm friendly one. This was the side he showed his patients."

In 1931, Sullivan moved to New York, where he entered private practice. From that time onward, he had greater opportunity to observe patients plagued by obsessional neuroses. Such patients had long interested him because of their possible connection to schizophrenia.

In 1938, Sullivan, preoccupied with "practical psychiatry" in the light of the coming international crisis, left New York to return to Washington, D.C. He became consultant in psychiatry for the Selective Service System in 1940, serving in this role for a year. In the 1930's and 1940's, Sullivan was a psychiatric consultant for numerous psychiatrists and clinical psychologists in both New York and Washington, D. C. During this period (in 1933), he and associates also established the William Alanson White Psychiatric Foundation. The Washington School of Psychiatry, one of the enterprises of the foundation, was established in 1938. (Soon after Sullivan's death in 1949, however, the school ceased to teach his brand of interpersonal psychiatry, and many of his former students returned to the fold of traditional psychoanalysis.)

After World War II, Sullivan moved toward a messianic role, calling upon psychiatrists to develop a "psychiatry of peoples" which would help reduce international tensions between nation-states. In this regard, Sullivan was influential in the founding of the World Federation for Mental Health and was an active participant in UNESCO. He had, in the meantime, suffered from heart disease for many years, and his international activities became, according to Thompson, a "fire within him." It was on such a mission, on January 14, 1949, that Sullivan died in Paris.

### Summary

Not only does Sullivan's life and work mark the personal victory of a troubled outsider; it was also a triumph for America. As Perry states, "At some level, Sullivan's final contribution was as American as Mark Twain." After absorbing the European masters of psychology, Sullivan reached out to American social science, incorporating the best of American sociology and anthropology into his theory of interpersonal relations. Furthermore, Sullivan's theory, with its practical emphasis on visible interpersonal relations, was deeply permeated with pragmatism, the one native American philosophy. The pragmatist philosophers of America were oriented toward lived experience, practical reality, life as it is sensed and felt, over lofty metaphysical abstractions.

Finally, Sullivan's theory of interpersonal relations is ripe with universal importance. Whereas the unconscious in Freudian theory is invisible and difficult to fathom concretely, Sullivan's emphasis on concrete, external interpersonal relations gave to the psychiatric world a new context for studying human behavior. Indeed, so profound was Sullivan's work that Arthur H. Chapman notes that he is recognized as "the most important American-born psychiatrist."

### Bibliography

Arieti, Silvano. *Interpretation of Schizophrenia*. 2d ed. London: Crosby, and New York: Basic, 1974. Places Sullivan's contributions on schizophrenia in the stream of the history of psychiatry and considers Sullivan to be the leading American contributor to knowledge of its pathology. A good place to start.

Chapman, Arthur H. *Harry Stack Sullivan: His Life and His Work*. New York: Putnam, 1976. An interesting and sympathetic biography, which confirms Sullivan's homosexuality. Analyzes Sullivan's concepts of interpersonal relations, the interpersonal approach to emotional development, and Sullivan's methods of psychotherapy. Concludes with the judgment that Sullivan's theories will one day rank alongside Freud's in importance.

Chrzanowski, Gerald. *Interpersonal Approach to Psychoanalysis: Contemporary View of Harry Stack Sullivan*. New York: Gardner Press, 1977. This volume presents a systemization, presentation, and evaluation of Sullivan's key concepts. The author, a Sullivanian clinician, treats the contemporary clinical applicability of Sullivan's theory. Considers Sullivan's One-Genus Postulate as the "leitmotif" of the interpersonal theory.

Doubt, Keith. "A Sociological Hermeneutics for Schizophrenic Language." *Social Science Journal* 31, no. 2 (April, 1994). The author creates a model for understanding the language of schizophrenics using the language of actors as a basis, and critiques the work of Sullivan and others on this subject.

Goldwert, Marvin. "The Psychiatrist as Shaman: Sullivan and Schizophrenia." *Psychological Reports* 70, no. 2 (April, 1992). Compares the emotional illness of the primitive shaman to the schizophrenic episodes experienced by Sullivan, which enabled him to treat others.

Mullahy, Patrick. *Psychoanalysis and Interpersonal Psychiatry: The Contributions of Harry Stack Sullivan*. New York: Science House, 1970. Attempts a "panoramic review" of all of Sullivan's important ideas. Although this volume is meant to fill the gap in the clinician's knowledge of Sullivan, the lay reader will find it a useful and comprehensive analysis.

Perry, Helen Swick. *Psychiatrist of America: The Life of Harry Stack Sullivan*. Cambridge, Mass.: Belknap Press of Harvard University Press, 1982. This is the definitive biography of Sullivan. Although it is a gold mine of information, setting Sullivan's life in the widest intellectual and environmental context, it is weak on theory. Furthermore, it glosses over Sullivan's homosexuality. This biography should be read with Chapman's, a work which Perry does not cite.

*Marvin Goldwert*

# SUN YAT-SEN

*Born:* November 12, 1866; Cuiheng, Xiangshan county, Guangdong Province, China
*Died:* March 12, 1925; Peking, China
*Areas of Achievement:* Government and politics
*Contribution:* Sun founded the Kuomintang (Chinese Nationalist Party) and led the Republican Revolution of 1911. He is honored by both the Communists and the Nationalists as the founding father of the Chinese republic.

## Early Life

Sun Yat-sen was born on November 12, 1866, in the village of Cuiheng, some eighty miles from Canton. His family was highly respectable, conservative, and ordinary. His father, a thin, ascetic man with a reputation for honesty, was a small landowner who also worked as a tailor. Sun's mother was conservative, observing ancestral rites, enduring bound feet, and teaching filial piety to her six children (Sun Yat-sen was the fifth). She was, however, literate, which was rare among Chinese women of the time. Sun apparently displayed a rebellious spirit from his early youth. He began attending his village school at the age of eight but also worked in the fields after school and during harvest season. By the age of ten, he had protested footbinding and criticized the traditional teaching methods of his school. A good student, Sun studied the Chinese language and the Confucian classics.

Sun's village was in the area of China most affected by Western influence. Two of his uncles had gone to the United States during the California Gold Rush and never returned, his grandmother told him stories about Westerners, and his elder brother, Ah-mei, emigrated in 1872 to Hawaii, where he became successful as a shopkeeper and as a rice and sugarcane grower. Sun joined his brother in Honolulu in 1879, working in his shop. He soon became bored, however, and went to the Church of England boarding school at Iolani in 1880. There he quickly learned English and became one of the first Chinese to obtain a Western education, studying geography, mathematics, science, and the Bible. He apparently became a convert of Christianity in 1882 and thereafter was an enthusiastic admirer of Western ways. All of this alarmed his elder brother, who sent him home in 1883.

Sun did not fit into village life, however, as he had learned to despise the old ways. He earned the enmity of the villagers by attacking the worship of idols. His father therefore sent him to another Christian school in Hong Kong to forestall further embarrassment. Between 1884 and 1892, Sun attended Queen's College, married a girl chosen by his parents, and earned a medical degree. His patron in medical school was the English dean of the college, James Cantlie. As the Western powers began to shear away China's peripheral territories, Sun turned to politics, hatching plots to reform or overturn the Ch'ing (Manchu) Dynasty. By 1894, he had decided to give up the practice of medicine and devote his life to revolutionary activities.

## Life's Work

During the Sino-Japanese War of 1894-1895, which the Chinese unexpectedly lost, Sun launched his first overt attempts at revolution. He founded his first revolutionary party, the Hsing Chung Hui ("Revive China Society"), in 1894 among overseas Chinese and plotted an uprising against the dynasty in October, 1895. Before the

revolt could be launched, however, the plot was discovered, the Ch'ing officials crushed the organization, and Sun fled the country, a price on his head. He spent most of the next sixteen years outside China, traveling around the world to raise money and popular support for his revolutionary activities from overseas Chinese.

Sun arrived in London in September, 1896, to visit his former mentor, Cantlie, and to raise support for his cause. On October 11, while walking near the Chinese embassy, he was abducted by the Chinese and held prisoner in the embassy. He was to be shipped back to China and executed. Eventually, he got word to Cantlie that he was being held prisoner, and Cantlie obtained his release by taking his case to the London newspapers. Overnight, Sun became famous. He spent the next two years in Europe, reading and studying Western political theory, including the writings of Karl Marx and Friedrich Engels. In 1898, he traveled to Japan, where he continued to build his revolutionary party and to argue against Chinese moderates who believed that the Ch'ing monarchy could be reformed. His organization launched an abortive attack on the dynasty after the Boxer Rebellion in 1900. Undaunted, he traveled around the world again, from 1903 to 1905, raising more support for his plans.

By 1905, Sun was back in Japan, where he founded a new revolutionary party, the T'ung Meng Hui ("Revolutionary Alliance"), with the goals of destroying the Ch'ing Dynasty, creating a republic, establishing full diplomatic relations with the world, and carrying out a social revolution. This was a significant political party, with branches in China and among overseas Chinese. Between 1906 and 1909, the party launched six revolutionary attempts, all of which failed. Sun's attempts at violent revolution made him unwelcome in most of Asia. He therefore went to the West again in 1909. In his absence, his party launched two more abortive attempts at revolution before finally succeeding in October, 1911. Sun returned to China in December, 1911, and assumed the office of president of a provisional Chinese republic on January 1, 1912.

Yet Sun's revolution was far from complete. The Ch'ing emperor still occupied the throne, and the foreign powers continued to recognize the Ch'ing as the legitimate government of China. Moreover, Sun's armies were small and poorly organized. His problem, then, was to develop a power base sufficient to overthrow the Ch'ing. In order to accomplish this overthrow, he made an alliance with a powerful Ch'ing general, Yuan Shih-k'ai, who agreed to support the republic in return for being made the provisional president. Sun hoped that Yuan could be converted to republicanism and that genuine representative institutions could be instituted. To further this end, Sun and his associates founded the Kuomintang ("Nationalist Party") in August, 1912. It soon became clear, however, that Yuan had no loyalty to republicanism and that he aspired to become a new emperor. Consequently, in the summer of 1913 the Kuominatang launched a so-called second revolution. It quickly failed, and Sun once again fled the country, arriving in Tokyo in early December, 1913.

Between 1913 and 1920, Sun struggled to find a formula for successful revolution. His attempts to gain control of the republican government by parliamentary means after Yuan's death in June, 1916, failed, and he concluded that his only recourse was to establish a rival government in south China. This was accomplished by April, 1921. Sun hoped to launch a "northern expedition" to unify the country, but this required a strong party organization built around Sun's ideology (the "Three Principles of the People") and outside military support. On January 26, 1923, Sun signed an agreement with the Soviet Union, whereby the Soviets agreed to help unify China. Sun was apparently not attracted by Communist doctrines but by the opportunity to obtain military and political assistance. The Soviets hoped to gain control of the Chinese revolution by working within the Kuomintang.

By 1924, the Kuomintang had been reorganized into a tightly disciplined party along the lines of the Soviet Communist Party, and the Chinese Communist Party had allied with the Kuomintang. The Soviets also supplied significant military assistance. Thus strengthened, Sun traveled to Peking in 1925 to consult with the Peking government leaders about potential unification of China. While there, in March, 1925, he fell seriously ill and died.

After his death, Kuomintang leaders took steps to ensure that his memory would be preserved. Eventually, he was honored as the father of the republic by both the Nationalists and the Communists. His thought, particularly the Three Principles of the People (San-min chu-i), was canonized. In the Three Principles of the People (nationalism, democracy, people's livelihood), Sun attempted to formulate a plan for China's national development. Nationalism initially demanded the overthrow of the Ch'ing Dynasty and then the ousting of the imperialist powers from China. Democracy called for the institution of a republican form of government through three stages of military government, political tutelage, and constitutional government. The people's livelihood was a quasi-socialist program that explicitly rejected Marxism while advocating such concepts as state ownership of industries. The Three Principles of the People were adopted as the official ideology of the Kuomintang and became the national ideology of the Republic of China on the mainland of China (1927-1949) and on the island of Taiwan after 1949.

### Summary

Sun Yat-sen was one of the most important political figures of twentieth century China. A short but strongly built man, with a broad face, wide-set eyes, and a high forehead, he had great personal magnetism and a commanding oratorical style. He was courageous, idealistic, and selfless. Yet his career as a revolutionary was marked by a continuous series of debacles and defeats. Many of his failures were attributable to his own limitations as a leader. Too often, he relied upon subordinates who flattered him but did not serve him well. His headstrong, impulsive nature led him into many foolhardy, unprofitable adventures. Nevertheless, most Chinese believe him to be the greatest man of China's twentieth century. He symbolizes honesty, sincerity, and idealism. His writings have exerted enormous influence in China. In spite of his personal and political shortcomings, he epitomizes China's long struggle to become a modern nation.

### Bibliography

Bergère, Marie-Claire. *Sun Yat-sen.* Stanford, Calif.: Stanford University Press, 1998. Balanced biography of Sun Yat-sen tempering the more radical approaches seen in other writings on his life.

Bruce, Robert. *Sun Yat-sen.* London and New York: Oxford University Press, 1969. A short, popular biography, this thin volume encapsulates the major events of Sun's life and provides a reliable introduction. Contains several pages of photographs.

Chen, Stephen, and Robert Payne. *Sun Yat-sen, A Portrait.* New York: Day, 1946. This book is an early attempt to record the essential outline of Sun's life and to place it within the context of twentieth century China. The authors received the assistance of Sun's family and the nationalist government, so it has the flavor of an authorized biography.

Elleman, Bruce A. "Soviet Diplomacy and the First United Front in China." *Modern China* 21, no. 4 (October, 1995). This article offers evidence that the Soviet motive for siding with Sun Yat-sen was to turn Chinese opinion against Beijing.

Leng, Shao Chuan, and Norman D. Palmer. *Sun Yat-sen and Communism.* New York: Praeger, 1960; London: Thames and Hudson, 1961. The authors explore the relationship between Sun and Communism, reviewing Sun's contacts with Western thought and the process of his ideological development. It compares the similarities and differences between his thought and Chinese Communism.

Schiffrin, Harold Z. *Sun Yat-sen: Reluctant Revolutionary.* Boston: Little Brown, 1980. Schiffrin provides a balanced appraisal of Sun's life and career in this well-written biography designed for general audiences. He presents Sun both as a man and as a symbol of China's national regeneration.

———. *Sun Yat-sen and the Origins of the Chinese Revolution.* Berkeley: University of California Press, 1968. This brilliant, scholarly book explores Sun's early career, particularly his exposure to Western thought and institutions, and his travels among the overseas Chinese communities. It is an indispensable source for understanding Sun's early years and his relationship to the larger Chinese revolution.

Sharman, Lyon. *Sun Yat-sen: His Life and Its Meaning.* New York: Day, 1934. Sharman witnessed the process by which Sun was turned into a national symbol and determined to write a biography that would penetrate beyond the ideological shibboleths to the man himself. As such, this is a "critical" biography that annoyed many Chinese nationalists. It is an early attempt to present a balanced image of the man.

Wilbur, C. Martin. *Sun Yat-sen: Frustrated Patriot.* New York: Columbia University Press, 1976. Wilbur focuses on the last years of Sun's career, particularly his efforts to find funding for his revolutionary activities, his search for foreign support, and his relationship with the Soviet Union. He demonstrates how Sun's hopes were frustrated by the intractable realities within China and by foreign manipulation.

Wong, J. Y. *The Origins of an Heroic Image: Sun Yat-sen in London, 1896-1897.* New York: Oxford University Press, 1986. Wong reexamines the events of Sun's abduction by the Chinese in London, attempting to clarify some of the mysteries surrounding the situation. It is a fascinating exploration of the events themselves and of the way they have entered into the popular image of Sun Yat-sen.

*Loren W. Crabtree*

# BILLY SUNDAY

*Born:* November 19, 1862; Ames, Iowa
*Died:* November 6, 1935; Chicago, Illinois
*Area of Achievement:* Religion
*Contribution:* Sunday was the most flamboyant and colorful of the many Christian revivalists of early twentieth century America. Born in poverty in a log cabin, he was a successful major league baseball player before becoming an evangelist. Sunday preached to more than a million persons in the days before radios and speaker systems; approximately one million of these persons came "down the sawdust trail" and were "saved" as a result of his efforts.

## Early Life

William Ashley Sunday was born November 19, 1862, in Ames, Iowa, the youngest of three sons of William Sunday, of Pennsylvania German descent, and Mary Jane Corey. The family name had been Sonntag in Germany but was Americanized to Sunday in the early nineteenth century. "Willie" Sunday never saw his father, a private in the Union army who died of pneumonia approximately a month after his third son's birth. The widowed mother and three children, in desperate financial straits, struggled to survive on a government pension and some limited assistance from her parents. After six years, Mrs. Sunday was remarried to a man named Heizer. After two more children were born, Heizer disappeared, and the mother and five children were forced to move in with the Coreys.

As an infant, Sunday was very sickly. He could barely walk at age three but was "cured" by an itinerant healer's syrup made from various roots, herbs, and leaves. (Sunday later claimed that nature provides a cure for every human ailment, if one can only discover it.) Young Sunday never got along with his stepfather Heizer, but he loved and admired his grandfather, Martin "Squire" Corey, very much. His youth was one of poverty and hard work. In 1874, he and his brother Edward were sent to the Soldiers' Orphans Home at Glenwood (later at Davenport), Iowa. It was there that Sunday learned the disciplines of hard work, neatness, and cleanliness which remained with him throughout his life.

Sunday's early educational and religious training was not impressive. Never an outstanding student, he did manage to complete the equivalent of grammar school at the orphanage. Religious training there consisted primarily of memorizing verses of Scripture, which made little impression on him until later in his life. He was better known for his running and fighting ability than his scholarship or religious interests. Soon after leaving the orphanage in 1876, he was employed by Colonel John Scott in Nevada, Iowa, as a stable boy and performer of various chores. Scott, who at one time had been lieutenant governor of Iowa, and his wife took him into their home in Nevada. Sunday attended high school there and also worked as a school janitor before drifting to Marshalltown in the next country, where he found employment as an undertaker's assistant and in the undertaker's furniture store.

It was at Marshalltown that Sunday's athletic ability as a runner in the local fire brigade and as a baseball player surfaced. When his baseball team won the state championship in 1883, Sunday caught the eye of A. C. "Pop" Anson, manager of the Chicago Whitestockings, a major league team owned by A. G. Spaulding, and Sunday was soon persuaded to join the Whitestockings at a salary of sixty dollars a month. Sunday's baseball career lasted eight years, from 1883 to 1991; he played for teams in Pittsburgh and Philadelphia as well as Chicago. He claimed to have set two major league records during his career: He circled the bases in fourteen seconds flat from a "standing start," and he once stole ninety-five bases in a single season, a record first surpassed by the legendary Ty Cobb in 1915. He also batted .359 one season, although his career batting average was a hundred points below that mark.

In Chicago, Sunday met and eventually married Helen A. "Nell" Thompson, daughter of a dairyman and ice-cream manufacturer. A staunch Presbyterian and devoted worker in the Christian Endeavor Society, Nell influenced Billy to begin attending the Jefferson Park Presbyterian Church. Her father, however, was not willing for her to marry a professional baseball player who worked during the winter as a locomotive fireman, and it took nearly three years for them to gain his permission to marry, on September 5, 1888. The couple had four children: Helen, George, William, and Paul. Nell eventually played a prominent role in Sunday's evangelistic crusades, handling much of the hiring and firing of personnel and other business decisions, as well as protecting his rest periods and smoothing over problems brought on by his quick temper and his overgenerosity with time and money. Unfortunately, Sunday's later years were marred by many personal problems associated with various family members. His mother was remarried and widowed a third time before her death in 1916. His best friend, Dr. J. Wilbur Chapman, died two years later. Two of Sunday's sons, George and William, were divorced and remarried, and George took his own life in 1933. In that same year, Sunday's only daughter, Helen, died, and, probably not coincidentally, Sunday suffered his first heart attack.

**Life's Work**

Billy Sunday's conversion took place in 1886. He and some baseball teammates, after getting "tanked up" in a Chicago saloon on a Sunday afternoon, stopped at the Pacific Garden Mission to listen to an evangelistic group singing "the gospel hymns that I used to hear my mother sing back in the log cabin in Iowa." Invited inside, Sunday liked what he heard; he returned again and again until one night he went forward and publicly accepted Jesus Christ as his savior. Subsequently, he gave up drinking, gambling, swearing, and going to the theater; he even refused to play baseball on Sunday. He began to take Bible courses at the Chicago Young Men's Christian Association (YMCA), then was offered and in 1891 accepted full-time employment with the YMCA.

Sunday's YMCA work brought him to the attention of J. Wilbur Chapman, later to become the most famous and successful professional evangelist of the early twentieth century. Sunday became Chapman's advance man, preparing various communities for the evangelist's revivals with meticulous attention to all the many details involved in assuring the success of such campaigns. He and Chapman became fast friends during the years Sunday worked for him, until Chapman abruptly decided to give up revivalism (temporarily, as it turned out) in December, 1895. Sunday's apprenticeship to Chapman served him well in later years. He began his own independent career as a revivalist in January, 1896, and during the next five years conducted more than sixty evangelistic campaigns in the Midwest, mostly from tents in the smaller towns of Iowa and Nebraska.

The years 1901-1906 were formative ones for Sunday and for his campaigns. He developed many of his most flamboyant techniques and perfected the businesslike approach to revivalism which became his trademark. He also began to attract criticism for these and other tactics, as well as what many local ministers thought was a growing tendency on his part to condemn their efforts in order to enhance his own. Sunday quit using tents for his revivals during this period, requiring instead that local wooden "tabernacles" be built for his meetings. (This followed a disastrous snowstorm in Salida, Colorado, in October of 1905, in which the snow was said to have fallen so fast that it piled up three feet deep on the tent until it broke the poles and "tore the tent into ribbons.") The tabernacles with which Sunday replaced his tents had wooden floors which were so noisy that he insisted on covering the floor with sawdust. Thereafter, "hitting the sawdust trail" became synonymous with dedicating one's life to Christ after coming to the front of the tabernacle during the "altar call" at one of his services.

Sunday was ordained by Chicago Presbytery on April 15, 1903, despite his lack of a theological education, ordinarily a strict Presbyterian requirement. He believed, correctly, as it turned out, that his success as an evangelist and "soul winner" would more than make up for any educational deficiencies. The presbytery's examination was less than demanding; one member of Sunday's examining board is said to have commented that "God has used him to win more souls to Christ than all of us combined, and must have ordained him long before we ever thought of it." After a few perfunctory questions, most of which Sunday reportedly could not answer, he was passed anyway and became an ordained Presbyterian minister, a position of some prestige and psychological value to him in his work.

When Sunday began his work as an independent revivalist in 1896, he was thirty-four years old, five feet, eight inches tall, and had a slim athletic build and an open, likable face. He wore his thin, prematurely balding hair parted in the middle. He had friendly, sparkling blue eyes, but his most impressive feature was probably his charming, infectious smile and boyishness. In his early efforts to imitate Chapman, he may have tried too hard to be dignified, but by 1900 he gave this up and began to develop his own sensational style, which entertained as well as moved his audiences. He had a definite talent for dramatization, and he blended his personal magnetism and sensational oratory with theatrical gestures which kept his audiences spellbound.

Sunday's salty, idiomatic slang and explosive preaching style in which he moved rapidly all over the podium led one biographer to call him a "gymnast for Jesus." It was conservatively estimated that he traveled more than a mile during the course of delivering a single sermon, and his athletic build and intensity of physical exertion both entertained the masses and stimulated the critics. He would race to and fro on the platform, stamping the floor, pounding the pulpit (during those rare occasions when he stood behind it); he would stand on a chair or the pulpit, swing a chair over his head, fall to the floor, slide, jump, whirl, and even do handsprings. A master of timing, he knew how to elicit applause or laughter. He spoke very rapidly, but in short, staccato sentences, and he acted out practically every word he uttered. Thus, even those who could not hear his words could see them, and he almost never failed to get the response he wanted. At the conclusion of his famous sermon "To Men Only," he parodied the comic poem "Slide, Kelly, Slide" by making a running dive across the length of the platform on his stomach, then imitating the "Great Umpire of the Universe" by jumping to his feet and yelling "You're out, Kelly!"—all this to dramatize a former baseball teammate named Kelly who had "taken to booze," and thus failed to make it "home to Heaven," according to Sunday.

### Summary

Among the many targets of Billy Sunday's ridicule and oratory was the theory of evolution, as well as science and learning in general whenever it conflicted with a literal interpretation of Scripture. Sunday railed against political corruption, slum housing, and oppressive labor conditions; yet he also attacked the Social Gospel movement of his day, which sought to alleviate such problems. Sunday sincerely believed that his "moral approach to reform" would change the hearts of individual men and women, who would subsequently set out to change the institutions of society.

Sunday believed that the root of virtually all evils of American society was "booze." He aided the amazingly successful Prohibition movement immeasurably through his most famous sermon of all, his "Booze Sermon." This sermon stirred millions of Americans in the dozens of cities where he preached it. Sunday closely allied himself with the Anti-Saloon League, founded in 1893 (although he never was on its payroll, as were many other evangelists of the day). He aroused public opposition to alcohol in many cities and states, and his followers were quick to claim credit whenever "dry" votes carried in local options or statewide referenda. Certainly the liquor industry expended enough money and energy in opposing Sunday's efforts to indicate that they considered him influential. After Prohibition became a reality in 1920, he presided over a mock funeral for "John Barleycorn" before ten thousand persons in Norfolk, Virginia.

Sunday probably reached the peak of his popularity during the years of World War I. Although he rarely mentioned the war prior to American involvement in 1917, his superpatriotism thereafter served to fan the flames of nationalism and, subsequently, nativism. In a famous prayer before the United States House of Representatives in 1918, Sunday reminded God that "we are in a life-and-death struggle with one of the most infamous, vile, greedy, avaricious, bloodthirsty, sensual, and vicious nations that has ever disgraced the pages of history." In countless similar jingoistic diatribes against the German "Hun" he railed on about "Kaiser Bill and his dirty bunch of pretzel-chewing, limburger-eating highbinders," much to the delight of largely sympathetic audiences. Sunday also encouraged young men to enlist or, at least, to register for the draft. Recruiting stations for both the army and the navy were placed near the entrance to his New York City tabernacle, and harsh vitriol was poured out on all who chose not to enlist or who opposed military conscription. Sunday also claimed credit for selling more than a hundred million dollars worth of Liberty and Victory bonds during the years of American involvement in the war.

Sunday's popularity declined rapidly after the war, as the public became aware that the Peace of Versailles had failed to achieve the moral aims for which most Americans believed the war had been fought. In the postwar years, Sunday's rhetoric and demagoguery did not change, although his audiences had changed. His great crusades for Prohibition and liberty were over; people tired of professional evangelism and soon turned for entertainment to films, radio, the automobile, and athletic events. Sunday continued to preach, mostly before smaller audiences, almost up to the time of his death, of a second heart attack, in 1935, but his later years were marred by remarks about the "social inequality" of whites and blacks, by his racially segregated services in the South, as well as by open support of his program by the Ku Klux Klan (neither solicited nor repudiated by Sunday), and by his increasingly shrill opposition to pacifism, socialism, labor "agitators," "liberals" of all stripes, Catholics, atheists, Unitarians, Moslems, Hindus, Mormons, and practically all nonnative-born Americans. As one biographer put it:

The fact that Sunday continued to find widespread support throughout the 1920's despite the reactionary extremism of his message indicates the extent to which the nation had turned aside from its principles. . . . Although Sunday was an almost forgotten man at his death, he had been a representative spokesman for the time in which he lived. He won recognition and fame precisely because he embodied so accurately the cultural pattern of his era. If Billy Sunday's career was, in the long run, a failure, it was a failure shared by a generation of Americans.

### Bibliography

Betts, Frederick W. *Billy Sunday: The Man and Method*. Boston: Murray Press, 1916. An anti-Sunday polemic based on a series of articles first published in the *Universalist Leader* by an opponent of a revival he held in 1915 in Syracuse, New York. This volume contains some interesting insights into Sunday's techniques but is of little value otherwise.

Brown, Elijah P. *The Real Billy Sunday*. New York: Revell, 1914. An authorized biography of the evangelist in midcareer by one of his early assistants, this volume is of limited value both because of its early date and its extreme pro-Sunday bias. Three of his complete sermons are included.

Ellis, William T. *"Billy" Sunday: The Man and His Message*. Philadelphia: Winston, 1914. Another "authorized" biography of Sunday in midcareer. More than half of this volume consists of excerpts from his sermons, topically arranged. The revised edition is somewhat less favorably biased than the original. The famous Booze Sermon is included in its entirety.

Frankenberg, Theodore T. *The Spectacular Career of Rev. Billy Sunday, the Famous Baseball Evangelist*. Columbus, Ohio: McClelland, 1913. Another midcareer biography, somewhat more revealing of personality than the two authorized ones. No material from his sermons is included.

Marin, Robert F. "Billy Sunday and Christian Manliness." *Historian* 58, no. 4 (Summer 1996). This article deals with Sunday's themes of physical strength and manliness, which were used to appeal to Americans' fears that too much culture would feminize the American male.

McLoughlin, William G. *Billy Sunday Was His Real Name*. Chicago: University of Chicago Press, 1955. The only real objective biography of Sunday available, this volume, by a skilled historian and professor at Brown University, is the result of extensive research and numerous interviews with Sunday's associates and his widow. Written in lively style, this book may be considered the definitive biography of Sunday.

———. *Modern Revivalism: Charles Grandison Finney to Billy Graham*. New York: Ronald Press, 1959. Another valuable work by McLoughlin, extensively researched and documented. Analyzes Sunday's life and career in its context of American religious revivalism since 1825.

Rodeheaver, Homer. *Twenty Years with Billy Sunday*. Nashville: Cokesbury Press, 1936. Written by the multitalented master of ceremonies, choirmaster, soloist, and trombonist for Sunday's campaigns, this volume describes some of his techniques as well as certain aspects of his personality. It is primarily interesting, however, for its insights into the musical aspects of mass evangelism.

Wright, Melton. *Giant for God*. Boyce, Va.: Carr, 1951. This volume is basically a rehash of the two 1914 authorized biographies. It is based on little, if any, independent research and thus is of extremely limited value.

*C. Fitzhugh Spragins*

# GRAHAM VIVIAN SUTHERLAND

*Born:* August 24, 1903; London, England

*Died:* February 17, 1980; London, England

*Area of Achievement:* Art

*Contribution:* Creatively fusing the English tradition of painting by the light of nature with the European practice of art, Sutherland earned his place as the most distinguished and original English artist of the mid-twentieth century.

## Early Life

Born August 24, 1903, in the London suburb of Streatham, Graham Vivian Sutherland was the first-born child of George Humphreys Vivian Sutherland and Elsie Sutherland (née Foster). During his youth, the family lived variously in Merton Park, Surrey; Rustington in Sussex; and Sutton in Surrey, where Graham attended preparatory school. He then attended public school at Epsom College until the age of sixteen, when Graham became an apprentice in the locomotive works in Derby. He hated being there. He was ill-equipped for the work both physically and mathematically. At a technical college which Sutherland concurrently attended, he discovered his penchant for drawing. The skill he acquired doing drafting assignments later resurfaced in his period as a war artist, when he made studies of steelworks and munitions factories.

Sutherland left Derby in 1920 and the following year enrolled in Goldsmith's College of Art, where he remained until 1926. There he prospered, learning drawing from work in numerous techniques taught at the school. He made frequent trips to the Kent and Sussex countryside, drawing from nature in the grand English tradition. During this period and for the next ten years, he also gave considerable time to engraving. He came under the influence of F. L. Griggs, a master engraver; his first etchings were issued, and *Barn Interior I* (1922) was exhibited at the Royal Academy in 1923.

In 1927, Sutherland married Kathleen Frances Barry and moved to Kent. Over the next several years, until 1939, he supplemented his income by teaching and for a time by designing commercial posters. Sutherland was an attractive, charming man who was modest about his work, often to the point of insecurity. As a result, throughout his life he was unwilling to reject any project offered him, and he was often woefully behind schedule.

In 1931, he began painting, although little is known of his earliest works because he destroyed most of them. In 1934, he made the first of many visits to Wales, and it was there that he developed the foundation of his body of work, although he did none of the painting there. Sutherland found it preferable to store the spaces and concentrations of land in his mind and then take them back to the studio, where he reformulated them in retrospect. He began to paint only after having sensed the emotion of being on the brink of some drama—much like William Wordsworth's "emotion recollected in tranquility"—and only by paraphrasing or condensing what he had seen. In this respect he was at one with William Blake and Samuel Palmer, and this creative method never altered over the next thirty years. Notable examples of these early Welsh paintings are *Green Tree Form* (1939), *Cliff Road* (1941), *Red Landscape* (1941-1942), and *Landscape with Pointed Rocks* (1944).

Sutherland's years as a war artist from 1940 to 1945 completed his rather long early development. Under the chairmanship of Sir Kenneth Clark, a corps of artists, Sutherland among them, was commissioned to make an artistic record of World War II. Sutherland painted bombed dwellings at Swansea, burned-out office buildings and factories in London and its suburbs, and open-cast coal mines and tin mines. Stylistically, these war paintings were more diverse than previously. What is seen in them is a further buttressing of Sutherland's ability to portray with maximum intensity his stored images, at times giving an ominous quality to the scene. He had by this time, nevertheless, matured enough to vary his treatments, utilizing the receding linear perspectives reminiscent of Blake's plates and alternatively painting such works as *Burnt-out Paper Rolls* (1941), which resembled in "death" their tree-trunk origins. No less important was his establishment at this time of a purely factual idiom; unlike his contemporaries, Sutherland projected the human implications of wartime scenes and in so doing selflessly suppressed his artistic ego.

## Life's Work

In 1944, Sutherland was commissioned to do a Crucifixion painting for St. Matthew's Church in Northhampton. Sutherland spent more than a year grappling with the stylistic difficulty of devising a painting which would express in twentieth century terms the traditional iconography, that is, the symbol of the precarious balanced moment, the hair's breadth between black and white. This struggle is evident in his studies and paintings *Thorn Trees* (1945) and *Thorn Heads* (1946), both then and several years later—abstractions of the tortured head of Christ. While Sutherland's *Crucifixion*, completed in 1946, is thought to be flawed by the weakness of the subject's legs, it proved to be a powerful depiction, at once stark, angular, pathetic, and horrible.

The great importance of this postwar period, however, was in the transition which took place in all of his work. It occurred gradually between 1944 and 1948. Sutherland gave up the effect of tunnel vision found in the earlier works and broadened his line of sight laterally. He also began experimenting with an interplay between the artificial and the natural so that natural growths appear to be on platforms. *Thistles* (1945) and *Thorns* (1945) are propped up on poles; the animal-like pieces of driftwood in *Turning Form* (1947) and *Articulated Form* (1947) are on pedestals. Also in 1947, Sutherland began spending time in the south of France, and his movement toward European art can be seen in his utilization of lighter tones and brighter colors, as well as in his incorporation of the imprint of man on nature in his landscapes. He was beginning to find his own way of expressing the influence upon him of Pablo Picasso, Henri Matisse, Joan Miró, and other Paris-based artists without abandoning his individuality. These influences can be seen in *Smiling Woman* (1945) and *Woman in a Garden* (1945).

Beginning in 1949 and continuing for the rest of his life, Sutherland undertook some forty-one portraits. For the casual art appreciator it is the work by which he is best known. The first was of W. Somerset Maugham in 1949, and perhaps the most notorious was of Winston Churchill in 1954. Sutherland's portraits were meticulous recordings, the product of patient observance of the gestures, attitudes, and facial expressions of the subject until his essence revealed itself to the artist. While Maugham eventually loved his portrait, Churchill, believing that his own made him appear half-witted, saw it as a plot to remove him from power. To exacerbate matters, the portrait received extraordinary coverage; it was carried in every newspaper in the country and in many abroad. A year later, Lady Clementine Churchill ordered it destroyed.

Thus, Sutherland was not without disappointments. The Churchill portrait and the Coventry tapestry, which was commissioned at about the same time in the early 1950's, and which was ten years in the making, represent the major setbacks in his career. He was commissioned to design the tapestry for the new Coventry Cathedral. The finished work was huge and overpowering; the treatment, however, was generally thought to be ineffective. It depicted a Christ in sitting position surrounded by the symbols of the four Evangelists: lion (St. Mark), eagle (St. John), calf (St. Luke), and man (St. Matthew). As one commentator has indicated, the Christ appeared mawkish and his feet were clumsily drawn.

In the last period of his life, from 1965 to 1980, a certain repetitiveness was noticeable in Sutherland's work. He began to be vigorously patronized by the Italians, and he spent the better part of his time in Italy. Much energy went into lithographs, which proved to be a lucrative business for him. Notable among them was *Bestiary* (1968), a series of twenty-six lithographs. Sutherland died in London, England, of cancer on February 17, 1980.

### Summary

Creatively, Graham Vivian Sutherland had brought to the body of English art a much-needed international diversity. Yet Sutherland's vision was completely individual; he was not dominated by any other artist or artistic movement. His work defied classification—he was neither expressionist nor realist, surrealist nor cubist. Rather, he sought always to make visual bridges between schools of artistic approach, in the same way that he made bridges between the natural, the animal, and the human.

In his investigative, rigorously honest style of portraiture, Sutherland showed a modesty which was admirable as well as courageous. More important, it is a measure of his breadth, for his Romantic tendencies formed the same kind of duality with his factual portraiture that is formed between hope and despair in his *Crucifixion*.

Sutherland's work did not go unappreciated during his lifetime. In 1960, he was awarded the highly distinguished Order of Merit and received numerous awards and accolades in England as well as around the world. Overall, Sutherland's work, the landscape painting, lithography, portraiture, posters, stained glass, tapestry designs, textile designs, watercolors, all have earned for him an honored place of artistic merit in the human community.

### Bibliography

Berthoud, Roger. *Graham Sutherland: A Biography.* London: Faber, 1982. An exhaustive biographical account based largely on taped interviews with Sutherland and his wife. Rich in contemporary settings for each work. Less useful for its critical content.

Cooper, Douglas. *The Work of Graham Sutherland.* London: Lund Humphries, and New York: McKay, 1961. Although this work was criticized when published for unrelated reasons as well as for the assessment of Sutherland as the only significant English painter since John Constable and J. M. W. Turner, on the whole the analysis of Sutherland's canon is unparalleled in its clarity.

Hayes, John. *The Art of Graham Sutherland.* Oxford: Phaidon Press, and New York: Alpine Fine Arts Collection, 1980. Thorough, but perhaps excessive in the author's unconditional love for Sutherland's work. Does contain one early 1930's painting not available in any other catalog.

Sackville-West, E. *Graham Sutherland.* Rev. ed. London: Penguin, 1955. Well-phrased discussion of Sutherland's connection to the Romantic poets. Articulate coverage of his artistic technique during the early years. Uneven quality in the reproduction of the plates.

Tassi, Roberto. *The Wartime Drawings.* London: Sotheby Parke Bernet, 1980. One of the numerous Italian books of criticism characterized by thorough detail but unswerving devotion. This work is recognized as one which helped thrust the wartime drawings into the limelight as one of Sutherland's most moving achievements.

Vine, Naomi. "Graham Sutherland at Guillaume Gallozzi." *Art in America* 82, no. 2 (February, 1994). The author reviews an exhibit of Sutherland's paintings at Guillaume Gallozzi in New York.

*Linda Fraser*

# ROBERT A. TAFT

*Born:* September 8, 1889; Cincinnati, Ohio
*Died:* July 31, 1953; New York, New York
*Area of Achievement:* Government and politics
*Contribution:* A third-generation member of one of America's most enduring political dynasties, Taft entered the United States Senate from Ohio in 1939 and there achieved a position of leadership as a spokesman for conservative Republicanism.

## Early Life

Robert Alphonso Taft was born September 8, 1889, the first of three children of William Howard and Helen Herron Taft. Robert's father, then a superior court judge in Ohio, became President of the United States in 1909; his paternal grandfather, Alphonso Taft, a successful lawyer, had served the Grant Administration as both secretary of war and attorney general prior to ending his years of public service with ministerial appointments to Austria-Hungary and Russia during the 1880's.

Robert Taft's youth was one of privilege; his first ten years were mainly spent in fashionable neighborhoods in Cincinnati or in Washington, D.C., while his father served as United States solicitor general from 1890 to 1892. In 1900, William Taft accepted an assignment in Manila as a commissioner and in 1901 became the first civilian governor of the recently acquired Territory of the Philippines. His family accompanied him.

From 1903 to 1906, Robert attended the Taft School, founded and run by his uncle Horace, in Watertown, Connecticut. The curriculum stressed academic rigor in the traditional subjects and the duty of young men of good family to take part in public service. At school, Robert excelled in academics. Nearly six feet in height and 170 pounds by the time he was graduated, he tried several sports with his customary earnestness but performed only passably.

In 1906, Robert Taft entered Yale, as family tradition dictated. In his junior year, his father became President of the United States, but by then, Robert, reserved and dignified, was immersed in his habits of diligent study and seemed little affected by his father's eminence. He had been first in his class at Taft, attained the same position at Yale, and finished first at Harvard Law School, still another step in the career progression that was expected of him and that he followed without question.

## Life's Work

In 1913, upon completion of his studies at Harvard, Taft was offered a clerkship with Supreme Court Justice Oliver Wendell Holmes. He declined it to join a prestigious Cincinnati law firm. Taft's workload allowed him ample time to take part in civic life: legal-aid work, charitable fund-raising, and support for a home-rule charter for Cincinnati. In October, 1914, he married Martha Bowers, sister of a Yale classmate. The Tafts had four sons.

Taft reluctantly came to favor American entry into World War I. He volunteered for military service only to be rejected because of poor eyesight. In July, 1917, he joined the Food Administration as one of the wartime agency's four assistant counsels. The work was tedious but satisfying compared with what he had been doing in Cincinnati, and for Taft personally, these years of public service seem to have brought about a new independence from his father's guidance of his career. Loyal to Herbert Hoover, the head of the Food Administration, Taft went with him to administer the Paris office of the American Relief Administration organized at the end of the war. While he was proud of his role in helping to bring relief to some 200 million people in war-ravaged Europe, Taft, like Hoover himself, soured on the diplomatic intrigues that were still part of the European scene. Taft did give his support to the League of Nations, albeit coolly, and he was not then or in the future the single-minded isolationist critics would later label him. Still, he came to regard European leaders as selfish and would always be wary when issues concerning American involvement in world affairs arose. He believed that international law rather than collective security could best be used to preserve peace.

In 1919, Taft returned home to establish a law practice, which his younger brother Charles soon joined. Their specialty was corporate law, much of the firm's business coming from their uncle Charles Taft, long a man of affairs in Cincinnati. In 1920, Robert Taft was elected to the Ohio assembly. He soon gained the respect of his peers for his expertise in tax problems and compiled a good record on civil liberties, supporting them even when it meant opposing the interests of the Ku Klux Klan, then a force in Ohio politics. In his participation in municipal reform in Cincinnati and in his service in the state assembly, Taft demonstrated his belief in party loyalty. Perhaps recalling how Republican factionalism had marred his father's administration, he remained a steadfast Republican even when various issues in Ohio, especially those concerning reform in Cincinnati, caused some to bolt the party.

Although his father, now Chief Justice of the United States, tried to interest him in running for the governorship of Ohio in 1926, Robert Taft showed no inclination to do so. In his six years in Columbus, he had come to enjoy legislative work but preferred to return home to Cincinnati and his law firm, known since 1924 as Taft, Stettinius, and Hollister. His practice boomed, and Taft represented many of Cincinnati's leading corporations, became a director of several, and took part in various protracted negotiations that involved streetcar service and Cincinnati's crying need for a union terminal to accommodate its large rail traffic. Taft handled these cases with a deftness that won praise from all sides. Other than his law practice, his chief interests were in raising money for the Taft School and for the arts in Cincinnati. His principal recreations were golf, fishing, and taking care of the affairs of the farm on which he and his family resided.

In 1930, Taft won election to the state senate, hoping to achieve tax reform in Ohio. An intangible property tax was enacted, but other measures he wanted, such as county zoning and planning commissions, gained insufficient support. Taft, at heart an efficiency-minded Progressive, found his political goals unappealing to others during a time when nationwide depression brought new demands for welfare and slum-clearance programs. Taft was by no means against all legislative action in these areas, and during his earlier stay in Columbus had shown moderation on several questions involving labor, but the priority he normally placed on a balanced budget and efficiency in government made him seem callously insensitive to human needs. A strong supporter of Hoover in 1932, he lost his own bid for reelection in that year of Democratic triumph. It was the only election he ever lost.

By the middle of the 1930's, Taft was ready to take an increased role in national Republican politics. He championed Republican presidential candidate Alf Landon in 1936 and was rumored to be a possible running mate for Landon. Two years later, Taft was elected to the United States Senate.

He quickly earned the respect of Senate colleagues for the care with which he studied legislative issues and, from the start of his tenure in Washington, served on such important committees as Education and Labor, propriations, and

Banking and Currency. During his first campaign for the Senate, he accepted important New Deal programs dealing with unemployment insurance and old-age pensions, but he never was comfortable with the New Deal's approach to government. Both from philosophy and his own experience, especially with the Food Administration, which had been involved in a host of complex and often disliked regulatory decisions, he opposed big government. He regarded the New Deal as seriously flawed in its careless administration, wasteful spending, and excessive interference with private enterprise. The forcefulness and intelligence with which he expressed his opinions quickly made him a prominent figure in the Republican Party.

As early as 1940, Taft was considered a possible presidential candidate. He was eager to enter the race and had assets as a campaigner: energy, ability to organize, and thorough knowledge of the issues. His chances were diminished, however, with the German conquest in the spring of 1940 of France and the Low Countries, for his previous insistence that Germany posed no threat to the United States now seemed shortsighted to many. He had other liabilities. Not only did he dislike mingling with a crowd, but also he was an uninspiring speaker. His talks were heavy with facts and often boring. Fortunately, his wife enjoyed campaigning on his behalf and brought to his campaigns an affability with the public that he lacked. She was, as Taft's most informed biographer states, the most helpful political wife since Jessie Benton Frémont nearly a century before. Republican Party leaders and the press, however, had already stereotyped Taft as a boring personality in an era increasingly dominated by charismatic politicians. Wendell Willkie, an internationalist and a more appealing candidate, gained the Republican nomination.

In the Senate, however, Taft became increasingly successful. He was reelected by a narrow margin in 1944 and, as a leader of a bipartisan conservative bloc in Congress, became one of the most powerful senators in modern American history. He was anathema to liberal Democrats because of his status among conservatives of both major parties. Because he spoke about public issues in forthright, often abrasive terms, he was easy to deride as an isolationist and a reactionary. In practice, his thought was more complex. He is perhaps best remembered for cosponsoring the Taft-Hartley Act of 1947, which to liberals and union spokesmen seemed a retrograde step in labor law. It did not, however, stifle unionism, as was feared by its opponents at the time; on many occasions since, Taft-Hartley's "cooling-off period" has been invoked when major strikes have been threatened. As he had in Ohio, Taft did work for some reformist measures—modest federal aid to education and public housing and federal grants to the states for improved health care. Fellow conservatives and liberals alike seemed puzzled by his support of such proposals, but in Taft's thinking the bills were consistent with his own conservative philosophy that all Americans deserved a fair start and that opportunity must be open to all.

In foreign affairs Taft also showed flexibility. Prior to Pearl Harbor, he had opposed Lend-Lease and other measures designed to aid Great Britain, but subsequently he supported American entry into the United Nations. With the emergence of the Cold War, he voted against American entry into the North Atlantic Treaty Organization (NATO), but once the United States had joined, he believed that American commitments to the alliance should be upheld. Like numerous other conservatives, he displayed more enthusiasm for American involvement in Asia; he derided the Truman Administration for "losing" China to Communism and called for a stronger American effort during the Korean conflict. To an extent his views had changed since his pre-World War II advocacy of noninvolvement, but basically he held that while the United States should oppose the expansion of Communism, American power had its limits and the United States should be wary of excessive commitments in distant areas of the world. Such views made him seem conservative in the early years of the Cold War. Ironically, they would make him a hero to some members of the succeeding generation's New Left, soured on America's interventionism in Vietnam and other Third World locations.

Disappointed by his failure to win the GOP presidential nomination in both 1940 and 1948, Taft was determined to make a strong effort in 1952. Taft and his supporters lashed out not only at the Truman Administration but also at his Republican rivals. Ordinarily a staunch supporter of civil liberties, he did not seek to curb the smear tactics of fellow Republican senator Joseph McCarthy of Wisconsin, who attributed setbacks in foreign affairs to Communist infiltration of the American government. Without regard for due process, McCarthy, and others who followed his lead, accused and brought ruin to many innocent people in government, the media, and in education. Taft seems to have hoped for the then-influential McCarthy's endorsement in 1952 and on several occasions seconded McCarthy's sweeping accusations. He did not, however, get McCarthy's backing. Neither did political newcomer Dwight D. Eisenhower, who had emerged as the chief obstacle to Taft's hopes. Prominent Republicans from the delegate-rich states of the East regarded the colorless Taft as a loser and backed the popular Eisenhower, who won the nomination on the first ballot.

The recriminations of the preconvention period had left Taft and Eisenhower at odds, but party figures attempted to reconcile the two. The effort worked, in part because Taft and Eisenhower were not that distant on domestic issues. Taft campaigned energetically for Eisenhower, and the two became friends and occasional golfing companions. Although Taft believed that he too could have won the election, he accepted Ike's triumph and became a strong backer of the new administration. Realizing that he would be too old to run again for president in 1960, Taft mellowed in his public appearances and praised Eisenhower, providing advice and able support in the Senate, where he secured the post of majority leader. He was determined to help make the first Republican administration in twenty years a success. Early in 1953, however, he was found to be suffering from a severe form of cancer. It spread rapidly, and he died in a New York City hospital.

### Summary

Robert Taft spent more than three decades in public life. He achieved leadership positions in his party in Cincinnati, in the Ohio assembly, and in the United States Senate. He was recognized as "Mr. Republican," widely quoted on both domestic and international issues. He was never as extreme as his rhetoric or that of his more vocal disciples made him appear. Yet the perception of him as a reactionary on domestic issues and as an isolationist made him unappealing as a presidential candidate to influential Republicans who wanted to back a winner. Inevitably measured against his political contemporaries such as Eisenhower and Franklin D. Roosevelt, he was found wanting in the personal flair that helped give them their widespread national following. He never received the nomination he sought so avidly. Taft's greatest distinction was therefore won in the legislative branch, where his diligent work habits and informed opinions won respect. He was one of the twentieth century's genuine masters of the legislative process.

### Bibliography

Alexander, Holmes Moss. *The Famous Five*. New York: Bookmailer, 1958. This is a book of sketches on the first five former senators inducted into the Senate's own hall of fame. Provides an introduction to Taft's career.

Ambrose, Stephen E. *Eisenhower.* 2 vols. New York: Simon and Schuster, and London: Allen and Unwin, 1983-1984. Valuable for its portrayal of the man whose candidacy kept Taft from getting the 1952 presidential nomination he coveted. Eisenhower was the only Republican to hold the presidency while Taft was in the Senate.

Harnsberger, Caroline Thomas. *A Man of Courage: Robert A. Taft*. Chicago: Wilcox and Follett, 1952. A laudatory popular biography of Taft. The author asks if Taft is qualified for the presidency and repeatedly answers yes. What he lacks in charisma, she argues, he more than makes up for in "integrity and courage."

Kirk, Russell, and James McClellan. *The Political Principles of Robert A. Taft*. New York: Fleet Press, 1967. Provides a brief and convenient guide to Taft's public career and a more extended discussion of his political principles.

Merry, Robert W. "The Last Stand of Senator Robert A. Taft, Republicans' Guiding Voice." *Congressional Quarterly Weekly Report* 53 (March 18, 1995). Merry reports on the last weeks of Taft's life.

Patterson, James T. *Mr. Republican: A Biography of Robert A. Taft*. Boston: Houghton Mifflin, 1972. Authorized by the Taft family but written by an outstanding academic historian. Detailed and judicious, it is a model of political biography and shows no effort by the late senator's family to censor the author's judgments. Provides an extensive bibliography.

Pringle, Henry F. *The Life and Times of William Howard Taft*. 2 vols. New York: Farrar and Rinehart, 1939. The most thorough biography of Taft's father, authorized by Robert Taft himself.

Robbins, Jhan, and June Robbins. *Eight Weeks to Live: The Last Chapter in the Life of Senator Robert A. Taft*. New York: Doubleday, 1954. The title of this twenty-three-page booklet makes the topic of this partial biography clear.

Robbins, Phyllis. *Robert A. Taft: Boy and Man*. Cambridge, Mass.: Dresser, Chapman and Grimes, 1963. Laudatory but helpful in that fully half the volume deals with Taft's youth.

Taft, Robert A. *A Foreign Policy for Americans*. New York: Doubleday, 1951. One of two books that contain Taft's own writings, it provides a guide to the senator's outlook on international affairs.

———. *The Papers of Robert A. Taft.* Edited by Clarence E. Wunderlin. Kent, Ohio, and London: Kent State University Press, 1998. The first of four planned volumes that will include selected speeches, letters, and other documents of Taft and the Taft political dynasty.

Taft, Robert A., and T. V. Smith. *Foundations of Democracy: A Series of Debates*. New York and London: Knopf, 1939. This helpful volume makes available the series of radio debates Taft conducted with T. V. Smith, a Democratic congressman from Illinois.

White, William S. *The Taft Story.* New York: Harper, 1954. Written by a reporter for *The New York Times* who knew Taft, this book deals primarily with Taft's career in the Senate.

*Lloyd J. Graybar*

# WILLIAM HOWARD TAFT

*Born:* September 15, 1857; Cincinnati, Ohio
*Died:* March 8, 1930; Washington, D.C.
*Area of Achievement:* Law, government and politics
*Contribution:* After serving as the twenty-seventh president of the United States, Taft finally achieved his personal goal and found both his greatest happiness and his greatest success as chief justice of the United States.

## Early Life

William Howard Taft was born September 15, 1857, the oldest son of Alphonso Taft and his second wife, Louise Torrey Taft. The Tafts were remarkably close; they all took a lively interest in Taft's career, and his brother Charles provided the financial subsidy which made Taft's public service possible. His father had served as secretary of war and as attorney general in the cabinet of President Ulysses S. Grant. Alphonso failed to win election as the Republican candidate for governor of Ohio but under President Chester A. Arthur was minister to Vienna and St. Petersburg.

The Puritan heritage of the Taft family emphasized hard work and the value of an education. Young Taft accepted these family values and, like his brothers, was a good student. He was graduated second in his class at Yale in 1878. He returned to Cincinnati to attend law school and in 1880 was appointed assistant prosecutor of Hamilton County (in which Cincinnati was situated). Not until 1913 did Taft leave the public service which he so enjoyed and for which he was so well-suited by temperament.

Taft was always large, and eventually fat. With his fair hair, blue eyes, and walrus mustache, the six-foot, three-hundred-pound Taft was a fine figure of a man. He was always good-natured and thoughtful, with an infectious chuckle which remained throughout his life as one of his most endearing characteristics. Though he described himself as lazy and a procrastinator, Taft was capable of prodigious effort and was always conscientious. Though he was a Unitarian, Taft was tolerant of the faiths of others. Like his father and most members of his social class, Taft was a staunch Republican, and he never deviated from a strong party loyalty and a belief that only the Republicans could keep the nation moving securely forward.

In 1885, Taft was appointed assistant county solicitor, a fact not nearly as important to Taft as the fact that he had fallen in love. In 1886, he married Nellie (Helen) Herron, an attorney's daughter of unusual intelligence, ambition, and strong convictions—qualities that Taft found admirable in a woman. After a European honeymoon, they built a home in Cincinnati. The following year, Taft was appointed judge of the superior court and in 1888 was elected to a full term. Already his judicial career had led Taft to cast his eyes and his hopes to the United States Supreme Court, a hope encouraged by his appointment as solicitor general in 1890 and to the federal circuit court in 1892. Taft's family, meanwhile, had grown to include a son, Robert (later to become a distinguished United States senator), a daughter, Helen, and six years later, their last son, Charles (later mayor of Cincinnati).

As a judge, Taft venerated the law and considered adherence to it a prerequisite for national stability. Though some of his decisions seemed antilabor, Taft was sympathetic to the workers and upheld their right to organize and to strike. He took a strong stand against the trusts, a position that drew him closer to one of his Washington friends, Theodore Roosevelt.

## Life's Work

In 1900, Taft was called to Washington, D.C., where President William McKinley urged him to take on the responsibility of chairman of the Philippine Commission, assuring him that it would not endanger his chances of elevation to the Supreme Court. Taft had originally opposed the United States' acquisition of the Philippines, but once it was an American possession, Taft saw it as his duty to guide the Philippines toward eventual self-government. With the encouragement of his beloved Nellie, Taft accepted the chairmanship and set sail for Manila.

Taft was well-suited to his task; he was patient, tolerant, affectionate, and stubborn when necessary (which it often was as he clashed with military governor General Arthur MacArthur). Taft came to love and respect the native population of the Philippines. His judicial mind and basic impartiality made him effective in his position, so much so that in 1901 he was sworn in as civilian governor of the island. The capture of Emilio Aguinaldo, leader of the native insurgents, and his oath of allegiance to the American government made Taft's job easier. Taft particularly concerned himself with organizing municipal government, establishing an honest judiciary, and finding sources of adequate revenue for the Philippines.

Taft was distressed by news of the death of President McKinley but rejoiced at the elevation of his dear friend Roosevelt to the presidency. Taft suffered from overwork and the debilitating climate and briefly returned to the United States after two operations. He next traveled to Rome to settle the ongoing dispute over land that had once belonged to the Spanish friars but that the native insurgents claimed as captured lands. Once again he brought order out of chaos and obtained a settlement satisfactory to both sides before returning to the Philippines. Taft was deeply committed to the Philippines and the development of a stable government there. On two separate occasions he declined appointment to the Supreme Court. For Taft, duty came always first, and he believed that his major responsibility at that time was in the Philippines. At last, however, President Roosevelt laid greater claim to Taft's abilities, and in 1903, he was named secretary of war in Roosevelt's cabinet. Roosevelt valued Taft's legal mind and often used him to act as president pro tempore while he was away. Taft's service in the Philippines lent great prestige to the 1904 campaign. As secretary of war, Taft traveled widely—again to the Philippines, to Japan, to Mexico, to Cuba, and to the Panama Canal. He briefly acted as provisional governor of Cuba in 1906 and used his influence to reestablish local government under new election laws. Again Taft was offered appointment to the Supreme Court, and again he declined, this time in order to pursue the presidency itself. He seemed more and more likely to be the party's choice to succeed Roosevelt (who had earlier announced that he would not be a candidate). He was indeed nominated and, with vigorous support from Roosevelt, was elected in 1908. He prepared to complete the work of reform begun by Roosevelt.

Taft and Roosevelt, however, differed in political experience, in style of government, and, most important, in their interpretation of the Constitution. Roosevelt had always believed that he and the government could do anything not specifically forbidden; Taft, with his legal background, was a strict constructionist who believed that he and the government ought to act only in those areas specifically authorized by the Constitution. Although Taft was as genuine a reformer as Roosevelt, his more limited view of presidential activism made him appear to his contemporaries as far more conservative than he really was.

In the area of foreign policy, Taft followed dollar diplomacy both in Asia and in Latin America. He supported Japan rather than China in the Pacific and stood aside while Mexico endured a series of revolutionary upheavals. Taft was devoted to the idea of peace and supported arbitration treaties among the nations as an alternative to war.

In his four years as president, Taft gained more than adequate Progressive credentials. He brought antitrust suits against ninety corporations, compared with only fifty-four in the nearly eight years of Roosevelt's administration. Taft, however, had none of Roosevelt's political skill, nor was he able to use the press to publicize his accomplishments. In an era in which support for Progressive reform still ran strong, Taft was seldom credited for what he did. Taft's administration was responsible for the establishment of a postal savings bank, a tax on corporate income, further regulation of the railroads, the creation of a budget surplus, civil service reform, the establishment of a children's bureau, and the admission of New Mexico and Arizona as states.

All these accomplishments, however, were overshadowed by major crises, or blunders, which together alienated Taft from Roosevelt and lost him much of the Progressive support necessary for successful reelection. The first crisis occurred when reformist congressional insurgents determined to reduce the extensive powers of Speaker of the House Joseph Cannon. Though largely in sympathy with this purpose, Taft remained aloof from the fight, believing in the separation of the executive and legislative branches of government. His private letters reveal his support for reform, but he was publicly identified with the conservative leadership. The second crisis occurred over the issue of tariff reform (a politically divisive issue which Roosevelt had avoided for eight years). Again, although Taft supported reform, the measure that he supported did not go far enough to satisfy Progressive reformers. The mixed rates of the heavily amended Payne-Aldrich Tariff Act were unwisely supported by Taft in such glowing terms that, once again, he alienated reformers who had hoped for more.

Specifically alienating not only Progressive reformers but also Roosevelt were Taft's actions in the Ballinger-Pinchot controversy and the United States Steel case. Interior Secretary Richard Ballinger was heavily criticized by Roosevelt's protégé Gifford Pinchot (who served under Ballinger), who accused Ballinger of corruption and misuse of federal lands in connection with territory in Alaska that had been set aside for government use but was later released for sale to the public. Pinchot's criticism continued publicly after Ballinger was exonerated of any wrongdoing, and Taft had no alternative but to fire him for insubordination. Roosevelt saw this as a personal affront. Similarly, Roosevelt viewed as a personal attack Taft's antitrust suit against the United States Steel Corporation for an earlier purchase of another steel company. Taft was unaware that in the economic crisis of 1907 Roosevelt had approved the purchase and given his word that there would be no government antitrust suit.

By 1912, Roosevelt had decided to challenge Taft for the Republican nomination, and Taft prepared to fight him for it, convinced that Roosevelt had become so radical that he was a danger to the nation. Taft controlled the party machinery and was renominated by the Republicans. Roosevelt turned to the Progressive Party and became their nominee. The bitter split between these two men made it all the easier for Democratic nominee Woodrow Wilson to be elected president. Taft ran a poor third, carrying only the states of Utah and Vermont. Taft was a gracious loser, and in his remaining months in office, he regained much of the personal popularity that he had enjoyed when he was first elected president.

When he left the White House, Taft accepted a position as a law professor at Yale University. In addition to his teaching responsibilities, he traveled widely and gave many speeches and wrote numerous articles to supplement his income. He also chaired the Lincoln Memorial Commission. By 1916, he had become reconciled with Roosevelt (in public at least) and ardently supported Hughes in opposition to Wilson, who by now was bitterly disliked by both Taft and Roosevelt.

When war broke out, Taft was eager to preserve neutrality but rallied to the nation's support after America entered the war in 1917. He supported the League of Nations as a logical successor to the League to Enforce Peace, which Taft had chaired in 1915. During the war, Taft was joint chairman (with Frank P. Walsh) of the National War Labor Board and its successor, the War Labor Conference Board. Once again, his judicial mind was a great asset as was his realistic approach to the needs of labor.

Taft rejoiced in the election of Republican Warren Harding as president in 1920. His lifelong ambition was at last fulfilled when he was appointed chief justice of the United States in 1921. Taft was a hardworking member of the Court, finally damaging his health by overwork. His tendency toward conservatism had grown more pronounced, especially in the areas of social legislation. Taft's radiant warmth and sincere desire for harmony did much to improve the efficiency of a court often divided on the issues. Taft was especially close to Oliver Wendell Holmes and relied on the intelligence of Louis Brandeis, in spite of their great differences on social issues.

The Court, under Taft, faced a heavy work load, primarily as a result of cases carried over from the war years, cases arising under the income tax laws, and cases involving Prohibition. Taft remained a conservative but was surprisingly sympathetic to labor. He consistently supported the right of labor to organize, to bargain, and to strike, but accorded labor no special privileges. He also supported a minimum wage for women and children. Taft supported a fairly broad interpretation of federal power to regulate business in the public interest, especially in cases under the Interstate Commerce Act. He was concerned as well over the general disrespect for the law engendered by the disregard of the Prohibition laws. As chief justice, Taft worked to preserve the harmony of the Court, seldom dissenting from the majority decision.

Taft was awarded an honorary degree from Oxford University in 1922, and he and his wife enjoyed the associations with royalty which the trip to England involved. He maintained a good Republican's interest in politics and privately supported the election of both Calvin Coolidge and Herbert Hoover. Gradually, however, Taft's health failed, and he resigned from the Supreme Court in February, 1930. He died on March 8, 1930, and was buried in Arlington Cemetery.

### Summary

William Howard Taft was a monumental man whose imprint on America was felt in many ways. He was a superb administrator of the Philippines, where his genuine affection for the people did much to assuage their dislike for a colonial overlord. He served well as secretary of war and was a valuable asset to Roosevelt's administration. As president, however, his weaknesses were more apparent. His judicial mind and temperament were ill-suited to the turbulent world of politics, particularly in the era of Progressive reform in which he governed. The public was never aware of Taft's concern and support for reform, and Taft never perceived the importance of public opinion or the value of publicity. He was inclined to let his accomplishments speak for themselves; thus, it has been posterity which has most accurately valued his contributions.

### Bibliography

Anderson, Donald F. *William Howard Taft: A Conservative's Conception of the Presidency.* Ithaca, N.Y.: Cornell University Press, 1973. This is a well-written, well-focused book covering only the presidential years and emphasizing Taft as a conservative. Excellent analysis of Taft's weaknesses, but less on his strengths.

Butt, Archibald W. *Taft and Roosevelt: The Intimate Letters of Archie Butt.* New York: Doubleday, 1930. The lively correspondence of a man who worked closely and intimately as a military aide to both Roosevelt and Taft.

Coletta, Paolo E. *The Presidency of William Howard Taft.* Lawrence: University Press of Kansas, 1973. An issue-oriented account of Taft's presidential years with a fair balance of both his strengths and his weaknesses.

Collin, Richard H. "Symbiosis Versus Hegemony: New Directions in the Foreign Relations Historiography of Theodore Roosevelt and William Howard Taft." *Diplomatic History* 19 no. 3, (Summer 1995). The author explores the views of several scholars with respect to diplomatic relations during the presidencies of Theodore Roosevelt and William Howard Taft.

Duffy, Herbert Smith. *William Howard Taft.* New York: Minton Balch, 1930. A memorial biography of the recently deceased president. Biased; lacks an evaluation of Taft's role in American political life.

Manners, William. *TR and Will: A Friendship That Split the Republican Party.* New York: Harcourt Brace, 1969. A scholarly approach to the theme of Archie Butt's letters and an acknowledgment that Roosevelt and Taft are best understood in contrast with each other rather than studied alone.

Mason, Alpheus Thomas. *William Howard Taft: Chief Justice.* London: Oldbourne, and New York: Simon and Schuster, 1965. As the title suggests, this book focuses on Taft on the Supreme Court with little mention of his presidential years.

Minger, Ralph E. *William Howard Taft and United States Foreign Policy: The Apprenticeship Years, 1900-1908.* Urbana: University of Illinois Press, 1975. A study of Taft as secretary of war and governor of the Philippines and the development of his opinions on the broad questions of foreign policy.

Post, Robert C. "Chief Justice William Howard Taft and the Concept of Federalism." *Constitutional Commentary* 9 no. 2, (Summer, 1992). The author argues that, contrary to popular opinion, Justice William Howard Taft supported aspects of federalism.

Pringle, Henry F. *The Life and Times of William Howard Taft.* New York: Farrar and Rinehart, 1939. Of the many books written about Taft, this massive, two-volume biography is the best, an indispensable beginning for any study of Taft. Splendidly written, it evokes not only the accomplishments but also the spirit of the man.

Rosenberg, Emily S. "Presidential Address Revisiting Dollar Diplomacy: Narratives of Money and Manliness." *Diplomatic History* 22 no. 2, (Spring, 1998). Rosenberg considers how William Howard Taft's dollar diplomacy continues to influence U. S. Foreign relations.

*Carlanna L. Hendrick*

# RABINDRANATH TAGORE

*Born:* May 7, 1861; Calcutta, India
*Died:* August 7, 1941; Calcutta, India
*Area of Achievement:* Literature
*Contribution:* The prolific author of more than one hundred books of verse, fifty dramas, forty works of fiction, and fifteen books of essays, Nobel laureate Tagore is recognized as a pioneer in Bengali literature, particularly the short story, and is internationally acclaimed as one of the world's finest lyric poets. The foundation for Tagore's literary achievements is his vision of the universal man, based on his unique integration of Eastern and Western thought.

## Early Life

Rabindranath Tagore was born on May 7, 1861, into a prosperous Bengali family in Calcutta, India. The fourteenth child and eighth son of Debendranath Tagore and Sarada Devi, he grew up surrounded by the artistic and intellectual pursuits of his elders. Agricultural landholdings in East Bengal supported the family's leisurely lifestyle, and their Calcutta mansion was a center for Bengalis who, like the Tagores, sought to integrate Western influences in literature, philosophy, arts, and sciences into their own culture. Young Tagore was a sensitive and interested child who, like his siblings, lived in awe of his father, a pillar of the Hindu reform group Brahmo Samaj. Cared for mainly by servants because of his mother's ill health, he lived a relatively confined existence, watching the life of crowded Calcutta from the windows and courtyards of his protected home.

From an early age, Tagore's literary talents were encouraged. Like the other Tagore children, he was thoroughly schooled in Bengali language and literature as a foundation for integrating culturally diverse influences, and, throughout his long career, Tagore composed most of his work in Bengali. In 1868, he was enrolled in the Oriental Seminary, where he quickly rebelled against formal education. Unhappy, transferring to different schools, Tagore nevertheless became appreciated as a budding poet during this time both in school and at home. In 1873, he was withdrawn from school to accompany his father on a tour of northern India and the Himalayas. This journey served as a rite of passage for the boy, who was deeply influenced by his father's presence and by the grandeur of nature. It also provided his first opportunity to roam in open countryside.

Returning to Calcutta, Tagore boycotted school and, from 1873 on, was educated at home by tutors and his brothers. In 1874, he began to recite publicly his poetry, and his first long poem was published in the monthly journal *Bhārati.* For the next four years, he gave recitations and published stories, essays, and experiments in drama. In 1878, Tagore went to England to prepare for a career in law at University College, London, but withdrew in 1880 and returned to India. Tagore's stay in England was not a happy one, but during those fourteen months, his intellectual horizons broadened as he read English literature with Henry Morley and became acquainted with European music and drama.

## Life's Work

Returning to India, Tagore resumed his writing amid the intellectual family life in Calcutta, especially influenced by his talented elder brothers Jyotirindranath (writer, translator, playwright, and musician) and the scholarly Satyendranath. Tagore's view of life at this time was melancholy; yet, with the metrical liberty of his poems in *Sandhya Sangit* (1882; evening songs), it became clear that he was already establishing new artistic and literary standards. Tagore then had a transcendental experience that abruptly changed his work. His gloomy introspection expanded in bliss and insight into the outer world, and Tagore once again perceived the innocent communion with nature that he had known as a child. This vision was reflected in *Prabhat Sangit* (1883; morning songs), and his new style was immediately popular. By his mid-twenties, Tagore had published devotional songs, poetry, drama, and literary criticism and was established as a lyric poet, primarily influenced by the early Vaishnava lyricists of Bengal and by the English Romantics. In 1883, he married Mrinalini Devi and continued to reflect his optimism in a burst of creativity that lasted for the next twenty years. During this period, he began to write nonsymbolic drama, and his verse *Kari O Komal* (1887; sharps and flats) is considered a high point in his early lyrical achievement.

In 1890, Tagore's father sent him to Shelaidaha, the family home in eastern Bengal, to oversee the family estates, and thus began the most productive period of Tagore's prolific career. His sympathetic observation of the daily activity of the Bengali peasant, as well as an intimacy with the seasons and moods of the rural countryside, sharpened Tagore's literary sensitivity and provided him with subject matter for his poems and essays during the 1890's. Tagore also wrote short stories—developing the genre in Bengali literature—and in 1891 started the monthly journal *Sadhana*, in which he published some of his work. In addition to literary output, Tagore began to lecture and write on his educational theories and the politics of Bengal, and he came more and more into public life. In 1898, he took his family to live in Shelaidaha, planning to spare his children the schooling against which he rebelled by educating them himself. The family soon moved to Santiniketan at Bolpur, where Tagore founded his experimental school, which became a lifelong commitment. He continued to write ceaselessly during this time: stories, poems, essays, textbooks, and a history of India. In 1901, he became editor of *The Bengal Review* and also launched into a period as a novelist, reflecting the political situation of the time in his work. Tagore's *Gora* (1910; English translation, 1924) is considered by many to be the greatest Bengali novel.

The year 1902 saw the school in serious financial condition and also brought the death of Tagore's wife. Others close to him passed away—his daughter in 1903, his favorite pupil in 1904, and his father in 1905—and Tagore experienced a time of withdrawal. In 1905, he was pulled back into public life by the division of Bengal. Tagore served as a highly visible leader in the antipartition nationalist movement and composed patriotic prose and songs popular with the people. In 1907, however, concerned about growing violence in the movement and its lack of social reform, Tagore suddenly withdrew from politics and retired to Santiniketan, where he resumed a life of educational and literary activity and meditation. Tagore's intuitive belief in the spirituality of life and the inherent divinity of all things was reflected in his work during this time: educational addresses at his school, a series of symbolic dramas that criticized monarchy, and an outpouring of religious poetry expressing his extremely intimate realization of God. A collection of such poems was published as *Gitanjali* (1910; *Gitanjali (Song of Offerings)* and other poems, 1912). During this time in relative seclusion, Tagore the individual poet became, more and more, Tagore the universal man. When next he emerged, it would be to international acclaim.

Tagore became known outside India through the influence of the English painter William Rothstein, the organizer of the India Society in London. Rothstein arranged to publish a private edition of *Gitanjali* for India Society members, and, in 1912, Tagore's English translation appeared with an introduction by William Butler Yeats. Tagore and his poetry were introduced to influential critics and writers such as George Bernard Shaw, H. G. Wells, John Galsworthy, John Masefield, Ernest Rhys, and Ezra Pound. His reputation spread to Europe and to the United States, where, in 1912, his work appeared in the journal *Poetry* and a public edition of *Gitanjali* was published in 1913. In 1912, and again in 1913, Tagore lectured in the United States on religious and social themes, bringing the wisdom of the East to the West in his desire to move the world toward a true humanity. In November, 1913, he was awarded the Nobel Prize in Literature. In December, the University of Calcutta conferred upon him an honorary doctorate of letters, and he was knighted by the British government in 1915. Underlying Tagore's success at this time was his apprehension about the future. Essentially a nonconformist and solitary soul, Tagore believed that he would have no peace from that time on; this, indeed, did prove to be true. Sudden international recognition brought Tagore intense public response, ranging from adulation to disenchantment, and he was an often misunderstood public figure for the rest of his life. At the height of his popularity, Tagore published *Balaka* (1916; *A Flight of Swans*, 1955), which enhanced his reputation as a mystical poet and is considered by many to be his greatest book of lyrics. He also toured Japan and the United States, giving a series of successful lectures later published as *Nationalism* (1919) and *Personality* (1917). Yet Tagore's reputation began to diminish almost as soon as it reached its peak. Some critics have proposed that the materialistic West was not able to appreciate the spiritual depth of the East, while others suggest that the poet and his publishers were themselves to blame for inept translation and unsystematic presentation. Forced to abandon his lecture tour in 1917 because of ill health, Tagore returned to India to a period of tragedy. Although he was greatly disturbed by World War I and denounced it in his writings, Tagore was also unable to endorse wholeheartedly the activities of his own culture. In 1918, with the money received from his writing, lectures, and the Nobel Prize, Tagore founded an international

university—Visva-Bharati—at Santiniketan. Yet in 1919, as he was forming the nucleus of the faculty, political turmoil in India caused Tagore to resign his knighthood in protest against the British massacre of Indians at Amritsar. As Tagore sought to unify humanity in a world that seemed at odds with his philosophy, he began to find himself less and less popular.

In 1920, Tagore undertook another international lecture tour to raise funds for the school, but the receptions in England and the United States were particularly disappointing. During the last two decades of his life, despite increasing ill health, which often forced him to cancel lectures, and problems with public relations, Tagore traveled widely in support of his ideals of a universal humanity and world peace. He also continued to write until the end of his life, mainly poetry—which critics perceive as uneven—and essays. In addition, Tagore began painting as a hobby in his later years and pursued it with increasing seriousness. In 1930, Tagore delivered the Hibbert Lectures at Oxford University, which were published in 1931 as the *Religion of Man*, and, in 1940, Oxford awarded him an honorary doctorate of letters. Because of frail health, Tagore received this honor at Santiniketan, which had become a permanent residence in his later years. On August 7, 1941, Tagore died at his family home in Calcutta.

## Summary

Internationally known as a humanist who sought to reconcile such apparent opposites as man and nature, materialism and spiritualism, and nationalism and internationalism, Rabindranath Tagore expressed a philosophy that was uniquely his own. His vision of the underlying wholeness of life was based on intuitive synthesis of classic Eastern religious texts and the works of early Indian poets and philosophers with Western thought and modern European literature. Although critics sometimes find it difficult to separate his distinguished literary career from his considerable role in transforming the Indian culture from the nineteenth to twentieth centuries, Tagore's place in history is nevertheless a literary one. In the East, he is known as a great poet and thinker; in the West, he is best known as the author of *Gitanjali*, which is characteristic of his work and considered to be his masterpiece. Recognized as a prolific and accomplished writer in all genres, Tagore is internationally acclaimed as one of the world's greatest lyric poets.

Tagore, a man of great courage and gentleness, of nobility and grace, is generally viewed as a symbol of the integration of East and West. Yet, many critics believe that the West has known him only superficially. They suggest that much of Tagore's best work remains accessible only in Bengali, and reading Tagore in translation—even his own translation—offers no real appreciation of his scope or the depth of his genius. Tagore's biographer, Kripalani, stated that "he lived as he wrote, not for pleasure or profit but out of joy, not as a brilliant egoist but as a dedicated spirit, conscious that his genius was a gift from the divine, to be used in the service of man." Although his writing is deeply rooted in Indian social history, Tagore's gift for expressing the unity of life and the grandeur of man gives it universal appeal.

## Bibliography

Banerjee, Hiranmay. *Rabindranath Tagore.* 2d ed. New Delhi: Government of India, 1976. One of a series about eminent leaders of India, this biographical narrative presents the depth and diversity of Tagore's character and his contributions to the heritage of India. It includes genealogical tables and a chronological list of his important works.

Ghose, Sisirkumar. *Rabindranath Tagore.* New Delhi: Sahitya Akademi, 1986. This short, interesting survey focuses on Tagore's life and his poetry, drama, short stories, and novels. It also includes chapters on Tagore's thoughts about religion, beauty, art, and education.

Henn, Katherine. *Rabindranath Tagore: A Bibliography.* Metuchen, N.J.: Scarecrow Press, 1985. This impressive, comprehensive bibliography will be useful both for general readers and for serious Tagore scholars. With short annotations, it includes Tagore's works—classified into nineteen categories—and works written in English about him up to the early 1980's.

Kripalani, Krishna. *Rabindranath Tagore.* 2d ed. Calcutta: Visva-Bharati, 1980. Written by a scholar well acquainted with the Tagore family, this interesting, 450-page work is considered the best English biography of Tagore. Includes twenty-three photographic illustrations as well as a detailed bibliography of Tagore's fiction, nonfiction, and musical compositions.

Lago, Mary M. *Rabindranath Tagore.* Boston: Twayne, 1976. This literary study concentrates on representative works by Tagore as a lyric poet and writer of short fiction. It suggests a perspective from which to view national and international response to Tagore's distinguished career and includes a chronology and selected bibliography.

Mukherjee, Kedar Nath. *Political Philosophy of Rabindranath Tagore.* New Delhi: Chand, 1982. In this volume, Mukherjee presents an analysis of Tagore's political philosophy—in order to fill what he perceives as a gap in the literature on Tagore—and emphasizes the value of Tagore's philosophy in contemporary political situations, both in India and the world.

Sen, Amartya. "Tagore and His India." *The New York Review of Books* 44 no. 11, (June 26, 1997). Profile of Rabindranath Tagore including information on his relationships with important figures such Jawaharlal Nehru and Mahatma Gandhi.

Sen, Suchismita. "Tagore's 'Lokashahitya': The Oral Tradition in Bengali Children's Rhymes." *Asian Folklore Studies* 55 no. 1, (April, 1996). This article includes a translation of Tagore's essay on Bengali children's rhymes, "Chhelebhulano Chharha," in which he maintains that they are created in a mental state similar to that of dreaming.

Singh, Ajai. *Rabindranath Tagore: His Imagery and Ideas.* Ghaziabad, India: Vimal, 1984. One of the few comprehensive considerations of Tagore's imagery available in English, this study relates Tagore's images to his thoughts on life, love, beauty, joy, and infinity. It also includes a selected bibliography.

Thompson, Edward. *Rabindranath Tagore: His Life and Work.* 2d ed. New York: Haskell House, 1974. A reprint of an earlier edition, this brief survey of Tagore's writing prior to 1921 includes commentary based on Thompson's own translations of Tagore's work.

———. *Rabindranath Tagore: Poet and Dramatist.* 2d ed. London: Oxford University Press, 1948; New York: Oxford University Press, 1991. This was among the first detailed literary studies of Tagore's work as poet and dramatist and is still considered to be one of the best.

*Jean C. Fulton*

# MARION TALBOT

*Born:* July 31, 1858; Thun, Switzerland
*Died:* October 20, 1948; Chicago, Illinois
*Areas of Achievement:* Education, sociology, and women's rights
*Contribution:* A leading authority on women's higher education, an author, the first dean of women in a coeducational institution, a cofounder of the American Association of University Women, and a charter faculty member at the University of Chicago, Talbot was also a significant leader of women in sociology and home economics.

## Early Life

Marion Talbot was born on July 31, 1858, while her American parents were visiting Thun, Switzerland. Her father, Israel Tisdale Talbot, practiced homeopathic medicine and served as the first dean of the medical school of Boston University. Her mother, Emily Fairbanks Talbot, was a leader in the struggle for women's higher education and women's work in the social sciences. She was active in establishing the Girls' Latin School in Boston, an endeavor she began partly to secure a forum for her daughter's training. The Talbots of Boston were located at the center of the city's intellectual and cultural life. Marion, the eldest of their six children, was always encouraged by her parents in her advocacy of women's rights in higher education.

After Marion's education at the Girls' Latin School, she was admitted conditionally to Boston University, where she earned a B.A. degree in 1880. After several years of social life and travel, she wanted more than the traditional life that was open to women at that time. Probably at the urging of a family acquaintance and one of the founders of human ecology, Ellen H. Richards, Marion was encouraged to study "domestic science." After several years of sporadic study, she completed a B.S. degree from the Massachusetts Institute of Technology in 1888.

In 1881-1882, Marion, her mother, Richards, and Alice Freeman Palmer, an early president of Wellesley College, cofounded the Association of Collegiate Alumnae (later renamed the American Association of University Women, AAUW). This organization spearheaded opportunities for educated women in the academy and in society. Marion was its first secretary and was its president from 1895 to 1897.

In 1890, Talbot was appointed an instructor in domestic science at Wellesley College (when Palmer was president).

## Life's Work

In March, 1892, Alice Freeman Palmer met with W. R. Harper, president of the University of Chicago, who offered her the position of dean of the women's colleges. Palmer wanted to keep her presidency at Wellesley and work part-time at Chicago, so she recommended Marion Talbot as her full-time assistant. With considerable anticipation mixed with fear, Talbot joined the University of Chicago faculty in 1892 as an assistant professor in the Department of Sociology and Anthropology. Shortly thereafter, she became the first full-time women's dean in a coeducational institution.

Talbot was included within the structure, teaching, and practice of sociology at the University of Chicago as the head of "women's work" throughout the institution. In 1895, she became an associate editor of *The American Journal of Sociology*, a

position she held until her retirement from Chicago in 1925. Talbot critiqued "women's work" in sociology and provided a "woman's perspective" for the most important journal in this discipline.

Talbot wrote in two major areas: the sociology of the home and the sociology of education. Talbot's study of the home was tied to its material reality, from its basic sanitary functioning to its aesthetic creation as an environment in which one lived. Thus, Talbot's pioneering work in women's education was complemented by her scholarly study of the application of science to the home.

Her study of the home was sparked by her association with Ellen H. Richards. Together, they edited *Home Sanitation: A Manual for Housekeepers* (1887) and wrote *Food as a Factor in Student Life* (1884), books that are now difficult to find and are outdated as sources of factual information. They were, however, crucial beginning steps in the study of nutrition and home economics. *The Modern Household* (1912), written with Talbot's former student Sophonisba Breckinridge, is an introductory text intended to help housewives and college students adapt to modern social changes affecting the home. The book covers a variety of topics, ranging from the mundane care of the house to ethics in consumerism and the community.

Anyone interested in the turbulent, innovative founding days of the University of Chicago will find Talbot's autobiography, *More than Lore* (1936), a delight to read. Talbot is forthright in her statements about discrimination against women professionals at the university. Unfortunately, this book is very hard to find and is out of print, so a brief summary is presented here.

Talbot's autobiography documents the segregation of the sexes at Chicago in 1902. Some professors wanted to "protect" young men against "dangerous" women. Her battle against this policy reflects her institutional struggle for coeducation and her bittersweet humor. Fortunately, the segregationist stance was never very successful, and it soon faded away.

Talbot's most important chapter on sexism at Chicago is called "The Weaker Sex." In it, she recounts women's long struggle to enter institutions of higher learning. Chicago was one of the few institutions that accepted women as graduate students in 1892, but few well-qualified women were hired over the next twenty-five years.

Although she was a powerful administrator, her intellectual leadership was severely limited at the University of Chicago. Talbot's continuing battles to make a department with its own funding, staff, journal, fellowships, library, and intellectual legitimacy is outlined in her personal papers at that institution, but this fascinating story has yet to be published.

Talbot was a charter member of the American Sociological Association and an early participant in the Lake Placid Conferences in Home Economics. She was also active in the American Historical Association, the American Public Health Association, the Labor Legislation Association, and the National Federation of Women's Clubs. In 1904, Talbot was awarded an honorary doctor of law degree by Cornell College in Iowa.

Talbot lived a woman-centered existence. She was surrounded in her youth by notable women such as Emily Talbot, Julia Ward Howe, and Louisa May Alcott. She then worked with Richards, Palmer, and the social settlement leader Jane Addams. She trained and worked for many decades with Sophonisba Breckinridge, with whom she shared her life. For years, they lived in women's dormitories as leaders, friends, and bulwarks against a world hostile to educated women. Talbot built institutional structures for women and carved a place for them in the academy. She helped dozens and dozens of female professionals find their first jobs.

She continued her work as dean of women at Chicago until her retirement in 1925. In 1927, she served as acting president of Constantinople Women's College in Turkey for a year, and she did so again in 1931 and 1932. In 1948, Talbot's health and fortunes changed rapidly. Breckinridge died in July, 1948, and her death was a severe blow to Talbot. Within four months, Talbot also died, at the end of a very productive life.

### Summary

Marion Talbot's administrative innovations at the University of Chicago and her analyses of women's work in that institution are major resources for scholars studying the history of women's higher education, especially in sociology. Talbot's policies on women's roles in universities laid the groundwork for similar programs throughout the country. Although she was not a radical, she consistently made decisions favoring equality between the sexes.

Concrete precedents favoring women are detailed in the administrative reports that Talbot made annually at the University of Chicago. In one report, for example, Talbot cited a number of statistics relating to women's low faculty status and the superior achievements of women students compared to those of men at Chicago. More women than men were also graduated Phi Beta Kappa. Female doctors (approximately 15 of graduates) were also very competitive in honorary awards and achievements. Women at Chicago built a sense of camaraderie through their participation in two organizations: The Club of Women Fellows for graduate women and The Women's Union for undergraduate women. These groups helped young women build social and professional networks when many people believed that women should not receive college degrees.

Despite Talbot's fights for women's equality, she believed that women should be "ladies," polite and well-bred, and that a higher education prepared women to be better wives and mothers. In this way, she supported the traditional roles of women. Her writings are interspersed, however, with an appreciation of women's contributions to society and the difficulty of managing a home, and these analyses sound similar to modern writings on housewives and housework. Most clearly, her critiques of discrimination against women in academia are still relevant and accurate.

Talbot was an immensely powerful woman who saw many of her dreams fulfilled during her lifetime. She helped establish the AAUW, with more than a hundred thousand members at the time of her death; saw women enter universities and college campuses across the country, and lived to see deans of women working on more than a thousand campuses. She was one of the recognized founders of home economics and had a pivotal role in the lives of early women in sociology.

### Bibliography


Deegan, Mary Jo. "'Dear Love, Dear Love': Feminist Pragmatism and the Chicago Female World of Love and Ritual." *Gender and Society* 10, no. 5, (October, 1996). The author considers the impact of the ideas of women professionals such as Marion Talbot on society and the development of sociology, using her correspondence with S. P. Breckinridge as a basis for discussion.

———. "Marion Talbot, 1858-1947." In *Women in Sociology: A Bio-bibliographical Sourcebook.* Westport, Conn.: Greenwood Press, 1991. This entry is a more scholarly version than the one included here. A longer bibliography on Talbot and scholarship on her is included.

Fish, Virginia K. "'More Than Lore': Marion Talbot and Her Role in the Founding Years of the University of Chicago." *International Journal of Women's Studies* 8, no. 3 (May/June, 1985): 228-249. This is an excellent analysis of Talbot's autobiography and her central role at the University of Chicago. Because *More than Lore* is difficult to find in libraries today, this article allows more people to learn about the book.

Fitzpatrick, Ellen. *Endless Crusade: Women Social Scientists and Progressive Reform.* New York: Oxford University Press, 1990. Talbot and some of the women she trained are discussed here. The Progressive Era and these women's impact on it are examined.

Palmer, George Herbert. *The Life of Alice Freeman Palmer.* Boston: Houghton Mifflin, 1908. George Palmer was the husband of Alice Freeman Palmer, and his biography is particularly informative regarding Talbot's era and one of her closest friends. The biography refers to Talbot in several places.

Rosenberg, Rosalind. *Beyond Separate Spheres: Intellectual Roots of Modern Feminism.* New Haven, Conn.: Yale University Press, 1982. This is a fine account of Talbot's early life and family and of her work in social science. Other women in the social sciences from Talbot's era are also discussed.

Schwartz, Robert A. "Reconceptualizing the Leadership Roles of Women in Higher Education: A Brief History on the Importance of Deans of Women." *Journal of Higher Education* 68 no. 5, (September-October, 1997). The author examines the contributions to higher education that have been made by women including Marion Talbot, Alice Freeman Palmer, and others, arguing that their roles are often overlooked.

Talbot, Marion. *The Education of Women.* Chicago: University of Chicago Press, 1910. This book describes the educational opportunities available to women in the United States in 1910. Talbot's defense of social hygiene, exercise, and training for rational thinking were "daring" ideas in her day.

———. *More than Lore: Reminiscences of Marion Talbot, Dean of Women, the University of Chicago, 1892-1925.* Chicago: University of Chicago Press, 1936. Although this book is hard to find, it is one of the most important books on women's entry into higher education and life at the University of Chicago from 1892 to 1925.

Talbot, Marion, and Lois Kimball M. Rosenberry. *The History of the American Association of University Women, 1881-1931*. Boston: Houghton Mifflin, 1931. This is a detailed account of the committees, work, and goals of the association that Talbot cofounded. It is a gold mine of information on the work and networks of early women professionals.

Wright, Gwendolyn. *Moralism and the Model Home: Domestic Architecture and Cultural Conflict in Chicago, 1873-1913*. Chicago: University of Chicago Press, 1980. This excellent analysis of the ideal home and its physical construction is an important resource for understanding Talbot's environment and role in the exciting world of Chicago architecture. Wright also explains Talbot's work with Ellen Richards and some professors at the University of Chicago.

*Mary Jo Deegan*

# MARIA TALLCHIEF

*Born:* January 24, 1925; Fairfax, Oklahoma
*Area of Achievement:* Dance
*Contribution:* Prima ballerina of the New York City Ballet for fifteen years, Tallchief symbolized American ballet for an entire generation of theater and television audiences.

## Early Life

Elizabeth Marie (Betty Marie) Tall Chief was born on January 24, 1925, in Fairfax, Oklahoma, a small community on the Osage Indian Reservation. Oil discovered on the reservation—and the tribal leaders' insistence on holding their mineral rights in common—had made the Osage the wealthiest tribe in the United States. Betty Marie's father, Alexander Tall Chief, a full-blooded Osage, was a well-to-do real estate executive whose grandfather, Chief Peter Big Heart, had negotiated the tribe's land agreements with the federal government. Her mother, Ruth Porter Tall Chief, came from Irish, Scottish, and Dutch ancestry. Her paternal grandmother, Eliza Big Heart Tall Chief, often took young Betty Marie to secret tribal dance ceremonies (the government had outlawed these "pagan" rituals at the turn of the century), but it was Ruth Tall Chief's culture and ambitions that ultimately prevailed. Betty Marie began taking piano and ballet lessons at age three; by the time she started school, she was performing before nearly every civic organization in Osage County.

Concerned about the lack of educational and artistic opportunities on the reservation, Ruth Tall Chief convinced her easygoing husband to move the family to Beverly Hills, California, in 1933. There, Betty Marie began a rigorous program of piano lessons and ballet classes, the latter taught by Ernest Belcher (whose talented daughter Marge would later team up with dancer/choreographer Gower Champion). Ruth Tall Chief was determined to groom her daughter for a career as a concert pianist, but it was dance that captivated both Betty Marie and her younger sister Marjorie. In 1938, Betty Marie and Marjorie began intensive training with David Lichine, Lichine's prima ballerina wife Tatiana Riabouchinska, and Bronislava Nijinska. Sister of the legendary dancer Vaslav Nijinsky, Nijinska was one of the foremost ballet teachers and choreographers in the United States. Both Tall Chief sisters impressed Nijinska, who cast them in her ballet *Chopin Concerto*, which was performed at the Hollywood Bowl in 1940.

## Life's Work

After her graduation from Beverly Hills High School in 1942, Betty Marie Tall Chief made her professional debut with the New York-based Ballet Russe de Monte Carlo, one of the two leading ballet companies in the country at that time. (The other, Ballet Theatre, hired Marjorie Tall Chief two years later.) Early in her five-year association with Ballet Russe, Betty Marie "Europeanized" her name to Maria Tallchief. Advancing rapidly from the corps de ballet to solo parts, she attracted favorable critical notice in a variety of classical productions, including Bronisuawa Nijinska's *Chopin Concerto* in 1943 and, in 1944, Michel Fokine's *Schéhérazade* and George Balanchine's *Bourgeois Gentilhomme* and *Danse Concertante*. By 1946, Tallchief's repertoire also included principal roles in Leonid Massine's *Gaîté Parisienne* and two more Balanchine ballets, *Baiser de la Fée* and *Ballet Imperial*. Critics and audiences alike now recognized her as a rising star in the ballet theater.

Balanchine's brief stint as ballet master with the Ballet Russe (1944-1946) marked a turning point in Tallchief's career. Trained in the Russian Imperial School of Ballet, Balanchine was one of the most brilliant choreographers and teachers of the twentieth century. His School of American Ballet, founded in 1936, trained many of the best performing artists on the American stage. He quickly recognized the young dancer's potential, made Tallchief his protégée, and created roles designed to exploit her strength, agility, and great technical proficiency. On August 16, 1946, Tallchief was married to the forty-two-year-old Balanchine. The following spring, she made her European debut with the Paris Opera, where her husband was guest choreographer. When she returned to the United States, Tallchief joined Balanchine's new company, the Ballet Society, which in 1948 became the New York City Ballet (NYCB).

From 1947 to 1965, Tallchief was the prima ballerina of the NYCB and created roles in most of Balanchine's repertoire. Two of these roles were destined to become classics of the ballet theater. In 1949, composer Igor Stravinsky revised his score especially for Balanchine's new version of *The Firebird*, with Tallchief in the title role. Her electri-

fying performance as the mythical bird-woman dazzled critics and audiences alike; for the rest of her career, she would be more closely identified with this role than with any other. In 1954, Balanchine choreographed the NYCB's most popular and financially successful production, a full-length version of Peter Ilich Tchaikovsky's *The Nutcracker*, with Tallchief as the Sugar Plum Fairy, which is regarded as the most difficult role in a classical dancer's repertoire. Tallchief's Sugar Plum Fairy earned for her the title of "America's prima ballerina" and helped to establish *The Nutcracker* as an annual Christmas season favorite in cities all over the country.

During the 1950's and early 1960's, Tallchief reached the pinnacle of her success as a classical dancer. She toured Europe and Asia with the NYCB, accepted guest engagements with other ballet companies, and gave numerous television performances on programs such as *Omnibus*, *Hallmark Hall of Fame*, and *The Ed Sullivan Show*. She played the famous Russian ballerina Anna Pavlova in a 1953 film, *Million Dollar Mermaid*, dancing the Dying Swan role from Balanchine's version of *Swan Lake*. Among the many honors awarded her, none pleased her more than those conferred by her home state: June 29, 1953, was declared Maria Tallchief Day by the Oklahoma State Senate, while the Osage Nation staged a special celebration during which she was made a princess of the tribe and given the name *Wa-xthe-Thonba*, Woman of Two Standards. A triumphal tour of Russia in 1960 with the young Danish ballet sensation Erik Bruhn cemented her international stardom. In 1961, Tallchief won for a second time (the first came in 1949) the coveted annual Dance Award. She resigned from the NYCB in 1965 and retired from the stage a year later.

Tallchief's marriage to Balanchine (though not her friendship or their professional association) was annulled in 1952, on the grounds that he did not want children. By her own admission, their age difference and his obsession with Tallchief the artist rather than the woman doomed their marital relationship. A brief second marriage to airline pilot Elmourza Natirboff ended in divorce in 1954 when Natirboff insisted that she give up her career. In June, 1956, Tallchief was married to Henry D. Paschen, a Chicago construction company executive who accepted her career ambitions. She gave birth to their only child, Elise Maria, in 1959. Retirement in 1966 allowed Tallchief to settle permanently in Chicago with her husband and daughter.

During the 1970's and 1980's, Tallchief brought to the Chicago artistic world the same energy and determination that had characterized her own dancing. In 1974, she formed the Ballet School of the Lyric Opera, where she passed on to younger dancers the Balanchine techniques and traditions that had shaped her own success. The school's original purpose was to provide a corps of dancers for the Chicago Lyric Opera. When financial problems forced the elimination of ballet from the Opera's budget, Tallchief engineered, in 1980, the creation of the Chicago City Ballet (CCB), using $100,000 in seed money from the state of Illinois and a building donated by her husband. Marjorie Tallchief, retired from her own highly successful career in Europe, moved to Chicago to direct her sister's school, while Maria became artistic codirector (with Paul Mejia) of the new ballet company. Following the demise of the CCB in 1988, Tallchief returned to the Lyric Opera to direct its ballet activities. In 1989, she appeared in *Dancing for Mr. B.: Six Balanchine Ballerinas*, a documentary film for PBS.

Despite her assimilation into Euro-American culture, Tallchief remained proud of her American Indian heritage. In 1967, she received the Indian Council of Fire Achievement Award and was named to the Oklahoma Hall of Fame. A longtime member of the Association on American Indian Affairs, she frequently spoke to American Indian groups about Indians and the arts, and participated in university programs to educate students about the first Americans. In 1991, Maria Tallchief became a charter member of the Honorary Committee of the National Campaign of the National Museum of the American Indian, whose members raised funds to assist the Smithsonian Institution in building the new museum on the National Mall in Washington, D.C. In 1998, Tallchief was among five Native American ballerinas designated "Oklahoma Treasures" in a ceremony at the state capitol.

## Summary

Maria Tallchief's primary contribution to American culture rests on her role as the first truly American prima ballerina. Four other American Indian ballet dancers enjoyed distinguished careers during Tallchief's era—Rosella Hightower (Choctaw), Yvonne Chouteau (Cherokee), Moscelyn Larkin (Shawnee), and Marjorie Tallchief—but none left her mark on the American ballet theater as did the elder Tallchief sister. Ballet as an art form in the United States was relatively new, and until the late 1940's, it relied heavily on European dancers. Even the Ballet Russe, with whom most of the "Indian ballerinas" began their careers, was a European company in exile, staffed largely with artists trained abroad. Not until the 1950's, when the NYCB came into its own as a major ballet company, did American ballet reach the standards set by the prestigious national ballets of Russia, France, and England. If it is true that George Balanchine and the NYCB created Tallchief's prima ballerina status, it is equally true that she, in turn, contributed significantly to that company's critical and financial success. American-born and American-trained, Tallchief fascinated audiences with her exotic beauty and her unmatched technical brilliance.

Gifted and driven, Tallchief made personal sacrifices in order to pursue her demanding career as a performing artist. Then, at age forty and still in peak form, she left the stage to devote more time to rearing her daughter. Like a number of Balanchine's former protégées, she ultimately went on to teach what she had learned from the master. She modeled her Chicago school after Balanchine's School of American Ballet in New York, and until his death in 1983, her former husband frequently hired dancers trained by Tallchief. A teacher, lobbyist, fund-raiser and publicist for the arts, Maria Tallchief remains a commanding force in the world of ballet.

## Bibliography

Gruen, John. *Erik Bruhn: Danseur Noble*. New York: Viking Press, 1979. Somewhat gossipy in tone, this biography of the superb Danish dancer contains useful insights into the artistic partnership (and alleged personal relationship) of Tallchief and Bruhn in the 1960's. It is especially useful in the absence of any Tallchief biography assessing her off-stage persona and later ballet achievements.

———. "Tallchief and the Chicago City Ballet." *Dance Magazine* 58 (December, 1984): HC25-HC27. Examines the progress of the CCB as a major American ballet company in the Balanchine tradition, including Tallchief's work with her artistic codirector, Paul Mejia, and NYCB star Suzanne Farrell (Mejia's wife).

Hardy, Camille. "Chicago's Soaring City Ballet." *Dance Magazine* 56 (April, 1982): 70-76. Details the origins of Tallchief's ballet company, focusing on the CCB's premier of Mejia's *Cinderella*.

Kokich, Kim Alexandra. "A Conversation with Maria Tallchief." *Ballet Review* 25 no. 1, (Spring 1997). Interview with Maria Tallchief in which she discusses her career including her struggles with the Ballet Russe.

Kufrin, Joan. *Uncommon Women: Gwendolyn Brooks, Sarah Caldwell, Julie Harris, Mary McCarthy, Alice Neel, Roberta Peters, Maria Tallchief, Marylou Williams, Evgenia Zukerman*. Piscataway, N.J.: New Century, 1981. One of nine performing artists profiled through extensive interviews, Tallchief speaks candidly about her career as a dancer, her professional debt to Balanchine, and her continuing commitment to ballet through teaching and creating the Chicago City Ballet.

Mason, Francis. *I Remember Balanchine: Recollections of the Ballet Master by Those Who Knew Him*. New York: Doubleday, 1991. Tallchief's contribution to this collection reveals her undiminished admiration for Balanchine's genius. She discusses their early association at Ballet Russe, describes the creation of her most famous role, *The Firebird*, and incorporates anecdotes of their life together.

Maynard, Olga. *Bird of Fire: The Story of Maria Tallchief*. New York: Dodd Mead, 1961. An incomplete and dated biography that lacks objectivity but gives the fullest account available of the dancer's early life and rise to stardom.

Myers, Elisabeth. *Maria Tallchief: America's Prima Ballerina*. New York: Grosset and Dunlap, 1966. A sentimental handling of Tallchief's stage career, based largely on the Maynard biography. Like Maynard's work, it reveals little about Tallchief the woman and nothing about her career after leaving the stage.

Tallchief, Maria, and Larry Kaplan. *Maria Tallchief: America's Prima Ballerina.* New York: Holt, 1997. Autobiography of Tallchief focusing on her years with choreographer George Balanchine. Best for those with serious interest.

*Constance B. Rynder*

# JUN'ICHIRŌ TANIZAKI

*Born:* July 24, 1886; Tokyo, Japan
*Died:* July 30, 1965; Yugawara, Japan
*Area of Achievement:* Literature
*Contribution:* Tanizaki admired Western literature early in his career but was drawn increasingly to traditional values and forms with the passage of time. His work is characterized by both intricate narratives and stylistic elegance.

## Early Life

Jun'ichirō Tanizaki was born in Tokyo, Japan, on July 24, 1886. His father, Sogoro Tanizaki, was a rice merchant by virtue of his marriage into the Tanizaki family, whose name he subsequently adopted. It was Jun'ichirō's grandfather, Hisaemon, who had built the business. Sogoro could not appropriate the Tanizaki business acumen as he had the name. When his father-in-law's fortune came into his hands, he grossly mismanaged it. As a result, the performance of the business fluctuated wildly, the long-term effect being a steady decline in the family fortune. The death of an elder brother left Jun'ichirō heir to the dissipated Tanizaki wealth. Although he was a brilliant student, there was at one point a serious problem regarding his tuition fee at the Tokyo Metropolitan First Middle School. Later, he would observe, in his typically paradoxical fashion, that his rearing in Tokyo's merchant class had left him with both a distaste for materialism and a strong sense of nostalgia.

Tanizaki studied classical Japanese literature at Tokyo Imperial University after first sampling English law and English literature. Very early, he had exhibited a talent for literary composition, and he published several pieces in small magazines during his years at the university. He was not graduated and, again, the lack of money was quite probably a contributing factor. In the autumn of 1910, he published two plays and two short stories in *Shinshicho*, a magazine that he and university friends were editing. The short story "Shisei" (1909; "The Tattooer," 1956) introduced one of Tanizaki's enduring themes—the erotic power of feminine beauty. Seikichi, a tattooer, becomes obsessed with a young geisha. He drugs the girl and tattoos an enormous spider sprawling across her back. When she awakens, however, she announces to Seikichi that he has become her victim.

## Life's Work

In January, 1911, Tanizaki's first paid piece, *Shinzei*, a play, was published in *Subaru*. In June and September, two of his stories appeared in the same periodical. The earlier of these, "Shōnen" (youth), attracted the attention of several prominent literary figures. In October, his first novel, *Taifū* (typhoon), appeared in *Mita-Bungaku*. He was married in 1915 to Chiyoko Ishikawa. The first decade of Tanizaki's career was an exciting period in Japanese literature. Japan, by virtue of its victory in the Russo-Japanese War, was now a force to be reckoned with internationally. Western literary influences had been growing since the previous century, and the hold of ancient conventions had been loosening. A controversy was in progress between the naturalist writers, who had commanded the literary field, and their opponents. Tanizaki embraced Westernism and fell under the spell of Edgar Allan Poe, Oscar Wilde, and Charles Baudelaire, especially the mixture of sensuousness and morbidity in their fiction. The critic Gwenn Boardman Petersen argues, on the other hand, that Tanizaki's Westernization has been overstated, that Japan's long tradition of ghost and horror tales is sufficient to account for the bizarre elements in his early work. These elements had by 1920 caused some critics to label him a "Satanist."

In 1923, a great earthquake struck Tokyo, and Tanizaki subsequently relocated to Okamoto, near Osaka. This move has been characterized as the turning point in Tanizaki's career. His simpler way of life, as he left the great metropolis behind, brought with it a reexamination of traditional Japanese customs and a disenchantment with industrialization and Western values. Some critics suggest that at this point Tanizaki ceased to be merely a good writer and became a great one. Again, Petersen sounds a cautionary note, pointing out that Tanizaki's residence in the Kansai area was not so very lengthy and that the writer, according to his own testimony, made no conscious break with Tokyo. Still, for whatever reasons, his writing underwent a noticeable change in the early 1920's. His themes were more surely developed. His narratives became more realistic. His style became more descriptive, less sensuously suggestive (he had been accused of disguising a lack of content with a complex and urbane style). *Chijin no ai* (1924; a fool's love), serialized in *Osaka*, reflects Tanizaki's gradual disillusionment with Western culture.

*Tade kuu mushi* (1928-1929; *Some Prefer Nettles*, 1955), set in Osaka, dramatizes the clash of East and West through a failing marriage. The husband, whose position the narrative seems to favor, has become a traditionalist, while the wife is chic and Westernized. As a result, the two are drifting further and further apart. The novel also contains a strong autobiographical element. Tanizaki's own marriage was failing. A choice bit of Tokyo literary gossip in 1928 had Tanizaki seeking to act as go-between in a proposed affair between his wife and the novelist Sato Haruo. In 1930, the marriage ended in divorce, and, in April, 1931, Tanizaki married Furukawa Tomiko. Within the next five years, he would be divorced and remarried again. Also by 1930, he had gained such distinction that his complete works were published.

An emphasis on physical mutilation and a strain of sadomasochism run through Tanizaki's work. Blindness is featured in "Momoku monogatari" (1931; "A Blind Man's Tale," 1963) and "Shunkin shō" (1933; "A Portrait of Shunkin," 1936). In the latter, a blind musician has such a profound effect upon her student that he blinds himself in order to share her suffering. Their relationship, however, despite its intensity, is very ambiguous (another quality that is characteristic of Tanizaki's fiction). Tanizaki's repeated use of unreliable narrators, multiple points of view, and peculiarly Japanese symbols often give to his narratives—especially for the Western reader—an oblique and problematical tone.

In 1937, Tanizaki was elected to membership in Japan's Imperial Academy of Arts. The coming of war had an effect upon Tanizaki, as it did upon all Japanese writers. Out of mixed feelings of nostalgia and despair, he began to re-create in *Sasame-yuki* (1943-1948; *The Makioka Sisters*, 1957) the world that after the war would never exist again. The progress of the serialized version was long and difficult and involved more than one periodical. The first installment appeared in January, 1943, the last in October, 1948. In between, Tanizaki even published a part of the novel himself, in July, 1944, after it was censured. It appeared in book form in December, 1948. *The Makioka Sisters* is set in the Kyōto-Osaka region. The regional differences that supposedly affected Tanizaki so deeply are dramatized in the novel when one sister is forced to move from her beloved Osaka to Tokyo. The novel contains a wealth of detail about daily life in Japan. Tanizaki received two prestigious awards for *The Makioka Sisters*: the Mainichi Prize for Publication and Culture in 1947 and the Asahi Culture Prize in 1949. In the latter year, he was awarded the Imperial Cultural Medal.

In 1962, more than fifty years after the appearance of "Tattoo," Tanizaki was still exploring the phenomenon of the self-willed victim of erotic desire in *Fūten rojin nikki* (*Diary of a Mad Old Man*, 1965). The diary of seventy-seven-year-old Utsugi Tokusuke makes up the bulk of the novel, but it is supplemented by his nurse's report, his physician's clinical record, and his daughter-in-law's note. These multiple points of view ambiguously interpret the old man's relationship with his ex-chorus girl daughter-in-law.

Tanizaki was elected to honorary membership in the American Academy and National Institute of Arts and Letters in 1964. He died on July 30, 1965, and two months later his last piece of writing appeared in the journal *Chuo Koron*.

**Summary**

Several themes recur in the work of Jun'ichirō Tanizaki throughout his long literary career: the artist's search for beauty, the fascinating quality—both erotic and aesthetic—of womanhood, and the clash of cultures—traditional and modern, Eastern and Western. Yet, often as Tanizaki has treated these themes in stories, novels, and plays, the reader must be careful in drawing generalizations from them. Tanizaki's narrative technique is habitually ambiguous, oblique, and ironic. He may use narrators who are dishonest or naïve. He may use multiple narrators. The narrator sometimes uses the authorial voice but without comment, forcing the reader to interpret for himself the actions, words, expressions, and gestures of the characters. Tanizaki has been called the chronicler of modern Japan, but for a long period he devoted himself to retelling the tales of ancient Japan. The view from ten centuries past gave him yet another perspective for his fiction. His scenes of perversity, especially in the early stories, have led some to include him in the "Satanist," or "demonic," school of writers. The autobiographical elements in his work have linked him to the "I-novelists," the confessional school of writers. His emphasis upon the erotic and his supposed worship of women have associated him with the "love-talk" school of writers. Yet Tanizaki cannot be fitted comfortably into any school or movement. The differences are always more striking than the similarities.

In his later years, Tanizaki was considered a strong and deserving candidate for the Nobel Prize. The rumor coming out of the Swedish Academy was that he was passed over because it was believed that too little of his work was available in translation. Still, he had succeeded in accomplishing what only the greatest writers can accomplish: He had converted his homeland, with all its cultural singularity, into a universal stage. Many agreed with the Asian scholar Donald Keene when he wrote in 1955 that *The Makioka Sisters* is "the most important Japanese novel published in the years following the war."

### Bibliography

Golley, Gregory L. "Tanizaki Junichiro: The Art of Subversion and the Subversion of Art." *Journal of Japanese Studies* 21 no. 2, (Summer 1995). The author argues that Tanizaki's fiction includes subtle subversive messages while the text appears to promote the very ideas he attacks.

Keene, Donald. *Dawn to the West: Japanese Literature of the Modern Era, Fiction.* New York: Holt Rinehart, 1984. A massive study of the fiction produced since the Japanese "Enlightenment" in the nineteenth century. Chapter 20, pages 720-785, is devoted exclusively to Tanizaki, and he is mentioned in the introduction and in several other chapters in association with other writers and literary movements.

———. *Dawn to the West: Japanese Literature of the Modern Era, Poetry, Drama, Criticism.* New York: Holt Rinehart, 1984. A companion volume to the entry cited above. Tanizaki's writing for the stage is discussed in "Part Three: The Modern Drama," and he is also mentioned in passing in "Part Two: Poetry in New Forms" and "Part Four: Modern Criticism."

———. *Japanese Literature: An Introduction for Western Readers.* London: Murray, 1953; New York: Grove Press, 1955. Unlike the comprehensive treatments cited above, this is a brief introduction to Japanese literature, designed for the neophyte reader. Tanizaki is only touched upon in the introduction and chapter 4, "The Japanese Novel," but is discussed throughout chapter 5, "Japanese Literature Under Western Influence."

Petersen, Gwenn Boardman. *The Moon in the Water: Understanding Tanizaki, Kawabata, and Mishima.* Honolulu: University Press of Hawaii, 1979. The first section of Petersen's book, "Contexts," is a brief summary of the rich literary tradition of Japan. The second section is a practical guide to the work of Tanizaki. A partial chronology and a general bibliography are provided.

Rimer, J. Thomas. *Modern Japanese Fiction and Its Traditions: An Introduction.* Princeton, N.J.: Princeton University Press, 1978. Indicates certain structural principles important in the tradition of Japanese narrative fiction and also discusses in detail works for which the author has a profound admiration. Treatment of Tanizaki occurs throughout the entire text, and copious excerpts from his *Seven Japanese Tales* are given a close analysis.

Ueda, Makoto. *Modern Japanese Writers and the Nature of Literature.* Stanford, Calif.: Stanford University Press, 1976. A study of eight major writers of modern Japan, those writers whose work constitutes the bulk of modern Japanese fiction available in English. Chapter 3 is devoted to Tanizaki. The work is indexed, contains a selected bibliography, and furnishes extensive source notes for those who read Japanese.

Yamanouchi, Hisaaki. *The Search for Authenticity in Modern Japanese Literature.* Cambridge and New York: Cambridge University Press, 1978. Tanizaki's much discussed attitude toward women is examined in chapter 5, "The Eternal Womanhood: Tanizaki Jun'ichirō and Kawabata Yasunari."

*Patrick Adcock*

# IDA TARBELL

*Born:* November 5, 1857; Erie County, Pennsylvania
*Died:* January 6, 1944; Bridgeport, Connecticut
*Area of Achievement:* Journalism
*Contribution:* Ida Tarbell became a prominent leader in American magazine journalism in a period when women were almost entirely absent from the field.

## Early Life

Ida Minerva Tarbell was born on her grandfather's farm in western Pennsylvania four years before the Civil War began. Her father, Franklin Sumner Tarbell, had earlier struck out for Iowa and its richer farming prospects; he would not see his daughter until she was eighteen months old. Ida's mother, Esther McCullough Tarbell, was a descendant of Massachusetts pioneers and had taught school for more than a decade before her marriage. She would ultimately bear four children, of whom Ida was the eldest.

When Ida was three, her father moved the family to the Pennsylvania oil region to take advantage of financial opportunities there. After the Civil War, the family would follow the oil boom to several towns in western Pennsylvania, settling ultimately in Titusville when Ida was thirteen. While her father made an increasingly comfortable living building wooden oil tanks, Ida studied in the local schools and attended Methodist church services and revival meetings with her family. When the time came for her to continue her studies, her father naturally selected Allegheny College, the Methodist coeducational college in nearby Meadville.

For the next four years, Tarbell combined diligent study in biology and languages with social activities, class offices, literary magazine editing, and public speaking. She was romantically linked with at least one young man, but the relationship did not survive college and Ida never married. After her graduation, she embarked on a short-lived career as a teacher at the Union Seminary in Poland, Ohio. A low salary and high expectations placed on her ability to teach all subjects led to her return to Titusville after two years.

The opportunity that led to her career in journalism appeared a few months after her return. She was hired as an editor for the *Chautauquan*, a magazine published to promote adult education and home learning by the Chautauqua Literary and Scientific Circle. Although the editorial work she was assigned initially was stultifying, she gradually expanded her responsibilities to include translating, reviewing manuscripts, and writing her own articles. The workload at first was light, and the magazine was located in Meadville, which enabled her to complete a master of arts degree at Allegheny College.

When Tarbell left the *Chautauquan* in 1891, she had no intention of accepting a mundane editorial post. Instead, she sailed to France determined to immerse herself in Parisian culture, support herself by submitting articles to American newspapers, and write a biography of Mme Manon Philipon de Roland, a heroine of the French Revolution. She did all of this and more. After reading some of her work, Samuel S. McClure, the publisher of *McClure's*, personally visited her in Paris to offer her a job. In the fall of 1894, she accepted his offer, which included money for the passage home.

## Life's Work

Ida Tarbell's first work at the magazine was the surprising assignment of producing a series of articles on the life of Napoleon, whose hundred-year-old military exploits produced a flurry of activity in the popular press of the 1890's. She had not expected to do a work of that sort, and she was astonished to be asked, after returning from Paris, to undertake a biography of a French subject using the comparatively limited sources to be found in American libraries. Nevertheless, her labors at the Library of Congress resulted in a distinctive and popular *McClure's* series that was subsequently published as a book, as was the practice at the time.

The resources of the Library of Congress were excellent, as Tarbell discovered, and so were the human resources in the nation's capital. She remained in Washington, D.C., until 1899, during which time she met influential politicians and public servants. She wrote articles about them and ghost-wrote the memoirs of other famous men. Her major work during her Washington years was another *McClure's* assignment, a biography of Abraham Lincoln. She conducted interviews in Washington and Illinois and established a wide network of correspondents who provided her with information. Her study of Lincoln's early years was published in 1896, with a complete two-

volume biography following in 1900, after its serialization in the magazine.

Called to the *McClure's* New York staff in 1899 as managing editor, Tarbell joined a talented group of writers and editors. Although McClure himself was seldom in the office, his partner, John Phillips, shrewdly managed the publisher's affairs. Among the writers McClure and Phillips published regularly were Ray Stannard Baker and William Allen White, both of whom were poised on the brink of fame as preeminent journalists of their time. Also on the staff then or shortly thereafter were Willa Cather, Finley Peter Dunne, and Lincoln Steffens. This group took the lead in a new journalistic enterprise—muckraking—and Ida Tarbell's series on the Standard Oil Company was in the forefront of that type of work.

The series that would later be published in book form as *The History of the Standard Oil Company* was launched in the November, 1902, *McClure's* magazine. Ida had undertaken it in response to Sam McClure's idea of detailing the rise of the trusts in the late nineteenth century; she had formulated the idea of tracing the history of one such enterprise and the great entrepreneur associated with it, John D. Rockefeller. Growing up in the oilfield districts had acquainted her with the industry and the geographic area in which the boom began. Her industrious methods of working and her indomitable spirit in researching her subject ensured a thorough product. If anyone in *McClure's* talented group of writers could master such a vast (and elusive) body of information, it was Ida Tarbell.

The Standard Oil series established two things: The first was that Ida Tarbell was a formidable author and one of the outstanding journalists of her time; the second was the fact that muckraking (as the reform journalists' movement was labeled in 1906 by Theodore Roosevelt) was a responsible enterprise that could produce thorough and dispassionate analyses of problems. Because of the efforts of Tarbell and her cohorts, *McClure's* became the leading voice of protest among the popular magazines.

This preeminence was short-lived, however, and Tarbell became the leader of a staff revolt against the magazine in 1906. At the center of the controversy was the mercurial Sam McClure. The publisher was famous for his ability to produce ideas for articles at a rapid-fire pace, but his erratic behavior in 1905 and 1906 seemed to Tarbell, Phillips, and others to threaten the magazine they had helped to build. They questioned his new, risky publishing ventures and wondered whether his commitment to reform had been undercut by his commitment to making money. Tarbell resigned from the magazine in April, 1906.

By June, the old *McClure's* group had formed a new venture. They founded the Phillips Publishing Company, raised money to purchase a failed magazine, and launched it in the fall as their own, *The American Magazine*. Tarbell remained a regular staffer and contributor until the group sold its interests in 1915, although she also submitted articles to other magazines. Her major series in *American Magazine* covered diverse topics: the protective tariff, the American woman, and the "golden rule" in business.

The first series highlighted the author at her best. She explained the complexities of the tariff to the general public, clarified controversies, and produced a reasoned analysis that clearly explained the costs of high tariffs to working people. Her golden rule series, her last extended writing for *The American Magazine*, was a defense of scientific management in industry, a work that demonstrated how efficiency could blend with humane treatment of labor. The third series—on the American woman—proved to be the most controversial and caused a rift between Tarbell and some of her suffragist friends.

Like may reformers during the early years of the twentieth century, Tarbell believed that the government, through protective legislation, could act in the general interest of laborers, women, and other minorities. Revolutionary change in the social or political system was not necessary. She was never truly a feminist. She did not support the woman suffrage movement, since she believed that a woman's influence was best exerted in the home, not in areas that were traditionally male preserves. Thus, for working women, she favored legislation that would limit their hours to allow them more time in the home. Raised by a suffragist mother, and herself a dominant force in a traditionally male profession, Ida Tarbell espoused an apparently contradictory philosophy relating to women and their roles in society.

After the sale of *The American Magazine* in 1915, Tarbell remained active as a freelance writer. She also traveled and lectured on topics about which she had written earlier. She worked briefly in Washington during World War I until she was sidetracked by a diagnosis of tuberculosis and by the subsequent treatment. She spent much time during her later years tending to family members, often at her farm in Connecticut which she had purchased in 1906 with her book earnings. Projects she completed in her sixties and seventies included biographies of steel magnate Elbert Gary and General Electric head Owen D. Young, a history of American business during the late nineteenth century, and her autobiography, *All in the Day's Work*. Her major magazine writings were series on the Florida land boom and on Italian dictator Benito Mussolini.

Her work progressed more slowly as she aged, but she kept doggedly at it. In her eighties, she used her own declining health as the subject of a work she never completed, *Life After Eighty*. Old age, Parkinson's disease (diagnosed about two decades earlier), and pneumonia brought about Tarbell's death in early January of 1944. At her request, she was buried in Titusville.

### Summary

Ida Tarbell exerted both a specific and a general influence on her times. The specific influence related to Standard Oil, whose illegal operations she documented as thoroughly as if she was preparing a legal brief. Legal action, in fact, was the result. When the attorney general filed a 1906 case against Standard Oil for violation of the Sherman Antitrust Act, the charges were essentially those that Ida Tarbell had made and documented in her book. The case was heard and appealed; when the Supreme court made its ruling in 1911, it ordered the dissolution of the giant corporation.

Tarbell's general influence concerned the status of women in public life. Although she, ironically, did not participate in feminist or suffragist activities, her whole career exemplified what activist women attempted to achieve—the opportunity for women to enter the professions.

### Bibliography

Brady, Kathleen. *Ida Tarbell: Portrait of a Muckraker*. New York: Seaview/Putnam, 1984. The most thorough treatment of the contradictions in Tarbell's writings and of the contrast between her own achievements and her views on women and public life.

Conn, Frances G. *Ida Tarbell, Muckraker*. Nashville, Tenn.: Nelson, 1972. Written especially for juveniles, the book is anecdotal but informative. There is no systematic discussion of Tarbell's works, but there are numerous quotes from her writings.

Lyon, Peter. *Success Story: The Life and Times of S. S. McClure*. New York: Scribner, 1963. Discusses Ida Tarbell's writings in the context of the magazine muckraking movement generally considered to have begun in *McClure's* magazine. Examines the complex relationship between Tarbell and McClure.

Tarbell, Ida M. *All in the Day's Work: An Autobiography*. New York: Macmillan, 1939. An unassuming autobiography made rather bland by the author's saccharine approach to describing the controversies in which she was involved.

———. *The History of the Standard Oil Company*. 2 vols. New York: Macmillan, 1904; London: Heinemann, 1905. Tarbell's magnum opus was not only the first great work of the muckrakers but also a solid history of the development of the oil industry in the United States. It is the main work upon which her literary reputation rests.

Tomkins, Mary E. *Ida M. Tarbell*. New York: Twayne, 1974. This book in Twayne's United States Authors series mainly considers Tarbell's writings and evaluates her contributions to literature.

*Richard G. Frederick*

# FREDERICK WINSLOW TAYLOR

*Born:* March 20, 1856; Germantown, Pennsylvania
*Died:* March 21, 1915; Philadelphia, Pennsylvania
*Area of Achievement:* Business
*Contribution:* Taylor studied the functions and practices of men and machinery in minute detail and drew up detailed plans for saving time and increasing productivity. Many of the principles upon which he worked have formed the basis of modern managerial practice.

## Early Life

Frederick Winslow Taylor was born March 20, 1856, just outside Philadelphia in the affluent community of Germantown. Both his father's and his mother's families were of old New England stock. Taylor's father was a lawyer who was interested more in literature than in the expansion of his practice. His mother was a prominent reformer—abolitionist, Transcendentalist, and female suffragist. It was from her that Taylor's early education came. Her qualities were transmitted to the young Taylor through rigorous drilling and training. From his mother, Taylor learned to be spartan, exacting, methodical, and extremely competitive. In the Taylor household, everyone had specific jobs. Throughout his life, Taylor was a most intense individual with an extraordinary power to arouse and inspire others, but he was temperamental, difficult to work with, and intolerant of the skepticism of others concerning his own theories. Friends testified to his great sense of humor, amiability, sociability, and sensitivity.

For three and a half years, Taylor's parents took him around Europe to complete the first stage of his education. While there, he became a fluent speaker of German. Upon their return to the United States in 1872, Taylor entered Philips Exeter Academy to prepare for Harvard Law School. Despite gaining honors in the entrance examination to Harvard, Taylor abandoned further study because of eye trouble. An independent young man, Taylor chose his own path and obtained a job as an apprentice with the Enterprise Hydraulics Works in Philadelphia, whose owners were family friends. Within four years, Taylor was a skilled machinist and pattern-maker.

## Life's Work

At the age of twenty-two, Taylor embarked upon his career in industry as a common laborer for the Midvale Steel Company of Philadelphia. His rise was meteoric. After only two months, he went from laborer to clerk, machinist, and gang boss. Within six years, he was promoted to foreman of the machine shop, master mechanic in charge of repairs and maintenance throughout the entire works, chief draftsman, and finally, chief engineer. In that time, Taylor developed a system of shop management never before known.

At first, Taylor merely goaded workers into working harder and producing more through a system of threats, wage cuts, fines, and inspirational exhortations. During his time as gang boss and foreman, Taylor was subjected to death threats, but because of his combination of imperiousness, personal courage, and rigorous honesty, as well as the power he could wield, he got his way: Machinery was speeded up and production increased.

Taylor observed minutely each function of work and set standards and times for each. If a man did not reach Taylor's standards, it was, according to Taylor, because the man was physically or mentally unfit for the job or because the man was shirking. It was during his time with Midvale that Taylor invented the time-and-motion study. It was the function of management, Taylor believed, to plan, and the function of workers to execute management's directives. There was no place in Taylor's scheme for the worker to have any role other than to do exactly as he was told. If he cooperated, then the worker should be well rewarded. Increases in production should be accompanied by increases in wages. Indeed, as a result of his systematic study, Taylor was able to increase production by three hundred percent and to raise wages by twenty-five to one hundred percent. During his time at Midvale, Taylor also produced a number of inventions which made improvements on machinery and on manufacturing methods. His outstanding achievement was the design and construction of the largest steam hammer ever built in the United States.

Shortly after he became chief engineer at Midvale, Taylor was married, on May 3, 1884, to Louise Spooner, a doctor's daughter and a friend since childhood. Taylor was of average height, blond, blue-eyed, about 145 pounds, with a slim, athletic build. Indeed, in 1881, he and a brother-in-law had won the United States National Championship in tennis. Typically, Taylor had used a racket of his own invention.

In 1890, Taylor resigned from Midvale to become general manager of the Manufacturing Investment Company, which operated large paper mills in Maine and Wisconsin. Taylor attempted to put his ideas into practice, but opposition from both workers and his group of financial backers made his job frustrating. In 1893, he opened his own consultancy business. His business card read "Systematizing Shop Management and Manufacturing Costs a Specialty." The business was not noticeably successful; he had few clients.

In 1898, another phase in Taylor's career began when he was retained exclusively by the Bethlehem Steel Company. It was at Bethlehem that he perfected his system and completed, with J. Maunsell White, a study he had begun while at Midvale of the treatment of tool steel. The resulting Taylor-White process increased steel-cutting capacities by between two hundred and three hundred percent and won national and international awards. The daily struggle which Taylor faced at Bethlehem, however, made the introduction of his system virtually impossible. He was not allowed the free rein he had demanded as a condition of accepting employment with the company, and, after being denied support by the company's president, Taylor was fired in 1901. He devoted the remainder of his life to expounding his principles and giving his services free to anyone sincerely desirous of carrying out his methods. These methods and principles were never comprehensively set out. Yet his publications, "A Piece-Rate System," "Shop Management," "On the Art of Cutting Metals," and *The Principles of Scientific Management* (1911), taken together with his testimony before a Special Committee of the House of Representatives to Investigate the Taylor and Other Systems of Shop Management, in January, 1912, offer a sample of his thoughts.

The resistance Taylor faced from workers, foremen, and managers in the companies where he attempted to introduce his system was replicated in his own professional body, the American Society of Mechanical Engineers (ASME). While his early work was published by the society and he was elected president of the ASME in 1906, Taylor had to go elsewhere to get *The Principles of Scientific Management* into print. Indeed, opposition to Taylor and his disciples proved so great that in 1911 a group of insurgent engineers founded the Society to Promote the Science of Management. After the death of its chief inspirer, it was renamed the Taylor Society.

Despite opposition, the reputation of "Taylorism" spread. His full system was most closely adopted by two small companies, Tabor and Link-Belt, where it was introduced by Taylor's associates. The system excited the interest of the ordnance department of the army and was adopted by it at the Watertown Arsenal near Boston in 1909. In 1910, the Taylor system was championed by Louis D. Brandeis during arguments over the level of freight rates before the Interstate Commerce Commission. The Taylor system was vindicated. Publicity surrounding these developments sparked a popular efficiency craze which, by 1912, reached into homes, schools, and churches.

While "efficiency" enjoyed enormous popularity among the population as a whole, industry continued to resist the Taylor system. Other forms of efficiency and many of Taylor's principles, if not his methods, were adopted. Abroad, Taylor's work enjoyed a greater reputation. His works were translated into almost every major European language, and attempts were made to adopt his methods. France especially seemed taken with Taylorism, particularly in the period following World War I. Russian leader Vladimir Ilich Lenin wrote enthusiastically and urged adoption of Taylorism throughout Russian industry. In Great Britain, eclectic as always, Taylor's system tended to be blended with other forms of efficiency-oriented systems of shop management but exercised great influence. Frederick Winslow Taylor died of pneumonia March 21, 1915, at his home in Philadelphia, but his work continued to reach wider audiences.

### Summary

Taylor was the leading figure in pioneering the rational management of industrial corporations. At a time when business was expanding in size, scope, and complexity, Taylor found a system to replace arbitrary and chaotic conditions with rational planning based on minute observation and study. He sincerely believed that once his system was introduced into industry, everyone could be duly rewarded and industrial harmony would result: The key was productivity.

Taylor was as much a visionary as a practical man. Resistance to his ideas was based on a number of factors. Workers were required to stop thinking altogether on the job. Foremen and supervisors were to be transformed from autonomous decision-makers with tremendous personal power over the workers under their command into enforcers of task definitions and production targets with little power of initiative (the concept of "functional foremanship"). Managers and employers were expected to relinquish much of their personal power to efficiency experts, who would take care of the detailed planning, preparation, and scheduling of work. None of these groups wished to do this. In addition, Taylor's personality induced resentment and even disbelief, especially his impatience with skeptics and his tendency to become carried away with his own rhetoric. Finally, his system did contain flaws, the major one of which was his crude conception of human motives, which led him to underestimate the importance of employee attitudes to work as a controlling variable in production.

Nevertheless, Taylor inspired a generation of young engineers with the concept of efficiency, and the tremendous success of American industry at home and abroad in the twentieth century is, in part, a result of his ideas and principles.

### Bibliography

Aitken, Hugh G. J. *Taylorism at Watertown Arsenal: Scientific Management in Action, 1908-1915.* Cambridge, Mass.: Harvard University Press, 1960. A most illuminating study which compares the theory of Taylorism with its practice in one case study. The author concludes that, although the Taylor system was not adopted in every detail, it did work at Watertown with various modifications and accommodations, the major one of which was the setting up of committees to ensure participation by employees in the determination of piece rates and standard times, the lack of which had led to serious conflicts and had strengthened labor unions in the facility.

Copley, Frank Barkely. *Frederick W. Taylor: Father of Scientific Management.* 2 vols. New York and London: Harper, 1923. This is the official biography. The author had access to all of Taylor's correspondence and papers; the full cooperation of relatives, friends, and professional organizations; and the support and counsel of a committee which included Taylor's widow, longtime associates, and the managing director of the Taylor Society. While it is highly favorable and claims rather too much for Taylor's achievement, the work is full of important detail and is the most exhaustive treatment.

Hoxie, Robert F. *Scientific Management and Labor.* New York and London: Appleton, 1915. Hoxie headed the investigation of Scientific Management for the United States Commission on Industrial Relations. This is his report. He concluded that, as applied, scientific management was crude and insufficiently sensitive to the human rights of workers, though it was certainly worth further experimentation. His fellow experts represented, respectively, management and labor, which accounts for the balanced nature of the findings. The report is based on field studies to plants operating the Taylor system. Well worth reading.

Kakar, Sudhir. *Frederick Taylor: A Study in Personality and Innovation.* Cambridge, Mass.: MIT Press, 1970. This is a psychohistorical interpretation of Taylor's life and work. Argues that the limitations of his ideas were to be found in his own obsessional neurosis, his love-hatred for his father, and his general ambivalence about people. Further, it suggests that his achievements were a result of the congruence of Taylor's own inner crisis with a historical crisis. Interesting, but to be avoided as an introduction to Taylor.

Merkle, Judith A. *Management and Ideology: The Legacy of the International Scientific Manage-*

*ment Movement*. Berkeley: University of California Press, 1980. An interesting study which analyzes Taylorism, distinguishes it from later, more polished approaches to scientific management, and places it in the context of social, political, and economic developments. The second part of the book discusses the adoption of the system in the Soviet Union, France, Germany, and Great Britain, and its metamorphosis in those countries.

Nadworny, Milton J. *Scientific Management and the Unions: 1900-1932*. Cambridge, Mass.: Harvard University Press, 1955. This was a pathfinding study which analyzed and chronicled the initial hostility of labor unions to Taylorism before World War I and examined the spectacular change that occurred afterward. Its final chapter, "Scientific Management in Retrospect," looks at the development and decline of Taylorism in the 1920's and 1930's. Well written and informative.

Nyland, Chris. "Taylorism, John R. Commons, and the Hoxie Report." *Journal of Economic Issues* 30 no. 4, (December, 1996). The author discusses John R. Common's assessment of Frederick Winslow Taylor's theories of scientific management.

Robinson, Thomas L. "Revisiting the Original Management Primer: Defending a Great Productivity Innovator." *Industrial Management* 34 no. 1, (January-February, 1992). Robinson discusses Frederick Winslow Taylor's scientific management principles, criticism of them, and the questions of authenticity that have been raised by Taylor's contemporaries.

Taylor, Frederick W. *Scientific Management*. New York: Harper, and London: Routledge, 1947. Consists of Taylor's two most important works, "Shop Management" and *The Principles of Scientific Management*, and his testimony to the special house committee. The first article quotes extensively from a previous work, "A Piece-Rate System," and also contains an exposition of the concept of functional foremanship, time-and-motion methods, and Taylor's attitudes toward workers. The second, an attempt to convince readers of the efficacy of scientific management, contains the famous illustration concerning pig-iron handlers and the workman Schmidt, as well as the mechanics of the system. The final part is a detailed exposition by Taylor of the principles and practicalities of his system and detailed, rigorous questioning by the chairman, William B. Wilson, concerning Taylor's ideas and their effects on workers.

Taylor Society. *Scientific Management in American Industry*. New York and London: Harper, 1929. A detailed statement by the devotees of the Taylor system of their beliefs and practices at the height of their influence. There are some substantial differences between the attitude of the Taylor Society and its mentor, but this represents the development of the movement Taylor founded.

*Stephen Burwood*

# SARA TEASDALE

*Born:* August 8, 1884; St. Louis, Missouri
*Died:* January 29, 1933; New York, New York
*Area of Achievement:* Literature
*Contribution:* One of the best-selling poets of the early twentieth century, Teasdale used traditional verse forms to express her own attitudes toward love, beauty, and solitude.

## Early Life

Sara Trevor Teasdale was born on August 8, 1884, in St. Louis, Missouri. At the time of her birth, St. Louis was experiencing a cultural and economic flowering, brought about in part by its mixed population of transplanted Easterners of Puritan ancestry and more recently immigrated Germans who stressed the importance of art and music. In 1884, the city was home to two universities, a museum, an art school, and numerous theaters where the great names in the acting and music worlds of the day sometimes performed.

The Teasdale family was of New England stock, descended from a dissenting Baptist who had emigrated from England in 1792. The poet's grandfather was a Baptist minister who had moved his family west to St. Louis in 1854. John Warren Teasdale, the poet's father, was a successful businessman. The ancestors of Sara's mother, Mary Elizabeth Willard, included the founders of Concord, Massachusetts, two presidents of Harvard, and a signer of the Declaration of Independence. Throughout her life, Sara would acknowledge the Puritan aspect of her character and its conflict with her more "pagan" poetic self.

Kept at home in early childhood because of her poor health, Sara began her formal education at the age of nine, attending a private school a block from her home, and she was graduated from a girls' school at the age of eighteen. In 1903, she became friends with an artistic and intellectual young woman named Williamina Parrish, with whom she and other friends formed a club called the Potters. These young women were products of the active women's club culture of the day and were themselves enthusiasts of and participants in the arts. For more than two years they produced a monthly hand-printed magazine known as *The Potter's Wheel*. Among their artistic influences were the Pre-Raphaelite poets and painters, particularly Christina Rossetti, the Celtic Revivalist Fiona MacLeod (actually, Scottish writer William Sharp), the Greek poet Sappho, and actress Eleonora Duse. Most of the poems in Sara's first book had originally appeared in *The Potter's Wheel*.

In 1905, Sara and her mother traveled to Europe and the Holy Land. Sara was depressed by the dirt and poverty of what was then Palestine but loved Seville, Spain, and Paris, France, where she pronounced the Venus de Milo "the most beautiful thing on earth." While in London, she sought out the homes of poets Elizabeth Barrett Browning and Algernon Charles Swinburne. The beauty that Teasdale found in Europe contributed subject matter for many of her later poems.

In 1906, *The Potter's Wheel* came to the attention of William Reedy, the publisher of a weekly newspaper known for its sponsorship of new artists. Reedy published one of Sara's prose sketches and a poem, thereby arousing her sense of professionalism and bringing her to the attention of poetry critics. The next year, the Poet Lore company published Teasdale's first book, *Sonnets to Duse and Other Poems*.

## Life's Work

On the surface, Sara Teasdale's life changed little following her initial publications, but she experienced a growing dissatisfaction with life in St. Louis and in her parents' home. This period saw the beginning of her lifelong pattern of periodic "rest cures" (then prescribed for many ailments of women) at various sanatoriums and hotels. She was proposed for membership in the Poetry Society of America in 1910, and in January of 1911, she made her first visit to New York City for the meeting of the society. Her second book, *Helen of Troy and Other Poems*, was published by Putnam in October of that year.

Poetry Society membership brought Teasdale friendships with influential poets, editors, and critics. Her work also brought her into contact with John Hall Wheelock, the young poet who became the unrequited love of her life and the subject of many of her finest lyrics of frustrated love. Although he never reciprocated Teasdale's romantic affection, Wheelock became the person to whom she turned in many of the later crises of her life.

In 1913, Teasdale visited Chicago and met Harriet Monroe, editor of the recently founded magazine *Poetry*. Monroe introduced her to Illinois poet Vachel Lindsay, then just becoming famous as the

author of "General William Booth Enters into Heaven." Lindsay's midwestern aesthetic was nearly the opposite of Teasdale's emphasis on careful craftsmanship in traditional verse forms, but he fell in love with his fellow poet and courted her with extravagant, lengthy letters and periodic visits. Teasdale remained fond of Lindsay throughout his life but found him exhausting and the prospect of a life of poverty with him terrifying. In December, 1914, she married St. Louis businessman Ernst Filsinger. Filsinger was passionately fond of the arts and a supporter of the twentieth century's new developments in poetry. In the early years of their marriage, he and Teasdale lived in St. Louis and occasionally wrote poetry together.

Teadale's 1915 volume *Rivers to the Sea* found her experimenting with free verse despite her original misgivings about the form. In this volume Teasdale found her poetic voice. *Sonnets to Duse* had been full of girlish enthusiasm, while *Helen of Troy* had consisted largely of dramatic monologues reminiscent of certain nineteenth century verse. *Rivers to the Sea* explored the moods of a love relationship from a woman's point of view and spoke as well of renunciation and of the need for solitude and natural beauty. The book was well received, and its first printing sold out in three months.

Ernst took a job in New York City, in late 1916, and he and Sara moved to the city where she would live for the rest of her life. To spare her the energy-sapping details of housekeeping, they lived in hotels, and she was able to devote herself exclusively to her writing and the promotion of her books. Her 1917 book, *Love Songs*, won the first Columbia University prize for poetry, an award that in 1922 would become the Pulitzer Prize. This volume contains some of her rare poems of fulfilled love; more important, however, the section "Interlude: Songs out of Sorrow" sounds a theme that would recur with increasing frequency in Teasdale's later work: that of using pain and grief as a means of attaining emotional independence from the accidents of life and love. In these poems, she also questions her Baptist upbringing, rejecting the notion of salvation through a personal god. The year 1917 also saw the publication of *The Answering Voice*, Teasdale's anthology of love poems written by women. The title is a clue to the volume's contents, largely poems detailing women's responses to men's love or lack of love. Most of the poets featured in the volume are such traditional favorites as Elizabeth Barrett Browning and Christina Rossetti, and even the more experimental writers sound the traditional women's themes of entrapment and escape.

Teasdale's next book, *Flame and Shadow* (1920), continues the development begun in *Rivers to the Sea* but adds the theme of the failure of love to provide meaning in life. Instead of seeking fulfillment through romantic love, the speaker in these poems banishes passion to the realm of memory and seeks salvation through beauty, conventional religions having failed. Beauty is perceived as the only meaningful thing that will outlast death, here seen as the great enemy of humankind. These poems also show Teasdale continuing to experiment with form, since even the seemingly conventional verses vary rhythms in unexpected ways.

The next five years were difficult ones for Teasdale because they held the deaths of both parents, a brother, and her friend Amy Lowell. The only book Teasdale wrote during this period, *Rainbow Gold* (1922), was an anthology of poetry for children. Teasdale's poor health and the overseas contacts required by her husband's business necessitated frequent separations, often of several months' duration. Despite Ernst's obvious devotion, marriage failed to provide an emotional foundation for Sara's life. Her 1926 publication, *Dark of the Moon*, expresses this darkening mood. Many of her familiar images—the sea, the stars, the wind—recur, but here they are not always positive. In one poem, the sea deceives humans into believing in their own immortality; in another, it erases all evidence of human presence. The speaker's attitude toward death changes in these poems as well; in "The Old Enemy" death is now, "save when he comes too late," a friend. The love poems here are calm and reminiscent, more recollections of past loves than celebrations of love's possibilities. Solitude is more and more accepted as the condition of life. Despite the book's essentially somber tone, its first edition sold out within two weeks.

This deepening solitude was typical of Teasdale's life as well as her work. She had long refused speaking engagements; now she no longer attended meetings of the Poetry Society. The death of long-time friend Marguerite Wilkinson in 1928 deprived her of an important daily contact. In 1929, she traveled to Reno, Nevada, and obtained a divorce; the news reached Filsinger on a business trip to South Africa. The divorce and a new friendship with college student Margaret Conklin, who eventually became her literary executor, brought some brief happiness to Teasdale, but these were not particularly productive years for her. Between 1926 and her death, she published only a revised and enlarged edition of *The Answering Voice* (1928) and a children's book, *Stars Tonight* (1930).

Possibly the most shattering event in Teasdale's life was the suicide of Vachel Lindsay in December, 1931. After a period of adjustment to Teasdale's marriage, the two had remained close friends, and the woman Lindsay married in 1926 had also become friendly with Teasdale. John Hall Wheelock, called by a hysterical Teasdale when she received the news of the suicide, viewed Lindsay's death as the event that inspired Teasdale to take her own life a little more than a year later.

Teasdale's last year found her writing poems again and working on a biography of Christina Rossetti. During a research trip to London, however, she became ill with pneumonia and was forced to return home still ill. Problems with high blood pressure and a broken blood vessel led her to fear that a stroke was imminent, and friends became concerned about her serous depression. On January 29, 1933, Sara Teasdale was found dead of an overdose of sleeping pills. Her last book, *Strange Victory* (1933), was published after her death.

### Summary

Sara Teasdale's work explores the moods and thoughts of a woman who studies her own reactions carefully. Furthermore, her writing explores the dilemma of a traditional woman in a transitional time, a time when formerly conventional notions about women and love have not died but are being found inadequate. Even Teasdale's early, seemingly derivative work contains a questioning of the traditional view of her female heroes; her Helen and Guenevere are not simply the creatures of popular imagination. In addition, Teasdale's best work has the musicality that distinguishes all good lyric poetry; she often claimed that the most important trait of poetry was melody, and she referred to her own works as "songs." This aspect of her work began receiving critical attention in the late 1980's.

Although her once-popular verse has fallen into oblivion among most professional literary critics, Sara Teasdale has continued to speak to a popular audience. Evidence for this is the continued reprinting of her *Collected Poems* and of *Mirror of the Heart*, William Drake's 1984 edition of her work, which included previously unpublished poems. Even feminist anthologies, which originally excluded Teasdale, began including her work in post-1990 editions.

### Bibliography

Carpenter, Margaret Haley. *Sara Teasdale: A Biography*. New York: Schulte, 1960. This early biography is particularly good in its treatment of Teasdale's early life, especially the Potter period. Its extensive use of letters to Teasdale also gives a vivid picture of her relationship with Vachel Lindsay.

Drake, William. *Sara Teasdale: Woman and Poet*. San Francisco: Harper, 1979. This psychologically oriented biography attempts to place Teasdale in the context of the transitional period between Victorianism and modernism. Although its conclusions about her motivations are speculative, this book's attention to Teasdale as a product of her time and its conflicts offers a reading of her character that is less idealized than that of the Carpenter book.

Gould, Jean. *American Women Poets: Pioneers of Modern Poetry*. New York: Dodd Mead, 1980. This collection of biographical reviews of early twentieth century poets gives a sympathetic overview of Teasdale's life and places her in the first rank of lyric poets.

Mannino, Mary Ann. "Sara Teasdale: Fitting Tunes to Everything." *Turn-of-the- Century Women* 5 (1990): 37-41. This brief study of Teasdale's metrics places her in the context of turn-of-the-century experimentation and argues that the formal aspects of her work deserve more attention than they have so far received.

Schoen, Carol B. *Sara Teasdale*. Boston: Twayne, 1986. This chronologically ordered overview is the first book-length study of Teasdale's work. Essentially sympathetic, it focuses on her use of images and on the development of her ideas about love, solitude, beauty, and death, arguing that the critical neglect of Teasdale's work is unjustified.

Walker, Cheryl. *Masks Outrageous and Austere: Culture, Psyche, and Persona in Modern Women Poets*. Bloomington: Indiana University Press, 1991. Feminist in its focus, this study views Teasdale as representative of one reaction to nineteenth century views of women and women's poetry. It holds that her treatment of the conflict between independence and the desire for love is archetypal.

*Rebecca Phillips*

# PIERRE TEILHARD DE CHARDIN

*Born:* May 1, 1881; Sarcenat, France
*Died:* April 10, 1955; New York, New York
*Areas of Achievement:* Theology, philosophy, geology, and anthropology
*Contribution:* Through his work as a geologist on the evolution of the earth and as a paleontologist on the evolution of life, Teilhard, a devout Jesuit priest, came to see human beings progressing toward a new consciousness and spiritual unity called the "Omega Point," which he identified with Jesus Christ.

## Early Life

From the perspective of his mature vision of the universe, Marie-Joseph-Pierre Teilhard de Chardin interpreted his own life in the light of his evolutionary doctrine. He saw as providential his birth in 1881 in a Sarcenat château amid the foothills of the Monts Dore in central France. Teilhard was the fourth child in a family that would eventually number eleven children, and on his mother's side he was distantly related to Voltaire and on his father's side to Blaise Pascal. His mother was a deeply religious Roman Catholic who ignited a spiritual fire in young Teilhard. His father was a gentleman farmer with interests in natural history, and he introduced his children to the delights of rocks, minerals, wildflowers, and animals. Thus, from an early age, Teilhard was able to combine two spheres of life—the material and the spiritual—commonly considered incompatible.

In 1892, a month before his eleventh birthday, Teilhard became a boarder at the Jesuit school of Nôtre-Dame de Mongré at Villefranche-sur-Saône, near Lyons. He was a good student, especially in science and literature, and in his free time he continued his interest in geology by collecting minerals. He eventually concluded that he had a vocation to the Jesuit life. On March 20, 1899, he entered the Jesuit novitiate in Aix-en-Provence, about twenty miles north of Marseilles, to begin a long period of spiritual and intellectual formation.

On March 25, 1901, Teilhard took his first vows of poverty, chastity, and obedience, and then began, at Laval, his studies in the Greek and Latin classics (the juniorate). These studies were interrupted when anticlerical legislation in France forced the Jesuits to transfer their juniorate to Jersey, one of the English Channel islands, in the summer of 1901. As a second-year junior in Jersey, Teilhard seriously considered abandoning the study of geology to devote himself completely to spiritual activities. One of his religious superiors wisely helped him put his spiritual evolution in perspective and guided him in a direction in which he could combine his love of matter, energy, and life (his cosmic sense) with his love of Christ and the supernatural (his Christic sense). From 1902 to 1905, he studied Scholastic philosophy at the Jesuit house on the Isle of Jersey, where he spent his free hours, geologist's hammer in hand, in scientific surveys, resulting in a paper on the island's mineralogy and geology.

In September, 1905, Teilhard was sent to teach chemistry and physics at the Jesuit College of the Holy Family in Cairo, Egypt. Although the science he taught was elementary, this experience of the chemical substances and physical forces of the universe helped him refine his still-crude understanding of the world. After three years as a teacher in Egypt, during which he published works on the Eocene period, he returned to England to complete his Jesuit training. He spent four years, from 1908 to 1912, studying theology at Hastings in southern England. While continuing his geological and paleontological research and writing, he also devoted time to the synthesis of his scientific and spiritual views.

During his theological studies at Hastings, Teilhard began to understand matter from the perspective of spirit, and this forced him to develop a new way of thinking and speaking about what he saw happening in the universe. He began to use the words of science (energy, force, radiation) to describe the previously unseen evolution of spirit that was taking shape in nature. This spiritual energy, already familiar to him in the evolution of his own consciousness, he now grasped as active in the universe, itself in the process of self-creation. Matter, as an evolutionary fact, had given birth to spirit; therefore, matter and spirit are not two separate substances but two aspects of a single evolving cosmos. Physical energy therefore contains something of the spiritual, since energy's upward trend is an observable fact in the increasing complexity of evolving organisms. By the time he was ordained, on August 14, 1911, he had discovered a vision by which he could understand scientific phenomena spiritually and spiritual phenomena scientifically. It therefore became the core of his vocation as a priest to show that evolutionism does not entail a rejection of Christianity, because Christ represented the crucial point in the universe's history at which matter and spirit met.

### Life's Work

Throughout the rest of his career, as priest and scientist, Teilhard devoted himself to the evolution of the universe (what he called cosmogenesis), whose ever-richening spirituality constantly became for him more real and resplendent. For him, salvation no longer meant abandoning the world but building it up. His scientific work therefore became something holy, to be undertaken not for its own sake but for the liberation of more spirit from matter.

After completing his theological studies in 1912, Teilhard went to Paris to study under Marcellin Boule, a professor at the Institute of Human Paleontology in the Natural History Museum. Boule was one of the leading experts on Neanderthal man, but Teilhard's work was mainly in the paleontology of Tertiary mammals in Europe. His scientific studies were interrupted by his tertianship (the final year of his Jesuit formation, a period of intense prayer, meditation, and ascetical training), and then by World War I. Although he could have chosen to be a chaplain, he joined the Eighth Regiment of the Moroccan Tirailleurs as a stretcher-bearer. Teilhard, whose bravery under fire and whose generosity of spirit throughout his military service were honored by medals both during and after the war, did not allow his experiences of the war's horrors to destroy the vision of human history he was constructing. Indeed, he found that his patriotic service on behalf of a great ideal had invigorated his life. Even in the trenches he believed that he was participating in the grand work of sanctifying humanity. In his personal writings during this time, his constant theme was spiritual evolution: When everything of value in the material world has passed into the souls of men, he believed that souls will pass into a new level. In 1917, he began describing this level as the mystic milieu.

After his demobilization, Teilhard returned to his scientific studies. He completed his academic requirements at the Sorbonne and then began work on a thesis about the mammals of the lower Eocene in France. In 1922, he successfully defended his thesis and was awarded his doctorate in paleontology. During the early 1920's, he served as an assistant professor of geology at the Catholic Institute of Paris, but his position there became untenable when he taught that evolution required a revision in the Church's doctrine of original sin. The discoveries of geologists, paleontologists, and paleoanthropologists had convinced Teilhard that no evidence existed for Adam, Eve, or Eden, and consequently the Fall was an event that could not be verified. Before Charles Darwin, Christians could believe that one man's sin (Adam's) had ruined everything and that another man's suffering (Christ's) had saved everything. After Darwin, Teilhard believed that Christians must realize that original sin is not a malady specific to the earth but an inevitable consequence of the limitations of evolving matter and spirit. Because of Teilhard's heterodox views on original sin, his Jesuit superiors asked him to leave the institute and take a research post in Tientsin, China, with Father Émile Licent, a Jesuit pioneer in paleontology. For the next twenty-three years, from 1923 to 1946, Teilhard's career would center on China. He would return to France periodically, but he led what he called a vagabond existence that would continue for the rest of his life.

During his first decade as a peripatetic priest, Teilhard worked mainly in the north of China. He participated in a French paleontological mission to the Ordos and Gobi deserts directed by Father Licent. On a visit to central Mongolia in the summer of 1923, the two priests found the first evidence for paleolithic man in China. After these research expeditions, Teilhard returned to Paris, hoping to continue teaching at the Catholic Institute while making occasional field trips to China, but his superiors continued to be bothered by his evolutionary views of original sin, and he was told to restrict himself to his scientific work (his position at the Catholic Institute was terminated at the end of 1926).

Returning to China in the spring of 1926, Teilhard obeyed the orders of his superiors not to disseminate publicly his theological speculations, and for the rest of his life, he confined himself to publishing his scientific work while privately developing his evolutionary vision (which he shared with friends and fellow Jesuits). During the late 1920's, he began using the term "noosphere" to describe the earth's sphere of thinking substances. The world of matter (the geosphere) had been the source of life (the biosphere), but now the human species was taking conscious control of evolution, and science, technology, and socialization were changing the earth more rapidly than natural selection ever had.

Teilhard's ideas about man's role in the universe found spiritual resonance his manuscript of *Le Milieu divin* (1957; *The Divine Milieu*, 1960), which he wrote in 1926 and 1927 (but which was not published until after his death). In this book, which many scholars see as a spiritual portrait of Teilhard himself, he tried to set down as simply as possible the religious life that he had been living. Through his scientific work, he had become convinced that man was at the spiritual center of the cosmos, and he wanted to show how Christianity was at the center of human history and should be the center of every person's spiritual life.

During this period of intense spiritual probing, Teilhard shifted the base of his operations from Tientsin to Cho-k'ou-tien, about thirty miles southwest of Peking. There, Davidson Black, a Canadian who was a professor of anatomy at the Peking Medical College, was engaged in an organized search for prehistoric man. In the decade from 1927 to 1937, many fossils of animals and man were found in the calcareous deposits of Cho-k'ou-tien. The human fossils were first called *Sinanthropus pekinensis*, then *Pithecanthropus pekinensis*, and now *Homo erectus*. Teilhard helped to date the fossils, to show that Peking man was a toolmaker, and to publicize the importance of the finds. Although he gained wide recognition for his account of the discovery, his principal paleontological work continued to be on non-human fossils—for example, on fossil carnivores.

During the late 1920's and through the 1930's, Teilhard went on several expeditions into northern and central China, made periodic trips to Europe and America, and continued to refine his synthesis of evolution and Christianity. He built up a network of friends and disciples in Paris and at the American Museum of Natural History in New York. In China, he had collaborators of many nationalities, and this contributed to his strongly cosmopolitan and internationalist views. His participation in various research trips to Africa, America, and especially China deepened his understanding of evolution.

In 1938, while he was in Peking, Teilhard began writing *Le Phénomène humain* (1955; *The Phenomenon of Man*, 1959), in which he tried to show how evolutionary data pointed to a Christian interpretation of the world. His approach was phenomenological; that is, he tried to bring out the meaning of phenomena by describing them as precisely as possible. By analyzing the problem of man in terms of evolution, he hoped to bridge the gap between Christians and non-Christians, for he believed that Jesus Christ, as God Incarnate, revealed himself not only in the New Testament but also in the evolution of man. In his book, Teilhard argued that consciousness evolves, and he located the origins of consciousness in preliving as well as living matter. Thresholds, such as the origin of life and of consciousness, are important examples of emergence, where something entirely new enters the universe. Traditional science, according to Teilhard, has not well served these threshold phenomena, and modern science has almost completely ignored what he calls "the within" of the world. This spiritual energy can be studied just as scientists study "the without," matter's external face, in terms of space and time. As the capstone of his evolutionary synthesis, Teilhard believed that, through an increase in knowledge and love, human consciousness can evolve to a new level. Noögenesis, the evolution of mind, is a stage on the way to Christogenesis, the evolution of the universe toward the Omega Point, Teilhard's term for the cosmic Christ.

Teilhard was composing this optimistic vision of the world against a background of world events that would have made pessimism a more natural response. The Japanese occupation of China interfered with his work at Cho-k'ou-tien and his attempt to establish a laboratory for advanced studies in human paleontology in Peking. When World War II began, he was trapped in China, a situation which continued for the war's duration. He abhorred both German Nazism and Japanese Fascism, both of which he interpreted as crudely and unjustifiably transferring the laws of natural selection (the survival of the fittest) from the biological to the human level, whereas, in his vision, mankind was clearly passing to a new level of existence in which a future of love and cooperation was being built. Nevertheless, beneath the human and national tragedies of this war, he believed that something spiritual was evolving. This vision of human evolution found expression in *The Phenomenon of Man*, which he completed in 1940 and sent to Rome in 1941 for approval by his superiors. Since his approach was phenomenological, he hoped that his book would pass the censors, but in 1944 he learned that it had been rejected.

After the war's end, he was able to return to Europe in 1946. He went to Paris, where, during the late 1940's, he was frustrated in his desire to teach at the Collège de France. A visit to Rome to seek permission to publish various works on his evolutionary synthesis was unsuccessful. In 1947, he was appointed director of research in the National Scientific Research Center, which subsidized his scientific work, but he was eager to communicate his evolutionary vision, for he found the existentialism that was spreading throughout France, with its pessimistic ideas of man and matter, dangerously anachronistic in a universe that was evolving toward Christ. On June 1, 1947, he suffered a sudden heart attack, and, though he recovered, his health remained precarious for the remainder of his life. These physical sufferings were followed by psychological ones, for in September his religious superiors forbade him again to write on philosophical or theological issues, thus squelching any hope that *The Phenomenon of Man* or any of his works on anthropogenesis would be published.

Refusing to be discouraged and undertaking no action that could be seen as disobedient, Teilhard nevertheless did everything he could to circulate his ideas privately. He was enthusiastic about the new United Nations, and he worked for some of its organizations that were concerned about the future of the human race. Through contacts made in these labors, for example, with Julian Huxley, he continued to develop his cosmogenetic vision. These efforts were further stimulated by his return to field work in the 1950's. With the financial support of the Viking Fund (soon to become the Wenner Gren Foundation for Anthropological Research), Teilhard made expeditions to various excavation sites in South Africa, where important prehuman fossils, especially the Australopithecines, had been discovered.

During the last period of Teilhard's life, from 1951 to 1955, his center of operations became New York City, where, as a fellow of the Wenner Gren Foundation, he concentrated on anthropogenesis (the evolution of the human species). In the summer of 1954, he made his last trip to France, and, though the visit aroused warm feelings for his native country, he was back in New York by September. He was denied permission by a superior to travel to a meeting at the Sorbonne in April, 1955, but he accepted this without bitterness, resolving to continue fighting to increase love in the world. Teilhard died on Easter Sunday, April 10, 1955.

### Summary

Pierre Teilhard de Chardin did more than any other thinker to help people understand evolution in the context of Christianity. Although he wrote nearly two hundred articles and technical papers in geology and paleontology, mainly on the early Cenozoic period in Europe and the late Cenozoic period in China, his name is most likely to be remembered for his radical view that evolution has a spiritual orientation. For him, the earth, which he so lovingly studied, was profoundly linked to Jesus Christ, since every created thing will find its fulfillment in him. In Teilhard's view, evolution is a purposeful process in which matter and energy progressively evolve in the direction of increasing complexity, consciousness, and spirituality. He so tightly identified Christ and the universe that many critics have interpreted his vision as a Christian pantheism. Although Teilhard often spoke of the universe as God's cosmic body, he also carefully distinguished pantheistic evolution, which destroys personalities in its union with matter, from Christian evolution, which culminates in a union with God that preserves personalities.

In the initial enthusiasm generated by the publication of many of Teilhard's works in the years after his death, some commentators compared the significance of his synthesis of evolutionism and Christianity with Thomas Aquinas' synthesis of Aristotelianism and Christianity. Now that most of Teilhard's writings and letters are in print, it is easier to see him as part of the intellectual development composed of such thinkers as Henri Bergson. These evolutionary philosophers were dissatisfied with the positivism and scientism of the twentieth century and attempted to provide an understanding of man's total experience, of the material as well as the spiritual, of the past and the future, of variety and unity. In this sense, Teilhard has much to teach both scientists and theologians. For scientists, his mystical temperament and loving grasp of positive values have given the world an interpretation of the universe that encourages love, progress, and unity. For theologians, his evolutionary view has necessitated a transposition of Christian revelation into a new key, where religion can profit from scientific insights.

Despite criticisms of his work, many of them justified, Teilhard did offer an alternative to the materialist vision of mankind as an accidental phenomenon, a random collection of molecules on an unimportant planet. In his view, mankind represented the culmination of the complex evolution of matter and life. It is doubtful that in the future Teilhard's evolutionary synthesis of Christianity and evolution will be completely accepted by Christians or by scientists, but as a product of a luminous mind and a loving heart, his conception of the universe as a unity in which all things work together for a final consummation in Christ has already found numerous followers, because this vision, which allows people to remain true to themselves while building union with God, reveals the deeply spiritual values in the innermost heart of mankind and the universe.

**Bibliography**


Browning, Geraldine O., Joseph L. Alioto, and Seymour M. Farber, eds. *Teilhard de Chardin: In Quest of the Perfection of Man*. Rutherford, N.J.: Farleigh Dickinson University Press, 1973. This book is the result of an international symposium held in San Francisco's Palace of Fine Arts in May of 1971. An international group of scholars analyzed the life and work of Teilhard from several perspectives—religious, scientific, psychological, and educational. This volume also contains a biographical sketch of Teilhard and a brief analysis of his philosophical beliefs.

Cuénot, Claude. *Teilhard de Chardin: A Biographical Study.* Edited by René Hague. Translated by Vincent Colimore. London: Burns and Oates, and Baltimore: Helicon Press, 1965. Cuénot, who was a close friend of Teilhard, has carefully documented his many travels. The evolution of Teilhard's ideas, in Cuénot's view, becomes clearer when seen against the background of his life as a Jesuit and a scientist. Contains an annotated bibliography.

Grenet, Paul. *Teilhard de Chardin: The Man and His Theories*. Translated by R. A. Rudorff. London: Souvenir Press, 1965; New York: Eriksson, 1966. Contains sections on Teilhard's life, personality, and scientific career, as well as on his philosophical and theological thought. A final section of selected writings from Teilhard is followed by a brief bibliography and an index. Scholars already familiar with Teilhard's ideas will find little new here, but Grenet's book is a good primer for novices.

Heller, Michael. "Teilhard's Vision of the World and Modern Cosmology." *Zygon* 30 no. 1, (March, 1995). Heller discusses how elements of modern physics affect Teilhard's theories.

Lubac, Henri de. *Teilhard de Chardin: The Man and His Meaning*. Translated by René Hague. London: Hawthorn, and New York: New American Library, 1965. One of the most enlightening studies of Teilhard's ideas. Lubac is a fellow Jesuit who bases his analysis on personal knowledge of Teilhard as well as on his mastery of the published and unpublished material by and about him. He presents both a spiritual portrait, in which he elucidates the interior life that animated Teilhard's work, and a modern apologetic, in which he shows how Teilhard tried to reinterpret Christianity for twentieth century man. Contains a bibliography, footnotes, and an index.

McDermott, Peter L. "Pierre Teilhard de Chardin: Being, Critical Thresholds, and Evolutionary Thought." *Perspectives in Biology and Medicine* 40 no. 4, (Summer 1997). The author reviews the work of Teilhard.

Mooney, Christopher F. *Teilhard de Chardin and the Mystery of Christ*. London: Collins, and New York: Harper, 1966. Mooney's basic theme is that what unifies the many facets of Teilhard's thought is the relationship between the evolving cosmos and the mystery of Christ. A Jesuit himself, Mooney is able to explicate with sensitivity and understanding the theological implications of Teilhard's ideas. Contains an extensive bibliography and a detailed index.

Speaight, Robert. *The Life of Teilhard de Chardin*. New York: Harper, 1967. Speaight, a British Catholic writer, presents a straightforward chronological account of Teilhard's life. He intended his work not to compete with Cuénot's definitive biography, but to make Teilhard's thought accessible and comprehensible to a wide readership. Contains a glossary, bibliography, and index.


*Robert J. Paradowski*

# EDWARD TELLER

*Born:* January 15, 1908; Budapest, Hungary

*Areas of Achievement:* Nuclear physics and public policy

*Contribution:* Teller helped to establish the theoretical groundwork for the production of the first atom bomb; he was also instrumental in the development of the hydrogen bomb in the United States. In the public policy arena, Teller promoted the peaceful uses of nuclear energy and urged the United States to develop new technologies to assure a strong defense.

## Early Life

Edward Teller, born in Hungary in 1908, was the second child of Max and Ilona Teller. His mother, née Ilona Deutsch, was an accomplished pianist and was fluent in Hungarian, German, French, Spanish, and Italian. Max Teller had a successful law practice in Budapest. As prosperous assimilationist Jews, Edward's parents emphasized the value of education. Edward and his sister, Emmi, were taught English by a governess; against a background of political upheaval in Hungary, Edward completed four years of training at the private Mellinger School and eight at the Minta gymnasium, or high school, both in Budapest. Edward's first year at the Minta was in 1918; it was the end of World War I and the beginning of the rise of Russian Bolshevism. A year later, the government of Hungary was in the hands of Béla Kun, a hard-line Communist and an inept leader. There was a reign of terror, and the Teller family was touched by food shortages and fears of violence. Kun was a Jew, and Max Teller sensed a growing resentment in his country of all Hungarian Jews; yet at the same time there was intellectual ferment in Hungary. Budapest, in the postwar years, produced Eugene Wigner, Nobel Prize-winning physicist; Leo Szilard, one of the pioneers of nuclear physics; and John von Neumann, one of the greatest mathematical minds of the century. Each, including Teller, would eventually emigrate to the United States.

Teller showed an exceptional mathematical ability, but his father insisted that his son study something practical. In 1926, just before his eighteenth birthday, Teller enrolled in the Karlsruhe Institute of Technology in Germany to study chemical engineering, which satisfied his father, and to take mathematics on the side.

Within two years, Teller was captivated by the field of quantum mechanics—a new way of theorizing about the inner workings of atoms—and continued his studies in 1928 at the University of Munich, not as a chemical engineer, but as a physicist. It was in that same year that Teller lost his entire right foot in a streetcar accident. He soon learned to walk with an artificial foot, but in later years his portly five-foot, nine-inch frame, great beetled brows, large ears, Hungarian accent, and uneven gait were the easy target of caricature. Teller could seem kindly but could as easily turn self-righteous and intimidating. Already, at the age of twenty, the gregarious Teller was developing a sense of self-assurance, of inner direction, that was counted by some as arrogance.

After the accident, Teller continued his doctoral studies at the University of Leipzig, studying under Werner Heisenberg, already famous for his "uncertainty principle" of quantum mechanics. Teller left the university in 1930 with a Ph.D. degree in theoretical physics; he stayed in Germany, working as a

research consultant at the University of Göttingen until Adolf Hitler came to power in 1933. Teller realized that he had no hope of continuing his academic career in Germany, so, in 1934, with his theoretical work in physics already highly regarded, he began a year's stay at the University of Copenhagen under a Rockefeller Foundation fellowship. This was a pivotal time in Teller's life. He studied with Niels Bohr and became part of a group of theoretical physicists who were looking at the atom with new eyes. Bohr had revolutionized physics with the "complementarity principle," which described the atomic structure as exhibiting both wave and particle characteristics; further, it stated that the two views of atomic structure, though seemingly mutually exclusive, were both correct.

In Copenhagen, Teller met the Russian expatriate George Gamow, who, two years later, invited Teller to George Washington University in Washington, D.C., as a professor of physics. Also in 1934, Teller married his childhood friend, Augusta Maria (Mici) Harkanyi, in a civil ceremony on February 26.

## Life's Work

Gamow is credited with encouraging Teller to focus on nuclear physics. In collaboration, they developed rules describing how certain subatomic particles could escape the atomic nucleus during radioactive decay. Both hosted a conference in January of 1939 that considered the possibility that an atomic nucleus, bombarded with subatomic particles, might actually split, releasing heat energy. Word had come from Berlin, via visiting lecturer Niels Bohr, that uranium had been bombarded with neutrons and that, chemically, part of the uranium had become barium, a lighter element. The uranium nucleus had been split, and a kind of alchemist's dream had been realized.

In March of that year, Teller was interrupted at home, in the midst of playing a Mozart sonata, by an urgent telephone call from Leo Szilard. Szilard had answered a question posed at the January conference: If neutrons could split atomic nuclei, would those atomic nuclei in turn emit neutrons? The answer was yes, and Teller remembered this answer as an ominous turning point of atomic physics. A chain reaction, with the release of immense amounts of explosive force, just might be possible.

President Franklin D. Roosevelt, in a speech to the Eighth Pan-American Scientific Conference in May, 1940, galvanized Teller into pouring his energies into the development of nuclear weapons. In the light of the recent Nazi invasions of the Low Countries, Roosevelt called on scientists to do what they could to preserve American freedom and civilization. Some months earlier, Roosevelt had established an advisory committee on uranium in response to a letter signed by Albert Einstein, detailing fears that Germany was making progress in developing nuclear technology. The letter urged the president to stimulate and coordinate the American research program. Teller himself worked closely with Enrico Fermi, first at Columbia University, then at the University of Chicago, to construct the first nuclear reactor, a demonstration of a controlled but sustained nuclear chain reaction.

The so-called Manhattan Project, conceived in 1942, served to bring the diverse research programs in nuclear fission (the splitting of the atomic nucleus) under control of the United States Army. In 1941, Teller and his wife had become American citizens; the next year, Teller joined with J. Robert Oppenheimer at the University of California at Berkeley, and, a year later, at Los Alamos Laboratory in New Mexico, to pursue theoretical studies and ultimately to deliver a working atom bomb. Teller was charged with proving that an atomic explosion would not destroy the earth in an uncontrollable chain reaction, setting the oceans on fire and consuming the world.

Yet according to Hans Bethe, who was in charge of the theoretical division at Los Alamos, Teller rankled at what he regarded as excessive secrecy and the lack of the long and open discussions to which he had been accustomed. Teller was more interested in what he called the "superbomb," a device that would mimic the sun in employing the fusion of atomic nuclei to create vast new energy. Such fusion could only be triggered by a fission explosion. Yet Teller's was a lonely voice; the push was on for a workable atom bomb, and Teller's interests were shunted aside. Then, on July 16, 1945, the world's first nuclear bomb was detonated, on top of a hundred-foot steel tower at Alamogordo, New Mexico. The force was equivalent to around twenty kilotons of TNT.

Though the war with Germany had ended, the newly produced atomic weapons were used against Hiroshima and Nagasaki. Teller had favored a demonstration, an explosion high over Tokyo with no casualties, to force the Japanese to surrender. Oppenheimer vetoed the idea, convincing Teller that scientists had no business making public policy. At the same time, Oppenheimer himself was pressing for the military use of the atomic devices.

With the end of World War II, Teller continued to lobby for the development of the fusion, or hydrogen, bomb, but there seemed little momentum at Los Alamos for more weapons work. Teller returned to teach at the University of Chicago, but when the Soviet Union exploded its first atom bomb in 1949, President Harry S Truman launched a formal drive to fashion an American fusion bomb—and Teller was ready.

He had returned to an assistant directorship at Los Alamos and proceeded with theoretical work on the superbomb. It appears that earlier calculations made by Teller relating to the fusion bomb had led to technical dead ends, but an idea by colleague Stanislaw Ulam, a mathematician, enabled Teller to overcome a major obstacle in the development of a trigger for the bomb's thermonuclear fuel. A hydrogen bomb was successfully tested at Eniwetok atoll in the Pacific, in 1952. Yet Teller, with his eye on the Soviet Union, was impatient with the pace of research at Los Alamos. He lobbied for a comparable laboratory under his guidance, which would pursue research in thermonuclear weapons to provide for a secure United States. In 1952, the Atomic Energy Commission established the Lawrence Livermore Laboratory in Livermore, California. In later years, Teller divided his time between work at Livermore and as a senior research fellow at the Hoover Institution on War, Revolution and Peace, at Stanford University in California.

In 1954, Teller found himself isolated from most of his other research colleagues after he testified against J. Robert Oppenheimer. Oppenheimer had been accused of disloyalty and of delaying the development of the hydrogen bomb. Though, in Teller's opinion, Oppenheimer was a loyal American, the former director of Los Alamos was a complicated man—and Teller said that he would prefer to see United States interests "in hands which I understand better and therefore trust more." After Teller's testimony, Oppenheimer was denied a security clearance. There was little rebuttal, since most of the reasons Oppenheimer might have cited for delay were still classified. Many of Teller's closest friendships were sundered over this seeming disloyalty to Oppenheimer.

In the 1950's Teller became the public advocate of a strong national defense and of the rational use of atomic power. He helped develop safety standards for nuclear reactors and championed the ill-fated Project Plowshare in the 1960's. One Plowshare proposal, for example, recommended that atomic bombs be used to dig a second "Suez canal" through the state of Israel. Ever an advocate for the continued development of technology, in the 1960's Teller argued against the proposed Comprehensive Test Ban Treaty with the Soviet Union, on the grounds that stopping atmospheric tests of nuclear weapons would cripple the United States' weapons program. Nevertheless, the Senate ratified the treaty in 1963.

With the election of Ronald Reagan to the American presidency in 1980, Teller found an ear for the idea of deterrence based not on retaliatory firepower (the Mutual Assured Destruction doctrine) but rather on more technologically sophisticated defensive mechanisms (the so-called Mutual Assured Survival doctrine). Teller endorsed President Reagan's 1983 speech advocating space-based lasers to form a protective shield above the United States, able to intercept incoming Soviet nuclear missiles.

Teller received the Enrico Fermi Award in 1962 for his contributions to national defense and thermonuclear research. Two children were born to the Tellers, Paul and Susan Wendy.

### Summary

Teller's optimistic vision of technology harnessed for the world's benefit is reflective of a strong current in American life, that American expertise can triumph over almost any problem. In the postwar years, Teller soon recognized that scientific progress in the United States was largely a product of public policy. In the late 1950's, he met then New York Governor Nelson Rockefeller and, through Rockefeller, began to take an active interest in national energy policies. For Teller, Rockefeller was an attractive model of a liberal Republican. Both men called for international control of nuclear energy; both were deeply suspicious of the closed Soviet society; and both called for a militarily strong United States and an emphasis on civil defense. Through books and lectures, Teller continued to press for an abandonment of what he saw as American guilt over Hiroshima and for the fashioning of defense and energy policies that would see the United States well into the twenty-first century.

Teller's scientific accomplishments include research into the functioning of molecules, development of insights into quantum mechanics, and a creative solution to the problem of the hydrogen-bomb trigger. Teller worked best when taking on cosmic theoretical questions; when he was convinced that his theories were accurate, he was content to let others do the detail work. He thrived on open discussion and, throughout his life, continued to call for the sharing of scientific findings.

Teller added several pieces to the puzzle of atomic fission and fusion; working with others (though sometimes reluctant to "go along with the crowd"), he fashioned weapons that would forever change the course of human history; he became an unreconstructed optimist about the technological future; and he worked in the public-policy arena to realize his vision of a strong America, strong enough to frighten away all predators.

### Bibliography

Anzovin, Steven, ed. *The Star Wars Debate*. New York: Wilson, 1986. Though Teller is mentioned only in passing, this volume brings together relevant speeches and article excerpts dealing with the Strategic Defense Initiative (Star Wars) enunciated by President Reagan in 1983 and supported by Teller.

Blumberg, Stanley A., and Gwinn Owens. *Energy and Conflict: The Life and Times of Edward Teller*. New York: Putnam, 1976. The standard biography of Teller, written by a science writer and a broadcast correspondent. It is based on extensive interviews with Teller and other atomic scientists, but its authors lacked access to classified information dealing with Teller's weapons-related activities and the Oppenheimer affair. Useful but dated.

Goodchild, Peter. *J. Robert Oppenheimer: Shatterer of Worlds*. London: BBC, 1980; Boston: Houghton Mifflin, 1981. This book is a companion to the British Broadcasting Corporation television series *Oppenheimer*, which was shown on public television in the United States. Based on extensive interviews and Federal Bureau of Investigation files on Oppenheimer, this volume humanizes Oppenheimer and is rather unfriendly to Teller. There are many photographs to illustrate Oppenheimer's career and extensive excerpts from the security hearings.

Holmes, Linda Goetz. "Dr. Teller Changes His Mind." *World Press Review* 42 no. 8, (August, 1995). Reprint of an article in the March 23, 1995 issue of *The Australian* wherein Teller is reported to have changed his opinion with respect to the use of the atomic bomb in Japan, believing now that its use saved the lives of prisoners of war.

Teller, Edward. *Energy from Heaven and Earth*. San Francisco: Freeman, 1979. Based on lectures delivered by Teller in Israel, the United States, and Nova Scotia in 1975. The chapters deal with petroleum, coal, fusion, and solar energies, in a lay guide to the value and quantity and prospect of energy sources for the future. Valuable chapter of Teller's reminiscences about his work at Los Alamos in the development of the atom bomb.

———. *The Pursuit of Simplicity*. Malibu, Calif.: Pepperdine University Press, 1981. Based on lectures given in 1978-1979, in which Teller rhapsodizes about the promise of technology in solving energy shortage problems and in freeing human beings to do more creative work. Teller repeats his call for openness in science, for a strong defense, and delivers a number of interesting anecdotes about his scientific colleagues.

Teller, Edward, with Allen Brown. *The Legacy of Hiroshima*. London: Macmillan, and New York: Doubleday, 1962. An extended account of Teller's work on the atom bomb; includes his prescriptions for being an optimist in the nuclear age. Teller maintains that proper civil defense procedures can ensure the survival of the United States in a limited nuclear war. He also calls for the establishment of a world government to guarantee freedom for the people of the world.

Wyden, Peter. *Day One: Before Hiroshima and After*. New York: Simon and Schuster, 1984. A dramatic account of the development of the first atom bomb, with an emphasis on the politics involved in the decision to use the weapons against Japan. There are extensive interviews with survivors of the Hiroshima bombing. Wyden is obviously critical of many of the weapons scientists but provides a dramatic and fairly accurate story, though the picture of Teller might be interpreted more as caricature than careful rendition.

York, Herbert F. *The Advisors: Oppenheimer, Teller and the Superbomb*. San Francisco: Freeman, 1976. York was the first director of the newly established Lawrence Livermore Laboratory and worked on the development of the hydrogen bomb. He believes that Teller was wrong in his insistence on building the fusion device and that Oppenheimer was correct in that the hydrogen bomb led to a dramatic and dangerous increase in the arms race with the Soviet Union. An insider's view, somewhat dated, at odds with Teller's recommendations.

*Dan Barnett*

# MOTHER TERESA
## Agnes Gonxha Bojaxhiu

*Born:* August 26, 1910; Shkup, Albania, Ottoman Empire (now Skopje, Macedonia)
*Died:* September 5, 1997; Calcutta, India
*Areas of Achievement:* Religion and social reform
*Contribution:* Mother Teresa spent most of her life caring for the "poorest of the poor." Her Missionaries of Charity have expanded their scope from the humblest beginnings on the streets of Calcutta to locations on every continent, including in the United States, New York's South Bronx. By 1987, the International Association of Co-Workers of Mother Teresa, formally established eighteen years before, numbered more than three million people. Mother Teresa was awarded the Nobel Prize in 1979.

### Early Life

The third child and second daughter of Nicholas and Rosa Bojaxhiu, wealthy parents of Albanian peasant stock, was christened Agnes Gonxha Bojaxhiu on August 26, 1910. In a town in what is now southern Yugoslavia, the Albanians were a minority, but the area, a historical meetingplace of East and West, was one that successfully blended many cultures. The Muslim influence was strong, as was that of the Eastern Orthodox church. Agnes' parents were devout Roman Catholics and saw to it that the children were given a strong background in that faith. The family prayed together each night. Rosa was particularly devout. It was she who prepared all three children, who attended the public school, to receive the sacrament of First Holy Communion. Nicholas Bojaxhiu was a well-educated man who owned a construction business. Agnes' parents were devoted to each other. Mother Teresa was later to recall that she and her brother and sister often teased their mother about her feelings for their father. Sadly, Nicholas died at age forty-two, a tragic blow to the family, who, in addition to the emotional loss, experienced a loss of income that drastically changed their circumstances but that brought them even closer.

As a young child, Agnes has been described as joyful and playful. Her childhood home was for the most part a happy one. She was educated in Croatian at the state high school and was a soprano soloist in the parish choir. At a very early age, Agnes felt the call of a religious vocation. She was twelve years old when she began seriously to meditate on her decision. Through her membership in the Sodality of Our Lady, she became aware of the missionary work being done in India by a group of Jesuit priests. After six years of soul-searching, she finally made her decision at eighteen while praying at the sanctuary of Our Lady of Letnice. She wanted to work with the Loretto Sisters in India.

Her mother was at first against Agnes' decision to enter the religious life but eventually gave her daughter her blessing with the admonition to remember to be true to God and Christ. Agnes applied to be admitted to the Loretto Order and left home on September 26, 1928, for Rathfarnam, Ireland, to learn English in preparation for her assignment to India. She spent six weeks as a postulant of the Institute of the Blessed Virgin Mary. Agnes took the name Teresa, for the "little Teresa," St. Teresa of Lisieux, who had led a painful and brief but pious life in France in the late nineteenth century. Sister Teresa arrived in India in January, 1929, and was sent to a novitiate in Darjeeling. She took her vows two years later and spent the next twenty years teaching geography to the daughters of middle-class Indians at St. Mary's High School, where she also became the principal.

### Life's Work

It was on a train to Darjeeling on September 10, 1946, that Sister Teresa received her second call from God. She called it a "call within a call," and it asked her to serve only the poorest of God's creatures, the destitute, the dying, the lonely, for the rest of her life. She accepted this summons without question, applying immediately for freedom from the Loretto Sisters to pursue her new duties. This was very difficult for her, as the convent and school had long been her home. She also loved teaching and was well loved by her students. With some difficulty, Teresa received permission to leave the order and work as a free nun in late 1948. She walked from the convent with only the clothes she wore. Her only real preparation was an elementary course in medicine with the American Medical Missionary sisters in Patna, India.

On December 21, 1948, Sister Teresa opened her first slum school in Moti Jheel in Calcutta. There, with absolutely no financial backing or supplies,

she began to teach poor Bengali children to read and write. She wrote with a stick in the dust and begged a place to stay among another order of sisters. The following March, Subhasini Das, a nineteen-year-old former student from St. Mary's joined Sister Teresa, taking the name Sister Agnes. Slowly Sister Teresa's group grew, living in the home of a wealthy Indian citizen, begging for food, and giving love and rudimentary medical care to Calcutta's sick and dying poor.

The Missionaries of Charity, with a membership of twelve, was approved and formally instituted by the Archdiocese of Calcutta on October 7, 1950. Sister Teresa became Mother Teresa. She and her novices took vows of poverty, chastity, obedience, charity, and an additional, special vow to serve the truly destitute. This vow proscribes any member of the order from working for the rich or from accepting money for services. All material resources are donated. Mother Teresa insisted on only four preconditions to becoming a sister in her order. Applicants must be healthy of mind and body, be able to learn, have plenty of common sense, and have a cheerful disposition. A novice can be no younger than seventeen. Once accepted into the order, a woman spends six months as an aspirant, six months as a postulant, two years as a novice, and six years under temporary vows. One year before temporary vows expire, the sister is sent back to the novitiate for an additional year of contemplation before taking her final, lifelong vows.

On March 25, 1963, the Archbishop of Calcutta formally blessed the new order of the Missionary Brothers of Charity. Six years and one day later, the International Association of Co-Workers of Mother Teresa, a secular group of volunteers active since 1954, received the blessing of Pope Paul VI. The Co-Workers were started by a wealthy Englishwoman named Ann Blaikie, who had begun helping Mother Teresa by gathering donated goods for Mother Teresa's poor. By 1987, the Co-Workers included a staggering three million people in seventy countries.

The Missionaries of Charity is the only religious order of its time that is actually growing in membership. By 1987, the group numbered three thousand sisters and four hundred brothers. These selfless people have treated tens of thousands of destitute sick and given the hopelessly dying the opportunity to die with dignity. In 1952, the Nirmal Hriday ("Place of the Pure Heart") Home for Dying Destitutes was opened at 1 Magazine Road in what was formerly a Kali temple, donated by the city of Calcutta. Nirmal Hriday is a last refuge for the dying. In 1957, the missionaries began treating India's large population of contagious lepers, first establishing a colony for lepers in West Bengal. As the order grew, they were also able to open an orphanage for abandoned children. Most of the children are adopted out to homes in Europe. In 1959, the first house of the Missionaries of Charity outside Calcutta was opened in Delhi. Since then, twenty-two other cities in India have become recipients of Mother Teresa's special brand of aid.

The decision to open houses outside India was a difficult one for Mother Teresa, who had become an Indian citizen in 1948. The first foreign country to welcome her help was Venezuela. Soon after, a house was established in Rome. Ceylon, Tanzania, and Australia followed. Perhaps most surprisingly, the missionaries found it necessary to establish the Queen of Peace Home in an area popularly known as Fort Apache in the South Bronx of New York. According to Mother Teresa, the spiritual poverty in the United States is greater than anywhere else on earth. Later the sisters expanded their efforts to Harlem. On December 24, 1985, a few short months after Mayor Ed Koch gave her his wholehearted permission, Mother Teresa opened a hospice for victims of acquired immune deficiency syndrome (AIDS) in Greenwich Village called Gift of Love. By 1987, the houses of the Missionaries of Charity numbered twenty-one in the United States alone. Other modern cities have not been forgotten. Houses of the Missionaries of Charity can be found in both London and Amman, Jordan. In Dacca, India, a home was opened to care for women from Bangladesh who had been raped by Pakistani soldiers.

All the houses follow the same rigid schedule. The sisters or brothers rise at 4:40 A.M. and have prayers from 5:00 until 6:00, when Mass is celebrated. At 6:45, the religious inmates are fed a light breakfast of unleavened bread and banana. The sisters are true to their vow of poverty. Each sister owns only two or three cotton saris, underclothes, bedding, a tin bucket (for laundry), prayer books, a pen, a pencil, and paper.

Mother Teresa was the recipient of many humanitarian prizes and honors. She was awarded the Pope John XXIII Peace Prize and the Joseph Kennedy, Jr., Foundation Award in 1971 and the Nobel Peace Prize in 1979. She also received awards from her own government, notably the Jawaharlal Nehru Award in 1969 for International Understanding and the Shiromani Award, which was presented to her personally by Indian President Giani Zail Singh. In April, 1990, Mother Teresa stepped down from the leadership of her order because of severe illness. In 1997, three months before her death, Mother Teresa received from the United States the Congressional Gold Medal.

## Summary

Attempts to write Mother Teresa's personal biography have been thwarted or replaced by the story of the Missionaries of Charity and their works. What her workers, sisters and brothers alike, give to the poor is much more than medical care. They give unconditional love to those who are shunned by the rest of the world. Mother taught that one may find Jesus in all persons, but he is especially present in the poor and grotesque. Recipients of the missionaries' aid are not proselytized, nor are they limited to the Catholic population. Unlike most missionaries, the Missionaries of Charity do not preach religion but teach by example.

Mother Teresa was an extremely practical woman with one goal in life: to serve the poor. While in charge of her order, she fed her sisters well, on the advice of the medical sisters who gave her her early training, so that they could resist contagion as they dress the sores of lepers or treat other sick people. Perhaps the most impressive phenomenon associated with Mother Teresa is the small social revolution that she instigated in her adopted homeland. In India, girls of very old and well-to-do castes are becoming sisters to give succor to the so-called Untouchables. They have said that they were first brought to the order by a desire to work beside Mother Teresa.

## Bibliography

Doig, Desmond, *Mother Teresa: Her People and Her Work.* London: Collins, and New York: Harper, 1976. Mother Teresa insisted that this book, originally intended to be a biography, be written instead about the Missionaries of Charity. The book does contain a useful chronological table of events relative to Mother Teresa. Illustrated with both color and black-and-white photographs.

Kwilecki, Susan, and Loretta S. Wilson. "Was Mother Teresa Maximizing her Utility? An Idiographic Application of Rational Choice Theory." *The Journal of the Scientific Study of Religion* 37 no. 2, (June, 1998). Innovative study on the work of Mother Teresa by authors with specialties in religion and economics. The authors use rational choice theory as a basis for their analysis and evaluate Mother Teresa as a "consumer of religious commodities" and as the proprietor of a religious business designed to maximize profit.

Le Joly, Edward. *Mother Teresa of Calcutta.* San Francisco: Harper, 1985. Written by a priest and close colleague of Mother Teresa, this book does not offer as much biographical information as its title promises. It does give detailed information on the Missionaries of Charity, along with much religious editorializing. Illustrated with black-and-white photographs.

Poplin, Mary. "No Humanitarian: A Portrait of Mother Teresa." *Commonweal* 124 no 22, (December 19, 1997). The author looks at the life and work of Mother Teresa based on personal observation while working with the Missionaries of Charity in Calcutta.

Rae, Daphne. *Love Until It Hurts.* New York: Harper, 1980; London: Hodder and Stoughton, 1981. This is primarily a pictorial tribute to the Missionaries of Charity. The book is aptly named; readers may find some photographs disturbing.

Teresa, Mother. *My Life for the Poor: Mother Teresa of Calcutta.* Edited by José Luis Gonzalez-Balado and Janet N. Playfoot. San Francisco: Harper, 1985. Mother Teresa's personality comes through in this book, because it is written in the words of Mother herself. She is shown to be a highly practical person with infinite faith in God. Readers will find her concise speech refreshing.

Tower, Courtney. "Mother Teresa's Work of Grace." *Reader's Digest* 131 (December, 1987): 163-75. Packed with information on Mother Teresa's work in India and around the world. Gives a clear picture of the organizational structure of the Missionaries of Charity. Pleasurable reading for a general audience.

*Joyce M. Parks*

## VALENTINA TERESHKOVA

*Born:* March 6, 1937; Maslennikovo, Yaroslavl region, Russia, U.S.S.R.

*Areas of Achievement:* Aviation, space exploration, government, and politics

*Contribution:* On June 16, 1963, Tereshkova became the first woman in space. During her 71-hour flight, she achieved an altitude of over 143.2 miles and traveled a distance of 1,222,020 miles. Upon her return to the Soviet Union, she became a national heroine who traveled the world extolling the virtues of the communist system.

### Early Life

Valentina Vladimirovna Nikolayeva Tereshkova was born on a collective farm about 200 miles from Moscow. Her father, a former tractor driver on a commune, died on the front during World War II when Tereshkova was just six years old. Her mother and older sisters worked in the Krasnui Perekop (Red Canal) textile factory during Tereshkova's school years. At seventeen, Tereshkova began working at the Yaroslavl tire factory while continuing her studies for Young Communist Workers. In 1955, she joined her mother and sisters as a spindler in the textile factory. At the same time, she completed studies during evening classes at the polytechnic institute in Yaroslavl. By 1961, Tereshkova had become a cotton-spinning technologist. She also headed the Textile Mill Workers' Parachute Club and had 126 jumps to her credit. She joined the Communist Party and became secretary of the local Komosol (Young Communist League).

In world politics, the Cold War began to intensify. On April 12, 1961, Yuri Gagarin successfully orbited the earth. U.S. astronaut Alan Shepard's suborbital flight followed on May 5. Gherman Titov flew aboard Vostok 2 on August 6, 1961, and was the first to experience space sickness. On August 11 and 12, 1962, Soviet premier Nikita Khrushchev arranged for two spacecraft to launch within 24 hours of each other for the world's first group flight. Vostok 3 contained Andrian G. Nikolayev, while Vostok 4 held Pavel R. Popovich. Though the two craft flew within 4 miles of each other, the craft could not maneuver without expending a great deal of fuel, so an actual rendezvous was not possible. Neither cosmonaut experienced space sickness during his three- to four-day journey, and Soviets began to feel better about the safety of longer flights. Space sickness apparently depended more upon the individual than upon the length of flight.

Following Gagarin's successful flight of Vostok 2, many women wrote to Moscow asking about spaceflight training. Air force majors Vera Sokolova and Marina Popovicha were rejected. Sokolova was a flight surgeon with many hours of flying experience. Popovicha, the wife of cosmonaut Pavel Popovich, was a qualified jet test pilot with an engineering degree. Khrushchev, however, decided that the woman selected to fly into space would not be an elite, highly trained specialist but rather an ordinary factory worker. He wanted to demonstrate that any woman could fly into space under socialism.

### Life's Work

In November, 1961, five selected trainees—Tatiana Kuznetsova, Valentina Ponamareva, Irena Solovyeva, Zhanna Yorkina, and Valentina Tereshkova—secretly reported to training camp. They trained as copilots and later progressed to piloting jets. The women received physical training, classroom lectures, and further jet flight orientation. They practiced parachute jumps because the Vostok spacecraft design required the pilot to bail out just before it made a hard-earth landing as opposed to the soft-water landing U.S. spacecraft made. Following their preflight training courses in jet aerobatics in a two-seater MIG trainer, the women received commissions as second lieutenants in the Soviet air force.

Andrian Nikolayev, pilot of Vostok 3, became a flight cadet in 1951. He was the only bachelor among the cosmonauts. The women were all single. Nikolayev was assigned as their training coach. Some reports claim that Tereshkova was chosen from the other candidates because of her subsequent engagement to Nikolayev. Other journalists wondered how much of a part Khrushchev played in matching the pair.

Tereshkova's flight, Vostok 6, which launched at 12:30 P.M. (Moscow time) on June 16, 1963, followed Valeri Bykovsky's Vostok 5 launch by 45 hours and 30 minutes. Both spacecraft were launched from the Baikonour space center in the central Asian republic of Kazakhstan. Tereshkova's radio call name was Chaika ("seagull"), while Bykovsky's was Yastreb ("hawk"). Both frequently

sent greetings to other nations while in orbit and appeared on Moscow television. Water from each cosmonaut's home area had been chemically treated to kill bacteria and was installed in each spacecraft. When the cosmonauts were thirsty, they pushed a button and water entered a mouthpiece through a rubber tube. For washing, they used pieces of cheesecloth soaked with a soap-and-water mix. Both were on a schedule of four meals per day. Meat, caviar sandwiches, and fruit were cut into small pieces to make eating easier. Vitamins were added to the rations to help normalize metabolism in the weightless state.

*Aviation Week and Space Technology* reported in their July, 1963, issue that perhaps the objective of Vostok 5 and 6 had been to make visual, optical, radio, and radar observations of their vehicles upon crossing courses. This exercise would give future cosmonauts an opportunity for inspection or even neutralization, if necessary, of a target vehicle. The Soviets agreed it was a wonderful space feat, but the flight mostly celebrated the fact that a woman had entered the space arena and that it had been the Soviet Union that had achieved it.

On the second day of Tereshkova's flight, Bykovsky became alarmed when he failed to rouse his travel companion. Tereshkova finally responded that she had overslept, and she reported promptly thereafter. Once again, both spacecraft flew within 3 miles of each other, but a true rendezvous was still not possible. Tereshkova was permitted to take manual control of her spacecraft for one orbit. She found it fascinating that such an intricate and complex machine responded so easily to her commands. After three days and forty-nine orbits, Tereshkova landed at 11:20 A.M. 386 miles northeast of Karaganda, a coal-mining and industrial city in Kazakhstan. Bykovsky completed eighty-one orbits and landed about 360 miles northwest of Karaganda.

Following their successful landing, Tereshkova and Bykovsky were warmly greeted by Premier Khrushchev at Moscow's airport. In his welcoming speech, Khrushchev compared Tereshkova's courage to that of Marina Raskova, the World War II heroine now buried in the Kremlin wall. Despite rumors of disorientation and space sickness, Tereshkova became an instant celebrity and began touring different countries extolling the virtues of her country and its values.

In October, 1963, it was announced that Tereshkova and Andrian G. Nikolayev were engaged to be married. On November 4, 1963, they were married in a simple ceremony at the Griboyedov Street Palace. Yuri Gagarin and his wife, and Valeri Bykovsky and his wife were witnesses for the couple. Acting as surrogate father for both bride and groom, Premier Khrushchev and his wife hosted a gala reception. Khrushchev reeled off a twenty-one-toast salute during the four-hour-long state splurge.

Following her honeymoon, Tereshkova continued her travels. She assumed dozens of ceremonial posts and moved into the office of chairwoman of the Committee of Soviet Women in Moscow. She also received the title of Hero of the Soviet Union and continued her studies at the Air Force Academy. On June 10, 1964, Tereshkova's healthy baby daughter, Yelena, was born. There had been some popular concern that the birth might be complicated and the health of the baby might be impaired since both parents had been in space. However, neither the child nor the parents seemed to suffer any ill effects from exposure to elements of space.

Tereshkova continued with studies at the Air Force Academy. A published account of the First U.S.S.R. Conference on Space Physics in June,

1965, announced that Tereshkova had determined the existence of a dust layer around earth at about 12 miles from its surface that seemed to play a major role in the development of enigmatic nacreous clouds. The crew of the Voskhod 1 confirmed Tereshkova's findings. In 1966, she received the rank of major in the Soviet air force. In September, 1969, she earned a diploma at the Zhukovsky Aircraft Engineering Academy, which qualified her as a full-fledged engineer. By April of 1977, Tereshkova had earned her doctorate in aeronautical engineering.

After the overthrow of Khrushchev, speculation that the marriage of Tereshkova and Nikolayev may have been orchestrated by the Soviet premier was fueled when the couple stopped living together and no longer stood near each other in official photographs of the cosmonauts. In 1982, their marriage ended in divorce.

### Summary

Aside from the biomedical information Tereshkova's spaceflight produced, there were at least two practical benefits. Her flight demonstrated that a healthy person can, with proper training, withstand the strains of launch, weightlessness, and reentry without having the highly specialized professional background of a military test pilot. Her successful flight also opened the way for the training of scientists for later, more complex, missions.

### Bibliography

Arnold, H. J. P., ed. *Man in Space*. New York: Smithmark, 1993. Arnold provides an excellent comparison of the space programs in the United States and the Soviet Union.

Clark, Phillip. *The Soviet Manned Space Program*. London: Salamander, and New York: Orion, 1988. This exhaustive analysis of the Soviet space program from Sputnik to the late 1980's includes chronological surveys. Consideration is given to future developments.

Department of the Air Force. *Soviet Aerospace Handbook*. Washington, D.C.: Government Printing Office, 1978. This booklet details the layout of Soviet armed forces organization, including ranks, structures, insignias, and decorations. It also describes the Zhukovsky Air Force Engineering Academy.

Hardesty, Von. *Red Phoenix*. Washington, D.C.: Smithsonian Institution Press, 1983. Hardesty gives an overview of the Soviet air force during World War II. Women played a very important part in many Soviet campaigns as medical personnel and as pilots.

O'Neil, Bill. "Whatever became of Valentina Tereshkova?" *New Scientist* 139 no. 1886, (August 14, 1993). Profile of Tereshkova including excerpts from her biography, *Valentina—First Woman in Space—Conversations with A. Lothian.*

Oberg, James E. *Red Star in Orbit*. London: Harrap, and New York: Random House, 1981. Oberg is considered one of the most accurate observers of and commentators on the Soviet space program. He analyzes Soviet statements, hardware, and orbital maneuvers of test flights, and reconstructs much of the hidden history of the Soviet space efforts.

Sharpe, Mitchell. *It Is I, Sea Gull*. New York: Crowell, 1975. Sharpe is a government analyst who has helped determine exactly what the Soviets have accomplished in space. He effectively captures the essence of Tereshkova's life.

*Lillian D. Kozloski*

# MEGAN TERRY

*Born:* July 22, 1932; Seattle, Washington
*Area of Achievement:* Theater and drama
*Contribution:* A founding member of the Open Theatre in the 1960's and playwright-in-residence at the Omaha Magic Theatre since 1974, Megan Terry is one of the most prolific American dramatists, having written more than sixty successful plays. She is one of the major pioneers in the development of transformational drama and is also considered one of America's first feminist dramatists.

## Early Life

Megan Terry was born Marguerite Josephine Duffy on July 22, 1932, in Seattle, Washington, to Harold Joseph Duffy, Jr., and Marguerite Cecelia Henry Duffy. She later recalled her interest in a film career when she was four years old, although "it changed to theatre when I was seven"—the result of a visit to the Seattle Repertory Playhouse. Except for theatrical activities—grade school plays, amateur theatricals in the Duffy backyard—her childhood was uneventful until 1942, when her father left to fight in World War II. During the war, young Marguerite played at defending the Duffy home with toy guns and bullets. In the seventh grade, she wrote, directed, and acted in her first musical and became convinced that she was destined for the theater.

When Harold Duffy returned to Seattle after the war, he and his wife were divorced; when Terry was fourteen, she and her sister left Seattle to live with their father. Harold Duffy did not encourage his daughter's theatrical aspirations—he called her Tallulah Blackhead and Sarah Heartburn—but he did instill in her a love of the outdoors and taught her carpentry and bricklaying. Returning to Seattle to live with her grandparents during her last year in high school, she rediscovered the Seattle Repertory Playhouse and came under the tutelage of Florence James, a Stanislavsky-trained director, and her husband, actor Burton James.

Terry later described her time at Seattle Repertory as her upbringing. At the theater she learned design, studied the work of Gordon Craig and Adolph Appia, and discovered the links between theater and politics from Florence James, who combined her work in theater with running for public office as a Progressive Party candidate. During those years, Terry also discovered classical drama. She spent the summer of 1950 as a scholarship student at the Banff School of Fine Arts, where she took the stage name of Maggie Duffy and played Hermia in *A Midsummer Night's Dream*. From 1950 to 1951, she studied at the University of Washington in Seattle, and when Seattle Repertory was closed in 1951 by the House Committee on Un-American Activities, she moved to Canada to study at the University of Alberta.

Her two years in Canada widened Terry's theatrical experience by exposing her to the work of Antonin Artaud and giving her the extensive backstage work that led her to decide to become a playwright instead of an actor. Her grandfather's illness forced her back to Seattle, and she reenrolled at the University of Washington. From 1954 to 1956, she taught at the Cornish School of Allied Arts, where she reorganized The Cornish Players, a theater group composed of students from the school as well as any others who wanted to act. She also wrote four children's plays that were performed under her direction in the Seattle area. After her graduation in 1956, she returned to the Banff School of Fine Arts, where she earned certificates in directing, acting, and design.

At some point during the early 1950's, Marguerite Josephine Duffy—briefly Maggie Duffy—became Megan Terry, a name she chose in honor of her Welsh heritage. The name "Megan" came from the Celtic version of "Marguerite," and "Terry" was a reference both to the actress Ellen Terry and to "terra," or the earth.

## Life's Work

In 1956, Megan Terry left the Pacific Northwest and moved to New York City. The move to New York unleashed Terry's playwriting talent, and for the next eighteen years she was a major figure in the New York theater scene. Her plays were produced by some of the major Off-Broadway and Off-Off-Broadway theaters—the Open Theatre, LaMama Experimental Theatre Club, Genesis Theatre, Cherry Lane Theatre, and the Manhattan Theatre Club, among others—as well as by the Firehouse Theatre in Minneapolis and the Mark Taper Forum in Los Angeles. She won the Stanley Drama Award for *Hot House* in 1965. Other fellowships and grants followed: two awards from the Office of Advanced Drama Research at the University of Minnesota (1965 and 1969), an ABC-Yale

University Fellowship (1966), Rockefeller grants (1968 and 1974), and a National Endowment for the Arts literature fellowship (1972). Her plays won a number of awards, including a 1970 Obie for *Approaching Simone*.

During her New York years, Megan Terry became a founding member of the New York Open Theatre, the brainchild of Joseph Chaikin, who brought together a group of young writers and actors—Jean-Claud van Itallie, Sam Shepard, Richard Gilman, Roberta Sklar, and others, in addition to Terry. The Open Theatre, which was to become a major influence on both experimental and traditional theater, focused on improvisation as the first step to developing a script and, ultimately, a performance piece. The emphasis was on the ensemble and on acting that combined the ideas of Stanislavsky with Chaikin's own "psycho-physical" technique.

Megan Terry was playwright-in-residence for the Open Theatre from 1963 to 1968—five years during which she created or revised for production eight plays. An important play from the Open Theatre years is *Calm Down Mother* (1965), which is often cited in discussions of transformational drama as an excellent example of the genre. Transformational drama is what critic Robert Pasolli describes as "a theatre of abstraction and illusion," in which actors "[delineate], consecutively and concurrently, concrete objects, stereotyped individuals, human relationships, impartial observers and abstract actions." *Calm Down Mother* involves three actresses who play several roles, transforming themselves into different characters and acting out new relationships from scene to scene. The most significant of Terry's Open Theatre plays is *Viet Rock: A Folk War Movie* (1966). The play grew out of her Open Theatre workshop, in which the actors improvised scenes from newspaper stories and television coverage of the war. It opened at La Mama Experimental Theatre Club on May 21, 1966, in New York, and later it was produced at Yale and at other theaters around the United States.

*Viet Rock* was the Open Theatre's first full-length production, and, like *Calm Down Mother*, it is a transformational piece with shifting characterization, episodic structure, and the subsuming of individual identity into the collective creativity of the ensemble. The play, a series of variations on war, was intended as an antiwar piece and a commentary on American involvement in Vietnam. Theatrical experimentation aside, *Viet Rock* is historically significant in a number of ways: It was the first full theatrical treatment of the Vietnam War, the first commercial production of a transformational play, the first American rock musical, and the first American play in which barriers between stage and house were broken down when the actors left the stage to make physical contact with the audience.

*Viet Rock* was Megan Terry's only collaborative creation with the Open Theatre, although that group produced seven of her other plays. Her formal connection with the Open Theatre lasted until 1968, after which she went on to help found the New York Theatre Strategy and the Women's Theatre Council, both in 1971. Meanwhile, Terry continued to experiment with the role-shaping transformations that had become an integral part of her work, and her plays were given productions both on the stage and on television. The most important work of Terry's late New York period would prove to be *Approaching Simone* (1970), which is still one of Terry's best-known plays.

Throughout her career, Terry has stressed repeatedly the need for strong role models for women. *Approaching Simone* is a dramatized biography of French philosopher, theologian, and mystic Simone Weil, whose life ended tragically when at thirty-four she committed suicide by starvation. Terry portrays the gradual development of Weil's political and theological beliefs—from Judaism through socialism and communism and finally to Catholicism—by creating a series of evolving supporting roles against which the character of Weil remains fundamentally a woman seeking ways to continue being a strong and responsible citizen of the world. *Approaching Simone* premiered in Boston before moving to New York, where it was honored with the Obie Award for Best New Play of 1969-1970. For Megan Terry, the production of the play set in motion the next phase of her career. Playing the role of Simone was a young actress named Jo Ann Schmidman, who had already—in 1968, before she came east to study for a B.F.A. at Boston University—founded the Omaha Magic Theatre in Nebraska. Schmidman's performance in *Approaching Simone* earned for her a place with the Open Theatre, with which Megan Terry was still loosely connected, and the two future collaborators briefly became Open Theatre colleagues.

Since 1974, Megan Terry has lived and worked in Omaha, Nebraska. Several circumstances impelled her to move away from New York: The

Open Theatre had disbanded in 1973; she was being blacklisted by Actors' Equity for withdrawing *Hothouse* from a showcase production; and, most important, she wanted to work with Jo Ann Schmidman and the Omaha Magic Theatre. As playwright-in-residence at the Magic Theatre, Terry has been productive and innovative, continuing her work with transformational drama and moving into new thematic territory.

*Babes in the Bighouse* (1974) has been one of Terry's most popular Magic Theatre plays, with its combination of documentary with musical theater and cross-gender casting to explore the lives of women in prisons and reformatories. Other plays treat equally disturbing subjects: sexism in language, domestic violence, and teenage alcoholism, among others.

Another item on Terry's creative agenda at the Magic Theatre is the creation of plays that address society's need for appropriate female role models. *Mollie Bailey's Traveling Family Circus: Featuring Scenes from the Life of Mother Jones* (1983) has received critical acclaim for its juxtaposition of the imaginary Mollie Bailey, a nineteenth century housewife and the center of a traveling "family" circus, and the historical Mother Jones, a political activist from the same century.

## Summary

Megan Terry's dramatic achievement is unique in the American theater. In her three decades as a playwright, she has produced a body of work that can be read as a history of American drama in the second half of the twentieth century. Her plays range from the realism of her Seattle period to the avant-garde experimentation of her New York plays; she has created ensemble pieces, naturalistic drama, performance art, musical theater, and transformational drama. Although she developed her transformational techniques out of the need to discover a theater that was relevant to the concerns of a 1960's audience, her experiments in theatrical image-making and the use of language have proved valid even for audiences in the closing years of the twentieth century.

Terry's continuing commitment to social change through the agency of a strong people's theater is responsible for two forms of drama into which she puts a great deal of creative energy: role model plays and public service community dramas. Critic Helen Keyssar has called Megan Terry the mother of feminist drama, a label that is particularly apt for the woman whose pioneering work in transformational drama is a major step toward breaking down gender stereotyping and freeing actors to play more varied roles. In her plays that highlight the activities and achievements of strong women characters, Terry not only provides American theater with excellent female roles but also gives audiences strong women with whom to identify. In her work with the Omaha Magic Theatre and its outreach programs, Terry is effecting social change by sparking dialogue about community concerns and political issues.

## Bibliography

Betsko, Kathleen, and Rachel Koenig, eds. *Interviews with Contemporary Women Playwrights*. New York: Beech Tree, 1987. Includes an informative interview in which Terry discusses her creative process, influences on her work, women in theater, sources of her ideas, and the state of American theater. In addition, she reminisces about her work with the Open Theatre and the Omaha Magic Theatre as well as with a number of America's most significant contemporary playwrights.

Fenn, Jeffery W. *Levitating the Pentagon: Evolutions in the American Theatre of the Vietnam War Era*. Newark: University of Delaware Press, and London: Associated University Presses, 1992. Contains an excellent analysis of Megan Terry's *Viet Rock* as transformational drama and as political commentary. Fenn studies the play in the contexts of both the experimental theater of the 1960's and the earliest American plays that focused on the Vietnam War.

Hart, Lynda, ed. *Making a Spectacle: Feminist Essays on Contemporary Women's Theatre*. Ann Arbor: University of Michigan Press, 1989. A wide-ranging collection of essays that includes Jan Breslauer's and Helen Keyssar's "Making Magic Public: Megan Terry's Traveling Family Circus," an analysis of Megan Terry's *Mollie Bailey's Traveling Family Circus: Featuring Scenes from the Life of Mother Jones* as new feminist drama. The other essays are equally valuable in that they provide a theatrical context for Terry's work and ideas.

Savran, David. *In Their Own Words: Contemporary American Playwrights*. New York: Theatre Communications Group, 1988. Features an in-depth interview with Megan Terry in which she describes the plays that have influenced her work and the emotions that lead to ideas for plays. She discusses specific plays and the genesis of each one, and she identifies her favorites among her plays. The interview closes with her speculations on the future of the American theater and her work with the Omaha Magic Theatre.

Schlueter, June. "*Keep Tightly Closed in a Cool Dry Place:* Megan Terry's Transformational Drama and the Possibilities of Self." *Studies in American Drama, 1945-Present* 2 (1987): 59-69. A lucid and interesting treatment of one of Megan Terry's more significant transformational dramas as an example of the Open Theatre's contribution to redefining the creation of dramatic character. Schlueter points out that *Keep Tightly Closed in a Cool Dry Place* is a work that strongly represents Terry's transformational experimentation and its impact on the definition of self in American drama.

*E. D. Huntley*

# U THANT

*Born:* January 22, 1909; Pantanaw, Burma
*Died:* November 25, 1974; New York, New York
*Area of Achievement:* Diplomacy
*Contribution:* Thant took over as acting secretary-general of the United Nations when Dag Hammarskjöld was killed in an airplane crash in 1961 and served until 1971. Thant therefore was the speaker for the United Nations during the many crises of the 1960's and early 1970's, including the Cuban Missile Crisis, the Arab-Israeli conflict, the crisis in the Congo and other parts of Africa, and the U.S. involvement in Vietnam, providing the U.N. with a strong neutral voice.

## Early Life

Thant ("U" is an honorific, and most Burmese do not use surnames) was born in the town of Pantanaw, Burma, which was then part of the British Indian Empire, the first of four sons. His home province is probably best known for the difficult traveling conditions within the area, for the many streams forming a delta in the almost totally flat area flood easily. Thant's family was one of the moderately wealthy ones in the town, since his paternal grandfather and great uncle were the owners of a prosperous rice mill and his maternal grandfather exported woven mats. The real wealth was held by other family members, however, rather than by Thant's father.

Thant's father had, however, been educated in Calcutta and is believed to have been the only person in town then able to read and speak English. He passed on his love of learning, as well as his knowledge of English, to his eldest son, and Thant started at the regional school at age six. At the age of fifteen, Thant impressed his family by having an article printed in the Burmese boy scout magazine *Burma Scout*, and he hoped to turn that small start into a career as a journalist.

Thant's father died in 1923, and much of the family's wealth was spent on a legal dispute between various members of the extended family. Thant therefore decided that he would be unable to spend the four years at the University of Rangoon he had planned on. Instead, he would stay two years and get a teaching certificate, which he did from 1926 to 1928. He returned to his hometown and taught in the high school, rising to the headmastership. He would later marry a distant relative, Thein Tin, in 1934.

In the tense political situation of Burma during the 1930's (nationalism and anticolonialism were both growing), Thant stood between the extremes of ardent nationalism and those who favored British policy. While this gained for him enemies, it also impressed a former university friend and short-term colleague at the Pantanaw High School. U Nu would always remember his friend when an intelligent moderate outlook was needed. As Nu rose through the ranks of the Burmese Nationalists, finally becoming prime minister of independent Burma in 1948, his need for Thant's opinions grew as well.

During the 1930's, Thant's influence grew within education circles as he became involved in various national committees. He also became a moderately well-known individual, as he started having articles published outside education journals. When the crisis of the Japanese invasion came in 1941, Thant was a respected, although not a very important, leader in Burmese society.

### Life's Work

The Burmese found themselves between Japanese and British imperialism during World War II. While a few still favored the British and some believed the Japanese propaganda of "Asia for the Asiatics," most Burmese nationalists joined or supported the Burmese Independence Army, led by one of Thant's former pupils, Aung San. Although it primarily fought against the British in 1942, a reorganized version would be instrumental in fighting the Japanese as well. In 1942, Thant left Pantanaw to help reorganize Burmese education under the Japanese occupation at the suggestion of San and Nu. This work, although ignored at the time, allowed the other leading nationalists to take a good look at the educator/journalist, even though Thant returned home after a few months' work.

When the British Indian Empire was dissolved in 1947, Burma was scheduled to become an independent nation. Thant moved his family to Rangoon, hoping to set up an independent magazine that would give the new nation a native literary forum. Instead, Thant first became press director of the nationalistic Anti-Fascist People's Freedom League (AFPF) and then held the same position in the Directorate of Information. During the next few troubled years, Thant became in turn the deputy to the information secretary, director of broadcasting, and then secretary of the information ministry and chair of the Burma film board. At the same time, he drew closer to his old friend Nu: accompanying him on a goodwill mission to India in 1950; leading missions to Indonesia, Thailand, and Great Britain in 1951; and then leading the Burmese mission to the United Nations in 1952. Returning in 1953, Thant became secretary of projects, secretary to the prime minister, and then secretary of the economic and social board. Finally, in 1957, he was sent to the United Nations as Burma's permanent representative, where he quickly made a reputation as a hardworking and impartial member of the General Assembly as well as for working in many of the committees and behind the scenes.

In September, 1961, the secretary-general of the United Nations, Dag Hammarskjöld, was killed in an airplane crash in Central Africa. The United States and the Soviet Union were unable to agree on any candidate put up by the other members of the Security Council, the Soviets going so far as to propose splitting the top position into three positions: one Communist, one from the West, and one from the third world, with each one having a veto. Over the next few weeks, the United Nations saw one of its greatest periods of political negotiation, as representatives from the smaller nations tried to mediate between the two superpowers and at the same time find somebody acceptable to the majority of the U.N. member nations.

Thant was one of the hardest workers in this process. Because of this, as well as all of his previous hard work, representatives started talking about having Thant fill out Hammarskjöld's term of office. Although there were some objections, based on a number of political reasons, few people had any personal objections to Thant. When the United States decided to back Thant as well, the Soviets joined in, and Thant was unanimously elected acting secretary-general of the United Nations in November, 1961. He was reelected in 1962 and 1966, serving until December 31, 1971.

Thant faced a number of problems during his tenure as secretary-general. Decolonialization was at its height during the early 1960's, and there were a number of violent and disruptive problems, both internal and external, associated with the process, particularly in the Congo, the area to which Hammarskjöld was on his way when his plane crashed. It was up to the secretary-general to keep as many of the disputants talking as possible.

Despite his many successes, such as helping to keep the United States and the Soviet Union talking during the Cuban Missile Crisis, Thant was not always seen in a favorable light by many of the world's national leaders. He was publicly critical of U.S. military policy in Vietnam, and he was also privately opposed to the U.S. armed intervention in the Dominican Republic in 1965. The American press responded with criticism of the secretary-general. Thant was also opposed to the Soviet invasion of Czechoslovakia in 1968, although as usual he kept his criticism private. Still, it was enough to upset the Soviets.

At all times, Thant was a defender of peace, trying to get various disputants to agree to arbitration of their problems. Quite often, however, at least one (and at times all) of those involved would refuse, gaining the secretary-general criticism for not actively taking the "correct" side. Besides the international disputes mentioned above, Thant's tenure also saw the 1967 Arab-Israeli Six-Day War, fighting between Pakistan and India over two different border areas and then the start of the war that resulted in the birth of Bangladesh, and numerous other, internal and smaller international disputes. Unable to serve as more than either an impartial adviser or uninvited observer despite the many demands that he take sides in controversial situations, Thant managed in general to maintain his position despite his critics and many temptations.

After his retirement, Thant was appointed senior fellow of the Adlai Stevenson Institute of International Affairs. He spent the last years of his life writing and speaking on the general themes he had tried to promote while he was secretary-general. He believed in the development of a true global community, which would mean not only the ending of armed conflict but also a true sharing of resources and technology as well.

Thant died of cancer in November, 1974. His body was returned to Rangoon for burial. A group of students seized the body on December 5, in order to bury it on the grounds of the university. When the police took the body back on December 11, it sparked days of riots.

### Summary

While U Thant contributed to maintaining the precarious balance of peace during the 1962 Cuban Missile Crisis, and much of the public portion of the confrontation was played out at the United Nations, he also helped turn the United Nations from what had been primarily a forum for the East/West Cold War conflict into an arena where the emerging less developed nations could express themselves on the world stage. His strong Buddhist beliefs, along with his own moral character, helped him defend his position as a leader of the global community, rather than a mere national figure speaking in an international setting. It was Thant's hope that the United Nations would continue to grow into that sort of an organization, a place in which the world would come together, rather than a forum to air disputes.

### Bibliography

The Asia Society. *Peacemaker from Pantanaw*. New York: Asia Society, 1977. A memorial tribute to Thant, this supplement to the journal *Asia* contains several articles assessing the historical importance of Thant to the history of Burma, the United Nations, and the world.

Bingham, June. *U Thant: The Search for Peace*. London: Gollancz, and New York: Knopf, 1966. An early but extremely good biography of the U.N. leader, concentrating on his pre-United Nations life. Bingham had the benefit of a number of interviews with Thant, which gives this work extra importance. It also includes a chronology and a reprint of a pre-World War II article that Thant wrote on the Burmese.

Butwell, Richard. *U Nu of Burma*. Stanford, Calif.: Stanford University Press, 1963. An in-depth study and biography of the main Burmese political leader during the 1940's through the early 1960's. Nu was a longtime friend and patron of Thant, and this work describes the effort made to establish an independent Burma and the home political situation with which Thant had to deal while he was Burma's representative at the United Nations.

Cordier, Andrew, and Max Harrelson, eds. *Public Papers of the Secretaries-General of the United Nations*. Vols. 6, 7, and 8. New York: Columbia University Press, 1976. These U.N. documents include not only official reports and speeches but also some of the behind-the-scenes memos and letters that formed Thant's positions, transcripts of press conferences, and public speeches during his tenure as secretary-general.

Johnstone, William C. *Burma's Foreign Policy: A Study in Neutralism*. Cambridge, Mass.: Harvard University Press, 1963. This work describes the political background that Thant brought with him to the United Nations and the neutralist policies that he espoused while he was working at the United Nations during the 1950's and early 1960's, which led to his being chosen secretary-general.

Nu, U. *U Nu, Saturday's Son: Memoirs of the Former Prime Minister of Burma*. Translated by Edward M. Law Yone. New Haven, Conn.: Yale University Press, 1975. Modern Burmese history as seen through the eyes of one of its nationalistic founders.

Thant, U. *Toward World Peace*. Edited by Jacob Baal Teshuva. New York: Yoseloff, 1964. This is a compilation of Thant's speeches and other public statements between 1957 and 1963, and therefore includes his opinions on the Cuban Missile Crises.

———. *View from the U.N.* Newton Abbott: David and Charles, 1977; New York: Doubleday, 1978. Thant's memoirs of his tenure as secretary-general of the United Nations, dealing in detail with the major crises of his tenure in office.

*Terrance L. Lewis*

# MARGARET THATCHER

*Born:* October 13, 1925; Grantham, Lincolnshire, England

*Areas of Achievement:* Politics and government

*Contribution:* Through fiscally conservative economic policies, Thatcher, the first woman prime minister in British history, has lessened public dependence on government and moved the nation in the direction of more competition and self-reliance.

## Early Life

Margaret Thatcher was born Margaret Hilda Roberts in Grantham, Lincolnshire, England, on October 13, 1925, the second daughter of Alfred and Beatrice Roberts. She grew up in a small apartment above her parents' grocery store in Grantham, a small town about one hundred miles from London. She and her older sister, Muriel, were reared in a very strict fashion by their parents, who were devout Methodists. Alfred Roberts had little formal education but was a prominent citizen of Grantham. He was well-read and served as mayor of his hometown. He was eager for his daughters to obtain the education he never had and encouraged them in their studies. Thatcher's family instilled in her the values of hard work, thrift, and self-reliance—instruction that had a lasting effect upon her. An outstanding student at the Huntingtower Road Elementary School, Thatcher passed the scholarship examination a year earlier than normal and attended the Kesteven and Grantham Girl's Grammar School.

Through hard work and diligence, Thatcher achieved what few women of her day achieved, entrance into Oxford University. In 1945, she was accepted to Somerville College, Oxford, where she majored in chemistry. She continued her hard work at Oxford, disdaining the frivolities of less serious students. At Oxford, she developed an interest in politics, joining the University Conservative Club, of which she became chairwoman in 1946. She received her degree in 1947, taking second-class honors.

Upon graduation, she went to work as a research chemist and also continued her interest in politics by joining the local Conservative Party. During her four years as a research chemist, Thatcher stood for Parliament twice. In 1949, at the age of twenty-four, she was chosen to run for the seat in Dartford, Kent. In the campaign, she criticized the Labour government's economic policies, insisting that taxes should be lowered to create incentives for the workingman. That position and her opposition to nationalization would be consistent themes throughout her political life. Although a very young and attractive candidate, she lost in this strong Labour constituency. In 1951, Thatcher ran again in the same constituency. Though she was unsuccessful, she made a favorable impression. On the day of the 1951 election, she became engaged to Denis Thatcher, a successful businessman ten years her senior. They were married the following December at Wesley Chapel in London. Two years later, their twins, Carol and Mark, were born.

Before becoming pregnant, Thatcher decided to pursue a law degree. She qualified as a barrister in 1954 and began practicing law, but she was eager to return to the political arena. Though eminently qualified for Parliament with a legal background, a strong, articulate manner of speaking, the experience of two campaigns behind her, and a penchant for hard work, she made several unsuccessful attempts, finally succeeding in 1959, within a week of her thirty-fourth birthday. She represented the North London constituency of Finchley.

Thatcher's persistence, hard work, patience, and singleness of purpose, values she acquired in her youth, paid dividends as she prepared to begin her new career in the House of Commons.

## Life's Work

Thatcher's introduction to the House of Commons was an auspicious occasion as she, in February, 1960, delivered an impressive speech without notes. In this initial speech she introduced a bill guaranteeing the press and the public the right to attend meetings of local government councils. Her colleagues were impressed, and her parliamentary reputation was established. She also proved to be a quick learner and an effective debater. Consequently, in 1962, Conservative prime minister Harold Macmillan made her a junior minister as joint parliamentary secretary to the Ministry of Pensions and National Insurance. She later served as opposition spokesperson in several areas, including pensions and education, during the tenure of the Labour government.

This experience proved valuable when the Conservatives won the next election in 1970, and the new prime minister, Edward Heath, appointed

Thatcher Minister of Education and Science in the new cabinet. Her educational philosophy was based on personal experience as well as her conservative inclinations. She strongly advocated improvement in education but opposed the controls placed on education by the former Labour government. Local governments, she insisted, should be able to choose the kind of secondary schools they wished to have and the specific programs they wished to offer based on the needs of the students. Her reputation suffered because of an economic measure in which the education ministry put a stop to free milk in schools except for the poor and then raised the price of school lunches. These measures aroused a storm of protest, and she was dubbed "Margaret Thatcher, the milk snatcher." Undaunted by the criticism, the determined Thatcher kept smiling and stoically bore the criticism of a cabinet decision not her own. She was praised, however, for her effective school construction and teacher-improvement programs.

In the February, 1974, election, the Conservatives were narrowly defeated. Once again in the opposition ranks, Thatcher was appointed opposition spokesperson for environment, treasury, and economic affairs. Trained as a tax lawyer, she proved to be a brilliant debater in the complex area of public finance. Heath at this time came under criticism from within his party, some seeing him as dictatorial, others as a loser without popular appeal. In 1974, the party adopted new rules for electing the party leader. Elections were to be held annually with three ballots. The winner must receive a majority of votes and total at least fifteen percent more votes than the closest rival. The election was held in February, 1975, and fortunately for Thatcher, the leading Conservative candidate, Sir Keith Joseph, a close friend of Thatcher, withdrew from the election, leaving an opening for her to run. She defeated Heath on the second ballot, becoming the first woman in British history to head a major political party. As leader of the opposition in the House of Commons, Thatcher's stirring speeches attacked socialism and continuously emphasized her strong faith in the virtues of self-reliance and independence.

Over the winter of 1978 and 1979, the Labour Party was beset by a crippling series of strikes for higher wages by public service workers. The government gave in to the unions' demands of a twenty-percent wage increase, which was met with scathing criticism by Thatcher, who called for a vote of no confidence in the Labour government. Since the government in power is the majority party, votes of no confidence seldom succeed. In this case, however, the March 28, 1979, vote of no confidence was carried by one vote. An election to form a new government was called for May 3.

During the campaign the Conservatives were strengthened by public concern over inflation, unemployment, and the power of the unions. Thatcher's promises to limit the power of the unions, cut taxes, and promote economic freedom were key planks in the Conservative platform. The Conservatives won by a 43-seat majority and Margaret Thatcher became Great Britain's, and Europe's, first woman prime minister.

During the first two years of her government, Thatcher's economic program of frugality and reduced government spending did not lead to an improved economy, since by early 1981 Great Britain suffered from the worst recession since the 1930's. Members of her own party, moderate Conservatives called "wets" (slang for those who do not stick to their principles), called on her to change her economic policies. She remained resolute, however, insisting that until competition was restored and government spending curtailed, the economy would never improve. Adding to the economic woes was a series of riots in 1981 in the inner cities, as young, frustrated blacks went on a rampage. Experts predicted certain defeat for Thatcher in the next election. In a surprising move, however, Argentina on April 2, 1982, invaded and captured the British-owned Falkland Islands and the situation changed. This event would reveal Thatcher's resolute character.

The invasion was condemned by Thatcher, who termed it an unprovoked attack without justification or legality. Her determination to use force met with much criticism in Great Britain and elsewhere. The surrender of Argentina two months later proved to be a tremendous boost to national morale—which had greatly diminished since World War II—and provided new political life for Thatcher, who called for elections in June, 1983. Thatcher's party won an overwhelming victory over the weak and disorganized Labour Party with a 144-seat majority. Unfortunately, a bitter coal miners' strike in 1985 and an unemployment of three million marred Thatcher's second term. She also survived an attempt in 1984 on her life in Brighton by Irish Republican Army (IRA) terrorists. Aided by the 1980's North Sea oil boom, her government survived these crises. Although she did not have to call for elections until June, 1988 (in Great Britain a government must call an election within five years), she decided that June, 1987, was the optimum time for elections. Aided again by divisions within and between the opposition parties, the Conservatives won the June election by a 101-seat majority, and Thatcher became the first prime minister in modern British political history to win three successive general elections. Following the election, she indicated that her third government would be dedicated to extending freedom of choice, particularly in housing and education. Control of inflation through sound financial policies, however, would remain Thatcher's highest priority. Regeneration of the inner cities was another central theme for the Thatcher government. Her government had effected tremendous change in Great Britain since 1979, and with this victory she could continue curbing socialism and make Great Britain a home-owning, share-owning democracy. The shopkeeper's daughter with old-fashioned values, extraordinary determination, and singleness of purpose had made history a second time.

Thatcher's third term, however, ended in her forced resignation. While she vigorously opposed any infringement of British sovereignty, she did support Europe's move toward a single market. The issue caused fracturing within her party. Thatcher's stubborn insistence on a poll-tax, which was imposed equally on rich and poor and was extremely unpopular, caused a critical weakening of her administration. She stepped down on November 22, 1990.

### Summary

Margaret Thatcher brought tremendous change to Great Britain in her term of office. In 1979, Great Britain, on the verge of economic ruin, had two years earlier sought a bailout loan from the International Monetary Fund. After Thatcher's term began, the economy became much stronger. Her policy of cutting back on inefficient industries and attacking inflation with tight money and reduced government spending caused Great Britain's economy to be the fastest-growing economy in the European Community. Many see her success as rooted in her appeal to the traditional middle-class values of hard work, self-reliance, thrift, and a commonsense approach to finances. These values undoubtedly are deeply ingrained in the British character. Her insistence that Great Britain is a great world power also struck a responsive chord in the minds of the British people as pride in their nation was restored.

Others see Thatcher in a different manner. They see her programs as having helped only the middle and upper classes, and they describe her as uncaring because of spending cuts in education, housing, and health care. To them, she truly is the "Iron Lady," as the Soviet press once dubbed her. Feminists also criticize her for not speaking out or doing more for women's rights. In fairness, Thatcher brought a positive change to Great Britain, though the price was unemployment and reduced social services. She was also successful because of her fierce determination and her enormous leadership talents.

Thatcher's personal and professional qualities were important in her rise to power, but good fortune and timing also played a role. The formation of the Social Democratic Party in 1981 and its alliance with the Liberal Party divided the Labour Party. The Conservatives failed to win fifty percent of the vote in three successive elections. The Falklands War also helped Thatcher, as did the North Sea oil boom. Yet successful leaders take advantage of good fortune, and Thatcher did just that, carving out a very prominent niche in her country's history.

### Bibliography

Bruce-Gardyne, Jock. *Mrs. Thatcher's First Administration: The Prophets Confounded.* London: Macmillan, and New York: St. Martin's Press, 1984. An analysis of the first Thatcher government by one of her former ministers. The author raises the question of whether with the decline of the Labour Party the Social Democrat-Liberal alliance might emerge as a more formidable opponent to the Conservatives.

Burton, John. "Privatization: The Thatcher Case." *Managerial and Decision Economics* 8 (March, 1987): 21-29. Scholarly analysis of the privatization process under the Thatcher government. Burton concludes that the result has been an increase in internal efficiency in the industries that have been privatized.

Cosgrave, Patrick. *Thatcher: The First Term.* London: Bodley Head, 1985. A study of Thatcher's first administration with two introductory chapters focusing on the 1975-1979 period, with emphasis on how Thatcher won the party leadership. Contains useful notes at the end and a helpful bibliography.

Garfinkel, Bernard. *Margaret Thatcher.* New York: Chelsea House, 1985; London: Burke, 1988.

Well-illustrated biography aimed at the younger reader. Contains an interesting introductory essay on leadership by Arthur M. Schlesinger, Jr. Brief suggested reading list included.

Hall, Stuart, and Martin Jacques, eds. *The Politics of Thatcherism*. London: Lawrence and Wishart, 1983. Based on articles that appeared in one of the journals of the Communist Party, *Marxism Today*. The articles are very critical of Thatcher's policies. Hall and Jacques believe, however, that critics underestimate the novelty of Thatcherism as a political force in Great Britain.

Lewis, Russell. *Margaret Thatcher: A Personal and Political Biography*. Rev. ed. London and Boston: Routledge, 1984. Informative, detailed, clearly written, interesting, although very sympathetic, biography of Thatcher. Contains no bibliography.

Manwaring, Tony, and Nick Sigler, eds. *Breaking the Nation: A Guide to Thatcher's Britain*. London: Pluto Press, 1985. Very critical attack on the Thatcher government written by researchers for the Labour Party. They point to inflation, unemployment, and pollution as examples of failure on the part of the government.

Riddell, Peter. *The Thatcher Government*. Oxford: Robertson, 1983; New York: Blackwell, 1985. Well-balanced account of the Thatcher government from 1979 to 1983. Emphasis is on the main economic themes of Thatcherism. Very helpful bibliography is included.

Royal, Robert. "The Character of Margaret Thatcher." *World and I* 13 no. 8, (August, 1998). In-depth look at Thatcher's character, attributing her success to her middle-class background, clear thinking, and humility.

Sherman, Alfred. "The Thatcher Interlude." *World and I* 13 no. 8, (August, 1998). Sherman considers the positive and negative elements of Thatcher's tenure as Prime Minister.

*James E. Southerland*

# AXEL HUGO TEODOR THEORELL

*Born:* July 6, 1903; Linköping, Sweden
*Died:* August 15, 1982; Stockholm, Sweden
*Area of Achievement:* Biochemistry
*Contribution:* Theorell received the 1955 Nobel Prize in Physiology or Medicine for his work on the nature and action of oxidation enzymes. He was the first to produce a pure enzyme in the laboratory and the first to produce myoglobin in a pure form.

## Early Life

Axel Hugo Teodor Theorell was born on July 6, 1903, in Linköping, Sweden, the son of the local military regiment's medical officer. Little has been written of the younger Theorell's early life. Like his father, he chose medicine as his vocation. He entered the Caroline Institute in Stockholm in 1921 and studied under Walther Nernst, who had won the Nobel Prize in 1920. Theorell was awarded his bachelor of medicine degree in 1924. He also studied at the Pasteur Institute in Paris.

Most of his academic work consisted of research into the chemistry of plasma lipids and their influence on red blood cells. He did this research under the direction of Einar Hammarstein at the Royal Caroline Medico-Surgical Institute. He was awarded his doctor of medicine degree by the Caroline Institute in 1930 and was preparing to embark on the career of medical practitioner when an attack of poliomyelitis left him crippled in both legs. Undaunted by this unfortunate turn of events, Theorell took up research and teaching.

Theorell was a short, stocky man, modest and reticent; for relaxation he enjoyed sailing. In 1931, he married a music teacher, Margit Alenius, who later became a professional musician. Theorell was himself a violinist and he appeared with the Academic Orchestra Society. He chaired the Stockholm Philharmonic Society. The Theorells had three sons.

## Life's Work

After receiving his doctorate, Theorell was appointed docent at the Caroline Institute. Using a new ultracentrifuge at the Svedberg in Uppsala, he investigated the molecular weight of myoglobin, an iron-containing protein of muscle tissue that has oxygen-carrying functions related to those of hemoglobin in the blood. Myoglobin is the pigment which makes muscles red. Theorell was an assistant professor of chemistry at Uppsala from 1932 to 1933 and from 1935 to 1936, taking leave to work in Berlin and Stockholm.

In 1933, Theorell was given a Rockefeller Fellowship to work at the Kaiser Wilhelm Institute in Berlin with Nobel Prize winner (1931) Otto Warburg. There, using electrophoretic methods which he had worked out himself, he purified a yellow enzyme, a feat Warburg had been attempting for years without success. Other enzymes had been isolated and crystallized by American Nobel Prize winner James Sumner, but the yellow enzyme, found in yeast, heart muscle, and milk, had remained problematic.

By dialysis of an acidified solution, Theorell separated the yellow enzyme into two fragments: the nonprotein coenzyme, which acts as a catalyst, and the apoenzyme, a colorless, pure protein, and determined that the yellow enzyme's essential ingredient is albumin. The coenzyme, a substance of low molecular weight, was identified as a monophosphate of vitamin B2. The substance is now

known as flavin mononucleotide and is believed responsible for the yellow coloration of the enzyme. The coenzyme and apoenzyme must exist together for enzyme activity to occur. In fact, Theorell found that the separation process was reversible. Theorell also discovered the chemical chain reaction by which enzymes enable living cells to breathe (oxidation).

From 1937 to 1970, Hugo Theorell was head of the biochemistry department of the Nobel Institute. The department had been established in 1936 by the Caroline Institute in Stockholm in order to give Theorell an opportunity to continue his research. Under Theorell's direction, the department became world-renowned as a "Mecca of biochemistry."

Upon returning from Berlin, Theorell began his research on the cytochrome C molecule, a heme-containing protein associated with cellular respiration. By 1936, he had been able to produce an 80 percent pure molecule, and by 1939 he succeeded in purifying cytochrome C 100 percent. His sometime associate and colleague Linus Pauling had discovered the "Alpha" spiral, or twisted atom chains of protein molecules. Theorell's work confirmed Pauling's findings. With Anders Ehrenberg, he constructed models of hemin peptides and was able to determine the precise nature of the chemical linkage between the iron-bearing, nonprotein porphyrin portion and the apoenzyme.

At the biochemistry department of the Nobel Institute, he directed studies of ADH enzymes, which break down alcohol in the kidneys. From this research, he was able to develop a new method of determining ethyl alcohol content in the bloodstream. These techniques were later adopted by the Swedish and West German governments for use in tests for drunkenness. Theorell's research resulted in the isolation of bacteria strains which were used in the treatment of tuberculosis. He also discovered an antibiotic called proaptin.

Articles by Theorell have appeared in many scientific journals, including *Biochemische Zeitschrift*, *Arkiv för Kemi*, *Journal of the American Chemical Society*, *Bulletin de la Société de Chimie Biologique*, *Acta Chemica Scandinavica*, and *Rendiconti Istituto di Sanità Publíca*. Theorell died on August 15, 1982.

### Summary

Axel Hugo Teodor Theorell's work helped create a modern understanding of enzyme action. His research shed light on the basic unit of life, the cell. Much of this work laid the groundwork for the creation of artificial life in the laboratory. His discoveries found wide scientific application in the study of cancer and tuberculosis, among other diseases.

Theorell was active in many professional organizations. He was secretary of the Swedish Society of Physicians and Surgeons from 1940 to 1946 and of the Swedish Society for Medical Research from 1942 to 1950, and he chaired the Swedish Chemists' Association from 1947 to 1949. He was a member of the Swedish Royal Academy of Sciences, the Scientific Council of the Swedish Board of Health, and the Swedish Academy of Engineering Science. He was a foreign associate of the United States National Academy of Sciences and a foreign member of Great Britain's Royal Society. He received honorary degrees from Belgium, Brazil, the United States, and France, including an honorary doctor's degree from the Sorbonne.

### Bibliography

Aaseng, Nathan. *The Disease Fighters: The Nobel Prize in Medicine.* Minneapolis: Lerner, 1987. In this brief book, Aaseng details the discoveries of several Nobel Prize-winning scientists. Written for high school or younger readers.

Candee, Marjorie Dent, ed. *Current Biography Yearbook, 1956.* New York: Wilson, 1957. Published annually, this book provides biographies of people in the news. Written in clear language for the lay reader.

Ludovici, Laurence James, ed. *Nobel Prize Winners.* London: Arco, and Westport, Conn.: Associated Booksellers, 1957. This book details the lives of fourteen well-known Nobel Prize winners, including many contemporaries of Theorell. Gives the student a perspective on the golden age of science of the late nineteenth and early twentieth centuries. For high school or beyond.

Schück, H., et al. *Nobel: The Man and His Prizes.* 2d ed. New York: Elsevier, 1962. A comprehensive account of the five major Nobel Prizes. Contains the life of Alfred Nobel as well as the rationale behind the establishment of the Nobel Foundation. A page-long description of the prize-winning work by Theorell on enzymes is included. Indexed. College-level material.

Schwert, George W., and Alfred D. Winer, eds. *The Mechanism and Action of Dehydrogenases: A Symposium in Honor of Hugo Theorell.* Lexington: University Press of Kentucky, 1970. Papers read at a conference held March 16-19, 1965, at the University of Kentucky. The foreword is by Theorell, who was visiting centennial professor in the biological sciences at the time. Includes bibliographies. College-level material.

Sourkes, Theodore L. *Nobel Prize Winners in Medicine and Physiology, 1901-1965.* London and New York: Abelard-Schuman, 1966. A compilation of short biographies of Nobel Prize winners in medicine and physiology and detailed descriptions of the scientific work which won for them the prize. Much of the section on Theorell is directly quoted from the scientist. This is a revision of an earlier work by Lloyd G. Stevenson. For advanced readers.

*Maureen Connolly*

# CLARENCE THOMAS

*Born:* June 23, 1948; Pin Point, Georgia
*Areas of Achievement:* Government and politics
*Contribution:* Confirmed by a narrow 52-48 Senate vote, Thomas became the second African American to serve as an associate justice of the United States. After his controversial nomination by President Bush and a brutal 1991 confirmation battle marked by accusations of sexual harassment against him in Anita F. Hill's testimony before the Senate Judiciary Committee, Thomas remained a controversial justice because of his refusal to support positions many believed were essential to African American well-being.

## Early Life

Clarence Thomas' life has many elements of traditional Horatio Alger stories, since he grew up in a poor African American household in segregated, rural Georgia. Thomas was one of three children born to M. C. Thomas and Leola Anderson Thomas, and his father left the family when Thomas was two. When Thomas was seven, a fire destroyed the family home, and he was sent to live with his maternal grandparents, Myers and Christine Anderson. Although Myers was semiliterate and of limited means, Thomas benefited from his grandparents' devotion to hard work and their encouragement of the values of self-help, thrift, and a search for educational attainment despite the fact that they were isolated enough from the American mainstream to use the African-influenced Gullah dialect.

The family members were committed Christians. Despite being Baptist, they sent Thomas to an all-black Roman Catholic school, St. Benedict the Moor. Even as an associate justice, Thomas spoke fondly of the white nuns who were his early teachers there. For his first two years of high school, Thomas attended St. Pius X High School. He later transferred to St. John Vianney Minor Seminary and aspired to the priesthood as he helped integrate the school, which he attended for three years because of his need for remedial work in Latin.

Leaving his Georgia roots behind, Thomas attended the Immaculate Conception Seminary in Conception, Missouri, in 1967-1968. After hearing classmates rejoice at the death of the Reverend Martin Luther King, Jr., Thomas left the seminary and abandoned his goal of ordination to the priesthood. After this searing experience, Thomas attended the Jesuit-run Holy Cross College in Worcester, Massachusetts, from 1968 to 1971 on a Martin Luther King scholarship. He graduated cum laude in 1971 with a degree in English literature.

After Holy Cross College, Thomas attended Yale Law School, from which he graduated in 1974. When he became a public figure, Thomas's supporters and adversaries disagreed on whether he had been a beneficiary of affirmative action. During his college years, Thomas married Kathy Ambush, whom he divorced in 1984. Their son, Jamal Adeen, was born in 1973. Thomas then married Virginia Bess Lamp, an accomplished conservative lawyer in her own right, in 1987. The marriage stimulated much adverse comment because of Virginia's wealthy white background and the preference Thomas has expressed for "women of a lighter complexion."

## Life's Work

After his Yale graduation, Thomas left behind the black power and liberal views he had expressed in college. Although he had supported George McGovern for president in 1972, Thomas's professional career soon moved him toward conservative Republican positions.

Thomas's first legal position was working in the office of Missouri attorney general John Danforth from 1974 to 1977. During that period, Thomas changed his party registration and adopted the Republican views of Danforth, who became a longtime mentor and friend. Thomas eventually became more conservative than Danforth. After leaving his position with Danforth, Thomas work for Monsanto Corporation from 1977 to 1979, serving as an in-house counsel to the firm in the area of environmental law. When he left Monsanto, Thomas moved to Washington, D.C., as a legislative assistant to Danforth, who had become a United States Senator. From then on, Thomas experienced rapid professional advancement. Under Danforth's sponsorship, Thomas became assistant secretary of Education for Civil Rights in 1981. In this position, Thomas met his fellow African American Yale Law School graduate Anita F. Hill, who followed him to the Equal Employment Opportunity Commission.

In 1982, Thomas became head of the Equal Employment Opportunity Commission (EEOC), a position he held for seven years. Critics com-

plained that he allowed many age discrimination claims to lapse that later had to be reinstated by Congress. During his EEOC period, Thomas became increasingly conservative. He became an advocate of limited government, emphasized individual rather than group rights, and opposed affirmative action. Thomas came to oppose the use of quotas, timetables, and even the use of statistics to prove patterns of discrimination. Although his views antagonized the civil rights community, Thomas accurately reflected the position of President Ronald Reagan, who had appointed him. In 1989, President George Bush appointed Thomas to the District of Columbia Court of Appeals seat vacated by Judge Robert Bork after the Senate refused to confirm Judge Bork's nomination to the supreme Court. Thomas joined the District of Columbia Court of Appeals in the spring of 1990.

Although Thomas had met no real opposition to his confirmation as head of the EEOC or judge of the District of Columbia Court of Appeals, his nomination to the Supreme Court proved extremely controversial. Liberal groups such as the Alliance for Justice had tasted success in defeating the nomination of Bork to the Supreme Court, and they quickly mobilized to block Thomas. In addition to his controversial views on civil rights issues of concern to the African American community, Thomas also aroused suspicion because of his Roman Catholic background and widespread suspicion among abortion rights groups that he was not fully supportive of abortion rights.

With the Senate and the country already bitterly divided about Thomas's fitness to serve on the Supreme Court, Anita F. Hill came forward with accusations that Thomas had sexually harassed her when she worked for him at the Department of Education and the EEOC. Hill received strong support, and buttons soon appeared saying, "I believe Anita." Thomas and Hill gave radically conflicting accounts of their relationship to the Senate Judiciary Committee. Hill's supporters saw her as conservative, religious, and a woman with nothing to gain by coming forward against Thomas. Thomas's supporters saw her as an ideologically committed liberal law professor at the University of Oklahoma who, by accusing Thomas, acquired overnight celebrity and access to professional acclaim and opportunity she would not otherwise have had.

Despite the seriousness of Hill's charges against Thomas, many of his supporters felt that, at worst, he had been guilty of being a single man with an unappetizing taste for sexually charged banter that was offensive to Hill but not sufficient to warrant jeopardizing his career. The African American community split on Thomas's nomination, but the received much support from African Americans in the South. Thomas avoided the humiliation of defeat that the Senate had inflicted on Bork, and he was able to join the court with a tarnished reputation but the conviction that a long tenure on the court would be his best revenge.

As an associate justice, Thomas became a polarizing figure. Supporters of Hill continued to take it as a given that her accusations of sexual harassment against him were true. In addition, many African Americans and Democratic liberals resented the fact that Thomas aligned himself with Antonin Scalia, who is generally considered to be the most conservative Supreme Court Justice.

**Summary**

Although President George Bush claimed that he appointed Thomas based on his qualifications, the claim lacked credibility. Bush wanted to replace liberal icon Thurgood Marshall with an African

American conservative Republican, and his choices were extremely limited because of the dearth of qualified black conservatives. Although he may have been appointed to the Supreme Court because of his race, Thomas has striven to acquire respect through diligence on the Court. As an African American conservative, Thomas has provided legitimacy to those who hold that, at least in the long run, African Americans must join the American mainstream based on merit rather than affirmative action.

### Bibliography

Brock, David. *The Real Anita Hill: The Untold Story.* New York: Free Press, 1993. Brock wrote this account as a slash-and-burn attack on Hill's credibility in an attempt to support Thomas. He portrayed Hill as an ideologically driven leftist.

Danforth, John C. *Resurrection: The Confirmation of Clarence Thomas.* New York: Viking, 1994. Danforth, a moderate Republican Senator from Missouri, was Thomas's mentor and friend from the 1970's until his appointment to the Supreme Court. An Episcopal priest as well as a lawyer, Danforth saw the confirmation battle in Christian terms. More balanced than most writers on Thomas's confirmation process, Danforth has written a book that ably supports Thomas without intemperate attack on those individuals and groups who opposed his confirmation.

Flax, Jane. *The American Dream in Black and White: The Clarence Thomas Hearings.* Ithaca, N.Y.: Cornell University Press, 1998. Flax, a professor of political science and practicing psychologist, examines the text of the Thomas hearings focusing in part on the differing accounts of events by Thomas and Anita Hill and the implications of the dispute for the United States.

Gerber, Scott D. *First Principles: The Jurisprudence of Clarence Thomas.* New York: New York University Press, 1999. Gerber presents Thomas's judicial work and legal philosophy based on his writings and speeches.

Hill, Anita Faye, ed. *Race, Gender, and Power in America: The Legacy of the Thomas-Hill Hearings.* New York: Oxford University Press, 1995. Hill has collected essays that support her and the stand she took against the confirmation of Thomas. Judge A. Leon Higginbotham contributed "The Hill-Thomas Hearings—What Took Place and What Happened: White Male Domination, Black Male Domination, and the Denigration of Black Women." Higginbotham describes Hill as a "friend," and he takes her harassment by Thomas as a given in an essay that briefly traces race and gender power relations from the antebellum era to the 1990's.

Morrison, Toni, ed. *Race-ing Justice, En-gendering Power: Essays on Anita Hill, Clarence Thomas, and the Construction of Social Reality.* New York: Pantheon, 1992; London: Chatto and Windus, 1993. Morrison, a noted African American novelist, has collected essays on the confirmation process that are uniformly hostile to Thomas. From a legal perspective, the most important contribution is Judge A. Leon Higginbotham's frigid admonishment of Thomas in "An Open Letter to Justice Clarence Thomas from a Federal Judicial Colleague." In 1998, Higginbotham crusaded to prevent Thomas from speaking before the National Bar Association.

Suskind, Ron. "And Clarence Thomas Wept." *Esquire* 130 (July, 1998): 70-73, 146. Suskind, a liberal observer, has written a book on Cedric Jennings' transition from an inner-city Washington, D.C., high school to undergraduate study at Brown University. This article details an interview between Thomas and Jennings, and it shows some sympathy for Thomas despite seeing him as tragically isolated.

Thomas, Susan. "Clarence Thomas." In *The Justices of the United States Supreme Court: Their Lives and Their Opinions.* Vol. 5. Edited by Leon Friedman and Fred L. Israel. New York: Chelsea House, 1997. Susan Thomas provides a scholarly summary of Thomas's career up to the 1992 term of the Supreme Court and a good bibliography, which includes publications by the associate justice. She views Thomas as an extreme conservative, especially in the area of criminal justice, and does not grant him the respect she accords his fellow archconservative associate justice Antonin Scalia.

*Susan A. Stussy*

# NORMAN THOMAS

*Born:* November 20, 1884; Marion, Ohio

*Died:* December 19, 1968; Huntington, New York

*Area of Achievement:* Social reform, government and politics

*Contribution:* Often called "the conscience of America," Thomas ran six times for president on the Socialist Party ticket and became one of the country's greatest critic-reformers.

### Early Life

Norman Mattoon Thomas was born November 20, 1884, in Marion, Ohio, the home of Warren Gamaliel Harding, where he earned pocket money by delivering the *Marion Star.* He was the eldest of six children sired by the Reverend Welling Thomas, a Presbyterian minister whose father, also a Presbyterian minister, had been born in Wales. Norman's mother, Emma Mattoon, was also the child of a Presbyterian clergyman. The Thomas household was Republican in politics, devout in religion, and conservative in conduct, opposed to dancing, cardplaying, and Sunday merrymaking. Emma Thomas was acknowledged by the family as its dominant force, emphasizing a keen sense of personal and social responsibility that her firstborn practiced all of his life.

After his 1905 graduation from Princeton University as valedictorian of his class, Thomas took his first full-time job as a social worker at New York City's Spring Street Presbyterian Church and Settlement House, located in a poverty-stricken area. In 1907, he became assistant to the pastor of Christ Church in Manhattan. There he met Frances Violet Stewart, active in Christian social service and born into a moderately wealthy family of financiers. They were married September 1, 1910, and led a notably happy marital life, in their turn having six children and fifteen grandchildren.

From 1910 to 1911, Thomas attended the heterodox Union Theological Seminary. There he was most impressed by the writings of Walter Rauschenbusch, one of the leading figures of the Social Gospel movement, who argued that the ethical precepts of Jesus did not harmonize with the selfish materialism of a capitalist society. Thirty years later, Thomas wrote, "Insofar as any one man . . . made me a Socialist, it was probably Walter Rauschenbusch." Ordained in 1911, Thomas became pastor of the East Harlem Presbyterian Church and chairman of the American Parish, a federation of Presbyterian churches and social agencies located in immigrant neighborhoods. In 1912, he declared, "The Christian Church faces no more burning question than the problem of making brotherhood real."

### Life's Work

The agonies of World War I crystallized Norman Thomas' social radicalism. He came to consider the war an immoral conflict between competing imperial powers, and in January, 1917, joined the Fellowship of Reconciliation, a religious pacifist group with a commitment to drastic social reform. Thomas came to regard resistance to the war as a clear choice of individual conscience over the dictates of an amoral state. His militant pacifism led him to support Morris Hillquit, the Socialist candidate, who ran on an antiwar platform in the 1917 New York City mayoralty race.

Thomas joined another pacifist, Roger Baldwin, in the 1917 establishment of the Civil Liberties Union, later renamed the American Civil Liberties Union. In the spring of 1918, he resigned from his church and the parish, aware that his radicalism was jeopardizing these institutions' chances for outside financial assistance. In October, 1918, he applied for membership in the American Socialist Party; he was motivated, he recalled later, by "grotesque inequalities, conspicuous waste, gross exploitation, and unnecessary poverty all around me."

The Party was led by three talented men: Victor Berger, Morris Hillquit, and Eugene V. Debs. The first two were its theoreticians and tacticians, but it was the populist, pragmatic Debs (1855-1926) who became American Socialism's greatest leader until Thomas' ascendancy. Debs grounded his convictions on emotional rather than philosophic premises: He had an evangelical devotion to social justice, a generous and sensitive temperament, sincerity, warmth, and an intuitive understanding of popular opinion.

In the 1920 election, Debs received 920,000 votes, but they were largely a tribute to his courage for having chosen imprisonment (from 1918 to 1921) to dramatize his pacifism; membership in the Socialist Party was down that year, from a 1912 peak of 108,000 to twenty-seven thousand. During the 1920's several conditions combined to keep the American Socialist Party's numbers and influence low: a dominant mood among the electorate of economic conservatism and intense nativism; hostility to organized labor by all three branches of government; a number of failed strikes; and the 1919-1920 "Red scare" mass arrests of radicals and labor leaders by the Department of Justice under Attorney General A. Mitchell Palmer. When Senator Robert M. La Follette campaigned for the presidency in 1924, he refused to run solely as the Socialist candidate, preferring to call himself a Progressive. Nevertheless, the Socialist Party energetically supported his campaign; 855,000 of La Follette's 3,800,000 votes were cast on Socialist levers.

Norman Thomas began his long career of seeking public office in 1924, running as a New York gubernatorial candidate on both the Socialist and Progressive tickets. Ironically, he had risen to Socialist leadership at a time when many people were leaving the Party. More ironically, the income his wife inherited from her conservative father enabled him to crusade for his causes on a full-time basis. He admitted that in this instance, "the critic of capitalism was its beneficiary."

By the mid-1920's, Thomas was the consensual choice to succeed Eugene V. Debs—who had never regained his health after his three-year imprisonment, and who died in 1926—as the leader of American Socialism. In 1928, he was chosen the party's presidential candidate—the first of six such nominations; he received 267,000 votes. In 1932 he was to poll 885,000; in 1936, 187,000; in 1940, 100,000; in 1944, 80,000; in 1948, 140,000.

Thomas attracted the deep affection and admiration of many people, often including ideological opponents. His physical appearance was impressive: He stood over six feet two, had strongly marked patrician features, vibrant blue eyes, well-bred manners, and an air of genteel self-confidence. Although a man of dignity, he could communicate warmth and cordiality to a wide range of people. His physical energy was phenomenal until his late seventies, when failing eyesight and crippling arthritis began to plague him. Since he had no hobbies, he focused his unflagging pace on not only campaigning, but also on writing sixteen books and scores of pamphlets, maintaining an enormous correspondence, attending countless conventions and committee meetings, and delivering thousands of speeches. Perhaps his only flaw as a leader was his remoteness—in contrast to Debs—from the rough-and-tumble realities of the American political panorama. He was by temperament an educator, moralist, and intellectual rather than a pragmatic accommodator of conflicting interests. Since he had no solid prospect of winning public office, he could afford to maintain an incorruptible integrity and the noblest of principles.

Thomas' virtuosity as a public speaker was his outstanding leadership asset. He was a masterful humorist, firing quick barbs at his targets. In 1932 he asked his listeners not to fix on Herbert Hoover as the person solely responsible for their economic suffering, since "such a little man could not have made so big a Depression" As for Harry S Truman, he "proves the old adage that any man can become President of the United States." Perhaps the best-known Thomas anecdote recounts a meeting he had with President Franklin D. Roosevelt in 1935. When Thomas complained to FDR about a particular New Deal measure, the president retorted, "Norman, I'm a damn sight better politician than you." Responded Thomas, "Certainly, Mr. President, you're on that side of the desk and I'm on this."

In 1932, with the country deeply mired in the Great Depression and capitalism seriously shaken, the Socialist Party hoped for a presidential vote of more than two million. The Socialist platform anticipated New Deal programs on many issues, demanding Federal appropriations for public works, reforestation, and slum clearance, increased public housing, a six-hour day and five-day working week, old-age pensions, health and maternity insurance, improved workmen's compensation and accident insurance, adequate minimum wage laws, and a compulsory system of unemployment compensation with adequate benefits derived from both government and employer contributions.

Contrary to Socialist expectations, the combined popular vote for all minority party candidates in 1932 barely exceeded one million, and Roosevelt embarked on an ambitious program to save capitalism by implementing a vast amount of social welfare legislation. Norman Thomas consistently chided the New Deal for what he regarded as its lack of any consistent underlying philosophy, for its opportunistic, helter-skelter improvisation and experimentation. This very pragmatism and daring, however, endeared FDR to the majority of the electorate—much to Thomas' frustration. In his *The Politics of Upheaval* (1979), the historian Arthur Schlesinger, Jr., considers that in the 1930's Thomas'

> essential contribution . . . was to keep moral issues alive at a moment when the central emphasis was on

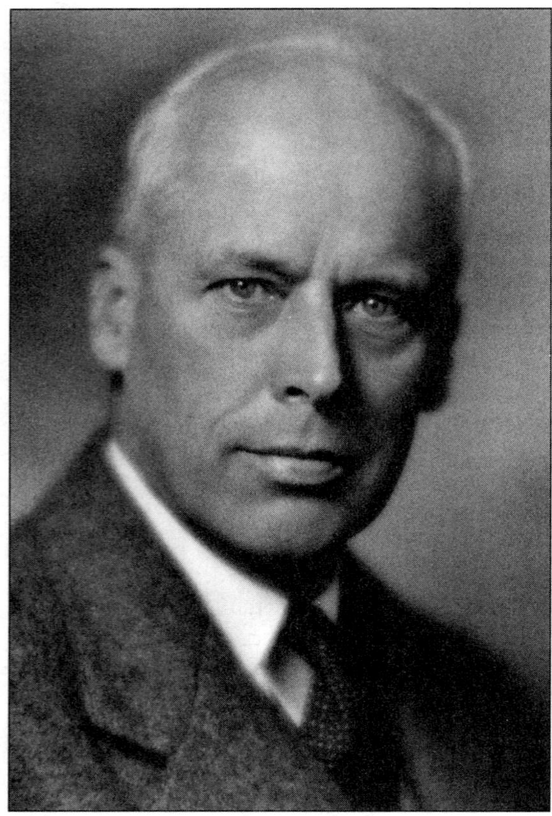

meeting economic emergencies. At his best, Thomas gave moving expression to an ethical urgency badly needed in politics. . . .

The 1930's witnessed an increasingly dangerous world situation, with Adolf Hitler's Germany, Benito Mussolini's Italy, and, late in the decade, Francisco Franco's Spain threatening the peace. Under the guise of opposing Fascism, communists in both Europe and the United States wooed liberals and radicals to form a united, "popular front." Norman Thomas temporarily flirted with the notion of such international solidarity in his 1934 book, *The Choice Before Us*. A 1937 trip he took to Europe, however, during which he witnessed Communist attempts to control Spain's Loyalist government through shabby betrayals and observed Stalin's purge trials of his former comrades, reaffirmed Thomas' mistrust of totalitarian Communism and his conviction of its basic incompatibility with democratic Socialism. The Moscow-Berlin Pact of August, 1939, outraged him as "a piece of infamy." Thomas made certain that, from 1939 on, the United States Socialist Party would vigorously oppose Communism, even when the Soviet Union was America's ally during World War II.

In the late 1930's and early 1940's Thomas' lifelong pacifist sentiments were in agonizing conflict with his detestation of Fascism and strong sympathy for the Spanish Republicans locked in civil warfare with Franco's Falangists. Thomas tried to solve this dilemma by backing aid for the Spanish government while opposing direct United States intervention on behalf of Great Britain and France after World War II had erupted in September, 1939. By late 1941, the Socialist Party's noninterventionist foreign policy, combined with Thomas' often acerbic criticism of the New Deal's socioeconomic program, had alienated many former members and well-wishers. Even though the Party fielded presidential tickets through 1956, it was never to recover its health from these losses. By the 1944 presidential campaign, Thomas' insistence on maintaining the fullest measure of civil liberties even amid a world war, and his opposition to the Allied demand on Germany and Japan for unconditional surrender had cost him much of his previous popularity: His vote total proved the lowest of his six national appeals.

In the 1948 presidential election, Thomas' main target was former vice president Henry Wallace, who had left the Democratic Party to run as an antimilitarist, radical candidate for president on the Progressive ticket. Thomas became convinced that the Progressive Party was controlled by communists, with Wallace serving as a naïve front man capable of such self-damning errors as describing the Soviet Union as a "directed democracy." When Thomas received less than 100,000 votes despite a spirited campaign, he became convinced of the futility of Socialist attempts to attract nationwide electoral support, and renounced further office seeking. In 1952 and 1956, the Party ran a Pennsylvania state legislator, Darlington Hoopes, for the presidency. He received twenty thousand votes in 1952, two thousand in 1956; no Socialist has since sought the presidency.

With his buoyant energy and sparkling mind, Thomas remained dynamically active through the 1950's and early 1960's. He resigned from various official posts in the Socialist Party in 1955, at the age of seventy-one, but remained its most magnetic advocate. The major party candidate to whom Thomas was most sympathetic during this period was Adlai Stevenson, with whom he shared a Princeton background, good breeding, and eloquent speech making. The American statesman with whom he disagreed most vehemently was John Foster Dulles, Eisenhower's secretary of state, also a fellow Princetonian as well as fellow Presbyterian. Thomas scorned Dulles' appeasement of demagogic Senator Joseph McCarthy; the bellicosity of his opposition to mainland China; his dismissal of Eleanor Roosevelt from the United States delegation to the United Nations; and his discharge of liberals and Socialists, no matter how talented, from foreign service posts.

Norman Thomas remained a morally consistent critic-commentator on American politics to the end of his fife. He voted for John Kennedy in 1960 and Lyndon Johnson in 1964, but with little enthusiasm for either candidate. In the former year, his favorite was an old friend, Hubert Humphrey, who lost the Democratic nomination to Kennedy. The Bay of Pigs fiasco shocked Thomas into an outraged telegram of protest, and thereafter he remained lukewarm through Kennedy's one thousand White House days, favoring the president's graceful style and careful separation of state from church, but worried about the moderate, cautious nature of Kennedy's liberalism. He voted for Johnson mainly to vote against the right-wing Barry Goldwater.

Though plagued by arthritic legs and a minor heart ailment, Thomas maintained a strenuous lecturing, debating, and writing schedule in the early 1960's, keeping in the fast lane of what his friends called the "Thomas Track Meet." The only debating opponent who succeeded in spoiling his usually good temper was William Buckley, Jr., whom he regarded as a cold-blooded imperialist and self-righteous reactionary. Thomas' preferred activity during his last years was spending several consecutive days as guest in residence on a college or university campus, not only lecturing but also making himself available as casual participant in bull sessions with students and faculty. On lecture platforms he would sometimes limp slowly to the podium, leaning on his cane, then address his audience with the opening line, "Creeping Socialism!"

By his eightieth birthday in late 1964 he was cast in the role of Grand Old Man, admired and loved for his integrity, dignity, intelligence, and wit, given standing ovations at his appearances. When he returned to his birthplace for a birthday tribute, the local paper printed one letter critical of Thomas' opposition to American military involvement in Vietnam. He was relieved: "I feel better not to be too respectable." In 1966, he shocked his oldest grandson, a pastor, by permitting *Playboy* to interview him at considerable length. Thomas expressed a frequent regret of his old age: that he had seen the American working class becoming increasingly middle-class in its materialism; this "dilution of labor's down-the-line militancy has been one of the greatest disappointments in my life." In 1965, ophthalmologists diagnosed his retinal arteriosclerosis; by 1966 he was legally blind, bent by his arthritis, and in pain much of the time. He never complained, however, and his voice retained its booming roar. He finished dictating his twenty-first book, *The Choices*, four weeks before his death in a nursing home a month after his eighty-fourth birthday.

### Summary

Norman Thomas devoted a long, honorable life to urging a largely uninterested American public to share his vision of democratic Socialism as a solution to social inequities and injustices. He served as a goad and gadfly in the Socratic tradition of appealing to his country's good sense and conscience. Some of the social welfare and civil rights legislation he sought was enacted into law during the administrations of Franklin Roosevelt and Lyndon Johnson—with Thomas given no or scant credit for having championed it. His great hope of building a strong Socialist movement in the United States was never realized, and he left his party, under circumstances beyond his control, weaker at his death than when he had joined it in young manhood.

Yet Norman Thomas' life can justly be called an extraordinary success story. He was a patrician moralist who maintained an unswerving passion for social justice, devotion to civil liberties, sympathy for the poor, deprived, and handicapped, hatred of war's wasteful slaughter, and faith in the ultimate wisdom of a free people. Profoundly reasonable and fair in temperament, he found expression for his evolving views first in humanitarian Christianity, then in a muted, non-Marxist Socialism. The personal esteem he gained was extraordinary: Thomas became not simply an adornment to hundreds of liberal and left-democratic causes but also an admirable member of the pantheon of great American dissenters that includes Henry Clay, Daniel Webster, Eugene V. Debs, Robert M. La Follette, and Martin Luther King, Jr.

**Bibliography**

Duram, James C. *Norman Thomas*. New York: Twayne, 1974. A concise study of Thomas' books and pamphlets, with comprehensive notes and references.

———. "Norman Thomas as Presidential Conscience." *Presidential Studies Quarterly* 20, no. 3 (Summer, 1990): 581-590.

Egbert, Donald D. *Socialism and American Life*. 2 vols. Princeton, N.J.: Princeton University Press, 1952. An incisive, lucidly written historical and sociological analysis, particularly useful for describing the background and development of marxist socialism in the United States.

Harrington, Michael. Review of two Thomas biographies in *The Reporter 25* (November 9, 1961): 64-66. A leading young socialist whom Thomas befriended portrays him as a representative of the American Protestant drive for social justice and moral improvement.

Rosenberg, Bernard. "The Example of Norman Thomas." *Dissent* 11 (Fall, 1964): 415-422. A review of two Thomas biographies. Rosenberg cogently analyzes Thomas' place in contemporary American society and urges fulfillment of Thomas' vision of a better world.

Seidler, Murray B. *Norman Thomas: Respectable Rebel*. Syracuse, N.Y.: Syracuse University Press, 1967. The most scholarly biographical-critical study to date, it focuses on Thomas' successes and failures as leader of the Socialist Party.

Swanberg, W. A. *Norman Thomas: The Last Idealist*. New York: Scribner, 1976. A vivid, well-written biography that emphasizes the warmth and courage of Thomas' character, has a multitude of illustrative photographs, but often gets so immersed in details that it loses sight of the larger ideological terrain.

*Gerhard Brand*

# TOM THOMSON

*Born:* August 4, 1877; Claremont, Ontario, Canada
*Died:* c. July 8, 1917; Canoe Lake, Ontario, Canada
*Area of Achievement:* Art
*Contribution:* In landscape paintings of vibrant color and energetic brushwork, Thomson helped steer a course toward an indigenous Canadian artistic expression.

## Early Life

Although Thomas John Thomson is one of Canada's leading cultural figures of the twentieth century, in popular imagination his life is as much based on myth as upon fact. His untimely death in 1917, in undetermined but almost certainly accidental circumstances, cut short a career that had begun to blossom only a decade earlier and lent a trace of mystery to his life's story.

Thomson was born to John and Margaret Thomson in a stone house in Claremont, Ontario, on August 4, 1877, and grew up on a farm named Rose Hill, near Leith, Ontario, on Georgian Bay of Lake Huron. He enjoyed a rural boyhood typical of the time, taking the usual interest in fishing and sports. His mother had a good library, and Thomson inherited her interest in literature, particularly Romantic poetry. The family enjoyed music, and Thomson seems to have played several instruments and later took voice lessons. In adult life, Thomson was not considered by his friends to be particularly literate or well educated, but he had a strong appreciation of fine things, both in the materials of his craft and in his life-style; he seems to have been the product of a relaxed and genteel home environment.

At age twenty-one, Thomson inherited approximately two thousand dollars, in those days a considerable sum, but the money was quickly spent. In 1899, he was apprenticed as a machinist, a career which lasted less than a year. A year's attendance at a business college in Chatham, Ontario, was followed by enrollment in a lettering and penmanship course in Seattle, Washington, at a business college cofounded by his eldest brother. After six months, Thomson left his studies to enter the photoengraving trade.

Thomson abruptly returned to Canada in 1904, apparently after his proposal of marriage to a girl of fifteen was rejected. For the next decade he continued his work as a commercial artist in various photoengraving houses in Toronto on a free-lance as well as a salaried basis. The scanty evidence of his earliest personal artistic endeavors shows little originality and only a modest range of skill. Part of his stock-in-trade as an illustrative artist were drawings of fashionable women in the manner originated by Charles Dana Gibson with the "Gibson Girl." Thomson himself was a tall, attractive man with a penchant for silk shirts and a good pipe, who appreciated unforced sophistication.

## Life's Work

Around 1908, Thomson began to associate with a group of creative men who stimulated his latent artistic genius. Most of these were colleagues in commercial art, including J. E. H. MacDonald, Frederick Varley, and others who were to come together in 1920 as the "Group of Seven." In the years just before the outbreak of World War I, Thomson and his congenial friends began to portray with fresh vision the landscapes of Southern Ontario, Algonquin Park, and the area of Thomson's boyhood home, Owen Sound.

Thomson had been sketching in pen-and-ink and in watercolor at least since his years in Seattle. His work was, at best, attractively conventional; at worst, it was clumsy and imitative. From his years as a commercial artist, there are numerous examples of competent design in an art nouveau manner, a style which was by that time so broadly disseminated as to be nearly exhausted. Yet beneath the mediocrity of his early commercial and personal artistic endeavors, Thomson was assimilating much from the broader world of art—though not, to be sure, from the most advanced styles of the day such as Cubism. Just how, and why, his association with such artists as MacDonald, Frank Johnston, and others liberated this growing store of knowledge is not well documented, but it is clear from the anecdotes and memoirs of his circle that Thomson was an energetic and adventurous painter and was able to grasp and extend artistic ideas with speed and insight. That he had the good fortune to associate with some of the strongest artistic personalities of the day in Canada, and to share ideas freely with them, is one of the signal events in the development of Canadian art and culture.

In the spring of 1912, Thomson began the final, brief phase of his career with a productive two-week sketching trip in Algonquin Park in the company of the painter H. B. Jackson. In late July, he began a tour by canoe of Spanish River with another colleague, William Broadhead, then went on by steamer at the end of September to Owen Sound. These and subsequent trips were both creative and recreational, for they were fit into a busy schedule of commercial work which occupied the greater part of the year. For Thomson as well as for many of his artist friends, these years initiated the discovery of an identifiably Canadian subject matter, the northern forest, and of an artistic language which, if not wholly original, was unique in flavor.

In the fall, Thomson was back in Toronto, employed by the firm of Rous and Mann for seventy-five cents per hour, a good wage for 1912. He had much to show for his summer's efforts, and it was no longer only his fellow workers who were excited by his sketches: He was soon to have a painting purchased by the Ontario government for $250.

Spring, 1913, found Thomson again in Algonquin Park, this time on his own. He first stayed at a lodge on Canoe Lake, then camped out when the weather warmed. It was likely in this season that he met Winnifred Trainor, who later was to be his fiancée. When he was not sketching with oil paints, he often indulged in a favorite pastime of fishing, for which he had an impressive reputation. Thomson is known to have been an expert maker of fly-fishing lures, which he characteristically gave away.

In Toronto in October, Thomson met the painter A. Y. Jackson, who had just arrived from Montreal; in January of 1914, they moved together into the first available studio of the Studio Building, which had been constructed partially with the support of Dr. James McCallum, an important patron of the arts. McCallum and to an extent Jackson are credited with helping keep Thomson's career in order, including looking after financial matters. Thomson was not indifferent to his own material well-being, but he was not a skilled organizer or promoter of his own activities. In 1914, the National Gallery of Canada purchased Thomson's *Moonlight, Early Evening*, a sign that his career was advancing and the day approaching when he might rely on sales of his paintings to sustain him.

The summer of 1914 was spent first on Georgian Bay and then in Algonquin Park, but this was the last excursion for which Thomson could rely on the companionship of his fellow artists, as the war would soon disperse many of his group. Thomson himself was rejected from the army, although he was accustomed to an energetic outdoor life during summers; he had also attempted unsuccessfully to enlist for the Boer War in 1899. The war also affected his opportunities for commercial work, and during the next two years he found occasional work as a ranger, a firefighter, and a guide. In the summer of 1915, he even thought of traveling to the prairies to work in the grain harvest, a plan which might have produced an interesting body of work had he found the time to paint the landscape there, but McCallum commissioned some decorative panels from him which kept him in Ontario for the season.

Thomson's summer painting consisted mostly of small oil sketches on birch panels. From a few of these he would derive larger paintings during the winter months when he was at work in his studio. Critics have had divided feelings about the strength of some of the more detailed studio compositions based on the vigorous sketches produced in the field, but it is clear that some of them are very fine, gaining in precision of color effect more than they may have lost in spontaneity of brushwork.

A productive winter in 1916-1917 was followed by Thomson's last spring and summer, which he spent at Canoe Lake. He was said to have produced then a series of sixty-two painted sketches depicting the unfolding of spring. It has not been possible to confirm this by correlating the body of his work, but such a series would not seem out of character for a painter whose skill and energy were at their height, and whose career was itself enjoying healthy growth.

Thomson's death just before his fortieth birthday has been interpreted speculatively in many ways over the years, but the known facts hardly support any dark theories. On July 8, he paddled off to fish at one of the lakes near Canoe Lake and was not seen alive again. His overturned canoe was found later that day, but his body was not recovered until July 16. There was a four-inch cut on his right temple and evidence of his having bled from his right ear. As in a large proportion of canoe drownings, Thomson probably stood up briefly in his canoe, lost his balance, fell, and struck his head on the gunwale. This mundane account of the circumstances of his death has often been rejected by worshipful commentators and public as holding no meaning for the culture. Apart from possible injury, under ordinary circumstances falling out of a canoe is merely embarrassing; when an acclaimed artist in the prime of his career dies in such a fashion, high tragedy must supplant embarrassment.

### Summary

Although Tom Thomson was an interesting personality and a major contributor to Canada's first important communal force in art—the loose association which later became the Group of Seven—it is in his paintings that one must seek the significance of his life. The myth of Thomson as a creative hero can be sustained only by a close appreciation of his works.

Thomson's greatest achievement as a painter was to evoke a powerful sense of the north woods through the use of strong color. The ultimate source of his sense of color was the art of the French Impressionists, but Thomson himself had little direct, sustained contact with any large body of Impressionist art or for that matter with any of the dominant styles of the previous half century. Jackson has been quoted as saying, "Tom Thomson never saw a good picture in Toronto, European or otherwise." Nevertheless, there are echoes in Thomson's work of the painting of the mid-nineteenth century Barbizon school of France, as well as strong influences from then-current German Expressionism; aspects of his style recall such varied artists as the Russian expatriate Wassily Kandinsky and the Austrian Gustav Klimt. In fact, the foreign as well as Canadian influences on Thomson are extensive enough to raise the question of his originality and individuality, but critical opinion is favorable on this point: Thomson turned what he inherited to excellent use, integrating the elements he borrowed into a style of his own.

Thomson's oil sketches are the largest of his work in the final years of his life. The characteristic subject matter is lakes, trees, and sky, and it is often the sky that is of central importance to a composition. Of Thomson's composition, David P. Silcox remarks that Thomson had "an easy, even casual approach to the construction of his painting" and that "it was the desire to paint, to mix colour and expeditiously get on with it that saved Thomson from the compositional fussiness that pervades the structure of some Group [of Seven] painting."

Much of Thomson's best work is characterized by an element of roughness both of color and paint application. Some viewers are inclined to see this roughness as an attempt to evoke the harshness of the North, but to Thomson and his colleagues the north woods were a paradise rather than a hostile environment, and they often painted in and near areas that were essentially summer resorts. A more convincing assessment of Thomson's gestural brushwork and turbulent color is that he was moving toward a concept of painting like that of Abstract Expressionism of the 1950's, in which the drama of the artist's physical deployment of paint on canvas mirrors an emotional involvement with the worlds of nature, society, and the human spirit. Seen in this light, Thomson's brief but productive career heralds the coming of age of a vigorous and indigenous Canadian art. Along with his colleagues in the Group of Seven and others, Thomson provided, in Harold Town's words, a "starting line" for all that was to follow.

### Bibliography

Addison, Ottelyn. *Tom Thomson: The Algonquin Years*. Foreword by A. Y. Jackson, drawings and an appendix by Thoreau MacDonald. Toronto: Ryerson Press, 1969. Contains many detailed anecdotes about Algonquin Park and Thomson's sojourns there from 1912. Plentiful photographs and records of conversations with friends and acquaintances give this small volume a feeling of authenticity and affection for the subject.

Carmichael, D. G. *The McMichael Canadian Collection*. Toronto: Matthews, 1973. This catalog of one of Canada's most unusual art galleries contains, in addition to color plates, a large selection of small black-and-white reference photographs of most of its remarkable collection. An indispensable introduction to the Tom Thomson era, and after, in the work of MacDonald, Harris, A. J. Casson, David Milne, Emily Carr, and others.

"The Genius of Tom Thomson." *Canadian Geographic* 113 no. 6, (November/December, 1993). This article focuses on the time spent by artist Tom Thomson in Ontario's Algonquin Park (1912-1917) and the work he produced there.

Harper, J. Russell. *Painting in Canada: A History*. 2d. ed. Toronto: University of Toronto Press, 1971. This standard survey is useful for viewing the scope of Canadian painting. Town and Silcox (below) contains a rebuttal, in passing, of a statement by Harper about the early reception of Thomson's work, but the work is still excellent for its intended purpose.

Murray, Joan. *The Art of Tom Thomson*. Toronto: Art Gallery of Ontario, 1971. A noted Canadian art curator surveys Thomson's work in this exhibition catalog.

Pattison, Jeanne L. *The Group of Seven and Tom Thomson*. Kleinburg, Ontario: McMichael Canadian Collection, 1977. The title of this paper-bound volume serves to remind readers both that Tom Thomson was not a member of the Group of Seven, since the Group came into being as such three years after his death, and that it is necessary to put Thomson into the context of the Group, as he was one of the leading exponents of landscape painting in the decade preceding its founding, and worked with many of its future members.

Peck, R.M. "Seasons of the Canadian Soul." *International Wildlife,* (May/June, 1989) The author discusses the "Group of Seven."

Town, Harold, and David P. Silcox. *Tom Thomson: The Silence and the Storm.* 3d ed. Toronto: McClelland and Stewart, 1989. An indispensable "appreciation" of the works of Thomson, this volume effectively juxtaposes essays by the perceptive Canadian artist Harold Town and those of art historian David P. Silcox. Both authors are straightforward in their praise and criticism of Thomson. The high-quality plates are well chosen and are supplied in generous numbers.

*Clyde S. McConnell*

# EDWARD L. THORNDIKE

*Born:* August 31, 1874; Williamsburg, Massachusetts
*Died:* August 9, 1949; Montrose, New York
*Areas of Achievement:* Psychology and education
*Contribution:* Often referred to as the "Father of Modern Educational Psychology," Thorndike incorporated measurement into education and psychology, as well as developing testing of animals and studies of learning in humans.

## Early Life

Edward Lee Thorndike was born August 31, 1874, in Williamsburg, Massachusetts. Thorndike was the second son and the second of four children of Edward Roberts Thorndike and Abigail Brewster (Ladd) Thorndike. His father had first practiced law and later became a Methodist clergyman. Reared in a clergyman's home, Thorndike and his siblings were expected to be models for the congregation and to strive for excellence.

The religious environment of the Thorndike home has been described as austere, and the children constantly participated in church activities. As an adult, Edward Thorndike financially supported the local Methodist church, but he did not attend or require attendance of his children. Thorndike guided his later life by nonsectarian ethical precepts, rather than by the religious precepts of his upbringing.

Intellectual pursuits were important in the home. Thorndike's mother, Abigail, was a highly intelligent woman, and the children were stimulated by their home environment as well as by contact with the sophisticated congregations of the Boston-Cambridge area. The four children all went on to earn excellent grades and scholarships, and all established academic careers. Ashley, the eldest son, became a professor of English; Lynn, the third son, a historian; and Mildred, the youngest child, a high school English teacher. All three of the Thorndike brothers were professors at Columbia University.

The elder Thorndike, as a minister, was forced to move his family frequently, and the disruption left young Thorndike with pronounced shyness and social uneasiness. This discontinuity of social contacts also may have contributed to his adult preference for the lonely privacy of research. His social contacts were with small groups of friends, and he disliked such routine gatherings as faculty meetings and national scientific conventions. Thorndike's work consumed his time and attention, and he found competition and the effort to influence others distasteful. To him, learning was essentially a private undertaking, something which happened under one's skin, in the nervous system.

## Life's Work

Thorndike attended Wesleyan University in Connecticut from 1891 to 1895 earning the B.A. degree, with honors, in the traditional classical curriculum, but had no firm career plans. While at Wesleyan, he held membership in Phi Beta Kappa. Thorndike stated in an autobiographical sketch that he had neither heard nor seen the word "psychology" until his junior year at Wesleyan. A required course taught by Andrew Armstrong in the subject and the text *Elements of Psychology* (1886) by James Sully did little to pique Thorndike's interest in psychology. While a senior, however, Thorndike studied parts of William James's *The Principles of Psychology* (1890) in connection with a prize examination and found them stimulating and interesting. An opportunity to study with James came the following year with a scholarship to Harvard. Study under James strengthened Thorndike's interest in psychology, and as he later wrote, "by the fall of 1897, I thought of myself as a student of psychology and a candidate for the Ph.D. degree."

Pioneering in the use of animals for psychological research, Thorndike, while studying with James, conducted several experiments on the instinctive and intelligent behavior of chickens. In 1897-1898, a substantial fellowship brought Thorndike to Columbia University in New York City to complete his doctoral study. While at Columbia, he received additional training in biology and statistics and worked primarily under James McKeen Cattell, who provided him with laboratory space. He completed his doctoral dissertation, "Animal Intelligence," in 1898; this work inaugurated the scientific study of animal learning and laid the foundation for study of stimulus-response connections (known as S-R bonds) as the central factors in all learning.

Upon graduation, Thorndike began teaching at Western Reserve University in Cleveland, Ohio. While there, teaching education courses in the 1898-1899 school year, he continued his investigations into animal learning. Then, on the recommendation of William James, he returned to Columbia

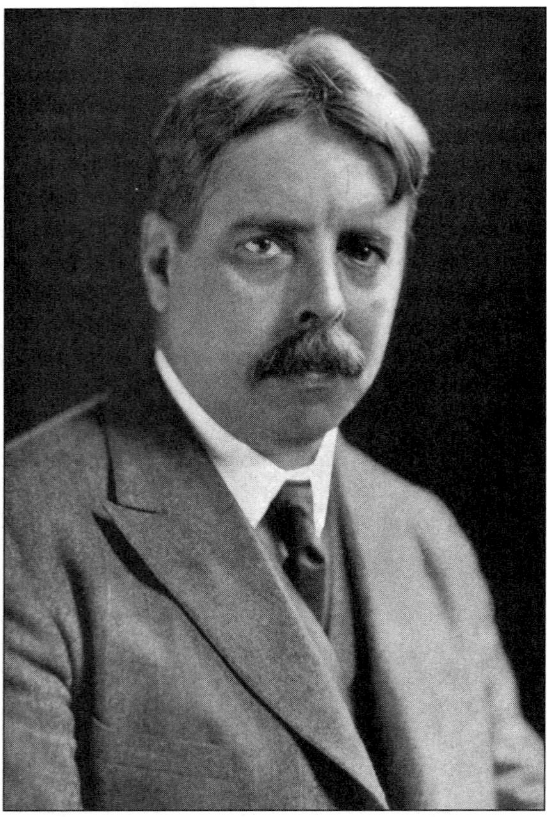

University in 1899 as instructor in genetic psychology and remained there for the rest of his life, earning the title adjunct professor in 1901, professor in 1904, and professor emeritus in 1941.

During the five decades of his career, Thorndike applied theoretical principles and empirical techniques to a vast range of educational problems. He attempted to rid psychology of such philosophical concepts as "soul" and "mental philosophy" and bring a more scientific approach to psychology and research. Thorndike believed that achievement and intellectual differences between people are quantitative, not qualitative. He believed heredity to be responsible for human differences and scorned environmental explanations. Thorndike also asserted the triumph of character over circumstances, arguing that the ingredients of success are in a man and not around him.

Thorndike became the educational world's major exponent of the use of science's universal language of description, numbers. All that exists, he affirmed, exists in some amount and can be measured. In 1902, he introduced the first university course in educational measurement, and two years later he wrote the first handbook for researchers in the use of social statistics, *An Introduction to the Theory of Mental and Social Measurements* (1904).

Thorndike's approach to research was observational; he would present the subject with a problem to solve—how to escape from a confining place, how to rank his attitudes, which response to select in order to avoid a mild shock—and then observe the behavior and report it in a quantitative form. Despite the simplicity of his approach, Thorndike is credited with creating two basic psychological research techniques: the maze and the problem box. Using this type of stimulus work in animal studies, Thorndike concluded that learning had taken place following the law of cause and effect. Thorndike also studied learning in human beings. His conclusions were that being right helped the student retain a correct response, but being wrong did not eliminate errors.

In work on more practical matters, Thorndike was active in the preparation of school materials and tools, various achievement scales, and a series of arithmetic texts for the elementary grades. His *The Teacher's Word Book* (1921), an alphabetical list of ten thousand words that occur most frequently in the general use of the English language, provided a foundation for a series of school readers. He also conducted large-scale statistical studies of mathematics, Latin, and other subjects that affected the later school performance of students. He was one of the first to devise tests to measure aptitudes and learning.

On August 29, 1900, Thorndike married Elizabeth Moulton of Boston; they had five children, four of whom lived to maturity and themselves followed scientific careers: Elizabeth Frances in mathematics, Edward Moulton in physics, Robert Ladd in educational psychology, and Alan Moulton in physics. Having enjoyed generally robust health throughout his life, Thorndike succumbed to a cerebral hemorrhage at his home in Montrose, New York, shortly before his seventy-fifth birthday. He was buried in Hillside Cemetery, Peekskill, New York.

Thorndike received much recognition during his lifetime for his efforts to help educational institutions capitalize upon learning potential. He received honorary degrees from many universities, was elected to the National Academy of Sciences, and held the presidencies and memberships in numerous American and international scientific and educational associations. In a 1925 tribute to Thorndike, Columbia University bestowed upon Thorndike the Butler Medal, "in recognition of his exceptionally significant contributions to the general problem of the measurement of human faculty and to the applications of such measurements to education."

### Summary

Thorndike wrote more than 450 books, monographs, and articles. His works include *Educational Psychology* (1903), *Elements of Psychology* (1905), *The Principles of Teaching* (1906), *Animal Intelligence* (1898), *The Original Nature of Man* (1926), *The Teacher's Word Book of Thirty Thousand Words* (1944), *Psychology of Arithmetic* (1922), *The Measurement of Intelligence* (1926), *Fundamentals of Learning* (1932), *Thorndike Century Junior Dictionary* (1935), *Human Nature and the Social Order* (1940), *Thorndike Century Senior Dictionary* (1941), and *Man and His Works* (1943).

Thorndike's work with educational testing has been a basis for subsequent quantitative testing in educational and psychological situations. Although many of his theories were not complete and were later superseded, Thorndike introduced the scientific method into these fields. This emphasis on scientific method is a reflection of the ideas and influence of the Industrial Revolution, of which Thorndike was a product.

Thorndike contributed significantly to the development of scientifically based schooling. Books such as *Notes on Child Study* (1901), *The Principles of Teaching Based on Psychology* (1906), and *Education: A First Book* (1912) directed teachers toward a more humane approach to teaching and to a support for the scientific movement in education. Thorndike also contributed to the growing awareness of individual differences and the main divisions of modern educational psychology—measurement, learning, and individual differences.

Thorndike's word-lists are the basis of the teaching of reading in all English-speaking schools. His impact on education has been diverse and practical. The Thorndike dictionary is still in use, and Thorndike's influence on education is still felt today.

### Bibliography

Beatty, Barbara. "From Laws of Learning to a Science of Values: Efficiency and Morality in Thorndike's Educational Psychology." *The American Psychologist* 53 no. 10, (October, 1998). Article commemorating Thorndike's work in educational psychology that discusses his methods, his development of tests, and his science of values.

Curti, Merle. "Edward Lee Thorndike: Scientist." In *Social Ideas of American Educators*. New York: Scribner, 1935. Curti disapproves of Thorndike and his methods.

Dewsbury, Donald A. "Celebrating E.L. Thorndike a Century after 'Animal Intelligence.'" *The American Psychologist* 53 no. 10, (October, 1998). A centenary tribute to the 1898 publication of Thorndike's doctoral dissertation on animal psychology.

Joncich, Geraldine. *The Sane Positivist: A Biography of Edward L. Thorndike*. Middletown, Conn.: Wesleyan University Press, 1968. A full-scale study of Thorndike and his work. The standard biography, covering Thorndike's personal as well as intellectual development.

Murchison, Carl. *A History of Psychology in Autobiography*. Vol. 3. Worcester, Mass.: Clark University Press, 1936; London: Russell, 1961. Autobiographical sketch of Thorndike with emphasis on his studies in psychology.

Thorndike, Edward Lee. *Man and His Works*. Cambridge, Mass.: Harvard University Press, 1943. Consists of the William James lectures given in 1942 at Harvard University. First three chapters present facts about humanity and the remaining chapters concern applications of psychology. Provides good insight into Thorndike's philosophy.

Woodworth, Robert S. *Biographical Memoir of Edward Lee Thorndike*. Washington, D.C.: National Academy of Sciences, 1952. Useful background material on Thorndike's personality.

*Annette Daniel*

## JIM THORPE

*Born:* May 22, 1888; near Prague, Oklahoma
*Died:* March 28, 1953; Lomita, California
*Area of Achievement:* Sports
*Contribution:* In 1950, the Associated Press voted Thorpe the best athlete of the first half of the twentieth century, a judgment based on his two gold medals won at the 1912 Olympic Games and on his athletic achievements as a football, track, and baseball star.

### Early Life

James Francis Thorpe and his twin brother Charlie were born on May 22, 1888, to Hiram and Charlotte Thorpe, in a small cabin on the banks of the North Canadian River near Prague, Oklahoma. Intermarriage among whites and Native Americans had become prevalent, and both Hiram and Charlotte were of mixed blood. Hiram's father, a blacksmith, was Irish; his mother was a Native American of Sac and Fox ancestry. Hiram eventually had nineteen children from five different women. Charlotte was his third wife; her great-grandfather had been Jacques Vieux, a French fur trader who had founded Milwaukee, Wisconsin. Charlotte was also the granddaughter of the Potawatomi Chief Louis Vieux. As a descendant of this multinational family tree of what might be considered the upper-class Indians of the Midwest, Jim Thorpe was of Irish, French, and Indian stock. His rugged looks were overwhelmingly Indian, and this fact would always be emphasized in his athletic life story.

Because of the government's desire for land, the Indians were moved about like so many checkers on a board. They were compensated with both financial allotments and new land farther west. Hiram and Charlotte lived under these conditions and received land and a stipend each month based on the number of children they had.

Thorpe's early childhood was filled with endless swimming, fishing, and hunting. At the age of six, however, he and his twin brother were sent to the mission boarding school. The white instructors there imposed strict discipline to indoctrinate the Indian children into the white culture. Students wore uniforms, the Indian language was forbidden, and the children's lives were regimented and time marked off by the ringing of bells. Thorpe eventually ran away, but his father forced him to return. Thorpe would never be a strong student, but he did benefit from the difficult experience: Without the basics he received in school, a college career would have been virtually impossible.

In 1897, Thorpe's schooling was sidetracked when his brother Charlie was stricken with pneumonia and smallpox and died in March. Thorpe returned to school, but, overcome with grief, he then ran away for the second time. The tragedy of the loss of his twin brother would remain with Thorpe throughout his life.

Hiram decided that his son had run away from school for the last time. At ten Thorpe was sent by train to Haskell Indian Junior College in Lawrence, Kansas, hundreds of miles from home. There, he would board with about six hundred other children of Indian parentage and receive much the same education he had received at the agency school, with one important addition: organized football.

Tragedy again struck in Thorpe's life when, on November 17, 1901, his mother died from complications while giving birth to her eleventh child. Again the smooth flow of events in Thorpe's life had been disrupted. Hiram remarried and young Thorpe's relationship with his father became strained. In January, 1900, the Carlisle Indian School football team had visited the students at Haskell. Thorpe dreamed of playing for Carlisle, and in February, 1904, he took the train to Carlisle, Pennsylvania.

### Life's Work

The administration at the Carlisle Indian School desired to increase their national recognition through a first-rate sports program. Public support was vital to Carlisle's future, and football was the sport with which to reach a vast number of people. The administration at Carlisle hired Glenn Scobey "Pop" Warner to be their head football coach. Almost as if the Fates had planned it, one of America's most skilled and, later, most famous coaches would have as his pupil one of the best athletes of the century.

Once again, however, the flow of life was interrupted for Thorpe as he received the news that his father had died of blood poisoning. Thorpe, too far from home to attend the funeral, was sixteen and had lost both his parents and his twin brother.

Soon Thorpe got a chance to demonstrate his track-and-field abilities. Competing against students in the upper class, Thorpe easily won the 120-yard hurdles and the high jump. He placed second in the 220-yard dash. From that point on,

Thorpe was assured a place on the varsity squad. Word quickly reached Pop Warner, and soon Thorpe received special coaching and an open summer schedule to work on athletics. Thorpe became a member of the varsity football team, having already lettered as a member of the varsity track team. In 1907, Thorpe proved to be an adept runner but, since he was still raw in terms of game skills, he was made a reserve.

During the 1908 football season, Thorpe, who now weighed 175 pounds, developed his famous placekick accuracy. His ability to kick field goals contributed to Carlisle's 10-2-1 season. That year, because of his kicking prowess, he was named a third-team all-American. During the summer of 1909, Thorpe made a decision that would prove very costly to him for the rest of his life. He loved baseball and decided to play for Rocky Mount in the East Carolina League for the princely sum of fifteen dollars a week, barely enough to cover living expenses. He enjoyed playing so much that he decided, in 1910, not to return to Carlisle and to play semiprofessional baseball instead.

In the summer of 1911, by sheer chance, Thorpe ran into a football teammate, Albert Exendine. Thorpe was now twenty-four, stood six feet tall, and weighed almost two hundred pounds. Exendine explained to Thorpe that the football team had fared poorly and that Thorpe was sorely missed. Thorpe cabled Carlisle, and with Pop Warner's influence he was readmitted. Coach Warner wanted Thorpe to return for two reasons: to play football and to be placed in training as a candidate for the 1912 Olympics.

Thorpe returned to football with almost no effort. In the first big game with the University of Pittsburgh, Thorpe kicked and ran with extraordinary results and the final score was Carlisle 17, Pittsburgh 0. Thirty thousand fans turned out for the Harvard game at Cambridge. The coaches at Harvard decided they could win with their reserves. Nursing a leg injury, Thorpe still managed to score a touchdown and kick field goals, and Carlisle led 15 to 9 as the Harvard Varsity finally came onto the field in the fourth quarter, but it was too late. Thorpe, with his ankle bandaged, kicked his fourth field goal (from a distance of forty-eight yards), Carlisle held Harvard to one touchdown, and the final score was Carlisle 18, Harvard 15. That afternoon, Thorpe had given one of his greatest game efforts, and historically it had been one of the greatest displays of football for all time.

Later that season, Thorpe punted against Brown for eighty-three yards, a new collegiate record. After that game, he was elected team captain. That same year Thorpe met Iva Miller, a Scotch-Irish Cherokee whom he would marry in October, 1913.

In the winter of 1912, Pop Warner began training Thorpe and Louis Tewanima, a Hopi Indian, for the Olympic tryouts. In the tryouts, Thorpe won eleven gold, four silver, and three bronze medals while Tewanima won most of the long-distance races in which he competed.

Both men qualified for the Olympics that spring. The team trained rigorously as it crossed the Atlantic aboard the specially outfitted SS *Finland*, and Thorpe, who was twenty-five, found the trip to Sweden to be one of the most exhilarating parts of the whole experience.

Thorpe's first event was the pentathlon. He won the broad jump with a distance of twenty-three feet, 2.7 inches. In the javelin he placed third, but that loss may have propelled him to win the discus, the two-hundred-meter dash, and the fifteen-hundred-meter race, where he stunned spectators with a time of four minutes, 44.8 seconds. Sweden's King Gustav V presented Thorpe with the gold medal for the pentathlon.

Thorpe's next event, the decathlon, was only a few days away. Competition would be spread over three days, and during the interval Thorpe returned to the *Finland* to train. While Thorpe trained and watched his teammates dominate the Games, Louis Tewanima won a silver medal in the ten-thousand-meter race. On a rainy afternoon, the decathlon's first three events were held. Thorpe finished third in the one-hundred-meter dash and second in the running broad jump. He won first place in the shot put, heaving it forty-two feet, 5.5 inches and was in a slight lead after the first day. On the second day, the weather was ideal. Thorpe easily took a first in the running high jump with a height of six feet, 1.6 inches. He also finished first in the 110-meter hurdles with a record time of 15.6 seconds, but finished fourth in the four-hundred-meter race. Nevertheless, his lead was maintained.

Only one day was left for both the decathlon and the Games. Jumping and running came naturally to Thorpe, but he lacked the experience and training that one would assume he needed for the discus, the javelin, and the pole vault on the final day. Yet he took second place in the discus, third in the javelin, and third in the pole vault. It was the final event, the fifteen-hundred-meter race, in which

Thorpe displayed the qualities of the famed athlete that he had become. Despite fatigue, Thorpe proceeded to run the fifteen-hundred-meter in four minutes, 40.1 seconds—an impressive finish in which Thorpe had bettered his own record.

Thorpe finished the decathlon with an incredible 8,412.96 points out of a possible ten thousand. This point record would not be beaten until 1926. For the second time, Thorpe stood before King Gustav V. The king placed a laurel wreath atop his head, hung the gold medal around his neck, shook hands with him, and proclaimed Thorpe to be the greatest athlete in the world.

In January, 1913, a newspaper reporter revealed that Jim Thorpe had played semiprofessional baseball prior to the 1912 Olympics, thus placing in question his status as an amateur athlete. After thorough investigations and extended testimony, the Amateur Athletic Union, despite a worldwide outcry, decided that Thorpe must return all medals won and have his name withdrawn from the record books for all athletic events in which he had taken part after his involvement in baseball. His two gold medals were returned to the International Olympic Committee, and King Gustav V awarded them to the runners-up in the pentathlon and decathlon.

To earn his living, Thorpe became a year-round professional athlete, playing baseball for the New York Giants and football for the Canton Bulldogs and later with other teams during the off-season. Thorpe and the Giant manager John McGraw never got along well, and one afternoon after an argument between the two, McGraw demoted Thorpe to the Giant Triple-A system. Thorpe would spend the rest of his baseball career being shuttled from team to team. He eventually returned to the major leagues and played with the Cincinnati Reds and the Boston Braves until 1919, but he never fulfilled his potential.

Throughout his life, Thorpe fought to regain reinstatement as an amateur, to no avail. Still, his fame did not fade, and he made a modest living lecturing and giving football exhibitions, one of which included a dropkicking demonstration at New York's Polo Grounds when he was sixty-one.

In 1945, Thorpe married Patricia Askew. She helped him organize his life and took up his cause after his death. In that same year, Thorpe supported the war effort by becoming a carpenter in the Merchant Marine. In 1952, Thorpe suffered his second heart attack. Seven months later, on March 28, 1953, the famed Native American athlete's heart gave out.

### Summary

In January, 1950, a poll of Associated Press reporters and broadcasters named Thorpe the greatest football player of the first half of the century. The next month, the Associated Press selected Thorpe as the "best male athlete of the half century." In 1963, he was elected a charter member of the Professional Football Hall of Fame. Thorpe's legendary abilities in sports had once again received recognition, and indeed he will always be remembered as one of America's greatest sports heroes.

What other American athlete could make such a diversified claim on the American sporting record? The honors continued throughout his life and after it. One honor of which he would have been particularly proud was his election in 1958 to the National Indian Hall of Fame.

Alongside his monumental sports career, however, Thorpe suffered more tragedies than the average person. His wife, his children, and his supporters fought for the reinstatement of his medals after his death. The fight was a long one, filled with ugly political bickering. Finally, justice was served and the International Olympic Committee restored Thorpe's honors at an official ceremony in 1983. Thorpe was named a cowinner for the two events which he won at the 1912 Olympics and his descendants were given replicas of his gold medals.

### Bibliography

Cutler, Gray. "Jim Thorpe: Native American Legend." *Films in Review* 47 no. 7-8, (July/August 1996). In-depth piece on Thorpe including his films, popularity, and his father's influence on his career.

"Greatest Athlete." *Time* 61 (April 6, 1953): 58. This obituary pays a tribute to Thorpe as the world's greatest athlete.

Hahn, James, and Lynn Hahn. *Thorpe! The Sports Career of James Thorpe*. Edited by Howard Schroeder. Mankato, Minn.: Crestwood House, 1981. A short paperback that covers the highlights of Thorpe's life.

*Jim Thorpe, All American*. Directed by Michael Urtiz. Hollywood, Calif.: Warner Bros., 1951. This film is worth viewing, but it glosses over the tragedies.

Masin, H. L. "Meet Jim Thorpe, Greatest Athlete of Them All." *Scholastic* 60 (May 7, 1952): 6.

Discusses Thorpe's feats as an athlete. Includes a photograph.

"Obituary." *Newsweek* 41 (April 6, 1953): 60. Thorpe's greatest moments as an athlete and a brief sketch of his life.

Richards, Gregory B. *Jim Thorpe: World's Greatest Athlete*. Chicago: Children's Press, 1984. Updated with story of reinstatement. Detailed and well written. Includes a foreword by Grace F. Thorpe, one of Thorpe's daughters. Contains photographs, a chronology, and an index.

Smith, Jane R. "Triumph and Tragedy." *American History* 32 no. 2, (May/June, 1997). Overview of Thorpe's life including his entry into football, his Olympic medals, and the cause of his death.

Wheeler, Robert W. *Jim Thorpe: World's Greatest Athlete*. Rev. ed. Norman: University of Oklahoma Press, 1979. Includes index and bibliography. Thorpe's athletic accomplishments are recounted.

*John Harty*

# JAMES THURBER

*Born:* December 8, 1894; Columbus, Ohio
*Died:* November 2, 1961; New York, New York
*Areas of Achievement:* Art, literature, theater, and entertainment
*Contribution:* Thurber pioneered an urbane and sophisticated style of humor that was markedly different from the bucolic, provincial, and often self-conscious American humor of the nineteenth century and that was far more appropriate to the complex, anxiety-ridden America being thrust into world leadership in the twentieth century.

## Early Life

James Grover Thurber was born and raised in Columbus, Ohio. Throughout his life, he often wrote about his memories of his early Ohio years. At age seven, Thurber was shot in the left eye by an arrow while playing cowboys and Indians with his two brothers. Through a sympathetic reaction, his right eye eventually became affected, and he became totally blind forty years later. His impaired vision prevented him from enjoying normal childhood activities; instead, he developed a rich fantasy life and became addicted to reading and watching motion pictures.

Thurber attended Ohio State University but did not graduate. He displayed early talent for humor by writing for the university's humor magazine and contributing skits to student theatrical productions. At college he was introduced to the highly polished fiction of Henry James, who became his most important literary influence. In a letter to his daughter in later years, Thurber wrote that other writers who "interested, inspired, or excited" him were Willa Cather, Evelyn Waugh, Nathanael West, Clarence Day, Ernest Hemingway, F. Scott Fitzgerald, and E. B. White. White, another great American essayist and humorist, later became Thurber's friend, mentor, and collaborator on a successful book titled *Is Sex Necessary?* (1929).

During World War I, Thurber served as a code clerk with the State Department in Washington, D.C., and later in Paris, France. He returned to Columbus in 1920, where he became a reporter for the *Columbus Dispatch* and a regional correspondent for *The Christian Science Monitor.* During 1924 and 1925, he reported for the European editions of the *Chicago Tribune* and supplemented his income with freelance contributions to the *New York Sunday World*, *Harper's Magazine*, the *New York Herald Tribune*, and the *Kansas City Star.* Later in 1925, he became a staff member of the *New York Evening Post.*

Thurber married Althea Adams in 1922. They had a daughter, Rosemary, who was to be Thurber's only child. He and Althea led a vagabond life while he was struggling to survive as a reporter and freelance writer in Columbus, Paris, and New York. However, Thurber and Althea were temperamentally incompatible, and they were divorced in 1935. Thurber married Helen Wismer, who remained with him for the rest of his life and became indispensable as a companion and literary assistant as his vision deteriorated.

## Life's Work

By far the most important event in Thurber's career came as a result of chance and timing. On February 19, 1925, the eccentric genius Harold W. Ross had started a sophisticated humor magazine called *The New Yorker*, which would ultimately discover and introduce many of America's best writers. On the recommendation of E. B. White, Thurber was hired as managing editor. However, he soon proved his managerial incompetence and was allowed to work with White as a staff writer. These two gifted men wrote most of the magazine's "Talk of the Town" section and set the high literary standards for which the magazine became internationally famous. They also created the magazine's sophisticated conversational style.

Thurber, who defined humor as "emotional chaos remembered in tranquility," always considered himself first and foremost a writer. He had, however, developed the habit of doodling. The men, women, and animals he drew looked very much like a child's drawings, but White saw that they often expressed the same quirky humor found in Thurber's writing. White submitted some of the discarded drawings to *The New Yorker*'s art department. To Thurber's great surprise, the magazine began publishing some of the drawings with appropriate captions added. The fact that they appeared to be so amateurish was a large part of their charm. White once warned Thurber, "If you ever got good you'd be mediocre." In time Thurber became almost better known as an artist than as a writer. His cartoons and "spots" became one of *The New Yorker*'s distinguishing features.

Thurber's drawings of dogs were his most popular creations. They usually looked something like bloodhounds and wore a brooding, troubled look, as if they were puzzled by the eccentric humans with whom they were forced to live. His dogs were as famous in his time as Snoopy, the happy-go-lucky beagle who originated in the *Peanuts* comic strip, was to become in later years. Thurber's distinctive style of drawing enabled him to obtain lucrative advertising jobs as a sideline. This added income helped the Thurbers enjoy a comfortable town-and-country lifestyle in the expensive New York area. His art achieved widespread acclaim. He held many exhibitions and was compared to such renowned artists as Henri Matisse.

Many of Thurber's books consist of stories, essays, cartoons, and drawings, most of which had originally appeared in *The New Yorker.* Among the best of these collections are *The Middle-Aged Man on the Flying Trapeze: A Collection of Short Pieces* (1935), *The Thurber Carnival* (1945), *The Beast in Me and Other Animals: A New Collection of Pieces and Drawings about Human Beings and Less Alarming Creatures* (1948), and *The Thurber Album: A New Collection of Pieces about People* (1952). Thurber also collaborated with Elliott Nugent on a successful play titled *The Male Animal* (1940) and personally starred in a show titled *The Thurber Carnival* (1960), a series of skits based on his *New Yorker* stories and humor pieces. *The Male Animal* was filmed by Warner Bros. in 1942, starring Henry Fonda and Olivia de Havilland. Thurber's most frequently anthologized, and perhaps most representative, short story, "The Secret Life of Walter Mitty," was filmed by Samuel Goldwyn Productions in 1947, starring Danny Kaye.

Thurber discovered another avenue of expression by creating books that have been variously described as fairy tales and romances for adults. He published *Many Moons* in 1943, *The Great Quillow* in 1944, *The White Deer* in 1945, *The Thirteen Clocks* in 1950, and *The Wonderful O* in 1957. They are ostensibly fantasy tales for children but can be read on an entirely different level by adults who see the fantasy characters as twentieth century men and women in thin disguise.

One of Thurber's favorite topics was what is often called "the battle of the sexes." He was one of the first to see that relations between the sexes were changing because of many complex factors. In his writing and cartoons, he depicted women who were chronically dissatisfied with their perplexed, anxiety-ridden husbands. In a famous set of drawings titled "The War Between Men and Women" (reprinted in *The Thurber Carnival*), Thurber depicts an actual war between the sexes reminiscent of the American Civil War. These works can now be interpreted as foreshadowing the women's movement in the late twentieth century.

In old age, Thurber was completely blind. He gave up drawing and began dictating his stories and essays. His work became bitter and cynical, reflecting growing depression, alcoholism, and loneliness. "I can't hide anymore behind the mask of comedy," he confessed to his old friend Nugent. "People are not funny; they are vicious and horrible—and so is life!" He found it increasingly difficult to get his work accepted, even by *The New Yorker.* He suffered a stroke in October, 1961, and died of pneumonia on November 2 of the same year. He was buried in his native Columbus, Ohio. Such was his worldwide fame that most of his previously rejected pieces appeared posthumously in collections such as *Credos and Curios* (1962), *Thurber & Company* (1966), and *Collecting Himself: James Thurber On Writing and Writers, Humor and Himself* (1990). All these books contain flashes of the old Thurber humor as well as insights into the complex personality of one of America's greatest and most influential literary geniuses.

### Summary

James Thurber was more than a humorist; he was a great writer. His works can be studied as examples of the best modern prose. He is always succinct, interesting, and crystal clear. His career spanned some of the most turbulent times in American history, including World War I, the Roaring Twenties with Prohibition and rampant gangsterism, the Great Depression and the specter of international Communism, World War II with its unspeakable crimes against civilians, and the seemingly interminable Cold War, which threatened global annihilation. The same period saw a dramatic decline in religious faith, a world population explosion, growing racial unrest, urban sprawl, environmental pollution, alcoholism, drug abuse, dysfunctional families, social alienation, and other characteristically modern phenomena. Thurber shared the anxiety experienced by most Americans but had the genius to convert his personal distress—even his blindness—into humor. His memories of Columbus, to which he frequently returned in his writing, represented a

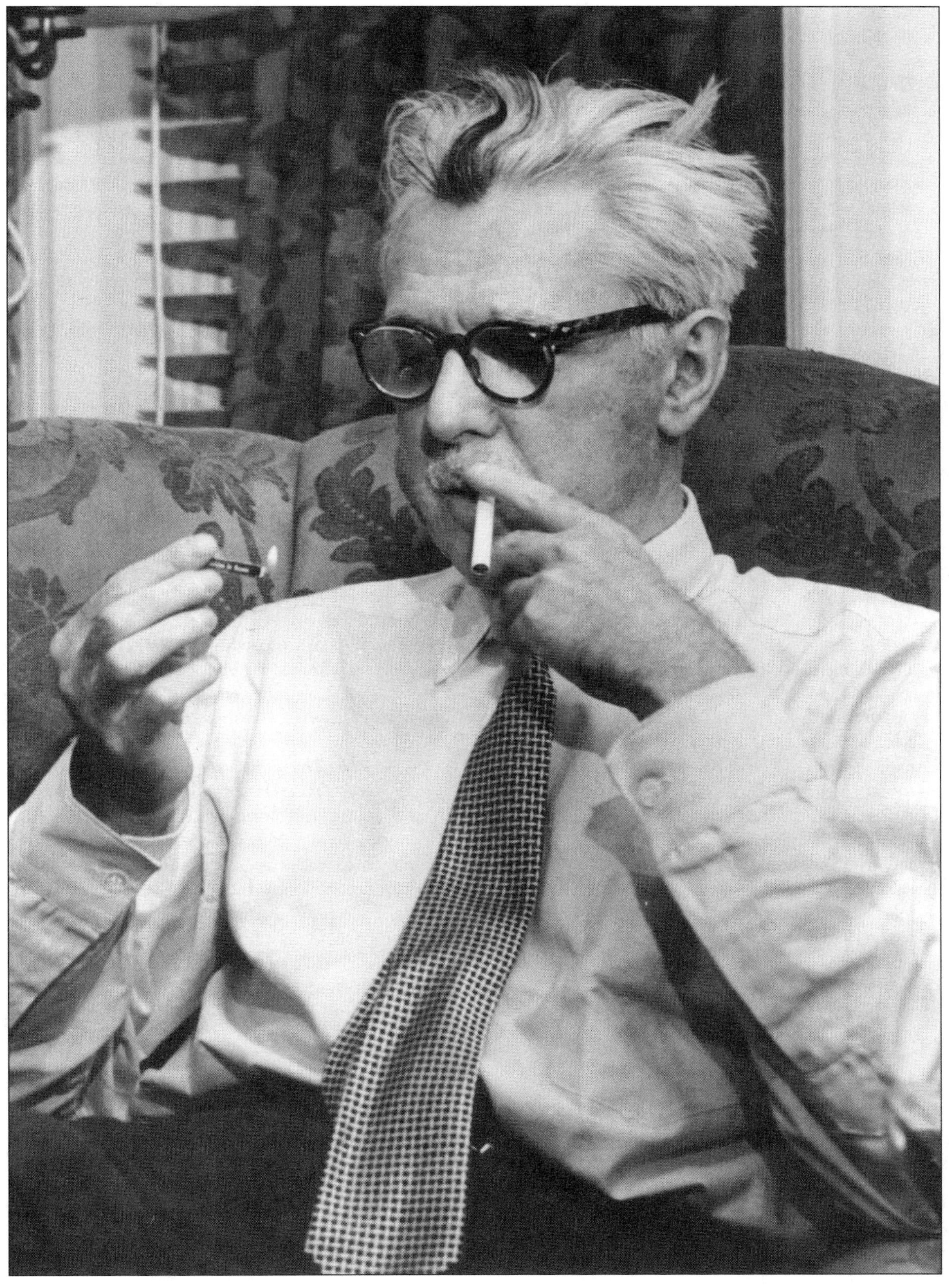

nostalgic longing for a saner, safer America that was being obliterated by the juggernaut called "progress."

Thurber helped Americans cope with radical change in their country and throughout the world. He taught people to laugh at their fears and perplexities. There has hardly been a humorist or comedian since his time who has not been influenced by Thurber's "sure grasp of confusion." His influence is conspicuous in such modern entertainers as Woody Allen and Jerry Seinfeld, who make audiences laugh at the angst and paranoia peculiar to modern times. Thurber was the voice of sanity in an insane world. He broadened American humor to reflect the increasing complexity of life and corresponding disorientation of the individual. With his conscientious craftsmanship—worthy of his great model Henry James—Thurber set an example of excellence from which countless writers throughout the world have profited.

**Bibliography**

Bernstein, Burton. *Thurber: A Biography.* London: Gollancz, and New York: Dodd Mead, 1975. This is the authorized biography of Thurber, written with the full cooperation of Thurber's widow Helen, who granted Bernstein access to all her husband's letters and papers. Well researched and well written, the book often reveals unflattering truths about the subject. Interesting black and white photographs.

Gopnik, Adam. "The Great Deflater." *The New Yorker* 70 no. 19, (June 27, 1994). The author explores Thurber's impact on American humor, touching on criticism of his work, his personal and his professional lives.

Grauer, Neil A. *Remember Laughter: A Life of James Thurber.* Lincoln: University of Nebraska Press, 1994. This excellent, short (203 pages) biography is written in an informal, entertaining fashion. It is full of amusing anecdotes and liberally illustrated with many of Thurber's best cartoons, including his famous "Seal in the Bedroom."

Holmes, Charles S., ed. *Thurber: A Collection of Critical Essays.* Englewood Cliffs, N.J.: Prentice-Hall, 1974. This book contains brief, illuminating essays on various aspects of Thurber's life and work by such famous authors as Dorothy Parker, W. H. Auden, Malcolm Cowley, John Updike, and Thurber's good friend and mentor, E. B. White.

Kinney, Harrison. *James Thurber: His Life and Times.* New York: Holt, 1995. This definitive biography, running to over 1200 pages, is based on exhaustive research. The book is written in a pleasant, informal style full of anecdotes and quotations and is generously illustrated with black and white photographs as well as many of Thurber's cartoons and line drawings.

Morsberger, Robert E. *James Thurber.* New York: Twayne, 1964. One of the distinguished series of Twayne's United States Authors Series, this small book presents a wealth of information about Thurber's life, philosophy, career, and the many interesting people he met during his lifetime. Includes many pages of notes and references, a chronology, and a select bibliography.

Tanner, Stephen L. "James Thurber and the Midwest." *American Studies* 33 no. 2, (Fall 1992). Tanner considers Thurber's feelings about his native Columbus, Ohio and how they were expressed in his writing.

Thurber, James. *My Life and Hard Times.* New York and London: Harper, 1933. This tremendously amusing, semifictional collection of autobiographical essays focuses on Thurber's early life in Columbus and his eccentric relatives. Russell Baker, a prominent *New York Times* columnist, called it "possibly the shortest and most elegant autobiography ever written."

———. *The Thurber Carnival.* London: Hamilton, and New York: Harper, 1945. This is the best collection of Thurber's memoirs, profiles, short stories, humor pieces, mood pieces, parodies, fables, and cartoons. It provides an overview of Thurber's themes, interests, talents, and life experiences. Publication of this potpourri made Thurber famous and financially secure.

———. *The Years with Ross.* London: Hamilton, and Boston: Little Brown, 1959. Thurber discusses his long association with the eccentric Harold Ross, the first editor of *The New Yorker.* Thurber's opportunity to become a staff writer was the most important event in his career, and he helped the struggling new magazine develop its unique style. Ross allowed him freedom to discover his own themes and aptitudes.

*Bill Delaney*

# BAL GANGADHAR TILAK

*Born:* July 23, 1856; Ratnagiri, India
*Died:* August 1, 1920; Bombay, India
*Areas of Achievement:* Government and politics
*Contribution:* Through his oratorical skill, political savvy, and editorship of several newspapers, Tilak showed the Hindu masses a connection between ancient tradition and twentieth century nationalism. His politics also were considerably more radical than those of other contemporary Indian leaders, giving the *swaraj* (self-government) movement a strong push forward.

## Early Life

Like two other well-known Indian nationalist leaders, Mahadev Govind Ranade and Gopāl Krishna Gokhale, Bal Gangadhar Tilak hailed from Maharashtra. This province boasted a poignant legacy: Its small army had defeated the powerful Muslim empire and, later, was the last Indian force to succumb to the British raj. Tilak also inherited the Chitpavan Brahman tradition, including caste-dictated leadership in religious and communal matters. Although his father's income remained modest, these priestly rights guaranteed the family some financial benefits, too.

Gangadharpant Tilak was a largely self-educated man who left school when his mother died. Eventually choosing a teaching career, he placed great value on learning and sent his son to class at the age of six. Bal proved to have a facile mind. Though not given to studying, he conducted intellectual debates with his teachers and supposedly even called on headmasters to settle these controversies. The Tilak family departed from village life in 1865 and moved to Poona, then considered an intellectual center of Maharashtra, where Gangadharpant became assistant deputy education inspector. His wife died the following year.

Bal continued his education and took a ten-year-old Chitpavan Brahman girl, Tapibai, to be his bride; the groom, himself, was fifteen. Neither the couple's ages nor the years between them proved at all unusual given the customs of the day. Yet, Bal soon was to experience an unexpected event—his father's death. Some scholars suggest that being orphaned at the age of sixteen may have sapped emotions from Tilak. While he possessed the passion to inspire masses of people, for example, he seemingly lacked a more personal empathy. Similarly, political solutions moved him in a way that social reform could not.

Following his graduation from high school in 1872, Tilak was enrolled in Deccan College. Sanskrit and mathematics came most naturally to him. Sometimes at the expense of his studies, however, he followed a rigorous daily exercise plan, which helped transform his formerly frail constitution into a vigorous one. Tilak appeared short and sturdy, with a broad, full mustache. In the traditional Brahman mode, he shaved his head, except for a central lock of hair. He wore orthodox garb, a beret-like *dhoti* cap perched on his head. This is the appearance he would maintain throughout his life.

While adhering to Hindu traditions, Tilak allowed himself to be shaped by other forces; indigenous political movements were starting to shake Maharashtra. Educated reformers, many admiring the advancements promised by Western civilization, formed the Poona Sarvajanik Sabha (public society) on April 2, 1870. Its leaders sought to en-

lighten the masses, while using the colonial system as a vehicle for social change. The brilliant jurist Ranade was at the forefront of this movement. A famine also ravaged the Deccan plateau during the late 1870's, propelling an insurrection by one Vasudeo Balwant Phadke. Though the British apprehended its leader, this rebellion proved inspirational to certain segments of the population who questioned various political aspects of colonialism.

Meanwhile, Tilak received his bachelor's degree with first-class honors and, as a senior, started to pursue legal studies. Though he never sought permanent, full-time law practice, he ably used the courtroom to further political causes. Tilak also appeared adept at integrating source material into his arguments and was forceful in presenting his viewpoint. During his law school days at Deccan College, Tilak befriended Gopal Ganesh Agarkar, another student motivated by progressive politics. The two men viewed education as a means of promoting change and sought to create a school that would conform to this ideal. While unable to secure the necessary funding for their venture, both ultimately were engaged to teach and help develop the fledgling New English School. Its founder, Vishnu Krishna Chiplunkar, favored broad learning but within a Hindu, rather than Christian or Western, cultural context.

### Life's Work

Both skilled educators, Tilak and Agarkar aided Chiplunkar in boosting the reputation of the New English School. The institute opened its doors with some thirty pupils in 1890 and, according to one source, boasted approximately five hundred two years later. This success spawned the Deccan Education Society (1894), dedicated to advancing the New English School model. Wealthy Indian families and royalty contributed heavily to this organization, as it reflected pride in the local heritage of which they were a part. Chiplunkar and his colleagues then founded Fergusson College, named for the retiring British governor of Bombay.

The New English School offered a collegial atmosphere, at least during its earliest days. A veteran publisher, Chiplunkar enlisted his two protégés in a new endeavor: providing political education to the older generation via weekly newspapers. Tilak became editor of the English-language *Mahratta* and Agarkar took charge of the Marathi *Kesari.* The next year, 1882, the neophyte journalists found themselves embroiled in a lawsuit. Their papers had criticized an Indian-born British official for unduly aggravating and subsequently trying to remove from power a rather unstable local prince. Convicted of slander, Agarkar and Tilak served brief prison sentences. Their bold, patriotic action, however, catapulted them into the public eye.

A new controversy, the Age of Consent debate, soon caused a rift between the young editors; it also gave Tilak his own political platform. In 1884, the reformer Behramji Merwanji Malabari called on British legislators to raise the age of marital consent for girls from the current age of ten to twelve. Reformers had long decried early marriage, citing premature death from childbirth, overpopulation, and poverty as social maladies which could be reduced, if not altogether alleviated. At around the same time, progressives debated education for women and changing the law to allow widows to remarry. Tilak vehemently opposed these measures. He believed that the imposition of British law unjustifiably tampered with Hindu culture, religion, and society; after all, Indians should govern their own lives. His editorials and speeches consequently were written to activate the religious masses. Tilak also argued that women should maintain their traditional roles in the home; education and Western, reformist ideas could turn them away from these values. While orthodox himself, however, Tilak occasionally indicated that social change would be acceptable, if publicly approved. Some scholars also cite his support of voluntary measures to raise the age of consent. Furthermore, he later sent his daughter to the Poona girls' school.

Tilak's nationalistic fervor was firmly rooted in his Brahman background. The inconsistencies that he demonstrated owed to personal dynamism, plus the ability to accept various political tactics as long as they led to the desired result: self-governance. Meanwhile, public debate manifested itself at the Deccan Education Society. Tilak left the organization in 1890, ostensibly over internal policy matters. Yet, by this time, a formal political schism had divided him from his erstwhile friend Agarkar and another faculty member, Gokhale. The latter would become a reformist leader, Indian National Congress president, and Tilak's foremost political adversary.

Having relinquished his formal teaching duties, Tilak spent more time influencing popular opinion. He became increasingly involved with Congress and helped to organize its 1895 Poona session.

Tilak objected to the fact that this meeting coincided and shared facilities with the National Social Conference. His editorials blared: "Whose is the Congress? Of the people of the Classes or of the Masses?" The Congress and Conference subsequently met in separate tents, a permanent split instituted between the two groups. Seeking new methods of rallying the masses behind his platform, Tilak had revived the Ganapti Festival, honoring a Hindu deity. Its success inspired a more politically focused activity: celebration of Shivaji, the Maharashtran who led his people to victory over the powerful Muslim empire. Combined with potent newspaper editorials (Tilak now managed *Kesari*, too), these events provided constantly growing forums for revolutionary agitation.

Right after the premier Shivaji Festival (1896), plague struck India. Walter Charles Rand, a British official, used strong-arm tactics and generally showed great insensitivity during this crisis. When he was assassinated, the government put Tilak on trial for sedition, citing his incendiary editorials as an agitating force. The gentle, reform-minded Gokhale and other Indian leaders had criticized Rand's administrative methods, but they typically apologized under pressure from British officials. Tilak, on the other hand, refused to amend his statements. In fact, one of his trial arguments was that the European-dominated jury had no business interpreting subtle nuances of a language they could not speak, read, or write. Although the defendant would serve a prison sentence, his case inspired the masses. He subsequently became known as the *Lokamanya*, or "Revered of the People."

The next major controversy to embroil India was the partition of Bengal, a British administrative action taken without consulting local leaders. This measure also diluted Hindu political power, carving out for the Muslim minority a territory in which they could prevail. Bengali Hindus then called for a boycott of British goods, and Tilak broadened the appeal to his native Maharashtra. He also would advocate for the development of Indian commerce and industry, plus a more nationalist-oriented education system that would reduce the emphasis on the English language and Western culture. Gokhale and those who favored constitutional methods of reform lobbied against the boycott and other measures that they believed might cause provocation. Emotions ran high; the 1907 Indian National Congress thus ended in the "Surat split" between nationalists (Tilak) and reformers (Gokhale).

The following year, a bomb intended for District Judge Douglas Kingsford accidentally killed a British barrister's wife and daughter. Tilak and other Indian leaders lamented the death, but a *Kesari* article stated: "The bomb party has come into existence as a result of the oppression practised by the official class, the harassment inflicted by them and their obstinacy in treating public opinion with recklessness. . . ." Tilak was arrested for sedition, his apartment searched. Police turned up one damaging piece of evidence: a postcard, written in the *Lokamanya*'s hand, listing four books on explosives.

The trial again questioned the ability of a primarily European jury to judge foreign language works. Tilak also raised freedom of press issues during his twenty-two hour closing speech. A guilty verdict was rendered: The *Lokamanya* would be confined to the Mandalay prison, Burma. Eighty textile mills in Bombay subsequently struck and some violence resulted; Tilak indeed had attained a hero's status.

Tilak finally emerged from prison in 1914, by most accounts a more subdued activist. Another legal complaint was lodged against him two years later, but this time, he won. Tilak proved to be a unifying force during the 1916 Lucknow Congress; there, nationalists and reformers coalesced, opening political representation to Muslims. Unfortunately, cross-culture agreement was only temporary and Hindu-Muslim friction continued to plague the *swaraj* movement.

Tilak's last legal battle took place on his own terms, when he went to England to prosecute Sir Valentine Chirol for slanderous remarks. Granted a passport on the condition that he refrain from political agitation, Tilak nevertheless lobbied Labor Party officials sympathetic to India's cause. He even invited some British political leaders to dinner. Although Tilak lost the lawsuit, his life continued—and concluded—in a poignant way. A new leader, Mahatma Gandhi, had chosen August 1, 1920, as the inaugural of a noncooperative movement for independence. Bal Gangadhar Tilak died on that day at the age of sixty-four.

## Summary

Bal Gangadhar Tilak consistently evoked Shivaji as a nationalistic metaphor. Yet, this analogy presented ethnical dilemmas. Shivaji allegedly met his Muslim adversary to discuss peace terms, then surprised him with a concealed weapon. Tilak, too, held that the ends justified the means: Western-style reform could not substitute for Indian self-rule, and the latter must override all other goals. Tilak's Shivaji revival inspired young people, but it also incited them to heckle reformist leaders whom they often unjustly perceived to be colluding with the British. Similarly, his proto-Hindu agitation at times exacerbated rifts between his coreligionists and the Muslims. When Tilak saw that the two peoples could unite for their common cause, however, he urged the concessions accepted at Lucknow. He also referred to the Indians as black and to the British as white. Indeed, an outspoken nature and political flexibility proved to be Tilak's trademarks. He considered all options, and scholars debate his links to a number of subversive activities. He attempted to develop ties with Nepal, for example, either to encourage that country's armed intervention or to establish a munitions factory there. Others point to his association with the men who murdered Walter Rand.

Many things have been said about or for Tilak, but his greatest contribution was a truly steadfast, pioneering devotion to Indian self-rule. He motivated his peers, and, though his political rhetoric could be harsh, he encouraged nationalistic involvement at all levels. Speaking on the 1915 death of his adversary, Gokhale, he said: "This diamond of India, this jewel of Maharashtra, this prince of workers, is taking eternal rest on the funeral grounds. Look at him and try to emulate him." Similarly, Tilak and Ghandhi differed tremendously in personality and outlook, yet on August 2, 1920, Gandhi eloquently eulogized his colleague: "For us, he will go down to the generations yet unborn as a maker of modern India."

## Bibliography

Brown, D. Mackenzie. *The Nationalist Movement: Indian Political Thought from Ranade to Bhave.* Berkeley: University of California Press, 1961. Chapters are devoted to the individual lives and writings of leading Indian nationalists. A twenty-page section on Tilak offers a good, concise biographical sketch, plus chronological excerpts from his articles urging *swaraj.*

Cashman, Richard I. *The Myth of the Lokamanya.* Berkeley: University of California Press, 1975. According to the author, Tilak proved an astute activist whose broad, popular appeal nevertheless was exaggerated by his followers for the purpose of defining consensus. Cashman argues that Tilak's legacy remains limited more to his caste and region than to India's larger nationalist movement. Several maps, a chart, tables, and appendices support this view.

Keer, Dhananjay. *Lokamanya Tilak: Father of the Indian Freedom Struggle.* 2d ed. Bombay: Popular Prakashan, 1969. This work depicts Tilak as one who politically roused the masses and brilliantly advocated workable revolutionary tactics, without helping to change social conditions. Debates among Indian leaders are vividly described. Here, Tilak usually appears to be more dynamic, committed, and effective than most of his peers.

Tahmankar, D. V. *Lokamanya Tilak: Father of Indian Unrest and Maker of Modern India.* London: Murray, 1956. Commemorating Tilak's centenary and written by one of his newspaper staff, this official biography stands loyal to its subject. Tilak, stresses Takmankar, was the first to defy boldly the British imperial presence in India. His personal powers charged the masses and inspired Asian emancipation movements for years to come.

Wolpert, Stanley A. *Tilak and Gokhale: Revolution and Reform in the Making of Modern India.* Berkeley: University of California Press, 1962. Wolpert theorizes that Indian nationalism reflects the often opposing views of Tilak, the revolutionary, and Gokhale, the reformer. By coming into contact with each other, the adversaries also refined their own strong philosophies. The book draws heavily on correspondence, articles, and Marathi sources. It also contains an excellent bibliography.

*Lynn C. Kronzek*

# PAUL TILLICH

*Born:* August 20, 1886; Starzeddel, Germany
*Died:* October 22, 1965; Chicago, Illinois
*Areas of Achievement:* Philosophy and theology
*Contribution:* Tillich introduced a unique and challenging approach to the area of theology.

## Early Life

Paul Johannes Tillich was born August 20, 1886, in Starzeddel, in the province of Brandenburg in eastern Germany, an area which later became part of Poland. His father, a Lutheran pastor from eastern Germany, instilled in his son a love for philosophy. Much of Tillich's later attitude toward traditional authority, however, was a negative reaction to the stern conservativeness of his father. Tillich was deeply fond of his mother, the more influential of his parents. She was from the progressive western part of Germany and encouraged her son to explore new ideas. The family also included two daughters.

Tillich loved the country life, where, although his family was in the upper class, he went to a public school and made most of his close boyhood friends from among the poorer classes. His later leanings toward socialism were begun in these friendships. When his father was called to a new position in Berlin in 1900, the fourteen-year-old Tillich found that he was also strongly attracted to the excitement of Berlin. In addition, he found great relaxation and contemplative value at the shore of the Baltic Sea, where the family vacationed each year.

When Tillich was seventeen, his mother died of melanoma, a painful form of cancer. This tragedy left him psychologically and spiritually destitute. The feeling of abandonment and betrayal, as if he had lost all direction, meaning, and stability, was to color his entire personal and professional life.

With his university work at Breslau, he earned a doctor of philosophy degree in 1910, going on to earn a licentiate of theology from Halle. He identified membership in a Christian student organization called the Wingolf Society as the most influential chapter in his life. This group of seventy men spent late nights in deep theological and philosophical debates, followed by smaller, quieter conversations continuing until nearly dawn. In August of 1912, he followed in his father's steps, receiving ordination in the Evangelical Lutheran Church.

When he was twenty-seven, Tillich married Grethi Wever, a woman much older than he. That same year, with the outbreak of war in Europe, he volunteered for service in the army as chaplain. During the next four years, he earned two Iron Crosses for valor, even though he suffered three nervous breakdowns during his service.

While Tillich was in the army, his wife had an affair with one of his friends and gave birth to a child. A child born earlier to the Tillichs had died in infancy. After a two-year separation, the couple was divorced in 1921.

In the meantime, Tillich became involved in the decadence and excesses that marked German society in the postwar period. Some even suggested that he resign from any further work in theology. It was in that social setting that he met Hannah Werner, who was already engaged to be married. Even so, they maintained a heated romance for a time, then resumed it after she left her new husband to return to Berlin to be with Tillich. She brought with her an infant child, whom she placed in a nursing home. When the child died there, her husband divorced her, and she married Tillich in 1924. A daughter, Erdmuthe, was born to them in 1926, and nine years later, a son, René Stephan.

Tillich was blond and possessed a face that seemed to have been chiseled from marble. He had tremendous personal charm and, as a public speaker, a commanding presence. Throughout his adult life, he took advantage of the fact that women found him very attractive. His second wife claimed that even on their wedding night he had an affair with another woman.

## Life's Work

Tillich began his career as a teacher in 1919, when he accepted a position as instructor at the University of Berlin. Because of the nature of the position, he needed the financial support of others during this time.

His private life was very much in turmoil during those years. In addition to his divorce and remarriage, he suffered the death of his older sister. Yet he was able to establish himself as a competent teacher and remained at Berlin until 1924. His lectures began to receive a somewhat wider audience, and he was able to publish a number of articles.

From Berlin, Tillich left with his wife for Marburg for a position as associate professor of theology at the university there. During this time, his first real success came with the publication of his book *The Religious Situation* (1925). Yet the Tillichs were unhappy in the smaller community of Marburg, and after three semesters, in 1925, they moved to the Dresden Institute of Technology, where he had full professorship. Over the next four years, he continued to publish and gain recognition as a speaker. He also took a position as adjunct professor of systematic theology at the University of Leipzig. In 1929, Tillich accepted a full professorship at the University of Frankfurt. There, he lectured on religion, culture, the social situation, and philosophy.

The growing power of Adolf Hitler and his National Socialist Party disturbed Tillich. He spoke and wrote with increasing strength against Nazi tactics. As a result, he lost his position at Frankfurt and was advised by friends and officials to go into exile. By the fall of 1933, he was being followed by members of the Gestapo.

His writings, however, had gained some international recognition. When efforts were made in New York City to bring to the United States those German intellectuals who were in trouble because of their resistance to Hitler, Union Theological Seminary in New York invited Tillich to join the faculty. Early in November, 1933, he arrived in New York and began an intensive study to learn the English language.

Tillich's early lectures at the seminary were interrupted by occasional outbursts of laughter among the students over the instructor's attempts to use the right words in the right order. He blushed easily and, for a while, had a difficult time dealing with the new environment. In Germany, it would have been unthinkable for students to laugh at the professor for any reason. Tillich's lectures introduced to the students some ideas which they had never heard presented in a classroom situation. His thinking very much reflected the influences of personal as well as social and political events. It was his contention that "truth is bound to the situation of the knower."

Tillich's view that God is unable to speak to man meant that He must therefore reveal truth, not only in the biblical records, or in Jesus Christ alone, but also through other means, including the human predicament and human expressions such as art and literature.

While for Tillich the Scriptures were the primary source for theological study, they certainly were not the only source. Church history, the Reformation, and the flow of culture were equally valid sources for his systematic theology. Tillich's study of theology thus began as an analysis of the human condition and the philosophical questions arising from it. This marked a keynote of his thinking. He maintained that any theological study originated in a philosophical question. Without philosophy, according to Tillich, theology had no questions, and therefore, nothing to study.

One of his statements, which led many to accuse him of being an atheist, was that God does not exist. His explanation was that God is existence itself, being itself, not some existing being who is simply higher than all other beings. He said that he did not know if there was a devil and that he was uncertain about his own salvation.

In the United States, Tillich did not participate in the local church and its programs. In fact, he often saw enemies of the church, who worked for social change, as more useful than the church.

Tillich's grasp of social issues, political viewpoints (he was a Socialist, but disavowed any political affiliation while in the United States), art, religion, and psychology, blended with his natural intelligence and almost actorlike quality of presentation, made him a favorite among the Union faculty. Seminary president Henry Sloane Coffin said, "I don't understand what he says, but when I look at his face I believe." In the twenty-two years he was in New York, Tillich also taught at Columbia University. In 1940, at age fifty-three, he became a citizen of the United States but maintained a deep love for his German homeland. In 1948, fifteen years after he left his native country, he made the first of several trips back to Germany.

Tillich moved to Harvard University Divinity School in 1995 and was soon named university professor, which freed him to study and teach in any discipline he chose. During this period, his growing reputation gained for him worldwide recognition. Some of his classes at the school were so popular that students would come an hour early simply to get a good seat in the lecture hall.

A position as professor of theology at the Divinity School of the University of Chicago was offered to him, and Tillich moved to the Midwest in the fall of 1962. He also conducted seminars in the winter quarters of 1963 and 1964 at the University of California at Santa Barbara.

His health began to fail while he was in Chicago. Even so, in the spring of 1965, Tillich received two offers—a full professorship at Santa Barbara, and an invitation to hold the chair of philosophy at the

New School for Social Research in New York City. Tillich accepted the position in New York, to begin the following year, but on October 12, 1965, he suffered a heart attack. He died in Chicago ten days later, after asking his wife, Hannah, to forgive him for his unfaithfulness to her.

His body was cremated, and after seven months in the East Hampton, New York, cemetery, his ashes were reinterred in a park named in his honor in New Harmony, Indiana.

### Summary

Paul Tillich believed orthodoxy to be intellectual Pharisaism, and he challenged many accepted tenets of Christianity. He rejected faith in a personal God, the historic fall into sin, the work of Christ, and the validity of prayer.

Tillich wanted to be a philosopher and called himself a theologian. It was this combination that determined his approach to religion and won for him many devoted followers as well as many severe critics. It also was the means to widespread recognition. His influence extends around the world. Scores of books and articles by Tillich and hundreds more about him and his views have been published on every continent.

### Bibliography

Bulman, Raymond F. "Paul Tillich and the Millennialist Heritage." *Theology Today* 53 no. 4, (January, 1997). Bulman considers Tillich's thoughts on the millennium as a rational source of hope.

Crossman, Richard C. *Paul Tillich: A Comprehensive Bibliography and Keyword Index of Primary and Secondary Writings in English*. Metuchen, N.J.: Scarecrow Press, 1983. A source book for titles of all of Tillich's writings in English and of articles, books, dissertations, theses, and reviews about Tillich.

Freeman, David Hugh. *Recent Studies in Philosophy and Theology*. Philadelphia: Presbyterian and Reformed Publishing Co., 1962. Compares Tillich's views with those of other liberal theologians.

———. *Tillich*. Philadelphia: Presbyterian and Reformed Publishing, 1962. An interesting work that fiercely assails Tillich's work in two areas: his view of God and his view of Revelation.

Johnson, Wayne G. *Theological Method in Luther and Tillich*. Washington, D.C.: University Press of America, 1981. Defends Tillich's approach to theology by making comparisons at different points with the theology of Martin Luther.

Lyons, James R. *The Intellectual Legacy of Paul Tillich*. Detroit, Mich.: Wayne State University Press, 1969. Printed versions of lectures by three scholars as they evaluate Tillich as philosopher and theologian and as an observer of psychiatry. Includes brief biographical notes and a letter Tillich wrote (to Thomas Mann) in 1943.

May, Rollo. *Paulus: Reminiscences of a Friendship*. New York: Harper, 1973; London: Collins, 1974. Extremely personal glimpses of Tillich by the man recognized as his best friend during his thirty-two years in the United States.

Newport, John P. *Paul Tillich*. Waco, Tex.: Word, 1984. One of the best and most complete books on Tillich. Includes an excellent biographical section, plus chapters on Tillich's views and evaluations of those views.

Thomas, John Heywood. *Paul Tillich*. London: Lutterworth Press, 1965; Richmond, Va.: John Knox Press, 1966. Gives critiques of Tillich in various areas of theology. Includes an excellent biographical section.

Tillich, Paul. *The Eternal Now*. New York: Scribner, 1963. Sixteen sermons delivered by Tillich give a good display of his views and of his ability to relate to a listener.

———. *On the Boundary: An Autobiographical Sketch*. New York: Scribner, 1966; London: Collins, 1967. A description of Tillich's view that he lived his life in tensions between conflicting forces.

Towne, Edgar. *Two Types of New Theism: Knowledge of God in the Thought of Paul Tillich and Charles Hartshorne*. New York: Lang, 1997. Towne examines the views of Tillich and philosopher Charles Hartshorne with respect to the manner in which God is perceived and the potential impact of Tillich and Hartshorne on religious faith in the modern world.

*John D. Wild*

# ALFRED VON TIRPITZ

*Born:* March 19, 1849; Küstrin, Brandenburg, Prussia

*Died:* March 6, 1930; Ebenhausen, Germany

*Area of Achievement:* The military

*Contribution:* Tirpitz, one of the ablest naval administrators in modern history, was the architect of the German High Seas Fleet that fought in World War I.

## Early Life

Alfred von Tirpitz was born March 19, 1849, of middle-class background. His father was a jurist and later county court judge in Brandenburg; his mother was the daughter of a physician. He joined the navy in 1865 when it was hardly a popular Prussian institution (the Prussian Navy in fact became a career for many ambitious young men of middle-class background who were barred from advancement in the army) and was commissioned four years later. Tirpitz rose rapidly in the navy. His leadership abilities were amply demonstrated when, in the 1880's, he headed the torpedo section of the German navy. Torpedoes were then coming into their own at sea, and Tirpitz worked to ensure their reliability. He was appointed captain in 1888 and gained practical experience at sea. From 1892 to 1896, he was chief of staff of the Naval High Command and was given responsibility for developing and codifying fleet tactics. He was promoted to rear admiral in 1895. His last assignment at sea was in 1896 to 1897, when he was chief of the cruiser squadron in East Asia. He was not a great success, as one of his vessels, the *Iltis*, sunk on a misson near Kiaochow, generating unfavorable publicity. Ironically, Tirpitz never commanded a modern battleship, much less a squadron of capital ships.

Tirpitz was a large man who had a strong personality. A trademark, and later a cartoonist's delight, was his great two-pronged beard. He radiated competence and leadership. A devoted family man, he liked to dress elegantly and had a polish lacking in many of his class. Patriotic and energetic, he could also be overbearing, ruthless, and domineering. Certainly he was an adroit politician and manipulator of men. He was also ambitious and very confident of his own abilities and came into office with a fully developed plan for naval expansion.

## Life's Work

On June 18, 1897, William II appointed Tirpitz as state secretary of the navy office, a post that he retained until he resigned all of his offices on March 15, 1916. In 1898, he became a voting member of the Prussian Ministry of State and two years later was raised to the hereditary Prussian nobility. In 1911, he was made admiral of the fleet. Tirpitz made his place in naval history on land, as the architect of the navy. Ironically, although Tirpitz built the German navy, in World War I he was not allowed to use it as he wished.

Tirpitz was appointed specifically to build up the size of the navy, which had languished under Chancellor Otto von Bismarck. In 1888, William II became kaiser. His mother, the Empress Frederick, wrote, "Wilhelm's one idea is to have a Navy which shall be larger and stronger than the Royal Navy." William was determined to pursue a more aggressive foreign policy (a chief reason for his break with Bismarck), and a strong navy was seen as a principal element in this *Weltpolitik.* The army had given Germany hegemony in Europe; the kaiser and Tirpitz saw the navy securing the same result for Germany in the world, elevating the nation to world power (*Weltmacht*) status. Justification for this view was provided by the timely publication of Alfred Thayer Mahan's *The Influence of Sea Power upon History, 1660-1783* in 1890. Mahan contended that history did not offer a single example of a world commercial power that was not also a sea power. Tirpitz agreed with the kaiser on the need for a strong fleet but disagreed that the emphasis should be on a *guerre de course* with commerce-raiding, cruiser-type vessels. Mahan had argued for the absolute primacy of the battleship, and Tirpitz won the kaiser to this viewpoint.

Tirpitz saw to it that the navy, unlike the army, came under the personal control of the Supreme War Lord. He assured the kaiser in February, 1898, that he would "remove the disturbing influence of the Reichstag upon Your Majesty's intentions concerning the development of the Navy," and he did precisely that. The Reichstag had no control over naval construction or organization. The Second Navy Bill of 1900 provided that a set number of vessels would be authorized, then built regardless of cost. Funds for personnel, maintenance, and training were all to be made available automatically based on the number of ships in service.

Tirpitz was able to take advantage of growing support in Germany for a strong navy, especially from the small but influential German Colonial League and the Pan-German League. Still, winning approval for a strong navy was in large part the result of Tirpitz' own extraordinary abilities as promoter and publicist. In March, 1897, the Reichstag rejected the modest naval building program advocated by his predecessor, Friedrich Hollmann. In April, 1898, the same body passed the much more ambitious Tirpitz program by a vote of two to one.

Tirpitz cultivated an alliance with the Rhineland industrialists, who embraced the navy as their vehicle to rival the old Prussian-Junker combination centered in the army. He supported the creation of the Navy League, which had its own publication and speakers who traveled throughout Germany. Although the Navy League had only about 100,000 members, it was quite influential. Tirpitz also did not hesitate to appeal to German nationalism, and he took advantage of foreign policy crises to push for additional naval construction.

Tirpitz relied on a program of steady expansion (*Etappenplan*) of the navy, or the "patient laying of brick upon brick." In part this was designed to deceive the Reichstag and German public as to his true aims. For public consumption Tirpitz announced only modest goals; Germany wanted a fleet capable of keeping the North Sea and Baltic shipping lanes open in time of war; a strong navy was also justified as necessary to protect steadily expanding German commerce and her overseas empire. By 1895, Germany was second in the world in the value of her foreign trade, but her navy was only the fifth largest.

For public consumption also, Tirpitz argued that the navy was to be a "risk" fleet, that is, only large enough that another major naval power would not "risk" doing battle with the German navy for fear that its strength might be crippled to the point at which it would be vulnerable to the fleet of another major naval power.

Tirpitz also argued that Germany did not need a fleet as large as that of Great Britain; her warships could be concentrated, whereas the Royal Navy had to dissipate its strength in worldwide commitments. Tirpitz also advanced the belief that the fleet would be a useful diplomatic tool, making Germany a more attractive ally. In private, Tirpitz spoke of a panic-stricken British government willing to surrender up to half of her colonial empire to Germany in return for an alliance.

Such arguments were, in fact, a smoke screen designed to mask Tirpitz' real intent of creating a fleet

strong enough to challenge Great Britain for control of the seas and world mastery. Tirpitz saw Great Britain as the enemy. He stated in 1897 that the navy had become "a question of survival" for Germany. He believed that the navy, supported by the middle-class industrial German state, was the future, to which eventually the army would have to give place. He opined in 1899 that if Germany could not, with her battle fleet, take advantage of shifts in world power, she "would sink back to the status of a poor farming country." In his view, Germany had to prepare for a showdown with the Anglo-Saxon powers. This would probably be in one great naval battle in the North Sea or Atlantic Ocean between Germany on the one side and either Great Britain or Great Britain and the United States on the other. Ironically, this was precisely the scenario anticipated by English navalists, and it almost came to pass at Jutland in World War I. Such a battle, Tirpitz believed, should take place only after 1920, when Germany would stand a good chance of winning it. His greatest concern was that the British might opt for a preemptive strike before that time, to "Copenhagen" his new creation before it was ready.

The first Tirpitz naval bill passed the Reichstag in April, 1898. It called for the construction, by April, 1904, of nineteen battleships, eight armored cruisers, and twelve large and thirty small cruisers. Taking advantage of the international situation (the impact of the Spanish-American War, sentiment against Great Britain aroused during the Boer War, and the Boxer Rebellion in China), Tirpitz introduced a second naval bill, which passed the Reichstag in June, 1900. It doubled the size of the projected navy to a total of thirty-eight battleships, twenty armored cruisers, and thirty-eight light cruisers—all to be built within twenty years. This was a direct challenge to the British Home Fleet, then about thirty-two battleships.

A naval building race between Great Britain and Germany ensued. In 1906, the British answered with the new super-battleship, *Dreadnought*, the first all big-gun ship, driven by steam turbines. Later they introduced the battle cruiser class as well. Tirpitz followed suit. Although the pace of construction subsequently slowed somewhat, Tirpitz used two crises over Morocco to secure the passage of supplementary German naval construction laws (*Novellen*) in 1906, 1908, and 1912. Six dreadnoughts were to be built by 1918; six large cruisers were also to be built, and additional funds were granted to expand dock facilities and widen existing canals so as to enable the warships to pass from the Baltic Sea to the North Sea. Battleship replacement was also to occur every twenty years instead of twenty-five as previously agreed. This meant, in effect, that new dreadnoughts would reach the fleet at a faster rate (four were to be built yearly from 1908 to 1911, and two per year from 1912 to 1917). The third *Novelle* of 1912 increased the projected size of the fleet to forty-one battleships (in five squadrons), twenty large cruisers, and forty light cruisers. It is by no means clear that Tirpitz intended to stop there. He was absolutely opposed to any reductions in the naval sphere and helped scuttle British war minister Richard Burdon Haldane's 1912 mission to Germany wherein he attempted to reduce the naval race between the two countries.

The quality of German construction was quite high. Naval historians generally concede that German range-finding optics were better than those of the British, and their armor-piercing shells were also superior. Although less heavily gunned than their British counterparts, German capital ships had excellent internal subdivision by watertight compartments, which at sea meant survivability. They also had better armor protection, and they were broader of beam and hence more stable as gun platforms.

With his attention fixed on battleships, Tirpitz was a late convert to submarines. The first German *Unterseeboot*, *U1*, was not completed until the end of 1906, and it was several years before its potential was realized. The budget of 1912 projected a total of seventy-two U-boats, but Germany entered World War I with only twenty-eight, compared with seventy-seven for France, fifty-five for Great Britain, and thirty-eight for the United States. There was no plan to employ them against commerce. By 1913, Tirpitz had also been won over to the use of naval airships.

At the beginning of World War I, Tirpitz offered to assume operational control over the navy, but this was rejected. He opposed keeping the fleet in port, where it spent most of World War I. He recognized the importance of the new U-boats in the war at sea but opposed their employment too early, judging 1916 as the right time. His advice was for the most part ignored, and he resigned his offices in 1916.

After leaving the Navy, Tirpitz went into politics. He was one of the founders of the Fatherland Party (*Vaterlandspartei*), and from 1924 to 1928 he was a nationalist deputy in the Reichstag. He supported the Dawes Plan but opposed the Locarno Pact and the reconciliation with France, as he believed that they would jeopardize cooperation with Great Britain and the United States. Tirpitz died on March 6, 1930.

### Summary

As the father of the German navy that fought World War I, Alfred von Tirpitz played a pivotal role in German history. The Tirpitz plan was, however, in the words of one historian, a "gruesome error" and a "monstrous error in judgment." Far from driving Great Britain to panic, the construction of German vessels simply goaded the British into action. Great Britain was dependent for its survival on imports of food and raw materials; British political leaders and the public long believed that the German fleet was a "luxury" designed to satisfy the kaiser's ego, whereas the Royal Navy was seen as a "necessity." The British government adopted the "two-power naval standard," which required a fleet as large as the next two naval powers combined. Although facing serious fiscal problems, the

British outspent the Germans in the naval sphere; one reason this was possible was that the British Army was so small.

As Bismarck predicted, the construction of a powerful German fleet drove Great Britain away from Germany and into alliance with France. Far from making Germany an attractive ally, the plan had the effect of further isolating Germany in Europe. The Entente Cordiale of 1904 was a direct result of German naval construction, as was the agreement in 1912 whereby the French agreed to take primary responsibility for the Mediterranean and concentrate their naval units there while the British did the same for the north Atlantic.

A treaty with Japan and the elimination of the Russian Navy in the Russo-Japanese War enabled the British to strengthen their position in Europe. As a result, the Home Fleet was able to overshadow the High Seas Fleet. Although by 1914 the German Navy was second in size only to that of Great Britain, the Royal Navy had in fact widened its advantage over Germany in most classes of ships (the capital ship ratio was thirty-two to eighteen), making the Tirpitz quest more illusory than ever.

There were limits to what Germany could do financially, particularly as it was at the same time maintaining the largest standing army in the world. By 1907-1908, the army was again getting priority in armaments expenditure. Seen in retrospect, had the bulk of assets spent on the navy gone to the army instead, Germany would have had a better chance at a land victory over France in 1914.

### Bibliography


Herwig, Holger. *"Luxury" Fleet: The Imperial German Navy, 1888-1918.* Rev. ed. London and Atlantic Highlands, N.J.: Ashfield Press, 1987. This is a well-balanced, lucid, dispassionate, short, and thoroughly researched study of the Tirpitz era. It is particularly strong in discussion of ship characteristics. Herwig also provides much useful information on Tirpitz.

Marder, Arthur J. *From the Dreadnought to Scapa Flow: The Royal Navy in the Fisher Era, 1904-1919.* 5 vols. London: Oxford University Press, 1961-1970. This is a comprehensive, often highly detailed, study of the Royal Navy of the period. There is much material here on Tirpitz' counterpart, Admiral John Arbuthnot Fisher, and his efforts to meet the German challenge.

Padfield, Peter. *The Great Naval Race: Anglo-German Naval Rivalry, 1900-1914.* London: Hart-Davis, and New York: McKay, 1974. While utilizing mostly secondary sources, Padfield nevertheless provides an introduction to the broader area of the development of German and British naval policies and the effects of their ensuing rivalry.

Scheer, Reinhard. *Germany's High Sea Fleet in the World War.* London and New York: Cassell, 1920. Although egocentric and often unreliable, this memoir by the admiral who commanded the High Seas Fleet at Jutland is useful for its discussion of the decision-making regarding tactical employment of the Tirpitz fleet in World War I.

Steinberg, Jonathan. *Yesterday's Deterrent: Tirpitz and the Birth of the German Battle Fleet.* London: Macdonald, 1965; New York: Macmillan, 1965. There is much useful material here on Tirpitz, especially on his early career. It lacks the documentation of Herwig's study but is particularly helpful in understanding the politics involved in the higher echelons of the German navy.

Tirpitz, Alfred von. *My Memoirs.* 2 vols. London: Hurst and Blackett, and New York: Dodd Mead, 1919. Tirpitz' own defense of his policies. Although these recollections are entirely self-satisfied and self-righteous, they are indispensable in understanding his point of view.


*Spencer C. Tucker*

# TITO
## Josip Broz

*Born:* May 7, 1892; Kumroveć, Croatia, Austro-Hungarian Empire
*Died:* May 4, 1980; Ljubljana, Yugoslavia
*Areas of Achievement:* The military, government, and politics
*Contribution:* Tito built and led the Yugoslav Communist Partisan army, which was the most successful guerrilla resistance force against the Nazis and Fascists in World War II. After the war, he broke away from Joseph Stalin and until his death led the country on an independent Communist path.

### Early Life

Josip Broz (Tito) was born of mixed Croatian-Slovenian ancestry in 1892 in Kumroveć, a Croatian village, which then was part of the Hungarian kingdom. He was the seventh child in a family of fifteen. His earliest political memories were of the peasant revolts against the Hungarian landlords in 1902. At seven he went to the new elementary school in Kumroveć, which had one teacher for three hundred and fifty pupils. At first he was a poor student but as time went on he improved. At twelve, as was customary, he stopped school and went to work for his uncle as a herder. At fifteen, although his father had hoped to send him to the United States, he went to work as a waiter. Shortly, however, he became an apprentice locksmith and learned about Marxism from a coworker.

At eighteen, Broz went to Zagreb, found work, and joined the Social Democratic Party of Croatia and Slavonia. In 1913, at twenty-one, he was drafted into the Austro-Hungarian army. At the beginning of World War I, he was briefly jailed for antiwar agitation but was acquitted and served with his regiment as an officer in the Carpathians on the Russian front. In 1915, Broz was wounded and captured by Russian troops and sent to a prisoner of war camp in the Ural Mountains, where he came in contact with the Bolsheviks. He escaped in May, 1917, during the Russian Revolution and made his way to Petrograd (now Leningrad), where he stayed briefly but was soon recaptured and returned to Siberia. After the October Revolution, he joined the international Red Guard and fought against the White forces of Admiral Aleksandr Kolchak. It was in Siberia that he married his first wife, Pelaghia Belousnova, the daughter of a Russian worker.

### Life's Work

In 1921, after the Russian Civil War, Broz returned to Croatia, where he joined the newly formed Communist Party of the Kingdom of the Serbs, Croats, and Slovenes. At this time, the Party was under the leadership of the old Serbian Social Democrats, and the young Croatian worker despite his experience in Soviet Russia was consigned to minor rules of propaganda and participation in demonstrations and strikes. The Party was declared illegal in 1921, and Broz was arrested in 1928 and spent five years in prison. There he came into contact with one of the most important influences in his life, the theoretical Marxist Moshe Pijade. Pijade helped Broz form his conception of Marxism. After his release from prison, Broz took the pseudonym "Tito" and went to the Soviet Union, where he witnessed the Stalinist purges of the 1930's that brought down the Serbian leadership of the Yugoslav Communist Party. Tito was now elevated to the supreme Party leadership. Tito returned to Yugoslavia and at a secret Party meeting in October, 1940, he was elected general secretary of the Party. When Nazi Germany invaded the Soviet Union in June, 1941, Tito organized the resistance that up to that time was chiefly led by the Serbian royalist nationalist Draža Mihajlović. It was as the commander in chief of the Yugoslav resistance army, the most successful in Europe, that Tito came into public renown.

As the leader of the Yugoslav forces, he built up a movement of 250,000 from all over the country including all nationalities. This gave him an advantage over his chief rival, the Serbian anti-Communist Mihajlović, and Stalin was able to convince his Western allies in 1942 to throw all support behind Tito. The guerrilla war against German, Italian, and Bulgarian occupation forces was complex and multifaceted, but it degenerated into a civil war between the partisans, as Tito's group was called, and the chetniks of Mihajlović. Both sides often made alliances with the occupiers, especially as a Fascist defeat seemed imminent and the struggle became more and more a fight for control of Yugoslavia after World War II. Although in December, 1945, Red Army troops moved into the country to fight the re-

*Tito (center) dancing with residents of Kola, Yugoslavia, while campaigning for office in 1950.*

treating German army, Tito won largely on his own efforts.

Thus after the conflict Tito was able to establish independent political authority over the country. Soviet leaders were anxious that they regain control of the international Communist movement and began to recruit Yugoslav agents to oppose Tito's independence. for his part, Tito not only wanted to establish independent Communist rule in Yugoslavia but also hoped to enlarge his own influence in an all-Balkan Communist federation and exerted pressure on Albanian Communist leaders, negotiated with the Communist leadership of Bulgaria, and armed the Communist insurgents in Greece. To the West, Tito appeared to be the most uncompromising of the new Eastern European Communist leaders. Therefore, it was a great surprise when the Soviets expelled Yugoslavia from the Communist Information Bureau in 1948.

Tito then decided to go his own way. He followed separate foreign and economic policies from the Soviet Union. At the time of the Cold War in the 1950's before the rupture of relations between China and the Soviet Union, Tito stood as the only Communist leader in power not allied to Moscow. He was able to use his position to gain aid from the West, and in November, 1950, the United States Congress passed the Yugoslav Emergency Relief Act. Along with Jawaharlal Nehru of India and Gamal Abdel Nasser of Egypt, he started the nonaligned nations movement in the international arena. In domestic policies, Tito advocated his own way toward socialism by emphasizing workers' control of factories. This permitted more economic liberalization in Yugoslavia than existed in other Communist-controlled countries. Although in the late 1940's Mihajlović was tried and executed as a war criminal and leading critics such as Milovan Djilas were imprisoned, more liberalism appeared in political and social life as well. As time went on, Yugoslavia enjoyed access to Western literature and freedom of travel long before the other socialist countries of Eastern Europe.

Tito could not solve all of Yugoslavia's problems. He was never able truly to unite the country, and hostility among the nationalities remained, although he was able to keep them under control while he lived. When he died, however, these burst forward with a new fury. The concept of workers' control of factories has also led to many economic problems—inflation as well as unemployment. The differences in the country from rich industrialized republics in the north to the agrarian ones in the south, combined with the national confrontations, has been one of Yugoslavia's critical issues since World War II.

Tito's dictatorial methods caused some of his closest allies to fall away. Djilas became a critic whom Tito threw in jail. Aleksander Rankovic, his chosen successor, also was jailed for abuse of power. Ironically, although Tito is best known for his clash with Stalin, he himself carried out his own "cult of personality" in Yugoslavia and became the glue to hold his fractious land together. When he died in 1980, there was no suitable successor. Under Tito's direction the League of Communists had established a system of rotating presidents to take into account the national differences—a method that was bound to fail and the consequences of which have not yet been resolved.

When asked by Vladimir Dedijer, his comrade and sympathetic biographer, to explain the differences between his system, what the West called "Titoism," and the Soviet system, Tito replied that Yugoslavia was building "genuine socialism" while the economic policies of the Soviet Union have "degenerated into state capitalism under the leadership of a dictatorial bureaucratic caste." Secondly, Yugoslavia was developing socialist democracy impeded only by the lack of technology. In the Soviet Union, there was not democracy, only a reign of terror and no freedom of thought or creative work in literature. Thirdly, Yugoslavia was a true federation of equal republics, while the Soviet Union was an equal federation on paper only. The Russian republic, through its Moscow bureaucrats, dominated everything. Critics of Tito, however, assert that the same charges could be leveled at him.

### Summary

Tito is one of the major political leaders of the twentieth century. His military and political accomplishments enabled him to defy both Adolf Hitler and Stalin. He had the rare gift of carrying out a revolution and leading a government. As a military commander Tito was able to organize a vast guerrilla army. While it is true that he was supplied by the Allies, the effort was still monumental. He took on one of the most successful war machines of the twentieth century and was able to maneuver through an extremely complex and multifaceted array of forces fighting both foreign enemies and domestic opponents.

As the leader of a small country he was in danger of being swallowed by the superpowers during the time of the Cold War. Yet he was most successful in playing one off the other. He was the first Communist leader after World War II to become diplomatically an ally of the West. Although a European and Communist head of state, he became a leader of the Third World. The force of his personality alone held his fragile government together. Using a combination of tyranny and liberalization, he established Yugoslavia as a country to be reckoned with in international and European politics. Because of his success, he also established himself as a major contributor to the field of socialist ideology. Maintaining that his was the true Marxism, he put into practice the economic principle of workers' control of factories. He was the first Communist leader to introduce a policy of openness into a Communist-led government since the 1930's.

Tito's faults cannot be overlooked. In many ways he was as egotistical in assuming personal command as his great opponent Stalin. His cult of personality rivaled that of the Georgian dictator. His intolerance of criticism, even from persons such as Djilas who were ideologically close to him, has tarnished his claim to have been a proponent of egalitarian democracy. His unwillingness to share power or introduce genuine multiopinion councils has led to chaotic national and political problems that linger in Yugoslavia today. Furthermore his economic policies have not all proved successful. While trying to implement the benefits of socialism, Yugoslavia has experienced both unemployment and inflation. Yugoslavia's postwar development under Tito was impressive, but in the 1970's it ran into economic snags and since then has been left behind. Tito's place in modern history rests with his war effort against Hitler and his defiance of Stalin. Perhaps he owes much to the fortunes of time and place, but no one can deny the magnitude of his achievement.

### Bibliography

Adamic, Louis. *The Eagle and His Roots.* New York: Doubleday, 1952. An early biography written by an American-Yugoslav collaborator with Tito. Partly propaganda, partly a friendly appraisal by an important historical figure himself, the president of the American Slavic Committee.

Auty, Phyllis. *Tito.* Rev. ed. London and Baltimore: Penguin, 1974. An excellent short biography by one of the leading scholars of Yugoslav history. Includes maps, notes, an index, and illustrations.

Campbell, John C. *Tito's Separate Road: America and Yugoslavia in World Politics.* New York: Harper, 1967. Part of the Policy Book series of the Council on Foreign Relations. A brief scholarly analysis of Tito's economics and politics especially in relation to its effect on international affairs. Contains bibliographical notes.

Clissold, Stephen. *Whirlwind: An Account of Marshal Tito's Rise to Power.* London: Cresset Press, and New York: Philosophical Library, 1947. A history of Tito's activities in World War II by a British officer who served alongside his partisans.

Dedijer, Vladimir. *Tito.* New York: Simon and Schuster, 1952; London: Weidenfeld and Nicolson, 1953. The semiofficial biography of Tito written by his comrade in arms and including extensive interviews with the man. An invaluable source. Contains an index.

Djilas, Milovan. *Tito: The Story from Inside.* Translated by Vasilije Kojić and Richard Hayes. New York: Harcourt Brace, 1980; London: Weidenfeld and Nicolson, 1981. An evaluation of Tito by a former ally and now Yugoslavia's most famous dissident. Contains a biographical appendix and illustrations.

Granville, Johanna. "Tito and the Nagy Affair in 1956." *East European Quarterly* 32 no. 1, (Spring 1998). The author presents a study of Tito, the Nagy Affair, and the revolution, based on research into newly available documents from Moscow archives.

Maclean, Fitzroy. *Eastern Approaches.* London: Cape, 1949; as *Escape to Adventure,* Boston: Little Brown, 1950. These memoirs are written by one of the British officers who served with Tito's partisans and are an important source of information about the man and his abilities. Includes an index, maps, and illustrations.

Rusinow, Dennison. *The Yugoslav Experiment, 1948-1974.* London: Hurst, and Berkeley: University of California Press, 1977. Published for the Royal Institute of International Affairs in London. Although dealing with the history of Yugoslavia after World War II, this work by a leading scholar gives an excellent survey and appraisal of Tito's contribution to the country. Includes an index and a bibliography.

Ulam, Adam B. *Titoism and the Cominform.* Cambridge, Mass.: Harvard University Press, 1952. An important scholarly monograph by a respected political scientist and critic of Marxism. This work analyzes the split between Stalin and Tito and examines its theoretical basis. Includes an index and a bibliographical note.

*Frederick B. Chary*

# J. R. R. TOLKIEN

*Born:* January 3, 1892; Bloemfontein, South Africa
*Died:* September 2, 1973; Bournemouth, England
*Area of Achievement:* Literature
*Contributions:* Tolkien communicated the sensibility of medieval epic and romance in his widely read mythopoetic fiction. With influential articles on the Anglo-Saxon epic *Beowulf* and the standard edition of the fourteenth century English Arthurian fantasy romance *Sir Gawain and the Green Knight*, he was an important medievalist long before he became much more famous and beloved for his widely read fantasy novels *The Hobbit*, *The Lord of the Rings*, and *The Silmarillion*.

### Early Life

John Ronald Reuel Tolkien was born on January 3, 1892, in Bloemfontein, South Africa, to Arthur and Mabel Suffield Tolkien. In 1895 they moved to Birmingham, England, to be near Mabel's family, but Arthur, a bank manager, died within the year. In 1900 Mabel scandalized the family by joining the Roman Catholic Church. After her early death in 1904, Tolkien and his brother, Hilary, lived in the house of a Mrs. Faulkner with another orphan named Edith Bratt. Tolkien and Bratt fell in love and were married in 1916 after Tolkien had completed his bachelor of arts at Exeter College, Oxford. He then served as a signalling officer during World War I as a second lieutenant in the Lancashire Fusiliers. In France he was felled by trench fever and was sent back to an English hospital, where he began his mythopoetic fiction. To the deaths of his parents and several other relatives while Tolkien was a young boy was added the loss of his fellow soldiers on and off the battlefields. The reality of mortality was established as one of the themes of both his scholarship and his fiction.

Following the war and the birth of his son, John, Tolkien worked for the *Oxford English Dictionary* and taught at Leeds University, where he and E. V. Gordon completed the definitive edition of the medieval romance *Sir Gawain and the Green Knight* (c. 1375). Ronald, Edith, and John Tolkien returned to Oxford in 1925 with two more sons, Michael and Christopher, where they lived until 1968. Fascinated and gifted with languages, Tolkien became the Rawlinson and Bosworth Professor of Anglo-Saxon and partly calmed the academic feuding in the English School between those more interested in early languages and those who studied the literature of later centuries. He continued his editing of medieval texts, including *The Pearl* (1375) and the *Ancrene Wisse* (1230; an advice book for nuns), and published influential essays on the Anglo-Saxon epic *Beowulf* (c. 1000). The essay "Beowulf: The Monsters and the Critics" (1936) has retained its power over the decades and stresses two key themes in Tolkien's work as both a medievalist and a writer of mythic narrative: mortality and the artist's role in honoring and transmitting a sense of the past (a partial response to that mortality). Such work led to Tolkien being named Merton Professor of English Language and Literature in 1945. At the same time, he was busy with other writings besides his scholarship.

The reclusive but "clubbable" Tolkien became friends with another influential writer and scholar of the Middle Ages, C. S. Lewis. Although more handsome, Tolkien was reclusive and not so athletic as Lewis, who was a vigorous walker and irrepressible talker. Both men, while generous of spirit, were argumentative and somewhat stubborn, especially during the weekly meetings of the Inklings, who gathered to discuss and critique their own writings. The group included Tolkien (Tollers), Lewis (Jack), Lewis's brother Warren (Warnie), R. E. Havard, Owen Barfield, Hugo Dyson, and Charles Williams. During these meetings, Tolkien first read, as he had to his wife and children, the early versions of his most beloved work, *The Hobbit* (1937).

### Life's Work

*The Hobbit* appeared after seventeen years of work, during which time its author was well known almost exclusively to academic medievalists for his scholarly editing and literary criticism, although many thought it too limited in scope and quantity. Two years later he published something of a bridge between his scholarship and his fantasy writing, "On Fairy Stories" (1939), which indicated the foundations (along with his fascination and expertise with the vocabulary and structure of languages as well as the northern European traditions of myth, epic, and saga) of the stories on which his fame among the general reading public continues to rest. This lecture, later published as a lengthy essay in *Tree and Leaf* (1964), is a charming, provocative, and essential essay for understanding the mythic foundations of Tolkien's fantasy fiction and the spirit of much of his medieval scholarship.

Although considered a work of fiction for youngsters, *The Hobbit* is Tolkien's most accessible narrative, perhaps because of the eccentric lovableness and inventive pluck of Bilbo Baggins and the wily cleverness of the dragon Smaug. Like the best of children's stories and the myths of all people, *The Hobbit* contains clearly delineated heroes and villains, gives attention to minute and realistic details that anchor and make credible the marvelous and often terrifying adventures, and provides certainty about the final outcome. It also features compelling examples of bravery, loyalty, and generosity rewarded and treachery, vanity, and selfishness punished. Above all, it is a convincing story about learning unselfishness in a menacing and predatory world—the necessary foundation of maturity.

Tolkien's greatest accomplishment, *The Lord of the Rings*, is sweeping work that was published in three volumes: *The Fellowship of the Ring* (1954), *The Two Towers* (1954), and *The Return of the King* (1955). Fifteen years in the making, the trilogy is structured as a "reverse quest," to deliver and destroy rather than find and possess. In *The Hobbit*, Bilbo Baggins finds the evil Sauron's "One Ring of Power." In *The Lord of the Rings*, he passes the ring down to his descendent Frodo, who must return it to the volcano where it was forged in order to destroy it and end its power over Middle Earth. Tolkien presents his familiar theme of quiet, heroic duty, which is often tested by the vicious evil of Sauron's minions (the Orcs) and the treacherous Gollum. The three books provide a panoramic narrative of vast and complex sweep. It is often most compelling in conveying the experience of fear or terror through expressionistic detail. Its epic heroism against difficult odds is sharpened by its emphasis on the essential powers of loyal love that eclipse weakness and failure, powerfully conveyed near the end of the narrative when Gollum seizes the ring from a weakened Frodo and his loyal friend Sam, only to fall to his and the ring's destruction in the volcano.

After Tolkien's death in 1973, his son Christopher edited *The Silmarillion* (1977), which had been started in a military hospital in 1917 and was essentially completed by 1923. It contains four shorter narratives and the "Quenta Silmarillion," an orderly arrangement of the chronicles of the Three Ages of Middle Earth. It is dense and difficult, with a staggering number of characters. Considered by many to contain essential background to a fuller understanding of *The Hobbit* and *The Lord of the Rings*, it cannot be read as an independent narrative.

Interspersed with these major fictions, and partly in response to their successes, came the lesser short narratives "Farmer Giles of Ham" (1949), "The Adventures of Tom Bombadil" (1962), "Leaf by Niggle" (1964), and "Smith of Wootton Manor" (1967). Their charm is accentuated by the writer's accompanying illustrations, but they are lesser accomplishments that demonstrate that Tolkien's narrative strengths are in sustained, multilayered, and lengthy stories with numerous competing characters.

The younger Tolkien also published his father's early drafts of *Unfinished Tales of Numenor and Middle-earth* (1980), *The Book of Lost Tales, Part I* (1983), *The Book of Lost Tales Part II* (1984), and *The Lays of Beleriand* (1985), but these have not had the remarkable popularity of the earlier works that Tolkien completed during his life.

## Summary

The success that J. R. R. Tolkien finally achieved as a fantasy writer in the late 1950's meant that a lifetime of financial worries and measured scorn from many of his academic colleagues were alleviated. Tolkien became famous. Among medievalists, his editing of *Sir Gawain and the Green Knight* and his essays on *Beowulf* continue to be instructive and persuasive in the midst of radical changes in the fashions of literary and medieval studies. However, his celebrity derives from his fantasy fiction.

In his heroic mythopoetic fiction, Tolkien has recreated something of the spirit of the best of medieval literature: a captivating release of the imagination tethered by details of the simple familiarities of essential living and interspersed with suggestions that heroism can make fleeting but radiant differences in a hostile world. For readers of all ages and tastes, Tolkien has been of enormous influence in demonstrating one of the traditional goals of the arts: to delight and instruct. As a solid medievalist, he managed to convey the ethos and spirit of medieval culture, to honor it for its charms and powers, and to present, in compelling narratives, the permanent attractions of heroism, duty, and loyal love in the inevitable human confrontations with fear, temptation, loss, and mortality.

## Bibliography

Carpenter, Humphrey. *Tolkien, A Biography*. London: Allen and Unwin, and Boston: Houghton Mifflin, 1977. This is the authorized biography based on full access to Tolkien's papers. Sound and thorough, it is perhaps too celebratory and fails to put Tolkien in the larger context of fantasy writers from the Middle Ages through the twentieth century. It has a very full appendix of Tolkien's scholarly and fiction writings through 1976.

Crabbe, Katharyn W. *J. R. R. Tolkien*. Rev. ed. New York: Continuum, 1988. Crabbe's book is the best single overview of Tolkien and his work. The writing is clear and succinct, and the observations are solid and thoughtful.

Critchett, David. "One Ring to Fool Them All, One Ring to Blind Them: The Propaganda of *The Lord of the Rings*." *Extrapolation* 38, no. 1 (Spring 1997). Comprehensive analysis of Tolkien's trilogy *The Lord of the Rings* focusing on the use of Christian symbolism.

Hammond, Wayne G. *J. R. R. Tolkien: A Descriptive Bibliography*. Winchester, Hants.: St. Paul's, and New Castle, Del.: Oak Knoll, 1993. This valuable and well-organized bibliography includes helpful annotations.

Johnson, Judith A. *J. R. R. Tolkien. Six Decades of Criticism*. Westport, Conn.: Greenwood Press, 1986. Johnson's thorough and well-annotated bibliography treats all phases of Tolkien's work. It is well indexed and especially good on the more obscure periodicals dealing with Tolkien's work.

*Mythlore. A Journal of J. R. R. Tolkien, C. S. Lewis, and Charles Williams, and the Genres of Myth and Fantasy*, 1969-current. This scholarly quarterly has absorbed earlier publications dealing with the "Oxford Fantasists," such as *The Tolkien Journal*. It regularly publishes articles on Tolkien.

Nitzsche, Jane Chance. *Tolkien's Art: A Mythology for England*. London: Macmillan, 1979. Nitzsche's provocative study examines the writer's dual roles in scholarship and fiction.

Obertino, James. "Tolkien's *The Fellowship of the Ring*." *The Explicator* 54, no. 4 (Summer 1996). Obertino discusses Tolkien's *The Fellowship of the Ring* and its treatment of the Christian precept of self-sacrifice.

Purtill, Richard. *J. R. R. Tolkien, Myth, Morality and Religion*. San Francisco: Harper, 1984. Purtill provides a solid exploration of the spiritual aspects of Tolkien and his work.

Rogers, Deborah Webster, and Ivor Rogers. *J. R. R. Tolkien*. Twayne's English Authors Series 304. Boston: Twayne, 1980. This is a competent and enthusiastic, but perfunctory, overview of Tolkien's life and work. It emphasizes, with limited criticism, a mythic approach to his writings.

Salu, Mary, and Robert T. Farrell, eds. *J. R. R. Tolkien, Scholar and Storyteller*. Ithaca, N.Y.: Cornell University Press, 1979. This book, the best of the collections of essays about Tolkien, emphasizes his work as a medievalist and its connection with his fiction.

*Xavier Baron*

## CLYDE WILLIAM TOMBAUGH

*Born:* February 4, 1906; Streator, Illinois
*Died:* January 17, 1997; Las Cruces, New Mexico
*Area of Achievement:* Astronomy
*Contribution:* After a systematic search based on the predictions of earlier astronomers, Tombaugh discovered the planet Pluto in 1930. He also discovered several star clusters and galaxies, studied the distribution of extragalactic nebulas, searched for small natural earth satellites, and made observations of the surfaces of several planets and of the moon.

### Early Life

Clyde William Tombaugh, the first of six children in his family, was born on a farm near Streator, Illinois, some seventy-five miles southwest of Chicago. His father, Muron, studied mechanical engineering at the University of Illinois but did not earn a degree. He took up farming on the family homestead and married Adella Chritton in 1905. On the farm, Muron maintained a well-equipped shop of hand-operated tools and encouraged his children to use them.

Young Clyde attended a two-room schoolhouse near the family farm. A fifth-grade teacher, Susie Szabo, encouraged his interests in history and geography, leading him to wonder about landscapes on other planets. High school was farther away, requiring a seven-mile bicycle ride each way. During the winter, he lived in Streator with his paternal grandmother and two "double" cousins, whose father, Clyde's brother Lee, had married Adella Chritton's sister.

In high school, Tombaugh became a voracious reader, completing the entire Bible and devoting many hours to the encyclopedia and his father's books on mathematics and physics. His uncle Lee gave him two astronomy books, one on eclipses and the other on the solar system. His interest in astronomy was further stimulated in 1920 when his father and uncle bought a refracting telescope with a 2.3-inch lens and a power of 45. This eventually became Clyde's first telescope, which he later installed as a finder on a 16-inch telescope.

A poor corn crop in 1921 led the Tombaughs to move to a farm near Burdett, Kansas, where they took up wheat farming. After the harvest of 1925, Tombaugh began the tedious process of grinding and polishing a mirror for an 8-inch reflecting telescope. After sending the mirror away for silvering, he was disappointed to learn that it had a poor figure and would not work well. He then built a testing chamber for mirrors in a family tornado cellar and began working on a 7-inch mirror for his uncle with much better results. In 1928, he completed a 9-inch reflecting telescope for himself and began serious observing.

Tombaugh's plans to attend Kansas State University in the fall of 1928 were ended by a summer hailstorm that destroyed the crops. In December he mailed his best astronomical sketches to Lowell Observatory in Flagstaff, Arizona, for some advice. A quick and unexpected response brought an inquiry about his training and abilities for an observing position to operate a new photographic telescope for a long-exposure survey of the sky. Director Vesto Slipher wanted a dedicated amateur astronomer willing to work long hours at low wages. In January of 1929, Tombaugh departed by rail for a ninety-day trial period at Lowell and the beginning of a new career.

## Life's Work

Tombaugh's most important achievement was the discovery of the planet Pluto, following up on predictions nearly thirty years earlier by astronomer Percival Lowell. Pluto was the last of the three planets discovered in modern times with the telescope. The planet Neptune was discovered in 1846 after small deviations in the orbit of Uranus (discovered in 1781) had led to predictions of a new and more distant planet. Since the orbital motion of Uranus did not appear to be totally explained by the presence of Neptune, Lowell, in 1905, calculated the position of an unknown object he called "Planet X" that might cause the presumed orbital discrepancies. He then initiated a series of three unsuccessful searches at his observatory in Flagstaff, Arizona.

Lowell died in 1916, and further searches were delayed when his widow challenged his will, which had designated funds for the Lowell Observatory. After the suit was settled one decade later, a new 13-inch refractor telescope and wide-angle camera were built. Late in 1928, Tombaugh was hired to conduct the fourth search for Planet X. His first duties after arriving in Flagstaff on January 15, 1929, included painting the new telescope, stoking the furnace, removing snow from the observatory domes, giving tours for visitors, and training for the planet search that began in earnest on April 26. Each 14 17-inch photographic plate required about an hour-long exposure to capture a 12-degree 14-degree region of the sky. Several plates could be exposed during a typical clear, moonless evening.

For two months, Tombaugh operated the 13-inch telescope and processed about one hundred plates, searching in the constellation Gemini as predicted by Lowell. The senior astronomers, brothers Earl and Vesto Slipher, examined the plates containing up to 300,000 stars each. They used a device called a "blink comparator" to try to detect any moving objects that might qualify as Planet X. For each small part of the sky, two identical photos were taken on two different days. By focusing the two plates on a screen in rapid alternation, the stars would remain in place, but any moving object would appear to shift back and forth. Several such moving objects appeared on each plate, but most had the faster motions of asteroids. In June, 1929, the Sliphers tired of this work and asked Tombaugh to take over the blink comparisons along with the telescope operations.

After a couple months of frustrating work, it occurred to Tombaugh that a new planet could best be identified near its opposition point (180 degrees from the sun). At this point, the outer planets appear to move backward in a western retrograde motion as the earth passes them, opposite from their usual eastward movement relative to the stars. The farther away a planet is, the slower it moves: An asteroid image would move about 7 millimeters in one day, while a planet beyond Neptune would move only about .5 millimeter per day. Now Tombaugh began to look at regions near the opposition point rather than concentrating on the predicted positions that Lowell had calculated. He could now eliminate most of the shifting images in the blink comparator and look for short retrograde tracks.

By January of 1930, the predicted region in Gemini was in opposition and could be rephotographed with better chances of success. On February 18, Tombaugh placed two plates from Gemini, one taken on January 23 and the other on January 29, into the comparator and observed a shifting retrograde image slow enough to be beyond Neptune. On February 19, he photographed the region again and found the object a bit west of its last position, where it was supposed to be after three weeks of motion, some 6 degrees from Lowell's prediction.

On February 20, the object was observed visually with the 24-inch refractor, but no hint of a disk was revealed, raising questions about whether it was big enough to affect the motions of Uranus and Neptune as calculated by Lowell. Further observations showed that the orbit was beyond Neptune, and the announcement of the planet's discovery was made on March 13, 1930, on the seventy-fifth anniversary of Lowell's birth and the 149th anniversary of the discovery of Uranus. Six weeks later, on May 1, Vesto Slipher proposed the name Pluto, the Greek god of the nether darkness, and a superposed *P* on *L* was chosen as its symbol, matching the initials of Percival Lowell.

For the next two years, Tombaugh continued his search program to be sure that no other planets might be missed. On June 1, 1932, he made his second major discovery when he identified a globular cluster of stars in our galaxy's central hub. In the fall of 1932, Tombaugh was given a leave from the observatory to take up a scholarship at the University of Kansas, where he met and married Patricia Edson in 1934 and completed an astronomy degree in 1936. Returning to Flagstaff, he continued his sky survey until 1943, interrupted only by his 1938-1939 master's degree work back in Kansas. In 1937, he discovered a supercluster of galaxies and measured its shape and size, eventually cataloguing nearly thirty thousand galaxies. He found five open-star clusters and identified a total of 3,969 asteroids, of which more than seven hundred had not been observed before.

In 1943, Tombaugh began teaching physics and navigation for the Navy at Arizona State Teachers' College in Flagstaff. In 1946, he moved to Las Cruces, New Mexico, to take a position as an optical physicist and astronomer at the White Sands Proving Grounds, designing optical equipment and supervising the tracking of V2 missile firings. In 1953, he proposed a project and received military funding to search for small natural earth satellites; for two years he divided his time between White Sands and Lowell Observatory, where the search began.

In 1955, Tombaugh transferred the natural satellite search project to New Mexico State University to facilitate observations from Quito, Ecuador. No such satellites were confirmed, but in 1957, Tombaugh made some of the first photos of Sputnik I, the first artificial satellite, and provided the observational basis for the safety of an extensive artificial satellite program. From 1961 to 1973, he was a professor in the Department of Earth Sciences and Astronomy at New Mexico State University, where he established a comprehensive observational program of the five nearest planets. After his retirement, he remained active in astronomy and continued to build telescopes. Over his lifetime, he ground thirty-six optical surfaces with diameters from 1.5 to 20 inches. Telescopes on which he worked are featured at the Tombaugh Observatories at both New Mexico State University and the University of Kansas.

### Summary

In many ways, Tombaugh was like his astronomer hero William Herschel, who discovered Uranus unexpectedly during a routine sky survey in 1781. Both were dedicated amateur astronomers and skilled telescope makers who devoted hours to tedious observations. Tombaugh, however, was only twenty-four years old when he discovered Pluto, while Herschel was nearly twenty years older. Furthermore, Tombaugh's year-long search for Planet X lasted much longer than that of either Herschel or Johann Galle, who discovered Neptune in 1846 on the first night he looked for it, lying less than 1 degree from its predicted position. The search for Pluto was complicated by the fact that its orbit is highly eccentric—sometimes even passing inside the orbit of Neptune—and has a large inclination of about 17 degrees from the mean plane of the other planets.

It is now known that Lowell's predictions for the position of Pluto were based on faulty calculations, and its discovery within 6 degrees of the predicted location was only a coincidence. Fortunately, Tombaugh did not limit his observations to the predicted area of the sky or to the region close to the mean orbital plane of the planets. When James Christy discovered Pluto's moon, Charon, in 1978, it was conclusively demonstrated that the mass of Pluto was far too small to cause observable deviations in the orbits of Uranus and Neptune; thus the two larger planets' orbits could not be used to predict Pluto's position. In the 1990's, several icy objects much smaller than Pluto were discovered just beyond its orbit in the Kuiper comet belt with periods of about three hundred years, compared to Pluto's 248-year period.

### Bibliography

Beebe, Reta. "Clyde William Tombaugh." *Physics Today* 50 no. 7, (July, 1997). Brief profile of Tombaugh with information on his discovery of Pluto.

Kaufmann, William J. *Universe*. 5th ed. New York: Freeman, 1999. This textbook is a good standard introduction to astronomy with accurate descriptions of the discovery of Pluto, its properties, and its moon Charon.

Levy, David H. *Clyde Tombaugh: Discoverer of Planet Pluto*. Tucson: University of Arizona Press, 1991. This is the only complete biography of Tombaugh; it is written by a fellow astronomer and based on thorough research and personal interviews.

———. "The Empty Chair." *Sky and Telescope* 93, no. 4 (April, 1997). Obituary for Tombaugh touching on his 1930 discovery of the planet Pluto and his development of telescopes used to track ballistic missiles.

Rath, Ida. *Boy Planet Seeker*. Dodge City, Kans.: Rollie Jack, 1963. This is a short (108 pages), illustrated children's book about the life of Tombaugh (with an emphasis on his Kansas roots), his planet search, and his discovery of Pluto.

Tombaugh, C. "The Discovery of Pluto." In *Source Book in Astronomy, 1900-1950*, edited by Harlow

Shapley. Cambridge: Harvard University Press, 1960. This excerpt is an accurate and readable first-person account of the discovery of Pluto.

Tombaugh, C., and Patrick Moore. *Out of the Darkness: The Planet Pluto*. Harrisburg, Pa.: Stackpole, 1980; Guildford: Lutterworth Press, 1981. This is an extended account of the discovery of Pluto written for the fiftieth anniversary of its discovery, with background information on asteroids, Uranus, and Neptune by astronomy writer Patrick Moore.

*Joseph L. Spradley*

# FERDINAND JULIUS TÖNNIES

*Born:* July 26, 1855; Oldenswort, Schleswig, Denmark

*Died:* April 9, 1936; Kiel, Germany

*Area of Achievement:* Sociology

*Contribution:* Tönnies was one of the founders of sociology as a field of scientific study. His major contribution lay in the distinction that he drew between two fundamentally different types of social orders—the realm of *Gemeinschaft* contrasted with that of *Gesellschaft*, or, in what has become the standard English translation, "community" versus "society." The continuing influence of this dichotomy upon sociological thought is shown in contemporary development theory with its distinction between traditional and modern societies.

## Early Life

Ferdinand Julius Tönnies was born July 26, 1855, on a farm in the parish of Oldenswort, district of Eiderstedt, Schleswig, then part of Denmark but incorporated into Germany during his boyhood. His father, of Frisian stock, was a prosperous farmer and cattle-raiser; his mother came from a family noted for its Lutheran ministers. Tönnies spent his boyhood first on the family farm and then, after his father retired in 1864, in the North Sea town of Husum. After graduating from the local *Gymnasium* in 1872, he entered the University of Strasbourg. Taking advantage of German students' freedom to travel, he spent time at the Universities of Jena, Bonn, Leipzig, and Tübingen. He received a doctorate in classical philology from Tübingen in 1877. By this time, however, the major focus of his interest had shifted to political theory and social problems. After postdoctoral work at the University of Berlin, he went on to London to continue his research on the seventeenth century English political thinker Thomas Hobbes. Tönnies gained his *venia legendi* (license to lecture) by submitting in 1881 a draft of what would become his major work, *Gemeinschaft und Gesellschaft*, as his *Habilitationsschrift* and became a *Privatdozent* in philosophy at the University of Kiel.

Tönnies had sufficient private means that he could devote the bulk of his time and energy to his own research and writing rather than to teaching. His most famous work, *Gemeinschaft und Gesellschaft*, was published in 1887. The revised and expanded definitive edition came out in 1912. An English translation by Charles P. Loomis first appeared in 1940 as *Fundamental Concepts of Sociology*; a new edition came out in 1955 under what has become the generally accepted English title, *Community and Association. Community and Association* is a work of immense erudition that reflects Tönnies' extensive reading in social and economic history, the political and social philosophers of the seventeenth through the nineteenth centuries, and nineteenth century anthropological writings. Two themes found in nineteenth century German thought were—along with his study of the philosophy of Hobbes—of crucial importance in shaping Tönnies' ideas. One was the distinction—inherited from the philosopher Georg Wilhelm Friedrich Hegel—between *Gesellschaft* ("society") and *Staat* ("state"): the first an organic reality, the second a mere artificial creation. The second was the concept of the *Volkgeist* ("spirit of a people"), with its corollary, the existence of a *Völkerpsychologie* (or collective psychology of a people) that was manifested in such social phenomena as customs, language, myths, and religion.

## Life's Work

In his mature work, Tönnies distinguished between broad and narrow conceptions of sociology. The broad conception included ancillary disciplines such as demography, physical anthropology, and social psychology. The narrow conception, which Tönnies took as his own primary interest, was limited to the study of social relationships and groups, their values, and their norms of conduct. He delineated three methodologically distinct levels of inquiry in this area. One was theoretical or pure sociology aimed at the formulation of an integrated system of basic concepts or ideal types. The second, which he termed applied sociology, applied the concepts of theoretical sociology to understand the development of concrete historical societies and explain the processes of social evolution, particularly the emergence of modern society. The third, empirical sociology, involved the description and analysis of contemporary human relationships and social phenomena.

The most complete available bibliography of Tönnies' writings lists more than six hundred items. His research on Hobbes resulted in the publication from previously unprinted manuscripts of the English political theorist's *Behemoth: Or, The Long Parliament* (1889) and *The Elements of Law, Natural and Politic* (1889) followed by a full-scale intellectual biography, *Hobbes Leben und Lehre* (1896), which would remain for many years the standard account. He undertook empirical studies dealing with population, the impact of business and seasonal cycles upon society, and such examples of deviant behavior as suicide, crime, and illegitimacy, partly because of his personal humanitarian sympathies and partly because of his conviction that sociological theory must rest upon a solid foundation of empirical research. He was a champion of the application of statistics for the illumination of contemporary social phenomena and processes; he even invented a new method of correlation, which he discussed in the article "Eine neue Methode der Vergleichung statistischer Reihen," which appeared in the journal *Jarbuch für Gesetzgebung, Verwaltung, und Volkswirtschaft im Deutschen Reich* in 1909.

Tönnies' major interest, however, lay in the elucidation and amplification of the concepts set forth in *Community and Association.* The more important of his writings along this line were: *Die Sitte* (1909; *Custom: An Essay on Social Codes*, 1961), *Kritik der öffentlichen Meinung* (1922; critique of public opinion); two collections of articles and papers, *Soziologische Studien and Kritiken* (1925-1929; sociological studies and reviews) and *Fortschritt und soziale Entwicklung: Geschichtsphilosophische Ansichten* (1926; progress and social evolution: views on the philosophy of history); and *Einführung in die Soziologie* (1931; introduction to sociology).

Tönnies regarded all social interactions and groups—what he called social entities (*soziale Wesenheiten*)—as the products of human thought or will. He distinguished three levels of social entities: social relationships (*soziale Verhältnisse*); social corporations (*soziale Körperschaften*), that is, groups that were able to act through representative organs or officers; and social corporations (*Samtschaften*), that is, unorganized groups such as social classes or nations that are large enough to be independent of specific individuals. Although he acknowledged that social relationships may have their source in biological relationships, or psychological relationships, or both (such as the relationship between parent and child), he emphasized the "voluntaristic" basis of all social relationships. A parent, for example, could disown his child. Marriage similarly could be terminated by divorce or, alternately, survive in name long after the psychological relationship had died. Social relationships thus exist because they are recognized, acknowledged, and willed by the participants via the acceptance of and adherence to certain norms or rules of conduct. A social entity, in other words, is the creation of the will of its members and, in turn, imposes upon them certain obligations and grants them certain rights.

Tönnies went on to distinguish between two different kinds of "will" involved in establishing a social entity. One was *Wesenwille* (variously translated by commentators as "natural will," "organic will," or "essential will"), wherein an action is willed for its own sake, or because of primarily unconscious drives or inclinations, or out of habit, or because of its own intrinsic value. The second kind he called *Kürwille* (translated as "rational will," "reflective will," or "arbitrary will"), a term from the old Germanic word for "choosing," because the actor chooses or wills a course of action from among possible alternatives to achieve a certain end or purpose.

The kind of will involved results in two fundamentally different types of social entity. *Gemeinschaft* is the type of social entity that is the project of *Wesenwille*; *Gesellschaft* is the type that results from *Kürwille.* Examples of the first include kin, neighborhood, and village networks social clubs, and religious sects, that is, relationships whose bonds grow out of mutual sympathy, habits, or common beliefs. Examples of the second include contractual arrangements, business associations, and special-interest organizations based upon the deliberate calculation of advantage and disadvantage and weighing ends against means. Although Tönnies took pains to deny that he was writing an "ethical or political treatise," the thrust of his analysis appeared to exalt "community" over "society." Community, he suggested, answered the "need of real and organic life" and was characterized by trust and intimacy. Society, in contrast, was "a mechanical and artificial aggregate" in which every person lived for himself "in a state of tension towards all the others."

Tönnies acknowledged that *Gemeinschaft* and *Gesellschaft* were ideal types that did not exist in pure form in the real world. Even *Gemeinschaften* had their rational aspect. Men's social conduct also could not be determined exclusively by intellect or reason. A given social entity must be ranked on a scale of more or less *Gemeinschaft*-like or more or less *Gesellschaft*-like. Yet Tönnies did see a long-term historical trend. It was his ambition to trace the evolution of human society from primitive agrarian communism through the individualistic society of modern capitalism to an ultimate socialistic-type order, which he envisaged as a higher-quality version of *Gemeinschaft.* Although he published only fragments of this planned universal history in his *Geist der Neuzeit* (1935; spirit of modern times), his article and papers show that he viewed the transition from a predominantly *Gemeinschaft*-like to a predominantly *Gesellschaft*-like social order as largely the result of three major forces: growing commercialization with its attendant corollaries of competition, the market, trade, and credit; the rise of the modern state; and the advance of science.

Tönnies was a German patriot who defended the German side during and after World War I. By the standard of his time and milieu, however, he was politically a liberal, even a radical. An active participant in the Verein für Sozialpolitik (Association for Social Politics) and the Gesellschaft für Soziale Reform (Society for Social Reform), Tönnies took a sympathetic interest in the trade union and socialist movements, workers' education, consumer cooperatives, and national independence movements in such places as Finland and Ireland. In 1932, he joined the Social Democratic Party in protest against the rising National Socialist strength. Hopeful about the possibility of a non-dogmatic universal religion that would unite all mankind, he was a leading figure in the Ethical Culture Society.

His pro-labor, pro-reform sympathies brought Tönnies into disfavor with the Prussian educational authorities and retarded his academic advancement. His growing international reputation, however, finally led to his appointment to a full professorship in political economy at the University of Kiel in 1913. He retired in 1916 but five years later resumed teaching as professor emeritus of sociology. His public denunciation of Nazism and anti-Semitism led to his dismissal from his professorship emeritus after Adolf Hitler came to power. He was with Max Weber, Werner Sombart, and George Simmel as one of the founders of the German Sociological Society in 1909, and he served as president from its founding to 1933. He died on April 9, 1936, at the age of nearly eighty-one, at Kiel.

## Summary

Ferdinand Julius Tönnies was one of the founding fathers of the modern discipline of sociology. Perhaps his major intellectual significance lay in how he offered a new way of looking at the relationship of the individual to society that could resolve the long-standing conflict between the mechanical and rationalistic view of the social contract theorists, on the one hand, and the organistic conception of the romantic and historical schools, on the other. Tönnies' point was that both positions were correct and complemented each other: Man was both a social and an asocial being, and there were both preexisting social relationships into which individuals were born and others that were the result of conscious agreement among formerly independent individuals. Tönnies, one of the leading students of the history of sociology, concludes,

> formulated and even inaugurated a typology of social relations which no sociologist can henceforth ignore, if he does not wish to pass for an amateur. . . . Indeed, all discussions on the opposition between competition and accommodation, conflict and association, cooperation and hostility, fusion and tension, integration and dissolution, solidarity and rivalry, communion and revolt, and all the other forms of social concord and discord, bring us back, directly or indirectly, to the work of Tönnies.

Although Tönnies' work attracted attention and controversy in scholarly circles from its first publication, he had not much influence outside the academic world until after World War I. A disillusioned post-World War I generation romanticized the supposed virtues of the close-knit rural and small-town community in contrast to the impersonality and anonymity of modern industrial, urban society. A more recent variant upon this same theme has been the popularity of the concept of "mass society" and its resulting "alienated man." Tönnies' work was first exploited to legitimize hostility to liberal capitalism and bourgeois society by the communitarian romantics of the German political right and had via this route an indirect influence on aspects of National Socialist ideology. In the 1960's and since, Tönnies has been drawn upon to justify the communitarian nostalgia of the so-called New Left.

## Bibliography

Bonner, Kiernan. "Reflexivity, Sociology and the Rural-Urban Distinction in Marx, Tönnies and Weber." *The Canadian Review of Sociology and*

*Anthropology* 35, no. 2 (May, 1998). The author provides analysis of the writings of Tönnies, Karl Marx, and Max Weber on ruralism versus urbanism.

Cahnman, Werner, ed. *Ferdinand Tönnies: A New Evaluation, Essays and Documents.* Leiden: Brill, 1973. A valuable collection of writings about and commentaries upon Tönnies—many of which could be found previously only in not always easily accessible scholarly journals.

Freund, Julien. "German Sociology in the Time of Max Weber." In *A History of Sociological Analysis*, edited by Tom Bottomore and Robert Nisbet. London: Heinemann, and New York: Basic, 1978. A brief but perceptive analysis that sketches the basic parameters of Tönnies' *Community and Association* distinction, places his work into the larger context of late nineteenth and early twentieth century social and philosophical thought, and offers a sympathetic appreciation of his contributions to the field of sociology.

Heberle, Rudolf. "Ferdinand Tönnies." In *International Encyclopedia of the Social Sciences*, edited by David L. Sills, 17 vols. New York: Macmillan, 1968. Despite (or perhaps because of) its brevity, Heberle's sketch is the most lucid and comprehensible introduction of Tönnies' ideas for the beginning student available.

Jacoby, E. G. "Tönnies." In *The McGraw-Hill Encyclopedia of World Biography*, vol. 10. New York: McGraw-Hill, 1973. A brief but good biographical source on Tönnies. Relates events from both his life and career and includes a bibliography.

Mitzman, Arthur. *Sociology and Estrangement: Three Sociologists of Imperial Germany.* New York: Knopf, 1973. A brilliant exercise in comparative intellectual biography focusing on Tönnies, Sombart, and Robert Michels. Mitzman's account is the fullest available exploration in English of the influences shaping Tönnies' thinking, the sources of his major concepts, and the evolution over time of his views.

Tönnies, Ferdinand. *Ferdinand Tönnies on Sociology: Pure, Applied, and Empirical.* Edited with an introduction by Werner J. Cahnman and Rudolf Heberle. Chicago and London: University of Chicago Press, 1971. The brief introduction by editors presupposes more background than the average undergraduate student is likely to have. The volume is invaluable, however, for its English translation of selections from Tönnies' previously untranslated writings. For students wishing to go further, there is a handy bibliography listing Tönnies' more important publications.

*John Braeman*

# ARTURO TOSCANINI

*Born:* March 25, 1867; Parma, Italy
*Died:* January 16, 1957; New York, New York
*Area of Achievement:* Music
*Contribution:* A genius among classical orchestral conductors, Toscanini is considered by many to be the most influential conductor of the twentieth century. His interpretive insights into the classical orchestral repertory and his development of the conductor's art made him a pivotal figure in the history of musical performance.

## Early Life

Arturo Toscanini was the first child of Paola and Claudio Toscanini. Claudio, a poor tailor, had fought alongside Italian military and nationalist leader Giuseppe Garibaldi and was often more preoccupied with politics than with providing for his family, to which he soon added three daughters—Narcisa (who died as a child), Zina, and Ada. Arturo was a sensitive and strong-willed child and, although sickly, grew strong enough to be sent to the famous Parma Conservatory when he was nine years old. To his father's relief, he received free board and education at the conservatory for nine years.

Trained primarily as a cellist, Toscanini also studied *solfeggio*, or music theory and composition. On his own, he also acquired some conducting experience by gathering his sometimes unwilling peers into small musical groups to play his arrangements. His musical sensitivity and memory for tone were remarkable from the start. Both characteristics, combined with his passion for precision and perfection, were important aspects of his development. As a conservatory student, he was invited to play for one year with the orchestra of the Teatro Regio in Parma. He graduated from the conservatory in 1885 with highest honors in both cello and composition. An excellent cellist, he played in the second cello section at La Scala in Milan in 1887 for the premiere of Giuseppe Verdi's opera *Otello*.

Toscanini's first major milestone as a professional musician came when he was nineteen years old and on tour in Brazil with an Italian opera company. Problems with a conductor in Rio de Janeiro led to his emergency appointment to conduct Verdi's opera *Aïda* (1871) on June 30, 1886. Conducting totally from memory (which turned out to be his custom), he achieved a resounding success that began one of the most remarkable conducting careers in history.

## Life's Work

Toscanini's career was long and varied. Following his recognition in South America, he worked in numerous theaters in Italy for the next ten years, where his reputation for emotional, exacting conducting became an institution. He despised anything routine or mediocre and worked mercilessly with his orchestras to achieve the desired effect. He became known for his interpretations of the works of verismo composers, whose art closely imitated real life. Toscanini's friendship with Alfredo Catalani caused him to often be associated with Catalani's music, especially the opera *La Wally* (1892). Toscanini was also responsible for the premieres of both Ruggero Leoncavallo's *Pagliacci* (1892) and Giacomo Puccini's *La Bohème* (1896). His relationship with Puccini lasted until Puccini's death. In the company of such great singers as Enrico Caruso, Toscanini brought life to many of Puccini's works, including *Madama Butterfly* (1904), *Tosca* (1900), *Manon Lescaut* (1893), and *La Rondine* (1917).

In addition to the Italian repertory, Toscanini had a particular affinity for both the symphonic and operatic music of Richard Wagner, whom he often called the "greatest composer of the [nineteenth] century." Teatro Regio in Turin appointed Toscanini music director in 1895, where he opened with Wagner's *Götterdämmerung* (1874). He was, at the same time, making guest appearances at La Scala and had made quite a name for himself in Milan. In 1898, La Scala's general manager Giulio Gatti-Casazza offered him the artistic direction of the famed opera house. On December 26, 1898, his reverence for the work of Wagner surfaced again as he bravely chose a German opera—*Die Meistersinger von Nürnberg* (1867)—for his first performance in an Italian theater. Toscanini had a commonality with Wagner in that he believed that opera should be a culmination of all the arts—visual, musical, and literary.

In addition to increasing the repertory to include German, Russian, and French works, Toscanini diligently strived to bring a seriousness to opera performance previously unknown: He asked women to remove their hats, deplored encores that stopped the dramatic motion, and would not tolerate egotis-

tical actions of singers onstage that undermined the artistic integrity of the work. The artistic conviction that made him demand total control was a point of struggle throughout his life; indeed, when, along with other small difficulties, the fight became too much for him at La Scala, he left in 1908.

At the same time, both he and his colleague Gatti-Casazza were engaged by the Metropolitan Opera in New York for what turned out to be the most outstanding artistic period yet experienced at the famous opera house. With the demanding temperament for which he was now well known, Toscanini ruled with an iron hand and brought performance standards to new heights. A dazzling roster of singers worked under his regime, including Emmy Destinn, Geraldine Farrar, Enrico Caruso, and Giovanni Martinelli. In seven seasons, he conducted 367 performances of thirty operas, adding works such as Wagner's *Tristan und Isolde* (1859) and *Götterdämmerung*, Georges Bizet's *Carmen* (1875), and Christoph Willibald Gluck's *Orfeo ed Euridice* (1762). Among the world or U.S. premieres were Modest Mussorgsky's *Boris Godunov* (1874), Gluck's *Armide* (1777), and Puccini's *La fanciulla del west* (1910). Unable to work out artistic disagreements with the management, Toscanini resigned from the Metropolitan Opera in 1915, never to conduct there again.

With war raging in his native Italy, Toscanini was restless to return home. During the next five years, he served a short term at the Teatro dal Verme in Milan and conducted many benefits for the war effort but had no permanent assignment. In 1920, Toscanini was appointed director of the newly organized La Scala and was given unprecedented artistic power. He built an orchestra of one hundred players and a chorus of 120 members. While the stage was being reconstructed according to his instructions, he took the troupe on European tours. Averaging five concerts per week, he remained at La Scala until 1929, when he resigned his post in the face of the growing menace of the Fascist regime and an inability to impose his rigid standards of excellence strongly enough to achieve what he felt was true integration of the arts. The politics of war caused him great concern as well, and, in the 1930's, he withdrew from his involvement with both the Bayreuth and Salzburg Festivals because he would not tolerate Nazi discrimination against Jewish performers.

From this point on, the maestro's emphasis was on the symphony orchestra, where demands were less complicated than in opera and where he felt he had more control over the artistic facets of his performances. From 1928 to 1936, he was the conductor of the New York Philharmonic, leading them on tours of Europe and the United States. These performances possessed a distinctive clarity and intensity new even to Toscanini, and some historians believe these years to be the zenith of his artistic life.

In 1938, Toscanini returned to New York at the invitation of David Sarnoff and Samuel Chotzinoff to lead the newly formed orchestra of the National Broadcasting Corporation (NBC). This became the venue for the majority of his recordings, and he remained with them for seventeen years. Although he did not always have the congenial relationship with the NBC players for which he was remembered at the New York Philharmonic, he was revered for his ability to bring an electric sense to the music that he loved and conducted. Although they were treasures in their own right, the recordings near the end of his career were probably not his best. They seem to reflect the impatience contained within in the driving tempos and sometimes harsh dynamics that were a direct consequence of his lifelong passion for perfection. After retiring from conducting after his last performance on April 4, 1954, Toscanini spent the final three years of his life editing the NBC recordings. He died in New York on January 16, 1956.

### Summary

Arturo Toscanini greatly valued his private life, from which his emotional support often came. Devoted to his friends and family, the formidable maestro was loving, unaffected, and playful at home. He was married to Carla de Martini for fifty-four years, and they had four children—two sons, Walter (his business manager) and Giorgio (who died from diphtheria at age five), and two daughters, Wanda (who married pianist Vladimir Horowitz) and Wally. He was a voracious reader and spent much of his quiet time with the classics, some of which he memorized. He also enjoyed entertaining friends at his restored Victorian home in Riverdale, New York.

Toscanini left a legacy that cannot be ignored. He was a man with a personality of extremes—passion, tenderness, exuberance, rage, sensitivity, devotion, and obsession. He recognized his own volatility and was often ashamed and apologetic following his outbursts. While these features made him the often difficult character that he was, they were also the same traits that made him able to express the genius that he possessed. An unyielding devotion to his ideals that even, at times, caused him physical pain gave him the ability to shape the history of music unlike few other conductors before his time.

**Bibliography**

Antek, Samuel. *This Was Toscanini.* New York: Vanguard Press, 1963. This is a simple, direct, yet moving biography from the point of view of a violinist who played under Toscanini. Includes beautiful photographs and reproductions of landmark programs.

Chotzinoff, Samuel. *Toscanini: An Intimate Portrait.* London: Hamilton, and New York: Knopf, 1956. As a music critic and the general musical director of NBC, Chotzinoff was one of the men responsible for bringing Toscanini to the network. Written in a very personal style, the book is important for the inside view it provides of the NBC years and Toscanini's personal life during that time.

Epperson, Gordon. "At the Hands of the Mighty." *Strad* 108, no. 1287 (July, 1997). A cellist's view of performing under the direction of larger-than-life conductors Toscanini, Thomas Beecham, and Serge Koussevitzky.

Ewen, David. *The Story of Arturo Toscanini.* Rev. ed. New York: Holt, 1960. This is simply written biography from the admiring standpoint of Ewen, who has written several other articles on Toscanini's life and work. A good overall history with personal insights.

Haggin, B. H. *Contemporary Reflections on the Maestro.* New York: DaCapo Press, 1989. A musician himself, Haggin offers good insight in defining Toscanini as a pivotal figure in the history of modern conducting. The book is filled with personal reflections, letters, and accounts of dialogues with Toscanini that give a close look at the conductor's perspectives on his personal and professional life.

Horowitz, Joseph. *Understanding Toscanini.* London: Faber, and New York: Knopf, 1987. This book is distinct from other works on Toscanini in that it is a nontheoretical but detailed case study that attempts to supply a broad sociocultural context out of which the "Toscanini phenomenon" emerged. Horowitz includes no personal impressions or interviews; the book contains more about the way in which the conductor was perceived than actual facts about his life.

Matthews, Denis. *Arturo Toscanini.* Turnbridge Wells, Kent: Midas, and New York: Hippocrene, 1982. Matthews attempts to give a balanced view on Toscanini's genius, including both criticism and admiration. He draws heavily on the biographies by Sachs and Sacchi for facts but includes many personal experiences and memories. Includes a lengthy bibliography and discography.

Sacchi, Filippo. *The Magic Baton: Toscanini's Life for Music.* Rev. ed. London and New York: Putnam, 1957. This somewhat wordy yet informative and elaborately detailed biography was published just after Toscanini's death; it served as a source of facts for later biographers.

Sachs, Harvey. *Reflections on Toscanini.* New York: Grove Weidenfeld, 1991; London: Robson, 1992. This is a different approach to biography in the form of collected essays, some previously published and revised, that are divided into six specific periods presented in chronological order. Includes a listing of family archives in the New York Public Library.

*Sandra C. McClain*

# AHMED SÉKOU TOURÉ

*Born:* January 9, 1922; Faranah, Guinea
*Died:* March 26, 1984; Cleveland, Ohio
*Areas of Achievement:* Government and politics
*Contribution:* A lifelong revolutionary nationalist, Touré led Guinea in 1958 to independence from French colonial rule by securing, in all of Francophone Africa, the only no vote against affiliation with the French Community. Guinea's president from independence in 1958 until his death twenty-six years later, he implemented radical sociopolitical transformations. A leading revolutionary African ideologue, Touré left the imprint of his socialist vision on all aspects of Guinean life.

## Early Life

Ahmed Sékou Touré was born on January 9, 1922, in the village of Faranah, situated on the bank of the Niger River, deep in the interior of Guinea. One of seven children born to Alpha and Aminata Touré, Malinke peasant farmers, Touré claimed to be the grandson of Samori Touré, the legendary Muslim state builder who waged a protracted resistance against French conquest until his capture in 1898. Reared a Muslim, the dominant religion in Guinea, Touré attended the École Coranique (Koranic school) and a French primary school in Kankan. In 1936, he was enrolled in the Georges Poiret Technical College in Conakry but was expelled at age fifteen for participation in a student food strike. Thereafter, Touré continued his education through correspondence courses and independent study. He became fluent in French and Soussou in addition to his native Malinké and a spellbinding orator in all three languages.

In 1940, Touré obtained a clerk's position with the Compagnie du Niger, a Unilever subsidiary, where he quickly became involved in labor union activities. The following year, after passing the qualifying exam for work with the Post, Telegraph and Telecommunications (PTT) service, he entered the colonial civil service as a postal clerk. While working in this capacity, he made his first remarkable impression as a constructive agitator by organizing the postal workers into a union. His talent and efficient work earned for him the admiration of his countrymen and the vigilance of the colonial authorities. At that time he formed connections with the Conféderation Générale de Travail (CGT), a Communist-dominated French labor organization.

By 1945 Touré was elected general secretary of the postal workers' union, the Syndicat du Personnel des PTT. A quick succession of upward moves in the trade union movement in both Guinea and French West Africa was to follow, establishing him between 1947 and 1956 as a leading West African trade unionist. In 1946 he became involved with intracolonial politics through the Rassemblement Démocratique Africain (RDA). By 1948, Touré was elected general secretary of the Territorial Union of the CGT, and two years later he was named general secretary of the coordinating committee of the CGT for French West Africa and Togoland. Touré's close relationship with the CGT was a significant influence upon the development of his skill as a mass organizer and political tactician and assisted in no small way in his mastery of Marxist-Leninist thought and practice

## Life's Work

Revolutionary political and socioeconomic change is the central theme of Touré's life. From his earliest years as a labor union organizer, through the decades he labored for independence and as President of Guinea and leader of the Parti Démocratique de Guinée (PDG), he sought to effect fundamental change in his country and create a model for other African nations to follow.

The first two decades of his work life centered on labor issues and the struggle for political independence. Although clearly a radical in the 1940's, he fought within the French colonial system to advance the causes of social justice and Guinean independence. During World War II, African nationalism developed rapidly, and in 1944, at Brazzaville (French Congo) General Charles de Gaulle, president of the French Committee of National Liberation, recognized that France's postwar relationship with French Africa must be revised. The Brazzaville recommendations, accepted by the Fourth French Republic formed in 1946, scrapped the French Empire and substituted the French Union, which allowed the African "overseas territories" administrative freedom, the right to form political parties, the creation of local assemblies composed of both Africans and Europeans, and the formation of regional assemblies for French West (AOF) and French Equatorial Africa (AEF).

In Guinea three parties arose, including the PDG in 1947; by 1952 Touré had become secretary gen-

eral, and the party had become dominant. That same year he became secretary general of the RDA and helped organize in September, 1953, the CGT-initiated, territory-wide strike that secured a significant increase in the minimum wage for workers in the AOF. Later that year Touré won a seat in the Territorial Assembly as the councilor for Beyla, Guinea. In 1955 he was elected mayor of Conakry, and in 1956, to a seat in the French National Assembly.

With the French government's promulgation of the *loi-cadre* for Francophone Africa in 1956, parties with a mass base such as the PDG-RDA obtained an ideal opportunity for greater support at the polls. The *loi-cadre* provided universal suffrage and home rule, with France retaining control over foreign affairs, defense, monetary affairs, justice, and higher education. Touré was elected vice president of the first Government Council of Guinea, the equivalent of prime minister and a position he used to eliminate the tribal chieftaincies, which he considered corrupt.

When the Fourth Republic collapsed and de Gaulle came to Africa in search of support for his Fifth Republic with a referendum on the French Community (an updating of the French Union), Touré urged a vote of no, asserting that the draft constitution provided neither liberty nor equality with France. A no vote meant automatic independence and the forfeiture of French economic and technical assistance. Ninety-five percent of the Guinean electorate complied; thus formal ties to France ended, and on October 2, 1958, the Republic of Guinea was proclaimed. Guinea was the only French African territory where a no vote was urged and overwhelmingly supported by the populace. Touré's and the PDG had demonstrated that they enjoyed virtually undisputed support of the Guinean people, and the future of Guinea fell squarely on their shoulders.

Under the new constitution, Guinea became a democratic and secular republic. Popular rule was to prevail through election of representatives to the National Assembly and the president, who was to serve a seven-year term. Economic development, Touré's prime objective, appeared brighter for Guinea than the other states of the AOF-AEF, for it was endowed with immense deposits of bauxite and iron ore, both already being exploited. For Touré the quandary was how to pursue development and fundamental social change while securing foreign investment and maintaining a foreign policy of positive neutralism. His strategies for realizing these goals were shaped by the dramatic rupture with France and Touré's own past in the CGT and PDG.

Economic decolonization, Touré quickly asserted, would be pursued by a planned economy and a noncapitalist path to development. This resulted in the nationalization of the export trade sector in 1959 and of internal trade in 1960. State agencies were created to control all aspects of marketing, and the civil service was completely Africanized. In March, 1960, he also announced that Guinea had created its own currency, which gave the state control over banking and insurance. Touré then designed an economic Triennial Plan, which was adopted at the PDG Congress in April, 1960, and which stressed developing public and social services while expanding mineral exploitation. Cooperation with foreign capital, however, was supported, and the mixed economic sector, in bauxite mining especially, became the most important source of revenue and foreign exchange.

Touré's political thinking, and hence the structure of the PDG, changed during the first decade of independence. Initially the party was conceived as a mass organization and thus voluntary associations were incorporated into it, such as the women's organizations, youth associations, and trade unions. He defined the party as the unity of Guinean people and rejected the concept of class struggle. By 1964, Touré claimed the revolution was threatened by corruption, inefficiency, smuggling, waste, and low morale. The 1964 *loi-cadre* was passed to correct this. It created standards for party membership and stiff party discipline and extended the party's reach into all factories, large businesses, the army, and the civil service, turning the PDG into a cadre party. Touré began to speak of class struggle and align himself ideologically more clearly with Marxism-Leninism. By the 1967 PDG Congress, he spoke of socialism as the official goal of the PDG and Guinea as divided into two opposing classes, the people (peasants and workers) and anti-people (their opponents).

Touré's political development placed him squarely in not only the camp of African Socialists but also the lead. Like Kwame Nkrumah, Julius Nyerere, and others who defined African Socialism, he redefined class struggle. His institutionalization of mass support through the one-party system went further than elsewhere in Africa, culminating in his declaration of a one-party state in 1978. His opponents have stressed that the evolution of the PDG as the focal institution engendering one-man, one-party rule was achieved through the creation of a permanent "state of plots" and the arrest, imprisonment, or execution of all opponents. Touré exposed nine major plots against the government between 1960 and 1976, which in each case were followed by suppression of the dissenters or protesters (that is, traditional chiefs and unionists in 1960, teachers in 1961, traders in 1965, and civil servants in 1967, 1969, and 1971). The largest crackdown occurred in 1971 after a Portuguese-backed mercenary force attacked Conakry and thousands were arrested and dozens hanged, including several former government ministers.

That invasion related to Touré's foreign policy, which emphasized African unity, support for national liberation struggles, anti-imperialism, and non-alignment. Touré extended support and refuge to the party waging a war for independence from Portuguese rule in neighboring Guinea-Bissau. Africa was the pivot of his foreign policy, but his international relations were characterized by militant rhetoric and flexible diplomacy. Thus, he sought good relations and aid from China, the Soviet Union, and the United States, receiving aid from all in the early years of independence. He nurtured strong relations with his ideological counterparts in Angola, Mozambique, Benin, Congo, and Algeria but failed to achieve good relations with his ideological opposites in the Ivory Coast, Sierra Leone, and Senegal until the late 1970's. His pan-African commitment was expressed two months after independence when Touré and Nkrumah, President of Ghana, signed a treaty of union—the Ghana-Guinea Union—as a nucleus for a union of West Africa. Mali joined two years later, uniting West Africa's most radical states, but it was a paper union and was disbanded in 1963 when the Organization of African Unity (OAU) was created.

### Summary

Throughout his life Ahmed Sékou Touré sought genuine independence and social transformation for Guinea. He will be forever remembered for his success in achieving Guinean independence and rejecting French neocolonialism. Although the imprint of his revolutionary vision was left in every area of Guinean life, his efforts at transforming Guinea may not be eventually judged as so successful. Within weeks of his death, there was a military coup led by Colonel Lansana Conte and the Military Committee for National Redress, which embarked on a course of liberalization and dismantling of the state sector of the economy; yet altering Touré's legacy will take a long time. When Touré died in a Cleveland hospital, flown there in the care of doctors sent by King Hassan of Morocco, much was made of his "opening to the West." In reality, during the last decade of his life he brought Guinea out of diplomatic isolation, improved Guinean and West African regional cooperation, advanced interstate mediation through his work as a peacemaker, and enticed foreign investors to Guinea with attractive financial terms.

Programmatic consistency was not always his forte, but genuine independence and economic development remained his goals. Touré's ideological shifts are spelled out in more than twenty books published between 1958 and 1977, works which clearly demonstrate his focus on radical social change, anti-imperialism, African unity, and national development. Even his many poems were politically charged paeans to the PDG, party militants, anti-colonial resistance, and hard work in the service of national development. His greatest achievement was, no doubt, in forging through a protracted process of national sacrifice an independent African Socialist path; African unity and development proved more elusive.

## Bibliography

Geiss, Imanuel. *The Pan-African Movement*. London: Methuen, and New York: Africana, 1974. An important and accessible work for understanding the development of pan-Africanism within African nationalism. Thus, Touré is seen as a representative of his generation in his pan-African concern.

Hanna, William J. *Independent Black Africa: The Politics of Freedom*. Chicago: Rand McNally, 1964. A helpful examination of independent African states in their early years, especially one-party systems such as that of Guinea.

Hargreaves, J. D. *Decolonization in Africa*. 2d ed. London and New York: Longman, 1996. A readily available work for the general reader to understand decolonization in Guinea and Africa in general.

Kaba, Lansine. "Guinean Politics: A Critical Historical Overview." *Journal of Modern African Studies* 15, no. 1 (1977): 25-45. The political evolution of Guinea and Touré is traced since World War II. A critical analysis of Touré, this article demonstrates that he created a tyranny in which he was the sole interpreter of correct politics and culture.

———. "A New Era Dawns in Guinea." *Current History* 84 (1985): 174-178. This article provides a succinct summary of the legacy of Touré in restructuring Guinea's society and economy. It also discusses the initial policies of his successors.

Langley, J. Ayo. *Ideologies of Liberation in Black Africa, 1856-1970*. London: Collings, 1979. A documentary study of African nationalism, this work places in context the revolutionary ideas of Touré as well as detailing the antecedents.

Touré, Sekou. "Speech to the Congress." *Black Scholar* 5, no. 10 (1974): 23-29. The President of Guinea's speech to the Sixth Pan-African Congress in Tanzania in June, 1974. An ode to African civilization and resistance to colonialism, it is a good example of his rhetorical style and his deep belief in African unity.

*Kathleen O'Mara*

# ARNOLD TOYNBEE

*Born:* April 14, 1889; London, England
*Died:* October 22, 1975; York, North Yorkshire, England
*Area of Achievement:* Historiography
*Contribution:* His challenge and response theory of history, set forth in his twelve-volume *A Study of History*, made Toynbee an important twentieth century philosopher of history.

## Early Life

Arnold Joseph Toynbee was born into a lower-middle-class family, rich intellectually if not socially. His family—including his grandfather, uncles, and parents—was scholarly, humanitarian, and pious. One uncle, also named Arnold Toynbee, earned distinction as a historian, philosopher, and reformer. Toynbee himself credited his mother, a historian and one of the first women to receive a degree from a British university, with first turning his thoughts to history. At Winchester and at Oxford, from which he was graduated in 1911, he received a traditional classical education. A product of late Victorian and Edwardian eras, Toynbee learned from men such as James Bryce and Sir Lewis Namier. During 1911 and 1912, Toynbee traveled in Greece and studied at the British Archaeological School in Athens. In 1912 at twenty-three, he became a Fellow and tutor at Balliol College, Oxford, in the field of ancient history. In 1913, he published a scholarly article on Sparta, and both his teaching and scholarship demonstrated promise.

World War I interrupted his academic career. Though a medical condition kept him from military service, he served in the Political Intelligence Department of the Foreign Office and engaged in propaganda activities. Toynbee's generations—hopeful before 1914—experienced the trauma of World War I, and that event stimulated the writing of his first two books by the age of twenty-six. Both *Nationality and the War* (1915) and *The New Europe* (1915) wrestled with two important themes that troubled civilization at the time: nationality and economics. With idealism similar to that of President Woodrow Wilson, Toynbee viewed self-determination as the remedy for nationalism and the League of Nations as the means of international cooperation. His works also revealed his skill as a writer. In 1919, as a member of the British delegation at the Paris Peace Conference as an expert on the Middle East, Toynbee encountered the rough-and-tumble of international politics.

In 1919, at the age of thirty, Toynbee became professor of Byzantine and modern Greek languages and history, an endowed chair at the University of London. This appointment recognized his reputation as a scholar and his ability to foster cultural ties between Great Britain and Greece. When fighting broke out between Greece and Turkey, Toynbee took a leave of absence and covered the war as a correspondent for *The Manchester Guardian*. The result was another book, *The Western Question in Greece and Turkey* (1922), a plea for understanding different civilizations. Toynbee's fairness to the Turks angered the Greeks in Great Britain who funded his endowed chair, and as a result, in 1924 he left the position. Thus far in his life, Toynbee's intellectual and professional interests focused on the ancient world and the Middle East, both of which shaped his view of history. His knowledge of the classics and his understanding of the world as it was since 1914 contributed to the broad conception of history evident in his later works.

## Life's Work

From 1925 until 1955 Toynbee served as Director of Studies for the Royal Institute of International Affairs and as Research Professor of International History at the University of London. In these capacities he made his most important contributions: his annual *Survey of International Affairs* and his monumental *A Study of History* (1934-1961). Beginning in the early 1920's and continuing through World War II, Toynbee wrote either all or part of, or edited, yearly volumes in the *Survey of International Affairs* series. Neither catalogs nor chronologies, these works discussed broad themes and analyzed world events. Toynbee displayed his historical imagination in these works; given the importance of events from the 1920's to the 1940's, his commentary was significant. In the 1933 volume, for example, Toynbee criticized Nazism as a triumph of paganism over Christianity. Adolf Hitler himself was impressed by Toynbee's grasp of world affairs, and in 1936, before he marched into the Rhineland, the führer conferred briefly with Toynbee.

The work for which Toynbee is most noted is *A Study of History*. Typically, he spent half the year working on the current volume of the *Survey of In-*

*ternational Affairs* and the other half on *A Study of History*, and the material and themes for the two often overlapped. He began serious work on *A Study of History* in 1927; the first three volumes were published in 1934, and the final one in 1961. His analytical world history examined the origin, growth, and decline of civilization. In the tumult of the interwar years, Western civilization, with its inability to deal with crises, appeared bankrupt politically and spiritually, and Toynbee sought answers. He wanted a synthesis in history, not the compartmentalized scholarship of the specialist. Rather than focus on nations as the unit of historical study, Toynbee insisted on studying civilizations, classifying and comparing them, and he proceeded to identify different societies in world history. At first, he distinguished twenty-one, but by the end of his *A Study of History*, he added several more to his list.

Toynbee's philosophy of history began with a discussion of the origins, or creation, of civilization. Rejecting race, God, and environment as explanations, he reasoned that societies emerged when a particular people responded successfully to a challenge, or adversity, such as climate or geography. The unpredictable human element was a major factor in this dynamic historical process of challenge and response. Next was the problem of a society's growth, and this second stage was not automatic. A people must continue to respond to challenges and meet problem after problem. The key to growth, and this was a virtual law of history for Toynbee, was spiritual. By spiritual he meant more than Christian religion, because he pointed to the influence of the creative individual or the creative community on the uncreative majority in the civilization. This psychic, ethereal quality in a people brought growth. His ideas about the importance of the spiritual and the creative individual showed the influence of Henri Bergson on Toynbee.

Toynbee further examined the breakdown of civilizations in *A Study of History*. Decline occurred when the creative power in the minority failed and social unity fractured. The key was a failure of a people to respond, and therefore it was self-failure or suicide. Societies could stop at this stage, and the next stage, disintegration, did not necessarily follow. Nevertheless, if social and individual schisms developed, disintegration ensued; the proletariat withdrew support from the ruling elites, and these divisions ruined the society. Promiscuity and a sense of purposelessness characterized this social decline. Toynbee ended his description of the downward spiral with a spiritual challenge: Western civilization could survive only by returning to its Christian heritage. By 1939, Toynbee had finished the first six volumes of his *A Study of History* and in a unified manner had delineated the process of growth and decline for civilizations as well as offered a solution.

During the 1940's and 1950's, Toynbee's stature as historian and prophet increased, and interest in his work mounted. Unwilling to rest on his achievements, he continued to write, but the remaining volumes of his work compared unfavorably with the previous ones. According to critics, the works were too long and offered little that was new. Toynbee began the seventh volume by discussing services that states provide, a pedestrian theme for his otherwise mystical tone. Yet with that volume, and through several of the remaining ones, he returned to the importance of religion. The chief purpose of history was the refinement of the higher religions; universal states provided universal churches, the highest type of civilization. Though a by-product of the disintegrating state, advancing religions always meant progress. Toynbee believed world religions eventually would achieve unity as one universal spiritual unit and man would come close to perfection. In this vein, Toynbee exhibited a Victorian view of progress. Ironically, after beginning his *A Study of History* on a very pessimistic note, he ended with an optimistic emphasis. His millennial view of history, which culminated with the kingdom of God, contrasted with the dark view of many modern thinkers.

In the last few volumes of *A Study of History*, Toynbee touched on miscellaneous topics. He analyzed the ways in which other civilizations have reacted to the West. In his examination of renaissances in European history—including those of Greece and Rome—he pointed to the origins of modern paganism, which led to war and dictatorships. On a personal note, in the tenth volume he acknowledged several influences on his own thinking: his mother, Edward Gibbon, Namier, Plato, Bergson, Augustine, the Bible, Johann Wolfgang von Goethe, and Carl Jung. In addition to *A Study of History*, Toynbee wrote numerous other books, including two which were autobiographical in nature: *Acquaintances* (1967) and *Experiences* (1969).

## Summary

Because of the massive range of subjects he covered, Arnold Toynbee was vulnerable to criticism, particularly from specialists and conservatives who attacked his unorthodox view of Christianity as well as his pacifism and internationalism. Critics charged him with distortion of the past and an arbitrary interpretation that forced history to fit a pattern. Historians labeled his method unscientific and unsupported by the evidence, and his classification of civilizations subjective and artificial. Some detractors pointed to factual errors, while others focused on Toynbee's overemphasis on religion and his moralizing conclusions. Scholars viewed Toynbee unfavorably because they distrusted simple generalizations about the past.

With *Reconsiderations* (1961), the last volume of *A Study of History*, Toynbee answered his critics. He defended his comparative historical method, his stress on religion, and his general laws, and stood by his interpretations. In a humble manner, however, he admitted errors and expanded his classification of civilizations to include several more. The best defense for Toynbee, however, remained the overwhelming mass and erudition of his writings. Though flawed, as critics proved, Toynbee ranks with the great historians for the impact of his provocative conclusions. In fairness to him, questions posed to Toynbee were issues for the entire historical profession. Like many intellectuals after World War I, he criticized Western secularism and rejected features of the modern world. Ironically, though an agnostic in his youth, he relied on religion in the end. He skillfully recognized the importance of myth in the historical process. In an age of scholarly specialization, Toynbee dared propose a total view of the past. His writings demonstrated his skill as a literary artist, as well as a historian. As a proponent of world unity, he revealed the romantic character typical of his life and work. Toynbee argued that history had meaning and was not irrational or deterministic. His challenge and response theory made him a major philosopher of history for the twentieth century.

## Bibliography

Ashley-Montagu, M. F., ed. *Toynbee and History*. Boston: Sargent, 1956. A general evaluation of Toynbee's work by thirty writers. Most are critical of his method, philosophy, and religious views.

Bagby, Philip. *Culture and History*. London: Longman, 1958; Berkeley: University of California Press, 1959. The author presents a theory of culture for understanding history. His comparative, anthropological approach to history is similar to Toynbee's philosophy of history.

Geyl, Pieter. *Debates with Historians*. London: Batsford, 1955; New York: Philosophical Library, 1956. Thirteen essays by the professor of history at the University of Utrecht on historians and historiography. Four critical essays on Toynbee.

Irwin, Robert. "Toynbee and Ibn Khaldun." *Middle Eastern Studies* 33, no. 3 (July, 1997). The author discusses Toynbee's introduction of philosopher-historian Ibn Khaldun to Western societies.

Jerrold, Douglas. *The Lie About the West*. London: Dent, and New York: Sheed and Ward, 1954. An attack on the thesis and evidence of Toynbee's *The World and the West* (1953), an abridgment of volume 8 of *A Study of History*.

Samuel, Maurice. *The Professor and the Fossil*. New York: Knopf, 1956. The author, a journalist and novelist, criticizes Toynbee for slighting Jewish civilization in his *A Study of History*. Asserts that Toynbee is guilty of factual errors and serious omissions.

Singer, C. Gregg. *Toynbee*. Philadelphia: Presbyterian and Reformed Publishing, 1974. A clear exposition and analysis of Toynbee's philosophy of history from the perspective of orthodox Christianity.

Stromberg, Roland N. *Arnold J. Toynbee: Historian for an Age in Crisis*. Carbondale: Southern Illinois University Press, 1972. An excellent discussion of Toynbee's career, writings, and philosophy, as well as an examination of criticisms of Toynbee.

*Douglas Carl Abrams*

# EIJI TOYODA

*Born:* September 12, 1913; Nagoya, Japan
*Areas of Achievement:* Business and industry
*Contribution:* For more than a half century, Toyoda has been a central management figure and a driving force in the development of a small family enterprise into one of the world's most successful corporate empires.

## Early Life

Eiji Toyoda was born in Nagoya, Japan, on September 12, 1913. Although the family name was eventually to gain international recognition and respect for automobile manufacturing, it was already a well-known name in Japan thanks to Eiji's uncle, Sakichi Toyoda, known as the "King of Inventors." Sakichi was a skilled carpenter, and most of the 150 domestic and international patents he eventually obtained were related to the weaving industry. In early 1895, he established in Nagoya the first of a series of successful ventures in the weaving and textile machinery industry. He was an aggressive entrepreneur with a blustery self-confidence and an early vision of doing commercial battle in order to project Japan's economic might into the world market. In his autobiography, Eiji warmly acknowledged his uncle's shaping influence on his early years. When Eiji was a second-grader, Sakichi took him to visit one of his weaving works in Shanghai and used the occasion of the trip abroad to acquaint the young Eiji with the intricacies of foreign exchange rates.

Shortly before his death in 1930, Sakichi enjoined his eldest son, Kiichirō Toyoda, Eiji's cousin, to explore the possibility of expanding the Toyoda Automatic Loom Works, Ltd., by that time the main firm in the family's growing textile complex, into automobiles. It was a risky venture. Japanese companies had manufactured autos—as early as 1914 a forerunner of the Nissan Company had turned out a DAT Model 1, a precursor to the Datsun—but so thoroughly did foreign motor car companies, notably Japan-Ford and Japan-General Motors, dominate the Japanese market that none of the corporate giants of Japan was willing to commit investments. Yet, since it was his father's last wish, Kiichirō ordered the Toyoda Automatic Loom Works to begin on automobile engines. An "automotive department" was established in 1931.

It was there, while studying as a mechanical engineering student at the prestigious Tokyo Imperial University in the mid-1930's, that Eiji began to spend his summer vacations tinkering with small engines. By the time Eiji was graduated in 1937, Toyoda Automatic Loom had produced three passenger cars with economical engines of Chevrolet design and the stylish lines of a DeSoto body. Eiji's father had plans for the young graduate at his own weaving mill, but Kiichirō, Eiji's strong-willed cousin, prevailed, and it was decided that Eiji would begin work in Toyoda's automotive facility. At about this same time, in August, 1937, the Toyota Motor Company was established. ("Toyota" is an alternate reading of the two ideographs that make up the family name; it was chosen for its phonetic clarity and potential advertising appeal.)

## Life's Work

The new company was barely on its feet when the eight-year-long Sino-Japanese War (1937-1945) began. Toyoda, who was in charge of product inspection and improvement, later conceded the poor quality of the company's early vehicles and candidly allowed that it was military procurements for the war effort that saved the company in its early years. Despite wartime procurement and production problems and an air raid that leveled a quarter of Toyoda's plant in the closing days of the war, the company tallied profits in every fiscal period during the war except for the first year. These wartime earnings were used to spin off several related companies. In 1940, for example, the Toyota Steel Corporation was founded in response to a need for locally produced, high-quality speciality steel. Toyoda eventually became director of this company after its name was changed to the Aichi Steel Works.

The immediate postwar years, 1945-1950, brought brutally harsh conditions to both industry and daily life for all Japanese. The initial policy of the U.S. occupation authorities was to "deconcentrate" Japanese industry (break up large industrial conglomerates such as Toyota), to ensure that they would remain forever weak and unable to contribute to any kind of revival of the expansionist drive that led to war. As production declined, management ordered layoffs and wage and benefit reductions without consulting the workers, and this touched off a wave of labor unrest and strikes that further damaged the country. In 1950, Toyota was close to bankruptcy.

By this time, however, the occupation authorities had come to reconsider their initial deconcentration policy. The onset of the Cold War had convinced the supreme commander, General Douglas MacArthur, of the merit in encouraging the revival of a strong industrial base that would in turn contribute to a rebuilding of a prosperous Japan that would be closely tied to U.S. strategic purposes in the Far East. One of the earliest beneficiaries of this new policy was Toyota. In the summer of 1950, at a time when few Japanese were allowed to travel abroad, U.S. occupation officials granted Toyoda permission to travel to the United States for three months to study production methods; half of this time he spent at the Ford Motor Company. The daily output of the various Ford plants was about eight thousand units, while Toyota's was a piddling forty.

As it turned out, the summer of 1950 was a watershed period for the Toyota Motor Company. By the time Toyoda returned to Japan in October, 1950, and was made the company's managing director, a "procurement boom" was under way as orders to supply U.S. forces in Korea with everything from gunny sacks to trucks flooded the offices of Japanese factories large and small. During the first year of the war, for example, the U.S. military ordered more than three thousand trucks from Toyota—equivalent to about one-fourth of the entire Toyota production in that year. By the end of the Korean War in 1953, the Japanese auto industry had surpassed the production record of the peak year of 1941, and Toyota had pulled ahead of Nissan in sales of both cars and trucks. Once again, a war had given the company a much-needed boost.

Another major turning point in the history of Toyota came in 1957 with the decision to establish Toyota Motor Sales, U.S.A. Volkswagen was demonstrating that foreign-made small cars could command a growing share of the U.S. market, and, while other Japanese manufacturers debated, Toyota acted. The first two Crown passenger cars arrived in California in September, 1957. They turned out to be a disaster. They were cars built for short hauls on crowded city streets, not for American high-speed roads, and for function rather than comfort. They lacked acceleration and strong brakes. Sales were so poor that the American franchise nearly collapsed, and it fell upon Toyoda, who was appointed as executive vice president of Toyota Motor Company in 1960, to travel to the United States in that year to handle the staff dismissals and reduce the scale of operations. The setback did not destroy the company's determination to break into the U.S. market, but rather it conveyed a "do or die" urgency to the need for radical improvement in the quality of Toyota's product. The urgency was heightened as American automakers introduced compact cars into their 1960 lines.

It would not be until 1964 that Toyota was ready to compete again in the United States. Two years later, the company introduced a new model, the Corolla, which met international standards of excellence for the mass market; exports began to climb rapidly. In the meantime, Japan's so-called economic miracle was rapidly increasing the purchasing power of the Japanese consumer, and, by the time Toyoda became president of Toyota in 1967, the era of private passenger car ownership, when an ordinary citizen could think about buying a car, had begun. One set of figures illustrates the dramatic growth of the auto industry in Japan in the decade of the 1960's. In 1960, the total output was 165,000 vehicles; by 1969 that figure had grown to 2,611,000 vehicles, and Toyota's share of the market had expanded from 25 percent to 37 percent. By 1982, when Toyoda retired from the presidency and became chairman of the board, Japan's automobile production had surpassed that of the United States, and Toyota remained well ahead of its eight domestic rivals in output. In 1984, Keidanren, the powerful federation of Japanese business organizations, elected Toyoda as its vice chairman.

### Summary

Eiji Toyoda's career in the industrial empire founded by his uncle and cousin spanned five decades that were as turbulent for Toyota as they were for Japan. The wartime years brought opportunity for a struggling new company, but Japan's defeat brought company and country to the brink of total economic collapse. The Korean War represented another opportunity for Toyota, but it was the drive for efficiency and quality control and improved labor-management relations that brought Toyota—and other automotive giants such as Nissan and Honda—to their world standing. By 1980, Japan's automobile industry had reached an annual production level of 11 million vehicles; Toyota had a third of that market, well ahead of Nissan, its nearest competitor. As the 1980's progressed, Toyota retained its premier position in the Japanese auto industry year after year.

Although personally very wealthy, neither Toyoda nor any other member of his family owns much of the company's assets anymore. The family's share of the holdings amounts to no more than 2 percent; banks and insurance companies own most of the company. The Japanese passion for anonymity and their belief that success is most likely to occur as a result of group rather than individual effort make it difficult to isolate the exact contribution that Toyoda personally made to the striking performance record of his company. Certainly, many of the management and production styles associated with Toyota were perfected while Eiji Toyoda was at the helm. The "just-in-time" system in which parts arrive from suppliers just in time to be part of the final assembly, thus reducing inventory costs, is an example. "There is no secret to how we learned to do what we do." Toyoda once confessed. "We learned it at the Rouge," he said, referring to the Ford plant he had visited in 1950. Toyoda deserves a large measure of the credit for the fact that the company has had no strikes since 1955. He thus illustrates the exemplary Japanese business executive who leads by building harmony and consensus among employees and instilling strong company loyalty.

**Bibliography**

Allinson, Gary D. *Japanese Urbanism: Industry and Politics in Kariya, 1872-1972.* Berkeley: University of California Press, 1975; London: University of California Press, 1976. A highly respected scholarly study of the relationship between the Toyota enterprises and the communities, in and around Nagoya, Japan, where they are located. It includes a good analytical discussion of the growth of the Toyota empire and the role of various family members including Eiji.

Cho, Yukio. "Keeping Step with the Military: The Beginning of the Automobile Age." *The Japan Interpreter* 7 (Spring, 1971): 168-178. A fascinating account of the early years of the automobile industry in Japan.

Cusumano, Michael A. *The Japanese Automobile Industry: Technology and Management at Nissan and Toyota.* Cambridge, Mass.: Harvard University Press, 1985. A scholarly examination of the history of the two companies and the personalities who helped to transform them into world-class auto manufacturers. Contains an immense amount of statistical data.

Kamata, Satoshi. *Japan in the Passing Lane: An Insider's Account of Life in a Japanese Auto Factory.* Translated by Tatsuru Akimoto. New York: Pantheon Books, 1982; London: Allen and Unwin, 1983. A controversial account of the Toyota Company by a freelance journalist who hired on at the company as a laborer. Kamata challenges the generally favorable view of Toyota's contented workers by depicting them as being driven as if they were machines under ferocious working conditions.

Kamiya, Shōtarō. *My Life with Toyota.* Translated by Thomas I. Elliott. Tokyo: Toyota Motor Sales Company, 1976. Although there is little mention of Toyoda in this book, it is a valuable study of the company by one of the founding members of the company and a president in the 1950's.

Singh, Ajay, and Murakami Mutsuko. "Autocrat." *Asiaweek* 22, no. 41 (October 11, 1996). Brief profile of Toyoda including how his robotics and manufacturing methods have influenced automaking.

Toyoda, Eiji. *Toyota: Fifty Years in Motion.* New York: Kodansha International, 1987. Originally published in Japanese in 1985. A rambling autobiography with many interesting anecdotes and numerous photographs from the early years of the company. Valuable for discussion of Toyoda's relationships with other leaders of the company.

*John H. Boyle*

# ERNST TROELTSCH

*Born:* February 17, 1865; Haunstetten, near Augsburg, Bavaria

*Died:* February 1, 1923; Berlin, Germany

*Areas of Achievement:* Theology, philosophy, historiography, and sociology

*Contribution:* Troeltsch pioneered in making the study of religion a phenomenon amenable to social and scientific analysis in contrast to the standard theological approach. His sociological method stimulated in turn the comparative study of religions and helped gain acceptance for sociology as an academic discipline. His reflections on the philosophy of religion also helped establish the credibility of that field of inquiry.

## Early Life

Ernst Peter Wilhelm Troeltsch was the eldest son of a physician of Augsburg, where the family was prominent among the local Lutheran burgher community. Through his father, young Ernst acquired early a fascination with scientific method and observation. He later recalled his ready access in the family home to botanical and geological specimens, anatomical charts, skeletons, and a library amply endowed with scientific books. Darwinism by the 1870's had found a welcome reception among the educated classes of Germany.

Nevertheless, after a solid grounding in the classical languages and literatures at local preparatory schools, Troeltsch gravitated toward the study of theology and particularly the relationship between Christian faith and human reason, a theme that would occupy most of his scholarly career.

Between 1884 and 1888, Troeltsch studied theology at three German universities. At Erlangen he pursued, in addition to courses in Lutheran theology, a general liberal arts curriculum that included studies in history, art history, psychology, and philosophy. The breadth and variety of this program, coupled with his enduring interest in the scientific method, led him to increasing dissatisfaction with what he regarded as the narrow, dogmatic Lutheranism of the Erlangen theology faculty.

Troeltsch therefore transferred to the more cosmopolitan University of Berlin and, within a year, to the University of Göttingen. There, after three further years of study, he received in 1888 the licentiate in theology. It was at Göttingen under the tutelage of the renowned liberal Lutheran theologian Albrecht Ritschl that Troeltsch's scholarly interests came into focus. Yet, while he learned much from Ritschl's neo-Kantian perspectives and his insights regarding Christian values as essentially independent of scientific verification, Troeltsch eventually broke with his mentor.

What Troeltsch could not accept was Ritschl's fully transcendent, ahistorical approach to the history of Christianity. Troeltsch had become convinced that theological study could no longer be based only on dogmatic authority. If theology were to be intellectually respectable it must, in his judgment, be subjected to the rigors of the scientific and historical methods. Troeltsch envisioned nothing less than a rational theory of religion rooted in concrete historical investigations. Since in his view religion had, like mankind, evolved across time, the Christian religion in particular should be studied within the framework of the comparative history of religions.

This was the message that the still obscure young scholar Troeltsch proclaimed at a meeting of German theologians in 1896. When his dramatic assertion that the old ways of theological study were tottering was sharply rebuked by a senior theologian present, Troeltsch angrily departed the assembly, slamming the door behind him. He was ready to carry forward the broad program of theological renewal that he had contemplated.

After a year as a Lutheran pastor, Troeltsch had in 1891 accepted his first academic position as a lecturer in theology at the University of Göttingen. The following year, he became associate professor of theology at the University of Bonn, where he remained until his elevation in 1904 to a full professorship in systematic theology at the University of Heidelberg. His final move came in 1915, when the now-renowned scholar became professor of philosophy at the University of Berlin. He developed his ideas within the framework of his teaching responsibilities at these institutions.

## Life's Work

Troeltsch identified the great spiritual dilemma of his time as the "dissolution of all norms and values under the endless turbulence of the currents of historical life." He related this crisis in coherence and meaning in large measure to the decline of religion as a vital force in society. A multifaceted intellectual movement called historicism had since the latter nineteenth century stressed the relentless relativity of things, both in nature and in history. Although Troeltsch shared many of the premises and conclusions of historicism, as a committed Christian he took it as his urgent scholarly task to confront the historicist challenge in order to provide a tenable new coherence to religion and to history.

Troeltsch's problem from the outset remained the great rift between the skepticism generated by what he called "the ceaseless flow and manifold contradictions within the sphere of history, and the demand of the religious consciousness for certainty, for unity and for peace." To bridge this gap and meet the challenge of historicism, Troeltsch determined to lay the foundations of a general theory of religion. He sought above all an extrahistorical basis for what he called "the morality of conscience . . . amid the flux and confusion of the life of the instincts."

In a series of essays beginning in 1895, Troeltsch tried to establish religion as a natural human phenomenon with its roots in the structure of the human mind, parallel to the various realms of reason affirmed in the famous critiques of Immanuel Kant. Troeltsch attempted to formulate a law that would, above any historical experience, attest the a priori existence of religious ideas such as a "morality of conscience" in human beings. If he could confirm the existence of a mental structure where religious ideas originated, he believed that he could demonstrate the actuality of the absolute in finite consciousness, a point at which the infinite and the finite would meet, thereby neutralizing permanently the acids of relativism on moral values. A "science of religion" could then be philosophically validated to protect objective norms of the religious consciousness. Yet because Troeltsch was ultimately unable to define convincingly the lines of the a priori connection of the finite with the infinite, he was forced to conclude that the human mind was capable of grasping only particular historical circumstances. In short, Troeltsch found his old historicist apprehensions reaffirmed.

Troeltsch was also compelled in the process to reject all arguments for the absoluteness and uniqueness of Christianity among the world's religions. While Troeltsch's early essays affirmed Christianity as the supreme faith, further study and reflection led him to quite another verdict. In his *Die Absolutheit des Christentums und die Religionsgeschichte* (1902; *The Absoluteness of Christianity and the History of Religions*, 1971), he surmised that "it is impossible to construct a theory of Christianity as an absolute religion on the basis of any historical way of thinking, or by the use of historical means." He had already rejected arguments for the primacy of Christianity based on dogma or on miracles: "Divine activity cannot be assumed to fill gaps in the causal sequence." For Troeltsch the baffling complexity of the problem lay precisely in the sheer interconnectedness of all that exists, what he described as "the relation of individual historical facts to standards of value within the entire domain of history" in his late work *Der Historismus und seine Probleme* (1922; *Historicism and Its Problems*, 1922).

Convinced in theory of the intrinsically conditional character of human experience, Troeltsch resolved increasingly after 1905 to test his abstract reflections on the philosophy of religion in a series of concrete historical investigations. In the process, he would generate significant new insights and methods for the scholarly study of religion. Inspired in part by the sociological studies of his celebrated friend Max Weber, Troeltsch began to examine in their historical contexts a number of questions previously raised solely from a theological vantage.

These investigations culminated in his massive *Die Soziallehren der christlichen Kirchen und Gruppen* (1912; *The Social Teaching of the Christian Churches*, 1931). Troeltsch here applied the new sociological perspective and method to the whole of Christian history over the first seventeen centuries of its existence to the age of the Enlightenment. He proposed to determine the extent to which the Christian religion had been influenced by the web of secular forces in its environment.

Drawing his evidence primarily from the ethical and social teachings of the Christian churches and sects within the context of each age, Troeltsch concluded that the religious teachings, beliefs, and organization of the premodern Christian past were demonstrably affected by the social milieu of their origins. The central moral and social doctrines of Christianity did not reflect either an absolute ethic or a pure religious spirit but simply various Christian social communities coming to terms with the world around them.

Troeltsch illustrated this interaction through a set of ideal types derived in large measure from Weber but modified to account for specific historical situations. Troeltsch found three main social expressions of Christianity's relationship with the world: a church type that encompassed the majority of Christians, a minority sect type that developed largely in reaction to the mainline church type structures, and, finally, a highly personal mystical type. For Troeltsch, the story of Christianity was essentially a series of responses or reactions that ranged across a continuum that included the various compromises made by the church-type communities through the outright rejection of the world's values as in the extreme sectarian type to the even more individualistic mystical form. Troeltsch's theory of church types has remained among the most influential of his ideas.

Although greatly discouraged by the failure of his historical research to provide a firmer foundation for his metaphysical conjectures, Troeltsch continued to seek clearer answers to the urgent question as to what one can know for certain in a situation whose subjective and contingent character remained insurmountable. He would remain disappointed. By the time of his death in early 1923, Christianity had become for him "a purely historical, individual, relative phenomenon," bound up inseparably with European culture. The concept of a pluralism of religions and of religious values became a dominant theme in his last writings.

If neither an a priori "science of religion" nor the absolute status of Christianity could be sustained by the methods of theology, philosophy, or history, what instruction or solace might Troeltsch offer to one adrift in the sea of relativism? To avert what he saw as the debacle of "absolute relativism," he devised a rationale based on the subjective value of Chistianity to the individual. Troeltsch, unable to achieve scientific verification for his investigations, related the validity of Christianity directly to the subjective judgment of each Christian: "No physics . . . biology . . . psychology or theory of evolution can take from us our belief in the living, creative purpose of God."

While Christianity remained for Troeltsch a relative phenomenon when considered in its purely historical dimensions, he insisted that there were still moral values to be derived from it, norms of conduct that are "true for us [in] the religion through which we have been formed, a part of our being." Each Christian encounters the truth of Christianity for himself within the context of the local cult or church community, or in his heart.

In short, the objective and universal validity of Christian ethics was mediated to individuals only in a subjective mode. The validity of Christianity as an ethical religion lies therefore in an ever-renewed commitment of each Christian, an act of will, based on faith. As he wrote in his last work: "In every cycle of cultural values it is faith that ultimately decides and here too it is faith that justifies." Troeltsch thus found the general validity he sought neither in philosophy nor in history but through his religious belief, a version of the justification by faith precept from the Lutheran heritage of his youth.

### Summary

Ernst Troeltsch was an extraordinarily prolific writer. His fourteen books and more than five hundred additional publications reflect the wide range of his scholarly interests, particularly in the philosophy and sociology of religion and in the historiography of Christianity. To the degree that he was never able to find a firm basis within history for the absolute values he sought, his life's work clearly fell short of his original aspirations. Yet the boldness and the magnitude of the issues that he raised and the continuing influence of his sociological approach to religious studies lend an enduring interest and merit to his major writings. He wrestled above all with a question that had long baffled theologians and philosophers alike, namely how to bridge the great chasm between the contingent realm of history and the domain of the absolute.

Compelled by his rigorous scientific methodology to remove the absolute from history, Troeltsch had to face the intellectual and spiritual consequences of his human predicament. Personally a man of deep religious convictions, he found himself caught between the need to believe and the pressing demands of the scientific method that he had imbibed from childhood. His friend Friedrich Meinecke ruefully described Troeltsch's plight as that of the ancient sages Heraclitus and Archimedes combined: "All is flux; give me a place to stand." It was in seeking a place to stand amid the historicist winds that appeared to have swept away all certainty in human affairs that Troeltsch identified the broad contours of the problem and the methods of scholarly inquiry through which to approach it. Subsequent generations have taken up the search where he left it.

### Bibliography

Antoni, Carlo. *From History to Sociology: The Transition in German Historical Thinking.* Translated by Hayden V. White. London: Merlin Press, and Detroit: Wayne State University Press, 1959. This work, originally published in

1939, contains an extensive pioneering essay on the dilemma of Troeltsch as theologian and as historian caught between the theologian's yearning for absolutes and the insistent counterclaims of historicism and the new sociology.

Clayton, John P., ed. *Ernst Troeltsch and the Future of Theology.* Cambridge and New York: Cambridge University Press, 1976. Contains six essays by Troeltsch scholars that focus primarily on the relevance of his thought to current theological concerns. A noteworthy feature of the bibliography is an extensive listing of Troeltsch's works that are available in English translation.

Honnefelder, Ludger. "Rationalization and Natural Law: Max Weber's and Ernst Troeltsch's Interpretation of the Medieval Doctrine of Natural Law." *The Review of Metaphysics* 49, no. 2 (December, 1995). The author comments on the analyses of Troeltsch and Weber with respect to the role of natural law in Christianity in the Middle Ages.

Pauck, Wilhelm. *Harneck and Troeltsch: Two Historical Theologians.* New York: Oxford University Press, 1968. Pauck's essay remains the best single introduction to Troeltsch's career. Having studied under Troeltsch at the University of Berlin, Pauck provides a balanced but sympathetic portrait of the man as well as the thinker. He stresses Troeltsch's abiding conviction that modern theology cannot survive without availing itself of the historical and sociological perspectives.

Reist, Benjamin A. *Toward a Theology of Involvement: The Thought of Ernst Troeltsch.* Philadelphia: Westminster Press, and London: SCM Press, 1966. Concentrating mainly on Troeltsch's two most celebrated works, *The Social Teaching of the Christian Churches* and *Historicism and Its Problems*, Reist analyzes Troeltsch's impressive attempt at laying the basis of a theology of culture and of Christian involvement in a pluralist social environment. He concludes that Troeltsch's failure to resolve his doubts about the uniqueness of Christianity was nevertheless a fertile failure in that it helped set the agenda for a continuing debate.

Rubanowice, Robert J. *Crisis in Consciousness: The Thought of Ernst Troeltsch.* Tallahassee: University Presses of Florida, 1982. This recent account of Troeltsch's development as teacher, as thinker, and as politician attempts to evaluate his career as a whole. The author places Troeltsch firmly and convincingly within the context of twentieth century intellectual history, especially in regard to his philosophy of history, his historical method, and his political thought.

Wyman, Walter E., Jr. "Revelation and the Doctrine of Faith: Historical Revelation within the Limits of Historical Consciousness." *The Journal of Religion* 78, no. 1 (January, 1998). The author compares the views of Ernst Troeltsch and Friedrich Schleiermacher on the history of religion.

*Donald Sullivan*

# LEON TROTSKY
## Lev Davidovich Bronstein

*Born:* November 7, 1879; Yanovka, Ukraine, Russian Empire

*Died:* August 20, 1940; Coyoacán, Mexico City, Mexico

*Areas of Achievement:* The military, journalism, government, and politics

*Contribution:* Trotsky was a preeminent leader of the 1917 Russian Revolution. Along with Vladimir Ilich Lenin, he directed and guided the revolution and became one of its leading political, military, and intellectual figures. Ousted from political power by Joseph Stalin in 1927 and exiled from the Soviet Union two years later, Trotsky continued to publish on a wide variety of political issues until his murder by a Soviet secret police agent in 1940.

### Early Life

The small farming village of Yanovka, in the southern Ukraine, was the birthplace of the Russian Revolutionary leader Leon Trostky. Trotsky was born Lev Davidovich Bronstein, in November, 1879, a period of considerable change in Imperial Russia. His parents were well-to-do farmers and, although barely literate, were committed to securing an education for their son. The Bronstein family was Jewish, although not particularly religious. While maintaining Jewish cultural traditions, they also assimilated much of the Russian and Ukrainian culture that surrounded them. By naming their son "Lev," the Russian word for lion and the Hebrew word for heart, they combined both Jewish and Russian traditions.

Lev Bronstein began his formal education in the port city of Odessa. One of the most Westernized of Russian cities, Odessa was a mecca for students and foreigners. Bronstein attended a German school, and it was at this school and in this cosmopolitan city that he developed an understanding of and appreciation for the West. He completed his schooling in the provincial city of Nikolayev. As Odessa had made him a man of the West, Nikolayev made him a man of politics. In Nikolayev, Bronstein met a group of young radicals and initially opposed their Marxist ideas. He maintained a passionate rivalry with Alexandra Lvovna Sokolovskaya, one of the most articulate Marxists in the group and the woman who became his first wife. In the spring of 1879, the radicals of Nikolayev, under Bronstein's leadership, organized the illegal and underground South Russian Workers' Union. The organization was short-lived, and in less than a year the members were arrested and exiled to Siberia. Before leaving for the Siberian wasteland, Bronstein and Sokolovskaya were married in a Moscow prison.

During his imprisonment and exile, Bronstein became increasingly convinced of the philosophical concepts of Marxism. During this time, he first encountered the works of Lenin. Exiled in the far reaches of Siberia, Bronstein read Lenin's plan for revolution, *Chto delat?* (1902; *What Is to Be Done?*, 1929). It was as if Bronstein had heard a calling. In 1902, leaving his wife and four-month-old daughter behind, Bronstein escaped from Siberia and journeyed to London to meet Lenin. In order to cross the Russian border undetected, Bronstein secured a false passport in which he penned the alias Trotsky, the name of his former jailer in Odessa, and the name that would be his for the remainder of his life.

### Life's Work

Trotsky's pen was his most valuable asset. In London, he joined the editorial board of *Iskra*, the newspaper and the organizational nucleus of the Russian Social Democratic Labor Party (RSDLP). Trotsky's fiery prose won for him praise among his fellow émigrés. He did not restrict his writing to revolutionary tracts. Trotsky was deeply interested in culture and literature. Later in life he wrote penetrating literary criticisms and critiques on the development of culture and its relationship to the proletariat. Trotsky was nicknamed "Pero" (the pen) by his contemporaries.

The year 1903 holds particular importance in Trotsky's life. He traveled to Paris on a lecture tour and met Natalia Sedova, who became his second wife and who remained with him in triumph and defeat until his death. It was also the year of the Second Congress of the RSDLP. During the congress, bitter disagreements between factions in the RSDLP caused a schism, creating two parties, the Bolsheviks, headed by Lenin, and the Mensheviks, headed by L. Martov. Trotsky sided with Martov and against Lenin on the issue of party structure.

An ideological opponent of Lenin and the Bolsheviks for more than a decade, Trotsky also had his differences with the Mensheviks, and, although he supported some of their programs, he remained independent, not joining either political party.

The 1905 revolution brought Trotsky back to Russia. Writing for both the Bolshevik and Menshevik presses, Trotsky became a popular spokesman for the revolution. In October, he was elected chairman of the Soviet of Workers' Delegates. By December, however, the revolution had run its course and the czarist regime regained authority and arrested leading members of the Soviets. Trotsky was again deported to Siberia, this time for life. Once again he escaped. Back in Europe, Trotsky turned to writing, composing his first major work.

Trotsky, now notorious, traveled from country to country as a political journalist. It was during this time that he developed his most important contribution to Marxist ideology, the theory of "permanent revolution." The theory rests on several basic principles: the application of Marxist ideas of revolution to backward or less developed nations, the constant or permanent relationship between democracy and socialism during and after the political phase of revolution, and the linkage between the fate of the revolution in Russia and a continued international revolution. In February, 1917, Trotsky was in New York writing for a Russian radical newspaper when he received news that the czarist government had collapsed.

Trotsky arrived in Petrograd on May 4, 1917; the revolution was already ten weeks old. Lenin had returned from exile one month earlier. Although in the past Lenin and Trotsky had had strong ideological differences, the paths of the two great political thinkers, so long divergent, now met. Upon Trotsky's return, Lenin asked him to join the Bolsheviks. Trotsky shared many views with the Bolsheviks; he opposed the new provisional government, wanted an immediate end to the war, supported redistribution of land to the peasantry, and believed that all power should rest in the hands of the Soviets. Trotsky did not immediately accept Lenin's offer; his was a gradual evolution to the Bolshevik Party. It was not until September that he openly referred to himself as a Bolshevik. From that time forward, Trotsky's name was synonymous with Bolshevism. He became the number two man in the Party. While many in the Bolshevik inner circle resented Trotsky's meteoric rise within the Party, they also had to acknowledge his firmness, clarity, intellect, and fiery oratory.

Trotsky assumed the leadership of the Military Revolutionary Committee of the Bolshevik Party in September, the same month he was elected President of the Petrograd Soviet. From the Smolny Institute, headquarters of the Bolshevik Party, Trotsky planned the overthrow of the provisional government. On October 25, 1917, radical soldiers led by the Military Revolutionary Committee stormed the Winter Palace, where the provisional government was meeting, and staged a successful *coup d'état.* That same evening the All-Russian Congress of Soviets, consisting of the divergent radical groups in Russia, convened. At the congress, Socialist groups opposed to the Bolsheviks denounced the seizure of power and withdrew from the congress, prompting Trotsky's famous comment: "To those who have left . . . [y]ou are miserable bankrupts, your role is played out; go where you ought to go: into the dustbin of history!"

The first aim of the revolution was to end Russia's involvement in World War I. Trotsky was named commissar of foreign affairs and went to Brest-

Litovsk to sign a peace treaty with Germany. No sooner was World War I over than the Russian Civil War began. The Bolsheviks faced their most serious challenge as anticommunist forces organized the White Army. Trotsky, who had no prior military experience except for leading the October coup, was placed in charge of the Red Army. From 1918 to 1921, Russia endured a long and bloody civil war. During this time of great chaos, Trotsky led the Red Army to a decisive victory over the Whites. He was hailed as the savior of the revolution. Never in his career was his reputation higher.

Shortly after the death of Lenin in 1924, Trotsky's political fortunes began to wane. It became clear that Trotsky's preeminence in the Party was the result of Lenin's support. Now with Lenin's death, the veteran functionaries of the Party such as Stalin, Lev Kamenev, and Grigori Zinovyev organized a "troika," a three-man political clique, to prevent Trotsky from taking power. Although Trotsky had a strong following in the rank and file of the Party, the leadership resented his rise to power, his arrogance, and his intellect.

In the years following Lenin's death, Trotsky continued to promote his own views for the continued development of the Soviet state. He advocated a move away from the New Economic Policy (NEP) adopted in 1921 and a more open, less bureaucratic party. The Left Opposition, organized by Trotsky and forty-six prominent Bolsheviks, opposed Stalin's troika and called for a more balanced economy and great democratization within the Party. Trotsky's political program came under scathing and brutal assault by Stalin and his followers.

Trotsky's personality was as much under attack as his political programs. His Western cosmopolitanism and Jewish background further alienated him from the Party leadership. Trotsky never fully understood that his late arrival into the Party and his vituperative disagreements with Lenin in the years prior to the Revolution would work against him. Although a powerful intellect, Trotsky was neither an adroit bureaucrat nor a skillful political opponent. By 1927, Stalin marshaled sufficient forces to oust Trotsky from the Party. He was exiled to Alma-Ata in Soviet Turkestan in 1928 and in 1929 was banished from the Soviet Union.

Even in exile Trotsky and his pen remained a threat to Stalin. On August 20, 1940, Roman Mercador, a Soviet secret police agent, under the direction of Stalin, assassinated Trotsky by a blow to the head with an ice pick.

### Summary

In exile Leon Trotsky continued to speak and write defiantly. His pen was once again his only weapon. He warned against the totalitarian model being applied in the Soviet Union by Stalin and railed against the evil of Fascism and its destructive forces. His analysis of the development of Stalinism and Fascism are classics of modern political theory. His most enduring works of this period are his autobiography *Moya zhizn: Opyt avtobiografi* (1930; *My Life: An Attempt at an Autobiography*, 1930), the monumental *Istoriya russkoy revolyutsii* (2 volumes, 1931-1933; *The History of the Russian Revolution*, 3 volumes, 1932-1933), and his prophetic exposé on the dangers of the Stalinist dictatorship, *The Revolution Betrayed: What Is the Soviet Union and Where Is It Going?* (1937).

Trotsky was a man of words and action and lacked political acumen. He found the business of politics, of manipulating men and creating self-promoting situations, crude and distasteful. His arrogance and his intolerance for the realities of political life made him vulnerable to the shrewder first secretary of the party, Stalin. Trotsky remains *persona non grata* in the Soviet Union. Much of his written work is banned. His role during the Revolution and Civil War are not officially recognized; not even his photograph is to be found in encyclopedias or textbooks. Outside the Soviet Union, Trotsky's many contributions are more widely recognized.

### Bibliography

Carr, E. H. *A History of Soviet Russia.* Vols. 1-3, *The Bolshevik Revolution.* London and New York: Macmillan, 1951. A comprehensive general account of Trotsky's role in the Russian Revolution.

Deutscher, Isaac. *The Prophet Armed.* New York: Oxford University Press, 1954; London: Oxford University Press, 1976.

———. *The Prophet Unarmed.* London and New York: Oxford University Press, 1959.

———. *The Prophet Outcast.* London and New York: Oxford University Press, 1963. Deutscher's trilogy is a historical classic. Based on extensive research at the Trotsky archives at Harvard University, this work is the most comprehensive biography on the life and works of Trotsky.

Geras, Norman. "Marxists before the Holocaust." *New Left Review* no. 224 (July-August, 1997). The author examines Trotsky's 1938 prediction with respect to the destruction of the Jews during World War II.

Howe, Irving. *Leon Trotsky.* New York: Viking Press, 1978; London: Penguin, 1979. A short and eloquently written biography.

Krasso, Nicolas, ed. *Trotsky: The Great Debate Renewed.* St. Louis, Mo.: New Critics Press, 1972. A book that reflects the continued controversy over Trotsky's ideas and his contribution to Marxist theory.

Thatcher, Ian D. "Trotsky Studies—after the Crash: A Brief Note." *Europe-Asia Studies* 48, no. 3 (May, 1996). Thatcher looks at Trotsky's role in the development of modern Russia, using Trotsky's correspondence with his wife and Lenin as well as his writings as a basis for analysis.

Trotsky, Leon. *History of the Russian Revolution.* Translated by Max Eastman. London: Gollancz, and New York: Simon and Schuster, 1932. This monumental three-volume work is considered Trotsky's greatest work. The book is an epical and passionate narrative and analyzes the events of the Russian Revolution.

———. *My Life.* New York: Grosset and Dunlap, 1960. Trotsky's autobiography written in 1930 while he was in exile in Turkey.

———. *The New Course.* Translation by Max Shachtman. New York: New International, 1943; London: New Park, 1956. Written in 1923, this series of articles is Trotsky's response to attacks made against his political views.

Wolfe, Bertram D. *Three Who Made a Revolution.* 4th ed. New York: Dial Press, 1964. A study of Lenin, Trotsky, and Stalin. Contains particularly good chapters on Trotsky's early life and his role in the revolution.

*Shlomo Lambroza*

# PIERRE ELLIOTT TRUDEAU

*Born:* October 18, 1919; Montreal, Canada
*Areas of Achievement:* Government and politics
*Contribution:* Through force of will and through his energetic efforts, Trudeau preserved the Canadian Confederation against the threat of Quebecois separatism.

## Early Life

Pierre Elliott Trudeau was born on October 18, 1919, in the wealthy Outremont neighborhood of Montreal, Quebec. His father, Charles-Émile Trudeau, was an ebullient lawyer-turned-entrepreneur of purely French-Canadian ancestry who had amassed a fortune out of selling gasoline and providing rescue services for stranded motorists. Pierre Elliott's mother, née Grace Elliott, had a Scottish-Canadian father and a French-Canadian mother. Thus, the young Pierre Elliott, one of three children, grew up bilingual; the fluency in English thus acquired would ultimately prove to be of great advantage to him.

Pierre Elliott, as a child and adolescent, had other advantages as well. Thanks to Charles-Émile's shrewd investments, son Pierre Elliott's pursuit of education was not interrupted even by his father's sudden death from pneumonia in 1935 at the age of forty-seven. Pierre Elliott attended Jean de Brébeuf College, a Jesuit institution, from his early teenage years until 1940.

As a law student at the Université de Montreal from 1940 to 1943, Trudeau gave little hint of the politician that he would later become. After he was graduated, Trudeau briefly worked for a Montreal law firm. From 1944 through 1948, he attended, successively, Harvard University, the Sorbonne in Paris, and the London School of Economics; this extended period of study enabled him to expand his horizons beyond the narrow bounds of French-Canadian provincialism. During his stay in Paris, he became close friends with a fellow French Canadian, Gerard Pelletier, whom he had first met in 1939; he would closely collaborate with Pelletier in the future. From late 1948 to early 1949, Trudeau, living frugally, took a tour around the world, visiting the Middle East, Eastern Europe, and India.

The turning point in Trudeau's life came after his return to Quebec in April of 1949. A strike of asbestos workers had stirred up controversy throughout the province, then ruled by the Union Nationale Party of Premier Maurice Duplessis. Appalled by the heavy-handed repression with which Duplessis responded to the strike, Trudeau became involved in legal defense work for the strikers. In the course of this activity, he met Quebec trade-union leader Jean Marchand, a man who would be a close political ally for many years. He also acquired the firm conviction that the hidebound conservatism of the Duplessis regime would have to go if Quebec were ever to achieve progress. The privileged youth had become something of a political radical, although one whose philosophy of change was democratic and nonviolent.

From 1949 to 1951, Trudeau served as an economic adviser in the Privy Council office in Ottawa, the Canadian capital. He quit this job, however, to meet the demands on his time made by another commitment: the journal *Cité Libre* (free community), founded in the spring of 1950 by Trudeau, his friend Pelletier, and other Quebec intellectuals dissatisfied with Duplessis and critical of what they saw as excessive Roman Catholic domination of the province's intellectual life. The intellectuals of the *Cité Libre* circle sharply criticized not only official conservatism but Quebec nationalism as well: Quebeckers, Trudeau insisted, had to eschew the backward-looking ideology of tribal nationalism if they wished to become part of the modern world.

In 1959, Duplessis died suddenly; in 1960, a Liberal Party electoral victory ousted his weak successor and inaugurated the so-called Quiet Revolution of provincial premier Jean Lesage. In the new, freer atmosphere, Trudeau was able, in 1960, to gain a professorship in law at the University of Montreal; he had been denied a teaching position fifteen years before. The Lesage regime loosened the Church's grip on intellectual life and introduced various social reforms. Yet Trudeau, ever the intellectual gadfly, criticized the Lesage cabinet for what he saw as its pandering to the rising power of French-Canadian nationalism. In 1966, the Union Nationale would return to power for a short time in Quebec; the effects of the Quiet Revolution on Quebec society, however, would never be undone.

For a long time, Trudeau and his fellows at *Cité Libre* remained independent leftists, critical of both of the major parties. They were closer to the Socialist-minded New Democratic Party (NDP) than to either the Liberals or the Progressive Conservatives. As late as 1963, Trudeau sharply attacked the national Liberal Party leader, Lester Pearson, for abandoning his earlier opposition to the stationing of American missiles on Canadian soil.

Only in September, 1965, did Trudeau begin to emerge from the relative obscurity of Quebec intellectual-journalistic circles. It was in that year that Liberal leader Prime Minister Pearson, lacking an absolute majority in Parliament and fearful of the rising wave of separatism in Quebec, decided that he needed the support of those who, although somewhat left-wing in their views, had staunchly defended federalism: the *Cité Libre* circle. The man the national Liberals most wanted on their team for the upcoming 1965 parliamentary elections was the trade unionist Marchand; Marchand, however, would neither join the Liberal Party nor run for Parliament unless Pelletier and Trudeau were also nominated as candidates for Parliament. Thus, Trudeau joined the Liberal Party. Liberal Party chieftains, fearful that Trudeau's personal eccentricity and bachelor lifestyle might lose votes among traditional-minded French Canadians, nominated him to run in a mostly Jewish (and thus largely English-speaking) seat in Montreal. The November, 1965, elections brought all three Quebeckers into Parliament but failed to give Pearson an absolute majority.

### Life's Work

Trudeau had entered Parliament thanks to the help of Jean Marchand; on April 4, 1967, Trudeau was appointed justice minister, again largely at Marchand's insistence. From the latter date onward, however, Trudeau's own star rose quickly. In December, 1967, Trudeau proposed a thoroughgoing revision of the Canadian legal code: The divorce law was to be reformed by broadening the grounds for divorce, and homosexuality was to be decriminalized. These reform proposals gave him the public image of a man determined to free the individual from the shackles of outdated restrictions on personal freedoms. Trudeau further attracted attention when, at a federal-provincial conference in February, 1968, he staunchly defended federalism against provincial premier Daniel Johnson's demand for a special status for Quebec. This incident established Trudeau's reputation throughout Canada as the one outspoken French-Canadian defender of national unity against all tendencies toward separatism within Quebec.

In December, 1967, the aging Pearson announced his plans to retire from politics. At the Liberal leadership conference of April 4-6, 1968, Trudeau won the position of Liberal Party leader over a field of several well-known contenders. After being sworn in as premier on April 20, 1968, he promptly called a snap election for June 25, 1968. The Liberal Party, under its new leader, won a clear majority over all the other parties combined, soundly defeating the Progressive Conservatives under Nova Scotia's Robert Stanfield.

Although he was forty-eight years old in 1968, the new premier projected an aura of youthfulness; his bachelor status, which did not end until his surprise marriage to twenty-two-year-old Margaret Sinclair in 1971, may have contributed to this youthful image as well. Contemporary observers, following Trudeau on the campaign trail in the spring of 1968, noted his extraordinary appeal to young women. With his well-publicized taste for such vigorous outdoor sports as high-diving and wilderness canoeing, his taste for unconventional clothing, his obvious worldliness and intelligence, and his knack for witty remarks, Trudeau at first impressed Canadians as a refreshing change from the bland and boringly conventional style of his predecessor. Canadians hoped he would project abroad an image of their country as youthful and vigorous. At five feet, ten inches tall and 160 pounds, Trudeau was indeed quite trim and athletic for a man of his age; yet he was by no means cinema-idol handsome. He had high cheekbones, a wide mouth, and a slightly hawklike nose. His sharp-featured face was pockmarked; he had to comb his hair forward, Roman-emperor style, to hide a growing bald spot.

During the long Trudeau era in Canadian politics, whose beginning the "Trudeaumania" electoral triumph of June, 1968, symbolized, there would be three major issues in Canadian politics: the relationship of Quebec with the Canadian Confederation of which it was a part; the deterioration of the economy; and the personality and behavior of the prime minister himself, a man who would arouse more extremes of both devotion and detestation than any of his recent predecessors had done.

The Quebec issue was the most urgent challenge facing Trudeau as he took office; it would occupy his mind throughout his years as prime minister. Ever since the British conquest of French Canada in 1763, the French had been in an economically subordinate position, despite the political autonomy gained through the creation of the province of Quebec in 1867. For a French-speaking Quebecker to advance in business in his own province, he had to learn English; all major banks and corporations were run by English speakers, leaving only small and medium-sized businesses to the French speakers. The separatist movement played on the frustrations of the growing class of educated French speakers.

The challenge of Quebec nationalism to Canadian Confederation first took a violent form: the activities of the underground organization known as the Front de Libération du Québec (FLQ), dedicated to achieving Quebec independence through force. Its members viewed Trudeau as a traitor to French Canada. In October, 1970, FLQ members kidnapped British diplomat James Cross and prominent Quebec Liberal and former provincial minister of labor Pierre Laporte. Acting decisively, Trudeau invoked the War Measures Act—federal troops patrolled Montreal, and police were authorized to arrest those suspected of being revolutionary separatists. Cross was eventually freed by the terrorists. This, the October Crisis, contained within it the potential for civil war; the immediate danger was defused, however, when news of the murder of Laporte provoked a wave of revulsion among French-speaking Quebeckers against the violent methods, although not necessarily the aims, of the FLQ.

In dealing with Quebecker discontent, Trudeau had to walk a tightrope. Trudeau sympathized with some of the linguistic grievances of French Canadians; trying to satisfy their grievances, however, risked the alienation of English-speaking Canada. The Official Languages Act of 1969, piloted through by Trudeau, required proficiency in both French and English from Canadian civil servants; it was intended to increase French-Canadian representation in the federal bureaucracy. The Conservative Party split over this act, although their leader accepted it; it was bitterly opposed by many English speakers, especially those of the prairie provinces. Other English Canadians, although not necessarily hostile to French-Canadian demands for parity, were indifferent to the entire issue; they would eventually come to view Trudeau as overly concerned with it to the neglect of other pressing matters.

Although the threat of violence abated, the threat of separatism remained strong. As early as 1974, a provincial Liberal administration, trying to appease the growing demand for Quebec rights, shocked English Canada by making French the sole official language of Quebec. In the summer of 1976, an attempt to introduce French as a language for air-traffic control provoked a strike by English-speaking air-traffic controllers; Trudeau caved in, shelving for the moment his plans to make the skies bilingual. In November, 1976, came the warning bell to the rest of Canada: the victory over the Liberals, in the provincial elections of that month, of the avowedly separatist Parti Québécois, led by the talented former radio-television journalist René Levesque. He soothingly promised that sovereign independence for Quebec could be gained without armed revolt and even without serious economic pain. Levesque pledged to hold a referendum to gain the voters' authorization to negotiate what he called "sovereignty-association" for Quebec.

On May 20, 1980, the referendum was finally held. With his persuasive oratory, Premier Trudeau turned the tide of voter opinion. He hammered again and again on one point: Quebec had little chance of holding on to the blessings of economic union with English-speaking Canada if it severed the political union, since such a purely economic union depended on the highly unlikely consent of the other provinces of Canada. French Canada could grow and prosper only within the Canadian Confederation, he argued. The vote ran nearly sixty percent against authorizing Levesque to negotiate for independence. Only a French Canadian such as Trudeau could have made such arguments persuasive to French Canadians.

Having won the referendum, Trudeau was able to succeed in his long-held goal of securing the "patriation" of the Canadian constitution. Up to 1982, Canada's only constitution was the British North America Act, which could be amended only by the British Parliament. In November 5, 1981, all provinces except Quebec approved a formula by which the constitution could be amended by Canadians; they also approved making a charter of rights part of the Canadian constitution. On April 17, 1982, a proud moment in Trudeau's life came when Queen Elizabeth II of Great Britain signed, in Ottawa, the act that finally gave Canadians the right to amend their own constitution: this "patriation" of the constitution symbolized the final stage of Canadian emancipation from England.

Another major challenge for Trudeau was the Canadian economy. When he took office, there was not a single cloud on the economic horizon. By the end of 1970, however, the country was beginning to experience stagflation, the previously unforeseen combination of high unemployment and high inflation. Throughout the decade, this unpleasant phenomenon would be made even more painful by the roller-coaster fluctuations of grain and energy prices, especially the latter. In the election of 1974, Trudeau promised not to impose wage and price controls; barely a year later, Trudeau imposed wage and price controls, not withdrawing them until 1978. By the end of the latter year, unemployment was 8.5 percent, while inflation ran at an annual rate of 8.6 percent. By the end of 1982, unemployment was 12.2 percent and inflation 10.6 percent. As late as early 1984, unemployment still stood at a discouraging 11 percent of the work force, although inflation had subsided somewhat as a result of worldwide recession.

Some of the widespread criticism of Trudeau and his handling of the economic issue was clearly unfair. The maturing of the post-World War II baby-boom generation was causing employment difficulties in other Western countries besides Canada. Trudeau had no control over the actions of the Organization of Petroleum Exporting Countries, which suddenly jacked up world oil prices in the autumn of 1973. Trudeau became the scapegoat for economic problems with which no Western government of the time was able to deal successfully. He was attacked in oil-rich Alberta for trying to hold down the price of oil; yet any other policy would probably have been attacked in other provinces as favoritism to Alberta. Trudeau was also attacked in the Western provinces when oil and grain prices began to slide downward in the early 1980's. Yet, while one must concede that Trudeau had no miracle-working powers over the economy, one must also point out that Trudeau's own abrasive personality made public criticism of his handling of the economy sharper than it need have been.

Trudeau's reputation as a man of good judgment was not helped by the collapse, in 1977, of his six-year marriage to the former Margaret Sinclair; in 1979, on the eve of a Canadian election, this flighty woman published, from her self-imposed exile in New York City, an indiscreet book about her adventures as a wayward wife. Trudeau kept custody of the three children of this marriage.

Besides personal scandals, Trudeau also had to face political scandal. The revelation in the late 1970's that the Royal Canadian Mounted Police had engaged in illegal breaking and entering in their surveillance of political extremism tarnished somewhat Trudeau's longtime reputation as a civil libertarian.

In May, 1979, a disgruntled Canadian electorate voted Trudeau out of office; in November of the same year, Trudeau announced his decision to retire from politics. In December, 1979, however, the new minority Progressive Conservative Party government, led by the young and inexperienced Joe Clark, lost a vote of confidence in Parliament after foolishly proposing a new excise tax on oil. Trudeau now yielded to pleas from the Liberal Party caucus that he resume party leadership for the upcoming electoral battle. In the election of February, 1980, Trudeau's party handily defeated Clark's Progressive Conservatives. Canadians had finally decided that they preferred Trudeau's cunning and toughness to Clark's apparent bungling and political ineptitude, even though Clark had the more pleasant personality.

By the beginning of 1984, however, Trudeau's popularity had once again begun to decline as a result of the failing economy. The prime minister's visit to Moscow, taken on his own initiative in an effort to ease Soviet-American tensions, had done little to restore his standing in the public-opinion polls. On February 29, 1984, Trudeau announced his retirement from politics; this time he stuck with his decision. In the election of September, 1984, the Liberal Party, under a new leadership, was soundly defeated by the Progressive Conservatives; the latter were now led not by Joe Clark but by a bilingual Irish-Canadian from Quebec, Brian Mulroney. Once out of politics, Trudeau kept a low profile, devoting himself to the practice of law and the upbringing of the three children from his failed marriage.

### Summary

Any assessment of Pierre Elliott Trudeau's record in office must necessarily be a mixed one. His term was marked by Canada's final achievement of symbolic emancipation from Mother England, in the form of the repatriation of the Canadian constitution. Trudeau will probably be remembered most favorably by future generations for his courageous fight to preserve Canadian unity against the threat of Quebec separatism. Through his success in this struggle, Trudeau showed the world that two distinct languages and cultures could indeed live peacefully under the same government. Trudeau warded off the kind of chaos that has paralyzed such ethnically mixed countries as Lebanon, Northern Ireland, South Africa, and Sri Lanka.

Perhaps such a political achievement prevented a drastic worsening of the economic situation; nevertheless, one must concede that Trudeau's record on economic questions was by no means as good as his record of achievement in constitutional matters. Trudeau shone in times of crisis, as in October, 1970; he was less adept at dealing with long-term problems. As a result, he left as a legacy to his successors not merely a strengthened feeling of Canadian unity but also a persistent economic malaise.

Despite their vocal complaints, Canadians always retained a modicum of respect for this unconventional but shrewd political leader. Pierre Elliott Trudeau represented the image of modernity and sophistication that Canadians, tired of the reputation of their country as dull and stodgy, wished to project to the outside world. Although he was by no means without flaws, he did demonstrate the kind of courage and decisiveness that Canadians value in their leaders.

### Bibliography

Basham, Richard Dalton. *Crisis in Blanc and White: Urbanization and Ethnic Identity in French Canada*. Cambridge, Mass.: Shenkman, 1977. An anthropologist argues that urbanization increased rather than decreased interethnic tensions in Quebec. Includes extensive discussion of the Front de Libération du Quebec, the October Crisis provoked by that group's actions, and the response of Quebec public opinion to the October Crisis.

Behiels, Michael D. *Prelude to Quebec's Quiet Revolution: Liberalism Versus Neo-Nationalism, 1945-1960*. Montreal: McGill-Queens University Press, 1985. Places Trudeau's ideas about Quebec nationalism, and those of the *Cité Libre* circle to which he belonged, within the context of Quebec intellectual history. This volume compares and contrasts Trudeau's early ideas with those of his Quebec contemporaries, who placed the preservation of French-Canadian identity above all else.

Fraser, Graham. *P.Q.: René Levesque and the Parti Québécois in Power*. Toronto: Macmillan of Canada, 1984. Tells the story of the political career of Trudeau's main rival for the soul of French Canada. Contains a good account of Trudeau's skillful campaign for a "no" vote in the referendum of May 20, 1980.

Graham, Ron. *One-Eyed Kings: Promise and Illusion in Canadian Politics*. Toronto: Collins, 1986. This Canadian journalist, in his survey of Canadian politics from 1980 to 1985, disputes the notion that Trudeau was elitist, arguing instead that he ran into trouble because he opposed the entrenched political influence of the old English-Canadian business elite. He sees Trudeau's political comeback in 1980 as the result of his appeal to the deep-rooted traditions of Canadian nationalism.

Iglauer, Edith. "Profiles: Prime Minister/Premier Ministre." *The New Yorker* 45 (July 5, 1969): 36-42, 44, 46-60. Gives a vivid word picture of Trudeau the man and a detailed account of his early political career. Based on interviews by Iglauer of both Trudeau and those who knew Trudeau over the years.

Lewis, Robert. "When We Were Young." *Maclean's* 111, no. 14 (April 6, 1998). Brief piece focusing on Trudeau, his many images, his charisma, and his thoughts on national unity.

McCall-Newman, Christina. *Grits: An Intimate Portrait of the Liberal Party*. Toronto: Macmillan of Canada, 1982. A portrait by a Canadian journalist of both Trudeau as a political leader and of the Liberal Party machine that he led. Takes the story up to the election of 1979. Argues that Trudeau's Frenchness and intellectualism created a gap in understanding between him and the English-Canadian wing of his party.

Radwanski, George. *Trudeau*. New York: Taplinger, 1978. The first attempt at a full-scale biography, by a journalist who was permitted to interview Trudeau extensively. Radwanski's approach is thematic rather than chronological. Although his assessment of Trudeau as a leader is generally positive, he is careful to point out his subject's faults as well as his virtues.

Stewart, Walter. *Trudeau in Power*. New York: Outerbridge and Dienstfrey, 1971. A bitter polemic, written by a journalist who worked for *Maclean's* magazine; accuses Trudeau of trying to become a dictator. This book is of value not as an objective assessment of the Canadian premier's record but as an example of the kind of violent animosity his personality and style of governing could arouse.

Trudeau, Pierre Elliot. "Trudeau Speaks Out." *Maclean's* 105, no. 39 (September 28, 1992). An essay by Trudeau attacking the push for more power by Quebec.

*Paul D. Mageli*

# FRANÇOIS TRUFFAUT

*Born:* February 6, 1932; Paris, France
*Died:* October 21, 1984; Neuilly-sur-Seine, France
*Area of Achievement:* Film
*Contribution:* A film critic whose auteur theory helped revolutionize film analysis, Truffaut was a leader of the New Wave directors who changed filmmaking itself.

## Early Life

François Truffaut was born February 6, 1932, in Paris, the only child of Roland Truffaut, a draftsman, and Janine de Montferrand, a typist. Young Truffaut was neglected by his parents, who were either working or engaged in his father's enthusiasm for camping. Truffaut spent his first eight years with his maternal grandmother, and, when she died, his parents reluctantly took him back. He frequently skipped school with his friend Robert Lachenay to go to see films, and, in 1943, he ran away from home but was eventually retrieved by his father.

Truffaut later ran away again and lived with Lachenay for a time. In 1947, they bought a print of Fritz Lang's *Metropolis* (1927) and launched a club for film enthusiasts. When this venture failed because of competition from another nearby club, Truffaut met its head, André Bazin, who became the most important influence on his life. They remained inseparable until Bazin's death at forty on November 10, 1958, the first day of shooting on Truffaut's *Les Quatre Cents Coups* (1959; *The 400 Blows*). Bazin's club folded shortly after Bazin and Truffaut met because of Bazin's poor health, and Truffaut became a petty thief. His father sent him to a reform school at Villejuif, but in March, 1948, he was released into the protective custody of Bazin, who had legal responsibility for him thereafter. After being rejected by a young woman, Truffaut joined the French army in December, 1950, but soon deserted. Bazin helped him obtain a dishonorable discharge in 1952.

Truffaut lived in the attic of the home of Bazin and his wife for the next year. Bazin helped Truffaut become film critic of the cultural magazine *Arts*, and Truffaut also began writing for *Cahiers du cinéma*, founded by Bazin and Jacques Doniol-Valcroze while Truffaut had been in the army and soon to be the world's most influential film journal. In his articles, Truffaut praised low-budget American films for their honesty and attacked recent French films as pedantic and artificial. These essays established his reputation as a confrontational critic and clearly stated his critical principles, influenced not only by Bazin but also by Henri Langlois, cofounder and director of the Cinémathèque Française. At the Cinémathèque, Truffaut and such friends as Jean-Luc Godard, Eric Rohmer, and Jacques Rivette, all future directors, saw silent films, the works of the German Expressionists and the Italian Neorealists, and the American films that had been banned during the Nazi Occupation. They were particularly impressed by the American *films noirs* of the 1940's.

Truffaut's passion for the cinema showed in his approach to reviewing, treating each film as if he were personally involved in determining its fate. In Truffaut's most famous essay, "Une Certaine Tendance du cinéma français;" (a certain tendency in French cinema), in January, 1954, he ridiculed the work of such directors as René Clement and Jean Delannoy as being too literary and for failing to recognize the visual aspects of film. According to Doniol-Valcroze, "What many uttered under their breaths he dared to say out loud." In contrast, Truffaut championed the efforts of such American B-film directors as Samuel Fuller and Edgar G. Ulmer for exploiting the relative freedom that low budgets provide to create films bearing the imprints of the director's personality and style.

Truffaut's affection for films was such that criticism could not satisfy him. Truffaut worked briefly for Max Ophüls during the making of *Lola Montès* (1955) and spent two years collaborating on three unproduced screenplays with Roberto Rossellini, the latter experience particularly helping him make the transition to filmmaker. He was to continue writing about films even after becoming a director. His best-known publication is *Le Cinéma selon Hitchcock* (1966; *Hitchcock*, 1967), based on fifty hours of interviews in 1962 with his favorite Hollywood director.

On October 29, 1957, Truffaut married Madeleine Morgenstern, daughter of Ignace Morgenstern, one of the most powerful film distributors in France. Their daughter Laura was born in 1959, and another daughter, Ewa, was born in 1961. They were later divorced.

## Life's Work

After directing two short films and codirecting a third with Godard, Truffaut made his first feature,

*The 400 Blows*, for slightly less than eighty thousand dollars. Because he had criticized people like his father-in-law so much, he was given a third of his budget by Ignace Morgenstern, who challenged him to prove he could make a theatrical film. This highly autobiographical account of the life of a young delinquent won the Grand Prix at the 1959 Cannes Film Festival. *The 400 Blows* stars thirteen-year-old Jean-Pierre Léaud, chosen from sixty boys who answered an advertisement in *France-Soir*. The son of a screenwriter and an actress, Léaud had a difficult childhood and developed a relationship with Truffaut similar to that between the director and Bazin. He was to appear in six additional Truffaut films, playing the Antoine Doinel character from *The 400 Blows* in four.

Truffaut did not savor this success and that of his friend Godard's *à bout de souffle* (1960; *Breathless*), which he cowrote, as much as he might have, because of the loss of his mentor. He was depressed by Bazin's death throughout the making of *Tirez sur le pianiste* (1960; *Shoot the Piano Player*), based on an American pulp novel by David Goodis. Packed with allusions to other films, especially American *films noirs*, and more visually experimental than *The 400 Blows, Shoot the Piano Player* was a commercial failure, disturbing the director, who believed himself in tune with public taste. Truffaut recovered with *Jules et Jim* (1962; *Jules and Jim*), which has since been considered his masterpiece. Based on an Henri-Pierre Roche novel, the film is a very unliterary adaptation, comprising almost a catalog of the visual language of the cinema. This depiction of the tragic relationship between two men and a woman was condemned by the Catholic church for its liberated attitude toward sex and adultery. It was an enormous popular success in France and confirmed Truffaut's international status as a major director.

Firmly established, Truffaut began imitating the American directors of whom he was so fond by becoming what critic Wheeler Dixon calls "a compulsive movie-maker." When the shooting of *Fahrenheit 451* (1966) was delayed, Truffaut hurriedly made *La Peau douce* (1964; *The Soft Skin*), a badly received tale of adultery and murder. *Fahrenheit 451*, from the Ray Bradbury novel, was another critical and commercial failure. Truffaut's only English-language film (made in England), it may have suffered from the director's discomfort with working in another language. (Truffaut turned down several Hollywood projects during this period because of the language barrier.) *La Mariée était en noir* (1968; *The Bride Wore Black*), another uneven film, is his most obvious homage to Hitchcock.

Truffaut recovered somewhat with a return to his autobiographical account of the young adult life of Antoine Doinel in *Baisers volés* (1968; *Stolen Kisses*). He and Léaud had previously continued the character's story in "Antoine et Colette" as part of the *L'Amour à vingt ans* (1962; *Love at Twenty*) anthology. He made the film during afternoons while spending his mornings protesting the firing by the Ministery of Culture of Langlois from the Cinémathèque. The Langlois dismissal helped set off massive student demonstrations against the Charles de Gaulle government in May, 1968, and Truffaut and Godard forced the Cannes Film Festival to close in sympathy with the demonstrators. Truffaut won Langlois's reinstatement by having other directors threaten to withdraw their films from the Cinémathèque.

After another failure, the glossy romance *La Sirène du Mississippi* (1969; *Mississippi Mermaid*), Truffaut realized he was not destined to be a director of commercial entertainments and decided to make only smaller, more personal films. The first of these, *L'Enfant sauvage* (1970; *The Wild Child*), represents a return to the stylistic simplicity and thematic sincerity of *The 400 Blows*. This account of the education of a boy discovered living wild in a forest tells virtually the same story of alienation, rebellion, and lost innocence as Truffaut's first film and seems almost a dramatization of the Bazin/Truffaut and Truffaut/Léaud relationships. Like his beloved Jean Renoir, Truffaut turned actor, playing the leading role of the doctor in charge of the boy. Short, thin, dark, intense, Truffaut was a good if limited actor. *The Wild Child* was better received by the critics than any of the director's efforts since *Jules and Jim*, with a new maturity and confidence found in his work.

After *Domicile conjugal* (1970; *Bed and Board*), focusing on Antoine Doinel's marriage and infidelity, Truffaut adapted another Henri-Pierre Roche novel. *Les Deux Anglaises et le continent* (1971; *Two English Girls*) is a somber treatment of doomed love. After *Une Belle Fille comme moi* (1972; *Such a Gorgeous Kid Like Me*), a low-key black comedy and perhaps his weakest film, Truffaut followed with one of his masterpieces, *La Nuit américaine (1973; Day for Night*). This story, loosely based on his experience with *Mississippi Mermaid* of the travails of making a hack film in a Nice studio with insecure, temperamental actors, is considered the best and most accurate film about filmmaking. Truffaut, who plays the director, uses the film to express his belief that films and life are inseparable, that he is alive only when making films. In spirit, if not in details, it is as autobiographical as *The 400 Blows*. *Day for Night* won the Academy Award as best foreign-language film of 1973.

Alternating between light and dark attitudes toward humanity, Truffaut next made *L'Histoire d'Adèle H.* (1975; *The Story of Adèle H.*), an account of the obsessive love of Victor Hugo's daughter for a soldier. After making *L'Argent de poche* (1976; *Small Change*), a much brighter picture of childhood than *The 400 Blows*, and playing a scientist (speaking French only) in Steven Spielberg's *Close Encounters of the Third Kind* (1977), he made *L'Homme qui aimait les femmes* (1977; *The Man Who Loved Women*), a romantic comedy; *La Chambre verte* (1978; *The Green Room*, an adaptation of Henry James's "The Altar of the Dead," with Truffaut as a man obsessed with death; *L'Amour en fuite* (1979; *Love on the Run*), the last and slightest of the Doinel series; *Le Dernier Métro* (1980; *The Last Métro*), a look at a Paris theatrical group during the Nazi Occupation; *Le Femme d' à côté* (1981; *The Woman Next Door*), another tale of adultery; and *Vivement dimanche* (1983; *Confidentially Yours*), a light tribute to *films noirs*. Truffaut spent his last years with Fanny Ardant, star of his final two films, and their daughter, Joséphine, was born in 1983. As with Bazin's fatal illness, he kept the fact that he was suffering from brain cancer from all but his closest friends. Truffaut died on October 21, 1984, at Neuilly-sur-Seine.

## Summary

By helping to create the auteur theory, François Truffaut pioneered recognition of the contribution of the film director to both obviously artistic films and low-budget genre films, bringing a new seriousness to film criticism. As auteur criticism became the most legitimate way of looking at films and works by Truffaut, Godard, Rohmer, and others in the New Wave showed the benefits of allowing directors the freedom to make personal statements, a new respect for the film director was created. The enthusiasm and humanity in such films as *The 400 Blows* and *Jules and Jim* have had a profound influence on directors throughout the world.

Except for his actions of 1968, Truffaut was a relatively nonpolitical person, saying he never voted because he did not think of himself as a citizen. His films have been attacked, especially in France, for lacking any political context. He has also been justifiably criticized for being too indiscriminate in his choice of material, for making more mediocre films that great ones. Ironically, despite the freedom he espoused for directors, Truffaut may have preferred working in the old Hollywood studio system in which he could have risen to the challenge of imposing his personality on formula films. He was being modest only to a degree when he called himself "the least modern and the least intellectual of all the New Wave directors."

Truffaut is clearly an auteur himself. The predominant theme in his films is his sympathy for outsiders. According to Truffaut, his "characters are on the edge of society" and he wants them "to testify to human fragility." His films illustrate how people, especially those in love, fail to make the necessary connections that could bring them happiness. Of all French directors, Truffaut most admired Jean Vigo, Jean Renoir, Jean Cocteau, and Robert Bresson. The compassion for human frailties in his films has made him their equal.

### Bibliography


Allen, Don. *Finally Truffaut*. London: Secker and Warburg, and New York: Beaufort, 1985. An analysis of Truffaut's films combined with biographical details. Based on fifteen years of interviews with the director.

Anzalone, John. "Heroes and Villains, or Truffaut and the Literary Pre/Text." *The French Review* 72, no. 1 (October, 1998). The author examines Truffaut's first film adaptation of a book and his opinions on the relationship between literature and film.

Crisp, C. G. *François Truffaut*. London: November, and New York: Praeger, 1972. A commentary on Truffaut's films emphasizing the autobiographical element, providing considerable information about the director's life. Sees Truffaut's characters as torn between dream and reality, art and life, savagery and civilization. Includes critical essays by Truffaut.

DalMolin, Eliane. "A Voice in the Dark: Feminine Figurations in Truffaut's *Jules and Jim*." *Literature-Film Quarterly* 22, no. 4 (October, 1994). This article provides analysis of Truffaut's 1962 film *Jules and Jim* focusing on the female character of Catherine who represents different things to the two men.

De Gramont, Sanche. "Life Style of Homo Cinematicus." *The New York Times Magazine*, June 15, 1969: 12-13, 34-47. An excellent profile revealing details of Truffaut's life, method of making films, and personality.

Dixon, Wheeler. "François Truffaut: A Life in Film." *Films in Review* 36 (1985): 331-336, 413-417. An excellent biographical sketch. One of the best sources of details about Truffaut's life.

Insdorf, Annette. *François Truffaut*. Rev. ed. Cambridge and New York: Cambridge University Press, 1994. A good overview of Truffaut's life and career. Discusses the influence of Renoir and Hitchcock.

Monaco, James. *The New Wave: Truffaut, Godard, Chabrol, Rohmer, Rivette*. New York: Oxford University Press, 1976. Analysis of Truffaut's films in context of the New Wave movement. Includes biographical details of his early life.

Roud, Richard. *A Passion for Films: Henri Langlois and the Cinémathèque Française*. London: Secker and Warburg, and New York: Viking, 1983. A biography of one of the most significant influences on Truffaut's life and career. Gives details of Truffaut's successful effort to save Langlois's job.

Truffaut, François. *The Films in My Life*. Translated by Leonard Mayhew. New York: Simon and Schuster, 1978; London: Allen Lane, 1980. A collection of Truffaut's reviews and essays written between 1954 and 1974. This is the best source of examples of his passion for American films. The introduction summarizes his career as a critic.

———. *Truffaut by Truffaut*. Compiled by Dominique Rabourdin. Translated by Robert E. Wolf. New York: Abrams, 1987. An illustrated account of Truffaut's career. Includes interviews with the director and essays, reviews, and letters by him.


*Michael Adams*

# HARRY S TRUMAN

*Born:* May 8, 1884; Lamar, Missouri
*Died:* December 26, 1972; Kansas City, Missouri
*Area of Achievement:* Government and politics
*Contribution:* As president of the United States from 1945 to 1953, Truman defended and institutionalized the New Deal reform program of Franklin D. Roosevelt and established the doctrine of containment that guided American policymakers in the Cold War era.

## Early Life

Harry S Truman, whose career enhanced Missouri's reputation for producing tough and stubborn individuals, was born in the southwestern part of that state on May 8, 1884, but grew up in rural Jackson County, in and around Independence. His parents, John Anderson and Martha Ellen Truman, were prominent, well-connected citizens of the area, and Harry looked back on his childhood years as happy, secure ones. He was captivated by the world of books, however, which revealed to him that there was a bigger, more rewarding realm within his reach. Success in that realm could be attained, he believed, by strictly adhering to the work ethic taught by his parents and by developing his ability to manipulate people by learning what motivated and pleased them. His parents also taught him a Victorian set of moral absolutes, a tendency to see the world in black and white terms, that later influenced his decision making.

When he was graduated from high school in 1901, his father's "entangled" finances prevented young Truman from going to college. He held several unsatisfying jobs in the next few years and then farmed until 1917, when he served in the army during World War I. After a small business firm he had opened in Kansas City failed in 1922, Truman, whose restless ambition had always left him with an edge of frustration, finally found the career that brought him fulfillment. He entered county politics with the backing of Thomas J. Pendergast, the "boss" of the Kansas City Democratic Party machine.

In 1934, after great success in local politics, Truman, with Pendergast's support, won election to the United States Senate. He strongly supported Franklin D. Roosevelt's New Deal program and then gained national recognition during World War II as head of a committee investigating defense contracts and mobilization bottlenecks.

In 1944, a number of Democratic Party leaders plotted to remove liberal Henry A. Wallace as vice president. Truman surfaced as one of the few prominent individuals acceptable to these bosses and to all the wings of the party. Roosevelt and the convention concurred, and the ticket won the 1944 election.

## Life's Work

President Roosevelt's death on April 12, 1945, gave Truman an opportunity to join the heroes who had enlivened his bookish world. The public initially responded favorably to the plainspoken Missourian, and the honeymoon continued as World War II ended, with Germany surrendering on May 7, 1945, and Japan on August 14. The end of the war brought reconversion problems, however, that would have challenged a political magician such as Roosevelt. They overwhelmed Truman. While searching for a chimerical formula that would allow him to please business, labor, consumers, and citizens hungry for scarce meat, Truman stumbled from policy to policy, convincing people that he was a bewildered throttlebottom.

Amid this turmoil, the beleaguered president formulated his domestic program. Operating within the reform legacy of the New Deal, he revealed to Congress on September 6, 1945, what later became the Fair Deal. His legislative requests included legislation requiring the government to maintain full employment, improved unemployment compensation benefits and minimum wages, major housing reforms, assistance to small business, and continued farm price supports. Later additions to the Fair Deal slate included national compulsory health insurance, federal ownership of atomic energy resources and development, aid to education, and civil rights legislation for blacks. Congressional response was disappointing. It gave Truman the watered-down Employment Act and created the Atomic Energy Commission under civilian control. Through executive orders, Truman forbade discrimination against blacks in the civil service and began to desegregate the armed forces. In his second term, Congress passed a housing act.

Perhaps his greatest reform contribution came when the Republicans won both houses of Congress in 1946 and set out to destroy much of the New Deal reform legacy. This allowed Truman to assume his most effective role: defender of the com-

mon man from the forces of reaction. He continued this role in the 1948 election, and further protected the New Deal by his upset victory over Republican New York Governor Thomas E. Dewey. No major New Deal program fell before the conservative onslaught, although the Taft-Hartley Act placed some restrictions on labor.

In foreign policy, Truman left a more perilous legacy. By 1947, the Cold War had started. Soviet leaders believed that since the birth of the Communist government in 1917, Western capitalist nations had been intent on destroying it. Soviet Premier Joseph Stalin intended to use his nation's great military strength, which had destroyed German dictator Adolf Hitler's armies, to build a buffer zone against these hostile Western powers. He hoped to work cooperatively with the West and cautiously refrained from meddling in areas the Western powers considered vital, but caution also compelled him to establish his nation's own sphere of dominance in Eastern Europe.

Truman was poorly suited to deal with the complexities of this situation. He had never been much interested in foreign affairs, and he held a black-and-white view of the world. He quickly came to two conclusions on which he based policy toward the Soviet Union: that Soviet leaders were breaking all of their wartime agreements, making future negotiations senseless, and that the only thing the Russians understood was force. Once committed to these propositions, he ignored all evidence to the contrary. He believed that he could use American military and economic power to coerce the Soviets into compliance with Washington's demands. The test explosion of the first atomic bomb in July, 1945, and use of the weapon against a collapsing Japan on August 6 and August 9 added to his confidence. He later claimed that his actions saved lives by eliminating the necessity of invading the Japanese mainland. The highest American military leaders believed that the bombing was unnecessary, however, especially since the Soviet Union's declaration of war on Japan, which took place on August 8, would, they believed, shock Japan into surrender. Truman dropped the bombs to force Japan to surrender and to intimidate the Soviet Union into accommodation with the United States.

By acting on the assumption that Russians only understood force, Truman convinced Stalin that the West was still intent on the Soviet Union's destruction. When Moscow countered what it viewed as a threat by, for example, tightening its control over Poland and other Eastern European nations, it confirmed Washington's belief that the Soviet Union intended world conquest. The cycle of suspicion and fear spiraled toward the Cold War, with each side taking defensive actions that appeared to be offensive threats to the other.

In 1947, Truman initialed the containment policy that became the fundamental American Cold War strategy. Abandoning serious negotiation, the United States moved to encircle the Soviet bloc, hoping such pressure would cause it to change, to mellow, internally. Over the next few years, one containment action followed another: the Truman Doctrine that promised support for free people facing totalitarian pressures, the Marshall Plan, the Berlin Airlift, and the North Atlantic Treaty Organization. Truman's decisions to fight the Korean War, to finance the French war in Vietnam, to rearm the United States and its Western European allies, and to incorporate West Germany and Japan into the anti-Soviet bloc further raised the containment barrier.

Domestic and foreign problems increasingly merged during Truman's second term, and together they unraveled the popularity he had gained during his 1948 election campaign. China had long been torn by civil war, and in 1949 it "fell" to Mao Tse-tung's Communists. Republican fury made Truman vulnerable to the bizarre charge of being soft on Communism and indifferent to growing fear of internal subversion. In 1946, Truman himself had initiated a loyalty program designed to eliminate Communists from government and had fed fear of subversion by using extreme anti-Communist rhetoric crafted to build public support for containment. Red hysteria, led by demagogues such as Senator Joseph R. McCarthy of Wisconsin, surged in 1950. Although Truman had been partly responsible for McCarthyism, it turned on his administration and undermined his ability to govern.

Truman confronted what he regarded as the greatest challenge of his presidency on June 24, 1950, when the army of North Korea swept across the thirty-eighth parallel into South Korea, an American ally. Truman interpreted this as a Soviet-directed attack on the West, a test of Western resolve. He ordered General Douglas MacArthur, commander of American forces in the Far East, to dispatch American troops to Korea. In September, 1950, MacArthur's forces, operating under the authority of the United Nations, first halted and then pushed the North Koreans back in disarray.

As the North Koreans retreated, Truman faced another major decision. Should he push them back across the thirty-eighth parallel and then halt, content with achieving the original war aim, or should the forces of the United Nations cross the parallel, destroy the North Korean army, and unify Korea? He chose the latter course, and MacArthur drove north toward the Chinese border. In November, 1950, after American leaders ignored China's clear warnings, 300,000 Chinese "volunteers" intervened, shattering the offensive and forcing the longest retreat in United States history. In 1951, the battlefront stabilized near the thirty-eighth parallel, but peace did not come until 1953, during Dwight D. Eisenhower's presidency.

By early 1951, public support for the war had eroded. Then, on April 11, 1951, after a number of public disagreements with MacArthur, Truman recalled the general, who was perhaps the American people's most admired military hero. This action, during an increasingly unpopular war, coupled with the growing force of McCarthyite attacks on the Administration, almost destroyed Truman's ability to govern. He had already decided not to run for reelection in 1952 and supported Adlai Stevenson for the nomination. Republican candidate Dwight D. Eisenhower, promising to clean up the "mess in Washington," easily defeated Stevenson.

### Summary

On January 20, 1953, Truman returned to Independence, Missouri, where he lived until his death on December 26, 1972. In retirement, Truman had the satisfaction of seeing many of his Fair Deal proposals take effect, including social security and housing expansion, government health-care programs, and civil rights legislation. Truman also watched his popularity rise to folk-hero status among the general public. Scholars concurred with this evaluation. In 1981, American historians ranked him as the nation's eighth greatest president, and one prominent Truman biographer predicted that he would take his place behind Abraham Lincoln as America's second most beloved president.

These admiring historians believed Truman's greatness rested on his foreign policy. Under his leadership, the United States committed itself to playing a continuing role in international affairs. His administration devised the containment strategy, which served as the foreign policy foundation for his successors in office, and established barriers, such as NATO, against the inundation of the "Free World" by aggressive Communism.

Other historians, however, questioned the wisdom of his policy. The Vietnam War compelled many scholars to reexamine the American past generally, and they often focused on the Cold War period specifically. These revisionists believed that either through an arrogant attempt to impose the American system on the world or through ignorance of Soviet desires and needs and overreaction to Stalin's cautious policy, the United States provoked the Cold War and initiated the dangerous tension that imperiled civilization. Many revisionists concluded that under Truman the United States began to build a national security state that led it to meddle in the affairs of other nations, while civil liberties eroded at home. This globalism diverted resources to military adventures, while American cities decayed and social problems mounted.

Thus, while many of the tumultuous conflicts that dominated the newspaper front pages during the Truman years later seemed petty and were largely forgotten, the man from Independence remained even after his death the center of controversy revolving around issues central to modern history.

### Bibliography

Cumings, Bruce. *The Origins of the Korean War: Liberation and the Emergence of Separate Regimes, 1945-1947*. Princeton, N.J.: Princeton University Press, 1981; Oxford: Princeton University Press, 1990. Excellent first volume in a projected two-volume study of the background of the Korean War. The roots of the war lay in 1945 and 1946, Cumings argues, when the United States undermined the democratic movements that were attempting to carry out needed reforms in South Korea.

Ferrell, Robert H. *Harry S Truman: A Life*. Columbia: University of Missouri Press, 1994.

Gaddis, John L. *Strategies of Containment: A Critical Appraisal of Postwar American National Security Policy*. Oxford and New York: Oxford University Press, 1982. A rich and provocative study of containment theory, arguing that the United States since 1947 has alternated between the limited containment theory of George Kennan and the more global conception of United States interests that Truman accepted in 1950 and afterward.

Hamby, Alonzo L. *Beyond the New Deal: Harry S Truman and American Liberalism*. New York:

Columbia University Press, 1973; London: Columbia University Press, 1974. Traces the tumultuous relationship between Truman and the liberals in the confusing years following Roosevelt's death.

———. *Man of the People: A Life of Harry S Truman*. New York: Oxford University Press, 1995; Oxford: Oxford University Press, 1999. Best account of Truman's personality in print. This impressive biography brings the man and his career to life, focusing on his presidency, the decision to drop the atomic bomb, and the Fair Deal domestic program.

Hogan, Michael J. *A Cross of Iron: Harry S Truman and the Origins of the National Security State*. Cambridge and New York: Cambridge University Press, 1998. This book provides the best account of the U. S. efforts in the area of national security in the first years of the Cold War. Examines the work of Truman and those after him to determine the structure of the national security state.

McCullough, David G. *Truman*. New York: Simon and Schuster, 1992.

Miller, Richard L. *Truman: The Rise to Power*. New York: McGraw-Hill, 1986. The best available study on Truman's prepresidential years. This is the starting place for an understanding of Truman.

Paterson, Thomas G. *On Every Front: The Making of the Cold War*. Rev. ed. New York: Norton, 1992. A short analytical survey of relations between the United States and the Soviet Union.

Pemberton, William E. *Bureaucratic Politics: Executive Reorganization During the Truman Administration*. Columbia: University of Missouri Press, 1979. A study of Truman's administrative reform program, the most extensive reorganization program in United States history.

Sherwin, Martin J. *A World Destroyed: The Atomic Bomb and the Grand Alliance*. New York: Knopf, 1975. Sherwin does not believe that the atomic bombs were dropped on Japan merely to frighten the Soviet Union, as some charge, but argues that possession of the bomb influenced United States policy toward Moscow. He also believes use of the bomb was probably unnecessary to bring peace.

Truman, Harry S. *Year of Decisions*. New York: Doubleday, 1955.

———. *Years of Trial and Hope*. New York: Doubleday, 1956. Truman's memoirs are a detailed description of his actions and policies, often quoting extensively from key documents. While an excellent source, they should be supplemented by additional reading.

Wainstock, Dennis D. *Truman, MacArthur and the Korean War*. Westport, Conn.: Greenwood, 1999. In-depth analysis of the first year of the Korean War focusing on the relationship between General Douglas MacArthur and President Truman.

Yeargin, Daniel H. *Shattered Peace: The Origins of the Cold War and the National Security State*. Boston: Houghton Mifflin, 1977; London: Deutsch, 1978. One of the best studies of the origins of the Cold War. It focuses on the ideology of United States decision makers.

*William Pemberton*

# MOÏSE TSHOMBE

*Born:* November 10, 1919; Musamba, Katanga, Belgian Congo

*Died:* June 29, 1969; under house arrest in a secret location near Algiers, Algeria

*Areas of Achievement:* Government and politics

*Contribution:* Tshombe believed that a confederation of provinces held together by a weak central government comprised the key to national unity in the postcolonial Congo. In spite of formidable opposition, Tshombe tried to carry out his unification program by emphasizing ethnicity over pan-Africanism and by using European money, men, and material.

## Early Life

Moïse Kapenda Tshombe was the eldest of eleven children of Joseph Kapenda Tshombe, a wealthy businessman. Tshombe was reared in a devout Christian atmosphere and educated in American Methodist mission schools in Katanga (now Shaba). He also earned a correspondence accounting degree. He married Ruth Matschik, the daughter of Paramount Chief Mbaku Ditende of the Lunda, and they had ten children. By the early 1950's, Tshombe's life had been shaped by business, religion, and royalty; these influences encouraged his European lifestyle. As the eldest son, Tshombe inherited his father's business at Elisabethville (now Lubumbashi) in 1951. Shortly thereafter, he was elected president of the African Chamber of Commerce. Tshombe's business success was hampered by his own mistakes and colonial restrictions. Realizing both shortcomings, he turned over what remained of the family business to his brothers and launched his political career.

## Life's Work

In 1951, Tshombe replaced his father as a member of the Katanga provincial council and began to expand his political base. Drawing on experience acquired from a variety of political offices, Tshombe helped form CONAKAT, the Lunda-dominated Confederation of Tribal Associations of Katanga, in October, 1958. CONAKAT was created to promote Lunda politicians, repatriate non-Lunda immigrants, create an autonomous Katanga within a loose confederation, and collaborate with European mining interests.

At decolonization talks in Brussels in January, 1960, Tshombe led the CONAKAT delegation and argued for autonomous provinces within a loose confederal state. He was opposed by African nationalists, who accused him of being in the pay of Belgian mining interests. Of Tshombe's two major opponents, Joseph Kasavubu led ABAKO, the Bakongo-dominated Alliance of the Bakongo, and also supported federalism. Tshombe's other opponent, Patrice Lumumba, led MNC, the multiethnic, Soviet-supported National Congolese Movement. Lumumba advocated a strong central government and pan-Africanism. The conference produced a compromise in which the state's unitary character was expressed through a president, prime minister, and bicameral legislature while the provinces joined in a federation of separate governments and legislatures. Independence was set for June 30, 1960.

Preindependence elections and Belgian support combined to make Tshombe president of Katanga. At the national level a coalition government was formed between Prime Minister Lumumba and President Kasavubu but ran into trouble immediately. By mid-July, army units, disillusioned with the slow pace of Africanization, mutinied. As violence spread throughout the Congo, the European-dominated civil service fled. Organized government collapsed. Lumumba appealed to the United Nations for help.

Tshombe also called on foreign intervention to end Katangan unrest. After Belgian paratroopers restored order, Tshombe proclaimed Katanga's secession on July 11, 1960. The weakness of Lumumba's central government, the encouragement from Belgian commercial and mining interests who preferred Western-oriented Tshombe over Soviet-supported Lumumba, and the ethnic desire to retain Katangan wealth within Katanga contributed to Tshombe's action. Katanga's major employer, Union Minière du Haut-Katanga, supported Tshombe's secession with armaments, taxes diverted from the central government, and the cover of employment for European mercenaries to prop up the secession. Lumumba broke diplomatic relations with Belgium because of that country's support for the secession. The Congo fragmented further when President Kasavubu and Prime Minister Lumumba quarreled over Soviet aid and dismissed each other. Mobutu Sese Sekou, head of the army, settled the dispute by seizing power on September 14, 1960.

By November, U.N. troops had entered a chaotic Congo, sided with Kasavubu's government, and

detained Lumumba in Léopoldville. Lumumba fled U.N. custody for his supporters in Stanleyville, but Kasavubu's soldiers captured him en route, interned him, and then transferred him to Katanga, where he was immediately executed under mysterious circumstances. His supporters continued his centralist, pan-Africanist government while accusing Tshombe of complicity in the execution.

From January 25 to February 16, 1961, national reconciliation talks took place at Léopoldville. Discussion continued from March 8 through March 12 in Tananarive (now Antananarivo), Madagascar, where Tshombe's influence was paramount. Delegates recommended a loose, autonomous confederation, a shared foreign policy, and a national president. Yet what Tananarive had been to Tshombe, Coquilhatville (now Équateur) would become to Kasavubu. During discussions from April 23 to May 30, the Tananarive accords were replaced with a federal structure composed of a strong central government, U.N. protection, and the U.N.-forced reintegration of Katanga. Tshombe walked out in protest, was arrested, and was threatened with trial. The agreement that Tshombe signed promising to reunite Katanga with the Congo was rejected by the Katangan government on the grounds that Tshombe had signed under duress.

Tshombe did not attend the central government convocation in Léopoldville (now Kinshasa) in July. Mobutu, Kasavubu, and Lumumba's successors accepted Cyrille Adoula as a compromise prime minister, restored constitutional government, and reestablished diplomatic relations with Belgium. With a central government now back in place, the U.N. could address the issue of mercenaries in Katanga. In late August, U.N. troops occupied key points in Katanga. After fighting broke out, Tshombe declared total war on U.N. forces. United Nations Secretary-General Dag Hammarskjöld was killed in an airplane crash en route to arrange a ceasefire.

Within weeks, the United Nations and Belgium took stronger measures against Tshombe. On November 24, 1961, the United Nations passed a resolution permitting U.N. forces to expel Katanga's mercenaries. Belgium ordered its nationals serving Katanga to leave, revoked the passports of Belgian mercenaries, condemned Katangan secession, and encouraged Tshombe to open negotiations with Adoula. Tshombe met Adoula on December 19, 1961, and agreed to recognize the indissoluble unity of the Congo, conceded the central government's authority over Katanga, and promised to help draft a new constitution. Yet Tshombe continued to delay. U.N. forces took control of most of Katanga on January 14, 1962. Tshombe marked the end of Katanga's secession and approval to the United Nations' reconciliation plan by going into exile.

Central government problems did not end with the reunification of Katanga. Kasavubu again fell out with a prime minister—this time over the draft of a new constitution. On September 29, 1963, Kasavubu prorogued parliament and declared a state of emergency. It was well timed—revolutionaries had captured about two-thirds of the Congo. Nevertheless, a special constituent assembly was convened in Luluabourg (now Kananga) on January 10, 1964, and established a U.N.-advised, unitary-federal constitution creating the Democratic Republic of the Congo.

Central government leaders invited Tshombe to return from exile and create a provisional government to implement the new constitution and end revolutionary activity. In July, 1964, Tshombe replaced Adoula as prime minister, created a coalition government in which he retained five of twenty portfolios, negotiated with rebel leaders, and released political prisoners.

Much of the country remained suspicious. In early August, Stanleyville (now Kisangani) fell to Lumumba's successors. Tshombe, now not so gregarious and exuberant, blamed corrupt centralized government and Chinese and Soviet aid for the success of the revolutionaries. Risking the opprobrium of African nationalists and the Organization of African Unity, Tshombe hired white mercenaries to restore order. By the end of 1964, Tshombe's combined mercenary-national forces had the revolutionaries in retreat. In response, Congolese revolutionaries held some eighteen hundred European hostages for bargaining purposes. Tshombe permitted Belgian paratroopers to fly in on U.S. airplanes to Stanleyville during November 24-26, 1964, to rescue them. The city was recaptured and most hostages freed, but about two hundred Europeans and many more Africans were killed before all revolutionary areas were liberated.

By May, 1965, Tshombe had gained the support of some African nations, reestablished international credit, met Charles de Gaulle and Pope Paul IV, held national elections, and, through his forty-nine-party CONACO coalition, the National Congolese Convention, won a majority in the forthcoming parliament. Tshombe seemed poised for an important role in shaping the Congo's future.

When the new parliament opened on October 13, 1965, Kasavubu, out of fear that Tshombe wanted the presidency, dismissed Tshombe and nominated another Katangan, Evariste Kimba, prime minister. When parliament rejected Kimba on November 14, 1965, Kasavubu nominated him again. Kasavubu's third constitutional deadlock was broken for the second time by Mobutu. On November 24, 1965, the general overthrew the government and declared himself temporary president. Shortly thereafter, Mobutu assumed the presidency for five years and appointed some of Tshombe's opponents to office. Tshombe returned to exile.

Mobutu further consolidated his power by seizing the property of Tshombe's longtime supporter, Union Minière, disbanding Tshombe's Katangan Regiment, and putting the former prime minister on trial in absentia. Tshombe was convicted of treason and sentenced to death by a three-man military court on March 13, 1967.

After almost two years of exile and intrigue, Tshombe's fortunes took another tumble. His airplane was hijacked over the Mediterranean and forced to Algiers on June 29, 1967. Still, the Algerian government refused to extradite Tshombe. Instead, Tshombe was confined to military barracks and various villas. He died of natural causes in his sleep ironically on double anniversaries: the independence date of the Congo and the date of his hijacking. Tshombe was buried at the Protestant church of Champ-de-Mars, Brussels, on July 4, 1969.

### Summary

Politics tossed Moïse Tshombe and controversy together. At one time or another he was praised and condemned by most major contributors to the Congo crisis. In fact, Tshombe symbolized both the Congo's hope and its hopelessness. Much of his complicated life remains mysterious. Tshombe's defenders, generally a combination of Lunda, neocolonial, imperial, collaborative, and Christian forces, argued that the United Nations and various self-serving nations had slandered him. To his supporters, Tshombe's diplomatic skills, Western education, wardrobe, entourage, and manners opened doors slammed shut to some African nationalists. Cultured and articulate, Tshombe was to many Europeans an intelligent, moderate African nationalist. His downfall was blamed more on the intrigue of the U.S. Central Intelligence Agency (CIA) than his own mistakes.

From the perspective of most African nationalists, however, Tshombe had betrayed Africa. Tshombe was accused of being out of touch with *négritude* and rising African nationalism by relying on white mercenaries and living like a European. Denounced by detractors as an embezzler and bribe-taking lackey of Belgian mining interests, Tshombe was seen as an opportunist who sought personal gain and Lunda supremacy over the Congolese people, an accomplice to the murder of Lumumba and perhaps Hammarskjöld, and a Cold War propagandist who slandered his political opponents with communist labels. Whether seen as a popular, pragmatic confederalist and diplomat or as a selfish sunderer of the Congo and collaborator with imperialists, Tshombe stirred strong feelings in everyone who knew him.

### Bibliography

Bouscaren, Anthony. *Tshombe.* New York: Twin Circle, 1967. Well-written, well-researched, and sympathetic from a Western perspective; contains a pro-Tshombe statement by Senator Thomas Dobb.

Bustin, Edouard. *Lunda Under Belgian Rule: The Politics of Ethnicity.* Cambridge, Mass.: Harvard University Press, 1975. An important study that places Tshombe and his ethnic group within Congolese and Katangan contexts. Last chapter considers Tshombe's activities in Katanga.

Colvin, Ian. *The Rise and Fall of Moïse Tshombe.* London: Frewin, 1968. Probably the most pro-Western, sympathetic account of Tshombe. Colvin interviewed him and blamed the CIA for his downfall. The book is considered reactionary by African nationalists.

Gordon, King. *The United Nations in the Congo.* New York: Carnegie Endowment for International Peace, 1962. Written by an employee of the United Nations who was in the Congo. Assessment of the relationship among Tshombe, the Congo, and the United Nations is splendid. Best when read in conjunction with Lefever.

Kaplan, Irving, ed. *Zaïre: A Country Study.* 3d ed. Washington, D.C.: American University, Foreign Area Studies, 1979. Contains the U.S. government's view of events in the Congo. CIA involvement in Tshombe's downfall is not considered. Important bibliographies are included.

Lefever, Ernest W. *Crisis in the Congo: A United Nations Force in Action.* Washington, D.C.: Brookings Institution, 1965. A fine summary of U.N. activity in the Congo. Tshombe is considered throughout. Contains useful appendices, including U.N. resolutions on the Congo. Best when read in conjunction with Gordon.

Nkrumah, Kwame. *Challenge of the Congo.* London: Nelson, and New York: International, 1967. Valuable from an African nationalist perspective of Tshombe. Particularly useful is Nkrumah's letter to African leaders that symbolically devastates Tshombe.

Tshombe, Moïse. *My Fifteen Months in Government.* Translated by Lewis Barnays. Plano, Tex.: University of Plano Press, 1967. Although Tshombe reflects on Africa, his premiership, and his resignation, he is very selective in recollecting his most controversial activities. Spotty and hastily written.

*Kenneth Wilburn*

# KONSTANTIN TSIOLKOVSKY

*Born:* September 17, 1857; Izhevskoye, Russia
*Died:* September 19, 1935; Kaluga, U.S.S.R.
*Area of Achievement:* Aeronautics
Contribution: Tsiolkovsky was the first scientist to discover the mathematical theories of rocketry and astronautics on which modern space travel is based. Along with contemporary scientists Hermann Oberth of Germany and Robert Goddard of the United States, he pioneered the concepts of reaction propulsion as a means to lift a rocket into space, liquid-fueled rocket engines, and manned space travel.

## Early Life

Konstantin Eduardovich Tsiolkovsky, a Russian schoolteacher who would become one of the founding fathers of modern astronautics, was born in the rural town of Izhevskoye, Russia, on September 17, 1857. Tsiolkovsky's father, Eduard Ignatyevich Tsiolkovsky, a forester, was a dominant figure in Konstantin's early life. The elder Tsiolkovsky's passion for invention led him to design and build model homes and machines that significantly influenced his son's interest in the inventive process. At the age of nine, Konstantin became ill with scarlet fever, which forced him into bed and into a process of disciplined self-study and experimentation that would be his primary means of education throughout his life. Using the books in his father's library, Tsiolkovsky taught himself the fundamentals of literature, history, and the subjects that he found most interesting, mathematics and physics.

Konstantin's passion for reading and study led him as a teenager to follow in his father's footsteps and become an inventor. By the age of sixteen, he had designed and built a miniature model of a wind-driven horseless carriage, windmills, pumps, and a unique device for measuring heights and distances, among other things. Tsiolkovsky would use his skills as an inventor and a craftsman to build equipment and conduct experiments to prove the theorems he would study in books. It was this practice that led him to the development of the theories of reaction propulsion and astronautics that would later make him world-famous.

Also at sixteen, Tsiolkovsky's father (his mother died when he was thirteen) sent him to Moscow to further his education. It was the elder Tsiolkovsky's hope that Konstantin would be able to gain admission to the Moscow Technical School to allow him to become a teacher. Unfortunately, Tsiolkovsky was unable to gain admittance to the school and was forced to continue his self-study efforts, using the books in the Moscow Technical School's library. Living on nothing but bread and water for months on end, Tsiolkovsky spent most of the meager allowance his father sent him on equipment and supplies for his experiments. Many of his experiments centered on designing new methods of construction of dirigibles, the airships of his day. One of his primary fascinations at this time, however, was the thought that humans could use the principles of physics to free themselves of gravity and move into the space beyond the atmosphere. His first unsuccessful experiment in this area left him shaken but emotionally challenged by the prospect of flight into space.

At the age of nineteen, Tsiolkovsky returned to his hometown to work as a tutor for young children in physics and mathematics. Two years later, he received a teaching certificate in arithmetic and geometry and was given a job as a teacher in Borovsk, in the Kaluga Province. He would live in Kaluga for the remainder of his life. In Kaluga, Tsiolkovsky continued to theorize and experiment in many areas of science. By the time he was twenty-four, the young schoolteacher had submitted a rudimentary technical paper to the St. Petersburg Society of Physics and Chemistry on the movement of gases. His second paper, which followed shortly after his first, gained for him full membership in the society—his first official recognition as a scientist and theorist. This development set the stage for his later successes in rocketry and astronautics.

## Life's Work

In 1883, Tsiolkovsky came upon the historic idea that one could use gases escaping from an opening in a pressurized chamber as a method of propelling an object through the air and, ultimately, through the airless, gravity-free void of interplanetary space. This theory, called reaction propulsion, uses Isaac Newton's laws of motion by throwing off particles of matter to propel an object through space. Tsiolkovsky explained his theory by noting that opening a hole in a cask or barrel filled with pressurized gas would push the cask through space. The number of holes in the cask would regulate the flow of escaping gas and control the di-

rection and speed of the cask's movement through the air. Tsiolkovsky's principle is also demonstrated by the way air released through the end of an inflated balloon causes the balloon to fly around a room.

By August, 1898, after years of experimentation into his theory, Tsiolkovsky had worked out the first mathematical formulas for the amount of thrust that would be necessary to lift objects into space and the speed at which the object would have to travel in order to develop the centrifugal force needed to balance the pull of Earth's gravity and remain in orbit. The following year he received a grant from the Academy of Sciences that he used to develop and refine his theories through rudimentary experiments and exhaustive computations.

While Tsiolkovsky was in the process of developing his theories on space travel, he began writing popular stories of science fantasy and fact that captured the imagination of the reading public in Russia. His fiction and narrative fantasies helped him communicate his dream of manned space exploration and the prospect of establishing colonies on other planets. These stories also helped the theorist to refine his scientific thought process and seek realistic applications for his theories. In 1903, Tsiolkovsky's first article on rocket-powered spaceflight, entitled "Issledovanie mirovykh prostranstv reaktivnymi priborami" (exploration of space with reactive devices), was published in *Naootchnoye Obozreniye* (scientific journal). This short article is considered the seminal work in the fields of rocketry and orbital mechanics. It would also, as the years passed, gain for Tsiolkovsky much recognition as a scientist within the Western world and what would later be the Soviet Union.

In the article "Issledovanie mirovykh prostranstv reaktivnymi priborami," Tsiolkovsky diagrammed his ideas for the construction of a rocket engine and the rocket it would power. Using liquid oxygen and hydrogen as fuels—the same materials that would later be employed by Robert Goddard, Wernher von Braun, Sergei Korolev, and other practical developers of manned and unmanned launch vehicles—Tsiolkovsky speculated that the mixing of the two substances in a narrow combustion chamber within the rocket would produce enough power through a nozzle at the rocket's end to power it through space.

In his most famous article, and in later published works, Tsiolkovsky would be the first scientist to explore the concept of stacking several rockets on top of one another to produce the momentum necessary to move into Earth orbit and beyond the planet's gravity. Tsiolkovsky developed this idea, the first multistage rocket, because his calculations showed him that a single-stage rocket would have to be of immense dimensions in order to place an object of any size into space. Tsiolkovsky's theory was that, after the first rocket had used its fuel, a second stage would be able to use the momentum developed by the first to increase the vehicle's speed to orbital, or escape, velocity. The second and later stages of the rocket would be succeedingly smaller, since less thrust would be required to push the vehicle as it got lighter after discarding each empty stage. Tsiolkovsky's first manned multistage design, called a passenger rocket train, included twenty rockets and was more than three hundred feet tall.

Two years after the Russian Revolution that brought Vladimir Ilich Lenin to power in what was now called the Union of Soviet Socialist Republics, Tsiolkovsky was elected to membership in that nation's premier scientific body, the Socialist Academy. This organization, the forerunner of the modern U.S.S.R. Academy of Sciences, was responsible for leading the development of scientific theory in the Soviet Union. Shortly after his election to the academy, Tsiolkovsky was given a pension to support his studies in Kaluga.

After his rise to fame, Tsiolkovsky became an icon for his contemporaries and for students of the budding science of rocket research. Oberth, the man who would later build upon Tsiolkovsky's theories and propose the first space-station design, began a substantial correspondence with the former schoolteacher. Korolev, the man who would later found the Soviet Union's missile and space programs, would also build a relationship with Tsiolkovsky, whom Korolev considered his scientific mentor. During much of the period of his earliest space travel computations, Tsiolkovsky continued to teach at the children's school in Kaluga. He had, it was said, a special rapport with the children he taught, and it is speculated that the young people's own imaginations helped their teacher continue to expand his own.

Although he never actually built a rocket or launch vehicle of any kind to substantiate his theories, Tsiolkovsky continued to promote the potential values of space travel and to work for a greater public understanding of the laws of physics and nature behind them. He was a strong role model for many of the young men who founded, in the 1930's, the first rocketry club in the Soviet Union, which built Russia's first successful liquid-fueled rocket. Among the members of the group were Friedrich Tsander, the famous Soviet aircraft designer, and Korolev, the future chief designer of the Soviet space program.

At the age of seventy-eight, in September, 1935, only two days after his birthday, Tsiolkovsky, still considering himself a humble but visionary schoolteacher, died in his home in Kaluga. At the time of his death, he had authored more than sixty works of fiction, fantasy, and fact. Numerous tributes to him have been established in the years following his death, most particularly since the establishment of the Soviet space program in the late 1950's.

## Summary

The mathematical theories and formulas developed by Konstantin Tsiolkovsky, coming as they did during the earliest days of aeronautic research, were part of a period of time in which one of the most rapid expansions of mankind's attainable horizons was occurring. In a space of less than twenty years, mankind went from being virtually earthbound to having the capacity to move through the skies and, in quantifiable theory, beyond the atmosphere into interplanetary space. Tsiolkovsky's studies essentially offered the blueprint for future reaction propulsion-powered travel by way of the rocket engine, the multistage rocket for launch vehicles and spacecraft, and the jet engine that would be used on modern aircraft. All major rocketry pioneers after Tsiolkovsky—Goddard, Oberth, von Braun, and Korolev—acknowledged him as the father of their fledgling science.

Tsiolkovsky was also part of a long series of events that allowed for the expansion and reshaping of the understanding of science and the world. Tsiolkovsky's popular writings showed the layperson the practical benefits of scientific endeavor, in much the same way that Jules Verne, Hermann Oberth, Isaac Asimov, and other scientists in the second half of the nineteenth century to modern times have done. He helped bring science, the study of the real world, and all the possibilities it holds into the frame of reference of laypersons.

### Bibliography

Braun, Wernher von, and Frederick I. Ordway III. *The History of Rocketry and Space Travel.* 3d ed. New York: Crowell, 1975. This compendium of information about the early days of the American space efforts and the history of rocketry gives an excellent, easy-to-read narrative by one of the pioneers in space travel.

Clark, Phillip. *The Soviet Manned Space Program: An Illustrated History of the Men, the Missions, and the Spacecraft.* London: Salamander, and New York: Orion, 1988. Clark is one of the acknowledged Western experts on the Soviet space program, and this is one of the most comprehensive books on the subject.

Daniloff, Nicholas. *The Kremlin and the Cosmos.* New York: Knopf, 1972. This book, by a noted American journalist, gives an insightful look at the early days of the Soviet space program and how space research developed in the closed society of the Soviet Union.

Kosmodemianskii, Arkadii Aleksandrovich. *Konstantin Tsiolkovsky: His Life and Work.* Moscow: Foreign Languages Publishing House, 1956. This book, one of the very few English-language biographies available in the West, is a propagandist view of Tsiolkovsky's life. It is interesting nevertheless and offers good information about his work.

McAleer, Neil. *The Omni Space Almanac: A Complete Guide to the Space Age.* New York: World Almanac, 1987. This book is an excellent beginner's resource on the history of space travel, from before Tsiolkovsky to modern times and beyond.

Oberg, James E. *Red Star in Orbit: The Inside Story of Soviet Failures and Triumphs in Space.* London: Harrap, and New York: Random House, 1981. Oberg is one of the Western world's leading experts on the Soviet space program. In this, his most famous book, he carefully details, in entertaining and informative language, the development of the cosmonauts' march to space. Through his discussions of Tsiolkovsky, Korolev, and other leading space figures in the Soviet Union, the reader is given a panoramic yet very human view of one of the world's two great space efforts.

Tsiolkovsky, Konstantin. *Beyond the Planet Earth.* Oxford, and New York: Pergamon Press, 1960. This English-language translation of one of Tsiolkovsky's popular accounts of space travel is a fascinating look at the work of the founder of modern rocketry principles.

*Eric Christensen*

# MARINA TSVETAYEVA

*Born:* October 9, 1892; Moscow, Russia
*Died:* August 31, 1941; Yelabuga, U.S.S.R.
*Area of Achievement:* Literature
*Contribution:* Tsvetayeva, whose life and work bridged the Bolshevik Revolution, was one of the greatest Russian poets of the twentieth century. Her poetry and her correspondence illuminate the time in which she lived, and her mastery of the technique of writing poetry led to innovative poetic forms and rhythms.

## Early Life

Marina Ivanovna Tsvetayeva was born in Moscow on October 9, 1982, the eldest daughter of Maria Alexandrovna, who was the second wife of Professor Ivan Vladimirovich Tsvetayev. Tsvetayeva had a stepsister, Valeria, who was ten years older, and a stepbrother, Andrei, only two years older. Two years after Tsvetayeva's birth, her sister Anastasia was born.

Tsvetayeva's mother was an outstanding pianist who not only had been forbidden to play professionally but also had been forced to marry a man she did not love. Tsvetayeva's father, a professor of Roman literature and of fine arts at the University of Moscow and director of the Rumyantsev Museum, was more interested in his work than in his children. He was also still in love with his dead first wife. Maria Alexandrovna was determined that her eldest daughter would become a concert pianist. Tsvetayeva was required to practice several hours daily and was punished for reading. Her mother feared that literature might distract her from the piano. Tsvetayeva's isolation in this family of emotionally detached people undoubtedly provided her with the inner strength that sustained her throughout her life.

At the age of nine, Tsvetayeva began school but was almost immediately removed to accompany her mother, suffering from tuberculosis, and sister to Italy for treatment. The two Tsvetayeva sisters were sent to boarding school in Lausanne, Switzerland, until they all returned to Moscow, where Maria Alexandrovna died in June, 1906.

Ivan Tsvetayeva then sent his young daughters to a boarding school, did not require Marina to pursue the piano, and in 1908 permitted her to study French literature at a Sorbonne summer school. During these years after her mother's death, Tsvetayeva began to write poetry reflecting her adoration of heroes such as the Russian poet Alexander Pushkin, Napoleon I and his son, the actress Sarah Bernhardt, and the playwright Edmund Rostand. Based on Russian folktales or everyday trivia, written in simple and clear language using traditional Russian meters, these early poems reveal Tsvetayeva's inherent talent and originality and her skillful use of language.

When Tsvetayeva published her first collection of poetry, *Vecherny albom* (1910; evening album), she was praised by Nikolai Gumilyov, husband of Anna Akhmatova and the leader of the Acmeist movement in Russian poetry, for her spontaneity and originality and by the eminent critic Max Voloshin. This praise and adulation opened up to Tsvetayeva and her sister Anastasia the society of poets in Moscow and at Voloshin's *dacha* at Koktebel in the Crimea. This was a passionate world not only of the mind but also of the heart and spirit, a world with powerful attraction for Tsvetayeva.

## Life's Work

Tsvetayeva's life's work was her poetry, but that was not her only life's work. Her energies were devoted to other people as well—lovers, children, husband, and friends. This intercourse was both the source of poetry for her and the source of life. At Koktebel in 1911, Tsvetayeva met Sergei Yaklovlevich Efron. Called Seryozha by his friends and family, he represented to Tsvetayeva a knight in shining armor. In January, 1912, Tsvetayeva and Efron married, and in September their first daughter, Ariadna, was born. Tsvetayeva also published her second book of verse, *Volshebny fonar* (1912; the magic lantern), but at this time writing was not her first priority. For the moment her family was.

During these years, Tsvetayeva's husband, Seryozha, was a student at the University of Moscow. When World War I broke out, he was eager to serve, partly for patriotic reasons and partly because Tsvetayeva's attention was focused elsewhere. As she continued to write in Moscow and the Crimea, Tsvetayeva met and cultivated infatuations with the Surrealist poet Tikhon Churilin and the Symbolist poet Osip Mandelstam as well as pursuing an openly lesbian relationship with Sophia Parnok, who became a poet only later. Even so, her attachment to her husband remained strong.

The 1917 February Revolution, which found Tsvetayeva in the Crimea, initiated a time of great confusion and hardship. Although Tsvetayeva was unconcerned with politics, Efron by chance fought in the White Army against the Bolshevik forces. From 1917 to 1922, Tsvetayeva lived in Moscow with her daughters, struggling to stay alive in the face of economic hardship and widespread famine, while her husband fought in the south on the losing side.

During these years on her own, Tsvetayeva's physical strength was tested by hunger that eventually led to the starvation death of her second daughter, born in April, 1917, and her emotional stamina was tested by the uncertainty about politics and Efron. Neverthelesss, she continued to write and to love passionately. Sophia Holliday, Pavlik Antokolsky, and other actors aroused her attention as she wrote verse plays. In 1920, she read her poem "Tsardevitsa" (1922; czar maiden) at the Palace of the Arts, home of the Moscow Writers' Union, and the following year she read poems from *Lebediny stan* (swan's encampment), which were composed between 1917 and 1921 but not published until 1957. The *Lebediny stan* poems praised the White Army, and, in Bolshevik Moscow, reading them was a considerable risk. Since 1916 Tsvetayeva had also been writing a series of poems dedicated to the great Russian Symbolist poet Aleksandr Blok. These poems, *Stikhi k Bloku* (1922; verses to Blok), were published in Berlin in 1922, a year after Blok's death.

The Bolshevik victory was consolidated in 1921, and liquidations of counterrevolutionaries began. Tsvetayeva was ecstatic to learn that Efron had survived the civil war and had escaped to Prague, where a sympathetic Czech government provided subsidies to a number of Russian émigrés. Tsvetayeva applied for a passport to leave Moscow in the spring of 1922 just as her poetry was beginning to be published; *Vertsty I* (1922; mileposts I) appeared and was greeted enthusiastically by Moscow writers, including Boris Pasternak.

On May 15, 1922, Marina and her daughter Ariadna or Alya, as she was called, arrived in Berlin, where they found a sizable Russian émigré population, three daily newspapers, five weeklies, and seventeen Russian publishing houses. Tsvetayeva worked feverishly and productively in spite of the harsh living conditions while she waited for Efron to arrive from Prague. During these months in Berlin, Tsvetayeva began a passionate correspondence with Pasternak that continued to fuel her creativity during the next years.

In August, Tsvetayeva, Efron, and Ariadna settled in Prague, where Efron received a government stipend to attend the university and Tsvetayeva received an allowance for her own writing. She entered the literary life of Prague and continued to write, while taking care of her husband and daughter even as she began to separate from them both emotionally and psychologically.

At thirty Tsvetayeva was entering her most vibrant and productive period both as a writer and as a lover. During the years in Prague, Tsvetayeva produced all the remaining poetry—lyrics, long poems, and verse drama—ever to be published during her lifetime. It is significant that during these years she continued the stimulating correspondence with Pasternak, initiated another equally sensual, although in the end platonic, correspondence with Aleksandr Bakhrahk, a critic in Berlin, and lived through a grand passion, certainly not platonic, with Konstantin Rodzevitch in Prague. Rodzevitch loved Tsvetayeva as she had always dreamed of being loved, but he could not live with the intensity of her passion or without the economic security that Tsvetayeva could not give him. In the end, Tsvetayeva transfigured the misery of this love affair into two poem cycles that are the most sophisticated of her lyric poetry: *Poema gory* (1925; poem of the mountain) and *Poema konca* (1926; poem of the end).

These poems and the epic poem "Molodec" (1924; the swain) show that Tsvetayeva had refined the intuitive and creative uses of language that had been apparent in the earlier *Versty I* poems: the mixture of meters in one poem and even in one line; the unusual rhythms and elliptic imagery; the verblessness, syntactic ellipsis, and one-word sentences; the use of archaisms and eighteenth century Russian words and images reminiscent of the Russian Symbolist and Acmeist poets as well as the use of colloquial, uneducated, and peasant speech forms characteristic of a peasant genre of poetry. Tsvetayeva's mature style, concise with an almost mystical bond between the shape and sound of a word and the object it designates, places her in the company of the European Futurist poets of the early 1920's while the musical richness and complexity of her verse ensures her uniqueness.

In February, 1925, Tsvetayeva and Efron's son was born and named Georgi after the patron saint of Moscow. Desperate to make a living, Efron moved his family to Paris. Although Tsvetayeva's poetry was well received, and Efron and Ariadna were able to get jobs on newspapers soon after their arrival, the émigré community began to distrust the Efrons. Efron became involved with a reformist Bolshevik group sympathetic to Bolshevism. In 1928, Tsvetayeva welcomed the Bolshevik Russian poet Vladimir Mayakovsky to Paris. A long poem about the civil war written in 1929 managed to offend both monarchist émigrés and revolutionary sympathizers. In 1932, Efron and Ariadna joined the Union for Repatriation of Russians Abroad; members were widely suspected of being Soviet agents. The Efrons were further tainted by Tsvetayeva's meetings with Sergei Prokofiev, a visiting Soviet composer, and Boris Pasternak, who came to Paris as a delegate to a Communist-sponsored Congress of Writers in Defense of Culture. Although art not politics was the subject of the conversations, the émigré community punished Tsvetayeva's political naïveté by refusing to publish her poetry and her prose. Living in Paris became more difficult as the Efron resources diminished. In 1937, Ariadna was finally granted a visa to return to Moscow; gladly she left Paris. Soon after that, Efron was accused of involvement in the assassination of a Soviet agent who had renounced Bolshevism. He, too, left for the Soviet Union.

On June 15, 1939, Tsvetayeva, with her son Georgi, followed her husband to Moscow—Tsvetayeva resigned but full of foreboding and Georgi eager to see his homeland for the first time. Shortly after their arrival, both Ariadna and Efron were arrested and sent to prison; Tsvetayeva's sister Anastasia had already been sent to a camp. Although Tsvetayeva was not arrested, she had difficulty getting anything but menial work even with the assistance of Pasternak. She and her son could find no suitable lodging. With the German invasion on June 22, 1941, Tsvetayeva became increasingly concerned about Georgi's safety and decided to emigrate to the Tatar region.

The burden had become too heavy. Rejected by the Writers' Union, without work or a place to live, with her husband and daughter far away in prison—by this time, Efron had been shot, although Tsvetayeva did not know it—she decided that her rebellious son would be better off without her. On Saturday, August 31, 1941, at the age of forty-eight in the village of Yelabuga in the Tartar Autonomous Republic, Tsvetayeva, lonely and exhausted, hanged herself.

### Summary

Throughout her life, Marina Tsvetayeva was passionately devoted to poetry and to people. During years of unbelievable hardship, she continued to write and to develop her poetic style without regard to politics or to fame. She wrote because she could do nothing else. Her poetry was personal, confessional, and both intuitive and intellectual in the way she used words. The passion she needed to inspire her creative soul she acquired from human relationships through conversation and correspondence.

After the death of Joseph Stalin in 1953, Tsvetayeva's sister and daughter were freed from the concentration camps. Tsvetayeva's friends arranged to have her writings, all banned in the Soviet Union, published in New York. From that time on, her work has appeared in Russian-language journals published abroad. Her poetry began to appear in anthologies within the Soviet Union in 1956 and to circulate secretly among the Russian population in manuscript. During the 1960's and 1970's, Tsvetayeva emerged as one of the poets most beloved by Soviet youth.

### Bibliography


Feinstein, Elaine. *A Captive Lion: The Life of Marina Tsvetayeva.* London: Hutchinson, and New York: Dutton, 1987. A popular biography with annotation and a selected bibliography, this work draws on material from scholars and presents Tsvetayeva as a humanist and feminist interested in art, not politics.

Hingley, Ronald. *Nightingale Fever: Russian Poets in Revolution.* New York: Knopf, 1981; London: Weidenfeld and Nicolson, 1982. An excellent collective biography of four contemporary Russian poets (Akhmatova, Pasternak, Mandelstam, and Tsvetayeva) in the context of their time. Includes a bibliography and notes.

Karlinsky, Simon. *Marina Cvetaeva: Her Life and Art.* Berkeley: University of California Press, 1966. The early version of the definitive biography divided into a biographical section and one of Tsvetayeva's poetry.

———. *Marina Tsvetaeva: The Woman, Her World, and Her Poetry.* Cambridge and New York: Cambridge University Press, 1985. A revised, updated, and definitive biography based on the poetry and prose of Tsvetayeva as well as the memoirs of her relatives. Material about her life and her writing are integrated in the text. Includes an excellent bibliography and notes.

McDuff, David. "Marina Tsvetayeva." *Parnassus: Poetry in Review* 12-13 (1985): 117-143. Good analysis of the poetry as it relates to biographical information about Tsvetayeva.

Pasternak, Boris, et al. *Letters, Summer 1926*. Edited by Yevgeny Pasternak, Yelena Pasternak, and Konstantin M. Azadovsky. Translated by Margaret Wettlin and Walter Arndt. San Diego: Harcourt Brace, 1985; London: Cape, 1986. The correspondence between Tsvetayeva, Pasternak, and Rainer Maria Rilke during the last year of Rilke's life. Discussion of poetry illuminated by the passion of relationship.

Proffer, Ellendea, ed. *Tsvetaeva: A Pictorial Biography.* Translated by J. Marin King. Introduction by Carl R. Proffer. Ann Arbor, Mich.: Ardis, 1980. An excellent collection of annotated photographs of Tsvetayeva throughout her life.

Razumovsky, Maria. *Marina Tsvetayeva: A Critical Biography.* Translated by Aleksey Gibson. Newcastle upon Tyne: Bloodaxe, 1994. The most detailed biography of Tsvetayeva in print. Based on memoirs and correspondence with friends, family, and literary contemporaries.

*Loretta Turner Johnson*

# WILLIAM V. S. TUBMAN

*Born:* November 29, 1895; Harper, Liberia
*Died:* July 23, 1971; London, England
*Areas of Achievement:* Government and politics
*Contribution:* Tubman, who was President of Liberia for twenty-seven years, held that office longer than anyone else in the history of Africa's first republic. During his tenure, he instituted several political, economic, and social reforms, which had important consequences for Liberian society.

## Early Life

William Vacanarat Shadrach Tubman was born in Harper, Maryland county, Liberia, on November 29, 1895. His ancestors were freed slaves, who emigrated from Georgia and settled in Liberia in the mid-nineteenth century. His father, a Methodist minister, also served as speaker of the House of Representatives and was later elected a senator. Tubman's parents were very religious and were strict disciplinarians; their six children were required to attend daily family prayers and weekly church services. Tubman attended Cape Palmas Seminary and Cuttington College and Divinity School. As a young man, he served with the Liberian militia and rose to the rank of colonel. He took part in several military encounters between forces of the Americo-Liberian government and the indigenous peoples. He founded a military unit known as the "Tubman Volunteers," which later became part of the Liberian National Guard. After his ordination as a Methodist minister in 1914, Tubman began teaching at the seminary he had attended, while studying law at the same time. He also served temporarily as collector of internal revenue for Maryland county. He was admitted to the bar in 1917 and two years later was appointed county attorney. He soon established a reputation for legal competence and eloquence in the courtroom. "The poor man's lawyer," as he became known, Tubman gave free legal advice and represented many poor clients who could not afford his fees. As a result, his popularity increased, and he developed friendships with ordinary men and women, which later served him well in his political career. Tubman joined the True Whig Party, which had been in power since 1878, in order to further his political aspirations. In 1923, he was elected to the senate, and at twenty-eight became the youngest senator in Liberian history. He was reelected for another six-year term in 1929.

## Life's Work

Tubman's political career received a temporary setback after the League of Nations inquiry into the Fernando Po scandal. In 1930, a Commission of the League concluded that Liberia (a member of the League of Nations) was guilty of selling its citizens to cocoa planters on the Spanish island of Fernando Po. This finding prompted the resignations of the President of Liberia, Charles D. B. King, and the vice president, Allen N. Yancy. Tubman, who had served as legal adviser to the vice president, resigned from the senate in 1931. Ironically, this incident afforded him the opportunity of gaining greater knowledge of the Liberian political system, when he defended the officials who were involved. Although Tubman returned to the senate in 1934, he again resigned three years later, when he was appointed an associate justice of the supreme court. Nevertheless, his responsibilities on the nation's highest court did not preclude him from remaining active in the ruling True Whig Party.

In 1943, Tubman was elected the eighteenth President of Liberia, for the first of seven successive terms. When Tubman, as president-elect, and President Edwin Barclay visited the United States as guests of President Franklin D. Roosevelt later that year, they became the first black guests to spend the night in the White House and the first to be entertained there since Booker T. Washington had visited President Theodore Roosevelt in 1901.

Tubman's inauguration in January, 1944, heralded major political, economic, and social changes in Liberia. Since the early nineteenth century, Liberian society had consisted of two distinct and separate societies: the Americo-Liberians, who were descended from freed American slaves who first arrived there in 1822, and the indigenous ethnic peoples. Although constituting only a small percentage of the total population, the Americo-Liberians soon became the ruling class and the established political and social elite. Tubman introduced two cardinal policies that were the pillars of his administration: the "Open Door Policy" and the "National Unification Policy." The Open Door Policy encouraged foreign investment and trade, and exploitation of the country's natural resources. This policy sought to reverse the policies of previous administrations, which isolated the indigenous peoples from economic development and modernization.

The National Unification Policy instituted by Tubman was aimed at improving the political and social relations between the Americo-Liberian minority and the indigenous majority. In his first inaugural address, he condemned the exploitation of the indigenous peoples and pledged himself to improving their political and educational opportunities. The constitution was amended to extend the suffrage to women and the ethnic majority, and legal barriers which prevented the latter from owning property on a freehold basis were eliminated. Non-Americo-Liberians were also represented in the legislature and were appointed to the cabinet. Tubman also traveled widely in the interior, forging personal contacts with the chiefs and ordinary people and listening to their grievances. Of symbolic importance was the deliberate policy to end public distinctions between Americo-Liberians and native, or tribal, peoples.

Liberia experienced rapid economic growth in the 1950's and early 1960's as a result of foreign investment and economic and technical assistance. Major concessions were given to foreign companies, such as the Firestone Corporation, for the exploitation of the country's natural resources. Many Liberians were employed in mines, plantations, and rapidly growing towns. The prices of Liberia's primary commodity exports—iron ore and rubber—also increased significantly. Between 1950 and 1970, the gross domestic product rose from $48 million to more than $400 million, and the national budget increased from $14 million to more than $60 million. With this relative prosperity, schools, bridges, markets, and hospitals were built. Monrovia, the capital, which had been a sleepy coastal town of 12,000 people in 1939, was transformed into a bustling city of 134,000 in 1970.

Yet, under Tubman's Open Door Policy, foreign entrepreneurs, rather than Liberians, controlled the economy. The terms of concession agreements were highly favorable to foreign investors, and there was no scrupulous enforcement of tax obligations and correct accounting practices by foreign companies. Most Liberians were employed as unskilled or semiskilled workers, and few provisions were made for the training and hiring of qualified Liberians for managerial positions. Nevertheless, the leading politicians and government officials benefited from increased foreign involvement in the economy, and many owned large rubber estates and shares in foreign companies. Starting in the late 1960's, Liberia faced severe economic problems and entered a period of stagnation as the international prices for iron ore and rubber slumped. Although Tubman instituted austerity measures, government officials continued their lavish life-styles, which put a further drain on the national treasury.

In the early years of his presidency, Tubman adroitly began to consolidate his political power. He undermined the bases of power of Americo-Liberian rivals, by coopting many of them into his administration. In addition, he broadened his base of support among the indigenous peoples. As his position became more secure, Tubman tolerated no challenges to his authority and used the police, army, and security forces to quell domestic opposition to his rule. Elections became a mere formality within the context of the single-party system of government.

As Liberia was one of only a few independent African countries at the end of World War II, Tubman became a leading spokesman for African independence. He used the major international forums to draw attention to the decolonization struggle and racial discrimination in southern Africa. In 1960, Liberia became the first African state to have a seat on the United Nations Security Council, and nine years later the Liberian delegate to the United Nations, Angie Brooks-Randolph, became the first African president of the General Assembly. On the continental level, Tubman hosted several important inter-African conferences, notably the Monrovia Conference of 1961. The conference brought together what at the time was the largest number of African states and favored functional cooperation over continental political unification, which was advocated by the more radical Casablanca Group of States. The Monrovia Conference played an important role in the creation of the Organization of African Unity in May, 1963. Having acquired the stature of an elder statesman, Tubman was often called upon to mediate disputes between African states.

## Summary

Throughout his long presidency, William V. S. Tubman proved to be the consummate politician: shrewd, astute, and tenacious. He was, in Niccolò Machiavelli's dictum, "a fox in order to recognize traps, and a lion to frighten off wolves." Although the True Whig Party, the only legitimate political party during his tenure, was still dominated by Americo-Liberians and the key positions in the government, judiciary, and bureaucracy remained in their hands, Tubman broadened the base of

Liberian politics and gave greater political and educational opportunities to the indigenous people. The political system during his presidency was not monolithic, and he developed and expanded the central and local institutions of government.

Although a member of the Americo-Liberian aristocracy, Tubman established strong personal ties with Liberians of different classes and ethnic backgrounds. Affable and accessible and with a dynamic personality, Tubman enjoyed wide support. He was largely responsible for bringing Liberia into the modern age. Tubman was able to maintain political stability in a period of tremendous political, economic, and social change, not only in Liberia but also throughout the African continent. He died in London on July 23, 1971.

### Bibliography

Liebenow, J. Gus. *Liberia: The Evolution of Privilege*. Ithaca, N.Y.: Cornell University Press, 1969; London: Cornell University Press, 1970. A readable, analytical, and dispassionate account of the political structure of Liberian society. It contains many insights into the emergence and nature of the Americo-Liberian elite.

———. *Liberia: The Quest for Democracy.* Bloomington: Indiana University Press, 1987. This is a discussion of Liberia's efforts at democracy and development. It has a stimulating interpretation of Tubman's contribution to the "cult of the presidency."

Lowenkopf, Martin. *Politics in Liberia: The Conservative Road to Development*. Stanford, Calif.: Hoover Institution Press, 1976. A competent treatment of Liberian development that blends politics, history, economics, and sociology. Includes a detailed discussion of the Tubman era. A major limitation is its use of the outdated "modernization school" approach to development.

Smith, Robert A. *William V. S. Tubman*. Amsterdam: Van Ditmar, 1967. A useful biography of Tubman. It conveys a good sense of the nature of the Tubman presidency.

Wreh, Tuan. *The Love of Liberty: The Rule of President William V. S. Tubman in Liberia*. London: Hurst, and New York: Universe, 1976. A short and lively biography that is critical of Tubman. Despite lapses in style, it focuses attention on some of the drawbacks of the Tubman era.

*Abiodun Williams*

## BARBARA TUCHMAN

*Born:* January 30, 1912; New York, New York
*Died:* February 6, 1989; Greenwich, Connecticut
*Area of Achievement:* Historiography
*Contribution:* Recipient of two Pulitzer Prizes in history and one of the most widely read American historians, Tuchman helped reintroduce history as an art to the reading public.

### Early Life

Barbara Wertheim would later recall having witnessed the first naval engagement of World War I when she was two years old. The event occurred in the Mediterranean as she traveled with her parents to visit her grandfather, who was then serving as U.S. Ambassador to Turkey. Her historical interests never wavered afterward, although they were reinforced during her childhood by the popular historical adventures recounted in Lucy Fitch Perkins' famous Twins series, as well as in books of the same genre by Sir Arthur Conan Doyle, Jane Porter, Alexandre Dumas, and George Alfred Henty. Her interests in place, imaginative research, and confident writing, however, required years of apprenticeship.

Wertheim's early background was marked by privilege and familial distinction. Maurice Wertheim, her father, was a leader in New York City's Jewish community, a successful international banker, publisher, and philanthropist. Her mother, Alma Morgenthau Wertheim, was a member of the prominent Morgenthau banking family. It was Henry Morgenthau, businessman turned diplomat, whom Barbara had been en route to see when elements of the British fleet attempted to intercept Germany's *Goeben* in August, 1914—one of the world's most memorable months, encapsulating the meltdown of a civilization whose ambience Barbara Tuchman later re-created in *The Guns of August* (1962). An uncle, Henry Morgenthau, Jr., served as Franklin Roosevelt's secretary of the Treasury, while cousin Robert Morgenthau gained repute as a U.S. federal attorney.

Barbara's formal education comported with her family's expectations and achievements: New York's Walden School and then, in 1929, Harvard's affiliate, Radcliffe College for women. In essays written decades later, she recalled the influences of Irving Babbitt, a specialist in French literature; Charles McIlwain, himself a Pulitzer Prize-winner for a historical study of American government; and John Livingston Lowe, an expert in comparative literature. Equally as memorable, she recounted, was her freedom to spend time in the magnificent stacks of Harvard's Widener Library, repository of one of the world's largest private book and manuscript collections. Meanwhile, her summers were spent with her family in Europe. Shortly after graduation, she joined her grandfather at the World Economic Conference of 1933.

Privileged as she was, Barbara Wertheim eagerly transmuted social advantage into cultivating her splendid background and temperament for historical writing. She commenced formal research working for the Institute of Pacific Relations soon after graduation. In 1935, she joined the staff of *The Nation*, which her father owned, writing on a variety of newsworthy subjects. The magazine dispatched her to Spain for coverage of that country's confused and savage civil war in 1937. Upon her return, she determined to work as a freelance correspondent for a British news journal. In the meantime, she witnessed the publication of her first book, *The Lost British Policy: Britain and Spain Since 1700* (1938), the precursor to eleven significantly better works.

### Life's Work

As for everyone of her generation and age, war and family for a time preempted Barbara Wertheim's other affairs. In 1940, shortly after the outbreak of World War II, and the year prior to America's direct involvement, she married the president of New York City Hospital's medical board, Dr. Lester Tuchman. In the acknowledgments of her final work, *The First Salute* (1988), she not only thanked him for aiding her with her failing eyesight but also acknowledged him as being "the rock upon which this house is built." From 1943 until 1945, both Tuchmans performed national service, she at the Far Eastern Office of the Office of War Information. Some of Barbara Tuchman's initial curiosities about life in the Far East, subsequently fleshed out in her *Stilwell and the American Experience in China* (1971), took shape.

Despite these early publications, her "first" book, as she described it, did not appear until 1956—*Bible and Sword: England and Palestine from the Bronze Age to Balfour*, a study of British policy in Palestine. It was, by her own admission, incomplete. The last six months of her research

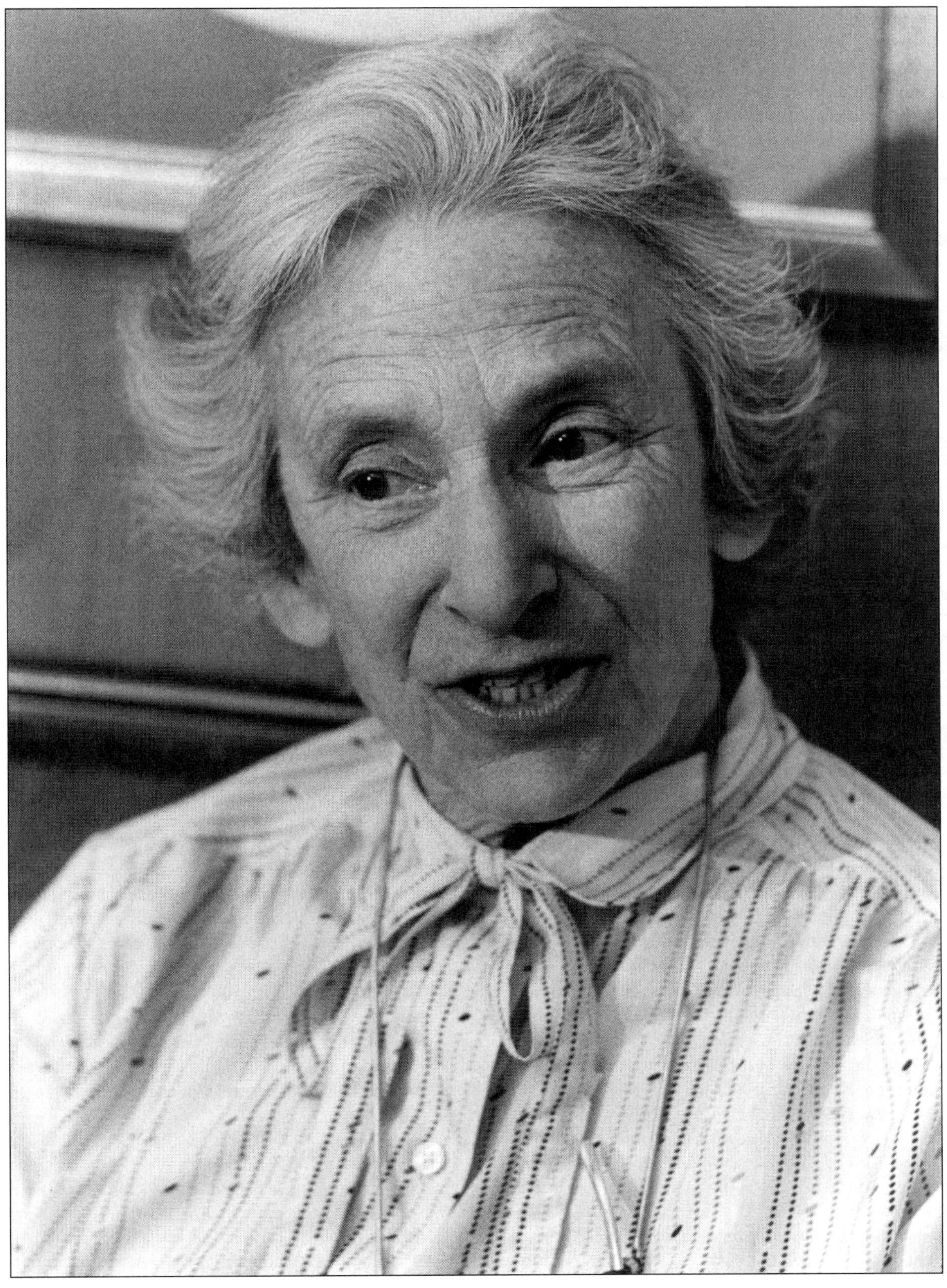

dealing with events from 1918 until 1948, a period of British Mandate over Palestine, of Arab uprisings, the Arab-Israeli War, and reestablishment of the state of Israel in 1948, so overwhelmed her with a sense of disgust and injustice that, contrary to her editor's wishes, she destroyed them. Her emotions had victimized her perception of scholarly discipline. The study thus ended in 1918. The lesson this experience conveyed to her persisted: Stay within the evidence and let the emotions come to the readers insofar as possible from the presentation itself.

In this regard, Tuchman readdressed an earlier canon of major historians, which had been eclipsed somewhat by historical writing like that of the distinguished and enormously influential Charles A. Beard. Beard and his wife, Mary Ritter Beard, in company with James Harvey Robinson and other Progressives, conceived of history as an important force in effecting social change, of molding civilization. They wrote the "New History," which questioned the older standard of objectivity, and their works raised their banners around the qualified relativism that became the trademark of their school.

Tuchman agreed that the goal of absolute objectivity was unattainable by historians. Nevertheless, in essays explaining her philosophy of history, she placed herself in the tradition of German historian Leopold von Ranke, the figure generally credited with founding the modern school of objective historiography known as "Scientific History." Inserting one's opinions into the hunchwork guiding research, as well as imposing these opinions on one's selection of materials for writing, she believed, was highly undesirable. Rather, self-conscious striving for objectivity, recording history "how it really was," as Ranke stated it, was Tuchman's goal. Thus, for the most part, contemporary history—evaluations of headline events of her own day or of recent decades—by choice lay outside her intellectual bailiwick. Such events were too immediate and too emotion-charged for her to analyze calmly and reflectively.

In a few essays, Tuchman did indeed ignore these tenets, but not in her major works. *Bible and Sword* thus closed in 1918; *The Zimmermann Telegram* (1958), *The Guns of August* (1962), and *The Proud Tower: A Portrait of the World Before the War, 1890-1914* (1966) all focused on events and personalities of World War I. *Stilwell and the American Experience in China* examined occurrences from which the passage of a full generation buffered her. Likewise, *A Distant Mirror: The Calamitous Fourteenth Century* (1978) focused on the excitement and upheaval of a distant European past and *The March of Folly: From Troy to Vietnam* (1984) sketched the timeless absurdities of warfare, while her last book, *The First Salute: A View of the American Revolution* (1988), assessed the impact of foreign involvement on the American Revolution. She agreed that contemporary history could be written, citing William L. Shirer's *The Rise and Fall of the Third Reich* (1960) as a superior example, but not by her.

Musing further on her own historical approach and style, Tuchman emphasized her distaste for history "in gallon jugs." By that she meant history wrestled into the service of a historian's grand explanatory or philosophical schemes, and therefore girdled with sweeping generalizations. The historian who after 1934 and through the 1960's had most recently fit this description was the English historian Arnold Joseph Toynbee, whose *A Study of History* (1934-1964), a twelve-volume theoretical analysis of the rise and decline of more than a score of notable civilizations, had proved surprisingly popular, particularly as made accessible to general audiences in excellent abridgments. For Tuchman, however, climbing "those Toynbeean heights" would have required her to soar from the ground impelled by theories of her own invention. That sort of endeavor, as she saw it, was not what a historian should do. Besides, however grand the view from a Toynbeean perspective, Tuchman lamented the inevitable disappearance of detail.

It was indeed an eye for telling detail that characterized Barbara Tuchman's histories—"corroborative detail," in her words. Such detail, she insisted, restrained historians and forced them to adhere to as much truth as could be gleaned from their materials. It was her view that while corroborative detail might not produce glittering generalizations, it still might reveal historical truths in addition to keeping research anchored in reality.

Tuchman's final work, *The First Salute*, was published in 1988, some months before her death at her home in Greenwich, Connecticut, in February of 1989.

## Summary

With the lengthy experience in research and writing that she had begun acquiring in her youth and with a firm grasp of the tenets of professional history, Barbara Tuchman made straightforward narrative history her genre. She embellished it with brilliantly selected detail—one of her trademarks—that made events and personalities vital for her readers. When she began her major works, narrative history was out of fashion, particularly in academia, and interpretive history seemed the route to reputation. Worse, as far as many academics were concerned, much of the best narrative history, and certainly the most readable—with notable exceptions—had been produced by nonacademics.

Despite the authority of academic historians, which had grown with the expansion of American universities, mass education, and the importance of the doctoral degree beginning in the 1950's, Tuchman chose an alternate course for herself. She earned no higher degrees, and she was faintly bemused by the overwhelmingly male- dominated mandarinate represented by academic historians. She certainly respected the standards that academics had set for the collection and accuracy of their research. Yet, academics essentially wrote for one another. To the extent that this was the case, historical writing became a busy closet enterprise to which reading publics were not privy. Tuchman consciously returned to the older tradition of history, writing "objective" narrative with literary merit—a tradition that had included such notables as Allan Nevins, Samuel Eliot Morison, and Douglas Southall Freeman, all of whom urged that while history should be judged by rigorous standards of accuracy it should also join hands with literature. Capitalizing on this advice and following her own artistic predilections, Tuchman became one of the most widely read of modern American historians. A best-selling author, she was an important figure in reviving history for the public. Two Pulitzer Prizes are testimonials to the high abilities she brought to bear in scholarly realms that into the 1990's were still overwhelmingly dominated by men.

### Bibliography

"Barbara Tuchman." *The Nation* 248, no. 9 (March, 1989): 252-253. A thoughtful, laudatory obituary by a periodical with which Tuchman was associated when she began her writing/research career, and one in which her family had owned an interest. This profile is valuable because while Tuchman's books were widely reviewed, there are few published materials about their author.

Beard, Mary Ritter. *Woman as Force in History: A Study in Traditions and Realities*. New York: Macmillan, 1946; London: Macmillan, 1973. Beard, who has been perceived as a founder of women's history and a champion of women writing history, was greatly admired by Tuchman. Neither Beard nor Tuchman fit into the academic historical guilds of their times. Brief annotated bibliography and useful index.

Hurwitz, Samuel T. "The Guns of August. Review." *American Historical Review* 7 (July, 1962): 1014-1015. Valuable as an appreciative academic review of Tuchman's first Pulitzer Prize-winning work. It credits Tuchman with vivid, imaginative, and passionate writing. It describes the work as a series of vignettes offering little new to professional specialists, but serving as a good example of how history can be written to appeal to a wide audience.

Marcus, Jacob R. *The American Jewish Woman, 1654-1980*. New York: Ktav, 1981. Briefly places Tuchman as a member of the Morgenthau-Wertheim families in context with other notable Jewish women of her generation.

Tuchman, Barbara W. *Practicing History: Selected Essays*. New York: Knopf, 1981; London: Macmillan, 1982. A collection of frank, often charming commentaries and examples of Tuchman's work and views. All are articles or lectures rather than selections from her books. Essays in part 1 are especially interesting and revelatory. Few notes, no bibliography or index. Her historical views should be juxtaposed to those male academic historians who reviewed her work. On balance they credited her with striking prose and good "popular" history, making clear that it was less thoroughly researched, profound, or interdisciplinary than they expected "reliable" history to be.

Zinsser, Judith P. *History and Feminism: A Glass Half Full*. New York: Twayne, 1993. A clear, cogent survey and comparative analysis of men's history, women's history, and the impact of feminism on each. Useful for placing Tuchman in the broader modern context of women writing history. An excellent work with annotated suggestions for further reading and a valuable index.

*Clifton K. Yearley*

# ANDREI NIKOLAYEVICH TUPOLEV

*Born:* November 10, 1888; Pustomazovo, Russia
*Died:* December 23, 1972; Moscow, U.S.S.R.
*Area of Achievement:* Aeronautics
*Contribution:* Tupolev was among the world's leading designers of military and civilian aircraft. He worked in the Soviet aircraft industry for half a century and designed more than 120 planes, many of which have held world records for being the heaviest, fastest, or largest built. He was first in the U.S.S.R. to build all-metal aircraft, was a member of the Academy of Sciences of the U.S.S.R., and was a recipient of many state prizes.

## Early Life

Andrei Nikolayevich Tupolev was born in Pustomazovo, Russia (modern Kalinin Oblast), on November 10, 1888. He was the son of the village notary public. In 1908, he entered the Moscow Higher Technical College (MVTU), from which he was graduated in 1918. There, he studied under Nikolay Yegorovich Zhukovsky, a lecturer in mechanical engineering. Zhukovsky, also known as "the father of Russian aviation," organized an aeronautical study group of interested students at MVTU, Tupolev being among them. While a student, Tupolev, working with Zhukovsky, was instrumental in developing the first wind tunnels. During the Russian Civil War, Leon Trotsky charged Tupolev and Zhukovsky with the task of creating a multiengine bomber to replace the very effective *Il'ya Muromets.* They designed a twin-engine triplane that failed, but the idea nevertheless did much to increase Soviet interest in building heavy bombers.

During his student years, Tupolev also worked on the Central Aero and Hydrodynamics Institute (TsAGI), established by Zhukovsky. From 1923 to 1938, he served as the chief engineer, and he continued an association with the institute during most of his career. In the early 1930's, this was the only organization in the Soviet Union dealing with aeronautics. Tupolev's first aircraft design, the ANT-1 (the letters were his initials), was a small, thirty-five-horsepower craft. It was built in 1922, the year that Zhukovsky died.

## Life's Work

Following his early research on wind tunnels and training gliders, Tupolev became involved in aerodynamics and the use of metal in aircraft construction. He was the first Soviet engineer to build an all-metal craft. In 1922, he organized a group at TsAGI for the purpose of working on all-metal planes and aerosleighs. In 1925, this group was named Aviation, Hydroaviation, and Special Design. The ANT-1 (1922) was made mostly of aluminum, and the ANT-2 (1924) was made entirely of metal. Both of these were single-engine monoplanes. These early aircraft were often used for propaganda purposes. The ANT-3, completed in 1926, received widespread acclaim when in late summer of that year Mikhail Gromov, in an ANT-3 named *Proletari*, made a forty-five-hundred-mile flight around various European capitals in approximately thirty-five hours of flying time. The next year, Semyon Shestakov flew *Nash otvet* (our reply) over Siberia to Tokyo.

Tupolev's ANT-4 first flew in 1925 and, despite protests from the Germans regarding infringed patents, was quickly put into series production. In 1929, an ANT-4 known as *Land of the Soviets* flew from Moscow to San Francisco to New York covering 13,600 miles in 153 flying hours. The wheels were replaced with floats before the flight across the Pacific. This twin-engine plane was developed by the military into a heavy bomber—the TB-1. It was also designed as a naval torpedo plane, the MTB-1. These were being built in the U.S.S.R. in the early 1930's, as were fighter planes, also designed by Tupolev. Having been instructed to design fighters in 1928, Tupolev produced the ANT-5 or I-4. The I-4 was in service to the Soviet air force until 1933. The ANT-6 or TB-3 was being produced by 1932, and by 1938 it had replaced the ANT-4 or TB-1 as the main Soviet bombing craft.

Tupolev was also a leader in developing planes for civilian transport, and several of his ANT designs were used for this purpose. The ANT-9 had three engines and carried nine passengers, and the ANT-14 had five engines and could seat thirty-six. The passenger plane of the early 1930's was the ANT-20 named *Maxim Gorky.* It could carry fifty passengers, making it the largest civilian plane in the world, and could be converted into a bomber or a military transport quite easily. It was developed primarily for propaganda purposes and received much news coverage. It had eight engines and weighed forty tons. It included a radio station, a printing press, a photographic laboratory, loudspeakers, a telephone switchboard, illuminated signs, and recording and projection equipment. It was taken, in 1935, for a demonstration flight and was escorted by a fighter plane that was painted red so people on the ground could easily compare the size of the two planes. The pilot of the fighter plane was a famous stunt pilot who was going through various dives and loops and in the process miscalculated and hit the *Maxim Gorky.* The plane crashed, killing the forty-nine passengers, all award-winning workers who were on the flight in recognition of their achievement.

Tupolev visited England in 1934 with other Soviet air force officers. In 1935, he completed designs for the ANT-22, a flying boat that set a record by reaching 6,370 feet carrying 22,000 pounds. His ANT-25, also designed in 1935, flew from Moscow to California by crossing the North Pole, traveling 6,262 miles in sixty-two hours and two minutes. The plane brought glory to the U.S.S.R. but never became the long-range bomber as had been intended.

Between 1933 and 1938, there were two aircraft design establishments serving the Soviet air force: Tupolev's Experimental Aero-Design Division and Sergey Ilyushin's Central Design Bureau. There was much rivalry and jealousy between these two establishments. Nikolai Polikarpov, who headed the Central Design Bureau, was, like Tupolev, an uncompromising person. Polikarpov modeled his management style after that of Joseph Stalin, who worked with a small group of loyal followers, while Tupolev insisted that only a large organization could effectively use the talent and have the experience necessary to succeed in the world of complex design. Polikarpov wanted to create aircraft that were superior to those in the West. That was the only way he would feel successful. Tupolev believed that such competition was pointless and that success was measured by designing a craft that served a function required by the Soviet air force.

Tupolev visited the United States and Germany in 1936. In the United States, he studied industrial design at both the Douglas plant in Santa Monica, California, and the Ford plant in Detroit, Michigan. Later that year, he was arrested during the Stalinist purges and was sentenced to five years in prison. He was charged with having sold plans for fighter planes to Germany. Supposedly the Germans used these plans for the construction of the Messerschmidt-109. Tupolev was also said to have opposed the purge trials, during which millions were

held without evidence, implying that he was willing to testify against Stalin. Tupolev was followed to prison by most of his senior staff; it is estimated that 450 aircraft designers from his bureau were arrested between 1934 and 1941, fifty being executed and one hundred dying in labor camps. Tupolev himself was originally sentenced to death, but Stalin recognized his value to the Soviet Union and established a design bureau in prison so he could continue to work for the good of his country. He later obtained his freedom for having produced a successful attack bomber, the TU-2, which was used extensively during World War II. For this he received a Stalin Prize in 1943. Later when Stalin wanted him to design an attack bomber that could reach the United States and return to the Soviet Union without refueling, Tupolev refused. While his stay in prison silenced his earlier criticism of the Soviet government and philosophy, he still dared to defy Stalin when he knew that he was being requested to perform an impossible task given the existing limits of technology. The arrest bothered Tupolev, and, after Nikita Khrushchev became head of the Party, Tupolev asked him if it would be possible to remove his arrest record as it was a black mark on the careers of his children as well as his own. Khrushchev, who considered Tupolev to be his country's greatest airplane designer, agreed. In 1953, after Stalin's death, Tupolev was given full membership in the Academy of Sciences.

After being released from prison in 1941, Tupolev served as a lieutenant general of the Engineering Technical Forces. In 1944, when three B-29's were impounded after being forced to land near Vladivostok following raids over Japan, Tupolev was assigned the task of producing a similar plane. In response, he designed the TU-4, which was put into production in less than a year. The Soviets built around fifteen hundred of these planes before they stopped production in 1954. The TU-4's could reach the United States and return to the Soviet Union if they were refueled in the air. Yet despite the superiority of the B-29 during World War II, by the time the TU-4 was in use it was outdated as the United States was already producing superior models.

Tupolev was a very practical person. Sometimes his airplanes did not turn out to be good for their intended use. The TU-95 was a turboprop bomber that could fly around 850 kilometers per hour and could not go higher than eighteen thousand meters. It had an excellent range, but its speed and altitude limitations would make it very easy to shoot down. Tupolev suggested that he be allowed to modify it for civilian uses. The TU-95 thus became the TU-114, the first nonstop passenger plane between Moscow and Washington.

Toward the end of World War II, Tupolev became concerned with developing jet-propulsion engines. He used British and German engines on his TU-2's to create a prop-jet. This was called a TU-2A and first appeared in 1947. Within two years, Tupolev was made a Hero of Socialism and received the Order of Lenin and two more Stalin Prizes. In 1948, his tactical jet bomber, TU-10, appeared, and in three years this plane was being used at bases in Eastern Europe. By the early 1950's Tupolev had developed a long-range strategic bomber, the TU-75, used in the Far East. In 1952, this brought Tupolev and his associates another Stalin Prize. His TxAGI-428 was similar to the B-52 and could deliver a hydrogen bomb. In 1956, his TU-104 transport was flown to England. It had a capacity of fifty persons and was considered well in advance of anything likely to be developed soon in the West. Tupolev visited England in 1956 with Khrushchev and announced that he was in the process of completing designs for a jet airliner. In September, 1957, his TU-114, capable of carrying 220 persons, was in operation. The culmination of his career came in 1968, when the supersonic TU-144 made its first flight. By 1971, it was in production. Foreign engineers had started work on the Concorde two and a half years before Tupolev began the project. On May 25, 1971, a TU-144 landed in Paris on its first flight West with its designer on board. A little more than a year later, at age eighty-four, Tupolev died.

### Summary

Born before the advent of flight, Andrei Nikolayevich Tupolev lived to witness and be a primary contributor to spectacular advances in aviation history. Having devoted more than fifty years of his life to keeping his country on the leading edge of aeronautical technology, he made a greater impact on the development of Russian aviation than anyone else. Tupolev had special problems as a Soviet designer. Not only did his planes have to be able to operate in and withstand the fierce winters of Siberia, but also, as late as 1960, there were still runways in major cities that were unpaved. Yet from monoplanes to fighters to supersonic jet transport, Tupolev's design bureau led the way. Because of his efforts, within a decade after the end of World War II, the Soviets had considerably diminished the United States' lead in air power.

Tupolev loved to travel to air shows in the West to obtain ideas to help him in his work. His last visit was to Paris in 1967. He also served as host to foreign visitors in his own country, graciously showing them his facilities near Moscow. Neil Armstrong was among the last of such guests, visiting with Tupolev in 1970. In a time when the Soviet Union remained quite isolated from capitalist societies, Tupolev did much to improve communications. Khrushchev, always an admirer of Tupolev for his enormous technical achievements, his passionate commitment to his work, and his personal warmth and humor, believed that while "there were other talented designers, Andrei Nikolayevich was head and shoulders above" the rest.

### Bibliography

Bailes, K. E. "Technology and Legitimacy: Soviet Aviation and Stalinism in the 1930's." *Technology and Culture* 17 (January, 1976): 55-81. Discusses Stalin's use of the aircraft industry for propaganda purposes and his establishment of a special design bureau in prison camp. Tupolev's work figures prominently in the article.

Boyd, Alexander. *The Soviet Air Force Since 1918.* London: Macdonald, and New York: Stein and Day, 1977. Includes considerable information about Tupolev but puts him in the context of the development of the Soviet air force, indicating the significance of his contribution in relation to the many other engineers and designers who were working during the same period.

Higham, Robin, and Jacob W. Kipp, eds. *Soviet Aviation and Air Power: A Historical Review.* London: Brassey's, and Boulder, Colo.: Westview Press, 1978. This is perhaps the best volume existing on the subject of Soviet air power, and it contains articles covering all aspects of Soviet aviation from the creation of the Central Aerohydrodynamic Institute to missile and cosmic research. Puts Tupolev's work in perspective.

Khrushchev, Nikita. *Khrushchev Remembers.* 2 vols. Translated and edited by Strobe Talbott. London: Deutsch, and Boston: Little Brown, 1970. In volume 2, chapter 3, Khrushchev gives a personal account of his association with Andrei Tupolev and discusses the accomplishments of the man he considers to be the Soviet Union's greatest aircraft designer. This is a very useful discussion.

Taylor, John W. R., ed. *Combat Aircraft of the World: From 1909 to the Present.* London: Ebury, and New York: Putnam, 1977. This allows comparisons of Tupolev's military craft designs with those of other Soviet and world designers, beginning with the ANT-3, the first mass-produced Soviet craft.

———. *Jane's All the World's Aircraft, 1970-1971.* London: Jane's and New York: McGraw-Hill, 1970. This volume includes complete descriptions and pictures of all aircraft designed by Tupolev from the TU-16 (*Badger*) in 1954 to the TU-154 (*Careless*), which went into production in the late 1960's.

*Nancy L. Ericksons*

# ALAN MATHISON TURING

*Born:* June 23, 1912; London, England
*Died:* June 7, 1954; Wilmslow, Cheshire, England
*Areas of Achievement:* Mathematics, computer science, and cryptology
*Contribution:* Through his research on computable functions and artificial intelligence, Turing prepared the foundation for modern computer science. His work during World War II breaking German codes for the British government was of major value to the Allied effort in Europe.

## Early Life

Alan Mathison Turing was born June 23, 1912, in London, England. His mother, née Ethel Sara Stoney, and his father, Julius Mathison Turing, were both of middle-class, Protestant British families. Both Turing and his brother John were educated in British boarding schools while their father served in the British civil service in India. Turing matriculated at the Sherbourne School in Dorset, rather than at one of the more fashionable public schools, because his family believed that the school would offer a more conducive environment for their socially awkward child. At Sherbourne, Turing distinguished himself in mathematics and science but was an indifferent student of other subjects. Already, his lifelong interest in scientific matters and passionate determination to learn by self-discovery rather than through reading were well established.

## Life's Work

Turing's most enduring scientific accomplishment was conceived during his undergraduate years at Cambridge University. Turing entered King's College, Cambridge, in 1931 and remained there until 1936, during which time he completed his baccalaureate and master's degrees with honors. Turing was tutored by mathematician M. H. A. Newman, who introduced him to the work of David Hilbert, Kurt Gödel, and others, on the logical foundations of mathematics—a subject of considerable mathematical interest and activity in the 1920's and early 1930's. Turing was attracted to one of the open questions in this subject: determining which mathematical functions are computable, that is, which functions can be calculated entirely in a machinelike way by a fixed set of deterministic rules. Following an independent and very clever line of reasoning, Turing found a solution. His answer involved defining an abstract machine, known today as the universal Turing machine, which could calculate all those functions that are computable. His machine embodied the concept of the general-purpose, stored program computer; thus the paper describing his result is regarded as a classic of both mathematical logic and computer science.

In 1936, Turing accepted a year's fellowship to visit Princeton University, where he could work with Alonzo Church and other mathematicians interested in the subject of computability. While at Princeton, Turing was persuaded to stay a second year and complete a Ph.D. in mathematics. His dissertation on ordinal logics made yet another important contribution to mathematics and computer science. Turing might have settled into a productive academic career as a mathematical logician, had World War II not intervened.

Turing returned to war-troubled Great Britain in 1938. He reassumed his fellowship at Cambridge, but soon he volunteered his services to the Government Code and Cypher School in Bletchley, a small town between Oxford and London, where a massive effort was under way to develop techniques and construct calculating machines capable of decoding machine-encrypted German diplomatic and military messages. Turing played a crucial role in the design of this equipment and in the development of procedures for breaking the codes: The work at Bletchley was critical to the Allied successes in Europe, and Turing was highly decorated for his contributions.

This wartime experience gave Turing a familiarity with electronics that complemented his mathematical training. In 1945, he moved to the National Physical Laboratory in Teddington, where he was given the responsibility for designing an electronic, stored program computer for use in government work. What Turing designed, in effect, was a physical embodiment of his universal Turing machine which used electronic circuitry. The plans he drew up called for an ambitious modern computer using vacuum tubes for logical switching and arithmetic calculations, and mercury delay lines (a radar technology) for storing information. A scaled-down version, known as Pilot Automatic Computing Engine (ACE), was completed in 1950—one of the first modern computers placed in operation—and used for important government and industrial research, including aircraft design.

Frustrated at the slow and somewhat political process of building the computer, Turing resigned from the National Physical Laboratory in 1947. After a short time at Cambridge, Turing accepted a position at Manchester University as the chief programmer for a powerful new computer, the Mark I, being built there. Joining this project, he was reunited with Newman, his college teacher and Bletchley colleague. His duties allowed him ample time and opportunity to pursue his main interest, what is now called "artificial intelligence." Turing became the champion of artificial intelligence research. He experimented with programming the Mark I computer to execute what he regarded as intelligent actions: proving mathematical theorems, translating from one language into another, breaking codes, and playing games such as chess. He also published a widely read paper setting out his counterarguments to the most popular objections to the possibility of artificial intelligence.

This paper introduced his "Imitation Game" better known today as the Turing Test. The test is the most frequently cited method for determining whether a computer has achieved intelligence and is based on Turing's belief in behaviorist philosophy: If a computer exhibits intelligent behavior, it is intelligent. In the test, an interrogator is connected by terminal to either a human or a computer at a remote location. The interrogator is allowed to pose any questions he wishes. Based upon the answers, the interrogator must decide whether a human or a computer is at the other end of the line. If the interrogator cannot distinguish between the two in a statistically significant number of cases, then Turing's test claims artificial intelligence to have been achieved.

Turing's productive and extraordinarily creative scientific career came to a sudden end in 1954 as the result of a fatal dose of cyanide poisoning. A few months earlier, Turing had been convicted of homosexual activity, at that time a felony in Great Britain. He had been sentenced to mandatory estrogen treatments, which caused strong physiological and psychological changes in him. These changes severely depressed Turing, and many people believe they caused him to take his life. At the time of his death, Turing had begun an ambitious investigation of the chemical basis of morphogenesis—that is, the information process in living organisms which determines why and how single cells grow into differentiated organs with specific functions.

### Summary

Alan Mathsion Turing made many contributions to mathematics, logic, and statistics, and was a marathon runner of world-class distinction. He is best remembered, however, for his contributions to computability, machine design, and artificial intelligence. His work on computability, especially the universal Turing machine concept, was the first modern work on the theory of computation and is a central idea in recursive function theory (an active area of research in mathematical logic) and in automata theory (an important theoretical discipline within computer science). The value of Turing's efforts in the design of code-breaking equipment to the war effort should not be underestimated. His postwar work on computer design is much harder to evaluate. His work at the National Physical Laboratory resulted in one of the first operating modern computers, which was used for important scientific and engineering applications in the 1950's. Turing's work also influenced the design of computers built by two companies, English Electric and Bendix, but his design ideas did not fall within the mainstream of computer design developments. Turing was the foremost champion of artificial intelligence research in the first decade of modern computing. He introduced the distinction between robotics and artificial intelligence research, arguing in opposition to researchers such as Grey Walter and W. Ross Ashby that the future of artificial intelligence research lay in the use of the stored program computer, not in the construction of special-purpose robots that could mimic vision or other human attributes. The Turing Test has endured as the principal test of success in artificial intelligence research.

### Bibliography

Carpenter, B. S., and R. W. Doran, eds. *A. M. Turing's ACE Report of 1946 and Other Papers*. Cambridge, Mass.: MIT Press, 1986. The volume reprints Turing's design report for the ACE computer, a 1947 lecture by Turing on computing, and a paper by M. Woodger on the history of computing at the National Physical Laboratory. The editors provide a historical introduction to computers that provides the context for these works.

Chesebro, James W. "Communication and Computability: The Case of Alan Mathison Turing." *Communication Quarterly* 41, no. 1 (Winter 1993). This article discusses the contributions of

Turing in the area of computer science and their implications for the field of communications.

Hodges, Andrew. *Alan Turing: The Enigma.* London: Burnett, and New York: Simon and Schuster, 1983. Hodges provides the definitive biography of Turing. It supplies detailed descriptions of his scientific accomplishments in computing equipment design, artificial intelligence, and cryptology. The effect of Turing's homosexuality and his social and personality traits on his career are investigated in detail.

Turing, Alan. "Computing Machinery and Intelligence." *Mind.* N.s. 59 (1950): 433-460. The paper gives Turing's counterarguments to common objections against artificial intelligence and introduces the Turing Test for deciding when a computer has achieved intelligence.

———. "On Computable Numbers, with an Application to the *Entscheidungsproblem.*" In *Proceedings of the London Mathematical Society.* 2d ser. 42 (1937): 230-265. This famous article sets forth the concept of the Turing machine and its application to problems in mathematical logic.

Turing, Sara. *Alan M. Turing.* Cambridge: Heffers, 1959. A memoir of Turing written by his mother when she was seventy-five. It provides useful information about his family life and a rather different interpretation of the facts surrounding his death, but it is weak on scientific matters.

Zabell, S. L. "Alan Turing and the Central Limit Theorem." *The American Mathematical Monthly* 102 no. 6, (June-July, 1995). Discusses the career of Turing, including his work in probability and decoding of German military codes.

*William Aspray*

# FREDERICK JACKSON TURNER

*Born:* November 14, 1861; Portage, Wisconsin
*Died:* March 14, 1932; Pasadena, California
*Area of Achievement:* History
*Contribution:* Developing a unique thesis based on the influence of the frontier in American history, Turner became the most dominant figure among professional historians in the United States for the first three decades of the twentieth century.

## Early Life

Frederick Jackson Turner, born in Portage, Wisconsin, on November 14, 1861, was the eldest son of Andrew Jackson and Mary Hanford Turner. His parents were both from New York, with ancestors among the early Puritan settlers of New England. In the same year that his first son was born, Andrew Jackson Turner purchased the small newspaper for which he worked and merged it with a rival to produce the weekly *Wisconsin State Register*, which he edited and published until 1878. An uncompromising Republican, the elder Turner was active in state politics and served four terms as mayor of Portage.

As son of a local political figure, young Turner grew up with firsthand knowledge of party politics and a healthy respect for the ability to influence men with words and ideas. In addition, an editor's son was perhaps predisposed to develop a love for the written word. As a boy, Turner read widely and, in 1876, when he was only fifteen, began to contribute to his father's newspaper through his Pencil and Scissors Department, where he printed quotations that had attracted his attention. His obvious intellectual ability and interest did not mean that the younger Turner became the stereotypical bookworm. On the contrary, when not reading his favorite author, Ralph Waldo Emerson, he could be found hunting and fishing with his father or engaging in the sort of activities that Mark Twain had imagined for Tom Sawyer.

Appropriately for a man who would have so much influence on American education, Turner excelled as a student and was graduated from Portage's only high school in June, 1878. His senior oration, "The Power of the Press," won first prize in the annual competition, and his reward was a set of Thomas Babington Macaulay's *History of England* (1849-1861). In spite of such foreshadowing, Turner entered the University of Wisconsin at Madison in September, with no idea that his future would be tied to the development of history as a profession. He had inherited a healthy interest in local history from his father, but, in the 1870's, history was not something that an enterprising young man would choose for a career. Not until 1881 would any American university establish a professorship in American history, and in 1884, the year Turner was graduated from college, there were only fifteen professorships and five assistant professorships in history throughout the nation.

On the surface, Turner appeared the typical undergraduate, except that he was actually enrolled as a subfreshman since his preparation in the classics at Portage High School was considered less than adequate. An enthusiastic fraternity man throughout his college career, extracurricular activities absorbed much of his time. In the summer of 1879, however, he underwent a forceful introduction to the more serious side of life. Contracting a nearly fatal case of spinal meningitis, he was unable to return to Madison until the spring of 1881. Turner used the enforced idleness well, studying Greek

and reading widely, and upon reentering college, he found a new love which he would never abandon—history. The matchmaker in this case was Professor William Francis Allen, a remarkable teacher whose ideas about education were extremely progressive for the time in which he lived. Viewing history as understanding the past rather than simply recording past events, Professor Allen was undoubtedly responsible for pushing his gifted student toward a career in history.

While academic life was clearly becoming more and more important to Turner himself, his fellow students knew him primarily as an outstanding orator. Public speaking played an important role in the educational system of the nineteenth century and would turn out to be very important for Turner's future. Winning the university's most prestigious oratorical contests in his junior and senior years made Turner something of a campus celebrity and prompted the offer of an assistant instructorship in rhetoric after his graduation. He initially declined and tried his hand at journalism, but newspaper work was simply not satisfying. In the spring of 1885, he seized the opportunity to return to the university as a temporary replacement for his mentor, Professor Allen, who had been given a temporary leave. Turner quickly recognized that he had found his true vocation; yet, unfortunately, there were no openings in history. At the beginning of the next academic year, he accepted an appointment as an assistant in the department of rhetoric and oratory.

Turner was a natural teacher, and his popularity with Wisconsin's students spread rapidly. At first, he had difficulty overcoming his youthful appearance. Five feet eight inches tall, slightly built with blue eyes and fair hair, the budding professor, according to Madison legend, was often mistaken for a freshman. Perhaps the well-trimmed mustache which he maintained for the remainder of his life was an attempt to add a few years to his appearance. Looks, however, could not hide his magnetic personality or detract from the deep voice and practiced delivery that made his lectures so popular. He soon added American history to his teaching duties and began work on a master's degree in history.

### Life's Work

On July 12, 1893, Professor Frederick Jackson Turner, a thirty-two-year-old teacher from a small, back-country state university, stepped before a group of professional historians meeting in conjunction with the World Columbian Exposition in Chicago. He was expected to present a paper much like the four other papers which had been given earlier that evening, and, certainly, none in the audience anticipated anything out of the ordinary. Indeed, when Turner had finished, the reaction was polite, and his colleagues returned to their hotels, blithely unaware that a revolution inside their profession had begun. This essay, "The Significance of the Frontier in American History," not only marked the introduction of Turner's famous "frontier thesis," which would dominate American historical debate for the next thirty years, but also signaled the emergence of the modern, academically trained, professional historian as the chief steward of the nation's past. For the remainder of his life, Turner's name would be associated with his particular interpretation of his country's history.

The frontier thesis grew in Turner's mind as a reflection of his background, his academic training, and his role as a college teacher. Already influenced by Allen as an undergraduate, Turner worked toward his master's degree under Allen's guidance. Though a classicist by training, Allen was sympathetic to Turner's interest in regional history and accepted "The Character and Influence of the Fur Trade in Wisconsin" as the subject of his master's thesis. Such research naturally drew Turner's attention to the development of the West, but his ideas were also influenced by his experience as a teacher. Modeling himself after Allen, Turner encouraged his students to seek to understand the past as well as ascertain the supposed "facts." In attempting to explain the "why" behind historical events to his students, Turner made his classes into a laboratory within which he could test new ideas.

There was also a very practical element in Turner's development: He wanted to make a career for himself. This element became much more important after he met Caroline Mae Sherwood of Chicago in 1887. His desire to marry the young woman, a feat which he accomplished in late 1889, motivated him to establish himself more firmly in the academic community. In the rapidly developing American system of higher education, this meant that he needed to acquire the coveted Ph.D. degree. In September, 1888, after receiving his master's degree in June, the loyal Midwesterner found himself in the exotic atmosphere of Baltimore as a graduate student at The Johns Hopkins University.

At the end of the nineteenth century, Johns Hopkins was the center from which a group of truly professional historians was beginning to emerge. The real point of origin was the famed historical seminar of Herbert Baxter Adams. Turner's experience at Johns Hopkins would be instrumental in completing his growth as a trained scholar, but ironically his own ideas ran counter to the Teutonic or "germ" school of history stressed by Adams himself. This school concentrated on the European origins of American institutions and could hardly be expected to appeal to a man whose heart never left the forests of Wisconsin. Adams, however, was tolerant enough to accept a revised version of Turner's master's thesis as a dissertation and wise enough to recognize his student's basic ability.

When Turner returned to Madison in 1889, he was awarded an assistant professorship in history and prepared to play the role of a junior faculty member. In December of that year, however, his career received a boost from an unwelcome event, the sudden death of Allen. Turner was soon made a full professor of history and chairman of the history department. For the next twenty years, he would dedicate himself to building Wisconsin's history department into one of the finest in the nation. His seminars in history soon eclipsed those of Adams and became the spawning ground for dozens of the young doctors of philosophy demanded by the expanding American university system.

The frontier thesis, which had caused so little immediate notice in Chicago, became the most important and controversial interpretation in American history during the first three decades of the twentieth century. Explaining the exact nature of Turner's analysis, however, is surprisingly difficult. His colorful rhetoric, which always reflected his background as an accomplished orator, led to vague generalizations rather than specific arguments. Moreover, Turner's many disciples often exaggerated their master's positions, converting what he intended as only a useful hypothesis into dogma. Basically, Turner believed that the existence of a continual frontier, especially cheap or free land, was the most significant element in American history and was largely responsible for the unique development of American institutions and the American character. The frontier, for example, supposedly created conditions which fostered the establishment of democracy and provided a "safety valve" which prevented labor unrest in the East.

The generally enthusiastic reception of Turner's ideas by professional scholars and their dominance of American history until the 1930's is in part a reflection of Turner's personal success as a colleague and teacher, but it also indicates the harmony between Turner's approach and the intellectual currents of his day. Turner's argument was rooted in Darwinian thought and was unabashedly environmentalist. Human society evolved from the physical conditions to which its members were forced to adapt. Such ideas also fit well with the philosophy of pragmatism being developed by William James and John Dewey and anticipated the relativist position in historical philosophy that would later emerge in the work of Charles Beard and Carl Becker. In fact, Carl Becker was one of Turner's many students.

Fortunately, the influence of Turner's thesis and the spread of his reputation did not depend on his production as a scholar. While he was a tireless researcher, he found writing a chore, and his most significant work is found in numerous short, provocative essays. He produced only one monograph during his lifetime, *The Rise of the New West, 1819-1829* (1906), as part of the American Nation Series. He also published two collections of essays, *The Frontier in American History* (1920) and *Significance of Sections in American History* (1932), the latter of which received the Pulitzer Prize. Another monograph which also received the Pulitzer Prize, *The United States, 1830-1850: The Nation and Its Sections* (1935), was published posthumously.

Part of Turner's difficulty with publishing stemmed from his dedication to his role as a college professor. In addition to spending an inordinate amount of his time and energy with his students, Turner always seemed to be involved in administrative tasks, particularly while at the University of Wisconsin. These duties were not only time consuming but also frustrating. For example, Turner, along with other faculty members, waged an unsuccessful struggle against the growing influence of big-time college football. Such activities, coupled with his commitment to academic excellence whatever the cost, produced friction between the university's board of regents and Wisconsin's most famous professor. In 1910, the same year he was elected president of the American Historical Association, Turner left his alma mater for the more rarefied atmosphere of Harvard, where he served as professor of history until his retirement in 1924. From 1927 until his death on March 14, 1932, Turner kept active as a research associate at Henry E. Huntington Library, San Marino, California.

### Summary

In the years after his death, Turner's famous frontier thesis suffered a barrage of criticism, much of it justified. By the 1950's, Turner's followers were fighting a rearguard action against the developing complexity of interpretation that his style of history had helped to create. Turner himself would not have been surprised; in fact, he would probably have applauded the new developments. He had always stressed the complexity of historical analysis and argued many times that each age must reinterpret the past in the light of present knowledge. Moreover, his frontier thesis had been put forward as a hypothesis rather than a final explanation. In Turner's view, qualification and even rejection of his arguments were part of the process by which human beings understood their past and, thereby, themselves.

Although there are few pure Turnerians left among professional historians in the United States, his legacy remains influential. While the frontier thesis can no longer be accepted as the primary explanation of America's past, there is little doubt that the frontier experience did play a crucial role in making the country unique. Perhaps most important, Turner himself stands as an example of what a professional scholar should be to those who would follow in his footsteps.

### Bibliography


Bennett, James D. *Frederick Jackson Turner.* Boston: Twayne, 1975. A short biography with an annotated bibliography. In addition to the usual biographical information, the author deals with the various criticisms of Turner's thesis and tries to place Turner within the context of American historiography.

Benson, Lee. *Turner and Beard: American Historical Writing Reconsidered.* New York: Free Press, 1960. A historiographical analysis of Turner and Beard and their economic interpretation of history. Provides an excellent examination of the origin of Turner's ideas and the influence of economic theory on his thesis.

Billington, Ray A. *Frederick Jackson Turner: Historian, Scholar, Teacher.* New York: Oxford University Press, 1973. The fullest biography of Turner, by one of his students. While the author is clearly an admirer of Turner, his careful scholarship provides a reasonably well-rounded picture.

Bogue, Allan G. *Frederick Jackson Turner: Strange Roads Going Down.* Norman: University of Oklahoma Press, 1998. Bogue presents a biography of Turner including his theories on the settlement of the western United States, his oratorical skills, and his critics.

Carpenter, Ronald H. *The Eloquence of Frederick Jackson Turner.* San Marino, Calif.: Huntington Library, 1983. An important study of Turner's rhetorical style. The author pays particular attention to the relationship of Turner's background as an orator to his historical analysis.

Hofstadter, Richard. *The Progressive Historians: Turner, Beard, Parrington.* New York: Knopf, 1968. A brilliant historiographical study of the Progressive Era. The author subjects the three most important historians of the period to careful critical analysis.

Jacobs, Wilbur R. *The Historical World of Frederick Jackson Turner, with Selections from His Correspondence.* New Haven, Conn.: Yale University Press, 1968. A selection of Turner's correspondence connected by biographical information. The author's comments are particularly helpful in placing Turner's voluminous correspondence in context.

Taylor, George Rogers, ed. *The Turner Thesis: Concerning the Role of the Frontier in American History.* 3d ed. Lexington, Mass.: Heath, 1972. A selection of articles attacking and defending Turner's thesis.

Turner, Frederick J. *Rereading Frederick Jackson Turner: "The Significance of the Frontier in American History" and Other Essays.* Commentary by John Mack Faragher. New York: Holt, 1994; London: Yale University Press, 1999. Faragher provides an introduction and commentaries on ten of Turner's most important essays on Western United States history.


*David Warren Bowen*

## DESMOND TUTU

*Born:* October 7, 1931; Klerksdorp, South Africa

*Areas of Achievement:* Religion, civil rights, and social reform

*Contribution:* Tutu became the first black Anglican Bishop of Johannesburg and head of the South African Anglican church. He is a leader of the antiapartheid movement, and his 1984 Nobel Peace Prize was a recognition of his contributions to nonviolent resistance to apartheid.

### Early Life

Desmond Mpilo Tutu was born in the gold-mining town of Klerskdorp, Witwatersrand, Transvaal, South Africa, on October 7, 1931. His father, Zachariah Tutu, was a schoolteacher, and his mother, Aletta, was a domestic servant. Although Tutu was baptized a Methodist, his parents later joined the Anglican church.

From an early age, he was profoundly influenced by the idealism of his parents. When he was twelve, the family moved to Johannesburg. His mother was employed as a cook at a missionary school for the blind, where Tutu's desire to serve the underprivileged was kindled. It was also at that school that he met the Anglican priest Father Trevor Huddleston, who had a profound influence on his life. Father Huddleston was a parish priest in Sophiatown, a black slum, and as Bishop Huddleston, became a leading antiapartheid activist in the United Kingdom.

When Tutu was graduated from Western High School in Johannesburg, he was unable to fulfill his ambition of becoming a doctor as his parents could not afford the tuition fees. As an adolescent, he earned money by selling peanuts at suburban railway stations and caddying at Johannesburg's exclusive Killarney golf course.

Having decided to pursue teaching as a career instead, he took a diploma at the Bantu Normal College in Pretoria and a B.A. degree at the University of Johannesburg. From 1954 to 1957, he taught high school in Johannesburg and Krugersdorp. A happy personal event occurred during this period, when he married Leah Nomalizo Shenxane in 1955. His career as a teacher was short-lived, for Tutu resigned in 1957 to protest the "Bantu Education Act," which introduced a discriminatory and inferior educational system for blacks.

Tutu subsequently joined the Community of the Resurrection, the religious order to which Huddleston belonged. Although Tutu has said that he was not motivated to join the ministry by high ideals, his religious conviction grew while studying theology at Saint Peter's Theological College in Johannesburg. He became a deacon in 1960 and was ordained as an Anglican priest in 1961.

### Life's Work

After serving as curate of two churches in Benoni and Alberton, Tutu left for England in 1962. During the four years he spent in London, he earned the bachelor of divinity and master of theology degrees from King's College. He was also assigned to St. Alban's parish in London and St. Mary's parish in Bletchingley, Surrey. When he returned to South Africa in 1967, he lectured at the Federal Theological Seminary in the Ciskei and from 1969 to 1971 at the University of Botswana, Lesotho, and Swaziland, which later became known as the National University of Lesotho at Roma. Tutu returned to England in 1972 as associate director of the Theological Education Fund based in Bromley,

Kent. During the next three years, he was responsible for administering scholarships for the World Council of Churches and traveled widely in sub-Saharan Africa and Asia.

Tutu was rising rapidly in the ranks of the church, and, when he returned to South Africa in 1975, he was appointed the first black Anglican dean of Johannesburg. The following year he was consecrated Bishop of Lesotho. Tutu was becoming more active in the struggle against apartheid, South Africa's oppressive system of institutionalized racism that denies the black majority any political rights. A few weeks before the Soweto riots on June 16, 1976, during which six hundred young blacks were murdered by the security forces, Tutu wrote an open letter to B. J. Vorster, then prime minister, warning him of the dangerous and volatile situation. Vorster dismissed the letter as a "propaganda ploy," and, since the uprising at Soweto, South Africa has faced continuing unrest and instability.

In 1978, Tutu became the first black general secretary of the South African Council of Churches (SACC). the largest ecumenical organization in the country, SACC represents thirteen million Christians (black and white) and is the national representative of the World Council of Churches. Under his leadership, SACC became an important force in the opposition to apartheid and filled the vacuum created by the banning of antiapartheid political parties. Tutu campaigned vigorously against the Pass Laws, the discriminatory and unequal educational system, and the forced relocation of blacks to Bantustans, or so-called homelands. Tutu began the call he has repeated over the years for the imposition of economic sanctions and an end to foreign investment in South Africa. Although the South African government confiscated his passport in 1979, Tutu continued his courageous opposition to its iniquitous system. Like Mahatma Gandhi and Martin Luther King, Jr., Tutu advocated civil disobedience and led many peaceful antigovernment demonstrations. With faith, resoluteness, and dynamism, he became a symbol of peaceful resistance to racial oppression and a leading apostle of interracial conciliation. He gained worldwide prominence, and his stature and reputation were enhanced internationally.

After the South African government restored his passport in 1981, Tutu traveled to the United States and Europe. In speeches and statements during his tour, Tutu reiterated the message that it was necessary for Western nations to apply diplomatic, political, and economic pressure on the South African government if there was to be peaceful change in South Africa. Upon his return to South Africa, his passport was again confiscated by the government. In 1982, Tutu was awarded an honorary doctorate of sacred theology by Columbia University but was denied permission to travel to New York to receive the degree. Michael Sovern, the president of Columbia, then traveled to Johannesburg to confer the degree on him. With his passport revoked, when permitted to leave South Africa, Tutu had to carry "travel documents" that stated that he was of "undetermined nationality."

In 1984, the South African government adopted a new constitution under which Parliament consisted of three segregated chambers, one each for whites, coloreds, and Asians. Blacks, who constitute 73 percent of the population, were still excluded from any political participation in their country. Tutu was an articulate spokesperson for the widespread opposition to the constitution. He denounced it as a "monumental hoax," a scheme to entrench further white minority rule and to give the impression to the world community that apartheid was being dismantled. Also in 1984, Tutu's efforts as a nonviolent crusader for civil and political rights received international recognition when he was awarded the Nobel Peace Prize. He received the news at General Theological Seminary in New York, where he was serving as a visiting professor. Tutu emphasized that the award was not for him alone but was a moving tribute to all those who had played a part in the struggle for racial equality and justice. He announced that he would put the $193,000 prize money into a trust fund for scholarships for black South Africans. Shortly after receiving the Nobel Prize, a synod of twenty-three bishops appointed Tutu the first black Anglican Bishop of Johannesburg.

South Africa had been in a state of turmoil since the introduction of the new constitution. As disenfranchised blacks vented their rage in protests across the country, the government imposed a state of emergency and a ban on mass funerals for the victims of apartheid in the summer of 1985. Tutu defied the government's ban on "political" funerals and continued his efforts to prevent civil war and massive racial bloodshed. He received increasing support from the international community as many companies and financial institutions disinvested in the South African economy. Members of the House of Representatives in the United States Congress adopted legislation banning the importation of Kruggerands into the United States, prohibiting new U.S. bank loans to South Africa and the export of computers and nuclear technology.

In 1986, Tutu set another milestone with his election as Archbishop of Cape Town and head of the Anglican church in South Africa. His installation ceremony at St. George's Cathedral was attended by more than fourteen hundred guests from around the world, including Coretta Scott King, widow of Martin Luther King, Jr., and John T. Walker, the Episcopal Bishop of Washington, D.C.

By 1994, international pressure, guided largely by Tutu, had forced South Africa to abandon the apartheid system. Free elections were held, and Nelson Mandela became South Africa's first black president. In subsequent years, Tutu led an unprecedented attempt to bring about a peaceful reconciliation between the country's bitterly divided populations. The Truth and Reconciliation Commission offered amnesty in return for testimony from participants in apartheid's atrocities. The commission sought to document the grim workings of the system, to shed light on the reasoning of the guilty, and to bring consolation to the bereaved. The commission's final report left some dissatisfied, but the transition had been accomplished without the bloodshed many had feared, thanks in large part to Tutu's dedications to peace and understanding rather than to retribution.

### Summary

For most of his life, Desmond Tutu has been in the vanguard of the struggle for racial justice and equality in South Africa. He has been courageous and outspoken in his denunciation of apartheid. In sermons, speeches, and other public statements, he has drawn attention to the inequalities in South African society and the urgent need of redressing them in order to prevent a catastrophe. He has been a familiar figure leading demonstrations, sometimes risking his own life in confrontations between protesters and security forces. As the Nobel citation stated, Tutu "has shown that to campaign for the cause of peace is not a question of silent acceptance, but rather of arousing consciences and a sense of indignation, strengthening the will and inspiring the human spirit so that it recognises both its own value and its power of victory."

Tutu has been a pathbreaker in a racially segregated society. He has helped to open doors previously closed to blacks, and as head of the Anglican church (to which 75 percent of the South African people belong) he has used his position to be a peacemaker as well. Although Tutu is first and foremost a religious leader, the scope of his activities and influence go far beyond the religious domain into the political and social spheres. When interpreting the Gospel, he stresses its revolutionary aspects; he believes that Christians have a special obligation to become involved in the liberation struggle. Tutu demonstrates that the struggle for political, social, and economic justice in South Africa has made politics and religion a "seamless garment."

### Bibliography

Brittain, James. "Healing a Nation." *Index on Censorship* 25, no. 5 (September-October, 1996). Interview with Tutu, Chairman of South Africa's Truth and Reconciliation Commission, which focuses on the commission's charter—helping the victimized African people.

Bunting, Brian. *The Rise of the South African Reich.* Rev. ed. London and Baltimore: Penguin, 1969. This book, which was first published in 1964, traces the origins and the rise to power of the Nationalist Party, showing the marked similarities between its ideology and that of Nazism. It gives a good illustration of the pillars of apartheid and the manner in which they were erected. It is well documented and highly readable.

Du Boulay, Shirley. *Tutu: Voice of the Voiceless.* London: Hodder and Stoughton, and Grand Rapids, Mich.: Eerdmans, 1988. This book is an excellent biography of Tutu. It contains many intriguing anecdotes.

Hope, Marjorie, and James Young. *The South African Churches in a Revolutionary Situation.* Maryknoll, N.Y.: Orbis, 1981. An insightful book that examines the role of churches within the context of South Africa's apartheid system. It includes a short but lucid portrait of Tutu.

Jaffrey, Zia. "Desmond Tutu." *The Progressive* 62, no. 2 (February, 1998). Interview with Tutu focusing on the hearings of South Africa's Truth and Reconciliation Commission.

Lodge, Tom. *Black Politics in South Africa Since 1945.* London and New York: Longman, 1983. A detailed history of black resistance to apartheid. Although it includes a chapter on early methods of resistance, its strength lies in its analysis of protest movements after World War II.

Murray, Martin J. *South Africa: Time of Agony, Time of Destiny.* London: Verso, 1987. An informed study of the roots and diversity of black opposition to apartheid. It is particularly useful on the new forces that have shaped the resistance groups since the Soweto uprising of 1976.

*Abiodun Williams*

# WALTER ULBRICHT

*Born:* June 30, 1893; Leipzig, Germany
*Died:* August 1, 1973; East Berlin, East Germany
*Areas of Achievement:* Government and politics
*Contribution:* As Moscow's loyal ally, Ulbricht helped to found East Germany and make it into the most stable and prosperous socialist state in Eastern Europe during his lifetime. His oppressive rule in the 1950's and 1960's, including the building of the Berlin Wall in 1961, prolonged the Cold War and cemented the political division of Germany.

## Early Life

Walter Ulbricht was born in Leipzig, Germany, on June 30, 1893. Son of an impoverished Social Democratic tailor, he learned about radical socialism at home and in the city's seamy Naundörfchen workers' district. The family's poverty forced "Red Walter"—as he was known to classmates—to leave school at the age of fourteen and apprentice himself to a cabinetmaker. Ulbricht's political education continued, however, first in Leipzig's Socialist youth movement, and, after his journeyman travels across Europe in 1911 and 1912, in the Social Democratic Party (SPD). It was in this prewar, proletarian environment that his dogmatic Marxist outlook took shape.

World War I pushed this shy but talented young Socialist in radical new directions. In August, 1914, he joined revolutionary Social Democrat Karl Liebknecht in condemning his party's support for the kaiser's war. Drafted in 1915, he served unwillingly on the Macedonian front and, in 1918, on the Western Front, where he twice tried unsuccessfully to desert. Following the November, 1918, revolution, Ulbricht returned to Leipzig, where he helped to found the local Communist Party (KPD).

The 1920's provided Ulbricht with the opportunity to work his way up through the ranks of the Communist Party. By 1921 he had been named to a salaried Party post in Thuringia; in 1923 he was elected to the KPD's central committee and transferred to Berlin as a paid Party functionary. By the end of the decade he had also taken charge of the Party's pivotal Berlin organization. In addition, Ulbricht was elected to the Thuringian State Assembly in 1926, and then in 1928 to the Reichstag, a seat he held until 1933.

Ulbricht's steady advance was the result in large part of his organizational talent, tireless capacity for work, and personal dedication. Another reason was his ability to avoid taking sides in factional disputes within the Party. By proclaiming his loyalty to Moscow and the Communist International (Comintern), he elevated himself above Party wrangling. Trips to Moscow in 1922 and 1924 sealed Ulbricht's allegiance. Thereafter he dutifully followed the Comintern line, including orders in the early 1930's to attack Social Democrats and the Weimar Republic rather than National Socialism.

## Life's Work

When Adolf Hitler came to power in January, 1933, Ulbricht was forced to emigrate, first to Paris, where he joined the KPD's exile organization, and eventually to Moscow, where he served as the KPD's permanent representative to the Comintern from 1938 to 1943. He loyally defended Joseph Stalin's every move, from the bloody purges to the Nazi-Soviet Nonaggression Pact of 1939, and thus survived the violence that eliminated so many other German exiles. During World War II, he distributed Soviet propaganda among German prisoners of war and prepared small groups of German Communists to implement Stalin's plans for a postwar bourgeois democratic republic in Germany.

The most crucial phase of Ulbricht's career began on April 30, 1945, when he and a small handpicked group of German Communists returned to Berlin in a Red Army plane. Subordinated to Soviet military directives and overshadowed by better known KPD survivors such as Wilhelm Pieck and Otto Grotowohl, Ulbricht nevertheless exercised considerable influence over postwar reconstruction in the Soviet occupation zone. He engineered the reorganization of local administration, helped to create the Communist-dominated Socialist Unity Party (SED) in 1946, and took charge of de-Nazification and economic recognization. When Moscow's plans for Germany changed and integration into the Soviet bloc became the top priority in 1947, Ulbricht ruthlessly pushed through the required Sovietization.

Ulbricht also used every opportunity to consolidate his own authority within the SED. During the occupation period (1945-1949), he outmaneuvered or neutralized political rivals who questioned his Moscow-backed authority. With the establishment of East Germany in 1949, Ulbricht stepped directly into the political spotlight, assuming the key post

of SED general secretary a few months later. A decade later he added the positions of head of state and chairman of the National Defense Council. Thereafter he controlled every major decision affecting central economic planning, forced socialization, military expansion, and Soviet East German relations.

Yet governing a socialist state in Eastern Europe during the height of the Cold War was no easy task, especially when that country was German. For Ulbricht it meant a difficult balancing act that required him to implement Moscow's orders, appease Eastern Europe's suspicions, and maintain strict controls over an untrusting East German citizenry. As long as Stalin lived, he could depend on Soviet backing and leadership. When the Soviet dictator died in 1953, however, Ulbricht encountered a series of challenges that tested his authority and demonstrated the precarious nature of socialist rule in Eastern Europe.

The most serious challenge came after Stalin's death in 1953. As a post-Stalinist political "thaw" swept Eastern Europe, disaffected construction workers in East Berlin staged a public protest against increased work norms, which, on June 17, 1953, mushroomed into a nationwide uprising against the East German state. Soviet troops had to be called in to suppress this workers' revolt against the workers' state. Coming at a time when rivals in the SED and their allies in Moscow were poised to replace the general secretary with a more reform-minded leader, the workers' revolt discredited the opposition and saved Ulbricht's political career. His harsh, Stalinist methods now seemed the only way to keep East Germany in the Soviet camp.

Another challenge to Ulbricht's authority came with de-Stalinization in 1956. Shocking revelations about Stalin's past raised new questions about the SED leader and forced relaxation of a number of arbitrary Stalinist controls. Before serious opposition to Ulbricht could form, however, revolts in Poland and Hungary once again undercut the reform movement, leaving the SED dictator free to restore his hard-line rule.

Economic problems also haunted Ulbricht in the late 1950's. He might boldly promise that rapid socialization would enable East Germany to overtake West Germany economically by the 1960's, but East Germans remained skeptical. In fact, lagging economic growth and ruthless agricultural collectivization in 1960 were driving thousands to flee the country through the open door of West Berlin. To halt this mass exodus of human resources, a flight that reached two thousand a day by mid-1961, Ulbricht demanded and received Soviet approval to begin building the Berlin Wall on August 13, 1961. The Berlin Wall provoked yet another Berlin Crisis, and it was heralded in the West as a monument to socialist failure, but it also began an economic turnaround in East Germany that rapidly transformed this nation of seventeen million into Eastern Europe's most prosperous state.

To Westerners, Ulbricht's strict rule changed little during the 1960's. His endless diatribes against West German imperialism, stern warnings to East European leaders about the dangers of reform, leading role in suppressing Czechoslovakia's 1968 reform movement, and ruthless elimination of dissent at home inspired little but enmity and disdain. Yet despite his well-deserved reputation as a servant of Moscow and Sovietization, Ulbricht spent the years after 1963 distancing East Germany from the Soviet model and emphasizing East Germany's independent achievements. Outsiders overlooked Ulbricht's flexibility in questions of economic reform, his progressive approach to education and social services, and the mounting respect he enjoyed in both Eastern Europe and the Soviet Union.

In the end, however, Ulbricht fell victim to his quest for independent leadership in the Soviet bloc. As Soviet Party leader Leonid Ilich Brezhnev sought to ease tensions with the West in the early 1970's, Ulbricht's rigid opposition to détente, especially with regard to Berlin, became intolerable to Moscow. His recalcitrance combined with mounting SED reservations about Ulbricht's grasp of contemporary problems (he was, after all, seventy-eight and ailing) led to his dismissal on May 3, 1971. He retained several ceremonial posts, including that of head of state, until his death on August 1, 1973, but his influence in these last years remained negligible. After a quarter century in power, not one foreign official mourner participated in his state funeral.

### Summary

Walter Ulbricht belonged to the first generation of European Communist leaders. More "apparatchik" than political revolutionary, he rose to prominence because of his close ties to the Soviet Union. Yet his success also resulted from exceptional personal diligence and political acumen. To be sure, he lacked the personal warmth, public charisma, and intellectual temper to give Communism a human face. He was too uninspiring, peremptory, and pitiless for that. Yet Ulbricht did possess the personal commitment, organizational talent, and administrative efficiency to make socialism work better in East Germany than in any other Soviet bloc country.

Despite his Moscow orientation, however, he always remained more German than socialist. Contemporaries remember him for his wiry goatee beard trimmed close in the imperial style, his fluting, sing-song voice, and his strong Saxon accent. His penchant for Prussian formality and order, and his clear feelings of national pride were also very German. He lived simply, devoting little time to family or personal interests—except sports. Almost every minute of every day was spent attending to the affairs of state, and as time passed it seemed as if no detail escaped his personal attention. His authoritative pronouncements in later years covered everything from architecture to fishing, from history to art, and they raised eyebrows even among loyal East Germans. Yet despite advancing age and mounting infirmities, he never weakened in his determination to keep the SED in power and East Germany in the vanguard of world socialism.

### Bibliography

Childs, David. *The GDR: Moscow's German Ally.* 2d ed. London and Boston: Unwin Hyman, 1988. This is the most comprehensive examination of East Germany available in English. Childs locates Ulbricht effectively in the context of his times and crises.

Kopstein, Jeffrey. "Ulbricht Embattled: The Quest for Socialist Modernity in the Light of New Sources." *Europe-Asia Studies* 46, no. 4 (1994). Examines East Germany's New Economic System (NES) implemented by Ulbricht in 1963 and the reasons for its demise.

Lippmann, Heinz. *Honecker and the New Politics of Europe.* Translated by Helen Sebba. New York: Macmillan, 1972; London: Angus and Robertson, 1973. A political biography of Ulbricht's chief protégé and successor by a former SED functionary who witnessed firsthand Ulbricht's dominant role in East Germany.

Ludz, Peter C. "Continuity and Change Since Ulbricht." *Problems of Communism* 21 (March/April, 1972): 56-67. This article provides an excellent analysis of Ulbricht's lasting political legacy at home and abroad. The author, a professor of political science at the University of Bielefeld in West Germany, has studied the East German political elite for a number of years.

Raack, R. C. "Stalin's Plans for World War Two Told by a High Comintern Source." *Historical Journal* 38, no. 4 (December, 1995). Discussion of Stalin's desires for the course of World War II as voiced by Ulbricht. Includes scenarios for wartime operations and information on Hitler's views of communism.

Sandford, Gregory W. *From Hitler to Ulbricht: The Communist Reconstruction of East Germany, 1945-46.* Princeton, N.J.: Princeton University Press, 1983. An excellent study of the origins of Communist rule in East Germany that explains the transition from Soviet military occupation to SED rule. Ulbricht's role is discussed only in broad outlines.

Sodaro, Michael J. "Ulbricht's Grand Design: Economics, Ideology, and the GDR's Response to Détente—1967-1971." *World Affairs* 142

(1980): 147-168. This article describes Ulbricht's unsuccessful attempt to develop an economic and political policy that would prevent détente with the West and preserve East German influence in the Soviet bloc.

Stern, Carola. *Ulbricht: A Political Biography.* London: Pall Mall Press, and New York: Praeger, 1965. The only full-scale biography available in English. The book attempts to assess Ulbricht evenhandedly but is limited by numerous gaps and its 1964 publication date.

Wilhelm, Berhard, "Walter Ulbricht: Moscow's Man in East Germany." In *Leaders of the Communist World*, edited by Rodger Swearingen. New York: Free Press, 1971. A short biographical article emphasizing Ulbricht's fanatical loyalty to Soviet Communism and dictatorial control in East Germany. It is based on East and West German sources and provides important information about Ulbricht's pre-1945 career and major challenges to his authority between 1949 and 1968.

*Rennie W. Brantz*

# MIGUEL DE UNAMUNO Y JUGO

*Born:* September 29, 1864; Bilbao, Spain
*Died:* December 31, 1936; Salamanca, Spain
*Area of Achievement:* Literature
*Contribution:* One of the outstanding Spanish men of letters of the twentieth century, Unamuno wrote everything from poetry and novels to philosophy, drama, and cultural criticism; he served the cause of Spanish republicanism, was a key figure in the expression of the existentialist tension between reason and faith, and influenced two generations of Spanish students at the University of Salamanca.

## Early Life

Miguel de Unamuno y Jugo was born September 29, 1864, in Bilbao, Spain, the first son and third of the six children of Félix de Unamuno and Salomé de Jugo. His father had gone to Mexico as a young man, accumulated some money, and then returned to marry his much younger niece, Salomé. He had also acquired several hundred books on philosophy, history, and the physical and social sciences, which helped form his son's mind. From an early age, death preoccupied Miguel. His father, two of Miguel's sisters, and a school friend died by 1873, producing a mysterious fear in the young boy. Unamuno's struggle to accept his own mortality became one of the major themes of his religious, philosophical, and literary work.

Miguel completed a traditional, Catholic secondary education at sixteen and then was enrolled in the Central University of Madrid, torn between his love for his childhood sweetheart, Concepción ("Concha") Lizárraga, and a mystical belief that God wanted him to become a priest. Fascinated with language since listening to his father talk with a Frenchman in French, Unamuno wrote his doctoral dissertation on the origins and prehistory of the Basque race. In Madrid he applied reason to his religious faith and lost it. He struggled for the remainder of his life to overcome his doubt. After receiving his doctorate in 1884, he returned to Bilbao, competed for a university teaching position, taught private classes, and wrote for local periodicals. Impatient to wait until securing a permanent teaching position, he married Concha on January 31, 1891, and, under the influence of his wife and his mother, began religious observance again. In 1891, he also won a competition for the chair in Greek language and literature at the University of Salamanca.

## Life's Work

In the provincial university town of twenty-three thousand, with the faded glory of its medieval university and magnificent, café-lined central plaza, Unamuno found the tranquillity to read voraciously and widely, ponder the human condition, write insatiably, and rear his family. Yet he soon lost interest in teaching Greek: given the desperate problems facing Spain, he decided that the nation really did not need more Hellenists. Although he conscientiously met his pedagogical responsibilities, Unamuno devoted the rest of his time to writing novels, poetry, and essays intended to illuminate the solution to Spain's problems and his own concerns about man's condition. He also associated himself with Spanish socialism, believing it offered man his best hope of liberty through a religion of humanity, but refused to join the party. In fact, his interest in socialism was primarily religious and ethical; Unamuno's heart was anarchist.

Transcendental questions troubled Unamuno. In 1896, Raimundo Jenaro, the third of his nine children, was born, but shortly after birth the infant contracted meningitis, which produced fatal encephalitis, although the child lingered until 1902. His child's condition agonized Unamuno. Why was God punishing an innocent child? Was it because of Unamuno's own sins, perhaps for having abandoned his Catholic faith? He was desperate for consolation, spent days in meditation and prayer, yet remained anguished. God did not answer, and Unamuno was obsessed with suicide and beset with angina, insomnia, and depression. Not only was reason unable to bring him to a knowledge of God, but it told him that God did not exist, that death brought the finality of nothingness. Yet Unamuno's despair at the inevitability of death forced him to hope and led him to the paradoxical solution of creating God for himself through his own faith. When he began reading the works of Søren Kierkegaard in 1900, he discovered a kindred being, although Unamuno had already developed the fundamentals of his own thought.

Meanwhile, Unamuno poured forth articles for Spanish and Latin American periodicals plus novels, plays, and criticism to supplement his meager academic salary. In 1895, he published a series of essays, later reedited as *En torno al casticismo*, which urged a return to the bedrock of tradition, to the study of the Spanish people, as the first step in confronting the nation's decadence. *Paz en la guerra* (1897; *Peace in War*, 1983), sometimes called the first existentialist novel, reflected his experiences during the Carlist siege of Bilbao (1874-1876). Two plays, *La esfinge* (1898) and *La venda* (1899), and an analysis of Spanish higher education, *De la enseñanza superior en España* (1899), soon followed, as did *Nicodemo el fariseo* (1899), which used Saint John's account of Nicodemus' meeting with Christ as a dramatic vehicle for stating the basic theme of all his remaining work: man's desire for God and his existential will to believe.

In 1900, Unamuno became rector of the university, despite opposition from conservatives who disliked the outsider from Bilbao for his socialist rhetoric and his unorthodox religious views. On taking office, he appointed himself to a new chair of the history of the Spanish language, declared that Spain was ready to be discovered, and urged that the students study popular culture. Dressed idiosyncratically in his "uniform," he appeared a cross between a Protestant minister and an owl; he wore a dark suit, with vest and white shirt buttoned to the top, but no tie, and metal-rimmed eyeglasses, and had an aquiline nose and a closely cropped and pointed graying beard.

Unamuno energetically joined in the campaign of the "Generation of 1898" to renew Spain following the loss of its last overseas colonies in 1898. Yet while others called for Spain to emulate the science, technology, and democracy of northern Europe and the United States, Unamuno rejected mass society and focused upon the potential of the individual. His essays entitled *La Vida de Don Quijote y Sancho* (1905; *The Life of Don Quixote and Sancho*, 1927) he considered genuine Spanish philosophy. Subjectively choosing parts of Cervantes' novel and ignoring relevant scholarship, Unamuno resurrected Quixote in his own image, a man who recreated the world around him through his own will to believe. Although some Spanish republicans looked to Unamuno to lead, or at least to participate in a revolution against the decadent monarchy, he opposed all revolution except in the individual heart. He found José Ortega y Gasset and other Spanish intellectuals too enamored of modern science and declared that Spain should let the northern Europeans invent and then apply their inventions.

Unamuno's religious thought received its fullest expression in *Del sentimiento trágico de la vida en los hombres y en los pueblos* (1913; *The Tragic Sense of Life in Men and Peoples*, 1921). Then, in 1914, the government unexpectedly and without explanation removed him as rector. Liberals and socialists supported him in the ensuing controversy. During World War I, he supported the Allied powers. His novel *Abel Sánchez: Una historia de pasión* (1917; *Abel Sánchez*, 1947) portrayed Cain as Abel's victim and questioned why God accepted the latter's smug offerings while rejecting those of his brother. In his powerful *El Cristo de Velásquez* (1920; *The Christ of Velázquez*, 1951), art and spiritual longing seek in Christ the possibility of redemption from death, while Unamuno eschews all dogma and cult.

For publishing in Valencia an article critical of the monarchy, a court there condemned Unamuno in 1920 to sixteen years' imprisonment. At the same time he was presented in both Bilbao and Madrid as a candidate for the national parliament but refused to campaign and was not elected. With his sentence under appeal, the faculty at Salamanca elected him vice-rector in 1922. Then, to the dismay of his supporters, he agreed to meet with the king, leading to criticism that he was self-serving and only wanted the rectorship. While awaiting appeal of his sentence, he took care to avoid offending the monarchy but became convinced that Spain was headed for dictatorship. Time bore out his forebodings, and General Miguel Primo de Rivera seized power with the connivance of Alfonso XIII. In early 1924, Primo de Rivera exiled Unamuno to the Canary Islands, stripping him of his salary and positions at Salamanca despite national and international protests. At Fuerteventura, he planned with some French friends to escape, but Primo de Rivera granted him amnesty, although subjecting him to certain restrictions upon his return. Unamuno refused to return and went into voluntary exile in France to wait for the fall of the dictatorship.

Unamuno passed the years of exile, first in Paris and then in Hendaye along the Basque border. They were years of despair and loneliness, since he refused to let members of his family take turns living with him, wanting his exile to be a moral protest. While in Paris, he published *L'Agonie du christianisme* (1925; *The Agony of Christianity*, 1928), a difficult but intense and poetical restatement of his anguish caused by loving an unreachable God, from which torment the only respite was death. With Primo de Rivera's fall, Unamuno reentered Spain on February 9, 1930, and returned to Salamanca. Faculty, students, and workers demanded his reinstatement as rector. His greatest novel, *San Manuel Bueno, mártir* (1933; *Saint Manuel Bueno, Martyr*, 1956), soon appeared. It tells the story of a priest who loses his faith but assumes the ethical obligation of protecting his parishioners from disbelief by setting an example of saintliness, teaching them to pray, and consoling himself by consoling them.

With the abdication of Alfonso XIII, Spain became a republic on April 14, 1931, and the municipal government of Salamanca named Unamuno an honorary magistrate for his role in the triumph of republicanism. The university cloister also appointed him rector, and some rumored that Unamuno wanted to be President of Spain. On April 27, the republic designated him president of the Council of Public Instruction, and Salamanca elected him as one of its representatives to the constituent assembly. In its deliberations Unamuno rarely participated except to stress unity, hoping to ward off regionalism. Increasingly disturbed by the factionalism and the anti- or irreligious stance of the leftists, he became openly critical of the republic, refused to be a candidate in the 1933 elections, and resigned from the Council of Public Instruction. Adding to his despondency were the deaths of his wife and eldest daughter in 1934. He retired from his university chair that September at age seventy, but the President of Spain decreed Unamuno rector of Salamanca for life and created a special chair in his name for him. The following year the republic named him a citizen of honor, and in 1936 the University of Oxford gave him an honorary doctorate.

After the outbreak of the civil war in July, 1936, the government removed Unamuno as rector because of his criticism of the republic. The Nationalists, however, soon captured Salamanca and rewarded Unamuno's support by reappointing him rector. Yet Unamuno had come to see the war as national insanity. In a ceremony on October 12 attended by faculty, some Nationalist military leaders, and townspeople, he courageously denounced the speech of a general who had exalted anti-intellectualism and death. Confined to his home for his protest, Unamuno died on December 31, 1936.

## Summary

Paradoxical and prickly, egocentric and sincere, Miguel de Unamuno y Jugo inevitably generated controversy. In his fiction and poetry, he sacrificed art to philosophical concerns, especially his religious despair and struggle for faith. Yet to Rubén Darío, the great Latin American poet, Unamuno was first and foremost a poet himself. His philosophy was not systematic and careful, and his assertions were sometimes outlandish and exaggerated. Scholars and critics even disagree regarding Unamuno's religious views, some arguing that he was an atheist and others that his belief was sincere. Certainly he constituted a thorny problem for Spanish Catholicism, which eventually banned several of his works.

Yet through the paradox, the rant, and the self-preoccupation, Unamuno's energy, determination, despair, and hope are unmistakable. The volume of his work was tremendous, and its breadth and weight placed him in the vanguard of Spanish intellectual life. With Kierkegaard and Friedrich Wilhelm Nietzsche, he laid out the existentialist dilemma, preparing the way for Martin Heidegger, Karl Jaspers, and Jean-Paul Sartre. He loved Spain deeply, despite its flaws, and became a sort of Quixote himself, tilting at transcendental windmills and giants that few had the courage or will to perceive.

## Bibliography

Callahan, David. "The Early Reception of Miguel de Unamuno in England, 1907-1939." *The Modern Language Review* 91, no. 2 (April, 1996). The author examines the reasons for Miguel de Unamuno's mediocre reception in English literary circles.

Ellis, Robert R. *The Tragic Pursuit of Being: Unamuno and Sartre.* Tuscaloosa: University of Alabama Press, 1988. A short comparison of the existentialism of Unamuno and Sartre.

Ferrater Mora, José. *Unamuno: A Philosophy of Tragedy.* Translated by Philip Silver. Berkeley: University of California Press, 1962. An excellent, brief survey of Unamuno's philosophy.

Ilie, Paul. *Unamuno: An Existential View of Self and Society.* Madison: University of Wisconsin Press, 1967. Considers Unamuno's contributions to existentialism in relation to Kierkegaard, Nietzsche, Heidegger, Jaspers, and Sartre.

Marías, Julían. *Miguel de Unamuno.* Translated by Frances M. López-Morillas. Cambridge, Mass.: Harvard University Press, 1942. Old but insightful, this work analyzes Unamuno's contribution to philosophy, with occasional biographical references.

Nozick, Martin. *Miguel de Unamuno.* New York: Twayne, 1971. Together with a short biography, this work is an analysis of Unamuno's thought and an evaluation of his literary art. Contains a good bibliography.

Rudd, Margaret Thomas. *The Lone Heretic: A Biography of Miguel de Unamuno y Jugo.* Austin: University of Texas Press, 1963. The most thorough biography in English but problematic in some of its details and interpretations.

*Kendall W. Brown*

# HAROLD C. UREY

*Born:* April 29, 1893; Walkerton, Indiana
*Died:* January 5, 1981; La Jolla, California
*Area of Achievement:* Science
*Contribution:* Urey discovered deuterium, the heavy isotope of hydrogen, as well as methods of isotope separation. He founded the modern science of cosmochemistry, devoted to understanding the origin and development of the solar system.

## Early Life

Harold Clayton Urey's life and career spanned a period of rapid change and development in the United States and the world. He grew up as a country boy, first in Indiana and later in Montana. By his own account, he was seventeen years old when he first saw an automobile; less than sixty years later, he held in his hand a rock from the surface of the moon, of which he was by then the leading student.

Growing up in the country and living mainly outdoors as an adolescent undoubtedly contributed to the rugged good health and stamina that he exhibited throughout his long life. At the same time, it did slow his entry into the world of scientific research. After he was graduated from high school, he did not go directly to college but spent three years as a teacher in country schools, one of which was a one-room school of the sort long since relegated to folklore. He was inspired by a friend to enter the University of Montana, where he majored in biology. He had to work to stay in college; this included periods as a waiter, as a construction worker, and finally as an instructor of biology. When the United States entered World War I, Urey found a job as an industrial chemist in Philadelphia. Apparently, he did not enjoy it much. He later said that this was one of the experiences that nudged him back toward a university career. He returned first to the University of Montana as an instructor for two years. Then came his first great break and the only one he ever needed: In 1921, he was admitted to graduate school in chemistry at the University of California, Berkeley.

The department chairman there was Gilbert Newton Lewis, the leading physical chemist in the United States, and, arguably, in the world. His colleagues were all eminent scholars. Urey's fellow graduate students were an incredibly bright bunch, most of whom were to be among the leaders of the next generation. Everyone worked very hard, including nights and weekends; (nearly) everyone helped his neighbor. At the same time, there was very little money for research, probably less than one percent of what such departments would have in the years to come. All apparatuses were home-built, mostly out of "sealing wax and string." The total population of staff and students was very small. The journals were thin and easy to keep up with, even though authors had much more freedom to ramble then. The center of the world of scientific research was in Europe, and nearly all of what there was in the United States was east of the Mississippi River. Berkeley was unique.

## Life's Work

Once Urey had entered this world and measured himself against it, he moved fast. He completed his Ph.D. work in 1923 and moved on to Niels Bohr's institute in Copenhagen on a fellowship. Bohr was already established as the central figure in atomic and nuclear physics. Urey met many other leaders in physics and chemistry while in Europe. He also

had his own first brush with fame, just missing out on the discovery that electrons, thought of as points with negative charge, actually spin on their axes like tops.

He returned to the United States to take a teaching position at The Johns Hopkins University. Because he was a chemist with a strong grasp of physics, many lines of work were open to him. His early papers were mainly related to the way molecules interact with light, using the then-new concepts of quantum theory to understand a wide range of phenomena. He formed a lifelong association with Joseph Mayer and Maria Mayer, who were also to enjoy distinguished scientific careers (Maria Mayer received the Nobel Prize in 1964). In 1929, he moved to Columbia University.

Urey's most important discovery came two years later. This was the period when the word "isotope" was new, and the whole periodic table was being searched for stable isotopes—atoms with the same place in the chemists' periodic table but with different weights. Urey followed this subject closely, since he foresaw the importance which these isotopes would come to have in many fields. After the discovery of the heavy isotopes of oxygen, he saw what had not been seen by others, namely, that this implied the existence of a rare heavy isotope of the lightest element, hydrogen. This had been searched for earlier, as part of a general survey, but not with the intensity and skill Urey and his collaborators then brought to the task. In a matter of months, they succeeded.

This isotope is so distinct from the usual, light hydrogen that Urey gave it a special name, deuterium (meaning "the second one"). Water made with it ("heavy water") boils at a temperature a few degrees higher than the usual kind and even looks slightly different. One of the first responses to the discovery was a murder mystery by S. S. Van Dine, in which the almost perfect crime involved poisoning the victim with a glass of heavy water. There is this much fact behind the fiction: The chemical properties of hydrogen and deuterium are different enough that aquatic organisms cannot live in pure heavy water.

The award of the Nobel Prize to Urey in 1934 sealed the recognition of his stature as a world-class figure in science. The time, in the midst of the Depression, must have made the money most welcome to a professor with a young family. His generosity and farsightedness were shown by two uses of the money: He loaned some of it to a colleague, Isidor Rabi, who used it for research that won for him the Nobel Prize a few years later, and he helped one of his graduate students, Mildred Cohn, to stay in school and complete her Ph.D. She, too, along with other students of his, has had a distinguished career.

In the remaining years before World War II, Urey centered his efforts on the practical separation of isotopes on a scale large enough to permit the power of isotopic methods to be exploited in physical and chemical research. He worked not only on deuterium but also on heavy isotopes of carbon, nitrogen, oxygen, and chlorine, all essential elements for life and for most important chemical reactions. He found time also to be the first editor of a new journal, the *Journal of Chemical Physics*, which became immediately the most widely read journal in the field.

When atomic energy and atomic weapons came into sight around 1940, Urey's Columbia colleagues Enrico Fermi and Leo Szilard were among the first to undertake work in the field. It seems to have been universally agreed that Urey should lead the effort to separate the fissionable isotope of uranium, U-235, from the much larger mass of U-238 in the natural element. Urey took up the challenge and became the director of the SAM Laboratory of Columbia, which developed the gas diffusion process used in the huge plant at Oak Ridge, Tennessee. The speed and success of this development were unmatched then, and probably would be quite impossible today.

Urey had always had a strong interest in politics, and the events at Hiroshima and Nagasaki gave him a feeling of personal responsibility which he never lost. Especially in the early postwar years, when he had moved to the University of Chicago together with Fermi, the Mayers, Szilard, Willard Libby, Edward Teller, and others, he spent much of his time writing, speaking, and lobbying in an effort to bring nuclear weapons and nuclear power under control in some internationally agreed-upon way. As hope waned that sanity would prevail, he turned back toward the laboratory. Like some others of that generation, however, he found that his prewar research interests had lost their excitement for him, and he looked around for new directions. He found them in the natural world.

His deep knowledge of isotopic processes was first applied to the "Urey temperature scale," a method of determining the temperatures at which organisms grew (or rocks formed) in ancient periods, using the subtle isotopic patterns of oxygen found in fossil shells or rocks. With his students, he pioneered studies which made clear the history of ice ages and even of the life cycles of species long extinct. He was fond of exhibiting a small fossil of an organism extinct for more than two hundred million years, a belemnite, and sharing his discovery that it had lived for four years and died in the spring.

Meanwhile, he broadened this historic interest to a general search for understanding of the earliest records of the origin of the earth, sun, and planets, and of the origin of life. Immersing himself in the literature of the subject, he quickly came to believe, correctly, that he could do better. The first great result was his book, *The Planets: Their Origin and Development* (1952), which raised the discussion of the subject to a new level and may be said to have begun the science of cosmochemistry. Two other landmark papers, one with his student Harmon Craig on meteorites and one with Hans Suess on the abundance of the elements, marked further progress. In this same period, his student Stanley Miller performed a classic experiment which gave support to Urey's ideas on the origin of life and has stimulated much further work. Many of the later leaders in cosmochemistry have been students of Urey or have otherwise been closely associated with Urey.

In 1958, on reaching the "normal" retirement age of sixty-five, Urey moved to the new campus of the University of California, San Diego. The rapid growth of this university to high standing in science owes much to his inspiration and efforts. At the age of eighty, he was still keeping to a full work schedule and publishing regularly. He published his last scientific paper at age eighty-four.

Urey thought much about the qualities needed to do great work in science, and his prescription may be worth recording. First, he said, one needs skills—intellectual, manual, and so on. These (including a high I.Q.) are not especially difficult to find. The second requirement is energy, drive, determination—this, in the required degree, is less common. Third is "problem sense," the ability to pick out the most important things that one is just able to do. This skill is really rare. Urey himself fit this analysis precisely. His influence on others was especially a result of this problem sense, which can apparently be learned to a degree by example.

There are many stories told about Harold Urey, and quite a few of them are true. They illustrate two of his most obvious qualities: his incredible powers of concentration and his bad memory. These qualities were linked, since a man thinking day and night about a scientific problem can hardly be expected to remember names and faces, or even whether he has eaten lunch. There were times when he literally could not hear people talking directly to him. There are fewer stories about his personal courage, his love of children, or how children loved him, yet these traits were equally striking to those who knew him.

He received many honors and medals and enjoyed them all. Like Mark Twain before him, he most enjoyed his honorary degree from Oxford University and the bright red academic robe that came with it, allowing him to outshine his black-robed colleagues on state occasions.

His personal life was simple and happy. Married for almost sixty years to Frieda Daum Urey, he had four children and numerous grandchildren. They had many friends and loved to socialize, enriching the lives of others.

### Summary

Harold Urey was one of a small handful of native-born American scientists whose abilities and achievements made them equals of the great Europeans who came to the United States after the rise of Adolf Hitler. Together, these brilliant scholars led the effort to produce first the atom bomb, radar, and other military devices in World War II and then had a part in the rapid growth of the United States to world leadership in science and technology in the years that followed. They did this both by their own achievements and by training a generation of students who followed them into positions of leadership.

Urey's own discoveries continue to have consequences. Deuterium is a key ingredient in the hydrogen (fusion) bomb, as is U-235 in fission weapons and nuclear power. Fusion power is not yet a reality, but if it can be harnessed, it may provide a source of power, available to all countries and sufficient for millions of years at current rates of usage. Stable isotopes have uses in every field of scientific research.

The personal qualities of pioneers also leave an imprint on later generations. Scientists who use Urey as a model, consciously or otherwise, are honoring qualities considered as characteristically American—generosity, neighborliness, hard work, and clean living.

### Bibliography

Cohen, S. K. P., S. K. Runcorn, H. E. Suess, and H. G. Thode. *Biographical Memoirs of the Royal Society.* Vol. 29, 623-659. London: Royal Society, 1983. This memoir, still fairly brief, is the most complete account yet in print of Urey's life and work.

Craig, Harmon, S. L. Miller, and G. J. Wasserburg, eds. *Isotopic and Cosmic Chemistry.* Amsterdam: North-Holland, 1964. This book of articles was published to celebrate Urey's seventieth birthday; the editors are all former students of his. There is some biographical material; of special interest is G. M. Murphy's account of the discovery of deuterium.

Ruark, Arthur Edward, and Harold Clayton Urey. *Atoms, Molecules and Quanta.* Rev. ed. New York: Dover, 1964. This textbook was one of the first to develop quantum ideas in chemistry.

Urey, Harold Clayton. *The Planets: Their Origin and Development.* New Haven, Conn.: Yale University Press, and London: Oxford University Press, 1952. This book by Urey is highly technical; it is only of historical interest, since experimental data have increased beyond recognition in both quality and quantity.

———. *Some Thermodynamic Properties of Hydrogen and Deuterium.* Stockholm: Norstedt, 1935. This is Professor Urey's Nobel Prize lecture, discussing his discovery of deuterium and its implications.

*James R. Arnold*

# PAUL VALÉRY

*Born:* October 30, 1871; Sète, France
*Died:* July 20, 1945; Paris, France
*Area of Achievement:* Literature
*Contribution:* Valéry was one of the most important French poets of the early twentieth century; he also made significant contributions to literary criticism.

## Early Life

Paul Valéry was born in Sète, France, in the western Mediterranean, on October 30, 1871. The family moved to the larger town of Montpellier in 1884 when Valéry was thirteen; he was already writing poems at this early age, but the family expected him to become a lawyer. The expectations of his family were increased when Valéry's father died in 1888, and so a year later Valéry entered the University of Montpellier to study law. After reading works by Stéphane Mallarmé, however, Valéry knew that his true vocation was as a poet not a lawyer. He began to acquire a circle of friends who shared his interests in literature, including his lifetime friend, André Gide. In 1891, he published two important poems, "La Fileuse" and the much praised "Narcisse parle," in a small review. He was established as a poet, and so he moved to Paris, where he became a friend of his master, Mallarmé.

## Life's Work

Valéry's early poems celebrate the wonders of nature; their major stylistic features are an evanescent mood and lush imagery. "Le Fileuse" portrays those powers of nature operating while an old woman who is spinning a thread falls asleep. Nature is the active agent; a spring waters the flowers and a stem bends to the wind. The human spinner dreams and sleeps.

> The rose, your sister, where a saint delights
> Perfumes your vague brow with her innocent breath;
> You languish . . . you are an innocent light
> At the blue window, where you spun the thread.

Nature, although invisible, is the real power and presence in the poem; the woman is a mere receptacle.

"Narcisse parle" is a longer and more important poem that uses the myth of Narcissus. Valéry was obsessed with the figure of Narcissus and wrote about him a number of times. In this early poem, Narcisse wanders in nature seeking "Some face that never wept." He is divided and incomplete, an early exploration by Valéry of consciousness and the failure to achieve unity. Once more, much of the poem is devoted to the force and activity of nature. For example, Narcisse speaks of the "waters" as a God. He cannot, however, find the peace of the old woman in "Le Fileuse"; he remains "restless" until the union with this shadowy other is consummated. At the end of the poem, he remains solitary and can only bid farewell to what cannot be.

> Alas: wretched flesh, it is time to be at one . . .
> Lean: Tremble in all thou art:
> Possessed, the love it has been thine to promise me
> Is passing; its tremor shatters Narcissus and fails . . .

After this early success, Valéry was forced to decide whether to continue with poetry or to "cultivate his mind." Should he be Orpheus or Narcissus? He had always been interested in the human consciousness and the best way to achieve the "true self," or unity, and poetry was only one aspect of the human mind. It has been suggested that this crisis came about as a result of an unhappy love affair. Whatever the reason, Valéry decided in 1892 to abandon poetry. He moved to Paris, began to study and to record his thoughts in notebooks. These labors led to a study of Leonardo da Vinci, a figure who was not restricted to one mode of creation, and to the books on his character Monsieur Teste.

"Introduction à la méthode de Léonard de Vinci" (1895; "Introduction to the Method of Leonardo da Vinci," 1929) is an attempt by Valéry to reconcile the conflicting claims of the artist and the thinker in the figure of Leonardo. Valéry had been forced to choose thought over art and could not reconcile them in his own person. The essay reveals much about Valéry's inner conflict. He contrasts the fragmented "consciousness" that can only end in "exhaustion" and despair, while the universal genius, such as Leonardo, can turn his hand to any activity and create something. He can accomplish this by restraining his ego. This formulation seems to be very similar to that of John Keats. Keats contrasted the poet of the "egotistical sublime," who could only create out of himself, with the one who had achieved "negative capability" and could, therefore, create any type of character. For Valéry, the best poetry was not a turning loose of emotion but a process of the mind.

The cycle on Monsieur Teste is a continuation of the Leonardo essay. Teste is seen as a thinking machine, a pure intellect. Teste is discovered, for example, doing material "gymnastics," discovering "angles" while others waste their time and minds and fail to perceive the patterns around them. Such an abstract thinking machine might seem repellent to those schooled in the Romantic tradition, but to Valéry it was an antidote to Romantic self-indulgence. He continually celebrated the discipline of the human mind and sought unity of consciousness.

In 1913, Valéry returned to poetry. He wrote a few minor poems, but he worked on one poem from 1913 to 1917 and published it as *La Jeune Parque* (1917; the young fate). The poem is very obscure but has a lulling sound and beautiful imagery; it also tantalizes the reader to decipher its meaning. For any or all these reasons, the poem became an immediate success, and Valéry was recognized as an important modern poet. One possible way to explicate the poem is to divide it into three parts. The first part is the awakening of the youngest Fate to sexual feelings, which are symbolized by the snake. This awakening is described with images of burning, coiling, and rioting; it is discomfiting but cannot apparently be resisted. The second part of the poem turns from the disturbances of the senses to a joyous celebration of nature. This moment of ecstasy, however, cannot be sustained, and the Fate accepts life with all its questions and uncertainties. This acceptance is a prominent theme in the major poems of Valéry and can be discovered in his own rejection of and return to poetry.

After the success of *La Jeune Parque*, Valéry published a collection of poems that he called *Charmes, ou poèmes* in 1922. There is one poem in *Charmes, ou poèmes* that has been recognized as Valéry's masterpiece—"Le Cimetière marin" ("The Graveyard by the Sea," 1946). The situation is one with which many poets have dealt: the poet in the graveyard. At first, Valéry notes the "forms" of nature surrounding him in the incessant activity. The moment of peace vanishes as he contemplates his self as a changing being and the dead as reduced to nothing. He then attempts to provide some compensation by seeing death as a "womb"; however, he quickly rejects that easy answer as mere feigning and falls into despair. He soon triumphs over the despair brought on by the "worm unanswerable" and the paradoxes of Zeno. He turns back to life, to nature, and resolves: "We must try to live!" The ending is very similar to the acceptance found at the end of *La Jeune Parque.*

In 1925, Valéry was elected to the Académie Française. Having thus achieved recognition as one of France's greatest poets, he set about to make himself a man of letters, not simply a poet. He published many essays, introductions, prefaces, and extracts from his *Les Cahiers* (1957-1961; notebooks). Perhaps of greatest interest are his essays on poetry and the nature of the poet. Valéry makes a distinction between the Romanticism of Victor Hugo and the classicism of Charles Baudelaire; the difference is that Baudelaire subjects the material in his poetry to an unrelenting criticism, an intellectual technique of analysis. Valéry, however, did not discount the importance of inspiration for the poet; he believed that, while feeling may be the origin of the poem, the poet must discipline and contain it by analysis, by the mind. In addition, on many occasions Valéry also insisted that poetry must be "pure." He tried to connect poetry to music and create a poetry in which the formal aspects, the internal relationships, are dominant.

In 1937, Valéry was appointed to the chair of poetics at the Collège de France, and he continued lecturing during the war years and German Occupation; he courageously resisted any attempts to censor his thought. A collection of poems written at various times was published in 1942. In 1945, Valéry, still busily at work, died on July 20. Two significant works were published after his death, *Mon Faust* (1946; *My Faust*, 1960) and "L'Ange."

*My Faust* is a fragment of a play in the form of a dialogue. In the early part of the play, Faust has reversed the traditional position and now dominates Mephistopheles. Mephistopheles attempts to tempt Faust by offering him, among other things, the glory of completing a book he has been contemplating. Faust rejects Mephistopheles by claiming that mankind has got beyond the narrow range of views that the devil represents. Even good and evil are to be questioned, although it is clear that the soul is immortal. In the last section, Faust leads Mephistopheles to the heights of a cliff to contemplate mankind below. Faust is uncertain that man can rise above his limited perspective and rise to the heights that only mind can give. It is a plea for a higher consciousness and a recognition of limitations. Valéry does not provide an answer but a goal to seek.

### Summary

Paul Valéry remains an important poet and thinker. He always doubted the value of poetry but must be ranked as one of the most important French poets of the early twentieth century. His masters and models, however, such as Baudelaire and Mallarmé, are of the nineteenth century. He was not an innovator as the Surrealists or Dadaists were; he was, in fact, one of the last poets to follow the classical rules of French verse. His poetry is marked by lush imagery and lulling sound effects. Within the "pure" poetry, Valéry is constantly exploring and seeking the unified self, the true self. The main concern of his life and his work is the human consciousness. He was not a Leonardo or a Monsieur Teste but one who was aware of the possibility of a higher and more complete human being. His major works from "Narcisse Parle" through *La Jeune Parque* to the final meditations of Faust deal with the conflict of a divided self and the search to attain a unified one.

### Bibliography

Bouveresse, Jacques. "Philosophy from an Antiphilosopher: Paul Valéry." *Critical Inquiry* 21, no. 2 (Winter 1995). The author delves into Valéry's thoughts on philosophy as a discipline.

Crow, Christine M. *Paul Valéry: Consciousness and Nature.* Cambridge: Cambridge University Press, 1972. A scholarly treatment of Valéry's various views on the human mind. The book is very good on the sources of Valéry's thought. It also deals in depth with Valéry's treatment of nature, which other critics ignore.

Gifford, Paul, and Brian Stimpson. *Reading Paul Valéry: Universe in Mind.* Cambridge and New York: Cambridge University Press, 1998. First collection of essays to provide a detailed, focused rendering of Valéry's work.

Grubbs, Henry A. *Paul Valéry.* New York: Twayne, 1968. A broad view of Valéry's life and works without much detailed discussion of specific works. While it does not significantly explore Valéry's theories of consciousness, this volume provides a useful introduction for students.

Hytier, Jean. *The Poetics of Paul Valéry.* Translated by Richard Howard. New York: Anchor, 1966. The best book on Valéry's poetics. There is a detailed discussion of the intellectual background of Valéry's work, the uses of inspiration, and Valéry's methods of composition.

Mackay, Agnes Ethel. *The Universal Self: A Study of Paul Valéry.* London: Routledge, and Toronto: University of Toronto Press, 1961. An excellent study of Valéry's major works. The author provides detailed, specific, and enlightening discussions of the major works. The discussion of consciousness is directly connected to the major works.

Thomson, Alastair W. *Valéry.* London: Oliver and Boyd, 1965. A very short though rather in-depth volume that traces Valéry's life and poetry from the early years to the late. Contains a bibliography.

*James Sullivan*

# EDGARD VARÈSE

*Born:* December 22, 1883; Paris, France
*Died:* November 6, 1965; New York, New York
*Area of Achievement:* Music
*Contribution:* Varèse was one of the first composers to appreciate the opportunities presented by electronic music and advanced recording techniques. His influence has been felt by many modern composers and has percolated into the rock music field.

## Early Life

Edgar Victor Achille Charles Varèse (he would later add a "d" to his first name) was born in Paris on December 22, 1883; his father was from the Piedmont region and his mother was a Parisienne. As his father's work entailed much travel, Varèse was several weeks old when he was entrusted to the care of his uncle Joseph and his wife, who lived in Villars. When Varèse was seven, his father moved his family to Turin. Varèse felt very isolated there and grew estranged from his father. Varèse attended his first concerts in Turin and was exposed to the music of Richard Wagner, Richard Strauss, Claude Debussy, and Jean Sibelius. Varèse began when he was seventeen to spend his pocket money secretly taking harmony and counterpoint lessons from the director of the conservatory, Giovanni Bolzoni.

When Varèse was eleven, he composed his first "opera," *Martin Paz*, based on a Jules Verne novel, to amuse his friends. His childhood was divided between Paris and relations in Burgundy. Varèse's father attempted to mold his son into following him in business, insisting that he take courses in engineering and mathematics. His father was not pleased with Varèse's choice of profession, preferring him rather to pursue a career in either mathematics or science. When Varèse found his son becoming too interested in the grand piano in the family home, he locked the keyboard shut. The strain between Varèse and his father grew so great that, after Varèse moved to Paris, he never saw his father again. By the age of fourteen, Varèse had already set his sights on being a composer.

In 1903, Varèse left home for Paris and the following year entered the Schola Cantorum. Varèse left the school in 1905 and entered the Conservatoire National de Musique et de Déclamation to study composition under Charles Widor. Varèse supported himself during these hard times by working as a musical copyist and later found employment in a library.

## Life's Work

While at the Schola Cantorum, Varèse met avant-garde artists from fields other than music; he numbered Max Jacob, Pablo Picasso, and Juan Gris among his acquaintances. Varèse's sources of inspiration frequently came from outside the musical sphere; he studied topics as diverse as alchemy and Leonardo da Vinci's notebooks. He later observed that music was the "art-science." Given his scientific education, he was particularly drawn to the work of physicists. Unfortunately, none of his works from this period has survived. In 1906, Varèse founded the choral society of the people's university, an educational establishment for working-class people in the faubourg Saint-Antoine. Varèse's personal life was also settling down; on November 5, 1907, he married Suzanne Bing.

Varèse in late 1907 left Paris for Berlin, where he would remain for most of the next six years; he had been impressed by Ferruccio Busoni's *A New Aesthetic of Music* and wanted to study under him. Busoni encouraged Varèse, and Varèse was later to state, "I owe him a debt of gratitude." He also met Debussy and Maurice Ravel around this time. In early 1909, Varèse finished his symphony *Bourgogne* and began work on a symphonic poem, *Gargantua.* He continued to support himself and his wife by copying music. He met Gustav Mahler and Strauss during this period, and Strauss made representations on Varèse's behalf to help him find work. In 1910, Varèse's daughter Claude was born. On December 15, 1910, *Bourgogne* was performed in Berlin, where its reception was stormy. Varèse would later destroy the score, his last link with his prewar past.

Despite the controversy, Varèse continued composing. Three years later, Suzanne Varèse decided to return to Paris to resume her acting career, and they were amicably divorced. The outbreak of World War I caught Varèse in Paris, and he was unable to return to Berlin until after the war in 1922, when he discovered that the warehouse in which his manuscripts had been stored had been completely destroyed by fire.

Varèse entered the military in April, 1915; after six months he asked for a transfer, but a medical examination showed that he was unfit for military service, and he was discharged. Varèse then decided to try his chances in the United States and arrived in New York on December 29, 1915, with ninety dollars in his pocket and knowing two words of English. He had originally planned to stay only a few weeks, but he eventually settled for good. The heady atmosphere of the Big Apple was introduced to him by a close friend from Berlin, Karl Muck, who was then conductor of the Boston Symphony Orchestra. Varèse's larger interests also put him on the edge of Dadaist groups. Once again, Varèse turned to music copying to keep body and soul together. Varèse was clear on what he wanted to achieve with his music, commenting to one reporter, "our musical alphabet must be enriched; we also need new instruments very badly."

Varèse made his New York conducting debut on April 1, 1917, with Hector Berlioz's *Requiem*; his performance was very favorably received. Conducting engagements now began to trickle in. Varèse remarried, taking as his bride Louise McCutcheon, a writer. In 1920, Varèse began to work on *Amériques*, which was premiered in 1926. It was scored for 142 instruments, including two sirens. Varèse also helped found the International Composers Guild with Carlos Salzedo at this time to encourage and support progressive composers. In the guild's six-year existence, it organized performances of works by Igor Stravinsky, Anton von Webern, Alban Berg, and many others.

In 1922, Varèse premiered *Offrandes*; the form of the work with soprano vocal and strings still had recognizable links with European tradition, but it was the last work Varèse composed that was so "conventional." The International Composers Guild staged the first performance on March 4, 1923, of Varèse's *Hyperprism*; scored for sixteen percussionists and ten wind instruments, the piece's debut was stormy. One listener, the London music publisher Kenneth Curwen, was sufficiently stirred to offer to publish Varèse's scores. One music critic observed of Varèse that he was the cause of peaceable music lovers coming to blows and using one anothers' faces for drums. Subsequent performances generated similar polarized criticism. When the British Broadcasting Company the following year broadcast a performance of *Hyperprism*, one critic complained of "musical Bolshevism." In reply to his critics, Varèse observed that "there has always been misunderstanding between the composer and his generation. . . . Music is antiquated in the extreme in its medium of expression compared to the other arts." One conductor who was to consistently champion Varèse's work was Leopold Stokowski, who premiered *Amériques* in 1926 in Philadelphia.

Despite maintaining his residency in the United States and eventually acquiring American citizenship, Varèse made a number of brief trips to Europe in the 1920's, and in 1928 began a long stay in Paris. One work was begun during this period, *L'Astronome*, but never completed. A second piece from this period, *L'Éspace*, was also never finished, although Varèse continued to tinker with it into the 1940's. As originally conceived, *L'Éspace* was a massive undertaking; in its most highly developed shape it was to involve simultaneous broadcasts by musicians scattered across the globe.

Varèse moved a step further to his concepts of *musique concrète* with his 1931 piece, *Ionisation*; the work explored more thoroughly than any other nonelectronic composition the structural values of all nonpitch properties of sound. The score was written for a thirteen-piece percussion ensemble. According to Louise Varèse, *Ionisation* was the piece of music that Varèse himself was most proud of and satisfied with. Varèse called the work, "cryptic, synthesized, powerful, and terse."

Varèse left Paris in 1933; before his departure he attempted to raise funds for a center of electronic instrument research from both the Bell Telephone Company and the Guggenheim Foundation, but the effort failed. Varèse's failure threw him into a deep depression which lasted for many years. In 1936, Varèse completed the work *Density 21:5*; he then wrote nothing for a decade. The following year, he gave classes in Santa Fe, New Mexico, at the Arsuna School of Fine Arts. Varèse moved in 1938 to Los Angeles and attempted to interest film producers in the possibilities of his concepts of "organized sound" for film scoring, but the conservatism of Hollywood doomed his efforts to failure. Returning to New York, Varèse organized the Great New York Chorus for performances of Renaissance and Baroque music. In 1948, he taught courses at Columbia on twentieth century music and composition. In 1950, he taught summer courses in Darmstadt, Germany.

In 1953, an anonymous donor provided Varèse with a tape recorder, a tool which finally allowed him to begin to explore more fully the possibilities of mixing live music and electronic prerecorded material. He began to record sounds for use in *Deserts*, a piece that he had begun to score three years previously for wind, percussion, and tape. In 1955, the work was broadcast in live concert form in stereo on French national radio, the first work to be so presented in France. At the Brussels Exhibition in 1958, Varèse had his *Poème électronique* performed. *Poème électronique* was a work for tape alone; relayed over four hundred loudspeakers and subsequently recorded, the work was very influential.

The last few years of Varèse's life brought him increasing recognition and renown. Performances of his works were staged much more frequently, and prominent younger composers such as Pierre Boulez and Robert Craft made recordings of his works. He received a number of academic and artistic honors, among them election to the National Institute of Arts and Letters and the Royal Swedish Academy. The one thing missing from this period of Varèse's life was new compositions. One of Varèse's confidants offered an explanation. In 1949, the composer Chou Wen-chung began to study with Varèse and eventually became his closest musical colleague as well as the executor of Varèse's musical estate. According to Chou, the reason for a lack of completed works by Varèse after 1960 is that he was "fundamentally writing a single work, despite the number of titles he worked with." Chou stated that shortly before Varèse's death he discarded a great number of manuscripts.

### Summary

Edgard Varèse's most important contributions to music began in the 1920's; like a number of his contemporaries, such as Stravinsky, he was aware that new modes of making music would be necessary to produce what he called organized sound. Varèse was one of the first composers to become interested in *musique concrète*, and as early as the 1950's he composed two of the earliest pieces in the classical mode employing taped effects. The great tragedy of Varèse's career was that his ideas outran the technology of the day; he would have been quite at home with the modern electronic revolution of synthesizers and digital sampling. Varèse did not leave a large body of work—total playing time for the pieces he wrote between 1920 and 1960 is about two hours; his influence nevertheless is immense. Varèse used rhythm as the primary base of his musical language at a time when other composers relied on melody and harmony.

### Bibliography

Austin, William W. *Music in the Twentieth Century.* London: Dent, and New York: Norton, 1966. This work fits Varèse and his accomplishments into the larger context of post-1900 musical development. While many surveys tend to concentrate on Varèse's earlier, more "heroic" works, Austin deals with Varèse's accomplishments as a unity.

Guck, Marion A. "The 'Endless Round.'" *Perspectives of New Music* 31, no. 1 (Winter 1993). Another chapter in Guck's ongoing debate with Jonathan Bernard with respect to analysis of the work of Varèse.

Julius, Ruth. "Edgard Varèse: An Oral History Project, Some Preliminary Conclusions." *Current Musicology* 25 (1978): 39-49. Julius conducted interviews with fourteen composers living in the New York metropolitan area, all of whom had known Varèse. Among the composers were John Cage, Charles Wuorinen, and Vladimir Ussachevsky. The article is an interpretive documentation of the interviews; the transcripts of the interviews are in the City University of New York Oral History Archives. Julius was interested not only in biographical information about Varèse but also in the composers' thoughts and observations on the music itself.

Mattis, Olivia. "Varèse's Multimedia Conception of 'Deserts.'" *Musical Quarterly* 76, no. 4 (Winter 1992). Compares the performance of Varèse's "Deserts," which premiered in 1954, with the composer's concept of the piece.

Ouellette, Fernand. *Edgard Varèse.* Translated by Derek Coltman. London: Calder and Boyars, and New York: Orion Press, 1968. Ouellette's work remains the best biography of Varèse. The author had the benefit of a number of conversations with Varèse, and Varèse's widow read and commented upon his manuscript before it went to press. The work contains an extensive bibliography of works on Varèse.

Van Solkema, Sherman, ed. *The New Worlds of Edgard Varèse.* Brooklyn: Institute for Studies in American Music, Brooklyn College, 1979. This monograph collects papers delivered at a symposium concerning Varèse's work conducted at the City University of New York in April, 1977. The papers are primarily analytical and technical; of particular interest is Chou Wen-chung's treatise on Varèse's *Ionisation.*

Varèse, Louise. *Varèse: A Looking-Glass Diary.* New York: Norton, 1972; London: Eulenberg, 1975. Mrs. Varèse calls this work "a personal remembering." The work was to be the first of several volumes and offers an intimate portrait of the composer up through 1928.

*John C. K. Daly*

# RALPH VAUGHAN WILLIAMS

*Born:* October 12, 1872; Down Ampney, Gloucestershire, England

*Died:* August 26, 1958; London, England

*Area of Achievement:* Music

*Contribution:* Through the use of folk songs and native idioms, Vaughan Williams helped bring about the twentieth century revival of English music and established himself as its foremost composer.

## Early Life

Ralph Vaughan Williams was born on October 12, 1872, in Down Ampney, Gloucestershire, England. His ancestry included lawyers and pastors on his father's side, and he was related to Charles Darwin on his mother's side. The youngest of three children, Vaughan Williams (he was always called by both names and is listed in references that way) was reared in an upper-middle-class environment at his mother's family home at Leith Hill Place in Surrey, having moved there in 1875 after the death of his father, the Reverend Arthur Vaughan Williams.

Vaughan Williams received private instruction in piano, violin, viola, and harmony and attended the Royal College of Music in London and Trinity College, Cambridge, completing his studies in 1896. This tall, heavyset man was often the recipient of stares and comments. He had a large head, with a pronounced square jaw and thin lips. Particularly noticeable were his sad eyes and his exaggerated air of absentmindedness. This seeming detachment from the realities of life was evident even during his student days, when he wrote music with a scrawling, sloppy script. His interest became the music of his native England, an interest that was heightened and encouraged by his lifelong friendship with fellow Englishman Gustav Holst. After marrying Adeline Fisher in 1897, Vaughan Williams traveled to Germany to study with the eminent composer Max Bruch. Returning to England, Vaughan Williams began a lifetime involvement with English folk music, as characterized by the songs "Linden Lea" (1901) and "Bushes and Briars" (1903). In 1904, he was given the opportunity to work on a project which would allow him to pursue his study of English music.

## Life's Work

From 1904 to 1906, Vaughan Williams served as music editor for a new edition of *The English Hymnal* (1906). Until this time, he had been generally frustrated with what he perceived as his country's willingness to accept hymnody of generally poor quality and replete with Victorian excesses. He discarded numerous hymn tunes, replacing them with more than forty of his own arrangements of folk tunes which he had gathered, or heard and written down, in many cases for the first time. Other hymnal insertions included his own compositions, notably "Sine nomine," known as "For All the Saints," and "King's Weston," known as "At the Name of Jesus." This immersion in English folk music was brought about by, and provided increased fervor to, Vaughan Williams' attitude toward both the everyday life and the work of the composers:

> The composer must not shut himself up and think about art; he must live with his fellows and make his art an expression of the whole life of the community.

This notion of music as "an expression of the whole life of the community" implied a very different course from that which was considered normal for musicians of his stature. In 1905, Vaughan Williams helped to organize and conduct the Leith Hill Musical Festival, a duty which he retained until 1953. This festival was by and for amateurs, with the exception of Vaughan Williams, and gained a reputation for the excellence and diversity of its musical offerings, ranging from folk music to the *Passion According to St. Matthew* of Johann Sebastian Bach.

In 1908, Vaughan Williams spent several months in Paris studying orchestration with Maurice Ravel. His lessons proved fruitful almost immediately, as Vaughan Williams combined Ravel's emphasis on instrumental combinations with his own English musical heritage, in *Fantasia on a Theme by Tallis* (1910). This piece, for double-string orchestra, would come to be considered his first masterpiece.

Although in his forties, Vaughan Williams felt compelled to participate in World War I, serving as an orderly with the Royal Army Medical Corps in France and, later, as a lieutenant operating heavy gunnery equipment. Upon returning to England, he resumed his affiliation with the Royal College of Music, this time as a teacher, a position he retained for the rest of his life. He demonstrated the rare ability to compose, revise, teach, write, conduct, and administrate, juggling these many positions at once. Early in the 1920's, he met the young conductor Adrian Boult. Boult became not only a close friend but also one of the foremost interpreters of the music of Vaughan Williams.

Throughout the 1920's and 1930's, Vaughan Williams continued to champion English folk music. Unlike the Hungarian composer Béla Bartók, to whom he is often compared, Vaughan Williams did not actually quote folk tunes in his compositions. Rather, through his gathering of folk tunes (he would gather more than eight hundred in the course of his lifetime) and arranging them for various occasions and publications, he came to write in a style that sounded like folk music without actually being folk music.

During the 1930's, Vaughan Williams began a period of his life that was disturbing to some of his followers. It was at this time that he became increasingly vocal in his opposition to the regime and practices of Adolf Hitler in Germany. In particular, Vaughan Williams became an advocate of German refugees, including Jews. An indication of the effect of his protest and of his international stature was Hitler's banning of all of Vaughan Williams' music, composed or arranged, effective in 1939.

World War II disturbed Vaughan Williams greatly and resulted in his most disturbing composition. The Sixth Symphony (1948) was not the flowing, melodic music of his past; rather, it was dissonant and unsettling. The symphony was seen by some as a shift in compositional goals and musical direction. In fact, it stands as an example that, even at the age of seventy-six, Vaughan Williams had not stopped growing. The Sixth Symphony was the musical outworking of his social conscience.

His last years were spent as he had spent most of his life. He continued his administrative and conducting responsibilities with the Leith Hill Musical Festival, and he continued composing and teaching at the Royal College of Music. Honors and accolades came his way, and he rather enjoyed his elder-statesman status. Following the death of his wife in 1951, Vaughan Williams married Ursula Wood, a longtime friend of the family, in 1953. He died in his sleep on August 26, 1958, and his ashes were interred in Westminster Abbey near the resting place of the seventeenth century English composer Henry Purcell.

### Summary

More than any of his contemporaries, Ralph Vaughan Williams wrote distinctively English music. This does not mean, as has sometimes been suggested, that he was so narrow that he could enjoy no appeal outside England. To the contrary, his music, in particular his *A Sea Symphony* (1910) for soloists, chorus, and orchestra, has been consistently popular internationally, especially in the United States, in part because of Vaughan Williams' use of Walt Whitman's poetry in the work. His *Pastoral Symphony* (1922) has gained a significant following on the Continent. Further evidence is the fact that he was the recipient of the Shakespeare Prize from the University of Hamburg, Germany, in 1937.

Vaughan Williams was accurately labeled as one who opposed the so-called Second Viennese School of atonal music as practiced by Arnold Schönberg and Alban Berg. Part of his opposition was his desire to make use of his native English musical resources. In addition, Vaughan Williams opposed the German school's emphasis on intellectualizing the art of composition. For him, composing was less an art than a craft, a practice, something that was natural to him. He thought of himself as an Englishman who happened to write music. His emphasis in his own work, and what he preached to his students, was to be more intuitive in writing music. Since he had so fully immersed himself in the folk music of England, it was natural to Vaughan Williams that his music should sound so distinctively English.

For some, Vaughan Williams stood as a Christian musician, with his extensive work on *The English Hymnal* and numerous church anthems. In fact, he was an agnostic who never embraced Christianity. Perhaps a better designation is that of a visionary, although not in the sense of one who ignores the past and looks only to the future. Rather, he can be seen as one who looked at the past and saw its usefulness in understanding and living life in the present.

### Bibliography

Day, James. *Vaughan Williams*. 3d ed. Oxford and New York: Oxford University Press, 1998. As part of the Master Musicians series, this is a very readable book. One nice feature is the year-by-year walk through the composer's life via highlights. In addition, Day provides individual chapter analyses of symphonies, choral works, chamber music, and so on. A good section on significant people in the composer's life adds breadth.

Dickinson, A. E. F. *Vaughan Williams*. London: Faber, 1963. This large (five-hundred-page) volume is probably the most thorough biography of Vaughan Williams. The author, who has written about the music of Vaughan Williams since 1928, not only covers all aspects of the composer's life and career but also includes much commentary about the way Vaughan Williams' music has affected England. Unfortunately, many American general readers will find this very British writing difficult reading.

Douglas, Roy. *Working with Ralph Vaughan Williams*. London: Oxford University Press, 1972. A close friend and associate of Vaughan Williams, Douglas served from 1944 to 1958 as chief copyist of Vaughan Williams' compositions, and this volume chronicles their times together. In this role he had a unique opportunity to observe the compositional process. The book is short (sixty-eight pages) and is very easy reading. Douglas obviously cared deeply for the composer, and that affection comes across in a pleasant style.

Ewen, David, ed. *The Book of Modern Composers*. 3d ed. New York: Knopf, 1961. A collection of essays by and about thirty-one composers of the twentieth century. The section on Vaughan Williams is only eighteen pages long, but is quite good in providing a thumbnail sketch of the man and his music. Includes a brief essay by the composer on nationalism and music.

Frogley, Alain. "Vaughan Williams and the New World: Manuscript Sources in North American Libraries." *Notes* 48, no. 4 (June, 1992). Discusses Vaughan Williams' fascination with North American music and the relationship of his visits there to some of his major works.

Vaillancourt, Michael. "Modal and Thematic Coherence in Vaughan Williams's *Pastoral Symphony*." *The Music Review* 52, no. 3 (August, 1991). Musical analysis of Vaughan Williams' *Pastoral Symphony* including its themes and tonal elements.

Vaughan Williams, Ralph. *National Music*. London and New York: Oxford University Press, 1934. This is a compilation of a series of lectures given by the author-composer at Bryn Mawr College in Pennsylvania in October and November of 1932. Most of the book deals with subjects pertaining to folk music, with two chapters spelling out Vaughan Williams' ideas on nationalism and music.

Vaughan Williams, Ursula (Wood). *R.V.W.: A Biography of Ralph Vaughan Williams*. London and New York: Oxford University Press, 1964. An anecdotal and intimate biography by the composer's second wife. Full of photographs, excerpts of conversations, and letters; the tone of the book is set by the author's use of the familiar "Ralph" to refer to her husband, the composer.

*David C. Stuntz*

# NIKOLAI IVANOVICH VAVILOV

*Born:* November 26, 1887; Moscow, Russia
*Died:* January 26, 1943; Saratov, U.S.S.R.
*Areas of Achievement:* Genetics and botany
*Contribution:* Vavilov is noted for his pioneering work on the origins, distribution, and genetics of crop plants. He postulated a law of homologous series in variation whereby variation (and thus characteristics of possible cultivars) of a plant could be predicted from variation in related species. He also mapped centers of origin and genetic diversity of cultivated plants on a worldwide scale as well as personally organizing and leading numerous botanical expeditions and establishing a network of agricultural experiment stations in the Soviet Union.

## Early Life

Nikolai Ivanovich Vavilov was born in Moscow on November 26, 1887, the eldest child of Ivan Vavilov, a prominent Moscow merchant. The Vavilovs were able to provide an excellent education for all three of their surviving children. Vavilov entered the Petrovsko Agricultural Institute (later the Timiraezev Academy) in Moscow in 1906, studying soils and plant chemistry. When he was graduated in 1910 his dissertation received an award from the Bogdanov Museum in Moscow.

After graduation Vavilov worked as an assistant at the Poltava Experiment Station, studying the immunity of plants to parasitic fungi and anatomical variation in grasses, subjects which were to continue to interest him throughout much of his professional career. In 1911, he moved to St. Petersburg, where he worked with the noted botanists R. E. Regel and A. A. Yachevsky, studying immunity and variability in plants. These men arranged for him to study in biological laboratories in continental Europe and in England, where in 1913-1914 he studied with Great Britain's pioneer geneticist William Bateson and Rowland Biffen, a noted cereal breeder.

In the early years of the twentieth century, botany was in the process of transition from a predominantly field-and-taxonomy-oriented discipline to a more experimental and laboratory-oriented science. Vavilov, who received an excellent education in both approaches, combined them successfully throughout his career. He returned to Russia in 1914, where he completed his M.S. dissertation. In 1917, he was appointed professor of genetics, plant breeding, and agronomy at the Agricultural Institute of Voronezh in central Russia and at the University of Saratov on the Volga. In these early years of the Soviet era, his legendary energy and devotion to agricultural science enabled him to carry on an ambitious program of research into the systematics and breeding of crop plants, despite the disruptions of revolution and civil war. In 1920, he organized a congress of plant breeders in Saratov, at which he presented his classic paper on the law of homologous series in variation, which was also presented at the International Agricultural Congress in the United States the following year and received immediate international acclaim. Some measure of Vavilov's zeal and vision can be deduced from the fact that the 1920 Saratov congress took place in a region devastated by famine and civil war, despite an almost complete breakdown of modern transport, while Vavilov was forming the groundwork for crop-breeding programs as ambitious as any being contemplated in the United States and Western Europe. Vavilov married Elena Ivanovna Barulina, a fellow plant scientist, and the couple had two sons.

## Life's Work

In 1920, Vavilov was appointed to succeed Regel as chairman of the department of economic botany and plant breeding in the Agricultural Institute of Petrograd. He held this appointment until the institute was reorganized in 1924 as the All-Union Institute of Economic Botany and New Cultures, with Vavilov as its head. In 1966, following Vavilov's rehabilitation, it was named the Vavilov Institute of Plant Industry.

Vavilov had a utopian vision of the transformation of Russian agriculture through plant breeding. His sweeping revolutionary views attracted favorable attention from Vladimir Ilich Lenin, which enabled him to establish a rapport with the Bolshevik hierarchy and obtain scarce funds for agricultural research. With energetic leadership and the full support of the government, agricultural research in Russia grew at a rapid pace. The number of research stations doubled from 1914 to 1929, and the number of trained specialists tripled. Vavilov undertook numerous expeditions to many parts of the world, including Central Asia, Afghanistan, the Mediterranean area, Italy, Ethiopia, China, Japan, Mexico, Central America, and South America to

collect stocks of cultivated plants and their wild relatives. These collections, grown in field plots and maintained as viable seed in various parts of the Soviet Union, provided a rich gene bank from which to draw useful characteristics for plant-breeding programs. Unfortunately, they were not well maintained following Vavilov's death, and many irreplaceable strains have been lost.

Vavilov drew on his experience as a field botanist and his work in plant breeding to propose two important principles of economic botany: the law of homologous series in variation and the definition of centers of origin of cultivated plants. The law of homologous series states that a variation found in one species is likely to be found in related species. Vavilov based his principle on observation of thousands of cultivars of grasses and legumes, species of wild plants, and even fungi. It is not a law in the sense of a physical principle (such as the laws of gravity), but it accurately summarized observations and provided a framework for systematic plant breeding.

Vavilov's main work on the centers of crop-plant origin and diversity was unpublished during his lifetime but has since been reconstructed from manuscripts by P. M. Zhukovsky, a younger colleague. He mapped eight (later increased to twelve) macrocenters of crop-plant origin, which in general coincide with the present areas of highest diversity of cultivars and the distributions of wild forebears, both important sources for useful genes, especially for resistance to diseases and pests. Vavilov was honored at home and abroad for his contributions to agricultural science. In 1923, he was elected corresponding member, and in 1929 a full member, of the U.S.S.R. Academy of Sciences and was director of its Institute of Genetics. He received the Lenin Prize for his work on plant-immunity breeding in 1926. Although not a Communist, he was a member of the Soviet Central Executive Committee. He participated in International Agricultural Congresses in the United States in 1922 and 1929, and in the International Genetics Conference in Ithaca, New York, in 1932.

As the foremost Russian geneticist of his day and a prominent figure in science and politics, Vavilov became involved with the scientific demagogue Trofim Denisovich Lysenko in a bitter controversy that ultimately destroyed both Vavilov and genetics in the Soviet Union. Ironically, Lysenko was aided in his early career by the growth of agricultural science under Vavilov's direction. Although he had some success in practical agricultural research, which gave him a certain plausibility, Lysenko was intellectually unable to master theoretical genetics. Instead, he became convinced that he had demonstrated inheritance of acquired characteristics (Lamarckian as opposed to Mendelian genetics), a position that was appealing to the new Soviet leadership under Joseph Stalin for a number of reasons. First, it promised a quicker route to producing improved varieties than laborious crossing experiments. Second, especially as applied to human genetics, inheritance of acquired characteristics was more palatable to Marxists than a doctrine teaching that one cannot by one's own actions change an offspring's genetic inheritance, which as a corollary admits at least the theoretical possibility that there are inherently genetically inferior classes or races of people. Finally, forced collectivization had been a disaster for Russian agriculture, and agricultural science provided a convenient scapegoat. At first, Vavilov attempted to compromise with Lysenko but found himself pushed into an increasingly untenable position. In 1935, he was dropped from the Central Executive Committee and in 1936 relieved of his duties as president of the All-Union Academy of Agricultural Sciences. An offer to chair the International Genetics Conference in Edinburgh in 1939 had to be declined, because he was no longer able to travel abroad, and a proposed International Genetics Congress in the U.S.S.R. in 1940 was abruptly and inexplicably dropped in the planning stages.

The stronger his enemies became, the harder he fought. In 1936, his criticism of Lysenkoism was mild; in 1939, he denounced it as ignorant and irrational. Finally, on August 6, 1940, while on a collecting trip in Moldavia, Vavilov was arrested as an enemy of the people. The charges against him consisted of fictitious allegations of sabotage and espionage in agricultural institutes, brought under duress by a subordinate who was himself in prison, plus a somewhat subtler charge of fascism based on association of Mendelian genetics with notions of racial superiority, a doctrine never espoused by Vavilov. He was interrogated in Moscow, then transferred to a prison in Saratov, on the Volga River, where he died of "dystrophy and edematous disease," according to the official death certificate, on January 26, 1943. Conflicting information appears in the literature regarding the date, place, and circumstances of his death, which only became known in the West after World War II. Mark Popovsky suggests that he may have been murdered at some earlier date when the Germans threatened Saratov, but the witnesses he quotes tend to support the official story. The hunger, cold, and brutality endemic in Soviet prisons at the time undoubtedly hastened the death of a vigorous, athletic man, who was only fifty-five years old.

## Summary

To his contemporaries, Nikolai Ivanovich Vavilov was a charismatic man, who seemed almost superhuman in his energies, persuasive, capable of inspiring loyalty, and capable, some might say, of working a miracle such as pulling Russian agriculture out of the dark ages into the twentieth century. He failed, not through an inappropriate approach or through lack of effort but through being unable to judge accurately the evolving political climate in which he worked. In retrospect, Vavilov's accomplishments as a geneticist are solid and were very influential in the period between the wars, although modern crop science looks to other models and his predictions about the future of genetics contained too much guesswork to be considered prophetic. It is a great misfortune that the collections he so laboriously built up did not survive intact and that the system of agricultural research he helped so much to foster was crippled by two decades of charlatanism.

In the end, then, it may well be in the unsought role of the most prominent martyr for science that Vavilov is longest remembered. His fate serves as a reminder that science and government are inextricably interconnected and that even in the twentieth century the rational can be overcome by the irrational in a scientific discipline when the wrong people are called upon to be judges.

## Bibliography

Bakhteev, F. T. "To the History of Russian Science: Academician Nicholas Ivan Vavilov on his Seventieth Anniversary (November 26, 1887-August 2, 1942)." *The Quarterly Review of Biology* 35: 115-119. A testimonial biography of a type commonly published in Soviet scientific journals on significant anniversaries in the life of prominent scientists, this paper coincides with efforts to rehabilitate Vavilov in the Soviet Union. It emphasizes the international character of his work and the respect with which Vavilov was regarded abroad and details his position and the honors he received in the Soviet Union.

Mangelsdorf, Paul C. "Nikolai Ivanovich Vavilov." *Genetics* 38, no. 1 (1953): 1-4. A belated obituary and testimonial in the leading American genetics journal. Vavilov's contributions to genetics are clearly summarized. Vavilov is characterized as Russia's most distinguished geneticist, and the writer comments on the irony that the free world was reaping substantial benefits from the work which the Soviet Union disdained.

Medvedev, Zhores A. *Soviet Science.* New York: Norton, 1978; Oxford: Oxford University Press, 1979. Medvedev concentrates his attention on the failures of Soviet science and conditions in the Soviet system that discourage scientific innovation. A considerable portion of the book is devoted to the flowering of genetics in the Soviet Union in the 1920's and its subsequent stifling under the influence of Lysenko. In Russia, Medvedev was among those responsible for defending and rehabilitating Vavilov; he subsequently emigrated to the United States.

Popovskii, Mark. *Manipulated Science: The Crisis of Science and Scientists in the Soviet Union To-*

*day.* New York: Doubleday, 1979. A Russian specialist in scientific journalism who emigrated to the United States, Popovsky presents a historical overview of the practice of science in the Soviet Union. The emphasis is on failures and weaknesses of the system and the dismal record of natural sciences under Stalin. An admirer of Vavilov, he devotes considerable space to the conflict between Vavilov and Lysenko and Vavilov's imprisonment.

———. *The Vavilov Affair.* Hamden, Conn.: Archon, 1984. The first two chapters of this book summarize Vavilov's contributions to genetics; the remainder is devoted to the conflict with Lysenko and Vavilov's arrest, trial, and imprisonment. Included are summaries of interviews with contemporaries and commentary on the position of scientists under a totalitarian regime.

Zirkle, Conway, ed. *Death of a Science in Russia.* Philadelphia: University of Pennsylvania Press, 1949. The conflict between Mendelian geneticists and Lysenko and his followers, who espoused a form of Lamarckianism, is documented chronologically in a series of excerpts from the Soviet press, interspersed with interpretive chapters by American scientists. The introductory chapter gives a clear explanation of the background of the controversy, the differences between the two views of inheritance, and factors in the Soviet Union that encouraged Lysenko.

*Martha Sherwood-Piked*

# THORSTEIN VEBLEN

*Born:* July 30, 1857; Cato Township, Manitowoc County, Wisconsin

*Died:* August 3, 1929; Palo Alto, California

*Areas of Achievement:* Economics and social theory

*Contribution:* Rejecting the classical view of economics as governed by "laws" of supply and demand, Veblen conceived a system in which production and distribution of goods would be controlled by engineers, foreshadowing a "technocracy."

## Early Life

Thorstein Bunde Veblen was born July 30, 1857, on an eighty-acre farm in Cato Township, Manitowoc County, Wisconsin. His father, Thomas Anderson Veblen, and his mother, Kari Bunde Veblen, immigrated to the United States from Norway in 1847. The sixth of twelve children, Veblen was named for his maternal grandfather, Thorstein Bunde. Eight years later, the family moved to a 290-acre farm in Wheeling Township near Nerstrand, Wisconsin.

When Veblen was seventeen, his father, without consulting him, enrolled him in Carleton College in nearby Northfield. He was graduated in 1880 and taught one year at the Monona Academy in Madison, 1880-1881, after which he enrolled in The Johns Hopkins University in Baltimore. He failed to get the fellowship he had hoped for to enable him to pursue his studies, and he left before the term was ended and enrolled at Yale to study philosophy under President Noah Porter and William Graham Sumner. He received his Ph.D. from Yale in 1884.

Veblen tried desperately to obtain a teaching appointment in the East, and finding none, he returned to Minnesota, married Ellen May Rolfe, and settled on a farm near Stacyville, Iowa. Since his degree in philosophy appeared to be unmarketable, he enrolled at Cornell in 1891 to study economics under J. Laurence Laughlin. The following year, when Laughlin was chosen to head the Economics Department at the new University of Chicago, he took Veblen along as a teaching fellow.

Veblen found advancement at Chicago slow and arduous. He was promoted to instructor after four years of teaching and assistant professor eight years after his first teaching assignment, in 1900. Veblen's reputation as a teacher was in no way commensurate with his scholarship. In his lectures, he rambled and repeated himself often, and only a handful of perceptive students were willing to complete his courses.

Another problem faced Veblen, causing his dismissal from two universities and the final separation from his wife. Women seemed attracted to him and he often found himself in compromising situations. One such affair brought his dismissal from the University of Chicago in 1904. He went to Stanford University in California at the invitation of President David Starr Jordan. His wife joined him for a time, but soon Veblen became involved with another woman and his wife left him permanently. He was also dismissed from Stanford.

Veblen was unemployed for two years when Herbert J. Davenport arranged for him to come to the University of Missouri in 1911. During his seven-year stay at Missouri, he became disillusioned with the whole process of higher education and left to become the managing editor of *The Dial* in New York. While in Missouri, he married Anne Fessenden in 1914, a divorcée with two daughters.

## Life's Work

Veblen's ideas began to surface early in his writings and caught the attention of scholars in the schools where he received his appointments. During his brief studies at Cornell in November, 1891, he published "Some Neglected Points in the Theory of Socialism" in the *Annals of the American Academy of Political and Social Science*, which earned for him a four-hundred-dollar fellowship at Chicago.

Veblen was of the transplanted European stock of agrarian Midwesterners who viewed with suspicion the world of urban finances during the Populist era. He came to believe that the production of the machine age should be for the use of all and not for the profit of a few. He questioned the classical model of Adam Smith and his disciples, which left moral decisions about the distribution of wealth to the impersonal mechanisms of the free market. Veblen was particularly distressed over what he viewed as the sabotage of the production system by entrepreneurs who created artificial shortages, controlled prices, and limited new entries into business in order to maximize their own gains.

Veblen was not content merely to identify the problem of the capitalistic system but wished to get to its historical source. He took a multidisciplinary approach by applying the principles of psychology and anthropology to economics. He saw modern capitalism as an anthropological problem rooted in man's barbaric past. Through study of archaeology and history, he developed a four-stage plan of the evolution of the human community in Western civilization: first, the peaceful savage economy of the Neolithic period, second, the predatory barbarian economy with its creation of the institutions of private property, war, masculine dominance, and the leisure class, third, the handicraft economy of the premodern period, and finally, the machine age of potentially unlimited production.

Veblen rejected the belief that the increasing wealth and power of the wealthy and the grinding poverty of the poor were the inevitable consequences of natural laws of economics. He believed economics needed an activist psychology to supplant hedonistic man, whom he believed acted from instincts and propensity, not from rationality.

Veblen was not a Marxist, although late in life he concluded that communism might offer a better course than unbridled capitalism. He agreed with Karl Marx that war was linked to private property. Marx looked to Georg Wilhelm Friedrich Hegel in the unfolding of history toward a predetermined goal of a class struggle and a classless society. Veblen looked to Charles Darwin and envisioned no foreordained goals but a ceaseless adaptation and continual change. Veblen did not believe the impoverishment of the industrial workers would lead to a proletarian revolution, since they do not act by a rational calculation of class interest. He believed misery brings deterioration and abjection, not rational counteraction.

The work which gave Veblen's ideas public exposure was *The Theory of the Leisure Class: An Economic Study in the Evolution of Institutions*, published in 1899. His writing was not graceful, but wordy, repetitive, and sustained argument. Early reviewers were infuriated over Veblen's depiction of businessmen as economic parasites who were dominated by a passion to amass fortunes to be spent on ostentatious living. The respected William Dean Howells, however, liked the work and gave it the favorable review which commended it to the world of scholars.

Veblen saw money not as a mere medium of exchange or standard of value but as an expression of power by means of its display value. With it, the captains of industry in the Gilded Age strove to outdo one another in what he called "conspicuous leisure" and "conspicuous consumption" of a pecuniary culture.

Veblen's next major work was entitled *The Theory of Business Enterprise* and was published in 1904. Based on the nineteen-volume *Reports* of the Industrial Commission (1900-1902), he showed how the entrepreneurs had manipulated the machine process to create their power base in law and politics to protect their prowess.

In 1919, Veblen joined the faculty of the New School for Social Research in New York City. The school was begun by a number of disenchanted scholars who had left Columbia, including Charles A. Beard and James Harvey Robinson. While there, Veblen published *The Engineers and the Price System* (1921), in which he called for a revolution through the organization of a soviet of technicians who would control production for the benefit of all by imposing on society their own instinct for rational process. He envisioned a technocracy of highly trained engineers holding power in a new economic order which would know no national frontiers. He believed there was a cultural lag created by an unreasoning resistance to change; therefore, it was the duty of technologists and engineers to manipulate developments and create a more efficient and equitable economic order.

At the outset of World War I, Veblen published his *Imperial Germany and the Industrial Revolution* (1915), in which he claimed that Germany had borrowed British technology and imposed it on its feudalistic state, and out of the fusion came dynastic imperialism aimed at world conquest. George Creel saw the book's propaganda value when the United States entered the war, although the Post Office Department labeled it subversive. The work was prophetic in that it envisioned the coming of national socialism with its racism, military caste, and expansionism. During the war, Veblen also wrote *An Inquiry into the Nature of Peace and the Terms of Its Perpetuation* (1917). He feared that the peacemakers would make the world safe for the vested interests and that continued national patriotism would be an obstruction to lasting peace. He accelerated his plea for peace and struggled against nativism as an editor of *The Dial* in New York City during the final year of the war.

In 1925, Veblen was offered the presidency of the American Economics Association, but he refused, claiming that he had not been offered the honor when he needed it most. He returned to his cabin near Palo Alto, California, where he was cared for by a stepdaughter until he died, on August 3, 1929.

### Summary

Veblen was both a genius and a failure. His ideas were revolutionary and possibly found overt expression in the New Deal programs of Franklin D. Roosevelt, but he possessed no talent for their promotion or organization. He chose to remain aloof from movements during the era of the intense activism of both the Populists and the Progressives. He was a wide-ranging scholar who grappled with some aspects of human behavior to the obvious neglect of others. He seemed obsessed with leisure-class sports, dress, and objects, and yet he omitted any study of the leisure industries as economic factors in the total productive process.

Although his ideas were brilliant, his human relations were nearly disastrous. He was a clumsy speaker, an awkward writer, and a poor conversationalist. He felt more at ease in a rustic cabin, surrounded by primitive furniture he had made himself and where he kept irregular hours, than with people.

His assault on the free-market theories of the classical economics of Adam Smith and his disciples were telling; he created an awareness that there are no immutable laws which govern economics, and that men acting out of primitive, acquisitive instincts have clothed themselves with the respectable mysticism of conspicuous consumption and leisure. Science and technology have unveiled this mysticism and made possible the evolution of a new era, wherein the production capacities of technology are not manipulated for the extravagance of the rich but for the benefit of all mankind.

### Bibliography

Diggins, John P. *The Bard of Savagery: Thorstein Veblen and Modern Social Theory.* Hassocks: Harvester Press, and New York: Seabury Press, 1978. A thorough analysis of the anthropological theories of Veblen in explaining the origins of man's current institutions in primitive instincts. The "barbarian status of women" and Veblen's affairs with women are treated judiciously.

"Display Cases: The Man Who Discovered Conspicuous Consumption Is Back in Style." *The New Yorker* 75, no. 9 (April 26, 1999). Examines the recent resurrection of interest in Veblen and his views on capitalism and economic class structure.

Dorfman, Joseph. *Thorstein Veblen and His America.* New York: Viking Press, 1934; London: Gollancz, 1935. Probably the most complete and thorough treatment of Veblen's life. The book puts him in his epoch and relates him to the main currents of American ideas.

Duffus, Robert L. *The Innocents at Cedro: A Memoir of Thorstein Veblen and Some Others.* New York: Macmillan, 1944. A firsthand account by one of his students of the conversations in which Veblen participated and shared some of his ideas, which never made it into any of his published works.

Ebv, Clare Virginia. "Veblen's Assault on Time." *Journal of Economic Issues* 32, no. 3 (September, 1998). Discusses the impact of time as an agent of change on society and the economy using Veblen's theories as a basis.

Lerner, Max, ed. *The Portable Veblen.* New York: Viking Press, 1948; London: Penguin, 1976. The selections from Veblen's writings provide the reader with the true essence of his theories. Lerner's comprehensive introduction is the most perceptive analysis of Veblen in print.

Mitchell, Wesley C., ed. *What Veblen Taught.* New York: Viking Press, 1936. Mitchell was a close friend who explains that Veblen was never quite sure of his work yet made no intellectual compromises with his opponents. Mitchell makes no attempt to place Veblen in the context of American social thought of his time.

Riesman, David. *Thorstein Veblen: A Critical Interpretation.* New York: Scribner, 1953. Riesman worked closely with Staughton Lynd, an enthusiastic Veblenite at the time, in writing this book. Riesman is cautiously critical of Veblen and raises many questions concerning the validity of his theories.

Rosenberg, Bernard. *The Values of Veblen: A Critical Appraisal.* Washington, D.C.: Public Affairs Press, 1956. Rosenberg is a sociologist/anthropologist who expertly deals with the underlying theories of Veblen and their roots in those disciplines. He is generally not sympathetic to Veblen's theories and faults him for his unwarranted assumptions.

*Raymond Lee Muncy*

# ELEUTHÉRIOS VENIZÉLOS

*Born:* August 23, 1864; Mournies, Crete, Ottoman Empire

*Died:* March 18, 1936; Paris, France

*Areas of Achievement:* Government and politics

*Contribution:* Venizélos is the outstanding national figure of modern Greece. In and out of power he was the country's leading statesman in the first part of the twentieth century.

## Early Life

Eleuthérios Venizélos was born in 1864 in the small village of Mournies near Canea in Crete. His father was the merchant Kiriakos Venizélos Krivatos, whose family had emigrated from Morea (the Peloponnesus) in 1770, and was a leader of the Greek national movement on the island attempting liberation from the Ottoman Empire and union to the Kingdom of Greece. The elder Venizélos had spent many years in exile on the island of Siros as a result of his activities. Eleuthérios was the fourth of six children born to the Venizéloses, the first to survive, and according to one account he was named for a local saint whose name derived from Eileithyia, the ancient goddess of childbirth. In 1866, after the great uprising of that year on Crete, the government deported Kiriakos Venizélos to Siros once again. The family, including Eleuthérios, then only two years old, followed. After the boy had finished elementary and part of secondary school in Siros, the family was allowed to return in 1872 to Canea, where Eleuthérios continued his education and then went on to private study in Athens and also classical studies at *lycées* in Athens and Siros. After Eleuthérios completed these studies, the elder Venizélos wanted his son to remain on Crete in the family business. Eleuthérios, however, wanted a career in law, and a friend of the family, the Greek consul at Canea, persuaded his father to allow it.

In 1881, Venizélos entered the University of Athens, where he gained public recognition when, as leader of the Cretan students' union, he put the island's cause for independence before Joseph Chamberlain, a leader of the British Liberal Party, then traveling in the Near East. While Venizélos was at the university, his father died, so in addition to his studies he was obliged to care for the family business. In 1886, he received his degree and went back to Crete to practice law and continue the struggle for independence. He also worked as a journalist and within a year was elected a deputy to the island's assembly and became the leader of the newly formed Liberal Party. Although he had planned to continue his studies in Germany in 1890, he chose instead to remain at home in order to marry Maria Catelouzu.

## Life's Work

Venizélos' real goal was the independence of Crete. When a new insurrection broke out in 1897, he was at the forefront. The Great Powers intervened and appointed a mixed international naval commission to oversee the governing of the island. Venizélos greeted the arrival of the Russian, French, English, and Italian admirals on behalf of the assembly. In December, 1898, Prince George, the younger son of the Greek king, George I, came as the High Commissioner of the Powers. Venizélos was appointed to the island's executive committee and soon became the dominant figure. Yet irreconcilable differences arose between him and Prince George.

Venizélos' anti-Turkish activities and insistence on pushing the government of the island to complete independence led to a new insurrection in 1905 against the wishes of the Great Powers and the commissioner. Prince George abdicated the following year. Venizélos emerged as a Greek hero, but Crete still remained in Turkish hands. In October, 1908, in the wake of the "Young Turk" revolution, Venizélos, without consulting Commissioner Alexandros Zaïmis, who had replaced Prince George, led the Cretans in declaring their independence with the hope of joining Greece; he also became prime minister of a provisional government.

Then an uprising by the junior officers of the Military League in Athens led to an invitation to Venizélos to become the Greek prime minister in 1910—the first of five times he held that post. Venizélos, with the support of the Military League and its backers, swept the elections of 1910. He assumed the leadership of the Greek Liberal Party and carried out major modernizing reforms in the constitution and government. Although he was very popular, he also had many bitter enemies, including the Conservative Party, members of the royal household, particularly the king's sons, and some members of the military.

Venizélos as prime minister also modernized the Greek army with British and French assistance and came to agreements with his Christian neighbors, Bulgaria, Serbia, and Montenegro, to prepare the final exodus of Turkey from Europe. The Balkan Wars of 1912-1913, the first against Turkey and the second against Bulgaria, gave Greece much of Macedonia, Thrace, and Epirus as well as Crete and the Aegean Islands.

In 1913, King George was assassinated and succeeded by his son, King Constantine I, who was less accommodating to Venizélos. The outbreak of World War I exacerbated relations between Venizélos and the monarch as the former wished Greece to join the Allies, but Constantine, loyal to his brother-in-law, William II of Germany, steadfastly chose to remain neutral. Venizélos resigned his post in March, 1915, but in the summer won a strong majority in parliament and began his second administration. His pro-Allied stance, however, caused the king to ask for his resignation within a few weeks.

The next year, the Allies, trying to establish a second front in Greece, invaded Athens and forced the government to expel the missions of the Central Powers. In September, Venizélos declared a Greek republic in Crete and then moved to Salonika, where large numbers of Allied troops were stationed. Great Britain and France enthusiastically recognized him. King Constantine persuaded the Metropolitan of Athens to swear a curse of anathema on Venizélos and then left the country with Prince George. In 1917, however, the royal family under Prince Alexander, Constantine's younger son, made its peace with Venizélos. The monarchy was restored and joined the Allied side.

After the war was over, Venizélos journeyed to Paris as the Greek representative at the peace conference and came away with great gains from Bulgaria and Turkey. Yet he had hoped to obtain Constantinople as well as more of Asia Minor for Greece. Although the Allies had promised this as a consideration, they were reluctant to hand the Turkish capital over to Athens. Venizélos returned from Paris in September, 1920. Despite his triumphs, his long absence and the continuation of wartime conditions in Greece pending the resolution of the Turkish dispute led to his loss of popularity. Furthermore, a month after his return, King Alexander died from illness contracted when bitten by his pet monkey. Then, in the November elections, the Conservative Party won a stunning upset. Constantine returned, and Venizélos went to Paris in self-imposed exile.

By this time the Greek army had moved into the interior of Asia Minor to enlarge its war gains. Mustafa Kemal (later Atatürk), however, organized the Turkish defense that delivered a stunning defeat to the Greek forces. An armed insurrection followed, and Constantine abdicated a second time. His son George became king, and Venizélos once more entered the Greek service, representing the monarchy at the peace talks at Lausanne between the Allies and Turkey.

Another insurrection in 1924 forced George into exile, and Venizélos became prime minister for the fourth time. He did not wish to end the monarchy as his associates did, however, and, using illness as an excuse, he resigned in four weeks and returned to Paris. Yet in 1928 he came back for his fifth term as prime minister and was confirmed when the country gave the Liberal Party a large electoral victory. These were turbulent years for Greece, with army insurrections, periods of military dictatorship, and the struggle between the monarchists and the republicans. Prime Minister Venizélos was able to come to peace terms with his neighbors, including Turkey, but the Great Depression had grievous economic effects for Greece, and the Conservatives swept him from power in 1932. After an unsuccessful run for the presidency in 1934, he went into exile a third time but continued to interfere in the chaotic politics of Greece, including another attempted *coup d'état.* In 1935, Ioannis Metaxas, a royalist general, reestablished the monarchy under his dictatorship. Venizélos died in March, 1936, at seventy-one from pneumonia after a short illness. He was survived by his second wife and two sons, Sophocles, who became prime minister of Greece in 1944, and Kyriakos.

**Summary**

Eleuthérios Venizélos is the towering figure of contemporary Greece. More than the monarchs whom he served and battled, he stands as the symbol of the twentieth century Hellenes. He was a nationalist who fought for the *Megali Idhea* (great idea) of great Greece but was willing to embrace the precepts of peace, equality, and justice. He was trained in the liberal tradition of the classics and law, and his ideas and deeds were a mixture of conservatism, progressivism, and radicalism that earned for him many friends and as many enemies. Under Venizélos, Greece fulfilled much of its dream of gaining Turkish territory, almost doubling in size. Venizélos' charisma and his political and oratorical gifts made him the ideal statesman to lead the Greek cause in the early twentieth century. His family tradition of Greek nationalism and rebellion as well as his nativity in Turkish-held Crete also aided his career. Much of Venizélos' success had a serendipitous aspect—being in the right place at the right time. He was a leader of Crete and then Greece during the final days of the Ottoman Empire. He chose the side of the winning Allies at a time when his monarch, a political rival, chose the losing Germans. He was out of power when Greece suffered its major defeat at the hands of Atatürk. Yet often fortune frowned on him. He lost his popular mandate after one of his greatest triumphs at the 1919 Peace Conference at Paris; he also bore the full brunt of censure for the unsuccessful military *coups d'état* of 1933 and 1935. (He actually was involved only in the latter.)

Venizélos was a stormy figure whose politics and actions called forth either unqualified adulation or bitter enmity. Like the monarchs he opposed, he alternated between holding the supreme rule in his state and living in exile. His political gifts of sagacity and moderation were also in part the cause of his downfall at a time when Greece, like many countries entering into the modern world, swung from one extreme to the other, from republicanism to monarchy, and indeed at a time when extremes of both Right and Left came to dominate much of European politics. As a national leader, Venizélos could only meet with success, but, when the boundaries of the new state had been won, he was unable to complete in the domestic political wars.

**Bibliography**

Alastos, Doros. *Venizélos: Patriot, Statesman, Revolutionary.* London: Lund Humphries, 1942; Gulf Breeze, Fla.: Academic International Press, 1978. A hagiographic biography of Venizélos that emphasizes his life to 1924 and has an appendix covering Greece from his death to the country's involvement in World War II. Includes maps.

Chester, Samuel Beach. *Life of Venizélos.* London: Constable, and New York: Doran, 1921. A sympathetic look at Venizélos' career to World War I. Contains a map of Greece.

Dakin, Douglas. *The Unification of Greece: 1770-1923.* London: Benn, and New York: St. Martin's Press, 1972. A history of Greece including the period of Venizélos' early political career, putting his role in context. Very sympathetic to the Greek point of view. Contains tables, notes, a bibliography, and an index.

Falls, Cyril. "The Greek Anatolian Adventure." *History Today* 16 (July, 1966): 452-458. An analysis of the Greco-Turkish war of 1919-1922 with an evaluation of Venizélos as well as the Turkish leaders.

Kerofilas, Costas. *Eleftherios Venizélos: His Life and Work.* Translated by Beatrice Barstow. London: Murray, 1915; New York: Dutton, 1979. A brief biography of Venizélos written for wartime propaganda.

*Frederick B. Chary*

## PANCHO VILLA
## Doroteo Arango

*Born:* June 5, 1878; Hacienda de Río Grande, San Juan del Río, Mexico

*Died:* July 20, 1923; near Parral, Mexico

*Area of Achievement:* The military

*Contribution:* Villa played a central role in the Mexican Revolution as a rough, crude, and sometimes brilliant general from 1910 to 1920. Villa's exploits on and off the battlefield have broadened into legends that remain an integral part of Mexican history and folklore.

### Early Life

Francisco "Pancho" Villa was born June 5, 1878, on a large estate, or "hacienda," in San Juan del Río, Durango, Mexico. His parents, who worked as laborers on the hacienda, named their son Doroteo Arango. Mexico at that time was ruled by Porfirio Díaz. Under the dictatorship of Díaz, landless peasants enjoyed few rights and remained caught in a cycle of poverty from which there was no escape.

As a young boy, Doroteo taught himself to ride horses, explored the mountainous terrain near his home, and acquired valuable skills that later enabled him to survive as a fugitive. Doroteo was only twelve years old when his father died and left him head of the family. At age seventeen, Doroteo was forced to leave his home after he killed a man who had attacked his sister. Although he was captured by police, Doroteo managed to escape into the mountains of northern Mexico. There he joined a group of bandits led by Ignacio Parra and adopted the name of a notorious, early nineteenth century bandit, Pancho Villa. After Parra was killed, Villa became leader of his own band of bandits and gained a reputation as a benevolent bandit who plundered the rich and shared his stolen goods with the poor. Villa's activities at this time included robbing banks and trains, and murdering those who challenged his outlaw existence.

From about 1896 to 1909, Villa extended his influence beyond Durango to Chihuahua, in the northern part of Mexico along the border with the United States. In 1910, however, Villa abandoned his outlaw career to join Francisco Madero in the revolution against the Díaz regime.

### Life's Work

The Mexican Revolution of 1910 to 1920 was a dramatic and convulsive period that became a revolt of the landless masses against oppressive rulers, cost millions of lives, and produced vast destruction of property and resources. From this struggle, Villa emerged as a folk hero to the Mexican people and became one of the most colorful personalities of the Revolution. Regional and personal conflicts as well as betrayals confused and symbolized the course of the Revolution.

When Madero rallied others against the despotic and dictatorial government of Díaz in 1910, Villa joined the movement to reform Mexico. Within a short period of time, Villa controlled a loosely organized force of men dedicated to the democratic ideals espoused by Madero. At the end of 1910, Villa led his troops in capturing the small town of San Andrés in Chihuahua. This victory, the first of many, established Villa as one of the most daring and competent military leaders of the Revolution. By May, 1911, Villa confirmed his reputation with a stunning victory over federal troops when he captured Ciudad Juárez. The control of this valuable border city by the rebel army forced the resignation and exile of Díaz and allowed Madero to assume the presidency.

Acquiescing to the demands of the new president, Villa reluctantly agreed to serve under the command of Madero's general Victoriano Huerta. Villa soon challenged the authority of Huerta, however, was arrested, and then sentenced to die. In June, 1912, while he was smoking the traditional last cigarette before he faced the firing squad, Villa won a reprieve when a last-minute pardon from Madero arrived. Transferred to the prison in Mexico City, Villa there sought the assistance of a fellow inmate to improve his reading and writing skills. In December of the same year, Villa and his tutor both escaped. Traveling north, Villa left Mexico and entered the United States at El Paso, Texas, where he organized supporters, plotted against Huerta, whom he believed had abandoned the ideals of the Revolution, and planned his return to Mexico.

In March, 1913, word reached Villa in El Paso that Huerta had murdered Madero and usurped the presidency. Acting on this information, Villa gathered his forces, reentered Mexico, and began to contest Huerta's control. By October, Villa emerged

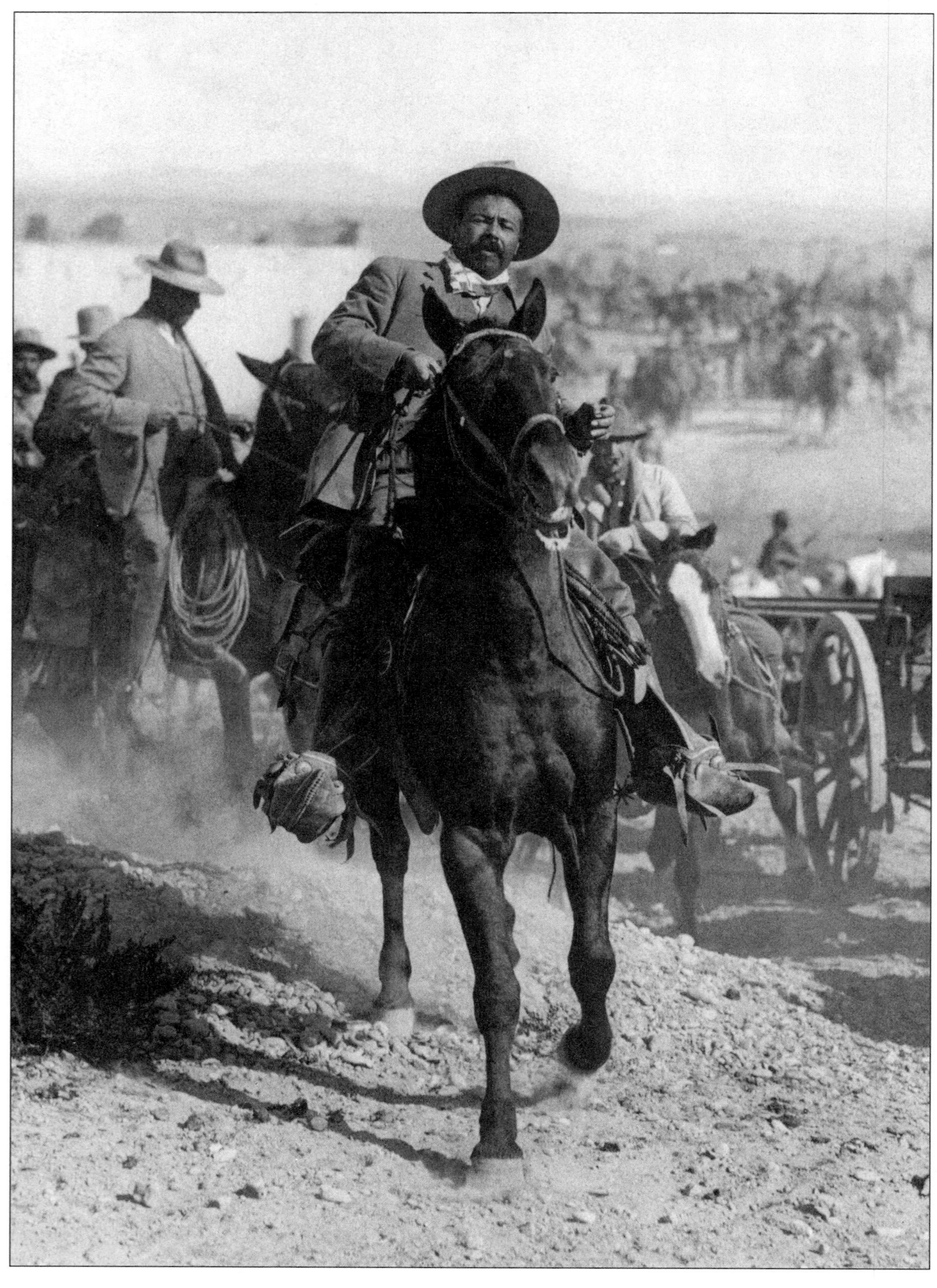

as the undisputed leader of the anti-Huerta forces in the north. Demonstrating remarkable military skills and utilizing daring strategies, Villa and his army, the Division of the North, cleared Huerta's forces from the state of Chihuahua. At the end of 1913, in one of the bloodiest battles of the Revolution, Villa recaptured Ciudad Juárez. While controlling that city, Villa undertook reforms that increased the food supply for the populace, improved the water system, and repaired the power plant to provide electricity for public and private use.

By 1914, Villa, now dubbed the "Centaur of the North," had become the symbol of the Revolution to his countrymen. Motivated by a desire to return Mexico to the Mexican people, and with few ideological purposes, Villa successfully commanded his forces in victories against the Huerta government. Although he brutally ordered foreigners to leave areas under his control, in the early stages of the Revolution Villa courted the friendship and goodwill of the United States. As an uneducated and unsophisticated general, Villa nevertheless understood the importance of propaganda and publicity to secure favorable public opinion in the United States. When President Woodrow Wilson in 1914 ordered the occupation of the port city of Veracruz after an affront to a ship of the United States Navy, Villa alone among Mexican leaders refused to condemn Wilson's actions. The United States at that time viewed Villa as the one revolutionary capable of establishing and maintaining order in Mexico, yet hesitated to recognize any clear leader.

In the middle of 1914, rebels supported by the United States overthrew the Huerta regime. At this point, the political climate in Mexico disintegrated into chaos. Although quarrels among the various factions had surfaced earlier, fundamental differences in direction and goals caused the Revolution by 1915 to degenerate into an anarchy characterized by civil wars in different regions of the country. During this period of intense bloodshed and destruction, a conflict between Venustiano Carranza and Villa dominated the Revolution. Carranza, as leader of a large rebel group that called themselves the Constitutionalists, and Villa, as commander in Chihuahua, both claimed control of Mexico. Failure to resolve this contest undermined the political stability of the country. Central to their dispute was a basic difference in attitude, education, and personality. Villa, a colorful, unorthodox, sometimes crude bandit-turned-general, denounced the supremacy of the courtly, well-bred Carranza. Yet, after General Álvaro Obregón, a supporter of Carranza, defeated the Centaur of the North at the Battle of Celaya in April, 1915, Villa's influence waned. Shortly thereafter, President Wilson recognized the government of Carranza as the legitimate authority in Mexico.

Resenting the official recognition of Carranza and attempting to demonstrate that his opponent did not control all of Mexico, Villa initiated attacks against the United States in towns along the border. These skirmishes culminated in a raid against Columbus, New Mexico, in March, 1916, when four hundred of Villa's men crossed the border before dawn, brutally murdered seventeen American citizens, then burned the center of the town before they escaped.

The reaction of the United States to Villa's wanton act of violence and disregard for international law was swift. Troops under the leadership of General John J. Pershing formed the Punitive Expedition that marched to Mexico in an attempt to capture Villa and disperse his forces.

Even though permission to enter Mexico remained a disputed issue between Carranza and Wilson, Pershing pursued Villa's army for more than ten months. Although never able to capture Villa, the Expedition succeeded in disrupting his organization and reducing his control in northern Mexico. Villa continued sporadic campaigns against the Carranza government until Carranza's murder in 1920. At that time, Villa surrendered his remaining army to the new president and retired to a ranch provided for him by the Mexican government. By then a hero to the Mexican people, Villa spent the next three years peacefully as a rancher in Chihuahua, outside the political sphere. On July 20, 1923, assassins hired by his old enemies murdered Villa and his bodyguards near the town of Parral.

### Summary

Pancho Villa, who began his career as an outlaw and bandit, became a symbol of the Revolution to Mexican peasants during and after his death. Despite documented evidence of his cruelty and perverse disregard for human life, Villa has dominated Mexican folklore as a champion of the poor and landless masses. Numerous myths and legends, popularized in songs and romanticized tales recount Villa's feats. Villa's support came from the lower classes, who saw in him a charismatic figure capable of winning for them an opportunity to gain a place in Mexican society and to improve their fortunes in life. As a military leader, Villa demonstrated extraordinary skill in routing his enemies on the battlefield. To his troops, Villa seemed to be the epitome of Mexican masculinity, with his fearless exploits and daring attacks against superior forces. Chased by Pershing's troops for more than ten months, Villa and his followers outwitted and eluded the more powerful and domineering United States. This feat not only brought Villa worldwide attention but also advanced Mexican nationalism during a period of violence and confusion. In the final analysis, Villa remained loyal to his cause during a time in Mexican history noted for betrayal and emerged as one of the foremost personalities of the Revolution. Yet Villa persists as an enigma. To some, Villa's brutality and atrocities inspired fear and hatred, while others responded to his leadership and acts of kindness with respect and adulation. Despite conflicting interpretations of his motives and actions, Villa influenced the course of Mexican history and has endured as a hero to his countrymen.

**Bibliography**

Braddy, Haldeen. *Cock of the Walk: The Legend of Pancho Villa.* Alberquerque: University of New Mexico Press, 1955.

———. *The Paradox of Pancho Villa.* El Paso, Tex.: Western Press, 1978. Both studies present a highly romanticized figure of Villa, with an emphasis on legends and myths that have developed since his death.

Clendenen, Clarence C. *The United States and Pancho Villa: A Study in Unconventional Diplomacy.* Ithaca, N.Y.: Cornell University Press, 1961. This work stresses that events in Mexico during the Revolution had a profound impact on the United States. The study is based on excellent research that explores Villa's actions and the diplomatic consequences.

Cumberland, Charles C. *Mexican Revolution: The Constitutionalist Years.* Introduction and additional material by David C. Bailey. Austin: University of Texas Press, 1972. This scholarly account of the Revolution, when Villa was most active, provides informative biographical information on the period's leading figures with insightful interpretations of the factional disputes during a very confusing time in Mexican history.

Katz, Friedrich. *The Life and Times of Pancho Villa.* Stanford, Calif.: Stanford University Press, 1998. Katz's book is based on years of research in the archives of seven countries and examines Villa's early life, his leadership in the Mexican Revolution, the theories of his revolutionary movement, his attack on the United States, and his ultimate decline.

Lansford, William Douglas. *Pancho Villa.* Los Angeles: Sherbourne Press, 1965. This fictional account, based closely on facts, provides insight into why Villa acted as he did before and during the Revolution.

Machado, Manuel A., Jr. *Centaur of the North: Francisco Villa, the Mexican Revolution, and Northern Mexico.* Austin, Tex.: Eakin Press, 1988. A well-written, well-researched, and favorable biography, with numerous pictures, that emphasizes Villa's pivotal role as a military leader in the Revolution.

Mason, Herbert Mollory, Jr. *The Great Pursuit.* New York: Random House, 1970. This detailed military history of the Punitive Expedition, with recollections by those involved on both sides, concentrates on the activities of the United States Army. The author claims the Expedition was successful because it dispersed Villa's troops and gave the United States experience to draw upon in World War I.

Peterson, Jessie, and Thelma Cox Knowles, eds. *Pancho Villa: Intimate Recollections by People Who Knew Him.* New York: Hastings House, 1977. These essays, composed by those who knew Villa as friend and enemy, capture the intensity of the Revolution and highlight his central role.

Thompson, Jessie L. "A Visit from Pancho." *American Heritage* 47, no. 8 (December, 1996). An account of Villa's 1916 raid on a small New Mexico town by a resident who was a child at the time and who lost relatives in the attack.

White, E. Bruce. "The Muddied Waters of Columbus, New Mexico." *The Americas* 32 (July, 1975): 72-98. This historiographical essay for the serious student explores why Villa raided Columbus, New Mexico. The author argues that the reason for the raid is less important than the result, since the Punitive Expedition helped the United States Army better prepare for World War I.

*Judith R. Johnson*

# HEITOR VILLA-LOBOS

*Born:* March 5, 1887; Rio de Janeiro, Brazil
*Died:* November 17, 1959; Rio de Janeiro, Brazil
*Area of Achievement:* Music
*Contribution:* Villa-Lobos' compositions number more than two thousand in authentic Brazilian style, which he cultivated and popularized throughout the world. He has also been a champion of Brazilian folk melodies, traveling through all areas of Brazil in search of melodies and rhythms that he has published and used as bases for compositions.

## Early Life

Heitor Villa-Lobos was born on March 5, 1887, in Rio de Janeiro, Brazil. He showed great interest in music as a young child and enjoyed sitting quietly as he listened to simple songs long before he could speak. At the age of six, Villa-Lobos began studying cello with his father as teacher. He held great interest in the sounds and technique of all musical instruments and learned throughout his life to play most, if not all, of the instruments commonly used in the symphony orchestra. Villa-Lobos attended school as a child in Rio de Janeiro, working on his music training after school with his father and anyone else he could find to teach him.

Tragedy struck the Villa-Lobos family when in 1898 Heitor's father died. The family was forced to find small jobs to provide income in a very depressed economy. Young Villa-Lobos, being only eleven years old, was forced to quit his formal schooling and perform in café and theater orchestras that were small and amateur. Rehearsal times made it impossible for Villa-Lobos to attend school, and he continued to study on his own, in what spare time he could find.

During this financially strained period of time, music became more of a means of survival than a course of study to Villa-Lobos, and, except for a few lessons in harmony and counterpoint from Agnello Franca and Francisco Braga, Villa-Lobos became a self-instructed musician and composer, as he spent many hours after his local jobs poring over borrowed scores and music texts. Because of his lack of training in traditional methods, Villa-Lobos ventured into his own realm of music construction. His originality and impatience with accepted harmonic rules manifested themselves very early in his career.

## Life's Work

In 1905, the interest that Villa-Lobos had found in Brazilian folk music led him on an extended trip through the northern states of Brazil, collecting popular folk songs and rhythmic patterns. Finally, in 1907, the financial position of his family had settled somewhat so that he could again enter school. Villa-Lobos began music composition studies at the National Institute of Music, where he studied intently with Frederico Nascimento. In between his studies, he continued to travel throughout Brazil in search of new songs and techniques.

In 1912, Villa-Lobos undertook his fourth and longest expedition deep into the interior of Brazil, accompanied by another musician named Gaetano Donizetti. During their three-year journey, they gathered a rich collection of folk songs from deep within the country, where the natives provided them with all the music they could gather. This experience in the Indian and Negro music forces influenced Villa-Lobos in many of his later compositions as he was able to call upon these remembered experiences for an almost unending source of musical suggestions. Returning to Rio de Janeiro in 1915, after three years of travel, Villa-Lobos presented a concert of his music on November 13, creating a sensation throughout the audience by the exuberance of his melodies and rhythms and the radical character of his idiom.

An ardent patriot of his homeland, Villa-Lobos resolved from his earliest steps in composition to use Brazilian song materials as the source of his thematic inspiration. Occasionally he used actual quotations from folk songs. Much more often, however, he used the folk songs as thematic germs, or suggestions, from which he wrote melodies in an authentic Brazilian style but of his own invention. In his desire to relate Brazilian folk resources to universal values, he wrote a unique series of compositions entitled *Bachianas brasileiras*, which consists of five suites. Number one is for the very unexpected instrumentation of eight celli; number two is for eight celli and soprano voice. Number three reaches the largest use of forces as it is composed for solo piano and orchestra, and number four begins to decline in numbers again, as it employs solo voice and small chamber orchestra. Number five, the last of the suites, returns to the use of eight celli and voice. Starting small, peaking in the middle, and shrinking to the end, these pieces are a fine example not only of Villa-Lobos' imagination but also of his orchestral techniques. Writing for eight celli is a challenge that Villa-Lobos completed very successfully. This set of five suites features Brazilian melo-rhythms being treated by almost Bach-like traditional counterpoint, which creates a sensation of exciting dance rhythms with flowing accompaniments.

In 1916, Villa-Lobos met the famous and artistically perfect pianist, Arthur Rubinstein, who became his ardent admirer. Rubinstein subsequently performed many of Villa-Lobos' pieces at concerts throughout Europe and the United States, including the very difficult composition *Rudepoema*, which Villa-Lobos had dedicated to Rubinstein. Through the worldwide success of Rubinstein, the compositions of Villa-Lobos began to have an impact on the international scene and were no longer kept within the borders of Brazil.

The five-year period from 1916 to 1921 saw the creation of Villa-Lobos' first six symphonies. The first three are written for traditionally organized symphony orchestra, while the fourth adds to the orchestra a large chorus. Symphony number five employs the orchestra, chorus, and symphonic band. Villa-Lobos' last symphony of this period, number six, is the only one of his first group of symphonies to be remembered by a subtitle, *The Indian Symphony.*

In 1923, Villa-Lobos was surprised to receive a stipend from the Brazilian government to study abroad. This government-sponsored opportunity was almost unheard of in most parts of the world and especially in Brazil, but with the surprise came an opportunity that Villa-Lobos had long secretly awaited: to study in Europe. His visit to Europe extended to nearly four years; he lived in Paris but enjoyed many excursions to London, Vienna, Lisbon, and Berlin. His main source of inspiration came through the French Impressionist musician Darius Milhaud, who introduced him to many other European composers.

A purely Brazilian form that Villa-Lobos successfully cultivated is the *choros*, a popular dance marked by incisive rhythm and songful balladlike melody. Villa-Lobos expanded the *choros* to embrace a wide variety of forms, from a solo instrumental to a large orchestral work with chorus. Villa-Lobos wrote his fourteen *choros* pieces between 1920 and 1929. According to Villa-Lobos, *choros* means "serenade," and is a synthesis of the various elements in Brazilian music, Indian, African, and popular folk melody, in which the harmonic treatment represents a stylization of the original material. These striking compositions are rhapsodic and free in structure.

Villa-Lobos returned home to Rio de Janeiro in 1926, determined to continue his career in composition with his new-found love of Impressionism. Composition had to take a backseat for some time, however, as he was engaged as director of musical education for the São Paulo public school system in 1930. After two successful years in this position, he assumed the important post of superintendent of musical and artistic education in Rio de Janeiro. In these positions he introduced bold innovations of using the cultivation of Brazilian songs and dances as the basis of music study in the public schools.

In 1929, after many careful years of study and categorization of pieces, Villa-Lobos published a book of Brazilian folk music under the title *Alma do Brasil*. He also compiled a selection of folk songs arranged for chorus, entitled *Guia Pratico*, which has been widely used in the public school system of Brazil and teaches music basics to students, while introducing them to their homeland culture.

An experimenter by nature, Villa-Lobos devised a graphic method of composition, using as material geometrical contours of drawings, shapes, structures, and the like. In 1940, Villa-Lobos used this method as he composed *The New York Skyline* for the World's Fair, in which he used as his source of inspiration a photograph of the city, from which he devised his melodic material.

In 1944, Villa-Lobos made his first tour of the United States, conducting many of his own works. During this period of personal unrest as well as world unrest, Villa-Lobos established the Brazilian Academy of Music in Rio de Janeiro in 1947. With this establishment came the desire to make Rio his permanent home, from which he continued to venture out on conducting tours but to which he always returned.

Between 1945 and 1956, Villa-Lobos wrote six more symphonies. His seventh, subtitled the *American* symphony was premiered in 1945. Villa-Lobos received praise throughout the United States when his eleventh symphony was premiered in Boston on March 2, 1956, with Villa-Lobos conducting. His last symphony, number twelve, followed close behind with the premier performance at the American Music Festival in Washington, D.C., April 20, 1958.

An exceptionally prolific composer, Villa-Lobos also wrote many operas, ballets, chamber pieces, choruses, piano works, solo songs, and instrumental solo pieces. His list of works numbers more than two thousand, and many of his most popular compositions are for massive and diverse musical forces. Villa-Lobos holds the record for the largest performance at any one time as he conducted more than forty thousand voices in a stadium outside Rio de Janeiro. For one composer to run the gamut of solo music to vast combinations of performers is remarkable enough but to be successful and competent in this endeavor is left to only a few composers, such as Wolfgang Amadeus Mozart, Ludwig van Beethoven, Gustav Mahler, and Villa-Lobos.

In addition to his work as a composer and conductor, Villa-Lobos was a champion of music education. He organized the Orfeao de Professores, a training school for teachers through which his system of music education has been carried throughout the nation of Brazil. He made enormous and exhaustive collections of folk and popular Brazilian music and arranged, classified, and traced to their original sources these melodies. Because of his care and interest in national musical pride, Villa-Lobos represented Brazil at the 1936 International Congress for Music Education in Prague, where he was honored for his nationalistic efforts. His music has long been known in Europe, and two festivals of his works were given in Paris in 1927 in conjunction with the Concerts Lamoureaux, and another concert was given in 1929. In 1938, Villa-Lobos was represented at the sixth International Festival of Contemporary Music in Venice.

### Summary

Heitor Villa-Lobos is one of the most original and imaginative composers of the twentieth century. His lack of formal academic training has never been considered a detriment to his work but rather the element that compelled him to create a technique all his own, curiously eclectic yet admirably suited to his musical ideas. In the ever-changing patterns and styles of the mixed-up twentieth century, it takes a determined artist to know what he wants to achieve and to know what to take from the popular society and what to discard in order to fulfill his purposes. Villa-Lobos was such an artist.

### Bibliography

Austin, William W. *Music in the Twentieth Century: From Debussy Through Stravinsky.* London: Dent, and New York: Norton, 1966. This source discusses the vast amount of music composed by Villa-Lobos and describes in detail some of his most famous works.

Chase, Gilbert. *The Music of Spain*. 2d ed. New York: Dover, 1959. This book provides a lengthy bibliography that provides further study into the life of Villa-Lobos and Spanish music in general.

Ewen, David. *David Ewen Introduces Modern Music*. Rev. ed. Philadelphia: Chilton, 1969. Ewen provides an interesting life sketch and a chronological list and description of Villa-Lobos' works. Good reading for young people.

Mariz, Vasco. *Heitor Villa-Lobos*. 2d rev. ed. Washington, D.C.: Brazilian American Cultural Institute, 1970. This book discusses the life and works of the great composer, providing insights, explanations, and detail from a Brazilian point of view.

Myers, Rollo H., ed. *Twentieth Century Music*. London: Calder and Boyars, and New York: Orion Press, 1968. A discussion of the various instruments and sounds needed to produce Villa-Lobos' music. It also discusses score techniques and musical comparisons to the works of other composers.

Peppercorn, Lisa M. *Villa-Lobos: Collected Studies.* Aldershot, Hants, England: Scolar Press, and Brookfield, Vt.: Ashgate, 1992. This book was written by the internationally recognized authority on Villa-Lobos and is a compilation of all the author's studies on the composer, his life, and music. Includes a sampling of letters and a chronology.

———. *The World of Villa-Lobos in Pictures and Documents.* Aldershot, Hants, England: Scolar Press, and Brookfield, Vt.: Ashgate, 1996. Unusual volume including a vast amount of source material on Villa-Lobos and the Brazil of his day. Includes reproductions of letters, newspaper articles, magazine pieces, and photographs and descriptions of old theaters where his works were originally performed.

Salzman, Eric. *Twentieth-Century Music: An Introduction*. 3d ed. Englewood Cliffs, N.J.: Prentice-Hall, 1988. This text compares Villa-Lobos' Brazilian nationalism with his studies in French Impressionism, providing a brief summary of the subject.

Slonimsky, Nicolas. *Music of Latin America*. New York: Crowell, 1945; London: Harrap, 1946. This book provides interesting reading about the sources of inspiration for much of Villa-Lobos' music as well as details into the composer's life that endear him to the reader.

*Robert Briggs*

# LUCHINO VISCONTI

*Born:* November 2, 1906; Milan, Italy
*Died:* March 17, 1976; Rome, Italy
*Areas of Achievement:* Film, theater, and entertainment
*Contribution:* Visconti helped create the neorealist movement in Italian cinema, by which Italians came to grips with the post–World War II world.

## Early Life

Don Luchino Visconti, count of Modrone, was born to one of Milan's and Italy's illustrious families, a fact that shaped his sensibilities and his films. Already artistic as a boy, he studied music and set design. From 1936 to 1940, Visconti assisted film director Jean Renoir in Paris. From 1945 to 1948, he introduced many plays by young European playwrights, particularly Jean Cocteau, at Rome's Teatro Eliseo. Thus he refined the art of directing actors to portray their characters as moving naturally through the time and place of the plot. In France Visconti adopted the politics of the French Popular Front against the Nazis, later joining the Italian resistance movement. In 1944 he escaped a Nazi death sentence for concealing escaped Allied prisoners and Italian partisans in his villa.

Under fascism (1928-1944), Italian film had leaned toward politically harmless, lavish costume period pieces and escapist comedies. The new social perspectives resulting from the fascist period and World War II fostered a national awakening to real problems that had endured since the *Risorgimento*, Italy's unification movement of the 1860's. Visconti became a leader among a group of intellectuals who wrote for the journal *Cinema* and who espoused a mix of realistic cinematic ideas that came to be known as neorealism. The term applies to many Italian films made between 1943 and 1971.

While neorealism dealt with Italian social problems during the immediate postwar period by means of real-life, even sordid, plots (its content), it was important, too, for its new cinematic aesthetics (its form): on-location shooting rather than studio sets and use of nonprofessional actors and documentary effects in which screen time reflected actual time. It became "a way of seeing reality without prejudice."

## Life's Work

Visconti was a prime theoretician and practitioner of neorealism. His films were characterized, moreover, by a visual richness often enhanced by gorgeous, evocative music. Though he outwardly espoused Marxism after World War II, he remained an aristocrat who harbored a paternalistic affection for the poor and whose most natural instinct was to enjoy their respect while assisting them in their needs and problems.

Visconti's first film, *Ossessione* (obsession), based on James Cain's novel *The Postman Always Rings Twice* (1934), appeared in 1942. This masterpiece helped establish the neorealist intellectual and aesthetic atmosphere. Indeed, the term was first used in the Rome review *Il Film* (June, 1943) to describe *Ossessione*. Three main characters propel the story, set in a wayside trattoria. Giovanna is tragically made to be used and cast aside. Bragana, her husband, is disgustingly unattractive but likeable. Gino, the lover, has used Giovanna without love but is full of guilt for betraying Bragana's kindness. Now persuaded to kill Bragana, he is over his head in a relationship with a woman he does not want. After the murder, which is officially regarded as an accident, pregnant Giovanna realizes she is not loved. Ironically, when Giovanna dies in a true auto accident, Gino is accused of murder. Visconti intrudes no moral judgment but allows "the wages of sin" theme to play itself out as the inevitable end of such an affair. In Italian cinema up to that time, raw passion and sex were nonexistent; bourgeois life was staid and stable. Visconti showed restlessness, adultery, and tragedy. It was the revelation of an Italy of poverty and suffering very different from what previous films had portrayed. Yet its characters were not protestors; rather, their passion was part of the poetry of real life.

*La Terra Trema* (1948; *The Earth Trembles*) was Visconti's next film. The talk of the 1948 Venice Festival, the film is, perhaps, the masterpiece of neorealism. Set in the Sicilian fishing village of Aci Trezza, it was intended by Visconti to be the first of a trilogy (fishermen, miners, and peasants) that was never completed. In nearly textbook neorealist style, the film has a documentary mood, using for its cast only the fishermen of Aci Trezza. Visconti himself described how his film virtually made itself. Every day he would tell the peasants what events were to be filmed, then incorporated their spontaneous reactions into the script, which thus evolved as the film progressed. According to the director, "They put what I asked them to say into their own words." Visconti kept their actual voices—and Sicilian dialect—introducing subtitles to translate the Sicilian where necessary to the plot. He also editorialized by means of an objective-sounding (but actually Marxist) voice-over narrative in Italian.

The theme of *La Terra Trema* is the misery of the working class, which serves an archaic sociopolitical system that does not serve it in return. The film is slow moving, but Visconti noted that this reflects the timeless ritual, the archetypal drama, the invariable slowness of life in Aci Trezza. The long takes of the men at work, of the women waiting for their men's daily return from the sea, and of the resplendent Sicilian landscape reflect his aesthetic ideal, which transmitted a natural beauty to the difficult lives of peasant fishermen. The plot is tragic. Wishing to better his family, Antonio dares to reject traditional village social hierarchy. As Antonio protests the prices he gets for his fish, the middlemen are seen standing by fascist slogans and grinning. The family mortgages their home to buy their own fishing boat. When it is destroyed in a storm, the family is destitute, and Antonio must humiliate himself by begging for work on the boats of others. Yet the film fails as pure Marxist propaganda. As a decent aristocrat, Visconti loved the old ways and saw beauty in the hierarchical society he condemned under the Marxist banner.

As if by an inner artistic necessity, Visconti followed the bleak *La Terra Trema* with a fresh stage adaptation of William Shakespeare's *As You Like It* (1599-1600) called *Rosalinda* (1948), which used Spanish surrealist Salvador Dali's set designs and Provençal choruses. Indeed, throughout his career Visconti directed numerous operas, plays with social messages, and innovative renderings of the classic drama.

In Visconti's film *Senso* (1954; *The Wanton Contessa*), Italy's overthrow of Austrian domination in the 1860's—the *Risorgimento*—became a symbol and a historical backdrop to the Italian resistance against the Nazis in 1944 and 1945. The film's realism was based on a mix of emotions: the war that the upper classes imposed upon the masses and the postwar Italian self-awareness that they had humbled and prostituted themselves to survive and had compromised their cherished ideal of honor. *Senso* was a color spectacle of undoubted visual beauty that attempted to blend theater, opera, and cinema. It opens with a demonstration by Italian patriots during a performance of Italian composer Giuseppe Verdi's *Il trovatore* (1852). As the chorus sings "To arms, to arms," the crowd chants "Viva Verdi!" The letters of Verdi's name were a nationalist acronym cheering the ruling Italian house of Savoy: "*V*ittorio *E*manuele, *R*e *d'I*talia (King of Italy)."

The characters are Countess Livia Serpieri; her husband, the count; her cousin, the patriot Ussoni; and her lover, Austrian officer Mahler. Livia betrays her husband, her country, her cousin, and her own honor. She has used money collected by Ussoni for the war against the Austrians to get Mahler released from the military, then learns that he has been unfaithful to her. Meanwhile, Livia's husband, Count Serpieri, aids the Austrians until they begin to lose, then turns his support to Ussoni. He is concerned only with protecting his status and property and not at all for the new nation about to be born. The refined but cowardly Austrian Mahler is as decadent as his country's effete aristocracy. While the beginning of the film is grandiose opera, its end is simple. The intense drama is suddenly depersonalized, and Mahler's execution by Austrian authorities is filmed dispassionately and distantly from above amid offstage singing.

In *Senso*, and frequently thereafter, Visconti presented a historical epic in which the lives of his characters embodied and defined the great historical events of the moment. He loved the decadent world of Livia and Mahler but knew it was doomed to pass away. The *Risorgimento* was the historical moment that signaled the birth of Italy as a modern nation. The victory of the resistance during World War II similarly marked the demise of the old ways and announced a kind of rebirth for Italy.

*Rocco e i suoi Fratelli* (1960; *Rocco and His Brothers*) was a violent film, almost a sequel to *La Terra Trema*, about the divisive effects of rapid cultural change upon a traditional southern Italian family attempting to modernize itself at the expense of ancient values and its archaic code of honor. *Il Gattopardo* (1963; *The Leopard*) was also set in Sicily during the *Risorgimento*. As the title implies, the plot involves one who "changes his spots" as the political climate unfolds. Burt Lancaster plays Don Fabrizio (the Leopard), Prince of Salina, Sicily, who represents the learning, grace, and culture of the old aristocracy. He permits his nephew to join Italian nationalist Giuseppe Garibaldi's Red Shirts in their takeover of Sicily. Now on the winning side, his survival in the new Italian nation is assured. However, Don Fabrizio hates the vulgarity of the middle class and the hypocrisy required for survival. In the cathedral, Visconti's ceiling camera pans over Fabrizio's whole family, now made up with chalk, sitting motionless like statues, symbolizing the death of an era.

*Morte a Venezia* (1971; *Death in Venice*) was an adaptation of Thomas Mann's novella, *Der Tod in Venedig* (1912; *Death in Venice*, 1925). Aschenbach is a maestro who has lost his ability to feel emotion. In Venice he experiences a revival of life in the form of a harmless homosexual attraction to a beautiful boy. However, a cholera epidemic (the cholera symbolizing the decay of an elegant prewar aristocratic society) fells Aschenbach. Visconti uses an effect also seen in *Il Gattopardo* and *La Caduta degli Dei* (1969; *The Damned*): Characters who are about to die or who symbolize death appear chalk-faced and ghastly. Thus does Aschenbach emerge from the barber's chair. Soon afterward he succumbs with a smile on his face while watching the boy at play. Throughout *Morte a Venezia*, Austrian composer Gustav Mahler's poignant music provides a leitmotif of death.

Again in *La Caduta degli Dei* Visconti studies the decadence of the values of prewar aristocracy. The German Essenbeck steel family, loosely based on the Krupps, produces incestuous child molesters, suicides, power seekers, and a Nazi officer while debating whether to support the Nazi war machine. The whole is a metaphor for Nazism's moral degradation.

## Summary

Luchino Visconti shared with other neorealists a sympathy for the lower classes of Italy. He had a penchant for adapting his films from books while moving the setting to Italy and altering the plot to suit his own sensibilities. His films are strong criticisms of the hypocrisy of "phony" liberalism, and they express a deeply felt regret for the disappearance of the simple and traditional times when great families like his own could exercise the role of godfather vis-à-vis the peasantry. While important for their sociopolitical messages, Visconti's films are rich in cinematic art. They are always visually powerful, and the astute viewer will perceive both subtle and patent symbolisms.

## Bibliography

Armes, Roy. *Patterns of Realism*. London: Tantivy Press, and Cranbury, N.J.: Barnes, 1971. General discussions of neorealism as a phenomenon of the 1940's and 1950's in both literature and film.

Bacon, Henry. *Visconti: Explorations of Beauty and Decay*. Cambridge and New York: Cambridge University Press, 1998. The first volume to consider Visconti's works in historical, cultural, and biographical contexts.

Bondanella, Peter. *Italian Cinema From Neorealism to the Present*. Rev. ed. New York: Continuum, 1990. The best overview of the period, with excellent characterizations and summaries of Visconti's films. Excellent bibliography for all important themes and Italian film figures.

Gray, Hugh, ed. and trans. *What is Cinema? Part II*. Berkeley: University of California Press, 1968. Includes André Bazin's essays on neorealism.

Leprohon, Pierre. *The Italian Cinema*. Translated by Roger Greaves and Oliver Stallybrass. London: Secker and Warburg, and New York: Praeger, 1972. The best broad history of Italian cinema.

Lopate, Phillip. "A Master Who Confounded the Categorizers." *New York Times* 147, no. 50978 (November 16, 1997). This article provides reviews of several of Visconti's films, including *The Earth Will Tremble* and *The Postman Always Rings Twice.*

Nowell-Smith, Geoffrey. *Visconti*. 2d ed. London: Secker and Warburg, and New York: Viking, 1973. An unfavorable biography that argues Visconti's shallowness. The author finds faults where most other treatments of Visconti find praise.

Overbey, David, ed. *Springtime in Italy: A Reader on Neo-realism*. London: Talisman, 1978; Hamden, Conn.: Archon, 1979. Overbey presents the many faces of neorealism.

Stirling, Monica. *A Screen of Time: A Study of Luchino Visconti*. New York: Harcourt Brace, 1979. The most complete English-language biography, written after Visconti's death.

*Daniel C. Scavone*

# VO NGUYEN GIAP

*Born:* 1911 or 1912; An Xa, Vietnam, French Indochina

*Areas of Achievement:* The military, government, and politics

*Contribution:* As chief Vietnamese Communist military strategist and expert guerrilla warfare tactician, Giap was architect of the Viet Minh victory over the French in 1954 (which ended French colonialism in Southeast Asia). Afterward he officially served as North Vietnam's defense minister and directed the military campaigns of the 1960's and 1970's that led to final victory over U.S. and South Vietnamese forces in 1975.

## Early Life

Vo Nguyen Giap, whose first name means "force" and last name means "armor," was born at An Xa in Quang Binh Province, a poor region of central Vietnam. He was reared in a lower-middle-class family of high educational attainment. His father, an ardent anticolonialist scholar who supported the family by cultivating rice, was determined to have his son educated and scraped together enough money to send him to a private school, Quoc Hoc Secondary School, in Hue. It was run by Ngo Dinh Kha, the father of Ngo Dinh Diem (future president of South Vietnam and enemy of Giap).

Quoc Hoc Secondary School was also attended by Ho Chi Minh, and there the young Giap began to read Ho's pamphlets, smuggled into Vietnam from abroad. Giap also acquired anticolonial and nationalistic political ideas from Phan Bio Chau, a veteran revolutionary who was then under house arrest at Hue but who was allowed to chat informally with interested parties. While still a student at Hue in 1926, Giap joined the Vietnamese Revolutionary Youth Association, known as the Thanh Nien, which Ho had helped to establish. At age fourteen, he was already becoming a bona fide revolutionary and disciple of Ho.

In 1930, at age eighteen, Giap was arrested by French security police as a supporter of revolutionary agitation. He had been helping to lay the groundwork for the Indochinese Communist Party, which was organized by Ho that year with the help of members of the Thanh Nien in Hanoi, Saigon, and Hue (where young Giap was involved). Giap was sentenced to three years in prison but was paroled after a few months. After his release from jail, he resumed his involvement in nationalistic anticolonial politics as well as the Communist Party, of which he became a recognized founding member.

Giap left Hue for Hanoi in order to study law at the French-run University of Hanoi. In 1937, he obtained a doctorate and went to work at Thang Long College, teaching history and writing articles in French and Vietnamese for nationalist newspapers. Giap converted many fellow teachers and students to his political views. In 1938, Giap married Minh Thai, daughter of the dean of the faculty of letters at the college; together they worked to further the Indochinese Communist Party. Their life together was not a long one In 1939, just before the Japanese occupation of Indochina, the Party was outlawed. Giap went to China to get military help, but his wife was arrested by the French and died in prison in 1941, along with their infant daughter. Giap's sister-in-law, arrested for terrorism, was guillotined in Saigon at the same time. Those events left Giap with profound anti-French feelings as he entered a new and intense phase of his life.

## Life's Work

As a teacher in Hanoi in 1937 and 1938, Giap developed a great admiration for Napoleon I, with whom, as a military leader, he later was said to identify. Decades afterward, former students recalled his lectures on Napoleon's campaigns, how he recounted the battles in brilliant detail as though he were the great commander himself or preparing to become one like him. After 1939, Giap would spend much of his life practicing the same profession as the man whom history had taught him to admire so much. It is ironic that the profession was practiced against Napoleon's homeland.

Once in China, Giap joined his political mentor, Ho, and became his military aide. When France was defeated by Germany in 1940, Ho, Giap, and Pham Van Dong worked out plans to advance Vietnamese nationalist goals. Crossing the border from China into Vietnam in January, 1941, the trio prepared to organize the League for the Independence of Vietnam, a coalition of various exile forces dedicated to liberating their country from foreign occupation or rule. Better known as the Viet Minh, the League was created in May of 1941. At Ho's direction, Giap also organized a Viet Minh army of liberation and trained it with China's help. By December, 1944, Giap's army began to wage guerrilla

warfare against the Japanese, who had completely overrun Indochina.

Described as a cynic in action, Giap first collaborated with the French when they were driven into the mountains by the Japanese. His commandos moved against Hanoi, the occupied Vietnamese capital, in the spring of 1945, but, after the bombing of Hiroshima (early August, 1945), Giap made overtures to the Japanese, from whom he hoped to get arms. Giap's brief collaboration with the Japanese paid off in late August, 1945, when they let his forces into Hanoi ahead of the Allies. The Allies were then put in the position of having to deal with Giap and Ho.

With the abdication of Emperor Bao Dai, Ho proclaimed Vietnamese independence in September, 1945. He became president of the new nation, and Vo Nguyen Giap was selected as minister of defense and state. Unfortunately, Giap, who was already viewed as being Moscow-oriented, could not refrain from passionately expressing hatred for France at a time when Ho was trying to foster a favorable public image of his government, especially on the international scene. Giap, therefore, was dropped briefly from the cabinet. Ultimately, however, the French were unwilling to give up their claims to Vietnam by recognizing its independence. When frustrating negotiations finally broke down altogether, Ho declared a national war of resistance. Giap, still commander in chief of the army, returned to the cabinet as minister of defense.

Actually, it was Giap who issued the first call to arms on December 19, 1945 (the official starting date for the French Indochina War), as Ho was sick in bed at the time. Outnumbered and poorly supplied at times, Giap took his ragtag army into the northern Tonkinese Mountains, built it into a sixty-thousand-man guerrilla force, and prepared a plan of calculated harassment of the French. In Giap's strategy, guerrilla resistance was to be the initial phase, preparatory to more conventional warfare which could culminate in a full-scale counteroffensive and final defeat of the enemy. Giap's training manual, a refinement of Mao Tse-tung's ideas, stressed the importance of surprise in guerrilla warfare. The feint, the ambush, and the diversion were important tactical elements. Though an army might be outnumbered ten to one strategically, careful use of guerrilla tactics could cause the opponent to disperse his force so widely that he then would become outnumbered ten to one at the point chosen for attack. Giap also taught the necessity of maintaining the allegiance and support of the peasantry.

General Giap began his drive against the French gradually by harassing the most isolated French garrisons, bottling up their defenders so as to leave the countryside open to the Viet Minh. As his strength increased, Giap accelerated the pace of his attacks and directed them against larger French garrisons. Sometimes the French would withdraw from positions, abandoning precious artillery, mortars, thousands of rifles, and thousands of tons of ammunition.

In 1951, Giap lost momentum by overstepping his own plans and attacking key sectors rashly and prematurely, aiming to dramatize his supremacy over the French. Yet after pulling back and learning from his errors, Giap's forces regained the initiative and enjoyed success. By late 1953, the French were tiring of a war which had already cost them 170,000 casualties and $10 billion. Their commanders decided that Dien Bien Phu would become the mooring point from which they could stop Giap and inflict a stunning defeat on the Vietnamese that would end the war.

The French fortress of Dien Bien Phu was located in a valley 180 miles west of Hanoi. By early 1954, the French had parachuted more than twelve thousand men into the area. Not knowing that Giap had acquired one hundred American-made 105-mm howitzers, that he had spent three months deploying fifty thousand men at the site, and that the Viet Minh had dragged the artillery up to the heights above the valley, the French hoped to lure the Vietnamese general into battle there. (They need not have worried about Giap failing to engage them.) Equally important was the fact that of the thirteen-thousand-man French fighting force, only half were qualified for combat, a fact discounted by French leadership because of their arrogance and vanity. Giap's army trapped the French within the bastion, and, after fifty-five days of bombardment, the few survivors surrendered to Giap, having lost four thousand dead and almost eight thousand missing. Giap thus became the first military leader to defeat a major Western army on the Asian continent and was known as the Tiger of Dien Bien Phu.

At Geneva, Switzerland, in July, 1954, the Vietnamese and French signed an official cease-fire agreement. Representatives of world powers also concluded that Vietnam was to be divided at the seventeenth parallel, into northern and southern sections. The Communist government of Ho Chi Minh would rule in North Vietnam (officially called the Democratic Republic of Vietnam), while the French would have some voice in a South Vietnamese government until the Vietnamese people themselves, voting in a 1956 national election, would decide the fate of their entire country. Those elections were never held, and gradually the United States replaced the weary French as the Western power in South Vietnam.

Despairing of ever reunifying Vietnam through legal means, nationalists in South Vietnam went underground and formed the so-called Viet Cong guerrilla force, which began conducting an armed revolt against the U.S.-sponsored regime of Ngo Dinh Diem. Upon the division of Vietnam in July, 1954, General Giap had become deputy prime minister, minister of defense, and commander of all the armed forces of North Vietnam. He began sending aid to the Viet Cong, and the United States reciprocated with aid to the south. This mutual intervention escalated into full-fledged war in 1965. Giap sent whole divisions of North Vietnamese regulars into the south to fight alongside the Viet Cong and assigned his associate, General Nguyen Chi Thanh, to direct operations in the south. Giap and Thanh often disagreed over the conduct of the war, and when the latter was killed in action in 1967 Giap took direct control of Communist military operations in the south.

Giap's masterstroke of 1968 was his execution of the Tet Offensive, in which he led the Americans to believe that he was planning a Dien Bien Phu-type attack on the Marine outpost at Khe Sanh. Then, during the Tet (lunar new year) holiday, while Americans were concentrating on Khe Sanh, Giap launched a sweeping offensive against cities as well as military and government compounds throughout South Vietnam with a Communist force of more than thirty-six thousand troops. Though his losses numbered some fifteen thousand, Giap's bold move was regarded as a moral and psychological victory, demonstrating that the Viet Cong, with the help of the peasantry (which Giap had advocated for many years), could strike at will all over South Vietnam against the world's mightiest military power. The Tet Offensive also reminded the world of Giap's brilliance and strength of will. From 1976 (when the two Vietnams were finally reunited) to 1980, Giap served as Vietnam's national defense minister and was confirmed as the united counfry's deputy prime minister. He was a full member of the Politburo of the Vietnamese Communist Party until 1982.

### Summary

Throughout the long years of his military service, Vo Nguyen Giap came to be seen as indispensable to the cause of an independent, unified Vietnam, even in the face of resentment from some Vietnamese. His successes boosted him to a position of popular hero second only to Ho but at the same time displayed the great brutality of which he was capable. In 1969, he admitted that North Vietnam had then already lost half a million troops against the United States and South Vietnamese regime, but he would have his forces continue to fight for another fifty years if necessary. Twenty-five years earlier, as he led his liberation army into the Dinh Ca Valley and liquidated government officials as well as wealthy farmers, he gave cruel force to his oft-repeated slogan: Every minute 100,000 men die all over the world—life and death of human beings means nothing.

Giap is to be regarded as Vietnam's most important modern military leader, theoretically and practically. He is universally recognized as an authority on and practitioner of modern guerrilla warfare. Giap's brilliance as a military strategist and tactician not only led to the end of the French colonialist regime in Vietnam but also was responsible for driving the Americans from the country and bringing about the fall of South Vietnam in 1975. Giap's genius lay in his ability to articulate and carry out the relationship of Communist ideology to military strategy. He was able to animate a conservative society and turn a group of medieval peasants into an army capable of defeating world powers.

Without question Giap was unbending on matters of duty. A veteran French officer of the first Indochinese War once summed up the tiny general (he was only five feet in height) succinctly when he said he was an implacable enemy and would follow to the end his dream and his destiny. Giap was more like Napoleon than the French themselves realized.

### Bibliography

Currey, Cecil B. *Victory at Any Cost: The Genius of Viet Nam's General Vo Nguyen Giap.* London: Aurum, and Washington, D.C.: Brassey's, 1997. This biography includes information on Vo Nguyen Giap's military campaigns and career.

Fall, Bernard B. *The Two Viet-Nams: A Political and Military Analysis.* Rev. ed. New York: Praeger, 1963; London: Pall Mall Press, 1965. Though written at a time when the U.S. military was beginning to escalate its involvement in South Vietnam, this scholarly work provides an excellent discussion of the conflicts and wars in Vietnam that arose out of colonialism and outside (especially Western) involvement in that country. Against this backdrop, Fall presents fascinating glimpses of Giap, his thinking, and his role in revolutionary activities.

Gerassi, John. *North Vietnam: A Documentary.* London: Allen and Unwin, and Indianapolis: Bobbs-Merrill, 1968. Written by a reporter and member of the first investigating team for the International War Crimes Tribunal, this book is a collection of documents (along with the author's observations) prepared by the North Vietnamese concerning U.S. aggression in North Vietnam. Its value for a study of Giap is its presentation of some twenty pages of material eloquently written by Giap detailing the United States violations of the 1954 Geneva Agreements. The book is polemical in nature in that it is antiwar.

Huyen, N. Khac. *Vision Accomplished? The Enigma of Ho Chi Minh.* New York: Macmillan, 1971. A native of Indochina, Huyen lived under Ho's regime for seven years. Though specifically not about Giap, the work nevertheless presents, in thorough fashion, the important association and points of contact between Giap and Ho—the twin pillars of Vietnamese nationalism. It is virtually impossible to understand Giap thoroughly without understanding something of his connection with Ho.

Karnow, Stanley. *Vietnam: A History.* Rev. ed. London and New York: Penguin, 1991. Perhaps the finest single volume on the history of war in Vietnam, Karnow does an excellent job of tracing Giap's role in fighting the first and second Indochinese wars against the background of the whole history of the country.

Kennedy, John, Jr. "The Master Mind." *George* 3, no. 11 (November, 1998). Interview with Vo Nguyen Giap in which he discusses the political aspects of the Vietnam War, his background, and his education.

O'Neill, Robert J. *General Giap: Politician and Strategist.* New York: Praeger, 1969. Though deficient in some respects, this modestly sized work (219 pages) represents the first book-length English-language biography on Giap. The author traces his intellectual, political, and military development against the background of the growth of nationalism and Communism in Indochina. The author served in the military in Vietnam from 1966 to 1967. The weakness of the book is its failure to discuss in greater detail Giap's contributions to guerrilla warfare by creating an army out of peasants.

Roy, Jules. *The Battle of Dienbienphu.* Translated by Robert Baldick. London: Faber, and New York: Harper, 1965. This outstanding work discusses what some consider to be Giap's greatest success—victory over the French. The most significant aspects of the book are not the details of the battle itself but the motives and reasoning of the leaders of the two combatants. Giap's ability comes through clearly in this well-written account.

Vo Nguyen Giap. *Banner of People's War: The Party's Military Line.* London: Pall Mall Press, and New York: Praeger, 1970. This short book written by the general himself constitutes a statement on Communist political and military strategy in the Vietnamese war against U.S. intervention. An important theme in Giap's text is that the Vietnamese Communist Party's military ideology is part of the two-thousand-year history of Vietnamese resistance to foreign aggression. He sees the struggle as a just war of national liberation against a bully.

*Andrew C. Skinner*

# ÉDOUARD VUILLARD

*Born:* November 11, 1868; Cuiseaux, France
*Died:* June 21, 1940; La Baule, France
*Area of Achievement:* Art
*Contribution:* Vuillard's wide experience in graphic art for the theater taught him to paint large-scale decorations, and, through his experiments with the formal elements of painting, he helped the Nabis school of painting to fulfill its primary ambition: to gain acceptance for decorative paintings.

## Early Life

Jean-Édouard Vuillard, the youngest of three children, was born at Cuiseaux, Saône-et Loire, in France, on November 11, 1868. After Édouard's father retired as a colonial officer, he married Marie Michaud, the daughter of a textile manufacturer. He died in 1883, and his wife, Marie, went into business as a corset maker in order to support the family. The household, though frugal, was not poverty-stricken. Marie, Vuillard's mother, worked hard and performed her daily duties with courage and a cheerful air. She remained close to her bachelor son until her death in 1928—when he was sixty years old—and she exerted a strong influence on him throughout her life.

Vuillard's habit of collecting colored boxes and pictures demonstrated an interest in art at an early age. He began his schooling under the stringently ascetic Marist Brothers, continued at the École Rocroy, then attended the Lycée Condorcet, where he met the two young painters who were to be the most important influences upon him: Ker-Xavier Roussel and Maurice Denis. (Denis is given credit for "recruiting" Vuillard into the Nabis.) Vuillard failed twice in his attempt to gain acceptance at the École des Beaux-Arts, but he was accepted on his third try. After two years of study in the crude barracks atmosphere there, the three young painters gradually began to spend more time at the Académie Julian, where they studied under Adolphe-William Bouguereau and Tony Robert Fleury. At this new school they met Pierre Bonnard and Paul Sérusier, the student monitor (*massier*) and leader of the Nabis, a secret brotherhood of discontented students. The Hebrew word, *nabis* means prophet, and these young men considered themselves to be prophets of Paul Gauguin's radical new synthetist discoveries.

## Life's Work

The year 1889 marked an important turning point in Vuillard's life. His first drawing was accepted for exhibition at the Salon, and this was the year that Gauguin, Émile Bernard, and their friends staged a significant exhibition at the Café Volponi. In 1889, he was still more interested in naturalism and the Barbizon school painters at the Palais des Beaux-Arts than in Gauguin's ideas, but a year later Denis had succeeded in recruiting him as a member of the Nabis.

Sérusier was the early spokesman for the Nabis: In reaction to photography's encroachment upon the domain once occupied by artists and in direct contrast to the attitude of the Impressionists, he maintained that painters—to avoid becoming machinelike copyists—should work only from memory. This practice was intended to simplify the forms and exaggerate the colors that nature inspired. This idea stems directly from the earlier concept that Bernard had persuaded Gauguin to accept. Bernard believed that the imagination retained only that which is essential and thus simplified the image because only the significant and the symbolic are retained by memory. This practice, he believed, generated a simplified, rather flat, silhouette and preserved the purity of color.

Denis had published an article, which came to exert an important influence on Vuillard's direction, in 1890 in which he argued for the primacy of formal elements over content in order to convey emotion in the New-Traditionism: "[A] painting, before it is a war horse, a nude woman or some anecdote, is first and foremost a flat surface covered with colours arranged in a certain order." Consequently, late in 1889 Vuillard wrote in his notebooks that he had begun to work from memory, painting what he called "little daubs" (*petites salissures*). He painted these little daubs quickly using a flat, simplified technique—sometimes with textured dots—on small panels or pieces of cardboard. In 1890 he began to use raw saturate color in some of his paintings and in the programs he designed for the Théâtre Libre, but he never entirely deserted his earlier use of low-key tones of color, carefully adjusted in value to avoid strong contrast in dark and light.

Vuillard, like the other Nabis, attempted to exploit the symbolic in order to express emotion and experience. He wrote that a woman's head created a certain emotion in him, and he wanted to paint only that emotion; he believed that details such as a nose or an ear were of no importance. Both the strong, raw color and the simplified silhouette—much like the Japanese woodblock prints which were so common in Paris during this period—were critical elements in this attempt to express emotion.

During the early 1890's, Vuillard began to enjoy some success; the critics were writing about him, and several collectors began to buy his work. He had his first two shows in 1892: the first at the offices of *La Revue blanche*, the second at le Barc de Boutteville's gallery. After 1894, his work was widely exhibited in galleries and exhibitions.

The graphic arts were enjoying a strong revival during the 1890's, and Vuillard worked in several media: prints, stained glass, colored lithographs, stage sets, and advertising playbills for the theater. The playbills and stage sets—including sets for Henrik Ibsen's plays—that he painted for the experimental Théâtre de l'Oeuvre are recognized as an important step in the development of his style.

During the last decade of the nineteenth century, Vuillard kept his pictorial space ambiguous and rather shallow—nearly flat—in the mode of the day: His designs and flat pictorial space often suggest tapestries. Like Gauguin, Pierre-Cécile Puvis de Chavannes, and most of the decorative painters of his time who sought to avoid the reflective surface and the illusion of depth associated with oil paint, Vuillard preferred a dry matte paint surface. Consequently, he used distemper as a medium in the four panels and continued thereafter to use this medium almost exclusively in both his decorative panels and his easel painting. This medium, coupled with his tendency to build up his surfaces quickly without allowing time for the first coats to dry, has led to severe cracking in some of his paintings.

Vuillard was not interested in painting posed figures or picturesque views, so he acquired a box camera in 1897 that he constantly used, as some painters use drawings, to record the candid, lifelike visual information that he painted: informal groupings and conversations, in public or at home. By 1898 his paintings were becoming more complex, rather than simplified and reductive. He began, perhaps with the help of the camera, to record the cluttered details and patterns of interior settings.

After the turn of the century, Vuillard abandoned the shallow, ambiguous pictorial space and flat figures of his earlier paintings and began to paint street scenes and landscapes in which he depicted a considerable amount of depth. These paintings featured a more volumetric treatment of the figure and a more realistic, wide-angle depiction of space, much like the fish-eye lens on an early camera. Influenced by Paul Valéry, he began to observe and paint details with more complexity.

The Nabis disbanded toward the end of the 1890's as the stronger talents achieved independent fame and no longer identified with the group. In 1899, at an exhibition of the Nabis and the Neo-impressionists at the Durand-Ruel Gallery, critics singled out Vuillard and Bonnard as the best artists in the exhibition. During the first years of the twentieth century, both Bonnard and Vuillard regularly exhibited and sold paintings at the Bernheim-Jeune Gallery and consequently enjoyed a great degree of financial security. Vuillard was given many commissions for both decorations and portraits between 1910 and 1914. In 1905, the year of the Fauves and their color revolution, the critic François Monot wrote that Vuillard was one of the first colorists of the time. Yet he was often criticized for carelessness in technique because of areas left blank or treated too quickly. He left blank areas of warm brown cardboard to harmonize with his color, and this was sometimes criticized as an affectation, a passing fad.

During the last twenty years of his life, Vuillard's work focused on portraiture. The composition in these portraits is often organized in traditional "compositional climax." The bottom and particularly the top sections of the painting are simplified and composed of large inactive areas, while a transition is made toward the middle area of smaller more complex shapes and details, creating an area of visual activity. Toward the end of his life, his paintings moved toward realism, complexity, and detail, finally to create a writhing surface of detailed and complex minutiae. Yet, when Vuillard was consulted about the selection of more than three hundred of his works to be shown at the major retrospective exhibition at the Pavillon de Marsan in 1938, almost half of the works included in this exhibition had been executed during that early reductionist period before 1900. At the age of seventy-one years, Vuillard died at La Baule, France, on June 21, 1940.

### Summary

Édouard Vuillard—the most famous member of the Nabis school of painting as well as an excellent realist painter—was best known for his "decorative" paintings of French gardens and interiors and his portraits of public men. Vuillard disliked theory and, influenced by Gauguin, relied on personal symbol, sensation, and instinct to express his emotional reaction to experience. During the course of his early career, Vuillard simplified his reductionist form and silhouette with ruthless discipline and relentless restraint to eliminate all unnecessary detail, but after the turn of the century he reversed priorities and direction to create a complex image of activity and detail.

During the first part of the twentieth century, the crucial split between the painters of classicism and the painters of genre in France was exemplified by Vuillard, the genre painter, and Denis, the classicist. Though Andy Warhol has been given credit for having reversed priorities in the relationship between fine art and graphic art, his accomplishment was preceded by the successes of Gauguin and Vuillard's group, the Nabis. Their efforts were directed primarily toward creating a decorative graphic art of such quality that it would have to be accepted in the same spirit, with the same respect, as the works of so-called fine artists. The success of this effort is demonstrated by the attention still accorded their work and their continuing influence upon painters during the twentieth century.

**Bibliography**

Boyer, Patricia Eckert, ed. *The Nabis and the Parisian Avant-Garde.* With essays by Patricia Eckert Boyer and Elizabeth Prelinger. New Brunswick, N.J.: Rutgers University Press and Jane Voorhees Zimmerli Art Museum, 1988. This 195-page book is an excellent catalog of the Voorhees Zimmerli Art Museum's exhibition of paintings from the Nabis group of painters. Several sections are devoted to Vuillard's place within the school, and it features a good chronology of the Nabis with 232 illustrations, forty in color.

Groom, Gloria L. *Édouard Vuillard: Painter-Decorator: Patrons and Projects 1892-1912.* New Haven, Conn.: Yale University Press, 1994. A comprehensive collection of information on Vuillard's decorative works.

Mauner, George L. *The Nabis: Their History and Their Art, 1888-1896.* New York: Garland, 1978. Though apparently a product of a subsidy press, this dissertation was written under the supervision of Meyer Shapiro. It is a solid scholarly work and the best-documented history of the Nabis school. Vuillard's contribution is well documented, and the book features 326 pages of text and 159 black-and-white illustrations—forty-seven by Vuillard.

Roger-Marx, Claude. *Vuillard: His Life and Work.* London: Elek, and New York: Éditions de la Maison Française, 1946. Marx was Vuillard's original biographer, an early champion of the applied arts, and he has written extensively on Vuillard, beginning in the 1890's. The book (212 pages, 204 illustrations, eight in color) is well written and accurate.

Sidlauskas, Susan. "Contesting Femininity: Vuillard's Family Pictures." *Art Bulletin* 79, no. 1 (March, 1997). Focuses on femininity in the works of Vuillard and addresses questions as to his gender orientation.

Thomson, Belinda. *Vuillard.* Oxford: Phaidon Press, and New York: Abbeville Press, 1988. Brief and easy to read but accurate and incisive, this is an excellent book for the general reader. Contains 139 illustrations (about half in color). Documents his early life and training, his relationship with the Nabis, his success, and his role in the theater. A good select bibliography is to be found at the end of the book.

Vuillard, Édouard. *Edouard Vuillard.* Text by Stuart Preston. New York: Abrams, 1972. This is an excellent picture book with forty-six pages of text interspersed with seventy-three black-and-white illustrations, followed by forty full-page color plates, each accompanied by a page of text about the painting. In the back is a select bibliography of books and articles; most are written in French.

*William V. Dunning*

# JOACHIM WACH

*Born:* January 25, 1898; Chemnitz, Germany
*Died:* August 27, 1955; Orselina, Switzerland
*Area of Achievement:* Religion
*Contribution:* Wach distilled the descriptive requirements for a scientific definition of religious experience from his general theory of knowledge and understanding. He created the modern academic field of the history of religions out of and in contrast to preceding notions of comparative religion.

## Early Life

Joachim Wach was born in 1898 at Chemnitz in Saxony, the eldest child of three, to Felix Wach, who was food comptroller of Germany during World War I, and his wife, Katharina von Mendelssohn-Bartholdy. Joachim's paternal grandparents were Adolf Wach, prominent juridical counsellor to the King of Saxony, and subsequently professor of law, first at the University of Rostock, later at the University of Leipzig, until his death in 1926; and Lily, the youngest daughter of the composer Felix Mendelssohn. Joachim's mother was the granddaughter of Paul, brother to the composer Felix. While the two lines were thus related, they distinguished by the hyphen in the name their common descent from the brothers' grandfather, the eminent Jewish philosopher Moses Mendelssohn.

The immediate family had means and influence in imperial Germany. Joachim, while of remote Jewish ancestry and prosperity, was reared Lutheran, though with a governess who was devoutly Roman Catholic. Through her he had a childhood audience with the Bishop of Wurzburg, who gave him religious pictures that entered into his play at mass with his brother and sister.

The Latin of that tradition came as easily into his formative years as did the variety of cultural influences of his exposures to international acquaintances connected with both the academic world and the royal courts of Saxony and, through an aunt, Sweden. The family estate overlooked the Elbe River near Dresden, but, with the family fortune, it was confiscated by Adolf Hitler.

Aside from familial contacts and activities, involving music, drama, literature, and poetry—read and performed—Joachim's early education included classical and modern languages. In 1916, he completed examinations at the Vitzhumsche Gymnasium in Dresden, was commissioned a German army officer, and was sent to the Russian front, accompanied by his boxes of books. He learned Russian and Arabic while on duty, completed a summary of the history of Greek philosophy for his sister, and was forced to encounter, both as a philosophical and as an existential issue, the matter of death. These ingredients came together in his personal religious life and in his intellectual development.

## Life's Work

At the end of World War I, Wach began his serious studies in the history and philosophy of religion at Leipzig. He spent the year 1919 at the University of Munich, under the tutorage of a slightly older, comparably minded instructor, Friedrich Heiler, with whom Wach, at the other's insistence, read Sanskrit, and by whom he was introduced to Rudolf Otto's *Das Heilige* (1920; *The Idea of the Holy*, 1923). After the year 1919, Heiler went to Uppsala, Sweden, to study with Archbishop Nathan Soderblom, who had previously held the chair of religions at Leipzig. Heiler returned in 1920 to the position at Marburg, which he held for the rest of his life, and remained a close friend and continuing influence on Wach.

Wach went on to Berlin, where he came into contact with the major historians of Christian thought and institutions, Adolf von Harnack and Ernst Troeltsch, before returning in 1922 to Leipzig to receive his doctor of philosophy degree for a dissertation begun with Heiler. The method, scope, and structure of Wach's mind were already in evidence in this preliminary work.

Wach's concern for phenomenology grew out of his contact with Edmund Husserl at Freiburg, and similar attentiveness to the history of literature was a by-product of his attending the lectures of Friedrich Gundolf at Heidelberg. By early 1924, Wach had completed a more systematic study on *Religionswissenschaft: Prolegomena zu ihrer wissenschaftstheoretischen Grundlegung* (1924; the science of religion: prolegomena to its epistemological foundations) and was appointed privatdocent in the faculty of philosophy at Leipzig, where his grandfather was still active. Successively thereafter, Wach published (1925) a summary of the fundamental notions of Mahayana Buddhism and a survey of the influence of Friedrich Adolf Trendelenburg upon Wilhelm Dilthey, whose philosophy of history was crucial to Wach's own thought.

Wach was ready to lay out his major study of human "understanding," *Das Verstehen: Grundzüge einer Geschichte der hermeneutischen Theorie im 19. Jahrhundert* (1926-1933), in a series of three volumes illustrative of sequential developments in general interpretive theory. The first volume appeared in 1926 and explained the general German intellectual situation in "hermeneutics," or theory of interpretation, at the outset of the nineteenth century, with focal attention upon the liberal Berlin court preacher and theologian, Friedrich Schleiermacher. The second volume followed in 1929 with a survey, after a lengthy and erudite introduction, of the divergent notions of interpretation applied to biblical materials from Schleiermacher, through twenty-two mid-century German academics, to the conservative proponent of the Erlangen "school," Johann Hofmann. In that same year, Wach gave his inaugural lecture as professor in Leipzig on the philosophical history of the nineteenth century and the theology of history, and, in 1930, he was awarded the degree of doctor of theology from Heidelberg. Volume three, dealing with "understanding in historical research" from before Leopold von Ranke at the outset of the nineteenth century to the positivistic Germans who dominated its mid-years, did not appear until 1933.

The interim had seen Wach's publication of *Einführung in die religionssoziologie* (1931; introduction to religious sociology) and *Typen religiöser Anthropologie* (1932; types of religious anthropology). The former was systematic, the latter comparative of Eastern and Western intellectual traditions. In 1934, Wach brought to fruition his consideration of *Das Problem des Todes in der Philosophie unserer Zeit* (1934; the problem of death in the philosophy of our times). All of this output, and much of its mode of treatment, suffered a severe and jarring impact from the Nazi movement, which forced the government of Saxony to dismiss Wach from his academic post on April 10, 1935.

Fortuitously, Wach had received but days before, from an old friend, Robert Pierce Casey of Brown University, Providence, Rhode Island, the invitation to be visiting professor. In spite of concern for his family and friends, whom he would have to leave behind to the terrible events of war and holocaust, Wach accepted. His family moved into a small villa at Orselina above Locarno in Switzerland, to which he could be a periodic visitor. His father died late in the war, his spirit broken by the tragedy of such vast destruction to all that had been their previous life; his brother survived to become a Lutheran pastor in the new East Germany.

Wach never turned back. He settled readily into the life of the United States and was naturalized as a citizen in 1946. He became an active communicant in the Protestant Episcopal church. His visiting professorial status was regularized in 1937 at Brown, and he was called to head a newly created department of the history of religions at the University of Chicago in 1946. At Chicago, Wach had doctoral candidates, and the desired involvement in the total life of a theological faculty. In both institutions, he displayed concern not merely for the relation of religion to the modern secular university but especially for the students under the impact of secular modernity. He gave generously of time and energy to collective student affairs and to individual counseling needs.

Wach was a devout churchman, though never ordained. He was ill-equipped to handle modern gadgets, even something as simple as the plugging in of a radio, for which he depended upon those students of whom he was most fond and whose company he enjoyed. He got acquainted easily and remained available—a most comforting figure among awesome faculty to the new student. He knew one by name from the first introduction. Yet his systematic mode when lecturing would not tolerate a late arrival.

Wach had the disciplined mind of one trained in the late nineteenth century's academic ideals of "abandoning the haphazard" in scholarship, with none of the arrogance of an elitist. He demanded a precision of time, of vocabulary, and of style—illustrating a touch of formality within a gentle warmth of humanity. He knew the key figures of the world's religions and tried to make them accessible to his students, not only in books but also in person—Hindu, Buddhist, Muslim, and the various kinds of Christian—at a level of both intellectual rigor and spiritual depth.

He was working on a major synthesis, *The Comparative Study of Religions* (1958), when he was stricken, while visiting his mother and sister, by a severe heart attack from which he succumbed within a few weeks. This study and other manuscripts survived and have received posthumous publication.

Ironically, only weeks before Wach's death, in an effort to recompense "that great injustice which the Nazi government had done to this outstanding representative of German science," as his lifelong friend Heiler expressed it, the state of Hesse offered Wach the chair of systematic theology at Marburg once held by Rudolf Otto. In commitment to all that had become the new repository for his life's work, he declined to accept.

### Summary

Joachim Wach tried to find those few unifying definitions by which the great variety of phenomena of religious experience could be understood. He perceived that it was not humanly possible to express with finality those dimensions that were traditionally described as godlike or divine or revelatory. He did think it conceivable to arrive at some generalizations indicative of the human responsive posture toward the essential and substantive activities. Encounters at Chicago with theologians and philosophers of emergent naturalism may have been at odds with Wach's inherent Kantianism, but, when mediated by the Anglican archbishop, William Temple, "process" thought provided the kind of medium through which his own bent toward historically conditioned sociology could be given its dynamic form.

Wach identified the descriptive requirements for a scientific definition of religious experience in a few fundamental propositions. Religious experience is the total response of the total human personality to that which is apprehended as ultimate reality. This experience is the most intense of which the human is capable, and this experience impels the human to act. In the analysis of the religious experience, all expression falls within three categories: theoretical, practical, and sociological. Wach affirmed that religion cannot be the perspective of one. Even the psychological dimension of the experience must have a communal component, if it is to qualify as religious.

In contrast to Mircea Eliade, who succeeded Wach at Chicago and who sought to create a "history of religions" from the diverse phenomena without reference to variations in time and space, Wach saw the unity and universality of all religious experience within a system of metaphysical principles whose fundamental ingredient was "understanding." That understanding required expression, with due reference to the whole history of human "modes of thought" and conscientious concern for a theory of human inquiry. Only then might one propound the nature of "revelation" as the empirical element in knowledge, which does not exclude but lies beyond human thought. Wach concluded that "the real history of man is the history of religion."

### Bibliography

Alles, Gregory D. "Wach, Eliade, and the Critique from Totality." *Numen* 35 (1988): 108-138. An evaluative essay reflecting upon the comparisons and contrasts between Wach and his successor.

Eliade, Mircea, and Joseph M. Kitagawa, eds. *The History of Religions: Essays in Methodology.* Chicago: University of Chicago Press, 1959. Within a volume collected in honor of Wach, Kitagawa's initial essay, "The History of Religions in America" (pages 1-30), places Wach within the context whereby a field of academic study was defined by his transitional role.

Georgia, Robert T. "Joachim Wach and the Study of Religion: A Comparative Approach." *Religious Education* 87, no. 2 (Spring 1992). The author discusses Wach's approach to the study of religion, which is based on comparison.

Kitagawa, Joseph Mitsuo. "The Life and Thought of Joachim Wach." In *The Comparative Study of Religions,* edited by Joachim Wach. New York: Columbia University Press, 1958; London: Columbia University Press, 1961. To accompany the posthumous publication of the manuscript, upon which Wach was working at the time of his death, his former student and colleague wrote a major biographical statement. The volume is an outgrowth of a series of lectures given in India in 1952 and in American universities in 1954-1955.

———. "The Nature and Program of the History of Religions Field." *The Divinity School News* 23, no. 4 (November 1, 1957): 13-25. The reconstruction of a department after the death of Wach and before the assumption of dominance by Eliade provided occasion to discuss Wach's understanding of "the history of religions" and the two kinds of "sociology of religion."

Wach, Joachim. "The Meaning and Task of the History of Religions (*Religionswissenschaft*)." In *The History of Religions: Essays on the Problem of Understanding*, edited by Joseph M. Kitagawa, Mircea Eliade, and Charles H. Long. Chicago: University of Chicago Press, 1967. In the first volume of a series of "Essays in Divinity," reflecting "the Chicago school," a translation of an article from Wach's German of 1935 was given priority of place to demonstrate the complete difference in method and interest of history of religions from comparative religion, whose transition Wach's appearance at Chicago had accomplished.

———. *Understanding and Believing: Essays.* Edited with an introduction by Joseph M. Kitagawa. New York: Harper, 1968. A series of minor writings on a variety of topics, some unpublished, some newly translated, were offered as memorial when Wach's manuscripts were gathered. A bibliography of Wach's works from 1922 to 1955 is included.

Wood, Charles Monroe. *Theory and Religious Understanding: A Critique of the Hermeneutics of Joachim Wach.* Missoula, Mont.: American Academy of Religion, 1975. Originally a doctoral dissertation at Yale (1972), this study examines Wach's method of interpretation as a derivative of his philosophical perspective on human knowledge and understanding.

*Clyde Curry Smith*

# SELMAN ABRAHAM WAKSMAN

*Born:* July 22, 1888; Priluka, Russia
*Died:* August 16, 1973; Hyannis, Massachusetts
*Areas of Achievement:* Medicine and microbiology
*Contribution:* Waksman's painstaking research into the nature of soil microorganisms, culminating in the discovery of streptomycin, helped to bring about the antibiotic age.

## Early Life

Selman Abraham Waksman was born on July 22, 1888, in Priluka, a small, bleak town in the Ukraine some two hundred miles from Kiev. His parents, Jacob and Fradia Waksman, were Russian-Jewish; his mother ran a dry-goods business, and his father's time was spent in managing his property and in study and attending synagogue.

Russia in the late nineteenth century was a place of poverty and prejudice. Waksman, however, remembered his childhood as a time of love and faith; his mother made considerable sacrifices to give him an education. At the age of five, Waksman entered a *cheder*, a private religious school; by the age of seven, he was studying Talmud, and at nine, he was entrusted to Jewish tutors knowledgeable not only in Talmud but also in Russian literature, history, arithmetic, and geography. What he learned, Waksman passed on to others; he taught eagerly in an unlicensed school that was regularly harassed by the czarist police.

The religious quotas of czarist Russia barred Waksman from the gymnasiums, which were the only institutions in which a secondary education could be obtained. Any individual who could pass monthlong competitive examinations, however, could earn a certificate that indicated that his level of knowledge was equivalent to that taught in the gymnasium. In 1907, at the age of nineteen, Waksman made his first attempt to obtain this valuable certificate. Although unsuccessful at the first attempt—a hostile examiner questioned him on the river that flows through Berlin (the Spree)—he succeeded in 1909 in obtaining the credentials.

His mother, however, had recently died, and with her, Waksman's ties to the Ukraine were gone as well. Some cousins had emigrated to the United States; one was a farmer in New Jersey who offered to board the young Waksman if he would emigrate. Although Waksman had won admission to the Polytechnic Institute of Zurich, he headed for the United States in 1910. After leaving the Ukraine in a train headed for the German border, he traveled from Bremen to Philadelphia in the steerage of an ocean liner. Waksman arrived in the United States on November 2, 1910, where his relative gave him a warm welcome.

Although he had never been in a scientific laboratory, Waksman determined that he would study biology or medicine. His gymnasium certificate allowed him admission to the Columbia University College of Physicians and Surgeons, but he was without financial aid. Rutgers University, a state school in New Jersey, however, could offer the young immigrant not only a state scholarship but also the tutelage of Dr. Jacob G. Lipman, head of the bacteriology department at the College of Agriculture and also a Russian immigrant.

Entering Rutgers in 1911, Waksman was at first uncomfortable in the American university. He met his living expenses by working as a greenhouse assistant, earning twenty cents an hour, living in a three-dollar-a-month room in the college farmhouse, and eating cracked eggs at eleven cents a dozen.

## Life's Work

Waksman's scientific career began during his undergraduate years at Rutgers. There, his fascination with the soil and earth began as he saw in a mere patch of earth a world teeming with life and energy. Waksman's senior project involved the enumeration of the organisms in the soil, and it was at about this time that he first came upon the microorganisms known as actinomyces. Even experts then knew little about the biology and chemistry of these microorganisms and about the roles these microscopic creatures played in the world of the soil. It was these actinomyces which ultimately were to be the source of some of the first major antibiotics.

Waksman received a bachelor of science degree in agriculture (Phi Beta Kappa) in 1915 from Rutgers, and was appointed research assistant in soil bacteriology under Lipman at the New Jersey Agricultural Experiment Station (a state-subsidized research facility). He continued to carry on graduate work at Rutgers, earning his master of science degree in 1916. In February of 1916, his first scientific paper was published. During this time, Waksman was granted United States citizenship and married the sister of a close friend from Priluka, Deborah Mitnik.

For his doctoral studies, Waksman accepted a fellowship offer from the University of California at Berkeley. There, he received a Ph.D. in biochemistry in 1918, working at Cutter Laboratories as well during the latter part of his tenure. He returned to Rutgers in July, 1918, taking a double position as lecturer in soil microbiology and microbiologist at the New Jersey Agricultural Experiment Station.

Waksman's firmly held scientific opinion was not only that it was the bacteria that played an important role in the microscopic worlds but also that the actinomyces, fungi, and other microbes had to be considered of equal importance. Waksman, firmly but diplomatically, pressed his views at scientific meetings and in learned journals. Slowly, recognition came. He was made associate professor at Rutgers in 1925 and professor in 1929. His monographs were eagerly read by workers in the field, and his huge textbook, *Principles of Soil Microbiology*, which was published in 1927, became accepted as a classic resource.

It was during this time that one of Waksman's students, René J. Dubos, a Frenchman who had worked with Waksman on the decomposition of cellulose by soil bacteria, was able in 1932 to isolate a soil microorganism that produced an enzyme that digested pneumonia organisms. Somewhat later, in 1938, Dubos found in enriched soil a bacterium active against several disease causing organisms. Isolating the active chemicals, Dubos termed the drug tyrothricin. Although tyrothricin was itself of limited usefulness, it showed the way for the development of other antibiotics.

Following Dubos' success, other scientists, particularly Howard W. Florey and Ernst B. Chain at Oxford, developed new antibiotics. Florey and Chain resurrected penicillin, which had actually been discovered more than a decade earlier by Alexander Fleming of London. With the beginning of World War II, the United States Department of Agriculture and the American pharmaceutical industry threw their weight into the development of penicillin, and by the end of World War II, enough penicillin was being produced to treat at least seven million patients.

It was at about this time that Waksman was called upon by the editor of *Biological Abstracts* to coin a word to describe these new "wonder drugs" that were cropping up in the professional literature. Waksman came up with the term "antibiotic," defining it as a chemical substance produced by a microbe which has the capacity to inhibit the growth of and even to destroy other microbes.

Waksman watched the development of penicillin from the sidelines, although with interest and enthusiasm. He still thought of himself as a soil microbiologist, devoted to the study of soils, composts, peat, and manure piles. With the way lighted by Dubos' 1938 success, however, Waksman was determined to isolate his own antibiotics, using the principles developed during years of research. Subsidized by the New Jersey Agricultural Experiment Station and by Merck and Company, he searched for disease-inhibiting chemicals produced by soil microorganisms. He turned to the actinomyces, those soil microorganisms that had so fascinated him from early in his career, with the certainty that they would prove to be a productive source of powerful new drugs. Indeed, by this time, he had already shown that as many as twenty to fifty percent of the actinomyces produced substances that had the ability to inhibit the growth of other microorganisms.

By 1940, Waksman had isolated his first antibiotic. Christened actinomycin, the drug had a wonderful capacity to destroy microbes but was toxic to experimental animals. Although then considered far too toxic to be used, a later modification of this chemical, actinomycin D (dactinomycin) continues to be employed in the treatment of cancer.

Waksman's laboratory undertook a comprehensive program of screening the actinomyces for their ability to produce antibiotics. Early isolates did not pass muster. In 1942, however, streptothricin seemed to show great promise. It seemed to kill infectious organisms and leave the experimental animals alive and well. Yet disappointment soon set in: Streptothricin had a delayed fatal effect that killed the experimental animals after the bacterial disease was cured.

The good news came in August, 1943. From two strains of streptomyces griseus, Waksman and his students isolated a substance which they dubbed streptomycin. This substance had a deadly effect on the tuberculosis bacilli. Streptomycin was also effective against the microorganisms causing dysentery, typhoid, plague, cholera, and certain types of meningitis and pneumonia, although it was later superseded by other, more effective, drugs. Waksman was also responsible for the discovery of neomycin, an antibiotic used to protect against infection of wounds. In later years, other investigators derived from Waksman's actinomyces a number of additional antibiotics. Following Waksman's discovery, Merck and Company embarked upon a crash program to develop and market streptomycin. By 1946, it was used worldwide, revolutionizing the treatment of tuberculosis. The discovery of this antibiotic, one of the first to be developed and marketed, led the way to the conquest of numerous diseases not before amenable to treatment.

Streptomycin brought Waksman both honors and public acclaim. He was awarded honorary degrees by twenty-two universities. In 1952, Waksman received the Nobel Prize for Medicine and Physiology. His Nobel address described the painstaking work that, in Waksman's own words, had brought the "conquest of the Great White Plague, undreamt of less than ten years ago . . . now virtually within sight."

The discovery also made Waksman a rich man. Waksman declined the greater part of his royalties, endowing the Foundation for Microbiology, a nonprofit corporation devoted to fostering research in microbiology. Patents were assigned to a Rutgers foundation that endowed the Rutgers Institute of Microbiology, founded in 1949 and headed by Waksman until his retirement in 1958. Following the scientist's death, the institution became known as the Waksman Institute.

Photographs of the Nobel laureate show a small, stocky man peering curiously at the world through shell-rimmed glasses. Despite fame and fortune, Waksman remained devoted not only to his science but also to his students. He noted in his autobiography that he owed his success not so much to what he taught his students but to what they taught him: René Dubos was one notable example. Waksman liked to paraphrase the words of an ancient Talmudic scholar, saying,

> I can truthfully say that I owe much to my professors, that I owe more to my colleagues, but that I owe most to my students, of whom I had a brilliant array. What greater joy can there be, in discussing certain scientific accomplishments, than to point to all these former students and say, "I have helped in shaping the minds of these so that they could become what they are today."

Waksman retired from his chair as head of the institute in 1958 but maintained an office and small laboratory at Rutgers. He died in 1973, survived by his widow, Deborah Waksman, and a son, Byron Waksman, also a professor of microbiology.

### Summary

The development of antibiotics revolutionized medical science. Waksman's 1943 discovery of streptomycin, combined with the development of penicillin during the same era, meant that once-fatal bacterial diseases were curable. Tuberculosis, the feared "consumption" of the nineteenth century, was no longer as frightening; it could now be readily treated with streptomycin.

Streptomycin, although still used in combination with other drugs in the management of tuberculosis, has been to some extent superseded by newer antibiotics. Yet the principles by which it was developed—the painstaking analysis of substances produced by naturally occurring microorganisms—formed the bedrock upon which the research that led to the development of even more effective drugs was based.

Waksman exemplified the man of science, devoted to teaching and research and to the painstaking analysis of a given problem. His study of soil microorganisms came to fruition when the actinomyces that he first noticed during his early student days at Rutgers proved to be the source of the valuable antibiotic streptomycin.

With the development of antibiotics such as streptomycin and penicillin, as well as those that came later, health and longevity became the norm rather than the exception.

Waksman's life shows that the promise of America for the early twentieth century immigrant was not merely a myth. A Russian Jew, fleeing prejudice and poverty, he arrived in the United States in 1910. Educated at a state university, he took the resources at hand—the soil upon which he stood—and transformed it into the "wonder drugs" of modern, scientific medicine.

### Bibliography

Carter, Richard. "Miracle Man of Wonder Drugs." In *Nine Who Chose America*. New York: Dutton, 1959. An excellent overview of Waksman's early life and later achievements, stressing Waksman's immigrant origins (part of a *Life* series on great immigrants).

"Obituary: Selman A. Waksman." *New York Times*, August 17, 1973: 1. This article-length overview of Waksman's life is a useful source of information where few sources exist.

Waksman, Selman A. *My Life with the Microbes*. London: Hale, and New York: Simon and Schuster, 1954. Waksman's autobiography. Although stylistically somewhat awkward, it is a major source of information on the scientist's life and work. To some extent a typical immigrant success story, it is redeemed by its honesty and sincerity. Nevertheless, it merely scrapes the surface, giving little insight into the real motivating forces behind Waksman's scientific genius.

———. *Scientific Contributions of Selman A. Waksman: Selected Articles Published in Honor of His Eightieth Birthday, July 22, 1968.* Edited by H. Boyd Woodruff. New Brunswick, N.J.: Rutgers University Press, 1968. A collection of Waksman's scientific contributions, including an introduction by H. Boyd Woodruff, one of his students, giving a brief biography of the scientist.

———. "Streptomycin: Background, Isolation, Properties, and Utilization." *Science* 118 (September 4, 1953): 259-266. Waksman's Nobel Prize address, describing the scientific work that led to the development of streptomycin.

*Adele Lubell*

# LILLIAN D. WALD

*Born:* March 10, 1867; Cincinnati, Ohio
*Died:* September 1, 1940; Westport, Connecticut
*Areas of Achievement:* Nursing and social reform
*Contribution:* Founder of the Henry Street Settlement and organizer of the first public health nursing system, Wald was a major social reformer during the Progressive Era.

## Early Life

Lillian D. Wald was born in Cincinnati on March 10, 1867, one of four children in a Jewish family. Her parents, Minnie Schwarz and Marcus Wald, emigrated from Germany and Poland, respectively, fleeing revolutions in central Europe. Since her father traveled often, selling optical supplies, Minnie was the major influence on Lillian. Minnie loved all forms of beauty—flowers, music, furnishings—and she brought warmth and good taste into the household as well as devotion to family ties.

In 1878, the family moved to Rochester, New York. The city was a center for optical supplies, which made Max Wald's work easier, and family relatives were well established there, people of wealth and status. Like many upper-middle-class girls, Lillian attended a boarding and day school, the School for Young Ladies and Little Girls. The nonsectarian school prepared young women to be wives and mothers, but Lillian aspired to more than a conventional life.

At sixteen, Wald applied to Vassar but was rejected as too young, so she stayed two more years at school, feeling closed in—no profession, no career, no training. Isolated from the larger world, Lillian knew little of the growing social unrest and demands for reform.

Wald spent much time with her married sister, Julia Barry. During Julia's pregnancy a nurse was hired, and Lillian questioned her extensively about her training at Bellevue Hospital School of Nursing in New York City. Wald saw an opportunity for a noble career, and, in 1889, she applied to the New York Hospital's School of Nursing and was accepted. With limited training gleaned from lectures, Wald learned to make bandages and dressings, and to sterilize instruments. Her patients and colleagues alike found Wald a cheerful, dedicated person with extraordinary energy and ability. After her graduation in March, 1891, Wald helped to train incoming students.

In August, 1891, she began her new job as staff nurse at the New York Juvenile Asylum. One thousand children between the ages of five and eighteen were housed in the asylum. Outraged by the poverty, injustice, and abuses the children faced, Wald left after one year, and, in the fall of 1892, she enrolled at Women's Medical College, which was part of the New York Infirmary for Women and Children. Her studies and work made the poor very visible to Wald. She began a volunteer class, teaching home-care and hygiene to immigrant women. Based in the Louis Technical School at 267 Henry Street, Wald was exposed directly to scenes of poverty and degradation so intense that her life was changed.

## Life's Work

Lillian Wald dropped out of medical college, determined to change the dreadful social conditions she encountered in New York's Lower East Side. She and a former schoolmate, Mary Brewster, planned to live among the poor, nursing them in their own homes. Support from wealthy patrons gave them economic security to do so. Wald and Brewster moved into a settlement house on Rivington Street with college graduates who were also willing to share their lives intimately with the poor. Classes were given in English, art, music, history, and economics, but Ward and Brewster focused on nursing the sick. The two nurses went from door to door in the tenements, handing out ointments, antiseptics, and advice. They wrote up their cases for a card file and reported monthly to their chief benefactor, Jacob Schiff, a senior partner in the international banking firm of Kuhn, Loeb, and Company.

Moving to a new address, the top floor of a six-story tenement, Wald and Brewster lived in the district in which they worked. They determined to remain independent and nonsectarian, resisting efforts to join forces with relief agencies. They visited homes, compiling statistics on the wretched situations and conditions they encountered. Immigrants poured into New York's Lower East Side. They clung together in religious and kinship groups, working twelve to fourteen hours daily, trying to survive. Wald wrote vivid reports to Jacob Schiff, describing these poverty-stricken people. Her experiences opened Wald to progressive thinkers and reformers such as Jacob Riis, Lincoln Steffens, and Josephine Lowell (founder of the Consumers' League of New York).

In April of 1895, Schiff bought a house on Henry Street that became Lillian's second home and the center for the Visiting Nurse Service. A second building next door was added later to accommodate the growing number of nurses asking to work with Wald. Henry House became a refuge for sick, needy neighbors who found nursing care as well as friendship there.

In 1900, the family of nurses grew to fifteen—an educated, middle-class, unmarried support network. Wald was the heart of this family, to which she also brought an executive ability to link Henry Street with the world of financial backers and with the larger reform movements. To save her patients' pride, Wald charged from ten cents to a quarter to those who could pay for personal health care, though no one was refused care. She wanted to treat the sick in their homes, referring only the extreme cases to dispensaries or the hospitals.

In 1899, the dynamic Florence Kelley joined Wald's inner circle of friends and advisers, becoming general secretary of the National Consumers' League. A lawyer and social activist, Kelley had served as special investigator of child labor conditions in Illinois. Wald and Kelley allied for social change, especially on behalf of children. Frequent visits by Jane Addams, head of Hull House Settlement, based in Chicago, further enlarged Wald's insights into the need for practical, political solutions to the economic and social problems of the day, which impinged heavily on health conditions. Addams' sharp mind and organizational skills were highly prized, and Wald and her coworkers often turned to her for advice.

Wald was moved particularly by the plight of children playing in crowded streets, attending crowded schools, and living in crowded homes. They faced hunger and disease daily, and Wald tried to awaken a social consciousness of their situation. She promoted neighborhood parks and more playgrounds, and she urged that public schools stay open after school hours and in summer as recreation centers. Wealthy patrons offered homes for day and weekend visits by the children, some bequeathing their estates as camps for Henry Street use.

Wald initiated the hiring of the first public school nurse. Worried that ill children were spreading contagious diseases, she offered to pay half the salary for a nurse if the Board of Education would pay the other half. A Henry Street nurse supervised four schools, identifying illnesses and visiting sick children's homes. When it was found that these schools had healthier children and better attendance than did all the others, the Board of Education agreed to make school nurses part of the system.

Forced to work to supplement their parents' wages, many children were not in school at all. In 1903, pressured by the National Consumers' League, settlement houses, and other reform organizations, New York established limits on child labor, although proper inspection was often absent. In 1905, Wald and Kelley proposed a federal bureau to care for the welfare of children. The proposal reached President Theodore Roosevelt, who discussed it with Wald and others. He supported a bill for a Federal Children's Bureau, and it was introduced in the 1906 Congress.

The bill was backed by prominent organizations and individuals such as women's clubs, state labor committees, newspaper publishers, and religious leaders. The bureau was envisioned as a national research center to collect and classify information on the nation's children. Because Congress refused to hold hearings on the bill, Roosevelt asked Wald to arrange what became, in January of 1909, a Conference on the Care of Dependent Children. When hearings on the bill began, Wald and Kelley testified in Washington, but Congress balked, and Wald and her colleagues kept up a barrage of writing and speaking to get the bill passed. In April of 1912, President William H. Taft signed the bill into law.

Expanding public health nursing into rural as well as urban areas, in 1908 Wald persuaded Schiff to give an initial grant of $10,000 to aid the Red Cross in establishing a Department of Town and Country Nursing. Realizing that there were too few nurses, she envisioned a corps of teachers to train more nurses. She persuaded another wealthy patron to bequeath a large sum to endow Teachers College of Columbia University with a postgraduate school for teacher nurses.

In 1913, the Henry Street Settlement and the Visiting Nurse Service celebrated twenty years of work in the Lower East Side. Wald could look back on twenty years of achievements, including improved status and increased self-esteem for all nurses.

The 1918 worldwide outbreak of influenza put new demands on Wald and her nurses. As head of the Nurses' Emergency Council, she created an effective administration to mobilize nurses, teachers, social workers, and volunteers to meet the health crisis. The Red Scare of 1919-1920, however, gripped the nation in a madness of violence, hatred, and intolerance. Dissent was dangerous, and Wald found herself censured as radical and unpatriotic because of her pacifist stand during World War I. Raising money became more difficult. Schiff died suddenly in September of 1920, ending the longest, steadiest, and most generous source of support for Wald's work.

The 1920's were a conservative age, and social reforms were not supported by the federal government as they had been in the past. Wald and her allies fought to retain progressive gains. She became vice president of the American Association for Labor Legislation, contributed to the American Anti-Imperialist League, and sponsored the American League to Abolish Capital Punishment. Wald remained very active on behalf of civil liberties, but her health declined with overwork.

During the Depression, Henry Street continued as a haven for the needy. The Visiting Nurse Service now had twenty centers, handling almost 100,000 cases annually. In 1933, Wald resigned as head of Henry Street but remained as president of the board of directors.

Wald died on September 1, 1940, and she was mourned by thousands. Her legacy would endure: the Visiting Nurse Service, the Henry Street Settlement, the Federal Children's Bureau, the public school nurse. Lillian Wald enriched the lives of many through her work as a pioneer public nurse, a settlement worker, a feminist, and a reformer—roles she imbued with a wealth of enthusiasm and charm.

### Summary

Lillian D. Wald, through her many efforts to improve health care and remedy the societal ills of poverty, ignorance, and inequality, had an immense impact on U.S. society, the effects of which can still be perceived. Her initial interest in social reform was sparked by the misery she witnessed in poor neighborhoods, but her special contribution to the field was perhaps her identification of the root causes of the problems she saw around her. She did seek to solve the immediate problems of those who required help by providing health care and education, but she also went further, calling for the establishment and support of human rights, civil liberties, and opportunities for all citizens to live decent lives.

### Bibliography

Daniels, Doris G. *Always a Sister: The Feminism of Lillian D. Wald*. New York: Feminist Press, 1989. A selective biography centered on Wald's feminist thinking and actions. Chapter notes, a bibliographical essay, and an index are included.

Duffus, Robert L. *Lillian Wald, Neighbor and Crusader*. New York: Macmillan, 1938. Written with Wald's cooperation, this is a glowing tribute to her and her career. Includes an index.

Rubenstein, A. T. "Fire, Grace, and Sisterhood: Two Women Activists of the Early 20th Century." *Science and Society* 55, no. 4 (Winter 1991-1992). Rubenstein discusses the lives and social works of Wald and Rose Pastor Stokes.

Siegel, Beatrice. *Lillian Wald of Henry Street*. New York and London: Macmillan, 1983. An excellent biography that captures the private Wald as well as the public figure. Chapter notes, sources, and an index are included.

Trolander, Judith A. *Settlement Houses and the Great Depression*. Detroit, Mich.: Wayne State University Press, 1975. The introduction and chapters one through three are superb regarding settlement houses and reform. Includes an appendix, chapter notes, and a bibliography.

Wald, Lillian D. *The House on Henry Street*. New York: Holt, 1915. An engrossing narrative of the famous settlement and its role in social reform.

Many stories illustrate conditions among the poor. Includes an index.

Williams, Beryl. *Lillian Wald, Angel of Henry Street*. New York: Messner, 1948. A lively biography meant mainly for young readers. Includes frequent dialogue and many anecdotes. A brief biography and an index are provided.

*S. Carol Berg*

# KURT WALDHEIM

*Born:* December 21, 1918; Sankt Andrä-Wördern, Austria

*Area of Achievement:* Diplomacy

*Contribution:* Following his tenure as an Austrian diplomat, Waldheim served as secretary general of the United Nations, where he distinguished himself by organizing massive relief operations. His subsequent election as president of Austria was overshadowed by controversies over his military service during World War II.

## Early Life

Kurt Josef Waldheim was born in Sankt Andrä-Wördern in Lower Austria, one of three children of Walter and Josefina Waldheim. Walter—he had changed the family name from Watzlawik to Waldheim shortly before his son's birth—was the local schoolmaster and would eventually advance to the position of superintendent of schools for the district of Tulln. Following his graduation from secondary school at Klosterneuburg near Vienna in 1936, Kurt enrolled at the Consular Academy in Vienna to study diplomacy. To fulfill his military obligation, he also enrolled as a one-year volunteer in the Austrian army, where he served in a cavalry unit.

The Waldheims were devout Roman Catholics, and both father and son were active supporters of Chancellor Kurt von Schuschnigg, who, as leader of the Christian Socialist Party, stood for an independent Austria. Following the Nazi annexation of Austria in 1938, the Waldheims' support for Schuschnigg resulted in considerable hardships for Walter, including arrests by the Gestapo. Young Waldheim still had to complete his military training with his original Austrian army unit, which by now had become part of the German army. At the same time, he managed to continue his studies and graduated from the Consular Academy in the spring of 1939. The question of whether Waldheim was at that time a member of National Socialist organizations such as the National Socialist Students League and an Equestrian Unit of the Sturmabteilung ("storm troopers," or SA) did not become an issue until his campaign for the presidency of Austria in the 1980's.

Between brief stints with his military unit and officer candidate training in Germany, Waldheim managed to attend law lectures at the University of Vienna, where he passed the basic examination in law in March of 1940. In June of 1941, Waldheim's cavalry unit participated in the German invasion of Russia, where, in December of the same year, he was wounded and sent to Vienna for physical therapy.

In the spring of 1942, Waldheim, now a lieutenant, was returned to active military service with the German 12th Army in the Balkans. Until the end of the war, he served in a number of capacities such as intelligence officer, interpreter, and liaison officer in at least ten different locations in Bosnia, Greece, and Albania, where German and Italian units were involved in partisan warfare and so-called pacification operations. Throughout this period, Waldheim managed to obtain several study leaves that enabled him to complete his doctorate in law at the University of Vienna in April of 1944. Following his marriage to Elisabeth Ritschel, he returned to duty in Greece with Army Group E, which became involved in the deportation of Jews.

## Life's Work

In June of 1946, Waldheim was appointed a career member of the Austrian Foreign Service. The pleasant and courteous young man impressed his superiors with his dedication and his abilities. In the years to come, he would serve in a variety of positions, including first secretary of the Austrian embassy in Paris (1948-1951), chief of the Personnel Division in the Austrian Foreign Ministry (1951-1955), and Austrian ambassador to Canada (1958-1960). Beginning in 1964, Waldheim served for four years as Austria's permanent representative to the United Nations and subsequently for two years as minister of foreign affairs. In 1971, he was narrowly defeated in his campaign for the presidency of Austria. In the same year, he was appointed secretary general of the United Nations for his first five-year term.

Like U Thant, his predecessor in the office of secretary general, Waldheim viewed the United Nations as a forum for communication and understood that the effectiveness of his office depended to no small degree on the support of the major powers. At the same time, he enjoyed support from Third World and nonaligned nations. A diplomat of the old school, he used his office to mediate conflicts and reconcile conflicting opinions that, given the inherently weak position of the secretary general, required considerable diplomatic skills.

In the course of his ten years as secretary general, Waldheim became involved in the mediation of numerous conflicts as well as in peace-keeping operations in such places as Cyprus and Yemen. In the early 1970's he began talks with the South African government and the South-West Africa People's Organization (SWAPO) over the future of Namibia. In the late 1970's, he played a major role in the establishment of the United Nations Interim Force in Lebanon (UNIFL). There were also failures; perhaps the most widely publicized was his trip to Tehran, Iran, to bring about the release of American hostages. Above all, Waldheim distinguished himself in organizing and implementing massive relief programs in Bangladesh, Cambodia, Nicaragua, and Guatemala. Although he generally preferred to work behind the scenes, he also voiced his concerns publicly when he appealed on humanitarian grounds for a cessation of U.S. bombing of dikes in North Vietnam.

Waldheim's election for an unprecedented third term as secretary general ran into opposition from the People's Republic of China, which favored a candidate from a Third World nation. In early 1983, he retired from his position at the United Nations and was succeeded by Javier Pérez de Cuéllar of Peru.

After a brief interlude as a research professor for diplomacy at Georgetown University in Washington, D.C., Waldheim again became a candidate for the presidency of Austria in 1986. Even before the electoral campaign was in full swing, however, an article in the Austrian weekly *Profil* revived old rumors and raised new questions about Waldheim's alleged membership in Nazi organizations and his wartime service in the Balkans. Waldheim continued to deny all allegations, even in the face of some documentary evidence to the contrary, and did not help matters by issuing vague and contradictory statements about his military service.

At the same time, the U.S.-based World Jewish Congress (WJC) took an increasingly aggressive role in the campaign to force Waldheim to reveal the details of his alleged Nazi past and military service during the war. However, other prominent Jews, such as the famous Nazi hunter Simon Wiesenthal, criticized the involvement of the WJC and argued that the available evidence was simply not sufficient to label Waldheim a Nazi or a war criminal. Many Austrians reacted angrily to the criticism from abroad as an unwarranted interference in Austria's internal affairs. The fact that much of the criticism was seen as coming from the WJC produced an upsurge of nationalism and anti-Semitism in Austria and helped solidify Waldheim's electoral support. In 1986, he handily won a run-off election against Kurt Steyrer, the candidate for the Socialist Party, and was inaugurated for a six-year term. However, the inaugural ceremonies were accompanied by protest demonstrations, while many European governments withheld the customary congratulations and distanced themselves from the newly elected president.

The turmoil over Waldheim's wartime activities continued and overshadowed his entire presidency. Under persistent pressure from the WJC, Attorney General of the United States Edwin Meese eventually agreed, in 1987, that Waldheim should be placed on the "Watch List" of undesirable aliens, thereby denying him entry into the United States as a private person. In 1988, a specially appointed international Commission of Historians was, on the basis of available evidence, unable to provide a final answer to the question of Waldheim's guilt. However, the commission also noted that he must have been aware of the illegal acts committed in the Balkans and that his own descriptions of his military past were at variance with the established facts. Waldheim's diplomatic isolation was at last broken when, on the invitation of Pope John Paul II in 1987, he made an official visit to the Vatican. In 1991, President Waldheim announced that he would not run for a second term in 1992.

### Summary

Had it not been for the public controversy initiated by Waldheim's presidential bid, he would, in all likelihood, be remembered as a skillful and effective Austrian diplomat and a competent and relatively efficient, if somewhat colorless, secretary general of the United Nations. As it turned out, however, his ambition to occupy the highest office his country had to offer brought about an unexpected public scrutiny of his past. Rather than squarely facing the various charges leveled against him, he pursued a course of action marked by a mixture of denials, contradictions, and changing versions of his military record. In many respects, Waldheim's defensive strategy reflected an attitude held by many of his fellow citizens, who felt that after the Nazi annexation of their country, they had little choice but to go along with the new political reality if they wanted to save their careers.

Increasing media involvement on both sides of the Atlantic, attended by a good measure of irresponsible rhetoric and sensationalist but baseless charges, produced a climate that seemed to rule out a rational dialogue. The outbreak of a number of anti-Semitic incidents reminiscent of the Nazi years and of openly anti-Semitic statements by several politicians clearly shocked a good number of Austrians and persuaded them to reexamine their nation's role during World War II.

### Bibliography

Bassett, Richard. *Waldheim and Austria*. London: Viking, 1988; New York: Viking, 1989. This slim volume by a journalist attempts to examine the Waldheim controversy in the broader context of Austria's recent history. Includes a brief appendix with documents, an index, and photographs.

Finger, Seymour Maxwell, and Arnold A. Saltzman. *Bending with the Winds: Kurt Waldheim and the United Nations*. New York: Praeger, 1990. Based, in part, on numerous interviews, this small volume by two former diplomats provides a useful assessment of Waldheim's tenure at the United Nations. Finger and Saltzman characterize Waldheim as an ambitious and mediocre secretary general. Includes a bibliography and an index.

Herzstein, Robert Edwin. *Waldheim: The Missing Years*. London: Grafton, and New York: Arbor House, 1988. This is a very readable and well-documented account of Waldheim's activities during the years between 1942 and the end of World War II that exonerates Waldheim of direct responsibility for war crimes in the Balkans and sees him as a bureaucratic facilitator. Includes an index, notes on sources, and photographs.

International Commission of Historians. *The Waldheim Report*. Copenhagen: University of Copenhagen and Museum Tusculanum Press, 1993. This report, submitted to the Austrian federal chancellor Dr. Franz Vranitzky on February 8, 1988, was unable to provide a final answer to the question of Waldheim's wartime guilt. The report concludes that while Waldheim had no command functions in the Balkans, he must have been aware of the nature of the German reprisals.

Levy, Alan. *The Wiesenthal File*. London: Constable, 1993; Grand Rapids, Mich.: Eerdmans, 1994. Part 4 of this volume offers a lucid and balanced discussion of Waldheim's career, his denazification, and Wiesenthal's view of the Waldheim question. Includes an index and photographs.

Mitten, Richard. *The Politics of Antisemitic Prejudice: The Waldheim Phenomenon in Austria*. Boulder, Co.: Westview Press, 1992. This scholarly and well-documented account of the Waldheim controversy in the context of Austrian politics offers an excellent critical analysis of the charges leveled against Waldheim and examines the arguments advanced by his defenders and his detractors. Extensive and very useful notes.

Rosenbaum, Eli M., and William Hoffer. *Betrayal: The Untold Story of the Kurt Waldheim Investigation and Cover-Up*. New York: St. Martin's Press, 1993. The authors present an accurate chronology of the war years preceding Waldheim's appointment as secretary general of the United Nations.

Waldheim, Kurt. *In the Eye of the Storm. A Memoir*. London: Weidenfeld and Nicolson, 1985; Bethesda, Md.: Adler and Adler, 1986. Waldheim attempts to explain his objectives and his actions in the course of the various conflicts he experienced during his ten years as secretary general of the United Nations. Includes an index.

*Helmut J. Schmeller*

## LECH WAŁĘSA

*Born:* September 29, 1943; Popowo, Poland

*Areas of Achievement:* Trade unionism, government, and politics

*Contribution:* Wałęsa's receipt of the Nobel Peace Prize in 1983 underlined his contributions to peaceful political evolution in the Eastern Bloc. Wałęsa's role since 1980 as leader of Solidarnost (Solidarity) in pressuring the Polish leadership for recognition of proletariat demands that were not addressed by the country's government-controlled trade unions was capped by the Polish authorities in 1989 with the holding of free elections and the subsequent victory of the Solidarity-led ticket.

### Early Life

Lech Michal Wałęsa was born in Popowo, Poland, north of Warsaw on September 29, 1943, the son of a carpenter, Boleslaw Wałęsa, and his wife, Fela Kaminska. His father died of deprivations suffered during World War II in a Nazi concentration camp when Lech was eighteen months old; his mother later married her deceased husband's brother, Stanisław. Lech was reared with seven siblings in the straitened circumstances of postwar Poland.

Wałęsa was trained in a state agricultural school at Lipno as an electrician and, after completing his studies, served two years in the army. Wałęsa moved to Gdańsk in 1966, where he began working in the Lenin Shipyards as an electrician. Wałęsa was working in the shipyards in 1970 when rioting erupted over the high cost of food; more than one hundred people were killed in the subsequent unrest. The demonstrations brought down Władysław Gomułka's government, but little was ultimately achieved. The same year, Wałęsa married, and he and his wife eventually had eight children.

### Life's Work

Wałęsa was dismissed in April, 1976, for participating in protests over the decline in living standard concessions made in 1970 by the authorities to the workers after riots over declining living standards. Wałęsa was unemployed for the next four years, during which time he supported his family by taking odd jobs. During this period he participated in meetings of the Workers Self-Defense Committee and edited an underground paper, *The Coastal Worker*, critical of the government. In 1978, Wałęsa also became a founding member of the Free Trade Union of the Baltic Coast, which would later provide many leaders and ideas for Solidarity. As Wałęsa's political awareness grew, so did his scrapes with the authorities; by his own estimate, he was detained more than one hundred times by the authorities during 1976-1980. Polish consciousness was heightened in October, 1978, with the election of Cardinal of Kraków Karol Wojtyła as Pope John Paul II. John Paul returned to Poland in June, 1979, for a nine-day visit to scenes of extraordinary national rejoicing.

Wałęsa's star again rose in August, 1980, when workers across Poland engaged in wildcat strikes protesting price increases. On July 1, the government had raised the prices of several types and cuts of meat 60 to 90 percent. In the Gdańsk Lenin Shipyards, events that summer were brought to a head by the dismissal for labor agitation of Anna Walentynowicz, an elderly woman who was six months short of receiving her retirement benefits. On August 14, the day that the strike began, Wałęsa climbed the fence and joined strikers in the Lenin Shipyards. The strike quickly spread throughout Poland, from the steelworkers at Nowa Huta to the Silesian coal mines. Intellectuals, peasants, and working men throughout Poland joined the labor unrest. More than 300,000 workers were shortly out on strike. The Gdańsk Lenin Shipyards' Inter-Factory Strike Committee, chaired by Wałęsa, presented a list of twenty-one demands to the government.

On August 31, 1980, the Polish government signed an accord with Wałęsa that granted unprecedented rights to labor organizations in a Communist country. Shortly thereafter, the first secretary, Edward Gierek, was dismissed. The right for workers to form independent trade unions was recognized, wage and benefit increases were granted, Catholic mass was broadcast on Sundays, censorship was eased, and political dissidents were freed. The 1980 strike that led to the formation of Solidarity drove Gierek's government from power. While Solidarity sought change from the authorities, it was careful not to offer challenges that would force the government's hand. Wałęsa and Solidarity called their innovations a "self-limiting revolution." As chairman of the National Commission of Solidarity, Wałęsa had enormous visibility.

Solidarity immediately attracted many followers; shortly before the imposition of martial law,

•

Wałęsa numbered its followers at ten million. Wałęsa once described his role as that of a "democratic dictator"; goals are developed in a democratic context, and Wałęsa then sets himself to realize them. Despite his prominence and popularity, Wałęsa as the head of a broad democratic movement spent much of his time attempting to calm militants within his organization and striking to head off confrontation with the authorities. Such a broad-based movement had many shades of opinion within it, and Wałęsa as a realist attempted to rein in its more extreme members.

The Soviet Union began to take an increasingly harsh line toward its unreliable Western neighbor and ally. Most menacing was the massing of fifty-five Soviet divisions near Poland's eastern frontier. The nervous Polish government began to see Soviet intervention as an increasingly likely possibility.

Events continued to show the increasing influence of Solidarity; on March 27, 1981, the biggest organized protest in the Eastern Bloc occurred when thirteen million workers staged a four-hour strike to protest the beatings in Bydgoszcz of several Solidarity activists. Solidarity's influence extended into the countryside with the formation of Rural Solidarity, making possible a coalition of workers and peasants. The government responded to the increasing unrest by appointing General Wojciech Jaruzelski Party leader in addition to premier on October 18, 1981.

After the imposition of martial law on December 13, 1981, the Polish authorities began a campaign of vilification against Wałęsa, describing him as the "former head of a former union." Nearly six thousand individuals were taken into immediate custody, among them Wałęsa and the rest of the Solidarity leadership. The number interned rose eventually to more than ten thousand. More than ninety thousand were tried by civil courts in the first six months of martial law. All labor unions, including Solidarity, were dissolved by a law introduced on October 6, 1982. A protest strike at the Lenin Shipyards in Gdańsk was ended when the authorities militarized the shipyard. When Solidarity attempted to organize a nationwide protest strike in November, it failed miserably.

On the day Wałęsa was released from prison he stated, "In my future conduct I will be courageous, but also prudent, and there is nothing negotiable in this regard. I will talk and act, not on my knees, but with prudence." Wałęsa was restored to the Lenin Shipyards' payroll in January, 1983, although he did not formally return to work until April. Wałęsa continued to work to restore Solidarity's role in national affairs; shortly after his return to work he prophetically declared that Solidarity "was a moral force without whose participation Poland could not get out of the crisis." He constantly reiterated that it was not Solidarity's intention to overthrow the government but to better workers' lives. Solidarity banners were unfurled at rallies, and, despite the authorities' best efforts, Solidarity's underground continued to keep the organization and its values alive.

Martial law was suspended on December, 1982, and lifted on July 22, 1983. Despite the government's attempts to bury him in oblivion, Wałęsa and his vision continued to thrive. His contributions to human values were recognized in 1983 when he was awarded the Nobel Peace Prize. The news was given to him by Western correspondents; Wałęsa observed, "The world recognizes Solidarity's ideals and struggles."

As the Polish government continued to grapple with its problems, it considered approaching Wałęsa for assistance. In 1987, Jaruzelski created a consultative council to include people of disparate political views and extended an invitation to Wałęsa, who declined to join. Wałęsa's refusal was based on his observation that the new council would only have the ability to debate issues and policy but lack the ability to legislate change.

Wałęsa again reemerged as a force in Polish politics in the autumn of 1988, when the government initiated talks with him. Faced by an outbreak of wildcat strikes, the government proposed to Wałęsa that it would open talks about relegalizing Solidarity if Wałęsa would persuade the workers to return to work. After hard bargaining, Wałęsa ended the strikes. Wałęsa's durability has proven remarkable; the loyalty that Solidarity retained during its period of repression combined with other factors to force the Polish government to hold elections in the summer of 1989, in which Solidarity candidates did remarkably well. Wałęsa proved himself a masterful and patient politician.

Despite official hostility, Solidarity continued to prove a potential alternative to the country's increasingly desperate financial problems. Wałęsa waited and on April 5, 1989, signed an agreement lifting the governmental ban on Solidarity, allowing the organization to participate in the upcoming elections for the Sejm. The government had proven itself unable to cope with its accumulated financial problems; inflation had reached 200 percent and the foreign debt stood at $39 billion. The result was a very unpleasant surprise for the Polish Communist Party; of 261 contested seats, Solidarity won 260.

A further element strengthening the forces of change was the visit of U.S. President George Bush to Poland in July, 1989. Both the Polish government and Wałęsa appealed to Bush to extend aid in the form of credits and loans to Poland to an eventual level of $10 billion in order to strenghten the forces pushing toward a mixed economy. Bush unfortunately offered about one hundredth of the amount requested, putting a severe strain on Polish reformers who wish to avoid seeking Eastern Bloc support. Wałęsa negotiated with the Polish president Jaruzelski throughout August and September, 1989, to prepare the way for forming a government led by a Solidarity activist. Solidarity proved its influence by largely halting strikes during this period.

In 1990 Wałęsa became Poland's first democratically elected president. His term, however, oversaw the difficult transition to a capitalist economy, and Wałęsa's ardent Catholocism was seen by many as tying Poland's government too closely to the church. By the next election, in 1995, Wałęsa's popular support had declined, and he did not win another term.

### Summary

Lech Wałęsa's contribution to the liberalization of Polish political life cannot be overstated. A proletarian from a working-class background, Wałęsa had the courage and skill to force a government holding power to admit by its actions that it simply represented a dictatorship. Wałęsa consistently showed the greatest courage from the beginning of his organizing activities, suffering punishment for his efforts. A deeply religious man, he consistently displayed moderation in the face of provocation by the authorities. In the early days of Solidarity, his abilities to compromise avoided splitting the movement between the moderate and more extreme elements.

The election on August 24, 1989, and subsequent appointment of longtime Solidarity supporter Tadeusz Mazowiecki, a lay Catholic lawyer and journalist, as prime minister represents the first time since 1945 that a government in Eastern Europe has been led by a non-Communist. While the Communist Party retains four influential ministerial portfolios to Solidarity's eight positions, Solidarity has been able to achieve the first coalition government in the Eastern Bloc led by non-Communists since 1945. The example that Solidarity provided to the rest of the Eastern Bloc had profound reverberations in 1989 in East Germany, Czechoslovakia, Hungary, Romania, and Bulgaria.

Wałęsa's and Solidarity's examples of nonviolent resistance will continue to influence Eastern European politics for many years to come. Despite Poland's crippling economic legacy from its Communist rulers, Solidarity's government has the immense advantage that it truly represents a "government of the people," the first that Poland has had since World War II. It is a mark of the high esteem in which Wałęsa is held worldwide that when he visited Washington in late 1989, he was invited to address a joint session of Congress, being only the second foreigner ever to be accorded this honor. Wałęsa promised to pursue a peaceful middle path; stating, "we want to take what is good from capitalism—what is good for the people, what the people will take from it, but we also want to take what is good from socialism."

### Bibliography

Ascherson, Neal. *The Polish August: The Self-Limiting Revolution.* London and New York: Penguin, 1986. Ascherson, a British correspondent, was in Poland during the heady days of Solidarity; the work covers the history of the country from 1939 to the imposition of martial law.

———, ed. *The Book of Lech Wałęsa.* London: Allen Lane, and New York: Simon and Schuster, 1982. A collection of various comments and statements of the leader of Solidarity with a good introduction providing some basic background.

Garton Ash, Timothy. *The Polish Revolution: Solidarity, 1980-1982.* Rev. ed. London: Granta, and New York: Penguin, 1991. Ash is a British historian specializing in Eastern Europe. His account is vivid and authoritative, covering the period from the beginnings of Solidarity to the imposition of martial law.

Labedz, Leopold, ed. *Poland Under Jaruzelski.* New York: Scribner, 1984. A collection of sixty-five articles by specialists on Eastern Europe analyzing Solidarity's influence and the immediate aftermath of martial law.

Mihas, D.E.M. "Poland: Two Years after Wałęsa." *Contemporary Review* 272, no. 1584 (January,

1998). Discussion of the reasons for Wałęsa's fall from power and information on his planned campaign against the reelection of Polish president Aleksander Kwasniewski in 2000.

Wałęsa, Lech. *A Way of Hope: An Autobiography.* New York: Holt, 1987. This work remains the best source for Wałęsa's early years and his experiences as leader of Solidarity. Despite its being published in 1987, Wałęsa's reminiscences end in 1984; as a result, the work does not contain his thoughts on the most recent dramatic changes in Poland.

Zubek, Voytek. "The Eclipse of Walesa's Political Career." *Europe-Asia Studies* 49, no. 1 (January, 1997). The author examines the end of Wałęsa's political career and his role in Poland's instability.

*John C. K. Daly*

# ALICE WALKER

*Born:* February 9, 1944; Eatonton, Georgia
*Area of Achievement:* Literature
*Contribution:* Walker, winner of the Pulitzer Prize and the American Book Award, has dedicated her life to establishing a literary canon of African American women writers and to encouraging the "survival whole" of all women. She has actively sought to win recognition for literary "foremothers" such as Zora Neale Hurston and to place their contributions within the fabric of her own artistry.

## Early Life

Alice Walker was born on February 9, 1944, into a family of sharecroppers near Eatonton, Georgia. Her father, Willie Lee Walker, was the grandson of slaves. Walker's enslaved paternal great-great-grandmother, Mary Poole, had walked from Virginia to Georgia carrying two of her children on her hips. Walker's relationship with her father became strained as she grew into adolescence and showed a proclivity for intellectual pursuits. Although her father was brilliant, his educational opportunities had been limited, and he feared that education would place barriers between him and his children. When Walker left her home for Spelman College in Atlanta, her relationship with her father ended.

Minnie Tallulah Grant Walker, Walker's mother, realized how important education was for her daughter. Minnie Walker, a farmhand and domestic worker, greatly desired an education for her daughter. She enrolled Walker in the first grade at the age of four and excused her from household chores so that she might have time for her reading and schoolwork. Minnie Walker saved the money she earned as a domestic in the town of Eatonton and bought several gifts that had a great impact upon her daughter's life. These gifts included a sewing machine that enabled Walker to make her own clothes, a suitcase, and a typewriter, of which she later made good use.

When Walker was eight years old, a shot fired from her brother's BB gun permanently blinded her right eye. Convinced that the resulting scar tissue in her eye was disfiguring and ugly, she retreated into solitude. She spent the next seven to eight years reading voraciously and writing poems. Walker was the valedictorian of her high school class, and when she was graduated in 1961, she was offered a scholarship to Spelman College in Atlanta. After traveling to Africa in 1964, Walker returned to the United States and entered Sarah Lawrence College. She soon discovered that she was pregnant, and just as quickly she found herself depressed and on the verge of suicide. Walker made a decision to end the pregnancy instead of her life and subsequently wrote her first published short story, "To Hell with Dying." She also produced *Once* (1965), her first published collection of poems, during her years at Sarah Lawrence.

While she was attending college, Walker spent her summers working for the Civil Rights movement in Georgia. She was graduated from Sarah Lawrence College in 1965, and after graduation, she became even more involved in the Civil Rights movement. In 1967, Walker was married to lawyer Mel Leventhal and moved with him to Mississippi. Leventhal worked as a civil rights attorney in the Jackson school desegregation cases, and Walker worked with Head Start programs and held writer-in-residence positions at Tougaloo College and Jackson State University. She subsequently taught at Wellesley College, the University of Massachusetts at Amherst, the University of California at Berkeley, and Brandeis University. In 1969, Walker's only child, Rebecca, was born.

## Life's Work

In 1970, while she was working on her short story "The Revenge of Hannah Kemhuff," Alice Walker discovered the works of Zora Neale Hurston. Her discovery of Hurston had a profound effect on Walker. Walker described Hurston as her literary "foremother," and in her essay "Zora Neale Hurston" (1979), Walker states that were she condemned to spend her life on a desert island with an allotment of only ten books, she would choose two of Hurston's books: *Mules and Men* (1935) and *Their Eyes Were Watching God* (1937). In August, 1973, Walker traveled to Florida to locate Hurston's grave. She had a marker placed on the spot that was most likely Hurston's grave and then dedicated herself to calling attention to Hurston's genius. Through Walker's efforts, Hurston's work received the critical acclaim that it deserved.

In 1970, Walker published her first novel, *The Third Life of Grange Copeland.* Although Grange Copeland is the protagonist of the novel, Walker focuses on his treatment of African American women. Walker's main concerns in her novels are the power-

lessness of African American women and sexist behavior on the part of men. In 1972, after the publication of *The Third Life of Grange Copeland*, Walker left Mississippi to teach at Wellesley College and the University of Massachusetts at Amherst.

The following year, Walker published a book of poetry, *Revolutionary Petunias* (1973), for which she won the Lillian Smith Award. This small volume of poems is a celebration of people who refuse to fit into other people's molds. She also published a book of short stories, *In Love and Trouble* (1973). The stories in this first collection depict African American women who are victimized by racism and/or sexism. They are women who are not whole, are often mute, and who are used and abused by the men they love.

In 1976, Walker published her second novel. *Meridian* is the story of a young woman's personal development in the midst of the Civil Rights movement. More autobiographical elements may be found in *Meridian* than in any other Walker narrative. Many of the struggles faced by Meridian were similar to struggles that Walker confronted in both her college years at a predominantly white women's college and in her interracial marriage to a civil rights lawyer. In 1976, Walker's marriage to Mel Leventhal ended in divorce, and two years later, Walker decided to move from New York City to San Francisco. A year after her move to the West Coast, Walker produced two more books. She published her second volume of African American women-centered poems, *Good Night, Willie Lee, I'll See You in the Morning* (1979), and she produced an anthology of Zora Neale Hurston's works, *I Love Myself When I Am Laughing* (1979).

Several literary critics, and even Walker herself, have compared Walker's stories and novels to crazy quilts. The bits and pieces that she weaves together have much in common; they originate in the South and they reveal the lives of African American women in various stages of development. In 1981, Walker produced *You Can't Keep a Good Woman Down*, a volume of fourteen stories that address the blossoming creativity of women. One year later, she produced her Pulitzer Prize-winning novel *The Color Purple* (1982). *The Color Purple* is a series of ninety letters that Celie, Walker's outwardly silent protagonist, addresses to God. These letters disclose Celie's development of self and voice, while providing the reader with a vision of how the societal intersection of sexism and racism affects the African American family.

The themes of forgiveness and reconciliation are prominent in Walker's writing. In Walker's next novel, *The Temple of My Familiar* (1989), her characters work toward forgiving one another. Walker reveals much of her personality in her book of essays *In Search of Our Mother's Gardens* (1983). Among other topics, she describes her discovery of and commitment to Zora Neale Hurston. Although Walker is a devoted mother, in her essay "One Child of One's Own," she openly and honestly describes her decision to have only one child. In *Living by the Word* (1988), her second volume of essays, her discussions range from the love she has for her daughter to her reactions to criticism of the treatment of men in her book *The Color Purple* (1985). In an interview with Oprah Winfrey in 1989, Walker discussed her critics' failure to recognize the development of nurturance and sensitivity in her male characters. In *The Color Purple*, Albert asks Celie to remarry him, and in *The Temple of My Familiar*, Suwelo realizes that Carlotta, and all women, are beings with feelings and spirits.

In several of her essays in *Living by the Word*, Walker moves her focus from the individual to larger issues between the peoples of this world—indeed, to unity within the universe. Walker's volumes of poetry *Horses Make a Landscape Look More Beautiful* (1984) and *Her Blue Body Everything We Know: Earthling Poems 1965-1990 Complete* (1991) reflect her larger concern for the cultures of this world and the planet itself. In her novel *Possessing the Secret of Joy* (1992), Walker moves from African American culture to detail the misogyny contained in the hideous practice of female circumcision. She continued her examination of that practice in the 1993 book *Warrior Marks: Female Genital Mutilation and the Sexual Blinding of Women*, which she wrote with Pratibha Parmas. Since the mid-1980's, Walker has lived in northern California. There she writes, communes with her friends, works in her garden, and prays to her Great Spirit.

### Summary

Alice Walker has had a tremendous impact on the African American literary canon. In addition to being a major author of notable literature, Walker has enlarged the canon by bringing the works of Zora Neale Hurston before the public, and she has both written within and revised the tradition of African American women writers. Her literary contribution includes novels, short stories, essays, and poetry. Walker moved to the North and then to the West, but her writer's soul returned to the South of her childhood; thence, she has given voice to previously silent and unseen generations of African American women. She has recognized their artistry and praised their resiliency and strength. Walker writes to and for women of all colors and cultures, urging them to know their inner selves and to bind up wounds resulting from centuries of silence and abuse. Walker believes in change, for the individual and for society, and for the "survival whole" of the African American woman. Although Walker has been labeled a feminist writer, she prefers the term "womanist" rather than "feminist," for she believes that the term "womanist" captures the spirit of the African American woman. The spirit of the African American woman remains Walker's primary commitment.

### Bibliography

Bloom, Harold, ed. *Alice Walker.* New York: Chelsea House, 1989. This volume includes much of the best current criticism of Walker's work. In his introduction, Harold Bloom discusses the impact of Zora Neale Hurston's work on Walker, and Dianne F. Sadoff and Deborah E. McDowell also discusses the import of the Walker-Hurston relationship.

Braendlin, Bonnie. "Alice Walker's *The Temple of My Familiar* as Pastiche." *American Literature* 68, no. 1 (March, 1996). Presents analysis of Walker's novel *The Temple of My Familiar,* which has been criticized as having a confusing narrative style.

Christian, Barbara. *Black Feminist Criticism: Perspectives on Black Women Writers.* New York: Pergamon Press, 1985. Christian includes two chapters about Alice Walker. "The Contrary Women of Alice Walker" is an analysis of the female protagonists of *In Love and Trouble*. "Alice Walker: The Black Woman Artist as Wayward" explores the ways in which Walker uses "forbidden" topics as a route to truth.

———. *Black Women Novelists: The Development of a Tradition, 1892-1976.* Westport, Conn.: Greenwood Press, 1980. Barbara Christian traces the historical development of the literature of African American women. She then critically analyzes the works of three contemporary African American writers who are building from the earlier tradition that preceded them and are developing that tradition in a critical way. Chapter 6, "Novels for Everyday Use," is an analysis of the early novels of Alice Walker.

Gates, Henry Louis, Jr., and K. A. Appiah, eds. *Alice Walker: Critical Perspectives Past and Present*. New York: Amistad Press, 1993. The most complete collec- tion of essays on Walker, this volume contains eleven reviews of her novels and sixteen critical essays on various aspects of her literature. The volume concludes with two well-regarded interviews in which Walker herself discusses her literary contributions.

Walker, Alice. *In Search of Our Mother's Gardens.* San Diego, Calif.: Harcourt Brace, 1983; London: Women's Press, 1984. A volume of Walker's essays in which she traces the development of her intellectual life, from her search for a literary model and gifts of empowerment, through the civil rights movement of the 1960's, toward what she terms "Breaking Chains and Encouraging Life." Her first essay deals with the importance of models in an artist's life, and one of her last essays is an account of how she wrote *The Color Purple*.

White, Evelyn C. "Activism on Campuses: Interview with Alice Walker." *The Black Collegian* 28, no. 1 (October, 1997). Interview with Walker in which she discusses the reasons for her rebellious character and how it has affected her writing and choice of subject matter.

Winchell, Donna Haisty. *Alice Walker*. New York: Twayne, 1992. Donna Winchell combines critical analysis with biographical information to provide a study of all Walker's works through 1991. Her comprehensive analysis includes Walker's novels, short stories, essays, and poetry.

*Yvonne Johnson*

# MADAM C. J. WALKER
## Sarah Breedlove McWilliams Walker

*Born:* December 23, 1867; Delta, Louisiana

*Died:* May 25, 1919; Irvington-on-Hudson, New York

*Areas of Achievement:* Business and industry

*Contribution:* Vastly successful as a self-made entrepreneur, Walker provided African American women with effective hair-care techniques and products as well as less arduous, higher paying employment as Walker Agents. She also made sizeable contributions to African American charities and educational institutions, supported African American architects, artists, and literary figures, and spoke out against injustices suffered by her people.

### Early Life

Sarah Breedlove was born to Owen and Minerva Breedlove, former slaves who remained as sharecroppers on the one-thousand-acre cotton plantation of Robert W. Burney in Delta, Louisiana (across the Mississippi River from Vicksburg). When Sarah was seven, her parents died during a major outbreak of yellow fever. She and her sister Louvenia soon moved to Vicksburg, Mississippi, and worked as laundresses. Louvenia married, so Sarah lived with her and her husband, Willie Powell. At age fourteen Sarah married Moses McWilliams, partly to escape her domineering brother-in-law. When she was seventeen, Sarah gave birth to her daughter, Lelia. Two years later, Sarah's husband was killed. She then moved to St. Louis, Missouri (which had one of the country's largest African American populations), because she had heard wages for laundresses would be higher there.

Sarah continued working as a laundress or cook for nearly twenty years while taking classes at night and saving money. She ensured that Lelia graduated from St. Louis public schools and then sent her to Knoxville College, a small, private African American school in Knoxville, Tennessee. She seemed unable to earn more than $1.50 per week, and she wondered how she would endure such hard, physical work when she got older.

Sarah joined the St. Paul African Methodist Episcopal Church, the National Association of Colored Women, and the Mite Missionary Society, which aided needy people in St. Louis. Through these organizations she met and came to admire such prosperous, influential African American women as Margaret Murray Washington, wife of educator Booker T. Washington. She longed for the poised, elegant demeanor they presented. Partly to advertise her skills as a laundress, she made sure her clothes were neat and crisp, but she disliked her hair, which was broken and had fallen out (especially at her temples), revealing patches of her scalp.

Like many African American women at the time, Sarah had strained her hair through the practice of dividing it into sections, wrapping string around each section, and twisting it to make it straighter. She and other women were also troubled by conditions such as dandruff and psoriasis, possibly caused by stress, poor diet, health problems, or use of damaging hair treatments. Sarah tried several products, including Poro's Wonderful Hair Grower, but was not helped by them. Around 1904, she worked briefly for the St. Louis-based Poro selling their products door to door. She experimented with her own formulas, trying them on herself. By early 1905 she was satisfied with her own Wonderful Hair Grower, which had her hair "coming in faster than it had ever fallen out."

### Life's Work

On July 21, 1905, with $1.50 in savings, Sarah moved to Denver, Colorado, to be near her recently widowed sister-in-law and to develop her business. She worked as a cook for E. L. Schoty, a pharmacist who may have helped her plan ingredients for her products. Her three basic products were Vegetable Shampoo; Wonderful Hair Grower, which contained medications to combat various conditions causing hair loss and dandruff; and Glossine, a light oil. Sarah also modified the steel comb popular in France, making the teeth wider and farther apart to suit African American hair. The comb was heated to press the oiled hair and soften the tight curls. She married Charles Joseph Walker, a sales agent for an African American newspaper who had become a close friend in St. Louis. She adopted the name Madam C. J. Walker for herself and her new company to convey an image of dignity in her business dealings and to evoke the glamour of France, where married women were called madame.

By September, 1906, Madam Walker had been advertising in local African American newspapers

(which generated some mail-order business) and doing personal treatments and door-to-door sales. She was making $10 per week and was ready to expand the business. She and her husband began an extended sales trip that covered nine states and lasted a year and a half.

Walker's business, the Madam C. J. Walker Company, grew at breakneck speed. She opened an office in Pittsburgh, Pennsylvania, where here daughter Lelia lived, in 1908. Lelia managed the mail-order business as well as the company's first beauty school, Lelia College, where hair stylists (who were called hair culturists) could learn the Walker System. Walker continued to travel extensively, stopping in towns of all sizes. She spoke at churches, public halls, and Masonic lodges on how women could achieve financial independence as Walker Agents or hair culturists.

Walker encountered resistance from some African American ministers when she asked to speak at their churches. They charged that she was trying to straighten women's hair and make them look white. Walker countered that she was trying to help women's hair grow and their scalps heal, as well as teaching them good grooming. More important to her was giving women alternatives to domestic work, even if they had no formal education. Her own appearance was one of her best tools for selling her products. Nearly six feet tall, the calm, dignified Walker was fashionably dressed and adorned by fine jewelry. She wore her long, beautifully groomed hair pinned up, often complemented by a hat. Unlike her competitors who used images of comely mulattos or white women on their products, Walker displayed her own likeness on her decorative tins.

In 1910 Walker consolidated her company's operations in Indianapolis, Indiana, by building a factory there and later hiring Freeman Briley Ransom as the company's attorney and general manager. Because of business differences, Walker and her husband divorced in 1912. By that point, the company employed 1,600 agents and earned $1,000 per week.

As Walker's success and visibility grew, she increasingly used her influence to help others. She lowered the cost of joining her business from $25 to $10 for women who could not afford the normal price but promised to repay her when they could. She organized her agents into Walker Clubs and later formed the Madam C. J. Walker Hair Culturists Union. Clubs that excelled at philanthropy in their communities won cash prizes. Two much-publicized gifts by Madam Walker herself were $1,000 to the African American Young Men's Christian Association (YMCA) in Indianapolis (1912) and $500 to the National Association of Colored Women (1918) for their fund to retire the mortgage on the home of African American abolitionist Frederick Douglass.

Walker also used her influence to combat injustice against her race. In 1915 she was charged 25 cents as a "colored person" rather than the usual dime for admission to a motion picture at the Isis Theater in Indianapolis. She sued the Central Amusement Company, which operated the theater, asking for a $100 fine against their "unwarranted discrimination." Race riots erupted in several cities during the summer of 1917, and African Americans were murdered, beaten, drowned, and driven from their homes, reportedly as white policemen watched. On July 28, 1917, many Walker Agents participated in the Negro Silent Protest parade, an event that Walker and other prominent African Americans had planned. Over ten thousand African Americans marched down Fifth Avenue in New York carrying banners protesting mob violence. Soon thereafter, Walker, along with African American leaders such as W. E. B. Du Bois, James Weldon Johnson, and Adam Clayton Powell, prepared a petition urging President Woodrow Wilson to make lynching a federal offense.

Walker's wealth drew her much acclaim, particularly when she began to build her thirty-five-room, three-story, Renaissance Revival home in Irvington-on-Hudson, New York. She purchased the four-and-one-half-acre lot in 1916 for $60,000. She was reportedly charged twice its worth when realtors discovered she was African American. She deliberately chose that area because of the prestige it enjoyed among New York industrialists and was determined that the house exemplify what could be achieved by someone of her race and sex. The mansion, named Villa Lewaro, was designed by Vertner Woodson Tandy, New York's first registered African American architect. It was completed in 1918 at a cost of $350,000. Walker had begun to experience fatigue during her travel. At her doctor's urging, she rested for several weeks at Hot Springs, Arkansas, but by then her high blood pressure had permanently damaged her kidneys. She died at Villa Lewaro on May 25, 1919, about seven months after its completion.

### Summary

Although Madam C. J. Walker was frequently described as a millionaire toward the end of her life, she denied this label. When federal taxes were paid in 1922, her total estate value was $509,864. Always thinking of others, she had willed over $100,000 to various charities. In 1927, her daughter Lelia opened a building in Indianapolis as a tribute to her mother, who had hoped someday to erect a movie theater where African Americans were welcome. The Walker Building was more like a city within a building; it housed a factory, a pharmacy, a theater, an auditorium, a restaurant, and offices for African American professionals. Renovated in the late 1980's as the Walker Urban Life Center, it is now on the state and national registers of historic places.

Walker's combination of accomplishments—as an employer and motivator of African American women, a social pioneer, a contributor to African American charities, and a beauty products innovator—led to much broader recognition. Noted African American novelist Alex Haley, with help from Walker's great-great-granddaughter, A'Lelia Perry Bundles, was writing a biography of her when he died. Haley's widow obtained the rights to complete the book. In 1922, Walker was elected to the National Business Hall of Fame. In February, 1998, Walker became the twenty-first African American and the first African American entrepreneur to be the subject of a commemorative stamp.

### Bibliography


Bundles, A'Lelia Perry. *Madam C. J. Walker, Entrepreneur.* New York: Chelsea House, 1991. Clear and readable, this copiously illustrated biography contains far more factual details and historical context than the other available sources, which are much briefer.

———. "Madam C. J. Walker—Cosmetics Tycoon." *Ms.* 12 (July, 1983): 91-94. This account opens with a description of Madam Walker's bold speech at the 1912 convention of the National Negro Business League. It also explains the hair conditions Walker sought to remedy with her products and outlines charities and causes to which she contributed.

Doyle, Kathleen. "Madam C. J. Walker: First Black Woman Millionaire." *American History Illustrated* 14 (March, 1989): 24-25. Doyle gives the essential facts of Walker's career and accomplishments, interspersed with quotations from Madam Walker.

Gates, Henry Louis, Jr. "Madam's Crusade: A Black Woman's Hair-Care Empire Set a Style and Smashed Barriers." *Time* (December 7, 1998). Short piece on Walker's hair care business.

Indiana Historical Bureau. "Focus—Madam C. J. Walker." *The Indiana Junior Historian* (February, 1992).

Indiana Historical Bureau. "Focus—Madam Walker—Entrepreneur." *The Indiana Junior Historian* (March, 1992). These two special issues of a juvenile magazine contain helpful, interestingly presented information on such topics as Walker's mail-order business, her involvement with the World War I recruitment of African Americans as soldiers, her protests against lynchings, her daughter A'Lelia's role in the Harlem Renaissance, and the Walker Building in Indianapolis.

Lathan, Charles C. "Madam C. J. Walker & Company." *Traces of Indiana and Midwest History* 2 (Summer, 1989): 29-36. Lathan, while working at the Indiana Historical Society, processed eighty-seven boxes and forty-nine ledgers of material on Walker and used this information to write his article. The article contains much useful and reliable information, particularly about Walker's real estate purchases, donations to charities, the intricacies of her will, and the company's progress after her death.


*Glenn Ellen Starr Stilling*

# GEORGE C. WALLACE

*Born:* August 25, 1919; Clio, Alabama
*Died:* September 13, 1998; Montgomery, Alabama
*Areas of Achievement:* Government and politics
*Contribution:* A four-time governor of Alabama and twice a candidate for the presidency, Wallace during the 1960's became a leading spokesman for continued segregation and southern conservativism.

## Early Life

George Corley Wallace was born on August 25, 1919, in Clio, Alabama. The Wallace family had been among the earliest settlers in Barbour County, where George spent his youth. His father was a farmer known for his quick temper and his passion for local politics. His mother, who came from a cosmopolitan neighborhood outside Birmingham, stoically accepted life in rural Alabama. Despite his family's relative poverty, George had a comfortable boyhood. The oldest of three boys and a girl, he was private and introspective, yet he was a good student and popular among his classmates. Throughout his youth, athletics played an important part in George's life. In high school, he quarterbacked his school football team and was runner-up in the state Golden Gloves boxing competition.

Politics was part of Wallace's life from an early age. One of his first memories was of watching local officials count votes; at seven, he helped his father hand out campaign material. Two years later, his grandfather was elected Barbour County probate judge after a campaign managed by George's father. Wallace later described the election as among his most exciting boyhood experiences. By his teen years, he was campaigning for candidates in state elections. Because of his political interests, he was encouraged to compete for an appointment as a page for the Alabama state senate. He was one of four winners, and he spent the summer of 1935 working in the state senate. Upon completion of his appointment, Wallace decided that he would one day like to serve as governor of Alabama.

During these early years, Wallace's political philosophy began to take shape. Most important in the molding process was his father. Blaming northern industrial interests for the problems of the agrarian South, the elder Wallace bemoaned federal regulations that, he contended, limited the South's ability to educate its people and to prosper. In reaction, he embraced the basic tenets of southern populism, including the principle of rigid segregation. During the early Depression years, he became an outspoken Roosevelt Democrat; at the same time, he vehemently opposed any federal intrusion into state or local matters. Young George accepted most of his father's political positions.

Upon graduation from Barbour County High School in 1937, Wallace enrolled in the pre-law program at the University of Alabama. Because his family could not afford to help with any of his academic expenses, he found several part-time jobs and began working his way through college. Two months into his freshman year, his father, who had suffered from chronic health problems for years, died. George immediately returned home and proposed withdrawing from the university to run the family farm. Yet his mother, who had always encouraged George's education, implored him to return to school, which he did. Two years later, he moved to advanced law studies, and he was graduated with a law degree in 1942.

The following October, Wallace was inducted into the Army Air Corps as an aviation cadet. Disenchanted with the training regimen, however, George requested reassignment. He spent the rest of his military service as a flight engineer and became part of a crew that flew numerous missions over Japan during the last weeks of World War II. While still an aviation cadet, he married sixteen-year-old Lurleen Burns.

## Life's Work

Upon his discharge from the Air Corps in December, 1945, Wallace, his young wife, and their new daughter returned to Alabama, where George began his political career in earnest. Among his first stops was the office of Governor Chauncey Sparks. He had met Sparks, who was also from Barbour County, during his days as a legislative page and had actively campaigned for him. The governor personally saw to it that Wallace was appointed as assistant attorney general; however, both men understood that the position was temporary and that George would soon pursue elective office. Two months after his appointment, Wallace took an unpaid leave of absence to run for the state legislature. Riding a wave of resurgent southern populism and aided by boundless energy on the campaign trail, he won election—making him, at twenty-seven, the state's youngest legislator.

Wallace served two terms in the state legislature. During those eight years, he spoke repeatedly about the need to raise Alabama's standard of living, one of the lowest in the nation. Among his more important initiatives was a call for the creation of a group of state-operated technical and vocational schools. He also became a champion of local government by introducing legislation designed to generate a bond issue that would help Alabama cities attract industry without sacrificing local control. Among his standard themes was a call to southern pride. Like his father, he warned about a northern post-Civil War legislative assault on the South. He advised southerners to remain vigilant and resist federal policies that might alter tradition. The federal policies he condemned most often involved civil rights issues.

While establishing himself as a capable and energetic legislator, Wallace also began to establish a base for his own statewide political organization. Among those he courted were former governor Sparks and current governor James "Big Jim" Folsom. Like Wallace, both generally took a progressive stand on economic issues. Both had also fought the "big mules" of Alabama politics—the local cliques of bankers, industrialists, and plantation owners who collectively had controlled much of the state's political structure for decades. In preparing his organization, Wallace also won support from several prominent businessmen and a few influential newspaper reporters.

Wallace first attracted national attention during the 1948 Democratic National Convention. Selected as an alternate delegate from Alabama, he got his chance to participate when a portion of the state's delegation walked out of the convention in reaction to the party's civil rights platform plank. Rather than join the "Dixiecrat" rebellion, he chose to stay and vehemently protest the plank as well as Harry Truman's presidential nomination. The episode enhanced Wallace's stature within Alabama and brought him national recognition. Eight years later, as he prepared to run for governor, Wallace again actively opposed his party's civil rights position. This time, key leaders from southern delegations chose him as their spokesman to the platform committee. With the help of several powerful southern Democrats, he was able to dilute the language of the plank, making it merely an ambiguous pledge to end discrimination.

In 1952, Wallace was elected judge of the Third Circuit of Alabama, a district that included Barbour County. During the election, he established a style that would characterize his future campaigns. Aggressive and confrontational, he encouraged polarization of his voters by appealing to their fears and prejudices. Generally considered a congenial and fair judge, Wallace in 1958 became known as the "fighting judge" during a showdown with federal authorities. As part of an investigation into discrimination against black voters, Wallace was ordered by the U.S. Civil Rights Commission to make available voter-registration books. He refused, claiming that the rights of Alabamians were being intruded upon by the federal government. Threatened with contempt charges and concerned about an approaching gubernatorial election, however, he eventually acceded to the commission's demands.

Wallace was defeated in the 1958 gubernatorial election, but he won the office four years later. Though economic issues constituted an important part of his platform, a resolute opposition to federally required integration of Alabama schools became his primary plank. In June, 1963, less than a year after becoming governor, he lived up to his pledge to "stand in the schoolhouse door" when he personally attempted to block the enrollment of African American students at the University of Alabama; he yielded only after he was challenged by National Guard troops. The confrontation brought a flood of media coverage and much notoriety to Wallace. Similar episodes at Tuskegee, Birmingham, Huntsville, and Mobile further established him as the nation's leading segregationist.

Rendered ineligible from running for reelection by his state's constitution, Wallace maneuvered the 1966 Democratic gubernatorial nomination to his wife Lurleen. Though she took a more active role as governor than most expected, there was little doubt that George continued to direct Alabama government. In 1968, two years into her term, however, Lurleen died from cancer. Despite the loss, Wallace maintained his grip on the state and was elected governor in 1970, 1974, and in 1982.

During his years as governor, Wallace steadfastly embraced several issues. Education, particularly at the postsecondary level, was always part of his agenda. Throughout his political career, he also advocated improving business conditions within the state. Likewise, road construction and the quality of the state's health-care facilities, especially in regard to the elderly and mentally disabled, were themes he regularly addressed. Yet segregation continued to be the issue most identified with him; from his earliest days in the state legislature, he defended the practice. When segregationist laws throughout the South were challenged in the 1960's, Wallace reacted aggressively against civil rights leaders and federally mandated integration. Only during his last term as governor did he begin to acknowledge that his earlier stance was wrong.

Wallace's political aspirations were not limited to Alabama. In 1964, despite being a lifelong Democrat, he considered becoming Republican Barry Goldwater's vice-presidential running mate. Four years later, Wallace captured forty-six electoral votes while running for the presidency as the candidate of the American Independent Party. He would run again in the 1972 Democratic primaries. It was at a campaign stop in Laurel, Maryland, in May, 1972, that Wallace was shot five times in an assassination attempt. The attack left him paralyzed below the waist.

Although he remained a political force to be reckoned with, Wallace's national influence eroded after the attack. In 1982, campaigning from a wheelchair, he won a fourth term as governor by publicly recanting much of his earlier segregationist rhetoric. Slowed by failing health and marital problems, he retired from politics five year later. On September 18, 1998, Wallace died of respiratory and cardiac arrest in Montgomery, Alabama.

### Summary

During the 1960's, George Wallace became the political voice of the traditional South. In many ways, his appeal recalled that of Populist candidates of the early twentieth century. Wallace advocated the interests of the small farmer, the blue-collar laborer, and the small business. At the heart of his appeal was a rejection of federal civil rights and school-integration policies. His fiery rhetoric and confrontational style aroused a grassroots conservatism throughout the South and elsewhere in the nation.

As a presidential candidate, Wallace tapped into a deep pool of voters who considered their interests to be underrepresented. In appealing to this constituency, he introduced several campaign themes that later became part of the conservative Republican agenda that carried Ronald Reagan into the White House. Among them was a call for massive tax reform, a pledge to support a school-prayer amendment to the constitution, an aggressive stance on law-and-order issues, and a promise to expand military programs. He also vowed to end federally required school busing. His appeals directly addressed an ever-deepening public distrust of the federal government and a concern about a disintegrating social order.

### Bibliography

Black, Earl. *Southern Governors and Civil Rights: Racial Segregation as a Campaign Issue in the Second Reconstruction*. Cambridge, Mass.: Harvard University Press, 1976. Provides a context for understanding Wallace's segregationist policies and identifies him as one of the most outspoken opponents of federal involvement in school integration.

Canfield, James Lewis. *A Case of Third Party Activism: The George Wallace Campaign Workers and the American Independent Party*. Washington, D.C.: University Press of America, 1984. While the author's focus is on the campaign, he provides much information about Wallace and his political philosophy during the 1968 presidential election.

Carter, Dan C. "Good Copy: George Wallace Understood that Media Thrived on Confrontation." *Media Studies Journal* 12, no. 3 (Fall 1998). Analysis of Wallace's use of confrontational techniques in gaining media attention during his presidential campaign.

Carter, Daniel T. *The Politics of Rage: George Wallace, the Origins of the New Conservatism, and the Transformation of American Politics*. New York: Simon and Schuster, 1995. A biographical investigation of Wallace's influence upon the rise of conservatism in American politics. Combines scholarly analysis and an appealing style.

Lesher, Stephan. *George Wallace: American Populist*. Reading, Mass.: Addison-Wesley, 1993. A thorough biography of Wallace. The author suggests that his subject reflected traditional southern values in the context of the mid-twentieth century.

Riley, Michael. "Confessions of a Former Segregationist." *Time* 139, no. 9 (March 2, 1992). Interview with Wallace in which he discusses how his attitudes toward black people have changed over time.

Taylor, Sandra Baxley. *Me 'n' George: A Story of George Corley Wallace and His Number One Crony, Oscar Harper*. Mobile, Ala.: Greenberry, 1988. Focuses on Wallace's early political years and his rise to governor.

*Paul E. Doutrich*

# HENRY A. WALLACE

*Born:* October 7, 1888; Adair County, Iowa
*Died:* November 18, 1965; Danbury, Connecticut
*Areas of Achievement:* Politics and journalism
*Contribution:* Wallace was an outspoken critic of post–World War II American foreign policy. He was also one of the principal architects of American farm policy and an eloquent spokesman for some of the most important ideas of twentieth century American liberalism.

## Early Life

Henry Agard Wallace was born on October 7, 1888, on a farm in Adair County, Iowa. His father, Henry Cantwell Wallace, was of Scotch-Irish origin; his mother, May Brodhead, was of English, Dutch, and French Huguenot background. Henry Agard's father, a farmer at the time of his birth, became, in 1893, a professor of agriculture at Iowa State College, his alma mater. Henry's paternal grandfather, "Uncle Henry" Wallace, a minister of the Gospel turned farmer and founder of the influential weekly newspaper *Wallace's Farmer* in 1895, was the greatest influence on young Henry Agard's intellectual development. Grandfather instilled in grandson a lively intellectual curiosity and a peculiar mixture of practicality and high idealism.

The young Wallace labored for many years in the shadow of his father and his grandfather, both well-known figures in rural journalism and in Iowa Republican politics; only after the two of them had died would he really begin to make his mark. Although Henry Agard's father was by no means wealthy, family circumstances were comfortable enough to permit Henry to attend Iowa State College, where he studied agricultural science. After he was graduated in 1910, Wallace conducted pioneering research in agricultural economics, producing the first charts of corn-hog ratios. He also continued his studies on the breeding of corn; the fruit of this research was the founding, in 1926, of a company for developing and selling hybrid corn seeds.

When Wallace's father, Henry Cantwell Wallace, became secretary of agriculture under Calvin Coolidge, Wallace became editor of *Wallace's Farmer*. As an editor, Wallace, a nominal Republican, became well-known during the 1920's for his relentless attacks on the ruling Republican Party's alleged indifference to the problems facing the American farmer. In 1932, he strongly supported Franklin D. Roosevelt's successful campaign for the presidency against Republican incumbent Herbert Hoover. In that election, the traditionally Republican state of Iowa, hard hit by the fall in agricultural prices that accompanied the Great Depression, voted for Roosevelt. As a reward for his help, Wallace received a high position in the new administration. Not until 1936, however, would he formally join the Democratic Party.

## Life's Work

When Wallace went to Washington, D.C., in March, 1933, at the age of forty-four, as Roosevelt's new secretary of agriculture, he was a most atypical cabinet member. About five feet, ten inches tall, he kept his weight to a trim 160 pounds through vigorous exercise. Although middle-aged, Wallace looked much younger; his boyish appearance was accentuated by his full head of still reddish-brown hair, which was often unkempt in appearance. He had gray eyes, a long, lantern-jawed face, a long nose, and a sensitive mouth. His voice was high-pitched, but he was often able to make up with his earnestness for any deficiencies of oratorical delivery. Wallace lacked the gift for small talk so prized at Washington social gatherings of the time. His strong religiosity, and his avoidance of smoking, drinking, or swearing, set him apart from many people in Washington political circles.

Wallace, despite his lack of previous experience in government, proved to be an effective administrator. He was aided by the large numbers of trained social scientists whom he brought with him into the department. Working together with such intellectuals not only enabled Wallace to carry out policy more efficiently; it also seems to have speeded his transition from a mere spokesman for agrarian interests to a proponent of a broader liberal economic philosophy. The New Deal farm policy devised by Wallace, embodied in the somewhat hastily prepared Agricultural Adjustment Act of 1933, tried to restore farm prosperity by getting American farmers to cooperate in cutting back on agricultural production, thereby raising prices. As an emergency measure to further this goal, millions of pigs were slaughtered; this action, coupled with the practice of paying farmers to grow less, caused many to criticize the policy as wasteful.

The reduction of crop surpluses through production cutbacks, although at first the most important part of Wallace's program, was by no means Wallace's only contribution to agricultural policy. Through the rural electrification program, electric power was brought to many farm families who had never before enjoyed its blessings. In the latter half of the 1930's, Wallace won the enactment of his plan for the so-called ever-normal granary, in which the federal government would store the surpluses from good years to help in times of poor harvests. It was in the latter half of the decade, too, that emphasis began to be placed on encouraging farmers to practice techniques of soil conservation; dust storms of the era had shown how necessary such techniques were. The food stamp program was devised by Wallace's subordinate Milo Perkins in 1938 to rebut accusations of wastefulness aimed at New Deal farm policy. Stamps would be issued enabling the poor to receive surplus food, thus at once combating crop surpluses on the land and relieving hunger in the Depression-stricken cities.

Wallace came to realize that the problem of agricultural overproduction could be resolved only by tackling the problem of underconsumption, both at home and abroad. Although he had briefly supported high tariffs in the 1920's, he had come to oppose protectionism by 1930, criticizing the high Smoot-Hawley Tariff enacted in that year. Convinced that a mutual lowering of tariff barriers by the nations of the world was necessary both to open new markets for American agriculture and to increase the chances of lasting peace in the world, Agriculture Secretary Wallace staunchly supported the efforts of Secretary of State Cordell Hull to negotiate reciprocal trade treaties with various nations. To increase consumption at home, Wallace came to advocate social security, minimum wage legislation, and better conditions for workers.

In February, 1935, Wallace abruptly dismissed various key officials of the department who had aroused resentment among white Southern landowners by trying to improve conditions for Southern black sharecroppers. It was not until the latter half of the 1930's that a conscience-stricken Wallace made some effort to help tenants and sharecroppers displaced by farm production cutbacks. At Wallace's urging, the Resettlement Administration and, later on, the Farm Security Administration were set up to aid the poorer segments of the farming community.

Although Wallace's record as agricultural secretary had thus not been particularly radical, he had, by 1940, gained a reputation within the Democratic Party as an extreme liberal ideologue. This reputation arose from Wallace's ceaseless attempts, from 1933 onward, to articulate through books, pamphlets, and speeches a coherent philosophy of New Deal liberalism, and to defend this philosophy against its enemies in the uncompromisingly biblical rhetorical style inherited from his preacher grandfather. Wallace's words were more doctrinaire than his acts; nevertheless, he aroused such suspicion in conservative Democratic Party circles that it took Roosevelt's emphatic personal insistence to secure Wallace's nomination for vice president in 1940.

As vice president from 1941 to 1945, Wallace was neither as busy nor as blessed with success as he had been as agricultural secretary. As head of the Board of Economic Warfare from 1941 to 1943, Wallace quarreled so heatedly with conservative Secretary of Commerce Jesse Jones that President Roosevelt, determined to soft-pedal ideological New Dealism for the sake of wartime unity, felt compelled to relieve the Iowan of that position. Wallace had insisted on decent conditions for workers in Latin American lands that were producing for the American war effort; the State and Commerce departments regarded such insistence as an unwarranted interference in other countries' internal affairs.

Unsuccessful in the bureaucratic wars, Wallace put more time than ever before into playing the role of spokesman for New Deal liberalism, a philosophy that he wished to see expanded from the domestic to the international arena. During World War II, Wallace advocated, as prerequisites for a lasting peace, both the creation of a strong world organization and the raising of living standards in Asia and Latin America through massive American aid. For Wallace, material well-being was a necessity if democracy was to thrive; democratic government, in turn, was necessary for peace among nations. Wallace's advocacy of massive foreign aid was widely ridiculed at the time, but his advocacy of a world organization did pay off: on July 28, 1945, the United States Senate ratified the United Nations Charter.

In 1944, a presidential election year, Roosevelt, in the interests of party unity, dropped Wallace from the ticket and accepted as his vice presidential running mate the Democratic senator from Missouri, Harry S Truman. Appointed secretary of commerce by an ailing President Roosevelt in 1945, Wallace retained that position after Roosevelt's death in April of that year.

As secretary of commerce, Wallace championed the cause of government planning for full employment, and he stated this belief vigorously in the book *Sixty Million Jobs* (1945). The Full Employment Act of 1946, embodying Wallace's ideas in a somewhat watered-down form, established a Council of Economic Advisers to aid the Federal government in its pursuit of the goal of full employment.

By 1945, Wallace had come to symbolize, within the Democratic Party, the aspirations of liberal intellectuals, blacks, and trade union members, as distinguished from the interests of the Northern big-city machine bosses and Southern conservative political chieftains who had so long dominated the party. Wallace squandered this vast reservoir of support, however, by his disastrous decision to oppose President Harry S Truman on issues of foreign policy.

By September, 1946, Wallace was troubled by the friction between the United States and her wartime ally, the Soviet Union. On September 12, 1946, in a speech in Madison Square Garden, Wallace publicly criticized the notion that the United States should take a tough line toward Soviet Russia. President Truman, preoccupied by both foreign and domestic problems and unsure how to deal with the Soviets, had approved Wallace's speech beforehand without realizing the impact it might have. Faced with the indignation of Secretary of State James F. Byrnes, who saw Wallace as undercutting his own negotiations with the Soviets, Truman was forced, on September 20, to dismiss Wallace from office.

After his resignation, Wallace served for about a year as editor of the liberal periodical *The New Republic*; from there he continued to criticize Truman's foreign policy. Wallace strongly condemned the Truman Doctrine, proclaimed in March, 1947. Despite his general approval of American aid to foreign countries, Wallace also opposed Marshall Plan aid to war-ravaged Western Europe. Because the Soviet Union was excluded and because it was not under the auspices of the United Nations, Wallace argued that such a program would only make Soviet-American relations worse and endanger world peace.

In 1948, Wallace ran for president of the United States on a third-party ticket, that of the Progressive Party. In the course of his presidential campaign, Wallace resolutely refused to criticize Soviet foreign policy. The Communist coup in Czechoslovakia in February, toppling a genuinely democratic regime, and the Russian imposition of the Berlin blockade in July both undermined the credibility of Wallace's approach to foreign policy, causing even liberal opinion to desert his candidacy. When the returns were counted in November, Truman had been reelected over his Republican opponent; Wallace had finished a poor fourth in the popular vote, slightly behind even Strom Thurmond, the candidate of the States' Rights Democratic (Dixiecrat) Party. The very elements to whom Wallace had hoped to appeal—liberal intellectuals, labor union members, black voters in the Northern states—had, by and large, resisted the Iowan's blandishments and remained loyal to Truman. Wallace's political career, ruined by his own lack of realism, was over.

In June, 1950, Wallace broke with the Progressive Party over the Korean War: He supported Truman's decision to send American troops to aid the South Koreans against the North Korean Communist invaders. Wallace had never really sympathized with Marxism as an ideology or with the authoritarian aspects of the Soviet system; his misguided defense of Soviet foreign policy had been inspired by a sincere love of peace, coupled with a serious misunderstanding of the true nature of Joseph Stalin's tyranny.

After 1950, Wallace devoted himself to nonpolitical pursuits, carrying out, at his country home just north of New York City, crossbreeding experiments on strawberries, chickens, and gladioli. On November 18, 1965, after prolonged suffering, he died of a degenerative disease of the nervous system.

### Summary

Although Wallace was a failure as a politician, he did leave behind a considerable legacy in the world of ideas. Wallace, through his preachings as country editor and through his actions as agriculture secretary, popularized the notion of intervention by the federal government to stabilize prices; the wisdom and value of such intervention has been upheld by later administrations, including some conservative Republican ones. The food stamp program, dropped with the coming of World War II, was ultimately revived under the John F. Kennedy Administration, and was continued and expanded under succeeding administrations. The attempts made under the Kennedy and Lyndon B. Johnson administrations (1961-1969) to fine-tune the national economy were inspired by the kind of Keynesianism popularized by Wallace in the 1940's. The creation of the Peace Corps and the Agency for International Development under the Kennedy Administration, and the pursuit of international tariff reduction by both the Kennedy and Johnson administrations reflect the enduring influence of Wallace's ideas; the Iowan had long stressed the need for both freer trade and expanded foreign aid if world peace and American economic well-being were to be furthered.

Wallace is especially significant as an early critic of post-World War II American foreign policy. America's involvement in a costly and losing conflict in Vietnam, from 1961 through 1975, has caused some scholars to reassess Wallace's criticism, for which he was so vilified in his lifetime. Such reassessment by no means redeems Wallace from the charge of naïveté; until 1950 he was as blind to Stalin's faults as he was acutely aware of his own country's errors.

In Wallace's career, one sees the peculiar difficulties faced by an American meliorist liberal when he tries to apply the lessons derived from his domestic political experience to the far different environment of international relations; this particular dilemma has reappeared in different forms in the careers of later American liberal leaders.

### Bibliography

Ezekiel, Mordecai. "Henry A. Wallace, Agricultural Economist." *Journal of Farm Economics* 48 (November, 1966): 789-802. A warmly favorable recollection of Wallace by an economist who was one of his principal advisers in the Department of Agriculture. Sets forth in considerable detail Wallace's scientific accomplishments and his intellectual legacy but passes over in one sentence Wallace's unsuccessful foray into third-party politics.

Hamby, Alonzo L. "Henry A. Wallace, the Liberals, and Soviet-American Relations." *Review of Politics* 30 (April, 1968): 153-169. Hamby shows that sympathy for Soviet Russia, a supposedly anti-Fascist power, had once been common to all liberal intellectuals; Wallace differed from the majority of them only in clinging to this viewpoint long after postwar realities had disillusioned others.

———. "Sixty Million Jobs and the People's Revolution: The Liberals, the New Deal, and World War II." *Historian* 30 (August, 1968): 578-598. Hamby ably explains how Wallace became the leading spokesman of American liberalism during the war years. The author sees, as one motive for the shift of liberals such as Wallace toward Keynesianism, a fear that mass unemployment after the war might provide the seedbed for a strong American Fascist movement.

Kelley, John L. "An Insurgent in the Truman Cabinet: Henry A. Wallace's Effort to Redirect Foreign Policy." *Missouri Historical Review* 77 (October, 1982): 64-93. Making full use of the recently opened diaries of President Truman and of Truman's press secretary, Charles G. Ross, Kelley provides a fresh look at the cabinet crisis that arose over Wallace's Madison Square Garden speech of September 12, 1946.

Kirkendall, Richard S. "Commentary on the Thought of Henry A. Wallace." *Agricultural History* 41 (April, 1967): 139-142. Sees Wallace as having evolved, during his years as secretary of agriculture, from a purely agrarian viewpoint to a broader liberal philosophy embracing urban as well as rural concerns. Asserts that the Iowan had lost the support of conservative farm organizations by 1940. Sees the influence of adviser

Mordecai Ezekiel as of crucial importance in Wallace's turn toward Keynesianism.

———. "Reflections of a Revolutionary on a Revolution." *Journal of the West* 31, no. 4 (October, 1992). Discusses the contributions of Wallace to farm products and technological advancement.

Lord, Russell. *The Wallaces of Iowa*. Boston: Houghton Mifflin Co., 1947. This contemporary study of Wallace is extremely detailed on the New Deal period but rather skimpy thereafter; it does, however, provide valuable information on Wallace's early life and family background.

Lowitt, Richard. "Henry A. Wallace and Irrigation Agriculture." Agricultural History 66, no. 4 (Fall 1992). Discussion of a series of articles written by Wallace for his grandfather's magazine, *Farmer,* which paint a clear picture of the lives and irrigation methods of farmers in the western United States.

Markowitz, Norman D. *The Rise and Fall of the People's Century: Henry A. Wallace and American Liberalism, 1941-1948*. New York: Free Press, 1973. Markowitz offers a revisionist scholarly view of Wallace, one apparently rooted in neo-Marxian socialism. Markowitz sees Wallace's view of Soviet-American relations as courageous and realistic; the Iowan's naïveté, the author believes, lay rather in thinking that capitalism could be transformed from within into a new type of society. Despite its somewhat questionable interpretation, Markowitz's book provides an excellent factual account of Wallace's activities during the Truman years, especially his dismissal from office in 1946 and his presidential bid of 1948.

Schapsmeier, Edward L., and Frederick H. Schapsmeier. *Henry A. Wallace of Iowa: The Agrarian Years, 1910-1940*. Ames: Iowa State University Press, 1968. Strongly sympathetic to Wallace. Although it provides many interesting factual details on Wallace's early years, it falls short as a work of analysis. Thus it fails to provide any satisfactory explanation of that peculiar mixture of idealism and pragmatism shown by Wallace during his years as secretary of agriculture.

Walker, J. Samuel. *Henry A. Wallace and American Foreign Policy*. Westport, Conn.: Greenwood Press, 1976. Walker traces Wallace's views on foreign policy from 1920 to the late 1940's; the material on the Iowan's early views on international trade is particularly interesting. Its treatment of Wallace's later political career, however, is flawed by the absence of a coherent argument.

*Paul D. Mageli*

# LÉON WALRAS

*Born:* December 16, 1834; Évreux, France
*Died:* January 5, 1910; Clarens, near Montreux, Switzerland
*Area of Achievement:* Economics
*Contribution:* Walras, along with Herman Heinrich Gossen, William Stanley Jevons, and Carl von Menger, discovered the concept of marginal utility. His long-term influence rests on his system of general equilibrium, which was a far more comprehensive analysis of value and price, demand and supply than any postulated up to his time. Many economists, however, believe that his pioneering use of mathematics in economic theory is his most lasting contribution to the science.

## Early Life

Marie-Esprit-Léon Walras was born in Évreux, a provincial town in Normandy, France, on December 16, 1834. His father, Antoine-Auguste Walras, though he never held an economic post, also wrote on economics and greatly influenced Léon throughout his life and career. The younger Walras later used many of his father's ideas and terms in his own works.

Léon received a standard education for a boy of his class and time, and was graduated from secondary school in 1852. He then attempted to enter an engineering school in Paris but failed the mathematics paper in the entrance examinations two years in a row. This is ironic in view of the fact that many think of him as the economist above all others who brought mathematical methodology into the theory of economics. While studying for these exams, he read the works of Augustin Cournot, who in 1838 had published a book on wealth using mathematical economics. Cournot, along with Walras' father, was the main influence on Walras' economic writings. Walras entered a less prestigious engineering school in 1854 but withdrew after a year and spent the following four years pursuing his interests in philosophy and literature. He published a novel in 1858 which is generally regarded as being very poor. That same year, he was finally persuaded by his father to devote himself to economics.

It took him twelve years to obtain an academic post in the discipline. His unwillingness to conform and his unpopular economic ideas, which included the nationalization of land, are usually cited as the reason for the many rejections. Meanwhile, he worked as a journalist for two publications and was dismissed from both for his independent viewpoints. Failing to establish his own journal, he worked with a railway company and afterward cofounded a bank, which went bankrupt in 1868.

Walras was very poor during this period and struggled constantly to support his wife and family. Indeed, only on his second marriage to a rich widow in 1884, his first wife having died, was he able to obtain financial security. Finally in 1870, he applied for the chair of political economy in the faculty of law at the Academy of Lausanne in Switzerland and was appointed to the post by a narrow majority. His financial situation was such that the academy had to advance him some money from his salary to meet his travel expenses.

## Life's Work

Walras held his position at Lausanne for twenty-two years, until 1892, when he retired for health reasons. His major work *Éléments d'économie politique pure* (1874; *Elements of Pure Economics*, 1954) was first published four years after his appointment and went through many revisions and additions. He intended it as the theoretical portion of a three-part study, the others being the application of economic theory and the social implications and ethics of this application. In philosophical terms, he referred to this division of the study of economics as the True, the Useful, and the Just. Yet it is as a theorist that he is remembered. His lasting contribution to economic theory was his analysis and outline of the concept of general equilibrium, that is, a situation in which the market and the economy show no tendency to move away from the current position. In this situation, each individual consumer receives the maximum possible satisfaction from exchange; the supply of each commodity equals the demand and the price of each product equals its cost of production.

Walras was the first economist to show the complete interdependence of all elements in an economic system. For example, a change in the demand for one commodity will affect the demand for all other commodities in the market, and it will also change the prices of the factors of production (land and labor, for example) used in producing the commodities. In his analysis, Walras used the term *rareté* (scarcity), which is now referred to as marginal utility. It signifies the utility or satisfaction obtained by the consumer from the last unit purchased of a commodity. This is in contrast to total utility, which is the satisfaction obtained from the total number of units of the commodity consumed. Walras assumed perfect competition for his analysis, that is, a market where a large number of small firms compete to sell their products to consumers who are perfectly rational in their buying and where full market information is freely available to all.

He thought of his marginal utility theory as the subjective theory of value to distinguish it from classical economics, which assumed all value comes from the supply side, that is, the sum total of the factors of production that are used in producing a commodity. Yet he also used marginal utility analysis on the supply side: The firms who produce the goods buy the factors of production, so they also gain a marginal utility from each unit of the factor they buy. Logically each firm on the supply side will also seek to maximize utility or satisfaction by equalizing the marginal utility gained from the purchasing of units of the different factors of production. For example, they will substitute land for labor if greater utility is obtained by doing this. Walras' great contribution was to demonstrate mathematically the tendency for market and prices to go toward equilibrium, where each firm and consumer gains maximum satisfaction. He did this with a series of simultaneous equations in which the price and quantity of the product and the factors of production are the unknown variables. *Tatonnements*, or gropings, was the catchword he used to express the idea of each price, each quantity produced and consumed in all markets tending to move toward the equilibrium value—the value wherein all of his equations are equalized and all satisfactions are maximized.

Walras corresponded with almost every economist of note before his death, mainly to convince them of the validity of his theories. On the whole, however, he met with little success in his advocacy. English economists, with the exception of Jevons, dismissed him out of hand, as indeed he did them. He was the recipient of even greater indifference in his native France, though he continued to try to obtain an economic post there with a view to a higher salary. The German universities and the Austrian school ridiculed his mathematics, and only in Italy, and to some extent in the United States, was he read and studied.

He was convinced of the need to develop economics as a pure science whose theory could be compared with the physical sciences. This was the reason he separated applied economics from the theory. He never wrote the systematic works he had planned on the social and applied aspects of economics. Instead, he published *Études d'économie sociale* (1896; studies in social economy) and *Études d'économie politique appliquée* (1898; studies in applied political economy), collections of his papers. His most controversial idea in applied economics was that of the nationalization of all land. In this theory, the state would rent land to people and businesses and the revenue obtained would eliminate the need for taxation. The proposition has led to Walras being labeled a communist, but this is inaccurate, since he strongly defended the idea of private property and emphasized the need for competition in the marketplace.

Walras resigned from his post at Lausanne in 1892 on the ground of exhaustion. He was succeeded by Vilfredo Pareto, one of his followers, who continued with the mathematical expression of economic theory. Eventually, however, Walras believed that Pareto had betrayed him and they quarreled publicly on many occasions. Walras was a difficult man to get along with, often suffering from paranoia and hypochondria. He was aggrieved when recognition of his achievements was not forthcoming. He put his name forward for the Nobel Peace Prize in 1906, but the award went instead to Theodore Roosevelt. Walras continued to work until his death in 1910 near Montreux, Switzerland.

### Summary

Léon Walras was one of the most controversial of all economists. Partly this was a result of his fiery, impatient, forceful personality and a strong propensity to engage in personal arguments. Yet his ideas were often unjustly represented and ignored. In some ways he was a man ahead of his time, with his insistence on the validity of using mathematics, an advocacy which has certainly been vindicated with the passage of time. Indeed Walras' stock has risen enormously since his death. Until the 1930's, he was hardly acknowledged in many textbooks, and his major work, *Elements of Pure Economics*, was not translated into English until 1954. Yet by the late 1940's, Milton Friedman could say: "We curtsy to [Alfred] Marshall, but we walk with Walras." Another great twentieth century economist, Joseph Schumpeter, wrote in 1952: "As far as pure theory is concerned, Walras is in my opinion the greatest of all economists."

He is most often compared to his contemporary Alfred Marshall, the great English economist. Marshall received the lion's share of the credit for equilibrium analysis both when he wrote, in the late nineteenth century, and afterward. This fact resulted mainly from the obscurity of much of Walras' writing with its strong mathematical content. Walras wrote for his fellow economists. By contrast, Marshall wrote for businessmen and the intelligent layperson, and, though he was the superior mathematician of the two, he consigned his mathematics to appendices. It has also been argued that Marshall is closer to life and that Walras is unduly abstract and too simplistic in his assumptions. Yet the economists of the 1920's and 1930's successfully related empirical data to Walras' model and gave it operational validity. What is certain is that, along with Jevons and Menger, Walras broadened the scope and methodology of economics and that only later was proper acknowledgment given to his achievements.

**Bibliography**

Blaug, Mark. *Economic Theory in Retrospect.* 5th ed. Cambridge and New York: Cambridge University Press, 1997. A difficult book for the layperson, with its detailed exposition of Walras' mathematics; nevertheless, it probably presents his mathematics in the simplest form possible, while doing justice to its complexity.

Burgenmeier, B. "The Misperception of Walras." *American Economic Review* 84, no. 1 (March, 1994). Examines Walras' theory of the interdependence of economic markets and social philosophies.

Cirillo, Renato. "Léon Walras and Social Justice." *American Journal of Economics and Sociology* 43 (January, 1984): 53-60. A very well-written and clear discussion of Walras' ideas on the best way to achieve justice for all through economic policies.

Deane, Phyllis. *The Evolution of Economic Ideas.* Cambridge and New York: Cambridge University Press, 1978. A brief, scholarly, but very readable overview of the history of economic ideas from Adam Smith to the modern times. It discusses Walras very much in his context among other theorists of this period rather than individually.

Ekelund, Robert B., Jr., and Robert F. Hebert. *A History of Economic Theory and Method.* 4th ed. New York: McGraw-Hill, 1997. Places Marshall and Walras in the same chapter and offers a very technical and exhaustive comparison and contrast of the two, though in their overview they also write in a nontechnical manner.

Gill, Richard T. *Evolution of Modern Economics.* Englewood Cliffs, N.J.: Prentice-Hall, 1967. Excellent short introduction to Walras and other major economists that is written in a simple, nontechnical style and could be understood by someone with no background in economics.

Jaffé, William. "The Antecedents and Early Life of Léon Walras." *History of Political Economy* 16, no. 1 (1984): 1-57. An interesting, anecdotal account of Walras' early life and that of his father.

———. *William Jaffé's Essays on Walras.* Edited by Donald A. Walker. Cambridge and New York: Cambridge University Press, 1983. A collection of essays varying from pure biography to Walras' correspondence to involved discussions of aspects of his theories. Written by the foremost authority on Walras.

Spiegel, Henry William. *The Growth of Economic Thought.* 3d ed. Durham: Duke University Press, 1991. A very well-written book that lies halfway between Gill's and Blaug's books in its treatment of Walras and its accessibility to the noneconomist.

Walker, Donald A. "Walras's Models of the Barter of Stocks of Commodities." *European Economic Review* 37, no. 7 (October, 1993). The author describes Walras' economic models.

*Philip Magnier*

# BARBARA WALTERS

*Born:* September 25, 1931; Boston; Massachusetts
*Area of Achievement:* Journalism
*Contribution:* As the first female cohost of the *Today Show* and the first female network news anchor, Walters broke ground for women in the top echelons of network news.

## Early Life

Barbara Jill Walters was born on September 25, 1931, in Boston, Massachusetts. She was the younger of the two daughters of Louis Edward Walters, a vaudeville booking agent, and his wife, Dena Seletsky Walters.

Lou Walters, of Lithuanian Jewish descent, had emigrated from London to the United States in 1910. The Seletskys were descended from Russian Jews who had come to the United States in the late nineteenth century. Although the Walters family was only minimally observant of major holidays, Barbara grew up in a succession of upper-middle-class Jewish milieus.

At the time of Barbara's birth, Lou Walters' highly successful booking business was failing as vaudeville disappeared with the advent of the talking motion picture. The family fortunes declined precipitously, and they would rise and fall several times during Barbara's youth.

Lou Walters was an energetic entrepreneur who founded and ran the celebrated Latin Quarter nightclubs, first in Boston, then in Miami, Florida, and New York City. The family moved from city to city, following Lou's successful and unsuccessful business ventures. Lou Walters was a celebrity, part of a vast entertainment network. Barbara grew up in a household where it was not unusual to be in contact with celebrities.

Barbara attended schools in Boston and Miami as well as the Fieldston School and Birch Wathen, private schools in New York. She is remembered by her peers as being shy and not particularly popular; she herself describes her youth as lonely. At Birch Wathen, Barbara showed a flair for writing and became active on the school literary magazine. Entering the elite and somewhat bohemian Sarah Lawrence College, Barbara set out to study acting, but she eventually turned to writing. She became the dramatics editor and theater and film critic for the college newspaper, as well as president of her dormitory.

## Life's Work

After she was graduated from Sarah Lawrence in 1951, Barbara Walters took a copywriting job with an advertising agency. In 1952, she was hired by a local New York City television station to write press releases. During a taxi strike, she got her first news scoop when she obtained an exclusive interview with an official of the taxi association. Walters then produced a children's program, *Ask the Camera*, and did production work for a network panel show, *Leave It to the Girls*. When these shows were canceled, Walters found herself unemployed.

In 1955, Walters was hired by the *Morning Show*, CBS's competitor against the highly successful *Today Show*, where Walters would eventually make her name. On the *Morning Show*, Walters' job was to book unusual guests, but the gimmicky show lasted only six months. Taking the initiative in her desire to get on the air, Walters began to produce fashion segments, doing commentary despite her slight speech impediment, and even modeling clothing. When the show was replaced with *Good Morning*, Walters was rehired.

Television was in its earliest stages, and the directors and producers with whom Walters worked, who were impressed by her, were in the process of forming an old-boy network of contacts that would eventually achieve important positions on all three television networks (ABC, NBC, and CBS).

In 1957, *Good Morning* was canceled, and in 1958, Walters' father's nightclub failed. Needing to support herself and her family, Walters took a job in a public relations firm. There she worked with William Safire, who would become a speechwriter for President Richard M. Nixon.

In 1961, CBS veteran Fred Freed, now the producer of NBC's *Today Show*, hired Walters as a writer. Walters began a campaign to get on camera, initiating stories involving fashion shows and a beauty makeover. When Shad Northshield, another CBS alumnus, was hired to produce *Today*, Walters began to write and edit short features, and she made a trip to Paris to cover the fashion shows. Walters convinced Northshield that she should narrate the piece, and so, on August 29, 1961, Barbara Walters first appeared on *Today* as a commentator.

In 1962, Walters received a plum assignment from Northshield; she would cover First Lady Jacqueline

Kennedy's goodwill visit to India and Pakistan. She had convinced him that the public would be interested in the woman's angle. When she managed to get a short interview with Jacqueline Kennedy, it was considered a journalistic coup, which gave Walters exposure and credibility.

The *Today Show* had a male host and a woman who was designated the "Today Girl." Since the show's inception, this position had been filled by a succession of thirty-three actresses or models. Walters had campaigned for the job but had been turned down by producer Al Morgan because of her "lateral lisp," which made it difficult for her to pronounce l's and r's. In 1964, Walters, with the help of *Today* host Hugh Downs, convinced Morgan to let her work several days a week on a probationary basis. In October of 1964, with no publicity and without any official designation, Barbara Walters appeared on the *Today Show*. She was the first woman not to be billed as the "Today Girl"; instead, she was referred to as "Today Reporter" Barbara Walters.

Morgan was not interested in promoting Walters, and Walters understood that her success depended on her being noticed. She hired a publicist to ensure that she was mentioned in the media. She also assembled a management team to represent her interests with the network. The publicity was successful, establishing Walters in her new position.

The persona that Walters created through her publicity efforts went beyond that of the anonymous journalist telling a story. She became a celebrity in her own right. Ironically, her own celebrity status aided in gaining access to the powerful and famous persons she would interview. Walters had an insider's view of publicity; she was never taken in by her own celebrity and treated herself as a working journalist. She is recognized in the industry for her preparation, persistence, and hard work, as someone who worked her way to the top.

In 1969, Walters was the first to interview former secretary of state Dean Rusk. The interview gave Walters credibility in Washington and led to more hard news assignments. In 1970, Walters published a book, *How to Talk with Practically Anybody About Practically Anything*, and took over a morning talk show, *Not for Women Only*, that focused on women's issues.

In 1971, Hugh Downs left the show to be replaced by NBC anchorman Frank McGee. Because he believed reporters should have a hard news background, McGee did not respect Walters, and his contract gave him control over interviews on the show. Walters could only question guests after McGee had asked three questions. When he was away from the show, he stipulated who would act as guest host, preventing Walters from performing that role.

Walters countered McGee by initiating her own interview segments, such as those with the Nixon Administration, in which he did not participate. Walters was well connected at the Nixon White House. Walters befriended National Security Adviser (later secretary of state) Henry Kissinger, whom she interviewed many times, as well as Nixon himself and Nixon's chief of staff H. R. "Bob" Haldeman. Walters broke the story of Nixon's 1972 trip to China and was invited to be one of the eighty-seven journalists to cover the historic opening of diplomatic relations with China.

The conflict ended when McGee died of bone cancer in 1974. Ironically, McGee's death led to Walters' becoming officially designated cohost of the *Today Show*. Her contract had stipulated that she would be promoted to cohost in the event that McGee left the show.

On April 22, 1976, Walters made television journalism history by signing with ABC to become the first woman news anchor. Her contract called for an annual salary of $1 million, half for her work on the *Evening News* and half for a series of four specials.

The publicity greeting the news of her salary was negative. Journalists publicly questioned her qualifications and decried the decline of journalism into show business. Even more of a problem was Harry Reasoner, who had been anchoring *ABC Evening News* alone. Like McGee, Reasoner had little respect for Walters, and the discord between the two was apparent to viewers. Eventually, they were never shown in the same camera shot. In June of 1978, Reasoner left ABC to return to CBS; Walters was assigned to special reporting assignments and interviews.

Although the anchor job was one of Walters' few failures, the *Barbara Walters Specials* were a huge success. The first program featured singer Barbara Streisand, President-elect Jimmy Carter and his wife Rosalynn, and a tour of Walters' own apartment. In November of 1977, Walters was the first to interview Israeli prime minister Menachem Begin and Egyptian president Anwar el-Sadat together. Barbara Walters' interviewing style, with its focus on the intimate revelations of celebrities and politicians, has influenced the direction of broadcast journalism. Walters' ingenuity, persistence, use of connections, and even her own celebrity have given her access to the powerful and famous that is unparalleled in the industry. By the end of the 1990's Walters was appearing in and producing a daytime talk show, *The View*, and had joined *20/20*, the ABC weekly news magazine program, as cohost.

### Summary

Barbara Walters made it to the top of broadcast journalism at a time when television news was essentially a man's domain. She was the first woman on *Today* to be treated as a serious journalist; before Walters, the role had essentially been decorative. As first woman news anchor at the national network level, she broke a barrier, achieving a position that was not matched by another woman until Connie Chung was named coanchor of the *CBS Evening News* in 1993. In 1976, critics questioned Walters' credentials, her high salary, and her show business orientation. In retrospect, most commentators believe that she was singled out for criticism because she was a woman entering a male preserve.

When Walters was passed over for promotion, she countered with hard work, initiating her own projects. When she was subjected to sexist dismissal of her work by critics and coworkers, she responded by going outside the system and producing her own interview segments. When she was given opportunities, she knew how to make use of publicity and a network of contacts that she cultivated throughout her career. Walters made sure that she understood how the system worked and used it to her own advantage.

### Bibliography

Bonderoff, Jason. *Barbara Walters: Today's Woman*. New York: Leisure, 1975. Containing short summaries of Walters' family background and early career, this biography ends before her move to ABC. It contains background information on many of her early interviews with such luminaries as singer Judy Garland, Great Britain's Prince Philip, and presidents Lyndon B. Johnson and Richard Nixon.

Lewis, Barbara, and Dan Lewis. *Barbara Walters: TV's Superlady*. New York: Pinnacle, 1976. This unauthorized biography provides inside information on Walters' career and the people with whom she worked through 1976, in a nonchronological format. It contains the complete text of the speech Walters gave to the ABC affiliates when she moved to that network.

Mansfield, Stephanie. "Barbara Walters, 1976: The First Woman to Anchor a Network-Television Evening News Show." *Working Woman* 21, no. 11 (November-December, 1996). Examines Walters's achievement as the first woman anchor of a network evening news program and how it has affected the fortunes of those who followed her.

Matusow, Barbara. *The Evening Stars: The Making of the Network News Anchor*. Boston: Houghton Mifflin, 1983. This analysis of the backgrounds and power struggles of news anchors contains a chapter on Walters and Reasoner that details the reasons for their failure. It also contains a good summary of Walters' career.

Oppenheimer, Jerry. *Barbara Walters: An Unauthorized Biography*. New York: St. Martin's Press, 1990. Despite its somewhat negative tone, this biography documents Walters' career in detail and provides much material on her family background and personal life.

Powers, Ron. *The Newscasters*. New York: St. Martin's Press, 1977. This analysis of the network news as moving from journalistic to entertainment values places ABC's decision to hire Walters in context. It also contains sections in which Walters discusses her career.

*Allison Carter*

# SIR WILLIAM WALTON

*Born:* March 29, 1902; Oldham, Lancashire, England

*Died:* March 8, 1983; Ischia, Italy

*Area of Achievement:* Music

*Contribution:* In the field of concert music, Walton created a small but remarkably effective group of masterpieces, heard throughout the world in public performances and by means of recordings. A wider public has heard his church music, his stirring ceremonial music, and his scores for radio and film—the latter including Sir Laurence Olivier's *Hamlet*, *Henry V*, and *Richard III*.

## Early Life

Like so many who have excelled in the field of music, William Turner Walton had musical parents: Charles, a choirmaster and teacher of singing, and Elizabeth, who played and taught piano. The composer was the second of their four children. Though introduced to piano and violin at an early age, Walton was no instrumental prodigy; only his outstanding ability as a boy soprano suggested musical gifts.

Through the persistence of his mother, the ten-year-old Walton auditioned successfully for a place in the choir school of Christ Church College, Oxford. By the time his voice had changed he had started on his lifetime career of musical composition; at sixteen, he published an anthem for four-part chorus, titled "A Litany." While not in the style of his most famous works, it is an excellent piece. Like so many of Walton's works, it has been recorded more than once, and it remains in the repertoire of many church, cathedral, and school choirs.

Admitted to Christ Church College as a regular undergraduate, Walton completed the next of his works to be published, a piano quartet. By this time he had the full support of the Reverend Thomas Banks Strong, dean of the college and later Bishop of Oxford. He neglected all but his musical studies, which he pursued under the wise and liberal guidance of Dr. Hugh Allen. When Allen became director of the Royal College of Music in 1919, Walton would normally have followed him there. Walton, however, disappointed his family and former teachers by leaving school altogether at age eighteen. He accepted the uniquely generous offer of patronage from his recently acquired friends Osbert and Sacheverell Sitwell, who, with their sister Edith, constituted a veritable modernist movement in poetry and the arts. Walton lived as a member of that eccentric family from 1920 until 1934. Through the Sitwells Walton met most of the leading personalities in British arts and letters—and many distinguished foreigners as well; they regularly took him along on their extensive trips to Spain and Italy, where their father, Sir George, owned an ancient castle. The circumstance was decisive in shaping Walton's career: Edith and Osbert Sitwell were collaborators on two of the early masterpieces that established him as a major composer, and he was so enchanted with southern Italy that years later, when circumstances permitted, he made it his permanent home.

As a young man, Walton was spare of build, somewhat below medium height, and quite handsome—his features suggested both strength and sensitivity. Though often in the company of brilliant and exhibitionistic people, he was himself almost, but not quite, taciturn. Throughout his life, Walton had a sharp and original wit, expressed in brief and pungent sayings.

## Life's Work

Walton's next two works were far from being instant successes. He collaborated with Edith Sitwell in composing *Façade* (1923). Osbert and Sacheverell were also helpful, as was a brilliant young student from the Royal College of Music, Constant Lambert (1905-1951), who had recently entered the Sitwell circle. *Façade* puzzled the guests who heard it first, in a private production at the Sitwell's house in Chelsea, and also failed to attract favorable notice in its first public performance in June, 1923. Walton's aggressively modern and dissonant string quartet similarly failed to make a great impression at the first Festival of the International Society for Contemporary Music in Salzburg. Yet *Façade* after much reworking, was a triumph in 1926, and has remained one of the most popular of modern pieces ever since. Modeled both on Arnold Schönberg's revolutionary *Pierrot Lunaire*, Op. 21 (1912) and the collaborative work by Jean Cocteau and Erik Satie, *Parade* (1917), *Façade* consisted of short poems, read rapidly through a megaphone whose bell formed the mouth of a comic face on a large screen. Speaker and instrumentalists were concealed behind the screen; this odd presentation and the use of words for sound and whimsy rather than sense made the experience unusually abstract and disorienting; Walton's music, influenced by popular tunes and Igor Stravinsky's *The Soldier's Tale* (1918), was both novel and yet familiar to self-consciously modern Londoners of the mid-1920's. The string quartet, on the other hand, enjoyed no such redemption. Walton abandoned it; even so, his trip to Salzburg had introduced him to leading composers from all over the world, and he began an association with Paul Hindemith, who a few years later gave the premier performance of Walton's Viola Concerto.

For the next several years, the most important influence on Walton seems to have been Constant Lambert. The two were close friends and had much in common: precocious musical gifts, a keen sense of humor, and sympathies that embraced French, Italian, and Russian music rather than German. There were striking differences as well: Lambert, however gifted as composer, had formidable gifts as artist, raconteur, critic, essayist, and finally conductor; unfortunately, he also had a self-destructive bent toward dissipation. The reticent and craftsmanlike Walton kept his good health and concentrated his creative energies on composition. Lambert, never entirely healthy, worked feverishly to make the Sadler's Wells Ballet one of the best in the world, giving it not only the finest in musical direction but also helping in all other aspects of performance and production—incidentally advancing the music of his contemporaries while neglecting his own talent for composition. Most of these events were still in the future when the two prodigies, still in their early twenties, most enjoyed each other's company. Through Lambert Walton became acquainted with Cecil Gray and Philip Heseltine, both of whom combined probing critical faculties with unconventional morals. Heseltine was especially gifted, published his music under the pseudonym Peter Warlock. Finally there was Gerald, fourteenth Lord Berners, who enjoyed success as a diplomat, painter, composer, novelist, and persistent practical joker. Among such people there was much frivolity and cynicism, but there was also a profound respect for the arts in general, and an approach to music that was original and exciting. One can savor it in Lambert's *Music Ho! A Study of Music in Decline* (1934). Original and captivating in argument, *Music Ho!* builds on the earlier iconoclastic writings of Gray, and like Gray finds hope for the modern composer precisely to the extent that he does not join a cult or school, or

even attempt self-consciously to be modern. Jean Sibelius was put forth (with good reason) as the exemplary composer content to go his own way in defiance of fads and trends. Yet Sibelius, though one could not yet be sure, had by 1934 essentially completed his life's work. If one reads *Music Ho!* carefully, one finds that the only young composer mentioned both frequently and favorably is William Walton.

By that time, Walton had enjoyed immense success with the Viola Concerto, first performed in October, 1929, with Hindemith as soloist and Walton himself, after lessons from Eugene Goossens, conducting. This was the wider public's first experience of Walton's extraordinary gift for long and heart-tugging melody. Lionel Tertis, England's foremost violist, had declined to perform the work, but after attending the premier changed his mind and subsequently played it many times.

The oratorio *Belshazzar's Feast*, for which Osbert Sitwell had arranged passages from the Old Testament and from the Revelation of St. John, caused a still greater stir in 1931. The English oratorio tradition was never so shallow musically or spiritually as its enemies have contended, but nothing in it—even masterpieces such as George Frideric Handel's *Israel in Egypt* (1739) or Felix Mendelssohn's *Elijah* (1846)—could rival Walton's music for expressing the bitter sorrow of Israel in the Babylonian captivity, the pagan rites and revels within the "mighty city," or the triumphant and vengeful songs of Israel after Babylon's destruction. With double chorus, a single baritone soloist serving as narrator, a huge battery of percussion and an extra brass band, the oratorio also offered a new and exciting range of sounds. Teeming with dissonance and complex rythms, *Belshazzar's Feast* nevertheless has a firm and clear sequence of tonalities, and for all its novelty made an immediate impression on the experienced concertgoers of England.

With *Façade*, the Viola Concerto, and *Belshazzar's Feast* all established as contemporary classics, Walton sealed his reputation in 1935 with his long and powerful First Symphony. So important had Walton become in English musical life that the great conductor Sir Hamilton Harty premiered the first three movements of the work before Walton had completed the finale; Harty also conducted a recording of the work shortly after the first public performance of the completed score. The last of Walton's serious works to become a "standard classic" was the Violin Concerto, commissioned by Jascha Heifetz, and premiered by that brilliant violinist with the New York Philharmonic in December, 1939. A recording by Heifetz and the Cincinnati Symphony under Eugene Goossens followed immediately.

During most of his career Walton was remarkable for the care he lavished on each composition, even disappointing some of his partisans by the relatively small number of works actually brought to performance and publication. The years from 1934 to about 1954, however, saw the composer rushing a variety of works to completion, almost always by invitation or commission. When necessary Walton could complete a score as quickly as Wolfgang Amadeus Mozart or Handel. One of his commissions came all the way from Illinois, where Frederick Stock conducted the high-spirited Scapino Overture while celebrating the fiftieth anniversary of the Chicago Symphony Orchestra in 1941. Many scores were for plays and films. In total, Walton composed music for fourteen films, including the celebrated Shakespearean works mentioned above, and the classic *Major Barbara* (1941) with Wendy Hiller and Rex Harrison. An opening sequence from the World War II film *The First of the Few* (1942) became independently famous as *Spitfire Prelude and Fugue*. In the tradition of Sir Edward Elgar, Walton composed grand symphonic marches: *Crown Imperial* for the coronation of George VI in 1936 and *Orb and Sceptre* for the coronation of Elizabeth II in 1953. For the latter he also composed the *Coronation te Deum* for large chorus and orchestra. He arranged several pieces by Johann Sebastian Bach, selected by Lambert, into music for the ballet *The Wise Virgins* (1940) and composed an original score for the ballet *The Quest* (1943). Returning to classical forms after the war, Walton completed his String Quartet in A Minor in 1947, his Sonata for Violin and Piano, commissioned by Yehudi Menuhin, in 1949, and his grand opera *Troilus and Cressida* in 1954. That much of this music was more facile than original, and some of it traditionally patriotic, led Lambert to refer to his gifted friend as "the late Sir William Walton" several years before Walton, alive and healthy, received the honor of knighthood in 1951.

Walton's personal life changed greatly during these years. He left Osbert Sitwell's house in 1934, to be sustained for the next few years by Lady Alice Wimbush. In 1948, Walton attended a conference in Buenos Aires where he met and courted Susana Gil. They were married in December and made their permanent home on the Italian island of Ischia in the Bay of Naples. This was not an early retirement: Walton continued to compose, but after *Troilus and Cressida* he attempted no more works on the grand scale and wrote relatively little occasional or incidental music. Though living far from the musical world he had so effectively conquered, Walton returned to England frequently to conduct concerts and recordings of his own music, to consult with collaborators on new works, and to negotiate with his publisher, the Oxford University Press. He also traveled to such remote but musical places as the United States, Australia, and the Soviet Union.

At home on Ischia he helped his wife develop a luxurious tropical garden and assisted her in building and maintaining several houses, which became a resort for friends and acquaintances as well as a source of income. Ralph and Ursula Vaughan Williams took one of those houses in January, 1958; the older composer was then eighty-five and in need of a vacation from his still-busy career. Ursula reminisces, "Everything had been done for us with imagination and practicality, there was food in the larder, and spring flowers in the sitting-room and bedroom. William was going to England so he very kindly lent Ralph his piano." Indeed, Walton personally supervised the moving of that piano, rolling it into the parlor just as a terrific storm broke.

Walton's later works have been less popular than the series of masterpieces that began with *Façade* and ended with the Violin Concerto. But they have hardly suffered neglect. In 1956 he completed a Cello Concerto for Gregor Piatagorsky. This work was followed by several excellent works for orchestra: *Johannesburg Festival Overture* (1956), *Partita for Orchestra* (1958), Symphony No. 2 (1960), Variations on a Theme of Hindemith (1963), and Improvisations on an Impromptu of Benjamin Britten (1970). With texts supplied by Christopher Hassall (1912-1962), his gifted librettist for *Troilus and Cressida*, Walton composed two elegant song-cycles: *Anon. in Love* (1960) for tenor with guitar accompaniment, and *A Song for the Lord Mayor's Table* (1962). *The Twelve* (1965), an anthem with words by W. H. Auden, was one of several choral works; *The Bear* (1967), a one-act chamber opera adapted from a play by Anton Chekhov, again displayed Walton's talent for comedy.

### Summary

In June, 1982, Sir William Walton attended a concert in London at which Mstislav Rostropovich performed his *Passacaglia* for solo cello. The audience turned to Walton's box and gave him a standing ovation. The enfant terrible of 1922 had become a figure as popular and beloved as Sir Edward Elgar in his latter years. Along the way he had received honorary doctorates from Oxford (1942) and other universities, the Gold Medal of the Royal Philharmonic Society (presented by Vaughan Williams at a concert in 1947), royal appointment to the Order of Merit (1967), and the American Benjamin Franklin Medal (1972). Walton had made his presence felt in every aspect of English musical life: in opera and song, symphony and concerto, art song and anthem, swaggering march and thrilling film score. If the output was small compared to a Vaughan Williams or a Benjamin Britten, it was still ample, memorable, and moving. Walton's music was performed all over the world during his eightieth anniversary year; since his death in early 1983, new performances and recordings have continued to pour forth. Combining the best in traditional musical language with an unmistakably modern touch, Walton has appealed to almost all sects within the world of music.

### Bibliography

A note on scores and recordings: Walton's music is available from the Oxford University Press, Music Division, London and New York. Recordings come and go too rapidly to permit even a short list here, but one can always find recordings of Walton's famous works, and many of the less familiar ones.

Craggs, Stewart R., ed. *William Walton: A Source Book.* Aldershot, Hants, England: Scolar Press, Brookfield, Vt.: Ashgate, 1993. A comprehensive collection of reference sources on Walton's life and works. Includes a day-by-day chronology of Walton's life, descriptions of more than 100 original manuscripts and first editions, and the locations of Walton's letter collections.

Howes, Frank. *The Music of William Walton.* 2d ed. London and New York: Oxford University Press, 1974. Brief as to the life, but outstanding on the music.

Kennedy, Michael. *Portrait of Walton.* Oxford and New York: Oxford University Press, 1989. Biography focusing on Walton's personality and work. Kennedy is Walton's biographer of choice and as such, has had access to the composer's personal correspondence with a number of notable individuals.

Lambert, Constant. *Music Ho! A Study of Music in Decline*. 3d ed. London: Faber, 1966; New York: October House, 1967. A wonderful book in its own right, this is indispensable for reconstructing the musical ideals of Walton's early years.

Motion, Andrew. *The Lamberts: George, Constant, and Kit*. London: Chatto and Windus, 1986; New York: Farrar Strauss, 1987. The exciting and tragic story of three generations of creative Lamberts. A good source for Walton's years in London.

Ottoway, Hugh. "Sir William Walton." In *The New Grove Dictionary of Music and Musicians*. Vol. 20. London: Macmillan, and Washington, D.C.: Grove's Dictionaries of Music, 1980. An excellent short musical biography, with a comprehensive catalog of works and a bibliography especially strong in journal articles.

Pearson, John. *The Sitwells: A Family's Biography.* New York and London: Harcourt Brace

Jovanovich, 1979. Walton contributed extensive reminiscences to this large and rich biography of his three friends and patrons, published in England as *Façades*.

Shead, Richard. *Constant Lambert*. With a memoir by Anthony Powell. London: Simon, 1973. This work has more details on the friendship of Lambert and Walton than Motion's wider-ranging book.

Sitwell, Sir Osbert. *Laughter in the Next Room: Being the Fourth Volume of Left Hand, Right Hand! An Autobiography*. Boston: Little Brown, 1948; London: Macmillan, 1949. Not the most objective of our authors, Sitwell was nevertheless a sharp observer and a trenchant writer. This volume covers the years of the Sitwells' close association with Walton.

*Robert McColley*

# WANG CHING-WEI

*Born:* May 4, 1883; Canton, China

*Died:* November 10, 1944; Nagoya, Japan

*Areas of Achievement:* Government and politics

*Contribution:* Wang, an early disciple of Sun Yat-sen and a founding member of the T'ung-meng hui, was contender for leadership of the Kuomintang after Sun's death in 1925. He was initially identified with the left wing of the party, then became an anticommunist and favored appeasement of Japan as leader of the government between 1932 and 1936; in 1937, he defected to form a puppet government in Japanese-occupied China in 1940.

## Early Life

The Wang family came from Shao-hsing in Chekiang Province. Wang Ching-wei was born in Canton, on May 4, 1883, the tenth and last child and fourth son of Wang Shu, and his second wife. His given name was Wang Chao-ming. The elder Wang, then sixty years old, was a government legal secretary and, because of his large family, was compelled to work until failing eyesight necessitated his retirement at age seventy. Although the family was not well-off, Wang had a happy childhood until he was twelve, when his mother died, followed by the death of his father the next year and of several siblings in the following years. Supported by his eldest brother, he continued his schooling and worked part-time as a tutor from age seventeen, in order to contribute to the family's income. His early education was typical for the time; it emphasized training in the classics, history, philosophy, and literature. He was later noted for his persuasive writing style and fine calligraphy. He also wrote poetry and published a volume of his poems.

In 1902, he placed third in the first level, or county, examination. Later that year he came in first in the provincial exam held at Canton, a great achievement considering his youth and the stiff competition. Despite this early scholarly success, Wang decided not to proceed to compete in the metropolitan exam but, influenced by new Western ideas, to pursue a modern education in Japan, for which he won a government scholarship in 1904. He quickly learned Japanese and attended the Tokyo Law College, where he obtained a degree in 1906. While in Japan he became attracted to anarchism, but, more important, he met Sun Yat-sen and other Chinese revolutionaries, joined Sun's T'ung-meng hui (United League) when it was formed in 1905, and contributed eloquent pro-republican articles to its publication, the *Min Pao*, waging pen battles with exiled supporters of a constitutional monarchy in Japan. His notoriety led his eldest brother to expel him from the family, lest its members in China should be blamed for his activities. When the Ch'ing government successfully persuaded Japanese authorities to expel Sun from Japan in 1907, Wang accompanied him on a recruiting and fund-raising trip to Southeast Asia. During this trip, he met Ch'en Pi-chun, the daughter of a wealthy overseas Chinese family in Malaya and an enthusiastic follower of Sun. He married her in 1912. She continued to be active in Kuomintang politics throughout her life. Against the advice of Sun and his other colleagues, Wang returned to China, was involved in a bungled attempt to assassinate the prince regent in 1910, was arrested, tried, and sentenced to death. The sentence was commuted to life imprisonment, but he was released in 1911 at the outbreak of the revolu-

tion. He and his wife lived in France from 1912 to 1917, during which time he wrote Chinese poetry but did not learn much French.

### Life's Work

Wang returned to China in 1917, again became active in Sun's movement, and served in various high positions in Sun's government in Canton. Although he had initially advised Sun against entering into an alliance with the Communists, once Sun embarked upon it, Wang, like other members of the Kuomintang, acquiesced in the decision. At the first Kuomintang Congress held in Canton in 1924, Wang was elected a member of the Central Executive Committee and was appointed as the party's minister of propaganda and to other key posts. He was among Sun's entourage when the latter made his final trip to Peking in 1924. Sun's aim was to negotiate with the warlords who ruled north China with the goal of establishing a unified government, but he fell terminally ill with cancer and died in 1925. Wang was the author of Sun's last will and testament.

After Sun's death, Wang became the leader of the left wing of the Kuomintang, which favored continuation of the alliance with the Soviet Union and cooperation with the Chinese Communist Party that Sun had forged in 1922, and contended for leadership of the party with right-wing leader Hu Han-min and centrist Chiang Kai-shek. Neither Wang nor Hu held military power, while Chiang, who was junior to both in the Kuomintang, became its rising star as commandant of the party's military academy and commander in chief of the new party army that he had been appointed by Sun to organize. In 1926, Chiang led the Kuomintang army in the successful Northern Expedition to unify China; Wang headed the Kuomintang civilian government, which had moved to Wu-han along the lower Yangtze River Valley at the beginning of 1927. In the spring of 1927, when Chiang and his right-wing allies, who had established themselves in Nanking, purged the Communists from lands that they controlled, Wang and his left-wing supporters in Wu-han refused to do so, and continued their cooperation with the Chinese Communists and Soviet advisers headed by Mikhail Borodin. They waited until July, 1927, when evidence proved beyond a doubt that the Soviet Union intended to use the Kuomintang to propel the Chinese Communist Party to power. The Wang-led Wu-han government dissolved itself after it, too, expelled the Soviet advisers and purged the Chinese Communists. From then until his death, Wang would be a staunch anticommunist; he regarded Communism and the Soviet Union as China's greatest threat. He left China in disgrace late in 1927 for France but soon returned to head a group called the Reorganizationists, and joined in various movements against the central government in Nanking headed by Chiang between 1928 and 1931, all of which, however, failed.

Japan's invasion of Manchuria in 1931 forced the factions of the Kuomintang to mend their differences and resulted in Wang's heading the civilian government as president of the executive yuan (premier) and foreign minister between 1932 and 1935, while Chiang led and modernized those units of the military under the central government's control and organized campaigns against the Communist insurgents. The cooperation between Chiang and Wang was an uneasy one. While Chiang and his allies controlled the major portions of the military and the party machinery, Wang, who had only a small corps of personal supporters, was clearly relegated to a junior position. Wang and Chiang were, however, agreed that weak and disunified China was in no condition to resist Japan and that, while they implemented programs to modernize China, they must negotiate with the Japanese and make concessions if necessary. Both men, but especially Wang, became targets of hostile public opinion, expressed in the press and in student demonstrations, for their nonresistance and concessions to Japanese aggression. In November, 1935, Wang was wounded in an attempted assassination by an army officer bitter about Wang's appeasement of Japan. He left for convalescence in Europe in early 1936, returned to China a year later, and found Chiang riding a crest of popularity as national leader in an incipient united front against Japan. When the Japanese invasion of north China in July, 1937, resulted in all out war, Chiang came to symbolize resistance and gained even greater power as commander in chief and as party leader in 1938; Wang was named deputy party leader, again superseded by Chiang, whom Wang regarded as a junior in party seniority.

Dissatisfied with his subordination to Chiang and pessimistic over the sufferings in a war against Japan that he saw as hopeless for China, Wang secretly left Chungking, China's wartime capital, in December, 1938. He surfaced in Hanoi in French Indochina and began actively to campaign for peace with Japan. He offered to lead that movement and placed himself and his supporters as alternatives to the Chinese government in Chungking led by Chiang. While he was in Hanoi, there was an attempt to assassinate him, probably instigated by some members of the Chungking government. Although he escaped unscathed, this event marked a point of no return for Wang's "peace movement." After two visits to Tokyo, Wang signed a secret treaty with Japan that permitted him to set up and head a "reform government" in Nanking in March, 1940. Aside from several long time associates, no one of note deserted the Chungking government to join Wang's puppet regime. Anti-Chiang politicians and dissident warlords alike denounced Wang for treason. He had clearly miscalculated disastrously; Chiang's prestige had soared as leader in a war of national salvation, and, among nationalistic Chinese, anti-Chiang did not mean pro-Japan. The Wang regime aped the legitimate Chinese government in its party structure and government organization, professed allegiance to Sun's ideology, and even used the same national flag, to which it added a yellow tab that read "peace, anti-Communism and reconstruction."

Japan had hoped that its installation of the Wang regime would bring about the collapse of the government at Chungking and continued Chinese resistance. When these things did not happen, Japanese support for Wang waned. Thus it did not formally recognize his Nanking regime until November, 1940, and conceded to it only nominal control of Japanese-occupied areas in central and south China, while earlier established puppet regimes in inner Mongolia and north China continued to exist separately. For its part, the Wang regime recognized Manchukuo, the first Japanese-created puppet state in China. It received diplomatic recognition from only the Axis powers and their client states.

The two most powerful offices in Nanking throughout the life of the Wang regime were Japan's Supreme Military and Economic Advisory Commissions, which supervised important activities in areas nominally under Chinese control. Several trips by Wang to Japan netted a treaty in 1943 in which Japan relinquished its extraterritorial rights in China and recognized the Wang regime as an ally in Japan's scheme of Greater East Asia. These were empty gestures, because Japanese troops remained in occupation of conquered China, where Japan continued to enjoy enormous economic and political privileges. Strains over the Pacific War led Japan to permit a greater role for Wang's puppet troops in the China theater after 1943, even as the same strains resulted in greater material demands on Chinese in occupied areas.

The turning tide of war enveloped the Wang regime in pessimism, evidenced by Wang's frequent raging temper outbursts and heavy drinking and a live-for-today attitude among his associates. Failing health and persistent trouble from the assassin's bullet wound led Wang to enter the Nagoya University Hospital in Japan in March, 1944. Even though he was given the best medical treatment available, Japanese authorities guarded his sick bed and prevented him from speaking to journalists. He died on November 10, 1944, from pneumonia. His body was flown back to Nanking, and he was given a huge public funeral and buried near to Sun's mausoleum outside Nanking. His demoralized regime ended with Japan's defeat and the end of World War II. After the war, Wang's tomb was destroyed by order of the Nationalist government. His associates and widow (who had been active politically and held high positions under the puppet regime) were tried by the Nationalist government for treason. Some were executed upon conviction, and Mrs. Wang was sentenced to life imprisonment, which she served out under the Communist government.

### Summary

Wang Ching-wei was a key figure in modern Chinese history. His eloquent writings in favor of the overthrow of the Ch'ing Dynasty and in support of Sun's ideology contributed to the cause of revolution, as did his willingness to sacrifice himself in the failed attempt to assassinate the prince regent. He was widely admired for his good looks, his elegant bearing, his charismatic speaking style, and his persuasive writing. The darker side of his personality includes his vaulting ambition, which drove him to sacrifice principle for personal political gain, and his mercurial temperament. His quest to be successor of Sun led him to oppose Hu Han-min, another leading disciple of Sun, and to espouse the alliance with the Soviet Union and the Chinese Communist Party. After the exposing of Joseph Stalin's goal in China and the discrediting of the left wing Kuomintang that he led, Wang joined in a series of makeshift alliances with warlords that waged civil wars against the new national government in Nanking led by Chiang. Even after his rapprochement with Chiang and installation as head of the civilian government in Nanking after 1932, he continued to chafe under Chiang's greater overall authority. He frequently used histrionics and real or pretended illnesses to threaten resignation and to gain political leverage. Popular opinion turned increasingly against him for his policy of nonresistance against Japanese aggression and for China's territorial losses to Japan under his stewardship; after he turned quisling and organized a puppet regime in Japanese occupied China in 1940, he became execrated as a traitor. Even those sympathetic to him condemned his collaboration with Japan as a hopeless and pointless endeavor. A revolutionary who had devoted much of his life in the cause of Chinese nationalism, he had disastrously misjudged its character when he deserted to the Japanese camp. In his last testament, he claimed that he acted to save the Chinese from the horrors of a prolonged war he saw as doomed and from the dangers of Communism that he saw as worse for China than Japanese imperialism.

**Bibliography**


Boyle, John Hunter. *China and Japan at War, 1937-1945: The Politics of Collaboration*. Stanford, Calif.: Stanford University Press, 1972. An analysis of why Wang and others collaborated with Japanese conquerors.

Bunker, Gerald E. *The Peace Conspiracy: Wang Ching-wei and the China War, 1937-1941*. Cambridge, Mass.: Harvard University Press, 1972. A sympathetic account of Wang's motives for collaborating with Japan. Examines the frustrations and achievements of his regime.

Shirley, James R. *Political Conflict in the Kuomintang: The Career of Wang Ching-wei to 1932*. Ann Arbor, Mich.: University Microfilms, 1965. Deals with Wang's rise and early career. Good explanation of the Kuomintang.

T'ang, Leang-li. *Wang Ching-wei: A Political Biography*. Peiping: China United Press, 1931. A laudatory account written by a Wang supporter, this book goes fairly in depth in biographical information.

Wang, Chao-ming. *China's Problems and Their Solution*. Shanghai: China United Press, 1934. Wang wrote these while he headed China's government to justify his policy. The listing of his name here is a variant spelling.


*Jiu-Hwa Lo Upshur*

# FELIX WANKEL

*Born:* August 13, 1902; Lahr, Germany
*Died:* October 9, 1988; Lindau, West Germany
*Areas of Achievement:* Invention and technology
*Contribution:* As early as 1924, Wankel began to sketch models for rotary piston engines; in 1929, he obtained his first patent for an engine that has a reciprocating piston housed in a horizontal cylinder, the earliest Wankel engine, that has since been perfected to the point that it can power automobiles and other motorized vehicles.

## Early Life

Felix Wankel was born in Lahr in that southwestern reach of Germany near the Alsace province of France, practically on the Swiss border. His father, Rudolf, a forest commissioner killed in the first month of World War I, left his wife, Gerty Heidlauff Wankel, and his twelve-year-old son, Felix Heinrich, to fend for themselves. They were financially comfortable. Their security, however, was sufficiently eroded by the raging postwar inflation that nineteen-year-old Wankel lacked the means to continue his education beyond the secondary level.

Wankel, leaving Lahr and its stolid people behind him, moved to Heidelberg and was employed there by a publisher of scientific books. Within three years, he had opened a mechanical shop and begun his early work with motors. He quickly learned the need for precision and meticulous craftsmanship in mechanical work. He began to dwell on the problem of finding more efficient engines than those then in common use: gas turbines, Diesel engines, free-piston engines, steam engines, electrically powered engines, fuel cells, Stirling engines, and combinations of these.

By 1924, he had conceived the basic idea for the Wankel engine. Working from his sketches of it, he eventually forged models that represented a dramatic departure from all engines of the past. The concept of such an engine was not new; mechanics and engineers had puzzled over the idea for more than a century, but Wankel was the first to conceive of a model that would work and that, providing the requisite power to propel vehicles, could function economically without undue wear.

The concept behind Wankel's engine was that energy could be conserved if an engine were developed that rotated rather than pumped vertically. Because the wheels of vehicles are round, the energy from piston-driven engines, once it is produced, must be converted to a rotary motion. Wankel found this conversion, with its accompanying loss of energy, inefficient.

The practical problem he had to solve was that of developing a working model of an engine that, housed in a horizontal chamber, would seal the gap created by the motion of the rotor. In piston engines, the only gap that has to be sealed is that between the piston rod and the walls of the cylinder into which it plunges. Wankel realized that if a rotor is packed into its chamber too tightly, it loses energy through friction. If the rotor is packed too loosely, the seal is not tight, so the cylinder leaks energy. Wankel packed the rotor in various materials, none of which worked.

## Life's Work

Unable to support himself from his workshop in Heidelberg, Wankel continued to work for a publisher of scientific books until 1926. By 1927, he had a detailed working sketch of his engine, but he had not solved the sealing problem. Despite this, he had progressed sufficiently by 1929 to obtain his first patent for a rotary engine.

The sealing problem, however, continued to plague Wankel for the next two decades. The substantial reputation he gained for his work grew during World War II, when he served Germany by working on torpedoes, although this work diverted him from his main purpose. As Adolf Hitler was rising to power, Wankel joined the Hitler Youth Movement, as did the woman he married. He remained a supporter of the dictator during the early years of Nazism but fell from grace, was arrested, and was imprisoned soon after he broke from the Nazi Party in 1932.

Wilhelm Keppler, a staunch supporter of Hitler, had become an enthusiastic advocate of Wankel and his invention. Through his intervention and that of the chief engineer of Daimler-Benz, Otto Nibel, Wankel was released from prison in 1933 and returned to his experimental work, now with Daimler-Benz, quitting a year later when he had a dispute with the general manager. He then went to work for Bayerischen Motoren Werke (BMW) in Munich, assigned to develop a piston engine with rotary valves.

The basic sealing problem Wankel encountered was that the seal edge in his previous designs was too wide. Every means he conceived of for sealing the cylinder resulted in lost energy and rapid wear, rendering the engine impractical.

Wankel's personality was such that people could not work easily with him, resulting in his usually having to attack problems independently that several minds working harmoniously might have resolved more quickly than Wankel alone could. Keppler, realizing his protégé's potential, used his influence to help Wankel receive a government subvention in 1936 that enabled him to establish a workshop that grew into an institute in the island town of Lindau, Bavaria, at the Lake of Constance, where he would settle permanently. There this man of average height, his hair growing thin and his eyes obscured behind thick glasses, proceeded with his solitary work.

Finally, after experimenting with various materials, Wankel devised thin strips of metal that represented a major step toward resolving the persistent sealing problem. His wartime work with the Goetz corporation, which made piston rings, added another possibility to Wankel's means of sealing his motor. Goetz developed an ultrastrong metal alloy, IKA, that would figure prominently in the development of sealing devices for rotary engines.

Wankel overcame another crucial obstacle when he discovered that he could use the gas pressure built up in the engine as the gas tries to escape to work for rather than against sealing it. He used this gas buildup to put pressure on the seals, thereby fixing them tightly enough to prevent significant leakage and obviating the need for springs beneath the plates of his engine.

At the war's end in 1945, the French occupied Lindau. Wankel was arrested, his institute disbanded, and most of the thousands of sketches for his engine destroyed. This seeming disaster turned into a blessing for Wankel, who was now forced to rethink his work from the beginning, unhindered by the lingering ghosts of his past work. By 1951, when he reestablished his institute, he began the tedious, gargantuan task of classifying the thousands of possible configurations for his engine, not publishing his results until 1963. By January, 1954, however, he had drawn the design for rotary engines that finally powered automobiles in the 1970's. It consisted of a double circle housing for a rotor with three convex sides, a fat, triangular figure rotating within a figure eight.

During the 1950's, automotive manufacturers in Japan, the United States, Germany, and France grew interested in Wankel's experiments, and with their help the first Wankel rotary engines stood endurance tests in 1959. Because such engines could deliver acceptable power economically with minimal air pollution, the idea was appealing to automobile manufacturers and environmentalists alike. The Wankel, half the weight of conventional six-cylinder engines but capable of delivering more power, had potential popular appeal.

General Motors committed fifty million dollars to buying the Wankel license but had difficulty bringing rotary-engine cars into production. Meanwhile, however, Toyo Kogyo of Japan produced an economically viable rotary engine car, the Mazda R-100 and later the Mazda RX-2, for the American market. The first of these cars reached the United States in May, 1970. Despite early customer skepticism and some negative reports, they enjoyed considerable popularity in the geographically limited market in which Toyo Kogyo first marketed them. Soon, Mazda's rotary engine models ranked fourth in sales in the markets where they were sold.

The only problem to emerge was that Wankel engines did not endure. Often the entire engine had to be replaced before thirty thousand miles. Enthusiasm for the Wankel engine waned as the end of the 1970's approached. Although several major automotive manufacturers bought the license to manufacture the engine, the piston engine still dominates the automobile industry.

### Summary

Despite its present lack of popular acceptance, the Wankel engine holds many appealing possibilities, particularly in its ability to produce sufficient power to propel automobiles smoothly and quietly at high speeds with much less air pollution than conventional engines create and with relatively modest consumption of fuel.

Felix Wankel became rich because he ensured that his early patents were airtight. Subsequent patents—more than thirty of them between 1955 and 1958 alone—were carefully drawn to protect Wankel's financial interests fully. His arrangement with the Necharsulm Strickmachinene Union (NSU), for example, gave him 40 percent of the profits from NSU's rotary engines, even though Wankel had been on their payroll when he developed them. Despite his wealth, Wankel always lived frugally and was not renowned for his beneficence, although he founded a refuge for dogs and cats and contributed money to cancer research.

### Bibliography

Ansdale, Richard F. *The Wankel RC Engine.* London: Iliffe, 1968; New Brunswick, N.J.: Barnes, 1969. This book by Wankel's translator is definitely for specialists although valuable general information can be gleaned from it. Ansdale's writing style is often unclear, resulting in an unnecessary complexity in a book whose subject is itself complex and highly technical in many of its essential aspects.

Burstall, Aubrey F. *A History of Mechanical Engineering.* London: Faber, and New York: Pitman, 1963. This book provides as solid a brief overview of Wankel and his work as any in print. Although written with an audience of engineers in mind, the book is not so technical as to bewilder more general readers. It makes a reasonable, well-focused starting point for those unfamiliar with Wankel and his inventions.

Faith, Nicholas. *Wankel: The Curious Story Behind the Revolutionary Rotary Engine.* New York: Stein and Day, 1975; London: Allen and Unwin, 1976. Faith's is the most accessible source for readers who do not require a highly technical approach. His exposition is lucid and appealing. Faith avoids scientific jargon, often defining key terms in context. His research is thorough and accurate. He is totally in control of all the basic writing by and about Wankel to the mid-1970's. The index is extensive and useful.

Inman-Hunter, Marcus C. *Rotary Valve Engines.* New York: Wiley, 1946. This book pays considerable homage to Wankel although it was published before his ideas had progressed to the point of making rotary engines reasonable alternatives to conventional piston engines. The book is interesting primarily for its historical review of Wankel's work at a time when the practicality of his inventions was questionable.

Norbye, Jan P. *The Wankel Engine: Design, Development, Applications.* Philadelphia: Chilton, 1971. Norbye, automotive editor of *Popular Science Monthly*, has produced a highly detailed book on the Wankel engine, profuse with clear, helpful illustrations. The book is more technical than Faith's, but it is generally comprehensible to nonspecialists. Norbye has an encyclopedic knowledge of the engines in general use and understands them technically. Although his emphasis is on engines rather than on the man, Norbye provides substantial biographical information.

Wankel, Felix. *Rotary Piston Machines.* Translated by Richard F. Ansdale. London: Iliffe, 1965. Wankel's own book provides an excellent resource for the specialist but is not valuable for beginners because it tends to be overly technical. Much of the material in this book is replicated in Ansdale's book cited above, but neither book is recommended for the novice.

Yamaguchi, Jack. "Mazda's Side-Intake, Side-Exhaust Rotary Engine Prototype." *Automotive Engineering* 104, no. 1 (January, 1996). The author describes Mazda Motor Corporation's prototype variation of Wankel's twin-rotor engine.

*R. Baird Shuman*

## ANDY WARHOL

*Born:* August 6, 1928(?); Pittsburgh(?), Pennsylvania

*Died:* February 22, 1987; New York, New York

*Area of Achievement:* Art

*Contribution:* More than any other artist of his time, Warhol created the world of American Pop Art. His many paintings and sculptures reflect the commercialism, affluence, and materialism of postwar American society, serving both as legitimate works of art and as artifacts of an era in America's development as a consumerist nation.

### Early Life

Andy Warhol's birth date and place are something of a mystery. Warhol (born Andrew Warhola) provides no information on the matter, so any definitive statement is dubious. Based on his early years and college dates, one can estimate that he was born in 1928 in Pennsylvania, to Czech immigrant parents, Ondrej and Julia Warhola, the second of their three sons. Ondrej Warhola worked for a coal-mining company, a job that often took him from home as he traveled to various mines in Pennsylvania and West Virginia. Warhol's interest in commercial art began when he spent his summers as a youngster in Pennsylvania copying newspaper and magazine advertisements; he pursued that interest throughout his high school and college years. He was graduated from Schenley High School in Pittsburgh in 1945 and worked in the summers for the Joseph Horne Company department-store chain in Pittsburgh, arranging window displays. In the autumn of 1945, he enrolled at the Carnegie Institute of Technology; the rigor of his academic courses there made college difficult for him but he met that challenge and was graduated from the school with a bachelor of fine arts degree in pictorial design in June of 1949.

With his college art degree in hand, Warhol hoped to find a position as an art teacher. During the summer of 1949, he moved to New York City to establish himself, an excellent draftsman, as a commercial artist. His style at that time was heavily influenced by fashion magazines, and his early commissions were illustrations for an article in *Glamour* and for women's shoe advertisements. Early in his career, Warhol lived among other artists who were also seeking a profession in New York and matured in that environment of avant-garde art.

By the early 1950's, Warhol gained some standing and success as a commercial artist. I. Miller Shoes chose him as the chief illustrator for their advertisements, and Warhol gained popularity in New York, becoming a very successful, well-paid artist. In addition to advertisements, he received commissions for book illustrations and jackets, for corporate designs, for magazine covers and illustrations, and for record-album covers. As his work became well-known, he won several design awards for his commercial art, including the Art Directors Club Medal. He invited himself along when a close friend took a tour around the world in 1956. That experience deepened Warhol's sources of ideas for his art and helped him to realize the uniqueness of America in the world.

At the same time that he was producing successful commercial art for advertisements and various publications, Warhol tried to exhibit and sell drawings and paintings which he viewed as serious art. Basically shy and quiet, Warhol shared his art with only a few close friends. These works used cartoon or comic-book figures as their subjects. His style at the time was mixed; some works reflected an abstract expressionist influence; others had hard edges, clear figures, and clean lines. To knowledgeable observers and art critics, the former style seemed trite and derivative and the latter seemed fresh and exciting. Warhol took the advice of others and concentrated on the new style as he and a few other New York artists developed the American Pop Art school in the late 1950's.

### Life's Work

Warhol stands foremost among American Pop artists. Although he was not the originator of Pop Art or the only Pop artist in the early 1960's, he is the archetypical Pop artist for many Americans. Part of Warhol's fame is a result of his outrageous behavior and part is a result of his superb and innovative art. His career has included achievements as a painter, sculptor, filmmaker, and celebrity. In each of these areas, he captured the spirit of affluent, postwar American society.

Warhol's first notoriety came with a show of his soup-can paintings in Los Angeles in 1961-1962. Along with Roy Lichtenstein, he established the American Pop Art world with canvases depicting ordinary objects such as soup cans or comic-book characters. By the fall of 1962, Warhol was noticed

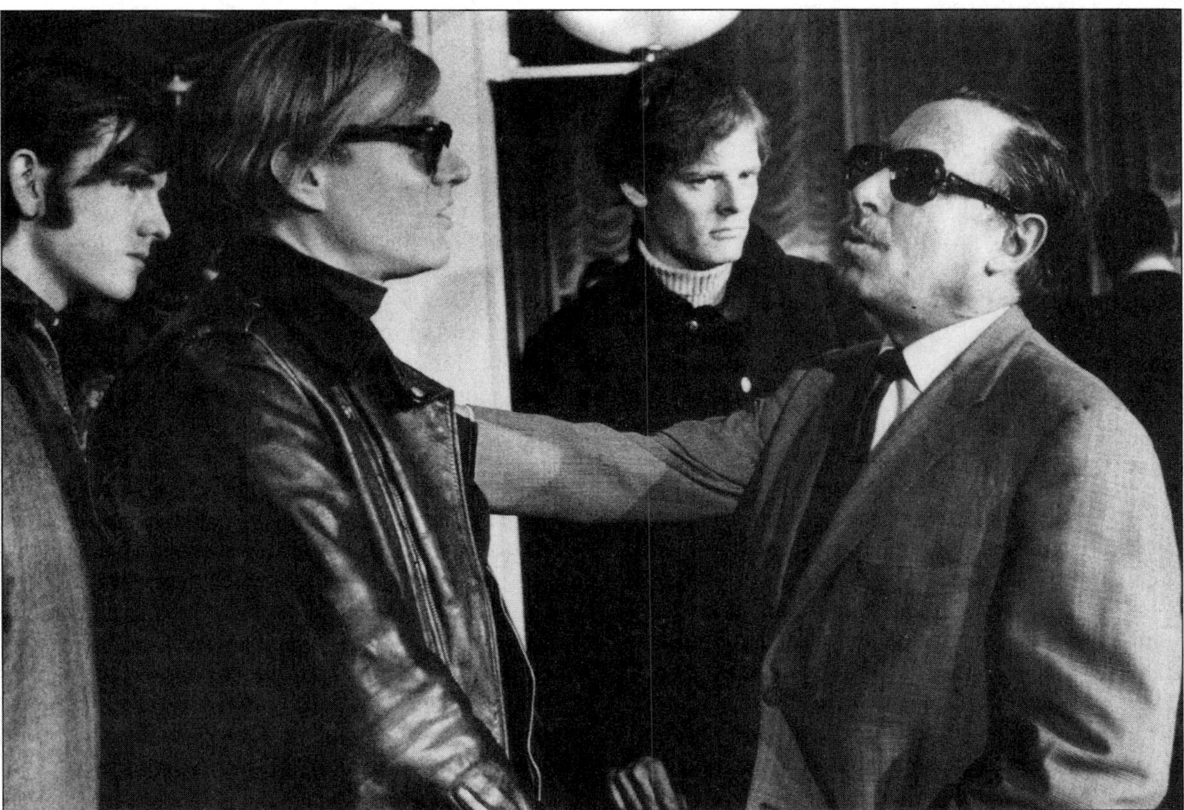

*Andy Warhol and Tennessee Williams*

enough by the art community to warrant a gallery show in New York City; this show, too, displayed paintings of Campbell's soup cans. His *Campbell's Soup Can* (1962) represented an advanced consumer-oriented technological society in the way that eighteenth century Dutch still lifes represented commonplace scenes of that era. Art critics were intrigued by Warhol's clear, clean, and superficial works, almost as laconic and unpretentious as their creator. Warhol's silk-screen technique of reproducing the images on his canvases further linked his work to the mechanical, technological world in which he and his viewers lived.

As he became more successful and renowned as a creative artist, Warhol established a studio loft known as The Factory (which had several addresses in New York City over the years from 1960 to 1985). This workplace attracted several celebrities and near-celebrities who engaged as much in theatrics as in the production of artworks. Warhol thrived on the interactions he had with various visitors to The Factory and found them a stimulus and an inspiration for his work.

In the early 1960's, his art increasingly depicted banal, ordinary, shocking, and vulgar scenes from American life. In addition to soup cans, his paintings included subjects such as popular film stars (as in *Marilyn Monroe*, 1962, and *Liz*, 1963), Coca-Cola bottles, race riots, automobile wrecks, cows, and flowers. By 1964, Warhol had exhibited Pop-sculpture replicas of such commercial items as a Brillo soap pad, Kellogg's corn flakes, and Mott's apple juice cartons. These paintings and sculptures served only to reinforce Warhol's reputation as an outrageous yet highly talented artist whose unusual subject matter brought him notoriety. By 1965, Warhol was as much of a celebrity as his artworks.

With his superstar status increasing by the mid-1960's, Warhol decided to retire from painting and to focus on filmmaking. He began making films with boring and banal themes as early as 1963, an activity which perpetuated his celebrity status. The Factory became a center for pop and would-be pop stars and attracted a wide variety of glamorous people, as well as an assortment of characters in the art and performing worlds. Although many of Warhol's films, such as *Sleep* (1963), *Eat* (1963), and *Empire* (1965), were lengthy depictions of the most mundane activity or object, some of his works anticipated future film themes or poked fun at certain subjects. *Lonesome Cowboys* (1968) treated homosexuality when it was taboo as a subject for commercial films and, at the same time, challenged the cowboy myth of courageous, macho riders of the range. With such works as *Flesh* (1968) and *Trash* (1970), Warhol focused on sexual themes in films which were precursors of the pornographic film market of the 1970's and 1980's. By the mid-1970's, his *Andy Warhol's Dracula* (1974) and *Andy Warhol's Frankenstein* (1974) enjoyed commercial success as satiric yet serious works. From 1963 to 1974, he had been involved in the production of more than sixty films of varying quality and subject matter.

In 1968, Warhol's celebrity status nearly cost him his life. A disturbed visitor to The Factory shot him, inflicting serious internal wounds. Warhol's slow recovery included a two-month hospital stay and a turn in a new direction, his post-Pop period. From 1970 onward, he increasingly turned to producing portraits of cult figures, prominent persons, and personal friends. These portraits, of figures such as Mao Tse-tung, Philip Johnson, Mick Jagger, Jimmy Carter, and Merce Cunningham display a softer, more delicate imagery than Warhol's earlier Pop Art paintings. His art of the 1970's moved closer to an abstract expressionist style and away from the figurative or realistic style of his work in the 1960's. In 1981, he undertook a series of myth paintings in which the subject matter treated mythical figures from popular-culture sources, such as advertisements, comic strips, and films. These works included *Dagwood, Mickey Mouse*, and *Superman*. Later, in 1983, he created a series of endangered-species paintings which depicted various threatened wildlife. As in all of his work, Warhol selected subjects with great popular imagery and treated the symbol and image as much as he does the real object itself.

## Summary

As the preeminent American Pop artist of the 1960's and 1970's, Andy Warhol enjoyed greater popularity in the public mind than his art. His treatment of ordinary subjects in an unemotional and passionless manner alienated many viewers and startled others. His nonchalant behavior and celebrity status convinced many Americans that Warhol was all style and no substance. Yet, for postwar American society, he stands as a significant figure—as both an artist and a social commentator.

Warhol fits into the vernacular art tradition of American culture. By celebrating the ordinary, the commonplace, and the unpretentious, he has created realistic works which reflect the surface and mundane aspects of a technological and democratic society. With that achievement, he stands with earlier realist American artists, such as Winslow Homer and Thomas Eakins, who chose contemporary, ordinary, unheroic themes for their art. Like them, Warhol emphasizes elements of everyday life.

As a social commentator (a role he denied), Warhol has the uncanny ability to mirror the trends and fads of his time. Recognizing the elements of an urban mass society heavily influenced by symbols, images, and the mass media, he has made those symbols and images the subjects of his art. For Warhol and other Pop artists, these images have taken on a reality of their own, not only shaped by but also reshaping popular culture. Warhol has therefore left social and cultural historians visual documents of the significant elements from America's consumerist society of the postwar era—an important legacy.

## Bibliography

Alloway, Lawrence. *American Pop Art*. New York and London: Macmillan, 1974. A well-illustrated treatise on significant American Pop artists, including Warhol, Jasper Johns, Robert Rauschenberg, Roy Lichtenstein, James Rosenquist, and Claes Oldenburg, by one of the leading interpreters of that art school. Places Warhol in the context of American Pop Art with a full discussion of that art movement.

Coplans, John. *Andy Warhol*. Greenwich, Conn.: New York Graphic Society, 1970; London: Weidenfeld and Nicolson, 1971. A thoroughly illustrated work on Warhol's painting, sculpture, and film of the 1960's. Useful for Coplans' perspectives on the whole of Warhol's work in that decade, although limited because it does not treat Warhol's later accomplishments.

Lippard, Lucy R. *Pop Art*. London: Thames and Hudson, and New York: Praeger, 1966. A fine survey of 1960's Pop Art with many illustrations. Includes chapters on the British origins of Pop Art, the New York and California schools, and the European scene. Helps to place Warhol in a national and international context.

Lucie-Smith, Edward. *Late Modern: The Visual Arts Since 1945*. Rev. ed. New York: Oxford University Press, 1975. Lucie-Smith presents developments in modern art after 1945 and places Pop Art in the larger context of Western art in the postwar world. Not limited to Pop Art, this work is a well-illustrated survey of various schools of art since 1945 and sets Pop Art into a larger framework of modern art.

Mattick, Paul. "The Andy Warhol of Philosophy and the Philosophy of Andy Warhol." *Critical Inquiry* 24, no. 4 (Summer 1998). The author argues that Warhol's work recognizes the relationship between creativity and commerce.

Ratcliff, Carter. *Andy Warhol*. New York: Abbeville Press, 1983. A thorough treatment of Warhol's life and work by a distinguished art critic and teacher. Contains an excellent bibliography, Warhol chronology, film list, and exhibition list. Particularly useful for information on Warhol's post-Pop activities. Fully illustrated.

Taylor, Joshua C. *America as Art*. New York: Harper, 1976; London: Harper, 1979. A fine survey of American art throughout the United States' history; a chapter on art of the 1960's and 1970's places Warhol's work in the larger context of American art. Useful for background about the developments in American art.

Warhol, Andy, and Pat Hackett. *POPism: The Warhol Sixties*. New York: Harcourt Brace, 1980; London: Hutchinson, 1981. Warhol's own musings about Pop Art and his activities as celebrity and artist in the 1960's. This year-by-year diary of Warhol's activities must be read with some skepticism, because Warhol is intentionally unreliable in his recollections.

Wilson, Simon. *Pop*. London: Thames and Hudson, 1974; Woodbury, N.Y.: Barron, 1978. A brief, well-illustrated survey of Pop Art in an inexpensive edition. Designed chiefly for classroom use, with an excellent, succinct text to accompany the illustrations.

Wolf, Reva. *Andy Warhol, Poetry and Gossip in the 1960s*. Chicago: University of Chicago Press, 1997. Innovative study of Warhol focusing on his relationships with writers, filmmakers, and other artists and their impact on his work.

*Harry J. Eisenman*

# EARL WARREN

*Born:* March 19, 1891; Los Angeles, California
*Died:* July 9, 1974; Washington, D.C.
*Area of Achievement:* Law
*Contribution:* Warren was Chief Justice of the United States between 1953 and 1969; under his leadership, landmark decisions were reached striking down existing practices in the areas of racial segregation, limitations on political association, voting apportionment, the investigation of criminal suspects, and other controversial issues.

## Early Life

On March 19, 1891, Earl Warren was born in Los Angeles, California. His father, Methias Warren, was a Norwegian immigrant who had come to the United States during his adolescence and for many years worked as a railroad car mechanic; the boy's mother, Christine Hernlund Warren, was of Swedish ancestry. Ethel Warren, Earl's sister, was four years older than he. In 1896, the family moved to Bakersfield. As a boy, Warren raised animals and worked at various jobs on the Southern Pacific Railroad; his best subjects in school were history, English, and French. His interest was aroused in 1903 when a deputy marshal killed two lawmen and was later tried in a local court; Warren saw the trial and also watched other trials. Although his father encouraged him to consider a career in engineering, Warren was intrigued by the examples of courtroom advocacy he had seen. By the time he completed high school, he had saved some eight hundred dollars, which he used to meet his expenses when he entered the University of California at Berkeley.

Warren's academic record was acceptable, if not outstanding; after his third year, he was allowed to take courses at the University's law school. He received a bachelor's degree in 1912, and two years later he was awarded his law degree. He was graduated at about the middle of his class and was not selected to serve on the school's *Law Review.* For some time thereafter, he practiced in a local law office; upon the United States's entry into World War I, he joined the army, serving as a bayonet instructor. After a period of service that took him to Fort Lee, Virginia, he was discharged in 1918 with the rank of first lieutenant in the infantry. He then began work for the city attorney in Oakland. In 1925, he became the district attorney for Alameda County, an area just east of San Francisco.

Slightly taller than six feet, Earl Warren weighed more than two hundred pounds; he had a strong build, though in later years he had to struggle somewhat to control his girth. His features were often described as typically Scandinavian: He had a long face with a straight nose and clear blue eyes, his complexion was fair, and he had blond hair which eventually became gray. Throughout his adult life he wore glasses, in time favoring those with rounded, dark-rimmed frames.

Although hither to he had not seriously concerned himself with women, Warren became deeply attached in 1921 to Nina Palmquist Meyers, whom he met at a morning swimming party. An attractive young widow whose husband had died shortly after their son was born, she returned Warren's affection; after a lengthy courtship, they were married in 1925. Over a period of seven years, two sons and three daughters were born to them, and Warren, as a proud father, became an archetypal family man, constantly concerned with his children's education and well-being.

## Life's Work

Warren became widely known for his relentless pursuit of lawbreakers, notably bootleggers, and he took vigorous action against gambling and vice. In 1931, Raymond Moley, an important political observer and later adviser to President Franklin D. Roosevelt, called Warren "the most intelligent and politically independent district attorney in the United States." On some cases Warren went to great lengths to obtain convictions; controversy arose in 1936, during his investigation of a shipboard homicide on the SS *Point Lobos*. Four defendants, who allegedly were Communist sympathizers, were brought to trial on evidence obtained partly through electronic eavesdropping and prolonged interrogation in the absence of defense counsel. Ultimately they were found guilty of second-degree murder. Violent crime affected Warren's life directly, as well: In 1938, his father was beaten to death at his home in Bakersfield. The assailant was never found.

Later that year, Warren was elected attorney general for the state of California; his tenure in that office was characterized by the same zeal he had displayed in local law enforcement. In 1939, drawing upon an extended legal definition of the state's coastal waters, he directed a major raid on the *Rex*, an offshore gambling ship. He also became involved in politics: He opposed the nomination of a noted legal scholar to the California Supreme Court, partly because of the latter's purported relations with the Communist Party. Claims of national security were invoked in 1942, when Warren supervised the forcible relocation of about 110,000 Japanese Americans; he depicted them as potential saboteurs and collaborationists. Although somewhat later many others denounced this measure, until the last years of his life Warren contended that it was necessary in view of the military situation at that time.

Warren's politics were Republican, but his positions on social issues had a wide appeal to voters at large. He campaigned for governor in 1942 and was elected overwhelmingly; four years later, under California's cross-filing system, he won the primaries of both major parties. In 1950, he became the only man to be elected to a third term as governor of that state. He supported measures to expand the state's educational system; he also advocated prison reform and improved mental health care. He was acutely conscious of the financial hardships imposed by medical expenses, which he and his family had incurred during periods of hospitalization; in 1945 he urged, unsuccessfully, that the state enact a form of health care insurance. In 1949, he signed a bill requiring that women receive equal pay for work performed on an equal basis with men.

Because of his demonstrated political appeal and the growing importance of California and the Western states in national politics, there were Republican political strategists who looked to Warren as one of the party's possible standard-bearers. In 1948, the Republican nominee for president, Governor Thomas E. Dewey of New York, chose Warren as his vice-presidential running mate. He campaigned with some vigor, and even after Dewey's unexpected defeat, some of the California governor's supporters held out hopes for the next election. At that time, however, Dwight D. Eisenhower announced his candidacy and in short order obtained the Republican nomination; he was then elected president by a convincing margin. In 1953, after the sudden death of Chief Justice Frederick M. Vinson created a vacancy on the United States Supreme Court, Eisenhower offered the position to Warren.

A major issue that Warren, and his colleagues, had to confront was the troubled question of racial segregation; in a landmark decision which he

wrote for a unanimous court, Warren found that public facilities described as "separate but equal" were inherently unequal and therefore were in violation of the Constitution. The case of *Brown v. Board of Education of Topeka* (1954) overturned rulings ultimately based upon a decision of 1896; once judicial decisions had eliminated distinctions on this level, a new era in racial relations was opened.

Political concerns also came before the Supreme Court, notably in connection with the government's efforts strictly to limit Communist and other left-wing activities. On constitutional grounds, Warren and his colleagues resisted such measures. On one Monday in June, 1957, the court handed down four separate decisions restricting powers to investigate individuals' political backgrounds or to cite political affiliations as grounds for the termination of employment.

Warren believed that the most important case to come before him was *Baker v. Carr* (1962), which challenged Tennessee's system of electoral apportionment as unduly favoring lightly populated rural districts. The court's decision, written by Justice

William J. Brennan, effectively established that federal judicial power could be exercised to ensure equal representation for voters participating in state elections. In another case, *Reynolds v. Sims* (1964), Warren wrote the opinion of a majority of justices in holding that both houses of the Alabama legislature had to be elected on an equal and proportional basis.

Rather different, and unsettling, questions arose when Warren became chairman of the commission that investigated the assassination of President John F. Kennedy. Although originally he had been reluctant to take this position, Warren conscientiously supervised the collection of evidence; after the commission's report was issued in 1964, he stoutly defended its conclusion that Lee Harvey Oswald had acted alone in killing the president.

Chief Justice Warren had often come under attack for the Supreme Court's decisions; desegregation and reapportionment had been denounced as intrusions upon states' rights, in areas not hitherto subject to the Court's rulings. Several United States senators contended that decisions upholding individual liberties actually were concessions to the Communists. Opposition arose in many quarters: In 1957, Warren resigned his membership in the American Bar Association in protest against lack of support from that organization. The militantly anticommunist John Birch Society mounted a wide-spread campaign calling for Warren's impeachment. During his later years on the Court, Warren became associated with controversial decisions affecting the rights of criminal suspects, for which he was castigated by many.

Cases such as *Mallory v. United States* (1957) and *Mapp v. Ohio* (1961) had overturned convictions obtained through improper interrogation or search and seizure without a warrant. *Gideon v. Wainwright* (1963) established the right of the indigent to obtain counsel for their defense during criminal trials. In *Escobedo v. Illinois* (1964), the court found that the accused has a right to counsel during initial questioning by the police; limitations on the direct investigation of suspects were stated specifically in *Miranda v. Arizona* (1966), a landmark decision which Warren wrote for a majority on the Court. The requirement that, prior to any questioning, the police must inform suspects of their rights under the Constitution established explicit guidelines for the treatment of accused persons but was bitterly attacked by many law enforcement officers and political figures.

Warren sometimes parted company with his fellow justices; thus, he sided with a majority on decisions involving the use of sit-ins to demonstrate for civil rights but dissented in cases in which claims of obscenity were contravened by those of free speech. Weary with advancing age, and in anticipation of his retirement from the bench, in 1968 he offered to resign upon the condition that a successor be found beforehand. Although his associate, Abe Fortas, was not confirmed by the Senate and ultimately resigned from the Supreme Court in the wake of a financial scandal, Warren renewed his offer and left the Court when Warren Burger was confirmed as chief justice in 1969. The last years of his life were spent writing, traveling, and lecturing; Warren continued to manifest a lively interest in political controversies where they affected judicial concerns. He suffered from angina pectoris and coronary occlusion, for which he was hospitalized several times. On July 9, 1974, he died of cardiac arrest at the Georgetown University Hospital in Washington, D.C.

### Summary

To friends, associates, and opponents alike, Earl Warren's career in public service posed contrasts and questions that were not readily resolved. During his work in law enforcement, Warren had shown some deference for the rights of the accused, but in exceptional cases he disregarded them; his active role in combating crime, in Alameda County and for the state of California, did not seem to foreshadow his efforts on behalf of individual rights after his appointment to the Supreme Court. In his native state he had denounced Communism, and he had carried out sweeping measures against Japanese Americans; as chief justice, he openly championed interpretations of the Constitution that ensured political liberties and promoted racial equality before the law. Although his views had been well within the political mainstream, the transition that later took place could not easily be ascribed to underlying features of continuity in his outlook, or indeed to the changed historical circumstances surrounding cases that arose during his tenure on the high court.

It was sometimes contended that Warren followed the lead of other justices, such as Hugo L. Black and William O. Douglas, in reaching major decisions, notably those that upheld individual rights. Warren had essentially a practical, rather than an abstract or academic, philosophy of the law; he reached decisions promptly and held fast once he had made them. Other justices, moreover, have readily attested the determined leadership he exercised, even in cases in which he assigned the Court's opinions to others of like mind. While occasionally, as in cases involving pornography, a majority voted against his positions, most major decisions reflected his colleagues' views as well as his own, and often he was able to win over those who wavered.

A final issue concerns the Supreme Court's role in American politics and society. More than any other institution, the Supreme Court brought about racial desegregation; it prescribed the forms by which criminal suspects are advised of their constitutional rights. Such decisions have tangibly affected the lives of millions. Supporters and critics have described this process as a form of judicial activism, by which the Court's interpretation of the Constitution was applied directly to state and local, as well as federal, concerns. Although often opposition centers upon the tenor and content of particular decisions, questions remain as to the nature and scope of the Court's powers within the framework of the Constitution. It is Earl Warren's legacy to have demonstrated the means and range by which the Supreme Court might intervene in major questions of American public life.

### Bibliography

Cox, Archibald. *The Warren Court: Constitutional Decision as an Instrument of Reform*. Cambridge, Mass.: Harvard University Press, 1968. Although generally in agreement with the Court's positions, the author displays an acute awareness of the constitutional dilemmas posed by judicial activism. Cox served as solicitor general of the United States from 1961 to 1965, between terms on the faculty at the law school of Harvard University.

Freyer, Tony A. "American Liberalism and the Warren Court's Legacy." *Reviews in American History,* (March, 1999). The author examines the expansion of legal rights during Warren's term as chief justice of the Supreme Court, using the writings of Morton Horowitz and Mark Tushnet as a basis.

Kurland, Philip B. *Politics, the Constitution, and the Warren Court*. Chicago: University of Chicago Press, 1970. In a series of lectures that are astringently critical of the Court's actions, Kurland, an important scholar specializing in the Supreme Court, contends that Warren and his colleagues found new and potentially hazardous interpretations of the Constitution.

Levy, Leonard W., ed. *The Supreme Court Under Earl Warren*. New York: Quadrangle, 1972. The divergent standpoints of defenders and responsible critics of the high court are presented in this collection of articles by various legal specialists.

Luban, David. "The Warren Court and the Concept of a Right." *Harvard Civil Rights-Civil Liberties Law Review* 34, no. 1 (Winter 1999). Discusses the concept of legal rights as redefined during Warren's tenure on the Supreme Court. Focuses on the protection of individuals from abuses by government.

Pollack, Jack Harrison. *Earl Warren: The Judge Who Changed America*. Englewood Cliffs, N.J.: Prentice-Hall, 1979. A brisk, favorable account of Warren's life which at each stage evokes the political atmosphere surrounding his work in law and government. The author emphasizes the social and political consequences of decisions handed down by the Warren Court.

Schwartz, Bernard. *Super Chief: Earl Warren and His Supreme Court, a Judicial Biography*. New York: New York University Press, 1983. Warren's sixteen terms on the high court are studied in this massive work by a noted legal scholar. The author reveals the extent to which differing positions and judicial infighting affected the court's deliberations; in the process, Warren's marked capacity for leadership is demonstrated. The unpublished papers of seven justices and a broad range of personal interviews were used in the composition of this work.

Schwartz, Bernard, and Stephan Lesher. *Inside the Warren Court*. New York: Doubleday, 1983. A colorful, crisply paced effort which provides a vivid and provocative treatment of decision making during Warren's tenure as chief justice.

Warren, Earl. *The Memoirs of Earl Warren*. New York: Doubleday, 1977. This work, which Warren composed during the last four years of his life, published posthumously, depicts Warren's work against crime, his actions as governor of California, and the concerns that guided him in reaching controversial decisions on the Supreme Court. Although not free from special pleading, some portions are lively, and there are also useful statements of his positions on racial issues, criminal investigation, and other important matters.

———. *The Public Papers of Chief Justice Earl Warren*. Edited by Henry M. Christman. New York: Simon and Schuster, 1959. Eleven of Warren's major opinions, from his first five terms on the Supreme Court, are published here, along with other addresses and statements on public issues.

———. *A Republic, If You Can Keep It*. New York: Quadrangle, 1972. This brief treatise sets forth, on a rather basic level, Warren's views on the constitution and its place in American history; from time to time he refers to major decisions in which he was involved.

White, G. Edward. *Earl Warren: A Public Life*. New York: Oxford University Press, 1982. This important scholarly examination of Warren's political career and judicial work points to the aspects of continuity and change in his outlook on major issues; the author provides, on a topical basis, a critical assessment of his opinions as chief justice.

*J. R. Broadus*

# ROBERT PENN WARREN

*Born:* April 24, 1905; Guthrie, Kentucky

*Died:* September 15, 1989; West Wardsboro, near Stratton, Vermont

*Area of Achievement:* Literature

*Contribution:* Warren, one of the foremost figures in twentieth century American literature, was widely admired for his novels, poetry, literary criticism, and writings on history and current events.

## Early Life

Robert Penn Warren was the oldest of three children born to Robert Franklin Warren and Anna Ruth Warren. As a young man, Robert Franklin had written poetry, but he had been forced to abandon his literary ambitions in order to work as a banker and shopkeeper to support his family. Still, the Warren household was filled with books, particularly books of poetry.

Guthrie, Kentucky, Warren's birthplace and childhood home, was a rough railroad town where acts of violence and bloodshed were common, as they would later be in Warren's fiction and poetry. The future writer was also influenced by his grandfather, Gabriel Thomas Penn, who owned a farm about 35 miles from Guthrie. Gabriel loved to tell stories, especially about his own exploits as a Confederate infantryman and cavalryman during the Civil War. Perhaps as a result of his grandfather's war stories, Warren's own early ambitions were military rather than literary. His goal in high school was to enter the U.S. Naval Academy and become an officer in the Navy. This dream was shattered in the spring of 1921 when his younger brother, Thomas, accidentally threw a piece of coal into his left eye. Although the tall, angular, red-haired Warren enjoyed generally good health through most of his long life, his eye was permanently damaged, and he eventually lost it altogether. No longer able to pass the physical for the Naval Academy, he enrolled at Vanderbilt University in Nashville, Tennessee, to study chemical engineering.

At Vanderbilt, he met teachers and friends who led him to decide on literature as his life's work. Allen Tate, later an eminent American poet, was one of his fellow students and a close friend. The poet John Crowe Ransom was one of Warren's professors. Warren and his fellow students and teachers formed a group known as the Fugitives, who founded a literary journal entitled *The Fugitive: A Journal of Poetry* in 1922. The Fugitives were dedicated to a social philosophy of southern agrarianism, a belief that the traditional values of the rural South could provide a way of life preferable to either communism or capitalism.

Concern over his future as a poet, anxiety over the worsening condition of his eye, and general depression pushed Warren to attempt suicide in the spring of 1924. However, he was still able to graduate from Vanderbilt with highest honors in 1925.

## Life's Work

Warren became known as both an academic commentator on literature and a writer. He prepared himself for his academic work through his graduate study at the University of California, Berkeley, where he earned a master of arts degree in English in 1927. He pursued further graduate study at Yale University and attended Oxford University on a Rhodes scholarship in 1928. He never completed a doctorate degree, a fact that kept him from getting a steady university job for a number of years.

While at Oxford, Warren wrote his first book, *John Brown: The Making of a Martyr* (1929), a biography of the antislavery crusader who died while trying to provoke a slave uprising just before the Civil War. Warren's analysis of the violence arising from conflicts between Brown's high ideals and psychological faults foreshadowed many of the themes in his later writings.

The year 1930 saw the publication of Warren's essay "The Briar Patch" in *I'll Take My Stand*, a collection of writings by the Fugitives from Vanderbilt and other southern writers. In that same year, he accepted a position as assistant professor at Southwestern College in Memphis, Tennessee, beginning two decades of wandering from one college teaching job to another. At this time, he also married a woman he had met in California, Emma "Cinina" Brescia. This proved to be a difficult marriage that would end in divorce in 1951.

After leaving Southwestern College, Warren taught at Vanderbilt and then, in 1935, became an assistant professor of English at Louisiana State University (LSU). In Louisiana, his reputation as a scholar and a writer grew, and he gathered material for some of his best-known works. Together with another LSU professor, Cleanth Brooks, he edited *The Southern Review*, which became an influential literary journal. His also established himself as a literary critic by writing *An Approach to Literature* (1936) and *Understanding Poetry* (1938). These works attempted to move the study of literature away from the examination of historical influences and toward an emphasis on the importance of the close, careful reading of the works themselves. While he was at LSU, Warren also published his first novel, *Night Rider* (1939), a dark, violent story about the tobacco war between big companies and independent tobacco growers in Kentucky in the first decade of the twentieth century.

Although he became a visiting professor at the University of Iowa in 1941, the state of Louisiana provided him with the inspiration for his best-known and most widely praised novel. Warren had been in Louisiana during the time that Huey P. Long was governor, senator, and the most powerful man in the state. Long, who was assassinated in 1936, provided Warren with many of the ideas for *All the King's Men* (1946), a novel about an idealistic politician who becomes corrupted by the pursuit of political power. Chosen as a Book-of-the-Month Club selection in 1946, *All the King's Men* was awarded the Pulitzer Prize for fiction in 1947 and was then made into a film, which won the Academy Award for Best Picture of 1949.

Warren's other novels included *At Heaven's Gate* (1943), a complex story of corruption and murder in Tennessee; *World Enough and Time* (1950), based on a murder trial in nineteenth century Kentucky; *Band of Angels* (1955), about a mixed-race woman at the time of the Civil War who had grown up believing herself to be white; *The Cave* (1959), about events surrounding a young Korean War veteran trapped in a Tennessee cave; *Wilderness* (1961), a novel of the Civil War; *Flood* (1964), the story of the obliteration of a Tennessee town by a flood; and *Meet Me in the Green Glen* (1971), a dramatic tale of love, betrayal, and murder. These novels were set in the South and showed deep knowledge of the people of the Kentucky-Tennessee region and a command of the local dialect. All of Warren's novels showed the same central concern with the painful and imperfect choices made by people who are faced with difficult moral dilemmas and who are trapped in conflicting desires and goals.

Changes in Warren's personal life accompanied success in his professional life. After a divorce from his first wife, Warren married a fellow writer, Eleanor Clark, in 1952. They had two children, and family became a frequent subject in Warren's poetry.

Although he achieved his greatest popular recognition as a novelist, Warren primarily regarded himself as a poet. He published numerous volumes of poetry and won the Pulitzer Prize for poetry twice, in 1958 for *Promises: Poems, 1954-1956* (1957) and in 1979 for *Now and Then: Poems 1976-1978* (1978). The 1958 prize made him the first person to win the Pulitzer Prize in both poetry and fiction. In addition to collections of relatively short poems, he also published *Brother to Dragons* (1953), a long narrative poem about the brutal murder of a slave by two nephews of Thomas Jefferson.

Although the young Warren and his fellow southern agrarians had idealized the pre-Civil War South, by the 1950's Warren became a staunch supporter of racial integration. His interest in the Civil Rights movement led him to write *Segregation: The Inner Conflict in the South* (1956). After intensive interviews with individuals involved in the civil rights struggle, he published another nonfiction book on African American efforts to achieve equal rights, *Who Speaks for the Negro?* (1965).

From 1963 to 1973, Warren taught at Yale University. He also traveled extensively and kept a vacation home in West Wardsboro, Vermont. He continued writing and publishing until near the end of his life, concentrating on his poetry in his later years. In 1986, he was selected as poet laureate by the U.S. Library of Congress.

The year before he died, Warren published a reminiscence of his father entitled *Portrait of a Father* (1988). As he was dying of cancer, he produced a new volume of critical writings, *New and Selected Essays* (1989). In his final days, he had friends and relatives read poetry to him. He died in his rural home in West Wardsboro and was buried in a graveyard by a small church in the nearby town of Stratton, Vermont.

## Summary

Robert Penn Warren made an enormous impact on several fields of American literature, including literary criticism, fiction, and poetry. Many teachers and literary historians have claimed that works such as *Understanding Poetry* revolutionized the teaching of literature. Before the time of Warren and colleagues such as Cleanth Brooks, teachers normally approached poems and other literary works by discussing events in a writer's personal life, political occurrences, or other matters outside the literary work itself. Warren and his colleagues maintained that any study of a poem or other literary work should begin with the words and images of the work itself rather than with questions of history or psychology surrounding the work. This type of approach, often labeled New Criticism, came to dominate American academic approaches to literature through the 1950's and early 1960's.

As a novelist, Warren advanced the concept of the "philosophical novel," fiction as a way of exploring the human condition. He was particularly effective in exploring the gap between political and moral ideals and human desires and ambitions. *All the King's Men* was an especially influential work. It was translated into many languages and was widely read outside the United States. It also became an established part of the American literary canon and required reading for many high school and college students. As a poet, Warren explored the relationship of human beings to the life around them, mixing personal and historical memories with meditations. Warren's long narrative poems, such as *Brother to Dragons*, *Audubon* (1969), and *Chief Joseph of the Nez Percé* (1983), are generally considered some of the finest poetic treatments of moral dilemmas in American history.

## Bibliography

Bloom, Harold, ed. *Robert Penn Warren*. New York: Chelsea House, 1986. This collection of essays on Warren's work considers both the poetry and the fiction.

Blotner, Joseph. *Robert Penn Warren: A Biography*. New York: Random House, 1997. Blotner's book, the most comprehensive biography of Warren available, is based on Warren's letters and papers and on extensive interviews with the writer's friends and family members.

Cutrer, Thomas W. *Parnassus on the Mississippi: The Southern Review and the Baton Rouge Literary Community*. Baton Rouge: Louisiana State University Press, 1984. Cutrer provides a history of the literary circle around the influential *Southern Review* at the time that Warren and Cleanth were the journal's editors.

Grimshaw, James A., Jr. *Cleanth Brooks and Robert Penn Warren*. Columbia: University of Missouri Press, 1998. A collection of more than 350 letters between lifelong friends Cleaneth Brooks and Warren. The letters provide information on their collaboration on two landmark textbooks, *Understanding Poetry* (1938) and *Understanding Fiction* (1943).

Guttenberg, Barnett. *Web of Being: The Novels of Robert Penn Warren*. Nashville, Tenn.: Vanderbilt University Press, 1975. This is a study of Warren's novels as expressions of philosophical ideas.

Millichap, Joseph R. *Robert Penn Warren: A Study of the Short Fiction*. New York: Twayne, 1992. Millichap examines fourteen stories and two essays by Warren and maintains that the short works provide a window into Warren's longer and better-known writings.

Warren, Robert Penn. *The Collected Poems of Robert Penn Warren*. Edited by John Burt. Baton Rouge: Louisiana State University, 1998. An important collection of Warren's published and previously unpublished poetry displaying an impressive range of styles and structures. Includes an introductory essay by Harold Bloom.

Watkins, Floyd C., John T. Hiers, and Mary Lou Weaks. *Talking with Robert Penn Warren*. Athens: University of Georgia Press, 1990. This collection of interviews with Warren covers literary and social topics.

Yarborough, Jane, and Robert Penn Warren. *Robert Penn Warren's All the King's Men*. New York: Barron's Educational Books, 1985. This guide to reading Warren's best-known work contains analyses of the novel's plot, style, form, and structure, and information about the author and his times.

*Carl L. Bankston III*

# JAMES D. WATSON

*Born:* April 6, 1928; Chicago, Illinois
*Area of Achievement:* Molecular biology
*Contribution:* Watson helped describe the structure of deoxyribonucleic acid (DNA), the molecule that is the basis of heredity, and has also done research on protein synthesis and the role of viruses in cancer.

## Early Life

James Dewey Watson was born in Chicago, Illinois, on April 6, 1928, the son of James Dewey and Jean (née Mitchell) Watson. His early life was spent in the Chicago area; he attended the University of Chicago Nursery School, Horace Mann Elementary School, and South Shore High School. An intellectually precocious youngster, Watson matriculated at the College of the University of Chicago when he was fifteen, after only two years of high school. As an undergraduate, he was drawn to the study of science, especially biology, in which he achieved very high grades. Two qualities of his mind showed early development during these years: sharp perception of the natural world and the ability to master and retain complex abstract information. One favorite early pastime was bird-watching, and Watson considered specializing in ornithology, the study of birds. (He later recommended bird-watching as good early training for the budding professional scientist.) Information mastery enabled him later to be at ease in discussions with colleagues and in lectures to students: After making careful notes, he developed a flow of talk without recourse to them.

Four years later, in 1947, Watson was graduated from Chicago with both Ph.B. and B.S. degrees. He then moved to the University of Indiana for graduate work. There, he studied with several distinguished scientists, including Tracy M. Sonneborn and Ralph Cleland. Two other scientists helped direct him to his field of greatest interest, genetics, the study of the ways in which an organism passes on its qualities to offspring. These professors were Hermann Joseph Muller, Nobel laureate in genetics, and Salvador Luria, an Italian-trained microbiologist. Under Luria's supervision, Watson wrote his doctoral thesis on bacteriophages—viruses which invade and multiply in bacteria. He was awarded the Ph.D. degree in 1950.

Viruses, thought at this time to be "naked genes," are intermediate in size between the giant molecules of organic chemistry and the even more complex ones of living matter; as a creative worker in genetics, Watson saw that he would have to learn more chemistry to supplement his firm grounding in biology. A "young man from the provinces," he yearned also to broaden his cultural outloook during this post-World War II era in which international cooperation was at a new high point. Clearly, postdoctoral work abroad was called for, and Luria, Watson's Indiana mentor, suggested Copenhagen University, where he knew people doing significant research in the biochemistry department. Watson was awarded a National Research Council Fellowship there for 1950-1951. Photographs of him around this time reveal a tall, slender, sharp-featured young man with bushy brown hair. A contemporary describes him as intense, energetic, usually moving feverishly around the laboratory, wearing a rumpled shirt with no tie.

## Life's Work

At Copenhagen, Watson studied chemistry and continued research on bacteriophages. An important turning point occurred in Naples, Italy, in the spring of 1951, during an international biological conference which he attended and at which he met Maurice H. F. Wilkins of the University of London. At this conference, Wilkins demonstrated his technique of X-ray diffraction, exhibiting pictures he had taken of the molecule deoxyribonucleic acid (DNA), believed to be crucially involved in the transmission of genetic information for all plants and animals. Watson formulated as his special goal the task of defining exactly the structure and function of this molecule. Wilkins' pictures were one form of evidence. At this point, Watson decided to leave Copenhagen for the Cavendish Laboratories of Cambridge University in England, where Francis Crick, well-grounded in mathematics and chemistry, was also trying to discover the structure of DNA. Between the fall of 1951 and the spring of 1953, Watson worked closely with Crick and intermittently with Wilkins, carefully watching the work of researchers on both sides of the Atlantic as well.

As Watson began this work, it was already known that DNA is composed of six kinds of subunits: sugars, phosphates, and four bases (complex molecules containing the important life elements carbon, hydrogen, and nitrogen): thymine, adenine,

cytosine, and guanine (T, A, C, G). For Watson and colleagues, the specific related problems were: What is the exact relationship among these six subunits? How do they look together physically and act chemically? How is reproduction accomplished through this structure?

Attempting to picture the DNA molecule more exactly than Wilkins' X rays had thus far been able to do, Watson and Crick, working in a shabby shack called The Hut, spent much of their time building three-dimensional models, working with pieces of wire, colored beads, steel rods, and oblongs of sheet metal. Across the Atlantic, help and competition came from California, where Linus Pauling was demonstrating, through similar models, that proteins have the form of a helix, or coil. Not yet determined, however, was the number of coils and how they are held together. For nearly two years they worked, often with Watson proposing a structural model and Crick checking its chemical and mathematical accuracy. They considered DNA structures of from one to four coils; finally, Watson became convinced of a double coil or helix, on the basis of his awareness of the repeated finding of twoness in biological systems—especially genetically, where one cell often divides and distributes its crucial contents to two offspring. This hypothesis about function, therefore, was crucial to Watson's discovery of the true model for structure. The DNA picture which Watson rightly affirmed to be too pretty not to be true turned out to be as follows: a double spiral staircase (sugar and phosphate units) with the stairs between consisting of specific sequences of pairs of the four bases T, A, C, and G. Functionally, during reproduction of the cell, this DNA molecule divides by having the two staircase parts uncoil, the stairs between split, and material from all six subunits distribute to the offspring. Each ladder half then becomes the mold, or template, for assembling new ladders.

In the spring of 1953, Watson and Crick published some of these findings in a nine-hundred-word article in *Nature*, a leading international journal. Their findings were greeted by immediate acclaim, followed by verification. In 1957, Dr. Arthur Kornberg of Washington University in St. Louis confirmed the Watson-Crick model by synthesizing DNA from its six constituents. The same year, Watson and Crick proposed a similar structure for viruses; this was confirmed by the electron microscope studies of Dr. Robert Horne, of Cambridge, England. In 1962, Watson, Crick, and Wilkins were jointly awarded the Nobel Prize for Medicine and Physiology for their work in DNA synthesis. In 1968, Watson published *The Double Helix*, a subjective account of his remarkable two years in England and a rare and skillful blending of scientific reportage with personal autobiography.

Between 1953 and 1955, Watson was a senior research fellow in biology at California Institute of Technology, the home base of his old friend and rival Linus Pauling. After 1955, he taught at Harvard University in Cambridge, Massachusetts, rising to the rank of full professor of biology in 1961. In 1968, he became director of the Cold Spring Harbor Laboratory on Long Island, New York. Also in that year, he married Elizabeth Lewis, with whom he had two sons, Rufus Robert and Duncan James.

Watson also made significant research contributions in the areas of sexuality and reproduction of bacteria; mechanisms of protein biosynthesis in which life molecules even larger than DNA are produced through the combining of nucleic acids; and induction of cancer through viruses. Impatience with conventional, single-discipline approaches to the solution of scientific problems is a continuing, unifying theme in Watson's work. His links to both basic and applied science and to the arts are underscored by the awards made to him, including the Eli Lilly Biochemistry Award in 1959 and the Presidential Medal of Freedom in 1977. He has also been a member of the National Academy of Sciences, the National Cancer Board, and the American Academy of Arts and Sciences, and is a past director of the Human Genome Project.

Some of Watson's other significant publications include *Origins of Human Cancer* (1977, edited with H. H. Hiatt and J. A. Winsten) and *The Molecular Biology of the Cell* (1983).

### Summary

Several themes relate James D. Watson's life and career to American culture in the mid-twentieth century. Watson's early life is a modern version of the Horatio Alger success story; a young man from the West who wins international fame through a combination of hard work, intellectual brilliance, and luck—as well as the blessings of good public education and generous availability of federal research funds in the years after World War II. He represents a new version of an old American heroic type, the questing scientist, descendant of the nineteenth century pioneer-inventor whose hallmark was self-reliance and ingenuity. Watson, however, has been no ivory-tower hermit; early in life, he demonstrated a flair for collaborative creative work with colleagues from different backgrounds. The progress of twentieth century science in general has been through such international, often American-inspired collaborations.

Watson's work has underscored the importance of interrelationship among different scientific disciplines, such as biology, chemistry, and physics, a concept pioneered in the United States and often a model for European and Asian researchers, many of whom were encouraged to move across subject-matter boundaries during an American apprenticeship. The international, interdisciplinary conference, in which scientists from many nations and fields of knowledge meet to share common concerns, has been a recurrent event in Watson's career as well as a symbol of political and intellectual involvement of twentieth century America. Another barrier to scientific communication has been lowered in the example of Watson's work: the distinction between pure and applied science and between the scientist and the technician; in the story of DNA identification, the photographer and the builder of mechanical models played significant roles, along with the mathematician and the theoretical physicist.

Watson's interests and achievements have also underscored the continuity between normal and abnormal. His work in genetics and molecular biology has had direct implications for poliomyelitis research and, even more significant, for the fight against cancer. Finally, Watson's career illustrates the successful combining of teaching with research, previously perceived as opposing interests.

If the image reflected by Watson's career has been that of the brash, competitive American, it has also been that of the unconventional, flexible facilitator, a creator cutting across traditional boundaries.

### Bibliography

Frankel, Edward. *DNA: Ladder of Life*. 2d ed. New York: McGraw-Hill, 1979. Lucid, well-illustrated book for readers with little scientific training. Excellent sections on the cell and on the relation of DNA to metabolism, reproduction, and disease. Fine context for appreciating Watson's special contribution.

Ibanez, Serafin Garcia. "James D. Watson Talks to Serafin Garcia Ibanez." *UNESCO Courier* (October, 1993). Interview with Watson in which he discusses his views on genetic research and his support of bioethics.

"Interviews on Genomics." *BioEssays* 21, no. 2 (February, 1999). Interview with Watson and Russell Doolittle in which they discuss the benefits of the Human Genome Project and the fears expressed by some bioethicists.

Kendrew, John C. *The Thread of Life: An Introduction to Molecular Biology.* London: Bell, and Cambridge, Mass.: Harvard University Press, 1966. Text by one of Watson's English colleagues with an important section on X-ray diffraction, one of the most important tools for the discovery and verification of components in a structure which cannot be seen by the naked eye.

Riedman, Sarah Regal, and Elton T. Gustafson. *Portraits of Nobel Laureates in Medicine and Physiology.* London and New York: Abelard-Schuman, 1963. Clearly written biographical study of Watson in the context of other honored scientists. Accessible to the nonscientist.

Schmeck, Harold M., Jr., and Philip M. Boffy. "Rapid Advances Point to the Mapping of All

Human Genes." *The New York Times*, July 15, 1986, sec. C:1. Summary of research in DNA decoding and some of the significant medical implications of this work. For the general reader.

Watson, James Dewey. *The DNA Story: A Documentary History of Gene Cloning*. San Francisco: Freeman, 1981. An updated, more technical account of DNA structure and function than the one in *The Double Helix*.

———. *The Double Helix: A Personal Account of the Discovery of the Structure of DNA*. New York: Atheneum Press, and London: Weidenfeld and Nicolson, 1968. A subjective, blow-by-blow account of the solution of the DNA riddle by Watson and his colleagues. An honest record of scientific cooperation and competition with two additional themes: the conflicts of an innocent young American abroad, and the difficulties of a brilliant young woman researcher in gaining acceptance from prejudiced mail colleagues. Few scientists have left such a vivid, personal account of their work.

———. *The Molecular Biology of the Gene*. 4th ed. Menlo Park, Calif.: Benjamin/Cummings, 1987. An undergraduate college textbook which explores in detail the implications of the discovery of DNA for the entire field of heredity. Watson's original area of scientific research.

*Sanford Radner*

## JOHN WAYNE

*Born:* May 26, 1907; Winterset, Iowa
*Died:* June 11, 1979; Los Angeles, California
*Area of Achievement:* Film
*Contribution:* Wayne, one of the most popular film actors of all time, achieved his greatest work in Westerns, many of which are among the finest Western films ever made. He also came to embody what many people saw as basic American values, such as strength, courage, patriotism, and willingness to accept personal responsibility.

### Early Life

John "Duke" Wayne was born Marion Michael Morrison on May 26, 1907, to Clyde and Mary (Molly) Morrison, of Winterset, Iowa. Five years later, the Morrisons had a second son, Robert. Clyde moved to California in 1913 after a Rexall drugstore he had purchased failed. He was joined by his wife and sons the following year, and the family settled in the Antelope Valley north of Los Angeles, where Clyde attempted farming. They moved to Glendale, California, in 1916, as young Marion's father returned to what he knew best, working in a drugstore. During these childhood years, Marion gained the nickname "Duke" after his dog, Little Duke.

At Glendale High School, Morrison excelled. He earned high grades, was a member of the Glendale High Dramatic Society, represented his school in a William Shakespeare competition, and was elected president of his senior class. He also starred at guard on the football team, earning an athletic scholarship to the University of Southern California (USC). During his Glendale years, two of his closest friends were the brothers Bob and Bill Bradbury, who were appearing in their father Robert's short films, *The Adventures of Bob and Bill.* Wayne would later act in about one dozen low-budget B-Westerns directed by the elder Bradbury.

Morrison entered USC in 1925, but his football success was limited; after his freshman year, he was cut from the team by the famous football coach Homer Jones. Morrison had begun working at Fox Film Corporation while attending college, and he continued after leaving USC in 1927, moving crates and furniture and appearing as an occasional extra in films. Six feet four inches tall, handsome, slim, and graceful in movement, Morrison drew the attention of John Ford, the legendary director who would earn six Academy Awards. Ford gave the young actor brief speaking roles in the films *Salute* (1929) and *Men Without Women* (1930). In *Salute,* the soon-to-be John Wayne began his association with Ward Bond, a USC football player who became one of Wayne's closest friends and who regularly appeared in Wayne's films.

### Life's Work

Although John Ford is the director most associated with John Wayne, it was Raoul Walsh who transformed Marion Michael Morrison into John Wayne, renaming the aspiring actor and teaching him how to ride a horse. Walsh made Wayne into a star by giving him the lead role in *The Big Trail* (1930), but the star would be clouded by a sky of B-Westerns for the next decade.

*The Big Trail* was an artistically successful film, and Wayne performed convincingly in his role as the noble hero scouting for a wagon train heading west. In his first major role, Wayne already demonstrated a professionalism that would permanently characterize his work. *The Big Trail* ultimately failed, primarily because of the onset of the Great Depression in 1929. Walsh filmed the story in both traditional 35 millimeter and the new 75 millimeter that permitted a wider camera range. Many theaters could not afford the new technology and were forced to show *The Big Trail* in the standard 35 millimeter version, which deprived the film of its sense of grandeur. Fox studios went into receivership, and although the studio continued to turn out motion pictures, it did not have the money to promote its new stars.

During the 1930's Wayne moved from studio to studio, spending most of his time making B-Westerns but at the same time learning and growing as an actor. He managed to stay employed throughout the Depression. Wayne's roles for Mascot, Warner Bros., and Monogram brought him into daily contact with Yakima Canutt, the legendary stuntman with whom he began a lasting friendship. From Canutt, Wayne learned to perfect his horsemanship and master the art of staging fistfights (a continuing staple of Wayne films). Throughout his career, even when age and declining health robbed him of his agility, Wayne insisted on performing many of his own stunts.

During the 1930's Wayne married Josephine Saenz, the first of his three wives, with whom he

*John Wayne (center) in* She Wore a Yellow Ribbon

had four children: Michael, Toni, Patrick, and Melinda. Subsequent marriages were to Esperanza "Chata" Bauer and Pilar Palette. Wayne had three children with Palette: Aissa, John Ethan, and Marissa. Several of Wayne's children appeared in his films, most notably Patrick in *The Searchers* (1956) and *The Comancheros* (1961).

Wayne's breakthrough film was a John Ford Western, *Stagecoach* (1939), which ended Wayne's long apprenticeship, reunited him with the director for whom he would make some of his greatest films, and introduced film fans to Monument Valley in Utah, soon to become a classic setting for Westerns. In *Stagecoach*, Wayne played the Ringo Kid, who was falsely accused of murder and who broke out of jail to return home and avenge his father's murderer.

*The Shepherd of the Hills* (1941) starred Wayne with one of his personal heroes, the cowboy star of silent films, Harry Carey, Sr. The film was directed by Henry Hathaway, who later directed Wayne in his only Oscar-winning performance, as Rooster Cogburn in *True Grit* (1969). Wayne acted with Carey three more times, in *The Spoilers* (1942), *Angel and the Badman* (1947), and *Red River* (1948). In one of the most famous scenes in all of Wayne's films, Wayne stood in the doorway of a cabin at the end of *The Searchers* (1956) holding his right forearm in his left hand in a typical Carey pose eight years after the older man's death. Wayne's friendship with Carey extended to his son, Harry Carey, Jr., who performed with Wayne in such films as *Red River*, *Three Godfathers* (1949), *She Wore a Yellow Ribbon* (1949), *Rio Grande* (1950), and *The Searchers*.

The year 1948 was a turning point for Wayne as two of the films released that year—*Fort Apache* and *Red River*—established their protagonist as one of Hollywood's leading stars. *Fort Apache*, with Henry Fonda, was the first of three Seventh Cavalry films in which John Ford directed Wayne (the others were *She Wore a Yellow Ribbon* and *Rio Grande*). Although Wayne played a cavalry officer in all three, his character changed with each film in an early indication of the versatility as an actor that Wayne possessed and for which he has often been given insufficient credit. *Rio Grande* introduced Wayne's successful acting partnership with the Irish actor Maureen O'Hara, whose flaming red hair, quick wit, and sharp tongue enabled her to hold her own in scenes with Wayne. They usually played spouses in initially antagonistic but ultimately loving relationships.

*Red River* offered Wayne the opportunity to work with the director Howard Hawks and play a character well removed from his usual roles. Tom Dunson, a middle-aged cattleman faced with financial reverses, set out to drive his herd to market accompanied by his adopted son, played by Montgomery Clift. The Wayne character became a tyrannical, obsessed trail boss who alienated his son, threatened to kill him, and beat him. The following year, Wayne made *Sands of Iowa Jima* (1949), where, as Sergeant Stryker, he established another Wayne persona, that of the powerful and courageous soldier whose tough love led his men at times to despise him but finally to respect his leadership and intentions.

Except for *The Quiet Man* (1952), directed by Ford and set in Ireland (and also starring Maureen O'Hara), most of Wayne's best films during the 1950's, 1960's, and 1970's were Westerns: *The Searchers*, in which Wayne, in perhaps one of his greatest performances, played Ethan Edwards, a man obsessed with his ten-year pursuit of revenge against the American Indians who kidnapped his nieces; *The Man Who Shot Liberty Valance* (1962), directed by Ford and costarring James Stewart; *True Grit*; *Big Jake* (1971), with Maureen O'Hara; *Rooster Cogburn* (1975), costarring Katharine Hepburn; and Wayne's final film, *The Shootist* (1976), with James Stewart.

Wayne, who had undergone surgery for cancer in 1964 and lost part of a lung, was again diagnosed with cancer in January, 1979. After stomach surgery on January 10, he regained enough strength to attend the Academy Awards on April 9, where he gave a moving speech to a rousing ovation. Wayne was hospitalized again early in May and remained at the University of California at Los Angeles (UCLA) Medical Center until his death on June 11, 1979.

### Summary

John Wayne's films (he made over 150) encompass many subjects and genres, but he remains best known for his war and Western films. In Westerns, Wayne became a symbol of the United States, the rugged, self-reliant, tough, but heart-of-gold American that millions of viewers imagined reflected their own behavior.

Wayne is also remembered for his conservative political views and ideological films. Both *The Alamo* (1960) and *The Green Berets* (1969), the latter released a few months after the Tet Offensive during the Vietnam War, were self-consciously patriotic and have often been viewed more as propaganda than as entertainment. Even as large numbers of the young and the intellectual elite turned against Wayne in the 1960's, his popularity with the general public remained high.

In his final films, Wayne continued to demonstrate his versatility as an actor. Deliberately using his age and growing waistline, he cemented his association with the American West as a way of life receding into the sunset. As the seriocomic and flawed Rooster Cogburn in *True Grit* and *Rooster Cogburn*, he portrayed an anachronism summoned to right a wrong that only he could correct; by doing so, he demonstrated the essential dignity and honor beneath his outdated veneer. In *The Man Who Shot Liberty Valance*, Wayne explicitly represented the past, in contrast to James Stewart, who learned to adjust and move into the future. Finally, in *The Shootist*, Wayne played the aging gunfighter J. B. Books, who was dying of cancer. Rather than wait for the cancer to kill him, Books ended his life by deliberately making himself a target for his enemies. The film was an eerily fitting conclusion to Wayne's career. *The Shootist* also emphasized the end of the Old West, although that West continues to live, and will continue to live, in John Wayne's films.

### Bibliography

Davis, Ronald L. *Duke: The Life and Image of John Wayne*. Norman: University of Oklahoma Press, 1998. Davis examines many aspects of Wayne's life and career, including his impact on American culture. Includes a filmography that lists Wayne films by year with principal participants.

Grenier, Richard. "The Cowboy Patriot." *The National Interest* no. 45 (Fall 1996). This article focuses on Wayne's patriotism and its effect on his life and work.

Roberts, Randy, and James Stuart Olson. *John Wayne: American*. New York: Free Press, 1995. This exhaustive and substantive biography written by experienced and accomplished historians is essential for an in-depth knowledge of Wayne's life and career.

Wayne, Aissa, with Steve Delsohn. *John Wayne, My Father.* New York: Random House, 1991; London: Hale, 1992. This intimate inside portrait of Wayne by one of his daughters gives a balanced account of the father's strengths and weaknesses as a parent. At times unclear regarding facts and dates, it nonetheless offers many insights into the character of Wayne.

Wayne, Pilar, with Alex Thorleifson. *John Wayne: My Life with the Duke*. New York: McGraw-Hill, 1987. Written by Wayne's third wife, this book is perhaps the most valuable primary source of knowledge about the actor because it includes much information known only by the author.

Wills, Garry. *John Wayne's America: The Politics of Celebrity.* New York: Simon and Schuster, 1997. Wills explores Wayne's accomplishments and friendships, including detailed accounts of his relationships with John Ford and Harry Carey. The author also examines the relationship between Wayne and his country, including his ideological films and his status as an American icon.

———. "John Wayne's Body." *The New Yorker* 72, no. 24 (August 19, 1996). Focuses on the enduring popularity of John Wayne and his lasting image as an icon of positive American qualities.

Zolotow, Maurice. *Shooting Star: A Biography of John Wayne*. London: Allen, and New York: Simon and Schuster, 1974. This was the most important biography of Wayne until the 1990's. Zolotow was the ghostwriter of Wayne's unfinished autobiography, which gave Zolotow access to a rich trove of personal information.

*Edward J. Rielly*

# BEATRICE WEBB and SIDNEY WEBB

## Beatrice Webb

*Born:* January 22, 1858; Gloucester, Gloucestershire, England

*Died:* April 30, 1943; Liphook, Hampshire, England

## Sidney Webb

*Born:* July 13, 1859; London, England

*Died:* October 13, 1947; Liphook, Hampshire, England

*Areas of Achievement:* Economics, sociology, social reform, and historiography

*Contribution:* The Webbs were leading figures in the Fabian Society and in the development of Labour Party policies. Founders of the London School of Economics and *New Statesman,* they also authored several important texts on trade unions, local government, and the Poor Laws.

### Early Lives

Beatrice Potter was born January 22, 1858, in Gloucester, Gloucestershire, England, the eighth of nine daughters in an upper-middle-class family. Her father, Richard Potter, was a wealthy industrialist; her mother, Laurencina Heyworth Potter, was a highly intelligent but increasingly reclusive woman, disappointed by a life of constant pregnancy rather than scholarly achievement. Beatrice's childhood was an unhappy one, marred by ill health, loneliness, and resentment. Her formal education was limited by chronic illness and psychosomatic complaints; it ended by the time she was thirteen. By then she had begun securing her own education through extensive reading. She had also begun her lifelong habit of keeping a diary in which she examined her own frailties and those of whomever came under her scrutiny.

At the age of sixteen, Beatrice lost her religious faith and was sorely troubled by that loss ever after. She remained an agnostic, dedicated to the religion of humanity, but she was much given to prayer. By the age of twenty-five, Beatrice had decided to become a social investigator, in spite of her belief that a woman's intellectual capacity was strictly limited. She hoped to apply the scientific method to the study of society, to understand and improve it.

Beatrice became a rent collector and tenant organizer at a housing project for the poor in London's East End. Later, she joined her cousin Charles Booth in his massive study of poverty in London; her first published article was "Dock Life in East London." To study sweated labor in the manufacturing trades, she worked briefly as a seamstress in several sweatshops. In 1888, five of her articles on sweated labor were published, and she began to enjoy a reputation as a knowledgeable social scientist.

It was in connection with her next project, a book on cooperative societies, that Beatrice first met Sidney Webb. Friends had recommended him as a useful resource for her work. Beatrice was thirty-two at the time, a tall, slim, dramatically attractive woman, with piercing brown eyes and long dark hair fashioned in a no-nonsense bun. She and Sidney were an unlikely match.

Sidney Webb was born on July 13, 1859, the second of three children, in a lower-middle-class family. His mother, Elizabeth Mary Stacy Webb, the more industrious and energetic partner, ran a millinery and hairdressing business. His father, a somewhat ineffectual but public-spirited man, reserved most of his energy for political debates and local politics. Educated to be a commercial clerk, Sidney continued taking courses, winning prizes, and passing examinations well after he had begun his career. He became a clerk in the colonial office in 1881 and was called to the bar in 1886.

Extremely bright and ambitious, Sidney also took advantage of the numerous debating clubs, study groups, and political societies which flourished in London in the 1880's. There he learned techniques for bringing people around to his point of view, mainly by mastering a subject and knowing far more about it than anyone else present. Thus, despite his rapid speech, slight lisp, and dropped aitches, Sidney was extremely persuasive, especially in a committee situation.

In 1885, Sidney joined the executive committee of the fledgling Fabian Society, a middle-class Socialist organization. The goals that Sidney helped to

establish as he, along with George Bernard Shaw and a few others, began to dominate the society were those of gradual change through the promotion of education and the permeation of other organizations and committees with collectivist ideas.

Sidney resigned from his position as a civil servant in 1892 and was elected as a Progressive member to the London County Council. By this time, he had wooed and won the illustrious Beatrice Potter, despite their class differences and despite the fact that he was far from attractive, with his bespectacled head atop a rotund little body and his unkempt appearance. Sidney had assured Beatrice that their marriage would be a working partnership, dedicated to the betterment of society, a relationship that would expand her own efforts along these lines rather than hinder them. That was certainly the case. Freed from the onus of earning a living by Beatrice's limited but adequate inheritance, the couple immersed themselves in researching and writing books and studying and formulating public policies.

### Lives' Work

For the first fifteen years of their married lives, the pattern established was one which kept Sidney in the public eye and Beatrice as the more private, research-oriented member of their team. Sidney continued to play a leading role in the Fabian Society as policymaker, speaker, and tract writer. In addition, he served on the London County Council for eighteen years, wielding his greatest influence as chairman of its Technical Education Committee. In this capacity he extended the number of scholarships to technical schools and universities, increased the number of such schools, and reformed the level of education practiced in these schools. Because of his expertise on education, Sidney was particularly influential in the drafting and passage of the Education Acts of 1902-1903, which expanded and consolidated public education. Sidney also served on various commissions and wrote a series of minority reports, such as one for the Royal Commission on Labour Disputes in 1894.

While Beatrice gave an occasional speech to the Fabians or served on a committee, her chief responsibility as a reformer and agitator was to hold select dinner parties for whichever political, intellectual, or philanthropic set of people they were most interested in knowing or influencing at the time. The meals, like the furnishings, were sparse at 41 Grosvenor Road—the home the Webbs rented for almost forty years—but the conversation was thick with ideas and plans for social reconstruction.

Administrative and social duties notwithstanding, the Webbs' joint research was carried on vigorously. For the most part, Beatrice planned their projects, formulated the questions to be asked, and did much of the interviewing, while Sidney concentrated his efforts on the analysis of their data. Their first joint venture, *The History of Trade Unionism* (1894), became the standard text on the subject. In their next effort, *Industrial Democracy* (1897), they argued that trade unions were necessary for the economic and moral benefit of workers and were needed to right the imbalance between powerful employers and their far weaker employees. Trade unions, they predicted presciently, would play a far more important role in the future.

By the beginning of the twentieth century, the Webbs had established themselves as respected and original investigators in the fields of economics and sociology. Their third major project, begun in this period, was a study of local government on which they worked sporadically. The motivation behind the work was their firmly held conviction that only government would or could be entrusted with the care and welfare of its citizens. The Webbs addressed their studies to the structure, function, and reform of parish and county governments in their first volume (1906), the manor and borough for their second and third volumes (1908), and completed the series in 1922 with the *Statutory Authorities for Special Purposes*. Along these lines, the Webbs produced occasional studies on specific local authorities such as "The History of Liquor Licensing" and "English Prisons Under Local Authorities," as well as three volumes on boards of guardians.

The Webbs' marriage remained childless, a fact which occasionally caused Beatrice some distress, the more so since she believed that motherhood was a woman's chief responsibility and greatest glory. Still, neither partner believed that the commitments to research and reform allowed sufficient time to rear a family. Instead, their progeny included their ideas, their books, and even more important, two influential British institutions. The Webbs founded the London School of Economics in 1895, a school devoted to research and teaching in the social sciences. In time, Sidney was able to secure the financial stability and independence of the London School of Economics by overseeing its incorporation into the University of London system. Both Webbs lectured at the school, and Sidney was chairman for several years. The second major offspring of the Webb partnership was *New Statesman*, a magazine which they founded in 1913 and which was to become a leading British weekly.

While the publication was Beatrice's idea, she had little time for it. Since her appointment to the Royal Commission on the Poor Laws in 1905, Beatrice had begun to play an active role in public life, both as commissioner and in the subsequent two-year campaign on behalf of her *The Minority Report of the Poor Law Commission* (1909). The report advocated not only the abolition of the Poor Laws but also of poverty itself, by such methods as public works, job-training programs, and labor exchanges. Beatrice and her thousands of supporters in the National Committee for the Prevention of Destitution were not successful in bringing about the specific changes advocated; they were effective, however, in awakening public opinion to the problems of poverty.

Remaining in the public eye, Beatrice next turned her energies to the Fabian Society, being elected to its executive in 1912 and founding the Fabian Research Department in 1913, drawing on many of the young talents from the National Committee and on her own expertise as a social investigator. Before returning to private life, Beatrice was appointed to the War Cabinet Committee on Woman in Industry in 1918. Again, she conducted research independent of the committee on which she served and produced her own minority report. This one championed equal wages for women, a reversal of policies she and Sidney had advocated earlier. Thereafter, Beatrice began to attend to private matters, in particular, turning her diaries into two volumes of autobiography. The first, *My Apprenticeship* (1923), was the story of her youth; the second, *Our Partnership* (1948), that of her marriage.

In the last two years of World War I, Sidney began to play a major role in the Labour Party, one which both he and Beatrice had eschewed in previous years. He, along with Arthur Henderson, not only drafted the new constitution for the party but also drew up its official policy, a policy of public ownership and welfare which strongly resembled the essence of Fabianism. He became the party's leading intellectual and key adviser on matters of economic and social reform, assuming the party's chairmanship in 1923. At long last, at age sixty-three, Sidney was elected to the House of Commons, and he held cabinet positions in Labour's first two ministries. Sidney was appointed president of the Board of Trade in 1924 and, elevated to the House of Lords as Baron Passfield, he served as secretary of state for the colonies in 1929. Unfortunately, as a Member of Parliament, and especially as cabinet minister, Sidney was less adroit, less effective, than he was as county councillor or resident intellectual.

Like Sidney's late-blooming political career, the Webbs' last major work was also of questionable quality. Distressed over worsening conditions in the 1930's, the Webbs looked to the Soviet Union for a solution. Given a royal welcome during their three-month stay in the Soviet Union, they produced a massive and adulatory volume, *Soviet Communism: A New Civilisation?*, in 1935. The Webbs were in their seventies by then and past the point of substantiating their theories with meticulous investigatory research.

In retirement at Passfield Corner, their country home on the Hampshire-Surrey border, the Webbs continued to view the Soviet Union as the embodiment of their own plans for a Socialist state, despite ominous reports to the contrary. Greatly distressed by the war and troubled by ill health, Beatrice died on April 30, 1943; Sidney, although weakened by an earlier stroke, lived for another four years. Their ashes were mixed at Westminster Abbey in 1947, an enormous honor and a fitting end to their extraordinary partnership.

**Summary**

The Webb partnership was remarkable for its continuous productivity, its long-term influence on British affairs, and the harmony with which the seemingly disparate partners worked. In the early years of their collaboration, the Webbs provided a program and a platform for the reformist middle class, whether as leaders of the early Fabian Society, as authors of the standard texts on trade unions, on local government and the Poor Laws, or as founders of the world-famous London School of Economics and *New Statesman*. After 1916, the Webbs became influential in the working-class movement and in Labour Party politics. Sidney Webb's role as the leading adviser to the Labour Party, as it reformulated itself into a party capable of winning elections and holding office, was crucial. The British Welfare State which emerged after World War II strongly resembled the collectivist state and the social welfare provisions outlined by the Webbs. Clearly, they cast an indelible stamp on British socialism in its formative years.

The Webbs' numerous honors included Beatrice Webb's election, as the first woman member, to the British Academy, and Sidney's being awarded the Order of Merit in 1944. Paradoxically, one important aspect of the Webbs' fame rests on work that they themselves underestimated. Beatrice's memoirs, *My Apprenticeship* and *Our Partnership*, and the full texts of her diaries, published posthumously, present a perceptive and beautifully written chronicle of the social, intellectual, and political climate of the late nineteenth and early twentieth centuries. Moreover, Beatrice's description of her own search for a moral creed to replace her lost religious certainty, as well as for an economic agenda to ameliorate the plight of the poverty stricken, recreates admirably two of the major issues of her time.

**Bibliography**

Cole, Margaret, ed. *The Webbs and Their Work.* London: Muller, 1949; New York: Barnes and Noble, 1974. Diverse essays on the major activities of the Webbs, covering a fifty-year span and dealing with their personalities, their thought, the institutions they founded, and their work as administrators. By a variety of contributors—all but two of whom knew the Webbs at firsthand—the essays attempt to assess the Webbs' influence on the modern world and to appraise, and at times criticize, their contributions to British society and social thought.

McBriar, A. M. *Fabian Socialism and English Politics, 1884-1918.* Cambridge: Cambridge University Press, 1962. Concerned with the doctrines of the early Fabian Society, this book attempts to estimate Fabian influence on the policies of local government and the policies of the Liberal Party and the Labour Party, both of whom the Fabians tried to permeate with their ideas. Given the importance of the Webbs in this phase of Fabian history, this is also an assessment of their ideas and their work. It is often more critical than congratulatory but gives them their due for their descriptive analyses of political institutions.

MacKenzie, Jeanne. *A Victorian Courtship.* London: Weidenfeld and Nicolson, and New York: Oxford University Press, 1979. A brief narrative of the two-year courtship that preceded the

Webbs' marriage in 1892. The author makes good use of Beatrice's diaries and the Webbs' letters to each other and to others to reconstruct the uneven relationships between the two and the working compact they formulated. A warm and sympathetic picture, short on psychological analysis.

MacKenzie, Norman, and Jeanne MacKenzie. *The Fabians*. London: Weidenfeld and Nicolson, and New York: Simon and Schuster, 1977. The most recent of the several books on the Fabian Society, covering the early years from 1884 to 1914, when the society was at its peak of influence. As leaders of the society, the Webbs' contributions to the Fabian, as well as their other activities, are discussed. The author offers a perceptive analysis of the ideas of the Webbs, their social and political milieu, and, especially, of the forces and conflicts that motivated them.

Nord, Deborah Epstein. *The Apprenticeship of Beatrice Webb.* London: Macmillan, and Amherst: University of Massachusetts Press, 1985. The most recent of the biographies of Beatrice Webb, this one is more concerned with Beatrice as diarist than as a social scientist. Still, there is much useful material here on Beatrice's other works and an insightful psychological analysis of her personal relationships as well. Placing Beatrice's diaries in a literary context, Nord underscores their value as literature and evaluates their place in the autobiographical literature, and in women's writings, of her period.

Radice, Lisanne. *Beatrice and Sidney Webb: Fabian Socialists*. London: Macmillan, and New York: St. Martin's Press, 1984. The most recent book on the Webbs, useful as an introduction to their lives and work.

Seymour-Jones, Carole. *Beatrice Webb: A Life.* Chicago: Dee, and London: Allison and Busby, 1992. The author explores the life of Beatrice Webb in the context of Victorian values and mores, especially with respect to women's roles and feminine repression.

"Sidney Webb, Fabian Intellectual and Reformer, Dies." *History Today* 47, no. 10 (October, 1997). Discusses the efforts of the Webbs in the development of the intellectual and philosophical bases for the British Labour Party.

Webb, Beatrice. *The Diary of Beatrice Webb.* Edited by Norman MacKenzie and Jeanne MacKenzie. 4 vols. London: Virago, 1882; Cambridge, Mass.: Belknap Press of Harvard University Press, 1982-1985. Based on Beatrice's first transcript of her fifty-seven manuscript books between 1873 and 1943. A fascinating chronicle of the Webbs' lives, their work, and their times. Few have known more important or interesting people than did Beatrice Webb, far fewer could write of them as perceptively as she did. Unlike the books she wrote with Sidney, *The Diary of Beatrice Webb* shows to advantage Beatrice's elegant prose style. Superbly edited and thoroughly annotated by the MacKenzies.

Webb, Sidney, and Beatrice Webb. *The Letters of Sidney and Beatrice Webb.* Edited by Norman MacKenzie. 3 vols. Cambridge and New York: Cambridge University Press, 1978. Volume 1 covers the period from 1873 to 1892; volume 2 covers from 1892 to 1912; volume 3 covers from 1912 to 1947. The letters of Beatrice and Sidney to each other and to others. Fascinating not only for what they impart of the Webbs themselves but also for the insight into the issues of their era and the personalities and concerns of the many, often famous, people with whom they corresponded. Edited with skill and meticulous attention to detail by MacKenzie.

*Reva Greenburg*

## MAX WEBER

*Born:* April 21, 1864; Erfurt, Prussia
*Died:* June 14, 1920; Munich, Germany
*Area of Achievement:* Sociology
*Contribution:* A German social scientist and theorist widely acclaimed as the "father of sociology," Weber is best known for his thesis of the Protestant ethic, which links the psychological effects of Calvinism with the development of modern capitalism.

### Early Life

Max Weber was the first child of Max and Helen Fallenstein Weber. His father was a prominent lawyer and aspiring politician whose family had attained considerable wealth in the German linen industry. An ardent monarchist and Bismarckian within the German Reichstag, the elder Weber was to his son the epitome of a patriarchal, amoral creature-of-pleasure who knew real politics and the art of compromise. His mother, on the other hand, was a highly educated, moralistic woman, intensely preoccupied with religious and social concerns, particularly with charity work for the poor. The hedonistic father and humanitarian mother shared little in common, and Weber grew to maturity in a household charged with open tension and hostility.

Weber received an excellent early education in select German private schools. In addition, because of the political prominence of his father, a considerable circle of famous personalities—such as Wilhem Dilthey, Heinrich von Treitschke, Levin Goldschmidt, and Theodor Mommsen—frequented the Weber household. Meeting and engaging in political discussion with such men of prestige not only stimulated young Weber's intellectual curiosity but also provided him with contacts who would help promote his career in later life.

Weber began his university studies in 1882 at Heidelberg—his mother's home during her youth—taking courses in law, history, and theology. At his father's suggestion (and against his mother's wishes), he also joined the student fraternity, an activity which consumed much of his time in drinking bouts and duels. In 1883, Weber moved to Strasbourg to fulfill his one-year military obligation in the National Service. There, Weber visited and developed a close attachment to his aunt and uncle: Ida Baumgarten, an intensely devout woman much like his mother, and Hermann Baumgarten, a professor of history who, unlike his father, was highly critical of the Bismarckian empire.

Hoping to extricate young Weber from the influence of the Baumgartens, the elder Weber encouraged his son to resume his studies back home at the University of Berlin. Weber returned to Berlin, and, except for one semester in school at Göttingen and several months away on military exercises, Weber spent the next eight years at home. In 1889, Weber was graduated magna cum laude and then began preparing for his *Habilitation* (a higher doctorate required to teach in German universities), which he received in 1891. While pursuing his advanced studies, Weber worked intermittently as a lawyer's assistant and a university assistant—two unremunerative apprenticeships. Hence at age twenty-nine, Weber was still residing in his parents' home, financially dependent on their income and continually subject to their conflicting claims on his loyalty.

In 1893, Weber married his second cousin, Marianne Schnitger, an intelligent woman who later achieved some prominence in the German feminist movement. The marriage lasted until Weber's death but never was consummated. Although their marriage was without affection, Weber and Marianne were intellectually compatible. Following Weber's death, Marianne published a seven-hundred-page biography of her late husband that contained not a negative word regarding their union.

### Life's Work

A workaholic with strong academic credentials and political contacts, Weber rose rapidly in the teaching profession. After a brief appointment in Berlin, Weber in 1894 became a full professor in economics at the University of Freiburg. Two years later, he was called to the University of Heidelberg to succeed the preeminent professor of political economy, Karl Knies. As a professor, Weber advocated what he called "freedom from value-judgment" in lecturing. This doctrine demanded that teachers present to their students the established empirical facts without expressing their evaluations as to whether the facts were satisfactory or unsatisfactory. Weber also was an avid researcher and writer. During these years, however, his research interests focused on rather mundane economic issues of immediate application.

Weber's academic career, however, was cut short in 1898 when he suffered a severe mental and physical breakdown that virtually incapacitated him for four years and prevented him from returning to the classroom until 1918. The symptoms of the illness included insomnia, inner tension, exhaustion, bouts of anxiety, and continual restlessness. Biographers have speculated that familial problems triggered this neurosis. In 1897, Weber had a violent dispute with his father over the authoritarian way his father treated his mother. Following the argument, his father stormed away from Weber's Heidelberg home, promising never to return. Shortly thereafter, the elder Weber died of a gastric hemorrhage. His mother quickly recovered from her grief, but Weber harbored intense feelings of guilt. Throughout his life, Weber had been intellectually torn between the moralistic idealism of his mother and the practical realism of his father. Outwardly, he resembled his father; inwardly, he aspired for the moral certitudes of his mother. Perhaps the tragic circumstances of his father's death locked the two sides of his personality in a paralyzing symbiosis.

Whatever the cause, Weber's neurotic breakdown had a dramatic impact upon his future thought and career. The prolonged agony of his personal crisis led him to develop insights into the relationship between religious ethics and social and economic processes that would distinguish his subsequent scholarship. His illness also freed him from the burden of the classroom. After a lengthy leave of absence, in 1903 Weber resigned from his university position and accepted the editorship of *Archiv für Sozialwissenschaft und Sozialpolitik* (social science and social political archives). This position provided Weber with a place to publish his own materials without passing an outside review. It also provided him with the leisure to write at his own pace. Except for a brief tenure as a German military hospital administrator during World War I, from the time of his partial recovery in 1903 until his return to academe in 1918, Weber was not obligated to any duties other than the editorial work he took on himself. All of Weber's most important works were written during these years between the worst part of his illness and his death. As tragic as his personal crisis was, without it he would not have achieved the greatness for which he is remembered.

Weber published his most famous piece, *Die protestantische Ethik und der Geist des Kapitalismus (The Protestant Ethic and the Spirit of Capitalism*, 1930), in the journal he edited during the years 1904 and 1905. In this work, Weber noted the correlation in German communities between the expansion of capitalism on the one hand and Protestant ideology on the other. He attributed this relationship to accidental psychological consequences of the Puritan doctrine of predestination. This doctrine, Weber postulated, produced an extreme condition of anxiety among Calvinist believers, which served to motivate them to discipline their lives in every respect. Calvinists worked hard, avoided idleness and waste, and, as a consequence, accumulated considerable wealth. Ironically, however, as capitalism grew and Calvinists became rich, puritanism began to fade. The Protestant ethic, in the end, transformed the world but in so doing eventually undermined itself.

After completing his study of Protestant ethics, Weber focused attention upon other world religions: Judaism, Confucianism, Taoism, Hinduism, and Buddhism. In all of his works on the sociology of religion, Weber emphasized the "universal historical relationship of religion and society." His studies attempted to show how different religious worldviews have affected the development of their cultures. In contrast with Karl Marx, who viewed religion as simply a reflection of the material basis of society, Weber argued that religious beliefs have significant impact upon economic actions and, in the case of Protestantism, were themselves the basis for the emergence of modern capitalism.

In 1909, Weber agreed to edit a new edition of an academic encyclopedia intended to cover every area of economics. In addition to arranging other contributors for the project, Weber planned to write for the volume a section on the relationship between economy and society. Although he never finished this work, Weber's involvement in the project provided him with the occasion to work out a comprehensive sociology. At the time of his death, he had written nearly fifteen hundred pages of text, but the work still was incomplete. The disordered and fragmentary manuscript was edited and published posthumously under the title *Wirtschaft und Gesellschaft* (1922; *Economy and Society*, 1968). This book contains many of Weber's thoughts on politics, law, bureaucracy, and social stratification.

Perhaps Weber's greatest impact on his contemporaries came near the end of World War I when he crusaded against Germany's annexationist war goals and policy of submarine warfare. His journalistic attacks at this time frequently placed him in conflict with the military censors. After Germany's defeat, Weber assisted in the drafting of the new constitution and in the founding of the German Democratic Party.

Weber briefly returned to the classroom, accepting in 1918 a professorship at the University of Vienna and the following year at the University of Munich. In early summer of 1920, Weber became ill with influenza, which soon turned into pneumonia. Weber died at his home in Munich on June 14, 1920.

### Summary

In a strictly scientific sense, Max Weber did not develop a new sociological theory. His works instead consisted of a cloud of axioms, hypotheses, suggestions, and a few theorems—the details of which generally have been discredited by specialists in their respective fields. Weber also did not discover any new problematic area which had not been discovered by others before him. Sociologists previous to and independent of him, for example, had delved into matters relating to the origins and effects of modern capitalism. Moreover, largely because little of his work was published in book form while he was alive, Weber did not stand in the center of sociological discourse during his own life. Much to his dismay, few of his peers welcomed his "freedom from value-judgment" doctrine, which was Weber's major methodological contribution to social science disciplines.

Yet, today Max Weber is almost the canonized saint of sociology who is widely acclaimed as the most influential and, perhaps, the most profound of twentieth century social scientists. His greatness does not lie in cerebral consistency, for much of his work is ambiguous and inconclusive, if not contradictory. Instead, Weber's fame is a result of his multisided, far-reaching intellect. Weber was a genius whose work crossed all the boundaries of sociology, law, economics, history, and religion. His multidimensional works influenced thinkers as diverse as C. Wright Mills, H. Richard Niebuhr, György Lukács, and Carl Schmitt. Weber's works remain "classic" because they call scholars away from the narrow perspectives of their individual disciplines to ask the grand questions about the meaning of human culture for which there are no easy answers.

### Bibliography

Bendix, Reinhard. *Max Weber: An Intellectual Portrait*. London: Heinemann, and New York: Doubleday, 1960. An older, but still one of the better single-volume portraits in English on the work of Weber.

Collins, Randall. *Max Weber: A Skeleton Key*. Beverly Hills, Calif.: Sage, 1986. An excellent brief introduction to Weber's life and thought. Beautifully written. Highly recommended for readers interested in a concise synopsis of Weberian thought.

Giddens, Anthony. "Marx, Weber and the Development of Capitalism." *Sociology* 4 (September, 1970): 289-310. An interesting summation of the works on the origins of capitalism of these two great thinkers.

Kasler, Dirk. *Max Weber: An Introduction to His Life and Work*. Translated by Philippa Hurd. Chicago: University of Chicago Press, and Cambridge: Polity Press, 1988. This English translation of Kasler's *Einfuhrung in das Studium Max Webers* is a scholarly interpretation of the work of Weber. Balanced and insightful, but definitely intended for the advanced reader. Includes an extensive bibliography of Weber's works listed in chronological order.

MacRae, Donald G. *Max Weber*. New York: Viking Press, 1974. A 111-page volume in the Modern Masters series edited by Frank Kermode. A very readable and informative work which briefly analyzes the components of Weber's genius and suggests some reasons for Weber's overrated reputation.

Ringer, Fritz K. *Max Weber's Methodology: The Unification of the Cultural and Social Sciences*. Illustrated by Jane Bendix. Cambridge, Mass.: Harvard University Press, 1997. Important study of Weber's work. The author provides examples in explanation of theories, which make this volume invaluable to students of Weber and social theory in general.

Swedberg, Richard. *Max Weber and the Idea of Economic Sociology*. Princeton, N.J.: Princeton University Press, 1998. The first critical analysis of Weber's economic theory termed "economic sociology."

Weber, Marianne. *Max Weber: A Biography*. Translated by Harry Zohn. New York and London: Wiley, 1975. A biography written by the wife of Weber. Although not to be taken at face value, this work is an interesting and sometimes entertaining volume that sheds considerable light on the humanness of this academic giant.

Weber, Max. *The Protestant Ethic and the Spirit of Capitalism*. Translated by Talcott Parsons, with an introduction by Anthony Giddens. London: Allen and Unwin, and Boston: Unwin Hyman, 1930. A translation of Weber's most famous work. Required reading for all students interested in the thought of Weber.

*Terry D. Bilhartz*

# ANTON VON WEBERN

*Born:* December 3, 1883; Vienna, Austro-Hungarian Empire

*Died:* September 15, 1945; Mittersill, Austria

*Area of Achievement:* Music

*Contribution:* Webern brought to the second Viennese school a unique and highly individual compositional approach. Like his mentor Arnold Schoenberg, Webern broke with existing musical traditions and developed a new compositional language and perspective. His adaptation of Schoenberg's twelve-tone method, based upon his own contrapuntal proclivity and concise musical rhetoric, proved to be the major influence on the subsequent generation of composers.

## Early Life

Anton Friedrich Wilhelm von Webern was born in Vienna on December 3, 1883. His father Karl, a mining engineer and government official, had an aristocratic lineage; vacations at the Preglhof, the family estate, fostered Anton's lifelong love of nature and mountain climbing, and provided a summer retreat for composition. Karl was well-read but not particularly artistic, and planned for his son to pursue an agricultural career. Webern's mother, Amalie (née Gehr), was an amateur pianist and singer. She taught her son piano from the age of five; with Webern's two sisters, the family often held impromptu concerts. Webern was particularly close to his mother and was deeply affected by her death in 1906; he later declared the majority of his works to be in her memory.

Because of Karl's career, the family moved from Vienna to Graz and finally settled in Klagenfurt in 1894. Webern received his first true music instruction there, studying cello, piano, and elementary harmony with Edwin Komauer, who also introduced Webern to contemporary works through piano reductions. Although Webern's musical inclinations were by now clear (his graduation from *Gymnasium* was celebrated with a pilgrimage to Bayreuth in 1902), his compositional proclivity was not as yet apparent. He entered the University of Vienna in 1902 to study musicology with Guido Adler; Webern's study of the Flemish composer Heinrich Isaac for his Ph.D. would later motivate the importance of counterpoint in his own compositional style. He continued to study cello and piano, and also studied harmony with Hermann Graedener and counterpoint with Karl Navrátil. Webern's work in composition to this point consisted of, for the most part, student efforts, but his increasing interest and productivity led him to seek out a true composition teacher. After a failed attempt to study with Hans Pfitzner, Webern began lessons in 1904 with Arnold Schoenberg, who, at nine years Webern's senior, was just beginning to attract attention, if not notoriety, in Viennese music circles. Schoenberg's instruction and the ensuing friendship that evolved proved to be the most crucial event in Webern's development; Schoenberg remained a profound artistic influence and close friend throughout Webern's life.

## Life's Work

The four years of Schoenberg's tutelage brought Webern's work to maturity, evident in the mastery of harmonic and formal considerations in the *Passacaglia* Op. 1 (1908). Yet the competence of the *Passacaglia* hardly foreshadows the unique traits that would evolve to characterize Webern's style: brevity, textural clarity, dynamic restraint, motivic conciseness, contrapuntal dexterity, harmonic stasis, and a delicate objectivity. While these traits evolved continually, Webern's oeuvre does not display the drastic changes of style that mark Schoenberg's evolution. Rather, Webern's development loosely paralleled that of his mentor, tempering each stylistic advance with his own compositional sensibilities.

This process is clearly evident in the evolution of the remarkable series of aphoristic instrumental miniatures, Opp. 5-11. The energetic terseness in the taut motivic construction of the Five Movements for String Quartet Op. 5 (1909) devolves into the fleeting ephemerality of the Six Bagatelles for String Quartet Op. 9 (1911-1913). Also, the surprisingly delicate, chamberlike scoring that belies the massive forces of the Six Pieces for Large Orchestra Op. 6 (1909) is distilled into the exotic instrumentation of the Five Pieces for Orchestra Op. 10 (1911-1913), which further explores the technique of *Klangfarbenmelodie* (tone-color melody, in which the progression of instrumental timbres becomes a prime developmental consideration), first developed in Schoenberg's Five Orchestral Pieces Op. 16 (1909). That coloristic effect has now become an integral aspect of development rhetoric and is apparent in the Four Pieces for Violin and Piano Op. 7 (1910) but is particularly so in the Three Little Pieces for Cello and Piano Op. 11 (1914), whose extreme brevity (the total of thirty-two measures lasts no more than two minutes) demonstrates the ultimate compression of musical development. While Webern's work would never again approach such extreme brevity, he found little need for extensive rhetoric in any of his work; at 269 measures (about ten minutes), the *Passacaglia* remained his most expansive single movement.

By 1910, his artistic development had convinced Webern of his compositional métier. Yet composition would never prove to be his livelihood nor the source of much local recognition. Rather, after receiving his Ph.D. in 1906, Webern embarked on a career as a conductor, a vocation that he appears to have taught himself. After a series of unsuccessful appointments in theater in Ischl, Teplitz, Danzig, Stettin, and Prague, he eventually settled in Mödling in 1918 in order to be near Schoenberg, conducting the Vienna Workers' Symphony Concerts and Chorus (1922-1934). Conducting did not prove lucrative, however, and recognition of his compositions was late in coming (it was not until 1921 that his music was published by Universal Edition); he found it necessary to supplement his income by consulting for the Austrian radio station and by making arrangements for Schoenberg and the Verein für Musikalische Privataufführungen (Society for Private Musical Performances, 1918-1922). Webern also taught piano at the Jewish Cultural Institute for the Blind (1925-1931); besides his periodic private students, this would be Webern's sole teaching position. Financial difficulties plagued Webern throughout his life; he periodically received loans and gifts from his publisher, friends, family, and patrons, often through Schoenberg's intercession. Financial constraints did not, however, markedly alter Webern's reserved and prudent lifestyle; he was throughout his life a dedicated family man, devoted to his wife Wilhelmine (née Mörtl), a cousin whom he married in 1911, and their four children.

Given the evident stylistic limitations of the aphoristic miniatures of 1909-1914, Webern turned in 1914 to writing songs, the use of text thus providing for and even dictating formal expansion. In fact, Opp. 12-18, spanning 1914-1925, are exclusively songs and accompaniments ranging from piano to small mixed ensembles to chamber orchestra. Yet genre and length are not the only aspects different from the preceding works. Stylistically, the songs tend toward a heightened emotional tension, reflecting attitudes prevalent in the expressionist movement as manifested in music by the second Viennese school (that is, Schoenberg, Webern, and Alban Berg, Webern's fellow pupil and close friend). Wide, dramatic leaps, exaggerated by sudden dynamic contrasts, mark the vocal lines, as they develop within an unsettling atonal harmonic context. Even with Webern's adoption of Schoenberg's twelve-tone method, consistently applied from the *Three Traditional Rhymes* Op. 17 (1924-1925) onward, no sudden stylistic change is apparent. Rather, Webern's individual style characteristics evolved throughout the series of songs. Leaps of major sevenths, minor ninths, and tritones become prominent, obscuring a sense of voice-leading. Melodic lines tend toward fragmentation, emphasizing motifs of only two to four notes. Natural and sacred imagery abounds in the texts (the authors range from Li T'ai-po to August Strindberg and Georg Trakl), reflecting Webern's deep spirituality that often expressed itself in his lifelong reverence of nature. Most characteristic, however, is the increasing importance of strict contrapuntal techniques, particularly evident from the *Five Canons on Latin Texts* Op. 16 (1923-1924) through the rest of his oeuvre. A lasting impression from his study of the Flemish composers, Webern's contrapuntal dexterity allowed for the coalescence of all of these varied traits into the unique style characteristic of his late works.

The ordering principles inherent in the twelve-tone method brought renewed structural coherence to Webern's work, which allowed for a return to purely instrumental works of greater expanse, beginning with the String Trio Op. 20 (1926-1927) and the Symphony Op. 21 (1927-1928). Beyond changes in length and genre, Webern's application of the technique explored its powerful structural possibilities, both within the tone-row itself and by using the row as the generator of the form of larger structures. Webern's general concern with contrapuntal clarity typically leads to the stratification of various row forms among the individual lines. Similarly, his predilection toward symmetrical and palindromic forms shaped not only the larger formal structures but also the internal structure of the rows as he devised them; internal motivic cells generate the row itself. Thus, the four-, three-, and even two-note motifs found within the rows carry on the motivic fragmentation characteristic of the earlier experiments in *Klangfarbenmelodie*, a process giving rise to musical pointillism. These formalistic concerns supersede earlier concerns of coloristic and melodic effect, giving late works such as the Piano Variations Op. 27 (1935-1936), the String Quartet Op. 28 (1937-1938), and the Variations for Orchestra Op. 30 (1940) a detached, objective quality. Yet Webern's eminently humanistic stance provides the motivation for his two Cantatas Op. 29 (1938-1939) and Op. 31 (1941-1943), the texts of which, written by his close friend Hildegard Jone, reflect his profound respect for nature through a simple spirituality.

The quantity of Webern's creative output steadily declined after the burst of compositional activity of 1909-1914, a decline balanced, however, by the continual development of his individual artistic voice. External economic, social, and political factors had their effect here; events such as the sale of the Preglhof retreat by Webern's father in 1912, Webern's volunteer efforts in World War I (along with his efforts to secure Schoenberg's release from duty), and his continual dependence on conducting for financial support all hampered his compositional activities. While his renown as a conductor was both local and international in scope (he made numerous conducting tours throughout Europe), his compositions sparked more interest abroad than at home. This situation worsened with the rise of the Nazi regime, which not only outlawed Webern's work as "degenerate art" but also disbanded the Vienna Workers' Concerts, Webern's major source of income. World War II brought numerous tragedies, including the death of Webern's son Peter in 1945, the emigration or death of numerous friends and colleagues (Schoenberg had fled to the United States in 1933), and the flight of his family to Mittersill to escape the bombings of Vienna. On September 15, 1945, Webern was accidentally shot and killed by a soldier from the occupying American forces during an attempt to arrest his son-in-law for black-marketeering.

## Summary

Much of the initial recognition of Anton von Webern's work was inextricably linked, often in a derogatory fashion, to his close relationship with Schoenberg as student, colleague, and friend. Webern's veneration of Schoenberg, at times carried to extremes of obsessive idolization, did little to diffuse misunderstanding about the development of their individual musical styles. Basic to the dynamics of their relationship were the marked differences of their personalities. With fierce independence garnered from enduring years of harsh criticism, Schoenberg demanded utter loyalty from his coterie; Webern, more reserved and reticent, thus often appeared subsumed. Schoenberg left a legacy of students, textbooks, and critical writings; Webern, who taught only occasionally and left few writings, often deferred what little recognition he did attain to his mentor. Yet the two continually exchanged reciprocal support throughout their lives on artistic, personal, and financial planes.

Such reciprocity extended to the musical plane as well, often leading to the conflation of their individual and communal (including Berg) stylistic development. Schoenberg is often characterized not only as the mentor but also as the sole innovator, which relegates Webern's development to a mere reinterpretation of Schoenberg's advances. Their creative interaction, however, was more symbiotic than this perspective implies. For example, while the exploration of *Klangfarbenmelodie* in Schoenberg's Five Orchestral Pieces Op. 16 (1909) predates Webern's Six Pieces for Large Orchestra Op. 6 (1909) by some months, the process of miniaturization seen in Webern's Opp. 5-11, begun in 1909, is only taken up by Schoenberg in his Three Orchestral Pieces (1910) and the Six Little Piano Pieces Op. 19 (1911). In similar fashion, Webern's application of Schoenberg's twelve-tone method is important not only as a demonstration of its stylistic flexibility but also for its deeper exploration of aspects of the method as reflected by Webern's own musical proclivities. Whereas Schoenberg viewed the tone row as able to provide compositional unity through motivic manipulation of the row, Webern turned to motivic connections within the row itself not only to generate the row but also to provide compositional unity, a significant shift in compositional perspective. To Webern, this reflected the balances he observed in nature, where each component works in perfect balance not only as part of a larger system but also as an individual, self-contained aspect.

The continual distillation and atomization apparent in the evolution of the various aspects of Webern's style grew to be of great influence to the succeeding generation of composers, particularly in Europe. Through courses taught by Webern's student René Liebowitz at the Kranichstein Summer School at Darmstadt, many younger composers of the 1950's took Webern to be their stylistic progenitor, most notably Karlheinz Stockhausen, Pierre Boulez, and Luciano Berio. These composers, whose compositional view in turn grew to great prominence, further distilled the serial, pointillistic, and objective aspects of Webern's style, to extremes perhaps far beyond Webern's broadest intentions, to a point at which musical rhetoric became solely an explication of compositional process. Thus, while in part construed in a manner seemingly at odds with his typically humanistic and deferential approach, Webern's influence on the development of music in the twentieth century has been pervasive.

**Bibliography**

Bailey, Kathryn. *The Life of Webern.* Cambridge and New York: Cambridge University Press, 1998. In contrast to other such works, Bailey focuses on Webern's personality and the manner in which it affected his work. Includes information on his dependence on Schoenberg and his instability in his early years.

Griffiths, Paul. "Anton Webern." In *Second Viennese School: Schoenberg, Webern, Berg.* Vol. 16 in *The New Grove Dictionary of Music and Musicians*, edited by Stanley Sadie. London: Macmillan, and Washington, D.C.: Grove's Dictionaries of Music, 1980. *Second Viennese School* is part of The New Grove Composer Biography series. This article provides a concise survey of Webern's life and work as well as a brief discussion of his style and ideas. A thorough list of works and bibliography is appended.

Kolneder, Walter. *Anton Webern: An Introduction to His Works.* Translated by Humphrey Searle. London: Faber, and Berkeley: University of California Press, 1968. Following a short biographical sketch, Kolneder examines Webern's works in chronological order, with emphasis on the evolution of stylistic traits. Chapters on Webern's personality and influence round out the study. Includes a list of works and an extensive, if somewhat outdated, bibliography.

Moldenhauer, Hans, and Rosaleen Moldenhauer. *Anton von Webern: A Chronicle of His Life and Work.* London: Gollancz, 1978; New York: Knopf, 1979. The most extensive and thorough biography available. Through interviews with Webern's family and associates, coupled with exhaustive gathering of surviving letters, documents, and manuscripts, the Moldenhauers augment existing information with important and insightful new research. Chapters alternate between Webern's life and works; the compendious detail is balanced by Moldenhauer's lively prose style. Includes Webern's own extensive analysis of his String Quartet Op. 28. The appended work lists are perhaps the most comprehensive available, and the select bibliography is also thorough.

Rognoni, Luigi. *The Second Vienna School.* Translated by Robert W. Mann. London: Calder, 1977. A study of the stylistic derivation of expressionism, as applied by Schoenberg, Berg, and Webern, and its relationship to other contemporaneous artistic trends. Webern's works are described in chronological order, with emphasis on stylistic evolution rather than biographical context.

Simms, Bryan R., ed. *Schoenberg, Berg and Webern: A Companion to the Second Viennese School.* Westport, Conn.: Greenwood, 1999. A collection of essays examining the development of modern Viennese composition in the early twentieth century including comparisons of music to other arts of the period.

Webern, Anton. *The Path to the New Music.* Edited by Willi Reich. Translated by Leo Black. London: Universal, and Bryn Mawr, Pa.: Presser, 1963. Given the dearth of Webern's extant critical prose, this transcription from shorthand of sixteen lectures given by Webern in 1932-1933 provides important insight into his aesthetic motivation. Traces the historic justification of the innovations in musical language developed by the second Viennese school. Includes as a postscript a number of personal letters from Webern to Reich.

Wildgans, Friedrich. *Anton Webern.* Translated by Edith Temple Roberts and Humphrey Searle. London: Calder and Boyars, 1966; New York: October House, 1967. Wildgans discusses the evolution of Webern's style in a biographical context, followed by a short critical description of the works in chronological order. Five tributes to and by Webern are appended. The short bibliography and discography have been surpassed.

*Paul A. Siskind*

# ALFRED WEGENER

*Born:* November 1, 1880; Berlin, Germany
*Died:* Winter of 1930; Greenland
*Areas of Achievement:* Geology and physics
*Contribution:* Wegener was a German meteorologist and Arctic explorer who received credit for the first clear statement of the hypothesis of continental drift. Although his ideas were scornfully dismissed by most geologists in his own time, they were enthusiastically revived by oceanographers in the mid-1960's as the precursor to the well-known plate tectonics theory.

## Early Life

Alfred Lothar Wegener was born in Berlin, Germany, on November 1, 1880, the son of a preacher in the Evangelical church. He was educated at the Köllnisches Gymnasium in Berlin and subsequently attended the Universities of Heidelberg, Innsbruck, and Berlin. He received his Ph.D. degree in astronomy from the University of Berlin in 1905, and his doctoral thesis was on the conversion of a set of thirteenth century tables of planetary motion from a number system based on multiples of sixty to the decimal system.

As a youth Wegener became fascinated with the vast, ice-covered island of Greenland. At that time nothing was known of Greenland's interior as exploration had been limited to the coastal areas only. In order to prepare himself for the longed-for trip to Greenland, Wegener spent much of his spare time in a rigorous program of endurance training, which consisted of gymnastics and all-day bouts of walking, ice skating, mountain climbing, and skiing.

Following his graduation from the University of Berlin in 1905, Wegener found that he had lost interest in the field of astronomy, and he turned his attention to the newly established science of meteorology instead, taking a position as an assistant at the Royal Prussian Aeronautical Observatory at Lindenberg. There he experimented with kites and balloons, and in 1906 he and his brother Kurt broke the world's record for long distance in a free balloon, drifting for fifty-two hours from April 5 to 7 across Germany, Denmark, and adjacent water bodies.

Also in 1906, the long-awaited opportunity to visit Greenland finally presented itself, and Wegener resigned his position at the observatory in order to join the 1906-1908 Danmark Expedition to Greenland. He served as official meteorologist to the expedition, which successfully explored the northeastern part of the island and made important weather measurements. Wegener returned safely to Germany at the expedition's end, but its leader, Ludvig Mylius-Erichsen, did not. He and two companions died while on a side trip northward toward the pole, a tragic premonition of Wegener's own death on the Greenland ice cap in 1930.

Upon his return to Germany in 1908, Wegener went to the University of Marburg as a lecturer. There he taught courses in meteorology, practical astronomy, and cosmic physics, meanwhile continuing his meteorological investigations. He also published a book on the thermodynamics of the atmosphere in 1911, but his academic career was abruptly halted in 1914 when World War I broke out, and he was called up as part of the general mobilization.

## Life's Work

Wegener is chiefly noted for the hypothesis of continental drift. In it he contended that the earth's continents had once been joined together but then had broken apart and begun drifting about the surface of the globe much as icebergs drift about the sea. The subject of drift had claimed his attention as early as 1903 when he pointed out the remarkable "fit" between the continents on the opposite sides of the Atlantic to a fellow student at the University of Berlin. Then in 1910, when he was examining world maps in a handsome new atlas, the idea of drifting continents came over him in its full force, but he relates that he instantly rejected the idea as being "too improbable." In 1911, however, he stumbled "quite by accident" on a study summarizing the similarities between the fossil animals found in Africa and in Brazil. The study attributed these similarities to a former land connection—now submerged—between the two continents; Wegener, however, believed otherwise. He was convinced that Africa and Brazil had once been joined together and subsequently had drifted apart.

Wegener presented his new ideas to the scientific community during January of 1912, first addressing the Geological Association in Frankfurt and then the Society for the Advancement of Natural Science in Marburg. A paper on the subject quickly followed, but next came two interruptions. The first was a return to Greenland in the spring of 1912, accompanied by J. P. Koch, a Dane whom he had met on the 1906-1908 expedition. After lengthy preparations, they made the first successful east-west crossing of the ice cap at its widest point, using sledges hauled by ponies for the 1,100-kilometer trip. The second interruption came in 1914 with the outbreak of World War I when Wegener was called into the army.

Wegener served with distinction and was wounded twice. In his spare time, however, he still managed to continue working on his Greenland data, to make meteorological observations, and to refine his thinking on the subject of continental drift. While on sick leave in 1915, he even managed to set down his ideas in a slender volume, which came out under the title *Die Entstehung der Kontinente und Ozeane* (1915; *Origin of Continents and Oceans*, 1922). This book spelled out the basic tenets of continental drift, along with supporting evidence. In essence, Wegener proposed that the continents had not always occupied their present positions but were originally gathered together as a large supercontinent, which he called Pangaea (literally, all-earth). Pangaea had occupied half the globe, with the other half being covered by water—the ancestral Pacific Ocean.

Beginning in the Mesozoic era, however—some 200 million years before the present—Wegener believed that the continents had begun detaching themselves from Pangaea and started drifting toward their new locations, much as icebergs plow through water. He proposed that the Atlantic Ocean had been formed when Pangaea split in two, with North America, South America, Antarctica, and Australia originating from the strip of continental crust on the west. As this strip plowed westward across the Pacific, Wegener believed that great wrinkles had appeared along its leading edge which now form the mountain chains that extend from the Andes to Alaska. He also proposed that the towering Himalaya Mountains had been created in a similar fashion when northward-drifting India crashed into the continent of Asia.

Wegener spent the years following 1915 marshaling the evidence to support his hypothesis. First there was the behavior of earthquake waves; they seemed to indicate that the continents were composed of lightweight rocks floating on the heavier rocks of the ocean floor. Then came the jigsaw-puzzle "fit" between continents on the opposite sides of the Atlantic; by including with the continents the submerged lands adjacent to their shoreline—the so-called continental shelves—he obtained an even better "fit" than was possible by merely juxtaposing coastlines.

A third line of evidence was the presence of similar geologic features on continents that are now widely separated. The rocks of Brazil strongly resemble those of Africa, for example, and mountain trends even seem to match when the continents are restored to their predrift positions. Wegener also cited similarities in fossil plants and animals found in continents that are now far distant from one another.

An ingenious line of evidence was based on glacial activity in pre-Mesozoic times. Distinctive deposits of ancient glacial debris are found in such diverse localities as southern South America, Antarctica, Australia, South Africa, and parts of India. Worldwide glaciation cannot explain these deposits, because tropical climates existed side by side with glaciated areas. Pangaea provided a likely explanation, however, because when the continents are restored to their predrift positions, all these glaciated areas become contiguous, suggesting a single large ice cap located at the South Pole. A final line of evidence was the apparent changes in the longitude of various localities on the globe. Such changes would have supported his hypothesis by demonstrating that the continents were still moving. Unfortunately, the methods used for measuring longitude in those days were not sufficiently precise to provide the confirmation he needed.

After the war's end, Wegener accepted a teaching post at the University of Hamburg and while there conducted experiments related to another one of his theories, namely that the moon's craters had originated as a result of meteoric bombardment, rather than through volcanic action. Continental drift remained his primary obsession, however, and he brought out revised and expanded editions of *Origin of Continents and Oceans* in 1920 and 1922. His hypothesis had attracted attention outside Germany by now, and French, English, Spanish, and Russian translations of the 1922 edition appeared in 1924. In the same year, Wegener was also appointed to the chair of meteorology and geophysics at the University of Graz in Austria, an important upward step in the academic world.

The growing attention to his ideas resulted in a swelling controversy, however, which reached its climax in 1926 when the American Association of Petroleum Geologists organized a symposium concerning continental drift as part of its annual meeting in New York City. Wegener attended, as did noted geologists from Europe and the United States. The hypothesis suffered a major setback as far as acceptance by the scientific world was concerned, however, because of the effective way in which his opponents presented their arguments. Undaunted, Wegener put out a fourth edition of his book in 1929, incorporating in it his rebuttals to the arguments advanced at the symposium. He also agreed to make another trip to Greenland, as leader of the German Inland Ice Expedition of 1930. The jet stream, that fast-moving current in the upper atmosphere which circles the earth in northern latitudes, had just been discovered, and the expedition's goal was to establish three year-round stations on the ice cap in order to study jet stream flow. The expedition was also to make pioneering measurements of the thickness of the ice cap using echo-sounding techniques.

Two of the three stations were to be on opposite coasts, and the third—named "Eismitte" (mid-ice)—was to be in the center of the ice cap at an elevation of 3,000 meters. Two members of the expedition had already set up a temporary camp there by the fall of 1930. Their quarters consisted of a pit dug into the ice and roofed over. Wegener and a fourth member followed with the necessary supplies but did not arrive until October 29 because of bad weather. Because most of the supplies had been lost en route, Wegener and his Eskimo companion decided to return to the coastal base before the polar night set in. They never made it. Wegener's body was later found halfway back, neatly sewn into his sleeping bag and buried in the snow with upright skis as a marker. His Eskimo companion apparently had gone on, but no trace of him or his sledge was ever found.

### Summary

Alfred Wegener's scientific reputation rests primarily on his advocacy of continental drift. Although he was not the first to speculate about drifting continents—Sir Francis Bacon had called attention to the similar shapes of Africa and South America in 1620—he was the first to present a unified hypothesis, together with evidence drawn from many scientific disciplines. This was a remarkable achievement in itself in that era of the Germanic tradition of specialization. Wegener was also the first scientist supporting continental drift who was taken seriously. His book went through four editions and was translated into as many languages. A symposium was even arranged by the prestigous American Association of Petroleum Geologists, and world-famous scientists met to discuss his ideas. Unfortunately, their verdict was negative, and this led to continental drift's being consigned to the academic scrap heap for the next thirty-five years.

Numerous factors led to the hypothesis' rejection. There were some flaws in his reasoning, to be sure, and some of the evidence proposed later proved to be inaccurate. More telling, however, was Wegener's inability to provide a convincing mechanism for moving continents around the globe. In fact, he was unable to demonstrate that the continents were moving at all. Being an "outsider" did not help either—his doctorate was in astronomy, his research had been in meteorology, and his professional reputation rested on his exploits as a balloonist and as an Arctic explorer. His credentials in geology were nonexistent. No wonder the reception that he received from the professional geologists at the New York City symposium ranged from politely skeptical to openly sarcastic.

After Wegener's death in 1930, the hypothesis of continental drift was no longer given serious consideration by the scientific world. It had been too radical a departure from the accepted thinking of the day. As one of the participants in the 1926 symposium put it, "If we are to believe in Wegener's hypothesis, we must forget everything which has been learned in the last seventy years and start all over again." That, of course, was exactly what was going to have to happen. A revolution in geological thinking was coming, but regrettably Wegener did not live to see it. It was not until the mid-1960's, when oceanographers proposed the radically new plate tectonics theory, that scientists around the world realized how forward-looking Wegener had been.

### Bibliography

Calder, Nigel. *The Restless Earth: A Report on the New Geology.* London: BBC, and New York: Viking Press, 1972. A concise overview of plate tectonics, suitable for high school level readers and the interested layperson. Well illustrated with diagrams, black-and-white photographs, and superb color plates. Wegener's contributions to the development of the plate tectonics theory are presented in summary form and are evaluated in terms of the overall framework of plate tectonics.

Dott, Robert H., and Roger Lyman Batten. *Evolution of the Earth.* 5th ed. New York: McGraw-Hill, 1994. A well-written and well-illustrated text. It presents an up-to-date account of earth history from the viewpoint of plate tectonics and describes the evidence that has been advanced to support this theory. Wegener's contributions are described and are compared with the contributions of others. Suitable for college-level readers.

Hughes, Patrick. "The Meteorologist Who Started a Revolution." *Weatherwise* 51, no. 1 (January-February, 1998). Profile of Wegener who proposed the concept of continental drift.

LeGrand, H. E. *Drifting Continents and Shifting Theories.* Cambridge and New York: Cambridge University Press, 1988. An up-to-date analysis of the thinking that led to the plate tectonics theory. Written for the college-level reader or layperson with some technical background. Wegener's work is described against the backdrop of the other theories of crustal evolution, and there is a very extensive bibliography of sources dealing with continental drift and plate tectonics.

Marvin, Ursula B. *Continental Drift: The Evolution of a Concept.* Washington, D.C.: Smithsonian Institution Press, 1973. A comprehensive study of the scientific debate on continental drift, with an exhaustive review of the evidence proposed by Wegener in support of his hypothesis and of the arguments advanced by his critics against it. The extensive bibliography contains a list of Wegener's publications dealing with continental drift.

Rupke, Nicolaas A. "Eurocentric Ideology of Continental Drift." *History of Science* 34, no. 3 (September, 1996). Focuses on the critics of Wegener's theory of continental drift, who found it too "Eurocentric" to accept.

Sullivan, Walter. *Continents in Motion: The New Earth Debate.* 2d ed. New York: American Institute of Physics, 1996. The author uses the historical approach to present the subject of plate tectonics in a manner that is both understandable and exciting for the average reader. A full chapter is devoted to Wegener, and the references accompanying this chapter list the important sources of bibliographical material pertaining to him.

Wyllie, Peter J. *The Way the Earth Works: The Introduction to the New Global Geology and Its Revolutionary Development.* New York: Wiley, 1976. An overview of the plate tectonic theory that is suitable for high school level readers and the interested layperson. Wegener's role is clearly described and much useful biographical information is included. The information relating to his Greenland expeditions is particularly useful, and there are also lists of suggested readings covering the various aspects of plate tectonics.

*Donald W. Lovejoy*

## SIMONE WEIL

*Born:* February 3, 1909; Paris, France
*Died:* August 24, 1943; Ashford, Kent, England
*Areas of Achievement:* Philosophy and religion
*Contribution:* Perhaps even more than her writing, the life of Weil, twentieth century French mystic and philosophical thinker, has for several generations both fascinated and perplexed many. Weil's passion and originality, her intense sense of commitment toward eternity and her fellowman, and her willingness to sacrifice her life for her truths remain her principal legacy.

### Early Life

Simone Weil was the second child and only daughter of a prosperous and highly cultured professional family. Her father, Bernard Weil, an eminent physician, was born in Strasbourg; Salomea Reinherz Weil, her mother, was from Rostov-na-Donu. The family was extremely close, and the influence of Weil's mother was particularly strong. Although Weil's parents were both of Jewish descent, they were agnostics and maintained no Jewish identity. Simone's attitude toward her own Jewishness was to remain problematical throughout her lifetime. A sickly child almost from birth, Weil experienced normal health for only a few years of her life. Although much of Weil's time was spent reading and studying, from a young age she also demonstrated an exceptionally acute moral sensibility and an unusual concern for the poor and oppressed.

An enlightened Parisian family, the Weils spared no expense in obtaining the best education for their children. They soon perceived, however, that André, Weil's brother, was the more intellectually gifted of the two children. Considered something of a genius, he passed the *baccalauréat* at the age of fourteen and later was to become one of the outstanding mathematicians of his time. Intimidated by her brother's achievements and discouraged by several unsympathetic teachers, Weil suffered through a period of deep depression in her early teens.

When Weil entered the Lycée Henri IV in 1925, she became acquainted with a man who was to exert the strongest and most lasting influence on her philosophy: Émile-Auguste Chartier, better known by his pseudonym, Alain. During her time at Henry IV (1925-1928), Weil continued her social activism. In particular, she became passionately committed to the revolutionary syndicalist, or trade unionist, movement. At this time she also began teaching in a type of free university organized for railroad workers. She was to devote much time and effort to this kind of project throughout her life because of her deep conviction that the proletariat—not merely the privileged few—could appreciate education and culture.

### Life's Work

In 1927 the École Normal Supérieure had only begun admitting women, but, when the results of the entrance examination in 1928 were announced, two women were at the top of the list. Weil was first, and Simone de Beauvoir was second, followed by thirty male students.

During her years at the École Normale Supérieure, Weil gained a reputation as an intransigent revolutionary and was nicknamed the "Red Virgin." Upon completion of the agrégation in philosophy in 1931 with a thesis on science and perception in the works of René Descartes, she was assigned to the position of professor of philosophy at the girls' *lycée* of Le Puy, a small town in the Massif Central. This was the first of her five teaching assignments in five different towns during the years of 1931 through 1937. Her organizing activities among the unemployed working classes of the area earned for her continual harassment—even arrest on several occasions—by the municipal authorities.

Believing that any political theory or plan of social action required a firsthand acquaintance with the moral and physical problems that confronted the proletariat, Weil, in 1934, took a one-year unpaid leave of absence from teaching in order to learn by direct contact what kinds of problems most seriously undermined the quality of working-class life. She took on a series of factory jobs to better her understanding. Weil's year of factory work is often regarded as a major turning point of her life. Her most ambitious goal during this year was to discover the means by which to reorganize industrial planning so as to create working conditions in which the proletariat could become truly free. Her probing essays on the subject, *La Condition ouvrière* (1951; factory journal), argued not for the conventional leftist change in ownership and political power but for a more profound transformation of modern work itself.

Pragmatically speaking, the answers that she found to freeing the proletariat were relatively vague. Yet the most lasting effect of the factory experience was one that she had not anticipated: a profound and irrevocable change in her character. She learned that, while the physical suffering of workers was deplorable, it was far less devastating than their slavelike humiliation and degradation. Another change was that a new pessimism about revolutionary activity began to surface in her thinking during this time.

Yet her dissociation from the revolutionary syndicalist movement as a result of this new pessimism was a process that had actually begun some time earlier. As early as 1933, Weil had written an article for the organ of La Révolution Prolétarienne (a humanitarian, anarchist, syndicalist movement with which she had become acquainted while at the École Normale Supérieure) in which she had criticized not only the Stalinist state in the Soviet Union but also the revolutionary syndicalist movement itself for excessive bureaucracy at the expense of the worker.

In August of 1936, Weil traveled to Barcelona to join the anarchist movement in the Spanish Civil War and volunteered for noncombatant service in the Confederación Nacional del Trabajo (CNT). Although she was in Spain only a few weeks, she witnessed enough of the conflict to learn that neither side could be trusted; in her opinion, the war was only a pretext for a battle between the interests of the Soviet Union and those of Germany and Italy.

Weil's involvement in the Spanish Civil War ended abruptly as the result of an injury (she accidentally spilled some boiling oil on her leg). Since Weil's general physical condition was already poor and the complications from her burns weakened her so severely, she was forced to take a medical leave of absence from teaching during the academic year 1936-1937. Although she returned to the classroom in October, 1937, at the Lycée of Saint-Quentin near Paris, by January of 1938 her health was so poor that she had to apply once again for sick leave. She was never to return to teaching.

From the time she ended her factory work in August, 1935, until the autumn of 1938, Weil was in spiritual crisis. One of the first revelations of her sympathy with Catholicism occurred during a visit to Portugal in September, 1935. It was in Santa Maria degli Angeli, in Italy, however, that a force far stronger than she, as the describes it, compelled her to go down on her knees for the first time in her life. Weil spent Holy Week of 1938 at the Benedictine monastery of Solesmes meditating, and it was

there, she recounts, that Christ himself came down and took possession of her. She had always admired Christ; from her *lycée* days she had read and used the Bible in her writing, teaching, and personal meditations on history, social justice, and philosophy. Yet her aversion for the Roman and Hebrew civilizations was a major obstacle that for years repelled her from the faith. As a result of her mystical experience, occurring in the autumn of 1938, Weil's life was suffused with a belief that she had encountered Christ and that she belonged to him. Thenceforth the person of Christ was to guide her philosophy.

During the years of Weil's spiritual crisis, she became more and more detached from the revolutionary syndicalist movement. While her faith in political parties had collapsed after her brief participation in the Spanish Civil War, she continued to demonstrate her concern for the working class in her articles on industrial reform. She also attended meetings of the Nouveaux Cahiers, a discussion group organized and attended by industrial executives for the purpose of planning a rational and equitable program of social reform in factory life.

The new emphasis in Weil's political thought at this time was on two rather unpopular causes: anticolonialism and pacifism. Although her views on a policy of gradual decolonization were similar to the policy eventually adopted by the French government in the 1950's, at that time the French public was not yet ready to give up its territorial claims. In retrospect, the pacifist stance in which Weil persisted right up to the German invasion of Czechoslovakia in March, 1939, was much less justified. She repeatedly underestimated Adolf Hitler's drive for conquest, and she insisted that almost anything was preferable to armed conflict. Yet when news reached France of German soldiers entering Prague, Weil was no longer able to support a pacifist position.

After a few months' stay in Vichy, in October of 1940 Weil moved to Marseilles, where she attended meetings of the Young Christian Workers' Movement and wrote for the French Resistance newspaper, *Témoignage chrétien.* One of the most important associations of Weil's Marseilles years, however, was her involvement with the group that published *Cahiers du sud*, including Jean Ballard, editor in chief, the poet Jean Torrel, and André Gide's son-in-law, Jean Lambert. It was in this journal that Weil published her essays on the *Iliad*, literature and morality, and Provençal Catharism (a form of Christian gnosticism widespread in the region known as Occitania in the eleventh and twelfth centuries).

Ever since her conversion experience, Weil had been exploring very carefully the doctrines and beliefs of the Catholic church. Yet, while she was drawn to Catholicism, she also criticized the Church as a bureaucratic establishment, especially in its inquisitional intolerance, ambiguous morality, anti-intellectualism, and otherworldly impurity. Because of these and other doubts, she never officially joined the Church and was never baptized.

Although she preferred to remain in France and share the hardship of her countrymen, in May, 1942, Weil reluctantly agreed to accompany her parents to New York, where she hoped to leave them in safety. After months of waiting in New York, Weil finally arranged passage to England, where she began working for the Free French movement. Assigned to the Ministry of the Interior, she was to submit written reports analyzing political documents received from unoccupied France. Since these documents concerned the postwar reconstruction of the new republic, they provided the occasion for some of Weil's most detailed political theorizing. While their tentative nature often led to impracticalities and excesses, the essays in *Écrits de Londres et dernières lettres* (1957) offer a useful look at the practical implications of her unusual speculative philosophy.

Ever since leaving France, Weil had drastically restricted her diet in order to share the privations of her countrymen in the Occupied zone. Her revulsion to the fallen material world had always included sexuality, comfort, and other desires—not the least of which was food. Eventually, however, her friends found it necessary to resort to subterfuge to keep her even minimally nourished. Negligent sleep habits also contributed to a general decline in her health involving an aggravation of her chronic migraines, progressive weakening of her physical stamina, and the onset of a tubercular condition.

As she felt her life ebbing away from her, Weil accelerated the pace of her writing. She reportedly spent her last months in a constant state of creativity, continually scribbling down notes on random topics as they occurred to her. The *Cahiers* (1951; *Notebooks*, 1952-1955) contain numerous examples of elliptical thoughts, outlines, and sketches of projects that she was unable to pursue. As such, these tentative explorations might be viewed as footnotes to the definitive formulation of her philosophy.

In April, 1943, Weil's body was no longer able to endure the demands she made upon it, and she was admitted to the hospital with tuberculosis and severe exhaustion. While the doctors believed that her chances of recovery were good, she persistently refused treatment and took food only infrequently. Clearly designed to transgress the boundaries of deprivation that could be reasonably attributed to solidarity with her countrymen, Weil's actions expressed her need for total personal affliction in the suffering world to which she was so sensitive.

On August 17, Weil was transferred to Grosvenor Sanatorium in Ashford, Kent, and on the afternoon of August 24, 1943, she lapsed into a coma and died later that evening. The newspapers in the area announced that the coroner's inquest had ruled her death a case of suicide by starvation, although medical reports were confusing and conflicting. At the age of thirty-four, Weil had reached the end of one of the most unusual and controversial pilgrimages in recent history.

## Summary

In her short life, Simone Weil was a striking teacher of philosophy, a dedicated left-militant, a provocative essayist on social and religious issues, and an exceptional, though controversial, personality. In her final years and posthumously for a much larger audience (when her essays, notes, fragments, poems, and letters were first published in book form), she gained an even more paradoxical notoriety as a "Catholic saint outside the church."

While her later social thought, exemplified in the political sociology of *L'Enracinement* (1949; *The Need for Roots*, 1952), still emphasized the centrality of the worker and his alienation and oppression, it demonstrates less of her earlier insight. The antipolitics and the libertarianism, egalitarianism, and pacifism had partly submerged themselves into a heightened spiritual quest that undercut merely human social questions. Weil's remarkable intensity and impassioned earnestness, combined with sophisticated philosophical and historical perceptions and abilities, made her a poignant witness to the possible social-religious transcendence of human suffering.

**Bibliography**

Coles, Robert. *Simone Weil: A Modern Pilgrimage.* Reading, Mass.: Addison-Wesley, 1987. In this intelligent and interpretive portrait written by a Harvard psychiatrist and humanities professor, the author describes Weil's major quests and obsessions in an effort to comprehend her inspiring and contradictory nature. Also contains notes and bibliography.

Dunaway, John M. *Simone Weil.* Boston: Twayne, 1984. This brief sketch is intended as an introduction to the subject, primarily for the use of the nonspecialist. A bibliography, extensive notes, and references are also provided.

Fiori, Gabriella. *Simone Weil: An Intellectual Biography.* Translated by Joseph K. Berrigan. Athens: University of Georgia Press, 1989. This lengthy and well-written synthesis of Weil's life and thought is based upon evidence solely provided by individuals closely familiar with Weil and her works. Extensive notes and a bibliography of primary and secondary works are included.

Grey, Christopher. "Towards a Critique of Managerialism: The Contribution of Simone Weil." *Journal of Management Studies* 33, no. 5 (September, 1996). The author considers Weil's writings on management and organizations, which have historically been ignored, and focuses on their relevance to contemporary forms of management.

Kazin, Alfred. "A Genius of the Spiritual Life." *The New York Review of Books* 43, no. 7 (April 18, 1996). Kazin examines Weil's search for spiritual meaning beyond traditional Jewish and Christian doctrines.

McFarland, Dorothy Tuck. *Simone Weil.* New York: Ungar, 1983. This brief but very readable study underscores the continuity of Weil's work beneath the seeming reversal of political positions. Also contains footnotes and primary and secondary bibliography.

Pétrement, Simone. *Simone Weil: A Life.* Translated by Raymond Rosenthal. New York: Pantheon, 1976; London: Mowbrays, 1977. Written by one of Weil's closest friends, this lengthy standard biography of Weil is particularly useful for the documents it contains and for the author's efforts at ordering and dating these documents. Numerous notes and illustrations are also included.

*Genevieve Slomski*

## KURT WEILL

*Born:* March 2, 1900; Dessau, Germany
*Died:* April 3, 1950; New York, New York
*Area of Achievement:* Music
*Contribution:* Weill was one of the outstanding composers of the generation that came to maturity after World War I. He broke away from the Romantic, emotional style of Wagnerian opera to create a revolutionary new form: the opera of sharp social satire. After his emigration to the United States, Weill turned away from his earlier "serious" works to become one of the top composers of Broadway musicals in the 1940's.

### Early Life

Kurt Julian Weill was born in Dessau, Germany, on March 2, 1900. His father, Albert, was the cantor at the synagogue in Dessau, and a composer in his own right. His mother, Emma (née Ackermann), loved literature and maintained an extensive library for the family. Weill was reared as an Orthodox Jew, along with his two elder brothers, Nathan and Hans Jacob, and his younger sister, Ruth. The Weill children were all taught music, and often attended performances of Wagnerian operas at the Ducal Court Theater, or Hofoper, in Dessau.

Weill had begun to compose by the time he was twelve years old. When he was fifteen, his father arranged for him to study with Albert Bing, a respected composer who served as the associate musical director of the Hofoper. In April, 1918, Weill went to Berlin to attend the Hochschule für Musik. There he studied composition under Wagner disciple Engelbert Humperdinck (composer of the opera *Hänsel und Gretel*, 1893), harmony and counterpoint with Friedrich E. Koch, and conducting with Rudolf Krasselt. He wrote a symphonic poem based on Rainer Maria Rilke's *Die Weise von Liebe und Tod des Cornets Christoph Rilke* (1906; *The Tale of the Love and Death of Cornet Christopher Rilke*, 1932). This piece was considered good enough to be performed by the Hochschule orchestra, and it won for him a scholarship given by the Felix Mendelssohn Foundation. Despite his success, however, Weill felt stifled by the old-fashioned musical ideas taught at the Hochschule, so he left it after one year to return to Dessau. There, he worked for three months as a repetiteur, or singing coach, at the Hofoper under his former teacher, Albert Bing. In December, 1919, he took a temporary staff conducting job with the tiny Lüdenscheid Civic Opera in Westphalia. There, he received a solid training in making music for the theater.

In September, 1920, Weill auditioned and was accepted into the master class in composition at the Berlin Academy of Art, which was taught by Ferruccio Busoni, an avant-garde composer who Weill greatly admired. Weill became one of Busoni's favorite students, and he studied under him for three years, until December, 1923. During that time, Weill wrote several works, including a children's ballet, *Die Zaubernacht*, which was performed in Berlin in 1922 and again two years later in New York under the title *Magic Night*; a *Divertimento* for orchestra and male chorus; his *Sinfonia Sacra* Op. 6; *Frauentanz* (women's dance), a cycle of seven songs for soprano and small instrumental ensemble, which was performed at the Salzburg Festival in 1924 and which won for him a contract with Universal Edition, a leading publisher of new music; and his String Quartet Op. 8. This piece was first performed for

the Novembergrüppe, an association of radical artists of which Weill was a member.

### Life's Work

In 1922, Weill met Georg Kaiser, perhaps Germany's most significant expressionist playwright. In January, 1924, Kaiser offered to collaborate with Weill on a ballet based on Kaiser's play *Der Protagonist* (1922; the protagonist). They worked for two months on the idea before they decided that the piece would work much better as an opera than a ballet. While Kaiser revised his libretto, Weill took the opportunity to compose his best instrumental work to date, a Concerto for Violin and Wind Orchestra, which was first performed in Paris in June, 1925.

Weill visited Kaiser at his country home during the rest of 1924 and early 1925 to complete the music for *Der Protagonist.* While he was there, in the summer of 1924, he became acquainted with an actress named Lotte Lenya (née Karoline Blaumauer). By the end of that year, they had taken an apartment together. They were married on January 28, 1926. Lenya was not Jewish, and Weill's parents disapproved of the match. By that time, however, Weill felt disaffected by the religion of his childhood and rebellious against middle-class conventions in life as well as music, and so his Bohemian, Gentile bride suited him very well. Their marriage was sometimes troubled, and once they divorced and remarried, but then they remained together until he died. Afterward, Lenya protected and promoted Weill's legacy until his music became well known around the world.

Weill and Kaiser completed the opera *Der Protagonist* in April, 1925. It was a fabulous success at its premier at the Dresden State Opera on March 27, 1926, and it marked the turning point in Weill's career. He was now considered one of the leading composers of theatrical music in Germany. Weill started writing another opera with Kaiser, a comic one-act piece called *Der Zar lässt sich photographieren* (1927; the czar has his picture taken) in March, 1927, the same month in which he began one of the most famous collaborations in twentieth century theater: his association with Marxist playwright Bertolt Brecht.

Weill and Brecht began with a plan for a full-length opera called *Aufstieg und Fall der Stadt Mahagonny* (1930; *The Rise and Fall of the City of Mahagonny,* 1957) based on part of Brecht's poetry collection, *Hauspostille* (1927, 1951; *A Manual of Piety,* 1966). In the meantime, however, Weill received a commission for a short, one-act opera to be performed at the Baden-Baden Festival of German Chamber Music that summer. He decided to use the commission to write five songs as a preliminary study for the opera. The result, *Mahagonny Songspiel*, premiered at the Baden-Baden Festival on July 17, 1927, with one of the female roles being sung by Lenya. Brecht then arranged to write the play that would open the new theater managed by impresario Ernst Robert Aufricht. *Die Dreigroschenoper* (*The Threepenny Opera*, 1949) was based on John Gay's *The Beggar's Opera* (1728) and featured songs by Weill. After a turbulent rehearsal period, it opened on August 31, 1928, at the Theater am Schiffbauerdamm in Berlin, to immense and immediate success.

*The Threepenny Opera* brought Weill popularity and financial security. He completed several other commissions before finishing the score for *Rise and Fall of the City of Mahagonny* in April, 1929. During that summer, he and Brecht collaborated on another musical play called *Happy End*, which premiered on September 2, 1929, at the Theater am Schiffbauerdamm. Before it opened, however, Brecht decided that the play was too frivolous, that it violated his belief that theater should teach, not entertain. He renounced his authorship of the play, and it closed after a few performances.

In the six months between the disastrous opening of *Happy End* and the premier of *The Rise and Fall of the City of Mahagonny* at the Leipzig Opera House on March 9, 1930, the stock market experienced its infamous crash that destroyed the economies of countries all around the world. The unemployment crisis in Germany had given the Nazis a new strength, and they put Weill, who was Jewish, on their list of artists that they reviled. On the opening night of *The Rise and Fall of the City of Mahagonny,* the Nazis interrupted the performance by starting fistfights in the aisles of the theater. Performances of *The Rise and Fall of the City of Mahagonny* in other cities were cancelled by Nazi-led town councils. By 1933, the Nazis had succeeded in their campaign to drive the works of Weill off the stages of Germany.

In the meantime, Brecht and Weill were growing apart. Brecht became increasingly autocratic and devoted to Marxism, whereas Weill grew more tolerant, exploring the tensions in his work between the atonality of the modern fashion and the traditional, romantic melodies he remembered from his youth. Their famous, productive partnership came to an end after only three years.

Weill wrote one more opera with Kaiser, *Der Silbersee* (silver lake), which opened simultaneously to good reviews in Leipzig, Erfurt, and Magdeburg on February 18, 1933. On February 27, Adolf Hitler began his crackdown on his political opponents. On March 21, Weill learned that he was about to be arrested by the Gestapo, so he packed a few belongings in a car and escaped to France. Weill's music was popular in Paris, and yet his exile there was unhappy. He felt betrayed by his homeland. Also, he had lost all of his money when he left Germany, and his relationship with his wife had become very strained. He reluctantly agreed to write a final piece with Brecht, a ballet called *Die sieben Todsünden der Kleinbürger* (*The Seven Deadly Sins of the Petit Bourgeois*, 1961), which premiered at the Théâtre des Champs Élysées on June 7, 1933. He composed several more pieces before being commissioned, late in the summer of 1934, to write the score for Franz Werfel's Biblical drama *Der Weg der Verheissung* (1935; *The Eternal Road*, 1936), which tells the story of the wanderings of the Jewish people toward their goal of the Promised Land. Weill's persecution at the hands of the Nazis caused him to reidentify with his Jewish ancestry, and he used the religious music of his youth as the basis for his score. The play was scheduled to open in New York in early 1936, and Weill was to conduct the performance. So, in September, 1935, he and Lenya, with whom he had recently reconciled, sailed for the United States.

For financial reasons, the production of *The Eternal Road* was delayed, so Weill took a commission from the Group Theatre to write the score for *Johnny Johnson*, an antiwar satire written by Paul Green, which opened in New York on November 19, 1936, and closed only sixty-eight performances later, the victim of bad reviews. *The Eternal Road* finally opened on January 7, 1937. Unfortunately, budget overruns doomed this lavish production to financial disaster, even though it played to packed houses.

Weill then collaborated with Maxwell Anderson on a political satire based on Washington Irving's book *A History of New York* (1809). Weill's first Broadway success, *Knickerbocker Holiday*, the score of which includes the famous "September Song," opened at the Ethel Barrymore Theater in New York on October 19, 1938. Weill teamed with Moss Hart and Ira Gershwin for his next Broadway hit. *Lady in the Dark*, starring Gertrude Lawrence and Danny Kaye, opened at the Alvin Theater in New York on January 23, 1941, and ran for two years. His next musical, called *One Touch of Venus*, was written with S. J. Perelman and Ogden Nash. It opened at the Imperial Theater in New York on October 7, 1943, starred Mary Martin, and was Weill's greatest Broadway success.

Weill wrote one more play with Gershwin, along with Gershwin's friend Edwin Justus Mayer, an operetta based on Mayer's play *The Firebrand* (1924). *The Firebrand of Florence*, starring Lenya in only her second American stage appearance, was a complete disaster when it opened on March 22, 1945. After this, Weill deliberately changed his musical style from a slick, Broadway idiom to a simpler, American folk sound. He collaborated with Elmer Rice to write the opera *Street Scene*, based on Rice's 1929 play of the same name. It opened in New York at the Adelphi Theater on January 9, 1947, to critical acclaim but only moderate box-office success. Weill wrote a folk opera, *Down in the Valley*, for the students at the University of Indiana at Bloomington, where it premiered on July 15, 1948. His next musical, *Love Life*, written with Alan Jay Lerner, opened on October 7, 1948, at the Forty-sixth Street Theater in New York, and received only mediocre critical reviews.

Weill's last work was written with his good friend Maxwell Anderson. It was a "musical tragedy" based on the novel *Cry, the Beloved Country* (1948) by Alan Paton. *Lost in the Stars* premiered at the Music Box Theater in New York on October 30, 1949. The production did very well, at first. Weill and Anderson began work on a musical based on Mark Twain's 1884 novel *The Adventures of Huckleberry Finn.* Then, in January, 1950, the box office for *Lost in the Stars* began to deteriorate. Weill became increasingly irritable, and he suffered a terrible attack of the psoriasis that had plagued him all of his life. On the night of March 16, he awoke with chest pains. He was admitted to Flower-Fifth Avenue Hospital in New York, where his condition gradually grew worse. He died there, at 7:00 P.M. on Monday, April 3, 1950, with Lenya and his friends Maxwell and Mab Anderson at his bedside.

### Summary

From 1924, with the premier of *Der Protagonist*, to 1935, when he emigrated to the United States, Kurt Weill was considered one of the leading composers in Europe. He worked to simplify music to make it more accessible to a popular audience and pioneered the technique of "alienation" in opera music, that is, writing music that goes against the stage action, thereby causing the listener to think about the message of the opera, rather than merely becoming emotionally involved with it. He believed that art should take a political stand against social injustice. In his music, there is always a tension between an atonal, intellectual sound and the melodious, emotional style of music that he heard as a child.

Weill fervently embraced his new home in the United States and totally rejected his German works, as he believed Germany had done to him. Indeed, after his arrival in New York, he never spoke German again. As he strove to write in an exclusively American idiom, his rebellion against sentiment in art mellowed, and his music became more rich and free. Although his American pieces lacked the intellectual sophistication of his European works, they nevertheless retained a sense of social consciousness that was very courageous, especially in the context of an American society that was growing increasingly nationalistic and conservative.

It is ironic that "Mack the Knife" from *The Threepenny Opera*, a play that denounces capitalism, has been used in an advertising campaign to sell McDonald's hamburgers. This fact testifies to Weill's extraordinary success as one of the few twentieth century composers whose music can be considered both "serious" and "popular."

**Bibliography**

Drew, David. *Kurt Weill: A Handbook.* London: Faber, and Berkeley: University of California Press, 1987. Drew is the foremost authority on Weill. He presents detailed chronologies of Weill's compositions, as well as a description of his method of composition.

Jarman, Douglas. *Kurt Weill: An Illustrated Biography.* London: Orbis, and Bloomington: Indiana University Press, 1982. This concise but complete biography serves as an ideal introduction to the composer's life and works.

Kowalke, Kim H., ed. *A New Orpheus: Essays on Kurt Weill.* New Haven, Conn.: Yale University Press, 1986. This is a collection of seventeen essays from the 1983 international conference on Weill held at Yale University. They are arranged according to the chronology of his career and are suitable for general readers.

Sanders, Ronald. *The Days Grow Short: The Life and Music of Kurt Weill.* London: Weidenfeld and Nicolson, and New York: Holt Rinehart, 1980. This detailed biography gives psychological insight to Weill's music. Sanders also outlines the backgrounds of the people and events who were important in Weill's life.

Schebera, Jurgen. *Kurt Weill: An Illustrated Life. Translated by Caroline Murphy.* New Haven, Conn.: Yale University Press, 1995. Balanced biographical study of composer Kurt Weill providing detailed information on his life, performances of his works, and critical reception of his compositions.

Spoto, Donald. *Lenya: A Life.* London: Viking, and Boston: Little Brown, 1989. Lenya's fame rests mostly on her interpretation of her husband's works. Along with that, however, she led a long and fascinating life. This book reveals some of the details of Weill's and Lenya's troubled marriage.

Weill, Kurt, and Lotte Lenya. *The Letters of Kurt Weill and Lotte Lenya.* Edited by and translated by Lys Symonette and Kim H. Kowalke. Berkeley: University of California Press, 1996. This volume includes 375 letters, 17 telegrams, and 18 postcards sent between Weill and Lotte Lenya. Supplemented by footnotes and explanations, this book provides an intimate look at their relationship and the times in which they lived.

*Pamela Canal*

# CHAIM WEIZMANN

*Born:* November 27, 1874; Motol, Poland, Russian Empire

*Died:* November 9, 1952; Rehovot, Israel

*Areas of Achievement:* Government, politics, statecraft, and chemistry

*Contribution:* Although a world-class chemist and scientific researcher, Weizmann's greatest contributions and achievements must be regarded as his leadership of the World Zionist Organization for twelve years and his central role in helping to forge the new State of Israel. He was the first president of that new nation from 1949 through 1952.

## Early Life

Chaim Azriel Weizmann was born in the small Russian (later Polish) village of Motol, near Pinsk, to a Jewish family that lived amid impoverished circumstances. Motol was situated in the Pale of Settlement, a region along Russia's western frontier and the only place in the country where Jews could reside legally. Even there, however, they existed under the constant threat of persecution and periodic massacres known as pogroms. Life was hard for everyone living within the Pale. Yet Chaim's large family, though of meager means, fared better than many other Russian Jews. Chaim was the third of fifteen children born to his parents, Ozer and Rachel Weizmann. Ozer supported the family as a timber merchant, a somewhat seasonal business that gradually improved over time.

The Weizmann children grew up in an enlightened atmosphere that encouraged learning but that also promoted reverence for tradition. Their home was filled with books written in the Yiddish, Hebrew, and Russian languages. Zionist periodicals also found their way into the house and influenced young Chaim. Ozer Weizmann was determined that his children should learn as much as they could about the world outside the Pale of Settlement. In an unprecedented step for a family living in a village like Motol, the elder Weizmann sent two sons, Chaim and an elder brother, twenty-five miles from home to study at the secondary school in Pinsk. There Weizmann's aptitude for science was fostered, and he decided on a career in chemistry.

At that time Pinsk was a center of Zionist beliefs and the home for an early Zionist group. Young Weizmann increasingly became involved with the movement and absorbed its beliefs. Upon his graduation from the Pinsk Gymnasium in 1891, he thought of himself as a committed Zionist.

After graduation, Weizmann left Russia for Germany and then Switzerland to continue his education, since his own country enforced university quotas restricting the admissions of Jewish students. After an unhappy and financially stressful year (1892) at the Darmstadt Polytechnic Institute, Weizmann returned home for a brief period only to set out again for the German capital, Berlin, where he was to attend the prestigious Charlottenberg Polytechnic Institute in 1893. In Berlin, Weizmann's Zionism matured as he joined with a group of intellectuals from the Russo-Jewish Academic Society, an organization he later regarded as the cradle of the modern Zionist movement. In 1896, he came under the influence of Asher Ginzberg, better known as Ahad Ha'am, a Hebrew essayist and an early Zionist theoretician. Weizmann adopted the approach of Ha'am, who advocated a slow and careful Jewish settlement process, making Palestine first a spiritual and cultural center for world Judaism, and who also stressed the importance of reaching an agreement with the Arabs of Palestine.

Because a favorite professor joined the staff of the University of Fribourg in Switzerland, Weizmann went there to study in 1897. After three more years of hard work, he obtained a Ph.D. magna cum laude (1900) and shortly thereafter was appointed *Privatdozent* (lecturer) in organic chemistry at the University of Geneva. The adult pattern of Weizmann's life was now established. He would blend a love of science with a passion for Zionism and end up directing the course of an entire race of people.

## Life's Work

For a half century, beginning in 1900, Weizmann devoted his life to considering the needs and aspirations of his people, deciding how the Jewish world should support Zionism and directing the desire for Jewish national rebirth. By the time of his graduation, he was becoming a well-known member of the World Zionist Organization. It had been created in 1897 by the First Zionist Congress, which Theodor Herzl had convened to bring about the establishment of a Jewish home in Palestine. Weizmann first served as a delegate to the Second Zionist Congress held in 1898 in Basel, Switzerland, while he was finishing his doctorate. At that time he was elected to the Congress Steering Committee (responsible for finances) and immediately began to make formal progress in the leadership of the movement. In 1900, Herzl convened the Fourth Zionist Congress in London, and Weizmann made his first visit to England.

By 1901, Weizmann, at age twenty-seven, found himself at odds with Herzl's ideas and efforts, which he considered too visionary, so he formed the first opposition group in the Zionist movement. This group greatly influenced Zionist affairs for a time and provided the vehicle through which Weizmann rose to prominence. Between 1904 and 1914, Weizmann devoted more time to his scientific career and personal life, though he remained an active Zionist. The death of Herzl in 1904 left the Zionist movement in a state of shock, and Weizmann, Herzl's as-yet-unrecognized heir, wanted time to think and to make a fresh start somewhere. So he set out for Great Britain, taking an academic position at the University of Manchester, where he also became the leader of the Manchester group of Zionists, which he headed for fifteen years. In 1905, in Manchester, he met Arthur Balfour (then Great Britain's prime minister) and convinced him that Palestine was the proper national homeland for Jews. Their meeting established a working relationship that eventually resulted in the Balfour Declaration of 1917.

In 1906, Weizmann married Vera Chatzman whom he had first met in Geneva six years before, when she was a medical student and he a doctoral candidate in chemistry. Two sons were born to them, and, though the marriage would be marked by many work-related separations, they shared a love that bridged these gaps.

In 1907, Weizmann took an important step toward assuming Herzl's mantle of leadership. At the Eighth Zionist Congress, he delivered a major speech on what he termed synthetic Zionism. He attempted to reconcile the two major schools of Zionist thought. Political Zionism, which Herzl advocated, promoted diplomacy and aimed at securing political guarantees for the establishment of a Jewish home in Palestine. While this was important, as Weizmann said, the achievements of practical Zionism—the actual establishment of settlers in the Yishuv (the Jewish Community in Palestine)—would create the strongest possible political base for a homeland. Therefore, Zionist leaders ought to strive for a synthesis between the two concerns.

Shortly after the speech, Weizmann made his first visit to Palestine. While there, he helped to

found the Palestine Land Development Company and stepped up his campaign for the Jewish settlement of Palestine when he returned to his home in England, which he had grown to appreciate. In 1910, Weizmann became a naturalized British subject and received two more doctoral degrees while at Manchester (a D.Sc. degree in 1909 and an LL.D. degree in 1919).

With the coming of World War I, international attention was diverted from the Zionist cause, and consensus broke down within the movement. Realizing the difficulty of conducting international Zionist politics under such circumstances, Weizmann focused his attention on helping England with the war effort through scientific research. He created a process for synthesizing acetone, which alleviated a shortage in the manufacture of explosives. He then directed the large-scale manufacture of the invaluable chemical. In 1916, Weizmann was appointed by Prime Minister David Lloyd George superintendent of the Admiralty Laboratories, a position that he retained until 1919.

Not satisfied with the direction taken by the secret Sykes-Picot Agreement of May, 1916 (a pact between the French and British that divided up the Middle East), Weizmann, when he learned of it, used his diplomatic talents to get the British to reconsider the pact as well as the plight of the Jewish people and their desire for a homeland. The result was the Balfour Declaration of November, 1917, a statement that seemed to throw full British support behind the Zionist cause.

By the end of 1917, Weizmann had become, in the eyes of many Jews (and deservedly so), a great emancipator and promoter of Jewish freedom. In 1920, he was elected unopposed as president of the World Zionist Organization. For twelve years Weizmann served as the president of that body (from 1920 to 1931 and again in 1935), trying to appease Zionist opponents and working on compromises between Zionists, Jewish settlers in Palestine, Arabs, and the British. From 1921 onward, he traveled the world at a dizzying pace, preaching Zionist ideology and raising funds at mass rallies. On April 2, 1921, Weizmann arrived in New York City on the first of many trips to the United States to drum up enthusiasm and financial support for his organization. Weizmann managed to turn the United States into Zionism's great provider during the 1920's.

Great Britain, in the 1920's, retreated from its commitment to support a Jewish national home in the face of Arab nationalism and civil strife. A summer-long Arab uprising in 1929 took the lives of more than one hundred Jews. Weizmann's years of negotiations only brought British policy changes unfavorable to Zionist aims. The British restricted Jewish immigration and limited Jews's land purchases. Ardent and extremist Zionists grew impatient and challenged Weizmann's leadership of the Zionist movement by submitting him to a vote of nonconfidence at the 1931 Zionist Congress. He was not reelected as president of the World Zionist Organization and Jewish Agency for Palestine, the expanded Zionist body he had helped form in 1929.

Weizmann returned to his science for a time, founding the Daniel Sieff Research Institute (1934) at Rehovot, Palestine—his second home. Yet, with the rise of Adolf Hitler's Germany and continued British limitation of immigrants to Palestine, Weizmann was returned to the presidency of the World Zionist Organization for one more year. He was surprised over, but happily supported, the recommendation of a 1937 British commission to partition Palestine into Jewish and Arab sectors. Ultimately the plan failed because the Arabs rejected it.

During World War II, Weizmann directed the Sieff Research Institute, which provided essential pharmaceuticals to the Allies; he also helped develop a method for producing synthetic rubber. Because of his denunciation (1945) of underground Jewish guerrilla groups such as the Irgun (led by Menachem Begin), which attacked British military posts and Arabs in Palestine in order to gain independence for a Jewish Palestine, Weizmann incurred the wrath of Zionist leaders. He again lost the presidency of his Zionist organization in 1946.

That the Jewish people as a whole, and many Zionist leaders in particular, continued to revere Weizmann is attested by the fact that he not only appeared before the United Nations as Zionism's most knowledgeable and articulate champion (1947) but also was sent to the United States in 1948 to reconfirm to President Harry S. Truman the rightness of an independent State of Israel and the importance of including the region known as the Negev within the boundaries of the Jewish state. His intervention led to U.S. recognition of the new State of Israel in May, 1948. In February, 1949, Weizmann was officially elected President of the State of Israel.

After 1949, his work as a theoretician having been accomplished, Weizmann was relegated in effect to a position of bystander in the government. Prime Minister David Ben-Gurion held all the real authority and expected Weizmann to be only a figurehead. The latter participated in no cabinet meetings and had little say in the practical affairs of state as his health and morale deteriorated.

Worn out by demanding itineraries, arduous political strife, and personal frustrations, Weizmann died in November of 1952, only days short of his seventy-eighth birthday. The fallen Zionist leader was mourned throughout the world and was buried on his estate at Rehovot, in the nation he was instrumental in bringing into being.

### Summary

Chaim Weizmann was a man of many attainments, and his impact on the world was great. The Weizmann legacy is really twofold: a new nation and scientific achievement. His scientific genius influenced the outcomes of two world wars. The Weizmann Institute of Science, built on the foundation of the Sieff Institute, became an important research facility for Israeli and world scientists. Weizmann wrote numerous important scientific papers (more than one hundred), many political essays, and left his memoirs in a book entitled *Trial and Error: The Autobiography of Chaim Weizmann* (1949). He was responsible for registering 110 patents, either singly or in collaboration.

Above all, however, Weizmann dedicated his life to the service of the Jewish people and to the quest of an ideal formulated in his youth. For more than half a century, he worked tirelessly, traveling around the world as leader of Zionism, to see that the Zionist ideal became a practical reality. Weizmann changed the course of history for an entire race of people. More than any other individual, Weizmann—with his powers of persuasion and negotiation, international contacts, passion, intelligence, and vision—enabled the Jewish people to realize a nearly two-thousand-year-old dream. It has been said that the State of Israel was constructed, in part, in the image of Weizmann—even though others tried to keep his influence on government from becoming too great after 1949. Accordingly, his name and ideas are recognized as being an important part of any discussion on Israel's future. Weizmann believed that the issue of Arab-Jewish relations was one of utmost importance. He reminded his followers that Zionism could exist only as it kept justice and the nonviolent resolution of disputes at the forefront of its concerns.

**Bibliography**

Amdur, Richard. *Chaim Weizmann.* New York: Chelsea House, 1988. Written especially for young adults, but by no means juvenile in its presentation, this succinct (one-hundred-page) biography is clearly written and chronicles the major events in the life of Weizmann. Contains many outstanding photographs.

Feis, Herbert. *The Birth of Israel.* New York: Norton, 1969. Of the voluminous literature on Zionism, this short, easy-to-read book puts Weizmann's life in the context of the birth of the nation over which he presided.

Kauffman, George B., and Isaac Mayo. "Chaim Weizmann (1874-1952): Chemist, Biotechnologist, and Statesman, the Fateful Interweaving of Political Conviction and Scientific Talent." *Journal of Chemical Education* 71, no. 3 (March, 1994). Profile of Chaim Weizmann including his efforts to gain support for Zionism.

Reinharz, Jehuda. *Chaim Weizmann: The Making of a Statesman.* New York: Oxford University Press, 1993. This is the second in a planned three-volume biography of Weizmann. This volume covers the years 1914-1922 and ends with the British mandate for Palestine.

———. *Chaim Weizmann: The Making of a Zionist Leader.* New York: Oxford University Press, 1985. This very scholarly volume of some length details and analyzes the first half of the life of Weizmann from his ancestry and birth to the outbreak of World War I. Its real strength lies in its extensive notes and its comprehensive bibliography and index.

Rose, Norman. *Chaim Weizmann, a Biography.* New York: Viking, 1986; London: Weidenfeld and Nicolson, 1987. This standard comprehensive one-volume presentation of Weizmann's life is balanced (presenting both successes and failures), well written, and well documented. The emphasis is on diplomatic and political history and makes extensive use of Weizmann's letters. Contains two sections of instructive and interesting photographs.

Weisgal, Meyer W., and Joel Carmichael, eds. *Chaim Weizmann: A Biography by Several Hands.* London: Weidenfeld and Nicolson, 1962; New York: Atheneum, 1963. Written by a group of Weizmann's disciples and admirers in Israel, England, and the United States, the work begins with a survey of the biographical facts of his life. Each following chapter describes and appraises a particular aspect of Weizmann's activity. His contribution to chemistry is well evaluated. The book is illustrated with thirty photographs of Weizmann from childhood to old age.

Weizmann, Chaim. *The Essential Chaim Weizmann.* Edited and compiled by Barnet Litvinoff. London: Weidenfeld and Nicolson, and New York: Holmes and Meier, 1982. This comprehensive source book presents selections of Weizmann's most significant and penetrating ideas as expressed in his letters, speeches, and writings. Particularly helpful is a succinctly annotated chronology, year by year, of Weizmann's life, which appears at the front of the book.

*Andrew C. Skinner*

## ORSON WELLES

*Born:* May 6, 1915; Kenosha, Wisconsin
*Died:* October 10, 1985; Hollywood, California
*Areas of Achievement:* Film, theater, and entertainment
*Contribution:* As an actor, director, and writer, Welles breathed fresh life into all the media he explored: stage, radio, and film. Most important, his innovative cinematic techniques in such areas as lighting, camera angles and focus, and sound continue to influence film directors.

### Early Life

George Orson Welles, the second son of Beatrice and Richard Welles, was born in Kenosha, Wisconsin. When he was three, the family moved to Chicago. His mother—an accomplished amateur pianist—saw to his education, immersing the precocious child in literature, the visual arts, and music as she sought to enter a Chicago society that boasted some of the United States' most prominent Midwestern families.

Doctor Maurice Bernstein, a man of varied medical interests and pioneering work, was a frequent visitor to the Welles home and the probable lover of Beatrice. When the family moved to Chicago, Bernstein moved with them. With the deaths of Beatrice when Orson was nine and Richard when he was fifteen, Bernstein became his legal guardian; indeed, Bernstein had acted as guardian for the boy since Beatrice's death. Bernstein and Richard had recognized the extraordinary talents and intellect of Orson and sent him to the famous Todd School in Woodstock, Illinois, where he received a more disciplined education.

After completion of his studies, the sixteen-year-old Welles took a trip to Ireland, where, after talking himself into an audition, he performed many plays at the Gate Theatre in Dublin. His performances earned him excellent reviews, made more remarkable by the fact that he often portrayed characters more than twice his age.

### Life's Work

After leaving Ireland, Welles arrived in New York in 1933 and became part of a touring company of William Shakespeare's *Romeo and Juliet,* headed by the husband-and-wife acting team of Guthrie McClintic and Katharine Cornell. His performance as Tybalt drew the attention of John Houseman, himself an actor and producer. Together they founded the Mercury Theater, their first production being a version of Shakespeare's *Julius Caesar* set in fascist Italy that became the talk of New York in 1937.

However, the production that made the Mercury Theater possible was the now infamous "voodoo" version of Shakespeare's *Macbeth* in 1936, staged at the Lafayette Theater in Harlem and later moved to Broadway. This adaptation of William Shakespeare's play set in the jungles of Haiti was produced by the Negro Theater Unit, part of the Federal Theater Project of the Depression-era 1930's and directed by the twenty-year-old Welles. A theatrical sensation that turned away thousands (an estimated ten thousand people crowded the streets of Harlem on opening night), *Macbeth* ran for ten weeks before moving to Broadway.

In the same year that *Macbeth* was staged, Welles began his famous radio adaptations of literary classics, which became known as Mercury Theater on the Air (later known as the Campbell Playhouse). He starred in the radio series *The Shadow* playing the mysterious Lamont Cranston. With several projects competing for his time—stage productions, radio adaptations, speaking engagements, and essays on the theater—he was quickly earning the nickname "Boy Wonder," which would follow him for much of his career. Welles enjoyed several theatrical successes over the next two years, but it was his notorious radio adaptation of H. G. Wells's *War of the Worlds* for Columbia Broadcasting System (CBS) that gave him national fame. The 1938 production, aired on Halloween night, dramatized a supposed invasion of Martians in Grovers Mill, New Jersey. Of the thousands who heard the program, many panicked, believing the United States (and the world) was under attack.

Although Welles and his cast were condemned by the press, disciplined by CBS, and threatened by the Federal Communications Commission (FCC) over the program, it led to an unprecedented offer by Radio-Keith-Orpheum (RKO) Pictures Corporation in 1939. Welles would be given total creative control over any project he might choose to develop—an offer unheard of in times when the studios "owned" stars, directors, and writers. After a disastrous first attempt at a motion picture project that never materialized, Welles followed up on RKO's unique offer by turning out a film perennially chosen as the finest film ever made, *Citizen Kane* (1941). Modeled after publishing magnate William Randolph Hearst, the film in fact draws its particulars from Welles's own youth. While *Citizen Kane* was not a commercial success, those knowledgeable about film marveled at the creativity and innovation found in Welles's cinematic technique.

The following year, Welles adapted Booth Tarkington's novel, *The Magnificent Ambersons* (1918), about life in a small Midwestern town at the beginning of the twentieth century, into a film of the same name. Although the film was nominated for an Academy Award, it too was unpopular with audiences. In fact, as measured by profit, Welles's artistic successes were few. Continually plagued with cost overruns, dangerous liberal views in an increasingly conservative business, and erratic behavior that alienated studio executives, he found himself with few opportunities and literally dozens of failed or unfinished projects.

However, Welles continued to find enough financial backing to turn out impressive films in which he both starred and directed, such as *The Stranger* (1946) and *The Lady From Shanghai* (1948), which costarred his second wife, Rita Hayworth. If Welles despaired as to where his career had taken him, he seemed intent on working on projects of his own choosing, which often had little commercial appeal. Thus he returned to Shakespeare, filming *Macbeth* (1948)—shot in three weeks for a film company best known for cheap westerns—and *Othello* (1952), a remarkable motion picture that took three years to complete. Although locations and cast members changed throughout the filming and stories abound about how the actors had to improvise scenes for lack of money, the critics once again recognized the talent of Welles: *Othello* was awarded the Grand Prix at the Cannes Film Festival.

During the 1950's, Welles toured Germany and performed on the London stage, then returned to the United States and directed and acted in Shakespeare's *King Lear* in New York. As busy as ever, he returned to Hollywood, once again using his cinematic art to psychologically profile authority corrupted and gone astray, a favorite theme of his. The result was *Touch of Evil* (1958), a *film noir* classic, which he directed and in which he starred as the rogue detective Hank Quinlan. In 1962, he adapted and directed Franz Kafka's *Der Prozess* (1925; *The Trial*, 1937), the nightmarish confrontation between the character Joseph K. and the nameless, faceless bureaucracy that condemns him. Four years later, Welles returned to his love for Shakespeare and filmed *Chimes at Midnight* (1966), an adaptation from Shakespeare's history plays of the fat knight Falstaff that he had staged in Belfast, Dublin, and London in 1960. The work of Welles in the 1970's and 1980's never achieved any of his former greatness. While he appeared as an actor in numerous films, his last completed film was *F For Fake* (1975), a part-documentary and part-scripted work that celebrates illusion and charlatans.

It remains unfortunate that many filmgoers are unfamiliar with Welles's work or unaware of the tremendous influence he had upon filmmaking. The last—and only—remembrance that many have of him is that of the perennial guest on late-night television talk shows or that of the corpulent, if elegant and refined, television spokesman for Paul Masson wines, in which his tag line on behalf of the company announced that they would "sell no wine before its time."

However, Welles's contribution to the arts, and film in particular, was not overlooked. He was honored with an Oscar for his life's work at the 1970 Academy Awards; in 1975, he received the Life Achievement Award from the American Film Institute; and in 1982, he was awarded the French Legion of Honor. At his death in Hollywood at the age of seventy, Welles left literally dozens of unfinished or unpublished screenplays and incomplete films.

### Summary

Virtually all work on the life and art of Orson Welles alludes to his failed genius, as if he came close but never quite made it, which is an unfortunate implication. While most studies accept the brilliance of the actor, director, playwright, and admitted self-promoter, the perceived "failure" of Welles is seen in his inability to maintain that excellence or to go beyond those promising years that led up to *Citizen Kane*. Perhaps his failure is that he achieved so much at a young age—he was twenty-six when *Citizen Kane* appeared—that he had nowhere to go or that, as an innovator and maverick in a film industry that was and is judged by the accepted norms and conventions of its business, he could not find the support and financial backing that more conventional filmmakers enjoyed.

*Orson Welles as the title character in* Macbeth

Certainly the strengths of Welles and strokes of brilliance were also his weaknesses. He had a restless, inexhaustible drive that could not be satisfied, even when numerous projects awaited completion. Indeed, several of his films were edited by others in his absence, and many scenes reshot with new directors because he was off on yet another venture. So too, his early successes merely confirmed the exceptional talents that he had been praised for since his childhood so that his extraordinary abilities became commonplace to a young man who knew he could do anything.

Yet his imagination and innovations on stage and especially in film are undeniable. He advanced the technique of "deep focus," wherein background action becomes as clear as that in the foreground (with the former commenting upon the latter); contrasted light and shadow for psychological effect; used a fluid camera technique of "long takes" to expand the dimensions of space beyond the limits of the screen; and developed the three-dimensional use of sound, which varied the audible range of voices and sounds according to their distance from the camera or viewer. These innovations, among others, still influence directors today and speak for the creative art of one of America's premiere talents.

## Bibliography

Brady, Frank. *Citizen Welles*. New York: Scribner, 1989; London: Hodder and Stoughton, 1990. An extensive, critical approach that is, even with its abundant anecdotes, an objective biography that credits Welles with a number of cinematic innovations.

Callow, Simon. *Orson Welles: The Road to Xanadu*. London: Cape, 1995; New York: Viking, 1996. An extensive biography by an actor, director, and writer who endeavors to look into the many influences that may have led to Welles's decline prior to his most famous film, *Citizen Kane*. The first of two proposed volumes, it covers Welles's life and career up to and including *Citizen Kane*.

Deleyto, C. "The Construction of Space and the Monstrous-Feminine in the Welles-Text." *Criti-*

*cal Survey* 10, no. 2 (May, 1998). Discusses the use and purpose of female characters in Welles' movies.

France, Richard. *The Theatre of Orson Welles*. Lewisburg, Pa.: Bucknell University Press, 1977. A study that concentrates on Welles's innovative and, at times, controversial stage work and its significant contributions to the theater.

Higham, Charles. *Orson Welles: The Rise and Fall of an American Genius*. New York: St. Martin's Press, 1985; London: Weidenfeld and Nicolson, 1986. A manageable biography that ends in the last year of Welles's life when the actor was preparing a film version of *King Lear*. Higham's biography clears away many of the repeated errors—begun by Welles himself—of the actor-director's life.

James, Howard. *The Complete Films of Orson Welles*. Secaucus, N.J.: Carol, 1985. A readable critique of the art and techniques of Welles's filmmaking, with some insightful comments on his innovations.

Leaming, Barbara. *Orson Welles, A Biography.* New York: Viking, and London: Weidenfeld and Nicolson, 1985. An "authorized" biography written in collaboration with Welles. While more intimate than other works on Welles, some of the events reported may, given Welles's penchant for misinformation about his past, be suspect.

McBride, Joseph. *Orson Welles*. Rev. ed. New York: Da Capo Press, 1996. A readable and manageable critical study by a former actor in Welles's unfinished film *The Other Side of the Wind*, which Welles was working on at the time of his death.

Naremore, James. *The Magic World of Orson Welles*. New York: Oxford University Press, 1978. One of the best critical examinations of Welles's work available; the criticism of Welles's films is excellent.

Rothwell, Kenneth S. "Orson Welles: Shakespeare for the Art Houses." *Cineaste* 24, no. 1 (Winter, 1998). Discusses Welles' body of Shakespearean work.

Thomson, David. *Rosebud: The Story of Orson Welles*. New York: Knopf, 1996; London: Abacus, 1997. An extensive account of Welles's life that is more critical than most written by an actor and authority on film. Thomson offers a number of personal observations, interpretations, and questions throughout the book that are, at times, bothersome.

*Wayne Narey*

## H. G. WELLS

*Born:* September 21, 1866; Bromley, Kent, England

*Died:* August 13, 1946; London, England

*Area of Achievement:* Literature

*Contribution:* Through his writings—both fiction and nonfiction—Wells became a significant shaper of liberal social thought in the first half of the twentieth century.

### Early Life

Herbert George Wells was born into a family struggling to maintain its place in the lower middle class. His father, Joseph, owned a shop but made more money coaching and playing professional cricket. After an injury prevented Joseph from playing cricket, Sarah, Herbert's mother, worked as a maid and housekeeper. A working wife ended the family's claim to middle-class status. Wells made much of, perhaps exaggerated, his family's struggles, and his characters often struggled with the conflicts of social respectability, personal satisfaction, and happiness.

One of the family's middle-class gestures was to send Wells to a private school, which was socially preferable to state schools even when, as in this case, the instruction was wretched. In 1874 Wells entered Thomas Morley's Commercial Academy. He learned little, but books supplied by his father during a six-month convalescence with a broken leg and access to the library of the estate where his mother was housekeeper provided him with an extensive, if haphazard, accumulation of knowledge.

In the early 1880's, Sarah arranged several apprenticeships for her son, twice with drapers and once with a pharmacist. Although his reading continued (at times in preference to his apprenticeship work) and he learned something of science from the pharmacist, Wells ultimately rejected the hopelessness of a career as a clerk. Out of concern that her son have a respectable occupation and to avoid forfeiting the apprenticeship fee, Sarah resisted. Finally, after coercing his mother with hints of suicide, Wells left the draper's trade and entered, in 1883, Midhurst Grammar School as a teaching scholar. As Wells remembers this time, he was expected to do most of the teaching and win government-sponsored scholarships to bring distinction and money to the school. Preparing for scholarship examinations helped expand his knowledge significantly.

More important, Wells discovered scholarships to study in the new government schools of science and technology. In 1884 he enrolled in the Normal School of Science in South Kensington, where he studied biology under the famous Thomas Henry Huxley, who has sometimes been called "Darwin's Bulldog" for his vigorous advocacy of evolution. Finally, the first-class intelligence of Wells met with first-class instruction and knowledge. Regrettably, illness kept Huxley from teaching after Wells's first year, and, not drawn to less inspired substitutes, he gave more and more attention to politics and writing for the *Science Schools Journal*, which he came to edit. Too late, he crammed for his exams and was forced to leave without a degree.

### Life's Work

To earn a living, Wells began teaching. In 1886 he met his cousin Isabel Mary Wells, whom he was to marry in 1891. Wells's relations with women were always problematic. His libido was strong, and although short (around 5 feet 6 inches) and a bit pudgy later in life, his chestnut hair and blue eyes were striking. Women were attracted to him, but he found respectable behavior difficult. Within one year of his marriage, he was enthralled by a student, Amy Catherine Robins. In 1895 his marriage ended in divorce, and he married Robins, whom he always called Jane. This marriage lasted until her death in 1927, but Wells had many affairs, most notably with Rebecca West, Moura Budberg, and Odette Keun. These relationships resulted in several illegitimate children. He frequently attacked restrictive sexual mores in his fiction. His novel *Ann Veronica* (1909), for example, was criticized because the heroine finds unwed bliss with her science teacher. The conventional view was that she should have suffered for such immoral behavior. He addressed this theme repeatedly but perhaps most effectively in *The Passionate Friends* (1913).

Wells continued to teach and earned a bachelor of science from the University of London in 1890. He also wrote more and more, first stories and articles, then the *Text-Book of Biology*, which was published in 1893. Wells moved steadily toward being a full-time writer. With four books, 1895 proved to be the breakthrough year. Most important was *The Time Machine*, which has been compared to Jonathan Swift's *Gulliver's Travels* (1726) for its satiric treatment of human foibles viewed through the eyes of a traveler. The struggle between the Eloi and Morlocks found by the traveler in the future has also been portrayed as a socialist class struggle. Whatever its ideological focus, it was a good story that sold well and gave Wells and his new bride the beginnings of financial stability. Of the other books published in 1895, *The Wonderful Visit*, the tale of an angel that appears in a small English village, is the most well known. Its comments about hypocrisy and people's failings are heavy-handed, and its fame has not lasted.

Over the next three years, Wells published four more novels, three of which are among his most famous works: *The Island of Dr. Moreau* (1896), *The Invisible Man* (1897), and *The War of the Worlds* (1898). He was, of course, drawing on his background in science for material, but he was also beginning to develop lifelong themes. He consistently asserted the importance of order and cooperation against individual extremes. He was also much concerned with the problems of class and respectability forcing men and women into socially acceptable but unsatisfying roles. As his fame grew, he began to make friends with prominent writers such as Henry James and Joseph Conrad.

During the first years of the twentieth century, Wells also began to make contact with the British socialist movement, particularly the Fabian Society. He became friends with leaders such as Sidney Webb, Beatrice Webb, and George Bernard Shaw. The Webbs were quite impressed with *Anticipations* (1902), which launched Wells on a tendency to prophesy for the future. His vision of human cooperation and creativity in the future fit Fabian thinking well. They did, however, think he lacked an understanding of institutions, particularly government, which they expected to be the means of solving society's problems. Wells joined the Fabian Society in 1903, but the association lasted only five years. Having experienced the frustrations of the British class structure—as detailed in the autobiographical novel *Kipps* (1905)—Wells found the efforts of the Fabians to work within existing institutions hopelessly dilatory. He wanted action. He criticized the Fabian movement not only indirectly in *Kipps* but also and more explicitly in *This Misery of Boots* (1906), in talks, and in shorter writings. He and his erstwhile friends were soon debating angrily. He could no longer, in good conscience, remain a Fabian and went his own way, as he so often did.

The years before World War I saw a flood of works from Wells. There were novels such as *Tono-Bungay* (1908) and *The History of Mr. Polly* (1910), and efforts to envision the future, including *A Modern Utopia* (1905), *The Future in America* (1906), and *The New Machiavelli* (1910). In the novels, often listed among his best works, the protagonists, respectively Edward Ponderevo and Alfred Polly, struggle to make their way despite social restrictions and poor education: Ponderevo makes and loses a fortune through sales of a worthless patent medicine called Tono-Bungay, while Polly eventually abandons a loveless, uninspiring marriage and middle-class life to be first a hobo and then to help a paramour run an inn. Like Wells himself, his fictional heroes found contentment outside the traditional bounds of society.

World War I had an enormous impact on England, and Wells was both unusual and lucky that he suffered no direct loss from it. He was, however, able to write one of his most popular books, *Mr. Britling Sees It Through* (1916), about the effects of the war. Hugh Britling, another of Wells's characters drifting through life looking for love and inspiration, loses his son and has to find ways to make life go on. Critics do not generally regard this as one of Wells's better efforts, and he expressed some regret at financial success arising from portraying wartime suffering in which he did not share. This led to some ruminations on religion in *God, the Invisible King*, published in 1917. More important, it motivated Wells to write his most influential book.

Wells resolved to write a survey of human history that would portray the patterns of growth and destruction in the hope that education would allow prevention of future catastrophes similar to the western front during World War I. The result was *The Outline of History* (1920). The volume was an instant success, with enough sales to make Wells financially secure. Although he sometimes grumbled that the number of buyers was dramatically higher than the number of readers, *The Outline of History* was a popular university textbook through the middle of the twentieth century and sold well among general readers. Its influence on the popular view of historical development was enormous. Wells's attempts to expand this influence into biological science with *The Science of Life* (1929-1930) and sociology with *The Work, Wealth, and Happiness of Mankind* (1931) proved less successful both commercially and intellectually.

The final two decades of Wells's life saw little change. He continued to write prolifically, but his production, as he acknowledged himself, was more polemic than literary. His conviction that humankind was blundering toward destroying itself and that life could be improved was overwhelming. He wrote again and again to try to influence the pattern. His best work after the mid-1920's was his *Experiment in Autobiography* (1934), an unusually candid autobiography. His had a worldwide reputation, and in 1944 he earned a doctorate from London University. His last novel, *You Can't Be Too Careful*, was published in 1941 and his last book, *Mind at the End of Its Tether*, in 1945. He died on August 13, 1946.

**Summary**

H. G. Wells's influence was both literary and political. His early works, called "scientific romances" at the time, helped develop the genre of science fiction. Works such as *The Time Machine* were not only good stories but they also proved that serious ideas might be conveyed in such a format. Wells was far more successful than most modern science fiction authors at mingling social and political commentary into speculative fiction, which perhaps explains the enduring interest in his books.

Wells was never successful in practical politics. His urgency and idiosyncratic ideas quickly made him uncomfortable in the Fabian Society, the only active political group of which he was ever a significant part. Nonetheless, he was very influential in political thought. His novels portrayed the restrictive British class system and made it clear that success did not depend on talent but social place. He also exposed the gender bias of his era in powerful but popular fiction. His nonfiction commentary was also effective and made the same points more explicitly. *The Outline of History* was one of the most widely read books of the mid-twentieth century, influencing students and general readers for two generations. Although he could find no place among its practitioners, Wells proved to be one of the true founders of modern British socialism, and the popularity of his works around the world indicates that his influence went far beyond his own nation. Justifiably, he continues to be studied by scholars in literature, political science, philosophy, and history.

**Bibliography**


Foot, Michael. *H. G.: The History of Mr. Wells*. London: Doubleday, and Washington, D.C.: Counterpoint, 1995. A wonderfully written, though impressionistic, biography. Foot, a socialist politician himself, is particularly interested in Wells as a founder of British socialism.

MacKenzie, Norman, and Jeanne MacKenzie. *The Life of H. G. Wells: The Time Traveller*. Rev. ed. London: Hogarth, 1987. The most detailed scholarly biography of Wells. The MacKenzies do an excellent job of covering the entire life.

Murray, Brian. *H. G. Wells*. New York: Continuum, 1990. Literary criticism effectively set into a biographical framework. Generally insightful but marred by an unfounded assertion that Wells was a racist.

Scheick, William J., ed. *The Critical Response to H. G. Wells*. Westport, Conn.: Greenwood, 1995. A collection of essays and reviews covering the critical response to the work of Wells over time. Includes an impressive bibliography of critical studies.

Simpson, Anne B. "H. G. Wells' 'Tono-Bungay': Individualism and Difference." *Essays in Literature* 22, no. 1 (Spring 1995). The author discusses Wells' *Tono-Bungay* and his use of Edwardian ideas of male white supremacy.

Wells, G. P., ed. *H. G. Wells in Love: Postscript to an Experiment in Autobiography*. London: Faber, and Boston: Little Brown, 1984. Edited by Wells's son, this volume includes writings about his personal and sexual relationships and how they influenced his life and work.

Wells, H. G. *Experiment in Autobiography*. 2 vols. London: Gollancz, and New York: Macmillan, 1934. Like most authors of autobiographies, Wells is sympathetic toward his subject, but these volumes are far more candid than most such works. Any serious study of Wells must start with the autobiography.

West, Anthony. *H. G. Wells: Aspects of a Life*. London: Hutchinson, and New York: Random House, 1984. West, Wells's illegitimate son by Rebecca West, provides a personal yet balanced and judicious account of his father's life and career.


*Fred R. van Hartesveldt*

# IDA B. WELLS-BARNETT

*Born:* July 16, 1862; Holly Springs, Mississippi
*Died:* March 25, 1931; Chicago, Illinois
*Areas of Achievement:* Civil rights, women's rights, and journalism
*Contribution:* An organizer of the antilynching movement, Ida B. Wells was an indefatigable crusader for equal rights for African Americans in the violent decades around the turn of the century, working on issues of education, social services, woman suffrage, and racial violence.

## Early Life

Ida Bell Wells was the eldest of eight children born in slavery to slave parents who were both of mixed racial parentage. (Her paternal grandfather was her grandmother's white owner, and her mother's father was an American Indian.) Both had learned trades during slavery—carpentry and cooking—which they were able to continue after the Civil War. In the yellow fever epidemic of 1878, both parents and the youngest child died, leaving Ida as the sole support of the younger children. Refusing offers from relatives and friends to parcel out the children, sixteen-year-old Ida decided to get a job as a schoolteacher. She had been educated at the Freedmen's School in Holly Springs (later Rust College). She successfully took the teacher's exam for the rural county schools and was able to "pass" for eighteen, teaching all week and riding a mule six miles home for the weekend. (A family friend stayed with the siblings during the week.) Later, she secured a better-paying position in Memphis. In 1886—after traveling to Fresno, California, with her aunt and siblings—she actually taught school in three different states: California, Missouri, and Tennessee.

Her activist career began in 1884, when she was forcibly ejected from the ladies' car on the Chesapeake and Ohio Railroad for refusing to sit in the segregated smoking car (Jim Crow segregation of transportation facilities was just beginning then). She sued the railroad and won $500 in damages; an appeal by the railroad to the Tennessee Supreme Court reversed the decision, however, and she had to pay court costs.

Her interest in journalism began in Memphis, where she participated in a weekly lyceum with other black schoolteachers, reading and discussing the weekly black newspaper *The Evening Star*, among other things. When she saw how much influence the newspapers had, she began writing a weekly column, which became popular and was printed in many newspapers across the country. She signed her articles "Iola." The name of the protagonist of fellow African American Frances Ellen Watkins Harper's popular novel *Iola Leroy* (1892) may have alluded to Wells. In 1889, she purchased a one-third interest in the Memphis *Free Speech and Headlight*, resigned her teaching job, and began organizing, writing, and selling subscriptions for the newspaper in black communities and churches throughout the South.

## Life's Work

In 1892, three black men who owned a successful grocery store that competed with the white-owned store in the black neighborhood were lynched in Memphis, Tennessee. Ida B. Wells not only editorialized against the lynching in her newspaper but also counseled black citizens to leave Memphis and move west to Arkansas and the newly opened Oklahoma Territory. Thousands took her advice. Those who remained heeded her call to boycott the streetcar system. In 1892, therefore, Ida B. Wells organized a successful public transportation boycott, sixty years before Rosa Parks began the Montgomery bus boycott after she refused to vacate her seat in the back of the bus to let a white person take it. Thus began Ida B. Wells's life work—her crusade for justice.

When she left Memphis for a speaking and writing trip to Philadelphia and New York, angry whites destroyed her offices and press and published notices that if she returned she herself would be lynched. She was hired by the important black paper the *New York Age* to gather lynching statistics and expose the fallacy that black men raped white women. Only one-fourth of all those who were lynched were even accused of sexually accosting or insulting a white woman. Women and children as well as white men were victims of lynch mobs. Most lynchings, she found, were economically motivated, designed to intimidate the black community if it attempted to become financially independent. She used white newspaper accounts to gather her evidence, publishing in 1892 her first feature story (later a pamphlet): "Southern Horrors: Lynch Law in All Its Phases." She listed all lynchings by name, state, alleged crime, method of killing, and month, continuing this practice in the following years.

Even in the North, her speeches and writings exposing lynch law were not well covered by a frightened white press, and she despaired of making any changes. She knew that international pressure could aid the cause, so she took her antilynching crusade worldwide, traveling to England to 1893 and again in 1894. She was warmly received by former abolitionists, and she published her stories in the mainstream press, lectured daily, and founded the first antilynching organizations. Her strategy worked—the American press picked up the stories from England, and the antilynching story was disseminated to a wider audience. When she attacked well-known white Americans Frances Willard (the president of the Women's Christian Temperance Union) and evangelist Dwight L. Moody for addressing segregated white audiences in the South and not speaking out against mob violence, Wells became the center of an international controversy but gained much publicity for her cause.

In 1893, she returned from England and, along with the venerable former slave Frederick Douglass and Ferdinand Barnett (a Chicago attorney to whom she was later married), organized the protest of excluded African Americans at the Chicago World Columbian Exposition. The three activists wrote and distributed 20,000 copies of their pamphlet, *The Reason Why the Colored American Is Not in the Columbian Exposition*, to people from all over the world. Douglass, the ambassador to Haiti at that time, was the only African American who was officially a part of the exposition. The pamphlet pointed out that without blacks there would be neither American civilization nor the industrial miracle so celebrated at the fair.

Remaining in Chicago after her second trip to England, Wells was married to Barnett and eventually gave birth to four children, but she continued her political organizing and journalism in Chicago's black newspaper *The Conservator* (which she purchased from Barnett). Although she was criticized by other women activists such as Susan B. Anthony for marrying and thus having "divided duty," Ida B. Wells-Barnett managed to be both a mother and an organizer, often traveling to lectures with one or another child, nursing between meetings. In Chicago, she founded the first black woman's club (later named the Ida B. Wells Club), the Alpha Suffrage Club (the first black woman's suffrage organization), and the Negro Fellowship League (which set up a reading room, job referrals, and a rooming house for black men newly arrived in Chicago). She helped to found a black kindergarten and a black orchestra, and she worked as a probation officer.

Her political position was very much opposed to that of accommodationists such as Booker T. Washington. She espoused a radical view akin to that of W. E. B. Du Bois and later the pan-Africanism of Marcus Garvey. She believed that African Americans should use both the law and agitation to gain equal rights in all areas, and that nothing was impossible. Along with Du Bois, she was one of the founding members of the National Association for the Advancement of Colored People (NAACP) in 1909, but she later broke with the organization because of its timid stance on racial issues.

As an Illinois delegate to the national woman suffrage parade in Washington in 1913, Wells-Barnett refused to march with the black delegates at the back of the procession; she quietly integrated the ranks of the Illinois delegates as the parade moved down Pennsylvania Avenue. She helped Chicago elect its first black alderman in 1915 and continued to work within the political structure, running herself unsuccessfully for the state senate in 1930.

She continued her investigative work in the South with a campaign to give justice to the black soldiers involved in the 1917 24th Infantry rebellion in Texas during World War I. She personally investigated the causes of the East St. Louis and Chicago riots of 1919 (which she predicted in print two weeks before they occurred). In 1922, she visited and wrote an exposé of the prison conditions of the Arkansas black farmers who had formed a cooperative and were attacked by whites—and then were arrested for starting a riot. For this journalistic work, she was hounded by the Federal Bureau of Investigation as a dangerous subversive during the Red Scare of the early 1920's.

Ida B. Wells-Barnett labored to the end of her life, leaving her autobiography unfinished in mid-sentence when she succumbed to her final illness, dying of uremic poisoning at the age of sixty-eight.

### Summary

Ida B. Wells-Barnett was radical, disputatious, angry, hard to get along with, and had arguments with nearly everyone with whom she worked. She said that she did not want publicity, but her autobiography makes it clear that she craved personal publicity. Still, she was a genius of an organizer: She had political savvy and a photographic memory. She was a powerful woman who played by the men's rules. She organized and carried out a successful economic boycott of public transportation facilities in the 1890's, she integrated the American woman suffrage movement, she single-handedly brought international attention to bear on the lynching scandal in the United States, and she kept the Chicago school system from being segregated by enlisting the help of social worker Jane Addams. She knew everyone and alienated everyone, and she took her issues personally to two presidents—William McKinley and Woodrow Wilson. She worked with, at various times, African Americans Booker T. Washington, W. E. B. Du Bois, Marcus Garvey, Madam C. J. Walker, Frederick Douglass, Anna Gaily Cooper, Fannie Barrier Williams, Mary Church Terrell, Mary McLeod Bethune, and many others. Although Wells-Barnett worked with whites when it was politically expedient to do so, she believed that a unified black community should band together for its own betterment. Her radical position and her refusal to compromise resulted in her near-erasure from American history, but Wells-Barnett has begun to garner more attention as the result of scholarly efforts in the fields of women's history and African American history.

### Bibliography


Bedermank, Gail. "'Civilization,' The Decline of Middle-Class Manliness, and Ida B. Wells's Antilynching Campaign (1892-94)." *Radical History Review*, no. 52 (1992): 5-30. An analysis of the racist evolutionary rhetoric of the end of the century, with special reference to Wells-Barnett's work in England and at the Chicago World Columbian Exposition of 1893.

Giddings, Paula. *When and Where I Enter: The Impact of Black Women on Race and Sex in America*. New York: Morrow, 1984. A history of black women in the United States, with large interpretive sections on Wells-Barnett's activist career, especially the antilynching campaign in England, the founding of the NAACP, and her activist work in Chicago. A good index and a bibliography are included.

Hendricks, Wanda. "Ida Bell Wells-Barnett." In *Black Women in America: An Historical Encyclopedia*, edited by Darlene Clark Hine. Brooklyn, N.Y.: Carlson, 1993. An important reference work that includes photographs and primary and secondary bibliographies.

"Ida B. Wells-Barnett: July 12, 1862." *Jet* 94, no. 8 (July 20, 1998). Brief profile of Wells-Barnett.

Loewenberg, Bert James, and Ruth Bogin, eds. *Black Women in Nineteenth Century American Life*. University Park: Pennsylvania State University Press, 1976. Includes the introduction and a selection from Wells-Barnett's antilynching writings published in London in 1892.

McMurry, Linda O. *To Keep the Waters Troubled: The Life of Ida B. Wells*. New York: Oxford University Press, 1998. The first full-length biography of Wells-Barnett. Based on diaries, letters, and published sources.

Sterling, Dorothy. "Ida B. Wells: Voice of a People." In *Black Foremothers: Three Lives*. 2d ed. New York: Feminist Press, 1988. A well-written and accessible narrative about all aspects of Wells's life. Contains a useful list of sources.

Wells-Barnett, Ida. *Crusade for Justice: The Autobiography of Ida B. Wells*. Edited by Alfreda M. Duster. Chicago: University of Chicago Press, 1970. This is Wells-Barnett's unfinished autobiography, which was edited and published by her daughter. It is the best source for biographical detail about Wells-Barnett's organizing and political work and is an important source for newspaper clippings and articles, many of which are printed verbatim.


*Margaret McFadden*

# MAX WERTHEIMER

*Born:* April 16, 1880; Prague, Austro-Hungarian Empire

*Died:* October 12, 1943; New York, New York

*Area of Achievement:* Psychology

*Contribution:* Wertheimer pioneered the development of Gestalt psychology, which he and his coworkers Kurt Koffka and Wolfgang Köhler introduced to the European and American psychological communities.

## Early Life

Max Wertheimer was born in Prague, which was then in the Austro-Hungarian Empire, on April 16, 1880, into an accomplished middle-class family. His mother was a respected musician, and his father was a school principal. Wertheimer contemplated a musical career and showed interest in writing poetry. Later, while ostensibly studying law at Prague University, he became intrigued by philosophy and psychology.

When Wertheimer was beginning his inquiries into man's ancient questions about the meaning of his life and its relation to the world around him—traditional philosophical issues—the methods of examining such profundities were changing dramatically. Many questions which previously had been the preserve of philosophy were coming under the purview of an increasingly empirical, evolving science subsequently known as psychology. This development led psychologists—Wertheimer among them—into many new areas, with physiological studies acquiring a significance equal to the older philosophies' vital, often rigorously logical yet nonempirical musings and reflections.

Leaving Prague University in 1901, Wertheimer proceeded to the University of Berlin to study philosophy and psychology, then to the University of Württemberg, where in 1904 he received his doctorate. Until 1909, he pursued postdoctoral studies in Prague, Vienna, and again in Berlin. Financial independence permitted such academic mobility. During World War I, he aided Germany's efforts in the development of acoustical devices for its submarines and the improvement of harbor fortifications. These services were short-lived, and he was never a combatant. Thus, from 1916 until 1929 he taught and conducted research at the University of Berlin, accepting a professorship at the University of Frankfurt in 1929 and maintaining it until he abandoned Adolf Hitler's Germany in 1933 for New York City's New School for Social Research. Meanwhile, in 1910, prior to his Frankfurt appointment, Wertheimer launched the psychological investigations that preoccupied the remainder of his life.

## Life's Work

Vacationing by train in 1910, Wertheimer made specific observations that gave initial shape to the school of psychology that shortly distinguished him as the founder of Gestalt (or Gestalten). Wertheimer did coin the term *Gestalt*, which had previously appeared in German philosophical-psychological literature, although with a meaning differing from his own. Wertheimer's Gestalt perceptions dealt with, or exposed, the overall configurations of shapes and forms existing prior to the mind's assimilating and making sense of myriad external sensory data imposed upon it. For Wertheimer, human perceptions occurred within an internal field; his evidence suggested that the totality of human perceptual observations constituted more than the sum of their tens of thousands of discrete, externally projected ele-

ments. Thus, Wertheimer aborted his 1910 vacation because of impressions drawn while watching scenery pass the train's windows that led him to assumptions about how people actually see "apparent" motion. Immediately afterward, he employed rudimentary tachistoscopes or stroboscopes to measure human perceptions of brief exposures to moving visual stimuli. Light was projected for viewers through two slits, one vertical, the other at an angle of twenty to thirty degrees. When light flashed briefly through the slits, they saw both lights continuously. With slower projections, they saw the lights moving from one place to another.

The results of this commonsensical experiment conflicted with assumptions and approaches of the dominant psychological schools of 1912. The prevalent presumption was that conscious observations could be analyzed into vast numbers of identifiable sensory elements. That is, viewers actually saw each of the bark, branches, and leaves of a tree and these parts imposed upon one's senses then converged in whole form or appeared to be in motion. Since that was deemed accurate, Wertheimer had to explain why, when one motionless object was added to another experimentally, the viewer perceived them to be in motion. Labeling his experimental discoveries the "phi phenomenon," he asserted that "apparent movement" simply existed a priori within the mind and was irreducible to a count of external stimuli affecting perception. "Apparent motion," for him, therefore required no explanation. Thus, although a square was composed of four lines joined in proper relation, the observer did not see four distinct lines; he saw squareness: the whole form instantly. Similarly, irrespective of the keys of instruments selected, when a melody was played, listeners heard neither the individual notes nor instruments. Whether the tune was "Yankee Doodle" or Ludwig van Beethoven's fifth symphony, listeners recognized a total composition. Such investigations were published by Wertheimer as "Experimentelle Studien über das Schen von Bewegung" (1912; "On the *Phi* Phenomenon as an Example of Nativism in Perception," 1965).

Wertheimer's advocacy of Gestalt initially contradicted the perspectives and assumptions of German structural and associationist psychologists, posing a challenge to such of their distinguished leaders as Wilhelm Wundt, who in Leipzig, Germany, then directed the world's first and most renowned psychological laboratory. Wundt was the quintessential elementalist. For him, psychology's task was to identify and calculate the tens of thousands of constituents of mental feelings, images, and sensations, hence the means by which they entered into combination as ideas, concepts, or images. Somewhat like contemporary chemists, Dmitry Mendeleyev, for example, or physicists such as Niels Bohr or Max Planck, Wundt sought to demonstrate that larger matter, forms, or shapes were composed of increasingly smaller, more distinct, and ultimately identifiable parts.

Wertheimer's Gestalt evidence convinced him on the contrary that such discrete elements were not the raw data of man's perceptions, feelings, images, or ideas. The fundamentals of human psychological activities were already structured within the mind and quite ready to assimilate assaults of external sensory stimuli. Men were therefore justified in simply saying "I see a horse" or "I see a house."

His continued investigations of perceptual constancies buttressed his confidence in Gestalt methodology. If, specifically, one stands directly before a window, it projects a rectangle onto the eye's retina. If one then stands to one side, in actuality the window becomes a trapezoid and that change is projected onto the retina. Yet, as Wertheimer's experiments—many along similar lines—demonstrated, one continued to perceive the window as a rectangle. Perception thus remained constant, despite alterations in the image projected onto the retina. He proffered further evidence that this same phenomenon occurs with regard to brightness and to the constancy of objects' sizes. Perceptual experience therefore possessed qualities of wholeness indiscernible in any part of that experience.

In 1922, Wertheimer professionally advanced his famous principles of perceptual organization in his *Untersuchungen zur Lehre von der Gestalt: I. Prinzipielle Bemerkungen* (1923; examination of objects as immediately given to consciousness). A person's perception of objects occurs in the identical simultaneous and unified manner as when he perceives apparent motion. The human mind possesses its own inner, dynamic principles for organizing perceptions.

Like many other psychologists, Wertheimer was interested in learning processes. His evidence, however, took him in different directions from those pursued by Wundt and associationists. Since Gestalt emphasized the salient importance of perceptual processes, Wertheimer consequently opposed the trial-and-error method of learning identified with E. L. Thorndike, as well as John Watson's stimulus-response approach. Ideally, Wertheimer would have teachers begin presentations with an overall view of their subject, proceeding then to their distinct parts.

Gradually, Gestalt psychology earned respect in Germany and much of Europe among psychologists as well as among other scientists who were dissatisfied with the purported sterility and mechanical qualities of Wundtian psychology. While this was occurring, Hitler's rise to power in Germany in 1933 persuaded Wertheimer and Köhler to immigrate to the United States. Wertheimer found a berth as professor of philosophy and psychology on the graduate faculty of the New School for Social Research in New York City. From then until his death on October 12, 1943, he continued experiments and sought to promulgate Gestalt psychology among American psychologists, although he was relatively unknown and, compared to Wundt's fifty-five thousand pages of publication, had published little. His expectations of greater influence were, however, ill-timed. By the 1920's and 1930's, American psychology was dominated by behavioral psychologists such as Watson and Raymond Cattell, and educational psychologists such as Thorndike. At the same time, the profession was assimilating the psychological theories of Sigmund Freud. Only after Wertheimer's death did the profound impact of his work become fully evident.

### Summary

Notwithstanding nineteenth century precedents for important Gestalt-like initiatives, there is little dispute that Max Wertheimer founded a new and permanent line of psychological and related physiological scientific inquiry. Because professional psychology recorded many significant attainments before and during Wertheimer's career, but in part because he broadly questioned the neglect or disdain of some of these previous endeavors, his conclusions challenged many fundamentals of the predominant psychological theories of his day and of some that preceded him. Traditional experimental psychology, like the natural sciences, had been premised on a reductionism, breaking down investigation of perception, memory, feeling, learning, and thought into distinct elements—indeed, when Wertheimer commenced experimenting, other psychologists had already counted forty-four thousand mental elements that combined to compose human perception and therefore on that basis were accounting for the way humans' minds functioned to make sense of themselves and their world.

Without ignoring physiological constituents of perception and comprehension, Wertheimer's evidence questioned, as the reigning theories did not, whether man was a mere apparatus, "a combination of cameras, telephone receivers, receptors for warmth, cold, pressure," which under external excitation produced a convergence descriptive of man's mental perceptions and reactions. He believed that such subsumptions ignored the basic and immanent human impulses of human actions: "a trend toward sensible, appropriate action, feeling, thought." Worse, from his viewpoint, traditionalists failed evidentially to explain elementary facts of human experiences: what people see when they open their eyes and look about them.

Starting with investigations of the retina, proceeding to explanations of the *phi* phenomenon, then to developing his principles of (mental) organization, advancing further to adducing physiological evidence for his principle of isomorphism, and finally to explications bearing upon productive and creative thought processes, Wertheimer produced substantial descriptions of a more human, thinking human species. These results he attributed to immanent psychological qualities allowing man to perceive himself, his environment, and his problems as wholes. Accordingly, Wertheimer has left a permanent imprint on the daily activities of psychologists.

### Bibliography

Asch, Solomon E. "Max Wertheimer's Contributions to Modern Psychology." *Social Research* 13 (1946): 81-102. A clearly written, readily comprehensible, authoritative, and professionally sound analysis. Contains a few information footnotes.

Fancher, Raymond E. *Pioneers of Psychology.* 3d ed. New York: Norton, 1996. Provides a fine contextual setting for a greater understanding of Wertheimer and his followers operating amid other psychological developments. Clearly written both for laymen and professionals alike. Contains several photographs, suggested readings at the end of major sections of this study, end-of-book notes for each chapter, and a very extensive, double-columned index.

Herrnstein, Richard, and Edward C. Boring, eds. *A Source Book in the History of Psychology.* Cambridge, Mass.: Harvard University Press, 1965.

A large, authoritative volume written with professional precision and intended for readers with some prior knowledge of psychology. Includes excerpts, abridgments, and translations of important psychological writings that are not easily found elsewhere. An invaluable and exhaustive work in its field. Excerpts are preceded helpfully by brief editorial abstracts. Thorough in its chronological, topical, and personality coverages. Includes an end-of-volume list of excerptions, plus extensive indexes of names and subjects.

King, D. Brett, and Michael Wertheimer. "The Legacy of Max Wertheimer and Gestalt Psychology." *Social Research* 61, no. 4 (Winter 1994). In-depth profile of Wertheimer including biographical information, career accomplishments, and information on Gestalt psychology.

Köhler, Wolfgang. "Max Wertheimer, 1880-1943." *The Psychological Review* 51 (May, 1944): 143-146. A tribute to Wertheimer's professional contributions by his distinguished coworker Köhler. The substance of the piece is professional and is devoid of personal information about Wertheimer. Includes an excellent photograph of the elderly Wertheimer. Useful, if not essential.

Neel, Ann. *Theories of Psychology.* Rev. ed. New York: Wiley, 1977. Part 4 deals with Gestalt psychology authoritatively and in its appropriate developmental setting. Excellent for understanding psychology's evolving theories. There are general but often extensive suggested readings at the end of major sections that relate to subject areas covered. Very useful reading for specialists and nonspecialists alike. Contains a very extensive index.

Rockman, I., and S. Palmer. "The Legacy of Gestalt Psychology." *Scientific American* 263, no. 6 (December, 1990). Discusses the development of Gestalt psychology by Max Wertheimer, Wolfgang Köhler, and Kurt Koffka. Includes information on perception theory, memory, thinking, and the impact of perception on learning.

Schultz, Duane P. *A History of Modern Psychology.* 6th ed. Fort Worth, Tex.: Harcourt Brace, 1996. Though the first two chapters provide useful historical background, the book's concentration is on late nineteenth and twentieth century psychologists and their work. A well-written, accurate, and useful survey. Chapter 12 features a fine discussion of Wertheimer and the Gestalt school and the nature and consequences of their work. Suggested readings close every chapter, and there is a useful bibliography and index.

*Clifton K. Yearley*

# MAE WEST

*Born:* August 17, 1893; Brooklyn, New York
*Died:* November 22, 1980; Los Angeles, California
*Areas of Achievement:* Film and theater and drama
*Contribution:* A memorable screen presence and wit, Mae West was also a breakthrough playwright in the handling of taboo subjects and a role model as a woman in control of her own sexuality.

## Early Life

Because her father was a prize fighter and her mother was a model, Mae West had an early familiarity with show business. Indeed, since she began her stage career as a child, she can hardly be said to have had an early life. By the time she left school at thirteen, she was an established vaudeville performer. While on tour but still under age (giving false information that has led to confusion about her age), she married a dancer named Frank Wallace—by implication gay—apparently as a way of protecting herself from scandal in the event of pregnancy. She never lived with Wallace—who entered into a bigamous marriage with someone else—and denied for many years that she was married.

When West made her Broadway debut in *À la Broadway* in 1911, she was already a seasoned trouper. Alert to her unique style, she retailored her songs for her earthy personality and was an immediate critical and popular success. Dividing her time between vaudeville and Broadway, she had trouble with the police on more than one occasion because of the suggestiveness of her dancing. In 1921, in *Sometime*, she introduced the shimmy dance to white audiences, creating a particular sensation.

## Life's Work

By 1926, Mae West realized that if she was to achieve star stature, she needed material tailored to her special personality and good-humored view of sex. Since no suitable star vehicle was available, she called upon her experience in writing her own vaudeville sketches and fashioned a play by adapting John J. Byrne's *Following the Fleet* (c. 1926). Even before opening, the show created more than one scandal, first when New York newspapers refused advertising because of the title she chose, *Sex* (1926), and then when the unprecedented enthusiasm of Yale undergraduates at the tryout in New Haven, Connecticut, and of sailors at the tryout in New London, Connecticut, caused the show to sell out even in previews. In New York, despite the advertising blackout and a plagiarism suit from Byrne, the show ran to packed houses for more than a year until suddenly the New York police decided that it was injurious to the morals of minors. She was convicted on that charge and spent ten days in prison.

The play itself is innocuous by later standards, which it helped to forge. It has no obscene language, nudity, or even suggested sex, all of which later became routine. *Sex*, which concerns the lives of prostitutes on the Bowery in New York, is a melodrama that presents a realistic view of sexuality with a light touch. The same could be said of all West's later vehicles.

At about this time, she began a long-term relationship with James Timony, an attorney who worked for West's mother and who later became West's business manager. While she was still performing in *Sex*, she wrote and produced another play that created a scandal on a different front. *The Drag* (1926), which had to be performed in Paterson, New Jersey—to packed houses—because of censorship restrictions in New York, was the first substantial, realistic picture of male homosexuality in the theater. It presents a somewhat naïve view of homosexuals as men who want to be women and advocates restraint of this impulse because it disrupts family life, but there is no doubt that the theme was heartfelt on the author's part and ahead of its time in terms of tolerance.

West wrote and performed with great success in several more plays along the same lines as *Sex*, including a beauty contest exposé, *The Wicked Age* (1927), and *Diamond Lil* (1928), a nostalgic view of the Bowery in the 1890's. West also wrote but did not appear in another play dealing with male homosexuality, *The Pleasure Man* (1928). Less provocative than *The Drag*, this work simply included homosexuality as a fact of backstage life in a melodrama about other relationships. Nevertheless, the police closed the show shortly after its Broadway opening and prosecuted the author for immorality. This time, however, West won the case, striking a blow for artistic freedom. Unfortunately, it was too late for the production to be resumed.

West toured with some of her plays, but the death of her mother and the 1929 stock market crash profoundly disrupted her life, and she wanted a change. She wrote a novel called *Babe Gordon* (1930; later reprinted as *The Constant Sinner*), the

first popular treatment of the social conditions in black Harlem. She also wrote a novelization of *Diamond Lil* (1932). Then, after a good Broadway run in a play she adapted from *The Constant Sinner* (1931), she accepted an offer from Paramount Studios to make films.

Allowed to rewrite her dialogue to fit her persona for her film debut in *Night After Night* (1932), West became an instant film star. Her next project was an adaptation of *Diamond Lil* into the legendary film *She Done Him Wrong* (1933), which featured Cary Grant in his first starring role. This film and its successor *I'm No Angel* (1933), for which she wrote the whole screenplay, were so successful that she brought Paramount Studios back from the brink of financial ruin. In *She Done Him Wrong* and *Belle of the Nineties* (1934; she also wrote the screenplay), she introduced costume drama to the talkies and started a Gay Nineties fashion trend. In the latter film, her insistence on using a black jazz band brought about the first instance of such integrated accompaniment.

At this point in her film career, however, West ran into the sort of trouble with the censors that had hounded her on the stage. The Hayes Office was introduced to monitor the language and plots of films while they were being made. *Klondike Annie* (1936), *Go West, Young Man* (1936), *Every Day's a Holiday* (1938), and other later pictures that West wrote and starred in were praised at the time for being clean yet amusing; most film historians, however, regard such later films as lacking the free spirit of her early ones. She was also banned from the radio for her supposedly too sensual reading of some innocuous lines in a sketch about Adam and Eve.

Her most memorable film, although not her best as either screenwriter or performer, is certainly *My Little Chickadee* (1940), costarring W. C. Fields, which she made for Universal. Although she found Fields unreliable because of his drinking and always maintained that he should not have been given a coauthor credit for the screenplay, the incongruous styles of the two meshed in this Western melodramatic spoof, apparently because she understood that giving Fields most of the laughs would mellow his usually misogynistic persona and because she saw that her eroticism could then effectively be directed away from her costar toward other men in the story.

Unhappy with the scripts she was offered and unable to convince anyone to finance a color costume epic of the Russian empress Catherine the Great, she was idle for several years. As a favor to actor-director Gregory Ratoff, she appeared in *The Heat's On* in 1943, but this unsatisfactory pastiche convinced her that she needed to return to the stage.

Turned into a play, *Catherine Was Great* received a lavish Broadway production from celebrated impresario Mike Todd in 1944. Critics found the play too historical and serious, but audiences loved it, and West followed the long Broadway run by taking the show on tour. She then adapted another play as *Come on Up* (1946) and played to great success in a production of *Diamond Lil* in the London West End, first on tour, and then in a revival on Broadway in 1949.

A number of scandals, personal problems, and lawsuits marred her later years. Frank Wallace surfaced and attempted to cash in on her fame, first by asking for separate maintenance, then by billing himself in a nightclub act as "Mae West's Husband," and finally by suing for divorce and alimony. She silenced him at last in 1942 in a divorce settlement by paying him an undisclosed amount of money. Her longtime companion James Timony died in 1954, as did Wallace. In 1955, *Confidential* magazine published a demonstrably untrue exposé. In 1950, 1959, and again in 1964, she was involved in complicated lawsuits in which she tried to defend the name Diamond Lil as a trademark, and two different writing teams accused her of plagiarism in *Catherine Was Great*.

Finally slowed down somewhat by advancing age and no longer able to carry a full play, West put together a nightclub act with a chorus of musclemen in 1954 and toured with great success, and she began a recording career. Yet there were troubles. Mickey Hargitay (Mr. Universe) and another muscleman in her act, Paul Novak, had a public fight over her when she played the Coconut Grove in 1955. When Hargitay turned his affections to Jayne Mansfield, a film star whose persona suggested West's sort of available sexuality but without the wit, West established a permanent liaison with Novak that was like the one she had had with Timony.

West made a spectacular television debut at the 1958 Academy Awards, singing "Baby, It's Cold Outside" (written in 1949, by Frank Loesser) with Rock Hudson, who was then at the height of his film career. Although a *Person to Person* interview with her on the occasion of the publication of her autobiography *Goodness Had Nothing to Do with It* (1959) was never shown because of the suggestiveness of some of her comments, she appeared on the television variety shows of Red Skelton and Dean Martin and as a guest star in the situation comedy *Mr. Ed*.

In 1970, the opportunity arose to return to film when a perfect part for her appeared in the screen adaptation of Gore Vidal's camp novel of sex change, *Myra Breckinridge* (1968). Her traditional parodic approach was exactly right for the material, and she was certainly the main reason people went to see the film. Excellent in parts and a *succès d'estime* for West, *Myra Breckinridge* was somewhat incoherent in its released form, since director Michael Sarne deleted most of the footage of rival auteur West. Its unauthorized use of clips of old films also caused legal trouble.

Nevertheless, the project convinced West that she still had a film public, and she set about refashioning a play adaptation she had appeared in briefly on tour into the film *Sextette* (1978). The time lag, however, was fatally damaging, and in the years between these last two films, anything that was left of her screen persona had passed with old age from parody and camp into caricature and grotesquerie. During the years between her two last films, she also wrote a novelization of *The Pleasure Man* (1975, "with the kind assistance of [her managing assistant] Lawrence Lee") and the self-help book *On Sex, Health and ESP* (also 1975), but both are believed to have been ghostwritten.

Although she was still active enough to record radio commercials in 1979, she died in 1980 after a series of strokes.

### Summary

Only Jean Harlow rivals Mae West in creating an indelible screen presence in a short career as a film star. Like Harlow's, West's screen persona works because she manages to be sexy without taking herself seriously. The combination led to her more than once being compared to a female impersonator and made her popular with women as well as men because the parody removed any chance that she would permanently divert men's attention. The strong impact of her physical presence is, however, attested by the inflatable life preserver that bears her name.

Although she was most famous as a personality, her enduring mark on theatrical history was made as a writer. By introducing straightforward and unpunished sexual situations, her plays and films defied the taboos of the time. It is particularly interesting that it was a woman who brought the subject of male homosexuality to Broadway. Her work made it possible for later—perhaps more technically interesting—playwrights to treat sexual themes. She suggested that sex without guilt is possible, even for women and gay men.

### Bibliography

Cashin, Fergus. *Mae West: A Biography*. London: Allen, and Westport, Conn.: Arlington House, 1981. This unconvincing exposé maintains that West was a man or was at least somehow biologically deformed.

Eells, George, and Stanley Musgrove. *Mae West*. New York: Morrow, 1982; London: Robson, 1984. A scholarly biography that corrects some of West's autobiographical memories, this is the best narrative work on West's career.

Malachosky, Tim, with James Greene. *Mae West*. Lancaster, Calif.: Empire, 1993. This lavish picture book of candid photographs was compiled by West's private secretary.

Pierpont, Claudia Roth. "The Strong Woman: What Was Mae West Really Fighting For?" *The New Yorker* 72, no. 34 (November 11, 1996). Discusses Mae West's body of work and her beliefs regarding women's sexuality and independence.

Schlissel, Lillian, ed. *Sex, The Drag, The Pleasure Man.* Edited by Lillian Schlissel. New York: Routledge, 1997. This is the first publication of three plays written by Mae West. Opening between 1926 and 1928, these plays closed as quickly as they opened, leading to charges of obscenity and several law suits.

Tuska, Jon. *The Complete Films of Mae West.* Secaucus, N.J.: Carol, 1992. A picture book that also contains full and remarkably accurate commentary on West's entire career, not only her films.

Ward, Carol M. *Mae West: A Bio-Bibliography.* Westport, Conn. and London: Greenwood Press, 1989. An annotated bibliography with a full career summary, this is the standard reference work on West.

West, Mae. *Goodness Had Nothing to Do with It: The Autobiography of Mae West.* Englewood Cliffs, N.J.: Prentice-Hall, 1959; London: Allen, 1960. Although sometimes obviously protective of her reputation, West is candid but not salacious in this chronological review of her career and private life. She is, however, strangely unreflective, and the transitions are often abrupt.

*Edmund Miller*

# EDITH WHARTON

*Born:* January 24, 1862; New York, New York
*Died:* August 11, 1937; St.-Brice-sous-Forêt, France
*Area of Achievement:* Literature
*Contribution:* Edith Wharton was a novelist who was noted for her portrayal of the decline of New York aristocracy and for her characters' trapped sensibilities.

## Early Life

Edith Newbold Jones, the daughter of George Frederic Jones and Lucretia Stevens Rhinelender Jones, was born into a society of aristocrats who led a leisured, proper life and disdained business and politics. Wharton's family was a prime example of "old" New York: moneyed, cultivated, and rigidly conventional.

According to custom, young Edith was educated by tutors and governesses. She also spent much of her childhood abroad with her family. Edith was forbidden to read literary "rubbish," so she fell back on the classics on her father's bookshelves. Despite her culture and education, Edith was expected to excel primarily in society, which involved rigid adherence to proper manners, dress, and lifestyle.

In 1885, Edith was married to another American socialite, Edward Wharton, an easygoing and unintellectual man. The Whartons led an affluent, social life in America and in Europe, uninterrupted by children or financial concerns.

Although Edith Wharton performed her social tasks well, her duties were not enough for her hungry mind. She began writing poems, stories, books on interior decorating, and travel pieces. Her husband was embarrassed by his wife's writing, and her friends also did not approve. Fortunately, Edith Wharton made the acquaintance of writer Henry James. James not only supported her writing but also served as her confidant throughout periods of emotional turmoil. Although Edith claimed that she wrote for distraction, her diary notes that only by creating another imaginary world through writing could she endure the "moral solitude" of her marriage. Despite obvious incompatibilities, Edith and Edward lived together for twenty-eight years. That they did not divorce until 1913 is probably because of conservative class traditions.

Wharton's divorce plus other personal tensions spurred her to do some of her best work. She converted her anguish into writing about the corrosive effects of social class upon a woman's identity. Young Edith Wharton found her society's indifference to anything but forms stultifying. Much of her writing examines the superfluous details of a refined class frozen in convention. Wharton also portrayed struggling characters trapped by larger social forces and, sometimes, by morally inferior individuals. Nevertheless, when Wharton grew old, she concluded that the "Age of Innocence" in which she was reared was preferable to the modern world, which valued nothing.

The declining aristocracy became Edith Wharton's principal subject matter. She most often depicted the society of "old" New York in conflict with nouveau riche capitalists of the Gilded Age, who respected only money.

## Life's Work

Edith Wharton's early literary output included poems, decorating books, short stories, and three novels. In 1899, a volume of short stories, *The Greater Inclination*, was published, followed by *The Touchstone* (1900). In 1901, *Crucial Instances* followed; these short books have a Jamesian influence. Wharton's three poetry collections are overserious and overornamented. Her first novel, *The Valley of Decision* (1902), another form of George Eliot's *Romola*, is notable because its descriptions capture the spirit of eighteenth century Italy. Wharton's novel *Sanctuary* (1903) and her short stories in *The Descent of Man* (1904) are still experimental. Nevertheless, in these early works appear two of Wharton's basic themes: the aristocratic, cold, egoistic male and the strong female, who eventually dominates the male.

*The House of Mirth* (1905) marked the beginning of Edith Wharton's mature artistic period. Wharton had discovered her medium and subject: the novel of manners and the invasion of old New York society by the millionaire "nouveau riche." Wharton indicated her realization that Knickerbocker society would eventually make peace with the "invaders." Her story concerned those who were trampled in this social clash. The novel's Lily Bart is similar to a Dreiser heroine in that she is doomed by heredity and a materialistic environment. Lily struggles to improve herself but is defeated by her embrace of a heartless social ideal and by scruples that prevent her from marrying only for money.

Despite the success of *The House of Mirth*, Wharton delayed for years before returning to the subject of society's clash with the invaders. *Madame de Treymes* (1907) is an innocents-abroad story with a Jamesian influence. *The Fruit of the Tree* (1907), a reform novel, considers labor reform and the morality of euthanasia, but it fails because of lack of unity. *The Hermit and the Wild Woman* (1908) is made up of slender stories of artists, but *Tales of Men and Ghosts* (1910) contains chilling ghost stories.

The novella *Ethan Frome* (1911) made Edith Wharton famous. Although *Ethan Frome* involves a poor New England farm family, Wharton's familiar themes predominate: a man under female domination and a human being crushed by circumstances and his own scruples. *Ethan Frome* is noted for its spare style, masterly details, tragic ending, and symbolism. Although Wharton used details, she did not often use symbolism. *Ethan Frome*'s theme is enhanced by landscape symbols that reflect Ethan's spiritual desolation. Suffocating snow symbolizes Ethan's financial and social trap, and withered apple trees on a slate hillside symbolize Ethan's emotional starvation.

*The Reef* (1912), although praised as a "Racinian" novel, puzzles readers because of its moral tone. The story involves a widow, who is at last to marry an old bachelor admirer, and her stepson, who is to marry the family governess. When she discovers that her fiancé and the governess have been lovers, the widow, Mrs. Leath, breaks her engagement. When she goes to the governess' sister's home to tell Sophy that she has given up her fiancé, she learns that Sophy has left for India in disreputable company. This departure leaves Leath free to return to her fiancé. The novel's problem is its implicit sense that social class determines justice. The governess' fate is semiprostitution precisely because she is a governess, but the bachelor's betrayal is forgivable because he is a gentleman.

In *The Custom of the Country* (1913), Wharton returns to the theme of rich, old New York and the "invaders." The heroine is not a delicate woman whom society crushes, but a predatory female invader who victimizes the society she crashes. Undine Spragg makes the same mistakes as Lily Bart, but unlike Lily, she uses street smarts and amorality to extricate herself. Some people consider *The Custom of the Country* to be Wharton's masterpiece because of its taut depiction of the invaders takeover of New York society and the resulting social and moral emptiness.

In 1913, the year in which *The Custom of the Country* was published, the Whartons were divorced. Edith Wharton, who had been spending most of her time in France, now settled there. The new francophile wrote books meant for tourists, for whom she had also written *A Motor-Flight Through France* (1908). Wharton also wrote about France's involvement in World War I in *Fighting France* (1915), *The Book of the Homeless* (1915), *The Marne* (1918), and *A Son at the Front* (1923), works more noted for their support of France than for their literary merit.

Ironically, the war made Edith Wharton long for the vanished, quiet world of her childhood. In "Autre Temps" (*Xindu*, 1916) and in *Twilight Sleep* (1927), Wharton expressed nostalgia for the once despised conventions, believing that these instilled fortitude and moral fiber.

In 1916 and 1917, Wharton published *The Bunner Sisters* and *Summer*. As in *Ethan Frome*, the characters are poor and working class. *The Bunner Sisters* contains a sensitive person trapped within an inferior human being, while *Summer* depicts squalid lives and characters struggling in a battle destined for defeat. Again, as in *Ethan Frome*, symbols signify the characters' fates, which are predetermined by forces beyond their comprehension.

Wharton's nostalgia culminated in *The Age of Innocence* (1920), a Pulitzer Prize-winning novel portraying the genteel New York of the 1870's and featuring characters trapped by their environment. No matter how much Newland Archer and Ellen Olenska are in love, society decrees that Archer shall marry May Welland, and so he does. Later, Archer even approves his dull marriage as part of good, traditional ways.

Edith Wharton's best literary period ended with *The Age of Innocence*, for her work declined after 1920. Wharton began publishing serial novels in American women's magazines to earn money to sustain her expensive lifestyle. *Glimpses of the Moon* (1922) shows a severe lapse in style and character. The short stories in *Old New York* (1924) successfully evoke that period, but Wharton also wanted to depict her contemporary age. This ambition, coupled with her need for money, resulted in inferior works. *The Mother's Recompense* (1925), *Twilight Sleep* (1927), and *The Children* (1928) unconvincingly lay the causes of the era's ills at

America's door. *Hudson River Bracketed* (1929) and *The Gods Arrive* (1932), novels set in the Midwest, a region she had never visited, make similar implausible criticisms.

Edith Wharton's posthumously published books are *Ghosts* (1937) and *The Buccaneers* (1938). *Ghosts* contains two superbly frightening stories, whereas *The Buccaneers* turns back again to "old New York." This unfinished work revives Wharton's forceful style but lacks the bitterness of her earlier works. Some critics believe that this book would have been her best had she completed it.

### Summary

Edith Wharton's place in literary history is secured by *Ethan Frome*. She will also be remembered for her depiction of the high society of old Knickerbocker New York. These works are almost historical novels because of their accurate rendering of an age. Through her exquisite use of detail, Wharton delineated not only the conventions of an unadventurous society but also its moral ambiguity. The stifling conventions of upper-class New York trap its members and often annihilate those who aspire to its society. This demanding social code also, however, produces people who have a strong moral fiber. Ironically, these strong characters whose values have been shaped by "high society" sometimes make unnoticed, and often needless, sacrifices. Although some readers find Wharton's characters lifeless, she is considered a superb novelist of manners.

Edith Wharton, though acclaimed in her lifetime, suffered from gender as well as class expectations. She began writing to escape her narrow social sphere as well as marital tensions. Edith Wharton endured artistic isolation partially because of her class. That class distrusted literature, particularly that written by women, because of the new and disquieting ideas that literature often advocated. That Edith Wharton's health improved and her publications increased after her divorce suggests that divorce separated her not only from a man but also from limiting gender roles. Edith Wharton triumphed over formidable obstacles of social position, wealth, and gender expectations. In this respect, she serves as role model for aspiring women with traditional familial and social obligations.

**Bibliography**

Auchincloss, Louis. *Edith Wharton.* Minneapolis: University of Minnesota Press 1961. This pamphlet covers Edith Wharton's biography and critically examines Wharton's plots, characters, themes, and style.

Bell, Millicent. *Edith Wharton and Henry James.* New York: Braziller, 1965; London: Owen, 1966. This scholarly account of the friendship between Edith Wharton and Henry James includes many of their letters.

Benstock, Shari. *No Gifts from Chance: A Biography of Edith Wharton.* London: Hamilton, and New York: Scribner, 1994. As the first substantial biography of Wharton to appear in nearly two decades, Benstock's study is informed by her investigation of a variety of primary sources that have become available in recent years.

Howe, Irving, ed. *Edith Wharton: A Collection of Critical Essays.* Englewood Cliffs, N.J.: Prentice-Hall, 1962. This anthology contains articles dealing with Wharton's overall achievement and others centering on specific works or aspects of her writing.

Jessup, Josephine Lurie. *The Faith of Our Feminists.* New York: Smith, 1950. A section on Wharton demonstrates how feminism is illustrated in Wharton's subtle portrayal of women's domination of men.

Kaye, Richard A. "Edith Wharton and the 'New Gomorrahs' of Paris: Homosexuality, Flirtation and Incestuous Desire in 'The Reef.'" *Modern Fiction Studies* 43, no. 4 (Winter 1997). Analysis of Edith Wharton's 'The Reef,' focusing on her interest in homosexuality and the tolerance for it on the part of the French.

Lewis, R. W. B. *Edith Wharton.* 2 vols. New York: Harper, and London: Constable, 1975. This Pulitzer Prize–winning work is essential reading for those interested in Wharton's life and how it informed her work.

Lubbock, Percy. *Portrait of Edith Wharton.* New York: Appleton-Century-Crofts, and London: Cape, 1947. This is an informal biography written by Edith Wharton's friend at the request of her literary executor. The biography portrays Edith Wharton through the perspectives of her friends as well as through the eyes of Percy Lubbock, with a nostalgic, sometimes gossipy tone.

Nevius, Blake. *Edith Wharton.* Berkeley: University of California Press, 1953. An excellent critical analysis of Wharton's works, plots, style, and themes—particularly the chapter "The Trapped Sensibility." The book follows Wharton's career chronologically, noting her artistic decline in the 1920's and her subsequent "tired writing."

Overton, Grant M. *The Women Who Make Our Novels.* New York: Dodd Mead, 1918. Written while Edith Wharton was still alive, Overton's book pronounces Wharton's overall literary achievement brilliant but lifeless, but he exempts *Ethan Frome*, *The House of Mirth*, and *Summer* from this verdict.

Shapiro, Charles, ed. *Twelve Original Essays on Great American Novels.* Detroit, Mich.: Wayne State University Press, 1958. This book is useful for Walter B. Rideout's essays on *The House of Mirth.* Rideout maintains that Edith Wharton has not received her just due because the major phase of her writing began just before World War I.

Wegener, Frederick. "Edith Wharton on French Colonial Charities for Women: An Unknown Travel Essay." *Tulsa Studies in Women's Literature* 17, no. 1 (Spring, 1998). A previously unpublished essay by Edith Wharton.

*Mary Hanford Bruce*

# GEORGE HOYT WHIPPLE

*Born:* August 28, 1878; Ashland, New Hampshire
*Died:* February 1, 1976; Rochester, New York
*Area of Achievement:* Medicine and physiology
*Contribution:* Using anemic dogs, Whipple studied the effects of many foods on the regeneration of hemoglobin. Along with two others, he won the Nobel Prize in Physiology or Medicine in 1934 for the discovery that liver was valuable in the treatment of pernicious anemia.

## Early Life

George Hoyt Whipple was born on August 28, 1878, in Ashland, New Hampshire, to Ashley Cooper Whipple and Frances Hoyt Whipple. Both his father and grandfather were physicians. Ashley Cooper died of typhoid fever when George was only two years old. Supportive of her son's desire to become a physician, Frances secured a first-rate education for him. He entered Phillips Academy, a preparatory school in Andover, Massachusetts, in 1892 and Yale University in 1896.

After graduating from Yale, Whipple chose to attend the Johns Hopkins University School of Medicine, which, though it had been founded only in 1893, had quickly become the best environment for medical students. At the beginning of his second year in medical school, Whipple began an association with the preeminent pathologist William Henry Welch and his six associates, all of whom had distinguished careers. This team ensured that the instruction of pathology was of the highest quality.

Graduating fourth in his class, Whipple qualified for one of twelve highly prized internships. He chose to become an assistant in pediatric pathology spending many hours performing autopsies and studying the effects that disease had upon bodily tissues. At the end of the year, he asked for and received a second appointment, which gave him the rank of instructor. Soon Whipple decided to devote his career to pathology.

One of the first diseases that he studied was tuberculosis, on which he authored his first paper in 1906. The following year, he accepted a position as assistant to the chief pathologist studying tropical diseases in Ancon Hospital in the Panama Canal Zone, alarming his mother, who expected him to open a private practice. In Panama he studied blackwater fever, an often fatal malarial disease, and published a paper that drew praise.

In 1909, Whipple returned to Johns Hopkins as the senior member of Welch's staff and also as the resident pathologist. That summer, he traveled to Heidelberg, Germany, and gained exposure to an outstanding European laboratory. Back at Johns Hopkins, he continued studies on the effects of chloroform, an anesthesia then widely used, and discovered that it interfered with blood clotting and damaged the liver. Chloroform poisoning also produced jaundice, which occurs when bile salts get into the blood in cases of liver damage.

In the following years, Whipple's interests changed from pathological anatomy, or the description and classification of disease-produced changes, to physiological pathology, the study of abnormal body states using chemistry and physiology. After another trip to Europe, Whipple researched liver function, blood coagulation, pancreatitis, and intestinal obstruction. During the period from 1912 to 1914, he and his coworkers published twenty-one research papers. In 1914, Whipple married Katherine Ball Waring, with whom he had two children, George Hoyt and Barbara.

## Life's Work

In 1914, Whipple left Johns Hopkins and accepted an invitation to organize the Hooper Foundation and become its director at the University of California Medical School in San Francisco, where, with Charles Hooper, he resumed research on the role that the liver played in the production of bile pigments. Experimenting on dogs that had bile fistulas (tubes surgically placed through the abdominal wall into the gall bladder), they found that bile secretion was influenced by dietary changes: Carbohydrates increased the production of bile pigments, and proteins diminished it. The dogs, however, did not thrive when deprived of their bile, and Whipple discovered that their health could be maintained by adding pig's liver to their diets. This unexpected discovery led Whipple to hypothesize that the liver made a prehemoglobin substance. He further speculated that if it could be established that liver cells formed such a substance, great progress would have been made toward understanding the complicated issue of hemoglobin metabolism.

Hooper then wondered if pernicious anemia, a fatal anemia, might result when the production of the hypothetical prehemoglobin was disturbed. He made an extract from liver tissue and gave it to

six patients. Some cases experienced remission. Since pernicious anemia cases did experience spontaneous remissions, hospital officials gave Hooper and Whipple no encouragement to continue this work. Whipple, however, continued his research on hemoglobin production with Hooper and Frieda Robscheit-Robbins. He and his coworkers bled dogs to make them anemic for a short time and then tested the effects of various foods and drugs to identify which best regenerated the depleted blood. Lean scrap meat regenerated the blood in two to four weeks, mixed table scraps in four to seven weeks, and high carbohydrate diets in four weeks to five months. Iron pills, contrary to expectations, did not help. They reported these results to the American Physiological Society in December, 1917, and published an abstract in 1918. In 1920, the *American Journal of Physiology* published a series of five papers that provided more details.

During his tenure at the Hooper Foundation, Whipple and his associates studied several other problems. They examined the formation of the bile salts and determined that their production was separate from that of the bile pigments. They also studied how the liver detoxifies poisonous metabolic products by combining them with other substances, thus rendering them harmless and promoting excretion in the urine. Finally, he studied toxicity resulting from injury to body tissues, extending the idea to the disease process. He discovered that septic states resulted not simply from the invading microorganism but were caused by the primary injury and autolysis (breakdown of the tissue) of the proteins in the injured tissue. Whipple then linked these results to radiation poisoning described in medical literature. On postmortem examination, he and a student, Charles Hall, discovered that there was only microscopic injury to the lining of the intestine in dogs exposed to intense radiation. In their 1919 report, Whipple and Hall gave the first warning that radiation affected the intestinal tract.

In 1920, Whipple became dean of the University of California Medical School. On July 1, 1921, he accepted the appointment as dean of the new School of Medicine and Dentistry at Rochester University in New York, which he held until 1953, and professor of pathology, which he held until 1955. He selected the faculty and designed a large tic-tac-toe-shaped building to house the entire medical school, thus fostering close communication among all departments. The first medical class entered in September, 1925.

During the early 1920's, Whipple remained in contact with his coworkers in San Francisco. He had left a large backlog of research, and during the transition years at Rochester, he continued to write and edit research papers. By 1923, Frieda Robscheit-Robbins and the dog colony had moved to Rochester. Unlike their earlier research, in which dogs were made anemic by a few large bleeds, the dogs in this research were kept in an anemic state by repeated small bleeds, thus eliminating the possibility of spontaneous recovery. A whole range of foodstuffs was tested to identify the substance that improved the anemia. Liver had the most beneficial properties, followed by beef heart and then meats. Milk did not improve the anemia. These studies resulted in a series of papers on "Blood Regeneration in Severe Anemia" published in the *American Journal of Physiology* in 1925 and 1927. Whipple and his coworkers attempted but failed to extract the specific hemoglobin-producing substances in the liver by making various fractions.

In 1926, Harvard University's George Richards Minot, with the help of pathologist William P. Murphy, tested a liver diet on patients with pernicious anemia. Keeping close records of the microscopic blood picture, they found the treatment effective. They published their findings in the *Journal of the American Medical Association* in August, 1926, attracting worldwide attention. Minot's group then was able to obtain a liver extract of high potency, which the pharmaceutical firm Eli Lilly mass produced. In 1934, Minot, Murphy, and Whipple received the Nobel Prize in Physiology or Medicine.

After he won the Nobel Prize, Whipple led three teams doing research on hemoglobin formation, iron metabolism, and the utilization of proteins. Whipple and Robscheit-Robbins continued to search for the specific dietary factors in the production of hemoglobin. He also undertook important investigations of iron absorption, discovering that the body takes only what it needs via the alimentary tract. At first, it was impossible to distinguish iron already present in the body from iron recently ingested. Developments in physics helped physiologists because the production of radioactive isotopes became possible, and, beginning in 1938, Whipple's team began to use the radioactive isotope Fe59 to trace the path of ingested iron.

Whipple's study of hemoglobin led him to investigate proteins in general. With his coworkers, he fed severely anemic dogs diets low in protein. They found that the dogs built up hemoglobin by taking protein from the blood plasma and other bodily tissues. Whipple called this give-and-take between body and plasma protein "the dynamic equilibrium of protein." Resuming his earlier line of research, Whipple tested the effects of various dietary substances on dogs with low protein levels. He linked this work to the study of amino acids done by other researchers. In 1944 Whipple's team began to use the radioactive isotope N15 in amino acid research and in studies of the dynamic equilibrium of protein.

Besides the Nobel Prize, Whipple was awarded the *Popular Science* Monthly Gold Medal and Annual Award in 1930 and the William Wood Gerhard Gold Medal of the Philadelphia Pathological Society in 1934. He died in Rochester, New York, on February 1, 1976, at age ninety-seven.

### Summary

The discoveries of Whipple, Minot, and Murphy did not completely explain pernicious anemia. Whipple was not surprised to discover that the liver extract prepared by Minot and Murphy worked for people with pernicious anemia but not for dogs with severe experimental anemia. He reasoned that there was a difference between primary (pernicious) and secondary (experimental or dietary) anemia and speculated that pernicious anemia was a deficiency disease. In 1948 the active principle was isolated from the liver simultaneously by investigators in Great Britain and the United States. This substance, cyanocolalamin or vitamin B12, became the standard treatment for pernicious anemia. Whipple studied the distribution of vitamin B12 labeled with Co60 and published papers on it with W. D. Woods and W. B. Hawkins in 1958 and 1960.

### Bibliography

Corner, George W. *George Hoyt Whipple and His Friends: The Life-Story of a Nobel Prize Pathologist.* Philadelphia: Lippincott, 1963. This useful biography published thirteen years before Whipple died details his scientific, administrative, and honorary accomplishments. It contains photographs, citations from personal correspondences, and a list of papers published through 1961.

Holmgren, I. "Presentation Speech by Professor I. Holmgren, Member of the Staff of Professors of the Royal Caroline Institute." In *Les Prix Nobel en 1934*. Stockholm: Imprimerie Royale, P. A. Norstedt and Soner, 1935. This is the speech presented at the ceremony awarding Whipple, Minot, and Murphy the Nobel Prize for their work on pernicious anemia. Presents the historical background of the nineteenth century and places Whipple's work in the context of Minot and Murphy.

Raju, Tonse N. K. "1934: George Hoyt Whipple (1878-1976); George Richard Minot (1885-1950); William Perry Murphy (1892-1987)." *The Lancet* 353 no. 9148, (January 16, 1999). Brief discussion of the co-recipients of the 1934 Nobel Prize in Physiology or Medicine.

Rapport, Samuel, and Helen Wright. *Great Adventures in Medicine*. 2d ed. New York: Dial Press, 1961. Contains a selection written by Minot, one of Whipple's corecipients of the Nobel Prize. Minot describes the symptoms of pernicious anemia and explains treatment of it in easily understandable language.

Wailoo, Keith. *Drawing Blood: Technology and Disease Identity in Twentieth-Century America.* Baltimore: Johns Hopkins University Press, 1997.

Wailoo discusses the history of the progress made in understanding several diseases of the blood. Contains a chapter on pernicious anemia, the disease Whipple's work helped to elucidate. The author interprets this disease in its social context and explores the role of the pharmaceutical industry in defining disease through manufacturing, packaging, advertising, and cure promotion.

Whipple, George H. "Autobiographical Sketch." *Perspectives in Biology and Medicine* 2 (Spring, 1959): 253-289. A short sketch outlining the main events in Whipple's life. Straightforward presentation of useful facts.

———. "Hemoglobin Regeneration as Influenced by Diet and Other Factors." In *Les Prix Nobel en 1934*. Stockholm: Imprimerie Royale, P. A. Norstedt and Soner, 1935. A nine-page account in Whipple's own words of the history of the work leading to the experiments on anemic dogs for which Whipple received the Nobel Prize. It includes citations of papers he published.

*Kristen L. Zacharias*

# WALTER WHITE

*Born:* July 1, 1893; Atlanta, Georgia
*Died:* March 21, 1955; New York, New York
*Area of Achievement:* Civil rights
*Contributions:* As the chief administrator of the NAACP during many of its formative years, White helped pave the way for the monumental changes that advanced U.S. civil rights and race relations in the second half of the twentieth century.

## Early Life

Walter White was born in Atlanta, Georgia, on July 1, 1893. In many ways, his youth differed from that of Atlanta's other black children. One of seven children born into a religiously devout middle-class family, he apparently experienced few material hardships. His father, who worked as a mail carrier, provided for his family a commodious and well-maintained home not far from Atlanta's downtown area. A family library exposed Walter to many of the great books and gave him an appreciation for literature that influenced him throughout his life. Attending grade school at Atlanta University afforded him an opportunity for formal education beyond the eight grades of public schooling open to the city's other black youths. He graduated college at the same institution in 1916.

In other ways, life for White in Atlanta paralleled that of other southern black people. Although White was blond, blue-eyed, and so fair-skinned that he could pass for white, he refused to do so and was himself subjected to Jim Crow indignities. Raised in an era when color and race truly mattered, White witnessed daily how the system emasculated black people. More traumatic, he experienced the terror of violent racism so frequently experienced by black people in the early twentieth century South.

In 1906 tensions in Atlanta erupted into bloody racial conflict. White Atlantans were already on emotional edge because of demagogue politicians who blatantly raised the "Negro question" for political advantage, and the effects of a rivalry for subscription between daily newspapers that preyed on their fears with sensational or fabricated stories of the so-called black rapist did not help matters. White people vented their anger after the showing of D. W. Griffith's film *The Birth of a Nation* further charged the atmosphere. During the evening of the outbreak, White had accompanied his father on his mail route and witnessed several black people being victimized in the rioting. The two escaped the wrath of the mob because of their near-white skin color and thus moved through the streets unmolested. More knowledgeable Caucasians, however, knew that they were African Americans, and, on a subsequent night of rioting, a mob gathered in front of their home to burn them out. However, thirteen-year-old White and his father had armed themselves and came close to firing on the frenzied crowd before neighbors interceded to prevent the Whites from losing their home or killing someone in the mob.

This violent outbreak deeply affected White. The Atlanta riot helped him through an identity crisis largely caused by his white physical features in what was "legally" a black body. After the event, White claimed to have understood and willingly accepted the reality of who he was. More important, the riot awakened in him a desire to prevent similar acts of lawlessness against African Americans. In many ways, this event, punctuated with subsequent random acts of violence against black people, helped to lay the foundation for a lifetime of service to the cause of civil rights.

## Life's Work

White's accomplishments in this regard essentially began in 1919 when he accepted National Association for the Advancement of Colored People (NAACP) executive secretary James Weldon Johnson's offer of a job in the New York City headquarters as his assistant. White had impressed Johnson as someone possessing good administrative skills and leadership potential during a recent visit to Atlanta in support of a local campaign to improve black education conditions. Although White had played only a minor role in the campaign, he quickly gained recognition as a gifted speaker and talented organizer.

From the outset of his association with the organization, White's work involved efforts to eradicate lynching. One of the nation's most disgraceful practices, especially prevalent in the South, lynching had been a perennial problem since the Reconstruction era. Between 1900 and 1919, nearly 1,300 African Americans had been victims of this form of vigilante justice; seventy-six lynchings occurred during the year that White joined the NAACP staff. As a Georgian, where hundreds of

these atrocities had occurred over the years, White was already sensitized to the problem. His antilynching efforts virtually became a personal crusade and easily dovetailed with years of NAACP campaigning to end the practice. He visited dozens of sites of some of the more horrific crimes and came close to becoming a victim himself while investigating the Helena, Arkansas, race riot during the 1919 Red Summer. He also spent a considerable amount of official time assisting in the drafting of legislative bills, testifying before congressional committees, and lobbying Congress for passage of federal antilynching laws. He influenced the introduction and passage of bills in the House of Representatives in 1935 and 1940, only to see them die in the Senate.

White's crusade against lynching failed to produce federal legislation outlawing the practice, though he worked doggedly for it until 1949. Gradually, however, lynching declined nationally as the appeal to the reason of potential vigilantes by numerous antilynching advocates, including journalists and organizations, began to pay off. In 1929, for example, only seven black people were murdered by lynchers, the lowest number since systematic record-keeping began in 1882 at the Tuskegee Institute. By then White had become a leading authority on lynching, as was made evident by his 1929 book *Rope and Faggot: A Biography of Judge Lynch*. Although its focus was an analysis on the causes of lynching—causes that White maintained included economic, political, social, religious, and sexual factors—his book was a telling, though predictable, indictment against the practice. Its publication, however, reflected a lifelong interest in literature. Prior to the appearance of *Rope and Faggot*, White had already published two novels, *Fire in the Flint* (1924) and *Flight* (1926). The two books, which dealt with themes consistent with the literary outpouring of the 1920's Harlem Renaissance—race conflict, color, and identity—brought White international recognition as a talented fiction writer. In the last decade of his life, three other books followed, one of which was an autobiography.

White's novels helped to validate his place in the black intellectual movement, but they were merely interludes in his larger civil rights career. Even the weekly newspaper columns and numerous journal articles that he published largely concerned improving the status of black Americans. White's opportunity to play a broader, more significant role in this regard began in 1930 when he served as the NAACP's acting executive secretary and permanently succeeded Johnson the next year. Only the second African American to hold the NAACP's top position, White led the organization until his death in 1955.

White's tenure encompassed some of the organization's greatest civil rights accomplishments and certainly its most significant judicial triumphs. Almost from the outset in his new position, White orchestrated a national campaign that prevented confirmation of President Herbert Hoover's appointee, Judge John J. Parker, a North Carolina segregationist and opponent of black voting rights, to the U.S. Supreme Court. The success helped to enhance White's reputation as a persuasive leader capable of influencing Congress in areas besides lynching. His involvement in formulating strategy in the support and legal defense of the nine famous Scottsboro boys falsely accused in two 1932 Alabama rape cases helped to focus international attention on southern injustice and prevented their execution—and perhaps lynching—if not their release from jail.

White guided the NAACP to the courts in its larger efforts to resolve racial discrimination and civil rights violations. A string of legal assaults addressing voting rights, which actually began prior to White's administration, culminated with a major Supreme Court decision in 1944 to declare all forms of the white Democratic primary unconstitutional. During much of White's tenure, the NAACP devoted considerable attention to breaking barriers of Jim Crow education, an area of interest that initiated his involvement in civil rights. The organization launched and won numerous lawsuits in the 1930's and 1940's that mandated pay equalization for black teachers in the South. During the same period, several cases backed by White's behind-the-scene's management and litigated by a team of talented NAACP lawyers (including Charles Houston, William Hastie, and Thurgood Marshall) won decisions that opened professional and graduate education for black students in southern white universities. The most notable victories were Thomas Hocutt's 1933 right to enter the University of Maryland's Pharmacy School, a 1938 Supreme Court decision to admit Lloyd Gaines into the University of Missouri Law School, and Ada Lou Sipuel's similar admission into the University of Oklahoma in 1948. These education advances set the stage for the most far-reaching legal decision under White's tenure, the 1954 *Brown v. Board of Education* ruling that declared segregated public schools unconstitutional and affected virtually every aspect of American life.

Politically, White supported Democrats Franklin Roosevelt and Harry Truman. He saw in Roosevelt's New Deal program real opportunity for black progress. However, as a part of the NAACP's dual agenda to fight for social welfare and economic justice for all people as well as black civil rights, he lobbied against some New Deal legislation that clearly excluded or discriminated against African Americans in employment, housing, and social security programs. Understandably, he played a leading role in the effort to acquire fair employment for black people in World War II defense plants, pushed for greater involvement of black soldiers as combatants in the war, and supported Truman's desegregation of the armed forces.

**Summary**

More than any other organization, the NAACP changed the South and thereby the state of U.S. race relations. Among the many leaders identified with this group, perhaps none played a more significant role in facilitating these changes than Walter White. He worked with other national and political leaders, managed behind the scenes, and used any available public forum to advance the rights of all Americans, especially African Americans. His interests, however, transcended the plight of black people in the United States as he supported ideas of Pan-Africanism, championed economic development in the Western Hemisphere, urged decolonization and independence movements in parts of West Africa, and served as an advisor to the U.S. United Nations delegation between 1945 and 1948. In many ways White was a precursor to the later reformers who sought to advance international human rights. It was, however, his stable and dedicated leadership of the NAACP, often overshadowed by the courtroom successes of his legal teams, that ultimately paved the way for many of the important civil rights gains that black people achieved during the twentieth century and that solidified his name as an enduring legacy.

**Bibliography**

Brooks, Neil. "We are not Free! Free! Free! *Flight* and the Unmapping of American Literary Studies." *CLA Journal* 41, no. 4 (June, 1998). Discussion of Walter White's novel *Flight* which deals with the protagonist's experiences with racial humiliation.

Hamilton, Dona Cooper, and Charles V. Hamilton, *The Dual Agenda: Race and Social Welfare Policies of Civil Rights Organizations*. New York: Columbia University Press, 1997. A valuable study of the efforts of civil rights organizations, especially the NAACP, to insure economic justice and social welfare for the poor, regardless of race.

Sitkoff, Harvard. *A New Deal for Blacks; The Emergence of Civil Rights as a National Issue: The Depression Decade*. New York: Oxford University Press, 1978; Oxford: Oxford University Press, 1981. A path-breaking book when it was published, Sitkoff's book contains numerous references to White, the NAACP, and New Deal issues.

Tushnet, Mark V. *The NAACP Legal Strategy Against Segregated Education, 1925-1950.* Chapel Hill: University of North Carolina Press, 1987. A law professor's brief look at how the NAACP legally undermined segregated public education prior to the momentous 1954 Supreme Court decision.

Waldron, Edward E. *Walter White and the Harlem Renaissance*. Port Washington, N.Y.: Kennikat Press, 1978. A brief analysis of White's creative work and his influence on the Harlem Renaissance.

White, Walter. *A Man Called White: The Autobiography of Walter White*. New York: Viking Press, 1948; London: Gollancz, 1949. Although this book is a good beginning to understanding White, especially the influences on his early life, it lacks real details on some of the major issues that consumed him.

Wilkins, Roy, with Tom Matthews. *Standing Fast: The Autobiography of Roy Wilkins*. New York: Viking Press, 1982. A revealing account of the life and times of White's longtime subordinate and eventual successor as NAACP executive secretary.

Wilson, Sondra K. *In Search of Democracy: The NAACP Writings of James Weldon Johnson, Walter White, and Roy Wilkins (1920-1977)*. New York: Oxford University Press, 1999. A collection of the writings of NAACP directors White, James Weldon Johnson, and Roy Wilkins, many published for the first time.

Zangrando, Robert. *The NAACP Crusade Against Lynching, 1909-1950*. Philadelphia: Temple University Press, 1980. Zangrando's book is one of the best publications detailing the work of the NAACP, and hence the efforts of White, on the subject of lynching. Contains valuable statistical data on lynchings.

*Robert L. Jenkins*

## ALFRED NORTH WHITEHEAD

*Born:* February 15, 1861; Ramsgate, Isle of Thanet, Kent, England

*Died:* December 30, 1947; Cambridge, Massachusetts

*Areas of Achievement:* Philosophy and mathematics

*Contribution:* Striving for a more comprehensive and unified system of human knowledge, Whitehead made major contributions to mathematical logic and produced a wholly original and modern metaphysics.

### Early Life

Alfred North Whitehead was born on February 15, 1861, in the town of Ramsgate on the Isle of Thanet, County of Kent, England. He was the last of four children born to Alfred Whitehead, a schoolmaster and clergyman, and Maria Sarah Buckmaster. Whitehead's father was a typical Victorian country vicar who tirelessly tended to the needs of the people of the island and was well loved by them. His grandfather, Thomas Whitehead, was more remarkable intellectually. The son of a prosperous farmer, he had single-handedly created a successful boys' school at Ramsgate, unusual for its time in its emphasis on mathematics and science.

Ramsgate was a small, close-knit community in which history was a physical presence in the form of many ancient ruins, including Norman and medieval churches and Richborough Castle, built by the Romans when they occupied Britain. The surrounding waters were notoriously treacherous, and Whitehead remembered as a child hearing at night the booming of cannon and seeing rockets rise in the night sky, signaling a ship in distress. He believed that over the generations this environment instilled in the people an obstinacy and a tendency toward lonely thought.

Because he was small for his age and appeared frail, young Whitehead was not allowed to attend school or participate in children's games. Instead, his father tutored him in Latin, Greek, and mathematics. Whitehead learned his lessons quickly and had free time for periods of solitary thought and rambles through the wild coastal countryside with its mysterious ruins.

In 1875, Whitehead left home and entered Sherborne in Dorsetshire, a well-regarded public school from which both of his brothers had been graduated. He had grown to love mathematics, and he excelled at it enough to be excused from some of the standard courses in classical languages and literature in order to study it more deeply. Ignoring his "frailty" he took up Rugby, developing his athletic skills with seriousness and tenacity. As captain of the team he compensated for his size with intelligence and leadership and became one of the best forwards in the history of the school. Later in life he said that being tackled in a Rugby game was an excellent paradigm for the "Real" as he meant the term philosophically.

Before his last year at Sherborne, he chose to take the grueling six-day scholarship examination for Trinity College, Cambridge, an examination that would determine not only entry and the needed financial assistance but, more important, eligibility for a fellowship and, therefore, his hopes for a career in mathematics. Whitehead took the examination a year earlier than he needed to, and passed.

Whitehead entered Trinity College in the autumn of 1880 as a participant in a special honors program which allowed him to study in his area of specialty, mathematics, exclusively for the full three years of undergraduate work. In the Cambridge of that time, however, perhaps more than today, important education also took place outside the classroom in lively, spontaneous discussions with other students, an experience which Whitehead described as being like "a daily Platonic Dialogue," and which sometimes ran late into the night and into the early morning, ranging over politics, history, philosophy, science, and the arts. For a time, Whitehead became intensely interested in Immanuel Kant's *Critique of Pure Reason* (1781), in which one of Kant's primary aims was to explain how arithmetic and geometry, which appear to be self-consistent deductive systems without need of empirical verification, can yet give knowledge that can be reliably applied in the real world. This question was a central theme in much of Whitehead's own work, though he became disenchanted with Kant's explanations.

While his mathematics teachers were all of the highest caliber, one in particular, William Davidson Niven, significantly influenced Whitehead's development by introducing him to the physics of James Clerk Maxwell, whose theories about electromagnetism called into question the all-encompassing explanatory power of the then-reigning Newtonian physics, opening the way to modern physics.

## Life's Work

Whitehead's high scores on final examinations and his dissertation on Maxwell's *Treatise on Electricity and Magnetism* (1873) won for him a six-year fellowship, allowing him free room and board at Cambridge and unlimited freedom for mathematical research.

Unlike most research fellows, however, Whitehead did not become immediately productive. By character he was not a piecemeal problem solver who worked in ever narrower and more refined areas of a subject, but rather an explorer seeking a wider and more unified perspective. He discovered and was impressed with the works of Hermann Günther Grassman, an all but forgotten German mathematician who had developed a new kind of algebra. Grassmann's *Die lineale Ausdehnungslehre, ein neuer Zweig der Mathematik* (1844), along with George Boole's *The Mathematical Analysis of Logic* (1847) and William Hamilton's *The Elements of Quaternions* (1866), seemed to Whitehead to portend a whole new field of algebras of logic not limited to number and quantity and with exciting unexplored applications. Whitehead envisioned a work in which all these ideas would be brought together in a general theory that would include giving a spatial interpretation to logic, which would provide a more powerful general theory of geometry. On a visit to his parents in Broadstairs in June of 1890, at a time when his great work did not seem to be going anywhere and he was contemplating conversion to Roman Catholicism, Whitehead was introduced to Evelyn Wade and fell in love. She was twenty-three years old, with black eyes and auburn hair and a vibrant personality. Though English, she spoke French as her native language, having been reared in a convent at Angers. Whitehead wasted no time and proposed to her romantically in a cave under the garden in his father's vicarage. They were married in December of 1891. Their marriage was to produce three children. The youngest would be tragically killed in aerial combat in 1918. Evelyn loved and cared for Alfred and always made a place where he could work without interruption wherever they lived, but she had no interest in science or mathematics. Yet she perfectly complemented his analytic temperament with a deep interest in people and a wonderful aesthetic sense. Her example, according to Whitehead, taught him that "beauty, moral and aesthetic, is the aim of existence: and that kindness, and love, and artistic satisfaction are among its modes of attainment"—logic and science being important because they are useful in providing the conditions for periods of great art and literature. Whitehead's later worldview incorporated these ideas.

Marriage was good for Whitehead. He soon began work in earnest on his project, the first volume of which was published in 1898 as *A Treatise on Universal Algebra*. The second volume was never written, partly because of another momentous event that occurred in the same year as Whitehead's marriage: In 1890, Bertrand Russell entered Cambridge.

Whitehead, who happened to be reading examinations at the time, recognized Russell's potential and, even though Russell's scores were disappointingly low, saw to it—some say by burning the scores—that Russell received a scholarship. Their future collaboration on *Principia Mathematica* (1910-1913) was to be one of the most fruitful in the history of mathematics.

By 1903, Russell and Whitehead were colleagues. Russell had won a fellowship to Trinity College with a dissertation on the foundations of geometry. The two men found their individual interests and aims increasingly converging. With their wives, they attended the First International Congress of Philosophy in Paris in 1900 and met the great mathematician Giuseppe Peano, who had devised a symbolic notation that he was applying to the clarification of the foundations of mathematics. Russell, in his own work, had extended some of Peano's ideas and in 1903 published *Principles of Mathematics*, in which he attempted to demonstrate that all mathematics, including geometry, could be deductively derived from a few concepts of logic. At the same time, Whitehead was working along similar lines in his projected second volume to his *A Treatise on Universal Algebra*. Their friendship and their intellectual excitement with what seemed to be a revolution in mathematics led inevitably toward collaboration, and they spent more and more time together.

At one point, the Russells even moved in with the Whiteheads. This, however, did not work out. Russell fell secretly and unrequitedly in love with Evelyn Whitehead—he was by then very unhappy with his own wife—and the Russells, without anything coming into the open, moved out amiably. The collaboration, however, was unaffected by this turn of events. The life of the mind was the greater passion for both men, and their work was proceeding well.

In 1903, they decided, rather than publish two separate additions to their own works, that they would concentrate on one joint work. This would become the monumental *Principia Mathematica*. They originally believed that it would take only about a year to complete. It took approximately nine. The manuscript ran to more than four thousand pages and required a four-wheeler to transport it to Cambridge Press. Whitehead, almost fifty, was now stooped from leaning over his desk for long periods. During the work on *Principia Mathematica*, Whitehead found time to write a short work which he considered to be his most original, "On Mathematical Concepts of the Material World." Published in 1906, it is concerned with "the possible relations to space of the ultimate entities which (in ordinary language) constitute the 'stuff' of space." Anticipating Albert Einstein's general theory of relativity, he criticized the classical concept of an absolute space occupied by pointlike atoms, defending instead a relativistic view that space is not independent of the things in it but is rather dependent for its structure on objects within it. Further, he proposed that the fundamental constituents of matter are not pointlike particles but are more complex entities such as lines of force, with particles being the result of the interactions of these lines. Neither this work nor *Principia Mathematica* met with great success when first published, being considered too philosophical by specialists.

In 1910, Whitehead rather mysteriously left his assured position at Trinity College and moved to London, where he had no position. Whitehead may have simply found himself in a rut; the reasons, however, are probably more complex. For one thing, he had become politically active in his last few years at Cambridge, speaking out for women's rights and adopting a liberal position which outraged the university elite with their bias toward the rich and titled—he and his wife were once pelted with oranges and rotten eggs while sitting behind a Labour Party speaker. A clue to his leaving Cambridge may also be found elsewhere. Years before, in 1887, as a member of the prestigious Cambridge Apostles discussion group, Whitehead had responded to the topic question, which asked which was more important in life, "Study or Marketplace?" with the terse comment, "Study with windows." Whitehead probably had begun to sense that he could not commit himself to the ivory tower life of a don without trying to make some connection between his work and the wider world.

Indeed, his subsequent actions bear out this inference. Soon after settling in London, he wrote a popular exposition of mathematics for the layman, *An Introduction to Mathematics*, which was published in 1911. From 1911 to 1914, he taught at University College, London, and from 1914 to 1924 he held a professorship at the Imperial College of Science and Technology in Kensington, all the while serving on various committees and councils setting the policies for London education. The aim of these institutions was to bring education to the masses, rationally adapting it to their needs and circumstances. Whitehead believed that the old elitist structure of the university must give way to new forms and that no less than the salvation of civilization was at stake. He compared this enterprise of mass education to the activities of the monasteries of the Middle Ages. His ideas on this subject appeared later in his books *The Aims of Education and Other Essays*, published in 1929, and *Essays in Science and Philosophy*, published in 1947. In 1923, another major shift occurred in Whitehead's life. While still at the Imperial College of Science and Technology, Whitehead received an invitation to come to Harvard University to join the philosophy department. This invitation was no doubt based on his reputation as a philosopher of science. Whitehead was then sixty-two years old, an age when most men are thinking of retirement. Whitehead, however, had never taught philosophy and liked the idea, and his wife wholeheartedly supported the move. It turned out to be the beginning of a massive creative surge in a new direction, reaching far beyond the specialized boundaries of the philosophy of science.

Beginning with *Science and the Modern World*, based on the Lowell lectures he gave in 1925 and published that year, Whitehead called into question the view that values have nothing to do with the basic constituents of nature, which, according to the prevailing view which he called "scientific materialism," consisted really only of matter in motion. In 1929, continuing this trend toward an all-inclusive worldview, there followed *Process and Reality*, which is considered to be one of the greatest works of metaphysics of all time, as well as one of the most forbidding. It propounds what Whitehead called "the philosophy of organism," in a novel terminology. *Adventures of Ideas*, published in 1933, was his last major work and probably his most accessible book on philosophy, with extensive explorations of sociology, cosmology, philosophy, and civilization as revealed from the perspective of his new metaphysical views.

Whitehead's reception in the United States was warm, and it provided him with an audience for the products of his far-ranging and independent intellect which he perhaps could not have had in his native England. He is remembered fondly by students and faculty as rosy-cheeked and cherubic, giving freely of his time, meeting with students often on Sunday evenings, and lecturing widely at Eastern and Midwestern universities. His last work, a small, lucid, and accessible work titled *Modes of Thought* (1938), was based on lectures he gave at Wellesley College and the University of Chicago. Whitehead died at Cambridge, Massachusetts, on December 30, 1947.

### Summary

For more than fifty years, Alfred North Whitehead applied his unique intellectual gifts successively to mathematics, education, and speculative philosophy and cosmology, always striving for an understanding of the nature of reality that could be applied to the betterment of man. Where he saw value in the ideas of others, he unselfishly helped those ideas to reach fruition. As a teacher, he brought out the best in his students, always with kindness and respect for their distinctive gifts. His later metaphysics is unique in the field for its scientific sophistication, yet it is free of the dogmatic rejection of the preeminence of human value in the world often found in the natural sciences.

### Bibliography

Emmet, Dorothy M. "Whitehead." *Philosophy* 71, no. 275 (January, 1996). Discusses several phases of Whitehead's life and his philosophical interests during those periods including mathematics, nature, and metaphysics.

———. "Whitehead, Alfred North." In *The Encyclopedia of Philosophy*, edited by Paul Edwards, vol. 7. New York: Macmillan, 1967. An excellent topical overview of Whitehead's philosophy.

Ford, Lewis S. "Structural Affinities between Kant and Whitehead." *International Philosophical Quarterly* 38, no. 3 (September, 1998). Compares the philosophies of Whitehead and Emmanuel Kant.

Lowe, Victor. *Alfred North Whitehead: The Man and His Work*. Vol. 1, *1861-1910*. Baltimore and London: Johns Hopkins University Press, 1985. The fullest available account of Whitehead's life through his tenure at Cambridge. A projected second volume will cover Whitehead's life in London and at Harvard. Lowe was a student of Whitehead and is an eminent authority on his work.

Russell, Bertrand. *The Autobiography of Bertrand Russell: 1872-1914*. London: Allen and Unwin, 1968; Boston: Little Brown, 1969. Valuable for its account of the writing of *Principia Mathematica*, even though it is related from Russell's somewhat biased point of view.

Schilpp, Paul Arthur, ed. *The Philosophy of Alfred North Whitehead*. New York: Tudor, 1941. A collection of critical essays on Whitehead which includes Whitehead's autobiographical sketch and Lowe's insightful essay "The Development of Whitehead's Philosophy." Contains complete bibliography of Whitehead's works.

Whitehead, Alfred North. *Alfred North Whitehead: An Anthology*. Compiled by F. S. C. Northrop and Mason W. Gross. New York: Macmillan, 1953. Contains selections from all Whitehead's major works and is thus an excellent starting point for anyone wishing to become familiar with his ideas.

———. *An Introduction to Mathematics*. London: Williams and Norgate, and New York: Holt, 1911. Rev. ed. London: Oxford University Press, 1948. For anyone interested in Whitehead or in an exposition of the power of mathematics.

*Scott Bouvier*

# GERTRUDE VANDERBILT WHITNEY

*Born:* January 9, 1875; New York, New York
*Died:* April 18, 1942; New York, New York
*Areas of Achievement:* Art and patronage of the arts
*Contribution:* Whitney was a distinguished American sculptor of figures, monuments, and reliefs for the public domain and an art patron and founder of the Whitney Museum of American Art in New York.

## Early Life

Gertrude Vanderbilt was born an heiress to the great family fortune established by her great-grandfather, Commodore Cornelius Vanderbilt. Gertrude was the second daughter and the fourth of seven children of Cornelius and Alice Claypoole Vanderbilt. Her father was a railroad magnate who indulged his interests as an art patron and collector. Gertrude was brought up in an atmosphere of wealth and luxury and spent most of her youth shuttling between her family's two homes: a luxurious mansion in New York City and a summer estate in Newport, Rhode Island. She was educated by private tutors both at home and in Europe. Later, she attended New York's exclusive, all-female Brearley School. During her youth, she wrote avidly in personal journals and showed promising skill in watercolor and drawing.

On August 25, 1896, Gertrude Vanderbilt was married to Harry Payne Whitney, an avid sportsman who spent his days traveling on hunting trips and playing polo. His father was William C. Whitney, a financier and secretary of the Navy under President Grover Cleveland. The couple maintained a town house on Fifth Avenue in New York City and a country estate at Westbury, Long Island. Gertrude bore three children, a son, Cornelius Vanderbilt Whitney, and two daughters, Flora Payne and Barbara. Over the years, Gertrude Whitney and her husband became estranged, yet they fostered a certain solidarity in times of crises and in relation to family obligations.

Gertrude Vanderbilt Whitney accepted the responsibility of rearing her three children and fulfilled her many social obligations. These obligations did not deter her from studying sculpture. She had three teachers from whom she learned her craft. The first was sculptor Hendrik Christian Andersen. Next, she studied with James Earle Fraser, who instructed her at the New Students League in New York City. Her last mentor, Andrew O'Connor, completed her education in Paris. Both Fraser and O'Connor were sculptors of public monuments and channeled her interests in the same direction. Her works soon became well known and highly regarded in the American and European art communities.

## Life's Work

During the first ten years of her work as a sculptor, Gertrude Vanderbilt Whitney exhibited under a pseudonym. She believed that her famous family name would never allow her the freedom of unbiased criticism from her viewers. It was not until 1910, when her statue, *Paganism Immortal*, won a distinguished rating at the National Academy that she began to exhibit under her own name. It was during these early years that Whitney set up her own studio in Greenwich Village. Though not taken seriously by the art community at first, she worked hard at perfecting her craft in her studio. Her dedication and perseverance soon won her the respect and companionship of other artists.

It was also during this time that Whitney became known as a patron of the arts. In 1908, when the "Eight of the Ash Can" group held an exhibit at the Macbeth Gallery, Whitney purchased four canvases from the exhibit. After witnessing the difficulties such young artists had in finding exhibition venues, she began to provide space in her studio where they could display their work. This temporary solution led her to establish the Whitney Studio in an adjacent building in 1914. It soon became a gathering place for various artists and developed into the Whitney Studio Club in 1918. Whitney stayed true to her original intentions for the gallery by continuing to exhibit and sell works by young artists who were either too poor or too unknown to afford dealers.

By this point, Whitney had built up her personal holdings in contemporary American art. In 1929, she chose to make her vast private art collection available to the public by offering her entire collection to New York City's Metropolitan Museum of Art, complete with an endowment to build a new museum wing in which to house her collection. After this offer was rejected, she established her own museum in 1931, known as the Whitney Museum of American Art. Whitney appointed Juliana Force, who had served as her assistant since 1914, as the museum's first director. For the remainder of

her life, Whitney continued to make private gifts to young artists in the hope of advancing their study and work.

The camaraderie Whitney experienced during her early years in Greenwich Village helped her to become more focused on her art and gave her great self-confidence in her abilities as a sculptor. Others, too, increasingly recognized her talent. In 1912, she was hired to construct the terra cotta fountain in the Aztec style for the patio of the Pan American Union Building in Washington, D.C. Also, her marble sculpture entitled *Fountain of El Dorado*, which depicted man's frantic search for gold, won a bronze medal at the 1915 Panama-Pacific Exposition in San Francisco. This fountain was later erected as a permanent fixture in Lima, Peru.

Whitney's next large-scale work was the result of a 1914 competition in which she won the $50,000 *Titanic Memorial* commission. Her design and its execution are considered by many critics to be her most important work. This monument to American citizens who lost their lives in the famous sea tragedy is eighteen feet high and was installed on the banks of the Potomac in Washington, D.C., in 1931. A seminude figure of a man, carved in granite, takes the shape of a cross atop the sculpture's pedestal, thus contributing to the sculpture's powerful symbolism of sacrifice and resurrection. Critics contend that the work of French sculptor Auguste Rodin profoundly influenced Whitney in her execution of this monument.

As it did for many of her generation, World War I had a profound influence on Whitney. The awful realities of the war and the resulting bloodshed prompted her to establish a field hospital at Juilly, France, in the fall of 1914. She personally administered to the wounded soldiers until the spring of 1915, when exhaustion and anguish compelled her to return home. The war forced her to turn away from aesthetic abstraction in her art work, and her later works expressed greater realism, particularly her memorials to the soldiers of World War I. These pieces bore titles such as *At His Post*, *His Last Charge*, *Gassed, Blinded*, *His Bunkie*, *Private in the 15th*, and *The Aviator*. After she returned to New York, she had begun throwing together masses of clay to re-create images of the soldiers she had seen, and these statues formed the foundation for her larger war memorials of the 1920's. Whitney completed two panels for the Victory Arch in New York City as well as the Washington Heights Memorial at 168th Street and Broadway. The latter won the New York Society of Architects' Medal as the most meritorious work of 1922. In 1926, Whitney designed a large memorial for the harbor of St. Nazaire, France, to commemorate the 1917 landing of the first American Expeditionary Forces. Sadly, the Germans destroyed this monument during World War II.

Most of Whitney's later work of the 1920's and 1930's was completed at her studio in Paris. Whitney produced significant works during these two decades that diverged from the war theme. In 1924, she produced a larger-than-life bronze equestrian statue of Colonel William F. Cody, better known as Buffalo Bill, which was eventually installed in Cody, Wyoming. Whitney then created the Columbus Monument, a 114-foot statue that was placed at the port of Palos, Spain, in 1933.

In 1934, Gertrude Vanderbilt Whitney attracted national attention—not as a result of her work, but because of a highly publicized child custody case concerning her niece, Gloria Vanderbilt. Gertrude Vanderbilt Whitney fought for, and won, custody of Gloria. The stress and publicity surrounding the prolonged case greatly undermined Whitney's already failing health. She refused to give in to her illness, however, and continued to exhibit her work publicly until after the unveiling of her sculpture *The Spirit of Flight* at the New York World's Fair of 1939. Three years later Whitney died, reportedly of a heart condition, at the age of sixty-seven.

**Summary**

Gertrude Vanderbilt Whitney is one of the few American women to hold such a prominent position in the history of American art as a traditional sculptor of public monuments. Her work as an artist is often downplayed in light of her munificence as patron of modern American art. Ironically, the founding of the Whitney Museum is often viewed as her greatest creation. Although her work as a philanthropist was crucial in generating greater respect and attention for modern American artists and their work, Whitney is equally notable for her own struggle to establish herself as a sculptor of public monuments in an era when her gender and her social background made the realization of her dream nearly impossible.

**Bibliography**

Auchincloss, Louis. *The Vanderbilt Era: Profiles of a Gilded Age*. New York: Scribner, 1989. Novelist and biographer Auchincloss examines the lives and accomplishments of the Vanderbilts of the period from 1880 to 1920. Although not focused exclusively on Gertrude Vanderbilt Whitney, this family history provides lively anecdotes and places her within her familial and historical context.

Dunford, Penny. *Biographical Dictionary of Women Artists in Europe and America Since 1850*. Philadelphia: University of Pennsylvania Press, 1989; London: Harvester, 1990. This work contains a brief biography covering Whitney's main works as a sculptor and her significant contributions as an art patron.

Fraser, Kennedy. "The Heiress." *Vogue* 188 no. 3, (March, 1998). Profile of Whitney.

Friedman, Bernard H. *Gertrude Vanderbilt Whitney*. New York: Doubleday, 1978. Biography of the sculptor written with the research assistance of the artist's granddaughter, Flora Miller Irving. This work is filled with many of Whitney's own writings but lacks much in the way of scholarly analysis and evaluation. The book details her life and relationships, but there is little information about her art.

Patterson, Jerry E. *The Vanderbilts*. New York: Abrams, 1989. Released in the same year as Auchincloss' work, this dynastic biography of the Vanderbilts examines the private and public lives of various family members, including their marriages, divorces, financial dealings and business investments, and their patronage of the arts. Illustrated with numerous photographs of Vanderbilt residences and personal art holdings. Helps place Whitney within the context of her family background.

Rubinstein, Charlotte Streifer. *American Women Artists: From Early Indian Times to the Present*. New York: Avon, 1982. This collection of biographical sketches includes a readable, comprehensive, yet brief sketch on Whitney. Contains delightful anecdotes, including the fact that Whitney often worked in turkish harem pants, turban, and turned up shoes.

Whitney Museum of American Art. *Memorial Exhibition: Gertrude Vanderbilt Whitney*. New York: Whitney Museum of Art, 1943. The introduction to this catalog is written by Juliana Force, Whitney's administrative assistant and her chosen director of the Whitney Museum. Force emphasizes Whitney's career as a creator of monumental sculpture and focuses on the Whitney Museum's works from her collection.

*Patricia McNeal*

# SIR FRANK WHITTLE

*Born:* June 1, 1907; Coventry, Warwickshire, England
*Died:* August 8, 1996; Columbia, Maryland
*Area of Achievement:* Aeronautical engineering
*Contribution:* With a background that included flight experience, training in power-plant design, and metalworking skills, Whittle designed and built the first jet engine in Great Britain.

## Early Life

Frank Whittle was born on June 1, 1907, in Coventry, England. His parents, of working-class background from Lancashire, had moved to Coventry, where Whittle's father worked in a cotton mill. The elder Whittle was fascinated by machinery and spent his spare time tinkering, often with his son at his elbow. Eventually, the elder Whittle was able to buy a small machine firm, the Leamington Valve and Piston Ring Company, which he ran for years as a one-man operation. As a boy, Whittle performed odd jobs in his father's business and eventually learned to use the various power tools, drilling valve stems and operating the lathe. In this way, he learned the fundamentals of drafting and metalworking, an understanding that proved to be valuable to designing and building the hand-tooled prototypes of jet engines.

At the age of eleven, Whittle won a scholarship to a secondary school which later became Leamington College. By his own account, Whittle did not set records as a scholar, but outside school he became an omnivorous reader of popular science books, spending hours in the public library. His chief interest lay in aviation, and this interest led to his decision to join the Royal Air Force (RAF) in 1922. He passed the RAF's written exams with high marks but was rejected because of his small size—he was only five feet tall. An active and competitive young man, Whittle sought out a friendly physical education instructor, who put him on a regime of exercises and a carefully planned diet. Whittle grew three inches and eventually became one of six hundred apprentices to the RAF training school at Cranwell in 1923.

For the next three years, Whittle studied the technicalities of rigging metal airplanes, a new specialty at that time, since aircraft construction was still dominated by wood and fabric. More important, he became very active in a local model airplane group which designed and built an impressive gas-engine aircraft with a wingspan of ten feet. This ambitious project caught the attention of his superiors, and Whittle was appointed as a cadet at the RAF College at Cranwell: He was on his way to becoming an RAF officer as well as a pilot. After Whittle was graduated second in his class from Cranwell in 1928, he was posted to a fighter squadron, then went on to a special school for flight instructors. During this time, the concept of using a gas turbine power plant for aircraft began to crystallize for him. He made some calculations, and the idea seemed feasible.

## Life's Work

Whittle's idea had first taken shape at Cranwell, where he wrote a thesis, "Future Developments in Aircraft Design," in which he concluded that high-speed, long-range aircraft would have to fly at very high altitudes, where low air density would enhance their performance. At a time when RAF fighters scuttled along at 150 miles per hour, Whittle was postulating speeds of five hundred miles per hour. As for power plants, his thesis discussed the possibility of rocket engines and gas turbines driving propellers. In the following months, after considering an arrangement in which a conventional piston engine was linked to a compressor and a low-pressure jet, he suddenly had the idea to substitute a turbine for the piston engine. He found that a high-pressure gas turbine could produce the energy to propel an aircraft. Although Whittle submitted sketches and calculations to appropriate offices in the Air Ministry, the response was disappointing. Nevertheless, he had sufficient faith in his proposal to take out a patent, which was filed in January, 1930.

Also during 1930, he was married to Dorothy Mary Lee and was posted to Felixstowe as a floatplane test pilot. Because of his flying skills and exemplary work at Felixstowe, Whittle went on to an officers' engineering course; a stellar performance in the class won for him a special appointment to take an honors course in mechanical engineering at the University of Cambridge. Throughout this time, Whittle periodically visited all the commercial firms he thought might have an interest in gas turbines. Unfortunately, it was the era of the Great Depression, and no business had money to sink into a radical new power system. Companies also complained that Whittle's design was ahead of the metallurgical state of the art by many years. Whit-

*Frank Whittle (left), beside the jet engine he designed, talks with Paul Garber*

tle was having a difficult time as well. His family now included two young children, and he was struggling to make ends meet on a young officer's salary. When his jet engine patent was due for renewal in 1935, he allowed it to lapse because he could not afford the renewal fee of five pounds.

At this point, his career took a dramatic turn. At Cambridge, two former RAF officers became convinced that Whittle's jet engine had merit. After reestablishing the basic patent and adding to it, they set out to find adequate financing to pursue the idea. Eventually a complex set of agreements was concluded which involved Whittle, his associates, the Air Ministry, a turbine engineering company, and an adventurous firm of investment bankers. In January, 1936, a contract was negotiated for the design and manufacture of an experimental jet engine. The Air Ministry allowed Whittle to work on the contract for six hours per week. The company organized to fabricate the engine was christened Power Jets Limited.

Meanwhile, Whittle received first-class honors in the engineering exams at Cambridge and was rewarded with a postgraduate year to conduct research on gas turbine engines. By 1937, he had been placed on the RAF's special duty list in order to work full-time on the jet engine. Coping with a multitude of problems, Whittle and the Power Jets team nevertheless built a full-sized bench-test engine and made a brief, though encouraging, run on April 12, 1937. This was a milestone and also won for the company a series of development contracts from the Air Ministry.

After an additional two years of experimental work, Power Jets received a government contract for a full-scale flight model of the Whittle engine, and Gloster Aircraft was to design the airplane, designated as E.28/39. The outbreak of World War II in September, 1939, added to the pressures of engine development. The strain took its toll on Whittle's health, and doctors were forced to hospitalize him more than once over the next few years.

Meanwhile, a series of combustion problems seemed to be resolved after liaison with engineers at Shell Group, who had been doing advanced research in fuels and combustion techniques. A series of endurance runs on a new engine design was successful, clearing the way for installation of a flight engine in the Gloster Aircraft model. Taxi trials were run during April, 1941, including some with Whittle at the controls. On May 15, 1941, as Whittle proudly looked on, the E.28/39 successfully took to the air, the hallmark of a new era in aviation.

During 1941, following a visit to Great Britain by American General Henry Harley "Hap" Arnold, it was decided to have the United States share in jet engine development. Because of its work on turbo superchargers, General Electric was selected for production in the United States. In October, 1941, a disassembled engine and a team from Power Jets flew across the Atlantic in the bomb bay of a B-24 Liberator. Whittle himself came to the United States the next year and stayed several months to advise the Americans on jet engine development. In October, 1942, the Bell P-59 made its first flight, beginning the jet age in the United States.

During the remaining years of the war, Whittle was closely involved in the development of the Gloster Meteor (a twin-engine jet fighter that shot down a number of V-1 Flying Bombs before the war's end) and spent considerable time in the coordination of jet engine manufacturing in Great Britain. Power Jets was not set up for volume production, and this task went to the large companies, such as Rolls Royce. Eventually, because of the government funds expended on Power Jets since 1939, the company was nationalized; the organization finally disintegrated, although its employees easily found positions in the many firms which were now entering the field. Whittle was later awarded £100,000, tax free, for his contributions. Because of medical problems, Whittle retired from the RAF in 1948, with the rank of air commodore. His contributions to the field of jet engineering were now well-known, and he received the honor of knighthood from George VI in the same year.

For the next two decades, Whittle became a technical adviser and consultant to leading aviation firms. After his first marriage ended, he married Hazel S. Hall in 1976. In 1977, Whittle accepted a position on the faculty of the United States Naval Academy, at Annapolis, Maryland, and while there he completed a technical book, *Gas Turbine Aero-Thermodynamics*, published by Pergamon Press in 1981.

### Summary

Although a German jet flew two years earlier than the British model, Sir Frank Whittle's pioneering efforts had major consequences for postwar military and civil aviation development. The leading German engineer in the field of jet propulsion was Hans von Ohain, who experimented with a jet engine fueled with gaseous hydrogen, early in 1937. As von Ohain himself has noted, dates and comparisons were "not meaningful," since Whittle's engine, tested in April of 1937, was operated with liquid fuel. In any case, the Germans surged ahead, because of the powerful influence of the Heinkel Corporation, one of the leading German aircraft manufacturers; the decision by military leaders to launch a crash program in jet engines; and the much less stringent reliability requirements of the German air ministry. The Heinkel He 178 took to the air on August 27, 1939. Like its Gloster counterpart, it was strictly an experimental airplane, quickly superseded by operational designs such as the Messerschmitt Me 262, a formidable opponent for Allied air forces over Europe late in the war.

In any event, American and British jets such as the Lockheed P-80 and the Gloster Meteor were in production by the war's end, ready to meet the Luftwaffe's jet challenge. The Allied jet fighters exemplified one of Whittle's most important legacies, stemming from the remarkable selflessness that had led the British to share this state-of-the-art technology and representing the expertise of the original Power Jets team. Commercially, Whittle's work led to the development of the famous de Havilland Comet jet transport of the 1950's and to its successors around the world. Commercial jet travel has been one of the most striking phenomena in transportation since World War II, with a major impact on business organization and the travel industry. In time-distance relationships, jet travel has literally brought all parts of the world closer together.

### Bibliography

Constant, Edward W., II. *The Origins of the Turbojet Revolution*. Baltimore: Johns Hopkins University Press, 1980. This prizewinning scholarly study traces jet technology in the early twentieth century. Constant's book includes an excellent, detailed survey of Whittle's work, as well as that of von Ohain. He also summarizes the transition from Whittle's centrifugal flow design to the modern axial flow turbojet.

Fulton, Kenneth. "Frank Whittle (1907-96)." *Nature* 383, no. 6595 (September 5, 1996). Brief profile of Whittle's career and life.

Heiman, Grover. *Jet Pioneers*. New York: Duell Sloan, 1963. A popular survey of several figures, including Whittle and von Ohain. Sprinkled with illustrations, this is a good introduction to Whittle and to the jet era.

Meher-Homji, C.B. "The Development of the Whittle Turbojet." *Journal of Engineering for Gas Turbines and Power* 120, no. 2 (April, 1998). Details Whittle's struggles to develop the turbojet.

Whittle, Sir Frank. "The Birth of the Jet Engine in Britain." In *The Jet Age*, edited by Walter Boyne and Donald Lopez. Washington, D.C.: Smithsonian Institute Press, 1979. An excellent essay by Whittle that closely follows his book (cited below).

———. *Jet: The Story of a Pioneer*. London: Muller, 1953; New York: Philosophical Library, 1954. An autobiographical review of Whittle's work that concludes with his retirement from the RAF in 1948. Valuable for its details on jet engine development and for details on the complex relationships of Power Jets to the Air Ministry as well as to other manufacturers.

*Roger E. Bilstein*

# NORBERT WIENER

*Born:* November 26, 1894; Columbus, Missouri
*Died:* March 18, 1964; Stockholm, Sweden
*Areas of Achievement:* Mathematics and cybernetics
*Contribution:* Wiener was a distinguished American mathematician credited with a founding of cybernetics, a science which facilitates comparison of biological and electronic systems by focusing on communication, feedback, and control.

## Early Life

In *Ex-Prodigy* (1964), the first volume of his two-volume autobiography, Norbert Wiener describes in detail his precocious youth and his relationship with his father, a brilliant and very forceful personality. Norbert Wiener's father, Leo Wiener, was born in the ghetto area of czarist Russia. At the age of thirteen, Leo became self-supporting. In spite of anti-Semitic laws and customs, he managed to be graduated from a Warsaw gymnasium. After emigrating to the United States, he worked in factories and on farms. He never received a university education, but he became a professor of Slavic languages, first at the University of Missouri and then at Harvard. Leo's wife and Norbert's mother, Bertha Kahn Wiener, was born in Missouri of German Jewish parents. Her family was in the process of being assimilated; each of her brothers had married a non-Jew. Norbert was not reared with an awareness of his own Jewish heritage and later bitterly resented what he came to believe was his mother's anti-Semitism.

Leo Wiener believed in beginning the education of children at a very early age and in expecting substantial intellectual progress during childhood. Coached by his father, Norbert learned to read by the time that he was three. His father educated him at home until he was nine, when he entered Ayer High School. At eleven, he entered Tufts College, where he became especially interested in physics, chemistry, and biology. After being graduated from Tufts, he enrolled before his fifteenth year in zoology at Harvard Graduate School. Since Norbert lacked the coordination and eyesight essential for laboratory work in the life sciences, at his father's suggestion, he shifted his program of study to philosophy. Norbert Wiener later resented his father's involvement in this decision.

Wiener's doctoral thesis involved a comparison of Ernst Schroeder's algebra of relatives with that of Alfred North Whitehead and Bertrand Russell. Of his thesis, he later commented, "When I came to study under Bertrand Russell in England, I learned that I had missed almost every issue of true philosophical significance."

During his last year at Harvard, Wiener was awarded a traveling scholarship, which he used to visit England and Germany. At Cambridge, his main course work was with Bertrand Russell. Wiener enjoyed his time in Cambridge, finding it a more sympathetic environment than Harvard because eccentricity and individuality were not only tolerated but even highly valued in this English university town. Since Russell was to be away from Cambridge during the spring term, Wiener visited Göttingen, where he met some of the greatest of the mathematicians and physicists of his day. His experiences in Göttingen also contributed to Wiener's social maturity, because he found that he could get along with many different types of people.

In 1919, after an instructorship at the University of Maine and service on the ballistic staff at Aberdeen Proving Ground, Wiener joined the faculty of Massachusetts Institute of Technology. In 1924, he was promoted to an assistant professor, and in 1926, he married Margaret Engemann; his parents strongly approved of this marriage, which they even promoted. The Wiener's two daughters were named Barbara and Peggy. The first volume of Wiener's autobiography concludes with his marriage in 1926 at the age of thirty-one.

Like his father, Wiener was a vegetarian. To his contemporaries he seemed highly eccentric in appearance. Stephen Toulmin, Director of the Nuffield Foundation Unit for the History of Ideas in London, described him in 1964 in the *New York Review* as "the most *peculiar* American in my experience, and even in England I can liken him only to the late Sir Thomas Beecham. . . . Both of them were short, myopic, tubby. . . . With it, there went a rotundity of expression in public conversation—I nearly said monologue—which was too puckish to be called pompous, and an assumed air of prejudice and self-importance so extreme it became a joy to observe."

Wiener described his father Leo as "brilliant," "absentminded," and "hot-tempered," adjectives which his contemporaries thought equally apt as a description of him. Wiener would go to sleep and even snore during discussions and classroom seminars. Since he was able to process information while sleeping, much to the surprise and even chagrin of his colleagues and students, he would sometimes awaken and make very perceptive comments concerning the topic being discussed.

### Life's Work

In 1929, Wiener was given the rank of associate professor, and after the appearance of important papers on generalized harmonic analysis (1930) and Tauberian theorems (1932), he was promoted to a professorship in 1932. Although he remained based at Massachusetts Institute of Technology, he welcomed opportunities to travel abroad, spending a year in Peking, China, during the academic year 1935-1936.

Throughout his career, Wiener experienced doubts concerning his reputation among other mathematicians. In 1933, however, he was awarded the Bôcher Prize, which is awarded only every five years by the American Mathematical Society. Since his work on generalized harmonic analysis and Tauberian theorems had appeared in 1930 and 1932, it is clear that the society recognized his achievements as soon as it was possible to do so.

During the war years, Wiener received a small grant to work on a design for an apparatus that would direct antiaircraft guns effectively. Solving this problem led Wiener to develop a theory of prediction and pointed the way toward cybernetics, the major contribution of his adult years. Wiener's prediction theory could have been synthesized from his previous work, but it was his solution to a concrete problem which prompted this important synthesis. He had to determine the position and direction of flight of airplanes and then extrapolate over the flight time of the projectile to be sure that the projectile would reach the airplane.

From a mathematical perspective, this theory was Wiener's principal contribution to cybernetics. When his book *Cybernetics: Or, Control and Communication in the Animal and the Machine* was published in 1948, Wiener became a public figure. Sometimes called the philosopher of automation, Wiener contributed to cybernetics as an organizer, popularizer, and enthusiastic interpreter.

The word "cybernetics" derives from the Greek for "helmsman." Wiener proposed the term as a replacement for the title Conference for Circular Causal and Feedback Mechanisms in Biological Systems. Cybernetics concerns the science of communication and control theory, especially in regard

to the comparative analysis of automatic control systems, the brain and nervous system as compared with mechanical-electrical communication systems. According to Wiener, the intellectual concerns of cybernetics distinguish modern civilization from that of previous centuries: "The thought of every age is reflected in its technique. . . . If the seventeenth and early eighteenth centuries are the age of the clocks, and the later eighteenth and the nineteenth centuries constitute the age of steam engines, the present time is the age of communication and control." As early as 1948, Wiener viewed the new concepts of message, information, feedback, and control as a supplement to physics which would facilitate a fully scientific description of an organism. These concepts now pervade neurobiology, biochemistry, genetics, psychology, and other disciplines concerned with organisms.

In 1964, in recognition of Wiener's contribution to theoretical mathematics and the sciences, President Lyndon B. Johnson awarded him the National Medal of Science. Shortly thereafter, while traveling in Sweden, Wiener died, on March 18, 1964.

### Summary

In the years preceding World War II, Wiener was plagued by continual doubts in regard to his productivity. His colleagues and students had to assure and reassure him that his current work was indeed excellent. This insecurity, which Wiener himself attributed to the pressures he experienced in early childhood, was never entirely overcome but did not keep Wiener from taking a very independent position on military contracts. Advocating noncooperation as a policy for scientists, Wiener commented: "It is perfectly clear also that to disseminate information about a weapon *in the present state of our civilization* is to make it practically certain that that weapon will be used." Wiener's position on noncooperation was supported by Albert Einstein, but as a consequence of his refusal to accept military grants and contracts, he had to discover other means of generating funds to maintain his research. His books on cybernetics and technology were addressed to the general public and were financially successful.

Norbert Wiener is acknowledged as the founder of cybernetics, although his contributions represented a synthesis of many concepts already implicit in the methodology of the social sciences. The basis for treating man and machine with the same theory derives not from analysis of physical constituents but from patterns of communication and control. Wiener was skeptical about the efficacy of quantitative description in these fields, but he did show that patterns of communication can be described mathematically by using statistics.

At the same time, Wiener opposed any simplistic application of the man/machine model. He opposed the use of game theory as a means of determining military or political strategy. In spite of the great impact that cybernetics had on the social sciences, Wiener remained skeptical about sociological and economic predictions, arguing that the statistical runs were too short and that the observations were conditioned by interaction between the social scientist and his subject.

Author of a number of books addressed to the educated general public, such as *The Human Use of Human Beings* (1950), Wiener set out to inform the public about both the potential and the pitfalls of communications and computation technology. He was concerned about the impact of automation upon the employment of laborers but recognized that machines might also help to improve working conditions. Advocating the independent and unbiased study of the relationship between man and machines, Wiener tried to assess what the relationship should be between a human and a mechanical translator, between a computerized diagnosis and a physician's diagnosis. He pointed out as well that the paradigm of "man as master" and "machine as slave" dangerously ignores the way in which machines may influence decisions and shape the course of events, if only because of their much greater speed of action.

### Bibliography

Galison, Peter. "The Ontology of the Enemy: Norbert Wiener and the Cybernetic Vision." *Critical Inquiry* 21, no. 1 (Fall 1994). Examines the development of Wiener's theories on cybernetics, which are based in part on his view that man's worst enemies are chaos and disorganization.

Grattan-Guiness, I. "Wiener on the Logics of Russell and Schroeder: An Account of His Doctor's Thesis, and of His Discussion of It with Russell." *Annals of Science* 32 (1975): 103-132. Discussion of Wiener's intellectual relation to Bertrand Russell.

Heims, Steve J. *John von Neumann and Norbert Wiener: From Mathematics to the Technologies of Life and Death.* Cambridge, Mass.: MIT Press, 1980. A biographical study lacking historical sensitivity, with an overriding bias against research in nuclear physics and military defense.

Levinson, Norman. "Wiener's Life." *Bulletin of the American Mathematical Society* 72 (1966): 1-32. Biographical description of Wiener and discussion of his contributions to mathematics. Levinson, Wiener's student and colleague, regards most of Wiener's work in cybernetics as not mathematical.

Simanaitis, Dennis. "Read about it in Road and Cybernetics." *Road and Track* 45, no. 10 (June, 1994). Profile of mathematician Wiener, whose studies included information transfer in machines and animals, which led to the development of the theory of cybernetics.

Struik, Dirk J. "Norbert Wiener: Colleague and Friend." *American Dialog* 3 (March, April, 1966): 34-37. Essay by a close personal friend of Wiener. As a result of his Marxist views, Struik was indicted during the anti-Communist crusades of the 1950's. Wiener strongly supported his friend, threatening to resign from the Massachusetts Institute of Technology if the institution failed to support Struik.

Wiener, Norbert. *Collected Works*. Edited by P. Masan. 3 vols. Cambridge, Mass.: MIT Press, 1976-1982. Three volumes of a projected four-volume set to comprise all of his scholarly publications other than books and some previously unpublished material. Organized to show the author's intellectual evolution and supplemented with commentaries by important scholars. Probably inaccessible to the lay reader. Includes a complete bibliography.

———. *Ex-Prodigy*. New York: Simon and Schuster, 1953. First volume of Wiener's autobiography, covering the years from 1894 to 1926.

———. *The Human Use of Human Beings*. London: Eyre and Spottiswoode, and Boston: Houghton Mifflin, 1950. Very popular nonmathematical treatment of cybernetics.

———. *I Am a Mathematician*. New York: Doubleday, and London: Gollancz, 1956. Second volume of Wiener's autobiography, covering the years from 1926 to 1964.

———. "A Scientist Rebels." *The Atlantic Monthly*. 179 (1947): 46. Proposes that scientists should refuse to engage in weapons research.

*Jeanie R. Brink*

# ELIE WIESEL

*Born:* September 30, 1928; Sighet, Romania

*Areas of Achievement:* Literature, philosophy, theology, and civil rights

*Contribution:* Wiesel is not only a prizewinning novelist, dramatist, and religious philosopher, but by writing and speaking out on behalf of the world's victims, he has become the conscience of modern times. For his work in this area he was awarded the Nobel Peace Prize.

## Early Life

Elie Wiesel was born on September 30, 1928, in Sighet, a small town in the Carpathian Mountains, in an area that belonged to Hungary during World War II but that was Romanian territory before and after the war. Wiesel's father, though a practicing member of the Jewish religious community, questioned traditional Judaism; a tolerant humanist, he emphasized the modern world at large and the need to be a part of it. Wiesel's mother had a lasting and, probably, deeper influence. A devout woman steeped in Hasidism, she hoped that her only son would become a rabbi. To that end, Wiesel studied the Torah and the Talmud in a local yeshiva known for its ascetic mysticism and Cabbalist teachers. This sheltered, bookish existence was irrevocably shattered in the spring of 1944, when the Nazis invaded Hungary and rounded up all its Jews, including Wiesel, his parents, and three sisters.

The fifteen-year-old Wiesel, along with his father, was sent first to Auschwitz and then to Buchenwald, from which he was liberated by American troops on April 11, 1945. (His two elder sisters survived as well.) The horrors he witnessed there, the despair he felt, the anger he directed at God were all to be incorporated in his literary and philosophical writings. Shortly after the war, the young adolescent went to a refugee home in France, where in two years he learned French by carefully reading the classics, especially Jean Racine, whose style he was later to adopt; indeed, French remains Wiesel's preferred written language. In addition, he was developing a life-long passion for philosophy (starting with Immanuel Kant and Karl Marx) and for philosophical fiction.

From 1948 to 1951, Wiesel studied philosophy, psychology, and literature at the Sorbonne, but, forced to work, he never finished his thesis on comparative asceticism. Instead, he began a career as a journalist, which allowed him to travel extensively; after emigrating to the United States in 1956, he became the United Nations correspondent of an Israeli newspaper, *Yediot Aharonot.*

At the urging of the French Catholic novelist François Mauriac, Wiesel agreed to bear witness to the six million Jews murdered in Europe's concentration camps. From a massive work which he wrote in Yiddish, *Un di Velt hot geshvign* (1956), Wiesel distilled a very brief but exceedingly powerful memoir of the Holocaust, published in French as *La Nuit* (1958; *Night*, 1960). Both a wrenching account of the presence of evil and a terrifying indictment of God's injustice, this book received international acclaim. Wiesel had found his voice and his themes.

## Life's Work

Following the success of *Night*, Wiesel wrote in rapid succession two short novels presenting the guilty anguish of those who survived the mass slaughter: *L'Aube* (1960; *Dawn*, 1961) and *Le Jour* (1961; *The Accident*, 1962). That every act is ambiguous and implies a loss of innocence and that "God commit[s] the most unforgivable crime; to kill without a reason" are central to the protagonists' conduct and outlook. Little by little, however, Wiesel's characters come to realize that friendship can help them live in the post-Holocaust world. This is especially true in *La Ville de la chance* (1962; *The Town Beyond the Wall*, 1964), where, despite society's indifference to persecution and cruelty, loving and being a friend allow man to attain a kind of equilibrium. Questions about God, evil, and suffering, while they cannot be satisfactorily answered, must nevertheless be asked, since from the begining such a dialogue has been established between God and His creation. By rejoining his religious community, Wiesel seems to suggest further, in *Les Portes de la forêt* (1964; *The Gates of the Forest*, 1966), that the survivor may finally create joy from despair.

At the same time that he was publishing his novels, Wiesel began writing eyewitness accounts and autobiographical pieces and stories of his life during the Hitler years. After a 1965 trip to the Soviet Union, he described in a series of articles originally published in Hebrew in *Yediot Aharonot* (collected and translated as *The Jews of Silence*, 1966) the plight of Soviet Jewry, as they try to maintain their ethnic and religious identity in the

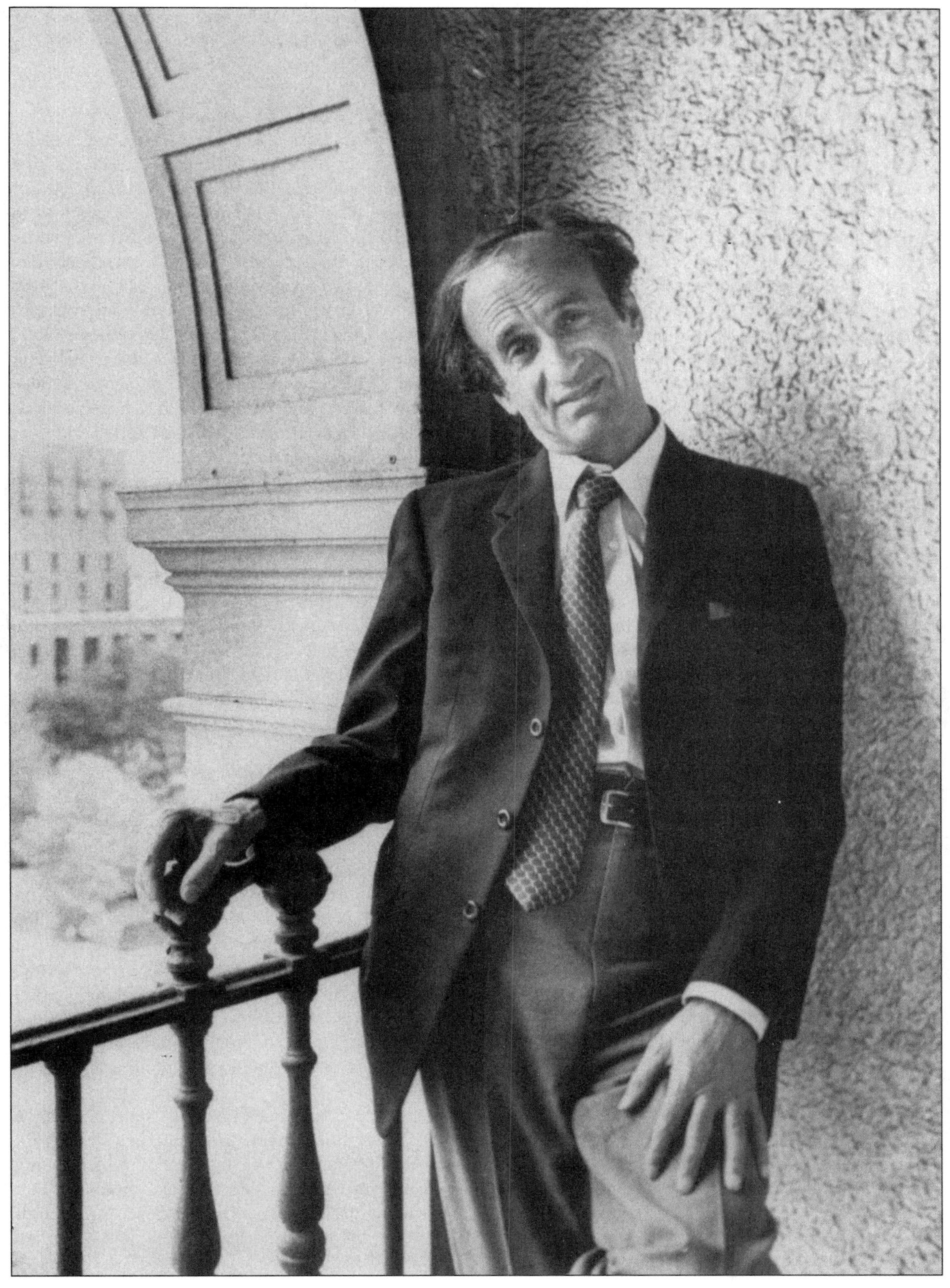

face of often implacable anti-Semitism. His yeshiva and Sorbonne studies, along with more mature and in-depth readings of biblical texts and exegeses, were to form the basis of other nonfiction works, including several studies of Hasidism and Hasidic masters.

The prizewinning novel *Le Mendiant de Jérusalem* (1968; *A Beggar in Jerusalem*, 1970) marked a turning point for Wiesel. The novel shows how, through Israel's victory in the Six Day War, a tormented people came of age; while celebrating this moment, the novel is both a memorial to the dead and an appeal on behalf of the world's "beggars." Although still haunted by the Holocaust, Wiesel could thereafter write about other human issues and problems faced by the next generation. For example, is madness, he asked in the first of several plays, an acceptable option for dealing with persecution (*Zalmen: Ou, La Folie de Dieu*, 1968; *Zalmen: Or, The Madness of God*, 1975)? Is silence a method for overcoming horror (*Le Serment de Kolvillàg*, 1973; *The Oath*, 1973)?

In 1969, Wiesel married Marion Erster Rose, who was to become his principal translator and with whom he would have one son. In the fall of 1972, he began his tenure at the City College of New York as Distinguished Professor of Judaic Studies. This endowed chair gave him the opportunity to teach young students (he considers himself to be an educator first) the celebrations and paradoxes of Jewish theology and the meaning of modern Jewishness and to continue writing in diverse genres. He left this position in 1976 to become the Andrew Mellon Professor of Humanities at Boston University. Meanwhile, Wiesel continued to publish plays, novels, and nonfiction at a prolific pace; in these he again wove post-Holocaust despair and divine cruelty, but above all he denounced the world's forgetfulness of and indifference to man's inhumanity to man.

During this period Wiesel was also involved in various social and political activities, from fighting against racism, war, fanaticism, apartheid, and violence to commemorating the Holocaust. (He was a member of the U.S. Holocaust Memorial Council until 1986, when he resigned in protest over President Ronald Reagan's controversial visit to the military cemetery in Bitburg, West Germany.) For his humanitarian work and his concern for the oppressed everywhere, as well as for his literary achievements, he has received numerous honorary degrees, prizes, and awards, including the Congressional Gold Medal, the rank of *Commandeur* in the French Legion of Honor, and, in 1986, the Nobel Peace Prize.

### Summary

The Holocaust and its remembrance, the nature of God and the terrible silence of God: These themes recur throughout Elie Wiesel's novels, plays, personal recollections, and nonfiction. In trying to understand the mystery of theodicy, this modern humanist has encompassed much of Jewish lore, tradition, and memory. In addition, by asking—but without answering—the hard questions that have always plagued man and by relating the Jews' unique experience to the universal legacy of humanity, he has succeeded in creating the quintessential Everyman: "What I try to do is to speak for man, but as a Jew. I make no distinction and I certainly make no restriction."

Against revisionist historians who deny the very existence of the Nazi extermination camps, Wiesel has written with contempt. He has passionately defended the conduct of the murdered and the survivors to his fellow Jews—those who are ashamed of the submissiveness of the victims and those who are skeptical of the survivors' integrity. He has no less passionately criticized novelists and playwrights, television and film directors for trivializing the tragedy of six million martyrs, whose greatest memorialist and bard he has become.

### Bibliography

Abramowitz, Molly, comp. *Elie Wiesel: A Bibliography.* Metuchen, N.J.: Scarecrow Press, 1974. Dated but still valuable annotated bibliography of works by and about Wiesel.

Berenbaum, Michael. *The Vision of the Void: Theological Reflections on the Works of Elie Wiesel.* Middletown, Conn.: Wesleyan University Press, 1979. Although discussing works published before 1979, this is an excellent study of the Jewish tradition as evident in Wiesel's religious writings and sociocultural position. The bibliography on theological philosophy is quite useful.

Cargas, Harry James. *Harry James Cargas in Conversation with Elie Wiesel.* New York: Paulist Press, 1976. In a series of fascinating and varied interviews, Wiesel speaks not only about the Holocaust but also about his audience, his craft, and his mission as a writer and witness.

———. ed. *Responses to Elie Wiesel.* New York: Persea, 1978. A stimulating collection of articles, interviews, and book chapters (a few are new, most are reprinted), which presents specific aspects of Wiesel's thought. Maurice Friedman's essay on "the Job of Auschwitz" is particularly perceptive; letters, written by Christian philosophers and theologians, show Wiesel's influence in the non-Jewish world as well.

Estess, Ted L. *Elie Wiesel.* New York: Ungar, 1980. In spite of its brevity, this general introduction is well argued and often insightful.

Mitterrand, Francois. *Memoir in Two Voices: Francois Mitterrand and Elie Wiesel.* Translated by Richard Seaver and Timothy Bent. New York: Arcade, 1996. Acclaimed by critics as "a special book, powerful at times," this volume includes Mitterrand's memoirs written as conversations between he and Elie Wiesel on subjects ranging from war to childhood; faith to power. Particularly interesting when Wiesel questions Mitterrand on his knowledge of the treatment of Jews during World War II.

Rosenfeld, Alvin H., and Irving Greenberg, eds. *Confronting the Holocaust: The Impact of Elie Wiesel.* Bloomington: Indiana University Press, 1978. A balanced collection of provocative essays, written by scholars from different disciplines. Also interesting is Wiesel's own short statement, "Why I Write." A highly selective and partly annotated bibliography of his writings is included.

Roth, John K. *A Consuming Fire: Encounters with Elie Wiesel and the Holocaust.* Atlanta: John Knox Press, 1979. This examination by a philosopher of ethics and religion, to which Wiesel contributed an informative prologue, is both thorough and intelligent.

Wiesel, Elie. *All Rivers Run to the Sea: Memoirs.* New York: Knopf, 1995; London: Harper Collins, 1996. The memoirs of Wiesel including his experiences at Auschwitz, the loss of his father and two of his sisters, and the quest for faith in a post-Holocaust world.

*Pierre L. Horn*

## SIMON WIESENTHAL

*Born:* December 31, 1908; Buczacz, Galicia, Austro-Hungarian Empire (now Buchach, Ukraine)
*Areas of Achievement:* Law and jurisprudence
*Contribution:* Wiesenthal, a survivor of a dozen Nazi concentration and death camps, became the world's leading independent Nazi hunter. Between 1945 and 1989, Wiesenthal investigated and brought charges against eleven hundred Nazi war criminals. Through his highly publicized cases and publications, he added significantly to the documentary record of the Holocaust—the Nazi destruction of the European Jews—and contributed more than any other individual to bringing the Nazi perpetrators to justice and keeping the historical memory of the Holocaust alive.

### Early Life

Simon Wiesenthal is the eldest of two sons of Rosa (Rapp) and Hans Wiesenthal, a prosperous wholesaler and reserve officer in the Austrian army, killed in action during World War I. Wiesenthal grew up in the deeply anti-Semitic Lvov Oblast, then a province of the Austrian Empire. During a pogrom in 1920, the twelve-year-old boy was slashed on the thigh by a mounted, saber-wielding Ukranian officer, leaving a lifelong scar.

Wiesenthal's mother remarried in 1925, restoring some security to the boys' lives. In 1928, Wiesenthal was graduated from the *Gymnasium.* Again, he experienced prejudice when his application to the Polytechnic Institute in Lvov was rejected because of Jewish quota restrictions. In 1932, he received a degree in architectural engineering from the Technical University of Prague. Returning to Lvov, he opened an architectural office and married his wife of more than fifty years, Cyla Muller, a distant relative of Sigmund Freud.

From 1939 to 1941, Wiesenthal practiced architecture in Lemberg, Poland. When the city was seized by the Soviets at the outbreak of World War II, the secret police arrested and killed his stepfather and brother, and the Wiesenthals barely avoided exile to Siberia. When the Germans invaded Russia in 1941, Wiesenthal was arrested and again narrowly escaped execution. He and Cyla were sent to the Janowska concentration camp, outside Lvov, where they worked in the repair shop for German eastern railroads. Wiesenthal was treated decently there by the secretly anti-Nazi German director and deputy director.

By 1942, the Holocaust had begun. Through a combination of luck, skill, friendship, and bribery, Wiesenthal was able to get Cyla out of the camp and, in 1943, to escape himself. Recaptured in June, 1944, Wiesenthal was a prisoner in more than a dozen Nazi concentration camps, escaping death on many occasions by the merest chance. At the end of the war, he arrived by forced march at the Mauthausen camp in Upper Austria, one of 34 prisoners of an original group of 149,000. When U.S. Army units liberated the camp in May, 1945, the six-foot-tall, thirty-seven-year-old Wiesenthal weighed less than one hundred pounds. His terrifying wartime experiences stamped his fearless character and formed the basis for his life's work.

### Life's Work

After a brief recovery, Wiesenthal assisted the newly arrived U.S. Army War Crimes Section in gathering and preparing evidence to prosecute Nazi war criminals. Wiesenthal worked in anger and despair during the first months of his work. He was amazed to learn that Cyla had survived, and the two were finally reunited late in 1945. They were the only survivors of ninety-one of their family members who perished in the Holocaust. Reunion and the birth of his daughter, Pauline, in 1947 softened his bitterness. He was soon employed by the Office of Strategic Services and the Counter-Intelligence Corps, and the evidence he assembled proved of great value in the preparation for war crimes trials held in the U.S. zone. At first he intended to devote a few years to bringing Nazi mass murderers to justice, and in 1947, he established the Jewish Historical Documentation Center on the Fate of Jews and Their Persecutors in Linz, Austria. Between 1947 and 1954, he built a vast network of informants and collected documentation to help bring Nazi war criminals to justice.

After the trial of the major war criminals at Nürnberg, Germany, however, the major Western powers, under the influence of Cold War ideology, gradually lost interest in prosecution of Nazi criminals and opened their doors to thousands of Nazis as "anti-Communists." By 1954, Wiesenthal, frustrated by lack of support from government authorities, had closed his documentation center and shipped his voluminous files to Yad Vashem Documentation Center in Israel, keeping only one for himself—that on Adolf Eichmann, the Nazi expert who supervised the genocidal destruction of the European Jews. Between 1955 and 1961, Wiesenthal held various social and welfare leadership posts in Austria, which further involved him in assisting Jewish victims of the Nazi regime. In his spare time, he searched for former Nazis, especially Eichmann.

Wiesenthal first gained international recognition for locating Eichmann in Buenos Aires, Argentina, where he was captured by Israeli agents in 1960, brought to Israel for trial, convicted of mass murder, and executed in 1961. Encouraged, Wiesenthal reopened his Jewish Documentation Center, this time in Vienna. Gifted with an extraordinary capacity for finding and evaluating evidence, Wiesenthal assembled, painstakingly scrutinized, analyzed, and cross-referenced every relevant document and survivor account available to him. He compiled a card index of 22,500 names on his Nazi wanted list, assembled dossiers on six thousand cases, and worked on as many as three hundred cases at a time.

In addition to Eichmann, Wiesenthal developed cases against Karl Babor, a Schutzstaffel (SS) captain at the concentration camp in Breslau, Poland, who committed suicide in 1964 after being discovered; sixteen Auschwitz SS officers, tried in Stuttgart, Germany, in 1966, the majority of whom Wiesenthal brought to trial; Joseph Mengele, who selected victims to be gassed at Auschwitz and died in Argentina before capture; Heinrich Müller, Heinrich Himmler's successor as chief of the Gestapo; Walter Kutschmann, former Gestapo leader; and many others.

With his strong interest in Holocaust public education, Wiesenthal has published a number of works on the Nazi perpetrators and their victims, including numerous newspaper and periodical pieces. Among his books are *KZ Mauthausen* (1946; concentration camp Mauthausen); *Grossmufti: Grossagent der Achse* (1947; head mufti, agent of the Axis); *Ich jagte Eichmann* (1961; I hunted Eichmann); and *Verjährung?* (1965; statute of limitations). In the media, books, and many articles, Wiesenthal has presented the philosophy behind his work. He is animated by a deep sense of compassion for the martyrs of the Nazi Holocaust and believes that all victims—Jews, Christians, Gypsies, and all nationalities—are brothers. He believes that forgiveness is a personal matter and that one has the right to forgive what was done to oneself but not what was done to

others. He does not condone assassination or other radical measures. Morality, he says, must remain on the side of the accusers, so proper punishment can come only from the courts. Nazi crimes can never be atoned, he believes, nor will all the murderers be caught, but he pursues them relentlessly so that time will not erase their guilt.

Until the 1970's, Wiesenthal rarely left Austria and Germany. Gradually, however, he became involved more directly in the work of Holocaust education, lecturing extensively in West Germany, The Netherlands, and the United States, primarily to university students. During the 1970's, Wiesenthal's activities became known worldwide through such films as *The Odessa File* (1974), for which he was a consultant, and *The Boys from Brazil* (1978), which glamorized the Nazi hunter, but for two decades he resisted all efforts to depict his life in film or biography, fearing distortion. Finally, in 1987, he agreed to give television rights for a documentary based on his memoirs. The production of *Murderers Among Us*, for which he was the primary consultant, was presented in 1988 with Ben Kingsley playing Wiesenthal. He also agreed to the 1990 television dramatization of his 1981 book, *Max und Helen* (*Max and Helen*, 1982), which recounts the intriguing story of a Nazi killer who Wiesenthal decided not to pursue. In April, 1977, he cooperated in the establishment of the Simon Wiesenthal Center for Holocaust Studies and Holocaust Museum at Yeshiva University in Los Angeles, California, with branch offices in New York, Chicago, Washington, D.C., Toronto, and Jerusalem. Its broad outreach program of Holocaust education and awareness, monitoring and combating neo-Nazi and anti-Semitic hate groups, and Nazi-hunting, reflects Wiesenthal's desire that his work continue.

In his pursuit of Nazis, Wiesenthal has made diverse enemies. Within the Communist Bloc, notably in Poland, a propaganda campaign surfaced in the 1960's against Wiesenthal's exposure of ex-Fascists placed high in the Communist Party apparatus who had instigated an "anti-Zionist" crusade against Israel.

Beginning in the 1970's, Wiesenthal's pursuit of former Nazis embroiled him in bitter disputes in his home country, threatening the future of his Jewish Documentation Center. In 1970, he revealed that some Socialist ministers in Austrian Chancellor Bruno Kreisky's government had Nazi backgrounds. The Socialist Party leadership responded with such vehement attacks that it was feared that the Austrian government was going to close down his Jewish Documentation Center. Only worldwide protests are credited with having saved it. Again, in 1975, antagonisms flared when Wiesenthal accused an Austrian politician of involvement in SS crimes of mass murder. Chancellor Kreisky, who was considering the politician for a governing coalition, attacked Wiesenthal severely. Relations between the two degenerated to personal invective, until Wiesenthal finally brought a libel suit against the chancellor. Only under threat of an official parliamentary investigation of his Jewish Documentation Center, did Wiesenthal finally settle out of court. In 1986, Wiesenthal again became enmeshed in Austrian politics when Kurt Waldheim, the Austrian presidential candidate, was accused by the World Jewish Congress and other organizations of membership in an SS unit implicated in deporting Jews to death camps. The sensational accusations caused a furor in Austria. Wiesenthal took a cautious line in the beginning, but finally in 1987 he called newly elected President Waldheim to resign if an international commission of historians, appointed by the Austrian government to study the case, proved that the military unit of which Waldheim was a member was involved in war crimes.

During the 1980's, Wiesenthal became increasingly an elder statesman of the Holocaust, traveling widely to publicize his Nazi-hunting message, while continuing to develop information on Nazi criminals. United States President Ronald Reagan was a strong supporter and met with him in 1984 to offer assistance. The next year Wiesenthal declined Reagan's invitation to Bitburg, West Germany, where a controversial wreath-laying ceremony to symbolize U.S.-German reconciliation was to mark the fortieth anniversary of the end of World War II. Wiesenthal declined because SS soldiers were buried in the cemetery where the ceremony took place.

In the second half of the 1980's, Wiesenthal expressed his increasing frustration with the Canadian government, which, after twelve years, had failed to prosecute several hundred known Nazis in Canada, many of whom Wiesenthal had identified. For a decade, Wiesenthal had brought increasing pressure on the government, including boycotting visits to Canada, until twenty key Nazis were brought to trial. In 1985, the government expressed its interest in pursuing the many Nazi criminals allegedly living in Canada, and in 1988 the Toronto branch of the Simon Wiesenthal Center presented evidence to the federal justice minister to indict twenty-one accused Nazi war criminals. Yet a Canadian government commission appointed to study the evidence concluded that the estimates of Nazi criminals in Canada had been grossly exaggerated and had made only one arrest by 1988. Toward the end of the 1980's, Wiesenthal and the Simon Wiesenthal Center had generated computer lists of thousands of suspects' names and addresses, which they presented to government authorities in Australia, Canada, England, the United States, and Sweden. These lists included police chiefs, Gestapo officials, and suspected collaborators.

Wiesenthal has received numerous honors and awards, including the Diploma of Honor from the League of the United Nations; a special Gold Medal of the American Congress from President Jimmy Carter in 1980; the Great Medal of Merit from the President of West Germany in 1985; a Nobel Peace Prize nomination in 1985; the French Legion of Honor in 1986; many honorary degrees; and honorary citizenship of many U.S. cities. The state of New

York declared June 13, 1984, as Simon Wiesenthal Day. During a trip to the United States in 1988, Chancellor Helmut Kohl of West Germany paid tribute to Wiesenthal at a banquet held by the Simon Wiesenthal Center in New York.

Wiesenthal knew he would never complete his work. The West German government has more than 160,000 names in its war-crimes files, most of them never tried. In the 1980's, it was estimated that fifty thousand Nazi criminals were still at large around the world. Wiesenthal, ailing with a heart condition and in his eighties, continued with a sense of urgency, realizing that he would not outlive all the criminals.

### Summary

Throughout a career spanning almost fifty years, Simon Wiesenthal dedicated his life to bringing Nazi war criminals to justice and publicizing the crimes of the Holocaust. With the patience of a great scholar, the structural sense of an architect, and the investigative genius of a keen detective, he developed a brilliant talent for investigative thinking. He brought eleven hundred Nazis to justice, making him the most successful Nazi hunter in the world.

He is motivated by a deep sense of outraged justice; a desire to keep faith with the millions of victims of the Holocaust; a desire that the murderers of 11 million Jews and Gentiles not be allowed "to get away with it"; a desire to deter future anti-Semitism and genocide; and a fear that the world will forget the Holocaust. Master investigator, avenger, prophet of justice, remarkable sleuth, few have become such symbols in the name of justice and loyalty to the victims of the Holocaust. His sense of justice, perseverance, and success evokes admiration and puzzlement, and the mass media has sometimes cultivated the legendary figure of a Jewish James Bond, scourge of Third Reich fugitives.

In 1988, at a reception honoring Wiesenthal, Reagan hailed Wiesenthal as "one of the true heroes" of the twentieth century and saluted the Nazi hunter for his "unswerving commitment to do honor to those who burned in the flames of the Holocaust by bringing their murderers and the accomplices of their murderers to the justice of a civilized world." He then announced his intention to sign into law the international "convention on the prevention and punishment of the crime of genocide," which had languished in the Senate for four decades. Wiesenthal's efforts contributed to the efforts of juridical justice to deal with genocide, the documentation of the Holocaust, Jewish self-identity, and Holocaust remembrance and education, all of which merge in his work.

### Bibliography

Ashman, Charles, and Robert J. Wagman. *The Nazi Hunters: The Shocking True Story of the Continuing Search for Nazi War Criminals.* Newton Abbot: David and Charles, and New York: Pharos, 1988. A competent and admiring treatment of Wiesenthal's life and work within the context of other Nazi hunters. Also presents the work of the Simon Wiesenthal Center and an appendix of selected war criminal cases.

Cooper, Abraham. "Simon Wiesenthal: The Man, the Mission, His Message." In *Genocide: Critical Issues of the Holocaust*, edited by Alex Grobman and Daniel Landes. Los Angeles: Simon Wiesenthal Center and Rossel Books, 1983. This work contains a brief introduction by Wiesenthal's close associate and director of the Simon Wiesenthal Center in Los Angeles.

Noble, Iris. *Nazi Hunter: Simon Wiesenthal.* New York: Messner, 1979. A dramatic, accessible biography of Wiesenthal's life, methods, and main cases, based primarily on his memoirs, for the general reader. Contains a brief bibliography of secondary sources.

Wiesenthal, Simon. *The Sunflower: On the Possibilities and Limits of Forgiveness.* Edited by Harry James Cargas and Bonnie V. Fedderman. Rev. ed. New York: Schocken, 1997. Wiesenthal recounts an experience from his time in a concentration camp that involved a dying Nazi's confession of remorse at his involvement in atrocities against the Jews. Wiesenthal then asks a symposium of 32 individuals (including Jacques Maritain, Cynthia Ozick, and Primo Levi) to put themselves in his place and answer the question "What would I have done?" The responses are enlightening, thought-provoking.

———. *The Murderers Among Us: The Simon Wiesenthal Memoirs.* Edited with a biographical profile by Joseph Wechsberg. New York: McGraw-Hill, and London: Heinemann, 1967. The most detailed memorialization of the author's life and work, told to Wechsberg, including the stories of many of the Nazi crimes that inspired Wiesenthal's searches. Contains illustrations.

"Wiesenthal Defends Swiss." *New York Times* 146, no. 50871 (August 1, 1997). Discusses

Wiesenthal's plea for restraint on the part of the international community in its criticism of Swiss dealings with Nazi assets during the war.

Wistrich, Robert S. "Bruno Kreisky and Simon Wiesenthal." *Midstream*, June/July, 1979: 26-35. A detailed, balanced assessment of the bitter conflict between Wiesenthal and the Austrian chancellor during the 1970's. For the general reader.

*Walter F. Renn*

## HAZEL HOTCHKISS WIGHTMAN

*Born:* December 20, 1886; Healdsburg, California

*Died:* December 5, 1974; Chestnut Hill, Massachusetts

*Area of Achievement:* Sports

*Contribution:* Labeled the "Queen Mother" of American tennis, Hazel Hotchkiss Wightman was a four-time national singles champion of the United States Lawn Tennis Association who paved the way for the acceptance of women's tennis as a reputable sport in the United States.

### Early Life

Hazel Virginia Hotchkiss was born in the northern California town of Healdsburg in 1886. On her mother's side, she was the descendent of Virginia expatriates who had moved west following the Civil War. Her father's parents had moved from Kentucky and settled in California shortly after it was admitted to the Union in 1850.

Hazel's father, William Joseph Hotchkiss, a respected and successful Sonoma Valley rancher and owner of a cannery, encouraged Hazel to play aggressive sports (perhaps as an antidote for her poor health as a child) with her three older brothers and her younger brother. Although frail and petite, Hazel played baseball and football with her four brothers and more than held her own. She would later recall that her mother, Emma Groves Hotchkiss, worried that Hazel might become too much of a tomboy and admonished her never to forget to act like a lady. She was encouraged by her mother to give up the rough sports she played with her four brothers and concentrate instead on playing tennis.

Shortly after her family moved to Berkeley, California, in 1900 when she was fourteen, Hazel began playing tennis. Her style of play was established early. Most of her practice was on the makeshift gravel court at her home, since girls were not permitted on the single asphalt court at Berkeley after eight in the morning. Because of the challenges of playing on a gravel surface, she developed a game that depended on hitting the ball before it had an opportunity to bounce, and she soon became accomplished at this technique of volleying.

### Life's Work

After six months of intensive preparation, Hazel Hotchkiss entered her first tournament. She and her partner, Mary Radcliffe, won the women's doubles championship in the Bay Counties tournament held in San Francisco. In the next seven years she not only helped change the prevailing belief that women should play a baseline rather than a volleying game, she also helped to popularize changes in tennis attire by wearing loose-fitting dresses when she played. She even popularized sleeveless dresses to provide greater freedom of movement for the arms. Combining tennis and academics while she attended the University of California at Berkeley, Hazel won the United States singles, doubles, and mixed doubles championships three consecutive years (1909-1911), an accomplishment equaled only by two other women (Alice Marble, 1938-1940; Margaret Osborne du Pont, 1948-1950). Her performance in the 1911 championships is even more remarkable because she won the singles, doubles, and mixed doubles championships on the same day. Her rivalry with May Sutton in the tournaments in California at this time was perhaps the first publicly recognized rivalry for women in tennis at the beginning of this century. Although she brought a strong spirit of competition to this intense rivalry, Hazel Hotchkiss quickly developed a reputation for authentic sportsmanship and was mentioned by subsequent women tennis players as a model they used in their careers.

Following her graduation from college in 1911, Hazel married George W. Wightman, a former Harvard tennis player and member of a prominent Boston family. The births of three children between 1912 and 1919 did not stop Hazel Wightman's activities as a competitive player on the national level. She resumed playing competitively after the birth of her first child, George, Jr., and added another United States Doubles Championship to her list of accomplishments in 1915. She also won the United States mixed doubles titles in 1918 and 1920, and in 1919, at the age of thirty-three, Hazel Hotchkiss Wightman captured her fourth and final U.S. National Championship singles title. She went on to win two more United States Doubles Championships in the 1920's, the last one coming in 1928 when at the remarkable age of forty-two she paired with twenty-three-year-old Helen Wills. Meanwhile, although she had become the mother of five children, Wightman captained the women's team in the 1924 Olympics, winning gold medals in the doubles and mixed double competition. She also demonstrated her skills in other racquet sports,

winning the National Squash Singles and finishing as a finalist in the National Badminton Mixed Doubles championships in 1927.

Her contributions to tennis were not restricted, however, to her performances as an individual player. In 1919, Hazel Wightman donated a silver vase to the United States Lawn Tennis Association (USLTA), attempting to create an "international cup" for women comparable to the international cup for men inaugurated by Dwight F. Davis in 1900. She met implacable resistance to her proposal to International Lawn Tennis Federation and temporarily was forced to withdraw her offer. The creation of the West Side Tennis Club in Forest Hills, New York, however, provided an opportunity for a renewal of her dreams and the first Wightman Cup match was played at that facility in 1923. The United States team, captained by Wightman herself, defeated the British team 7-0. The following year, the Wightman Cup was played at the newly created Center Court at Wimbledon in Great Britain, and the British team won 6-1. The evenness of the competition in the next six years assured the success of the Wightman Cup. Even though the American teams dominated the British teams between 1931 and 1958, the Wightman Cup became a respected part of tennis competition and helped to improve the image of women's tennis in the world. The decision to move the competition indoors in 1974 coincided with the tennis boom of that decade and increased the appeal of the Wightman Cup competition; it was not uncommon for the matches to draw between ten and fifteen thousand spectators, figures that were comparable to Davis Cup matches.

Meanwhile, Wightman herself continued to remain involved with the promotion and development of tennis in the United States. She played on five Wightman Cup teams between 1923 and 1931, and she captained thirteen Wightman Cup teams in all, making her final appearance as captain in 1948. She continued to compete in national tournaments, playing in her last national championship when she was seventy-three years old.

Had these been her only accomplishments in tennis, Hazel Hotchkiss Wightman might still have earned her title as the "Queen Mother of Tennis," but she also contributed to tennis in several other ways. After her divorce from George Wightman in 1940, Hazel Wightman graciously opened her home near the Longwood Cricket Club in Chestnut Hill, Massachusetts, as a home away from home for aspiring women players who went east to prepare for the summer tournaments that culminated in the United States Nationals at Forest Hills. Wightman developed a reputation for a quick recognition of talent, and she aided several prominent tennis players, including Sarah Palfrey, Helen Wills, and Helen Jacobs. She became a respected tennis teacher and promoter, giving free clinics at the Longwood Cricket Club, running tournaments for players of all skill levels, and writing a manual which became a guide for many players.

As a tennis instructor, Wightman had a particular fondness for ordinary players. The awkward and shy players, she claizmed, gained "confidence and poise" by being able to do "something well that other people admire." Her approach to the teaching of tennis emphasized the mental as well as the physical and technical sides of the game. She encouraged her students to "cultivate a buoyant spirit" as well as develop good footwork. She emphasized the fact that tennis was a sport that helped in the development of personal as well as physical grace. She always noted that she believed that ordinary players could gain as much from perfecting their skills as could the more accomplished players. Moreover, she argued long before the tennis boom of the 1970's that tennis should be a sport open to the entire public, not simply the wealthy members of elite private clubs. *Better Tennis* (1933), an instruction book that Wightman composed during the hours she waited in the car to pick up her children from school, became a standard teaching book during the 1930's.

Her contributions to tennis were recognized in 1957, when she was inducted into the Tennis Hall of Fame at Newport, Rhode Island. She also was recognized on the fiftieth anniversary of the Wightman Cup in 1973, when Queen Elizabeth II made Hazel Hotchkiss Wightman an honorary Commander of the British Empire. Wightman died in 1974 at the age of eighty-seven in Chestnut Hill, Massachusetts.

### Summary

Hazel Hotchkiss Wightman's life mirrors in several ways the development of women's tennis in the United States. Her performance on the court as a national champion came at a time when few sports other than tennis were open to women. She excelled during an era in which women's tennis was dominated primarily by women whose wealth permitted them to have the travel and leisure time necessary for capturing championships. She changed the style of play for women by emphasizing a more aggressive game that combined volleying with the traditional ground stroke elements, and she was an active participant in the dress reform movement in women's tennis. She introduced the Wightman Cup during the Golden Age of Sports in the 1920's, supported and encouraged the development of international competition in tennis for women, advocated the acceptance of tennis as an Olympic sport, and helped nurse women's tennis through the Depression and World War II years. Although she at first was opposed to the professionalization of women's tennis, Hazel Hotchkiss Wightman became one of its strongest supporters. It was therefore appropriate that she was chosen to present the first monetary award for women that was equal to the men's prize—an award Wightman presented to Margaret Court at the United States Tennis Association championship in 1973.

### Bibliography

Carter, Tom. "Stamp of Approval: Hazel Wightman Commemorated on Olympic Stamp." *Inside Tennis* (October, 1990): 28. A brief overview of Wightman's career is included in this column commenting on her selection as the first American tennis player to be featured on a stamp commemorating the participation of the United States in the Olympic Games.

Jacobs, Helen Hull. *Gallery of Champions*. New York: Barnes, 1949; London: Redman, 1951. Originally published in 1949, this collection of essays about many of the champion women's tennis players was written by Jacobs, a leading player who competed directly against many of the women she profiled. Includes a discussion of Hazel Hotchkiss Wightman's career during the years between World War I and World War II.

Klaw, Barbara. "Queen Mother of Tennis: An Interview with Hazel Hotchkiss Wightman." *American Heritage* 26 (August, 1975): 16-24, 82-86. Conducted only a few weeks before her death, Klaw's interview with Hazel Wightman reveals an individual who was capable of change but who remained true to the values which she had learned in the first quarter of the twentieth century.

Wightman, Hazel Hotchkiss. *Better Tennis*. London: Allen and Unwin, and Boston: Houghton Mifflin, 1933. Written in longhand while she juggled her roles as social director and chauffeur for her school-aged children, Hazel Wightman used this popular manual of the 1930's to promote the mental as well as the technical aspects of the game.

Wind, Herbert W. "From Wimbledon to Forest Hills: A Summer to Remember." *The New Yorker* 51 (October 13, 1975): 116-120. Although quite brief, this article was used by Wind as a means to reminisce about women's tennis in general and Wightman in particular.

Woolum, Janet. *Outstanding Women Athletes: Who They Are and How They Influenced American Sports*. 2d ed. Phoenix, Ariz.: Oryx Press, 1998. A thoroughly researched collection of sports biographies that includes a sketch on Wightman. Provides a thorough assessment of Wightman's career as a player and explains her role in popularizing a more aggressive style of play for women, in advocating dress reform for women in the sport, and in promoting greater opportunities and equality for women in the world of tennis.

*Robert L. Patterson*

## LAURA INGALLS WILDER

*Born:* February 7, 1867; Pepin, Wisconsin
*Died:* February 10, 1957; Mansfield, Missouri
*Area of Achievement:* Literature
*Contribution:* As a newspaper columnist in the 1910's and 1920's, Wilder espoused traditional values. Through the widely acclaimed fictionalized account of her youth in the "Little House" novels, she presented a picture of pioneer and homesteading life from the 1860's to the 1880's.

### Early Life

Laura Ingalls was born in Pepin, Wisconsin, the second of four daughters of Charles Phillip Ingalls and his wife, Caroline Quiner Ingalls. They moved around frequently before finally settling in De Smet, South Dakota, in 1879. Because of an economic depression, the Ingalls family moved to Missouri in 1868, which Laura's father found too crowded, and then in 1869 to Osage Indian Territory in Kansas, as recounted in *Little House on the Prairie* (1935). Returning to the woods of Wisconsin, the family found that it had become too populous for good hunting, so in 1874 the family settled in Walnut Grove, Minnesota, in a dugout house described in *On the Banks of Plum Creek* (1937). On November 1, 1875, a brother, Charles Frederick, was born. The family decided to move again, to Burr Oak, Iowa, where Charles and Caroline ran the Masters Hotel. Baby Freddie died, and in 1877, sister Grace Pearl was born. In the fictionalized account of her life, Laura omitted the two years at Burr Oak and, to compensate, placed the events of the first book, *Little House in the Big Woods* (1932), in 1870. After Burr Oak, the Ingalls returned to Walnut Grove, where the eldest daughter, Mary, became severely ill and lost her sight.

With sickness and debt haunting them, the Ingalls moved to the Dakota Territory in 1879, prompted by Charles's brother-in-law, who worked for the railroad and who needed someone to help him take care of the books and payroll of the store. Though Charles filed a homestead claim, the family lived in the surveyor's house at first and moved into town the next spring. Charles built a store there but soon moved the claim because of the threat of claim jumpers.

In De Smet, the Ingalls endured the hardships detailed in *The Long Winter* (1940). Laura met her husband, Almanzo Wilder, and earned her teacher's certificate at the age of fifteen. Her first position was at the Bouchie school, called the Brewster school in *These Happy Golden Years* (1943). By then, Almanzo was courting her, and after she taught two more terms, they married on August 9, 1885. Almanzo filed a homestead claim and a tree claim. On December 9, 1886, daughter Rose was born. The young couple, however, had to endure many troubles. Almanzo contracted diphtheria, which left him with a permanent limp. A son died shortly after birth in 1889. They lost the homestead claim, their house on the tree claim burned down, crops failed, and the trees on the claim died. The family was deeply in debt.

Laura, Almanzo, and Rose left De Smet in 1890, spent a year in Spring Valley, Minnesota, with Almanzo's parents, and then lived for two years in Florida. They returned to De Smet in 1892. Laura sewed to earn enough money for the family to leave Dakota. By covered wagon, they moved to Missouri, "The Land of the Big Red Apple," and settled near Mansfield. Wilder's diary of the trip was published in *On The Way Home* (1962). In Missouri they established Rocky Ridge Farm, where they remained for the rest of their lives.

### Life's Work

Wilder's writing career began when she was in her forties. Until this point, she had been a farmer's wife. As she had become an expert in raising chickens, agricultural groups occasionally invited her to speak. One time in 1911, she was unable to attend the meeting, so she had someone read her talk. It impressed the editor of the *Missouri Ruralist*, who was in the audience, and he invited her to submit essays for publication. With this invitation, the author Laura Ingalls Wilder was born. Her first article, "Favors the Small Farm Home," appeared on February 18, 1911, and developed several themes often appearing in her work: the virtues of the rural life and small farm; the benefits of technological developments such as the telephone, news delivery, and transportation innovations; and the necessity of cooperation between husband and wife in farm management. From the beginning, detailed descriptions applied to broader lessons characterized her writings. Between 1911 and 1915, she wrote only nine articles, some of which were signed not with Mrs. A. J. Wilder, as was the first one, but with Almanzo Wilder, to give them more authority.

In 1915 she went to San Francisco, California, a trip detailed in letters in *West From Home* (1974), to visit her daughter Rose Wilder Lane, herself an experienced writer. Lane recognized that her mother was highly skilled in description and helped her with stylistic and organizational matters. With Lane's encouragement, Wilder found other places to publish her farm articles, including the *Missouri State Farmer* and the *St. Louis Star*. She became a regular columnist for the *Ruralist*, with her column appearing in almost each of the bimonthly issues. These nonfiction articles focused on values that appeared later in her novels: hard work, thrift, honesty, and self-help, all within a balanced life. With Lane's help, she published the article "Whom Will You Marry" in the June, 1919, issue of *McCall's* magazine using the pen name Laura Ingalls Wilder.

In December, 1922, Lane arrived in Mansfield and again encouraged her mother to write for a larger audience. Wilder produced two pieces, which Lane edited, and sold them for $150 each to *Country Gentleman*. Wilder confessed that Lane's emendations took some joy away from the achievement. Lane in turn assured her mother that the reworking was minimal and that she could teach her to write in a style suitable for national publication with six months of instruction. Part of Lane's motive seems to have been to increase her parents' income. Lane had a rock house built for her parents on the Mansfield farm, which they inhabited for eight years, while Lane settled down in the original farmhouse.

During the first half of 1930, Wilder finally wrote a two-hundred-page memoir, "Pioneer Girl," which Lane sent to her agent. Of all the national publications, only *The Saturday Evening Post* expressed an interest in "Pioneer Girl," though only if it was reworked in fictional form. Lane abstracted some early material and worked it into a twenty-page story called "When Grandma Was a Little Girl," which a friend of Lane then sent to Alfred A. Knopf publishers. The editor observed that little in general, and almost nothing for children, had been written about that period in American history. Wilder was advised to expand the manuscript to 25,000 words and to write for children aged eight to twelve. She wrote the additional material in first person, and Lane spent a week reworking it into the third person and making other editorial changes. Knopf, meanwhile, had closed its children's division, leaving the book without a publisher. At the end of 1931, Virginia Kirkus at Harper Brothers took on the project, and when *Little House in the Big Woods* was chosen as the Junior Literary Guild selection for April, 1932, Harper Brothers published it. Wilder was then sixty-five years old.

Wilder next took up her husband's youth in *Farmer Boy* (1933). Midway through editing this book, Lane became acutely distressed over her own loneliness and frustrations at writing but recovered sufficiently to complete the task in August, 1932. Because the depression had affected book sales, Harper Brothers initially turned down the manuscript and suggested extensive revisions. Lane redid the manuscript in early 1933, and Harper Brothers published the book later that year.

The relationship between Lane and her mother was complex. On one hand, they helped each other, Lane by reworking Wilder's manuscripts and Wilder by giving Lane details of her life, which Lane then used in works such as her successful *Let the Hurricanes Roar* (1933). However, Lane's relationship with her mother during the collaborative years was often strained, and her own writing suffered. Wilder in turn was particularly upset by Lane's critique of *By the Shores of Silver Lake* (1939). Nevertheless, the two continued to collaborate, and Wilder generally acquiesced to Lane's suggestions. During Wilder's lifetime, Harper Brothers published eight of her books; a ninth, *The First Four Years* (1971), was probably written during the 1930's. Untouched by Lane, its style is quite different from the others, as it is mainly a bare narrative, adult fare realistically detailing the early years of Wilder's marriage.

### Summary

*Little House in the Big Woods* was an immediate success, and it and the subsequent books won wide praise. *By the Shores of Silver Lake* was a Newberry Honor Book and the Pacific Northwest Library Young Reader's Choice Award in 1942. Four other books were also Newberry Honor Books: *On the Banks of Plum Creek*, *The Long Winter*, *Little Town on the Prairie* (1941), and *These Happy Golden Years*. In 1954 the Association for Library Services created the Laura Ingalls Wilder Medal for authors who have made a lasting contribution to children's literature and presented Wilder with the first award.

The Little House books are instructive from several viewpoints. They provide a sustained, though perhaps romanticized and sanitized, view of pioneer and homesteading life and provide a comparison with the works of such authors as Willa Cather. They also illustrate the process of women writing about girls. At first Pa was the dominant character, but as the series progressed, Wilder and Lane developed Laura's voice. The books also illustrate the conflicts between independence and conformity to late nineteenth century gender roles that Laura experienced. Finally, the books may be seen as excellent historical fiction, for Wilder and Lane made every effort to ensure historical accuracy, resorting to research on events and places that Wilder could no longer clearly remember.

**Bibliography**

Anderson, William. *Laura Ingalls Wilder Country.* New York: Harper, 1990. A photographic essay, this attractive book illustrates the lives of the Ingalls and Wilder families and people they knew. Included are pictures of the places where the Ingalls lived during Wilder's childhood, including markers and replicas of some of their cabins. Also contains a map and a chronology.

Holtz, William. "Ghost and Host in the Little House Books." *Studies in Literary Imagination* 29, no. 2 (Fall 1996). This article discusses the fact that Wilder's daughter, Rose Wilder Lane, rewrote the "Little House" book series and argues that ghostwriters deserve as much credit as original creators.

———. *The Ghost in the Little House: A Life of Rose Wilder Lane.* Columbia: University of Missouri Press, 1993. This 425-page biography of Wilder's daughter contains extensive discussions on the relationship between the mother and daughter, including the collaborative effort involved in publishing the Little House books.

Jameson, Elizabeth. "In Search of the Great Ma." *Journal of the West* 37, no. 2 (April, 1998). Discusses Wilder's eight-volume Little House series.

Miller, John E. *Becoming Laura Ingalls Wilder: The Woman Behind the Legend.* Columbia: University of Missouri Press, 1998. A 306-page biography detailing the major periods of Wilder's life. Personal events are placed within a historical and economic context, and the nature of the collaboration between Wilder and her daughter is examined.

———. *Laura Ingalls Wilder's Little Town: Where History and Literature Meet.* Lawrence: University Press of Kansas, 1994. A literary analysis of Wilder's books as history, focusing on life in De Smet. The author examines themes such as place and community in De Smet and love and affection in the writing and life of Wilder, and compares the prairie depicted by Wilder and artist Harvey Dunn.

Romines, Ann. *Constructing the Little House: Gender, Culture, and Laura Ingalls Wilder.* Amherst: University of Massachusetts Press, 1997. Written by an English professor interested in women's writing and gendered culture, this 287-page book examines how Wilder and Lane overcame patriarchal commitments in the first two books and succeeded as women writing about girls. It also studies the problem of racial and ethnic discourse, the importance of material culture in Wilder's youth, gendered roles in adolescence, and the expansion of female possibilities in a patriarchal culture.

Spaeth, Janet. *Laura Ingalls Wilder.* Boston: Twayne, 1987. Spaeth's book identifies themes in the Little House books such as family folklore, the woman's role in the family, and the representation of Wilder's growth through languages.

*Kristen L. Zacharias*

# MAURICE H. F. WILKINS

*Born:* December 15, 1916; Pongaroa, New Zealand

*Areas of Achievement:* Physics and biophysics

*Contribution:* Wilkins' X-ray diffraction studies were instrumental in the structure determination of DNA.

## Early Life

Maurice Hugh Frederick Wilkins was born on December 15, 1916, in Pongaroa, New Zealand, to Edgar Henry and Eveline Constance Jane (Whittaker) Wilkins. His parents came from Dublin, Ireland, but his Irish heritage had little influence on him. His father was a doctor in the School Medical Service and was very interested in research but had little chance to do it. In his life Maurice would fulfill this dream of his father.

At the age of six, Maurice was brought to England and educated at King Edward's School in Birmingham. He went to study physics at St. John's College, Cambridge University, where he was a fencer (his lack of speed led him later to give up the sport) and where he learned some crystallography from J. D. Bernal. He obtained his B.A. degree in 1938. Then he attended Birmingham University, where he became research assistant to Dr. John T. Randall in the physics department. Together they developed the electron-trap theory of phosphorescence and thermoluminescence. Wilkins' doctoral thesis was concerned with studies of phosphorescence, in particular as applied to various wartime needs, such as the improvement of cathode-ray screens for radar. He received his Ph.D. for this work in 1940.

During World War II, Wilkins moved from radar screens to weapons. He joined the physicists under Sir Marcus Oliphant in their work using the mass spectrograph to separate uranium isotopes for the atom bomb. When nuclear research was transferred to the United States, Wilkins was one of the scientists who went with it. He traveled to the University of California at Berkeley to become part of the Manhattan Project. There he continued to use the mass spectrograph to build up quantities of uranium-235 for the American atom bomb. As the war neared its end and the atom bombs were dropped, Wilkins' interest in nuclear physics waned. He read *What Is Life? The Physical Aspect of the Living Cell* (1944), by the Nobel Prize-winning physicist Erwin Schrödinger, and became eager to apply his understanding of physics to the complexities of living things.

In 1945, Wilkins returned to Great Britain and began a career in biophysics at St. Andrew's University in Scotland, where he was again under the direction of his old teacher, Randall. Wilkins was a tall, thin, bespectacled man with a straight nose and long neck. He took the strict scientific approach not only to physics and biology but also to life. Conclusions were acceptable to him only after rigid experimental observation.

## Life's Work

In 1946, Wilkins and Randall moved to King's College, London, which was then reconstructing buildings and staff left in ruins by the war. The money for the biophysics unit came from the Medical Research Council, a governmental agency which had been established after World War I to promote research in medicine. By the time Wilkins went to King's College, scientists at the Rockefeller Institute in New York had proved that genes were made of deoxyribonucleic acid (DNA). Wilkins became fascinated with this substance, and he started doing research on it, at first indirectly, by trying to cause mutations in fruit flies with ultrasonic vibrations, then directly, by developing a special microscope for studying the amount of DNA in cells. While Wilkins was using the ultraviolet microscope to study quantities of nucleic acid in cells, Randall and his associates were investigating the sperm of rams by means of the electron microscope and X-ray diffraction. Wilkins decided to leave the analysis of DNA in intact cells to the biologists; he believed that he could contribute more effectively by using his specialized skills to study the DNA molecule in isolation, outside the cell.

One of the techniques physicists had developed by that time was the analysis of dichroism patterns. Wilkins placed the specimen of DNA under the microscope and then subjected it to two colors of light simultaneously: One color was transmitted directly and the other was reflected. From the contrast of the colors, some information about the structure of DNA could be inferred.

These optical studies of DNA molecules eventually convinced Wilkins that DNA fibers would be ideal material for X-ray diffraction studies. While examining DNA gels prepared for his dichroism work, Wilkins observed, through a microscope,

that each time he touched the gel with a glass rod and then removed it, a thin fiber of DNA was drawn out and suspended between the rod and the gel. The uniformity of the fibers suggested that the DNA molecules were arranged in some kind of regular pattern, and therefore they might be suitable material for analysis by X-ray diffraction. This technique, developed by Henry and Lawrence Bragg forty years before, used X rays scattered by the regular spacing of atoms in a crystal to determine their arrangement in three dimensions.

Wilkins took the DNA fibers to Raymond Gosling, who had the department's only X-ray equipment. The first diffraction patterns of DNA obtained with their makeshift equipment were very encouraging. Before long, Wilkins and his colleagues got much sharper diffraction photographs of DNA. The sharpness showed that the DNA molecules were highly regular; the pattern indicated that they were helical. Wilkins had learned from John Bernal that it was important to keep the fibers moist to get good diffraction patterns. This proved to be a key to obtaining experimental data that were useful in clarifying the structure of DNA. When the material was dried, there was no pattern; when high humidity was restored, there was a detailed pattern in the form of a cross.

While this experimental work was going on at King's College, Wilkins realized that theoretical work needed to be done on the X-ray diffraction of helices. To meet this need, Alex Stokes and others formulated a theory that predicted the absence and presence of certain reflections, which appeared as spots in the X-ray photographs. The precise location and intensity of these spots depended on the characteristics of the helix—that is, its repeat distance and its diameter. By 1951, then, Wilkins had come to realize that the X-ray diffraction pattern of DNA exhibited helical characteristics. The matter was far from clear, however, and it was at this point that Randall invited Rosalind Franklin to join the group at King's College. This brought about a personality conflict, since Franklin believed that the DNA problem had been given to her, whereas Wilkins believed that the problem was his and that she would be working for him. Matters were not helped by the extended absence of Wilkins on visits to Naples in May of 1951 and to the United States in September. On his return, Wilkins found that Franklin and Gosling, using more advanced X-ray equipment with which they were able to attain higher humidities than previously, had made much progress. Since collaboration was no longer possible, the work was divided, and Wilkins and Franklin studied different problems. Wilkins was able to show the existence of helical DNA in certain living cells. He also showed that DNAs from different biological sources were basically the same; this was important evidence for the generality of the DNA structure. Meanwhile, Franklin found that the crystalline patterns of DNA that Wilkins had described earlier were attributable to what was called the A (or low-humidity) form, but she also observed for the first time at high humidities a less crystalline form, called the B form, that was to be instrumental in elucidating DNA's structure.

During this period, Wilkins maintained personal contact with his friend Francis Crick, a physicist whose interest in DNA intensified when James Watson, a young American postdoctoral fellow, arrived at the Medical Research Council Unit in Cambridge. Watson-Crick and Wilkins-Franklin were not the only groups attempting to find the structure of DNA; in California, Linus Pauling was also thinking about the problem. Toward the end of 1952, Watson and Crick heard, via Pauling's son

Peter, who was working with John Kendrew at Cambridge, that his father had come up with a structure for DNA. This proved to be a triple helix with the phosphate groups on the inside and the bulky base groups on the outside of the molecule.

Early in 1952 Watson visited London to discuss the Pauling structure with Franklin and Wilkins. Watson's talk with Franklin was abortive, but he spent time with Wilkins, who showed him a good B-structure photograph, which he probably had obtained from Franklin. It immediately struck Watson that DNA must have a helical structure. He also learned from Wilkins that two chains were not inconsistent with Franklin's results. He was also reminded by Wilkins that Franklin had concluded that the bases were in the center and the phosphate groups on the outside of the DNA molecule. After his return to Cambridge, Watson saw, with some help from Pauling's former colleague, Jerry Donohue, that the bases could be paired in the center of the molecule, and by using this and several other clues, Watson and Crick were able to construct their famous double helix for the structure of DNA.

It remained for Wilkins to demonstrate that the structure of DNA was not merely an artifact resulting from the manipulation of the material once it had been removed from the cell. He found that X-ray diffraction photographs taken of intact biological systems bore a close resemblance to the photographs obtained from purified DNA, thus proving that DNA was the same highly structured double-helical molecule before and after isolation.

After the publications in *Nature* by the two groups in 1953, Wilkins proved that the Watson-Crick model was unique—that is, no other model would give the same X-ray diffraction pattern. His data also allowed Wilkins to readjust and refine the Watson-Crick model. In 1962, he obtained the first clear X-ray diffraction patterns of ribonucleic acid (RNA), and he showed that it had a helical structure very similar to the Watson-Crick double helix.

In 1955, Wilkins became deputy director of the Biophysics Research Unit of the Medical Research Council. He married Patricia Ann Chidgey in 1959; they have a daughter, Sarah, and a son, George. In 1963, Wilkins was made professor of molecular biology at King's College, and in 1970 he became professor of biophysics as well. He shared the 1962 Nobel Prize with Watson and Crick, but he suffered under the duress of changes in his life brought by the award. The strain he felt came from altered schedules and too many social obligations and too little time for the science that he loved the best.

### Summary

There are many ironies in Maurice H. F. Wilkins' life. He won the Nobel Prize for his work with nucleic acids, but as late as 1950 he wondered why they were in the cell at all. Much of the information and some of the ideas about DNA's structure derived from the work of Rosalind Franklin, a collaborator with whom he had difficulty communicating. James Watson, the biologist, realized the decisive importance of the DNA molecule, whereas the physicists Wilkins and Crick emphasized the technicalities of the X-ray data.

Despite the complications and human foibles surrounding the discovery of the double helix, the structure itself proved to be a simple and a beautiful one. Wilkins was impressed by this simplicity, and he came to regard DNA's simplicity as symbolizing the underlying simplicity of all biological phenomena. In his later career, he believed that science's search for simple principles could also be used to resolve social conflicts. For him science represented rationality, and in the 1960's and 1970's Wilkins warned of the growth of antirational attitudes in the world. This is not to say he was unaware of science's potential for dehumanization. He recognized that objective thinking could reduce moral sensitivity. According to Wilkins, modern man lives with a dilemma: Science is the only way for human beings to avoid starvation, disease, and premature death, but science can be used to accelerate human annihilation. To reduce these dangers, science must be carefully interrelated to technology, politics, art, and the rest of society.

### Bibliography

Judson, Horace Freeland. *The Eighth Day of Creation: Makers of the Revolution in Biology.* New York: Simon and Schuster, and London: Cape, 1979. Judson interviewed Wilkins several times, and his book contains a good description of Wilkins' work in the context of the evolution of modern biology. It also has much interesting information on the other participants in the discovery of the double helix.

Olby, Robert. *The Path to the Double Helix.* London: Macmillan, and Seattle: University of Washington Press, 1974. This is the best detailed scientific and historical account of the discovery of DNA's structure, and Wilkins' work is given ample treatment.

Portugal, Franklin H., and Jack S. Cohen. *A Century of DNA: A History of the Discovery of the Structure and Function of the Genetic Substance*. Cambridge, Mass.: MIT Press, 1977. This book traces the story of DNA from the time of its discovery in 1869 to the solution of the genetic code in the 1960's, and so it provides a good background for the work of Wilkins on DNA.

Sayre, Anne. *Rosalind Franklin and DNA*. New York: Norton, 1975. This book takes Rosalind Franklin's view of the controversy over the discovery of the double helix, but it, too, has its mistakes and distortions. Nevertheless, it presents an account of Wilkins from another perspective, albeit an unflattering one.

Schrödinger, Erwin. *What Is Life? The Physical Aspect of the Living Cell*. Cambridge: Cambridge University Press, and New York: Macmillan, 1944. This widely read book converted Wilkins and many other physicists to biology. The most important point it makes is that the gene is an information carrier.

Stent, Gunther, ed. *The Double Helix: A Personal Account of the Discovery of the Structure of DNA by James Watson*. London: Weidenfeld and Nicolson, and New York: Norton, 1980. Wilkins and others succeeded in preventing Harvard University Press from publishing Watson's book by objecting to many of his interpretations. This edition, which, besides the complete text of the book, has much other material, in the form of reviews, commentaries, original scientific papers, and discussions, helps to put this famous work in a more objective context.

Wilkins, Maurice H. F. "The Molecular Configuration of Nucleic Acids." In *Nobel Lectures, Physiology or Medicine, 1942-1962*. New York: Elsevier, 1964. Wilkins' Nobel lecture gives a good overview not only of his prizewinning work but also of the basic themes of his other scientific accomplishments.

*Robert J. Paradowski*

# SIR GEORGE HUBERT WILKINS

*Born:* October 31, 1888; East Mount Bryan, South Australia, Australia

*Died:* December 1, 1958; Framingham, Massachusetts

*Area of Achievement:* Natural science, cinematography, and exploration

*Contribution:* Wilkins was able to utilize new technological developments and to apply aviation, cinematography, and meteorology in order to understand the diverse conditions of the polar regions during his explorations.

## Early Life

George Hubert Wilkins was born at East Mount Bryan, near Adelaide, South Australia, on October 31, 1888. He was the thirteenth and youngest child of Harry Wilkins and the former Louisa Smith. Harry Wilkins had failed to find his fortune in the Ballarat, Victoria, gold strikes in 1851 and turned to the open range as one of the earliest drovers to bring cattle into South Australia. It was on his sheep and cattle ranch that Wilkins lived and worked as a young boy. Although he received a diploma qualifying him to enter a state high school, Wilkins had no formal secondary education because he spent nearly three years helping his father through a devastating drought. His years of living in the vastness of the country, observing and camping with the neighboring aborigines and experiencing the destructive forces of nature, influenced Wilkins' lifetime interest in natural sciences, anthropology, climatology, and meteorology.

In 1903, his parents retired to Adelaide, where Wilkins worked in the mornings and attended classes at both the University of Adelaide and the South Australian School of Mines and Industries. Although he studied electrical and general engineering, his interests diversified to include music, botany, zoology, geology, and particularly photography. While attending school, Wilkins served as an apprentice to a mechanical engineer and later spent nearly a year in charge of the electric lighting for a touring carnival company. It was during his years with the carnival that he developed his love for travel and his expertise in the new technology of motion pictures.

In 1908, Wilkins was offered a position with the Gaumont Motion Picture Company in London, England, as a cinematographic cameraman. He stowed away on a ship, was caught and forced to work on the ship's dynamo, and eventually arrived in England after an adventurous journey through the Mediterranean and North Africa. In London, his rare skills with cameras and motion pictures enabled him to work for both the Gaumont company and the London *Daily Chronicle*. While on assignment at Hendon Aerodrome, Wilkins met Claude Grahame-White, the pioneer English aviator, who took him on his first flight and arranged for him to take flying lessons. Wilkins' flight training was interrupted when his employers jointly sent him to cover the brutal Balkan War in 1912-1913 as a cinematographer. He was briefly captured during the war and at great personal risk became the first photographer to obtain motion pictures of actual combat. After the war, Wilkins continued to build a reputation in the photographic and cinematographic fields in Europe and the West Indies while continuing his flying lessons in both airplanes and dirigibles. In 1913, his career suddenly changed when he was invited to join an expedition to the Arctic.

## Life's Work

In 1913, Wilkins joined the Vilhjalmur Stefansson Arctic Expedition, sponsored by the Canadian government. During the following three years, he walked thousands of miles across the Arctic ice and acquired great expertise in the techniques of living, traveling, and working under Arctic conditions. Although Wilkins was the expedition's photographer, he added greatly to his knowledge of natural sciences, studied Eskimo ethnology, and carried out oceanographic and meteorological experiments. He also developed plans to utilize airplanes in polar explorations and mapping and for establishing permanent weather stations in those regions as part of a worldwide weather forecasting program.

Because of World War I, Wilkins left the expedition in 1916 to accept a commission in the Royal Australian Flying Corps. He was assigned to the military history department as a photographer, navigator, and pilot. During this assignment, he was wounded nine times and received the Military Cross with Bar for his bravery. When the war ended, Wilkins returned to flying. In 1919, he participated in the England-to-Australia air race, but a fuel leak forced his Blackburn Kangaroo airplane to land in Crete.

In 1920-1921, Wilkins made his first trip to Antarctica as second in command of John Lachlan Cope's British Imperial Expedition to survey the coastline of Graham Land. On his second visit, he served as naturalist with Sir Ernest Shackleton and John Quiller Rowett's *Quest* expedition of 1921-1922, during which Shackleton died. Wilkins discovered several new species of vegetation, birds, and insects, while continuing his meteorological study of the polar regions.

Wilkins spent 1922 and 1923 in Europe and the Soviet Union with the Society of Friends, filming the effects of drought and famine. Upon his return to London, he was selected by the British Museum to lead a natural history expedition in 1923-1925 to collect plant and animal specimens in tropical Northern Australia. He summarized his results in his book *Undiscovered Australia* (1928), which showed the extent and quality of his studies of plants, birds, insects, fish, mammals, fossils, and archaeological artifacts.

Unable to secure funding for an Antarctic expedition, Wilkins, with support from several private sources, such as the *Detroit News* and the American Geographical Society, returned to his earlier goal of exploring the Arctic by airplane. After two abortive efforts in 1926 and 1927, Wilkins and Carl Ben Eielson in 1928 flew their Lockheed Vega monoplane twenty-one hundred miles across previously unexplored territory between Point Barrow, Alaska, and Spitsbergen, Norway. In his book *Flying the Arctic* (1928), Wilkins explained that the flight was made to prove the value of airplanes for polar exploration and to further his plans for polar meteorological stations.

Wilkins was knighted by King George V on June 14, 1928, at Buckingham Palace, in recognition of his pioneer flights and other accomplishments. He won several other honors, including the Patron's Medal of the Royal Geographic Society and the Samuel Finley Breese Morse Gold Medal of the American Geographical Society.

Wilkins next launched his project for the aerial exploration of the Antarctic as the leader of the Wilkins-Hearst Expedition sponsored by the American Geographical Society and financier William Randolph Hearst. From Deception Bay in the South Shetland Islands, he and Eielson made the first flight in the Antarctic on November 16, 1928. On subsequent flights from 1928 to 1930, Wilkins flew over Graham Land, discovering Crane Channel, Stefansson Strait, and the Lockheed Mountains. He claimed the island known as Charcot Land for Great Britain and mapped more than eighty thousand square miles of Antarctica.

Wilkins' reputation as a pioneer aviator in polar regions was firmly established. Handsome, six feet tall, and possessing a grace that belied his solid two hundred pounds, Wilkins was highly respected for his scholarship, professionalism, amiability, and integrity. In 1929, he married Suzanne Bennett, an Australian actress who lived in New York. Theirs was a childless but happy marriage which by mutual agreement permitted them to pursue their individual careers.

In all of his flights over the Arctic Sea, Wilkins had found no land on which to build his projected weather stations. Unwilling to accept ice floes as station platforms and doubting that surface ships could penetrate the icy seas to suitable locations, he turned to the submarine as an experimental weather station. Converting an obsolete navy submarine, which he named the *Nautilus*, into an oceanographic laboratory, Wilkins proposed crossing the Arctic basin using the vessel both above and below the ice to radio weather information to the world. A series of mishaps and malfunctions forced the *Nautilus* expedition of 1931 to be abandoned, but not before the feasibility of using submarines under the polar ice cap had been demonstrated. This was the first submarine trip under the Arctic ice and preceded the atomic-powered *Nautilus* by twenty-seven years.

From 1933 to 1937, Wilkins commanded the ship *Wyatt Earp* and managed four Antarctic flights by the American Lincoln Ellsworth. In November, 1935, Ellsworth, utilizing Wilkins' planning, succeeded in the first flight across the Antarctic continent, rendezvousing with Wilkins aboard the *Wyatt Earp*. In August, 1937, the Soviet Union gave Wilkins the command of a search expedition to locate Soviet aviator Sigesmund Levanevsky, who had disappeared between Moscow and Alaska. During the following months, Wilkins and Herbert Hollick-Kenyon combined the search with pioneer moonlight flying in winter conditions while covering more than 150,000 square miles of the uncharted polar basin, but Levanevsky was never found.

The Levanevsky search was Wilkins' last great feat of exploration. During World War II, Wilkins was utilized as a geographer, climatologist, and Arctic adviser to the United States Quartermaster Corps and the Office of Strategic Studies. He was specifically involved in developing clothing and equipment for troops engaged in rugged environments. Wilkins designed special parkas and underwear for troops assigned to polar regions and personally tested them in the Aleutian Islands.

After the war, Wilkins worked with the United States Navy Office of Scientific Research from 1946 to 1947 and served as an adviser to the United States Weather Bureau (1946-1948) and the Arctic Institute of North America (1947). He was a guest lecturer in geography at McGill University in Montreal, Canada, in 1947-1948 and at the National Defense College of Canada in 1948.

Wilkins was an active participant in the Antarctic studies conducted during the International Geophysical Year, 1957-1958. Wilkins died of a heart attack on December 1, 1958, in Framingham, Massachusetts, where he had worked as a consultant on polar regions for the Research and Development Command of the Department of Defense since 1953. On March 17, 1959, the American nuclear submarine *Skate*, the first vessel to surface at the exact geographical North Pole, honored Wilkins' lifetime wish by scattering his ashes over the icy terrain.

### Summary

Sir George Hubert Wilkins was primarily a field explorer who had an inquisitive mind and the outlook of a true pioneer. He was at home with primitive people whose reverence for nature he shared. His adaptability to extreme environmental conditions made him an ideal polar explorer. At the same time, he was one of the least publicly recognized expedition leaders because he cared less for headlines than for genuine advances in knowledge of mankind's environment. He was never interested in the races to either pole, and it was only after thousands had preceded him that he visited either one, even though he had spent five summers and twenty-six winters in the Arctic and eight summers in the Antarctic.

In addition to his pioneering efforts in cinematography and the *Nautilus* expedition, Wilkins was the first to fly in the Antarctic, the first to fly over the Arctic Ocean, and the first to prove the feasibility of landing a plane on packed ice. Respect from his colleagues and honors from governments were bestowed on him for his feats and scientific contributions. His greatest successes and rewards were the reorientation of geographic thought that the airplane engendered, the development of submarines capable of exploring the polar waters, and the establishment of the polar weather stations for which he had worked during his lifetime.

Wilkins was as much at home with the scientific world world of the International Geophysical Year in 1957 as he had been with his early experiences in cinematography and flight. His ability to utilize new technology and ideas and to realize their long-term significance made him the consummate explorer that he was.

### Bibliography

Bertrand, Kenneth J. *Americans in Antarctica, 1775-1948*. New York: Lane Press, 1971. An American Geographical Society special publication. Excellent information about Wilkins with particular emphasis on the Ellsworth flights.

Grierson, John. *Sir Hubert Wilkins: Enigma of Exploration*. London: Hale, 1960. A factual and informative biography of an admirable individual whose adventurous life was lived in near obscurity.

Kirwan, Laurence P. *A History of Polar Exploration*. London: Penguin, 1959; New York: Norton, 1960. Comprehensive narrative with references to Wilkins in the context of polar exploration.

MacLean, John Kennedy, and Chelsea Fraser. *Heroes of the Farthest North and Farthest South*. New York: Crowell, and London: Chambers, 1913. Good chapters on the early expeditions and accomplishments of Wilkins and Stefansson.

Mill, Hugh Robert. "The Significance of Sir Hubert Wilkins' Antarctic Flights." *The Geographical Review* 19 (July, 1929): 377-386. A contemporary and professional analysis of the importance of Wilkins' early aeronautical achievements in the Arctic.

Stefansson, Vilhjalmur. *Unsolved Mysteries of the Arctic*. New York: Macmillan, 1938; London: Harrap, 1939. An entire chapter is devoted to Wilkins' involvement in the Levanevsky search. Comprehensive narrative by an expert in polar history.

Thomas, Lowell. *Sir Hubert Wilkins, His World of Adventure*. New York: McGraw-Hill, 1961; London: Barker, 1962. Informative biography in which the author has Wilkins narrate his life from their thirty years of conversations. Excellent photographs.

Wood, Walter A. "George Hubert Wilkins." *The Geographical Review* 49 (July, 1959): 411-416. Brief but informative biographical account of Wilkins' life and accomplishments.

*Phillip E. Koerper*

# WILLIAM II

*Born:* January 27, 1859; Berlin, Prussia
*Died:* June 4, 1941; Doorn, The Netherlands
*Areas of Achievement:* Government and politics
*Contribution:* After a quarter of a century of straining the patience and tolerance of his fellow rulers with his ill-advised antics, it was William II's misfortune to lead the German Empire during World War I. Although certainly not solely responsible for that conflict, it is hard to deny that his inability to cope with the demands of the modern state helped to create the climate of instability that eventually led to the rise of Adolf Hitler.

## Early Life

Born on January 27, 1859, Prince Friedrich Wilhelm Viktor Albert was the eldest son of Prince Frederick William of Prussia and his wife, Princess Victoria, the eldest child of Queen Victoria and Prince Albert. The delivery was difficult and William's left arm was severely injured. The hand and arm, although healthy, never grew to normal size, thereby producing a lack of bodily balance. This handicap drove the young prince to try harder than his fellows to succeed in areas that required physical stamina, and especially in athletics.

In contrast to his autocratic grandfather, who would in 1871 become the first emperor of Germany, William's parents were liberals who were determined that their son would be educated to govern a democratic state, not an absolute monarchy. Consequently, at the age of sixteen he became the first member of his family to attend a school open to the general public. Having been carefully prepared for entry into the *Gymnasium* at Kassel, William did quite well academically, but he was carefully isolated from his fellow students. Beginning in 1877, he spent four semesters at the University of Bonn, but his real interest lay with the army and not the university.

William began his military training late in 1879 at Potsdam, near Berlin. There William came in close contact with the most conservative elements in German society, the Prussian nobility and the corps of professional officers. At last he could rebel against the ideas and concepts that his parents had tried to instill in him since childhood. His rebellion brought him into conflict with his mother, who was as willful and determined as he was. This tension continued until her death in 1901 and gave rise to a number of unfounded rumors about relations between William and other members of his mother's family.

As was the custom among European royalty, William's marriage was arranged for him, and in February, 1880, he was engaged to Augusta Victoria of Schleswig-Holstein-Sonderburg-Augustenberg, Dona to her family. Reared to concern herself with children and home, she did not provide William with either the intellectual companionship or direction that he so desperately needed. Yet the marriage, which was solemnized in February, 1881, proved a happy one, and the couple had six sons and one daughter.

During the years that followed his marriage, William was rarely in the public eye, but he was considered important enough to be cultivated by his grandfather's chancellor, Otto von Bismarck. The young prince was flattered by the attention from one whom he greatly admired, and during the last years of the old emperor's life, he seemed to grow closer to the man whom neither his father

nor his mother trusted. Then on March 9, 1888, William I died and Fredrick III ascended the throne. His reign was brief; on June 15, 1888, he died of cancer of the throat. At the age of twenty-nine, William II inherited the crown of Germany and began a reign that would last until 1918.

## Life's Work

Almost completely ignorant of foreign affairs and uncertain of his ability to understand the endless ramifications of his ministers' domestic policies, William II was nevertheless determined to bring under his personal control every aspect of government. Bismarck was equally convinced that to entrust such weighty matters to the care of an immature monarch whose impatience and lack of tact were proverbial might endanger the continued peaceful evolution of the German state. Resolved to manage the young kaiser, and sure of his own indispensable position, Bismarck invoked a long-forgotten cabinet order of 1850 that forbade individual ministers to report to the monarch save in the presence of the chancellor. Having endured Bismarck's arrogance for almost two years, William dismissed him on March 10, 1890.

With the departure of Bismarck, William II assumed complete control of the government, but the only thing consistent bout his policies was their inconsistency. Often his instincts were correct, but, aware of his lack of real experience, he repeatedly allowed himself to endorse a course of action that eventually proved injurious to the interests of Germany. Thus, shortly after Bismarck left office, the kaiser was persuaded not to renew the vital Reinsurance Treaty with Russia. This rejection of one of the cornerstones of Bismarck's foreign policy forced Russia into an alliance with France in 1894. This blunder ended the diplomatic isolation of France and left Germany surrounded by potential enemies. The climate of opinion thus created allowed proponents of a two-front war, such as Alfred von Schlieffen, the opportunity to convince William of the inevitable armed conflict with France and Russia.

Determined to counter the Franco-Russian alliance with a diplomatic coup of his own, William used every device at his disposal to form a permanent arrangement with Great Britain. Instead of creating a lasting friendship with the foreign power he most admired, William seemed to lurch from one crisis to another. The African and Asian policies of the two countries were not incompatible, but, when the kaiser finished his diplomatic offensive, relations between the two countries were almost openly hostile. As the possibility of an Anglo-German rapprochement became increasingly remote, William encouraged the passage by the Reichstag of a naval bill that would create a German war fleet. While it was intended to protect Germany's merchant fleet and serve the empire, the British regarded the naval building program as a threat to their continued hegemony on the high seas. All hope of an alliance, formal or informal, was destroyed by the kaiser's continued public support of the Boers in South Africa and his enthusiastic endorsement of the building of a railroad from Berlin to Baghdad.

William's grasp of domestic affairs during the first decade of his reign was equally unsuccessful. In the early days of the empire, Berlin was slowly transformed from a mere royal capital into a city of world stature. Unfortunately, William was completely out of touch with the cultural trends that were sweeping Germany into the mainstream of European life. He turned from the exciting new Berlin of artists and intellectuals, poets and playwrights, politicians and reformers to an older Berlin that still celebrated the martial virtues. Surrounding himself with military personnel, William became increasingly remote from his civilian advisers, a trend that had dire consequences in the early years of the twentieth century.

To their dismay, German diplomats learned of the Entente Cordiale between France and Great Britain in 1904. Undaunted, William proceeded the following year to execute his plan for dislodging the British from their potential alliance with the Third French Republic. Bismarck had encouraged the French to develop a sphere of influence in North Africa, but now William sought to reverse that policy while reawakening British distrust of French colonial ambitions. He recognized the Sultan of Morocco as an independent ruler and paid a visit to Tangier in 1905. To prevent an escalation of this manufactured crisis, the great powers assembled at Algeciras in Spain the following year. The conference was a diplomatic victory for France. It received a free hand in Morocco, the arrangement with Great Britain was strengthened, and in 1907, after months of negotiations begun at Algeciras, Russia was persuaded to settle a number of long-standing differences with Great Britain.

William provoked a second Moroccan crisis in 1911 by sending a German warship to the port of

Agadir to protest the French occupation of the city of Fez. The European powers came very close to war, but somehow peace was maintained. Actual fighting in the Balkans the following year had a sobering effect on Europe's leaders, and even the kaiser began to work for the maintenance of peace. The months that followed saw an easing of tensions, and the gala wedding of William's daughter, Viktoria Luise, to Ernst August of Hannover in May, 1912, seemed to mark the beginning of a new era of tranquillity and cooperation. It was to be the last time that the royalty of Europe would assemble socially, but on that happy occasion war was far from their minds. The development of a rational and peaceful approach to the Continent's problems was welcomed by people of every nationality.

In June, 1914, the kaiser was on holiday when the Archduke Francis Ferdinand was assassinated. Shocked at the loss of an old friend, he promised Germany's moral support to Austria-Hungary, never dreaming that his ally would use that offer to force Serbia into a diplomatic position that could only result in a declaration of war. Ignorant of the exact details of the ultimatum, William nevertheless felt honor-bound to defend Austria-Hungary. Once committed to war, albeit reluctantly, the kaiser threw himself into the fray with his usual energy. His fits of bombastic rhetoric gave the Allies grist for their propaganda mills, but the German people remained loyal until the end. Like all the belligerent powers, Germany censored the news from the front and successfully edited the truth to convince the people of their ultimate victory. The rumor of the armistice and Germany's subsequent admission of defeat seemed to paralyze the nation. Republican elements then seized the opportunity to overthrow the monarchy, which was tainted with failure. On November 10, 1918, William, the last member of the House of Hohenzollern to govern in Germany, crossed the frontier into The Netherlands, an exile.

For more than twenty years, William pursued the life of a country gentleman in the charming castle at Doorn, which he purchased in 1920. Despite repeated Allied demands, the Dutch government refused to extradite him as a war criminal. To ensure his safety, William had only to promise his Dutch hosts that he would abstain from all political activity. This he did, although he never ceased to hope for a restoration. Unfortunately, the suicide of his son Joachim in 1920 and the death of the empress in 1921 made his early years of exile bleak. His marriage to Hermine, the widow of Prince Schonaich-Carolath in November, 1922, marked the beginning of a much happier phase of his life. As the years passed, the former kaiser's public image began to soften, and, with the rise of Hitler, many in Germany and abroad longed for his return. Forgotten were the diplomatic blunders and his open hostility to liberal trends and ideas; instead, his integrity, his patriotism, and his devotion to duty were remembered. When, in November, 1938, William denounced the savagery of Kristallnacht, many of his critics revised their opinions of their former adversary.

When war came in September, 1939, William declined the offer of sanctuary in England, preferring to remain at Doorn. He spent his last months a virtual prisoner of his Nazi guards, but he refused to allow his death on June 4, 1941, to be used to serve the propaganda aims of the Hitler government. He was buried at Doorn and not Berlin. The notice of his death was lost amid the war news, but for those who longed for the return of order and honor he became a symbol of better times.

### Summary

Although William II was hardly the quintessence of evil portrayed in Allied propaganda during World War I, he does bear a portion of the blame for the outbreak of that most tragic of modern conflicts. Nevertheless, he was also a victim of the system that sucked the great powers into the vortex of war in the second decade of the twentieth century. The last kaiser of Germany was a man of intelligence with the potential for a depth of understanding of the workings of the modern state unparalleled among his fellow rulers, but his erudition was a façade and his learning superficial. William had flair but no substance. By rebelling against the ideals of his parents, he rejected the chance to aid in the transformation of Germany into a modern constitutional monarchy and chose instead to ally himself with those who espoused the outmoded and potentially dangerous military virtues that had helped to unite Germany in 1871. With the death of his father in 1888, William assumed the responsibility of leading his nation into the new century. He was neither professionally trained nor emotionally prepared to bear that burden. Indecisive and hopelessly naïve when it came to international relations, blind to the forces that were transforming Germany, he clung to the past and refused to embrace the future. He was a good man, a courageous man who was chosen to perform a task beyond his capacity. He might have been one of the great men of his time; instead he was one of its greatest failures.

### Bibliography

Annan, Noel. "The Abominable Emperor." *The New York Review of Books* 43, no. 10 (June 6, 1996). Profile of Kaiser Wilhelm II including his evil activities, homosexual escapades, and unbalanced behavior.

Balfour, Michael. *The Kaiser and His Times.* London: Cresset Press, and Boston: Houghton Mifflin, 1964. Written in the decade when historians first began to examine World War I and the years that preceded it with real objectivity, this biography remains one of the best treatments of William and his time. The exceptional bibliography, the careful notation, and the charts provided at the end of this work tend to enhance a very scholarly and yet readable book.

Cowles, Virginia. *The Kaiser.* London: Collins, and New York: Harper, 1963. Relying on the scholarship of contemporary historians, this popular biography was written with only a passing reference to changing views and attitudes toward the kaiser and his era. Yet it is lively, well written, and very readable, and serves well as an introduction to the subject.

Hull, Isabel V. *The Entourage of Kaiser Wilhelm II.* Cambridge, and New York: Cambridge University Press, 1982. This fascinating study explores in detail the influence exercised upon the kaiser by his friends, family, and government officials during the thirty years of his reign. Particular attention is given to the often destructive nature of the military elements in William's government and household. The kaiser emerges not as a monster but as a man plagued by indecision and the legacy of Bismarck.

Rohl, John C. G., and Nicolaus Sombart, eds. *Kaiser Wilhelm II, New Interpretations: The Corfu Papers.* Cambridge, and New York: Cambridge University Press, 1982. This collection of eleven essays covers a number of topics ranging from William's relations with his parents and his family in Germany and England to the nature of the empire that he governed for a generation. The questions raised by these scholarly papers delivered at Corfu, the kaiser's favorite vacation retreat, will provide a new generation of historians with subjects for a whole new series of books.

Tuchman, Barbara. *The Guns of August.* New York: Macmillan, 1962. This is without a doubt one of the finest books ever written dealing with the crisis that led to the beginning of World War I. It is the product of thorough scholarship, but it reads like a work of fiction, proving that history is more exciting than any novel.

———. *The Proud Tower.* New York: Macmillan, 1965; London: Hamilton, 1966. In this fascinating portrait of an age, Tuchman explores the glittering world that existed in the years before the tragedy of World War I. It is, however, a work of limited depth and intended more for the general reader than the serious scholar. Both of these works by Tuchman are useful supplements for the student who wishes to place William in the context of his age.

Viktoria Luise, Duchess of Brunswick and Lüneburg. *The Kaiser's Daughter.* Edited and translated by Robert Vacha. London: Allen, and Englewood Cliffs, N.J.: Prentice-Hall, 1977. This one volume is the English version of the three-part autobiography of the kaiser's only daughter, and it presents an entirely different view of William. In a frank and lively style, Princess Viktoria Luise portrays her father as a devoted husband and father and a patriot with high standards of morality who was anything but the "Beast of Berlin."

*Clifton W. Potter, Jr.*

# TENNESSEE WILLIAMS

*Born:* March 26, 1911; Columbus, Mississippi
*Died:* February 24, 1983; New York, New York
*Area of Achievement:* Literature
*Contribution:* Williams' plays, to a large extent drawn from his own experiences, brought new realism and compelling originality to the American theater.

## Early Life

Tennessee Williams was born Thomas Lanier Williams on Palm Sunday, 1911, the second child of Cornelius Coffin Williams and Edwina Dakin Williams. Columbus, the eastern Mississippi town in which he was born, was still small and quite rural in the early years of the twentieth century. Social attitudes of the Old South and feelings engendered by the Civil War remained strong, and Williams grew up hearing stories about his father's volunteer service in the Spanish-American War, as well as stories about his mother's numerous beaux, the forty-five "gentlemen callers" who had courted her in the years before her marriage.

His parents' marriage was never a happy one, though social custom precluded divorce. After only two years together and before the birth of their first child, Rose, in November, 1909, Williams' mother left Gulfport, Mississippi, where the couple had lived since their marriage, and returned to her father's Columbus rectory. Though the elder Williams visited regularly and though a third child, Walter Dakin Williams, would be born in 1919, Williams came to feel a special affection for his grandparents, the Reverend Mr. Walter Dakin and Rose Otte Dakin. Indeed, Williams came to dread his father's visits. He seemed overcritical, insensitive, and rough-hewn to the boy, and these tensions would increase as Williams grew older.

When the elder Williams obtained a managerial position with the Friedman-Shelby branch of the International Shoe Company in the summer of 1918, he was able to convince his wife to join him in St. Louis, Missouri. Williams' mother left her parents' home—at this time in Clarksdale, Mississippi—with reluctance. She feared a recurrence of her husband's drinking, gambling, and womanizing, which had separated them nine years earlier, but she was expecting the birth of their child and had hopes for a more normal life.

Her worst fears were justified in every sense. Thomas, though only nine, came to detest St. Louis. His Mississippi accent was ridiculed by boys his own age, and he and his sister often absented themselves from school. He read several of Charles Dickens' works, the Waverly novels of Sir Walter Scott, and selections from the plays of William Shakespeare until he could return home. Meanwhile, his mother also waited, often for long hours in the dark, for her husband's vices continued and worsened in the St. Louis years.

Williams found outlets for this family tension in occasional visits to "Grand," as he called his grandmother, in Clarksdale, and in the writing of poems and short stories. Several of these were published while he was still in junior high school from 1923 to 1926. The 1925 yearbook of Ben Blewett Junior High School contained "Demon Smoke," his essay on the factories of St. Louis. He continued to write after he transferred to Soldan High School, and his review of the silent film *Stella Dallas* (1925) was the talk of his English class.

Though he read and wrote insatiably, Williams was never a successful student, and his poor academic performance, right through his college years, was a never-ending cause of friction in relations with his father. His grades at the University of Missouri grew worse each term, and his consistently poor, and ultimately failing, grades in the required Reserve Officers' Training Corps (ROTC) courses there particularly mortified his father, for whom military life and masculinity were synonymous. After a devastating spring term in 1932, Williams' father insisted that his son take some job, but the Depression, then at its worst, precluded this, and it was not until June, 1934, that Williams spent a brief time—until April, 1935—at the International Shoe Company, his father's employer. Thus, Williams passed at least two years out of school and unemployed, though this frustrating period of his early life would in time be exorcised in *The Glass Menagerie* (1944), the most autobiographical of all of his plays.

## Life's Work

In September, 1935, Williams returned to school as a nonmatriculated student at Washington University, St. Louis. He continued to write, mostly short stories and poetry, but it was not until he was accepted at the University of Iowa, in Iowa City, in the fall of 1937—when he met E. C. Mabie and E. P. Conkle, who taught drama there—that Williams

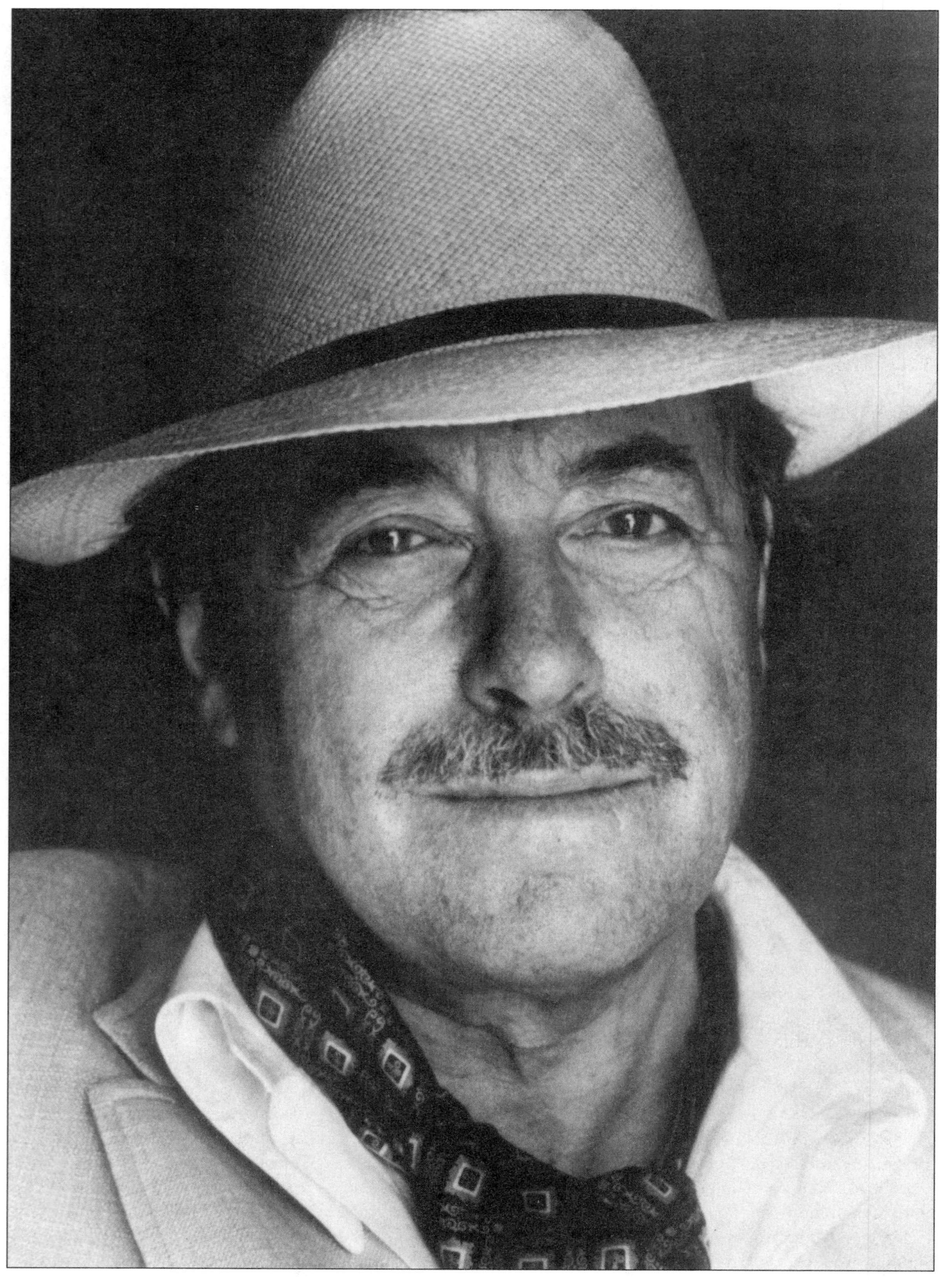

realized where his special talents lay. Williams' first play, *Spring Storm* (1938), though given a cool reception in Mabie's drama production class, nevertheless inspired him to write others, and *Not About Nightingales* (1939), a play about prison life, received Mabie's praise. It was during his student years at Iowa that Williams would acquire his lifelong habit of reusing titles and revising plays completely, even after performance or publication.

Williams had just arrived for the fall term at Iowa when he learned of his sister's deteriorating mental state and of his mother's decision to allow a leucotomy, or prefrontal lobotomy, to be performed on her. This procedure was experimental and at the time was considered the only way of rendering violently schizophrenic patients harmless to themselves. Williams never forgave either his mother for allowing the operation or himself for not having prevented it. Rose imagery would pervade his works—*The Rose Tattoo* (1951); the "blue roses" of *The Glass Menagerie*; Aunt Rose of *The Unsatisfactory Supper* (1948); roses "of yesterday, of death, and of time" in *The Milk Train Doesn't Stop Here Anymore* (1963), *Camino Real* (1953), *The Last of My Solid Gold Watches* (1943), and *Something Unspoken* (1958); wild roses in *The Case of the Crushed Petunias* (1948); roses of Picardy in *Moony's Kid Don't Cry* (1941); the mystic rose of *Now the Cats with Jewelled Claws* (1981); the smell of roses in *The Mutilated* (1966); wild roses in *Will Mr. Merriwhether Return from Memphis?* (wr. 1969, pr. 1979); crushed roses in *Suddenly Last Summer* (1958), the play which deals most explicitly with Rose's operation—and Williams would regularly visit his sister to the last months of his life. She would survive her younger brother by two years.

It was after his graduation from Iowa in August, 1938, that Williams changed his first name to "Tennessee." He considered his given name more appropriate for a poet (he was indeed distantly related to the poet Sidney Lanier), and he followed the lead of classmates who for some time had called him Tennessee as a nickname. Tennessee was also, however, the state in which his grandparents resided by this time, and Memphis held pleasant associations for him. In interviews, Williams sometimes quipped that his ancestors had fought Indians in Tennessee and he often found himself in a stockade fighting off his attackers.

In the autumn of 1938, Williams found his way to New Orleans, hoping to find support for his writing through the Works Progress Administration (WPA) project there; he came to love the bohemian atmosphere of the city's French quarter. He had his first homosexual experience in New Orleans and gave free rein to the insatiable passions which increasingly governed his life. In later years, he would say that he felt as though two elements, intellectual and sensual, were constantly at war within him, and this dichotomy appears in many of his tragic protagonists. When it became clear early in 1939 that no WPA aid would be forthcoming, Williams submitted four of his one-act plays as well as his full-length works *Not About Nightingales* and *The Fugitive Kind* (1939) to the Group Theatre in New York, which was sponsoring a competition. In order to satisfy the age requirement, he gave his date of birth as March 26, 1914, thus starting a fiction concerning his age that would continue well into the 1950's.

While awaiting a decision from the Group Theatre, Williams and a companion left New Orleans for Los Angeles with the vague idea of writing screenplays, but Molly Day Thacher of the Group Theatre soon wrote to praise the one-act works he had sent under the collective title *American Blues* (1948). She also enclosed a check for one hundred dollars and sent the plays to Audrey Wood, the famed theatrical agent who would work tirelessly in Williams' behalf.

It was Wood who would bring Williams to New York, advance him money with no sure hope of repayment, oversee his personal affairs, continue to champion his works, and, in late December, 1940, bring his play *Battle of Angels* to its Boston premiere. Though *Battle of Angels* was hardly a resounding success, it brought Williams' work to the attention of important critics who recognized the young playwright's promise. In late March, 1957, its revision, called *Orpheus Descending*, would be given a Broadway production.

Williams first took the theatrical world by storm with the premiere in Chicago of his compelling "memory play" *The Glass Menagerie* on December 26, 1944. Though not written as autobiography, it nevertheless reflects the strains of Williams' life in St. Louis during the Depression. Tom, the play's narrator, is Williams' persona; Tom presents a subjective remembrance of Amanda Wingfield (an incisively accurate portrait of Williams' mother) and his shy, fragile sister Laura (identifiable with Williams' sister Rose). This was a painful and difficult play for Williams to write, but it was immediately heralded as a landmark of the American theater and was quickly brought to Broadway, where it enjoyed immense success.

Other triumphs followed, each more astounding than the last for its innovative realism: *A Streetcar Named Desire* (1947), *Summer and Smoke* (1947), *The Rose Tattoo*, *Camino Real*, *Cat on a Hot Tin Roof* (1955), *Suddenly Last Summer*, *Sweet Bird of Youth* (1959), *The Night of the Iguana* (1961), and *The Milk Train Doesn't Stop Here Anymore*. Not all were given enthusiastic critical reaction, and *Camino Real*, Williams' foray into political drama, has never been a popular favorite; nevertheless, each reveals some distinctive aspect of Williams' genius.

Williams was fortunate to have, from the beginning of his career, the support of both good friends and professional associates. Harold Clurman of New York's Group Theatre; Elia Kazan, famed for his direction of *A Streetcar Named Desire* and other Williams plays; outstanding actors such as Marlon Brando, Laurette Taylor, and Maureen Stapleton; and selfless friends, such as his agent Audrey Wood and longtime companion Frank Merlo, helped to foster Williams' fragile genius, bolster his always shaky self-confidence, and control his self-destructive indulgence in drugs and in promiscuous sex.

It is a tragic but undeniable fact that Williams found his work increasingly difficult and ultimately impossible as these individuals were taken from him, either by death, by other commitments, or by petty disagreements. Though Williams was fabulously wealthy at the time of his death, he died a lonely man. Found at his bedside on February 25, 1983, the morning his body was discovered, was an assortment of capsules, tablets, eye and nose drops, and the half-empty bottle of wine he had brought to his room upon retiring the evening before. The New York City medical examiner reported that a barbiturate safety cap had somehow lodged in Williams' throat. Williams had either been unable or unwilling to call for aid.

At the peak of his career in the 1940's and 1950's, Williams was the image of the successful playwright: sensitive features, neat mustache, immaculately groomed in well-cut English-tailored suits and bow ties, often sporting a cigarette in an onyx holder. Significantly, later pictures often show him in white or light-tan suiting, Panama hat, and a full beard or goatee added to a fuller mustache. He appears heavier in the latest of these, and in retrospect, considering what is now known about the unhappiness of his final years, his lighteartedness seems forced. It is the paradox of Williams' art that he drew his greatest triumphs from his deepest pain.

### Summary

Williams, a true poet of the American theater, was noted for the tension of his brilliant dialogue. His characters, like their creator, have strong passions and overwhelming frustrations. Mythic interplay of Apollonian intellect and Dionysian passion often shares the stage with Southern settings and characterizations; Williams looks beyond genteel stereotypes, however, to reveal disturbed and frequently brutal people.

Apparent outward control but inner turmoil characterized Williams' life and was the basis for the most striking characterizations of his plays. He aspired to the ascetic while being simultaneously drawn to the sensual. For him, it was a mystical coupling, one which he often explored in his works. Alma Weinmiller and John Buchanan in *Summer and Smoke*, Sebastian Venable in *Suddenly Last Summer*, Val Xavier in *Orpheus Descending* all illustrate Williams' own duality, and each is a projection of the playwright's complex personality. Certainly, it is true that no playwright ever searched more deeply than Williams into family history and personal background. In one sense, this explains the increasingly abstract nature of his plays, for symbol eventually came to overwhelm plot. His constant revisions of already published material, including works which enjoyed popular success, represented an attempt to reclaim elements of his life from the public domain, to reconstitute them in abstractions only he could completely fathom. Williams saw his life in terms of a daily battle between these ascetic and sensual impulses. He often hurt those who deeply loved him, and the loneliness felt by many homosexuals was for him exacerbated by his inclination toward self-destruction.

Though honored by the National Institute of Arts and Letters, the National Arts Club, though twice awarded the Pulitzer Prize and given numerous other recognitions, Williams remained an insecure genius throughout his career, almost as fragile as the sister he so dearly loved.

### Bibliography

Donahue, Francis. *The Dramatic World of Tennessee Williams*. New York: Ungar, 1964. Contains biographical information and reliable analyses of the most important plays. Good introduction to Williams, written just after his greatest period of productivity.

Hirshhorn, Clive. "When I'm Alone It's Just Hell." *London Sunday Express*, March 28, 1965. A frank interview conducted during the period of Williams' psychoanalysis. Williams candidly reveals his fears and loneliness.

Kolin, Philip C., ed. *Tennessee Williams: A Guide to Research and Performance.* Westport, Conn.: Greenwood Press, 1998. Comprehensive reference work bringing together voluminous research on Williams. Expert contributors provide chapters on each of his works. Includes an introductory essay and bibliography.

Leavitt, Richard, ed. *The World of Tennessee Williams*. London: Allen, and New York: Putnam, 1978. Contains biographical information based on the recollections of those who knew Williams best. These are neatly drawn together with a minimum of critical speculation.

Leydon, Joe. "Alley Brings Williams Play Home." *Variety* 371, no. 6 (June 15, 1998). A previously unproduced Williams play, *Not About Nightingales* is produced in Houston, Texas. The play is set in a prison during the Depression where a hunger strike is staged to protest inhumane treatment of prisoners.

Spoto, Donald. *The Kindness of Strangers: The Life of Tennessee Williams*. London: Bodley Head, and Boston: Little Brown, 1985. A well-reviewed biography, documented but designed for the general reader. Spoto's major theme is how Williams' warring passions and intellect paradoxically allowed creation of his greatest works and equally hastened his death.

Vidal, Gore. "Selected Memories of the Glorious Bird and an Earlier Self." In *Matters of Fact and Fiction: Essays 1973-1976*. London: Heinemann, and New York: Random House, 1977. Vidal here sees similarities in the experience of all artists and makes comparisons between himself and Williams. Vidal was one of Williams' friends and was responsible for the screenplay of *Suddenly Last Summer.*

Williams, Dakin, and Shepherd Mead. *Tennessee Williams: An Intimate Biography.* New York: Arbor House, 1983. Interesting because of its coauthor, Williams' younger brother, rather than because it supplies new insights into the playwright's life. The brothers' contrasting views of their father and their different personalities emerge clearly.

Williams, Ewina Dakin, as told to Lucy Freeman. *Remember Me to Tom.* New York: Putnam, 1963; London: Cassell, 1964. The classic but quite idealized and often inaccurate memoir by Williams' mother, the original Amanda of *The Glass Menagerie*. It is best to read this volume after Donahue, Leavitt, or Spoto.

Wood, Audrey, with Max Wilk. *Represented by Audrey Wood*. New York: Doubleday, 1981. Reflections on Wood's famous clients, who included William Inge, Carson McCullers, Maurice Valency, and Williams. Wood often involved herself personally with those whom she represented, encouraging them when necessary to help them create their greatest works.

*Robert J. Forman*

# EDMUND WILSON

*Born:* May 8, 1895; Red Bank, New Jersey
*Died:* June 12, 1972; Talcottville, New York
*Areas of Achievement:* Literary criticism and literature
*Contribution:* Combining an acute literary sensibility with both a social and a historical point of view, Wilson became an influential force in twentieth century literature and literary criticism.

## Early Life

Edmund Wilson was born May 8, 1895, an only child of well-to-do parents. His father had been attorney general under the Democratic administration of Woodrow Wilson, even though he had been a lifelong Republican. Edmund went to the Hill School in Pottsdown, Pennsylvania, where he distinguished himself by his precocious interest in, and knowledge of, literature. He continued his education at Princeton, where he formed enduring friendships with John Peale Bishop and F. Scott Fitzgerald. Wilson was never to be the poet Bishop was or the novelist Fitzgerald was, but he impressed both of them with his critical powers. Fitzgerald always referred to Wilson as "my literary conscience." Wilson's own "literary conscience" was a teacher he met at Princeton, Christian Gauss.

Christian Gauss was the one professor at Princeton who influenced Wilson. First, Gauss was not a dry academic but was passionately interested in the works he taught. Gauss's specialty was European literature, and he helped Wilson with the new avant-garde works coming out of Europe. As Wilson later observed, Gauss's teaching of Gustave Flaubert and Dante "admirably prepared us for Joyce and Proust." In addition, Gauss introduced Wilson to the historical method of looking at literature. A specific work needed to be connected to its time, its milieu, and its race, in the famous formula of Hippolyte-Adolphe Taine. Gauss was to remain "a spiritual and intellectual force" throughout Wilson's life.

After he was graduated from Princeton, Wilson joined the army, where he was exposed to people from different classes and backgrounds. It was at this time that he decided to reject his family's class and social position: "It suddenly became very clear to me that I could never go back to the habits and standards of even the most cultivated elements of the world in which I had lived." He became, instead, a reporter for the New York *Evening Sun* and a book reviewer for the politically radical *The New Republic*, and he also at this time became a Socialist. Although Wilson rejected the way of life of his family, some influences remained. Later in life, he settled into the family house in Talcottville, and he retained his father's detached attitude even when he wrote on subjects in which he was deeply involved. One can see this quality in Wilson's treatment of those figures whom he admired the most, Karl Marx and Abraham Lincoln. Wilson always managed to retain a critical reserve.

## Life's Work

In 1920, having been discharged from the army the year before, Wilson joined the staff of *Vanity Fair.* The next year, he joined the staff of *The New Republic*, with which he would be associated for nineteen years. During this period, Wilson married actress Mary Blair, and they had a daughter, Rosalind. He divorced Blair in 1928. Wilson published *I Thought of Daisy* (1929) and *Poets, Farewell!* (1929). Two years later, he published the work which established his reputation as a literary critic, *Axel's Castle* (1931).

In the 1930's, Wilson traveled around the United States, studying the effects of the Depression on the American people. Also during this period, Wilson married Margaret Canby, who died in 1932. Wilson's interest in socialism attracted him to study in the Soviet Union in 1935, under a Guggenheim Fellowship. *Travels in Two Democracies* (1936), in which he contrasted the Soviet and the American environments, was a result of that journey. In 1938, Wilson married Mary McCarthy, with whom he had a son, Reuel.

In the 1940's, his relationship with *The New Republic* having ended, Wilson became literary editor of *The New Yorker.* In 1946, Wilson divorced McCarthy and was married for the last time, to Elena Mumm Thornton, with whom he had a daughter, Helen Miranda. During this period, Wilson continued with his writing, producing several important works during the 1950's and the 1960's.

In 1963, Wilson was awarded the Presidential Medal of Freedom, the highest civilian honor given by the United States government. The next year, he received the Edward MacDowell Medal for his "outstanding contribution to literature." In 1966, he was awarded the National Medal for Literature and the Emerson-Thoreau Medal. Having returned to the family home in Talcottville, Edmund Wilson died there on June 12, 1972, and was buried in Wellfleet, Massachusetts, on June 15, 1972.

Edmund Wilson was a "man of letters" in the tradition of Samuel Johnson, Matthew Arnold, and William Dean Howells. The range of a man of letters is not limited to one type of writing. Wilson, for example, wrote poetry, plays, and fiction, as well as occasional book reviews and major studies of Symbolism, Marxism, Freudianism, and the literature of the American Civil War. His literary works are of less importance than his literary criticism, but they are worth discussion.

Wilson published three collections of poetry: *Poets, Farewell!, Notebooks of Night* (1942), and *Night Thoughts* (1961). While he was a technically proficient poet, he could not escape the poetic models he celebrated in his criticism. As one critic said, "Wilson was the master of every poetic aspect except originality." The one exception to this difficulty is his satires or parodies. With these, originality was not to be desired, and "The Omelet of A. MacLeish," with its Eliotic parody, remains fresh and amusing while his evocative lyrics seem hopelessly dated.

Wilson's fiction has had a better critical reception than his poetry, but there are some problems. For example, Wilson later criticized his first novel, *I Thought of Daisy*, as "having been subjected to a preconceived scheme." That scheme was the Proustian and symphonic form that he had noticed and admired in Marcel Proust's *Remembrance of Things Past* (1913-1927) and pointed out in *Axel's Castle*, Wilson's first major book of literary criticism. In *I Thought of Daisy*, the form gets in the way of the action, although there are many good things in the book, such as the trip to Coney Island with Daisy. *Memoirs of Hecate County* (1946) is less structured—six short stories are brought together into one book—but is more successful. One of the major reasons for the success of the book is its social dimension. "The Man Who Shot Snapping Turtles," for example, is an allegory of capitalist exploitation in which the pursuit of beauty represented by destroying the turtles (because the turtles are destroying the beautiful ducks in his pond) is abandoned for the profit those turtles will bring when sold. It also shows the impact made by advertising in the character of Clarence, who kills the old-fashioned capitalist and is left to spend his days in Southern California, filled with dread. The most important story is "Princess with the Golden Hair," a much deeper version of the paired women characters of *I Thought of Daisy*. In "Princess with the Golden Hair," Wilson contrasts the upper-class Imogen with the lower-class Anna. He is ironic in his descriptions of Imogen and her environment, but the main character is also ashamed of Anna and her poverty, so the easy contrast of *I Thought of Daisy* is avoided. The story is resolved when the main character suddenly sees beyond his social prejudices. "It was Anna who had made it possible for *me* to recreate the actuality; who had given me that life of the people which had before been but prices and wages. . . ." Yet this revelation is mixed with a sense of loss over the fact that "we should never make love again."

Wilson's later fiction can be impressive, but his real achievement was in literary and social criticism. In *Axel's Castle*, he used a historical and comparative method, tracing Symbolism to its origins in Romanticism and describing it as being a "second flood of the same tide" with its roots "in the individual." He saw Symbolism as a reaction against mechanistic views of the universe. Wilson was better at applying theories to specific works than he was in defining a movement, and he was much better with fiction than with poetry.

Wilson found much to praise in the poetry of Paul Valéry, William Butler Yeats, and T. S. Eliot. Yet, in his opinion, their works are not as connected to the real world as they should be; he preferred the "wide knowledge of human affairs" of Anatole France to the "introspection" of the Symbolist poets. He saw a similar problem in the poetic prose of Gertrude Stein and claimed that "she has gone so far she no longer even suggests."

Wilson was a better critic when he dealt with the prose fiction of Proust and James Joyce. He traced both the "symphonic" structure of *Remembrance of Things Past* and the "mythic" structure of *Ulysses* (1922) and found in both novels the subjectivity of Symbolism and the objectivity of naturalism. He even suggested that *Ulysses* is a successful blending of the two. Wilson did have some reservations about both novels. He found Proust's novel to be morbid and Joyce's novel to suffer from an excessive use of technical devices.

*Axel's Castle* ends with a chapter on "Axel and Rimbaud," which is a warning to future writers. Here, Wilson not only traced the development of Symbolism but also evaluated it, warning his readers that to follow Villiers de l'Isle-Adam's *Axël* (1890) is to be removed from "common life." Yet if one follows Arthur Rimbaud, one ends up embracing primitivism. Wilson had many reservations about Symbolism, but he also found much of value; Wilson's value to his readers was to make them aware of this new movement.

Wilson was also instrumental in making Sigmund Freud and Freudian literary criticism available in Great Britain and the United States with his essays and with *The Wound and the Bow* (1941). The thesis of *The Wound and the Bow* is that the artist receives a wound in childhood that later becomes a central part of his imaginative "bow." What Wilson does not explain is how a great artist can make use of his wound while an ordinary person cannot. The book, however, is useful in showing how Charles Dickens and Rudyard Kipling were affected by their early experiences and how they incorporated them into their work.

Wilson was also deeply interested in Socialist and Marxist thought. In *To the Finland Station* (1940), he traced Marxist thought from its origins in Jules Michelet and Charles Fourier to its implementation by Vladimir Ilich Lenin in the Revolution of 1917. The method is historical and biographical, and the center of the book is the biographies of Karl Marx and Lenin.

Wilson's portrait of Marx is balanced. Marx is portrayed not only as a rebel Prometheus who brought light to mankind but also as a Lucifer who treated his enemies with scorn and allowed his family to sink into poverty while he concentrated his energies on his work. According to Wilson, Marx was afflicted with disease and neglect, yet Marx made use of his "wounds." Marx once said, "I hope the bourgeoisie as long as they live will have cause to remember my carbunkles." Wilson did criticize Marx's antidemocratic tendencies, and he was very dubious about Marx's Hegelian dialectic. Yet all the faults and doubts are washed away by Marx's creation of a "truly human world" in *The Communist Manifesto* (1848) and *Das Kapital* (1867).

Wilson's chapters on Lenin emphasize the practical steps that Lenin took to bring about change; Lenin was not a theoretician such as Marx. Nor did Lenin possess Marx's reverence for culture. Lenin loved Ludwig van Beethoven's *Appassionata* Sonata but refused to listen to it because he feared that it might weaken him. Wilson seemed to be less skeptical about Lenin than about Marx; he excused Lenin's undemocratic and autocratic ways and suggested that they were necessary at the time. Lenin is, for Wilson, the instrument that is used to complete the process begun by Michelet; Wilson stated that Lenin uses "the weapons that had been hung up by Marx and Engels."

Wilson's last major work, *Patriotic Gore* (1962), is an analysis of some major and less-important figures of the American Civil War. In the introduction, Wilson justified the rebellion of the Confederacy and debunked the moral claims of the North, calling them disguises for power politics. Wilson, at the time of the book's publication, was troubled by the growth of the central government in the United States and elsewhere. Thus, the book is both a tracing of the origins of modern centralized government and a warning against such growth.

One of the most important portraits in *Patriotic Gore* is that of Abraham Lincoln. Wilson saw Lincoln as a convert to the cause of the Union. In that conversion, according to Wilson, lies the growth of centralized government. For example, Wilson saw a marked change in Lincoln's views on slavery and religion from his early skeptical days to the mystical views he held as president. Wilson praised Lincoln's moral authority even though that authority was used to further what Wilson saw as an illegitimate growth of government.

Two other important chapters deal with the opposing views of Alexander Stephens, the vice president of the Confederacy, and Oliver Wendell Holmes, the famous justice of the Supreme Court. Wilson praised Stephens' attack upon the central government and saw his usefulness in his raising "certain fundamental issues." Holmes was the opposite of Stephens; he was skeptical of all absolute views and remained aloof from all sects and parties. His skepticism seems very similar to that of Edmund Wilson.

### Summary

Edmund Wilson was a very influential figure. He introduced the ideas of Symbolism, of Freud, and of Marx to American and British audiences and then made Americans take another look at their history in *Patriotic Gore*. In addition, he did important work on Russian literature and the Dead Sea Scrolls. No one has written so cogently on so many diverse topics in the twentieth century. Furthermore, Wilson was often the first one to notice the importance of these movements or writers.

Wilson's later work is marred by an increasing irascibility. He referred to himself in those years as an "old curmudgeon," and that role came to replace the earlier pioneering one. One can see this irascibility in his attacks upon the Internal Revenue Service and the Modern Language Association (MLA). The attack upon the MLA is especially important because, at that time, the universities were turning out specialists in the fields in which Wilson had been a pioneer. He hated the specialization and narrowness that he saw coming, but he could not prevent it. There is no "first man of American letters" with whom to replace Edmund Wilson. His role has been usurped by university specialists, but his influence remains.

### Bibliography

Castronovo, David. *Edmund Wilson*. New York: Ungar, 1984. A full-length study of all of Wilson's major works. Especially good on the fiction and social criticism.

Dabney, Lewis M., ed. *Edmund Wilson: Centennial Reflections.* Princeton, N.J.: Princeton University Press, 1997. A collection of views on Wilson's work and personality by participants in a 1995 symposium at the Mercantile Library at Princeton University.

Frank, Charles P. *Edmund Wilson*. New York: Twayne, 1970. Frank is critical about the limitations in Wilson's literary criticism, but he barely touches on the social criticism.

Hyman, Stanley Edgar. *The Armed Vision*. New York: Knopf, 1948. Hyman devotes a chapter of his book to Wilson's literary criticism, and he finds little to praise in that criticism. He sees Wilson as only a "translator" of others' work.

Kriegel, Leonard. *Edmund Wilson*. Carbondale: Southern Illinois University Press, 1971. A complete if somewhat uncritical discussion of the major works.

March, Thomas. "Wilson's 'The Jumping-Off Place.'" *The Explicator* 57, no. 2 (Winter 1999) March provides analysis of Edmund Wilson's essay "The Jumping-Off Place," focusing on representations of wealth and destitution.

Paul, Sherman. *Edmund Wilson: A Study of the Literary Vocation in Our Time*. Urbana: University of Illinois Press, 1965. The first full-length study of Wilson remains a useful introduction to his works.

Wain, John. *Edmund Wilson: The Man and His Work*. New York: New York University Press, 1978. The best essays in this collection are on Wilson's fiction and poetry and the memoirs of his life; the essays on the criticism are less useful.

Wilson, Edmund. *Axel's Castle: A Study in the Imaginative Literature of 1870-1930*. New York and London: Scribner, 1931. The book that introduced Symbolism to American and English readers.

———. *Patriotic Gore: Studies in the Literature of the American Civil War.* London: Deutsch, and New York: Oxford University Press, 1962. An analysis of some important figures of the Civil War.

———. *To the Finland Station*. New York: Harcourt Brace, and London: Secker and Warburg,1940. An analysis of Socialist thought from its beginnings to the triumph of Lenin.

———. *The Wound and the Bow: Seven Studies in Literature*. Boston: Houghton Mifflin, 1941; London: Secker and Warburg, 1942. An application of Freudian criticism to writers such as Dickens and Kipling.

*James Sullivan*

## SIR HAROLD WILSON

*Born:* March 11, 1916; Huddersfield, Yorkshire, England
*Died:* May 24, 1995; London, England
*Areas of Achievement:* Government and politics
*Contribution:* As prime minister for eight years, from 1964 to 1976, Wilson became the most successful politician of the postwar era, winning four general elections of the five he contested as leader of the Labour Party.

### Early Life

James Harold Wilson was born on March 11, 1916, in Huddersfield, England. His father, Herbert Wilson, was an industrial chemist; his mother, Ethel, had been trained as a teacher. Wilson attended the local grammar school until he was fourteen, when the family moved to Cheshire. Wilson was an outstanding student at his new school, Wirral Grammar, and also a good sportsman, captaining the Rugby football team. In 1934, he won a partial scholarship to Oxford, where he studied philosophy, politics, and economics. Studious and brilliant, Wilson won a number of prizes and was graduated in 1937 with first-class honors, the highest degree available; his was widely thought to be the best academic performance for fifty years. Then, at the age of twenty-one, he became a lecturer in economics at New College, Oxford, an extraordinary feat for one so young.

When World War II erupted, Wilson joined the civil service. After serving in two minor posts, his reputation as an economist secured for him a position as an economic assistant to the War Cabinet Secretariat. During this time, he married Gladys Mary Baldwin, the daughter of a Congregationalist minister. They had first met in 1934.

In 1941, Wilson became chief of the Statistical Department of the Mines Department. A year later, the stocky, pipe-smoking young man, who had grown a mustache to make himself appear older, advanced once more to become director of economics and statistics at the newly established Ministry of Fuel and Power.

Wilson had been considering entering a career in politics, and in 1944, he was adopted as Labour candidate for the Northwest constituency of Ormskirk. In July, 1945, he was elected to Parliament in the landslide Labour victory. He immediately took a junior position in the government, and his dynamism and efficiency ensured that he was soon to rise again. In 1947, he was appointed president of the Board of Trade, a huge department which made up one-tenth of the entire civil service. At the age of thirty-one, he had become the youngest cabinet member of the century.

### Life's Work

In the general election of 1950, Wilson won the Lancashire seat of Huyton, which he was to represent in Parliament for more than thirty years. Yet his ministerial career as president of the Board of Trade, in which he had traveled widely and proved himself to be a skilled negotiator, was voluntarily cut short in 1951. Following the lead of left-wing minister Aneurin Bevan, Wilson resigned in protest upon the introduction of prescription charges in the National Health Service, and the excessive pace of the rearmament program at a time when raw materials were in short supply.

Labour lost the general election of 1951, and Wilson spent three years on the back benches as a rebel against the official Labour leadership. Then, in 1954, he returned to the forefront as a member of the "Shadow Cabinet," and in 1956, he became the shadow Chancellor of the Exchequer, gaining a reputation as a witty and formidable parliamentary performer. In 1960, he unsuccessfully challenged Hugh Gaitskell for the party leadership, and the following year he became shadow foreign secretary and party chairman.

When Gaitskell died in 1963, Wilson was elected leader of the party as the man best able to preserve unity between the left- and right-wing factions. In the general election of October, 1964, Wilson campaigned against what he repeatedly called "thirteen years of Tory misrule," promising that Labour would create a new, dynamic society which would push Great Britain into "the white heat of the technological era." The election produced an overall majority for Labour of only five seats in the House of Commons, but it was enough to make Wilson prime minister, the youngest since William Pitt the Younger in the nineteenth century.

Wilson had promised, as had President John F. Kennedy, a hundred days of dynamic activity, and in his first year of office he established himself as a credible, although not especially popular or inspiring, national leader. The new government was faced with a balance-of-payments deficit and a sterling crisis, one of a number which were to trouble it for the next five years. There was also the crisis which culminated in the unilateral declaration of independence by Rhodesia in November, 1965, after successive British governments had refused to allow the former colony independence unless it made rapid progress toward black majority rule. Wilson himself took a strong stand on the issue, but over the next few years his handling of the crisis did not enhance his reputation.

Eighteen months after the 1964 general election, Wilson called another. Capitalizing on the widespread belief that the government should be given a fair chance to make its policies work, Labour was returned in March, 1966, with a much-increased overall majority. Yet the resulting period of office was not an unqualified success. The Rhodesia problem proved intractable, despite the application of economic sanctions against the rebel regime and Wilson's statement that they "might bring the rebellion to an end within a matter of weeks" (a remark which was often thrown scornfully back at him as the rebellion dragged on for years).

The years of 1967 and 1968 were especially difficult for Wilson. The worst setbacks were the devaluation of the pound in November, 1967, and the French veto of Great Britain's attempt to join the European Economic Community. One notable event during this time was the visit of Soviet premier Aleksey Kosygin in February, 1967, and the attempt by him and Wilson to spearhead a solution to the Vietnam War. Wilson was later to claim in his memoirs that the plan came near to success, although this was not generally known at the time. The following year, Wilson's popularity went into a sharp decline. There were calls from within his own party for his resignation, and opinion polls showed the lowest-ever approval rating for a prime minister. In part, this was a result of the Labour government's failure to stabilize the economy, over which Wilson had assumed personal control. Also, many people disliked what they perceived as Wilson's deviousness, opportunism, and lack of principle.

In June, 1970, encouraged by favorable opinion polls and local election results, Wilson called a general election, but the government was surprisingly defeated, and the Conservatives, under Edward Heath, took office. The Labour government's economic record had counted against them, as well as their failure to deal effectively with strikes and inflationary pay awards to the powerful trade unions.

The following year, Wilson found time to write his own lengthy record of his five and a half years in office. As leader of the opposition, he faced heavy criticism for his *volte face* on the question of British membership of the European Economic Community. When the Conservatives successfully negotiated Great Britain's entry, Wilson, conforming to a change of opinion within his own party, opposed the move.

In February, 1974, the Conservative government, unable to find a solution to a damaging miners' strike, called a general election. No party gained an overall majority, but as the leader of the largest party, Wilson was once again invited to form a government. Another election was held in October, in which Labour won a small overall majority. It was Wilson's fourth general election victory out of five fought as Labour's leader. He had made a remarkable comeback after the defeat of 1970.

In 1976, at the age of sixty, he surprised almost everyone by announcing his retirement, saying that he feared that he might no longer be able to bring a fresh approach to the problems the country faced. Wilson had served a total of eight years as prime minister, at that time longer than anyone else in peacetime in the twentieth century. On his retirement, he was created a Knight of the Garter, and he continued to serve as a Member of Parliament until 1983.

### Summary

For thirteen years, Harold Wilson was one of the dominant figures in British politics. He was a brilliant tactician, a pragmatic politician rather than an inspiring leader. His reputation for deviousness was probably caused by nothing more than his necessarily wily approach to the difficult task of placating rival factions in a party which is known for the fierce divisiveness of its internal quarrels. Wilson would often refer to the Labour Party as a "broad church," and the maintenance of at least a semblance of unity between the far left, which grew rapidly during the 1970's, and the right-wing social democrats was always one of his highest priorities. A remark he once made gives insight into his strategy: "Any fool can have a confrontation. You can press at the wrong time and get the wrong answer. Or you can work on people. You've got to have a sense of timing." It is significant that after his retirement, divisions within the party grew wider, resulting in a group of right-wing Labour Members of Parliament forming the breakaway Social Democratic Party in 1981. It should also be remembered that since Wilson's retirement, the Labour Party has lost three successive general elections.

Although Wilson was unable to reverse fundamentally the decline in Great Britain's economic fortunes and her diminishing role in world affairs, he did have occasional successes. In foreign affairs, he was instrumental in mediating a territorial dispute between India and Pakistan, and on the domestic scene his handling of the 1975 referendum on Great Britain's entry into the European Economic Community ended the long and divisive national debate over the issue. For much of his ministry, Wilson was faced with a hostile Conservative press, anxious to discredit him. His resilience, and his ability to extricate himself from the most difficult situations, caused him to be known as the Houdini of British politics.

### Bibliography

Crossman, R. H. S. *Diaries of a Cabinet Minister.* 3 vols. London: Hamilton, and New York: Holt Rinehart, 1975-1977. A journalist, an indefatigable diarist, and a minister in the Labour government of 1964-1970, Crossman gives an outstanding, detailed, and shrewd account of how British politics really works, including a highly critical portrait of Wilson as prime minister.

Dembrell, John. "The Johnson Administration and the British Labour Government: Vietnam, the Pound and East of Suez." *Journal of American Studies* 30, no. 2 (August, 1996). The author considers the relationship between Lyndon Johnson and Prime Minister Harold Wilson in the 1960s and its affect on British economic and political policies.

Falkender, Marcia. *Inside Number 10.* London: Weidenfeld and Nicolson, and New York: Coward McCann, 1972. Wilson's personal and political secretary since 1956 describes her five and a half years (1964-1970) at the center of British political life. A valuable account, although it says little that Wilson himself has not said in his own record of the period.

Howard, Anthony, and Richard West. *The Road to Number 10.* New York: Macmillan, 1965. In a swiftly moving, highly readable account, modeled on T. H. White's *The Making of the President* (1960), two top British political journalists tell the story of the British election campaign of 1964 and the events and issues leading up to it.

Mitchell, Austin. "Don't Do It Wilson's Way. What can Labour in the Sixties Teach Labour in the Nineties? Those Who Were There are Keen to Give Their Advice." *New Statesman* 126, no. 4323 (February 28, 1997). This article discusses the British Labour Party in the 1960s and the 1990s and criticizes Wilson's ineffective government.

Roth, Andrew. *Sir Harold Wilson: Yorkshire Walter Mitty.* London: Macdonald and Jane's, 1977. The format of this uneven and disappointing biography is curious, beginning with chapters on Wilson's resignation and his controversial honors list, followed by a chronological biography which stops, without explanation, at the 1964 election. The author's frequent attempts to denigrate his subject are unpleasant and unnecessary, and they spoil some otherwise sound research.

Smith, Leslie. *Harold Wilson: The Authentic Portrait.* London: Hodder and Stoughton, 1964; New York: Scribner, 1965. An authorized, largely uncritical biography by a BBC producer, based on taped interviews with Wilson.

Wilson, Harold. *The Governance of Britain.* London: Weidenfeld and Nicolson, and New York:

Harper, 1976. An inside account, much of it anecdotal, of how British parliamentary democracy works, the first ever written by a prime minister. Analyzes the role of the prime minister from the eighteenth century to the present, and his relations with cabinet, Parliament, and party. Includes a comparison of the British and American systems.

———. *A Personal Record: The Labour Government, 1964-70*. London: Weidenfeld and Nicolson, and Boston: Little Brown, 1971. A detailed, week-by-week account of Wilson's first period in office. Includes details of the secret negotiations in England in 1967 between Wilson and Kosygin to end the Vietnam War.

———. *Purpose and Power: Selected Speeches by Harold Wilson*. London: Weidenfeld and Nicolson, and Boston: Houghton Mifflin, 1966. A collection of fifteen speeches given during the first year of the Labour government in 1964. Subjects include the economy, Rhodesia, and two tributes to Sir Winston Churchill.

*Bryan Aubrey*

## WOODROW WILSON

*Born:* December 28, 1856; Staunton, Virginia
*Died:* February 3, 1924; Washington, D.C.
*Area of Achievement:* Government and politics
*Contribution:* As twenty-eighth president of the United States (1913-1921), Wilson was responsible for American entry into World War I, was one of the formulators of the Paris peace settlement, and was the principal architect of the League of Nations.

### Early Life

Thomas Woodrow Wilson's passion for constitution-making came from his childhood experience in drafting a set of rules for a neighborhood club that met in a hayloft. From then on, he tried to reform any organization he joined, crafting new sets of procedures and aims and then going on to repeat the procedure somewhere else. He rarely let himself get involved with practical application; he was essentially a policymaker. Also from his early days, or more specifically from his stern father, Joseph Ruggles Wilson, a Presbyterian minister and theologian, came his highly developed sense of moral righteousness. This was reinforced by his mother, the daughter of a minister, Thomas Woodrow, pastor of a church in Carlisle, England, before he migrated to the United States in 1836. As President of the United States, Wilson would have the privilege of preaching a sermon from his grandfather's old pulpit in 1919. It was one of the high points of his life.

When Wilson was a year old, his family moved to Augusta, Georgia, where he lived during the Civil War, a conflict which influenced his later determination to create an organization to guarantee international peace and cooperation. When he was fourteen, his father was appointed professor at the theological seminary in Columbia, South Carolina, and several years later became pastor of a church in Wilmington, North Carolina. In 1874, Wilson entered college, first at nearby Davidson College, then, the following year, at the College of New Jersey (later Princeton University), where he participated in literary activities and in debate. Upon graduation in 1879, he enrolled in the University of Virginia law school, which led him to a brief and unsuccessful legal practice in Atlanta, Georgia. In 1883, he entered The Johns Hopkins University, receiving his Ph.D. in government and history three years later.

Over the next decade and a half, Wilson held a variety of academic positions, at Bryn Mawr College, Wesleyan University in Connecticut, and Princeton University, of which, in 1902, he became president. He devoted himself to reshaping undergraduate education, working to institute a preceptorial system whereby students and professors would live together in quadrangles to follow common scholarly pursuits; the plan, however, was opposed by the trustees and never adopted. Wilson also failed to gain control of the graduate school, a loss to his self-esteem that made him turn to politics as compensation.

In 1910, Wilson accepted the Democratic nomination for the governorship of New Jersey and ran on a Progressive platform, promising to reform the election system with direct primaries, to introduce antitrust legislation, and to wipe out corruption. He was elected by a plurality of forty-nine thousand votes and immediately proceeded to enact his program despite the fact that the Republicans enjoyed a majority in both houses of the New Jersey congress. His success brought him wider attention, and in 1912, he was persuaded to become a contender for the Democratic nomination for President of the United States, winning on the forty-sixth ballot against the party favorite, Speaker of the House Champ Clark.

Wilson brought his Progressivism into national politics as the New Freedom. He ran against a badly divided Republican Party—split between the candidacies of William Howard Taft and Theodore Roosevelt—and won forty-two percent of the national vote, one million votes less than the combined tally of his opponents. In the electoral college, however, he got 435 votes to their ninety-six. With both houses of Congress now under Democratic control, Wilson looked forward to carrying out the major reforms for which he had fought during his campaign.

### Life's Work

Wilson's entire political experience had been with domestic politics, and once in the White House, he took a direct role in the presentation of his legislative program to Congress. In short order, he saw adopted a federal income tax, the Federal Reserve Board to control the nation's currency, and the Clayton Anti-Trust Act, which strengthened labor's right to strike. It was Wilson's role in foreign affairs, however, for which he is best known.

His inauguration coincided with the outbreak of a revolt in Mexico against General Victoriano Huerta, who had become president with the connivance of the American ambassador Henry Lane Wilson. Woodrow Wilson considered the Mexican strongman a bloody usurper and denied him United States recognition. He decided to arrange Huerta's downfall. To this end, he authorized aid to Huerta's opponents. When this failed to do the job, he opted for direct military intervention. In April, 1914, after a bloody battle with the Mexicans, the marines occupied the port of Vera Cruz. The city remained under American control for the next half year, finally being handed over to Venustiano Carranza, one of the contenders for national power whom Wilson thought a more acceptable Mexican president. Wilson professed to be turning over a new leaf in American relations with the countries of Latin America, replacing the crass dollar diplomacy practiced by his predecessors with a policy of high moral purpose; intervention by any other name, however, still smelled the same. Wilson clearly did not shy away from meddling in the affairs of other countries if he found a suitable rationale for doing so. His confidence that he knew what was best for others led him to establish a virtual protectorate over Haiti in 1915 and to institute United States military government over Santo Domingo the following year. Wilson might have expressed a desire to prepare the Philippines for self-government, but this hardly prevented the United States from being seen as an imperialistic bully. Wilson's concern for the fate of Third World nations was minor, however, compared to his preoccupation with the major conflict now going on in Europe.

On August 4, 1914, the day Germany invaded Belgium, Wilson officially admonished the American people to remain neutral in both thought and deed. The declaration was willingly accepted as the magic formula for nonparticipation; yet American neutrality was a sham from the beginning. Wilson's one-sided enforcement of American neutrality rights showed that he was clearly committed to the victory of the Entente. Moreover, Wilson saw nothing wrong with putting the industrial capacity of the United States at the service of the British and the French, something the Germans could not tolerate for long. Yet when German submarines began sinking merchant ships in the war zone around the British Isles, Wilson was outraged. He even believed that Americans traveling on belligerent ships should be free from attack. He was not yet willing, however, to let his indignation develop into a declaration of war.

Wilson won the election campaign of 1916 with the slogan "He kept us out of the war." He continued to talk peace but now emphasized preparedness and, in a speech given on January 22, 1917, started to enumerate war aims. He emphasized the necessity of establishing "a peace that will win the approval of mankind," a peace based on "an equality of rights" and on the "principle that governments derive all their just powers from the consent of the governed." He also endorsed freedom of the seas, disarmament, and collective security. By these vague and impressionistic "principles of mankind," Wilson committed the United States to a role in peacemaking that could only be achieved if the nation participated directly in the war. Thus, he clearly separated himself from his previously alleged policy, and indeed from a majority of his own people. He already had an excuse for entry as the Germans had committed themselves to unrestricted submarine warfare.

On April 2, 1917, Wilson delivered his war message to Congress, claiming that "the world must be made safe for democracy." American participation proved crucial to Allied victory and gave Wilson his great opportunity to write a constitution for the world. The establishment of the League of Nations was the fulfillment of a boyhood dream. The most important part of the League of Nations Covenant lay in Article 10, in which the members undertook to preserve against aggression the integrity and political independence of the others. To assure acceptance, the league was made an integral part of the Treaty of Versailles with Germany.

Article 10 struck some United States senators, however, as a danger to American sovereign rights, and they insisted that before ratification certain modifications be made. Wilson, though, fought all change, believing that this would only weaken the moral authority of the United States to protect other states from aggression. In an effort to improve the treaty's chances, he made a direct appeal to the American people in a nationwide speaking tour. He collapsed in Pueblo, Colorado, and was rushed back to Washington paralyzed and without the power to speak. His wife Edith became his main link with the outside world.

The treaty, containing the reservations on the league, was offered for ratification twice, on November 19, 1919, and on March 19, 1920. It failed both times, mainly because Wilson urged his supporters to vote against it. Thus, it was killed on his orders. The United States never joined the League of Nations and later made a separate peace with Germany.

Wilson's administration ended on March 4, 1921. Wilson continued to live in Washington but took no further part in the city's political or social fife. When he died, on February 3, 1924, he was buried in the non-Presbyterian National Cathedral, his wife being Episcopalian.

### Summary

Wilson had come to the Paris Peace Conference on a crusade, convinced that he alone of all Allied leaders represented the general will of the people. It made no difference that his own Democratic Party had lost both houses in the recent November elections, and he took no steps to make his peace delegation bipartisan. He had told the American people that the armistice had given them everything for which they had fought, but he believed that the defeat of Germany was not enough because it was now his duty to assist in the establishment of just democracy throughout the world. Such knight-errantry was not favored by his fellow countrymen, who believed that the defeat of the Kaiser meant that it was really over "over there."

Wilson was correct in assuming that the United States had a stake in the war, though he did not enter to preserve the balance of power. He defined his goals in terms of destroying the whole international system upon which that equilibrium had been based. The United States emerged from the war the strongest power in the world, but if the pursuit of a new world order involved, as Wilson maintained that it should, the destruction of the sovereignity of the nation-state, the Americans could lose what they had acquired. Wilson was convinced, however, that all problems and threats to national security could be solved through participation in the League of Nations.

The president believed that this organization would have a chemical effect on mankind, making people "drunk with the spirit of self-sacrifice." He saw its responsibilities to extend beyond peacekeeping, even obliging all states to guarantee equality to their racial and religious minorities and to require them to apply universal standards of work, including the eight-hour day.

Unfortunately, Wilson saw things in moral terms while the Europeans saw them in strategic. They looked upon the League of Nations as a device through which they could project their power, not as, in Georges Clemenceau's words, "a bridge leading to the new Jerusalem." Wilson was torn between two contradictory positions: He professed a belief in the sovereign equality of states, but he believed in the use of force for the good of civilization. Unfortunately, not everybody trusted the United States to act in any interest but its own. What appeared to Wilson as "unalterable lines of principle" frequently struck others as American realpolitik. Wilson was a persuasive orator, and his idealistic sloganeering had great appeal. The conduct of foreign affairs along lines of high morality had a lofty attraction, but often, too often, it could become the refuge of a scoundrel.

### Bibliography

Bailey, Thomas A. *Woodrow Wilson and the Great Betrayal*. New York: Macmillan, 1945. Concentrates on the attempts to get the Treaty of Versailles, containing the League of Nations, ratified by the Senate. Particularly good in describing the differing points of view of Wilson's opponents as well as the president's own stubbornness. In his conclusions, though, Bailey is a bit simplistic in assuming that the United States, as a member of the League of Nations, would have played a great role in European politics.

Baker, Ray Stannard. *Woodrow Wilson and World Settlement.* New York: Doubleday, 1922; London: Heinemann, 1923. The author draws heavily on his own experiences as Wilson's press secretary at the Paris conference. Although he holds Wilson in high esteem and his account lacks analysis, Baker deserves credit for being one of Wilson's first biographers, his presentation furnishing a basis on which other more thoughtful accounts were written.

Bragdon, Henry W. *Woodrow Wilson: The Academic Years.* Cambridge, Mass.: Belknap Press of Harvard University Press, 1967. Shows how Wilson's style of leadership in academe presaged his later career as president. Traces Wilson's transition from conservatism to Progressivism through an analysis of his published writings, speeches, and lecture notes. Maintains that earlier mild attacks of arteriosclerosis accounted for his aggressiveness and refusal to compromise.

Buehrig, Edward H. *Woodrow Wilson and the Balance of Power.* Bloomington: Indiana University Press, 1955. One of the few studies that gets at this subject and with good reason, since balance-of-power considerations were never essential elements in Wilson's thinking, his concept being the projection of world power by the English-speaking nations.

Daniels, Josephus. *The Life of Woodrow Wilson: 1856-1924.* London: Allen and Unwin, and Philadelphia: Winston, 1924. Essentially a panegyric written by a member of Wilson's cabinet who was one of the most dubious of political creatures: a Southern liberal.

Devlin, Patrick. *Too Proud to Fight: Woodrow Wilson's Neutrality.* London and New York: Oxford University Press, 1974. Shows how American entry into the war related to Wilson's sense of morality and his desire to gain representation at the peace conference as a ticket to remaking the world order. Devlin, a British jurist, has largely relied on the primary research of others, but he mastered the intricacies of Wilson's day-to-day diplomacy, which he presents in great detail.

Esposito, David M. *The Legacy of Woodrow Wilson: American War Aims in World War I.* Westport, Conn.: Praeger, 1996. Focuses on Wilson's actions during World War I and his opinions with respect to Imperial Germany as a threat to the United states.

Heckscher, August. *Woodrow Wilson.* New York: Macmillan, 1991.

Knock, Thomas J. *To End All Wars: Woodrow Wilson and the Quest for a New World Order.* New York: Oxford University Press, 1992; London: Princeton University Press, 1995.

Link, Arthur Stanley. *Wilson.* 5 vols. Princeton, N.J.: Princeton University Press, 1947-1965. A painstakingly researched and meticulously documented study, letter by letter, memoir by memoir, document by document. Seldom is heard a discouraging word, however, on Wilson himself. For example, Link gushingly calls Wilson's preposterous note to the Germans following the sinking of the *Lusitania* (the one upholding the rights of Americans to travel anywhere they want on the high seas) so "bold as to be almost breathtaking."

Mulder, John M., et al. *Woodrow Wilson: A Bibliography.* Westport, Conn.: Greenwood Press, 1997. The last in the 69-volume set of Woodrow Wilson's papers, this volume covers the secondary literature on Wilson.

Saunders, Robert M. *In Search of Woodrow Wilson: Beliefs and Behavior.* Westport, Conn.: Greenwood Press, 1998. Saunders presents a comprehensive analysis of Wilson's personal relationships with family, friends, and professional associates and describes his beliefs, behavior, dreams, and accomplishments from a historical perspective.

Schulte Nordholt, J. W. *Woodrow Wilson: A Life for World Peace.* Translated by Herbert H. Rowen. Berkeley and Oxford: University of California Press, 1991.

Smith, Gene. *When the Cheering Stopped: The Last Years of Woodrow Wilson.* London: Hutchinson, and New York: Morrow, 1964. A journalistic account of the year and a half following Wilson's stroke. Smith, a reporter for the *New York Post*, describes the "petticoat presidency" presided over by Wilson's dedicated but often spiteful wife in colorful detail and with great sympathy. Wilson's stature was enhanced through suffering, and, despite incapacitation, his popularity with the American people remained strong.

Weinstein, Edwin A. *Woodrow Wilson: A Medical and Psychological Biography.* Princeton, N.J.:

Princeton University Press, 1981. Despite the obvious handicap of not having had direct contact with the subject, nor access to a professional case history, this provocative study by a former professor of neurology at Mount Sinai Medical School in New York is the best attempt to explain Wilson's behavior clinically.

*Wm. Laird Kleine-Ahlbrandt*

# DUKE OF WINDSOR
## Edward VIII

*Born:* June 23, 1894; Richmond, Surrey, England
*Died:* May 28, 1972; Paris, France
*Area of Achievement:* Monarchy
*Contribution:* By abdicating the throne in order to marry a twice-divorced American commoner, Edward VIII, the Duke of Windsor, seriously tested the resilience of the British monarchy and created a modern romantic myth known the world over as "the love story of the century."

### Early Life

The man who would eventually become the Duke of Windsor was born His Royal Highness Prince Edward Albert Christian George Andrew Patrick David, the first son of the Duke and Duchess of York (later King George V and Queen Mary). Four more sons and a daughter would eventually be born to the couple, but from the beginning, "David" (as he was known to his family and later to his wife), as heir apparent to the throne then occupied by his grandfather, King Edward VII, was given the special treatment and saddled with the special responsibilities unique to the person who will someday reign. He enjoyed a privileged childhood at his family's various official residences (York Cottage at the royal estate of Sandringham, Frogmore House at Windsor, and Marlborough House in London), but he seems never to have had a particularly close relationship with either of his parents, both of whom were traditionalists who placed duty to king and country ahead of personal happiness. From early childhood he showed signs of being temperamentally unsuited to the position that he was destined to occupy.

Prince Edward never showed great scholastic promise, and, like most young men in the Royal Family, he was prepared very early for a career in the military. In 1907, he was enrolled in the Naval College at Osborne, where an atmosphere of stern and even brutal militarism ensured that the young prince was treated no differently than were the other boys. From there he was sent to the Naval College at Dartmouth, and during his time there King Edward VII died, making way for the young prince's father to ascend the throne as King George V. In the summer of 1911, Prince Edward was officially invested by his father as Prince of Wales in a ceremony at Caernarvon Castle in Wales.

After serving briefly as a midshipman in the Royal Navy, the Prince of Wales was sent to Oxford University to complete his formal education, but his undergraduate career was interrupted in 1914 by the outbreak of World War I. It was during his service in this war that the prince's immense international popularity first began. Rather than taking advantage of his privileged position by assuming a comfortable desk job in England, the prince insisted upon being sent to the front in France and later saw action in the Middle East and in Italy. He behaved with unquestionable bravery throughout the war, and for the rest of his life he would be approached by grateful veterans who remembered his selfless and valorous service.

After the war, the prince undertook a series of state visits that established him as the most popular Prince of Wales in history. During highly publicized visits to Canada, India, Australia, and the United States, cheering crowds greeted him wherever he went, and the press followed him everywhere. He seemed to many the embodiment of the "flaming youth" of the 1920's, with his incomparable social skills, his easygoing, unaffected manner, his modish clothes, and his weakness for tennis matches and cocktail parties. Throughout the 1920's and the early 1930's, his photogenic smile and his attractiveness to women earned for him the title "The World's Most Eligible Bachelor." Not only did he garner the type of press attention usually reserved for film stars, but also he knew how to use it to his and his family's advantage. This genius for public relations was thought by some to foreshadow a new image for the British monarchy, a "democratic" kingship uniquely suited to the twentieth century, but other observers (including, for the most part, his parents) found this latter-day Prince Charming shallow and irresponsible, more concerned with late nights and polo matches than with his hereditary duties as the future King of England.

### Life's Work

The Prince of Wales had met Mrs. Wallis Warfield Simpson, an American socialite then living in London with her second husband, as early as 1930, but it was not until King George V died in January of 1936 that the relationship became troublesome to the government and to the Royal Family. Following in the footsteps of his grandfather, King Edward VII, the prince had had a series of love affairs with married women, each of which had run its course without causing scandal. Yet the new king showed no signs of ending his relationship with Mrs. Simpson; in fact, he privately announced his intentions to marry her as soon as she could obtain a divorce from her husband. Even in the more liberal years to come, a commoner with two living husbands would be deemed unsuitable as Queen of England, but in the 1930's, following so closely upon the reign of the traditional and popular King George V and Queen Mary, it was unthinkable. Though the British press maintained a gentlemanly silence on the issue, American newspapers and wire services were full of the story when Mrs. Simpson filed a divorce petition against her husband in May of 1936.

The carefree disregard for propriety that had been so attractive in the young Prince of Wales began to seem tiresome and immature in the forty-one-year-old King Edward VIII. In the late 1930's, Europe was on the brink of World War II: In Spain, Germany, and Italy, Fascist dictators were consolidating their power, and the island nation of Great Britain seemed imperiled as never before. England more than ever needed the continuity and sense of duty symbolized by the monarchy, but the new king discharged his official duties with alarming haphazardness, looking bored and behaving boorishly when circumstances forced him to be separated from Mrs. Simpson. In addition, it was suspected in some quarters that Adolf Hitler's Nazi regime in Germany had a potential ally in King Edward. The king, though constitutionally prohibited from meddling in politics, let it be known that he wanted to avoid war at all costs, even if it meant instituting a policy of appeasement with Nazi Germany.

To the end of his life, the Duke of Windsor would blame then prime minister Stanley Baldwin for plotting against him, but there is little evidence that Baldwin had anything but the national interest in mind during the ensuing abdication crisis. The British Parliament, the majority of the leaders of the British Dominions (Canada, Australia, New Zealand, India, South Africa, and Ireland), and even Queen Mary and the rest of the Royal Family, were united in their opposition to Mrs. Simpson's being crowned queen. The possibility of a morganatic marriage, under the terms of which Mrs. Simpson could marry the king without becoming queen, was proposed but deemed unacceptable by the cabinet. On December 2, the British press broke its long silence on the issue, and on December 3, Mrs. Simpson, disturbed by popular resentment and frightened by threats against her life, left England for France. At length, it became clear to the increasingly self-absorbed king that he faced a choice between the Crown and marriage to Mrs. Simpson. His once-enormous popular support had eroded, and his only two influential allies were Winston Churchill and the press magnate Lord Beaverbrook. On December 10, King Edward VIII officially abdicated in favor of his younger brother, the Duke of York, who ascended the throne as King George VI. That evening, after making a now-famous radio broadcast to his former subjects, the former king left England for Austria, having been made Duke of Windsor by his brother. He married Mrs. Simpson in France on June 3, 1937, soon after her divorce became final.

Even after his abdication, the Duke of Windsor continued to attract unfavorable press attention and to bring embarrassment upon the British monarchy. His political naïveté made him easy prey for the political apparatus of Nazi Germany, and in 1937 he and the duchess undertook a tour of Germany that culminated in an audience with Hitler. In 1940, the Windsors again became the subject of Nazi intrigue. Hitler was still convinced that a bloodless takeover of Great Britain was possible, and there were rumors of a Nazi plan to kidnap the Windsors and to restore the duke to the throne as an ally of the Third Reich. This plan was abandoned only when, in August of 1940, the Germans realized that Great Britain would not under any circumstances capitulate without a fight.

The Duke of Windsor's final official station was as governor of the Bahamas from August, 1941, to April, 1945. Though he was still as adept as ever at ceremonial functions, his insistence on meddling in political matters that he but vaguely understood offended many of the islands' leading residents and led to charges of racism and incompetence. He resigned his post several months before his term ended and never again sought employment in the spheres of government or international relations.

### Summary

When the Duke of Windsor died of throat cancer in Paris in 1972, his body was flown back to Great Britain to be interred in the royal burial ground at

Frogmore, near Windsor Castle. The duchess, invited by Queen Elizabeth II to stay at Buckingham Palace, was flown to and from England in a jet belonging to the Queen's Flight, the queen's personal fleet. In death, the duke received all the ceremonial honors due a former King of England. To many observers, however, this official recognition came too late. For some thirty-five years, the British Royal Family had snubbed the Windsors, and not until 1966 had the duchess been officially recognized by her niece-in-law, the queen. Though the duke had been allowed to keep the designation of "His Royal Highness" after the abdication, his wife had never been granted royal status (though the case against the legality of withholding it from her is strong), and the duke was never able to forgive or forget his family's treatment of the wife to whom he was truly devoted. Especially in the United States and in France, the two republics where the Windsors had spent most of their time for the last quarter of a century and where their romance had long been mythologized as the "love story of the century" the unyielding attitude of the British Royal Family seemed reactionary and coldhearted.

Still, many observers in Great Britain remembered the blow that the duke had dealt the fragile institution of the constitutional monarchy by refusing to put his duty to country before the considerations of personal happiness. As it happened, King George VI and his wife (later Queen Elizabeth the Queen Mother) and their daughter Queen Elizabeth II, were in all respects more suited to the crown than was the duke and were to bring the monarchy to new heights of popularity. The resentment fostered in 1936 died hard, however, especially in the light of the high press visibility that the Windsors enjoyed to the end of their lives. They seemed always to be on the move, traveling with thirty pieces of luggage and an army of servants to Palm Beach, to Biarritz, to New York, international socialites whose sole purpose in life seemed to be attending parties and nightclubs.

On the one hand, the story of the Duke of Windsor is one of wasted potential, of a natural genius for public relations squandered in a life of imposed exile. One can see, however, how to some it remains a love story with a happy ending: the story of a king who gave up his empire for love.

### Bibliography

Beaverbrook, Lord. *The Abdication of King Edward VIII*. London: Hamilton, and New York: Atheneum, 1966. Completed by the powerful newspaper magnate toward the end of his life and published posthumously, this account is written almost wholly from memory and is thus less than scrupulously accurate in places. Still, extremely valuable as an insider's record of the events leading up to the abdication crisis.

Donaldson, Frances. *Edward VIII*. London: Weidenfeld and Nicolson, and Philadelphia: Lippincott, 1974. The most authoritative biography available, exhaustively researched and documented. Donaldson writes with detachment and honesty, refusing to sentimentalize her subject. Very little attention given to the last twenty-five years of the duke's life, but invaluable in its treatment of his early life and of his reign as King Edward VIII.

Inglis, Brian. *Abdication*. London: Hodder and Stoughton, and New York: Macmillan, 1966. Though partially outdated and only sketchily documented, this is still the best book-length study of the abdication crisis. Especially useful is the background information on Prime Minister Stanley Baldwin and the cabinet ministers.

Lacey, Robert. *Majesty: Elizabeth II and the House of Windsor*. London: Hutchinson, and New York: Harcourt Brace, 1977. Essential to the understanding of the British monarchy in the twentieth century, especially for American readers mostly unfamiliar with the subject. Though it is primarily concerned with Queen Elizabeth II, it links the abdication of Edward VIII both with the manner in which Elizabeth has conducted her reign and with such later royal crises as the affair between Princess Margaret and Group Captain Peter Townsend.

Oursler, Fulton, Jr. "Secret Treason." *American Heritage* 42, no. 8 (December, 1991). The author, son of journalist Fulton Oursler, Sr., reveals his father's secret 1940 interview with the Duke of Windsor in which Edward asked that the United States arrange peace between Germany and the United Kingdom.

Sweet, Paul R. "The Windsor File." *The Historian* 59, no. 2 (Winter 1997). Discusses documents released in 1957 which include evidence of Edward's apathy with respect to Nazi activities.

Thornton, Michael. *Royal Feud*. London: Joseph, and New York: Simon and Schuster, 1985. A fascinating study of the enmity between Queen Elizabeth the Queen Mother and the Duchess of Windsor, this carefully documented book chronicles the personal side of the abdication, the events leading up to it, and its aftermath. Particularly useful is the information on the later years of the Windsors' marriage.

Windsor, Prince Edward. *A King's Story.* London: Cassell, and New York: Putnam, 1951.

Windsor, Wallis. *The Heart Has Its Reasons.* London: Joseph, and New York: McKay, 1956. Though the memoirs of both the duke and the duchess are highly opinionated and factually inaccurate, they deserve to be read for the insights they provide into the couple's temperaments and personalities. Both books provide highly idiosyncratic coverage of the abdication crisis; both were runaway best-sellers when first published.

*J. D. Daubs*

# OPRAH WINFREY

*Born:* January 29, 1954; Kosciusko, Mississippi
*Areas of Achievement:* Film and television
*Contribution:* A talk-show host, actor, producer, and one of the richest women in the entertainment business, Winfrey is the first African American to own a television and film studio.

## Early Life

*The Oprah Winfrey Show* is watched every day by millions of people throughout the world. The woman behind the award-winning show is so famous and so popular that she is known as "Oprah" by her legions of fans, yet her position belies the struggles, heartaches, and disappointments of her past.

Oprah Gail Winfrey was born on January 29, 1954, in Kosciusko, Mississippi, the child of a young unmarried couple. Vernita Lee and Vernon Winfrey were barely out of their teens when they became parents. Vernon Winfrey was in the armed forces when a postcard from Vernita Lee notified him that he had become a father. Oprah Gail Winfrey's first name was to have been Orpah, but a misspelling on her birth certificate renamed the child Oprah.

Vernita Lee, who had become a single mother, began to seek employment. She opted to relocate to the North in an attempt to find work. Intent on settling in Milwaukee, Lee left Oprah in the care of the child's paternal grandmother. The influence of her elderly caretaker, according to Winfrey, is still an important element in her life. As Winfrey describes her, her grandmother was disciplined, strong, and religious. Oprah was reared to be a churchgoer. She proved herself to be intelligent, articulate, and animated. She learned to read early and became a voracious reader. Her quick mind was never idle; she craved mental challenges. Her school environment soon proved to be restrictive to the intelligent child, who found the lack of adequate mental stimuli stifling and confining.

At home, Oprah was under the strict care of her grandmother, whose caretaking techniques included living by the adage that children were "to be seen and not heard." The rod was not to be spared, if the occasion warranted its use. The strong-willed child resented her restrictive environment, and she began to believe that the best way out of her predicament was to become white. She believed that white children were adequately challenged and were not subject to corporal punishment. She fantasized about having lighter skin and a straight nose, and this fantasy was a source of comfort to her. She continued to be a high-spirited young girl, and ultimately she proved to be too difficult and recalcitrant for her grandmother to handle. Her grandmother decided that Oprah would have to move to Milwaukee to live with her mother.

Life in Milwaukee was very different from the kind of life Oprah had known in rural Mississippi. Vernita Lee, who had little money, lived an uncomfortable life in a single room. Living without enough money and the comforts of her grandmother's home made Oprah more rebellious. Vernita Lee soon decided that because both she and Oprah's paternal grandmother had been unable to handle what they deemed a recalcitrant child, it would be best for everyone for Oprah to live with her father. Oprah was to move yet again.

Life in Tennessee with her father and stepmother proved to be good for Oprah. They encouraged her in her academic work and provided a loving yet firm environment. Oprah thrived in her new surroundings, excelling academically and socially. After a year, Oprah went to visit her mother for summer vacation. When it was time for Oprah to return to Tennessee, Vernita Lee refused to permit her to return to her father. Vernita Lee wanted Oprah back. Reluctantly, Vernon gave in.

Life immediately turned sour for Oprah. Her self-esteem suffered badly. She felt unwanted and believed that her lighter-skinned sister was treated better than she was. She took refuge in reading books. The quality of Oprah's academic work never decreased, although she suffered from many years of sexual abuse by male relatives and acquaintances. She suffered in silence. She manifested her inner suffering and rage by lying and destroying property. Her mother's confusion and exasperation with Oprah increased, and soon it was decided that alternate living arrangements would have to be made. It was then decided that another visit to Vernon was needed. The move to back Tennessee in 1968, however, did not work out as well as the move in 1962 had. She had difficulty readjusting to her new environment.

In her senior year at Nashville's East High School, Oprah decided that she wanted her future to be in entertainment. Her aspirations were well on the way to being realized. She excelled academically and also won several titles, including

that of Miss Black Tennessee. She read the news for the local radio station while she was still in her teens. Despite her decision to attend college outside Tennessee, her father insisted that she enroll in Tennessee State University in Nashville. With an oratorical scholarship in hand, Oprah entered Tennessee State as an English major.

### Life's Work

During her college years, Oprah Winfrey worked for several media organizations. She was employed in Nashville by the radio stations WVOL and WLAC, and later she worked as a television reporter-anchor for WLAC-TV. Only a few months before she was to have been graduated from Tennessee State University, she accepted a position with WJ2-TV in Baltimore, Maryland. Her enthusiasm and personality attracted many admirers within the journalistic community, and she quickly became a favorite with the public. She became the cohost of a local morning show, *People Are Talking*.

Winfrey's popularity soon extended outside Baltimore. After having sent demo tapes to media markets throughout the country, Oprah was asked to host *A.M. Chicago*. She was now in the national arena, competing with television talk-show hosts such as Phil Donahue. She quickly won the ratings war against Donahue, who left Chicago in 1985 to relocate in New York.

It was at this time that Winfrey began to gain weight. She became concerned about her health and her appearance, and she tried many diets. Dieting, however, did not solve her weight problem. She found that she always regained any weight that she had been able to lose by dieting. Winfrey underwent extensive psychoanalysis, and she finally concluded that her weight problem was the result of her lack of a positive self-image, which in turn was the result of her childhood experiences. Despite the fact that she continued to be successful as a media personality, Winfrey continued to gain weight. Her popularity, Emmy awards, and increased respect within the industry did not halt her eating binges.

Winfrey soon decided that she wanted to work as an actor. In 1985, she requested a leave of absence from her show to costar in Steven Spielberg's film *The Color Purple*, which went on to garner extensive critical acclaim. The film, which was based on Alice Walker's novel of the same title, portrayed strong African American females but depicted many of its African American male characters as abusive and weak.

Winfrey was nominated for an Academy Award for her role in *The Color Purple*, and she followed that role with the role of the mother in a film version of Richard Wright's novel *Native Son*. Although the role was a relatively small one and the film was not widely distributed, Winfrey was satisfied with her performance. She hoped to continue portraying women of strength and character. Consequently, she pursued other acting projects in an effort to stretch her acting skills as well as to inform and educate her audience.

Because of Winfrey's popularity, *A.M. Chicago* was renamed *The Oprah Winfrey Show* and was widely distributed. By 1988, Winfrey was the most highly paid entertainer in show business. At that time, Winfrey also revealed that she had lost the weight she had wanted to lose for so long. Only a few months later, however, she had regained all of her former weight and more besides. The public became obsessed with her weight, and it became a frequent subject of tabloid journalism.

Yet Oprah remained the quintessential host and entertainer. She continued to break records in areas never before ventured into by any African American woman. In addition to owning and producing *The Oprah Winfrey Show*, Winfrey formed her own company, which she called Harpo (Oprah spelled backward), and purchased a studio. She ventured into film production, producing and costarring in African American author Gloria Naylor's *The Women of Brewster Place*, which was a ratings hit. The made-for-television film became a short-lived television series. Winfrey has won several Emmy Awards as Best Talk Show Host, and *The Oprah Winfrey Show* has won several Emmys as Best Talk Show. In 1998, Winfrey produced and starred in a film version of Toni Morrison's Pulitzer Prize-winning novel *Beloved* (1987).

Oprah Winfrey frequently gives lectures to youth groups and universities, and she has made multimillion-dollar donations to several causes. She supports the United Negro College Fund, and she has formed a Tennessee State University Scholarship Fund that awards ten students annually who are deemed economically disadvantaged as well as academically talented. She writes each student personally on a regular basis. She also serves as their mentor and provides them with moral as well as financial support, encouraging them to excel and to maintain grade-point averages of 3.0 or above. If they do so, she finances their education to its completion.

Winfrey also serves as a spokesperson against child abuse. A victim of sexual and mental abuse as a child, she has dedicated herself to helping those in similar situations. She has testified on the subject of child abuse in front of a congressional committee, and she continues to enlighten the public about the many problems that children face in the United States, such as abuse, homelessness, and illness.

### Summary

Oprah Winfrey's rise to stardom may seem to many people to have been quick and easy. Despite her youth, however, Winfrey has paid her dues. Her achievements are the results of her effort and tenacity. Oprah has demonstrated that one's dreams and aspirations can be realized if they are supported by diligence and persistence. Her rise, despite seemingly insurmountable odds, has inspired many people. She affects millions of individuals daily through her television show, which has focused on a wide variety of topics. Her programs inform, enlighten, and influence a large sector of the populace. She has examined on her show such issues as racism, sexism, spousal abuse, acquired immune deficiency syndrome (AIDS), violence in schools, drunk driving, political corruption, and child abuse. She continues to make journalistic history by interviewing elusive luminaries. Her exclusive interview with superstar Michael Jackson in 1993 was a ratings coup.

Winfrey has expanded her business horizons by opening a restaurant in Chicago and by bringing to the screen inspiring stories such as *Kaffir* and *Beloved*. She is always pursuing projects of substance and causes that will affect the masses. Still unmarried, Winfrey has been engaged for many years to entrepreneur Stedman Graham. She has also resolved the problem of her vacillating weight with proper nutrition, exercise, and medical supervision. Determined to keep the weight off, Winfrey has become an inspiration to many women who have experienced similar problems. Lauded by her employees for her generosity, Oprah Winfrey remains accessible to her public and continues to be one of the most famous people in the world.

### Bibliography

King, Norman. *Everybody Loves Oprah!* New York: Morrow, 1987. This book chronicles the life and work of Oprah Winfrey. It also deals with her ability to elicit admiration and love from those around her.

Long, Richard A. *African Americans*. New York: Random House, and London: Prion,1993. This text celebrates the role African Americans have played and continue to play in the history of the United States. Oprah Winfrey is discussed and analyzed in the chapter "The African-American Age."

Smith, Jessie Carney, ed. *Notable Black American Women*. Detroit: Gale Research, 1992. The biographical sketch on Winfrey contained in this book covers her life, achievements, and struggles in a definitive and informative manner.

Steyn, Mark. "Comic Oprah: American's Talker-in-Chief is the Perfect Embodiment of the Virtual Culture of the Nineties." *National Review* 50, no. 5 (March 23, 1998). The author discusses Oprah Winfrey's influence on the American people and the concept of "Oprahfication," which the author defines as "public confession as a form of therapy."

Van Meter, Jonathan. "Ophrah's Moment." *Vogue* 188, no. 10 (October, 1998). Interview with Oprah Winfrey in which she discusses her movie *Beloved* based on the novel by Toni Morrison, a study of the desperation felt by slaves in 1873.

Waldron, Robert. *Oprah!* New York: St. Martin's Press, 1987; London: Futura, 1991. A popular biography of Winfrey that includes a sixteen-page photograph section.

Woods, Geraldine. *The Oprah Winfrey Story: Speaking Her Mind, an Authorized Biography.* Minneapolis, Minn.: Dillon Press, 1991. This biography, which bears Winfrey's stamp of approval, focuses on the significance of Winfrey's success as an African American woman. Includes an index and bibliographical references.

*Annette Marks-Ellis*

# STEPHEN SAMUEL WISE

*Born:* March 17, 1874; Budapest, Austro-Hungarian Empire (now Hungary)
*Died:* April 19, 1949; New York, New York
*Areas of Achievement:* Religion, and social reform
*Contribution:* One of the most influential rabbis in U.S. history, Wise was a social and moral reformer, a Zionist, a leader in Jewish-Christian relations, and the founder of the Free Synagogue.

## Early Life

Stephen Samuel Wise was born in Budapest in the Austro-Hungarian Empire (now Hungary) on March 17, 1874. He moved to the United States as a one-year-old infant with his parents, Aaron and Sabine De Fischer Wise. His paternal grandfather, the Reverend Joseph H. Wise, had been a well-known Hungarian rabbi. After the death of her husband, Stephen's paternal grandmother went to Palestine to pray, die, and be buried in a grave facing the site of the Holy of Holies rather than opting to join her only surviving son, Aaron, in the United States. Her example no doubt influenced Stephen's later Zionism.

Upon arriving in the United States, Aaron settled his family in New York City, where he became rabbi of Temple Rodeph Sholem. He served there until his death in 1896. Stephen later paid tribute to his father as the one who had enabled him to see that the rabbinate was a noble and high calling. Wise earned a bachelor of arts degree from Columbia University in 1892 and then received private rabbinic training. He was ordained by Adolf Jellineck of Vienna. His first appointment was at the Conservative B'nai Jeshurun Temple in New York City, where he served from 1893 to 1900. During this period he first identified himself with the Zionist movement. He also continued his education, receiving his Ph.D. from Columbia University in 1901.

In 1900 Wise married Louise Waterman. In that same year he received a call to become rabbi of a Reform congregation in Portland, Oregon. He accepted the call and served there until 1906. The congregation more than doubled in size during his stay and became known for its generous contributions to Jewish causes. However, the young rabbi's vision did not stop at the doors of his synagogue. He tirelessly devoted his energies and abilities to works of social reform. Upon arriving in Oregon, he quickly recognized that child labor was one of the unchecked evils of that state. There was no law regarding this practice on the statute books. Rabbi Wise drafted a law of such high caliber that it made Oregon a leader in child labor legislation. He was one of the founders of the Oregon State Board of Charities and Correction and was its first vice president. He also worked for the recognition of the importance of the Juvenile Court, the institution of the indeterminate sentence, and the parole of first offenders.

In addition to his congregational duties and his service to the state of Oregon, Wise was responsible for establishing, in the city of Portland, the People's Forum, reminiscent in many ways of the old New England town meeting. At the weekly meetings of the People's Forum, matters of civic interest were brought to a free platform for discussion. Rabbi Wise's service as founder and president of the forum brought him an invitation to become one of the members of Portland's executive Board of Nine, in whom, under the mayor, the municipal government of the city was vested.

### Life's Work

News of Wise's groundbreaking reform work trickled back to New York City. In 1905 he was invited to preach a series of sermons in Temple Emanu-El, New York's greatest and richest synagogue. The sermons would enable the trustees to determine whether to recommend him for the position of rabbi. The trustees proposed to extend a call to him, but one clause in the offer drew Wise's attention and elicited a reply that attracted nationwide attention. The clause stated that the pulpit of Temple Emanu-El "shall always be subject to, and under the control of the Board of Trustees." When, in answer to his frank question concerning the meaning of this condition, he was given the equally frank answer that "should the rabbi in his sermons or addresses offend the opinion of the lay heads of the congregation, he would be expected either to retract the offending remarks or to maintain a discreet silence on the subject thereafter," Wise declined the pulpit in an open letter to the congregation of Temple Emanu-El. The letter, which became a classic defense of free speech in the pulpit, stated:

> The chief office of the minister . . . is not to represent the views of the congregation, but to proclaim the truth as he sees it . . . A free pulpit, worthily filled, must command respect and influence; a pulpit that is not free, howsoever filled, is sure to be without potency or honor. A free pulpit will sometimes stumble into error; a pulpit that is not free can never powerfully plead for truth and righteousness. In the pursuit of the duties of his office, the minister may from time to time be under the necessity of giving expression to views at variance with the views of some, or even many, members of the congregation. Far from such difference proving the pulpit to be in the wrong, it may be, and ofttimes is, found to signify that the pulpit has done its duty in calling evil evil and good good . . . Difference, and disquiet, even schism at the worst, are not so much to be feared as the attitude of the pulpit which never provokes dissent because it is cautious rather than courageous, peace-loving rather than prophetic, time-serving rather than right-serving.

Thus it was that Wise lost his opportunity to become rabbi of the richest synagogue in New York City. Yet some Jews of influence responded favorably to his insistence upon religious freedom within the synagogue. With their support, he founded the Free Synagogue in New York in 1907, which emphasized a free pulpit and the preaching of a vital and prophetic Judaism. Its constitution states:

> Believing that the power of the synagogue for good depends in part upon the inherent right of the pulpit to freedom of thought and speech, the founders of the Free Synagogue resolve that its pulpit shall be free to preach on behalf of truth and righteousness in the spirit and after the pattern of the prophets of Israel.

Wise also believed that the synagogue must again become democratically managed and that there could be no synagogue democracy as long as the "pews and dues" system remained. Hence the constitution also states that the Free Synagogue "shall not at any time nor for any reason impose any pecuniary due, tax, or assessment upon its members, but shall be supported wholly by voluntary contributions."

As was the case with the young Rabbi Wise in Oregon, the mature Wise served far beyond the boundaries of his congregation, championing the causes of interfaith cooperation, social reform, and moral reform in government. He was peripherally involved in the founding of the National Association for the Advancement of Colored People (NAACP) in 1909 and the American Civil Liberties Union (ACLU) in 1920. He and a fellow New York clergyman, John Haynes Holmes, garnered national publicity for their exposure of graft in city administration. Throughout his life, he sought better relations between Christians and Jews.

Wise was both admired and condemned for his discussion of controversial topics, one notable example of which was his series of sermons on "The Life, Teachings, and Death of Jesus the Jew," which were summarized in the June 7, 1913, issue of *Outlook* magazine (which Wise founded and edited). Wise not only asserted the Jewishness of Jesus, but also and much more controversially claimed for Jews a preeminent right to interpret Jesus: "When the processes of the resurrection of the body of the teachings of Jesus from the tomb of dogmatic Christianity shall have been completed, we of the House of Israel know that a figure will emerge who is our own, long hidden from us rather than by us."

Despite his interfaith and social interests, Wise did not neglect Jewish causes and concerns. In 1922, he established the Jewish Institute of Religion, a seminary offering training for rabbis of all branches of the faith. He was largely responsible for the establishment of the American Jewish Congress (1916) as well as the World Jewish Congress (1936), presiding over both from their inception until his death in 1949.

Perhaps his best-known Jewish cause was that of Zionism. He was one of the first Jewish leaders in the United States to become active in the Zionist movement. He attended the Second Zionist Congress in Basel, Switzerland, in 1898 and helped to found the Zionist Organization of America in the same year, for which he served as president in 1917 and from 1936 to 1938. As a prominent member of the Democratic Party and an acquaintance of President Woodrow Wilson, Wise influenced the U.S. government toward approval of the Balfour Declaration. He was a leader in the struggle to marshal American public opinion against Adolf Hitler in the 1930's. However, he was not a supporter of the growing militancy of the Zionist movement during the war years, and this led to difficult conflicts with other Zionist leaders. Happily, at the time of his death in 1949, the state of Israel had just been established, fulfilling a dream that Wise had pursued for half a century.

### Summary

Many have considered Stephen Samuel Wise to be the outstanding rabbi of American Jewish history. Fellow rabbi P. S. Bernstein lauded him as the person who almost single-handedly transformed liberal Judaism in the United States. Finding it "conventional, smug, fettered and barren," he infused it with new life through "his passion for social justice, his intense love of freedom, and his devotion to the Jewish masses." It was largely through his efforts, Bernstein claimed, that the liberal Jewish pulpit was freed, that the rabbis became earnestly concerned with the social and economic implications of their religion, and that the Reform synagogue was democratized in form and spirit.

In addition to the internal reforms he brought to Judaism, Wise gave Jewishness increased visibility in the United States. He brought the destruction of Jews in Europe to the attention of the American government and people. He preached to large audiences, including many non-Jews, in Carnegie Hall. He founded the magazine *Opinion*, and his name appeared often in the pages of *The Christian Century*. He spoke about Jesus as a Jew, and both Christians and Jews listened even if all did not agree with what he said. He was a Jew for all people, indelibly Jewish but concerned about the good of all.

### Bibliography

Urofsky, Melvin I. *A Voice That Spoke for Justice*. Albany: State University of New York Press, 1982. This is the only book-length biography of Wise in existence, and fortunately it is a good one. An extensively researched and brilliantly analyzed portrayal of its subject.

Voss, Carl Hermann. *Rabbi and Minister*. Cleveland: World, 1964. This book chronicles the joint endeavors of Wise and Unitarian minister John Haynes Holmes in championing social reforms. Offers insight into an influential Jewish-Christian friendship strong enough to allow differences of opinion on issues that mattered to both.

Wise, James Waterman. *Jews Are Like That*. New York: Brentano's, 1928. Rather than being a straightforward biography, James Waterman Wise provides a chapter-long character sketch of his father, Stephen S. Wise.

Wise, Stephen Samuel. *As I See It*. New York: Jewish Opinion Publishing Corporation, 1944. Contains articles penned by Wise for the magazine *Opinion* and collected by its editors. Gives the reader an opportunity to hear Wise's reaction to historical events as they were unfolding. Arranged chronologically within each of five topics: Jewishness, Hitlerism, Zionism, contemporary Jews, and war and its lessons.

———. *Challenging Years: The Autobiography of Stephen Wise*. New York: Putnam, 1949; London: East and West, 1951. Wise's autobiography reveals much about his personality, telling, as it does, the main stories of his life in his own words. It is less helpful in terms of objective biographical information, but an introductory essay by his daughter and son helps to compensate for that deficiency.

*Ann Marie B. Bahr*

# LUDWIG WITTGENSTEIN

*Born:* April 26, 1889; Vienna, Austro-Hungarian Empire

*Died:* April 29, 1951; Cambridge, England

*Area of Achievement:* Philosophy

*Contribution:* Wittgenstein is one of the most important and influential philosophers of the twentieth century and perhaps of all time. In his later, mature period, he did not produce a systematic philosophy or even claim to teach new doctrines. Instead, he professed to offer new methods and techniques for work in philosophy.

## Early Life

Ludwig Josef Johann Wittgenstein was born into a prominent and highly cultured family in turn-of-the-century Vienna. His father, Karl Wittgenstein, was a leading Austrian industrialist and had in fact made a fortune in the iron and steel industry. Originally educated at home, at the age of fourteen Wittgenstein entered school at Linz in Upper Austria and later attended the Technische Hochschule in Berlin-Charlottenburg. Wittgenstein developed a strong interest in physics, technology, and engineering. In 1908, he went to England, where he experimented with kites at the Kite Flying Upper Atmosphere Station and became a student at the University of Manchester. His early studies took him into airplane engine design, mathematics, and the philosophical and logical foundations of mathematics. He went to Jena, Germany, to visit Gottlob Frege (the "father of modern logic"), where he was advised to study with Bertrand Russell at the University of Cambridge. Russell had published *The Principles of Mathematics* in 1903, and, together with Alfred North Whitehead, had published in 1910 the first volume of their *Principia Mathematica*, a monumental and definitive work in modern logic. In 1912, Wittgenstein was accepted at the University of Cambridge and took up his formal studies there under Russell.

Although Russell and Wittgenstein later drifted apart, there was at this early period a closeness and a mutual seriousness that show themselves in many stories, still told, that date from this time. According to Russell, at the end of Wittgenstein's first term at Cambridge he came to Russell and asked, "Do you think I am a complete idiot?" The idea was that Wittgenstein was thinking about becoming a pilot (if he was an idiot) and a philosopher (if he was not). Russell said to write a paper during the term break. Wittgenstein did, and when Russell saw it he immediately said that Wittgenstein should not become a pilot. On another occasion, Wittgenstein came to Russell's rooms late one night and paced up and down, in a distraught mood, for hours. Russell asked him whether he was thinking about logic or his sins, and Wittgenstein answered "Both!" Russell was convinced that, although Wittgenstein was eccentric, he was a genius.

In 1913, Wittgenstein's father died and left him a huge fortune. This Wittgenstein gave away, some of it in the form of anonymous benefactions to Austrian poets and writers. Wittgenstein himself assumed a rather austere lifestyle, which he maintained for the rest of his life. He ate simply, dressed simply, had no family, and lived in very humble rooms.

## Life's Work

Wittgenstein's early masterpiece, and the only philosophical book that he published during his lifetime, is best known by the title *Tractatus Logico-Philosophicus*—or, for short, the *Tractatus.* This was published in the original German in 1921 and first appeared in an English-German bilingual edition in 1922. Wittgenstein stated in the preface that the gist of the book lies in the following statement: "What can be said at all can be said clearly, and what we cannot talk about we must pass over in silence." The book is quite terse and follows a special numbering system in which each section (sometimes only a single sentence) receives a number based on its relative importance to the whole. The main statements are given the numbers one through seven. Number one says "The world is all that is the case"—that is, the world is the totality of facts or situations. One of the essential features of Wittgenstein's early philosophy, as expressed in the *Tractatus*, is that the most basic statements (or elementary propositions) of language achieve meaning by picturing facts. More complicated factual statements are built up from these. Thus, when all the true propositions have been stated, everything that can be said has been said; the rest is silence. As Wittgenstein claimed in the *Tractatus*, there are some things that are inexpressible—he spoke here of things that are mystical—and to try to express these in language will only result in nonsense.

Wittgenstein claimed that his *Tractatus* solved the problems of philosophy. So, he left philosophy and pursued various other professions. He became a village schoolteacher in the Austrian mountains, a gardener in a monastery, and a worker at sculpture and architecture. In 1929, however, Wittgenstein returned to Cambridge and to philosophy. His *Tractatus*, already acknowledged as a classic work, was accepted as his Ph.D. dissertation, and he became first a research fellow and later a professor. Until his death in 1951, Wittgenstein wrote many volumes of philosophy (almost always in German) but did not publish any of these (or have them translated into English). He taught philosophy at Cambridge, but, instead of lecturing, he used a method of discussion and thinking aloud. Most of his influence—and it was considerable—occurred through the students who attended his discussions and those who took dictation from him (in English). Wittgenstein, however, found the atmosphere of Cambridge life to be sterile. He would sometimes leave to spend weeks and months in out-of-the-way places in Norway and Ireland and would write philosophy there.

The new philosophy that Wittgenstein developed in the 1930's and 1940's retained its focus on language but gave up the monolithic idea that language always functions in merely one way, that is, via the picturing relation. He now came to emphasize the great variety of uses of language and the fact that language is intertwined with the rest of human life. His later work, best seen in his posthumously published *Philosophical Investigations* (1953), provides some explicit criticism of the views earlier taken in the *Tractatus*. Wittgenstein went on to develop his thoughts in new and positive directions.

Wittgenstein's view of the nature of philosophical problems changed. He now came to see problems as tied to individuals. Thus he said, for example, that the philosopher's treatment of a problem is like the treatment of an illness. Just as in medicine there is always a patient (and never an illness alone) who is to be cured, in philosophy there is a person who is the bearer of philosophical questions or confusions. The doctor does not treat diseases in the abstract, and the philosopher does not treat problems in the abstract.

The later philosophy of Wittgenstein has been characterized as a therapeutic approach. A philosophical problem is seen as a sort of difficulty. A person who has such a problem is lost, in a sense, and Wittgenstein's aim is to show this person how to get out of the difficulty. One image he used was that of knots. Although philosophy should be simple, he said, in order to untie the knots of our thinking it must be at least as complicated as those knots.

Wittgenstein believed that language itself was exceedingly tricky and often extremely misleading. At one point he said that philosophy is a battle against the bewitchment of intelligence by means of language. In emphasizing the variety of ways in which language is used, Wittgenstein opposed the idea that any one form of language or thought—the scientific, for example—is in some sense basic or foundational. If anything is foundational, according to Wittgenstein, it is one's practice or way of life.

Wittgenstein believed that some of the occasions on which people are most likely to be misled occur in thinking and talking about mathematical abstractions, psychological concepts, and language itself. Although he did not confine his thought and writing to these areas, he did concentrate his attention on what he regarded as the temptations that are likely to appeal to thinkers in these areas and on the means of overcoming these temptations.

**Summary**

Ludwig Wittgenstein's influence spread rapidly from Cambridge to other areas of the English-speaking world and to Scandinavia. This influence operated largely through his students and by word of mouth. Since his death in 1951, more and more of his philosophical writings have been published, and his influence has spread, although it remains significantly stronger in English-speaking countries and in Scandinavia and weaker on the European continent, Latin America, and elsewhere.

It is not an exaggeration to say that Wittgenstein was a leader in a philosophical revolution. The revolution focuses particular attention on language and on the ways in which people can be confused or misled, especially by ordinary language.

One recent movement that takes its inspiration from Wittgenstein is known as "ordinary language" philosophy. Herein, the emphasis is on the ordinary meanings of customary terms, clarity of expression, and down-to-earth common sense rather than special philosophical or technical terminology, impressive-sounding but vague language, and high-flown metaphysical notions.

Although it is true that Wittgenstein's own views and practice in philosophy changed over time, and many scholars distinguish sharply between the earlier and the later approaches, one constant concern of his focuses on the idea that clarity of thought and expression is of the first importance and nonsense is always to be rejected, and sometimes even fought against.

## Bibliography

Cavell, Stanley. *The Claim of Reason: Wittgenstein, Skepticism, Morality and Tragedy.* New York: Oxford University Press, 1999. Cavell discusses "ordinary language philosophy" as seen in the work of J.L. Austin and Wittgenstein.

Fann, K. T., ed. *Ludwig Wittgenstein: The Man and His Philosophy.* New York: Dell, 1967; Hassocks, Sussex: Harvester Press, 1978. A collection of articles by friends, students, and scholars of Wittgenstein. Included are articles on Wittgenstein as a person, a teacher, and a philosopher, and treatments of various aspects of Wittgenstein's philosophical work.

Janik, Allan, and Stephen Toulmin. *Wittgenstein's Vienna.* London: Weidenfeld and Nicolson, and New York: Simon and Schuster, 1973. An illustrated survey showing the many connections between Wittgenstein's philosophical development and modern movements in architecture, literature, music, psychoanalysis, and other fields, in the setting of late nineteenth century Viennese culture.

Marion, Mathieu. *Wittgenstein, Finitism, and the Foundations of Mathematics.* Oxford: Clarendon Press, Oxford and New York: Oxford University Press, 1998. Based on research into Wittgenstein's unpublished papers, this volume presents the development of his philosophy from his early theories through later revisions.

McGinn, Colin. *Wittgenstein on Meaning: An Interpretation and Evaluation.* Oxford and New York: Blackwell, 1984. The long first chapter of this work is especially useful in providing a large-scale view of the later Wittgenstein views on meaning, understanding, and language.

McGuinness, Brian. *Wittgenstein, A Life: Young Ludwig, 1889-1921.* London: Duckworth, and Berkeley: University of California Press, 1988. The first volume of a projected two-volume authorized biography, providing by far the fullest account to date of Wittgenstein's early life. This first volume concludes with a discussion of the *Tractatus.* Includes illustrations.

Malcolm, Norman. *Ludwig Wittgenstein: A Memoir.* 2d ed. Oxford and New York: Oxford University Press, 1984. This book is a gem, written by Wittgenstein's most prominent American philosophical student. Malcolm allows the reader to see the force of Wittgenstein's personality as well as his particular way of practicing philosophy. The second edition includes numerous letters that Wittgenstein wrote to Malcolm.

Pears, David. *The False Prison.* 2 vols. Oxford: Clarendon Press, 1987; New York: Oxford University Press, 1988. The first volume covers Wittgenstein's early philosophy; the second covers the time from 1929 to his death. Pears focuses clearly on Wittgenstein the philosopher rather than on Wittgenstein the person. His treatment of Wittgenstein's work is scholarly and reliable.

Wittgenstein, Ludwig. *Culture and Value.* Edited by G. H. von Wright, in collaboration with Heikki Nyman. Translated by Peter Winch. 2d ed. Oxford: Blackwell, and Chicago: University of Chicago Press,1980. A bilingual edition of sentences and paragraphs taken from all periods of Wittgenstein's life, arranged chronologically, addressing a wide range of topics in art, music, philosophy, religion, science, and the like.

*Stephen Satris*

# MAX WOLF

*Born:* June 21, 1863; Heidelberg, Baden
*Died:* October 3, 1932; Heidelberg, Germany
*Area of Achievement:* Astronomy
*Contribution:* Wolf was the first astronomer to use an astronomical camera to discover asteroids by combining the camera with a mechanical telescope. During his very full career, Wolf discovered 582 asteroids with 228 of these receiving general recognition. This figure is a personal record of discoveries in astronomy which has been difficult to surpass.

## Early Life

Max Wolf was the son of Franz Wolf and Elise Halwerth. He was attracted to astronomy at an early age and, while a student at Heidelberg, erected his own small observatory. Since his father was a wealthy physician, Wolf was able to afford this private facility. In 1884, he discovered the comet which bears his name. This discovery so fired his interest in astronomy that he gave up all of his other studies to pursue a career in this field, earning a Ph.D. from Heidelberg with a dissertation in celestial mechanics.

In 1891, Wolf discovered his first asteroid, using photography. For this discovery, he was awarded the Lalande Prize of the Paris Academy of Sciences. After a visit to the United States, during which he received financial support for a sixteen-inch double telescope, Wolf returned to Heidelberg to work with the Grand Duke of Baden to build a new observatory at Königstuhl. In 1893, Wolf was named director of this new observatory and, simultaneously, became extraordinary professor of astrophysics at the University of Heidelberg. In 1902, he was elected to the chair of astronomy at the same university. Wolf remained at Heidelberg for the rest of his life, discovering his last asteroid, 1219 Britta, there only a few months prior to his death.

## Life's Work

Wolf had two major accomplishments during his career. The first was the use of an astronomical camera in connection with a telescope to hunt for asteroids. To accomplish this search, the telescope was centered on a conveniently located bright star. The clockwork of the telescope kept track with the movement of the star so that photographs showed the star as a dot of light. Asteroids and comets moving across the field around the star would appear on the photograph as lines. Visual observation with the telescope alone would then determine whether the line was a comet or an asteroid. Because the clockwork drive for telescopes was not entirely accurate, the photographic session had to be monitored constantly to keep the star in the crosshairs of the telescope. Wolf developed the technique for this method of sky search to a high degree. His methods were adapted widely by other astronomers.

The second great accomplishment of Wolf's career was the discovery of the Trojan asteroids, a large number of asteroids outside the asteroid belt and in the orbit of Jupiter. In 1906, Wolf observed an asteroid, which he called Achilles, whose orbit seemed unusual. Mathematical computations showed that Achilles was in the orbit of Jupiter. Although this seems impossible, an eighteenth century mathematician, Joseph-Louis Lagrange, had determined that, in theory, a small object can travel in the same orbit as a large object if the two objects and the sun form an equilateral triangle. In order to do this, the small object must be about sixty degrees ahead of or behind the large one. Wolf was searching sixty degrees ahead of Jupiter when he discovered Achilles. The name "Achilles" was chosen by Wolf because other asteroids had feminine names, but this one was outside the asteroid belt.

The discovery of Achilles suggested that one should search sixty degrees behind Jupiter, and there other bodies were found. The first of these was named Patroclus. This established a pattern; all these asteroids were named for heroes of the Trojan War, and the two groups are collectively called the Trojan asteroids. All of those in the Achilles group, except one, Hector, are named for the Greeks, and, except for Patroclus, the second group are named for the defenders of Troy. Some seven hundred Trojan asteroids have been identified.

## Summary

By combining the best technology of his time with accepted theories, Max Wolf was able to demonstrate the factuality of the Lagrange theory with respect to Jupiter. No other planets have asteroids at the Lagrange points of sixty degrees ahead or behind. By demonstrating an effective method of searching for asteroids, Wolf advanced early twentieth century knowledge of astronomy. The technology of astronomy of the late twentieth century has led to so many asteroid discoveries that one astronomer has called them "vermin of the skies." In Wolf's day, they were a new and exciting field of observation and discovery.

## Bibliography

Freiesleben, H.-Christ. "Maximilian Franz Joseph Cornelius Wolf." In *Dictionary of Scientific Biography*, edited by Charles Coulston Gillispie, vol. 14. London: Macmillan, and New York: Scribner, 1976. This reference work has a biographical sketch of Wolf and includes a short bibliography of his astronomical articles, most of which are in German and are untranslated.

Gehrels, Tom. *Asteroids.* Tucson: University of Arizona Press, 1979. This textbook on asteroids has several references to Wolf and his work. It explains the significance of asteroids in the planetary scene.

Kowal, Charles T., ed. *Asteroids: Their Nature and Utilization.* 2d ed. New York: Wiley, and London: Praxis, 1996. Kowal describes Wolf's discovery of the Trojan asteroids and discusses the Lagrange theory in layperson's terms.

Mitton, Simon, ed. *The Cambridge Encyclopedia of Astronomy.* New York: Crown, 1977. A basic reference work, this book has good articles on asteroids and the Trojan asteroids. Includes a brief biographical sketch on Wolf that focuses on his work.

Tenn, Joseph S. "Max Wolf." *Mercury* 23, no. 4 (July/August, 1994). Profile of Max Wolf including information on his photography of meteors, asteroids, and comets.

Vaucouleurs, Gérard Henri de. *Astronomical Photography: From the Daguerrotype to the Electron Camera.* London: Faber, and New York: Macmillan, 1961. A history of the photographing of asteroids. Contains numerous references to Wolf's work and several photographs and charts of asteroids.

*Michael R. Bradley*

# THOMAS WOLFE

*Born:* October 3, 1900; Asheville, North Carolina
*Died:* September 15, 1938; Baltimore, Maryland
*Area of Achievement:* Literature
*Contribution:* Wolfe was a master of characterization who, particularly in his first two novels, created memorable characters drawn directly from his family. He was an effusive, gargantuan writer, often uncontrolled, often poetic, but always imbued with the sense of what it meant to be American; he sought to achieve in prose what Walt Whitman had achieved in poetry.

## Early Life

Thomas Clayton Wolfe, the son of William Oliver and Julia Elizabeth Westall Wolfe, was always larger than life. Six and a half feet tall, somewhat stooped, Wolfe had a roundish head that was covered by a mop of dark hair, often disheveled. His dark eyes were animated and kindly. His shirttail usually stuck out, and his clothing hung loosely from his oversized, raw-boned limbs.

Asheville, North Carolina, the town in which he was born, was a somewhat isolated mountain community of about fifteen thousand inhabitants in 1900. The town was a popular summer resort where people could escape from the heat and humidity of the piedmont and coastal South, and it was also gaining popularity as a winter resort.

Wolfe was the youngest of his parents' eight children. Julia Wolfe, his mother, the elder Wolfe's third wife, was interested in music and had taught school before her marriage. She also had a keen interest in real estate and was considered avaricious. In 1904, she packed up her family and left her husband, whose heavy drinking bothered her. She went to St. Louis, where she opened a boardinghouse to accommodate visitors to the World's Fair. It was there that her son, the twin brother of Wolfe's brother Ben, succumbed unexpectedly to typhoid fever.

Returning to Asheville, Julia, in 1906, opened a boardinghouse called The Old Kentucky Home (Dixieland in *Look Homeward, Angel*, 1929), which she ran until after Wolfe's death in 1938. The elder Wolfe lived a few blocks away, and the children moved freely between the two houses. Thomas Wolfe always resented the lack of privacy that being brought up in a boardinghouse involved, but his youth was not an unhappy one.

He began his education in 1905, at the Orange Street Public School, which he attended until 1912. In that year, J. M. Roberts, former principal of the Orange Street Public School, and his wife, Margaret, persuaded Julia to allow her son to attend the North State Fitting School, a private establishment, which they had opened. In this school, Wolfe received a sound basic education, developing a great love of the classics and of reading. The school is depicted quite favorably in *Look Homeward, Angel*, as is Margaret Roberts, who becomes Margaret Leonard in the book.

In 1916, Wolfe entered the University of North Carolina at Chapel Hill, then a school with about eleven hundred students. He had wanted to go to the University of Virginia, but his father vetoed that plan, as he did Wolfe's attempt to transfer to Princeton University at the end of his freshman year. At Chapel Hill, Wolfe became editor of the school newspaper, the *Tar Heel*, and worked with Frederick H. Koch, director of the Carolina Playmakers, who had studied at Harvard in George Pierce Baker's famed 47 Workshop.

In 1918, Wolfe was called home by the death of his favorite brother, Ben, whose death Wolfe chronicles in *Look Homeward, Angel* in an extended passage that represents some of Wolfe's finest writing. By the time Wolfe was graduated from the University, his father was mortally ill with cancer, which finally killed him in 1922. In 1920, diploma in hand, Wolfe turned down several job offers and went to Harvard to study for the master's degree in English and to participate in Baker's 47 Workshop in drama. He remained at Harvard until 1923, a year after he had completed the A.M. degree in English, so that he could continue his involvement with the 47 Workshop.

In 1924, Wolfe went to New York City to teach at the Washington Square Campus of New York University, and he taught freshman composition there on and off until the publication of his first novel in 1929, making trips to Europe as often as he could during that period. On his return voyage from his first such trip in 1925, he met Aline Bernstein, a married woman eighteen years older than he, with whom he had a protracted affair and who is the model for Esther Jacks in *The Web and the Rock* (1939). Aline Bernstein helped Wolfe financially so that he could take time off from his teaching to write and travel.

It was not until 1926 that Wolfe turned from writing plays to writing novels. A number of the

plays he wrote for the Carolina Playmakers and in the 47 Workshop were produced on campus; yet, despite Baker's strong support, the Theater Guild rejected the drama he submitted to them, and he apparently believed that he would do better as a novelist and short-story writer, a conclusion that history has borne out.

### Life's Work

With the publication of *Look Homeward, Angel* by Scribner's in October, 1929, Wolfe gained immediate celebrity. By March of the next year, he had been awarded a Guggenheim fellowship, which enabled him to give up his teaching and to make his fifth trip to Europe. *Look Homeward, Angel*, an often inchoate, overwritten manuscript, fortuitously had fallen into the hands of Maxwell Perkins, who was able to impose an order upon it that was not inherent in the original work.

In Europe, F. Scott Fitzgerald sought out Wolfe. He was also mentioned favorably in Sinclair Lewis' acceptance speech when, in 1930, Lewis became the first American author to be awarded the Nobel Prize for Literature. *Look Homeward, Angel* was badly received in Asheville because Wolfe had not taken great pains to disguise the people about whom he had written in it. Several lodged lawsuits against him.

*Look Homeward, Angel* is a romantic, autobiographical outpouring, huge both in its conception and in its execution. In the novel, Eugene Gant, the narrator based on Wolfe himself, is taken from birth to his graduation from college. The final version of the book ran to 200,000 words. From 1929 until 1934, Wolfe worked steadily on his new book, another autobiographical novel, in which Eugene would go from his native North Carolina to Harvard University, then to New York and to Europe, and would end with meeting Esther Jacks.

From another inchoate manuscript filled with extremely skillful writing but interspersed with flagrantly bad writing, Perkins sought to create a second Thomas Wolfe novel. He reduced the 400,000-word manuscript to something manageable, although still considerably longer than the typical novel, and Scribner's published it under the title *Of Time and the River* (1935). In this book, Wolfe had tried to control his romanticism and to be more realistic. His gargantuan effusiveness and essential enthusiasm, however, made it difficult for him to achieve the objective realism to which he aspired. *Of Time and the River*, which the reading public received enthusiastically, was the last Wolfe novel to be published during his lifetime.

When he was in New York, Wolfe worked almost daily with Perkins, and the two had considerable differences of opinion about crucial artistic matters relating to Wolfe's work. The relationship, as necessary as it was to Wolfe, became strained to the point that, in September of 1937, Wolfe bolted from Scribner's and, on the last day of that year, signed a contract allowing Harper and Brothers to publish his subsequent books.

Between *Look Homeward, Angel* and *Of Time and the River*, Scribner's had published *From Death to Morning* (1935), a collection of Wolfe's short stories, followed by *The Story of a Novel* (1936), a long, detailed lecture he had delivered the year before at the Colorado Writers' Conference.

Wolfe was now working on another large manuscript, essentially a retelling of his first two novels, which were to appear posthumously as *The Web and the Rock* and *You Can't Go Home Again* (1940). In May, 1938, he lectured at Purdue University, after which he left by automobile on a trip through the national parks of the West. In Seattle, he fell ill and then recovered. In September, however, he entered The Johns Hopkins Hospital in Baltimore, where he underwent brain surgery on September 12. He was found to have an incurable miliary tuberculosis of the brain, and he died on September 15, less than a month short of his thirty-eighth birthday.

Aside from the two novels that were published after his death, *The Face of a Nation* (1939), *The Hills Beyond* (1941), *A Stone, a Leaf, a Door* (1945), *Mannerhouse* (1948), and his unrevised *A Western Journal* (first published shortly after his death as "A Western Journey"; published in book form in 1951) have been published, as well as editions of some of his plays and collections of his letters, short novels, and selected works. *The Face of a Nation* reproduces poetic passages from Wolfe's work; *The Hills Beyond* is a collection of his stories that had previously been published in periodicals; *A Stone, a Leaf, a Door* is a collection of his poetry; *Mannerhouse* is a play that Wolfe wrote in the 47 Workshop; and *A Western Journal* is the unrevised notes he made on his final trip in 1938.

### Summary

In retrospect, it is surprising that *Look Homeward, Angel* and Ernest Hemingway's *A Farewell to Arms* (1929) were both the literary sensations of 1929. No two major American authors could have been more different in their approach to their art than Wolfe and Hemingway. Hemingway was the meticulous reviser who turned out a thousand words on a particularly good day; Wolfe was the effusive giant, the "hungry Gulliver," as Pamela Hansford Johnson dubbed him, who in two or three years filled enough ledgers with his writing that the accumulated pile reached to the top of his refrigerator.

Wolfe was trying to define the American experience in much the way that Whitman had tried to do a generation earlier. For Wolfe, defining the American experience was synonymous with defining himself. Consequently, many of his weaknesses—his subjectivity, his effervescent if naïve enthusiasm, his lack of real invention of plot—become his strengths and his hallmarks.

It is impossible to say in what direction Wolfe might have developed literarily had he lived longer. His last two novels leave one with the feeling that he was repeating himself like a broken record. Nevertheless, some of America's finest writing is to be found in his work, and his writing has held much of its popular appeal through the years.

### Bibliography

Everton, Michael. "American Exodus: Movement as Motive and Structure in Thomas Wolfe's *Of Time and the River*." *The Southern Literary Journal* 30, no. 2 (Spring, 1998). The author discusses Thomas Wolfe's attempt to write the definitive American epic and the criticism that it fell short of its mark.

Field, Leslie A., ed. *Thomas Wolfe: Three Decades of Criticism*. London: University of London Press, and New York: New York University Press, 1968. This overview of Wolfe criticism is organized into discussions of major themes, style, specific novels, and short stories. It presents a checklist of Wolfe criticism and includes an important essay by Maxwell Perkins, Wolfe's editor at Scribner's.

Holman, C. Hugh. *The Loneliness at the Core: Studies in Thomas Wolfe*. Baton Rouge: Louisiana State University Press, 1975. Holman provides valuable insights into the catalytic effect that Europe had on Wolfe's writing and thinking. Discusses intelligently Wolfe's problems with point of view.

McElderry, Bruce R., Jr. *Thomas Wolfe*. New York: Twayne, 1964. A straightforward critical biography with a particularly useful annotated bibliography of secondary sources. Contains a brief but helpful consideration of Wolfe's plays and of his short stories.

Magi, Aldo P., and Richard Walser, eds. *Thomas Wolfe Interviewed: 1929-1938*. Baton Rouge: Louisiana State University Press, 1985. A valuable primary resource which reproduces twenty-six newspaper interviews that Wolfe gave between the publication of *Look Homeward, Angel* and his death.

Nowell, Elizabeth. *Thomas Wolfe: A Biography*. New York: Doubleday, 1960; London: Heinemann, 1961. This carefully researched biography is based upon Nowell's 1956 edition of Wolfe's letters and is authoritative though dated.

Reeves, Paschal, ed. *Thomas Wolfe: The Critical Reception*. New York: Lewis, 1974. Reeves presents, in chronological order, reproductions of significant reviews of Wolfe's books as well as assessments published immediately after his death in 1938.

Roberts, Terry. "'By the Wind Grieved': The Poem of 'Look Homeward, Angel.'" *The Southern Literary Journal* 29, no. 1 (Fall 1996). Roberts discusses symbolism in "Look Homeward, Angel."

Rubin, Louis D., Jr. *Thomas Wolfe: The Weather of His Youth*. Baton Rouge: Louisiana State University Press, 1955. Rubin considers the question of autobiography as a fictional form. He also writes of the effect that Wolfe's premonitions of death had on his art.

Walser, Richard. *Thomas Wolfe: An Introduction and Interpretation*. New York: Barnes and Noble, 1961. This brief book follows a chronological order and gives a solid basic understanding of Wolfe to readers not otherwise familiar with him. The illustrations are worthwhile.

*R. Baird Shuman*

# GRANT WOOD

*Born:* February 13, 1891; near Anamosa, Iowa
*Died:* February 12, 1942; Iowa City, Iowa
*Area of Achievement:* Art
*Contribution:* Wood was one of the central figures of Midwestern regionalism, a visual and literary arts movement in the United States during the 1920's and 1930's that emphasized the history, lifestyles, and folkways of specific geographic areas.

## Early Life

Grant Devolson Wood was born to Francis and Hattie (Weaver) Wood on a farm near Anamosa, Iowa. Two years later, Wood's father died, whereupon his mother moved her three sons and one daughter to Cedar Rapids, about twenty-five miles away. As a child, Wood drew and made watercolor studies of birds, flowers, and tree branches with an innate sense of proportion and composition. Upon graduation from Washington High School in 1910, Wood enrolled for two consecutive summers at the Minneapolis School of Design and Handcraft to study design. Such instruction seemed to encourage Wood to continue exploring his interest in landscapes for several years, which was expressed in small-panel oil paintings.

During the next academic year or two, Wood taught various courses at a country school near Cedar Rapids. Nevertheless, he also found time to enroll in a night life-drawing class at the University of Iowa in Iowa City. In 1913 Wood traveled to Chicago, Illinois, worked as designer for Kalo Silversmiths Shop, and then opened his own silversmith business, the Wolund Shop, with a partner. While in Chicago, Wood attended night classes at the School of Art Institute. By 1915, the Wolund Shop had closed, whereupon Wood returned to Cedar Rapids.

The years 1916 through 1918 saw Wood primarily involved in nonart activities, including building a home for his immediate family and enlisting in the United States Army, where his duties included designing artillery camouflage in Washington, D.C. By September, 1919, Wood was again teaching art, this time at Jackson Junior High, a Cedar Rapids public school. In October he showed twenty-three paintings in a two-person exhibit at a Cedar Rapids department store.

The next summer Wood traveled to Europe and painted in and around Paris with fellow Iowa artist Marvin Cone. Rather than seeking formal training or attempting to join the avant-garde artists who lived in Paris, they instead roamed the city searching for subject matter. The resulting sketches and finished compositions recorded unspectacular vignettes of Paris and the countryside around it. The paintings were generally composed with a central focus and painted with large brush strokes and palette-knife work. Returning to the United States that September, Wood began teaching at McKinley High School.

In 1923 Wood returned to France and attended classes at the prestigious Académie Julian in Paris. When not in class, he again painted rather nondescript areas of Paris, certain French provinces, and Belgium. Several works evidenced an interest in medieval portals and doorways in areas such as Brittany. In the fall of 1924, Wood returned to the United States and resumed high school art instruction in Cedar Rapids but retired from it altogether in May, 1925. His goal was to be an independent, full-time artist. He continued painting Iowa landscapes and also created several handsome portraits. There had been no radical shifts or deviations in his work since late adolescence. Instead, Wood's early development seemed to be toward a competent, rather comfortable realism that was respectful of the expectations of his small town and rural Iowa clientele. That viewpoint continued through the 1920's in spite of trips to Europe.

## Life's Work

Another voyage to Europe in 1928 involving a stained-glass window commission unexpectedly precipitated a major stylistic change in Wood's paintings. He traveled to Munich, Germany, where he supervised the creation of a 24-foot by 20-foot window for the American Legion building in Cedar Rapids. While there, Wood visited the city's famous museum collections, where he was captivated by the late Gothic and early Renaissance paintings of Dutch and German artists. Wood was already acquainted with this period in art history by faithfully reading *Craftsman* magazine.

It was not the traditional iconographic content and symbolism that intrigued Wood. Rather, his attention was caught by the highly organized, preplanned, and linear compositions; the symmetrically formal design; the refined figure and landscape elements; and the meticulous details. Of special

note was Wood's awareness that even in this centuries-old art, artists often incorporated city views, landmarks, dress, and other contemporary features—not for illustrative story sensibility but as a matter of integrated form and composition. Soon Wood began to think of ways to introduce pattern and design from his own historical period into his paintings.

In 1929 Wood's portrait work continued with the introduction of thematic elements. *Woman with Plants*, a portrait of the artist's mother, was one of his first attempts at creating a subtle narrative through symbolism as an emulation of the German and Flemish Renaissance masterpieces he had seen in Munich. His mother was rendered with unflattering frankness and spartan but precise description with modest attire (including an apron over a black dress) and weathered face and hands, the latter clutching a plant in a clay pot. The rural landscape presence in this painting and in a similar thematic figurative painting, *Appraisal* (1932), reflected agrarian and small-town living, which became Wood's major area of exploration for the rest of his career.

The best remembered of the thematic portraits evolved into a classic work of American satire—*American Gothic* (1930). It presents a farm couple standing in front of a modest frame house with touches of the Gothic Revival style. The unforgettable imagery is anchored in the foreground, where the scrupulously clean, plain-featured, and plain-dressed couple stands and firmly, resolutely, and quietly returns the viewer's gaze. The thin, small-framed man, bespectacled and balding, wears a dress shirt minus its starched collar, bib overalls, and a dark suit jacket. His right hand grips the handle of an upturned, three-pronged pitchfork. Standing to his right and slightly behind him is a woman both younger and shorter yet equally plain and somber. She is, one assumes, his wife. This woman, with blond, straight hair parted in the middle and gathered at the back, wears a dark dress with a white collar and a cameo brooch at the neckline. The pointed, arched window over the porch roof, divided into three sections by slender, pointed mullions, likewise echoes the three tines of the pitch fork. Together they may refer, in an ironic way, to the Trinity of the Christian faith. Hence, by inference, the image suggests a nonmaterial ethic of hard-working people rooted in an endless agricultural cycle of planting and harvesting complimented by a simple, unwavering, stoic spiritual faith.

*American Gothic* was essentially an overnight success, catapulting Wood into national awareness. His gentle satire and irony, balanced by a nostalgic longing for the Iowa of his youth, found a receptive audience among cosmopolitan viewers. Soon Wood was in demand as a lecturer. He traveled across the nation encouraging regional-based artists to focus upon the indigenous qualities of their areas rather than importing European subjects and mainstream modernism.

Somewhat concurrent with *American Gothic* came Wood's first major landscape painting in his signature manner. *Stone City, Iowa* (1930) depicts an aerial view of a tiny village with a deep vista of rolling hills under a cloudless sky. The viewer is introduced to the artist's summarized, simplified, and regularized hills, trees, and fields, both planted and stacked with hay or cornshocks. The open land is skintight and smooth with peach-like cleavage. The landscape also includes a young corn crop in the lower foreground, the full green foliage of late spring along a river bank, highway windbreaks, and one sizable wooded area. The overall impact is arresting to the point of fantasy. Wood's soft, glowing chiaroscuro painting influenced animated cartoons of the 1940's as well as two background set designs of farm landscapes in the 1939 movie *The Wizard of Oz*. Wood painted many more landscapes with rural life or agricultural themes after *Stone City, Iowa*, all of which were touched by it without becoming thin restatements. Complimenting those paintings was a series of meticulously rendered and masterfully printed lithographs.

Wood's sensitive perception of life was not limited to agriculture and livestock. In 1936, his satirical gifts resulted in a set of commissioned illustrations in charcoal pencil and chalk for a new edition of Sinclair Lewis's 1920 novel *Main Street*. Yet the best-remembered satirical works beyond *American Gothic* tackled several of the myths of American history, namely *Midnight Ride of Paul Revere* (1931), *Daughters of Revolution* (1932), and *Parson Weems' Fable* (1939). In the first painting, Paul Revere rides at breakneck speed through a dark colonial hamlet rousing the citizenry to alarm and action with no concern on the artist's part about whether the event was painted factually. In *Parson Weems' Fable*, young George Washington (with a child's body but an adult head that is probably based upon the Gilbert Stuart portrait on the U.S. one dollar bill) faces his father's wrath after cutting down a young cherry tree. Finally, in *Daughters of*

*Revolution*, three matronly women with rather masculine faces and sober expressions seem to gaze at viewers with skepticism as if the ladies' monthly meeting has been interrupted by an uninvited visitor. They stand in front of a framed print of George Washington's crossing of the Delaware River in advance of his daring raid on the English troops at Trenton, New Jersey.

Despite Wood's stature as a painter in the 1930's the urge to multiply the numbers of regionalist painters led him to cofound the Stone City Colony and Art School and to teach there during the two summers of its existence (1932-1933). Teaching remained part of his life as he was appointed associate professor of fine arts at the University of Iowa in 1934. That year he was also named director of the Public Works of Art Project for Iowa and personally launched two murals for the Iowa State University library in Ames.

In 1935 Wood wrote a lengthy essay called "Revolt against the City," published independently in Iowa City by Frank L. Mott as a pamphlet. Wood's essay formally outlined his primary beliefs in what became known as regionalism and promoted family farm life, local dress, and the landscape of one's region as highly worthwhile materiasl for American art. During the same year, Wood married Sara Maxon (they were divorced four years later) and had important one-person exhibitions in Chicago and New York. About six months after Wood's death in 1942, the Art Institute of Chicago mounted a memorial exhibition for him, which included forty-eight works.

### Summary

Grant Wood is remembered as the Depression-era artist from Iowa who, clad in bib overalls, made paintings and lithographs that extolled and sometimes ribbed rural and small-town life. He emerged as the leading spokesperson for the realistic style called regionalism. The art world of Wood's later years (1930-1942) was increasingly dominated by European modernism. Its exponents considered Wood's art and that of other notable regionalists, such as John Steuart Curry of Kansas and Thomas Hart Benton from Missouri, as regressive and isolationist. By the 1970's, modernism itself had been declared passé, resulting in a postmodern period. Ironically, the last quarter of the twentieth century witnessed the flourishing of regional studies programs in academia that stressed indigenous qualities of America's regions just as Grant Wood had promoted in the 1930's.

### Bibliography

Brinkley, Douglas. "Grant Wood's Road." *American Heritage* 49, no. 7 (November, 1998). This is an essay adapted from the author's book, *The American Heritage New History of the United States,* in which he considers Wood's treatment by the art world since his death.

Corn, Wanda. *Grant Wood, the Regionalist Vision.* New Haven, Conn.: Yale University Press, 1983; London: Yale University Press, 1985. This well-researched exhibition catalogue contains reproduced paintings accompanied by good notes of decent length. Also noteworthy is a thirteen-page section titled "American Gothic: The Making of a National Icon."

Dennis, James M. *Grant Wood: A Study in American Art and Culture.* New York: Viking Press, 1975. A thorough critical study of Wood's development, his major paintings and prints, the rise of regionalism, and his resistance to the mechanization of farming and the creeping standardization of American life. The appendix includes a reprint of Wood's essay "Revolt against the City."

Garwood, Darrell. *Artist in Iowa: A Life of Grant Wood.* New York: Norton, 1944. Surely the first biography of Wood, Garwood's book was published just two years after the artist's death. It is perceptive and well written, filling out the personal forces that shaped the painter.

Jennings, Kate. *Grant Wood.* London: Magna, and New York: Crescent, 1994. A thoughtfully written and exceptionally well-illustrated study keeps this publication from being a slender coffee table book. Contains some rare biographical photographs and source works for Wood's paintings.

Wooden, Howard E. "Grant Wood: A Regionalist's Interpretation of the Four Seasons." *American Artist* 55, no. 588, (July, 1991). The author discusses Grant Wood's values as reflected in his works.

*Tom Dewey II*

# TIGER WOODS

*Born:* December 30, 1975; Cypress, California
*Area of Achievement:* Sports
*Contribution:* Woods has laid the foundation for the sport of golf to open its doors to minorities and has a chance to become the best golfer and ambassador of the game in its history.

## Early Life

Eldrick "Tiger" Woods was born on December 30, 1975, in Cypress, California, to Earl and Kultida Woods. Earl was from Manhattan, Kansas, while Kultida was from Bangkok, Thailand. They were married in 1969 and dreamed of having a child. After six years, the baby boy that Earl thought would never arrive was born. He named his healthy son Tiger in honor of his South Vietnamese Army combat partner Nguyen Phong. Earl had nicknamed Phong "Tiger" for his unrelenting prowess and bravery on the battlefield. In fact, Phong had saved Earl's life several times. It was also during his years in the service that Earl became hooked on golf.

As a toddler, Woods quickly picked up the game of golf, and his father knew from the beginning that he had talent and potential. He soon became a champion golfer, doing exceptionally well in local junior golf tournaments. One of the reasons that Woods succeeded in the sport was the mental toughness that his father gave him. Earl never forced Woods to play; it was always the youngster's choice. His father taught him to take the initiative in the sport and helped him develop the skills and techniques he needed to win in the game. Earl, a great teacher and motivator to Woods, had some impressive qualifications. For instance, Earl's love of baseball enabled him to become the first African American baseball player in the Big Eight Conference, playing for Kansas State University. Later, he began to work on a career as an educator and was a Green Beret in Vietnam. He retired from the Army in 1974.

Woods had two significant coaches during his childhood years. One, of course, was his dad, and the other was Rudy Duran, who was an exceptional golf instructor. Duran coached Woods from the ages of four to ten. Woods's wizardry on the links during his childhood and early teens enabled him to appear on such national television shows as *The Mike Douglas Show*, *That's Incredible*, *The Today Show*, and *Good Morning America*. After gaining the attention of the media at an early age, Woods began gaining the interest of universities by the age of thirteen. Stanford University's golf coach wrote Woods a letter suggesting that maybe someday he would consider playing golf for the university. Woods wrote back and reported that he was thankful for the letter and that he would seriously consider the offer in the future. In the meantime, Woods was planning on going to Western High School in Anaheim, California.

## Life's Work

By the early 1990's Woods was a junior golf phenomenon who had won several junior titles. When he was only sixteen and still in high school, Woods was invited to play in the Los Angeles Open. It was his first Professional Golfers' Association (PGA) tournament, and he became the youngest golfer to play in one. Though he did not win, he rightfully acknowledged that the event was a significant learning tool for him. His experiences in professional golf tournaments as an amateur were, for the most part, uneventful. He did make the cut in some tournaments but usually finished well behind the leaders. The important thing was that he gained knowledge of how the pro game was played, and it gave him the opportunity to learn what he had to work on to take his game to another level.

By the time Woods enrolled at Stanford, he was already a celebrity. One of the major stepping stones to greatness for Woods was becoming the first African American and, at age eighteen, the youngest player in history to win the United States Amateur Championship. He went on to win the championship for three consecutive years. In 1995 Woods made his Masters debut, in which he finished in forty-first place with a score of five over par. He competed in other tour events as an amateur: the United States Open (where he had to withdraw in the second round because of a wrist injury), the Scottish Open, and the British Open. Again, there is no doubt that he came out of these PGA Tour events a much better golfer. Yet Woods seemed to be disassociating himself from Stanford golf. He did not appear to care about the weekly competition in college, just how he could make his game better. After two years, Woods left Stanford and turned professional in August of 1996 at the age of twenty. He was by far the best National Collegiate Athletic Association (NCAA) golfer that the sport had ever seen. He vowed to his par-

ents that he would return to college someday and get his degree.

A little over one month after Woods turned professional, he won his first professional tournament: the Las Vegas Invitational. Just a couple of weeks later, he won again at the Disney Classic in Orlando, Florida. Nobody other than Jack Nicklaus had such a quick impact on the sport. Indeed, his first year as a professional was extraordinary. Beginning in August, he competed in only eight tournaments in 1996 and won two of them. His winnings for all of those tournaments was $790,594, which put him in twenty-fifth place on the PGA Tour money list for 1996. In addition to more calls for autographs and interviews, Woods was soon signing endorsement contracts that were worth millions of dollars.

Unfortunately, one theme that kept following Woods around was racism. The media labeled him the "Great Black Hope" for African Americans in the sport of golf. African Americans felt that Woods offered a chance to finally put an end to the discrimination against them prevalent in the golf world, especially in the American South. Woods was quick to point out that his heritage included not only African American but also Chinese, American Indian, Thai, and Caucasian. The media, however, continued to portray Woods as a black man. Woods, on the other hand, wanted to be known as the best golfer in the history of the sport, not just the best black golfer. Still, some of Woods's fan mail has been littered with racial slurs and remarks that really have no place in or out of the sport. Like a true champion, Woods let his golf game do the talking for him.

The highlight of Woods's young professional career was his victory at the Masters in Augusta, Georgia, on April 13, 1997. On the way to victory, he broke numerous records: He won by a phenomenal twelve strokes, came in with the lowest score ever (270), and finished eighteen under par. At the age of twenty-one, he was also the youngest player ever to win the event. He had dreamed of winning the Masters since he was a child and celebrated the victory with his parents. By winning this prestigious event, Woods perhaps did more for the game of golf than any other player before him. African Americans and other minority groups began playing the game en masse, and Woods became an idol to millions of children who also began playing the sport. He was overwhelmed by the publicity he received, but he had the support and guidance of his parents, his managers, and other star athletes such as Michael Jordan, who reached out to give him much-needed advice on how to handle the situation.

In 1997, Woods also won the GTE Byron Nelson Classic and the Mercedes Championships and signed a whopping $30 million contract with American Express. Woods also set the record for achieving $1 million in winnings faster than any other PGA player by doing so in just nine events (the previous record of twenty-seven had been held by Ernie Els). Although Woods cannot win every golf tournament, he can be a very effective ambassador of the game who reaches out to people of all ages and races. Perhaps, in the long run, this will be his supreme achievement.

### Summary

By the age of twenty-two, Tiger Woods had refined the way golf was played and viewed by the general public. His impact on the sport was swift and immediate. His young career has been nothing short of spectacular, and his achievements have been unmatched by anyone except perhaps Jack Nicklaus. However, even Nicklaus did not have the impact that Woods has had on golf and its fans during his rise to the top. Woods continues to thrill and amaze the galleries that follow him on the links. He influences nearly every youngster who sees him play, and he has helped popularize golf in the United States. Only with time will it be seen to what extent his legend will grow and how far it will reach.

**Bibliography**

Abrahams, Jonathan. "Golden Child or Spoiled Brat." *Golf Magazine* 40, no. 4 (April, 1998). This article discusses the problems Tiger Woods has experienced in adapting to high profile media coverage.

Diaz, Jaime. "Masters Plan." *Sports Illustrated* 88, no. 15 (April 13, 1998). Diaz examines the pressures of success that have started to affect Woods.

Edwards, Nicolas. *Tiger Woods: An American Master*. New York: Scholastic, 1997. Edwards provides a solid account of Woods's life from childhood through his Masters victory. Includes photographs, an assembling of Woods's career highlights, general achievements, and scores of all his tournaments, as well as a glossary of golf terms and addresses of golf-related web sites on the Internet.

Sports Illustrated. *Tiger Woods: The Making of a Champion*. New York: Simon and Schuster, 1996. This book contains a compilation of articles excerpted from the pages of *Sports Illustrated* over the years that cover Woods's rise to golfing stardom. Includes an introduction, photographs, rich commentary, and an epilogue.

Strege, John. *A Biography of Tiger Woods*. New York: Broadway, 1997. This behind-the-scenes look at Woods's rise to the top of the sports world was written by a golf writer and friend of the Woods family. Includes photographs and interesting personal anecdotes from Woods, his parents, and others.

Teague, Allison L. *Prince of the Fairway: The Tiger Woods Story*. Greensboro, N.C.: Avisson Press, 1997. Teague's engaging biography contains a good opening chapter on Woods and the background of his parents. Includes photographs, a chronology of his life, a bibliography, and a glossary of golf terms.

Woods, Earl, with Pete McDaniel. *Training a Tiger: A Father's Guide to Raising a Winner in Both Golf and Life*. New York: HarperCollins, and London: Hodder and Stoughton,1997. This interesting work takes an in-depth and personal view at the training and mental philosophy that went into raising Woods to become a golf champion. Equally important, it shows how parents can teach their kids to play the game correctly and love it at the same time. Includes a foreword by Tiger Woods, photographs, and diagrams.

*David Trevino*

## ROBERT BURNS WOODWARD

*Born:* April 10, 1917; Boston, Massachusetts
*Died:* July 8, 1979; Cambridge, Massachusetts
*Area of Achievement:* Chemistry
*Contribution:* Woodward was the preeminent organic chemist in the postwar United States. Renowned for the total synthesis of complex natural products, for more than thirty years he achieved syntheses of unparalleled creativeness and elegance.

### Early Life

Robert Burns Woodward was the only child born to Margaret Burns and Arthur Chester Woodward. His father died in October of 1918 at the age of thirty-three. His mother was a native of Glasgow, Scotland, and claimed descent from the poet Robert Burns. Young Woodward grew up in Quincy, near Boston, and attended its public schools. Chemistry attracted him from an early age, although he was vague on what started the interest. He indulged in this hobby in a home laboratory, fascinated from the start by the beauty of molecular structures. A gifted child, Woodward skipped grades three times, which enabled him to enroll at the Massachusetts Institute of Technology in 1933 at the age of sixteen. Possessing a staggering amount of chemical knowledge, he earned a Ph.D. from MIT within four years.

Woodward's experiences at MIT were not positive at first. The slow pace of the curriculum led to boredom and inattention to his studies, to such an extent that he was requested not to return for his sophomore year. Some of the faculty, however, recognized his unusual capabilities and arranged a reinstatement which allowed him to forgo all requirements and class attendance as long as he took the course examinations. This unusual arrangement enabled him to devise his own program and take as many as fifteen courses in a semester. Furthermore, he requested laboratory space, then permitted only for graduate students; the faculty agreed to consider this if he would supply a list of experiments. His list was so original that he was given his own laboratory for the remainder of his stay at MIT. His attendance at a lecture inspired his doctoral dissertation the professor was discussing the difficulties in synthesizing a sex hormone. Woodward, at the end of the lecture, showed the professor at the blackboard how it might be done.

After a brief period in 1937 as instructor at the University of Illinois, Woodward returned to Boston, rising from Harvard University instructor to full professor in 1950, Morris Loeb Professor of Chemistry in 1953, and Donner Professor of Science in 1960, the latter position freeing him from lecturing.

Woodward was married twice, to Irja Pullman, whom he had known for many years, in 1938, and to Eudoxia Muller, a Polaroid consultant, in 1946; there were two children from each marriage. His passion for chemistry and his habit of pursuing it during all hours of the day and night made him difficult to live with, and both marriages ended in divorce.

Woodward was a tall, powerfully built man, very neat and well-groomed, his daily attire being a dark blue suit and a plain, light-blue necktie. He was addicted to puzzles and games and enjoyed being the life of a party, taking great pleasure as a storyteller. He developed a deep interest in literature of all types, especially biography. Woodward was an inveterate smoker and a heavy drinker of whiskey. From his youth onward, he normally slept only three hours a day. This ability to do without sleep, coupled with his incessant smoking and heavy consumption of alcohol, led him to believe that he was different from other people and would not be subject to the frailties of his fellowmen. A lone wolf throughout his life, he made few intimate friends, and, despite appearances, he was a very lonely human being.

### Life's Work

When Woodward began his research at Harvard, synthetic organic chemistry had major limitations. Chemists were still using the same techniques of separation and purification of natural products as had chemists of 1890. To obtain a total synthesis of a natural product was an enormous challenge, especially with the lack of control over the essential three-dimensional arrangement of atoms in space (stereochemistry). Yet Woodward chose to specialize in this realm of naturally occurring animal and plant substances because it was one of endless fascination and unlimited opportunities.

Woodward's success lay in combining two contemporary developments in chemistry. An instrumental revolution was taking place during his research career, with ultraviolet, infrared, and nuclear magnetic resonance spectroscopy coming into general use by chemists as well as novel methods of chromatography for the separation and purification of substances. He combined these and other tools of the instrumental revolution with a master plan based on theoretical developments involving electronic reaction mechanisms. He could determine theoretically how chemical bonds form, break, and rearrange, and the stereochemical configurations which would result, and envisage the entire synthetic route before any laboratory work was done. In this way, Woodward made organic synthesis into both an art of creative planning and design and an experimental science involving hard, tedious laboratory work. A typical Woodward synthesis was noted for its planning. In the execution of the plan, he rarely took a physical part. His reputation assured him of coworkers of high quality; his role was to direct and inspire them.

The revolution in organic synthesis was first announced in 1944 when Woodward, along with another brilliant young chemist, William Doering, synthesized the antimalarial drug quinine. It was important enough to make page one of *The New York Times*, since it was part of the World War II effort to find quinine substitutes. (Natural quinine came from cinchona tree bark and the plantations were in Japanese control.) Woodward and Doering achieved the synthesis in fourteen months, starting with a common coal-tar derivative, and showed what could be done with an original plan, the mapping of every step, and resourceful experimental work.

Following the quinine synthesis, Woodward turned to another important wartime project: penicillin, then a strategic material desperately needed to combat infections. In 1945, he was the first to propose, defend, and show the consequences of the fused ring structure basic to all penicillins. He continued to make important contributions to antibiotic research over the years. He investigated the broad spectrum antibiotics terramycin and aureomycin following their discovery, establishing the complete structures of these tetracyclic molecules by 1952.

After the war, Woodward continued to pursue problems of structure determination and synthesis. In 1947, he solved the structure of the complex natural poison strychnine in a brilliant interpretation of an array of experimental data and transformations. He also synthesized strychnine in 1954; it was one of several important syntheses of alkaloid drugs.

Woodward made headlines again in 1951 with the first total synthesis of a natural steroid. After sixteen months of hard work, involving twenty steps from a coal-tar derivative, he obtained the steroid nucleus, which, since many steroids had already been interconverted, represented a synthesis of many of them, such as cortisone and cholesterol. *Time* and *Newsweek* featured stories and interviews with him. Cortisone, made with difficulty from oxbile, was scarce and expensive. His synthesis was from relatively cheap coal tar and promised an abundance of the antiarthritis drug. Woodward tried to dampen the enthusiasm; his was only a laboratory synthesis. In fact, his feat was practical, and cortisone came to be provided to arthritis sufferers in synthetic form.

While most of his synthetic work concerned natural products, Woodward made important contributions to other areas. In 1952, in one of his most inspired insights, he revealed the structure of dicyclopentadienyl iron or "ferrocene," as he named it. Discovered in 1951, its nature was intensely debated, and Woodward daringly proposed the famed sandwich structure of an atom of iron sandwiched between two cyclopentadienyl rings. This was a new type of organometallic substance and the basis of a new class of molecules having unique pi electron binding. (Pi bonding refers to modern molecular orbital theory in organic chemistry.)

One brilliant synthesis after another marked the 1950's. Woodward followed the 1954 synthesis of lysergic acid, the basis for the hallucinogenic drug LSD, with a masterful synthesis in 1956 of reserpine—the first of the tranquilizing drugs. The reserpine synthesis stood out for its complete stereospecificity and high yield; it was the most elegant synthesis ever achieved and, as with cortisone, so well done that his plan could be adapted to commercial production.

Woodward kept reaching for higher levels of complexity and took on the challenge of chlorophyll, the green pigment in plants responsible for the conversion of solar energy into the basic materials of life. The synthesis took four years (1956-1960) of work by his dedicated research group of Harvard graduate students and postdoctoral fellows.

The year 1965 was noteworthy for two developments. The first was his winning the Nobel Prize "for his outstanding achievement in the art of organic synthesis." The wording is significant; the honor was not only for the synthesis of natural products but also for the distinctive way that the synthesis was achieved. Interestingly, in his address on receiving the prize, Woodward did not reflect on his past accomplishments but used the occasion to illuminate the "art" of synthesis by reporting on his latest work, the synthesis of the antibiotic cephalosporin C.

The cephalosporin work was not done at Harvard, for in 1963 he acquired a second research group with the creation of the Woodward Research Institute in Basel, Switzerland, by Ciba Limited, with Woodward as director; like Harvard, it became a center of impressive achievements.

Also in 1965 came what may have been Woodward's most significant contribution to organic chemistry. He was deeply interested in theoretical chemistry and had published in this area from time to time. With a distinguished collaborator, Roald Hoffmann (a Cornell professor and Nobel Prize winner in 1981), Woodward disclosed a new principle, the conservation of orbital symmetry. This discovery has been quoted more frequently than anything else he published. The conception came out of his synthetic work in which some puzzling stereochemical phenomena appeared. Baffled, he and Hoffmann eventually realized that something fundamental was behind the unexpected results. The explanation was the conservation of orbital symmetry, a quantum mechanical description of chemical bonding and reactivity, extending it to the course and stereochemistry of organic reactions and allowing for the prediction of both the way a reaction would proceed and the stereochemistry of the products. This principle stands as one of the most basic theoretical advances in the history of organic chemistry and almost immediately changed profoundly the thinking of chemists.

The most formidable problem undertaken by Woodward was the total synthesis of vitamin B12; its complexity was greater than anything he had ever encountered. With another collaborator, Albert Eschenmoser of Zurich, and about one hundred coworkers, Woodward devised a strategy involving a pyrotechnic display of appearing and disappearing rings with the vitamin appearing at the end of an eleven-year hunt in 1972.

Woodward never stopped working; there were always more challenges. From his Basel group came the synthesis of a prostaglandin in 1973, a member of the relatively new and fascinating class of biologically active substances. He even joined with Hoffman after a ten-year interval in an attempt to design some molecular systems with novel conducting properties, a new field to both men and testimony to his versatility. At the time of his death following a heart attack at his Cambridge home, he was planning the synthesis of another antibiotic.

In addition to the achievements which appeared in his publications, Woodward's lectures and seminars were a major source of influence. He held lectureships worldwide, and few scientists could match the elegance, precision, and great artistic quality of his talks at the blackboard, with formulas and reaction sequences outlined in a unique graphic style that produced both clarity and aesthetic satisfaction. Every presentation was dramatic, creative, and lucid. Woodward enjoyed the attention that he commanded, relishing holding an audience enthralled for hours.

By the end of his life, Woodward had become the most honored American scientist in history. In addition to the Nobel Prize, there was the National Medal of Science presented by President Johnson in 1964 and some thirty international awards, including the Pius XI Gold Medal of the Pontifical

Academy of Sciences (1961) and the Order of the Rising Sun from Japan (1970). Some twenty-five universities in North America, Europe, Asia, and Australia awarded him honorary degrees and almost all major scientific societies made him an honorary member. In 1979, in the announcement of his death released by Harvard, Woodward was described as "the greatest organic chemist of modern times."

### Summary

Woodward's mastery of all available physical, instrumental, and theoretical methods guided him through the pathways of organic reactions and his astonishing array of achievements. He combined the three major strands in modern organic chemistry, the structural and synthetic, the physical and theoretical, and the instrumental, and set new standards of quality with his syntheses and structural elucidations of complex natural products. He taught others how to think and plan in detail; he taught theoreticians how to interact with experimentalists in the quest for solutions. Woodward represented a new generation of organic chemists who combined the best of modern theoretical and experimental methods in highly original and creative ways to solve incredibly complex and difficult problems.

### Bibliography

Dolphin, David. "Robert Burns Woodward: Three Score Years and Then?" *Heterocycles* 7 (December, 1977): 29-35. This issue of a Japanese journal was dedicated to Woodward on the occasion of his sixtieth birthday. Dolphin, a former student, gives a more detailed picture of the man, his character and habits, than does any other essay.

Nobelstiftelsen, Stockholm. *Chemistry*. New York: Elsevier, 1972. This volume includes the brief speech that accompanied the presentation of the Nobel Prize to Woodward; a biographical sketch; and the full text of Woodward's lecture at the Nobel Prize ceremony.

Ollis, W. D. "Robert Burns Woodward—An Appreciation." *Chemistry in Britain* 16 (April, 1980): 210-216. Ollis, another former associate, gives the most lucid scientific account of Woodward's researches in all major areas of endeavor.

Tarbell, D. Stanley. "Organic Chemistry: The Past 100 Years." *Chemical and Engineering News* 54 (April 6, 1976): 110-123. This is an excellent account of the development of organic chemistry in the United States, considering Woodward's predecessors and contemporaries, the development of methods and instruments, and how Woodward used these as well as what was novel and important about his work.

Todd, Lord Alexander R., and Sir John Cornforth. "Robert Burns Woodward." *Biographical Memoirs of Fellows of the Royal Society of London* 27 (1981); 629-695. The only extensive study of Woodward. It contains listings of appointments, medals and awards, honorary degrees, and society memberships, and a seven-page bibliography of his 196 publications. Todd wrote the biographical section, and Cornforth wrote an analysis of the scientific work. While the biographical section is suitable reading for the layman, the scientific analysis part is probably too difficult for most readers.

Wassermann, Harry H. "Profile and Scientific Contributions of Professor R. B. Woodward." *Heterocycles* 7 (December, 1977): 1-28. Like the Dolphin entry, this article appeared in a Japanese journal, in an issue dedicated to Woodward. Includes a bibliography and lists of awards and achievements comparable to those provided in the Royal Society article, as well as a coherent description of Woodward's accomplishments.

*Albert B. Costa*

## VIRGINIA WOOLF

*Born:* January 25, 1882; London, England
*Died:* March 28, 1941; near Rodmell, Sussex, England
*Area of Achievement:* Literature
*Contribution:* Woolf contributed significantly to prose fiction through her experiments with stream of consciousness and characterization; she also influenced critical thought through her analytical essays and reviews.

### Early Life

Virginia Woolf was born on January 25, 1882, into a Victorian world and family. The third child and second daughter of Leslie and Julia Stephen, she was reared in an environment of many people and many privileges. Both her parents had been married before and widowed; therefore, the household consisted not only of Virginia and her two full brothers and sister but also of Leslie's daughter, Laura, who was retarded, and Julia's children, George, Stella, and Gerald Duckworth.

Leslie and Julia Stephen, though not rich, were nevertheless financially comfortable and well connected. Leslie, who had been a don at Cambridge, moved to London in his mid-thirties and became editor of a significant literary journal and eventually wrote an important work on the history of English thought. Additionally, he edited and contributed to the *Dictionary of National Biography*, a project that established him as one of the leading intellectuals of England. Julia was known for her remarkable physical beauty as well as her attractive and nurturing character. Together, Leslie and Julia created what Virginia later described as a happy childhood for their large family. When Julia died, however, that existence ended for Virginia, and her father's domineering personality shaped the household and molded Virginia's character, in a mostly painful fashion.

Following Julia's death, Virginia suffered her first bout with mental illness. Approximately ten years later, following her father's death and sexual attention from her half brother George, she suffered her second nervous breakdown and also attempted to kill herself by jumping from a window. Her pattern of mental imbalance was thus established by the time she and her full brothers and sister moved to a house in the Bloomsbury section of London.

Photographs of Virginia Woolf during this time and later reveal an elegant woman, graceful, tall, and fragile, a reflection of her mother's intense physical beauty. Despite this attractiveness, which included deep-set eyes and an ethereal presence, Woolf never saw herself in that light, believing instead that she was unattractive. Uncomfortable with herself in that respect, she was nevertheless unselfconscious about her ability to converse with people, and she became one of the most famous conversationalists of London, entertaining people with her wit, provocative questions, and fantastic stories.

Because of these qualities, Woolf was an integral part of what came to be known as the Bloomsbury Group, which included Lytton Strachey, the biographer; John Maynard Keynes, the economist; Roger Fry, the art critic; and novelist E. M. Forster, who once called Woolf the Invalid Lady of Bloomsbury. Both admired and condemned by their contemporaries, this group of gifted individuals earned the reputation for being bohemian intellectuals who, in the words of their friend Stephen Spender, nourished themselves "on a diet of the arts, learning, amusement, travel, and good living." Their relationships with one another and with Woolf became a significant part of her life and her literature.

### Life's Work

The year 1917 was an important one for Woolf, ushering in her time of literary activity. After several painful years, during which Woolf suffered from extreme depression and found herself unable to write in the way she was coming to expect from herself, she resumed contributing reviews to the *Times Literary Supplement* and began to write a diary which is now considered one of her major works. In 1917, Woolf and her husband, Leonard, whom she had married in 1912, also founded The Hogarth Press, which published Virginia Woolf's novels and the works of other significant contemporaries, including T. S. Eliot. The Woolfs and Virginia herself were assuming a leadership role in the London literary world.

The first novel published by The Hogarth Press was Woolf's *Jacob's Room*, in 1922. While that book suggested some of the technical virtuosity that was to be her hallmark and contribution to modern literature, it was her subsequent work, particularly that written in the second half of the 1920's, that most critics consider to be her greatest. The novels *Mrs. Dalloway* (1925) and *To the Lighthouse* (1927) reveal Woolf's concern with lit-

erary experimentation and characterization, and her critical essays collected in the first series of *The Common Reader* (1925) demonstrate her interest in not only writing literature but also writing about it. Still another dimension of her remarkable literary output during this time was *A Room of One's Own* (1929), a series of lectures Woolf had delivered during which she made the famous comment that, to be a writer, a woman must have five hundred pounds and a room of her own.

During the 1930's, Woolf was extremely well-known, enjoyed great prestige, and was offered many honors for her contributions to the world of letters. She continued to write novels, despite her persistent bouts with mental illness, publishing *The Waves* (1931), *Flush: A Biography* (1933), and *The Years* (1937), and she also produced an important feminist long essay, *Three Guineas* (1938). Following each publication, she was besieged by severe depression, and after writing her last book, *Between the Acts* (1941), she committed suicide, on March 28, by drowning herself in the River Ouse.

### Summary

Virginia Woolf's relationship to the Victorian and modern eras is dramatized by her chronology: She was born in 1882, and she died in 1941. Her literary life was spent in reacting against the nineteenth century, into which she was born, and in ushering in the twentieth century, during which she lived most of her life. In one of her most famous statements, she said that on or about December, 1910, human nature had changed, and she spent her literary career exploring and depicting that change.

In her essays she attacked what she called the "materialism" of novelists such as Arnold Bennett, H. G. Wells, and John Galsworthy, who, in her view, adhered to the traditional form of the novel and emphasized externals instead of the inner life of the self. She called for a new kind of literature that explored the consciousness through new techniques which recognized the complexities and aberrations of the psyche.

Woolf's best novels demonstrate the ways in which she translated this theory into practice through her use of the "stream of consciousness" technique. *Mrs. Dalloway, To the Lighthouse*, and *Between the Acts* rely upon interior monologues and a prose style that re-creates the mental processes of the characters, usually with rhythms and images of lyric poetry. The books thus emphasize the disjointed, illogical quality of the mental-emotional life, and replicate, rather than describe, that quality.

Concerned with questions of identity, relationships, time, change, and human personality, Virginia Woolf helped shape literary history by writing about, for, and of the modern mind in the modern world.

### Bibliography

Beja, Morris, ed. *Critical Essays on Virginia Woolf.* Boston: Hall, 1985. This collection is divided into two sections: reviews of Woolf's major works and essays on Woolf's art and artistic vision. The various interpretations reflect the editor's premise that Virginia Woolf, though claimed by several ages and schools of criticism, was unique and thus cannot be pigeonholed in any specific way.

Bell, Quentin. *Virginia Woolf: A Biography.* 2 vols. London: Hogarth Press, and New York: Harcourt Brace, 1972. Written by Virginia Woolf's nephew, this definitive biography is based upon Woolf's memoirs, journals, and correspondence. While it is invaluable for its storehouse of information, it says little about Woolf's fiction and the ways in which her life and work were interrelated.

Bennett, Joan. *Virginia Woolf: Her Art as a Novelist.* Cambridge: Cambridge University Press, and New York: Harcourt Brace, 1945. Though a slim volume, this book offers a useful overview of Woolf's innovations and her continuity with tradition. Chapters on Woolf's fictional techniques are followed by chapters on her contributions to nonfiction through *A Writer's Diary* (1953) and her many critical essays.

Bloom, Harold, ed. *Virginia Woolf.* New York: Chelsea House, 1986. This volume is a collection of essays and excerpts ranging from 1951 to the time of the book's publication. Arranged chronologically, the volume offers various interpretations of Woolf's work, including the editor's introduction, with its discussion of Woolf's aesthetic ideas and several essays which offer feminist interpretations of Woolf's novels.

Goldman, Jane. *The Feminist Aesthetics of Virginia Woolf: Modernism, Post-Impressionism, and the Politics of the Visual.* Cambridge and New York: Cambridge University Press, 1998. The author considers Virginia Woolf's work from a feminist perspective.

———. *Virginia Woolf--To the Lighthouse, The Waves.* Duxford, Cambridgeshire: Icon, 1997; New York: Columbia University Press, 1998. Goldman considers two of Woolf's works and examines the critical reception to both along with Woolf's own thoughts on them.

Gordon, Lyndall. *Virginia Woolf: A Writer's Life.* Oxford and New York: Oxford University Press, 1984. In this biography, Gordon looks not only at Woolf's life in Bloomsbury but also at her works, including the unfinished memoirs, the drafts of novels, and some lesser-known and unpublished pieces. Divides Woolf's life into three phases: her childhood, her time of literary apprenticeship and recurring illness, and her mature period of artistic achievement.

Guiguet, Jean. *Virginia Woolf and Her Works.* London: Hogarth Press, and New York: Harcourt Brace, 1965. This book begins with a study of Woolf's world, the cultural milieu which shaped her and within which she wrote. It then focuses on specific works, beginning with the nonfiction and working through the novels, stories and sketches, and biographies. The final section considers basic problems Woolf faced in her search for a new literary form.

Marcus, Jane, ed. *Virginia Woolf: A Feminist Slant.* Lincoln: University of Nebraska Press, 1983. In this second volume of feminist essays (the first, *New Feminist Essays on Virginia Woolf*, was published in 1981 and was also edited by Marcus), the diversity within the discipline of feminist scholarship is apparent. The editor writes about Woolf's aunt, Caroline Emelia Stephen; Louise De Salvo explores Virginia Stephen at fifteen; Emily Jensen examines the lesbian content of *Mrs. Dalloway;* and other essays consider still more diverse aspects of Woolf's life and works.

Rose, Phyllis. *Woman of Letters: A Life of Virginia Woolf.* London: Routledge, and New York: Oxford University Press, 1978. In this biography, Rose assumes a feminist perspective, asserting that Woolf's feminism was the crux of her life and literature. Explores in great detail Woolf's recurrent bouts with madness.

*Marjorie Smelstor*

# FRANK LLOYD WRIGHT

*Born:* June 8, 1867; Richland Center, Wisconsin
*Died:* April 9, 1959; Phoenix, Arizona
*Area of Achievement:* Architecture
*Contribution:* Strongly individualistic, flamboyant, and arrogant, Wright designed and built more than four hundred structures which reflect his architectural genius. Wright, directly and indirectly, heavily influenced twentieth century architecture with his diverse use of geometry in his designs.

## Early Life

The life of one of America's most eccentric, dramatic personalities began simply enough on June 8, 1867, when Frank Lloyd Wright was born in the small town of Richland Center, Wisconsin, the eldest of three children born to William C. Wright, a Baptist preacher, and his young wife, Anna Lloyd-Jones. After his parents were divorced in 1885, Wright was reared by his mother, and he sustained a close relationship with her during her lifetime. Anna Wright's use of the Froebel kindergarten method, which introduced children to pure geometric forms and their patterns on grids, provided Wright with the foundations of sophisticated geometric design so evident in his later architecture.

Wright grew up in a rather comfortable, middle-class home during the 1870's and 1880's. With the hope of studying at the University of Wisconsin, he moved to Madison in 1885, seeking part-time employment and admission to the university. A local contractor took Wright on as an apprentice, and he worked his way up to construction supervisor within two years. At the same time, Wright took engineering and graphics courses in 1886, his only year at the university. To further his architectural apprenticeship and training, Wright left Madison in 1887 for Chicago, where he secured a position with a family friend, the successful residential architect, Joseph Lyman Silsbee.

Wright's position with Silsbee exposed him to the architects who were transforming Chicago in the 1880's. With Silsbee's permission, he soon took on his own commissions and gained confidence as a residential architect. In 1888, he moved to the firm of Adler and Sullivan, where he was given the firm's home designs. This position introduced him to Louis H. Sullivan, the most innovative and influential architect of Chicago at the time, and established Wright's talents as an architect specializing in houses. He collaborated with Sullivan on the seminal Transportation Building for the 1893 Chicago World's Fair, a design which testified to the innovative talent of each man. As Wright's position became more secure, he married and built a home for his new wife in the Chicago suburb of Oak Park, Illinois, where he lived until the marriage dissolved in 1909.

In 1893, at the age of twenty-six, Wright left the firm of Adler and Sullivan and established a full-time private practice. The break with Sullivan was uneasy, especially because Sullivan had developed a close personal relationship with Wright, treating him as a son. Wright, however, had learned all he could from Sullivan by the early 1890's and believed that the time was right to launch his own independent career.

## Life's Work

As he began his independent career, Wright had an established reputation as an excellent domestic architect. From 1893 to 1910, he created many houses in the prairie-house style, an amalgam of Japa-

nese and American influences. A style which he perfected, the prairie house epitomized Wright's perspective of America, which was rooted deeply in the nineteenth century. In contrast to crowded urban Europe, America's was an open, expanding society. Wright believed that American architecture should reflect that environment of the frontier, of an abundance of land; thus, he created homes with strong horizontal shapes, with large roof overhangs, and with a dynamic asymmetry to create a sense of the horizon, of motion, and of spaciousness. His interior designs, influenced by the Japanese style of large open spaces using modular units, called for expansive central rooms, few closed corners, ample windows, and a geometric emphasis in the rooms' decor. For the most part, the exterior of Wright's prairie houses was unadorned, although he often created an ornate entranceway in homes otherwise characterized by bold simplicity. To complete the dramatic design, Wright integrated the house into the landscape so that the building seemed to grow out of the ground and to belong on its site.

One of the best extant examples of Wright's prairie-house style is the Robie House (1909), adjacent to the University of Chicago. This red-brick-and-stone structure contains many innovations which were pioneering techniques and designs in American domestic architecture. Features Wright used in the prototype prairie house included the casement window, the corner window, cathedral ceilings, built-in furniture and lighting, a concrete slab foundation with radiant heat, and the carport. Many of these ideas appeared in mass housing almost a half century after Wright incorporated them as trademarks of his successful prairie style.

Wright's professional success in the first decade of the twentieth century, with more than 140 houses and buildings to his credit, did not translate into a successful home life. In 1909, as had his father before him, he abandoned his wife and family and traveled in Europe with Mamah Borthwick Cheney, the wife of a former client. Europeans were beginning to discover Wright at that time, and he and his new companion escaped much of the scandal in the United States over their affair by remaining in Europe for more than a year. Upon their return to the United States, Wright settled at Spring Green, Wisconsin, near his birthplace, and built Taliesin ("shining brow" in Welsh) for himself and for Cheney. Professionally, Wright fell from favor as a domestic architect, obtaining fewer commissions and enduring the continuing scandal about his personal life. Although he continued to receive commercial projects, his overall work declined. In 1914, personal tragedy struck when a newly hired chef murdered Mamah Cheney and six other occupants of the Wright home and set fire to Taliesin. Shattered emotionally and physically, Wright secluded himself in the remains of Taliesin. Fortunately, a major commission abroad took him away from Wisconsin and its tragedy.

Wright's design of Tokyo's Imperial Hotel enhanced his reputation as an architectural genius. This large-scale project kept him in Japan for much of the time from 1915 to the hotel's completion in 1922. Forgoing the striking simplicity of his prairie-house designs, Wright devised an intricate, ornate, complex building in Tokyo. Because of earthquake danger, the hotel he designed consisted of many independent sections which could move separately. Each floor was suspended from a center post, or cantilever. When a major earthquake struck Tokyo in 1923 and Wright's Imperial Hotel was one of the few buildings to suffer no damage, he gained even greater esteem in architectural circles.

The 1920's were unhappy times for Wright. A second and short-lived marriage failed; another fire at Taliesin in 1925 further sapped his dwindling finances. Although he received a few commissions each year in that decade, Wright turned to writing and to addressing his personal problems in the 1920's. Late in the era, partly to raise revenue and partly to direct his creative energies, he established the Taliesin Fellowship. There, under Wright's direction, students would develop their creative energies through craftsmanship and physical labor on the land.

The stock-market crash of 1929 and the resultant Depression of the 1930's also took its toll on Wright and his finances. Potential commissions were cancelled, and Wright, never very careful about money, was more deeply in debt. Yet his work and personal life did improve. His successful marriage, in 1928, to Olgivanna (Olga Milanoff Hinzenberg) steadied his domestic world.

Four major projects of the 1930's reconfirmed his originality and leading position among American architects: the Kaufmann House (1936), the Johnson Wax Company headquarters buildings (1936-1937, 1947-1950), Taliesin West (1938), and the Usonian houses.The Kaufmann house, also known as Fallingwater, was prairie-house architecture at its most dramatic. Built over a waterfall in the mountains of southern Pennsylvania, this multilevel residence, daring in design and spectacular in setting, consisted of several cantilevered balconies in a building of stone, concrete, and glass.

Equally dramatic and unique is the Johnson Wax Company headquarters complex in Racine, Wisconsin. An administration building with surfaces supported by thin disc-topped pillars, it mirrored Wright's growing interest in continuity and plasticity. With the research tower, Wright demonstrated his structural solution for the skyscraper in an organic way, patterning his design of brick and opaque-glass walls and cantilevered floors after a tree with a solid trunk and several supporting branches, thus avoiding the rigid rectilinear forms of the standard skyscraper design pioneered by Ludwig Mies Van Der Rohe.

Taliesin West, begun in 1938, was Wright's winter headquarters near Scottsdale, Arizona. A building of stone, concrete, redwood, and canvas, this desert home conveyed the essence of Wright's organic architecture, with its use of natural materials and its low profile in the arid landscape. With the simplicity and boldness he used at Fallingwater, Wright had created another dramatic addition to an attractive natural setting with Taliesin West.

The Usonian houses, introduced in the late 1930's and named for the United States, were modest versions of the prairie-house style. Usually one story with a concrete-slab foundation and carport, these homes influenced suburban tract architecture for at least two decades. Horizontal in profile, with walls and spaces based on modular construction, the Usonian design provided owners with efficient, economical, and easily maintained homes.

After World War II, Wright came into his own again in the United States. Americans recognized his genius and his daring; by the 1950's, he was a popular, though eccentric, hero. From 1939 to 1945, he moved away from the horizontal motif to the circle and spiral as signatures of his work. The most famous of these structures is the Solomon R. Guggenheim Museum (1956-1959) on New York's Fifth Avenue. Its circular form and concrete construction reaffirm Wright's interest, late in his life, in continuous shapes and plastic forms. Wright, now in his eighties, delighted in eccentricity, drama, flamboyance, and unconventionality; yet he continued his prolific output even in his senior years. When he died from complications following surgery in a Phoenix hospital on April 9, 1959, he had built in his long lifetime more than four hundred homes and other buildings which carried the Wright hallmark of originality, drama, and innovation.

### Summary

Frank Lloyd Wright was America's most creative architect. His artistic genius is evident in the variety of styles he created, from the horizontal prairie house to the plastic, circular forms of his last works. Rooted in the nineteenth century, Wright perceived an America of unlimited opportunity, abundant land, and strong individualism. His buildings, in harmony with nature, made of natural materials with dramatic and dynamic designs, mirrored the energy, youth, and promise of a democratic American society.

Never conventional, usually eccentric and flamboyant, and strongly individualistic, Wright influenced hundreds of architects through his designs and his Taliesin Fellowship program. Although his disciples seldom replicated his originality and genius, they and other designers did learn from Wright's examples the diversity and potential of architecture and its relationship to the larger culture of American society. At a time when many other architects were relying on European influences or historical styles, Wright was enclosing and defining space in unique and artistic ways, far in advance of the conventions of his time. His buildings had the distinctive mark of newness in a New World and of the spirit of individual creativity he hoped to nurture in the United States.

Like many men of great talent, Wright experienced an unsettled personal life. Extravagance and indebtedness were twin conditions for him. Failed marriages, unconventional behavior, and tragedy marred his private world. His uncompromising nature, outspokenness, and arrogance cost him popular acclaim throughout much of his life. Only in the last decade of his life did Americans claim him warmly as a distinguished citizen.

Wright's legacy of more than four hundred structures is a testament to his genius and prodigious talent. Ironically, the modern flavor of Wright's works owed more to his nineteenth century attitudes about the United States than to the twentieth century urban, industrial country which embraced them. Yet, more than any other American architect, he has left a tangible record of buildings that defy the conventional, that remain fresh and vital years after their construction, and that anticipated many building innovations and designs considered modern long after he introduced them.

**Bibliography**

Blake, Peter. *Frank Lloyd Wright: Architecture and Space*. Baltimore: Penguin, 1964. Excellent brief treatment of Wright's life and work. Serves as a very good introduction to Wright's architecture.

Brooks, H. Allen. *The Prairie School: Frank Lloyd Wright and His Midwestern Contemporaries*. Toronto: University of Toronto Press, 1971. A thorough treatment of Wright and his influence in domestic architecture, especially the derivative prairie-style houses in the United States.

———. ed. *Writings on Wright*. Cambridge, Mass.: MIT Press, 1981. Selected comments on Wright's work and life by his contemporaries, by his clients, by Europeans, and by later evaluators. Provides a fascinating portrait of Wright through others' thoughts and words.

Heinz, Thomas A. *Frank Lloyd Wright Field Guide*. Vols. 1-3. London: Academy, 1996; New York: Wiley, 1999. These guides provide information on all of Wright's buildings, his planned, but unexecuted sites, and razed structures. All include maps of the sites, directions to them, information on accessibility and available tours.

Jencks, Charles. *Modern Movements in Architecture*. 2d ed. London and New York: Penguin, 1985. Jencks puts Wright in the context of modern architecture.

Kaufmann, Edgar, and Ben Raeburn, eds. *Frank Lloyd Wright: Writings and Buildings*. New York: New American Library, 1960. One of several books reprinting Wright's own writings. Well illustrated with a map showing the location of his buildings in the United States.

Russell, James S. "One of Frank Lloyd Wright's Great Visions, Monona Terrace, is Transformed and Opens after 50 Tumultuous Years." *Architectural Record* 186, no. 3 (March, 1998). Russell discusses the completion of Wright's project—the Monona Terrace Conference and Convention Center—38 years after the architect's death.

Storrer, William A. *The Architecture of Frank Lloyd Wright: A Complete Catalog*. 17th ed. Newark, N.J.: WAS, 1997. The most complete photographic and descriptive catalog of Wright's buildings; includes locator map, listing by state, and alphabetical index.

Twombly, Robert C. *Frank Lloyd Wright: His Life and His Architecture*. New York and London: Wiley, 1979. A first-rate biography of Wright; well illustrated.

Wright, Frank Lloyd. *An Autobiography*. New York: Duell Sloan, 1943; London: Faber, 1945. A rather unconventionally written autobiography which gives the reader a sense of Wright's distinctive personality and character.

*Harry J. Eisenman*

# WILBUR WRIGHT and ORVILLE WRIGHT

## Wilbur Wright

*Born:* April 16, 1867; near Millville, Indiana *Died:* May 30, 1912; Dayton, Ohio

## Orville Wright

*Born:* August 19, 1871; Dayton, Ohio *Died:* January 30, 1948; Dayton, Ohio

*Area of Achievement:* Invention

*Contribution:* The Wright brothers invented the first practical manned powered aircraft, thereby initiating the Air Age.

### Early Lives

The Wrights belonged to a sturdy Midwestern family of five children. Wilbur and Orville were the third and fourth boys, respectively; their younger sister, Katherine, was the only girl. Their father, the Reverend Milton Wright of the Evangelical United Brethren Church in Christ, had a large personal library, particularly of scientific and mechanical books. Their mother, née Susan Catherine Koerner, had been college educated and, with her husband, had invented several practical household items. As children, Wilbur, Orville, and Katherine established a closeness which became lifelong, especially after 1889, when Katherine took over running the home upon their mother's death. The Wright brothers initially fashioned and sold toys; later they made tools, including a lathe, a newspaper-folding device, and a printing press. Between 1889 and 1894, they used the latter to produce a small local journal; Wilbur did the writing. Since their father's calling required the family to move often, the boys attended public schools in Iowa, Indiana, and Dayton. Wilbur and Orville were the only Wright children not to attend college.

The two brothers shared a remarkable genius for mechanics and complemented each other so closely as to give the appearance of being practically of one mind. Both had serious, no-nonsense, and reserved personalities. Wilbur was more pragmatic, had a steadier business sense, read much, and wrote for his father's church bulletin. Orville was more meticulous, temperamental, and full of ideas; he became a fairly successful bicycle racer. Late in 1892, the two young men opened a shop for the sale and repair of bicycles, utilizing their own mechanical skills to ensure quality workmanship. They were so successful that within three years they had sold their printing press, had expanded their bicycle business, and had begun to assemble their own cycles, using improved designs and tools of their own making. Orville even devised a crude calculating machine. An early gift from their father of a toy helicopter stimulated a gradual interest in the rudiments of flight.

### Lives' Work

By the mid-1890's, the Wright brothers were closely following the successful experiments of the German Otto Lilienthal with gliders, only to be stunned by news of his death in a gliding mishap in 1896. The tragedy, however, served as a catalyst for both men, who thereupon embarked on a common quest to solve the problem of manned flight. At first they read the scanty scientific literature on aerodynamics. From 1899, they experimented with kites and gliders in their spare time, usually to the derision of witnesses. The task came to dominate both their lives, and neither one ever married. From 1900, Wilbur corresponded extensively with the French expert in gliders, Octave Chanute, who was endeavoring to discover where Lilienthal had erred. Chanute greatly encouraged the Wright brothers and promoted their work.

The approach of the Wrights toward mastering the air was novel. They differed from the experimenters in Europe, who, ever since the adoption of the internal combustion engine to the automobile in the 1880's, had concentrated on developing power plants. Instead, the two brothers—after observing birds in flight in 1899—believed that pilot control of the vehicle under wind power had to be established before mechanical power could be applied. Orville theorized that lateral balance held the key. (Lateral balance is the ability of the pilot to adjust air pressure against the wing tips to his right and left at different angles to the wind in order to bank to either side.) Wilbur provided the means: a twisting or "warping" of the wings at correspondingly opposing angles. They built and tested a

*Wilber (left) and Orville Wright.*

small kite-like glider in 1899 which proved their thinking correct. They discovered that a manned "aeroplane" not only had to be controlled simultaneously along the horizontal axis to bank right or left but also had to be steered vertically to climb or descend. The plane also had to be directed to turn right or left.

Concurrent control of flight along these three axes thus dominated the Wrights' subsequent experiments before a motor could ever be mounted. Solution of the three-axis control problem was their greatest contribution to the science of aerodynamics. Between 1899 and 1903, they constructed and tested a succession of biplane gliders, incorporating the horizontal wing-warping mechanism, a forward elevator for vertical control, and a movable rear rudder tail for turning. The latter became standard for all subsequent aircraft. Because existing tables of air pressure and drift proved inaccurate, Orville devised two small wind tunnels to make his own innumerable correct measurements of wing surfaces. Wilbur revealed these figures to the world of aeronautics in 1901. Though the Wrights' scientific work was undertaken at Dayton, their glider flights were made in the ideal breezes over the sand dunes on the beach at Kitty Hawk and nearby Kill Devil Hills, North Carolina.

By 1903 the brothers had not only solved the three-axis challenge but had also calculated the amount of engine power required to lift their most advanced biplane glider. Their talents as mechanics enabled them that year to build a superb lightweight four-cylinder engine with approximately four horsepower. They also constructed an unprecedentedly efficient airscrew propeller for the engine to drive. They then joined these two inventions with bicycle chains, which drove two propellers mounted aft of the wings as pushers. Skids rather than wheels ensured stable landings. The entire flying machine was to be launched by a weight-dropping catapult. With Orville at the controls, the completed aircraft, the *Flyer I*, made its first flight at Kill Devil Hills on December 17, 1903. It flew 120 feet in twelve seconds, but by the end of the day Wilbur had achieved a flight of 852 feet. Only five other people, all local citizens, witnessed the epic event.

The world took no notice of the Wright brothers' monumental achievement, especially since the Wrights discouraged publicity until after their pending patents had been granted in 1906. Returning to Dayton, they devoted all of their time to creating and testing the first practical airplane. They were frustrated in their attempts to sell it to the United States or foreign governments; only in 1908 did their success become known. That summer, Orville dazzled United States Army observers at Fort Myer, Virginia, while Wilbur did the same in France for European observers. The effect was electric, and aviation enthusiasts now adopted the Wright method of aerodynamical control. Although a United States Army officer was killed and Orville seriously injured in a crash at Fort Myer, the army accepted a Wright plane. European governments made similar purchases. In 1909, the Wright Company was incorporated, with Wilbur as president. Orville was content to be vice president and leave the business to his brother while he taught flying and improved aircraft designs.

Their fame assured, the Wrights now prospered, yet the adoption of their wing-warping techniques by competitors led them to institute legal action against many manufacturers. In the United States, their chief rival was Glenn H. Curtiss, who, like many other manufacturers, had adopted the European-invented aileron in preference to the full warped wing for lateral control. The Wrights protested that any wing-warping device owed ultimate credit to themselves. The bitter lawsuits did not endear them to the world's aviation community, and they absorbed much of their energies. Furthermore, after 1909, they were quickly bypassed by advancing technology in Europe, and several of their army planes suffered fatal crashes. Then, in May, 1912, Wilbur succumbed to typhoid fever, and this blow sapped much of Orville's enthusiasm.

Succeeding to the presidency of the company, Orville carried on. He continued to test every improvement to his planes, even though whenever a plane vibrated in flight he suffered pains stemming from his 1908 injuries. Because his interest was in research and not business, he sold out his interest in the company late in 1915 and gave his final flying lesson. Orville remained thereafter a consulting engineer with the company. The lawsuits, and countersuits, were not resolved until the United States entered World War I in 1917, at which time all the aircraft manufacturers agreed to a cross-licensing system whereby their patents were pooled to enable the United States to produce unlimited numbers of warplanes. Orville served as a major in the Army Air Service, primarily as a technological adviser at Dayton. He gave up flying in 1918 and spent the rest of his life devising aeronautical equipment, mechanical toys, and other ingenious gadgets. He also for many years lent his expertise as a member of the National Advisory Committee on Aeronautics (NACA).

Despite rival claims and ensuing controversies that did not abate until the early 1940's, Wilbur and Orville Wright are firmly recognized as the undisputed inventors of the airplane.

## Summary

The Wright brothers exemplified the great era of individual invention which preceded the massive team research efforts funded by large corporations, foundations, governments, and universities. Their discovery of the key to manned, powered flight—pilot control over the free-flying aircraft—stemmed largely from the mechanical "Yankee know-how" passed on to them by their parents and honed in their bicycle business. Their practical experiments, therefore, succeeded whereas those of the theoretical scientist Samuel Pierpont Langley (1834-1906) of the Smithsonian Institution did not. Similarly, the bicycle and motorcycle racing and manufacturing of their major American competitor, Curtiss, yielded the same results as those of the Wrights—after Curtiss profited from their basic discovery. Also, the Wrights did not succumb to the European fascination with engines until the fundamental aerodynamical problems had been solved. Nor were they air sportsmen, like many enthusiasts of the day.

The historical timing was right. Technology and science were merging in all aspects of the rapidly industrializing Western world, enabling the Wrights to apply existing knowledge in the creation of the first airplane. In addition, the conquest of the air had become but one aspect of the last phase of modern terrestrial exploration and discovery—of the polar regions, remote jungles, and "lost" civilizations—a preoccupation of the public that the Wrights shared. They also exploited the public's craving for adventure with an exhibition team of stunt-flyers, though they did this only in response to competitors; by nature, neither man enjoyed popular hoopla of any kind. Finally, the drift of the European powers toward world war brought the Wrights the contracts they needed to continue their work with formal companies at home and in Europe.

The American military had no such sense of urgency and adopted early Wright flying machines only slowly, turning to the brothers to teach several officers to fly. The United States Army relied most heavily on Wright planes in the early years, 1908-1912, but several crashes led the army to turn increasingly to other manufacturers. By contrast, the United States Navy initially preferred "hydroaeroplanes" that took off from and landed on the water, machines which Curtiss provided since the Wrights opted for landplanes. To compete in seaplanes, however, the Wright brothers subcontracted with the only other airplane manufacturer of the early days, W. Starling Burgess (1878-1947), who used Wright blueprints but designed his own pontoon floats. Still, the Wright control mechanism of levers proved too cumbersome and was eventually overshadowed by the Deperdussin method, another example of the brothers' failure to innovate beyond their basic design. Ironically, the Wright Company merged with the Curtiss firm in 1929 to become Curtiss-Wright.

The tragic aspect of the Wright brothers was their attempt, through litigation, virtually to patent powered flight itself with their claims over the wing-warping concept. Whatever the legal merits of their case, the airplane was one of those inventions that belonged to humanity as a whole and could not be controlled through patents. They did not object to others imitating their design, but they steadfastly opposed any who used it for profit without recompense to them. The ensuing lawsuits inhibited much aeronautical progress in Europe and the United States in the early years. The principal focus of their anger was Curtiss, a man of almost identical character, integrity, and mechanical genius whose seaplanes and flying boats provided the bulk of Allied naval aviation during World War I. Orville's resentment only deepened after Wilbur's untimely death, which he attributed partly to his brother's exhaustion from the dispute. Another source of irritation was the insistence of the Smithsonian Institution that its pioneer scientist, Langley, really deserved the credit for the key initial discoveries in aeronautics—a claim not abandoned until World War II.

The Wrights conquered the problems of manned flight and by so doing initiated the Air Age, that essential historic bridge between the final conquest of the planet's surface and the ultimate leap into outer space.

## Bibliography

Brown, Ben L. "The Man Who Asked Smart Questions." *American Heritage* 44, no. 6 (October, 1993). The author, a World War II transport pilot, recounts his story of a man he met in Dayton, Ohio who asked particularly intelligent questions about the plane the author was flying at the time. He later found out the man was Orville Wright.

Freudenthal, Elsbeth Estelle. *Flight into History: The Wright Brothers and the Air Age*. Norman: University of Oklahoma Press, 1949. An adequate popular biography of the two men.

Gibbs-Smith, Charles H. *Aviation*. 2d ed. London: HMSO, 1985. A historical survey of flight from its origins in antiquity to the end of World War II, this work is the best single volume on the subject, giving a balanced treatment of the Wrights' key role. It is dedicated to them, their entry in the *Encyclopedia Britannica* also being written by Gibbs-Smith.

———. *The Wright Brothers: A Brief Account of Their Work, 1899-1911*. 2d ed. London: HMSO, 1987. A well-illustrated booklet on the crucial years.

Kelly, Fred C. *The Wright Brothers*. New York: Harcourt Brace, 1943; London: Harrap, 1944. The closest volume to an autobiography, this work was authorized by Orville Wright, who contributed heavily to it. It remains the standard work on their lives, though it is weak on the technological aspects and on the rivalry with Glenn Curtiss.

Renstrom, Arthur G., comp. *Wilbur and Orville Wright: A Bibliography Commemorating the Hundredth Anniversary of the Birth of Wilbur Wright*. Washington, D.C.: Library of Congress, 1968. An essential listing of books and articles down to 1968.

Wright, Orville, and Wilbur Wright. *Miracle at Kitty Hawk: The Letters of Wilbur and Orville Wright*. Edited by Fred C. Kelly. New York: Farrar Straus, 1951. A very complete collection of the personal and technical correspondence of the brothers.

Wright, Wilbur, and Orville Wright. *The Papers of Wilbur and Orville Wright*. Edited by Marvin W. McFarland. 2 vols. New York: McGraw-Hill, 1953. An exhaustive, meticulously annotated compendium of all papers relating not only to the Wrights' careers but to that of Octave Chanute as well.

*Clark G. Reynolds*

## WILHELM WUNDT

*Born:* August 16, 1832; Neckerau, Baden
*Died:* August 31, 1920; Grossbothen, Germany
*Areas of Achievement:* Psychology and physiology
*Contribution:* Wundt did much to develop psychology as an independent discipline. Beginning in 1879, Wundt established a psychological institute at the University of Leipzig, where he directed many experiments in which subjects studied their sensations and feelings. He was an effective teacher, who trained many of the next generation's leading psychologists.

### Early Life

Wilhelm Wundt was born in Neckerau, Baden, on August 16, 1832. He came from a distinguished family that included two university presidents as well as theologians and other scholars. Wundt's father was a Lutheran pastor. Wundt's childhood was apparently lonely; indeed, even as an adult with a successful career, Wundt was generally shy and withdrawn. When Wundt was eight, he came under the tutelage of his father's assistant, a young vicar whose guidance supported Wundt for several years. After failing his first year at the Catholic *Gymnasium* at Neckerau, Wundt transferred to the Heidelberg *Gymnasium*, where he was more comfortable, and was graduated in 1851.

Wundt's scholastic record was mediocre, but with the help of his maternal uncle he gained admission to the premedical program at the University of Tübingen, where he stayed for only a year before transferring to the University of Heidelberg. His diligence earned for Wundt a summa cum laude in three years and a first place on the state board medical examination.

After a year of study at the University of Berlin, Wundt returned to Heidelberg in 1857 as a lecturer in physiology, but he overworked himself preparing lectures on experimental psychology and contracted a serious illness that forced him to recuperate for a year in the Swiss Alps. In 1858, Wundt took a position as assistant to the distinguished physiologist Hermann von Helmholtz, who had been appointed head of the Institute of Physiology at the University of Heidelberg. Wundt wearied of his tenure with Helmholtz and resigned in 1863, but by that time he had published his first book and launched what was to become an astonishingly prolific scholarly career.

Wundt became active in politics in the 1860's, serving as president of the Heidelberg Working-men's Educational Association and completing two terms in the Baden parliament. In 1871, however, he returned to the University of Heidelberg for three more years; during this period, he published one of the most important books in the history of psychology, *Grundzüge der physiologischen Psychologie* (2 vols., 1873-1874; *Principles of Physiological Psychology*, vol. 1, 1904). Wundt revised this work in six more editions through 1911, and it remained the basis for his work in experimental psychology.

After three final years at Heidelberg, Wundt left there for the University of Zurich. His stay at Zurich was brief; after one year, he moved to the University of Leipzig to accept the chair in philosophy. He remained at Leipzig for the remainder of his life, establishing and lecturing in the Psychological Institute, from which he derived his fame as an educator.

### Life's Work

The Psychological Institute began in 1879 in makeshift quarters, and, before it was given better housing in 1897, Wundt had trained a large number of the best-known experimental psychologists of the next generation. Wundt's institute was especially influential in its nurturing of the most prominent American psychologists, among them Granville Stanley Hall and the English-born Edward Bradford Titchener. In 1881, Wundt founded a journal, *Philosophische Studien*, as the voice of the new institute. In the same decade, he published a series of philosophical tomes: *Logik*, in two volumes (1880-1883), *Ethik: Eine Untersuchung der Tatsachen und Gesetze des sittlichen Lebens* (1886; *Ethics: An Investigation of the Facts and Laws of the Moral Life*, 1897-1901), and *System der Philosophie* (1889). His scholarly output in the 1880's was prodigious. Besides the three long philosophical works, Wundt published numerous articles in *Philosophische Studien* as well as the second and third revised editions of the two-volume *Principles of Physiological Psychology*. This huge work was an attempt to explain the mind in a series of elements interrelated by the principle of association, a holdover from earlier theorizing about the mind in England. This period in Wundt's career culminated in his appointment in 1889 as rector of the University of Leipzig.

The 1890's were no less fruitful, producing a fourth edition of *Principles of Physiological Psy-*

*chology* (1893), an important theory of feeling presented in *Grundriss der Psychologie* (1896; *Outlines of Psychology*, 1897), several revisions of the earlier philosophical works, and more articles. In *Outlines of Psychology*, Wundt built upon the *Principles of Physiological Psychology* and tried to demonstrate a three-part structure to explain feelings. Wundt believed that feelings can be measured in terms of their pleasantness or unpleasantness, their degree of strain or relaxation, and their components of excitement or calm. The basis for this analysis was the unverifiable record of personal experience and its effect was to enrich the theoretical understanding of the workings of the mind. Wundt's efforts to find experimental evidence for this new theory led to strenuous testing by others in Germany and the United States, and although the results were equivocal the work was important in fostering the studies of the new laboratories.

The century ended with the publication of the first volume of Wundt's *Völkerpsychologie* (1900; cultural psychology), an immense undertaking that reached ten volumes by 1920. *Völkerpsychologie* occupies a problematic position in the huge corpus of Wundt's work. Two of its volumes treat aspects of language, two are on myth and religion, two on society, and one each on art, law, culture, and history.

The special nature of the *Völkerpsychologie* can be explained by the German differentiation between *Naturwissenschaften*, or natural science, and *Geisteswissenschaften*, the less rigorous observation that does not depend on experimental evidence. Historians of experimental psychology have understandably slighted *Völkerpsychologie*, but Wundt obviously saw the work as an integral part of his complete vision of the study of the mind's workings and not as a late interest attached as a huge footnote to his experimental work. He had indeed defined the topic as early as 1862, explaining it more fully in 1904 in a reference to "other sources of psychological knowledge, which become accessible at the very point where the experimental method fails us."

### Summary

Wilhelm Wundt's major contribution was his establishment of the psychological institute that put psychology on a firm experimental basis, dividing it from metaphysics. The use of such instruments as tachistoscopes, pendulums, and sensory mapping apparatus put psychology into the laboratory, and it is now difficult to imagine the intensity of some of Wundt's opponents. There were those, for example, who predicted that self-conscious examination of one's mental and emotional responses would lead to insanity. Wundt's laboratory studies involved the recording by trained subjects of their mental reactions to controlled events, and from these studies Wundt isolated two elements of the mind, sensation and feeling. In *Outlines of Psychology*, Wundt went beyond the associationist theory that influenced him in *Principles of Physiological Psychology* to advance a picture of the mind's creative vitality: The mind was to be seen not as a mechanical manipulator of static elements but as an organic and dynamic synthesis of the mental and the physical.

Wundt was a teacher of great influence and authority who assigned research projects to students and directed dissertations. In the roughly four decades that he ran his laboratory, Wundt directed 186 doctoral theses, seventy in philosophy and the others in psychology. (His most famous student, however, was not a psychologist but Hugo Eckener, commander of the *Graf Zeppelin.*) The list of Wundt's students who founded their own psychology laboratories in the United States includes Frank Angell, Edward A. Pace, and Edward Scripture. Lightner Witmer started the first psychological clinic in the United States in 1896, three years after he received his degree under Wundt. Harry Kirke Wolfe founded the department of psychology at the University of Nebraska; Charles Judd, who translated Wundt's *Outlines of Psychology* into English, founded both the department of educational psychology at the University of California at Berkeley and the psychology laboratory at New York University. Wundt's influence was so strong that, by 1900, twelve of the forty-three psychological laboratories in the United States had been started by former students of Wundt.

Wundt was not a flamboyant man, but he drew large gatherings of students to his lectures and taught more than twenty-four thousand students during his long career. He continued to be interested in politics throughout his life and spoke ardently in support of the German cause in World War I, judging France, Russia, and especially England to be coconspirators against Germany.

### Bibliography

Blumenthal, Arthur. "A Reappraisal of Wilhelm Wundt." *American Psychologist* 30 (1975): 1081-1083. A much-praised fresh look at Wundt that takes *Völkerpsychologie* seriously and sees Wundt's work as more of a piece.

Boring, Edwin G. *A History of Experimental Psychology.* 2d ed. New York: Appleton-Century-Crofts, 1950. A standard history of the subject but lopsided in its treatment of Wundt in that it slights *Völkerpsychologie.*

Cahan, Emily D., and Sheldon H. White. "Proposals for a Second Psychology." *The American Psychologist* 47, no. 2 (February, 1992). Discusses the proposals by writers such as Wundt and Auguste Comte for an alternative approach to psychology based on the behaviors that result from the culture in which the individual lives.

Hilgard, Ernest R. *Psychology in America: A Historical Survey.* San Diego: Harcourt Brace, 1987. Chapter 2 gives a succinct account of Wundt as a "systematic psychologist," treating him with William James.

Hothersall, David. *History of Psychology.* 3d ed. New York: McGraw-Hill, 1995. Chapter 4, "Wilhelm Wundt and the Founding of Psychology" is divided into sections such as "Wundt the Man," "Wundt as Advisor," and "Wundt's Research" that provide an excellent overview of the man and his career.

Littman, Richard. "Social and Intellectual Origins of Experimental Psychology." In *The First Century of Experimental Psychology*, edited by Eliot Hearst. Hillsdale, N.J.: Erlbaum, 1979. A useful look at Wundt's work from a modern perspective.

Mandle, George. "The Situation of Psychology: Landmarks of Choicepoints." *American Journal of Psychology* 109, no. 1 (Spring 1996). In-depth examination of the relationship between major political and social events and the psychologies of the period.

Rieber, Robert W., ed. *Wilhelm Wundt and the Making of a Scientific Psychology.* New York: Plenum Press, 1980. A valuable collection of eight essays on Wundt plus two selections in translation from Wundt's own work. The essays include "Personal History Before Leipzig," four articles about Wundt's influence, and three appreciations by Wundt's contemporaries.

Robinson, Daniel N. *Toward a Science of Human Nature: Essays on the Psychologies of Mill, Hegel, Wundt, and James.* New York: Columbia University Press, 1982. Superb essays in intellectual history, elaborating the approach in Wundt's time to such issues as the mind-body problem and definitions of the self. Very stimulating but not for beginners.

Wertheimer, Michael. *A Brief History of Psychology.* 3d ed. New York: Holt Rinehart, 1987. The two chapters "Wilhelm Wundt" and "The Contemporary Scene in the Age of Wundt" offer a convenient introduction to the subject.

*Frank Day*

# ANDREW WYETH

*Born:* July 12, 1917; Chadds Ford, Pennsylvania
*Area of Achievement:* Art
*Contribution:* Wyeth, one of the most famous and best-loved American painters throughout the world, created a body of work that many consider to embody the essence of American representational art.

## Early Life

Andrew Newell Wyeth and his four older siblings grew up in a family dominated by the dynamic personality of their father, Newell Convers (N. C.) Wyeth, one of America's greatest illustrators, whose work included drawings for Scribner's Illustrated Classics. The world of heroic, daring action that his father depicted for such epic tales as Robert Louis Stevenson's *Treasure Island* (1881-1882) and *Kidnapped* (1886), James Fenimore Cooper's *The Last of the Mohicans* (1826), Daniel Defoe's *Robinson Crusoe* (1719), and the anonymous *Robin Hood's Adventures* (c. 1490) was very real to young Andrew, who saw the paintings and props in his father's studio and heard his father relate the stories again and again. In the rural atmosphere of Chadds Ford, Pennsylvania, the young Wyeths received most of their education from tutors and their father, who saw that his children had access to good music, literature, and all kinds of creative activities. Andrew's childhood was a mixture of fantasy and reality combined with the security of a warm, close-knit family in which children were encouraged to express themselves. Newell believed that a successful life demanded total emotional involvement in both work and play.

Wyeth's only art training came from his father. In his early teenage years, he began regular studies in his father's studio along with other students that Newell occasionally accepted. Newell took an academician's approach to teaching by stressing that the fundamentals of drawing and painting must be mastered before one was capable of individual interpretation. He required beginners to draw from plaster casts, still lifes, and landscapes in order to train the hand and eye before being allowed to work in oils. Always avoiding rules or formulas, Newell believed that artists must intimately and spiritually experience the people or things they paint to the extent that they almost become the subject of the painting. Wyeth has said that his father was a great teacher because he made students feel things in their own way, giving them a curiosity about the quality and character of an object.

## Life's Work

Wyeth's relationship with his extroverted, famous father did not keep him from developing a distinctive personality and style of his own as an artist. More introverted and less gregarious than his father, he enjoyed solitary painting excursions. By the mid 1930's, he had achieved public success with his exhibitions of watercolors, but his serious career began with his discovery of tempera paint in the late 1930's. Wyeth has explained that he and his father took up the medium at the same time but, even though they believed absolutely the same things, each went about it in a different way. Newell used tempera very much as he used oils; Wyeth, however, saw it as a way of controlling any latent tendencies toward expressionism (or "messiness," as he said) that might appear in his work with watercolors or oils.

Significantly, although both artists wanted their works to allow the viewer to experience the artists' own feelings about their subjects, Newell's methods were always more literary and relied upon strong narrative. Wyeth, on the other hand, usually avoided his father's literary description, preferring to rely upon color and perspective to set the mood. An early example of his success in this regard is *Public Sale* (1943), in which the cold, gray sky and the vastness of a landscape with only two buildings separated by an anonymous crowd, barren trees, and two men leaning against a truck combine with the plunging diagonal of a dirt road to effectively convey the idea of sadness and tragedy.

Wyeth has said that the turning point in his life was his father's accidental death in a car-train collision in 1945. Before that, he thought of himself as just a "clever watercolorist with lots of swish and swash." After the accident, however, he felt the need to prove himself, to live up to his father's teachings. In the first tempera he painted after Newell's death, *Winter* (1946), the emotion that Wyeth had always felt toward the landscape was stronger because he chose to depict a landscape that he identified with his father. There is an autobiographical quality to this painting of a young boy, seemingly at a loss, running down a hill near the spot where Newell was killed.

As his style developed toward maturity, Wyeth, concerning himself with problems of conveying emotion and drama without resorting to his father's use of narrative details, found that he could achieve the results he wanted by limiting the panorama of nature and closely focusing upon a few details. In *Spring Freshet* (1942), for example, he brings a section of a tree trunk growing on the bank of the river up close to the picture plane, foreshortens the distance between the tree and the water, and focuses on the swirling, rough textures of the tree's bark. This technique, which he often used throughout his career (*Spring Beauty* and *The Hunter*, 1943; *Northern Point*, 1950; *The Pantry* and *Thin Ice*, 1969), is based upon the principle that a detail of nature, when it is examined microscopically and when its proportion is subtly altered, generates a kind of mysterious energy. As one writer stated, an isolated fragment of nature becomes a magical presence, and the ordinary seems to become extraordinary.

In the late 1940's, Wyeth experimented briefly with another technique in which he made use of ghostly figures, dilapidated interiors, condensed and claustrophobic spaces, and almost supernatural lighting (*Christmas Morning*, 1943; *Seed Corn*, 1948; *The Revenant*, 1949). He was searching for a way to express a sensation of the infinite within the context of the commonplace, but he realized that perhaps he was overstating the drama in these works.

Many writers consider that Wyeth reached the high point of his early period with *Wind from the Sea* (1947), *Karl* (1948), and *Christina's World* (1948). These three paintings represent the kind of resolution that occurs when an artist has found the elements of style that become a trademark. Wyeth combined an arid, explicit realism and a sparseness of compositional elements with oblique or unexpected viewpoints. Although *Christina's World* is still tied to a more obvious drama or symbolism as the woman strains toward the house in the distance, *Karl* and *Wind from the Sea* substitute a gesture or a moment as the defining element in achieving the picture's expression—the tilt of Karl's head or the gust of wind blowing through torn curtains. These simple, sometimes totally unexpected moments and gestures became the most important stylistic feature of Wyeth's mature style.

Another significant aspect of Wyeth's mature style is his attraction to objects that broadly symbolize the passage of time and the transitory nature of life. The theme of death and decay, which became a major motif in his mature work, is apparent in earlier pictures of dried vegetation, dead birds, and decrepit buildings. Later, he substituted cracked walls, torn curtains, worn clothing, and dented buckets as metaphors for the brevity of life. Consequently, he seems to prefer the winter and fall as seasons for his paintings; as he has commented, during these seasons one feels the bone structures, the loneliness, and the dead feeling in the landscape.

Although Wyeth has often been thought of as the portraitist of the average American, he has never considered himself to be a portraitist of any kind and has rarely accepted a portrait commission. His reasons for choosing the people he paints are complicated and have to do with his being drawn for his own private reasons to certain kinds of personalities, physiognomies, and situations.

Wyeth's art cannot be simply defined by referring to any one theme or stylistic device. There are a number of thematic series to be found in his body of work, although these have never been fully recognized by most critics. Many times throughout his career, he has returned to explicate the same person, scene or idea, thus creating a situation in which viewers must look at more than just a single work in order to fully grasp Wyeth's meaning.

## Summary

Andrew Wyeth's great popularity as an artist has partly been responsible for the many inaccurate labels that have been attached to him. In the 1950's and 1960's, some critics characterized him as a kind of dinosaur, the last exponent of nineteenth century realism in an art world ruled by abstract expressionism, while others claimed that he was only a self-appointed interpreter of rural America. Still others have dismissed him as a mere illustrator. Wyeth himself has been well aware that placing a label on his work is difficult, if not impossible, explaining with good humor, "I'm so conservative I'm radical." Most scholars today acknowledge the futility of trying to pigeonhole every artist and recognize that even though Wyeth's art is essentially representational, it does not simplistically fit into the category of realism.

The most enlightened view of Wyeth's art is that it may be far more accurate to see his individualized, unique preoccupation with his own circumscribed surroundings as an exploitation of a psychic universe rather than a physical one. *Thin Ice* is an example of just such a psychic universe, with its juxtaposition of the opposites of light and dark, solid and void, surface and depth, life and death. Viewers look through the ice but are then forced to confront their own subconscious feelings or fears. Wyeth's own words are, however, the best summation of his art. He has said that emotion is his bulwark. In the end, that is the only thing that endures.

**Bibliography**

*The Brandywine Heritage*. Greenwich, Conn.: New York Graphic Society, 1971. This catalog of an exhibit of the works of Howard Pyle, N. C. Wyeth, Andrew Wyeth, and James Wyeth includes a short introduction and many illustrations of each artist's work.

Corn, Wanda M. *The Art of Andrew Wyeth*. Greenwich, Conn.: New York Graphic Society, 1973. Corn's monograph is the most complete and insightful analysis of Wyeth's work. She considers his development from his early training in his father's studio to his mature period. The book is well-illustrated with examples of Wyeth's work and interesting family photographs and also contains a chronology of exhibitions and an extensive bibliography.

Hoving, Thomas. *Andrew Wyeth: Autobiography.* Boston and London: Bulfinch Press, 1950. This is Wyeth's commentary as told to Thomas Hoving and includes reproductions of 133 works in a variety of media, a personal chronology, a chronology of exhibitions, and a bibliography.

———. *Two Worlds of Andrew Wyeth*. Boston: Houghton Mifflin, 1978. This book contains a penetrating, in-depth interview with Wyeth by Hoving, who was the director of the Metropolitan Museum of Art on the occasion of a Wyeth exhibit. Profusely illustrated.

Logsdon, Gene. *Wyeth People*. New York: Doubleday, 1971. Logsdon provides a different approach to the consideration of the artist and his work by exploring the Brandywine Valley and Chadds Ford and interviewing Wyeth's friends and neighbors. Illustrated with a few black and white photographs of the people and places.

McCord, David, and Frederick A. Sweet. *Andrew Wyeth*. Boston: Museum of Fine Arts, 1970. This is a catalog of the works that Wyeth completed in Chadds Ford and Cushing, Maine. Includes an introductory essay, and color and black and white illustrations.

Severens, Martha. *Andrew Wyeth, America's Painter*. New York: Hudson Hills Press, 1996. This catalog of a 1996 Wyeth exhibition at the Greenville County Museum in South Carolina contains an informative essay on Wyeth's work by the museum's curator and many excellent color plates of Wyeth's work from 1988 through 1994.

Venn, Beth, and Adam D. Weinberg. *Unknown Terrain: The Landscapes of Andrew Wyeth*. New York: Whitney Museum, 1998. Catalog and essays based on an exhibit at the Whitney Museum of American Art. Includes many unknown works in a variety of media and techniques.

*LouAnn Faris Culley*

# IANNIS XENAKIS

*Born:* May 29, 1922; Brăila, Romania

*Areas of Achievement:* Music, architecture, engineering, and mathematics

*Contribution:* Xenakis is one of Europe's most prestigious avant-garde composers. His works exhibit a new and individual kind of musical thinking based on physics, mathematics, and architecture. Especially important for Xenakis has been the mathematics of probability. He introduced the term "stochastic music" for music utilizing probabilistic processes, and he has sometimes used computers to aid in the elaborate calculations demanded.

## Early Life

Of Greek parentage, Iannis Xenakis was born on May 29, 1922, in Brăila, Romania. His father, Charcos Xenakis, was a wealthy businessman; his mother was Fantins Parlou Xenakis. Xenakis early became familiar with the rich folk music of his native region of the Lower Danube, and he was influenced considerably by the Byzantine music of the Orthodox rite. As a boy, he also demonstrated a fascination with unpitched sounds. In 1932, his family returned to Greece. There, he was reared and educated, eventually attending a Greek-English college on the island of Spetsai. Xenakis' first exposure to music from Ludwig van Beethoven to Johannes Brahms dates from this period. In 1934, he began studying composition with Aristotle Koundourov, a former pupil of Mikhail Ippolitov-Ivanov.

Deciding to divide his time and energy between the sciences and music, Xenakis successfully passed the entrance examinations for the Polytechnic Institute in Athens in 1940. His studies in Athens were prolonged by the Nazi invasion of Greece, for he spent much of his time fighting with the resistance. Xenakis became secretary of a resistance group at the Polytechnic Institute in 1941, and he was jailed and tortured several times. His face was disfigured, and he lost completely the vision in one eye when struck by a tank during street fighting in Athens on New Year's Day, 1945. He was captured, imprisoned, and sentenced to die as a terrorist but managed to escape. Completing his studies at the Polytechnic Institute in 1947, he received his degree in engineering. In September of that year, he left Greece on a forged passport, eventually entering France illegally as a political refugee and a stateless person. Xenakis would become a French citizen in 1965.

In Paris, Xenakis became interested in architecture, studying with Le Corbusier, one of France's best-known modern architects. From 1948 to 1959, he worked as Le Corbusier's assistant and closest collaborator in planning housing projects in Nantes and Marseilles and a number of ambitious structures in Europe and elsewhere, including the assembly building at Chandigarh, India, and the Baghdad Stadium. Though Xenakis earned his living from achitecture during this period, music was not put aside. Both Arthur Honegger and Nadia Boulanger turned him down as a pupil in composition in 1949, but he managed to get advice and criticism from Darius Milhaud. In 1950, he entered the Paris Conservatoire, where he studied composition under Olivier Messiaen. Messiaen was struck by the fecundity and originality of his largely self-taught pupil's musical ideas. In 1953, Xenakis married Françoise, a novelist and a former heroine in the French Resistance. Her Christian name, Françoise, is all she would take from her family, choosing to be known by her married name only. Iannis and Françoise Xenakis have one child, a daughter.

## Life's Work

The key to Xenakis' creative awakening is an identity of approach to architecture and music; indeed, he sees no cleavage between the theories of music and architecture. In order to satisfy the unity of thought and the sense of cohesion that his intellect demanded, Xenakis located problems that were common to both architecture and music. He could develop his architectural ideas by articulating them in space, while in music he could arrange his ideas in time. Xenakis was also concerned with a major difference between architecture and music: The experience of space in the former is reversible, but time in the latter is not. In 1954, within a month of starting design work on the Couvent de St. Marie de la Tourette—a Dominican monastery and the most ambitious project assigned him thus far by Le Corbusier—he jotted down ideas for *Métastasis*, the first of a major series of compositions that would challenge the existing body of contemporary music.

The remarkable parallel in method of design between *Métastasis* and the monastery is clear from the hundreds of plans and sketches drawn and signed by Xenakis and scattered with notes by Le Corbusier. Different functions were allotted to the various portions and levels of the ensemble. Extraordinary sculptural forms were designed for the different elements, severe geometric solids, arranged in a free, flowing open form around the basic square. Space was used dynamically, freeing elements such as the sharp pyramid of the oratory to soar into the sky from the hollowed square of the courtyard surrounded by flat roofs, in a vigorous display of positive and negative space. No chronological order emerges in the design work for the monastery. Xenakis worked on several parts at the same time, stopping to develop a new idea and returning months later to make modifications. He found such an approach—attacking problems from both ends, detail and general—useful in music as well as architecture.

In 1954, while working on the designs for the Couvent de St. Marie de la Tourette, Xenakis began to develop his own method of musical composition, one that he called "stochastic," from the Greek root meaning "straight aim." In actuality, it involved controlled improvisation. As a mathematician, he evolved his method from the laws of mathematical probability, probability calculus, set theory, and symbolic and mathematical logic. Thus, his music was worked out according to the probabilities of certain notes, sonorities, and rhythms recurring in a given work. Instead of thinking in terms of harmony, which composers have done for centuries, Xenakis thinks in terms of sound entities that have the characteristics of intensity, pitch, and duration, as associated to one another by and within time.

The stochastic method is related to Jacques Bernoulli's Law of Large Numbers, which maintains that as the number of repetitions of a given chance trial (such as flipping a coin) increases, the probability that the results will tend to a determinate end approaches certainty. A stochastic process, then, is one that is probabilistic in the sense of tending toward a certain goal. Though John Cage and others who use the contingency process in music have sought to undercut the primacy of the composer by pursuing the ideal of indeterminacy, Xenakis has maintained the principle of indeterminacy and the dominance of the composer. His goal is the expression in music of the unity he sees as underlying all activity, human and nonhuman, scientific and artistic.

Xenakis' first important composition in his stochastic method was *Métastasis* (1954), for an orchestra of sixty-one instruments, each required to play its own music. Clear musical ideas occur and merge into nebulous, unidentifiable states to give birth to new phenomena in an uninterrupted chain of destruction-construction, or metastasis. The piece begins with the strings sustaining several measures of the note G; meanwhile, gliding glissandi in the rest of the orchestra and expanding dynamics help to create an eerie effect and to arrive at a dramatic climax. The possibilities of simulating electronically produced sounds with conventional instruments is explored. Textures are dense, and sonorities are overpowering.

In October of 1955, at the Donaueschingen Festival in Germany, Hans Rosbaud introduced *Métastasis.* Many in the audience were scandalized, and Xenakis had to wait another four years before his work could be performed in Paris. A second work, *Pithoprakta* (1955-1956), for an orchestra of fifty musicians and similar in nature to *Métastasis*, was first performed in Munich in March, 1957, under the direction of Herman Scherchen. Xenakis received the Geneva Prix de la Fondation Européenne pour la Culture for these two compositions in 1957; both were used by the New York City Ballet in 1968 for a ballet entitled *Métastasis and Pithoprakta*, choreographed by George Balanchine.

*Diamorphoses*, developed in the studios of the Groupe de Recherche Musicale de la Radio-Télévision Française in Paris in 1957, marks Xenakis' earliest experiment with electronic music on magnetic tape. His interest in electronic music increased after meeting Edgard Varèse in 1958 at the Brussels World Exposition. Still working in Le Corbusier's office, Xenakis designed the Philips Pavilion at the exposition, where Varèse's *Poème Électronique* on magnetic tape was regularly projected through four hundred or more speakers. Xenakis wrote *Concret PA*, a short electronic piece for magnetic tape, intended as a welcoming piece at the Philips Pavilion.

From its very inception, the Philips Pavilion raised one controversy after another: It vexed its sponsor by its extreme conceptions; it annoyed Le Corbusier, who came into conflict with Xenakis over its authorship; it outraged critics with its weirdness; yet, it delighted the public by the thousands. In conceiving the form and mathematical expression of the Philips Pavilion, Xenakis invented an architecture constructed entirely from surfaces derived from the hyperbolic paraboloid. A graph of ruled surfaces plotting the string glissandi of *Métastasis* demonstrates that the architecture of the pavilion orginated in Xenakis' composition.

Having not seen eye to eye with Le Corbusier for some time, Xenakis decided to strike out on his own in 1960. Though still intermittently active in the field of architecture, he has devoted himself almost entirely to music since that time. By the early 1960's, he had considerable support among the more radical of contemporary musicians and found himself a focal center at modern music festivals and the recipient of a number of commissions.

From magnetic tape, Xenakis went to the computer. He found the computer valuable in stochastic computations. Between 1956 and 1962, *ST/4* for string quartet, *ST/10* for ten instruments, and *ST/48* for forty-eight musicians playing forty-eight different parts were produced. "ST" represents stochastic; the adjoining number indicates the number of instrumentalists required. In these pieces, the program is basically a complex of stochastic laws by which the composer orders the electronic brain to define all the sounds, one after the other, in a previously calculated sequence. In reviewing a performance of *ST/48*, one critic noted that bowed glissandi were used so frequently that the listener soon became saturated with the device. He noted that *ST/48* has enough going on in it to hold one's attention at first hearing, but repeated exposure caused the novelty to wear off. Xenakis' *Atrées* (1956-1962), for ten instruments, was programmed and calculated on the computer.

Xenakis also experimented in the area of "games." First performed in 1971 by Radio Hilvershum in Germany, *Duel* (1959) was a competitive "game" for two orchestras and two conductors. Each orchestra played different music mathematically devised from a single theory. The audience picked the winner. *Stratégie* (1962), which was premiered in April of 1963, was similarly constructed. Awarded the Prix Manos Hadjidakis in 1962, Xenakis also came to the United States for the first time. At the invitation of Aaron Copland, he taught composition at the Berkshire Music Center at Tanglewood, Massachusetts. Later in 1962, he served as artist-in-residence in Berlin at the invitation of the West Berlin Senate and the Ford Foundation.

Xenakis' *Eonta* (1963-1964) was premiered in Paris in 1964 under the direction of Pierre Boulez. In this piece, the motor energy is provided by the piano, while the brass harnesses it. Similarly controlled power is generated by *Akrata* (1964-1965), commissioned by the Koussevitzky Music Foundation and written for fifteen wind instruments and vibraphone. *Terretektorh* (1965-1966) and *Vamos Gamma* (1967-1968) required that orchestra members be scattered among the unsuspecting audience. A variety of sonorities, including noise elements, are then unleashed on the audience.

In 1965, the first Xenakis Festival was held at the Salle Gaveau in Paris. The following year, Xenakis was invited to participate in the Musicological Congress in Manila and to attend the Japanese premiere of *Stratégie* in Tokyo. In 1960, he also founded Équipe de Mathématique et Automatique Musicales in Paris. For Montreal's Expo 67, he conceived and realized a light and sound spectacle entitled *Polytope de Montréal* for the French Pavilion. In 1967, Xenakis was appointed associate professor of music at Indiana University, where he founded and directed for five years the Center for Mathematical and Automated Studies.

In 1969, Xenakis received a commission for a ballet by the Canadian Arts Council. He wrote not only his own music but also his own story. *Kraanerg* is set in the year 2069, when the youth who now control the world decree all persons over the age of thirty must be exterminated. It is filled with architectural buildings into aural space and with strange and chilling sonorities. Xenakis commented on his own music at the Composers Showcase in New York on May 11, 1971. His *Bohor I* (1962), for magnetic tape, elicited a strong unfavorable response. One woman screamed throughout the final few minutes.

The 1970's were to be productive and glamorous years for Xenakis. Commissioned by the Gulbenkian Foundation in Lisbon, his *Cendrées* (1974), for chorus and orchestra, is a wordless chant. *Erikhthon* (1974), for piano and orchestra, *Noomena* (1975), for large orchestra, *Empreintes* (1975), for orchestra, *Phlegra* (1975), for eleven instruments, and *Retours-Windungen* (1976), for twelve cellos all received premieres in the mid-1970's. During the 1970's Xenakis was the recipient of the Bax Society Prize in London, the Maurice Ravel Gold Medal in Paris, the Grand Prix National de la Musique in Paris, and the Prix Beethoven in Bonn. He was made an honorary member of the British Computer Art Society in 1972, and, in 1975, he was made an honorary member of the American Academy and Institute of Arts and Letters. Xenakis was finally permitted to return to Greece in 1974; there, he received a hero's welcome. In 1976, the Sorbonne conferred on him an honorary doctorate in humane letters and sciences.

Works of Xenakis in the 1980's include *Shar* (1983), for large string orchestra; *Khall Perr* (1983), for brass quintet and percussion; *Tetras* (1983), for string quartet; *Naama* (1984), for harpsichord; *Lichens* (1984), for orchestra; and *Thallein* (1985), for orchestra. In 1980, Xenakis was elected a member of the European Academy of Sciences and of Arts and Letters in Paris and a member of the National Council of Hellonie Resistance in Greece. He became a member of the Académie des Beaux Arts in Paris in 1984. Xenakis has continued to compose and teach.

### Summary

Despite a plurality of approaches, Iannis Xenakis' music is characterized by coherence and unity. The beginning point of each new phase of composition is analytic. Because his creative work is based on a strong theoretical foundation, analysis and creation are inseparable for Xenakis. In various compositions, he has attacked the hierarchic structure of the orchestra, giving each player equal responsibility; in others, he has pushed instrumentation to extremes, making nearly impossible demands on the players. It has been argued that Xenakis' influence has grown to the point that it has changed popular understanding of what is "musical" in music to include the unthinkable and unplayable within its boundaries. The results of such a change now seem so natural and even necessary that few have taken the trouble to identify the specific influences of Xenakis and his work on this process.

Xenakis was one of the first of his contemporaries to reevaluate and articulate in writing and music the force of science, mathematics, logic, and philosophy in the center of a modern conception of the arts. He succeeded in clearing new ground for music in restoring it as a serious experimental discipline, one with a substantial body of theory that has vital connections with different branches of learning. In his work, he has rendered a dynamic depiction of the universe informed by modern science. Within the bounds of the same composition, this depiction may be developed in sounds that are brutal, harsh, and jarring, yet also poetic, musical, and beautiful.

### Bibliography

Bois, Mario. *Iannis Xenakis: The Man and His Music.* London: Boosey and Hawkes, 1967; Westport, Conn.: Greenwood Press, 1980. Record of an extended conversation with Xenakis, along with a description of Xenakis' works.

Grifiths, Paul. "He Composes Differently, Therefore He Exists." *New York Times* 146, no. 50684 (January 26, 1997). Examines the music of Xenakis.

Hiller, Lejaren. *The Computer and Music.* Ithaca, N.Y.: Cornell University Press, 1970. Chapter 4, on French experiments in computer composition, sets Xenakis' work in this area prior to 1970 in perspective.

Matossian, Nouritza. *Xenakis.* London: Kahn and Averill, and New York: Taplinger, 1986. The best treatment in English of Xenakis and his work to date. Includes a list of musical compositions, a catalog of architectural projects, a list of distinctions received by Xenakis, a bibliography of books and articles by and about Xenakis, and a discography.

Russcol, Herbert. *The Liberation of Sound: An Introduction to Electronic Music.* Englewood Cliffs, N.J.: Prentice-Hall, 1972. A good overview of developments in electronic music that leads to a better understanding of Xenakis' work in this medium.

"Xenakis, Iannis." *Current Biography* 66, no. 9 (September, 1994). Short biography of Xenakis including his childhood, family, education, interest in architecture, and hobbies and pastimes.

Xenakis, Iannis. *Formalized Music.* Rev. ed. Stuyvesant, N.J.: Pendragon Press, 1992. First published in Paris in 1963 as *Musique formelles*, this is a collection of previously published essays. Now recognized as one of the most important theoretical contributions on composition to emerge from the postwar period.

*L. Moody Simms, Jr.*

# AHMAD ZAKI YAMANI

*Born:* June 30, 1930; Mecca, Saudi Arabia

*Areas of Achievement:* Diplomacy and politics

*Contribution:* Between 1962 and 1986, Yamani was the best-known spokesman for Middle Eastern oil producing countries' interests in the Organization of Petroleum Exporting Countries (OPEC). He built a considerable reputation as a moderate interested in reconciling strong nationalist demands among producers and the expectations of Western industrialist consuming countries.

## Early Life

Ahmad Zaki Yamani was born in Mecca, Saudi Arabia, on June 30, 1930. The Yamani family name derives from its probable origin among the tribes of southern Arabia, or the Yemen. Genealogically the family descends from the Hashemite clan within the Quraysh tribe. The Hashemite clan is especially noble in Islamic tradition, having been the clan of the Prophet Muhammad.

Yamani's father was at the time of his birth *qadi*, or chief judge, of the Islamic Supreme Court of the Hejaz district of the new Saudi kingdom. This post represented a continuation of a long family tradition: Yamani's grandfather had been a grand mufti, or jurisprudent, in the late Ottoman Turkish period (to 1914). During the early years of Yamani's childhood, his father was absent from the family home, serving as grand mufti in Indonesia. Later he filled the same prestigious post in Malaysia.

The young Yamani received his early education in Mecca. When he was seventeen, his father sent him to study law, not at the Azhar, which was the main institution of learning in Islamic subjects, but at the law faculty of the University of Cairo. Yamani was so successful in his study of law that the Saudi government awarded him a scholarship to study at the New York University Comparative Law Institute. It was during his stay in New York that Yamani met and married his first wife, Laila Faidhi, a Ph.D. student in education at New York University and daughter of a well-known Iraqi author and lawyer.

After earning his M.A. in comparative jurisprudence, Yamani and his wife spent a year at the Harvard Law School, where he focused his studies on international legal dimensions of capital investment. This led to a second American master's degree.

Yamani returned to Saudi Arabia in 1956, after nine years of study abroad. He was soon appointed to his first governmental post in the ministry of finance's newly formed department of *zakat* (religious alms tax) and income tax. Within a year, the first child of the Yamani family, their daughter Mai, was born. A second daughter, Maha, followed in 1959. Their son, Hani, was born in 1961.

## Life's Work

Yamani's exposure to technical questions relating to the Saudi petroleum industry began even while he was an official in the ministry of finance. In 1957, the controversial director of the Saudi Office of Petroleum and Minerals (Petromin), Abdullah Tariki, called upon the young Yamani to draft complicated oil exploration contracts, most notably the one governing Japanese offshore concessions. His skillful work attracted the attention of Crown Prince Faisal, who summoned him to his personal residence. Yamani's biographer suggested that Faisal already had an important political strategy in mind: to replace the rather brash Abdullah Tariki, who had pioneered successful Saudi renegotiation of the internationally dominant Arabian American Oil Company (ARAMCO) concession, with the calm and professional lawyer Yamani.

Following creation of the Organization of Petroleum Exporting Countries (OPEC) in 1960, Faisal's preference for Yamani took on concrete form. In March, 1962, Yamani was appointed minister for petroleum. One of the major internal development projects Yamani would support fully soon after becoming minister was Arabia's unique University of Petroleum and Minerals in the "oil capital" at Dhahran. This specialized school had been set up with the cooperation of American professors who designed a curriculum based on engineering, science, and industrial management.

Beyond these types of supportive activities, Yamani's reputation as a moderate but determined representative of Arabian oil interests came to the fore in the late 1960's. Particularly after the 1967 Arab-Israeli War, world attention focused on the Middle Eastern members of OPEC to see if an effort would be made to use oil exports as a political weapon. Following the January, 1971, Tehran meeting of OPEC—after an organization-wide call for a 55 percent tax on foreign concessionaires' production profits and a uniform price increase—

Yamani's role became key. After a crisis was averted by compromising on a five-year interim tax of 35 percent, OPEC raised the ante, demanding either direct participation by each exporting country in the total operations of the companies or nationalization (Libya's solution in mid-1971). When ARAMCO tried to strike a bilateral deal with Arabia that would put other OPEC members at a disadvantage, Yamani refused to cooperate: Within a short time, 20 percent participation, based on Saudi compromises, became standard among the moderates. Arabia held the line even after Iraq's nationalization of the British-controlled Iraq Petroleum Company, offering another compromise: an immediate adjustment to 25 percent participation, to rise to 51 percent in stages by 1982.

Even then, there was clear dissatisfaction among some OPEC members, who suspected that Yamani's moderation spelled a willingness to cooperate with Western oil consumers. This view was dispelled at the time of the October, 1973, Middle East War and the Saudi-backed Arab decision to impose an oil embargo on supporters of Israel. In this matter, Yamani took the lead in condemning the West, including the United States. In an interview with *Newsweek* in December, 1973, Yamani indicated that he was not opposed to cooperation with Washington and the oil companies but expected some concrete signs of U.S. aid in making Israel compromise politically and militarily. He even went so far as to open splits in the oil consuming world by offering to deal separately with "preferred" importers, especially Japan.

On the whole, however, Yamani came out of the petroleum turmoil of the mid- to late 1970's with his moderate image intact. This was in part a result of the fact that the Saudi oil giant, under Yamani's guidance, frequently found itself offsetting (by increasing its own share of world production, thus easing supply and demand pressures) the extreme inflationary price demands of the Iranian oil giant across the Persian Gulf. In an OPEC meeting in late 1976, for example, Yamani made a special trip back to Riyadh to obtain (then) Crown Prince Fahd's agreement that, no matter what Iran's extreme increase demands might be, Arabia and the United Arab Emirates (representing 40 percent of OPEC production) would keep their price more than a dollar under other members. Experts looking back on the oil price bonanza to 1980 suggest that, had it not been for Yamani's moderating influence, the price per barrel would have been in the fifty dollar range, at least ten dollars over the peak reached before trends went in the other direction.

The period between 1976 and 1986—the year of Yamani's dismissal as oil minister—was anything but a calm and secure one for Yamani. First, he would be personally affected by the chaotic politics of the Palestine/Israel question: In December, 1975, he and a number of other oil negotiators narrowly escaped death when terrorists captured their plane following an OPEC meeting in Vienna. Even before these events, however, a less dramatic but ultimately more definitive source of turmoil in the next ten years of his career occurred: On March 25, 1975, only two days after Yamani's second marriage was concluded with Tammam al-Anbar, daughter of a former Saudi ambassador, King Faisal was assassinated. Although King Khālid occupied the throne for the next few years, the crown prince, Fahd, began already to demonstrate his opposition to Yamani's obvious dominance in making Saudi oil policy. When Khālid died in 1982, and during the first few years of Fahd's reign, the oil price boom was over, making it essential for OPEC's members to readjust. Readjustments had to do not only with relations with oil consumers but also with internal budgets that had become immensely inflated and dependent on continued high levels of revenue from oil. By October, 1986, King Fahd's disagreements with his oil minister, especially following a clash between the Iranian and Saudi delegates to an OPEC summit in Geneva, led to Yamani's dismissal after twenty-four years in office.

### Summary

Ahmad Zaki Yamani represents, like Egyptian President Anwar el-Sadat, a familiar face and symbol of apparent rationalism in the troubled late twentieth century scenario of Middle East politics. In part this stemmed from his relaxed technocratic style, which allowed him to engage Western diplomats and politicians in a way that did not alienate them. Lack of external signs of nationalistic fervor, however, did not mean that Yamani was willing to compromise easily on the critical issue of defending oil as the Middle East's only, or nearly only, important raw material for export. In short, during his long tenure as Saudi oil minister, he showed again and again that maintaining a political and economic balance in adjusting clashing interests between producers and consumers must be recognized as a necessity in Middle East-Western relations.

### Bibliography

Collin, Jane. "Regardless of Quotas, Saudis Will Boost Output in 1998, Yamani Says." *The Oil Daily* 47, no. 222 (November 20, 1997). Examines a speech delivered by Yamani in which he discussed OPEC and the future of oil markets.

Kelly, John B. *Arabia, the Gulf and the West*. London: Weidenfeld and Nicolson, and New York: Basic, 1980. After offering two general historical chapters, this book analyzes the international politics of oil and, very important, the way petroleum fits into the economy and society of Saudi Arabia. There is very substantial coverage of Yamani's dealings with ARAMCO and his policies toward European and Japanese oil consumer interests.

Robinson, Jeffrey. *Yamani: The Inside Story*. London: Simon and Schuster, 1988; New York: Atlantic Monthly Press, 1989. This is the only full-length biography of Yamani available in English. It is highly informative and contains all essential details, but tends to be overly journalistic in style, with uneven jumping from personal impression to personal impression.

"Working Hard for Yamani." *New Republic* 195 (September 29, 1986): 4. This is an unsympathetic account of Yamani's speech given at the time of the 350th anniversary celebration of Harvard University. The observations came at a time when oil prices were dropping rapidly, and Yamani was calling for actions to halt the slump, to safeguard both consumers' and producers' interests.

Yamani, Ahmad Zaki. "The Man Who Has What Makes the World Go Round." Interview by Wendy O'Flaherty, in *Maclean's* 91 (June 26, 1978): 46-47. This Canadian interview with Yamani covers three main questions: how long Arabia can continue its policy of keeping oil prices down by increasing its share of world production, Yamani's suggestion that Soviet oil reserves may be seriously diminishing, the views on Canada's oil producing potential in the 1980's.

———. "Yamani on Oil—and Israel." Interview by Armand de Borchgrave, in *Newsweek* 94 (July 9, 1979): 21. *Newsweek*'s senior editor Borchgrave spoke with Yamani following the momentous Geneva conference of OPEC, a meeting that raised oil prices per barrel from $18 to $23.50. In this interview, Yamani implies that a serious world economic catastrophe (an increase to $50) could occur if something happened in the Middle East to further exacerbate the world shortage of oil. This "something" was tied to Israel's increasingly hostile actions against Arab states and U.S. lack of reaction to the same.

———. "The Gulf Crisis: Oil Fundamentals, Market Perceptions and Political Realities." *Energy Journal* 12, no. 2 (1991). Yamani discusses the Gulf crisis of August, 1990, and its impact on oil prices. Provides information on the oil industry and its relationship to politics.

*Byron D. Cannon*

## WILLIAM BUTLER YEATS

*Born:* June 13, 1865; Sandymount, near Dublin, Ireland

*Died:* January 28, 1939; Cap Martin, France

*Area of Achievement:* Literature

*Contribution:* Yeats transformed himself from a minor late Romantic poet into the complex artist who became the greatest poet of the twentieth century.

### Early Life

William Butler Yeats was born in Sandymount, near Dublin in 1865. His father was an unsuccessful painter who encouraged his son to pursue a life in the arts. William attempted to follow his father and attended art school in Dublin for a short while. He disliked the form of instruction, however, and found that his talents lay in poetry rather than painting. Yeats's roots were in Ireland, but he spent an equal amount of time in London. While he was in London, he came in contact with William Morris and other adherents of the Pre-Raphaelite movement; this connection increased his already latent Romanticism. He published a long narrative poem, "The Wanderings of Oisin," in 1889, and the poem shows the influences on his early poetry. It evokes a legendary Irish hero, Oisin (Ossiah), and is written in the Romantic style of the Pre-Raphaelites. In another early poem, Yeats declares, "Words alone are certain good." Reality and facts are seen as enemies of the life of the imagination and need to be overcome by "words." One of the reasons that Yeats turned to Romanticism was that he was poor, badly clothed, and obsessed with the fame and sex that seemed to be so far out of his reach.

Yeats was also seeking to replace the religion that his father and other skeptics had driven out. He was associated for a while with the Theosophists and Madame Blavatsky and later joined the Order of the Golden Dawn. This interest in mysticism had an effect on his poetry; his second book, *The Rose* (1893), has a number of poems that allude to Rosicrucianism and a mystical union after death with the beloved. It was during this period that Yeats met the woman he was to love for the rest of his life, Maud Gonne. She was interested in Irish affairs but not in the same way as Yeats was; he wanted to make "an Ireland beautiful in the memory" with his poems, but she was interested in radical political action. He wrote many poems to and about her, and he proposed to her a number of times, but she continued to refuse him. Even after she married John MacBride in 1903, she remained an inspiration for his poems.

Yeats became interested in the theater in the late 1890's after he met Lady Gregory, and he founded the Irish National Theatre with her in 1899. As a result of his involvement with the theater and Irish culture and politics, Yeats's style and subject matter began to change from the shadowy Romanticism of the early poems to the satiric and realistic poems found in the 1914 volume, *Responsibilities*. The last poem of that volume, "A Coat," makes his change clear.

> I made my song a coat
> Covered with embroideries
> Out of old mythologies
> From heel to throat;
> But the fools caught it,
> Wore it in the world's eyes
> As though they'd wrought it.
> Song, let them take it,
> For there's more enterprise
> In walking naked.

### Life's Work

By 1914, Yeats had published several books of poetry and a number of well-received plays. If he had died at that time, he would be remembered as an important but minor poet of the late nineteenth and early twentieth centuries. Beginning with *Responsibilities*, Yeats began to remake himself as a modern poet. The first aspect of that modernity is a satiric rather than a Romantic approach. In poems such as "Paudeen," "To a Shade," and "To a Wealthy Man," Yeats takes on the Irish middle class and scorns them for not knowing excellence when it comes before them. The style is also much leaner and tighter; Yeats's description of "the fumbling wits, the obscure spite/ Of our old Paudeen in his shop" has a hard edge not to be found in the other-worldly early poems. There are, to be sure, poems on Maud Gonne in the book, but they have changed as well. For example, in "The Cold Heaven," he describes the relationship with Gonne as one that "should be out of season"; the only reward he receives for his loyalty in love is to be "sent/ Out naked on the roads. . . ."

During this period, Yeats met Ezra Pound, who helped him change his style. Pound also introduced him to Japanese Nō drama, and Yeats was immediately taken with this symbolic theater. He wrote and produced *At the Hawk's Well* in 1916 with Japanese-like masks. Another event that altered Yeats was not a literary one but a political one: the Easter Uprising of 1916. The revolutionary politics that he hated had suddenly blossomed and, as a poet, he had to respond. The response is found in "Easter 1916." The poem describes how everything has been "changed, changed utterly" by the actions of a few heroic fanatics. Moreover, while Yeats celebrates the "terrible beauty" that was born by this revolution, he also makes the political action into a myth and himself into a bard; in that mythic and apolitical dimension, it does not matter whether "England" keeps faith or not. Political action fades before the timelessness of myth.

In 1917, Yeats married Georgia Hyde-Lees, and she gave him some of the stability that he had lacked until this point. They lived at Coole on the estate of Lady Gregory, who had helped and been helped by Yeats for a number of years. His wife also helped Yeats by engaging in automatic writing that was later to produce *A Vision* (1925) as well as many of the occult symbols and the fascination with history that began to become prominent in Yeats's poetry.

In *The Wild Swans at Coole* (1919) and *Michael Robartes and the Dancer* (1921), some of these new directions in Yeats's poetry are apparent. There is now an interest in the heroic man who puts by tragedy in "In Memory of Major Robert Gregory" and in "An Irish Airman Foresees His Death." Gregory is portrayed as an ideal man who combines "Soldier, Scholar, Horseman," and his death is not tragic but an escape from old age, another of Yeats's prominent themes. "A Deep-Sworn Vow" is about Maud Gonne, but it is about loss more than love.

> Others because you did not keep
> That deep-sworn vow have been friends of mine;
> Yet always when I look death in the face,
> When I clamber to the heights of sleep,
> Or when I grow excited with wine,
> Suddenly I meet your face.

We also find the first signs of the system of *A Vision* appear in the poetry in such poems as "The Phases of the Moon," although they are at this time less successful than the love poems and the heroic ones.

Yeats's greatest book is certainly *The Tower* (1928), and it reflects much of the bitterness he perceived in the civil war in Ireland and the breakdown of old traditions after World War I. The first poem in that volume, "Sailing to Byzantium," opens with a rejection of a society that has no concern for "Monuments of unageing intellect" since it is caught in its own "sensual music" that is ensnared in the process of "Whatever is begotten, born, and dies." His solution is to turn himself into an art object that escapes this cycle. In the poems that follow, however, Yeats returns to confront once more the problems of old age and history. These themes can be seen in the title poem, "The Tower," in "Nineteen Hundred and Nineteen," and, above all, in "Among School Children." In that poem, Yeats again confronts the problems of old age, love, and the life of the artist. He seems to conclude that "passion, piety, and affection" are only temporary and "mockers of man's enterprise." The last stanza, however, moves to a transcendent union of all things: "O body swayed to music, O brightening glance,/ How can we know the dancer from the dance?" The last poem in the volume is "All Souls' Night: Epilogue to 'A Vision.' " It is also a poem of transcendence, but not the natural one of "Among School Children"; it is, instead, a victory of "meditation" and of the cycles of history that Yeats thought he controlled in *A Vision*.

Yeats believed that "The Tower" was a "distortion" because its bitterness showed only one side. In his next volume, *The Winding Stair and Other Poems* (1933), the poems celebrate life and the victory of the "Self" over the abstraction of the "Soul" in "A Dialogue of Self and Soul" and "Vacillation." In addition, there is a new emphasis on sexuality in the "Crazy Jane" poems. In 1934, Yeats had a Steinach operation performed to rejuvenate his sexual powers, and an emphasis on the sexual rather than the earlier ideal love began to become more important in his poetry.

In 1938, Yeats moved to France, where he wrote some of his best plays, including *Purgatory*, and the poems that would later be collected in *Last Poems and Plays* (1940). His powers did not flag, and while *Last Poems and Plays* is more uneven than the earlier volumes, it does contain such great poems as "Lapis Lazuli" and "The Circus Animals Desertion." On January 26, 1939, Yeats suddenly fell ill and died soon after. He was buried in France, but his body was returned to his beloved Ireland in 1948 and was met by Sean MacBride, Minister for External Affairs and the son of Maud Gonne.

### Summary

William Butler Yeats described some of the stages he went through in "The Circus Animals' Desertion"; the first stage was "that sea-rider Oisin led by the nose/ Through three enchanted islands"; the next was the political stage of the "counter-truth" and its play, *The Countess Cathleen*, and Maud Gonne, who played the title role; the last was a recognition that his perfect art grew out of imperfect material and needed the realism that the earlier stages lacked:

> Now that my ladder's gone
> I must lie down where all the ladders start,
> In the foul rag-and-bone shop of the heart.

Yeats began as a gifted late Romantic poet whose poems were more sound than sense, and the doctrine they pronounced was that only the imagination is real. He made himself into a modern poet by changing his subject matter and technique. The middle and last phases of Yeats's poetry are marked by poems that connect and relate more closely to the concerns of the audience than did the earlier ones. Such great poems as "A Prayer for My Daughter," "The Municipal Gallery Revisited," and "Easter 1916" deal intimately with such concerns as the future of one's child, friendship, and revolution and would have been impossible in his earlier style.

His life as well as his art changed from about 1914 onward. The pursuit of Gonne continued but became angry and realistic rather than Romantic. Yeats became involved in such historical events as the Easter Uprising and World War I, and history itself became prominent in his thought. His position as a senator in the Irish Free State as well as a founder or leader of various Irish cultural groups testifies to his involvement in the world. He may have defied the world in his epitaph ("Cast a cold eye/ On life, on death/ Horseman, pass by"), but he was a part of it. As Richard Ellmann said, "Few poets have found mastery of themselves and their craft so difficult or have sought such mastery, through conflict and struggle, so unflinchingly."

### Bibliography

Ellmann, Richard. *Yeats: The Man and the Masks.* New York: Macmillan, 1948; London: Macmillan, 1949. One of the first "life and works" books on Yeats and still a useful introduction to the poet.

Sung, Hae-Kyung. "The Poetics of Purgatory: A Consideration of Yeats's Use of Noh Form." *Comparative Literature Studies* 35, no. 2 (Spring 1998). Sung examines the influence of the Japanese noh form of drama on Yeats' work, in particular the play Purgatory.

Unterecker, John. *A Reader's Guide to William Butler Yeats*. New York: Farrar, Straus and Giroux, 1959. A useful interpretive guide for readers of the poems.

Wenthe, William J. "'It Will Be a Hard Toil': Yeats's Theory of Versification, 1899-1919." *Journal of Modern Literature* 21, no. 1 (Summer 1997). The author examines the influence of the philosophies of Nietzsche on Yeats' work in the early twentieth century.

Whitaker, Thomas R. *Swan and Shadow.* Chapel Hill: University of North Carolina Press, 1964. An excellent study of Yeats's ideas about history and how they are incorporated into the poems.

Yeats, William B. *Memoirs: Autobiography, First Draft Journal*. London and New York: Macmillan, 1972. An excellent edition of Yeats's *Autobiography* and *Journal* in one volume, in which Yeats describes his development and his relationship with other poets and Maud Gonne.

*James Sullivan*

# BORIS N. YELTSIN

*Born:* February 1, 1931; Butka, Sverdlovsk region, U.S.S.R.

*Area of Achievement:* Government and politics

*Contribution:* From within the Soviet establishment, Yeltsin led the increasingly radical forces that first sought to reform the Soviet Union then engineered its demise. Yeltsin became the first president of the post-Soviet Russian Federation.

## Early Life

Boris Nikolayevich Yeltsin was born in the town of Butka, in the Soviet Union's Sverdlovsk region, in 1931. His family was politically unexceptional. As a youth, Yeltsin displayed a combination of intelligence and impertinence. He was once expelled from school but later returned and, in 1955, earned an engineering degree from Ural Kirov Technical College.

Yeltsin joined the Communist Party of the Soviet Union (CPSU) in 1961 at the age of thirty. The Soviet Union, at that time led by Premier Nikita Khrushchev, was embroiled in a Cold War with the United States. The Soviet Union defined its international role as leading the communist world against the Washington-led capitalist world. Focusing more on domestic economic issues, Yeltsin steadily rose through the ranks of the regional party and became first secretary of Sverdlovsk's CPSU committee in 1976. In 1985, the reformist Soviet leader Mikhail Gorbachev personally selected Yeltsin to serve as the chairman of the party committee for the Soviet Union's capital city, Moscow. The following year, Gorbachev elevated Yeltsin to the CPSU's top body, the Politburo.

## Life's Work

Gorbachev's selection of Yeltsin for the Politburo position was part of his larger attempt to place more liberal (reformist) allies in positions of authority. Gorbachev had concluded that his country had been severely weakened by the unrelenting international competition of the Cold War, and so he sought to modify long-standing economic and social policies as a way of reversing the Soviet Union's decline. Gorbachev clearly hoped that Yeltsin and the other reformers would support his various reform efforts. Yeltsin did just this, endorsing reform on a number of fronts, including marketization of the economy, loosening of censorship, and decentralization of authority. He took a vigorous, public stand against conservatives in the Politburo and elsewhere who opposed liberalization. Soon, however, Yeltsin was criticizing Gorbachev himself for being too timid in pursuing his own reform program. Events came to a head at a Central Committee meeting in the fall of 1987, when Yeltsin accused the Soviet leadership of hypocrisy in its sham reform efforts. Shortly thereafter, Yeltsin was dismissed from the Politburo.

The political and societal forces unleashed by Gorbachev continued to spin out of control. In March, 1989, Gorbachev allowed semifree elections to be held for the first time in Soviet history; in these elections, Yeltsin was overwhelmingly elected to the Soviet parliament (representing a district centered on Moscow). In addition to nationwide liberalization, popular forces pressed for a decentralization of power from Moscow to the regional governments. Concurrently, Yeltsin came to be associated less with the goal of reforming the Soviet Union and more with the objective of gaining greater freedom for the Russian Soviet Federat-

ed Soviet Republic (RSFSR), the largest of the fifteen constituent republics of the Soviet Union. By the late 1980's, similar independence drives were gaining ground in most of the Soviet republics.

In the face of mounting public pressure, political intransigence, and worsening economic conditions, Gorbachev's reforms became increasingly desperate in the late 1980's. Again hoping to defuse popular dissatisfaction and propel like-minded allies to power, Gorbachev authorized popular elections in the country's republics in March, 1990. Again, one of the main beneficiaries of those elections was Yeltsin, who secured a seat in the RSFSR's parliament, which in turn elected him leader of the republic.

Yeltsin had become Gorbachev's most potent rival. As the leader of the RSFSR, Yeltsin's constituency included over one-half of the Soviet Union's population, and his authority extended across three-quarters of the country's territory. Several months after attaining the RSFSR's top political position, Yeltsin dramatically relinquished his membership in the Communist Party. As a political maverick frequently at odds with Gorbachev, Yeltsin enjoyed the support of most of the country's liberals, capitalists, and national liberationists. His mandate was strengthened in June, 1991, when, in free elections, Russian voters decisively elected him to the newly created Russian presidency.

Gorbachev had been trying to occupy the middle of the political spectrum, but the rush of events in the late 1980's and early 1990's polarized society. Now, the two main groups were old-guard communists who wanted to preserve the union and the political system, and liberal reformers who sought varying degrees of capitalism, democracy, and decentralization of power. Yeltsin became the standard-bearer for the latter group. The climactic clash between the two groups occurred in August, 1991, when a small cabal of communists and conservative military leaders placed Gorbachev under house arrest and attempted to seize control of the government. They hoped to preserve the Soviet Union, which they believed Gorbachev had endangered with his reforms.

On August 18, the coup leaders arrived at the dacha where Gorbachev was vacationing and demanded that he turn over power to them. When Gorbachev refused, the coup plotters had him placed under house arrest and assumed emergency executive powers. Early in the morning of August 19, the Soviet press agency claimed that Gorbachev had an "illness" and announced that Vice President Gennady Yanayev had assumed presidential powers. Yanayev led an eight-member "State Committee for the State of Emergency in the U.S.S.R.," which began issuing decrees that suspended various civil freedoms.

Significantly, Yeltsin, who inexplicably had not been detained by the coup plotters, rallied the anticoup forces. He proclaimed his own control of the RSFSR and called for general strikes and public resistance. Thousands of Muscovites heeded Yeltsin's call and surrounded the central government building, dubbed the "White House," where Yeltsin and his loyal lieutenants were staying. Soldiers refused orders from the State Committee to fire on the building, and the coup dissolved after only three days.

From that point onward, Yeltsin was seen as the country's liberator. Not only did he become the new leader for the reform movement begun by Gorbachev six years earlier, but he also became the central figure who defeated the reactionary forces that opposed reform. Gorbachev never recovered politically from the coup and spent his remaining months as Soviet president in the shadow of Yeltsin. Moreover, the coup attempt precipitated the final unravelling of the Soviet Union. Within four months, all fifteen republics had declared their independence. On December 25, 1991, Gorbachev resigned as Soviet president, and the Soviet Union was declared defunct. The RSFSR was renamed the Russian Federation upon the collapse of the Soviet Union. Yeltsin now led a country that possessed the world's second-largest nuclear arsenal, held one of the five permanent seats on the United Nations Security Council, and otherwise represented the "successor" to the Soviet Union.

Notwithstanding the Soviet Union's collapse, Yeltsin could not entirely escape the problems that had earlier beset Gorbachev. Many elites, including a majority of Russia's parliamentary members, opposed Yeltsin's efforts to proceed with market reforms. The growing tension between Yeltsin and the parliament reached a climax in the fall of 1993, when Yeltsin ordered the military to attack the parliament building. Victorious, Yeltsin wrote a new constitution that strengthened the presidency. He also ordered new parliamentary elections in December, 1993, but the new parliament was no less ideologically hostile to Yeltsin than the last. The following year, Yeltsin found it necessary to order the army to fight secessionists in Chechnya, one of

Russia's many ethnic-based republics. A tentative peace was achieved in 1996, but Chechens and other ethnic people of the Russian Federation remained restive.

Yeltsin faced reelection in the summer of 1996. He failed to achieve 50 percent in the first electoral round against one dozen candidates. He faced communist leader Gennady Zyuganov in a run-off one week later and won the race comfortably. Although the Russian constitution limits the president to two terms, Yeltsin would not rule out the possibility of running again in the year 2000. He hinted that his first election occurred before the current constitution was written and thus did not count toward his two-term limit.

Yet the largest obstacle to Yeltsin's future leadership was his health. Frequently beset by heart troubles and bouts of apparent alcohol abuse, Yeltsin's tenure was marked by periodic health-related absences. A serious heart attack shortly after his reelection, followed by quadruple bypass surgery and pneumonia, kept Yeltsin out of the public eye for much of 1996 and 1997. Yeltsin appeared in public with a bit more frequency in 1998, but he clearly was becoming more physically frail and mentally weak. Spending much of his time in hospitals and sanatoriums, Yeltsin had largely removed himself from the day-to-day operations of the Russian government

Like his health, Yeltsin's popularity plummeted in the months and years after his re-election. By early 1999, Yeltsin's public approval rating had dropped to about one percent. This was in large measure due to the near free-fall of the Russian economy and the worsening chaos within the Russian government. Like Mikhail Gorbachev before him, Boris Yeltsin had, in the space of a few years, gone from being a worshipped public hero to a despised politician, blamed—rightly or wrongly—for destroying a once-proud country.

### Summary

There is no question that Boris Yeltsin has been one of the twentieth century's most influential world leaders. While Gorbachev began the Soviet Union's liberalization, Yeltsin led the country's turn from communism and its disaggregation into sovereign republics. Moreover, Yeltsin helped shape the new, post-Soviet Russia during a time of global and national upheaval. He was directly responsible for the country's 1993 constitution, hand-picked the country's top cabinet officials, saw the country through a two-year civil war in Chechnya, and crafted a new foreign policy in the post-Cold War world. Although he earned his share of criticism in carrying out these tasks, Yeltsin deserves credit for managing a turbulent, nuclear-armed ex-superpower during one of the world's most critical periods.

### Bibliography

Buzgalin, Alexander, and Andrei Kolganov. *Bloody October in Moscow: Political Repression in the Name of Reform*. New York: Monthly Review Press, 1994. As suggested by the title, the authors seek to portray Yeltsin as a tyrant masquerading as a democrat. The central event of the book is Yeltsin's clash with the parliament in 1993, culminating in the military assault during "Bloody October."

Daniels, Robert V. "The End of the Yeltsin Era." *Dissent* 46, no. 1 (Winter 1999). The author examines the problems that have occurred during Yeltsin's term, which have been described as reversing much of what his predecessor Mikhail Gorbachev accomplished. Discusses inflation in the new free-market economy and mistakes made in privatizing business.

Fedorov, Velentin P. *Yeltsin: A Political Portrait*. Bellevue, Wash.: Imperial, 1996. Federov provides an overview of Yeltsin and his political background.

Konstantinova, Natalya, et al. "Yeltsin Illness Spurs Search for Legal Remedies." *The Current Digest of the Post-Soviet Press* 50, no. 43 (November 25, 1998). Although Yeltsin attempts to dispel rumors of his inability to lead due to illness, proposals have been made to amend Russia's constitution so that someone can be appointed to a position as "acting president."

Rutland, Peter. "Yeltsin: The Problem, Not the Solution." *The National Interest* 49 (Fall, 1997). This is an analysis of Yeltsin's leadership of the Russian Federation. Rutland, an expert in the field, is highly critical of Yeltsin, particularly regarding his social and economic policies and his imperialistic governing style.

Solovev, Vladimir, and Elena Klepikova. *Boris Yeltsin: A Political Biography*. London: Weidenfeld and Nicolson, and New York: Putnam, 1992. Although written before Russia became truly sovereign with the collapse of the Soviet Union in December, 1991, the authors cogently describe Yeltsin's rise to power.

Yeltsin, Boris N. *Against the Grain: An Autobiography.* London: Cape, and New York: Summit, 1990. These are Yeltsin's first memoirs, documenting his rise to the Politburo under Gorbachev and his fall from grace in 1997. The book focuses on the *perestroika* years and concludes before the Soviet Union collapses.

———. *The Struggle for Russia.* New York: Belka, 1994. The second installment of Yeltsin's memoirs, this book focuses on the leading of Russia from a republic of the Soviet Union to a sovereign state. It describes events from the August, 1991, coup through his clash with the parliament in the fall of 1993. The writing is in the form of diary entries, subsequently edited and reorganized.

*Steve D. Boilard*

## HIDEKI YUKAWA

*Born:* January 23, 1907; Tokyo, Japan
*Died:* September 8, 1981; Kyoto, Japan
*Area of Achievement:* Physics
*Contribution:* Yukawa's most important work concerned the nature of elementary particles making up the universe and the nuclear forces controlling their interactions. He formulated the theory of the short-range strong nuclear force, predicting the pion particle as an intermediate transference medium.

### Early Life

Hideki Yukawa was born in Tokyo, Japan, on January 23, 1907. His father, a professor of geology at Kyoto University, played an important role in developing his son's interest in science. Early ability in mathematics led him to attend Kyoto University, where he specialized in physics and theoretical mathematics, astounding his professors with his brilliant insights into interpretations of physical theories.

He was graduated in 1929 with a basic science degree. For his graduate education, he decided on Osaka University, where, because of his physics record, he was able both to teach, joining the faculty in 1933, and to study for his advanced degree. The doctorate in physics was awarded to him in 1938 from Osaka University. In 1932, he married a classical Japanese dancer, Sumi, with whom he had two sons.

In October, 1934, at the age of twenty-seven Yukawa, after giving his imagination free rein on numerous sleepless nights, read his first and most celebrated paper, "On the Interaction of Elementary Particles, I," to the Physico-Mathematical Society meeting in Osaka. Unfortunately, the article and presentation were not well received by the attending Japanese physicists. Yukawa's wife, however, encouraged him to publish it because she believed in his enthusiasm. The epoch-marking paper appeared in 1935 in the society's *Proceedings of the Physico-mathematical Society of Japan*.

### Life's Work

In his first original work, Yukawa had derived equations he believed would solve the contemporary problem of what held the atomic nucleus together. In his theory of nuclear forces, he postulated the existence of a new elementary particle, one possessing a mass several hundred times greater than that of the electron. Without such a particle acting, as he theorized, as an extremely strong form of nuclear glue, the positively charged protons would all immediately repel one another so fiercely that all nuclei beyond simple hydrogen nuclei would cease to exist. It had previously been thought that the neutron, discovered in 1932 by Sir James Chadwick, might be part of the solution, but Yukawa showed that an entirely different exchange force had to be present to counteract the mutual repulsion of the protons. His predictions included an unknown particle's acting as the transfer agent for this force, an effective range for the force of very short distance, a strength vastly greater than that of the electrical repulsion force between like charges, but a force whose strength decreased so quickly over space as not to have any significant effect on the inner-shell electrons. He predicted a mass for the new particle of 270 times the electron, and that it should be spontaneously radioactive, self-destructing with an extremely short life span.

Yukawa's theory of a particle that is emitted and reabsorbed too quickly to be detected showed that, in the exchange process, protons become neutrons, and neutrons change to protons, with the same phenomena occurring for antimatter particles. These changes required two charged particles, a positive meson and negative meson, the negative one for antimatter, the positive one for normal matter. Also, since exchange forces could work between proton-proton or neutron-neutron, a neutrally charged meson was necessary, one acting as its own antiparticle.

In 1936, Carl D. Anderson found in cosmic ray tracks a particle that at one time was thought to be the meson but that was soon shown not to be, weighing only 207 electronic masses, bearing only positive or negative charges, and not reacting with protons or neutrons (it is now known as a mu-meson). In 1947, Cecil Frank Powell discovered a new meson, of mass 273, which fit the description for Yukawa's predicted particle. The new meson was called a pi-meson, or pion. With the construction of high-energy cyclotrons, it became possible to produce pions in large enough numbers to study their behavior and nature. In the 1950's, Robert Hofstadter, using his 600-million-electron-volt linear accelerator, showed both the neutron and proton as consisting essentially of clouds of pions.

In 1936, Yukawa further advanced elementary-particle physics with his prediction that a nucleus could absorb one of the innermost shell electrons, a process equivalent to emitting a positron (a positively charged electron). Since those electrons were in the K-shell, the process became known as K-capture.

Yukawa became a professor of physics at Kyoto University in 1939, continuing his theoretical work there through World War II, even after the American occupation forces destroyed his small cyclotron. In 1948, as a guest of J. Robert Oppenheimer, he went to the Institute for Advanced Study at Princeton, staying for a year before going to Columbia University as a visiting professor. In 1949, he received the Nobel Prize in Physics. In 1953, he left the United States to return to Kyoto University as the first director of Japan's Research Institute of Fundamental Physics. He had donated most of his Nobel Prize money to Osaka and Kyoto universities, to thank them for their encouragement and to motivate younger students. He remained as director there until 1970.

After his first pioneering work, Yukawa contributed greatly to the detailed theory of particle physics. By his advances and his teaching ability, he built an advanced school of theoretical physicists. He had declined the invitation of Columbia University to stay there because he wanted to train new people in his field, which had few specialists in Japan. He became the editor of a new journal, *Progress of Theoretical Physics*, providing a much-needed outlet for important contributions in all areas of physics from his own school and his colleagues.

Yukawa always preferred to pursue fundamental problems, using insights based on intuitive methods found often among great geniuses such as Albert Einstein, a close acquaintance of Yukawa until Einstein's death in 1955. Yukawa did not, he maintained often, seek immediate appreciation of his work, because he believed that his work would eventually be understood and appreciated. By 1954, he had begun to stress the importance of scientists' accepting social responsibility. He became highly visible in scientific and other groups working for the cause of peace and against nuclear armaments. That year, 1954, he broke his own imposed silence to denounce atom bomb tests. He tried to establish the role of scientists from a perspective of integrity and independence. In 1962, he was vocal at the First Kyoto Conference of Scientists, noting that "physics cannot be separated from humanity. The results of physics are inevitably connected with the problems of humanity through their application to human society."

After setting out to discover the innermost secrets of nature, to explain the atom and the universe, Yukawa died at his home in Kyoto at the age of seventy-four. Many physicists grieved at his death, many publicly becoming even more fiercely determined to obtain Yukawa's objective of world peace.

## Summary

Although he was interested in theoretical physics from all viewpoints, Hideki Yukawa was principally committed to increasing the depth of Japanese contributions to physics by the training and influencing of new physicists. His great work, of elucidating the nature of the nuclear force using a virtual particle, the meson, to cement the nucleus together, provided the step necessary to break the deadlock in understanding the atom's place in the universe. Based solely on theoretical calculations, he explained how the atom fixed its stability and why the proton and neutron were stable within the central core. Without any experimental justification, he predicted a new fundamental particle, the first of the exchange particles, mathematically determining its size, nature, and the fact that there should be three different ones, differing in charge, decay mode, and half-lives. His contributions to elementary-particle physics and quantum mechanics have revolutionized the entire nature of the field.

In addition, Yukawa helped formulate his country's viewpoints on world peace, nuclear disarmament, and the social responsibilities of scientists toward the rest of civilization. He strongly believed that physicists and others, instead of being concerned only with the technical feasibility of discoveries or advances, needed also to develop criteria for using good judgment to further the cause of humanity instead of harming it.

**Bibliography**

Alfvén, Hannes. *Worlds-Antiworlds: Antimatter in Cosmology.* San Francisco: Freeman, 1966. A delightfully written book dealing with the structure of the universe based on the interaction of regular and antimatter. Starting with what the world consists of, the nature of the fundamental particles is discussed, along with their importance in formulating a plasma, the most abundant form of matter. For beginners in physics and cosmology.

Brown, Laurie M., and Yoichiro Nambu. "Physicists in Wartime Japan." *Scientific American* 279, no. 6 (December, 1998). Discusses theoretical physics in Japan from 1935 to 1955 including the work of Yukawa, Yoshio Nishina, and others.

Davies, P. C. *The Forces of Nature.* 2d ed. Cambridge and New York: Cambridge University Press, 1996. A well-written description of the forces controlling the universe and their associated particle natures. Traces the works of gravity, electromagnetism, and the strong and weak nuclear forces, identifying their associated exchange particles. Mesons are discussed as they pertain to Yukawa's ideas and subsequent discoveries. For laypersons.

Dodd, James. *The Ideas of Particle Physics.* 2d ed. Cambridge and New York: Cambridge University Press, 1991. A well-written overview of the current ideas on basic particles and the forces that control them. Fundamental forces are identified, and the interactions of particles under weak and strong nuclear forces are discussed. Covers intermediate transfer particles to present ideas of quarks. Contains a good glossary and additional references.

Gueller, Sam. *Frontiers of Physics.* New York: Vantage Press, 1987. An all-encompassing work, covering the range of problems in modern physics. Extremely interesting discussions on the nature of gravity, particles, and the possibility of a unified theory of the forces of nature. For the layperson. Gives an insight into philosophical problems of modern development.

Mauldin, John H. *Particles in Nature: The Chronological Discovery of the New Physics.* Blue Ridge Summit, Pa.: Tab, 1986. A quantitative overview of the particle view of the universe, starting with basic physics and reaching to principles of invariance, fields, and matter waves. Identifies all the currently known particles, their interactions with one another and the nucleus. Mesons as exchange bodies are studied, and their relationship to quarks is clarified. Includes good pictures and extensive references.

Nambu, Y. *Quarks.* Philadelphia: World Scientific, 1985. Written as an introduction, this work explains what elementary particles are and how the various quarks and leptons act to control the universe. Detailed section on the birth and development of the Yukawa theory and how it gave rise to the newer models of particle construction. Discusses chromodynamics, gauge theories, and unified theories. Well written and well illustrated.

Segrè, Emilio. *From X-Rays to Quarks: Modern Physicists and Their Discoveries.* San Francisco: Freeman, 1980. Written for the layperson, this work traces the history of elementary particles in the twentieth century, from Wilhelm Röntgen's discovery of X rays to modern ideas on the quarks as fundamental building blocks. Deals with the mesons and their roles in nature, along with the other forces present in the atom. Well written with additional references.

Trefil, James S. *From Atoms to Quarks.* London: Athlone Press, and New York: Scribner, 1980. A well-written introduction to the discovery of particles and the structure of the nucleus. Starting with the simplified physics of the atom, cosmic-ray experiments are identified, leading to the discovery of the mesons. The importance of accelerators in understanding the nature of the particle proliferation is stressed. Includes a glossary.

*Arthur L. Alt*

# SA'D ZAGHLŪL

*Born:* June 1, 1859; Ibyanah, Egypt
*Died:* August 23, 1927; Cairo, Egypt
*Areas of Achievement:* Government and politics
*Contribution:* Zaghlūl was modern Egypt's outstanding politician before Gamal Abdel Nasser. He led the 1919 revolution against the British and founded the Wafd Party.

## Early Life

Sa'd Zaghlūl Pasha ibn Ibrahim was born in July, 1857, at Ibyānah, Egypt. His parents were Sheikh Ibrahim Zaghlūl and Miriam. Of peasant extraction, Ibrahim possessed wealth and his village's Muslim leadership. When Ibrahim died during Sa'd's early youth, Miriam and her stepson, Shanaui, arranged for Sa'd's education so he would become, like his father and grandfather, a Muslim sheikh. In 1864, Sa'd began study at Ibānāh's mosque school. In 1870-1873, he studied recitation of the Koran under a famous teacher at Dusuq's main mosque.

In 1873, Zaghlūl entered al-Azhar University, exhibiting independence by lodging outside the student inhabited area. At al-Azhar Zaghlūl met Jamāl ad-Dīn al-Afghānī and Muhammad 'Abduh. The former's stress on anti-imperialism, constitutionalism, and revitalized Arabic captivated Zaghlūl. In 1880, Zaghlūl left al-Azhar without a degree. In October, 1880, Muhammad 'Abduh, chief editor of the Egyptian government's official gazette, hired Zaghlūl. They used the publication to mold public opinion. In May, 1882, Zaghlūl shifted to the ministry of the interior as an aide and then to Giza province's legal department as an overseer.

In 1881-1882, Zaghlūl vocally supported the Urabi Revolt. This caused loss of his position, deprivation of civil rights, and barring from governmental service. He now represented some of the accused in the revolt. In June, 1883, Zaghlūl was arrested as a member of the Society of Revenge, an organization pledged to end Great Britain's occupation and the khedivial regime. In October, 1883, he was freed on bond. In 1884, Zaghlūl became a lawyer in the new national court system. He rose rapidly because of his courtroom eloquence. In 1892, his reputation brought an unprecedented appointment as a deputy judge in the appellate court. His legal success also led to entrée into Egypt's Turco-Circassian aristocracy. In 1896, he married a member of this class, Safiyya, daughter of Prime Minister Mustafa Pasha Fahmī. The marriage was arranged by Princess Nazli, cousin to Khedive 'Abbās II. She was Zaghlūl's mentor in Egyptian high society and he her lawyer. Following her advice, he studied French. At Nazli's salon, Zaghlūl met the head of the British occupation in Egypt, Sir Evelyn Baring (later Lord Cromer).

## Life's Work

In 1904, Cromer made Zaghlūl Egypt's first minister of education, the title "pasha" being awarded by the khedive. Zaghlūl checked the autocratic British adviser in his ministry, assigned to Egyptians several jobs formerly always reserved for Britons, founded the School of Qadis (judges in Islamic law courts), enlarged the Training College and added a section for training secondary school teachers, expanded the use of Arabic in schools, established free education in governmental institutes for poverty-stricken students, and disciplined a British headmistress.

In 1910, Zaghlūl became minister of justice. His efforts to make the cabinet effective in governing Egypt aroused the British, 'Abbas, and his prime minister. Zaghlūl sought vainly to render three repressive bills ineffective. In March, 1912, he resigned upon his failure to prevent prosecution of Muhammad Farid, the nationalist leader. In December, 1913, Zaghlūl was the only candidate elected to represent two constituencies in the new Legislative Assembly, winning easily. In January, 1914, by sixty-five to fourteen votes, he became the elected vice president of the Legislative Assembly, which he dominated. He helped to bring down Prime Minister Muhammad Sa'īd and sought to replace him with Fahmī. Since the latter had fallen under the influence of his son-in-law Zaghlūl, the British agent, Lord Horatio Herbert Kitchener, vetoed him. Because of World War I's outbreak, the British authorities prorogued the assembly *sine die*. The British refused refused three times, 1914-1918, to allow Prime Minister Husain Rushdi to take Zaghlūl into his cabinet.

On November 13, 1918, Zaghlūl and two colleagues sought permission to go to London to present their demands for Egypt's complete autonomy. When the British government refused, Zaghlūl organized the Wafd to gain Egyptian independence. He secured thousands of signatures throughout Egypt giving the Wafd power of attorney to act for the nation. The British adviser to the ministry of the interior sought to break this campaign. Zaghlūl composed a long, eloquent appeal to the president of the Paris Conference, Georges Clemenceau, protesting the British protectorate. These and other actions by Zaghlūl led the British on March 9, 1919, to deport Zaghlūl to Malta. Revolutionary fervor now gripped students, workers, lawyers, government clerks, and others throughout Egypt. The British squelched the revolt, but Special High Commissioner Edmund Allenby, sensing a dangerous undercurrent of bitterness and nationalism, on April 7, 1919, freed Zaghlūl and three associates and allowed them to travel to Europe.

Frustration plagued Zaghlūl in Europe. The Paris Peace Conference shunned him. In 1920 in London, Lord Alfred Milner met with him informally, but Zaghlūl refused terms that legalized and strengthened Great Britain's position in Egypt. Thinking he would obtain better terms through backing by the Egyptian people, Zaghlūl agreed to the Wafd's submitting Milner's proposals to them. The public disliked the proposals, whereupon Zaghlūl demanded more from Milner, who then canceled negotiations. Zaghlūl returned to Egypt in March 1921.

Violence erupted in Egypt. Prime Minister 'Adlī Pasha Yakan rejected Zaghlūl's demand that he head the Egyptian delegation going to London to negotiate with Great Britain. Riots and demonstrations supported Zaghlūl. 'Adlī failed in negotiations in London and resigned. In December, 1921, Allenby deported Zaghlūl to Aden, then to the Seychelles, and finally to Gibraltar. In exile Zaghlūl keenly watched developments. He condemned Great Britain's 1922 declaration of Egypt's independence, claiming it was a sham. He denounced the Constitution of 1922 because of its vast royal powers and the difficulty in changing it.

In March, 1923, Allenby released Zaghlūl. The Egyptian people gave him a tumultuous reception. A dislike for other politicians led King Fu'ād I to a temporary rapprochement with Zaghlūl. In the 1923-1924 elections, Zaghlūl led the Wafd to victory, winning 90 percent of the seats in the Chamber of Deputies. On January 27, 1924, Zaghlūl became prime minister. Optimism engulfed Egypt, being best reflected in the self-confidence and deep sense of responsibility shown by the deputies under Zaghlūl's guidance. In September, 1924, Zaghlūl went to London to negotiate a treaty with Prime Minister James Ramsay MacDonald. The latter rejected Zaghlūl's demands: withdrawal of British forces, no control by the British government over Egypt and abolition of the two offices of judicial and financial advisers, no limitation on Egypt's conduct of foreign affairs, abandonment of Great Britain's claim to protect foreigners and to defend the Suez Canal, and unity of Egypt and the Sudan.

Anglo-Egyptian relations soon reached a boiling point. Zaghlūl gave cabinet positions to two noted extremists. In November, 1924, in Cairo, Sir Lee Stack, Governor-General of the Sudan and commander in chief of Egyptian forces, was assassinated. Zaghlūl expressed profound regret, and his government put a price of ten thousand pounds on the assassins' heads. High Commissioner Allenby issued an ultimatum to Egypt, asking for an apology, punishment of the assassins, prohibition of political demonstrations, payment of 500,000 Egyptian pounds, withdrawal within twenty-four hours of Egyptian troops in the Sudan, immediate removal of all restrictions on irrigation in the Sudan El-Gezira, and withdrawal of all objections to Great Britain's assumption of responsibility for foreigners in Egypt. Zaghlūl accepted only the first, second, and fourth demands. Allenby held firm and took over the Alexandria customs. Then, on November 23, 1924, Zaghlūl resigned. His successor accepted all the demands, and the king dissolved parliament. Zaghlūl temporarily left politics, discouraged by politicians' opportunism and reactionary monarchy.

Zaghlūl soon returned to public life, however, determined to preserve the constitution because it would allow his party to recover power, to avoid clashes with Great Britain for fear it would nullify the constitution, and to form a Wafd-Liberal Constitution coalition to overthrow the cabinet. In the 1926 elections, Zaghlūl led the Wafd to outstanding victory, but the high commissioner vetoed Zaghlūl's becoming prime minister. Zaghlūl headed the chamber and quieted anti-British agitation. Soon, however, on August 23, 1927, Zaghlūl died. His death deepened the cynicism in society.

## Summary

Sa'd Zaghlūl's life became synonymous with obtaining Egypt's independence. His pre-1914 career involved a cautious course through service in the British Occupation. As minister of education and minister of justice he sought to prepare Egypt for freedom through moderate reform and Egyptianization of the administration. Thus he advanced secularism in education and law and promoted modernization of al-Azhar University.

By 1914, Zaghlūl emerged as Egypt's leading nationalist. This position he maintained in World War I, counseling loyal opposition. In 1919, Zaghlūl led Egypt's greatest revolution between that of 'Urābī Pasha and Nasser. Nothing, not two exiles, illnesses, attempts on his life, British imperial might, King Fu'ād I's machinations, or politicians' intrigues, deflected Zaghlūl from working for a truly independent Egypt. Perhaps had he lived longer he would have succeeded, because he had modified his extremism toward Great Britain as his life ebbed.

Welding peasants and townspersons together, Zaghlūl created the Wafd, Egypt's largest mass party. This legacy would bode ill for the future. As Wafd chief, Zaghlūl became, in 1924, the first prime minister of the modern Kingdom of Egypt. His administration brought direct suffrage but established a pattern of spoils system by party and continued the practice of muzzling the press. Zaghlūl gained reverence as "The Grand Old Man of Egypt." Tallness, leanness, noble mien, and quick wit characterized him. His oratory captivated audiences. His wife was called "Mother of the Egyptians." Zaghlūl's home became a national museum.

### Bibliography

Ahmed, Jamal Mohammed. *The Intellectual Origins of Egyptian Nationalism.* London and New York: Oxford University Press, 1960. Emphasizes Zughlūl's many years of apprenticeship in Egypt's social and political life. Stresses that Zughlūl's long service and association with Muhammad 'Abduh produced qualities of leadership and intellect that he used skillfully and intelligently.

Harris, Christina Phelps. *Nationalism and Revolution in Egypt.* Stanford, Calif.: Hoover Institution on War, Revolution, and Peace, 1964. Objective treatment of Zughlūl. Contrasts Zughlūl's conciliatory attitude toward Great Britain in 1920 with the British government's intransigent stand. Criticizes Great Britain for the harsh ultimatum of 1924 imposed upon Egypt at the dawn of her first democratic experiment.

Hourani, Albert. *Arabic Thought in the Liberal Age, 1798-1939.* London and New York: Oxford University Press, 1962. In his activities before 1914, Zughlūl reflected the beliefs of Jamal ad-Din al-Afghani and Muhammad 'Abduh. After 1914 Zughlūl became more exacting in his dealings and more exclusive in his conception of the Egyptian nation.

McIntyre, John D., Jr. *The Boycott of the Milner Mission: A Study in Egyptian Nationalism.* New York: Lang, 1985. In 1919, Egypt developed the idea of "complete independence" during the boycott campaign against the Milner Mission. Zughlūl got Milner to include recommendations in his report that would cause the British cabinet to dismiss them.

Marlowe, John. *A History of Modern Egypt and Anglo-Egyptian Relations 1800-1956.* 2d ed. Hamden, Conn.: Archon Books, 1965. Denies that Zughlūl was a statesman. Asserts he had no interest in the Egyptians' welfare or any enthusiasm for reforming the Egyptian administration.

Sayyid-Marsot, Afaf Lutfi al-. *Egypt's Liberal Experiment: 1922-1936.* Berkeley: University of California Press, 1977. Holds that Zughlūl galvanized and united the nationalist movement until he became synonymous with it. Believes that Zughlūl sowed and nurtured the seeds of many political ills that beset political life for decades to come.

Smith, Russell Yates. *The Making of an Egyptian Nationalist.* Ann Arbor, Mich.: University Microfilms, 1973. Sympathetic doctoral dissertation on Zughlūl's pre-1919 political career. States that Zughlūl's outlook was based on his assumption that Great Britain was avoiding preparing Egypt for self-government.

Vatikiotis, P. J. *The Modern History of Egypt.* London: Weidenfeld and Nicolson, and New York: Praeger, 1969. Notes Zughlūl's achievements as minister of education and then as minister of justice. Clearly delineates the strengths and weaknesses in Zughlūl's political activity.

Zayid, Mahmud Y. *Egypt's Struggle for Independence.* Beirut: Khayats, 1965. Affirms that Zughlūl's political role before 1918 was the prelude to his later leadership. Observes that initially after World War I Zughlūl "was ready to forget the Sudan."

*Erving E. Beauregard*

## "BABE" DIDRIKSON ZAHARIAS

*Born:* June 26, 1914; Port Arthur, Texas
*Died:* September 27, 1956; Galveston, Texas
*Area of Achievement:* Sports
*Contribution:* Participating in numerous sports in which she excelled and set several records, Zaharias is recognized as the greatest woman athlete of the first half of the twentieth century.

### Early Life

Mildred Ella Didriksen was born June 26, 1914, in Port Arthur, Texas. Her mother, née Hannah Olson, was born in Norway and emigrated to the United States in 1908; her father, Ole Didriksen, also born in Norway, came to Port Arthur in 1905 and worked as a sailor and carpenter. Throughout her adult life she was known as Babe Didrikson, taking the name "Babe" from the sports hero Babe Ruth and the spelling of her surname, Didrikson, to emphasize that she was of Norwegian rather than Swedish ancestry.

After the 1915 hurricane which devastated Port Arthur, the family, which included her sister and two brothers, moved to nearby Beaumont. Growing up in the rugged south end of the city, Didrikson was a tomboy who shunned feminine qualities and excelled at a variety of athletic endeavors. She was slim and of average height but had a muscular body and was exceptionally well coordinated. Her hair was cut short like a boy's, and she usually wore masculine clothing. As a youth, Didrikson had a belligerent personality and was constantly involved in fights and scrapes.

At Beaumont High School, Didrikson was outstanding at a number of sports, including volleyball, tennis, baseball, basketball, and swimming, but she was not popular with her classmates. Didrikson was a poor student, usually passing only enough courses to remain eligible for athletic competition. All of her energy was directed toward accomplishment on the athletic field, where she had no equal. Didrikson's best sport was basketball, which was the most popular women's sport of the era. During her years in Beaumont, her high school team never lost a game—largely because of her aggressive, coordinated play.

### Life's Work

In February, 1930, Colonel Melvin J. McCombs of the Casualty Insurance Company recruited Didrikson to play for the company's Golden Cyclone basketball team in Dallas. She dropped out of high school in her junior year and took a job as a stenographer with the company with the understanding that she would have time to train and compete in athletics. During the next three years, 1930-1932, Didrikson was selected as an All-American women's basketball player and led the Golden Cyclones to the national championship in 1931. She often scored thirty or more points in an era when a team score of twenty for a game was considered respectable. While in Dallas, she competed in other athletic events, including softball. Didrikson was an excellent pitcher and batted over .400 in the Dallas city league. Increasingly, however, her interest was drawn to track and field and she became a member of the Golden Cyclone track team in 1930. Profiting from coaching provided by the Dallas insurance company and relying on her innate athletic ability, Didrikson soon became the premier women's track and field performer in the nation.

Between 1930 and 1932, Didrikson held American, Olympic, or world records in five different track-and-field events. She stunned the athletic world on July 16, 1932, with her performance at the national amateur track meet for women in Evanston, Illinois. Didrikson entered the meet as the sole member of the Golden Cyclone team and by herself won the national women's team championship by scoring thirty points. The Illinois Women's Athletic Club, which had more that twenty members, scored a total of twenty-two points to place second. In all, Didrikson won six gold medals and broke four world records in a single afternoon. Her performance was the most amazing feat by any individual, male or female, in the annals of track-and-field history. The outstanding performance at Evanston put Didrikson in the headlines of every sports page in the nation and made her one of the most prominent members of the United States Olympic team of 1932.

Although Didrikson had gained wide recognition in her chosen field of athletics, many of her fellow athletes resented her. They complained that she was an aggressive, overbearing braggart who would stop at nothing in order to win. During the trip to Los Angeles for the Olympic Games, many of her teammates came to detest her, but her performance during the Olympiad made her a favorite among sportswriters and with the public. At Los Angeles,

Didrikson won two gold medals and a silver medal, set a world's record, and was the co-holder of two others. She won the javelin event and the eighty-meter hurdles and came in second in the high-jump event amid a controversy which saw two rulings of the judges go against her. Didrikson came very close to winning three Olympic gold medals, which had never been accomplished before by a woman. She became the darling of the press, and her performance in Los Angeles created a springboard for Didrikson's lasting fame as an athlete.

After the 1932 Olympic Games, Didrikson returned to Dallas for a hero's welcome. At the end of 1932, she was voted Woman Athlete of the Year by the Associated Press, an award which she won five additional times, in 1945, 1946, 1947, 1950, and 1954. After a controversy with the Amateur Athletic Union concerning her amateur status, Didrikson turned professional in late 1932. She did some promotional advertising and briefly appeared in a vaudeville act in Chicago, where she performed athletic feats and played her harmonica, a talent she had developed as a youth. Struggling to make a living as a professional athlete, Didrikson played in an exhibition basketball game in Brooklyn, participated in a series of billiard matches, and talked about becoming a long-distance swimmer. In 1933, she decided to barnstorm the rural areas of the country with a professional basketball team called Babe Didrikson's All-Americans. The tour was very successful for several years, as the team traveled the backroads of America playing against local men's teams. In 1934, Didrikson went to Florida and appeared in major league exhibition baseball games during spring training and then played on the famous House of David—all the men on the team sported long beards— baseball team on a nationwide tour. As a result of her many activities, Didrikson was able to earn several thousand dollars each month, a princely sum during the depths of the Depression.

During the mid-1930's, Didrikson's athletic interests increasingly shifted to golf. Receiving encouragement from sportswriter Grantland Rice, she began intensive lessons in 1933, often hitting balls until her hands bled. She played in her first tournament in Texas in 1934 and a year later won the Texas Women's Amateur Championship. That same year, Didrikson was bitterly disappointed when the United States Golf Association (USGA) declared her a professional and banned her from amateur golf. Unable to make a living from the few tournaments open to professionals, Didrikson toured the country with professional golfer Gene Sarazen, participating mainly in exhibition matches.

On December 23, 1938, Didrikson married George Zaharias, a professional wrestler; they had no children. Her marriage helped put to rest rumors that she was in fact a male and other attacks on her femininity. Zaharias became her manager and under his direction she won the 1940 Texas and Western Open golf tournaments. During World War II, Babe Zaharias gave golf exhibitions to raise money for war bonds and agreed to abstain from professional athletics for three years in order to regain her amateur status. In 1943, the USGA restored her amateur standing.

After the war, Babe Zaharias emerged as one of the most successful and popular women golfers in history. In 1945, she played flawless golf on the amateur tour and was named Woman Athlete of the Year for the second time. The following year, she began a string of consecutive tournament victories, a record which has never been equaled by man or woman. During the 1946-1947 seasons, Zaharias won seventeen straight tournaments, including the

British Women's Amateur. She became the first American to win the prestigious British championship. In the summer of 1947, Zaharias turned professional once again, with Fred Corcoran as her manager. She earned an estimated $100,000 in 1948 through various promotions and exhibitions, but only $3,400 in prize money on the professional tour, despite a successful season. In 1948, Corcoran organized the Ladies Professional Golfer's Association (LPGA) in order to help popularize women's golf and increase tournament prize money. During the next several years, the LPGA grew in stature and Zaharias became the leading money winner on the women's professional circuit.

In the spring of 1953, doctors discovered that Zaharias had cancer, and she underwent radical surgery in April, 1953. Although many feared that her athletic career was over, Zaharias played in a golf tournament only fourteen weeks after the surgery. She played well enough the remainder of the year to win the Ben Hogan Comeback of the Year Award. In 1954, Zaharias won five tournaments, including the United States Women's Open, and earned her sixth Woman Athlete of the Year Award. During 1955, doctors diagnosed that the cancer had returned, and she suffered excruciating pain during her final illness. Despite the pain, Zaharias continued to play an occasional round of golf and through her courage served as an inspiration for many Americans. She died in Galveston on September 27, 1956.

## Summary

Babe Didrikson Zaharias was a remarkable woman in many respects. Her place in American sports history is secure in her athletic accomplishments alone: In addition to her six Woman Athlete of the Year Awards, she was named the Woman Athlete of the Half Century by the Associated Press in 1950. No other woman has performed in so many different sports so well. She is arguably the greatest woman athlete of all time.

Beyond this, however, Zaharias was a pioneer who struggled to break down social customs which barred women from various segments of American life. During an era when society dictated that women conform to a particular stereotype, Zaharias persisted in challenging the public's view of woman's place in society. She not only insisted on pursuing a career in sports but also participated in sports considered in the male domain. In her dress, speech, and manner, Zaharias refused to conform to the ladylike image expected of female athletes. She did it successfully because she was such an outstanding athlete. It nevertheless took courage, because she was subjected to the most insidious rumors and innuendos concerning her sex and femininity, attacks which she suffered without complaint.

During her final illness, Zaharias displayed the kind of strength and courage which was a trademark of her career. She was a great athlete, but beyond that she was a courageous pioneer blazing a trail in women's sports which others have followed.

## Bibliography

Cayleff, Susan E. *Babe: The Life and Legend of Babe Didrikson Zaharias.* Urbana: University of Illinois Press, 1995. A well-researched biography in which the author makes use of journalistic sources and extensive interviews with the athlete's family, other sports figures, and close friends.

De Grummond, Lena Young, and Lynn de Grummond Delaune. *Babe Didrikson: Girl Athlete.* Indianapolis: Bobbs-Merrill, 1963. A brief account of Didrikson's life for very young readers.

Gallico, Paul. *The Golden People.* New York: Doubleday, 1965. A moving tribute to Didrikson is part of this anthology by a sportswriter who covered her career.

Johnson, William O., and Nancy P. Williamson. *Whatta-Gal: The Babe Didrikson Story.* Boston: Little Brown, 1975. This popular biography offers the fullest account of Didrikson's life but tends to be uncritical.

Miller, Helen Markley. *Babe Didrikson Zaharias: Striving to Be Champion.* Chicago: Britannica, 1961. A juvenile book aimed at high school students; glorifies Didrikson's life.

Rader, Benjamin G. *American Sports: From the Age of Folk Games to the Age of Spectators.* 4th ed. Upper Saddle River, N.J.: Prentice-Hall, 1999. Gives an overview of American sports history, in the context of which Didrikson's career can be best understood. Rader attempts an assessment of Didrikson's place in history.

Roberts, David. "The Babe Is Here." *Women's Sports and Fitness* 12 no. 8, (November-December, 1990). Profile of Zaharias including her many accomplishments and her provocative nature.

Schoor, Gene. *Babe Didrikson: The World's Greatest Woman Athlete.* New York: Doubleday,

1978. Strictly a popular account which adds a few details and stories omitted by Johnson and Williamson.

Zaharias, Babe Didrikson, as told to Harry Paxton. *This Life I've Led: My Autobiography.* New York: Barnes, 1955; London: Hale, 1956. Avoids the rough spots in Didrikson's life but is good on her family and personality. Useful when read in conjunction with other sources.

*John M. Carroll*

# DARRYL F. ZANUCK

*Born:* September 5, 1902; Wahoo, Nebraska
*Died:* December 22, 1979; Palm Springs, California
*Area of Achievement:* Motion pictures
*Contribution:* As the head of production at two major Hollywood studios, Zanuck was the youngest, fiercest, and most flamboyant of the tycoons who controlled the American film industry.

## Early Life

Darryl F. Zanuck was born September 5, 1902, in Wahoo, Nebraska, a town of two thousand inhabitants, thirty-five miles west of Omaha. His mother, Louise, was the daughter of Henry Torpin, the owner of Wahoo's only hotel, and was a descendant of the legendary English outlaw Dick Turpin. His father, Frank Zanuck, a former Iowa farm boy of Swiss heritage, worked as a night clerk in the Wahoo hotel.

Zanuck's father had a problem with gambling and alcoholism, which drove Louise away from him. She moved to the area around Los Angeles, where she remarried. At that time she invited her seven-year-old son to join her. Zanuck alternated living with his mother and stepfather (with whom he did not get along) in California and with his grandparents in Nebraska until he was able to pass the army physical examination. He passed on September 4, 1916, one day before his fourteenth birthday, having lied about his age.

Zanuck's career in the army lasted two years. He was shipped overseas after the United States entered World War I. Zanuck was sent to the front lines but was saved from actual combat by the armistice. He returned to Nebraska, but he stayed only a few days. Zanuck wanted to be a writer and thought that California was the place to start.

While continuing to write short stories, which he hoped to sell to pulp magazines, Zanuck tried an assortment of odd jobs—eighteen in one year—in the Los Angeles area. After several of his stories were sold, Zanuck realized he could make more money by writing screenplays for motion pictures. He found work as a gag writer for several Hollywood comics (including Mack Sennett, Harold Lloyd, and Charlie Chaplin) before teaming up with director Mal St. Clair to make two-reelers for the Film Booking Offices of America (which later became RKO) and Universal studios.

Zanuck and St. Clair, both of them young and ambitious, happened to see a German shepherd named Rinty in *Where the North Begins* (1923). Thinking the dog wonderful but the film terrible, they convinced the film's producers, Jack and Harry Warner, that they could do better. The result was a six-picture contract at the Warner Bros. studio for both screenwriter (Zanuck) and director (St. Clair), which led to a series of hits starring the dog, renamed Rin Tin Tin.

The Warners' studio, which at the time was approaching bankruptcy, was badly in need of someone like Zanuck. He could write scripts faster and better than anyone else around, and he was a source of new ideas and new energy at the studio. In 1924, Zanuck married Virginia Fox, an actress who had appeared with Buster Keaton. He was on his way up in Hollywood.

## Life's Work

By 1925, Zanuck was earning one thousand dollars a week as the top screenwriter at Warner Bros. When the studio's head of production was fired that year, Zanuck knew the job would be his. He demanded a salary of five thousand dollars a week and got it.

At twenty-three, Zanuck was the youngest head of production in Hollywood. He looked even younger than his age: He stood only five feet, six inches, and was slim and trim at 140 pounds. To look older, he grew a thin mustache and took to smoking large cigars. Always self-confident, Zanuck became even more self-assured in his new position. There was a distinctive air of authority about him, enhanced by a swaggering walk and a sawed-off polo mallet swinging in his hands. His voice retained the nasal Nebraska twang of his youth, but it was a voice that commanded respect and attention.

As head of production, Zanuck ultimately was responsible for all motion pictures released by Warner Bros. He did not take this responsibility lightly, and he plunged himself into all aspects—writing, casting, directing, editing, and more—of dozens of films each year. He is credited with introducing numerous innovations.

For example, when *The Jazz Singer* (1927) was in production, it was Zanuck who urged the use of spoken dialogue, not only singing, in the film. The result—thanks also to Al Jolson's dynamic screen presence—was a hit that ended the era of silent pictures. It was also Zanuck who started the cycle of gangster films at Warner Bros., with *Little Caesar* (1930) and *The Public Enemy* (1931); it was Zanuck who was credited with creating the grapefruit-shoving scene in the latter film.

Zanuck was about to start a new cycle of musicals—beginning with *42nd Street* (1933)—when he quarreled with Jack Warner about the necessity of salary cuts during the Depression. He resigned his post as head of production on April 15, 1933.

A man of Zanuck's talent, however, could not remain idle for long. Joseph Schenck, a longtime Hollywood producer, offered Zanuck the position of production chief at a new studio called Twentieth Century Films. Zanuck accepted. Two years later, when the new studio merged with the failing Fox Films, he was named vice president in charge of production at Twentieth Century-Fox, a position he would hold until 1956.

In his first years at Twentieth Century-Fox, Zanuck was not as bold as he had been at Warner Bros. Shirley Temple was the studio's biggest star in the 1930's, and Zanuck dared not alter the formula that had made her Hollywood's biggest box-office attraction. Zanuck also produced so many costumed romantic epics that the studio earned the sobriquet "Sixteenth Century Fox."

By 1940, Twentieth Century-Fox was on solid enough ground for Zanuck to try more challenging productions. *The Grapes of Wrath* (1940) and *How Green Was My Valley* (1941) were two films that some people had thought too radical for a major Hollywood studio.

In 1942, Zanuck was commissioned a colonel in the United States Army Signal Corps and was sent overseas to make films for the war effort. He took part in the invasion of North Africa before resigning his commission in May, 1943. He returned to Twentieth Century-Fox and embarked on an even more adventurous program of filmmaking.

Under Zanuck's leadership, Twentieth Century-Fox became known as a studio that was not afraid to address problems such as anti-Semitism (*Gentleman's Agreement*, 1947), insanity and mental institutions (*The Snake Pit*, 1948), racial prejudice (*Pinky*, 1949, and *No Way Out*, 1950), and the psychological pressures of war (*Twelve O'Clock High*, 1949).

As a result of a variety of factors—including the advent of television, the effect of a Supreme Court decision against the major studios, and demographic changes in the population of the United States—the filmgoing audience began to dwindle in the 1950's. In response, Twentieth Century-Fox produced the first wide-screen film, *The Robe* (1953). This new process, called CinemaScope, was not, however, enough to stop the inevitable decline of Hollywood's fortunes.

On March 22, 1956, at the age of fifty-three, Zanuck left his wife and family and resigned as head of production to start his own independent company, DFZ productions, operating out of Paris. Over the next five years, Zanuck produced only five films, none of them particularly successful. DFZ's parent corporation, Twentieth Century-Fox, was not doing much better. In 1962, as Zanuck was on his way to developing a big hit, *The Longest Day*, Twentieth Century-Fox was being forced into bankruptcy by continually escalating costs in its production of *Cleopatra* (1963). A major battle of stockholders was under way, and Zanuck was in the thick of it. On July 25, 1962, the company's board of directors ousted Spyros Skouras as president and elected Zanuck as his replacement. Zanuck promptly named his son, Richard, as head of production.

The success of *The Longest Day* (1962) was sufficient to get Twentieth Century-Fox back on its feet. Under Richard Zanuck's guidance, other hits followed, notably *The Sound of Music* (1965) and *Planet of the Apes* (1968). Darryl Zanuck, working in New York as chairman of the board, missed the creative side of the studio and perhaps also was jealous of his son's position. On December 29, 1970, Zanuck fired Richard and took control of the studio. The move, however, backfired. Several major stockholders declared war against Zanuck and on May 18, 1971, he was forced to resign as chairman of the board. He kept only the honorary title of president emeritus.

Zanuck was reunited with his wife in January, 1974, on the occasion of their fiftieth wedding anniversary. He was no longer working, and his health declined quickly over the next five years. Following a heart attack in October, 1979, he died of pneumonia on December 22, 1979.

### Summary

From the 1920's through the 1950's, the American film industry was controlled largely by a handful of men who ran the major Hollywood studios with an iron hand: Louis B. Mayer at Metro-Goldwyn-Mayer, Jack L. Warner at Warner Bros., Harry Cohn at Columbia, Adolph Zukor at Paramount, and Darryl F. Zanuck at Twentieth Century-Fox.

Of this group of studio heads, Zanuck was the youngest, fiercest, and most flamboyant. Unlike some of the others, who preferred quiet anonymity, Zanuck relished his public image as a big-time Hollywood producer. With his ever-present cigar and a lovely (preferably young) actress at his side, Zanuck became the quintessential Hollywood mogul in the minds of many Americans.

Yet there was much more to Zanuck than surface image. He had started out as a screenwriter and knew the motion-picture business from top to bottom. More than any other producer, he was able to immerse himself in all aspects of production; he knew (with a sixth sense) the best way to write, cast, edit, and direct the films released by his studio. He is the only producer to have won the Irving Thalberg Memorial Award three times.

During Zanuck's reign in Hollywood, there were two major developments in motion-picture technology: sound films in the 1920's and wide-screen films in the 1950's. It is not surprising that Zanuck played a pivotal role in presenting both of these innovations to the public. He was fearless, energetic, and intelligent. He used these attributes to make the best films he could during the best years of the American film industry.

The era of the all-powerful movie mogul who controlled the release of several dozen films a year is over. By outliving his rivals, Zanuck was the last of this distinctively American breed: the last of the Hollywood tycoons.

## Bibliography

Behlmer, Rudy. *Memo from Darryl F. Zanuck: The Golden Years at Twentieth Century-Fox.* New York: Grove Press, 1993. A collection of letters, memos, and meeting minutes provide a glimpse into the day-to-day life of the mastermind of Twentieth Century-Fox studios in the 1930s, 1940s, and 1950s.

Campbell, Russell. "The Ideology of the Social Consciousness Movie: Three Films of Darryl F. Zanuck." *Quarterly Review of Film Studies* 3 (Winter, 1978): 49-71. Discusses Zanuck's role in producing *The Grapes of Wrath*, *Gentleman's Agreement*, and *Pinky.* These three films are seen as epitomizing Hollywood's concern for social issues.

Custen, George F. *Century's Fox: Darryl F. Zanuck and the Culture of Hollywood.* New York: Basic, 1997. Custen argues that Zanuck has never been fully recognized because of his lack of polish in a Hollywood culture where such behavior was expected. The author focuses on movie-making and ends with Zanuck's departure for France in 1956. Not a full biography, but interesting reading.

Dunne, John Gregory. *The Studio.* New York: Farrar Straus, 1969. Dunne spent a year observing all aspects of life (from top executives down to stagehands) at Twentieth Century-Fox. The result is one of the most fascinating and revealing looks at an old-style Hollywood studio.

Guild, Leo. *Zanuck: Hollywood's Last Tycoon.* Los Angeles: Holloway House, 1970. A breezy, popular biography of Zanuck, but with a fair assessment of his motion-picture career within the larger context of the Hollywood studio system.

Gussow, Mel. *Don't Say Yes Until I Finish Talking: A Biography of Darryl F. Zanuck.* New York: Doubleday, and London: Allen, 1971. Written with Zanuck's cooperation, but (according to Gussow) not an "authorized biography." Because Zanuck talked to Gussow more than to anyone else, this is an invaluable resource for understanding Zanuck's point of view.

Mosley, Leonard. *Zanuck: The Rise and Fall of Hollywood's Last Tycoon.* London: Granada, and Boston: Little Brown, 1984. This is the most thorough and carefully researched biography of Zanuck to date. Mosley makes a special effort to understand Zanuck's personality, particularly his competitiveness and his view of women as objects to be conquered sexually.

Schrank, Joseph. "Facing Zanuck." *American Heritage* 35 (December, 1983): 40-44. A brief but revealing firsthand account of working with Zanuck at Twentieth Century-Fox on the film *Song of the Islands* (1942).

Zierold, Norman. *The Moguls.* New York: Coward-McCann, and London: Hamilton, 1969. This history of film tycoons includes a chapter on Zanuck and Twentieth Century-Fox. It emphasizes the fact that Zanuck was a Gentile in a business that was dominated by Jewish immigrants.

*James I. Deutsch*

## EMILIANO ZAPATA

*Born:* August 8, 1879; Anenecuilco, Morelos, Mexico

*Died:* April 10, 1919; Hacienda Chinameca, Morelos, Mexico

*Areas of Achievement:* Social reform and the military

*Contribution:* Zapata was a notable rebel leader of peasant guerrillas in the Mexican Revolution who became a legendary folk hero among the poor Mexican farmers of Morelos because of his idealistic devotion to land reform and his brilliant guerrilla tactics during the Revolution.

### Early Life

Emiliano Zapata, born in the small village of Anenecuilco in the tiny Mexican state of Morelos on August 8, 1879, was the ninth of ten children, only four of whom survived, born to Cleofas and Gabriel Zapata. The Zapatas were a proud family of primarily Indian heritage. They owned a modest ranch and lived in a small adobe-and-stone house, but they were better off than many of their neighbors who, owning no land, had to work on the lands of the wealthy sugar plantation owners in a state of virtual peonage. Zapata, with little formal education, attended an inadequate school at the nearby village of Ayala. When he left school at the age of twelve, he could barely read and write.

Orphaned at the age of fifteen, Zapata and his elder brother, Eufemio, inherited the ranch although his brother soon left home as did his two sisters. Zapata worked the land and even sharecropped a few acres from the local hacienda, supplementing his earnings by buying and selling mules and occasionally horses. Zapata developed into a skilled horseman and a well-respected horse trainer. The characteristics of the native peoples were reflected in the young Zapata—he was quiet, honest, courteous, gentle, and distrustful of strangers. Zapata's own attachment to the land and village was evidenced by his people, who saw the land as belonging to the villagers since they, like their Indian ancestors, had no clear concept of private land ownership.

As a young boy, Zapata learned to hate the rich landowners in Morelos as he witnessed evictions of peasants from their huts and small plots of land. The sugar planters, who needed more land for expansion into world markets, were supported by the Mexican government, which was headed by the despotic dictator, Porfirio Díaz. Zapata was a popular young man; he was something of a dandy and often dressed on holidays in black with tight-fitting trousers completed by an enormous sombrero. His appreciation for the fine life extended to riding a black or white, silver-saddled horse. His single life would end with his marriage, at the age of thirty-two, in 1911. His wife, Josefa Espejo, was the daughter of a successful livestock dealer from Ayala.

Conflict with authority was not unusual for Zapata, as he often defended fellow villagers against the oppressive landowners or the rural police. This conflict not only hardened him and won for him respect from the villagers but also helped to prepare him for the leadership role that was thrust upon him in 1909 when he was elected, at the age of thirty, president of the village council and defense committee of Anenecuilco. He was about to participate in the cataclysmic Mexican Revolution, which would forge for him a place in Mexican history.

### Life's Work

Zapata became immersed in regional politics in 1909, when he supported an anti-Díaz candidate for the governorship of Morelos. The corrupt Díaz, however, used his influence along with federal troops to get his own candidate "elected." Zapata continued to fight for peasant land rights and unsuccessfully sought legal assistance on behalf of the villages. In 1909, unrest in Morelos led to the formation of small, poorly armed guerrilla bands seeking redress against the oppressive policies of the government. Disappointed at the futility of legal means, Zapata urged direct action and led villagers in taking the disputed fields. Others in the area followed Zapata's example and began reclaiming disputed lands.

In 1910, the ruthless Díaz, swept aside by the tide of revolution, was replaced by Francisco Madero, who promised sweeping reforms for Mexico. Madero called for the various revolutionary leaders, including Zapata, to disband their guerrillas and support him. Zapata was willing to comply with Madero's request, but, when Madero's promised land distribution did not occur, he and other dissatisfied leaders throughout Mexico rose in rebellion against Madero. The guerrilla chieftains elected him supreme chief of the revolutionary movement in the south. He later became General

Zapata, head of the Liberation Army of the South. His efficiency, honesty, and popular appeal led to large numbers of followers in the ranks of his ragtag army. He proved to be a strong leader, who inspired his troops through quiet persuasion.

Unlike Madero, who seemingly wanted only middle-class political and economic reform for Mexico, and other revolutionary leaders who supported narrow self-interest, Zapata passionately sought social justice for the mistreated landless peasants of Morelos and neighboring states in the south. This position placed him out of the mainstream of the Revolution with its emphasis on middle-class values and made him the target of Madero and later leaders such as Victoriano Huerta and Venustiano Carranza, who saw him as a troublemaker and radical. Zapata nevertheless persisted in his passion for the rural poor.

In 1913, the sadistic and brutal General Huerta seized control of the government and had Madero murdered. Zapata had hoped to lay down his arms and go home and farm his lands, but, after initially offering support to Huerta, he soon found himself in conflict with the new president. Zapata, the "Attila of the South" as the Mexican newspapers called him, was one of four guerrilla leaders who opposed Huerta along with Carranza in the northeast, the infamous Pancho Villa in Chihuahua to the north, and Álvaro Obregón in Sonora to the northwest. Huerta was also opposed by the President of the United States, Woodrow Wilson. In the face of such opposition, Huerta fell from power in 1914.

Carranza, in an attempt to take power, invited all the revolutionary leaders to a convention in order to solicit their support, but Villa and Zapata refused to participate. Zapata was willing to quit the Revolution if Carranza would adopt his Plan of Ayala, which called for distribution of land to the landless peasants. According to the plan, a portion of land would be expropriated from each hacienda with the landowners receiving compensation. Landowners who would not cooperate would lose their entire lands. Stolen lands, furthermore, would be returned to the proper owners. Zapata had one of his chief aides, Otilio Montaño, a former schoolteacher, compose the plan, which was proclaimed by Zapata and his leading chiefs in November, 1911. Some suggested that Zapata had the plan written to counter charges from Mexico City that the Zapatistas were simply bandits who looted and pillaged in the countryside and not revolutionaries fighting for a true cause. Carranza found Zapata's demands to be too inflexible and did not agree to them.

Five years of brutal civil war ensued as General Obregón allied himself with Carranza against the recalcitrant Villa and Zapata. Mexico City, a virtual no-man's-land with generals coming and going, on one occasion was occupied by the forces of Villa and Zapata. The citizens of Mexico City expected the Zapatistas to wreak havoc in the city but were amazed at their timidness and gentleness. Later, Zapata and his followers quietly left the city to Villa.

In 1915, Obregón's forces defeated Villa, leaving Zapata in opposition to Carranza. Carranza denounced Zapata as a renegade and bandit who knew nothing about government. Zapata's followers continued to threaten the capital and in areas under their control confiscated land without using the legal procedures advocated by Carranza. Even though they were unorganized, Zapata's men were effective fighters who laid traps and ambushes, cut supply lines, took small towns while avoiding larger ones, and always avoided open formal battles unless they had a good assurance of victory. These tactics proved frustrating to the large government forces of Carranza.

For several years, Carranza attempted, without success, to defeat Zapata in Morelos. General Pablo González commanded Carranza's troops there and carried on a "scorched earth" policy against the Zapatistas by destroying those villages that he believed might give sanctuary to Zapata. The corrupt González showed little respect for Zapata and his troops, labeling them as uneducated, country hicks. In 1919, González, with the help of one of his colonels, Jesús M. Guajardo, had Zapata killed through treachery and deceit. González had Guajardo pretend to defect to Zapata in order to kill him. On April 10, Guajardo invited Zapata to dine with him at his hacienda, and, after some hesitation, Zapata accepted. When Zapata reached the door, Guajardo's men fired two volleys at point blank into him. The beloved leader of the peasants was dead. His body was strapped to a mule and taken to Cuautla, the capital of Morelos, and openly displayed. Though thousands came to see the body, many of his supporters refused to believe he was dead; they thought that it was a trick to fool the authorities and that Zapata had actually escaped. People later reported that they saw Zapata riding across the fields of Morelos on his white horse. Yet the hero who could do no wrong in the eyes of the landless peasants was gone; his ideals, however, did not die with him because the farmers of Morelos continued their cry for "land and liberty" long after 1919.

### Summary

Emiliano Zapata occupies a controversial place in Mexican history. To his followers, he was a romantic folk hero who died for a noble cause. To his enemies, he was a savage villain, the leader of wild revolutionary bandits who committed atrocities on the Mexican populace. Being a radical revolutionary in their eyes, he also did not conform to their notion of middle-class revolution. The truth no doubt lies somewhere in between. Zapata was an honest and simple man who reluctantly became an effective leader of disorganized guerrillas who adapted his military tactics to fit the situation at hand and avoid defeat by larger and better armed forces. (Interestingly enough, these same tactics would later be used in limited wars following World War II.) He was a born leader who used his natural abilities to try to right the wrongs he saw in his native land. The provincial Zapata pales in comparison to revolutionary leaders such as Vladimir Ilich Lenin and Mao Tse-tung, who were worldly intellectuals who brought about a radical transformation in their respective societies. It is interesting to note that Zapata did not break with the Church as did other Mexican revolutionaries, who criticized the Church for doing little to ease social ills in Mexico. Nevertheless, he remains a legend and an inspiration to the downtrodden and unfortunate natives of Mexico.

### Bibliography

Brenner, Anita. *The Wind That Swept Mexico: The History of the Mexican Revolution, 1910-1942.* New York and London: Harper, 1943. This book contains one hundred concisely written pages of text, and it contains 184 historical photographs, which present the Mexican Revolution in all of its drama and poignance. The author witnessed the Revolution as a child.

Brunk, Samuel. "Remembering Emiliano Zapata: Three Moments in the Posthumous Career of the Martyr of Chinameca." *Hispanic American Historical Review* 78, no. 3 (August, 1998). The author considers the role played by Zapata in Mexican land reform in the early twentieth century.

———. "'The Sad Situation of Civilians and Soldiers': The Banditry of Zapatismo in the Mexican Revolution." *American Historical Review* 101, no. 2 (April, 1996). Examination of grassroots revolutions, in particular that led by Zapata in Mexico, and the internal conflicts that often plagued them.

Dunn, H. H. *The Crimson Jester: Zapata of Mexico.* New York: McBride, 1933; London: Harrap, 1934. A sensationalized account of Zapata's life written in dialogue form. The author compares Zapata to Geronimo and Julius Caesar. Contains no bibliography.

Newell, Peter E. *Zapata of Mexico.* Somerville, Mass.: Black Thorn, 1979. A simply written, straightforward biography of Zapata. Contains interesting photographs and illustrations. Written primarily from secondary sources.

Parkinson, Roger. *Zapata.* New York: Stein and Day, 1980. A very interesting and scholarly book that builds on Womack's biography. Contains a helpful index, a bibliography, and end notes.

Ruiz, Ramón Eduardo. *The Great Rebellion: Mexico, 1905-1924.* New York: Norton, 1980; London: Norton, 1982. A scholarly reinterpretation of the Mexican Revolution. The author emphasizes the middle-class nature of the Revolution. Contains an excellent chapter on Zapata.

Womack, John. *Zapata and the Mexican Revolution.* New York: Knopf, 1968; London: Thames and Hudson, 1969. Probably the definitive work on Zapata. A scholarly analysis of Zapata and his role in the Revolution. Contains a very helpful bibliography, footnotes, and appendices.

*James E. Southerland*

# FERDINAND VON ZEPPELIN

*Born:* July 8, 1838; Konstanz, Baden
*Died:* March 8, 1917; Charlottenburg, Germany
*Area of Achievement:* Aeronautics
*Contribution:* Zeppelin developed the concepts and designs for the construction of the first practical airships capable of navigating over long distances. The success of Zeppelin's rigid dirigibles served to stimulate experimentation in all areas of aeronautics and paved the way for military and commercial applications of airships.

## Early Life

Ferdinand von Zeppelin was born into a family with a long history of military and diplomatic service. His grandfather, Ferdinand Ludwig Zeppelin, was minister of foreign affairs for the King of Württemburg; his father, Count Frederich von Zeppelin, was in the diplomatic service of a German prince. In 1834, Count Frederich married Amelie Macaire d'Hogurre, then living in her grandparents' house in Konstanz, Baden; it was there that Ferdinand, his brother Eberhard, and his sister Eugenie were born. In 1840, Count Frederich retired from his diplomatic post, purchased a large estate near Girsberg, on the shores of Lake Constance, and devoted his life to managing his estate, rearing his children, and caring for his invalid wife.

Ferdinand's mother and father were gentle, loving parents, and they provided for their children a home that was harmonious and completely free of ostentation. When Ferdinand entered a preparatory school in Stuttgart, he concentrated on studies in physics, chemistry, and mathematics, a course that was a significant departure from the one normally followed by boys intent on a military career. It was an early indication, however, that Zeppelin's career would not follow a predictable pattern.

In 1857, at age nineteen, Zeppelin was graduated from the War Academy at Ludwigsburg and joined an infantry regiment as a lieutenant. After only a year, he became disenchanted with the monotony of the army's discipline and asked for a leave of absence to continue his engineering studies at the University of Tübingen. He then elected to join an engineer corps stationed at Ulm—a post considered inappropriate for a count, but one which he believed was more suited to his interests and sense of adventure. In less than a year, he was promoted to the rank of first lieutenant and was assigned to the general staff.

With little prospect of being involved in military action on the home front, young Zeppelin turned his attention to the Civil War being fought in the United States. He conceived the idea of acting as a military observer for the German army, ostensibly to study the organization of volunteer armies that were being used extensively in the American conflict; he believed, moreover, as he prophetically noted in his request to the king: "The Americans are especially inventive in the adaptation of technical developments for military purposes. I do not have to mention the benefits such a journey promises to have for the general enlightenment."

In May of 1863, Zeppelin's leave of absence was approved and he set sail for the United States. He obtained letters of introduction from President Abraham Lincoln that enabled him to travel freely among the Union armies; he also participated in several campaigns, including the battles of Fredericksburg and Ashby's Gap in Virginia. Desiring to learn as much as possible about this new world, he then embarked on a journey westward, traveling first by

train through the northeast from New York City through Buffalo, Erie, Cleveland, and Detroit. From Detroit he explored Lake Huron and Lake Superior by steamer. In Superior, Wisconsin, Zeppelin joined a small party intent on exploring the headwaters of the Mississippi River; after a journey of twenty-one days, the party arrived at Fort Snelling in St. Paul, Minnesota.

During his visit at Fort Snelling Zeppelin was able to observe the flight of a captive hot-air balloon. The Union Army had been experimenting with the use of balloons as observation posts and, at Fort Snelling, was in the process of evaluating the merits of a new design. Zeppelin seized the opportunity for a flight and purchased enough gas to ascend several hundred feet. It was there that the military advantages of an aerial reconnaissance platform became evident to him; it was there, too, that he first started thinking of ways to control the flight of a free-floating balloon.

### Life's Work

Ten years would pass before Zeppelin began to work seriously on his designs for a controllable balloon, although he did continue to research the literature then available on the subject. He returned to Germany with a rank of captain and served on the personal staff of King Charles I of Württemberg during the war between Austria and Prussia. He received his first decoration for bravery—the Knight's Cross—during the Battle of Aschaffenburg in 1866; he earned a second commendation—the Royal Cross, First Class—for his exploits during the war with France in 1870. During the siege of Paris, he again had the opportunity to observe the effective use of free-floating balloons during a military operation. The siege lasted for four months, but more than a hundred influential military and political leaders were able to escape from the city using a total of sixty-four hot-air balloons. Convinced that this exploit had seriously prolonged the war, Zeppelin renewed his studies of balloons and began developing some preliminary designs for a rigid dirigible.

The specifications that he chose for his airship were to remain practically unchanged over the course of his career. He envisioned an elongated, aerodynamically shaped airship with an internal, lightweight skeletal framework supported by a number of separate gas-filled cells attached to the framework. The payload and the engines would be contained in separate gondolas suspended below the main structure; the control surfaces, such as rudders, would be attached to the exterior of the airship in a position that would provide maximum control over direction and attitude. In 1887, he sent a letter to the king describing his designs and outlining the various applications that he could foresee for such an airship. Zeppelin believed that his invention would be very important in warfare, suitable for civilian transport, and beneficial for voyages of exploration and discovery.

Although his political and military career had flourished (he was promoted to the rank of brigadier general in 1888), Zeppelin decided to devote more of his time to his family; thus, in 1890 he retired from the army and returned to his home in Stuttgart. This early retirement allowed him to continue the development of his airship.

The realization of his dream of powered, controlled flight would not be fulfilled for another decade. He hired Theodore Kolb, an experienced engineer, and together they began a series of tests on engines, propellers, and construction materials. The most serious problem confronting Zeppelin—one that would continue to impede his work throughout the next fifteen years—was financing the construction of his design. He appealed to his friends in court, but the government was not interested in funding his experiments; the war ministry believed that Zeppelin's ideas were too radical. In 1896 Zeppelin sent a report on his designs and experiments to the German Association of Engineers with the request that they review his designs and perhaps support his request for funds from the government. The society reported favorably on the project; as a result, a company was formed for the construction of the airship, and solicitations were made to the public for support. Approximately 90 percent of the $250,000 required for the project was obtained through public subscriptions and the remainder came from Zeppelin's personal funds. The Daimler Motorworks was contracted to design and build a lightweight gasoline engine. The company also needed to find a supplier of the then-scarce metal aluminum.

On July 2, 1900, Zeppelin's dream became a reality: The first rigid, engine-powered airship was ready for its first flight. The floating hangar was turned into the wind and the airship was pulled out by a small steamer. To the crowd of spectators on the shore, it was an impressive sight. The LZ-1 was a cigar-shaped airship 419 feet long and thirty-eight feet in diameter, supported by seventeen gas cells containing eleven thousand cubic meters of gas. Suspended below the airship were two gondolas connected by a long gangplank; the rear gondola supported two Daimler gasoline engines turning four propellers. At 8:03 A.M., the airship was freed of its restraining ropes, and, driven by its propellers, the ship moved away at a speed of about eight miles per hour. The flight lasted about fifteen minutes, and the ship landed safely near Immenstaad. Although there had been some difficulties with the directional controls, Zeppelin declared that the flight was a success. In the next four months, the LZ-1 made two more flights, during which refinements to the engines and steering mechanisms were tested. Airspeed approached eighteen miles per hour and control of the airship improved. By then, however, the funds had become depleted and the company could no longer pay for material and gas. As a result, the LZ-1 was dismantled and the hangar torn down.

During the next five years Zeppelin used his entire personal fortune to begin construction of a second ship. Through lotteries and other public appeals he was able to raise enough money to finish the LZ-2. It flew successfully in 1906 and demonstrated the increased speed and control that the new eighty-five-horsepower engines provided. Unfortunately, the ship was destroyed by fire during a storm shortly after its first flight. Completely destitute and disheartened by the disaster, Zeppelin thought that his work was at an end. Public sentiment had turned in his favor, however, and, as a result, the Parliament voted to subsidize the construction of the LZ-3. It proved to be such a success that the government authorized a sum to be included in the annual budget for the construction and testing of airships.

For the next eleven years, Zeppelin worked tirelessly on the design and testing of more than a hundred airships. He was at the helm of the LZ-4 during its flight from Lake Constance to Switzerland. The airship carried eleven passengers at the amazing speed of forty miles per hour. In 1912, he piloted the navy's first ship (LZ-12) on its historic trip of more than a thousand miles to and from Denmark. He helped to develop the airships used in the first commercial airline routes, and during World War I he supervised the construction of more than a hundred airships for the army and navy.

### Summary

The first decade of human flight is representative of human ingenuity in its most adventuresome and audacious form. In particular, the sight of the massive airships that appeared in the skies over Germany, Great Britain, France, and the United States seemed to symbolize the inevitable mastery of humankind over the forces of nature. It is not often remembered that three years before the flight of Orville and Wilbur Wright, Ferdinand von Zeppelin and a crew of three had piloted a four-hundred-foot-long airship on a flight over southern Germany for a distance of four miles and at an altitude of thirteen hundred feet. Furthermore, in the year 1910, when a single American pilot took forty-nine days to fly thirty-two hundred miles across the United States, Zeppelin's dirigible (LZ-6) had flown thirty-four trips carrying a total of eleven hundred passengers for a distance of thirty-one hundred miles.

The technological innovations that accompanied the development of the airship found applications in aircraft design and other areas of engineering. Zeppelin was responsible for the development of the alloy Duralumin in his search for lighter and stronger structural materials. Zeppelin was convinced that his airships would be an important asset to the army in the event of war but, ironically, it was the German navy that derived the most benefit from his Zeppelins. At the outbreak of World War I, several of Zeppelin's airships were armed with machine guns and fitted with bomb racks, but they proved to be susceptible to the vagaries of the weather and attacks by enemy aircraft; thus, they were only marginally effective as weapons. Yet the navy found that their long range made them ideally suited to scout the location of enemy warships and eventually had more than sixty airships in service during the war. In January, 1915, two army airships did succeed in crossing the English Channel to discharge their small loads of bombs on two English cities, but the damage was more psychological than real. This air raid demonstrated one important fact: Cities and civilians could no longer rely on fortifications or oceans to protect them from feeling the effects of war. The Zeppelins were perceived to be more of a threat than they actually proved to be, but their existence prompted the British to develop more effective anti-aircraft weapons and stimulated the development of high-performance aircraft capable of flying to the high altitudes at which the airships operated.

On the occasion of his seventieth birthday, Zeppelin expressed the hope that one day his airships would provide the means to bring together the peoples of the world; in fact, he did live long enough to see the establishment of regular air routes between a number of cities in Europe. His airship, the

*Victoria Luise*, made nearly five hundred scheduled flights carrying a total of ninety-eight hundred passengers. Unfortunately, he did not live to see the great flights of the 1920's and 1930's: the flight of the British R34 across the Atlantic Ocean in July of 1919, of the *Norge*, four thousand miles across the North Pole in 1926, and of the *Graf Zeppelin* around the world in 1929.

The culmination of Zeppelin's work was the magnificent airships—the *Hindenburg* and the *Graf Zeppelin*. From 1928 to 1937, they carried a total of forty thousand passengers on regularly scheduled flights between Germany, New York, and Buenos Aires, providing accommodations and service comparable to those of the finest ocean liners. For a time it appeared that the airship would dominate long-distance air travel, but the explosion of the *Hindenburg* at Lakehurst Naval Station in 1937 ended that possibility; thereafter, production of rigid airships ceased.

### Bibliography

Goldsmith, Margaret. *Zeppelin: A Biography*. London: Cape, and New York: Morrow, 1931. A general biography containing many personal anecdotes that illustrate the unique personality of the subject.

Hoyt, Edwin P. *The Zeppelins*. New York: Lothrop Lee, 1969. An abbreviated account of the development of the Zeppelins with an emphasis on the use of the airship as a military weapon.

Karwatka, Dennis. "Technology's Past." *Tech Directions* 56, no. 8 (March, 1997). Focuses on Zeppelin and his airships.

Le Tissier, Tony. *Zhukov at the Oder: The Decisive Battle for Berlin*. Westport, Conn.: Greenwood Press, 1996. The author examines the last major land battle in Europe in World War II, having researched both official sources and information from those involved. Includes maps and detailed illustrations of operations.

Lehmann, Ernst A., and Howard L. Mingos. *The Zeppelins*. London: Putnam, and New York: Sears, 1927. An account of the wartime activities of Germany's airship squadrons by two of Zeppelin's associates.

Nitske, W. Robert. *The Zeppelin Story*. South Brunswick, N.J.: Barnes, 1977. A general history of the development of the rigid airship, beginning with the experiments with free-floating balloons and concluding with the development of successful long-range airships capable of transoceanic travel.

Ventry, Lord, and Eugène M. Koleśnik. *Airship Saga: The History of Airships Seen Through the Eyes of the Men Who Designed, Built, and Flew Them*. Poole, Dorset: Blandford Press, and New York: Sterling, 1982. A pictorial history of the airship, containing numerous personal accounts of the inventors and aviators who flew them.

*C. D. Alexander*

# CLARA ZETKIN

*Born:* July 5, 1857; Wiederau, Saxony

*Died:* June 20, 1933; Arkhangelskoye, near Moscow, U.S.S.R.

*Areas of Achievement:* Women's rights, politics, social reform, trade unionism

*Contribution:* With Friedrich Engels and August Bebel, Zetkin pioneered a Marxist analysis of women's status in a capitalist society. Her objective was to create a new social order free of political and economic oppression.

## Early Life

Clara Eissner, the eldest of three children, was born in Wiederau near Leipzig in Saxony, a small town of textile workers and small farmers. Her father, Gottfried Eissner, poor but educated, was the village schoolteacher and church organist. His second wife, Josephine Vitale Eissner, was the widow of a doctor in Leipzig, a believer in the French Revolutionary ideals of liberty, equality, and fraternity. Frau Eissner founded in Wiederau a *Frauenverein*, or women's educational society, to teach local women to expect and get economic equality.

Women's educational societies of this type were offshoots of the bourgeois German Women's Association and the Federation of German Women's Associations, led by feminist idealists such as Auguste Schmidt and Luise Otto. In 1872, when Herr Eissner retired, the family moved to Leipzig so that Clara could attend the Van Steyber Institute founded by Schmidt and Otto. While at the institute from 1875 to 1878, Clara read social democratic newspapers and other socialist writings and attended meetings of the Leipzig Women's Education Society and the National Association of German Women.

In 1878, Clara met some local Russian students and émigrés, who introduced her to Wilhelm Liebknecht's German Social Democratic Party (SPD), and her political education began. One of the émigrés from Odessa, Russia, Ossip Zetkin, introduced Clara to scientific socialism and the writings of Karl Marx and Friedrich Engels. He also encouraged her to live a working-class life-style and to attend lectures of the Leipzig Worker's Education Society. In 1879, she visited Russia, and during an extensive stay she developed a strong appreciation of Russian revolutionary spirit. Clara's newly raised proletarian consciousness led to a break with her family and her mentor, Schmidt.

When Ossip was expelled from Germany for illegal political activity under the government's 1878 Anti-Socialist Law, Clara left Germany. First, she went to Linz, Austria, where she tutored factory workers. In 1882, she moved to Zurich with leaders of the exiled SPD to write propaganda for Party literature to be smuggled into Germany. In November, 1882, after five months in Zurich, Clara moved to Paris to join Zetkin. Although she did not marry him, for fear of losing her German citizenship, Clara took Ossip's name and had two sons by him, Maxim (1883) and Konstantine (1885).

## Life's Work

During these years in Paris, Clara Zetkin began her life's work of using scientific socialism to improve the condition of the proletariat and to achieve equality for proletarian women. Ironically, the second stage in her evolution from political theorist to activist resulted from a reconciliation with her bourgeois family. In 1886, Zetkin succumbed to the harsh poverty of the Paris years and, suffering from tuberculosis, was invited by her family to return to Leipzig to convalesce. In Leipzig, she gave her first public speech to explain Bebel's ideas in his book *Die Frau und der Sozialismus* (1879; *Woman and Socialism*, 1910). Bebel's theory was that class revolution would end the oppression of both workers and women and lead to women's economic development and equality with men. This was Zetkin's view as well.

Returning to Paris, Zetkin nursed Ossip until his death in January, 1889, from spinal tuberculosis. Zetkin's grief was cut short by the need to prepare for the Second International Congress, which met in Paris on the centennial of Bastille Day (July 14, 1889). As one of only eight official woman delegates, Zetkin represented working-class women of Berlin and had clearly moved from theory to activism. Zetkin's speech, published later as *Die Arbeiterinnen und Frauenfrage der Gegenwart* (1889; *Working Women and the Contemporary Woman Question*, 1984), stated clearly that the issue of women's emancipation is a question of work. Blaming capitalism for women's oppression, Zetkin declared that women's work outside the home would not result in an improvement of the family income or independence until women's labor no longer resulted simply in profits for capitalists. Neither political equality nor access to education and the benefits of capitalism would solve the problem; only a social revolution and the end of the capitalist system would. At the congress, however, Zetkin's view that women should have no special privileges was vetoed. The delegates favored equal pay for equal work and opposed dangerous work for women.

At this Second International, Zetkin was named one of seven women to create the Berlin Agitation Committee responsible for educating and recruiting women into the SPD. This committee became the executive of a Socialist women's movement. Zetkin accepted this appointment only because women were by German law forbidden membership in political parties; she believed that women should be equal members of the party.

In 1890, the Reichstag did not renew Otto yon Bismarck's Anti-Socialist Laws, and the SPD exiles returned to Germany. In Stuttgart, Zetkin was named editor of *Die Gleichheit*, the SPD's journal for women. The first issue, in January, 1892, defined the journal's policy and purpose as educating enlightened women about Marxism and Social Democratic principles and the need for economic equality while opposing bourgeois feminist emphasis on reforms of the law.

During these years when women could not belong to the SPD, the trade union movement served as a means of recruiting women. Zetkin printed handbills, gathered strike funds, and set up international communication networks among the unions. She gave more than three hundred speeches, and, by 1896 and the SPD Congress at Gotha, her position on women had changed in response to the contemporary German political context. Although Zetkin still believed that the needs of proletarian women were different from those of bourgeois women and that only the destruction of the capitalist system would relieve women's oppression, she conceded that women needed special protections to allow them to be mothers as well as workers. Zetkin did not claim special privilege, however, and, while working for the SPD, she also reared her two sons. Zetkin also conceded that women's suffrage would make socialism stronger in the fight against capitalism.

Such concessions were the exception not the rule. As early as 1890, Zetkin was fighting the battle against Eduard Bernstein's revisionist interpretation of Marx's doctrine that approved compromise with capitalism and the abandonment of the class struggle. The years after 1900 saw the SPD and the women's movement become more concerned with protective legislation—insurance benefits, education, and suffrage. Zetkin found herself under attack as well. Revisionists complained that *Die Gleichheit* under Zetkin's leadership was too theoretical and demanded that the journal appeal to a more general audience. In 1905, as the circulation began to grow, she added supplements for housewives and for children, until by 1914, with a readership of 125,000, these features became a regular part of the paper.

Complaints against Zetkin were difficult to act upon because she had become an important leader in the SPD. Although women could not be members of the SPD until 1908, after 1890 women were elected to party congresses, and in 1895 Zetkin was the first woman elected to sit on the SPD governing body. In 1906, she was appointed one of seven members of the central committee on education at a time when the German government was trying to strengthen religious influence in the schools.

In 1908, when women were finally permitted to participate legally in political party activity, Zetkin fought hard to preserve an autonomous women's movement both to prevent decisions about women from being made by a predominantly male SPD executive committee and to preserve a radical enclave within the party. Again Zetkin's perspective had changed. She saw not only that proletarian women had different needs from those of bourgeois women but also that proletarian women had different needs from proletarian men. In 1907, the First International Women's Conference was held in Stuttgart at the same time that the International Socialist Congress was meeting there. A separate International Women's Bureau was created with Zetkin as Secretary and *Die Gleichheit* as the official organ of communication. The Second International Women's Conference met in 1910 in Copenhagen, where Zetkin led the fight to oppose socialist support for a restricted female suffrage as proposed in Great Britain and Belgium.

As Europe moved closer to war, Zetkin, along with Rosa Luxemburg and other radical socialists, found their struggle against revisionism becoming more difficult and unpopular. They had to fight not only the German government and capitalism but also a more conservative SPD that favored parliamentary methods and officially opposed the mass strike. In 1911, at the SPD Congress in Jena, Zetkin and Luxemburg fought unsuccessfully to get the party to condemn all imperialism, including that of Germany. On August 4, 1914, Zetkin, Luxemburg, Franz Mehring, and Karl Liebknecht denounced the party's decision to vote for war credits. In March, 1915, Zetkin, without party permission, organized another women's conference to protest the war. After spending a few months in protective custody for continuing to oppose the government in *Die Gleichheit* against party orders, Zetkin was finally removed as editor by the SPD in May, 1917. They claimed her views in support of the Bolshevik Revolution and against war were unpalatable to women.

By this time Zetkin had transferred her political allegiance first to the Independent Social-Democratic Party, or antiwar socialists, and then had joined Liebknecht, Luxemburg, and Mehring as a founding member of the Gruppe Internationale, or the Spartacus League, which in November, 1918, became the German Communist Party (KPD).

Zetkin's message, however, did not change. In 1919, addressing the Comintern (the Third International Congress), Zetkin reminded the party that a dictatorship of the proletariat could not work without proletarian women. She warned the Communist Party to educate women for their role in the international struggle. Elected international secretary of Communist women in 1920, Zetkin proclaimed again that the woman question was part of the worker question.

Zetkin's new postwar political duties required her to live part of the time in the Soviet Union, where she worked with Vladimir Ilich Lenin and Aleksandra Kollontai, the only Russian woman on the Comintern. Although her health was not good, Zetkin continued to write and speak out against persecution, including racist acts in the United States. In addition, she represented the German Communist Party in the Reichstag as long as Adolf Hitler allowed it to meet. In the summer of 1932, she went to Berlin to convene the Reichstag, a privilege traditionally exercised by the eldest living member. She took the opportunity to denounce Fascism and Hitler and to appeal for the creation of a United Front of Workers to include the millions of laboring women. Within a year, she died, on June 20, 1933, in the Soviet Union.

### Summary

Although Clara Zetkin was estranged from Soviet politics after the death of Lenin, she was buried with great ceremony in the Kremlin wall. Attending her funeral and eulogizing her were Soviet and Eastern European Communist officials, including Joseph Stalin, Nadezhda Krupskaya (Lenin's widow), Kollontai, Nikolai Ivanovich Bukharin, Andrei Marti of Czechoslovakia, Karl Radek of Germany, and Béla Kun of Hungary.

Zetkin had little personal life, but she reared her two sons and, in 1899, she married the painter Georg Friedrich Zundel, eighteen years younger. This marriage lapsed during World War I and ended in divorce in 1927, when Zetkin was seventy. Politics was the core of her being. In this political struggle, it was Zetkin's dynamic personality that allowed her to carry on simultaneously the struggle with and against socialist men, fighting with them for class and party solidarity and against them for women's autonomy and power. A staunch defender of the proletariat, from first to last, she saw women's liberation in the larger historical context of the workers' drive for socialism. Women's problems, she believed, would be solved only by socioeconomic change and through class struggle. An internationalist to the end, she opposed war as a capitalist tool against the workers. Clear-sighted and committed, Zetkin lived and died devoted to her causes.

### Bibliography

Boxer, Marilyn J., and Jean H. Quataert, eds. *Socialist Women: European Socialist Feminism in the Nineteenth and Early Twentieth Centuries*. New York: Elsevier, 1978. A collection of articles on the relationship of women's issues and socialism linking Zetkin to the movement in several European countries.

Evans, Richard J. "Theory and Practice in German Social Democracy, 1880-1914: Clara Zetkin and the Socialist Theory of Women's Emancipation." *History of Political Thought* 3 (Summer, 1982): 285-304. Contrasts Zetkin's views about the women's movement in 1889 with those of 1896 seen in the contemporary German political context. Her new position favored a separate Socialist women's organization and women's suffrage.

Nettl, J. P. *Rosa Luxemburg*. 2 vols. London and New York: Oxford University Press, 1966. There is also a one-volume abridged edition (London: Oxford University Press, 1969). Illuminates the significant relationship between Zetkin and Luxemburg.

Pore, Renate. *A Conflict of Interest: Women in German Social Democracy, 1919-1933*. Westport, Conn.: Greenwood Press, 1981. Attributes the character of women's involvement in the SPD to Zetkin, lauding her unswerving adherence to the twofold fight for socialism and women's rights.

Porter, Cathy. *Alexandra Kollontai: The Lonely Struggle of the Woman Who Defied Lenin*. London: Virago, and New York: Dial Press, 1980. Contains some discussion of the relationship of Zetkin and the Soviet government after World War I.

Zetkin, Clara. *Clara Zetkin: Selected Writings*. Edited by Philip S. Foner. Translated by Kai Schoenhals. Foreword by Angela Y. Davis. New York: International Publishers, 1984. The introduction supplies the most complete analytical survey published in English of Zetkin's life and ideas. It draws substantially on an unpublished Ph.D. thesis by Karen Honeycutt.

*Loretta Turner Johnson*

# GEORGY KONSTANTINOVICH ZHUKOV

*Born:* December 2, 1896; Strelkovka, Russia
*Died:* June 18, 1974; Moscow, U.S.S.R.
*Areas of Achievement:* The military, government, and politics
*Contribution:* Zhukov was the most important Soviet staff and field commander throughout World War II and was involved in the planning and/or execution of all the primary battles and campaigns against the Germans. Zhukov was the first career military man to be selected as a member of the Presidium (Politburo) of the Communist Party, came to be feared as a rival by both Joseph Stalin and Nikita S. Khrushchev, and was decisive in preventing Khrushchev's ouster in 1957.

## Early Life

Georgy Konstantinovich Zhukov was born December 2, 1896, in the village of Strelkovka, Kaluga Oblast, Russia. Strelkovka is approximately one hundred miles southwest of Moscow. Zhukov was born to poor peasants, his father serving as the village shoemaker. At eleven years of age, since his parents could no longer afford to pay for his education, he was taken in to be reared by his grandfather. His grandfather lived in Moscow, where he was a laborer in a metallurgical plant. Zhukov worked at several menial jobs and then apprenticed himself to a furrier and leather dresser. He continued his schooling and became a master at his trade. Then, in 1915, the military was calling up those born in 1896, so he was inducted into the czarist army.

Zhukov was placed in the Tenth Novgorod Dragoon Regiment, which received a short training period before being ordered to the front lines. From 1915 to 1917, the regiment was almost constantly engaged in battle. He became known throughout the unit for his enthusiasm and bravery, and was promoted through the ranks until he attained the highest noncommissioned rank. He was presented twice with the Cross of St. George, the highest military award given to noncommissioned officers. Soon after the February Revolution in 1917, the soldiers of his unit elected him to be chairman of the Squadron Soviet (council) and their representative on the regimental soviet of deputies. The Soviets exerted control over the army, allowing the officers to do only what they approved, and therefore Zhukov's leadership role was significant.

After the October Revolution that same year brought the Bolsheviks to power, Zhukov helped in the organization of the Red Army, and, during the Russian Civil War (1918-1920) and Polish War (1920), he served in the Red Cavalry. He began as platoon commander and then advanced to squadron commander in the important First Cavalry Army, which was the shock force of the Red military. The commander of his brigade was Semyon K. Timoshenko, future marshal and defense minister, who became Zhukov's sponsor during the interwar period. Zhukov was wounded but recovered to fight anew, and for his many contributions he received many citations in Orders of the Day, an engraved saber from the group commander, a gold watch with an inscribed commendation from the Defense Council of the Soviet Republic, and the highest army military decoration, the Order of the Red Banner.

Zhukov chose a professional military career at the end of the wars. He had joined the Communist Party in March, 1919, and was a member the rest of his life. He was graduated from an advanced training program for cavalry officers in 1925. From 1928 to 1931, he attended the Frunze Military Academy, specializing in armored operations. He also traveled to Germany in the 1920's to study armor. In 1936 and 1937, Stalin had him and other astute observers gather information from the Spanish Civil War, including the testing of Soviet tank tactics in actual combat. He was able to survive the massive military purge in 1937, perhaps because he was out of the country. Thus, he and other junior officers were blessed subsequently with the opportunity to rise rapidly in rank and position because of the vacancies created. Zhukov already had served successively as commander of a cavalry regiment, brigade, and division, and in 1937-1938 he was commander of the Third, then the Sixth Cavalry Corps. In 1938-1939, he was designated the deputy commander of cavalry, Belorussian Military District. In 1939, he was ordered to head the Far East First Army Group with the mission of driving Japanese invaders out of the Mongolian People's Republic. His success caused the Presidium of the Supreme Soviet to bestow on him the highest military award of his country, the Golden Star with title of Hero of the Soviet Union. In January, 1940, he was appointed chief of staff of the Soviet forces fighting the Finns. In May, 1940, Zhukov was promoted to general of the army and was assigned

*Soviet commander Georgy Konstantinovich Zhukov (seated, left) with American general Dwight D. Eisenhower and British field marshal Bernard Law Montgomery*

commander of the Kiev Military District. From February to the end of July, 1941, he was given the positions of chief of the general staff of the Soviet army and deputy people's commissar of defense of the Soviet Union. Thereby, at age forty-four, Zhukov occupied the second-highest military offices of his country, with the top positions of marshal of the Soviet Union and minister of defense entrusted to his benefactor, Timoshenko. He also was designated an alternate member of the Central Committee of the Communist Party in February, 1941.

### Life's Work

During World War II, Zhukov personally and directly was important to the planning or the implementation, or both, of all the main battles and campaigns. Often he was in Moscow serving as a leading figure in the supreme command headquarters. At such times, his chief occupation was with overall strategy and the formulation of specific campaign plans. In several instances, he was selected by Stalin personally to represent him and supreme headquarters on field duty at the front line. When acting in such a capacity, he was endowed with virtually unlimited powers of command and decision-making. When Leningrad was threatened so quickly in 1941, Zhukov hurriedly was dispatched there in September to halt the invading forces and to organize more adequate and permanent defenses. In October, he moved quickly to Moscow to direct the frantic preparations for saving that most important city, preparations that continued on into 1942. His skillful use of reserve troops undoubtedly saved Moscow from being taken. As commander in chief of the Western Front during the winter of 1941-1942, he also took advantage of the Russian weather to direct offensive actions against the climatically unprepared enemy. When the Nazis resumed offensive operations from spring to fall of 1942, Zhukov was in charge of defensive actions and acted with particular significance in planning the defense of the Caucasus. In August, he was appointed first deputy people's commissar of defense and deputy supreme commander in chief, second only to Stalin.

The struggle for Stalingrad had already begun, and Zhukov became responsible for planning its defense and coordinating the movements of the various forces. He deserves much credit for the ultimate victory that finally came in January, 1943, in this greatest battle of World War II and its turning point in the European theater. For his achievement he was named marshal of the Soviet Union, which was the country's highest military title. He then planned and commanded the largest tank battle of the war at Kursk-Orel, was in charge of devising the strategies for the offensives of 1944 and overseeing their execution, and personally commanded the final drive on Berlin. In both 1944 and 1945, he again was designated Hero of the Soviet Union. It seemed fitting that in Berlin on May 8 of the latter year, it was Marshal Zhukov, in the name of the Soviet Union, who accepted the unconditional German surrender from Field Marshal Wilhelm Keitel.

From the end of the war until January of the following year, Zhukov stayed in Germany as the commander of the Soviet occupation forces and the Soviet representative on the Allied Control Commission. Then he was recalled to the Soviet Union to serve as deputy minister of defense and commander in chief of the Soviet ground forces. Yet his great popularity as the returning war hero apparently caused Stalin to view him as a potential threat, for soon Zhukov was relieved of both positions and given assignments outside the capital city. First he was relegated to the position of commander of the Odessa Military District. Then his appointment to command the Ural Military District was even more of a demotion. From 1946 through 1952, therefore, Zhukov was removed from significant and highly visible government activities. Even historical writings on the war years made mention of his name much less frequently, and his accomplishments were described in a fashion similar to that used to describe those of many other leaders. Almost unlimited praise and credit were given to Stalin for every important decision and activity of the war.

Zhukov's role in affairs changed immediately, however, with Stalin's death in March, 1953. When a new government was formed three days later, he was named first deputy to Minister of Defense Nikolai Bulganin, who was a Communist Party and Soviet government politician. Zhukov was listed as the highest ranking Soviet military officer, and his position was indicative of the importance that the new leaders attributed to the military establishment. The army cooperated in July in the arrest and death of Lavrenti Beria, secret police chief, and Zhukov was given full membership in the Party's Central Committee. Military leaders, particularly Zhukov, were important political activists in the power struggle that ensued between Khrushchev and Georgi M. Malenkov. Zhukov backed Khrushchev because of their long friendship and the support by Malenkov of a reduction in military expenditures. In February, 1955, following his success, Khrushchev replaced Malenkov with Bulganin as chairman of the council of ministers and gave to Zhukov the position of minister of defense.

Thereafter, Zhukov's power and influence in not only the military but also the political and governmental activities of the Soviet Union were enormous. That same year he went with Khrushchev and Bulganin to the Geneva Conference and in 1957 visited Yugoslavia and Albania. At the Twentieth Party Congress in February, 1956, he was selected for alternate membership in the Presidium. That December, on the occasion of his sixtieth birthday, he became the only man to be awarded his fourth Golden Star and designated four times Hero of the Soviet Union. The apex of his political power and influence occurred the next spring and summer as a majority of the Presidium attempted to remove Khrushchev as top leader. Zhukov stated that the armed forces would "not permit anyone to bid for power" and then provided planes for Central Committee members to come quickly to Moscow to settle the crisis by reversing the decision of the Presidium. In addition, the Central Committee elected Zhukov a full member of the Party Presidium, a position of leadership and an honor that no other career military man has attained.

Circumstances changed abruptly, however, and on October 26, 1957, Zhukov was removed as minister of defense. A week later he was dismissed from his Presidium and Central Committee positions "for violating Leninist principles concerning the administration of the armed forces." He had implemented programs to enhance military professionalism that lessened control from the Party's political advisers. This brought him into fundamental disagreement with Khrushchev and most other leading Party officials. Zhukov was accused of fostering a personality cult within the armed forces, and, along with his removal from all Party and government positions, he was publicly disgraced for allegedly questioning Party leadership of the military. He retired from active military service.

Zhukov completely disappeared from Soviet public affairs until after Khrushchev's tenure as top Party and government leader ended in the fall of 1964. In addition, few saw him in a private capacity. Official publications stated little in a positive sense about him during this time. In 1965, however, at the twentieth anniversary celebration of the victory over Germany, he made his first major public appearance. He was seen by thousands with other noted Soviet figures atop Vladimir Ilich Lenin's tomb in Red Square. On December 1 of the following year, he was awarded for the sixth time the Order of Lenin in recognition of "services to the armed forces." Three years later, his youth and military memoirs, *Vospominaniia i razmyshleniia* (1969; *The Memoirs of Marshal Zhukov*, 1971), were published in the official magazine of the ministry of defense, five years before his death.

### Summary

Georgy Konstantinovich Zhukov's greatest achievements were in the realm of military leadership. In this area, his plans, decisions, and influence directly affected the lives of millions of combatants and the survivability of his country during its period of crisis. They impacted as well on the power levels and relationships between nations. The full significance of his impact can be appreciated even more by the fact that a leading Soviet officer wrote later that Zhukov at times even corrected Stalin, something no one else dared even to try to do. It was during the mammoth struggle of World War II that Zhukov made such a major difference. His strategical and tactical plans were often very bold and innovative. Thus, it can readily be assumed that, in his absence, other actions, even very different ones at times, would have been undertaken. He was the top military figure throughout the conflict, second in power to only Stalin himself, was involved with all the great battle areas, and was the dominant general in both defensive and offensive actions against the Nazis. As such, his achievements are difficult to overestimate.

Second only to his military contributions were those Zhukov made in the area of politics and government. After the death of Stalin, in a time of great uncertainty, the military leaders became a powerful political force. Certain of them, most especially Zhukov, were key players in the triumph of Khrushchev over Malenkov in their struggle for power. The height of Zhukov's political power and influence came in 1957, when he worked successfully with others to prevent a majority of the Presidium from ousting Khrushchev as top Party leader. He became the first professional military man to become an alternate member, then a full member, of the Presidium of the Communist Party.

In addition to the awards and honors previously mentioned, a host of others were bestowed upon Zhukov in his lifetime. He became the most decorated military person in Soviet history. After his death in 1974, he was accorded the final great honor of being buried beside the Kremlin Wall in Red Square with his country's other leading heroes.

### Bibliography

Bialer, Seweryn, ed. *Stalin and His Generals: Soviet Military Memoirs of World War II.* New York: Pegasus, 1969; London: Souvenir, 1970. This book is authored by military officers, from the top ones down to the regimental level. Zhukov is the author of three articles and is the object of much comment by his contemporaries. Contains maps, notes, and a biographical index.

Chaney, Otto Preston, Jr. *Zhukov.* Rev. ed. Norman: University of Oklahoma Press, 1996. This is probably the best and most useful of all books on Zhukov. It is fair and judicious, researched thoroughly, and comprehensive. Contains maps, illustrations, notes, a bibliography, appendices, and an index.

Clark, Alan. *Barbarossa: The Russian-German Conflict, 1941-1945.* London: Hutchinson, and New York: Morrow, 1965. This work is a detailed and balanced account done in a scholarly manner after much research. There is much about Zhukov. It is a good source to begin with to get the overall picture. Contains maps, illustrations, charts, notes, a bibliography, and an index.

Erickson, John. *The Soviet High Command: A Military-Political History, 1918-1941.* London: Macmillan, and New York: St. Martin's Press, 1962. Zhukov appears a surprising amount in this exhaustive narrative. It is well researched and is a good source for Zhukov in the 1918-1941 years. Contains maps, notes, appendices, a bibliography, and an index.

Kerr, Walter. *The Russian Army: Its Men, Its Leaders, and Its Battles.* London: Gollancz, and New York: Knopf, 1944. Kerr was a correspondent in the Soviet Union during World War II and observed much and interviewed many. He writes in a down-to-earth fashion. Zhukov appears often. Contains maps and an index.

Shtemenko, Sergei M. *The Soviet General Staff at War, 1941-1945.* Translated by Robert Daglish. Moscow: Progress, 1970. Shtemenko served on the general staff, but he was also knowledgeable about front-line activities. His book is written from the perspective of a devoted nationalist and Communist, but it contains much good inside information. Zhukov is mentioned often. Contains maps and illustrations.

Werth, Alexander. *Russia at War, 1941-1945.* New York: Dutton, 1964; London: Pan, 1965. Extensive treatment is given to Zhukov in this balanced account of Soviet events from 1939 to 1945. Werth experienced many of the matters he writes about, presented in an easy, flowing style. He allows the reader to see Zhukov's role within the full perspective of Soviet affairs. Contains maps, a chronological table, a bibliography, and an index.

Zhukov, Georgy. *The Memoirs of Marshal Zhukov.* London: Cape, and New York: Delacorte Press, 1971. Zhukov writes of his childhood and youth and of his military life to April, 1946. It is a detailed account that contains much not found elsewhere. Contains maps and illustrations.

*James G. Nutsch*

# ELLEN TAAFFE ZWILICH

*Born:* April 30, 1939; Miami, Florida
*Area of Achievement:* Music
*Contribution:* One of America's foremost composers of art music, Zwilich became the first woman to win the Pulitzer Prize in music.

### Early Life

Born in Miami, the cultural mecca of Florida, Ellen Taaffe was adopted by Ruth Howard Taaffe and Edward Taaffe. Her surname is Irish in origin, although many of her father's ancestors can be traced to Austria. While neither parent had a musical background, they did own a piano, which immediately attracted Ellen and on which she began to explore the keys at the age of three. By the age of five, she was studying with a neighborhood piano teacher, but she rebelled at having to play the customary children's pieces. When she was seven or eight years old, she heard the Symphony No. 5 in C minor by Ludwig van Beethoven and was deeply impressed by it.

By the age of thirteen, Ellen came under the tutelage of Bower Murphy, who taught her to play the trumpet, to transpose music into different keys, and to perform in chamber ensembles. He also guided her in learning the orchestral repertoire and in devising ways in which to overcome technical problems in trumpet performance.

At Coral Gables High School, Ellen became an accomplished violinist. Soon she was serving as concertmistress of the school orchestra, as principal trumpeter in the band, and as student conductor. In addition, she composed pieces for band and for orchestra. Music was clearly to be her vocation. After graduating from high school, she entered Florida State University in Tallahassee as a music education major. In her sophomore year, she changed her area of emphasis to composition. Her undergraduate years, which culminated in a bachelor's degree in 1960, found her performing as concertmistress in the university orchestra under the direction of the Hungarian composer and pianist, Ernst von Dohnanyi; as first trumpeter in the symphonic band; and as a jazz trumpeter. Violin was her principal instrument, and she had the good fortune to study violin with Richard Burgin, former concertmaster of the Boston Symphony Orchestra, who had joined the Florida State faculty. Her composition teachers were John Boda and Carlisle Floyd. Following graduation, Ellen stayed at Florida State and pursued graduate work in composition. She received her master's degree in 1962.

### Life's Work

After a somewhat less than satisfying year of teaching in a small community in South Carolina, Ellen Taaffe arrived in New York City. She resumed her violin studies with Ivan Galamian and his assistant, Sally Thomas. Taaffe also worked as a freelance musician, and in 1965, began a seven-year relationship as a violinist with the American Symphony Orchestra under its founder and conductor, Leopold Stokowski. She gained experience and seasoning by playing under a variety of guest conductors, some of whom were composers; they included Ernest Ansermet, Luciano Berio, Karl Bohn, Eugen Jochum, Hans Werner Henze, Paul Kletzki, Aram Khachaturian, Yehudi Menuhin, Igor Markevitch, Gunther Schuller, and Andre Previn. On June 22, 1969, she married the Hungarian-born violinist Joseph Zwilich, who played with the Metropolitan Opera Orchestra. These years solidified her intention to pursue a career as a composer rather than as a performer, and, indeed, she began to try her hand at the creation of art songs, producing, for example *Einsame Nacht*, a setting of six poems by Herman Hesse, which explore the theme of loneliness; this song cycle is stylistically beholden to the Second Viennese School and exhibits both craftsmanship and expressivity within the parameters of this sometimes restrictive school.

When Stokowski relocated to London in 1972, Ellen Taaffe Zwilich left her orchestral position and entered the doctoral program in composition at the Juilliard School. Her principal teachers there were Roger Sessions and Elliott Carter. During her three years at this esteemed institution, she formed the core of her creative personality, much of which is related directly to her extensive background as a performer. Music, for Zwilich, is a unique form of communication; therefore, its sheer sound and how that sound is perceived by an audience illuminate her approach to composition.

By the time she received the Doctor of Musical Arts degree, the first woman ever to achieve this distinction at Juilliard, Zwilich had created an impressive array of works that established her as a powerful new voice in the world of music. Her Sonata in Three Movements for Violin and Piano, written in 1973 for her husband and performed by him on a

European tour that year, won a gold medal at the G. B. Viotti International Composition Competition in 1975. *Symposium for Orchestra* (1973), introduced by Pierre Boulez and the Juilliard Orchestra in Alice Tully Hall in New York's Lincoln Center during the summer of 1975, was declared an official United States entry for the International Society for Contemporary Music "World Music Days" Festival in Paris; it was also performed in 1978 in Carnegie Hall by the American Symphony Orchestra under Kazuyoshi Akiyama. As the title suggests, this twelve-minute work in one movement takes an academic point of view wherein the various members of the orchestra offer musical commentary on the subject (theme) under consideration.

Zwilich's String Quartet (1974), recipient of the Coolidge Chamber Music Prize, was premiered by the New York String Quartet at Jordan Hall in Boston, Massachusetts, on October 31, 1976. It received subsequent renderings at Alice Tully Hall, Carnegie Hall, and in 1977, at the Aspen Music Festival in Colorado. The composition's essential materials are set forth in the first movement, a type of prologue, and are incorporated in diverse manner through each of the four movements, the last of which is to be regarded as a closing epilogue. Zwilich's String Quartet is to be thought of as musical conversation among four equals, the drama of which impels the divergent exchanges of the four strings.

While Ellen Taaffe Zwilich was working on *Chamber* Symphony on a commission from the Boston Musica Vera, conducted by Richard Pittman, in 1979, her husband Joseph died suddenly of a heart attack while he and Ellen were attending a performance by the Stuttgart Ballet in the Metropolitan Opera House shortly after their tenth wedding anniversary. When the young widow resumed composition on the work, the symphony had evolved into one in which long musical lines are derived from shorter ideas. The solo capacities of the individual instruments are contrasted with a fuller sound created by such devices as instrumental doubling. The Boston premiere on November 30, 1979, was followed by performances in major American and European musical centers including one which was shown on television in Sofia, Bulgaria.

Only two years prior to the *Chamber* Symphony, Zwilich was composing a very different type of chamber music: her Clarino Quartet, dedicated to the memory of her high school trumpet teacher, Bower Murphy. In this unusual work, the piccolo trumpet, playing largely in the clarino register, is exploited handsomely along with the peculiar qualities of the D, C, and B-flat trumpets. The premiere, which took place at Hamline University in St. Paul, Minnesota, during March of 1979, featured members of the Minnesota Orchestra's trumpet section; Charles Schlueter played the clarino part on his personally designed valved instrument. The Clarino Quartet received subsequent performances at the Festival of Contemporary Music at Tanglewood in Lenox, Massachusetts, and in Paris, France, by the Pierre Thibaud Ensemble.

Zwilich received a Norlin Foundation Fellowship from the MacDowell Colony in Peterborough, New Hampshire, in 1980, and a Guggenheim Memorial Foundation Fellowship in 1980-1981. These fellowships enabled her to create such works as *Passages*, a setting of six poems by A. R. Ammons, for soprano and chamber ensemble. Commissioned by Boston Musical Vera, the work concerns the various forms of the passage of life and of time. The *Three Movements for Orchestra*, which includes serial techniques as well as traditional tonality, was retitled Symphony No. 1 and was premiered by the American Symphony Orchestra under the baton of Gunther Schuller in New York on May 5, 1982. It was this composition that made musical history when it was awarded the Pulitzer Prize in music in 1983; it competed against seventy-nine other entries. Zwilich was the first woman ever to win this prestigious award in its forty-year history. The symphony was recorded by John Nelson and the Indianapolis Symphony Orchestra in 1986.

During the next decade, Zwilich firmly established herself as one of America's most respected composers. In May of 1991, she received the Ernst von Dohnanyi Citation from her alma mater, Florida State University, and saw her works featured in the university's Festival of New Music. Her productivity continued at a staggering pace throughout the 1980's and included both large and small compositions. The Fantasy for Harpsichord received its first hearing in Linda Kobler's debut recital at Carnegie Hall in 1984. The Double Quartet for strings, commissioned by the Emerson Quartet and the Chamber Music Society of Lincoln Center, was premiered on October 21, 1984. (The two quartets are treated as separate but equal entities competing and cooperating with each other.) In the same year, Zwilich completed the Concerto for Trumpet and Five Players.

Symphony No. 2, known as the *Cello* Symphony because of the prominence given to that section of the orchestra, was introduced by the San Francisco Symphony Orchestra on November 13, 1985. The Piano Concerto, commissioned by the Detroit Symphony Orchestra and the American Symphony Orchestra League, was premiered on June 26, 1986, at Michigan's Meadowbrook Festival. *Tanzspiel*, Zwilich's only ballet, was commissioned by the New York City Ballet in 1987. *Symbalom*, commissioned by the New York Philharmonic and its conductor, Zubin Mehta, was first heard in the city of Leningrad on June 1, 1988, on the Philharmonic's tour of the Soviet Union. Other works include *Trio* for piano, violin, and cello commissioned by the Kalichstein-Laredo-Robinson Trio (1987), Trombone Concerto (1988), Flute Concerto (1990), Oboe Concerto (1991), Bass Trombone Concerto (1993), and Symphony No. 3 (1993). Symphony No. 3 was commissioned by the New York Philharmonic and premiered by that orchestra under the baton of Jahja Ling, who substituted for the indisposed Kurt Masur. This work seems to sum up the principles upon which Zwilich's art is founded. It is a creation whose roots in the Romantic tradition are clearly discernible. The music communicates an oft-told tale, to speak metaphorically, but it does so with such verve and enthusiasm that the listener retains his or her interest throughout. In short, the expressive power that is contained within the confines of traditional symphonic form is such that it holds in its grip an audience that is eager to accept its message.

### Summary

Ellen Taaffe Zwilich has had a profound impact upon twentieth century American music and has been a beacon of inspiration for aspiring women composers and young composers in general. Her success continues to breed success, and it allows her to lead her life solely as a composer; she does not supplement her income by teaching in a university or by conducting or by performing (as she had done early in her career). Although she was trained by such "advanced" composers as Roger Sessions and Elliott Carter, she has discovered and cultivated a musical language which is comprehensible to large numbers of people. For that reason, she is very much a part of the world in which she lives, in opposition to the "ivory tower" creator who lives apart from society at large.

Ellen Zwilich's long list of commissions from eminent musicians and organizations is a testament to the impact she has made on both professional musicians and the public. While her earlier efforts show a linkage to such Viennese masters as Alban Berg and Arnold Schoenberg, her more recent compositions seem to meld classical and Romantic traits. Her large-scale works also call to mind composers such as Dmitri Shostakovitch and Carl Nielsen. Inspiration comes to her through a thorough knowledge and command of her craft. Her career is a testament to the rewards that follow on the heels of prodigious talent, discipline, and the recognition that a composer needs to create not in a vacuum but with a view to addressing one's fellow inhabitants on the planet.

### Bibliography

DeLorenzo, Lisa C. "An Interview with Ellen Taaffe Zwilich." *Music Educators Journal* 78, no. 7 (March, 1992). Interview with Zwilich in which she discusses the popularity of her music and her background and development.

Dreier, Ruth. "Ellen Taaffe Zwilich." *High Fidelity* (Musical America edition) 33 (September, 1983): 4. Dreier, a cellist, interviewed Zwilich shortly after she had won the Pulitzer Prize. Zwilich offers her views on the composer's relationship to the community of humankind, her assessment of the influence of performance on her creativity, and her opinion on the state of orchestras in the early 1980's.

Griffiths, Paul. "Zwilich in F-Sharp." *The New Yorker* 69 (March 15, 1993): 113–116. A discussion of Zwilich's *Third Symphony* in relation to her previous work, this essay concludes with the view that the composer is perhaps too beholden to the past in her musical expression.

LePage, Jane Weiner. "Ellen Taaffe Zwilich." In *Women Composers, Conductors, and Musicians of the Twentieth Century: Selected Biographies*. 3 vols. Metuchen, N.J. and London: Scarecrow Press, 1980-1988. In the absence of a book-length work, this article provides the most complete source of biographical information on Zwilich. Traces her life from childhood through the early 1980's and includes excerpts of reviews of her musical works.

Moor, Paul. "Ellen Taaffe Zwilich." *High Fidelity* (Musical America edition) 33 (March, 1989): 16-18. Focuses on Zwilich's ideas concerning the role of women in music in the late twentieth century and in the past. In addition, Zwilich articulates her notions about the relationship between composer and performer.

Page, Tim. "The Music of Ellen Zwilich." *The New York Times Magazine*, July 14, 1985, 26-32. A wide-ranging interview with Zwilich that provides a good overview of her career. Conveys the breadth of her work, the depth of her commitment to musical composition, and the genesis of her musical inspiration.

*David Z. Kushner*

# VLADIMIR ZWORYKIN

*Born:* July 30, 1889; Mourom, Russia
*Died:* July 29, 1982; Princeton, New Jersey
*Area of Achievement:* Electronics
*Contribution:* Frequently called the "father of television," Zworykin invented both the iconoscope camera tube and the kinescope picture tube, which together form the electronic television system.

## Early Life

Vladimir Kosma Zworykin was born July 30, 1889, in Mourom, Russia, on the Oka River, where his father, Kosma Zworykin, owned a fleet of steamboats. Since many family members were engineers, young Vladimir manifested an interest in engineering. As an undergraduate student at the St. Petersburg Institute of Technology, he first became interested in television. There, Professor Boris Rosing was working on a cathode-ray tube for use as the picture-forming device. In Rosing's system, the camera depended on mechanically moving parts. Zworykin, assisting the professor in the evenings, came to the conclusion that television could be perfected only if the camera were also a cathode-ray tube.

After he was graduated in 1912, Zworykin entered the College of France in Paris. There, he gained an understanding of theoretical physics while studying X rays under the renowned Professor Paul Langevin until the beginning of World War I in 1914. Returning home, Zworykin became an officer in the Russian Signal Corps, in which he was assigned work on radio transmission. On April 17, 1916, he married Tatiana Vasilieff. They had two children, Nina and Elaine, the latter of whom was named after Zworykin's mother. This marriage was later to end in divorce. In 1951, he married Dr. Katherine Polevitzky, who survived him.

At the time of the Bolshevik Revolution in 1917, Zworykin was in Moscow at the factory of the Russian Marconi Company. He decided to escape from the Soviet Union. The journey of eighteen months took him down the Ob River to the Arctic Ocean and then to Norway, Denmark, Great Britain, and finally, in 1919, the United States. Unable to find an appropriate position, he worked as a bookkeeper for the financial agent of the Soviet Embassy.

## Life's Work

In 1920, Zworykin entered the employ of the Westinghouse Electric Corporation in Pittsburgh, Pennsylvania. This was most fortunate, as Westinghouse was a world leader in the development of radio. In addition, its research interests were expanding. Except for a brief absence, Zworykin spent the 1920's at Westinghouse, and while there, he pursued a great variety of scientific problems that the burgeoning field of electronics presented: radio receiving valves, mercury rectifiers, and photoelectric cells.

It was television, however, that compelled Zworykin's interest. Earlier experimental television systems had handled only an element of the picture at a time, requiring an intense illumination of the scene, impractical since most of the light was wasted. Zworykin conceived of a camera that would store the light from an entire picture until it could be measured by a rapidly scanning electron beam. The sensitivity and detail of such a camera would be far higher than those of previous systems. Zworykin developed his first functioning iconoscope, as he called it, in 1923 (from the Greek *eikon*, meaning "image," and *skopon*, "to watch"). This television-camera tube equipped for rapid scanning of an image-storing photoactive mosaic was demonstrated in Pittsburgh in 1924, but the images were dim and shadowy. The Westinghouse executives were unimpressed, and Zworykin was permitted to work on television only intermittently.

Meanwhile, he had been building his reputation and career in the United States. In 1924, Zworykin became a naturalized citizen of the United States. In 1926, he earned a Ph.D. from the University of Pittsburgh.

Zworykin's work on television attracted the attention of a fellow Russian immigrant, David Sarnoff, general manager and vice president (later president) of the Radio Corporation of America (RCA). Westinghouse and RCA were closely allied at the time, and Sarnoff urged Westinghouse to devote more effort to research on television. It did, but only modestly. Improved versions of the iconoscope were demonstrated in 1927 and again in 1929. It was in 1929 that Zworykin obtained his first patent on color television.

Sarnoff, a visionary who believed in the commercial feasibility of television, persuaded Westinghouse (which was then a major stockholder in RCA) to move the effort to RCA. Zworykin accordingly transferred, along with several other sci-

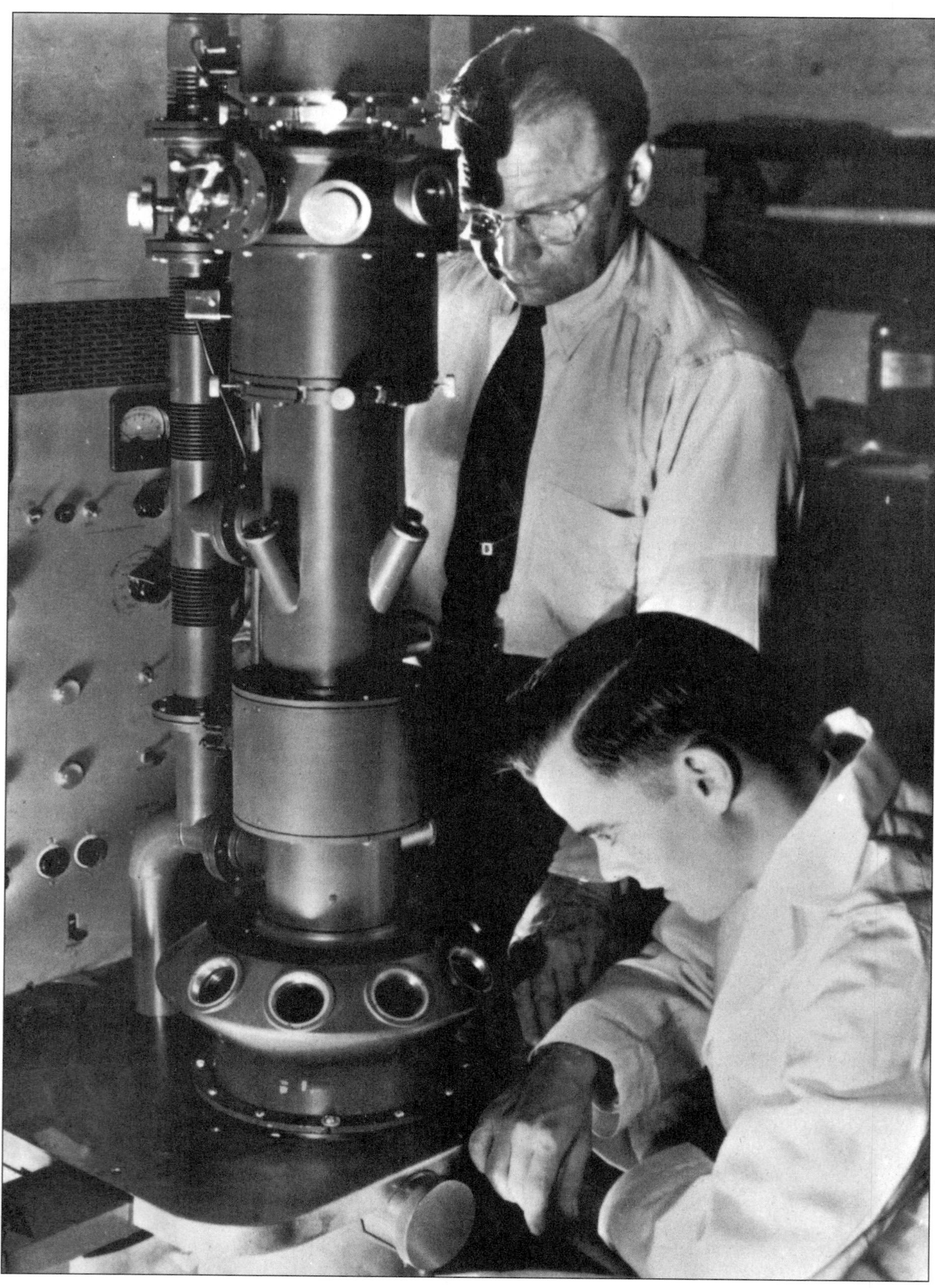

entists, and became director of eletronics research at RCA in Camden, New Jersey, in 1929. Famous in the history of RCA was a meeting between Sarnoff and Zworykin in which the RCA president asked how much it would cost to perfect a television system. "About $100,000," Zworykin replied. As Sarnoff was later fond of telling, RCA was to spend fifty million dollars before realizing a cent of profit from television.

At RCA, Zworykin was able to develop further what he called the kinescope ("kine" from the Greek *kinesis*, "motion"), the picture tube of the television set. Zworykin's kinescope was a cathode-ray tube in which electrons bombard a screen of fluorescent material. This system gave a clearer picture than systems using a mechanically rotating scanning disc yielding only 120 lines on the screen. Zworykin's kinescope image was steadily improved, 240 lines, 343, 441, and so forth. (Modern televisions have 525 lines.) In addition, the size of the picture-tube screen was enlarged. One test in 1936 utilized a "large" 7.5-by-12-inch screen. In what was the first showing of a complete program originating in NBC studios in the RCA Building but broadcast from the top of the Empire State Building, a consistent picture was received forty-five miles away.

By 1938, RCA deemed Zworykin's system commercially feasible, but the required approval of the federal government did not come until July of 1941. In 1940, Zworykin recruited Dr. James Hillier, and in three months' time, they developed the electron microscope. The United States' entry into World War II curtailed commercial broadcasting, but RCA continued to fund television research. During the war, a research team headed by Zworykin developed a camera tube one hundred times more sensitive than the iconoscope. After the war, RCA began to market commercially a television with a ten-inch screen. A table model went on sale in the fall of 1946 for $375. Meanwhile, Zworykin became the world leader in the development of color television.

Zworykin retired from RCA in 1954, having served as director of electronic research from 1929 to 1942 and again from 1946 to 1954; associate research director from 1942 to 1945; and vice president, technical consultant, from 1947 to 1954. Zworykin was especially proud of this last title and listed his occupation in *Who's Who in America* as business executive.

Upon his retirement, Zworykin was given a small research laboratory near Princeton, New Jersey, at which he was able to pursue his own interests. There, he envisioned an electronic warning system for automobiles to avert accidents, a "televoter" by which citizens could render instantaneous decisions on public matters, and most important, medical electronics. Becoming the director of the electronics center at the Rockefeller Institute for Medical Research and a founder of the International Federation of Medical Electronics, Zworykin foresaw the potential for the wider use of electronics in medicine. In the 1950's, the "Endoradiosonde," or radio pill, was developed. It utilized a compact transistor oscillator powered by a minute cell to transmit physiological data from inside the human body. Following this development was an ultraviolet microscope using color television in which features in the body appeared in their complexity on the screen of the picture tube. His work on medical electronics was to herald numerous breakthroughs in the use of electronic devices in medicine.

Zworykin coauthored four books: *Photocells and Their Application*, originally published in 1930 and later, in 1949, under the title *Photoelectricity and Its Application; Television: The Electronics of Image Transmission* (1940); *Electron Optics and the Electron Microscope* (1945); and *Television in Science and Industry* (1958). He also received dozens of awards, including the National Medal of Science, the nation's highest, in 1966.

### Summary

Zworykin was never comfortable with the appellation "father of television," insisting that he was but one of many who worked on its development. Although further refined, his system remains the basis of modern television.

In an accent that remained discernibly Russian after half a century in the United States, the inventor lamented the far-reaching changes his invention wrought, calling it one of the leading causes of juvenile delinquency. Although Zworykin seldom watched television, the American people did. Television changed enormously the entertainment and information-gathering habits of Americans and, in the process, their perception of the world in which they live.

### Bibliography

Abramson, Albert. "Pioneers of Television: Vladimir Kosma Zworykin." *SMTE Journal* 90 (July, 1981): 579-590. This highly technical article, published in the journal of the Society of Motion Picture and Television Engineers, lists Zworykin's patents from 1927 to 1965. Also gives patent specifications. Contains numerous reference sources and a bibliography.

MacLaurin, William Rupert. *Invention and Innovation in the Radio Industry.* New York: Macmillan, 1949. The chapter on the beginning of the television industry describes Zworykin's work at Westinghouse Electric and RCA. Largely nontechnical—it relates who decided what and why they did—it does, however, explain the iconoscope.

Lear, John. "Merchant of Vision." *Saturday Review* 40 (June 1, 1957): 43-45. Traces Zworykin's leadership role in the development of television. Nontechnical.

Udelson, Joseph H. *The Great Television Race: A History of the American Television Industry, 1925-1941.* University: University of Alabama Press, 1982. Although mainly concerned with the early technological development of television, this work does treat personalities involved. The book ends with the early commercialization of television in 1941.

*Joseph F. Rishel*

# Dictionary of World Biography

# The 20th Century

## Indices

## AREA OF ACHIEVEMENT

**PHOTOGRAPHY.** ***See also*** **ART**



**PHYSICS.** ***See also*** **ASTRONOMY**



**PHYSIOLOGY.** ***See also*** **MEDICINE**



**POETRY.** ***See*** **LITERATURE**

**POLITICAL SCIENCE.** ***See also*** **GOVERNMENT AND POLITICS**



**POLITICS.** ***See*** **GOVERNMENT AND POLITICS**

**PSYCHIATRY AND PSYCHOLOGY**

**ZOOLOGY**

## GEOGRAPHICAL LOCATION

# NAME INDEX

## PHOTO CREDITS

All photos in these volumes are courtesy of the Library of Congress except for the following:

Agence France Presse/Archive Photos: 1380, 2990
AIP, Niels Bohr Library: 3367
Amanda Saunders: 1469
AP/Wide World Photos: 87, 1372
Archive Photos: 42, 231, 492, 507, 561, 658, 891, 1049, 1138, 1194, 1276, 1452, 1567, 1635, 1646, 1684, 1836, 1863, 1946, 1978, 2247, 2277, 2350, 2426, 2552, 2580, 2703, 2729, 2736, 2885, 2950, 3067, 3542, 3608, 3712, 4102
Archive Photos/AGIP: 903
Archive Photos/AMW Pressedienst: 2385
Archive Photos/Archive France: 1099, 1360
Archive Photos/Camera Press: 674, 2535, 3133
Archive Photos/David Lees: 2610, 2721
Archive Photos/DPA: 445
Archive Photos/Express Newspapers: 46, 924, 1240, 1817, 2370, 3064, 3178
Archive Photos/Horst Tappe: 910
Archive Photos/Imapress: 92, 880, 2559, 4086
Bantam Books: 1581
Bernard Gotfryd/Archive Photos: 2333, 2770, 3923
CNP/Archive Photos: 2010, 3169, 3658
D.C. Public Library: 372, 1464, 2116, 3302, 3566, 3893, 3981, 4057
Deutsche Presse/Archive Photos: 359, 499
Frank Capri/Archive Photos: 80
Frank Driggs/Archive Photos: 1218
Franklin D. Roosevelt Memorial Library: 3219
International Tennis Hall of Fame: 1365
Jerry Bauer: 2305
Joe McTyre: 2786
John Kings: 2518
Kim Kurnizki: 184, 661, 1921, 3681
Korea Society/Los Angeles: 3166
Lawrence Radiation Laboratory, AIP, Niels Bohr Library: 3631
Leo Baeck Institute/Archive Photos: 484
Maclean Dameron: 2676
Maria Mulas: 2628
Michael Dorris: 1092
Mikhail Lemkhin/Archive Photos: 596
Museum of Modern Art, Film Stills Archive: 425, 654, 844, 1305, 1392, 1598, 1638, 2580, 2809, 3077, 3902, 3936
Museum of the City of New York/Archive Photos: 1412
NASA: 442
National Archives: 173, 1022, 1033, 1037, 1040, 1113, 1210, 1267, 1495, 1693, 1700, 1763, 2273, 2296, 2402, 2466, 2467, 2669, 2694, 2805, 2834, 2898, 2958, 3018, 3269, 3306, 3388, 3392, 3418, 3564, 3571, 3650, 3673, 3727, 3780, 3850
National Baseball Library: 3195
National Institutes of Health: 189
National Library of Medicine: 1840
National Portrait Gallery, Smithsonian Institution: 998

Nobel Foundation: 75, 161, 215, 240, 244, 248, 276, 302, 346, 350, 380, 411, 464, 473, 487, 502, 514, 526, 554, 612, 636, 692, 746, 799, 813, 814, 928, 952, 1009, 1059, 1134, 1167, 1236, 1368, 1425, 1428, 1503, 1510, 1515, 1618, 1625, 1648, 1651, 1656, 1752, 1760, 1828, 1871, 1872, 1907, 1914, 2028, 2052, 2063, 2074, 2132, 2176, 2190, 2236, 2239, 2282, 2330, 2393, 2337, 2593, 2638, 2653, 2700, 2707, 2714, 2820, 2856, 2924, 2927, 2934, 3014, 3074, 3102, 3110, 3230, 3232, 3247, 3278, 3285, 3297, 3362, 3372, 3377, 3401, 3457, 3459, 3471, 3490, 3498, 3516, 3636, 3654, 3775, 3787, 3845, 3898, 3958, 3999, 4021, 4084, 4091
Nordisk Pressefoto/Archive Photos: 2
Photo File/Archive Photos: 3240
Popperfoto/Archive Photos: 1712, 1969, 3332, 3737, 3926
Ralph W. Miller Golf Library: 3041
Reuters/Aladin/Archive Photos: 2356
Reuters/Archive Photos: 727
Reuters/Eric Miller/Archive Photos: 681
Reuters/Mike Blake/Archive Photos: 4050
Reuters/Peter Mueller/Archive Photos: 2931
Reuters/Wolfgang Rattay/Archive Photos: 2507
RGS: 2322
Rocon/Enuu, Nigeria: 14
Schomberg Center for Research, New York Public Library: 3113
Smithsonian Institution: 103, 3973
Sophia Smith Collection, Smith College: 3037
Supreme Court Historical Society: 3142
Supreme Court of the United States: 3547
United Nations: 618
University of Illinois, Chicago: 2766
Victor Malafronte/Archive Photos: 4030